THE INDEX LIBRARY

General Editor (Probate): Cliff Webb, M.A. (Cantab), F.S.A., F.S.G.

WILLS AT SALISBURY

1464-1858

THE BRITISH RECORD SOCIETY
INDEX LIBRARY VOL.122

INDEX LIBRARY VOLUME 122

Published by the British Record Society
c/o Patrick Dickinson,
The College of Arms,
Queen Victoria Street,
London EC4V 4BT

ISBN 0-901505-49-8 978-0-901505-49-1 Volume 1
ISBN 0-901505-50-1 978-0-901505-50-7 Volume 2
ISBN 0-901505-52-8 978-0-901505-52-1 Set of 2 volumes

CONTENTS

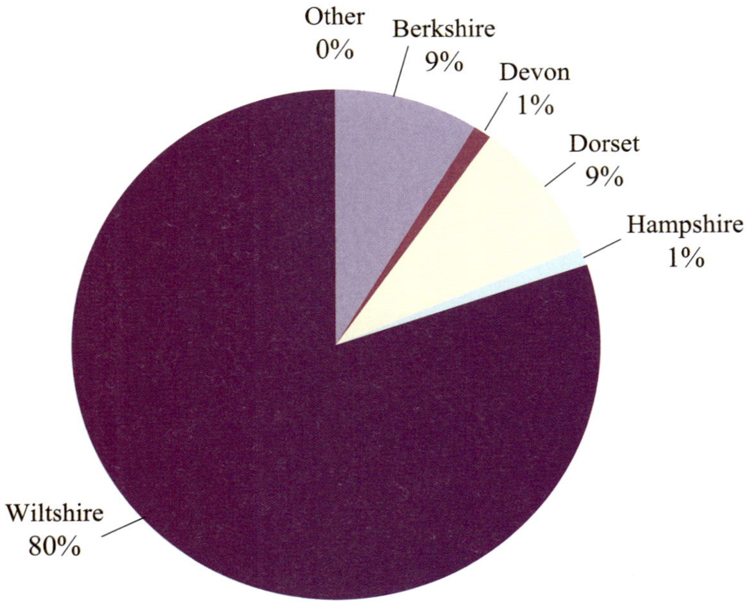

Chart 1 Proportion of wills by county

Abbreviations used in the text

AB	administration bond
a/c	account
admon	administration
aff	affidavit
alleg	allegation
alias	alias
All C.	All Cannings
Alton B.	Alton Barnes
Alton P.	Alton Pancras
Alton Pr.	Alton Priors
Amesb.	Amesbury
And.	Andrew
Anth.	Anthony
Ashton G.	Ashton Giffard
Ashton K.	Ashton Keynes
Aston U.	Aston Upthorpe
Barford St M.	Barford St Martin
Beam.	Beaminster
Benj.	Benjamin
Bere R.	Bere Regis
Berks.	Berkshire
Berwick B.	Berwick Bassett
Bower C.	Bower Chalke
Bps. C.	Bishops Cannings
Bradford A.	Bradford on Avon
Brinkw.	Brinkworth
Brixton D.	Brixton Deverill
Broad B.	Broad Blunsdon
Broad C.	Broad Chalke
Broad H.	Broad Hinton
Brokenb.	Brokenborough
Broughton G.	Broughton Gifford
Bulk.	Bulkington
Calstone W.	Calstone Wellington
Castle C.	Castle Combe
Cath.	Catherine
Chards.	Chardstock
Charl. nr. P.	Charlton near Pewsey
Chas.	Charles
Chilton F.	Chilton Foliat
Chipp.	Chippenham
Chitterne AS	Chitterne All Saints
Chris.	Christopher
Chr. M.	Christian Malford
clothw.	clothworker
Clyffe P.	Clyffe Pypard
Codf.	Codford
Collingbourne D.	Collingbourne Ducis
Collingbourne K.	Collingbourne Kingston
Compton B.	Compton Bassett
Compton C.	Compton Chamberlayne
Coombe B.	Coombe Bissett
Crick.	Cricklade
Crick. St S.	Cricklade St Sampson
D	deposition
Dan.	Daniel
Dilton M.	Dilton Marsh
Donhead St A.	Donhead St Andrew
Draycot C.	Draycot Cerne
E.	East
Edmd.	Edmund
Edwd.	Edward
Eliz.	Elizabeth
Figh.	Figheldean
Fisherton A.	Fisherton Anger
Fisherton D.	Fisherton Delamere
Fonthill B.	Fonthill Bishop
Fonthill G.	Fonthill Gifford
Fugg.	Fugglestone
Geo.	George
Geoff.	Geoffrey
Gilbt.	Gilbert
Grn	Green
Gt.	Great
GVD	Granted at the Metropolitan Visitation to Dorchester
GVS	Granted at the Metropolitan Visitation to Salisbury
Hampstead N.	Hampstead Norris
Hanging L.	Hanging Langford
Hants.	Hampshire
Heytes.	Heytesbury
Highworth	Highw.
Hill D.	Hill Deverill
Hilp.	Hilperton
Hy.	Henry
inty	interrogatory
I	inventory
Jas.	James
Jn.	John
Jos.	Joseph
Kingston D.	Kingston Deverill
Kington L.	Kington Langley
Kington St M.	Kington St Michael
L	letter
LA	letters of admon
Lawr.	Lawrence
Littleton P.	Littleton Pannell
Lt.	Little

Longbridge D.	Longbridge Deverill
Ludg.	Ludgershall
Lydiard M.	Lydiard Millicent
Lydiard T.	Lydiard Tregoze
Lyme R.	Lyme Regis
Maiden B	Maiden Bradley.
Malm.	Malmesbury
Manningford A.	Manningford Abbots
Marl.	Marlborough
Mart.	Martin
Melk.	Melksham
Mgt.	Margaret
Milton L.	Milton Lilborne
Mkt.L.	Market Lavington
Monkton D.	Monkton Deverill
Monkton F.	Monkton Farleigh
Motc.	Motcombe
My.	Mary
N.	North
NBI	Place suggested by National Burial Index
NEP	No evidence of probate
Netherb.	Netherbury
Nether C.	Nether Compton
Netherh.	Netherhampton
Newton T.	Newton Tony
Nich.	Nicholas
Norton B.	Norton Bavant
nr	near
NW	nuncupative will
O	oath
Ogbourne St A.	Ogbourne St Andrew
Over C.	Over Compton
PCC	Prerogative Court of Canterbury
Pott.	Potterne
Quidh.	Quidhampton
Rams.	Ramsbury
Rd.	Richard
ren	renunciation
req	requisition
Robt.	Robert
Rodbourne C.	Rodbourne Cheney
Ryme I.	Ryme Intrinsica
S.	South
Sal.	Salisbury
Sam.	Samuel
Sherb.	Sherborne
Somerford K.	Somerford Keynes
Stanton St B.	Stanton St Bernard
Stanton St Q.	Stanton St Quintin
Steeple A.	Steeple Ashton
Steeple L.	Steeple Langford
Steph.	Stephen
Stoke F.	Stoke Farthing
Stratfield M.	Stratfield Mortimer
Stratford sub C.	Stratford sub Castle
Sutton B.	Sutton Benger
Sutton C.	Sutton Courtenay
Sutton M.	Sutton Mandeville
Sutton V.	Sutton Veny
T	tuition bond
Teffont E.	Teffont Evias
Teffont M.	Teffont Magna
Thos.	Thomas
Tilsh.	Tilshead
Tinh.	Tinhead
Tisb.	Tisbury
Trowb.	Trowbridge
Tytherton L.	Tytherton Lucas
Uffc.	Uffculme
Upton L.	Upton Lovell
Upton S.	Upton Scudamore
Urchfont	Urchf.
vict.	victualler
W	will
W.	West
Wanb.	Wanborough
Warm	Warminster
Wedh.	Wedhampton
Westb.	Westbury
Westb. L.	Westbury Leigh
Whitep.	Whiteparish
Winterborne K.	Winterborne Kingston
Winterborne M.	Winterborne Muston
Winterbourne D.	Winterbourne Dauntsey
Winterbourne E.	Winterbourne Earls
Winterbourne G.	Winterbourne Gunner
Winterbourne M.	Winterbourne Monkton
Winterbourne S.	Winterbourne Stoke
Wm.	William
Wokm.	Wokingham
Woodb.	Woodborough
Wootton B.	Wootton Bassett
Wootton R.	Wootton Rivers
Wr	wrapper
Wrou.	Wroughton
Yetm.	Yetminster

INTRODUCTION

Probate jurisdictions included

One of the best collections of local probate records is held by the Wiltshire and Swindon Archives. These 105,000 records, comprising over 400,000 individual papers the archive of the various probate courts of the diocese of Salisbury. The main courts were the Bishop's Consistory Court, the two Archdeaconry courts (the Archdeaconry of Wiltshire in the north; the Archdeaconry of Sarum in the south of the county), the Sub-Dean's Court covering Salisbury and Stratford sub Castle, and the Dean's Court. In addition, there were several small jurisdictions covering either a single parish or group of parishes, attached to various lay or clerical dignitaries. As a result, there are records for 29 different jurisdictions at the Record Office, covering the whole of Wiltshire, parts of Dorset, Hampshire and Berkshire and the Devon parish of Uffculme. There are a small number of strays from Somerset, Gloucestershire and a number of other counties. In spite of the transfer of the deaneries of Malmesbury and Cricklade to Bristol Diocese in 1836, wills from these areas continued to be proved in the courts of the Archdeacon of Wiltshire and Bishop of Salisbury. A parish map of these jurisdictions is appended to this introduction.

The situation is complicated by the 'inhibition' or taking-over of the jurisdiction of most of the lower level courts every three years by the Bishop's or Dean's courts for a period of about six months. Thus the Consistory Court of Salisbury inhibited the jurisdiction of the Archdeacon of Berkshire. During the Bishop's visitation, wills that were normally proved at the Archdeacon's Court had to be proved in the Bishop's Court. The Dean's Court 'inhibited' those of nearly all the peculiar jurisdictions, the main exception being that of the Dean and Chapter.

Chart 1 shows the proportion of wills from each county. As will be seen, fully one in five of the wills have non-Wiltshire testators.

Salisbury Probate Documents

As elsewhere Salisbury diocesan probate records are concerned generally with people of a lower social status than those whose wills were proved in the Prerogative Court of Canterbury. They are therefore mostly from the ranks of farmers, yeomen, tradesmen and artisans.

Most of the records are original wills and bonds, that is those actually signed by the testator or administrator, although some wills survive as (and sometimes only as) copies entered in registers. Where a person died leaving no will, the right to administer the estate might be applied for to the court. The court required a bond to be entered into (to distribute the estate properly) before granting this. In addition, administrations could be granted even where there was a will, when the executor had died, refused to act (by renouncing their rights) or where the heirs were under age or lunatics, for example. Administration bonds give only the names of next-of-kin and of two or three bondsmen or sureties, who might or might not be relatives. However, they may be made many years after the death, and give details of the surviving family not easily obtainable elsewhere. Inventories of the dead person's goods and chattels also survive, though these are rarely found after about 1750. They vary greatly in length and detail. There are also about 2,000 16th and 17th century administrators' accounts.

The relationship between a master or mistress and servants is an interesting one. Popularly supposed to be exploitative or even cruel, the many bequests in wills from masters to servants, often stated in affectionate terms, shows that this was not always the case. Even more touching is the will of Gilbert Pether of Arborfield, who in 1569 left all his estate to his master, Richard Bullocke 'for seeing me kept and cherished while I was sick'. It was not uncommon, indeed, for servants to leave bequests to their masters.

A very interesting will is that of Elizabeth Martyn, the last Prioress of Wintney Priory, Hampshire. Since the priory was suppressed in 1536 at the latest, Elizabeth must have been quite an age when she died in 1587. Although she died at Wokingham, she left money for her body to be conveyed to, and buried at, Hartley Wintney. She gave directions that "a stone should be layd over my grave, with a picture made of a plate of a woman in a long garment with wyde sleves hir handes ioyned together holdinge upon her brest and figured over her head In te domine speram non confundor in aeternam. In iustica tua libera me, et salva me." She also directs that "an herse should be standinge over my grave by the space of an whole yere covered with black cotton with a croisse of white fustyan."

Life was very hard for many nuns forced to leave their religious houses, for they had taken lifelong vows of celibacy, and could not marry; Elizabeth Martyn, indeed, describes Jesus as "the only spouse of my sowle", but luckily she had had relatives to turn to in Wokingham, many of whom were remembered in her will. One of her bequests is of her "great ringe with the crapowlde (toadstone) in itt", and she also left a jacinth ring. She must have given one of them away before her death, though, as her inventory refers to only one ring "that was uppon her fynger when she dyed." It was valued at 2s 6d.

William Payne of Winterslow in his will proved in 1558 left to Thomas Bundy a harness girdle decorated with 62 silver fleur de lys which was to be passed down among future generations of the Bundy xfamily. In 1558 the vicar of Chitterne St Mary made a bequest of his horse with a glass eye. Rather then referring to a cosmetic device it is far more probable that the animal had a cataract which made his eye glazed.

The History of the Documents

In January 1858 civil registries became responsible for probate matters. The Diocesan probate records were sent from Salisbury to the new Principal Probate Registry at Doctors' Commons in London. Conditions there were far from ideal, as Charles Dickens described in *David Copperfield*:

"I replied ... that perhaps it was a little nonsensical that the Registry of the Court, containing the original wills of all persons leaving effects within the immense province of Canterbury, for three whole centuries, should be an accidental building, never designed for the purpose, leased by the registrars for their own private emolument, unsafe, not even ascertained to be fire-proof, choked with the important documents it held, and positively, from the roof to the basement, a mercenary speculation of the registrars, who took great fees from the public, and crammed the public's wills away anyhow and anywhere, having no other object than to get rid of them cheaply."

In 1874 the wills were moved to Somerset House, home of the General Register Office. Somerset House was not able to cope with the volume of documents it received. Undertaking research there was a challenge: the search room was below ground level and had no artificial light. It closed for 6 weeks in the summer and for a further six weeks it was only open between 11am and 2.30pm. Furthermore, you were not allowed to visit on more than two days per week!

After the Second World War, the development of a network of county record offices provided a sensible alternative place of deposit for the probate material. The Salisbury wills and administrations were transferred to the Wiltshire and Swindon Record Office (renamed Wiltshire and Swindon Archives in 2007) which became the official repository for the records of the diocese of Salisbury.

Wiltshire and Swindon History Centre in Cocklebury Road, Chippenham, opened in Autumn 2007 and comprises Wiltshire and Swindon Archives and also Local Studies, Archaeology, Conservation and Museum services and the Wiltshire Buildings Record.

The Wiltshire Wills Project

For many years the collection of probate documents had been poorly stored. Instead of lying flat in boxes of a suitable size, they were folded into small parcels and forced into inadequate containers. A significant quantity of the material was in poor condition.

Until recently there was no comprehensive, all-embracing index to the records. Each of the courts had its own manuscript index, some arranged chronologically and others by the initial letter of the testator's surname and then by date.

The Wiltshire Wills Project (in fact covering all probate records of the whole diocese of Salisbury), supported by a grant from the Heritage Lottery Fund (HLF) of £200,000 and funding from other charitable bodies and individuals, was developed to catalogue and repair the documents and compile a database of them, to be made available freely on the Internet. Once the database was published the Record Office foresaw an increased demand for the collection from researchers. As increased usage would make the material even more vulnerable to damage, it was decided to produce surrogate images of the collection by digitisation.

The documents were flattened and repackaged by a team of volunteers (led by the conservation team), conserved where necessary, and filmed using the digital camera. A state of the art "leaf-casting" machine was used to repair damaged documents. A paper pulp mixture was drained through the holes in the will. The pulp filled the gaps and, as it dried, paper patches formed in the document. In order to ensure that the images produced by the Project are those most suitable for researchers, the Record Office conducted a user evaluation of images of wills, digitised at different levels of colour and resolution. Over 200 readers were consulted and the results of the survey defined the specification for the images. The images were then checked to ensure they were of the highest quality. Full colour images have been made available on DVDs at the Wiltshire and Swindon Archives, and at the Central Reference Library in Swindon. Some 25% of the wills have images available on the online catalogue.

Work progressed steadily, and cataloguing was completed in early 2006. During the cataloguing many misplaced documents were found. A marriage licence bond was discovered with the Dean's wills and has been placed in the main licence series. An administration bond for the goods of Elizabeth Pratt of Faringdon, issued by the Peculiar Court of Faringdon, was sent to the Berkshire Record Office where it was reunited with Elizabeth Pratt's nuncupative will - the documents had probably been apart for centuries.

Series P30 originally contained over 2,000 documents which while they were transferred to the District Probate Registry had remained in diocesan custody. An index to the Wiltshire documents was published by C.R. Everett in Wiltshire Archaeology Magazine volume 45, 1930 and to the non-Wiltshire material in the Genealogists' Magazine. Some documents were lost between 1930 and 1958 when they came into the Record Office. As the work progressed items from this series were returned to their appropriate court and in many cases matched up with other documents relating to a particular testator. At the conclusion of cataloguing only about 200 documents remained in class P30.

As the printed index was prepared, a large number of further errors and discrepancies were noticed and where necessary corrections made. Indeed this process is one, though only one, of the justifications for the continued production of printed indexes.

Publication History

It had always been intended that the database be published in traditional book form as well as online. Discussions were had between the Wiltshire Record Society and the British Record Society as to which of them should publish the work, or whether it should be a joint publication.

The size of the database made it clear that the index would occupy more tha one volume. The Wiltshire Record Society already had a full programme of publications, into which more than one volume could only be inserted at an interval of several years. This would delay not only the second half of the alphabet, but also the apparatus of supplementary indexes, necessary for many users. Many members, especially the institutional, would be shared, and would not want two copies. The British Record Society had, as one of its series, will indexes. Since the index could be fitted into two (albeit large) volumes, they could be published by them simultaneously. It was therefore decided that the British Record Society alone would publish the printed text.

In May 2006, the computer files were delivered to the British Record Society Probate Series general editor.

Editorial Method

The initial task was to make the Excel files more standardised, and check for obvious discrepancies. The index compilers had not attempted to bring together documents appertaining to a single testator thus, as a simple example, a filed copy and a registered copy of the same will had generated two entries which needed conflating. While it is to be hoped that no conflated entries belong to different testators, there is the certainty that many administration bonds, for example, have not been linked to the original will.

Seemingly innumerable queries arose, which were cheerfully dealt with by Wiltshire Record Office. Marks had to be introduced that would enable the supplementary indexes of places, trades, etc. to be created.

Using pivot tables, the Excel spreadsheets were made to generate various statistical data (to be found later in this introduction). This is the first British Record Society work (but will undoubtedly not be the last) to use technology to map and analyse willmaking patterns in ways difficult or impossible in the pre-computer age. This information is presented here, because it cannot be obtained readily from the printed volumes.

The Excel spreadsheets had to then be converted into Word files so that the text proper could be constructed.

Number of wills over time.

The number of documents by year is shown in table 1 and chart 2.

Table 1 Number of wills by year

Early oddments: 1464 – 1 1479 – 1 1519 – 1 1526 – 1 1528 – 1 1530 – 2 1534 - 1

1537	5	1549	48	1561	159	1573	163	1585	151	1597	283
1538	11	1550	80	1562	136	1574	183	1586	125	1598	189
1539	18	1551	70	1563	171	1575	190	1587	183	1599	123
1540	28	1552	77	1564	158	1576	175	1588	229	1600	175
1541	34	1553	53	1565	108	1577	73	1589	151	1601	184
1542	30	1554	63	1566	121	1578	120	1590	174	1602	236
1543	42	1555	68	1567	175	1579	193	1591	206	1603	272
1544	15	1556	59	1568	88	1580	166	1592	206	1604	218
1545	49	1557	205	1569	203	1581	170	1593	247	1605	313
1546	82	1558	261	1570	280	1582	162	1594	223	1606	343
1547	71	1559	270	1571	234	1583	141	1595	128	1607	240
1548	51	1560	145	1572	150	1584	110	1596	163	1608	294

Table 1 Contd.

1609	351	1651	22	1693	464	1735	467	1777	266	1819	230
1610	386	1652	25	1694	445	1736	317	1778	235	1820	274
1611	348	1653	12	1695	486	1737	373	1779	267	1821	209
1612	357	1654	12	1696	393	1738	483	1780	248	1822	225
1613	376	1655	5	1697	347	1739	347	1781	253	1823	289
1614	405	1656	6	1698	432	1740	411	1782	272	1824	241
1615	298	1657	2	1699	341	1741	492	1783	290	1825	252
1616	400	1658	7	1700	339	1742	395	1784	231	1826	275
1617	292	1659	7	1701	439	1743	396	1785	266	1827	280
1618	293	1660	68	1702	335	1744	451	1786	248	1828	250
1619	396	1661	253	1703	335	1745	318	1787	198	1829	300
1620	325	1662	452	1704	369	1746	319	1788	190	1830	248
1621	299	1663	417	1705	416	1747	370	1789	262	1831	224
1622	329	1664	373	1706	382	1748	332	1790	201	1832	287
1623	315	1665	331	1707	327	1749	298	1791	188	1833	214
1624	316	1666	295	1708	386	1750	383	1792	248	1834	203
1625	397	1667	453	1709	390	1751	358	1793	204	1835	282
1626	359	1668	477	1710	387	1752	281	1794	175	1836	254
1627	303	1669	494	1711	539	1753	352	1795	252	1837	295
1628	436	1670	574	1712	405	1754	261	1796	162	1838	211
1629	334	1671	526	1713	377	1755	264	1797	255	1839	204
1630	378	1672	452	1714	456	1756	356	1798	306	1840	197
1631	468	1673	376	1715	382	1757	263	1799	252	1841	208
1632	354	1674	390	1716	443	1758	294	1800	264	1842	231
1633	372	1675	375	1717	427	1759	322	1801	258	1843	189
1634	333	1676	418	1718	371	1760	282	1802	274	1844	231
1635	395	1677	415	1719	408	1761	243	1803	264	1845	215
1636	405	1678	375	1720	567	1762	311	1804	293	1846	202
1637	340	1679	429	1721	437	1763	385	1805	209	1847	216
1638	572	1680	482	1722	417	1764	259	1806	246	1848	226
1639	524	1681	587	1723	479	1765	265	1807	250	1849	189
1640	438	1682	566	1724	457	1766	331	1808	279	1850	213
1641	375	1683	523	1725	352	1767	346	1809	240	1851	206
1642	168	1684	620	1726	438	1768	245	1810	222	1852	232
1643	143	1685	592	1727	399	1769	298	1811	272	1853	238
1644	168	1686	533	1728	493	1770	316	1812	213	1854	221
1645	156	1687	472	1729	713	1771	267	1813	229	1855	209
1646	186	1688	420	1730	531	1772	250	1814	287	1856	212
1647	166	1689	484	1731	453	1773	347	1815	236	1857	195
1648	151	1690	443	1732	512	1774	227	1816	220	1858	7
1649	75	1691	392	1733	433	1775	284	1817	213		
1650	46	1692	452	1734	350	1776	325	1818	212		

Probate business, or rather the number of surviving probate documents rises steadily until the onset of the Civil War when it drops precipitously (as one would expect). With the Restoration numbers immediately recover to pre-Civil War levels. From the 1740s, numbers slowly drop until the 1780s, after which there is little change. Unlike some courts nearer the Metropolis, business never dries up completely until the end of ecclesiastical probate jurisdiction.

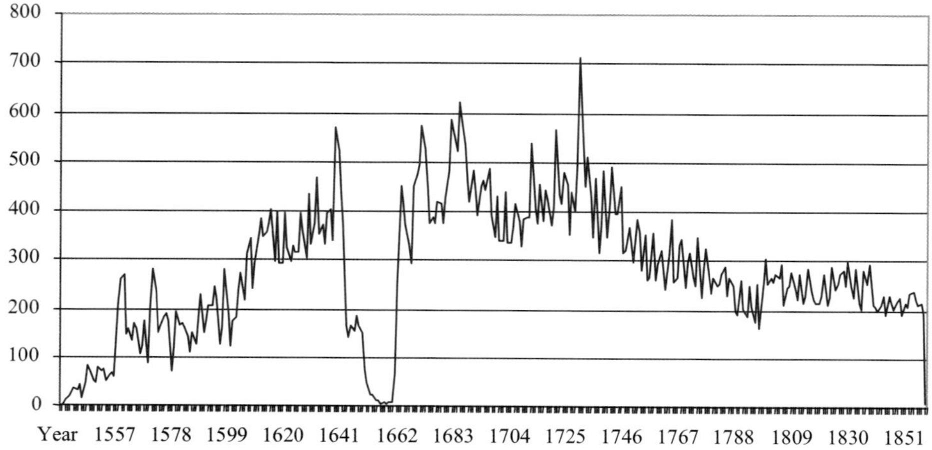

Chart 2 Will Numbers

Christian names

Of the testators just under 70,000 were men (77.17%) and just over 20,000 female (22.83%). Some 500 different male christian names are represented and just under half that number of female.
The distribution of the commonest christian names seems little different from normal. Table 2 shows the ten commonest male and female christian names. More than 75% of male and 70% of female testators had one of the ten commonest names.

Table 2 The ten commonest male and female christian names

John	15780	22.71%	Mary	3121	15.19%
William	10420	15.00%	Elizabeth	2940	14.31%
Thomas	8748	12.59%	Ann(e/a)	2182	10.62%
Richard	4547	6.54%	Joan(na)	1573	7.65%
Robert	4099	5.90%	Sarah	1062	5.17%
Henry	2343	3.37%	Jane	994	4.84%
James	2336	3.36%	Alice	978	4.76%
Edward	2279	3.28%	Margaret	789	3.84%
George	1732	2.49%	Agnes	559	2.72%
Joseph	1172	1.69%	Susan(na)	511	2.49%

Such tables of other counties will be needed before we can say which middling common names are more or less common in Wiltshire than normal. However, some names occur which are definitely unusual. Praxey (variously Praxed and Praxy) is the name of eight women (the earliest in 1618) mainly of apparently different families; the only name in the Oxford Dictionary of Christian Names to which it may be related is Protasia. Similarly, there are five women called Warborough, the earliest in 1571.

As would be expected, only a very small proportion of testators had 2 or more christian names. Just 0.59% of male and 0.78% of female testators had more than one christian name, a gender difference entirely and, interestingly, exactly explained by Mary Ann, which with Anna Maria, are the only combinations for either sex with more than a handful of examples.

Occupations

Wiltshire and its surrounding areas is and was primarily an agricultural society. Just over half of male testators were engaged in primary industry, while nearly 10% worked with wood.

Although one would expect most gentry to prove their wills in the Prerogative Court of Canterbury, in fact 7% of the wills came from this group. There was, again as would be expected a smattering of professionals and merchants, mainly in Salisbury and the other market towns.

Chart 3 and Table 3 show the distribution of occupational groups among male testators.

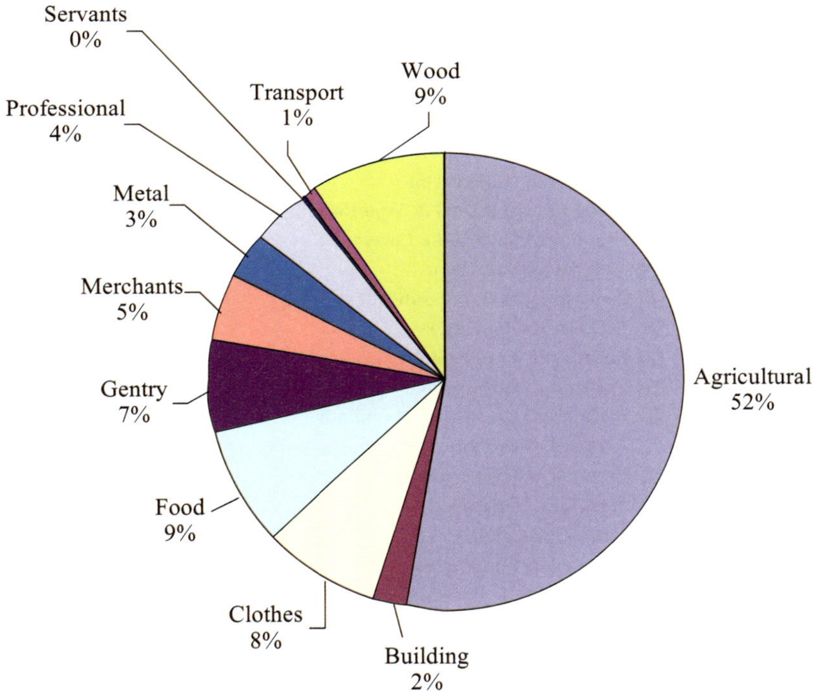

Chart 3 Occupations of Wiltshire male testators

Table 3 Occupations of male testators

Agricultural	23581	52.60%
Builders	1002	2.23%
Clothes & Weaving	3501	7.81%
Food & Drink	3812	8.50%
Gentry	3009	6.71%
Merchants & Traders	2130	4.75%
Metalworkers	1474	3.29%
Professionals & Officials	1735	3.87%
Servants	144	0.32%
Transport	309	0.69%
Wood, Leather Etc. Workers	4131	9.21%
Unidentified	7	0.02%
Total	44835	100.00%

Key to Map of Probate Jurisdictions in Wiltshire and the Diocese of Salisbury

- Archdeaconry of Wiltshire
- Archdeaconry of Salisbury (Sarum)
- Deanery of Salisbury
- Prebend of Chute & Chisenbury
- Archdeaconry of Winchester
- Peculiar of Corsham
- Peculiar of Castle Combe
- Peculiar of the Treasurer
- Peculiar of Precentor
- Dean & Chapter of Salisbury
- Deanery of Windsor
- Prebend of Hurstbourne & Burbage
- Prebend of Netheravon
- Prebend of Wilsford & Woodford
- Peculiar of Savernake Forest
- Peculiar of Sub-Dean
- Consistory Court of Salisbury
- Diocese of Gloucester
- Peculiar of Trowbridge
- Prebend of Bishopstone
- Prebend of Coombe & Harnham
- Prebend of Durnford
- Prebend of Highworth
- Peculiar of Uffculme
- Extra-parochial
- Prebend of Fordington
- Peculiar of the Prebend of Lyme and Halstock
- Prebend of Chardstock and Wambrook
- Prebendal Court of Netherbury
- Prebendal Court Preston and Sutton Poyntz
- Prebend of Yetminster
- Royal Peculiar of Gillingham

Wiltshire Probate Jurisdictions

For key see facing page

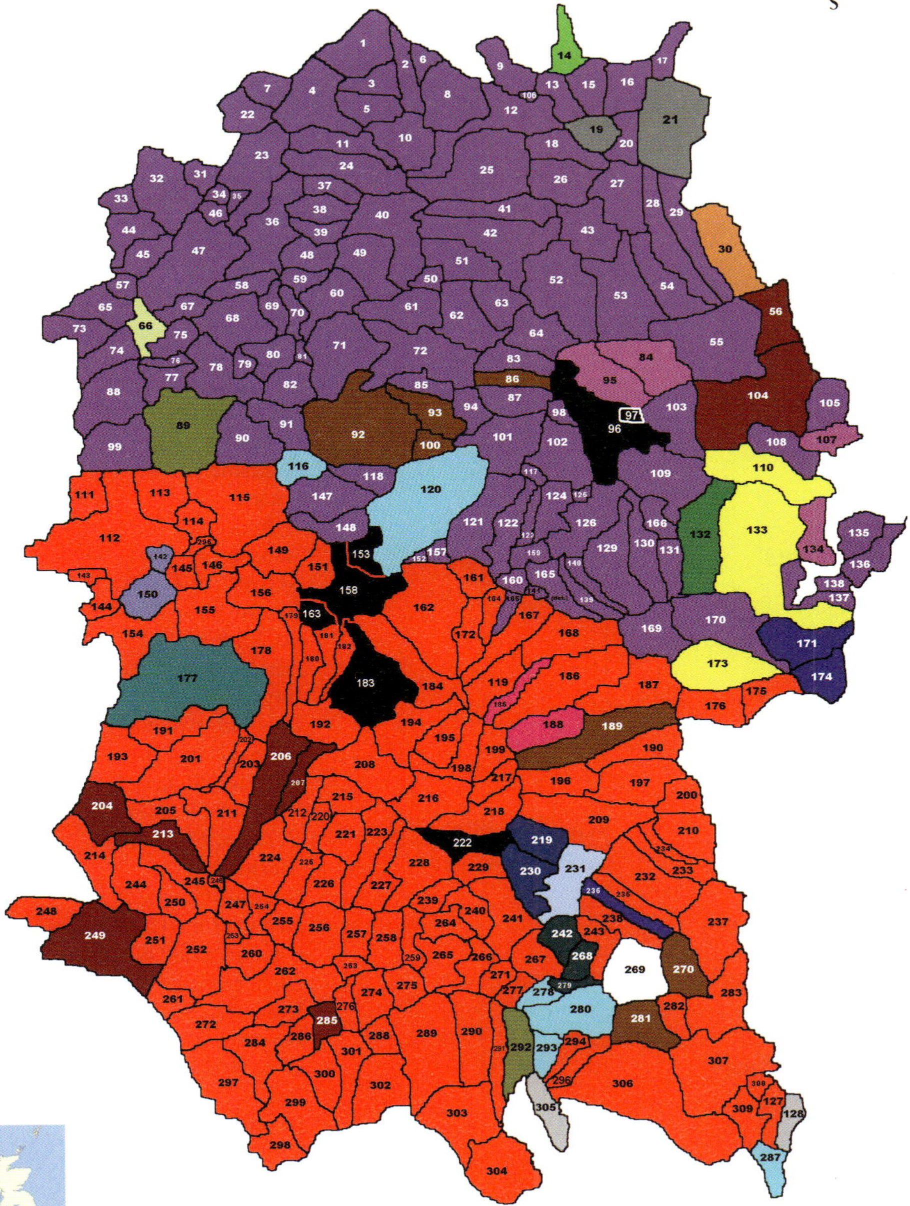

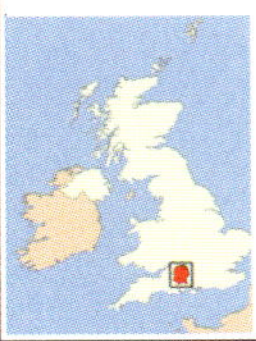

Places

The following Table 4 shows the number assigned to each parish on the parish map. There are two sequences, one in parish order, one in number order. It should be noted that for the compilation of statistics, it has not been possible to distinguish Fyfield from Fifield Bavant, or the different Charlton and Wilsford parishes. Blackland and Bowood are included in Calne, Bratton in Westbury, Chalfield in Atworth, Ditteridge in Box, Draycot Foliat in Chisledon, Fisherton Anger and No Man's Land in Salisbury, Grittleton in Hullavington, Highway in Hilmarton, Standlynch in Downton and Westport St Mary in Brokenborough.

Table 4 Key to Wiltshire parishes

Parishes by numerical order		Parishes by name	
Kemble	1	Aldbourne	55
Somerford Keynes	2	Alderbury	281
Poole Keynes	3	Alderton	45
Crudwell	4	All Cannings	121
Oaksey	5	Allington	234
Shorncote	6	Alton Barnes	123
Ashley	7	Alton Priors	124
Ashton Keynes	8	Alvediston	300
Latton	9	Amesbury	209
Minety	10	Ansty	286
Hankerton	11	Ashley	7
Cricklade St Sampson	12	Ashton Keynes	8
Eisey	13	Atworth & Chalfield	113
Marston Meysey	14	Avebury	101
Castle Eaton	15	Barford	265
Hannington	16	Baverstock	259
Inglesham	17	Baydon	56
Blunsdon St Andrew	18	Beechingstoke	160
Broad Blunsdon incl.Highworth	19	Berwick Bassett	86
Stanton Fitzwarren	20	Berwick St James	222
Highworth	21	Berwick St John	299
Long Newnton	22	Berwick St Leonard	254
Brokenborough	23	Biddestone	77
Charlton (Hankerton)	24	Bishops Canning	120
Purton	25	Bishopstone (Little Hinton)	30
Rodbourne Cheney	26	Bishopstone (Wilton)	290
Stratton St Margaret	27	Bishopstrow	202
Wanborough	28	Blunsdon St Andrew	18
Little Hinton	29	Boscombe	233
Bishopstone (Little Hinton)	30	Bowerchalke	302
Grey Easton	31	Box	99
Sherston Magna	32	Boyton	224
Sopworth	33	Bradford on Avon	112
Foxley	34	Bramshaw	287
Bremilham	35	Bremhill	71
Malmesbury	36	Bremilham	35
Garsdon	37	Brinkworth	40
Lea and Cleverton	38	Britford	280
Little Somerford	39	Brixton Deverill	245

Table 4 Contd.

Parishes by numerical order		Parishes by name	
Brinkworth	40	Broad Blunsdon incl.Highworth	19
Lydiard Millicent	41	Broad Chalke	289
Lydiard Tregoze	42	Broad Hinton	64
Swindon	43	Broad Town	63
Luckington	44	Brokenborough	23
Alderton	45	Bromham	147
Norton Coleparle	46	Broughton Gifford	114
Hullavington	47	Bulford	197
Great Somerford	48	Burbage	132
Dauntsey	49	Burcombe	266
Tockenham	50	Buttermere	136
Wootton Bassett	51	Calne	92
Wroughton	52	Calstone Wellington	100
Chisledon	53	Castle Coombe	66
Liddington	54	Castle Eaton	15
Aldbourne	55	Charlton (Hankerton)	24
Baydon	56	Charlton (Rushall)	167
Littleton Drew	57	Cherhill	93
Stanton St Quintin	58	Chicklade	247
Seagry	59	Chilmark	256
Christian Malford	60	Chilton Foliatt	105
Lyneham	61	Chippenham	78
Clyffe Pypard	62	Chirton	172
Broad Town	63	Chisenbury	185
Broad Hinton	64	Chisledon	53
Nettleton	65	Chitterne All Saints	208
Castle Coombe	66	Chitterne St Mary	215
Leigh Delamere	67	Chittoe	116
Kington St Michael	68	Cholderton	200
Draycot Cerne	69	Christian Malford	60
Sutton Benger	70	Chute	171
Bremhill	71	Chute Forest	174
Hilmarton	72	Clarendon Park	269
West Kington	73	Clyffe Pypard	62
North Wraxall	74	Codford St Mary	221
Yatton Keynell	75	Codford St Peter	220
Slaughterford	76	Colerne	88
Biddestone	77	Collingbourne Ducis	173
Chippenham	78	Collingbourne Kingston	170
Hardenhuish	79	Compton Bassett	85
Langley Burrell	80	Compton Chamberlain	275
Tytherton Kellaways	81	Coombe Bisset	292
Tytherton Lucas	82	Corsham	89
Winterbourne Bassett	83	Corsley	193
Ogbourne St George	84	Cricklade St Mary	106
Compton Bassett	85	Cricklade St Sampson	12
Berwick Bassett	86	Crudwell	4
Winterbourne Monkton	87	Dauntsey	49
Colerne	88	Devizes	153

Table 4 Contd.

Parishes by numerical order		Parishes by name	
Corsham	89	Dinton	258
Lacock	90	Donhead St Andrew	284
Pewsham	91	Donhead St Mary	297
Calne	92	Downton	306
Cherhill	93	Draycot Cerne	69
Yatesbury	94	Durnford	231
Ogbourne St Andrew	95	Durrington	196
Preshute	96	East Coulston	179
Marlborough	97	East Kennett	117
Fyfield	98	East Knoyle	252
Box	99	Easton Royal	131
Calstone Wellington	100	Ebbesbourne Wake	301
Avebury	101	Edington	178
Overton	102	Eisey	13
Mildenhall	103	Enford	186
Ramsbury	104	Erlestoke	180
Chilton Foliatt	105	Etchilhampton	152
Cricklade St Mary	106	Everleigh	169
Hungerford	107	Fifield Bavant	288
Froxfield	108	Figheldean	189
Savernake	109	Fisherton Delamere	223
Little Bedwin	110	Fittleton	187
Monkton Farleigh	111	Fonthill Bishop	255
Bradford on Avon	112	Fonthill Gifford	260
Atworth & Chalfield	113	Fovant	274
Broughton Gifford	114	Foxley	34
Melksham	115	Froxfield	108
Chittoe	116	Fugglestone St Peter	267
East Kennett	117	Fyfield	98
Heddington	118	Garsdon	37
Rushall	119	Great Bedwin	133
Bishops Canning	120	Great Cheverell	181
All Cannings	121	Great Somerford	48
Stanton St Bernard	122	Great Wishford	240
Alton Barnes	123	Grey Easton	31
Alton Priors	124	Groveley Wood	264
Huish	125	Ham	135
Wilcot	126	Hankerton	11
Plaitford	127	Hannington	16
West Wellow	128	Hardenhuish	79
Pewsey	129	Heddington	118
Milton Lilborne	130	Heytesbury	206
Easton Royal	131	Highworth	21
Burbage	132	Hill Deverill	213
Great Bedwin	133	Hilmarton	72
Shalbourne	134	Hilperton	145
Ham	135	Hindon	253
Buttermere	136	Hippenscombe	137
Hippenscombe	137	Homington	293

Table 4 Contd.

Parishes by numerical order		Parishes by name	
Tidcombe	138	Horningsham	204
Manningford Bruce	139	Huish	125
Manningford Abbots	140	Hullavington	47
North Newnton	141	Hungerford	107
Staverton	142	Idmiston	232
Westwood	143	Imber	192
Hilperton	145	Inglesham	17
Semington	146	Keevil	156
Bromham	147	Kemble	1
Rowde	148	Kingston Deverill	244
Seend	149	Kington St Michael	68
Trowbridge	150	Knook	207
Poulshot	151	Lacock	90
Etchilhampton	152	Landford	309
Devizes	153	Langley Burrell	80
North Bradley	154	Latton	9
Steeple Ashton	155	Laverstock and Ford	243
Keevil	156	Lea and Cleverton	38
Stert	157	Leigh Delamere	67
Potterne	158	Liddington	54
Woodborough	159	Little Bedwin	110
Beechingstoke	160	Little Cheverell	182
Patney	161	Little Hinton	29
Urchfont	162	Little Langford	239
Worton and Marston	163	Little Somerford	39
Marden	164	Littleton Drew	57
Wilsford (Pewsey)	165	Long Newnton	22
Wootton Rivers	166	Longbridge Deverill	205
Charlton (Rushall)	167	Luckington	44
Upavon	168	Ludgershall	175
Everleigh	169	Lydiard Millicent	41
Collingbourne Kingston	170	Lydiard Tregoze	42
Chute	171	Lyneham	61
Chirton	172	Maddington	216
Collingbourne Ducis	173	Maiden Bradley	214
Chute Forest	174	Malmesbury	36
Ludgershall	175	Manningford Abbots	140
North Tidworth	176	Manningford Bruce	139
incl.Bratton	177	Marden	164
Edington	178	Market Lavington	184
East Coulston	179	Marlborough	97
Erlestoke	180	Marston Meysey	14
Great Cheverell	181	Martin	303
Little Cheverell	182	Melchet Park	308
West Lavington	183	Melksham	115
Market Lavington	184	Mere	249
Chisenbury	185	Mildenhall	103
Enford	186	Milford	268
Fittleton	187	Milston	190

Table 4 Contd.

Parishes by numerical order		Parishes by name	
Netheravon	188	Milton Lilborne	130
Figheldean	189	Minety	10
Milston	190	Monkton Deverill	250
Upton Scudamore	191	Monkton Farleigh	111
Imber	192	Netheravon	188
Corsley	193	Netherhampton	277
Orcheston St Mary	195	Nettleton	65
Tilshead	195	Newton Tony	210
Durrington	196	North Bradley	154
Bulford	197	North Newnton	141
Orcheston St George	198	North Tidworth	176
Shrewton	199	North Wraxall	74
Cholderton	200	Norton Bavant	203
Warminster	201	Norton Coleparle	46
Bishopstrow	202	Nunton and Bodenham	296
Norton Bavant	203	Oaksey	5
Horningsham	204	Odstock	294
Longbridge Deverill	205	Ogbourne St Andrew	95
Heytesbury	206	Ogbourne St George	84
Knook	207	Orcheston St George	198
Chitterne All Saints	208	Orcheston St Mary	195
Amesbury	209	Overton	102
Newton Tony	210	Patney	161
Sutton Veny	211	Pertwood	246
Upton Lovell	212	Pewsey	129
Hill Deverill	213	Pewsham	91
Maiden Bradley	214	Pitton and Farley	270
Chitterne St Mary	215	Plaitford	127
Maddington	216	Poole Keynes	3
Rollstone	217	Potterne	158
Winterbourne Stoke	218	Poulshot	151
Wilsford (Amesbury)	219	Preshute	96
Codford St Peter	220	Purton	25
Codford St Mary	221	Ramsbury	104
Berwick St James	222	Rodbourne Cheney	26
Fisherton Delamere	223	Rollstone	217
Boyton	224	Rowde	148
Sherrington	225	Rushall	119
Stockton	226	Salisbury	279
Wylye	227	Savernake	109
Steeple Langford	228	Seagry	59
Stapleford	229	Sedgehill	261
Woodford	230	Seend	149
Durnford	231	Semington	146
Idmiston	232	Semley	272
Boscombe	233	Shalbourne	134
Allington	234	Sherrington	225
Winterbourne Gunner	235	Sherston Magna	32
Winterbourne Dauntsey	236	Shorncote	6

Table 4 Contd.

Parishes by numerical order		Parishes by name	
Winterslow	237	Shrewton	199
Winterbourne Earls	238	Slaughterford	76
Little Langford	239	Somerford Keynes	2
Great Wishford	240	Sopworth	33
South Newton	241	South Damerham	304
Stratford Subcastle	242	South Newton	241
Laverstock and Ford	243	Stanton Fitzwarren	20
Kingston Deverill	244	Stanton St Bernard	122
Brixton Deverill	245	Stanton St Quintin	58
Pertwood	246	Stapleford	229
Chicklade	247	Staverton	142
Stourton	248	Steeple Ashton	155
Mere	249	Steeple Langford	228
Monkton Deverill	250	Stert	157
West Knoyle	251	Stockton	226
East Knoyle	252	Stourton	248
Hindon	253	Stratford Subcastle	242
Berwick St Leonard	254	Stratford Tony	291
Fonthill Bishop	255	Stratton St Margaret	27
Chilmark	256	Sutton Benger	70
Teffont Magna	257	Sutton Mandeville	276
Dinton	258	Sutton Veny	211
Baverstock	259	Swallowcliffe	285
Fonthill Gifford	260	Swindon	43
Sedgehill	261	Teffont Evias	263
Tisbury	262	Teffont Magna	257
Teffont Evias	263	Tidcombe	138
Groveley Wood	264	Tilshead	195
Barford	265	Tisbury	262
Burcombe	266	Tockenham	50
Fugglestone St Peter	267	Tollard Royal	298
Milford	268	Trowbridge	150
Clarendon Park	269	Tytherton Kellaways	81
Pitton and Farley	270	Tytherton Lucas	82
Wilton	271	Upavon	168
Semley	272	Upton Lovell	212
Wardour	273	Upton Scudamore	191
Fovant	274	Urchfont	162
Compton Chamberlain	275	Wanborough	28
Sutton Mandeville	276	Wardour	273
Netherhampton	277	Warminster	201
West Harnham	278	West Dean	283
Salisbury	279	West Grimstead	282
Britford	280	West Harnham	278
Alderbury	281	West Kington	73
West Grimstead	282	West Knoyle	251
West Dean	283	West Lavington	183
Donhead St Andrew	284	West Wellow	128
Wingfield	144	Westbury incl.Bratton	177

Table 4 Contd.

Parishes by numerical order		Parishes by name	
Swallowcliffe	285	Westwood	143
Ansty	286	Whaddon	295
Bramshaw	287	Whiteparish	307
Fifield Bavant	288	Whitsbury	305
Broad Chalke	289	Wilcot	126
Bishopstone (Wilton)	290	Wilsford (Amesbury)	219
Stratford Tony	291	Wilsford (Pewsey)	165
Coombe Bisset	292	Wilton	271
Homington	293	Wingfield	144
Odstock	294	Winterbourne Bassett	83
Whaddon	295	Winterbourne Dauntsey	236
Nunton and Bodenham	296	Winterbourne Earls	238
Donhead St Mary	297	Winterbourne Gunner	235
Tollard Royal	298	Winterbourne Monkton	87
Berwick St John	299	Winterbourne Stoke	218
Alvediston	300	Winterslow	237
Ebbesbourne Wake	301	Woodborough	159
Bowerchalke	302	Woodford	230
Martin	303	Wootton Bassett	51
South Damerham	304	Wootton Rivers	166
Whitsbury	305	Worton and Marston	163
Downton	306	Wroughton	52
Whiteparish	307	Wylye	227
Melchet Park	308	Yatesbury	94
Landford	309	Yatton Keynell	75

Table 5 shows the number of wills for each Wiltshire place, that place's population in 1801, the number of wills per 100 population in 1801, the number of wills for that place proved in the Prerogative Court of Canterbury, and the total of wills per 100 of 1801's population. The final column therefore indicates how far a given parish's inhabitants were likely to leave a will. This information is repeated in Table 6 for non-Wiltshire parishes in the diocese of Salisbury

The Wiltshire table has also been mapped. This shows a pattern of will-making being more concentrated in the south-east of the county, with another area in the north-west, and with a broad swathe of low activity across the county from south-west to north-east.

The market towns of Salisbury, Marlborough etc. generally had a higher rate of will-making than the more rural parishes. These results need to be compared with several other areas before any more than this can be said.

Wiltshire Will-Making

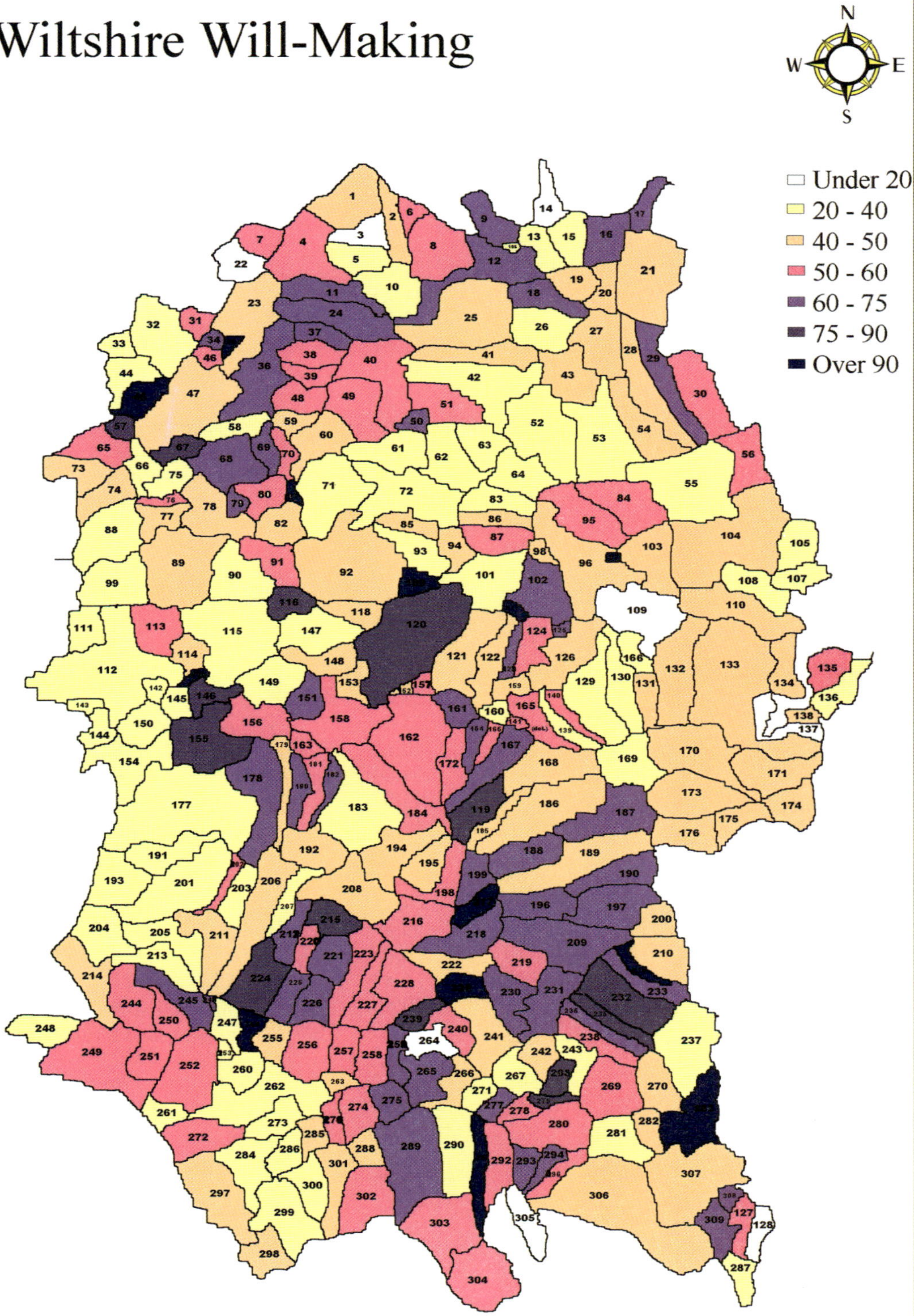

Table 5 Willmaking by Place in the Diocese of Salisbury (Wiltshire)

Parish	**Local Wills**	**1801 Pop.**	**Local Wills Per 100 Pop.**	**PCC Wills Per 100. Pop.**	**PCC + Local Wills Per 100 Pop.**	**Pro-portion per 100 Pop.**
Aldbourne	322	1280	25.16	49	371	28.98
Alderton	74	103	71.84	22	96	93.20
All Cannings	403	911	44.24	27	430	47.20
Allington	67	75	89.33	8	75	100.00
Alton Barnes	43	83	51.81	13	56	67.47
Alton Priors	83	178	46.63	10	93	52.25
Alvediston	47	217	21.66	12	59	27.19
Amesbury	423	721	58.67	102	525	72.82
Ansty	65	242	26.86	8	73	30.17
Ashley	18	75	24.00	23	41	54.67
Ashton Keynes	438	938	46.70	114	552	58.85
Avebury	202	689	29.32	51	253	36.72
Barford St Martin	234	450	52.00	45	279	62.00
Baverstock	62	120	51.67	18	80	66.67
Baydon	120	290	41.38	31	151	52.07
Beechingstoke	47	174	27.01	10	57	32.76
Berwick Bassett	57	158	36.08	12	69	43.67
Berwick St James	86	226	38.05	10	96	42.48
Berwick St John	85	357	23.81	26	111	31.09
Berwick St Leonard	27	36	75.00	8	35	97.22
Biddestone	133	331	40.18	27	160	48.34
Bishops Cannings	714	1108	64.44	146	860	77.62
Bishopstone (North)	228	530	43.02	81	309	58.30
Bishopstone (South)	199	535	37.20	*	*	*
Bishopstrow	85	227	37.44	36	121	53.30
Blackland	1	48	2.08	8	9	18.75
Blunsdon St Andrew	16	65	24.62	32	48	73.85
Boscombe	52	103	50.49	16	68	66.02
Bower Chalk	156	320	48.75	19	175	54.69
Bowood	15	237	6.33	6	21	8.86
Box	243	1165	20.86	111	354	30.39
Boyton	186	248	75.00	32	218	87.90
Bradford on Avon	1674	7302	22.93	543	2217	30.36
Bremhill	407	1303	31.24	88	495	37.99
Bremilham	7	14	50.00	6	13	92.86
Brinkworth	398	923	43.12	77	475	51.46
Britford	300	675	44.44	57	357	52.89
Brixton Deverill	68	144	47.22	23	91	63.19
Broad Chalke	354	625	56.64	44	398	63.68
Broad Hinton	142	550	25.82	45	187	34.00
Brokenborough	99	211	46.92	22	121	57.35
Bromham	352	1154	30.50	93	445	38.56
Broughton Giffard	214	613	34.91	48	262	42.74
Bulford	131	228	57.46	27	158	69.30
Burbage	421	1008	41.77	49	470	46.63

Table 5 Contd.

Parish	**Local Wills**	**1801 Pop.**	**Local Wills Per 100 Pop.**	**PCC Wills Per 100. Pop.**	**PCC + Local Wills Per 100 Pop.**	**Pro-portion per 100 Pop.**
Burcombe	87	253	34.39	17	104	41.11
Buttermere	40	129	31.01	10	50	38.76
Calne	1479	3767	39.26	372	1851	49.14
Calstone Wellington	55	21	261.90	9	64	304.76
Castle Combe	116	567	20.46	33	149	26.28
Castle Eaton	66	295	22.37	33	99	33.56
Chalfield	21	63	33.33	15	36	57.14
Charlton near Malmesbury	235	428	54.91	57	292	68.22
Charlton near Pewsey	131	168	77.98	*	*	*
Cherhill	72	304	23.68	15	87	28.62
Chicklade	44	150	29.33	11	55	36.67
Chilmark	191	406	47.04	39	230	56.65
Chilton Foliat	191	616	31.01	24	215	34.90
Chippenham	1033	3366	30.69	352	1385	41.15
Chirton	159	347	45.82	29	188	54.18
Chiseldon	261	904	28.87	27	288	31.86
Chitterne All Saints	116	314	36.94	19	135	42.99
Chitterne St Mary	100	155	64.52	21	121	78.06
Cholderton	37	127	29.13	15	52	40.94
Christian Malford	413	938	44.03	50	463	49.36
Chute	183	488	37.50	59	242	49.59
Clarendon Park	42	129	32.56	23	65	50.39
Clyffe Pypard	209	624	33.49	40	249	39.90
Codford St Mary	105	187	56.15	15	120	64.17
Codford St Peter	180	393	45.80	31	211	53.69
Colerne	125	693	18.04	53	178	25.69
Collingbourne Ducis	158	457	34.57	37	195	42.67
Collingbourne Kingston	284	731	38.85	65	349	47.74
Compton Bassett	104	366	28.42	46	150	40.98
Compton Chamberlayne	140	283	49.47	30	170	60.07
Coombe Bissett	142	271	52.40	18	160	59.04
Corsham	885	2402	36.84	311	1196	49.79
Corsley	317	1412	22.45	91	408	28.90
Cricklade St Mary	70	376	18.62	38	108	28.72
Cricklade St Sampson	490	957	51.20	141	631	65.94
Crudwell	175	512	34.18	82	257	50.20
Dauntsey	138	357	38.66	45	183	51.26
Devizes	1427	4747	30.06	540	1967	41.44
Dinton	169	421	40.14	44	213	50.59
Ditteridge	16	101	15.84	2	18	17.82
Donhead St Andrew	131	607	21.58	39	170	28.01
Donhead St Mary	373	945	39.47	71	444	46.98
Downton	878	2426	36.19	183	1061	43.73
Draycot Cerne	66	141	46.81	24	90	63.83
Draycot Foliat	12	38	31.58	3	15	39.47
Durnford	219	399	54.89	42	261	65.41

Table 5 Contd.

Parish	**Local Wills**	**1801 Pop.**	**Local Wills Per 100 Pop.**	**PCC Wills Per 100. Pop.**	**PCC + Local Wills Per 100 Pop.**	**Pro-portion per 100 Pop.**
Durrington	217	339	64.01	37	254	74.93
East Coulston	35	90	38.89	3	38	42.22
East Kennett	47	102	46.08	2	49	48.04
East Knoyle	467	853	54.75	70	537	62.95
Easton Grey	64	149	42.95	15	79	53.02
Easton Royal	130	391	33.25	27	157	40.15
Ebbesborne Wake	93	225	41.33	15	108	48.00
Edington	440	834	52.76	78	518	62.11
Eisey	29	124	23.39	8	37	29.84
Enford	353	814	43.37	41	394	48.40
Erlestoke	181	342	52.92	35	216	63.16
Everleigh	65	321	20.25	18	83	25.86
Fifield Bavant	9	42	21.43	10	19	45.24
Figheldean	148	367	40.33	24	172	46.87
Fisherton Anger	312	865	36.07	95	407	47.05
Fisherton Delamare	131	270	48.52	13	144	53.33
Fittleton	150	251	59.76	17	167	66.53
Fonthill Bishop	81	194	41.75	11	92	47.42
Fonthill Gifford	114	493	23.12	29	143	29.01
Fovant	266	514	51.75	28	294	57.20
Foxley	24	50	48.00	10	34	68.00
Froxfield	119	492	24.19	55	174	35.37
Fugglestone St Peter	111	590	18.81	33	144	24.41
Garsdon	72	143	50.35	18	90	62.94
Great Bedwyn	692	1632	42.40	66	758	46.45
Great Cheverell	228	457	49.89	25	253	55.36
Great Somerford	158	358	44.13	21	179	50.00
Great Wishford	163	346	47.11	40	203	58.67
Grittleton	117	340	34.41	25	142	41.76
Grovely Wood	3	33	9.09	3	6	18.18
Ham	73	188	38.83	34	107	56.91
Hankerton	154	286	53.85	31	185	64.69
Hannington	156	363	42.98	69	225	61.98
Hardenhuish	20	55	36.36	13	33	60.00
Heddington	107	287	37.28	36	143	49.83
Heytesbury	382	1072	35.63	97	479	44.68
Highway	43	104	41.35	4	47	45.19
Highworth	635	2328	27.28	325	960	41.24
Hill Deverill	44	146	30.14	14	58	39.73
Hilmarton	250	717	34.87	19	269	37.52
Hilperton	211	748	28.21	31	242	32.35
Hippenscombe	2	47	4.26	2	4	8.51
Homington	88	148	59.46	8	96	64.86
Horningsham	253	1030	24.56	36	289	28.06
Huish	32	82	39.02	22	54	65.85
Hullavington	160	395	40.51	28	188	47.59

Table 5 Contd.

Parish	**Local Wills**	**1801 Pop.**	**Local Wills Per 100 Pop.**	**PCC Wills Per 100. Pop.**	**PCC + Local Wills Per 100 Pop.**	**Pro-portion per 100 Pop.**
Idmiston	289	422	68.48	31	320	75.83
Imber	133	331	40.18	25	158	47.73
Inglesham	44	89	49.44	13	57	64.04
Keevil	405	792	51.14	30	435	54.92
Kemble	122	400	30.50	57	179	44.75
Kilmington	1	504	0.20	0	1	0.20
Kingston Deverill	107	292	36.64	47	154	52.74
Kington St Michael	405	729	55.56	65	470	64.47
Knook	48	194	24.74	6	54	27.84
Lacock	424	1408	30.11	101	525	37.29
Landford	95	186	51.08	35	130	69.89
Langley Burrell	152	333	45.65	36	188	56.46
Langley Wood	3	15	20.00	0	3	20.00
Latton	188	349	53.87	36	224	64.18
Laverstock	121	373	32.44	18	139	37.27
Lea and Cleverton	118	252	46.83	28	146	57.94
Leigh Delamere	43	65	66.15	13	56	86.15
Liddington	134	337	39.76	31	165	48.96
Little Bedwyn	165	428	38.55	45	210	49.07
Little Cheverell	104	159	65.41	10	114	71.70
Little Hinton	106	239	44.35	38	144	60.25
Little Langford	10	25	40.00	11	21	84.00
Little Somerford	111	255	43.53	24	135	52.94
Littleton Drew	57	87	65.52	20	77	88.51
Long Newnton	30	196	15.31	11	41	20.92
Longbridge Deverill	327	1228	26.63	69	396	32.25
Luckington	79	304	25.99	29	108	35.53
Ludgershall	170	471	36.09	36	206	43.74
Lydiard Millicent	96	300	32.00	30	126	42.00
Lydiard Tregoze	144	578	24.91	61	205	35.47
Lyneham	229	833	27.49	53	282	33.85
Maddington	152	327	46.48	31	183	55.96
Maiden Bradley	226	611	36.99	65	291	47.63
Malmesbury	806	1491	54.06	140	946	63.45
Malmesbury Abbey	17	80	21.25	6	23	28.75
Manningford Abbots	65	131	49.62	9	74	56.49
Manningford Bruce	51	213	23.94	23	74	34.74
Marden	82	162	50.62	25	107	66.05
Market Lavington	491	1238	39.66	166	657	53.07
Marlborough	1106	1122	98.57	543	1649	146.97
Melchet Park	10	22	45.45	6	16	72.73
Melksham	1396	5006	27.89	309	1705	34.06
Mere	893	2091	42.71	234	1127	53.90
Mildenhall	129	376	34.31	46	175	46.54
Milston	76	139	54.68	15	91	65.47

Table 5 Contd.

Parish	Local Wills	1801 Pop.	Local Wills Per 100 Pop.	PCC Wills Per 100. Pop.	PCC + Local Wills Per 100 Pop.	Pro-portion per 100 Pop.
Milton Lilborne	152	573	26.53	6	158	27.57
Minety	151	479	31.52	9	160	33.40
Monkton Deverill	68	168	40.48	20	88	52.38
Monkton Farleigh	69	264	26.14	28	97	36.74
Netheravon	272	479	56.78	38	310	64.72
Netherhampton	105	167	62.87	8	113	67.66
Nettleton	158	338	46.75	42	200	59.17
Newton Tony	110	286	38.46	32	142	49.65
No Man's Land	6	149	4.03	0	6	4.03
North Bradley	534	2068	25.82	114	648	31.33
North Newnton	76	221	34.39	39	115	52.04
North Tidworth	79	240	32.92	25	104	43.33
North Wraxall	71	304	23.36	64	135	44.41
Norton	18	94	19.15	10	28	29.79
Norton Bavant	111	264	42.05	31	142	53.79
Nunton and Bodenham	110	221	49.77	18	128	57.92
Oaksey	45	363	12.40	36	81	22.31
Odstock	65	118	55.08	8	73	61.86
Ogbourne St Andrew	166	434	38.25	54	220	50.69
Ogbourne St George	197	406	48.52	42	239	58.87
Orcheston St George	76	160	47.50	10	86	53.75
Orcheston St Mary	45	133	33.83	10	55	41.35
Patney	93	130	71.54	4	97	74.62
Pertwood	7	15	46.67	4	11	73.33
Pewsey	373	1179	31.64	60	433	36.73
Pewsham	68	139	48.92	5	73	52.52
Pitton and Farley	5	468	1.07	112	117	25.00
Plaitford	108	232	46.55	14	122	52.59
Poole Keynes	24	169	14.20	6	30	17.75
Potterne	558	1304	42.79	112	670	51.38
Poulshot	185	308	60.06	9	194	62.99
Poulton	63	306	20.59	40	103	33.66
Preshute	233	618	37.70	61	294	47.57
Purton	489	1467	33.33	115	604	41.17
Ramsbury	660	1963	33.62	224	884	45.03
Rodbourne Cheney	117	451	25.94	49	166	36.81
Rollestone	31	34	91.18	5	36	105.88
Rowde	283	796	35.55	53	336	42.21
Rushall	116	157	73.89	15	131	83.44
Salisbury	3619	7126	50.79	2246	5865	82.30
Seagry	94	233	40.34	19	113	48.50
Sedgehill	64	199	32.16	7	71	35.68
Semley	196	493	39.76	51	247	50.10
Shalbourne	294	774	37.98	45	339	43.80
Sherrington	91	134	67.91	7	98	73.13

Table 5 Contd.

Parish	Local Wills	1801 Pop.	Local Wills Per 100 Pop.	PCC Wills Per 100. Pop.	PCC + Local Wills Per 100 Pop.	Pro-portion per 100 Pop.
Sherston	284	992	28.63	109	393	39.62
Shorncote	9	29	31.03	8	17	58.62
Shrewton	181	269	67.29	15	196	72.86
Slaughterford	54	124	43.55	17	71	57.26
Somerford Keynes	53	203	26.11	45	98	48.28
Sopworth	27	180	15.00	20	47	26.11
South Newton	229	541	42.33	32	261	48.24
Standlynch	2	41	4.88	7	9	21.95
Stanton Fitzwarren	63	181	34.81	19	82	45.30
Stanton St Bernard	93	297	31.31	27	120	40.40
Stanton St Quintin	56	193	29.02	17	73	37.82
Stapleford	195	233	83.69	15	210	90.13
Steeple Ashton	741	1136	65.23	117	858	75.53
Steeple Langford	252	523	48.18	25	277	52.96
Stockton	136	224	60.71	30	166	74.11
Stourton	130	649	20.03	52	182	28.04
Stratford sub Castle	113	352	32.10	32	145	41.19
Stratford Tony	98	119	82.35	14	112	94.12
Stratton St Margaret	199	596	33.39	65	264	44.30
Sutton Benger	179	420	42.62	36	215	51.19
Sutton Mandeville	117	252	46.43	26	143	56.75
Sutton Veny	237	622	38.10	49	286	45.98
Swallowcliffe	78	217	35.94	14	92	42.40
Swindon	415	1198	34.64	166	581	48.50
Teffont Evias	62	143	43.36	8	70	48.95
Teffont Magna	105	199	52.76	11	116	58.29
Tidcombe and Fosbury	89	220	40.45	20	109	49.55
Tilshead	124	327	37.92	24	148	45.26
Tisbury	557	1961	28.40	30	587	29.93
Tockenham	57	124	45.97	29	86	69.35
Tollard Royal	89	238	37.39	15	104	43.70
Trowbridge	752	5799	12.97	409	1161	20.02
Tytherton Kellaways	41	12	341.67	28	69	575.00
Upavon	165	430	38.37	9	174	40.47
Upton Lovell	134	242	55.37	22	156	64.46
Upton Scudamore	115	409	28.12	23	138	33.74
Urchfont	690	1320	52.27	75	765	57.95
Wanborough	250	793	31.53	69	319	40.23
Warminster	1240	4932	25.14	585	1825	37.00
West Dean	182	221	82.35	23	205	92.76
West Grimstead	85	179	47.49	4	89	49.72
West Harnham	88	186	47.31	20	108	58.06
West Kington	68	221	30.77	38	106	47.96
West Knoyle	92	184	50.00	13	105	57.07
West Lavington	347	958	36.22	33	380	39.67

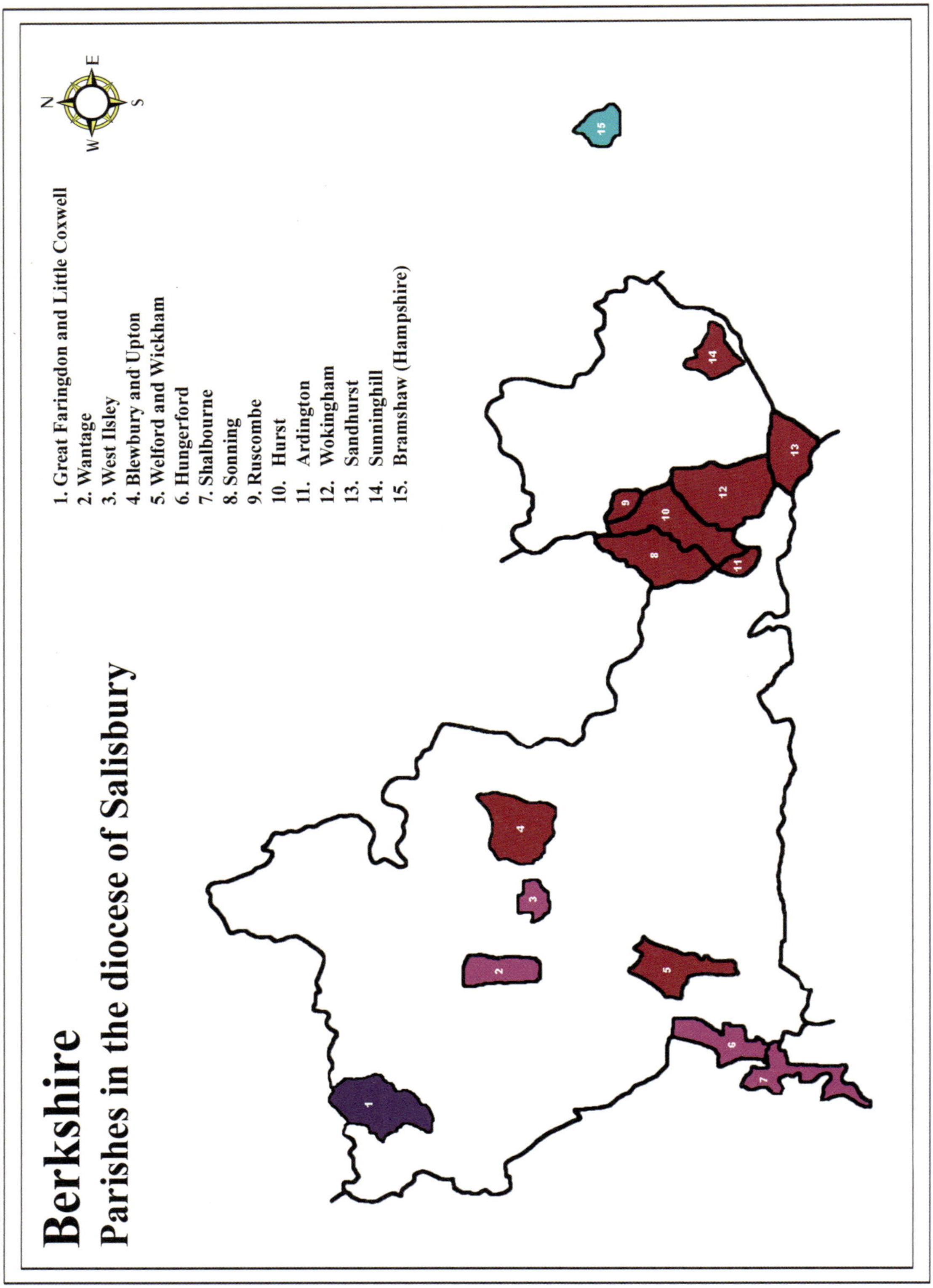
Berkshire
Parishes in the diocese of Salisbury
1. Great Faringdon and Little Coxwell
2. Wantage
3. West Ilsley
4. Blewbury and Upton
5. Welford and Wickham
6. Hungerford
7. Shalbourne
8. Sonning
9. Ruscombe
10. Hurst
11. Ardington
12. Wokingham
13. Sandhurst
14. Sunninghill
15. Bramshaw (Hampshire)
N
E
S
W
1
2
3
4
5
6
7
8
9
10
11
12
13
14
15

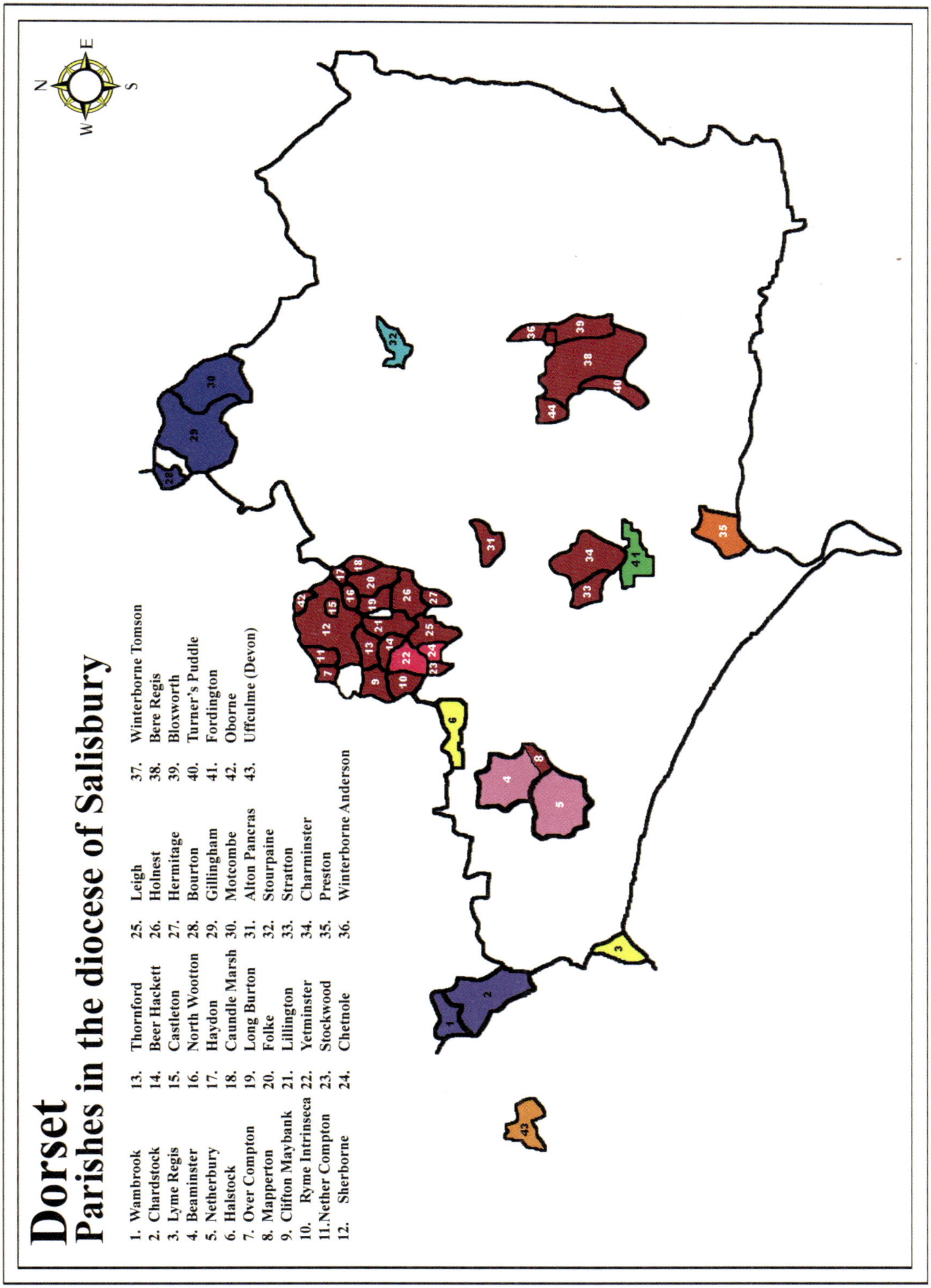
Dorset
Parishes in the diocese of Salisbury
1. Wambrook
2. Chardstock
3. Lyme Regis
4. Beaminster
5. Netherbury
6. Halstock
7. Over Compton
8. Mapperton
9. Clifton Maybank
10. Ryme Intrinseca
11. Nether Compton
12. Sherborne
13. Thornford
14. Beer Hackett
15. Castleton
16. North Wootton
17. Haydon
18. Caundle Marsh
19. Long Burton
20. Folke
21. Lillington
22. Yetminster
23. Stockwood
24. Chetnole
25. Leigh
26. Holnest
27. Hermitage
28. Bourton
29. Gillingham
30. Motcombe
31. Alton Pancras
32. Stourpaine
33. Stratton
34. Charminster
35. Preston
36. Winterborne Anderson
37. Winterborne Tomson
38. Bere Regis
39. Bloxworth
40. Turner's Puddle
41. Fordington
42. Oborne
43. Uffculme (Devon)
N
E
S
W

Table 5 Contd.

Parish	Local Wills	1801 Pop.	Local Wills Per 100 Pop.	PCC Wills Per 100. Pop.	PCC + Local Wills Per 100 Pop.	Pro-portion per 100 Pop.
West Overton	446	640	69.69	9	455	71.09
West Wellow	6	345	1.74	18	24	6.96
Westbury	1504	4836	31.10	425	1929	39.89
Westport St Mary	241	702	34.33	49	290	41.31
Westwood	84	446	18.83	31	115	25.78
Whaddon	61	36	169.44	10	71	197.22
Whiteparish	353	877	40.25	56	409	46.64
Whitsbury	3	132	2.27	13	16	12.12
Wilcot	190	567	33.51	41	231	40.74
Wilsford near Pewsey	160	387	41.34	35	195	50.39
Wilsford with Lake	31	99	31.31	*	*	*
Wilton	625	2144	29.15	145	770	35.91
Wingfield	89	290	30.69	25	114	39.31
Winterbourne Bassett	38	218	17.43	6	44	20.18
Winterbourne Dauntsey	66	120	55.00	18	84	70.00
Winterbourne Earls	97	189	51.32	15	112	59.26
Winterbourne Gunner	94	136	69.12	10	104	76.47
Winterbourne Monkton	84	177	47.46	12	96	54.24
Winterbourne Stoke	159	256	62.11	31	190	74.22
Winterslow	180	694	25.94	28	208	29.97
Woodborough	124	326	38.04	19	143	43.87
Woodford	167	345	48.41	50	217	62.90
Wootton Bassett	447	1244	35.93	190	637	51.21
Wootton Rivers	94	313	30.03	24	118	37.70
Wroughton	347	1100	31.55	83	430	39.09
Wylye	193	352	54.83	18	211	59.94
Yatesbury	74	234	31.62	25	99	42.31
Yatton Keynell	101	353	28.61	14	115	32.58
Total	64758	178842	36.21	17476	82234	45.98

Table 6 Willmaking by Place in the Diocese of Salisbury (Non-Wiltshire)

Parish	County	Local Wills	1801 Pop.	Local Wills Per 100 Pop.	PCC Wills	PCC + Local	Pro-portion per 100 Pop.
Arborfield	Berkshire	82	171	47.95	41	123	71.93
Blewbury (incl. Aston Upthorpe & Upton)	Berkshire	293	770	38.05	100	393	51.04
Hungerford	Berkshire[1]	514	2292	22.43	344	858	37.43

[1] Partially in Wiltshire

Table 6 Contd

Parish	County	Local Wills	1801 Pop.	Local Wills Per 100 Pop.	PCC Wills	PCC + Local	Pro-portion per 100 Pop.
Ruscombe	Berkshire	94	170	55.29	47	141	82.94
Sonning	Berkshire	2281	1669	136.67	546	2827	169.38
Wantage	Berkshire	690	3288	20.99	371	1061	32.27
Wokingham	Berkshire	475	7666	6.2	613	1088	14.19
Uffculme	Devon	585	1837	31.85	270	855	46.54
Alton Pancras	Dorset	61	184	33.15	11	72	39.13
Beaminster	Dorset	408	1545	26.41	255	663	42.91
Bere Hackett	Dorset	55	87	63.22	6	61	70.11
Bere Regis with Winterborne Kingston	Dorset	601	936	64.21	104	705	75.32
Bloxworth	Dorset	98	182	52.75	26	124	68.13
Caundlemarsh	Dorset	32	46	69.57	10	42	91.30
Castletown	Dorset	48	125	38.40	9	57	45.60
Chardstock	Dorset[2]	422	1095	38.54	158	580	52.97
Charminster	Dorset	109	416	26.20	79	188	45.19
Clifton Maybank	Dorset	6	40	15	3	9	22.50
Folke	Dorset	87	182	47.80	23	110	60.44
Fordington	Dorset	276	888	31.08	115	391	44.03
Halstock	Dorset	150	397	37.78	63	213	53.65
Haydon	Dorset	65	83	78.31	13	78	93.98
Hermitage	Dorset	29	123	23.58	22	51	41.46
Holnest	Dorset	143	160	89.38	9	152	95.00
Lillington	Dorset	45	128	35.16	26	71	55.47
Long Burton	Dorset	124	216	57.41	14	138	63.89
Lyme Regis	Dorset	666	1451	45.90	445	1111	76.57
Mapperton	Dorset	25	72	34.72	17	42	58.33
Motcombe	Dorset	302	917	32.93	73	375	40.89
Nether Compton	Dorset	140	371	37.74	21	161	43.40
North Wootton	Dorset	50	67	74.63	7	57	85.07
Oborne	Dorset	43	132	32.58	21	64	48.48
Over Compton	Dorset	94	135	69.63	26	120	88.89
Ryme Intrinsica	Dorset	39	123	31.71	2	41	33.33
Sherborne	Dorset	1116	3159	35.33	645	1761	55.75
Stockwood	Dorset	14	56	25.00	4	18	32.14
Stourpaine	Dorset	99	380	26.05	23	122	32.11
Stratton	Dorset	64	233	27.47	33	97	41.63
Thornford	Dorset	163	256	63.67	24	187	73.05
Turner's Puddle	Dorset	43	82	52.44	13	56	68.29
Wambrook	Dorset[3]	66	138	47.83	34	100	72.46
Winterborne Thompson	Dorset	6	97	6.19	2	8	8.25
Yetminster	Dorset	211	947	22.28	111	322	34.00
Bramshaw	Hampshire	209	490	42.65	29	238	48.57
South Damerham	Hampshire	345	716	48.18	17	362	50.56

[2] Later in Devonshire [3] Later in Somerset

No attempt has been made to map these non-Wiltshire patterns, as it will be much preferable to do so when all the parishes in the counties concerned can be subjected to this sort of analysis.

Table 7 Probate Jurisdictions in the Diocese of Salisbury

Reference	Title of Court	Description	Date
P1	Consistory Court of Salisbury	The Archdeaconry of Berkshire was transferred to the Diocese of Oxford in 1836. After this date the Consistory Court ceased to have jurisdiction over the Archdeanery.	1557–1858
P2	Archdeaconry of Salisbury		1537–1858
P3	Archdeaconry of Wiltshire	The jurisdiction extended to the Archdeaconry of Wiltshire, except when the court was inhibited by the Bishop. The inhibition extended for six months once every 3 years.	1557–1858
P4	Peculiar of the Sub-Dean of Salisbury	The Sub-Dean's jurisdiction extended the five parishes in and near Salisbury: St Thomas, St Edmund, St Martin, Stratford-sub-castle and Milford (the inhabitants of the latter, having no church, used St Martin's). The court was inhibited by the Bishop for six months during every three years. There are almost no surviving records for the years 1589–1610.	1581–1857
P5	Dean of Salisbury	The Dean's jurisdiction extended to The Close, Salisbury, eight Wiltshire parishes, seven Berkshire parishes and twenty seven Dorset parishes. The Wiltshire parishes were: Baydon, Heytesbury, Hill Deverill, Horningsham, Knook, Mere, Ramsbury and Swallowcliffe. The Berkshire parishes were: Arborfield, Blewbury, Hurst, Ruscombe, Sandhurst, Sonning and Wokingham, with the Chapels of Upton and Aston Upthorpe. The Dorset parishes were: Alton Pancras, Anderston, Bere Hackett, Bere Regis with Winterborne Kingston, Bloxworth, Candlemarsh, Castletown, Charminster, Folke, Haydon, Hermitage, Holnest, Lillington, Long Burton, Mapperton, Nether Compton, North Wootton, Oborne, Over Compton, Ryme Intrinsica, Sherborne, Stockwood, Stratton, Thornford, Turner's Puddle & Winterborne Thompson. Clifton Maybank was also included in this jurisdiction until 1824 when it was united with Bradford Abbas and thereafter it was under the jurisdiction of the Bishop of Bristol and the Archdeacon of Dorset. For six months every three years the Dean also inhibited the Prebendaries.	1539–1858
P6	Prebend of Bishopstone	This Court had jurisdiction in the parish of Bishopstone, North Wiltshire. It was inhibited by the Dean of Salisbury for six months in every three years.	1625–1854
P7	Prebend of Chute and Chisenbury	This jurisdiction extended to the parishes of Chute, Winterbourne Dauntsey and Chisenbury, Dorset. The Court was inhibited by the Dean of Salisbury for six months in every three years.	1609–1857

Table 7 Contd.

Reference	Title of Court	Description	Date
P8	Prebend of Coombe and Harnham, Wiltshire	This jurisdiction extended to the parishes of Coombe Bisset and Harnham Chapel, Wiltshire. The Court was inhibited by the Dean of Salisbury for six months in every three years.	1648–1856
P9	Prebendal Court of Durnford	This Court had jurisdiction in the parish of Durnford, Wiltshire. It was inhibited by the Dean of Salisbury for six months in every three years.	1634–1857
P10	Peculiar of the Prebend of Highworth	This Court had jurisdiction in the parish of Highworth with the chapels of South Marston, Sevenhampton and Broad Blunsden. It was inhibited by the Dean of Salisbury for six months in every three years.	1623–1775
P11	Prebend of Hurstbourne and Burbage	This jurisdiction extended to the parish of Burbage, Wiltshire, but not that of Hurstbourne Tarrant, Hampshire. The Court was inhibited by the Dean of Salisbury for six months in every three years.	1635–1856
P12	Prebend of Netheravon	Jurisdiction in the parish of Netheravon, Wiltshire, including the hamlet of Chisenbury de la Foley. The Court was inhibited by the Dean of Salisbury for six months in every three years.	1594–1854
P13	Prebend of Wilsford and Woodford	This jurisdiction extended to the parishes of Wilsford (near Amesbury) and Woodford, Wiltshire. The Court was inhibited by the Dean of Salisbury for six months in every three years. Only 6 items date before 1628.	1588–1854
P14	Prebend of Chardstock and Wambrook, Dorset	Jurisdiction extended to the Dorset parishes of Chardstock (transferred to Devon, 1896), and Wambrook (transferred to Somerset, 1896). The Court was inhibited by the Dean of Salisbury for six months in every three years.	1639–1857
P15	Prebend of Fordington and Writhlington	This Court had jurisdiction in the parish of Fordington, Dorset, but not in Writhlington, Somerset. It was inhibited by the Dean of Salisbury for six months in every three years.	1660–1855
P16	Peculiar of the Prebend of Lyme and Halstock	This jurisdiction extended to the parishes of Lyme Regis and Halstock in Dorset. The Court was inhibited for six months in every three years by the Dean of Salisbury.	1594–1857
P17	Prebendal Court of Netherbury, Dorset	This jurisdiction extended to the parishes of Netherbury and Beaminster, Dorset. The Court was inhibited for six months in every three years by the Dean of Salisbury.	1608–1857
P18	Prebendal Court of Preston and Sutton Poyntz	This jurisdiction extended to the parishes of Preston and Sutton Poyntz, Dorset. The Court was inhibited by the Dean of Salisbury for six months in every three years.	1761–1834

Table 7 Contd.

Reference	Title of Court	Description	Date
P19	Prebend of Yetminster and Grimstone	This jurisdiction extended to the parish of Yetminster, Dorset. The Court was inhibited by the Dean of Salisbury for six months in every three years.	1654–1857
P20	Prebend of Uffculme	This Court had jurisdiction in the parish of Uffculme, Devon. It was inhibited by the Dean of Salisbury for six months in every three years. There are no records for the years 1554-1574 and 1576-1622. The earliest records are contained in a small register kept by John Toser, Prebendary of Uffculme, containing notes and memoranda relating to a variety of prebendal and personal matters. This volume, although repaired, remains very fragile.	1545–1857
P21	Peculiar of the Lord Warden of Savernake Forest	Jurisdiction extended to the parishes of Collingbourne Ducis, Great Bedwyn and Little Bedwyn. In some records the official is described as the official of Sir Edward Seymour, within the parishes of Trowbridge, Collingbourne Ducis and Great Bedwyn. Collingbourne Ducis was inhibited by the Bishop for six months in every three years. The Bedwyns were inhibited by the Dean of Salisbury for six months in every three years. After 1829 the court ceased to function. Subsequent records from the Bedwyns will be found in the Dean's court (P5) and from Collingbourne Ducis in the Consistory Court (P1).	1613–1829
P22	Peculiar of Trowbridge	At some time before 1717, Trowbridge became a Bishop's peculiar. After 1717, the probate work of this court was absorbed by the Bishop's Court, the Consistory Court of Salisbury (P1). No records survive after 1646.	1574–1646
P23	Dean and Canons of Windsor	This jurisdiction extended to the following parishes: Hungerford, Berkshire (including Charnham Street, Eddington, Hidden, Newtown and Sanden Fee); Wantage, Berkshire (including Charlton, Grove, Tulwick & West Lockinge); Shalbourne, part in Wiltshire, part in Berkshire (including Bagshot); Ogbourne St Andrew, Wiltshire (including Ogbourne Maizey and Rockley); Ogbourne St George, Wiltshire. After 1840 this court was in abeyance as there was no official; the wills were proved in the Dean of Salisbury's court. There are several gaps in the series, notably for the years 1613-1639 and 1642-1667.	1604–1840
P24	Dean and Chapter of Salisbury	This peculiar's jurisdiction extended to the parishes or chapelries of Stourpaine in Dorset, Bramshaw in Hampshire, and Bishops Cannings, Britford, Homington and Southbroom in Wiltshire.	1574–1857
P25	Peculiar of the Precentor or Chanter	This Court had jurisdiction in the parish of Westbury, Wiltshire, with the chapelries of Bratton and Dilton. A few records dealt with in the Dean's court remain in P5.	1575–1857

Table 7 Contd.

Reference	Title of Court	Description	Date
P26	Peculiar of the Treasurer of the Cathedral Church of Salisbury	The jurisdiction extended to the parishes of Alderbury (with the chapelries of Pitton and Farley), Berwick Bassett, Calne, Calstone Wellington, Cherhill and Figheldean. There are 2 entries for 1574 and 1599.	1609–1858
P27	Royal Peculiar of Gillingham	This jurisdiction extended to the parishes of Gillingham (including the chapelries of Milton on Stour and Bourton) and Motcombe, Dorset.	1560–1858
P28	Peculiar of Castle Combe	This Court had jurisdiction in the parish of Castle Combe, Wiltshire. For later records, see the Archdeaconry of Wiltshire probate indexes. Some items (the latest of which was dated 1786) included in the original index have been missing for many years, and are not given in this index.	1669–1770
P29	Peculiar Court of the Perpetual Vicar of Corsham	This jurisdiction extended to the parishes of Corsham and Stratton St Margaret, Wiltshire. The place of residence of the deceased is frequently not given, but has been assumed to be Corsham (this is usually indicated by other evidence); only a small proportion of the wills (less than 3%) are from Stratton St Margaret. The earliest entries in the first register (1Reg) are later, 17th century, transcriptions. In addition to the three registers containing copies of wills, etc, there is a series of original, unbound wills, arranged alphabetically by surname, which partially overlap in date; many individuals therefore appear in both a register and the alphabetical series. The second register (2Reg) contains 54 marriage licence entries, as well as wills.	[1464]–1857
P30	Miscellaneous probate records	This series comprises probate records that were never sent to the General or District Probate Registries after 1857 but remained with the diocesan archives. Originally it numbered about 2000 items of almost entirely unprobated wills and inventories but many documents have been placed into their appropriate series (P1-P29), in many instances being reunited with associated papers. Among the records is a series of copies of wills and inventories dated around 1540 from parishes in the Archdeaconry of Salisbury. A box containing unidentified fragments has not been indexed or digitised.	1530–1776

Acknowledgments

I should like to acknowledge the work of the large body of volunteers, who must remain anonymous, who worked on these wills as part of the project to re-catalogue them. Without the many hours of work they gave, this index could never have been compiled. My son, Mark, helped very considerably with the maps and colouring thereof.

It is always very dangerous to compile indexes to material from geographical areas outside one's own knowledge. Steven Hobbs, archivist at Wiltshire and Swindon Archives, and Christopher Elrington, doyen of Wiltshire historians, both made many useful suggestions and comments on the introduction and saved me from some mistakes. Naturally, any errors remain entirely my own responsibility.

Cliff Webb, September 2008.

WILLS AT SALISBURY

Aaron, Chris., capital burgess, Malm., 1830, W, Wr, P3/1830/30
Abarrow *see* Abery
Abath, Clement, yeo., Bishopstrow, 1610, I, W, Wr, P2/A/83
Robt., sen., miller, Smallbrook Mills, Upton S., 1708, I, W, P2/A/360
see also Bath *or* A.
Abbott, Alice, widow, Stratford Tony, 1583, I, W, P2/A/17, P2/6Reg/96B
Chas., yeo., Corsley, 1708, AB, W, P2/A/362
Christian, widow, Semley, 1545, W (NEP), P2/1Reg/60A
Chris., tailor, Sal., 1630, I, W, P4/1630/3
Chris., Halstock, Dorset, 1694, AB, comm, I, P5/1693/1
David, yeo., Bloxworth, Dorset, 1754, W, P5/1754/1
David, yeo., Bloxworth, Dorset, 1769, W, P5/1769/1
Edmd., Martin, Hants, 1576, AB, I, P2/A/11, P2/5Reg/273B
Edmd., Winterbourne D., 1771, AB, P7/166
Edwd., Semley, 1585, W, P2/7Reg/10B
Eliz., sp., Sutton V., 1679, I, NW (2), P2/A/271
Eliz., widow, Halstock, Dorset, 1683, comm, I (detailed), W, P16/72
Eliz., widow, Godswell Grove, Dilton, Westb., 1696, I, W, P25/1696/7
Francis, husb., Halstock, Dorset, 1706, AB, I, P16/167
Geo., tanner, Mere, 1612, AB, I, P5/1612/2, P5/9Reg/78A
Geo., Winterborne K., Dorset, 1663, AB, I, P5/1663/1
Geo., shopkeeper, Sutton V., 1849, comm, W, Wr, P2/1849/57
Hester *see* Edwd. Fricker
Jas., gent., Sal., 1665, I, W, P4/1664/2
Abbett, Jas., thatcher, Fovant Stroud, 1710, W, P2/A/367
Abbett, Jas., yeo., Wambrook, Somerset, 1791, W, P5/1791/1, P5/18Reg/168C
Joan, widow, Donhead St My., 1614, I, W, P2/A/102, P2/8Reg/238B
Joan, widow, Mere, 1619, AB, I, P5/1619/3, P5/9Reg/223A
Joanna, sp., Sal., 1712, W, P4/1711/4
Jn., Semley, 1543, W (NEP), P2/1Reg/46
Jn., jun., Stratford Tony, 1552, AB, P2/2Reg/156C
Jn., dyer, Lyme R., Dorset, 1570, W, P5/2Reg/75A
Jn., husb., Charlton, Donhead St My., 1574, W, P2/5Reg/213A
Jn., Martin, Hants, 1587, W, P2/7Reg/85C
Jn., Sutton V., 1597, AB, I, P2/A/46
Jn., blacksmith, Bower C., 1623, I, W, P2/A/130
Jn., Rushall, 1639, AB, I, P2/A/185
Jn., brewer, Sal. St Thos., 1639, I, NW, P4/1639/6
Jn., Halstock, Dorset, 1661, comm, I, W, P5/1661/1
Jn., yeo., Coombe, Donhead St My., 1741, W, P2/A/446

Jn., thatcher, Heytes., 1756, I, W, P5/1756/1
Jn. *see also* Agnes Gooding
My., widow, Sal., 1621, I, W, P4/1621/6
My., Winterborne K., Dorset, 1687, AB, I, W, P5/1687/2
My., widow, Stockley, Bere R., Dorset, 1687, I, W, P5/1687/1
My., widow, Winterbourne D., 1716, W, P7/104
My., Heytes., 1765, W, P5/1765/4
Matthew, yeo., Bloxworth, Dorset, 1768, AB, I, P5/1768/1
Nich., husb., Sutton V., 1625, AB, comm, I, P2/A/137
Abbett, Reynold, yeo., Winterborne K., Dorset, [1625], W, copy W, P5/1625/112
Rd. *see* Agnes Gooding
Robt., clerk and minister, Hungerford, Berks., 1678, AB, I, P23/76
Roger, Halstock, Dorset, 1567, W, P5/2Reg/20C
Steph., Warm., 1592, AB, P1/A/2
Thos., Donhead St A., 1591, I, W, P2/A/25
Thos., Donhead St My., 1611-14, AB, a/c, P2/A/87, 101, P2/8Reg/154A
Valentine, Donhead St My., 1669, AB, P2/A/249
Wm., husb., Filford, Netherb., Dorset, 1642, comm, I, W, P5/1642/1
Wm., yeo., Beer Hackett, Dorset, 1723, AB, I, P5/1723/1
Wm., thatcher, Sutton V., 1780, AB, P2/A/533
see also Bartlett als A.; Beegle als A. (Habbott)
Abdy, Ebdy, Jn., shopkeeper, Abingdon, Berks., 1738, W, P1/E/218, P1/8Reg/243B
Wm., yeo., Grove, Wantage, Berks., 1674, AB, I, P23/47
Abeare, Abeary *see* Abery
A'Beckett, Thos., gent., Littleton P., 1792, W, P1/A/468, P1/14Reg/360B
Abell, Jn., Mkt. L., 1637, I, W, P2/A/172
Abery, Abarrow, Ann, yeo.'s wife, Lillington, Dorset (form. of Stalbridge, Dorset), 1837, AB, O, W, Wr, P5/1837/19
Abrey, Chris., cooper, Compton C., 1595, W, P2/A/560
Chris., Reading St Lawr., Berks., 1717, AB, I, P1/A/242
Aborough, Edwd., Stourton, 1577-78, AB, I, P2/A/12, P2/5Reg/298D
Edwd., broad weaver, Chittoe, Bps. C., 1716, AB, I, P24/658
Eliz., widow, Reading, Berks., 1826, AB, Wr, P1/1826/79
Abrey, Geo., tailor, woollen draper and mercer, Sal., 1815, W, P4/1815/3
Abrey, Hester, widow, Chittoe, Bps. C., 1728, W, P24/891
Joan, Farley, Alderbury, 1574, I, P5/1574/1
Jn., husb., Whitep., 1559, W, P2/3Reg/160A
Jn., Farley, Alderbury, 1574, W, P5/3Reg/34B
Abrey, Jn., butcher, Downton, 1589, I, P2/A/22
Abeare, Jn., jun., yeo., Wargrave, Berks., 1625, I, W, P1/A/47
Abrey, Jn., yeo., Deptford, Wylye, 1787, W, P2/A/544
Abrey, Jn., wheelwright, Chitterne AS, 1788, D, W, P2/A/546
Abery form. Lawes, My., wheelwright's wife, Chitterne AS, 1773, AB, P2/A/514
My., widow, Chitterne AS, 1830, AB, comm, P2/1830/15
Aborough, Thos., Mere, 1579, I, W, P5/1578/1, P5/3Reg/118A
Abeary, Wm., yeo., Chipp., 1570, W (NEP), P1/1Reg/51B
Wm., wheeler, Shrewton, 1683, AB, I, ren, P2/A/292
Abrey, Wm., wheelwright, Chitterne AS, 1766, W, P2/A/495
Wm., carp., Chitterne AS, 1829, comm, W, Wr, P1/1829/41
see also DeBeare *or* A.
Abethell, Abethell als Biffen, Geoff., sen., husb., Charl. nr. P., 1643, I, W, P2/A/194
Abethell als Biffin, Joan, widow, Charl. nr. P., 1666, I, W, P2/A/226
Joan, widow, Chisenbury, Enford, 1670, W, P2/A/253
Jn., husb., Upavon, 1557, W, P2/3Reg/22C
Abethell als Biffen, My., sp., Upavon, 1673, I, NW, P2/A/260
Rd., husb., Fyfield, Milton L., 1681, I, W, P3/A/166
Abethell als Biffen, Thos., husb., Charl. nr. P., 1646, AB, I, NW, P2/A/203
A'Bevyn, Elias, yeo., Town, Wilton, 1549, W, P2/2Reg/90A
Abington, And., esquire, Over C., Dorset, 1636, AB, comm, I, P5/1636/1, P5/12Reg/253D
Francis, Beam., Dorset, 1686, W, P17/226
Jn., captain and esquire, Over C., Dorset, 1685, AB, I (very detailed), P5/1685/3

My., widow, Over C., Dorset, 1599, AB, I, W, P5/1599/1, P5/6Reg/229A
Roger, Over C., Dorset, 1670, AB, comm, P5/1670/1
Thos., gent., Over C., Dorset, 1583, AB, P5/4Reg/69C
see also Tomkins als A.
Aborne, Thos., Pott., 1623, AB, I, P1/A/42
Aborough *see* Abery
Abraham, Abram, Agnes, widow, N. Bradley, 1574, W, P2/5Reg/186A
Alexander, [tallow chandler], Devizes St Jn., 1632, AB, I, P1/A/60
Edwd., Westb., 1808, AB, P25/1808/6
Eliz., widow, N. Bradley, 1550, W, P2/2Reg/110A
Abram, Joan, widow, Southwick, N. Bradley, 1614, W, P2/8Reg/243
Abram, Jn., husb., Southwick, N. Bradley, 1614, I, W, P1/A/26
Abram, Jn., husb., Southwick, N. Bradley, 1663, AB, W, P1/A/103
Abram, Jn., gent., Wootton B., 1705, W (on reverse are signatures of legatees), Wr, P3/A/250
Lewis, Corsley, 1663, AB, P2/A/219
My., sp., Sal., 1820, AB, P4/1820/7
My., sp., Bedborough, Bps. C., 1845, AB, O, Wr, P24/1380
Abram, Rebecca, sp., N. Bradley, 1667, AB, P2/A/231
Abram, Robt., sen., market spinner, Southbroom, 1671, I, W, P24/380
Sarah, widow, Bps. C., 1699, AB, I, P24/563
Thos., husb., Southwick, N. Bradley, 1640, I, W, P2/A/190
Wm., N. Bradley, 1558, W, P2/3Reg/99C
Abram, Wm., husb., N. Wootton, Dorset, 1610, W, P5/9Reg/39A
Abram, Wm., husb., Southwick, N. Bradley, 1611, I, W, P2/A/90
Wm., husb., Whitbourne, Corsley, 1620, I, W, P2/A/119
Abram, Wm., sen., labourer, Wick, Bps. C., 1702, I, NW, P24/548
Abrahams, Wm., dyer, Bradford A., 1729, W, P1/A/292, P1/7Reg/337B
Wm., gardener, Wick, Bps. C., 1757, comm, W, P24/1014
Wm., shopkeeper, Bradford A., 1758, W, P2/A/477
Abrey *see* Abery
Absolon, Abraham, sen., husb., Woodley, W. and Sandford, Berks., 1703, W, P5/1703/1
Abraham, jun., Midgham, Thatcham, Berks., 1735, AB, I, P1/A/311
Abraham, husb., Sonning, Berks. (form. of St My. Newington, Surrey), 1737, W, P5/1737/2
Cath., Anfields Cross, Hurst, Berks., 1583, W, P5/4Reg/72C
Edith, widow, Cholsey, Berks., 1622, I, W, P1/A/40
Hy., Aston Tirrold, Berks., 1723, AB, I, P1/A/264
Absolom, Jas., dairyman, Downton, 1777, W, P2/A/523
Absolom, Jas., Sal., 1820, AB, W, P4/1820/6
Absolon als Hobbs, Jn., yeo., Gt. Durnford, 1668, AB, W (NEP), P9/11
Rd., Aston U., Blewbury, Berks., 1729, AB, P5/1729/1, P5/16Reg/218B
Rd., husb., Bulmershe, Sonning, Berks., 1767, W, P5/1767/1
Seth, carp., Wallingford, Berks., 1763, W, P1/A/396, P1/12Reg/75B
Absolon als Hobbs, Thos., husb., Gt. Durnford, 1625, AB, I, P5/1624/1
see also Hobbs als A.
Aburges, Thos., weaver, Bradford A., 1588, W, P2/7Reg/129A
A'Burrowe, Wm., Trowb., 1570, W, P1/1Reg/125B
Abyn, Alice, widow, S. Newton, 1598, I, T, W, P2/A/51
Cath., sen., widow, Wilton, [1667], I, W, P2/A/230
Chas., weaver, Wilton, [1679], I, W, P2/A/273
Frances, Wilton, 1669, AB, P2/A/248
Geoff., shearman and clothw., Wilton, 1646, AB, a/c, I, P2/A/205
Jn., husb., S. Newton, 1565, W, P2/4Reg/194C
Jn., Wilton, 1595, AB, P2/A/40, P2/7Reg/142A
Jn., broad weaver, Wilton, 1641, AB, a/c, P2/A/191
Jn., sen., weaver, Wilton, 1699, I, W, P2/A/341
Jn., Wilton, 1708, W, P2/A/361
Rebecca, widow, Wilton, 1682, AB, I, P2/A/284
Wm., S. Newton, 1611, AB, I, P2/A/89
Wm., gent., Wilton, 1663, court paper, I, W, P2/A/220
Acceley *see* Ackley

Ackerman *see* Akerman
Ackers *see* Akers
Ackley, Eliz., sp., Wrou., 1741, W, P1/A/339, P1/9Reg/151
Akerley, Jn., husb., Hurst, Berks., 1668, AB, I, ren, P5/1667/5
Acceley form. Hughes, Sarah, widow, Burghfield, Berks., 1744, W, P1/A/349, P1/9Reg/349A
Wm., husb., Knighton, Rams., 1662, AB, I, NW, P5/1662/1
Acloughe, Brian, innholder, Sal., 1587, W, P4/Reg/33
Acourt, Ann, wife, Sal., 1692, AB, a/c, P4/1692/4
Ann, sp., Sal., 1728, AB, P4/1728/12
Acott, Edwd., blacksmith, Hannington, 1730, W (NEP), P3/A/322
Isaac, minor, Sal., 1693, T (no decd named), P4/1692/9
Acott, Jn., sen., blacksmith, Coleshill, Berks., 1759, W, P1/A/392, P1/11Reg/396
Acutt, Martha, widow, Crickl. St S., 1782, AB, P3/A/466
Acutt, Robt., Crickl. St S., 1764, AB, revoked LA, P3/A/425
Acutt, Robt., blacksmith, Crickl. St S., 1782, AB, comm, W, P3/A/467
A'Court, Susanna, widow, Pensbury, Motc., Dorset, 1854, aff, O, W, Wr, P27/1/771
Acutt, Wm., blacksmith, Crickl. St S., 1697, AB, I, P3/A/229
Acreman *see* Akerman
Acres *see* Akers
Acrigg, Geo., Laverstock, 1583-89, T (child: Jn. A.), W, P2/A/21, P2/6Reg/99A
Joan, widow, Stockton, 1613, I, W, P2/A/99, P2/8Reg/187
Aylerugg, Maurice, gent., Sal., 1661, AB, P4/1660/6
Rd., blacksmith, Fisherton A., 1701, W, P2/A/346
Wm., sen., Serrington, Stapleford, 1606, I, W, P1/A/19
Acutt *see* Acourt
Adams, Abraham, Hurst, Berks., 1820, AB, Wr, P5/1820/1
Adam, sen., yeo., Wantage, Berks., 1771, W, P23/731
Agnes, widow, Netheravon, 1652, I, W, P1/A/94
Addams, Agnes, widow, Bloxworth, Dorset, 1663-64, AB, app. of admr, comm, I, NW (2), P5/1663/2, P5/1664/1
Alice, widow, Sherb., Dorset, 1588, W, P5/5Reg/25C
Alice, widow, Poulton, 1703, I, W, P3/A/244
Amy, widow, Stapleford, 1737, AB, P2/A/433
And., innholder, Sal., 1725, W (NEP), P4/1725/17
Ann, widow, Poulton, 1631, I, W, P1/A/59
Ann, wife, Crickl. St S., 1690, AB, comm, P3/A/207
Ann, widow, Farnborough, Berks., 1705, W (probate copy), P1/A/201
Ann, widow, *The King's Head*, Downton, 1768, W, P2/A/501
Ann, sp., Wootton R., 1781, W, P3/A/462
Addams, Anth., yeo. *or* husb., Barford St Mart., 1668-71, I, W, P1/A/122, P2/A/240
Addams, Anth., grocer, Gt. Bedwyn, 1678, AB, a/c, I, P21/2/53
Anth., husb., Rowde, 1684, I, W, P3/A/180
Anth., yeo., W. Shefford, Berks., 1701, I, W, P1/A/189, P1/4Reg/99
Addams, Bridget, widow, Enford, 1618-20, AB, I, NW, P2/A/111, 116
Bridget, widow, Downton, 1738, W, P1/A/320, P1/8Reg/219
Chas., rector, Manningford A., 1771, W, P1/A/417, P1/12Reg/393A
Addams, Cicely, widow, Bere R., Dorset, 1639, AB, I, P5/1639/6, P5/13Reg/216A
Dan., sen., carp., Highw., 1712, W, P10/1712/7
Dan., carp., Highw., 1727, W, P10/1727/3
Dan., Atworth, Bradford A., 1808, W, Wr, P1/1808/26
Edith, widow, Trowb., 1625, I, W, P1/A/48
Edmd., yeo., Poulton, 1675, I, W, P3/A/144
Edmd., Poulton, 1709, I, W (NEP), P3/A/263
Addams, Edmd., Newtown, Shalbourne, 1715, AB, comm, P5/1715/1
Edwd., labourer, Steeple A., 1728, W, P2/A/412
Edwd., Speenhamland, Berks., 1826, comm, W, Wr, P1/1826/85
Eleanor, widow, Westrop, Corsham, 1621, W, copy W, P29/A/9, P29/1Reg/89, 91A
Eleanor, sp., Poulton, 1712, W, P3/A/270
Addams, Eliz., widow, Enford, [1670], I, NW (2), P2/A/250
Eliz., widow, Sherrington, 1684, I, W, P2/A/300
Eliz., widow, Enford, 1697, I, W, P2/A/338

Eliz., widow, Milton L., 1761, AB, I, P3/A/417
Eliz., widow, Sal. The Close, 1782, W, P5/1782/1, P5/17Reg/217B
Eliz., widow, Winterslow, 1800, AB, P2/1800/57
Frances, widow, Sal., 1828, AB, P4/1828/3
Gabriel, Enford, 1693, AB, I, P2/A/323
Gabriel, maltster, Marl., 1724-25, W, P1/A/269, P1/7Reg/54
Addams, Geo., Aldbourne, 1649, I, W, P1/A/89
Geo., husb., Downton, 1662, AB, I, P1/A/97
Addams, Geo., mason, Broad B., Highw., 1672, I, W, P10/1672/3
Geo., E. Garston, Berks., 1689, AB, I, P1/A/168
Geo., sen., yeo., Aldbourne, 1694, I, W, P3/A/221
Geo., Halstock, Dorset, 1736, AB, P5/1736/1
Geo., butcher, Uffc., Devon, 1807, W, P20/1/285
Geo., gent., Crickl. St S., 1813, AB, W, Wr, P3/1813/2
Heber, clothw., Gt. Trowle, Bradford A., 1717, AB, I, P2/A/388
Hy., husb., Fonthill B., 1586, W, P2/7Reg/64
Hy., stuff maker, Reading St Giles, Berks., 1756, W, P1/A/384, P1/11Reg/215
Hy., minor, Winterslow, 1800, T (son of Eliz. A., decd), P2/1800/56-57
Hester, widow, Sherb., Dorset, 1766, W, P5/1766/1
Isabel, widow, Sherb., Dorset, 1750, W, P5/1750/2
Jas., Sal., 1721, I, W, P4/1720/14
Jeremiah, shopkeeper, Corsley, 1813, W, Wr, P2/1813/52
Joan, widow, Sutton V., 1575, W, P2/5Reg/228A
Joan, widow, Sherrington, 1625, W, P2/A/138
Jn., Sutton V., 1542, W (NEP), P2/1Reg/39C
Jn., clothier, N. Bradley, 1559, W, P2/3Reg/164A
Jn., husb., Sherb., Dorset, 1581, I, W, P5/1580/1, P5/4Reg/15A
Addams, Jn., Sutton V., 1596, AB, P2/A/42
Jn., husb., Radway, Preston, Dorset, 1601, AB, I, W, P5/1601/2, P5/7Reg/26B
Jn., husb., Poulton, [1610], W (NEP), P3/A/12
Jn., carp., Sonning, Berks., 1631, I, W, P5/1631/4, P5/12Reg/70
Jn., yeo., Poulton, 1649, I, W, P1/A/90
Jn., sen., yeo., Berwick St Jas., 1680, AB, a/c, app of admr (2), I, P1/A/146
Addams, Jn., husb., Fittleton, 1682, I, NW, P2/A/290
Jn., yeo., Netheravon, 1683, AB, I, ren, P12/120
Jn., yeo., Poulton, 1684, I, W, P3/A/181
Addams, Jn., jun., gent., Beer Hackett, Dorset, 1705, comm, I, P5/1705/1
Jn., Bere R., Dorset, 1709-11, AB, P5/1709/1, P5/1711/1
Jn., sen., yeo., Poulton, 1714, AB, W, P1/A/228, P1/5Reg/400
Addams, Jn., sen., innholder, Crickl. St S., 1716, W, P3/A/279
Jn., husb., Enford, 1717, AB, I, P2/A/387
Jn., Collingbourne D., 1718, AB, comm, P21/7/36
Jn., yeo., Beer Hackett, Dorset, 1720, I, W, P5/1720/1, P5/16Reg/49A
Jn., schoolmaster and yeo., Stapleford, 1721, I, W, P2/A/398
Jn., blacksmith, Sal., 1729, AB, I, P1/A/277
Jn., yeo., Easton, 1729, W, P1/A/290, P1/7Reg/327A
Jn., yeo., Kingston Lisle, Sparsholt, Berks., 1729, AB, I, P1/A/280
Jn., Wilton, 1730, AB, P2/A/417
Jn., Enford, 1735, AB, P2/A/431
Jn., husb., Poulton, 1737, W, P3/A/353
Jn., Broad B., Highw., 1747, AB, P10/1747/1
Jn., baker, Gt. Bedwyn, 1758, W, P5/1758/1
Jn., plumber and glazier, Mkt. L., 1769, W, P2/A/503
Jn., plumber and glazier, Aldermaston, Berks., 1773, W, P1/A/426, P1/12Reg/496
Jn., minister of the Independent meeting, Sal., 1805, receipt, req, W, P4/1805/1
Jos., tailor and draper, Sal., 1837, W, Wr, P4/1837/3
Jos., stonemason, Alcombe, Box, 1840, comm, W, Wr, P3/1840/3
Julian, widow, Enford, 1557, W, P2/3Reg/38D
Mabel, sp., Milton L., 1760, W, P3/A/411
Addams, Margery, Fifield, Enford, 1644, I, W, P2/A/199

Mark, yeo., Aldbourne, 1669, AB, comm, I, ren, P3/A/120
Addams, My., widow, Enford, [1677], I, W, P2/A/267
My., widow, Fifield, Enford, 1696, AB, I, ren, P2/A/334
Adams nee West, My., widow, Devizes, 1700, AB, P1/A/187
My., Somerford K., 1714, AB, P3/A/277
My., sp., Steeple A., 1840-41, AB, comm, Wr, P2/1840/46, P2/1841/15
Matthew, Poulshot, 1808, AB, comm, Wr, P2/1808/38
Maud, N. Bradley, 1565, W, P2/4Reg/200A
Nich., weaver, Keevil, 1598, I, W, P2/A/54
Addams, Nich., yeo., Corsley, 1696, W, P2/A/336
Nich., husb., Aldbourne, 1722, AB, ren, W, P3/A/292
Addams, Paul, Norton B., 1575, AB, I, P2/A/10, P2/5Reg/244B
Philip, Grittleton, 1629, I, W, P3/A/47
Ralph, collarmaker, Sherb., Dorset, 1827, W, Wr, P5/1827/43
Rees, sen., yeo., Sherrington, 1666, I, W, P2/A/227
Rees, sen., clerk and rector, Donhead St My., 1738, W, P1/A/319, P1/8Reg/346B
Reynold, Twyford, Hurst, Berks., 1550, W, P5/20Reg/106B
Addams, Rd., Newnham, Sutton V., 1566, W, P2/4Reg/226C
Rd., Fifield, Enford, 1597, I, W, Wr, P2/A/48
Rd., ploughwright, Blewbury, Berks., 1626, AB, I, P5/1626/2, P5/10Reg/318A
Addams, Rd., Fifield, Enford, 1640, I, W, P2/A/187
Rd., yeo., Enford, 1643, I (detailed), W, P2/A/196
Rd., maltster, Sal., 1662, I, W, P1/A/102
Addams, Rd., husb., Stockley, Bere R., Dorset, 1665, AB, I, P5/1665/1
Addams, Rd., sen., butcher, Crickl. St S., 1721, W, P3/A/290
Rd., butcher, Crickl. St S., 1761, W, P3/A/414
Rd., butcher, Crickl. St S., 1815, AB, P3/1815/12
Robt., Sonning, Berks., 1555, W, P5/20Reg/136
Addams, Robt., husb., Compton, Enford, 1652, I, W, P1/A/95
Addams, Robt., husb., Stockley, Bere R., Dorset, 1663, comm, I, W, P5/1663/3
Roger, sen., carp., Rams., 1726, W, P5/1726/5, P5/16Reg/137B
Addams, Ruth, widow, Gt. Faringdon, Berks., 1674, W, P5/1674/1
Sam., bach., Homington, 1686, AB, P24/801
Steph., husb., Sutton V., 1584, W, P2/6Reg/138B
Addams, Thos., Fonthill G., 1543, W (NEP), P2/1Reg/45A
Thos., Fonthill B., 1556, W, P2/1Reg/109B
Thos., Bratton, Westb., 1573, W, P5/3Reg/8D
Thos., husb., Enford, 1600, AB, I, W, P2/A/60
Thos., husb., Bulmershe, Sonning, Berks., 1603, W, P5/7Reg/54
Addams, Thos., husb., Fifield, Enford, 1605, I, W, P2/A/70
Addams, Thos., Sherb., Dorset, 1606, AB, I, draft I, W, P5/1606/1, P5/8Reg/73A
Addams, Thos., miller, Warm., 1613, W, P2/8Reg/206B
Thos., husb., Letcombe Regis, Berks., 1614, I, W, P1/A/27
Thos., sen., husb., Sherrington, 1623, I, NW, P2/A/127
Thos., Wootton B., 1627, AB, comm, P3/A/41
Addams, Thos., husb., Chisenbury, Enford, 1628, I, W, P12/55
Thos., yeo., Bulmershe, Sonning, Berks., 1632, I, W, P5/1632/4, P5/12Reg/95B
Addams, Thos., husb., Bere R., Dorset, 1639, I, P5/1639/1
Thos., husb., Enford, 1644, I, W, P2/A/200
Addams, Thos., husb., Enford, 1668, I, NW, P2/A/241
Thos., husb., Crockerton, Longbridge D., 1689, comm, I, W, P1/A/169
Thos., yeo., Stert, Urchf., 1702, AB, I, P1/A/193
Thos., yeo., Amesb., 1704, I, W, P2/A/350
Addams, Thos., gent., Enford, 1733, I, W, P2/A/422
Thos., yeo., Poulton, 1761, AB, ren, W, P3/A/415
Thos., yeo., Limpley Stoke, Bradford A., 1763, W, P1/A/398, P1/12Reg/121A
Thos., yeo., Corsham, 1770, W, P29/A/33
Thos., yeo., Corsham, 1775, W, P29/2Reg/156
Thos., collarmaker, Milborne Stileham, Bere R., Dorset, 1780, W, P5/1780/1, P5/17Reg/184
Thos., Corsham, 1782, AB, P29/2Reg/166A

Thos., gent., W. Lavington, 1793, comm, W, P1/A/474, P1/14Reg/482
Thos., tailor, woollen draper and mercer and undertaker, Sal., 1814, AB, W, Wr, P1/1814/145
Thos., Rams., 1822, AB, Wr, P5/1822/8
Thos., Martin, Hants, 1827, AB, Wr, P2/1827/83
Thos., labourer, Swindon, 1832, comm, W, Wr, P1/1832/143
Addams, Uriah, widower, Corsley, 1800, W, Wr, P2/1800/91
Wm., Sutton V., 1552, I, W, P2/A/2, P2/2Reg/154A
Wm., Blackland, Calne, 1601-02, I, W, P5/1601/1, P5/7Reg/33C
Wm., Seend Row, Melk., 1611, AB, a/c, P2/A/88, P2/8Reg/159A
Adams als Taylor, Wm., yeo., Stourpaine, Dorset, 1622, I, W, P24/197
Wm., yeo., Bonnishe, Sonning, Berks., [1629-30], W (made 1629, date of probate given as 1634, although context would suggest 1630; no original copy of W appears to exist), P5/11Reg/146
Wm., Greenham, Thatcham, Berks., 1683, AB, I, P1/A/152
Wm., Bulford, 1684, I, W, P1/A/156
Wm., Corsham, 1691, AB, I, P29/A/22, P29/1Reg/252D
Wm., Downton, 1715, AB, P2/A/567
Wm., vict., Calne, 1832, W, Wr, P26/1404
Wm., maltster, Corsham, 1841, W, Wr, P3/1841/36
see also Jones als A.; Scory als A.; Taylor als A.
Adamson, Robt., Hurst, Berks., 1549, W, P5/20Reg/101B
Adcock, Wm., gent., Wilton, 1779, AB, P2/A/532
Addams *see* Adams
Addis, Adis, Thos., Burton, Charminster, Dorset, 1593, AB, P5/6Reg/52A
Wm., Reading, Berks., 1708, AB, P1/A/208
Addison *see* Adyson
Addy *see* Ady
Adeane, Aden, Jn., yeo., Allweston, Folke, Dorset, 1622, AB, I, P5/1622/2, P5/10Reg/116B
Jn., husb., Hurst, Berks., 1747, W, P5/1747/1
Adyn, Methusalah, vintner, Lyme R., Dorset, 1630, W, P5/11Reg/127B
Steph., Gt. Bedwyn, 1620, I, NW, P5/1620/1, P5/10Reg/12A
Thos., tailor, Sonning, Berks., 1796, W, P5/1796/1, P5/18Reg/224B
Wm., Wedh., Urchf., 1557, W, P2/3Reg/42D
Wm., Rams., 1572, AB, P5/2Reg/117A
Wm., Axford, Rams., 1597, I, W, P5/1597/2, P5/6Reg/185A
Adee *see* Ady
Aden *see* Adeane
Adey *see* Ady
Adis *see* Addis
Adkins, Jeremiah, Wytham, Berks., 1807, AB, comm, Wr, P1/1807/14
Robt., maltster, Wantage, Berks., 1734, W, P5/1734/1
Robt., Liberty of Newland, Hurst, Berks., 1785, AB, ren of estate, P5/1785/1, P5/18Reg/22
Wm., yeo., Sandford, Woodley and S., Berks., 1720, comm, W, P5/1720/2, P5/16Reg/50A
Adlam, Adam, Calne, 1638, AB, P26/82
Adlam *or* Adland, Agnes, widow, Reading St Giles, Berks., 1662, AB, I, P1/A/99
Ambrose, Westb., 1565, W, P5/1Reg/62
Bridget, Corsham, 1609, AB, I, W, P29/A/3, P29/1Reg/66A
Edmd., clothw., S. Burcombe, 1664, AB, W, P2/A/222
Edmd., yeo., Crockerton, Longbridge D., 1817, comm, W, Wr, P2/1817/9
Edwd., Edington, 1585, W, P2/7Reg/2D
Edwd., Longbridge D., 1585, AB, P2/7Reg/1A
Edwd., yeo., Westb. L., 1721, I, W, P25/1721/3
Eliz., widow, Devizes, 1711, I, W, P1/A/217, P1/5Reg/247
Eliz., sp., Westb., 1836, declaration, O, W, Wr, P25/1836/2
Frederick, weaver, Dilton M., Westb., 1820, W, Wr, P25/1820/5
Gertrude, Westb., 1573, W, P5/3Reg/29D
Hannah, widow, Bower C., 1819, W, Wr, P2/1819/25
Jas., glover, Dilton M., Westb., 1842, W, P25/1842/3
Jane, widow, Sal., 1852, W, Wr, P4/1852/11
Joan, widow, Crockerton, Longbridge D., 1566, W, P2/4Reg/234B
Joan, widow, Crockerton, Longbridge D., 1617, I, W, P2/A/108

Joan, widow, Horningsham, 1751, AB, P5/1751/1
Jn., Edington, 1557, W, P2/3Reg/49A
Jn., Corsham, [1581], W (NEP), P29/1Reg/20B
Jn., broad weaver, Horningsham, 1610, I, W, P5/1610/1, P5/9Reg/43C
Jn., S. Newton, 1610-13, AB, a/c, I, P2/A/79, 96, P2/8Reg/82E
Jn., yeo., Crockerton, Longbridge D., 1612, I, W, P2/A/95
Jn., sen., fuller, Dilton, Westb., 1648, AB, P25/1648/2
Jn., Horningsham, 1680, I, T (re Edmd. A., a minor), P5/1680/2
Jn., N. Tidworth, 1681, AB, P2/A/279
Jn., Alvediston, 1695, AB, I, P2/A/331
Jn., weaver, Rowde, 1717, AB, ren, P3/A/280
Jn., tanner, Warm., 1718, W, P2/A/390
Jn., woolstapler, Devizes, 1739, W, P1/A/330, P1/8Reg/403
Jn., minor, Westb., 1743, AB, T, P25/1743/4, 8
Jn., Chicksgrove, Tisb., [1745], NW (2), P2/A/452
Jn., bach., St Nich.'s Hospital, The Close, Sal., 1808, AB, Wr, P1/1808/12
Jn., maltster, Westb., 1832, O, W, Wr, P25/1832/5
Eadleam, Jos., yeo. and husb., Seend, Melk., 1719, I, W, P2/E/288
Jos., Horningsham, 1819, AB, O, W, Wr, P5/1819/9
Julian, widow, Warm., 1614, W, P2/8Reg/223A
Louisa, sp., Sal., 1855, aff, W, Wr, P1/1855/45
Adlam als Clevelodd, Magdalen, widow, Longbridge D., 1558, W, P2/3Reg/119C
My., Corsley, 1712, AB, P2/A/375
Matthew, husb., Melk., 1601, I, W, P2/A/62
Matthew, Horningsham, 1822, AB, W, Wr, P5/1822/20
Patience, widow, Longbridge D., 1817, W, Wr, P1/1817/41
Reynold *or* Rendell, Bratton, Westb., 1685, AB, I, P25/1685/12
Rd., Imber, 1587, AB, P2/A/19, P2/7Reg/103A
Rd., weaver, Horningsham, 1636, I, W, P5/1636/4, P5/13Reg/12B
Rd., Sal., c1668, AB, P4/1668/3
Robt., Westb., 1570, W, P5/2Reg/82
Sam., N. Bradley, 1679, AB, comm, I, P2/A/272
Sam., sen., Crockerton, Longbridge D., 1768, AB, P2/A/500
Thos., Longbridge D., 1588, W, P2/7Reg/134A
Thos., fuller, Crockerton, Longbridge D., 1605, AB, I, P2/A/72
Thos., Crockerton, Longbridge D., 1619, AB, I, P1/A/34
Thos., Heytes., 1627, I, W, P5/1627/2, P5/11Reg/7G
Thos., Leighs Marsh, Dilton, Westb., 1640, AB, I, P25/1640/16
Thos., Melk., 1692, AB, I, P2/A/320
Thos., weaver, Horningsham, 1710-11, W, P5/1710/1, P5/15Reg/223
Thos., Warm., 1752, AB, P2/A/470
Thos., labourer, Warm., 1792, W, P2/A/552
Thos., Longbridge D., 1804, AB, P1/1804/112
Thos., Horningsham, 1839, AB, W, Wr, P5/1839/23
Timothy, draper, Sal., 1671, I (detailed), W, P4/1670/22
Valentine, clothier, Crockerton, Longbridge D., 1611, I, W, Wr, P2/A/86
Wm., Longbridge D., 1638, AB, P2/A/181
Wm., jun., tanner, Warm., 1682, I, W, P2/A/288
Wm., maltster, Warm., 1690-91, I, W, P2/A/318
Wm., Corsley, 1706, AB, I, P2/A/353
Wm., sen., gent., Devizes, 1751, W, P1/A/370, P1/10Reg/469
Wm., maltster, Devizes, 1759, W, P1/A/393, P1/11Reg/465
Wm., Warm., 1772, AB, P2/A/510
Wm., clerk, Hullavington, 1792, W, P3/A/489
Wm., weaver, Crockerton, Longbridge D., 1813, comm, W, Wr, P2/1813/34
Adley, Hy., yeo., Durley, Burbage, 1687, I, W, P11/59
Theophilus, yeo., Aldbourne, 1698, AB, comm, I, P3/A/237
Wm., Durnford, 1748, AB, Wr, P5/1748/1
Adlington, Rd., Devizes St My., 1605, AB, I, W, P1/A/9
Wm., Devizes, 1624, AB, comm, P1/A/45

Adnam, Hannah, sp., Chieveley, Berks., 1776, AB, comm, P1/A/436
Admans, Jas., Chieveley, Berks., 1729, AB, I, P1/A/285
Jn., yeo., Leckhampstead, Chieveley, Berks., 1779, W, P1/A/441, P1/13Reg/261
Adman, My., widow, Farnborough, Berks., 1747, I, W, P1/A/361, P1/10Reg/116
Adnams, My., widow, Pound's Farm, E. Garston, Berks., 1792, W, P1/A/473, P1/14Reg/423
Rd., yeo., Leckhampstead, Chieveley, Berks., 1714, AB, I, P1/A/226
Sarah, sp., Newbury, Berks., 1829, AB, O, Wr, P1/1829/129
Wm., Leckhampstead, Chieveley, Berks., 1668, I, W, P1/A/117
Adnams, Wm., yeo., Oare, Chieveley, Berks., 1804, W, P1/1804/14
Adson, Ann, widow, Devizes, 1745, W, P1/A/354, P1/10Reg/12
Jn., gent., Devizes, 1737, AB, P1/A/318
Ady, Adye, Ann, Cowage Farm, Foxley, 1680, AB, P3/A/165
Ann, Malm., 1744, W, P3/A/378
Adye, Arthur, gent., Sherston, 1783, W, P3/A/469
Cath., widow, Sutton B., 1665, AB, comm, P3/A/103
Adee als Hedges, Cath., clerk's wife, Rodbourne C., 1669, AB, comm, I, NW, P3/A/121
Adye, Edwd., sen., gent., Seagry, 1663, I, W, P3/A/97
Adye, Edwd., cooper, Seagry, 1768, W, P3/A/434
Adye, Eliz., widow, Easton Grey, 1634, I, W, P1/A/66
Eliz., widow, Melk., 1706, I, W, P2/A/354
Hy., yeo., Lt. Somerford, 1811, W, Wr, P1/1811/101
Hy., yeo., Yatesbury, 1829, W, Wr, P3/1829/20
Jas., yeo., Brinkw., 1838, O, W, Wr, P3/1838/12
Adye, Jewell, yeo., Seagry, 1671, AB, a/c, comm, I, P3/A/133
Adee, Jn., mercer, Aldbourne, 1686, I, W, P3/A/194
Adye, Jos., gent. and bach., Easton Grey, 1703, AB, P3/A/245
Adye, Jos., yeo. and innholder, Sherston, 1804, W, P1/1804/89
Addy, Julia, rector's widow, Imber, 1738, comm, W, P2/A/435
My., widow, Malm., 1676, I, W, P3/A/150
My., widow, Melk., 1832, comm, D, W, Wr, P1/1832/125
Adye, Nathaniel, innholder, Sherston, 1791, W, P3/A/486
Adee, Nich., clerk and vicar, Rodbourne C., 1713, W, P3/A/272
Adey, Susanna, widow, Crickl. St S., 1727, W, P3/A/305
Adee, Swithin, husb., Even Swindon & Rodbourne C., 1623, I, W, P3/A/36
Adye, Thos., husb. and yeo., Chr. M., 1606, I, W, P1/A/13
Adye, Thos., yeo., Sal., 1616, I, P4/1616/9
Adee, Thos., Aldbourne, 1620, I, W, P3/A/27
Adye, Thos., jun., yeo., Seagry, 1664, I, W, P3/A/100
Thos., grocer, Aldbourne, 1680, AB, I, P3/A/164
Adye, Thos., yeo., Seagry, 1686, AB, I, P3/A/193
Adye, Thos., Coleshill, Berks., 1726, AB, P1/A/273
Adye, Walter, yeo., Hullavington, 1729, AB, I, W, Wr, P3/A/318
Adye, Wm., yeo., Seagry, 1630, I, W, P3/A/53
Wm., sen., husb., Seagry, 1640, I, W, P3/A/79
Adye, Wm., mercer, Chipp., 1668, AB, comm, I, P3/A/115
Adye, Wm., Melk., 1680, AB, I, P2/A/274
Adey, Wm., E. Garston, Berks., 1698, AB, P1/A/184
Wm., Melk., 1730, AB, P2/A/416
Wm., cooper, Seagry, 1745, AB, ren, P3/A/379
Adye, Wm., miller, Kingsmead Mill, Lt. Somerford, 1750, W, P1/A/366, P1/10Reg/402
Wm., jun., yeo., Malm. (late of Ashford), 1812, W, Wr, P3/1812/50
Wm., butcher, Melk., 1831, comm, W, Wr, P2/1831/22
see also Ody
Adyn *see* Adeane
Adyson, Rd., slater, Wilton, 1576, W, P2/5Reg/253B
Afforde, Rd., Colerne, 1641, AB, I, P3/A/84
Afoord, Thos., husb., Ruscombe, Berks., 1636, AB, I, P5/1636/2, P5/13Reg/1B
Agnew, And. *see* Thos. Hellier
Ailes *see* Eyles
Ailford *see* Alford

Ailworth *see* Allworth
Ainsworth *see* McIntosh nee A.
Aish *see* Ash
Aislye, Thos., clerk and parson, Fisherton A., 1618, AB, I, P1/A/32
Akerley *see* Ackley
Akerman, Acreman, Cath., widow, Burbage, 1631, I, NW, P5/1631/3, P5/12Reg/41
Ackerman, Eliz., widow, Chirton, 1841, O, W, Wr, P2/1841/58
Ackerman, Frances, widow, Collingbourne D., 1742, W, P21/9/42
Geo., sen., Wilsford nr Pewsey, 1615, I, W, P2/A/103, P2/8Reg/256A
Geo., Amesb., 1618, I, W, P2/A/112
Geo., grocer, Wylye, 1683, I, W, P1/A/154
Geo., yeo., Eisey, 1790, W, P3/A/483
Geo., jun., Crickl. St S., 1847, AB, comm, Wr, P3/1847/6
Hester, sp., Collingbourne D., 1769-76, AB (2), P21/10/73, P21/11/13
Jane, widow, Wilsford nr Pewsey, 1623, AB, I, NW, P2/A/129
Jn., Chilton F., 1685, I, W, P3/A/188
Acreman, Jn., Holt, Bradford A., 1703, AB, I, P2/A/347
Jn., turner, Holt, Bradford A., 1751, W, P2/A/463
Jn., weaver, Bromham, 1815, comm, W, Wr, P3/1815/20
Jn., baker, Calne, 1837, W, Wr, P26/1435
Jn., innkeeper, Bromham, 1854, AB, aff, O, Wr, P3/1854/66
Jn., farmer, Calne, 1855, comm, O, W, Wr, P26/1465
Jonathan, Wylye, 1744, AB, P1/A/347
Margery, widow, Stanton Fitzwarren, 1629, comm, I, W, P3/A/48
Acreman, My., widow, Goatacre, Hilmarton, 1714, I, W, P1/A/230, P1/5Reg/435
My., widow, Wylye, 1781, W, P2/A/534
My., widow, Eisey, 1798, AB, comm, P1/A/484, P1/15Reg/130A
My., widow, Calne, 1839, AB, Wr, P5/1839/16
Matthew, labourer, S. Marston, 1758, AB, W, P5/1758/4
Moses, husb., Blunsdon St And., 1761, W, P3/A/416
Moses, Leigh, Ashton K., 1770, AB, P1/A/413
Moses, Blunsdon St And., 1849, D, O, W, Wr, P3/1849/4
Rd., husb., Wilsford nr Pewsey, 1611, AB, court papers (5), I (2), P2/A/91
Rd., yeo., Wilsford nr Pewsey, 1677, I, W, P2/A/265
Acreman, Rd., farmer, Patney, 1772, W, P2/A/511
Acreman, Robt., Lyme R., Dorset, 1679, AB, I, P5/1679/2
Ackerman, Roger, sen., shepherd, Coate, Bps. C., 1668, I, W, P24/369
Roger, sen., yeo., Bedborough, Bps. C., 1685, AB, I, W, P24/807
Roger, yeo., Bedborough, Bps. C., 1693, I, W, P24/531
Sarah, sp., Breamore, Hants, 1757-76, AB, W, P2/A/475
Sarah, widow, Patney, 1775, W, P2/A/518
Sarah, widow, Crockerton, Longbridge D., 1857, aff, W, Wr, P2/1857/53
Silvester, Stanton Fitzwarren, 1642, AB, I, P3/A/89
Acreman, Susanna, widow, Bedborough, Bps. C., 1716, W, P24/661
Susanna, sp., Newbury, Berks. (leaving effects at Patney), 1839, AB, comm, Wr, P2/1839/41
Thos., yeo., Hampton, Highw., 1708, W, P5/1708/1, P5/15Reg/95
Thos., Collingbourne D., 1714, AB, I, P1/A/227
Thos., yeo., Bromham, 1848, O, W, Wr, P1/1848/73
Acreman, Wm., husb., Wilsford nr Pewsey, 1586, W, P2/7Reg/51B
Wm., sen., husb., Stanton Fitzwarren, 1609, W, P3/A/10
Wm., Horningsham, 1621, AB, P5/1621/1, P5/10Reg/23A
Wm., yeo., Goatacre, Hilmarton, 1669, I, P3/A/122
Wm., yeo., Goatacre, Hilmarton, 1687, I, W, P3/A/197
Wm., bach., Broad B., Highw., 1849, AB, O, Wr, P10/1849/2
Wm., yeo., Urchf., 1850, W, Wr, P2/1850/68
see also Grammet als A.
Akers, Geo., blacksmith, Collingbourne K., 1807, W, Wr, P3/1807/8
Joan, widow, Sunton, Collingbourne K., 1676, I, W (damaged), P3/A/149
Acres, Jos., labourer, E. Hagbourne, Berks., 1716, W, P1/A/238, P1/6Reg/59
Jos., collarmaker, Devizes, 1771, W, P1/A/418, P1/12Reg/403A

Acres, Mark, Coscote, E. Hagbourne, Berks., 1617, AB, I, P1/A/144
Ackers, My., widow, Abingdon, Berks., 1747, I, quitclaim, W, P1/A/356, P1/10Reg/71B
Rd., vicar, Bps. C., 1565, W, P5/1Reg/55A
Thos., Collingbourne K., 1686, AB, I, P1/A/164
Wm., Brightwalton, Berks., 1692, AB, I, P1/A/173
Wm., yeo., Water Eaton (Eisey), Latton, 1829, O, W, Wr, P3/1829/22
Akery, Jas., yeo., Farley, Alderbury, 1716, I, W, P26/604
Aland, Cath., widow of tallow chandler, Chipp., 1713, I, W, P3/A/273
Chas., Langley Burrell, 1638, I, W (damaged), P1/A/75
Chas., tobacconist, Chipp., 1688, AB, comm, I, P3/A/200
Chas., yeo., Langley Burrell, 1692-93, I, W (2 - 1 a copy), P3/A/212, 214
Chas., yeo., Langley Burrell, 1743, W, P3/A/374
Chas., tailor, Melk., 1748, W, P2/A/456
Chas., bach., Bradford A., 1788, AB, comm, P2/A/547
Chas., gent., Conigree, Trowb., 1818, AB, comm, P1/1818/10
Dan., yeo., Kington L., 1696, comm, I, W, P3/A/225
Dorothy, widow, Bromham, 1644, AB, I, P1/A/81, P3/A/80
Edwd., bach., Lacock, 1711, AB, I, P3/A/268
Eleanor, widow, Gt. Somerford, 1757, W, P3/A/403
Eliz., sp., Langley Burrell, 1662, W, P3/A/94
Eliz., yeo.'s widow, Langley Burrell, 1717, I, W, P3/A/281
Eliz., widow, Cherhill & Chipp., 1840, AB, Wr, P3/1840/36
Frideswide, widow, Bromham, 1633, I, W, P3/A/61
Hy., yeo., Gt. Somerford, 1706, W, P3/A/255
Hy., cordw., Gt. Somerford, 1752, comm, W, P3/A/396
Hy., blacksmith, Bradford A., 1819, W, Wr, P2/1819/38
Hugh, Langley Burrell, 1631, I, W (damaged), P3/A/57
Isaac, clothw., Turleigh, Winsley, Bradford A., 1740, W, P2/A/443
Jane, widow, Kington St M., 1672, AB, I, P3/A/138
Jane, widow, Langley Burrell, 1697, AB, comm, I, P3/A/230
Jn., sen., broad weaver, Langley Burrell, 1665, I, W, P3/A/104
Jn., sen., yeo., Langley Burrell, 1667, I, W, P3/A/113
Jn., yeo., Langley Burrell, 1693, comm, I, W, P3/A/215
Jn., yeo., Cook St., Chipp., 1771, comm, W, P3/A/441
Matthew, yeo., Beanacre, Melk., 1772, W, P3/A/445
Peter, yeo., Gt. Somerford, 1677, AB, I, P3/A/153
Rebecca, widow, Chipp., 1681, I, note of probate, W, P3/A/168
Rd., fuller, Langley Burrell, 1664, comm, I, W, P3/A/101
Rd., yeo., Langley Burrell, 1705, I, W, P3/A/251
Richmond, Melk., 1724, AB, I, P2/A/403
Richmond, maltster, Chipp., 1776, comm, W, P3/A/451
Robt., yeo., Chipp., 1675, I, W, P3/A/145
Robt., baker and maltster, Chipp., 1782, AB, comm, ren, P3/A/468
Sarah, widow, Chipp., 1807, W, Wr, P3/1807/36
Sipram, Bearfield, Bradford A., 1814, AB, comm, LA, P1/1814/100
Thos., Langley Burrell, [1617], I, W (NEP), P3/A/24
Wm., jun., husb., Melk., 1620, I, W, P2/A/115
Wm., sen., yeo., Bromham, 1621, I, W, P3/A/30
Wm., yeo., Melk., 1621, W, P2/A/121
Albert, Dorothy, sp., Winterborne K., Dorset (form. of Poole), 1733, W, P5/1734/2
Essex, grocer, Sal., 1770, W, P1/A/408, P1/12Reg/298A
Albin, Albyn, Ann, widow, Sherb., Dorset, 1633, comm, I, W, P5/1632/1, P5/12Reg/84D
Frances, linen weaver's widow, Mere, 1679, I, W, P5/1679/1
Jos., Sal., 1719, AB, L, ren, P4/1719/10
Albyn, Robt., parchment maker, Sherb., Dorset, 1580, I, W, P5/1580/2, P5/4Reg/5B
Alborne, Ann, sp., Biddestone St Nich., 1827, W, Wr, P3/1827/63
Geo., yeo., Nettleton, 1678, I, W, P3/A/155
Geo., Biddestone St Nich., 1785, AB, comm, P3/A/473
Jane, sp., Biddestone St Nich., 1810, W, Wr, P3/1810/50
Joan, widow, Seend, Melk., 1603, I, W, P2/A/65

Paul, baker, Slaughterford, 1787, comm, W, P3/A/475
Thos., Seend Row, Melk., 1602, AB, I (fragment), P1/A/7
Albright, Eliz., widow, Whitehorn Hill, Whitep., 1697, I, W, P2/A/337
Robt., rector, Landford, 1671, AB, I, P1/A/123
Allbright, Robt., yeo., Hamptworth, Downton, 1741, I, W, P1/A/338, P1/9Reg/196A
Wm., gent., Hamptworth, Downton, 1699, I, W, P1/A/185, P1/3Reg/225
Albyn *see* Albin
Alcock, Sarah, widow, Broad H., 1689, I, W, P3/A/206
Thos., clerk and minister, Broad H., 1665, comm, I, W, P3/A/105
see also Elcock
Alden, Eliz., mercer's widow, Sopworth, 1698, I, W, P3/A/238
Alding, Jos., widower, Woodford, 1848, AB, Wr, P13/6/17
Aldin, Lawr., Alderton, 1626, I, W, P3/A/40
Aldin, Marian, widow, Alderton, 1635, I, W, P3/A/65
Aldens, Rd., Amesb., 1561, I, P30/5
Robt., baker, Gastard, Corsham, 1662-63, I, W, P29/A/14, P29/1Reg/167
Thos., mercer, Sopworth, 1689, I, W, P3/A/201
see also Olden
Alder, Brian, rector, Peasemore, Berks., 1678, AB, comm, I, P1/A/145
Chas., Reading, Berks., 1747, AB, P1/A/360
Chas., retail beer seller, Rams., 1857, aff, O, W, Wr, P5/1857/9
Denis, Blewbury, Berks., 1735, AB, P5/1735/1
Geo., schoolmaster, Abingdon, Berks., 1792, AB, W, P1/A/470, P1/14Reg/405A
Jane, widow, Pewsey, 1772, W, P3/A/446
Joan, widow, S. Denchworth, Berks., 1720, W, P1/A/255, P1/6Reg/298
Jn., Highw., 1606, I, P1/A/12
Jn., Gt. Bedwyn, 1610, AB, P5/9Reg/27B
Jn., Denchworth, Berks., 1735, AB, P1/A/306
Judith, widow, E. Challow, Letcombe Regis, Berks., 1729, W, P1/A/286, P1/7Reg/275B
Peter, yeo., E. Grafton, 1716, I, W, P5/1716/1, P5/15Reg/348B
Sarah, minor, Ogbourne St And., 1751, app. of guardian, P5/1751/2
Thos., husb., Crofton, Gt. Bedwyn, 1670, I, NW, P21/2/15
Thos., Grove, Wantage, Berks., 1721, AB, P23/404
Thos., Crofton, Gt. Bedwyn, 1735, AB, P21/9/12
Thos., yeo., Marl. St My. (comm. admd at Hereford), 1750, cert, comm, W, P1/A/365, 394, P1/10Reg/380
Thos., yeo., Marl. St My., 1759, W, P1/11Reg/477B
Thos., yeo., Pewsey, 1771, W, P3/A/442
see also Aldworth *or* A.
Alderman, Arthur, Goatacre, Hilmarton, 1758, W, P3/A/407
Jas., husb., Goatacre, Hilmarton, 1668, AB, I, ren, P3/A/116
Jn., yeo., Goatacre, Hilmarton, 1733, AB, I, W, P3/A/330
Rd., yeo., Goatacre, Hilmarton, 1697, I, W, P3/A/231
Thos., jun., Lyneham, 1764, AB, comm, P3/A/426
Thos., innholder, Lyneham, 1773, W, P1/A/427, P1/13Reg/1A
Wm., shopkeeper, Marl., 1753, W, P1/A/380, P1/11Reg/142
Alderwick, Eleanor, Bradford A., 1724, AB, P2/A/404
Rd., plumber, Woolley, Bradford A., 1691, comm, W, P2/A/319
Robt., weaver, Broughton G., 1608-13, AB, a/c, I, P2/A/75, 97, P2/8Reg/27A
Alderwitt, Robt., Sal. The Close, 1741, AB, Wr, P5/1741/1
Thos., yeo., Broughton G., 1624, I, W, P2/A/132
Wm., yeo., Woolley, Bradford A., 1636, I, W, P2/A/169
Aldin, Alding *see* Alden
Aldridge, Adam, widower, Warm., 1844, AB, O, Wr, P2/1844/13
Adam, labourer, Stratford sub C. & Amesb., 1852, W, Wr, P2/1852/28
Agnes, widow, Bratton, Westb., 1609, I, W, P25/1609/2
And., yeo., Plaitford, 1683, AB, a/c, I, P2/A/296
Aldrick, Ann, widow, no abode stated, 1640?, W, valuation, P2/A/188
Aldredge, Chris., Westb., 1636, AB, P25/1636/10
Aldredge, Chris., blacksmith, Porton, Idmiston, 1720, W, P1/A/248, P1/6Reg/231A
Edith, Bps. C., 1619, a/c, comm, I, W, P5/1619/1, P24/57

Edwd., Bere R., Dorset, 1723, I, W, P5/1723/2, P5/16Reg/85A
Eleanor, widow, Bratton, Westb., 1668, comm, I, NW, P25/1668/2
Eleanor, widow, Stratford sub C., 1721, AB, W, P4/1721/13
Eliz., widow, Amesb., 1786, AB, P1/A/451
Eliz., widow, Amesb., 1843, AB, Wr, P2/1843/19
Aldridge *or* Aldright, Frances, widow, Earley, Sonning, Berks., 1669, AB, I, W, P5/1669/1
Geo., Beenham Valence, Berks., 1668, AB, P1/A/116
Grace, widow, Erlestoke, 1721, W, P2/A/396
Hy., Hankerton, 1738, comm, W, P3/A/359
Isaac, yeo., Erlestoke, 1740, AB, a/c, comm, I (2 very detailed), P2/A/440
Isaac, yeo., Erlestoke & Poulshot, 1805, AB, P2/1806/5
Jas., Warm., 1805, AB, comm, P2/1805/17
Joan, widow, Melbourne, Bratton, Westb., 1629, I, W, P25/1629/6
Jn., Westb., 1569, AB, P5/2Reg/41A
Jn., jun., yeo., Bratton, Westb., 1616, I, W, P25/1615/12
Jn., Stapleford, 1636, AB, I, P2/A/168
Jn., fuller, Stratford sub C., 1680, AB, a/c, I, P1/A/149
Jn., Wilton, 1694, AB, I, P2/A/329
Jn., gardener, Bratton, Westb., 1710, I, W, P25/1710/5
Jn., labourer, Netton, Durnford, 1710, AB, I, P5/1710/2
Jn., innholder, Amesb., 1748, AB, a/c, I, P2/A/458
Jn., yeo., Ham, 1753, W, P1/A/381, P1/11Reg/141
Jn., gent., Warm., 1775, W, P2/A/519
Jn., innholder, Baydon, 1783, W, P5/1783/1, P5/17Reg/245B
My., sp., Winterslow, [1687], NW, P2/A/312
My., widow, Warm., 1762, W, P2/A/487
Millicent, widow, W. Lavington, 1628, AB, a/c, I, P1/A/51
Morgan, Stapleford, 1619, I, W (2), P2/A/114
Aldredge, Nich., gent., Bramshaw, Hants, 1709, I, W, P24/568
Ralph, husb., Upton S., 1604, AB, I, P2/A/68
Aldredge, Ralph, jun., clothier, Edington, 1632-33, AB, a/c, comm, I (2), NW, P2/A/156, P2/9Reg/23A
Ralph, sen., clothier, Bratton, Westb., 1640, I (detailed), W, P25/1640/3
Ralph, Compton B., 1676, AB, I, NW, P3/A/151
Rd., Bratton, Westb., 1566, W, P5/1Reg/81A
Rd., yeo., Stapleford, 1706, I, W, P2/A/356
Rd., baker, Wootton B., 1833, comm, W, Wr, P3/1833/15
Robt., yeo., Cookham, Berks., 1723, W, P1/A/266, P1/7Reg/4A
Sarah, widow, Cookham, Berks., 1729, W, P1/A/281, P1/7Reg/270A
Sarah, widow, Cookham, Berks., 1738, AB, P1/A/325
Steph., yeo., Gt. Bedwyn, 1730, W, P21/8/61
Aldredge, Susan, maid, Bratton, Westb., 1640, I, W, P25/1640/13
Thos., Bourton, Bps. C., 1617, I, W, P24/76
Aldredge, Thos., Westb., 1684, I, P25/1684/11
Thos., Westb., 1695, I, W (NEP), P25/1695/6
Thos., yeo., Erlestoke, 1712, W, P2/A/376
Wm., Bratton, Westb., 1609, a/c, P25/1609/3
Wm., yeo., Bratton, Westb., 1698, I, NW, P25/1698/5
Wm., maltster, Marl., 1711, I, W, P1/A/219, P1/5Reg/251
Wm., yeo., Erlestoke, 1721, I, W, P2/A/397
Wm., yeo., Lt. Bedwyn, 1730, W, P21/8/65
Wm., sen., yeo., Cookham, Berks., 1738, AB, W, P1/A/321, P1/8Reg/291
Wm., Burrs, Lt. Bedwyn, 1811, AB, comm (conditional on mortgage of B., L.B. made 1707), P21/12/26-27
Wm., labourer and shopkeeper, Figh., 1825, AB, W, Wr, P26/1358
see also Annetts als A.; Finch als A.
Aldwin, Thos., Hullavington, 1620, I, W, P3/A/28
Aldworth, Alexander, sen., shoemaker, Wantage, Berks., 1628, I, W, P5/1628/1, P5/11Reg/90A
Alexander, maltster, Marl., 1713, I, W, P1/A/221, P1/5Reg/293A
Eliz., widow, Charlton, Wantage, Berks., 1638, I, W, P5/1638/1, P5/13Reg/139C
Joan, widow, Barwell, Grove, Wantage, Berks., 1665, I (detailed), W, P5/1665/2
Jn., yeo., Grove, Wantage, Berks., 1691, I, W, P5/1691/1

Jn., yeo., Duxford, Hinton Waldrist, Berks., 1804, W, P1/1804/63
Lydia, widow, Reading, Berks., 1701, comm, W, P1/A/192, P1/4Reg/168
Mgt., widow, Tanners St., Wantage, Berks., 1685, I, W, P5/1685/1
Margery, Childrey, Berks., 1613, AB, I, P1/A/22
Margery, widow, Wantage, Berks., 1688, I (shoes & leather listed), W, P5/1688/1
Aldworth *or* Alder, Mark, Drayton, Abingdon, Berks., 1677, I, W, P1/A/143
My., widow, Wantage, Berks., 1740, W, Wr, P5/1740/2
Peter, Compton Beauchamp, Berks., 1595, a/c, P1/A/5
Rd., gent., Manor House, Hinton Peppard, Hurst, Berks. (to be buried at Ruscombe), 1639, comm, I (detailed), W, P5/1639/5, P5/13Reg/199E
Rd., sen., shoemaker, Wantage, Berks., 1678, I, W, P23/77
Robt., gent., Wantage, Berks., 1641, AB, I, P5/1641/2, P5/14Reg/2C
Robt., gent., Frilford, Marcham, Berks., 1808-10, receipt, req, copy W, Wr, P1/1808/96
Thos., clerk, Wantage, Berks., 1681, AB, P23/103
Thos., gent., Wantage, Berks., 1682, bond to return W, I, W, copy W, P5/1682/1
Thos., husb., Grove, Wantage, Berks., 1694, AB, I, P23/201
Thos., yeo., Wantage, Berks., 1709, I, W, P23/303
Wm., shoemaker, Reading, Berks., 1732, W, P1/A/300, P1/7Reg/476
Wm., Frilford, Marcham, Berks., 1759, W, P1/A/391, P1/11Reg/399B
see also Pope als A.
Alexander, Elisander, Agnes, widow, Sherston, [1608], W (NEP), P3/E/5
Agnes, widow, Maiden B., 1632, I, W, P2/A/155
Alice, widow, Sherston, 1639, I, W, P3/A/75
Alice, widow, Compton B., 1733, I, NW, P3/A/331
Alice, widow, Urchf., 1757, W, P2/A/474
Ann, widow, Seagry, 1737, W, P3/A/356
Ann, wife, Upavon, 1807, AB, Wr, P2/1807/77
Anth., blacksmith, Kington St M., 1622, I, W, P3/A/33
Benj., yeo., Old Park, Devizes St Jn., 1772, W, P1/A/420, P1/12Reg/423
Cath., widow, Cleverton, Lea and C., 1613, I, W, P3/A/20
Chapman, Mynte, Corsham, 1755, AB, ren, P3/A/399
Chas., barber, Devizes, 1731, AB, ren, P1/A/296
David, yeo., Rodbourne, Malm., 1720, W, P1/A/259, P1/6Reg/359B
David, Rodbourne, Malm., 1748, AB, comm, P3/A/385
Edith, widow, Tilsh., 1638, I, W, P1/A/74
Edwd., [blacksmith], Hurst, Berks., 1616, I, T, P5/1616/2
Edwd., yeo., Manningford Bruce, 1645, comm, I, W, P3/A/497
Edwd., bach., Hilcott, N. Newnton, 1673, AB, alleg, P1/A/134
Edwd., farmer *or* yeo., Manningford Bruce, 1675, I, W, P3/A/146
Edwd., yeo., Preshute, 1704, I, W, P1/A/195
Edwd., sen., yeo., Urchf., 1711, I, W, P1/A/214, P1/5Reg/207
Edwd., yeo., Lt. Cheverell, 1742, I, W, P2/A/448
Edwd., Durnford, 1782, AB, P9/85
Edwd., sen., yeo., Rams., 1807, W, Wr, P5/1807/17
Edwd., yeo., Westport St My., 1824, W, Wr, P3/1824/54
Eleanor, widow, Rushall, 1789, W, P2/A/548
Eliz., widow, Preshute, 1711, W, P1/A/213, P1/5Reg/140
Eliz., widow, Castle Eaton, 1747, AB, I, P1/A/355
Eliz., sp., Sal., 1816, W, P4/1816/2
Eliz., widow, Urchf., 1822, W, Wr, P2/1822/64
Eliz., widow, Fisherton A., 1828, AB, P2/1828/14
Geoff., weaver, Dauntsey, 1666, I, W, P3/A/109
Geo., vict., Tilsh., 1777, AB, P2/A/526
Geo., Cholderton, 1807, W, Wr, P2/1807/57
Giles, labourer, Tilsh., 1731-32, I, W, P2/A/419
Elisander, Gillian, widow, Durrington, 1626, W, P2/E/96
Harry Head, Malm., 1842, AB, O, Wr, P3/1842/32
Helen, widow, Netheravon, 1631, I, W, P12/65
Helen, farmer's wife, Gt. Somerford, 1685, AB, P3/A/189
Hy., Amesb., 1615, I (2 - 1 a copy), W, P2/A/105

Hy., fellmonger, Malm., 1717, I, W, P3/A/284
Hy., clothw., Turleigh, Winsley, Bradford A., 1720, W, P1/A/251, P1/6Reg/262B
Hillier, yeo., Wrou., 1737, AB (3), P3/A/345
Humphrey, Chipp., 1665, AB, P3/A/106
Jas., Seend, Melk., 1630, AB, I, P2/A/148, P2/9Reg/77D
Elixander, Jas., no abode stated, [1633], I, P2/E/114
Jas., yeo., Newbury St., Preshute, 1714, W, P1/A/229, P1/5Reg/410
Elisander, Joan, widow, Chirton, 1563, W, P1/2Reg/145C
Joan, widow, Arborfield, Berks., 1592, I, W, P5/1592/2, P5/6Reg/12C
Joan, widow, Luckington, 1671, comm, I, W, P3/A/134
Joan, widow, Marden, 1694, comm, I, W, P2/A/328
Jn., Tidcombe, T. and Fosbury, 1572, W, P1/1Reg/44A
Elisander, Jn., husb., Cleverton, Lea and C., 1601, W, P3/1Reg/63B
Jn., sen., Cleverton, Lea and C., 1603, I, W, P3/A/1
Jn., N. Newnton, 1613, I, W, P1/A/25
Jn., Tilsh., 1624, AB, I, P2/A/131
Jn., Easton, 1634, I, W, P1/A/67
Jn., shepherd, Maddington, 1638, I, W, P2/A/176
Jn., Gt. Cheverell, 1641, comm, W, P1/A/79
Alexander als Symons, Jn., Codf. St P., 1648, I, W, P2/A/208
Jn., yeo., Hilcott, N. Newnton, 1663, AB, I, NW, P3/A/98
Jn., yeo., Sherston, 1665, AB, I, P3/A/108
Jn., yeo., Maddington, 1667, I, W, P2/A/237
Jn., yeo., E. Coulston, 1669, I, W, P2/A/245
Jn., husb., Hurst, Berks., 1671, AB, I, P5/1671/1
Jn., yeo., W. Stowell, Alton Pr., 1675, I, W, P3/A/147
Jn., sen., yeo., Compton B., 1695, I, W, Wr (fragile & damaged documents), P3/A/222
Jn., Stockley, Calne, 1724, AB, P26/686
Jn., day labourer, Froxfield, 1724, W, P3/A/297
Jn., yeo., Rodbourne, Malm., 1727, W, P3/A/306
Jn., yeo., Wrou., 1733, W, P3/A/332
Jn., cordw., Shrewton, 1735, W, P2/A/429
Jn., sen., yeo., Manningford Bruce, 1735, W, P1/A/312, P1/8Reg/42
Jn., yeo., W. Lavington, 1744, W, P1/A/352, P1/9Reg/406
Jn., sen., yeo., Manningford Bruce, 1750, AB, W, P1/A/369, P1/10Reg/439
Jn., cordw., S. Newton, 1751, W, P2/A/461
Jn., yeo., Rams., 1758, AB, W, P5/1758/2
Jn., bach., Buttermere, 1764, AB, P3/A/427
Jn., Sal., 1772, AB, P4/1772/15
Jn., husb., Castle Eaton, 1775, W, P3/A/449
Jn., Winterbourne M., 1780, AB, P3/A/459
Jn., yeo., W. Wellow, 1789, W, P1/A/463, P1/14Reg/315
Jn., yeo., Wrou., 1791, W, P3/A/487
Jn., gent., Manningford Bohun, 1797, AB, ren, W, P2/A/563
Jn., sen., Donnington, Berks., 1798, AB, comm, P1/A/481, P1/15Reg/57B
Jn., baker, Trowb., 1802, W, P1/1802/9, P1/15Reg/366
Jn., Woolley, Bradford A., 1803, W, P2/1803/53
Jn., yeo., Wedh., Urchf., 1815, O, W, P2/1815/70
Jn., Wrou., 1827, W, Wr, P3/1827/29
Jn., gent. (form. carp. & wheelwright), Lambourn, Berks. (describes himself as late of Rams.), 1835, comm, W, P3/1835/37
Jn., grocer, Rams., 1842, W, Wr, P5/1842/15
Jn., yeo., Ogbourne St Geo., 1852, comm, W, Wr, P5/1852/12
Jos., Norton, 1706, AB, I, P3/A/256
Jos., cooper, Rams., 1790, W, P5/1790/1, P5/18Reg/149
Jos., sen., vict., *The Royal Oak*, Devizes Grn, Bps. C., 1799, W, P24/1197
Joyce, sp., Rodbourne, Malm., 1749, W, P3/A/387
Mgt., Seend Row, Melk., 1645, I, W, P2/A/201
Mgt., widow, Charlton nr Malm., 1661, I, W, P3/A/93, P3/3Reg/8B
Mgt., widow, Rodbourne, Malm., 1750, comm, W, P1/A/368, P1/10Reg/438A

Martha, sp., Gt. Somerford, 1743, W, P3/A/375
Ellisander, My., widow, Sandhurst, Berks., 1662, AB, I, P5/1662/41
My., widow, Shrewton, 1673, I, W, P2/A/262
My., widow, Manningford Bruce, 1684, W, P3/A/182
My., Allington, Chipp., 1710, I, W (NEP), P3/A/266
My., widow, Rangebourne, Pott., 1733, AB, P24/947
My., widow, Swinley Farm, Kington St M., 1736, AB, P3/A/346
My., widow, Sal., 1768, W, P4/1768/4
My., sp., Gt. Cheverell, 1797, W, P2/A/565
Nathaniel, yeo., Manningford Bruce, 1706, W, P3/A/258
Nathaniel, yeo., Pott., 1714, W, P1/A/234, P1/5Reg/464A
Nathaniel, schoolmaster, Ogbourne St Geo., 1784, W, P23/775
Nich., Maiden B., 1630, I, P2/A/147
Paget, Elcombe, Wrou., 1740-53, AB (2), comm, P1/A/373, P3/A/366
Rd., weaver, Arborfield, Berks., 1596, AB, a/c, I, P5/1596/1, P5/6Reg/138E
Rd., Rodbourne, Malm., 1608, AB, P3/A/8
Rd., Marl., 1693, NW, P1/A/176
Rd., Avebury, 1720, AB, P1/A/252
Rd., yeo., Chedglow, Crudwell, 1733, I, W, P3/A/333
Rd., grocer, The Shambles, Chipp., 1839, O, W, Wr, P3/1839/10
Rd., silversmith, Chipp., 1852, comm, W, Wr, P3/1852/9
Robt., Arborfield, Berks., 1575, I, W, P5/1575/1, P5/3Reg/69C
Robt., yeo., Rodbourne, Malm., 1637, I, W, P3/A/70
Robt., yeo., Manton, Preshute, 1722, W, P1/A/260, P1/6Reg/391
Robt., sen., dyer, Bps. C., 1731, W, P24/817
Robt., yeo., Castle Eaton, 1736, W, P1/A/315, P1/8Reg/151
Robt., Old Park, Devizes St Jn., 1783, W, P1/A/448, P1/14Reg/9
Robt. *see also* Jas. Henley
Roger, shepherd, Marden, 1649, comm, I, W, P1/A/91
Ruth, widow, Marl., 1674, I, W, P1/A/138
Sam., Marl., 1671, AB, I, P1/A/124
Solomon, husb., Manton, Preshute, 1669, I, W, P1/A/121
Susanna, E. Coulston, 1766, W, P2/A/498
Susanna, sp., Swindon, 1820, comm, W, Wr, P1/1820/26
Susanna, sp., Luckington, 1826, comm, W, Wr, P1/1826/122
Thos., husb., Rockley, Ogbourne St And., 1667, I, W, P5/1667/2
Thos., yeo., Wedh., Urchf., 1670, I, W, P2/A/252
Elixander, Thos., serge maker *or* serge weaver, E. Coulston, [1688], I, W, P2/E/220
Thos., yeo., Elcombe, Wrou., 1713, I, W, P3/A/274
Thos., yeo., Hilcott, N. Newnton, 1717, I, W, P3/A/282
Thos., E. Coulston, 1730, AB, I, P2/A/418
Thos., yeo., Upavon, 1746, ren, W, P2/A/455
Thos., shepherd, Upavon, 1761, W, P2/A/486
Thos., Winterbourne M., 1775, W, P3/A/450
Thos., sen., oatmeal maker, Malm., 1789, W, P3/A/481
Thos., yeo., Bromham, 1795, W, P1/A/475, P1/14Reg/543
Thos., S. Farm, All C., 1813, AB, comm, note, Wr, P3/1813/20
Thos., Rams., 1836, aff, comm, W, Wr, P5/1836/3
Ursula, widow, Amesb., 1635, AB, P1/A/68
Walter, husb., Hilcott, N. Newnton, 1621, I, W, P3/A/31
Walter, yeo., Seend, Melk., 1668, I, W, P1/A/118
Walter, Hilcott, N. Newnton, 1674, AB, I, P1/A/139
Wm., jun., husb. and bach., Charlton nr Malm., 1627, I, W, P3/A/42
Wm., husb., Charlton nr Malm., 1641, I, W, P3/A/85
Wm., yeo., Allington, Chipp., 1678, AB, I, P3/A/156
Wm., blacksmith, Gt. Cheverell, [1680], I, NW, P2/A/277
Wm., yeo., Chedglow, Crudwell, 1693, I, W, P3/A/216
Wm., yeo., Gt. Cheverell, 1715, I, W, P2/A/382
Wm., jun., yeo., Gt. Somerford, 1717, AB, I, ren, P3/A/283
Wm., shoemaker, Shrewton, 1741, W, P1/A/331, P1/9Reg/70B

Wm., sen., capital burgess, Malm., 1757, W, P3/A/404
Wm., Stert, Urchf., 1759, W, P1/A/389, P1/11Reg/372
Wm., yeo., Beversbrook, Hilmarton, 1764, W, P3/A/428
Wm., blacksmith, Devizes, 1768, AB, W, P1/A/407, P1/12Reg/283
Wm., Gt. Wishford, 1784, AB, P2/A/540
Wm., gent., Upavon, 1786, W, P2/A/542
Wm., shopkeeper, Calne, 1824, W, Wr, P5/1824/8
Wm., Wilsford nr Pewsey, 1825, comm, W, Wr, P2/1825/59
Wm., Marl., 1828, AB, aff, O, Wr, P1/1828/16
see also Green als A.
Aley *see* Alley
Alford, Abraham, linen weaver, Mere, 1726, W, P5/1726/1, P5/16Reg/131C
Agnes, widow, Mere, 1591, I, W, P5/1591/1, P5/5Reg/106B
Amariah, Mere, 1831, AB, Wr, P5/1831/12
And., maltster, Tisb., 1740, W, P2/A/442
And., Tisb., 1769, AB, P2/A/504
Benj., linen weaver, Bourton, Gillingham, Dorset, 1802, comm, W, P27/1/569
Chas., Marl., 1839, AB, O, Wr, P1/1839/8
Chris., sen., linen weaver, Mere, 1690, I, W, P5/1690/1
Chris., Mere, 1742, I, NW, Wr, P5/1742/2
Chris., higler, Sherrington, 1769, W, P2/A/505
Chris. *see also* Jn. Lambe
Aulford, Edwd., broad weaver, Mere, 1587, AB, I, P5/1587/2, P5/4Reg/148B
Edwd., Lydiard T., 1672, AB, a/c, P3/A/139
Eliz., widow, Tisb., 1813, W, Wr, P2/1813/66
Grace, widow, Lyme R., Dorset, 1693, AB, I, W, P16/114
Hy., Chards., Devon, 1691, AB, I, P14/73
Jas., Mere, 1630, AB, I, P5/1629/1, P5/11Reg/133D
Jas., yeo., Mere, 1710, I, W, P5/1710/3, P5/15Reg/213
Jas., yeo., Tisb., 1726, W, P2/A/408
Jas., maltster, Tisb., 1773, W, P2/A/513
Jas., yeo., Place Farm, Tisb., 1782, W, P2/A/535
Jas., Tisb., 1794, W, P2/A/558
Jas., yeo., Sherrington, 1841, W, Wr, P2/1841/66
Joan, widow, Hincke's Mill, Mere, 1612, I, W, P5/1612/1, P5/9Reg/81C
Joan, widow, Lyme R., Dorset, 1634, AB, comm, I, W (GVS), P5/1634/18
Jn., Mere, 1590, W, P5/1590/1, P5/5Reg/80B
Jn., [hatter], Chipp., 1665, AB, comm, I, P3/A/107
Eaylford, Jn., [Marl.] (NBI), 1668, W, P26/157
Ailford, Jn., husb., Overton, 1670, I, ren, W, P3/A/132
Alfield, Jn., sen., yeo., Winkfield, Berks., 1750, W, P1/A/363
Jn., yeo., Tisb., 1785-92, AB, W, P2/A/541
Jn., Warm., 1807, AB, Wr, P2/1807/67
Jn., poulterer, Sal., 1848, W, Wr, P1/1848/34
Jos., Tisb., 1806, AB, Wr, P2/1806/52
Lucy, widow, Mere, 1729, AB, I, W, P5/1729/2, P5/16Reg/221C
Mgt., widow, Mere, 1588, W, P5/5Reg/27D
Mgt., widow, Mere, 1742, W, Wr, P5/1742/1
Margery, sp., Mere, 1633, I, W, P5/1633/1, P5/12Reg/146E
My., widow, Lyme R., Dorset, 1673, AB, comm, P16/31
My., widow, Mere, 1710, W, P5/1710/4, P5/15Reg/212
My., sp., Devizes, 1798, AB, comm, P1/A/480, P1/15Reg/35A
Rd., clothman, Mere, 1567, W, P5/2Reg/21A
Rd., Stourton, 1578, W, P2/A/13, P2/5Reg/299B
Robt., Motc., Dorset, 1664, AB, P27/1/13
Robt., Mere, 1675, AB, I, P5/1675/4
Robt., sen., Sherb., Dorset, 1685, AB, I, P5/1685/2
Sam., cordw., Devizes, 1796, comm, W, P1/A/479, P1/15Reg/7B
Sam., yeo., Witheyslade, Tisb., 1832, W, Wr, P2/1832/24
Susan, widow, Limpers Hill, Mere, 1713, AB, I, P5/1713/4

Susanna, sp., Tisb., 1776, W, P2/A/521
Susanna, widow, Tisb., 1792, AB, P2/A/553
Thos., Bradford A., 1570, AB, P2/5Reg/101B
Thos., carp., Mere, 1580, AB, a/c, I, P5/1580/3, P5/4Reg/5A
Thos., miller, Pitteridge, Mere, 1619, I, W, P5/1619/5, P5/10Reg/59
Thos., Mere, [1620?], a/c, P5/1620/45
Thos., wheeler, Mere, 1623, AB, I, P5/1623/1, P5/10Reg/212A
Thos., Mere, 1630, AB, P5/11Reg/132C
Thos., yeo., Barrow St., Mere, 1696, I, W, P5/1696/40
Thos., yeo., Mere, 1739, W, Wr, P5/1739/1
Thos., husb., Sherrington, 1807, W, Wr, P2/1807/39
Aulford, Walter, sen., wheeler, Mere, 1587, AB, I, W, P5/1587/1, P5/4Reg/148C
Walter, wheeler, Mere, 1618, I, W, P5/1618/1, P5/10Reg/34A
Walter, sen., blacksmith, Mere, 1690, I (detailed), W, P5/1690/2
Walter, blacksmith, Mere, 1704, W, P5/1704/1
Walter, Mere, 1731, AB, P5/1731/2
Wm., Mere, 1588, AB, P5/5Reg/27E
Wm., mariner, Lyme R., Dorset, 1614, comm, I, NW, P5/1614/1, P5/9Reg/155B
Wm., Mere, 1630, AB, P5/11Reg/133C
Wm., mariner, Lyme R., Dorset, 1641, AB, I, P5/1641/1, P5/14Reg/33C
Wm., merchant, Lyme R., Dorset, 1648, AB, comm, P5/1648/1, P5/14Reg/106B
Wm., bodice maker, Sal., 1662, AB, ren, W, P4/1662/2
Wm., linen weaver, Mere, 1667, AB, I, P5/1666/1
Wm., hatter and gent., Devizes, 1672, I, W, P1/A/130
Wm., mariner, Lyme R., Dorset, 1691, AB, I, P16/108
Wm., glover, Tisb., 1733, W, P2/A/423
see also Elford
Alines *see* Allen
Allam, Benet, widow, Wokm., Berks., 1643, W, P5/1642/2, P5/14Reg/57C
Rd., bach., Wantage, Berks., 1788-99, AB (3 - 2 re goods left unadmd by his brother Jn. A.), comm (2), P5/1788/1, P5/18Reg/103A, 286A, P23/815
Sarah, widow, Abingdon, Berks., 1767, W, P1/A/405, P1/12Reg/250A
Thos., Wokm., Berks., 1643, AB, P5/1642/3
Allambridge, Jn., yeo., Enmore Grn, Motc., Dorset, 1701, I, W, P5/1701/4
My., widow, Enmore Grn, Motc., Dorset, 1819, W, L (2), Wr, P19/225
Thos., minor, Sherb., Dorset (form. of Yetm., Dorset), 1750, app. of guardians, T, P5/1750/1
Thos., gent., Enmore Grn, Motc., Dorset, 1792, comm, W, P5/1792/1, P5/18Reg/177B
Allaway *see* Alloway
Allbright *see* Albright
Allen, [female], no abode stated; proved at Boyton, 1611, W, P2/A/92
Agnes, widow, Yatton K., 1623, I, W, P3/A/37
Ann, sp., Pewsey, 1728, AB, comm, W, P3/A/323
Ann, widow, Rams., 1728, AB, P5/16Reg/168A
Ann, sp., Upavon, 1734-45, AB (2), P2/A/426
Ann, widow, Clewer, New Windsor, Berks., 1738, AB, I, P1/A/322
Ann, widow, Easton, 1745, W, P3/A/380
Ann, widow, Sal., 1797, cert, comm, W, P4/1797/10
Ann, widow, Didcot, Berks., 1798, AB, W, P1/A/483, P1/15Reg/87
Ann, widow, Hurst, Berks., 1828, AB, Wr, P5/1828/15
Allin, Ann, widow, Rams., 1728, AB, P5/1728/1
Anna, widow, Pewsey, 1802, W, P3/1802/36
Allen als Kember, Anth., yeo., Badbury, Chiseldon, 1708, I, W, P3/A/262
Anth., bach., Wrou., 1750, AB, P3/A/392
Anth., gent., Whitley, Melk., 1826, comm (endorsed with L from Sal. Probate Registry to solicitors, on unconnected business), W, Wr, P2/1826/15
Barbara, widow, Devizes, 1686, I, W, P1/A/157
Benedict, gent., Calne, 1623, AB, I (2), P5/1623/2, P5/10Reg/159A
Cath., widow, Wokm., Berks., 1676, a/c, T (re Jos. & Cath. A., minors), P5/1676/2
Allen als Barker, Cath., wife, Wokm., Berks., 1676, AB, I, P5/1675/1
Allens, Christian, collarmaker's widow, Fovant Stroud, 1683, I, W, P2/A/293

David, butcher, Amesb., 1835, W, Wr, P1/1835/63
Dorothy, widow, Durrington, 1664, I, W, P2/A/223
Dorothy, widow, Holnest, Dorset, 1712, W, P5/1712/2, P5/15Reg/291
Edborough, widow, Reading, Berks., 1735, W, P1/A/307, P1/8Reg/8
Edith, widow, Wedh., Urchf., 1582, W, P2/6Reg/62B
Edith, widow, Warm., 1685, AB, I, P2/A/302
Edmd., Wilsford nr Pewsey, 1566, W, P2/4Reg/239B
Edmd., husb., Charlton, Charminster, Dorset, 1671, AB, ren, P5/1671/2
Edwd., jun., vict., Amesb., 1672, I, NW, P2/A/258
Edwd., butcher, Sal., 1675, AB, I, W, P4/1675/2
Edwd., sen., bargemaster, Reading, Berks., 1683, AB, I, ren, W, P1/A/153
Edwd., gent., Reading, Berks., 1717, I, W, P1/A/243, P1/6Reg/94
Allin, Edwd., carp., Pewsey, 1722, AB, ren, W, P3/A/293
Edwd., Pewsey, 1730-37, AB (3), P3/A/324, 341, 357
Edwd., Rowde, 1750, AB, P3/A/393
Edwd., horse driver, Hinton, Steeple A., 1764, W, P2/A/489
Allen als Kimber, Eleanor, widow, Coate, Liddington, 1669, comm, I, W, P3/A/125
Eleonora, widow, Bradford A., 1822, O, W, Wr, P2/1822/70
Eliz., widow, Charminster, Dorset, 1582, AB, I, W, P5/1582/1, P5/4Reg/34A
Eliz., widow, Sandhurst, Berks., 1613, I, P1/A/24
Eliz., widow, Stert, Urchf., 1635, I, W, P2/A/165, P2/9Reg/101A
Eliz., widow, Sandhurst, Berks., 1636, I, W, P5/1636/3, P5/13Reg/5C
Eliz., widow, Warm., 1682, AB, NW, P2/A/287
Eliz., widow, Marl., 1723, AB, P1/A/268
Eliz., sp., Grittleton, 1795, AB, P3/A/493
Frances, widow, Hinton, Steeple A., 1765, AB, P2/A/492
Francis, sen., Stratfield M., Berks., 1773, W, P1/A/424, P1/12Reg/487B
Geo., baker, Warm., 1663, comm, I, W, P2/A/218
Geo., sen., butcher, Sal., 1719, W, P4/1719/12
Geo., gent., Sal., 1770, W, P1/A/409, P1/12Reg/300
Geo., vict., Thatcham, Berks., 1783, W, P1/A/445, P1/13Reg/476
Allin, Hannah, widow, Cumnor, Berks., 1811, W, P1/1811/79
Hy., husb., Rough Down, Preshute, 1675, comm, I, NW, P1/A/140
Hy., Hodson, Chiseldon, 1683, I, W, P3/A/177
Hy., sen., cooper, Upavon, 1711, I, W, P1/A/215, P1/5Reg/220
Hy., Upavon, 1735-45, AB (2), P1/A/314
Jacob, husb., Warm., 1672, I, NW, P1/A/125
Jas., Fordington, Dorset, 1743, AB, ren, P15/134
Jas., miller, Bishopstrow, 1766, W, P1/A/402, P1/12Reg/172A
Jas., Chipp., 1778, AB, comm, P3/A/456
Jas., horse chapman, Devizes, 1786, W, P1/A/450, P1/14Reg/77B
Jas., sackcloth weaver, Wantage, Berks., 1788, W, P5/1788/3, P5/18Reg/100B
Jas., wheelwright, Hurst, Berks., 1823, W, Wr, P5/1823/23
Jas., Sal., 1842, AB, I, Wr, P1/1842/23
Jas., yeo., Landford, 1842, W, Wr, P1/1842/67
Jas., labourer, Box, 1843, W, Wr, P3/1843/47
Jane, widow, Kellaways, 1757, AB, W, P3/A/405
Allin, Joan, Tinh., Edington, 1567, W, P2/5Reg/12A
Joan, widow, Marl., 1691, I, W, P1/A/170
Joanna, widow, Bradford A., 1775, comm, W, P2/A/516
Allin, Jn., husb., Stourpaine, Dorset, 1564, W, P5/1Reg/52B
Allin, Jn., Mere, 1600, AB, I, W, P5/1600/2, P5/6Reg/256A
Jn., baker, Warm., 1611, AB, I, P1/A/20
Jn., Southbrook, Bere R., Dorset, [1619], W, P5/1619/4
Jn., blacksmith, Chiseldon, 1637, I, W, P3/A/69
Alines, Jn., yeo., Trowle, Bradford A., 1669, AB, a/c, I (2), P2/A/244, 247
Jn., yeo., W. Compton, Berks., 1680, AB, comm, I, P1/A/147
Jn., clothier, Fordington, Dorset, 1698, I, W, P5/1698/1
Jn., Sal., 1701, AB, P4/1701/2
Jn., yeo., Devizes, 1701, AB, I, P1/A/190

Allen als Chapp, Jn., [maltster], Thickwood, Colerne, 1709, AB, I, P3/A/264
Jn., yeo., Holnest, Dorset, 1712, AB, I, W, P5/1712/1, P5/15Reg/290
Jn., fellmonger, Devizes, 1713, W, P1/A/220, P1/5Reg/291
Jn., sen., yeo., Upton, Blewbury, Berks., 1713, W, P5/1713/2, P5/15Reg/369A
Jn., sen., butcher, Durrington, 1716, W, P1/A/237, P1/6Reg/12A
Jn., Upton, Blewbury, Berks., 1717, L, W, copy W, P5/1717/2, P5/15Reg/397A
Jn., sen., yeo., Countess Farm, Amesb., 1726, W, P2/A/409
Jn., Pewsey, 1738-40, AB, W, P3/A/360, 367
Jn., apothecary, Devizes, 1743, comm, W, P1/A/345, P1/9Reg/235
Jn., Pewsey, 1748, AB, P3/A/386
Jn., labourer, Thatcham, Berks., 1753, W, P1/A/372, P1/11Reg/27
Jn., Durrington, 1754, AB, P2/A/472
Jn., sen., miller, Meerhay, Beam., Dorset, 1754, W, P17/526
Jn., Kellaways, 1757, AB, W, P3/A/406
Allen als Chapp, Jn., carp. and widower, Slaughterford, 1758, AB, comm, ren, P3/A/408
Jn., yeo., E. Kennett, 1764, W, P3/A/429
Jn., sen., vict., Devizes, 1766, W, P1/A/403, P1/12Reg/183
Jn., Amesb., 1776, AB, P1/A/429
Jn., horse driver, Hilp., 1777, W, P2/A/527
Jn., Devizes, 1795, AB, P1/A/478, P1/14Reg/634B
Jn., yeo., Binknoll, Broad H., 1799, W, P3/A/496
Jn., carp., Pewsey, 1800, W, P3/1800/21
Jn., brazier, Chipp., 1816, W, Wr, P3/1816/30
Jonathan, Sherb., Dorset, 1780, AB, P5/1780/2, P5/17Reg/199A
Jos., Wokm., Berks., 1675, AB, I, P5/1675/3
Allin, Jos., yeo., Bremhill, 1724, AB, I, P3/A/298
Jos., Draycot C., 1756, AB, comm, P3/A/401
Jos., glover, Hungerford, Berks., 1762, W, P23/695
Jos., Peasemore, Berks., 1767, AB, P1/A/404
Mgt., widow, Devizes, 1709, AB, P1/A/207
Mgt., widow, E. Kennett, 1789, W, P1/A/460, P1/14Reg/284
Margery, widow, Warm., 1598, AB, I, P2/A/55
Martha, sp., Sal., 1679, AB, P4/1679/14
My., sp., Charminster, Dorset, 1698, AB, comm, W, P5/1698/2
My., Pewsey, 1713, AB, P3/A/275
My., widow, Wantage, Berks., 1733, W, P23/494
My., widow, Devizes, 1744, comm, W, P1/A/346, P1/9Reg/276
My., widow, Devizes Grn, Bps. C., 1761, comm, W, P24/1106
My., sp., Thatcham, Berks. (form. of Newbury, Berks.), 1776, W, P1/A/433, P1/13Reg/118B
My., widow, Woodb., 1790, W, P1/A/467, P1/14Reg/352
My., wife, W. Wellow, 1832, AB, Wr, P2/1832/29
Matthew, gent., Devizes, 1693, bond to return W, W, P1/A/177
Matthew, gent., Nursteed, Bps. C., 1752, W, P24/1038
Philip, tanner, Wantage, Berks., 1691, I, W, P5/1691/3
Phoebe *see* Phoebe Wilkins
Allin, Rd., Tinh., Edington, 1559, W, P2/3Reg/148B
Rd., husb., W. Ashton, Steeple A., 1575, W, P2/5Reg/228C
Rd., yeo., Tinh., Edington, 1624, I (detailed), W, P2/A/133
Allen als Chapp, Rd., Malm., 1640, I, W, P3/A/81
Rd., bricklayer, Newbury, Berks., 1686-87, AB, I, W, P1/A/158, 165
Rd., Pewsey, 1697, AB, P3/A/232
Rd., butcher, Trowb., 1712, I, W, P2/A/374
Rd., yeo., Cuttenham Farm, N. Newnton, 1723, AB, comm, P3/A/294
Rd., husb., Clewer, New Windsor, Berks., 1735, W, P1/A/309, P1/8Reg/13
Rd., watchmaker, Pangbourne, Berks., 1820, W, Wr, P1/1820/105
Rd., carp., Pewsey, 1842, AB, Wr, P3/1842/42
Robt., vicar, Liddington, 1557, AB, P1/1Reg/14B
Robt., husb., Charminster, Dorset, 1614-19, I, W, P5/1619/2, P5/9Reg/223B
Robt., husb., Boreham, Warm., 1661, AB, comm, I, P2/A/215
Allin, Robt., glover, Marl., 1715, W, P1/A/235, P1/5Reg/479A

Robt., yeo., Trowb., 1800, W, P1/1800/1, P1/15Reg/198B
Sam., fellmonger, Malm., 1723, I, W, P3/A/295
Sam., d. at sea on HMS *Elizabeth*, Hawkeridge, Westb., 1746, W, P25/1746/5
Sarah, sp., Sal., 1678, NW, P4/1678/1
Sarah, widow, Dilton M., Westb., 1826, AB, O, Wr, P25/1826/1
Seth, sen., horse chapman, Devizes, 1738, W, P1/A/328, P1/8Reg/318
Seth, horse dealer, Warm., 1776, W, P1/A/431, P1/13Reg/150
Simon, tailor, Highw., 1576, AB, I, W, P5/1576/2, P5/3Reg/89E
Simon, sen., yeo., Pewsey, 1635, I (detailed), W, P3/A/66
Allin, Simon, Dauntsey, 1670, AB, I, P3/A/127
Simon, sawyer, Pewsey, 1714, AB, I, P3/A/278
Allin, Simon, gent., Dauntsey, 1728-33, W (2), P3/A/311, 334
Steph., Everleigh, 1777, AB, comm, P3/A/453
Steph., Pewsey, 1832, AB, O, Wr, P1/1832/31
Steph., yeo., Southcott, Pewsey, 1853, comm, W, Wr, P3/1853/19
Allin, Thos., vicar, Downton, 1559, T (child: Rd. A.), W, P2/4Reg/12B
Thos., sen., smith, Mere, 1570, W, P5/2Reg/89A
Thos., husb., Pewsey, 1604, I, W, P3/A/3
Thos., sen., yeo., Durrington, 1692, I, W, P1/A/172
Thos., yeo., Durrington, 1715, comm, W, P2/A/383
Thos., Rams., 1716, AB, P5/1716/2
Thos., fellmonger, Pott., 1718, W (draft), NW, P1/A/245, P1/6Reg/170A
Thos., sen., yeo., Grove, Wantage, Berks., 1731, W (& cod), P5/1731/1
Thos., Bradford A., 1764, AB, comm, P2/A/490
Allin, Thos., Thatcham, Berks., 1770, W, P1/A/414, P1/12Reg/342
Thos., Southbroom, 1771, AB, P24/1150
Thos., broad weaver, Winsley, Bradford A., 1776, W, P1/A/432, P1/13Reg/93B
Thos., retired fellmonger, Newbury, Berks., 1820, comm, W, Wr, P1/1820/44
Thos., wheelwright, Hurst, Berks., 1844, W, Wr, P5/1844/9
Timothy, Devizes, 1682, AB, comm, P1/A/151
Walter, clerk, Reading St My., Berks., 1625, AB, I, P1/A/46
Allin, Wm., husb., E. Knoyle, 1559, W, P2/3Reg/183E
Allin als Hutchins, Wm., Gillingham, Dorset, 1577, W, P27/1Reg/34A
Wm., weaver, Iford, Westwood, 1601, AB, I, P2/A/61
Wm., yeo., Tinh., Edington, 1615, W, P2/A/104
Wm., Boreham, Warm., 1624, AB, I, P2/A/135
Allens, Wm., no place visible but overseers are of Etchilhampton & Urchf., [1627], I, W (badly damaged), P1/A/50
Wm., Beam., Dorset, 1671, AB, P5/1671/3
Allin, Wm., yeo., Kepnal, Pewsey, 1687, I, W, P3/A/198
Wm., Pewsey, 1728, AB, P3/A/310
Wm., cooper, Upavon, 1737-44, AB (2 - left unadmd), ren, W, P2/A/434
Wm., sen., yeo., Pewsey, 1738, W, P3/A/361
Wm., yeo., Everleigh, 1764, W, P3/A/430
Wm., Warm., 1770, AB, P2/A/507
Wm., besom maker, Speen, Berks., 1776, W, P1/A/434, P1/13Reg/146B
Wm., butcher, Sal., 1776, W, P1/A/435, P1/13Reg/149B
Wm., sen., gent., Amesb., 1796, W, P2/A/561
Wm., broad weaver, Westb., 1816, W, Wr, P25/1816/9
Wm., yeo., Boreham, Warm., 1831, W, Wr, P2/1831/37
Wm., sen., carp., Pewsey, 1835, comm, W, Wr, P3/1835/22
see also Chapp als A.; Ellen
Alley, Aley, Agnes, widow, Homington, 1623, deed of gift, P24/190
Alye, Geo., yeo., Homington, 1605, I, W (both dated 1592), P24/1
Hy., weaver, Wantage, Berks., 1628, I, W, P5/1628/2, P5/11Reg/89
Elly, Isaac, Pott., 1789, AB, P1/E/285
Jas., miller, Hawkeridge, Westb., 1770, W, P25/1770/2
Elloy, Wm., Highw., 1638, AB, P5/1638/38, P5/13Reg/134A
Wm., Beedon, Berks., 1795, AB, P1/A/477, P1/14Reg/583A
Allin *see* Allen
Allis, Alice, widow, Charlton nr Malm., 1736, W, P3/A/348

Eliz., widow, Charlton nr Malm., 1670, I, W, P3/A/126
Eliz., widow, Poole Keynes, 1724-25, AB, comm, P3/A/299, 302
Jn., Long Newnton, 1620, AB, P3/A/29
Jn., yeo., Horton, Bps. C., 1697, comm, I, W, P24/503
Jn., yeo., Charlton nr Malm., 1736, AB, W, P3/A/347
Julian, widow, Charlton nr Malm., [1619], I, W (NEP), P3/A/25
Robt., husb., Charlton nr Malm., 1647, W, P1/A/86
Susanna, [widow], Charlton nr Malm., 1706, W, P3/A/257
Thos., yeo., Charlton nr Malm., 1641, I, W, P3/A/86
Thos., yeo., Charlton nr Malm., 1664, I, W, P3/A/102
Allison, Jn., cordw., Winkfield, Berks., 1756, W, P1/A/385, P1/11Reg/213A
Mgt., widow, Devizes, 1852, AB, O, Wr, P1/1852/12
Rd., husb., Elcombe, Wrou., 1623, I, P3/A/34
Allnut, My., maltster's widow, Sutton C., Berks., 1770, W, P1/A/415, P1/12Reg/362
Nich., tailor, Reading St Lawr., Berks., 1664, AB, I, P1/A/107
Alloway, Allway, Alice, widow, Sherston, 1770, AB, P1/A/411
Ann, widow, Wokm., Berks., 1701, W, P5/1701/3
Allaway, Cath., widow, Brokenb., 1745, W, P3/A/381
Allway, Chris., weaver, Keevil, 1598, I, W, P2/A/53
Allway, Denise, widow, Keevil, 1604, I, W, P2/A/69
Allway, Edith, widow, Keevil, 1593, AB, I, W, P2/A/33
Allaway, Edwd., yeo., Bulk., Keevil, 1672-76, AB, a/c, I, P2/A/257
Jacob, farmer, Aldermaston, Berks., 1817, W, Wr, P1/1817/64
Allway, Jas., yeo., Keevil, 1686, comm, I, W, P1/A/160
Jas., Sonning, Berks., 1749, AB, P5/1749/2
Allaway, Jas., Malm., 1838, AB, O, Wr, P3/1838/6
Allaway, Jane, Hilp., 1769, AB, W, P2/A/506
Joan, widow, Reading, Berks., 1738, W, P1/A/323, P1/8Reg/284A
Allway, Jn., weaver, Keevil, 1574, W, P2/5Reg/207A
Allway, Jn., husb., Keevil, 1579, AB, I, Wr, P2/A/15, P2/5Reg/353C
Allaway, Jn., blacksmith, Brokenb., 1708, I, W, P3/A/261
Allaway, Jonas, yeo., Brinkw., 1743, W, P3/A/376
Jonas, yeo., Lt. Somerford, 1781, W, Wr, P3/A/463
Moses, Rams., 1761, AB, P5/1761/1
Allway, Nathaniel, Sherston, 1711, AB, P1/A/216
Allway, Nathaniel, yeo., Willesley, Sherston, 1742, W, P3/A/371
Rd., gardener *or* cook, Wokm., Berks., 1678, I, W, P5/1678/20
Rd., Wokm., Berks., 1700, AB, I, P5/1700/2
Rd., blacksmith *or* yeo., Lt. Somerford, 1717, I, W, P3/A/285
Allaway, Robt., Chipp., 1646, AB, I, P1/A/84
Allaway, Robt., broad weaver, Chipp., 1662, comm, I, W, P3/A/95
Allway, Robt., Malm., 1770, AB, P1/A/412
Alloway *or* Allway, Sarah, widow, Trowb., 1838, O, W, Wr, P1/1838/15
Allaway, Thos., Keevil, 1633, I, W, P2/A/158
Thos., yeo., Lt. Somerford, 1668, I, W, P3/A/117
Thos., yeo., Wokm., Berks., 1692, W, P5/1692/2
Thos., yeo., Wokm., Berks., 1740, W, Wr, P5/1740/1
Walter, clerk and curate, Maddington, 1634, AB, I, P1/A/62
Walter, Tilehurst, Berks., 1741, W, P1/A/336, P1/9Reg/126
Allway, Wm., weaver, Bulk., Keevil, 1621, AB, I, W, P2/A/120
Wm., yeo., Lt. Somerford, 1631, I, W, P3/A/58
Allaway, Wm., sen., Bulk., Keevil, 1667-69, AB, a/c, I, P2/A/234
Allaway, Wm., sen., yeo., Hilp., 1700, AB, I, P2/A/342
Allaway, Wm., Hilp., 1753, AB, W, P1/A/375, P1/11Reg/104B
Allaway, Wm., yeo., Stowford, Wingfield, 1797, AB, W, P2/A/566
Wm., glazier, Sonning, Berks., 1825, W, Wr, P5/1825/10
see also Elloway *or* A.
Allsey, Awsey, Jn., yeo., Dunsden, Sonning, Berks., 1622-23, I, W, P5/1622/87, P5/10Reg/208
Thos., bricklayer, Winkfield, Berks., 1628, I, W, P1/A/54
Allston *see* Elstone

Allsup *see* Alsop
Allsworth *see* Allworth
Allway *see* Alloway
Allwood, Ayleward, Agnes, widow, Sandhurst, Berks., 1569, W, P5/2Reg/36B
Eylward, Christian, widow, Rowde, 1608, W, P3/E/6
Edwd., mason, Shrewton, 1598, I, W, P2/A/50
Hy., Motc., Dorset, 1703, AB, P27/1/146
Jas., Enmore Grn, Motc., Dorset, 1690, AB, I, P19/58
Jn., hellier, Motc., Dorset, 1570, W, P27/1Reg/21C
Aylverd *or* Aylford, Jn., Oare, Wilcot, 1639, I, W, P3/A/77
Jn., Holnest, Dorset, 1758, W, P5/1758/3
Aylward, Wm., bucket maker, Sandhurst, Berks., 1592, I, W, P5/1592/3, P5/6Reg/13A
Allworth, Ailworth, And., W. Hanney, Berks., 1741, W, P1/A/333, P1/9Reg/96
Giles, gent., Savernake Park, 1679, W, P3/A/159
Hy., yeo., W. Ashton, Steeple A., 1759, W, P2/A/481
Hy., yeo., Westb., 1844, O, W, Wr, P25/1844/1
Allsworth, Jn., husb., Swindon, 1640, I, W, P3/A/82
Jn., yeo., W. Ashton, Steeple A., 1714, W, P1/A/232, P1/5Reg/440
Wm., yeo., Hilp., 1811, comm, W, Wr, P2/1811/1
Allwright, Eliz., widow, Reading St Giles, Berks., 1792, W, P1/A/472, P1/14Reg/416
Francis, sen., yeo., Arborfield, Berks., 1632, I, W, P5/1632/3, P5/12Reg/98
Francis, sen., husb., Arborfield, Berks., 1695, I, W, P5/1695/3
Jas., yeo., Barkham, Berks., 1747, W, P1/A/359, P1/10Reg/96
Jn., Liberty of Newland, Hurst, Berks., 1776, W, P5/1776/1, P5/17Reg/122A
My., wife, Reading, Berks., 1829, AB, comm, D, Wr, P1/1829/67
Matthew, smith, Arborfield, Berks., 1567, W, P5/2Reg/27C
Matthew, Anfields Cross, Hurst, Berks., 1573, I, P5/1573/4, P5/3Reg/24C
Matthew, Hurst, Berks., 1576, AB, P5/1576/1, P5/3Reg/88F
Rd., clothier, Reading St My., Berks., 1671, AB, W, P1/A/126
Sarah, sp., Letcombe Regis, Berks., 1789, AB, P1/A/461
Thos., yeo., Liberty of Newland, Hurst, Berks., 1695, I, W, P5/1695/1
Thos., sen., yeo., Liberty of Newland, Hurst, Berks., 1709, W, P5/1709/2, P5/15Reg/127
Thos., Arborfield, Berks., 1719, AB, P5/1719/1
Wm., yeo., Arborfield, Berks., 1668, I, NW, P5/1668/1
Wm., blacksmith, Arborfield, Berks., 1743, W, Wr, P5/1743/1
Wm., Wokm., Berks., 1752-55, AB, comm, P5/1752/1, P5/1755/1
Wm., innholder, Tinh., Edington, 1763, AB, a/c, comm, I, P1/A/399
Wm., shopkeeper, Hurst, Berks., 1827, comm, W, Wr, P5/1827/10
Alner, Olner, Alice, widow, Thornford, Dorset, 1581, I, W, P5/1580/43, P5/4Reg/16B
Olner, Ann, widow, Thornford, Dorset, 1581, I, W, P5/1580/44, P5/4Reg/16A
Caleb, bach., Bere R., Dorset, 1850, comm, D (2), W (& cod), Wr, P5/1850/10
Chris., [Dawlish, Dorset] (NBI), 1682, I, P30/2
Eliz., widow, Bloxworth, Dorset, 1734, W, P5/1734/3
Eliz., widow, Milford, Sal. St Mart., 1818, W, Wr, P4/1818/15
Jas., sen., schoolmaster, Dinton, 1793, W, P2/A/554
Jas., clerk, Milford, Sal. St Mart., 1814, W, Wr, P1/1814/12
Jn., blacksmith, Bere R., Dorset, 1809, AB, W, P5/1809/40
Jos., Turners Puddle, Dorset, 1778, AB, P5/1778/1, P5/17Reg/159C
Rd., yeo., Ebbesborne Wake, 1638, I, W, P2/A/179
Robt., yeo., Bloxworth, Dorset, 1702, comm, W, Wr, P5/1701/2
Robt., Turners Puddle, Dorset, 1760, W, P5/1760/1
Robt., yeo., Bloxworth, Dorset, 1762, W, P5/1762/1
Robt., Bloxworth, Dorset, 1773, AB, P5/1773/1
Thos., yeo., Bloxworth, Dorset, 1780, AB, ren, P5/1780/3, P5/17Reg/187A
Wm., Bloxworth, Dorset, 1712, I, W, P5/1712/4, P5/15Reg/299
Alnewick, Alnewick, Amon, clerk and parson, Didcot, Berks., 1621, AB, a/c, I, P1/A/38
Alow, Eylowe, Agnes, widow, Gt. Cheverell, 1578, I, T, W, P2/E/17, P2/5Reg/308A
Eylowe, Jn., husb., Gt. Cheverell, 1575, I, T, W, P2/E/15, P2/5Reg/239C
Aylowe, Jn., husb., Gt. Cheverell, 1627, I, W, P2/A/142
Aylowe, Jn., Gt. Cheverell, 1629, AB, P2/A/146

Jn., Rams., 1693, AB, I, P5/1693/3
Mgt., widow, E. Coulston, 1592, I, W, P1/A/3
Wm., husb., E. Coulston, 1603, I, W, P2/A/66
Alridge, Alridge als Annatt, Thos., Upavon, 1557, AB, P2/3Reg/21C, P2/3Reg/24D
Alrith, Cath., Wokm., Berks., 1683, AB, comm, P5/1682/4
Alshare, Rd., Maddington, 1552, I, W, P2/A/1, P2/2Reg/147A
Wm., husb., Mkt. L., 1630, AB, I, P2/A/150
Alsop, Ann, sp., Long Newnton, 1823, AB, Wr, P1/1823/75
Chas., yeo., Hullavington, 1835, O, W, P3/1835/14
Allsup, Chris., surgeon, Pewsey, 1738, AB, deed of gift, P3/A/362
Jos., no abode stated; proved at Warm., 1735, W, P2/A/430
Awsopp als Marks, Wm., W. Harnham, 1573, W, P5/3Reg/7A
Alston *see* Allston
Alt *see* Ault
Alvin, Rd., gent., Sal., 1830, AB, O, LA, P4/1830/7
Alye *see* Alley
Aman, Amans, Cath., widow, Castleton, Dorset, 1773, comm, W, P5/1773/2, P5/17Reg/74C
Awman, Deodatus, glover, Wantage, Berks., 1693, AB, I, W, P23/182
Awman, Hy., Ruscombe, Berks., 1616, AB, I, P5/1616/1
Thos., mason, Sherb., Dorset, 1607, AB, comm, I, P5/1607/2, P5/8Reg/87B
Amans, Walter, mason, Sherb., Dorset, 1613, AB, I, T, P5/1613/1, P5/9Reg/110B
Wm., Winterborne K., Dorset, 1739, AB, Wr, P5/1739/2
Ambrose, Ann, sp., Abingdon, Berks., 1747, W, P1/A/358, P1/10Reg/76A
Chas., sen., gent., Abingdon, Berks., 1723, W, P1/A/262, P1/6Reg/465B
Eliz., Milston, 1681, AB, P2/A/280
Eliz., widow, Letcombe Regis, Berks., 1773, AB, comm, P1/A/421
Jn., glover, Donhead St My., 1630-34, AB, a/c (1634), I (2), P2/A/149
Jn., yeo., Milton, E. Knoyle, 1639, I, W (2 - 1 a copy), P2/A/183
Jn., weaver, Compton C., [1678], court papers, W, P2/A/269
Jn., maltster, Newbury, Berks., 1729, NW, P1/A/287, P1/7Reg/281
Thos., Haywood Farm, Chilton F., 1725, I, W, P3/A/303
Wm., Corton, Boyton, 1592, I, W, P2/A/31
Wm., yeo., Compton C., 1669, AB, I, P2/A/243
Wm., yeo., Stratfield M., Berks., 1723, W, P1/A/265, P1/7Reg/4B
Amer *see* Amor
Amery, Wm., Wokm., Berks., [1550], W, P5/20Reg/105B
Ames, Agnes, Netton, Durnford, 1596, AB, I, W, P5/1596/2, P5/6Reg/123A
Alice, widow, Kingston D., 1583, W, P2/6Reg/108B
Ann, Salterton, Durnford, 1632-35, AB, I, P9/2
Amis, Edwd., husb., Gt. Durnford, 1614, I, W, P5/1614/2, P5/9Reg/140B
Frances, widow, Ford, Laverstock, 1644, I, W, P2/A/198
Amis, Geo., Semley, 1553, AB, P2/2Reg/180A
Geo., clothw., Westb., 1742, W, P25/1742/2
Amos, Geo., yeo., Malm. Abbey, 1851, O, W, Wr, P3/1851/14
Hy., baker, Sal. St Thos., 1646, I, W, P1/A/83
Amis, Isabel, widow, Bulford, 1557, W, P2/3Reg/33A
Jn., Semley, 1581, W, P2/6Reg/33B
Amos, Jn., chandler, Sopworth, 1686, I, W, P3/A/195
Jn., saddletree maker, Wilton, 1694, AB, I (2), ren, P2/A/325
Amos, Jn., soap boiler, Sherston, 1718, I, W, P3/A/287
Amis, Lawr., husb., Semley, 1541, I, W (NEP), P30/3
Amos, Rd., tallow chandler, Sopworth, 1733, W, P3/A/335
Sam., Sal., 1686, AB, I, P4/1685/31
Aymes, Thos., Hindon, 1598, AB, I, P2/A/56
Thos., husb., Gt. Durnford, 1621, AB, I, T, W, P5/1621/2, P5/10Reg/24A
Amis, Wm., Broad C., 1557, AB, P2/3Reg/33E
Wm., Durnford, 1588, AB, I, W, P5/1588/1, P5/5Reg/45C
Wm., baker, Sal., 1633, I, W, P4/1632/3
Wm., husb. *or* yeo., Lt. Woodford, 1680, I, W, P13/3/1
Amesbury, Amesbury als Horn, Cath., widow, Yarnbrook, N. Bradley, 1585, I (detailed), W, P2/A/18, P2/7Reg/16D

Cath., widow, Yarnbrook, N. Bradley, 1587, W, P2/7Reg/67
Geo., Bradford A., 1787, AB, comm, W, P2/A/545
Jn., yeo., N. Bradley, [1680], I, W, P2/A/276
Jos., tailor, Limpley Stoke, Bradford A., 1767, comm, W, P2/A/499
My., widow, Holt, Bradford A., 1752, W, P2/A/467
Emsbury als Hurne, Rd., broad weaver, N. Bradley, 1637, I, W, P2/E/128
Amesbury als Hurne, Robt., Westb., 1576, AB, I, P25/1576/1, P5/3Reg/84B
Wm., [chandler], Limpley Stoke, Bradford A., 1732, AB, I, P1/A/302
Wm., Bradford A., 1760, AB, P2/A/483
Amey, Sarah, sp., Sherb., Dorset, 1781, W, P5/1781/1, P5/17Reg/212A
Ameyrs *see* Amor
Amiat *see* Emmett
Amills, Geo., weaver, Westb., 1719, comm, W, P25/1719/1
Geo., shopkeeper, Hawkeridge, Westb., 1762, W, P25/1762/5
Hy., Hawkeridge, Westb., 1704, I, P25/1704/12
Amill, Jn., sen., Chitterne AS, 1552, I, W, P2/A/3, P2/2Reg/155A
Jn., yeo., Westb., 1632, I (ref. to looms), W, P25/1632/4
Jn., sen., yeo., Westb., 1638, I, W, P25/1638/11
Jn., sen., clothw., Westb., 1724, AB, I, W, P25/1724/13
Mgt., widow, Westb., 1642, I, W (part missing) (NEP), P25/1642/7
Nich., sen., yeo., Westb., 1635, I (detailed), W, P25/1635/7
Nich., yeo., Westb., 1673, I, W, P25/1673/4
Robt., weaver, Westb., 1678, I, NW, P25/1678/2
Wm., [weaver], Westb., 1642, comm, I, W, P25/1642/5
Wm., Westb., 1715, AB, I, P25/1715/5
Wm., broad weaver, Westb., 1733, W, P25/1733/2
Wm., Westb., 1739, AB, P25/1739/3
Amis *see* Ames
Amiser *see* Phillips als A.
Amor, Aldhelm, yeo., Bps. C., 1732, AB, I, ren, P24/963
Amer, Ann, widow, Charl. nr. P., 1707, W, P1/A/203
Ann, sp., Rushall, 1741, W, P1/A/341, P1/9Reg/179
Benj., Trowb., 1779, AB, W, P1/A/440, P1/13Reg/236A
Chas., husb., Burdens Ball, Wilton (described as in S. Newton), 1682, I, W, P2/A/286
Amor als Somerset, Chas., publican, Pewsey, 1841, comm, W, Wr, P3/1841/31
Deborah, sp., Avebury, 1818, AB, Wr, P3/1818/35
Edmd. *or* Edwd., yeo., Rushall, 1705, I, W, P2/A/352
Edmd., yeo., Lt. Wishford, S. Newton, 1711, I, W, P2/A/371
Edmd., Pewsey, 1753, AB, P3/A/398
Amer, Eleanor, sp., Trowb., 1842, comm, W, Wr, P1/1842/7
Eliz., widow, Damerham, Hants, 1603, AB, I, NW (2), P2/A/67
Eliz., widow, Rushall, 1741, W, P1/A/340, P1/9Reg/180
Eliz., widow, Wilsford nr Pewsey, 1749, W, P2/A/459
Eliz., widow, Laverstock, 1821, W, Wr, P2/1821/16
Eliz., widow, Devizes, 1836, O, W, Wr, P1/1836/15
Ameyrs, Ellen, widow, Over C., Dorset, 1587, I, W, P5/1587/4, P5/4Reg/153C
Ameyrs, Geo., yeo., Over C., Dorset, 1590, I, T, W, P5/1590/2, P5/5Reg/83B
Amer, Gregory, Rushall, 1602, AB, I, NW, P2/A/63
Harry, Avebury, 1777, AB, P3/A/454
Harry, Avebury, 1807, AB, Wr, P3/1807/53
Isaac, yeo., Gt. Cheverell, 1739, W, P2/A/436
Amer, Jas., Bramshaw, Hants, 1630, AB, a/c, I, P24/210
Joan, widow, Bourton, Bps. C., 1671, AB, I, P24/383
Joan, widow, Charl. nr. P., [1693], I, W, P2/A/324
Amer, Joanna, widow, N. Bradley, 1837, W, Wr, P2/1837/41
Amoore, Jn., Damerham, Hants, 1586, W, P2/7Reg/57B
Amer, Jn., sen., yeo., Charl. nr. P., 1636-38, cert, court paper, I, T, W, P1/A/76, P2/A/170
Jn., yeo., Charl. nr. P., 1721, W, P2/A/395
Jn., yeo., Patney, 1741, AB, W, P2/A/447
Jn., sen., yeo., Rushall, 1752, W, P2/A/468

Jn., sen., yeo., Patney, 1753, W, P2/A/471
Amer, Jn., yeo., Lower Studley, Trowb., 1777, W, P1/A/438, P1/13Reg/181B
Amer, Jos., yeo., Drynham, N. Bradley, 1810, comm, W, Wr, P1/1810/16
Martha, wife, Charl. nr. P., 1632, AB, P2/A/153
My., widow, Marden, 1695, I, W, P2/A/330
My., minor, Wilsford nr Pewsey, 1791, W, P2/A/551
Matthew, sen., tailor, Rushall, 1639, comm, W, P2/A/184
Amer, Nich., husb., Poulshot, 1582, W, P2/6Reg/72A
Amer, Osmund, Charl. nr. P., 1602, AB, I, W, P2/A/64
Praxey, widow, Gt. Cheverell, 1732, W, P2/A/420
Rd., Charl. nr. P., 1618, AB, I, P2/A/113
Rd., glover, Gt. Cheverell, 1668, comm, I, W, P1/A/119
Rd., yeo., Charl. nr. P., [1688], I, W, P2/A/317
Rd., Damerham, Hants, 1703, AB, P2/A/348
Rd., sen., Crookwood, Urchf., [1706], I, W, P2/A/355
Rd., Chirton, 1709, AB, P2/A/365
Rd., gent., Woodb., 1729, W, P1/A/293, P1/7Reg/355
Rd., yeo., Chilton F., 1737, I, W, P3/A/354
Rd., Pewsey, 1738, AB, P3/A/363
Rd., yeo., Crookwood, Urchf., 1738, W, P1/8Reg/210
Rd., yeo., Marston, Pott. (form. of Crookwood, Urchf.), 1738, I, W, P1/A/317
Rd., gent., Chirton, 1757, W, P2/A/476
Rd., yeo., Urchf., 1768, W, P2/A/502
Rd., builder, Sal., 1801, W, P4/1801/1
Rd., bach., Worton, Pott., 1820, AB, ren (in form of L from decd's mother to friend, asking her to act), Wr, P1/1820/124
Robt., husb., Charl. nr. P., 1560, I, W, P2/A/5, P2/4Reg/51C
Amer, Robt., Damerham, Hants, 1595, W, P2/7Reg/147C
Amer, Robt., Bourton, Bps. C., 1602, I, P24/2
Robt., yeo., Marden, 1683, I, W, P2/A/295
Robt., yeo., Patney, 1685, AB, I, P2/A/303
Robt., yeo., Gt. Cheverell, [1706], I, W, P2/A/357
Robt., Chirton, 1728, AB, P2/A/411
Robt., maltster, W. Lavington, 1734, W, P1/A/304, P1/7Reg/597A
Robt., gent., Rushall, 1740, comm, W, P2/A/444
Robt., sen., Woodb., 1772, AB, comm, P3/A/447
Robt., gent., W. Lavington, 1772, W, P1/12Reg/421
Robt., yeo., Laverstock, 1777, W, P2/A/525
Robt., Wilsford nr Pewsey, 1782, AB, P1/A/444
Sam., Gt. Cheverell, 1777, AB, P2/A/528
Sam., Bromham, 1792, receipt for AB, P3/A/498
Sarah, sp., Littleton P., 1753, W, P1/A/378, P1/11Reg/126
Sarah, W. Lavington, 1787, AB, P1/A/455
Susanna, widow, Woodb., 1731, W, P3/A/328
Amoore, Thos., Damerham, Hants, 1630, AB, a/c, I, P2/A/151
Thos., yeo., N. Newnton, 1630, AB, a/c, I, P3/A/54
Thos., glover, Gt. Cheverell, 1666, AB, I, P2/A/228
Thos., glover, Gt. Cheverell, 1711, W, P1/A/209, P1/5Reg/30
Amer, Thos., Bourton, Bps. C., 1712, AB, P24/696
Thos., Bromham, 1778, AB, comm, P3/A/457
Thornehill, Charl. nr. P., 1688, AB, I, P2/A/316
Wm., husb., Charl. nr. P., 1562, I, W, P2/A/6, P2/4Reg/103D
Wm., Charl. nr. P., 1568, W, P2/5Reg/45A
Wm., husb., Pewsey, 1605, I, W, P3/A/4
Wm., Bromham, 1669, AB, comm, I, P3/A/123
Wm., Gt. Wishford, 1684, AB, P2/A/298
Wm., Charl. nr. P., 1707, AB, P2/A/359
Wm., husb., Pewsey, 1738, W, P3/A/364
Wm., yeo., Wilsford nr Pewsey, 1745, comm, W, P2/A/451
Wm., Bromham, 1792, AB, P3/A/490
Eamor, Wm., Broomfield, Yatton K., 1820, AB, Wr, P1/1820/73

Wm., Laverstock, 1834, AB, Wr, P2/1834/24
Wm., Chitterne, 1843, O, W, Wr, P3/1843/35
Amos *see* Ames
Amyatt *see* Emmett
Anderson, Edwd., tailor, Wokm., Berks., 1576, AB, I, P5/1576/3, P5/3Reg/88B
Jn., Wokm., Berks., 1603, W, P5/7Reg/53
Rd., labourer, Aldbourne, 1752, W, P3/A/397
Robt., Marl., 1826, AB, Wr, P1/1826/96
Wm., clerk and rector, Sutton M., 1715, AB, I, W, P1/A/236, P1/5Reg/488
Wm., husb., Britford, 1722, AB, I, P24/884
Wm., gardener, Marl., 1806, W, Wr, P1/1806/10
Anderton, Edwd., Pott., 1759, AB, P1/A/390
Jas., clerk and rector, Boxford, Berks., 1698, I, W, P1/A/180, P1/3Reg/145
Peter, gent., W. Lavington, 1699, comm, W, P1/A/186, P1/3Reg/251
Andrews, Agnes, Amesb., 1566, AB, P2/4Reg/239E
Amos, carp. and joiner, Mere, 1801, W, P5/1801/17, P5/18Reg/321
And., bach., Alderton, 1855, AB, aff, O, Wr, P3/1855/45
Ann, widow, Collingbourne K., 1679, AB, I, P3/A/160
Ann, sp., Lydiard M., 1736, AB, comm, ren, P3/A/349
Ann, sp., Amesb., 1791, W, P2/A/550
Anna, Landford, 1853, AB, aff, Wr, P2/1853/63
Betty, widow, Sherb., Dorset, 1777, W, P5/1777/1, P5/17Reg/144
Androws, Cath., E. Knoyle, 1608, W, P2/8Reg/9B
Androws, Cath., Hankerton, 1736, W, P3/A/351
Chas., shopkeeper, Bremhill, 1826, comm, W, Wr, P3/1826/2
Christian, widow, Bramshaw, Hants, 1711, AB, I, P24/695
Andrew, Edmd., Upton L., 1624, AB, I (detailed), P2/A/134
Edmd., Chiseldon, 1642, W, P3/A/90
Andrew, Edwd., white baker, Uffc., Devon, 1666, AB, I, P20/1/52
Edwd., Cloatley, Hankerton, 1686, comm, I, W, P1/A/159
Edwd., blacksmith, Wilton, 1739, W, P2/A/437
Edwd., Bramshaw, Hants, 1751, W, P24/1046
Edwd., Bramshaw, Hants, 1792, AB, P24/1222
Eliz., Allington, All C., 1612, W, P3/A/16
Eliz., widow, Dilton, Westb., 1640, I, W, P25/1640/6
Andrew, Eliz., widow, Uffc., Devon, 1647, AB, I, P20/1/36
Eliz., widow, Burbage, 1725, I, W, P5/1725/1, P5/16Reg/118B
Eliz., widow, Burbage, 1763, W, P11/218
Eliz., widow, Landford, 1828, W, Wr, P2/1828/41
Androws als Boy, Ellen, widow, Marl. St My., 1594, AB, I, W, P1/A/4
Andrew, Florence, sen., widow, Lyme R., Dorset, 1713, I, W, P5/1713/3, P5/15Reg/377D
Francis, carp., Gt. Cheverell, 1667, comm, I, W, P2/A/236
Francis, gent., Collingbourne K., 1679, AB, comm, I, P3/A/161
Geo., bach., Overton, [1611], NW (NEP), P3/A/14
Androws, Geo., sen., yeo., Ashton K., 1640, I, W, P3/A/83
Geo., Bourton, Gillingham, Dorset, 1808, comm, W, Wr, P27/1/599
Giles, capital burgess, Malm., 1776, W, P1/A/430, P1/13Reg/96
Hannah, blacksmith's wife, Rams., 1825, AB, Wr, P5/1825/5
Hy., barber surgeon, Warm., 1646, AB, I, NW, P2/A/207
Hy., Aldermaston, Berks., 1704, AB, P1/A/197
Hester, widow, All C., 1728, W, P3/A/312
Hester, widow, Pott. (form. of Coate, Bps. C.), 1728, AB, comm, W, P1/A/275, P1/7Reg/195
Andrew, Hugh, Amesb., 1569, W, P2/5Reg/51E
Isaac, Overton, 1742, AB, P3/A/372
Androws, Jas., clothier, Wokm., Berks., 1632, I, W, P5/1632/2, P5/12Reg/103
Androws, Jas., husb., Wootton B., 1632, I, W, P3/A/59
Jas., Wootton B., 1688, AB, comm, ren, P3/A/202
Jas., jun., yeo., Oak Hill, Froxfield, 1749, AB, I, P3/A/388
Jas., yeo., Wingfield, 1753, W, P1/A/377, P1/11Reg/119A
Jas., Oak Hill, Froxfield, 1761, W, P3/A/418

Jas., Chipp., 1807, AB, Wr, P3/1807/41
Jas., Tisb., 1809, AB, Wr, P2/1809/27
Jane, minor, Bps. C., 1683, guardianship bond, P24/756
Jane, widow, Gt. Cheverell, 1792, W, P1/A/469, P1/14Reg/383
Jeremiah, Netherh., 1834, AB, I, Wr, P2/1834/7
Androws, Joan, widow, Amesb., 1555, W, P2/1Reg/86B
Joan, Stockton, 1593, AB, I, P2/A/35
Andrew, Joan, widow, Warm., 1611, I, P2/A/93
Joan, widow, Collingbourne K., 1630, I, W, P3/A/55
Joan, sp., Fisherton D., 1638, I, W, P2/A/174
Joan, widow, no abode stated, but proved at Collingbourne D., 1639, I, W, P21/1/38
Joan, widow, Sal., 1675, AB, I, P4/1675/1
Joan, widow, Southwick, N. Bradley, 1682, I, W, P2/A/289
Joan, Collingbourne K., 1695, AB, I, P3/A/223
Androws, Jn., Amesb., 1547, W, P2/2Reg/43A
Andrew, Jn., Amesb., 1566, W, P2/4Reg/231C
Andrew, Jn., sen., Fisherton D., 1591, AB, W, P2/A/26
Androws, Jn., Maiden B., 1596, I, W, P2/A/45
Andrew, Jn., sen., Fisherton D., 1598, AB, I, memo, T, W, P2/A/49
Androws, Jn., carrier, Chapmanslade, Corsley, 1616, AB, I, P2/A/107, P2/8Reg/302A
Androws, Jn., sen., husb., Maiden B., 1620, I, W, P2/A/117
Jn., yeo., W. Grimstead, 1622, AB, I, W, P1/A/41
Androws, Jn., baker, Ashton K., 1625, I, W, P3/A/39
Jn., Tockenham, 1627, AB, a/c (on reverse a/c for Rd. Ody of T.), I, P3/A/43
Jn., yeo., Collingbourne K., 1629, AB, a/c, I, P3/A/49
Andrews als Stevens, Jn., sen., yeo., Allington, All C., 1629, I, W, P3/A/50
Androws als Miller, Jn., Holnest, Dorset, 1631, AB, P5/12Reg/28A
Andres, Jn., carrier, Chapmanslade, Dilton, Westb., 1635, I, P25/1635/6
Jn., husb., Long Wittenham, Berks., 1635, comm, I, W, P1/A/71
Jn., husb., Fisherton D., 1638, AB, I, ren, P2/A/173
Jn., Burbage, 1664, I, W, P11/18
Jn., yeo., Maiden B., 1668, AB, I, NW, P2/A/239
Andrew, Jn., sen., Amesb., 1671, I, W, P1/A/131
Jn., clothier, Devizes, 1673, AB, a/c, I, P1/A/133
Jn., sen., yeo., Mkt. L., [1680], I, W, P2/A/275
Jn., Collingbourne K., 1682, AB, I, P3/A/171
Jn., yeo., Coate, Bps. C., 1682, AB, a/c, I (detailed), P24/769
Jn., husb., Sevenbridges Farm & Water Eaton, Latton, 1684, AB, I, ren, P3/A/183
Jn., Kingston D., 1685, AB, I, W, P2/A/304
Jn., Calne, 1686, AB, I, P26/341
Jn., miller, Port Mill, Preshute, 1687, AB, I, P1/A/166
Jn., Charl. nr. P., 1696, AB, I, P2/A/335
Jn., Calne, 1701, AB, I, P5/1701/6
Jn., yeo., Burbage, 1710, I, W, P11/98
Jn., Mkt. L., 1715, AB, P2/A/384
Jn., husb., Upavon, 1719, I, W, P2/A/394
Jn., Quidh., 1728, AB, P2/A/413
Jn., sen., Bramshaw, Hants, 1741, AB, W, P24/989
Jn., shoemaker, Gt. Cheverell, 1750, I, W, P2/A/460
Jn., gent., S. Burcombe, 1793, O, W, Wr, P2/A/555
Jn., innkeeper, Melbury Abbas late of Mere, 1797, comm, W, P5/1797/41, P5/18Reg/256C
Jn., Baydon, 1800, AB, comm, P5/1800/1, P5/18Reg/286B
Jn., cordw., Malm., 1802, W, P3/1802/49
Jn., yeo., Bramshaw, Hants, 1811, W, P24/1274
Jn., yeo., Leigh, Yetm., Dorset, 1820, W, Wr, P19/226
Jn., gent., Deptford, Wylye, 1829, W, Wr, P1/1829/31
Jn., yeo., Plaitford, 1846, D, W, Wr, P2/1846/20
Jn., yeo., Gillingham, Dorset, 1849, aff, O, W, Wr, P27/1/762
Jos., yeo., Collingbourne K., 1781, W, P3/A/464
Jos., yeo., Semley, 1795, comm, W, P2/A/559

Joshua, husb., Winterbourne D., 1766, AB, W, P7/170
Leah, Shaw cum Donnington, Berks., 1789, AB, P1/A/458
Leonard, Teffont E., 1600, I (2 - 1 a copy), W, P2/A/59
Marmaduke, yeo., Sunton, Collingbourne K., 1691, AB, comm, I, Wr (all damaged & fragile), P3/A/209
Marmaduke, Collingbourne K., 1729, AB, P3/A/320
Martha, sp., Winterbourne D., 1785, W, P7/177
My., widow, Gt. Cheverell, 1686-87, AB, I, ren, P2/A/308
My., widow, Catcomb, Hilmarton, 1728, W, P3/A/313
My., widow, Hindon, 1751, comm, W, P2/A/465
My., sp., Durrington, 1759-60, AB, I, copy I, P2/A/482
My., Collingbourne D., 1760, court paper, I, P30/6
My., sp., Hamptworth, Downton, 1856, aff, D, W, Wr, P2/1856/43
My. Cousins, Amesb., 1758, AB, P2/A/480
Andrew, Nich., husb., Amesb., 1631, AB, I, P2/A/152
Androws, Peter, Marl. St My., 1691, I, W, P1/A/171
Philip, labourer, Fisherton D., 1623, I, W, P2/A/128
Philip, yeo., Maiden B., 1712, W, P2/A/373
Philip, yeo., Charlcote, Bremhill, 1747, W, P1/A/362, P1/10Reg/157
Phyllis, labourer's wife, Aston Tirrold, Berks., 1741, W, P1/A/332, P1/9Reg/94
Androwe, Rd., W. Dean, 1558, W, P2/3Reg/85B
Androws, Rd., [blacksmith], Donhead St My., 1565, W, P2/4Reg/216A
Androwe, Rd., Bramshaw, Hants, 1574, W, P5/3Reg/46C
Androwe, Rd., sen., Burnford, Bramshaw, Hants, 1580, I, W, P5/1580/5, P5/3Reg/155D
Rd., Brook, Bramshaw, Hants, 1613, I, W, P24/106
Andrew, Rd., Amesb., 1614, AB, a/c, P2/A/100, P2/8Reg/206A
Rd., husb., Blewbury, Berks., 1623, I, W, P5/1622/3, P5/10Reg/143C
Andrews als Tayler, Rd., fellmonger, Hagbourne, Berks., 1674, AB, I, P1/A/137
Rd., shepherd, Amesb., 1675-76, AB, I, P2/A/264
Rd., Upton L., [1677], I, P2/A/266
Rd., Stop, Fonthill G., 1682, I, W, P2/A/283
Rd., Bramshaw, Hants, 1684, AB, I, P24/738
Rd., yeo., Corsham, 1699, AB, I, P29/A/26, P29/1Reg/272B
Andrew, Rd., sen., yeo., Amesb., 1714, W, P2/A/380
Rd., Avebury, 1719, AB, P3/A/288
Rd., sen., yeo., Bramshaw, Hants, 1742, W, P24/980
Rd., sen., gent., Amesb., 1748, W, P2/A/457
Rd., Bramshaw, Hants, 1762, comm, W, P24/1101
Rd., Overton, 1784, AB, P3/A/470
Andrew, Rd., Amesb., 1794, AB, comm, P2/A/557
Rd., maltster, Teffont M., 1800, W, P2/1800/39
Rd., yeo., Enmore Grn, Motc., Dorset, 1815, W (& cod), Wr, P5/1815/18
Rd., Monkton D., 1846, AB, comm, Wr, P2/1846/25
Rd., plasterer, Enmore Grn, Motc., Dorset, 1847, O, W, Wr, P19/254
Rd. Miller, yeo., Leigh, Yetm., Dorset, 1843, O, W, Wr, P19/250
Androws, Robt., husb., Mkt. L., 1598, I, W, P2/A/52
Androws, Robt., Rushall, 1609, I, W, P2/A/77, P2/8Reg/58A
Androws, Robt., yeo., W. Grimstead, 1640, I, W, P2/A/186
Androws, Robt., yeo., Rushall, 1669, I, W, P2/A/242
Robt., minor, Wedmore, Somerset, 1678, T, P2/A/268
Robt., carp., Manton, Preshute, 1719, W, P1/A/246, P1/6Reg/178
Robt., Ogbourne St Geo., 1722, W, P5/1722/1, P5/16Reg/70A
Robt., carp. and innholder, Overton, 1769, W, P3/A/436
Robt., carp., Overton, 1771, W, P3/A/443
Roger, Sunton, Collingbourne K., 1634, I, W, P1/A/64
Androws, Roger, yeo., Brokenb., 1672, I, W, P3/A/140
Roger, yeo., Collingbourne D., 1758, W, P21/10/39
Androws, Rowland, weaver, Corsham, 1616, AB, I, P29/A/6
Rowland, husb., Lynleys, Corsham, 1682, AB, I, W, P29/A/18, P29/1Reg/216
Sam., cutler, Wantage, Berks., 1677, I, W, P23/65
Sam., yeo., Maunditts Park, Lt. Somerford, 1820, W, Wr, P1/1820/78

Sarah, widow, Charlcote, Bremhill, 1727, W, P3/A/307
Sarah, Semley, 1800, AB, P2/1800/75
Androws, Sibyl, widow, W. Dean, 1549, W, P2/2Reg/72B
Simon, yeo., Collingbourne K., 1695, I, W, P3/A/224
Simon, Collingbourne D., 1719, AB, P21/7/43
Androws, Steph., husb., Kingston D., 1645, AB, I, P2/A/202
Steph., N. Hut, Fovant, 1724, AB, I, P2/A/402
Susan, widow, Upton L., 1666, I, W, P2/A/229
Androws, Susanna, widow, Coate, Bps. C., 1663, comm, I, W, P1/A/104
Susanna, widow, Berwick St Jn., 1665, I, W, P1/A/109
Susanna, widow, Enmore Grn, Motc., Dorset, 1847, O, W, Wr, P19/255
Thos., hosier, Sherb., Dorset, 1593, AB, I, P5/1593/3
Androws, Thos., Ogbourne St And., 1606, AB, I, P1/A/17
Thos., husb., Ashton K., [1612], W (NEP), P3/A/17
Thos., sen., gent., Collingbourne K., 1627, I (detailed), W, P3/A/44
Thos., husb., Collingbourne D., 1632, I, W, P21/3/18
Thos., Alderbury, 1669, AB, P26/175
Thos., labourer, Kingston D., 1671, I, W, P1/A/128
Thos., Burbage, 1676, I, P11/38
Thos., Preshute, 1684, I, P1/A/155
Thos., Charlcote, Bremhill, 1698, AB, I, P1/A/181
Thos., cordw., Gt. Cheverell, 1701, I, W, P2/A/345
Thos., yeo., Eisey, 1705, I, W, P3/A/252
Thos., sen., yeo., Rushall, 1708, comm, W, P1/A/205
Thos., vict., Malm., 1709, I, W, P3/A/265
Thos., cooper, Hindon, 1712, W, P2/A/377
Thos., Newbury, Berks., 1723, AB, I, P1/A/267
Thos., yeo., Charlcote, Bremhill, 1727, W, P3/A/308
Thos., sen., Collingbourne K., 1728, W, P3/A/314
Thos., yeo., Stratton St Mgt., 1729, W, P3/A/321
Thos., schoolmaster, Amesb., 1734, W, P2/A/427
Thos., cordw., Gt. Cheverell, 1740, I, W, P2/A/445
Thos., Collingbourne K., 1751-62, AB (2), P3/A/394, 420
Thos., schoolmaster, Amesb., 1771, W, P2/A/509
Thos., yeo., Baverstock, 1772, W, Wr, P2/A/512
Thos., innholder, *The Black Boy*, Calne, 1774, W, P26/1068
Thos., Bramshaw, Hants, 1790, W, P24/1160
Thos., innkeeper, Lt. Bedwyn, 1804, W, P21/12/9
Thos., Landford, 1807, AB, Wr, P2/1807/4
Thos., Overton, 1828, AB, Wr, P3/1828/20
Tristram, carp., Bramshaw, Hants, 1689, AB, I, P24/730
Androws, Walter, Maiden B., 1586, AB, P2/7Reg/47C
Androws, Walter, yeo., Bulford, 1633, I, W (2), P2/A/162, P2/9Reg/33B
Walter, vict., Calne, 1697, I, P26/453
Walter, Chipp., 1807, AB, Wr, P3/1807/42
Androws, Wm., Winsley, Bradford A., 1550, W (incomplete & struck through), P2/2Reg/115B
Androws, Wm., Damerham, Hants, 1557, W, P2/3Reg/46C
Andrew, Wm., Fisherton D., 1586, W, P2/7Reg/45C
Androws, Wm., Chitterne St My., 1591, I, W, P2/A/27
Wm., Allington, All C., 1602, W, P3/1Reg/68B
Androws als Hicks, Wm., husb., Coombe B., 1608, I, W, P5/1608/1, P5/8Reg/121
Androws, Wm., Overton, 1614, I, W, P1/A/28
Andrew als Stevens, Wm., yeo., Allington, All C., 1635, I, W, P3/A/67
Andrew, Wm., jun., shepherd, Amesb., 1638, I, W, P2/A/178
Andrew, Wm., sen., tailor, Broad C., 1664, AB, I, P1/A/108
Andrew, Wm., Amesb., 1668, I, P2/A/238
Wm., blacksmith, Wilton, 1681, AB, I, W, P2/A/281
Wm., yeo., Upavon, [1685], I, W, P2/A/305
Wm., [sen.], Broad C., 1716-17, AB, P1/A/240, P2/A/386
Wm., W. Amesb., 1718, W, P2/A/391

Wm., yeo., Burbage, 1728, AB, I, P5/1728/2, P5/16Reg/160A
Wm., Burbage, 1733, AB, P5/1733/1
Wm., carp., Overton, 1736, W, P3/A/350
Wm., sen., miller, Shaw cum Donnington, Berks., 1786, W, P1/A/453, P1/14Reg/115
Wm., yeo., Bramshaw, Hants, 1813, W, P24/1263
Wm., gent., Reading, Berks., 1835, D, O, W, P1/1835/48
Andrew, Wm. Hockmore, Lyme R., Dorset, 1719, AB, P16/213
see also Diment als A.; Lake als A.; Miller als A.; Ring form. A.
Aneve, Cath., widow, Keevil, 1558, AB, P2/3Reg/97D
Francis, husb., Edington, 1594, I, W, P2/A/39
Mgt., widow, Edington, 1592, I, P2/A/30
Roger, Edington, 1584, W, P2/6Reg/129A
Thos., Edington, 1548, W, P2/2Reg/76B
Angell, Anth., husb., Westport St My., 1690, AB, cit, W, P3/A/208
Benj., clothw., Trowb., 1857, aff, O, W, Wr, P1/1857/18
Cath., widow, Draycot C., 1789, W, P1/A/466, P1/14Reg/336
Angle, Edmd., Crickl. St S., 1610, AB, P3/A/13
Hy., gent., Westrop, Highw., 1788, AB, W, P10/1788/1
Isaac, soldier in 31st Regt. of Foot, bach., Trowb., 1798, AB, P1/A/486
Jas., butcher, Trowb., 1784, app. of guardian, comm, T, W, P1/A/449, P1/14Reg/164
Jas., Trowb., 1798, AB, P1/15Reg/173A
Angle, Jn., Corsham, 1616, AB, P29/A/7
Angell als Anniar, Jn., broad weaver, Chipp., 1666, I, W, P1/A/111
Angle, Jn., husb., Ford, N. Wraxall, 1683, comm, W, P3/A/178
Jn., sen., husb., Calne, 1690, I, W, P26/392
Jn., Melk., 1800, AB, comm, P2/1800/87
Jn., scribbler, Trowb., 1808, W, Wr, P1/1808/52
Jn., gent., Calne, 1837, comm, ren, W, Wr, P26/1429
Martha, widow, Greenway Farm, Tockenham, 1745, AB, I, W, P3/A/382
Martha, widow, Draycot C., 1783, W, P1/A/447, P1/14Reg/64
My., Devizes, 1814, AB, comm, P1/1814/147
Angle, Rd., Corsham, 1625, AB, I, P29/A/11
Rd., yeo., Draycot C., 1766-70, W (2), P3/A/432, 439
Thos., yeo., Pewsham Forest, 1684, AB, I, P3/A/184
Thos., Welford, Berks., 1732, AB, comm, P1/A/303
Thos., Hilmarton, 1735, AB, P1/A/313
Thos., baker, Rowde, 1736, AB, comm, P3/A/352
Thos., broad weaver, Trowb., 1742-70, AB (2), comm, I, ren, P1/A/344
Thos., tailor, Chipp., 1771, W, P3/A/444
Thos., Calne, 1806, AB, comm, P26/1259
Thos., yeo., Steeple A., 1850, W, Wr, P2/1850/69
Angle, Wm., Avill's Farm, Corsham, 1625, W, P1/A/49
Wm., sen., yeo., Chipp., 1758, W, P3/A/409
Wm., Draycot C., 1770, AB, P3/A/440
see also Anger *or* A.
Anger, Anth., blacksmith, Watchfield, Shrivenham, Berks., 1676, I, W, P1/A/142
Anth., blacksmith, Watchfield, Shrivenham, Berks., 1723, ren, W, P1/A/263, P1/6Reg/465A
Aunger, Jn., husb., Bray, Berks., 1686, I, W, P1/A/162
Jn., yeo., Watchfield, Shrivenham, Berks., 1701, W, P1/A/188, P1/4Reg/126
Jn., innholder, Highw., 1718, W, P10/1718/6
Nich., Wantage, Berks., 1571, W, P5/2Reg/100A
Robt., Calne, 1628, I, P5/1628/3
Sarah, wife, Bishopstone N., 1765, AB, comm, P5/1765/3
Anger *or* Angell, Thos., clothw. and ale holder, Highw., 1690, I, W, P10/1690/3
Thos., Bishopstone N., 1806, AB, comm, Wr, P5/1806/16
Wm., yeo., Wickfield, Lydiard T., 1783, W, P1/A/446, P1/13Reg/493
Wm., vict., Broad B., Highw., 1819, comm, W, Wr, P10/1819/2
Angle *see* Angell
Angod, Michael, butcher, Broad C., 1605, AB, I, W, P2/A/73
Robt., shepherd, Tilsh., 1636, AB, a/c, I, P2/A/167, P2/9Reg/92B

Wm., sen., Broad C., 1635, I, W, P2/A/164
Anley, Anlie *see* Annerly
Annats, Annetts als Aldridge, Alice, widow, Bourton, Bps. C., 1627, I, W, P24/226
Annetts, Ann, widow, Chute, 1735, I, W, P7/130
Edmd., yeo., Chute, 1715-16, AB, comm, I, ren, W, P5/1715/2, P5/15Reg/332A
Edwd., husb., N. Tidworth, 1635, I, P2/A/166
Annets, Edwd., Marten, Grafton, 1685, I, W, P21/4/18
Annatts, Edwd., yeo., Collingbourne D., 1733, W, P21/8/72
Annets, Jas., Ludg., 1724, W, P2/A/405
Annetts, Jas., blacksmith, Sunton, Collingbourne K., 1854, aff, D, O, W, Wr, P3/1854/63
Annets, Jn., husb., Chute, 1616, I, W, P7/9
Annets, Jn., sen., husb., Marten, Grafton, 1633, I, W, P21/3/26
Annatt, Jn., Chetnole, Yetm., Dorset, 1721, AB, I, P19/106
Annets, Jn., Collingbourne K., 1785, AB, P3/A/474
Annetts, Jn., yeo., Idmiston, 1853, aff, D, I, W, Wr, P2/1853/61
Annatt, Rd., warrener, Warm., 1718, W, P2/A/393
Annatt, Robt., shepherd, Odstock, 1670, AB, I, P2/A/251
Annett, Robt., jun., husb., Wokm., Berks., 1735, W, P5/1735/2
Annatt, Sarah, sp., Horningsham, 1765, W, P5/1765/2
Annetts, Susanna, widow, Marten, Grafton, 1721, W, P21/8/2
Thos., husb., Wilsford nr Pewsey, 1640, I, W, P2/A/189
Annetts, Thos., Idmiston, 1662, I, W, P2/A/216
Annett, Walter, yeo., Netherh., [1693], W, P2/A/322
Wm., Collingbourne D., 1632, AB, a/c, I, P21/3/19
Annets, Wm., sen., Collingbourne K., 1676, I, W, P3/A/152
Wm., husb., Chute, 1716, I, W, P7/109
Annatt, Wm., Sal., 1735, AB, Wr, P4/1734/15
Annetts, Wm., cutler, Kintbury, Berks., 1773, W, P1/A/425, P1/12Reg/491A
see also Alridge als A.; Jacob als A.
Anne, Edwd., gent., [surgeon and physician], Devizes, 1687, I, W, P1/A/167
Francis, Grovely Wood, 1710, AB, P2/A/369
Anns, Jane, widow, Westrop, Highw., 1806, W, P10/1806/2
Anns, Joan, widow, Lt. Coxwell, Gt. Faringdon, Berks., 1722, I, W, P5/1722/2, P5/16Reg/75C
Anns, Jn., sack and rope maker, Highw., 1827, W, Wr, P5/1827/26
My., sp., Sutton M., 1726, W, P2/A/407
Rd., barber surgeon, Highw., 1593, I, W, P5/1593/1, P5/6Reg/37A
Rd., Highw., 1667, AB, comm, I, P10/1667/1
Anns, Rd., blacksmith, Steventon, Berks., 1770, W, P1/12Reg/350A
Rd., blacksmith, Steventon, Berks., 1779, W, P1/A/410
Thos., clerk and vicar, Urchf., 1671, AB, I, ren, P2/A/255
Thos., surgeon, Marl., 1673, AB, P1/A/132
Anns, Thos., Westrop, Highw., 1794, W, Wr, P5/1794/1, P5/18Reg/197A
Annerly, Hy., Yarnfield, Maiden B., Somerset, 1673, I, NW, P2/A/261
My., widow, Maiden B., [1692], I, W, P2/A/321
Ralph, husb., Maiden B., 1626, I (detailed), W, P2/A/140
Anlie, Thos., Devizes, 1612, AB, P1/A/21
see also Auley *or* A. (Anley)
Annets, Annett, Annetts *see* Annats
Anniar *see* Angell als Anniar
Anns *see* Anne
Ansell, Dorothy, Sal., 1619, I, P4/1619/10
Jn., peruke maker, Highw., 1822, W, P10/1822/1
My., widow, S. Marston, 1807, comm, W, P10/1807/1
Thos., yeo., S. Marston, 1778, W, P10/1778/3
see also Withier als A.
Anslo, Jas., Bradford A., 1733, AB, P2/A/421
Anson, Wm., Marl., 1774, AB, ren, P1/A/428
Anstie *see* Anste
Anstell, Jn., Basildon, Berks., 1616, I, W, P1/A/30
Anstey *see* Anstie

Anstice, Edwd., Thornford, Dorset, 1825, AB, comm, Wr, P5/1825/28
Anstie, Abigail, gentlewoman, Heddington, 1699, I, W, P3/A/241
Benj., clothier, Devizes, 1758, AB, comm, P1/A/388
Anste, Hy., husb., Marston, Pott., 1612, W, P1/A/23
Isabel, W. Lavington, 1623, AB, P1/A/43
Anstey, Jas., W. Lockinge, Wantage, Berks., 1719, AB, comm, P23/375
Anstey, Jos., yeo., Bromham, 1638, AB, I, W, P3/A/73
Anstey, Jos., yeo., Nether St., Bromham, 1698, I, W, P1/A/182, P1/3Reg/192
My., widow, W. Lavington, 1631, AB, a/c, I, P1/A/57
My., sp., Heddington, 1703, I, W, P3/A/246
My., widow, Devizes, 1799, copy req, copy W (cods incomplete), P1/A/487, P1/15Reg/185B
Rd., Devizes, 1763, AB, P1/A/400
Anstey, Sarah, widow, Alvediston, 1664, I, W, P2/A/224
Anstey, Thos., yeo., Alvediston, 1660, I, W, P2/A/214
Answorth, Wm., yeo., Clarendon Park, 1812, W, P4/1813/15
Antell, Thos., husb., Charminster, Dorset, 1712, I, W, P5/1712/3, P5/15Reg/302B
Anthony, Arthur, yeo., Preston, Dorset, 1607, AB, comm, I, P5/1607/1
Arthur, Sutton Poyntz, Dorset, 1607, AB, P5/8Reg/92D
Dorothy, widow, Sutton Poyntz, Dorset, 1622, AB, I, P5/1622/1, P5/10Reg/130A
Eliz., widow, Preston, Dorset, 1586, AB, P5/1586/1, P5/4Reg/134C
Wm., Sutton Poyntz, Dorset, 1584, AB, I, P5/1584/1, P5/4Reg/79A
see also Burchall als A.
Antram, Aaron, general shopkeeper, Downton, 1851, D, W, Wr, P1/1851/36
Alice, widow, S. Burcombe, 1599, AB, I, P2/A/58
Elias, husb., S. Burcombe, 1593, I, W, P2/A/32
Eliz., widow, Broad C., 1638, I (detailed), W, P2/A/182
Eliz. *see also* Edmd. Sainsbury
Hy., W. Knoyle, 1557, W, P2/3Reg/17B
Isaac, Sal., 1696, W, P4/1696/13
Joan, widow, Sal. St Mart., 1670, I, ren, W, P4/1670/1
Joan, widow, Sal., 1686, W, P4/1685/26
Jn., Sal. St Mart., 1620, AB, a/c, expenses, I, P1/A/37
Jos., Sal., 1693, AB, I, P4/1692/14
Priscilla, widow, Sal., 1672, AB, I, P4/1672/14
Robt., Wilton, 1594, I, T, W, P2/A/569
Robt., yeo., Broad C., 1642, AB, I (detailed), NW, P2/A/193
Robt., Sal., 1723, AB, P4/1723/6
Thos., sen., miller, Sal., 1619, I, T, P4/1619/2
Wm., sen., clothier, Sal., 1670, AB, a/c, I (detailed), W, P4/1669/10, P4/1670/15
Wm., sen., parchment maker, Sal., 1676, AB, a/c, I, P4/1676/9
Wm., clothw., Sal., 1689, AB, I (detailed), P4/1689/10
Wm., clothier, Sal., 1702, W, P4/1702/10
see also Baskerville als A.
Anway, Jn., weaver, Marl. St My., 1584, W, P1/A/1
ap David, Edwd., priest, Blunsdon St And., 1557, institution to rectory, P1/1Reg/6D
Aplin, Eliz., widow, Lyme R., Dorset, 1795, comm, W, P16/354
Applin, Jas., E. Harnham, Britford, 1778, AB, P24/1126
Jn., Bere R., Dorset, 1692, AB, P5/1692/1
Applin, Sarah, widow, Farnham, Tollard Royal, Dorset, 1766, I, W, P2/A/494
Apperry, Peter, blacksmith, W. Harnham, 1737, W, P5/1737/1
Appleby, Hy., Donhead St My., 1530, W (NEP), P30/52B
Jas., Woolhampton, Berks., 1786, W, P1/A/452, P1/14Reg/110
Jane, Trowb., 1827, W, Wr, P1/1827/19
Jn., husb., Donhead St My., 1575, W, P2/5Reg/233D
Wm., Halstock, Dorset, 1636, I, W, P5/1636/5, P5/13Reg/21A
Appledore *see* Applegate *or* A. als Grant
Appleford, Ann, sp., Sal. St Edmd., 1740, cit, I, NW, P4/1739/15
Ann, widow, Newbury, Berks., 1829, W, Wr, P1/1829/121
Anth., tailor, Axford, Rams., 1704, I, W, P5/1704/2
Anth., Axford, Rams., 1726, AB, P5/1726/4

Anth., innholder, Reading, Berks., 1744, W, P1/A/350, P1/9Reg/339B
Cath., widow, Biddestone St Nich., 1724, I, W, P3/A/300
Cath., widow, Marl., 1754, AB, P1/A/382
Dan., sen., yeo., Rockley, Ogbourne St And., 1736, W, P23/518
Dan., labourer, Sutton V., 1787, comm, W, P2/A/543
Dorothy, widow, Axford, Rams., 1670, I, W, P5/1670/2
Edwd., Axford, Rams., 1675, AB, comm, I, P5/1675/2
Edwd., yeo., Axford, Rams., 1695, I, W, P5/1695/4
Edwd., yeo., Rams., 1705, AB, I, P5/1705/2
Edwd., yeo. and wheelwright, Axford, Rams., 1730, AB, I, W, P5/1730/1
Edwd., Ogbourne St And., 1742, AB (2 - George A., ex. & minor d. before admg father's estate), comm, W, P23/551-52
Joan, sen., widow, Axford, Rams., 1639, I, W, P5/1639/3, P5/13Reg/184C
Joanna, widow, Combe, Rams., 1680, I, W (NEP), P5/1680/1
Joanna *see also* Alice West
Jn., maltster, Biddestone St Nich., 1703, I, W, P3/A/247
Jn., yeo., Axford, Rams., 1782, AB, ren, W, P5/1782/2, P5/17Reg/218B
My., sp., Ogbourne St Geo., 1849, D, O, W, Wr, P5/1849/13
Rebecca, widow, Axford, Rams., 1770, W, P5/1770/1, P5/17Reg/14B
Roger, yeo., Axford, Rams., 1686, I, W, P5/1686/1
Roger, Marl., 1724, W, P1/A/270, P1/7Reg/45A
Simon, yeo., Combe, Rams., 1727, W, P5/1727/1, P5/16Reg/148C
Simon, Axford, Rams., 1787, AB, P5/1787/1, P5/18Reg/71B
Steph., yeo., Rams., 1597-98, W, P5/1598/1, P5/6Reg/198C, P30/4
Steph., Rams., 1617, AB, comm, P5/1616/3, P5/9Reg/213E
Steph., husb., Axford, Rams., 1648, AB, comm, I, NW, P5/1647/1, P5/14Reg/101A
Steph., yeo., Rams., 1713, AB, I, P5/1713/1
Steph., maltster, Marl., 1741, W, P1/A/343, P1/9Reg/207
Steph., yeo., Axford, Rams., 1765, W, P5/1765/1
Thos., Axford, Rams., 1631, AB, P5/1631/2, P5/12Reg/75A
Thos., yeo., Combe, Rams., 1676-77, AB, a/c, app. of proctors, comm, I (detailed), P5/1676/1, P5/1677/1
Thos., Axford, Rams., 1708, AB, P5/1708/2
Thos., yeo., Axford, Rams., 1729, I, W, P5/1729/3, P5/16Reg/231
Thos., jun., gent., Rams., 1790, W, P5/1790/2, P5/18Reg/144
Thos., Rams., 1805, note, req, W, copy W, P5/1805/18, P5/19Reg/141
Ursula, wife of Dan., wheelwright, Axford, Rams., 1724, W, P5/1724/1, P5/16Reg/97A
Applegarth, Alexander, Pott., 1776, AB, P1/A/437
Applegath, Chas., baker, Wallingford, Berks., 1747, W, P1/A/357, P1/10Reg/74A
Joan, sen., widow, Wallingford, Berks., 1720, I, summary I, W, P1/A/257, P1/6Reg/293
Applegate, Jas., innkeeper, Newtown, Trowb., 1847, D, I, O, W, Wr, P1/1847/19
Applegate *or* Appledore als Grant, Joan, widow, Bratton, Westb., 1639, I, W, P25/1639/7
Jn., yeo., N. Bradley, 1848, D, O, W, Wr, P2/1848/33
Jn., sawyer, Chalford, Westb., 1849, comm, declaration, W, Wr, P25/1849/2
Sam., shopkeeper, Chalford, Westb., 1820, O, W, Wr, P25/1820/3
Steph., yeo., Brown Close, Westb., 1750, W, P25/1750/2
Steph., Westb., 1769, AB, P25/1769/5
Steph., collier, Westb., 1780, W, P25/1780/4
Steph., yeo., Chalford, Westb., 1823, W, Wr, P25/1823/2
Tabitha, widow, Chalford, Westb., 1816, W, Wr, P25/1816/4
Thos., serge weaver, Chalford, Westb., 1738, W, P25/1738/3
Thos., narrow weaver, Westb. (lately lived in Westb. L.), 1798, W, P25/1798/1
Thos., yeo., Westb. L., 1816, W, Wr, P25/1816/7
Thos., Westb., 1838, AB, O, ren, Wr, P25/1838/3
Wm., vict., Marl., 1613, I, W, P1/A/29
Applegath *see* Applegarth
Appleton, Jn., labourer, Bucklebury, Berks., 1764, W, P1/A/401, P1/12Reg/146B
Martha, widow, Marl. (form. of Shoreditch, Middlesex), 1682, AB, W, P1/A/150
Wm., carp., Stratfield M., Berks., 1695, W, P1/A/178
Wm., jun., yeo., E. Hendred, Berks., 1823, W, Wr, P1/1823/83
Wm., sen., yeo., E. Hendred, Berks., 1823, W, Wr, P1/1823/84
Appleyard, Sam., [bridle and saddle maker], Sal., 1671, AB, I, P4/1670/26

Applin *see* Aplin
ap Powell, Evan, Westport St My., 1569, W, P1/1Reg/121A
Appowell, Jn., Tisb., 1589, AB, L (2), P2/A/23
Apprice *see* Aprice
Approbine, Jn., husb., Rushall, 1588, W, P2/7Reg/131A
Aprice, Apprice als Price, Hy., yeo., Tinh., Edington, 1766, comm, W, P2/A/493
Jn., priest, Wilsford nr Pewsey, 1548, institution to vicarage, P2/2Reg/59B
Apprice, Jn., yeo., Tinh., Edington, 1679, I, W, P2/A/270
Jn., yeo., Edington, 1729, W, P1/A/291, P1/7Reg/320A
Wm., miller, Byde Mill, Corsham, 1699, I, W, P29/A/25, P29/1Reg/277B
Wm., innholder, Melk., 1758, comm, W, P2/A/479
see also Jones als A.
ap Richard, Joan, widow, Twyford, Hurst, Berks., 1545, W, P5/20Reg/69C
Jn., Twyford, Hurst, Berks., 1545, W, P5/20Reg/69B
Apsey, Robt., husb., Halstock, Dorset, 1634, AB, comm, I(GVS), P5/1634/19
Sam., miller, Chards., Devon, 1799, comm, W, P14/195
Sam., labourer, Chards., Devon, 1835, O, W, P14/219
Thos., miller, Chards., Devon, 1735, W, P14/151
Arch, Alice, widow, Malm., 1667, W, P3/A/114
Ann, widow, Dauntsey (late of Calne), 1704, I, W, P3/A/249
Ann, widow, Chipp., 1705, AB, P3/A/253
Edith, widow, Alderton, 1638, I, W, P3/A/74
Eliz., widow, Kington St M., 1698, I, W, P1/A/183, P1/3Reg/186
Jn., yeo., Fowlswick Farm, Chipp., 1630, I, W, P3/A/56
Jn., yeo., Bremilham, 1641, I, W, P1/A/80
Jn., clothier, Malm., 1670, AB, comm, I, P3/A/128
Jn., yeo., Fowlswick Farm, Chipp., 1693, I, W, P3/A/218
My., Fowlswick Farm, Chipp., [1666?], comm, I, W (damaged), P1/A/110
Nich., yeo., Kington St M., 1667, AB, comm, I, P3/A/111
Rd., priest, Fisherton A., 1554, institution to rectory, P2/1Reg/18B
Wm., yeo., Norton, 1607, W, P3/2Reg/16
Wm., [shopkeeper], Chipp., 1681, AB, comm, I, P3/A/169
Wm., cordw., Brinkw., 1696, AB, I, P3/A/226
Archar *see* Archard and Archer
Archard, [male], abode lost through damage, c1630s, a/c (date & name lost through damage, but mentions bequests to Alice & Joyce A.), P1/A/61
Agnes, widow, Lyneham, 1615, I, W, P3/A/21
Alexander, Devizes, 1705, AB, P1/A/200
Ann, widow, Castle C., 1756, I, W, P3/A/402
Anth., Broad C., 1696, AB, P2/A/332
Arthur, Purton, 1683, AB, I, P3/A/179
Arthur, Wedh., Urchf., 1734, W, P2/A/425
Archard als Hayes, Cath., widow, Crudwell, 1763, comm, W, P3/A/423
Edwd., mason, Kington L., 1800, W, P3/1800/33
Eliz., Spirthill, Bremhill, 1609, W, P3/A/11
Archard *or* Archar, Eliz., widow, Corsham, 1622, AB, W, copy W, P29/A/10, P29/1Reg/90, 91B
Eliz., widow, Etchilhampton, 1790, W, Wr (NEP), P3/A/484
Francis, jun., baker, Gt. Coxwell, Berks., 1720, W, P1/A/256, P1/6Reg/288
Geo., feltmaker & hatter, Corsham, 1689, AB, I, W, P29/A/21, P29/1Reg/242
Grace, widow, Pott., 1814, W, Wr, P1/1814/74
Archard als Pinchin, Hy., Corsham, 1619, AB, P29/A/8
Hy., sen., tiler, Calne, 1781, W, P26/1113
Jas., yeo., Corsham, 1767, W, P29/2Reg/111
Jas., yeo., Pott., 1826, W, Wr, P1/1826/3
Joan, widow, Ashton K., [1606], W (NEP), P3/A/6
Jn., weaver, Lambourn, Berks., 1628, I, W, P1/A/52
Archard als Hayes, Jn., yeo., Crudwell, 1675, I, W, P3/A/148
Jn., sen., tiler, Gate Croft, Corsham, 1677-78, I, W, P29/A/17, P29/1Reg/208A
Jn., Corsham, 1684-85, I, ren, P29/A/20
Jn., Corsham, 1691, AB, I, P29/A/23

Archard als Hay, Jn., sen., yeo., Crudwell, 1696, I, W, P3/H/759
Jn., cooper, Castle C., 1741, AB, W, P28/18
Jn., broad weaver, Corsham, 1747, W, P29/A/31
Jn., yeo., Etchilhampton, 1761, W, P3/A/419
Archard als Hayes, Jn., yeo., Crudwell, 1763, comm, W, P3/A/424
Jn., Castle C., 1787, AB, P3/A/476
Jn., yeo., Derry Hill, Pewsham, 1792, W, P5/1792/2, P5/18Reg/174B
Jn., yeo., Pott., 1798, comm, W, P1/A/485, P1/15Reg/136
Archard als Hay, My., widow, Crudwell, 1684, I, W, P3/A/185
Matthew, yeo., Avill's Farm, Corsham, 1674, I, W, P3/A/142
Matthew, yeo., Urchf., 1797, O, W, P2/A/564
Robt., weaver, Devizes, 1629, I, W, P1/A/55
Thos., yeo., Whores, Corsham, 1614, AB, I, P29/A/5
Thos., sen., Stanford in the Vale, Berks., 1792, W, P1/A/471, P1/14Reg/409
Archar, Wm., Corsham, 1596-97, I, W, P29/A/2, P29/1Reg/44
Wm., sen., Bradford A., 1632, I, W, P2/A/154
Wm., yeo., Broad Mead, Lacock, 1634, I, W, P1/A/65
Wm., broad weaver, Corsham, 1671-72, I, NW, P29/A/16, P29/1Reg/198A
Wm., Purton, 1685, AB, I, P3/A/190
Wm., thatcher, Corsham, 1728, marriage licence, P29/2Reg/54D
Wm., tailor, Castle C., 1767, AB, W, P28/28
Wm., carrier, Redhill, Pewsham, 1775, W, P5/1775/1, P5/17Reg/90A
Archard als Hayes, Wm., yeo., Dean Farm, Oaksey (form. of Crudwell), 1856, aff, O, W, Wr, P3/1856/59
see also Hay/Hayes/Hays als A.; Orchard; Pinchin als A.

Archer, Adam, gent., Lyneham, 1637, AB, I, ren, P3/A/71
Archar, Ann, sp., Crickl. St S., 1733, AB, P3/A/336
Ann, sp., Castle C., 1806, W, Wr, P3/1806/61
Benj., Crickl. St S., 1728, AB, I, P3/A/315
Edwd., Swindon, 1743, W, P3/A/377
Eliz., sp., Calcutt, Crickl. St S., [1642], I, NW (NEP), P3/A/91
Archar, Eliz., sp., Crickl. St S., 1733, AB, P3/A/337
Eliz., sp., Crickl. St S., 1835, O, req, W, P3/1835/12
Francis, yeo., Purton, 1615, AB, a/c, I, P3/A/22
Francis, weaver, Chelworth, Crickl. St S., 1686, I, W, P3/A/196
Geo., staymaker, Crickl. St S., 1777, comm, W, P3/A/455
Geo., Thornhill, Clyffe P., 1813, AB, comm, Wr, P3/1813/43
Archar, Guy, mason, Swindon, 1763, AB, W, P3/A/422
Hannah, sp., Turleigh, Winsley, Bradford A., 1852, O, W, Wr, P2/1852/61
Jacob, yeo., Thornhill, Clyffe P., 1808, comm, W, Wr, P1/1808/129
Jas., Broad Town, Broad H., 1814, W, Wr, P1/1814/33
Jas., yeo., Broad Town, Clyffe P., 1831, comm, W, Wr, P3/1831/42
Jn., clerk and vicar, Broad C., 1622, I, NW, P2/A/123
Jn., weaver, Wootton B., 1673, I, W, P3/A/141
Jn., labourer, Leigh, Ashton K., 1682, I, W, P3/A/172
Jn., sen., yeo., Crickl. St S., 1682, I, W, P3/A/173
Jn., yeo., Ansty, 1763, W, P1/A/395, P1/12Reg/60A
Jn., Corsham, 1814, AB, comm, P3/1814/14
Martha, widow, Broad C., 1633, AB, I, P2/A/159, P2/9Reg/13B
Martha, widow, Crickl. St S. (form. of Down Ampney, Gloucs), 1719, I, W, P3/A/289
Martha, widow, Wootton B., 1781, W, P3/A/465
Archar, My., widow, Lyneham, 1642, AB, I, P3/A/92
My., gent.'s wife, Crickl. St S., 1809, AB, Wr, P3/1809/23
My., sp., Corsham, 1843, W, P29/1800-1857/38, P29/3Reg/306
Matthew, yeo., Ansty, 1756, W, P1/A/387, P1/11Reg/272B
Archar, Moses, Crickl. St S., 1670, AB, I, P3/A/129
Rebecca, sp., Crickl. St S., 1728, AB (2), P3/A/316
Archar, Rd., sen., yeo., Bramshaw, Hants, 1668, W, P24/367
Robt., Bramshaw, Hants, 1637, I, W, P24/286
Robt., sen., yeo., Calcutt, Crickl. St S., 1639, I, W, P3/A/76
Archar, Robt., yeo., Calcutt, Crickl. St S., 1682, AB, I, W, P3/A/174

Sam., Crickl. St S., 1830, AB, comm, Wr, P3/1830/14
Thos., vict., Melk., 1777, W, P2/A/529
Wm., weaver, Broad C., 1660, I, W, P2/A/213
Wm., clothier, Broad C., 1663, I, W, P2/A/217
Archar, Wm., yeo., Crickl. St S., 1729, W, P1/A/288, P1/7Reg/287B
Wm., sen., yeo., Crickl. St S., 1780, W, P3/A/460
Wm., shopkeeper, Castle C., 1800, W, P3/1800/34
Archar, Wm., yeo., Chelworth, Crickl. St S., 1807, W, Wr, P3/1807/48
Wm., carp., Crickl. St S., 1809, W, Wr, P3/1809/1
Wm., labourer, Purton, 1817, W, Wr, P1/1817/115
Wm., collarmaker, Grittleton, 1841, W, Wr, P3/1841/7
see also Wells form. A.
Arden, Agnes *or* Ann, widow, Hampton, Highw., 1626, I, W, P10/1626/3
Alice, widow, Lt. Coxwell, Gt. Faringdon, Berks., 1639, I, W, P5/1639/2
Ann *see* Agnes
Grace, widow, Sevenhampton, Highw., 1746, W, P5/1746/1
Joan, widow, Broad B., Highw., 1606, I, W, P1/A/16
Joan, widow, Westrop, Highw., 1634, I, W, P10/1634/2
Jn., husb., Broad B., Highw., 1682, I, W, P5/1682/2
Jn., yeo., Sevenhampton, Highw., 1694, AB, I, P10/1694/10
Jn., yeo., Highw., 1761, W, Wr, P5/1761/2
Nich., Sevenhampton, Highw., 1662, AB, I, P5/1662/2
Nich., innholder, Gt. Faringdon, Berks., 1662, AB, I, P5/1662/3
Oliver, goldsmith, Sherb., Dorset, 1684, AB, comm, I, P5/1684/1
Rebecca, widow and feltmaker, Broad B., Highw., 1689, AB, I, P10/1689/2
Rd., labourer, Rams., 1616, I, NW, P5/1616/4
Robt., husb., Rams., 1682, I, W, P5/1682/3
Robt., yeo., Broad B., Highw., 1778, W, P10/1778/4
Ruth, sp., Broad B., Highw., 1693, AB, I, P10/1693/3
Thos., Broad B., Highw., 1580-96, AB, a/c, I, P5/1580/6, P5/3Reg/153C
Thos., Gt. Faringdon, Berks., 1588, AB, P5/1587/5, P5/5Reg/4D
Thos., husb., Latton, 1641, I, W, P3/A/87
Thos., sen., yeo., Broad B., Highw., 1667, I, W, P5/1667/3
Thos., slater, Westrop, Highw., 1670, I, W, P10/1670/1
Thos., tailor, Broad B., Highw., 1686, I, W, P10/1686/4
Walter, labourer, Buscot, Berks., 1635, I, W, P1/A/72
Wm., yeo., Broad B., Highw., 1667, I, W, P5/1667/4
Wm., feltmaker, Broad B., Highw., 1687, I, W, P10/1687/2
Wm., sen., Harwell, Berks., 1692, I, NW, P1/A/174
Arding, Wm., yeo., E. Ilsley, Berks., 1832, comm, W, Wr, P1/1832/46
see also Gale als A.
Arderne, Wm. Hy., clerk, Crickl. St S., 1778, W, P3/A/458
Arding *see* Arden
Arelsmyth *see* Arrowsmith
Arenburg, Matteas, Sherb., Dorset, 1823, AB (2), P5/1823/10
Aris, Edwd., boatman, Abingdon, Berks., 1732, W, P1/A/297, P1/7Reg/465A
Arkill, Chas., yeo., Chelworth, Crickl. St S., 1794, W, P3/A/492
Arkis, Thos., husb. *or* labourer, Hurst, Berks., 1636, I, W (on reverse of bond to pay £10), P5/1636/6, P5/13Reg/1A
Arlett, Arlot, Jas., Padworth, Berks. (form. of Aldermaston, Berks.), 1744, I, W, P1/A/351, P1/9Reg/365A
Julian, Ashley, Box, 1678, I, W, Wr, P3/A/157
Reynold, yeo., Ashley, Box, 1669, I, W, P3/A/124
Arman *see* Harman
Armany, Jn., blacksmith, Compton C., 1667, I, W, P2/A/232
Jn., Compton C., 1709, AB, P2/A/366
Armens, Jn., W. Lavington, 1601, I, P1/A/6
Armsby, Jn., Barford St Mart., 1760, AB, P2/A/485
Armstrong, Wm., joiner, Wantage, Berks., 1673, I, W, P23/40
Arndell, Ann, sp., W. Shefford, Berks., 1701, receipt of legacy, W, P1/A/191
Arndell, My., sp., Wantage, Berks., 1749, AB, P5/1749/1
Arneley, Joan, Wokm., Berks., 1543, court proceedings (libel case), P5/20Reg/46A

Arnell *see* Arnold
Arnett *see* Arnott
Arney, Ann, Downton, 1854, aff, W, Wr, P2/1854/10
Deborah *see* Deborah Barksdale
Edmd., plumber, Chipp., 1724, AB, comm, ren, P3/A/301
Eleanor, widow, Bere R., Dorset, 1704, I, W, P5/1704/17
Eliz., widow, Urchf., 1765, W, P2/A/491
Jn., sen., weaver, Gillingham, Dorset, 1785, AB, W, P27/1/522, P27/3Reg/244
Rd., Downton, 1617, AB, comm, I, P2/A/110
Robt., apothecary, Highw., 1680, AB, I, P10/1680/2
Robt., jun., Highw., 1686, AB, comm, P10/1686/11
Robt., surgeon, Swindon, 1693, I, W, P3/A/217
Sam., Woodfalls, Downton, 1852, aff, W, Wr, P2/1852/52
Arnne, Sarah, widow, Knighton, Rams., 1759, W, P5/1759/1
Sarah, widow, Sal. St Edmd., 1846, W (on pre-printed form), Wr, P4/1846/3
Wm., Bere R., Dorset, 1696, I, W, P5/1696/2
Wm., gent., Bere R., Dorset, 1771, W, P5/1771/1, P5/17Reg/33
Wm., Sal., 1816, AB, P4/1816/3
Wm., Alderstone, Whitep., 1854, aff, D, W, Wr, P2/1854/19
Arnold, Agnes, widow, Over C., Dorset, 1582, I, W, P5/1582/2, P5/4Reg/40B
Agnes, Bishopstone S., 1606, AB, P1/A/18
Alexander, yeo., W. Winterslow, 1664, I, W, P2/A/225
And., Over C., Dorset, 1726, AB, P5/1726/2
Arnoll, Ann, sp., Lacock, [1680], AB, I, P3/A/167
Arnoll, Ann, widow and shopkeeper, Lacock, 1701, alleg, D, inty, I, sentence, W, P3/A/243
Ann, scrivener, Winterborne K., Dorset, 1762, W, P5/1762/2
Ann, widow, Sutton B., 1774, AB, P3/A/448
Cath., widow, Clevancy, Hilmarton, 1646, AB, I, P1/A/85
Chas., Mere, 1821, AB, comm, Wr, P5/1821/41
Charlotte, wife of Steph., yeo., Gillingham, Dorset, 1811, AB, P27/1/610
Chris., Winterborne K., Dorset, 1744, AB, Wr, P5/1744/1
Chris., yeo., Winterborne K., Dorset, 1803, W, P5/1803/39, P5/19Reg/70B
Deborah, widow, Yatesbury, 1697, AB, I, P3/A/234
Dorothy, widow, Ogbourne St Geo., 1695, AB, I, P5/1695/2, P5/1696/1
Edith, widow, Winterslow, 1579, I, W, P2/A/14, P2/5Reg/323A
Edith, widow, Ogbourne St Geo., 1692, cert, I, W, P5/1691/4
Arnold als Groves, Edmd., yeo., Malm., 1692, AB, I, P3/A/213
Eliz., widow, Yatesbury, 1751, W, P3/A/395
Gabriel, maltster, Ogbourne St Geo., 1693, I, W, P23/202
Geo., [leather worker], Avebury, 1706, AB, I, P3/A/259
Arnoll, Hy., mercer, Lacock, 1628, I (detailed), W, P3/A/45
Hy., sen., yeo., Winterborne K., Dorset, 1731, W, P5/1731/3
Hugh, Wootton B., 1641, AB, I, P3/A/88
Jas., yeo., Berwick B., 1684, I, W, P26/315
Jas., Abbot's Court, Winterborne K., Dorset, 1717, AB, I, P5/1717/1
Jas., labourer, Motc., Dorset, 1804, W, P27/1/577
Jas., innkeeper, Corsley (form. of Fovant), 1850-51, court proceeding, W, Wr, P2/1850/4, P2/1851/25
Arnoll, Jane, widow, Abbot's Court, Winterborne K., Dorset, 1701, comm, I, W (damaged), P5/1700/1
Arnoll, Jane, widow, Corsham, 1725, AB, I, W, P29/A/30, P29/2Reg/47
Jane, sp., Corsham, [1761], W, P29/A/32
Jane, sp., Corsham, 1783, W, P29/2Reg/177
Jasper, Sherb., Dorset, 1710, AB, P5/1710/5
Arnold als Palmer, Joan, widow, Collingbourne D., 1639, W, P21/1/15
Arnoll, Joan, widow, [Corsham] (NBI), 1640, I, P30/1
Jn., gent., W. Hatch, Tisb., 1542-64, AB (re unadmd goods), W, P2/1Reg/31A, P2/4Reg/185C
Jn., Enford, 1553, W, P2/2Reg/170B
Arnoll, Jn., no abode stated, 1606, AB, P1/A/14
Jn., sen., husb., Over C., Dorset, 1625, I, W, P5/1625/1, P5/10Reg/281C
Arnold als Groves, Jn., vict., Malm., 1663, AB, I, NW, P3/A/99
Jn., gent., Alton P., Dorset, 1681, AB, comm, I, P5/1681/1

Arnoll, Jn., husb., Wootton B., 1684, I, W, P3/A/186
Jn., mason, Wootton B., 1691, AB, I, ren, P3/A/210
Jn., Westb., 1693, AB, I, P25/1693/7
Jn., jun., Fordington, Dorset, 1695, AB, P15/52
Jn., cordw., Malm., 1711, AB, comm (dispute between mother of decd & his wife over AB), I, P1/A/210
Arnell, Jn., sen., yeo., Farley, Alderbury, 1729, W, P26/745
Jn., sen., yeo., Pitton, Alderbury, 1757, W, P26/953
Jn., Motc., Dorset, 1764, AB, P27/1/440, P27/3Reg/118
Jn., yeo., Muston Farm, Winterborne K., Dorset, 1770, W, P5/1770/2, P5/17Reg/20B
Jn., yeo., Farley, Alderbury, 1788, W, P26/1159
Jn., fuller, Bull Mill, Longbridge D., 1793, W, P2/A/556
Jn., yeo., Kemble (of Bristol, 1817), 1822, O, W, Wr, P3/1822/4
Jn., Motc., Dorset, 1849, D, O, W, Wr, P27/1/760
Laura, widow, Over C., Dorset, 1638, I, W, P5/1638/2, P5/13Reg/81B
Martha, widow, Sherb., Dorset, 1672, comm, I, W, P5/1672/1
My., sp., Corsham, 1783, W, P29/2Reg/176
My., widow, Mere, 1788, W, P5/1788/2, P5/18Reg/123
Melior *or* Mille, Chipp., 1750, AB, I, P1/A/367
Nich., husb., Milford, Sal. St Mart., 1666, I, NW (plague victim), P4/1666/11
Arnold als Gerard, Nich., thatcher and labourer, Warm., 1687, comm, I, W, P2/A/310
Rd., shepherd, Winterslow, 1563, AB, I, P2/A/7, P2/4Reg/138B
Arnell, Rd., Langley Burrell, 1725, W, P3/A/304
Arnoll, Robt., Bishopstone N., 1635, I, W, P6/18
Robt., husb., Charminster, Dorset, 1636, AB, comm, I, T (re Thos. A., minor), W, P5/1636/7, P5/12Reg/257
Robt., Heywood, Westb., 1638, AB, I, P25/1638/7
Arnoll, Robt., sen., husb., Farley, Alderbury, 1668, I, W, P26/141
Robt., sen., yeo., Over C., Dorset, 1724, W, P5/1724/2, P5/16Reg/101B
Robt., yeo., Farley, Alderbury, 1734, W, P26/780
Robt., cordw., Nether C., Dorset, 1846, W, Wr, P5/1846/13
Sam., yeo., Downton, 1742, W, P2/A/449
Sam., mason, Zeals, 1788, comm, W, P5/1788/4, P5/18Reg/97
Sarah, widow, Nether C., Dorset, 1693, I, W, P5/1693/2
Sarah, sp., Over C., Dorset, 1726, AB, W, P5/1726/3, P5/16Reg/133A
Sarah, widow, Bloxworth, Dorset, 1807, W, Wr, P5/1807/15
Sarah, widow, Farley, Alderbury, 1807, W, P26/1266
Sarah, widow, Park Hill, Horningsham, 1812, W, Wr (incorrectly labelled), P5/1812/29
Steph., shoemaker, Downton, 1593, AB, I (detailed), W, P2/A/34
Steph., Gillingham, Dorset, 1704, AB, P27/1/578
Thos., husb., Nether C., Dorset, 1579, I, W, P5/1578/2, P5/3Reg/114B
Arnold als Groves, Thos., gent., Malm., 1671, AB, a/c, I, P3/A/135
Arnold als Groves, Thos., sen., butcher, Malm., 1705, I, W, P3/A/254
Thos., ragman, Chipp., 1734, I, W, P3/A/342
Thos., stonemason, Stourton, 1820, comm, W, Wr, P1/1820/133
Valentine, husb., Laverstock, 1667, AB, I, P2/A/235
Wm., husb., Langsheate, Enford, 1608, W, P2/8Reg/18A
Wm., husb., Yatesbury, [1617], I, W, P3/A/26
Wm., Clevancy, Hilmarton, 1641, comm, I, W, P1/A/78
Wm., husb., Sal., 1661, I, W, P4/1661/5
Arnoll, Wm., sen., mercer, Lacock, 1697, comm, I, W, P3/A/235
Wm., Corsham, 1716, marriage licence, P29/2Reg/19E
Arnoll, Wm., sen., mercer, Corsham, 1720, AB, W, P29/A/29, P29/2Reg/32
Wm., bach., Yatesbury, 1721, AB, P5/1721/1
Wm., Laverstock, 1775, AB, P4/1775/14
Wm., yeo., Wootton B., 1787, comm, W, P3/A/477
Wm., Aston Tirrold, Berks., 1789, AB, P1/A/456
Wm., esquire, Corsham, 1802, AB, comm, ren, W, P3/1802/21
Wm., tailor, Bucklebury, Berks., 1835, W, P1/1835/98
Wm., cooper, Motc., Dorset, 1840, O, W, Wr, P27/1/727
see also Aynoll; Mason als A.; Palmer als A.
Arnott, Abraham, yeo., Broad H., 1740, W, P3/A/368

Arnett, Edwd., Englefield, Berks., 1686, AB, I, P1/A/163
Arputt *see* Orpett
Arr, Joan, widow, Allweston, Folke, Dorset, 1579, I, W, P5/1579/1, P5/3Reg/134A
Arrowsmith, Anth., yeo., Wokm., Berks., 1667, comm, W, P5/1667/1
Dorothy, widow, Wantage, Berks., 1724, AB, note, P5/1724/3
Jane, widow, Newbury, Berks., 1789, L, comm, W, P1/A/462, P1/14Reg/332
Arelsmyth, Thos., Wokm., Berks., 1540, W, P5/20Reg/16
Wm., brickmaker, Wokm., Berks., 1707, W, P5/1707/1, P5/15Reg/6
Arscott *see* Escott
Art, Art als Teague, Wm., clothw., Sal. St Mart., 1634, AB, NW, P4/1633/7
Arthur, Arter, Anth., husb., Allington, 1638, I, W, P2/A/175
Arter *or* Arthur, Ferdinand, W. Kington, 1628, I, NW, P3/A/46
Jn., [sen.], Idmiston, 1716, AB, P1/A/239
My., widow, Brook, Westb., 1668, W, P25/1668/11
Arther, My., sp., Crickl. St S., 1730, AB, P1/A/295
Arter, Wm., Amesb., 1605, I, W, P2/A/71
Wm., sen., wheelwright, Idmiston, 1683, I, W, P2/A/294
Wm., Idmiston, 1744, AB, P1/A/353
Artlett, Thos., Box Quarries, 1797, AB, comm, P3/A/494
Arundell, (Lord) *see* Jas. Wheble; Wm. Yates
Ann, sp., W. Shefford, Berks., 1701, W, P1/4Reg/82
Chas. Jn., gent., Brinsham, Netherb., Dorset, 1717, W, P17/372
Jn., yeo., Shefford, Berks., 1668, AB, comm, ren, W, P1/A/113
Jn., yeo., Manton, Preshute, 1711, I, W, P1/A/212, P1/5Reg/138
Julian, widow, Enborne, Berks., 1602, I, W, P1/A/8
Rd., Sutton B., 1739, W, P3/A/365
Wm., joiner and vict., Pangbourne, Berks., 1738, AB, I, P1/A/326
Asey, Asey, Alice, widow, Dunsden, Sonning, Berks., 1639, I, W, P5/1639/4, P5/13Reg/190
Ash, Aish, And., husb., Beckhampton, Avebury, 1799, note of probate, W, P3/A/495
Aish, Ann, widow, Calne, 1846, O, W, Wr, P5/1846/10
Ashe, Benj., weaver, Chipp., 1800, note, W, Wr, P3/1800/66
Ashe, Edwd. *see* Jn. Masters
Aish, Jas., dealer and chapman, Chipp., 1800, W, P3/1800/36
Jas., Bere R., Dorset, 1830, W, Wr, P5/1830/31
Ashe, Jas., Chr. M., 1851, AB, O, Wr, P3/1851/12
Jn., esquire, Heywood, Westb., 1709, monition, W (proved again in PCC, 1710), P25/1709/4
Jn., Bere R., Dorset, 1724, AB, I, P5/1724/4
Jn., fuller, Studley, Bremhill, 1732, AB, I, W, P1/A/301, P1/7Reg/511A
Aish, Jn., vict., Lacock, 1760, W, P3/A/412
Ashe, Margery, blacksmith's widow, Old Windsor, Berks., 1622, AB, I, P1/A/39
My., widow, Malm., 1755, W, P3/A/400
Rd., yeo., Edington, 1617, AB, I, P2/A/109
Robt., jun., shopkeeper, Bere R., Dorset, 1784, AB, ren, P5/1784/1, P5/17Reg/258B
Robt., yeo., Bere R., Dorset, 1793, W, P5/1793/1, P5/18Reg/193A
Ashe, Robt., esquire, Langley House, Langley Burrell, 1830, comm, W, Wr, P3/1830/6
Aish, Robt. Hyde, plumber and glazier, Sherb., Dorset, 1855, aff, W, Wr, P5/1855/12
Ashe, Wm., Preston, Dorset, 1585, AB, P5/4Reg/105C
Ashe, Wm., husb., Burton, Charminster, Dorset, 1586, I, W, P5/1585/1, P5/4Reg/128B
Aish, Wm., Sal., 1728, AB, P4/1728/22
Ashe, Wm., draper, Causeway, Chipp., 1836, W, Wr, P3/1836/66
Aish, Wm., yeo., Calne, 1844, O, W, Wr, P5/1844/4
Ashborne, Jn., Sal., 1581, W, P4/Reg/4
Ashby, Jn., Hurst, Berks., 1542, W, P5/20Reg/38A
Jn., weaver, Wilton, 1593-1610, T, W, P2/A/568
Wm., labourer, Reading, Berks., [1619], I, schedule, W, P1/A/33
Ashe *see* Ash
Ashelford, Adrian, mason, Uffc., Devon, 1675, W, P20/1/78
Hy., Netherb., Dorset, 1707, I, W, P5/1707/2, P5/15Reg/37
Asher, Ann, widow, Rowde, 1839, W, Wr (late Ann Kite), P1/1839/50
Eliz., widow, Maddington, 1558, W, P2/3Reg/134A

Sarah, widow, E. Grimstead, W. Dean, 1751, W, P2/A/462
Thos., tailor, Maddington, 1646, AB, I, W, P2/A/206
Ashey, Joan, widow, Wokm., Berks., 1595, AB, I, P5/1595/1
Ashfield, Dorothy, widow, Wantage, Berks., 1727, W, P23/449
Ashford, Jn., Wambrook, Somerset, 1722, AB, P5/1722/3
Jn., jun., gent., Broadclist, Devon (& Waldron's Ashill, Uffc.), 1840, AB, comm, P20/1/322
Ashley, Ambrose, yeo., Hamptworth, Downton (form. of W. Wellow), 1810, W, P2/1810/53
Ann, widow, Corsham (form. of Chilvester Hill, Calne), 1817, AB, Wr, P3/1817/15
Anth., carp., Purton, 1681, I, W, P3/A/170
Edwd., gent., Nash Hill, Lacock, 1617, I, W, P1/A/31
Eliz., sp., Calne, 1807, AB, comm, P26/1261
Geo., weaver, Corsham, 1629, I, W, P29/A/12, P29/1Reg/118C
Gracious, gardener, Edington, 1841, O, W, Wr, P2/1841/63
Isaac, yeo., Semington, Steeple A., 1813, W, Wr, P2/1813/38
Jacob, maltster, Calstone W., 1760, W, P26/979
Ashly, Joan, widow, Wokm., Berks., 1595, W, P5/6Reg/96B
Ashly, Joan, widow, N. Bradley, 1622, I, NW, P2/A/124
Joan, widow, Stockley, Calne, 1689, I, W, P26/372
Jn., N. Bradley, 1580, W, P2/A/16, P2/6Reg/9A
Jn., gent., Notton, Lacock, 1633, I, W, P3/A/62
Jn., carp., Purton, 1634, I, W, P3/A/64
Ashly als Launder, Jn., sen., fuller, Kington L., 1648, I, W, P1/A/87
Jn., Bps. C., 1686, AB, I, P24/799
Jn., maltster, Downton, 1711, AB, I, P2/A/370
Ashly, Jn., yeo., Stockley, Calne, 1731, AB, NW, P26/764
Jn., tanner, Rams., 1843, AB, note, ren, W, Wr, P5/1843/19
My., widow, Nash Hill, Lacock, 1632, AB, W, P3/A/60
My., widow, Calstone W., 1768, W, P26/1023
My., Devizes, 1812, AB, Wr, P1/1812/17
Matthew, Sulham, Berks., 1741, AB, P1/A/337
Rd., Sal. St Mart., 1674, AB, a/c, I, P4/1674/1
Rd., labourer, Dauntsey, 1677, I, W, P3/A/154
Robt., bach., Westb., 1818, AB, comm, O, Wr, P25/1818/1
Sarah, widow, Aldbourne, 1811, AB, Wr, P1/1811/61
Ashly, Sarah, widow, Hamptworth, Downton, 1821, W, Wr, P2/1821/43
Thos., Sherb., Dorset, 1604, AB, I, P5/1604/1, P5/8Reg/11C
Thos., sen., yeo., Stockley, Calne, 1684, I, W, P26/323
Ashly, Timothy, Kington St M., 1671, AB, I, P1/A/127
Ashly, Walter, Sal., 1628, AB, P4/1627/2
Walter, Bps. C., 1721, AB, I (2 - 1 a copy), P24/893
Walter, Bps. C., 1789, AB, comm, P24/1163
Walter, gent., Bps. C., 1830, W, P24/1319
Wm., clothw., Kington L., 1623, I, W, P3/A/35
Wm., yeo., Melk., 1827, aff, comm, W, Wr, P2/1827/7
see also Ashlock *or* A.
Ashlock, Agnes, widow, Heytes., 1590, AB, I, W, P5/1590/3, P5/5Reg/91E
Alice, Ashton G., Codf. St P., 1581, W, P2/6Reg/43C
Eliz., widow, Marston, Pott., 1669, I, W, P1/A/120
Geoff., yeo., Gt. Cheverell, 1687, AB, I, W (2), P2/A/313
My., widow, Heytes., 1601, AB, I, W, P5/1600/1, P5/7Reg/8
Ashlock *or* Ashly, My., widow, Gt. Cheverell, 1694, I, W, P2/A/326
Thos., Heytes., 1593, AB, I, T, P5/1593/5, P5/6Reg/52B
Thos. *see also* Humphrey Hayward
Ashly *see* Ashley
Ashman, Chris., husb., N. Bradley, 1638, I, W, P2/A/180
Edwd., Hilp., 1806, AB, Wr, P2/1806/58
Eliz., widow, Trowb., 1635, I, W, P22/1/33
Hy., cutler, Trowb., 1613, AB, I, P22/2/10
Jn., Trowb., 1624, AB, I, P22/1/5
Thos., currier, Warm., 1851, comm, W, Wr, P1/1851/60

Ashon *see* Ashton
Ashridge, Jn., Lt. Bedwyn, 1720, I, W, P21/8/8
Jos., yeo., Grafton, 1751, W, P21/10/14
Thos., husb., Urchf., 1620, I, W, P2/A/118
Wm., husb., Chute, 1576, I, W, P5/1576/4, P5/3Reg/84E
Ashton, Alice, Sal., 1695, AB, ren, W, P4/1695/9
Anth., broad weaver, N. Bradley, 1705, I, W, P2/A/351
Anth., broad weaver, Hilp., 1776, W, P2/A/520
Cath., Chr. M., [1602], W, P3/1Reg/110B
Dan., Pewsey, 1703, AB, I, P3/A/248
Dan., weaver, N. Bradley, 1720, AB, W, P1/A/249, P1/6Reg/252
Hy., husb., N. Bradley, 1594, I, W, P2/A/38
Humphrey, Fifield Bavant, 1668, AB, comm, I, P1/A/115
Ashton als Sarshall, Joan, widow, Pewsey, 1717, W, P3/A/286
Ashon als Sharshill, Jn., Pewsey, 1606, AB, I, NW, P1/A/11
Jn., N. Bradley, 1610, AB, I (very detailed), P2/A/85, P2/8Reg/148B
Jn., Pewsey, 1734, AB, P3/A/343
Jn., maltster, Pewsey, 1740, W, P3/A/369
Jn., Pewsey, 1769, AB, P3/A/437
My., weaver's widow, N. Bradley, 1720, W, P1/A/250, P1/6Reg/253A
My., widow, N. Bradley, 1722, W, P2/A/399
My., widow, Biddestone St Nich., 1730, W, P3/A/325
Moses, N. Bradley, 1648, comm, I (2), NW (2), P2/A/209
Moses, broad weaver, N. Bradley, 1744, W, P2/A/450
Rd., clerk, Bramshaw, Hants, 1639, I, W, P24/290
Rd., yeo., Pewsey, 1737, W, P3/A/355
Rd., Pewsey, 1779, AB, P1/A/442
Ashton als Sarshall, Thos., joiner, Pewsey, 1707, I, W, P3/A/260
Wm., sen., yeo., Broad H., 1687, I, W, P3/A/199
Wm., Sal., 1689, AB, P4/1689/3
Wm., sen., yeo., All C., 1693, I, W, P3/A/219
Wm., minor, All C., 1696, AB, comm, P3/A/227
Wm., Biddestone St Nich., 1724, AB, P3/A/296
Ashwell, Ashwell als Carter, Hy., husb., Wokm., Berks., 1585, I, W, P5/1585/9, P5/4Reg/116
Wm., Gt. Cheverell, 1561, W, P2/4Reg/69B
Ashwick, Joan, widow, Dauntsey, 1680, I, W, P1/A/148
Martha, Dauntsey, 1713, AB, I, P3/A/276
Ashwin, Alexander, innholder, Devizes, 1711, I, W, P1/A/218, P1/5Reg/248
Alexander, marine in Gen.Lord's Regt, Devizes, 1751, AB, P1/A/371
Justiniana, Devizes, 1713, AB, P1/A/222
Askew, Paul, Littleton Drew, 1712, I, W, P3/A/269
Robt., innholder, Fisherton A., 1815, W, Wr, P2/1815/61
Aslett, Alan, feltmaker, Wokm., Berks., 1626, I, W, P5/1626/1, P5/10Reg/314
Edwd., yeo., Padworth, Berks., 1619, I, W, P1/A/36
Aslat, Walter, Sal., 1822, AB, ren, P4/1822/4
Aspeck, Louis, yeo., Bremhill, 1852, comm, W, Wr, P3/1852/21
Aste, Anth., cardmaker, Bradford A., 1676, I, W, P2/A/263
Eliz., widow, Woodrow, Melk., 1648, AB, W, P2/A/211
Jn., broad weaver, Woodrow, Melk., 1643, I, W (2 - 1 a copy), P2/A/197
Jn., broad weaver, Woodrow, Melk., 1648, AB, P2/A/212
Astell, Agnes, Hurst, Berks., 1551, W, P5/20Reg/112
Jn., Tilehurst, Berks., 1704, AB, I, P1/A/198
Astewood, And., husb., Binfield, Berks., 1630, W, P5/11Reg/143A
Astins *see* Bland form. A.
Astley, Edwd., gamekeeper, Bloxham Lodge, Tottenham Park, Gt. Bedwyn, 1841, O, W, Wr, P5/1841/18
Aston, Susanna, Abingdon, Berks., 1732, AB, I, P1/A/298
Astwick, Edwd., smith, Mere, 1578, I, W, P5/1578/3, P5/3Reg/109C
Atfield, Jn., sen., yeo., Winkfield, Berks., 1750, W, P1/10Reg/337
Thos., sen., Wokm., Berks., 1603, AB, I, W, P5/1603/1, P5/7Reg/77A
Athearn, Wm., shoemaker, Marl., 1771, W, P1/A/419, P1/12Reg/403B

Atheath, Humphrey, clothier *or* shearman, Warfield, Berks., 1635, I, W, P1/A/70
Atherton, Jane, sp., Abingdon, Berks., 1704, AB, I, P1/A/196
Athwaight *see* Atwhaite
Atkins, Abraham, Bulford (form. of Warm.), 1853, aff, W, Wr, P2/1853/49
Agnes, widow, Kingston D., 1632, I, W, P2/A/157, P2/9Reg/29A
Hatkins, Ann *see* Thomas Hilary
Hatkins, Cath., widow, Chapmanslade, Corsley, [1618], I, W, P2/H/323
Cath., widow, Sutton B., 1714, copy req, copy W, P1/A/223, P1/5Reg/325
David, Winsley, Bradford A., 1575, W, P2/5Reg/218D
Atkins als Cock, Edwd., carp., Kingston D., 1570, W, P2/5Reg/95E
Edwd., Corsham, 1595, AB, W, P29/A/1, P29/1Reg/41
Edwd., sen., fellmonger, Hungerford, Berks., 1720, W, P23/379
Eliz., widow, Heale, Woodford, 1686, I, W, P13/3/2
Eliz., Heale, Woodford, 1721, W, P13/4/18
Joan, widow, Codf. St P., 1610, I, W, P2/A/84, P2/8Reg/140B
Hatkins, Joan, widow, Stapleford, 1728, AB, P2/H/1222
Jn., Heytes., 1597, AB, I, NW, P5/1597/1, P5/6Reg/191B
Jn., Kingston D., 1610, I, W, P2/A/80, P2/8Reg/102A
Jn., sen., Over St., Stapleford, 1612, I, W, P2/A/94, P2/8Reg/164
Jn., gent., Sutton B., 1629, AB, a/c, comm, I, P3/A/51
Jn., [sawyer], Sal., 1667, I, W, P4/1666/2
Hatkins, Jn., sen., Barford St Mart., 1684, AB, I, P2/A/299, P2/H/833
Hatkins, Jn., Stapleford, 1709, AB, I, P2/H/1075
Jn., Gt. Woodford, 1711, I, W, P13/4/1
Jn., Sal., 1734, AB, Wr, P4/1734/9
Jn., sen., carp., Donhead St A., 1746, W, P2/A/453
Jn., breeches maker, Wargrave, Berks., 1795, AB, W, P1/A/476, P1/14Reg/576
Jn., Landford, 1851, W, Wr, P1/1851/64
Leonard, gent., Sutton B., 1668, I, W, P3/A/119
My., sp., Sal. St Thos., 1670, AB, I, P4/1670/18
My., widow, Sutton B., 1674, I, W, P3/A/143
My., widow, Chards., Devon, 1685, I, W, P14/62
Nich., Sal. The Close, 1571, W, P5/2Reg/108D
Nich., W. Dean, 1615, deed of gift, P2/A/106
Rd., fuller, Winsley, Bradford A., 1593, AB, I, P2/A/36
Rd., rough mason, N. Bradley, 1624, AB, I, P2/A/136
Rd., yeo., W. Hatch, Tisb., 1638, AB, a/c, I, P2/A/177
Rd., W. Dean, 1716, AB, P2/A/385
Rd., bach., Mkt. L., 1830, AB, comm, P2/1830/8
Robt., husb., Plaitford, 1569, W, P2/5Reg/53B
Robt., millwright, Turleigh, Winsley, Bradford A., 1634, I, P2/A/163
Robt., gent., Sutton B., 1664, comm, D, I, NW, P1/A/105
Robt., gent., Sutton B., 1671, AB, comm, I (detailed), W, P3/A/136
Robt., Chards., Devon, 1674, AB, I, P14/38
Robt., yeo., Woodford, 1714, W, P13/4/4
Atking, Thos., Stapleford, 1567, W, P2/5Reg/11A
Thos., Corsham, 1632, AB, LA, P29/A/13
Thos., innkeeper, Sal., 1678, AB, I (detailed), W, P4/1678/26, P4/1718/12
Thos., hair cutter, Mkt. L., 1847, aff, O, W, Wr, P2/1847/22
Wm., broad weaver, Winsley, Bradford A., 1722, W, P2/A/400
Wm., yeo., Britford, 1785, W, P24/1177
Wm., gent., Westb., 1847, W, Wr, P25/1847/2
see also Hardikin als A.
Atkinson, Anth., Codf. St P., 1593, AB, I, P2/A/37
Jn., saddler, Sal., 1773, AB, promise to pay debts, ren, W, P1/A/422, P1/12Reg/458
Nich., embroiderer, Sal. St Thos., 1618, I, W, P4/1618/18
Thos., clerk and vicar, Overton, 1650, I, T, W, P1/A/92
Atneve, Jn., yeo., Marston, Pott., 1708, I, W, P1/A/206
Attneave, Jn., sen., yeo., Marston, Pott., 1723, I, note of I, W, P1/A/261, P1/6Reg/441A
Atnoke, Thos., Alvediston, 1567, I, W, P2/A/8, P2/5Reg/27C

Atrithe, Joan, widow, Sandhurst, Berks., 1592, AB, I, W, P5/1592/1, P5/1593/4, P5/5Reg/140C
Atrithe, Thos., yeo., Sandhurst, Berks., 1572, W, P5/2Reg/112A
Atrithe, Wm., wheeler, Sandhurst, Berks., 1572, W, P5/2Reg/112B
Attlee, Robt., yeo., Old Windsor, Berks., 1662, I, W, P1/A/98
Thos., basket maker, Hurst, Berks., 1724, W, P5/1724/5, P5/16Reg/93B
Thos., Winkfield, Berks., 1741, AB, P1/A/342
Attneave *see* Atneve
Attry *see* Ettry
Attwater, Atwater, Alice, widow, Bishopstone S., 1573, W, P2/5Reg/170F
Ambrose, Britford, 1630, AB, a/c, I, P24/209
Atwater, Arthur, Britford, 1633, I (detailed), W (buried at B. 26 Jan 1633), P24/259
Betty, widow, Britford, 1764, W, P24/1093
Caleb, yeo., Britford, 1756, W, P24/1015
Atwaters, Jn., sen., Britford, 1670, I, W, P24/391
Jn., sen., yeo., Britford, 1707, comm, I, W, P24/585
Jn., yeo., Britford, 1751, W, P24/1047
Martha, sp., Britford, 1738, W, P24/913
My., widow, Britford, 1718, AB, P24/644
Atwater, Nich., Hurst, Berks., 1548, W, P5/20Reg/99
Atwaters, Paul, yeo., Hurst, Berks., 1611-12, I, W, P5/1611/1, P5/9Reg/69B
Atwaters, Robt., Westb., 1569, W, P5/2Reg/40C
Atwaters, Sibyl, Britford, 1672, I, W, P24/461
Atwaters, Thos., Britford, 1570, W, P5/2Reg/59D
Atwaters, Thos., Bishopstone N., 1580, W, P5/4Reg/7A
Atwaters, Thos., husb., Britford, 1580, I, P5/1580/4
Atwaters, Thos., yeo., Hurst, Berks., 1609, I, W, P5/1609/1, P5/8Reg/146B
Atwater, Wm., yeo., Bishopstone S., 1559, W, P2/3Reg/171D
Atwaters, Wm., husb., Sal., 1690-91, AB, I, ren (2), W, P4/1690/4, P4/1691/3
Attwell, Attwell als Turner, Edwd., sen., yeo., Swallowfield, Shinfield, Berks., 1714, I, W, P1/A/224, P1/5Reg/354
Jas., yeo., Eaton Hastings, Berks., 1783, W, P1/A/443, P1/13Reg/431
Atwell, Jane, widow, Rowde, 1833, W, Wr, P3/1833/29
Rd., labourer, Heytes., 1811, W, Wr, P5/1811/24
Attwood, Atwood, Cicely, widow, Keevil, 1560, I, W, P2/A/4, P2/4Reg/43C
Edwd., lath maker, Downton, 1791, app. of guardian, W, P2/A/549
Atwood, Eliz., widow, Crookham, Thatcham, Berks., 1756, W, P1/11Reg/206
Atwood, Eliz., widow, Cookham, Berks., 1756, W, P1/A/386
Attwoods, Eliz., widow, Biddestone St Nich., 1766, W, P3/A/433
Atwood, Francis, apprentice, Malm., 1612, W, P3/A/19
Atwood, Francis, husb., W. Wellow, 1723, I, W, P2/A/401
Geo., baker, Devizes, 1787-89, W, P1/A/465, P1/14Reg/180
Atwood, Hy., weaver, Seend, Melk., 1627, I, NW, P2/A/143
Atwood, Jn., husb., Chitterne St My., 1610, I (detailed), W, P2/A/81, P2/8Reg/102B
Atwood, Jn., butcher, Upavon, 1668, AB, I, ren, P1/A/112
Atwood, Jn., yeo., Chitterne St My., 1688, AB, I, NW, P2/A/314
Atwood, Jn., S. Wraxall, 1714, AB, P1/A/231
Jn., sen., yeo., Bromham, 1848, O, W, Wr, P3/1848/11
Atwood, Lawr., aged 14, Chitterne St My., 1621, AB, a/c, I, P2/A/122
Lawr., blacksmith, S. Wraxall, 1714, W, P2/A/381
Atwood, Rd., weaver, Seend, Melk., 1591, AB, I, W, P2/A/28
Atwood, Rd., parson, Gt. Somerford, 1606, AB, comm, O, P1/A/10
Atwood, Rd., Devizes St My., 1623, AB, I, P1/A/44
Rd., yeo., Keevil, 1751, W, P2/A/464
Atwood, Sam., yeo., Keevil, 1777, ren, W, P2/A/524
Sarah, widow, Bromham, 1814, W, Wr, P1/1814/149
Atwood, Susanna, yeo.'s widow, Devizes, 1777-78, comm, W (mentions marriage settlement), P1/A/439, P1/13Reg/183B
Thos., blacksmith, Biddestone, 1684, I, W, P3/A/187
Thos., sen., blacksmith, Biddestone St Nich., 1728, I, W, P3/A/317
Atwood, Thos., Cookham, Berks., 1738, AB, P1/A/324
Atwood, Thos., Keevil, 1752, AB, P2/A/469
Thos., sen., blacksmith, Bromham, 1835, W, Wr, P3/1835/24

Vincent, Donhead St My., 1714, AB, P1/A/233
Atwood, Wm., Sonning, Berks., 1593, AB, a/c, I, P5/1593/2, P5/6Reg/52C
Atwood, Wm., husb., Winterbourne E., 1682, AB, I, P2/A/291
Wm., butcher, Upavon, 1696, I, W, P2/A/333
Wm., husb., Steeple A., 1712, W, P2/A/372
Atwood, Wm., sen., gent., Netheravon, 1739, W, P12/172
Wm., yeo., Amesb., 1746, AB, ren, W, P2/A/454
see also Southernwood als A.; Woods als A.
Attworth, Rd., Wantage, Berks., 1696, W, P5/1696/3
Atwater, Atwaters *see* Attwater
Atwell *see* Attwell
Atwhaite, Atwhaite als Sweet, Edith, Wilsford nr Pewsey, 1595, I, W, P2/A/41
Athwaight als Sweet, Jn., Wilsford nr Pewsey, 1626, W, I (detailed), P2/A/139
Atwhaite als Sweet, Wm., labourer, Wilsford nr Pewsey, 1609, I, T, P2/A/76
Atwood *see* Attwood
Aubert, Lewis, grocer, Bracknell, Warfield, Berks., 1811, W, Wr, P1/1811/71
Aubery *see* Aubrey
Aubin, Edwd., Redlynch, Downton, 1784, W, P2/A/539
Aubrey, Awbrey, Ann, shoemaker's widow, Bodenham, Nunton and B., 1757, W, P2/A/473
Aubury, David, innkeeper, Twyford, Hurst, Berks., 1822, W, Wr, P5/1822/17
Awbery, Edwd., husb., Cholsey, Berks., 1628, I, NW, P1/A/53
Awbery, Jn., sen., yeo., Snelsmore, Chieveley, Berks., 1716, comm, W, P1/A/241, P1/6Reg/80
Aubery, Jn., yeo., Yattendon, Berks., 1729, AB, comm, I, P1/A/276
Awbrey, Jn., Bodenham, Nunton and B., 1771, AB, P2/A/508
Awbery, Rd., sen., yeo., Beenham Valence, Berks., 1729, AB, ren, W, P1/A/282, P1/7Reg/262A
Thos., doctor of divinity and vicar, Ashton K., 1623, I, W, P3/A/38
Awbrey, Thos., gent. and esquire, Chaddenwick, Mere, 1635, I, W, copy W, P5/1635/1, P5/12Reg/170D
Awbery, Thos., gent., Broad C., 1682-86, AB (2), I, P2/A/282, 309
Awbrey, Thos., shoemaker, Bodenham, Nunton and B., 1752, W, P2/A/466
Awbery, Wm., Reading, Berks., 1729, AB, P1/A/284
Audley, Jn., Turners Puddle, Dorset, 1591, I, W, P5/1591/2, P5/5Reg/98B
Lewis, innholder, Marl., 1661-74, AB, court papers, I, W, P1/A/96
Maud, widow, Bradford A., 1593, AB, I, W, P2/A/570
Roger, priest, Stourton, 1561, institution to rectory, P1/1Reg/77A
Thos., Bradford A., 1588, AB, P2/A/20, P2/7Reg/138B
Wm., sen., mercer, Bradford A., 1633, AB, a/c, I (very detailed), P2/A/160
see also Ludwell als A.
Augustine, Jn., husb., Wrou., 1571, W (NEP), P1/1Reg/83B
Wm., priest, 1550, institution to vicarage on death of Fryar, P2/2Reg/111A
Wm., priest, Bishopstrow, 1554, institution to rectory on deprivation of Locke, P2/2Reg/193A
Auley, Auley *or* Anley, Robt., shoemaker, Warm., 1565, W, P2/4Reg/196C
Aulford *see* Alford
Ault, Alt, Eliz., Tockenham, 1729, W, P3/A/319
Francis, hair weaver, Sal., 1614, I, W, P4/1614/2
Aunger *see* Anger
Ause *see* Awse
Auseman, Eliz., widow, Welford, Berks., 1804, W, P1/1804/62
Ausgood *see* Osgood
Aust, Alice, sp., Gt. Somerford, 1621, AB, a/c, comm, I, NW, P3/A/32
Anth., tiler, Corsham, 1669, AB, I, P29/1Reg/187
Anth., yeo., Marl. St Peter and St Paul, 1676, AB, comm, I, P1/A/141
Arthur, Broughton G., 1710, AB, P2/A/368
Dan., yeo., Colerne, 1853, W, Wr, P3/1853/31
Edith, widow, Colerne, 1639, I, W, P3/A/78
Edwd., husb., Broughton G., 1541, W (NEP), P2/1Reg/42A
Edwd., carp., Pickwick, Corsham, 1614, AB, I, P29/A/4
Edwd., weaver, Broughton G., 1631, I, W, P1/A/58
Eleanor, Colerne, 1635, AB, I, P1/A/69
Eliz., widow, Corsham, 1700, AB, P29/A/27, P29/1Reg/274D
Geo., builder and mason, Corsham, 1856, AB, aff, O, ren, Wr, P3/1856/2

Gerard, E. Coulston, 1566, W, P2/4Reg/231A
Hy., gent., Urchf., 1717, AB, ren, P2/A/389
Isabel, E. Coulston, 1567, W, P2/5Reg/12B
Jn., sen., Broughton G., 1621, W, P2/A/571
Jn., yeo., Biddestone St Nich., 1697, comm, I, W, P3/A/236
Jn., husb., Chipp., 1740, I, W, P3/A/370
Jn., tile raiser, S. Wraxall, 1789, W, P1/A/457, P1/14Reg/265
Jn., yeo., Corsham, 1834, W, Wr, P3/1834/37
Judith, widow, Corsham, 1701, I, W, P29/A/28, P29/1Reg/279
Martha, wife, Walcot, Bath, Somerset (leaving her effects at Calne), 1834, AB, comm, Wr, P26/1409
My., widow, Sal. St Thos., 1635, I (detailed), W, P4/1635/1
My., widow, Biddestone, 1679, I, W, P3/A/162
My., yeo.'s wife, Lacock, 1784, AB, comm, ren, P3/A/471
Nich., yeo., Semington, Steeple A., 1607, I (detailed), W, P2/A/74
Rd., Broughton G., 1626, AB, I (detailed), P2/A/141
Rd., yeo., Biddestone St Nich., 1629, I, W, P3/A/52
Rd., fuller, Slaughterford, 1637, AB, I, W, P3/A/72
Rd., Easton, Corsham, 1697, I, P29/A/24
Rd., yeo., Allington, 1727, W, P3/A/309
Rd., carp., Colerne, 1732, W, P3/A/329
Thos., carrier, Colerne, 1753, W, P1/A/374, P1/11Reg/86
Thos., Melk., 1753, AB, P1/A/379
Thos., Colerne, 1822, AB, comm, W, Wr, P3/1822/29
Thos., yeo., Streets Grn, Gt. Chalfield, 1826, W, Wr, P1/1826/108
Uriah, tiler, S. Wraxall, 1775, W, P2/A/517
Uriah, Mount Scylla, Colerne, 1806, W, Wr, P3/1806/34
Wm., husb., Slaughterford, 1612, W, P3/A/18
Wm., clerk and rector, Beechingstoke, 1631, I, W, P1/A/56
Wm., sen., yeo., Biddestone St Nich., 1633, AB, I, NW, P3/A/63
Wm., tiler, Pickwick, Corsham, 1671-72, I, W, P29/A/15, P29/1Reg/196
Wm., Biddestone, 1691, I, W, P3/A/211
Wm., Pickwick, Corsham, 1827, AB, comm, Wr, P3/1827/6
see also Buckland als A.

Austin, Amos, yeo., Wrou., 1844, comm, W, Wr, P3/1844/58
Ann, S. Newton, 1758, AB, P2/A/478
Austin als Drew, Dan., wheelwright *or* carp., Leverton, Chilton F., 1710, I, W, P3/A/267
Dan., blacksmith, Wrou., 1787, W, P3/A/478
Austen, Edgar Francis, gent., Calne, 1804, note, W, P26/1245
Eliz., widow, Sal., 1710, AB, I, P4/1710/5
Eliz., widow, Wrou., 1791, W, P3/A/488
Austin als Drew, Jas., wheelwright, Leverton, Chilton F., 1720, comm, W, P1/A/247, P1/6Reg/225
Jas., chimney sweep, Timber St., Chipp., 1846, O, W, Wr, P3/1846/6
Jane Tanner, widow, Chipp., 1856, aff, W, Wr, P3/1856/36
Jason, farmer, Chilton F., 1855, aff, O, W, Wr, P1/1855/49
Austen, Jn., Turners Puddle, Dorset, 1568, W, P5/2Reg/30D
Jn., milliner *or* mercer, Pewsey, 1667, AB, I, ren, W, P3/A/112
Jn., carp., Elcombe, Wrou., 1670, AB, I, P3/A/131
Jn., Ditchampton, Wilton, 1673, a/c, P2/A/259
Jn., sen., butcher, Westb., 1746, AB, W, P25/1746/4
Jn., Longworth, Berks., 1750, AB, P1/A/364
Jn., sen., carp. and wheelwright, Wrou., 1763, W, P1/A/397, P1/12Reg/103B
Austen, Jn., butcher, Wilton, 1766, W, P2/A/496
Jn., yeo., Highw., 1826, W, P10/1826/1
Jn., wheelwright, Wrou., 1827, W, Wr, P3/1827/27
Jn., ironfounder, Wantage, Berks., 1833, W, Wr, P5/1833/15
Jonathan, shoemaker, Marl. St My., 1720, I, W, P1/A/254, P1/6Reg/284A
Jos., clothw., Chalford, Westb., 1705, AB, I, P25/1705/6
Austin als Drew, Jos., labourer, Chilton F., 1760, W, P3/A/413
Austen, Lawr., yeo. of Her Majesty's larder, Hurst, Berks., 1593, I, T, P5/1593/6
Martha, widow, Eastrop, Highw., 1840, comm, W, Wr, P10/1840/1

Austen, Martha, widow, Wrou., 1852, comm, W, Wr, P3/1852/59
My., widow, Pewsey, 1749, W, P3/A/390
My., widow, Westb., 1761, W, P25/1761/1
Paul, Westb., 1770, AB, L, P25/1770/3
Rd., carp., Wrou., 1828, W, Wr, P3/1828/34
Sam., yeo., Chilton F., 1672, AB, I, P3/A/137
Sam., innholder, Pewsey, 1745, W, P3/A/383
Sam., yeo., Wrou., 1819, W, Wr, P3/1819/23
Susanna, Marl., 1672, AB, P1/A/129
Thos., yeo., S. Newton, 1713, AB, I, P2/A/378
Thos., butcher, Westb., 1799, W (note includes request for return of W), P25/1799/2
Thos., bach., Compton B., 1829, AB, comm, Wr, P1/1829/43
Thos., butcher, Westb., 1829, O, W (bequest to Lower Meeting House), P25/1829/5
Thos. *see also* James Hall
Austen, Wm., blacksmith, Brinkw., 1615, AB, a/c, I, P3/A/23
Wm., Uffcott, Broad H., 1749, AB, P3/A/391
Wm., scribbler, Chipp., 1789, AB, D, W, P1/A/459, P1/14Reg/278
Wm., butcher, Westb., 1816, O, W, Wr, P25/1816/2
Wm., yeo., Westb., 1828, O, W, P25/1829/1
Wm., labourer, Highw., 1856, aff, O, W, Wr, P10/1856/1
Wm., private in the 10th Regt of Hussars, and bach., Chilton F., 1856, AB, aff, D, O, Wr, P3/1856/12
Auther, Eliz., widow, Kirkstall, Leeds, Yorkshire (leaving effects at Marl.), 1842, comm, court paper, W, Wr, P1/1842/22
Aven, Ann, widow, Erlestoke, 1667-69, AB, a/c, I, W, P2/A/233
Edwd., glover, Marl., 1674, AB, I, P1/A/135
Jn., husb., Erlestoke, 1596, I, W, P2/A/43
Jn., Erlestoke, 1619, I, W, P1/A/35
Jn., yeo., Erlestoke, 1694, I, W, P2/A/327
Avons, Jn., vict., Studley, Trowb., 1847, AB, D, O, ren, W, Wr, P1/1847/15
Rd., broad weaver, Erlestoke, [1683], I, W, P2/A/297
Sibyl, widow, Erlestoke, 1622, I, W, P2/A/126
Susan, Coulston, Edington, 1596, I, W, P2/A/44
Avon, Wm., Allington, 1608, W, P2/8Reg/16B
Avenell, [...], Sevenhampton, Highw., 1561-70?, W (damaged), P5/1561/1
Hy., sen., blacksmith, Wanb., 1745, W, P3/A/384
Jn., yeo., Badbury, Chiseldon, 1836, comm, W, Wr, P3/1836/18
Mgt., sp., Wanb., 1789, W (NEP), P3/A/482
Sarah, widow, Wanb., 1825, AB, O, Wr, P3/1825/13
Steph., yeo., Westrop, Highw., 1686, AB, L, I, P10/1686/10
Averad *see* Everard
Averis, Agnes, widow, Slaughterford, 1569, W, P1/1Reg/102C, P1/2Reg/97B
Avery, Ann, widow, Newbury, Berks., 1738, W, P1/A/329, P1/8Reg/346A
Edwd., husb., Upper Stratton, Stratton St Mgt., 1662, I, W, P1/A/100
Edwd., husb. and yeo., Walcot, Swindon, 1686, I, W, P1/A/161
Eliz., widow, Stratton St Mgt., 1737, W, P3/A/358
Frances, sp., Compton B., 1666, I, W, P3/A/110
Hy., husb., All C., 1698, comm, I, W, P3/A/240
Avsey, Jn., Sonning, Berks., 1539, W, P5/20Reg/6
Jn., Swindon, 1708, W, P1/A/204
Jn., Studley, Calne, 1740, W, Wr, P5/1740/3
Jn., bricklayer, Enborne, Berks., 1741, AB, I, P1/A/334
My., widow, Beanacre, Melk., 1736, W, P2/A/432
My., widow, Watchfield, Shrivenham, Berks., 1826, AB, comm, Wr, P1/1826/20
Noah, Charlton nr Malm., 1736, AB, P3/H/1131
Priscilla, trunk and fishing tackle maker, Reading, Berks., 1823, W, Wr, P1/1823/95
Rd., Sonning, Berks., 1586, AB, P5/1586/3, P5/4Reg/133B
Rd., Newbury, Berks., 1704, AB, P1/A/199
Robt., labourer, Upper Stratton, Stratton St Mgt., 1685, I, W, P3/A/191
Robt., yeo., Stratton St Mgt., 1733, W, P3/A/338
Every, Sarah, sp., The Close, Salisbury, 1825, W, Wr, P5/1825/26
Thos., bricklayer, Reading, Berks., 1744, W, P1/A/348, P1/9Reg/342B

Timothy, Speenhamland, Berks., 1720, copy req, copy W (original W transmitted to PCC), P1/A/258, P1/6Reg/339
Walter, Stratford Tony, 1547, AB, P2/2Reg/29B
Wm., sen., blacksmith, Charl. nr. P., 1695, I, L, W, P1/A/179
Wm., blacksmith, Charlton nr Malm., 1733, I, W, P3/A/339
Avis, Havis, Edwd., sen., husb., Wilton, Gt. Bedwyn, 1713, I, W, P5/1713/40, P5/15Reg/362A
Jn., carp., Old Windsor, Berks., 1732, W, P1/A/299, P1/7Reg/480B
Robt., priest, Cholsey, Berks., 1560, institution to vicarage, P1/1Reg/80A
Susan, widow, Wokm., Berks., 1629, AB, comm, P5/1629/2, P5/11Reg/26A
Thos., clothw., Wokm., Berks., 1630-31, AB, a/c, P5/1631/123, P5/11Reg/145B
Wm., [weaver], Wokm., Berks., 1587, I, W, P5/1587/3, P5/4Reg/149B
Avoake, Cath., widow, Sherb., Dorset, 1708, W, P5/1708/3, P5/15Reg/92
Jos., Sherb., Dorset, 1690, AB, P5/1690/3
My., widow, Sherb., Dorset, 1701, AB, P5/1701/5
Robt., sen., gent., Sherb., Dorset, 1714, W, P5/1714/1, P5/15Reg/389C
Wm., currier, Sherb., Dorset, 1708, W, P5/1708/4, P5/15Reg/97
Wm., yeo., Sherb., Dorset, 1722, comm, W, P5/1722/4, P5/16Reg/61B
Avon, Avons *see* Aven
Avsey *see* Avery
Awbery, Awbrey *see* Aubrey
Awcolt, Jn., blacksmith, Broad B., Highw., 1714, W, P10/1714/5
Awdry, Ambrose, mercer, Melk., 1701, W, P2/A/344
Ambrose, esquire, Seend, Melk., 1802, AB, comm, P3/1802/31
Ambrose, esquire, Seend, Melk., 1810, AB, comm, P3/1810/2
Eliz., widow, Seend, Melk., 1852, W, Wr, P2/1852/31
Geo., Maiden B., 1703, AB, I, ren, P2/A/349
Godwin, mercer, Melk., [1636-77], W, P1/A/73
Jane, sp., Melk., 1784, comm, W, P2/A/536
Jn., jun., clerk, Melk., 1637, I (very detailed), W, P2/A/171
Jn., mercer, Melk., 1698, I, W, P2/A/340
Jn., Marl., 1800, AB, P1/1800/6, P1/15Reg/207A
Jos., mercer, Steeple A., 1669, AB, I, P2/A/246
Awman *see* Aman
Awndeley, Rd., Warm., 1551, AB, P2/2Reg/133C
Awse, Ause, Jn., husb., Wokm., Berks., 1546, W, P5/20Reg/72A
Awsis, Radegund, widow, Wokm., Berks., 1583-84, AB (in minority of Jn., Robt. & Mgt. A.), I, T, P5/4Reg/96A
Rd., parchment maker, Sherb., Dorset, 1627, I, NW, P5/1627/1
Rd., parchment maker, Sherb., Dorset, 1691, I, P5/1691/2
Robt., Sherb., Dorset, 1627, NW, P5/11Reg/39B
Thos., Sherb., Dorset, 1614, AB, P5/9Reg/117B
Awsey *see* Allsey
Awsis *see* Awse
Awsopp *see* Alsop
Axam, My., sp., Woodb., 1688, AB, comm, P3/A/204
Robt., sen., Preshute, 1789, AB, swearing in of admr, P1/A/464
Axbridge, Thos., baker, Corsham, 1684, AB, I, P29/A/19, P29/1Reg/221A
see also Hooper als A.
Axden, Nich., Sutton V., 1569, W, P2/5Reg/60D
Rd., Sutton V., 1558, AB, P2/3Reg/120C
Axford, Aaron, Berwick B., 1735, W, P26/786
Aldhelm, husb., Chitterne AS, 1590, I, W, P2/A/24
Alice, widow, Erlestoke, 1572, W, P2/5Reg/154C
Ambrose, no abode stated, 1713, W, P2/A/379
Ann, widow, Gt. Cheverell, 1651, AB, I, P1/A/93
Ann, widow, Berwick B., 1709, I, W, P26/560
Ann, widow, Gt. Cheverell, 1725, I, W, P2/A/406
Betty, widow, Upton L., 1773, AB, P2/A/515
Buckett, husb., Chitterne AS, 1670, I, NW, P2/A/254
Cath., widow, Erlestoke, 1672, AB, I, P2/A/256
Edwd., vict., Streatley, Berks., 1798, W, P1/A/482, P1/15Reg/63B
Eliz., widow, Erlestoke, [1686], I, W, P2/A/306

Ephraim, sen., rugmaker, Melk., 1688, AB, I, P2/A/315
Hy., husb., Gt. Cheverell, 1633, I, W, P2/A/161
Hy., yeo., Erlestoke, 1664, comm, I, W, P1/A/106
Hy., yeo., Gt. Cheverell, 1668, AB, comm, P1/A/114
Hy., yeo., Erlestoke, 1682, court paper, I, W, P2/A/285
Hy., Gt. Cheverell, 1686, comm, I, W, P2/A/307
Hy., Pott., 1771, AB, I, P1/A/416
Isaac, Fisherton A. (form. of Erlestoke), 1739-40, AB, cert, I, P2/A/439
Isaac, farmer, Warm. & Erlestoke, 1740, a/c, I, W, P2/A/441
Isaac, Erlestoke, 1784, AB, comm, P2/A/537
Isaac, Erlestoke, 1828, AB, comm, P2/1828/6
Jas., carp., Gt. Cheverell, [1706], I, W, P2/A/358
Jas., Westb., 1765, AB, P25/1765/2
Jas., woolstapler, Warm., 1813, comm, W, Wr, P2/1813/13
Jane, widow, Rowde, 1682, I, W, P3/A/175
Jane, sp., Steeple A., 1850, W, Wr, P2/1850/52
Jane, widow, Warm., 1852, AB, D, O (2), W, Wr, P2/1852/21
Joan, Erlestoke, 1709, I, W, P2/A/364
Joan, widow, Gt. Cheverell, 1730, I, W, P2/A/415
Jn., husb., Erlestoke, 1598, I, W, Wr, P2/A/57
Jn., husb., Chitterne AS, 1606, AB, I, W, P1/A/15
Jn., yeo., Rowde, 1679, I, W, P3/A/163
Jn., Whitep., 1681, W, P2/A/278
Jn., linen weaver, Bratton, Westb., 1695, I, W (NEP), P25/1695/5
Jn., Whitep., 1718, AB, P2/A/392
Jn., Erlestoke, 1727, AB, P2/A/410
Jn., maltster, Lt. Cheverell, 1734, W, P2/A/428
Jn., yeo., Erlestoke, 1778, W, P2/A/530
Jn., sen., gent., Mkt. L., 1784, W, Wr, P2/A/538
Jn., yeo., Steeple A., 1802, W, P2/1802/71
Jn., sen., gent., Eastcott, Urchf., 1807, comm, W, Wr, P2/1807/34
Jonathan, yeo., Erlestoke, [1687], I, W, P2/A/311
Jonathan, Westb., 1704, AB, P25/1704/1
Jos., Worton, Pott., 1767, AB, P1/A/406
Jos., bach., Worton, Pott., 1802, AB, Wr, P1/1802/2, P1/15Reg/361B
Mgt., widow, Chitterne AS, 1643, I, W, P2/A/195
Mgt., widow, Erlestoke, 1729, W, P1/A/294, P1/7Reg/361A
Axford form. Williams, My., Devizes, 1755, AB, P1/A/383
Rd., Erlestoke, 1641, I (detailed), W, P2/A/192
Robt., cordw., Upton L., 1726, I, W, P1/A/272, P1/7Reg/67A
Robt., Erlestoke, 1809, AB, comm, Wr, P2/1809/9
Roger, yeo., Edington, 1609-10, AB (in minority of Hy. A.), I, memo, W, P2/A/82, P2/8Reg/53D
Sarah, sp., Devizes, 1717, W, P1/A/244, P1/6Reg/121
Sarah, sp., Lt. Cheverell, 1776, AB, P2/A/522
Sarah, widow, Worton, Pott., 1786, W, P1/A/454, P1/14Reg/138A
Sarah, widow, Steeple A., 1825, W, Wr, P2/1825/46
Susanna, sp., Bremhill, 1730, AB, W, P3/A/326-27
Thos., husb. and bach., Chitterne AS, 1646, I, W (2 - 1 is NW), P2/A/204
Thos., yeo., Gt. Cheverell, 1648, comm, I, W, P2/A/210
Thos., sen., yeo., Erlestoke, 1708, I, W, P2/A/363
Thos., yeo., Gt. Cheverell, 1711, W, P1/A/211, P1/5Reg/103
Thos., yeo., Erlestoke, 1752-53, W, P1/A/376, P1/11Reg/106
Thos., gent., Lt. Cheverell, 1778, W, P2/A/531
Thos., gent., Westb. L., 1782, W, P25/1782/4
Thos., gent., Trowb., 1845, O, W, Wr, P1/1845/10
Wm., husb., Erlestoke, 1575, I, W, P2/A/9, P2/5Reg/239B
Wm., Winterbourne M., 1696, I, W, P3/A/228
Wm., tailor, Upton L., 1760, W, P2/A/484
Wm., yeo., Mkt. L., 1762, AB, comm, ren, P2/A/488
Wm., sen., gent., Erlestoke, 1773, W, P1/A/423, P1/12Reg/465A

Wm., Sutton V., 1797, W, Wr, P2/A/562
Wm., Erlestoke, 1828, AB, aff, comm, P2/1828/17
Wm., property in Easterton & E. Lavington ; no abode stated, 1830, AB, O, P1/1830/1
Axford als Burge, Wolstan, W. Knoyle, 1597, grant of AB, P2/A/47,
Axton, Axton, Edmd., Westport St My., 1712, AB, I, P3/A/271
Ayers, Eyres, Alice, widow, Netheravon, 1591, I, W, P5/1591/23, P5/5Reg/125B
Eyres, Alice, widow, Durrington, 1663, court paper, I, T, W, P2/E/157
Eyres, Ann, widow, Chapmanslade, Corsley, 1678, I, W, P2/E/189
Eyre, Ann, widow, Stratford sub C., 1681, W (bequests include Luther's Sermons & surgery & physic books), P4/1681/1
Eyers, Ann, widow, Westb. L., 1761, W, P25/1761/3
Eyers, Anth., gardener, Rams., 1703, I, W, P5/1703/8
Augustine, yeo., Eastcott, Swindon, 1662, comm, W, P3/A/96
Eyers, Charity, widow and maltster, Warm., 1691, AB, I, P2/E/227
Eyre, Chris., gent., Orcheston St My., 1561-89, AB, I, P2/E/27, P2/4Reg/87B
Eyre, Chris., Sal. St Mart., 1602, AB, I, W, P1/E/3
Eyre, Chris., Sal. St Thos. & London, [1617-1801], comm (1801, to grant LA to Susanna Harriet E. next of kin of Chris. E. of S. & L. merchant enabling alteration to trust fund created by W of 1617 to provide additional weekly sermon at St Thos. S.), P4/1801/4
Eyre, Cicely, widow, Bromham, 1617, I, W, P3/E/27
Ayres, Cornelius, boot and shoemaker, Lyneham, 1838, W, Wr, P3/1838/38
Eyre, Cuthbert, gent., Sal., 1629, AB, a/c, I (detailed), P4/1629/9
Eyre, Darius, clerk, Poulshot, 1636, I, W, P2/E/119
Eyre, Dorothy, wife, Brickworth, Whitep., 1668, AB, P2/E/170
Eyre, Edmd., Durrington, 1574, AB, P2/5Reg/182B
Eyers, Edmd., broad weaver, Dilton M., Westb., 1820, W, Wr, P25/1820/2
Edwd., Blunsdon St And., 1788, AB, comm, P3/A/479
Eyers, Edwd., labourer, Durrington, 1804, W, P2/1804/16
Eyres, Eleanor, Westb. L., 1759, W, P25/1759/4
Eyres, Eliz., sp., Sal. St Thos., 1675, AB, NW, P4/1674/14
Eliz., widow, Groundwell, Blunsdon St And., 1765, W, P3/A/431
Eyres, Eliz., housekeeper, Sal. (form. of Ringwood, Hants), 1820, AB, cert, P4/1820/3
Eyres, Francis, yeo., Wrou., 1765, W, P3/E/269
Eyre, Geo., Atworth, Bradford A., 1681, AB, P2/E/198
Eyre, Giles, yeo., Sal. St Edmd., 1629, AB, a/c, I, T (children: Rd. & Giles E.), P4/1629/2, 4
Eyre, Grace, Sal., 1724, AB, P4/1724/4
Eyre, Hy., yeo., Wokm., Berks., 1619, I, W, P5/1619/19, P5/10Reg/39
Hy., yeo., Lydiard T., 1742, W, P3/A/373
Eyres, Hy., Burbage, 1807, AB, P11/262
Eyres, Isaac, yeo., Hodson, Chiseldon, 1789, W, P3/E/304
Ayres, Jas., tallow chandler, Reading, Berks., 1741, W, P1/9Reg/114
Ayres, Jas., labourer, Gt. Bedwyn, 1760, W, P21/10/48
Eyers, Jn., Marl. St Peter and St Paul, 1602, AB, I, P1/E/2
Eyers, Jn., husb., Swindon, 1602, W, P3/1Reg/45A
Eyre, Jn., yeo., Seend, Melk., 1610, I, W, P2/E/430, P2/8Reg/135B
Ayres *or* Eyres, Jn., sen., yeo., Ogbourne St Geo., 1613, I, W, P5/1613/78
Eyre, Jn., yeo., Bromham, 1620, I, W, P3/E/36
Eyre, Jn., weaver, Sal. St Edmd., 1622, I, W, P4/1621/3
Eyre, Jn., weaver, Nether St., Bromham, 1661, I, W, P3/E/71, P3/3Reg/27B
Ayres, Jn., husb., Pewsey, 1692, W, P1/A/175
Jn., bach., Shaw, Lydiard M., 1720, W, P1/A/253, P1/6Reg/281B
Eyres, Jn., Corsley, 1728, AB, P2/E/304
Jn., yeo., Blunsdon St And., 1729, I, W, P1/A/289, P1/7Reg/293B
Jn., Hurley, Berks., 1735, AB, P1/A/308
Ayres, Jn., vict., Burghfield, Berks., 1735, I, W, P1/A/310, P1/8Reg/9A
Ayres, Jn., tallow chandler, Reading, Berks., 1741, W, P1/A/335
Ayres, Jn., brickmaker and farmer, Marcham, Berks., 1811, W, Wr, P1/1811/77
Ayres, Jn., Coped Hall, Wootton B., 1842, AB, comm, Wr, P3/1842/9
Eyres, Jos., Ludg., 1758, AB, P2/E/357
Ayres *or* Eyres, Kinborough, widow, Westb., 1674, I, NW, P25/1674/2
Ayres, Martha, sp., Broad B., Highw., 1797, W, P5/1797/1, P5/18Reg/250B

Eyre, My., widow, Hawk St., Bromham, 1687, AB, I, ren, W, P3/E/143
Eyres, My., widow, Chain St., Warm., 1744, W, P1/E/236, P1/9Reg/441B
Ayres, Nich., yeo., Sonning, Berks., 1637, I, W, P5/1637/1, P5/13Reg/33B
Eayers, Nich., wheelwright, Chapmanslade, Corsley, [1696], I, W, P2/E/240
Nich., sen., yeo., Pewsey, 1726, W, P1/A/274, P1/7Reg/103B
Ayres, Nich., Marcham, Berks., 1729, AB, I, P1/A/279
Eyre, Prudence, widow, Sal., 1637, I, W, P4/1636/1
Eyre, Rd., husb., Poulshot, 1605, AB, I, ren, P2/E/60
Eyre, Rd., Wokm., Berks., 1616, I, W, P5/1616/21
Eyre *or* Arie, Rd., Sonning, Berks., 1624, AB, I, P5/1624/15, P5/10Reg/229A
Eyre, Rd., Bromham, 1636, I, W, P3/E/59
Eyre, Rd., druggist, Sal., 1728, W, P4/1728/3
Rd. Croft, bach., Blunsdon St And., 1762, AB, P3/A/421
Ayre, Robt., clothier, Bromham, 1603, I, W, P3/A/2
Eyers, Robt., Wrou., 1610, W, P3/E/9
Eyre, Robt., weaver, Rowde, 1633, I, W, P3/E/55
Eayres, Robt., husb., Preston, Dorset, 1641, I, W, P5/1641/29, P5/14Reg/26D
Eyres, Robt., broad weaver, Westb. L., 1678, I, W, P25/1678/10
Eyres, Robt., shopkeeper, Chapmanslade, Corsley, 1762, W, P2/E/367
Eayears, Robt., Southwick, N. Bradley, 1763, AB, I, P1/E/255
Ayres, Robt., gent. *or* linen draper, Bewley, Lacock, 1784, W, P3/A/472
Eyers, Sam., yeo., Hinton, Steeple A., 1737, I, W, P2/E/320
Eyres, Sam., cooper, Hinton, Steeple A., 1825, W, Wr, P2/1825/24
Eyres, Thos., Durrington, 1603, AB, I, W, P2/E/59
Thos., Elcombe, Wrou., [1606], I, W (NEP), P3/A/7
Eyres, Thos., Swindon, 1610, AB, P3/E/10
Eyre, Thos., jun., Bromham, 1616, AB, a/c, I, P3/E/24
Eyre, Thos., grocer, Sal., 1631, I, W, P4/1631/19
Eyre, Thos., gent., Bromham, 1636, I, W, P3/E/60
Eyre, Thos., Sutton Poyntz, Dorset, 1673, AB, comm, P5/1673/14
Eyres, Thos., jun., Sherb., Dorset, 1684, AB, comm, I, P5/1684/16
Thos., yeo., Ogbourne St Geo., 1687, I, W, P23/157
Eayers, Thos., Chapmanslade, Corsley, 1697, AB, I, P2/E/242
Eyre, Thos., gent., Sal., 1699, W, P4/1699/8
Eyres, Thos., Elcombe, Wrou., 1734, AB, P3/A/344
Ayres, Thos., basket maker, Hungerford, Berks., 1742, ren, W, P23/563
Eyres, Thos., Westb. L., 1760, AB, P25/1760/4
Thos., yeo., Minety, 1768, W, P3/A/435
Ayres, Thos., Everleigh, 1769, W, P3/A/438
Eyers, Thos., carp., Steeple A., 1773, W, P2/E/385
Eyres, Thos., property in Corsley ; no abode stated, 1841, AB, comm, P2/1841/23
Eyres, Wm., Durrington, 1575, AB, P2/5Reg/220C
Eyres, Wm., husb., Durrington, 1597-98, W (incomplete), P1/2Reg/165B
Wm., husb., Swindon, [1609], W (NEP), P3/A/9
Eyre, Wm., no abode stated, 1638, I, P30/64
Eyres, Wm., yeo., Westb., 1644, comm, I, W, P25/1644/7
Eyre, Wm., gent., Wedh., Urchf., 1667, AB, comm, P2/E/166
Eyres, Wm., no abode stated, 1669, I (NEP), P1/E/100
Eyre, Wm., clothier, Bromham, 1669, AB, comm, I, P3/E/84
Eyre, Wm., maltster, Warm., 1673, AB, I, P2/E/183
Ayres, Wm., yeo., Aldbourne & Ogbourne St Geo., 1682, I, W, P3/A/176
Eyre, Wm., esquire, Neston, Corsham, 1684, I (very detailed), W, P3/E/128
Eyre, Wm., Wanb., 1685, AB, comm, P3/E/137
Eyre, Wm., gent., Henley, Box, 1700, W, Wr, P3/E/162
Eyre, Wm., apothecary, Sal., 1703, AB, I, P4/1703/9
Eyers, Wm., clothw., Westb. L., 1710, I, W (NEP), P25/1710/7
Eyres, Wm., Bishopstrow, 1748, AB, P2/E/338
Eyres, Wm., yeo., Burbage, 1775, AB, P11/236
Eyers, Wm., cooper, Steeple A., 1787, W, P2/E/412
Eyers, Wm., Bulford, 1847, AB, Wr, P2/1847/53

Ayler, Aylor, Jn., yeo., Gt. Cheverell, 1698, L, W, P2/A/339
Aylor, Jn., yeo., Gt. Cheverell, 1730, AB, I, P2/A/414
Robt., husb., Gt. Cheverell, 1664, comm, I, W, P2/A/221
Aylerugg *see* Acrigg
Ayles *see* Eyles
Aylesbury, Elsbury, Eliz., sp. and servant, The Close, Salisbury, 1762, AB, W, P5/1762/11
Thos., rector, Corsley, 1725, AB, P1/A/271
Ayleward, Aylford *see* Allwood
Ayliff, Ann, sp., Sal. St Thos., 1799, W, P4/1799/3
Ayliffe, Arthur, gent., Brinkw., 1646, comm, I, W, P1/A/82
Ayliffe, Benj., Brinkw., 1693, AB, comm, P3/A/220
Chris., slaymaker, Rowde, 1819, W, Wr, P3/1819/31
Ayliffe, Edwd., yeo., Eastrop, Highw., 1624, AB, a/c, I, W, P10/1624/2
Ayliffe, Geo., gent., Grittenham, Brinkw., 1685, AB, I, P3/A/192
Ayliffe, Geo., cook, Marl., 1704, AB, I, ren, P1/A/194
Ayliffe, Geo., Lea, L. and Cleverton, 1733, AB, I, P3/A/340
Ayliffe, Hester, widow, Grittleton, 1824, W, Wr, P3/1824/34
Humphrey, yeo., Norton, 1738, W, P1/A/327, P1/8Reg/321B
Joan, widow, Eastrop, Highw., 1603, AB, P5/1603/2, P5/7Reg/88C
Ayliffe, Joan, widow, Sherston, 1611, AB, P3/A/15
Ayliffe, Joan, widow, Grittenham, Brinkw., 1688, AB, P3/A/205
Ayliffe, Jn., esquire, Grittenham, Brinkw., 1635, W, P3/A/68
Ayliffe, Jn., Sandhurst, Berks., 1682, I, W, P5/1682/5
Ayliffe, Jn., schoolmaster, Lyneham, 1735, AB, comm, I, P1/A/305
Ayliffe, Jn., Atworth, Bradford A., 1768, AB, P2/A/497
Ayliffe, Jn., blacksmith, Holt, Bradford A., 1809, AB, comm, W, P2/1809/47
Ayliffe, Jn., late of Plymouth, but leaving effects at Corsham, 1811, AB, Wr, P1/1811/81
Jn., yeo., Latton, 1816, W, Wr, P3/1816/49
Ayliffe, My., widow, Smithcot Farm, Dauntsey, 1699, AB, I, W, P3/A/242
Ayliffe, Peter, husb. *or* yeo., Didcot, Berks., 1729, I, W, P1/A/278, P1/7Reg/251B
Ayliffe, Rachel, widow, Luckington, 1793, AB, P3/A/491
Robt., Marl., 1844, AB, comm, W, P1/1844/34
Ayliffe, Rowland, Sherston, 1606, I, W, P3/A/5
Sarah, yeo.'s wife, Gt. Somerford, 1813, ren, W, Wr, P3/1813/45
Ayliffe, Steph., sen., yeo., Sonning & Sindlesham, Berks., 1672, I, W, copy W, P5/1672/2
Ayliffe, Steph., Woodley, W. and Sandford, Berks., 1687, AB, I, P5/1687/3
Ayliffe, Steph., yeo., Gt. Joldings Farm, Woodley and Sandford, Berks., 1711, comm, W, P5/1711/2, P5/15Reg/274
Susan, Wokm., Berks., 1699, W (damaged), P5/1699/1
Thos., Bagshot, Shalbourne, 1605-06, AB, comm, I, P5/1606/2, P5/8Reg/56A
Ayliffe, Thos., yeo., Atworth, Bradford A., 1739, W, P2/A/438
Ayliffe, Thos., Luckington, 1790, AB, P3/A/485
Ayliffe, Thos., blacksmith, Corsham, [1799], W, P29/A/34, P29/2Reg/229
Ayliffe, Thos., baker and maltster, Grittleton, 1811, W, Wr, P3/1811/26
Ayliffe, Wm., sen., blacksmith, Box, 1788, W, P3/A/480
Ayliffe, Wm., blacksmith, Westrop, Highw., 1828, W, P10/1828/2
Ayliffe, Wm., blacksmith, Box, 1836, W, Wr, P3/1836/39
Aylor *see* Ayler
Aylowe *see* Alow
Aylward *see* Allwood
Aymes *see* Ames
Aynoll, Alice, widow, Croucheston, Bishopstone S., 1592, AB, I, W, P2/A/29
Chris., Bishopstone S., 1609, AB, P2/A/78, P2/8Reg/61B
Jn., sen., Bishopstone S., 1567, W, P2/5Reg/2B
Eynells, Jn., Barford St M., 1636, AB, P2/E/125
Nich., Damerham, Hants, 1554, AB (with unrelated notes from ecclestiastcal text), P2/2Reg/195B
Rd., sen., yeo., Bishopstone S., 1662, I, W, P1/A/101
Rd., sen., yeo., Netton, Bishopstone S., 1701, I, W, P2/A/343
Wm., weaver, Bishopstone S., 1574, W, P2/5Reg/183A
Wm., shepherd, Bishopstone S., 1685, AB, a/c, I, P2/A/301
Wm., Bishopstone S., 1734, AB, I, P2/A/424

see also Arnold
Ayre, Ayres *see* Ayers
Ayscough, Jas., clerk, Highw., 1745, W, P10/1745/7
Ayton, Jas., Toyd Farm, Martin, Hants, 1831, W, Wr, P5/1831/6

Baalam *see* Ballam
Babault, Babault als Newburgh, Thos., Downton, 1734, AB, P2/B/1537
Babb, Bernard, vicar, Inglesham, 1702, AB, P3/B/1012
Babbidge, Geo., soldier in HM Royal Regt of Horse Guards Blues, Upavon, 1786, AB, P2/B/2012
Baber, Edwd., Bradford A., 1755, W, P2/B/1719
Jn., innholder, Bradford A., 1749, W, P2/B/1673
My., sp., Bradford A., 1793, W, P2/B/2084
Rd., cordw., Bradford A., 1747, W, P1/B/1216, P1/10Reg/160
Rd., cooper, Bradford A., 1774, W, P2/B/1902
Sam., innholder, Bradford A., 1740, W, Wr, P2/B/1587
Sam., innholder, Bradford A., 1821, AB (re property in B.), comm, P2/1821/54
Sarah, wife, Bradford A., 1720, AB, comm, P2/B/1393
Sarah, sp., Bradford A., 1740, W, P2/B/1586
Baberstock, Baberstocke, Baberstoke, Babstock *see* Baverstock
Babthorpe, Jn., clerk and parson, Winterbourne Bassett, 1608, I, W, P1/B/63
Baby, Wm., sen., Bramshaw, Hants, 1760, W, P24/1109
Wm., sen., Bramshaw, Hants, 1822, AB, Wr, P24/1292
Baccaller *see* Backoller
Bachelor *see* Pearce/Peirce als B.
Backan *see* Bacon
Backer *see* Baker
Backhouse *see* Bakehouse
Backlett *see* Bartlett
Backoller, Eliz., widow, Chards., Devon, 1841, aff, O, W, Wr, P5/1841/4
Baccaller, Jn., tiller, Chards., Devon, 1567, W, P5/2Reg/18D
Bacon, Agnes, widow, Compton C., 1552, AB, P2/2Reg/166C
Agnes, widow, Britford, 1570, W, P5/2Reg/61D
Alice, widow, Broad C., 1567-68, I, W, P2/B/45, P2/5Reg/31B
Cath., widow, Lyme R., Dorset, 1722, AB, comm, P16/220
Dorothy, widow, Lacock, 1663, I, W, P3/B/483
Edwd., yeo., Aldbourne, 1684, comm, W, P3/B/781
Eliz., widow, Chiseldon, 1662, I, W, P1/B/373
Eliz., widow, Aldbourne, 1705, I, W, P3/B/1032
Eliz., widow, Netherh., 1721, W, P2/B/1402
Ellen, Bishopstone S., 1570, W, P2/5Reg/103A
Emmot, widow, Mkt. L., 1552, NW, P2/B/11
Francis, Oak Hill, Froxfield, 1741, AB, I, P1/B/1125
Backon, Geo., yeo., Quidh., 1662-75, I, W, P2/B/737, 883
Geo., no abode stated, 1677, I, P2/B/917
Heath, grocer, Wantage, Berks., 1718, W, P23/365
Hy., Highw., 1631, AB, I, P5/1631/16, P5/12Reg/71
Hy., paper maker, Nunton, N. and Bodenham, 1653, I, P2/B/727
Jane, widow, no abode stated, 1663, I, P1/B/383
Joan, widow, Stanton Fitzwarren, [1591], W (NEP), P3/1Reg/39A
Joan, widow, Highw., 1634, I, NW, P10/1634/4
Jn., Downton, 1575, NW, P2/5Reg/215C
Jn., Fugg. St Peter, 1586, W, P2/7Reg/31B
Jn., sen., Quidh., 1599, W, P2/B/194
Jn., weaver, Orcheston St Geo., 1601, AB, court paper, I, W, P2/B/207
Jn., yeo., Stanton Fitzwarren, 1638, I, W, P1/B/279
Jn., Stourton, 1642, AB, I, W, P2/B/673
Jn., sen., yeo., Sanden Fee, Hungerford, Berks., 1678, I, W, P23/78
Jn., Lyme R., Dorset, 1692, AB, P16/115
Jn., sen., yeo., Aldbourne, 1713, W, P3/B/1109
Jn., bach., Lyme R., Dorset, 1726, AB, P16/238

Jn., sen., yeo., Aldbourne, 1741, W, P3/B/1394
Jn., Sal., 1756, W, P4/1756/5
Jn., Speenhamland, Berks., 1770, W, P1/B/1394, P1/12Reg/346
Jn., yeo., Rams., 1771, W, P5/1771/2, P5/17Reg/27B
Jos., Newbury, Berks., 1726, AB, comm, P1/B/935
Josias, Pott., [1629], I, W, P1/B/219
Mgt., widow, Enford, 1594, AB, I, note, P2/B/155
Martha, widow, Sal., 1779, W, P4/1779/4
My., Quidh., 1630, AB, I, P2/B/528, 549
My., widow, Netherh., 1681, I, W, P2/B/963
My., widow, Broad H., 1714, W, P1/B/790, P1/5Reg/444
My., sp., Gt. Wishford, 1771, W, P2/B/1869
Middleton, Blewbury, Berks., 1731, AB, P5/1731/7
Nich., Stratton St Mgt., 1615, AB, a/c, I (2 - 1 a copy), P3/B/116
Noah, yeo., Aldbourne, 1667, I, W, P3/B/517
Phyllis, widow, Sal., 1763, W, P1/B/1367, P1/12Reg/138A
Rachel, Rams., 1812, W, Wr, P5/1812/32
Rebecca, widow, Marl., 1791, AB, W, P1/B/1518, P1/14Reg/363
Rd., Whitep., 1558, W, P2/3Reg/140D
Rd., husb., Quidh., 1558, W, P2/3Reg/76B
Rd., husb., Quidh., 1564, I, W, P2/B/2151, P2/4Reg/185B
Rd., Mkt. L., 1572, W, P2/5Reg/139A
Backan, Rd., husb., Quidh., 1618, I, W, P2/B/389
Rd., smith, Bishopstone N., 1627, I, W, P6/4
Rd., mariner (made at sea - on reverse says his clothes found on *The Lark*, day & time of death, & following day sewn into shroud & put overboard weighted with a stone as had begun to smell), Lyme R., Dorset, 1684, AB, I, NW, P16/77
Rd., Quidh., 1702, AB, P2/B/1225
Robt., Sal., 1753, AB, P4/1753/1
Robt., clerk, Sal. The Close, 1762, W, P5/1762/3
Robt., glover, Sal., 1765, W, P4/1765/2
Sibyl, Quidh., 1640, I, W, P2/B/656
Simon, Enford, 1556, AB, P2/3Reg/40B
Steph., husb., Quidh., 1559, W, P2/4Reg/10A
Steph., Netherh., 1610, AB, I, W, P2/B/297, P2/8Reg/87D
Steph., Netherh., 1695, I, W, P1/B/649
Steph., yeo., Aldbourne, 1794, comm, W, P3/B/1741
Theophilus, mariner, Lyme R., Dorset, 1680, I, NW, P16/53
Thos., Mkt. L., 1552, I, W, P2/B/12, P2/2Reg/166B
Thos., husb., Netherh., 1557, W, P2/3Reg/48
Thos., Mkt. L., 1577-78, I, W, P2/B/65-66, P2/5Reg/308B
Thos., Stourton, 1604, I, W, P2/B/252
Thos., husb., Enford, 1640, I, W, P2/B/648
Thos., Mkt. L., 1647, AB, I, P2/B/716
Thos., yeo., Aldbourne, 1668, AB, comm, I, P1/B/447
Thos., paper maker, Downton, 1679, I, W, P2/B/949
Thos., yeo., Plaitford, 1717, W, P2/B/1353
Thos., pin maker, E. Harnham, Britford, 1720, W, P1/B/851, P1/6Reg/200B
Thos., yeo., Membury, Rams., 1729, W, P5/1729/4, P5/16Reg/241B
Ursula, Whitep., 1607, AB, comm, I, note, P2/B/279
Wm., carp., Mere, 1580, I, T, W, P5/1580/13, P5/3Reg/152C
Wm., husb., Bemerton, Fugg. St Peter, 1647, AB, I, W, P2/B/709
Wm., husb., Quidh., 1682, I, W, P2/B/1000
see also Cooper form. B.; Sayer als B.; Sotwell als B.
Badcock, Benj., innkeeper, Yarnbrook, N. Bradley, 1851, O, W, Wr, P2/1851/1
Jos., yeo., Garford, Marcham, Berks., 1729, W, P1/B/970, P1/7Reg/247A
My., widow, Abingdon, Berks., 1738, AB, P1/B/1085
Badder, Jn., Sutton V., 1676, AB, I, ren, P2/B/900
Matthew, Heytes., 1666, AB, I, P5/1665/4
Thos., Sutton V., 1668, AB, I, P2/B/796
Wm., gent., Heytes., 1731, comm, W, P5/1730/9

Baddum, Thos., yeo., Pewsham Forest, 1669, I, W, P3/B/542
Baden, Alexander, hellier, Sal. St Mart., 1716, I, W, P4/1716/16
Alice, widow, Burbage, 1772, W, P11/232
And., sen., gent., Burbage, 1766, W, P11/221
Ann, sp., Longstreet, Enford, 1832, AB, comm, ren, Wr, P2/1832/9
Eliz., gent.'s wife, Broad B., Highw., 1791, app. of proctor, W, P10/1791/1
Frances, widow, Enford, 1734, W, P2/B/1534
Hy., hellier, Sal., 1736, W, P4/1736/7
Baden *or* Bawden, Jn., hellier, Sal., 1680, AB, I, P4/1680/20
Jn., gent., Enford, 1726, W, P2/B/1449
Jn., bricklayer, Sal., 1773, W. Not proved, P4/1773/9
Jn., yeo., Ganhill Farm, Chiseldon, 1801, comm, W, Wr, P1/1801/121, P1/15Reg/340
Mgt., sp., Sal. (now sojourner at Bemerton), 1726, W, P1/B/934, P1/7Reg/149
My., widow, Sal., 1707, W, P4/1707/3
Baydon, My., Wantage, Berks., 1713, AB, P5/1713/10
My., yeo.'s widow, Fifield, Enford, 1753, AB, comm, ren, W, P1/B/1271, P1/11Reg/60
Baydon, Maud, widow, Burbage, 1626, I, W, P5/1625/3, P5/10Reg/192
Nathaniel, Chisenbury, Enford, 1720, AB, P5/1719/3
Baydon, Nich., yeo., Grove, Wantage, Berks., 1709, W, P23/304
Robt., hellier, Sal., 1723, AB, I, P4/1723/7
Robt., gent., Littlecott, Enford, 1732, W, P2/B/1511
Robt., Fifield, Enford, 1740, AB, comm, P2/B/1590
Thos., clerk, Fisherton D., 1673, I, W, P2/B/866
Thos., notary public, Sal., 1734, W, Wr, P1/B/1034, P1/7Reg/598
Virtue, widow, Sal. St Mart., 1681, W, P4/1680/12
Wm., Chisenbury, Enford, 1663, I, W, P2/B/752
Wm., gent., Dayhouse, Chiseldon, 1814, comm, W, Wr, P3/1814/12
Wm., Longstreet, Enford & Burbage, 1817, AB (re leasehold property in B.), comm, P11/266
Badenell *see* Badnoll
Badger, Bagior, Ann, widow, Sherb., Dorset, 1618, I, W, P5/1618/4, P5/10Reg/31A
Wm., Norton B., 1791, AB, P2/B/2065
Badgin, Michael, Sal., 1667, AB, I, P4/1666/24
Badmington, Jn., Pascroft, Whaddon, 1758, W, P2/B/1743
Badnoll, Thos., yeo., Littleworth, Gt. Faringdon, Berks., 1588, I, T, W, copy W, P5/1588/3, P5/5Reg/40
Badenell, Thos., Eisey, 1713, AB, ren, P3/B/1110
Wm., Littleworth, Gt. Faringdon, Berks., 1564, W, P5/1Reg/53
Baggs, Agnes, widow, Rams., 1633, I, W, P5/1633/8, P5/12Reg/124A
Edwd., husb. *or* yeo., Caundle Bishop, Dorset, 1669, I, W, P5/1669/13
Bagg, Geo.?, Netherb., Dorset, 1632, I, P17/16
Geo., Steeple A., 1712, AB, I, P2/B/1308
Jas., W. Hagbourne, Berks., 1750, AB, P1/B/1242
Jas., yeo., Steeple A., 1802, W, P2/1802/40
Bagg, Jn., vict., Chards., Devon, 1597, I, copy I, P5/1597/8
Jn., husb., Aston U., Blewbury, Berks., 1626, I, W, P5/1626/3, P5/10Reg/316
Bagg, Jn., Netherb., Dorset, 1632, AB, W, P17/10
Jn., yeo., Steeple A., 1759, W, P1/B/1324, P1/11Reg/453A
Jn., weaver, Broughton G., 1827, O, W, P1/1827/6
Jn., yeo., Shaw Hill, Melk., 1857, aff, O, W, Wr, P2/1857/14
Bagg, Mgt., widow, Chards., Devon, 1641, AB, I, P14/8
Martha, widow, Rams., 1810, AB, W, P5/1810/24
Rd., Duxford, Hinton Waldrist, Berks., 1631, AB, I, P1/B/236
Bagg, Rd., cordw., Lyme R., Dorset, 1668, AB, I, P5/1668/5
Bagg, Rd., Lyme R., Dorset, 1695, AB, P16/133
Wm., broad weaver, Rams., 1613, AB, I, P1/B/95
Wm., Heytes., 1855, AB, aff, O, Wr, P5/1855/13
see also Selwood form. B.
Bagior *see* Badger
Bagley, Cicely, widow, Reading St Lawr., Berks., 1628, I, W, P1/B/216
Geo., husb., Hurst, Berks., 1677, AB, I, P5/1677/3
Thos., yeo., Ufton Nervet, Berks., 1738, AB, copy W, P1/B/1082, P1/8Reg/290

Bagster, Wm., mariner, Lyme R., Dorset, 1631, I, W, P5/1631/11, P5/12Reg/10A
Bagus, Alice, widow, Martin, Hants, 1809, W, Wr, P2/1809/60
Jane, widow, Martin, Hants, 1797, I, W, Wr, P2/B/2118
Jn., Martin, Hants, 1781, AB, P2/B/1981
Jos., wheelwright, Martin, Hants, 1797, AB, W, P2/B/2119
Bagurste, Nich., Stratfield M., Berks., 1613, I, W, P1/B/87
see also Lawrence als B.
Bagwell, Isabel, widow, Keevil, 1632, AB, court paper, P2/B/559, P2/9Reg/112C
Jn., Stratton, Dorset, 1564, W, P5/1Reg/38A
Jn., tallow chandler, Beam., Dorset, 1681, I, W, P17/260
My., widow, Chards., Devon, 1725, I, W, P5/1725/8, P5/16Reg/115B
Baich *see* Batch
Bailey, (Miss) *see* Ann Hussey
Baily, Abraham, glazier, Sal. St Thos., 1618, AB, a/c, I, P4/1618/4
Baily, Adam, yeo., Hurst, Berks., 1743, W, Wr, P5/1743/6
Baylie, Agnes, widow, Grittleton, 1613, W, P3/B/101
Baylie, Alice, widow, Corsham, [1582], W (NEP), P29/1Reg/22B
Bayly, Alice, Chittoe, Bps. C., 1607, AB, I, P24/163
Baylie, Alice, widow, Cumberwell, Bradford A., 1607, AB, I, W, P2/B/271
Bayley, Alice, Stourpaine, Dorset, 1612, AB, P24/119
Bayley, Alice, widow, Sal. St Edmd., 1612, I, W, P4/1612/5
Bayley, Alice, widow, Goatacre, Hilmarton, 1622, I, W, P1/B/181
Baily, Alice, widow, Corston, Malm., 1624, I, W, P3/B/244
Bayly, Alice, Lyneham, 1638, AB, P1/B/268
Baily, Alice, widow, Westport St My., 1715, I, W, P3/B/1125
Baily, Alice, widow, Enford, 1731, AB, NW, P2/B/1498
Alice, widow, Kington L., 1776, W, P3/B/1640
Baylie, And., feltmaker, Maiden B., 1647, AB, caveat, I, P2/B/713
Bayly, Ann, widow, Kington L., 1680, I, W, P3/B/724
Bayly, Ann, widow, Box, 1728, W, P3/B/1265
Baily, Ann, widow, Calne, 1729, I (detailed), W, P26/742
Bayly, Ann, sp., Box, 1737, W, P3/B/1359
Bayley, Ann, widow, Marl., 1743, AB, P1/B/1158
Bayly, Ann, sp., Marl., 1749, W, P1/B/1227, P1/10Reg/251A
Ann, widow, Westrop, Highw., 1816, comm, W, P10/1816/1
Baily, Ann, wife, Warm., 1854, AB, aff, Wr, P2/1854/30
Bayly, Anth., yeo., Hampton, Highw., 1700, AB, I, P10/1700/4
Baily, Anth., labourer, Gt. Somerford, 1736, AB, I, P3/B/1348
Bayly, Arthur, no abode stated, 1597, I, W, P2/B/186
Baker, yeo., Preston, Lyneham, 1761, comm, W, P3/B/1535
Benj., labourer, Hurst, Berks., 1724, AB, I, W, P5/1724/8, P5/16Reg/96B
Baily, Betty, sp., E. Town, W. Ashton, Steeple A., 1808, W, Wr, P2/1808/41
Betty, widow, Kington L., 1810, W, Wr, P3/1810/49
Betty, widow, Kington L., 1833, W, Wr, P3/1833/31
Cath., widow, Corston, Malm., [1612], I, W (NEP), P3/B/76
Bayly, Cath., widow, Maiden B., 1685, AB, I, ren, W, P2/B/1054
Bayley, Cath., innholder's widow, Gt. Faringdon, Berks., 1719, I, W, P5/1719/8, P5/16Reg/26A
Baily, Cath., widow, Kington St M., 1762, W, P3/B/1542
Cath., widow, Calne, 1845, AB, Wr, P5/1845/15
Bayly, Christian, widow, Boreham, Warm., 1646, W, P2/B/701
Christine, widow, Wardour, Tisb., 1848, comm, D, W, Wr, P1/1848/22
Baily, Chris., Wingfield, 1603, AB, P2/B/230
Bayly, Chris., husb., Maiden B., 1626-30, AB, a/c, I, P2/B/462, 508
Baily, Chris., Warm., 1684, AB, I, P2/B/1033
Bayly, Chris., gent., Trowle, Bradford A., 1688, AB, I, P2/B/1093
Bayly, Chris., Compton C., 1690, AB, I, P2/B/1118
Baylie, Chris., Gt. Trowle, Bradford A., 1714, AB, P2/B/1328
Bayly, Damaris, Marl., 1740, AB, P1/B/1121
Baylie, Dan., physician, Horningsham, 1670, comm, I, W, P5/1670/5
Baily, Dan., broad weaver, Bromham, 1675, AB, comm, I, W, P3/B/648

Bayly, Dan., weaver, Westbrook, Bromham, 1733, AB, ren, W, P3/B/1321
Bayly, Dan., yeo., Seend Park, Melk., 1755, W, P2/B/1718
Dan., gent., Chipp., 1842, O, W, Wr, P3/1842/6
Dan., gent., Chipp., 1857, AB, aff, O, W, Wr, P3/1857/38
Bayly, Dorothy, widow, Winsley, Bradford A., 1665, comm, I, W, P2/B/775
Baily, Dorothy, widow, Sutton V., 1702, I, NW, P2/B/1223
Bayly, Dulcibella, Netherb., Dorset, 1664, AB, P17/32
Bayly, Edith, widow, Newnham, Sutton V., 1597, AB, I, W, P2/B/180
Bayly, Edith, Maiden B., 1612, AB, P2/B/335
Baylie, Edith, widow, Chards., Devon, 1628, I, W, P5/1628/9
Bayly, Edith, widow, Broughton G., 1673, I, W, P2/B/862
Beilie, Edmd., yeo., Holt, Bradford A., 1603, I, W, P2/B/234
Edmd., husb., Westport St My., 1637, I, W, P3/B/378
Baylie als Derrenc, Edmd. *or* Edwd., Lacock, 1663, AB, I, W, P3/B/488
Baylie, Edmd., sen., clothier, Bradford A., 1706, W, P2/B/1261
Edmd., Marl., 1796, AB, P1/B/1545, P1/15Reg/7A
Baylie, Edwd., Boreham, Warm., 1610, I, W, P2/B/308, P2/8Reg/127A
Bayly, Edwd., labourer, Bromham, 1629, I, W, P3/B/303
Bayly, Edwd., Devizes St Jn., 1646, AB, comm, I, P1/B/321
Baylie als Derrenc, Edwd. *see* Edmd. *or* E., 1663
Bayly, Edwd., Highw., 1685, AB, I, P10/1685/2
Bayly, Edwd., gent., Etchilhampton, 1690, comm, I, W, P3/B/863
Baily, Edwd., husb., Bromham, 1700, AB, I, P3/B/990
Bayly, Edwd., yeo. *or* husb., Kington L., 1712, I, W, P3/B/1103
Baily, Edwd., yeo., Stitchcombe, Mildenhall, 1733, W, P3/B/1317
Baily, Edwd., Bradford A., 1760, AB, P2/B/1768
Baily, Edwd., S. Wraxall, 1788, AB, comm, P2/B/2030
Edwd., yeo., Seagry, 1798, W, P3/B/1759
Edwd., miller, Upavon, 1821, W, Wr, P2/1821/39
Edwd., vict. and maltster, Devizes, 1837, O, W, Wr, P1/1837/10
Edwd., Nettleton, 1851, AB, Wr, P3/1851/46
Bayly, Eleanor, maid, Westport St My., 1606, L, P1/B/40
Eliza, minor, Kington L., 1850, AB, O, Wr, P3/1850/53
Baylie, Eliz., widow, Box, 1673, I, W, P3/B/624
Bayly, Eliz., widow, Axford, Rams., 1685, I, W, P5/1685/8
Bayly, Eliz., widow, Box, 1702, AB, I, P3/B/1015
Baily als Wilton, Eliz., Bishopstrow, 1714, AB, P1/B/806
Bayly, Eliz., widow, Warm., 1719, W, P2/B/1380
Baily, Eliz., Bps. C., 1758, AB, P24/1011
Eliz., widow, Etchilhampton, 1769, comm, W, P3/B/1596
Eliz., Waltham St Lawr., Berks., 1820, W, Wr, P1/1820/42
Eliz., widow, Upavon, 1832, W, Wr, P1/1832/26
Baylie, Emanuel, sen., yeo., Bishopstrow, 1677, I, W, P2/B/923
Bayly, Emanuel, Boreham, Warm., 1690, AB, P2/B/1121
Emanuel, yeo., Upavon, 1807, comm, W, Wr, P1/1807/31
Bayley, Emma, widow, Damerham, Hants, 1692, I, W, P1/B/616
Bayly, Fanny, widow, Devizes, 1817, AB, comm, Wr, P1/1817/105
Bayly, Frances, widow, Overton, 1745, W, P3/B/1424
Baylie, Frances, widow, Bradford A., 1775, W, P2/B/1919
Baily, Francis, tanner, Westb., 1647, AB, a/c, comm, I (detailed with copy made 1648), P25/1647/2
Bayly, Francis, rector and clerk, Woodb. (some goods at the Red Lion, Devizes), 1667, AB, comm, I, P1/B/431
Bayly, Francis, [weaver], Gt. Bedwyn, 1715, AB, I, P21/7/21
Bayly, Francis, miller, Poulton Mill, Mildenhall, 1715, I, W, P3/B/1128
Bayly, Francis, gent., Devizes, 1762, comm, W, P1/B/1339, P1/12Reg/20
Francis, tailor, E. Ilsley, Berks., 1804, W, P1/1804/70
Bayly, Geoff., yeo., Lt. Somerford, 1672, I, W, P3/B/604
Bayly, Geo., Devizes, 1681, AB, P1/B/550
Bayly, Geo., sen., farrier, Devizes Grn, Bps. C., 1725, I, W, P24/859
Bayly, Geo., labourer, Warm., 1733, W, P2/B/1519
Bayly, Geo., vict., Sherb., Dorset, 1735, AB, W, P5/1735/5

Bayly, Geo., barber and peruke maker, Marl., 1740, W, P1/B/1119, P1/8Reg/439
Baily, Geo., corn and coal dealer, Calne, 1832-43, AB, comm, W, Wr, P26/1403, P5/1843/5
Baily, Giles, yeo., Westport St My., 1714, I, W, P1/B/801, P1/5Reg/408
Bayly, Hannah, widow, Broom Farm, Swindon, 1800, O, W, P3/1800/26
Bayly, Hannah, widow, Sutton V. (form. of Sal.), 1844, comm, W, Wr, P2/1844/17
Hannah, widow, Malm., 1847, O, W, Wr, P3/1847/29
Bayly, Hy., husb., Minety, 1627, I, W, P3/B/287
Baily, Hy., Chittoe, Bps. C., 1638, AB, I, P24/303
Baylie, Hy., Westb., 1662, AB, I, P25/1662/3
Bayly, Hy., vict., Hermitage, Dorset, 1743, I, W (& cod), Wr, P5/1743/2
Bayly, Hy., yeo., Kington L., 1769, comm, W, P3/B/1599
Hy., yeo., Kington L., 1802, comm, W, P3/1802/25
Hy., jun., minor, Kington L., 1850, AB, O, Wr, P3/1850/52
Beyly, Hugh, W. Ashton, Steeple A., 1564, I, P30/17
Baylie, Humphrey, Dunsden, Sonning, Berks., 1628, AB, I, P5/1628/7, P5/11Reg/82A
Bayly, Isaac, Bromham, 1727, AB, I, P3/B/1252
Bayly, Jacob, innholder, Box, 1737, W, P3/B/1360
Bayly, Jacob, bach., Box, 1769, AB, P3/B/1600
Baily, Jas., Bradford A., 1618, AB, P2/B/390
Bayly, Jas., sen., feltmaker, Trowb., 1731, AB, W, P1/B/988-89, P1/7Reg/416A
Bayly, Jas., Box, 1741, W, P3/B/1395
Bayly, Jas., mercer, Warm., 1744, W, P1/B/1188, P1/9Reg/441A
Bayly, Jas., yeo., Wadswick, Box, 1753, W, P1/B/1275, P1/11Reg/90B
Bayly, Jas., hosier, Warm., 1763-73, AB, req, copy W, P2/B/1789
Jas., tailor, Kington St M., 1768, W, P3/B/1587
Baily, Jas., Melk., 1777, AB, P2/B/1950
Baily, Jas., Holt, Bradford A., 1824, AB, comm, Wr, P2/1824/75
Baily, Jas., labourer, Lt. Somerford (form. of Chr. M.), 1835, O, W, P3/1835/18
Jas., gent., Lea and Cleverton, 1844, O, W, Wr, P3/1844/40
Bayly, Jane, widow, Longbridge D., 1682, AB, comm, W, P2/B/1006
Bayly *or* Green, Jane, baker's wife, Preston, Lyneham, 1740, AB, P3/B/1384
Bayly, Jane, sp., Devizes, 1773, W, P1/B/1422, P1/13Reg/14B
Baylie, Jasper, yeo., Stourpaine, Dorset, 1608, I (detailed, 1604), W, P24/153
Bayly, Jeremiah, tailor, Devizes, 1770, W, P1/B/1391, P1/12Reg/318
Jeremiah, Bridzor, Tisb., 1834, AB, Wr, P2/1834/10
Baylie, Jeremy, sen., fuller, Calne, 1674, I, P5/1674/10
Bayley, Joan, widow, Maiden B., 1561, I, W, P2/B/23, P2/4Reg/82B
Bayly, Joan, Gt. Somerford, 1603, I, W, P3/B/4
Bayly, Joan, widow, Bromham, 1632, I, W, P3/B/340
Baylie, Joan, sp., Chards., Devon, 1635, I, NW, P5/1635/2, P5/12Reg/221
Bayly, Joan, widow, W. Lavington, 1642, I, W, P1/B/299
Bayly, Joan, widow, Hidden, Hungerford, Berks., 1666, comm, I, W, P5/1666/5
Bayly, Joan, widow, Malm., 1670, I, NW, P3/B/565
Bayley, Joan, widow, Crowlway, Chards., Devon, 1680, I, W, P14/49
Baylie, Joan, widow, Boreham, Warm., 1682, W, P2/B/998
Baily, Joan, widow, Fifield, Enford, 1695, AB, comm, P1/B/644
Bayly, Joan, widow, Calne, 1696, W, P26/439
Bayly, Joan, widow, Highw., 1698, I (mentions a shuffle-board room), W, P5/1698/13
Bayly, Joan, widow, Wilton, 1715, W, P2/B/1336
Bayly, Joan *or* Joanna, Mildenhall, 1734, AB, NW, P3/B/1335
Baily, Joanna, sp., Calne, 1816, W, Wr, P26/1306
Bayly, Jn., Upavon, 1544, W (NEP), P2/1Reg/48C
Bayly, Jn., husb., Imber, 1558, W, P2/3Reg/79B
Bayly, Jn., husb., Wilsford nr Pewsey, 1562, I, W, P2/B/31, P2/4Reg/101A
Baylie, Jn., yeo., Chirton, 1575, W, P2/5Reg/238C
Baylie, Jn., husb., Crowlway, Chards., Devon, 1579, I, W, P5/1579/4, P5/3Reg/128C
Bayley, Jn., Sal. St Thos., 1581, W (much loss of text), P4/Reg/37A
Bayly, Jn., labourer, Urchf., 1581, W, P2/6Reg/26A
Jn., yeo., Cumberwell, Bradford A., 1598, AB, I, W, P2/B/193
Baylie, Jn., husb., W. Lavington, 1605, I, W, P1/B/32

Bayley, Jn., Crowlway, Chards., Devon, 1606, W, P5/1606/5, P5/8Reg/78A
Bayly, Jn., Maiden B., 1606, AB, comm, I, record of ex. of comm, W, P1/B/56
Jn., butcher, Highw., 1607, AB, W, P5/1607/9, P5/8Reg/104A
Bayley, Jn., husb., Malm., 1608, W, P3/B/30
Bayly, Jn., yeo., Rodbourne, Malm., [1611], I, W (NEP), P3/B/77
Bayly, Jn., broad weaver, Malm., 1613, I, W (2 - 1 a copy), P3/B/102
Baylie, Jn., husb., Gt. Bedwyn, 1613, I, W, P1/B/91
Baylie, Jn., weaver, Dunsden, Sonning, Berks., 1614, AB, I, P5/1614/12, P5/9Reg/117C
Bayley, Jn., husb., Upton L., 1615-16, AB, a/c, I, W, P2/B/354, P2/8Reg/261
Baylie, Jn., yeo., Horningsham, 1619, I (damaged), W, P5/1619/11, P5/10Reg/64A
Baily, Jn., husb., Collingbourne D., 1621, W (NEP), P21/1/7
Baily, Jn., sen., Chittoe, Bps. C., 1624, AB, a/c, I, W, P24/177
Baylie, Jn., husb., Urchf., 1627, AB, I, W, P2/B/478
Bayly, Jn., husb., Wokm., Berks., 1629, AB, I, P5/1629/5, P5/11Reg/117C
Bayly, Jn., sen., husb., Malm., 1630, I, W, P3/B/318
Bayly, Jn., Warm., 1631, AB, P2/B/532
Bayly, Jn., Maiden B., 1636, AB, I, L, P2/B/594, P2/9Reg/102C
Bayly, Jn., sen., husb., N. Tidworth, 1638, I, W, P2/B/622
Baily, Jn., weaver, Wilton, 1639, I, W, P2/B/633
Bayly als Clerk, Jn., tanner, Box, 1646, AB, I, P1/B/322
Bayley, Jn., Crawley, Chards., Devon, 1666, AB, a/c, comm, I, P14/20
Baylie, Jn., yeo., Maiden B., 1666, I, W, P2/B/777
Bayly, Jn., Stourton, 1671, AB, P1/B/480
Baylie, Jn., Littleton P., [1671], I, P1/B/481
Bayly, Jn., broad weaver, Bromham, 1675, I, W, P3/B/647
Bayly, Jn., yeo., Lacock, 1677, AB, ren, P3/B/678
Baily, Jn., burler, Westb., 1678, I, W, P25/1678/9
Bayly, Jn., yeo., E. Grimstead, W. Dean, 1680, AB, I, P2/B/961
Bayly, Jn., sen., broad weaver, Rowde, 1685, I, W, P3/B/810
Bayly, Jn., Dilton, Westb., 1686, AB, comm, P25/1686/6
Bayly, Jn., yeo., Stitchcombe, Mildenhall, 1686, AB, I, P1/B/1567
Baily, Jn., sen., husb., Malm., 1691, AB, I, W, P3/B/879
Bayly, Jn., yeo., Crookwood, Urchf., [1692], I (2), W, P2/B/1147
Bayly, Jn., innholder and vict., Highw., 1694, I, W, P10/1694/11
Baily, Jn., sen., yeo., Box, 1697, comm, I, W, P3/B/960
Bailey als Denslow, Jn., Netherb., Dorset, 1699, AB, P17/126
Bayley, Jn., yeo., Stratfield M., Berks., 1701, W, P1/4Reg/160
Baily, Jn., husb., Hurst, Berks., 1702, I, W, P5/1702/7
Bayly, Jn., fuller, Quemerford, Calne, 1707, I, W, P5/1707/5, P5/15Reg/13
Baily, Jn., Lower Seagry, 1709, W, P1/B/1557
Bayly, Jn., Horton, Bps. C., 1711, AB, P24/699
Baily, Jn., sen., gent., Holt, Bradford A., 1712, W, P2/B/1304
Baily, Jn., gent., Monkton F., 1712, W, P2/B/1305
Baily, Jn., sen., sergemaker, Chittoe, Bps. C., 1720, AB, I, P24/621
Bayly, Jn., yeo., Tytherton L., Chipp., 1722, AB, ren, W, P3/B/1202
Bayly, Jn., vicar, Cookham, Berks., 1723, AB, P1/B/897
Bayly, Jn., cordw., Westport St My., 1725, I, W, P3/B/1237
Bayly, Jn., innholder, Box, 1726, W, P3/B/1244
Bayly, Jn., yeo., Overton, 1730, I, W, P3/B/1284
Baily, Jn., yeo., Wilsford with Lake, 1735, AB, W, P13/4/29
Bayly, Jn., Westb., 1737, AB, P25/1737/7
Baily, Jn., yeo., Streatley, Berks., 1741, W, P1/B/1130, P1/9Reg/91A
Baily, Jn., yeo., Wingfield, 1750, W, P1/B/1230, P1/10Reg/265
Bayly, Jn., Etchilhampton, 1752, comm, W, P3/B/1476
Baily, Jn., yeo., Brokenb., 1757, W, P3/B/1506
Bayly, Jn., innholder, Pickwick, Corsham, 1760, W, P3/B/1525
Bayly, Jn., Overton, 1764, W, P3/B/1559
Baily, Jn., Horse Lane, Bromham, 1769, W, P3/B/1597
Jn., innholder, *Crown Inn*, Highw., 1770, W, P5/1770/3, P5/17Reg/10
Jn., yeo., Collingbourne D., 1784, W, P21/11/27

Bayly, Jn., tailor, Melk., 1785, AB, aff, comm, NW, P2/B/2004
Baily, Jn., Lower Seagry, 1798, W, P1/15Reg/107
Baily, Jn., Steeple A., 1802, AB, comm, ren, P2/1802/48
Bayly, Jn., Devizes, 1803, AB, comm, Wr, P1/1803/11, P1/15Reg/392B
Baily, Jn., yeo., Holt, Bradford A., 1804, comm, W, P1/1804/25
Baily, Jn., weaver, Dilton M., Westb., 1808, W, P25/1808/5
Baily, Jn., Wingfield, 1814-16, AB, comm, Wr, P1/1814/154, P2/1816/63
Bayley, Jn., yeo., Sutton V., 1820, W, Wr, P2/1820/8
Baily, Jn., timber merchant, Redlynch, Downton, 1821, W, Wr, P2/1821/3
Jn., labourer, Trowb., 1826, AB, comm, ren, W, Wr, P1/1826/142
Baily, Jn., woolstapler, Wood St., Calne, 1833, comm, W, Wr, P5/1833/31
Baily, Jn., bach., Downton, 1846, AB, Wr, P2/1846/28
Baily, Jn., yeo., Holt, Bradford A., 1848, comm, W, Wr, P1/1848/12
Baily, Jn., gent., London Road, Calne, 1858, W, Wr, P26/1474
Jn. Coles, yeo., Wingfield, 1837, O, W, Wr, P2/1837/37
Baily, Jn. Oriel, gent. and clothier, Calne, 1799, AB, note, W, P26/1219
Bayley, Jonathan, Bradford A., 1721, comm, W, P2/B/1399
Bayley, Jonathan, Cleverton, Lea and C., 1723, AB, I, P3/B/1217
Baily, Jonathan, maltster, Streatley, Berks., 1756, W, P1/B/1293, P1/11Reg/208
Bayly *or* Baily, Jos., Horningsham, 1683, AB, I, P5/1683/5
Baily, Jos., baker and maltster, Chipp., 1738, W, P1/B/1098, P1/8Reg/324
Bayly, Jos., yeo., Dauntsey Park, 1740, W, P3/B/1385
Baily, Jos., Corsley, 1751, AB, P2/B/1685
Bayly, Jos., yeo., Lydiard M., 1763, W, P1/B/1363, P1/12Reg/101
Baily, Jos., Bromham, 1804, AB, comm, P3/1804/28
Bayly, Joyce, widow, Westb. L., 1669, AB, I, P25/1669/13
Bayly, Joyce, sp., Warm., 1762, W, P2/B/1779
Baylie, Leonard, husb., Southridge, Streatley, Berks., 1619, I, W, P1/B/157
Magor, Cadley, Chute, 1827, aff, O, W, Wr, P5/1827/34
Bayly, Mgt., Imber, 1560, W, P2/4Reg/31A
Baylie, Mgt., widow, Sal., 1581, W, P4/Reg/5
Bayly, Mgt., Wrou., 1610, W, P3/B/60
Bayly, Mgt., widow, Corston, Malm., 1666, AB, P3/B/514
Bayly, Mgt.?, Sal., 1666, W (fragment; name taken from modern annotation), P1/B/425
Bayly, Mgt., widow, Chittoe, Bps. C., 1675, comm, I, W, P24/441
Mgt., yeo.'s wife, Malm., 1771, AB, P3/B/1612
Bayly, Mgt., sp., Etchilhampton, 1789, AB, ren, P3/B/1719
Baily, Margery, Warm., 1699, AB, W, P2/B/1204
Bayly, My., widow, Etchilhampton, 1633, AB, I, W, P3/B/347
Bayley, My., widow, Marden, 1662, cert, W, P2/B/739
Bayly als Denslow, My., widow, Ash, Netherb., Dorset, 1669, I, W, P17/93
Bayly, My., Rams., 1701, AB, I, P5/1701/8
Baylie, My., widow, Gt. Trowle, Bradford A., 1714, comm, NW, P2/B/1326
Bayly, My., sp., Westb., 1716, a/c, P25/1716/4
Bayly, My., widow, Devizes, 1721, W, P1/B/873, P1/6Reg/377
My., widow, Hurst, Berks., 1724, I, W, P5/1724/6, P5/16Reg/94B
Baily, My., widow, Boreham, Warm., 1726, W, P2/B/1447
Bayly, My., sp., Marl., 1727, W, P1/B/938, P1/7Reg/171B
Bayly, My., widow, Kington St M., 1738, W, P1/B/1099, P1/8Reg/327
Baily, My., widow, Calne, 1738, W, P26/804
My., Bewley, Lacock, 1743, alleg, D, inty, sentence, W, P3/B/1407
Bayly, My., widow, Sherston, 1769, W, P3/B/1602
Bayly, My., sp., Norton Ferris, Kilmington, 1771, W, P2/B/1876
My., widow, Collingbourne D., 1796, W, P21/11/41
My., widow, Wantage, Berks., 1799, AB, comm, P23/816
My., widow, Trowb. (form. of Wingfield), 1816, W, Wr, P1/1816/13
My., widow, Wingfield, 1822, comm, O, W, Wr, P2/1822/68
My., widow, E. Ilsley, Berks., 1823, AB, comm, ren, W, Wr, P1/1823/26
My., wife, Malm., 1847, AB, Wr, P3/1847/54
My. Ann, widow, Devizes, 1855, aff, comm, W, Wr, P1/1855/18

Baily, Matthew, tailor, Lyme R., Dorset, 1620, AB, comm, I, P5/1620/6, P5/10Reg/13B
Bayly, Michael, carrier, Marl., 1680, AB, I, P1/B/543
Bayly, Michael, baker, Wadswick, Box, 1699, I, W, P3/B/980
Bayly, Michael, yeo., Wadswick, Box, 1699, W, P3/B/979
Bayly, Michael, yeo., Hazelbury, Box, 1757, AB, comm, ren, W, P3/B/1507
Bayly, Michael, Pickwick, Corsham, 1808, AB, Wr, P1/1808/78
Bayly, Michael, Melk., 1844, AB, comm, Wr, P2/1844/75
Baylie, Nathaniel, yeo., Kington L., 1670, I, O, W, P3/B/566
Bayly, Nathaniel, sen., yeo., Kington L., 1709, W, P3/B/1076
Bayly, Nathaniel, cardmaker, Chipp., 1732, AB, W, P1/B/1017, P1/7Reg/504A
Bayly, Nathaniel, Kington L., 1740, W, P3/B/1386
Nehemiah, gent., Upavon, 1821, W, Wr, P2/1821/18
Bayley, Nich., Tilsh., 1610, I, W, P2/B/2158, P2/8Reg/135A
Bayly, Nich., Nettleton, 1611, I, P2/B/322
Baylie, Nich., yeo., N. Tidworth, 1620, I, W, P1/B/164
Bayly, Nich., shoemaker, Chipp., 1638, AB, I, P3/B/397
Bayley, Nich., Broughton G., 1671, AB, I, P1/B/473
Bayly, Owen, husb., Bishopstone S., 1579, I, T, NW, P2/B/73, P2/5Reg/337B
Baylie, Owen, Frome Whitfield, Dorset, 1593, AB, P5/1593/19, P5/6Reg/34B
Bayly als Denslow, Peter, yeo., Ash, Netherb., Dorset, 1668, I, W, P5/1668/3
Bayly, Philip, Garsdon, 1569, W, P1/1Reg/100A
Baily, Ralph, yeo., Wokm., Berks., 1631, I, W, P5/1631/17, P5/12Reg/57B
Baily, Ralph, Maiden B., 1696, AB, I, P2/B/1180
Baily, Rebecca, widow, Chipp., 1752, W, P3/B/1473
Bayly, Rd., Maiden B., 1556, W, P2/3Reg/5B
Bayly, Rd., husb., Broughton G., 1575, W, P2/5Reg/225B
Baily, Rd., tailor, Holt, Bradford A., 1606, I, P1/B/35
Bayly, Rd., sen., yeo., Etchilhampton, 1610, W, P3/B/61
Rd., husb., Corston, Malm., [1611], W (NEP), P3/B/74
Baylie, Rd., mason, Sherston, 1620, I, W, P3/B/187
Baylie, Rd., yeo., Bradford A., 1627, AB, I (list of debts), P2/B/470
Baylie, Rd., Hawkeridge, Westb., 1630, AB, I, P25/1630/2
Bayly, Rd., gent., Etchilhampton, 1643, AB, comm, I, P1/B/301
Bayley, Rd., husb., Foxham, Bremhill, 1678, I, W, P3/B/679
Bayly, Rd., gent., Etchilhampton, 1688, comm, I, W, P3/B/841
Baily *or* Bayliffe, Rd., broad weaver, Bromham, 1690, AB, I, P3/B/858
Bayley, Rd., yeo., Stourton, 1694, W, P2/B/1164
Bayly, Rd., carp., Burton Hill, Malm., 1699, AB, I, Wr (fragile items), P3/B/981
Baylie als Stoks, Rd., slaymaker, Bradford A., 1701, AB, I, P1/B/685
Bayly, Rd., yeo., Hurst, Berks., 1701, AB, I, P5/1701/11
Bayly, Rd., weaver, Compton C., 1707, AB, I, P2/B/1271
Baily, Rd., gent., Leigh, Bradford A., 1709, AB, I, P2/B/1282
Bayly, Rd., yeo., Spirthill, Bremhill, 1709, I, W, P3/B/1077
Bayly als Denslow, Rd., yeo., Beam., Dorset, 1719, AB, I, P5/1719/2
Bayly, Rd., Bromham, 1720, AB, I, P3/B/1179
Bayly, Rd., Westport St My., 1726, AB, I, P3/B/1245
Bayley, Rd., Chittoe, Bps. C., 1727, AB, I, P24/849
Rd., yeo., Maiden B., 1747, W, P1/B/1218, P1/10Reg/191
Baily, Rd., maltster, Avebury, 1783, AB, W, P3/B/1679
Robt., Bps. C., 1605, AB, I, P24/3
Bayly, Robt., sen., yeo., Easton Town, Sherston, 1621, I, W, P3/B/202
Bayley, Robt., Rowhayes, Yetm., Dorset, 1631, I, W, P5/1631/13, P5/12Reg/25B
Bayly, Robt., husb., Nettleton, 1635, AB, I, P1/B/257
Bayly, Robt., husb., Corston, Malm., 1646, I, copy W (original sent to PCC), P1/B/329
Baily, Robt., yeo., N. Tidworth, 1648, I, W, P2/B/719
Bayly, Robt., gent., Etchilhampton, 1661, AB, comm, I, P3/B/468, P3/3Reg/7C
Bayly, Robt., mercer, Crickl. St S., 1670, AB, I, P3/B/564
Bayley, Robt., clothw., Quemerford, Calne, 1674, I, W, P5/1674/11
Bayly, Robt., N. Tidworth, 1675, I, P2/B/891
Bayly, Robt., baker, Bradford A., 1684, comm, I, W, P2/B/1034

Bayley, Robt., tanner, Leigh, Yetm., Dorset, 1696, I, W, P19/76
Bayly, Robt., Marl. St My., 1715, AB, I, P1/B/811
Bayly, Robt., Mildenhall, 1719, I, W, P3/B/1164
Baily, Robt., fuller, Calne, 1720, AB, I, P26/637
Baily, Robt., Sal., 1736, AB, W, P1/B/1062, P1/8Reg/148B
Baily, Robt., yeo., Leigh, Bradford A., 1746, AB, comm, ren, P2/B/1646
Baily, Robt., Cleverton, Lea and C., 1754, W, P3/B/1485
Baily, Robt., Chute, 1810, AB, P7/187
Baily, Robt., gardener, Calne, 1825, W, Wr, P26/1352
Robt., gent., Calstone W., 1829, comm, req, W, Wr, P3/1829/15
Baily, Robt., woolstapler, Calne, 1830, W, Wr, P5/1830/19
Baily, Robt., Calne, 1835, AB, comm, Wr, P26/1419
Bayly, Roger, yeo., Fifield, Enford, 1695, I, W, P1/B/645
Bayly, Rolf, Marl., 1704, AB, comm, P1/B/707
Baily, Ruth, widow, Eastbrook, Avebury, 1744, W, P1/B/1164, P1/9Reg/284A
Bayley, Sam., linen draper, Rams., 1669, I, W, P5/1669/8
Bayly, Sam., weaver, Marl., 1698, AB, I, P1/B/663
Bayly, Sam., clothier, Pickwick, Corsham, 1741, comm, W, P3/B/1396
Sam., yeo., Brokenb., 1755, W, P3/B/1495
Baily, Sam., Westb., 1757, AB, P25/1757/5
Sam., innholder, Marl., 1771, AB, ren, P1/B/1407
Sam., sen., yeo., Charlton, Downton, 1792, AB, W, P1/B/1520, P1/14Reg/367
Sam., fisherman, Charlton, Downton, 1795-1806, AB, W, P1/B/1534, P2/1806/22, P1/14Reg/524A
Bayly, Sarah, widow, Warm., 1691, I, W, P2/B/1133
Bayly, Sarah, widow, Etchilhampton, 1694, I, W, P3/B/917
Bayly, Sarah, widow, Devizes, 1707, W, P1/B/729
Baily, Sarah, Bps. C., 1726, W, P24/853
Baily, Sarah, widow, Startley, Gt. Somerford, 1734, I, W, P3/B/1332
Bayly, Sarah, widow, Pickwick, Corsham, 1762, W, P3/B/1545
Baily, Sarah, Calne, 1799, AB, note, P26/1218
Sarah, widow, Kington L., 1817, W, Wr, P1/1817/49
Bayly, Simon, Boreham, Warm., 1703, AB, I, P2/B/1234
Bayly, Steph., mercer, Devizes, 1684, comm, I, NW, P1/B/573
Bayley, Susanna, widow, Bromham, 1679, I, W, P3/B/708
Baily, Susanna, sp., Netherh., 1717, W, P2/B/1352
Bayly, Susanna, Chirton, 1729, AB, P1/B/947
Sydenham Wood, yeo., Kington L., 1851, D, W, Wr, P3/1851/53
Bayley, Thos., Wexcombe, Grafton, 1569, W, P5/2Reg/44B
Bayly, Thos., yeo., Baldham, Keevil, 1569, W, P2/5Reg/78A
Baylie, Thos., Shalbourne, 1571, AB, P5/2Reg/92C
Thos., Flamston, Bishopstone S., 1571, W, P2/5Reg/124B
Baylie, Thos., husb., Tilsh., 1571, W, P2/5Reg/121B
Bayly, Thos., N. Tidworth, 1581, AB, P2/6Reg/48D
Baylie als Westrope, Thos., husb., S. Marston, 1590, I, T, W, P5/1590/6, P5/5Reg/76
Bayly, Thos., broad weaver, Rowde & Chittoe, 1635, I, W, P1/B/255
Bayly, Thos., [Netherb., Dorset], [1639], W, P17/40
Bayly, Thos., Bps. C., 1642, AB, I, ren, P24/274
Bayley, Thos., yeo., Compton C., 1648, AB, I, P2/B/726
Bayly, Thos., no abode stated, 1663, W, P1/B/399
Bayly, Thos., tailor, Devizes, 1679, I, W, P1/B/525
Bayly, Thos., yeo., Pickwick, Corsham, 1682, AB, I, W, P29/B/25, P29/1Reg/212B
Bayly, Thos., sen., yeo., Compton C., 1696, I, W, P2/B/1174
Bayly, Thos., yeo., Holt, Bradford A., 1704, I, W, P1/B/710
Baily, Thos., glover, Box, [1704], W, P1/B/708
Baylie, Thos., sen., yeo., Bps. C., 1721, W, P24/899
Baily, Thos., Wantage, Berks., 1729, AB, P23/460
Bayly, Thos., sen., yeo., Compton C., 1732, W, P1/B/1002, P1/7Reg/450
Baily, Thos., yeo., Upper Richardson, Winterbourne Bassett, 1734, AB, a/c (2 - ex's detailed), I (2), ren, W, P3/B/1333
Bayly, Thos., jun., butcher, Marl., 1739, AB, W, P1/B/1113, P1/8Reg/390A
Baily, Thos., farmer, Streatley, Berks., 1744, W, P1/B/1175, P1/9Reg/354B

Baily, Thos., sen., translator, Westport St My., 1745, W, P3/B/1422
Bayly, Thos., cordw., Devizes, 1747, W (2), P1/B/1196, P1/10Reg/39, 62
Baily, Thos., yeo., Trowle, Bradford A., 1749-50, AB (2), ren, P2/B/1676
Baily, Thos., yeo., Chittoe, Bps. C., 1752, W, P24/1032
Bayly, Thos., innholder, Pickwick, Corsham, 1754, W, P3/B/1486
Baily, Thos., yeo., N. Bradley, 1758, W, P2/B/1739
Bayly, Thos., Pickwick, Corsham, 1767, AB, P29/2Reg/106
Baily, Thos., Compton C., 1770, AB, P2/B/1867
Baily, Thos., Wargrave, Berks., 1789, AB, W, P1/B/1509, P1/14Reg/234A
Baily, Thos., yeo., Pomeroy, Wingfield, 1792, W, P2/B/2075
Bayley, Thos., soldier, form. member of the 7th Regt of Dragoon Guards & *also* pensioner of Chelsea Hospital, Sherb., Dorset, 1813, AB, Wr, P5/1813/16
Thos., tailor, E. Ilsley, Berks., 1820, W, Wr, P1/1820/69
Thos., broad weaver, Dilton M., Westb., 1821, W, Wr, P25/1822/2
Baily, Thos., Nursteed, Bps. C., 1822, AB, Wr, P24/1288
Thos., farmer, Snelsmore, Chieveley, Berks., 1829, O, W, Wr, P1/1829/37
Thos., Netheravon, 1834, AB, O, Wr, P12/220
Thos., miller, Upavon, 1837, O, W, Wr, P2/1837/26
Thos., yeo., Langley Fitzurse, Kington St M., 1841, comm, W, Wr, P3/1841/6
Thos., gent., Marl., 1843, O, W, Wr, P1/1843/2
Thos., Malm., 1845, AB, O, Wr, P3/1845/33
Thos., yeo., Bradford A. (form. of Wingfield), 1846, O, W, Wr, P2/1846/49
Bayly, Walter, Bodenham, Nunton and B., 1552, W, P2/2Reg/157B
Bayly, Wm., jun., Maiden B., 1552, W, P2/2Reg/156B
Bayly, Wm., Holt, Bradford A., 1559, W, P2/3Reg/181B
Bayly, Wm., Maiden B., 1560, W, P2/4Reg/31C
Bayly, Wm., clothman, Keevil, 1560, W, P2/4Reg/36B
Bayly, Wm., Westwood, 1566, W, P2/4Reg/225C
Beyley, Wm., Gt. Wishford, 1566, W, P2/4Reg/228A
Bayly, Wm., Frome Whitfield, Dorset, 1579, AB, W, P5/1579/6, P5/3Reg/124C
Bayly, Wm., husb., Stratfield Saye, Hants, 1602, I, W, P1/B/22
Baylie, Wm., Horningsham, 1606, AB, P5/1606/4
Bayly, Wm., sen., Goatacre, Hilmarton, 1610, W, P3/B/62
Bayly, Wm., Chittoe, Bps. C., 1610, I, W, P24/143
Bayley, Wm., clothier, Boreham, Warm., 1614, AB, a/c, comm, W, P2/B/342, P2/8Reg/232
Bayly, Wm., husb., Chittoe, Bps. C., 1614, comm, I, W, P24/95
Bayley, Wm., bach., Chisenbury, Enford, [1614], I, W, P12/24

Bayly, Wm., husb., Maiden B., 1630-32, I, W, P2/B/506, 551
Baily, Wm., husb., 1632, I, P30/227
Bayly, Wm., Stourton, 1633, a/c, I, P2/B/570
Baylie, Wm., sen., husb., Inglesham, 1635, I, W, P1/B/260
Bayley als Pick, Wm., husb., Easton, 1638, I, W, P3/B/395
Bayly, Wm., Catcomb, Hilmarton, 1676, AB, comm, P3/B/661
Bayly, Wm., husb., Broad B., Highw., 1676, I, W, P5/1676/6
Bayly, Wm., no abode stated, 1678, W, P1/B/522
Bayly, Wm., Bere R., Dorset, 1681, AB, P5/1681/3
Bayley, Wm., weaver, Chittoe, Bps. C., 1681, comm, I, NW, P24/410
Bayly als Hussey, Wm., yeo., Netherb., Dorset, 1681, AB, I, P17/252
Bayly, Wm., sen., husb., Maiden B., 1682, I, W, P2/B/997
Bayly, Wm., yeo., Boreham, Warm., 1682, AB, I, P2/B/995
Baily, Wm., Longbridge D., 1684, AB, P2/B/1031
Bayly *or* Bayliffe, Wm., gent., Chipp., 1685-91, AB (2), comm (2), I, P3/B/811
Baily, Wm., yeo., Boreham, Warm., 1691, W (unproved per later annotation), P2/B/1129
Bayly, Wm., yeo., Goatacre, Hilmarton, 1692, comm, I, W, P3/B/888
Baily, Wm., cordw., Steeple A., 1696, AB, a/c, I, ren, P2/B/1173
Bayley, Wm., carp., Hilmarton, 1699, W, P3/B/982
Baily, Wm., physician, S. Marston, 1702, W. Not proved, P10/1702/5
Baily, Wm., Keevil, 1704, AB, I, P1/B/713
Baily, Wm., Boreham & Bishopstrow, 1707, AB, comm, P2/B/1262

Bayley, Wm., Ogbourne St And., 1709, AB, I, P23/306
Bayley als Derrenc, Wm., Kington St M., 1717, I, W, P3/B/1143
Bayly, Wm., Marl., 1718, AB, P1/B/842
Wm., yeo., Broad B., Highw., 1721, W, P10/1721/4
Bayly, Wm., vict., Pott., 1724, W, P1/B/907, P1/7Reg/53A
Bayly, Wm., yeo., Upton L., 1725, AB, I, P2/B/1440
Baily, Wm., mercer, Ludg., 1729, I, W, P2/B/1470
Bayly, Wm., tanner, Westb., 1729, W, P25/1729/4
Bayly, Wm., Marl. St Peter and St Paul, 1731, AB, P1/B/991
Baily, Wm., gent., Semington, Steeple A., 1735, W, P1/B/1041, P1/7Reg/641
Bayly, Wm., Westb., 1747, AB, P25/1747/4
Baily, Wm., yeo., Trowle, Bradford A., 1756, W, P2/B/1723
Bayly, Wm., Warm., 1759, AB (2), comm, P2/B/1751
Wm., sen., butcher, Kington St M., 1761, comm, W, P3/B/1536
Baily, Wm., midshipman on the Dolphin, Sherb., Dorset, 1762, AB, P5/1762/4
Baily, Wm., Maiden B., 1770, AB, P1/B/1404
Bayly, Wm., shopkeeper, Ludg., 1776, comm, W, P1/B/1437, P1/13Reg/140A
Wm., yeo., Sevington, Leigh Delamere, 1785, W, P3/B/1694
Baily, Wm., bach., N. Bradley, 1796, AB, P2/B/2112
Wm., fisherman, Charlton, Downton, 1797, copy req, copy W, P2/B/2129
Wm., yeo., Somerford K., 1800, W, P3/1800/62
Wm., weaver, Hilp., 1821, W, Wr, P2/1821/45
Bayley, Wm., Westb., 1829, AB, O, Wr, P25/1829/7
Wm., gent., Collingbourne D., 1833, req, W, Wr, P1/1833/5
Wm., horsekeeper, Devizes, 1846, O, W, Wr, P1/1846/40
Wm., innkeeper, Durrington, 1846, D, W, Wr, P2/1846/66
Wm., shoemaker, Chipp., 1848, W, Wr, P3/1848/28
Baily, Wm., yeo., Corsley, 1852, note, req, W, Wr, P2/1852/44
Wm., Westb., 1857, AB, declaration, O, Wr, P25/1857/1
Bayly, Wm. Lewis, Box, 1762, AB, P3/B/1546
see also Balley; Bayle *or* B.; Bayleffe *or* B.; Denslow als B.; Heath als B.; Hudson als B.; Hussey als B.; Laverstock als B.; Smith als B.; Taunton als B.
Bailiff *see* Bailey *or* B.
Bailward, Benj., Trowb., 1844, W, Wr, P1/1844/21
Bainbridge, Robt., priest, Warfield, Berks., 1561, institution to vicarage, P1/1Reg/78C
Baines, Bayones, Edwd., Edington, 1648, AB, comm, I, W, P2/B/715
Bane, Hugh, Calne, 1705, AB, I (detailed), P26/511
Jas., yeo., Trowb., 1853, D, O, W, Wr, P1/1853/2
Jn., yeo., Gt. Trowle, Bradford A., 1801, comm, W, P2/1801/37
Bayne, Lawr., yeo., Chetnole, Yetm., Dorset, 1688, I, W, P19/54
Bayne, Lawr., jun., Leigh, Yetm., Dorset, 1694, AB, I, P19/67
Baynes, Matthew, yeo., Easton, 1849, AB, I, Wr, P3/1849/14
Bayne, Thos., Enmore Grn, Motc., Dorset, 1748, AB, P19/147
Thos., Bradford A., 1803, AB, comm, P2/1803/58
Bainton, Bayntun, Cath., widow, Erlestoke, 1717, AB, ren, P2/B/1360
Baynton, Edwd., gent., Rowde, 1614, I, W, P3/B/108
Baynton, Edwd., clothier, Durlett Farm, Rowde, 1616, AB, a/c, I, P3/B/132
Baynton, (Sir) Edwd. *see also* Roger Long
Baynton, Eliz., widow, Bremhill, 1611-12, AB, cit, comm, note of ren, P1/B/68, P3/B/103
Eliz., widow, Burbage, 1721, AB, I, P11/125
Eliz., minor, Westcourt, Burbage, 1723-32, T (2 - 1 electing father Wm. B. & kinsman Steph. Dore as guardians), P11/128, 145
Baynton, Eliz., sp., Burbage, 1734, AB, I, P5/1734/4
Frances, widow, Westcourt, Burbage, [1668], W (NEP), P11/19
Jane, widow, Wootton R., 1685, AB, comm, P3/B/804
Baynton, Jn., gent., Bremhill, [1602], W, P3/1Reg/70
Jn., yeo., Westcourt, Burbage, 1644-45, comm, I (2 - 1 draft), W, P5/1644/5, P5/14Reg/76B
Jn., yeo., Burbage, 1693, I, W, P11/75
Jn., yeo., Burbage, 1741, W, P11/179
Bayntun, Lucy, widow, Spye Park, Bromham, 1730, W, P3/B/1285

My., widow, Burbage, 1777, W, P11/238
Bayntun, My., dame & wife of baronet, Spye Park, Bromham, Chittoe, Bps. C., 1799, comm, W, Wr, P3/B/1766
Baynton, Nich., Loxwell Farm, Pewsham, 1700, AB, P3/B/994
Ralph, husb., Wootton R., 1665, comm, NW, P3/B/503
Baynton, Sarah, widow, Burbage, 1740, W, P11/172
Steph., butcher, Corsley, 1846, W, Wr, P2/1846/39
or Ramton?, Thos., no abode stated, c1629, I, P2/B/503
Bayntun, Wm., Hungerford, Berks., 1637, a/c (2), P30/24
Wm., Westcourt, Burbage, 1711, W, P11/106
Baynton, Wm., Burbage, 1735, W, P11/132
see also Banning
Baish, Rd., blacksmith, W. Lavington, 1739, AB, I, P1/B/1110
Wm., mariner on HMS *Hampton Court*, Wilton, 1745, AB, P2/B/1631
Baiss *see* Bass
Baitch *see* Batch
Bakehouse, Backhouse, Jn., husb., Pinkney, Sherston, 1672, I, W, P3/B/599
Rd., Pinkney, Sherston, 1696, AB, I, P3/B/939
Baker, Abraham, Hilp., 1829, AB, comm, P2/1829/31
Adam, wheelwright, Ufton Nervet, Berks., 1720, W, P1/B/863, P1/6Reg/304B
Agnes, Hurst, Berks., 1545, W, P5/20Reg/68B
Alice, widow, Sonning, Berks., 1640, I, W, P5/1640/2, P5/13Reg/253
Alice, widow, Netherh., 1676, I, W, P2/B/911
Ambrose, Fovant Stroud, 1617, AB, I, P2/B/374
Amy, widow, Bere R., Dorset, 1570, W, P5/2Reg/88B
And., Hindon, 1702, I, W, P2/B/1227
Ann, sen., widow, Monkton F., 1670, I, W, P2/B/828
Ann, widow, Semley, 1767, W, P2/B/1837
Ann, sp., Sal., 1816, W, Wr, P4/1816/6
Ann, sp., Semley, 1850, W, Wr, P2/1850/66
Ann, widow, Dinton, 1855, AB, aff, Wr, P2/1855/6
Anna, widow, Lyme R., Dorset, 1711, I (detailed), W, P16/187
Anth., labourer and husb., Bracknell, Warfield, Berks., 1620, I, W, P1/B/168
Anth., husb., Monkton F., 1632, AB, a/c, I, P2/B/560, P2/9Reg/114A
Bridget, widow, Uffc., Devon, 1666, I, W, P5/1665/6
Cath., sp., Sal., 1633, AB, P4/1633/11
Cath., Longbridge D., 1696, AB, I, P2/B/1178
Chas., baker, Longbridge D., 1691, I, W, P2/B/1132
Chas., chair maker, Lacock, 1743, W, P3/B/1410
Chris., Fovant, 1670, AB, I, P2/B/829
Chris., Mildenhall, 1713, AB, P3/B/1111
Chris., sen., innholder, Uffc., Devon, 1802, W, P20/1/279
Cicely, widow, Fovant, 1666, AB, W, P2/B/776
Edmd., husb., Wylye, 1562, I, W, P2/B/29, P2/4Reg/100D
Edwd., yeo., Chitterne AS, 1628, AB, I, W, P2/B/493
Edwd., shepherd, Tilsh., 1668, AB, a/c, comm, I, P2/B/788
Edwd., Tilsh., 1711, AB, P1/B/756
Edwd., gent., Chipp., 1712, I, W, P3/B/1100
Edwd., husb., Sunninghill, Berks., 1738, W, P1/B/1076, P1/8Reg/285
Edwd., Cocklebury, Langley Burrell, 1756, AB, comm, ren, P3/B/1500
Elias, yeo., Fisherton A., 1558, W, P2/3Reg/103C
Elias, gent., Mkt. L., 1702, I, W, P2/B/1222
Eliz., widow, Chitterne AS, 1635, I, W, P2/B/584, P2/9Reg/49C
Eliz., widow, Crockerton, Longbridge D., 1682, W, P2/B/996
Baker als Williams als Winterne, Eliz., Chetnole, Yetm., Dorset, 1693, AB, P19/66
Eliz., widow, Tilsh., 1723, W, P1/B/881, P1/6Reg/426A
Eliz., widow, Cocklebury, Langley Burrell, 1725, W, P3/B/1231
Eliz., widow, Wanb., 1739, I, W, P3/B/1376
Eliz., widow, Quidh., 1753, a/c, I, W, P1/B/1280, P1/11Reg/125
Eliz., widow, Oaksey, 1851, aff, D (2), O, W, Wr, P3/1851/11
Esau, Longbridge D., 1850, AB, comm, Wr, P2/1850/63

Francis, poulterer, Holt, Bradford A., 1832, O, W, Wr, P2/1832/12
Francis, poulterer, Holt, Bradford A., 1848, O, W, Wr, P2/1848/17
Gabriel, sen., vict., Newbury, Berks., 1732, I, W, P1/B/1014, P1/7Reg/493A
Geo., glover, Beam., Dorset, 1623, comm, I, W, P5/1623/4, P5/10Reg/157B
Geo., yeo., Monkton F., 1623-24, AB, a/c, I, P2/B/438
Geo., yeo., Steeple L., 1683, I, W, P2/B/1015
Geo., yeo., Chipp., 1690, I, W, P3/B/860
Geo., yeo., Asserton, Berwick St Jas., 1761, W, P1/B/1336, P1/12Reg/13
Geo., maltster, Tilsh., 1762, W, P2/B/1780
Geo., Inkpen, Berks., 1801, AB, W, P1/1801/45, P1/15Reg/265A
Geo., vict., Sal., 1813, W, Wr, P4/1813/6
Geo., farmer and nursery & seedsman, Stapleford, 1847, AB, ren, W, Wr, P2/1847/18
Geo. Rodbourn, Clyffe P., 1854, AB, aff, comm, Wr, P3/1854/59
Hannah, sp., Wantage, Berks., 1784, W, P23/776
Hy., woollen draper, Trowb., c1616, copy W, W, P22/2/21
Hy., yeo., Dunsden, Sonning, Berks., 1629, comm, I, W, P5/1629/4, P5/11Reg/116
Hy., Crockerton, Longbridge D., 1767-78, AB (2), comm, P2/B/1836, 1956
Hy., yeo., Tilsh., 1797, W, P2/B/2123
Hy., form. soldier in 2nd Regt of Dragoon Guards, Chelsea Hospital, London (form. of Bulford), 1818, AB, P2/1818/17
Hy., Longbridge D., 1836, comm, W, P2/1836/21
Hy., Sal. (form. of Homington), 1851, AB, Wr, P4/1851/3
Jacob, yeo., Snap, Aldbourne, 1819, W, Wr, P3/1819/16
Jas., husb., Melk., 1558, W, P2/3Reg/116A
Jas., yeo., Stapleford, 1670, W, P2/B/830
Jas., parchment maker, Burton Hill, Malm., 1685, I, W, P3/B/805
Jas., yeo., Westport St My., 1689, AB, I, P3/B/850
Jas., gent., Preston, Lyneham, 1716, W, Wr, P3/B/1134
Jas., Steeple L., 1760, AB, P2/B/1761
Jas., Uffc., Devon, 1767, W, P5/1767/2
Jas., Uffc., Devon, 1773, AB, O, P20/1/257
Jas., sen., labourer, Long Burton, Dorset, 1812, W, Wr, P5/1812/21
Jas., gent., Bradford A., 1832, O, W, Wr, P2/1832/35
Jas., innkeeper, Crickl. St S., 1848, comm, D, W, Wr, P3/1848/37
Jane, sp., Broad H., 1618, I, NW, P3/B/154
Jane, widow, E. Coulston, 1679, I, W, P2/B/946
Jane, widow, Devizes St My., 1706, AB, I, T, P1/B/727
Jane, widow, Steeple L., 1741, W, P1/B/1129, P1/9Reg/72
Joan, Woodford, 1574, I, W, P5/1574/18, P5/3Reg/35A
Joan, widow, Netherh., 1576, I, T, W, P2/B/51, P2/5Reg/247B
Joan, Stapleford, 1616-19, AB, a/c, I, P2/B/359, P2/8Reg/298B
Joan, sp., Charlton nr Malm., 1622, I, W, P3/B/215
Joan, widow, Halstock Leigh, Dorset, 1681, I, W, P16/54
Jn., husb., Netherh., 1559, W, P2/4Reg/14D
Jn., Warm., 1572, AB, P2/5Reg/156C
Jn., husb., Stapleford, 1579, AB, I, W, P2/B/72, P2/5Reg/327D, 338A
Baker als Vincent, Jn., Sonning, Berks., 1582, W, P5/4Reg/50A
Jn., Blewbury, Berks., 1610, AB, P5/9Reg/36
Baker als Coate, Jn., butcher, Calne, 1612, AB, a/c, I, surety bond (1599), P26/14
Jn., yeo. and bach., Uffc., Devon, 1632, comm, I, W, P5/1632/8, P5/12Reg/89A
Jn., yeo., Ford, Sal. St Mart., 1664, AB, I, P4/1663/3
Jn., sen., fisherman, Moulsford, Cholsey, Berks., 1668, AB, I, P1/B/446
Jn., E. Coulston, 1673, W, P2/B/863
Jn., sen., Stapleford, 1674, I, exhibited I, W, P2/B/877
Jn., carp., Stanton Fitzwarren, 1682, I, W, P3/B/748
Jn., yeo., Pitton, Alderbury, 1690, I, W, P26/387
Jn., sen., clothw., Wantage, Berks., 1706, I, W, P23/281
Jn., weaver, E. Harnham, Britford, 1708, I, W, P24/579
Jn., Beam., Dorset, 1711, AB, P17/200
Jn., Dauntsey, 1713, AB, I, P3/B/1112
Jn., Shalbourne, 1718, AB, I, P23/366

Jn., clerk, Rowde, 1719, W, P3/B/1158
Jn., Chards., Devon, 1722, AB, comm, P5/1722/5
Jn., innholder, Sal., 1723, W, P4/1722/6
Jn., yeo., Hidden, Hungerford, Berks., 1727, W, P23/450
Jn., innholder, Bradford A., 1729, W, P2/B/1474
Jn., Sal., 1730, AB, P4/1730/7
Jn., vict., Reading, Berks., 1741, AB, comm, ren, P1/B/1148
Jn., yeo., Brimpton, Berks., 1741, W, P1/B/1138, P1/9Reg/107
Jn., yeo., Wanb., 1743, W, P3/B/1408
Jn., grocer, Abingdon, Berks., 1747, W, P1/B/1200, P1/10Reg/76B
Jn., jun., sailor, Lyme R., Dorset, 1757, AB, O, P16/316
Jn., carp., Uffc., Devon, 1760, W (on same piece of paper is L from incumbent of Uffculme to Mr Wm. Boucher at Sal. Registrar's office, requesting extract from W of Thos. Percy [1715] on behalf of a poor old fellow in parish), P20/1/238
Jn., clothier, Wantage, Berks., 1760, W, P23/686
Jn., gent., Shalbourne, Berks., 1766, W, P23/712
Jn., tailor, Uffc., Devon, 1766, W, P20/1/247
Jn., Wootton B., 1769, AB, P3/B/1601
Jn., yeo., Somerford K., 1773, W, P1/B/1417, P1/12Reg/511
Jn., jun., Bradford A., 1800, W, P2/1800/61
Jn., shopkeeper, Uffc., Devon, 1802, W, P20/1/278
Jn., cooper, Newbury, Berks., 1817, W, Wr, P1/1817/75
Jn., cooper, Box, 1819, W, Wr, P3/1819/35
Jn., yeo., Lt. Somerford, 1830, AB, O, ren, W, Wr, P3/1830/5
Jn., gent., Maddington, 1835, W, Wr, P2/1835/18
Jn., carp., Fisherton A., 1841, W, Wr, P2/1841/53
Jn., shopkeeper, Crudwell, 1842, O, W, Wr, P3/1842/39
Jn., Dinton, 1855, AB, aff, D (2), W, Wr, P2/1855/7
Jn. Totty, gardener, Milford, Sal. St Mart., 1726, W, P4/1726/13
Jn. Totty, gardener, Fisherton A., 1772, W, P2/B/1893
Lawr., Wilton, 1616, AB, P2/B/363
Lawr., sen., yeo., Tilsh., 1664, I, W, P1/B/413
Lawr., grocer, Devizes, 1726, comm, W, P1/B/913, P1/7Reg/76A
Levi, Tilsh., 1830, W, Wr, P2/1830/41
Lucy, Lyme R., Dorset, 1694, AB, P16/125
Malachi, sen., yeo., Halstock Leigh, Dorset, 1735, W, P5/1735/3
Mgt., widow, Sonning, Berks., 1607, AB, W, P5/1607/3, 8, P5/8Reg/101A
Baker als Marlin, Mgt., Monkton F., 1623, AB, P2/B/440
Backer, Mgt., widow, Fonthill B., 1730, W, P2/B/1489
Mgt., widow, Sal., 1732, AB, P1/B/1022
Mgt., widow, Uffc., Devon, 1773, AB, P20/1/256, P5/17Reg/48A
Margery, widow, Stapleford, 1701, I, W, P1/B/696, P1/4Reg/175
Margery, widow, Martin, Hants, 1704, valuation, W, P1/B/720
Martha, sp., W. Lavington, 1842, O, W, Wr, P1/1842/18
My., sp., Bere R., Dorset, 1706, AB, I, P5/1706/1
My., Longbridge D., 1729, AB, P1/B/977
My., widow, Malm., 1733, AB, I, P3/B/1318
My., sp., Sal. The Close, 1739, W, Wr, P5/1739/3
My., [widow], Chards., Devon, 1749, comm, W, P14/170
My., widow, Lyme R., Dorset, 1771, W, P16/335
My., widow, Littleton P., 1787, W, P1/B/1503, P1/14Reg/171
My., widow, Maddington, 1801, W, Wr, P2/1801/28
My., widow, Teffont M., 1826, AB, Wr, P2/1826/12
My., widow, Chumleigh & E. Row *or* Ford, Uffc., Devon, 1835, AB (re lease of house in U.), comm, P20/1/318
Backer, Matthew, Elcombe, Wrou., 1726, W, P1/B/926, P1/7Reg/117B
Matthew, Halstock, Dorset, 1741, AB, P16/277
Maud, Wylye, 1577, I, W, P2/B/60, P2/5Reg/291E
Millicent, Fisherton A., 1558, W, P2/3Reg/110D
Miriam, widow, Malm., 1777, W, P3/B/1644
Nich., Lt. Bedwyn, 1563, AB, P5/1Reg/20C
Nich., yeo., Stapleford, 1687, I, W, P2/B/1082

Nich., sen., Lacock, 1712, W, P3/B/1101
Philip, Corsham, 1714, marriage licence, P29/2Reg/10C
Rd., Stapleford, 1558, W, P2/3Reg/106C
Rd., Uffcott, Broad H., [1568], W (19th C. transcript - damaged, date of probate illegible), P1/2Reg/83A
Rd., Marridge Hill, Rams., 1584, AB, I, W, P5/1583/3, P5/4Reg/91A
Rd., husb., Northcott, Uffc., Devon, 1635, AB, a/c, I, P5/1635/4, P5/12Reg/219A
Rd., yeo., Eastcott, Swindon, 1687, I, W, P3/B/828
Rd., Pott., 1697, AB, P1/B/662
Rd., servant to the Duke of Somerset, Mere, 1791, AB, W, P5/1791/2, P5/18Reg/165A
Rd., blacksmith, W. Lavington, 1823, W, P1/1823/156
Rd., Charlton nr Malm., 1835, AB, O, P3/1835/11
Rd., innkeeper, Sherb., Dorset, 1844, comm, W, Wr, P5/1844/19
Robt., husb., Netherh., 1563, a/c, I (2), W, P2/B/28, 42, P2/4Reg/156B
Robt., Cocklebury, Langley Burrell, 1621, I, W, P3/B/197
Robt., yeo., Cocklebury, Langley Burrell, 1682, I, ren, NW, P3/B/767
Robt., Enmore Grn, Motc., Dorset, 1685, AB, comm, P19/47
Baker als Williams, Robt., yeo., Chetnole, Yetm., Dorset, 1758, AB, ren, P5/1758/5
Robt., Purton, 1762, AB, P3/B/1543
Robt., chair maker, Reybridge, Lacock, 1765, W, P3/B/1567
Robt., yeo., Semley, 1767, AB, comm, P2/B/1833
Robt., Semley, 1778, AB, I, P2/B/1964
Roger, labourer, Shalbourne, 1567, W, P5/2Reg/23B
Roger, Devizes, 1613, AB, P1/B/85
Roger, sen., yeo., Monkton F., 1615, I, W, P2/B/351
Roger, sen., yeo., Monkton F., 1649, comm, I, W, P1/B/349
Roger, clothw., Bradford A., 1683, I, W, P2/B/1016
Sam., chair maker, Reybridge, Lacock, 1719, I, W, P3/B/1159
Sam., yeo., Horningsham, 1775, W, P5/1775/2, P5/17Reg/88B
Sam., yeo., Semley, 1807, W, Wr, P2/1807/76
Sarah, widow, Sal., 1756-57, AB, W, P4/1756/1, P4/1757/14
Sarah, Oaksey, 1768, W, P3/B/1588
Sarah, dairyman's wife, Bulbridge, Wilton, 1796, proxy of consent, W, P2/B/2110
Sarah, widow, Semley, 1833, W, Wr, P2/1833/41
Sarah, widow, Holt, Bradford A., 1848, AB, O, Wr, P2/1848/27
Steph., husb., Winterbourne E., 1648, AB, I, P2/B/723
Susan, widow, Newnham, Sutton V., 1630, AB, I, W, P2/B/530, P2/9Reg/125A
Susanna, wife, Purton, 1857, AB, aff, D, O, Wr, P3/1857/28
Baker als Cull, Thos., Idmiston, 1571, W, P2/5Reg/109B
Thos., husb., Stapleford, [1594], W, P2/B/156
Baker als Cheate, Thos., husb., Gt. Wishford, [1623], W, P2/B/433
Thos., labourer, Newnham, Sutton V., 1624, I, W, P2/B/447
Thos., butcher, Chipp., 1625, I, P3/B/261
Thos., yeo., E. Coulston, 1665, I, W, P2/B/766
Thos., Draycot C., 1674, AB, I, P3/B/634
Thos., Wilton, 1691, AB, a/c, I, P2/B/1128
Thos., miller, Gt. Wishford, 1699, AB, I, P1/B/678
Thos., broad weaver, Ashley, Bradford A., 1729, I, W, P2/B/1469
Thos., yeo., Steeple L., 1730, W, P1/B/985, P1/7Reg/396
Thos., sen., yeo., Wanb. (form. of Ogbourne St Geo.), 1732, W, P3/B/1312
Thos., sen., Draycot C., 1736, W, P3/B/1350
Thos., Steeple L., 1737, AB, comm, P2/B/1563
Thos., yeo., Quidh., 1738, AB, app. of admr, W, P1/B/1106, P1/8Reg/349
Thos., yeo., Quidh., 1748, W, P1/B/1226, P1/10Reg/239
Thos., Conkwell, Winsley, Bradford A., 1754, comm, W, P2/B/1711
Thos., Melk., 1765, AB, P2/B/1811
Thos., chair maker, Malm., 1777, AB, W, P3/B/1645
Thos., Bramshaw, Hants, 1799, W, P24/1196
Thos., Tisb., 1803, AB, P2/1803/8
Thos., blacksmith, W. Lavington, 1812, W, Wr, P1/1812/5
Thos., carp., Compton C. (form. of Quidh.), 1812, AB, W, Wr, P2/1812/29

Thos., Fifield, 1824, comm, W, Wr, P3/1824/9
Thos., Maddington, 1831, AB, P2/1831/42
Thos., Shalbourne, 1841, AB, O, Wr, P5/1841/17
Thos., yeo., Semley, 1855, aff, W, Wr, P1/1855/36
Walter, horner, Calne, 1684, I, W, P26/321
Wm., Netherh., 1551-52, I, W, P2/B/4, P2/2Reg/142B
Wm., Wantage, Berks., 1569, AB, P5/2Reg/48C
Wm., Haxton, Fittleton, 1591, I, W, P2/B/128
Wm., yeo., Sonning, Berks., 1593, AB, I, draft I, W, P5/1593/8, P5/6Reg/47A
Wm., husb., Bere R., Dorset, 1625, I, W, P5/1625/8, P5/10Reg/293
Wm., clothw., Bishopstone N., 1626, a/c, P6/2
Wm., tailor, Brinkw., 1635, I, W, P3/B/359
Wm., blacksmith, Wilton, 1637, AB, I, P2/B/619
Wm., Netherh., 1669, W, P2/B/803
Wm., gardener, Marl., 1669, I, W, P1/B/457
Wm., tailor, Uffcott, Broad H., 1672, comm, I, W, P3/B/600
Wm., yeo., Stanford in the Vale, Berks., 1672, I, W, P1/B/486
Wm., husb. and yeo., Zeals, 1674, I, W, P5/1674/3
Wm., Marl., 1678, AB, NW, P1/B/518
Wm., Gt. Bedwyn, 1682, I, W, P5/1682/16
Wm., gardener and husb., Milford, Sal. St Mart., 1683, AB, I, P1/B/569
Wm., yeo., Paven Hill, Purton, 1687, AB, I, P3/B/829
Wm., W. Coulston, Edington, 1711, AB, I, P1/B/761
Wm., Teffont M., 1712, AB, I, P2/B/1316
Wm., jun., innholder, Sal., 1726, W, P4/1726/1
Wm., Werg, Mildenhall, 1729, AB, P3/B/1275
Wm., cutler, Sal., 1730, W, P4/1730/10
Wm., Hopgrass, Hungerford, Berks., 1733, AB, P5/1733/2
Wm., drover, Gillingham, Dorset, 1735, AB, I, Wr, P27/1/336
Wm., cooper, Box, 1737, W, P3/B/1358
Wm., joiner, E. Hagbourne, Berks., 1750, W, copy W, P1/B/1243, P1/10Reg/351
Wm., labourer, Bromham, 1750, AB, I, P1/B/1237
Wm., yeo., Purton, 1758, W, P3/B/1514
Wm., Littleton P., 1761, AB, P1/B/1335
Wm., woollen draper, Sal., 1774, W, P4/1774/7
Wm., sen., yeo., Woodshaw, Wootton B., 1785, comm, W, P3/B/1695
Wm., gent., Sal., 1792, W, Wr, P4/1792/9
Wm., cooper, Box, 1832, comm, W, Wr, P3/1832/14
Wm., Dinton, 1837, W, Wr, P2/1837/7
Wm., Fisherton A., 1837, AB, Wr, P2/1837/92
Wm., blacksmith, Chilmark, 1850, W, Wr, P2/1850/56
Wm., yeo., Stanley, Bremhill, 1850, note, O, W, Wr, P3/1850/5
Wilmot, esquire, Moulsford, Cholsey, Berks., 1783, W, P1/B/1474, P1/13Reg/406B
see also Brewer als B.; Ellis als B.; Hall als B.; Poole als B.; Shefford als B.; Vincent als B.
Balch, Alice, widow, N. Wootton, Dorset, 1587, I, W, P5/1587/8, P5/4Reg/149A
Hugh, husb., N. Wootton, Dorset, 1580, I, W, P5/1580/8, P5/3Reg/155B
Jacob, husb., N. Wootton, Dorset, 1620, AB, I, P5/1620/3
Jas., N. Wootton, Dorset, 1620, AB, P5/10Reg/77A
Jas., Corsham, 1831, AB, Wr, P3/1831/70
Jn., bread and biscuit maker, Devizes, 1842, O, W, Wr, P1/1842/14
Jn. Morris, Corsham, 1838, AB, comm, ren, Wr (record of decree in Archdeaconry court), P3/1838/24, 66
Jos., yeo., Chards., Devon, 1753, W, P14/166
Thos., yeo., Lt. Langford, 1558, W, P2/3Reg/139B
Wm., husb., Fonthill G., 1571, AB, P2/B/48, P2/5Reg/125E
see also Batch
Baldchild *see* Jumper als B.
Balden *see* Baldwin
Balderie *see* Bawdry
Baldwin, Alexander, Sal. St Mart., 1628, AB, a/c, I, P4/1627/9
Chris., yeo., Corsham, 1689-90, AB, I, W, P29/B/30, P29/1Reg/244A

Dorcas, widow, Corsham, 1687, AB, I, P29/B/28, P29/1Reg/238A
Edwd., Ditteridge, 1799, W, Wr, P3/B/1764
Balden, Eleanor, widow, Chipp., [1608], I, W (NEP), P3/B/28
Eliz., widow, Twyford, Hurst, Berks., 1663, W (damaged), P5/1663/4
Eliz., widow, Charlcote, Bremhill, 1684, AB, I, P3/B/782
Eliz., widow, Crickl. St S., 1719, AB, I, P3/B/1176
Eliz., widow, Edington, 1786, W, P2/B/2015
Eliz., sp., Marl., 1842, AB, Wr, P1/1842/60
Baldveene, Frideswide, widow, Avebury, 1631, W, P1/B/230
Hy., maltster and yeo., Crickl. St S., 1720, I, W, P1/B/856, P1/6Reg/281A
Baldveene, Jas., yeo. *or* husb., Avebury, 1628, I, W, P3/B/294
Jn., Chr. M., 1617, AB, P3/B/155
Jn., weaver, Corsham, 1618, I, P29/B/15
Bolwin, Jn., tailor, Seend, Melk., 1632, W, P2/9Reg/109B
Jn., yeo., Charlcote, Bremhill, 1669, I, W, P3/B/543
Balden *or* Bauldwin, Jn., yeo., Charlcote, Bremhill, 1682, AB, I, P3/B/749
Bawden, Jn., Sal., 1686, AB, I, P1/B/588
Jn., sen., innholder, Calne, 1745, W, P26/866
Jn., Edington, 1777, AB, P2/B/1944
Jn., yeo., Chiseldon, 1815, W, Wr, P3/1815/71
Jn., farmer, Chiseldon, 1850, comm, W, Wr, P3/1850/11
Jonathan, shopkeeper, S. Marston, 1778, AB, ren, P10/1778/1
Jonathan, shopkeeper, Stratton St Mgt., 1807, W, Wr, P3/1807/65
Jos., Corsham, 1602-03, I, W, P29/B/9, P29/1Reg/53
Jos., Avill's Farm, Corsham, 1617, AB, P1/B/146
Jos., yeo., Easton, Corsham, 1672, I, NW, P29/B/23, P29/1Reg/195D
Jos., yeo., W. Kington, 1771, W, P3/B/1613
My., widow, Tinh., Edington, 1774, W, P2/B/1907
My., widow, Axford, Rams., 1833, O, W, Wr, P5/1833/32
My., widow, Edington, 1842, W, Wr, P1/1842/71
Bealding, Matthew, yeo., Ansty, 1691, AB, I, copy W, P1/B/607
Balden, Maud, widow, Winterbourne M., 1615, I, W, P3/B/117
Nathaniel, yeo., Tinh., Edington, 1771, W, P2/B/1879
Nathaniel, Tinh., Edington, 1810, AB, Wr, P2/1810/69
Nathaniel, gardener, Edington, 1840, W, Wr, P2/1840/50
Bawden, Rd., husb., Chisenbury, Enford, 1564, I, W, P2/B/2152, P2/4Reg/181A
or Balden, Rd., miller, Gatcombe, Littleton Drew, 1641, I, W, P3/B/450
Rd., yeo., Purton, 1673, AB, I, P3/B/620
Rd., yeo., W. Kington, 1693, I, W, P3/B/894
Rd., Crickl. St S., 1707, AB, I, P3/B/1061
Rd., plumber, Twyford, Hurst, Berks. (form. of Bath, Somerset), 1727, W, P5/1727/3, P5/16Reg/153A
Balding, Rd., Hungerford, Berks., 1823, AB, comm, Wr, P23/907
Balden, Robt., Westrop, Corsham (in Caernarvon, Wales at making W; directs body be buried in church of Llandegwin), [1580], W (NEP), P29/B/5
Balding *or* Baulden, Robt., Laverstock, 1609, I, T, P2/B/292
Robt., husb., Slaughterford, 1634, I, W, P3/B/355
Robt., Calne, 1701, AB, I (detailed), P26/479
Robt., Yatesbury, 1701, AB, I, P3/B/999
Robt., yeo., Calne, 1791, comm, W, P5/1791/3, P5/18Reg/160B
Roger, parchment maker, Sal., 1697, W, P4/1696/4
Roger, yeo., W. Kington, 1722, I, W, P3/B/1197
Sampson, Rushall, 1618, AB, L, P2/B/387
Thos., Chisenbury, Enford, 1625, AB, I, P2/B/460
Thos., baker, Crickl. St S., 1690, AB, I, P3/B/859
Thos., Crickl. St S., 1714, AB, P3/B/1121
Wm., Corsham, 1593, W, P29/B/7, P29/1Reg/38A
Wm., clerk and parson, Arborfield, Berks., 1606, I, O, W, P5/1606/6, P5/8Reg/55A
Bawden *or* Baldwin, Wm., yeo., Chisenbury, Enford, 1619, I, W, P1/B/151
Wm., yeo., Charlcote, Bremhill, 1691, AB, I, W, P3/B/877
see also Baden *or* B.

Bale *see* Bayle
Ball, Alexander, yeo., Broad B., Highw., 1736, W, P10/1736/4
Ball als Stride, Alice, tailor's wife, Gt. Wishford, 1648, AB, P2/B/724
Ambrose, labourer, Donnington, Berks., 1767, W, P1/B/1378, P1/12Reg/234A
Ann, widow, Dilton M., Westb., 1794, W, Wr, P25/1794/1
Ann, widow, Berwick B., 1844, comm, W, Wr, P3/1844/17
Anth., vict., Rode, N. Bradley, 1742, W, P2/B/1603
Barbara, sp., Whitley, Reading, Berks., 1695, I, W, P1/B/647
Chris., yeo., Garsdon, 1670, I, W, P3/B/560
Denis, Britford, 1579, AB, I, T, P5/1578/4, P5/3Reg/115A
Drew, shepherd, Heytes., 1719, deed of gift, P5/1719/94
Edith, Chards., Devon, 1628, W, P5/11Reg/67
Edmd., Dinton, 1745, W, P2/B/1639
Edwd., clothshear grinder, Trowb., 1728, W, P1/B/943, P1/7Reg/199A
Edwd., gent., Sal. (form. of Barford St Mart.), 1812, W, Wr, P4/1812/2
Edwd., yeo., Boreham, Warm., 1836, O, W, P2/1836/17
Eliz., widow, Warm., 1717, W, P2/B/1361
Eliz., widow, Leigh, Yetm., Dorset, 1740, W, Wr, P5/1740/10
Eliz., widow, Broad B., Highw., 1811, W, P10/1811/3
Eliz., sp., Trowb., 1830, comm, W, Wr, P1/1830/4
Frances, wife, Fisherton A., 1809, AB, Wr (form. Frances Carter, sp.), P2/1809/88
Geo., Swindon, 1677, AB, a/c, I, P3/B/674
Geo., Mere, 1713, AB, I, P5/1712/17
Geo., yeo., Steeple A., 1778, W, P2/B/1959
Geo., grazier, Broad B., Highw., 1810, W, P10/1810/4
Geo., tailor, Rams., 1839, W, Wr, P5/1839/20
Harry, porter, Devizes, 1836, W, P1/1836/5
Hy., Rams., 1743, AB, Wr, P5/1743/3
Hugh, sen., clothier, Wokm., Berks., 1593, I, W, P5/1593/16, P5/6Reg/27
Ball als Rogers, Hugh, linen weaver, Mere, 1669, I (detailed), W, P5/1669/3
Ball als Rogers, Hugh, linen weaver, Mere, 1718, W, P5/1718/1, P5/16Reg/2B
Isaac, shoemaker, Hungerford, Berks., 1699, AB, I, ren, P23/232
Jacob, grocer, Marl., 1763, AB, P1/B/1348
Jas., cordw., Longbridge D., 1712, W, P2/B/1310
Jas., maltster, Warm., 1837, W, Wr, P2/1837/40
Jas., innkeeper, Tilsh., 1855, AB, aff, Wr, P1/1855/34
Jane, widow, Calne, 1709, W, P26/561
Joachim, gent., Trowb., 1828, W, Wr, P1/1828/8
Joan, widow, Tytherington, Heytes., 1571, W, P5/2Reg/93B
Joan, widow, Tytherington, Heytes., 1612-13, AB, I, P5/1612/6, P5/9Reg/112B
Jn., N. Bradley, 1568, W (detailed list of clothes), P2/5Reg/32B
Jn., smith, Hungerford, Berks., 1570, W, P5/2Reg/63C
Jn., yeo., Knights, Wokm., Berks., 1592, AB, I, W, P5/1592/14, P5/1593/21, P5/6Reg/12B
Jn., Wokm., Berks., 1599, AB, I, W, P5/1599/4, P5/6Reg/233A
Jn., yeo., Burbage, 1613, W, P1/B/94
Jn., basket maker, Hinton, Hurst, Berks., 1617, AB, I, P5/1617/5
Jn., Sonning, Berks., 1619, AB, P5/10Reg/42B
Jn., Tytherington, Heytes., 1638, AB, P5/1638/3, P5/13Reg/111
Jn., blacksmith, Longbridge D., 1674, I, NW, P2/B/880
Jn., blacksmith, Longbridge D., 1700, I, W, P2/B/1210
Jn., carp., Hungerford, Berks., 1713, AB, I, P5/1713/6
Jn., wheelwright, Abingdon, Berks., 1804, W, P1/1804/69
Jn., porter, Devizes, 1826, W, Wr, P1/1826/113
Jn., yeo., Corsley, 1840, W, Wr, P2/1840/53
Jos., yeo., Malm., 1748, AB, W, P3/B/1449
Josiah, Quidh., 1835, AB, P1/1835/61
My., widow, Broad B., Highw., 1712, I, W, P10/1712/8
My., widow, Steeple A., 1724, W, P2/B/1425
My., widow, Wargrave, Berks., 1732, W, P1/B/1006, P1/7Reg/481
My., widow, Rams., 1744, W, Wr, P5/1744/2

My., widow, Malm., 1801, AB, P3/1801/15
Nich., husb., Calne, 1707, I, W, P5/1707/3, P5/15Reg/46
Ralph, Sonning, Berks., 1554, W, P5/20Reg/122A
Ralph, carp., Woodley, W. and Sandford, Berks., 1594, I, W, P5/1594/1, P5/6Reg/76A
Rebecca, sp., Sherb., Dorset, 1707-08, W, P5/1707/4, P5/15Reg/53
Rd., weaver, Wilton, 1727, W, P2/B/1455
Robt., baker, *The King's Arms*, Swindon, 1712, I, W, P3/B/1102
Robt., Swindon, 1731, AB, P3/B/1300
Sam., yeo., Tytherington, Heytes., 1602, I, W, P5/1602/9, P5/7Reg/46C
Sam., yeo., Kingston D., 1676, I, W, P2/B/904
Sam., clothier, Bishopstrow, 1700, AB, I, ren, P2/B/1213
Sarah, sp., Devizes, 1822, W, Wr, P1/1822/10
Steph., husb., Tytherington, Heytes., 1582, T (children: Jn., Thos., Sam., Steph., Edith & My. B.), W, P5/1582/4, P5/4Reg/44
Susan, Sandhurst, Berks., 1663, AB, I, P5/1663/5
Ball als Rogers, Susan, Mere, 1674, AB, P5/1674/4
Susanna, widow, Bishopstone S. (form. of Sal.), 1846, W, Wr, P2/1846/15
Thos., husb., Sonning, Berks., 1539, W, P5/20Reg/5B
Thos., Crudwell, 1634, AB, P3/B/356
Thos., jun., yeo., Wokm., Berks., 1635, AB, comm, I, P5/1634/2, P5/12Reg/169A
Thos., yeo., Wokm., Berks., 1637, I, W, P5/1637/2, P5/13Reg/33A
Thos., Mere, 1674, AB, P5/1674/5
Thos., mason, Hungerford, Berks., 1682, comm, I, W, P5/1682/17
Thos., husb. and cordw., Swindon, 1684, I, W, P1/B/570
Thos., Swindon, 1711, AB, P3/B/1094
Thos., sen., baker, Sonning, Berks., 1711, W, P5/1711/3, P5/15Reg/263
Thos., yeo., Warm., 1715, W, P2/B/1333
Thos., scribbler, Heytes., 1720, AB, I, P5/1720/6
Thos., jeweller, Sal., 1721, AB, I (2 - detailed - 1 a draft), P4/1720/9
Thos., Clewer, New Windsor, Berks., 1741, AB, I, P1/B/1140
Thos., collarmaker, Steeple L., 1797, aff, W, P2/B/2124
Thos., Trowb., 1805, AB, comm, P1/1805/3
Thos., collarmaker, Codf. St P., 1815, W, Wr, P2/1815/76
Thos., E. Knoyle, 1853, D, W, Wr, P2/1853/28
Virtue, widow, E. Knoyle, 1717, W, P2/B/1355
Walter, husb., Tytherington, Heytes., 1579, AB, I, P5/1579/2, P5/3Reg/119B
Wm., husb., Wokm., Berks., 1550-51, W, P5/20Reg/113
Wm., Tytherington, Heytes., 1566, W, P5/1Reg/71B
Wm., Haydon Wick, Rodbourne C., 1617, I, W (2 - 1 a copy), P3/B/139
Wm., yeo., Tytherington, Heytes., 1673, I, W, P5/1673/3
Wm., yeo., Bremhill, 1674, I, W, P3/B/635
Wm., Crockerton, Longbridge D., 1676, I, W, P2/B/902
Wm., miller, Sherb., Dorset, 1681, AB, I, P5/1681/4
Wm., Dilton, Westb. (estates at Coldharbour & Penleigh), 1687, AB, I, P25/1687/2
Wm., grocer, Steeple A., [1718?], W (buried 1717), P2/B/1379
Wm., Gt. Faringdon, Berks., 1719, AB, P5/1719/6
Wm., Calne, 1743, AB, P26/849
Wm., Dilton M., Westb., 1768, W, P25/1768/2
Wm., yeo., Bapton, Fisherton Delamare, 1793, W, P2/B/2088
Wm., yeo., Broad B., Highw., 1810, AB, comm, W, P10/1810/2
Wm., vict., Bradford A., 1818, comm, W, Wr, P2/1818/73
Wm., vict., Westport, Malm. (but late of Measham, Derbyshire), 1822, W, Wr, P3/1822/21
Wm., yeo., Semley, 1832, W, Wr, P2/1832/37
see also Balley *or* B.; Rogers als B.
Ballam, Baalam, Joshua, Winterborne K., Dorset, 1746, W, P5/1746/2
Martha, widow, Winterborne K., Dorset, 1797, W, P5/1797/2, P5/18Reg/256B
Ballard, Anth., Marridge Hill, Rams., 1674, AB, a/c, I, P5/1674/6
Anth., yeo., Marridge Hill, Rams., 1729, I, W, P5/1729/5, P5/16Reg/232A
Cath., widow, Dilton, Westb., 1682, AB, I, P25/1682/5
Denise, Rams., 1606, W, P1/B/54

Edwd., Rams., 1662, AB, I, W, P5/1662/7
Edwd., broad weaver, Bromham, 1675, comm, I, W, P3/B/642
Edwd., Marridge Hill, Rams., 1686, I, W, P5/1686/9
Edwd., blacksmith, Hilcott, N. Newnton, 1733, W, P3/B/1319
Edwd., vict., Chiseldon, 1749, W, P3/B/1454
Eleanor, widow, Edington, 1732, AB, I, W, P2/B/1509
Eliz., widow, Bromham, 1628, I, W, P1/B/213
Eliz., doctor of divinity's wife, Old Windsor, Berks., 1767, W, P1/B/1379, P1/12Reg/247B
Ballard als Upshall, Grace, Bratton, Westb., 1636, AB, P25/1636/2
Hy., yeo., Bratton, Westb., 1688, I (detailed), W, P25/1688/2
Hy., yeo., Frankleigh, Bradford A., 1690, AB, comm, I, P2/B/1115
Hy., yeo., Bratton, Westb., 1754, AB, ren, P25/1754/6
Jas., yeo., Bratton, Westb., 1680, I, W, P25/1680/7
Jas., Steeple A., 1718, AB, P2/B/1371
Jas., plumber and glazier, Warm., 1764, AB, comm, W, P2/B/1801
Joan, widow, Bromham, 1611, I, W, P1/B/70
Jn., husb., Hilp., 1560, W, P2/4Reg/35A
Jn., Rams., 1565, W, P5/1Reg/59B
Jn., husb., Bratton, Westb., 1609, I, W (NEP), P25/1609/1
Jn., Steeple A., 1614, W, P2/8Reg/240B
Jn., Dilton, Westb. (& Leigh tanpits), 1671, I, W, P25/1671/5
Jn., husb., Eastridge, Rams., 1677, I, W, P5/1677/5
Jn., husb., Buttermere, 1680-81, I, W, P1/B/545, P3/B/720
Jn., Rams., 1693, AB, I, P5/1693/5
Jn., yeo., Steeple A., 1723, comm, W, P2/B/1417
Jn., doctor, Sal., 1725, W, P4/1725/2
Jn., butcher, Box, 1731, W, P3/B/1301
Jn., yeo., Rams., 1768, W, P5/1768/2
Jn., vict., Chiseldon, 1776, AB (2), comm, ren (2), W, P3/B/1641
Jn., Warm., 1803, AB, P2/1803/63
Jn. Aldridge, gent., Bratton, Westb., 1740, AB, ren, P25/1740/7
My., Bratton, Westb., 1714, W, P25/1714/2
My., widow, Steeple A., 1761, W, P2/B/1777
Philip, gent., Bratton, Westb., 1724, I, L, req (of 1736), copy W, P25/1724/11
Robt., Rams., 1565, W, P5/1Reg/59C
Robt., husb., Bratton, Westb., 1581-82, I, W, P5/1581/2, P5/4Reg/29B
Roger, Marridge Hill, Rams., 1686, AB, I, P5/1686/13
Sarah, Bratton, Westb., 1728, W (NEP), P25/1728/4
Steph., husb., Marridge Hill, Rams., 1628-29, AB, I, P5/1628/13, P5/11Reg/18A
Thos., yeo., Preston, Rams., 1589, AB, I, W, P5/1588/6, P5/5Reg/49D
Thos., husb., Bromham, 1602, W, P3/1Reg/51A
Thos., weaver, Bromham, 1626, I, W, P3/B/272
Ballerd, Thos., husb., Preston, Rams., 1626, I, W, P5/1625/4, P5/10Reg/191
Thos., husb., Hurst, Berks., 1670, AB, I, P5/1670/4
Thos., yeo., Edington, 1729, W, P1/B/961, P1/7Reg/338
Thos., tailor, Rams., 1753, W, P5/1753/2
Ballerd, Timothy, yeo., Bratton, Westb., 1675, I (detailed), W, P25/1675/1
Wm., Bulbridge, Wilton, 1551, W, P2/2Reg/125A
Wm., Wilton, 1591, AB, P2/B/127
Wm., Buttermere, c1604?, I, W, Wr (badly damaged), P3/B/10
Wm., sen., broad weaver, Bromham, 1673-77, AB, I (2), W, P3/B/621, 675
Wm., Uffington, Berks., 1708, AB, I, ren, P1/B/736
Wm., sen., yeo., Steeple A., 1709, AB, I, ren, P2/B/1286
Wm., broad weaver, Bromham, 1733, I, W, P3/B/1320
Baller *see* Bowler
Balley, Balley *or* Ball, Jn., shepherd, Bratton, Westb., 1692, I, W, P25/1692/4
Jos., jun., Gt. Bedwyn, 1743, AB, Wr, P5/1743/4
Jos., maltster, Gt. Bedwyn, 1755, W, Wr, P21/10/31
Jos., shopman, Chipp., 1782, W, P1/B/1470, P1/13Reg/380
Thos., Seend, Melk., 1638, AB, I, P1/B/276

Wm., yeo., Seend, Melk., 1560, W, P2/4Reg/45A
Wm., Bps. C., 1569, AB, P5/2Reg/38C
Balliman, My., widow, Uffc., Devon, 1703, ren, W, P20/1/141
Ballinger, Alice, Bere R., Dorset, 1683, AB, I, P5/1683/6
Ann, widow, Bere R., Dorset, 1633, I, W, P5/1633/3, P5/12Reg/153B
Going, Bere R., Dorset, 1632, I, W, P5/1632/9, P5/12Reg/122C
My., yeo.'s widow, Cleverton, Lea and C., 1758, W, P3/B/1516
Rd., yeo., Long Newnton, 1720, AB, I, P3/B/1177
Sarah, widow, Devizes St My., 1838, comm, W, Wr, P1/1838/8
Ballow, Eliz., widow, Hannington, 1700, I, W, P3/B/991
Joan, widow, Hannington, 1663, I, W, P3/B/484
Jn., husb., Hannington, 1613, I, W, P1/B/96
Jn., labourer, Chelworth, Crickl. St S., 1713, AB, I, P3/B/1113
Millicent, widow, Swindon, 1625, I, W, P1/B/195
Sam., yeo., Hannington, 1695, AB, I, ren, Wr (all fragile), P3/B/933
Thos., yeo., Hannington, 1663, comm, I, W, P1/B/398
Balster, Anstis, widow, N. Wootton, Dorset, 1696, AB, comm, P5/1696/5
Jas., N. Wootton, Dorset, 1779, AB, P5/1779/1, P5/17Reg/179B
Bolster, Jas., Sal., 1823, AB, Wr, P4/1823/3
Bolster, Jn., yeo., N. Wootton, Dorset, 1692, AB, I, P5/1692/4
Jn., sen., yeo., N. Wootton, Dorset, 1757-59, AB, req, W, copy W, P5/1757/1, P5/1759/2
Wm., yeo., Uffc., Devon, 1715, W, P20/1/151
Balston, Eliz., widow, Charminster, Dorset, 1800, W, P5/1800/22, P5/18Reg/296C
Jane, widow, Wilton, 1809, AB, Wr, P2/1809/73
Bamfield *see* Banfield
Bampton, Abraham, yeo., Bramshaw, Hants, 1796, W, Wr, P24/1211
Ambrose, yeo., Homington, 1663, I (detailed), W, P24/320
Eliz., widow, Nunton, N. and Bodenham, 1677, AB, comm, I, W, P2/B/918
Geo., clerk, Chards., Devon, 1731, AB, P5/1731/10
Joan, widow, Nunton, N. and Bodenham, 1578, I, W, P2/B/64, P2/5Reg/302C
Jn., gent., Nunton, N. and Bodenham, 1668, W, P2/B/794
Jn., sen., weaver, Sal., 1674, AB, I, NW, P4/1674/2
Jn., layer, Sal., 1677, AB, I, P1/B/508
Jn., Downton, 1689, AB, P2/B/1105
Jn., Downton, 1767, AB, P2/B/1835
My., sp., Sal. The Close, 1744, W, Wr, P5/1744/3
Sarah, sp., Downton, 1789, AB, P2/B/2045
Thos., brewer, Downton, 1638, AB, P2/B/613
Bance, Eliz., widow, Henley, Buttermere, 1697, I, W, P3/B/957
Geoff., Highw., 1636, AB, I, P10/1636/4
Hy., Henley, Buttermere, 1690, AB, I, P3/B/861
Joan, widow, Westrop, Highw., 1625, I, W, P10/1625/2
Jn., Sevenhampton, Highw., 1609, W (NEP), P10/1609/1
Jn., cooper, Inkpen, Berks., 1741, W, P1/B/1136, P1/9Reg/108B
Jn., husb., Tilehurst, Berks., 1773, W, P1/B/1414, P1/12Reg/489
Jn., Inkpen, Berks., 1823, AB, Wr, P1/1823/105
Matthew, cooper, Kintbury, Berks., 1779, W, P1/B/1453, P1/13Reg/265
Rd., cordw., Highw., 1685, comm, I, W, P10/1685/4
Wm., Gomeldon, Idmiston, 1611, court papers, W, P2/B/321
Wm., hosier and haberdasher, Newbury, Berks., 1804, W, P1/1804/61
Bancroft, Dorothy, widow, Bradford A., 1637, comm, I, W, P2/B/606
Jas., broad weaver, Bearfield, Bradford A., 1807, AB, comm, ren, W, Wr, P1/1807/10
Wm., Devizes, 1665, AB, P1/B/420
Band, Cath., widow, Hindon, 1710, W, P2/B/1293
Edwd., servant, Bulford, [1684?], W (date suggested in later annotation), P2/B/1030
Margery, widow, Chr. M., 1627, AB, a/c, W, P3/B/283
Matthew, vict., Reading St Lawr., Berks., 1638, AB, I, P1/B/270
Walter, miller, Lacock, [1574], W (NEP), P3/1Reg/20B
Bane *see* Baines
Banfield, Bamfield, Dorothy, gentlewoman and widow, W. Lavington, 1571, W, P1/1Reg/19

Jn., yeo., Chards., Devon, 1803, W, P5/1803/48, P5/19Reg/81
Bonfield, Wm., Woodb., 1682, AB, I, P3/B/756
Banger *see* Benger
Banghurst, Wm., carp., Midgham, Thatcham, Berks., 1723, AB, W, P1/B/900, P1/7Reg/16B
Banks, [...], widow, Upavon, 1646, L (requests cav. on behalf of widow B.), P2/B/706
Agnes, Milton L., 1613, I, W, P3/B/98
Agnes, widow, Rams., 1676, I, W, P5/1676/3
Alice, widow, Milton L., 1617-18, AB, a/c, I, W, Wr, P3/B/140, 156, 182
Bank, Ann, Upavon, 1695, AB, I, P1/B/653
Ann, widow, Bromham, 1805, AB, P3/1805/42
Barbara, Clench, Milton L., 1689, W (NEP), P3/B/851
Bridget, widow, Compton, Enford, 1682, AB, I, P2/B/1003
Denise, widow, Whittonditch, Rams., 1611, I, P5/1611/2
Dorothy, widow and vict., Lacock, 1738, W, P1/B/1097, P1/8Reg/321A
Edith, widow, Odstock, 1676, I, W, P2/B/908
Edwd., Rams., 1673, AB (damaged and incomplete), I, P5/1673/6
Edwd., yeo., Bradford A., 1715, W, P2/B/1345
Edwd., shoemaker, Lacock, 1717, W, P3/B/1140
Edwd., Sonning, Berks., 1734, W, P5/1734/7
Edwd., yeo., Bewley, Lacock, 1769, W, P3/B/1598
Eliz., widow, Rams., 1705, I, W, P5/1705/3
Eliz., sp., Netheravon, 1725, I, W, P12/152
Eliz., widow, Castle C., 1769, AB, W, P28/31
Eliz., widow, Corsham, 1840, W, Wr, P3/1840/30
Emma, widow, Devizes St Jn., 1668, comm, I, NW, P1/B/434
Francis, linen draper, Upavon, 1693, W, P2/B/1152
Francis, widow, Sal., 1732, W, P4/1731/20
Geoff., Milton L., 1637, AB, P3/B/379
Geo., Milton L., 1614, AB, P3/B/109
Geo., innholder, Sal., 1639, I, W, P4/1639/8
Hy., stapler, Devizes, 1667, AB, comm, I, P1/B/430
Hy., woolstapler, Devizes, 1681, AB, comm, I, P1/B/553
Hy., sen., yeo., Easton, Corsham, 1797-1880, L (2 - between Somerset House & Sal. Registries re 1797 W which should be in this register, but is not), W, P29/B/56, P29/2Reg/226
Hy., vict., Corsham, 1821, W, Wr, P3/1821/29
Humphrey, sen., yeo., Inkpen, Berks., 1677, I, W (NEP), P1/B/509
Humphrey, sen., yeo., Inkpen, Berks., 1708, W, P1/B/733, P1/4Reg/292
Humphrey, Inkpen, Berks., 1717, AB, P1/B/834
Joan, widow, Rams., 1663, AB, comm, I, P5/1663/6
Joan, widow, Longstreet, Enford, 1699, I, W, P2/B/1207
Jn., shepherd, Ogbourne St And., 1615, AB, alleg, I, P5/1615/1, P5/9Reg/160C
Jn., innholder, Chilton F., 1636, I, W, P3/B/363
Jn., vict., Chipp., 1672, NW, P3/B/601
Jn., husb., Rams., 1673, AB, I, P5/1673/5
Jn., innholder, Swan, Rams., 1678, I (detailed), W, P5/1678/22
Jn., yeo., Britford, 1684, AB, I, P24/751
Bank, Jn., sen., gent., E. Challow, Letcombe Regis, Berks., 1686, I, W, P1/B/1570
Jn., butcher, Homington, 1690, AB, I, ren, P2/B/1119
Jn., sen., blacksmith, Milton L., 1703, AB, I, W, P3/B/1022
Jn., common brewer, Bromham, 1824, comm, W, Wr, P3/1824/24
Jos., no abode stated, 1613, AB, P2/B/338
Margery, widow *or* sp., Milton L., 1663, AB, I, W, P3/B/485
My., sp., Corsham, 1828, W, Wr, P3/1828/16
Rd. Silk, gent., Chipp., 1853, O, W, Wr, P3/1853/26
Roger, yeo., Crowood, Rams., 1597, AB, W, P5/1597/16, P5/6Reg/156E
Roger, yeo., Rams., 1699, AB, I, P5/1699/7
Roger, grocer, Rams., 1717, W, P5/1717/7, P5/15Reg/397B
Roger, yeo., Rams., 1718, comm, W, P5/1718/4, P5/16Reg/9B
Sam., yeo., Whittonditch, Rams., 1685, I, NW, P5/1685/11
Sam., saddler, Beam., Dorset, 1743, W, P17/479

Steph., Rams., 1633, AB, I, P5/1633/7, P5/12Reg/127A
Steph., sen., butcher, Odstock, 1638, I, W, P2/B/627
Steph., Sal., 1695, AB, I, P4/1695/7
Steph., Britford, 1708, AB, P24/584
Thos., yeo., Whittonditch, Rams., 1597, I, T, W, P5/1597/6, P5/6Reg/184
Thos., yeo., Odstock, 1670, W, P2/B/833
Thos., Longstreet, Enford, 1688, AB, I, P2/B/1101
Thos., Lacock, 1689, AB, I, P3/B/852
Uriah, clerk, Bemerton, Fugg. St Peter, 1668, I, W, P1/B/453
Walter, yeo., Horton, Bps. C., 1600, I, W, P24/4
Wm., Netheravon, 1616, AB, P12/32
Wm., Foghamshire, Chipp., 1636, AB, I, P3/B/364
Wm., Compton, Enford, 1676, I, P2/B/907
Wm., yeo., Manningford A., 1684, I, W, P3/B/783
Wm., yeo., Milton L., 1692, I, W, P3/B/886
Wm., vict. and hairdresser, Chipp., 1816, W, Wr, P3/1816/25
Wm., Chipp., 1827, AB, Wr, P3/1827/2
Banne, Robt., Chipp., 1723, AB, comm, P3/B/1223
Banner *see* Bonner
Banning, Agnes, widow, Huish, 1670, I, NW, Wr, P3/B/561
Alice, widow, Sal., 1612, AB, I, W, P4/1612/8
Ann, widow, Winterbourne G., 1845, W, Wr, P1/1845/20
Anth., husb. *or* yeo., Wootton R., 1707, I, W, P3/B/1062
Augustine *or* Austin, Clench, Milton L., 1664, AB, I, P3/B/491
Cath., sp., Burbage, 1605, AB, D (2), I, W, P5/1605/6, P5/8Reg/41A
Chas., cook, Charlton nr Malm., 1732, W, P1/B/1018, P1/7Reg/506A
Chas., blanket maker, Avill's Farm, Corsham, 1760, AB, app. of guardian, comm, W, P3/B/1522
Dan., New Mill, Milton L., 1833, AB, Wr, P3/1833/55
Edmd., Durley, Burbage, 1588, AB, I, P5/1587/6, P5/4Reg/156B
Eliz., widow, Westcourt, Burbage, 1594, I, W, P5/1594/4, P5/6Reg/73A
Eliz., widow, Milton L., 1721, AB, NW, P1/B/871, P1/6Reg/369B
Jas., bach., Avill's Farm, Corsham, 1762, AB, P3/B/1544
Jas., smith, Collingbourne D., 1835, W, P1/1835/127
Joan, Cules Parcill, Burbage, 1597, W, P5/1597/15, P5/6Reg/155B
Jn., Clench, Milton L., 1614, I, P3/B/110
Jn., yeo., Westcourt, Burbage, 1646, comm, I, W, P11/17
Jn., maltster, New Mill, Milton L., 1774, W, P3/B/1628
Jn., yeo., Milton L., 1814, W, Wr, P3/1814/9
Jn., yeo., Wootton R., 1825, W, Wr, P3/1825/71
Jn., gent., Ogbourne St Geo., 1837, comm, W, Wr, P23/990
Jn., shoemaker, Pewsey, 1853, comm, W, Wr, P3/1853/4
Philip, Burbage, 1835, W, Wr, P11/290
Ralph, yeo., Wootton R., 1636, I, W, P3/B/365
Robt., Burbage, 1575, I, W, P11/304, P5/3Reg/55A
Robt., Westcourt, Burbage, 1596, I, W, P5/1595/2, P5/6Reg/118
Ruth, widow, Chipp., 1837, W, Wr, P3/1837/57
Sarah, widow, Collingbourne D., 1792, W, P21/11/38
Steph., innholder, Sherston, 1766, W, P3/B/1575
Thos., Burbage, 1568, W, P5/2Reg/8A
Thos., Burbage, 1590, I, W, P5/1590/4, P5/5Reg/71B
Thos., Sopworth, 1688, I, W, P1/B/595
Thos., yeo., Clench, Milton L., 1705, AB, I, ren, P3/B/1033
Thos., sen., cordw., Pewsey, 1818, W, Wr, P3/1818/33
Thos., gent., Wootton R., 1844, O, W, Wr, P3/1844/66
Wm., Clench, Milton L., 1571, W, P1/1Reg/84A
Wm., Brunton, Collingbourne K., 1629, I, W, P3/B/299
Wm., Westcourt, Burbage, 1645, AB, I, P5/1645/3, P5/14Reg/84B
Wm., Sal. St Thos., 1798, W, P4/1798/9
Wm., gent., Chipp., 1835, W, P3/1835/36
see also Bainton

Bannister, Ann, widow, Woodlands, Mere, 1597, AB, I, W, P5/1597/13, P5/6Reg/177A
Ann, sp., Bramshaw, Hants, 1735, AB, comm, I, P24/931
Edmd., husb., Bramshaw, Hants, 1719, AB, I, P24/634
Edwd., Abingdon, Berks., 1692, AB, I, P1/B/627
Eleanor, widow, Stourton, 1740, AB, P2/B/1582
Eliz., widow, Hungerford, Berks., 1822, comm, W, Wr, P23/898
Geo., sen., baker, Hindon, 1669, I, W, P2/B/801
Geo., Hindon, 1684, AB, P2/B/1045
Grace, widow, Melk., 1774, AB, P2/B/1901
Hy., Wokm., Berks., 1605, AB, I, P5/1605/1
Hy., shoemaker, Wokm., Berks., 1638, I, W, P5/1638/10, P5/13Reg/118C
Jas., Sal., 1739, AB, Wr, P4/1739/2
Jas., dyer, Trowb., 1827, comm, W, Wr, P1/1827/8
Jn., sen., yeo., Bramshaw, Hants, 1617, I, W, P24/82
Jn., labourer, Bramshaw, Hants, 1689, AB, I, P24/729
Jn., collarmaker and sadler, Hungerford, Berks., 1803, W, P5/1803/40, P5/19Reg/72
Lucy, sp., Mere, 1673, comm, I, W, P5/1673/1
My., sp., Gillingham, Dorset, 1716, W, P27/1/208
Nich., sen., W. Knoyle, 1693, I, W, P2/B/1154
Bannister als Foster, Randall, linen weaver, Mere, 1583, I, T, W, P5/1583/5, P5/4Reg/66B
Thos., yeo., Woodlands, Mere, 1647, AB, I, W, P5/1646/1, P5/14Reg/92D
Wm., sen., husb., Bramshaw, Hants, 1717, W, P24/648
Wm., Stourton, 1733, AB, P2/B/1524
Wm., woolstapler, Charlton, Donhead St My., 1742, W, P2/B/1602
Bannock, Alice, widow, Westb., 1641, I, W, P25/1641/6
Bannock als Taunton, And., butcher, Westb., 1669, AB, comm, I, ren, P25/1669/12
Jn., Bratton, Westb., 1588, AB, I, T, P5/1587/7, P5/5Reg/29A
Jn., Westb., 1640, AB, I, P25/1640/11
Banstone, Banstone als Masey, Rd., clothier, Cutteridge, N. Bradley, 1702, I, W, P1/B/700, P1/4Reg/220
see also Macy als B.
Banton, Banting, Chas., Sal. (form. of E. Tytherley, Hants), 1838, W, Wr, P4/1838/9
Banting, Jas., blacksmith, Childrey, Berks., 1823, W, Wr, P1/1823/85
Banten *or* Baunton, Joan, widow, Sherb., Dorset, 1590, AB, I, W, P5/1590/5, P5/5Reg/90
Baunton *or* Banton, Joan, widow, Sherb., Dorset, 1638, comm, I, W, P5/1638/12, P5/13Reg/150
Jn., sen., haberdasher, Warm., 1630, I, NW, P2/B/514, P2/9Reg/81C
Banting, Jos., Standen, Chute, 1850, AB, comm, D, ren, W, Wr, P7/211
Baunton, Rd., yeo., Sherb., Dorset, 1588, AB, I, W, P5/1588/5, P5/5Reg/7C
Banton *or* Baunton, Rd., sen., vict., Sherb., Dorset, 1637, AB, comm, I, P5/1637/5, P5/13Reg/60A
Robt., yeo., Folke, Dorset, 1773, W, P5/1773/4, P5/17Reg/66A
Baunton, Thos., Folke, Dorset, 1781, AB, comm, P5/1781/2, P5/17Reg/215A
Wm., vict., Sherb., Dorset, 1634, AB, I. Granted at Metropolitan visitation to Dorchester, P5/1634/20
Banwell, Banwell *or* Bauwell, Geo., Westb., 1565, AB, P5/1Reg/63B
Bapshin, Eliz., widow, Bradford A., 1592, AB, I, P2/B/139
Hy., husb., Bradford A., 1586, I, W, P2/B/93, P2/7Reg/34B
Hy., Bradford A., 1631, AB, P2/B/548
Bapton, Alice, Amesb., 1564, W, P2/4Reg/201A
Barber, Adam, tailor, Wilcot, 1813, W, Wr, P3/1813/4
Agnes, widow, Ashton K., [1616], W (NEP), P3/B/131
Ann, widow, Wilton, Gt. Bedwyn, 1670, I, W, P21/2/3
Benj., Horningsham, 1801, W, P5/1801/23, P5/18Reg/324B
Edwd., yeo. *or* husb., Froxfield, 1680, AB, comm, I, ren, P3/B/721
Edwd., husb., Gt. Bedwyn, 1698, W, P21/5/43
Eleanor, widow, Coombe B., 1685, AB, I, P5/1685/80
Eliz., widow, S. Newton, 1730, W, P1/B/984, P1/7Reg/391B
Francis, E. Grafton, 1699, I, NW, P21/5/48
Francis, cutler, Sal., 1748, W, P4/1747/8
Grace, widow, Enmore Grn, Motc., Dorset, 1694, I, W, P19/68
Jane, widow, Westb., 1693, AB, I, P25/1693/4
Jean, widow, Froxfield, 1665, I, W, P3/B/499
Joan, Wilton, Gt. Bedwyn, 1614, I, W, P5/1614/6, P5/9Reg/143B

Joan, widow, Wilton, Gt. Bedwyn, 1703, I, W, P21/6/11
Barber als Hore, Jn., Southbroom, 1585, AB, I, P24/1429, P5/4Reg/101C
Jn., yeo., Ruscombe, Berks., 1596, I, T, W, P5/1596/3, P5/6Reg/134
Jn., Coombe B., 1603, I, P5/1603/5
Jn., yeo., Ashton K., 1606, I, W, P1/B/55
Jn., Sal., 1626, AB, I, P4/1625/10
Jn., husb., Wilton, Gt. Bedwyn, 1638, I, W, P21/1/34
Jn., Ryme I., Dorset, 1728, AB, I, P5/1728/3, P5/16Reg/209A
Jn., Coombe B., 1732, W, P5/1732/1
Jn., Odstock, 1762, AB, P2/B/1778
Jn., gent., Coombe B., 1788, W, P5/1788/5, P5/18Reg/91B
Jn., Coombe B., 1793, W, P8/66
Jn., tallow chandler, Sal., 1794, W, P4/1794/10
Jn., yeo., Wilcot, 1819, D, W, Wr, P3/1819/1
My., widow *or* sp., Horningsham, 1733, I, W, P5/1733/4
Matthew, fuller, Swindon, 1604, I, NW, P3/B/11
Ralph, curate, Fugg. St Peter, 1549, W, P2/2Reg/73A
Barber als Watkins, Rd., husb., Wingfield, 1633, I, W, P2/B/572
Rd., sen., narrow weaver, Horningsham, 1726, W, P5/1726/9, P5/16Reg/141A
Robt., Ruscombe & Hurst, Berks., 1619, comm, I, P5/1619/6
Robt., Burbage, 1628, AB, I, P5/1628/14, P5/11Reg/13B
Robt., jun., broad weaver, Horningsham, 1719, W, P5/1719/4, P5/16Reg/23A
Robt., Horningsham, 1826, W, Wr, P5/1826/5
Roger, gent., Sal. The Close, 1631, I, W, P5/1631/6, P5/11Reg/162B
Sarah, sp., Stratford Tony, 1742, AB, I, P2/B/1605
Thos., husb., Froxfield, 1621, I, W, P3/B/183
Wm., Froxfield, 1562, W (NEP), P1/2Reg/114B
Barber als Weller, Wm., sen., Coombe B., 1617, I, W, P5/1616/9, P5/9Reg/184A
Wm., yeo., Ruscombe, Berks., 1663, I, NW, P5/1663/7
Wm., Coombe B., c1670, I, P30/15
Wm., Uppington, Stapleford, 1671, I, W, P2/B/839
Wm., yeo., Coombe B., 1695, AB (in minority of Wm., Sarah & Eliz. B.), I, P8/4
Wm., glover, Wantage, Berks., 1714, I, W, P23/347
Wm., Stratford Tony, 1756, I, W, P2/B/1727
Wm., bach., Boscombe, 1811, AB, Wr, P1/1811/122
Wm., carp. and joiner, Horningsham, 1843, D, W, Wr, P5/1843/8
see also Laurence als B.; Waylett als B.
Barby *see* Burrow als Barby
Barcroft, Jn., clerk, Melk., 1665, AB, I, P2/B/770
Bard, Thos., chapman, Sal., 1613, AB, I, P4/1613/4
Barefoot *see* Barfoot
Barens *see* Baron
Barfield, Alice, Calne, 1604, AB, P5/8Reg/11A
Joan, Calne, 1611, I, P5/1611/3
Rd., Cherhill, 1614, AB, I, T, P5/1613/2, P5/9Reg/131C
Barfoot, Edwd., mason, Lt. Coxwell, Gt. Faringdon, Berks., 1674, AB, I, P5/1674/7
Edwd., Chetnole, Yetm., Dorset, 1813, AB, comm, P19/219
Eliz., wife, Beam., Dorset, 1773, AB, comm, P17/564, P5/17Reg/72B
Jn., yeo., Upton, E. Knoyle, 1687, I, W, P2/B/1085
Barefoot, My., patten maker, Newbury, Berks., 1750, AB, W, P1/B/1244, P1/10Reg/373
Maud, Sonning, Berks., 1575, I, W, P5/1575/3, P5/3Reg/60C
Barefoot, Rd., soap boiler, Chetnole, Yetm., Dorset, 1796, W, P19/198
Barefoot, Roger, Sonning, Berks., 1555, W, P5/20Reg/143
Sam., tallow chandler, Chetnole, Yetm., Dorset, 1783, comm, W, P19/181
Barefoot, Thos., Lt. Coxwell, Gt. Faringdon, Berks., 1591, I, NW, P5/1591/3, P5/5Reg/120A
Thos., jun., husb. and tailor, Sonning, Berks., 1620, I, W, P5/1620/7, P5/10Reg/67B
Barefoot, Thos., patten maker, Newbury, Berks., 1744, I, W, P1/B/1172, P1/9Reg/337
Thos., innholder, Newbury, Berks., 1753, W, P1/B/1266, P1/11Reg/30
Thos., tallow chandler, Chetnole, Yetm., Dorset, 1804, comm, W, P19/207
Wm., Sonning, Berks., 1550, W, P5/20Reg/106A

Barrfoot, Wm., husb., Woodley, W. and Sandford, Berks., 1600, W, P5/6Reg/242B
Wm., gent., Sal. The Close, 1667, I, W, P5/1666/2
Barford, Ann, sp., Sal., 1732, W, P4/1732/3
Frances, widow, Sal., 1729, W, P4/1729/2
Jn., apothecary, Warm., 1704, AB, ren, W, P1/B/712
Rd., clerk and rector, Chilmark, 1769, AB, W, P1/B/1388, P1/12Reg/295A
Bargare, Giles, white baker, S. Bowood, Netherb., Dorset, 1731, I, W, P5/1731/11
Barge, Jos., farmer, Halstock, Dorset, 1767, W, P16/330
Roger, sen., Halstock, Dorset, 1639, comm, I, L, W, P5/1639/7, P5/13Reg/160B
Roger, Halstock, Dorset, 1796, AB, comm, P16/355
Wm., sen., yeo., Halstock, Dorset, 1594, AB, I, W, copy W, P16/468
Bargeman, Jn., sen., weaver, Wantage, Berks., 1694, W, P23/183
Bargent, Jas., sen., gardener, Reading, Berks., 1717, W, P1/B/837, P1/6Reg/91, 154
Bargett, Jn., yeo., Haydon Wick, Rodbourne C., 1711, I (2 - 1 a copy), W, P3/B/1095
Rd., Haydon Wick, Rodbourne C., [1588], W (NEP), P3/1Reg/38B
Thos., husb., Highw., 1589, I, W, P10/1589/2, P5/5Reg/60C
Thos., yeo., Haydon Wick, Rodbourne C., 1633, I, W, P3/B/345
Thos., Haydon Wick, Rodbourne C., 1662, comm, I, W, P1/B/375
Barham, Thos., sen., husb., Sal., 1663, AB, W, P4/1663/13
Barkelman *see* Bartholomew als Johnson
Barker, Barbara, Wokm., Berks., 1687, AB, P5/1687/9
Eliz., widow, Sonning, Berks., 1746, AB, P5/1746/3
Hy., husb., Winterslow, 1691, I, P2/B/1134
Hy., tallow chandler, Westb., 1714, AB, I, ren, P25/1714/4
Hy., innholder, Westb., 1737, W, P25/1737/3
Hy., innholder, Westb., 1766-71, a/c (2), comm, I (very detailed), NW, note, P25/1766/2
Jas., surgeon and apothecary, Highw., 1763, W, P10/1763/1
Jane, widow, Calne, 1665, I, W, P5/1665/7
Jn., sen., tallow chandler, Westb., 1674, I (detailed), W, P25/1674/1
Jn., grocer, Westb., 1685, AB, I (very detailed), P25/1685/2
Jn., [mercer and haberdasher], Westb., 1698, AB, comm, I (very detailed), P25/1698/1
Jn., yeo., Stratfield M., Berks., 1716, W, P1/B/818, P1/6Reg/51
My., sp., Devizes, 1744, W, P1/B/1162, P1/9Reg/273
Rd., Devizes, 1664, AB, comm, I, P1/B/418
Rd., joiner, Devizes, 1703, I, W, P1/B/705, P1/4Reg/250
Robt., gent., Sutton M., 1562, I, P2/B/30
Thos., maltster, Devizes, 1689, I, W, P1/B/596
Thos., tinman, Wokm., Berks., 1692, AB, I (detailed), ren, P5/1692/9
Thos., baker, Devizes, 1726, W, P1/B/929, P1/7Reg/127
Wm., Sonning, Berks., 1742, AB, Wr, P5/1742/5
see also Allen als B.
Barkleman *see* Bartholomew
Barksby, Barkesby, Alice, widow, Chipp., [1604], I, W (2 - 1 a copy) (NEP), P3/B/12
Wm., Lt. Somerford, 1639, AB, P3/B/405
Barksdale, Deborah (form. wife of Robt. Arney, jun.), wife, Highw., 1686, AB, comm, P10/1686/12
Isabel, widow, Keevil, 1559, W, P2/3Reg/172D
Jn., no abode stated, 1561, AB, P2/4Reg/83C
Barsdale, Jn., clothier, Seend Head, Melk., 1606, I, P1/B/59
Jn., yeo., Kilmersdon, Somerset, 1719, I, W, P2/B/1386
Robt., gent., Keevil (bequest of *The Bear*, Reading), 1558, I, W, P2/B/15, P2/3Reg/93C
Thos., clerk and vicar, Britford (leaving effects at Ham), 1608, I (3), NW, P24/155
Thos., yeo., Seend Head, Melk., 1614-16, AB, a/c, I, W, P2/B/343, P2/8Reg/230B
Barkstall, Thos., yeo., Seend Head, Melk., 1698, I, W, P2/B/1197
Wm., Highw., 1694, AB, comm, P10/1694/2
Barkshire, Jn., W. Grimstead, 1559, W, P2/4Reg/9B
Thos., husb., E. Grimstead, W. Dean, 1568, W, P2/5Reg/31A
Wm., W. Grimstead, 1547, W, P2/2Reg/47C
see also Harway/Harraway als B.
Barkstall *see* Barksdale
Barley, Ann, widow, Chilton F., 1749, W, P3/B/1455

Benj., sen., yeo., Baydon, 1686-89, AB, I, P3/B/853, P5/1686/10, P5/1688/12
Cath., widow, Fifield, Enford, 1629, W, P2/B/507
Chris., Burbage, 1721, AB, P11/123
Hy., farmer, Burbage, 1785, W, P5/1785/5, P5/18Reg/12
Jn., Shrewton, 1571, W, P2/5Reg/110B
Jn., Ogbourne St And., 1640, AB, W, P23/1009
Jn., yeo., Chilton F., 1743, W, P3/B/1409
My., sp., Baydon, 1690, I, W, P5/1690/5
Ralph, Enford, 1587, AB, P2/7Reg/90A
Rd., husb. *or* yeo., Fifield, Enford, 1641, I, W, P1/B/294
Rd., Fifield, Enford, 1722, I, W, P2/B/1408
Rd., husb., Burbage, 1798, W, P11/231
Robt., yeo., Pewsey, 1736, W, P3/B/1349
Robt., yeo., Burbage, 1756, W, P11/208
Steph., yeo., Baydon, 1710, AB, I, P5/1710/7
Steph., gent., Wrou., 1742, AB, ren, W, P3/B/1400
Thos., Fifield, Enford, 1589, I, W, P2/B/101
Thos., Mkt. L., 1601, I, W (NEP), P30/26
Thos., Fifield, Enford, 1611, AB, I, NW, P2/B/315, P2/8Reg/158A
see also Barlow *or* B.
Barling, Chris., Burbage, 1690, I, W, P11/74
Eliz., Burbage, 1689, I, W, P11/73
Jn., sen., yeo., Whitep., 1732, W, P1/B/999, P1/7Reg/445
Moses, yeo., Whitep., 1739, W, P2/B/1579
Robt., Burbage, 1675, I, P11/23
Barlow, Agnes, widow, Shrewton, 1575, I, W, P2/B/50, P2/5Reg/242F
Ann, servant, Wokm., Berks., 1829, W, Wr, P5/1829/1
Chas., Heytes., 1710, W, P5/1710/6, P5/15Reg/188
Chas., Sal., 1726, AB, P4/1726/6
Hy., Shrewton, 1602, AB, P2/B/218
Jn., Mkt. L., 1614, I, W, P2/B/344
Jn., Burbage, 1694, comm, I, ren, P11/76
Lawr., clerk and parson, Nettleton, 1637, AB, a/c, I, P1/B/267, P3/B/380
Maud, widow, Mkt. L., 1612, I, W, P2/B/332, P2/8Reg/173C
Rd., yeo., Rams., 1739, W, Wr, P5/1739/4
Barlow *or* Barly, Robt., husb., Fifield, Enford, 1623-24, AB, a/c, I, P2/B/443
Robt., husb., Fifield, Enford, 1685, AB, I, W, P2/B/1056
Roger, innholder, Mkt. L., 1766, W, P2/B/1822
Sarah, widow, Reading, Berks., 1789, W, P1/B/1508, P1/14Reg/220
Thos., Mkt. L., 1661, I, W, P2/B/730
Thos., Netheravon, 1687, AB, I, P12/128
Thos., blacksmith, White Waltham, Berks., 1720, W, P1/B/864, P1/6Reg/302
Wm., blacksmith, White Waltham, Berks., 1686, comm, I, W, P1/B/586
Barn *see* Barnes
Barnaby, Edwd., Amesb., 1686, AB, P2/B/1073
Jn., gent., Chitterne St My., 1620, I, W, P1/B/172
Jn., Amesb., 1802, AB, ren, Wr, P1/1802/1, P1/15Reg/361A
My., widow, Chitterne St My., 1622, AB, a/c, I, P2/B/418, 426
Susanna, sen., widow, Gt. Amesb., 1701, AB, NW, P2/B/1216
Barneby, Wm., husb., Codf. St P., 1601, AB, I, W, P2/B/213
Wm., gent., Amesb., 1638, I, W, P1/B/283
Wm., cordw., Trowb., 1840, O, W, Wr, P1/1840/19
see also Hayward als B.
Barnard, Alice, Sutton B., 1635, I, W, P1/B/258
Ann, widow, Swindon, 1620, I, W, P3/B/184
Ann, widow, Wargrave, Berks., 1625, I, W, P1/B/193
Ann, widow, Stourton, 1665, AB, P2/B/774
Ann, widow, Sutton B., 1669, I, W, P3/B/544
Ann, widow, Sutton B., 1697, I, W, P3/B/958
Ann, widow, Littleton Drew, 1782, AB, P3/B/1678

Anna, widow, Sutton B., 1728, W, P3/B/1262
Barnald, Brice, husb., Swindon, [1605], W (NEP), P3/B/15
Bridget, widow, Chr. M., 1683, W, P3/B/768
Cath., Wokm., Berks., 1682, W, P5/1682/19
Clement, shepherd, Winterbourne Bassett, 1682, AB, I, ren, P3/B/750
Edith, sp., Sherb., Dorset, 1627, I (draft), I, W, P5/1626/5, P5/11Reg/3C
Barnard als Hayward, Edmd., mason, Garsdon, 1614, I, W, P1/B/110
Edwd., Sutton B., 1627, I, W, P3/B/284
Edwd., Littleton Drew, 1701, W, Wr (very fragile), P3/B/1000
Edwd., yeo., Oakley, Tisb., 1719, W, P2/B/1388
Edwd., Marl., 1726, AB, I, P1/B/923
Edwd., sen., weaver, Calne, 1728, AB, comm, I, P26/732
Edwd., yeo., Sutton B., 1783, W, P1/B/1490, P1/14Reg/23
Eliz., widow, Crickl. St S., 1619, I, W, P1/B/156
Eliz., widow, Mere, 1686, I, W, P5/1686/3
Eliz., widow, Leigh Grn, Bradford A., 1714, W, P2/B/1327
Eliz., widow, Charlton, Wantage, Berks., 1836, O, W, Wr, P5/1836/12
Gabriel, Chisbury, Lt. Bedwyn, 1600, I, W, P5/1600/6, P5/6Reg/260
Geo., Chr. M., 1711, AB, I, P3/B/1096
Geo., Burton Hill, Malm., 1760, AB, I, P3/B/1523
Gervase, husb., Sherb., Dorset, 1583, I, T, W, P5/1583/2, P5/4Reg/61B
Hy., husb., Sherb., Dorset, 1602, AB, I, W, P5/1602/5, P5/7Reg/42
Hy., sen., gent., Crickl. St S., 1617, I (detailed), W, P3/B/141
Hy., Goatacre, Hilmarton, 1636, AB, a/c, I, P3/B/366
Hy., yeo., Burton, Mere, 1690, I, W, P5/1690/7
Hy., sen., Goatacre, Hilmarton, 1700, AB, I, P3/B/992
Hugh, Sonning, Berks., 1541, W, P5/20Reg/23A
Humphrey, yeo., Goatacre, Hilmarton, 1681, comm, I, W, P3/B/734
Isaac, yeo., Littlecott, Hilmarton, 1684, I, W, P3/B/784
Jane, widow, Halstock Leigh, Dorset, 1698, I, W, P16/153
Jerome, yeo., Berwick St Jn., 1592, app. of notary public, I, W, P2/B/140
Joan, widow, Leigh, Ashton K., 1617, I, W, P3/B/142
Joan, widow, Sutton B., 1637, I, W, P3/B/381
Joan, widow, Goatacre, Hilmarton, 1661, AB, I, P3/B/466
Joan, widow, Hurst, Berks., 1673, I, W, P5/1673/2
Jn., shoemaker, Marl. St My., 1557, W (NEP), P1/2Reg/156C
Jn., husb., Leigh, Ashton K., 1611, comm, I, W, P3/B/75
Jn., husb., Sutton B., [1614], I, W (NEP), P3/B/111
Jn., Stockwood, Dorset, 1622, AB, I, P5/1622/4, P5/10Reg/141B
Jn., jun., husb., Sutton B., 1633, I, W, P3/B/346
Jn., sen., weaver, Bromham, 1640, I, W, P3/B/431
Jn., Ogbourne St And., 1671, comm, I, W, P5/1671/13
Jn., yeo., Chr. M., 1673, I, W, P3/B/622
Jn., husb., Horningsham, 1675, I, NW, P5/1675/10
Jn., yeo., Halstock Leigh, Dorset, 1676, I, P16/45
Jn., yeo., Hilmarton, 1694, I, W, P3/B/913
Jn., Sutton B., 1703, AB, I, P3/B/1023
Jn., gent., Wilton, 1749, I (very detailed), W, P2/B/1668
Jn., Maidenhead, Berks., 1759, AB, P1/B/1318
Jos., Marl., 1734, AB, P1/B/1033
Mgt., widow, servant to Wm., 5th Baron Digby, Sherb. Lodge, Dorset, 1716, W, P5/1716/10, P5/15Reg/347A
My., sp., Reading, Berks., 1638, I, W, P1/B/271
My., sp., Littleton Drew (form. of Grittleton), 1851, W, Wr, P3/1851/49
Ralph, yeo., Sutton B., 1677, AB, a/c, I, P3/B/676
Ralph, Langley Burrell, 1721, AB, I (2 - 1 a copy), P3/B/1184
Barnard *or* Bernard, Rebecca, sp., Sal., 1670, a/c, I, W, P4/1670/14
Rd., Kingston D., 1558, W, P2/3Reg/138C
Rd., Goatacre, Hilmarton, 1606, W, P1/B/51
Rd., yeo., Burton, Mere, 1684, I, W, P5/1684/5
Rd., Bremhill, 1722, AB, P3/B/1198

Robt., Sonning, Berks., 1539, W, P5/20Reg/5A
Robt., husb., Hurst, Berks., 1610, W, P5/9Reg/29B
Robt., Hullavington, 1624, I, W, P3/B/240
Robt., sen., glazier, Crickl. St S., 1667, I, W, P3/B/518
Robt., glazier, Crickl. St S., 1679, I, W, P3/B/702
Simon, yeo., Hurst, Berks., 1638, I, W, P5/1638/11, P5/13Reg/120B
Susanna *or* Susan, sp., Wokm., Berks., 1682, AB, comm, P5/1682/18
Thos., Garsdon, 1569, W (NEP), P1/1Reg/105C
Thos., clothman, Mere, 1593-94, AB, I, W, P5/1593/12, P5/6Reg/54C
Thos., sen., husb., Sutton B., 1635, I, NW, P3/B/360
Thos., yeo., Stourton, 1681, comm, I, NW, P2/B/990
Thos., Littleton Drew, 1682, AB, comm, I, P3/B/751
Thos., yeo., Staverton, Trowb., 1704, I, W, P2/B/1241
Thos., Staverton, Trowb., 1752, AB, comm, P1/B/1259
Thos., yeo., Sherb., Dorset, 1776, AB, W, P5/1776/2, P5/17Reg/123A
Thos., yeo., Mere, 1705, W, P5/1705/4
Barnarde, Wm., bailiff to the bishop of Sal., Sherb., Dorset, 1583, W, P5/4Reg/57A
Wm., Sal. The Close, 1604, AB, P24/5
Wm., chandler, Sherb., Dorset, 1626, AB, I, P5/1626/4, P5/10Reg/325A
Wm., husb., Hurst, Berks., 1682, I, W, P5/1682/11
Wm., sen., yeo., Mere, 1685, I, W, P5/1685/15
Wm., weaver, Hurst, Berks., 1686, AB, I, ren, P5/1686/11
Wm., yeo., Mere, 1724, W, P5/1724/7, P5/16Reg/100A
Wm., sen., cordw., Sutton V., 1760, W, P2/B/1763
Wm., broad weaver, Frankleigh, Bradford A., 1776, comm, W, P1/B/1429, P1/13Reg/80
Wm., shopkeeper, Wilton, 1808, comm, W, P2/1808/49
Wm., bach., Charlton, Wantage, Berks., 1812, AB, Wr, P5/1812/8
Wm., yeo., Charlton, Wantage, Berks., 1831, comm, W, Wr, P23/958
see also Cole als B.; Fryer als B.; Stratford als B.
Barncott, Barncott, Thos., yeo., Clewer, New Windsor, Berks., 1694, W, P1/B/636
Barneby *see* Barnaby
Barnes, Barns, Adam, Whitep., 1776, AB, P2/B/1937
Agnes, widow, Wexcombe, Grafton, 1608, I, W, P5/1608/5, P5/8Reg/124A
Agnes, W. Kington, 1610, AB, P3/B/55
Alexander, carp., Chipp., 1845, aff, W, Wr, P3/1845/24
Alice, widow, Wexcombe, Grafton, 1575, AB, I, P5/1575/4, P5/3Reg/58A
Alice, Brinkw., 1615, AB, P3/B/118
Alice, widow, Sal., 1619, I, W, P4/1619/1
Alice, widow, Shalbourne, Berks., 1640, I, W, P23/1019
Alice, widow, Gillingham, Dorset, 1704, AB, P27/1/154
Ambrose, apothecary and surgeon, Warm., 1782, W, P2/B/1996
And., Brinkw., 1563, W (value of I given), P1/2Reg/148A
And., Melk., 1669, AB, P2/B/823
And., Devizes, 1677, AB, P1/B/506
Ann, Corsham, 1635?, note of probate, NW, P29/1Reg/132B
Ann, widow, Brinkw., 1667, I, W, P3/B/519
Ann, widow, Idmiston, 1767, W, P1/B/1383, P1/12Reg/266
Ann, Hazeldon, Tisb., 1820, AB, P2/1820/12
Ann, widow, Chirton, 1821, W, Wr, P2/1821/37
Ann, sp., Sal., 1830, W, Wr, P4/1830/9
Anth., sen., chapman, Wick, Bps. C., 1670, comm, I, ren, W, P24/386
Anth., Latton, 1680, AB, P3/B/722
Anth., silk weaver, Devizes Grn, Bps. C., 1680, I, W, P24/416
Benj., innkeeper, Sal., 1836, W, Wr, P4/1836/9
Bridget, widow, Boyton, 1638, W (NEP), P2/B/626
Barns, Chris., labourer, Overton, 1747, W, P1/B/1197, P1/10Reg/40, 64A
Dan., Seend, Melk., 1762, AB, P2/B/1785
Barns, Dan., baker and yeo., Seend, Melk., 1806, W, P2/1806/46
Denise, widow, Wylye, 1715, I, W, P2/B/1343
Dorothy, widow, Stourton, 1727, AB, deed of gift, W, P1/B/939, P1/7Reg/177B

Edgar, yeo., Fovant, 1573, W, P2/5Reg/165A
Edith, widow, Trowb., 1613, I, W, copy I & NW, P22/2/12
Edwd., Southbroom, 1588, W, P5/5Reg/12B
Edwd., Devizes Grn, Bps. C., 1588, I, W, P24/1440
Edwd., Sal., 1672, AB, I, P4/1672/10
Edwd., husb., Urchf., 1696, AB, I, P2/B/1177
Barns, Edwd., yeo., Broad B., Highw., 1734, W, P5/1734/5
Barns, Edwd., yeo., Widhill, Crickl. St S., 1809, W, Wr, P3/1809/43
Eleanor, widow, Lyneham, 1684, AB, I, P3/B/785
Eliz., widow, W. Knoyle, 1703, W, P2/B/1236
Emanuel, yeo., Bowden Hill, Lacock, 1818, AB, comm, W, Wr, P3/1818/8
Barnes als Carter, Frances, widow, Long Wittenham, Berks., 1735, AB, P1/B/1044
Francis, innholder, Chipp., 1635, I, W, P3/B/361
Francis, cordw., Calne, 1725, AB, I, P5/1725/4
Francis, Sal., 1767, AB, P4/1767/4
Gabriel, jun., broad weaver, Chipp., 1692, AB, a/c, comm, I, P3/B/887
Geo., Sunninghill, Berks., 1704, AB, comm, I, P1/B/722
Giles, husb., Poulton, 1617, I, W, P3/B/143
Hannah, Bugley, Warm., 1824, W, Wr, P2/1824/83
Hy., gent., Snelling, Turners Puddle, Dorset, 1619, AB, I, ren, P5/1619/7, P5/9Reg/229B
Hy., yeo., Holnest, Dorset, 1624, AB, I, P5/1624/4, P5/10Reg/234B
Hy., Downton, 1630, AB, I, P2/B/527
Hy., yeo., W. Kington, 1675, I, W, P3/B/643
Hy., sen., Bodenham, Nunton and B., 1683, AB, P2/B/1018
Barns, Israel, widow, Gt. Somerford, 1770, W, P1/B/1392, P1/12Reg/327B
Jacob, yeo., Gt. Somerford, 1825, W, Wr, P3/1825/37
Barn, Jas., freemason, Winsley, Bradford A., 1608, W, P2/8Reg/1B
Jas., yeo., Cowesfield, Whitep., 1688, I, W, P2/B/1102
Jas., shepherd, Winterbourne Bassett, 1709, W, P3/B/1074
Jas., yeo., Cowesfield, Whitep., 1730-34, AB, a/c, I, ren, P2/B/1485
Jane, widow, Fonthill B., 1800, AB, P2/1800/49
Jerome, gent., Madjeston, Gillingham, Dorset, 1698, AB, P27/1/135
Joan, widow, Chipp., 1666, I, W, P3/B/500
Barns, Joan, widow, Gillingham, Dorset, 1689, I, P27/1/111
Jn., Fordington, Dorset, 1567, W, P5/2Reg/15B
Jn., Brook, Bramshaw, Hants, 1584, AB, I (detailed), P24/1442, P5/4Reg/92C
Jn., husb., Blewbury, Berks., 1600, AB, I, P5/1600/5, P5/7Reg/2B
Jn., husb., Deptford, Wylye, 1603, AB, I, W, P2/B/240
Jn., Fordington, Dorset, 1609, I, W, P5/1609/3, P5/8Reg/163B
Jn., husb., Charlton, Downton, 1610-19, bond to pay legacy, I, W, P2/B/306, P2/8Reg/124
Jn., Sal., 1611, AB, P4/1611/2
Jn., husb., Stourpaine, Dorset, 1612, I, W, P24/118
Jn., Southbroom, [1612], I (buried 3 May 1612), P24/113
Jn., innholder, Sal., 1615, W, ?copy W, P4/1615/21
Jn., joiner, Sal., 1639, I, W, P4/1638/10
Barns, Jn., yeo., Wilton, Gt. Bedwyn, 1639, I, W, P21/1/49
Jn., yeo., Teffont M., Dinton, 1669, I, W, P2/B/815
Jn., butcher, Heddington Wick, 1670, comm, I, W, P3/B/562
Jn., yeo., Wylye, 1672, W, P2/B/850
Jn., clerk and vicar, Lacock, 1676, AB, I, P3/B/659
Jn., Shalbourne, 1692, AB, I (detailed), P5/1692/14
Jn., Colthrop, Thatcham, Berks., 1698, AB, I, P1/B/677
Jn., sen., shoemaker, Sal., 1703, AB, ren(2), P4/1703/8
Jn., gent., Marl., 1704, I, W, P1/B/715
Barns als Carter, Jn., yeo., Long Wittenham, Berks., 1711, I, W, P1/B/765, P1/5Reg/165B
Jn., carp., Teffont E., 1717, AB, I, P2/B/1358
Jn., carp., Sal., 1718, AB, I, P4/1718/11
Jn., clothier and drugget maker, Rode, N. Bradley, 1723, W, P1/B/887, P1/6Reg/434
Jn., yeo., Wylye, 1723, W, P2/B/1421
Jn., carp., Dinton, 1729, W, P1/B/974, P1/7Reg/350B

Barns, Jn., tailor, Gt. Bedwyn, 1730, AB, W, P21/8/53
Barns, Jn., sen., yeo., Shalbourne, 1751, W, P23/630
Jn., yeo., Steeple L., 1752, AB, ren, P2/B/1692
Jn., yeo., Seend, Melk., 1755, W, P2/B/1716
Jn., sen., yeo., Gt. Somerford, 1761, W, P3/B/1537
Jn., labourer, Crickl. St S., 1765, W, P3/B/1568
Jn., Froxfield, 1766, AB, P3/B/1576
Jn., sen., carp., Clack, Lyneham, 1767, W, P3/B/1582
Jn., tailor, Codf. St P., 1796, note of AB, W, P2/B/2113
Jn., surgeon, Heytes., 1797, W, P5/1797/5, P5/18Reg/234B
Barns, Jn., gardener, Tisb., 1819, W, Wr, P2/1819/54
Jn., yeo., Dinton, 1820, W, Wr, P2/1820/15
Jn., gent., Dinton, 1822, W, Wr, P2/1822/9
Barns, Jn., yeo., Seend, Melk., 1827, O, W, Wr, P2/1827/53
Jn., carp., Malm., 1832, AB, O, ren, W, Wr, P3/1832/5
Jn., Tisb., 1853, AB, Wr, P2/1853/27
Jn., labourer, Oaksey, 1857, AB, aff, D, O, W, Wr, P3/1857/2
Jonathan, gent., Porton, Idmiston, 1785, W, P2/B/2006
Jonathan, Marston Meysey (& goods in Crickl. St S.), 1839, AB, O, Wr, P3/1839/1
Jos., rector and clerk, E. Ilsley, Berks., 1671, comm, I, W, P1/B/468
Jos., yeo., Damerham, Hants, 1681, I, W, P2/B/967
Barns, Jos., yeo., Moor Down, Buttermere, 1827, W, Wr, P3/1827/23
Jos., grocer, Dilton M., Westb., 1852, O, W, Wr, P25/1852/2
Joyce, widow, Urchf., 1696-97, I, W, P2/B/1183
Mgt., widow, Downton, 1592, AB, I, W, P2/B/129
Mgt., Enmore Grn, Motc., Dorset, 1712, AB, I, P19/99
Martha, widow, Sal., 1834, AB, Wr, P4/1834/5
My., widow, Studley, Calne (but d. at Castle C.), 1634, I, W, P1/B/249
My., widow, Chipp., 1663, I, W, P3/B/486
My., widow, Studley, Bremhill, 1732, W, P3/B/1313
My., widow, Idmiston, 1748, W, P2/B/1663
My., widow, Dinton, 1828, W, Wr, P2/1828/1
Matthew, cordw., Redhill, Pewsham, 1727, W, P3/B/1250
Maud, widow, Halstock, Dorset, 1595, AB, a/c, I, P5/1595/9, P5/6Reg/103C
Mercy, widow, Dauntsey, 1724, AB, I, P3/B/1224
Barns, Michael, butcher, Longbridge D., 1578, I, T, P2/B/63
Michael, mercer, Urchf., 1669-72, bond to pay legacy, I, W, P1/B/485, P2/B/816
Michael *or* Mink, yeo., Fordington, Dorset, 1681, I, W, P15/33
Barns, Miriam, widow, Overton, 1752, W, P3/B/1474
Moses, Broad B., Highw., 1810, AB, P10/1810/1
Barns, Nich., Longbridge D., 1578, AB, P2/5Reg/300B
Nich., yeo., Theale, Tilehurst, Berks., 1622, I, W, P1/B/186
Olivia, sp., Sal., 1844, W, Wr, P1/1844/25
Rebecca, widow, Shitterton, Bere R., Dorset, 1803, note, note of AB, W, Wr, P5/1803/51, P5/19Reg/84
Barn, Rd., Silton, Dorset, 1570, AB, P27/1Reg/21A
Barns, Rd., husb., Brinkw., 1570, W (NEP), P1/1Reg/50B
Rd., Wexcombe, Grafton, 1575, I, T, W, P5/1575/5, P5/3Reg/57E
Rd., yeo., Wylye, 1595-1603, AB, I, note, W, P2/B/164, 242, P2/7Reg/152B
Rd., husb., Wexcombe, Grafton, 1630, I, NW, P21/3/14
Rd., husb., Wexcombe, Grafton, 1638, I, NW, P21/1/35
Rd., Ashley, 1640, AB, I, P3/B/432
Rd., husb., Hawkeridge, Westb., 1641, I, NW, P25/1641/5
Rd., Bourton, Gillingham, Dorset, 1695, I (re Rd. B. & Rebecca, his wife), P27/1/130
Rd., Winterbourne D., 1774, W, P7/168
Robt., Fordington, Dorset, 1588, I, W, P15/191, P5/5Reg/8A
Robt., Tisb., 1630, AB, I, NW, P2/B/522, P2/9Reg/84C
Robt., smith, Devizes St Jn., 1638, I, W, P1/B/287
Robt., clerk and rector, E. Ilsley, Berks., 1701, I, W, P1/B/689, P1/4Reg/112
Robt., gilder, Stourton, 1729, W, P1/B/976, P1/7Reg/358
Robt., Westb., 1736, AB, ren, P25/1736/4

Robt., bach., Kington St M., 1849, AB, O, Wr, P3/1849/6
Roger, yeo., Gurston, Broad C., 1699, AB, I, ren, W, P2/B/1200
Roger, farmer, Broad C., 1750, W, Wr, P1/B/1233, P1/10Reg/305
Roger, shopkeeper, Dinton, 1820, W, Wr, P1/1820/25
Sam., sen., yeo., Hyde, Bere R., Dorset, 1759, W, P5/1759/3
Sarah, widow, Winterbourne D., 1813, W, P7/190
Steph., yeo., Wylye, 1714-26, AB (2), I, W, P2/B/1332
Thos., husb., Hilp., 1559, W, P2/3Reg/183A
Thos., smith, Sonning, Berks., 1594, AB, a/c, I, P5/1594/2
Thos., W. Kington, 1618, a/c, P3/B/157
Thos., Poulton, 1621, AB, a/c, I, ren, P3/B/198
Thos., yeo., Lyneham, 1640, I, W, P3/B/433
Barnes *or* Barrons, Thos., chandler, Mere, 1662, AB, I, P5/1662/10
Thos., yeo., Nettleton, 1674, I, W, P3/B/636
Thos., husb., Hurst, Berks., 1683, AB, I, P5/1683/2
Thos., yeo., Wylye, 1692, AB, I, P1/B/630
Thos., Knighton, Beer Hackett, Dorset, 1710, I, W, P5/1710/8, P5/15Reg/209
Thos., broad weaver, Newnham, Sutton V., 1740, I, W, P2/B/1593
Thos., innholder, Fovant, 1797, W, P2/B/2126
Thos., sen., gent., Chute (form. of Woodhouse, Southampton), 1800, W, P7/183
Thos., gent., Lt. Cheverell, 1814, W, Wr, P2/1814/20
Barns, Thos., Shalbourne, 1822, AB, W, Wr, P23/896
Thos., Widhill, Crickl. St S., 1843, AB, comm, Wr, P3/1843/7
Thos., maltster, Kington St M., 1851, O, W, Wr, P3/1851/13
Vincent, Bodenham, Nunton and B., 1698, AB, I, P2/B/1190
Walter, sen., yeo., Chipp., 1637, I, W, P3/B/382
Walter, clothier, Chipp., 1669, comm, I, W, P3/B/545
Wm., husb., Hilp., 1565, T (grandchildren of the decd: Thos. B., sen. & jun.), W, P2/4Reg/207A
Wm., yeo., Charlton, Downton, 1587, I, W, P2/B/96, P2/7Reg/108B
Wm., Wylye, 1603, AB, I, W, P2/B/241
Wm., husb., W. Kington, 1609, I, W, P3/B/40
Wm., jun., linen draper, Urchf., 1619, I, W, P2/B/397
Barns, Wm., chandler, Urchf., 1624, I, NW, P2/B/450
Wm., yeo., Brinkw., 1638, I, W, P3/B/394
Wm., Chr. M., 1639, I, NW, P3/B/406
Wm., Wilton, Gt. Bedwyn, 1648, comm, I, L (2), W, P21/1/71
Wm., yeo., Fordington, Dorset, 1660, I, W, P15/2
Wm., Beechingstoke, 1661, AB, I, P3/B/467, P3/3Reg/11B
Wm., carp., Winterbourne E., 1661, AB, comm, I, P2/B/732
Wm., chandler, Urchf., 1672, comm, I, W, P2/B/852
Wm., yeo., Ridge, Chilmark, 1682, I, W, P2/B/1008
Wm., yeo., Eddington, Hungerford, Berks., 1696, AB, I, P5/1696/6
Wm., Aldbourne, 1699, AB, I, P3/B/977
Wm., yeo., Dauntsey, 1699, I, W, P3/B/978
Wm., yeo., Wylye, 1707, I, W, P2/B/1264
Wm., yeo., Bowood, 1730, W, P3/B/1280
Wm., gent., Mkt. L., 1760, W, P2/B/1770
Barns, Wm., Chirton, 1773, AB, W, P1/B/1424, P1/13Reg/20B
Wm., broad weaver, N. Bradley, 1773, W, P2/B/1899
Wm., gent., Chirton, 1781, W, P2/B/1987
Wm., shopkeeper, Letcombe Regis, Berks., 1783, comm, W, P1/B/1475, P1/13Reg/411
Barns, Wm., yeo., Chilton F., 1791, W, P3/B/1728
Wm., Lyneham, 1802, AB, comm, P3/1802/75
Wm., yeo., Seend, Melk., 1809, W, Wr, P2/1809/85
Wm., gent., Coombe Farm, Enford, 1811, W, Wr, P2/1811/14
Wm., keeper, Dinton, 1848, W, Wr, P1/1848/15
Wolstan, clothier, Sal., 1680, W, P4/1679/25
see also Waldron als B.
Barnett, Ann, Mildenhall, 1822, AB, Wr, P3/1822/7
Dan., butcher, Dinton, 1753, W, P1/B/1282, P1/11Reg/133B

Edwd., yeo. and dairyman, N. Leaze, Highw., 1696, I, W, P10/1696/1
Edwd., yeo., Croucheston, Bishopstone S., 1776, W, P2/B/1935
Geo., yeo., Brightwalton, Berks., 1759, W, P1/B/1321, P1/11Reg/408
Geo., broker, Sal., 1844, W, Wr, P1/1844/36
Jas., yeo., Marsh Benham, Speen, Berks., 1747, I, W, P1/B/1210, P1/10Reg/113
Jas., sen., cordw., Stourpaine, Dorset, 1857, aff, W, Wr, P24/1423
Jas., dealer, Stapleford, 1857, aff, W, Wr, P2/1857/17
Jn., Tilehurst, Berks., 1720, AB, I, P1/B/850
Jn., butcher, Wylye, 1742, AB, a/c, I (2), ren, W, P2/B/1614
Jn., Seend, Melk., 1815, AB, Wr, P2/1815/37
Margery, widow, Broad C., 1847, W, Wr, P2/1847/25
Sophia, sp., Stapleford, 1846, AB, Wr, P2/1846/14
Thos., sen., Calne, 1666, AB, P3/B/513
Thos., Bishopstone N., 1680, I, P6/51
Thos., Wantage, Berks., 1804, AB, P23/839
Thos., gardener, Calne, 1814, W, P26/1299
Thos., gardener, W. Grafton, 1829, O, W, Wr, P5/1829/7
Thos., yeo., Broad C., 1835, req, W, Wr, P1/1835/10
Thos., gent., Wantage, Berks., 1836, comm, W, P23/989
Wm., husb., Leighs Marsh, Dilton, Westb., 1730, W, P25/1730/18
Wm., Stapleford, 1781, AB, P2/B/1984
Barnfather, Wm., sen., Sal., 1690, AB, P4/1689/17
Barnfield, Jn., sen., husb., Uffc., Devon, 1687, I, W, P20/1/106
Mgt., widow, Uffc., Devon, 1694, I, W, P20/1/126
Barnows, Thos., Wokm., Berks., 1546, W, P5/20Reg/79A
Barns *see* Barnes
Barnshow, Rd., cordw., Highw., 1764, O, W, P10/1764/1
Baron, And., tailor, Bourton, Gillingham, Dorset, 1680, I, W, P27/1/58
Barren, Jane, widow, Pewsey, 1720, W, P1/B/849, P1/6Reg/199
Jane, widow, Sal. St Thos., 1725, AB, P4/1725/5
Jn., Hilp., 1553, AB, P2/2Reg/169D
Barens, Jn., Trowb., 1613, I, W, P22/2/8
Jn., gent., Mere, 1644, I, W, P5/1644/6, P5/14Reg/69A
Jn., Crickl. St S., 1686, AB, I, P2/B/1061
Jn., surgeon, Pewsey, 1690, AB, I, P3/B/862
Mgt., sp., Mere, 1676, comm, I, NW, P5/1675/5
Barens, Wm., maltster, Sal. St Mart., 1618, a/c (very brief), I, P4/1618/22
Wm., sen., gent., Mere, 1684-85, AB, I, P5/1684/4, P5/1685/17
Wm., clerk and rector, Enborne, Berks., 1714, AB, P1/B/807
Wm., gent., Sal., 1758, W, P4/1758/6
Barens, Wm., gardener, Tollard Royal, 1776, W, P2/B/1933
see also Barnes *or* B. (Barrons)
Barr, Ann, servant, Kemble, 1621, I, W, P3/B/199
Jn., husb., Odstone, Ashbury, Berks., 1744, W, P1/B/1170, P1/9Reg/325
Peter, ironmonger, Wantage, Berks., 1692, AB, P23/179
Rd., yeo., Winkfield, Berks., 1631, I, W, P1/B/238
Rd., Grove, Wantage, Berks., 1696, AB, I, P5/1696/7
Robt., yeo., Wantage, Berks., 1571, W, P5/2Reg/100B
Steph., Grove, Wantage, Berks., 1711, I, W, P23/314
Thos., Sonning, Berks., [1603], W, P5/1603/10
Barrs, Thos., husb., Sonning, Berks., [1660], I, P5/1660/2
Thos., wheelwright, Speen, Berks., 1716, I, W, P1/B/831, P1/6Reg/81
Thos., Grove, Wantage, Berks., 1720, AB, I, P23/380
Wm., yeo., Charlton, Wantage, Berks., 1699, I, W, P23/230
Barraker, Wm., White Hill, Mere, 1598, AB, a/c, I, P5/1598/4, P5/6Reg/199A
Barrar *see* Barter
Barratt *see* Barrett
Barrell, Jn., Broad H., 1855, AB, aff, O, Wr, P1/1855/42
Barren *see* Baron
Barrett, Alexander, Donhead St My., 1712, AB, P2/B/1312

Alexander, Donhead St A., 1749, AB, P2/B/1670
Barratt, Alexander, stonemason, Donhead St My., 1845, W, Wr, P2/1845/17
And., Donhead St A., 1628, AB, I, P2/B/492
Barratt, And., mason, Donhead St My., 1772, W, P2/B/1891
Barratt, Ann, widow, Donhead St My., 1807, comm, W, Wr, P2/1807/35
Berrett, Anth., Coate, Bps. C., 1627, AB, I, P24/225
Anth., blacksmith, E. Garston, Berks., 1770, W, P1/B/1396, P1/12Reg/340
Bridget, widow, Langley Burrell, 1622, I, W, P3/B/216
Chas., sen., rough mason, Kellaways, 1745, AB, W, P3/B/1423
Chas., yeo., Swindon, 1802, AB, comm, ren, W, P3/1802/32
Chas., blacksmith, Sevenhampton, Highw., 1805, W, P10/1805/4
Chas., free stonemason, Box, 1814, W, Wr, P1/1814/125
Chas., publican, Fisherton A., 1854, aff, I, W, Wr, P2/1854/48
Cornelius, mason, Donhead St A., 1672, I, W, P2/B/845
Barratt, Deborah, widow, Donhead St My., 1836, W, P2/1836/27
Edmd., Eisey, 1613, comm, I, W, P3/B/99
Edmd., carp., Fovant Stroud, 1683, I, W, P2/B/1019
Barratt, Edwd., husb., Halstock, Dorset, 1674, comm, I, W, P5/1674/9
Edwd., Goatacre, Hilmarton, 1679, AB, court note, P3/B/703
Berrett, Edwd., Allington, All C., 1681, AB, I, P1/B/547
Edwd., gent., Eisey, 1721, AB, comm, I (2 - 1 a copy), P3/B/1185
Edwd., innholder, Marl., 1729, W, P1/B/952, P1/7Reg/286B
Edwd., innholder, Gt. Bedwyn, 1758, W, P21/10/40
Edwd., widower, Tisb., 1843, AB, Wr, P2/1843/20
Elias, Halstock, Dorset, 1603, AB, I, P5/1603/7
Barratt, Eliz., widow, Donhead St My., 1735, AB, P1/B/1059
Eliz., widow, Compton B., 1817, AB, comm, Wr, P3/1817/8
Gabriel, yeo., Donhead St My., 1709, W, P2/B/1285
Berrett, Geo., All C., 1608, AB, P3/B/31
Geo., yeo., Minety, 1665, I, W, P3/B/501
Geo., gent., Calcutt, Crickl. St S., 1725, W, P3/B/1232
Geo., mason, Semley, 1812, comm, W, Wr, P2/1812/59
Barratt, Grace, sp., Donhead St My., 1801, W, Wr, P1/1801/102, P1/15Reg/320
Hy., tailor, Broughton G., 1633, AB, comm, I, L, P2/B/569
Hugh, gent., Tytherton L., Chipp., 1627, W, P3/B/285
Barratt, Hugh, maltster, Donhead St A., 1808, W, P1/1808/59
Barratt, Isaac, Donhead St My., 1777, W, P2/B/1942
Isaac, Donhead St My., 1820, AB, Wr, P2/1820/10
Israel, Kington St M., 1729, AB, P1/B/956
Jas., mason, Kington St M., 1702, I, W, P3/B/1014
Jas., mason, Kington St M., 1784, W, P3/B/1685
Jas., Wingfield, 1829, AB, comm, P2/1829/18
Jane, widow, Bradford A., 1725, AB, I, P2/B/1439
Jane, widow, Sal., 1839, AB, Wr, P1/1839/38
Jerome, weaver, Knights Marsh, Stockley, Calne, 1716, I, W, P5/1716/13, P5/15Reg/348D
Joan, widow, Stanton Fitzwarren, 1622, I, W, P3/B/217
Joan, widow, Halstock, Dorset, 1633, comm, I, W, P5/1633/4, P5/12Reg/152
Joan, widow, Baydon, 1662, comm, I, W, P5/1662/5
Joan, widow, Crickl. St S., 1722, AB, P3/B/1199
Joan, wife, Notton, Lacock, 1732, AB, comm, P1/B/1027
Job, yeo., Moordown Farm, Henley, Buttermere, 1782, W, P3/B/1674
Berrett, Jn., shepherd, Winterbourne M., [1576], W (NEP), P3/1Reg/21B
Jn., yeo., Stratton St Mgt., 1596, AB, W, P29/B/8, P29/1Reg/43
Barratt, Jn., sen., yeo., Ham, [1603], W (NEP), P3/B/13
Jn., yeo., Nettleton, 1603, I, W, P3/B/2
Jn., Gt. Bedwyn, 1606, AB, I, P5/1606/3
Jn., husb., Halstock, Dorset, 1609, AB, I, W, P5/1609/6, P5/8Reg/166
Berrett, Jn., tailor, Chipp., [1619], I, W (NEP), P3/B/173
Jn., sen., husb., Snelsmore, Chieveley, Berks., 1622, I, W, P1/B/184
Berrett, Jn., dyer, Chipp., 1623, I, W, P3/B/230

Jn., husb., Stratton St Mgt., 1636, I, W, P3/B/367
Jn., rector, clerk and minister, Ashley, 1667, AB, agreement, I, P1/B/433
Barratt, Jn., husb., Bagshot, Shalbourne, 1686, AB, I, P23/147
Jn., Donhead St My., 1687, AB, P2/B/1086
Jn., chandler, Lacock, 1688, AB, I, P3/B/839
Jn., glover, Devizes, 1688, I, W, P1/B/594
Jn., Donhead St My., 1706, AB, P2/B/1251
Jn., Donhead St My., 1723, AB, P2/B/1419
Jn., Hungerford, Berks., 1735, AB, P5/1735/4
Jn., baker, Devizes, 1761, W, P1/B/1334, P1/12Reg/4A
Barratt, Jn., innholder, Marl., 1763, W, P1/B/1359, P1/12Reg/95
Jn., Semley, 1787, AB, P2/B/2020
Jn., baker, Devizes, 1806, AB, LA, P1/1806/9
Jn., Devizes, 1813, AB, comm, P3/1813/16
Jn., dealer, Upper Stratton, Stratton St Mgt., 1837, AB, O, W, Wr, P3/1837/13
Barratt, Jn., mason, W. Tisb., 1850, comm, W, Wr, P2/1850/67
Barratt, Jn., Teffont M., 1856, aff, W, Wr, P2/1856/53
Barratt, Jn. Hearn, late an innholder and maltster, but now out of business, Beam., Dorset, 1853, comm, W, Wr, P17/625
Barratt, Jos., More Crichel, Dorset (property at Donhead St My.), 1791, comm, W, P2/B/2069
Berrett, Mgt., widow, Bps. C., 1617, I, W, P24/77
Mgt., Swindon, 1806, AB, comm, Wr, P3/1806/39
Martha, sp., Crickl. St S., 1706, AB, I, P3/B/1052
Martha, widow, Sal. (form. of Gratelv, Hants), 1803, W, P4/1803/2
My., widow, Snelsmore, Chieveley, Berks., 1602, I, W, P1/B/17
My., widow, E. Garston, Berks., 1708, AB, I, P1/B/740
My., sp., Devizes, 1782, W, P1/B/1464, P1/13Reg/351
Barratt, My., sp., Rams., 1828, AB, O, W, Wr, P5/1828/23
Nich., gent. [and shopkeeper], Devizes, 1635, AB, I, P1/B/265
Nich., yeo., Lacock, 1663, I, W, P3/B/487
Nich., sen., yeo., Lacock, 1693, W, P3/B/895
Nich., yeo., Lacock, 1728, W, P3/B/1263
Nich., sen., gent., Notton, Lacock, 1734, I, W, P3/B/1334
Nich., gent., Lacock, 1783, W, P1/B/1487, P1/13Reg/504
Peter, blacksmith, Winterborne K., Dorset, 1851, aff, I, W, Wr, P5/1851/15
Barratt, Rachel, widow, Rams., 1771, W, P5/1771/3, P5/17Reg/30C
Rd., gent., Ford, N. Wraxall, [1602], W (NEP), P3/1Reg/110A
Berrett, Rd., Allington, All C., 1603, I, W, P3/B/5
Rd., saddler, Sal., 1617, AB, I, P4/1617/2
Berrett, Rd., tailor, Chipp., 1649, I, NW, P1/B/346
Rd., Wilton, 1683, AB, I, P2/B/1027
Rd., Alex Farm, Eisey, 1687, AB, I, P3/B/830
Rd., mason, Donhead St A., [1699], W, P2/B/1206
Rd., Berwick St Jn., 1707, AB, P2/B/1270
Barratt, Rd., mason, Sutton M., 1718, I, W, P2/B/1374
Rd., Lambourn, Berks., 1738, AB, P1/B/1094
Rd., carp., Berwick St Jn., 1745, comm, W, P2/B/1645
Rd., yeo., Appleton, Berks., 1795, W, P1/B/1539, P1/14Reg/564
Berrett, Robt., husb., Steeple A., 1688, I, W, P2/B/1099
Robt., sen., husb., All C., 1700, I, W, P3/B/993
Robt., thatcher, Steeple A., 1721, AB, I, P2/B/2145
Robt., yeo., All C., 1743, I, W, P3/B/1411
Berrett, Robt., thatcher, Hilp., 1745, AB, ren, W, P2/B/1644
Robt., cordw., Crickl. St S., 1775, AB, W, P3/B/1635
Robt., lay vicar of Sal. Cathedral, Sal. The Close, 1801, W, P5/1801/1, P5/18Reg/311
Berrett, Robt., thatcher, Steeple A., 1809, W, Wr, P2/1809/10
Roger, husb., Wokm., Berks., 1618-19, I, W, P5/1618/2, P5/9Reg/205
Sarah, widow, Pewsey, 1693, AB, I, P3/B/896
Sarah, Halstock, Dorset, 1798, W, P16/356
Sarah, widow, Melk., 1811, AB, comm, Wr, P1/1811/21
Steph., Sal., 1623, AB, I, W, P4/1623/6

Steph., sen., yeo., All C., 1706, I, W, P3/B/1053
Steph., yeo., All C., 1729, W, P1/B/982, P1/7Reg/368A
Steph., tailor, Swindon, 1856, aff, O, W, Wr, P3/1856/60
Susanna, widow, Donhead St My., 1725, W, P2/B/1443
Susanna, widow, Kington St M., 1787, AB, comm, ren, P3/B/1706
Berrett, Thos., sen., Bps. C., 1603, AB, I, NW, P24/8
Barratt, Thos., husb., Latton, 1612, I, W (2 - 1 a copy), P3/B/85
Thos., slaymaker, Warm., 1625, AB, I, P2/B/456
Thos., Nettleton, 1626, AB, P3/B/273
Thos., husb., Stratton St Mgt., 1639, I, W, P3/B/407
Thos., innholder, Calne, 1668, I, W (NEP), P5/1668/13
Thos., yeo., Hartham, Corsham, 1680, comm, I, W, P3/B/723
Thos., Kington St M., 1694, I, W, P3/B/914
Thos., Bradford A., 1723, AB, comm, P1/B/891
Thos., yeo., Donhead St My., 1727, W, P2/B/1456
Thos., sen., baker, Calne, 1759, AB, ren, W, P26/967
Barratt, Thos., yeo., Donhead St My., 1766, W, P2/B/1830
Barratt, Thos., yeo., Henley Farm, W. Shefford, Berks., 1770, W, P1/B/1397, P1/12Reg/343B
Thos., tailor, Castle C., 1779, W, P3/B/1656
Thos., baker, Crickl. St S., 1784, note, W, Wr (NEP), P3/B/1686
Walter, husb., Moordown Farm, Henley, Buttermere, 1640, I, W, P3/B/434
Walter, yeo., Buttermere, 1709, AB, P3/B/1075
Walter, yeo., Moordown Farm, Henley, Buttermere, 1799, W, P3/B/1765
Wm., Stratton St Mgt., [1605], I, W (NEP), P3/B/16
Wm., jun., tucker, Compton B. & Clack, 1615, AB, I, P3/B/119
Wm., Halstock, Dorset, 1625, comm, W, copy W, P5/1625/2, P5/10Reg/188A
Wm., yeo., Stratton St Mgt., 1679, I, W, P3/B/704
Barratt, Wm., Beam., Dorset, 1697, AB, I, P17/119
Wm., Cherhill, 1725, I, W, P26/693
Wm., joiner, Hungerford, Berks., 1755, W, P5/1755/3
Wm., yeo., Bailey Ridge, Lillington, Dorset, 1804, W, P5/1804/5, P5/19Reg/97B
Wm., Wanb., 1809, AB, Wr, P3/1809/30
Wm., schoolmaster, Swindon, 1824, W, Wr, P3/1824/18
Berrett, Wm., sen., thatcher, Steeple A., 1833-38, AB, comm, court proceeding, O, W, Wr, P2/1833/25, P2/1838/49
Berrett, Wm., thatcher, Steeple A. Common, 1853, comm, W, Wr, P2/1853/19
Barrfoot *see* Barfoot
Barrington, Berington, Cath., widow, Beenham Valence, Berks., 1744, W, P1/B/1178, P1/9Reg/358B
David, labourer, Stanton St Q., 1826, AB, aff (2), W, Wr, P1/1826/61
Joan, Sal., 1619, AB, P4/1618/10
My., widow, Stanton St Q., 1826, AB, W, Wr, P1/1826/62
Barrons *see* Baron
Barrow, Barbara, sp., Charlton, Downton, 1788, AB, ren (covers all 3 sisters Barbara, Cath. & Phyllis B.), P2/B/2033
Cath., sp., Charlton, Downton, 1788, AB, ren, P2/B/2032-33
Humphrey, husb., Long Newnton, 1641, I, W (NEP), P3/B/451
Jas., sen., yeo., Fritham, Bramshaw, Hants, 1715, I, W, P24/670
Jas., yeo., Fritham, Bramshaw, Hants, 1726, W, P24/855
Jane, widow, Rowde, 1721, I (2 - 1 a copy), W, P3/B/1186
Jn., Highway, 1629, I, W, P3/B/300
Jn., yeo., Highway, 1668, I, W, P3/B/531
Jn., yeo., Barford, Downton, 1671, comm, I, W, P2/B/842
Jn., gent. [and innholder], Sal., 1682, I, W, P4/1682/15
Jn., Melk., 1716, AB, comm, P2/B/1347
Jn., Highway, 1719, AB, I, P3/B/1160
Jn., maltster, Rowde, 1720, AB, I (2 - 1 a copy), P3/B/1178
Jos., yeo., Forest Gate, Melk., 1732, I, W, P1/B/1025, P1/7Reg/541
My., widow, Highway, 1685, I, W, P3/B/806
My., widow, Blackland, Calne, 1709, W, P26/550
My., minor, Lacock, 1740, T, P3/B/1383
Phyllis, sp., Charlton, Downton, 1788, AB, ren, P2/B/2031, 2033
Ralph, husb., Steeple L., 1622, AB, I, W, P2/B/422

Robt., husb. *or* yeo., Highway, 1670, I, W, P3/B/563
Thos., Calne, 1625, I, NW, P5/1625/6, P5/10Reg/306B
Thos., sen., husb., Beechingstoke, 1662, AB, I, P1/B/369
Tristram, husb., Bramshaw, Hants, 1668, I, P24/356
Barrow *or* Borrow, Wm., Teffont M., 1628, I, W, P2/B/488
Barrowby, Thos., Wokm., Berks., 1543, court proceedings (libel case), P5/20Reg/42B
Barrs *see* Barr
Barry, Edwd., Bramshaw, Hants, 1562, AB, P5/1Reg/13B
Eliz., sp., Fordingbridge, Hants (leaving effects at Sal.), 1835, W, Wr, P4/1835/3
Eliz., Fisherton A., 1849, AB, aff, Wr, P2/1849/5
Jas., yeo., Fritham, Bramshaw, Hants, 1631, I, W, P24/265
Jn., husb., Redlynch, Downton, 1555, W, P2/1Reg/90A
Jn., Bramshaw, Hants, 1562, AB, P5/1Reg/13C
Jn., jun., Fritham, Bramshaw, Hants, 1597, AB, W, P24/6
Mgt., widow, Sal., 1740, W, P4/1739/16
Rd., clerk and rector, Upton S., 1749, comm, W, P1/B/1229, P1/10Reg/263
Sam., currier, Trowb., 1637, I, W, P22/2/36
Sam., Stratford sub C., 1788, AB, P4/1788/1
Walter, widow, Sal., 1722, AB, P4/1722/13
Wm., husb., Winterbourne S., 1559, W, P2/3Reg/146A
see also Wright form. B.
Barryman *see* Berryman
Barsdale *see* Barksdale
Barsh, Wm., Stratford sub C., 1686, I, W, P4/1686/14
Barsley *see* Basely
Barston, Bastian, Edwd., yeo., Sulhamstead Bannister, Berks., 1692, I, W, P1/B/628
Barston als Rundle, Eliz., widow, Hankerton, 1639, AB, I, P3/B/430
Baston, Geo., rope maker, Marl., 1647, W, P1/B/333
Barston als Rundle, Jn., Hankerton, 1650, AB, comm, I, P1/B/357
Barston als Rundle, Jn., yeo., Latton, 1705, I, W, P3/B/1034
Buston, My., widow, Downton, 1695, W, P2/B/1169
Barston als Rundle, Walter, husb., Hankerton, 1619, comm, I, W, P1/B/153
Barston als Randall, Wm., yeo., Minety, 1672, I, W, P3/B/602
see also Rundell als B.
Bartellme *see* Bartholomew
Barter, Agnes, widow, Fovant, 1564, I, P2/B/43
Agnes, Fovant, 1631, AB, P2/B/523
Alice, widow, Gt. Wishford, 1559, W, P2/3Reg/151D
Edith, sp., Fovant, 1589, AB, I, W, P2/B/110
Edwd., yeo., N. Bradley, 1641, AB, a/c, I, P2/B/671
Edwd., sen., gent., Fiddington, W. Lavington, 1718, comm, W, P1/B/845, P1/6Reg/167A
Edwd., sen., yeo., Hamptworth, Downton, 1813, W, Wr, P2/1813/7
Edwd., yeo., Fovant, 1817, comm, W, P1/1817/18
Bartor, Eliz., widow, Fovant, 1570, W, P2/5Reg/103D
Eliz., widow, Fovant, 1597, W, P2/B/173
Eliz., widow, Fiddington, W. Lavington, 1728, comm, W, P1/B/942, P1/7Reg/184B
Eliz., widow, Hamptworth, Downton, 1764, W, P2/B/1803
Francis, Fovant, 1597, I, T (2), W, P2/B/172
Francis, husb., Fonthill G., 1681, I, W, P2/B/976
Bartar, Geo., husb., Dinton, 1557, W, P2/3Reg/40D
Hy., husb., Fovant, 1600, AB, I, P2/B/205
Hy., husb., Fovant, 1677, I, W, P2/B/921
Hy., Fovant, 1728, AB, P2/B/1468
Hy., yeo., Enford, 1759, W, P2/B/1753
Hy., bricklayer and husb., Hamptworth, Downton, 1761, W, P2/B/1771
Hy., millwright, Sherb., Dorset, 1798, W, P5/1798/3, P5/18Reg/266
Jas., Fovant, 1565, W, P2/4Reg/210A
Jas., Broad C., 1800, AB, P2/1800/78
Jane, widow, Stratford Tony, 1675, I, W, P2/B/892
Barter form. Wadworth, Jane, Sal., 1756, AB, P1/B/1303

Joan, widow, proved at Sal. but no abode stated, 1690, I, W, P2/B/1117
Jn., husb., Fovant, 1585, I, W, P2/B/88, P2/7Reg/19A
Jn., Stratford Tony, 1592, AB, I, P2/B/132
Jn., husb., Compton C., 1605, AB, NW, P2/B/254
Bartar, Jn., sen., yeo., Stratford Tony, 1665, I, W, P2/B/763
Jn., [weaver], Wilton, 1681, I, P2/B/975
Jn., yeo., Stratford Tony, 1693, I, W, P2/B/1149
Jn., architect, Swallowcliffe, 1730, W, P5/1730/6
Jn., Gillingham, Dorset, 1742, W, Wr, P27/1/364, P27/3Reg/21B
Barrar, Jn., vict., Sherb., Dorset, 1787, comm, W, P5/1787/2, P5/18Reg/72A
Jn., Broad C., 1856, aff, D, W, Wr, P2/1856/48
Jos., yeo., Sal., 1755, W, P4/1755/10
Bartar, Julian, widow, Dinton, 1561-62, I, W, P2/B/22, P2/4Reg/94A
Mgt., widow, Fovant, 1589, I, W, P2/B/109
Martha, widow, Chapmanslade, Dilton, Westb., 1844, AB, O, Wr, P25/1844/6
My., widow, Sal. St Mart., 1682, I, W, P4/1682/9
My., sp., Sherb., Dorset, 1839, AB, Wr, P5/1839/9
Rd., Sutton M., 1576, W, P2/5Reg/247A
Rd., yeo., Homington (form. of W. Harnham), 1726, I, W, P24/856
Bartar, Robt., husb., Gt. Wishford, 1553, W, P2/2Reg/172A
Robt., gent., Sutton M., 1563, W, P2/4Reg/120
Robt., Dinton, 1572, AB, P2/5Reg/150C
Robt., innholder, Sal., 1678, I, W, P4/1678/4
Sarah, sp., W. Lavington, 1753, AB, comm, P1/B/1272
Sarah, widow, Holnest, Dorset, 1835, W, Wr, P5/1835/13
Sarah, Whitep., 1857, aff, D, W, Wr, P2/1857/58
Solomon, woolsorter, Sutton V., 1854, aff, O, W, Wr, P2/1854/11
Thos., yeo., Tisb., 1582, W, P2/6Reg/75A
Thos., W. Knoyle, 1610, AB, T (unnamed children), P2/B/303, P2/8Reg/114B
Thos., yeo., Holnest, Dorset, 1823, W, Wr, P5/1823/9
Thos., yeo., Chapmanslade, Dilton, Westb., 1844, AB, O, W, Wr, P25/1844/7
Wm., Stratford Tony, 1596-1601, I, T, W, P2/B/216
Wm., yeo., E. Hatch, Tisb., 1610, W, P2/8Reg/145D
Wm., sen., husb., Throope, Bishopstone S., 1636, I, NW, P2/B/589, P2/9Reg/93A
Wm., blacksmith, Ansty, 1703, AB, I, W, P2/B/1229
Wm., sen., yeo., Stratford Tony, 1713, I, W, P2/B/1322
Wm., yeo., Stratford Tony, 1718, I, W, P2/B/1364
Wm., Corsley, 1729, AB, P1/B/981
Wm., wheelwright, Gillingham, Dorset, 1731, W, P27/1/308
Wm., Sutton V., 1827, AB, I (merely notes a clock & a table), Wr, P2/1827/30
Barterton *see* Batterton
Bartholomew, Bartlemore *or* Bartellme als Check, Alexander, yeo., Sunton, Collingbourne K., 1696, I, W, P3/B/940
Ann, widow, W. Hendred, Berks., 1729, I, W, P1/B/971, P1/7Reg/247B
Edwd., yeo., W. Hendred, Berks., 1759, W, P1/B/1320, P1/11Reg/406
Edwd., clockmaker, Sherb., Dorset, 1767, W, P5/1767/3
Edwd., Streatley, Berks., 1783, AB, P1/B/1481
Edwd., yeo., Aldworth, Berks., 1789, W, P1/B/1511, P1/14Reg/241
Francis, innkeeper, Wantage, Berks., 1809, W, P23/857
Barkelman *or* Bartholomew als Johnson, Hugh, yeo. *or* glazier, Malm., 1672, I, W, P3/B/603
Bartholemew, Isabel, widow, Pangbourne, Berks., 1611, I, W, P1/B/72
Jean, widow, Purton Stoke, 1713, I, W, P3/B/1114
Joan, widow, Boxford, Berks., 1607, I, W, P1/B/61
Joan, widow, Hurst, Berks., 1635, I, T (re Rd. & Edwd. B.), W, P5/1635/12, P5/12Reg/199B
Jn., yeo. *or* husb., Hurst, Berks., 1633, AB, a/c, I, note, NW, P5/1633/5, P5/12Reg/139A
Jn., Purton Stoke, 1687, I, W, P3/B/831
Jn., labourer, Gt. Bedwyn, 1733, W, P5/1733/5
Jn., yeo., E. Ilsley, Berks., 1744, W, P1/B/1168, P1/9Reg/331
Jn., blacksmith, Sherb., Dorset, 1749, AB, deed of gift, Wr, P5/1749/6
Jos., tailor, Rams., 1674, I, W, P5/1674/8
Jos., Sal., 1718, AB, I, P4/1718/17

My., widow, Wantage, Berks., 1802, W, P23/827
Reynold, Blewbury, Berks., 1614, T (child: Joan B.), P1/B/121
Sarah, widow, Sherb., Dorset, 1766, W, P5/1766/3
Thos., Welford, Berks., 1728, AB, I, P1/B/964
Thos., sen., yeo., Thatcham, Berks., 1732, W, P1/B/1013, P1/7Reg/487
Thos., marine, Gt. Bedwyn, 1749, AB, P5/1749/11
Thos., whitesmith, Sherb., Dorset, 1766, AB, W, P5/1766/2
Wm., yeo., Gt. Bedwyn, 1815, W, Wr, P5/1815/16
Wm., Sonning, Berks., 1837, AB, O, Wr, P5/1837/7
see also Clifford als B.; Johnson als B.
Bartle *see* Bartley
Bartlemew, Bartlemore *see* Bartholomew
Bartlett, Agnes, widow, Conock, Chirton, 1615-16, I, NW, P2/B/358, P2/8Reg/295
Alexander, E. Knoyle, 1670, I, W, P2/B/826
Alice, widow, Gt. Cheverell, 1730, W, P2/B/1488
Ambrose, husb., W. Lavington, 1606, I, W, P1/B/43
Ann, widow, Mkt. L., 1619, I, W, P1/B/152
Ann, vict.'s widow, Westb., 1771, AB, ren, W, P25/1771/6
Anth., gent., S. Farm, All C., 1674, AB, a/c, I, W, P3/B/637
Anth., All C., 1720, AB, P1/B/857
Audrey, Lyneham, 1612, AB, P3/B/86
Cath., sp., Sherb., Dorset, 1805, comm, W, P5/1805/5, P5/19Reg/119C
Chris., W. Lavington, 1617, AB, P1/B/143
Bartlett *or* Bartly, Deborah, widow, Gt. Cheverell, 1686, I, W, P1/B/1569
Dorothy, widow, Lyneham, 1612, AB, I, W, P3/B/87
Edith, Ludg., 1635, I, W, P1/B/254
Edwd., gent., Fittleton, 1643, I, W, P1/B/306
Eliz., widow, Clack, Lyneham, 1647, AB, P1/B/337
Eliz., Fordington, Dorset, 1739, W, P15/126
Eliz., widow, Gt. Cheverell, 1756, AB, P1/B/1307
Bartlett lately called Dyke, Eliz., Netheravon, 1768, AB, O, P12/190
Eliz., sp., Sal., 1848, AB, Wr, P1/1848/16
Emma, widow of Wm., late vicar of Yetminster, Enmore Grn, Motc., Dorset, 1670, I, W, P19/21
Esther, sp., Donhead St My., 1768, W, P2/B/1847
Francis, widow, Stockwood, Dorset, 1633, AB, I, P5/1632/5, P5/12Reg/83
Gabriel, presser, Devizes, 1773, comm (endorsed with affirmation taken in place of O by an ex.), W, P1/B/1413, P1/12Reg/453
Geo., Donhead St My., 1748, AB, W, P2/B/1665
Geo., yeo., Steeple A., 1846, W, Wr, P2/1846/67
Hy., yeo., Tockenham, Lyneham, 1608, I, W, P3/B/29
Hy., Leigh, Yetm., Dorset, 1740, AB, comm, ren, P19/130
Hy., Bere R., Dorset, 1816, W, Wr, P5/1816/12
Hester, sp., Mkt. L., 1833, W, Wr, P2/1833/77
Hugh, Bromham, [1602], W (NEP), P3/1Reg/111A
Hugh, husb., Hinton, Steeple A., 1669, AB, comm, I, P2/B/820
Hugh, Seend, Melk., 1709, AB, P2/B/1283
Isaac, Warm., 1714, AB, P2/B/1331
Jas., official named in document endorsed 'of Trowb., *also* of Bedwyn & Collingbourne '; abode of decd not stated, 1615, I, P1/B/125
Jas., sen., yeo., Semington, Steeple A., 1703, I, W, P2/B/1232
Jas., sen., gardener, Chalford, Westb., 1705, I, W, P25/1705/5
Jas., yeo., Gt. Cheverell, 1752, comm, W, P2/B/1697
Jas., yeo., Crockerton, Longbridge D., 1793, W, P2/B/2085
Jas., Hinton, Steeple A., 1815, AB, comm, ren, Wr, P2/1815/22
Jas., yeo., Hinton, Steeple A., 1821, W, Wr, P2/1821/44
Jas., farmer, Keevil, 1823, W, Wr, P2/1823/6
Jas., sen., yeo., Littleton P., 1828, O, req, W, Wr, P1/1828/15
Jas., yeo., Steeple A., 1857, aff, W, Wr, P2/1857/48
Jn., servant to Wm. Hussey, esquire, Ebbesborne Wake, 1563, W, P5/1Reg/17C
Jn., Longbridge D., 1579, W, P2/B/77, P2/5Reg/348A

Bartlett als Hancock, Jn., carp., Long Burton, Dorset, 1589, I, W, P5/1589/3, P5/5Reg/56B
Bartlett als Warr, Jn., sen., Enmore Grn, Motc., Dorset, 1593, I, W, P5/1593/11, P5/6Reg/24B
Jn., surgeon, Crockerton, Longbridge D., 1611, I, W, P2/B/319
Jn., yeo., Stockwood, Dorset, 1616, I, W, P5/1616/5
Jn., Enmore Grn, Motc., Dorset, 1628, AB, I, P5/1628/11
Jn., Yetm., Dorset, 1628, AB, P5/11Reg/62C
Jn., vict., Sherb., Dorset, 1640, I, W, P5/1640/4, P5/13Reg/235A
Jn., carp., Crofton, Gt. Bedwyn, 1695, AB, I, W, P21/5/31
Jn., Over C., Dorset, 1700, AB, comm, P5/1700/52
Jn., Pott. Park, 1721, AB, P1/B/874
Jn., Corsley, 1728, AB, P2/B/1461
Jn., yeo., Damerham, Hants, 1729, W, P1/B/949, P1/7Reg/225B
Jn., gardener, Devizes, 1731, AB, I, ren, P1/B/994
Jn., Heytes., 1731, AB, P5/1731/14
Jn., yeo., Gt. Cheverell, 1736-56, AB, I, W (2 - 2nd probate after widow's remarriage), P2/B/1552, 1728
Jn., yeo., Keevil, 1737, W, P2/B/1554
Jn., yeo., Haydon, Dorset, 1743, W, Wr, P5/1743/5
Jn., yeo., Alton P., Dorset, 1749, W, P5/1749/7
Jn., shepherd, S. Moreton, Berks., 1753, W, P1/B/1263, P1/11Reg/1A
Jn., schoolmaster, Sherb., Dorset, 1757, AB, ren, P5/1757/2
Jonas, linen draper, Broad B., Highw., 1834, W, Wr, P10/1834/2
Jonathan, sen., gent., Butterwick aka Boyes Hill, Haydon, Dorset, 1703, comm, I, L, W, P5/1703/3
Jonathan, yeo., Haydon, Dorset, 1712, AB, NW, P5/1712/6, P5/15Reg/294
Jos., Fordington, Dorset, 1726, AB, W, P15/109
Joshua, Whitep., 1732, W, P1/B/996, P1/7Reg/443A
Mgt., Charl. nr. P., 1555, W, P2/1Reg/99A
Bartlett als Warr, My., sp., Netherb., Dorset, 1633, AB, I, P5/1633/9, P5/12Reg/159A
My., widow, Seend, Melk., 1737, AB, P2/B/1560
My., sp., Haydon, Dorset, 1739, W, Wr, P5/1739/5
My., widow, Tinh., Edington, 1745, W, P2/B/1638
My., widow, Keevil, 1839, comm, W, Wr, P2/1839/11
Maud, widow, Maiden B., 1571, T (child: Ann B.), W, P2/B/49, P2/5Reg/129B
Michael, Calne, 1712, AB, NW, P26/577
Rd., shoemaker, Sherb., Dorset, 1574, W, P5/1573/1, P5/3Reg/31D
Bartlett als Abbutt, Rd., Sherb., Dorset, 1609, I, P5/1609/8
Rd., Fordington, Dorset, 1679, I, P15/29
Robt., Fordington, Dorset, 1579, AB, I, W, P5/1579/8, P5/3Reg/124B
Robt., husb., Chetnole, Yetm., Dorset, 1593, AB, I, W, P5/1592/4, P5/6Reg/17B
Robt., Whitecliff, Brixton D., 1634, AB, NW, P2/B/580
Robt., Fordington, Dorset, 1661, AB, I, P15/5
Robt., yeo., All C., 1691, AB, comm, I, P3/B/878
Robt., All C., 1694, comm, I, W, P3/B/915
Robt., yeo., Steeple A., 1782, W, P2/B/1994
Roger, Leigh, Yetm., Dorset, 1700, I, W, P19/84
Roger, sen., yeo., Holnest, Dorset, 1736, W, P5/1736/2
Roger, yeo., Keevil, 1857, aff, O, W, Wr, P2/1857/39
Steph., yeo., Whistley, Pott., 1813, W, Wr, P1/1813/10
Thos., tanner, Mere, 1561, W, P5/1Reg/1B
Thos., jun., potter, Crockerton, Longbridge D., 1580, W, P2/6Reg/13C
Thos., carp., Crofton, Gt. Bedwyn, 1670, I, W, P21/2/5
Thos., yeo., Alton P., Dorset, 1725, comm, W, P5/1725/7, P5/16Reg/126B
Thos., sen., Chetnole, Yetm., Dorset, 1752, AB, P5/1752/2
Thos., scribbler, Westb. L., 1755, AB, a/c, I (detailed), P25/1755/3
Thos., brazier, Marl. St Peter and St Paul, 1756, W, P1/B/1305, P1/11Reg/323
Thos., Enmore Grn, Motc., Dorset, 1756, AB, P19/155
Tristram, Mkt. L., 1628, AB, a/c, I, proclamation, P1/B/214
Bartlett als Curme, Virtue, sp., Holnest, Dorset, 1598, AB, I, W, P5/1597/5, P5/6Reg/197A
Wm., day labourer, Chetnole, Yetm., Dorset, 1594, AB (2), I, W, P5/1594/5, 10, P5/6Reg/72B, 88B
Wm., gent., All C., 1623, I (detailed), W, P3/B/226
Wm., servant, Dinton, 1624, I, NW, P2/B/446

Backlett, Wm., Devizes, 1633, AB, I (part missing), P1/B/242
Wm., sen., yeo., Hilp., 1645, comm, W, P2/B/695
Wm., tailor, Devizes, 1662, AB, comm, I, P1/B/382
Wm., yeo., Sonning, Berks., 1663, I, W, P5/1663/8
Wm., clerk [vicar of Yetminster], Enmore Grn, Motc., Dorset, 1665, I, W (leaves books & manuscripts worth Ł50), P19/2
Wm., Corsley, 1681, AB, I, P2/B/977
Wm., weaver, Over C., Dorset, 1688, AB, I, W, P5/1688/6, P5/1689/1
Wm., yeo., Kemble Wick, 1696, I, W, P3/B/941
Bertlett, Wm., yeo., Gt. Cheverell, 1701, AB, W, P2/B/1217
Wm., yeo., Fordington, Dorset, 1727, W, P15/112
Wm., Gt. Cheverell, 1733, AB, I, P2/B/1528
Wm., butcher, Fordington, Dorset, 1742, W, P15/133
Wm., yeo., Nether C., Dorset, 1770, W, P5/1770/4, P5/17Reg/15C
Wm., W. Lavington, 1779, W, P1/B/1454, P1/13Reg/230B
Wm., Keevil, 1793, AB, comm, P2/B/2089
Wm., Beam., Dorset, 1818, AB, comm, Wr, P5/1818/4
Wm., yeo., S. Marston, 1837, O, W, Wr, P10/1837/2
Wm., widower, Sal., 1855, AB, D, Wr, P4/1855/5
see also Martin als B.
Bartley, Eliz., sp., N. Bradley, 1731, AB, P2/B/1496
Henrietta Maria, widow, Tilsh., 1820, W, Wr, P2/1820/39
Hugh, [weaver], Gt. Cheverell, 1614, AB, a/c, I, P1/B/109
Hugh, Gt. Cheverell, 1674, AB, I, P2/B/881
Jas., clothw., Trowb., 1715, AB, I, P2/B/1337
Jane, sp., N. Bradley, 1731, AB, P2/B/1497
Joan, widow, Gt. Cheverell, 1631, I, W, P2/B/546
Bartley als Taber, Jn., Gt. Cheverell, 1558, W, P2/3Reg/101B
Jn., carp., Calne, 1569, W, P5/2Reg/56A
Jn., husb., Gt. Cheverell, 1636, I, W, P2/B/603
Jn., yeo., Teffont M., 1693, I, W, P2/B/1153
Bartle, Jn., farmer, Chitterne St My., 1730, W, P2/B/1487
Bartle, Martha, widow, Tinh., Edington, 1791, W, P2/B/2057
Maud, Gt. Cheverell, 1599, I, W, P2/B/198
Melior, widow, Gt. Cheverell, 1616, I, T, W (2 versions), P1/B/141
Robt., Baynton, Edington, 1686, AB, comm, P2/B/1072
Bartle, Robt., yeo., Tinh., Edington, 1719, I, W, P2/B/1385
Bartle, Robt., yeo., Baynton, Edington, 1731, W, P2/B/1500
Sam., yeo., Bishopstrow, [1718], NW, P2/B/1368
Bartley als Taber, Steph., Gt. Cheverell, 1553, W, note (about searching for will, probably by Francis Roberts, registrar, c1630), P2/2Reg/179D
Steph., no abode stated, 1638, I, W, P2/B/631
Thos., husb., Gt. Cheverell, 1569, W, P2/5Reg/76B
Thos., husb., Edington, 1686, AB, I, P2/B/1065
Thos., sen., shopkeeper and tallow chandler, Southwick, N. Bradley, 1718, I, W, P2/B/1370
Wm., Gt. Cheverell, 1559, W, P2/3Reg/175C
Bartley als Taber, Wm., Gt. Cheverell, 1567, W, P2/5Reg/18C
Wm., Upton L., 1601, AB, I, note, P2/B/206
Wm., Leigh Delamere, 1708, AB, I, W, P3/B/1069
Bartle, Wm., Tinh., Edington, 1718, AB, I, P2/B/1376
Bartle, Wm., gent., Tinh., Edington, 1772, W, P2/B/1885
see also Bartlett *or* B.
Barton, Benj., shopkeeper, Lacock, 1817, W, Wr, P1/1817/46
Betty, widow, described as late of Turleigh, Bradford A., but not clear whether decd was living at Turleigh *or* Corsham at death, 1808, W, Wr, P2/1808/11
Chas., weaver, Bradford A., 1818, W, Wr, P2/1818/23
Chas., baker, Monk's, Corsham, 1848, AB, comm, ren, W, Wr, P3/1848/25
Barton *or* Burton, Dorothy, Donhead St My., 1648, I, W, P2/B/725
Edith, widow, Haxton, Fittleton, 1576, I, W, P2/B/56, P2/5Reg/273C
Edwd., Fittleton, 1548, W, P2/2Reg/70
Edwd., Haxton, Fittleton, 1575, W, P2/5Reg/231B

Edwd., shopkeeper, Bewley, Lacock, 1781, W, P3/B/1669
Edwd., Corsham, 1819, AB, comm, W, Wr, P3/1819/39
Eleanor, widow, Bradford A., 1616, AB, I, NW, P1/B/140
Eleanor, widow and baker, Lacock, 1784, W, P3/B/1687
Eliz., widow, Westb. L., 1738, W, P25/1738/5
Eliz., widow, Upton L., 1742, AB, W, P2/B/1608
Eliz., widow, Corsley, 1848, D, O, W, Wr, P2/1848/25
Geo., husb., Sherb., Dorset, 1608, I (3), P5/1608/7
Hy., All C., 1605, W, P3/B/17
Hester, sp., Atworth, Bradford A., 1832, O, W, Wr, P2/1832/11
Isaac, maltster, Goblins Pit, Corsham, 1782, W, P29/B/54, P29/2Reg/167
Jas., Widbrook, Bradford A., 1570, W, P2/5Reg/81C
[Jn.], Bradford A., 1605, I (fragment - information taken from Wr), P2/B/256
Jn., cordw., Devizes, 1617, I, NW, P1/B/145
Jn., husb., Widbrook, Bradford A., 1629, I, W, P2/B/502
Jn., mercer, Warm., 1717, AB, ren, NW, P2/B/1359
Jn., cordw., Newbury, Berks., [1725-26], W, P1/B/910, P1/7Reg/111
Jn., broad weaver, Cocklebury, Langley Burrell, 1811, comm, W, Wr, P3/1811/2
Jn., baker and maltster, Atworth, Bradford A., 1828, O, W, Wr, P2/1828/44
Martha, widow, Newbury, Berks., 1723, W, P1/B/901, P1/7Reg/16A
My., widow, Widbrook, Bradford A., 1643, I, W, P2/B/682
My., widow, Brook, Westb., 1735, W, P25/1735/4
My., Easterton, Mkt. L., 1794, W, P2/B/2095
Michael, priest, Foxley, 1561, institution to rectory, P1/1Reg/77D
Nathaniel, cordw., Newbury, Berks., 1735, W, P1/B/1049, P1/8Reg/27
Robt., tailor, Chipp., 1620, I, W, P3/B/185
Robt., Pott., 1693, AB, I, P1/B/635
Robt., sen., tobacconist, Wokm., Berks., 1742, W, Wr, P5/1742/7
Robt., Trowb., 1851, D (2), O, W, Wr, P1/1851/4
Wm., Pott., 1593, AB, I, W, P1/B/6
Wm., husb., Haxton, Fittleton, 1611, W, P2/B/2159, P2/8Reg/159D
Wm., yeo., Lt. Coxwell, Gt. Faringdon, Berks., 1639, I, W, P5/1639/11
Wm., Pott., 1646, comm, I, W, P1/B/328
Wm., sen., yeo., Haxton, Fittleton, 1678, I, W, P2/B/937
Wm., broad weaver, Pott., 1680, I, W, P1/B/529
Wm., yeo., Lt. Coxwell, Gt. Faringdon, Berks., 1688, AB, I, W, P5/1688/10
Wm., Upton S., 1769, AB, P2/B/1858
Wm. Kington, Chipp., 1801, AB, ren, P1/1801/83
see also Brown als B.; Gauntlet form. B.; Giddings als B.
Bartor *see* Barter
Bartram, Chas., tailor, Netherb., Dorset, 1725, W, Wr, P5/1725/10, P5/16Reg/113B
Faith, Netherb., Dorset, 1638, I, NW, P5/1638/4, P5/13Reg/78C
Joan, widow, Netherb., Dorset, 1636, I, W, P17/31
Jn., smith, Fonthill B., 1558, W, P2/3Reg/82B
Jn., miller, Bere R., Dorset, 1621, AB, I, W, P5/1621/3, P5/10Reg/18
Steph., Tisb., 1572, W, P2/5Reg/159A
Thos., miller, Broad C., 1628, I, W, P2/B/495
Thos., Netherb., Dorset, 1664, AB, I, P17/77
Thos., tailor, Netherb., Dorset, 1709, W, P17/187
Wm., Netherb., Dorset, 1641, AB, I, P17/51
Barwell, Ann, widow, Coulston, Edington, 1833, W, Wr, P2/1833/65
Barwis, Wm., bach. of physic [physician], Devizes, 1792, AB, comm, P1/B/1519
Bascombe, Cath., widow, Fordington, Dorset, 1675, I, P15/23
Chas., widower, Bere R., Dorset, 1844, D, O, W, Wr, P5/1844/18
Francis, sen., miller, Dodding, Bere R., Dorset, 1705, I, W, P5/1705/5
Jas., Bere R., Dorset, 1773, AB, comm, P5/1773/5, P5/17Reg/51A
Jn., miller, Bere R., Dorset, 1713, I, W, P5/1713/16, P5/15Reg/379A
Jn., Bere R., Dorset, 1767, AB, P5/1767/9
Jn., yeo., Bere R., Dorset, 1809, W, Wr, P5/1809/3
Marian, widow, Fordington, Dorset, 1592, I, W, P5/1592/11, P5/5Reg/143D

Wm., Shitterton, Bere R., Dorset, 1621, I, W, P5/1620/10
Base, Nich., husb., Orcheston St Geo., 1560, W, P2/4Reg/38A
Wm., Orcheston St Geo., 1548, AB, value of I given, P2/2Reg/61A
Baseing *see* Basing
Basely, Bessley, Agnes, widow, Ashbury, Berks., 1614, W, P1/B/115
Bosley, Ann, widow, Charnham St., Hungerford, Berks., 1717, W, P23/358
Besly, Ann, widow, Stratton St Mgt., 1770, W, P1/B/1405, P1/12Reg/382A
Bazely, Benj., sen., butcher, Lyme R., Dorset, 1758, AB, O, W, P16/320
Beasely, Charlotte, minor, Aldbourne, 1826, O, T, P1/1826/138
Besley, Edmd., labourer, Blewbury, Berks., 1635, W, P5/12Reg/234
Bazely, Edwd., yeo., Besselsleigh, Berks., 1638, I, W, P1/B/272
Edwd., gent., Fonthill G., 1680, AB, P1/B/532
Bizley, Edwd., carp., Brocale Terrace, Swindon, 1836, W, Wr, P3/1836/21
Jas., Lyme R., Dorset, 1667, AB, P16/8
Beezley, Jas., bach., Marl. St Peter and St Paul, 1798, AB, P1/B/1548, P1/15Reg/168A
Joan, Lyme R., Dorset, 1667, AB, P16/9
Bosely, Joanna, widow, Theale, Tilehurst, Berks., 1759, W, P1/B/1316, P1/11Reg/385
Basley, Jn., Shrewton, 1581, AB, P2/6Reg/48C
Bazely, Jn., Lyme R., Dorset, 1641-42, I (2), P30/27
Bazely, Jn., carp., Lyme R., Dorset, 1680, I, W, P16/57
Bazely, Jn., ship's carp., Lyme R., Dorset, 1712, I, W, P16/192
Besley, Jn., yeo., Braydon, Crickl., Purton, 1725, I, W, P3/B/1239
Bazely, Jn., mariner and bach. (late of *The Mermaid* man of war), Lyme R., Dorset, 1746, AB, P5/1746/6
Beezley, Jn., yeo., Stratton St Mgt., 1763, AB, ren, W, P1/B/1360, P1/12Reg/96B
Bosley, Jos., E. Hagbourne, Berks., 1783, AB, P1/B/1484
Beasely, Martha, Tisb., 1709-12, AB (2), P2/B/1284, 1306
Beessly, My., widow, Upton, Blewbury, Berks., 1640, I, W, P5/1640/3, P5/13Reg/236B
Bosley als Mascall, My., wife, Bucklebury, Berks., 1708, AB, comm, P1/B/737
Beasely, My., widow, Besselsleigh, Berks., 1741, AB, P1/B/1133
Bosley, Rachel, yeo.'s wife, Hurst, Berks., 1832, AB, O, Wr, P5/1832/5
Barsley, Rd., yeo., E. Knoyle, 1550, W, P2/2Reg/121C
Bestly, Rd., blacksmith, Westbrook, Gt. Faringdon, Berks., 1639, I, NW, P5/1639/12
Bestley, Robt., sen., widow, Stratton St Mgt., 1638, AB, I, P1/B/285
Bestly, Thos., husb., Upper Stratton, Stratton St Mgt., 1629, I, W, P3/B/308
Besly, Thos., jun., husb., Over Stratton, Stratton St Mgt., 1682-83, AB, I, W, P29/B/26, P29/1Reg/215
Bestly, Thos., sen., weaver, Westbrook, Gt. Faringdon, Berks., 1695, I, W, P5/1695/6
Bestly, Thos., weaver, Gt. Faringdon, Berks., 1719, AB, I, P5/1719/7
Besley, Valentine, husb., Upper Stratton, Stratton St Mgt., 1629, I, W, P3/B/310
Bosely, Walter, carp., Charnham St., Hungerford, Berks., 1697, I, W, P23/221
Basely, Wm., E. Knoyle, 1559, AB, P2/3Reg/183B
Bestley, Wm., Westbrook, Gt. Faringdon, Berks., 1641, AB, I, P5/1641/5, P5/14Reg/3B
Besly, Wm., husb. *or* labourer, Over Stratton, Stratton St Mgt., 1695, AB, I, P29/B/32
Besley, Wm., Stratton St Mgt., 1830, W, Wr, P3/1830/26
see also Tripe als B.
Basford, Jas., Boxford, Berks., 1720, AB, comm, I, P1/B/846
Sarah, widow, Boxford, Berks., 1756, W, P1/B/1300, P1/11Reg/233B
see also Bastard *or* B.
Basing, Alice, widow, Shalbourne, 1635, AB, P5/1635/7, P5/12Reg/240A
Jane, widow, Curridge, Chieveley, Berks., 1814, note, W, Wr, P1/1814/90
Baseing, Joan, widow, Boxford, Berks., 1635, AB, I, P1/B/264
Basing *or* Bazing, Jn., yeo., Bagshot, Shalbourne, 1683, I, W, P23/121
Jn., yeo., Chieveley, Berks., 1723, comm, W, P1/B/877, P1/6Reg/415
Jn., yeo., Curridge, Chieveley, Berks., 1779, req, copy W, P1/B/1452, P1/13Reg/264
Jn., Newbury, Berks., 1814, AB, P1/1814/89
Jn., Newbury, Berks., 1832, AB, O, Wr, P1/1832/44
Jos., sen., yeo., Boxford, Berks., 1711, I, W, P1/B/771, P1/5Reg/197
Jos., Faircross, Hampstead N., Berks., 1823, AB, comm, Wr, P1/1823/133
Baseing, Robt., W. Woodhay, Berks., 1683, AB, I, P1/B/561
Baseing, Sarah, widow, Bagshot, Shalbourne, 1711, I, W, P23/322
Wm., husb., Rams., 1716, AB, I, P5/1716/3

Bazing, Wm., yeo., Easthampstead, Berks., 1763, W, P1/B/1352, P1/12Reg/70A
Wm., Boxford, Berks., 1763, AB, P1/B/1356
Baskerville, Baskerville als Antram, Alice, wife, Sal., 1708, AB, P1/B/746
Ann, widow, Woolley, Bradford A., 1787, W, P2/B/2025
Christian, Berwick B., 1767, W, P5/1767/4
Ezekiel, gent., Burton Hill, Malm., 1756, W, P3/B/1501
Francis, gent., Lt. Somerford, 1725, comm, I, W, P3/B/1233
Francis, clothier, Malm., 1731, W, P3/B/1302
Geo., sen., gent., Winterbourne Bassett, 1755, W, P3/B/1496
Hannah, widow, Sal., 1790, AB, W, P4/1790/1
Jane, widow, Sal., 1772, AB, P4/1772/7
Jn., yeo. *or* gent., Malm., 1682, AB, comm, I, P3/B/752
Jn., Burton Hill, Malm., 1732, W, P3/B/1314
Judith, widow, Pewsey, 1714, I, W, P1/B/786, P1/5Reg/317
Mgt., widow, Marl., 1696, comm, W, P1/B/657
My., sp. and gentlewoman, Broad H., 1679, I, W, P3/B/705
My., widow, Richardson, Winterbourne Bassett, 1725, W, P3/B/1234
Rd., gent., Berwick B., 1739, req, W, P26/812
Sam., yeo., Malm., 1717, I, W, P3/B/1141
Thos., jun., gent., Richardson, Winterbourne Bassett, 1695, AB, W, Wr, P3/B/942
Thos., Sal., 1726, AB, P1/B/930
Thos., gent., Woodside, Lymington, Hants, 1782, W, P4/1782/9
Wm., gent., Berwick B., 1768, AB, D, W, P26/1026
Baskett, Hussey, sp., Sal., 1672, W, P4/1672/11
Jn., Bere R., Dorset, 1574, AB, I, P5/1574/3, P5/3Reg/33A
Thos., clerk, Bere R., Dorset, 1665, AB, comm, I, P5/1665/8
Basley *see* Basely
Basnett, Nathaniel, Wokm., Berks., 1728, AB, P5/1728/5, P5/16Reg/200B
Bason, Ann, widow, Winterborne K., Dorset, 1720, AB, I, P5/1720/9
Eleanor, widow, Winterborne K., Dorset, 1670, AB, I, P5/1670/3
Jn., Winterborne K., Dorset, 1679, AB, I, W, P5/1679/4
Jn., yeo., Winterborne K., Dorset, 1747, W, P5/1747/3
Thos., Winterborne K., Dorset, 1692, AB, I, P5/1692/6
Bass, Baiss, Eliz., widow, W. Lavington, 1744, AB, P1/B/1185
Baiss, Jas., Sal., 1812, AB, D, ren, P4/1812/5
Baiss, Jane, widow, Fonthill G., 1816, W, Wr, P2/1816/38
Jeremiah, innholder, E. Harnham, Britford, 1775, W, P24/1139
Basse, Joan, widow, Idmiston, 1556, W, P2/1Reg/101A
Basse, Jn., Winterslow, 1555, W, P2/1Reg/104
Baiss, Jn., sen., blacksmith, Fonthill G., 1767, W, P1/B/1381, P1/12Reg/257
Baiss, Jn., Fonthill B., 1808, AB, Wr, P1/1808/45
Michael, Idmiston, 1550, W, P2/2Reg/98A
Nanny, widow, E. Harnham, Britford, 1784, W, P24/1179
Baiss, Rachel, widow, Fonthill B., 1772, AB, W, P2/B/1881
Rd., Hamptworth, Downton, 1573, W, P2/5Reg/166D
Bays, Thos., husb., Ogbourne St Geo., 1625, AB, I (2), P2/B/459
Baiss, Thos., Fonthill B., 1808, comm, W, Wr, P2/1808/18
Bays, Thos., bricklayer, Sal., 1855, AB, aff, ren, W, Wr, P1/1855/7
Vincent, husb., Plaitford, 1582, W, P2/6Reg/57A
Baiss, Wilks, W. Lavington, 1750, AB, P1/B/1253
Wm., Fonthill G., 1730, AB, P2/B/1490
Bassett, Benj., vict., Marl. St Peter and St Paul, 1716, I, W, P1/B/814, P1/6Reg/1B
Dorothy, widow, Codf. St P., 1636, I, W, P2/B/600
Eliz., sp., Westrop, Highw., 1803, O, W, P5/1803/28, P5/19Reg/57
Giles, Westbrook, Gt. Faringdon, Berks., 1698, AB, I, P5/1698/14
Jn., yeo., Midgham, Thatcham, Berks., 1726, comm, W, P1/B/931, P1/7Reg/143B
My., widow, Tittle Row, Bray, Berks., 1753, W, P1/B/1269, P1/11Reg/34
Nich., Chipp., 1624, I, P3/B/241
Rd., husb., Sal. St Thos., 1633, I, W, P4/1632/4
Rd., Winsley, Bradford A., 1730, W (2), P2/B/1491

Wm., sen., baker, Box, 1715, W, P3/B/1126
Wm., baker, Box, 1728, I, W, P3/B/1264
Wm., carp., Crickl. St My., 1743, W, P3/B/1412
Bassingey, Augustine, Stourton, 1553, W, P2/2Reg/167D
Mgt., Stourton, 1571, AB, P2/5Reg/135D
Bastard, Adam, barber, Beam., Dorset, 1628, AB, I, P5/1628/10, P5/11Reg/62D
Eliz., mason's wife, Sherb., Dorset, 1736, AB, P5/1736/3
Baster, Geo., sen., Shalbourne, 1702, AB, I, P5/1702/12
Baster, Jas., Collingbourne D., 1791, AB, P21/11/35
Jn., yeo., Fisherton A., 1595, AB, I, W, P2/B/165
Jos., Shalbourne, Berks., 1750, AB, P23/619
Baster, Jos., glover and breeches maker, Rowde, 1765, W, P3/B/1569
Busterd, Rd., Damerham, Hants, 1768, AB, I, ren, P2/B/1846
Susanna, widow, Shalbourne, Berks., 1750, AB, P23/620
Thos., clerk and vicar, Bere R., Dorset, 1618, AB, I, P5/1618/3, P5/9Reg/211B
Walter, yeo., Littlecote, Rams., 1666, AB, comm, I, P5/1666/4
Bastard *or* Basford, Walter, Soley, Chilton F., 1705, I, W, P3/B/1035
Bastian, Baston *see* Barston
Batch, Baitch, Ann, widow, Netheravon, 1691, I, NW, P12/134
Edmd., husb., Netheravon, [1661], I, O, W (NEP), P12/89
Hy., yeo., Netheravon, 1645, I, W, P12/86
Jn., Keevil, 1566, W, P2/4Reg/230A
Baitch, Jn., yeo., Netheravon, 1665, I, W, P5/1665/5
Baitch, Jn., Netheravon, 1686, I, P12/126
Jn., Durrington, 1767, AB, P1/B/1373
Jn., yeo., Netheravon, 1827, W, Wr, P5/1827/9
Batch als Bennett, My., wife, Netheravon, 1632, AB, P5/1632/13, P5/12Reg/87
My., widow, Netheravon, 1665, I, W, P5/1665/3
Baitch, My., widow, Netheravon, 1668, AB, NW, P12/100
My., widow, Homington, 1715, W, P24/671
My., widow, Durrington, 1734, W, P2/B/1544
Thos., husb., Netheravon, 1645, I, W, P12/85
Baich, Thos., Gomeldon, Idmiston, 1698, AB, I, P2/B/1194
Thos., sen., yeo., Durrington, 1716, AB, I, W, P1/B/815, P12/149
Thos., Durrington, 1727, AB, P2/B/1450
Wm., yeo., Netheravon, 1789, W, P12/201
see also Balch
Batchelor, Agnes, Burcombe, 1578, I, W, P2/B/70, P2/5Reg/321A
Alice, Durrington, 1577, I, W (damaged), P2/B/61, P2/5Reg/295C
Alice, widow, Broughton G., 1715, W, P2/B/1335
Benj., Sal., 1716, AB, P1/B/823
Benj., Sal., 1760, AB, P4/1760/10
Bridget, Durrington, 1623, I, copy I, W, copy W, P2/B/437
Chris., husb., Stratfield Saye & Mortimer, Hants, 1613, I, W, P1/B/103
Dan., clothw., Sal., 1726, W, P4/1726/4
Edwd., yeo., S. Wraxall, 1686, comm, I, W, P1/B/1568
Edwd., yeo., Wilton, 1718, W, P2/B/1365
Eliz., widow, Gt. Bedwyn, 1622, W, P5/10Reg/27A
Eliz., widow, Wexcombe, Grafton, 1622, I, W, P5/1622/9
Eliz., widow, Greenhill, Wootton B., 1701, I, W, P3/B/1001
Eliz., widow, Sal., 1718, W, P4/1718/22
Enoch, yeo., Monkton F., 1830, comm, W, P2/1830/2
Geo., gent., N. Bradley, 1814, comm, W, Wr, P1/1814/152
Gilbt., mercer, Melk., 1687, AB, I, P2/B/1081
Hy., yeo., Durrington, 1609, AB, I (2), P2/B/293, P2/8Reg/81C
Hy., yeo., Durrington, 1643, I, W, P2/B/684
Hy., sen., yeo., Durrington, 1705, I, W, P2/B/1244
Jas., Wrou., 1677, AB, I, P1/B/510
Jas., Chute, 1818, AB, Wr, P7/193
Jas., clothw., Bradford A., 1856, aff, comm, W, Wr, P2/1856/70

Jane, widow, N. Bradley, 1758, AB, P2/B/1738
Joan, Alderbury, 1693, I, W, P26/407
Jn., husb., Wexcombe, Grafton, 1611, I, W, P5/1611/4
Jn., husb., Newtown, Durnford, 1661, I, W, P5/1661/2
Jn., yeo., Westwood, 1679, I, W, P2/B/947
Jn., Alderbury, 1688, AB, I, P26/367
Jn., sen., yeo., Bramshaw, Hants, 1745, AB, ren, NW, P24/970
Jn., Pewsey, 1753, AB, P3/B/1481
Jn., cordw., Sal., 1769, W, P4/1769/20
Jn., Sal., 1831, AB, P4/1831/9
Jos., shoemaker, Sal., 1735, I, W, P1/B/1058, P1/8Reg/119
Julian, widow, Gt. Chalfield & Broughton G., 1691, I, W, P2/B/1130
Matthew, yeo., Bramshaw, Hants, 1752, W, P24/1036
Nich., Wexcombe, Grafton, 1575, I, W, P5/1575/2, P5/3Reg/71B
Nich., Atworth, Bradford A., 1727, AB, W, P2/B/1451
Repentance, widow, Chute, 1853, comm, W, Wr, P7/213
Robt., husb., Keevil, 1641, I, W, P2/B/666
Robt., shopkeeper, Box, 1749, W, P3/B/1456
Robt., Monkton F., 1828-29, AB (2), comm (2), P2/1828/5
Susan, widow, Grittleton, 1687, I, W, P3/B/827
Thos., Durrington, 1559, W, P2/3Reg/156B
Thos., Ratfyn, Amesb., [1620?], a/c, P2/B/402
Thos., husb., Newtown, Durnford, 1627-28, I, W, P5/1627/6, P5/11Reg/35B
Thos., Wilton, Gt. Bedwyn, 1646, I, W, P21/1/60
Thos., yeo., Ratfyn, Amesb., 1685, AB, a/c, I, P2/B/1052
Thos., Sal., 1709, AB, P4/1709/7
Thos., carp., Seend, Melk., 1778, comm, W, P2/B/1951
Wm., husb., Amesb., 1558, W, P2/3Reg/100E
Wm., N. Burcombe, 1572, AB, P2/5Reg/158C
Wm., Wexcombe, Grafton, 1613-14, comm, I, W, P5/1613/7, P5/9Reg/140A
Wm., tanner, Edington, 1639, AB, I, P2/B/643
Wm., husb., Marl., 1670, comm, I, W, P1/B/465
Wm., yeo., Pewsey, 1830, comm, W, Wr, P3/1830/13
Batcher *see* Butcher
Bateman, Jn., gent., Wokm., Berks., 1702, W, P5/1702/10
Bates, Jn., Dauntsey, 1688, I, W, P1/B/591
Jn., yeo., Erlestoke, 1775, W, P2/B/1917
Jos., E. Harnham, Britford, 1693, AB, I, P5/1693/7
Wm., yeo., Dauntsey, 1679, court papers, I, W, P3/B/706
Batesby, Robt., Monkton F., 1594, I, W, P2/B/152
Bath, Ann, widow, Hook, Lydiard T., 1696, I, W, P3/B/944
Ann, widow, Purton, 1696, AB, I, W, P3/B/943
Ann, Wootton B., 1722, I, W, P3/B/1200
Anth., yeo., Purton, 1665, AB, I, P3/B/502
Anth., Purton, 1694, AB, I, P3/B/916
Anth., sen., yeo., Purton, 1743, W, P3/B/1413
Anth. Mortimor, innkeeper, Wootton B., 1856, aff, comm, W, Wr, P3/1856/50
Betty *see* Eliz.
Edwd., chapman, Sal., 1772, W, P4/1772/12
Eliz., sp., Sal., 1701, W, P4/1701/8
Eliz., widow, Purton, 1814, comm, W, Wr, P1/1814/142
Eliz. *or* Betty, widow, Chr. M., 1817, W, Wr, P1/1817/48
Geoff., husb., Bushton, Clyffe P., 1625, AB, I, NW, P3/B/262
Geoff., blacksmith, Clyffe P., 1730, W, P3/B/1281
Beath, Geoff., yeo., Bromham, 1798, comm, W, P3/B/1760
Geo., Wootton B., 1663, AB, comm, I, P1/B/392
Beath, Geo., Chr. M., 1710, I, W, P3/B/1083
Giles, yeo., Purton Stoke, 1620, I, W, P3/B/186
Hy., yeo., Brinkw., 1773, W, P1/B/1419, P1/13Reg/2
Jas., Sal., 1765, AB, P4/1765/4

Jas., gent., Purton, 1798, comm, W, P1/B/1546, P1/15Reg/163
Jas., Purton, 1816, AB, comm, Wr, P3/1816/37
Jas., Hayes Knoll, Purton, 1825, O, W, Wr, P3/1825/4
Jane, widow, Heytes., 1738, AB, W, copy W, P5/1738/1
Jane, sp., Purton Stoke, 1809, W, Wr, P3/1809/3
Joan, widow, Wootton B., 1620, I, W, P3/B/181
Joan, widow, Chr. M., 1627, AB, I, P3/B/286
Jn., sen., Purton, 1609, AB, P3/B/42
Jn., husb., Wootton B., 1609, W, P3/B/43
Jn., yeo., Hook, Lydiard T., 1610, W, P3/B/56
Jn., husb., Purton, 1641, I, W, P3/B/452
Jn., Chr. M., 1643, comm, I (damaged), W (damaged), P1/B/307
Jn., Hook, Lydiard T., 1667, AB, I, P3/B/520
Jn., yeo., Leigh, Ashton K., 1687, AB, I, P3/B/832
Jn., maltster, Purton, 1705, I, W, P3/B/1036
Jn., widower, Purton, 1714, W, P1/B/787, P1/5Reg/324B
Jn., Purton, 1723, AB, comm, P1/B/879
Jn., carp., Purton, 1744, AB, W, P3/B/1420
Jn., carp., Purton, 1750, comm, W, P3/B/1465
Jn., yeo., Brinkw., 1801, W, P1/1801/84, P1/15Reg/303C
Jn., yeo., S. Wraxall, 1845, O, W, Wr, P1/1845/55
Jn. Ings, S. Wraxall, 1842, AB, comm, Wr, P2/1842/19
Bath *or* Abath, Joshua, yeo., Warm., 1683, I, W, P2/B/1021
My., sp., Wrou., 1725, W, P3/B/1235
My., widow, Purton Stoke, 1831, comm, W, Wr, P3/1831/10
Milborough, widow, Purton, 1774, W, P3/B/1629
Nich., yeo., Chr. M., [1613], I, W, P3/B/100
Nich., yeo., Melchet Park, 1730, W, P2/B/1479
Nich., yeo., Chr. M., 1750, W, P1/10Reg/401A
Rd., sen., yeo., Purton, 1610, W, P3/B/57
Rd., Wootton B., 1615-18, AB, a/c, I, P3/B/120, 158
Rd., Marl., 1668, W, P1/B/438
Rd., yeo., Wootton B., 1675, I, W, P3/B/644
Rd., yeo., Plaitford, 1681, I, W, P2/B/987
Rd., Chr. M., 1756, AB, P3/B/1502
Rd., baker, Purton, 1783, W, P1/B/1485, P1/13Reg/494
Robt., yeo., Wootton B., 1673, I, W, P3/B/623
Robt., Lydiard M., 1778, AB, P3/B/1650
Roger, bach., Lydiard M., 1688-90, AB (2), P3/B/840
Sarah, widow, Purton, 1760, W, P3/B/1524
Sarah, sp., Corsham, 1839, O, W, Wr, P3/1839/15
Susanna, widow, Crickl. St S., 1791, W, P3/B/1730
Thos., Wootton B., 1686, AB, I, P3/B/822
Thos., yeo., Littlecott, Hilmarton, 1722, AB, W, P3/B/1216
Thos., Brinkw., 1753, AB, P3/B/1482
Thos., yeo., Chr. M., 1782, AB, W, P1/B/1471, P1/13Reg/381
Thos., Chr. M., 1791, W, P3/B/1729
Wm., husb., Purton Stoke, [1610], W (NEP), P3/B/58
Wm., husb., Corton, Boyton, 1633, I, NW, P2/B/567
Wm., yeo., Purton, 1695, AB, I, P3/B/934
Wm., clerk, Purton Stoke, 1715, W, P3/B/1127
Wm., yeo., Purton, 1729, W, P3/B/1276
Wm., gent., Brinkw., 1829, AB, W, Wr, P1/1829/84
Bathe, Wm., labourer, Wrou., 1841, W, Wr, P3/1841/5
Batson, Alice, widow, Hannington, 1730, W, P3/B/1282
Francis, jun., brickmaker, Lydiard M., 1693, AB, I, P3/B/897
Hy., gent., Court House, Thornford, Dorset, 1663, I, W, copy W, P5/1662/104
Jn., sen., yeo., Hannington, 1624, I, W, P3/B/242
Jn., sen., yeo., Hannington, 1702, I, W, P3/B/1013
Jn., Sherb., Dorset (form. of Trent, Somerset), 1838, AB, Wr, P5/1838/9

Jn., yeo., Nether C., Dorset, 1844, D, W, Wr, P5/1844/14
Mgt., widow, Hannington, 1629, I, W, P3/B/301
Mgt., widow, Wanb., 1679, AB, I, W, P3/B/707
Michael, labourer, Sherb., Dorset, 1838, W (& cod), Wr, P5/1838/8
Nich., Hannington, 1722, W, P3/B/1201
Nich., brickmaker, Purton, 1791, W, P3/B/1731
Sibyl, Highw., 1693, I, W, P10/1693/5
Susanna, widow, Thornford, Dorset, 1667, I, W, P5/1666/3
Wm., chandler, Highw., 1624, I, NW, P10/1624/3
Batt, Alexander, gent., Easton, 1766, W, P3/B/1577
Alice, widow, Burbage, 1698, I, W, P5/1698/11
Ann, sp., Durley, Burbage, 1677, I, W (made 1673), P11/37
Ann, sp., Sal., 1742, AB, W, P4/1741/2
Anth., husb. *or* yeo., Idmiston, 1680, I, W, P2/B/960
Augustine, bach., Marl., 1682, AB, P1/B/557
Augustine, yeo., Easton, 1685, I, W, P3/B/807
Augustine, yeo., Westcourt, Burbage, 1698, I, W, P11/83
Augustine, yeo., Westcourt, Burbage, 1712, I, W, P11/108
Augustine, yeo., Pewsey, 1748, W, P3/B/1450
Benj., Marl., 1823, AB, comm, Wr, P1/1823/47
Batt als Cowslade, Bridget, widow, Sal., 1716, AB, P4/1716/2
Cath., widow, Collingbourne D., 1611, AB, I, W, P1/B/74
Cath., widow, Wilton, Gt. Bedwyn, 1740, I, W, Wr, P5/1740/4
Cath., widow, Allington, 1780, W, P2/B/1968
Chris., Sal., 1717, AB, P4/1717/9
Dorothy, widow, Bulford, 1667, I, W, P2/B/786
Edmd., W. Grafton, 1694, AB, I, P5/1694/31
Edmd., yeo., Collingbourne D., 1695, I, W, P1/B/652
Edwd., yeo., Chute, 1624, W, P7/16
Edwd., Hungerford, Berks., 1702, AB, comm, P5/1702/11
Edwd., yeo., Allington, 1753, W, P2/B/1703
Edwd., yeo., Ludg., 1759, W, P1/B/1326, P1/11Reg/433A
Edwd., Marl., 1835, W, P1/1835/134
Eliz., widow, Collingbourne D., 1681, W, P21/2/78
Eliz., sp., Wilton, Gt. Bedwyn, 1721, W, P21/8/13
Eliz., widow, Sal., 1739, W, P4/1739/12
Eliz., widow, Marl., 1740, AB, req, W, P1/B/1122, P1/9Reg/8
Eliz., Ogbourne St Geo., 1759, W, P23/680
Eliz., widow, Marl., 1786, AB, comm, copy W, P1/B/1496
Eliz., widow, Wilton, Gt. Bedwyn, 1800, W, P21/12/1
Eliz., widow, Town Farm, Buttermere, 1801, W, P1/1801/28, P1/15Reg/251
Frances, sp., Sal., 1684, AB, P4/1684/3
Francis, Wilton, Gt. Bedwyn, 1672, AB, I, O, P21/2/32
Francis, widow, Burbage, [1677], I, W, P11/41
Francis, Wilton, Gt. Bedwyn, 1710, AB, I, P21/7/7
Francis, yeo., N. Tidworth, 1778, W, P2/B/1953
Francis, yeo., Ludg., 1783, W, P2/B/2001
Francis, yeo., Wilton, Gt. Bedwyn, 1832, O, W, Wr, P5/1832/4
Geo., yeo., Durley, Burbage, 1672, I, W, P11/33
Hy., Kingston D., 1615, AB, I, NW, P2/B/347, 361
Jas., innholder, Sal., 1753, W, P1/B/1283, P1/11Reg/137B
Jas., Sal., 1777, AB, P4/1777/11
Jean, sp., Ludg., 1829, O, W, Wr, P2/1829/19
Joan, Urchf., 1602, I, NW, P2/B/224
Joan, widow, Devizes, 1662, AB, I, P1/B/367
Joan, widow, Easton, 1697, I, W, P3/B/959
Joan, Westcourt, Burbage, 1713, I, W, P5/1713/7, P5/15Reg/367A
Joan, widow, Allington, 1716, W, P1/B/828, P1/6Reg/34B
Jn., Erlestoke, 1558, I, P2/B/14
Jn., yeo., Melk., 1559, W, P2/3Reg/150F

Jn., sen., husb., E. & W. Grafton, 1587, AB, I, W, P5/1587/42, P5/4Reg/144C
Jn., Ashgrove, Donhead St My., 1597, AB, I, W (2), P2/B/184
Jn., E. Grafton, 1613, AB, I, P1/B/90
Jn., sen., gent., Sal., 1643, AB, I, NW, P1/B/308
Jn., sen., husb., Urchf., 1645, I, W, P2/B/697
Jn., Burbage, 1646, AB, I, P11/16
Batts, Jn., Burbage, 1664, AB, I, P5/1664/2
Jn., Sal., 1666, AB, P4/1666/16
Jn., sen., yeo., Urchf., 1674, AB, I, W, P2/B/874
Jn., tanner, Sal., 1680, W, P4/1680/7
Jn., yeo., Collingbourne D., 1685, I, W, P21/4/15
Jn., yeo., Ludg., 1695, I, W, P2/B/1170
Jn., yeo., Burbage, 1698, I, W, P5/1698/10
Jn., yeo., Easton, 1698, AB, W, P3/B/973
Jn., mason, Urchf., 1705, W (NEP), P30/25
Jn., Sal., 1712, AB, ren, P4/1711/13
Jn., Urchf., 1715, AB, I, P2/B/1339
Jn., sen., maltster, Ludg., 1733, W, P2/B/1521
Jn., sen., innholder, Marl., 1734, AB, W, P1/B/1032, 1109, P1/7Reg/593B
Jn., Ogbourne St Geo., 1748, W, P23/605
Jn., yeo., Allington, 1765, W, P2/B/1814
Jn., yeo., Town Farm, Buttermere, 1801, AB, W, P1/1801/27, P1/15Reg/250
Jn., Buttermere, 1806, AB, T, Wr (children: Sarah, Francis, George, Eleazar, Jas. & Eliz. B.), P3/1806/19
Jn., yeo., Collingbourne D., 1821, W, Wr, P1/1821/16
Manuel, gent., Lt. Hinton, 1797, W, P3/B/1754
My., sp., Marl., 1682, AB, P1/B/556
My., minor, Sal., 1692, app. of guardian, T (no decd named), P4/1691/18
My., widow, Sal., 1693, W, P4/1693/6
My., widow, Urchf., 1731, W, P2/B/1501
My., widow, Urchf., 1754, I, W, P2/B/1707
My., widow, Collingbourne K., 1771, W, P3/B/1614
Michael, Monkton D., 1689, I, W, P2/B/1122
Nathan, bach., Easton, 1771, AB, P3/B/1615
Nich., yeo., Chr. M., 1750, W, P1/B/1246
Peter, Kingston D., 1631, I, W, P1/B/224
Rd., yeo., Collingbourne D., 1633-35, bonds (2) to pay legacies, I, note (gives ages of grandchildren), W, P21/1/17, P21/3/21
Rd., yeo., Devizes, 1669, I, W, P1/B/458
Rd., Wilton, Gt. Bedwyn, 1794, AB, P5/1794/6, P5/18Reg/196B
Robt., husb., Shalbourne, 1602, I, P5/1601/54
Robt., husb., Manton, Preshute, 1610, comm, O, NW, P1/B/66
Robt., yeo., Pewsey, 1675, I (damaged), W, P3/B/645
Robt., Burbage, 1687, AB, I, P11/60
Robt., sen., yeo., Urchf., 1691, AB, I, P2/B/1137
Robt., sen., yeo., Savernake Park, 1718, I (2), W, P1/B/843, P1/6Reg/160B
Robt., yeo., Pewsey, 1725, W, P3/B/1236
[Roger], Urchf., 1596, I, P2/B/169
Roger, yeo., Wedh., Urchf., 1663, I, W, P2/B/749
Sam., minor, Sal., 1690, T (no decd named), P4/1690/7
Sam., rector, E. Coulston, 1690, AB, W, P4/1690/6
Thos., sen., Burridge Heath, Lt. Bedwyn, 1623, AB, I, P21/3/4
Thos., Devizes St My., 1631, AB, P1/B/241
Thos., innholder, Hindon, 1639, AB, a/c, I, P2/B/637
Thos., husb., Bulford, 1642, AB, I, P2/B/674
Thos., sen., tanner, Sal., 1687, I, W, P4/1687/8
Thos., husb., Burridge Heath, Lt. Bedwyn, 1711, I, W, P21/7/12
Thos., innholder, Sal., 1733, W, P4/1733/2
Thos., Lt. Bedwyn, 1741, I, W, P21/9/35
Thos., tanner, Sal., 1748, W, P4/1748/13
Thos., yeo., Ludg., 1779, W, P2/B/1967

Thos., yeo., Ludg. & Allington, 1818, AB (re property in A.), W, Wr, P2/1818/30, 53
Thos., gent., Rams., 1836, AB, comm, W, Wr, P5/1836/5
Wm., husb., Crofton, Gt. Bedwyn, 1639, I, W, P21/1/47
Wm., husb., Burridge Heath, Lt. Bedwyn, 1682, I, W, P5/1682/15
Wm., yeo., Collingbourne D., 1707, W, P21/6/39
Wm., yeo., W. Grafton, 1709, W, P21/6/46
Wm., yeo., Collingbourne D., 1760, comm, W, P21/10/49
Wm., bach., Marl., 1769, AB, P1/B/1387
Wm., Fonthill G., 1771, AB, P2/B/1872
Wm., gent., Sal., 1808, AB, LA, P1/1808/17
Wm., brewer, Rams., 1825, I, O, W, Wr, P5/1825/7
Wm. *see also* Jas. Grist
Zebulon, Wilton, Gt. Bedwyn, 1812, W, P21/12/29
Zebulon, yeo., Wilton, Gt. Bedwyn, 1847, D, form of O, O, W, Wr, P5/1847/25
see also Godding als B.
Battar *see* Batter
Battel *see* Batwell
Batten, Alice, widow, Beam., Dorset, 1595, I, W, P5/1595/7, P5/6Reg/99A
Battyn, Alice, widow, Sal., 1660, AB, I, P4/1660/3
Alice, Collingbourne D., 1693, AB, P21/5/8
Ann, widow, Kintbury, Berks., 1789, W, P1/B/1507, P1/14Reg/209A
Caesar, innholder, Wokm., Berks., 1679, I (mentions Angel & Princes chambers), W, P5/1679/9
Edwd., husb., Ashton K., [1619], I, W (NEP), P3/B/171
Edwd., yeo., Longcott, Shrivenham, Berks., 1720, W, P1/B/858, P1/6Reg/299B
Eleanor, Allington, Chipp., 1605, W, P1/B/29
Eleazar, yeo., Crofton, Gt. Bedwyn, 1719, I (detailed), W, P21/7/41
Eleazar, Hidden Farm, N. Hidden, Hungerford, Berks., 1772, AB, comm, P23/745
Elias, husb., Plaitford, 1681, I, W, P2/B/982
Eliz., widow, Langley Burrell, 1681, W, P3/B/735
Eliz., wife, Donhead St My., 1827, AB, comm, Wr (seems to have been d. a wife not widow), P2/1827/76
Ephraim, weaver, Manchester, Lancashire (leaving effects at Bradford A.), 1818, comm, court proceeding, W, Wr, P2/1818/10
Frances, sp., Wantage, Berks., 1770, W, P5/1770/5, P5/17Reg/6
Francis, Allington, Chipp., 1717, AB, I, P3/B/1142
Geo., Chr. M., 1696, AB, I, P3/B/945
Hy., Farley, Alderbury, 1687, AB, I, W, P26/351
Hy., labourer, Longcott, Shrivenham, Berks., 1747, AB, W, P1/B/1201, P1/10Reg/94
Isaac, mason, Bradford A., 1789, W, P2/B/2040
Jas., Lyme R., Dorset, 1759, AB, comm, P16/321
Jas., collarmaker, Ludwell, Donhead St My., 1796, W, P2/B/2114
Jas., collarmaker, Ludwell, Donhead St My., 1829, AB, comm, D (2), W, P2/1829/9
Jas., No Man's Land, 1845, AB, aff, D, W, Wr, P1/1845/49
Jeremiah, builder, Bradford A., 1832, O, W, Wr, P1/1832/140
Jn., yeo., Allington, Chipp., 1640, I, W, P3/B/435
Jn., yeo., Chr. M., 1641, I, W, P3/B/453
Jn., yeo., Haxton, Fittleton, 1667, I, W, P2/B/778
Jn., broad weaver, Langley Burrell, 1676, I, W, P3/B/660
Jn., Sutton B., 1701, AB, I, P3/B/1002
Jn., Beam., Dorset, 1714, AB, P17/217
Jn., yeo., Langley Burrell, 1719, W, P3/B/1162
Jn., yeo., Dauntsey, 1719, AB, I, P3/B/1161
Jn., yeo., Ardington, Berks., 1720, I, W, P1/B/859, P1/6Reg/296
Jn., tailor, Enford, 1729, I, W, P1/B/957, P1/7Reg/322A
Jn., Clarendon Park, 1755, AB, P1/B/1290
Jn., yeo., Allington, Chipp., 1765, W, P3/B/1570
Jn., Quidh., 1793, AB, P2/B/2083
Jn., weaver, Bradford A., 1795, W, P2/B/2102
Jn., yeo., S. Wraxall, 1819, comm, W, Wr, P2/1819/17
Jn., yeo., Wantage, Berks., 1821, comm, W, Wr, P23/891
Jn., yeo., Whitep., 1826, W, Wr, P1/1826/35

Jn., mason, Bradford A., 1827, W, Wr, P2/1827/33
Jn., Sal. St Mart., 1829, D, W, Wr, P4/1829/1
Jos., minor, Milford, Sal. St Mart., 1738, T (no decd named), P4/1738/5
Mgt., sp., Ashley, [1609], W (NEP), P3/B/59
Mgt., widow, Ardington, Berks., 1708, I, W, P1/B/741
Margery, widow, Sal., 1663, AB, I, P4/1663/6
My., sp., Chr. M., 1695, AB, I, ren, P1/B/641
Batting, Matthew, yeo., Chilton F., 1719, I, W, P3/B/1163
Matthew, sen., yeo., Hidden, Hungerford, Berks., 1759, W, P23/681
Matthew, yeo., Enborne, Berks., 1792, AB, W, P1/B/1521, P1/14Reg/380A
Philip, yeo., Gt. Somerford, 1605, I, W, P3/B/18
Philip, yeo., Chr. M., 1646, comm, I, W, P1/B/330
Batteyne, Rd., Sal. The Close, 1579, I, W, P5/1579/3, P5/3Reg/145B
Battyn, Rd., joiner, Sal., 1619, W, P1/B/162
Rd., yeo., Beam., Dorset, 1694, AB, I, P17/340
Rd., gardener, Wokm., Berks., 1782, W, P5/1782/3, P5/17Reg/223A
Robt., Lyme R., Dorset, 1567, AB, P5/1Reg/80D
Robt., gent., Wokm., Berks., 1662, AB, I, ren, W, P5/1662/18
Robt., Bradford A., 1811, AB, Wr, P1/1811/82
Roger, [blacksmith], Urchf., 1556, W, P2/3Reg/1D
Sarah, widow, Allington, Chipp., 1752, W, P3/B/1475
Sarah, widow, Bradford A., 1829, comm, ren, req, W, P2/1829/2
Simon, joiner, Sal., 1663, AB, I, P1/B/393
Susanna, widow, Bradford A., 1797, AB, comm, P2/B/2127
Thos., Kington L., 1603, AB, I, W, P3/B/3
Thos., sen., yeo., Chr. M., 1624, I, W, P3/B/243
Thos., weaver, Blackland, Calne, 1628, I (draft), I, W, P5/1628/4, P5/11Reg/97B
Thos., husb., Allington, Chipp., 1629, I, W, P3/B/302
Thos., husb., Farley, Alderbury, 1693, W, P26/419
Thos., yeo., Farley, Alderbury, 1693, W, P26/409
Thos., Avon, Chr. M., 1701, comm, W, Wr, P3/B/1003
Thos., yeo., Tulwick, Grove, Wantage, Berks., 1732, AB, W, P23/480
Thos., yeo., Ardington, Berks., 1735, W, P1/B/1043, P1/7Reg/655
Thos., sen., tailor, Gt. Bedwyn, 1740, W, Wr, P5/1740/8
Thos., yeo., Bucklebury, Berks., 1763, W, P1/B/1357, P1/12Reg/88B
Thos., mealman, Downton, 1771-74, AB, W, P2/B/1870, P2/B/1906
Thos., tailor, Gt. Bedwyn, 1789, W, P21/11/33
Thos., Holnest, Dorset, 1810, AB, Wr, P5/1810/3
Walter, husb., Allington, Chipp., [1605], W (NEP), P3/B/19
Walter, Draycot C., 1632, I, NW, P3/B/339
Wm., Ditchampton, Wilton, 1558, W, P2/3Reg/87A
Batten als Welsted, Wm., butcher, Biddestone, 1571, W (NEP), P1/1Reg/39B
Wm., husb., Collingbourne D., 1681, AB, I, P21/2/73
Wm., Farley, Alderbury, 1716, AB, P26/599
Wm., sen., yeo., Alderbury, 1758, W, P26/960
Wm., maltster, Quidh., 1778, W, P2/B/1952
Wm., yeo., S. Wraxall, 1780, W, P2/B/1971
Wm., maltster, Quidh., 1801, W, P2/1801/34
Wm., shoemaker, Farley, Alderbury, 1831, W, P26/1388
Wm., No Man's Land, 1853, aff, D, W, Wr, P5/1853/5
see also Perrin/Perom als B.
Batter, Alice, sp., Winterbourne E., 1630, AB, note with L (from Hercules Stourton to accompany his churchwarden's presentation at visitation; been churchwarden for the year & hopes another parishioner will now be found to do same), P2/B/519
Edwd., husb., Fiddington, W. Lavington, 1677, AB, comm, I, P1/B/517
Geo., yeo., Winterbourne D., 1609, W (conveyance from George B. to son Giles) (NEP), P7/4
Geo., Sal. St Edmd., 1664, I, P4/1664/14
Giles, Winterbourne E., 1618-19, a/c, copy AB, a/c, P2/B/391
Battar, Joan, widow, Amesb., 1559, W, P2/4Reg/6A
Joan, Amesb., 1599, AB, I, W, P2/B/197

Jn., Amesb., 1558, W, P2/3Reg/104A
Jn., Sutton Poyntz, Dorset, 1571, W, P5/2Reg/107D
Jn., Sutton Poyntz, Dorset, 1597, W, P5/6Reg/148B
Jn., Idmiston, 1601, AB, I, note, P2/B/210
Mart., Amesb., 1593, AB, I, W, P2/B/149
Robt., Sutton Poyntz, Dorset, 1573, W, P5/3Reg/19E
Battar, Thos., jun., Amesb., 1547, W (2), P2/2Reg/35A-B
Thos., Sutton Poyntz, Dorset, 1593, AB (1595), I, T (children: Michael, Edith, Mgt., Eliz., My., Jane & Rd. B.), P5/1592/5, 17, P5/6Reg/21A
Thos., innholder, Sal., 1650, I (detailed), W, P1/B/358
Batterton, Rd., Blunsdon St And., [c1600?], W, Wr (badly damaged), P3/B/1
Barterton, Thos., yeo., N. Bradley, 1622, comm, I, copy I, W, copy W, P2/B/427
Batteyne, Batting *see* Batten
Battington, Chris., yeo., Avebury, 1636, AB (2), court papers (2), I, NW, P3/B/368
Battington, Eleanor, widow, Marl., 1692, AB, P1/B/611
Bottenton, Eliz., sp., Upton, Blewbury, Berks., 1711, W, P5/1711/9, P5/15Reg/255
Bottendon, Wm., yeo., Blewbury, Berks., 1591, AB, I, P5/1591/5, P5/5Reg/97B
Battrick, Geo., sen., Bere R., Dorset, 1717, W, P5/1717/3, P5/15Reg/403B
Robt., currier, Bere R., Dorset, 1746, W, P5/1746/4
Robt., yeo., Bere R., Dorset, 1783, AB, ren, W, P5/1783/2, P5/17Reg/248A
Batts *see* Batt
Batty, Jn., Sutton Poyntz, Dorset, 1597, AB, I, W, P5/1596/4
Battyn *see* Batten
Batwell, Ann, widow, Sal., 1641, AB, P4/1641/6
Botwell, Ephraim, Gillingham, Dorset, 1751, AB, P27/1/399, P27/3Reg/61B
Battel, Jn., yeo., Norton B., 1815, W, Wr, P2/1815/44
Buttell, Rd., day labourer, Woodley, W. and Sandford, Berks., 1688, AB, I, P5/1688/2
Battel, Simon, Sindlesham, Hurst, Berks., 1588, I, W, P5/1588/2, P5/5Reg/38A
Botwell, Thos., husb., Mere, 1570, W, P5/2Reg/80C
Thos., glover, Sal., 1633, AB, a/c, I, P4/1633/10
Bottwell, Thos., linen weaver, Bourton, Gillingham, Dorset, 1700, I, P27/1/138
Baugh, Alexander, Winterslow, 1739, W, P2/B/1573
Edwd., glover, Devizes, 1683, I, W, P1/B/559
Jn., yeo., Winterslow, Idmiston, 1637, I, partial copy I (2), W, P2/B/605, 609
Jn., sen., yeo., Chalke Rudd Farm, Idmiston, 1691, I, W, P2/B/1138
Jn., yeo., Winterslow, Idmiston, 1712, I, W, P2/B/1301
Jos., Winterslow, 1772, W, P2/B/1882
My., sp., Sal., 1849, W, Wr, P4/1849/20
Sam., bach., Milbourne, Malm., 1771, AB, P3/B/1616
Thos., Milbourne, Malm., 1730, W, P3/B/1283
Walter, yeo., Idmiston, 1610, W, P2/B/312, P2/8Reg/148D
Walter, Idmiston, [1630], I, P2/B/2156
Baughurst *see* Banghurst
Bauler *see* Bowler
Baun, Baune *see* Bowne and Bourne
Baunton *see* Banton
Bauth, Walter, tanner, Sal. St Edmd., 1671, AB, I, P4/1671/8
Bauwell *see* Banwell *or* B.
Baverster *see* Beverster
Baverstock, Beverstock, Anth., broad weaver, Bradford A., 1637, comm, I, NW, P2/B/607
Benj., Stockton, 1782, AB, W, P1/B/1466, P1/13Reg/347A
Chas., Teffont M., 1734, AB, P2/B/1543
Baberstock, Dan., Teffont M., 1698, AB, I, P2/B/1193
Dorothy, Tisb., 1570, AB, W, P2/5Reg/94B
Beverstock, Geo., sen., broad weaver, Leigh, Bradford A., 1688, I, W, P2/B/1106
Jas., yeo., Stockton, 1742, AB, W, P2/B/1607
Jas., tailor, Mere, 1826, W, Wr, P5/1826/14
Jas., farmer, Soley, Chilton F., 1853, AB, O, W, Wr, P3/1853/6
Jas., tailor, Mere, 1855, aff, comm, W, Wr, P5/1855/5
Jane, sp., Teffont M., 1641, AB, P2/B/664

Baberstock, Joan, Teffont, 1572, W, P2/5Reg/149D
Baberstoke, Jn., Teffont M., 1559, W, P2/4Reg/15C
Baberstocke, Jn., Dinton, 1569, AB, P2/5Reg/63C
Jn., no abode stated, 1710, W, P2/B/1295
Beverstock, Jn., broad weaver, Bradford A., 1721, I, W, P2/B/1401
Babstock, Jn., Haydon, Dorset (form. of Stoke, Somerset), 1841, AB, comm, D, W, Wr, P5/1841/16
Lucy, widow, Teffont M., 1670, I, W, P2/B/831
Mgt., widow, Rode, N. Bradley, 1798, AB, comm, P2/B/2134
My., widow, Teffont M., 1646, AB, I, W, P2/B/704
My., widow, Sal., 1746, AB, P4/1746/6
Nich., sen., yeo., Stockton, 1740, W, P2/B/1592
Nich., yeo., Stockton, 1767, W, P2/B/1839
Sarah, widow, E. Knoyle, 1828, AB, W, Wr, P2/1828/24
Thos., Porton, Idmiston, 1606, I, W, P2/B/265
Thos., husb., Porton, Idmiston, 1629, AB, a/c, I, draft a/c, P2/B/504
Walter, sen., yeo., Teffont M., 1618, I, W, P2/B/384
Walter, yeo., Dinton, 1641, I, W, P2/B/667
Wm., Teffont M., 1640, I, W, P2/B/659
Wm., husb. *or* yeo., Swallowcliffe, 1675, I, W, P5/1675/11
Wm., husb., Netherh., 1681, I, W, P2/B/983
Bawden *see* Baldwin
Bawdry, Balderie, Joan, widow, Clevancy, Hilmarton, 1623, I, W, P3/B/225
Rd., yeo., Seagry, 1621, I, W, P3/B/200
Rd., husb., Easton Grey, 1675, I, W, P3/B/646
Robt., yeo., Seagry, 1640, I, NW, P3/B/436
Wm., yeo., Sherston, 1650, W, P1/B/355
Bawler *see* Bowler
Bawn, Bawne, Bawnse *see* Bowne
Baxter, Alexander, Mkt. L., 1730, AB, P2/B/1481
Edwd., gent., Mkt. L., 1733, W, P2/B/1516
Rd., innholder, Reading, Berks., 1698, I, W, P1/B/669, P1/3Reg/78
Robt., Sal. St Edmd., 1571, W, P1/1Reg/30C
Susanna, widow, W. Lavington, 1706, comm, I, W, P1/B/726
Thos., gent., W. Lavington, 1692, comm, I, W, P1/B/614
Baydon *see* Baden
Bayland, Baylond, Rd., Maiden B., 1612, I, NW, P2/B/333, P2/8Reg/183A
Baylod, Thos., Maiden B., 1546, W, P2/2Reg/8B
Wm., clothw., Sal. St Mart., 1692, AB, I, ren, P1/B/620
Bayle, Bale, Ann, widow, Uffc., Devon, 1733, W, P5/1733/3
Bale, Anth., sen., sergemaker, Uffc., Devon, 1722-33, AB (in minority of joint execs, Ann & Sarah B., daus of decd.), W, P20/1/172, 188
Bayle *or* Bayley, Edmd., Wokm., Berks., 1542, W, P5/20Reg/36B
Eustace, husb. and joiner, Ash, Stourpaine, Dorset, 1580, I, W, P5/1580/11, P5/3Reg/152B
Frances, Hurst, Berks., 1728, W, P5/16Reg/202A
Francis, Hurst, Berks., 1728, I, W, P5/1728/6
Joan, sp., Malm., 1624, AB, I, W, P3/B/245
Jn., yeo., Stratfield M., Berks., 1701, I, W, P1/B/694
Baylie, Bayly *see* Bailey
Bayliffe, Agnes, widow, Monkton, Chipp., 1623, I, W, P3/B/227
Ann *or* Agnes, Slaughterford, 1637, caveat, P3/B/383
Ann *or* Agnes, widow, Chipp., 1638, AB, I, P3/B/396
Bayliffe als Jefferys, Ann, gent.'s wife, Calne, 1732, AB, comm, P5/1732/2
Edwd., tailor, Chipp., 1689, AB, comm, P3/B/854
Eliz., widow, Monkton, Chipp., 1705, I, W, P3/B/1037
Eliz., sp., Chipp., 1735, AB, P1/B/1051
Frances, widow, Tytherton L., Chipp., 1640, I, W, P3/B/437
Frances, gent.'s wife, Chipp., 1673, AB, P3/B/625
Hannah, widow, Chipp., 1684, comm, I, W, P3/B/786
Hy., [glover], Chipp., 1684, AB, I, P3/B/787
Bayleffe *or* Bailey, Jn., Pott., 1603, AB, I, P1/B/25

Judith, widow, Chipp., 1727, W, P3/B/1251
Matthew, gent., Weaver's Mill, Slaughterford, 1626, AB, a/c, court paper, I, P3/B/274
Wm., Lt. Somerford, 1621, I, W, P3/B/201
Wm., gent., Monkton, Chipp., 1673, I, W, copy W, P3/B/626
Baylod *see* Bayland
Baylond *see* Bayland
Bayly *see* Bailey
Bayman, Bayman als Pithouse, Ann, widow, Rams., 1661, comm, I, W, P5/1661/3
Eliz., widow, Rams., 1796, AB, comm, ren, W, P5/1796/2, P5/18Reg/228
Joan, widow, Rams., 1630, W, P5/11Reg/151
Lionel, yeo., Rams., 1617, comm, I, W, P5/1616/10, P5/9Reg/184B, 213D
Bayman als Pithouse, Roger, Rams., 1687, AB, I, P5/1687/7
Roger, labourer, Rams., 1785, W, P5/1785/2, P5/18Reg/24
Thos., tanner and shopkeeper, Sal., 1769, W, P4/1769/7
Thos., Hungerford, Berks., 1822, AB, Wr, P23/897
Wm., labourer, Rams., 1774, W, P5/1774/1, P5/17Reg/76
Baynard, Jas., Lackham, Lacock, 1638, AB, P3/B/398
Bayne *see* Baines
Bayner *see* Bonner
Baynes *see* Baines
Baynger *see* Benger
Baynham, Jn., Malm., 1726, AB, I, P3/B/1246
Jn., mason, Malm., 1803, W, P3/1803/34
Baynton, Bayntun *see* Bainton
Baynye, Roger, Bridmore, Berwick St Jn., 1629, AB, I, P2/B/501
Bayones *see* Baines
Bays *see* Bass
Bazely *see* Basely
Bazing *see* Basing
Beacer *see* Beaker
Beach, Agnes, widow, Horningsham, 1605, I, P5/1605/7
Cath., sp., Steeple A., 1738, comm, W, P2/B/1568
Eliz., sp., Monkton D., 1732, W, P1/B/1028, P1/7Reg/554A
Francis, sen., Sonning, Berks., 1762, AB, P5/1762/5
Francis, sen., yeo., Sonning, Berks., 1799, W, P5/1799/2, P5/18Reg/285A
Grace, widow, Devizes, 1685, W, P1/B/581
Grace, sp., Steeple A., 1733, comm, W, P2/B/1515
Hy., clerk and vicar, Coombe B., 1668, I, W, P5/1667/11
Joan, widow, Sal., 1665, W, P1/B/419
Jn., Wilton, Gt. Bedwyn, 1639, I, W, P21/1/41
Beech, Jn. *see* Hy. Jackson
Beech, Julian, widow, Warm., 1583, W, P2/6Reg/82
Beech, Mgt., former nun, Amesb. (Priory), 1553, W, P2/2Reg/175A
Matthew, Alderbury, 1774, AB, P26/1065
Nich., Sal. & Trowb., 1659, I (detailed), P4/1659/1
Rd., yeo., Sonning, Berks., 1827, aff, comm, W, Wr, P5/1827/63
Thos., Warm., 1576, AB, I, P2/B/57, P2/5Reg/272C
Thos., gent., Lt. Somerford, 1815, AB, Wr, P3/1815/5
Wm., sen., gent., Fittleton, 1686, I, W, P2/B/1068
see also Coker als B.
Beacham *see* Beauchamp
Beachy *see* Beechey
Beadell *see* Biddle
Beak, Chas., gent., Stanton St Q., 1783, W, P3/B/1680
Chas., vict., Ford, N. Wraxall, 1835, W, Wr, P1/1835/84
Beak *or* Berke, Eliz., sp., Stanton St B., 1646, AB, I, NW, P1/B/325
Beke, Francis, [clerk], St Nich. Earley, Sonning, Berks. (& manor of Whiteknights), 1547, institution as rector *or* chaplain, on resignation of Hugh B.; Joan B., widow, patron of the living, P5/20Reg/95A
Humphrey, yeo., Stanton St Q., 1765, AB, W, P3/B/1571
Isaac, Hullavington, 1790, AB, comm, P3/B/1723

Jane, sp., All C., 1695, AB, bundles of court papers (3 including include W, alleg, inty & D), I, P3/B/935
Joanna, widow, Calne (form. of Chipp.), 1827, W (& cod), Wr, P5/1827/31
Jn., All C., [1582], W (NEP), P3/1Reg/20A
Jn., husb., All C., 1625, I, W, P3/B/263
Jn., sen., yeo., All C., 1665, I, W, P3/B/504
Jn., yeo., Allington, All C., 1684, I, W, P3/B/788
Jn., jun., yeo., All C., 1694, I, W, P3/B/918
Jn., sen., yeo., All C., 1701, comm, I, W, P3/B/1004
Jn., gent., E. Kennett, 1741, W, P3/B/1397
Jn., All C., 1767, AB, P3/B/1583
Jn., sen., yeo., Bradfield, Hullavington, 1774, comm, W, P3/B/1630
Jn., Box, 1806, AB, Wr, P3/1806/57
Margery, widow, All C., 1679, I, W, P3/B/709
My., widow, Wokm., Berks., 1681, I, NW, P5/1681/7
My., widow, Allington, All C., 1767, a/c, I, W, P3/B/1584, P1/12Reg/196B
My., widow, Seagry, 1795, AB, P3/B/1744
Rd., Manton, Preshute, 1777, AB, P1/B/1446
Thos., esquire, no abode stated; to be buried in St Giles' church, Reading, Berks. ; W proved at Sonning, 1546, W, P5/20Reg/84C
Beke, Thos., gent., Earley, Sonning, Berks., 1600, AB, W, P5/1600/7, P5/6Reg/243A
Thos., yeo., Allington, All C., 1735, W, P1/B/1057, P1/8Reg/108
Wm., husb., Stanton St Q., 1615, I, W, P3/B/121
Wm., sen., Stanton St Q., 1675, I, W, P3/B/649
Wm., Easton Grey, 1740, AB, P3/B/1387
Wm., Stanton St Q., 1742, AB, P3/B/1401
Wm., gent., Priory Farm, Kington St M., 1784, comm, W, P3/B/1688
Wm., yeo., Stert, Urchf., 1840, W, Wr, P1/1840/24
Beaker, Eliz., widow, N. Wraxall, 1639, AB, I, P3/B/409
Isaac, yeo., Nettleton, 1803, W, P3/1803/47
Jane, widow, Castle C., 1762, AB, W, P28/23
Jn., husb., W. Kington, [1613], I, W (NEP), P3/B/104
Jn., husb., Malm., 1634, AB, a/c, I, P3/B/357
Jn., yeo., Hullavington, 1729, W, P3/B/1277
My., sp., Castle C., 1770, AB, W, P28/32
My., widow, Nettleton, 1780, AB, P3/B/1661
Nich., sen., yeo., Nettleton, 1722, I, W, P3/B/1203
Nich., gent., Nettleton, 1745, W, P3/B/1425
Nich., gent., Nettleton, 1763, comm, W, P3/B/1556
Philip, yeo., Nettleton, 1739, W, P3/B/1377
Sarah, wife of cooper, Castle C., 1682, AB, P3/B/753
Thos., Nettleton, 1616, I, W, P1/B/139
Thos., sen., yeo., W. Kington, 1688, I, W, P3/B/842
Thos., yeo., Littleton Drew, 1718, I, W, P3/B/1149
Thos., sen., yeo., W. Kington, 1729, W, P3/B/1278
Thos., yeo., W. Kington, 1746, W, P3/B/1435
Thos., W. Kington, 1760, AB, P3/B/1526
Ursula, widow, Westport St My., 1616, I, W, P3/B/133
Beaket *see* Beckett
Beakhurst, Thos., vict., Hampstead Marshall, Berks., 1814, W, Wr, P1/1814/24
Bealding *see* Baldwin
Beale, Alice, widow, Idmiston, 1560, AB, W, P2/4Reg/39A
Ann, widow, Clyffe P., 1674, AB, P3/B/638
Anth., husb., Brinkw., 1639, I, W, P3/B/410
Edith, widow, Idmiston, 1617, I, W, P2/B/371, P2/8Reg/320C
Eleanor, widow, Brinkw., [1605], W (NEP), P3/B/20
Eliz., widow, Grove Farm, Mildenhall, 1671, I, NW, P3/B/584
Eliz., sp., Crickl. St S., 1758, AB, P3/B/1515
Emma, Brinkw., 1747, I, W, P1/B/1214, P1/10Reg/155A
Frances, widow, Brinkw., 1694, I, W, P3/B/919
Giles, Hankerton, 1696, AB, I, P3/B/946

Hy., Idmiston, 1565, W, P2/4Reg/204B
Hy., sen., Hankerton, 1685, AB, I, P3/B/812
Hy., cordw., Binfield, Berks., 1714, AB, I, P1/B/793
Hy., gent., Malm. (late of Murcott), 1802, comm, W, P3/1802/34
Jn., tailor, Brinkw., 1606, I (2), W, P1/B/41
Jn., sen., [haberdasher], Wantage, Berks., 1682, I, W, P5/1682/13
Jn., sen., yeo., Hankerton, 1807, W, Wr, P3/1807/61
Jn., Crudwell, 1828, AB, O, P3/1828/41
Jn., vict., Marl., 1848, W, Wr, P1/1848/54
Mgt., widow, Swallowcliffe, 1561, AB, P5/1Reg/1C
Mgt., widow, Brinkw., 1651, I, W, P1/B/361
My., widow, W. Grimstead, 1734, W, P2/B/1541
My., widow, Crudwell, 1803, comm, W, P3/1803/52
Maud, widow, Porton, Idmiston, 1584, AB, W, P2/6Reg/118B
Beale als King, Rd., husb., Beam., Dorset, 1632, AB, I, P17/7
Rd., cutler, Calne, 1638, AB, I, P26/67
Robt., yeo., Brinkw., 1619, a/c, bonds to pay sums of money (5 - 2 cancelled), I, note of court charges, proceedings (in King's Bench), P3/B/172
Robt., Lea and Cleverton, 1630, AB, a/c, I, P3/B/319
Robt., Beechingstoke, 1698, AB, I, P3/B/974
Sam., Chiseldon, 1718, AB, I, P3/B/1150
Thos., Brinkw., 1602, W, P3/1Reg/108
Thos., yeo., Broad H., 1648, I, W, P1/B/343
Thos., E. Grimstead, W. Dean, 1733, W, P2/B/1520
Tobias, yeo., Brinkw., 1688-90, comm, I, W, P3/B/843, 864
Walter, Porton, Idmiston, 1581, W, P2/6Reg/36B
Wm., yeo., Idmiston, 1584, W, P2/6Reg/117B
Wm., husb., Dunnington, Wootton B., 1606, W, P1/B/50
Wm., sen., yeo., Brinkw., 1628, AB, I, W, P1/B/209
Wm., Hankerton, 1685, AB, I, P3/B/813
Wm., W. Grimstead, 1732, AB, P2/B/1512
Wm., maltster, Crickl. St My., 1742, W, P3/B/1402
Wilson, Sal., 1786, AB, P4/1786/3
Bealing, Edith, Swallowcliffe, 1570, W, P5/2Reg/61A
Bealyn, Edmd., Swallowcliffe, 1585, AB, I, P5/1585/10, P5/4Reg/121B
Eliz., widow, Swallowcliffe, 1622, I, W, P5/1622/5, P5/10Reg/28A
Eliz., Ansty, 1694, AB, P2/B/1163
Geo., yeo., Gillingham, Dorset, 1717, AB, I, P27/1/219
Hy., yeo., Sutton M., 1680, I, W, P2/B/957
Hy., yeo., Sutton M., 1722, W, P2/B/1412
Jane, widow, Sutton M., 1679, AB, I, copy I, P2/B/953
Joan, widow, Sutton, 1615, W, P2/B/357
Joan, sp., Sal. The Close, 1688, W, P5/1688/8
Jn., husb., Swallowcliffe, 1562, W, P5/1Reg/28B
Jn., husb., Sutton M., 1613, I, W, P1/B/89
Jn., cook, Winterborne K., Dorset, 1673, I, W, P5/1673/4
Beelen, Jn., Sutton M., 1679, I, W, P2/B/948
Jn., linen weaver, Woodlands, Mere, 1685, AB, I, P5/1685/19
Mgt., sp., Sutton M., 1714, I, W, P1/B/791, P1/5Reg/346A
Matthew, gent., Ansty, 1743, AB, ren, P1/B/1161
Ralph, husb., no abode stated, 1620, W, P2/B/406
Sarah, widow, Mere, 1751, I, W, P5/1750/3
Steph., husb., Sutton M., 1639, I, W, P2/B/635
Steph., Gillingham, Dorset, 1826, comm, W, Wr, P27/1/671
Steph., yeo., Milton upon Stour, Gillingham, Dorset, 1834, W, Wr, P27/1/706
Thos., linen weaver, Mere, 1742, W, Wr, P5/1742/3
Wm., husb., Swallowcliffe, 1616, I, W, P5/1616/8, P5/9Reg/178D
Wm., yeo., Mere, 1745, W, P5/1745/1
Wm., yeo., Mere, 1748, W, Wr, P5/1748/2
Bealy, Armanel, sp., Sherb., Dorset, 1733, AB, ren, P5/1733/6

Belly, Hy., husb., Wylye, 1620, AB, I, W, P2/B/394, 409
Belley, Joan, widow, E. Kennett, 1623, I, W, P3/B/228
Belly, Jn., husb., Wylye, 1598, AB, I, W, P2/B/192
Jn., weaver, Short St., Dilton, Westb., 1672, AB, I, W, P25/1672/11
Jn., innholder, Sherb., Dorset, 1698, AB, I, P5/1698/6
Robt., Sherb., Dorset, 1588, AB, P5/5Reg/27A
Robt., yeo., Sherb., Dorset, 1644, comm, I, W, P5/1644/2, P5/14Reg/73B
Belle *or* Belley, Thos., Wylye, 1640, I, NW, P2/B/658
Thos., vict., Sherb., Dorset, 1714, W, P5/1714/2, P5/15Reg/387A
Belley, Wm., husb., Wylye, 1675, I, W, P2/B/890
Bealyn *see* Bealing
Beaman *see* Beaumont
Beames, Abigail, widow, Alderton, 1707, W, P3/B/1063
Agnes, widow, Littleton Drew, [1665], I, W (NEP), P3/B/505
Beems, Alice, widow, Holt, Bradford A., 1856, aff, O, W, Wr, P2/1856/59
Edith, sp., Wootton B., 1723, AB, ren, W, P1/B/886, P1/6Reg/425
Edwd., cordw., Hook, Lydiard T., 1734, W, P3/B/1336
Geo., yeo., Stanley, Bremhill (& Tytherton L.), 1673, I, W, P3/B/627
Geo., yeo., Lowden, Chipp., 1776, W, P1/B/1431, P1/13Reg/97B
Geo., gent., Allington, Chipp., 1838, O, W, Wr, P3/1838/27
Hugh, yeo., Stanley, Chipp., 1699, I, W, Wr, P3/B/983
Hugh, yeo., Lowden, Chipp., 1754, W, P3/B/1487
Jas., bach., Sal., 1800, AB, P4/1800/2
Jane, vict. and widow, Kington St M., 1788, W, P3/B/1709
Jn., Coped Hall, Wootton B., 1743, AB, I, P3/B/1414
Jn., Kemble, 1790, AB, comm, P3/B/1724
Jn., labourer, Grittleton, 1852, comm, W, Wr, P3/1852/54
Jonathan, patten maker, Sal., 1791, W, P4/1791/5
Jos., Grittleton, 1716, W, P1/B/822, P1/6Reg/24A
My., widow, Biddestone St Nich., 1756, W, P3/B/1503
Beems, Robt., grocer, Holt, Bradford A., 1842, O, W, Wr, P1/1842/103
Rosamond, sp., Chipp., 1810, AB, P3/1810/28
Steph., yeo., Alderton, 1701, I, W, P3/B/1005
Thos., yeo., Latton, 1692, comm, I, W, P3/B/889
Thos., yeo., Tytherton L. & Stanley, Chipp., 1713-14, I, W, P1/B/803, P1/5Reg/431
Thos., yeo., Hardenhuish, 1776, W, P3/B/1642
Walter, baker and maltster, Chipp., 1773, W, P1/B/1418, P1/13Reg/3
Wm., butcher, Crickl. St My., 1702, I, W, P3/B/1016
Wm., yeo., Lydiard T., 1808, W, Wr, P1/1808/84
Beamon, Beamond, Beamont, Beamount *see* Beaumont
Beanlands, Jn., innholder, Melk., 1781, comm, W, P2/B/1988
Bear *see* Beare
Beard, Alexander Sealy, blacksmith, Malm., 1856, aff, O, W, Wr, P3/1856/49
Ann, widow, Highw., 1698, I, W, P5/1698/12
Ann, widow, Castle C., 1810, AB, Wr, P3/1810/48
Deborah, widow, Corsham, 1702, I, W, P29/B/35, P29/1Reg/282B
Edwd., yeo., Gt. Somerford, 1690, I, W, P3/B/865
Eliz., widow, Sal., 1715, W, P4/1715/5
Hy., E. Grimstead, W. Dean, 1732, AB, P1/B/997
Jas., innholder, Reading, Berks., 1664, I, W, P1/B/405
Jas., Chipp., 1792, AB, P3/B/1736
Joan, widow, Alderbury, 1676, W, P26/240
Jn., sen., Yetm., Dorset, 1596, W, P5/6Reg/138A
Jn., sen., Enmore Grn, Motc., Dorset, 1596, I, W, P5/1596/5
Jn., Trowb., 1615, I (2), P22/2/19
Jn., E. Grimstead, W. Dean, 1667, AB, I, P1/B/429
Jn., miller, Westb., 1728, W, P25/1729/2
Jn., blacksmith, Malm. St Peter & St Paul, 1838, W, Wr, P3/1838/39
Jos., farmer, Maiden B., 1803, W, P2/1803/90
Margery, widow, E. Grimstead, W. Dean, 1699, I, W, P2/B/1202

Martha, sp., Sevenhampton, Highw., 1682, I, W, P10/1682/1
My., sp., Hurst, Berks., 1674, I, W, P5/1674/2
My., widow, Chapmanslade, Dilton, Westb., 1713, W, P25/1713/6
My., widow, Worton, Pott., 1738, AB, I, P1/B/1107
My., widow, Sherb., Dorset, 1760, W, P5/1760/2
Matthew, mariner, Lyme R., Dorset, 1606, I, W, P5/1606/9, P5/8Reg/60B
Rd., Eastrop, Highw., 1668, AB, I, P5/1668/7
Rd., Edington, 1673, I, NW, P2/B/869
Rd., Wargrave, Berks., 1698, AB, P1/B/670
Rd., Sevenhampton, Highw., 1721, AB, P10/1721/2
Robt., Leigh, Yetm., Dorset, 1564, W, P5/1Reg/44B
Berd, Robt., Corsham, [1569], W (NEP), P29/1Reg/12
Robt., clerk, Hilmarton, 1627, I, P3/B/288
Susanna, wife, Malm., 1827, AB, O, Wr, P3/1827/20
Thos., Sonning, Berks., 1568, AB, P5/2Reg/28F
Thos., broad weaver, Semington, Steeple A., 1641, I, W, P1/B/300
Thos., jun., yeo., Sevenhampton, Highw., 1669, I, W, P10/1669/4
Thos., sen., yeo., Sevenhampton, Highw., 1671, I, NW, P10/1671/1
Thos., labouring man, Warren Row, Hurley, Berks., 1744, W, P1/B/1174, P1/9Reg/361B
Thos., carp., Warm., 1746, AB, P2/B/1649
Thos., yeo., Allington, Chipp., 1820, AB, comm, ren, W, Wr, P1/1820/145
Berd, Wm., Hurst, Berks., 1582, AB, a/c, I, P5/1582/7, P5/4Reg/50C
Wm., weaver, Semington, Steeple A., 1630, I, W, P2/B/531
Wm., jun., husb., Hurst, Berks., 1639, AB, comm, I, P5/1639/10, P5/13Reg/161B
Wm., sen., yeo., Hurst, Berks., 1639, AB, comm, I, P5/1638/5, P5/13Reg/160A
Wm., husb., Allington, Chipp., 1666, I, W, P1/B/426
Wm., yeo., Avill's Farm, Corsham, 1699, I, W, P3/B/984
Wm., yeo., Wokm., Berks., 1706, comm, W, P5/1706/3, P5/15Reg/1A
Wm., fisherman, Cookham, Berks., 1708, AB, I, P1/B/742
Wm., yeo., Yatton K., 1730, W, P3/B/1286
Wm., gent., Yatton K., 1796, W, P3/B/1749
Wm., sen., yeo., Yatton K., 1815, W, Wr, P3/1815/42
Wm., yeo., Yatton K., 1819, comm, W, Wr, P3/1819/43
see also Biggs als B.; King als B.
Beardon *see* Burdon
Beare, Alice, widow, Chisbury, Lt. Bedwyn, 1679, I, W, P5/1679/7
Beer, Ann, sp., Calne, 1799, note, W, P26/1224
Beere, Benj., jun., merchant, Lyme R., Dorset, 1725, W, P5/1725/9, P5/16Reg/115A
Beere, Benj., sen., merchant, Lyme R., Dorset, 1733, comm, W, P16/268
Beere, Benj., Lyme R., Dorset, 1735, AB, comm, P16/275
Beer, Chas., sen., roper, Chards., Devon, 1774, W, P14/184
Christian, widow, Everleigh, 1739, W, P3/B/1378
Bear, Edwd., Patney, 1706, AB, P2/B/1258
Edwd., yeo., Everleigh, 1735, W, P1/B/1040, P1/7Reg/627A
Beer, Edwd., miller, Sherrington, 1763, comm, W, P2/B/1795
Eliz., widow, Calne, 1671, I, W, P26/179
Beere, Eliz., widow, Holnest, Dorset, 1737, I, W, Wr, P5/1737/4
Beer, Eliz., sp., Stockwood, Dorset, 1773, AB, comm, P5/1773/6, P5/17Reg/49B
Beer, Eliz., sp., Calne, 1799, note, W, P26/1223
Bear, Francis, shoemaker, Hungerford, Berks., 1817, comm, req, W, Wr, P23/878
Beere, Gideon, yeo., Halstock, Dorset, 1686, I, W, P16/85
Hector, husb. *or* yeo., W. Everleigh, 1706, I, W, P3/B/1054
Beere, Hippolyte, Holnest, Dorset, 1634, AB, comm, I, P5/1634/3, P5/12Reg/166A
Hy., cordw., Calne, 1707, I, W, P5/1707/6, P5/15Reg/15
Beere, Jas., Westb., 1757, AB, P25/1757/6
Beere, Jane, widow, Halstock, Dorset, 1710, W, P5/1710/9, P5/15Reg/187
Beer, Jane, widow, Sherrington, 1781, AB, comm, W, P2/B/1980, P1/13Reg/319
Joan, widow, Over C., Dorset, 1613, I, W, P5/1613/8, P5/9Reg/108B
Jn., sen., yeo., Bullands, Calne, 1582, AB, I, W, P5/1582/9, P5/4Reg/51B
Jn., sen., husb., Over C., Dorset, 1610, W, P5/9Reg/38B

Beere, Jn., yeo., Over C., Dorset, 1631, I, W, P5/1631/14, P5/12Reg/26
Jn., W. Lavington, 1639, AB, P1/B/288
Beere, Jn., serge weaver, Lacock, 1684, I, W, P3/B/789
Beer, Jn., woolcomber, Holnest, Dorset, 1695, AB, I, P5/1695/5
Bear, Jn., Horton, Bps. C., 1717, AB, I, P24/651
Jn., Calne, 1722, AB, I, P5/1722/6
Beere, Jn., tailor, Holnest, Dorset, 1724, I, W, P5/1724/10, P5/16Reg/101A
Beere, Jn., sen., gent., Ford, Netherb., Dorset, 1730, W, P17/438
Jn., Everleigh, 1737, AB, P3/B/1361
Beer, Jn., Netherb., Dorset, 1747, AB, P17/502
Beere, Jn., Ryme I., Dorset, 1766, AB, comm, P5/1766/8
Jn., Sal. St Thos., 1838, D, W, Wr, P4/1838/10
Beere, Mgt., widow, Over C., Dorset, 1685, AB, I, P5/1685/13
My., minor, Over C., Dorset, 1588, T (dau of Wm. B.), P5/5Reg/27B-C
Beer, My., sp., Milston, 1766, W, P2/B/1832
Beer, My., widow, Sherrington, 1771, comm, W, P2/B/1874
Rachel, widow, W. Everleigh, 1723, W, P1/B/883, P1/6Reg/426B
Rd., husb., E. Everleigh, Everleigh, 1675, AB, I (re both Rd. & Joan), W, P3/B/650
Robt., glover, Eddington, Hungerford, Berks., [1608], W (NEP), P5/1608/39
Beere, Robt., husb., Chisbury, Lt. Bedwyn, 1678, comm, I, W, P21/2/54
Beer, Sam., carp., Sal., 1852, W, Wr, P4/1852/7
Beere, Sarah, Holnest, Dorset, 1708, W, P5/1708/5, P5/15Reg/78
Thos., Fittleton, 1608, AB, I, W, P2/B/283, P2/8Reg/30C
Thos., Fittleton, 1630, AB, I, P2/B/516
Beere, Thos., husb., Halstock, Dorset, 1710, comm, W, P5/1710/10, P5/15Reg/186
Beer, Thos., yeo., Netherb., Dorset, 1746, AB, comm, W, P5/1746/5
Beere, Thos., gent., Ryme I., Dorset, 1771, comm, W, P5/1771/5, P5/17Reg/28
Walter, servant to Wpful Mr Wm. Brouncker, Tilsh., 1592, W, P1/B/5
Beere, Wm., Upavon, 1546, W, P2/2Reg/4B
Wm., husb., Over C., Dorset, 1588, W, P5/5Reg/27B
Wm., husb., W. Everleigh, 1639, AB, I, P3/B/411
Wm., Sunton, Collingbourne K., 1670, AB, I, P3/B/567
Beere, Wm., jun., cordw., Holnest, Dorset, 1677, I, W, P5/1677/8
Beere, Wm., sen., yeo., Holnest, Dorset, 1692, comm, I, W, P5/1692/3
Bear, Wm., collarmaker, Pewsey, 1741, W, P1/B/1146, P1/9Reg/165A
Bear, Wm., Sherrington, 1773-80, AB (2), P2/B/1894
Bear, Wm., soldier in E. India Co. service, Melk. (form. of Bromham), 1794, AB, comm, P2/B/2096
Beer, Wm., accountant, Sal., 1851, W, Wr, P4/1851/13
Bearley *see* Burley
Bearn, Bearns *see* Burne
Beasely *see* Basely
Beaser *see* Beazer
Beast *see* Best
Beat, Wm., Bodenham, Nunton and B., 1581, W, P2/B/2150, P2/6Reg/34A
Wm., Sal. St Thos., 1621, AB, I, P4/1621/8
Beath *see* Bath
Beaton, Edwd., husb., Nether C., Dorset, 1705, W, P5/1705/6
Francis, yeo., Over C., Dorset, 1686, AB, I, W, P5/1686/6
Geo., gardener and clerk, Nether C., Dorset, 1815, W, Wr, P5/1815/19
Jn., Nether C., Dorset, 1675, AB, I, P5/1675/6
Jn., yeo., Nether C., Dorset, 1738, I, W, Wr, P5/1738/2
Nehemiah, clerk, Lillington, Dorset, 1689, AB, comm, ren, P5/1689/2
Nich., yeo., Nether C., Dorset, 1668, I, P5/1668/8
Robt., gent., Halstock, Dorset, 1676, AB, comm, I, P16/46
Robt., sen., Nether C., Dorset, 1724, AB, P5/1724/9
Thos., husb., Nether C., Dorset, 1674, I, W, P5/1674/12
Beaty, Jn., grocer, Abingdon, Berks., 1747, W, P1/B/1199, P1/10Reg/81
Beauchamp, Beacham, And., yeo., Winterslow, 1756, W, P2/B/1724
Beecham, Hy., sen., Whitep., 1640, AB, a/c, comm, I, P2/B/662
Beacham, Hy., yeo., The Earldoms, Whitep., 1681, I, NW, P2/B/966

Beacham, Hy., The Earldoms, Whitep., 1690, AB, I, P5/1690/4
Beacham, Hy., The Earldoms, Whitep., 1724, AB, I, P2/B/2149
Honour, Lady, Sal. St Edmd., 1615, I, W, P4/1615/10
Beacham, Jas., tanner and innholder, Semington, Steeple A., 1805, W, P2/1805/78
Jn., Plaitford, 1557, W, P2/3Reg/39D
Beacham, Jn., Newbury, Berks., 1711, AB, P1/B/751
Sam., yeo., Whitehorn Hill, Whitep., 1847, D, W, Wr, P2/1847/26
Wm., publican and maltster, W. Dean, 1854, AB (2), court proceeding, D (2), O, W, Wr, P2/1854/28
Beaumont, Beamond, Cath., widow, New Windsor, Berks., 1708, AB, I, P1/B/743
Bemant, Edmd., maltster, Warm., 1768, W, P2/B/1848
Beaman, Edwd., Bowerhill, Melk., 1744, AB, P2/B/1628
Beamond, Eliz., widow, Melk., 1626, I, W, P2/B/464
Beaman, Eliz., widow, Bradford A., 1679, comm, I, W, P2/B/951
Beaman, Gerard, miller, Bradford A., 1671-76, AB, comm, I, P2/B/836, 898
Beamont, Hannah, widow, Seend Row, Melk., 1722, AB, P2/B/1406
Beamon, Hy., Rams., 1582, I, W, P5/1582/5, P5/4Reg/48B
Bemond, Jn., husb., Whitep., 1613, AB, I, W, P1/B/82
Bemond, Jn., Newton T., 1618, I, W, P2/B/382
Beaman, Jn., husb., Cholderton, 1676, I, W, P2/B/906
Beaman, My., sp., Bradford A., 1730, I, W, P2/B/1495
Peter, Winterbourne G., 1764, W, P2/B/1799
Beymonde, Rd., curate, Fovant, 1547, W, P2/2Reg/48A
Beamount, Robt., Newton T., 1639, I, W, P2/B/646
Beamon, Robt., Woodrow, Melk., 1663, AB, comm, I, P2/B/755
Bemont [Beamont], Robt., Newton T., 1728, AB, P2/B/1460
Robt., yeo., Allington, 1778, W, P2/B/1955
Beamont, Sarah, widow, Cholderton, 1752, AB, I, P2/B/1698
Beaumont *or* Beaman, Wm., cook, Devizes, 1667, I, P1/B/436
Beaven, Abraham, farmer, Pewsey, 1842, AB, comm, Wr, P3/1842/19
Ann, widow, E. Town, W. Ashton, Steeple A., 1809, W, Wr, P2/1809/22
Ann, wife, Poulshot, 1825, W, Wr, P2/1825/56
Ann Sarah, widow, Hilp., 1843, O, W, Wr, P2/1843/37
Charity, widow, Holt, Bradford A., 1830, O, W, Wr, P2/1830/50
Bevan, Chris., Bradford A., 1665, AB, P2/B/773
Chris., jun., yeo., Littleton Mill, Steeple A., 1706, I, W, P2/B/1253
Chris., yeo., Littleton, Steeple A., 1724, W, P2/B/1426
Chris., farmer, Bulk., Keevil, 1775, W, P2/B/1923
Chris., Hinton, Steeple A., 1778, AB, P2/B/1960
Chris., yeo., Littleton, Steeple A., 1798, W, P1/B/1547, P1/15Reg/153
Chris., yeo., Hilp., 1815, W, Wr, P2/1815/36
Beeven, Hannah, sp., Calne, 1729, I (detailed), W, P26/743
Jas., Edington, 1759, AB, P2/B/1757
Jas., dairyman and grazier, Whaddon, 1775, comm, W, P2/B/1914
Jas., clothw., Melk., 1792, cert of AB, P2/B/2073
Jas., yeo., Steeple A., 1838, O, W, Wr, P2/1838/36
Jas., gent., Gore Farm, Mkt. L., 1848, O, W, Wr, P1/1848/13
Jeremiah, Melk., 1726, AB, P2/B/1445
Joan, widow, Hinton, Steeple A., 1748, I, W, P2/B/1666
Jn., Melk., 1684, AB, I, P2/B/1040
Bevan, My., widow, Bristol, but effects at Melk., 1752, AB, affirmation (W believed lost, destroyed *or* mislaid & ex. bankrupt & abroad), P2/B/1696
Bevan form. Gowen, My., wife, Melk., 1758, AB, P2/B/1748
Bevan, My., widow, Bristol but with property at Devizes, 1761, AB, W, P1/B/1337
My., widow, Hinton, Steeple A., 1785, W, P2/B/2010
Bevan, Mercy, widow, Enborne, Berks., 1747, AB, P1/B/1220
Philip, yeo., S. Wraxall, 1676, AB, comm, I, P2/B/897
Rebecca, sp., Melk., 1782, comm, W, P2/B/1998
Rd., Lt. Cheverell, 1855, aff, D, W, Wr, P1/1855/39
Beven, Robt., tailor, Melk., 1601, I, W, P2/B/212
Bevin, Robt., tailor, Melk., 1669, AB, comm, I, P2/B/821

Roger, Melk., 1686-95, AB (2), comm, P2/B/1074, 1167
Bevan, Roger, Tinh., Edington, 1752, AB, P2/B/1693
Sam., yeo., Semington, Steeple A., 1811, W, Wr, P2/1811/30
Sam., yeo., Littleton, Steeple A., 1845, D, O, W, Wr, P2/1845/15
Steph., Avoncliff, Westwood, 1799, AB, comm, P2/B/2141
Susanna, widow, Calne (form. of Melk.), 1835, comm, W, P26/1423
Thos., Devizes, 1736, AB, P1/B/1066
Thos., cordw., Keevil, 1754, W, P2/B/1710
Bevan, Thos., merchant, Marl., 1755, W, P1/B/1286, P1/11Reg/172
Thos., gent., St Jas., Bristol, Gloucs, 1761, W, P1/12Reg/15
Thos., innholder, Melk., 1771, W, P2/B/1873
Thos., Holt, Bradford A., 1811, AB, comm, Wr, P1/1811/39
Thos., gent., Semington, Steeple A. (form. of Whaddon), 1820, W, Wr, P1/1820/15
Thos., Pewsey, 1847, AB, comm, Wr, P3/1847/42
Bevan, Wm., minor, Melk., 1744, T, P2/B/1630
Wm., yeo., Hilp., 1810, W, Wr, P2/1810/37
Wm., Melk., 1811, AB, comm, Wr, P2/1811/28
Bevan, Wm., Queenfield, Melk., 1836, AB, comm, P2/1836/25
Wm., gent., E. Town Farm, W. Ashton, Steeple A., 1852, O, W, Wr, P2/1852/33
Worthy, gent., Sutton V., 1837, comm, W, Wr, P2/1837/2
Beaver, Eleanor, Stratfield M., Berks., 1619, I, P1/B/149
Bever, Joan, widow, Stratfield M., Berks., 1668, I, NW, P1/B/445
Oliver, labourer, Sal. St Mart., 1633, I, W, P4/1633/4
Bever, Wm., Hurst, Berks., 1569, W, P5/2Reg/53B
see also Feltham als B.
Beavis, Bevis, Agnes als Ann, widow, Gillingham, Dorset (d. of Bulford), 1646, AB, NW, P2/B/708
Bevis, Alice, sp., Netheravon, 1696, AB, P12/137
Bevis, Ann, widow, Bishopstone S., 1803, W, P2/1803/30
Bevis, Ann *see* Agnes
Bevis, Edwd., Newton T., 1602, AB, I, note, P2/B/220
Bevis, Edwd., blacksmith, Sal. St Mart., 1713, AB, I, P4/1713/10
Eliz., widow, Trowb. (form. of Chilmark), 1816, comm, W, Wr, P1/1816/10
Bevis, Hy., husb., Bulford, 1638, I, W, P2/B/618
Bevis, Hy., W. Amesb., 1707, AB, ren, P2/B/1272
Hy., carp., Southwick, N. Bradley, 1778, W, P2/B/1963
Bevis, Jas., sen., stonemason, Tisb., 1854, aff, W, Wr, P2/1854/29
Bevis, Jn., Lyme R., Dorset, 1691, ren, P16/109
Bevis, Jn. *or* Rd., clothw., W. Harnham, 1671, AB, I, NW, P5/1671/14
Bevis, Mgt., widow, Wambrook, Somerset, 1825, comm, W, P14/212
My., Bulford, 1610, I, W, P2/B/305, P2/8Reg/111B
Bevis, My. *see also* Jonathan Symes
Bevis, Nathan, Boscombe, 1731, W, P2/B/1492
Bovis *or* Bevis, Rd., husb., Newton T., 1630, a/c (partly missing), I (badly damaged), NW, P2/B/520
Bevis, Rd., Bulford, 1681, I, W, P2/B/972
Bevis, Rd. *see also* Jn. *or* Rd.
Bevis, Robt., Bulford, 1599, I, W, P2/B/195
Bevis, Robt., blacksmith, Stratford Tony, 1632, AB, I, P2/B/552
Bevis, Robt., Newton T., 1639, AB, a/c, I, P2/B/640
Bevis, Robt., tailor, Bulford, 1646, I, W, P2/B/711
Bevis, Robt., yeo., Newton T., 1720, I, W, P1/B/865, P1/6Reg/345
Bevis, Sam., jun., seaman (d. on HMS *Victory*), Lyme R., Dorset, 1744, AB, P16/285
Bevis, Thos., Newton T., 1668, I, P2/B/787
Bevis, Wm., husb., Milford, Sal. St Mart., 1595, AB, W, P1/B/10
Bevis, Wm., Landford, 1631, AB, a/c, P2/B/545
Wm., shopkeeper, Codf. St P., 1803, W, P2/1803/62
Wm., yeo., Chilmark, 1814, W, Wr, P2/1814/24
Beazer, Bezer, Cath., widow, Warm., 1792, W, P2/B/2078
Beycer, Chris., Corsham, 1576, W, P29/B/3
Beaser *or* Beacer, Edwd., yeo., S. Wraxall, 1638, AB, I, P2/B/615
Besser, Edwd., Hilp., 1824, AB, Wr, P2/1824/42

Besar, Geo., yeo., Cumberwell, Bradford A., 1600, I, W, P2/B/204
Bezar, Geo., button maker, Cumberwell, Bradford A., 1677, AB, comm, ren, P2/B/916
Beaser, Geo., husb., Wadswick, Box, 1678, I, W, P3/B/680
Bezar, Grace, sp., Warm., 1690, AB, P2/B/1126
Beaser, Jn., Corsham, mid to late 16th century, W (date missing), P29/B/1
Maria, wife, Corsham, 1850, AB, O, Wr, P3/1850/47
My., widow, W. Yatton, Yatton K., 1685, I, W, P3/B/814
Beaser, Rd., yeo., S. Wraxall, 1633, I, W, P2/B/568, P2/9Reg/10B
Bezer, Robt., sen., mason, Rams., 1675, I, W, P5/1675/7
Bezar, Robt., mason, Rams., 1682, I, W, P5/1682/14
Beecer, Thos., yeo., Slaughterford, 1763, comm, W, P1/B/1345, P1/12Reg/46B
Beacer, Wm., yeo., Cumberwell, Bradford A., 1632, I, W, P2/B/555, P2/9Reg/24
Wm., Rams., 1690, AB, P5/1689/3
Bezer, Wm., grocer, Warm., 1854, aff, O, W, Wr, P2/1854/69
Beck, Agnes, wife of Thos., Mere, 1597, AB, NW, P5/1596/6, P5/6Reg/149D
Giles, New Windsor, Berks., 1628, AB, I, P1/B/218
Jasper, yeo., Gillingham, Dorset, 1682, I, P27/1/65
Jn., yeo., S. Marston, 1724, W, P10/1724/2
Jn., wheelwright, Remenham, Berks., 1770, W, P1/B/1403, P1/12Reg/371
Jos., yeo., N. Town, Maidenhead, Berks., 1711, AB, I, P1/B/770
Sam., carp., Lyme R., Dorset, 1824, W, Wr, P5/1824/32
Thos., tanner, Mere, 1603, W, P5/7Reg/73A
Thos., husb., Gillingham, Dorset, 1684, I, P27/1/73
Thos., Pewsey, 1826, W, Wr, P1/1826/100
Beckett, Alice, sp., Sal., 1683, AB, W, P4/1682/14
And., butcher, Hindon, 1706, I, W, P2/B/1254
Benj., Hindon, 1820, AB, Wr, P2/1820/14
Chas., S. Newton, 1596, I, T (children: Thos. & Wm. B.), W, P2/B/163, 166
Edith, S. Newton, 1614, W, P2/B/345
Edith, Urchf., 1703, AB, P2/B/1237
Eliz., widow, Hannington, 1670, I, W, P3/B/568
Beaket, Frances, sp., Castle Eaton, 1638, I, W, P1/B/280
Geo., Walcot, Bath, but left effects at Hindon, 1849, O, D, W, Wr, P2/1849/52
Jn., Lyneham, 1662, AB, comm, P3/B/477
Jn., yeo., Bushton, Clyffe P., 1663, AB, comm, I, P1/B/391
Jn., Devizes, 1691, AB, P1/B/609
Jn., Hindon, 1754, W, P2/B/1704
Jn., innholder, Hindon, 1791, W, P2/B/2056
Jn., butcher, Mere, 1803, W, P5/1803/41, P5/19Reg/73
Jn., Hindon, 1803, AB, P2/1803/72
Jn., butcher, Chilmark, 1808, W, Wr, P2/1808/8
Jn., sievemaker, Upton L., 1815, W, Wr, P2/1815/32
Jos., tailor, Hindon, 1785, W, P2/B/2003
Jos., carp., Mere, 1791, W, P5/1791/18, P5/18Reg/166A
Luke, collarmaker, Mkt. L., 1820, comm, W, Wr, P1/1820/125
Becketts, My., widow, Mere, 1817, W, Wr, P5/1817/5
Michael, husb., Stert, Urchf., 1686, I, W, P1/B/583
Thos., S. Newton, 1638, I, W, P2/B/628
Thos., maltster, Urchf., 1690, I, W, P2/B/1120
Thos., innkeeper, Stapleford, 1853, D, W, Wr, P2/1853/58
Wm., husb., Blackland, Calne, 1584, AB, I, W, P5/1583/1, P5/4Reg/73A
Wm., husb., S. Newton, 1598, AB, I, W, P2/B/191
Wm., sen., gent., Littleton P., 1606, I, W, P1/B/36
Wm., gent., Littleton P., 1678, AB, I, W, P1/B/520
Wm., gent., Littleton P., 1705, AB, I, W, P1/B/725
Wm., gent., Littleton P., 1755, W, P1/B/1287, P1/11Reg/176
Wm., innholder, Hindon, 1793, W, P2/B/2090
Wm., Hindon, 1805, AB, P2/1805/71
Wm., cordw., Mere, 1819, W, Wr, P5/1819/2
Beckford, Wm., yeo., Knowl Hill, Hurley, Berks., 1674, I, W, P1/B/497

Wm. *see also* Jn. Collins
Beckham, Benj., joiner, Sal., 1683, W, P4/1683/16
Humphrey, joiner, Sal., 1672, I, W, P4/1671/14
Jn., Sal., 1645, I, W, P1/B/320
Nathaniel, joiner, Sal., 1678, AB, I, P4/1678/24
Beckingham, Anth., yeo., Upton, Blewbury, Berks., 1674, AB, a/c, I, P5/1674/13
Anth., yeo., Upton, Blewbury, Berks., 1702, W, P5/1702/4
Archibald, innholder and gent., *Three Swans Inn*, Sal., 1672, AB, I, P4/1671/11
Benj., Lambourn, Berks., 1808, AB, Wr, P1/1808/119
Eliz., widow, Baydon, 1771, AB, comm, P5/1771/4, P5/17Reg/30A
Hy., E. Garston, Berks., 1692, AB, I, P1/B/625
Jas., yeo., Upton, Blewbury, Berks., 1794, W, P5/1794/3, P5/18Reg/200B
Jn., Upton, Blewbury, Berks., 1698, I, W, P5/1698/15
Jn., Upton, Blewbury, Berks., 1739, AB, I (detailed), Wr, P5/1739/6
Jn., Overton, 1847, AB, Wr, P3/1847/18
My., widow, Whittonditch, Rams., 1814, comm, W, Wr, P5/1814/10
Roger, husb. and yeo., Gt. Hidden, Hungerford, Berks., 1674, I, W, P5/1674/14
Seymour, sen., wheelwright, Baydon, 1753, W, P5/1753/1
Thos., sen., yeo., Baydon, 1794, W, P5/1794/5, P5/18Reg/198B
Thos., yeo., Baydon, 1806, W, P5/1806/4, P5/19Reg/151
Beckingsale, Dan., Sal., 1818, W, Wr, P4/1818/3
Geo., auctioneer, Sal., 1856, aff, D, W, Wr, P4/1856/1
Jn., gent., Milford, Sal. St Mart., 1854, aff, W, Wr, P4/1854/9
Beckington, Gilbt., yeo., W. Amesb., 1616, AB, I, W, P2/B/362, P2/8Reg/302E
Melior, yeo., W. Amesb., 1573, W, P2/5Reg/174E
Thos., Steeple A., 1574, AB, P2/5Reg/180C
Wm., Britford, 1570, W, P5/2Reg/60A
Wm., Winterbourne S., 1571, W, P2/5Reg/114C
Beckley, Hy., Marl., 1641, AB, P1/B/296
Nathaniel, yeo., Boscombe, 1683, I, W, P2/B/1017
Nathaniel, Durrington, 1753, W, P2/B/1702
Thos., Ludg., 1599, AB, I, note, P2/B/196
Wm., Durrington, 1688, I, W, P2/B/1090
Bedborough, Agnes, widow, Tytherington, Heytes., 1593, AB, I, W, P5/1592/16, P5/6Reg/16B
Agnes, widow, Alton Pr., 1612, W, P3/B/88
Alice, widow, Alton Pr., [1621], I (NEP), P3/B/203
Alice, widow, Alton Pr., 1639, AB, a/c, P3/B/412
Edith, widow, Longbridge D., 1588, W, P2/7Reg/134D
Jn., Longbridge D., 1569, AB, P2/5Reg/60C
Jn., husb., Longbridge D., 1610, I, W, P2/B/302, P2/8Reg/106B
Kinborough, widow, Longbridge D., 1634, I, W, P1/B/246
Leonard, husb., Longbridge D., 1565, W, P2/4Reg/195A
Thos., Longbridge D., 1557, W, P2/3Reg/64B
Bedbury, Amy, widow, Sal., 1688, AB, P4/1688/8
Amy, widow, Sal., 1721, AB, P4/1721/2
Jn., yeo., Sal. St Edmd., 1645, I, W, P1/B/317
Bedell *see* Beadle
Bedford, Chas., innkeeper, Sal., 1854, aff, W, Wr, P4/1854/15
Christian, widow, Burdens Ball, Wilton, 1747, I (very detailed), W, P2/B/1656
Eliz., widow, Alderbury, 1646, I, W, P26/94
Eliz., widow, Winterslow, 1832, W, Wr, P1/1832/58
Geo., vict., Abingdon, Berks., 1750, W, P1/B/1231, P1/10Reg/290
Hy., builder and stone mason, Warm. Common, 1853, D, W, Wr, P2/1853/29
Bedford *or* Betford, Jn., Lyme R., Dorset, 1609, AB, I, P5/1609/4, P5/8Reg/167B
Jn., weaver, Calne, 1639, I, P26/90
Jn., miller, Wrou., 1813, W, Wr, P3/1813/22
Jn., cordw., Clyffe P., 1851, comm, W, Wr, P1/1851/5
Jos., yeo., Wrou., 1857, aff, comm, W, Wr, P3/1857/12
My., Maidenhead, Berks., 1664, I, W, P1/B/407
My., widow, Sonning, Berks., 1833, W, Wr, P5/1833/16

Rachel, widow, Wrou., 1820, W, Wr, P1/1820/119
Rd., Lyme R., Dorset, 1607, AB, comm, I (2), P5/1607/10, P5/8Reg/92B
Betford, Robt., husb., Halstock, Dorset, 1609, AB, I, W, P5/1609/5, P5/8Reg/167A
Thos., Burdens Ball, S. Newton, 1748, AB, P2/B/1664
Thos., yeo., Warm., 1774, W, P2/B/1908
Thos., shopkeeper, Warm., 1801, W, Wr, P1/1801/125, P1/15Reg/343B
Thos., Winterslow, 1818, AB, W, Wr, P2/1818/67
Thos., yeo., Wantage, Berks., 1829, W, P23/947
Thos., miller, Wrou., 1852, comm, W, Wr, P3/1852/36
Wm., broad weaver, Calne, 1619, NW, P5/1619/88, P5/10Reg/50A
Betford, Wm., weaver, Corsley, 1625, AB, I, NW, P1/B/203
Wm., gent., Sal. St Edmd., 1635, I, W, P4/1634/4
Wm., sen., slaymaker, Chipp., 1667, comm, I, W, P3/B/521
Wm., Lambourn Woodlands, Berks., 1701, W, P1/4Reg/114
Wm., Blagrave, Lambourn, Berks., 1701, I, W, P1/B/688
Wm., slaymaker, Chipp., 1705, I (detailed), W, P3/B/1038
Wm., Stratford sub C., 1812, AB, P4/1812/7
see also Clerke als B.; Grant als B.
Bedlegge, Adrian, priest, Stanton St B., 1561, institution to vicarage, P1/1Reg/76A
Bedler, Wm., Bromham, 1610, AB, P3/B/63
Bedloe, Moses, clothier, Fordington, Dorset, 1703, AB, I, P15/70
Bedmead *see* Bidmead
Bedwell, Ann, widow, Calne, 1760, AB, W, P26/977
Bidwell, Anna, widow, Devizes St My., 1846, W, Wr, P1/1846/3
Harry, sen., yeo., Calne, 1760, W, P26/978
Bidwell, Jn., gent., Sherb., Dorset, 1721, W, P5/1721/2, P5/16Reg/57D
Thos., gent., Poulton, 1728, W, P3/B/1266
Bedwin, Ann, widow, N. Moreton, Berks., 1756, W, P1/B/1301, P1/11Reg/252
Bee, Jn., gent., Downton, 1682, AB, I, P2/B/1007
My., Britford, 1664, AB, W, P24/342
Matthew, gent., Charlton, Downton, 1671, AB, I, P1/B/478
Beebee *see* Biby
Beecer *see* Bezer
Beech *see* Beach
Beecham *see* Beacham
Beechey, Gregory, husb., Wootton B., 1621, AB, I, P3/B/204
Jas., Highw., 1714, AB, I (miscellaneous notes on reverse), P10/1714/2
Beachy, Jn., Highw., 1733, AB, P10/1733/4
Beegle, Beegle als Habbott, Roger, tailor, Downton, 1628, I, W, P1/B/208, P2/B/483
Beelen *see* Bealing
Beems *see* Beames
Been, Geo., Atworth, Bradford A., 1763, W, P1/B/1353, P1/12Reg/72
Wm., yeo., Shaw, Melk., 1794, comm, W, P2/B/2092
Beer, Beere *see* Beare
Bees, Margery, widow, Grittleton, 1630, I, W, P3/B/320
Beesy *see* Bysy *or* B.
Beessly *see* Basely
Beeston, Wm., Mkt. L., 1743, AB, P2/B/1618
Beeven *see* Beaven
Beezley *see* Basely
Befford, Thos., Sal. St Edmd., 1584, AB, P4/Reg/23E
Thos., butcher, Sal., 1686, I, W, P4/1685/28
Wm., fishmonger, Sal., 1785, W, P4/1785/1
Wm., Sal., 1787, AB, P4/1787/4
Beilie *see* Bailey
Beke *see* Beak
Belben, Wm., Fordington, Dorset, 1742, AB, P15/129
Belch, Belck, Robt., Fordington, Dorset, 1702, AB & comm, P15/84
Wm., carp., Sonning, Berks., 1635, I, W (2 - 1 informal & 1 formalised version), P5/1635/13, P5/12Reg/198
Belcher, Alice, widow, Gt. Faringdon, Berks., 1634, comm, I, W (GVS), P5/1634/21, P5/12Reg/320

Amy als Ann, widow, Sonning, Berks., 1639, AB, I, P5/1639/13, P5/13Reg/199C
Anth., Dilton M., Westb., 1741, AB, I, P25/1741/12
Edwd., maltster, Chipp., 1854, aff, W, Wr, P3/1854/23
Francis, sen., yeo., Denchworth, Berks., 1732, W, P1/B/1000, P1/7Reg/447A
Francis, yeo., S. Denchworth, Berks., 1770, W, P1/B/1400, P1/12Reg/364
Geo., shoemaker, Wantage, Berks., 1641, I, W, P5/1641/4, P5/14Reg/2A
Belshaw, Geo., Fisherton A., 1668, AB (blank AB on reverse), P2/B/790
Geo., Wantage, Berks., 1716, I, W, P5/1716/4, P5/15Reg/351B
Hy., husb., E. Hanney, W. Hanney, Berks., 1741, W, P1/B/1132, P1/9Reg/97
Isaac, yeo., Chr. M., 1714, W, P1/B/800, P1/5Reg/428B
Isolde, widow, Highw., 1726, AB, P10/1725/1
Belshire, Jn., broad weaver, Westb., 1706, I, W, P25/1706/2
Jos., yeo., Goosey, Stanford in the Vale, Berks., 1747, W, P1/B/1202, P1/10Reg/93
My., sp., Kington L., 1854, D, O, W, Wr, P3/1854/2
Rd., gent., Wantage, Berks., 1838, O, W, Wr, P23/994
Belsheire, Thos., Fisherton A., 1667, AB, P2/B/781
Belshire, Thos., Sal., 1677, AB, I, P4/1677/15
Thos., yeo., Eastrop, Highw., 1723, W, P10/1723/7
Thos., sen., cordw., Eastrop, Highw., 1740, W, Wr, P5/1740/11
Wm., husb. *or* yeo., Denchworth, Berks., 1631, I, W (probate copy, proved in Archdeaconry of Berkshire), P1/B/234
Wm., wheelwright, W. Hanney, Berks., 1729, I, W, P1/B/969, P1/7Reg/246
Wm., Hannington, 1734, AB, P3/B/1337
Wm., Charlton, Wantage, Berks., 1739, W, P23/532
Wm., maltster, Chr. M., 1745, comm, W, P3/B/1426
Wm., Chr. M., 1785, AB, P3/B/1696
Wm., sen., baker and maltster, Chr. M., 1798, W, P1/B/1556, P1/15Reg/113
Wm., maltster, Kington L., 1836, W, Wr, P3/1836/66
Wm., maltster, Langley Fitzurse, Kington St M., 1848, O, W, Wr, P3/1848/7
Wm., maltster, Kington L., 1854, aff, O, W, Wr, P3/1854/51
Belck *see* Belch
Belde *see* Bold
Bell, Alan, tanner, Sal., 1674, I, W, P4/1674/7
Alan, currier, Sal., 1701, AB, I, P4/1701/3
Alice, widow, Zeals, 1669, I, W, P5/1669/4
And., yeo., Upton S., 1728, W, P2/B/1463
Ann, sp., Marl., 1756, W, P1/B/1306, P1/11Reg/330
Anna, widow, Enford, 1771, ren, W, P1/B/1406, P1/12Reg/399
Anth., Chisenbury, Enford, 1776, W, P5/1776/3, P5/17Reg/130
Chas., sen., husb., Luckington, 1771, W, P3/B/1617
Chas., baker, Trowb., 1800, comm, W, P1/1800/3, P1/15Reg/201
Chas., gent., Luckington, 1835, W, P3/1835/29
Chris., Zeals, 1668, AB, I, P5/1668/11
Dan., yeo., Kington L., 1710, AB, I, P3/B/1084
David, chapman, Reading, Berks., 1708, comm, W, P1/B/747
Edith, Kington St M., [1611], W (NEP), P3/B/78
Edwd., Kington L., 1630, I, W, P3/B/321
Edwd., yeo., Priory Farm, Kington St M., 1641, AB, a/c, I, ren, P3/B/454
Edwd., husb., Donhead St A., 1689, I, W, P2/B/1103
Edwd., sen., gent., Marl., 1714, I, W, P1/B/805, P1/5Reg/461
Edwd., Easton Grey, 1842, AB, O, W, Wr, P3/1842/40
Eliz., widow, Gillingham, Dorset, 1790, comm, W, P27/1/538, P27/3Reg/265
Essex, jun., sp., Rams., 1754, AB, W, P5/1754/3
Essex, widow, Rams., 1754, W, P5/1754/2
Francis, [draper], Wokm., Berks., 1703, AB, I, P5/1703/2
Francis, innholder, Rams., 1708, AB, comm, ren, W, P5/1708/6, P5/15Reg/88
Geo., husb., Trowb., 1630, I, P22/1/17
Geo., yeo., Clatford, Preshute (form. of Broughton ; effects at Winterslow), 1846, W, Wr, P2/1846/45
Hy., Langley Burrell, 1620, I, W, P3/B/188
Isaac, yeo., S. Burcombe, 1638, AB, I, P2/B/629
Jas., yeo., Chisenbury, Enford, 1764, W, P2/B/1798

Jane, widow, Trowb., 1776, W, P1/B/1445, P1/13Reg/163
Joan, widow, Foxham, Bremhill, 1629, I, W, P3/B/304
Joanna, minor, Luckington, 1783, app. of guardian, P3/B/1681
Jn., Sal. St Mart., 1639, I, NW, P4/1639/5
Jn., yeo., Luckington, 1725, I, W, P3/B/1238
Jn., fellmonger, Marl., 1727, W, P1/B/940, P1/7Reg/183A
Jn., miller, Seend Head, Melk., 1777, comm, W, P2/B/1941
Jn., Trowb., 1785, AB, P1/B/1495
Jn., yeo., Allington, 1799, W, P2/B/2139
Jn., yeo., Luckington, 1853, O, W, Wr, P3/1853/63
Jonathan, glazier, Corsham, 1727, I, W, P29/B/42, P29/2Reg/49
Jos., yeo., W. Harnham, 1818, W, Wr, P8/82
Margery, Kington L., 1606, I, W, P1/B/52
Margery, Foxham, Bremhill, 1629, AB, a/c, P3/B/305
My., widow, Westb., 1695, AB, I, P25/1696/5
My., widow, Bulford, 1749, AB, P2/B/1669
My., widow, Reading, Berks., 1750, W, P1/B/1241, P1/10Reg/346
Rd., tailor, Kington L., 1624, I, W, P3/B/246
Rd., Foxham, Bremhill, 1625, I, W, P3/B/264
Rd., husb., Chr. M., 1641, I, W, P3/B/455
Rd., tanner, Eddington, Hungerford, Berks., 1699, I, W (NEP), but W (1685) & I (undated) both endorsed 1699, P23/231
Robt., husb., Maiden B., 1623, AB, I, P2/B/429
Robt., gent., W. Harnham, 1856, aff, W, Wr, P8/100
Sarah, innkeeper & widow, Hungerford, Berks., 1715, I, W, P23/348
Sarah, widow, Devizes, 1743, W, P1/B/1160, P1/9Reg/256
Sarah, sp., Gillingham, Dorset, 1802, AB, comm, P27/1/583
Sarah, widow, Farley, Alderbury, 1827, AB, Wr, P26/1364
Steph., yeo., Zeals, 1681, I, W, P5/1681/5
Steph., hairdresser, Devizes, 1826, O, W, Wr, P1/1826/43
Steph., yeo., W. Harnham, 1846, AB, Wr, P8/95
Susanna, widow, Warm., 1759, W, P2/B/1755
Thos., Devizes St Jn., 1639, AB, P1/B/290
Thos., [maltster], Warm., 1723, AB, I (very detailed), P2/B/1420
Thos., The Earldoms, Whitep., 1735, AB, I, P2/B/1547
Thos., miller, Baldham Mill, Keevil, 1788, comm, W, P2/B/2028
Thos., Luckington, 1818, AB, comm, Wr, P3/1818/37
Thos., shopkeeper, Winterslow Common, 1826, W, Wr, P2/1826/14
Thos., Winterslow, 1856, AB, aff, D, I, W, Wr, P2/1856/38
Wm., husb., Hamptworth, Downton, 1555, W, P2/1Reg/99B
Wm., Hungerford, Berks., 1693, AB, comm, P5/1693/9
Wm., barber, Devizes, 1699, I, W, P1/B/681, P1/3Reg/240
Wm., vintner, Hungerford, Berks., 1702, I, W, P23/245
Wm., blacksmith, Mkt. L., 1723, W, P2/B/1422
Wm., Zeals, 1732, AB, I, P5/1732/3
Wm., miller, Steeple L. (form. of Bulford), 1733, W, P2/B/1522
Wm., yeo., W. Grimstead, 1766, AB, I, a/c, P2/B/1825
Wm., sen., baker, Trowb., 1768, W, P1/B/1385, P1/12Reg/278
Wm., yeo., Farley, Alderbury, 1783, W, P26/1128
see also Belle *or* B.; Jackson form. B.
Bellamy, Abraham, Gt. Cheverell, 1807, AB, comm, Wr, P2/1807/75
Ann, widow, Hermitage, Dorset, 1802, note of AB, W, P5/1802/22, P5/19Reg/21
Eliz., wife, Netherb., Dorset, 1760, AB, P17/545
Belle *see* Bealy
Bellett *see* Billett
Belley *see* Bealy
Belling, Jn., priest, W. Grimstead, 1552, institution to rectory on death of Bowman., P2/2Reg/146A
Bellinger, Eliz., blacksmith's widow, Shippon, Abingdon, Berks., 1741, AB, comm, I, P1/B/1124
My., widow, Chilton, Berks., 1732, W, P1/B/1004, P1/7Reg/466
Bellman, Benj., yeo., Fordington, Dorset, 1731, AB, I, P15/79
Jn., blacksmith, Motc., Dorset, 1699, W, P27/1/134

My., Calne, 1671, AB, P26/180
Robt., weaver, Mill St., Fordington, Dorset, 1741, I, W, P15/128
Thos., Fordington, Dorset, 1573, I, W, P5/1573/6, P5/3Reg/19A
Bellot, Bellott *see* Billett
Bellow, Bellows, Wm., draper, Bere R., Dorset, 1815, W, Wr, P5/1815/26
Wm., Durrington, 1823, W, Wr, P1/1823/21
Belly *see* Bealy,
Belott *see* Billett
Belsheire, Belshire *see* Belcher
Belton, Eleanor, widow, Westb., 1629, I, W, P25/1629/2
Eliz., Westb., 1704, I, W, P25/1704/6
Hy., sen., yeo., Westb., 1697-1702, AB, I, W, P25/1697/5, P25/1702/7
Hy., Westb., 1718, AB (d. c1705), P25/1718/7
Philip, gent., Westb., 1710, I, ren, W, P25/1710/6
Robt., joiner, Westb., 1679, AB, I, P25/1679/7
Thos., linen draper, Westb. L., 1636, I, NW, P2/B/599
Bemant *see* Beaumont
Bemister, Ann, sp., Sal. The Close, 1708, W, P5/1708/15, P5/15Reg/102A
Christian, Sal. The Close, 1689, I, W, P5/1688/15
Bimister *or* Binister, Jn., yeo., Alderbury, 1776, W, P26/1084
Jn., Rushall, 1826, AB, Wr, P2/1826/4
Bemond, Bemont *see* Beaumont
Benbery, Jn., Tollard Royal, 1602, AB, I, W, P1/B/13
Bence, Alice, widow, Biddestone St Nich., 1845, aff, W, Wr, P3/1845/21
Hy., weaver, Corsham, 1607, W, P29/B/12
Hy., yeo., Biddestone St Nich., 1840, W, Wr, P3/1840/34
Isaac, yeo., Lacock, 1733, comm, W, P3/B/1322
Jn., Bere R., Dorset, 1733, AB, P5/1733/7
Thos., Hullavington, 1826, AB, Wr, P1/1826/66
Bench, Wm., yeo., Tollard Royal, 1774, W, P2/B/1904
Wm., yeo., Tollard Royal, 1810, W, Wr, P2/1810/21
Bendall, Bendoll, Ann, widow, Heytes., 1704, I, W, P5/1704/8
Benj., Wootton R., 1770, W, P3/B/1608
Cath., Mere, 1610, AB, I, T, P5/1609/11, P5/9Reg/14A
Chas., shopkeeper, Teffont M., 1717, I, NW, P2/B/1362
Grace, widow, Codf. St My., 1823, W, Wr, P1/1823/55
Hy., Kingston D., 1597, I, W, P2/B/182
Joan, Marl., 1696, AB, I, P1/B/658
Jn., Sutton V., 1565, AB, P2/4Reg/191C
Jn., Marl., 1710, AB, P1/B/750
Jn., Horningsham, 1789, AB, comm, P5/1789/1, P5/18Reg/132A
Jn., bach., Netheravon, 1846, AB, Wr, P1/1846/6
Matthew, labourer, Knook, 1637, I, NW, P5/1637/4, P5/13Reg/48
Susanna, sp., Warm., 1797, AB, comm, P2/B/2117
Thos., Dilton, Westb., 1619, I, W (both are lacking parts), P25/1619/2
Thos., husb., Leighs Marsh, Dilton, Westb., 1628, I, W, P25/1628/5
Thos., sen., husb., Heytes., 1638, I, W, P5/1638/6, P5/13Reg/89C
Bendoll, Thos., Dilton M., Westb., 1682, AB, comm, P25/1682/2
Thos., husb., Heytes., 1685, I, W, P5/1685/14
Thos., innholder, Chilton F., 1729, W, P1/B/951, P1/7Reg/285B
Thos., Sherrington, 1788, AB, P2/B/2036
Thos., Netheravon, 1808, AB, P12/210
Valerian, yeo., Corton, Boyton, 1631, I, W, P2/B/539
Wm., Tytherington, Heytes., 1560, AB, P5/1Reg/34D
Wm., carp., Boreham, Warm., 1791, AB, comm, W, P2/B/2058
Bendery *see* Bendry
Bendin, Jane, widow, Horningsham, 1611, I, W, P5/1612/4, P5/9Reg/53B,
Bendoll *see* Bendall
Bendry, Francis, yeo., Chr. M., 1671, AB, a/c, I, ren, P3/B/585
Bendery, Jane, gent.'s wife, Elcombe, Wrou., 1775, app. of proctor, W (2 - 1 a copy), P3/B/1636

Jn., yeo., Grittenham, Brinkw., 1616, comm, I, W, P3/B/134
Jn., sen., yeo., Chr. M., 1705, I, W, P3/B/1039
Jn., sen., gent., Chr. M., 1737, comm, W, P3/B/1362
Bendery, Jn., gent., Elcombe, Wrou., 1776, W, P3/B/1643
Jn., yeo., Wrou., 1800, comm, W, P3/1800/11
Jn., bach., Rowde, 1820, AB, comm, Wr, P3/1820/6
Margery, widow, Grittenham, Brinkw., 1629, I, W, P3/B/306
My., widow, Dauntsey, 1705, I, W, P3/B/1040
Ralph, yeo., Dauntsey, 1701, comm, I, W, P3/B/1006
Bendery, Thos., sen., blacksmith, Lyneham, 1712, I, W, P3/B/1104
Thos., vict., Chipp., 1831, W, P3/1831/40
Bendery, Wm., yeo., Wrou., 1780, W, P3/B/1662
Bendy, Jas., blacksmith, Steeple A., 1771, AB, comm, W, P2/B/1871
Jas., blacksmith, Keevil, 1802, W, P2/1802/69
Jn., Semington, Steeple A., 1803, W, P2/1803/48
Jn., glazier, Trowb., 1804, W, Wr, P1/1804/1, P1/15Reg/394
Jn., Melk., 1855, aff, comm, W, Wr, P2/1855/23
Rd., Semington, Steeple A., 1807, AB, comm, Wr, P2/1807/81
Thos., Steeple A., 1765, AB, P2/B/1812
Benfield *see* Binfield
Bengeman, Rd., husb., Stapleford, 1557, W, P2/3Reg/28A
Benger, Ann, widow, Elcombe, Wrou., 1692, I, W, P1/B/624
Ann, widow, Roundway, Bps. C. (form. of Manningford Bohun), 1695, I, W, P24/514
Banger, Bernard, rector, Mapperton, Dorset, 1698, I, W, P5/1698/5
Edith, widow, Alton B., 1614, I, W, P1/B/116
Banger, Eliz., widow, Alton B., 1662, AB, I, W, P3/B/476
Eliz., sp., Westb., 1820, O, W, Wr, P25/1820/1
Banger, Frances, Turners Puddle, Dorset, 1616, AB, gift, P5/1616/11
Geoff., yeo., Milton L., 1615, I, W, P3/B/122
Geo., yeo., Oare, Wilcot, 1614, AB, W (consists of nunc. cod to W now lost), P1/B/120
Geo., yeo., Oare, Wilcot, 1680, W, P1/B/528
Hy., yeo., Longcott, Shrivenham, Berks., 1631, I, W, P1/B/235
Hy., yeo., Alton B., 1640, AB, I, P3/B/438
Banger, Hy., yeo., Longcott, Shrivenham, Berks., 1671, I, W, P1/B/476
Jane, widow, Gt. Wishford (place missing - taken from later annotation), 1675, I, P2/B/887
Jane, widow, Manningford Bohun, 1702, AB, I, P2/B/1228
Jane, widow, Oare, Wilcot, 1783, W, P3/B/1682
Jane, widow, no abode stated but property in Devizes, 1831, AB, Wr, P1/1831/1
Joan, widow, Gt. Wishford, 1669, W, P2/B/813
Jn., Bulford, 1550-51, AB, W, P2/2Reg/106B, 125B
Jn., Rushall, 1576, I, copy I, W, P2/B/54, P2/5Reg/259A
Jn., Oare, Wilcot, 1609, AB, W, P3/B/44
Jn., yeo., Alton B., 1610, W, P3/B/64
Jn., bach., Overton, 1618, I, W, P3/B/159
Jn., gent., Pewsey, 1636, comm, I, NW, P3/B/369
Jn., Lt. Woodford, 1669, AB, I, P13/1/24
Benger *or* Benjor, Jn., husb., Quidh., 1683, I, W, P1/B/566
Jn., husb., Barford St Mart., 1704, AB, I, P2/B/1243
Jn., Newtown, Durnford, 1706, AB, I, P9/34
Jn., Manningford Bruce, 1711, AB, P1/B/763
Jn., yeo., Oare, Wilcot, 1722, W, P3/B/1204
Jn., sen., yeo., Oare, Wilcot, 1763, AB, comm, W, P3/B/1557
Jn., Wilcot, 1781, AB, P3/B/1670
Jn., Manningford Bruce, 1784, AB, P3/B/1689
Joyce, widow, Manningford Bruce, 1718, I, W, P3/B/1151
Mgt., widow, Manningford Bohun, 1662, I, W, P3/B/478
Baynger, My., widow, Woodb., 1639, I, W, P3/B/408
My., widow, Upavon, 1763, AB, app. of guardian, P2/B/1794
Banger, Moses, cheesemonger, Sal., 1785, W, P4/1785/6
Rd., sen., Bratton, Westb., 1685, I, P25/1685/16

Bonger, Robt., husb., Turners Puddle, Dorset, 1611, I, W, P5/1612/3, P5/9Reg/52B
Robt., Overton, 1631, I, P3/B/335
Banger, Sam., yeo., Thornford, Dorset, 1802, W, P5/1802/17, P5/19Reg/16
Banger, Sam., postman, Chetnole, Yetm., Dorset, 1828, O, W, P19/238
Banger, Susanna, sp. *or* widow, Over C., Dorset, 1744, W, Wr, P5/1744/4
Thos., Manningford Bohun, 1673, I, W, P2/B/865
Thos., yeo., Lt. Woodford, 1676, I, W, P5/1676/4
Thos., yeo., Manningford Bohun, 1687, comm, I, W, P3/B/833
Thos., husb., Manningford Bruce, 1694, I, W, P3/B/920
Thos., clerk, Manningford Bohun, 1710, W, P2/B/1292
Banger, Thos., Lillington, Dorset, 1718, AB, W, P5/1718/2, P5/16Reg/3A
Wm., sen., yeo., Upavon, 1703, I, W, P2/B/1231
Wm., sen., yeo., Manningford Bohun, 1743, comm, W, P2/B/1625
Wm., [jun.], Manningford Bohun, 1744, AB, comm, P2/B/1624
Wm., yeo., Upavon, 1745, W, P2/B/1636
Banger, Wm., blacksmith, Sal., 1786, W, P1/B/1501, P1/14Reg/149
Wm., sen., labourer, Pewsey, 1808, W, Wr, P1/1808/44
Wm., baker, Pewsey, 1837, comm, W, Wr, P3/1837/5
see also Banger; Stevens form. B.
Benham, Eleanor, widow, Swallowfield, Shinfield, Berks., 1638, I, W, P1/B/282
Mgt., widow, Reading, Berks., 1753, O, W, P1/B/1261, P1/10Reg/502B
Thos., former wheelwright, Speen, Berks., 1835, W, Wr, P1/1835/107
Benill *see* Benwell
Benjamin, Chris., yeo., Broad B., Highw., 1721, W, P10/1721/6
Chris., Norton, 1727, AB, P3/B/1253
Chris., Seagry, 1766, AB, P3/B/1578
Benjaman als Gabbett, Jane, widow, Broad B., Highw., 1743, W, Wr, P5/1743/7
My., widow, Seagry, 1797, W, P3/B/1755
Benjamen als Gabbet, Wm., yeo., Broad B., Highw., 1686, I, W, P10/1686/9
Wm., yeo., Norton, 1793, W, P3/B/1739
see also Gabbett als B.
Benjor *see* Benger
Benkin *see* Benskin
Bennall *see* Benwell
Bennett, [lost], widow, no abode stated, [1647], I, W (damaged), P1/B/334
Agnes, widow, Collingbourne Valence, Collingbourne K., 1606, AB, I, P3/B/24
Agnes, widow, Ashton K., 1624, I, W, P3/B/247
Alexander, husb., Scowte Lane, Winterslow, 1586, W, P2/7Reg/65A
Alexander, yeo., E. Grimstead, W. Dean, 1672, I, W, P2/B/843
Alexander, surgeon, E. Grimstead, W. Dean, 1681, AB, I, W, P1/B/544
Ann, widow, Steeple A., 1677, W, P2/B/920
Ann, sp., Ashton K., 1706, W, P3/B/1055
Ann, widow, Melk., 1710, W, P2/B/1290
Ann, widow, Seagry, 1791, AB, P3/B/1732
Ann, sp., Bradford A., 1851, D, O, W, Wr, P1/1851/31
Anth., no abode stated, [1602?], W, P3/1Reg/88
Barbara, widow, Fisherton D., 1671, I, NW, P1/B/471
Benj., farrier, Sherb., Dorset, 1811, comm, W, Wr, P5/1811/20
Bridget, widow, Ashton K., 1626, I, W, P3/B/275
Bridget, widow, Codf. St My., 1839, W, Wr, P2/1839/43
Cath., sp., Sal., 1755, W, P4/1755/5
Christian, brazier's wife, Malm., 1749, AB, P3/B/1457
Chris., vicar, Mkt. L., 1668, I, P2/B/795
Cuthbert, husb., Biddestone, 1632, AB, a/c, I, P3/B/341
Dan., yeo., Nettleton, 1765, W, P3/B/1572
Dan., Alderton, 1783, AB, app. of guardian, P1/B/1489
Dorothea, Devizes St Jn., 1633, I, W, P1/B/244
Dorothy, widow, Foxley, 1639, I, W, P3/B/413
Dorothy, widow, Tollard Royal, 1786, W (NEP), P2/B/2013
Edith, sp., N. Wraxall, 1810, AB, P3/1810/33

Edmd., S. Marston, 1603, AB, P5/1602/4, P5/7Reg/59B
Edwd., Hindon, 1631, AB, P2/B/541
Edwd., Gurston, Broad C., 1631-32, a/c, I, T, W, P2/B/538, 2161
Edwd., Stockton, 1692, W, P2/B/1143
Edwd., Brinkw., 1718, I, W, P3/B/1152
Edwd., innholder, Fisherton A., 1732, W, P2/B/1505
Eleanor, sp., Ashton K., 1677, W, P3/B/690
Eliz., widow, Warm., 1551, W, P2/2Reg/131B
Eliz., widow, Devizes St Jn., 1620, I, W, P1/B/173
Eliz., widow, Upper Stratton, Stratton St Mgt., 1623, I, W, P3/B/229
Eliz., widow, E. Knoyle, 1662, I, W, P2/B/745
Eliz., widow, Tidcombe and Fosbury, 1673, AB, I, P3/B/628
Eliz., widow, Sherb., Dorset, 1689, I, W, P5/1689/4
Eliz., white baker, Sherb., Dorset, 1698, AB, I, P5/1698/4
Eliz., widow, Burbage, 1711, AB, I, P11/100
Eliz., widow, Martin, Hants, 1788, W, P2/B/2026
Eliz., sp., Wantage, Berks., 1791, AB (2), P5/1791/4, P5/18Reg/170A
Elizeus, Halstock, Dorset, 1603, AB, P5/7Reg/72A
Francis, Burbage, 1703, AB, I, P11/93
Francis, (Revd), Sal., 1736, W, Wr, P4/1735/3
Geo., yeo., Ashton K., 1621, I, W, P3/B/205
Geo., Westb., 1663, AB, I, P25/1663/7
Geo., widower, Chute, 1816, AB, T (re decd's children: Abraham, Ann & My. B.), Wr, P7/192
Geo., clothier, Ditchampton, Wilton, 1819, W, Wr, P2/1819/76
Gilbt., thatcher, Codf. St P., 1662, I, W, P1/B/380
Hy., tallow chandler, Sal., 1743, D, W, P4/1743/8
Hy., bach., Sal., 1757, AB, P4/1757/11
Hy., bach., Barford St Mart., 1856, AB, aff, Wr, P2/1856/21
Hester, widow, Milton L., 1782, AB, P1/B/1463
Hugh, gent., Aylesbeare, Devon (& estate at Buckham Mill, Beam.), 1683, W, P17/641
Jacob, jun., S. Moreton, Berks., 1677, AB (not completed), I, P1/B/507
Jas., S. Marston, 1591, I, W, P5/1591/49, P5/5Reg/121A
Jas., yeo., Newton, Whitep., 1683, I, W, P2/B/1024
Jas., husb., Fordington, Dorset, 1716, W, P5/1716/11
Jas., Melchet Park (buried in Whitep.), 1717, W, P30/23
Jas., yeo., Tollard Royal, 1825, W, Wr, P2/1825/13
Jane, widow, Urchf., 1580, AB, W, P2/6Reg/6A
Jane, Leverton, Chilton F., 1713, AB, P1/B/784
Jane, widow, Sal. St Mart., 1727, AB, W, P4/1726/14
Jane, widow, Fordington, Dorset, 1767, W, P5/1767/5
Jane, gentlewoman, Wokm., Berks. (form. of Ramslade, Winkfield, Berks.), 1805, W, P5/1805/7, P5/19Reg/121
Jane, widow, Tollard Royal, 1849, AB, comm, Wr, P2/1849/43
Joan, widow, Winterslow, 1557, W, P2/3Reg/22B
Joan, Urchf., 1564, I, W, P2/B/2167, P2/4Reg/175B
Joan, widow, Urchf., 1580, I, T, W, P2/B/81
Joan, clothier's widow, Stockton, 1616, I, W, P1/B/142
Joan, widow, Sal. St Thos., 1686, I, W, P4/1686/16
Jn., Winterbourne S., 1550, W, P2/2Reg/95A
Jn., Urchf., 1560, I, W, P2/B/16, P2/4Reg/52B
Jn., husb., Codf. St My., 1561, W, P2/4Reg/77D
Jn., Norton B., 1565, AB, P2/4Reg/216C
Jn., Boyton, 1568, AB, P2/5Reg/48
Jn., Figh., 1572, AB, P5/2Reg/116A
Jn., gent., Haygrove, Warm., 1585, I, T, W, P2/B/89, P2/7Reg/21
Jn., husb., E. Grimstead, W. Dean, 1603, AB, I, W, P2/B/239
Jn., clerk and vicar of Sal. Cathedral, Sal. The Close, 1606, W, Wr, P24/7
Jn., sen., husb., Stratton St Mgt., [1609], W (NEP), P3/B/45
Jn., husb., Compton B., [1612], W (NEP), P3/B/79
Jn., smith, Shalbourne, 1614, I, W, P5/1614/4, P5/9Reg/143C
Jn., Codf. St My., 1614, AB, a/c, P2/B/341, P2/8Reg/218C

Jn., Aldbourne, 1620, I, W, P3/B/189
Jn., esquire, Sal. St Edmd., 1628, AB, I, P4/1628/13
Jn., sen., yeo., Earley, Sonning, Berks., 1647, comm, I, W, P5/1647/2, P5/14Reg/95
Jn., cardmaker, Bromham, 1649, I, W, P1/B/345
Jn., Sonning, Berks., 1662, AB, I, P5/1662/17
Jn., sen., yeo., Pewsham Forest, 1672, AB, I, W, P3/B/606
Jn., sen., tanner, Ashton K., 1672, AB, a/c, I, P3/B/605
Jn., sen., yeo., E. Winterslow, 1677, I, W, P2/B/927
Jn., yeo., Sal., 1677, I, W, P4/1677/4
Jn., Coulston, Edington, 1678, I, W, P2/B/933
Jn., gent., Smallbrook, Warm., 1678, AB (to deliver W), I, W, P2/B/931
Jn., sen., yeo., Ebbesborne Wake, 1691, I, W, P2/B/1131
Jn., Sherb., Dorset, 1694, AB, I, request to transfer W, P5/1694/38
Jn., yeo., Winterslow, 1708, D, sentence, W, P1/B/749
Jn., yeo., Liberty of Newland, Hurst, Berks., 1708, comm, W, P5/1708/7, P5/15Reg/90
Jn., weaver, Ashton K., 1712, I, W, P3/B/1105
Jn., blacksmith, Lyneham, 1716, W, P3/B/1135
Jn., tanner, Ashton K., 1719, AB, I, P3/B/1165
Jn., yeo., Ebbesborne Wake, 1719, AB, I, P2/B/1387
Jn., Stockton, 1723, W, P1/B/876, P1/6Reg/401
Jn., husb., Sonning, Berks., 1728-29, AB, W, P5/1728/7, P14/196, P5/16Reg/201A
Jn., yeo., Tollard Royal, 1747-53, AB, a/c, I, W, P2/B/1655
Jn., Ogbourne St Geo., 1757, AB, P23/672
Jn., clothw., Bradford A., 1758, W, P2/B/1742
Jn., weaver, Devizes, 1772, W, P1/B/1409, P1/12Reg/433
Jn., grocer, Chipp., 1780, W, P1/B/1500
Jn., gent., Smallbrook, Warm., 1782, W, P2/B/1993
Jn., grocer, Chipp., 1786, W, P1/14Reg/142
Jn., Ogbourne St Geo., 1790, AB, comm, P23/789
Jn., gent., Smallbrook, Warm., 1799, W, P2/B/2142
Jn., Barford St Mart., 1799, AB, P2/B/2140
Jn., Warm., 1819, AB, comm, Wr, P2/1819/26
Jn., Lyme R., Dorset, 1838, AB, O, Wr, P16/420
Jn., gent., Ebbesborne Wake, 1851, W, Wr, P2/1851/5
Jn. Litchfield, Pickwick, Corsham, 1802, AB, P3/1802/57
Jos., Yarnbrook, N. Bradley, 1775, W, P2/B/1922
Jos., Chute, 1804, AB, P7/185
Josiah, Sal., 1723, AB, P4/1723/2
Josiah, wine merchant, Sal., 1818, W, Wr, P4/1818/1
Julian, widow, Steeple L., 1772, W, P2/B/1886
Lawr., clothw., Newbury, Berks., 1605, AB, I, P1/B/37
Mgt., widow, Alton P., Dorset, 1579, I, W, P5/1579/9, P5/3Reg/123B
Mgt., widow, Stratton St Mgt., 1621, I, W, P3/B/206
Mgt., widow, Highw., 1667, AB, I, P10/1667/2
Margery, widow, Devizes, 1681, W, P3/B/737
Maria, esquire's widow, Pythouse, Tisb., 1618, I, P2/B/377
Martha, widow, Liberty of Newland, Hurst, Berks., 1730, W, P5/1730/3
My., widow, Tisb., 1543, W (NEP), P2/1Reg/47
My., [Netheravon] (NBI), 1632, I, P30/22
My., Sherb., Dorset, 1640, AB, P5/1640/7, P5/13Reg/267C
My., sp., Lyme R., Dorset, 1692, W, P5/1692/5
My., widow, Lyme R., Dorset, 1723, I (detailed), W, P16/228
My., widow, Mkt. L., 1733, AB, P2/B/1527
My., sp., Sal., 1745-46, AB, I, W, P4/1744/4, P4/1746/15
My., widow, N. Wraxall, 1831, AB, comm, P3/1831/45
My., widow, Littleworth, Milton L., 1850, comm, W, Wr, P3/1850/56
Maurice, Boreham, Warm., 1598, AB, I, P2/B/190
Maurice, yeo., Leigh, Ashton K., 1692, W, P3/B/890
Nathaniel, husb., W. Kington, 1727, W, P3/B/1254
Nich., husb., Stratton St Mgt., 1618, AB, comm, I, P3/B/160

Norton, yeo., Tollard Royal, 1849, D, O, W, Wr, P2/1849/6
Peter, yeo., Foscote, Grittleton, 1720, I, W, P3/B/1180
Philip, husb. *or* yeo., Codf. St P., 1615, I, W, P2/B/352
Philip, Tilsh., 1683, AB, I, W, P2/B/1025
Philippa, widow, Broad C., 1675, I, W, P2/B/884
Ralph, husb., Bapton, Fisherton Delamare, 1627, I, W, P2/B/476
Rebecca, widow, Reading St Giles, Berks., 1808, W, Wr, P1/1808/102
Renatus, E. Knoyle, 1739, AB, P2/B/1574
Rd., priest, Yetm. Secunda, Dorset, 1561, collation to the prebend, P1/1Reg/78B
Rd., Codf. St P., 1571, W, P2/5Reg/119C
Rd., Fisherton D., 1574, W, P2/5Reg/208D
Rd., labourer, Urchf., 1590, I, W, P2/B/118
Rd., husb., W. Kington, [1613], I, W (NEP), P3/B/105
Rd., husb., Laverstock, 1614, W, P2/8Reg/208
Rd., baker, Sherb., Dorset, 1623, I, W, P5/1623/5, P5/10Reg/213
Rd., tailor, Sherb., Dorset, 1629, AB, I, T, W, copy W, P5/1629/7, P5/11Reg/105
Rd., yeo., W. Kington, 1663, AB, I, P3/B/489
Rd., yeo., Winterslow, 1665, I, W, P2/B/764
Rd., cutler, Devizes, 1669, I, W, P1/B/456
Rd., yeo., E. Grimstead, W. Dean, 1746, I, W, P2/B/1650
Rd., labourer, Chute, 1765, W, P7/160
Rd. Edmd., gent., Westport St My., 1831, W, P3/1831/32
Robt., Winterslow, 1545, W (NEP), P2/1Reg/59A
Robt., Chilmark, 1612, I, T, W, P2/B/327
Robt., husb., Ashton K., [1612], I, NW, P3/B/90
Robt., Wilton, 1623, I, W, P2/B/439
Robt., Stratton, Dorset, 1635, I, NW, P5/1635/3, P5/12Reg/227B
Robt., Highw., 1664, comm, I, W (damaged), P10/1664/1
Robt., Wilton, 1664, AB, P2/B/762
Robt., husb., Winterbourne G., 1671, W, P2/B/832
Robt., Mkt. L., 1686, AB, P2/B/1066
Robt., carp., Devizes, 1693, agreement, W, P1/B/633
Robt., labourer, Wootton R., 1694, AB, I, P3/B/921
Robt., tallow chandler, Sal., 1729, W, P4/1728/30
Robt., Sal., 1750, AB, ren, P4/1750/7
Robt., collarmaker, Thatcham, Berks., 1770, W, P1/B/1395, P1/12Reg/337A
Robt., yeo., Upper Seagry, 1786, W, P3/B/1704
Robt., yeo., The Laundry, Gt. Bedwyn, 1847, W, Wr, P5/1847/20
Sam., heelmaker, Wokm., Berks., 1790, W, P5/1790/3, P5/18Reg/152
Sarah, sp., Eastrop, Highw., 1760, W, P10/1760/1
Sarah, Ashton K., 1773, AB, P1/B/1415
Sarah, sp., W. Kington, 1811, AB, Wr, P1/1811/92
Sarah, widow, Sherb., Dorset, 1839, AB, note, Wr, P5/1839/3
Steph., shepherd, Corton, Boyton, 1599, I, W, P2/B/199
Steph., miller, Broad H., 1760, W, P3/B/1527
Susanna, yeo.'s widow, Stockton, 1664, I, W, P1/B/414
Susanna, widow, Smallbrook, Warm., 1763, comm, W, P2/B/1791
Thos., yeo., Bishopstrow, 1607, AB, I, W, P2/B/269
Thos., gent., Heytes., 1612, I, W, P5/1612/5, P5/9Reg/76
Thos., no abode stated, but widow is of Wilton, Gt. Bedwyn, 1617, AB, P21/1/3
Thos., shepherd, Coombe B., 1624, I, W, P5/1624/6, P5/10Reg/180B
Thos., husb., Sopworth, 1632, I, W, P3/B/342
Thos., carp., Ashton K., 1638, AB, a/c, I, P3/B/399
Thos., yeo., Grittenham, Brinkw., 1648, I, W, P1/B/340
Thos., Collingbourne K., 1660, W, P3/B/463, P3/3Reg/3B
Thos., gent., Berwick St Jn., 1671, W, P1/B/459
Thos., labourer and husb., Milton L., 1671, I, NW, P1/B/475
Thos., yeo., Broad C., 1674, AB, I, NW, P2/B/879
Thos., clerk, Hungerford, Berks., 1681, AB, comm, I, P5/1681/2
Thos., yeo., E. Knoyle, 1688, I, W, P2/B/1097

Thos., sen., blacksmith, Calne, 1689, I, W, P26/384
Thos., cordw., Ham, 1692, AB, comm, I, P3/B/891
Thos., Hindon, 1692, AB, P2/B/1144
Thos., carp., Ham, 1693, AB, I, P3/B/898
Thos., labourer, Reading, Berks., 1704, I, W, P1/B/717
Thos., Ebbesborne Wake, 1707, AB, I, P2/B/1263
Thos., gent., Semley, 1712, W, P2/B/1315
Thos., yeo., Alderbury, 1729, I, W, P26/746
Thos., Hindon, 1738, AB, P1/B/1077
Thos., vict., Fovant, 1750, AB, ren, P2/B/1679
Thos., Sal., 1753, AB, P4/1753/2
Thos., Limpley Stoke, Bradford A., 1774, AB, P2/B/1911
Thos., yeo., Quidh., 1790, W, P2/B/2052
Thos., collarmaker, Thatcham, Berks., 1795, W, P1/B/1543, P1/14Reg/623C
Thos., Tollard Royal, 1802, W, P2/1802/18
Thos., gardener, Littleworth, Milton L., 1850, comm, W, Wr, P3/1850/23
Thos. Headly, gent., Pickwick, Corsham, 1807-10, W, P29/1800-1857/14, P29/3Reg/275
Ursula, widow, Foscote, Grittleton, 1739, W, P3/B/1379
Walter, cardmaker, Devizes, 1667, AB, comm, I, P1/B/432
Walter, yeo., Ebbesborne Wake, 1716, W, P2/B/1351
Warborough, Stockton, 1604, AB, P2/B/246
Wm., gent., Norton B., 1559, W, P2/3Reg/159D
Wm., vicar, Westb., 1560, comm (by archbishop for visitation of dioceses of Sal. & Bristol; presented to bishop by Wm. B.), P1/1Reg/73
Wm., husb., Urchf., [1561], I, P2/B/27
Wm., Codf. St P., 1576-77, AB, I, T, P2/B/58, P2/5Reg/280C
Wm., Sal., 1594, AB, P1/B/8
Wm., Sal. St Mart., 1613, AB, I, P4/1613/11
Wm., carp., Ashton K., 1620, AB, I, P3/B/190
Bennett als Tyler, Wm., husb., Grove, Wantage, Berks., 1628, I, W, P5/1628/5, P5/11Reg/92
Wm., shepherd, Collingbourne K., 1659-60, AB, I, W, P3/B/464, P3/3Reg/3A
Wm., yeo., Hopgrass, Hungerford, Berks., 1665, comm, I (damaged), W, P5/1665/10
Wm., yeo., Downton, 1668, I, W, P2/B/793
Wm., Devizes, 1668, AB, P1/B/439
Wm., E. Winterslow, 1671, I, P2/B/2164
Wm., yeo. and husb., Thatcham, Berks., 1689, AB, I, ren, P1/B/599
Wm., Lyme R., Dorset, 1721, AB, P16/221
Wm., sen., yeo., Maiden Earley, Sonning, Berks., 1728-32, AB, I (detailed), W, P5/1728/8, P5/1732/4, P5/16Reg/200D
Wm., jun., d. at Manston, effects at Semley, 1737, AB, ren, P2/B/1559
Wm., yeo., Chilton F., 1737, AB, I, P3/B/1363
Wm., bach., W. Woodhay, Berks., 1750, AB, P5/1749/10
Wm., Bloxworth, Dorset, 1761, AB, P5/1761/3
Wm., Steeple L., 1770, AB, W, P2/B/1866
Wm., Wylye, 1791, AB, P2/B/2067
Wm., cabinet maker, Wokm., Berks., 1808, W, Wr, P5/1808/9
Wm. Biggs, draper, Hindon, 1824, W, Wr, P2/1824/15
see also Batch als B.
Benoll *see* Benwell
Benskin, Jos., vict., Biddestone St Nich., 1822, W, Wr, P3/1822/27
Benkin, Thos., late of Bath but with effects at Inkpen, Berks., 1744, W, P1/B/1171, P1/9Reg/327
Benson, Binson, Geo., carp., S. Burcombe, 1724, W, P2/B/1424
Jn., coachman, Reading, Berks., 1744, W, P1/B/1177, P1/9Reg/347
Robt., [husb.], Wexcombe, Grafton, 1619, AB (2), comm (2), I, P5/1619/9, P5/1620/9, P5/9Reg/228B
Robt., Gt. Bedwyn, 1620, AB, P5/10Reg/9B
Bent, Rd., Sonning, Berks., 1605, W, P5/1605/2, P5/8Reg/50B
Rd., sen., Calne, 1647, AB, P26/98
Rd., husb., Calne, 1681, I, W, P26/290
Rd., husb., Bagnor, Speen, Berks., 1689, I, W, P1/B/601
Bents, Thos., yeo., Sheldon, Chipp., 1711, W, P1/B/759, P1/5Reg/67
Bently, Joan, widow, Chards., Devon, 1690, I, W, P14/70

Jn., husb., Chards., Devon, 1580-81, I, W, P5/1580/7, P5/4Reg/24A
Jn., sen., Chards., Devon, 1699, AB, I, P14/86
Jn., yeo., Chards., Devon, 1735, W, P14/150
Mgt., widow, Chipp., 1615, I, W, P3/B/123
Robt., yeo., Chards., Devon, 1830, W, P5/1830/35
Wm., husb. and servant, Chards., Devon, 1695, I, NW, P5/1695/12
Bents *see* Bent
Benwell, Benoll, Edith, widow, Chards., Devon, 1594, I, W, P5/1594/9, P5/6Reg/66B
Frances, widow, Sonning, Berks., 1678, I, W, P5/1678/21
Hannah, minor, Wargrave, Berks., 1763, AB, P1/B/1344
Hy., miller and farmer, Twyford, Hurst, Berks., 1799, W, Wr, P5/1799/1, P5/18Reg/271A
Jos., Stratfield M., Berks., 1701, AB, I, P1/B/693
Mgt., widow, Chapelrow, Bucklebury, Berks., 1692, AB, I, P1/B/619
Benill *or* Benwell, Martha, widow, Chilton F., 1730, W, P3/B/1287
Thos., yeo., Oxenwood, Shalbourne, 1740, AB, I, ren, W, P5/1740/9
Wm., Chilton F., 1685, AB, I, P3/B/815
Benwell *or* Bennall, Wm., yeo., Chilton F., 1727, AB, I, P3/B/1255
Benyon, Jn., vicar and clerk, Malm., 1702, AB, I, W, P3/B/1017
Berd *see* Beard
Bereman, Rd., Calne, 1598, AB, T (children: Jn. & Joan B.), P5/1598/5, P5/6Reg/202A
Beriett, Robt., Grimstone, Stratton, Dorset, 1562, T (children: Jn., Wm. & Eliz. B.), P19/5
Berington *see* Barrington
Berjew, Jn., clerk, vicar, Norton B., 1676, AB, I, P2/B/903
Jn., Kingston D., 1719, AB, P2/B/1378
Jn., clerk and rector, Over C., Dorset, 1743, AB, comm, Wr, P5/1743/8
Jos., Mere, 1728, AB (2), comm, P5/1728/9, P5/16Reg/208B
Berke *see* Beak *or* B.
Berkley, Cath., widow, Chards., Devon, 1728, AB, I, P5/1728/4, P5/16Reg/178A
Edwd., Tinh., Edington, 1608-11, AB, a/c (incomplete), P2/B/316, P2/8Reg/6A
My., Tinh., Edington, 1627, I, W, P2/B/480
Wm., husb., Tinh., Edington, 1637, I, W, P2/B/610
Berkshire *see* Barkshire
Bernard, Benedict, Froxfield, 1768, AB, P3/B/1589
Chas., Devizes, 1748, W, P1/B/1222, P1/10Reg/209B
Christian, yeo., Chr. M., 1726, W, P1/B/925
Edwd., gent., Eastcourt, Crudwell, 1677, AB, a/c, comm, I, P3/B/681
Burnard, Edwd., Lyme R., Dorset, 1730, AB, P16/259
Jn., yeo., Sutton B., 1638, I, W, P1/B/275
Jn., yeo., Chr. M., 1726, W, P1/7Reg/113
Jos., Sutton B., 1710, AB, I, P3/B/1085
Mgt., widow, Bowood, 1678, ren, W, Wr, P3/B/700
Martha, miller's widow, Kingswood, Gloucs, 1736, AB, I, W, P3/B/1351
Rebecca, sp., Sal., 1671, AB, P4/1670/23
Rd., Sal. (form. of London), 1677, AB, P4/1677/6
Robt., glazier, Crickl. St S., 1693, AB, I, P3/B/899
Bernar (Barnarde), Thos., chantry priest, Tisb., 1547, W, P2/2Reg/28A
Wm., Devizes St My., 1617, AB, I, P1/B/144
Wm., weaver, Hurst, Berks., 1685, I, P5/1685/9
see also Barnard *or* B.; Burnett *or* B. (Burnard)
Berrett *see* Barrett
Berriman *see* Berryman
Berrow, Alice, Bremhill, 1571, W, P1/1Reg/87C
Jn., clerk and vicar, Inglesham, 1719, comm, I, W, P3/B/1166
Berry, Bridget, widow, Lt. Hinton, 1695, I, W, Wr (very fragile items), P3/B/936
Cyrenes, millwright, late of Westport but now of Malm., 1813, W, Wr, P3/1813/27
David, miller, Sherston, 1811, W, Wr, P1/1811/94
Edwd., maltster, Keevil, 1706, W, P2/B/1255
Edwd., maltster, Keevil, 1727, W, P2/B/1453
Eliz., Castle C., 1710, AB, P28/6
Eliz., widow, Kintbury, Berks., 1738, W, P1/B/1081, P1/8Reg/235

Guy, Fisherton A., 1715, AB, W, P2/B/1341
Hy., mercer, Chipp., 1636, I (detailed), W, P3/B/370
Hy., sen., mercer, Castle C., [1667], I, W (NEP), P3/B/522
Isaac, Castle C., 1725, AB, W, P28/14
Berry als White, Isaac, gent., Corston, Malm., 1831, comm, W, Wr, P3/1831/5
Jas., butcher, Sonning, Berks., 1697, I, W, P5/1697/3
Joan, widow, The Mill, Lt. Hinton, 1685, I, W, P3/B/816
Jn., parson, Wasing, Berks., 1622, I, W, P1/B/187
Jn., mercer, Tinh., Edington, 1673, AB, I (detailed), P2/B/870
Jn., sen., cordw., Lt. Hinton, 1722, I, W, P3/B/1205
Jn., W. Harnham, 1727, AB, P8/27
Jn., labourer, Stratford sub C., 1779, W, P4/1779/2
Jn., yeo., Chiseldon, 1784, W, P3/B/1690
Jn. Lovell, Milford, Sal. St Mart., 1835, AB, P1/1835/38
Martha, widow, Sonning, Berks., 1739, AB, comm, Wr, P5/1739/7
Martha, widow, Sal., 1853, AB, Wr, P4/1853/10
Martha Freak, minor, Milford, Sal. St Mart., 1835, O, T (dau of Jn. Lovell B., decd), P1/1835/37-38
My., widow, Castle C., 1730, I, W, P3/B/1288
Rd., gent., Compton C., 1677, AB, I, P2/B/928
Robt., miller, Lt. Hinton, 1602, W, P3/1Reg/80B
Robt., yeo., Malm., 1629, AB, a/c, I, P3/B/307
Robt., Lt. Hinton, 1631, AB, a/c, I, P3/B/322
Robt., sen., baker, S. Marston, 1707, I, W, P5/1707/7, P5/15Reg/12
Sam., Preston, Aldbourne, 1855, AB, aff, O, Wr, P1/1855/50
Sarah, widow, Lt. Hinton, 1730, I, W, P3/B/1289
Thos., Lt. Hinton, 1665, I, W, P3/B/506
Thos., mercer, Castle C., 1708, W, P3/B/1070
Thos., Kington St M., 1811, AB, Wr, P1/1811/90
Thos., Chiseldon, 1828, AB, note, O, Wr, P3/1828/46
Thos. Freke, Sal., 1839, AB, Wr, P1/1839/25
Wm., clerk parson, Langley Burrell, 1638, I, W, P1/B/278
Wm., sen., yeo., Lt. Hinton, 1679, comm, I, W, P3/B/710
Wm., gent., Draycot C., 1697, I, W, P3/B/961
Wm., sen., miller, Lt. Hinton, 1710, I (2 - 1 a copy), W, P3/B/1086
Berryman, Berriman, Agnes, widow, Hannington, 1635, I, W, P1/B/262
Anth., Downton, 1762, AB, P2/B/1782
Berriman, Chris., brickmaker, Burridge Heath, Lt. Bedwyn, 1649, AB, I, P21/1/73
Berriman, Edwd., dairyman, Whitehall Farm, Crickl. St S., 1857, aff, comm, W, Wr, P3/1857/37
Berriman, Jas., innholder, Beam., Dorset, 1748, W, P17/505
Jn., Steeple L., 1618, I, W, P2/B/386
Berriman, Jn., Hannington, 1621, AB, a/c, comm, I, P1/B/163
Jn., mariner on HMS *Dorsetshire* later steward on HMS *Ludlow Castle*, hulks, Downton, 1746-53, req, W, P2/B/1654
Jn., Downton, 1766, W, P2/B/1826
Berriman, Jos., yeo., Nether C., Dorset, 1755, AB, P5/1755/6
Barryman, Mgt., Calne, 1599, I, P5/1598/3
My., widow, Downton, 1804, W, P1/1804/123
Peter, freemason, Steeple L., 1662, I, W, P2/B/744
Berriman, Robt., Minety, 1683, I, W, P3/B/769
Steph., yeo., Sonning, Berks., 1644, comm, I, W, P5/1644/4, P5/14Reg/71B
Thos., yeo., Garsdon, 1617, I, W, P3/B/135
Wm., servant to Roger Fynamorry, Whetham, Calne, 1569, W (NEP), P1/1Reg/98C
Berriman, Wm., wheelwright, Clack, Lyneham, 1821, W, Wr, P3/1821/26
Bert *see* Burt
Bertlett *see* Bartlett
Bertram, Alice, widow, Lyme R., Dorset, 1672, W, P16/32
Besant, Bezant, Alice, Wilsford nr Pewsey, 1580, AB, W, P2/5Reg/360B
Edwd., vict., Charminster, Dorset (form. of Dorchester), 1735, W, P5/1735/6
Eliz., widow, Gt. Bedwyn, 1764, AB, P5/1764/1
Grace, widow, Enmore Grn, Motc., Dorset, 1808, W, P19/216

Hy., Shitterton, Bere R., Dorset, 1586, AB, T (children: George B., & child which Hy.'s widow, Edith, expecting), P5/1585/11, P5/4Reg/124A
Hubert, Winterborne K., Dorset, 1619, AB, I, P5/1619/8, P5/9Reg/229A
Bessant, Jn., collarmaker, Upavon, 1672, comm, I, W, P2/B/851
Jn., Stourpaine, Dorset, 1678, AB, comm, I (dated 1675), P24/434
Jn., Stourpaine, Dorset, 1697, AB, I, P24/502
Jn., Chetnole, Yetm., Dorset, 1719, AB, I, P5/1719/12
Jn., gent., Winterborne K., Dorset, 1819, W, Wr, P5/1819/16
Bezant, Lucy, sp., Devizes, 1678, AB, comm, I, draft NW, P1/B/519
Nich., labourer, Winterborne K., Dorset, 1598, I, W, P5/1597/4, P5/6Reg/195C
Besontes, Rd., Wilsford nr Pewsey, 1569, AB, P2/5Reg/63D
Rd., shepherd, Wilsford nr Pewsey, 1640, I, W, P2/B/651
Rd., vict., Winterborne K., Dorset, 1715, W, P5/1715/3, P5/15Reg/327
Thos., yeo., Winterborne K., Dorset, 1739, AB, I, Wr, P5/1739/8
Thos., yeo., Enmore Grn, Motc., Dorset, 1804, comm, W, P19/208
Thos., yeo., Winterborne K., Dorset, 1841, W, Wr, P5/1841/15
Wm., husb., Winterborne K., Dorset, 1666, I, W, P5/1666/6
Bezant, Wm., mariner on *The Young Factor*, bach., Quidh. & Sal., 1814, AB, P1/1814/64
Besent, Wm., sen., yeo., Court Farm, Bere R., Dorset, 1841, aff, comm, W, Wr, P5/1841/3
Besar *see* Beazer
Besent *see* Besant
Besley, Besly *see* Basely
Besontes *see* Besant
Bessant *see* Besant
Besser *see* Beazer
Bessey *see* Bissey
Bessley *see* Basely
Bessy *see* Bissey
Best, And., Sonning, Berks., 1824, AB, Wr, P5/1824/19
Ann, widow, Lyme R., Dorset, 1775, W, P16/341, P5/17Reg/100A
Edith, widow, Shrewton, 1625-35, I, W, P2/B/582, P2/9Reg/46B
Edmd., yeo., Zeals, 1637, AB, a/c, I, P5/1636/11, P5/12Reg/252C
Edmd., sen., yeo., Mere, 1700, W, P5/1700/4
Edwd., shipwright, Lyme R., Dorset, 1608, I, W, P5/1607/7, P5/8Reg/168B
Edwd., shepherd, Fovant, 1649, AB, I, P1/B/348
Eliz., widow, Sutton V., 1747, W, P2/B/1659
Eliz., widow, Shrewton, 1781, AB, P2/B/1989
Giles, yeo., Farley, Alderbury, 1722, AB, I, W, P26/664
Hy., Fovant, 1645, I, W, P2/B/700
Hy., tailor, Ebbesborne Wake, 1701, I, W, P2/B/1219
Hy., W. Dean, 1746, W, P2/B/1652
Hy., shepherd, Shrewton, 1763, AB, W, P2/B/1793, P1/12Reg/64B
Jas., bach., Corsham, 1720, marriage licence, P29/2Reg/43A
Jane, widow, Bemerton, Fugg. St Peter, 1682, I, W, P2/B/993
Joan, widow, Swallowcliffe, 1583, AB, I, W, P5/1582/10, P5/4Reg/58B
Jn., Sutton M., 1561, I, W, P2/B/19, P2/4Reg/74C
Jn., yeo., Ansty (d. at Stert), 1674, AB, I, NW, P1/B/492
Jn., Swallowcliffe, 1702, AB, I, P5/1702/14
Jn., jun., Bower C., 1711, AB, I, P2/B/1298
Jn., shepherd, Shrewton, 1724, W, P2/B/1432
Jn., Bemerton, Fugg. St Peter, 1738, AB, I, P2/B/1569
Jn., gent., Whaddon, Alderbury, 1806, AB, W, Wr, P26/1254
Jos., Swallowcliffe, 1690, AB, I, P5/1689/5
Jos., Ansty, 1748, AB, P2/B/1660
Martha, widow, Sal., 1799, W, P4/1799/1
Martha, sp., Sal., 1806, W, P4/1806/2
My., widow, Sutton V., 1795-96, comm, W, P1/B/1544, P1/14Reg/636
Matthew, gent., Fisherton A., 1672, I, W, P2/B/856
Matthew, gent., Sal., 1734, W, Wr, P4/1734/19
Michael, Sutton M., 1573, W, P2/5Reg/163C

Nich., shepherd, Shrewton, 1759, W, P2/B/1752, P1/11Reg/423
Philip, Grimstone, Stratton, Dorset, 1603, AB, I, W, P5/1603/3, P5/7Reg/64C
Rd., husb., Swallowcliffe, 1576, I, W, P5/1576/5, P5/3Reg/96C
Robt., sen., Ansty, 1682, AB, P1/B/555
Robt., blacksmith, Sutton V., 1728, W, P2/B/1464
Robt., Sal., 1780, W, P4/1780/11
Sarah, sp., Grimstone in Charminster, Stratton, Dorset, 1661, comm, NW, P5/1661/4
Steph., sen., shepherd, Shrewton, 1745, W, P2/B/1634
Steph., shepherd, Shrewton, 1760, W, P2/B/1766
Susanna, widow, Shrewton, 1724, I, W, copy W, P2/B/1433
Thos., husb., Swallowcliffe, 1603, AB, I, T, P5/1602/1, P5/7Reg/60A
Thos., shepherd, Shrewton, 1671, I, W, P2/B/835
Thos., yeo., E. Knoyle, 1682, AB, I, P2/B/1004
Thos., yeo., Knighton, Broad C., 1717, W, P2/B/1357
Thos., Sal., 1742, AB, Wr, P4/1741/1
Thos., tailor, Sal., 1747, W, P4/1747/3
Thos., yeo., Clarendon Park, 1779, W, P26/1100
Thos., Bere R., Dorset, 1812, AB, Wr, P5/1812/16
Thos., yeo., Fovant, 1839, W, Wr, P2/1839/24
Bist, Tristram, shepherd, Mere, 1694, I, W, P5/1694/39
Walter, husb., Longbridge D., 1597, AB, I, W, P2/B/179
Wm., Winterslow, 1555, W, P2/1Reg/95A
Wm., Donhead St My., 1557, W, P2/3Reg/34B
Wm., Ebbesborne Wake, 1559, W, P2/3Reg/168A
Wm., husb., Ebbesborne Wake, 1585, I, W, P2/B/87, P2/7Reg/17A
Wm., cartwright, Winterslow, 1604, I, W, P2/B/248
Beast, Wm., sen., Winterslow, 1634, I, W, P2/B/578, P2/9Reg/41A
Wm., yeo., Farley, Alderbury, 1697, I, W, P26/446
Wm., jun., yeo., Thingley Bridge, Corsham, 1725, I, W, P3/B/1240
Wm., shepherd, Shrewton, 1781, AB, W, P2/B/1990
see also Biss als B.,
Bestley, Bestly *see* Basely
Beswick, Rd., vicar, Westport St My., 1705, W, P3/B/1041
Besy *see* Bissey
Beterton *see* Betterton
Betford *see* Bedford
Bethell, Ann, widow, Nettleton, 1803, W, P3/1803/60
Eliz., widow, E. Tytherton, Bremhill, 1850, AB, Wr, P3/1850/25
Jn., sen., Nettleton, 1761, AB, cert, W, P3/B/1538
Jn., sen., husb., Nettleton, 1800, note, W, P3/1800/45
My., sp., Bradford A., 1758, W, P2/B/1746
Sam., gent., Bradford A., 1805, W, Wr, P2/1805/18
Thos., labourer, Colerne, 1834, aff, W, Wr, P3/1834/29
Thos., linen draper, Calne, 1841, AB, Wr, P26/1455
Bether, Jn., Bapton, Fisherton Delamare, 1587-88, I, W, P2/B/98, P2/7Reg/116A
Bett *see* Bott *or* B.
Betteridge, Adam, collarmaker, Hungerford, Berks., 1727, AB, I, ren, P5/1727/6
Cornelius, labourer, Lt. Bedwyn, 1767, W, P5/1767/6
Jn., sen., collarmaker, Hungerford, Berks., 1726, I, W, P23/437
Jos., yeo., Urchf., 1745, W, P2/B/1637
My., widow, Hungerford, Berks., 1743, W, Wr, P5/1743/9
Wm., husb., Chiseldon, 1629, I, W, P3/B/309
Wm., Chisbury, Lt. Bedwyn, 1808, AB, P21/12/19
Betterton, Agnes, widow, Crickl. St S., 1614, I, W, P1/B/122
Edmd., blacksmith, Poulton, 1832, comm, W, Wr, P1/1832/105
Eliz., widow, Chelworth, Crickl. St S., 1720, I, W, P3/B/1181
Beterton, Francis, Crickl. St S., 1679, AB, comm, P3/B/711
Geoff., Crickl. St My., 1730, AB, I, P3/B/1290
Jn., husb., Crickl. St S., 1606, W, P3/2Reg/8A
Jn., Crickl. St S., 1758, AB, P3/B/1517

Mark, Crickl. St My., 1690, AB, I, P3/B/866
My., widow, Crickl. St My., 1709, I, W, P3/B/1078
Tobias, Highw., 1723, AB, comm, P10/1723/1
Wm., butcher, Crickl. St S., 1704, I, W, P3/B/1028
Bettiscombe, Eliz., widow, Beam., Dorset, 1730, W, P17/439
Robt., sen., carp., Beam., Dorset, 1693, W, P17/332
Bevan, Beven *see* Beaven
Bever *see* Beaver
Bevercombe, Hy., Bere R., Dorset, 1667, AB, I, P5/1667/6
Wm., mariner on *The Guernsey*, bach., Bere R., Dorset, 1705, AB, cert, P5/1705/7
Wm., Bere R., Dorset, 1782, W, P5/1782/4, P5/17Reg/218C
Beverly, Jas., bargeman, Wallingford St My. le More, Berks., 1614, I, W, P1/B/108
Beverster *see* Beverstone *or* B.
Beverstock *see* Baverstock
Beverstone, Beverston, Chris., weaver, Wootton B., 1619, I, W, P1/B/155
Beverston, Edith, widow, Wootton B., 1621, I, W, P3/B/207
Jn., husb., Stockley, Calne, 1602, AB (during minority of Edith, Eleanor, Agnes, Alice, Eliz. & Thos. B.), I, P5/1602/7, P5/7Reg/46B
Jn., Highway, 1623, I, W, P3/B/231
My., widow, Highway, 1629, I, W, P3/B/311
Beverstone *or* Beverster, Thos., Devizes St Jas., Devizes, 1560, W (NEP), P1/2Reg/118A
Bevin *see* Beaven
Bevington, Edmd., brewer, Downton, 1620, I, W, P2/B/408
see also Simper als B.
Bevis *see* Beavis
Bew, Bew als Harris, Cath., Whittonditch, Rams., 1724, AB, P5/1724/11
Bews, Hy., weaver, Corsham, 1607, W, P29/1Reg/61
Rd., yeo., Rams., 1728, AB, I, P5/1728/10, P5/16Reg/209C
Thos., yeo., Oare, Chieveley, Berks., 1716, AB, comm, I, P1/B/816
Thos., Leckhampstead, Chieveley, Berks., 1786, AB, comm, P1/B/1502
Bewdon, Agnes, widow, Milton, Berks., 1664, I, W, P1/B/408
Bewley, Agnes, Chirton, 1582-83, I, W, P2/B/83, P2/6Reg/84C
Agnes, widow, Wedh., Urchf., 1589, AB, I, W, P2/B/100, 105
Bewly, Alice, widow, Coombe, Enford, 1681-82, AB, I, W, P2/B/968, 981
Benj., yeo., Lydiard M., 1808, W, Wr, P3/1808/26
Benj., yeo., Lydiard M., 1837, comm, note, W, Wr, P3/1837/3
Edwd., yeo., Calne, 1776, W, P5/1776/4, P5/17Reg/108
Bewly, Fabian, Rushall, 1610, AB, I, P2/B/304
Jn., husb., Rushall, 1562, I, W, P2/B/32, P2/4Reg/102B
Jn., Conock, Chirton, 1574, AB, P2/5Reg/212A
Jn., sen., husb., Urchf., 1603, AB, I, P2/B/238
Bewly, Jn., husb., Urchf., 1614, W, P2/8Reg/216A
Bewly, Jn., sen., husb., Urchf., 1644, a/c, I, T, P2/B/691
Jn., husb., Coombe, Enford, 1664, I, P2/B/756
Bewly, Jn., carp., Melk., 1677, AB, I, P2/B/922
Jn., Calne, 1773, AB, comm, P26/1061
Jos., farmer, Bremhill, 1836, W, Wr, P3/1836/35
Julian, widow, Urchf., 1630, I, W, P2/B/512, P2/9Reg/80A
Margery, widow, Urchf., 1607, AB, I, P2/B/275
Bewly, My., E. Tytherton, Bremhill, 1837, W, Wr, P3/1837/46
Osmund, husb., Coombe, Enford, 1620, AB, I, W, P1/B/129, P1/B/165
Bewly, Robt., Conock, Chirton, 1623, I, W, P2/B/441
Susan, widow, Calne, 1832, comm, W, Wr, P26/1399
Thos., husb., Chirton, 1557, W, P2/3Reg/30A
Thos., Rushall, 1569, W, P2/5Reg/58B
Bewly, Wm., Wrou., 1667, AB, I, W, P3/B/523
Bewly, Wm., sen., yeo., Wedh., Urchf., 1686, I, W, P1/B/1566
Wm., jun., yeo., Quemerford, Calne, 1786, W, P26/1148
Wm., sen., yeo., Broad's Grn, Calne, 1819, W, Wr, P26/1328
Wm., shoemaker, Calne, 1827, AB, comm, W, Wr, P26/1363

Bews *see* Bew
Bewsey, Arthur, sen., yeo., Holnest, Dorset, 1682, I, W, P5/1682/6
Chas., Leigh, Yetm., Dorset, 1838, AB, Wr, P5/1838/6
Edmd., Thornford, Dorset, 1631, AB, a/c, I, P5/1631/9, P5/12Reg/4A
Eliz., widow, Holnest, Dorset, 1716, I (NEP), P5/1716/5
Francis, bodice maker, Chetnole, Yetm., Dorset, 1742, comm, T (re decd's children: Thos. & Eliz. B.), W, P19/132
Hy., yeo., Hermitage, Dorset, 1689, AB, comm, I, P5/1688/14
Jn., Holnest, Dorset, 1593, I, NW, P5/1593/9, P5/6Reg/50A
Rd., Thornford, Dorset, 1602, AB, I, W, P5/1602/8, P5/7Reg/46A
Robt., Holnest, Dorset, 1715-16, AB, I, ren, P5/1715/5, P5/1716/6
Bewshen, Anth., S. Wraxall, 1552, AB, I, P2/B/9, P2/2Reg/166F
Jn., gent., Smallbrook, Warm., 1574, W, P2/5Reg/202A
Bewton, Anth., Tilehurst, Berks., 1625, I, W, P1/B/194
Beycer *see* Beazer
Beyley, Beyly *see* Bailey
Beymonde *see* Beaumont
Bezant *see* Besant
Bezar, Bezer *see* Beazer
Biby, Beebee, Anth., clerk, Dinton, 1687, AB, I, P2/B/1084
Jn., fuller, Sal., 1642, AB, P4/1641/7
Bickerton, Jn., clerk, W. Knoyle, 1604, AB, I, P2/B/247
Bicknell, Alice, widow, Over C., Dorset, 1621, I, W, P5/1621/5, P5/10Reg/94
Barbara, widow, Over C., Dorset, 1669, I, W, P5/1669/6
Edwd., Over C., Dorset, 1691, AB, I, P5/1691/9
Bucknoll, Isaac, Sherb., Dorset, 1738, AB, ren, Wr, P5/1738/6

Jn., carp., Over C., Dorset, 1715, W, P5/1715/6, P5/15Reg/324A
Jn., Over C., Dorset, 1733, AB, P5/1733/10
Jos., grocer, Cheap St., Sherb., Dorset, 1827, W, Wr, P5/1827/40
Mgt., sp., Nether C., Dorset, 1762, W, P5/1762/6
Rd., yeo., Over C., Dorset, 1668, AB, comm, I, P5/1667/7, P5/1667/12
Biddle, Alice, W. Amesb., 1550, W, P2/2Reg/99B
Beadell, Edith, widow, Bulford, 1620, I, W, P2/B/400
Beadell *or* Biddle, Edwd., Bulford, 1551, I, W, P2/B/2, P2/2Reg/135B
Edwd., Bulford, 1615, I, W, P2/B/356
Edwd., yeo., Liberty of Newland, Hurst, Berks., 1711, AB, W, P5/1711/4, P5/15Reg/261B
Bidell, Eliz., Bulford, 1567, AB, P2/5Reg/4C
Eliz., widow, Liberty of Newland, Hurst, Berks., 1711, AB, I, P5/1711/5
Beadell, Geo., tanner, Devizes, 1671, I, W, P1/B/467
Biddell, Hannah, sp., Swallowfield, Shinfield, Berks., 1741, W, P1/B/1142, P1/9Reg/117
Jane, widow, Westport St My., 1710, I, W, P3/B/1087
Jn., Amesb., 1566, W, P2/4Reg/232A
Jn., cordw., Malm., 1705, I, W, P3/B/1042
Justinian, husb., Cloatley, Hankerton, 1624, I, W, P3/B/248
Rd., husb., Bulford, 1586, W, P2/7Reg/65C
Rd., tanner, Westport St My., [1615], I, W (NEP), P3/B/124
Robt., W. Amesb., 1549, W, P2/2Reg/86B
Biddell, Robt., haberdasher, Devizes, 1681, I, W, P1/B/548
Beadell, Roger, yeo., Bulford, 1628, I, W, P2/B/487
Beadell, Sam., clerk and rector, Tollard Royal, 1696, AB, I, P1/B/659
Thos., tanner, Devizes, 1681, I, W, P1/B/551
see also Venny als B.
Biddlecombe, Chas., labourer, Landford, 1857, I, W, Wr, P2/1847/69
Duran, Downton, 1704, AB, P2/B/1240
Edwd., husb., Milston, 1711, W, P2/B/1297
Frances, widow, Broad C., 1689, I, W, P2/B/1078
Hy., barber, wig-maker and mariner on Grafton, warship, Sal. St Mart., 1762, req, W, copy W, P4/1762/14
Jn., yeo., Compton C., 1559, W, P2/4Reg/13C
Rd., sen., yeo., Sutton M., 1628, I, W, P2/B/498
Rd., yeo., Ashton G., Codf. St P., 1676, I, W, P2/B/909

Thos., husb., Dinton, 1609-11, AB, a/c (fragment), I, T, P2/B/287, 318, P2/8Reg/47
Thos., Compton C., 1632, AB, a/c, I, P2/B/562, P2/9Reg/37B
Thos., tanner, Sal., 1667, AB, I, P4/1667/5
Thos., hairdresser, Sal., 1783, W, P4/1783/4
Wm., woodman, Redlynch, Downton, 1843, AB, D, W, Wr, P2/1843/21
Bide, Bide *or* Bides, Edith, widow, Sal. St Edmd., 1625, I, W, P4/1625/7
Bidell *see* Biddle
Biden, Bydon, Cath., widow, Manton, Preshute, 1698, I, W, P1/B/674, P1/3Reg/148
Hy., Lockeridge, Overton, 1639, I, W, P3/B/414
Bydon, Jn., Preshute, 1694, AB, I, P1/B/640
Bides *see* Bide *or* B.
Bidgood, Bidgard *or* Bidgwood, Jn., gardener, Bratton, Westb., 1710, I, W, P25/1710/2
Bidggood *or* Bidgood, Robt., jun., clothier, Fordington, Dorset (exhibited at Sal.), 1631-33, AB, a/c, I, P5/1631/10, P5/1633/2, P5/12Reg/82B
Bidmead, Dan., Lea, L. and Cleverton, 1836, AB, O, Wr, P3/1836/3
Bedmead, Geo., innholder, Crickl. St S., 1744, AB, W, P3/B/1421
Bidwell *see* Bedwell
Biffin, Anth., husb., Figh., 1664, I, W, P26/120
Chris., Mkt. L., 1832, W (dated Mar 1832 - endorsed 'unproved'), P2/1832/42
Edwd., plumber, Devizes, 1739, W, P1/B/1111, P1/8Reg/385
Frances, sp., Chitterne St My., 1791, AB, P2/B/2063
Jeremiah, Melk., 1692, AB, I, P1/B/622
Jn., Stratford Tony, 1681, AB, I, ren, P2/B/986
Jn., innholder, Sal., 1713, W, P4/1713/7
Biffin als Jeffrey, Nich., husb., Urchf., 1630, I, NW, P2/B/513, P2/9Reg/80B
Nich., husb., Furleigh Cross, Netherb., Dorset, 1701, AB, L, W, copy W, P5/1700/3
Thos., Devizes, 1740-42, AB, P1/B/1118, P1/B/1156
Wm., Wootton R., 1699, AB, P3/B/985
Biffin *see also* Abethell als B.
Biggood *see* Bigwood
Biggs, Abigail, widow, Rollestone, 1730, AB, P2/B/1484
Agnes, widow, Pomeroy, Wingfield, 1640, I, W, P2/B/654
Agnes, widow, Serrington, Stapleford, 1644, I, copy I, W, copy W, P2/B/685
Alice, Atworth, Bradford A., 1733, AB, I, P2/B/1513
Bigges, Ann, widow, Marl. St Peter and St Paul, 1626, AB, I, W, P1/B/205
Ann, widow, Rams., 1680, I, W, P5/1680/4
Ann, widow, Worton, Pott., 1690, AB, I, P1/B/605
Ann, widow, Worton, Pott., 1741, I, W, P1/B/1147, P1/9Reg/186
Ann, widow, Sal., 1780, W, P4/1780/1
Bigges, Anth., yeo., Gt. Woodford, 1638, I, W, P5/1638/7, P5/13Reg/143B
Anth., bach., Gt. Durnford, 1693, AB, I (2 - 1 includes desperate debts), P9/27
Christian, widow, Newtown, Durnford, 1721, I, W, P5/1720/10, P5/16Reg/52A
Bigges, Chris., Stapleford, 1612, AB, P2/B/331
Bigges, Chris., husb., Lt. Wishford, S. Newton, 1612, I, W, P2/B/330
Chris., sen., yeo., Worton, Pott., 1696, I, W, P1/B/656, P2/B/1172
Bigges, Chris., sen., yeo., Worton, Pott., 1717, I, W, P1/B/840, P1/6Reg/114
Chris., yeo., Pott., 1792-93, W, P1/B/1530, P1/14Reg/478
Chris., dairyman, Pott. Park, 1845, O, W, Wr, P1/1845/4
Edmd., Chirton, 1667, I, W, P2/B/782
Edmd., gent., Chisenbury, Enford, 1735, W, P2/B/1545
Edmd., Farleigh Wick, Monkton F., 1765, W, P2/B/1813
Edwd., husb., Easton, 1680, I, W (damaged) (NEP), P2/B/958
Edwd., yeo., Monkton F., 1747, AB, a/c, I (2), P1/B/1215
Eliz., linen draper's wife, Sal., 1720, W, P1/B/848, P1/6Reg/193
Eliz., widow, Worton, Pott., 1756, W, P1/B/1304, P1/11Reg/289
Eliz., widow, Poulshot, 1802, W, P2/1802/3
Ellen, widow, Stapleford, 1663, AB, I, P1/B/397
Frances, sp., Sal., 1780, W, P4/1780/2
Geo., yeo., Seend Row, Melk., 1721, I, W, P2/B/1405
Geo., tiler, Bradford A., 1797, W, P2/B/2122

Geo., yeo., Seend, Melk., 1818, comm, W, Wr, P2/1818/7
Grace, widow, Pott., 1803, AB, Wr, P1/1803/5, P1/15Reg/388A
Hannah, sp., Rollestone, 1762, AB, comm, P2/B/1787
Hannah, sp., Sal., 1812, W, Wr, P4/1812/4
Harry, gent., Amesb., 1743, W, P2/B/1615
Bigges, Hy., yeo., Gt. Woodford, 1663-71, I, W, P13/1/23, P30/21
Hy., sen., Lake, Wilsford with L., 1694, I, W, P13/3/19
Hy., yeo., Wokm., Berks., 1699, AB, comm, I, P5/1699/8
Hy., Deptford, Wylye, 1700, AB, I, P2/B/1215
Hy., yeo., Durnford, 1727, W, P9/46
Hy., Sal., 1755, AB, W, P4/1755/11
Hy., bach., Woodford, 1770, AB, P5/1770/6, P5/17Reg/5B
Hy., gent., Gt. Woodford, 1776, W, P13/5/1
Hy. Sam., gent., Devizes, 1803, W, Wr, P1/1803/2, P1/15Reg/379B
Bigges, Hester, no abode stated, 1674, I, P2/B/882
Hugh, weaver, Sal., 1759, W, P4/1759/3
Jas., Eastcott, Urchf., 1684, I, W, P2/B/1032
Jas., yeo., Seend, Melk., 1699, AB, I, P2/B/1208
Jas., sen., Worton, Pott., 1795, W, P1/B/1532, P1/14Reg/513
Jas., gent., Worton, Pott., 1852, O, W, Wr, P1/1852/18
Jane, widow, Crofton, Gt. Bedwyn, 1632, AB, I, P21/3/20
Jane, sp., Woodford, 1683, AB, I, P13/3/8
Joan, widow, Bradford A., 1559, W, P2/4Reg/1A
Jn., yeo., Warm., 1562, W, P2/4Reg/91B
Jn., yeo., Serrington, Stapleford, 1585, I, W, P2/B/86, P2/7Reg/16A, 25B
Bigg, Jn., husb., Serrington, Stapleford, 1602, AB, a/c, I, P2/B/229
Jn., Seend, Melk., 1630, AB, P2/B/524
Jn., yeo., Burbage, 1637, I, W, P11/3
Bigge, Jn., clerk, Pewsey, 1646, AB, P1/B/326
Jn., Stapleford, 1662, AB, I, P2/B/741
Jn., innholder, Marl. St Peter and St Paul, 1663, AB, comm, I, P1/B/387
Bigges, Jn., Southwick, N. Bradley, 1669, I, W, P2/B/806
Bigg, Jn., innholder, Lyme R., Dorset, 1679, I, W, P5/1679/6
Jn., Sonning, Berks., 1683, AB, I, P5/1683/4
Bigges, Jn., thatcher, Winsley, Bradford A., 1684, I, W, P2/B/1042
Jn., yeo., Newtown, Durnford, 1704, I (over Ł1,300), W, P5/1704/7
Jn., yeo., Trowle, Bradford A., 1705, comm, NW, P2/B/1246
Jn., gent., Worton, Pott., 1732, W, P1/B/1020, P1/7Reg/521
Jn., yeo., Atworth, Bradford A., 1733, W, P2/B/1517
Jn., Hawkeridge, Westb., 1745, AB, P25/1745/11
Jn., gent., Chirton (form. of Codf. St P.), 1757, AB, ren, P2/B/1736
Jn., yeo., Codf. St P. (form. of Chirton), 1759, I (2), W, P2/B/1750
Jn., yeo., Poulshot, 1774, W, P2/B/1912
Jn., Berwick B., 1780, W, P26/1106
Jn., Trowb., 1789, AB, comm, P1/B/1504
Biggs als Beard, Jn., Marston, Pott., 1827, AB, comm, L (3), Wr, P1/1827/28
Jn., labourer, Waltham St Lawr., Berks., 1829, W, Wr, P1/1829/111
Jn., farmer, Etchilhampton, 1837, O, W, Wr, P3/1837/71
Jn., farmer, Etchilhampton, 1846, O, W, Wr, P3/1846/8
Jos., soldier in the Parliamentarian service, no abode stated but made at Devizes, 1647, NW, P1/B/338
Mgt., widow, Hawkeridge, Westb., 1679, comm, I (ex.'s a/c at foot), W, P25/1679/6
Margery, widow, Lt. Bedwyn, 1632, I, W, P5/1631/5, P5/11Reg/177
Maria, sp., *The Ivy Mill*, Edington, 1835, W, P2/1835/23
My., sp., Rollestone, 1762, AB, comm, P2/B/1786
My., sp., Sherb., Dorset, 1821, AB, actuary's note, Wr, P5/1821/29
Bigges, Nich., Crofton, Gt. Bedwyn, 1621, I, W, P5/1620/8, P5/10Reg/14
Rd., Hankerton, 1615, AB, P3/B/125
Rd., Westb., 1674-75, AB, comm, L, P1/B/490, P25/1675/10
Rd., sen., yeo., Broughton G., 1698, I, W, P1/B/676, P1/3Reg/179
Rd., Burbage, 1712, AB, P11/105

Rd., sen., maltster, Westb., 1720, W (NEP), P25/1720/6
Rd., yeo., Broughton G., 1729, I, W, P1/B/958, P1/7Reg/331
Rd., Earley, Sonning, Berks., 1732, AB, I, P5/1732/5
Rd., farmer, Berwick B., 1771, W, P26/1041
Rd., yeo., Atworth, Bradford A., 1777, AB, ren, P2/B/1946
Robt., yeo., Lt. Durnford, 1694, AB, I, P9/28
Robt., gent., Gt. Durnford, 1752, AB, ren, W, P9/65
Roger, yeo., Deptford, Wylye, 1707, AB, ren, P2/B/1267
Sam., yeo., Winterslow, 1754, AB, ren, W, P2/B/1709
Sam., gent., Chitterne St My., 1798, W, P2/B/2135
Sarah, sp., Seend Row, Melk., 1715, W, P2/B/1338
Sarah, widow, Pott., 1801, AB, comm, ren, Wr, P1/1801/129, P1/15Reg/354B
Bigges, Steph., Lt. Bedwyn, 1625, AB, P3/B/265
Steph., yeo., Rams., 1680, I, W, P5/1680/3
Steph., yeo., Holt, Bradford A., [1699], I, W, P2/B/1203
Steph., yeo., Wantage, Berks., 1797, W, P5/1797/4, P5/18Reg/238
Thos., Stapleford, 1551, AB, I (with list of debts owed by decd), P2/B/6, P2/2Reg/135C
Thos., Hawkeridge, Westb., 1629, I, W, P25/1629/1
Bigges, Thos., yeo., Pewsey, 1671, I, W, P1/B/479
Thos., Sonning, Berks., 1683, AB, I, P5/1683/3
Thos., yeo., Fisherton A., 1685, a/c (2), I, W, P2/B/1062
Thos., yeo., Worton, Pott., 1687, I, W, P1/B/589
Thos., W. Lavington, 1691, AB, I, P1/B/621
Thos., yeo., Berwick St Jas., 1694, I, W, P1/B/639
Bigg, Thos., yeo., New Windsor, Berks., 1695, I, W, P1/B/648
Thos., yeo., Heywood, Westb., 1705, I, W, P25/1705/9
Thos., Broughton G., 1706, AB, P2/B/1259
Thos., yeo., Chisenbury, Enford, 1709, W, P2/B/1279
Thos., Winsley, Bradford A., 1730, AB, P2/B/1478
Thos., Amesb., 1734, AB, P2/B/1542
Thos., tallow chandler, Westb., 1735, W, P25/1735/1
Thos., Seend, Melk., 1750, W, P2/B/1677
Thos., sen., Fisherton A., 1784-87, AB, a/c, I, T, P2/B/2002, 2024
Thos., Atworth, Bradford A., 1785, AB, comm, P2/B/2007
Thos., yeo., Burderop, Chiseldon, 1788, W, P3/B/1710
Thos., bach., Devizes, 1845, AB, O, Wr, P1/1845/89
Tristram, sen., yeo., Steeple L., 1721, W, P2/B/1398
Ursula, widow, Westb., 1724, W, P25/1724/8
Whitfield Bourn, gent., Bramshaw, Hants, 1772, W, P24/1144
Wm., sen., Marl., 1661, AB, comm, I, P1/B/363
Wm., yeo., Heywood, Westb., 1680, I, W, P25/1680/11
Wm., gent., Gt. Woodford, 1688, AB, I, ren, W (& cod), P5/1688/9
Wm., Westb., 1721, AB, I, P25/1721/4
Bigg, Wm., yeo., New Windsor, Berks., 1723, W, P1/B/896, P1/7Reg/11
Wm., tallow chandler, Hungerford, Berks., 1733, AB, a/c, comm, I (detailed), ren, W, P5/1733/8
Wm., yeo., Gt. Wishford, 1742, W, P1/B/1155, P1/9Reg/220B
Wm., yeo., Poulshot, 1748, W, P1/B/1224, P1/10Reg/225B
Wm., Farleigh Wick, Monkton F., 1758, W, P2/B/1741
Wm., Winterbourne Bassett, 1789, AB, P1/B/1505
Wm., yeo., Seend, Melk., 1804, W, P1/1804/23
Wm., Binfield, Berks., 1811, AB, comm, Wr, P1/1811/68
Wm., Worton, Pott., 1819, AB, Wr, P1/1819/5
Bignell, Chas., Wilton, 1737, W, P2/B/1557
Geo., sen., innholder, Wilton, 1699, I, W, P2/B/1205
Geo., farrier, Wilton, 1750, W, P1/B/1252, P1/10Reg/436A
Hugh, jun., E. Harnham, Britford, 1752, AB, guardianship bond, P24/1037
Jane, sp., Wilton, 1729, AB, P2/B/1471
My., widow, Wilton, 1718, I, W, P2/B/1366
Walter, sen., clothier, Trowb., 1742, AB, ren, P1/B/1154
Wm., porter to the Earl of Pembroke, Wilton, 1742, AB, I, P2/B/1601

Bigwood, Dorothy, widow, Bishopstrow, 1622, I, W, P2/B/419
Eliz., widow, Westb., 1739, W, P25/1739/5
Geo., blacksmith, Westb., 1812, W, P25/1812/1
Hannah, widow, Westb., 1788, W, P25/1788/1
Jane, Westb., 1691, AB, P25/1691/2
My., sp., Devizes, 1831, W, Wr, P1/1831/6
Biggood, Nich., yeo., Westb., 1642, I, W (NEP), P25/1642/6
Rd., vict., Westb., 1757, W, P25/1757/4
Sam., Westb., 1747, AB, P25/1747/1
Sam., Westb., 1771, AB, O, P25/1771/7
Thos., Westb., 1736, AB, I, ren, P25/1736/6
Wm., sen., scribbler, Westb., 1687, I, NW, P25/1687/9
Wm., sen., scribbler, Dilton M., Westb., 1701, AB, I, P25/1701/7
Wm., book keeper, Westb., 1803, O, W, P25/1803/5
Wm., Pott., 1835, W, P1/1835/133
Biles, Jn., Stourpaine, Dorset, 1716, I, L, W, P24/668
Byles, Wm., Sal. St Mart., 1675, AB, P4/1675/11
Wm., blacksmith, Bere R., Dorset, 1853, aff, comm, D, W, Wr, P5/1853/26
Bilke, Jn., husb., Perhay, Netherb., Dorset, 1572, W, P5/2Reg/118B
Bill, Chris., Haydon Wick, Rodbourne C., 1571, W, P1/1Reg/35D
Billett, Anth., carrier, Lacock, 1630, AB, a/c, I, P3/B/323
Anth., jun., baker, Lacock, 1704, AB, I, ren, W, P3/B/1029
Anth., joiner, Lacock, 1708, I, W, P3/B/1071
Bellett, Cicely, widow, Stratton, Dorset, 1573, I, W, P5/1573/5, P5/3Reg/18B
Edwd., Corsham, 1718, marriage licence, P29/2Reg/25B
Edwd., wheelwright, Seend, Melk., 1723, AB, ren, W, P2/B/1418
Edwd., yeo., Chr. M., 1779, W, P3/B/1657
Francis, yeo., Gt. Chalfield, 1672, I, W, P2/B/849
Hilary, Sal., 1612, app. of proctor, court paper, I, T, P1/B/83
Bellett, Joan, widow, Stratton, Dorset, 1597, AB, I, W, P5/1597/10, P5/6Reg/166A
Bellett, Jn., Stratton, Dorset, 1564, W, P5/1Reg/37C
Jn., sen., carp., Corsham, 1617, AB, W, P29/B/14, P29/1Reg/79
Jn., sen., carp. *or* joiner, Corsham, 1673, AB, P29/1Reg/198C
Jos., bach., N. Wraxall, 1855, AB, aff, O, Wr, P3/1855/15
Belott, Michael, Chipp., 1746, W, P3/B/1436
Ralph, husb., Corsham, [1566], W (NEP), P29/1Reg/10B
Bellott, Rd., gent., Corsham, 1558, W, P29/B/2
Rd., Langley Burrell, 1664, AB, comm, I, P3/B/492
Rd., Corsham, 1719, marriage licence, P29/2Reg/28D
Bellett, Robt., husb., Stratton, Dorset, 1594, I, W, P5/1594/6, P5/6Reg/60A
Sam., Corsham, 1672, AB, I, P29/B/22, P29/1Reg/195B
Sarah, Lacock, 1713, AB, P3/B/1115
Thos., Pickwick, Corsham, [1641], W, P29/B/18
Thos., tanner, Lacock, 1715, I, W, P3/B/1129
Thos., wheelwright, Melk., 1723, AB, comm, ren, P2/B/1416
Thos., tanner, Lacock, 1735, I, W, P1/B/1052, P1/8Reg/76
Thos., vict., Lacock, 1754, AB, ren, P3/B/1488
Wm., yeo., N. Wraxall, 1801, W, P1/1801/73, P1/15Reg/287C
Billing *see* Billings
Billinghurst, Ann, widow, Sonning, Berks., 1752, W, P5/1752/3
Jane, Sonning, Berks., 1713, AB, P5/1713/12
Jn., mealman, Sonning, Berks., 1741, AB, comm, ren, Wr, P5/1741/2
Billings, Billing, Ann, widow, Hindon, 1790, AB, P2/B/2047
Hannah, sp., S. Newton, 1766, W, P2/B/1829
Robt., Wilton, 1765, W, P2/B/1807
Billingsley, Jos., yeo. and waggoner, Timbridge, Lt. Bedwyn, 1716, I, W, P21/7/26
Billson, Thos., Reading St Lawr., Berks., 1753, AB, I, P1/B/1268
Bimister *see* Bemister
Binder, Alice, Idmiston, 1694, AB, I, P2/B/1162
Edmd., yeo., Idmiston, 1638, I, W, P1/B/281

Eliz., widow, Idmiston, 1685, I, W, P2/B/1049
Jn., sen., yeo., Edington, 1662, I, W, P2/B/747
Jn., husb., Idmiston, 1671, I, W, P1/B/466
Rd., yeo., Idmiston, 1678, I, W, P2/B/935
Byndar, Robt., Idmiston, 1568, W, P2/5Reg/44C
Robt., husb., Idmiston, 1637, AB, a/c, I, T, P2/B/611, P2/9Reg/106A
Wm., yeo., E. Grimstead, W. Dean, 1697, I, W, P2/B/1188
Binfield, Augustine, Wokm., Berks., 1710, AB, I, P5/1710/11
Eliz., Reading, Berks., 1726, AB, P1/B/918
Frances, widow, Sonning, Berks., 1742, W, Wr, P5/1742/6
Hy., husb., Eye and Dunsden, Sonning, Berks., 1697, I, W, P5/1697/4
Martha, widow, Wokm., Berks., 1756, W, P5/1756/2
Nich., Sonning, Berks., 1547, W, P5/20Reg/90B
Rd., yeo., Wokm., Berks., 1769, W, P5/1769/2
Benfield, Robt., Wokm., Berks., 1636, AB, I, P5/1636/10, P5/13Reg/5A
Robt., yeo., Eye and Dunsden, Sonning, Berks., 1665, I, W, P5/1665/9
Robt., yeo., Sonning, Berks., 1730, W, P5/1730/4
Robt., barber surgeon, Wokm., Berks., 1734, W, P5/1734/6
Wm., Hurst, Berks., 1630, AB, P5/11Reg/128A
Bingham, Eliz., widow, Over C., Dorset, 1801, W, P5/1801/18, P5/18Reg/322
Jn., husb., Lyme R., Dorset, 1692, I, W, P16/116
Jonathan, buttonmaker, Sherb., Dorset, 1702, AB, comm, W, P5/1701/1
Nathaniel, Sherb., Dorset, 1740, AB, P5/1740/13
Bingley, Michael, clerk and vicar, Latton, 1710, AB, I, P3/B/1088
Binister *see* Beminster
Binson *see* Benson
Bint, Rd., yeo., Sonning, Berks., 1641, I, W, P5/1641/3, P5/14Reg/15A
Birch, Burch, Ambrose, clothw., St Nich.'s Hospital, The Close, Sal., 1699, W, P5/1699/5
Ambrose, E. Harnham, Britford, 1733, AB, P5/1733/9
Burch, Ambrose, haberdasher, Sal., 1745, W, P4/1745/1
Burch, Ambrose, apothecary's apprentice, Romsey, Hants (form. of Sal.), 1775, W, P4/1775/13
Burch, Ambrose, apothecary, Sal. & Whitep., 1819, AB, Wr, P2/1819/47
Burch, Ann, widow, Leigh, Ashton K., 1728, AB, I, P3/B/1273
Burch, Ann, widow, Sal., 1765, W, P4/1765/8
Cath., widow, Lyneham, 1698, W (NEP), P3/B/975
Burch, Eliz., widow, Theale, Tilehurst, Berks., 1756, W, P1/B/1296, P1/11Reg/207
Geo., Catcomb, Hilmarton, 1697, W, P3/B/962
Burch, Geo., labourer, Barford St Mart., 1790, AB, W, P2/B/2048
Burch, Hy., yeo., Axford, Rams., 1718, AB, I, L, P5/1718/3
Burch, Jane, widow, Rams. (form. (1774) of Feltham, Middlesex), 1792, W, P5/1792/3, P5/18Reg/180
Jane, widow, Sotwell, Wallingford St Leonard, Berks., 1798, W, P1/B/1555, P1/15Reg/83
Burch, Joan, widow, Chilton F., 1702, AB (she d. c40 years ago), P3/B/1021
Burch, Joan, widow, Chilton F., 1709, AB, comm, I, P3/B/1080
Burch, Jn., Oak Hill, Froxfield, 1626, AB, a/c, comm, I, P3/B/282
Burch, Jn., yeo., Leigh, Ashton K., 1724, AB, I, P3/B/1230
Jn., clerk, Wantage, Berks., 1728, W, P5/1728/11, P5/16Reg/193
Burch, Jn., yeo., Chards., Devon, 1753, W, P14/165
Burch, Mgt., Gt. Faringdon, Berks., 1710, AB, P5/1710/18
My., widow, gentlewoman, Baydon, 1764, W, P5/1764/2
Rd., labourer, Aldbourne, 1795, W, P1/B/1538, P1/14Reg/558
Burch, Robt., Oak Hill, Froxfield, 1636, I, W, P3/B/376
Burch, Robt., blacksmith, Aldbourne, 1667, comm, W, P3/B/530
Sam., husb., Winterbourne Bassett, 1740, W, P3/B/1388
Burch, Steph., yeo., Baydon, 1741, W, Wr, P5/1741/4
Steph., yeo., Weston, Welford, Berks., 1786, W, P1/B/1497, P1/14Reg/119B
Burch, Susanna, widow, Leigh, Ashton K., 1693, I, W, P3/B/909
Birche, Thos., Burbage, 1591, AB, I, W, P11/310, P5/5Reg/95D
Burch, Thos., Leigh, Ashton K., 1670, AB, I, ren, P3/B/581
Burch, Thos., Isbery, Lambourn, Berks., 1698, I, W, P1/B/666, P1/3Reg/10
Burch, Thos., yeo., Leigh, Ashton K., 1773, W, P3/B/1627

Burch, Wm., yeo., Sal., 1847, W, Wr, P4/1847/11
Birchill *see* Burchall
Bircombe *see* Burcombe
Bird, Agnes, widow, Wilton, 1631, I, W, T, P2/B/534
Burd, Alice, sp., Devizes, 1678, AB, NW, P1/B/523
Ann, widow, Durley, Burbage, 1740-50, AB (exx, decd's dau Eliz. Ralfe, d.1750, leaving mother's goods unadmd; AB issued to her husband, Jas. R.), W, P11/174
Ann, widow, Hindon, 1793, W, P2/B/2087
Byrd, Bernard, Uffc., Devon, 1808, AB, comm, P20/1/290
Edith, widow, Fordington, Dorset, 1642, AB, I, L (sends 10s in silver therefore so recipient is not defrauded with light gold), P5/1642/4, P5/14Reg/48C
Burd *or* Buerd, Edmd., husb., Allington, All C., 1569, W, P1/1Reg/96A, P1/2Reg/90A
Edwd., Amesb., 1684, AB, P2/B/1041
Burd, Eleanor, widow, Avill's Farm, Corsham, 1677, AB, W, P3/B/687
Burd, Eliz., widow, Winterbourne G., 1587, W, P2/7Reg/94D
Geo., husb., Wilton, 1628-36, AB, I, W, P2/B/494, 595
Hannah, widow, Ogbourne St And., 1736, W, P23/520
Herbert, vict., Hilp. Marsh, 1844, O, W, Wr, P1/1844/3
Burd, Jane, sp., Fordington, Dorset, 1718, AB, P15/99
Joan, sp., Shrewton, 1669, AB, I, P2/B/814
Byrde, Jn., Fordington, Dorset, 1575, I, W, P15/187, P5/3Reg/68B
Burd, Jn., haberdasher, Devizes, 1594, AB, I, W, P1/B/9
Jn., yeo., Devizes, 1615, I, P1/B/124
Jn., Savernake, 1722, AB, P1/B/875
Jn., vict., Trowb., 1807, W, P1/1807/1
Byrd, Jonathan, sen., labourer, Sanden Fee, Hungerford, Berks., 1694, I, W, P23/203
Jos., bach., Hungerford, Berks., 1793, AB, comm, P23/796
Lydia, widow, Trowb., 1814, comm, W, Wr, P1/1814/66
Burd, Mgt., widow, Fordington, Dorset, 1592, AB, a/c, I, P5/1592/10, P5/5Reg/143A
My., sp., Gt. Amesb., 1684, AB, I, W, P2/B/1029
My., Amesb., 1686, AB, P2/B/1060
My., Gt. Bedwyn, 1705, AB, P21/6/22
My., sp., Liddington, 1705, AB, comm, I, P3/B/1043
Matilda, sp., Bathford, Somerset], but leaving effects at Chipp., 1855, AB, aff, O, Wr, P3/1855/49
Nathan, yeo., Leigh, Yetm., Dorset, 1825, W, P19/231
Byrd, Peter, broad weaver, Kington L., 1701, comm, I, W, Wr, P3/B/1011
Phyllis, widow, Winterbourne G., 1605, W, P2/B/258
Burd, Rd., gent., Chards., Devon, [1772], W (NEP), P14/186
Byrd, Robt., husb., Amesb., 1588, W, P2/7Reg/126C
Burd, Robt., yeo., Gt. Amesb., 1628, W, P2/B/481, P2/9Reg/61
Robt., husb., Winterbourne S., 1639, I, W, P2/B/645
Burd, Robt., sen., yeo., Gt. Amesb., 1668, I, W, P2/B/792
Burd, Robt., Amesb., 1680, AB, I, P1/B/540
Robt., innholder, Beam., Dorset, 1759, W, P17/541
Robt., Froxfield, 1832, O, W, Wr, P1/1832/4
Byrd, Thos., Sonning, Berks., 1562, W, P5/1Reg/29A
Thos., husb., Winterbourne S., 1616, I, W, P2/B/360, P2/8Reg/300B
Thos., husb., Hidden, Hungerford, Berks., 1674, AB, comm, I, P5/1674/15
Burd, Walter, Winterbourne S., 1595, I, W, P2/B/161, P2/7Reg/147A
Byrd, Wm., Winterbourne G., 1579, I, W, P2/B/71, P2/5Reg/324B
Burd, Wm., tanner, Pott. Wick, 1643, I, W, P1/B/305
Wm., gent., Gt. Amesb., 1684, AB, I, P2/B/1028
Byrd, Wm., esquire, Stock, Gt. Bedwyn, 1692, AB, a/c, comm, I, P1/B/618
Wm., wheelwright, Ogbourne St And., 1736, AB, P23/519
Byrde, Wm., gent., Gt. Bedwyn, [1746], W, P21/9/56
Wm., groom to the Duke of Queensberry, Amesb., 1766, W, P2/B/1827
Wm., Beer Hackett, Dorset, 1767, AB, comm, P5/1767/7
Birt *see* Burt
Bishop, [...], Brixton D., 1616, a/c, P2/B/2160
[male], abode lost, 1638, a/c (damaged: christian name lost; has son Jn. & dau Mgt.), P2/B/616

Aaron, baker, Bradford A., 1842, O, W, Wr, P1/1842/101
Agnes, widow, Yatton K., 1605, I, W, P1/B/31
Agnes, widow, Sutton B., 1679, AB, I, W, P3/B/712
Alan, clerk, Ashton K., 1664, I, W, P3/B/493
Alice, widow, W. Grimstead, 1561, W, P2/4Reg/79A
Alice, widow, All C., [1581], W (NEP), P3/1Reg/11C
Busshopp, Alice, Sal. St Thos., 1588, AB, P4/Reg/34
[Alice], Newnham, Sutton V., 1596, I, W, P2/B/170
Alice, widow, Malm., 1789, W, P3/B/1720
Ann, widow, Tytherton Kellaways, Bremhill, 1683, I, W, P3/B/770
Ann, sp., Mere, 1711, W, P5/1711/6, P5/15Reg/226
Ann, widow, Sal., 1778, W, P4/1778/9
Ann, sp., Brinkw., 1780, W, P3/B/1663
Avis, widow, S. Bowood, Netherb., Dorset, 1593, I, W, P17/635, P5/6Reg/44B
Benj., husb., Fordington, Dorset, 1730, W, P15/114
Betty, widow, Sherb., Dorset, 1837, W, Wr, P5/1837/15
Cath., sp., Calne, 1777, W, P26/1088
Cath., widow, Devizes, 1820, AB, W, Wr, P1/1820/121
Chris., yeo., E. Tytherton, Bremhill, 1667, I, NW, P3/B/524
Chris., yeo., Uffc., Devon, 1720, I, W, P20/1/169
Dan., Damerham, Hants, 1630, I, W (NEP), P2/B/526
Dan., yeo., Beam., Dorset, 1845, W, Wr, P5/1845/22
David, Alderbury, 1785, AB, P26/1143
Edwd., Winterborne K., Dorset, 1613, AB, P5/1612/9, P5/9Reg/79B
Edwd., physician and apothecary, Calne, 1663, AB, I, NW, P5/1663/11
Edwd., husb., Uffc., Devon, 1670, I, W, P20/1/58
Bishop als Cru, Edwd., surgeon, Lacock, 1678, I, W, P3/B/682
Edwd., Crockerton & Mount Mill, Longbridge D., 1681, I, W, P2/B/978
Edwd., Warm., 1748, W, P2/B/1667
Elbright, Alderton, 1571, W (NEP), P1/1Reg/84/B
Elias, miller, Sherb., Dorset, 1720, W, P5/1720/7, P5/16Reg/46A
Eliz., widow, Tytherington, Heytes., 1613, I, W, P5/1612/7, P5/9Reg/112C
Eliz., E. Tytherton, Bremhill, 1668, AB, I, P1/B/451
Eliz., widow, Uffc., Devon, 1688, AB, comm, I, ren, W, P5/1688/7
Eliz., sp., d. Collingbourne D. but lived in Gt. Bedwyn 40 years, 1693, I, W, P21/5/24
Bishop als Yeamans, Eliz., wife, Fritham, Bramshaw, Hants, 1724, AB, P24/862
Eliz., sp., Hinton, Steeple A., 1749, W, P2/B/1674
Eliz., widow, Uffc., Devon, 1761, W, P5/1761/4
Eliz., sp., Charminster, Dorset, 1782, W, Wr, P5/1782/5, P5/17Reg/216A
Eliz., widow, Reading, Berks., 1832, AB, O, Wr, P1/1832/136
Busshopp, Geo., Kingston, Dorset, 1568, W, P5/2Reg/30B
Geo., husb., Draycot C., 1639, W, P3/B/415
Geo., sen., yeo., Easterton, Mkt. L., 1709, I, W, P2/B/1281
Geo., yeo., Trowb., 1764, AB, a/c, I (2), P1/B/1369
Geo., yeo., Easterton, Mkt. L., 1767, W, P1/B/1376, P1/12Reg/226
Geo., plumber and glazier, Devizes, 1841, comm, W, Wr, P1/1841/14
Giles, S. Bowood, Netherb., Dorset, 1585-1606, D, W, P5/1606/10, P5/8Reg/65D
Giles, yeo., Uffc., Devon, 1709, I, W, P20/1/166
Giles, yeo., Uffc., Devon, 1749, W, Wr, P5/1749/4
Busshopp, Hy., jun., Poulshot, 1558, W, P2/3Reg/95B
Hy., sen., shoemaker, Chipp., 1637, I, W, P3/B/384
Hy., shoemaker, Chipp., 1640, I, W, P3/B/439
Hy., yeo., Devizes, 1668, NW, P1/B/437
Hy., yeo., E. Tytherton, Bremhill, 1669, I, W, P3/B/546
Hy., husb., Devizes St Jn., 1685, I, W, P1/B/578
Hy., yeo., Over C., Dorset, 1708-09, AB, I, ren, W, P5/1708/16, P5/15Reg/103
Humphrey, Calne, 1633, I, P30/20
Humphrey, yeo., Uffc., Devon, 1705, I, W, P20/1/142
Humphrey, Uffc., Devon, 1751, W, P20/1/220
Isaac, innholder, Sherb., Dorset, 1834, W, Wr, P5/1834/10

Bishops, Isabel, widow, Kingston, Dorset, 1568, W, P5/2Reg/30C
Jas., Enmore Grn, Motc., Dorset, 1677, AB, P19/36
Jas., yeo., W. Lavington, 1697, I, W, P1/B/661
Jas., yeo., Easterton, Mkt. L., 1743, W, P2/B/1621
Jas., Woodb., 1759, AB, P1/B/1322
Jas., husb., Westport St My., 1813, W, Wr, P3/1813/28
Jane, widow, Fordington, Dorset, 1683, a/c, I, P30/19
Jane, sp., Sal., 1821, AB, P4/1821/6
Jn., Winterborne K., Dorset, 1566, W, P5/1Reg/67B
Jn., Pickwick, Corsham, [1568], W (NEP), P29/1Reg/10A
Jn., sen., labourer, Downton, 1571, W, P1/1Reg/32B
Jn., The Borough, Downton, 1612, I, W, P2/B/323
Jn., husb., Berwick St Jn., 1616, AB, a/c, I, P1/B/135
Jn., yeo., Poulshot, 1617, I, W, P2/B/375
Jn., Mere, 1617, AB, I, P5/1617/3, P5/9Reg/216C
Jn., W. Kington, 1630, AB, I, P3/B/324
Jn., husb., Imber, 1639, I, W, P2/B/636
Jn., Sherrington, 1640, I, T, W, P2/B/652
Jn., Poulshot, 1644, AB, comm, P2/B/692
Jn., Sal., 1667, AB, I, P4/1667/12
Jn., yeo., E. Tytherton, Bremhill, 1669, I, W, P3/B/547
Jn., sen., yeo., Eastmanstreet, Calne, 1684, I, W, P26/320
Jn., Barford St Mart., 1709, AB, P2/B/1278
Jn., sen., yeo., Uffc., Devon, 1710, W, P5/1710/12, P5/15Reg/200
Jn., yeo., Easterton, Mkt. L., 1713, I, W, P2/B/1323
Jn., yeo., Semley, 1719, W, P2/B/1384
Jn., sen., gent., Eastmanstreet, Calne, 1728, W, P26/734
Jn., Marl., 1731, AB, P1/B/992
Jn., bargeman, Speenhamland, Berks., 1732, W, P1/B/1009, P1/7Reg/491B
Jn., sen., gent., Eastmanstreet, Calne, 1744, W, P26/862
Jn., gent., Uffc., Devon, 1751, W, P20/1/218
Jn., vict., Quemerford, Calne, 1763, W, P26/1000
Jn., Fritham, Bramshaw, Hants, 1764, W, P24/1094
Jn., Chr. M., 1768, AB, P3/B/1590
Jn., yeo., Gt. Somerford, 1800, AB, O, ren, W, Wr, P3/1800/9
Jn., gent., Calne, 1816, W, Wr, P26/1309
Jn., tallow chandler, Sherb., Dorset, 1827, W, Wr, P5/1827/39
Jn., gardener, Sutton B., 1829, O, W, P1/1829/34
Jn., farmer, Worton, Pott., 1847, I, W, Wr, P1/1847/12
Jos., butcher, Malm., 1815, W, Wr, P3/1815/34
Judith, widow, Chr. M., 1684, I, W, P3/B/790
Judith, widow, Eastmanstreet, Calne, 1693, I, W, P26/408
Judith, sp., Calne, 1709, AB, P26/551
Lawr., Sherb., Dorset, 1579, I, W (damaged), P5/1579/12, P5/3Reg/119A
Leonard, sen., yeo., Easterton, Mkt. L., 1672, comm, I, W, P2/B/858
Leonard, yeo., Easterton, Mkt. L., 1719, W, P2/B/1381
Mgt., Calne, 1637, AB, a/c, I, P26/61
Mgt., widow, Sherrington, 1643, LA, W, P2/B/680
Mgt., widow, Nettleton, 1675, I, W (both damaged), P3/B/651
Martha, widow, Heytes., 1705, I, W, P5/1705/9
Martha, sp. form. milliner & haberdasher, Sal., 1809, W, P4/1809/4
My., sp., Pickwick, Corsham, [1641], W, P29/B/17
My., widow, Tytherington, Heytes., 1661, I, W, P5/1661/7
My., widow, S. Bowood, Netherb., Dorset, [1668], W, P17/84
My., widow, S. Bowood, Netherb., Dorset, 1691, I, W, P5/1691/5
My., widow, Sal., 1714, AB, I, ren, W, P4/1714/10
My., yeo.'s wife, Sydling St Nich., Dorset, 1739, AB, W, P5/1739/9
My., widow, Rams., 1742, W, Wr, P5/1742/4
My., sp., Uffc., Devon, 1774, W, P20/1/260
My., sp., Sal., 1787, W, P4/1787/11

My., sp., Sal., 1810, AB, P4/1810/7
Matthew, labourer, Fritham, Bramshaw, Hants, 1726, W, P24/852
Matthew, yeo., Sherb., Dorset, 1757, W, P5/1757/3
Matthew, smith, Enmore Grn, Motc., Dorset, 1843, W, Wr, P19/249
Nich., Netherb., Dorset, 1603, AB, I, T, P5/1603/4, P5/7Reg/64B
Nich., Aldbourne, 1608, W, P3/B/32
Nich., yeo., Nettleton, 1634, I, W, P1/B/248
Nich., sen., Amesb., 1718, AB (2), W, P2/B/1377
Peter, W. Lavington, 1682, AB, comm, draft I, I, P1/B/558
Peter, cordw., Pewsey, 1730, W, P3/B/1291
Philip, fuller, Mount Mill, Sutton V., 1718, W, P2/B/1375
Ralph, yeo., Nettleton, 1649, AB, I, W, P1/B/347
Ralph, husb., Nettleton, 1686, I, W, P3/B/823
Rebecca, widow, Sherb., Dorset, 1856, aff, O, W, Wr, P5/1856/11
Rd., Sherb., Dorset, 1591, AB, I, P5/1591/13, P5/5Reg/129A
Rd., husb., Fordington, Dorset, 1634, I, W (GVS), P5/1634/22, P5/12Reg/292
Rd., slaughterman, Chr. M., 1683, AB, comm, I, P3/B/771
Rd., yeo., Calne, 1748, AB, ren, P26/884
Rd., sen., farmer, Cowesfield, Whitep., 1776, W, P2/B/1928
Rd., sen., sievemaker, Amesb., 1788, W, P2/B/2027
Rd., Allington, 1805, W, P2/1805/28
Rd., sen., yeo., Calne, 1823, W, Wr, P26/1344
Rd., Charlton nr Malm., 1841, W, Wr, P3/1841/45
Robt., husb., Tytherington, Heytes., 1588, W, P5/5Reg/30B
Robt., Corsham, 1605, AB, P29/B/10
Busshop, Robt., Netherb., Dorset, 1613, I, T, P5/1613/4
Robt., husb., W. Kington, 1613, AB, I, W, P1/B/93, P5/9Reg/94B
Robt., sen., tailor, Nettleton, [1613], I, W (NEP), P3/B/106
Robt., yeo., Bray, Berks., 1616, I, W, P1/B/132
Robt., yeo., Bowood Park, Bowood, 1684, AB, I, P3/B/791
Robt., husb., Calne, 1689, AB, I, P26/385
Robt., cordw., Studley, Calne, 1714, I (detailed), W, P26/585
Robt., Bratton, Westb., 1773, AB, P25/1773/1
Robt., shoemaker, Sal., 1784, W, P4/1784/10
Robt., Worton, Pott., 1793, AB, P1/B/1531, P1/14Reg/485A
Ruth, sp., Calne, 1758, W, P5/1758/6
Sam., yeo., Uffc., Devon, 1677, I, W, P20/1/80
Sam., Fordington, Dorset, 1693, AB, I, P15/50
Sam., yeo., Uffc., Devon, 1696, I, W, P20/1/130
Sam., gent., Uffc., Devon (of Milbrook, Axminster, Devon, 1784), 1816, O, W, Wr, P20/1/304
Sarah, widow, Uffc., Devon, 1713, W, P5/1713/15, P5/15Reg/376C
Thos., Boyton, 1555, AB, P2/1Reg/22B
Thos., Bere R., Dorset, 1564, W, P5/1Reg/36D
Thos., Alderton, 1626, I, W, P3/B/276
Thos., Pickwick, Corsham, [1637], W, P29/B/16
Thos., Studley, Calne, 1641, I, W, P5/1641/6, P5/14Reg/8A
Thos., sen., yeo., Chr. M., 1671, I, W, P3/B/587
Thos., Fordington, Dorset, 1691, AB, I, P15/47
Thos., soap boiler and chandler, Chr. M., 1723, AB, W, P3/B/1218
Thos., sen., tailor, Garsdon, 1789, W, P3/B/1721
Thos., sen., wigmaker, Winchester St., Sal. St Edmd., 1818, W, Wr, P4/1818/8
Thos., yeo., Melplash, Netherb., Dorset, 1827, comm, W, Wr, P17/605
Thos., sen., hairdresser, Sal., 1832, W, Wr, P4/1832/7
Thos., yeo., Melplash, Netherb., Dorset, 1845, AB, comm, W, Wr, P17/617
Thomasine, sp., Uffc., Devon, 1775, W, P20/1/265
Valerian, husb., Tytherington, Heytes., 1601, I, W, P5/1601/7, P5/7Reg/26A
Walter, Kellaways, 1631, I, W, P3/B/336
Walter, Calne, 1638, AB, I, P26/77
Walter, cordw., Sherb., Dorset, 1672, AB, I, P5/1672/4
Bishopp, Walter *see also* Philip Tyser

Wm., jun., labouring man, W. Grimstead, 1561, I, W, P2/B/21, P2/4Reg/79B
Wm., sen., labouring man, W. Grimstead, 1561, W, P2/4Reg/79C
Wm., yeo., Yatton K., [1615], I, W (NEP), P3/B/130
Wm., S. Bowood, Netherb., Dorset, 1663, I, memo, P30/18
Wm., yeo., Fordington, Dorset, 1668, I, W, P15/13
Wm., Draycot C., 1670, comm, I, W (2 - 1 a copy), P3/B/569
Wm., husb., Nettleton, 1676, I, W, P3/B/662
Wm., sen., collarmaker, Sal., 1680, AB, P4/1680/6
Wm., woollen draper, Westb. L., 1681, AB, comm (unexecuted), I (detailed), W, P25/1680/2
Wm., yeo., W. Yatton, Yatton K., 1684, I, W, P3/B/792
Wm., Mere, 1699, AB, P5/1699/3
Wm., carp., Nettleton, 1704, W, P3/B/1030
Wm., Sal., 1706-08, AB, I, P4/1705/4, P4/1708/10
Wm., shoemaker, Sal., 1733, W, P4/1733/8
Wm., Yatton K., 1740, AB, comm, P3/B/1389
Wm., shoemaker, Sal., 1741, W, P4/1741/5
Wm., husb., Coombe B., 1745, I, W, P8/36
Wm., Hullavington, 1760, AB, P3/B/1528
Wm., shopkeeper, Sherb., Dorset, 1777, comm, W, P5/1777/2, P5/17Reg/138B
Wm., Sal., 1788, AB, P4/1788/9
Wm., Sal., 1797, AB, P4/1797/13
Wm., woolcomber, Uffc., Devon, 1800, W, P5/1800/30, P5/18Reg/302A
Wm., plumber and glazier, Devizes, 1807, W, P1/1807/35
Wm., Fritham, Bramshaw, Hants, 1814, W, P24/1265
Wm., plumber, Devizes, 1821, comm, W, Wr, P1/1821/4
Wm., Devizes, 1824, AB, comm, P1/1824/20
Wm., capital burgess, Malm., 1848, O, W, Wr, P3/1848/24
Bisly, Edmd., labourer, Upton, Blewbury, Berks., 1635, I, W, P5/1635/78
Biss, Bess, Edwd., mariner, Lyme R., Dorset, 1686, I, W, P16/86
Frances, widow, Warm., 1738, comm, NW, P1/B/1078, P1/8Reg/221A
Hannah, sp., Westb., 1682, AB, comm, P25/1682/12
Jerome, Maiden B., 1631, NW, P2/B/542, P2/9Reg/68D
Bysse, Jn., husb., Tisb., 1557, W, P2/3Reg/27D
Bysse, Jn., Warm., 1574, AB, P2/5Reg/183B
Jn., sen., husb., Chicksgrove, Tisb., 1592, I, T, P2/B/134
Jn., husb., Crockerton, Longbridge D., 1606, I, W, P2/B/267
Jn., broad weaver, Leighs Marsh, Dilton, Westb., 1671, I, W, P25/1671/11
Jn., yeo., E. Hatch, Tisb., 1672, AB, I, P2/B/847
Jn., yeo., Tisb., 1716, W, P1/B/826, P1/6Reg/35A
Bess, Jn., cordw., Lyme R., Dorset, 1736, AB, comm, ren, P5/1736/4
Jos., grocer, Marl., 1703, W, P1/B/702, P1/4Reg/233
Jos., Hungerford, Berks., 1710, AB, I, P5/1710/13
Lawr., Tisb., 1694, AB, I, P2/B/1160
Bess, Lucy, widow, Turners Puddle, Dorset, 1729, W, P5/16Reg/226A
Nich., Chicksgrove, Tisb., 1599, AB, P2/B/200
Nich., Berwick St Leonard, 1711, AB, P1/B/776
Roger, Dilton, Westb., 1616, AB, I, P25/1616/1
Roger, tailor, Hungerford, Berks., 1689, AB, I (detailed), P23/167
Roger, grocer, Hungerford, Berks., 1732, W, P5/1732/6
Thos., E. Harnham, Britford, 1698, AB, I, P5/1698/17
Ursula, widow, Marl., 1725, W, P1/B/909, P1/7Reg/63A
Walter, rector and clerk, Bishopstrow, 1665, comm, I, W, P1/B/421
Wm., husb., Dinton, 1606, AB, I, P2/B/264
Wm., yeo., N. Bradley, 1635, I, NW, P2/B/583
Biss als Best, Wm., yeo., Berwick St Leonard, 1638, comm, I, W, P2/B/625
Wm., yeo., Tisb., 1690, I, W, P2/B/1123
Bess, Wm., yeo., Turners Puddle, Dorset, 1717, AB, I, P5/1717/4
see also Bussie *or* B.; Cuin als B.; Thomas als B.
Bissey, Anth., fuller, N. Bradley, 1669, I, W, P2/B/805
Bizey, Anth., N. Bradley, 1742, AB, P2/B/1613

Bissie, Anth., gent., Southwick, N. Bradley, 1838, comm, W, Wr, P2/1838/6
Bustey *or* Busten, Edmd., labourer, Netheravon, 1623, I & W, P12/47
Bissie, Eliz., widow, N. Bradley, 1805, W, P2/1805/10
Burssy, Geo., yeo., Burbage, 1741, AB, P11/182
Jas., gent., Broughton G., 1805, W, P2/1805/79
Bysy, Joan, widow, Holt, Bradford A., 1613, I, W, P2/B/340, P2/8Reg/191B
Besy, Jn., Pumbray, Monkton F., 1575, W, P2/5Reg/226B
Bysy, Jn., jun., Pomeroy, Wingfield, 1623, AB, a/c (2), I, LA, NW, P2/B/435, 485
Bessey, Jn., yeo., Pomeroy, Wingfield, 1645, comm, W, P2/B/698
Bussy, Jn., gardener, Rams., 1686, AB, I, P5/1686/2
Jn., clothier, Southwick, N. Bradley, 1694, AB, W, P2/B/1165
Nathaniel, Trowb., 1806, note, W, P1/1806/6
Bussie *or* Besse, Peter, Westb., 1631, AB, I, P25/1631/2
Busie, Philip, button mould cutter, Sherb., Dorset, 1712, AB, I, P5/1712/16
Bussey, Robt., yeo. and sergeant major in Berkshire Regt of Militia quartered at Ipswich, Suffolk, Liberty of Newland, Hurst, Berks., 1808, comm, W, Wr, P5/1808/2
Bissy, Sibyl, yeo., Westb., 1638, AB, I, P25/1638/5
Byssey *or* Bysie, Thos., Holt, Bradford A., 1598, AB, I, P2/B/189
Thos., yeo., Staverton, Trowb., 1800, W, P1/1800/19, P1/15Reg/221
Bissie, Wm., yeo., N. Bradley, 1635, W, P2/9Reg/49A
Bysy *or* Beesy, Wm., yeo., Holt, Bradford A., 1650, I, T, W, P1/B/356
Bissy, Wm., yeo., Colerne, 1677, I, W, P3/B/683
Bessy, Wm., husb., Stratton St Mgt., 1695, AB, P29/1Reg/263B
Buissy, Wm., yeo., N. Bradley, 1707, I, W, P2/B/1269
Bist *see* Best
Bitfield, Martha, widow, Whitley, Melk., 1676, I, NW, P2/B/905
My., sp., Whitley, Melk., 1703, W, P2/B/1238
Wm., baker, Whitley, Melk., 1708, I, W, P2/B/1275
Bitham, Bithum *see* Bytham
Bittle, Bittill, Agnes, widow, Amesb., 1583, W, P2/6Reg/90B
Bythell, Jn., husb., Nether St., Bromham, 1648, comm, I, NW, P1/B/344
Wm., Devizes St My., 1699, I, W, P1/B/680, P1/3Reg/234
Bizey *see* Bissey
Bizley *see* Basely
Blacden *see* Blagden
Blach *see* Blatch
Blachford *see* Blackford
Blachley, Blachly *see* Blatchley
Black, Block, Frances, yeo., Bray, Berks., 1689, I, W, P1/B/602
Jn., husb., Chilhampton, S. Newton, 1564, W, P2/4Reg/170
Jn., sen., carp., S. Newton, 1682, I, W, P2/B/1001
Black *or* Blake, Jn., [yeo.?], Gt. Durnford, 1762, I, W, P9/74
Rd., husb., Ruscombe, Berks., 1554, W, P5/20Reg/120B
Robt., husb., S. Newton, 1564, W, P2/4Reg/179B
Thos., yeo., Trowle, Bradford A., 1643, I, W, P2/B/683
Black *or* Blake, Thos., jun., Sal., 1675, AB, a/c, I, P4/1674/13
Wm., sen., yeo., Warm., 1618, AB, NW, P2/B/379
Bluck, Wm., Sonning, Berks., 1714, AB, I, P5/1714/3
Blackaller, Jn., Uffc., Devon, 1715, AB, I, P20/1/153
Robt., gent., Abingdon, Berks., 1714, W, P1/B/796, P1/5Reg/391
Blackborrow, Alice, widow, Edington, 1612, I, W, P2/B/328
Ann, widow, Tinh., Edington, 1693, I, W, P2/B/1151
Blackborough, Chris., Melk., 1682, I, W, P2/B/1011
Hy., yeo., Tinh., Edington, 1640, AB, P2/B/660
Jn., Tinh., Edington, 1678-82, I, NW, P2/B/938, P2/B/1005
Matthew, fellmonger, Devizes, 1665, AB, comm, I, P1/B/417
Nathaniel, shoemaker, Devizes, 1667, AB, comm, I, P1/B/435
Robt., yeo., Tinh., Edington, 1619, I, W, P2/B/393
Thos., Devizes, 1647, AB, P1/B/335
Wm., yeo., Edington, 1608-09, I, W, P2/B/284, P2/8Reg/53C

Blackbury, Mgt., widow, Devizes, 1685, AB, I, P1/B/577
Blackeden *see* Blagden
Blacker, Cicely, widow, Donhead St My., 1617, I, NW, P2/B/373
Jn., Heytes., 1591, AB, I, P5/1591/4, P5/5Reg/129D
Jn., Donhead St My., 1592, I, W, P2/B/135
Jn., Donhead St My., 1614, a/c, P2/B/346
Nich., Donhead St My., 1564, W, P2/4Reg/218B
Thos., Coombe, Donhead St My., 1622, AB, I, NW, P2/B/421
Blackett, Jn., Sal. St Mart., 1668, AB, I, P4/1667/30
Blackford, Ann, widow, Malm., 1814, W, Wr, P1/1814/120
Cath., Somerford K., 1696, comm, W, P1/B/655
Eleanor, sp., Somerford K., 1674, I, W, P3/B/639
Geo., sen., husb., Somerford K., 1669, AB, I, W, P3/B/549
Geo., sen., yeo., Ashton K., 1719, I, W, P3/B/1167
Jn., innkeeper, Malm., 1806, W, Wr, P3/1806/31
Jn., butcher, Swindon, 1825, W, Wr, P3/1825/22
Rd., yeo., Somerford K., 1737, W, P3/B/1364
Rd., Ashton K., 1803, AB, P3/1803/16
Blachford, Robt., cabinetmaker, Sal., 1836, W, Wr, P4/1836/15
Sarah, widow, Somerford K., 1729, comm, W, P1/B/950, P1/7Reg/230
Thos., yeo., Somerford K., 1726, W, P1/B/924, P1/7Reg/112
Thos., Somerford K., 1776, AB, comm, P1/B/1438
Thos., Somerford K., 1815, W, Wr, P3/1815/61
Wm., carp., Calne, 1846, O, W, Wr, P5/1846/5
Blackhall, Rd., labourer, Hurst, Berks., 1614, AB, I, P5/1614/7, P5/9Reg/119C
Blackhead, Chas., Milford, Sal. St Mart., 1728, AB, W, ren, P4/1728/23
Jn., sen., yeo., Sal., 1667, I, P4/1667/35
Blackman, Chris., husb., Chicklade, 1582, W, P2/6Reg/61C
Chris., Chicklade, 1630, AB, I, P2/B/511, P2/9Reg/84A
Edwd., sen., Ludg., 1634, AB, I, P1/B/250
Edwd., sen., yeo., Tilehurst, Berks., 1729, I, W, P1/B/966, P1/7Reg/267A
Eliz., widow, Sal., 1681, I, W, P4/1681/20
Eliz., widow, Amesb., 1715, W, P2/B/1334
Geo., Gt. Amesb., 1696, I, W, P2/B/1176
Hy., Marston, Pott., 1660, AB, comm, I, P1/B/364
Hy., yeo., Sal., 1679, I, W, P4/1679/9
Jas., bach., Corsham, 1853, AB, O, Wr, P3/1853/29
Jn., Arborfield, Berks., 1595, AB, a/c, I, P5/1594/7, P5/1595/8
Jn., maltster, Amesb., 1687, I, W, P2/B/1077
Jn., yeo., Clewer, New Windsor, Berks., 1738, W, P1/B/1086, P1/8Reg/288
My., widow, Marl. St My., 1715, AB, I, P1/B/809
Nich., sen., yeo., Tilehurst, Berks., 1645, comm, I, W, P1/B/314
Rd., Bulford, 1725, AB, P2/B/1436
Robt., vict., Chipp., 1783, W, P1/B/1486, P1/13Reg/503
Solomon, sen., yeo., Wokm., Berks., 1727, W, P5/1727/4, P5/16Reg/153C
Solomon, Wokm., Berks., 1740, W, Wr, P5/1740/7
Thos., Sonning, Berks., 1686, AB, I, P5/1686/12
Thos., Marl., 1758, AB, P1/B/1314
Wm., yeo., Hawkridge, Bucklebury, Berks., 1701, I, W, P1/B/683, P1/4Reg/105
Wm., Charlton, 1840, AB, Wr, P2/1840/51
Blackmore, Aaron, yeo., Bradford A., 1851, D, O, W, Wr, P2/1851/32
Adriana, widow, Collingbourne K., 1629, I, W, P3/B/312
Ann Perry, widow, Longbridge D., 1760, W, P2/B/1764
Cornelius, broad weaver, Bearfield, Bradford A., 1818, W, Wr, P2/1818/29
Edith, Seagry, [1617], I, W (NEP), P3/B/144
Edwd., yeo., Collingbourne K., 1631, AB, a/c, I, P1/B/239
Edwd., yeo., Collingbourne D., 1639, I, W, P21/1/37
Eleanor, widow, Uffc., Devon, 1831, W, P20/1/317
Eliz., widow, Uffc., Devon, 1635, AB, I, P5/1635/5, P5/12Reg/218A
Eliz., widow, Collingbourne D., 1639, I, W, P21/1/39

Hy., husb., Lower Seagry, 1639, I, W, P1/B/284
Hy., Longbridge D., 1750, AB, P2/B/1681
Jas., shepherd, Everleigh, 1829, AB, O, ren, W, Wr, P1/1829/18
Jn., Collingbourne D., 1629, AB, I, P21/3/11
Jn., sergemaker, Uffc., Devon, 1742, comm, W, P20/1/202
Jn., yeo., Uffc., Devon, 1801, W, P20/1/277
Jn., miller, Uffc., Devon, 1803, W, P5/1803/47, P5/19Reg/79
Jonathan, jun., Longford, Britford, 1701, AB, I, P24/555
Jonathan, innholder, Longford, Britford, 1703, I, W, P24/617
Martha, widow, Collingbourne D., 1742, W, P21/9/40
My., widow, Collingbourne D., 1693, I, W, P21/5/19
My., widow, Longford, Britford, 1730, I, W, P24/824
Bleckmore, My., Easthampstead, Berks., 1747, AB, P1/B/1206
Philip, servant, Fittleton, 1768, W, P2/B/1844
Rd., Collingbourne D., 1627, a/c, I (agreement re portions to children), P21/3/8
Rd., no abode stated; proved at Sal., 1647, I, W, P1/B/331
Rd., Collingbourne D., 1706, AB, P21/6/34
Robt., husb., Collingbourne D., 1626, W, P21/1/13
Robt., gent., Corsham, 1681, AB, P29/B/24, P29/1Reg/211A
Robt., Sal., 1732, AB, ren, P1/B/1026
Robt., Donhead St My., 1790, AB, P2/B/2046
Sarah, widow, Collingbourne D., 1744, W, P1/B/1166, P1/9Reg/303B
Wm., husb., Collingbourne D., 1605, I, W, P1/B/30
Wm., Collingbourne K., 1606, AB, P1/B/53
Wm., sen., Collingbourne D., 1673, I, W, P21/2/33
Wm., yeo., Marl., 1673, I, W, P1/B/488
Wm., Wilton, Gt. Bedwyn, 1812, AB, comm, Wr, P5/1812/33
Winifred, Everleigh (form. of Manningford Bruce), 1810, W, Wr, P3/1810/34
Blackney, Jn., Ruscombe, Berks., 1602, AB, P5/1602/10
Blackwell, Edmd., yeo., Kemble, 1741, W, P1/B/1150, P1/9Reg/209A
Eliz., Castle Eaton, 1723, AB, P1/B/893
Hy., yeo., Castle Eaton, 1644, I, W, P1/B/311
Hy., Kemble, 1770, AB, P3/B/1609
Humphrey, Kemble, 1672, AB, a/c, I, P3/B/607
Humphrey, sen., yeo. *or* husb., Castle Eaton, 1684, AB, a/c, I, W, P3/B/793-94
Jean, widow, Hurst, Berks., 1699, I, W, P5/1699/6
Jn., gent., Abingdon, Berks., 1631, AB, I, P1/B/233
Jn., sen., gent., Devizes, 1841, comm, W, Wr, P1/1841/23
Peter, labourer, White Waltham, Berks., 1668, AB, I, P1/B/444
Sarah, Kemble, 1742, AB, P3/B/1403
Thos., sen., cordw., Crickl. St My., 1665, I, W, P3/B/507
Thos., [shoemaker], Crickl. St My., 1676, comm, I, NW, P3/B/663
Blafford, Robt., Sal., 1742, AB, Wr, P4/1742/6
Blagbury, Matthew, yeo., Holt, Bradford A., 1732, W, P2/B/1506
Thos., labourer, Devizes, 1729, I, W, P1/B/983, P1/7Reg/383A
Blagden, Ann, widow, Keevil, 1769, comm, W, P2/B/1861
Edwd., gent., Keevil, 1733, comm, W, P2/B/1523
Eliz., widow, Marl., 1679, comm, I, W, P1/B/521
Geo., yeo., Norton B. (late of Sutton V.), 1821, W, Wr, P2/1821/20
Blackeden als Chiverson, Isaac, Yatesbury, 1660, AB, comm, I (2), P3/B/465, P3/3Reg/5A
Isaac, husb., Erlestoke, 1686, AB, I, W, P2/B/1064
Joan, widow, Devizes, 1682, AB, comm, P1/B/554
Margery, Trowb., 1572, W, P5/3Reg/1E
Rebecca, Keevil, 1631, I, NW, P1/B/226
Blacden, Robt., sen., yeo., Keevil, 1635, I, W, P2/B/587
Roger, yeo., Keevil, 1630, I, W, P2/B/521, P2/9Reg/74A
Roger, mercer and gent., Marl., 1674, I, W, P1/B/493
Sarah, widow, Malm., 1711, I, W, P1/B/758, P1/5Reg/71
Thos., Dinton, 1817, AB, comm, Wr, P1/1817/101
Wm., chandler, Malm., 1668, AB, comm, I, P1/B/442

Wm., gent., Littleton, Steeple A., 1698, AB, I, P2/B/1192
Wm., widower, Pewsey, 1828, W, Wr, P3/1828/36
Blagne *see* Blague
Blagrave, Blagrove, (Dr) *see* Jn. Grove
Edwd., Earley, Sonning, Berks., 1680, AB, I, P5/1680/6
Edwd., Wantage, Berks., 1698, AB, I, P5/1698/3
Eliz., sp., Reading, Berks., 1747, W, P1/B/1205, P1/10Reg/100
Blagrove, Frances, widow, Sevenhampton, Highw., 1711, I, W, P10/1711/1
Giles, Purley, Berks., 1738, AB, P1/B/1091
Hugh, baker, Aldbourne, 1682, W, P3/B/754
Hugh, innholder, Marl., [1707], W, P1/B/731
Blagrove, Isaac, yeo., Draycot C., 1774, W, P3/B/1631
Blagrove, Jas., gent., Sevenhampton, Highw., 1700, AB, I (detailed), W, P10/1700/6
Jn., labourer, Wokm., Berks., 1827, W, Wr, P5/1827/14
Blagrove, My., widow, Sevenhampton, Highw., 1680, W, P10/1680/1
My., widow, Marl., 1729, W, P1/B/980, P1/7Reg/361B
Blagrove, My., widow, Wantage, Berks., 1730, W, P23/469
Blagrove, Nanny, Sutton C., Berks., 1789, AB, P1/B/1512
Blagrove, Oliver, Sonning, Berks., 1702, AB, P5/1702/6
Oliver, Sonning, Berks., 1734, AB, I, P5/1734/8
Blagrove, Rd., yeo., Wantage, Berks., 1677, AB, I, P23/66
Rd., gent., Speenhamland, Berks., 1747, W, P1/B/1209, P1/10Reg/114
Thos., clerk, Purley, Berks., 1671, I, W, P1/B/477
Blagrove, Wm., yeo., Lambourn, Berks., 1606, AB, I, P1/B/49
Blagrove, Wm., Lambourn, Berks., 1717, AB, P1/B/833
Blagrove, Wm., maltster, Bishopstone N., 1790, AB, W, P6/134
Blague, Joan, widow, Sandford, Woodley and S., Berks., 1632, W, P5/1632/7, P5/12Reg/96
Blake, Abigail, widow, Pinhill, Calne, 1665, W, P5/1665/11
Adelaide, minor, Paxcroft Farm, Steeple A., 1851, app. of guardian, court proceeding, O, T (dau of Jas. B., decd), P2/1851/28-29
Agnes, widow, Ruscombe, Berks., 1554, W, P5/20Reg/119
Agnes, widow, Martin, Hants, 1563, I, W, P2/B/39, P2/4Reg/115A
Agnes *see also* Ann *or* Agnes
Alice, Stoford, S. Newton, 1566, W, P2/5Reg/2C
Alice, widow, Stoford, S. Newton, 1607, I, W, P2/B/278
Alice, widow, Gt. Wishford, 1676, I, W, P2/B/912
Alice, widow, Devizes, 1676, D, I, sentence, W, P1/B/503
Alice, sp., Porton, Idmiston, 1685, I, W, P2/B/1047
Alice, widow, Purton, 1733, AB, P3/B/1323
Ann *or* Agnes, widow, Porton, Idmiston, 1677, I, W, P2/B/913
Ann, widow, Chipp., 1826, comm, W, Wr, P1/1826/10
Ann, widow, Biddestone St Nich., 1846, W, Wr, P3/1846/26
Anth., Stoford, S. Newton, 1663, AB, comm, I, P2/B/753
Anth., Purton, 1730, AB, P3/B/1292
Benj., yeo. *or* clothw., S. Newton, 1684, I, W, P2/B/1044
Benj., Ford, Laverstock, 1838, AB, W, Wr, P2/1838/7
Benj., yeo., Winterbourne G., 1841, W, Wr, P2/1841/19
Chas., [weaver], Baynton, Edington, 1670, AB, I, P1/B/474
Chas., Kingston D., 1676, AB, I, P2/B/901
Chas., yeo., Chilhampton, S. Newton, 1706-07, AB, app. of guardian, W, P2/B/1265
Chas., Kingston D., 1715, I, W, P2/B/1344
Chas., tailor, Trowb., 1802, W, Wr, P1/1802/8, P1/15Reg/365B
Chas., shopkeeper, Keevil, 1813, W, Wr, P2/1813/53
Chris., turner, Marl., [1690], comm, W, P1/B/597
Chris., gent., Chilhampton, S. Newton, 1724, I, W, P2/B/1431
Edith, widow, Chilhampton, S. Newton, 1621, I, NW, P2/B/412
Edmd., no abode stated, 1612, I, P1/B/76
Edmd., Wootton R., 1702, AB, I, P3/B/1018
Edwd., tailor, Amesb., 1602, I, W, P2/B/223
Edwd., husb., Baynton, Edington, 1627, I, W, P2/B/477

Edwd., Lyme R., Dorset, 1641, AB, P5/1641/8, P5/14Reg/33B
Edwd., merchant, Lyme R., Dorset (d. in France), 1642, I, P5/1642/5
Edwd., Fisherton A., 1662, I, W, P2/B/736
Edwd., yeo., Purton, 1679, I, W, P3/B/713
Edwd., weaver, Sal., 1738, W, P4/1738/13
Edwd., rector of Tortworth, Gloucestershire, Sal., 1765, W, P4/1765/12
Eliz., widow, Martin, Hants, 1583, I, W, P2/B/84, P2/6Reg/90D
Eliz., widow, Wootton R., 1673, I, W, P1/B/489
Eliz., widow, Sal., 1724, W, P4/1724/16
Eliz., widow, Stratford sub C., 1725, W, P4/1725/4
Eliz., sp., Sal., 1749, AB, W, P4/1748/17
Eliz., sp., Maddington, 1821, W, Wr, P2/1821/40
Emma, widow, Sandford, Woodley and S., Berks., 1692, note, W, P5/1692/12
Fanny, sp., Netherh., 1830, AB, P2/1830/49
Francis, Harwell, Berks., 1829, O, W, Wr, P1/1829/23
Geoff., Stratford sub C., 1730, AB, P4/1730/19
Geo., yeo., Fugg. St Peter, 1646, AB, P2/B/705
Geo., carp., Gt. Amesb., 1678, I, W, P2/B/929
Geo., carp., Amesb., 1761, W, P2/B/1776
Geo., cordw., Keevil, 1802, W, P2/1802/70
Geo., innholder, Milford, Sal. St Mart., 1817, W, Wr, P1/1817/25
Gertrude, sp., Wootton R., 1676, AB, a/c, I, P3/B/665
Hy., Smallbrook, Warm., 1571, AB, P2/B/47, P2/5Reg/121C
Hy., Warm., 1626, AB, a/c, I, P2/B/463
Hy., Chilhampton, S. Newton, 1639, I, W, P2/B/644
Hy., sen., yeo., S. Newton, 1663, AB, comm, I, W (W is Alice's & the I Hy.'s), P1/B/396, P2/B/748
Hy., sen., yeo., Chilton F., 1708, I, W, P1/B/738
Hy., yeo., Stoford, S. Newton, 1720, AB, ren, P2/B/1391
Hy., yeo., Rams., 1732, W, P5/1732/7
Hy., yeo., Knighton, Rams., 1767, W, P5/1767/8
Hy., vict., Charnham St., Hungerford, Berks., 1798, W, P23/809
Hester, widow, Sal., 1719, W, P4/1719/15
Isaac, chandler, Sal., 1708, copy W, W, P1/B/735, P1/4Reg/276
Isaac, yeo., Quidh., 1763, W, P1/B/1347, P1/12Reg/59
Isaac, vict., Manton, Preshute, 1849, W, Wr, P1/1849/10
Jas., Burbage, 1733, W, P11/139
Jas., sen., yeo., Knighton, Rams., 1738, W, Wr, P5/1738/3
Jas., yeo., Littlecote, Rams., 1765, W, P5/1765/7
Jas., baker, Hinton, Steeple A., 1800, comm, W, P2/1800/79
Jas., [innkeeper], *The Rising Sun Inn*, Milford, Sal. St Mart., 1803, W, P4/1803/7
Jas., Inmarsh, Seend, Melk., 1819, W, Wr, P2/1819/39
Jas., vict., Downton, 1845, W, Wr, P1/1845/56
Jas., relieving officer, Stratford sub C., 1849, W, Wr, P4/1849/15
Jas., farmer, Paxcroft Farm, Steeple A., 1851, AB, court papers (2), D, O (2), copy W, Wr (W destroyed by his children, between whom subsequent disagreement), P2/1851/29
Jas., sen., gent., Hindon (form. of W. Harnham), 1853, W, Wr, P2/1853/26
Jane, widow, Sal., 1736, W, P4/1735/7
Jane, widow, Sal., 1830, W, Wr, P4/1830/4
Jane, Stratford sub C., 1839, W, Wr, P4/1839/3
Jane, sp., Tilsh., 1840, W, Wr, P2/1840/30
Jane, widow, Wylye, 1855, aff, D, W, Wr, P2/1855/40
Joan, widow, Purton, 1622, AB, a/c, I, P3/B/220
Joan, widow, Stratford Tony, 1682, bond to pay legacies, I, copy I, W, P2/B/971
Joan, widow, Stoford, S. Newton, 1687, AB, I, copy I, ren, P2/B/1079
Joan, widow, Milford, Sal. St Mart., 1694, AB, I, W, P4/1693/13
Joan, Purton, 1740, AB, P3/B/1390
Joan, widow, Chilhampton, S. Newton, 1744, W, P2/B/1627
Jn., Stoford, S. Newton, 1546, W (NEP), P2/1Reg/62
Jn., husb., S. Newton, 1554, W, P2/2Reg/186A
Jn., Stoford, S. Newton, 1572, W, P2/5Reg/160A

Jn., yeo., Erlestoke, 1574, W, P2/5Reg/188A
Jn., Martin, Hants, 1582, W, P2/6Reg/58
Jn., yeo., Stoford, S. Newton, 1607, I, W, P2/B/276
Jn., sen., husb., Chilhampton, S. Newton, 1610, I, W, P2/B/313, 2157, P2/8Reg/149
Jn., Sherston, 1619, AB, a/c, I, P3/B/174
Jn., Gt. Woodford, 1637, AB, a/c, I, P13/1/18
Jn., carp., Marl., 1639, I, P1/B/289
Jn., yeo., Warm., 1639, I, W, P2/B/634
Jn., carp., S. Newton, 1645, AB, cit, I, L, P2/B/694, P2/B/721
Jn., Stoford, S. Newton, 1664, I, W, P1/B/412
Jn., yeo., Gt. Woodford, 1671, AB, I, ren, P5/1671/4
Jn., sen., husb., Downton, 1675, AB, I, P2/B/888
Jn., Stoford, S. Newton, 1689, AB, I, P2/B/1104
Jn., sawyer, Fritham, Bramshaw, Hants, 1689, W, P24/737
Jn., yeo., Baynton, Edington, 1692, AB, I, P2/B/1140
Jn., Westcourt, Burbage, 1704, comm, I, W, P11/94
Jn., S. Newton, 1710, AB, P2/B/1296
Jn., S. Newton, 1716, W, P1/B/829, P1/6Reg/37B
Jn., blacksmith, Purton, 1722, AB, W, P3/B/1206
Jn., sen., yeo., Pitton, Alderbury, 1727, I, W, P26/718
Jn., Newtown, Durnford, 1744, AB, P9/61
Jn., Sal., 1750, AB, P1/B/1232
Jn., yeo., Bowden, Burbage, 1758, W, P11/211
Jn., husb., Gt. Woodford, 1763, W, P13/4/37
Jn., gent., Ford, Laverstock, 1767, W, P1/B/1382, P1/12Reg/264B
Jn., Stratford sub C., 1776, AB, P4/1776/2
Jn., farmer, Biddestone St Nich., 1778, W, P3/B/1651
Jn., jun., Stratford sub C., 1792, AB, P4/1792/4
Jn., blacksmith, Purton, 1808, comm, W, Wr, P3/1808/1
Jn., Burbage, 1815, AB, Wr, P5/1815/6
Jn., S. Newton, 1840, W, Wr, P2/1840/21
Jn., S. Newton, 1845, AB, Wr, P2/1845/8
Jos., husb., Chilhampton, S. Newton, 1639, I, T, W, P2/B/642
Jos., baker, Marl., 1670, AB, comm, W, P1/B/462
Jos., maltster, Winterslow, Idmiston, 1731, W, P2/B/1494
Jos., jun., Marl. St Peter and St Paul, 1737, AB, I, P1/B/1071
Jos., sen., labourer, Marl. St My., 1737, AB, W, P1/B/1072, P1/8Reg/196
Jos., shopkeeper, Trowb., 1829, W, Wr, P1/1829/143
Kitty, sp., Sal., 1767, AB, ren, P4/1767/8
Mgt., sp., Ludg., 1648, AB, I, W, P2/B/718
Maria Matilda, widow, Hindon, 1857, aff, D, W, Wr, P2/1857/21
Marmaduke, yeo., Porton, Idmiston, 1611, I, W, P2/B/320
My., widow, Pinhill, Calne, 1570, W, P5/2Reg/85
My., widow, Wootton R., 1687, I, W, P3/B/835
My., widow, Kingston D., 1688, I, NW, P2/B/1107
My., widow, Reading, Berks., 1701, W, P1/B/687, P1/4Reg/151
Blake form. Scott, My., wife, Warm., 1789, AB, P2/B/2043
My., widow, Homington, 1791, W, P24/1155
My., widow, Westcourt, Burbage, 1826, W, P11/280
My., widow, Hinton, Steeple A., 1853, AB, aff, O, Wr, P2/1853/57
My., innkeeper and widow, *The Marquess of Aylesbury's Arms*, Preshute, 1855, aff, O, W, Wr, P1/1855/23
My., widow, Downton, 1855, aff, L, W, Wr, P2/1855/31
Maud, Stoford, S. Newton, 1616, I, W, P2/B/364, P2/8Reg/307
Michael, widow, Flamston, Bishopstone S., 1713, I, W, P2/B/1319
Moses, tailor, Stratford Tony, 1668, I, W, P2/B/791
Moses, E. Harnham, Britford, 1698, AB, I, P24/501
Nich., Ruscombe, Berks., 1568, W, P5/2Reg/28D
Nich., husb., Purton, 1640, I, W, P3/B/440
Nich., staymaker, Sal., 1709, W, P4/1709/11
Nich., yeo., Coleshill, Berks., 1720, W, P1/B/860, P1/6Reg/291B

Nich., vict., Imber, 1745, AB, I, W, P2/B/1643
Philip, yeo. and husb., Flamston, Bishopstone S., 1701, I, W, P1/B/695, P1/4Reg/178
Rd., husb., Plaitford, 1572, W, P2/5Reg/156A
Rd., vicar of Little Bedwyn, Lt. Bedwyn, 1601, AB, P5/1601/8, P5/7Reg/28A
Rd., yeo., Manningford Bruce, 1669, AB, I, P3/B/550
Rd., hellier, Sal., 1685, W, P4/1685/5
Rd., [draper], Sal., 1697, AB, I, P4/1687/5
Rd., yeo., Woodsend, Aldbourne, 1705, I, W, P3/B/1044
Rd., husb., Purton, 1710, I, W, P3/B/1089
Rd., jun., Didcot, Berks., 1729, AB, I, P1/B/978
Rd., Harwell, Berks., 1729, AB, P1/B/979
Rd., surgeon, Hungerford, Berks., 1770, W, P5/1770/7, P5/17Reg/13C
Rd., yeo., Wootton B., 1800, W, P3/1800/25
Rd., Aldbourne, 1814, W, P1/1814/84
Rd., labourer, S. Newton, 1837, AB, W, Wr, P2/1837/1
Blake als Jaques, Robt., husb., Paven Hill, Purton, 1617, AB, I, P3/B/145
Robt., yeo., Stoford, S. Newton, 1662, I, W, P2/B/734
Robt., glover, Sal., 1679, I, W, P4/1679/15
Robt., yeo., Amport, Hants & Stoford, S. Newton, 1688, AB, I, W, P2/B/1098
Robt., tailor, Purton, 1694, AB, I, P3/B/922
Robt., cordw., Crickl. St S., 1737, W, P3/B/1365
Robt., yeo., Imber, 1745, W, P2/B/1642
Robt., Tilsh., 1837, AB, O, ren, Wr, P2/1837/86
Robt., Tilsh., 1840, AB, comm, court proceeding, P2/1840/14
Robt., yeo., Chicklade, 1854, aff, O, W, Wr, P3/1854/57
Roger, sen., esquire, Melk., 1621, I, NW, P2/B/417
Roger, yeo., Durley, Burbage, 1635, AB, comm, I, W, P11/1
Sam., broad weaver, Bearfield, Bradford A., 1769, W, P2/B/1860
Sam., poulterer, Sal., 1824, a/c, W, Wr, P4/1824/1
Sarah, widow, S. Newton, 1851, W, Wr, P1/1851/72
Steph., yeo., Road, Collingbourne K., 1631, I, W, P3/B/337
Steph. Hyett, gent., Hilp., 1855, aff, O, W, Wr, P2/1855/3
Thos., Stoford, S. Newton, 1550, W, P2/2Reg/100B
Thos., husb., Plaitford, 1565, W, P2/4Reg/203A
Thos., W. Lavington, 1571, W, P1/1Reg/28A
Thos., Uppington, Stapleford, 1583, AB, I, T, P2/B/85, P2/6Reg/101A
Thos., Warm., 1584, W, P2/6Reg/132C
Thos., Wilton, 1669, AB, P2/B/800
Thos., wheelwright, Sal., 1683, W, P4/1683/7
Thos., yeo., Dinton, 1688, I, W, P2/B/1096
Thos., chandler, Milford, Sal. St Mart., 1693, AB, bond to secure goods, I, ren, W, P4/1692/17, P4/1693/11
Thos., Imber, 1712, AB, NW, P1/B/782, P1/5Reg/273A
Thos., yeo., Burbage, 1758, W, P11/212
Thos., yeo., Upton, Blewbury, Berks., 1813, W, Wr, P5/1813/7
Thos., carrier, Bramshaw, Hants, 1842, W, Wr, P24/1368
Thomasine, widow, Ogbourne St And., 1573, W, P5/3Reg/6A
Wm., Warm., 1538, W (dated 1539), P2/1Reg/1B
Wm., Martin, Hants, 1545, W (NEP), P2/1Reg/56B
Wm., Mere, 1581, AB, a/c, I, P5/1580/9, P5/4Reg/9B
Wm., husb., Winterbourne S., 1597, AB, NW, P2/B/174
Wm., sen., husb., Stoford, S. Newton, 1600, AB, I, W, P2/B/202
Wm., Chilhampton, S. Newton, 1610, I, W, P2/B/307, P2/8Reg/125B
Wm., Amesb., 1616, AB, a/c, I, P2/B/367, P2/8Reg/312A
Wm., husb., Bishopstone S., 1618, AB, I, P2/B/388
Wm., husb., Cotmarsh, Broad H., 1637, AB, a/c, I, W, P3/B/385
Wm., husb., Stoford, S. Newton, 1638, I, W, P2/B/621
Wm., sen., yeo., Porton, 1667, comm, I, W, P2/B/783
Wm., yeo., W. Amesb., 1681, I, W, P2/B/965
Wm., gent., Bugley, Warm., [1688], W, P2/B/1089
Wm., saddler, Hungerford, Berks., 1700, AB, I (detailed), P23/240

Wm., yeo., Gt. Woodford, 1700, I, W, P13/3/30
Wm., grocer, Warm., 1701-02, I, W, copy W, P1/B/697, P1/4Reg/186
Wm., husb., Stratford sub C., 1721, W, P5/1721/4, P5/16Reg/60B
Wm., yeo., Chicklade, 1722, W, P2/B/1411
Wm., turner, Marl., 1724, W, P1/B/906, P1/7Reg/49B
Wm., sen., Pitton, Alderbury (form. of Idmiston), 1732, W, P26/768
Wm., Keevil, 1738, AB, P1/B/1102
Wm., yeo., Snap, Aldbourne, 1742, W, P3/B/1404
Wm., yeo., Gt. Woodford, 1745, W, P13/4/32
Wm., innholder, Crockerton, Longbridge D., 1787, W, P2/B/2018
Wm., yeo., Chicklade, 1791, W, P2/B/2064
Wm., shopkeeper, Keevil, 1810, W, Wr, P2/1810/75
Wm., Landford, 1819, AB, Wr, P2/1819/14
Wm., yeo., Biddestone St Nich., 1821, comm, W, Wr, P3/1821/14
Wm., yeo., Biddestone, 1832, W, Wr, P3/1832/21
Wm., Fisherton A., 1833, AB, Wr, P2/1833/81
Wm., carp., W. Lavington, 1848, W, Wr, P1/1848/29
see also Black *or* B.
Blampin, Rd., coal merchant, Calne, 1836, comm, W (& cod), Wr, P5/1836/11
Blanch, Henrietta, sp., Stratfield M., Berks., 1808, W, Wr, P1/1808/7
Margery, widow, Gt. Wishford, 1673, I, W, P2/B/860
Thos., Heywood, Westb., 1684, AB, P25/1684/6
Thos., Hawkeridge, Westb., 1696, AB, I, P25/1696/1
Blanchard, Cath., widow, Holt, Bradford A., 1613, I, W, P1/B/104
Edwd., tailor, Amesb., 1739, W, P2/B/1571
Eliz., widow, Budbury, Bradford A., 1630, I, W, P2/B/515
Eliz., widow, Burbage, 1732, AB, I, P11/142
Gabriel, Wolf Hall, Gt. Bedwyn, 1670, W (NEP); described of as at laundry house, P30/16
Gabriel, sen., yeo., Durley, Burbage, 1723, I, W, P11/129
Gabriel *see also* Jn. Church
Geo., sen., cordw., Marl., 1669, comm, W, P1/B/460
Geo., sen., yeo., Sunton, Collingbourne K., 1708, I, W, P3/B/1072
Geo., carp., Rowde, 1820, comm, W, Wr, P1/1820/141
Jas., Wilton, 1833, W, Wr, P2/1833/3
Jn., Norrington, Broughton G., 1614, W, P2/8Reg/213
Jn., Collingbourne K., 1625, AB, a/c, I, NW, P3/B/266
Jn., broad weaver, Steeple A., 1634, I, W, P1/B/247
Jn., jun., yeo., Collingbourne K., 1690, I, W, P3/B/867
Jn., sen., yeo., Alton P., Dorset, 1696, W, P5/1696/8
Jn., yeo., Collingbourne K., 1696, I, W, P3/B/947
Jn., yeo., Alton P., Dorset, 1708-09, AB, I, P5/1708/8, P5/1709/3
Jn., blacksmith, Swindon, 1721, W, P3/B/1188
Jn., maltster, Collingbourne K., 1728, I, W, P3/B/1267
Jn., yeo., Alton P., Dorset, 1730, I, W, P5/1730/8
Jn., collarmaker, Collingbourne D., 1740, I, W, P1/B/1115, P1/8Reg/427
Jn., Rowde, 1754, AB, I, P3/B/1489
Jn., yeo., Durley, Burbage, 1758, I (2) (detailed - 1 gives appraisers' valuations, other actual prices fetched at sale), W, P11/209
Jn., carp., Rowde, 1798, AB, cert, P1/B/1553, P1/15Reg/50A
Jn., yeo., N. Bradley, 1808, W, Wr, P2/1808/29
Jos., husb., Corsham, 1752, W, P29/B/50, P29/2Reg/73
My., Collingbourne D., 1755, AB, P21/10/30
My., Burbage, 1760, AB, P11/213
My., widow, N. Bradley, 1839, O, W, Wr, P2/1839/35
Nich., Steeple A., 1572, AB, P2/5Reg/141A
Philip, Rowde, 1835, W, Wr, P1/1835/79
Rd., sen., yeo., Alton P., Dorset, 1711, W, P5/1711/7, P5/15Reg/230
Sarah, widow, Collingbourne K., 1732, I, W, P3/B/1315
Sarah, sp., N. Tidworth, 1810, W, P2/1810/20
Steph., Donhead St My., 1739, AB, I, W, P2/B/1578

Thos., priest, Bloxworth, Dorset, 1560, institution to rectory, P1/1Reg/80C
Thos., Holt, Bradford A., 1584, W, P2/6Reg/135
Thos., Chute, 1616, AB, I, W, P5/1616/7
Thos., yeo., Holt, Bradford A., 1620, AB, a/c, I, W, P2/B/403
Thos., Box, 1639, AB, I, P3/B/416
Thos., yeo., Collingbourne K., 1676, I, W, P3/B/664
Thos., gent., Corsham, 1689, note of probate, P29/1Reg/243B
Thos., Newbury, Berks., 1750, AB, ren, P1/B/1245
Thos., wharfinger, Bourton, Shrivenham, Berks. (effects at Swindon), 1827, W, Wr, P3/1827/60
Thos. Tanner, yeo., Chipp., 1851, comm, W, Wr, P3/1851/41
Walter, [miller], Bromham, 1746, AB, a/c, I (detailed), P3/B/1437
Wm., husb., Steeple A., 1567, W, P2/5Reg/6B
Wm., Holt, Bradford A., [1628?], I, W, P2/B/484
Wm., Alton P., Dorset, 1710, AB, P5/1710/14
Wm., yeo., E. Everleigh, Everleigh, 1763, W, P1/B/1343, P1/12Reg/38
Wm., yeo., Wingfield, 1783, W, P1/B/1476, P1/13Reg/415
Wm., yeo., N. Bradley, 1791, W, P2/B/2059
Wm., blacksmith, Lt. Woodford, 1814, W, P13/6/7
Blanchet, Chas., Winterbourne E., 1692, AB, schedule, P1/B/617
Blanchett, Frances, widow, Mkt. L., 1688, AB, I, P2/B/1092
Jn., Eastcott, Urchf., 1671, I, W, P2/B/837
Blanchett, Robt., woodman, Wootton B., 1830, W, Wr, P3/1830/51
Walter, miller, Bromham, 1668, I, W, P1/B/449
Bland, Alice, widow, Edington, 1719, I, W, P2/B/1383
Ann, widow, Chitterne AS, 1683, AB, I, P2/B/1023
Edwd., Southcott, Pewsey, 1645, AB, comm, I, P1/B/316
Geo., plumber and glazier, Wilton, 1775, AB, P2/B/1924
Jas., plumber and glazier, Wilton, 1787, W, P2/B/2023
Bland form. Astins, My., Wilton, 1758, AB, P2/B/1749
Blandford, Aaron, Bower C., 1855, AB, aff, D, ren, W, Wr, P2/1855/1
Abraham, sen., cordw., Devizes, 1738, AB, W, P1/B/1104, P1/8Reg/330A
Blanford, Alice, widow, Semley, 1602-03, AB, I, W, P1/B/14, P2/B/236
Alice, Semley, 1621, W (in form of deed poll) (NEP), P30/200
Blanford, Alice, widow, Semley, 1630, NW, P2/B/509
Ann, sp., Oborne, Dorset, 1711, W, P5/1711/8, P5/15Reg/232
Ann, Sal., 1714, AB, P1/B/785
Ann, widow, Sal., 1722, AB, P4/1722/16
Bernard, Farley, Alderbury, 1720, W, P26/640
Chas., yeo., Poole Keynes, 1746, W, P3/B/1438
Edwd., yeo., Even Swindon, 1813, W, Wr, P3/1813/18
Blanford, Frances, sp., Crickl. St S., 1752, W, P3/B/1477
Hy., late of Hatherop, but effects at Poole Keynes, 1811-12, D (dated 1812), W, Wr, P1/1811/46
Hester, Swindon, 1695, AB, P3/B/937
Blanford, Isaac, maltster, Semley, 1722, W, P2/B/1409
Isaac, yeo., Motc., Dorset, 1823, comm, W, Wr, P27/1/662
Isaac, cordw., Berwick St Jn., 1837, W, Wr, P2/1837/91
Blanford, Jas., Tisb., 1680, AB, a/c, I, P2/B/955
Jas., gent., Semley, 1766, W, P2/B/1831
Jas., Donhead St A., 1793, AB, P2/B/2086
Blanford, Joan, widow, Highw., 1637, I, NW, P10/1637/4
Joan, widow, Martin, Hants, 1744, I, W, P2/B/1629
Blanford, Jn., yeo., Stourton, 1575, W, P2/5Reg/216D
Blanford, Jn., husb., Semley, 1606, I, W, P2/B/262
Jn., sen., cordw., Devizes, 1621, AB, a/c, I, proclamation, P1/B/174
Jn., sen., E. Martin, Hants, 1665, AB, I, P2/B/765
Blanford, Jn., butcher and vict., Devizes, 1670, I, W, P1/B/464
Blanford, Jn., yeo., Semley, 1674, AB, I, P1/B/494
Jn., blacksmith, Crickl. St S., 1725, I, W, P3/B/1241
Jn., yeo., Toyd Farm, Martin, Hants, 1726, I, W, P2/B/1446
Blanford, Jos., yeo., Semley, 1690, I, W, P2/B/1124

Jos., Downton, 1815, AB, Wr, P2/1815/3
Joshua, yeo., Toyd Farm, Martin, Hants, 1737, AB, W, P2/B/1555
Lawr., Semley, 1630, AB, a/c, I, NW, P2/B/517
Mgt., widow, Toyd Farm, Martin, Hants, 1741, AB, a/c (2), I (4), T, P2/B/1596
Martha, widow, Martin, Hants, 1690, AB, I, P2/B/1125
Blanford, Martha, widow, Sedgehill, 1708, AB, I, P1/B/744
My., widow, Semley, 1701, W, P2/B/1218
Blanford, Maud, widow, Semley, 1580, W, P2/B/82, P2/6Reg/14
Nehemiah, yeo., Donhead St A., 1791, AB, W, P2/B/2060
Blanford, Rd., silk weaver, Devizes, 1689, I, W, P1/B/598
Robt., Stourton, 1606, AB, I, ren, P1/B/47
Blanford, Robt., butcher, Sal., 1691, I, W, P4/1691/7
Sam., dairyman, Tisb., 1813, W, Wr, P2/1813/8
Blanford, Sarah, widow, Barford St Mart., 1765, W, P2/B/1805
Blanford, Silas, tallow chandler, Hindon, 1675, I, P2/B/894
Steph., yeo., Semley, 1732, W, P2/B/1510
Blanford, Susan, widow, Devizes, 1665, I, W, P1/B/422
Susanna, widow, Semley, 1713, W, P2/B/1325
Thos., woollen draper, Highw., 1590, I, T, W, P5/1590/7, P5/5Reg/75C
Blanford, Thos., yeo., Semley, 1624, I, W, P2/B/451
Blanford, Thos., maltster, Semley, 1677, I, P1/B/511
Thos., E. Martin, Hants, 1721-25, AB, I, W, P2/B/1403, 1435
Thos., Semley, 1743, W, P2/B/1620
Thos., yeo., Poole Keynes, 1743, W, P3/B/1415
Blanford, Walter, Semley, 1558, W, P2/3Reg/101C
Blanford, Walter, Semley, 1573, W, P2/5Reg/164C
Blanford, Walter, Semley, 1596, AB, I, W, P2/B/171
Walter, Semley, 1598, W, P2/B/217
Blanford, Walter, yeo., Semley, 1673, I, W, P2/B/861
Blanford, Walter, yeo., Semley, 1683, W, P2/B/1022
Blanford, Wm., Semley, 1552-53, I, W, P2/B/7, P2/2Reg/147B
Wm., yeo., Semley, 1611, I, W, P1/B/67
Wm., yeo., Martin, Hants, 1681, I, W, P2/B/973
Wm., Martin, Hants, 1712, AB, P2/B/1314
Wm., yeo., Ansty, 1778, W, P2/B/1958
Wm., Berwick St Leonard, [1866], Wr, W (date not given) unproved; transferred to Sal. District Probate Registry (and proved there). Nov 1866, P2/1857/73
Blandy, Ann, sp., Gt. Bedwyn, 1690, AB, comm, I, P21/5/1
Ann, widow, E. Grafton, 1693, I, W, P21/5/18
Ann, minor, Wexcombe, Grafton, 1709, T (*see also* P21/6/31), P21/7/3
Benj., yeo., Grafton, 1708, AB, I (detailed) [copy], P21/6/44
Chas., yeo., Pewsey, 1708, I (2 - 1 a copy), W, P3/B/1073
Eliz., widow, Marl., 1731, W, P1/B/993, P1/7Reg/424
Eliz., sp., Appleford, Sutton C., Berks., 1763, O, W, P1/B/1346, P1/12Reg/56
Ellen, widow, E. Grafton, 1585, AB, a/c, I, P5/1585/7
Grace, widow, W. Woodhay, Berks., 1625, I, W, P1/B/191
Helen, widow, E. Grafton, 1585, AB, P5/4Reg/102B
Jn., husb. *or* yeo., E. Grafton, 1584, AB, I, W, P5/1584/4, P5/4Reg/96B
Jn., gent., Purley, Chaddleworth, Berks., 1744, ren, copy W, P1/B/1189, P1/9Reg/443
Jos., Wexcombe, Grafton, 1706, W, P21/6/31, P21/7/3
Steph., yeo., Grafton, 1705, I, W, P21/6/23
Thos., sen., [1623-25], I, W, P5/1624/5, P5/10Reg/170C
Thos., maltster, Marl., 1717, I, W, P1/B/841, P1/6Reg/151
Thos., Devizes St My., 1823, AB, Wr, P1/1823/152
Wm., Grafton, 1579, I, NW, P5/1579/5, P5/3Reg/138B
Blanford *see* Blandford
Blanket, Alice, widow, Urchf., 1636, I, W, P2/B/596
Anth., Harding, Gt. Bedwyn, 1647, AB, I, L (2), P21/1/67
Jn., husb., Urchf., 1617, I, W, P2/B/372
Jn., yeo., Urchf., 1685, AB, I, P2/B/1055

Philip, husb., Ebbesborne Wake, 1593, I, W, P2/B/143
Wm., yeo., Urchf., 1669, W, P2/B/822
Blann, Wm., Sal., 1705, AB, P4/1704/6,
Blashford, Rd., Martin, Hants, 1685, AB, I, ren, P2/B/1048
Blatch, Deborah, Bratton, Westb., 1730, W, P25/1730/9
Denise, [sp.], Bratton, Westb., 1671, I, W, P25/1671/4
Hy., yeo., Westb., 1718, AB, P25/1718/3
Hy., baker, Westb. L., 1805, note, W, P25/1805/3
Hy., yeo., Westb. L., 1825, O, W, Wr, P25/1825/6
Blach, Jas., Bratton, Westb., 1618, I, W, P25/1618/3
Jas., baker, Westb. L., 1687, AB, a/c, I, P25/1687/1
Jas., yeo., Bratton, Westb., 1702, I (detailed), W, P25/1702/1
Jas., yeo., Dilton M., Westb., 1709, AB, I, P25/1709/7
Jane, widow, Bratton, Westb., 1844, comm, declaration, W, Wr, P25/1844/8
Joan, widow, Westb., 1711, I, W, P25/1711/7
Joan, widow, Westb. L., 1763, W, P25/1763/5
Jn., yeo., Westb., 1682, I, W, P25/1682/6
Jn., sen., yeo., Westb. L., 1715, I (2), W (2), P25/1715/2-3
Jn., yeo., Bratton, Westb., 1716, I, W (NEP), P25/1716/1
Jn., Westb. L., 1754, AB, P25/1754/1
Jn., sen., gent., Bratton, Westb., 1773, W, P25/1773/3
Jn., gent., Bratton, Westb., 1785, W, P25/1785/3
Jn., baker, Chalford, Westb., 1800, O, W, Wr, P25/1800/1
Jos. Goodenough, gent., Bratton, Westb., 1840-44, comm, W, Wr, P25/1840/3, P25/1844/5
Blach *or* Blatch, My., widow, Bratton, Westb., 1636, I, W, P25/1636/9
Philip, yeo., Bratton, Westb., 1669, comm, W, P25/1669/11
Philip, yeo., Bratton, Westb., 1728, W, P25/1728/2
Philip, yeo., Westb. L., 1795, W, P25/1795/2
Philip, yeo., Westb., 1807, O, W, P25/1807/2
Sarah, sp., Bratton, Westb., 1854, comm, declaration, W, Wr, P25/1854/4
Susanna, sp., Westb., 1730, W, P25/1730/7
Blatche, Thos., clerk, Chitterne AS, 1584, AB, W, P2/6Reg/116A
see also Pearce lately B.
Blatchley, And., yeo., Conkwell, Winsley, Bradford A., 1752, W, P2/B/1695
Blachly, And., Haugh, Winsley, Bradford A., 1758, AB, W, P2/B/1740
Ann, widow, Winsley, Bradford A., 1759, AB, P2/B/1758
Dan., sow gelder and yeo., Eastrip, Colerne, 1744, AB, I, ren, W, P1/B/1167, P1/9Reg/313
Jas., Haugh, Winsley, Bradford A., 1786, AB, comm, ren, P2/B/2016
Joan, widow, Hilp., 1597, I, W, P2/B/181
Bleachly, Jn., yeo., Winsley, Bradford A., 1679, I, W, P1/B/539
Bleachly, Jn., yeo., Haugh, Winsley, Bradford A., 1737, I, W, P2/B/1562
Jn., Atworth, Bradford A., 1803, W, P2/1803/18
Robt., husb., Hilp., 1591, I, W, P2/B/126
Blachly, Thos., baker, Colerne, 1669, I, NW, P3/B/548
Thos., yeo., Conkwell, Winsley, Bradford A., 1771, W, P2/B/1878
Blachley, Wm., broad weaver, Trowb., 1726, W, P1/B/914, P1/7Reg/78
Wm., yeo., Eastrip, Colerne, 1728, I, W, P3/B/1269
Wm., Colerne, 1772, comm, W, P3/B/1620
Blathwaite, Jn., Sal., 1627, AB, P4/1626/24
Blathatt *or* Blathwaite, Wm., sen., butcher, Sal., 1686, I, W, P4/1686/19
Bleachly *see* Blatchley
Bleaden, Chas., sen., innholder, *The White Hart*, Calne, 1783, W, P26/1135, 1178
Edith, sp., Calne, 1831, AB, comm, P26/1393
Geo., miller and baker, Calne, 1845, O, W, Wr, P5/1845/4
Rd., baker and maltster, Calne, 1825, comm, W, Wr, P26/1350
Bleathman, Eliz., widow, Sal., 1736, NW, Wr, P4/1736/10
Joan, widow, Stratford Tony, 1727, I, W, P2/B/1454
Jn., tailor, Stratford Tony, 1720, AB, I, P2/B/1395
Bleckmore *see* Blackmore
Bledwin *see* Blewden

Bleeke *see* Blick
Bletso, Wm., farmer, Monkton D., 1809, W, Wr, P2/1809/62
Blevin, Agnes, widow, Imber, 1586, I, W, P2/B/92, P2/7Reg/35C
Jas., Imber, 1584, W, P2/6Reg/127A
Blew, Alice, widow, Brokenb., [1607], W (NEP), P3/B/26
Blewden, Ann, widow, Shrewton, 1826, W, Wr, P1/1826/32
Dorothy, widow, Elston, Orcheston St Geo., 1706, I, W, P2/B/1257
Eliz., widow, Shrewton, 1675, I, P2/B/896
Jn., Shrewton, 1676, AB, P2/B/915
Jn., sen., wheelwright, Elston, Orcheston St Geo., 1703, I, W, P2/B/1235
Jn., labourer, Maddington, 1768, W, P2/B/1843
My., gardener's wife, Sal. (form. of Warm.), 1857, AB, aff, Wr, P4/1857/2
Robt., yeo., Shrewton, 1853, D, W, Wr, P2/1853/13
Sam., Maddington, 1736, AB, P2/B/1549
Blowden, Thos., Maddington, 1742, AB, P2/B/1604
Thos., Sal., 1850, AB, Wr, P4/1850/13
Walter, yeo., Shrewton, 1665, AB, P2/B/769
see also Hazard als B.
Blewett, Evan, Aston U., Blewbury, Berks., 1662, I, W, P5/1662/15
Blewett, Wm., clerk and parson, Newnton, 1616, T, W, P1/B/136
Blick, Bleeke, Anth., yeo., Hullavington, 1697, I, W, P3/B/963
Anth., Westwood, 1742, AB, P2/B/1612
Blick *or* Bleek, Avis, widow, Lea and Cleverton, 1696, I, W, P3/B/948
Bleeke, Clement, tailor, Lt. Somerford, [1614], I, W (NEP), P3/B/112
Eliz., widow, Lt. Somerford, [1612], I, W (NEP), P3/B/89
Bleeke, Hy., yeo., Hindon, 1628, I, NW, P2/B/489
Jn., sen., Burton Hill, Malm., 1661, AB, comm, I, P3/B/469, P3/3Reg/11A
Bleeke, Jn., jun., hellier, Holnest, Dorset, 1712, comm, I, W, P5/1712/13, P5/15Reg/309B
Jn., yeo., Dauntsey, 1730, W, P3/B/1293
Jn., yeo., Dauntsey, 1753, W, P3/B/1483
Jn., Hullavington, 1800, AB, P3/1800/58
My., sen., widow, Lt. Somerford, 1678, I, W, P3/B/684
Bleeke, Rebecca, widow, Stop, Fonthill G., 1610, W, P2/B/309, P2/8Reg/127C
Robt., sen., yeo., Lt. Somerford, 1668, I, W, P3/B/532
Robt., Lt. Somerford, 1683, I, W, P3/B/772
Robt., Malm., 1746, AB, P3/B/1439
Bleeke, Robt., Warm., 1769, AB, P2/B/1857
Simon, yeo., Chipp., 1673, I, W, P3/B/629
Bleeke, Simon, yeo., Langley Burrell, 1680, W, P3/B/725
Bleeke, Simon, Langley Burrell, 1741, AB, P1/B/1143
Bleeke, Thos., husb., Blackland, Calne, 1631, I, W, P5/1631/7, P5/12Reg/37B
Bleeke, Thos., yeo., Milbourne, Malm., 1640, I, W, P3/B/441
Bleeke, Thos., Bishopstone S., 1706, AB, P2/B/1256
Thos., yeo., W. Dean, 1775, AB, P2/B/1927
Blike, Wm., butcher, Fonthill G., 1589, I, T, W, P2/B/108
Bleeke, Wm., shoemaker, Milbourne, Malm., 1631, I, W, P1/B/222
Bleeke, Wm., surgeon, Bradford A., 1776, AB, comm, P2/B/1931
Blinckerne, Roger, Manningford A., [1612], I (only part present), W (NEP), P3/B/91
Blissett, Giles, stationer, Snelsmore, Chieveley, Berks., 1622, I, W, P1/B/183
Jn., Blewbury, Berks., 1662, AB, I, P5/1662/16
Jn., yeo., Wanb., 1696, I, W, P3/B/949
Jn., sen., Marl., 1719, req, P1/B/847
Jn., Marl., 1753-55, W, P1/B/1289, P1/11Reg/186
Jn., Marl., 1762, AB, P1/B/1342
Jn., yeo., Poulton, Mildenhall, 1788, W, P3/B/1712
Jn., clothier, Reading, Berks., 1801, AB, O, LA, P1/1801/119
Jos., yeo., Stanley, Bremhill (late of Hazeland, Bremhill), 1782, W, P1/B/1472, P1/13Reg/435
Jos., Broughton G., 1802, AB, P2/1802/23
My., sp., Marl., 1776, AB, P1/B/1432
My., widow, Marl., 1846, D, O, W, Wr, P1/1846/13

Rebecca, widow, Marl., 1791, W, P1/B/1515, P1/14Reg/356
Robt., yeo., Poulton, Mildenhall, 1762, AB, ren, W, P3/B/1547
Robt., publican, Marl. St Peter and St Paul, 1837, AB, Wr, P1/1837/19
Thos., Marl., 1642, AB, comm, I, P1/B/298
Thos., yeo., Upton, Blewbury, Berks., 1772, W, P5/1772/1, P5/17Reg/43
Wm., yeo., Streatley, Berks., 1729, AB, I, P1/B/965
Wm., Marl., 1755, AB, P1/B/1285
Wm., Wantage, Berks., 1818, AB, Wr, P5/1818/19
see also Hall als B.
Block *see* Black
Blockeley, Margery, widow, Keevil, 1596, I (2), W, copy W, P2/B/168
Thos., weaver, Keevil, 1615, I, W, P2/B/349
Blomer *see* Bloomer
Blondey, Isaac, Rams., 1694, NW, P5/1694/32
Bloomer, Ann, sp., Downton, 1785, W, P2/B/2005
Jane, widow, Devizes, 1747, AB, comm, ren, W, P1/B/1195, P1/10Reg/36B, 59A
Blomer, Jn., apothecary, Downton, 1773, W, P1/B/1411, P1/12Reg/446
Blose *see* Blowes
Blowden *see* Blewden
Blowes, Alice, widow, E. Harnham, Britford, 1628, AB, NW, P24/214
Blose, Jn., Lyme R., Dorset, 1571, AB, P5/2Reg/92F
Bloxham, Eliz., widow, Gt. Bedwyn, 1803, AB, P21/12/7
Thos., Stratton St Mgt., 1623, AB, P29/1Reg/94A
Wm., Amesb., 1803, AB, comm, P2/1803/81
see also Fry als B.
Bluck *see* Black
Bluding *see* Blewden
Blundell, Francis, gent., Fovant, 1805, W, P2/1805/60
Hy., Sal. (of Cockey More, Ainsworth, Lancashire), 1829, AB, P4/1829/3
Jn., gent., Fovant, 1796, W, P2/B/2115
My., sp., Fovant, 1818, AB, Wr, P2/1818/62
Rd., Kintbury, Berks., 1613, I, W, P1/B/92
Sam., clerk, Codf. St My., 1741, W, P1/B/1151, P1/9Reg/210
Blunden, Frances, Bere R., Dorset, 1612, AB, I, P5/1612/8, P5/9Reg/63A
Blunt, Alice, widow, Durnford, 1738, AB, Wr, P5/1738/4
Anth., Charlton nr Malm., 1678, I, W, Wr, P3/B/692
Denise, widow, Gt. Wishford, 1713, I, W, P2/B/1321
Jn., yeo., Gt. Wishford, 1701, W, P1/B/698, P1/4Reg/197
My., Keevil, 1592, AB, I, P2/B/137
My., widow, Gt. Wishford, 1742, W, P2/B/1606
Rd., Gt. Wishford, 1662, I, W, P2/B/735
Wm., waterman, Lt. Durnford, 1727, W, P5/1727/5, P5/16Reg/156C
Wm., cordw., Gt. Wishford, 1741, W, P1/B/1126, P1/9Reg/34A
Blyde, Jos., Wardour Castle, Tisb., 1792, W, P2/B/2076
Blythe, Giles, Tilehurst, Berks., 1628, I, W, P1/B/217
Jn., carp., Dunsden, Sonning, Berks., 1645, comm, I, W, P5/1644/1, P5/14Reg/75
Blytheman, Jas., yeo., W. Harnham, 1575, I, T, W, P5/1575/6, P5/3Reg/58C
Board, Jas., Trowb., 1813, W, Wr, P1/1813/6
Bocher *see* Butcher
Bockelman *see* Johnson als B.
Bodenham, Ann, gentlewoman, Hilldrop, Rams., 1690, AB, comm, I, ren, W, P5/1690/8
Edwd., servingman, Whaddon, 1677, AB, I, P1/B/516
Edwd., Tollard Royal, 1729, AB, P2/B/1472
Geo., gent., Gt. Wishford, 1602, AB, I, P2/B/228
Jn., Throope, Bishopstone S., 1615, I, W, P2/B/353, P2/8Reg/256B
Bodingham, Thos., Heytes., 1684, AB, I, P5/1684/6
Wm., Heytes., 1691, AB, P5/1691/7
see also Bodman *or* B.
Bodman, Benj., butcher, Calne, 1749, comm, W, Wr, P5/1749/8
Benj., yeo., Compton B., 1825, W, Wr, P3/1825/50

Bodman *or* Bodnam, Edwd., Worton, Pott., 1716, AB, NW, P1/B/832
Edwd., Calne, 1725, AB, I, W, P5/1725/3, P5/16Reg/117C
Edwd., cordw., Church St., Calne, 1783, W, P26/1134
Eliza, minor, Melk., 1837, app. of guardian, comm, T (sisters & brother of Jas. B., decd), Wr, P2/1837/69-70
Hy., Shaw, Melk., 1640, AB, comm, P2/B/649
Hy., Keevil, 1747, AB, comm, I, P1/B/1221
Hy., bach., Rowde, 1829, W, Wr, P1/1829/74
Humphrey, sen., sergemaker, Calne, 1697, I (detailed), W, P26/450
Humphrey, serge weaver, Calne, 1722, I, W, P26/669
Jas., bach., Melk., 1837-39, AB, comm, court proceeding, Wr, P2/1837/70, P2/1839/19, 22
Boudmayne, Jn., alien [?French], Sutton Poyntz, Dorset (debtors in Normandy, France), 1579, AB, I, W, P5/1579/7, P5/3Reg/125
Jn., husb., Elston, Orcheston St Geo., 1601, AB, I, P2/B/215
Jn., husb., Westb., 1731, AB, bill of sale (1712), brief schedule of house contents, P25/1731/2
Jn., butcher, Box, 1822, W, Wr, P3/1822/17
Sarah, widow, Worton, Pott., 1732, AB, ren, P1/B/1001
Sarah, widow, Worton, Pott., 1742, AB, comm, P1/B/1153
Thos., Calne, 1710, AB, I, P5/1710/15
Thos., Calne, 1733, AB, P26/774
Thos., sen., cordw., Calne, 1807, note, W, P26/1269
Timothy, labourer, Chalford, Westb., 1825, comm, W, Wr, P25/1825/4
Bodnam, Wm., husb., Keevil, 1599, AB, I, W, P2/B/201
Wm., Fosbury, Tidcombe and F., 1606, AB, I, P1/B/58
Bodnam, Wm., no abode stated, c1631?, I, P2/B/535
Wm., serge weaver, Calne, 1695, I, W, P5/1695/11
Wm., Warm., 1741, W, P2/B/1598
Wm., yeo., Beanacre, Melk., 1816, comm, W, P2/1816/11
Body, Dorothy, widow, Sal., 1688, AB, P4/1688/3
Jas., blacksmith, Waltham St Lawr., Berks., 1714, I (2), W, P1/B/794, P1/5Reg/360
Jn., Norton, 1731, I, W, P3/B/1303
Thos., maltster, Sal., 1678, I, W, P4/1678/14
Boham, Jn., farmer, Bramshaw, Hants, 1849, aff, W, Wr, P24/1394
Sarah, widow, Marl., 1802, W, P1/15Reg/367
Boland, Jn., Laverstock, 1550, AB, P2/2Reg/97A
Jn. *see also* Jn. Hall
Bolch *see* Balch
Bold, Belde, Edwd., Idmiston, 1558, W, P2/3Reg/134D
Eliz., Sonning, Berks., 1570, W, P5/2Reg/68B
Bowlde, Geo., yeo., Hurst, Berks., 1594, AB, I, W, P5/1594/11, P5/6Reg/56
Jn., clerk and parson, Broughton G., 1621, AB, a/c, I, NW, P1/B/178
Bouldes, My., widow, Hurst, Berks., 1702, I (may not relate, 1671), W, P5/1702/5
Bouldes, Thos., yeo., Hurst, Berks., 1645, comm, I, L, W, P5/1645/5, P5/14Reg/84C
Bolding, Boulding, Frances, jun., sp., Clapton, Kintbury & Eddington, Hungerford, Berks., 1711, AB (2), comm, I, ren, W, P1/B/778, P1/5Reg/231
Boulding, Frances, sen., widow, Clapton, Kintbury, Berks., 1711-29, AB (2), comm, I, L, W, P1/B/777, P1/5Reg/229
Boulden, Jn., yeo., Eddington, Hungerford, Berks., 1670, AB, I, P23/16
Rd., Alderbury, 1685, W, P26/332
Robt., Laverstock, 1609, AB, P2/8Reg/80A
Bolden, Ruth, sp., Fyfield, Milton L., 1692, comm, I, W, P1/B/623
Bolden, Ruth, widow, Fyfield, Milton L., 1695, comm, I, W, P1/B/654
Steph., Fyfield, Milton L., 1704, court papers (2), W, P3/B/1031
Steph., Milton L., 1713, AB, I, P3/B/1116
Boulden, Wm., labourer, husb. and servant, Donnington, Berks., 1674, AB, comm, I, NW, P1/B/495
Boldy, Agnes, widow, Lt. Woodford, 1632-33, I, W, P5/1632/6, P5/12Reg/82C
Alice, Wilton, 1554, AB, P2/2Reg/184B
Bouldy, Edith, yeo.'s widow, Lt. Woodford, 1605, AB, I, W, P5/1605/4, P5/8Reg/36C
Edwd., husb., Lt. Woodford, 1628, AB, W, P13/1/8
Jn., husb., Stoford, S. Newton, 1562, I, P2/B/33
Jn., Chilhampton, S. Newton, 1606, AB, I, NW, P2/B/263
Jn., husb., Lt. Woodford, 1615, I, W, P13/1/5

Bouldie, Roger, husb., Fyfield, Milton L., 1610, W, P3/B/65
Simon, tailor, Shrewton, 1567, W, P2/5Reg/27D
Bouldie, Steph., yeo., Fyfield, Milton L., [1618], I, note of legacies, W (NEP), P3/B/161
Steph., Amesb., 1673, AB, I, P2/B/864
Thos., Stoford, S. Newton, 1594, AB, P2/7Reg/140A
Wilmot, widow, S. Newton, 1567, AB, P2/5Reg/30B
Boldyer, Thos., S. Newton, 1594, AB, I, P2/B/159
Boles *see* Bowles
Boling *see* Bollen
Boll, Bolle *see* Boles
Bollen, Ambrose, rug weaver, Sherb., Dorset, 1729, W, P5/1729/6, P5/16Reg/240A
Edwd., weaver, Chipp., 1681, AB, I, P3/B/745
Bullen, Helen, Codf. St My., 1559, AB, P2/3Reg/179D
Humphrey, sen., yeo., Seend, Melk., 1697, I, W, P2/B/1187
Humphrey, weaver, Seend Row, Melk., 1622, I, W, P2/B/428
Bollin, Joan, widow, Hinton, Steeple A., 1636, I, W, P3/B/371
Bollyn, Jn., Kington L., 1601, W, P3/1Reg/62B
Bollinge, Jn., yeo., Long Burton, Dorset, 1620, AB, deed of gift, I, T, W (grant of property to dau Ann, 1609), P5/1620/4, P5/10Reg/79A
Jn., Hinton, Steeple A., 1627, I, W, P2/B/467
Jn., tailor, Seend, Melk., 1632, I, W, copy W, P2/B/558
Boling, Jn., no abode stated, but proved at Gt. Bedwyn, 1636, I, P21/1/23
Jn., husb., Rowde, 1640, I, W, P3/B/442
Bullen, Jn., schoolmaster, Sherb., Dorset, 1767, W, P5/1767/10
Phineas, dairyman, Clifton Maybank, Dorset, 1801, comm, W, P5/1801/10, P5/18Reg/317
Rebecca, widow, Littleton, Steeple A., 1688, I, W, P2/B/1087
Rd., Rowde, 1612, W, P1/B/81
Bullen, Robt., Collingbourne K., 1687, comm, I, W, P3/B/837
Bollin, Sarah, widow, Westrop, Corsham, 1709, I, W, P29/B/37
Thos., sen., weaver, Seend, Melk., 1638, I, W, P1/B/277
Bollyn, Wm., husb., Holnest, Dorset, 1593, AB, I, P5/1593/10, P5/6Reg/41A
Bolles *see* Bowles
Bollin, Bollinge *see* Bollen
Bollock *see* Bullock
Bollwell, Bolwell, Agnes, widow, Mkt. L., 1635-36, I, W, P2/B/592, P2/9Reg/101B
Anth., yeo., Box, 1626, I, W, P3/B/277
Anth., miller, Box, 1705, I, W, P1/B/723
Dan., chemist, Poulshot, 1766, W, P2/B/1823
David, husb., Box, 1707, W, P3/B/1064
Bolwell, Isaac, carp., Melk., 1822, W, Wr, P2/1822/41
Bolwell, Isaac, Melk., 1838, AB, comm, Wr, P2/1838/31
Boollwell, Joan, widow, no abode stated, 1557, I, P2/B/13
Bolwell, Joel, wheelwright, Westrop, Corsham, 1698-99, I, W, P29/B/33, P29/1Reg/271
Jn., Hinton, Steeple A., 1548, W, P2/2Reg/69A
Bolwell, Jn., Steeple A., 1678, AB, I, P2/B/936
Bolwell, Jn., carp., Westrop, Corsham, 1728-29, W, P29/B/44, P29/2Reg/55A
Bolwell, Jn., jun., yeo., Rowde, 1735, AB, W, P1/B/1055, P3/B/1345, P1/8Reg/93
Jn., mail contractor, N. Bradley, 1829, comm, W, Wr, P1/1829/159
Bolwell, Maud, widow, Wingfield, 1586, AB, I, T, W, P2/B/94, P2/7Reg/47A
Rd., yeo., Poulshot, 1718, W, P2/B/1369
Robt., Holt, Bradford A., 1738, AB, comm, P1/B/1083
Bolwell, Thos., husb., Semington, Steeple A., 1568-69, AB, W, P2/5Reg/44D, 70B
Bolwell, Wm., husb., Wingfield, [1582], W (NEP), P3/1Reg/16A
Bolwell, Wm., blacksmith, Rowde, 1683, I, W, P3/B/773
Bollyn *see* Bollen
Bolsom, Bolsom als Vowell, Rd., Hurst, Berks., 1547, W, P5/20Reg/94
Bolster *see* Balster
Bolt, Edwd., Turners Puddle, Dorset, 1594, AB, I, P5/1593/15, P5/6Reg/54B
Francis, Reading, Berks., 1738, AB, P1/B/1087
Hy., Bere R., Dorset, 1564, AB, P5/1Reg/36A

Boult, Joan, widow, Bere R., Dorset, 1590, AB, I, W, P5/1590/9, P5/5Reg/78B
Boult, Jn., husb., Bere R., Dorset, 1596, AB, I, W, P5/1596/8, P5/6Reg/125A
Boult, Jn., Winkfield, Berks., 1756, AB, P1/B/1292
Boult, Jn., yeo., Bray Wick, Berks., 1783, W, P1/B/1483, P1/13Reg/466
Bowlte, Rd., husb., Sutton Poyntz, Dorset, 1578, I, W, P5/1578/5, P5/3Reg/110C
Boult, Rd., Shitterton, Bere R., Dorset, 1614, I, W, P5/1614/5, P5/9Reg/133B
Thos., miller, Alton P., Dorset, 1699, I, W, P5/1699/4
Boult, Wm., yeo., Warfield, Berks., 1738, W, P1/B/1090, P1/8Reg/274B
Bolter, Bowlter, Alice, widow, Gt. Cheverell, 1579, I, W, P2/B/75, P2/5Reg/344C
Chris., tailor, Lt. Cheverell, 1605, I, note, T, P2/B/261
David, Lt. Cheverell, 1830, AB, L, O, P2/1830/42
Bowlter, Eliz., sp., Winterbourne M., 1631, I, W, P1/B/231
Boulter, Francis, tailor, Sal., 1670, NW, P4/1669/2
Boulter, Geo., Staverton, Trowb., 1758, AB, P1/B/1313
Boulter, Geo., Urchf., 1829, AB, W, P2/1829/12
Hy., Edington, 1779, AB, P2/B/1965
Boulter, Hy., mason, Chipp., 1837, W, Wr, P3/1837/55
Boulter, Hy., Trowb., 1852, O, W, Wr, P1/1852/19
Hugh, Melk., 1610, AB, I, T, P2/B/295, P2/8Reg/82D
Bowlter, Hugh, Lt. Cheverell, 1641, AB, P1/B/297
Boulter, Hugh, clothw., Sal. St Thos., 1670, AB, a/c, I, ren, W, P4/1670/12
Jas., labourer, Lt. Cheverell, 1820, AB, W, Wr, P1/1820/37
Jas., brickmaker, Lt. Cheverell, 1833, AB, comm, W, Wr, P2/1833/63
Boulter, Jane, bricklayer's widow, Edington, 1773, W, P1/B/1423, P1/13Reg/17
Boulter, Jane, Nursteed, Bps. C., 1806, W, P24/1244
Jn., Erlestoke, 1597, a/c, I, T, P2/B/177
Boulter, Jn., yeo., Chisbury, Lt. Bedwyn, 1775, W, P21/11/11
Jos., Edington, 1760, AB, P2/B/1769
Mgt., widow, Lt. Cheverell, 1623, I, W, P2/B/445
My., Marston, Pott., 1642, I, W, P1/B/302
My., widow, Lt. Cheverell, 1833, AB (seq), O, Wr, P1/1833/9
Boulter, Peter, husb., Tilehurst, Berks., 1747, W, P1/B/1208, P1/10Reg/105B
Boulter, Rd., yeo., Hilp. Marsh, 1835, comm, W, Wr, P1/1835/51
Boulter, Robt., widower, Hurst, Berks., 1723, AB, P5/1723/3
Sam., Atworth, Bradford A., 1768, AB, P2/B/1845
Boulter, Sam., Tinh., Edington, 1799, note of AB, ren, Wr, P2/B/2144
Sarah, widow, Lt. Cheverell, 1758, I, W, P2/B/1745
Sarah, sp., Worton, Pott., 1848, O, W, Wr, P1/1848/72
Thos., Tinh., Edington, 1774, AB, P2/B/1903
Thos., sen., labourer, Lt. Cheverell, 1775, AB, W, P2/B/1921
Thos., mason, Tinh., Edington, 1780, W, P2/B/1977
Boulter, Wm., sen., Bere R., Dorset, 1669, AB, I, P5/1669/5
Wm., innholder, Mkt. L., 1750, W, P2/B/1678
Boulter, Wm., Gt. Cheverell, 1767, AB, comm, P2/B/1834
Bolton, Boulton, Abraham, baker, Newbury, Berks., 1726, AB, comm, I, P1/B/911
Boulton, Alfred, cordw., Ashton K., 1857, aff, D, O, W, Wr, P3/1857/61
Boulton, Alice, widow, Hannington Wick, 1620, I, W, P3/B/191
Boulton, Alice, Wootton B., 1648, AB, P1/B/339
Boulton, Alice, widow, Hannington, 1679, I, W, P3/B/714
Boulton, Edith, widow, Hannington, 1605, W, P3/B/21
Boulton, Edwd., gent., Pinkney, Sherston, 1843, W, Wr, P3/1843/28
Boulton, Edwd., Pinkney, Sherston, 1850, W, Wr, P3/1850/39
Boulton, Eliz., widow, Hannington, 1640, I, W, P3/B/443
Boulton, Eliz., sp., Malm., 1799, W, P3/B/1767
Boulton, Grace, widow, Ashton K., 1832, aff, O, Wr, P3/1832/15
Boulton, Hannell, carp., Holt, Bradford A., 1688, NW, P2/B/1088
Boulton, Harry, glover, Hankerton, 1840, W, Wr, P3/1840/39
Boulton, Hy., cordw., Ashton K., 1767, W, P3/B/1585
Boulton, Hy., husb., Ashton K., 1768, W, P3/B/1591
Boulton, Humphrey, yeo., Hannington, 1639, I, W, P3/B/417

Boulton, Isaac, labourer, Ashton K., 1857, aff, O, W, Wr, P3/1857/18
Boulton, Jacob, bach., Ashton K., 1843, O, W, Wr, P3/1843/3
Boulton, Jn., Crickl. St S., 1773, AB, P1/B/1416
Boulton, My., widow, Kingston Bagpuize, Berks., 1747, I, W, P1/B/1203, P1/10Reg/92B
Boulton, Nich., yeo., Wootton B., 1715, I, W, P3/B/1130
Boulton, Obadiah, yeo., Ashton K., 1759, W, P1/B/1325, P1/11Reg/435
Boulten, Philip, Edmondsham, Dorset (exhibited at Calne), 1641, I, P5/1641/7
Boulton, Rd., husb., Hannington, 1602, I, W, P1/B/18
Boulton, Rd., blacksmith, Hannington, 1667, I, W, P3/B/525
Boulton, Rd., farmer, Garsdon (form. of Tetbury, Gloucs), 1785, W, P3/B/1697
Bowlton, Robt., husb., Hannington Wick, 1633, I, W, P3/B/348
Boulton, Robt., Malm., 1760, AB, P3/B/1530
Simon, Poulton Mill, Mildenhall, 1672, AB, comm, P1/B/484
Thos., sen., husb., Sulhamstead Abbots, Berks., 1747, W, P1/B/1207, P1/10Reg/106
Boulton, Thos., yeo., Somerford K., 1814, W, P3/1814/8
Boulton, Walter, Hannington, 1631, AB, I, P1/B/229
Wm., Wilton, 1642, AB, I, P2/B/676
Boulton, Wm., Ewen, Kemble, 1693, W, P3/B/900
Boulting, Wm., sen., linen weaver, Silton, Dorset, 1770, W, P27/1/472, P27/3Reg/155
Boulton, Wm., matmaker, Ashton K., 1835, comm, W, P3/1835/38
Bolwell *see* Bollwell
Bolwin *see* Baldwin
Bombe, Wm., Speen, Berks., 1726, AB, I, P1/B/922
Bonam *see* Bonham
Bonar *see* Bonner
Bond, Ann, widow, Chipp., 1841, W, Wr, P3/1841/38
Benj., shopkeeper, Calne (form. of Biddestone St. Nich.), 1742, W, P26/836
Dolly, widow, Rams., 1798, W, P5/1798/4, P5/18Reg/257C
Dyer, Lacock, 1708, I, W, P1/B/734
Edwd., broad weaver, Lacock, 1688, AB, I, ren, W, Wr, P3/B/844
Edwd., sen., Pott., 1785, W, P1/B/1494, P1/14Reg/70B
Eleanor, widow, Wambrook, Somerset, 1729, W, P14/140
Eliz., widow, Donhead St My., 1794, AB, P2/B/2091
Eliz., gent.'s wife, Corsham, 1807, AB, comm, Wr, P3/1807/54
Eliz., sp., Trowb., 1839, AB, O, W, Wr, P1/1839/67
Ferdinand, yeo., Chards., Devon, 1844, comm, W, Wr, P14/225
Hy., rugmaker, Lacock, 1687, I, W, P3/B/836
Hopeful, gardener, Westport St My., 1803, W, P3/1803/39
Isaac, Wambrook, Somerset, 1729, AB, comm, P14/142
Isaac, gent., Chards., Devon (form. of Ottery St My. & late of Exeter, Devon), 1839, AB, W, Wr, P5/1839/6
Isolde, sp., Chards., Devon, 1714, comm, W, P14/121
Jas., yeo., Chards., Devon, 1670, I, W, P14/29
Jas., weaver, Chipp., 1738, AB, comm, I, P3/B/1370
Jas., Westb. L., 1755, AB, P25/1755/2
Jas., Westport St My., 1759, comm, W, P1/B/1323, P1/11Reg/427B
Jas., carp., Westport St My., 1801, W, P1/1801/78, P1/15Reg/298
Jn., Quemerford, Calne, 1610, I, P5/1610/4
Jn., Chards., Devon, 1626, comm, I, W, P5/1625/5, P5/10Reg/189
Jn., butcher, Chipp., 1653, W, P3/B/462
Jn., Bere R., Dorset, 1668, AB, I, W, P5/1668/2
Jn., husb., Gt. Somerford, 1682, I, W, P3/B/755
Jn., Alston, Chards., Devon, 1691, AB, comm, I, P14/76
Jn., yeo., Pott., 1694, I, W, P1/B/637
Jn., husb., Marcham, Berks., 1698, I, W, P1/B/672, P1/3Reg/99
Jn., yeo., Chards., Devon, 1710, I, W, P5/1710/16, P5/15Reg/198A
Jn., Chipp., 1721, AB, I, P3/B/1189
Jn., Donhead St My., 1813, AB, Wr, P2/1813/10
Jn., Crawley, Chards., Devon, 1848, AB, comm, O, Wr, P14/230
Jos., tailor, Bromham, 1706, I, W, P3/B/1056
Jos., Gillingham, Dorset, 1720, AB (endorsed: 'some ABs & probates not paid nor called for'), P27/1/239

Jos., blacksmith, Sutton C., Berks., 1744, W, P1/B/1180, P1/9Reg/371B
Mark, joiner, Worton, Pott., 1748, I, W, P1/B/1223, P1/10Reg/224
My., widow, Chipp., 1686, AB, I, P3/B/824
My., sp., Leigh, Ashton K., 1759, AB, P3/B/1521
My., widow, Westport St My., 1760, AB, comm, W, P3/B/1529
My., sp., Calne, 1800, affirmation, W, P26/1228
Nich., Homington, 1747, AB, ren, P24/1064
Nich., gent. and capital burgess, Malm., 1765, AB, W, P3/B/1573
Rd., Holnest, Dorset, 1598, AB, I, P5/1598/7, P5/6Reg/206D
Rd., husb., Pott., 1619, I, NW, P1/B/160
Rd., yeo., Charney Bassett, Longworth, Berks., 1680, I, W, P1/B/531
Rd., sen., rugmaker *or* rug weaver, Bromham, 1683, I, W, P3/B/774
Rd., cordw., Chipp., 1700, I, W, P3/B/995
Robt., innholder, Chipp., 1672, AB, comm, I, P3/B/630
Robt., Chards., Devon, 1703, AB, I, P14/99
Robt., sen., Bowden Hill, Lacock, 1713, AB, I, P3/B/1117
Robt., yeo., Lacock, 1723, W, P1/B/890, P1/6Reg/453B
Sarah, widow, Chipp., 1701, AB, P1/B/684
Sarah, Sutton B., 1829, W, Wr, P1/1829/93
Thos., weaver, Reybridge, Lacock, 1609, W, P3/B/47
Thos., Chards., Devon, 1662-63, I, W, P5/1662/11, P5/1663/12
Thos., sen., Sutton B., 1802, W, P3/1802/55
Thos., Bower C., 1823, W, Wr, P1/1823/23
Wm., Holnest, Dorset, 1598-1600, AB, a/c, I, P5/1598/6, P5/1600/83, P5/6Reg/206E
Wm., Lacock, 1609, AB, P3/B/46
Wm., milliner, Notton, Lacock, 1628, I, W, P1/B/206
Wm., sen., husb., Quemerford, Calne, 1639, I, W, P26/83
Wm., Chards., Devon, 1685, AB, a/c, I, P14/59
Wm., rector, Bradfield, Berks., 1744, W, P1/B/1179, P1/9Reg/355B
Wm., vict., Pott., 1749, W, P1/B/1228, P1/10Reg/260A
Wm., yeo., Sutton B., 1774, W, P3/B/1632
Wm., vict., Malm., 1777, W, P3/B/1646
Wm., yeo., Sutton M., 1808, W, Wr, P2/1808/5
Bondy *see* Bundy
Bone, And., gardener, Downton, 1757, W, P2/B/1734
Eliz., widow, New Windsor, Berks., 1753, AB, P1/B/1267
Geo., gardener, Downton, 1772, W, P2/B/1892
My. Ann, sp., Sal. The Close, 1844, AB, D, Wr, P5/1844/13
Bones, Roger, shopkeeper, Upavon, 1692, AB, I, P2/B/1142
Boners *see* Bowers
Bones *see* Bone
Boney *see* Bonny
Bonfield *see* Banfield
Bonger *see* Benger
Bonham, Jn., sen., W. Lavington, 1571, W, P1/1Reg/29B
Jn., Amesb., 1669-74, AB, a/c, P2/B/819, 875
Jn., maltster, Sal., 1683, I, W, P4/1683/2
My., widow, W. Lavington, 1633, I, W, P2/B/571
Bonam, Nich., Wokm., Berks., 1575, I, W, P5/1575/7, P5/3Reg/60B
Sarah, widow, Marl., 1802, W, P1/1802/10
Bonhan, Walter, Sal., 1616, AB, P1/B/134
Boniface, Charlotte, sp., Sherb., Dorset, 1829, comm, W, Wr, P5/1829/6
Bonifant, Sam., Uffc., Devon, 1712, W, P20/1/147
Bonnell, My., widow, Nether C., Dorset, 1704, AB, comm, P5/1704/6
Nich., weaver, Netherb., Dorset, 1634, I, NW. Proved at the Metropolitan visitation to Dorchester, P5/1634/23, P5/12Reg/288A
Bonner, Alice, widow, Sal., 1665, AB, I, W, P4/1664/3
Alice, widow, Rams., 1685, ren, W, P5/1685/4
Ann, widow, Lyme R., Dorset, 1642, AB, comm, P5/1642/20, P5/14Reg/49A
Ann, widow, Upavon, 1706, I, W, P2/B/1250

Edmd., Lyme R., Dorset, 1686, AB, I, P16/87
Edmd., yeo., Upavon, 1734, W, P2/B/1533
Edwd., Upavon, 1669, AB, P2/B/808
Edwd., husb., Upavon, 1677, AB, a/c, I, P2/B/919
Eliz., widow, Lyme R., Dorset, 1703, I, W, P16/163
Eliz., sp., Winterslow, 1780, W, P2/B/1973
Jas., glover, Wantage, Berks., 1725, W, P5/1725/5, P5/16Reg/122B
Jn., baker, Lyme R., Dorset, 1641, AB, comm, I, P5/1641/9, P5/13Reg/276A
Jos., carp., Dauntsey, 1837, W, Wr, P3/1837/43
Sarah, sp., Lyme R., Dorset, 1752, AB, Wr, P5/1752/5
Thos., husb., Upavon, 1557, W, P2/3Reg/25C
Thos., Sal., 1663, AB, I, P1/B/386
Thos., Eddington, Hungerford, Berks., 1675, I, W, P23/51
Bunner, Thos., widower, Melk. Wharf, 1857, AB, aff, O, Wr, P2/1857/24
Bayner, Wm., shepherd, Lt. Bathampton, Steeple L., 1624, I, P2/B/453
Bonnett, Isaac, mariner (made before going on board the brigantine William & Jane, Wm. Japlin, master), Fordington, Dorset, 1754, W (engraving of warships at head), P15/141
Jas., husb., Fordington, Dorset, 1716, I, W, P15/165, P5/15Reg/344B
Jas., Fordington, Dorset, 1749, AB, P5/1749/3
Bonnet, Jn., Fordington, Dorset, 1693, AB, I, P15/51
Bonnet, Jn., cloth weaver, Fordington, Dorset, 1705, I, W, P15/74
Jos., sen., clothier, Fordington, Dorset, 1740, W, P15/127
Robt., clothier, Fordington, Dorset, 1730, W, P15/118
Sarah, widow, Fordington, Dorset, 1787, W, P15/164
Bonney *see* Bonny
Bonniwell, Adriana, widow, Sutton C., Berks., 1680, AB, I, P1/B/536
Wm., maltster, Sutton C., Berks., 1729, W, P1/B/968, P1/7Reg/242
Bonny, Bony, Dorothy, widow, Fisherton A., 1682, AB, W, P2/B/1010
Bonney, Dorothy, widow, Rams., 1700, AB, I, P5/1700/5
Bonny als Noad, Jane, sp., Swindon, 1722, I, W, P3/N/189
Boney, Thos., Fisherton A., 1734, AB, P2/B/1530
Boney, Thos., Fisherton A., 1775, W, P2/B/1915
Boney, Wm., Fisherton A., 1791, AB, P2/B/2061
see also Mason als B.
Boocher *see* Butcher
Bookings, Jonathan, yeo., Langley Whire, Cumnor, Berks., 1783, W, P1/13Reg/453
Booles *see* Bowles
Boollwell *see* Bollwell
Boon, Boone *see* Bowne
Boorn, Boorne *see* Bourne
Boote, Jn., Wantage, Berks., 1569, AB, P5/2Reg/48E
Peter, gent., Wantage, Berks., 1729, W, P23/461
Booth, Booth als Joyner, Thos., carp., Warm., 1605, I, W, P2/B/260
Booy, Buoy, Betty, widow, Steeple A., 1852, D, W, Wr, P2/1852/47
Edwd., tiler and plasterer, Castle C., 1807, W, Wr, P3/1807/58
Boy, Eliz., widow, Nettleton, 1693, I, W, P3/B/901
Francis, husb., Luckington, 1619, I, W, P1/B/154
Francis, yeo., Nettleton, 1739, W, P3/B/1380
Isabel, widow, Nettleton, 1630, I, W, P3/B/325
Boy, Jn., sen., yeo., Nettleton, 1707, I, W, P3/B/1066
Booy *or* Boy, Jn., yeo., Nettleton, 1753, W, P1/B/1276, P1/11Reg/94
Jn., yeo., Steeple A., 1840, W, Wr, P2/1840/27
Boy, Jos., bach. and yeo., Luckington, 1707, AB, I, P3/B/1067
Boy, My., widow, Nettleton & Littleton Drew, 1731, I, W, P3/B/1304
Sarah, widow, Nettleton, 1764, W, P3/B/1560
Boy, Simon, Luckington, 1735, W, P3/B/1346
Thos., Marl. St My., 1648, AB, P1/B/342
Boy, Wm., labourer, Chipp., 1676, AB, comm, I, P3/B/666
see also Androws als B.
Bordeman, Agnes, sp., Marl. St My., 1619, AB, I, P1/B/161

Bordock, Jn., weaver, Horningsham, 1609, AB, I, T, P5/1609/9, P5/9Reg/6B
Bordon, Rd., Chirton, 1584, AB, P2/6Reg/119A
Boreman, Robt., miller, Sherb., Dorset, 1636, comm, I, W, P5/1635/14, P5/12Reg/258B
Borne *see* Bourne
Borrow, Borrough, Enion, yeo., Woodford, 1710, W, P5/1710/19, P5/15Reg/184
Jn., miller, Donhead St A., 1752, W, Wr, P2/B/1694
Thos., Charlton nr Malm., 1684, I, W, P3/B/795
see also Barrow *or* B.
Bory, Edwd., Biddestone St Peter, 1728, AB, P3/B/1268
Boscombe *see* Bascombe
Bosden, Rd., gent., Shute, Longbridge D., 1589, I, P2/B/111
Bosely *see* Bosley
Boshear, Bosher *see* Boucher
Bosley *see* Basely
Boss, Lucy, widow, Turners Puddle, Dorset, 1729, W, P5/1729/7
Silvester, weaver, Wick, Bps. C. (d. at Malm.), 1608, AB, I (2 - 1 deals with effects found with him at M. where taken ill), NW, P24/161
Wm., Horningsham, 1608, I, W, P5/1608/6, P5/8Reg/114B
Bossawsack, Rd., gent., Bishopstone N., 1637, AB, I, P6/22
Boston, Mgt., widow, Homington, 1610, AB, I, P24/139
Robt., physician, Devizes St My., 1621, AB, I, W, P1/B/175
Boswell, Oliver *see* Joan Hether
Simon, husb., Beenham Valence, Berks., 1613, AB, I, W, P1/B/99
Wm., no abode stated but probably Lt. Bedwyn, 1625-1649, AB. No date given except temp.Chas. I., P21/3/29
Bosworth, Jn., Lacock, 1570, W (ref. to book *'Cranmer upon the Sacraments*'), P1/1Reg/110B
Botcher *see* Butcher
Botley *see* Botly
Botlore *see* Butler
Botly, Eliz., sp., Sal., 1853, W, Wr, P4/1853/8
Rd., Plaitford, 1638, AB, I, P2/B/630
Thos., Sal., 1681, AB, I, P4/1681/21
Wm., Plaitford, 1593, I, note, T, P2/B/147
Botley, Wm., husb., Plaitford, 1627, I, W, P2/B/471
Wm., Sal., 1757, AB, P1/B/1308
Botrell, Geo., Sonning, Berks., 1545, W, P5/20Reg/62
Bott, Bott *or* Bett, Thos., Mkt. L., 1612, W, P1/B/79
Bottemley, Edwd., yeo., Kingston Bagpuize, Berks., 1625, I, W, P1/B/190
Bottendon, Bottenton *see* Battington
Bottwell *see* Batwell
Bottyfield, Peter, gent., Warm., 1629, I, W, P2/B/505
Botwell *see* Batwell
Boucher, Bosher, Agnes, widow, Longbridge D., 1639, NW, P2/B/647
Bowsher, Alice, Mildenhall, 1625, I, NW, P3/B/267
Bowsher, Ann, widow, Avill's Farm, Corsham, 1799, W, P3/B/1768
Benj., clothw., Trowb., 1778, W, P1/B/1449, P1/13Reg/188B
Bowsher, Chas., Biddestone, 1770, AB, P3/B/1610
Bowsher, Chas., Corsham, 1801, AB, P3/1801/21
Bowsher, Chas., farmer, Allington, Chipp., 1822, W, Wr, P3/1822/25
Bousher, Chris., yeo., Lambourn, Berks., 1729, AB, I, ren, P1/B/963
Bowsher, Eliz., widow, Marl., 1736, comm, W, P1/B/1061, P1/8Reg/148A
Bowsher, Francis, innholder, Marl., 1720, AB, I, W, P1/B/853, P1/6Reg/201
Boshear, Francis, miller, Greenham, Thatcham, Berks., 1792, W, P1/B/1525, P1/14Reg/432B
Hy., husb., W. Ashton, Steeple A., 1600, I, P30/14
Bowsher, Hy., husb., Lambourn Woodlands, Berks., 1756, W, P1/B/1299, P1/11Reg/239
Bosher, Jane, widow, [Marl.] (NBI), [1697], I, P1/B/660
Bowsher, Jn., sen., Mildenhall, [1609], W (NEP), P3/B/48
Bowsher, Jn., husb. *or* yeo., Longbridge D., 1636, I, W, P2/B/602
Bowsher, Jn., yeo., Ogbourne Maizey, 1662, I, W, P5/1662/4
Bowsher, Jn., sen., baker, Marl., 1694, I, W, P1/B/638
Bowsher, Jn., innholder *or* innkeeper, Biddestone St Nich., 1717, I, W, P3/B/1144

Bowsher, Jn., baker, Marl. St My., 1720, comm (2), W, P1/B/869, P1/6Reg/355
Bowsher, Jn., Marl., 1739, AB, P1/B/1112
Bowsher, Jn., Lambourn, Berks., 1747, AB, P1/B/1211
Bosher, Jn. Mart., farmer, Hurst, Berks., 1809, W, Wr, P5/1809/12
Jos., gent., Trowb., 1826, O, W, Wr, P1/1826/143
Mgt., widow, Bemerton, Fugg. St Peter, 1724, I, W, P2/B/1428
Bowsher, My., widow, Biddestone St Nich., 1751, W, P3/B/1466
My., widow, Wilton, 1774, AB, P2/B/1910
My., widow, Corsham, [1790], W, P29/B/57, P29/2Reg/212
Bouchier, Nich., gent., Sherb., Dorset, 1705, AB, I, P5/1705/10
Rd., sen., Corsham, 1790, W, P29/B/55, P29/2Reg/184B
Bowsher, Robt., Mildenhall, 1638, I, W, P3/B/400
Boushere, Robt., Lambourn Woodlands, Berks., 1672, comm, I, W, P1/B/483
Bowsher, Robt., yeo., Lambourn Woodlands, Berks., 1738, W, P1/B/1075, P1/8Reg/216
Bowsher, Roger, Chilton F., 1671, AB, a/c, comm, I, P3/B/588
Bowsher, Ruth, widow, Biddestone, 1689, AB, I, P3/B/855
Bowcher, Susanna, Corsham, 1832, W, Wr, P1/1832/34
Boutcher, Thos., innholder, Sherb., Dorset, 1787, comm, W, P5/1787/3, P5/18Reg/72B
Bowsher, Thos., Avill's Farm, Corsham, 1797, AB, comm, P3/B/1757
Bowsher, Timothy, baker, Marl., 1691, W, P1/B/608
Bowsher, Wm., Longbridge D., 1616, AB, I, P2/B/366
Bowsher, Wm., [Marl.] (NBI), 1681, I, W, P1/B/552
Bowsher, Wm., innholder, Biddestone St Nich., 1682, AB, comm, I, P3/B/758
Wm., Sal. The Close, 1692, AB, P5/1692/10
Bowsher, Wm., butcher, Avill's Farm, Corsham, 1792, W, P3/B/1737
Bowsher, Wm., yeo., Devizes, 1834, D, W, Wr, P1/1834/6
Wm., baker, Trowb., 1836, AB, O, ren, W, P1/1836/12
Wm. *see* Jn. Baker
see also Butcher; Eglen als B.
Bouckley *see* Buckley
Boudler, Boudly *see* Bowdley
Boudmayne *see* Bodman
Bouggis *see* Buggis
Boughey, Ann, sp., Lacock, 1852, O, W, Wr, P3/1852/17
Boulden *see* Bolding
Bouldes *see* Bold
Bouldie *see* Boldy
Boulding *see* Bolding
Bouldy *see* Boldy
Boules *see* Bowles
Bouller *see* Bowler
Boulse *see* Bowles
Boult *see* Bolt
Boulten *see* Bolton
Boulter *see* Bolter
Boulting, Boulton *see* Bolton
Bound, Bownde, Agnes, widow, Teffont E., 1614, W, P2/8Reg/222B
Betty, sp., Lydiard T., 1806, comm, W, Wr, P3/1806/15
Edmd., sen., yeo., Boulsbury, Damerham, Hants, 1730, AB, W, P2/B/1483
Edmd., yeo., Tidpit, Martin, Hants, 1841, W, Wr, P2/1841/33
Edwd., Downton, 1566, AB, P2/4Reg/238B, P2/4Reg/239D
Eliz., widow, Downton, 1776, W, P2/B/1936
Hannah, widow, Charlton, Downton, 1819, W, Wr, P2/1819/9
Hy., Dinton, 1605, AB, P2/B/255
Hy., Teffont E., 1636, I, W, P2/B/598
Jas., Wylye, 1755, AB, W, P2/B/1717
Jos., yeo., Damerham, Hants, 1798, W, P2/B/2136
Bownde, Lawr., Chitterne AS, 1555, W, P2/1Reg/25C
Maria Emily, wife, Fisherton A., 1848, D, W, Wr, P2/1848/43
Bownde, Rd., Downton, 1545, AB, P2/B/1

Sarah, sp., Lydiard T., 1806, comm, W, Wr, P3/1806/50
Thos., husb., Teffont E., 1606, I, W, P1/B/46
Bownde, Thos., husb., Dinton, 1608, I, W, P2/B/281
Thos., husb., Alvediston, 1610, I, W, P2/B/296
Thos., yeo., Lydiard T., 1789, W, P1/B/1514, P1/14Reg/330
Walter, Semley, 1594, AB, I, note, P2/B/154
Walter, weaver, Codf. St My., 1648-49, AB. No month given, P2/B/720
Wm., yeo., Compton C., 1561, I, W, P2/B/24, P2/4Reg/85D
Wm., carp., Fovant, 1590, I, T, NW, P2/B/113
Wm., shopkeeper, Maiden B., [1692], I (very detailed), W, P2/B/1148
Wm., Damerham, Hants, 1789, AB, P1/B/1506
Wm., dealer, Downton, 1792, W, P2/B/2072
Boundy *see* Bundy
Bouner *see* Bonner
Bounsall, Jas., mariner on HMS *Grafton*, Sal., 1761, req, W, copy W, P4/1761/6
Bounty, Edith, widow, Crickl. St S., 1639, I, W, P3/B/418
Bourcheir *see* Burchall *or* B.
Bourgoine *see* Burgoin
Bourne, Boorne, Ann, widow, Amesb., 1745, AB, ren, W, P2/B/1640
Avis, widow, Hinton St. George, Somerset (effects left to relatives at Beam., Dorset), 1755, W (NEP), P5/1755/4
Benj., Westb., 1718, AB, comm, I, P25/1718/1
Geo., clothier, Westb., 1777, W, P25/1777/1
Hannah, widow, Westb., 1777, AB, ren, W, P25/1777/5
Joan, [Mere] (NBI), 1612, I, P2/B/325
Jn., sen., husb., Mere, 1569, W, P5/2Reg/43A
Jn., Mere, 1590, I, W, P5/1590/8, P5/5Reg/80A
Boorne, Jn., Amesb., 1697, AB, P2/B/1184
Jn., Bramshaw, Hants, 1786, AB, P24/1174
Baun, Jn., innholder, Pickwick, Corsham, 1774-75, W, P29/B/53, P29/2Reg/135
Boorne, Jos., N. Bradley, 1622, AB, a/c, I, W, P1/B/182
Jos., linen draper, Sal., 1758, W, P4/1758/11
Borne, Leonard *see* Isabel Wastell
Boorn, Moses, Bulford, 1778, W, P2/B/1954
Rd., tailor, Mere, 1600-01, AB, I, W, P5/1600/8, P5/7Reg/9B
Rd., yeo., Heywood, Westb., 1828, O, W, P25/1828/9
Rd., farmer, Fillingbridge, Westb., 1844, O, W, Wr, P25/1844/11
Rd., Horsecroft Farm, Westb., 1853, AB, O, Wr, P25/1853/1
Steph., barber and perukemaker, Westb., 1798, W. note, P25/1798/3
Thos., husb., Ogbourne Maizey, 1612, I, P5/1612/45
Baune, Thos., baker, Luckington, 1679, AB, comm, I, P3/B/701
Thos., husb. and yeo., Burton, Mere, 1702, I, W, P5/1702/3
Thos., Middle Pickwick, Corsham, 1820, comm, W, Wr, P1/1820/12
Thos., farmer, Penleigh Farm, Dilton, Westb., 1856, declaration, O, W, Wr, P25/1856/5
Boorne, Whitfield, surgeon, Amesb., 1734, W, P2/B/1532
Wm., vict., Westb., 1757, W, P25/1757/2
Wm., bach., Westb., 1762, AB, P25/1762/3
Wm., jun., Brook Farm, Westb., 1848, AB, comm, Wr, P25/1848/1
Wm., yeo., Dunge Farm, Steeple A., 1852, comm, W, Wr, P2/1852/34
Bourton *see* Burton
Bousher, Boushere, Boutcher *see* Boucher
Bovet, Rd., Lyme R., Dorset, 1597, AB, I, P5/1597/12, P5/6Reg/168D
Bovis *see* Bevis
Bow, Wm., yeo., Stockwood, Dorset, 1821, W, Wr, P5/1821/30
Bowcher *see* Boucher
Bowden, Eliz. *or* Betty, widow, Poulshot, 1819, W, Wr, P2/1819/8
Geo., clerk, Mapperton, Dorset, 1640, I, W, P5/1640/1, P5/13Reg/256C
Geo., innholder, Lacock, 1805, W, Wr, P3/1805/43
Geo., Poulshot, 1818, AB, comm, ren, Wr, P2/1818/19
Geo., The Earldoms, Whitep., 1824, AB, Wr, P5/1824/2
Gregory, clothier, dated at Exeter but proved at Warm., 1714, W, P1/B/808, P1/5Reg/467

Jn., Bps. C., 1805, AB, comm, P24/1237
Jn., Bps. C., 1823, AB, Wr, P24/1294
My., Westb., 1751, W, P25/1751/2
Rd., fishmonger, Sal., 1662, W, P4/1661/5, P4/1662/5
Robt., clothw., Westb., 1638, AB, I (ref. to Spanish wool), W (part missing), P25/1638/3
Thos., E. Harnham, Britford, 1814, AB, P24/1270
Wm., sen., Warm., 1766, AB, P2/B/1818
Wm., Bps. C., 1806, AB, P24/1243
Wm., Poulshot, 1830, W, P2/1830/12
Bowditch, Agnes, widow, Chards., Devon, 1676, I, W, P14/41
Bowdich, Ann, widow, Chards., Devon, 1723-24, comm, W, P5/1723/4, P5/16Reg/91B
Bridget, widow, Chards., Devon, 1704, I, W, P14/104
Bowdich *or* Bowditch, Geo., sen., gent., Chards., Devon, 1682, AB, I, P5/1682/7
Geo., clerk, Farley, Alderbury, 1768, D, W, P26/1024
Bowdich, Hy., gent., Chards., Devon, 1645, AB, comm, I, P5/1645/1, P5/14Reg/80A
Joan, widow, Lyme R., Dorset, 1713, W, P5/1713/14, P5/15Reg/377A
Bowdidge, Jn., Lyme R., Dorset, 1694, AB, P16/126
Bowdidge, Jn., sen., mercer, Lyme R., Dorset, 1727, W, P16/244
Jn. Snow, woolsorter, Wilton, 1836, W, P2/1836/22
Bowdich, Rd., gent., Chards., Devon, 1665, I, W, P14/17
Bowdidge, Sarah, widow, Lyme R., Dorset, 1695, I (very detailed), NW, P16/134
Sarah, wife, Beam., Dorset, 1818, AB, comm, Wr, P17/601
Steph., yeo., Chards., Devon, 1709, I, W, P14/109
Bowdidge, Thos., yeo., Lyme R., Dorset, 1699, W (printed & illuminated heading), P16/155
Bowdidge, Thos., mariner on HMS *Litchfield*, Lyme R., Dorset, 1723, AB, P16/229
Thos., woolsorter, Codf. St P., 1837, W, Wr, P2/1837/16
Bowditch *or* Bowdidge, Wm., mariner, Lyme R., Dorset, 1675, I (2) (detailed - 1 draft), ren, P16/43
see also Harrison als B.
Bowdley, Boudly *or* Boudler, Jn., husb., Highway, 1621, I, W, P3/B/208
Miles, husb., Highway, 1637, I, W, P3/B/386
Boudly, Robt., Compton B., 1726, I, W, P1/B/912, P1/7Reg/75A
Bowell, Margery, widow, Mere, 1685, I, W, P5/1685/16
Rd., linen weaver, Mere, 1641, AB, I, P5/1641/10, P5/14Reg/40A
Bowen *see* Bowne
Bower, Agatha, widow, Donhead St A., 1664, I, NW, P2/B/759
Ann, clerk's wife, Wylye, 1618, AB, comm, P2/B/378
Ann, widow, Norton B., 1681, I, NW, P2/B/964
David, tanner, Mere, 1572, W, P5/3Reg/2D
David, Wylye, 1604, AB, I, note, P2/B/245
Bowers, Edwd., husb., Binfield, Berks., 1717, I, W, P1/B/836, P1/6Reg/106
Eliz. *see* Edwd. Hart
Ellen, Donhead St A., 1632, I, W, P2/B/550
Francis, shoemaker, Chute, 1762, AB, comm, P7/159
Gabriel, miller *or* millwright, Winterbourne G., 1641, I, NW, P2/B/665
Geo., Everleigh, 1803, AB, P3/1803/19
Hy., shoemaker, Sal., 1669, W (NEP), P4/1669/19
Hy., [Fisherton A.] (NBI), 1672, I, P2/B/853
Hester, widow, Coombe, Donhead St My., 1794, AB, app. of guardian, P2/B/2101
Jas., yeo., Farnham, Tollard Royal, Dorset, 1633-34, I, W, P2/B/574, P2/9Reg/9B
Jane, widow, Donhead St A., 1587, W, P2/7Reg/75B
Jane, widow, Castle St., Sal., 1799, W, P4/1799/2
Jeremiah, Sal., 1759, AB, P4/1759/2
Joan, widow, W. Lavington &, Seend, Melk., 1645, I, W, P2/B/696
Jn., glazier, Beam., Dorset, 1622, AB, I, P5/1622/6, P5/10Reg/117A
Jn., clerk parson, Gt. Wishford, 1637, AB, I, W, P1/B/266
Jn., Winterbourne G., 1732, AB, P1/B/995
Jn., gent., Coombe, Donhead St My., 1742, W, P2/B/1610
Jn., Winterbourne G., 1791, AB, P2/B/2055
Jos., Donhead St My., 1685, AB, I, P2/B/1051
Margery, widow, Beam., Dorset, 1623, AB, I, NW, P5/1623/6, P5/10Reg/222B

My., widow, Coombe, Donhead St My., 1721, W, P2/B/1397
Nich., innholder, Mkt. L., 1642, I, W, P2/B/678
Rd., barber, Gt. Faringdon, Berks., 1662, I, W, P5/1662/20
Rd., glover, Donhead St A., 1739, AB, ren, W, P2/B/1580
Robt., clerk, Gt. Wishford, 1664, I, W, P1/B/403
Robt., Bemerton, Fugg. St Peter, 1711, AB, I, P1/B/774
Thos., Mkt. L., 1558, AB, a/c, P1/1Reg/16B
Thos., yeo., Donhead St A., 1620, I, W, P1/B/167
Thos., gent., Donhead St A., 1644, AB, I (2), P2/B/688
Thos., Beam., Dorset, 1696, AB, P17/358
Thos., sen., Stourpaine, Dorset, 1732, W, P24/959
Thos., Stourpaine, Dorset, 1788, AB, comm, P24/1167
Wm., Donhead St A., 1568, W, P2/5Reg/38A
Wm., yeo., Donhead St A., 1608, AB, W, P2/B/282, P2/8Reg/9C
Wm., W. Lavington, 1611, comm, I, W, P1/B/73
Wm., Plaitford, 1721, W, P2/B/1404
Bowering, Benj., Devizes, 1851, AB, D, W, Wr, P1/1851/1
Bowren, Eleanor, widow, Mere, 1586, I, W, P5/1586/4, P5/4Reg/134D
Bowring nee Ironside, My., widow, Charminster, Dorset, 1843, comm, W, Wr, P5/1843/4
Robt. Edwd. Rodd, baker, Southbroom, 1834, W, Wr, P24/1341
Roger, mercer, Beam., Dorset, 1697, AB, I, P17/123
Bowring, Steph., Sal., 1844, AB, Wr, P1/1844/8
Bowren, Thos., husb., Mere, 1578, I, W, P5/1578/6, P5/3Reg/110B
Bowerman, Anstis, Uffc., Devon, 1673, AB, P20/1/73
Jn., E. Knoyle, 1722, AB, P2/B/1415
Sarah, scrivener's wife, Uffc., Devon, 1827, AB, O, Wr, P5/1827/55
Wm., blacksmith, Uffc., Devon, 1845, D, W, Wr, P5/1845/23
Bowers *see* Bower
Bowes, Eliz., widow, Haydon Wick, Rodbourne C., 1745, W, P3/B/1427
Wm., Haydon Wick, Rodbourne C., 1734, AB, P3/B/1338
Bowgis *see* Buggis
Bowlde *see* Bold
Bowle *see* Bowles
Bowler, Bouller, Ann, Westb., 1565, W, P5/1Reg/56C
Bauler, Ann, maid, Beer Hackett, Dorset, 1621, I, W, P5/1621/4, P5/10Reg/92
Bauler, Eliz., widow, Beer Hackett, Dorset, 1588, W, P5/5Reg/26A
German, Whitep., 1635, I, NW, P2/B/586, P2/9Reg/90B
Bawler, Jn., husb., Beer Hackett, Dorset, 1600, I, W, P5/1600/3, P5/6Reg/255A
Bawler, Jn., Bere R., Dorset, 1629, AB, P5/11Reg/106B
Bowler *or* Baller, Jn., Beer Hackett, Dorset, 1629-32, AB, a/c, deed of gift (copy) (NEP), I, P5/1629/6, P5/1631/124, P5/1632/12
Jn., innholder, Maidenhead, Berks., 1680, AB, I, P1/B/535
Bawler, Wm., husb., Beer Hackett, Dorset, 1616, I, W, P5/1616/6
Bowles, Bole, Alice, widow, Bower C., 1560, W, P2/4Reg/58A
Alice, widow, Winterbourne G., 1683, I, W, P2/B/1014
Ann, widow, Ansty, 1842, W, Wr, P5/1842/10
Boles, Bart., husb., Chilmark, 1688, AB, I, W, P2/B/1094
Cath., widow, Idmiston, 1686, AB, I, P2/B/1071
Bowle, Chas., gent., Idmiston, 1704, I, W, P2/B/1239
Chris., yeo., Winsley, Bradford A., 1844, O, W, Wr, P2/1844/49
Bowle, Culpepper, sp., Boscombe, 1734, W, P2/B/1536
Edith, widow, Donhead St My., 1608, W, P2/8Reg/11A
Edith, gent.'s wife, Barford St Mart., 1683, W, P2/B/1013
Edmd., Gillingham, Dorset, 1687, I, P27/1/99
Booles, Edwd., freemason, Totterdale, Tisb., 1592, I, W, P2/B/136
Edwd., glover, Fovant, 1647, AB (2 - 2nd cancelled), I, P2/B/714
Edwd., woodman, Plaitford, 1853, W, Wr, P2/1853/3
Boles, Eleanor, widow, Gomeldon, Idmiston, [1694], W, P2/B/1157
Boles, Eliz., Chilmark, 1613, AB, P1/B/88
Bowle, Eliz., widow, Kintbury, Berks., 1723, cert (2), comm, L, W, P1/B/905, P1/7Reg/32

Eliz., widow, Sal., 1732, AB, I, P4/1732/4
Eliz., sp., W. Hanney, Berks., 1786, AB, ren, W, P1/B/1498, P1/14Reg/120
Eliz., widow, Plaitford, 1809, W, Wr, P2/1809/17
Geo., Tisb., 1574, AB, P2/5Reg/200A
Boles, Geo., Fovant, 1622, AB, P2/B/414
Geo., cordw., Chilmark, 1768, W, P2/B/1841
Giles, silk weaver, Ham, 1700, AB, I, P3/B/996
Boles, Helen, widow, Tisb., 1603, AB, note, P2/B/232
Hy., Tisb., [1593], note, P2/B/141
Hy., [Tisb.] (NBI), 1620, I, P1/B/147
Hy., gent., Burcombe, 1678, ren, W, P2/B/941
Hy., yeo., Winterbourne G., 1684, I, W, P2/B/1036
Hy., jun., mason, Fovant Stroud, 1685, AB, a/c, I, P2/B/1058, 1155
Bowle, Hy., yeo., Longcott, Shrivenham, Berks., 1704, I, W, P1/B/716
Hy., Burcombe, 1781, AB, P2/B/1985
Jas., Mere, 1575, I, W, P5/1575/8, P5/3Reg/64A
Jas., glover, Fovant, 1625, I, W, P2/B/458
Boles, Jas., Sherb., Dorset, 1728-29, AB, P5/1728/12, P5/16Reg/214B
Joan, widow, Fovant Stroud, 1683, I, W, P2/B/1020
Bole, Jn., Nether C., Dorset, 1602, AB, I, W, P5/1602/6, P5/7Reg/44C
Jn., Gomeldon, Idmiston, 1689, a/c (2), AB, I, P2/B/1111
Jn., sen., baker, Sal., 1699, W, P4/1698/5
Jn., clerk, Woodford, 1714, W, P5/1713/17, P5/15Reg/384A
Jn., baker, Hindon, 1746, W, P2/B/1651
Bowle, Jn., clerk, Idmiston, 1789, W, P2/B/2038
Jn., yeo., Plaitford, 1791, W, P2/B/2068
Jn., yeo., Ansty, 1835, AB, D, W, Wr, P5/1835/19
Judith, Gillingham, Dorset, 1837, AB, comm, W, Wr, P27/1/716
Leonard, Winterbourne G., 1720, W, P2/B/1394
Mgt., widow, Marl., 1686, comm, I, W, P1/B/582
Martha, widow, Winterbourne G., 1727, W, P2/B/1459
My., widow, Winterbourne G., 1685, I, W, P2/B/1050
My., widow, Gt. Durnford, 1735, AB, P9/51
My., sp., Crickl. St S., 1762, W, P3/B/1548
Matthew, Woodford, 1714, AB, P13/4/9
Maud, widow, Chilmark, 1595, AB, I, W, P2/B/162, P2/7Reg/150A
Nich., miller, Urchf., 1671, comm, I, W, P2/B/841
Rd., Pierston, Gillingham, Dorset, 1583, W, P27/2Reg/18A
Boles, Rd., Donhead, 1631, I, P2/B/547
Rd., yeo., Winterbourne G., 1664, AB, I, P1/B/402
Rd., tanner, Blewbury, Berks., 1674, I, W, P5/1674/16
Bowle, Rd., esquire, Idmiston, 1678, I, W, P2/B/942
Boll, Robt., Donhead St My., 1558, W, P2/3Reg/124B
Boulse, Robt., Norton B., 1574, W, P2/5Reg/190A
Rowland, S. Newton, 1570, W, P2/5Reg/107C
Ruth, Downton, 1763, W, P1/B/1350, P1/12Reg/65
Bowle, Sandys, widow, Idmiston, 1723, W, P1/B/903, P1/7Reg/31A
Simon, Stapleford, 1718, AB, P2/B/1372
Susanna, Winterbourne D., 1738, W, P7/134
Bolles, Thos., Peasemarsh, Gillingham, Dorset, 1571, W, P27/1Reg/25A
Thos., gent., Edington, 1632, AB, I, P2/B/556
Thos., sen., yeo., Gillingham, Dorset, 1687, I, W, P27/1/100
Thos., yeo., Gillingham, Dorset, 1708, I, W, P27/1/171
Thos., sen., turner, Maiden B., 1710, I, W, P2/B/1291
Thos., yeo., Hanging L., 1750, AB, ren, P1/B/1239
Bowle, Walter, husb., E. Knoyle, 1578, NW, P2/B/67
Boles, Walter, Tisb., 1602-03, AB, I, note, W, P2/B/219, 231
Wm., husb., Gillets, Gillingham, Dorset, 1551, W, P27/2Reg/5C
Bolle, Wm., husb., Tisb., 1552-53, I, W, P2/B/8, P2/2Reg/155B
Bole, Wm., husb., Bower C., 1554, W, P2/2Reg/182A

Wm., yeo., Gillingham, Dorset, 1566, W, P27/1Reg/17B
Bowle, Wm., husb., E. Knoyle, 1578, W, P2/5Reg/311B
Wm., Tisb., 1590, AB, I, P2/B/122
Wm., sen., Mere, 1596, AB, a/c, I, P5/1596/10, P5/6Reg/122A
Wm., Chilmark, 1612, T (unnamed children), P2/B/324
Wm., Barford, Downton, 1612, I, W, P2/B/329
Wm., innholder, Fisherton A., 1636, AB, a/c, I, P2/B/597
Boles, Wm., Upton, E. Knoyle, 1673, AB, I, P2/B/871
Boules *or* Bowly, Wm., haberdasher, Hankerton, 1678, I, W, P3/B/685
Wm., mason, Fovant, 1695, AB, I, P2/B/1168
Wm., sen., Winterbourne G., 1702, W, P2/B/1221
Wm., yeo., W. Hanney, Berks., 1711, I, W, P1/B/779, P1/5Reg/151
Wm., Lt. Woodford, 1713, AB, P5/1713/5
Wm., Lt. Woodford, 1717, AB, P13/4/12
Wm., Pewsey, 1723, AB, P1/B/894
Wm., Winterbourne G., 1731, comm, W, P2/B/1504
Wm., yeo., Winterbourne E., 1734, AB, W, P2/B/1539
Wm., maltster, Luckington, 1741, AB, W, P3/B/1398
Wm., clerk, Sal. (late of Church Oakley, Hants), 1760, W, P4/1760/9
Wm., yeo., Pickernels, Plaitford, 1798-1805, D, W, Wr, P1/B/1561, P1/15Reg/145B
Wm., gent., Alvediston, 1809, W, P2/1809/61
Bowle, Wm., Mere, 1827, AB, Wr, P5/1827/60
Wm., sen., yeo., Plaitford, 1839, W, Wr, P2/1839/32
Wm. *see also* Alice Extin
see also Reeks als B.
Bowley *see* Bowly
Bowlinge, Agnes, widow, Durley, Burbage, 1595, AB, I, W, P5/1595/4, P5/6Reg/94
Geo., Durley, Burbage, 1587, AB, I, W, P5/1587/9, P5/4Reg/153A
Bowlings, Joan, widow, Marl., 1615, I, W, P1/B/130
Jn., yeo., Durley, Burbage, 1597, I, T, W, P5/1596/9, P5/6Reg/146A
Bowlin, Jn., Horningsham, 1599, AB, I, W, P5/1599/3, P5/6Reg/234C
Bowlte *see* Bolt
Bowlter, Bowlters *see* Bolter
Bowlton *see* Bolton
Bowly, Hugh, weaver, Sal., 1708, I, W, P4/1708/5
Oliver, sen., labourer, Crudwell, 1707, I, W, P3/B/1065
Wm., gent., Woodford, 1711, AB, P13/4/3
Bowley, Wm., Somerford K., 1797, AB, P3/B/1756
see also Boules *or* B.
Bowmaker, Dan., Biddestone, 1773, AB, P1/B/1421
Bowman, Ann, widow, Church St., Calne, 1804, req, W, P26/1246
Benj., Calne, 1701, AB, I, P26/483
Chris., yeo., Chelworth, Crickl. St S., 1682, I, W, P3/B/757
Edwd., jun., sergemaker, Devizes, 1699, AB, ren, P1/B/682
Jas., linen draper, Devizes, 1830, I (just note of value of estate), W, Wr, P1/1830/9
Jas., linen draper, Devizes, 1851, AB, comm, court proceeding, W, Wr, P1/1851/2
Jn., sen., butcher, Calne, 1775, W, P26/1074
Jn., Devizes, 1806, AB, Wr, P1/1806/11
Jn., Devizes, 1822, AB, comm, P1/1822/22
Rd., vicar of Potterne and prebend of Uffculme, Pott., 1692, W (holograph), P1/B/612
Rd., yeo., Edington, 1741, W, P2/B/1599
Steph., gent., Compton C., 1677, W, P1/B/515
Bown *see* Bowne
Bownde *see* Bound
Bowne, Bawnse, Alice, widow, Winterbourne G., 1640, I, W, P2/B/657
Eliz., Semley, 1609, AB, I, W, P2/B/290, P2/8Reg/64
Boon, Eliz., sp., Sal., 1846, AB, note, Wr, P1/1846/5
Bowns, Geo., innholder, E. Harnham, Britford, 1851, W, Wr, P24/1400
Jas., yeo., Whitfield, Lillington, Dorset, 1648, AB, comm, I, ren, P5/1648/2, P5/14Reg/107B
Baune, Jane, widow, Chipp., 1677, AB, I, P3/B/677

Joan, widow, Semley, 1559, W, P2/3Reg/152A
Jn., Semley, 1559, W, P2/3Reg/151C
Bowen, Jn., Sal., 1611, AB, P4/1611/9
Bawne, Jn., carp., Chipp., 1685, AB, I, P3/B/808
Boone, Jn., maltster, Hungerford, Berks., 1714, W, P5/1714/4, P5/15Reg/393C
Bown, Jn., Motc., Dorset, 1744, W, P27/1/376, P27/3Reg/34
Bown, Jn., labourer, Redlynch, Downton, 1806, W, P2/1806/9
Bowen, My., widow, Poole St Jas. and St Paul, Dorset, 1692, I (exhibited in Archdeaconry of Sarum - Poole in peculiar of Great Canford, diocese of Bristol), P2/B/1146
Bawne, My., widow, Chipp., 1721, AB, P3/B/1187
Bown, My., widow, Waltham St Lawr., Berks., 1744, W, P1/B/1173, P1/9Reg/353
Peter, Sedgehill, 1673, AB, I, P2/B/867
Peter, gent., Sal., 1793, W, P4/1793/4
Philip, sen., yeo., Motc., Dorset, 1680, I, W, P27/1/59
Bown, Philip, yeo., Motc., Dorset, [1708], W, P27/1/172
Boon, Rd., Fordington, Dorset, 1567, W, P5/2Reg/16B
Thos., yeo., Semley, 1625, comm, I, W, P1/B/201
Bawne, Thos., carp., Chipp., 1681, comm, I, W, P3/B/736
Bawne, Thos., weaver, Chipp., 1685, I, W, P3/B/809
Bowen, Thos., vict., Melk., 1799, comm, W, P2/B/2143
Bownes, Thos., Berwick St Jas., [1825], W (notes re legacies), Wr (wanting), P1/1826/38
Walter, husb., Dinton, 1629, deed of gift, P2/B/472
Wm., Alvediston, 1558, AB, P2/3Reg/100C
Wm., Semley, 1559, W, P2/4Reg/15B
Boone, Wm., Fordington, Dorset, 1582, AB, I, W, P15/189, P5/4Reg/28C
Bawnse, Wm., Winterbourne G., 1639, AB, I, P2/B/641
Wm., tailor, Maiden B., 1664, AB, I, P2/B/757
Wm., wheelwright, Gt. Amesb., 1688, I, W, P2/B/1100
Bawn, Wm., Chipp., 1744, AB, P1/B/1163
Bowren, Bowring *see* Bowering
Bowsher *see* Boucher
Bowyer, Agnes, widow, Hurst, Berks., 1609, I, W, P5/1609/7, P5/8Reg/153A
Alice, Upton S., 1547, W, P2/2Reg/47A
And., husb., Upton S., 1545, W (NEP), P2/1Reg/60B
Ann, widow, Calne, 1638, AB, I, P26/71
Hy., yeo., Winkfield, Berks., 1704, comm, I, W, P1/B/721
Hy., yeo., Winkfield, Berks., 1756, W, P1/B/1294, P1/11Reg/212
Jas., yeo., Bradford A., 1729, W, P2/B/1473
Jn., Britford, 1638, AB, P24/294
Jn., sen., S. Wraxall, 1734, AB, I, P2/B/1529
Jn., yeo., Frankleigh, Bradford A., 1821, W, Wr, P2/1821/36
My., widow, Westb. L., 1633, I, W, P25/1633/2
Matthew, yeo., Dilton M., Westb., 1639, AB, a/c, I (detailed), P25/1639/13
Rd., blacksmith, Calne, 1611, AB, I, W, P26/2
Rd., [cutler], Newbury, Berks., 1614, I, W, P1/B/114
Sarah, widow, Lyme R., Dorset, 1854, D, O, W, Wr, P16/454
Thos., husb., Chipp., 1668, AB, I, NW, P3/B/533
see also Hoare/Hore/Whore als B.
Box, Alice, widow, Sutton B., [1571], W (NEP), P1/1Reg/131C
Ann, widow [and weaver], Bradford A., 1593, I, W, P2/B/142
Ann, widow, Fiddington Farm, W. Lavington, 1822, W, Wr, P2/1822/73
Ann, sp., Reading, Berks., 1826, AB, comm, Wr, P1/1826/23
Cath., widow, Sutton, 1560, W, P1/2Reg/114C
Chas., Melk., 1802, AB, comm, Wr, P2/1802/2
Chas., gent., Westport St My., 1846, aff, D, W, Wr, P3/1846/31
Edwd., husb., Sutton B., 1609, W, P3/B/49
Edwd., husb., Sutton B., 1618, I, W, P3/B/162
Edwd., yeo., Sutton B., 1684, AB, I, P3/B/796
Eliz., widow, Seagry, 1670, AB, I, P3/B/570
Faith, widow, Sutton B., 1636, I, W, P3/B/372

Frances, widow, Wokm., Berks., 1764, W, P5/1764/3
Grace, widow, Sutton B., 1745, W, P3/B/1428
Hy., yeo., Corsham, 1753-58, W, P29/B/51, P29/2Reg/90
Isabel, widow, Sutton B., [1619], I, W (NEP), P3/B/175
Joan, widow, Sutton B., 1662, I, W, P3/B/479
Jn., husb., Sutton B., [1570], W, P1/1Reg/131B
Jn., husb., Chr. M., 1634, I, W, P3/B/358
Jn., husb., Chr. M., 1648, AB, I, ren, P1/B/341
Jn., sen., carp., Sutton B., 1667, AB, I, W, P3/B/526
Jn., Melk., 1769-70, AB (2), comm, P2/B/1865
Jn., yeo., Fiddington Farm, W. Lavington, 1805, W, Wr, P1/1805/5
Jos., yeo., Malm., 1712, I, NW, P3/B/1106
Jos., Thornhill Farm, Westport St My., 1761, W, P3/B/1539
Margery, widow, Rodbourne, Malm., 1605, I, W, P1/B/38
Philip, blacksmith, Chr. M., 1632, I, W, P3/B/343
Rd., Sutton B., [1570], W, P1/1Reg/122B
Rd., weaver, Seagry, 1637, I, W, P3/B/387
Rd., gent., Chipp., 1853, AB, D, O, W, Wr, P3/1853/9
Robt., Bradford A., 1560, W, P2/4Reg/36D
Robt., Sutton B., 1624, AB, a/c, I, ren, P3/B/249
Robt., yeo., Holt, Bradford A., 1722, I, W, P2/B/1410
Thos., yeo., Enford, 1681, W, P2/B/988
Thos., wheelwright, Wilsford nr Pewsey, 1795, W, P2/B/2105
Walter, carp., Calne, 1638, I, W, P26/62
Wm., Monkton F., 1572, W, P2/5Reg/155C
Wm., Cumberwell, Bradford A., 1583, AB, W, P2/6Reg/79A
Wm., weaver, Seagry, [1609], W (NEP), P3/B/33
Boxwell, Hannah, widow, Swindon, 1751, W, P3/B/1467
Julian, widow, Crickl. St My., 1614, NW, P3/B/113
Wm., yeo. *or* innholder, Swindon, 1705, I, W, P3/B/1045
Boy *see* Booy
Boyce, Boyse, Agnes, widow, no abode stated, 1624, AB, I, NW, P2/B/448
Boyes, Alice, widow, Chitterne St My., 1625, I, W, P2/B/457
Ann, widow, Lt. Coxwell, Gt. Faringdon, Berks., 1710, I, W, P5/1710/17, P5/15Reg/176
Benj., yeo., Lt. Coxwell, Gt. Faringdon, Berks., 1688, AB, I, P5/1688/11
Boyes, Eliz., widow, Tilsh., 1560, W, P2/4Reg/30C
Boys, Eliz. Ann, sp., Sherb., Dorset, 1852, comm, W, Wr, P5/1852/11
Boyse, Florence, widow, Trowb., 1615, I, W, P22/2/17
Geo., sen., Warfield, Berks., 1744, AB, P1/B/1176
Boyes, Giles, yeo., Colston, Chards., Devon, 1589, AB, I, P5/1590/10, P5/5Reg/93A
Boyse, Harry, husb., Chitterne St My., 1603, I, W, P2/B/235
Boys, Joanna, Sherb., Dorset, 1732, W, P5/1731/9
Boys, Jn., Sherb., Dorset, 1724, W, P5/1724/12, P5/16Reg/103B
Boyes, Jn., Sherb., Dorset, 1772, AB, comm, P5/1772/2, P5/17Reg/40A
Boyse, Jos., Warm., 1631, AB, I (2), ren, P2/B/537
Boyse, My., widow, Malm., 1680, comm, W, P1/B/533
Boyse, Rd., innholder, Trowb., 1613, I, W, P22/2/13
Boyes, Robt., Shitterton, Bere R., Dorset, 1615, I, W, P5/1614/11, P5/9Reg/152B
Boys, Sampson, jun., Sherb., Dorset, 1793, AB, comm, P5/1793/2, P5/18Reg/188A
Boys, Sampson, sen., surgeon, Sherb., Dorset, 1793, comm, W, P5/1793/3, P5/18Reg/188B
Boyse, Simon, innholder and yeo., Malm., 1677, comm, I, W, P1/B/514
Timothy, physician, Wantage, Berks., 1721, W, P23/406
Boyse, Wm., Chitterne, 1619, I, NW, P2/B/395
see also Wake form. B.
Boyd, Geo., Steeple A., 1687, AB, I, P2/B/1075
Robt., sergemaker, Steeple A., 1730, W, P2/B/1480
Roger, Wingfield, 1662, AB, comm, P2/B/740
Sarah, widow, Chipp., 1741, W, P1/B/1145, P1/9Reg/155A
Boyer, Asenath, Bradford A., 1777, AB, P2/B/1949
Chris., bach. and husb., Winkfield, Berks., 1714, I, W, P1/B/795, P1/5Reg/361

Edwd., husb., Easthampstead, Berks., 1720, W, P1/B/861, P1/6Reg/310A
Jn., yeo., Easthampstead, Berks., 1692, I, W, P1/B/629
Boyes *see* Boyce
Boyette, Jn., tanner, Gillingham, Dorset, 1580, W, P27/2Reg/4A
Boyland, My., widow, N. Mapperton, Dorset, 1669, W, P17/86
Boylon, Thos., Norrington, Alvediston, 1566, W, P2/4Reg/236B
Thos., yeo., Mythe, Mapperton, Dorset, 1770, W, P5/1770/8, P5/17Reg/18B
Boyle, Giles, Enmore Grn, Motc., Dorset, 1671, AB, comm, I, P5/1671/15
Boylon *see* Boyland
Boys, Boyse *see* Boyce
Boyte, Jn., Bere R., Dorset, 1596, AB, I, P5/1596/12, P5/6Reg/148C
Boyter, And., clothw., Sal., 1740, W, P4/1740/15
And., jun., alehouse keeper, Sal., 1824, AB, LA, P4/1824/8
Edwd., Fonthill G., 1766, W, P2/B/1820
Brabam, Isaac, Baverstock, 1750, AB, P2/B/1683
Brabant, Cath., Compton C., 1558, AB, P2/3Reg/128D
Gabriel, Chr. M., 1724, AB, P3/B/1242
Brabin, Jas., tailor, Winterbourne M., 1724, I, W, P3/B/1225
Brabance, Rd., Calne, 1608, W, P5/1608/2, P5/8Reg/131A
Rd., Shaw, Melk., 1734, AB, comm, P2/B/1540
Roger, butcher, Calne, 1680, AB, comm, I, P26/268
Thos., Dauntsey, 1754, AB, P3/B/1490
see also Nowell als B.
Brace, Jane, widow, Sherston, 1745, W, Wr, P3/B/1429
Wm., Wokm., Berks., 1846, note, W, Wr, P5/1846/20
Bracefield, Joyce, Downton, 1730, AB, I, P1/B/987
Bracher, Alice, widow, Tisb., [1611], NW (proved by witnesses but not in common form), P2/B/314
Ann, widow, Wallmead, Tisb., 1718, W, P2/B/1373
Ann, Sal., 1740, AB, Wr, P4/1740/18
Ann, widow, Shrewton, 1756, AB, P2/B/1726
Ann, widow, Sutton M., 1797, AB, P2/B/2116
Ann, sp., Chicksgrove, Tisb., 1807, AB, comm, Wr, P2/1807/51
Betty, widow, Tisb., 1808, W, Wr, P1/1808/28
Charlotte, sp., Bower C., 1848, AB, Wr, P1/1848/7
Dan., bach., Fovant, 1844, AB, Wr, P2/1844/60
Diana, sp., Wardour, Tisb., 1857, AB, aff, Wr, P2/1857/23
Edwd., Semley, 1713, AB, I, P2/B/1324
Edwd., yeo., Chicksgrove, Tisb., 1715, W, P2/B/1342
Edwd., yeo., Tisb., 1740, W, P2/B/1585
Edwd., gent., Chicksgrove, Tisb., 1756, W, P2/B/1725
Edwd., yeo., Semley, 1780, W, P2/B/1974
Edwd., gent., Wallmead, Tisb., 1785-87, AB, comm, ren, req, W, P2/B/2009
Edwd., gent., Sutton M., 1792, W, P2/B/2074
Edwd., gent., Bathampton, Steeple L., 1796, W, P2/B/2111
Edwd., Chicksgrove, Tisb., 1804, AB, P1/1804/132
Edwd., farmer, Chicksgrove, Tisb., 1815, W, Wr, P2/1815/46
Edwd., gent., Place Farm, Tisb., 1819, W, Wr, P2/1819/48
Edwd., gent., Place Farm, Tisb., 1836, W, Wr, P2/1836/67
Edwd., Sal., 1847, AB, note, Wr, P4/1847/12
Edwd., Sal., 1851, AB, Wr, P4/1851/11
Edwd. Jukes, Sutton M., 1823, AB, P2/1823/14
Eliz., widow, Chicksgrove, Tisb., 1773, W, P2/B/1895
Eliz., widow, Sal., 1802, W, P4/1802/4
Eliz., widow, Tisb., 1833, W, Wr, P2/1833/49
Geo., Bower C., 1846, AB, Wr, P2/1846/47
Hy., Sutton M., 1686, I, W, P2/B/1114
Hy., Wylye, 1812, AB, Wr, P2/1812/26
Jas., Semley, 1739, AB, P2/B/1576
Jas., gent., Tisb., 1839, W, Wr, P1/1839/28
Jane, widow, Bower C., 1837, W, Wr, P2/1837/34

Joan, widow, Sutton M., [1690], W, P2/B/1108
Jn., yeo., Tisb., 1642, I, W, P2/B/681
Jn., yeo., Duck St., Tisb., 1686, I, NW, P1/B/1565
Jn., E. Hatch, Tisb., 1714, AB, I, P1/B/792
Jn., Duck St., Tisb., 1721, I, W, P2/B/1400
Jn., Semley, 1722, W, P2/B/1407
Jn., Sal., 1738, AB, P1/B/1105
Jn., sen., Hindon, 1765, W, P2/B/1809
Breashur, Jn., yeo., Elmdown, Rams., 1785, W, P5/1785/3, P5/18Reg/25B
Jn., gent., Hatch, Tisb., 1793, AB, W, P2/B/2082
Jn., yeo., Sedgehill, 1803, W, P2/1803/12
Jn., Semley, 1819, AB, Wr, P2/1819/32
Jn., carp., Odstock, 1824, AB, W, Wr, P2/1824/56
Jn., gent., Duck St., Tisb., 1825, comm, W, Wr, P2/1825/55
Jn., yeo., Semley, 1828, W, P2/1828/35
Brasher, Jn., clothier, Ditchampton, Wilton, 1836, D, W, P2/1836/3
Jn., Semley, 1837, AB, comm, ren, Wr, P2/1837/89
Lawr., Tisb., [1594], AB, W, P2/B/2154
Lawr., sen., farrier, Tisb., 1686, comm, I, ren, NW, P1/B/587
Lawr., Tisb., 1708, W, P2/B/1273
Martha, widow, Hazeldon, Tisb., 1718, W (NEP), P30/8
Martha, Tisb., 1729, AB, P1/B/975
Martha, widow, Bourton, Gillingham, Dorset, 1765, W, P27/1/448, P27/3Reg/120
My., widow, Tisb., 1697, I, W, P2/B/1182
My., widow, Hindon, 1737, W, P2/B/1561
My., widow, Sutton M., 1793, W, P2/B/2080
My., sp., Fovant, 1844, W, Wr, P2/1844/30
My. Ann, widow, Wardour, Tisb., 1844, W, Wr, P2/1844/10
Matthew, wheelwright, Tisb., 1739, AB, I, P2/B/1581
Braysher, Rd., Quidh., 1771, W, P2/B/1875
Robt., blacksmith, Tisb., 1578, I, T, W, P2/B/62, P2/5Reg/300A
Sam., blacksmith, Tisb., 1642, AB, a/c (3 - 2 badly damaged, 3rd list of funeral expenses), P2/B/679
Sam., yeo., Tisb., 1714, I, W, P1/B/788, P1/5Reg/344
Sam., maltster, Hindon, E. Knoyle, 1734, W, P2/B/1538
Sam., sen., farrier, Tisb., 1736-37, a/c, I, W, P2/B/1550
Sam., yeo., Tisb., 1740, AB, ren, W, P2/B/1589
Sam., yeo., Sutton M., 1754, W, P2/B/1714
Sam., Tisb., 1757, W, P2/B/1733
Sam., currier, Hindon, 1760, W, P2/B/1762
Sam., gent., Sutton M., 1768, W, P2/B/1850
Sam., yeo., Duck St., Tisb., 1780, W, P2/B/1975
Sam., farmer, Semley, 1788, W, P2/B/2034
Sam., Sutton M., 1796, AB, P2/B/2107
Sam., gent., Chicksgrove, Tisb., 1810, W, P2/1810/10
Brasher, Sam., Ditchampton, Wilton, 1811, AB, Wr, P1/1811/43
Sam., Fovant, 1835, AB, P2/1835/9
Sarah, sp., Sal., 1849, D, W, Wr, P4/1849/6
Thos., husb., Semley, 1711-12, AB, W, P1/B/775, P2/B/1313, P1/5Reg/217
Thos., Semley, 1729, AB, P2/B/1475
Brasher, Thos., carp., S. Burcombe, 1735, W, P2/B/1546
Thos., Wanb., 1752, AB, P3/B/1478
Thos., yeo., Semley, 1781, W, P2/B/1978
Thos., bach., Semley, 1789, AB, ren, P2/B/2042
Thos., Sal., 1797, AB, P4/1797/7
Brasher, Wm., Newton T., 1636, AB, I, P2/B/590, P2/9Reg/102B
Bratcher, Wm., yeo., Biddestone, 1717, I, W, P3/B/1146
Wm., Chicksgrove, Tisb., 1724, AB, P2/B/1434
Wm., yeo., Sutton M., 1765, W, P2/B/1816
Wm., bach., Sutton M., 1794, AB, P2/B/2097
Wm., Sal., 1800, AB, label, note, W, P4/1800/6

Wm., Bower C., 1816, AB, Wr, P2/1816/46
Wm., gent., Sutton M., 1817, W, Wr, P2/1817/17
Wm., gent., Fovant, 1839, W, Wr, P1/1839/33
Wm., gent., Bishopstone S., 1839, comm, W, Wr, P2/1839/38
see also Frith als B.
Brackley, Edwd., chapman, Newbury, Berks., 1729, W, P1/B/946, P1/7Reg/211
Jn., clerk, Wrou., 1716, W, P1/B/821, P1/6Reg/64
Brackstone, Aaron, labourer, Newtown, Rams., 1740, W, Wr, P5/1740/6
Ann, widow, Rams., 1690, AB, comm, I, P5/1689/6
Ann, widow, Whitep., 1720, I, W, P1/B/854, P1/6Reg/227B
Eliz., widow, Newtown, Rams., 1719, W, P5/1719/5, P5/16Reg/23C
Brackstone, Giles, sen., husb., Rams., 1671, I, W, P5/1671/8
Giles, sen., husb., Rams., 1713, W, P5/1713/8, P5/15Reg/364C
Giles, labourer, Rams., 1715, W, P5/15Reg/394A
Giles, yeo., Rams., 1790, W, P5/1790/4, P5/18Reg/148
Brackstone, Hester, Froxfield, 1821, AB, Wr, P3/1821/11
Jeremiah, hot presser, Devizes, 1723, I, W, P1/B/885, P1/6Reg/431A
Jn., tanner, Sal. St Mart., 1623, I, NW, P4/1623/5
Jn., husb., Rams., 1698, AB, I, P5/1698/8
Jn., Rams., 1708, I, W, P5/1708/9, P5/15Reg/75A
Jn., Fisherton A., 1711, AB, P1/B/752
Jonathan, husb., Rams., 1702, comm, I, W, P5/1702/9
Bragstone, My., Sherb., Dorset, 1719, AB, P5/1719/11
Brackstone, My., labourer's wife, Rams., 1735, AB, P5/1735/7
My., widow, Rams., 1751, W, P5/1751/5
My., sp., Marl. (d. Rams.), 1763, AB, W (NEP), P5/1763/1
Brackstone, My., widow, Easton, 1785, W, P3/B/1698
Moses, labourer, Rams., 1712, W, P5/1712/11, P5/15Reg/307B
Moses, labourer, Rams., 1745, AB, I, P5/1745/2
Rd., Sal. St Edmd., 1628, AB, P4/1627/17
Brackstone, Rd., husb., Rams., 1690, AB, I, P5/1690/6
Rd., vict., Sherb., Dorset, 1711, I, W, P5/1711/10, P5/15Reg/228
Brackstone, Rd., yeo., Wokm., Berks., 1715, I, W, P5/1715/7, P5/15Reg/317B
Rd., labourer, Rams., 1731, W, P5/1731/8
Rd., Rams., 1745, W, P5/1745/3
Brackstone, Rd., Rams., 1755, AB, P5/1755/5
Brackstone, Thos., butcher, Whitep., 1640, I, W, P2/B/655
Thos., husb., Warm., 1664, AB, I, P1/B/411
Brackstone, Thos., Rams., 1671, AB, P5/1671/9
Brackstone, Wm., ironmonger, Devizes, 1816, W, Wr, P1/1816/7
see also Branston *or* B.
Bradbury, Brodbury, Cicely, widow, Dauntsey, 1663, AB, comm, I, P1/B/390
Clementina, widow, Chipp., 1786, W, P3/B/1705
Bradbury als Segry, Dan., butcher, Chipp., 1737, AB, I, P3/B/1357
Bradbery, Eliz., widow, Hurst, Berks., 1573, W, P5/3Reg/14C
Jas. Ambrose, draper, Chipp., 1851, W, Wr, P3/1851/47
Bradbery, Oliver, Sindlesham, Hurst, Berks., 1569, W, P5/2Reg/54C
Unite, carp., Westport St My., 1631, I, W, P3/B/338
Bradbury *or* (alias ?) Zachary, Wm., butcher, Chipp., 1764, W, P3/B/1561
Zachariah, sergemaker, Charlcote, Bremhill, 1730, I, W, P3/B/1294
see also Innot als B.; Seagry als B.
Bradden, Braddon, Edwd., carp., Chaddenwick, Mere, 1604-05, W, P5/1604/3, P5/8Reg/38C
Braddon, Jn., Stourton, 1649, AB, I, P1/B/354
Braden, Jn., sen., husb., Gasper, Stourton, 1680, AB, I, ren, P2/B/959
Jn., widower, Stourton, 1729-33, AB (2), P2/B/1476, 1518
Jn., yeo., Gasper, Stourton, 1761, AB, comm, ren, W, P2/B/1775
Bradden *or* Bradder, Steph., Stourton, 1590, I, T, P2/B/115
Braden, Thos., sen., Gillingham, Dorset, 1709, AB, P27/1/176
Braden, Thos., yeo., Milton upon Stour, Gillingham, Dorset, 1724, I, W, P27/1/264
Bradin, Thos., innholder, Warm., 1735, W, P1/B/1056, P1/8Reg/113

Valentine, cordw., Stourton, [1690], W, P2/B/1127
Bradfield, Eliz., sp., Colerne (form. of Littleton Drew), 1855, aff, L, O, W, Wr, P3/1855/1
Jas., Sal., 1783, AB, P1/B/1477
Jas., carp., Derry Hill, Pewsham, 1827, W, Wr, P5/1827/61
Bradfield *or* Bratfield, Jane, widow, Cherhill, 1750, AB, W, P26/901
Jane, sp., Devizes, 1836, AB, O, P1/1836/7
Brodfield, Jn., husb., Cherhill, 1581, AB, I, W, P5/1581/1, P5/4Reg/25B
Jn., sen., miller, Milton, Berks., 1759, W, P1/B/1317, P1/11Reg/397
Jn., carp., Yatesbury, 1841, comm, W, Wr, P3/1841/17
Jos., Pott., 1768, AB, P1/B/1386
Rd., Bromham, 1726, AB, I, P3/B/1247
Rd., gardener, Pewsham Forest, 1798, W, P5/1798/1, P5/18Reg/268B
Bradfield *or* Bratfield, Robt., yeo., Cherhill, 1750, AB (2), certified burial entry (d. Jul 1740), D, I, W, P26/899
Thos., Ashton G., Codf. St P., 1621-22, AB, a/c, I, P2/B/416
Thos., gardener, Pewsham, 1832, W, Wr, P3/1832/22
Wm., yeo., Yatesbury, 1696, I, W, P3/B/950
Wm., yeo., Manningford A., 1730, W, P3/B/1295
Wm., carp. and wheelwright, Pewsham, 1818, W, Wr, P5/1818/39
Bradford, Agnes, widow, Hurst, Berks., 1617-19, I, W, P5/1617/4, P5/10Reg/38A
Bradford als Butler, Alice, widow, Crickl. St S., 1624, I, W, P3/B/250
And., yeo., Upland, Wokm., Berks., 1571, W, P5/2Reg/104A
Ann, widow, Sal., 1667, I, W, P4/1667/4
Anth., yeo., Rams., 1786, W, P5/1786/1, P5/18Reg/51
Chris., carp., Beam., Dorset, 1631, AB, I, P5/1631/12, P5/12Reg/17B
Cornelius, carp., Wrou., 1713, I, W, P3/B/1118
Cornelius, yeo., Can Court, Lydiard T., 1734, W, P3/B/1339
Eliz., widow, Bradford A., 1720, comm, W, P2/B/1392
Jn., [Hurst, Berks.] (NBI), 1613, comm, P1/B/86
Jn., Sal. St Mart., 1691, I, W, P4/1691/2
Jn., innholder, Bradford A., 1718, comm, W, P2/B/1367
Jn., carp., Elcombe, Wrou., 1722, I, W, P3/B/1207
Mgt., widow, Bere R., Dorset, 1686, I, W, P5/1686/8
My., Lydiard T., 1759, W, P1/B/1329, P1/11Reg/433B
Nathaniel, Lyme R., Dorset, 1738, AB, I, Wr, P5/1738/5
Nich., Sutton Poyntz, Dorset, 1585, AB, P5/1585/12, P5/4Reg/122A
Oliver, Hurst, Berks., 1554, W, P5/20Reg/129
Rd., Sutton Poyntz, Dorset, 1585, AB, P5/1585/13, P5/4Reg/122B
Rd., Lydiard T., 1769, AB, P3/B/1603
Rd., gent., Bushton, Clyffe P., 1800, W, Wr, P3/1800/63
Rd., gent., Midgehall, Lydiard T., 1811, comm, W, Wr, P1/1811/142
Broadford, Thos., Sutton Poyntz, Dorset, 1639, AB, I, P5/1639/8, P5/13Reg/161A
Wm., Hurst, Berks., 1575, AB, I, T, P5/1575/9, P5/3Reg/62A
Wm., Hurst, Berks., 1579, AB, T (children: Susan & Eliz. B.), P5/1579/10, P5/3Reg/139E
Wm., yeo., Hurst, Berks., 1585, a/c, I, T, W, P5/1585/16, P5/4Reg/115C
Wm., clerk, Turners Puddle, Dorset, 1686, AB, I, P5/1686/7
Bradin *see* Bradden
Bradley, Clement, Ogbourne St And., 1570, W, P5/2Reg/72C
Dan., mariner, Wilton (d. in the E. Indies), 1807, W, Wr, P2/1807/10
Edwd., Wokm., Berks., 1671, AB, I, P5/1671/11
Eliz., widow, Donhead St My., 1620, I, W, P2/B/405
Eliz., widow, Sal. The Close, 1817, Wr (original AB delivered to PCC following monition), P5/1817/4
Geo., Sutton C., Berks., 1735, AB, P1/B/1042
Jn., weaver, Highw., 1588, AB, I, P10/1588/1, P5/5Reg/8B
Michael, yeo., Leigh, Yetm., Dorset, 1856, aff, comm, W, Wr, P19/263
Steph., Leigh, Yetm., Dorset, 1807, AB, P19/212
Thos., Pickwick, Corsham, 1628, W, P29/1Reg/115A
Thos., husb., Hannington, 1733, W, P3/B/1324
Wm., tailor, Broad B., Highw., 1745, W, P10/1745/3
Bradock, Jn., mariner, Lyme R., Dorset, 1642, AB, comm, I, P5/1642/6, P5/14Reg/56B
Bradshaw, Alice, widow, Long Burton, Dorset, 1676, comm, I, W, P5/1676/7

Edwd., yeo., Crickl. St S., 1639, I, W, P3/B/419
Jn., New Windsor, Berks., 1635, AB, P1/B/253
Rd., Ludg., 1601, AB, P2/B/211
Robt., clerk, Gt. Chalfield, 1629, I, W, P1/B/220
Susanna, sp., Compton B., 1668, AB, I, P3/B/534
Susanna, widow, Imber, 1830, AB, comm, Wr, P2/1830/25
Wm., Imber, 1828, AB, O, P2/1828/37
Bradway *see* Broadway
Brady, Eliz., wife, Bradford A., 1810, W, Wr, P2/1810/32
Jn., Gillingham, Dorset, late 16th/early 17th C., I (previously filed with P27/1/63, (Jn. B., d. 1682) but does not relate to him), P27/1/64
Jn., Huntingford, Gillingham, Dorset, 1682, I, P27/1/63
Braffield, Jn., Redlynch, Downton, 1593, I, T, W, P2/B/144
Bragge, Chas., clerk, Oborne, Dorset, 1639, I, W, P5/1639/9, P5/13Reg/177B
Eliz., widow, Lyme R., Dorset, 1751, O, W, P16/307
Jn., Chards., Devon, 1746, AB, P5/1746/7
Matthew, sen., gent., Lyme R., Dorset, 1667, I, W, P16/3
Robt., mercer, Lyme R., Dorset, 1736, comm, W, P5/1736/5
Walter, Holnest, Dorset, 1588, AB, I, P5/1588/4, P5/5Reg/10B
Wm., yeo., Ford, Laverstock, 1669, AB, a/c, I, P2/B/817
Bragstone *see* Brackstone
Braine, Alice, widow, Malm., 1706, I, W, P3/B/1057
Bart., husb., Latton, 1637, I, W, P3/B/388
Edwd., yeo., Charlton nr Malm., 1730, W, P3/B/1296
Eliz., widow, Charlton nr Malm., 1670, AB, I, P3/B/571
Geo., gent., Malm., 1693, AB, comm, I, ren, P3/B/902
Hy., Latton, 1701, AB, I, P3/B/1007
Hugh, husb., Calcutt, Crickl. St S., 1616, AB, a/c, comm, I (2 - 1 a copy), O, Wr, P3/B/136
Joan, widow, Latton, 1685, I, W, P3/B/817
Jn., Ogbourne St Geo., 1571, W, P5/2Reg/102B
Jn., Ogbourne St Geo., 1573, W, P5/3Reg/31A
Robt., Charlton nr Malm., 1623, AB, P3/B/232
Robt., mercer, Mere, 1662, I, W, P5/1662/6
Robt., yeo., Greenhill Farm, Wootton B., 1779, W, P1/B/1451, P1/13Reg/245
Sam., yeo., Charlton nr Malm., 1670, I, W, P3/B/572
Thos., Latton, [c1600?], W (NEP), P3/1Reg/48A
Thos., Chelworth, Crickl. St S., 1668, I, W, P3/B/535
Thos., mason, Latton, 1678, I, W, P3/B/693
Wm., Wootton B., [1581], W (NEP), P3/1Reg/8B
Wm., Poulton, [1606], W (NEP), P3/2Reg/7
Wm., butcher, Ashton K., 1773, W, P3/B/1625
Braithwaite *see* Brathwaite
Brake, Chas., yeo., Enmore Grn, Motc., Dorset, 1828, comm, W, P19/240
Chas., yeo., Leigh, Yetm., Dorset, 1851, comm, W, Wr, P19/259
David, yeo., Enmore Grn, Motc., Dorset, 1783, W, P19/183
Jn., Enmore Grn, Motc., Dorset, 1773, AB, O, P19/172, P5/17Reg/74B
My., widow, Enmore Grn, Motc., Dorset, 1786, W, P19/186
Susanna, sp., Enmore Grn, Motc., Dorset, 1845, aff, O, W, Wr, P19/252
Brambach, Peter, Castleton, Dorset, 1596, AB, I, P5/1596/7, P5/6Reg/124B
Bramble, Edith, sp., Chipp., 1829, W, Wr, P1/1829/101
Eliz., widow, Lacock, 1847, AB, Wr, P3/1847/28
Geo., wheelwright, Chipp., 1830, comm, W, Wr, P3/1830/19
Jas., miller, Norton B., 1764, W, P2/B/1802
Bremble, My., widow, Sal., 1663, I, W, P1/B/388
My., widow, Chipp., 1849, AB, O, Wr, P3/1849/11
Rd., miller, Preshute, 1680, AB, ren, P1/B/527
Robt., carp., Chipp., 1808, W, Wr, P1/1808/81
Sarah, sp., Chipp., 1827, W, Wr, P3/1827/36
Bremble, Thos., Corsham, 1593, W, P29/1Reg/38B
Bremble, Thos., Winterborne K., Dorset, 1683, I, NW, P5/1683/1

Bremble, Wm., sen., Mere, 1597, AB, I, P5/1597/3, P5/6Reg/191A
Wm., miller, Norton B., 1706, I, W, P2/B/1249
Wm., Warm., 1797, AB, P2/B/2131
Wm., innkeeper, Chiseldon, 1856, aff, comm, W, Wr, P3/1856/21
see also Bromley
Bramham *see* Bromham
Bramley, Bramly *see* Bromley
Brampton, Jn., Broad C., 1541, I, W (NEP), P30/13
Branch, Edwd., Uffc., Devon, 1641, AB, I, P5/1641/11, P5/14Reg/33E
Brandis, Ann, widow, Wylye, 1806, W, P2/1806/25
Caroline, sp., Sherrington, 1857, AB, aff, D, W, Wr, P2/1857/52
Chris., householder, Wylye, 1853, D, W, Wr, P2/1853/34
Branker *see* Brunker
Branston, Ann, widow, Sonning, Berks., 1702, AB, I, W, P5/1702/8
Branston *or* Braxtone, Giles, labourer, Rams., 1714, AB, I, W, P5/1714/5
Branstone, Jn., yeo., Woodley and Sandford, Berks., 1773, W, P5/1773/7, P5/17Reg/59
Branstone, Robt., cordw., Sonning, Berks., 1662, AB, I, P5/1662/21
Brant, Brante, Guy, Yatesbury, 1601, AB, I, P5/1601/6, P5/7Reg/25A
Robt., yeo., Liberty of Newland, Hurst, Berks., 1695, I, W, P5/1695/8
Robt., Hurst, Berks., 1731, I, W, P5/1731/5
Thos., proved at Sonning, Berks., 1631, I, W, P5/1631/18, P5/12Reg/59A
Brasher *see* Bracher
Brashford, Lawr., tailor, Stratford Tony, 1575, W, P2/5Reg/218B
Brasier *see* Brazier
Brassfield, Ann, sp., Sal., 1821, W, Wr, P4/1821/7
Bratcher *see* Bracher
Bratfield *see* Bradfield *or* B.
Brathat *see* Brathwaite
Brathod, Jn., sen., hatmaker, Sal. St Edmd., 1617, I, W, P4/1617/3
Brathwaite, Chris., cutler, Sal., 1666-67, AB, I, W, P4/1666/4, P4/1666/10
Chris., cutler, Marl., 1691, I, NW, P1/B/610
Braithwaite, Eliz., sp., Marl., 1751, W, P1/B/1257, P1/10Reg/477
Eliz., widow, Marl., 1770, W, P1/B/1393, P1/12Reg/336B
Braithwaite, Francis, Marl., 1686, W, P1/B/584
Francis, Marl., 1823, AB, comm, Wr, P1/1823/36
Jane, Marl. St Peter and St Paul, 1715, AB, P1/B/810
Jn., cutler, Sal., 1666, AB, I, P4/1666/12
Jn., clerk, Milton L., 1812, AB, P1/1812/12
My., sp., Devizes & Cornhill, London, 1755, W, P1/B/1288, P1/11Reg/185
Brathat *or* Brathwait, Thos., Sal., 1628, AB, P4/1628/12
Braxton *see* Brackstone
Bray, Ambrose, carp., Rushall, 1743, W, P2/B/1617
Ambrose, Rushall, 1776, AB, P1/B/1427
Anna, widow, Marl., 1851, W, Wr, P1/1851/57
Bray nee Mould, Eliz., gardener's wife, Sal. (form. of Quarley, Hants), 1857, AB, aff, Wr, P4/1857/1
Harriet, widow, Devizes, 1829, AB, comm, Wr, P1/1829/162
Humphrey, weaver, Uffc., Devon, 1640, I, W, P20/1/25
Jas., husb., Uffc., Devon, 1716, I, W, P5/1716/9, P5/15Reg/341
Jas., labourer, Marl., 1784, W, P1/B/1493, P1/14Reg/57
Jas., yeo., Uffc., Devon, 1800, comm, W, P5/1800/6, P5/18Reg/290A
Jas., Uffc., Devon, 1814, AB, comm, P20/1/300
Jas., bach., Fisherton A., 1856, AB, aff, Wr, P2/1856/6
Jn., Winsley, Bradford A., 1559, W, P2/4Reg/18B
Margery?, Avebury, 1666-67, AB (fragment - name taken from modern annotation), P1/B/424
My., sp., Marl. St My., 1838, W, Wr, P1/1838/11
Rd., tailor, Avebury, 1670, I, W, P3/B/573
Sarah, widow, Winterbourne M., 1745, AB, P3/B/1430
Susanna, sp., Charl. nr. P., 1775, W, P2/B/1918
Thos., Winsley, Bradford A., 1557, W, P2/3Reg/50A
Thos., jun., Avebury, 1639, AB, I, W, P3/B/420-21

Thos., Avebury, 1662, comm, W, P3/B/480, P3/3Reg/41A
Thos., Purton, 1734, AB, comm, P3/B/1341
Wm., yeo., Avebury, 1699, I, W, P3/B/986
Wm., Warm., 1852, AB, O, Wr, P2/1852/23
Braysher *see* Bracher
Brazant, Mark, vict., Devizes, 1838, AB, note, O, Wr, P1/1838/14
Brazenton, Jane, widow, Calcutt, Crickl. St S., 1717, I, W, P3/B/1145
Wm., Crickl. St S., 1697, AB, I, P3/B/964
Brazier, Brasier, Alice, widow, Wilton, 1706, W, P2/B/1252
Eliz., widow, Wilton, 1842, AB, Wr, P2/1842/1
Geo., painter, Wilton, 1837, W, Wr, P2/1837/14
Hy., carp. and builder, Wilton, 1839, W, Wr, P2/1839/40
Herbert, carp., Wilton, 1839, W, Wr, P2/1839/1
Brazyer, Jn., cooper, Wallingford, Berks., 1614, I, W, P1/B/107
Brasier, My., Wilton, 1728, W, P2/B/1467
Rd., carpet weaver, Wilton, 1789, W, P2/B/2041
Sarah, widow, Wallingford, Berks., 1750, AB, I, P1/B/1238
Brasier, Walter, W. Dean, c1551, I, P2/B/5
Brasier, Wm., vict., Lacock, 1678, I, W, P2/B/932
Brasier, Wm., clothw., Wilton, 1694, W, P2/B/1156
Breach, Aaron, Cherhill, 1717, AB, P5/1716/12
Aaron, Poulshot, 1807, AB, comm, W, P2/1807/13
Aaron, yeo., Melk., 1835, comm, W, P2/1835/2
Alice, Eye and Dunsden, Sonning, Berks., 1687, AB, P5/1687/5
Breche, And., Sonning Eye, Berks., 1546, W, P5/20Reg/75A
Chas., gent., Sonning, Berks., 1669, AB, I, P5/1669/2
Edwd., yeo., Eye and Dunsden, Sonning, Berks., 1662, I, W, copy W, P5/1662/19
Edwd., Barkham, Berks., 1732, AB, P1/B/1008
Eliz., widow, Borough, Sonning, Berks., 1636, AB, I, W, P5/1636/9, P5/13Reg/16
Eliz., widow, Poulshot, 1815, comm, W, Wr, P2/1815/60
Hy., yeo., Sonning Eye, Berks., 1625, I, W, P5/1625/11, W, P5/10Reg/262B
Humphrey, yeo., Sonning, Berks., 1667, I (damaged), W, P5/1667/8
Humphrey, Eye and Dunsden, Sonning, Berks., 1709, AB, P5/1709/4
Humphrey, yeo., Sonning, Berks., 1719, W, P5/1719/10, P5/16Reg/30A
Humphrey, yeo., Sonning, Berks., 1726, W, P5/1726/10, P5/16Reg/140C
Jas., yeo., Aldermaston, Berks., 1756, W, P1/B/1298, P1/11Reg/220
Jas., cooper, Broken Brow, Earley, Sonning, Berks., 1800, W, P5/1800/15, P5/18Reg/294A
Jn., Stratfield M., Berks., 1592, I, P1/B/3
Jn., yeo., Burbage, 1596, W, P5/6Reg/115B
Jn., husb., Borough, Sonning, Berks., 1596, AB, I, W, P5/1595/3
Jn., fisherman, Sonning Eye, Berks., 1645, comm, I, W, P5/1645/2, P5/14Reg/83B
Jn., yeo., Sonning, Berks., 1714, AB, I, P5/1714/6
Jn., Melk., 1722, AB, P2/B/1414
Jn., Sonning, Berks., 1729, AB, P5/1729/8, P5/16Reg/236B
Jn., yeo., Ashampstead, Basildon, Berks., 1750, W, P1/B/1240, P1/10Reg/339
Jos., Compton B., 1733, W, P3/B/1325
Lawr., yeo., Compton B., 1784, note, W, P3/B/1691
Moses, Selves, Melk., 1775, W, P2/B/1925
Nich., Sonning, Berks., 1600, W, P5/6Reg/242C
Peter, yeo., Eye and Dunsden, Sonning, Berks., 1722, I, W, P5/1722/7, P5/16Reg/80B
Ralph, Sonning Eye, Berks., 1596, I, W, P5/1595/5, P5/6Reg/120B
Rd., husb., Earley, Sonning, Berks., 1614, AB, I, P5/1614/9, P5/9Reg/119A
Rose, widow, Sindlesham, Hurst, Berks., 1801, W, P5/1801/28, P5/18Reg/325D
Sarah, wife, Bradfield, Berks., 1826, comm, W, Wr, P1/1826/91
Thos., Sonning, Berks., 1566, W, P5/1Reg/72B
Walter, baker, Broughton G., 1755, comm, ren, W, P2/B/1721
Wm., husb., Borough, Sonning, Berks., 1604, AB, I, W, P5/1603/12, P5/8Reg/3C
Wm., yeo., Borough, Sonning, Berks., 1668, AB, I, P5/1667/10
Wm., yeo., Sonning, Berks., 1711, W, P5/1711/11, P5/15Reg/261A
Bread, Bredd, Cath., widow, Devizes St Jn., 1572, W, P1/1Reg/56D, P1/2Reg/92A

Breede als Sansom, Edmd., sen., Malm., 1608-19, AB, a/c, I, P3/B/34, 176
Joan, sp., Wick, Bps. C., 1670, I, W, P24/388
Bryd, Thos., priest, 'Major Pars Altaris Prebend', 1558, collation to prebend, P1/1Reg/8B
Breads, Thos., Arborfield, Berks., 1614, AB, comm, I, P5/1614/10, P5/9Reg/117E
Bredds, Wm., trenchermaker, Sandhurst, Berks., 1619, AB, I, W, P5/1619/40, P5/10Reg/44
Wm., Bps. C., 1622, AB, I, P24/204
Bryd, Patrick, yeo., Gt. Bedwyn, 1742, W, P21/9/38
see also Sansome als B.
Breadmore, Bredmar, Joan, Pott., 1613, AB, a/c, I, P1/B/84
Brydmore, Jn., Tisb., 1572, AB, P2/5Reg/159B
Bredmar, Jn., Pott., 1612, I, W, P1/B/75
Bridmore als Brown, Jn., carrier, Pott., 1791, AB, W, P1/B/1516, P1/14Reg/358
Breadmair, Robt., husb., Southbroom, 1575, I, W, P24/1439
Brydmore, Robt., husb., Bps. C., 1575, W, P5/3Reg/62C
Bridmore, Roger, yeo., Pott., 1731, W, P1/B/990, P1/7Reg/417
Breedmore, Roger, Pott., 1768, W, P1/B/1384, P1/12Reg/277A
Breadmore als Workman, Thos., yeo., Marston, Pott., 1723, W, P1/B/880, P1/6Reg/433B
see also Brown als B.
Breads *see* Bread
Breame, Clement, Ogbourne St Geo., 1602, AB (re Clement B. & Ellen his wife), P5/7Reg/36C
Ellen, Ogbourne St Geo., 1602, T (children: Vincent & Eliz. B.), P5/1602/3
Breashur *see* Bracher
Breather, Breathers *see* Brether
Breche *see* Breach
Bredd, Bredds *see* Bread
Bredmar *see* Breadmore
Breede *see* Bread
Breedmore *see* Breadmore
Breffell, Wm., Hornington, Stratford Tony, 1578, I, W, P2/B/69, P2/5Reg/317B
Bremble *see* Bramble
Bremblecombe *see* Brimblecombe
Bremer, Jas., butcher, Reading St Lawr., Berks., 1735, W, P1/B/1045, P1/8Reg/20
Brimmer, Rd., Inglewood, Kintbury, Berks., 1735, AB, P1/B/1047
see also Peremer als B.
Brende *see* Brind
Brendy, Agnes, widow, Roundway, Bps. C., 1615, AB, I, P24/84
Brenham *see* Brensham
Brenit *see* Brent
Brenn, Eliz., widow, Hampstead Marshall, Berks., 1723, I, W, P1/B/899, P1/7Reg/15
Brensham, Jn., Lyme R., Dorset, 1603-10, AB, a/c, I, T, P5/1603/6, P5/1610/5, P5/7Reg/67A
Brent, Jacob, clerk and vicar, Ashton K., 1672, AB, I, P3/B/608
Jn., husb., Shinfield, Berks., 1738, W, P1/B/1088, P1/8Reg/240A
Mgt., widow, Haydon, Dorset, 1613-28, AB, a/c, I, P5/1613/3, P5/1628/12, P5/9Reg/79D
Brenit, Rd., yeo., Warm., 1561-62, I, W, P2/B/25, P2/4Reg/91A
Bretell *see* Brettell
Brether, Brothers, Ambrose, carp. *or* wheelwright, Mkt. L., 1678, I, W, P2/B/930
Brethers, Ambrose, carp., Berwick St Jas., 1705, I, W, P1/B/724
Brothers, Jane, sp., Breamore, Hants, 1845, note, W, Wr, P1/1845/64
Edith, widow, E. Knoyle, 1555, W, P2/1Reg/21A
Edith, widow, E. Knoyle, 1570, W, P2/5Reg/91C
Edith, E. Knoyle, 1622, AB, a/c, I, P2/B/420
Brothers, Geo., Stratford Tony & Bower C., 1676, AB, P2/B/910
Brothers, Geo., Farley, Alderbury, 1722, I, W, P26/667
Brothers, Hannah, widow, Ludwell, Donhead St My., 1814, AB, P1/1814/148
Brethers, Hy., husb., Mere, 1662, AB, I, W, P5/1662/9
Joan, widow, E. Knoyle, 1573, W, P2/5Reg/171B
Brethren *or* Brethern, Jn., Mkt. L., 1561-62, I, W, P2/B/35, P2/4Reg/103A
Breather, Jn., gent., E. Knoyle, 1633, I, NW, P2/B/563
Jn., Shrewton, 1639, I, NW, P2/B/639
Brothers, Jn., vict. *or* yeo., Westport St My., 1719, I, W, P3/B/1171

Brothers, Jn., Sal., 1756, AB, P1/B/1291
Brethers, Margery, Nunton, N. and Bodenham, 1569, W, P2/5Reg/77E
Brothers, Nancy White, widow, Coombe, Donhead St My., 1852, W, Wr, P2/1852/30
Brothern, Peter, Urchf., 1616, I, W, P2/B/365
Bryther, Rd., E. Knoyle, 1602, AB, I, W, P2/B/221
Brethers, Robt., Maddington, 1622, AB, a/c, I, P2/B/425
Brethers, Thos., husb., Poulshot, 1615-16, AB, a/c, I, P2/B/350
Brothers, Thos., sen., butcher, Farley, Alderbury, 1702, AB, I, W, P26/491
Walter, husb., E. Knoyle, 1561-63, I, W, P2/B/37, P2/4Reg/113A
Bryther, Wm., Steeple L., 1554, W, P2/2Reg/189B
Brethers, Wm., Woodrow, Melk., 1564, I, W, P2/B/2155, P2/4Reg/176B
Wm., Damerham, Hants, 1592, AB, I, W, P2/B/133
Brethers, Wm., broad weaver, Hungerford, Berks., 1606, I, NW, P1/B/45
Brethers, Wm., Chute, 1619, AB, I, P5/1619/44, P5/10Reg/37C
Breathers, Wm., Mere, 1685, AB, I, P5/1685/18
Brothers, Wm., carp., Easterton, Mkt. L., 1698, I, W, P2/B/1198
Brothers, Wm., Ludwell, Donhead St My., 1792, AB, comm, P2/B/2079
Bretsch, Edwd., mealman, Speen, Berks., 1823, W, Wr, P1/1823/103
Brett, And., yeo., Oborne, Dorset, 1822, W, Wr, P5/1822/10
Ann, widow, N. Wootton, Dorset, 1664, AB, I, P5/1664/3
Dorothy, sp., N. Wootton, Dorset, 1678, I, W, P5/1678/2
Frances, widow, Thornford, Dorset, 1693, AB, W, P5/1693/11
Jn., gent., N. Wootton, Dorset, 1644, AB, a/c, comm, I, P5/1644/3, P5/14Reg/73A
Jn., gent., Caundle Marsh, Dorset, 1702, AB, ren, W, P5/1702/2
Jn., sen., yeo., Caundle Marsh, Dorset, 1704, comm, I, W, P5/1703/5
Jn. Homan, bricklayer and innkeeper, Winterborne K., Dorset, 1857, aff, O, W, Wr, P5/1857/2
Peter, Allweston, Folke, Dorset, 1675, I, W, P5/1675/9
Thos., yeo., Haydon, Dorset, 1804, comm, W, P5/1804/18, P5/19Reg/114C
Wm., yeo., Stratton, Dorset, 1786, W, P5/1786/3, P5/18Reg/62
Brettell, Simon, Sal., 1727, AB, W, P4/1727/13
Thos., tailor, Sal., 1782, declaration (by widow, granting share to husband's nephew), W, P1/B/1462, P1/13Reg/341
Brewer, Alice, widow, Hardenhuish, 1616, AB, I, W, P1/B/137
Brewer als Dowers, Alice, widow, Gomeldon, Idmiston, 1644, I, copy I, W, P2/B/690
And., [shoemaker], Highw., 1662, AB, I, P5/1662/13
Ann, Rowde, 1720, W, P3/B/1182
Ann, widow, Rowde, 1723, I, W, P3/B/1219
Ann, widow, Wantage, Berks., 1776, W, P5/1776/5, P5/17Reg/112A
Bridget, widow, Penn, Hilmarton, 1723, I, W, P3/B/1220
Cath., Hardenhuish, 1620, I, W, P3/B/193
Chris., N. Wraxall, 1620, AB, a/c, P3/B/192
Dorcas, widow, Bromham, 1732, AB, I, P1/B/1029
Edwd., Crickl. St S., 1806, AB, Wr, P3/1806/55
Edwd., Crickl. St S., 1815, AB, Wr, P3/1815/81
Brewer als Vuckes, Eliz., Steeple A., 1631, AB, note, P1/B/227
Eliz., widow, Westb., 1670, I, NW, P25/1670/3
Frances, widow, Amesb., 1697, W, P2/B/1189
Francis, Padworth, Berks., 1668, I, copy NW, P1/B/443
Geo., Trowb., 1844, AB, O, Wr, P1/1844/10
Bruar, Hy., weaver, Langley Burrell, 1569, W (NEP), P1/1Reg/52C
Hy., Sal. St Edmd., 1587, AB, P4/Reg/29B
Hy., husb., Ford, N. Wraxall, 1610, W, P3/B/68
Hy., Hardenhuish, 1639, I, W, P3/B/422
Hy., yeo., Hardenhuish, 1711, I, W, P3/B/1097
Hy., horse dealer, Pott., 1740, AB, a/c, I, P1/B/1120
Isaac, husb., Sevington, Leigh Delamere, 1618, I, W, P3/B/163
Jas., Kington St M., 1807, AB, Wr, P3/1807/60
Jas., Kington St M., 1815, AB, comm, Wr, P3/1815/53
Jas., saddler and harnessmaker, Trowb., 1844, comm, W, Wr, P1/1844/31
Jane, sp., Calne, 1711, NW, P26/569
Jeremiah, Sal., 1782, W, P4/1782/1

Joan, widow, Calne, 1613, I, W, P26/30
Joan, widow, Penn, Hilmarton, 1630, I, W, P3/B/326
Joan, sp., Rowde, [1704], W, P1/B/709
Jn., Peasemarsh, Gillingham, Dorset, 1569, W, P27/1Reg/19B
Jn., husb., Norton B., 1610, I, W, P2/B/300, P2/8Reg/106A
Jn., N. Wraxall, 1612, AB, P3/B/92
Jn., Hardenhuish, 1616, I, W, P3/B/137
Jn., sen., weaver, Rowde, [1665], I, W (NEP), P3/B/508
Bruar, Jn., Wootton B., 1668, I, W, P1/B/450
Jn., husb., Rowde, 1672, AB, I, P3/B/609
Jn., glover, Avill's Farm, Corsham, 1676, AB, I, P3/B/667
Jn., cordw., Wootton B., 1681, I, W, P3/B/738
Jn., broad weaver, Ford, N. Wraxall, 1691, I, W, P3/B/880
Jn., Wick, Downton, 1698, AB, I, P2/B/1191
Jn., tailor, Colerne, 1700, I, W, P3/B/997
Jn., Calne, 1708, AB, P26/543
Jn., Avon, Chr. M., 1713, AB (re Jn. & his wife Martha), I, P3/B/1119
Jn., jun., cordw., Wootton B., 1721, AB, I (2 - 1 a copy), ren, P3/B/1191
Jn., husb., Hermitage, Dorset, 1727, W, P5/1727/2, P5/16Reg/146B
Jn., carp., Shrewton, 1751, W, P2/B/1689
Jn., mason, Calne, 1755, AB, W, P5/1755/2
Jn., gent., Wootton B., 1776, comm, W, P1/B/1443, P1/13Reg/155
Jn., yeo., Ford, N. Wraxall, 1782, W, P3/B/1675
Jn., Marl. St My., 1822, AB, P1/1822/11
Mgt., widow, Grittleton, 1635, I, W, P1/B/256
My., Sherb., Dorset, 1610, AB, P5/1610/2, P5/9Reg/45B
My., widow, Gt. Cheverell, 1794, AB, comm, P2/B/2094
Nich., Pierston, Gillingham, Dorset, 1571, W, P27/1Reg/24B
Paul, stonemason, Kington St M., 1834, W, Wr, P3/1834/22
Peter, Amesb., 1691, AB, I, P2/B/1135
Peter, Amesb., 1700, AB, P2/B/1212
Philip, widow, Calne, 1632, I, W, P26/43
Rebecca, widow, Rowde, 1681, AB, I, W, P3/B/739
Rd., Hardenhuish, 1638, I, W, P3/B/401
Rd., jun., baker, Malm. Abbey, 1662, I, W, P1/B/374
Rd., husb., Burghfield, Berks., 1662, AB, I, P1/B/372
Rd., mason, Upper Combe, Castle C., 1738, W, P3/B/1372
Rd., fellmonger, Castle C., 1796, W, P3/B/1750
Robt., Wilton, 1609, AB, T (unnamed children), P2/B/288, P2/8Reg/63B
Robt., vict., Wootton B., 1762, W, P3/B/1549
Sam., Colerne, 1749, AB, P3/B/1458
Sarah, widow, Devizes, 1740, AB, P1/B/1116
Sarah, grocer's wife, Chipp., 1804, AB, comm, P3/1804/19
Steph., Pierston, Gillingham, Dorset, 1571, W, P27/1Reg/24C
Susanna, widow, Pott., 1764, W, P1/B/1370, P1/12Reg/148
Thos., S. Wraxall, 1542, W (NEP), P2/1Reg/27A
Thos., husb., Berwick B., 1570, W, P5/2Reg/66
Thos., sen., innholder, Avill's Farm, Corsham, 1664, comm, I, W, P3/B/494
Thos., fuller, Hardenhuish, [1667], I, W (NEP), P3/B/527
Thos., coachman, Whitley Farm, Calne, 1669, I, W, P26/156
Thos., yeo., Penn, Hilmarton, 1669, I, W, P3/B/551
Thos., Hardenhuish, 1675, I, NW, P3/B/652
Thos., Devizes, 1723, AB, P1/B/884
Thos., tailor, Devizes, 1731, comm, W, P1/B/986, P1/7Reg/414
Thos., clerk, Wantage, Berks., 1755, comm, W, P23/660
Thos., Melk., 1835, AB, O, P2/1835/33
Walter, Westb., 1642, I, W, P25/1642/2
Brewer als Baker, Wm., Beam., Dorset, 1576, I, W, P5/1576/6, P5/3Reg/95A
Wm., sen., yeo., Ford, N. Wraxall, 1620, I, W, P3/B/194
Wm., Rowde, 1629, AB, I, P3/B/313

Wm., Seagry & Stanton, 1637, I (2), W, P3/B/389
Wm., broad weaver, Corsham, 1654, I, NW, P29/B/20, P29/1Reg/151B
Wm., sen., yeo. and husb., Bromham, 1662, AB, comm, I, W, P1/B/381
Wm., weaver, Langley Burrell, 1663, I, W, P3/B/490
Wm., broad weaver, Bromham, 1675, I, W, P3/B/653
Wm., Langley Burrell, 1677, AB, I, P3/B/686
Wm., Penn, Hilmarton, 1686, AB, I, P3/B/825
Wm., labourer, Colerne, 1697, AB (2), I, P3/B/965
Wm., Kington L., 1747, ren, W, P3/B/1446
Wm., scribbler, Calne, 1776, W, P26/1083
Wm., Kington St M., 1829, AB, Wr, P1/1829/88
see also Dawers als B.; Doosell als B.; Edwards als B.; Open als B.; Robbince als B.
Brewet, Nich., carp., Idmiston, 1708, I, W, P2/B/1274
Brewford, My., widow, Lyme R., Dorset, 1747, AB, P16/292
Wm., seaman (d. on HMS *Lennox*), Lyme R., Dorset, 1747, W, P16/293
Brewlie, Wm., Marl., 1640, I, W, P1/B/293
Brewston, Wm., Ruscombe, Berks., 1617, AB, P5/1617/1
Brewstow *see* Bristow
Brian *see* Bryan
Briant *see* Bryant
Briar, Brier, Chris., Preston, Dorset, 1583, I, W, P5/1583/4, P5/4Reg/68B
Bryer, Chris., weaver, Wingfield, 1601, I, P2/B/208
Bryar, Edwd., weaver, Uffc., Devon, 1639, I, NW, P20/1/27
Bryar, Geo., Sherb., Dorset, 1699, AB, comm, I, P5/1699/2
Jn., Keevil, 1603, AB, P2/B/237
Bryer, Jn., Preston, Dorset, 1609, AB, I, T, P5/1609/2, P5/8Reg/164A
Bryer, Robt., yeo., Sutton Poyntz, Dorset, 1641, I, W, P5/1641/12, P5/14Reg/27A
Brice, Ann, widow, Trowb., 1795, comm, W, P1/B/1536, P1/14Reg/611
Edwd., carp., Heytes., 1693, definitive sentence, D, I, W, P5/1692/11
Edwd., maltster, Uffc., Devon, 1816, W, Wr, P20/1/303
Eliz., widow, Stockton, 1685, I, W, P2/B/1046
Evans, carp., Beam., Dorset, 1632, AB, I, P17/6
Francis, Durrington, 1678, AB, I, P2/B/939
Geo., yeo., Fordington, Dorset, 1736, comm, W, P5/1736/6
Hy. Smith, surgeon, Sherb., Dorset, 1810, comm, W, Wr, P5/1810/5
Jane, widow, Sherb., Dorset, 1835, W (& cod), Wr, P5/1835/15
Joan, widow, Netherb., Dorset, 1686, AB, I, P17/228
Jn., Durrington, 1624, AB, a/c, I, P2/B/452
Jn., Redlynch, Downton, 1628, AB, P2/B/2163
My., widow, Durrington, 1630, I, W, P2/B/518
My., widow, Heytes., 1724, AB, I (3 - 1 lists price for which goods sold), P5/1724/13
Nathaniel, Netherb., Dorset, 1663, I, W (NEP), P30/12
Philip, carp., Quidh., 1693, W, P2/B/1150
Brisse *or* Bryse, Thos., miller, Longbridge D., 1580, I, W, P2/B/79, P2/6Reg/1A
Thos., carp., Stockton, 1679, I, NW, P2/B/944
Thos., Heytes., 1715, AB, P5/1715/4
Thos., broad weaver, Heytes., 1778, W, P5/1778/3, P5/17Reg/156B
Bryce, Wm., yeo., Longbridge D., 1557, W, P2/3Reg/40A
Wm., Durrington, 1602, AB, I, W, P2/B/225
Wm., Longbridge D., 1620, I, W, P1/B/170
Wm., Old Windsor, Berks., 1738, AB, P1/B/1089
Wm., Bradford A., 1777, AB, comm, ren, P2/B/1947
Brickell, Brickle, Eliz., widow, Motc., Dorset, 1687, I, copy I, P27/1/98
Brickle, Frances, widow, Mere, 1775, W (& cod), P5/1775/3, P5/17Reg/95
Giles, gardener, Enmore Grn, Motc., Dorset, 1797, W, P27/1/560
Jas., Shaftesbury St Rumbold *or* Cann, Dorset, 1763, AB, P27/3Reg/108A
Jas., bach., Motc., Dorset, 1763, AB, W, P27/1/435
Brickill, Jn., servant, Ashton G., Codf. St P., 1705, I, W, P2/B/1247
Brickle [Brickell], Jn., Stourton, 1710, AB, I, P2/B/1288
Rd., sen., Motc., Dorset, 1660, AB, I, W, P27/1/8

Brickle, Robt., Littleton P., 1762, AB, P1/B/1338
Brickle, Robt., Fovant, 1798, W, P2/B/2132
Sam., grazier, Shaftesbury, Dorset & Fisherton A., 1822, AB, P2/1822/51
Steph., yeo., Semley, 1672, I, P2/B/855
Susanna, sp., Sal., 1765, W, P4/1765/11
Thos., sen., yeo., Motc., Dorset, 1719, W, P27/1/237
Thos., baker, Sal., 1760, W, P4/1760/2
Wm., gent., Enmore Grn, Motc., Dorset, 1806, comm, W, P27/1/588
Bricker, Amos, cordw. *or* day labourer, Corsham, 1738, W, P29/B/47-48
Christian, widow, Corsham, 1606, AB, W, P29/B/11, P29/1Reg/59A
Jas., butcher, Corsham, 1715, AB, ren, P29/B/40, P29/2Reg/12
Job, N. Bradley, 1792, AB, comm, P2/B/2070
My., widow, Southwick, N. Bradley, 1795, comm, W, P2/B/2104
Rd., N. Bradley, 1822, AB, comm, Wr, P2/1822/2
Thos., N. Bradley, 1785, AB, comm, P2/B/2008
Wm., yeo., Southwick, N. Bradley, 1795, comm, W, P2/B/2103
Brickett, Jn., cutler, Sal., 1587, W, P4/Reg/32
Patecon, Sal. St Edmd., 1627, AB (re both Patecon & his wife Thomasine; 1st name given as 'Patison' on contemporary endorsement), P4/1627/21
Peter, joiner, Sal., 1593, I, P1/B/7
Brickill, Brickle *see* Brickell
Briddell *see* Bridle
Bridden, Ann, widow, Wantage, Berks., 1745, W, P23/586
Bridge *see* Bridges
Bridgeman, Bridgman, Constance, widow, Ogbourne St Geo., 1688, AB, I, P5/1688/5
Edwd., yeo., Bremhill Wick, 1682, AB, I, W, P3/B/759
Bridgman, Edwd., Chr. M., 1792, AB, P3/B/1738
Edwd., yeo., Seagry, 1847, W, Wr, P3/1847/25
Bridgman, Eliz., widow, Hungerford, Berks., [1735], W (NEP), P23/505
Eliz., widow, Calne, 1798, W, P26/1212
Bridgman *or* Burgeman, Hy., yeo., Pewsham Forest, 1681, I, W, P3/B/746
Bridgman, Hy., yeo., Chipp., 1705, I, W, P3/B/1046
Jn., gent., Marl., 1734-35, W, P1/B/1035, P1/7Reg/601
Jn., Hullavington, 1826, AB, Wr, P3/1826/24
Jn., gardener, Lt. Somerford, 1834, AB, Wr, P3/1834/56
Jn., boat builder, Honey St., Woodb., 1857, aff, W, Wr, P3/1857/24
Jos., sen., yeo., Sutton C., Berks., 1792, W, P1/B/1528, P1/14Reg/439
Bridgman, Ralph, carp., Corsham, 1615, AB, I, note, W, copy W, P29/B/13
Rd., Bradford A., 1557, W, P2/3Reg/72B
Bridgman, Roger, vict., Newbury, Berks., 1741, AB, I, P1/B/1134
Thos., stationer, Marl., 1751, AB, ren, W, P1/B/1256, P1/10Reg/476
Bridgman, Wm., labourer, N. Hidden, Hungerford, Berks., 1681, AB, I, P23/104
Bridgman, Wm., yeo., Chipp., 1706, AB, I, P3/B/1058
Bridgman, Wm., Savernake Forest, 1744, AB, Wr, P5/1744/5
Bridges, Ann, sp., Melk., 1743, AB, P2/B/1622
Edwd., rector, N. Wraxall, 1666, I, W, P1/B/428
Edwd., yeo., Gt. Somerford, 1669, AB, I, ren, P3/B/552
Eleanor, widow, Newton, 1643, I, W, P1/B/309
Frances, widow, Seend, Melk., 1737, W, P3/B/1366
Hy., broad weaver, Bradford A., 1632, AB, comm, I, NW, copy NW, P2/B/554
Isaac, Devizes, 1737, AB, P1/B/1070
Jn., husb., Long Newnton, 1641, I, W, P3/B/456
Jn., yeo., Chipp., 1721, W, P3/B/1192
Bridge, Jonathan, Kington St M., 1745, W, P3/B/1432
My., widow, Highw., 1608-09, AB, W, P5/1607/5, P5/8Reg/113
Michael, Chirton, 1641, I, W, P2/B/669
Michael, maltster, Eastrop, Highw., 1671, AB, I, P5/1671/6
Rd., yeo., Bushton, Clyffe P., 1697, I, W, P3/B/966
Rd., farmer, Gotshill, Bremhill, 1809, comm, W, Wr, P3/1809/14
Sam., Botley, Hants, 1817, AB, comm, Wr, P1/1817/14

Sibyl, widow, Eastrop, Highw., 1675, I, W, P10/1675/2
Steph., N. Wraxall, 1680, I, W, P3/B/726
Steph., seaman (late of HMS *Nassau*, man of war), Box, 1749, AB, P3/B/1459
Steph., tailor, Box, 1799-1802, AB, comm, W, Wr, P3/B/1769, P3/1802/60
Bridge, Thos., husb., Isbery, Lambourn, Berks., 1732, W, P1/B/1012, P1/7Reg/494
Wm., gent. *or* yeo., Eastrop, Highw., 1586, I, W, P5/1585/14, P5/4Reg/122D
Wm., Semington, Steeple A., 1648, comm, I, W, P2/B/717
Wm., yeo., Broad B., Highw., 1709, W, P10/1709/2
Wm., yeo., Foxham, Bremhill, 1788, W, P3/B/1713
Wm., labourer, Chiseldon, 1835, W, P1/1835/111
Bridgewater, Edwd., Sonning, Berks., 1748, AB, ren, Wr, P5/1748/3
My., widow, Shinfield, Berks., 1720, I, W, P1/B/862, P1/6Reg/309
Robt., yeo., Shinfield, Berks., 1795, W, Wr, P1/B/1541, P1/14Reg/568
Bridgman *see* Bridgeman
Bridle, Briddell, Edwd., yeo., Holnest, Dorset, 1705, I, W, P5/1704/3
Jas., Brixton D., 1775, AB, P2/B/1913
Job, Bere R., Dorset, 1832, AB, comm, Wr, P5/1832/13
Jn., yeo., Motc., Dorset, 1759, W, P27/1/422, P27/3Reg/82
Jn., yeo., Long Burton, Dorset, 1780, W, P5/1780/4, P5/17Reg/196A
Jn., sen., yeo., Holnest, Dorset, 1708-09, AB, ren, W, P5/1708/17, P5/15Reg/104
Jonathan, yeo., Motc., Dorset, 1687, I, P27/1/97
Josias, yeo., Motc., Dorset, 1758, W, P27/1/419, P27/3Reg/79
Judith, widow, Pott., 1674, AB, I, W, P1/B/498
Philip, husb., Leigh, Yetm., Dorset, 1593, AB, I, W, P5/1593/20, P5/6Reg/30A
Rd., sen., yeo., Holnest, Dorset, 1640, I, W, P5/1640/5, P5/13Reg/229
Briddell, Thos., sen., yeo., Holnest, Dorset, 1686, I, W, P5/1686/5
Wm., sen., yeo., Hermitage, Dorset, 1612, I, W, P5/1612/10, P5/9Reg/65A
Wm., sen., Hermitage, Dorset, 1638, AB, I, NW, P5/1638/8, P5/13Reg/86C
Wm., Pott., 1671, AB, I, P1/B/469
Wm., husb., Tisb., 1691, I, W, P2/B/1136
Bridmore *see* Breadmore
Briend *see* Brind
Brient *see* Bryant
Brier *see* Briar
Briggs, Jn., yeo., Stapleford, 1585, I (very detailed), P2/B/91
Thos., Burton, Nettleton, 1853, AB, D, O, W, Wr, P3/1853/23
Bright, Abraham, bach., Kington L., 1797, AB, comm, P3/B/1758
Alice, widow, Winterbourne S., 1607, AB, I, W, P2/B/270
Ambrose, weaver, Seend Row, Melk., 1635, I, W, P1/B/259
Ann, widow, Kingston D., 1680, AB, I, L with cert, P1/B/530
Bright als Lucas, Ann, widow, Crickl. St S., 1686, I, W, P2/B/1063
Bright als Lucas, Ann, sp., Chicklade, 1852, aff, O, W, Wr, P2/1852/72
Dan., Easton Town, Sherston, 1795, W, P3/B/1745
Bright als Lucas, Edith, widow, Berwick St Jn., 1769, ren, W, P2/B/1862
Elias, Kingston D., 1661, AB, I, P2/B/731
Bright als Lucas, Elias, yeo., Norton B., 1713, W, P2/B/1318
Francis, Berwick St Jn., 1769-70, AB, declaration, W (admr unable to submit I, as many goods have been seized following d. of widow, such info as she can give is in declaration), P2/B/1863
Hy., husb., Seend, Melk., 1628, I, W, P2/B/490
Bright als Lucas, Hepzibah, widow, Chicklade, 1831, AB, O, W, Wr, P2/1831/1
Jane, wife, Stoke F., 1817, AB, P1/1817/103
Joan, widow, Kington L., 1739, W, P3/B/1381
Bright als Lucas, Jn., Berwick St Jn., 1551, W, P2/2Reg/127A
Jn., shearman, Sal. St Edmd., 1582, W, P4/Reg/7
Jn., husb., Winterbourne S., 1603, I, W, P2/B/233
Jn., yeo., Mkt. L. (& of E. Lavington & Codf.), 1644, I, W, P2/B/689
Jn., yeo., Woodrow, Melk., 1664, I, W, P2/B/761
Jn., husb., Shalbourne, Berks., 1723, AB, W, P23/417
Jn., yeo., Melk., 1734, W, P2/B/1531
Jn., tailor, Tytherton L., Chipp., 1780, W, P3/B/1664

Jos., clothw., Melk., 1733, W, P1/B/1030, P1/7Reg/575
Margery, widow, Woodrow, Melk., 1612, I, W, P1/B/78
My., widow, E. Grimstead, W. Dean, 1763, W, P2/B/1792
Rd., weaver, Melk., 1592, I, W, P2/B/138
Rd., labourer, Compton B., 1608, W, P3/B/35
Rd., husb., W. Dean, 1694, AB, I, W, P2/B/1158
Rd., E. Grimstead, W. Dean, 1737, W, P2/B/1558
Robt., sen., yeo., Ham, 1666, comm, I, W, P3/B/515
Robt., sergemaker, Chr. M., 1701, AB, W, P1/B/686, P1/4Reg/65
Robt., yeo., Ham, 1717, W, P3/B/1147
Robt., gent., Trowb., 1776, comm, W, P1/B/1444, P1/13Reg/160B
Sarah, widow, Ebbesborne Wake, 1793, W, P2/B/2081
Bright als Lucas, Thos., Berwick St Jn., 1587-88, AB, T (children: Robt., Thos., Jerome, Jn. & Eliz. B. als L.), P2/B/97, P2/7Reg/113A
Thos., sen., yeo., Marden, 1669, I, W, P2/B/807
Thos., yeo., Woodrow, Melk., 1675, comm, I, W, P2/B/893
Bright als Lucas, Thos., yeo., Crickl. St S., 1677, I, W, P2/B/925
Thos., yeo., Holt, Bradford A., 1703, AB, I, W, P2/B/1233
Brite, Wm., serge weaver, Kington L., 1722, I, W, P3/B/1208
Bright als Lucas, Thos., yeo., Chicklade, 1728, W, P2/B/1462
Thos., Burbage, 1748, W, P11/200
Thos., gardener, Collingbourne K., 1777, W, P3/B/1647
Wm., Aldbourne, 1569, W, P1/1Reg/108B
Wm., tailor, Chipp., 1769, AB, ren, P3/B/1604
see also Lucas als B.
Brightwell, Benj., yeo., Hurst, Berks., 1693, AB, I, P5/1693/8
Frances, widow, Hurst, Berks., 1693, AB, comm, P5/1693/4
Thos., yeo., Bulmershe, Sonning, Berks., 1702, comm, I, W, P5/1701/7
Brimblecombe, Bremblecombe, Edith, widow, W. Kington, [1611], W (2 written a year apart, the later one being NW), P3/B/80
Rd., husb., W. Kington, 1608, I, W, P3/B/36
Brimbley, Wm., miller, Hill D., 1681, I, W, P5/1681/6
Brimmer *see* Bremer
Brimsdon, Brimsen *see* Brinsden
Brimsmeade *see* Brinnsmead
Brimson *see* Brinsden
Brimstone, Jn., vicar, Coombe B., 1605, I, W, P5/1605/5, P5/8Reg/36B
Brincknell, Robt., tailor, Bromham, 1619, AB, a/c, comm, I, lists of debts (2), P3/B/177
Brinckworth *see* Brinkworth
Brind, Abigail, labourer's widow, Aldbourne, 1738, W, P1/B/1095, P1/8Reg/306
Abraham, yeo., Earlscourt, Wanb., 1688, I, W, P3/B/845
Ann, sp., Westrop, Highw., 1635, I, NW, P5/1635/6, P5/12Reg/179A
Ann, widow, Wanb., 1674, I (2), W, P3/B/640
Ann, sp., Wrou., 1792, W, P1/B/1523, P1/14Reg/398
Anth., husb., Wanb., 1685, AB, I, P3/B/818
Bart., yeo. *or* husb., Wrou., 1671, I, W, P3/B/589
Benj., gent., Malm., 1837, W, Wr, P3/1837/40
Chas., yeo., Wanb., 1736, W, P3/B/1352
Edwd., Wanb., 1688, AB, P3/B/846
Edwd., yeo., Wanb., 1738, W, P3/B/1373
Eliz., widow, Whitemorley, Aldbourne, 1686, I, W, P1/B/1564
Eliz., sp., Liddington, 1808, W, Wr, P3/1808/22
Geo., husb., Aldbourne, 1721, I (2 - 1 a copy), W, P3/B/1190
Geo., yeo., Liddington, 1723, W, P1/B/892, P1/6Reg/463A
Geo., yeo., Liddington, 1799, W, Wr, P3/B/1770
Geo., Liddington, 1842, AB, comm, Wr, P3/1842/38
Hy., innholder, Highw., 1723, W, P10/1723/2
Hy., gent. and widower, Hannington, 1757, req, W, copy W, P3/B/1509
Hy., Stratton St Mgt., 1778, W, P3/B/1652
Jane, sp., Wanb., 1666, comm, I, W (2 - 1 a copy), P3/B/516

Brende, Jn., yeo., Westrop, Highw., 1606-07, I, W, P2/B/268, P5/1607/6, P5/8Reg/105C
Jn., yeo. and husb., Westrop, Highw., 1634, comm, I, W (GVS), P5/1634/24, P5/12Reg/324B
Jn., sen., gent., Wanb., 1641, comm, W, P1/B/295
Jn., yeo., Wrou., 1671, I, W, P3/B/590
Jn., gent., Wanb., 1684, AB, I, P3/B/798
Jn., yeo., Wanb., 1690-99, AB, I, W, P3/B/868
Jn., husb., Lt. Hinton, 1694, I, W, P3/B/923
Jn., shepherd, Aldbourne, 1703, comm, I, W, P3/B/1024
Briend, Jn., Westrop, Highw., 1726, W, P10/1726/1
Jn., Stratton St Mgt., 1727, AB, comm, I, P3/B/1256
Jn., Aldbourne, 1730, I, P3/B/1298
Jn., Wanb., 1730, AB, P3/B/1297
Jn., gent., Wanb., 1743, W, P3/B/1417
Jn., yeo., Wanb., 1763, W, P1/B/1362, P1/12Reg/100
Jn., yeo., Wanb., 1777, W, P3/B/1648
Jn., innkeeper, Codf. St P., 1852, comm, W, Wr, P2/1852/60
Jos., yeo., Liddington, 1845, comm, O, ren, W, Wr, P3/1845/14
My., widow, Wanb., 1699, I, W (very fragile), P3/B/987
My., widow, Liddington, 1736, W, P3/B/1353
My., widow, Lt. Hinton, 1751, W, P3/B/1468
My., widow, Crickl. St S., 1780, W, P3/B/1665
Matthea, widow, Lt. Hinton, 1697, I, W, P3/B/968
Nich., gent., S. Marston, 1635, AB, I, P5/1635/11, P5/12Reg/178
Owen, Lt. Hinton, 1684, I, W, P3/B/799
Rd., husb., Whitemorley, Aldbourne, 1677, comm, I, W, P1/B/512
Rd., Sal., 1728, AB, P4/1728/17
Sarah, widow, Marl., 1834, AB, W, Wr, P1/1834/9
Thos., Aldbourne, 1637, AB, a/c, I, P3/B/390
Thos., shepherd, Aldbourne, 1739, W, P3/B/1382
Thos., yeo., Liddington (form. of Wanb.), 1851, comm, D (2), W, Wr, P3/1851/9
Vincent, Ogbourne St Geo., 1607, AB, NW, P5/1608/4
Walter, Liddington, 1762, AB, P3/B/1550
Walter, Wrou., 1826, AB, Wr, P3/1826/25
Wm., innholder, Highw., 1732, AB, copy req, copy W, P10/1732/1
Wm., labourer, Aldbourne, 1801, W, P1/1801/116, P1/15Reg/335B
Wm., yeo., Malm., 1812, W, Wr, P3/1812/48
Brindell, Eleanor, sp., Lydiard M., 1721, W, P3/B/1193
Brindley, Ann, clerk's wife, Lacock, 1809, AB, Wr, P3/1809/7
Brine, Alice, widow, Collingbourne K., 1615, I, W, P3/B/126
Bryne, And., yeo., Coombe B., 1671, I, NW, P5/1671/12
Bryne, Cath., widow, Coombe B., 1688, AB, I, P5/1688/13
Cath., widow, Sal., 1718, AB, W, P4/1718/13
Edmd., Pewsey, 1696, AB, I, ren, P3/B/951
Edwd., husb., Stoke F., 1675, I, P2/B/895
Edwd., husb., Pewsey, 1676, AB, I, P3/B/668
Eliz., widow, Whaddon, 1611, I, W, P2/B/317
Eliz., widow, Bere R., Dorset, 1687, AB, I, P5/1687/4
Gabriel, sen., Aughton, Collingbourne K., 1609, W, P3/B/50
Gabriel, Collingbourne K., 1682, AB, I, P3/B/760
Joan, widow, no abode stated, 1561, I, P2/B/20
Bryne, Joan, widow, Broad C., 1563, W, P2/4Reg/146A
Bryne, Joan, widow, Whaddon, 1585, W, P2/7Reg/4B
Bryne, Jn., Fordington, Dorset, 1570, AB, W, P5/2Reg/74A-B
Bryne, Jn., husb., Stoke F., 1591, I, T, W, P2/B/123
Jn., joiner, Sal. St Edmd., 1612, AB, I, W, P4/1612/4
Bryne, Jn., yeo., Whaddon, 1667, comm, I, NW, P2/B/784
Jn., yeo., Coombe B., 1682, AB, I, P5/1682/8
Bryne, Julian, widow, Stoke F., 1593, AB, I, W, P2/B/145
My., widow, Damerham, Hants, 1825, W, Wr, P2/1825/66
Robt., Sal. St Edmd., 1628, AB, a/c, I, P4/1628/11

Sarah, widow, Downton, 1735, W, P1/B/1039, P1/7Reg/620
Thos., jun., husb., Stoke F., 1619, W, P2/B/398
Walter, Broad C., 1640, AB, P2/B/650
Bryne, Wm., Broad C., 1562, W, P2/4Reg/103B
Wm., Stoke, 1563, I, P2/B/34
Wm., yeo., Cranborne, Dorset, 1701, a/c, W, P4/1700/2
Wm., sen., yeo., Homington, 1704, I, W, P24/615
Wm., butcher, Sal., 1709, I, W, P4/1709/2
Wm., yeo., Standlynch, 1713, W, P2/B/1320
Brinkworth, Ann, widow, Lacock, 1835, W, P1/1835/86
Benj., Lacock, 1766, W, P3/B/1579
Geo., carp., Langley Burrell, 1830, aff, comm, W, Wr, P3/1830/7
Jas., bach., Lacock, 1746, AB, I, P3/B/1440
Jas., gent., Langley Burrell, 1853, comm, W, Wr, P3/1853/18
Luke, baker, Lacock, 1808, comm, W, Wr, P3/1808/3
Brinckworth, Mgt., widow, Alderton, [1611], I, W, Wr (NEP), P3/B/81
My., widow, Chipp., 1824, W, Wr, P3/1824/28
Rebecca, widow, Lacock, 1750, W, P1/B/1235, P1/10Reg/315
Robt., yeo., Lacock, 1697, AB, I, P3/B/967
Thos., baker, Chipp., 1807, W, P3/1807/59
Thos., gent., Devizes, 1844, W, Wr, P1/1844/23
Wm., baker, Lacock, 1833, W, Wr, P3/1833/48
Brinnsmead, Roger, freemason, Sherb., Dorset, 1623, AB, I, P5/1623/7, P5/10Reg/216C
Brinsden, Brunsden, Alice, sp., Collingbourne K., 1672, AB, P3/B/615
Brimsdon, Alice, widow, E. Stowell, Wilcot, 1718, I, W, P3/B/1153
Brinsdon, Ann, widow, Steeple L., 1711, W, P1/B/781, P1/5Reg/260
Brunsden, Ann, widow, Snodshill, Chiseldon, 1776, AB, P1/B/1442
Brimson, Ann, sp., Maiden B., 1806, W, Wr, P2/1806/44
Brunsden, Benj., glazier, Devizes, 1681, comm, I, W, P1/B/549
Brunsdon, Benj., yeo., Tottenham Park, Gt. Bedwyn, 1693, AB, I, P21/5/22
Betty, widow, Marl., 1825, W, Wr, P1/1825/13
Chas., clothier, Chr. M., 1721, AB, ren, P3/B/1194
Christian, widow, Hunt Mill, Wootton B., 1609, W, P3/B/51
Brunsdon, Edith, Marl., 1616, I, P1/B/127
Brunsden, Edith, widow, Lt. Hinton, 1801, W, P3/1801/13
Brunsden, Edmd., yeo., E. Grafton, 1614, I, W, P5/1614/8, P5/9Reg/138
Brunsden, Edmd., yeo., Gt. Bedwyn, 1661, I, NW, P5/1661/6
Brunsdon, Edmd., Fisherton A., 1672, AB, I, NW, P2/B/854
Brunsden, Edwd., husb., Stratton St Mgt., 1621, I, W, P3/B/213
Brinsdon, Edwd., yeo., Winterbourne Bassett, 1683, AB, comm, I, P3/B/776
Brunsdon, Edwd., Stratton St Mgt., 1684, AB, comm, P3/B/801
Brunsdon, Edwd., yeo., Gt. Bedwyn, 1727, AB, I, P21/8/36
Brunsden, Edwd., bach., Ogbourne St Geo., 1802, AB, P23/833
Brunsdon, Eliz., Urchf., 1669, AB, I, P1/B/455
Brunsdon, Eliz., widow, Sal., 1680, AB, I, P4/1680/2
Eliz., widow, Gt. Somerford, 1746, W, P3/B/1441
Brunsden, Eliz., sp., Inholmes, Lambourn, Berks. (late of Ogbourne St Geo.), 1802, W, P23/834
Brunsden, Frances, sp., Ogbourne St Geo., 1694, I, W, P23/204
Brunsden, Hy., yeo., Ogbourne St Geo., 1771, AB, W, P23/733
Brunsden, Hy., yeo., Ogbourne St Geo., 1803, AB (decd's goods left unadmd by his dau, Eliz., at time of her death), comm, W, P23/835
Brunsden, Isaac, Preshute, 1802, AB, Wr, P1/1802/5, P1/15Reg/363
Jane, widow, Winterbourne Bassett, 1693, AB, comm, I, P3/B/903
Brunsdon, Jane, widow, Stratton St Mgt., 1724, I, W (2 different, dated 1714 & 1724, with no evidence of probate), P3/B/1229
Brunsden, Joan, widow, E. Grafton, 1615, I, W, P1/B/126
Brimsdon, Jn., yeo., Bathampton, Steeple L., 1566, W, P2/5Reg/3
Brunsdon, Jn., Stratton St Mgt., [1602], W (NEP), P3/1Reg/99A
Brunson als Bronsdon, Jn., Ogbourne St Geo., [1606], W (NEP), P5/8Reg/135B
Brinsen, Jn., sen., husb., Urchf., 1627, I, W, P2/B/468

Brunsden, Jn., sen., yeo., E. Grafton, 1645, I, W, P21/1/57
Brunsden, Jn., Aughton, Collingbourne K., 1651, I, W, P1/B/359
Brunsden, Jn., Fosbury, Tidcombe and F., 1661, AB, P3/B/472
Jn., sen., gent., Wootton B., 1664, comm, I, W, P3/B/495
Brunsden, Jn., yeo., Urchf., 1665, AB, I, P2/B/767
Brunsdon, Jn., jun., labourer, Stratton St Mgt., 1671, AB, comm, I, P3/B/594
Brinsdon *or* Brunsden, Jn., husb., Urchf., 1674, AB, I, P2/B/876
Brunsdon, Jn., husb. *or* labourer, Stratton St Mgt., 1681, I, W, P3/B/744
Brunsden, Jn., sen., yeo., Fosbury, Tidcombe and F., 1681, I, W, P3/B/743
Brimsdon, Jn., glazier, Devizes, 1692, AB, I, P1/B/613
Brunsden, Jn., sen., yeo., Ogbourne St Geo., 1694, I, W, P23/205
Brunsdon, Jn., yeo., Manton, Preshute, [1702], W, P1/B/699
Brunsden, Jn., yeo., Aughton, Collingbourne K., 1705, I, W, P3/B/1049
Brinson als Miller, Jn., husb., Strong Gate, Netherb., Dorset, 1709, AB, I, P17/188
Jn., clerk and vicar, Winterbourne M., 1719, I, W, P3/B/1169
Brunsden, Jn., sen., yeo., Ogbourne St Geo., 1733, W, P23/495
Brunsden, Jn., yeo., Ogbourne St Geo., 1740, W, P23/548
Brunsden, Jn., Manton, Preshute, 1747, AB, P1/B/1212
Brunsdon, Jn., yeo., Stratton St Mgt., 1749, W, P3/B/1463
Brunsden, Jn., Lambourn, Berks., 1754, AB, P1/B/1260
Brunsdon, Jn., baker, Marl., 1762, W, P1/B/1340, P1/12Reg/22
Brunsden, Jn., labourer, Ogbourne St Geo., 1762, comm, ren, W, P23/832
Jn., sen., Marl., 1782, W, P1/B/1465, P1/13Reg/344
Brunsdon, Jn., Stratford sub C., 1788, AB, P4/1788/11
Brunsden, Jn., yeo., Lt. Hinton, 1789, W, P1/B/1513, P1/14Reg/274
Brunsden, Jn., dairyman, Snodshill, Chiseldon, 1804, W, P1/1804/81
Brunsdon, Jn., gent., Newbury, Berks., 1817, W, copy W, P1/1817/79
Brinson, Jn., Beam., Dorset, 1820, AB, O, Wr, P17/602
Brunsdon, Jn., Stratford sub C., 1826, AB, Wr, P1/1826/15
Brunsden, Jos., yeo., Ogbourne St Geo., 1774, W, P23/756
Brunsdon, Jos., carp., Stratford sub C., 1803, W, P4/1803/10
Brunsden, Letitia, sp., Ogbourne St Geo., 1832, W, Wr, P23/963
Brinsen, Lisken, widow, Urchf., 1628, I, W, P1/B/210
Brunsdon, Mgt., widow, Marl., 1668, comm, I, W, P1/B/454
My., widow, Wootton B., 1683, AB, I, P3/B/777
Brinson als Miller, My., widow, Strong Gate, Netherb., Dorset, 1717, AB, I, P17/373
Brunsdon, My., widow, Marl., 1763, W, P1/B/1361, P1/12Reg/99A
Brinson als Brunsdon, My., Chitterne (living in Imber), 1777, W, P2/B/1939
Brinsdon, Nich., labourer, Imber, 1788, W, P2/B/2029
Brinsom als Miller, Philip, mason, Netherb., Dorset, 1696, AB, I, P17/303
Brimsdon, Philip, yeo., Woodb., 1757, W, P3/B/1508
Brunsdon, Rd., Ogbourne St Geo., 1603, AB, I (2), T, P5/1603/11, P5/7Reg/89C
Brinsdon, Rd., yeo., E. Stowell, Wilcot, 1665, AB, I, P1/B/448
Bronsdon, Rd., husb., Manton, Preshute, 1725, W, P1/B/908, P1/7Reg/56
Brunsden, Rd., sen., yeo., Ogbourne St Geo., 1725-64, AB (of unadm.goods), comm, W, P5/1725/6, P5/1764/5, P5/16Reg/126A
Brunsdon, Rd., Preshute, 1748, AB, P1/B/1225
Brunsdon, Rd., yeo., Ogbourne St Geo., 1762, AB, W, P5/1762/7
Brunsdon, Rd., gent., Rams., 1763, O, W, P5/1763/2
Brunsden, Rd., dairyman, Snodshill, Chiseldon, 1774, W, P3/B/1633
Brunsdon, Rd., Marl., 1823, AB, comm, Wr, P1/1824/2
Brunsden, Robt., sen., yeo., Crofton, Gt. Bedwyn, 1671, I, W, P5/1671/7
Roger, Gt. Somerford, 1745, W, P3/B/1431
Brinsdon, Sarah, widow, Yatton K., 1850, L, note, W, P3/1850/62
Simon, husb., Eddington, Hungerford, Berks., 1678, AB, I, P23/79
Brunsdon, Steph., Ogbourne St Geo., 1740, AB, P23/549
Brunsdon, Susanna, sp., Stratton St Mgt., 1687-88, AB, I, W, P29/B/29, P29/1Reg/233
Brimsdon, Thos., Barford St Mart., 1550, AB, P2/2Reg/100A, 112C
Brunsdon, Thos., Berwick B., 1576, I, T, W, P5/1576/7, P5/3Reg/90B
Brunsdon, Thos., yeo., Steeple L., 1597, AB, I, W, P2/B/176

Brinsdon, Thos., Collingbourne D., 1619, AB, W, P21/1/5
Brunsdon, Thos., Urchf., 1669, AB, P2/B/812
Brunsdon, Thos., Marl. St Peter and St Paul, 1715, AB, P1/B/812
Brimsdon, Thos., husb. *or* yeo., E. Stowell, Wilcot, 1715, I, W, P3/B/1131
Brunsdon, Thos., yeo., Manton, Preshute, 1735, W, P1/B/1053, P1/8Reg/59
Brunsden, Thos., Ogbourne St Geo., 1736, I, W, P5/1736/7
Brimsdon, Thos., Wilcot, 1743, W, P3/B/1416
Brunsdon, Thos., mercer, Marl., 1743, W, P1/B/1157, P1/9Reg/249
Brunsden, Thos., vintner, Newbury, Berks., 1808, W, Wr, P1/1808/120
Brunsdon, Toby, yeo., Stratton St Mgt., 1703, I, W, P3/B/1025
Bromesden, Walter, husb., Urchf., 1596, I, P2/B/167
Brunsdon, Wm., bach., Aldbourne, 1624, AB, I, L, P3/B/254
Brunsdon, Wm., husb., Lambourn, Berks., 1625, I, W, P1/B/192
Brimsen, Wm., carp., Urchf., 1632, I, P2/B/557
Brunsdon, Wm., Marl., 1662, AB, I, P1/B/385
Brunsdon, Wm., tailor, Easton, 1662, I, W, P3/B/482
Brimsdon, Wm., yeo. *or* husb., Alton Pr., 1690, I, W, P3/B/872
Brinson als Miller, Wm., mason, Beam., Dorset, 1693, I, W, P17/335
Brunsdon, Wm., yeo., Tottenham Park, Gt. Bedwyn, 1694, W, P21/5/29
Brimsdon, Wm., tailor *or* yeo., Wilcot, 1719, I, W, P3/B/1168
Brunsdon, Wm., Amesb., 1722, AB, P2/B/2148
Brinson, Wm., Beam., Dorset, 1724, AB, P17/403
Brunsdon, Wm., butcher, Denchworth, Berks., 1726, AB, I, P1/B/919
Brunsdon, Wm., sen., yeo., S. Denchworth, Berks., 1770, AB, ren, P1/B/1399
Brunsdon, Wm., yeo., Charlton nr Malm., 1773, AB, W, P3/B/1626
Brunsdon, Wm., Imber, 1777, AB, P2/B/1940
Brunsdon, Wm., Wootton B., 1835, W, P1/1835/110
see also Miller als B.

Briscoe, Hy., Uffington, Berks., 1747, W, P1/B/1204, P1/10Reg/80
Robt., Newbury, Berks., 1732, AB, I, P1/B/1011,

Brisse *see* Brice

Bristow, Ann, widow, Leigh Delamere, 1670, I, W, P3/B/574
Ann, widow, Milford, Sal. St Mart., 1730, AB, W, P4/1730/21
Ann, Foscote, Grittleton, 1738, W, P1/B/1108, P1/8Reg/373
Ann, wife, Devizes, 1851, AB, comm, D, Wr, P1/1851/34
Anth., yeo., Sand Furlong Farm, Broad H., 1727, W, P3/B/1257
Anth., yeo., Liddington, [1591], W (NEP), P3/1Reg/27
Benj., yeo., Biddestone, 1688, I, W, P3/B/847
Benj., yeo., Edington, 1711, I, W, P2/B/1300
Benj., Edington, 1744, AB, P1/B/1184
Bristow, ironmonger, Wood St., Swindon, 1845, comm, req, copy W, Wr, P3/1845/11
Cath., sp., Sal., 1736, AB, P1/B/1065
Dorcas, widow, Chipp., 1762, W, P3/B/1551
Dorothy, Devizes, 1703, AB, P1/B/703
Edith, widow, Winsley, Bradford A., 1621, I, W, P2/B/415
Edith, widow, Marston, Pott., 1639, AB, I, P1/B/292
Edwd., sen., yeo., Grittleton, 1618, I, W, P3/B/164
Edwd., yeo., Pott., 1662, I, W, P1/B/377
Edwd., yeo., Nettleton, 1688, I, W, P3/B/848
Edwd., yeo., Pott., 1703, I, W, P1/B/706, P1/4Reg/235
Edwd., Biddestone St Nich., 1733, AB, I, P3/B/1326
Edwd., yeo., Pott., 1740, W, P1/B/1123, P1/9Reg/1B
Edwd., labourer, Lowden, Chipp., 1835, comm, W, Wr, P1/1835/112
Eliz., widow, Sal., 1758, W, P4/1758/14
Francis, yeo., Crickl. St S., 1704, I, W, P1/B/714
Hannah, widow, Biddestone, 1759, I, W, P1/B/1328, P1/11Reg/441
Hy., Coate, Liddington (described as of Coate, Swindon), 1661, AB, comm, P3/B/470
Hy., innholder, Fisherton A., 1743, W, P2/B/1616
Hy., blacksmith, Swindon, 1812, W, Wr, P3/1812/35
Hy., vict., Marl., 1822, comm, W, Wr, P1/1822/14

Isaac, yeo., Ryley's Farm, Leigh Delamere, 1668, I, W, P3/B/536
Isaac, yeo., Grittleton, 1719, AB, I, P3/B/1170
Isaac, yeo., Nettleton, 1749, W, P3/B/1460
Isaac, Nettleton, 1767, AB, P3/B/1586
Isaac, N. Wraxall, 1812, AB, comm, P3/1812/14
Jacob, Pott., 1717, AB, P1/B/839
Jacob, blacksmith, Lacock, 1633, AB, a/c, I, P3/B/349
Jas., Fisherton A., 1747, W (in his 84th year), P1/B/1219, P1/10Reg/194
Jas., Grittleton, 1747, AB, W, P3/B/1447
Jas., yeo., Edington, 1802, W, P2/1802/36
Jas., shopkeeper, Warm., 1849, AB, aff, O, Wr, P2/1849/58
Jane, widow, Nettleton, 1741, W, P1/B/1144, P1/9Reg/164
Joan, widow, Notton, Lacock, 1639, I, W, P3/B/423
Jn., Slaughterford, 1571, W (NEP), P1/1Reg/82C
Bristow als Panter, Jn., husb., Clatford, Preshute, 1614, I, W, P1/B/106
Jn., husb., Pott., 1620, I, W, P1/B/179
Jn., Manton, Preshute (has a room in Marl.), 1664, I, W (damaged), P1/B/409
Jn., yeo., Coate, Liddington, 1673, AB, a/c, comm, I, ren, P3/B/618
Bristow *or* Bristoll, Jn., [farmer], Clarendon Park, 1684, a/c, I (over Ł1,000), W, P4/1684/6
Jn., Axford, Rams., 1687, AB, P5/1686/16
Jn., sen., yeo., Broad H., 1689, I, W (NEP), P3/B/856
Jn., jun., yeo., Nettleton, 1707, I, W, P1/B/730
Jn., soldier, Sal., 1713, AB, P4/1712/11
Jn., yeo., Elcombe, Wrou., 1726, comm, W, P1/B/928, P1/7Reg/136
Jn., yeo., Charl. nr. P., 1727, W, P2/B/1457
Jn., yeo., Nettleton, 1730, I, W, P3/B/1299
Jn., yeo., Kington L., 1766, W, P3/B/1580
Jn., jun., yeo., Cholsey, Berks., 1776, AB, comm, W, P1/B/1434, 1440, P1/13Reg/122A
Jn., gent., Speen, Berks., 1846, W, Wr, P1/1846/15
Jn., traveller for iron founders, Upper Clatford, Hants (goods in Swindon), 1846, AB, alleg, comm, note, W, Wr, P3/1846/18, 35
Judith, widow, Chelworth, Crickl. St S., 1681, I, W, P3/B/740
Judith, widow, Pott., 1685, W, P1/B/576
Lucy, Leigh Delamere, 1674, AB, P1/B/500
My., widow, Pott., 1676, I, W (NEP), P1/B/505
My., widow, Pott., 1728, W, P1/B/944, P1/7Reg/199B
My., widow, Cholsey, Berks., 1741, W, P1/B/1131, P1/9Reg/93
My., widow, Alderton, 1855, aff, D, W, Wr, P3/1855/28
Nich., Nettleton, 1649, AB, P1/B/351
Rebecca, widow, Edington, 1744, AB, P1/B/1186
Rd., husb., Pott., 1558, W (NEP) but before 1562 (AB of supervisor's estate 1562), P1/1Reg/40C
Rd., sen., tucker *or* clothw., Sal. St Edmd., 1621, AB, I, W, copy W, P4/1620/1
Rd., tailor, Devizes, 1688, I, W, P1/B/592
Rd., maltster, Sal., 1728, W, P4/1728/27
Rd., Chilton F., 1749, AB, P3/B/1461
Rd., The Broyle, Gt. Bedwyn, 1712-30, I, release (re house in T.B., 1712), ren, P21/8/55
Robt., yeo., Chelworth, Crickl. St S., 1769, W, P3/B/1605
Sarah, Ogbourne St Geo., 1716, W, P5/1716/15, P5/15Reg/350C
Sarah, widow, Foscote, Grittleton, 1733, I, W, P3/B/1327
Sarah, sp. *or* widow, Crickl. St My., 1795, W, P3/B/1746
Steph., Broad H., 1788, AB, P3/B/1714
Steph., carp., Crickl. St S., 1798, W, P3/B/1761
Susanna, widow, Crickl. St S., 1718, AB, I, ren, P3/B/1154
Thos., husb., Marston, Pott., 1605, AB, I, note of debts, W, P1/B/33
Thos., Swindon, 1636, AB, P3/B/362
Thos., innholder, Fisherton A., 1732, W, P1/B/1023, P1/7Reg/534B
Thos., Sal., 1752, AB, W, P4/1752/4
Timothy, clothw. *or* husb., Sal. St Edmd., 1674, AB, W, P4/1673/11
Timothy, Sal., 1728, AB, P4/1728/11
Wm., husb., Notton, Lacock, 1603, I, W, P3/B/6

Brewstow, Wm., Ruscombe, Berks., 1617, AB, P5/9Reg/215E
Wm., Chute, 1634, AB, comm(GVS), P5/1634/25
Wm., Preston, Lyneham, 1680, I, P3/B/727
Wm., yeo., Honey Hill, Broad H., 1752, W, P3/B/1479
Wm., Swindon, 1814, AB, P3/1814/22
Britain *see* Britten
Brite *see* Bright
Britt, Thos., Langley Fitzurse, Kington St M., 1691, AB, I, P3/B/881
Britten, Baldwin, husb., Winterbourne S., 1559, W, P2/4Reg/3C
Betty, yeo.'s widow, Pewsham, 1852, AB, aff, O, Wr, P5/1852/2
Edwd., Stourton, 1571, AB, P2/5Reg/135A
Brittan, Eliz., cooper's widow, Devizes, 1747, W, P1/B/1217, P1/10Reg/175
Brittan, Eliz., sp., Devizes, 1805, AB, P1/1805/6
Brittan, Eliz., widow, Devizes St My., 1814, W, Wr, P1/1814/20
Brittan, Francis, ironmonger, Devizes, 1780, W, P1/B/1457, P1/13Reg/307
Brittan, Francis, ironmonger, Devizes, 1822, W, Wr, P1/1822/13
Geo., Sal., 1848, W, Wr, P4/1848/1
Brittan, Grizel, widow, Sonning, Berks., 1744, comm, W, Wr, P5/1744/6
Britton, Hannah, widow, Sal., 1843, AB, Wr, P1/1843/26
Hy., Stourton, 1567, AB, P2/4Reg/239H
Britton, Hy., yeo., Avill's Farm, Corsham, 1753, W, P3/B/1484
Britton, Hy., baker and shopkeeper, Kington St M., 1790, AB, comm, ren, P3/B/1725
Britton, Jn., Semley, 1558, W, P2/3Reg/114A
Jn., Sutton M., 1580, AB, P2/B/80, P2/6Reg/2B
Britain, Jn., cordw., Shrewton, 1789, W, P2/B/2039
Britain, Jos., collarmaker, Crickl. St S., 1696, I, W, P3/B/952
Britain, Jos., yeo., Letcombe Regis, Berks., 1817, comm, W, Wr, P1/1817/91
Jos., widower, Pewsham, 1852, AB, O, Wr, P5/1852/9
Britton, Lucinda Rebecca Watts, widow, Devizes, 1853, AB, aff, O, Wr, P1/1853/4
Margery, widow, Chirton, 1582, AB, P2/6Reg/75C
Brittan, My., widow, Bulk., Keevil, 1749, AB, W, P2/B/1675
Brittan, My., widow, Devizes, 1777, AB, app. of attorney with ren, W, P1/B/1448, P1/13Reg/171B
Brittan, Meshach, cooper, Devizes, 1740, comm, W, P1/B/1114, P1/8Reg/423
Brittan, Meshach, Devizes, 1777, AB, comm, P1/B/1447
Britain, Reynold, no abode stated, 1607, I, W, P2/B/277
Rd., Stourton, 1627, AB, I, P2/B/469
Rd., husb., Horningsham, 1632, W, P5/1632/11, P5/12Reg/88
Robt., yeo., Pewsham, 1852, AB, O, W, Wr (2), P5/1852/3
Thos., yeo., Lockshill, Chipp., 1818, W, Wr, P3/1818/21
Wm., husb., Stourton, 1563, W, P2/4Reg/132B
Brittane, Wm., blacksmith, Sherb., Dorset, 1636, AB, I, P5/1636/8, P5/13Reg/26B
Brittan, Wm., sen., [blacksmith], Sherb., Dorset, 1668, AB, I, P5/1668/10
Britain, Wm., edge toolmaker, Sherb., Dorset, 1695, AB, I, P5/1695/9
Brittan, Wm., butcher, Sonning, Berks., 1741, W, Wr, P5/1741/3
Wm., Stanley, Bremhill, 1848, comm, D, W, Wr, P3/1848/48
see also Oak form. B.
Brivate, Chris., dealer, bread seller to Jn. Sweetland baker of Bratton, Heywood, Westb., 1720, AB, I, ren, P25/1720/4
Brixey, My., widow, Bourton, Gillingham, Dorset, 1797, W, P27/1/559
Rd., feltmaker, Mere, 1677-78, AB, a/c, I, P5/1677/7, P5/1678/1
Robt., widower, Bourton, Gillingham, Dorset, 1801, AB, P27/1/571
Broad, Abel, vict., Turleigh, Winsley, Bradford A., 1775, W, P2/B/1920
Abel, yeo., Winsley, Bradford A., 1786, W, P2/B/2014
Ann, widow, Gt. Bedwyn, 1685, AB, I, P5/1685/10
Cornelius, Winsley, Bradford A., 1704, I, W, P2/B/1242
Cornelius, butcher, Winsley, Bradford A., 1757, W, P2/B/1735
Cornelius, yeo., Bradford A., 1780, W, P2/B/1976
Edwd., jun., carver, Pewsey, 1711, AB, I, P3/B/1098
Eleanor, widow, Kemble, 1714, W, P3/B/1122
Eleazar, farming bailiff, Cadley, Chute, 1851, W, Wr, P7/212
Isabel, widow, Garsdon, 1625, I, W, P1/B/197

Jane, Winsley, Bradford A., [1717], W, P2/B/1363
Jn., carp., Trowb., 1685, AB, I, P1/B/579
Jn., yeo., Charlton nr Malm., 1693, AB, agreement, I, Wr, P3/B/904
Jn., yeo., Winsley, Bradford A., 1776, W, P2/B/1934
Jos., blacksmith, Whitep., 1723, W, P1/B/878, P1/6Reg/406
Jos., Upton L., 1730, AB, P2/B/1482
Jos., labourer, Wantage, Berks., 1824, comm, W, Wr, P5/1824/4
Brode, My., widow, Charlton nr Malm., 1731, W, P3/B/1305
Rd., yeo., Hazelbury, Box, 1694, I, W, P3/B/924
Robt., yeo., Clench, Milton L., 1685, AB, I, P3/B/819
Robt., yeo., Coleshill, Berks., 1726, I, W, P1/B/920, P1/7Reg/101A
Thos., yeo., Garsdon, 1603, I, W, P3/B/7
Thos., yeo., Wadswick, Box, 1633, I, W, P3/B/350
Thos., rough mason, Wadswick, Box, 1693, I, W, P3/B/905
Thos., rough mason, Wadswick, Box, 1698, AB, W, P1/B/668, P1/3Reg/36
Thos., carp., Winsley, Bradford A., 1707, comm, I, W, P2/B/1266
Thos., blacksmith, Collingbourne K., 1837, W, Wr, P3/1837/30
Tobias, clothw., Holt, Bradford A., 1728, W, P2/B/1465
Wm., sen., yeo., Gt. Bedwyn, 1675, AB, I, NW, P21/2/43
Wm., sen., Gt. Bedwyn, 1729, I, W, P21/8/48
Wm., yeo., Charlton nr Malm., 1731, AB, W, P3/B/1306
Wm., labourer, Hatchet, Chute, 1827, O, W, Wr, P7/199
Broadford *see* Bradford
Broadhead, Rd., clerk and rector, Lt. Cheverell, 1703, comm, I, W, P1/B/704, P1/4Reg/242
Susanna, widow, Westb., 1724, W, P25/1724/2
Broadhurst, Jn., yeo., Alton Pr., 1680, AB, I, P3/B/728
Jn., cordw., Bremhill, 1783, W, P3/B/1683
Phyllis, widow, Alton Pr., 1681, I, W, P3/B/741
see also Littleworth als B.
Broadly, Jasper, Netherb., Dorset, 1678, AB, P17/89
Broadmead, Eliz., widow, Devizes, 1737, W, P1/B/1074, P1/8Reg/175
Broadrib, Jos., yeo., Southwick, N. Bradley, 1735, AB, W, P1/B/1036, P1/7Reg/615A
My., Southwick, N. Bradley, 1735, ren, W, P1/B/1037, P1/7Reg/614
Thos., yeo., Southwick, N. Bradley, 1697, I, W, P2/B/1186
Thos., narrow weaver, N. Bradley, 1734, W, P2/B/1535
Broadrib *or* Brodripp, Walter, Pitton, Alderbury, 1580, I, P5/1580/10, P5/4Reg/6D
Broadshall, And., weaver, Broughton G., 1594, I, W, P2/B/158
Broadwater, Rd., Abingdon St Helen, Berks., 1605, AB, I (damaged), P1/B/39
Broadway, Anth., weaver, Crickl. St S., 1748, W, P3/B/1451
Edwd., Motc., Dorset, 1706, AB, ren, P27/1/160
Brodeway, Geoff., Motc., Dorset, 1577, W, P27/1Reg/34B
Hy., yeo., Crickl. St S., 1789, W, P3/B/1722
Keturah, widow, Gillingham, Dorset, 1838, req, W, P27/1/713
Bradway, Luke, clothier, Semington, Steeple A., 1558, W, P2/3Reg/112D
My., widow, Swindon, 1755, W, P3/B/1497
My., wife of Hy., druggist, Gillingham, Dorset, 1830, comm, ren, W, Wr, P27/1/690
Nehemiah, Quidh., 1828, AB, D, W, Wr, P2/1828/25
Ralph, sen., Woodley, W. and Sandford, Berks., 1671, I, W, P5/1671/10
Ralph, Sonning, Berks., 1712, W, P5/1712/9, P5/15Reg/303
Rd., tailor, Kington St M., 1622, I, W, P3/B/219
Sarah, widow, Landford, 1841, W, Wr, P2/1841/4
Thos., Motc., Dorset, 1719, AB, I, P27/1/229
Wm., Motc., Dorset, 1718, AB, P27/1/227
Wm., bach., Crickl. St S., 1727, AB, comm, ren, P3/B/1258
Wm., yeo., Motc., Dorset, 1764, W, P27/1/441, P27/3Reg/111
Wm., Motc., Dorset, 1780, AB, P27/1/506, P27/3Reg/218
Brock, David, Imber, 1783, W, P1/B/1480, P1/13Reg/424
Dennis, husb., Martin, Hants, 1591, W, P2/B/124
Brock *or* Brooke, Geo., Leighs Marsh, Dilton, Westb., 1644, AB, I, W, P25/1644/1
My., sp., Shrewton, 1853, aff, W, Wr, P2/1853/47

Rd., husb., Hilmarton, 1572, W, P1/1Reg/51A
Walter, husb., Gillingham, Dorset, 1567, W, P27/1Reg/18A
see also Brooks *or* B.
Brockway, Brokeway, David, Donhead St My., 1554, AB, P2/2Reg/187B
Eleanor, widow, Donhead St My., 1772, W, P2/B/1883
Jas., jun., wheelwright, Charlton, Donhead St My., 1661, I, W, P2/B/728
Jas., yeo., Charlton, Donhead St My., 1680, I, W, P2/B/952
Jas., Charlton, Donhead St My., 1729, W, P1/B/973, P1/7Reg/350A
Jn., Donhead St A., 1588, W, P2/7Reg/125A
Jn., Corsham, 1691, AB, P29/B/31, P29/1Reg/252A
Jn., sen., yeo., Charlton, Donhead St My., 1732, W, P1/B/1024, P1/7Reg/539
Jn. White, maltster, Marl., 1824, W, Wr, P1/1824/18
My., sp., Winterslow, 1772, AB, P2/B/1887
Rd., Donhead St My., 1804, W, P2/1804/3
Thos., Coombe, Donhead St My., 1829, AB, comm, ren, W, Wr, P2/1829/3
Wm., vict., Donhead St My., 1763, W, P1/B/1349, P1/12Reg/63B
Wm., Donhead St My., 1773, AB, P2/B/1896
Brodbury *see* Bradbury
Brode *see* Broad
Brodeway *see* Broadway
Brodey *see* Brodie
Brodfield *see* Bradfield
Brodie, Brodey, Hugh, linen weaver, Milton, Gillingham, Dorset, 1687, I, P27/1/92
Louisa, esquire's wife, Sal. The Close, 1816, AB, Wr, P5/1816/14
Brodripp *see* Broadrib *or* B.
Broke *see* Brooks
Brokeman *see* Brookman
Brokenborow, Brokenborough, Alice, widow, Kington L., 1630, I, W (NEP), P3/B/328
Brokenbrow, Alice, widow, Sevington, Leigh Delamere, 1705, I, W, P3/B/1047
Brokenbury, Ann, wife, Nettleton, 1683, I, W, P1/B/568
Brokenbrow, Ann, widow, Gt. Somerford, 1785, W, P3/B/1699
Brokenbrow, Anna, sp., Grittleton, 1856, AB, aff, comm, O, Wr, P3/1856/4
Chris., no abode stated but proved at Hungerford, Berks., 1597, I, P5/1597/117
Brokenbrow, Dorothy, sp., Wantage, Berks., 1789, AB, P23/785
Brokenbrow, Jas., labourer, Grittleton, 1856, aff, O, W, Wr, P3/1856/63
Jn., carp., Kington St M., 1621, I, NW, P3/B/209
Jn., husb., W. Kington, 1636, I, W, P3/B/373
Brokenbury, Jn., yeo., Nettleton, 1694, I, W, P3/B/925
Brokenbrow *or* Brokenbury, Jn., carp., Grittleton, 1715, I, W, P3/B/1132
Brokenbrow, My., widow, Grittleton, 1768, comm, W, P3/B/1592
Brokenbrow, Nich., Castle C., 1719, AB, I, P28/9
Brokenbrow, Nich., vict. and maltster, Grittleton, 1778, W, P3/B/1653
Brokenbrow, Prudence, sp., Malm., 1805, AB, P3/1805/20
Brokenbrow, Rebecca, innkeeper's and maltster's widow, Grittleton, 1728, W, P3/B/1270
Brokenbrow, Robt., yeo., Colerne, 1825, comm, W, Wr, P3/1825/43
Brokenbrow, Roger, yeo., Alderton, 1736, W, P3/B/1354
Brokenbrow, Roger, Alderton, 1762, W, P3/B/1552
Brokenbrow, Roger, Gt. Somerford, 1791, comm, W, P3/B/1733
Simon, Long Newnton, 1609, AB, P3/B/52
Brokenbrow, Simon, yeo., Grittleton, 1671, I, W, P3/B/591
Brokenbrow, Thos., maltster and yeo., Grittleton, 1714, I, W, P1/B/802, P1/5Reg/434
Walter, yeo. *or* wheeler, Grittleton, 1690, I, W, P3/B/869
Brokenbrow, Walter, sen., yeo., Grittleton, 1769, W, P3/B/1606
Brokenbrow, Walter, yeo., Foscote, Grittleton, 1838, comm, W, P3/1838/13
Wm., day labourer, Long Newnton, 1610, W, P3/B/66
Brokenburrow, Wm., Kington L., 1623, AB, a/c, I, P3/B/233
Brokeway *see* Brockway
Brokwell *see* Broxwell
Bromage *see* Bromwich
Broman, Brooman, Jane, widow, Kingston Bagpuize, Berks., 1711, I, W, P1/B/766, P1/5Reg/170

Robt., Amesb., 1695, AB, I, P2/B/1166
Brome *see* Broom
Bromeley *see* Bromley
Bromesden *see* Brinsdon
Bromewich *see* Bromwich
Bromham, Ann, widow, Figh., 1726, AB, P26/712
Chris., husb., Figh., 1696, I, W, P26/443
Geo., maltster, Upavon, 1711, AB, W, P1/B/755, P1/5Reg/49
Brumham, Geo., yeo., Chitterne St My., 1741, W, P2/B/1595
Jacob, Compton, Enford, 1669, AB, a/c, I, P2/B/802
Jacob, yeo., Haxton, Fittleton, 1753, W, P1/B/1277, P1/11Reg/110
Bramham, Jas., Lacock, 1738, W, P3/B/1371
Jn., sen., husb., Coombe, Enford, 1634, I, W, P2/B/577, P2/B/608
Brumham, Jn., husb., Coombe, Enford, 1663, I, W, P2/B/760
Bromham als Phelps, Jn., yeo., Avebury, 1664, I, W, P1/B/416
Jn., yeo., Fittleton, 1682, AB, I, P2/B/1002
Brumham, Jn., husb., Compton, Enford, 1711, W, P1/B/762, P1/5Reg/120B
Jn., yeo., Fittleton, 1720, I, ren, W, P1/B/867, P1/6Reg/348B
Jn., yeo., Fittleton, 1762, AB, comm, P2/B/1783
Jn., Sudley Brook, Calne, 1847, AB, I, note (2), Wr, P5/1847/12
My., widow, Netheravon, 1622, AB, P12/44
Bromham als Phelps, Sarah, sp., Bromham, 1673, AB, comm, I, W, P3/B/631
Steph., baker, Calne, 1705, AB, comm, I (detailed), ren, P26/509
Brumham, Thos., Sutton V., 1790, AB, P2/B/2051
see also Phelps als B.
Bromhead, Thos., priest, Newbury, Berks., 1560/1561, institution to rectory, P1/1Reg/79B
Bromley, Bromiley, Arthur, clerk, Blewbury, Berks., 1833, note, O, W, Wr, P5/1833/5
Bartholemew, curate of Wokingham, Wokm., Berks., 1572, AB, P5/2Reg/114C
Geo., carp. and builder, Pickwick, Corsham, 1840, W, Wr, P3/1840/20
Browmlaye, Jn., Wokm., Berks., [1574?], I (2), Wr (endorsed in later hand 'Ex Court of the Chancellor of the University of Oxford'), P5/1574/2
Jn., sen., carrier, Wokm., Berks., 1682, AB, I, P5/1682/12
Bramly, Martha, wife, Preshute, 1676, AB, P1/B/504
My., widow, Littlewick Grn, White Waltham, Berks., 1756, W, P1/B/1297, P1/11Reg/204
Bromeley, Rd., Wokm., Berks., 1541, W, P5/20Reg/21A
Brumley, Robt., Wokm., Berks., 1543, W (probate given as May 1542 which error for 1543 as W dated Mar 1542/3), P5/20Reg/42C
Thos., parson, Manningford A., 1620, AB, I, NW, P1/B/171
Bramly, Thos., keeper, New Windsor, Berks., 1711, AB, I, P1/B/769
Bramley, Wm., Wantage, Berks., 1573, W, P5/3Reg/12A
Wm., jun., Sonning, Berks., 1805, W, P5/1805/10, P5/19Reg/128
Wm., sen., fisherman, Sonning, Berks., 1805, W, P5/1805/11, P5/19Reg/129
see also Bramble
Bromsgrove, Ann, widow, Corston, Malm., 1804, W, P1/1804/91
Broomsgrove, Rd., Startley, Gt. Somerford, 1832, AB, Wr, P1/1832/76
Broomsgrove, Thos., Malm., 1785, AB, P3/B/1700
Bromwich, Arthur, gent., Seend, Melk., 1670, AB, a/c, comm, ren, P2/B/827
Rachel, widow, Seend, Melk., 1677, AB, I, P1/B/513
Rd., gent., Malm., 1753, W, P1/B/1274, P1/11Reg/84
Susanna, widow, Malm., 1764, W, P3/B/1562
Bromage, Thos., Sal., 1798, AB, W, P1/B/1552, P1/15Reg/49
Bromewich, Wm., Bratton, Westb., 1665, AB, comm, P25/1665/9
Bronsdon *see* Brinsden
Brook, Brooke, Brookes *see* Brooks
Brookeman *see* Brookman
Brooker, Christian, Crickl. St S., 1696, AB, I, P3/B/953
Henrietta, sp., Thatcham, Berks., 1729, I, W, P1/B/962, P1/7Reg/277A
Broucker, Hy., labourer, Whitley, Melk., 1633, I, NW, P2/B/565
Jn., gent., Abingdon, Berks., 1671, note of probate at PCC, P1/B/472
Jn., woolstapler, Burcombe, 1774, W, P2/B/1905

Brucker, Martha, widow, Warnhill, Longworth, Berks., 1795, W, P1/B/1533, P1/14Reg/518
My., widow, Wilton, 1780, W, P2/B/1970
Thos., wheelwright, Newtown, Hungerford, Berks., 1828, W, Wr, P23/934
Brookings, Jonathan, yeo., Langley Whire, Cumnor, Berks., 1783, W, P1/B/1482
Brookman, Hy., husb., Stanford Dingley, Berks., 1711, AB, I, P1/B/768
Jn., yeo., Stoke F., 1770, W, P1/B/1389, P1/12Reg/304
Brokeman, Thos., yeo., Eastrop, Highw., 1676, I, W, P5/1676/8
Brokeman, Wm., Wylye, [1551], I (2), P2/B/3
Brookeman, Wm., yeo., The Parsonage, Eastrop, Highw., 1629, I, W, P10/1629/5
Wm., bach., Tilehurst, Berks., 1811, AB, Wr, P1/1811/34
see also Newman als B.
Brooks, Aaron, widower, Longworth, Berks., 1783, AB, P1/B/1478
Abel, yeo., Hodson, Chiseldon, 1798, comm, W, P3/B/1762
Abel, bach., Uffcott, Broad H., 1802, AB, P3/1802/1
Abraham, shopkeeper, Bremhill, 1781, W, P3/B/1672
Broke, Alice, widow, Wokm., Berks., 1540, AB, P5/20Reg/13A
Brookes, Alice, widow, Melk., 1647, AB, P2/B/710
Broke, Alison, widow, Uffc., Devon, 1570, W, P5/2Reg/86B
Brookes, Ambrose, mason, Uffington, Berks., 1776, comm, W, P1/B/1428, P1/13Reg/79A
Ann, widow, Marl., 1674, AB (to pay legacy), P1/B/502
Brook, Ann, widow, Wantage, Berks., 1688-91, AB, I, P23/165, 177
Ann, widow, Calne, 1698, AB, I, W, P26/458
Ann, sp., Chipp., 1711, comm, W, P1/B/754, P1/5Reg/48
Brooke, Ann, widow, Calne, 1754, AB, W, P26/930
Ann, widow, Seend, Melk., 1769, W, P2/B/1859
Ann, widow, Devizes, 1772, W, P1/B/1408, P1/12Reg/428
Ann, widow, Wootton B., 1779, AB, comm, P3/B/1658
Brooke als Butstone, Anth., yeo., Rull, Uffc., Devon, 1623, comm, I, W, P5/1622/11, P5/10Reg/153
Anth., yeo., Aston, Remenham, Berks., 1732, W, P1/B/1007, P1/7Reg/483A
Brooke, Anth., sen., Heddington, 1742, W, P3/B/1405
Brooke, Christian, sp., Chards., Devon, 1640, AB, P5/1640/6, P5/13Reg/225B
Browke, David, Donhead St My., 1558, W, P2/3Reg/103B
Deborah, sp., Sherb., Dorset, 1776, comm, W, P5/1776/6, P5/17Reg/102B
Broke, Edmd., husb., Hullavington, 1617, NW, P3/B/146
Edwd., yeo., Fordington, Dorset, 1770, W, P5/1770/9, P5/17Reg/20A
Elias, Chilmark, 1694, AB, I, P2/B/1161
Brooke, Eliz., widow, Donhead St A., 1561, W, P2/4Reg/87A
Broke, Eliz., widow, Wantage, Berks., 1574, W, P5/3Reg/40C
Brooke, Eliz., widow, Kington L., 1633, I, W, P3/B/351
Brookes, Eliz., widow, Norton, 1737, AB, comm, P1/B/1079
Brookes, Geo., yeo., E. Hatch, Tisb., 1716, AB, W, P1/B/827, P1/6Reg/36
Geo., yeo., Flamston, Bishopstone S., 1797, W, P2/B/2130
Brook, Giles, husb., Uffc., Devon, 1754, I, W, P20/1/223
Brook *or* Brock, Hy., clerk parson, Fisherton A., 1605, AB, I, P1/B/27
Brookes, Hy., vict., Calne, 1695, comm, I (detailed), W, P26/434
Hy., butcher, Chipp., 1724, AB, P3/B/1226
Hy., yeo., Seend, Melk., 1762, AB, comm, P2/B/1788
Brooke, Hy., sen., plumber, glazier and painter, Marl., 1857, aff, O, W, Wr, P1/1857/3
Jas., Chilmark, 1738, AB, P2/B/1567
Brooke, Jas., tailor, Uffc., Devon, 1758, W, P5/1758/7
Jas., jun., vict., Charminster, Dorset, 1844, comm, W, Wr, P5/1844/17
Brooke, Jane, widow, Clevancy, Hilmarton, 1681, AB, P3/B/742
Brooke, Jane, sp., Stert, Urchf., 1744, W, P1/B/1183, P1/9Reg/423B
Jane, widow, Sherb., Dorset, 1818, comm, W, Wr, P5/1818/3
Brooke, Joan, widow, Bishopstone N., 1667, I, W, P6/28
Joan, widow, E. Hanney, W. Hanney, Berks., 1680, I, W, P1/B/538
Brookes, Joanna, sp., Wantage, Berks., 1712, AB, P23/323
Broyke, Jn., Uffc., Devon, 1552, W, P20/Reg/56
Brooke, Jn., Chicksgrove, Tisb., 1563, I, W, P2/B/41, P2/4Reg/152B
Brook, Jn., Easton Grey, 1626, AB, I, P3/B/278

Brooke, Jn., husb., Goatacre, Hilmarton, 1630, I, W, P3/B/327
Brooke, Jn., Stop, Fonthill G., 1634, I, P2/B/575
Brooke, Jn., husb., Clack, Lyneham, 1643, AB, comm, I, P1/B/304
Brook, Jn., sen., butcher, Calne, 1663, I, W, P5/1663/10
Brookes, Jn., innkeeper, Marl., 1671, comm, I, NW, P1/B/482
Brookes, Jn., vict., Chipp., 1672, I, W, P3/B/611
Brookes, Jn., Liddington, 1683, AB, I, P1/B/563
Jn., sen., vict., Calne, 1683, I (detailed), W, P26/309
Jn., yeo., Burghfield & Sulhamstead, Berks., 1683, I, W, P1/B/560
Jn., yeo., Chieveley, Berks., 1704, I, W, P1/B/718
Jn., Barford St Mart., 1708, AB, ren, P2/B/1276
Brookes, Jn., sen., currier, Chipp., 1727, I, W, P3/B/1260
Jn., Chipp., 1736, AB, P3/B/1355
Jn., cordw., Marl., 1738, W, P1/B/1096, P1/8Reg/311A
Jn., yeo., E. Grimstead, W. Dean, 1738, W, P2/B/1570
Brooke, Jn., sen., gent., Calne, 1742, AB, comm, ren, W, P26/831
Jn., yeo., E. Hanney, W. Hanney, Berks., 1773, W, P1/B/1412, P1/12Reg/472
Brooke, Jn., schoolmaster, Nether C., Dorset, 1777, W (& cod), P5/1777/3, P5/17Reg/142B
Brooke, Jn., brewer, Malm., 1822, comm, W, Wr, P3/1822/37
Brooke, Jn., no abode stated; property in Blackland, 1826, AB, comm, P1/1826/37
Jonah, joiner, Wootton B., 1766, W, P3/B/1581
Jos., mason, Uffington, Berks., 1698, I, W, P1/B/673, P1/3Reg/86
Brookes, Jos., Wantage, Berks., 1752, AB, P5/1752/4
Jos., innholder, Devizes, 1765, W, P1/B/1371, P1/12Reg/159B
Mgt., sp., Devizes, 1743, AB, P1/B/1159
Brooke, Margery, sp., Wantage, Berks., 1668, AB, P5/1668/9
Brooke, My., widow, Farnham, Tollard Royal, Dorset, 1682, AB, I, P2/B/994
My., widow, Calne, 1716, W, P5/1716/14, P5/15Reg/349A
Brook, My., widow, Sherb., Dorset, 1734, W, P5/1734/9
My., widow, Chipp., 1737, W, P3/B/1367
My., widow, Corsham, 1770, W (cod), P29/B/52, P29/2Reg/132
Brookes, My., widow, Uffington, Berks., 1779, W, P1/B/1456, P1/13Reg/299
My., wife of Chas., Wokm., Berks., 1795, AB, comm, P5/1795/1, P5/18Reg/210A
My., sp., Bath, Somerset, 1801, AB (2), comm (2), P4/1801/3
Brooke, Nich., carp., Easton Grey, 1618, I, W, P3/B/165
Philip, Sutton B., 1726, AB, P3/B/1248
Brooke, Rd., Fonthill G., 1574, W, P2/5Reg/203C
Brooke, Rd., yeo., Uffc., Devon, 1625, AB, I, P5/1625/10, P5/10Reg/270C
Brooke, Rd., Nether St., Bromham, 1647, I, W, P1/B/336
Brookes, Rd., husb., Snelsmore, Chieveley, Berks., 1664, AB, I, P1/B/406
Brook, Rd., gent., Wantage, Berks., 1672, AB, I, P23/27
Brooke, Rd., gent., Wantage, Berks., 1692, AB, P23/180
Brook, Rd., Wantage, Berks., 1696, AB, P23/217
Brookes, Rd., miller, Clatford Mill, Preshute, 1698, I, W, P1/B/665
Rd., W. Hanney, Berks., 1701, AB, P1/B/690
Brooke, Rd., yeo., Brokenb., 1801, req, copy W, P1/1801/79, P1/15Reg/299
Rd., bach., Pangbourne, Berks., 1807, AB, comm, Wr, P1/1807/22
Brooke, Robt., mason, Lyneham, 1637, I, W, P3/B/391
Brook, Robt., labourer, Hullavington, 1707, I, NW, P3/B/1068
Robt., vict., Sandy Lane, Calne, 1709, comm, W, P3/B/1079
Robt., butcher, Chipp., 1782, W, P1/B/1469, P1/13Reg/385
Robt., Chipp., 1807, AB, Wr, P1/1807/34
Brooke, Roger, Sherb., Dorset, 1609, AB, a/c, I, T, P5/1609/10, P5/8Reg/143B
Sarah, widow, E. Grimstead, W. Dean, 1753, W, P2/B/1700
Brooke, Susanna, wife of Jn. B., Nether C., Dorset ; he now *or* late of London, 1786, comm, W, P5/1786/2, P5/18Reg/54
Brooke, Thos., Wantage, Berks., 1573, W, P5/3Reg/12B
Brooke, Thos., gent., Wilton, 1641, I, draft W (unsigned - re-written later as NW), W, P2/B/670
Brooke, Thos., gent., Wantage, Berks., 1678, I, P5/1678/3
Brook, Thos., Wantage, Berks., 1692, AB, P5/1692/13
Brookes, Thos., cardmaker, Warm., 1705, I, W, P2/B/1245

Thos., sen., butcher, Chipp., 1710, I, W, P3/B/1090
Brookes, Thos., butcher, Chipp., 1726, W, P1/B/917, P1/7Reg/119A
Thos., yeo., Wargrave, Berks., 1726, W, P1/B/927, P1/7Reg/95A
Thos., Norton, 1729, AB, P3/B/1279
Thos., cardmaker, Warm., 1743, AB, ren, P2/B/1619
Brooke, Thos., [linn man], Nether C., Dorset, 1785, comm, W, P5/1785/6, P5/18Reg/9
Broke, Tristram, gent., Wantage, Berks., 1569, W, P5/2Reg/47B
Broox, Walter, weaver, Chipp., 1724, W, P3/B/1227
Walter, butcher, Chipp., 1763, W, P3/B/1558
Brooke, Wm., sen., broad weaver, Malm., 1610, W, P3/B/67
Wm., W. Hanney, Berks., 1698, AB, P1/B/671
Wm., yeo., Brinkw., 1713, I, W, P3/B/1120
Wm., yeo., N. Moreton, Berks., 1723, W, P1/B/895, P1/7Reg/3A
Brook, Wm., sen., miller, Uffc., Devon, 1749, W, Wr, P5/1749/5
Brook, Wm., Uffc., Devon, 1772, AB, O, P20/1/255
Wm., carp., Sal., 1782, W, P4/1782/12
see also Brock *or* B.
Broom, Ann, widow, Calne, 1830, AB, O, Wr, P26/1384
Brome, Bartlett, apothecary, Marl., 1763, W, P1/B/1364, P1/12Reg/125A
Chas., yeo., Yatton K., 1728, I, W, P3/B/1271
Broome, Chas., Old Park Farm, Devizes St Jn., 1854, AB, aff, O, Wr, P1/1855/5
Broome, Chris., Bushton, Clyffe P., 1716, AB, comm, I (all fragile), P3/B/1136
Broome, Eliz., widow, Lyneham, [1665], I, NW (NEP), P3/B/510
Brome, Francis, yeo., Lyneham, 1740, W, P3/B/1391
Francis, sen., carp., Castle C., 1784, W, P3/B/1692
Giles, joiner, Castle C., 1849, W, Wr, P3/1849/19
Jas., baker and maltster, Castle C., 1811, W, Wr, P1/1811/87
Jane, widow, Castle C., 1852, O, W, Wr, P3/1852/6
Joan, widow, Chards., Devon, 1745, comm, W, P14/174
Broome, Jn., Wrou., 1668, AB, comm, I, P1/B/441
Broome, Jn., jun., Lyneham, 1699, AB, comm, I (2 - 1 a copy), P3/B/988
Broome, Jn., sen., yeo., Chards., Devon, 1705, AB, I, P14/103
Broome, Jn., Woolley, Bradford A., 1720, AB, I, P2/B/1390
Broome, Jn., yeo., Lyneham, 1724, W, P3/B/1228
Brome, Jn., yeo., Crowlway, Chards., Devon, 1729, AB, ren, P14/143
Broome, Jn., gent., Avill's Farm, Corsham, 1781, W, P3/B/1673
Jn., thatcher, Uffc., Devon, 1800, comm, W, P5/1800/39, P5/18Reg/309
Jn., Calne, 1829, O, AB, P26/1377
Love, widow, Castle C., 1813, AB, comm, Wr, P3/1813/19
Paul, farmer, Castle C., 1825, W, Wr, P3/1825/32
Broome, Ralph, yeo., Spirthill, Bremhill, 1672, I, W, P3/B/612
Ralph, yeo., Nuthills, Calne, 1748, W, P26/876
Broome, Ralph, gent., Bushton, Clyffe P., 1768, W, P3/B/1593
Broome, Rd., Kington St M., 1638, AB, a/c, I, P3/B/402
Broome, Rd., yeo., Cowitch Farm, Compton B., 1716, comm, I, W, P3/B/1137
Broome, Thos., husb., Kington St M., 1617, I, W, P3/B/147
see also Browne *or* B.
Brooman *see* Broman
Broome *see* Broom
Broomsgrove *see* Bromsgrove
Broox *see* Brooks
Brossier, Jas., Longbridge D., 1792, AB, comm, ren, P2/B/2071
Brothern *see* Brethren
Brothers *see* Brethers
Brotherton, Wm., sen., fishmonger, Sal., 1624, W, P4/1624/4
Wm., fishmonger, Sal., 1629, AB, a/c, I, P4/1628/15
Broucker *see* Brooker
Broughton, Benj., Wambrook, Somerset, 1818-20, AB, comm, O, W, Wr, P5/1818/28, P5/1820/17
Eliz., widow, Tubney, Berks., 1811, W, Wr (2), P1/1811/78
Mgt., widow, Wokm., Berks., 1600, AB, W, P5/1600/4, P5/6Reg/266B

Brouncker *see* Brunker
Broune *see* Brown
Brounjohn *see* Brownjohn
Brounker *see* Brunker
Brouse *see* Browse
Browen *see* Brown
Browke *see* Brooks
Browmlaye *see* Bromley
Brown, Browne, Agnes, widow, Brokenb., 1570, W (NEP), P1/1Reg/89B
Browne, Agnes, widow, Semley, 1744, W, P1/B/1187, P1/9Reg/439A
Algernon, farmer, Broad H., 1840, W, Wr, P3/1840/47
Browne, Alice, widow, Idmiston, 1560, W (NEP), P2/4Reg/63E
Browne, Alice, widow, Sherb., Dorset, 1592, AB, I, W, P5/1592/15, P5/5Reg/129E
Brown als Clement, Alice, Shaw, Semley, 1593, I, W, P2/B/148
Browne, Alice, widow, Gt. Somerford, 1620, I, W, P1/B/169
Browne, Alice, widow, Watchfield, Shrivenham, Berks., 1622, I (part missing), W, P1/B/185
Browne, Alice, widow, Figh., 1664, AB, I, P26/122
Alice, widow, Pertwood, 1712, W, P2/B/1307
Alice, widow, W. Lavington, 1805, comm, W, P1/1805/8
Browne, And., husb., Devizes Grn, Bps. C., 1568, W, P5/2Reg/4B
Browne, And., Marden, 1610, a/c, comm, I, T, P2/B/311
And., Sunton, Collingbourne K., 1633, I, W, P3/B/352
Browne, And., yeo., Cowesfield, Whitep., 1670, I, W, P2/B/825
Browne, Ann, widow, Play Hatch, Eye and Dunsden, Sonning, Berks., 1627, I, W, P5/1627/4, P5/11Reg/45
Browne, Ann, widow, Gt. Somerford, 1639, I, W, P3/B/424
Browne, Ann, widow, Sunton, Collingbourne K., 1670, I (2), W, P3/B/575
Ann, widow, Winterbourne G., [1684], I, W, P2/B/1035
Browne, Ann, widow, Cherhill, 1689, AB, a/c, D, I, P26/379
Browne, Ann, sp., Castle Eaton, 1732, W, P3/B/1316
Browne, Ann, sp., Malm., 1738, W, P3/B/1374
Ann, sp., Bratton, Westb., 1750, AB, P25/1750/5
Ann, widow, Wilton, 1770, W, P1/B/1390, P1/12Reg/305A
Ann, sp., Steeple A., 1796, W, P2/B/2108
Ann, widow, Chipp., 1825, W, Wr, P3/1825/30
Ann, widow, Sal., 1834, W, Wr, P4/1834/4
Ann, sen., sp., Semley, 1855, aff, W, Wr, P1/1855/12
Anna, wife, Horton, Bps. C., 1835, AB, comm, P24/1343
Anna My. (*or* Maria), sp., Kellaways, 1826, AB, comm, Wr, P3/1826/11
Browne, Anth., yeo., Ashton K., 1570, W (NEP), P1/1Reg/49B
Browne, Anth., butcher, Steeple A., 1573, W, P2/5Reg/161A
Browne, Anth., gent., Broad C., 1640, AB, a/c, I, P2/B/653
Browne, Arthur, husb., Semley, 1611, I, W, P2/B/298, P2/8Reg/151C
Bro[wn], Avis, [Marl.] (NBI) (1618), c1616, I, W (dated 1616 but endorsed 'ex bundle 1620-1622'), P1/B/133
Browne, Benj., innholder, Biddestone, 1672, I, W, P3/B/613
Browne, Benj., gent., Wokm., Berks., 1837, comm, W, Wr, P5/1837/10
Betty, widow, Pott., 1791, W, P1/B/1517, P1/14Reg/357
Betty, widow, Seend, Melk., 1828, W, Wr, P2/1828/46
Browne, Cath., Devizes, 1611, AB, a/c, P1/B/77
Browne, Cath., widow, S. St., Avebury, 1623, I, W, P3/B/236
Cath., widow, Gt. Wishford, 1702, I, W, P2/B/1224
Cath., sp., Gt. Wishford, 1714, I, NW, P2/B/1329
Chas., sen., yeo., Kington St M., 1760, W, P3/B/1531
Browne, Chas., sen., yeo., Minety, 1769, W, P3/B/1607
Chas., Easton Grey, 1852, O, W, Wr, P3/1852/48
Charlotte, Sal., 1824, W, P4/1824/2
Browne, Chris., Whistley, Hurst, Berks., 1668, AB, I, P5/1669/7
Chris., yeo., Liberty of Newland, Hurst, Berks., 1751, W, P5/1751/4
Chris., Draycot C., 1764, AB, P3/B/1563
Dan., Beenham Valence, Berks., 1738, AB, comm, P1/B/1084
Browne, David, tiler, Kington St M., 1686, I, W, P3/B/826

Browne, Denise, widow, Purton, 1627, I, W, P3/B/290
Browne, Dorothy, widow, Milton, E. Knoyle, 1698, I, W, P2/B/1196
Browne, Edith, Sutton V., 1597, I, P2/B/183
Browne, Edmd., husb., Figh., 1574, W, P5/3Reg/49A
Edmd., husb., Wilcot, [1607], NW (NEP), P3/B/27
Browne, Edmd., husb., Hankerton, 1619, I, W, P3/B/178
Browne, Edmd., Purton, 1623, AB, a/c, I, P3/B/235
Browne, Edmd., yeo., Wilton, Gt. Bedwyn, 1661, comm, I, W, P5/1661/5
Browne, Edmd., tailor, Blackland, Calne, 1693, AB, I, P26/410
Browne, Edmd., barber, Devizes, 1712, I, W, P1/B/783, P1/5Reg/277A
Browne, Edwd., Cherhill, 1669, NW, P26/171
Browne, Edwd., yeo., Bulford, 1681, I, W, P2/B/984
Browne, Edwd., Lyneham, 1689, AB, comm, P1/B/600
Edwd., yeo., Purton, 1693, AB, I, P3/B/906
Browne, Edwd., tailor, Purton, 1719, W, P3/B/1172
Browne, Edwd., innholder, Devizes, 1720, AB, P1/B/870
Edwd., bodicemaker, St Edmd.'s St., Sal. St Edmd., 1742, W, P4/1742/10
Edwd., Collingbourne D., 1773, I, W, P21/11/6
Browne, Eleanor, widow, Overton, 1617, I, W, P3/B/148
Browne, Eleanor, widow, Marl. St My., 1640, I, NW, P1/B/291
Browne, Eleanor, widow, Collingbourne D., 1701, I, W, P21/6/2
Eleanor, widow, Calne, 1763, W, P26/994
Eleanor, widow, Manningford A., 1803, W, P3/1803/13
Browne, Eliza, widow, Trowb., 1844, AB, O, Wr, P1/1844/4
Browne als Humphry, Eliz., sp., Imber, 1627, AB, I, P2/B/475
Browne, Eliz., widow, Sunton, Collingbourne K., 1639, I, W, P3/B/425
Browne, Eliz., widow, Semley, 1674, I, W, P2/B/878
Eliz., widow, Tinh., Edington, 1698, I, W, P2/B/1195
Eliz., widow, Steeple A., 1712, W, P2/B/1311
Browne, Eliz., widow, Devizes, 1716, comm, W, P1/B/813, P1/5Reg/493C
Eliz., widow, Devizes, late husband of Cutteridge, N. Bradley, 1723, W, P1/B/888, P1/6Reg/439
Eliz., sen., widow, Steeple A., 1733, W, P2/B/1514
Eliz., sen., widow, Upavon, 1736, W, P2/B/1551
Eliz., minor, Salterton, Durnford, 1739, T, P9/55
Eliz., widow, Sal., 1739, AB, I, Wr, P4/1739/5
Eliz., widow, Kington St M., 1754, AB, P3/B/1491
Eliz., widow, Wantage, Berks., 1759, ren, W, P23/682
Eliz., widow, Devizes, 1799, AB, app. of guardian, P1/B/1551, P1/15Reg/198A
Eliz., wife, Malm., 1816, AB, P3/1816/5
Eliz., sp., Broad H., 1831, W, Wr, P3/1831/22
Eliz., widow, Aldbourne, 1837, AB, comm, Wr, P3/1837/19
Esau, labourer, Stapleford, 1725, AB, I, ren, P2/B/1437
Browne, Francis, Spirthill, Bremhill, 1638, a/c, P3/B/403
Browne, Francis, baker, Clack, Lyneham, 1680, I, W, P3/B/729
Browne, Francis, Welford, Berks., 1720, AB, P1/B/866
Brown als Brownjohn, Francis, stonemason, Sal. The Close, 1765, W, P5/1765/5
Francis, Sal. The Close, 1835, AB, Wr, P5/1835/4
Browne, Geoff., Gt. Somerford, 1638, AB, I, P3/B/404
Browne, Geo., Avebury, 1619, AB, comm, I, P3/B/179
Browne, Geo., butcher, Sal., 1633, I, W, P4/1633/2
Browne, Geo., Hilmarton, 1671, AB, I, P3/B/592
Geo., Tisb., 1672, a/c (2), AB, I, P2/B/846
Browne, Geo., yeo., Overton, 1711, I, W, P3/B/1099
Geo., Downton, 1754, AB, P2/B/1705
Geo., yeo., Manton, Preshute, 1759, W, P1/B/1327, P1/11Reg/431
Geo., yeo., Manton, Preshute, 1781, W, P1/B/1459, P1/13Reg/321
Geo., yeo., Avebury, 1794, W, P3/B/1742
Geo., Seend, Melk., 1795, AB, P1/B/1537, P1/14Reg/544A
Browne, Gerard, sen., tailor, Durnford, 1713, W (NEP), P9/38
Browne, Giles, yeo., Brinkw., 1698, comm, court papers (2), D (several), L (5), W (2 - 1 a copy), Wr, P3/B/976

Giles, vict., Warm., 1782, comm, W, P2/B/1999
Browne, Gregory, husb., Hill D., 1607, AB, I, W, P5/1607/11, P5/8Reg/87C
Hannah, widow, Britford, 1730, AB, P24/822
Hannah, widow, Malm., 1785, W, P3/B/1701
Hannah, widow, Sal., 1839, W, Wr, P4/1839/2
Browne, Hannell, Hilp., 1670, comm, I, W, P2/B/834
Browne, Harry, husb., Semley, 1589, I, copy I, W, P2/B/103
Browne, Hy., E. Knoyle, 1587, AB, P2/7Reg/90B
Browne, Hy., jun., Lyneham, 1624, AB, I, P3/B/252
Browne, Hy., E. Kennett, 1624, I, W, P3/B/251
Browne, Hy., sen., yeo., Lyneham, 1644, comm, I, T, W, P1/B/310
Browne, Hy., husb., Basildon, Berks., 1668, comm, I, W, P1/B/452
Browne, Hy., husb., Netheravon, 1683, I, W, P12/119
Browne, Hy., yeo., Longbridge D., [1685], W, P2/B/1053
Browne, Hy., yeo., Steeple A., 1703, I, W, P2/B/1230
Hy., gardener, Steeple A., 1711, W, P1/B/760, P1/5Reg/111
Hy., gardener, Steeple A., 1757-60, AB, a/c, comm, I, copy I, ren, W, P2/B/1731
Hy., yeo., Downton, 1758, W, P2/B/1747
Hy., sen., yeo., Britford, 1762, W, P24/1069
Hy., Oaksey, 1796, AB, P3/B/1751
Hy., gent. and innholder, Sal., 1818, W, Wr, P4/1818/7
Browne, Hy., Trowb., 1830, AB, Wr, P1/1830/14
Hy., Sal., 1852, AB, Wr, P4/1852/2
Browne, Hugh, husb., Mere, 1564, W, P5/1Reg/45B
Isaac, Speen, Berks., 1776, AB, W, P1/B/1441
Browne, Jas., Stratton, Dorset, 1662, AB, I, NW, P5/1662/8
Browne *or* Brownjohn, Jas., blacksmith, Porton, Idmiston, 1683, I, W, P2/B/1012
Jas., Gt. Durnford, 1731, AB, P9/48
Jas., Dilton M., Westb., 1750, AB, a/c, I, P25/1750/6
Jas., gardener, Wilton, 1757, W, P2/B/1737
Browne, Jas., yeo., S. Wraxall, 1760, W, P2/B/1765
Jas., yeo., Upavon, 1761, W, P2/B/1774
Jas., yeo., Stratton, Dorset, 1773, W, P5/1773/8, P5/17Reg/70
Jas., Trowb., 1781, AB, P1/B/1473
Jas., Hungerford, Berks., 1785, W, P5/1785/4, P5/18Reg/28
Jas., yeo., Baynton, Edington, 1801, W, P1/1801/95, P1/15Reg/312
Jas., tallow chandler, Trowb., 1804, comm, W, P1/1804/147
Jas., widow, Pott., 1828, O, W, P1/1828/13
Jas., yeo., Sutton V., 1840, W, Wr, P2/1840/7
Jas., labourer, Sal., 1844, W, Wr, P1/1844/16
Jas., labourer, Semley, 1844, D, note, O, W, Wr, P2/1844/16
Jas., gardener, Southbroom, 1849, O, W, Wr, P24/1391
Browne, Jas., farmer, Bromham, 1850, comm, W, Wr, P3/1850/41
Jas., gardener, Littleton P., 1850, D, O, W, Wr, P1/1850/23
Jas. *see also* Phineas
Browne, Jane, widow, Whitep., 1677, I, P2/B/914
Jane, widow, Castle C., 1749, W, P3/B/1462
Jane, widow, Steeple A., 1808, AB, comm, Wr, P1/1808/143
Jane, widow, Minety, 1839, O, W, Wr, P3/1839/9
Jeremiah, Westb., 1714, AB, I, P25/1714/6
Browne, Jeremiah, Sal., 1807, AB, P4/1807/2
Browne, Joan, servant, Damerham, Hants, 1563, AB (in minority of Agnes B.), P2/4Reg/139A
Browne als Knight, Joan, widow, Yatesbury, 1608, AB, P3/B/37
Browne, Joan, widow, Manton, Preshute, 1614, I, NW, P1/B/113
Browne als Clement, Joan, Semley, 1620, AB, I, P2/B/407
Browne, Joan, Ogbourne St And., 1635, AB, I, P5/1635/8, P5/12Reg/239A
Browne, Joan, widow, Gt. Wishford, 1641, I, W, P2/B/661
Browne, Joan, widow, Charlton nr Malm., 1646, I, W, P1/B/324
Browne, Joan, Lockeridge, Overton, 1680, AB, P3/B/730
Browne, Jn., Sonning, Berks., 1544, W, P5/20Reg/54C

Browne, Jn., husb., Rushall, 1547, W, P2/2Reg/48B
Browne, Jn., E. Knoyle, 1558, W, P2/3Reg/94C
Browne, Jn., Wilton, 1570, AB, P2/5Reg/107B
Browne, Jn., husb., Gillingham, Dorset, 1575, W, P27/1Reg/30B
Browne, Jn., shepherd, Imber, 1575, W, P2/5Reg/227B
Browne, Jn., yeo., Netherh., [1594], W, P2/B/153
Browne, Jn., sen., Bradford A., 1598, I, P2/B/187
Browne, Jn., Wokm., Berks., 1613, I, W, P5/1613/6, P5/9Reg/101A
Browne, Jn., sen., husb., Kennet, Overton, 1616, I, W, P1/B/131
Browne, Jn., jun., Hankerton, 1617, AB, I, P3/B/149
Browne, Jn., Netton, Durnford, 1618, AB, P5/1617/2, P5/9Reg/217D
Browne, Jn., Dinton, 1621, I, W, P2/B/411
Broune, Jn., Westbrook, Avebury, 1622, I, W, P3/B/218
Browne, Jn., husb., Spirthill, Bremhill, 1623, I, W, P3/B/234
Browne, Jn., sen., Lyneham, 1626, AB, I, P3/B/281
Browne, Jn., Charlton nr Malm., 1626, AB, I, P3/B/280
Browne, Jn., husb., Marl., 1629, I, W, P1/B/221
Browne, Jn., husb., Charlton nr Malm., 1629, AB, I, P3/B/314
Browne, Jn., sen., yeo., Kemble, 1633, I, W, P3/B/353
Browne, Jn., labourer, Corston, Malm., 1636, I, W, P3/B/374
Browne, Jn., husb., Calne, 1638, AB, a/c, I, P26/46
Browne, Jn., yeo., Charlton nr Malm., 1639-40, a/c, I, W, P3/B/426, 444
Browne, Jn., butcher, Purton, 1645, comm, I, W, P1/B/315
Browne, Jn., husb., Hindon, 1661, I, W, P2/B/733
Browne, Jn., Pott., 1663, AB, court paper, I, P1/B/400
Browne, Jn., yeo. and shoemaker, Overton, [1664], I, W (NEP), P3/B/496
Browne, Jn., sen., stone cutter, Swindon, 1670, AB, I, W, P3/B/577
Jn., sen., yeo., Gt. Somerford, 1670, I, W, P3/B/576
Jn., sen., yeo., Semley, 1670, comm, I, W, P2/B/824
Browne, Jn., Mildenhall, 1671, I, W, P3/B/593
Browne, Jn., bricklayer, Gt. Bedwyn, 1681, AB, I, P21/2/74
Browne, Jn., Salterton, Durnford, 1682, AB, P9/18
Browne, Jn., serge clothier, Devizes St My., 1684, AB, I, P1/B/565
Browne, Jn., yeo., Sandford, Woodley and S., Berks., 1687, comm, I, W, P5/1687/6
Browne, Jn., Gt. Amesb., 1688, AB, I, P2/B/1095
Browne, Jn., sen., butcher, Pott., 1688, I, W, P1/B/593
Browne, Jn., jun., yeo., Brinkw., 1689, AB, I, P1/B/604
Browne, Jn., yeo., Cloatley, Hankerton, 1693, I, W, P3/B/907
Jn., husb., Ashton K., 1696, I, W, P3/B/954
Browne, Jn., maltster, Collingbourne D., 1697, AB, W, P21/5/39
Browne, Jn., yeo., Semley, 1697, I, W, P2/B/1185
Browne, Jn., gent. *or* yeo., Lt. Somerford, 1712, AB, I, P3/B/1107
Broune, Jn., yeo., Easton, Welford, Berks., 1714, W, P1/B/798, P1/5Reg/393A
Browne, Jn., Grove, Wantage, Berks., 1720, W, P23/381
Browne, Jn., yeo., N. Bradley, 1720, comm, W, P1/B/868, P1/6Reg/352
Jn., Ogbourne St And., 1721, AB, comm, P23/405
Jn., yeo., Bratton, Westb., 1721, AB, I, P25/1721/1
Jn., sen., tailor, Slaughterford, 1722, I, W, P3/B/1209
Browne, Jn., barber, Devizes, 1723, W, P1/B/882, P1/6Reg/432
Jn., sen., Semley, 1726, AB, P1/B/936
Browne, Jn., yeo., Chapel Plaster, Box, 1728, NW, P3/B/1272
Jn., Box, 1731, AB, P3/B/1307
Jn., Avebury, 1731, AB, P3/B/1308
Jn., bach., Hermitage, Hampstead N., Berks., 1732, AB, I, P1/B/1010
Jn., yeo., Overton, 1734, W, P3/B/1342
Jn., Newton T., 1737, AB, P2/B/1556
Browne, Jn., Newton T., 1741, AB, W, P2/B/1597
Jn., grocer, Wilton, 1742, W, P2/B/1611
Browne, Jn., yeo., Aldbourne, 1743, W, P3/B/1418
Jn., yeo., Manton, Preshute, 1746, I, W, P1/B/1194, P1/10Reg/22

Jn., Slaughterford, 1747, comm, W, P3/B/1448
Jn., Sedgehill, 1750, W, P2/B/1680
Jn., yeo., Crudwell, 1751, AB, comm, ren, P3/B/1469
Jn., Mere, 1766, AB, comm, P5/1766/4
Jn., Steeple A., 1768, AB, P2/B/1852
Browne, Jn., yeo., Roundway, Bps. C., 1769, W, P24/1082
Jn., Alton B., 1771, AB, P3/B/1618
Jn., Warm., 1773, AB, P2/B/1900
Jn., innkeeper, Trowb., 1778, W, P1/B/1450, P1/13Reg/193
Jn., labourer, Whitep., 1778, W, P2/B/1957
Jn., gent., Aldbourne, 1779, comm, W, P3/B/1659
Jn., Durnford, 1783, AB, P9/86
Jn., baker, Chipp., 1787, W, P3/B/1707
Jn., tailor, Netton, Durnford, 1792, W, P9/90
Jn., soap boiler and chandler, Devizes St My., 1799, W, P1/B/1549, P1/15Reg/184
Jn., Whitep., 1805, AB, P2/1805/48
Jn., Semley, 1811, AB, Wr, P1/1811/5
Jn., bach., Semley, 1817, AB, Wr, P1/1817/38
Jn., yeo., Atworth, Bradford A., 1823, comm, W, Wr, P1/1823/17
Jn., gent., Broad H., 1826, W, Wr, P3/1826/26
Jn., Sutton Poyntz, Dorset, 1834, O, W, Wr, P18/24
Jn., basketmaker, Chapmanslade, Corsley, 1836, W, P2/1836/31
Jn., Stapleford, 1844, W, Wr, P2/1844/47
Jn., linen draper, Sal., 1850, AB, app. of guardian, note, O, T (children of the decd: Jn. George Rontree, Robt. Hy. & Eliz. B.), Wr, P4/1850/8, 18, 20
Jn., labourer, Mill Lane, Donhead St A., 1854, AB, aff, O, W, Wr, P2/1854/6
Jn., Lyme R., Dorset, 1857, AB, D, W, Wr, P16/465
Browne, Jonathan, mason, Woolley, Bradford A., 1782, W, P2/B/1992
Jonathan, gardener, Littleton P., 1857, aff, O, W, Wr, P1/1857/9
Browne, Jos., broad weaver, Slaughterford, 1672, comm, I, W, P3/B/614
Browne, Jos., day labourer, Seagry, 1695, AB, I, W, P1/B/643
Jos., tailor, Chipp., 1714, AB, W (2 - 1 a copy), P3/B/1123
Jos., yeo., Stanton St Q., 1729, AB, W, P1/B/955, P1/7Reg/304
Jos., W. Grimstead, 1736, W, P2/B/1548
Jos., labourer, Oaksey, 1815, W, Wr, P3/1815/36
Browne, Jos., yeo., Chittoe, Bps. C., 1845, aff, O, W, Wr, P24/1379
Jos., widower, Sutton V., 1853, AB, Wr, P2/1853/1
Browne, Julian, widow, Lyneham, 1626, I, NW, P3/B/279
Kitty, widow, Amesb., 1855, aff, W, Wr, P2/1855/17
Lawr., tailor, Broad H., 1624, I, W, P3/B/253
Lawr., Bps. C., 1754, AB, I, P24/1023
Browne, Leonard, yeo., Winterbourne G., 1633, I, W, P2/B/573, P2/9Reg/17
Browne, Lionel, Beer Hackett, Dorset, 1624, AB, I, P5/1624/3, P5/10Reg/234A
Lionel, yeo., Enmore Grn, Motc., Dorset, 1708, I, W, P5/1708/11
Browne, Lionel, yeo., Yetm., Dorset, 1708, W, P5/15Reg/80
Browne, Lucian, husb., Cloatley, Hankerton, 1622, I, W, P3/B/221
Browne, Lucian, Cloatley, Hankerton, 1705, AB, I, P3/B/1048
Browne, Lucian, Windmill House, Minety, 1788, W, P3/B/1716
Browne, Mgt., widow, Winterbourne G., 1582, W, P2/6Reg/59B
Browne als Clement, Mgt., widow, Semley, 1630, AB, P2/B/525
Browne, Mgt., gentlewoman, Aldbourne, 1647, comm, I, W, P1/B/332
Browne, Mgt., Westport St My., 1692, AB, P3/B/892
Browne, Margery, widow, Avebury, 1620, I, W, P3/B/195
Mark, vict., Steeple A., 1716, W, P2/B/1349
Mark, Aldbourne, 1748, AB, P3/B/1452
Mark, yeo., Aldbourne, 1829, comm, W, Wr, P1/1829/76
Browne, Martha, Devizes, 1631, AB, P1/B/223
Martha, widow, Warm., 1808, W, Wr, P2/1808/26
Browne, Mart., Farnham, Tollard Royal, Dorset, 1590, AB, I, L, P2/B/116
Browne, My., widow, Highw., 1628, AB, I, P10/1628/1

Browne als Humphry, My., widow, Imber, 1628, AB, I, W, P2/B/496
Browne, My., widow, Hankerton, 1640, AB, I, P3/B/445
Browne, My., widow, Shinfield, Berks., 1662, AB, I, NW, P1/B/371
Browne, My., sp., Kington St M., 1675, I, W, P3/B/654
Browne, My., widow, Warm., 1682, AB, I, P2/B/1009
Browne, My., widow, Wootton R., 1684, I, W, P3/B/800
My., widow, Charlton nr Malm., 1717, I, W, P3/B/1148
Browne, My., widow, Lt. Somerford, 1722, AB, P3/B/1210
My., widow, Lyme R., Dorset, 1730, AB, comm, ren, W, P16/252
My., Hankerton, 1733, W, P3/B/1328
My., sp., Sal., 1740, AB, Wr, P4/1740/4
My., widow, Netheravon, 1743, W, Wr, P5/1743/10
My., widow, Woodb., 1771, AB, P3/B/1619
Browne, My., yeo.'s wife, Overton, 1775, AB, comm, P3/B/1637
My., sp., Steeple A., 1797, comm, W, P2/B/2128
My., sp., Sutton Poyntz, Dorset, 1823, AB, cert, O, P18/21
My., Littleton P., 1843, AB, O, Wr, P1/1843/7
My., sp., Warm., 1847, D, W, Wr, P2/1847/9
My., widow, Warm., 1850, comm, D, W, Wr, P2/1850/2
My., widow, Sal., 1850, AB, Wr, P4/1850/19
My., widow, Wilton, 1855, AB, aff, Wr, P1/1855/10
My. Ann, Marl., 1823, AB, Wr, P1/1823/4
Browne, Matthew, Lt. Bedwyn, 1634, I, W. Proved at archiepiscopal visitation at Sal.., P21/3/28, P5/12Reg/285A
Browne, Michael, weaver, Frankleigh, Bradford A. (form. of Trowb.), 1802, W, P2/1802/8
Browne, Nich., yeo., Rockley, Ogbourne St And., 1668, AB, I, ren, P5/1668/12
Browne, Oliver, gent., Calne, 1673, AB, comm, I (detailed), P26/213
Browne, Oswald, Tinh., Edington, 1635, I, P2/B/588
Oswald, sen., yeo., Tinh., Edington, 1696, I, W, P2/B/1175
Paul, Slaughterford, 1828, AB, Wr, P3/1828/18
Browne als Clement, Peter, Chicklade, 1609, AB, a/c, I, W, P2/B/294, P2/8Reg/80D
Browne, Peter, yeo., Donhead St My., 1714, AB, I, P1/B/804
Browne, Philip, yeo., Sandford, Woodley and S., Berks., 1690, comm, I, W, P5/1690/10
Philip, labourer, N. Tidworth, 1741, W, P2/B/1600
Phineas als Jas., yeo., Seend, Melk., 1781-98, AB, note (shows pedigree, to explain later bond), NW, P2/B/1991
Priscilla, widow, Malm., 1753, W, P1/B/1270, P1/11Reg/58A
Browne, Ralph, Wrou., 1563, W, P1/2Reg/125B
Browne, Ralph, E. Stowell, Wilcot, 1636, I, NW, P3/B/375
Browne, Rebecca, widow, Sandford, Woodley and S., Berks., 1705, W, P5/1705/11
Rebecca, widow, Sedgehill, 1767, W, P1/B/1374, P1/12Reg/196A
Browne, Rees, stone cutter, Swindon, 1668, I, W, P3/B/537
Broune, Rd., Sonning, Berks., [1542-43], W (NEP), P5/20Reg/50
Browne, Rd., sen., Winterbourne E., 1549, W, P2/2Reg/72A
Browne, Rd., Calstone W., 1560, W (NEP), P1/2Reg/113A
Browne, Rd., Avebury, c1570, W (NEP), P1/1Reg/82B
Browne, Rd., Hungerford, Berks., 1579-80, AB, I, P5/1579/11, P5/3Reg/148C
Browne, Rd., husb., Ogbourne St And., 1597, I, W, P5/1597/7, P5/6Reg/194A
Browne, Rd., clerk and curate, Semington, Steeple A., 1610, I, NW, P2/B/299, P2/8Reg/100A
Browne, Rd., husb., Sunton, Collingbourne K., 1611, I, W, P1/B/71
Browne, Rd., husb., Shrewton, 1612, I, W, P2/B/334, P2/8Reg/181A
Browne, Rd., shepherd, Lt. Woodford, 1616, W, P13/1/6
Browne, Rd., husb., Purton Stoke, 1618, AB (2), I, P3/B/166
Browne *or* Broome, Rd., yeo., Lyneham, 1627, AB, a/c, I, P3/B/289
Browne, Rd., jun., Sunton, Collingbourne K., 1633, I, W, P3/B/354
Browne, Rd., Marl. St My., 1633, AB, I, P1/B/243
Browne, Rd., gent., Broad C., 1641, AB, I, P2/B/672
Browne, Rd., Eye and Dunsden, Sonning, Berks., 1665, AB, I, P5/1665/12
Browne, Rd., Fisherton A., 1665, AB, P2/B/771
Browne, Rd., Chilton F., 1680, AB, I, P3/B/731
Browne, Rd., Lockeridge, Overton, 1680, AB, P3/B/732
Browne, Rd., clerk and vicar, Minety, 1682, I, W, P3/B/761

Rd., Wilton, Gt. Bedwyn, 1686, I, W, P21/4/21
Browne, Rd., tailor, Avebury, 1695, I, W, P1/B/646
Browne, Rd., yeo., Quemerford, Calne, 1700, AB, I, P26/467
Browne, Rd., clothw., Westb., 1709, I, W, P25/1709/1
Browne, Rd., sen., yeo., Quemerford, Calne, 1718, I, W, P26/624
Rd., sen., yeo., Hungerford, Berks., 1723, I, W, P23/418
Browne, Rd., Downton, 1732, AB, P1/B/998
Rd., yeo., Woolhampton, Berks., 1732, W, P1/B/1005, P1/7Reg/477A
Rd., Gt. Wishford, 1760, AB, P2/B/1760
Rd., sen., pikemaker, N. Heath, Chieveley, Berks., 1763, W, P1/B/1354, P1/12Reg/84
Rd., Stapleford, 1782, AB, P2/B/1997
Rd., shopkeeper, Baydon, 1816, W, Wr, P5/1816/4
Browne, Robt., Cherhill, 1544, W (NEP), P1/1Reg/95C
Browne, Robt., husb., Bradford A., 1566, W, P2/4Reg/223B
Browne, Robt., yeo., E. Knoyle, 1576, W, P2/B/55, P2/5Reg/273A
Broune, Robt., labourer, Sonning, Berks., 1591, I, W, P5/1591/6, P5/5Reg/113A
Browne, Robt., Winterbourne E., 1602, AB, I, W, P2/B/227
Robt., mason, Westport St My., 1615, AB, I, P3/B/127
Browne, Robt., yeo., Rockley, Ogbourne St And., 1619, I, W, P5/1619/87, P5/10Reg/43
Browne, Robt., weaver, Slaughterford, 1621, I, W, P3/B/210
Browne, Robt., Bradford A., 1623, AB, I, P2/B/442
Browne, Robt., Bradford A., 1627, AB, a/c, I, P2/B/473
Browne, Robt., blacksmith, Highw., 1627, W, P10/1627/4
Browne, Robt., Castleton, Dorset, 1638, comm (*also* applies to Mabel Tizer, widow, decd), I, W, P5/1638/13, P5/13Reg/94
Browne, Robt., yeo. *or* husb., S. Wraxall, 1646, comm, I, W, P2/B/712
Robt., yeo., Cherhill, 1666, comm, I, W, P26/131
Browne als Sanders, Robt., Hankerton, 1678-79, AB, a/c, I, P3/B/694, 715
Browne, Robt., Overton, 1679, AB, P3/B/716
Browne, Robt., yeo., Manton, Preshute, 1689, I, W, P1/B/603
Robt., Sonning, Berks., 1708, AB, I, P5/1708/10
Browne, Robt., yeo., Sal., 1708, W, P1/B/745
Browne, Robt., gent., Minety, 1731, W, P3/B/1309
Robt., blacksmith, Castle C., 1732, AB, I, P1/B/1019
Robt., Ogbourne St And., 1737, AB, P5/1737/5
Robt., bricklayer, Borough, Gt. Bedwyn, 1742, W, P21/9/39
Robt., Wantage, Berks., 1755, AB, P23/661
Browne, Robt., sen., yeo., Minety, 1758, W, P3/B/1518
Robt., Minety, 1764, AB, P3/B/1564
Robt., Baverstock, 1764, AB, P2/B/1797
Robt., Warm., 1767, AB, P2/B/1838
Robt., yeo., Brightwalton, Berks., 1789, W, P1/B/1510, P1/14Reg/239
Robt., vict., Chipp., 1790, AB, comm, W, P3/B/1726
Robt., gardener, Nether C., Dorset, 1832, W, Wr (not labelled), P5/1832/10
Browne, Roger, day labourer, Eddington, Hungerford, Berks., 1605, I, NW, P5/1605/3, P5/8Reg/42A
Browne, Roger, husb., Ashton K., 1613, AB, I, P3/B/107
Browne, Roger, tailor, Lt. Bedwyn, 1632, I, W, P21/3/17
Roger, sen., weaver, Aldbourne, 1694, I, W, P3/B/926
Roger, Heytes., 1730, W, P5/1730/7
Browne, Sam., Marl. St Peter and St Paul, 1601, I, P1/B/12
Browne, Sam., broad weaver, Leigh Delamere, 1621, AB, I, P3/B/211
Browne, Sam., Steeple A., 1705, I, W, P2/B/1248
Sam., sen., baker, Castle C., 1813, W, Wr, P3/1813/64
Sam., Bere R., Dorset, 1827, W, Wr, P5/1827/51
Sam., painter and glazier, Landford, 1827-44, AB, court papers, court proceeding, req, W, Wr, P2/1827/27, P2/1844/74
Sarah, widow, Overton & Preshute, 1690, I, W, P3/B/870
Sarah, widow, Kington St M., 1762, W, P3/B/1553
Brown als Breadmore, Sarah, widow, Poulshot, 1776, AB, P1/B/1430
Sarah, widow, Warm., 1809, W, Wr, P2/1809/79
Browne, Simon, Netheravon, 1630, I, P12/60

Browne, Steph., husb., Play Hatch, Eye and Dunsden, Sonning, Berks., 1625, I, W, P5/1625/12, P5/10Reg/250
Browne, Steph., Longbridge D., 1710, AB, P2/B/1294
Browne, Steph., Marl., 1711, AB, P1/B/780
Browne, Steph., feltmaker, Mkt. L., 1722, W, P2/B/1413
Steph., farmer and innholder, Warm., 1797, W, P2/B/2121
Browne, Steph., sen., maltster, Westb. L., 1798, W, P25/1798/5
Steph., Aldbourne, 1843, AB, comm, Wr, P3/1843/4
Steph., gent., Westb. L., 1848, comm, W, Wr, P25/1848/2
Browne, Susan, S. Wraxall, 1665, AB (2), comm (2), P2/B/772
Browne, Thos., Wylye, 1577, I, W, P2/B/59, P2/5Reg/292A
Browen, Thos., Figh., 1580, I, W, P5/1580/12, P5/3Reg/151E, P26/1480
Browne, Thos., husb., Dinton, 1590, I, W, P2/B/114
Browne, Thos., Kington L., 1592, I, W, P1/B/4
Browne, Thos., Lyneham, 1606, W, P3/2Reg/11B
Browne, Thos., gent., Marl., 1608, I, W, P1/B/64
Browne, Thos., Sal. St Thos., 1619, AB, I, P4/1619/7
Browne, Thos., Eye and Dunsden, Sonning, Berks., 1622, I, W, P5/1622/10, P5/10Reg/103
Browne, Thos., Highw., 1625, AB, I, P5/1625/7, P5/10Reg/301A
Browne als Humphrey, Thos., Imber, 1627, I, W, P2/B/479
Browne, Thos., Castleton, Dorset, 1628, AB, P5/1628/15, P5/11Reg/15B
Broune, Thos., husb., Quemerford, Calne, 1631, I, W, P5/1631/8, P5/12Reg/38
Browne, Thos., shepherd, Blewbury, Berks., 1631, AB, comm, I, P5/1631/19, P5/11Reg/172B
Browne, Thos., Leigh, Ashton K., 1635, I, W, P1/B/261
Browne, Thos., husb., Brokenb., 1644, AB, I, P1/B/312
Browne, Thos., sen., cooper, Clack, Lyneham, 1661, comm, I, W, P3/B/471, P3/3Reg/12B
Browne, Thos., yeo., Minety, 1665, AB, I, P3/B/509
Browne, Thos., husb., N. Hidden, Hungerford, Berks., 1666, I, ren, W, P5/1666/7
Browne, Thos., yeo., Kemble, 1666, comm, I, W, P1/B/427
Browne, Thos., yeo., Blackland, Calne, 1667, I (detailed), W, P26/135
Browne, Thos., weaver, Wilton, 1679, I, W, P2/B/945
Browne, Thos., yeo., Sutton B., 1682, AB, court paper, ren, W, P3/B/762
Broune, Thos., Burbage, 1684, AB, I, P11/53
Browne, Thos., stone cutter, Swindon, 1685, I, W, P3/B/820
Browne, Thos., yeo., Clack, Lyneham, 1690, I, W, P3/B/871
Browne, Thos., miller and bach., Somerford K., 1695, AB, I, ren, P3/B/938
Browne, Thos., sen., yeo., Sunton, Collingbourne K., 1697, I, W, P3/B/969
Thos., yeo., Sutton B. (d.1682), 1702, AB, comm (2), W, P3/B/1019
Thos., yeo., Aughton, Collingbourne K., 1706, W, P3/B/1059
Browne, Thos., rector, Rollestone, 1708, AB, comm, P1/B/748
Browne, Thos., Gt. Bedwyn, 1710, AB, I, P21/7/5
Browne, Thos., Wilton, 1711, AB, I, P2/B/1299
Thos., yeo., Wilton, Gt. Bedwyn, 1715-16, I, W, P5/1715/8, P5/15Reg/331
Thos., yeo., Castle C., 1723, W, P1/B/904, P1/7Reg/31B
Thos., Westb., 1740, I, W, P25/1739/11
Browne, Thos., yeo., Minety, 1747, W, P1/B/1213, P1/10Reg/136
Thos., yeo., Kington St M., 1750, W, P1/B/1249, P1/10Reg/404
Thos., Easton, 1754, AB, I, P3/B/1492
Thos., maltster, Kington St M., 1755, W, P3/B/1498
Thos., Rams., 1759, AB, P5/1759/4
Thos., Minety, 1763, AB, P1/B/1368
Thos., Halstock, Dorset, 1764, W, P5/1764/4
Thos., yeo., Rockley, Ogbourne St And., 1771, W, P23/732
Thos., Sal., 1780, NW, P4/1780/4
Thos., Warm., 1792, AB, P2/B/2077
Thos., printer, Marl. (late of London), 1792, W, P1/B/1522, P1/14Reg/380B
Thos., gent., Edington, 1807, W, Wr, P2/1807/42
Thos., yeo., Lockeridge, Overton, 1809, comm, W, Wr, P3/1809/6
Thos., labourer, Beenham Valence, Berks., 1814, W, Wr, P1/1814/18
Thos., possibly of Speen, Berks., 1836, Wr (contents missing), P1/1836/9
Thos., yeo., Grove, Wantage, Berks., 1836, O, W, P23/988

Thos., yeo., Stock Cross, Speen, Berks. (left goods in Chiseldon), 1836, comm, W, Wr, P3/1836/11
Browne, Thos. Warne, ironmonger, Warm., 1853, D, W, Wr, P2/1853/36
Timothy, Edington, 1744, AB, P2/B/1623
Browne, Walter, Idmiston, 1550, W, P2/2Reg/108E
Browne als Clement, Walter, Semley, 1562, AB, P1/2Reg/128A
Browne, Walter, Ogbourne St Geo., 1599, AB, T (children: Wm. & Nich. B.), P5/1598/2, P5/6Reg/218A
Walter, husb., Biddestone St Nich., 1625, I, W, P3/B/268
Browne, Wm., Arborfield, Berks., 1550, W, P5/20Reg/107B
Browne, Wm., Crudwell, 1570, W, P1/1Reg/122C
Browne, Wm., Sonning, Berks., 1589, I, W, P5/1589/2, P5/5Reg/64B
Browne, Wm., yeo., Sherb., Dorset, 1590, AB, I, W, P5/1589/1, P5/5Reg/68A
Browne als Clement, Wm., sen., husb., Semley, 1602, AB, I, copy I, W, copy W, P2/B/226
Wm., S. Wraxall, 1604, I, W, P2/B/249
Browne, Wm., Mere, 1611, AB, I, P5/1610/6, P5/9Reg/52A
Browne, Wm., sen., yeo., Tisb., 1614, W, P2/8Reg/229B
Browne, Wm., sen., husb., Kington St M., 1615, I, W, P3/B/128
Browne, Wm., husb., Charlton nr Malm., 1620, I, W, P3/B/196
Browne, Wm., husb., Bedborough, Bps. C., 1621, AB, I (2), P24/59
Browne, Wm., shoemaker and apprentice, Wootton B., 1621, AB, I, NW, P3/B/212
Browne, Wm., Hankerton, 1622, AB, I, P3/B/222
Wm., husb., Stanton St Q., 1622, AB, I, NW, P3/B/223
Browne, Wm., husb., Wrou., 1625, I, W, P3/B/269
Browne, Wm., sen., Imber, 1626, I, W, P2/B/465
Browne, Wm., [blacksmith], Kington St M., 1628, I, W, P3/B/296
Browne, Wm., labourer, Leigh, Ashton K., 1631, AB, a/c, comm, I, P3/B/329
Browne, Wm., butcher, Gt. Somerford, 1637, AB, a/c, I, P3/B/392
Browne, Wm., clerk, Nether C., Dorset, 1637, AB, I, P5/1637/3, P5/12Reg/246A
Browne, Wm., Dunsden, Sonning, Berks., 1639, I, W, P5/1639/14, P5/13Reg/192
Browne, Wm., husb., Longbridge D., 1639, AB, I, P2/B/638
Browne, Wm., Leigh, Ashton K., 1662, AB, comm, I, P3/B/481
Browne, Wm., carp., Porridge Hill, Gillingham, Dorset, 1664, W, P27/1/15
Browne, Wm., yeo., Purton, 1668, I, W, P3/B/538
Browne, Wm., Mildenhall, 1670, AB, I, P3/B/578
Browne, Wm., [innkeeper], Wilton, 1673, a/c (2), AB, I (detailed including chambers called the Crown, Swan, Squirrel & Bell), P2/B/872
Browne, Wm., yeo., Quemerford, Calne, 1674, I, W, P5/1674/17
Wm., Bishopstone N., 1677, AB, I, P6/44
Browne, Wm., dyer, Westb., 1678, comm, I (detailed), W, P25/1678/5
Browne, Wm., miller, Dauntsey, 1678, AB, a/c, I, P3/B/695
Browne, Wm., sen., yeo., Collingbourne D., 1680, I, W, P1/B/541
Browne, Wm., sen., Warm., 1681, AB, I, P2/B/979
Browne, Wm., Wilton, 1681, AB, a/c, I, P2/B/985
Browne, Wm., sen., husb., Rockley, Ogbourne St And., 1693, AB, I, P23/184
Browne, Wm., tailor, Blackland, Calne, 1699, I, W, P26/464
Browne, Wm., tailor, Collingbourne D., 1703, AB, I, W, P21/6/10
Browne, Wm., gardener, Abingdon, Berks., 1711, W, P1/B/767, P1/5Reg/171
Wm., Stratford Tony, 1714, I, W, P2/B/1330
Wm., yeo., Burbage, 1731, I, W, P5/1731/4
Browne, Wm., Wrou., 1733, comm, W, P3/B/1329
Wm., farmer, Trowb., 1733, comm, W, P1/B/1031, P1/7Reg/580
Wm., Durnford, 1740, O (2), W, P9/57
Wm., Mere, 1740, AB, Wr, P5/1740/12
Wm., wheelwright, Bucklebury, Berks., 1741, W, P1/B/1137, P1/9Reg/103A
Wm., Sal., 1745, AB, P1/B/1190
Wm., Berwick St Jas., 1746, AB, W, P1/B/1193, P1/10Reg/32, 53
Wm., Newton T., 1751, W, P2/B/1687
Wm., yeo., Steeple A., 1751, W, P2/B/1686
Wm., husb., Limmerhill, Wokm., Berks., 1756, W, P5/1756/3
Wm., miller, Bremilham, 1762, W, P3/B/1554
Wm., sen., yeo., Overton, 1764, W, P3/B/1565

Wm., sen., yeo., Aldbourne, 1765, W, P3/B/1574
Wm., gent., Aldbourne, 1773, comm, W, P1/B/1425, P1/13Reg/48
Wm., tailor, Box, 1788, AB, W, P3/B/1715
Wm., gent., Nunton, N. and Bodenham, 1794, W, P2/B/2099
Browne, Wm., yeo., Ewen, Kemble, 1804, W, Wr, P3/1804/17
Wm., Whitep., 1805, AB, P2/1805/49
Wm., shopkeeper, Devizes, 1812, AB, ren, W, Wr, P1/1812/1
Wm., gardener, Littleton P., 1813, W, Wr, P1/1813/9
Wm., weaver, Sal., 1816, W, Wr, P4/1816/5
Wm., baker, Westb., 1826, O, W, Wr, P25/1826/4
Wm., Warm., 1828, AB, comm, P2/1828/54
Brown als Barton, Wm., yeo., Eastcott, Urchf., 1834, O, W, Wr, P2/1834/19
Wm., hairdresser and shopkeeper, Pewsey, 1838, comm, W, Wr, P3/1838/60
Wm., yeo., W. Lockinge, Wantage, Berks., 1840, O, W, Wr, P23/999
Wm., carp., Sutton V., 1849, O, W, Wr, P2/1849/11
Wm. Geoff., yeo., Wadswick, Box, 1827, W, Wr, P3/1827/47
see also Bridmore als B.; Clements als B.; Edwards als B.; Smith als B.; Weare als B.; Wier als B.
Browning, Ambrose, Bishopstone N., 1604, AB, comm, I, O, P5/1604/2, P5/8Reg/22B
Ann, wife, Kington St M., 1853, AB, comm, D, Wr, P3/1853/1
Betty, widow, Sal., 1781, W. Not proved, P4/1781/13
Betty, widow, Sal., 1790, W, P4/1790/5
Elbright, smith, Calne, 1576, I, T (re Wm., Christian, Eliz. & Edith B., minors), W, P26/1477, P5/3Reg/74B
Eliz., sp., Sevington, Leigh Delamere, 1851, O, W, Wr, P3/1851/32
Geo., yeo., Stanton St Q., 1808, comm, W, Wr, P1/1808/140
Hy., vict., Swindon, 1809, W, Wr, P3/1809/27
Hester, widow, Charlton nr Malm., 1718, AB, P3/B/1155
Jas., Westport St My., 1750, AB, P1/B/1248
Jas., yeo., Leigh Delamere, 1791, W, P3/B/1734
Jas., yeo., Slaughterford, 1812, W, Wr, P3/1812/8
Joan, Sevenhampton, Highw., 1592, AB, I, NW, P5/1592/9, P5/5Reg/141A
Joan, widow, Nettleton, 1614, I, NW, P1/B/111
Joan, widow, Bishopstone N., 1687, I, W, P6/67
Jn., Nettleton, 1609, AB, P3/B/53
Jn., Gt. Somerford, 1667, AB, P3/B/528
Jn., husb., Bishopstone N., 1680, AB, I, P6/47
Jn., Brokenb., 1691, AB, I, ren, P3/B/882
Jn., yeo., Castle C., 1723, W, P3/B/1221
Jn., mason, Bishopstone N., 1728, AB, P6/114
Jn., weaver, Westport St My., 1744, I, W, P1/B/1182, P1/9Reg/401A
Jn., Leigh Delamere, 1751, AB, P3/B/1470
Jn., wheelwright, Newton T., 1755, W, P2/B/1720
Jn., sen., farmer, Church Yatton, Yatton K., 1811, comm, W, Wr, P1/1811/40
Jn., Lambourn, Berks., 1832, AB, comm, Wr, P1/1832/24
Jos., yeo., Hankerton, 1741, AB, P3/B/1399
Jos., blacksmith, Sal. St Edmd., 1778, AB, W, P4/1778/3
Mgt., widow, Chelworth, Crudwell, 1605, I, W, P1/B/42
My., widow, Sevington, Leigh Delamere, 1815, W, Wr, P3/1815/44
Nich., yeo., Foulcombe, Bere R., Dorset, 1685, I, W, P5/1685/12
Philippa, widow, Bere R., Dorset, 1732, AB, comm, P5/1732/8
Rd., mason, Littleton Drew, 1603, I, W, P3/B/8
Rd., husb., Barford St Mart., 1684, I, W, P2/B/1038
Rd., sen., Sevington, Leigh Delamere, 1810, W, P3/1810/25
Rd., yeo., Kington St M., 1838, W, Wr, P3/1838/40
Roger, Chelworth, Crudwell, 1571, W, P1/1Reg/34B
Thos., Lt. Hinton, 1682, AB, I, P3/B/763
Walter, gent., Chipp., 1851, O, W, Wr, P3/1851/23
Wm., husb., Barford St Mart., 1605, AB, I, W, copy W, P2/B/257
Wm., rugmaker, Minety, 1670, AB, I, W, P3/B/579
Wm., carp., Dinton, 1684, AB, I, P2/B/1043
Wm., Malm., 1750, AB, P1/B/1247

Wm., sen., parchmentmaker, Malm., 1751, W, P3/B/1471
Brownjohn, Alice, widow, Idmiston, 1561, AB, P2/B/18
Alice, [Idmiston] (NBI), 1618, AB, P2/B/385
Alice, Idmiston, 1663, AB, I, P2/B/751
Edwd., sen., yeo., Idmiston, 1621, AB, I, W, P2/B/413
Edwd., husb., Allington, 1635, I, W, P1/B/252
Edwd., Laverstock, 1644, I, W, P2/B/686
Edwd., Idmiston, 1675, AB, P2/B/886
Eliz., widow, Idmiston, 1662, I, NW, P2/B/746
Hannah, widow, Sal., 1830, W, Wr, P4/1830/14
Jas., yeo., Ownham, Boxford, Berks., 1695, I, W, P1/B/650
Jas., Fisherton A., 1800, AB, P2/1800/76
Jas., timber merchant, W. Dean, 1801, W, P2/1801/12
Jerome, yeo., Idmiston, 1620, I, W, P2/B/399
Jn., N. Tidworth, 1585, AB, I (2), T, W, P2/B/90, P2/7Reg/25A
Jn., yeo., Idmiston, 1604, AB, I, W, P2/B/243, 251
Jn., Idmiston, 1634, I, W, P1/B/251
Jn., sen., Cutteridge, N. Bradley, 1646-47, AB, P2/B/702
Jn., Wilton, 1706, AB, I, P2/B/1260
Jn., Holt, Bradford A., 1711, AB, I, P1/B/772
Jn., Stratford sub C., 1780, AB, P4/1780/17
Jn., wheelwright, Bulford (form. of Newton T.), 1785, aff (2), W (2), P2/B/2011
Jn., bach., W. Dean, 1808, AB, Wr, P1/1808/138
Jos., yeo., Porton, Idmiston, 1733, W, P2/B/1526
Jos., shoemaker, Sal., 1818, W, Wr, P4/1818/11
Mgt., widow, Gomeldon, Idmiston, 1696, I, W, P2/B/1171
My., widow, Idmiston, 1604, AB, I, W, P2/B/250
My., widow, Porton, Idmiston, 1766, AB, W, P2/B/1824
Rd., Winterbourne G., 1574, W, P2/5Reg/179B
Rd., husb., Allington, 1639, I, W, P2/B/632
Rd., yeo., Middle Winterslow, 1739, W, P2/B/1572
Rd. Goldfinch, tailor, Sal., 1799, W, P4/1798/2
Robt., gardener, Milford, Sal. St Mart., 1790, W, P4/1790/21
Sally, sp., Fisherton A., 1846, W, Wr, P2/1846/7
Sam., widower, Sal., 1849, AB, note, O, Wr, P4/1849/9, 12
Sarah, widow, Milford, Sal. St Mart., 1804, W, P4/1805/7
Steph., yeo. *or* husb., Allington, 1663, AB, I, W, Wr, P1/B/401
Steph., wheelwright, Milford, Sal. St Mart., 1679, W, P4/1679/13
Steph., yeo., Allington, 1711, W, P1/B/757, P1/5Reg/60
Susanna, sp., Milford, Sal. St Mart., 1790, W, P4/1790/18
Thos., Porton, Idmiston, 1617, I, NW, P2/B/370
Thos., yeo., Heytes., 1668, AB, I (over Ł800), W, P5/1667/9
Thos., gent., Sal., 1677, AB, P4/1677/10
Thos., Britford, 1718, AB, I, P24/639
Thos., gardener, Fisherton A., 1854, aff, W, Wr, P2/1854/31
Timothy, Marl., 1840-41, AB, comm, court proceeding, O, Wr, P1/1840/6, P1/1841/6
Walter, yeo., Gomeldon, Idmiston, 1731, W, P2/B/1503
Wm., weaver, Southwick, N. Bradley, 1664, comm, I, W, P1/B/404
Wm., Wilton, 1682, AB, I, P2/B/999
Wm., gent., Fisherton A., 1840, W, Wr, P2/1840/35
see also Brown alias/*or* B.
Brownsay, Jn., blacksmith, Chards., Devon, 1638, AB, I, P5/1638/14, P5/13Reg/74B
Brownson, Edwd., bricklayer, Caversham, Oxfordshire but left effects at Wokm., Berks., 1748, W, Wr, P5/1748/4
Browse, Hy., Lt. Woodford, 1686, I, W, P13/3/11
Brouse, Jos., hatter, Trowb., 1728, AB, ren, P1/B/941
Broxhead, Hy., Bourton, Maddington, 1623, AB, I, P2/B/432
Broxholm, Jn., dealer in china and glasswares, Calne, 1842, comm, W, Wr, P26/1459
Thos., sen., auctioneer and appraiser, Calne, 1841, W, Wr, P26/1456
Broxwell, Hy., husb., Bourton, Maddington, 1558, W, P2/3Reg/134B
Rd., Winterbourne E., 1597, AB, I, P2/B/175

Brokwell, Steph., Goatacre, Hilmarton, 1672, AB, comm, I, P3/B/610
Wm., husb., Maddington, 1591, I, W, P2/B/125
Broyke *see* Brooks
Bruar *see* Brewer
Bruce, Jas., Devizes St My., 1804, AB, P1/1804/77
Brucker *see* Brooker
Bruges, Betty, gent.'s wife, Semington, Steeple A., 1804, W, P1/1804/106
Gifford, Conock, Chirton, 1765, AB, P2/B/1808
Gifford, Conock, Chirton, 1800, AB, comm, P2/1800/101
Gifford Holloway, gent., Haxton, Fittleton, 1838, O, W, Wr, P2/1838/28
Bruges *or* Burges, Hy., gent., Hawkeridge, Westb., 1698, AB, I, P25/1698/10
Matthew, Paxcroft, Steeple A., 1729, W, P1/B/959, P1/7Reg/333A
Rebecca, sp., Devizes, 1818, W, Wr, P1/1818/5
Brugis, Rebecca Harris, Conock, Chirton, 1725, W, P2/B/1442
Robt., Devizes, 1816, AB, Wr, P1/1816/2
Thos., farmer, Semington, Steeple A., 1782, W, P1/B/1468, P1/13Reg/372
Wm., gent., Devizes, 1818, comm, W, Wr, P1/1818/6
Wm., bach., Semington, Steeple A., 1848-49, AB, comm, court proceeding, O, Wr, P1/1848/63, P1/1849/14
Brumham *see* Bromham
Brumley *see* Bromley
Brumsdon *see* Brinsden
Brunker, Branker, Agnes, widow, Whaddon, 1619, I, W, P1/B/150
Brounker, Ann, widow, Bradford A., 1634, AB, a/c, I, P2/B/579
Anth., tiler, Corsham, 1652, AB, I, W, P29/B/19, P29/1Reg/148
Hy., weaver, Broughton G., 1625, I, W, P1/B/200
Jn., sen., Whaddon, 1612, I, W, P1/B/80
Jn., Broughton G., 1638, I, W, P2/B/617
Thos., Atworth, Bradford A., 1574, AB, P2/5Reg/177A
Brounker, Wm., husb., Whaddon, 1573, W, P2/5Reg/168A
Bruncker, Wm., sen., Whaddon, 1607, AB, I, W, P2/B/273
Brounker, Wm., fuller, Bradford A., 1631, I, W, P2/B/536
Brounker, Wm., sen., esquire, Erlestoke, 1686, AB, I (detailed), P2/B/954, 1059
Brouncker, Wm. *see also* Walter Beare
Brunsden, Brunsdon *see* Brinsden
Brunsell, Oliver, clerk, Wrou., 1641, I, W, P3/B/457
Brunson *see* Brinsden
Bruorton, Wm., widower and collector of excise duty, St Ann's St., Sal. St Mart., 1838, W, Wr, P4/1838/16
Bruton, Geo. Nelson, Devizes St Jn., 1828, AB, comm, ren, Wr, P1/1828/14
Jn., Sal., 1689, AB, I, P4/1689/11
Robt., Sal., 1832, AB, Wr, P4/1832/2
Bryan, Brian, Elias, chapman, Westbrook, Gt. Faringdon, Berks., 1613, AB, I, P1/B/98
Eliz., widow, Newtown, Shalbourne, 1705, I, W, Wr, P23/272
Brian, Jn., Oborne, Dorset, 1632, AB, I, P5/1632/10, P5/12Reg/116A
Jn., yeo., Pinkney, Sherston, 1670, I, W, P3/B/580
Brian, Jn., carp., Winterborne K., Dorset, 1693, I, W, P5/1693/10
Wm., Stratford Tony, 1715, I, W, P2/B/1346
Wm., Winterbourne D., 1820, AB, Wr, P7/195
Bryant, Briant, Benj., sen., butcher, Rushall, 1790, W, P2/B/2054
Briant, Bridget, widow, Devizes, 1663, I, W, P1/B/389
Briant, Cath., widow, Whitsbury, 1778, W, P2/B/1961
Briant, Chas., miller, Bradford A., 1771, W, P2/B/1877
Christian, Lyme R., Dorset, 1628, I, W, P5/1628/8, P5/11Reg/66
Briant, Edith, Pewsey, 1614, AB, I (drowned by misfortune), P1/B/105, P3/B/114
Edmd., husb., Whaddon, 1579, W, P2/5Reg/332A
Briant, Edwd., Devizes, 1699, AB, P1/B/679
Edwd., yeo., Dauntsey, 1783, ren, W, P1/B/1488, P1/13Reg/499
Eliz., widow, Axnoller, Beam., Dorset, 1742, W, P17/485
Briant, Eliz., widow, Fisherton A., 1750, AB, I, P1/B/1251
Eliz., widow, Sutton B., 1761, W, P3/B/1540
Eliz., widow, Bradford A., 1857, AB, aff, O, Wr, P2/1857/59

Francis, yeo., Chipp., 1842, O, W, Wr, P3/1842/25
Geo., labourer, Woodb., 1722, AB, P3/B/1211
Geo., yeo., Holnest, Dorset, 1723, AB, I, ren, P5/1723/5
Geo., jun., Axnoller, Beam., Dorset, 1736, I, P17/464
Geo., bach., Beam., Dorset, 1756, AB, P17/531
Briant, Geo., Shalbourne, Berks., 1813, AB, P23/863
Hy., serge weaver, Uffc., Devon, 1698, W, P5/1698/7
Hy., linen weaver, Gillingham, Dorset, 1710, I, W, P27/1/183
Hy., carp., Morgan's Vale, Downton, 1843, W, Wr, P2/1843/43
Briant, Jas., Whitsbury, 1776, W, Wr, P2/B/1932
Jas., yeo., Warm. Grn, Downton, 1837, W, Wr, P2/1837/75
Briant, Jeremiah, Pitton, Alderbury, 1806, AB, P26/1258
Briant, Jeremiah, Pitton, Alderbury, 1820, AB, Wr, P26/1330
Briant, Jerome, yeo., Chilhampton, S. Newton, 1739, W, P2/B/1577
Brient, Joan, widow, Hullavington, 1684, I, W, P3/B/797
Joan, widow, Lacock, 1693, I, W, P3/B/908
Briant, Jn., husb., W. Lavington, 1561, W (NEP), P1/2Reg/144A
Briant, Jn., husb. and innholder, Steeple L., 1633, I, W, P2/B/566
Jn., chandler, Devizes, 1646, I, W, P1/B/327
Briant, Jn., S. Marston, 1662, AB, I, P5/1662/14
Brient, Jn., labourer, Hullavington, 1683, comm, I, W, P3/B/775
Jn., S. Marston, 1687, AB, P5/1686/15
Briant, Jn., sen., fuller, Worton, Pott., 1688, I, W, P1/B/590
Jn., yeo., Langley Burrell, 1697, AB, comm, P3/B/970
Briant, Jn., Fisherton A., 1745, AB, P2/B/1632
Briant, Jn., All C., 1772, AB (2), P3/B/1621
Jn., miller, Hunt Mill, Wootton B., 1813, W, Wr, P3/1813/24
Jn., gent., Fisherton A. & Sal., 1835, AB, comm, P2/1835/22
Jn., coal merchant, Bradford A., 1839, O, W, Wr, P2/1839/3
Jn., bricklayer, Sal., 1844, W, Wr, P1/1844/39
My., Chr. M., 1614, I, P1/B/117
My., widow, Lyme R., Dorset, 1622, AB, I, P5/1622/8, P5/10Reg/127C
My., Littleton, Steeple A., 1638, AB, P2/B/623
Briant, My., yeo.'s widow, Chilhampton, S. Newton, 1742, W, P2/B/1609
My., sp., Fisherton A., 1762, AB, W, P2/B/1784
Briant, My., sp., Fisherton A., 1792, AB, P1/B/1529, P1/14Reg/468A
My., widow, Chipp., 1844, O, W, Wr, P3/1844/36
Briant, Philip, broad weaver, Yatton K., 1735, I, W, P1/B/1050, P1/8Reg/74
Rd., Inglesham, 1641, AB, I, P3/B/458
Briant, Rd., heelmaker, Rushall, 1777, W, P2/B/1943
Rd. Wayte, yeo., Langley Burrell, 1835, W, P3/1835/34
Robt., Durnford, 1591, AB, I, P5/1591/7, P5/5Reg/127B
Briant, Robt., Rowde, 1628, AB, I, P3/B/295
Robt., Whitley, Melk., 1775, AB, P2/B/1926
Sam., carp., Holt, Bradford A., 1815, AB, comm, ren, W, Wr, P2/1815/20
Sarah, sp., Sal., 1825, W, Wr, P4/1825/12
Sarah, widow, Grittleton, 1832, W, Wr, P1/1832/94
Thos., yeo., Calne, 1602, I (part missing), W, P5/1601/5, P5/7Reg/32C
Briant, Thos., Broad B., Highw., 1678, AB, P10/1678/3
Thos., yeo., Lacock, 1688, AB, I, P3/B/849
Thos., broad weaver, Cumberwell, Bradford A., 1796, W, Wr, P2/B/2106
Briant, Thos., Folly Lane, Melk., 1841, O, W, Wr, P2/1841/50
Walter, Sal., 1788, AB, P4/1788/5
Bryants, Wm., Bradford A., 1569, AB, P2/5Reg/77C
Wm., tailor, Damerham, Hants, 1619, I, NW, P1/B/148
Briant, Wm., husb., Durnford, 1620, I, W, P5/1619/43, P5/9Reg/229F
Briant, Wm., keeper, Rams. (form. of Catherington, Hants), 1634, AB, I, NW, P5/1634/4, P5/12Reg/166C
Bryant als Richards, Wm., [miller], Brokenb., 1639, I, W, P3/B/427
Wm., Yattendon, Berks., 1741, AB, P1/B/1135
Wm., yeo., Seagry, 1742, AB, W, P3/B/1406

Wm., innholder, Sal., 1769, I, W, P4/1769/15
Wm., dairyman, Dauntsey, 1809, W, Wr, P3/1809/64
see also Witnam als B.
Bryar *see* Briar
Bryce *see* Brice
Bryd *see* Bread
Brydmore *see* Breadmore
Bryent *see* Bryant
Bryer *see* Briar
Bryne *see* Brine
Bryse *see* Brice
Bryther *see* Breather,
Buck, [...], tanner, Marl., c1603, I, P1/B/24
Geo., Sherb., Dorset, 1705, AB, I, P5/1705/13
Jn., wheelwright, Chr. M., 1736, AB, I (2), W, P3/B/1356
Judith, widow, Rowde, 1665, comm, I, W, P3/B/511
Nich., tucker, Turners Puddle, Dorset, 1583, AB, I, W, P5/1583/6, P5/4Reg/66A
Thos., Wokm., Berks., 1594, AB, P5/6Reg/79A
Thos., miller, Wokm., Berks., 1603, AB, a/c (2), I, W, P5/1603/8, P5/7Reg/80C
Thos., Chr. M., 1734, AB, P3/B/1343
Wm., Sutton V., 1557, W, P2/3Reg/72C
Buckaridge *see* Buckeridge
Buckell *see* Buckle
Buckerfield, Edwd., yeo., Marl. (form. of Ogbourne St Geo.), 1751, W, P1/B/1254, P1/10Reg/465
Edwd., sen., Chiseldon, 1782, AB, P3/B/1676
Eliz., widow, Marl., 1757, AB, P1/B/1312
Hy., yeo., Ogbourne St Geo., 1708, AB, I (detailed), ren, W, P5/1708/12, P5/15Reg/98
Joanna, sp., Marl., 1753, W, P1/B/1273, P1/11Reg/79B
Philip, gent., Ogbourne St Geo., 1743, W, Wr, P5/1743/11
Thos., bach., Marl., 1757, AB, P1/B/1311
Buckeridge, Buckaridge, Ann, widow, Aston U., Blewbury, Berks., 1628, I, W, copy W, P5/1628/6, P5/11Reg/83C
Ann, sp., Tilehurst, Berks., 1729, I, W, P1/B/948, P1/7Reg/225A
David, potter, Inkpen, Berks., 1835, W, Wr, P1/1835/105
Giles, Purton, 1667, AB, I, P3/B/529
Buckridge, Jas., potter, Inkpen, Berks., 1801, W, P1/1801/39, P1/15Reg/259
Jane, widow, Eastcourt, Crudwell, 1630, I, W, P3/B/330
Buckridge, Jn., yeo., Tilehurst, Berks., 1602, I, W, P1/B/20
Jn., yeo., Chaddleworth, Berks., 1711, comm, I, W, P1/B/773, P1/5Reg/212
Jn., Inkpen, Berks., 1759, AB, P1/B/1315
Rachel, gent.'s wife, Garsdon, 1734, AB, P3/B/1344
Rd., Aston U., Blewbury, Berks., 1608, record of execution of AB, P5/1608/3
Buckridge, Rd., sen., Aston U., Blewbury, Berks., 1677, I, W, P5/1677/4
Rd., yeo., Aston U., Blewbury, Berks., 1711, I, W, P5/1711/12, P5/15Reg/257
Sarah, widow, Aston U., Blewbury, Berks., 1713, AB, I, P5/1713/11
Thos., yeo., Eastcourt, Crudwell, [1619], I, W (NEP), P3/B/180
Buckridge, Thos., yeo., Bisham, Berks., 1622, I, W, P1/B/180
Thos., Eastcourt, Crudwell, 1675, AB, I, P3/B/655
Thos., yeo., Purton Stoke, 1680, I, W, P3/B/733
Thos., Chute Forest, Chute, 1813, AB (relating only to lease in C. F.), comm, P7/189
Buckaridge, Wm., yeo., Sonning, Berks., 1620, I, W, P5/1620/2, P5/10Reg/74
Wm., yeo., Lydiard M., 1623, AB, a/c, I (very detailed), P3/B/237
Buckett, Thos., Milford, Sal. St Mart., 1838, AB, D, W, Wr, P4/1838/3
Buckford, Rd., merchant, Lyme R., Dorset, 1594, AB, I, P16/469
Buckingham, Robt., vict., Sandford, Woodley and S., Berks., 1797, W, P1/15Reg/129A
Robt., vict., Stanford in the Vale, Berks., 1798, W, Wr, P1/B/1559
Thos., Marl., 1632, AB, I (fragment), P1/B/240
Buckland, Abraham, sen., yeo., Brinkw., 1757, W, P3/B/1510
Agnes, widow, Broad B., Highw., 1669, AB, comm, I, NW, P10/1669/1
Ann, widow, Netheravon, 1672, I, W, P12/107
Ann, sp., Beer Hackett, Dorset, 1720, W, P5/1720/3, P5/16Reg/37A

Anth., sen., yeo., Brinkw., 1691, I, W, P3/B/883
Anth., Lt. Somerford, 1718, AB, I, P3/B/1156
Anth., Liddington, 1815, W, Wr, P3/1815/33
Barbara, widow, Standlynch, Downton, 1625, AB, I, P2/B/454
Buckland als Down, Cath., widow, Charlton nr Malm., 1632, I, W, P3/B/344
Edwd., yeo., Netheravon, 1751, W, P12/179
Eliz., widow, Wrou., 1605, W, copy W, P3/B/22
Geo., Wrou., 1628, I, W, P1/B/215
Geo., sen., surgeon and vict., Ryme I., Dorset, 1751, W, P5/1751/3
Geo., surgeon, Enmore Grn, Motc., Dorset, 1795, W, P19/196
Geo., whitesmith, Sal., 1838, AB, ren, W, Wr, P4/1838/12
Hy., yeo., Garsdon, 1661, AB, comm, I, P3/B/473, P3/3Reg/11D
Hugh, Lyme R., Dorset, 1676, NW (NEP), P30/11
Jacob, yeo., Grittleton, 1802, note, W, P3/1802/9
Jacob, yeo., Kington St M., 1846, W, Wr, P3/1846/25
Jas., sen., dairyman, Cleverton, Lea and C., 1777, W, P3/B/1649
Jas., yeo., Rowde, 1780, W, P3/B/1666
Jas., toolmaker, Netheravon, 1845, court paper, O, W, Wr, P12/230
Jas., edge toolmaker, Netheravon, 1849, AB, court paper, Wr, P12/233
Jas. Brooke, Crickl. St My., 1839, W, Wr, P3/1839/19
Jeremiah, gardener, Melk., 1772, AB, NW, P2/B/1884
Jeremiah, cutler, Netheravon, 1823, grant of probate, W, Wr, P12/217
Joan, widow, Lyme R., Dorset, 1679, AB, I, W, P5/1679/8
Jn., husb., Beam., Dorset, 1641, AB, I, P17/67
Jn., sen., yeo., Wrou., 1661, comm, I, W, P3/B/474, P3/3Reg/17B
Buckland als Horne, Jn., husb., Aldbourne, 1678, I, ren, P3/B/696
Jn., yeo., Dauntsey, 1678, I, NW, ren, P3/B/697
Jn., yeo., Crudwell, 1722, I, W, P3/B/1212
Jn., Bemerton, Fugg. St Peter, 1724, AB, I, P2/B/1427
Jn., yeo., Wrou., 1772, comm, W, P3/B/1622
Jn., yeo., Norton, 1798, comm, W, P3/B/1763
Jn., innkeeper, Melk., 1847, O, W, Wr, P2/1847/60
Lucy, widow, Netheravon, 1849, AB, O, Wr, P12/232
Margery, widow, Brinkw., 1711, AB (endorsed with Quaker declaration), certs (2), ren, P1/B/753
My., widow, Lydiard M., 1679, I, W, P3/B/717
Maurice, bach., Downton, 1559, W, P2/4Reg/23A
Obed-edom, shoemaker, Melk., 1848, W, Wr, P1/1848/47
Priscilla, widow, Trowb., 1835, comm, W, Wr, P1/1835/44
Buckland als Down, Robt., husb., Charlton nr Malm., 1621, I, W, P3/B/214
Buckland als Down, Robt., husb., Garsdon, 1639, I, W, P3/B/428
Buckland als Down, Robt., sen., yeo., Garsdon, 1669, AB, comm, I, NW, P3/B/553
Ruth, widow, Beanacre, Melk., 1780, W, P2/B/1972
Sam., yeo., Brinkw., 1708, AB, L, ren, P1/B/732
Steph., yeo., Wrou., 1824, W, Wr, P3/1824/15
Thos., Rams., 1593-94, AB, P5/1593/7, P5/6Reg/14A
Thos., weaver, Melk., 1627, I, W, P2/B/474
Buckland als Aust, Thos., sen., baker, Calne, 1636, W, P26/55
Thos., Brinkw., 1698, AB, I, P1/B/675
Thos., broad weaver, Shaw Hill, Melk., 1769, W, P2/B/1854
Thos., yeo., Wrou., 1785, W, P3/B/1702
Walter, esquire, Standlynch, 1638, AB, I, P2/B/624
Wm., husb., Netherb., Dorset, 1595, I, W, P5/1595/10, P5/6Reg/116
Wm., Beanacre, Melk., 1777, comm, W, P2/B/1948
Wm., maltster, Chr. M., 1782, comm, W, P3/B/1677
Wm., cordw., Canonhold, Melk., 1844, comm, W, Wr, P2/1844/68
see also Horne als B.
Buckle, Buckell, Ann, widow, Upton, Blewbury, Berks., 1645, I, W, P5/1645/4, P5/14Reg/86A
Hy., tanner, Upton, Blewbury, Berks., 1644, I, W (NEP), P5/1643/1
Robt., carp., Devizes, 1841, W, Wr, P1/1841/20
Simon, Wantage, Berks., 1695, AB, I, P5/1695/7

Buckell, Thos., blacksmith, Chilton, Berks., 1817, W, Wr, P1/1817/63
Walter, farmer, Nettleton, 1786-87, W, P1/B/1499, P1/14Reg/145B
Wm., Barford St Mart., 1664, AB, ren, P1/B/410
Buckler, Ann, widow, Rowde, 1716, W, P3/B/1138
Austin, gent., Warm., 1680, comm, W, P1/B/542
Edwd., yeo., Warm., 1650, comm, W, P1/B/360
Eleanor, widow, Warm., 1723, W, P2/B/1423
Eleazar, innholder, Devizes, 1727, W, P1/B/937, P1/7Reg/167
Eliz., widow, Warm., 1743, W, P2/B/1626
Fanny, widow, Warm., 1845, W, Wr, P2/1845/28
Grace, widow and innholder, Sal., 1675, I (detailed), W, P4/1675/6
Humphrey, yeo., Rowde, 1714, W, P1/B/789, P1/5Reg/345
Jn., Thornford, Dorset, 1697, AB, comm, P5/1696/4
Robt., Thornford, Dorset, 1597, AB, P5/1597/14, P5/6Reg/158C
Robt., Thornford, Dorset, 1623, AB, a/c, ren, P5/1623/3, P5/10Reg/154B
Ruth, widow, Devizes, 1754, AB, P1/B/1284
Walter, innholder, Sal., 1673, I, W, P4/1673/6
Wm., miller, Sherb., Dorset, 1633, I, W, P5/1633/6, P5/12Reg/149B
see also Bugler *or* B.
Buckley, Edith, widow, Melk., 1725, AB, P2/B/1438
Geo., Melk., 1772, AB, P2/B/1880
Jn., S. Wraxall, 1559, W, P2/3Reg/172B
Jn., sen., husb., Woodrow, Melk., 1652, I, W, P1/B/362
Bouckley, Mgt., widow, S. Wraxall, 1570, W, P2/5Reg/88B
Wm., Whitep., 1559, W, P2/4Reg/28A
Wm., Whitep., 1565, T (child: Robt. B.), P2/4Reg/213B
Buckleyn, Edwd., shepherd, Netheravon, 1689, AB, I, P12/131
Bucknoll *see* Bicknell
Bucknor, Benj., farmer, Charlton, Wantage, Berks., 1818, AB, W, Wr, P5/1818/18
Buckpitt, Geo., carp., Trowb., 1827, W, Wr, P1/1827/18
Geo., timber merchant and carp., Trowb., 1839, O, ren, W, Wr, P1/1839/65
Buckridge *see* Buckeridge
Budd, Ann, widow, Westport St My., 1731, W, P3/B/1311
Ann, widow, Bradford A., 1759, W, Wr, P1/B/1330, P1/11Reg/457A
Edwd., husb., Idmiston, 1618, AB, I, P2/B/383
Budd als Bugg, Eliz., widow, Inglesham, 1783, W, P3/B/1684
Eliz., widow, Ditchampton, Wilton, 1824, I, W, Wr, P2/1824/51
Jn., mason, Westport St My., 1692, I, W, P3/B/893
Jn., tailor, Westport St My., 1716, I, W, P3/B/1139
Jn., yeo., Edington, 1831, W, Wr, P2/1831/59
Robt., mason, Bradford A., 1766, AB, comm, P2/B/1817
Thos., tailor, Malm. Abbey, 1691, I, W, P3/B/884
Thos., Bradford A., 1738, AB, P1/B/1101
Thos., husb., Inglesham, 1778, W, P3/B/1654
Thos., Stratford Tony, 1830, W, P2/1830/29
Wm., no abode stated, 1571, W. Proved by Archdeacon of Wiltshire, P1/1Reg/130A
Wm., sen., yeo., Winterbourne G., 1608, W, P2/8Reg/11B
Wm., tailor, Winterbourne G., 1637, W, P2/B/612
Wm., rector and clerk, Alton B., 1685, I, W, P1/B/580
Wm., sen., yeo., Penleigh, Dilton, Westb., 1762, W, P25/1762/6
Wm., Westb., 1771, AB, O, P25/1771/4
Wm., gent., Westb., 1850, declaration, O, W, Wr, P25/1850/4
see also Butt als B.
Budden, Ann, widow, Hyde, Bere R., Dorset, 1726, W, P5/1726/8, P5/16Reg/134A
Deborah, widow, Damerham, Hants, 1748, AB, comm, P2/B/1661
Deborah, sp., Damerham, Hants, 1825, AB, Wr, P2/1825/52
Edmd., bach., Sal., 1744, AB, a/c, D, I, ren, P4/1744/2
Geo., gent., Bower C., 1776, W, P2/B/1930
Hugh, Damerham, Hants, 1641, I, W, P2/B/668
Hugh, gent., Downton, 1724, AB, W, P2/B/1429

Jane, widow, Bower C., 1773, W, P2/B/1898
Jn., sen., Donhead St My., 1573, W, P2/5Reg/169A
Jn., husb., Damerham, Hants, 1646, AB, I, W, P2/B/707
Jn., yeo., Bere R., Dorset, 1704, I, W, P5/1704/5
Jn., sen., husb., Filholds, Bere R., Dorset, 1712, W, P5/1712/8, P5/15Reg/298
Jn., Homington & Sal., 1851, AB, Wr, P1/1851/22
Patience, widow, Lyme R., Dorset, 1719, W, P5/1719/13, P5/16Reg/15B
Susanna, widow, Donhead St My., 1803, W, Wr, P2/1803/77
Thos., bookkeeper, Sal., 1829, req, W, Wr, P1/1829/75
Budge, Thos., sen., yeo., Halstock Leigh, Dorset, 1666, I, W, P16/4
Budget, My., widow, Mere, 1768, W, P5/1768/3
Buerd *see* Burd
Buffing, Jn., cordw., Mere, 1728, W (very lengthy religious preamble), P5/1728/13, P5/16Reg/169A
Buffington, Robt., gent., Melk., 1590, I, T, W, P2/B/120
Bufford *see* Bulford
Bufton, Bufton als Scholler, Ann, widow, Stratton St Mgt., 1712, I, W, P29/B/38
Bufton als Scholler, Jn., Stratton St Mgt., 1660-61, I, W, P29/B/21, P29/1Reg/163
Buffton, Jn., yeo., Templeton, Kintbury, Berks., 1686, I, W, P1/B/1563
Jn., Stratton St Mgt., 1701, I, W, P29/B/34, P29/1Reg/276
Thos., yeo., Hungerford, Berks., 1712, I, W, P23/324
Bugden, Ann, Donhead St My., 1747, W, P2/B/1657
Charlotte, sp., Coombe, Donhead St My., 1812, W, Wr, P2/1812/6
Edmd., yeo., Donhead St My., 1609, AB, I, P2/B/291, P2/8Reg/68B
Edmd., carp., Donhead St My., 1621, I, NW, P2/B/410
Bugden als Peirce, Eliz., wife, Sal., 1672, AB, P4/1671/13
Geo., weaver, Sal., 1722, W (NEP), P4/1722/22
Jesse, Tisb., 1831, W, P2/1831/17
Jn., Hindon, 1552, app. of attorney, I, W, P2/B/10, P2/2Reg/154C
Jn., glover, Donhead St My., 1602, W, I, P1/B/15
Jn., woollen weaver, Donhead St My., 1613, W, P2/8Reg/204B
Jn., husb., Donhead St My., 1626, AB, a/c, I, P2/B/466
Jn., Sal., 1724, AB, I, P4/1723/14
Matthew, Donhead St My., 1615, AB (fragment), I, P2/B/348
Philip, gent., Sal., 1720, W, P1/B/852, P1/6Reg/206
Rd., yeo., Donhead St My., 1638, I, W, P2/B/614
Robt., sen., husb., Donhead St My., 1717, I, W, P2/B/1356
Robt., sen., yeo., Donhead St My., 1745, W, P2/B/1635
Simon, clerk curate, Donhead St My., 1635, I, W, P2/B/585, P2/9Reg/53
Thos., weaver, Sal., 1734, W, Wr, P4/1734/3
Thos., W. Harnham, 1845, W, Wr, P8/93
Wm., mariner in Col.Jeffrey's Regt., Col.Down's Co. and HMS *Worcester*, Sal. St Edmd., 1748, W, P4/1748/12
Bugg, Jn., miller, Dinton, 1834, W, Wr, P2/1834/3
see also Budd als B.
Buggis, Eliz., widow, Mere, 1590, I, W, P5/1590/11, P5/5Reg/80C
Bowgis *or* Bouggis, Wm., clerk, Mere, 1596-97, W, P5/1596/11, P5/6Reg/178C
Bugler, Bugler *or* Buckler, Betty, widow, Sherb., Dorset, 1846, AB, comm, Wr (form. Betty Warr, widow), P5/1846/1
Jos., Beam., Dorset, 1729, AB, P17/436
Thos., tanner, Beam., Dorset, 1830, W, Wr, P5/1830/34
Buissy *see* Bissey
Bulford, Jas., shearman, Crockerton, Longbridge D., 1589-1613, I, a/c, app. of proctor, T, P2/B/106, 337
Bufford, Wm., Crockerton, Longbridge D., 1579, I, T, W, P2/B/78, P2/5Reg/347A
Bulgin, Jas., baker, Bradford A., 1796, comm, W, P2/B/2109
Thos., clothier, Rowde, 1807, W, Wr, P3/1807/14
Bull, Abraham, sen., weaver, Broughton G., 1732, W, P2/B/1508
Alexander, cardmaker, Westb. L., 1698, W, I, P25/1698/2
Benj., farmer, Westb., 1838, AB, O, W, Wr, P25/1838/1
Cath., widow, Broughton G., 1569, W, P2/5Reg/70A
Cath., widow, Sherb., Dorset, 1773, W, P5/1773/9, P5/17Reg/65B
Dennis, broad weaver and bach., Seend, Melk., 1611, I, W, P1/B/69
Edwd., yeo., Westb. L., 1679, AB, a/c, I, P25/1679/4

Eliz., widow, Broughton G., 1590, I (fragment), W, P2/B/119
Eliz., widow, Keevil, 1603, I, P2/B/222
Eliz., widow, Lacock & Pott., 1710, I, W, P3/B/1091
Eliz., widow, Chipp., 1787, W, P3/B/1708
Frances, Pott., 1707, W, P1/B/728
Francis, weaver, Biddestone St Nich., 1610, W, P3/B/69
Grace, widow, Bere R., Dorset, 1704, I, W, P5/1704/4
Hy., sievemaker, Chards., Devon, 1582, I, W, P5/1582/3, P5/4Reg/38F
Hy., sen., yeo., Marston, Pott., 1674, I, W, P1/B/499
Isaac, weaver, Melk. Forest, 1821, W, Wr, P2/1821/65
Jane, wife of Jn., gent., Calne & Corsham, 1783, W (made 1748, mentions manorial property in Co.), P29/B/49, P29/2Reg/171
Jane, Westb. L., 1812, W, P25/1812/2
Jn., Stratford Tony, 1546, AB, P2/2Reg/18E
Jn., husb., Broughton G., 1557, W, P2/3Reg/43A
Jn., Gt. Bedwyn, 1565, W, P5/1Reg/61B
Jn., husb., Broughton G., 1567, W, P2/5Reg/7C
Jn., Melk., 1597, I, W, P2/B/185
Jn., husb., Broughton G., 1613, comm, W, P2/B/336
Jn., Hermitage, Dorset, 1620, AB, comm, I, P5/1620/5, P5/10Reg/11B
Jn., Chipp., 1628, AB, P1/B/212
Jn., fuller, W. Lavington, 1633, I, W, P1/B/245
Jn., Sal. St Edmd., 1633, AB, I, P4/1633/15
Jn., tailor, Lyme R., Dorset, 1643, I (3 - 1 draft, 2 unsigned copies), W (2 - 1 signed & witnessed, 1 copy with formalised wording). Not proved., P5/1642/7
Jn., clothier, Whitley, Melk., 1675, AB, a/c, I, W, P2/B/885
Jn., clothier, Broughton G., 1694, AB, I, P2/B/1159
Jn., yeo., Chipp., 1733, W, P3/B/1330
Jn., vict., Chipp., 1752, W, P3/B/1480
Jn., tile digger, Yatton K., 1758, W, P3/B/1519
Martha, widow, Sal., 1769, W, P4/1769/14
My., widow, Trowb., 1745, comm, W, P1/B/1192, P1/10Reg/13A
My., wife, Melk., 1808, AB, comm, Wr, P2/1808/24
Philip, gent., Chipp., 1628, I, NW, P1/B/207
Philip, vict., Devizes, 1808, O, W, Wr, P1/1808/145
Rd., Broad C., 1567, AB, P2/5Reg/15A
Rd., Broad C., 1579, T (child: Thos. B.), P2/B/74
Rd., yeo., Rowde, 1684, I, W, P3/B/802
Rd., Bere R., Dorset, 1703, AB, I, P5/1703/4
Robt., husb., Broughton G., 1625, I, W, P2/B/455
Robt., tailor, Sal., 1769, AB, P4/1769/13
Robt., linen weaver, Mere, 1784, W, P5/1784/2
Sarah, widow, Bearfield, Bradford A., 1761, W, P2/B/1772
Sarah, widow, Folly Lane, Melk., 1847, comm, W, Wr, P2/1847/54
Thos., husb., Broughton G., 1574, W, P2/5Reg/183C
Thos., Melk., 1576, W, P2/5Reg/269B
Thos., broad weaver, Broughton G., 1628, AB, I, P1/B/211
Thos., yeo., Marston, Pott., 1679, I, W, P1/B/526
Thos., Seend Row, Melk., 1732, W, P1/B/1021, P1/7Reg/524B
Wm., Barford St Mart., 1595, I, T, W, P2/B/160, P2/7Reg/141A
Wm., weaver, Trowb., [1616], I (2), copy W, W, P22/2/20
Wm., yeo., Staverton, Trowb., 1630, comm, I, W, P22/1/18
Wm., Bradford A., 1758, AB, comm, P2/B/1744
Wm., labourer, Allington, Chipp., 1778, AB, W, P3/B/1655
Wm., yeo., Kellaways, 1815, W, Wr, P3/1815/41
Bullen *see* Bollen
Bullmore *see* Bulmer
Bullock, Adam, baker, Hullavington, 1702, AB, I, P3/B/1020
Adam, yeo., Hullavington, 1816, W, Wr, P3/1816/28
Agnes, widow, Alderton, 1624, I, W, P3/B/255

Agnes, widow, Hullavington, 1630, I, W, P3/B/331
Alice, widow, Hullavington, 1614, I, W, P1/B/118
Arthur, Hullavington, 1690, AB, I, P3/B/873
Bollock, Chas., bach., Chetnole, Yetm., Dorset, 1832, AB, Wr, P19/243
Edwd., yeo., Fyfield, Berks., 1756, W, P1/B/1302, P1/11Reg/251
Eliz., Yatesbury, 1727, AB, P3/B/1259
Francis, sen., yeo., Garford, Marcham, Berks., 1801, W, P1/1801/57, P1/15Reg/272
Francis, yeo., Garford, Marcham, Berks., 1832, O, W, Wr, P1/1832/25
Gilbt., gent., Arborfield, Berks., 1606, AB, I (detailed), W, P5/1606/8
Giles, Hullavington, [1618], I, W (NEP), P3/B/167
Giles, husb., Hullavington, 1640, I, W, P3/B/446
Jacob, baker, Hullavington, 1813, W, P3/1813/57
Jacob, Corston, Malm., 1842, AB, comm, Wr, P3/1842/36
Jacob, Corston, Malm., 1848, AB, O, Wr, P3/1848/51
Bollock, Jesse, bach., Chetnole, Yetm., Dorset, 1832, AB, Wr, P19/242
Joan, widow, Newbury, Berks., 1613, I, NW, P1/B/102
Joan, widow, N. Bradley, 1631, I, P2/B/544
Joan, widow, Sandhurst, Berks., 1684, comm, I, W, P5/1684/9
Jn., husb., Grittleton, [1614], I, W, P3/B/115
Jn., Hullavington, 1614, I (2), W (2), P1/B/119
Jn., yeo., Grittleton, 1675, AB, I, ren, P3/B/656
Jn., gent., Wokm., Berks., 1684, comm, W, P5/1683/7
Jn., yeo., Nettleton, 1723, AB, I, P1/B/889
Jn., yeo., Yatesbury, 1727, W, P3/B/1261
Jn., yeo., Kingsclere, Hants (property in Ludg.), 1732, W, P2/B/1507
Jn., Yatesbury, 1757, AB, P3/B/1511
Jn., Broughton G., 1825, AB, O, Wr, P2/1825/26
Jn., Yatesbury, 1837, AB, comm, O, Wr, P3/1837/10
Jn. Alexander, Bradford A., 1825, AB, comm, Wr, P2/1825/25
Judith, widow, Yatesbury, 1757, W, P3/B/1512
Lucy, widow, Anfields Cross, Hurst, Berks., 1593, I, W, P5/1593/14, P5/6Reg/51
Lydia, sp., Sandhurst, Berks., 1733, W, P5/1733/11
Maria, widow, Corston, Malm., 1848, AB, D, O, ren, W, Wr, P3/1848/12
Martha, widow, Kington L., 1843, AB, comm, notification, Wr, P3/1843/30, 38
Rd., [miller], Warm., 1563, W, P2/4Reg/142
Rd., yeo., Warm., 1592, W, P2/B/131
Rd., gent., Halcombe, Westport St My., 1703, AB, I, ren, P3/B/1026
Rd., sen., yeo., Netherton, Fyfield, Berks., 1753, W, P1/B/1264, P1/11Reg/10
Rd. *see* Gilbt. Pether
Robt., Barkham, Berks., 1592, W, P5/6Reg/8B
Robt., Avell Cross, Hurst, Berks., 1592-93, AB, I, W, P5/1592/13, P5/6Reg/12A
Robt., labourer, Westbrook, Gt. Faringdon, Berks., 1679, I, W, P5/1679/10
Robt., yeo., Yatesbury, 1756, W, P3/B/1504
Roger, carp., Hullavington, 1704, I, W, P1/B/711
Roger, joiner, Corsham, 1727, AB, I, P29/B/43, P29/2Reg/51
Roger, yeo., Hullavington, 1788, W, P3/B/1717
Sarah, widow, Hullavington, 1725, AB, W, P3/B/1243
Sarah, sp., Hullavington, 1744, W, P1/B/1181, P1/9Reg/399A
Simon, Hurst, Berks., 1556, W, P5/20Reg/149B
Steph., yeo., Yatesbury, 1793, I, W, P3/B/1740
Susanna, widow, Nettleton, 1732, I, W, P1/B/1016, P1/7Reg/500A
Thos., esquire, Arborfield, Berks., 1596, AB, I, P5/1596/14, P5/6Reg/126C
Thos., Urchf., 1610, AB, P2/B/310, P2/8Reg/128A
Thos., Notton, Lacock, 1733, W, P3/B/1331
Thos., sen., silversmith, Reading, Berks., 1756, W, P1/B/1295, P1/11Reg/217B
Thos., Lt. Cheverell, 1798, AB, P1/B/1558, P1/15Reg/124
Walter, yeo., Clapcote, Grittleton, 1669, AB, I, P3/B/554
Wm., Sonning, Berks., 1572, W, P5/2Reg/112C
Wm., gent., Arborfield, Berks., 1590, I (detailed), T, W, P5/1590/12, P5/5Reg/91C
Wm., Alderton, 1610, AB, P3/B/70

Wm., Sandhurst, Berks., 1684, AB, I, P5/1684/8
Wm., Lt. Cheverell, 1804, AB, P1/1804/21
Wm., yeo., Dunsden Grn, Sonning, Berks., 1816, W, Wr, P5/1816/6
Wm., yeo., Leigh, Bradford A., 1850, D, O, W, Wr, P2/1850/26
Zephaniah, clock and watchmaker, Box, 1832, W, Wr, P1/1832/6
Bulmer, Bulmer *or* Bullmore, Jas., Sherb., Dorset, 1595, AB, I, T, NW, P5/1595/6, P5/6Reg/95A
Jn., N. Bradley, 1559, W, P2/3Reg/166A
Bulpit, Dorothy, widow, Tidcombe, T. and Fosbury, 1743, W, P3/B/1419
Jn., husb., Tidcombe, T. and Fosbury, 1624, I, list of debts, W, P3/B/256
Jn., yeo., Shalbourne Down, 1729, W, P5/1729/9
Lawr., Tidcombe and Fosbury, 1618, note concerning PCC W, P3/B/168
Lawr., Fosbury, Tidcombe and F., 1700, AB, I, P3/B/998
Rd., husb., Hampstead Marshall, Berks., 1683, I, W, P1/B/562
Robt., Patney, 1553, W, P2/2Reg/172C
Thos., yeo., Gt. Bedwyn, 1682, I, W, P21/4/4
Thos., husb. and bach., Tidcombe and Fosbury, 1710, AB, I, P3/B/1092
Wm., husb., Patney, 1616, I, W, P1/B/128
Wm., sen., yeo. *or* husb., Tidcombe and Fosbury, 1690, I, W, P3/B/874
Wm., yeo., Tidcombe and Fosbury, 1715, comm, I, W, P3/B/1133
Bulston, Wm., Beam., Dorset, 1639, AB, I, P17/37
Bulstrode, Jn., Reading, Berks., 1723, AB, P1/B/898
Bumford *see* Burnford
Bun *see* Bunn
Bunce, Alice, widow, Broad B., Highw., 1681, I, W, P10/1681/1
Augustine, chandler, Swindon, 1690, W, P3/B/875
Eliz., widow, late of E. Woodhay, but leaving effects at Newbury, Berks., 1804, AB, P1/1804/133
Francis, sen., yeo. and husb., Letcombe Regis, Berks., 1680, AB, deed of gift, I, P1/B/537
Francis, husb., Shippon, Abingdon, Berks., 1753, W, P1/B/1262, P1/10Reg/512B
Jacob, bricklayer, Warfield, Berks., 1767, req, copy W, P1/B/1380, P1/12Reg/244
Jn., yeo., Eastbury, Lambourn, Berks., 1631, I, W, P1/B/232
Jn., tailor, Shalbourne, 1695, AB, I, P5/1695/10
Jn., Wokm., Berks., 1700, AB, I, P5/1700/7
Jn., potter, Wokm., Berks., 1708, AB, I, P5/1708/14
Jn., Frilford, Marcham, Berks., 1726, AB, comm, P1/B/915
Jn., barber, Westbrook, Gt. Faringdon, Berks., 1728, W, P5/1728/17, P5/16Reg/192B
Jn., Garford, Marcham, Berks., 1753, AB, P1/B/1265
Jn., wheelwright, Chute, 1760, W, P7/158
Jn., yeo., Milton L., 1768, AB, comm (2), W (2 - 1 a copy), P3/B/1594
Jn., plumber and glazier, Abingdon, Berks., 1770, W, P1/B/1402, P1/12Reg/367
Jn., Wootton R., 1808, AB, Wr, P1/1808/41
Bunse, My., widow, Wokm., Berks., 1719, W, P5/1719/9, P5/16Reg/28A
My., widow, Childrey, Berks., 1729, W, P1/B/954, P1/7Reg/295
Robt., yeo., Broad B., Highw., 1672, I, W, P10/1672/1
Robt., Buttermere, 1697, AB, I, P3/B/971
Sam., potter, Wokm., Berks., 1737, W, Wr, P5/1737/3
Sam., yeo., Wokm., Berks., 1746, W, P5/1746/8
Sarah, widow, Moordown Farm, Henley, Buttermere, 1737, W, P3/B/1368
Sarah, sp., Paven Hill, Purton, 1772, W, P3/B/1623
Sarah, widow, Milton L., 1775, comm, W, P3/B/1638
Thos., potter, Hurst, Berks., 1629, I, W, P5/1629/8, P5/11Reg/119B
Thos., yeo., Childrey, Berks., 1716, I, W, P1/B/820, P1/6Reg/61
Thos., yeo., Woodsend, Aldbourne, 1801, W, P3/1801/8
Wm., wheeler, Purton, 1671, AB, P3/B/595
Wm., yeo., Aldbourne, 1720, I, W, P3/B/1183
Wm., sen., Purton, 1751, AB, P3/B/1472
Wm., yeo., Purton, 1810, comm, W, Wr, P3/1810/13
Bunch, Thos., Wokm., Berks., 1666, AB, comm, I, P5/1665/13
Buncombe, Wm., gent., Beam., Dorset, 1762, W, P17/549
Bundy, Ann, widow, Poulshot, 1661, I, W, P2/B/729
Edith, widow, Allington, 1593, I, W, P2/B/146

Edwd., yeo., Amesb., 1661, AB, P2/B/738
Edwd., collarmaker, Amesb., 1669, I, W, P2/B/799
Eleanor, widow, Amesb., 1628, I, W, P2/B/486
Eliz., Amesb., 1726, AB, P1/B/932
Geo., labourer, Stratford sub C., 1702, W, P5/1702/13
Geo., blacksmith, Pitton, Alderbury, 1837, W, Wr, P26/1428
Geo., labourer, Redlynch, Downton, 1850, cert, D, W, Wr, P2/1850/5
Jas., woodman, Redlynch, Downton, 1841, W, Wr, P2/1841/31
Jane, widow, Gt. Amesb., 1663, I, copy I, W, P2/B/754
Jn., yeo., Amesb., 1564-66, AB, W (note of probate 1559 crossed out), P2/4Reg/13A, P2/4Reg/229C
Bondy, Jn., carp., Chirton, 1594, I, W, P2/B/151
Boundy, Jn., Chirton, 1613, a/c (2), AB, I, P2/B/339, P2/8Reg/189C
Jn., Coate, Bps. C., 1659, I (detailed), P24/314
Jn., collarmaker, Broad C., 1683, AB, I, ren, P2/B/1026
Jn., Amesb., 1751, AB, P2/B/1688
Martha, Downton, 1855, AB, aff, Wr, P2/1855/10
Mart., Gt. Amesb., 1576, I, T, W, P2/B/52, P2/5Reg/254A
Mart., Winterslow, 1739, W, P2/B/1575
My., widow, Gt. Amesb., 1671, I, W, P2/B/840
My., sp., Amesb., 1712, AB, I, P2/B/1303
Nich., jun., Downton, 1678, AB, I, P2/B/940
Nich., yeo., Pensworth, Downton, 1690, I, W, P2/B/1116
Rd., yeo., Amesb., 1556, W, P2/3Reg/2C
Rd., Amesb., 1564, W, P2/4Reg/160A
Rd., Winterslow, 1753, AB, P1/B/1281
Robt., Bulford, 1614-16, AB, a/c, P2/B/2168, P2/8Reg/246A
Robt., collarmaker, Amesb., 1712, AB, I, P2/B/1302
Steph., Allington, 1567, W, P2/5Reg/5B
Steph., shepherd, Ogbourne St And., 1619, I, W, P5/1619/10, P5/9Reg/227A
Thos., vict., Gt. Amesb., 1642, AB, a/c, I, P2/B/675
Wm., Amesb., 1559, AB, P2/4Reg/25F
Wm., Allington, 1586, W, P2/7Reg/32C
Wm., yeo., Amesb., 1616, I, W, P2/B/369, P2/8Reg/313B
Wm., sen., yeo., Amesb., 1620, I, W, P2/B/401
Wm., husb., Gt. Amesb., 1646, I, W, P2/B/703
Wm., collarmaker, Gt. Amesb., 1689, AB, I, L, ren, P2/B/1109
Wm., wheelwright, Amesb., 1692, AB, ren, P1/B/631
Wm., baker, Amesb., 1783, W, P1/B/1479, P1/13Reg/433
Wm., Amesb., 1799, AB, P2/B/2138
Bungey, Amy, widow, Alderbury, 1719, W, P26/626
Anth., innholder, Fisherton A., 1667, I, W, P2/B/779
Chris., husb., Elston, Orcheston St Geo., 1618, I, W, P2/B/392
Bungey nee Fleetwood, Eliz., wife, Alderbury, 1756-58, AB, P26/950, 964
Eliz., widow, Fisherton A., 1770, W, P2/B/1868
Harry, Dinton, 1752, AB, P2/B/1691
Hy., Chipp., 1617, AB, I, P3/B/150
Jas., labourer, Downton, 1768, W, P2/B/1849
Jn., sen., husb., Berwick St Jas., 1668, I, W, P1/B/440
Jn., Downton, 1746, I, W, P2/B/1653
Jn., yeo., Alderbury, 1752, W, P26/911
Jn., innholder, Fisherton A., 1769, W, P2/B/1855
Jn., gent., Alderbury, 1791, W, P26/1176
Jn., Redlynch, Downton, 1798, AB, W, P2/B/2137
Joshua, Downton, 1759, W, P2/B/1754
My., Downton, 1760, W, P2/B/1767
Milly, widow, Shalbourne, 1806, AB, Wr, P5/1806/30
Sam., labourer, Redlynch, Downton, 1853, W, Wr, P2/1853/25
Steph., Timbury Lane, Downton, 1738, AB, W, P2/B/1566
Steph., gent., Alderbury, 1758, W, P26/963
Tabitha, widow, Redlynch, Downton, 1836, W, P2/1836/24

Thos., Imber, 1721, AB, P2/B/2147
Thos., Fisherton A., 1745, AB, a/c, I, ren, P1/B/1191
Walter, Alderbury, 1679, I, W, P26/262
Wm., Grittleton, 1624, AB, I, W, P3/B/257
Wm., Alderbury, 1789, AB, P26/1175
Wm., W. Grimstead (form. of Alderbury), 1852, ren, W, Wr, P2/1852/3
Wm. Steph., Whaddon, Alderbury, 1856, AB, ren, Wr, P26/1469
Bunn, Arthur, wheelwright, Fordington, Dorset, 1711, comm, W, P15/89
Bun, Edith, Fordington, Dorset, 1660, I, W (documents dated 1654 but not proved until 1660), P15/1
Jn., labourer, Fordington, Dorset, 1729, W, P15/116
My., Zeals, 1677, AB, P5/1677/6
My., widow, Zeals, 1686, I, W, P5/1686/4
My., widow, Ansty, 1816, comm, W, Wr, P5/1816/11
Bun, Philip, husb., Fordington, Dorset, 1662, AB, I, P15/8
Robt., sen., Fordington, Dorset, 1640, I, W, P5/1639/15, P5/13Reg/219B
Robt., vict., Burton, Charminster, Dorset, 1712, AB, W, P5/1712/14, P5/15Reg/311A
Wm., Fordington, Dorset, 1680, I, W, P15/30
Wm., vict., Burton, Charminster, Dorset, 1712, W, P5/1712/15, P5/15Reg/311B
Bunner *see* Bonner
Bunny, Ann, widow, Pott., 1740, W, P1/B/1117, P1/8Reg/433
Jn., husb., Sherrington, 1557, W, P2/3Reg/67B
Wm., yeo., Pott., 1672, AB, comm, I, P1/B/487
Wm., yeo., Pott., 1737, comm, W, P1/B/1067, P1/8Reg/173
Wm., basketmaker, Pott., 1784, AB, W, P1/B/1492, P1/14Reg/50B
Bunse *see* Bunce
Bunston, Hy., clockmaker, Lyme R., Dorset, 1733, W, P16/271
Bunter, Chris., tailor, Donhead St My., 1763, W, P1/B/1366, P1/12Reg/130B
Jas., yeo., Donhead St My., 1740, AB, ren, P2/B/1588
Jas., labourer, Marden, 1842, O, W, Wr, P2/1842/18
Jn., Donhead St My., 1551, W, P2/2Reg/132A
Jn., Donhead St A., 1569, W, P2/5Reg/73C
Jn., Donhead St A., 1797, AB, comm, P2/B/2120
Robt., Bower C., 1664, AB, I, P2/B/758
Robt., Bower C., 1674, a/c (2), L, P2/B/873
Robt., Donhead St A., 1676, I, W, P2/B/899
Thos., Donhead St My., 1687, AB, I, P2/B/1080
Thos., innholder, Donhead St A., 1736, W, P2/B/1553
Buoy *see* Booy
Burbage, Burbidge, And., yeo., Bulk. Mill, Keevil, 1830, W, Wr, P2/1830/40
Burbidge, Ann, widow, E. Knoyle, 1667, I, W, P2/B/780
Burbidge, Ann, widow, Bulk., Keevil, 1781, comm, W, P2/B/1979
Ann, sp., Easterton, Mkt. L., 1781, W, P2/B/1982
Burbidge, Ann, widow, Sherb., Dorset, 1802, comm, W, P5/1802/23, P5/19Reg/22
Burbidge, Anna, sp., W. Dean, 1847, D, W, Wr, P2/1847/30
Burbidge, Anth., E. Knoyle, 1702, AB, P2/B/1226
Burbidge, Anth., butcher, E. Knoyle, 1794, W, P2/B/2093
Burbidge, Chas., yeo., Semington, Steeple A., 1768, comm, W, P2/B/1840
Burbidge, Chas., bach., Melk., 1787, AB, P2/B/2017
Burbidge, Edwd., Whistley, Pott., 1852, AB, O, Wr, P1/1852/14
Elias, yeo., Bulk., Keevil, 1721, I, W, P2/B/1396
Burbidge, Elias, yeo., Bulk., Keevil, 1789, W, P2/B/2037
Ellen, widow, E. Knoyle, 1578, I, W, P2/B/68, P2/5Reg/313B
Burbidge, Geo., baker, Trowb., 1849, comm, D, W, Wr, P1/1849/3
Burbidge, Geo., gent., Sal., 1853, aff, W, Wr, P4/1853/13
Burbidge, Grace, sp., Bulk., Keevil, 1767, W, P1/B/1372, P1/12Reg/188
Grace, Worton, Pott., 1854, D, O, W, Wr, P1/1854/12
Burbidge, Hy. Beaven, innholder, E. Knoyle, 1791, W, P2/B/2066
Burbidge als Harrel, Jacob, yeo., Bromham, 1826, W, Wr, P1/1826/117
Burbidge, Jas. Chas., yeo., E. Knoyle, 1835, W, Wr, P2/1835/29
Burbidge, Jane, widow, E. Knoyle, 1800, W, P2/1800/50

Jn., E. Knoyle, 1558, W, P2/3Reg/111B
Jn., Sherrington, 1589, I, T, NW, P2/B/104
Jn., yeo., E. Knoyle, 1663, I, ren, W, P2/B/750
Burbidge, Jn., tailor, Chilmark, 1667, AB, I, P2/B/789
Burbidge, Jn., yeo., Bulk., Keevil, 1700, I, W, P2/B/1214
Burbidge, Jn., shopkeeper, E. Knoyle, 1740, W, P2/B/1591
My., widow, Homington, 1684, I, P24/749
Burbidge, My., sp., Boscombe, 1731, AB, P2/B/1499
Matthew, E. Knoyle, 1583, W, P2/6Reg/88B
Rd., Sutton Poyntz, Dorset, 1611, I, P5/1611/45
Robt., Tisb., 1588, AB, I, P2/B/99, P2/7Reg/138E
Robt., Box, 1612, AB, P3/B/93
Burbidge, Roger, Bulk., Keevil, 1759, AB, comm, P2/B/1756
Burbidge, Roger, jun., wheelwright, Bulk., Keevil, 1764, AB, ren, W, P2/B/1796
Burbidge, Sam., Sherb., Dorset, 1794, AB, P5/1794/2, P5/18Reg/201B
Burbidge, Sarah, widow, Bulk. Mill, Keevil, 1840, W, Wr, P2/1840/48
Burbidge, Susanna, widow, Westb. & Warm., 1790, AB, W, P2/B/2053
Thos., Donhead St A., 1567, I, W, P2/B/44, P2/5Reg/30C
Thos., yeo., Sherrington, 1586, I, W, P2/B/95, P2/7Reg/40A
Burbadge, Thos., Coombe B., 1610, AB, I, draft I, P5/1610/3, P5/9Reg/21B
Wm., Milton, E. Knoyle, 1585, W, P2/7Reg/11A
Wm., innholder, Sal., 1716, AB, I (detailed), P4/1716/7
Burbidge, Wm., maltster, E. Knoyle, 1794-95, req, copy W, P2/B/2100
Burbidge, Wm., E. Knoyle, 1829, W, Wr, P2/1829/30
Burbank, Burbanck, Eliz., sp., E. Harnham, Britford, 1684, AB, I, W, P5/1684/7
Jas., yeo., Britford, 1670, T (children: Eliz., My., Jas., Wm., Ann, Thos. & Amy B.), P24/384
Burbanck, Jas., Britford, 1680, AB, I, P24/430
Burbanck, My., Britford, 1684, AB, I, P24/744
Burbidge *see* Burbage
Burch *see* Birch
Burchall, Burchell, Adam, innholder, Atworth, Bradford A., 1741, AB, ren, P2/B/1594
Burchell, Agnes, Nettleton, [1605], W, copy W (NEP), P3/B/23
Ann, widow, Preston, Lyneham, 1616, I, W, P3/B/138
Cath., widow, Compton B., 1673, W, P3/B/632
Clement, gent., Compton B., 1740, comm, W, P3/B/1392
Clement, yeo., Calne (form. of Compton B.), 1785, W, P3/B/1703
Edmd., husb., Preston, Lyneham, 1562, W. No date of probate, P1/2Reg/107B
Edmd., Lyneham, 1646, AB, I, P1/B/323
Edwd., sen., Wootton R., 1669, AB, comm, P3/B/555
Edwd., yeo. *or* gent., Wootton B., 1701, I, W, P3/B/1008
Byrchall, Edwd., gent., Over Stratton, Stratton St Mgt., 1758, W, P3/B/1520
Eleanor, widow, Brinkw., 1676, I, W, P3/B/669
Hy., Preston, Lyneham, 1706, AB, I, P3/B/1060
Isaac, yeo., Brinkw., 1671, I, W, P3/B/597
Jane, widow, Grove, Wantage, Berks., [1786], W (NEP), P23/782
Joan, widow, Preston, Lyneham, [1612], I, W (NEP), P3/B/94
Jn., Bps. C., 1567, W, P5/1Reg/82A
Jn., yeo., Preston, Lyneham, 1641, I, P3/B/459
Jn., yeo., Avebury, 1672, AB, comm, W, P3/B/619
Burchell, Jn., Goatacre, Hilmarton, 1685, I, NW, P3/B/821
Jn., yeo., Preston, Lyneham, 1692, I, W, P1/B/615
Jn., tailor, Wantage, Berks., 1705, AB, I, P23/273
Jn., Grove, Wantage, Berks., 1745, AB, P23/587
Burchell, My., sp., Lyneham, 1722, I, W, P3/B/1213
My., widow, Compton B., 1746, comm, W, P3/B/1442
Rd., carp., Wootton B., 1679, I, W, P3/B/718
Byrchall, Rd., sen., gent., Sevenhampton, Highw., 1735, W, P10/1735/4
Byrchall, Rd., gent., Sevenhampton, Highw., 1745, W, P10/1745/4
Rd., Bencroft Farm, Bremhill, 1768, comm, W, P3/B/1595
Rd., jun., sackcloth weaver, Grove, Wantage, Berks., 1771, W, P23/734

Birchill, Rd., gardener, Preston, Lyneham (late of Bethnal Green), 1781, W, P3/B/1671
Robt., Wantage, Berks., 1607, AB, I, P5/1607/4, P5/8Reg/102C
Robt., sen., yeo., Quemerford, Calne, 1708, W, P26/548
Robt., Compton B., 1723, AB, comm, P3/B/1222
Susanna, widow, Wootton B., 1694, AB, P3/B/927
Thos., yeo., Preston, Lyneham, [1611], I, W (NEP), P3/B/82
Thos., tailor, Brinkw., 1671, I, W, P3/B/596
Thos., tailor, Brinkw., 1682, AB, I, P3/B/764
Burchall *or* Bourcheir, Thos., gent., Highw., 1698, AB, I, P10/1698/1
Thos., sen., Lyneham, 1721, AB, I, P3/B/1195
Thos., gent., Lyneham, 1735, W, P3/B/1347
Birchill, Thos., labourer, Preston, Lyneham, 1788, AB, W, P3/B/1711
Burchell, Thos., Brinkw., 1794, AB, comm, P3/B/1743
Burchell, Thos., carp., Grittenham, Brinkw., 1834, W, Wr, P3/1834/55
Burchall als Anthony, Wm., husb., Preston, Lyneham, 1625, I, NW, P1/B/198
Wm., Pewsey, 1627, I, W, P3/B/291
Wm., Preston, Lyneham, 1669, AB, caveat, P3/B/556
Burchell, Wm., blacksmith, Nettleton, 1719, AB, I, P3/B/1173
Burchell, Wm., minor, Lyneham, 1732, T, P1/B/1015
Burchesse, Robt., Mkt. L., 1624, I, W, P2/B/449
Burchett, My., widow, Winkfield, Berks., 1606, I, W, P1/B/34
Burcombe, Bircombe, And., Hungerford, Berks., 1705, AB, comm, P5/1705/8
Ann Eliz., Bradford A., 1819, W, Wr, P2/1819/55
Eliz., widow, Bradford A., 1762, W, P2/B/1781
Jn., Lacock, 1610, AB, P3/B/71
Jn., baker and confectioner, Devizes, 1823, W, Wr, P1/1823/5
Nancy, widow, Devizes, 1823, W, Wr, P1/1823/53
Rd., Holt, Bradford A., 1813, AB (re property in H.), comm, P2/1813/2
Thos., Lacock, 1608, AB, P1/B/62
Wm., innholder, Charnham St., Hungerford, Berks., 1685, AB, I (mentions names of rooms in inn), P5/1685/7
Wm. Goodall, yeo., Bradford A., 1816, W, Wr, P2/1816/42
Burd *see* Bird
Burden, Alice, widow, Tisb., 1617-18, I, W, P2/B/376, P2/8Reg/322B
Alice, sp., Upavon, 1626, court paper (2), NW, P2/B/461
Burdon, Ann, widow, Stanton St B., [1591], W (NEP), P3/1Reg/33A
Ann, widow, Hilcott, N. Newnton, 1759, AB, ren, W, P1/B/1331, P1/11Reg/471
Anth., Collingbourne K., 1663, AB, I, note of NW, P1/B/384
Benj., farmer, Wedh., Urchf., 1769, W, P2/B/1853
Chas., yeo., Snelling Farm, Turners Puddle, Dorset, 1855, aff, I, W, Wr, P5/1855/9
Dan., yeo., Etchilhampton, 1748, W, P3/B/1453
Edith, widow, Marden, 1680, I, W, P2/B/956
Edwd., Bourton, Bps. C., 1607, AB, I, P24/169
Eliz., widow, Sherb. Causeway, Motc., Dorset, 1855, aff, D, O, W, Wr, P27/1/775
Burdon, Geoff., gent., Stanton St B., 1661, I, W, P3/B/475, P3/3Reg/25A
Geo., husb., Semley, 1607, AB, I, NW, P2/B/274
Geo., Etchilhampton, 1684, AB, I, P3/B/803
Hy., tailor, Bere R., Dorset, 1597, AB, I, W, P5/1597/9, P5/6Reg/164B
Hy., Semley, 1624, AB, comm, I, P2/B/444
Hy., yeo., Etchilhampton, 1818, W, Wr, P3/1818/28
Isaac, Charl. nr. P., 1672, AB, I, P2/B/848
Jas., Downton, 1811, AB, comm, Wr, P2/1811/10
Jas., farrier, Rockley, Ogbourne St And., 1823, comm, W, Wr, P23/913
Jas., Semley, 1828, W, P2/1828/68
Jeremiah, husb., Marden, 1681, AB, I, P2/B/969
Joan, widow, Donhead St My., 1576, I, W, P2/B/53, P2/5Reg/257A
Burdon, Job, carp., Landford, 1829, AB, W, Wr, P1/1829/73
Jn., Semley, 1563, W, P2/4Reg/135
Jn., Wilsford nr Pewsey, 1571, W, P2/5Reg/109A
Jn., husb., Coombe, Donhead St My., 1612, I, NW, T, P2/B/326
Jn., tailor, Fyfield, Milton L., 1629, I, W, P3/B/315

Jn., husb., Fyfield, Milton L., 1642, I, W (NEP), P3/B/461
Jn., Landford, 1682, AB, I, P2/B/991
Jn., yeo., Coombe, Donhead St My., 1684, AB, I, P2/B/1037
Jn., sen., yeo., Etchilhampton, 1689, I, W, P3/B/857
Jn., yeo., Gt. Bedwyn, 1709, AB, I, P21/6/48
Jn., yeo., Etchilhampton, 1710, I, W (2 - 1 a copy), P3/B/1093
Beardon, Jn., woolcomber, N. Bradley, 1715, I, W, P2/B/1348
Jn., Etchilhampton, 1760, AB, P3/B/1532
Burdon, Jn., yeo., Ansty, 1803, W, P5/1803/12, P5/19Reg/37
Jn., yeo., Pott., 1835, W, Wr, P1/1835/128
Mgt., widow, Gt. Bedwyn, 1713, AB, I, P5/1712/18
Margery, Bourton, Bps. C., 1607, I, P24/166
My., sen., widow, Amesb., 1668, I, W, P2/B/804
My., widow, Coombe, Donhead St My., 1692, AB, I, P2/B/1139
Nich., weaver, Tisb., 1598, I, NW, P2/B/188
Rd., All C., [1581], W (NEP), P3/1Reg/11A
Rd., Wilsford nr Pewsey, 1605, I, P2/B/259
Robt., husb., Wilsford nr Pewsey, 1662, AB, I, W, P2/B/742, P2/4Reg/92A
Robt., yeo., Lyneham, 1694, W, P3/B/928
Robt., wheeler, Marden, 1710, W, P2/B/1289
Sarah, widow, Charl. nr. P., 1673-79, I, W, P2/B/868, 950
Steph., yeo., Semley, 1620, I, W, P2/B/404
Steph., Wilsford nr Pewsey, 1782, AB, P2/B/2000
Steph., widower, Berwick St Jn., 1858, AB, aff, comm, Wr, P2/1857/69
Thos., Charl. nr. P., 1616, AB, P2/B/368
Thos., yeo., Coombe, Donhead St My., 1677, I, W, P2/B/926
Thos., blacksmith, Sutton V., 1840, comm, W, Wr, P2/1840/6
Walter, Donhead St My., 1565, W, P2/4Reg/216B
Wm., husb., Donhead St My., 1569, W, P2/5Reg/62C
Wm., tailor, Donhead St My., 1608, I, W, P1/B/65
Wm., husb., Donhead St My., 1662, AB, I, P1/B/378
Wm., Marl., 1681, AB, P1/B/546
Wm., Etchilhampton, 1682, I, W, P3/B/765
Wm., yeo., Etchilhampton, 1774, W, P3/B/1634
Burdett, Frances, husb., Upton, Blewbury, Berks., 1687, I, W, P5/1687/8
Jn., yeo., Upper Stratton, Stratton St Mgt., 1845, W, Wr, P3/1845/30
Burdge *see* Burge
Burdgman *see* Burgeman
Burdon *see* Burden
Burford, Alice, Bower C., 1586, W, P2/7Reg/62A
Amy, widow, Sonning, Berks., 1720, I, W, P5/1720/4, P5/16Reg/39B
Francis, clerk, Clyffe P., 1614, AB, a/c, I, note of legacies, P1/B/112
Burfott *or* Burford, Gabriel, husb., Aldbourne, 1694, I, W, P3/B/929
Gabriel, yeo., Downton, 1754, AB, I, P2/B/1712
Geo., Fisherton A., 1853, W, Wr, P2/1853/41
My., Downton, 1717, AB, P2/B/1354
My., sp., Kemble, 1779, W, P3/B/1660
Peter, yeo., Nether C., Dorset, 1627, AB, I, T, W, P5/1627/5, P5/11Reg/41B
Burfitt, Wm., yeo., Westb. L., 1825, W, Wr, P25/1825/3
see also Rose als B.
Burge, Amy, sp. and servant, Bath, Somerset (leaving effects at Trowb.), 1846, O, W, Wr, P1/1846/39
Ann, minor, Sal., 1681, T (no decd named), P4/1681/9
Anth., Moredon, Rodbourne C., 1669, I, W, P3/B/557
Benedict, husb., Crickl. St S., 1639, I, P3/B/429
Cath., widow, Calcutt, Crickl. St S., 1603, I, W, P3/B/9
Cath., minor, Sal., 1688, T (no decd named), P4/1688/13
Edmd., Stratton St Mgt., [1600], W (NEP), P3/1Reg/45B
Elias, cordw., Sal., 1775, W, P4/1775/1
Jane, widow, Leigh, Ashton K., 1640, I, W, P3/B/448
Jane, widow, Purton, 1694, comm, I, W, P3/B/930

Jn., Long Newnton, 1569, W (NEP), P1/1Reg/103A, P1/2Reg/97A
Jn., glover, Crickl. St S., 1611, bond to pay legacy, P3/B/83
Jn., glover, Crickl. St My., 1624, I, P3/B/258
Burdge, Martha, widow, Isbery, Lambourn, Berks., 1738, W, P1/B/1093, P1/8Reg/301
Ralph, yeo., Crickl. St My., 1623, AB, a/c, I, P3/B/238
Robt., yeo., Leigh, Ashton K., 1662, I, W, P1/B/376
Sam., yeo., Moredon, Rodbourne C., 1683, AB, I, P3/B/778
Thos., husb., Norton B., 1610, I, W, P2/B/301, P2/8Reg/105B
Thos., yeo., Leigh, Ashton K., 1617, AB, I, W, P3/B/151
Thos., yeo., Purton, 1678, AB, I, P3/B/698
Thos., jun., Crickl. St My., 1693, AB, I, NW, P3/B/910
Wm., husb., Calcutt, Crickl. St S., 1602, I (damaged), W, P1/B/19
Wm., shoemaker, Crickl. St S., [1612], W (NEP), P3/B/95
Wm., Calcutt, Crickl. St S., 1668, AB, comm, P3/B/539
Wm., Chelworth, Crickl. St S., 1673, I, W, P3/B/633
see also Axford als B.; Hilsden als B.
Burgeman, Edwd., Durrington, 1574, W, P2/5Reg/191C
Burgman, Jn., labourer, Eastcourt, Crudwell, 1734, W, P3/B/1340
Burdgman, Margery, widow, Lacock, 1640, I, W, P3/B/447
Burgman, Roger, husb., Goatacre, Hilmarton, 1623, I, NW, P3/B/239
see also Bridgman *or* B.
Burgess, Abraham, yeo., Long Burton, Dorset, 1757, W, P5/1757/4
Burges, Agnes, N. Tidworth, 1587, AB, P2/7Reg/66B
Burges, Alice, Collingbourne K., 1570, W (NEP), P1/1Reg/116B
Burges, Alice, widow, S. Marston, 1592, AB, I, P5/1592/12, P5/6Reg/1B
Burges, Alice, widow, Brook, Westb., 1640, I, NW, P25/1640/12
Burges, Anchoret, widow, Stapleford, 1641, I, NW, P2/B/663
Burges, Ann, widow, W. Ashton, Steeple A., 1637, I, W, copy W, P2/B/620
Burges, Ann, widow, Devizes, 1674, W, P1/B/496
Burges, Ann, Leighs Marsh, Dilton, Westb., 1759, W, P25/1759/2
Ann, widow, Haugh Farm, Haugh, Winsley, Bradford A., 1774, AB, P2/B/1909
Burges, Anth., Sawser's Ashton, E. Town, W. Ashton, Steeple A., 1592, I, W (part missing), P2/B/130
Burges, Augustine, sen., yeo., Stapleford, 1649, AB, a/c, I, note (2), W, P1/B/352-53
Burges, Chas., Aston U., Blewbury, Berks., 1672, AB, comm, I, P5/1672/3
Burgish, Chas., yeo., Plaitford, 1692, I, W, P2/B/1145
Christian, widow, Steeple A., 1623, I, W, P2/B/434
Burges, Clement, Bere R., Dorset, 1666, AB, I, P5/1666/8
Burges, Damaris, widow, Brimpton, Berks., 1708, W, P1/B/739, P1/4Reg/297A
Burges, Dan., gent., Wantage, Berks., 1679, AB, comm, I, P23/80
Burges, Dan., yeo., Aston U., Blewbury, Berks., 1697, AB, I, P5/1697/2
Burges, Edmd., S. Marston, 1590, I, T, P5/1589/4
Burges, Edmd., sen., carp., Devizes, 1670, W, P1/B/463
Burges, Edwd., Laverstock, 1574, W, P2/5Reg/181B
Burges, Edwd., husb., Pitton, Alderbury, 1613, W, P26/28
Burgis, Edwd., yeo., Stapleford, 1638, I (name from parish register), P2/B/2166
Burgis, Edwd., weaver, Wilton, 1695, AB, I, P1/B/642
Burges, Elias, yeo., Earley, Sonning, Berks., 1698, W, P5/1698/16
Burges, Eliz., widow, E. Grafton, 1638, I, W, P21/1/36
Burges, Eliz., widow, Pitton, Alderbury, 1708, AB, I, P26/539
Eliz., widow, Bere R., Dorset, 1798, AB, P5/1798/2, P5/18Reg/267C
Eliz., widow, Wilsford nr Pewsey, 1800, W, P2/1800/67
Eliz., widow, Erlestoke, 1829, AB, O, Wr, P1/1829/59
Eliz. *see also* Eliz. Wallis
Burges, Gabriel, butcher, Eastcott, Urchf., 1618, W, P2/B/381
Burgis, Geo., tailor, Aston U., Blewbury, Berks., 1700, AB, I, P5/1700/6
Giles, yeo., Chilton Farm, Chilton F., 1817, W, Wr, P1/1817/67
Burges, Hannah, sp., Sal., 1674, NW, P4/1674/19
Burges, Hy., husb., W. Ashton, Steeple A., 1632-36, I (2), W, P2/B/553, 601
Burges, Hy., Bratton, Westb., 1693, AB, I, W, P25/1693/6
Hy., broad weaver, Westb. L., 1696, I, W (NEP), P25/1696/9

Burges, Hy., Bradford A., 1719, AB, deed (mortgage making over estate from widow & her dau to principal creditor & admr as security for payment of Ł12 debt plus interest), I, P2/B/1389
Burges, Hy., Devizes, 1774, AB, P1/B/1426
Hy., mason, Calne, 1855, comm, W, Wr, P26/1464
Burges, Hugh, Grafton, 1622, I, W (damaged), P5/1622/7, P5/10Reg/136A
Isaac, sen., gent., Rockley, Ogbourne St And., 1716, comm, I (detailed), W, P5/1716/7, P5/15Reg/359
Isaac, Gt. Bedwyn, 1758, AB, P5/1758/8
Burges, Jas., Steeple A., 1568, T (children: Harry, Wm., Jn., Philip, Lewis, Rd. & Joan B.), P2/B/46
Jas., coal hauler, Edington, 1853, O, W, Wr, P2/1853/18
Burges, Jane, Drayton, Abingdon, Berks., 1606, AB, I, P1/B/48
Burges, Jane, widow, Sal. St Mart., 1639, I, W, P4/1639/11
Burgis, Joan, widow, Stapleford, 1606, I, W, P2/B/266
Burges, Joan, widow, Stanford Dingley, Berks., 1613, I, W, P1/B/97
Burgis, Joan, widow, Newbury St., Preshute, 1693, comm, I, W, P1/B/632
Burges, Jn., Uffington, Berks., 1558, dispensation re marriage against laws of consanguinity, P1/1Reg/59
Burgis, Jn., yeo., Warm., 1561, I, P2/B/26
Burges, Jn., Marl., 1616, AB, a/c, bonds to pay Ł5 & Ł4, copy of borough of M. court paper re debt, P1/B/138
Burges, Jn., Steeple A., 1618, I, W, P2/B/380
Burges, Jn., sen., broad weaver, Leigh, Bradford A., 1620, I, W, P2/B/2162
Burgis, Jn., Wilton, 1623, AB, P2/B/431
Burgis, Jn., cooper, Hankerton, 1624, I, W, P3/B/259
Burges, Jn., sen., Devizes, 1626, AB, P1/B/204
Jn., yeo., W. Grimstead, 1628, I, W, P2/B/482
Burges, Jn., carp., Tisb., 1649, I, W, P1/B/350
Burges, Jn., yeo., Plaitford, 1669, I, W, P2/B/810
Burges, Jn., sen., yeo., Mildenhall (form. of Rockley, Ogbourne St And.), 1671, W, P3/B/598
Burges, Jn., yeo., Hawkeridge, Westb., 1672, AB, a/c, comm, I (detailed), P25/1672/4
Jn., freemason, Box, 1676, AB, I (re both Jn. & Eliz. his wife), P3/B/670
Burges, Jn., weaver, Studley, Trowb., 1688, I, W, P2/B/1091
Burges, Jn., husb. and yeo., Rockley, Ogbourne St And., 1690, I, W (damaged), P5/1690/9
Burgis, Jn., Oare, Chieveley, Berks., 1704, AB, P1/B/719
Burgis, Jn., yeo., Sanden Fee, Hungerford, Berks., 1709, W, P23/305
Burgis, Jn., sen., Durrington, 1712, AB, I, W, P2/B/1309
Burges, Jn., sen., yeo., E. Grafton, 1721, W, P21/8/14
Burges, Jn., glover, Malm., 1746, W, P3/B/1443
Jn., carp., Devizes, 1762, W, P1/B/1341, P1/12Reg/23B
Jn., farmer, Chieveley, Berks., 1792, AB, W, P1/B/1526, P1/14Reg/420
Jn., yeo., Chirton, 1810, W, Wr, P2/1810/9
Jn., sen., farmer and widower, Bourton, Bps. C., 1856, aff, O, W, Wr, P24/1420
Joy, maltster, Bere R., Dorset, 1775, W, P5/1775/4, P5/17Reg/98C
Lucy, widow, Redhill, Pewsham, 1754, W, P3/B/1493
Burgis, Mgt., sp., W. Ashton, Steeple A., 1669, W, P2/B/818
Mgt., widow, Winterborne K., Dorset, 1835, W, Wr, P5/1835/8
Burges, Margery, widow, Westrop, Highw., 1593, AB, I, P5/1593/18
Burges, Margery, Patney, 1607-36, comm, I (d. 1607 but I dated 1636), P2/B/593
Burges, My., Urchf., 1672, AB, I, P2/B/857
Burges, My., wife, Marl., 1684, AB, P1/B/571
My., widow, Keevil, 1749, AB, T, P2/B/1672
My., widow, Devizes St My., 1781, AB, app. of guardian, comm, T, P1/B/1461
My., widow, Devizes, 1799, AB, P1/B/1550, P1/15Reg/185A
My., widow, Chieveley, Berks., 1811, comm, W, Wr, P1/1811/45
Burges, Matthew, yeo., Keevil, 1746, W, P2/B/1647
Matthew, Keevil, 1754, AB, I, P2/B/1708
Burgis, Michael, sen., yeo., Chirton, 1686, I, W, P2/B/2165
Michael, yeo., Chirton, 1766, W, P2/B/1821
Michael, yeo., Etchilhampton, 1813, W, Wr, P3/1813/21
Milly *see* Eliz. Wallis
Burges, Nich., Chipp., 1741, AB, comm, P1/B/1127
Burgis, Olive, widow, Hankerton, 1630, I, W, P3/B/333
Burges, Philip, yeo., Heywood, Westb., 1644, I, W, P25/1644/3

Burges, Philip, W. Ashton, Steeple A., 1669, AB, comm, I, P2/B/798
Burgis, Philip, blacksmith, Quidh., 1710, I, T, W, P2/B/1287
Philip, sen., blacksmith, Durrington, 1772, W, P2/B/1888
Burges, Prosper, carp.'s wife, Devizes, 1757, W, P1/B/1309, P1/11Reg/335
Ralph, clothw., Dilton, Westb., 1738, W, P25/1738/7
Burges, Rd., butcher, N. Tidworth, 1560-61, I, W (2), P2/B/17, P2/4Reg/54C, 81E
Burges, Rd., miller, Westb., 1616, I, W, P25/1616/5
Burges, Rd., Westb., 1637, I, W, P25/1637/2
Burges, Rd., husb., Collingbourne K., 1641, AB, I, ren, P3/B/460
Burgis, Rd., broad weaver, Dilton M., Westb., 1696, I, W, P25/1696/10
Rd., yeo., Hurst, Berks., 1724, I, W, P5/1724/14, P5/16Reg/94A
Burges, Rd., yeo., Compton, Enford, 1757, W, P2/B/1730
Burgis, Robt., husb., Paxcroft, Steeple A., 1579, I, T, W, P2/B/76, P2/5Reg/344A
Burges, Robt., husb., Ham, 1630, I, W, P3/B/332
Burges, Robt., Chilmark & ' Stoverd', 1636, AB, a/c, I, P2/B/591
Burges, Robt., slater, Rams., 1664, AB, app. of admr, I, P5/1664/4
Burges, Robt., Urchf., 1700, AB, I, P2/B/1211
Robt., Sal., 1736, AB, I, Wr, P4/1735/8
Robt., Everleigh, 1772, AB (2), P3/B/1624
Robt., labourer, Chipp., 1773, W, P1/B/1420, P1/12Reg/509
Burges, Roger, tailor, Mildenhall, 1672, AB, I, W, P3/B/616
Burges, Sam., Inglesham, Berks., 1622, I, W, P3/B/224
Burges, Sam., Fordington, Dorset, 1672, AB, NW, P15/19
Burges, Sarah, widow, Aston Tirrold, Berks., 1729, AB, I, P1/B/967
Sarah, clothw.'s wife, Westb., 1813, AB, O, P25/1813/2
Sarah *see also* Eliz. Wallis
Burgis, Silas, blacksmith, Bulford, 1681, AB, I, P2/B/970
Burges, Susanna, widow, Corsham, 1669, W, P29/1Reg/188A
Thos., [rector], Rampisham, Dorset, 1570, W (NEP), P1/1Reg/37A
Burgis, Thos., husb., Purton, [1580], W (NEP), P3/1Reg/17A
Burges, Thos., yeo., Marl., 1592, I, W, P1/B/1
Burgis, Thos., Fisherton A., 1615, AB, I, P2/B/355, P2/8Reg/274D
Burges, Thos., husb., Eastcourt, Crudwell, 1615, I, W, P3/B/129
Burges, Thos., Devizes, 1642, I, W, P1/B/303
Burges, Thos., husb., Stapleford, 1662, I, W, P2/B/743
Burges, Thos., yeo., Marl., 1678, W, P1/B/524
Burges, Thos., cooper, Chipp., 1681, court paper, NW, P3/B/747
Burgis, Thos., Pitton, Alderbury, 1683-87, AB, I (detailed), ren, P26/307, 338
Burges, Thos., sen., joiner, Malm., 1697, AB, I, P3/B/972
Burges, Thos., yeo., Keevil, 1716, W, P1/B/830, P1/6Reg/79
Burges, Thos., Calne, 1735, AB, P26/785
Burges, Thos., sen., Everleigh, 1750, comm, W, P1/B/1234, P1/10Reg/312
Thos., rector, Dauntsey, 1751, AB, P1/B/1255
Thos., Lockeridge, Overton, 1756, AB, P3/B/1505
Thos., yeo., Heywood, Westb., 1781, AB, ren, W, P25/1781/5
Burges, Thos., yeo., Westb. L., 1852, O, W, Wr, P25/1852/5
Burges, Ursula, widow, Plaitford, 1674, I, W, P1/B/501
Burges, Walter, W. Grimstead, 1690, AB, I, P2/B/1112
Burgis, Wm., husb., Stapleford, 1590, I, W, P2/B/117
Burges, Wm., minor, S. Marston, 1590, T (children of Edmd. B.), P5/5Reg/69B
Burgis, Wm., no abode stated, [1602], W (NEP), P3/1Reg/111B
Burgis, Wm., Hampstead Marshall, Berks. & Wiltshire, 1613, AB, a/c, I, P1/B/100
Burges, Wm., husb., W. Ashton, Steeple A., 1635, comm, I, W, P2/B/581
Burges, Wm., yeo., Over St., Stapleford, 1663, I, W, P1/B/395
Burges, Wm., yeo., Hannington, 1678, comm, I, W, P3/B/699
Burgis, Wm., clothier, Beam., Dorset, 1679, AB, comm, I, P17/286
Burges, Wm., Studley, Calne, 1685, AB, I, P5/1685/5
Burges, Wm., blacksmith, Ludg., 1686, I, W, P2/B/1067
Wm., Chards., Devon, 1717, W, P14/124
Wm., Wilton, 1730, AB, P2/B/1486

Wm., yeo., Pewsham Forest, 1738, W, P3/B/1375
Wm., vict., Quemerford, Calne, 1746, W, P5/1746/9
Wm., gent., Marl., 1757, W, P1/B/1310, P1/11Reg/342
Wm., yeo., N. Newnton, 1780, W, P2/B/1969
see also Bruges *or* B.
Burgh, Burgh als Hooper, Jn., Beam., Dorset, 1563, AB, P5/1Reg/4F
Jn., gent., Chards., Devon, 1644, AB, I, NW, P14/14
Burgis, Burgish *see* Burgess
Burgman *see* Burgeman
Burgoin, Peter, sen., Sal. The Close, 1689, AB, P5/1689/7
Bourgoine, Peter, Sal. The Close, 1730, AB, P5/1730/2
Buris *see* Burris
Burk, Thos., Wokm., Berks., 1594, T (children: Thos., Ursula, Ann & Margery B.), P5/1594/8
Burleigh *see* Burley
Burleton, Joan, Motc., Dorset, 1683, I, P27/1/72
Burlton, Jos., Motc., Dorset, 1717, AB, P27/1/217
Burlton, Martha, widow, Bourton, Gillingham, Dorset, 1798, W, P27/1/562
Burlton, My., widow, Compton C., 1766, AB, P2/B/1819
Robt., gent., E. Knoyle, [1698], W, P2/B/1199
Robt., yeo., Motc., Dorset, 1719, W, P27/1/235
Burlton, Robt., butcher, Fovant, 1769, W, P2/B/1864
Walter, Motc., Dorset, 1675, a/c, P27/1/781
Wm., yeo., Kingston D., 1768, W, P2/B/1842
Burlton, Wm., innholder, Sal., 1795, W, P1/B/1540, P1/14Reg/616A
Burley, Alice, widow, Bere R., Dorset, 1711, I, W, P5/1711/13, P5/15Reg/239
Burly, Amy, widow, Turners Puddle, Dorset, 1679, AB, I, P5/1679/3
Burleigh, And., husb., Fordington, Dorset, 1725, AB, comm, W, P5/1725/2, P5/16Reg/108A
Edwd., Sutton V., 1546, W (NEP), P2/1Reg/66
Burleigh, Eliz., widow, Stockley, Bere R., Dorset, 1627, I, T, W, P5/1627/3, P5/11Reg/9B
Burly als Measure, Hy., Winterbourne D., 1620, W, P7/10
Burly, Jn., rector, Milston, 1570, W (NEP), P1/1Reg/99A, P1/2Reg/92B
Jn., gent., Upavon, 1634, AB, ren, P2/B/576, P2/9Reg/9A
Burleigh, Jn., gent., Stockley, Bere R., Dorset, 1689, AB, comm, I, P5/1689/8
Burleigh, Luke, shopkeeper, S. Newton, 1825, AB, note, W, Wr, P2/1825/67
Bearley, Robt., Rushall, 1546, W, P2/2Reg/3
Thos., gent., Bere R., Dorset, 1697, AB, I, P5/1697/1
Burlton *see* Burleton
Burly *see* Burley
Burman, Cath., Aston U., Blewbury, Berks., 1634, I, W. Proved at the Metropolitan visitation to Newbury, P5/1634/27, P5/12Reg/302A
Burnam, Jn., husb., Aston U., Blewbury, Berks., 1603, I, W, P5/1603/9, P5/7Reg/82B
Burnand, Hannah, brewer's wife, Sal., 1757, W, P4/1757/3
Burnard *see* Bernard
Burne, Bearn, Amelia, sp., Netherb., Dorset, 1811, AB, comm, P17/596
Jn., Fordington, Dorset, 1567, AB, P5/1Reg/76E
Bearns, Jn., yeo., Bere R., Dorset (form. of Milborne Stileham, Dorset), 1747, W, P5/1747/2
Robt., Fordington, Dorset, 1566-67, AB, P5/1Reg/66E, P5/1Reg/76D
Bearn, Wm., yeo., Salwayash, Netherb., Dorset, 1821, comm, W, Wr, P5/1821/46
Burneham *see* Burnham
Burnell, Hy., gent., Biddestone, 1624, I, W, P3/B/260
Burnell als Oats, Hy., cordw., Chipp., [1606], W, copy W (NEP), P3/B/25
Rd., yeo., Midgham, Thatcham, Berks., 1726-27, L, req, copy W (2), P1/B/921, P1/7Reg/106A
Burnett, Amy, widow, Berwick St Leonard, 1754, W, P2/B/1713
Eliz., Sal. St Edmd., 1637, AB, P4/1636/10
Eliz., widow, Chicklade, 1740, AB, P2/B/1584
Frances, Deptford, Wylye, 1669, I, W, P2/B/811
Hy., sen., yeo., Berwick St Leonard, 1725, W, P2/B/1444
Burnet, Hy., yeo., Chicklade, 1756, W, P2/B/1729
Hy., yeo., Berwick St Leonard, 1769, AB, P2/B/1856
Burnette, Jn., husb., Shalbourne, 1631, W (NEP), P30/10

Jn., licensed vict., Sal. St Thos., 1855, aff, D, I, W, Wr, P1/1855/13
Martha, widow, Chipp., 1814, comm, W, Wr, P3/1814/20
Peter, cordw., Blewbury, Berks., 1722, I, W, P5/1722/8, P5/16Reg/77B
Reuben, yeo., Mere, 1768, W, P5/1768/4
Burnett *or* Burnard, Robt., Deptford, Wylye, 1668, I, W, P2/B/797
Susanna, widow, Lyme R., Dorset, 1795, comm, W, P16/352
Wm., vict., Sal. St Edmd., 1612, AB, a/c, I (damaged), P4/1612/3
Wm., shoemaker, Blewbury, Berks., 1680, AB, a/c, I, T (re Wm. B., minor), P5/1680/5
Wm., Blewbury, Berks., 1736, W, P5/1736/8
Wm., sen., yeo., Berwick St Leonard, 1751, comm, W, P1/B/1258, P1/10Reg/478
Wm., gent., Sal., 1761, W, P4/1761/10
Burnford, Burnford *or* Bumford, Eliz., widow, Hurst, Berks., 1708, I, W, P5/1708/13, P5/15Reg/65
Wm., Hurst, Berks., 1733, AB, P5/1733/12
Burnham, Burneham, Thos., husb., Hagbourne, Berks., 1592, I, W, P1/B/2
Wm., yeo., Hagbourne, Berks., 1711, I, W, P1/B/764, P1/5Reg/165A
Burningam, Burningam, Joan, widow, Wokm., Berks. (form. of Wargrave, Berks.), 1691, W, P5/1691/6
Burnley, Jn., rector, Winterbourne G., 1685, I, W, P1/B/575
Rd., linen weaver, Luckington, 1710, AB, I, P1/B/817
Burow *see* Burrow
Burre, Agnes, widow, Corsley, 1590, I, W, P2/B/121
Burreat *see* Burrett
Burree *see* Burry
Burrell, Thos., husb., Aldbourne, 1609, W (damaged), P3/B/41
Thos., clerk, Bulford, 1644, comm, I, W, P2/B/687
Burrett, Benj., sen., labourer, Swallowfield, Shinfield, Berks., 1744, AB, I, W, P1/B/1165, P1/9Reg/286B
Edwd., Gt. Bedwyn, 1639, AB, I, P21/1/51
Burreat, Jn., Gt. Bedwyn, 1606, AB, P5/8Reg/56B
Burritt, Thos., husb., Wokm., Berks., 1794, W, P5/1794/4, P5/18Reg/199
Wm., Oxenwood, Shalbourne, 1575, I, W, P5/1575/10, P5/3Reg/67B
Burret, Wm., husb., Fosbury, Tidcombe and F., 1625, AB, I, P1/B/189
Burrey *see* Burry
Burridge, Geo., servant, Heytes., 1844, O, W, Wr, P5/1844/1
Jn., cordw., Donhead St My., 1810, comm, W, Wr, P2/1810/46
Sophia, widow, Heytes., 1850, AB, D, W, Wr, P5/1850/5
Walter, merchant, Lyme R., Dorset (d. in Virginia), 1721, AB, I (detailed), P16/222
Burris, Buris, Jn., Biddesden, Ludg., 1697, AB, I, ren, P2/B/1181
Thos., serge weaver, Whitley, Melk., 1763, W, P1/B/1365, P1/12Reg/116A
Burritt *see* Burrett
Burrow, Burrow als Barby, And., Uffc., Devon, 1681, AB, I, P20/1/91
Ann, widow, Sherb., Dorset, 1713, I, W, P5/1713/13, P5/15Reg/373C
Burrough, Ann, widow, Sal., 1783, AB, P4/1783/1
Burrough, Ann, widow, Westb. L., 1821, W, Wr, P25/1821/7
Burrows, Anna, sp., Beer Hackett, Dorset, 1769, AB, P5/1769/3
Burrows, Charlotte, widow, Melk., 1831, comm, W, Wr, P2/1831/39
Chris., broad weaver, Calne, 1611, AB, I, P26/5
Burrough, Edwd., yeo., Gt. Woodford, 1674, I, W, P5/1674/18
Edwd., Gt. Woodford, 1676, AB, a/c, I, P5/1676/5
Edwd., yeo., W. Grimstead, 1707, W, P2/B/1268
Burrough, Eliza, sp., Gt. Chalfield, 1822, AB, Wr, P2/1822/15
Eliz., widow, W. Grimstead, 1709, AB, P2/B/1280
Burrough, Eliz., widow, Alton Pr., 1790, W, P3/B/1727
Burrough, Eliz., widow, Barford St Mart., 1848, D, W, Wr, P2/1848/31
Emanuel, husb., Blewbury, Berks., 1624, AB, I, P5/1624/2, P5/10Reg/224
Francis, husb., Gt. Durnford, 1601, AB, I, T, P5/1601/3, P5/7Reg/20A
Geo., husb., Sutton M., 1708, I, W, P2/B/1277
Burrows, Giles, Shaw Hill, Melk., 1777, W, P2/B/1938
Burrough, Grace, widow, Bower C., 1642, AB, I, P2/B/677
Jas., Gt. Woodford, 1682, AB, I, P5/1682/9
Burrough, Jas., Sal., 1792, AB, P1/B/1524, P1/14Reg/469C
Burrough, Jas., weaver, Ditchampton, Wilton, 1814, W, Wr, P2/1814/18

Burrough, Joan, Uffc., Devon, 1690, AB, P20/1/114
Burrowes, Jn., husb., Norton B., 1604, I, W, P2/B/253
Jn., yeo., Gt. Woodford, 1634, I, W, P13/1/15
Jn., yeo., W. Grimstead, 1672, I, W, P2/B/859
Jn., sen., Teffont E., 1681, I, W, P2/B/980
Jn., yeo., Uffc., Devon, 1707, W, P5/1707/8, P5/15Reg/40
Jn., Sherb., Dorset, 1711, AB, P5/1711/14
Jn., yeo., Chards., Devon, 1712, comm, W, P14/117
Burow, Jn., labourer, Teffont E., 1714, W, P1/B/797, P1/5Reg/458
Burrough, Jn., sen., yeo., Bathampton, Steeple L., 1726, W, P1/B/933, P1/7Reg/145
Burrough, Jn., gent., Laverstock, 1735, W, P1/B/1038, P1/7Reg/615B
Jn., Bower C., 1763, W, P2/B/1790
Burrough, Jn., Avon, Stratford sub C., 1769, W, P4/1769/10
Burrows, Jn., Beer Hackett, Dorset, 1769, AB, P5/1769/4
Jn., yeo., Uffc., Devon, 1808, W, P20/1/288
Burroughs, Jn., labourer, Bishopstone S., 1857, aff, W, Wr, P2/1857/38
Jos., Old Windsor, Berks., 1701, AB, P1/B/692
Burrough, Jos., Reading, Berks., 1726, AB, P1/B/916
Lucy, widow, Sutton M., 1715, I, W, P2/B/1340
Burrows, Martha, wife, Bristol, Gloucs (leaving effects at Warm.), 1833, AB, Wr, P2/1833/22
Burrough, My., widow, Gt. Woodford, 1698, I, W, P13/3/24
Burrough, My., widow, Farley, Alderbury, 1726, AB, W, P26/705
Ninian, jun., yeo., Gt. Woodford, 1639, AB, a/c, I (2), W, P13/1/20
Prudence, widow, Uffc., Devon, 1649, W, P20/1/42
Rd., husb., Teffont M., 1678, I, W, P2/B/934
Burrough, Rd., sen., yeo., Bower C., 1681, I, W, P2/B/989
Rd., yeo., Woodminton, Bower C., 1687, I, W, P2/B/1083
Rd., yeo., Bower C., 1798, W, P2/B/2133
Burrough, Robt., sen., weaver, N. Burcombe, 1789, W, P2/B/2044
Roger, sen., tailor, Sherb., Dorset, 1668, I, W, P5/1668/4
Burrough, Sam., Shrewton, 1761, AB, P2/B/1773
Burrough, Susanna, sp., Devizes, 1845, AB, O, Wr, P1/1845/14
Burrough, Thos., yeo., Woodford, 1675-77, AB, I, P13/1/25, P13/2/7
Thos., yeo., Beer Hackett, Dorset, 1678, comm, I (including pair of virginals), W, P5/1678/4
Burrough, Thos., Woodford, 1719, W, P13/4/14
Thos., Farley, Alderbury, 1723, I, W, P26/676
Burrough, Thos., yeo., Sherb., Dorset, 1728, AB, W, P5/1728/14, P5/16Reg/213A
Thos., Bower C., 1781, AB, P2/B/1983
Burrough, Thos., goldsmith, stationer and bookbinder, Devizes, 1781, W, P1/B/1460, P1/13Reg/325
Wm., Everington, Yattendon, Berks., 1635, I, NW, P1/B/263
Wm., husb., Blewbury, Berks., 1675, AB, I, P5/1675/8
Burrough, Wm., Clarendon Park, 1717, W, P5/1717/6, P5/15Reg/399A
Burrough, Wm., Woodford, 1728-29, AB, P5/1728/15, P5/16Reg/217A
Burrough, Wm., yeo., Avon, Stratford sub C., 1760, W, P4/1760/3
Burrough, Wm., cordw., Sal., 1780, W, P4/1780/14
Burrough, Wm., baker, Shrewton, 1794, W, P2/B/2098
Burrough, Wm., Bower C., 1800, AB, P2/1800/48
see also Hayward als B.
Burry, Dan., Lockeridge, Overton, 1679, comm, NW, P3/B/719
Bury, Eliz., widow, N. Wraxall, 1719, W, P3/B/1174
Burrey, Jane, sp., Martin, Hants, 1684, AB, I, W, P2/B/1039
Bury, Jane, widow, Etchilhampton, 1815, AB, comm, Wr, P3/1815/57
Jane, widow, Etchilhampton, 1831, W, Wr, P3/1831/73
Jn., Beechingstoke, [1604], W (NEP), P3/B/14
Millicent, widow, Lockeridge, Overton, 1699, I, W, P3/B/989
Rd., Wylye, 1550, W, P2/2Reg/93B
Simon, Etchilhampton, 1813, AB, Wr, P3/1813/48
Simon, yeo., Stert, Urchf., 1820, W, Wr, P1/1820/1
Burrey, Thos., sen., Bottle, Beechingstoke, 1610, W, P3/B/72
Thos., Marl., 1693, AB, P1/B/634

Thos., sen., innholder, Lydeway (in Stert), Urchf., 1772, AB, W, P1/B/1410, P1/12Reg/434
Burree, Thos., servant to Hy. Hoare, Stourton, 1772, W, P2/B/1890
Wm., husb., Rushall, 1557-60, AB, W, P2/3Reg/25A, P2/4Reg/47D, 50D
Burson *see* Busson
Burssy *see* Bissey
Burt, Byrt, Agnes, widow, Caundle Marsh, Dorset, 1602, AB, I, W, P5/1602/2, P5/7Reg/34A
Byrte, Alexander, husb., Studley, Trowb., 1567, W, P5/2Reg/4A
Alice, widow, Brook, Westb., 1626, a/c, P25/1626/4
Ann, widow, Bere R., Dorset, 1721, I, W, P5/1721/3, P5/16Reg/60A
Ann, widow, Sal., 1767, W, P4/1767/5
Benj., sen., shoemaker, Long Burton, Dorset, 1731, I, W, P5/1731/12
Edwd., Enmore Grn, Motc., Dorset, 1662, I, W, P19/3
Bert, Eleanor, widow, Grove, Wantage, Berks., 1670, AB, I, P23/15
Eleanor, widow, Littleton P., 1736, W, P1/B/1064, P1/8Reg/155
Eliza, minor, Gillingham, Dorset, 1813, T (dau of George B., decd), P27/1/623
Burte, Eliz., widow, Britford, 1565, W, P5/1Reg/39B
Birt, Eliz., widow, Allweston, Folke, Dorset, 1603, W, P5/7Reg/57
Burte, Eliz., widow, Butterwick, Folke, Dorset, 1625, I, NW, P5/1625/9, P5/10Reg/281B
Eliz., sp., Gillingham, Dorset, 1816, AB, comm, Wr, P27/1/637
Emma, widow, Long Burton, Dorset, 1678, comm, I, W, P5/1678/5
Birt, Frances, sp., Mere, 1663, I, W, P5/1663/9
Geo., sen., broad weaver, Semington, Steeple A., 1665, I, W, P2/B/768
Geo., Gillingham, Dorset, 1813, AB, P27/1/622
Byrte, Hy., yeo., Caundle Marsh, Dorset, 1600, AB, a/c, I, T, P5/1600/9, P5/7Reg/7B
Burte, Jas., Mere, 1635, AB, P5/1634/1, P5/12Reg/203B
Byrt, Jas., Thornford, Dorset, 1706, AB, P5/1706/4
Jas., blacksmith, Berwick St Jn., 1830, W, P2/1830/45
Jas., Semley, 1850, W, Wr, P2/1850/22
Joan, widow, Long Burton, Dorset, 1635, I, W, P5/1635/9, P5/12Reg/211C
Birt, Jn., Caundle Marsh, Dorset, 1583, AB, P5/1582/8, P5/4Reg/58E
Burte, Jn., gent., Caundle Marsh, Dorset, 1587, AB, I, W, P5/1587/44, P5/4Reg/142A
Jn., husb., Stockley, Bere R., Dorset, 1593, I, T, W, P5/1593/13, P5/6Reg/45B
Jn., gent., Caundle Marsh, Dorset, 1629, I, W, P5/1629/3, P5/11Reg/109
Burte, Jn., yeo., Long Burton, Dorset, 1629, I, W, P5/1628/16, P5/11Reg/108
Jn., Shrewton, 1630, I, W, P2/B/529, P2/9Reg/126
Jn., Studley, Trowb., 1631, AB, I, P22/1/20
Jn., yeo., Grove, Wantage, Berks., 1668, I, W, P23/3
Jn., yeo., Brook, Westb., 1689, I, W, P25/1689/6
Byrt, Jn., yeo., Holnest, Dorset, 1691, AB, I, P5/1691/8
Jn., yeo., Halstock Leigh, Dorset, 1718, W, P16/209
Jn., tailor, Poulshot, [1719?], NW, P2/B/1382
Birt, Jn., clothier, 1734, W, Wr, P4/1734/4
Jn., sen., collarmaker, Tisb., 1765, AB, W, P2/B/1815
Jn., Leigh, Yetm., Dorset, 1774, W, P19/174
Jn., yeo., Poulshot, 1790, W, P2/B/2049
Byrt, Jn., gent., Crickl. St S., 1796, AB, W, P3/B/1753
Birt, Jn., clothier, Sal., 1818, AB, LA, P4/1818/9
Jn., yeo., Swallowcliffe, 1848, W, Wr, P5/1848/10
Jn. *see also* Sam. Harris
Jos., sen., Long Burton, Dorset, 1706, AB, comm, I, P5/1706/2
Birt, Jos., Corsham, 1714, marriage licence, P29/2Reg/8A
Jos., yeo., Sal., 1808, W, P4/1808/2
Jos., gent., Damerham, Hants, 1822, W, Wr, P2/1822/60
Mgt., widow, Westb., 1733, W, P25/1733/1
Birt, Martha, widow, Sal., 1737, W, Wr, P4/1737/8
Birt *or* Burt, Martha, sp., Everleigh, 1829, AB, O, W, Wr, P3/1829/17
My., widow, Tollard Royal, 1622, I, W, P2/B/423
My., widow, Long Burton, Dorset, 1720, I, W, P5/1720/8, P5/16Reg/47B
Byrt, My., gent.'s wife, Crickl. St S., 1721, AB, P3/B/1196
My., Corsham, 1733, AB, P29/B/45

My., widow, W. Lavington, 1737, AB, comm, P1/B/1069
Birt, My., widow, Leigh, Yetm., Dorset, 1739, comm, W, P19/129
My. Ann, wife, Hook Farm, Semley, 1856, AB, aff, O, Wr, P2/1856/56
Birt, Matthew, Coltleigh, Mapperton, Dorset d. in Dorchester Prison, 1697, AB, I, P17/121
Nich., Shrewton, 1623-28, AB, comm, I, W, copy W, P1/B/188, P2/B/430, 491
Nich., yeo., Westb., 1649, AB, I, NW, P25/1649/1
Nich., husb. and labourer, Shrewton, 1699, I, W, P2/B/1201
Nich., labourer, Wylye, 1811, W, Wr, P1/1811/16
Paul, yeo. *or* gent., Ashton K., 1687, AB, I, ren, P3/B/834
Peter, farmer, Leighs Marsh, Dilton, Westb., 1736, W (NEP), P25/1736/8
Peter, broad weaver, Sutton V., 1787, AB, app. of guardian, W, P2/B/2021
Burte, Philip, Letcombe Regis, Berks., 1631, AB, I, P1/B/237
Byrt *or* Burtt, Rd., Southbrook, Bere R., Dorset, 1692, AB, I, P5/1692/7
Birt, Rd., Westb., 1705, AB, P25/1705/8
Byrt, Rd., yeo., Holnest, Dorset, 1717, I, W, P5/1717/5, P5/15Reg/401C
Rd., cooper, Devizes, 1760, AB, ren, P1/B/1333
Byrt, Rd., gent., Crickl. St S., 1764, W, P3/B/1566
Byrte, Robt., shepherd, Chitterne AS, 1632, I, W, P2/B/561
Robt., yeo., Littleton, Steeple A., 1690, AB, I, W, P2/B/1113
Robt., cordw., W. Lavington, 1728, W, P1/B/945, P1/7Reg/200
Robt., maltster, Mkt. L., 1747, W, P1/B/1198, P1/10Reg/69B
Burte, Roger, Long Burton, Dorset, 1591, AB, I, P5/1591/8, P5/5Reg/106A
Byrt, Roger, shoemaker, Hermitage, Dorset, 1668, AB, I (detailed), P5/1668/6
Roger, yeo., Long Burton, Dorset, 1676, AB, I, P5/1676/10
Burt *or* Byrt, Sam., yeo., Holnest, Dorset, 1712, AB, I, P5/1712/7
Byrt, Simon, Holnest, Dorset, 1702, I, W, P5/1702/1
Susanna, widow, Ashton K., 1693, AB, I, Wr (very fragile items), P3/B/911
Susanna, widow, Enmore Grn, Motc., Dorset, 1745, AB, P19/143
Burte, Thos., Studley, Trowb., 1613, I, W, P22/2/9
Thos., Alderbury, 1828, AB, P26/1368
Thos., ironmonger, Mkt. L. (form. of Devizes), 1832, court proceeding (prohibits anything to be done re decd's estate without consulting principal creditor), O, W, Wr, P1/1832/20
Thos., Sandleys, Gillingham, Dorset, 1852, comm, W, Wr, P27/1/765
Thomasine, widow, Sal., 1680, I, W, P1/B/534
Birt, Unity, widow, Dunsden Grn, Sonning, Berks., 1682, I, W, P5/1682/10
Walter, yeo., Leigh, Yetm., Dorset, 1673, I, W, P19/30
Byrte, Wm., husb., Caundle Marsh, Dorset, 1576, AB, I, W, P5/1576/8, P5/3Reg/83B
Burte, Wm., husb., Allweston, Folke, Dorset, 1587, AB, I, W, P5/1587/43, P5/4Reg/141C
Birt, Wm., husb., Shrewton, 1601, AB, I, note, P2/B/209
Wm., blacksmith, Tollard Royal, 1614, W, P2/8Reg/244B
Wm., labourer, Eye and Dunsden, Sonning, Berks., 1724, I, W, P5/1724/15, P5/16Reg/96A
Burton, Alexander, blacksmith, Charnham St., Hungerford, Berks., 1634, I, W. Proved at the Metropolitan visitation to Newbury, P5/1634/26, P5/12Reg/302B
Alexander, [blacksmith], Charnham St., Hungerford, Berks., 1684, AB, comm, I, P5/1684/2
Alexander, carp., Ebbesborne Wake, 1721, I, W, P1/B/872, P1/6Reg/372B
Alexander, innholder, Charnham St., Hungerford, Berks., 1750, W, P23/621
Alice, widow, Studley, Trowb., 1631, I, W, P1/B/228
Amos, chandler, Ansty, 1736, I, W, P1/B/1063, P1/8Reg/154A
Arthur Francis Thos., vicar, Hampstead N., Berks., 1820, AB, comm, W, Wr, P1/1820/49
Edith, Lyme R., Dorset, 1693, AB, P16/119
Eliz., widow, Tisb., 1753, W, P2/B/1701
Eliz., widow, Enborne, Berks., 1829, W, Wr, P1/1829/128
Bourton, Hannah, widow, Maiden B., 1821, W, Wr, P2/1821/41
Hy., blacksmith, Charnham St., Hungerford, Berks., 1700, AB, I, P23/241
Hy., blacksmith, Charnham St., Hungerford, Berks., 1744, W, P23/575
Bourton, Hester, Gillingham, Dorset, 1818, AB (2), comm, D, O, Wr (case involves relinquishment of AB to decd's husband, Steph. B. He had returned to G. from abroad where it had been thought that he had d.), P27/1/641
Jasper, tailor, Hurst, Berks., 1712, W, P5/1712/10, P5/15Reg/305
Jn., Warm., 1548, W, P2/2Reg/60A
Jn., sen., mariner, Lyme R., Dorset, 1679, W, P5/1679/5

Jn., husb., Bradfield, Berks., 1686, AB, I, P1/B/1562
Jn., Netheravon, 1714, I, W, P12/147
Jn., yeo., Fisherton D., 1724, W, P2/B/1430
Jn., painter stainer, Fisherton A., 1726, W, P2/B/1448
Jn., sen., Ruscombe, Berks., 1728, AB, comm, P5/1728/16, P5/16Reg/211C
Jn., Compton C., 1755, AB, P2/B/1722
Jn., yeo., Tisb., 1818, W, Wr, P2/1818/64
Jn., Chittoe, Bps. C., 1822, AB, Wr, P24/1289
Jn., Wardour, Tisb., 1842, AB, I, W, Wr, P1/1842/97
Jn., yeo., E. Tisb., 1851, W, Wr, P1/1851/25
Jos., miller and yeo., Ansty, 1661, comm, I, W, P1/B/365
Jos., yeo., Tisb., 1727, AB, ren, W, P2/B/1452
Lawr., carp., bound on a voyage to sea, Ebbesborne Wake, 1745, W (pre-printed naval form), P2/B/1641
My., widow, Boreham, Warm., 1601, I, W, P2/B/214
My., sp., Semley, 1686, AB, P1/B/585
My., widow, Ansty, 1687, AB, I, P2/B/1076
My., sp., Wilsford nr Pewsey, 1831, AB, comm, Wr, P2/1831/3
Robt., yeo., Wambrook, Somerset, 1717, I, W, P14/125
Robt., Crickl. St My., 1722, AB, P3/B/1214
Ruth, widow, Charnham St., Hungerford, Berks., 1686, comm, I, W, P5/1686/14
Steph. Pope, Chittoe, Bps. C., 1846, AB, comm, ren, Wr, P24/1381
Thos., Newnham, Sutton V., 1553, W, P2/2Reg/171C
Wm., Sutton Poyntz, Dorset, 1591, I, W, P5/1591/9, P5/5Reg/101A
Wm., husb., Burghfield, Berks., 1716, W, P1/B/819, P1/6Reg/53B
Wm., sen., bricklayer, Kintbury, Berks., 1776, W, P1/B/1433, P1/13Reg/110B
Wm., Durrington, 1845, AB, Wr, P1/1845/72
see also Barton *or* B.; Gravell als B.
Bury *see* Burry
Busfield, Jn., gent. *or* yeo., N. Burcombe, 1672, I, W, P2/B/844
Bush, Adam, husb., Tockenham, 1645, comm, T, W, P1/B/319
Adam, husb., Lyneham, 1669, AB, I, P3/B/558
Amelia, widow, Bath, Somerset (leaving effects at Chipp.), 1856, AB, aff, D, O, W, Wr, P3/1856/64
Damon, Tockenham, 1645, AB, I, P1/B/318
Edwd., Calne, 1780, AB (2), P26/1110
Edwd., chaise driver, Calne, 1857, W, Wr, P26/1473
Eleanor, widow, W. Tockenham, Lyneham, 1683, I, W, P1/B/564
Jane, widow, Lacock, 1676, I, W, P3/B/671
Joan, widow, Quemerford, Calne, 1770, W, P26/1035
Jn., husb., Paxcroft, Steeple A., 1597, I, W, P2/B/178
Jn., broad weaver, Sal. St Edmd., 1615, AB, W, P4/1615/20
Jn., tailor, Zeals, 1712, I, W, P5/1712/5, P5/15Reg/287
Jn., Fisherton A., 1721, AB, I, P2/B/2146
Jn., sen., yeo., Childrey, Berks., 1759, W, P1/B/1319, P1/11Reg/402
Jn., stonemason, Warm. Common, 1848, W, Wr, P2/1848/1
Jonathan, yeo., Childrey, Berks., 1770, W, P1/B/1401, P1/12Reg/352
Mgt., widow, Chitterne St My., 1589, I, W, P2/B/102
Mgt., sp., Chr. M., 1755, W, P3/B/1499
Michael, widow, Bradford A., 1791, W, P2/B/2062
Miles, yeo., Lacock, 1664, court papers, I, W, P3/B/497
Nathaniel, Dauntsey, 1709, comm, I, W, P3/B/1081
Oswald, Lacock, 1664, AB, P3/B/498
Peter, clothw., Corsham, 1715, I, W, P29/B/39, P29/2Reg/10G
Busshe, Robt., husb., Longbridge D., 1562, W, P2/4Reg/107D
Busshe, Robt., Chitterne St My., 1563, I, P2/B/36
Thos., Calne, 1612, AB, P26/21
Thos., clerk, Sal., 1739, AB, Wr, P4/1739/4
Thos., sen., yeo., Leigh, Yetm., Dorset, 1795, W, P19/197
Thos., yeo., Leigh, Yetm., Dorset, 1827, W, Wr, P5/1827/37
Thos. *see also* Dan. Shipman
Wm., yeo., Nethermore, Pewsham, 1626, I (detailed), W, P3/B/270

Wm., husb., Lacock, 1670, comm, I, W, P3/B/582
Wm., sen., baker, Lacock, 1672, AB, I, ren, W, P3/B/617
Wm., Lacock, 1705, I, W, P3/B/1050
Wm., Mere, 1711, AB, I, P5/1711/15
Wm., jun., Calne, 1716, AB, ren, P5/1716/8
Wm., sen., carp., Calne, 1723, W, P26/681
Wm., innholder, Bradford A., 1747, AB, I (very detailed), W, P2/B/1658
Wm., gardener, Fisherton A., 1751, W, P2/B/1690
Bushbe, Anth., tailor, W. Shefford, Berks., 1723, I, W, P1/B/902, P1/7Reg/17B
Wm., W. Shefford, Berks., 1741, AB, comm, P1/B/1128
Bushell, Alice, Welford, Berks., 1602, I, W, P1/B/21
Ann, yeo., Crofton, Gt. Bedwyn, 1733, W, P21/9/3
Cath., widow, Netheravon, 1618, I, copy I, W, P12/37
Chris., yeo., Lt. Bedwyn, 1698, I, W, P5/1698/9
Chris., yeo., Lt. Bedwyn, 1746, W, P5/1746/10
Dan., sen., yeo., Wilton, Gt. Bedwyn, 1776, W, P5/1776/7, P5/17Reg/120B
Dan., yeo., Gt. Bedwyn, 1781, W, P21/11/22
Edwd., husb., Willesley, Sherston, 1610, NW, P3/B/73
Edwd., Mildenhall, 1613, AB, P3/B/96
Edwd., yeo., Wilton, Gt. Bedwyn, 1699, I, W, P21/5/46
Edwd., Chipp., 1712, AB, comm, I, P3/B/1108
Edwd., bach., Wilton, Gt. Bedwyn, 1733, AB, P5/1733/13
Eliza, widow, Langley Burrell, 1839, comm, W, Wr, P3/1839/30
Eliz., widow, Crofton, Gt. Bedwyn, 1711, W, P21/7/10
Eliz., widow, Chipp., 1735, W, P1/B/1054, P1/8Reg/62
Eliz., widow, Littleton P., 1753, W, P1/B/1278, P1/11Reg/112
Eliz., sp., Lacock, 1757, W, P3/B/1513
Francis, clerk, Sal., 1678, AB, I, ren, P4/1678/2
Giles, yeo., Alderton, 1676, I, NW, P3/B/672
Busshell, Hy., husb., Winterbourne M., [1572], W, P1/1Reg/132A
Jas., blacksmith, Lyneham, 1853, comm, W, Wr, P3/1853/46
Busshell, Joan, widow, Fyfield, Overton, 1606, AB, I, P1/B/57
Jn., miller, Netheravon, 1588, I, W, P12/238, P5/5Reg/18A
Jn., miller, Netheravon, 1614, AB, I, P12/26, 29
Jn., jun., yeo., Lt. Bedwyn, 1675, AB, a/c, I, P21/2/45
Jn., gent., Gt. Bedwyn, 1720, W (very detailed), P21/8/1
Jn., yeo., Wilton, Gt. Bedwyn, 1753, W, P21/10/18
Jn., Lt. Bedwyn, 1758, AB, P5/1758/9
Jn., sen., Crofton Fitzwarren, Gt. Bedwyn, 1765, W, P21/10/63
Jos., labourer, Yatton K., 1745, I, W, P3/B/1433
Bushell *or* Tawbott, Mgt., widow, Netheravon, 1592, AB, I, P5/1592/82
Margery, widow, Netheravon, 1641, I, NW, P5/1641/13, P5/13Reg/278A
My., widow, Crofton, Gt. Bedwyn, 1798, W, P21/11/44
Matthew, yeo., Littleton P., 1741, W, P1/B/1152, P1/9Reg/212
Busshell, Rd., husb., Crofton, Gt. Bedwyn, 1592, I, T, W, P5/1591/10, P5/5Reg/136
Rd., Gt. Bedwyn, 1630, AB, I, W, P5/1629/9, P5/11Reg/27A
Rd., yeo., Crofton, Gt. Bedwyn, 1711, comm, W, P21/7/8
Rd., husb., Avebury, 1716, W, P1/B/825, P1/6Reg/45B
Robt., husb., Abingdon, Berks., 1638, AB, I, P1/B/274
Robt., farrier, Lyneham, 1856, aff, comm, D, W, Wr, P3/1856/44
Ruth, Wilton, 1729, W, P21/8/49
Sam., sen., cordw., Reading, Berks., 1717, W, P1/B/835, P1/6Reg/101
Sarah, sp., Burbage, 1744, AB, I, W, P5/1744/7
Sarah, widow, Westport St My., 1791, W, P3/B/1735
Thos., jun., Netheravon, 1618, AB, I, copy I, P12/36
Thos., gent., Netheravon, 1634, I, NW, P12/74
Thos., sen., yeo., Fittleton, 1662, comm, I, W, P1/B/370
Thos., yeo., Fittleton, 1671, I, P1/B/470
Thos., Netheravon, 1688, I, NW, P5/1688/3
Thos., Purley, Berks., 1701, AB, P1/B/691

Thos., yeo., Crofton, Gt. Bedwyn, 1707, W, P5/1707/9, P5/15Reg/50
Thos., broad weaver, Rowde, 1750, W, P1/B/1250, P1/10Reg/419
Thos., broad weaver, Rowde, 1780, AB, ren, P3/B/1667
Thos., yeo., Crofton, Gt. Bedwyn, 1786, W, P21/11/28
Wm., Ludg., 1594, AB, I, L, P2/B/157
Wm., labourer, Wilton, Gt. Bedwyn, 1744, W, P21/9/53
Wm., bach., Sal., 1802, AB, P4/1802/6
see also Simons als B.
Bushnell, Christian, widow, Blewbury, Berks., 1730, W, P5/1730/5
Dan., yeo., Reading, Berks., 1804, W, P1/1804/46
Jn., sen., tailor, Sulham, Berks., 1735, I, W, P1/B/1060, P1/8Reg/130
Sarah, widow, Bucklebury, Berks., 1763, W, P1/B/1358, P1/12Reg/93
Walter, gent., Avill's Farm, Corsham, 1694, W, P3/B/931
Wm., sen., yeo., Blewbury, Berks., 1720, W, P5/1720/5, P5/16Reg/43B
Bushrod, Robt., cordw., Castleton, Dorset, 1610, AB (fragment), I, P5/1610/8, P5/9Reg/39B
Wm., cordw., Sherb., Dorset, 1677, W, P5/1677/2
Busie *see* Bissey
Busley, Rd., Bulford, 1589, AB, I, draft I, P2/B/112
Buss, Jn., vict., Chitterne St My., 1782, req, copy W, P2/B/1995
Bussell, Jane, sp., Urchf., 1802, AB, P2/1802/37
Jn., yeo., Uffc., Devon, 1597, I, W, P5/1597/11, P5/6Reg/168E
Jn., Oborne, Dorset, 1610, I, W, P5/1610/7, P5/9Reg/39C
Jn., sen., maltster, Marden, 1809, O, W, Wr, P2/1809/24
My., wife, Wilsford nr Pewsey, 1813, AB, Wr (form. My. Strong, spinster), P2/1813/59
Rd., yeo., Firstead, Netherb., Dorset, 1723, I, W, P17/410
Wm., husb., Caundle Marsh, Dorset, 1710-13, comm, NW, P5/1710/20, P5/15Reg/381A
Bussey *see* Bissey
Busshe *see* Bush
Busshell *see* Bushell
Busshop, Busshopp *see* Bishop
Bussie *see* Bissey
Bussington, Fortune, widow, Whitley, Melk., 1603, I, W, P1/B/23
Busson, Burson, Chas., wheeler, Grove, Wantage, Berks., 1766, W, P23/713
Chas., wheelwright, Grove, Wantage, Berks., 1813, W, P23/865
Geo., yeo., Hilmarton, 1853, AB, aff, comm, Wr, P3/1853/53
Bussy, Busten *see* Bissey
Busterd *see* Bastard
Bustey *see* Bissey
Buston *see* Barston
Butcher, Alice, widow, Warm., 1760, AB, P2/B/1759
Ambrose, yeo., Highw., 1706, W, P10/1706/1
Ann, widow, Wanb., 1675, I, NW, P3/B/657
Ann, N. Bradley, 1776, AB, P1/B/1439
Benj., postmaster, Marl., 1737, W, P1/B/1068, P1/8Reg/180
Chas., glover, Highw., 1697, W, P10/1697/5
Cicely, widow, Henley, Box, 1625, I, W, P1/B/196
Dan., Crockerton, Longbridge D., 1746, AB, P2/B/1648
Dorothy, widow of yeo., Boxford, Berks., 1698, I, W, P1/B/667, P1/3Reg/134
Edmd., husb., Woodrow, Melk., 1624, I, W, P2/B/436
Edwd., Grittenham, Brinkw., [1612], I, W (NEP), P3/B/97
Edwd., Urchf., 1768, W, P2/B/1851
Edwd., Bromham, 1784, W, P3/B/1693
Edwd., Burbage, 1798, AB, W, P11/255
Edwd., tailor, Crockerton, Longbridge D., 1800, D, W, P2/1800/4
Bocher, Eliz., widow, Shalbourne, 1567, AB, P5/2Reg/7C
Eliz., widow, Eastrop, Highw., 1592, I, T, W, P5/1592/8, P5/5Reg/141B
Eliz., widow, E. Coulston, 1609, AB, court paper, I, W, P2/B/286, P2/8Reg/43B
Eliz., widow, Eastrop, Highw., 1664, I, W, P5/1664/5
Eliz., widow, N. Bradley, 1787, W, Wr, P2/B/2019
Eliz., wife, Mkt. L., 1802, L, W, P2/1802/61

Eliz., wife, N. Bradley, 1807, AB, Wr, P2/1807/16
Eliz., sp., Milton L., 1821, AB, comm, W, Wr, P3/1821/7
Eliz., widow, Easton, 1823, W, Wr, P1/1823/9
Frances, widow, Beam., Dorset, 1744, W, P17/489
Botcher, Gabriel, [tucker?], no abode stated, c1595, I, P1/B/11
Gabriel, sen., fuller, Devizes, 1718, W, P1/B/844, P1/6Reg/164
Gabriel, gent., Rowde, 1799, W, P3/B/1771
Geo., yeo., Damerham, Hants, 1670, I, P30/9
Geo., yeo., Bowden Hill, Lacock, 1850, O, W, Wr, P3/1850/59
Geo. Wheeler, Melk., 1836, AB, P2/1836/34
Hy., sen., yeo., Hannington, 1687, I, W, P3/B/838
Bocher, Isabel, widow, Rivar, Shalbourne, 1570, W, P5/2Reg/64C
Jas., maltster, Fisherton A., 1806, W, Wr, P2/1806/53
Jas., yeo., Gt. Cheverell, 1857, AB, aff, Wr, P2/1857/66
Jeremiah, yeo., Southwick, N. Bradley, 1830, comm, W, P2/1830/13
Joan, widow, Warm., 1685, I, W, P2/B/1057
Joan, widow, Hannington, 1705, W, P3/B/1051
Bocher als Shephard, Jn., Bratton, Westb., 1559, I, P5/1558/3
Jn., Beam., Dorset, 1596, AB, I, W, P5/1596/13, P5/6Reg/126A
Jn., husb., Edington, 1645, AB, I, copy I, P2/B/699
Jn., Hannington, 1677, I, W, P3/B/688
Jn., carrier, N. Bradley, 1686, AB, comm, I, P2/B/1069
Jn., butcher, Worton, Pott., 1720, W, P1/B/855, P1/6Reg/254
Jn., mercer, Warm., [1728], W, P2/B/1466
Jn., potter, Crockerton, Longbridge D., 1730, W, P2/B/1477
Jn., yeo., Quidh., 1731, W, P2/B/1502
Jn., vict., Warm., 1733, W, P2/B/1525
Jn., yeo., Leekshedge, Bremhill, 1753, W, P1/B/1279, P1/11Reg/119B
Jn., yeo., Erlestoke, 1753, AB, comm, P2/B/1699
Jn., broad weaver, Southwick, N. Bradley, 1757, W, P2/B/1732
Jn., All C., 1770, AB, P3/B/1611
Jn., broad weaver, N. Bradley, 1776-78, W, P2/B/1929, 1962
Jn., Mkt. L., 1781, AB, comm, P2/B/1986
Jn., wick yarnmaker, Quemerford, Calne, 1799, note, W, P26/1222
Jn., gent., Mkt. L., 1803, W, P2/1803/17
Jn., Sutton V., 1816, AB, Wr, P2/1816/60
Jn., gent., Easton, 1817, W, Wr, P3/1817/5
Jn., yeo., Gt. Cheverell, 1825, D, W, Wr, P2/1825/37
Jn., weaver, N. Bradley, 1832, O, W, Wr, P2/1832/5
Jn., gent., Gt. Cheverell, 1852, W, Wr, P2/1852/80
Jos., Newbury, Berks., 1735, AB, I, P1/B/1048
Jos., blacksmith, Brixton D., 1754, W, P2/B/1706
Jos., yeo., N. Bradley, 1766, W, P2/B/1828
Judith, wife, Marl., 1684, AB, P1/B/572
Leonard, Wilton, 1567, AB, P2/5Reg/4A
Butcher als Marchant, Lucy, widow, Warm., 1631, I, W, P2/B/543, P2/9Reg/66B
Bocher, Mgt., Bratton, Westb., 1564, W, P5/1Reg/25B
Margery, widow, N. Bradley, 1607, I, W, P2/B/280
Margery, widow, Westrop, Highw., 1693, AB, P10/1692/4
Butcher late Morse, My., gent.'s wife, Liddington, 1694, AB, P3/B/932
My., widow, Brixton D., 1765, W, P2/B/1810
My., widow, Easton, 1806, W, Wr, P3/1806/6
Moses, Urchf., 1700, AB, I, P2/B/1209
Moses, yeo., Gt. Cheverell, 1788, W, P2/B/2035
Moses, farmer, Gt. Cheverell, 1807, W, Wr, P2/1807/27
Philip *see* Jn. Davenant
Reuben, Longbridge D., 1772, AB, P2/B/1889
Rd., husb. and carrier, N. Bradley, 1619-21, AB (remarks on widow's plans to remarry), bond (2) to pay Ł25 6s, I, W, P1/B/159, 176
Rd., husb., Beam., Dorset, 1634, AB, I, W, P17/22, P5/12Reg/286

Rd., widower, N. Bradley, 1770, W, P1/B/1398, P1/12Reg/368B
Batcher als Pannell, Robt., Wilton, 1622, AB, P2/B/424
Robt., Woodrow, Melk., 1628, NW, P2/B/497
Robt., sen., carp., Shaw, Tockenham Wick, 1636, I, W, P3/B/377
Robt., fuller, Devizes, 1661, AB, comm, I, P1/B/366
Robt., fuller, Devizes, 1674, I, W, P1/B/491
Robt., yeo., Dauntsey, 1683, I, W, P3/B/779
Robt., jun., yeo., Aldermaston, Berks., 1695, comm, I, W, P1/B/651
Robt., sen., grocer, Marl., 1697, W, P1/B/664
Robt., broad weaver, N. Bradley, 1745, W, P2/B/1633
Robt., yeo., N. Bradley, 1787, AB, comm, W, P2/B/2022
Robt., Warm., 1820, AB, Wr, P2/1820/33
Robt., yeo., Corsley, 1850, court proceeding, D, W, Wr, P2/1850/36
Sarah, widow, Warm., 1751, ren, W, P2/B/1684
Thos., butcher, Sparsholt, Berks., 1732, AB, W, P1/B/1003, P1/7Reg/455
Thos., yeo., Quidh., 1755, AB, ren, P2/B/1715
Thos., yeo., Courtoak Farm, Boxford, Berks., 1798, AB, W, P1/B/1560, P1/15Reg/130B
Thos., gent., Crockerton, Longbridge D., 1804, W, P1/1804/110
Thos., yeo., Gt. Cheverell, 1808, W, Wr, P1/1808/56
Thos., jun., maltster, Steeple A., 1831, comm, D, W, Wr, P2/1831/55
Thos., sen., maltster, Steeple A., 1831, W, Wr, P2/1831/4
Thos., yeo., Gt. Cheverell, 1833, I (summary), O, W, Wr, P2/1833/9
Walter, Colerne, 1795, AB, Wr, P3/B/1747
Bocher, Wm., W. Ashton, Steeple A., 1563, T (children: Jn., Alice, Joan, Maud & Mgt. B.), W, P2/4Reg/128B, P2/4Reg/153A
Bocher, Wm., Bratton, Westb., 1564-65, W, P5/1Reg/26A, P5/1Reg/57B
Wm., blacksmith, Bradford A., 1588, W, P2/7Reg/130B
Wm., yeo., Henley, Box, 1619, I, W, P1/B/158
Wm., N. Bradley, 1621, bond to pay Ł35 4s, P1/B/177
Wm., Westport St My., 1674, AB, I, W, P3/B/641
Wm., mercer, Warm., 1682, comm, W, P2/B/992
Wm., clothier, Warm., 1713, W, P2/B/1317
Wm., Longbridge D., 1727, AB, P2/B/1458
Wm., Burbage, [1738], W (year of probate not given), P11/167
Wm., sen., potter and tilemaker, Crockerton, Longbridge D., 1821, comm, W, Wr, P2/1821/15
Wm., Crockerton, Longbridge D., 1828, note, W, Wr, P2/1828/62
Wm., weaver, N. Bradley, 1837, O, W, Wr, P2/1837/73
Wm., shopkeeper, Sevenhampton, Highw., 1849, comm, W, Wr, P10/1849/1
see also Boucher; Jenkins als B.; Marchant als B.; Torles als B.
Butler, Agnes, widow, Corsham, 1592, draft W (2), W, P29/B/6, P29/1Reg/30
Agnes, Milton L., 1629, AB, I, NW, P3/B/316
Alice, sp. *or* widow, Staverton, Trowb., 1626, I, W, P22/1/7
Ann, widow, Bishopstone N., 1688, I, W, P5/1688/4
Ann, [sp.], Wokm., Berks., 1705, AB, P5/1705/12
Butler als Hawksworth, Ann, yeo.'s widow, Lambourn, Berks., 1744, W, P1/B/1169, P1/9Reg/334
Butler form. Jacob, Ann, wife, Warm., 1765, AB, P2/B/1806
Ann, widow, Wootton B., 1788, AB, P3/B/1718
Ann, widow, Holt, Bradford A., 1815, AB, comm, W, Wr, P2/1815/57
Ann, widow, Lyneham, 1843, comm, W, Wr, P3/1843/27
Cath., widow, Stratton St Mgt., 1628, I, W, P3/B/297
Cath., widow, Erlestoke, 1738, W, P1/B/1103, P1/8Reg/338
Cath., widow, Swallowfield, Shinfield, Berks., 1741, W, P1/B/1141, P1/9Reg/116
Chas., carp., Colerne, 1854, aff, D, O, W, Wr, P3/1854/35
Christian, widow, Longbridge D., 1600, I, W, P2/B/203
Cicely, widow, Haxton, Fittleton, 1630, I, W, P2/B/510
Cornelius, yeo., Inglesham, 1703, W, P3/B/1027
Cornelius, Tockenham, 1714, AB, I, P3/B/1124
Cornelius, yeo., Tockenham, 1731, AB, ren, P3/B/1310
Cornelius, gent., Malm. (form. of Garsdon), 1814, W, Wr, P1/1814/121
Dan., slaymaker, Bromham, 1760, W, P3/B/1533

Dan., yeo., Bromham, 1837, comm, W, Wr, P3/1837/88
David, grocer, Reading, Berks., 1820, W, Wr, P1/1820/98
David, builder, Hullavington, 1847, comm, D, W, Wr, P3/1847/32
Diana, widow, Melk., 1853, O, W, Wr, P2/1853/20
Ebenezer, gent., Sutton V., 1775, AB, W, P2/B/1916
Edith, widow, Alton Pr., 1716, W, P1/B/824, P1/6Reg/47
Edith, widow, Upton, E. Knoyle, 1716, W, P2/B/1350
Botlore, Edmd., Donhead St A., 1608, I, W, P2/B/285, P2/8Reg/32
Edmd., Bremhill, 1609, AB, P3/B/54
Edwd., carp., Wantage, Berks., 1705, AB, I, P23/274
Eliz., sp., Blewbury, Berks., 1585, AB, I, W, P5/1585/15, P5/4Reg/119A
Eliz., widow, Blewbury, Berks., 1591, AB, P5/1591/12, P5/5Reg/119C
Eliz., widow, Bishopstone N., 1638, AB, I, W, P5/1638/9, P5/13Reg/134B
Eliz., wheelwright's wife, Swindon, 1719, AB, P3/B/1175
Eliz., widow, Farleigh Wick, Monkton F., 1748, W, P2/B/1662
Eliz., widow, Tockenham, 1749, W, P3/B/1464
Eliz., widow, Bromham, 1760, W, P3/B/1534
Eliz., widow, Long Wittenham, Berks., 1776, W, P1/B/1435, P1/13Reg/122B
Eliz., widow, Lattins Down Farm, Wantage, Berks., 1799, W, P23/817
Ferdinand, Devizes St Jn., 1606, AB, comm, I, O, P1/B/60
Frances, widow, E. Hendred, Berks., 1692, W, P1/B/626
Frances, widow, Corsham, 1790, AB, P29/B/58, P29/2Reg/184A
Francis, glover, Chipp., 1626, AB, I, P3/B/271
Francis, carp., Lyneham, 1728, W, P3/B/1274
Geo., Pewsey, 1627, AB, I, P3/B/292
Geo., Bishopstone N., 1635, AB (widow renounces probate), articles of agreement, ren, I, W, P5/1635/10, P5/12Reg/179B
Geo., Damerham, Hants, 1670, W (NEP), P30/28
Geo., yeo., Damerham, Hants, 1703, AB, I, P1/B/701
Geo., Rodbourne C., 1828, AB, Wr, P3/1828/32
Geo., yeo., Lains Farm, Aldbourne, 1834, W, Wr, P3/1834/15
Giles, Crickl. St S., 1640, AB, I, P3/B/449
Hannah, widow, Sal., 1739, W, P4/1739/10
Hannah, widow, Tockenham, 1767, W, P1/B/1375, P1/12Reg/229B
Hy., weaver, Rudloe, Box, 1637, I, W, P3/B/393
Hy., broad weaver, Gastard, Corsham, 1684, AB, I, P29/B/27, P29/1Reg/222A
Hy., Wokm., Berks., 1692, AB, P5/1692/8
Hy., shoemaker, Blewbury, Berks., 1715, AB, ren, W, P5/1715/9, P5/15Reg/315B
Hy., serge weaver, Devizes Grn, Bps. C., 1727, I, W, P24/916
Butlar, Hy., carp., Broughton G., 1749, W, P2/B/1671
Hy., innholder, Broughton G., 1779, comm, W, copy W, P2/B/1966
Hy., sen., yeo., Chilton, Berks., 1779-82, AB, W, P1/B/1455, 1467, P1/13Reg/294
Hy., Lopshill Farm, Damerham, Hants, 1810, W, Wr, P2/1810/56
Hy., Greenhill, Corsham, 1826, AB, W, P29/3Reg/322
Hy., sen., yeo., Greenhill, Corsham, 1850, AB, D (2), O, W, P29/1800-1857/46
Hester, grocer's wife, Warm., 1686, AB, comm, W, P2/B/1070
Jacob, Sal., 1709, AB, NW, P4/1709/9
Jacob, Rowde Hill, 1852, AB, Wr, P3/1852/61
Jas., yeo., Blewbury, Berks., 1613, W, P5/1613/5, P5/9Reg/97C
Jas., Charlton nr Malm., 1737, AB, P3/B/1369
Jas., carp., Broughton G., 1767, AB, ren, P1/B/1377
Jas., sen., W. Tockenham, Lyneham, 1819, W, Wr, P3/1819/33
Jas., labourer, Hudswell, Corsham, 1832, W, Wr, P1/1832/70
Jas., butcher and mealman, Tockenham, Lyneham, 1836-44, a/c of fees, comm, O, W, Wr, P3/1836/17, P3/1844/35
Jas., tailor, Sal., 1840, W, Wr, P4/1840/3
Jean, sp., W. Field, Corsham, 1726, W, P3/B/1249
Joan, gentlewoman, Foxley, 1617, AB, I, P3/B/152
Joan, widow, Donhead St A., 1648, AB, P2/B/722
Jn., Fittleton, 1559, W, P2/3Reg/184D
Jn., Donhead St A., 1563, I, W, P2/B/40, P2/4Reg/133C
Jn., Corsham, [1566], W (NEP), P29/1Reg/6A

Jn., Bishopstone N., 1593, I, W, P5/1593/17, 29, P5/6Reg/38B
Jn., Speen, Berks., 1605, AB, P1/B/28
Jn., Westrop, Highw., 1606, AB, P5/1606/7, P5/8Reg/82A
Butlar, Jn., weaver, Toghill, Box, 1618, I, W, P3/B/169
Jn., Monkton F., 1625, AB, I, P1/B/199
Jn., yeo. *or* husb., Stratton St Mgt., 1630, I, W (both damaged), P3/B/334
Jn., Staverton, Trowb., 1636, AB, I, P22/2/27
Jn., Manton, Preshute, 1662, comm, I, W, P1/B/368
Jn., Highw., 1662, AB, I, P5/1662/12
Jn., husb., Boscombe, 1662, I, W, P1/B/379
Jn., collarmaker, Marl., 1670, I, W, P1/B/461
Jn., stapler, Haxton, Fittleton, 1681, AB, I, P2/B/974
Jn., carp., Bishopstone N., 1684, AB, I, P6/60
Jn., maltster, Woodb., 1690, I, W, P3/B/876
Jn., yeo., Monkton F., [1702], I, W, P2/B/1220
Jn., yeo. *or* maltster, W. Field, Corsham, 1714, I, W, P29/B/41, P29/2Reg/7
Jn., sen., clothw., Limpley Stoke, Bradford A., 1729, W, P1/B/960, P1/7Reg/335
Jn., Reading, Berks., 1741, AB, P1/B/1139
Jn., Woodb., 1754, AB, P3/B/1494
Jn., clerk and rector, Lydiard M., 1760, comm, W, P1/B/1332, P1/11Reg/481C
Jn., Wootton B., 1761, AB, P3/B/1541
Jn., gent., Broad C., 1790, W, P2/B/2050
Jn., maltster, Newbury, Berks., 1792, W, P1/B/1527, P1/14Reg/426
Jn., labourer, Beedon, Berks., 1798, W, P1/B/1554, P1/15Reg/74
Jn., Melk., 1807, AB, comm, Wr, P2/1807/28
Jn., jun., yeo., Allington, 1845, O, W, Wr, P3/1845/6
Jn., yeo., Allington, Chipp., 1851, O, W, Wr, P3/1851/36
Jonas, sen., yeo., Westbrook, Gt. Faringdon, Berks., 1713, W, P5/1713/9, P5/15Reg/367C
Jonathan, gent., Wantage, Berks., 1749, W, Wr, P5/1749/9
Jos., bach., Sal., 1763, AB, ren, P1/B/1351
Jos., innholder, Hare Hatch, Wargrave, Berks., 1776, W, P1/13Reg/133
Mgt., widow, Monkton F., [1692], I, W, P2/B/1141
Maria Emma, sp., Swindon, 1856, aff, O, W, Wr, P3/1856/58
Mark, yeo., Tinh., Edington, 1845, W, Wr, P1/1845/41
My., widow, Stratton St Mgt., 1638, I, W, P1/B/286
My., widow, Woodb., 1722, I, W, P3/B/1215
My., widow, Limpley Stoke, Bradford A., 1750, comm, W, P1/B/1236, P1/10Reg/319
Nich., Corsham, [1586], W (NEP), P29/B/4
Nich., husb., Donhead St A., 1604, AB, I, note, P2/B/244
Nich., labourer, Abingdon, Berks., 1638, AB, I, P1/B/273
Nich., tailor, E. Knoyle, 1764, AB, W, P2/B/1800
Peter, E. Knoyle, 1677, I, NW, P2/B/924
Philip, Longbridge D., 1619, I, W, P2/B/396
Ralph, yeo., Stanton Fitzwarren, 1676, I, W, P3/B/673
Rebecca, widow, Marl., 1841, comm, W, Wr, P1/1841/25
Rd., clothier, Monkton F., 1569, W, P2/5Reg/56D
Rd., Wantage, Berks., 1571, AB, P5/2Reg/101A
Rd., labourer, Stapleford, 1580, W, P2/6Reg/17A
Rd., jun., husb., Blewbury, Berks., 1604, I, W, P1/B/26
Rd., gent., Crickl. St S., 1668, AB, I, P3/B/540
Rd., broad weaver, Corsham, 1703, I, W, P29/B/36, P29/1Reg/283A
Rd., gardener, Wokm., Berks., 1734, W, P5/1734/10
Rd., Ogbourne St Geo., 1737, AB, P5/1737/7
Rd., Streatley, Berks., 1738, AB, P1/B/1092
Rd., clothw., Limpley Stoke, Bradford A., 1741, comm, W, P1/B/1149, P1/9Reg/196B
Robt., husb., Compton C., 1564, I, W, P2/B/2153, P2/4Reg/186A
Robt., Arborfield, Berks., 1566, W, P5/2Reg/9B
Robt., Stratton St Mgt., 1608, W (damaged), P3/B/38
Robt., Haxton, Fittleton, 1625, AB, a/c, I, proclamation, P1/B/202
Robt., sen., yeo., Haxton, Fittleton, 1679, I, NW, P2/B/943

Robt., Downton, 1725, AB, P2/B/1441
Robt., yeo., Fowlswick Farm, Chipp., 1805, W, P3/1805/26
Robt., butcher, Melk., 1835, comm, W, Wr, P2/1835/15
Roger, yeo., Stratton St Mgt., 1691, I, W, P3/B/885
Roger, yeo., S. Marston, 1707, W, P5/1707/10, P5/15Reg/47
Sally, widow, Castle Eaton, 1796, W, P3/B/1752
Silvester, millwright, Wantage, Berks., 1757, W, P23/673
Susan, wife, Donhead St My., 1620, AB (draft L from bishop on reverse), P1/B/166
Susanna, widow, Gt. Faringdon, Berks., 1821, comm, W, Wr, P5/1821/40
Susanna, widow, W. Kennett, Avebury, 1825, AB, Wr, P3/1825/69
Thos., Donhead St My., 1565, W, P2/4Reg/193A
Thos., husb., Hurst, Berks., 1591, I, T, NW, P5/1591/11, P5/5Reg/114A
Thos., Allington, 1607, AB, I, note, P2/B/272
Thos., Donhead St A., 1609, I, W, P2/B/289, P2/8Reg/57A
Thos., Staverton, Trowb., 1618, AB, P3/B/170
Thos., shepherd, Ashton K., 1627, I, W, P3/B/293
Thos., Monkton F., 1631, AB, a/c, I, req, P2/B/533
Thos., yeo., Bishopstone N., 1663, I, W, P6/37
Thos., husb., Lyneham, 1682, AB, I, P3/B/766
Thos., husb., Bishopstone N., 1685, I, W, P5/1685/6
Thos., sen., wheelwright, Swindon, 1701, I, W, P3/B/1009
Thos., yeo., Stratton St Mgt., 1714, W, P1/B/799, P1/5Reg/414
Thos., yeo., Long Wittenham, Berks., 1729, I, W, P1/B/972, P1/7Reg/258B
Thos., gent., Wantage, Berks., 1731, W, P5/1731/6
Thos., Grove, Wantage, Berks., 1758, AB, P5/1758/10
Thos., Chaddleworth, Berks., 1763, AB, P1/B/1355
Thos., yeo., Holt, Bradford A., 1814, W, Wr, P1/1814/161
Thos., gent., Wokm., Berks., 1829, W, Wr, P5/1829/17
Wm., Cholderton, 1571, W, P1/1Reg/28B
Wm., sen., tanner, Hungerford, Berks., 1576, W, P5/3Reg/87B
Wm., weaver, Longbridge D., 1593, I, W, P2/B/150
Wm., Blewbury, Berks., 1599, AB, P5/1599/2
Wm., weaver, Middlehill, Box, 1628, I, W, P3/B/298
Wm., Boscombe, 1681, AB, I, P2/B/962
Wm., yeo., Badbury, Chiseldon, 1696, comm, I, W, Wr, P3/B/955
Wm., cordw., Reading, Berks., 1717, I, W, P1/B/838, P1/6Reg/95
Wm., Corsham, 1733, AB, P29/B/46
Wm., yeo., Erlestoke, 1737-38, comm, I, W, P1/B/1073, P1/8Reg/205
Butler als Hawksworth, Wm., yeo., Hungerford, Berks., 1740, W, Wr, P5/1740/5
Wm., yeo., Tockenham, 1762, W, P3/B/1555
Wm., yeo., Mere, 1774, W, P5/1774/2, P5/17Reg/83C
Wm., innholder, Castle Eaton, 1795, comm, W, P3/B/1748
Wm., yeo., Spittle Farm, Chipp., 1806, comm, W, P3/1806/2
Wm., Sherston, 1817, AB, Wr, P3/1817/19
Wm., widower, Melk., 1819, AB, comm, Wr, P2/1819/49
Wm., yeo., Chilton, Berks., 1826, W, Wr, P1/1826/71
Wm., yeo., Hazeland, Bremhill, 1840, comm, W, Wr, P3/1840/6
Wm., yeo., Beanacre, Melk., 1844, comm, W, Wr, P2/1844/36
see also Bradford als B.; Rawlins als B.
Butson, Amos, yeo., Uffc., Devon, 1737, W, P5/1737/6
Jn., husb., Uffc., Devon, 1671, I, W, P5/1671/5
Jn., [shopkeeper], Uffc., Devon, 1683, AB, I (of Jn. B. & Eliz. his wife, both decd), P20/1/98
Jn., Uffc., Devon, 1694, comm, I, W, P20/1/127
Thos., Uffc., Devon, 1593, AB, I, P5/1592/7
see also Brooke als B.
Butt, [...], Leigh, Yetm., Dorset, 1669, I, P19/12
Abraham, Mere, 1747, AB, P5/1747/4
Agnes, widow, Bishopstone N., 1628, AB, I, P5/1628/17, P5/11Reg/97A
Ambrose, silk throwster, Hincke's Mill, Mere, 1852, grant of probate, O, W, Wr, P5/1852/6
Ann, wife, Sutton V., 1664, AB, P1/B/415

Ann, widow, Mere, 1797, W, P5/1797/3, P5/18Reg/247A
Ann, widow, Allweston, Folke, Dorset, 1832, AB, comm, Wr, P5/1832/1
Cath., sp., Gillingham, Dorset, 1737, AB, Wr, P27/1/344
Chas., shopkeeper, Calne, 1820, comm, W, Wr, P26/1332
Butt nee Fiander, Christiana, wife, Clarendon Park, 1804, AB, P1/1804/129
Chris., sen., linen weaver, Mere, 1743, W, Wr, P5/1743/12
Dorothy, sp., Gillingham, Dorset, 1765, AB, P27/1/447, P27/3Reg/125
Edwd., Mere, 1693, AB, comm, I, P5/1693/6
Edwd., sen., linen weaver, Mere, 1730-35, W (2), P5/1735/8
Edwd., bach., Mere, 1764-65, AB (2), P5/1764/6, P5/1765/6
Edwd., Mere, 1810, AB, ren, Wr, P5/1810/2
Butt als Budd, Eleanor, tailor's wife, Malm. Abbey, 1668, AB, I, P3/B/541
Emma, jun., Gillingham, Dorset, 1847, D, O, W, Wr, P27/1/752
Harry, Mere, 1731, AB, P5/1731/13
Hy., Gillingham, Dorset, 1664, AB, P27/1/14
Hy., yeo., Malm., 1701, I, W, P3/B/1010
Honour, widow, Bourton, Gillingham, Dorset, 1815, W, P27/1/633
Hugh, Milton, Gillingham, Dorset, 1733, AB, I, P27/1/317
Jacob, yeo., Sutton V., 1667, NW (NEP), P2/B/785
Jas., yeo., Gillingham, Dorset, [1707], W, P27/1/163
Jas., linen weaver, Mere, 1743, AB, W, P5/1743/13
Jas., Milton upon Stour, Gillingham, Dorset, 1809, W, Wr, P27/1/600
Jas., Ansty, 1837, AB, W, Wr, P5/1837/1
Jas., confectioner, Warm., 1840, AB, comm, W, Wr, P1/1840/14
Jeremiah, clerk, Sherston, 1746, W, P3/B/1444
Joan, widow, Westport St My., 1669, AB, I, W, P3/B/559
Jn., joiner, Sherb., Dorset, 1598, AB, I, W, P5/1598/8, P5/6Reg/213B
Butt als Knowles, Jn., blacksmith, Westport St My., 1683, AB, I, W, Wr, P3/B/583, 780
Jn., sen., butcher, Gillingham, Dorset, 1712, AB, I, W, P27/1/178, 198
Jn., linen weaver, Mere, 1738, W, Wr, P5/1738/7
Jn., yeo., Milton, Gillingham, Dorset, 1767, W, P27/1/457, P27/3Reg/131
Jn., Chipp., 1780, W, P3/B/1668
Jn., yeo., Rodbourne C., 1783, W, P1/B/1491, P1/13Reg/502
Jn., innholder, Sal., 1794, W, P4/1794/1
Jn., gent., Warm., 1795, W, P1/B/1535, P1/14Reg/597
Jn., Ansty, 1809, AB, Wr, P5/1809/34
Jn., Heddington, 1822, W, Wr, P3/1822/35
Jn., Milton upon Stour, Gillingham, Dorset, 1823, W, Wr, P27/1/663
Jn., shopkeeper, Calne, 1831, W, P26/1390
Jn., Gt. Wishford, 1857, AB, aff, Wr, P2/1857/45
Jonathan, Wilton, 1696, AB, P2/B/1179
Lawr., yeo., Gillingham, Dorset, 1717, W, P27/1/216
Mgt., sp., Gillingham, Dorset, 1725, W, P27/1/276
Martha, widow, Sherb., Dorset, 1783, W, P5/1783/3, P5/17Reg/256A
Mart., Tisb., 1801, W, P1/1801/24, P1/15Reg/246
Mart., Trowb., 1818, AB, Wr, P1/1818/12
My., widow, Etchilhampton, 1740, W, P3/B/1393
My., widow, Warm., 1824, W, Wr, P2/1824/39
My., Bishopstone S., 1845, cert, D, W, Wr, P2/1845/12
Michael, Mere, 1753, W, P5/1753/3
Prudence, Mere, 1712, W, P5/1712/12, P5/15Reg/308B
Butt als Yard, Rd., joiner, Sherb., Dorset, 1617, AB, I, P5/1617/41, P5/9Reg/215C
Robt., merchant tailor, Boreham, Warm., 1764, W, P2/B/1804
Robt., linen weaver, Mere, 1784, W, P5/17Reg/263A
Robt., gent., Warm., 1822, comm, W, Wr, P2/1822/48
Sarah, widow, Heddington, 1816, comm, W, Wr, P3/1816/11
Sarah, widow, Calne, 1823, W, Wr, P26/1346
Steph., Mere, 1815, AB, Wr, P5/1815/29
Thos., husb., Lambourn Woodlands, Berks., 1613, I, W, P1/B/101
Thos., servant (to Mr Mildmay of Sherborne) and bach., Sherb., Dorset, 1726, AB, I, P5/1726/6

Thos., cordw., Gillingham, Dorset, 1731-38, AB, W, Wr, P27/1/309, 347
Thos., Gillingham, Dorset, 1758, AB, P27/1/420
Thos., Sherb., Dorset, 1782, AB, P5/1782/6, P5/17Reg/229A
Thos., saddler, Sherb., Dorset, 1811, comm, W, Wr, P5/1811/5
Thos., Gillingham, Dorset, 1822, W, Wr, P27/1/659
Walter, Gillingham, Dorset, 1709, AB, I, P27/1/177
Walter, yeo., Langham, Gillingham, Dorset, 1751, AB (in minority of ex.), NW, P27/1/400, P27/3Reg/64
Wm., Gillingham, Dorset, 1567, W, P27/1Reg/18B
Wm., sen., yeo., Pierston, Gillingham, Dorset, [1663], W, P27/1/12
Wm., Gillingham, Dorset, 1724, AB, P27/1/268
Wm., yeo., Milton, Gillingham, Dorset, 1753, W, P27/1/407, P27/3Reg/67
Wm., Plaitford, 1797, AB, P2/B/2125
Wm., Wyke, Gillingham, Dorset, 1803, AB, P27/1/574
Wm., yeo., Peasemore, Berks., 1811, W, Wr, P1/1811/62
Wm., bach., Sal., 1814, AB, P1/1814/135
Worthy, Cleverton, Lea and C., 1851, D, O, W, Wr, P3/1851/31
Buttell *see* Batwell
Butten *see* Button
Butter, Eliz., sp., Lyme R., Dorset, 1728, AB, comm, ren, P5/1728/18, P5/16Reg/211A
Jas., clerk, Ditteridge (in ren d. 5 years prev. in HMS overseas), 1709-12, I, W, P3/B/1082, P30/7
Jas., apothecary, New Windsor, Berks., 1738, AB, I, ren, P1/B/1080
Jos., innholder, Hare Hatch, Wargrave, Berks., 1776, W, P1/B/1436
Susanna, widow, Hare Hatch, Wargrave, Berks., 1795, W, P1/B/1542, P1/14Reg/573A
Wm., Wokm., Berks., 1778, AB, P5/1778/2, P5/17Reg/155B
Butterworth, Alfred, gent., Bradford A., 1851, O, W, Wr, P2/1851/7
Jas. Hy., linen and woollen draper, Melk., 1841, comm, W, Wr, P2/1841/52
Jn., gent., Bradford A., 1835, O, W, Wr, P1/1835/125
Jos., Chapmanslade, Dilton, Westb., 1804, O, W, P25/1804/5
Buttery, Rd., curate, Bower C., 1548, W (NEP), P2/2Reg/58D
Button, Agnes *see* Ann *or* Agnes
Alice, Throope, Bishopstone S., 1683, AB, P1/B/567
Ann, widow, Foxham, Bremhill, 1617, I, W, P3/B/153
Ann, widow, dame, Tockenham, 1666, W, P1/B/423
Ann *or* Agnes, widow, Chr. M. (form. of Fovant), 1606, I, W, P1/B/44
Chas., sen., Over C., Dorset, 1758, I, W, P5/1758/11
Butten, Dan., gent., Friar St., Reading St Lawr., Berks., 1808, W, Wr, P1/1808/110
Edith, sp., Godsell Farm, Bremhill, 1629, I, W, P3/B/317
Edwd., husb., Heytes., 1631, I, W, P5/1631/15, P5/12Reg/33B
Butten, Edwd., sen., tailor, Calne, 1712, W, P26/573
Edwd., bach., Corsham, 1829, AB, comm, Wr, P3/1829/14
Edwd., carp., Calne, 1843, O, W, Wr, P5/1843/22
Eliz., Bishopstrow, 1740, AB, P2/B/1583
Geo., yeo., Throope, Bishopstone S., 1675, I, W, P2/B/889
Geo., clerk, S. Newton, 1773, AB, W, P2/B/1897
Geo., yeo., Corsham, 1810, W, Wr, P3/1810/27
Geo., gent., Calne, 1824, comm, W, Wr, P26/1347
Hannah, widow, Calne, 1858, W, Wr, P26/1475
Harry *or* Hy., husb., Ebbesborne Wake, 1563, I, W, P2/B/38, P2/4Reg/112B
Jacob, Calne, 1705, AB, I, P26/512
Jas., excise officer, Melk., 1777, W, P2/B/1945
Joan, sp., Foxham, Bremhill, 1608, I, W, P3/B/39
Butten, Joan, widow, Bishopstone S., 1645, copy NW, P2/B/693
Joan, widow, Bishopstone S., 1669, AB, a/c, I, P2/B/809
Jn., Maddington, 1574, W, P2/5Reg/192C
Jn., husb., Gt. Cheverell, 1602, I, W, P1/B/16
Jn., gent., Throope, Bishopstone S., 1731-38, AB, W, P2/B/1493, 1564
Jn., Beenham Valence, Berks., 1735, AB, P1/B/1046
Jn., Heytes., 1739, AB, Wr, P5/1739/10
Jn., sen., mason, Calne, 1793, W, P26/1196
Jn., gent., Calne, 1821, W, Wr, P5/1821/13

Jn., yeo., Chipp., 1822, W, Wr, P3/1822/48
Jn., bach., Corsham, 1829, AB, comm, Wr, P3/1829/13
Martha, widow, Calne, 1784, AB, P26/1140
Matthew, Heytes., 1574, W, P5/3Reg/49C
Michael, widow, Wilton, 1738, W, P2/B/1565
Nanny, sp., Calne, 1815, W, Wr, P5/1815/9
Nich., Ebbesborne Wake, 1589, I, W, P2/B/107
Nich., Ebbesborne Wake, 1631, W, P2/B/540
Rd., Sonning Eye, Berks., 1601, AB, I, W, P5/1601/4, P5/7Reg/15B
Rd., yeo., Knook, 1616, AB, NW, P5/1615/2, P5/9Reg/169A
Rd., yeo., Heytes., 1664, I, W, P5/1664/6
Rd., labourer, Corsham, 1829, comm, W, Wr, P3/1829/12
Robt., husb., Bishopstone S., 1629, I, W, P2/B/500
Robt., yeo., Bower C., 1689, I, W, P2/B/1110
Sarah Ann, minor, Calne, 1850, admission to guardianship, O, proxy of guardianship, ren, T, P5/1850/1
Steph., yeo., Ebbesborne Wake, 1671, I, W, P2/B/838
Thos., Foxham, Bremhill, [1570], W (NEP), P1/1Reg/132B
Thos., sen., gent., Calne, 1838, W, Wr, P26/1443
Thos., plumber and glazier, Calne, 1840, W, Wr, P26/1448
Thos., widower, Calne, 1850, AB, O, Wr, P5/1850/2
Wm., Brimpton, Berks., 1814, W, Wr, P1/1814/91
Wm., widower, Stratford Tony, 1847, AB, Wr, P2/1847/1
Buy, By *see* Bye
Byam, Geo., esquire, Pott. (d. Antigua), 1780, AB, ren., P1/B/1458
My., widow, Sherston, 1746, W, P3/B/1445
Sam., yeo., Willesley, Sherston, 1745, W, P3/B/1434
Sarah, sp., Westport St My. (form. of Kings Stanley, Gloucs), 1718, W, P3/B/1157
Bydon *see* Biden
Bye, Buy, Arthur, husb., Pewsey, 1677, AB, P3/B/689
Buy, Chas., Reading St Giles, Berks., 1804, AB, comm, ren, P1/1804/17
Chas., carp., Hindon, 1834, W, Wr, P2/1834/28
Hannah, sp., Crickl. St S., 1807, W, Wr, P3/1807/10
Hy., sen., tailor, Poulton, 1696, W, P3/B/956
Hy., yeo., Poulton, 1729, W, P1/B/953, P1/7Reg/294
Buy, Jasper, carp., Calne, 1718, I (detailed), W, P26/620
Buy, Jn., yeo., Bulmershe, Sonning, Berks., 1710, W, P5/1710/21, P5/15Reg/152
Buy, Jos., broad weaver, Sutton B., 1693, AB, I, P3/B/912
By, Rd., Leigh, Ashton K., [1611], W (NEP), P3/B/84
Rd., yeo., Poulton, 1677, I, W, P3/B/691
By, Sam., husb., Lydiard T., 1665, I, W, P3/B/512
Thos., Urchf., [1628], W, P2/B/499
By, Thos., Lt. Somerford, 1671, AB, a/c, I, P3/B/586
Thos., sen., yeo., Bulmershe, Sonning, Berks., 1760, W, P5/1760/3
Wm., Seagry, 1614, I, W, P1/B/123
Buy, Wm., yeo., Buck Hill, Calne, 1720, I (detailed), W, P26/635
Buy, Wm., yeo., Langley Burrell, 1738, AB, ren, P1/B/1100
Buy, Wm., Swindon, 1775, AB, P3/B/1639
see also Crapon als B.
Byfield, Cornelius, gent., Bradford A., 1824, W, Wr, P2/1824/21
Emanuel, brewer, Turleigh, Winsley, Bradford A., 1856, aff, O, W, Wr, P2/1856/13
Geo., broad weaver, S. Wraxall, 1750, W, P2/B/1682
My., widow, Biddestone St Nich., 1834, W, Wr, P3/1834/27
Byforrest, Ann, widow, Hurst, Berks., 1743, AB, Wr, P5/1743/14
Byles *see* Biles
Byndar *see* Binder
Byrchall *see* Burchall
Byrd, Byrde *see* Bird
Byrt *see* Burt
Bysie *see* Bissey
Bysse *see* Biss

Byssey, Bysy *see* Bissey
Bytham, Bythombe, Grace, widow, Amesb., 1638, I, W, P1/B/269
Hy., clothw., Milford, Sal. St Mart., 1685, AB, I, P4/1684/15
Jn., yeo., Amesb., 1572, W, P2/5Reg/149C
Bitham, Jn., jun., yeo., Gt. Amesb., 1633, I, W, P2/B/564, P2/9Reg/20B
Jn., weaver, Sal., 1758, AB, ren, P4/1758/1
My., wife, Milford, Sal. St Mart., 1803, AB, P4/1803/6
Bitham, Wm., yeo., Gt. Amesb., 1636, comm, I, W, P2/B/604, P2/9Reg/105D
Bithum, Wm. *see also* Hy. Crouch
Bythell *see* Bittle
Bythesea, Edwd., Mapperton, Dorset, 1687, comm, I, NW, P5/1686/17
Bythewater, Wm., husb., Netton, Durnford, 1594, I, W, P5/1594/12, P5/6Reg/88C
Bythewood, Thos., Bere R., Dorset, 1726, AB, P5/1726/7
see also Strode als B.
Bythombe *see* Bytham

Cabell, Alice, widow, Berwick St Jas., 1716, AB, I, P1/C/564
Ann, Haydon, Dorset, 1726, W, P5/1726/11, P5/16Reg/129B
Cath., widow, Upton S., 1597, AB, I (for both husband & wife), P2/C/145
Christian, widow, Warm. (described as Lt. Corsley), [1668], I, W, P2/C/578
Chris., husb., Upton S., 1594, I, T, W, copy W, P2/C/129
Chris., Trowb., 1630, AB, I, P22/1/16
Chris., husb., Horningsham, 1710-11, I, W, P5/1710/22, P5/15Reg/221
Chris., Horningsham, 1735, AB, P5/1735/9
Eliz.?, Bradford A., 1694, AB (from burial register), P2/C/842
Giles, servant, Downton, 1587, W, P2/7Reg/74B
Cabel, Harry, shopkeeper, Sal., 1787, W (NEP), P4/1787/13
Hy., Warm., 1551, W, P2/2Reg/131A
Cabel, Hy., shepherd, Gt. Durnford, 1763, W, P9/76
Cabble, Jas., barber, Westb., 1671, AB, I, P25/1671/8
Joan, widow, Gt. Corsley, 1597, I, W, P2/C/148
Jn., Longbridge D., 1580, I, W, P2/C/58, P2/6Reg/12A
Jn., husb., Upton S., 1599, AB, I, P2/C/167
Jn., dyer, Sal., 1679, bond to deliver W, I, W, P4/1679/8, 11
Cabble, Jn., clothw., Limpley Stoke, Bradford A., [1688], I, W, P2/C/787
Jn., dyer, Sal., 1713, AB, ren, P4/1713/6
Cable, Jn., labourer, Stapleford, 1837, W, Wr, P2/1837/74
Jos., sen., baker, Rode, N. Bradley, 1763, W, P2/C/1313
My., widow, Warm., 1705, W, P2/C/919
Cabble, Nich., Westb. L., 1668, I, NW, P25/1668/7
Nich., Warm., 1730, W, P2/C/1121
Robt., [weaver], Devizes St Jn., 1562, I, W, P2/C/24, P2/4Reg/97C
Robt., clothier, Southwick, N. Bradley, 1612, AB, I, W, P2/C/263
Roger, yeo., Haydon, Dorset, 1711, AB, I, P5/1711/16
Cabel, Ruth, sp., Woodford, 1802, AB, P13/6/2
Sibyl, widow, Sal., 1713, W, P4/1713/3
Thos., innholder, Warm., 1588, W, P2/C/74, P2/7Reg/116C
Cable, Thos., gent., Whelpley, Whitep., 1635-37, AB, a/c, deed of gift, I, P2/C/432, 453
Cabel, Thos., yeo., Gt. Durnford, 1808, W, P9/102
Wm., yeo., Boreham, Warm., 1572, W, P2/5Reg/156B
Wm., yeo., Norridge, Upton S., 1632, I, W, P2/C/411, P2/9Reg/117A
Wm., sen., yeo., Warm., 1704, AB, comm, I (detailed), P1/C/484
Wm., Warm., 1735, AB, I, P1/C/725
Wm., Warm., 1739, AB, I, P2/C/1192
Cable, Wm., sen., broad weaver, Trowb., 1757, W, P1/C/890, P1/11Reg/349B
Cable, Wm., yeo., Winterbourne S., 1763, W, P2/C/1314
Cable, Wm., shopkeeper, Wilton, 1816, W, Wr, P2/1816/19
see also Harris als C.
Cadbury, Jn., Uffc., Devon, 1625, AB, P20/1/3
Matthew, Uffc., Devon, 1627, AB, a/c, comm, I, P20/1/14

Cadby, Jas., plumber and glazier, Trowb., 1808, W, Wr, P1/1808/142
Maria, widow, Trowb., 1819, W, Wr, P1/1819/8
Philip, sen., joiner, Devizes, 1683, I, W, P1/C/359
Philip, shopkeeper, Trowb., 1830, W, Wr, P1/1830/12
Philip, Trowb., 1856, AB, aff, O, Wr, P1/1856/10
Robt., carp., Bradford A., 1815, W, Wr, P2/1815/16
Wm., sen., gardener, Bedborough, Bps. C., 1729, W, P24/835
Caddell *see* Cadle
Caddy, Cadey, Cath., widow, Wantage, Berks., 1773, W, P5/1773/10, P5/17Reg/55
Keady als Cadey, Eliz., widow, S. Wraxall, 1818-23, AB, comm (2), ren, W, Wr, P2/1818/71, P2/1823/17
Jn., husb., Beam., Dorset, 1631, AB, I, P5/1631/28, P5/12Reg/18A
Jn., wool breaker, Uffc., Devon, 1720, I, W, P20/1/170
Cade, Hester, widow, Sal., 1628, I, W, P4/1627/7
Cadey *see* Caddy
Cadle, Cowdall, Eliz., sp., Westb., 1741, W, P25/1741/11
Cowdall, Eliz., sp., Westb., 1850, declaration, O, W, Wr, P25/1850/3
Giles, Hungerford, Berks., 1641, AB, P23/1011
Caudell, Jas., Waltham St Lawr., Berks., 1829, W, Wr, P1/1829/112
Caddell, Jn., husb., Shinfield, Berks., 1635, I, W, P1/C/172
Jn., Calstone W., 1683, AB, I, quitclaim, P26/305
Robt., Nettleton, 1608, I, W, P3/C/27
Caudell, Thos., husb., Swindon, 1609, W, P3/C/36
Cadman, Jeremiah, vict., Kintbury, Berks., 1776, W, P1/C/998, P1/13Reg/114
Thos., currier, Sal., 1731, AB, I (detailed), P4/1730/25
Cadwallader, Jn., Sal. St Edmd., 1615, I, W, P4/1615/18
Caeser, Alice, widow, Ludg., [1675], I, NW, P2/C/650
Benj., yeo., Swallowfield, Shinfield, Berks., 1801, W, P1/1801/38, P1/15Reg/258
Jn., farrier, Hinton, Hurst, Berks., 1746, W, P5/1746/11
Caffe *see* Cave
Cafil, Edwd., Gt. Wishford, 1733, W, P2/C/1154
Caines, Cains *see* Keynes
Caissons *see* Cousins
Cake, Agnes, Sutton Poyntz, Dorset, 1594, I, W, P5/1594/13, P5/6Reg/63A
Robt., husb., Sutton Poyntz, Dorset, 1578, I, W, P5/1578/7, P5/3Reg/111A
Wm., Coltleigh, Mapperton, Dorset, 1625, I, W, P5/1625/21, P5/10Reg/268A
Calbreath, Sarah, widow, Uffc., Devon, 1763, W (ex., Stevenson Dunsford, Quaker), P20/1/242
Caldron, Robt., no abode stated; issued at Wokm., Berks., 1613, comm, P1/C/48
Cale, Jn., sen., tiler, Calne, 1744, W, P26/855
Jos., tiler, Church St., Calne, 1790, W, P26/1164
My., widow, Calne, 1757, W, P26/956
Robt., cordw., Calne, 1783, W, P26/1127
Wm., collarmaker, Calne, 1759, W, P26/969
Caleway *see* Callaway
Calfey, Caulfey, Ann, widow, Purton, 1623, I, W, P3/C/119
Anth., yeo., Purton, 1602, I (top part missing), W (damaged), Wr, P1/C/15
Cawfey *or* Calfway, Jn., husb., Somerford K., 1642, comm, I, W, P3/C/269
My., servant, Crickl. St S., 1729, AB, NW, P1/C/689, P1/7Reg/379A
Callaway, Ann, sp., Amesb., 1780, W, P2/C/1410
Edmd., tailor, Winterbourne D., 1681, AB, I, P7/48
Geo., Malm., 1854, AB, aff, O, Wr, P3/1854/69
Calloway, Jas., Westb., 1747, AB, P25/1747/3
Jn., fellmonger, Amesb., 1776, W, P2/C/1386
Jn., Hurdcott, Winterbourne E., 1809, AB, Wr, P2/1809/31
Caleway, Roger, broad weaver, Bratton, Westb., 1720, I, W, P25/1720/1
Calloway, Sarah, widow, Britford, 1738, AB, P24/911
Calloway, Thos., no abode stated but widow of Collingbourne D., 1618, AB, P21/1/4
Wm., shepherd, Winterbourne E., 1809, W, Wr, P2/1809/28
Wm., shepherd, Winterbourne D., 1837, W, Wr, P7/206
Calley, Agnes, widow, Highway, 1619, app. of proctors, I (2 detailed), W, P3/C/103
Agnes, Norton, 1684, AB, P3/C/475

Ann, sp., Rowde, 1696, I, L, W, P3/C/587
Ann, widow, Catcomb, Hilmarton, 1700, comm, W, P3/C/616
Ann, sp., Speenhamland, Berks., 1826, AB, comm, Wr, P1/1826/46
Chas., gent., Catcomb, Hilmarton, 1678, comm, I (2 - 1 a copy), W, P3/C/404
Coely, Edwd., clothw., Bradford A., 1677, I, W, P1/C/331
Coley, Edwd., Chipp., 1678, AB, comm, P3/C/409
Judith, sp., Rowde, 1696, AB, P3/C/588
My., widow, Lyneham, 1833, W, Wr, P3/1833/24
Michael, gent., Catcomb, Hilmarton, 1637, I, W, P3/C/222
Oliver, Lyneham, 1771, AB, P3/C/1017
Ralph, gent., Langley Burrell, 1619, I, W, P1/C/93
Roger, gent., Hilmarton, 1670, I, W, P3/C/335
Wm., sen., gent., Clack, Lyneham, 1663, AB, comm, I, P3/C/287
Callimore *see* Cullimore
Callow, Ann, widow, matron of the Sal. Infirmary, Sal., 1804, W, P1/1804/125
Hy., serge weaver, Uffc., Devon, 1731-38, I, W, P20/1/171, 197
Honour, widow, Collingbourne D., 1728, I (detailed), note, W, P21/8/39
Rd., Collingbourne D., 1679, W (77 years old in 1677), P21/2/58
Rd., gent., Collingbourne D., 1692, AB, a/c (2), I (2 - 1 dated 1695), O, P21/5/12
Rd., gent., Collingbourne D., 1741, comm, W, P1/C/772, P1/9Reg/27A
Rd., former currier, d. 1820 in Winchester St Almshouses, Sal., 1843, AB, L, Wr, P1/1843/35-36
Rd. *see also* Ann Sheppard
Sam., yeo., Uffc., Devon, 1800, W, P5/1800/28, P5/18Reg/300B
Calloway *see* Callaway
Calsay *see* Kelsey
Calverley, Geo., innholder, *The Bell Inn*, Thatcham, Berks., 1720, W, P1/C/603, P1/6Reg/319
Cam *see* Came
Cambridge, Ann, widow, Devizes, 1806, AB, comm, Wr, P1/1806/4
Anth., Milbourne, Malm., 1632, I, W, P3/C/179
Eliz., widow, Chipp., 1807, W, P3/1807/57
Jas., Langley Burrell, 1715, AB, I, P3/C/693
Jane, widow, Pickwick, Corsham, 1711, I, W, P29/C/14
Jn., Chipp., 1753, W, P3/C/923
Jn., Castle C., 1762, AB, P28/20
Robt., vict., Pickwick, Corsham, 1722, AB, I, W, P29/C/16, P29/2Reg/38
Robt., Avill's Farm, Corsham, 1753, AB, P1/C/861
Robt., Easton, Corsham, 1800, I, W, P29/1800-1857/1
Wm., carp., Chipp., 1754, W, P3/C/929
Wm., gent., Chipp., 1833, W, Wr, P3/1833/38
Camden, Comden, Anth., yeo., Holnest, Dorset, 1830, W, Wr, P5/1830/3
Giles, Minety, 1636, AB, a/c, comm, I, P3/C/209
Comden, Robt., husb., Forston, Charminster, Dorset, 1562, W, P5/1Reg/18
Came, Cam, Hy., Marl., 1769, AB, P1/C/954
Matthew, cordw., New Windsor, Berks., 1611, AB, I, P1/C/47
Wm., Over Zeals, 1639, AB, I, P5/1639/16
Wm., Mere, 1639, AB, P5/13Reg/176A
Camelford, Nich., tailor, Lyme R., Dorset, 1628, AB, I, P5/1628/23, P5/11Reg/71A
Camery, Robt., clerk, Dauntsey, 1697, I, W, P3/C/596
Camfick *see* Kenfick
Cammell, Wm., yeo., Bere R., Dorset, 1687, AB, I, P5/1687/10
Campbell, Betty, sp. and physican's daughter, Sutton B., 1756, L, req, W, copy W, P1/C/889, P1/11Reg/313
Betty, widow, Sutton B., 1765, W, P3/C/984
Jn., Sutton B., 1762, W, P3/C/963
Campeny, Jn., clothier, Uffc., Devon, 1546, W, P20/Reg/34
Camphy, Wm., Sherb., Dorset, 1689, AB, comm, P5/1688/22
Cande *see* Candy
Candell, Candill, Francis, Swallowcliffe, 1622, AB, P5/1621/6, P5/10Reg/25B
Jn., yeo., Fovant, 1546, W, P1/2Reg/129, P2/1Reg/75B
Jn., Fovant Stroud, 1610, AB, I, P2/C/233, P2/8Reg/82A
Michael, Fovant, 1593, I, W, P2/C/121

Peter, Tisb., 1584, W, P2/6Reg/136A
Rd., husb., Bower C., 1648, cit, court papers (3), booklet of D (several), inty, NW, P2/C/481, 542
Robt., husb., Fovant, 1569, W, P2/5Reg/81A
Thos., labourer, Sal., 1581, NW, P4/Reg/6B
Thos., husb., Fovant, 1587-89, AB, I (2), T, W, P2/C/85, P2/7Reg/71B
Thos., husb., Fovant, 1625, I, W, P1/C/122
Wm., Fovant, 1610, AB, I, P2/C/236, P2/8Reg/84C
Candill, Wm., yeo., Bower C., 1644, I, W, P2/C/515
Candy, Chas., Donhead St My., 1850, AB, O, Wr, P2/1850/8
Christian, sp., Fovant Stroud, 1774, AB, W, P2/C/1373
Chris., Bishopstrow, 1612, a/c, P2/C/1508
Eliz., widow, Linley Farm, Tisb., 1628, I, W, P1/C/125
Eliz., servant to Viscount Weymouth at Longleat, Longleat, Horningsham, 1737, W, P2/C/1177
Eliz., Gillingham, Dorset, 1839, AB, P27/1/726
Hercules, yeo., Fovant, 1645, AB, I, P2/C/521
Humphrey, Fovant, 1638, I, W, P2/C/462
Jas., bach., Donhead St My., 1827, AB, Wr, P2/1827/34
Jane, widow, Fovant, 1763, W, P2/C/1316
Joan, widow, Fovant, 1604, W, P2/C/203
Leonard, Gillingham, Dorset, 1716, AB, P27/1/210
Mgt., widow, Horningsham, 1723, AB, I, P5/1723/6
Margery, widow, Fovant, 1669, I, W, P2/C/590
My., widow, Sedgehill, 1739, AB, P2/C/1190
Nich., carp., Fovant, 1630, I, NW, P2/C/390
Rd., E. Knoyle, 1685, AB, ren, P2/C/747
Rd., Fovant, 1728, AB, I, P2/C/1087
Robt., Tisb., 1724, AB, P2/C/1061
Robt., Sedgehill, 1808, AB, W, P2/1808/42
Robt., yeo., Fonthill G., 1813, W, Wr, P2/1813/60
Thos., E. Knoyle, 1668, AB, P2/C/580
Cande, Wm., sen., Fovant, 1645, I, W, P2/C/518
Wm., freemason, Fovant, 1668, comm, I, W, P1/C/289
Wm., Bere R., Dorset, 1675, AB, a/c, I, P5/1675/14
Wm., Semley, 1695, AB, I, P1/C/448
Wm., sen., yeo., Fovant, 1720, I, W, P1/C/590, P1/6Reg/231B
Wm., Motc., Dorset, 1770, AB, P27/1/473, P27/3Reg/157A
Wm., gent., Hindon, 1848, D, O, W, Wr, P2/1848/19
see also Gandy *or* C.
Cane, Eliz., widow, Maidenhead, Berks., 1773, W, P1/C/969, P1/12Reg/488A
Joan, widow, Winterbourne E., 1597, I, W, P2/C/146
Jn., husb., Winterbourne E., 1582, W, P2/6Reg/62A
Jn., Broad C., 1583, I, W, P2/C/60, P2/6Reg/94A
Jn., husb., Broad C., 1600, AB, I, W, P2/C/181
Jn., Broad C., 1616, AB, P2/C/292, P2/8Reg/304A
Rd., Winterbourne E., 1626, AB, P2/C/356
Robt., Broad C., 1617, T (unnamed children), P2/C/298
Robt., Alderbury, 1775, AB, P26/1079
Roger, Winterbourne E., [1628], NW, P2/C/384
Thos., husb., Winterbourne E., 1592, I, W, P2/C/112
Thos., weaver, Stratfield M., Berks., 1602, I, W, P1/C/17
Thos., yeo., Swallowfield, Shinfield, Berks., 1814, AB, D, W, Wr, P1/1814/98
Canfick *see* Kenfick
Canin *see* Cannings
Cannaway, Jn., yeo., Pewsham Forest, 1671, AB, a/c, I, P3/C/347
Maud, widow, Reading St Giles, Berks., 1608, AB, I, P1/C/38
Steph., yeo., Pewsham Forest, 1668, AB, I (detailed), ren, P1/C/291
Cannens *see* Cannon
Cannings, Agnes, widow, Charl. nr. P., 1577, I, W, P2/C/43, P2/5Reg/290B
Alexander, New Mill, Milton L., 1700, I, W, P3/C/617
Alexander, miller, New Mill, Milton L., 1745, W, P3/C/882

Eliz., widow, Milton L., 1710, W, P3/C/676
Canning, Eliz., minor, Collingbourne K., 1837, app. of guardian, O, T, Wr, P3/1837/76
Frances, Preshute, 1705, AB, P1/C/493
Jacob, clothw., Trowb., 1840, O, W, Wr, P1/1840/2
Jane, widow, Milton, E. Knoyle, 1811, comm, W, P1/1811/35
Canning, Jane, sp., Ogbourne St And., 1812, AB, comm, Wr, P5/1812/31
Canin, Jn., Hungerford, Berks., 1711, AB, P23/315
Jn., Preshute, 1723, AB, P1/C/627
Jn., sen., wool scribbler, Newbury, Berks., 1738, W, P1/C/758, P1/8Reg/292B
Canning, Jn., yeo., Richardson, Winterbourne Bassett, 1751, W, P3/C/907
Jn., yeo., Fyfield, Milton L., 1761, W, P3/C/956
Jn., Pewsey, 1806, AB, Wr, P3/1806/10
Canning, Jn. Davis, gent., Ogbourne St Geo., 1818, comm, W, Wr, P5/1818/37
Cannen *or* Canning, Mark, Pewsey, 1674, I, W, P1/C/317
Canning, My., gent.'s widow, Ogbourne St Geo., 1848, comm, W, Wr, P5/1848/3
Rd., servingman, Monkton F., 1567, I, W, P2/C/36, P2/5Reg/19B
Sam., Orcheston St My., 1835, AB, W, Wr, P2/1835/1
Sarah, sp., Hungerford, Berks., 1776, AB, P5/1776/8, P5/17Reg/120A
Thos., miller, Milton L., 1785, W, P3/C/1084
Canning, Thos., gent., Rams. Park Farm, 1841, note, W, Wr, P5/1841/7
Violetta, widow, Milton L., 1774, W, P3/C/1035
Wm., yeo., Marl., 1689, W, P1/C/395
Canning, Wm., gent., Ogbourne St And., 1827, comm, W, Wr, P5/1827/5
Canning, Wm., Collingbourne K., 1837, AB, O, Wr, P3/1837/77
Cannon, Abigail, widow, Kintbury, Berks., 1704, I, W, P1/C/482
Chas., Hungerford, Berks., 1771, AB, P23/735
Canon, Christian, widow, Shalbourne, Berks., 1575, I, W, P23/1017, P5/3Reg/72C
Edwd., husb., Winkfield, Berks., 1698, I, W, P1/C/458, P1/3Reg/68
Eliz., widow, Hungerford, Berks., 1824, AB, comm, Wr, P23/919
Hannah, Shalbourne, 1802, AB, P23/861
Canon, Jn., husb., E. End, Shalbourne, Berks., 1575-76, I, T (re Agnes C., minor), W, P23/1015-16, P5/3Reg/68C, 86D, 93C
Jn., Aughton, Collingbourne K., [1591], W (NEP), P3/1Reg/39B
Jn., husb., Figh., 1695, AB, I, P26/429
Jos., Marl., 1706, AB, ren, P1/C/497
Nathaniel, sen., weaver, Figh., 1645, I, W, P26/93
Rd., husb., Hungerford, Berks., 1618, W (NEP), P30/45
Cannens *or* Canons, Rd., sen., yeo., Porton, Idmiston, 1747, W, P1/C/818, P1/10Reg/67A
Robt., Hungerford, Berks., 1696, AB, I, P5/1696/13
Sarah, widow, Charnham St., Hungerford, Berks., 1773, AB, comm, P23/761
Thos., yeo., Ham, 1641, I, W, P1/C/188
Thos., sen., weaver, Figh., 1646, I, W, P26/96
Thos., sen., husb., Figh., 1710, I, W, P26/564
Cannon *or* Cannings, Thos., yeo., Grafton, 1767-79, AB, W, P21/10/72, P21/11/17
Wm., Overton, 1641, AB, I, P3/C/260
Wm., Holt, Kintbury, Berks., 1689, I, P1/C/1106 (found with P1/C/395)
Wm., sen., yeo., Figh., 1739, W, P26/811
Cannons, Wm., yeo., Figh., 1746, AB, I (detailed), P26/865
Wm., yeo., Speen, Berks., 1756, W, P1/C/877, P1/11Reg/243A
Wm., gent., Grafton (form. of Sal.), 1780, W, P21/11/19
Cannopp, Joan, widow, Charlton nr Malm., 1627, AB, a/c, I, P3/C/148
Canon, Canons *see* Cannon
Canter, Alice, widow, Chedglow, Crudwell, 1609, W, P3/C/37
Giles, Westport St My., 1778, W, P3/C/1055
Giles, gent., Burton Hill, Malm., 1839, O, W, Wr, P3/1839/33
Jas., Westport St My., 1739, AB, P3/C/844
Jn., husb., Corston, Malm., 1630, I, W, P3/C/164
Jn., husb., Chelworth, Crudwell, 1669, I, W, P3/C/323
Jn., Brokenb., 1687, I, W, P3/C/512
Jn., yeo., Brinkw., 1745, W, P3/C/883

Jn., Brokenb., 1782, AB, P3/C/1074
My., widow, Brokenb., 1723, W, P3/C/743
My., Westport St My., 1821, W, Wr, P3/1821/40
Thos., Chedglow, Crudwell, 1628, AB, I, P3/C/154
Wm., husb., Chedglow, Crudwell, 1624, I, W, P3/C/126
Canterbury, Jn., mason, Beam., Dorset, 1747, W, P17/508
My., widow, Beam., Dorset, 1696, W, P17/362
Cantloe, Amy, widow, Fonthill G., 1680, I, W, P1/C/342
Cath., widow, Fonthill G., 1612, AB, a/c, I, P2/C/260
Geo., surgeon, Linley, Tisb., 1681, I, W, P2/C/704
Hugh, Fonthill G., 1562, AB, I, P2/C/23, P2/4Reg/95D
Humphrey, Fonthill G., 1630, L, P2/C/398
Jas., Tisb., 1839, AB, ren, Wr, P2/1839/42
Jn., husb., Chitterne AS, 1612, W, P2/8Reg/182A
Jn., sen., maltster, Tisb., 1707, W, P2/C/945
Margery, widow, Damerham, Hants, 1665, I, W, P2/C/563
Thos., yeo., Stop, Fonthill G., 1610, I, W, P2/C/245, P2/8Reg/143B
Thos., Fonthill B., 1677, I, P2/C/668
Thos., husb., Hindon, 1693, AB, I, P2/C/834
Walter, glover, Hindon, 1673, I, W, P2/C/632
Walter, maltster, Tisb., 1703, W, P2/C/907
Wm., vict., Tisb., [1675], W, P2/C/653
Cantrell, Humphrey, gent., Wokm., Berks., 1689, note, T (re Humphrey C., jun., minor), W, P5/1689/9
Cantwell, Wm., yeo., Hillend Farm, Cumnor, Berks., 1711, I, W, P1/C/521, P1/5Reg/163B
Canworth, Arthur, Uffc., Devon, 1589, AB, T (child: Chris. C.), P5/1589/8, P5/5Reg/54B
Cape, Wm., Uffc., Devon, 1647, AB, a/c, I, P20/1/39
Capell, Chas., Cumnor, Berks., 1814, AB, comm, P1/1814/63
Capell, Geo., Fonthill G., 1731, W, P2/C/1131
Caplin, Caplin *or* Saplin, Rd., Sal., 1631, a/c, I (detailed), P4/1631/17
Wm., Woodley, W. and Sandford, Berks., 1815, W, Wr, P5/1815/2
Capp, Denise, widow, Melk., 1611, I, W, P2/C/257
Hy., weaver, Melk., 1606, I, W, P1/C/26
Jn., sen., weaver, Quemerford, Calne, 1663, I, W, P26/112
Nich., weaver, Melk., 1555, W, P2/1Reg/83B
Robt., weaver, Melk., 1598, I, W, P2/C/160
Robt., maltster, Calne, 1776, W, P26/1081
Card, Alice, sp., Ashton G., Codf. St P., 1687, AB, I, P2/C/777
Ann, widow, Codf. St My., 1631, I, W, P2/C/407
Cath., widow, Codf. St My., 1703, I, W, P2/C/910
Chas., yeo., Sal., 1709, W, P4/1709/13
Chris., yeo., Wylye, 1686, I, W, P2/C/772
Chris., maltster, Wylye, 1729, W, P2/C/1101
Edmd., clockmaker, Codf. St P., 1702, I, W, P2/C/901
Edwd., W. Hatch, Tisb., 1574, W, P2/5Reg/181A
Edwd., miller, Gillingham, Dorset, 1733, W, P27/1/323
Edwd., maltster, Gillingham, Dorset, 1788, W, P27/1/532, P27/3Reg/257
Edwd., Milton upon Stour, Gillingham, Dorset, 1810, W, P27/1/605
Humphrey, Codf. St My., 1617, AB, I, T, P2/C/295, P2/8Reg/316B
Jane, Sherb., Dorset, 1697, AB, I, P5/1697/12
Joan, widow, Tisb., 1543, W (NEP), P2/1Reg/48A
Jn., [shoemaker], Sal., 1621, I (includes bequests to shoemakers' company & chamber of S.), P4/1621/18
Jn., husb., Winterbourne D., 1673, I, W, P7/43
Jn., yeo., Tisb., 1677, I, NW, P1/C/326
Jn., Codf. St My., 1697, AB, P2/C/867
Jn., Ashton G., Codf. St P., 1705, W, P2/C/916
Jn., Sal., 1721, I, W, P4/1720/12
Jn., Milton upon Stour, Gillingham, Dorset, 1802, O, W, P27/1/576
Jos., yeo., Donhead St A., 1788, W, P2/C/1446
Jos., Donhead St A., 1813, AB, P2/1813/42
Martha, sp., Chipp., 1725, AB, comm, P3/C/754

My., widow, Gillingham, Dorset, 1725, W, P27/1/277
Maud, widow, Tisb., 1619, I, W (NEP), P1/C/86
Michael, W. Hatch, Tisb., 1558, I, W, P2/K/418, P2/3Reg/92B
Prudence, widow, Ashton G., Codf. St P., 1675, I, W, P2/C/648
Rawlins, husb., Tisb., 1604, AB, I, W, P2/C/202
Robt., sen., Calne, 1722, I, W, P5/1721/10, P5/16Reg/60C
Robt., hatter, Calne, 1737, AB, W, P5/1737/11
Roger, Tisb., 1541, W (NEP), P30/46B
Sampson, Maiden B., 1740, AB, P2/C/1203
Sam., baker, Gillingham, Dorset, 1743, W, P27/1/368, P27/3Reg/30B
Sam., sen., Mere Down Farm, 1833, comm, W, Wr, P5/1833/29
Steph., Chitterne AS, 1576, I, W, P2/C/39, P2/5Reg/255B
Thos., W. Hatch, Tisb., 1603, AB, P2/C/199
Thos., Downton, 1639, AB, I, P2/C/477
Thos., butcher, Gillingham, Dorset, 1687, I, P27/1/101
Thos., yeo., Gillingham, Dorset, 1722, W, P27/1/254
Thos., cooper, Wilton, 1728, AB, NW, P2/C/1099
Thos., miller, Donhead St A. (form. of Romsey, Hants), 1798, AB, ren, W, P2/C/1489
Thos., gent., Pierston, Gillingham, Dorset, 1824, W, Wr, P27/1/666
Walter, yeo., Wylye, 1671, I, W, P2/C/615
Wm., sen., yeo., Lt. Wishford, S. Newton, 1678, W, P2/C/678
Wm., wheelwright, Fisherton A., 1683, AB, a/c, I, P2/C/730
Wm., yeo., Calne, 1793, comm, W, P26/1189
Carden, Joan, widow, Benham Valence, Speen, Berks., 1619, I, W, P1/C/95
Jn., yeo., Beenham Valence, Berks., 1608, I, W, P1/C/37
Rd., Sal., 1637, AB, I, P4/1636/9
Wm., cordw., Sal., 1679, AB, a/c, I (2), P4/1679/6
Cardiff, Chas., Brokenb., 1672, AB, P3/C/353
Care *see* Keer als C.
Careles, Hy., miller, Warfield, Berks., 1664, AB, I, P1/C/272
Corless, Jn., labourer, Swindon, 1694, AB, I, P3/C/581
Carent, Eliz., widow, Wilton, 1547, W, P2/2Reg/32
Jas., surgeon, Sal., 1734, I (detailed), W, Wr, P4/1734/7
Jane, widow, Sal., 1762, AB, P4/1762/11
Wm., Sal., 1754, AB, P1/C/867
Careway *see* Carraway
Carey, Cary, Alice, widow, Corsley, 1671, I, W, P1/C/310
Cary, Anna, sp., Dragon St., Sal. St Mart., 1776, W, P1/C/990, P1/13Reg/87B
Edwd., yeo., E. Knoyle, 1802, W, Wr, P2/1802/28
Cary, Eliz., widow, Westport St My., 1758, W, P3/C/948
Eliz., sp., Sal., 1762, W, P4/1762/6
Geo., Durley, Burbage, 1680, AB, I, P11/51
Geo., sen., tiler and plasterer, Lacock, 1848, D, O, W, Wr, P3/1848/15
Cary, Hy., Milton L., 1571, AB, P1/1Reg/23H
Hester, widow, Lacock, 1855, aff, O, W, Wr, P3/1855/20
Cary, Jane, widow, Sal. The Close, 1756, W, P5/1756/4
Jn., Sal. The Close, 1628, I, P5/1627/9
Cary, Jn., Grimstone, Stratton, Dorset, 1634, I, NW. Proved at the Metropolitan visitation to Dorchester, P5/1634/28, P5/12Reg/289A
Jn., sen., yeo., Milton L., 1634, I, W, P1/C/149
Jn., yeo., Ash, Netherb., Dorset, 1733, I, W, P17/457
Jn., cordw., Wrou., 1829, W, Wr, P1/1829/136
Cary, My., widow, Whitbourne, Corsley, 1705, W, P2/C/918
Cary, My., sp., Chr. M., 1749, AB, W, P3/C/899
Cary, Robt., clerk, Fovant, 1724, W, P1/C/632, P1/7Reg/47B
Cary, Robt., clerk (of the Dunkirk man of war), Sal. The Close, 1738, AB, Wr, P5/1738/8
Cary, Susanna, widow, Dauntsey, 1687, I, W, P3/C/514
Cary, Susanna, sp., Dauntsey, 1718, AB, I, P3/C/709
Thos., Pewsey, 1606, I, W, P1/C/34
Cary, Thos., yeo., Haverings Heath, Burbage, 1631-32, I, NW, P5/1631/32, P5/12Reg/40C

Cary als Cur, Thos., yeo., Horton, Bps. C., 1675, AB, I, P24/435
Cary, Thos., gent., Gt. Bedwyn, 1689, AB, I, P21/4/34
Cary, Thos., clothw., Corsley, 1697, I, W, P2/C/863
Cary, Thos., Hindon, 1769, AB, P2/C/1347
Cary, Wm., sen., Dauntsey, 1670, AB, I, P3/C/337
Cary, Wm., carp., Lower Seagry, 1790, W, P3/C/1104
Wm., Lacock, 1855, AB, aff, O, Wr, P3/1855/26
Wm. Gilbt., attorney, Calne, 1849, O, W, Wr, P5/1849/15
Carkpatrick *see* Kirkpatrick
Carle *see* Curle
Carley, Jn., labourer, Alderbury, 1729, AB, I, ren, P26/730
Cearley, Mgt., sp., Brook Common, Dilton, Westb., 1722, W, P25/1722/2
Carman, Wm., Sherb., Dorset, 1776, AB, P5/1776/9, P5/17Reg/131A
Carnal, Jas., carp. and builder, Devizes, 1839, O, W, Wr, P1/1839/39
Carpenter, Abraham, farmer, Blackland, Calne, 1847, comm, W, Wr, P5/1847/9
Agnes, Corsley, 1549, W, P2/2Reg/83B
Alice, widow, Warm., 1551, W, P2/2Reg/137
Alice, widow, Britford, 1668, I, W, P24/370
Ann, widow, S. Newton, 1628, I, W, P2/C/379
Ann, widow, Conock, Chirton, 1683, I, W, P2/C/729
Ann, wife, Sal., 1724, W, P4/1724/14
Ann, widow, Crickl. St My. (form. of Toot Hill), 1838, AB, comm, ren, W, Wr, P3/1838/53
Ann, widow, Foxham, Bremhill, 1840, AB, comm, Wr, P3/1840/12
Bridget, widow, Upton S., 1674, I, W, P1/C/314
Cath., widow, Barford St Mart., 1564, W, P2/4Reg/159D
Chris., Corsley, 1590, I, W, P2/C/87
Chris., Upton S., 1618, AB, I, P2/C/304
Chris., yeo., Upton S., 1636, I, W, P2/C/446
Dan., yeo., Monkton D., 1750, AB, W, P2/C/1257
Dorothy, widow, Bugley, Warm., [1626], I, W, P2/C/365
Dorothy, widow, Lt. Bedwyn, 1693, I, W, P21/5/16
Edith, widow, Bulk. & Mannings Hill, Calne, 1740, W, P2/C/1206
Edmd., S. Newton, 1620, I, W, P2/C/320
Edwd., yeo., Warm., 1674, AB, comm, I, P2/C/640
Edwd., Seend, Melk., 1701, AB, P2/C/890
Edwd., sen., yeo., Chiseldon, 1733, W, P3/C/811
Edwd., Horningsham, 1735, AB, P5/1735/10
Carpenter als Wheeler, Eleanor, widow, Charlton, Downton, 1615, AB, I, P2/C/283, P2/8Reg/274E
Eliz., widow, Barford St Mart., 1579, W, P2/5Reg/351
Eliz., widow, Corsley, 1612, AB, a/c, P2/C/262
Eliz., widow, Bucklebury, Berks., 1671, AB, W, P1/C/309
Eliz., sp., Bradford A., 1714, AB, I (detailed), P1/C/543
Emma, Newton T., 1632, I, W, P2/C/413, P2/9Reg/59B
Geo., yeo., Barford St Mart., 1642, AB, copy AB, I, NW, P2/C/505
Geo., yeo., Barford St Mart., 1685, AB, I, W, P2/C/763
Geo., innkeeper, Wrou., 1815, W, Wr, P3/1815/70
Gerard, Bremhill, 1709, AB, P3/C/670
Hector, clerk and gent., Barford St Mart., 1662, I, T, W, P2/C/549
Hy., carp., Fovant, 1665, I, W, P2/C/560
Hy., yeo., Blackland, Calne, 1848, comm, W, Wr, P5/1848/1
Isabel, widow, Marden, 1596, I, W, P2/C/138
Jas., Lyme R., Dorset, 1588, AB, P5/5Reg/23F
Jas., yeo., Barford St Mart., 1625, I, W, P2/C/348
Jas., Hurdcott, Barford St Mart., 1689, AB, I, P2/C/796
Jas., Westb., 1726, AB, P25/1726/2
Jane, widow, Monkton D., 1750, W, P2/C/1258
Joan, widow, Conock, Chirton, 1557, W, P2/3Reg/18B
Joan, widow, Wokm., Berks., 1667, I, W, P5/1667/16
Jn., sen., Barford St Mart., 1545, W (NEP), P2/1Reg/64B
Jn., Chirton, 1551, W, P2/2Reg/128E

Jn., ale brewer, Fisherton A., 1551, W, P2/2Reg/134
Jn., Barford St Mart., 1558, W, P2/3Reg/122A
Jn.?, no abode stated but later endorsement mentions Conock, 1589, I (damaged, name & date missing), P2/C/81
Jn., husb., Charlton, Downton, 1592, I, T, W, P2/C/104
Carpenter als Wheeler, Jn., Bodenham, Nunton and B., 1593, T (children: Roger, Ambrose, Edith, Rd., Jn. & Eleanor C.), P2/C/1517
Jn., yeo., Barford St Mart., 1600, AB, I, W, P2/C/182
Jn., husb., S. Newton, 1605, AB, I, NW, P2/C/208
Jn., Bishopstrow, 1610, AB, P2/C/248, P2/8Reg/148A
Carpenter als Wheeler, Jn., Downton, 1616, AB, I, T, P2/C/289, P2/8Reg/302B
Jn., yeo., Warm., 1618, AB, I, P2/C/310
Jn., yeo., S. Newton, 1624, I, W, P2/C/342
Jn., tailor, Chapmanslade, Corsley, 1626, I, W, P2/C/366
Jn., Sal., 1632, indemnity bond, P1/C/145
Jn., Britford, 1638, AB, I, P24/299
Jn., sen., Barford St Mart., 1639, I, P2/C/467
Jn., carp., Norridge, Upton S., 1669, W, P2/C/597
Jn., thatcher, Thoulstone, Upton S., 1687, I, W, P1/C/379
Jn., sen., yeo., Mannings Hill, Calne, 1690, I, W, P26/393
Jn., yeo., Clyffe P., 1697, AB, I, P3/C/597
Jn., Manningford Bruce, 1700, AB, I, P3/C/618
Jn., porter to the Dean & Canons of Sal. Cathedral, Sal. The Close, 1717, I, W, P5/1717/8, P5/15Reg/407B
Jn., roper, Swindon, 1717, W, P3/C/704
Jn., yeo., Nether St., Bromham, 1724, I, W, P3/C/748
Jn., jun., gent., Sal. St Thos., 1748, AB, W, P4/1748/3
Jn., Dilton M., Westb., 1762, AB, P25/1762/4
Jn., Minety, 1769, AB, P3/C/1012
Jn., yeo., Corston, Malm., 1769, W, P3/C/1011
Jn., gent., Sal., 1771, W, P4/1771/2
Jn., Hungerford, Berks., 1774, AB, P23/757
Jn., weaver, Wilton, 1775, AB, P2/C/1378
Jn., yeo., Rudge, Froxfield, 1781, W, P3/C/1068
Jn., yeo., Blackland, Calne, 1789, W, P5/1789/4, P5/18Reg/155
Jn., yeo., Corston, Malm., 1796, W, P3/C/1127
Jn., Wanb., 1813, W, Wr, P3/1813/40
Jn., cooper, Warm., 1855, aff, O, W, Wr, P2/1855/26
Jos., yeo., Horningsham, 1733, AB, I, P5/1733/14
Jos., Newton T., 1763, W, P2/C/1315
Jos., yeo., Tossell's Farm, Calne, 1820, comm, W, Wr, P26/1334
My., widow, Edington, 1668, AB, comm, I, NW, P2/C/583
My., widow, Warm., 1678, AB, I, P2/C/673
Carpenter als Downer, My., Sal. The Close, 1680, AB, P5/1680/7
My., widow, Seend, Melk., 1700, comm, I, W, P2/C/883
My., Barford St Mart., 1703, AB, P2/C/903
My., sen., widow, Marden, 1765, W, P2/C/1322
Maud, widow, Charlton, Downton, 1552, I, W, P2/C/2, P2/2Reg/152B
Moses, yeo., Barford St Mart., 1690, AB, I, P2/C/806
Nathaniel, Marl., 1676, AB, I, P1/C/321
Nich., gent., Edington, 1633, AB, a/c, I, P2/C/416
Nich., Upton S., 1693, AB, I, P2/C/833
Oliver, husb., Chenys Farm, Warm., 1554, W, P2/2Reg/193B
Peter, vict., Warm., 1830, W, P2/1830/35
Philip, clerk, Seend, Melk., 1682, comm, I, W, P2/C/719
Philip, yeo., Gt. Somerford, 1794, W, P3/C/1121
Philip, servingman, Maunditts Park, Lt. Somerford, 1822, W, Wr, P3/1822/46
Ralph, Corsley, 1558, W, P2/3Reg/94B
Rebecca, widow, Rams., 1797, comm, W, P5/1797/11, P5/18Reg/229B
Rd., husb., S. Newton, 1564, I, W, P2/C/33, P2/4Reg/182D
Rd., yeo., Newton T., 1592, I, W, P2/C/103
Rd., Newton T., 1614, W, P2/8Reg/226

Rd., Woodb., 1626, I, W, P3/C/143
Rd., husb., Aughton, Collingbourne K., 1646, I, W, P1/C/211
Rd., yeo., Marden, 1670, W, P2/C/605
Rd., husb., Horningsham, 1671, comm, W, P5/1671/23
Rd., yeo., Witcomb, Hilmarton, 1676, AB, I, P3/C/385
Rd., blacksmith, Lt. Bedwyn, 1684, comm, I, W, P5/1683/15
Rd., Marden, 1763, AB, comm, P1/C/916
Rd., sen., Marden, 1766, AB, P2/C/1328
Robt., husb., Upton S., 1545, W (NEP), P2/1Reg/77B
Carpenter als Wheeler, Robt., Boscombe, 1554, W, P2/1Reg/18A
Carpenter als Wheeler, Robt., Downton, 1596, AB, I, P2/C/136
Robt., yeo., Newton T., 1620, I, W, P1/C/105
Carpenter als Wheeler, Robt., husb., Charlton, Downton, 1630, I, W, P2/C/397
Robt., husb., S. Newton, 1669, AB, I, P2/C/596
Robt., yeo., Conock, Chirton, 1670, W, P2/C/607
Robt., Marl., 1689, W, P1/C/406
Robt., yeo., Cherhill, 1689, I, W, P26/380
Robt., Penleigh, Dilton, Westb., 1711, AB, I (ref to weaving loom, but probably husbandman *or* yeoman), P25/1711/15
Robt., Rushall, 1713, AB, P2/C/983
Sam., scrivener, Lyme R., Dorset, 1625, AB, I, W, P5/1625/18, P5/10Reg/285
Steph., Newton T., 1603, AB, I, W, P2/C/200
Steph., Newton T., 1702, AB, P2/C/900
Thos., Barford St Mart., 1558, W, P2/3Reg/122B
Carpenter als James, Thos., husb., Enford, 1559, T (children: Thos., Agnes, Alice & Maud C. als J.), W, P2/C/10, P2/4Reg/11D
Thos., W. Dean, 1596, AB, P2/C/1521
Thos., husb., S. Newton, 1605, AB, I, copy W, W, P2/C/209
Thos., husb., Chapmanslade, Corsley, 1607, I, W, P2/C/219
Thos., Bodenham, Nunton and B., 1611, I, P2/C/252
Thos., fuller, Warm., [1622], I, W, P2/C/326
Thos., yeo., Hungerford, Berks., 1626, AB, I, T, P5/1625/23, P5/10Reg/242A
Thos., S. Newton, 1638, AB, a/c, I, P2/C/461
Carpenter als Wheeler, Thos., yeo., Nunton, N. and Bodenham, [1641], AB, I, P2/C/498
Thos., husb., Bishopstrow, 1646, I, W, P2/C/529
Thos., sen., yeo., Chittoe, Bps. C., 1698, AB, I, W, P24/498
Thos., Seend, Melk., 1735, AB, P2/C/1171
Thos., S. Newton, 1746, AB, P2/C/1234
Thos., yeo., Rams., 1773, AB, comm, ren, P5/1773/11, P5/17Reg/49A
Thos., gent., S. Newton, 1775, W, P2/C/1376
Wm., Charlton, Downton, 1547, W (NEP), P2/1Reg/81A
Wm., Barford St Mart., 1552, AB, I, P2/C/4, P2/2Reg/156A
Wm., sen., Marden, 1587, W, P2/7Reg/71D
Wm., Netherh., 1591, AB, I, W, P2/C/96
Wm., yeo., Bugley, Warm., 1625, AB, I, P1/C/120
Wm., Fovant, 1638, AB, a/c, I, P1/C/184
Wm., sen., yeo., Barford St Mart., 1638, I, W, P2/C/459
Wm., husb. and yeo., Shute, Horningsham, 1663, comm, I, W, P5/1663/13
Wm., Horningsham, 1665, I, W, P5/1665/14
Wm., Fovant, 1690, AB, P2/C/802
Wm., sen., maltster, Crockerton, Longbridge D., 1730, W, P2/C/1116
Wm., Longbridge D., 1746, AB, P2/C/1238
Wm., yeo., Avon, Stratford sub C., 1754, W, P4/1754/12
Wm., Wanb., 1819, AB, Wr, P3/1819/18
Wm., parish clerk, Calne, 1837, comm, W, Wr, P26/1427
Wm., farmer, Roughlease Farm, Calne, 1857, D, note, W (2), Wr, P26/1472
see also Hale als C.; James als C.; Jes als C.; Wheeler als C.

Carr, Bennet, vict., Upton S., 1759, AB, W, P2/C/1304
Geo., Wilton, 1743, AB, P2/C/1221
Joan, widow, Poulshot, 1586, W, P2/7Reg/42E
Jn., sen., yeo., Corsley, 1624, T, W, P2/C/346

Jn., yeo., Dilton, Westb., 1644, AB, I, P25/1644/4
Jn., Hungerford, Berks., 1666, AB, comm, P5/1666/11
Susan, Corsley, [1639], I, W, P2/C/468
Wm., husb., Corsley, 1553, W, P2/2Reg/176C
Wm., Horningsham, 1713, W, P5/1712/20, P5/15Reg/313A
Carraway, Rd., merchant, Horningsham, 1673, AB, comm, I, P5/1673/7
Robt., blacksmith, Lacock, 1696, AB, I, P3/C/589
Careway, Walter, Imber, 1575, AB, P2/5Reg/227C
Wm., yeo., Heytes., 1667, I, W, P5/1666/10
Wm., tailor, Longbridge D., 1726, W, P1/C/640, P1/7Reg/79A
Carret *see* Carrot
Carrick, Jn., living at N. Waltham, Hants, but W proved at Reading, Berks., 1767, W, P1/C/946, P1/12Reg/242B
Carrier, Eliza, wife, Bradford A., 1850, AB, O, Wr, P2/1850/29
Eliz., widow, Warm., 1740, W, P2/C/1202
Hannah, widow, Gillingham, Dorset (form. of Buckhorn Weston, Dorset), 1855, aff, D, W, Wr, P27/1/776
Hy., husb., Warm., 1678, I, W, P2/C/674
Wm., Seend, Melk., 1676, AB, P2/C/667
Carrington, Edwd., sen., yeo., Staverton, Trowb., 1759, W, P1/C/906, P1/11Reg/464A
Jn., husb., Holt, Bradford A., 1585, W, P2/7Reg/5D
Thos., weaver, Atworth, Bradford A., 1611, I, W, P1/C/43
Thos., Holt, Bradford A., 1721, AB, P2/C/1035
Thos., sen., blacksmith, Trowb., 1769, W, P1/C/955, P1/12Reg/288
Carrot, Chris., sen., Devizes, 1644, I, W, P1/C/203
Thos., hellier, Devizes St Jn., 1661, AB, comm, I, P1/C/240
Thos., Devizes, 1698, AB, P1/C/465
see also Garret als C.
Carruthers, Wm., brandy merchant, Wantage, Berks., 1831, aff, comm, W, Wr, P23/953
Carslake, Eliz., widow, Uffc., Devon, 1691, I, W, P20/1/117
Kerslake, Wm., yeo., Uffc., Devon, 1689, I, W, P20/1/111
Carson, Jos., Trowb., 1847, AB, O, Wr, P1/1847/22
Carswell, Carswell als Cole, Jn., Uffc., Devon, 1549, W, P20/Reg/39
Kerswell als Cole, Rd., Uffc., Devon, 1686, I, P20/1/137
Carswell als Cole, Robt., Uffc., Devon, 1549, W, P20/Reg/38
Robt., Lyme R., Dorset, 1693, AB, I, P16/120
Robt., gent., Lyme R., Dorset, 1740, W, Wr, P5/1740/22
Steph., fuller, Lyme R., Dorset, 1625, AB, I, P5/1625/19, P5/10Reg/274A
see also Cole als C.l; Cole als Kerswell als Cashere
Carter, [...], Enford, 1590, W, P2/C/1514
Alexander, sen., shepherd, Ablington, Figh., 1741, I, W, P26/821
Alice, Newbury, Gillingham, Dorset, 1563, W, P27/1Reg/14B
Alice, widow, Butterwick, Folke, Dorset, 1679, I, W, P5/1679/17
Alice, sp., Ashton K., [1714], W (NEP), P3/C/687
Alice, widow, Crickl. St My., [1720], W (NEP), P3/C/728
Ambrose, shoemaker, Sal., 1691, AB, I, P4/1691/8
Ann, widow, Boreham, Warm., 1727-30, AB, alleg, I, NW, P2/C/1082, 1120
Ann, widow, Remenham, Berks., 1729, AB, comm, P1/C/664
Ann, widow, Winterbourne E., 1747, AB, ren, P1/C/816
Ann, widow, Zeals, 1803, comm, W, P5/1803/9, P5/19Reg/35
Ann, widow, Ashton K., 1806, AB, Wr, P3/1806/44
Ann, widow, Fisherton A., 1812, W, Wr, P2/1812/13
Anth., yeo., Odstock, 1618, AB, I, P2/C/307
Anth., Sal., 1669, I, W, P4/1669/8
Benj., sen., husb., Boreham, Warm., 1695, I, W, P2/C/856
Benj., miller, Boreham, Warm., 1721, W, P2/C/1043
Chas., Stratford sub C., 1755, AB, P1/C/869
Chas., Sal., 1848, AB, Wr, P1/1848/62
Christian, Rowde, 1623, I, W, P3/C/120
Chris., shoemaker, Sal., 1712, W, P4/1712/3
Drewse, Bradford A., 1560, W, P2/4Reg/36C
Edith, widow, Patney, 1607, I, W, P2/C/218

Edmd., husb., Westbrook, Gt. Faringdon, Berks., 1613, I, W, P1/C/60
Edmd., husb., Ashton K., 1625, I, W, P1/C/116
Edmd., mercer, Ashton K., 1705, W, P3/C/650
Edmd., innholder, Longbridge D., 1757, W, P2/C/1293
Edmd., sen., yeo., Crickl. St S., 1775, AB, W, P3/C/1041
Edmd. Morgan, tiler and plasterer, Crickl. St S., 1819, W, Wr, P3/1819/53
Edwd., yeo., Marl., 1637, I, W, P1/C/173
Edwd., sen., husb., Wilcot, 1638, I, W, P1/C/181
Edwd., saddler, Marl. St Peter and St Paul, 1684, AB, I (detailed), P1/C/368
Edwd., Wilcot, 1686, AB, I, P1/C/1121
Edwd., sen., saddler, Calne, 1706, I, W, P26/536
Edwd., yeo., Gt. Durnford, [1707], I, W (NEP), P9/36
Edwd., yeo., Leigh, Ashton K., 1805, W, P3/1805/1
Elias, husb., Fittleton, 1619, I, W, P1/C/87
Eliz., widow, Ashton K., 1611, I, W (NEP), P3/C/54
Eliz., sp., Berwick St Jas., 1662, AB, comm, P1/C/241
Eliz., widow, Durrington, 1701, AB, I, ren, W, P1/C/469, P1/4Reg/3
Eliz., sp., Idmiston, 1738, W, P2/C/1184
Eliz., widow, Leigh, Ashton K., 1782, W, P3/C/1075
Eliz., sp., Zeals, 1803, AB, comm, P5/1803/38, P5/19Reg/70A
Eliz., widow, Wilton, Gt. Bedwyn, 1817, AB, P21/12/37
Frances, widow, W. Dean, 1685, I, W, P2/C/751
Frances, sp., Hagbourne, Berks., 1729, W, P1/C/667, P1/7Reg/250
Frances *see* Frances Ball
Francis, gent. and innholder, Abingdon St Nich., Berks., 1689, I (detailed), W, P1/C/405
Francis, cordw., Upton, Blewbury, Berks., 1757, W, P5/1757/5
Geo., Ashton K., 1682, AB, I, P3/C/442
Geo., gent., Clarendon Park, 1790, W, P4/1790/3
Giles, tailor, Ashton K., 1639, I, W, P3/C/237
Giles, Orcheston St Geo., 1722, AB, P2/C/1503
Grace, widow, Winterbourne S., 1621, AB, a/c, P1/C/107
Gratian, no abode stated, 1650, I, W, P1/C/229
Hy., Ashton K., 1608, AB, P3/C/28
Hy., Ashton K., 1630, AB, a/c, P3/C/165
Hy., Cleverton, Lea and C., 1664, AB, comm, P3/C/295
Jas., husb., Boyton, 1616, I, W, P2/C/293
Jas., gent., Melchet Park, 1685, I, W, P2/C/753
Jas., Haxton, Fittleton, 1700, AB, P2/C/887
Jas., shoemaker, Berwick St Jas., 1807, W, P1/1807/26
Joan, Enford, 1561, I, P2/C/17
Joan, widow, Imber, 1599, AB, W, P2/C/169
Joan, widow, Fifield, Enford, [1613], I, W, P2/C/271
Joan, widow, Ash, Netherb., Dorset, 1662, I, W, P17/246
Joan, widow, Ashton K., 1663, I, W (damaged), P3/C/288
Joan, widow, Winterbourne G., 1673, I, W, P2/C/637
Joan, sp., Ashton K., 1721, W, P3/C/733
Jn., Coombe, Enford, 1543, W (NEP), P2/1Reg/64A
Jn., yeo., Chitterne AS, 1552, I, W, P2/C/3, P2/2Reg/154B
Jn., husb., Chitterne St My., 1553, W, P2/2Reg/180C
Jn., sen., Fifield, Enford, 1555, W (NEP), P2/1Reg/98B
Jn., husb., Tilsh., 1564, AB, I, W, P2/C/34, P2/4Reg/187C
Jn., yeo., Blewbury, Berks., 1588, I, T, W, P5/1588/9, P5/5Reg/39A
Jn., husb., W. Ashton, Steeple A., 1594, I, W, P2/C/124
Jn., Imber, 1598, W, P2/C/1522
Jn., husb., Chitterne AS, 1600, W, P2/C/176
Jn., sen., Stratton St Mgt., 1602, I, W, P1/C/14
Jn., sen., husb., Ashton K., 1602, I, W, P1/C/13
Jn., husb., W. Ashton, Steeple A., 1603, I, W, P2/C/194
Jn., husb., Moulsford, Cholsey, Berks., 1628, I, W, P1/C/132
Jn., horner, Sal., 1673, AB, a/c, court proceeding, I, P4/1673/5

Jn., collarmaker, Winterbourne G., 1681, I, W, P2/C/696
Jn., Ashton K., 1682, AB, I, P3/C/443
Jn., husb., Fittleton, [1684], I, W, P2/C/740
Jn., Durnford, 1688, AB, I, P9/23
Jn., Whitep., 1703, AB, P2/C/902
Jn., gent., Downton, 1709, W, P2/C/951
Jn., carp., Hurdcott, Winterbourne E., 1711, W, P2/C/972
Jn., clothw., Newbury, Berks., 1711, I, W, P1/C/526, P1/5Reg/202
Jn., yeo., Pincent's Farm, Tilehurst, Berks., 1717, AB, I (detailed), P1/C/579
Jn., Remenham, Berks., 1729, AB, comm, P1/C/662
Jn., Newtown, Enford, 1733, AB, P2/C/1146
Jn., gent., Tilehurst, Berks., 1735, W, P1/C/736, P1/8Reg/21
Carter als May, Jn., yeo., Wilcot, 1735, W, P3/C/825
Jn., carp., Sal., 1735, AB, a/c (in minority of Jn. C., jun.), I, W, P4/1734/18
Jn., tailor, Castle St., Sal., 1739, W, P1/C/769, P1/8Reg/401
Jn., vict. *or* innholder, Chipp., 1741, AB, alleg, answers to alleg, D (2), I (2), W, P3/C/859
Jn., collarmaker, Fisherton A., 1743, W, P2/C/1223
Jn., innholder, Longbridge D., 1744, W, P2/C/1224
Jn., miller, Sandford, Woodley and S., Berks., 1746, W, P5/1746/12
Jn., yeo., Wrou., [1751], W (NEP), P3/C/908
Jn., yeo., Leigh, Ashton K., 1753, W, P1/C/859, P1/11Reg/78
Jn., collarmaker, Fisherton A., 1765, W, P2/C/1327
Jn., Whaddon, Alderbury, 1793, AB, P26/1190
Jn., yeo., Horningsham, 1803, comm, W, P5/1803/6, P5/19Reg/28
Jn., vict., Ashton K., 1809, W, Wr, P3/1809/18
Jn., sen., sack carrier, Warm. Common, 1822, comm, W, Wr, P2/1822/23
Jn., yeo., Westport St My., 1822, W, Wr, P3/1822/45
Jn., Haxton, Fittleton, 1831, AB, P2/1831/68
Jn., pig dealer, Crickl. St S., 1851, O, W, Wr, P3/1851/42
Jn., yeo., Ashton K., 1857, aff, O, W, Wr, P3/1857/9
Jonathan, woodman to the Marquess of Bath, Horningsham, 1826, W, Wr, P5/1826/9
Jos., Sal., 1829, AB, P1/1829/62
Jos., Horningsham, 1840, AB, Wr, P5/1840/16
Julian, widow, W. Ashton, Steeple A., 1680, AB, I, P1/C/336
Leonard, Littlecott, Enford, 1632, AB, I, P2/C/410
Lucy, widow, Calne, 1717, AB, P26/614
Mgt., Chitterne St My., 1559, W, P2/3Reg/185B
Mgt., widow, W. Knoyle, [1685], I, W, P2/C/754
Mgt., widow, Figh., 1706, I, W, P26/524
Carter form. Walker, Martha, labourer's wife, Warm., 1789, AB, P2/C/1452
My., widow, Leighs Marsh, Dilton, Westb., 1617, I, W, P25/1617/1
Carter als Simpkins, My., Lea and Cleverton, 1663, AB, comm, I, P1/C/260
My., widow, Moulsford, Cholsey, Berks., 1717, I, W, P1/C/575, P1/6Reg/140A
My., widow, Bucklebury, Berks., 1729, W, P1/C/679, P1/7Reg/275A
My., widow, Crickl. St S., 1778, AB, P3/C/1056
My., widow, White St., Horningsham, 1841, AB, W (& cod), Wr, P5/1841/21
Matthias, poulterer, Holt, Bradford A., 1833, O, W, Wr, P2/1833/57
Neville, cooper, Crickl. St S., 1753, AB, P3/C/924
Neville, gent., Sherston, 1837, W, Wr, P3/1837/80
Carter als Williams, Nich., husb., Durnford, 1636, I, W, P9/4
Olive, widow, Broad H., 1636, AB, a/c, P3/C/210
Olive, widow, Ashton K., 1851, O, W, Wr, P3/1851/28
Oliver, yeo., Leigh, Ashton K., 1682, I, W, P3/C/444
Oliver, gunsmith, Wootton B., 1784, comm, W, P3/C/1079
Oliver, gunmaker, Wootton B., 1822, AB, comm, P3/1822/31
Peter, clothier, Sal., 1692, AB, I, P1/C/414
Philip, Pitton, Alderbury, 1710, W, P2/C/967
Philip, yeo., Pitton, Alderbury, 1748, W, P26/880
Prudence, widow, Britford, 1730, W, P24/819
Rachel, cooper's wife, Wokm., Berks., 1724, AB, P5/1724/16

Rachel, widow, Wokm., Berks., 1743, W, Wr, P5/1743/15
Ralph, Fittleton, [1578], T (children: Thos., Jn., Elias, Leonard & Ralph C.), P2/C/47
Ralph, tailor, Fittleton, 1609, AB, T, W, P2/C/229, P2/8Reg/52A
Reynold, Stratton St Mgt., 1670, AB, I, P3/C/336
Rd., Enford, 1579-80, AB, I, W, P2/C/48, 53, P2/5Reg/340B, 354A
Rd., husb., W. Ashton, Steeple A., 1591, I, W, P2/C/92
Rd., Southbroom, 1609, I, W, P24/147
Rd., yeo., Odstock, 1617, I, W, P2/C/301
Rd., yeo., Idmiston, 1707, I, W, P2/C/947
Rd., Sherston, 1714, AB, P1/C/540
Rd., Ashton K., 1773, W, P3/C/1031
Rd., yeo., Preshute, 1797, W, P1/C/1090, P1/15Reg/29B
Robt., husb., Odstock, 1557, W, P2/3Reg/66
Robt., husb., Fittleton, 1562, I, W, P2/C/25, P2/4Reg/101B
Robt., husb., Over C., Dorset, 1593, I, W, P5/1593/22, P5/6Reg/40B
Robt., yeo. *or* husb., Calcutt, Crickl. St S., 1603, I, W, P3/C/6
Robt., yeo., W. Grimstead, 1609, AB, I, P2/C/228, P2/8Reg/39A
Robt., Fifield, Enford, 1630, W, P2/C/387
Robt., husb., Sherston, 1632, I, W, P3/C/180
Robt., sen., Enford, 1642, AB, P2/C/509
Robt., sen., yeo., Longstreet, Enford, 1648, I, note of probate, W, P2/C/540
Robt., [maltster?], Westbrook, Gt. Faringdon, Berks., 1685, AB, I, ren, P5/1685/21
Robt., yeo., Buckland, Berks., 1716, AB, I (detailed), P1/C/568
Robt., tailor, E. Harnham, Britford, 1717, W, P24/645
Robt., Wood Street Lane, Wootton B., 1741, AB, W, P3/C/860
Robt., yeo., Purton Stoke, 1761, W, P3/C/957
Robt. *see also* Sam. Monk
Roger, Sherston, 1634, I, W, P3/C/199
Roger, yeo., Eastrop, Highw., 1772, W, P10/1772/5
Rose, widow, Hurst, Berks., 1566, AB, P5/1Reg/75C
Rudolph, Fifield, Enford, 1562, W, P2/4Reg/90B
Sam., yeo., Hurst, Berks., 1728, W, P5/1728/19, P5/16Reg/201B
Simon, husb., Fifield, Enford, 1626, AB, I, W, P2/C/362
Simon, husb., Bagshot, Shalbourne, 1677, AB, I, P23/67
Simon, Bagshot, Shalbourne, 1743, AB, Wr, P5/1742/9
Simon, farmer, Liddington, 1796, W, P3/C/1128
Carter als Gyllett als Smith, Steph., Warm., 1588, I, T, P2/C/75
Susanna, widow, Gt. Durnford, 1714, I, W, P9/39
Thos., Enford, 1561, AB, P2/4Reg/88C
Thos., tanner, Mere, 1571, W, P5/2Reg/102D
Thos., husb., Hurst, Berks., 1585, I, W, P5/1585/18, P5/4Reg/113B
Thos., clerk and vicar, Chards., Devon, 1585, AB, I, P5/1585/19, P5/4Reg/142B
Carter als Williams, Thos., Bemerton, Fugg. St Peter, 1592, I, W, P2/C/105
Thos., husb., Coombe, Enford, 1606, AB, I, W, P1/C/27
Thos., Fifield, Enford, 1610, I, W, P2/C/235, P2/8Reg/120A
Thos., Odstock, 1615, AB, I, P2/C/288, P2/8Reg/292A
Thos., Winterbourne S., 1616, AB, comm, I, T, P2/C/294, P2/8Reg/325B
Thos., husb., Hilp., [1639], I, P2/C/475
Thos., yeo., Sal., 1651, AB, I, L, P1/C/233
Thos., yeo., W. Dean, 1663, AB, comm, I, ren, P1/C/256
Thos., husb., Butterwick, Folke, Dorset, 1664, I, NW, P5/1664/7
Thos., labourer, Swindon, 1667, AB, I, P3/C/314
Thos., sen., glover, Crickl. St My., 1678, I, W, P3/C/405
Thos., sen., husb., Ashton K., 1681, I, W, P3/C/430
Thos., sen., miller, Stanton Fitzwarren, 1682, I, W, P3/C/445
Thos., Durrington, 1682, AB, I, P2/C/705
Thos., yeo., Coombe, Enford, 1684, I, W, P2/C/739
Thos., gent., Cowesfield, Whitep., 1684, AB, I, P2/C/741
Thos., sen., Netheravon, 1686, AB, I, P12/127
Thos., Whitep., 1686, a/c, P2/C/769

Thos., sen., yeo., Ashton K., 1687, I, W, P3/C/513
Thos., gent., Winterslow, 1692, AB, W, P2/C/822
Thos., Crickl. St My., 1699, AB, P3/C/604
Thos., yeo., Ashton K., 1704, I, W, P1/C/487
Thos., yeo., Seend, Melk., 1717, ren, W, P2/C/1015
Thos., yeo., Shellingford, Berks., 1720, W, P1/C/596, P1/6Reg/295
Thos., yeo., Leigh, Ashton K., 1728, I, W, P3/C/773
Thos., labourer, Shrewton, 1760, I, W, P2/C/1307
Thos., cordw., Fisherton A., 1798, W, P2/C/1486
Thos., gent., Bradford A., 1802, comm, W, Wr, P2/1802/9
Thos., yeo., Chapmanslade, Dilton, Westb., 1829, W, P25/1829/8
Thos., tiler and plasterer, Malm., 1842, O, W, Wr, P3/1842/33
Thomasine, [shopkeeper and widow], Uffc., Devon, 1663, AB, I, P20/1/46
Vincent, husb., Odstock, 1559, W, P2/4Reg/1C
Walter, Bucklebury, Berks., 1671, AB, I, P1/C/307
Walter, Tinh., Edington, 1724, AB, P2/C/1504
Walter, yeo., Warm., 1729, W, P2/C/1102
Walter, vict., Tinh., Edington, 1753, comm, W, P2/C/1275
Wm., Fittleton, 1581, W, P2/6Reg/50A
Carter als Smith, Wm., yeo., Warm., 1607, AB, comm, I, P2/C/216
Wm., yeo., Purton Stoke, 1621, I, W, P3/C/111
Wm., husb., Enford, 1624, I, W, P2/C/341
Wm., husb., Uffcott, Broad H., 1636, I, W, P3/C/211
Wm., fustian weaver, Sherston, 1639, I, W, P3/C/238
Wm., saddler, Marl. St Peter and St Paul, 1644, AB, comm, NW, P1/C/198
Wm., yeo., Lt. Durnford, 1668, I, W, P9/10
Wm., bricklayer, White Waltham, Berks., 1671, AB, I, P1/C/306
Wm., husb., Ashton K., 1672, I, W, P3/C/354
Carter als May, Wm., husb., Wilcot, 1674, I, W, P3/C/370
Wm., Calcutt, Crickl. St S., 1681, I, W, P3/C/431
Wm., Ashton K., 1699, AB, P3/C/605
Wm., yeo., Winterbourne M., 1711, AB, I, P1/C/516
Wm., scrivener, Sal., 1733, AB, I, P4/1733/10
Wm., yeo., Ashton K., 1744, W, P1/C/798, P1/9Reg/290
Wm., carp., Hurdcott, Winterbourne E., 1747, W, P2/C/1240
Wm., innholder, Zeals, 1749, W, Wr, P5/1749/14
Wm., marine of the 47th Company on HMS *Barfleur*, Barford St Mart., 1759, W (printed naval form with attractive headings), P2/C/1301
Wm., Zeals, 1790, AB, P5/1790/5, P5/18Reg/157A
Wm., yeo., Horningsham, 1798, W, P5/1798/6, P5/18Reg/261C
Wm., builder, Fisherton A., 1801, W, P1/1801/107, P1/15Reg/325
Wm., shopkeeper, Crickl. St S., 1811, W, Wr, P3/1811/3
Wm., bach., Fisherton A., 1815, AB, Wr, P2/1815/10
Wm., yeo., Crickl. St S., 1820, W, Wr, P1/1820/53
Wm., sack carrier, Warm. Common, 1835, W, P2/1835/28
Wm., sen., clock and watchmaker, Sal., 1854, AB, aff, W, Wr, P4/1854/11
Wm., husb., Shrewton, [1686], I, W, P2/C/765
Zebulon, Sunton, Collingbourne K., 1702, AB, I, P3/C/636
Zebulon, carp., Tidcombe and Fosbury, 1761, AB, I, P3/C/958
Zebulon, bach., Wilton, Gt. Bedwyn, 1797, AB, P21/11/43
Zebulon, husb., Gt. Bedwyn, 1809, W, P21/12/23
Zebulon, Wilton, Gt. Bedwyn, 1848, AB, comm, Wr, P5/1848/12
see also Ashwell als C.; Barnes/Barns als C.; Edmonds/Edmund als C.; May als C.; Palmer als C.; Williams als C.
Cartrowll *see* Courtroll
Cartwright, Martha, widow, Wantage, Berks., 1718, W, P23/367
My., Wantage, Berks., 1730, AB, P23/470
Thos., gent., Shrewton, 1700, W, P2/C/886
Thos., yeo., Charlton, Wantage, Berks., 1705, I, W, P23/275
Thos., Lyme R., Dorset, 1764, AB, P16/326
Carver, Ann, widow, Shalbourne, 1720, comm, W, P5/1719/19, P5/16Reg/36A

Corver, Francis, husb., Shalbourne, 1702, I, W, P23/248
Corver, Jas., yeo., Shalbourne, 1719, comm, NW, P5/1719/18, P5/16Reg/34A
Geo., Horningsham, 1702, W, P5/1702/15
Jas., Shalbourne, 1794, W, P23/798
Corver, Jn., innkeeper, Bagshot, Shalbourne, [1735], W (NEP), P23/507
Curver?, Thos., Hungerford, Berks., 1566, AB, P5/1Reg/50B
Thos., Sonning, Berks., 1663, AB, I, P5/1663/14
Carver als Lewis, Thos., labourer, Compton, Berks., 1668, I, W, P1/C/293
Corver, Thos., labourer, Collingbourne K., 1742, AB, ren, P3/C/870
see also Tayler als C.
Carway, Wm., Pott., 1570, W, P1/1Reg/37C
Carwood, Wm., gent., Abingdon, Berks., 1750, W, P1/C/838, P1/10Reg/348
Cary *see* Carey
Casbeard, Christian, widow, Aston U., Blewbury, Berks., 1603, I, W, P5/1603/17, P5/7Reg/83
Chris., yeo., Blewbury, Berks., 1625, AB, a/c, I, P5/1625/14, P5/10Reg/304B
Edwd., Aston U., Blewbury, Berks., 1722, AB, P5/1722/9
Eleanor, widow, Blewbury, Berks., 1748, W, Wr, P5/1748/5
Eliz., widow, Blewbury, Berks., 1775, W (& cod), P5/1775/5, P5/17Reg/92
Jn., sen., carp., Blewbury, Berks., 1683, I, W, P5/1683/13
Jn., sen., Blewbury, Berks., 1713, W, P5/1713/21, P5/15Reg/368B
Jn., sen., yeo., Blewbury, Berks., 1762, W, P5/1762/8
Casebert, Jos., clerk, Westport St My., 1696, AB, I, P3/C/590
Sarah, sp., Blewbury, Berks., 1739, W, Wr, P5/1739/11
Thos., Aston U., Blewbury, Berks., 1628, I, W, P5/1628/19, P5/11Reg/86A
Case, Abiah, yeo., Enmore Grn, Motc., Dorset, 1810, comm, W, Wr, P27/1/607
Bart., sen., yeo., Cowesfield, Whitep., [1674], I, W, P2/C/646
Bart., barber, Sal., 1715, AB, a/c, cert of surrender of goods, P4/1715/6
Bart., yeo., Cowesfield, Whitep., 1718, I, W, P2/C/1019
Benj., clothier, Kershay, Netherb., Dorset, 1750, W, P17/516
Benj., carp., Lyme R., Dorset, 1831, comm, W, Wr, P16/405
Christian, Chilmark, 1559, W, P2/4Reg/20B
Christian, widow, Hole, Lyme R., Dorset, 1614, comm, I, W, P5/1614/13, P5/9Reg/146
Dan., clothier, Kershay, Netherb., Dorset, 1779, W, P5/1779/4, P5/17Reg/166
Hy., Sal., 1730, AB, P4/1729/11
Hy., grocer, Amesb., 1788, W, P2/C/1449
Hugh, labourer, Netherb., Dorset, 1716, AB, I, P5/1716/19
Jas., baker, Lyme R., Dorset, 1838, AB, comm, Wr, P16/418
Joanna, widow, Beam., Dorset, 1775, W, P17/567
Jn., yeo., Chilmark, 1558, W, P2/3Reg/102C
Jn., yeo., Compton C., 1693, I, W, P2/C/827
Jn., Fole, Netherb., Dorset, 1696, AB, I, P17/354
Jn., Sal., 1723, AB, P1/C/610
My., widow, Lanchitcraste, Lyme R., Dorset, 1635, AB, I, P5/1635/17, P5/12Reg/222A
Rd., yeo., Compton C., 1669, I, W, P2/C/585
Sam., button mould cutter, Motc., Dorset, 1799, W, P27/1/563
Sam., E. Knoyle, 1832, AB, W, Wr, P2/1832/21
Sarah, sp., Strode, Netherb., Dorset, 1781, comm, W, P17/572
Susan, hempdresser's wife, Beam., Dorset (form. of Whitchurch, Dorset), 1815, AB, P5/1815/5
Thos., husb., Gt. Somerford, 1616, AB, I, P3/C/81
Thos., yeo., Hole, Lyme R., Dorset, 1631, comm, I, W, P5/1631/35, P5/11Reg/173B
Thos., butcher, Lyme R., Dorset, 1712, W, P16/193
Wm., yeo., Cowesfield, Whitep., 1739, AB, W, P2/C/1189
Wm., Amesb., 1798, W, P1/C/1102, P1/15Reg/144
Casebert *see* Casbeard
Caselman, Edith, widow, Bulford, 1620-21, a/c, I, T, W, P2/C/315
Castlemain, Enoch, Milston, 1798, AB, P1/C/1094, P1/15Reg/57A
Jn., husb., Bulford, 1619, I, NW, P2/C/313
Jn., Bulford, 1729, AB, NW, P1/C/665, P1/7Reg/231
Robt., husb., Bulford, 1631, I, copy I, W, P2/C/401
Casement, Jn., husb., Sonning, Berks., 1718, W, P5/1718/5, P5/15Reg/412A

Caseway *see* Cawsey
Casher, David, shepherd, Charminster, Dorset, 1710, W, P5/1710/23, P5/15Reg/195B
Edwd., innholder, Bere R., Dorset, 1809, W, Wr, P5/1809/16
Edwd., husb., Charminster, Dorset, 1702, AB, comm, I, W, P5/1702/20
Eliz., widow, Leigh, Yetm., Dorset, 1737, W, P5/1737/10
My., widow, Bere R., Dorset, 1817, W, Wr, P5/1817/7
see also Cole als Kerswell als C.
Caslake, Edwd., carrier, Corsham, 1696, AB, I, P29/C/13, P29/1Reg/265A
Geo., Corsham, [1735], W, P29/C/19
Hy., gunsmith, Corsham, 1716, I, W, P29/C/15, P29/2Reg/21
Hester, sp., Corsham, 1753, I, W, P29/C/20, P29/2Reg/82
Castlack, Jas., Corsham, 1717, marriage licence, P29/2Reg/25A
Castlack, Jane, sp., Jaggards, Corsham, [1766], W, P29/2Reg/138
My., sp., Corsham, 1738, I, P29/C/21
Robt., carrier, Corsham, 1695, AB, I, P29/C/12, P29/1Reg/262B
Thos., Corsham, 1685, AB, I, P29/C/9
Casmore, Rd., priest, Alvediston, 1557, W, P2/3Reg/47A
Cass, Eliz., widow, Heytes., 1583-84, AB, P5/1584/5, P5/4Reg/93A
Cass, Jas., tailor, Sherb., Dorset (form. of Middlemarsh, Dorset), 1830, W, Wr, P5/1830/28
Cassell, Cussell, Rd., Sonning, Berks., 1841, W, Wr, P5/1841/9
Wm., yeo., Overton, 1763, AB, P1/C/918
Cassey, Jn., collarmaker, Wilton, 1829, W, Wr, P2/1829/16
Wm., Ashton K., 1724, AB, P3/C/749
Casswell *see* Caswell
Castan *see* Caston
Castlack *see* Caslake
Castle, Eliz., sp., Worlds End, Hampstead N., Berks., 1753, AB, W, P1/C/851, P1/10Reg/498A
Castel, Frances, widow, Reading, Berks., 1698, ren, W, P1/C/460, P1/3Reg/80
Hester, widow, Cherhill, 1741, W, P26/827
Jeremiah, tailor, Whitley, Melk., 1779, AB, W, P2/C/1400
Jn., Ludwell, Donhead St My., 1628, AB, I, P2/C/383
Jn., blacksmith, Wantage, Berks., 1696, I, W, P5/1696/11
Castel, Jn., tailor, Shaw, Melk., 1763, W, P1/C/922, P1/12Reg/116B
Lawr., gent., Wantage, Berks., 1676, I, W, P23/61
Paul, Box, 1809, comm, W, Wr, P3/1809/47
Rd., Sal. The Close, 1760, AB, W, P5/1760/4
Rd., Abingdon, Berks., 1786, AB, P1/C/1047
Castel als Williams, Sam., carp., Aldbourne, 1705, I, W, P3/C/651
Susanna, sp., Gillingham, Dorset, 1743, AB, P27/1/369, P27/3Reg/23A
Wm., yeo., Wytham, Berks., 1823, comm, W, Wr, P1/1823/143
Wm., farmer, Gillingham, Dorset, 1826, W, Wr, P27/1/674
Wm., yeo., Hodson, Chiseldon, 1854, comm, O, W, Wr, P3/1854/42
see also Penn form. C.
Castlemain *see* Caselman
Caston *see* Costen
Caswell, Agnes, sp., Castle Eaton, 1628, I, W, P1/C/128
Casswell, Jas., vict., Trowb., 1795, comm, W, P1/C/1080, P1/14Reg/604
Jn., Beckhampton, Avebury, 1731, W, P3/C/789
Jn., sen., joiner, Beckhampton, Avebury, 1735, W, P1/C/734, P1/8Reg/43
Jn., sen., yeo., Cherhill, 1788, comm, W, P26/1158
Jn., vict., Melplash, Netherb., Dorset, 1792, AB, comm, W, P17/581
My., clothw.'s wife, Kington L., 1722, AB, P3/C/738
My., widow, Cherhill, 1834, comm, W, Wr, P26/1408
Philip, widow, Bourton, Bps. C., 1664, comm, I, W, P24/337
Rd., husb., Cherhill, 1667, AB, comm, I, P26/136
Casswell, Rd., yeo., Rowde, 1730, AB, ren, P3/C/797
Robt., Yatesbury, 1626, I, W, P3/C/139
Robt., yeo., Yatesbury, 1752, W, P3/C/916
Thos., husb., Castle Eaton, 1626, I, W, P3/C/140
Thos., yeo., Bremhill, 1768, comm, W, P3/C/1002

Timothy, yeo., Ogbourne St And., 1808, W, P23/855
Timothy, blacksmith, Ogbourne St And., 1824, W, P23/916
Timothy, blacksmith, Avebury, 1836, O, W, Wr, P3/1836/7
Wm., yeo., Cherhill, 1707, W, P5/1707/11, P5/15Reg/24B
Wm., W. Kennett, Avebury, 1740, AB, P3/C/852
Wm., Yatesbury, 1765, AB, P3/C/985
Wm., yeo., Brinkw., 1826, W, Wr, P1/1826/145
see also Oswell als C.
Catcet *see* Catcott
Catchmay, Thos., Calstone W., 1737, AB, P3/C/832
Wm., yeo., Cherhill, 1763, W, P26/1002
Catcott, Catcote, [...] *see* Rd. Ivy, clerk, Mkt. L.
Agnes, Steeple L., 1566, W, P2/4Reg/228B
Catcet *or* Catkit, Alexander, Stratford sub C., 1633, AB, I, W, P4/1633/9
Alice, widow, Steeple L., 1597, AB, I, W, P2/C/143
Edith, Gt. Wishford, 1565, W, P2/4Reg/202D
Eliz., minor, Alderbury, 1722, T, P26/666
Joan, widow, Gt. Wishford, 1615, I, W, P2/C/286, P2/8Reg/284B
Jn., W. Lavington, c1540, W (NEP), P30/201A
Jn., Orcheston St Geo., 1592, I, T, W, P2/C/111
Jn., Gt. Wishford, 1640, I, W, P2/C/484
Leonard, Gt. Wishford, 1602, AB, I, W, P2/C/188
Steph., Gt. Wishford, 1613, I, W, P1/C/55
Wm., Steeple L., 1557, W, P2/3Reg/56B
Wm., husb., Gt. Wishford, 1585, W, P2/7Reg/12A
Wm., Steeple L., 1589, I, W, P2/C/78
Cate, Agnes, widow, Chards., Devon, 1627, comm, I, W, P5/1626/9, P5/11Reg/12
Geo., yeo., Chards., Devon, 1605, W, P5/1605/15, P5/8Reg/78B
Mgt., widow, Chards., Devon, 1582, I, W, P5/1582/13, P5/4Reg/39A
Thos., Leigh, Yetm., Dorset, 1695, I, NW, P19/70
Wm., husb., Chards., Devon, 1568, W, P5/2Reg/33B
Wm., Chards., Devon, 1596, I, T, W, P5/1596/15, P5/6Reg/127
Wm., weaver, Chards., Devon, 1670, I, W, P14/32
see also Keate
Cater, Keator, Eliz., widow, Holt, Bradford A., 1674, I, W, P1/K/77
Jn., husb., Holt, Bradford A., 1574, W, P2/5Reg/206B
Cator, Jn., draper, Sal., [1580], W (incomplete - end & note of probate wanting), P4/Reg/9
Lawr., yeo. and gent., Shurnhold, Melk., 1702, I, W, P2/C/898
My., sp., Leigh, Bradford A., 1707, I, W, P2/C/944
My., widow, Westb., 1739, W, P25/1739/2
Rd., Downton, 1583, AB, I, P2/C/63, P2/6Reg/94B
Rd., Gt. Faringdon, Berks., 1725, AB, I, P5/1725/12
Roger, yeo., Westb., 1643, AB, I, P25/1643/1
Roger, maltster, Westb., 1694, I, ren, W (NEP), P25/1694/8
Roger, clothw., Melk., 1698, AB, comm, I, P2/C/878
Roger, sen., yeo., Westb., 1725, AB, comm, ren, W (NEP), P25/1725/4
Roger, yeo., Westb., 1772, W (to be buried in Old Meeting House yard), P25/1772/2
Thos., glazier, Trowle, Bradford A., 1725, comm, W, P2/C/1072
Wm., husb., Holt, Bradford A., 1589, I, T, W, P2/C/80, P2/4Reg/1B
Wm., plumber, Bradford A., 1701, W, P1/C/470, P1/4Reg/15
Cathens, Ann, widow, Hoe Benham, Welford, Berks., 1747, W, P1/C/823, P1/10Reg/187
Cathringham, Thos., pewterer, Wokm., Berks., 1598, AB, I, W (2 attached but not clear whether *or* not 2nd one re Thos. C.), P5/1598/11, P5/6Reg/209
Catkate, Catkit *see* Catcott
Catley, Thos., husb., Bugley, Warm., 1591, I, W, P2/C/95
Cator *see* Cater
Cattle, Alexander, mason, Swindon, 1662, AB, I, P1/C/250
Cattell, Jn., Sherb., Dorset, 1614, AB, I, P5/1614/15, P5/9Reg/117A
Wm., stone cutter, Swindon, 1742, comm, W, P3/C/864
Caudell *see* Cadle

Cauderay *see* Cowdry
Caulfey *see* Calfey
Caull, Jn., Bramshaw, Hants, 1570, AB, P5/2Reg/90C
Caupin *see* Cawpin
Causon, Edwd., yeo., W. Crudwell, 1712, AB, I, P3/C/680
Causten *see* Costen
Causway *see* Cawsey
Cave, Abraham, yeo., Long Burton, Dorset, 1796, W, P5/1796/3, P5/18Reg/226A
Caffe, Agnes, Gillingham, Dorset, 1560, W, P27/1Reg/7A
Ann, sp., Winterslow (living at Longfleet, Poole, Dorset, 1825), 1825, W, Wr, P2/1825/65
Augustine, Gillingham, Dorset, 1577, W, P27/1Reg/32C
Edith, widow, Stockwood, Dorset, 1773, W, P5/1773/12, P5/17Reg/68B
Edwd., Langham, Gillingham, Dorset, 1577, W, P27/1Reg/32A
Edwd., butcher, Chetnole, Yetm., Dorset, 1755, W, P5/1755/8
Eliz., widow, Chetnole, Yetm., Dorset, 1733, W, P19/126
Francis, Norton B., 1735, AB, P1/C/726
Geo., vict., Sal., 1785, I, W, P4/1785/8
Hy., Langham, Gillingham, Dorset, 1574, W, P27/1Reg/29B
Caffe, Joan, widow, Langham, Gillingham, Dorset, 1570, W, P27/1Reg/22B
Joan, widow, Leigh, Yetm., Dorset, 1707, AB, P5/1707/12
Caffe, Jn., Hamp, Gillingham, Dorset, 1563, W, P27/1Reg/13B
Jn., husb., Madjeston, Gillingham, Dorset, 1571, W, P27/1Reg/25B
Jn., Mere, 1576, AB, I, P5/1576/9, P5/3Reg/92A
Jn., bodicemaker, Chetnole, Yetm., Dorset, 1700, NW, P19/82
Jn., cutter, Sal., 1709, I, P4/1709/22
Jn., Thornford, Dorset, 1788, W, P5/1788/7, P5/18Reg/112
Jn., yeo., Long Newnton, 1813, W, Wr, P3/1813/26
Luke, Sherb., Dorset, 1715, AB, P5/1715/10
Martha, widow, Sal., 1787, AB, P4/1787/10
Nich., labourer, Gillingham, Dorset, 1756, AB, I, P27/1/413, P27/3Reg/73A
Peter, Lotborne, Gillingham, Dorset, 1582, W (& cods), copy W, P27/2Reg/14
Robt., butcher, W. Woodhay, Berks., 1616, AB, a/c, I (killed by fall from cart), P1/C/78
Silas, farmer, Chetnole, Yetm., Dorset, 1712, W, P19/97
Thos., tanner, Chetnole, Yetm., Dorset, 1719, AB, I, P5/1719/20
Thos., gent., Leigh, Yetm., Dorset, 1747, NW, P19/146
Thos., Stockwood, Dorset, 1750, W, P5/1750/5
Thos., Holnest, Dorset, 1756, AB, P5/1756/5
Wm., Gillingham, Dorset, 1566, W, P27/1Reg/17A
Wm., Lotborne, Gillingham, Dorset, 1577, W, P27/1Reg/32B
Wm., vict., Stockwood, Dorset, 1738, W, P5/1738/9
Wm., jun., Fordington, Dorset, 1804, AB, P15/174
Wm., labourer, Langham, Gillingham, Dorset, 1818, W, Wr, P27/1/638
see also Langford als C.
Cavey, Cavies, Rd., Corsham, 1656, AB, P29/1Reg/159B
Robt., Medbourne, Liddington, 1784, W, P3/C/1080
Cawfey *see* Calfey
Cawlie *see* Cowley
Cawood, Wm., jun., servant to Wm. C., Sandhurst, Berks., 1582, I, W, P5/1582/11, P5/4Reg/50B
Cawpin, Cawpin *or* Caupin, Wm., yeo., Nether Zeals, 1619, AB, I, P5/1619/15, P5/10Reg/61B
Cawsey, Causway, Ann, sp., Devizes, 1707, AB, P1/C/499
Causway, Geo., brazier, Devizes St Jn., 1728, W, P1/C/658, P1/7Reg/188
Cowsey, Hy., yeo., Ogbourne St Geo. (of Stratton St Mgt., 1668), 1669, I, W, P23/5
Cowsey, Hy., Wootton R., 1738, AB, P1/C/751
Jas., Bratton, Westb., 1562, W, P5/1Reg/9A
Cowsey, Jane, widow, Froxfield, 1745, AB, P3/C/886
Cowsey, Rowland, Wootton R., 1684, AB, I, P1/C/367
Caseway, Wm., Bratton, Westb., 1614, AB, I, P25/1614/4
Caxesden *see* Coxesden
Cayford, Nich., yeo., Maiden B., 1747, W, P1/C/819, P1/10Reg/74B
Cayney, Francis, yeo., Lockeridge, Overton, 1811, W, Wr, P1/1811/53

Caynis *see* Keynes
Cearle *see* Curle *or* C.
Cearley *see* Carley
Cecil, Edmd., gent., Sal., 1608, I (detailed), W, P1/C/39
Cicell, Joan, widow, Purton, 1619, I, W, P1/C/89
Robt., saddler, Sal. St Thos., 1614, AB, I, P1/C/69
Cissell, Wm., Trowb., 1611, I, W, P22/2/4
Cew *see* Kew
Chaderton, Wm., Lydiard M., 1609, AB, L, P3/C/38
Chadsey, Jn., labourer, Tidcombe and Fosbury, 1626, I, W, P3/C/141
Jn., blacksmith, Ogbourne St And., 1678, AB, I, P5/1677/14
Jn., bricklayer, Shalbourne, 1727, W, P5/1727/11, P5/16Reg/157B
My., widow, Newbury, Berks., 1695, W, P1/C/446
Chudsey, My., sp., Coombe B., 1729, AB, P8/30
Chadwell, Ann, widow, Ebbesborne Wake, 1619, I, W, P2/C/314
Edmd., gent., Wrou., 1682, comm, W, Wr, P3/C/446
Honour, widow, Swindon, 1685, comm, W (2 - 1 a copy), P3/C/502
Chadwick, Robt., vict., Trowb., 1832, W, Wr, P1/1832/92
Chaffe *see* Chaffey
Chaffen *see* Chaffin
Chaffey, Ambrose, yeo., Langham, Gillingham, Dorset, 1734, I, ren, W, P27/1/328
Chassey, Ann, sp., Long Burton, Dorset, 1842, W, Wr, P5/1842/21
Barter, Sherb., Dorset, 1734, AB, I, P5/1734/11
Edwd., currier, Dorchester, Dorset (property at Fordington, Dorset), 1779, W, P5/1779/3, P5/17Reg/165B
Ephraim, Long Burton, Dorset, 1772, AB, P5/1772/3, P5/17Reg/47A
Geo., Allweston, Folke, Dorset, 1753, AB, W, P5/1753/6
Hannah, sp., Allweston, Folke, Dorset, 1759, W, P5/1759/5
Jane, Sherb., Dorset, 1785, AB, P5/1785/7, P5/18Reg/42
Jn., Chicklade, 1613, AB, P1/C/53
Jn., yeo. *or* husb., Halstock, Dorset, 1678, comm (2 - 1 a draft), L, NW, ren, P5/1678/46, P16/52
Chaffe, Jn., yeo., Butterwick, Folke, Dorset, 1704, I, W, P5/1704/12
Jn., mercer, Sherb., Dorset, 1734, W, P5/1734/12
Josias, Sherb., Dorset, 1706, W (tobacco engine & press to son), P5/1706/5
Rd., Lillington, Dorset, 1641, AB, a/c, I, P5/1641/14, P5/14Reg/35B
Robt., Sherb., Dorset, 1803, W, P5/1803/44, P5/19Reg/77A
Walter, Sherb., Dorset, 1740, AB, Wr, P5/1740/19
Chasy, Wm., priest, 1553, institution to vicarage on death of Ernley, P2/2Reg/167C
Wm., Gillingham, Dorset, 1734, AB, P27/1/329
Chaffin, (Lady), widow, Sal. The Close, 1692, W (badly damaged), P5/1691/18
Ann, widow, Timbrell Lane, Downton, 1622, I, T, W, P2/C/328
Chas., gent., Sal. The Close, 1657, a/c, P5/1657/1
Dorothy, widow, Sal. St Thos., 1562, W (to be buried in St T. church by 1st husband Jn. Newman; several bequests of clothes & jewels) (NEP), P1/2Reg/119
Edwd., Mere, 1614, AB, T (unnamed children), P5/1613/9, P5/9Reg/131D
Essex, sp., Rams., 1756, W, P5/1756/6
Mgt., widow, Sal. St Thos., 1631, AB, P1/C/137
My., widow, Zeals, 1713, comm, W, P5/1712/21, P5/15Reg/314
Rd., priest, 1553, institution to rectory on death of Nelson, P2/2Reg/177D
Thos., esquire, Sal. The Close, 1688, I, W, copy W, P5/1688/19
Thos., baker, Sherb., Dorset, 1852, O, W, Wr, P5/1852/28
Wm., gent., Bulford, 1558, W, P2/3Reg/141B
Wm., mercer, Mere, 1619-20, AB, comm, I, P5/1619/12, P5/9Reg/229E
Chaffen, Wm., Stourton, 1808, AB, Wr, P2/1808/48
Chair *see* Cheer
Chalcott *see* Chamberlain als Chalcott
Chaldecott, Geo., jun., bach., Bere R., Dorset, 1746, AB, P5/1746/13
Geo., tanner, Shitterton, Bere R., Dorset, 1752, W, P5/1752/6
Jn., Lyme R., Dorset, 1724, I, P30/42
Rebecca, widow, Shitterton, Bere R., Dorset, 1764, W, P5/1764/7
Chalk, Ann, widow, Leverton, Chilton F., 1697, AB, I, P3/C/598

Anna, widow, Downton, 1811, W, P2/1811/34
Benj., Chilton F., 1743, AB, I, P3/C/871
Chas., tailor, Maddington, 1740, AB, ren, W, P2/C/1208
David, yeo., Downton, 1784, W, P2/C/1428
Eliz., Donhead St A. (written at Barford), 1623, AB, NW, P2/C/333
Ellen, Barford St Mart., 1555, W (NEP), P2/1Reg/26A
Geo., minor, Bulford, 1811, T (children of Jas. C., decd), P1/1811/6-7
Chalke, Hannah *see* Hannah Morgan
Harry, yeo., Winterbourne S., 1789, W, P2/C/1451
Jacob, Downton, 1813, AB, Wr, P2/1813/5
Jas., Bulford, 1811, AB, Wr, P1/1811/7
Joan, widow, S. Burcombe, 1569, W, P2/5Reg/51C
Jn., Woodfalls, Downton, 1641, I, W, P2/C/496
Jn., husb., S. Burcombe, 1669, deed of gift, P2/C/586
Jn., Woodfalls, Downton, 1672, AB, I, P2/C/620
Jn., husb., Barford St Mart., 1691, AB, I, P2/C/815
Jn., husb., Hurdcott, Barford St Mart., 1711, AB, I, P1/C/514
Jn., [brewer], Leverton, Chilton F., 1718, I, W, P3/C/710
Jn., Wilton, 1773, AB, ren, P2/C/1363
Jn., yeo., Woodfalls, Downton, 1853, W, Wr, P2/1853/42
Jos., woodman and husb., Woodfalls, Downton, 1735, I, W, P2/C/1170
Jos., yeo., Downton, 1809, W, P2/1809/42
Jos., Downton, 1822, AB, Wr, P2/1822/59
Martha, vict., Leverton, Chilton F., 1749, W, P3/C/900
Rd., husb., Upton, Blewbury, Berks., 1600, I, W, P5/1600/12, P5/7Reg/1
Rd., yeo., Leverton, Chilton F., 1695, comm, I, W, P1/C/443
Rd., Wilton, 1812, AB, W, Wr, P2/1812/48
Rd., labourer, Morgan's Vale, Downton, 1844, W, Wr, P2/1844/23
Rd., labourer, Whitep., 1844, W, Wr, P2/1844/63
Robt., Burcombe, 1558, W, P2/3Reg/129A
Robt., Barford St Mart., 1589, AB, I, W, P2/C/79
Sam., Downton, 1776, W, P1/C/988, P1/13Reg/73A
Sam., labourer, Morgan's Vale, Downton, 1843, W, Wr, P2/1843/15
Sam., brickmaker, Fisherton A., 1847, cert, W, Wr, P2/1847/59
Thos., Barford St Mart., 1557, W, P2/3Reg/14B
Wm., S. Burcombe, 1558, W, P2/3Reg/87C
Wm., yeo., Downton, 1776, W, P1/C/999, P1/13Reg/139
Wm., labourer, Bower C., 1832, W, Wr, P2/1832/18
Challen, Jn., gent., Marl., 1856, aff, O, W, Wr, P1/1856/7
Challis, Jn., clothdrawer, Warm., 1700, AB, I, P2/C/885
Challis, Jn., Hungerford, Berks., 1709, I, W (small holograph), P5/1709/5, P5/15Reg/140
Challis, Jn., Speen, Berks., 1747, W, P1/C/822, P1/10Reg/120A
Challis, Jos., servingman, Benham Valence, Speen, Berks., 1773, W, P1/C/971, P1/12Reg/497A
Chalver, Robt., Garsdon, 1571, W, P1/1Reg/52B
Chamber *see* Chambers
Chamberlain, Alice, widow, Boreham, Warm., 1574, W, P2/5Reg/209B
Alice, widow, Brokenb., 1673, AB, I, P3/C/360
Alice, widow, Baydon, 1709, I, W, P5/1709/6, P5/15Reg/116
Ann, widow, Manton, Preshute, 1662, I, W, P1/C/253
Ann, widow, Woodford, 1729, W, P13/4/24
Anth., sen., yeo., Brokenb., 1664, I, W, P3/C/296
Austin, sen., Lyme R., Dorset, 1776, AB, O, P16/342
Benj., yeo., Marsh Benham, Speen, Berks., 1823, W, Wr, P1/1823/108
Caleb, Westport St My., 1755, AB, P3/C/936
Chas., Chicklade, 1752, W, P2/C/1270
Edith, Chitterne St My., 1558, W, P2/3Reg/118A
Eleanor, widow, Sal., 1632, I, W, P4/1632/2
Eliz., Warm., 1558, W, P2/3Reg/144B
Eliz., widow, Sevenhampton, Highw., 1733, W, P10/1733/1
Eliz., widow, Arborfield, Berks., 1792, note of AB, W, P5/1792/4, P5/18Reg/184B

Erasmus, husb., Chitterne St My., 1605, I, W, P2/C/212
Frances, widow, Lacock, 1687, I, W, P3/C/516
Giles, yeo., Idmiston, 1709-11, I, legacy a/c, T, W, P1/C/512, P2/C/963
Hy., sen., E. Garston, Berks., 1759, W, P1/C/902, P1/11Reg/410
Hy., yeo., Newtown, Hungerford, Berks., 1789, W, P23/786, P1/14Reg/232
Humphrey, yeo., Sal., 1616, W, P4/1615/2
Jas., husb. and woollen weaver, Over Zeals, 1619, I, NW, P5/1619/16, P5/10Reg/63A
Jas., Reading, Berks., 1747, AB, quitclaim, P1/C/831
Joan, widow, Tytherington, Heytes., 1619, I, W, P5/1619/17, P5/10Reg/64B
Joan, widow, Idmiston, 1684, AB, I, P2/C/742
Jn., Chitterne St My., 1550, W, P2/2Reg/94A
Jn., yeo., Sutton V., 1558, W, P2/3Reg/112B
Jn., Chitterne St My., 1559, W, P2/3Reg/175A
Chamberlain als Chalcott, Jn., Chitterne St My., 1564, AB, P2/4Reg/165A
Jn., Lacock, 1611, AB, P3/C/55
Jn., yeo., Tytherington, Heytes., 1619, I, W, P5/1619/14, P5/10Reg/66
Jn., husb., Chitterne St My., 1625, I, W, P1/C/119
Jn., collier, Frilsham, Berks., 1628, I, W, P1/C/131
Jn., yeo., Tytherington, Heytes., 1642, I, W, P5/1642/8, P5/14Reg/55A
Jn., yeo., Tytherington, Heytes., 1644, I, NW, P5/1644/8, P5/14Reg/63A
Jn., husb., Badbury, Chiseldon, 1661, I, W, P3/C/273, P3/3Reg/8A
Jn., labourer, Chilton F., 1727, W, P3/C/763
Jn., yeo., Bemerton, Fugg. St Peter (described as of Bedhampton), 1729, W, P2/C/1106
Jn., carp., Bucklebury, Berks., 1763, W, P1/C/920, P1/12Reg/91A
Jn., Fosbury, Tidcombe and F., 1788, AB, comm, P3/C/1099
Jn., yeo., All C., 1819, W, Wr, P3/1819/48
Jn., *The Shoulder of Mutton*, Wantage, Berks., 1827, W, Wr, P5/1827/23
Lawr., gent., Broad B., Highw., 1823, W, Wr, P10/1823/1
My., widow, Malm., 1775, AB, P3/C/1042
My., Preshute, 1781, AB, P1/C/1022
Maurice, Bps. C., 1638, I (buried 14 Jan 1638), P24/301
Nich., Boreham, Warm., 1552, I, W, P2/C/1, P2/2Reg/148A
Noah, Stratfield M., Berks., 1704, AB, I, P1/C/490
Rd., Monkton D., 1557, W, P2/3Reg/57C
Rd., yeo., Sevenhampton, Highw., 1730, AB, I, P10/1730/3
Robt., sen., Warm., 1543, W (NEP), P2/1Reg/39A
Robt., Boreham, Warm., 1572, W, P2/5Reg/159H
Robt., yeo., Imber, 1586, W, P2/7Reg/48B
Robt., yeo., Boreham, Warm., 1607, I, W, P2/C/225
Robt., Winterbourne G., 1614, W, P2/8Reg/211
Robt., Kingston D., 1627, AB, a/c, P2/C/369
Robt., husb., Aldbourne, 1688, I, W, Wr, P3/C/526
Robt., farmer, Arborfield, Berks., 1765, W, P5/1765/8
Steph., husb., Kingston D., 1590, I, W, P2/C/89
Susanna, widow, Crickl. St S., 1670, I, W, P3/C/338
Thos., Figh., 1581, AB, I, P26/1482, P5/4Reg/18C
Thos., husb., Tytherington, Heytes., 1597, I, W, P5/1597/23, P5/6Reg/179B
Thos., Wootton R., 1661, comm, I, NW, P3/C/274, P3/3Reg/28A
Thos., husb., Baydon, 1685, AB, I, P5/1685/23
Thos., shoemaker, Marl., 1693, I, W, P1/C/433
Thos., yeo., Clatford Park, Preshute, 1705, comm, I, W, P5/1705/14
Thos., sen., yeo., Aldbourne, 1707, I, W, P3/C/661
Thos., husb., Baydon, 1726, W, P5/1726/12, P5/16Reg/136
Thos., yeo., Bemerton, Fugg. St Peter, 1731, AB, I, P2/C/1126
Thos., innholder, Mkt. L., 1737, W, P2/C/1180
Thos., Lambourn Woodlands, Berks., 1738, W, P1/C/759, P1/8Reg/300A
Thos., yeo., Wantage, Berks. (of Shifford, Oxfordshire, 1743), 1745, W, P23/588
Thorp, yeo., Lockeridge, Overton, 1718, I, W, P3/C/711
Walter, husb., Tytherington, Heytes., 1569, W, P5/2Reg/42
Wm., sen., Boreham, Warm., 1572, W, P2/5Reg/155B

Wm., husb., Boreham, Warm., 1576, I, W, P2/C/40, P2/5Reg/255A
Wm., jun., tailor, Idmiston, 1662, AB, I, P1/C/254
Wm., woollen draper, Crickl. St S., 1667, comm, I, NW, P3/C/310
Wm., Clatford Park, Preshute, 1674, AB, I, W, P1/C/312
Wm., weaver, W. Harnham, 1688, NW, P5/1688/18
Wm., yeo., Tilehurst, Berks., 1689, AB, I, P1/C/407
Wm., sen., carp., Westport St My., 1699, AB, I, P3/C/606
Wm., husb., Estcourt, Lt. Hinton, 1714, W, P3/C/688
Wm., carp., Westport St My., 1720, I, W, P3/C/729
Wm., yeo., Milton L., 1721, I (2 - 1 a copy), W, P3/C/734
Wm., sen., yeo., Uffington, Berks., 1732, W, P1/C/705, P1/7Reg/460B
Wm., innholder, Mkt. L., 1748, W, P2/C/1246
Wm., carp., Malm., 1774, W, P3/C/1036
Chambers, Ann, widow, Erlestoke, 1571, W, P2/5Reg/124C
Bridget, widow, Poulshot, 1691, I, W, P2/C/812
Chas., vict., Yarnbrook, N. Bradley, 1842, W, Wr, P2/1842/33
Chris., yeo., Erlestoke, 1569, W (to be buried in church porch where father was), P2/5Reg/58D
Edmd., Wokm., Berks., 1579, AB, I, T, P5/1579/14, P5/3Reg/139D
Edwd., broad weaver, Poulshot, 1680, I, W, P1/C/343
Eliz., widow, Kingston D., 1734, W, P2/C/1163
Eliz., widow, Chipp., 1753, W, P1/C/862, P1/11Reg/90A
Hannah, gent.'s wife, Biddestone, 1815, AB, comm, Wr, P3/1815/4
Jane, widow, Castle C., [1709], W, P28/5
Jn., smith, Kemble, 1697, I, W, P3/C/599
Jn., sen., Norton B., 1736, AB, W, P2/C/1175
Jn., feltmaker, Chipp., 1743, comm, W, P3/C/872
Jn., Heytes., 1750, AB, P5/1750/4
Jn., carp., Heytes., 1792, W, Wr, P5/1792/6, P5/18Reg/181B
My., widow, Norton B., 1782, AB, P2/C/1423
Chamber als Smith, Nich., Amesb., 1543, W (NEP), P2/1Reg/29
Philippa, widow, Sutton V., 1627, AB, I, W, P2/C/373
Rachel, sp., Norton B., 1685, AB, comm, I, P2/C/750
Chamber, Rd., Norton B., 1585, W, P2/7Reg/8B
Rd., Norton B., 1684, AB, P2/C/743
Robt., weaver, Sutton V., [1628], I, W, P2/C/381
Simon, Imber, 1751, AB, P2/C/1266
Thos., weaver, Norton B., [1629], I, W, P2/C/385
Thos., Imber, 1722, W, P2/C/1049
Thos., Norton B., 1726, AB, P2/C/1075
Thos., sen., carp., Norton B., 1781, AB, ren, W, P2/C/1416
Thos., carp., Norton B., 1812, W, P2/1812/51
Walter, yeo., Norton B., 1669, I, W, P2/C/591
Wm., Stanton Fitzwarren, 1623, AB, P3/C/121
Wm., shoemaker, Sal., 1787, W (NEP), P4/1786/7
Wm., Sal., 1805, AB, P4/1805/8
Chambury, Jos., clothw., Trowb., 1854, aff, O, W, Wr, P1/1855/1
Champ, Ann, widow, Durnsford Mill, Mildenhall, 1683, AB, I, P3/C/466
Charity, widow, Beam., Dorset, 1697, I, W, P17/117
Edwd., Stratton St Mgt., 1694, AB, I, P3/C/567
Edwd., yeo. *or* husb., Stratton St Mgt., 1703, I, W, P3/C/644
Gregory, husb., Compton, Berks., 1619, AB, a/c, I, P1/C/94
Champ als Helliar, Joan, Sal., 1712, AB, P4/1712/14
Jn., miller, Mildenhall, 1682, comm, I, W, P3/C/447
My., yeo.'s widow, E. Hendred, Berks., 1735, W, P1/C/728, P1/8Reg/4
Rd., Amesb., 1611, I, W, P1/C/42
Sam., grocer, Lyme R., Dorset, 1834, O, W, Wr, P16/408
Thos., clothw., Reading St My., Berks., 1680, comm, I, W, P1/C/338
Wm., shepherd, E. Hendred, Berks., 1766, W, P1/C/939, P1/12Reg/171B
Champernown, Ann, widow, Calcutt, Crickl. St S., 1764, W, P3/C/976
Edwd., husb., Crickl. St S., 1613, I, W, P1/C/58

Jennifer, husb., Crickl. St S., 1607, W, P3/C/25
Champernown als Slatter, Moses, yeo., Calcutt, Crickl. St S., 1662, I, W (damaged), P3/C/283, P3/3Reg/39B
Champernown als Slatter, Rd., Calcutt, Crickl. St S., 1696, AB, I, P3/C/591
Champernown als Slatter, Rd., gent., Calcutt, Crickl. St S., 1787, W, P3/C/1092
Champernown als Slatter, Wm., yeo., Calcutt, Crickl. St S., 1690, I, W, P3/C/541
Champion, Champin, Agnes, widow, Alderbury, 1569, AB, P5/2Reg/37A
Champin, Agnes, widow, Downton, 1613, AB, I, P1/C/52
Alice, widow, Arborfield, Berks., 1631, I, NW, P5/1630/22, P5/11Reg/154
And., yeo., Blewbury, Berks., 1632, I, W, P5/1632/15, P5/12Reg/93
Ann, sp., Beam., Dorset, 1668, AB, I, P5/1668/19
Cath., Dunsden, Sonning, Berks., 1640, I, W, P5/1640/11, P5/13Reg/247
Champin, Denise, widow, Sonning, Berks., 1607, I, W, P5/1607/16, P2/C/215, P5/8Reg/100B
Denise, widow, S. Newton, 1641, NW, P2/C/499-500
Dorothy, widow, Wantage, Berks., 1694, AB, P23/206
Champion als Clark, Francis, butcher, Beam., Dorset, 1748, copy W, P17/506
Champion als Clark, Francis, butcher, Beam., Dorset, 1812, AB, comm, ren, W, Wr, LA, P5/1812/39
Hugh, yeo., Hurst, Berks., 1602, AB, I, P5/1602/11, P5/7Reg/52B
Hugh, Fisherton A., 1620-21, a/c, I, P2/C/321
Jas., Peasemore, Berks., 1744, AB, P1/C/800
Jn., Corsham, 1590, AB, P29/C/1, P29/1Reg/26A
Jn., husb., Mynte, Corsham, 1615, I, W, P29/C/3, P29/1Reg/74B
Jn., S. Newton, 1641, AB, court paper, I, W, P2/C/499-500
Jn., Corsham, 1719, marriage licence, P29/2Reg/29
Maud, widow, Easton, Corsham, [1567], W (NEP), P29/1Reg/14A
Philip, yeo., Corsham, [1633], W, P29/1Reg/132C
Thos., yeo., Sonning, Berks., 1585, I, T, W, P5/1585/20, P5/4Reg/117B
Thos., yeo., Arborfield, Berks., 1630, AB, W, P5/1630/1, P5/11Reg/153
Thos., yeo., Dunsden, Sonning, Berks., 1644, comm, I, W, P5/1644/7, P5/14Reg/71A
Thos., yeo., Eye and Dunsden, Sonning, Berks., 1688, I, W, P5/1688/17
Champin, Wm., husb., Walton, Downton, 1558, W, P2/3Reg/142A
Wm., yeo., Steeple L., 1558, W, P2/3Reg/108B
Wm., Melk., 1611, I, W, P2/C/256
Wm., millwright, Beam., Dorset, 1619, W, P5/1619/48, P5/10Reg/51C
Wm., Britford, 1672, I, W, P24/463
Champlate *see* Hellier als Champlate
Champneys, Jn., gent., Uffc., Devon, 1631, AB, I, P5/1631/26, P5/12Reg/17A
My., Uffc., Devon, 1635, I, W, P5/1635/19, P5/12Reg/213D
Chancellor, My., sp., Abingdon, Berks., 1729, W, P1/C/671, P1/7Reg/243A
Wm., Swallowfield, Shinfield, Berks., 1625, AB, I, P1/C/114
Chandler, Agnes, widow, Hilp., 1562, I, W, P2/C/19, P2/4Reg/92C
Alice, widow, Hilcott, N. Newnton, 1640, I, W, P3/C/250
Ann, widow *or* sp., Mildenhall, 1636, AB, a/c, I, P3/C/212
Ann, widow, All C., 1737, I, W, P3/C/833
Ann, widow, Rushall, 1754, W, P2/C/1286
Ann, widow, Woodb., 1754-66, AB (2), comm, P3/C/930
Ann, widow, Preshute, 1780, AB, P1/C/1021
Ann, sp., Burbage, 1808, W, P11/263
Anth., weaver, Bromham, 1606, I, W, P1/C/31
Bart., Crickl. St My., 1641, AB, I, W, P3/C/261
Betty, widow, All C., 1828, O, W, Wr, P3/1828/17
Brian, gent., Sudden Park, Gt. Bedwyn, 1800, W, P5/1800/32, P5/18Reg/304
Chas., husb., Stourton, 1611, W, P2/8Reg/168B
Chas., no abode stated, 1638, I, P1/C/175
Dan., yeo., Hilcott, N. Newnton, 1706, I (2 - 1 a copy), W, P3/C/657
Dan., sen., thatcher, All C., 1723, I, W, P1/C/611, P1/6Reg/441B
Dan., All C., 1779, W, P1/C/1011, P1/13Reg/231
Dan., maltster, Marden, 1791, comm, W, P2/C/1462
Dan., Chirton, 1796, AB, P2/C/1478
Dan., Pewsey, 1837, AB, comm, Wr, P3/1837/21
Edith, widow, Manningford Bohun, 1660, AB, I, W, P1/C/238

Edmd., farmer, Gomeldon, Idmiston, 1647, I, W, P2/C/533
Edmd., yeo., Netherh., 1721, AB, ren, P2/C/1501
Eleanor, widow, Sonning, Berks., 1665, I, W, P5/1665/15
Eliz., Bradford A., 1613, AB, ren, P2/C/272, P2/8Reg/196A
Eliz., widow, Castle Eaton, 1662, W, P1/C/249
Eliz., wife, Marl., 1687, AB, ren, W, P1/C/387
Eliz., widow, Durrington, 1693, I, W, P2/C/832
Eliz., Amesb., 1714, W, P1/C/546, P1/5Reg/351
Eliz., widow, Hilcott, N. Newnton, 1739, W, P3/C/845
Eliz., sp., Collingbourne K., 1761, W, P3/C/959
Eliz., widow, Marden, 1813, AB, Wr, P2/1813/63
Eliz., Manningford Bohun, 1819, AB, Wr, P2/1819/52
Eliz., widow, Clapcote Farm, Grittleton, 1827, W, Wr, P3/1827/66
Francis, Marl. St Peter and St Paul, 1694, W, P1/C/434
Francis, Snap, Aldbourne, 1694, AB, comm, I, P3/C/568
Geoff., Compton, Enford, 1638, I, W, P2/C/464
Geo., tailor and woollen draper, Bradford A., 1606, AB, a/c, P1/C/25
Chanlor, Geo., Sopworth, 1611, W, P3/C/56
Geo., weaver, Melk., 1620, I, W, P1/C/104
Geo., miller, Hurst Mill, Worton, Pott., 1850, O, W, Wr, P1/1850/17
Good, Bps. C., 1638, AB, I, P24/305
Grace, widow, Woodb., 1682, I, W, P3/C/448
Grace, sp., Alton B., 1771, W, P3/C/1019
Hy., Kepnal, Pewsey, 1613, AB, I, P1/C/59
Hy., Collingbourne K., 1734, AB, P3/C/821
Hy., yeo., Collingbourne K., 1756, W, P3/C/941
Isaac, Manton, Preshute, 1781, AB, comm, W, P1/C/1026, P1/13Reg/329B
Jas., [farmer], Clapcote Farm, Grittleton, 1836, aff, O, W, Wr, P3/1836/45
Joan, Ruscombe, Berks., 1541, W, P5/20Reg/23C
Jn., freemason, N. Bradley, 1556, W, P2/1Reg/108B
Jn., W. Lavington, 1597, AB, I, W (damaged), P1/C/11
Chandler als Pearce, Jn., fellmonger, Urchf., 1598, I, W, P2/C/162
Jn., sen., husb., Seend Row, Melk., 1672, I, W, P2/C/626
Jn., sen., yeo., Collingbourne K., 1680, I, W, P3/C/427
Jn., yeo., Sal., 1682, AB, I, P4/1681/4
Jn., sen., yeo., Oare, Wilcot, 1684, I, W, P3/C/476
Jn., chandler, Collingbourne K., 1694, I, W, P3/C/569
Jn., Hilp., 1706, AB, I, P2/C/936
Jn., [blacksmith], Wokm., Berks., 1710, AB, I, P5/1710/24
Jn., Sal. St Mart., 1715, AB, I, P4/1715/14
Jn., sen., yeo., Rushall, 1721, W, P2/C/1042
Jn., yeo., Rushall, 1729, AB, D, I, NW, P1/C/660, P1/7Reg/212A
Jn., Rushall, 1751, AB, W, P2/C/1265
Jn., gent., Idmiston, 1760, W, P2/C/1308
Jn., Burbage, 1823, AB, P11/274
Jos., gent., Wick, Bps. C., 1771, W, P24/1152
Jos., gent., Lake, Wilsford with L., 1793, W, P13/5/11
Lawr., sen., yeo., Hullavington, 1769, W, P3/C/1013
Lawr., Hullavington, 1849, O, W, Wr, P3/1849/35
Margery, widow, Milton L., 1693, I, W (NEP), P3/C/561
My., Clapcote Farm, Grittleton, 1838, W, Wr, P3/1838/70
My., widow, Hullavington, 1851, AB, O, Wr, P3/1851/24
Matthew, yeo., Bps. C., 1628, AB, I, W, P24/218
Matthew, Woodb., 1684, I, W, P3/C/481
Matthew, jun., yeo., Hilcott, N. Newnton, 1684, AB, I, P3/C/477
Matthew, yeo., Hilcott, N. Newnton, 1689, I, W, P1/C/398
Matthew, Winterbourne E., 1692, AB, I, P2/C/823
Nathaniel, beer brewer, Sonning, Berks., 1713, W, P5/1713/22, P5/15Reg/370B
Philip, vintner, Amesb. (now resident in London), 1693, W, P2/C/830
Chandler als Perse, Prudence, Calne, 1638, AB, I, T (re Thos. & Jn. Perse, minors), P5/1638/15

Rd., priest, Grimston, Dorset & Odstock, 1558, collation to prebend; institution to rectory, P1/1Reg/7B, 7C
Rd., sen., yeo., Woodb., 1672, I, W (damaged), P3/C/355
Rd., yeo., Woodb., 1693, comm, I (2), W, P3/C/554
Rd., Manningford Bruce, 1737, W, P3/C/834
Rd., Rushall, 1741, W, P1/C/785, P1/9Reg/165B
Rd., Southbroom, 1758, AB, P24/1008
Rd., Southbroom, 1766, AB, P24/1086
Rd., gent., Lake, Wilsford with L., 1784, W, P13/5/5
Rd., yeo., Wilsford nr Pewsey, 1800, AB, W, P2/1800/93
Rd., sen., Pewsey Wharf, 1838, AB, comm, ren, Wr, P3/1838/4
Rd., gent., Southbroom, 1839, O, W, Wr, P24/1359
Robt., Everleigh, 1620, I, W, P3/C/106
Robt., yeo., Chute, 1631, I, W, P5/1631/30, P5/11Reg/166B
Robt., yeo., Collingbourne K., 1646, AB, comm, I, P1/C/210
Robt., esquire, Netheravon, 1681, W, P12/115
Robt., Fittleton, 1709, AB, P2/C/957
Robt., grocer and yeo., Collingbourne K., 1711, AB, I, W, P1/C/513, P1/5Reg/33
Steph., yeo., Cothill, Marcham, Berks., 1717, I, W, P1/C/572, P1/6Reg/129B
Susanna, widow, Fisherton A., 1799, W, P2/C/1499
Thos., yeo., Woodb., 1620, I, W, P3/C/107
Thos., Oare, Wilcot, 1630, I, NW, P3/C/166
Thos., sen., glover, Studley, Calne, 1638, I, W, P26/70
Thos., Amesb., 1726, AB, P2/C/1074
Thos., sen., gent., Upavon, 1753, W, P1/C/865, P1/11Reg/105
Thos., gent., Woodb., 1781, W, P3/C/1069
Thos., gent., Alton B., 1790, req, W, copy W, P3/C/1105
Thos., Mkt. L., 1797, AB, Wr, P2/C/1481
Thos., labourer, Woodley, W. and Sandford, Berks., 1830, O, W, Wr, P5/1830/38
Thos. Hicks, gent., Aldbourne (form. of Stockton), 1852, comm, W, Wr, P3/1852/43
Thomasine, widow, Stourton, 1615, I, W, P2/C/279
Walter, yeo., Hilcott, N. Newnton, 1636, W, P3/C/213
Walter, husb., Fyfield, Milton L., 1664, AB, I, P3/C/297
Wm., husb., Seend, Melk., 1634, AB, I, W, P2/C/425
Wm., basketmaker, Sonning, Berks., 1641, I, W, P5/1641/15, P5/14Reg/16
Wm., bach., Devizes, 1660, AB, P1/C/237
Wm., jun., Berwick St Jas., 1668, AB, I, W, P1/C/284, 286
Wm., yeo., Rushall, 1677, I, W, P1/C/324
Wm., yeo., Woodb., 1689, I, W, P1/C/402
Wm., yeo., Rushall, 1693, comm, W, P2/C/831
Wm., yeo., Rushall, 1696, I, W, P2/C/859
Wm., sen., yeo., Bugley, Warm., 1702, W, P2/C/899
Wm., yeo., Bugley, Warm., 1719-21, AB, W, P2/C/1028, 1046
Wm., sen., yeo., Woodb., 1728, W, P3/C/774
Wm., yeo., Collingbourne K., 1729, AB, I, P3/C/779
Wm., yeo., Idmiston, 1731, W, P2/C/1125
Wm., yeo., Rushall, 1735, W, P1/C/737, P1/8Reg/109
Wm., yeo., Baydon, 1735, AB, I, W, P5/1735/11
Wm., Rushall, 1751, AB, W, P2/C/1264
Wm., gent., Rushall, 1754, comm, W, P2/C/1281
Wm., yeo., W. Grimstead, 1783, W, P2/C/1427
Wm., woodmonger, Milton L., 1788, W, P3/C/1100
Wm., Whitep., 1796, W, P2/C/1479
Wm., Whitep., 1820, AB, Wr, P1/1820/34
Wm., carp., Burbage, 1834, O, W, Wr, P11/288
Wm., innkeeper, Devizes Grn, Bps. C., 1840, W, Wr, P24/1362
Wroughton, yeo., Hullavington, 1759, W, P1/C/905, P1/11Reg/440B
see also Coke als C.; Pearce als C.
Channon, Dan., jun., blacksmith, Lyme R., Dorset, 1821, W, Wr, P16/390
Jas., miller, Uffc., Devon, 1769, W, P20/1/252
Jas. Somers, mariner, Coombe St., Lyme R., Dorset, 1847, comm, D, W, Wr, P16/444

Cheanen, Rachel, Stourton, 1672, I, P2/C/629
Susan Cuming, widow, Lyme R., Dorset, 1846, comm, W, Wr, P16/440
Chant, Ambrose, sen., Fisherton A., 1729, I, W, P2/C/1111
Benj., innholder, Milford, Sal. St Mart., 1747, W, P4/1746/10
Roger, butcher, Sherb., Dorset, 1644, I, P5/1644/29
Thos., tailor, Sherb., Dorset, 1630, I, W, P5/1629/15, P5/11Reg/27B
Chanter, Ann, sp., Avill's Farm, Corsham, 1781, W, P3/C/1070
Betty, widow, Corsham, 1760, W, P29/C/22, P29/2Reg/94
Dan., Corsham, 1720, marriage licence, P29/2Reg/30A
Edwd., clothw., Corsham, [1723], W, P29/C/17
Edwd., clothw., Corsham, 1753, W, P29/2Reg/78
Jn., Corsham, 1716, marriage licence, P29/2Reg/24A
Wm., cook, Corsham, 1730, W, P29/C/18, P29/2Reg/55B
Wm., clothw., Avill's Farm, Corsham, 1749, W, P3/C/901
Chantrell, Jas., sen., yeo., Aldermaston, Berks., 1692, I, W, P1/C/420
Jas., yeo., Thatcham, Berks., 1712, AB, comm, I, P1/C/534
Thos., clerk, Sal. The Close, 1739, AB, Wr, P5/1739/12
Chapel *see* Chappell
Chaper, Edmd., husb., Martin, Hants, 1587-1603, AB, I, quitclaim, P2/C/73, P2/7Reg/114B
Eliz., widow, Martin, Hants, [1581], W (NEP), P3/1Reg/13A
Joan, widow, Maiden B., 1570-71, W (NEP), P1/1Reg/127C
Ralph, weaver, Maiden B., [1623], I, NW, P2/C/329
Robt., Martin, Hants, 1568, W, P2/5Reg/50A
Chaplin, Ann, widow, Sherb., Dorset, 1593, AB, I, P5/1593/23, P5/6Reg/42A
Dorothy, widow, Lyme R., Dorset, 1625, I, W, P5/1625/20, P5/10Reg/271
Edith, widow, Ham, 1615, I, W, P3/C/76
Eliz., widow, Mere, 1744, AB, Wr, P5/1744/8
Jn., sen., husb., Over C., Dorset, 1598, AB, I, W, P5/1598/12, P5/6Reg/210A
Mgt., widow, Crickl. St S., 1684, I, W, P3/C/478
My., Penleigh, Dilton, Westb., 1681, I, W, P25/1680/4
My., widow, Mere, 1769, W, P5/1769/5
Nich., Brook, Westb., 1679, AB, I, P25/1679/5
Robt., Crickl. St S., 1683, comm, NW, P3/C/467
Thos., yeo., Crickl. St S., 1663, W, P3/C/289
see also Chapperlin
Chapman, Adam, broad weaver, Holt, Bradford A., 1664, AB, I, P1/C/273
And., gardener, Sal. St Mart., 1734, W, Wr, P4/1734/13
And., bach., Milford, Sal. St Mart., 1766, AB, P4/1766/14
Ann, sp., Tytherton L., Chipp. (form. of Stanley, Bremhill), 1689, I, W, P1/C/400
Ann, widow, Milton L., 1746, AB, I, P3/C/890
Anth., Limpley Stoke, Bradford A., 1764, AB, comm, P2/C/1318
Chapman als Hitchcock, Christian, sp., Marl., 1637, I, W, P1/C/174
Davis, Sherston, 1805, AB, P3/1805/21
Dorothy, widow, Littleton Drew, 1687, I, W, P3/C/517
Ebenezer, vict., Bradford A., 1766, W, P2/C/1332
Cheapman, Edmd., weaver, no abode stated, 1632, I, P30/43
Edwd., yeo., Horningsham, 1802, comm, W, P5/1802/4, P5/19Reg/3
Eleanor, sp., Holt, Bradford A., 1681, AB, I, P2/C/701
Eleanor, sp., Aldermaston, Berks., 1801, AB, Wr, P1/1801/117, P1/15Reg/336A
Eliz., widow, Holt, Bradford A., 1634, I, W, P1/C/146
Cheapman, Eliz., widow, Wilton, 1671, I, W, P2/C/613
Eliz., sp., Biddestone, 1737, W, P3/C/835
Eliz., widow, Horningsham, 1794, W, P5/1794/7, P5/18Reg/196A
Eliz., widow, Sonning, Berks., 1803, W, P5/1803/23, P5/19Reg/52
Faith, widow, Haydon, Dorset, 1672, definitive sentence, W, P5/1671/98
Grace, widow, Tytherton L., Chipp., 1680, comm, I, W, P3/C/426
Hy., Horningsham, 1637, AB, I, P5/1637/7, P5/13Reg/57A
Hy., vict. and butcher, Westport St My., 1650, I, W, P1/C/230
Hy., shoemaker, Leigh, Bradford A., 1667, AB, comm, I, P2/C/575
Hy., slaughterman, Milbourne, Malm., 1675, I, W, P3/C/374

Hy., Holt, Bradford A., 1676, AB, I, P2/C/664
Hy., Melk., [1686], I, W, P2/C/764
Hy., Westport St My., 1699, AB, P3/C/607
Hy., husb., Earley, Sonning, Berks., 1715, AB, I, P5/1715/11
Hy., weaver, Sal., 1723, AB, I, P4/1722/5
Hy., yeo., Sherston, 1841, O, W, Wr, P3/1841/14
Chepman, Jas., horse driver, Southwick, N. Bradley, 1753, W, P1/C/857, P1/11Reg/68
Jas., Hilp., 1785, AB, comm, P2/C/1435
Chepman, Jas., yeo., Heywood, Westb., 1802, O, W, P25/1801/2
Jane, Ashton K., 1755, W, P3/C/937
Jeremy, weaver, Sal., 1612, AB, I, P4/1612/15
Joan, widow, Calstone W., 1581, I, W, P5/1581/5, P5/4Reg/26B
Job, woolcomber, Calne, 1782, AB, P26/1125
Jn., bach., Shalbourne, Berks., 1576, W, P5/3Reg/76C
Jn., Trowle, Bradford A., 1597, I, W, P2/C/152
Jn., carp., Tytherton L., Chipp., 1625, I, W, P3/C/135
Jn., sen., yeo., Haydon, Dorset, 1628, cert, comm, I, W, copy W, P5/1628/27, P5/11Reg/19
Jn., Hurst, Berks., 1665, AB, comm, P5/1665/16
Cheapman, Jn., Calne, 1668, AB, comm, I, P26/146
Jn., yeo., Littleton Drew, 1677, I, W, P3/C/398
Jn., yeo., N. Wootton, Dorset, 1689, I, W, P5/1689/10
Jn., weaver, Horningsham, 1708, AB, I, ren, P5/1708/18
Jn., sen., yeo., Biddestone St Nich., 1712, I, W (2 - 1 a copy), P3/C/681
Jn., yeo., Haydon, Dorset, 1729, W, P5/1729/10, P5/16Reg/219
Jn., sen., yeo., Littleton Drew, 1741, W, P1/C/783, P1/9Reg/156
Jn., tilemaker, Warfield, Berks., 1741, W, P1/C/782, P1/9Reg/133
Jn., yeo., Holt, Bradford A., 1747, comm, W, P2/C/1242
Jn., Haydon, Dorset, 1751, AB, P5/1751/9
Jn., Gt. Bedwyn, 1756, AB, P5/1756/7
Jn., sen., yeo., Wick, Sherston, 1762, W, P3/C/964
Jn., gent., Littleton Drew, 1780, W, P3/C/1062
Jn., sen., yeo., Thornford, Dorset, 1792, W, P5/1792/5, P5/18Reg/182B
Jn., linen draper, Sal., 1796, cert, comm, W, P4/1796/8
Jn., yeo., Wick, Sherston, 1800, W, P3/1800/30
Jn., gent., Littleton Drew, 1814, AB, comm, P1/1814/156
Jn., gardener, Littleton P., 1836, O, W, P1/1836/11
Jn., yeo., Wick, Sherston, 1844, W, Wr, P3/1844/32
Jonathan, butcher, Arborfield Cross, Berks., 1740, W, Wr, P5/1740/14
Lawr., Holt, Bradford A., 1669, I, W, P2/C/594
Lawr., yeo., Biddestone St Nich., 1753, W, P3/C/925
Mgt., widow, Mill St., Wantage, Berks., 1824, comm, W, Wr, P5/1824/5
Chapman als Hitchcock, My., widow, Preshute, 1570, W, P1/1Reg/24
Maud, widow, Haydon, Dorset, 1636, I, W, P5/1636/12, P5/13Reg/23
Peter, clothier, Frome Selwood, Somerset (property in Chapmansdale, Corsley), 1816, AB, comm, P2/1816/43
Phyllis, widow, Castle St., Sal., 1841, W, Wr, P1/1841/22
Rachel, widow, Westport St My., 1667, I, W, P3/C/315
Rd., husb., Holt, Bradford A., 1583, W, P2/6Reg/87A
Rd., weaver, Calne, 1597, W, P5/1597/118, P5/6Reg/189C
Rd., yeo., Holt, Bradford A., [1624], I, W, P2/C/340
Rd., Sevenhampton, Highw., 1629, AB, P10/1629/2
Rd., husb., Wingfield, 1638, I, W, P1/C/182
Rd., tailor, Studley, Trowb., 1639, I, W, P22/2/40
Rd., yeo., Swindon, 1708, W, P3/C/667
Rd., sen., Littleton P., 1744, AB, W, P1/C/811, P1/9Reg/435C
Rd., jun., Littleton P., 1758, AB, W, P1/C/891, P1/11Reg/353A
Rd., maltster, Coulston, Edington, 1760, W, P2/C/1305
Rd., sen., yeo., W. Lavington, 1765, comm, W, P1/C/934, P1/12Reg/160B
Rd., yeo. & widower, Lillington, Dorset, 1835, W (& cods), P5/1835/10
Rd., yeo., Littleton P., 1845, W, Wr, P1/1845/44

Chapman als Hitchcock, Robt., Marl., 1609, AB, court papers (with copy of NW), I, Wr (damaged) (d. of plague), P1/C/40
Robt., husb., Studley, Trowb., 1636, I, W, P22/2/26
Robt., sen., yeo., Littleton Drew, 1751-54, AB, W, P3/C/909, 931
Robt., clerk, Trowb., 1763, AB, P1/C/928
Sam., yeo., Sherb., Dorset, 1793, W, P5/1793/5, P5/18Reg/192
Sam., clerk, Holt, Bradford A., 1838, O, W, Wr, P2/1838/46
Sarah, yeo.'s widow, Littleton Drew, 1767, W, P3/C/999
Sarah, Hurst, Berks., 1797, W, P5/1797/9, P5/18Reg/241B
Sibyl, Ashton K., 1756, W, P3/C/942
Steph., Reading St Giles, Berks., 1723, AB, I, P1/C/625
Steph., china man, Devizes, 1846, W, Wr, P1/1846/17
Thos., Trowle, Bradford A., 1597, I, NW, P2/C/153
Thos., yeo., Littleton Drew, 1617, I, W, P3/C/84
Thos., yeo., Holt, Bradford A., 1624, I, W, P2/C/337
Thos., yeo., Haydon, Dorset, 1629, I, W, P5/1629/10, P5/11Reg/107
Chapman als Hitchcock, Thos., yeo., Marl. St My., 1640, I, W, P1/C/186
Thos., butcher, Westport St My., 1673, I, W, P3/C/361
Thos., yeo., Littleton Drew, 1684, I, W, P3/C/479
Thos., sen., tailor, Sherb., Dorset, 1724, AB, I, P5/1724/17
Thos., yeo., Sherston, 1733, W, P3/C/812
Thos., yeo., Chards., Devon, 1737, AB, I, P5/1737/9, 12
Thos., handle setter, Bradford A., 1738-40, comm, W (2), Wr, P2/C/1183, 1204
Thos., maltster, Sherston, 1784-86, AB, W, P1/C/1049, P3/C/1081
Thos., Lt. Cheverell, 1827, O, W, Wr, P2/1827/4
Thos., blacksmith, Stanford Dingley, Berks., 1832, W, Wr, P1/1832/123
Cheapman, Wm., sen., husb., Studley, Trowb., 1615, I, W, P1/C/193
Wm., yeo., Holt, Bradford A., 1678, I, W, P2/C/676
Wm., Marl., 1683, AB, P1/C/358
Wm., sen., husb., Clench, Milton L., 1684, I, W, P3/C/482
Wm., broad weaver, Holt, Bradford A., 1692, AB, I, ren, W, P2/C/820
Wm., Haydon, Dorset, 1695, AB, comm, I, P5/1695/18
Wm., broad weaver, Melk., 1709, W, P2/C/962
Wm., yeo., Clench, Milton L., 1729, W, P3/C/780
Wm., clothw., Bradford A., 1756, W, P2/C/1292
Wm., Lattin Down, Wantage, Berks., 1760, AB, I, P23/687
Wm., collarmaker, Avebury, 1804, W, P1/1804/108
Wm., Sherston, 1806, AB, Wr, P3/1806/29
Wm., weaver, Trowb., 1828, W, Wr, P1/1828/7
Chapp, Chapp als Allen, Margery, widow, Malm., 1663, I, W, P3/C/290
Sam., [fellmonger], Malm., 1684, AB, I, P3/C/480
see also Allen als C.
Chappell, Agnes, Sutton Poyntz, Dorset, 1570, W, P5/2Reg/74C
Ambrose, yeo., Brokerswood, N. Bradley, 1662, comm, W, P1/C/244
Ambrose, clothw., Sal., 1684, I, W, P4/1684/2
Ambrose, clothw., Sal., 1720, W, P4/1720/3
Ambrose, Byde, Pott., 1743, W, P1/C/793, P1/9Reg/255
Ambrose, tucker, Sal., 1757, W, P4/1757/6
Anna, sp., Malm., 1744, AB, I, P3/C/880
Avis, widow, Sutton Poyntz, Dorset, 1613, AB, I, T, W, P5/1613/10, P5/9Reg/89C
Chas., Marl., 1752, AB, P1/C/848
Dan., Lyme R., Dorset, 1684, AB, P16/78
David, maltster, Winterborne K., Dorset, 1766, W, P5/1766/5
Eliz., widow, Sal., 1737, W, Wr, P4/1737/7
Jas., Sutton Poyntz, Dorset, 1593, AB, I, W, P5/1592/6, P5/6Reg/14B
Joan, sp., Fovant, 1664-71, bond, I, W, P1/C/276, 300
Joan, widow, Brokerswood, N. Bradley, 1687, comm, I, W, P1/C/378
Jn., husb., Fovant, 1571, W, P2/5Reg/123A
Chapel, Jn., husb., Gt. Wishford, 1615, I, W, P2/C/287, P2/8Reg/287A
Jn., Norrington (in Broad C.), Alvediston, 1642, AB, P2/C/510

Jn., yeo., Fovant, 1714, I, W, P2/C/994
Jn., mason, Fovant Stroud, 1747, W, P2/C/1245
Martha, sp., Stert, Urchf., 1779, AB, P1/C/1017
My., widow, Sutton Poyntz, Dorset, 1692, I, W, P5/1692/16
My., widow, Byde Mill, Pott., 1704, W, P1/C/485
My., widow, Sal., 1766, W, P4/1766/13
Michael, husb., Sutton Poyntz, Dorset, 1615, AB, I, T, W, P5/1615/4, P5/9Reg/165C
Michael, yeo., Bedborough, Bps. C., 1688, W, P24/779
Rd., yeo., Fovant, 1639, I, W, P2/C/478
Sam., salesman, Calne, 1857, aff, comm, W (& cod), Wr, P5/1857/1
Thos., husb., Gt. Wishford, 1626, I, W, P2/C/357
Thos., cutler, Sal. St Mart., 1628, AB, I, P4/1627/6
Thos., maltster, Chipp., 1700, I (detailed), W, P3/C/619
Thos., sen., Pott., 1703, AB, P1/C/481
Thos., yeo., Fullaway, All C., 1766, W, P3/C/992
Wm., Sutton Poyntz, Dorset, 1638, I, W, P5/1638/16, P5/13Reg/86D
Wm., [Chieveley, Berks.] (NBI), 1663, I, P30/31
Wm., groom, Sherb. Lodge, Dorset, 1689, I, W, P5/1689/11
Wm., innholder, Town, Malm., 1840, O, W, Wr, P3/1840/23
Chapperlin, Eliz., widow, Ashton K., 1670, AB, I, P3/C/339
Giles, potter, Ashton K., 1739, W, P3/C/846
Joan, widow, Langley Burrell, 1634, I, W, P3/C/200
Jn., sen., Ashton K., [1580], W (NEP), P3/1Reg/7C
My., widow, Ashton K., 1795, comm, W, P1/C/1086, P1/14Reg/630B
Maurice, husb., Ashton K., 1624, I, W, P3/C/127
Maurice, sen., yeo., Ashton K., 1687, I, W, P3/C/518
Maurice, yeo., Ashton K., 1766, W, P3/C/993
Robt., yeo., Ashton K., 1716, W, P3/C/702
Robt., yeo., Ashton K., 1777, W, P3/C/1053
Wm., husb., Ashton K., 1637, I, W, P3/C/223
Wm., pipemaker, Malm., [1710], I, W (NEP), P3/C/677
see also Chaplin
Chard, Rd., miller, Chards., Devon, 1808, comm, W, P14/203
Robt., yeo., Chards., Devon, 1830, W, Wr, P14/215
Sarah, widow, Netherb., Dorset, 1777, W, P17/569
Wm., Sal., 1642, AB, P4/1642/1
Charker *see* Charter
Charles, Charlotte, sp., Bradford A., 1792, AB, comm, P2/C/1466
Jane, sp., Bradford A., 1786, note of AB, P2/C/1440
Jn., carp., Atworth, Bradford A., 1691, AB, I, P2/C/813
Jn., sen., Atworth, Bradford A., 1720, AB, I, P2/C/1033
Sarah, sp., Baydon, 1844, comm, W, Wr, P5/1844/2
see also Shadwell als C.
Charlett, My., widow, Fisherton A., 1634, W, P2/C/424
Nich., tailor and yeo., Fisherton A., 1616, I (detailed), W, P1/C/76,
Charlton, Edwd., Warm., 1585, W, P2/7Reg/9A
Francis, yeo., Swallowfield, Shinfield, Berks., 1789, W, P1/C/1056, P1/14Reg/222
Hy., surgeon, Mere, 1829, W, Wr, P5/1829/13
Joan, widow, Warm., 1619, AB, I, P1/C/90
Jn., yeo., Eye and Dunsden, Sonning, Berks., 1794-95, W, P5/1795/3, P5/18Reg/218B
Jn., farmer, Longbridge D., 1814, W, Wr, P2/1814/33
Jos., yeo., Nether Zeals, 1744, W, Wr, P5/1744/9
Jos., maltster, Warm., 1833, aff, cert, W, Wr, P2/1833/17
My., widow, Longbridge D., 1821, W, Wr, P2/1821/58
Paul, Mere, 1724, AB, P5/1724/18
Paul, yeo., Over Zeals, 1733, W, P5/1733/15
Rachel, widow, Zeals, 1738, W, Wr, P5/1738/10
Rd., Stourton, 1692, AB, I, P1/C/424
Thos., blacksmith, Zeals, 1731, AB, I, P5/1731/19
Wm., husb., Stourpaine, Dorset, 1695, AB, I, P24/512

Wm., Zeals, 1813, AB, comm, Wr, P5/1813/4
Charman, Eliz., widow, Sal. The Close, 1728-29, W, P5/1728/20, P5/16Reg/215B
Charmbury, Betty, widow and vict., *The White Horse Inn*, Biddestone St Nich., 1780, W, P3/C/1063
Wm., husb., Sutton V., 1706, I, W, P2/C/933
Charter, Jn., tailor, Reading, Berks., 1729, W, P1/C/673, P1/7Reg/264
Charker, Thos., Sherb., Dorset, 1806, AB, P5/1806/5, P5/19Reg/152
Chase, Mgt., widow, Wambrook, Somerset, 1691, AB, comm, I, P14/77
Walter, tanner, Wambrook, Somerset, 1606, W, P5/1606/11, P5/8Reg/81B
Chassey, Chasy *see* Chaffey
Chater, Edmd., Damerham, Hants, 1620, AB, I, P2/C/319
Edwd., husb., Damerham, Hants, 1627, AB, I, P2/C/370
Eliz., widow, S. Damerham, Hants, 1638, I, W, P2/C/465
Harry, husb., Damerham, Hants, 1565, W, P2/4Reg/213E
Harry, Damerham, Hants, 1586, W, P2/7Reg/33A
Hy., Barford St Mart., 1609, AB, I, W, P2/C/230, P2/8Reg/70A
Jn., sen., husb., Damerham, Hants, 1603, AB, I, W, P2/C/198
Jn., sen., husb., Damerham, Hants, 1615, I, W, P2/C/285, P2/8Reg/281
Ralph, Damerham, Hants, 1593, I, W, P2/C/1516
Robt., husb., Damerham, Hants, 1598, AB, I, P2/C/157
Thos., Damerham, Hants, 1632, I, W, P2/C/412
Thos., Damerham, Hants, 1634, AB, a/c, comm, I, P1/C/151
Chatter, Timothy, clothier, Sal., 1729, AB, W, P4/1729/16
Chatterton, Hy., Tinh., Edington, 1575, W, P2/5Reg/229A
Hy., gent., Minety, [1602?], W (NEP), P3/1Reg/109A
Mgt., widow, Tinh., Edington, 1575, W, P2/5Reg/229C
Chatwell, Cath. *see also* Joan Davis
Jn., vintner, Wilton, 1585, W, P2/C/67, P2/7Reg/23B
Jn., yeo., Wilton, 1610, AB, I (Cath. C., Jn.'s widow, admr for Joan Davis, her mother in law), P2/C/249, P2/D/99
Jn. *see also* Joan Davis
Chawner, Jn., Wilcot, 1563, W (value of I given), P1/2Reg/147B
Cheanen *see* Channon
Cheapman *see* Chapman
Chearch *see* Church
Cheate *see* Baker als Cheate
Cheater, Chas., jun., vict., Devizes, 1732, comm, W, P1/C/701, P1/7Reg/437
Dan., grocer, Chipp., 1843, aff, W, Wr, P3/1843/49
Edwd., weaver, Devizes, 1810, W, Wr, P1/1810/1
Edwd., Devizes, 1815, AB, P1/1815/7
Eliz., widow, Deptford, Wylye, 1831, AB, W, P2/1831/6
Geo., shepherd, Easterton, Mkt. L., 1799, W, P2/C/1495
Hy., serge weaver, Devizes, 1720, AB, P1/C/606
Jn., chairmaker, Easterton, Mkt. L., 1753, W, P1/C/856, P1/11Reg/121B
Jn., W. Dean, 1808, AB, Wr, P2/1808/21
Rd., butcher, W. Dean, 1804, W, P1/1804/142
Sarah, widow, W. Dean, 1812, W, Wr, P2/1812/49
Simon, shepherd, Idmiston, 1709, AB, I, P2/C/953
Simon, Idmiston, 1731, AB, P2/C/1123
Chitter, Thos., sen., tailor, Devizes, 1651, I, W, P1/C/235
Thos., husb. and labourer, Idmiston, 1662, I, W, P2/C/548
Wm., Deptford, Wylye, 1829, AB, W, Wr, P2/1829/6
Checete *see* Huce als Checete
Check *see* Bartlemore *or* Bartellme als C.
Checker, Eliz., widow, Lt. Bedwyn, 1670, AB, I, P21/2/8
Eliz., widow, Lt. Bedwyn, 1689, AB, I, P21/4/40
Jas., husb., Lt. Bedwyn, 1679-81, AB, I, NW, P21/2/61, 75
Jane, widow, Lt. Bedwyn, 1748, W, P21/10/6
Jn., Burbage, 1676, I, P11/26
Chequer, Jn., Burbage, 1732, AB, I, P11/143
Thos., husb. and yeo., Lt. Bedwyn, 1662, I, W, P5/1662/28
Thos., husb., Lt. Bedwyn, 1680, I, W, P21/2/65

Thos., Lt. Bedwyn, 1689, a/c, I, P21/4/30
Thos., labourer, Lt. Bedwyn, 1736, I, W, P21/9/16
Wm., sen., yeo., Oak Hill, Froxfield, 1639, I, W, P1/C/185
Wm., servant to Sir Thos. Dolman of Shaw, Shaw cum Donnington, Berks., 1662, AB, I, NW, P1/C/247
Wm., Burbage, 1680, AB, I, P2/C/691, P11/46
Wm., sen., yeo., Westcourt, Burbage, 1731, AB, W, P5/1731/20
Ched, Wm., Sherb., Dorset, 1615, AB, comm, W, P5/1615/7, P5/9Reg/168C
Cheeke, Christian, sp., Marl., 1766, AB, comm, P1/C/936
Joan, sp., Uffc., Devon, 1628, AB, I, NW, P5/1628/28, P5/11Reg/64A
Jn., butcher, Craddock, Uffc., Devon, 1635, I, W, P5/1635/20, P5/12Reg/214
Jn., carp., Whitmore, Uffc., Devon, 1662, AB, I, P5/1662/30
Jn., yeo., Uffc., Devon, 1665, AB, I, LA, P5/1665/17
Oliver, husb., Bloxworth, Dorset, 1767, W, P5/1767/11
Cheer, Ann, wife, Drayton, Abingdon, Berks., 1714, AB, P1/C/555
Eliz., widow, Drayton, Abingdon, Berks., 1770, W, P1/C/963, P1/12Reg/354B
Jane, widow, E. Hendred, Berks., 1720, W, P23/382
Jn., sen., yeo., W. Lockinge, Wantage, Berks., 1716, I, W, P5/1716/23, P5/15Reg/352B
Jn., yeo., Drayton, Abingdon, Berks., 1823, W, Wr, P1/1823/82
Chair, Rd., Frilsham, Berks., 1726, AB, I, W, P1/C/648, P1/7Reg/105B
Sam., Abingdon, Berks., 1814, AB, P1/1814/104
Thos., sackclothmaker, Abingdon, Berks., 1820, W, Wr, P1/1820/89
Chair, Wm., yeo., W. Lockinge, Wantage, Berks., 1730, I, W, P23/471
Cheeseman, Christian [male], Enmore Grn, Motc., Dorset, 1665, AB, P19/4
Chisman, Chris., sen., clothier, Upton, E. Knoyle, 1679, I, W, P2/C/680
Chisman, Chris., yeo., E. Knoyle, 1750, W, P1/C/843, P1/10Reg/441
Eliz., sp., Newbury, Berks., 1717, comm, W, P1/C/570, P1/6Reg/86
Geo., miller, Alton P., Dorset, 1665, I, W, P5/1665/18
Geo., labourer, Enmore Grn, Motc., Dorset, 1850, aff, W, Wr, P19/258
Chisman, Jas., gent., E. Knoyle, 1845, W, Wr, P1/1845/29
Jn., tucker, Mkt. L., 1557, W, P2/3Reg/26A
Jn., yeo., Woodshaw, Wootton B., 1637, I, W, P3/C/224
Jn., blacksmith, Bower C., 1639, I, W, P2/C/473
Jn., yeo., Enmore Grn, Motc., Dorset, 1679, AB, I, P5/1679/14
Jn., yeo., Enmore Grn, Motc., Dorset, 1715, W, P5/1715/12
Jn., yeo., Yetm., Dorset, 1716, W, P5/15Reg/330B
Letitia *see* Leititia Wilton
My., widow, Mildenhall, 1779, W, P1/C/1004, P1/13Reg/217A
Patrick, Rams., 1709, AB, P5/1709/7
Robt., gent., Sal., 1825, W, Wr, P4/1825/7
Thos., sen., tanner, Enmore Grn, Motc., Dorset, 1730, W, P19/120
Thos., farmer, Mildenhall, 1779, AB, W, P1/C/1006, P1/13Reg/217B
Thos., labourer, Lucas's Hospital, Wokm., Berks., 1832, W, Wr, P5/1832/15
Chisman, Wm., maltster, E. Knoyle, 1766, W, P2/C/1346
Chisman, Wm., yeo., E. Knoyle, 1811, W, Wr, P2/1811/7
Cheeslett *see* Chislett
Cheesley, My., widow, Hampton, Highw., 1821, W, Wr, P10/1821/3
Steph., Hampton, Highw., 1804, AB, P10/1804/3
Cheetham, Sam., vict., Clarendon Park, 1795, W, P1/C/1077, P1/14Reg/590
Chefers *see* Chivers
Chegey, Edwd., Atworth, Bradford A., 1664, comm, W, P2/C/558
Cheltenham, Jn., sen., Alcombe (in Ditteridge), Box, 1617, I, W, P3/C/83
Mgt., widow, Ditteridge, 1618, I, W, P3/C/92
Chelton *see* Chilton
Cheney, Cheyney, Ann, Oare, Wilcot, 1742, W, P3/C/866
Cheyney, Barbara, widow, Oare, Wilcot, 1713, W, P3/C/683
Cheyney, Jn., husb., Everleigh, 1616, I, W, P3/C/82
Cheyney, Jn., Oare, Wilcot, 1669, AB, I, NW, P3/C/326
Cheyney, Jn., gent., Oare, Wilcot, 1681, AB, I, P3/C/432
[Jn.], tailor, Hurst, Berks., 1700, I, W [chr.name from burial entry], P5/1700/9
Cheyney, Jn., yeo., E. Challow, Letcombe Regis, Berks., 1735, W, P1/C/727, P1/7Reg/660

Nich., Marl. St Peter and St Paul, 1638, AB, P1/C/183
Robt., sen., feltmaker and hatter, Wallingford, Berks., 1714, I, W, P1/C/553, P1/5Reg/378
Cheyney, Sarah, widow, Oare, Wilcot, 1720, W, P3/C/730
Simon, gent., Porton, Idmiston, 1630, I, W, P2/C/394, P2/9Reg/123
Simon, Oare, Wilcot, 1725, W, P3/C/755
Cheyney, Thos., Oare, Wilcot, [1590], W (NEP), P3/1Reg/35
Thos., husb., Milton L., 1631, AB, I, P1/C/138
Cheyney, Thos., yeo., Easton, 1664, AB, I, P3/C/298
Cheyney, Thos., gent., Oxenwood (in Tidcombe), Shalbourne, 1675, AB, a/c, I, ren, NW, P3/C/375
Cheyney, Thos., Oare, Wilcot, 1743, W, P3/C/868
Cheyney, Wm., gent., Abingdon, Berks., 1686, W, P1/C/1118
Chepman *see* Chapman
Cheppenham *see* Chippenham
Chequer *see* Checker
Cherington, Hugh, yeo., Charlton nr Malm., 1617, I, W, P3/C/85
Cherry, Edith, widow, Winterborne K., Dorset, 1607, AB, I, W, P5/1607/17, P5/8Reg/86C
Rd., vicar, Burbage, 1695, AB, ren, P5/1695/15
Wm., husb., Winterborne K., Dorset, 1593, I, W, P5/1593/24, P5/6Reg/46B
Cheselden *see* Chisleton
Cheshire, Alice, widow of doctor in divinity, Dauntsey, 1673, court paper, I (2), W, P3/C/362
Dan., yeo., Rodbourne, Malm., 1730, I, W, P3/C/798
Cheshire als Young, Edwd., Ham, 1642, I, W, P3/C/270
Geo., minor, Dauntsey, 1675, T, P3/C/386
Robt., yeo., Collingbourne Woods & Bentley Woods, Idmiston, 1701, AB, I, ren (2), P2/C/896
Susanna, sp., Rodbourne, Malm., 1669, I, W, P3/C/325
see also Young als C.
Chesterman, Benj., vict., Reading, Berks., 1804, comm, W, P1/1804/76
Chris., shoemaker, Devizes Grn, Bps. C., 1611, AB, I, P24/129
Edwd., confectioner, Marl., 1832, W, Wr, P1/1832/145
Frances, Clack, Lyneham, 1634, AB, P1/C/154
Grace, widow, Wood St., Clyffe P., 1704, I (detailed), W, P1/C/486
Jas., sen., gent., Lyford, W. Hanney, Berks., 1729, W, P1/C/663, P1/7Reg/221
Jn., yeo., Clyffe P., 1790, W, P3/C/1106
Jn., yeo., Clyffe P., 1812, W, Wr, P3/1812/31
My., widow, Bradford A., 1774, W, P2/C/1370
Michael, yeo., Clyffe P., 1691, comm, I, NW, P3/C/549
Michael, Bradford A., 1739, AB, P2/C/1193
Michael, weaver, Woolley, Bradford A., 1840, O, W, Wr, P2/1840/40
Rd., Avebury, 1611, AB, I, P3/C/57
Rd., Avebury, 1639, I, W, P3/C/239
Thos., yeo., Kellaways, 1836, W, Wr, P3/1836/64
Wm., waggoner, Chipp., 1715, AB, I, W, P3/C/694
Chestle, Jn., Alderbury, 1703, AB, I, P26/495
Cheston, Steph., priest, Bishopstone S., 1558, institution to rectory, P1/1Reg/8A
Chestrow, Alice, widow, Purton, 1615, AB, I, W, P3/C/77
Chetmill, Arthur, weaver, Sherb., Dorset, 1683, I, NW, P5/1683/9
Eliz., widow, Sherb., Dorset, 1675, I, W, P5/1675/15
Jn., sen., Sherb., Dorset, 1595, AB, I, W, P5/1594/23, P5/6Reg/93B
Chetnoll, Jn., sen., [weaver], Sherb., Dorset, 1606, AB, I, T, P5/1606/13, P5/8Reg/74C
Chetnell, Jn., Sherb., Dorset, 1715, AB, I, P5/1715/13
Robt., Sherb., Dorset, 1611, I, P5/1611/5
Chetnill, Wm., Sherb., Dorset, 1667, AB, comm, P5/1667/17
Chettel *see* Chittle
Chever *see* Chivers
Cheverell, Chiverell, Alice, Tisb., 1587, W, P2/7Reg/88B
Eliz. *see* Wm. Pearce
Jn., yeo., Urchf., 1570, W, P2/5Reg/87B
Chiverell, Jn., mason, Tisb., 1633, I, W, P2/C/420, P2/9Reg/31A
Chiverill, Jn., Hindon, 1721, AB, P2/C/1040
Robt., Burbage, 1640, I, W, P11/13

Thos., Tisb., [1571], AB, P1/1Reg/23G
Thos., yeo., Marston, Pott., 1627, comm, I, W, P1/C/165
Thos., yeo., Tisb., 1827, W, Wr, P2/1827/13
Chiverell, Wm., sen., labourer, Hindon, [1676], I, W, P2/C/660
Chiverill, Wm., Tisb., 1741, AB, W, P2/C/1213
Chevers *see* Chivers
Chew, Wm., labourer, Purton, 1694, I, W, P3/C/570
Wm., yeo., Charlton nr Malm., 1705, I, W, P3/C/652
Cheyney *see* Cheney
Chick, Hy., Furleigh Cross, Netherb., Dorset, 1685, I, W, P5/1685/24
Chickes, Jas., Beam., Dorset, 1593, T, W, I, P5/1593/28, P5/6Reg/44C
Jas., husb., Beam., Dorset, 1634, I, W. Proved at the Metropolitan visitation to Dorchester, P5/1634/29, P5/12Reg/287
Jas., sen., husb., Beam., Dorset, 1698, I, W, P5/1698/19
Jas., sen., potter, Beam., Dorset, 1718, W, P17/376
Jas., potter, Beam., Dorset, 1770, W, P5/1770/10, P5/17Reg/18A
Rd., Ludg., 1581, W, P2/6Reg/38A
Roger, carp., Furleigh Cross, Netherb., Dorset, 1670, I, W, P17/95
Thos., Chards., Devon, 1815, W, O, Wr, P14/208
Wm., Beam., Dorset, 1570, AB, P5/2Reg/78A
Wm., husb., Beam., Dorset, 1683, I, P17/243
Chiddeock, Hugh, husb., Wexcombe, Grafton, 1563, W, P5/1Reg/20D
Chidwick, Jn., yeo., Gt. Bedwyn, 1754, W, P21/10/21
Thos., Gt. Bedwyn, 1635, AB, P5/12Reg/262D
Thos., husb., Wexcombe, Grafton, 1635, AB, I, P5/1635/27
Chidick, Thos., yeo., Gt. Bedwyn, 1702, I, W, P21/6/6
Chiddoke, Wm., husb., Chute, 1563, W, P5/1Reg/19B
Chiffence, Chiffinch, Edmd., husb., Stert, Urchf., 1557, W, P2/3Reg/40C
Chissing, Eleanor, sp., Stert, Urchf., 1628, I, W, P1/C/127
Eliz., widow, Devizes St My., 1793-94, W, P1/C/1076, P1/14Reg/471B
Jas., grazier, Rowde, 1824, comm, W, Wr, P3/1824/39
Jane, widow, Nursteed, Bps. C., 1855, AB, aff, app. of guardian, O (2), T (re Eliza Jane C.), Wr, P24/1413
Joan, widow, Stert, Urchf., 1619, I, W, P1/C/100
Chiffins, Joan, widow, Melk., 1638, I, NW, P1/C/180
Chiffins, Jn., husb., Stert, Urchf., 1616, I, W, P1/C/83
Chiffesin, Jn., labourer, Ogbourne St Geo., 1689, AB, I, P23/168
Jn., weaver, Melk., 1737-48, AB, I (1737), P2/C/1247
Lewis, gent., Dunkirk, Rowde, 1818, W, Wr, P3/1818/27
Chiffing, Nich., fellmonger, Bedborough, Bps. C., 1622, I, NW, P24/203
Nich., sen., gardener, Devizes, 1705, I, W, P1/C/495
Robt., nurseryman, Pott., 1807, W, Wr, P1/1807/32
Chiffinch, Thos., innholder, Sal., 1649, W, P1/C/224
Chiffinch, Thos., yeo., Pott. Wick, 1724, W, P1/C/635, P1/7Reg/53B
Thos., gardener, Nursteed, Bps. C., 1855, AB, aff, O, W, Wr, P24/1414
Chilcott, Ann, wife, Hooke, Dorset (effects at Netherb., Dorset), 1749, AB, Wr, P5/1749/17
Jos., weaver, Melk., 1843, comm, W, Wr, P2/1843/56
Jos., widower, Melk., 1844-45, AB, comm, court proceeding, Wr, P2/1844/7, P2/1845/14
Robt., yeo., Beam., Dorset, 1686, AB, I, P17/297
Robt., Beam., Dorset, 1724, AB, P17/420
Susanna, widow, Winterborne St Mart., Dorset (but effects held at Beam., Dorset), 1740, W, Wr, P5/1740/18
Wm., yeo., N. Mapperton, Dorset, [1687], I, W, P17/304
Wm., Avebury (late of St Jn. the Baptist's Hospital, Bath, commonly called the Blue Alms House), 1783, comm, W, P3/C/1078
Child, Chills, Ann, widow, Boscombe, 1716, W, P1/C/569, P1/6Reg/69B
Childs, Ann, sp., Gillingham, Dorset, 1764, W, P27/1/442, P27/3Reg/108B
Ann, widow, Hurst, Berks., 1824, O, W, Wr, P5/1824/40
Anth., Newbury, Berks., 1628, AB, I, P1/C/123
Childs, Asa, carp., Amesb., 1758, W, P2/C/1294
Chas., husb., Hurst, Berks., 1711, AB, comm, I, P5/1711/17
Childs, Eliz., widow, Heytes., 1738, W, Wr, P5/1738/11
Eliz., widow, Hurst, Berks., 1764, AB, P5/1764/8

Eliz., widow, Heddington, 1819, req, W, Wr, P3/1819/36
Francis, Melk., 1767, AB, comm, W, P2/C/1341
Francis, gent., Castle C., 1820, W, Wr, P1/1820/79
Francis, yeo., Castle C., 1852, W, Wr, P3/1852/30
Geo., husb., Hurst, Berks., 1720, AB, I (detailed), P5/1720/12
Geo., yeo., Hurst, Berks., 1745, AB, I (detailed), P5/1745/4
Hy., baker, Calne, 1790, W, P26/1166
Childs, Hugh, Sutton C., Berks., 1729, AB, P1/C/668
Childs, Hugh, E. Hagbourne, Berks., 1747, AB, P1/C/829
Jas., Winnersh, Hurst, Berks., 1799, AB, P5/1799/5, P5/18Reg/277A
Jas., yeo., Waltham St Lawr., Berks., 1820, W, Wr, P1/1820/3
Jane, widow, Heddington, 1690, W, P3/C/542
Jane, Ludg., 1701, AB, P2/C/892
Jane, sp., Sal., 1810, W, P4/1810/5
Joan, widow, Heddington, 1629, I, W, P3/C/159
Chiles, Jn., Nether C., Dorset, 1606, I, W, P5/1606/14, P5/8Reg/74A
Chiles, Jn., shepherd, Idmiston, 1661, AB, I, P2/C/546
Jn., yeo., Long Wittenham, Berks., 1689, I, W, P1/C/404
Jn., cordw., E. Hagbourne, Berks., 1747, W, P1/C/827, P1/10Reg/79
Jn., husb., Beech Hill, Stratfield Saye, Hants, 1783, W, P1/C/1038, P1/13Reg/459
My., sp., Newton T., 1729, AB, P1/C/688
My., sp., Sal., 1772, W, P4/1772/10
Chiles, Nich., maltster, Nether C., Dorset, 1666, I, W, P5/1666/9
Childs, Nich., yeo., Milton, Berks., 1770, W, P1/C/962, P1/12Reg/357A
Rd., Thornford, Dorset, 1640, AB, I, P5/1640/12, P5/13Reg/233A
Rd., yeo., Newton T., 1692, I, W, P2/C/825
Rd., carp., Bourton, Gillingham, Dorset, 1767, W, P27/1/459, P27/3Reg/140
Robt., clothier, Heddington, 1688, comm, I, W, P3/C/527
Childs, Robt., innholder, Fisherton A., 1738, W, P1/C/766, P1/8Reg/355
Childs, Roger, labourer, Blewbury, Berks., 1635, AB, I, P5/1635/23, P5/12Reg/236B
Simon, Newton T., 1636, I, W, P2/C/447
Childs, Steph., yeo., Boscombe, 1708, W, P2/C/949
Steph., S. Newton, 1718, W, P2/C/1020
Childs, Steph., sen., Heytes., 1721, AB, I, P5/1721/6
Childs, Steph., yeo., Mere, 1743, AB, NW, P5/1743/16
Chiles, Thos., yeo., Thornford, Dorset, 1637, AB, a/c, comm, I, P5/1636/17, P5/12Reg/252B
Thos., gent., Sal., 1661, I, W, P4/1661/2
Childs, Thos., yeo., Yattendon, Berks., 1720, I, W, P1/C/604, P1/6Reg/325
Thos., Castle C., 1773, AB, P1/C/974, P3/C/1032
Chiles als Waggen, Walter, tanner, Warm., 1595, I, W, P2/C/133, P2/7Reg/153A
Wm., E. Hagbourne, Berks., 1677, AB, I, P1/C/329
Childs, Wm., sen., yeo., Newton T., 1681-82, I, W, P2/C/702, 724
Childs, Wm., husb., Bourton, Gillingham, Dorset, 1685, I, P27/1/89
Wm., yeo., Allington, All C., [1688], I, W, P2/C/786
Childs, Wm., yeo., S. Newton, 1707, I, W, P2/C/946
Wm., sen., yeo., Allington, 1729, W, P1/C/685, P1/7Reg/353B
Childs, Wm., Heytes., 1760, AB, P5/1760/5
Childs, Wm., Heytes., 1768, AB, P5/1768/5
Wm., glazier, Castle C., 1831, W, Wr, P3/1831/68
Chilford, Geo., yeo., Shrewton, 1766, W, P2/C/1329
Chills *see* Childs
Chilton, Eliz., widow, Maiden B., 1624, I, P2/C/336
Chelton, Gilbt., labourer, Westport St My., 1739, AB, I, P3/C/847
Chelton, Theodore, Gt. Somerford, 1669, comm, W, P3/C/324
Chilvester, Alice, widow, W. Lavington, 1690, AB, I, W, P1/C/410
Chilvester, Ann, widow, W. Lavington, 1701, W, P1/C/468, P1/3Reg/275
Chilvester, Edmd., yeo., Charnham St., Hungerford, Berks., 1707, W, P5/1707/13, P5/15Reg/49
Chilvester, Joan, widow, Yatesbury, 1594, AB, I, W, P5/1594/18, P5/6Reg/85B
Chilvester, Jn., Enford, 1622, AB, P2/C/325
Chilvester, Jn., sen., husb., Yatesbury, 1628, I, W, P3/C/155

Chilvester, Jn., husb., Calne, 1636, I, W, P26/56
Chilvester, My., wife, Charnham St., Hungerford, Berks., 1695, AB, P5/1695/17
Chilvester, Steph., husb., Heytes., 1631, I, NW, P5/1631/22, P5/12Reg/39A
Chinn, Geo. Thos., Sal., 1850, AB, Wr, P4/1850/5
Jos. Jas., innholder, Sal., 1833, W, Wr, P4/1833/1
Chinock, Agnes, widow, Winterborne K., Dorset, 1612, W, P5/1612/16
Edwd., carp., Fisherton A., 1640, I, W, P2/C/489
Jn., husb., Baynton, Edington, 1598, W, P2/C/165
Robt., Edington, 1559, W, P2/3Reg/148C
Thos., Winterborne K., Dorset, 1611, I, W, P5/1610/9, P5/9Reg/52C
Chipman, Jn., yeo., N. Wootton, Dorset, 1693, I, W, P5/1693/16
Chipp, Abel, Preston, Dorset, 1625, AB, I, P5/1625/13, P5/10Reg/289B
Eliz., widow, Charminster, Dorset, 1662, I, W, P5/1662/25
Jas., Bere R., Dorset, 1777, AB, P5/1777/5, P5/17Reg/138C
Thos., Alton P., Dorset, 1597, AB, I, W, P5/1597/19, P5/6Reg/165B
Thos., sievemaker, Knook, 1669, I, W, P5/1669/11
Thos., sen., yeo., Corsley, 1696, AB, I, W, P2/C/860
Wm., husb., Charminster, Dorset, 1623-24, I, W, P5/1623/8, P5/10Reg/167D
Wm., husb., Charminster, Dorset, 1639, I, W, P5/1639/17, P5/13Reg/217
Wm., yeo., Alton P., Dorset (effects at Southwick, N. Bradley), 1733, AB, comm, I, W, P5/1733/16
Chippenham, Cheppenham, Jane, widow, Holt, Bradford A., 1603, I, W, P2/C/193
Chisholme, Jas., gent., Sal., 1849, D, W, Wr, P4/1849/5
Chisleton als Hellier, Chas., Heddington, 1731, AB, P3/C/790
Cheselden als Hiller, Thos., husb., Cherell, Calne, 1574, W, P5/3Reg/48B
Thos., Calne, 1638, AB, a/c, P5/1638/17, P5/13Reg/131D
see also Hellier als C.
Chislett, Cheeslett, Anchoret, widow, Mere, 1578, I, W, P5/1578/10, P5/3Reg/106C
Cheeslett, Edith, widow, Mere, 1576, AB, P5/1576/10, P5/3Reg/92B
Eleanor, widow, Mere, 1618, I, W, P5/1617/42, P5/9Reg/195B
Jas., innholder, Sherb., Dorset, 1798, W, P5/1798/5, P5/18Reg/264B
Cheeslett, Jn., husb., Mere, 1568, W, P5/2Reg/6A
Lambert Tree, bach., Upton S., 1846, AB, comm, Wr, P2/1846/65
Lawr., yeo., Sandhurst, Berks., 1606, AB, I (detailed), W, P1/C/29
Cheeslett, Margery, widow, Mere, 1581, I, W, P5/1580/16, P5/4Reg/17C
Cheeslett, Robt., husb., Mere, 1579, I, W, P5/1578/9, P5/3Reg/115B
Cheeslett, Robt., tailor, Warm., 1619, I, W, P1/C/97
Cheeslett, Robt., [blacksmith], Mere, 1682, AB, I, P5/1682/20
Cheeslett, Thos., yeo., Sandhurst, Berks., 1596, AB, I, W, P5/1596/16, P5/6Reg/133
Thos., Mere, 1716, AB, P5/1716/17
Thos., yeo., Mere, 1738, AB, I, W, P5/1738/12
Cheeslett, Wm., butcher, Mere, 1572, W, P5/3Reg/3A
Wm., Mere, 1614, AB, I, P5/1614/14, P5/9Reg/148B
Chisman *see* Cheeseman
Chissing *see* Chiffence
Chittel *see* Chittle
Chitter *see* Cheater
Chitterne, Jn., Sal., 1685, AB, I, P4/1685/6
Chittle, Chittle als May, Ann, wife, Speenhamland, Berks., 1732, AB, comm, P1/C/707
Chittel, Ann, widow, Beedon, Berks., 1770, W, P1/C/960, P1/12Reg/347B
Wm., sen., blacksmith, Blewbury, Berks., 1605, I, W, P1/C/23
Wm., blacksmith, Blewbury, Berks., 1624, AB, a/c, I, notes, P5/1624/8, P5/10Reg/225A
Chittel, Wm., salesman, Speenhamland, Berks., 1726, comm, W, P1/C/638, P1/7Reg/74
Chitts, Joan, widow, Blewbury, Berks., 1589, I, W, P5/1589/10, P5/5Reg/53
Robt., husb., Blewbury, Berks., 1628, I, W, P5/1628/20, P5/11Reg/84
Chitty, Jn., yeo., Cadley, Chute, 1781, W, P7/174
Chiver *see* Chivers
Chiverell, Chiverill *see* Cheverell
Chivers, Alexander, Brokerswood, N. Bradley, 1753, AB, P2/C/1274
Chiver, Alice, widow, Chittoe, Bps. C., 1616, I, W, P24/90
Alice, widow, Gt. Amesb., 1630, I, W, P2/C/388

Ann, widow, Bromham, 1682, AB, I, P3/C/449
Chevers, Anth., tailor, Devizes, 1680, AB, I, W, P1/C/346
Anth., maltster, Devizes, 1743, W, P1/C/794, P1/9Reg/257
Chefers, Bart., broad weaver, Dilton, Westb., 1687, I. No evidence of being exhibited, P25/1687/11
Dorothy, widow [and innholder], Sal., 1671, a/c (detailed), AB, D, I (detailed), NW, P4/1671/6
Chever, Edmd., Blackland, Calne, 1612, I, W, P26/25
Chiver, Eleanor, Calne, 1604, AB, P5/1603/22
Eliz., Upton S., 1679, AB, P2/C/682
Eliz., widow, Chipp., 1723, W, P3/C/744
Gabriel, farmer, Holt, Bradford A., 1729, I, W, P2/C/1105
Geo., Kington St M., 1763, AB, P1/C/921
Chiver, Hy., Chittoe, Bps. C., 1628, AB, memo, P24/216
Hy., Bromham, 1628, AB, I, P3/C/156
Hy., sen., fuller, Slaughterford, 1662, I, W, P1/C/251
Hy., weaver, Bromham, 1673, AB, comm, I, W, P3/C/364
Hy., innholder, Calne, 1740, W, Wr, P5/1740/17
Chever, Hy. *see also* Eliz. Francis
Humphrey, yeo., Sandridge Hill, Melk., 1729, W, P2/C/1107
Jacob, yeo., Compton B., 1801, W, P3/1801/5
Jas., Upton S., 1759, AB, comm, P2/C/1302
Jas., yeo., Kington L., 1828, req, W, Wr, P3/1828/19
Jane, widow, Marl., 1694, I, W, P1/C/435
Joan, widow, Westb. L., 1729, W, P25/1729/12
Joan, widow, Kington L., 1785, comm, W, P3/C/1085
Chevers, Jn., no abode stated, [1597], I, P2/C/149
Chiver, Jn., husb., Heddington, 1599, W, P3/C/3
Chever, Jn., yeo., Chittoe, Bps. C., 1610, I, W, P24/142
Chever, Jn., Chittoe, Bps. C., 1612, I, W, P24/56
Jn., Westb. L., 1700, AB, I, P25/1700/2
Chevers, Jn., broad weaver, Chittoe, Bps. C., 1702, I, W, P3/C/637
Jn., tailor, Heddington, 1738, W, P3/C/842
Jn., Chipp., 1798, AB, P1/C/1098, P1/15Reg/116A
Jn., Preshute, 1811, AB, comm, Wr, P1/1811/139
Jn., Avebury, 1845, AB, W, Wr, P3/1845/38
Jn., bach., Barbary Farm, Ogbourne St And., 1850, AB, comm, Wr, P5/1850/13
Jos., yeo., Compton, Berks. (form. of E. Ilsley, Berks.), 1798, W, P1/C/1092, P1/15Reg/35C
Chever, Mgt., Bromham, 1608, I, W (NEP), P3/C/30
Mgt., widow, Shaw, Melk., 1618, I, W, P2/C/309
Mgt., widow, Heddington, 1743, W, P3/C/873
Marian, Heddington, 1634, court paper, P3/C/201
Martha, sp., Marl., 1733, W, P1/C/716, P1/7Reg/572
Marvin, chairmaker, Trowb., 1785, AB, comm, ren, P1/C/1044
Chevers, Nich., broad weaver, Trowb., 1639, I, W, P22/2/37
Philip, hosier, Marl., 1697, I, W, P1/C/453
Rd., yeo., Brokerswood, N. Bradley, 1833, aff, comm, W, Wr, P2/1833/4
Robt., Marl., 1726, AB, P1/C/643
Robt., maltster, Foxham, Bremhill, 1727, W, P3/C/764
Chever, Roger, Trowb., 1574, AB, P5/3Reg/47A
Roger, Devizes, 1714, AB, P1/C/558
Roger, broad weaver, Bradford A., 1719, I, W, P2/C/1027
Sam., yeo., Slaughterford, 1718, I, W, P3/C/712
Sam., weaver, Melk., 1800, W, Wr, P2/1800/15
Sarah, widow, Compton, Berks., 1807, comm, req, W, copy W, Wr, P1/1807/27
Susanna, widow, Hilmarton, 1762, AB, P3/C/965
Thos., Bps. C., 1622, AB, I, P24/201
Chever, Thos., sen., weaver, Bromham, 1631, I, W, P3/C/176
Chiver, Thos., weaver, Bromham, 1635, I, W, P3/C/204
Thos., [innholder], Sal., 1664, AB, I, P4/1663/4
Chevers, Thos., sen., sievemaker, Calne, 1700, I, W, P26/470
Thos., sen., yeo., Upton S., 1742, W, P2/C/1215

Timothy, currier, Marl., 1687, I, W, P1/C/388
Walter, farmer, Dauntsey, 1827, comm, W, Wr, P3/1827/13
Chever, Wm., fuller, Quemerford, Calne, 1580, W (lists of debts owing to decd on dorse), P26/1478, P5/3Reg/151B
Chiver, Wm., clothier, Bromham, 1614, comm, I, W, P1/C/71
Wm., cordw., Goatacre, Hilmarton, 1707, I, W, P3/C/662
Wm., barber, Chipp., 1713, I, W, P3/C/684
Wm., Calne, 1723, AB, I, P26/680
Wm., sen., baker, Goatacre, Hilmarton, 1773, W, P1/C/973, P1/13Reg/7B
Wm., Compton B., 1820, comm, W, Wr, P1/1820/21
Wm., Seend, Melk., 1825, AB, comm, Wr, P2/1825/57
Wm., Corsham, 1828, AB, Wr, P3/1828/66
Wm., ironmonger, Calne, 1830, comm, W, Wr, P26/1382
Chiverson, Alexander, husb., Winterbourne M., 1741, AB, W, P1/C/774, P1/9Reg/47
Bridget, widow, Yatesbury & Clyffe P., 1715, AB, W, P3/C/695
see also Blackeden als C.
Chocke, Wm., Hurst, Berks., 1573, W, P5/3Reg/14D
Cholesey *see* Cholsey
Cholet, Jemima, widow, Bridzor, Tisb., 1781, comm, W, P2/C/1418
Cholls *see* Choules
Cholsey, Jn., Stockton, 1574, W, P2/5Reg/195B
Jn., vict., Norton B., 1626, I, W, P2/C/363
Choulsie, Jn., jun., yeo., Longbridge D., [1636], I, P2/C/444
Cholesey, Jn., Hindon, 1694, AB, P2/C/846
My., widow, Longbridge D., 1677, AB, P2/C/670
Rd., sawyer, Hindon, 1723, I, W, P1/C/628, P1/7Reg/35
Choules, Cholls, Agnes, widow, Baydon, 1566, W, P5/2Reg/11B
Benj., yeo., Chiseldon, 1811, W, Wr, P3/1811/10
Benj., Gt. Bedwyn, 1813, AB, P21/12/30
Chowles, Christian, Rams., 1605, AB, P5/1605/17
Chowles, Ellen, widow, Baydon, 1607, AB, I, W, P5/1607/12, P5/8Reg/96
Chowles, Hugh, Baydon, 1636, AB, comm, I, P5/1635/26, P5/12Reg/259A
Chowles, Jn., yeo., Baydon, 1605, I, W, P5/1605/8, P5/8Reg/43A
Chowles, Jn., yeo., Minety, 1636, I (2 - 1 a copy), W, P3/C/214
Chowles, Jn., labourer, Rams., 1668, AB, I, NW, P5/1668/21
Chowles, Jn., yeo., Baydon, 1678, AB, comm, I, P5/1678/7
Chowles, My., widow, Bishopstone N., 1721, I, P6/81
Robt., sen., yeo., Hodson, Chiseldon, 1789, comm, W, P1/C/1063, P1/14Reg/322
Robt., yeo., Badbury, Chiseldon, 1826, comm, W, Wr, P1/1826/123
Sarah, sp., Collingbourne D., 1850, comm, W, Wr, P1/1850/22
Chowles, Thos., Minety, 1607, AB, P3/C/26
Chowles, Thos., husb., Baydon, 1661, comm, I, W, P5/1661/8
Thos., yeo., Baydon, 1678, I, W, P5/1678/8
Chowles, Thos., yeo., Bishopstone N., 1705, I, W, P6/93
Chowles, Thos., yeo., Baydon, 1711, I, W, P5/1711/18, P5/15Reg/251
Chowles, Wm., labourer, Wanb., 1760, W, P3/C/951
Chowles, Wm., yeo., Badbury, Chiseldon, 1782, W, P3/C/1076
Wm., carp., Chiseldon, 1813, W, Wr, P3/1813/41
Chowles, Wm., baker and shopkeeper, Donnington, Berks., 1823, W, Wr, P1/1823/98
Wm., yeo., E. Leaze Farm, Aldbourne, 1841, comm, W, Wr, P3/1841/28
Young, yeo., Badbury, Chiseldon, 1803, comm, W, P3/1803/54
Choulsie *see* Cholsey
Chount, Rd., husb., Fordington, Dorset, 1640-41, I, W, P5/1641/16, P5/14Reg/29B
Chownt, Robt., husb., Sutton Poyntz, Dorset, 1579, I, W, P5/1579/17, P5/3Reg/127B
Chowles *see* Choules
Chown, Agnes, Uffc., Devon, 1553, W, P20/Reg/61
Christian, Berwick St Jn., 1842, I, W, Wr, P2/1842/24
Chownt *see* Chount
Chreasby *see* Crosby
Chresbin *see* Cresbin
Christian, Jane, widow, Earley, Sonning, Berks., 1719, W (NEP), P5/1719/16

Jn., Sonning, Berks., 1720, AB, P5/1720/11
Rd., sen., Hurst, Berks., 1627, I, W, copy W, P5/1627/10, P5/11Reg/50
Christmas, My., widow, Sonning, Berks., 1710, W, P5/1710/25, P5/15Reg/154A
Christopher, (Mr) *see* Roger Pinckney
Anth., Fisherton A., 1668, AB, I, P2/C/581
Judith, widow, Sonning, Berks., 1708, W, P5/1708/19, P5/15Reg/71
Thos., Bray, Berks., 1744, AB, P1/C/802
Wm., Fisherton A., 1722, AB, P2/C/1502
Christophers, Thos., cooper, Sal., 1680, I, P4/1680/22
Chritchell *see* Crichell
Chubb, Abraham, husb., Chards., Devon, 1839, W, Wr, P5/1839/13
Alice, widow, Odstock, 1734, AB, P2/C/1161
Anth., yeo., Odstock, [1639], I, W, P2/C/469
Barbara, widow, Sal., 1717, W, P4/1717/6
Bennet, Downton, 1682, AB, P2/C/720
Betty, sp., Hindon, 1772, AB, P2/C/1362
Betty, sp., Sal., 1849, W, Wr, P4/1849/14
Edith, widow, Nunton, N. and Bodenham, 1554, W, P2/2Reg/182D
Edmd., Sal., 1764, AB, P4/1764/5
Edwd., rector, Brixton D., 1713, W, P1/C/535, P1/5Reg/293B
Eliz., widow, Chards., Devon, 1631, AB, W, copy W, P5/1631/25, P5/12Reg/12
Eliz., sp., Berwick St Jas., 1716, W, P2/C/1005
Eliz., Winterbourne S., 1741, W, P1/C/776, P1/9Reg/60A
Geo., yeo., Odstock, 1682, I, W, P2/C/722
Geo., miller, Swallowcliffe, 1852, W, Wr, P5/1852/27
Hy., Coombe B., 1612, AB, I, T, P5/1612/15, P5/9Reg/77A
Hy., sen., maltster, E. Harnham, Britford, 1689, AB, I, W, P24/733
Hy., clothier, Downton, 1700, I, W, P2/C/888
Hy., maltster, E. Harnham, Britford, 1760, W, P24/1107
Jas., sen., yeo., Odstock, 1726, comm, I, W, P1/C/641, P1/7Reg/79B
Jas. *see also* Wm. Hiscock
Joan, Heddington, [1583], W (NEP), P3/1Reg/9A
Joan, widow, Coombe B., 1598, AB, I (fragment), W, P5/1598/9, P5/6Reg/201C
Joan, Alston, Chards., Devon, 1631-32, I, W, P5/1631/24, P5/12Reg/13
Joan, widow, Bloxworth, Dorset, 1724, AB, I, P5/1724/22
Jn., husb., Nunton, N. and Bodenham, 1551, W, P2/2Reg/119D
Jn., husb., Nunton, N. and Bodenham, 1592, I, T, W, P2/C/108
Jn., Chards., Devon, 1629, AB, comm, I, P5/1628/32, P5/11Reg/18B
Jn., yeo., Charlton, Downton, 1635, I, W, P2/C/427, P2/9Reg/45A
Jn., Gt. Amesb., 1638, AB, a/c, P2/C/460
Jn., sen., yeo., Nunton, N. and Bodenham, 1670, comm, W, P2/C/602
Jn., innholder, Sal., 1696, AB, P4/1696/5
Jn., shoemaker, Sal. St Thos., 1709, W, P4/1708/12
Jn., yeo., Coombe B., 1710, I, W, P5/1710/26, P5/15Reg/194
Jn., Odstock, 1717, AB, P2/C/1009
Jn., yeo., Bemerton, Fugg. St Peter, 1731, W, P2/C/1134
Jn., Shrewton, 1830, W, Wr, P2/1830/19
Jos., Nunton, N. and Bodenham, 1714, AB, P2/C/995
Jos., sen., yeo., Nunton and Bodenham, 1717, AB, I, P2/C/1010
Jos., clothier, Downton, 1725, AB, I, P2/C/1068
Jos., wheelwright, Charlton, Downton, 1786, W, P2/C/1437
Lawr., cheesemonger, Sal., 1719, W, P4/1719/14
Lawr., sen., cheesemonger, Sal., 1759, W, P1/C/904, P1/11Reg/430
My., widow, Nunton, N. and Bodenham, 1689, I, W, P2/C/799
My., widow, E. Harnham, Britford, 1724, AB, I, P24/863
My., sp., E. Harnham, Britford, 1728, AB, P24/840
My., sp. & leatherseller, Castle St., Sal. (form. of Exeter, Devon), 1841, W, Wr, P1/1841/7
Melior, Sal., 1780, AB, P1/C/1020
Rd., Damerham, Hants, 1815, AB, Wr, P2/1815/72
Robt., husb., Gt. Cheverell, 1685, I, W, P2/C/761

Roger, yeo., Bodenham, Nunton and B., [1686], I, P2/C/770
Roger, Odstock, 1727, AB, P1/C/657
Sarah, sp., Sal., 1802, AB, P4/1802/9
Susanna, widow, Downton, 1738, W, P2/C/1182
Susanna, sp., Sal., 1798, req, W, copy W, P4/1798/3
Thos., husb., Coombe B., 1575, T, W, P5/1575/11, P5/3Reg/64D
Thos., husb., Coombe B., 1601, I, T, W, P5/1601/11, P5/7Reg/23C
Thos., yeo., Odstock, 1731, AB, I, ren, W, P2/C/1135
Thos., Sal., 1747, AB, P4/1746/12
Walter, husb., Sal. St Edmd., 1584, W, P4/Reg/24
Walter, yeo., Nunton, N. and Bodenham, 1612, W, P2/C/261
Wm., husb., Odstock, 1592, I, W, P2/C/109
Wm., Odstock, 1670, AB, I, P2/C/612
Wm., blacksmith, Bloxworth, Dorset, 1695, comm, I, W, P5/1695/14
Wm., gent., Sal., 1701, W, P1/C/475, P1/4Reg/195
Wm., yeo., Coombe B., 1705, W, P8/11
Wm., Odstock, 1726, AB, I, P1/C/639
Wm., sen., The Mill, Swallowcliffe, 1825, W, Wr, P5/1825/9
Chudsey *see* Chadsey
Chun, Ann, widow, Lt. Bedwyn, 1696, AB, I, P21/5/36
Jn., collarmaker, Lt. Bedwyn, 1692, AB, I, P21/5/10
My., sp., Marl., 1841, D, O, W, Wr, P1/1841/12
Thos., sen., yeo., Shalbourne, 1692, I, W, P5/1692/19
Church, Ann, widow, Charlton nr Malm., 1673, AB, I, P3/C/363
Ann, widow, Chaddington, Lydiard T., 1695, AB, I, P3/C/582
Ann, widow, Westrop, Highw., 1702, I, W, P10/1702/3
Ann, widow, Cleverton, Lea and C., 1720, I, W, P3/C/731
Ann, butcher's widow, Malm., 1806, W, Wr, P3/1806/4
Cath., widow, E. Stowell, Wilcot, 1639, I, W, P3/C/240
Edwd., sen., Hinton Waldrist, Berks., 1729, AB, P1/C/669
Edwd., tallow chandler, Rams., 1781, W, P5/1781/3, P5/17Reg/214A
Edwd., gent., Hunts Coppice, S. Marston (late of Blunsdon St And.), 1784, W, P10/1784/2
Eliz., widow, Durley, Burbage, 1571, W, P5/2Reg/105
Eliz., widow, Tockenham, 1692, AB, I, W, P3/C/555
Eliz., widow, Milbourne, Malm., 1765, W, P3/C/986
Eliz., widow, Newbury, Berks., 1814, note, W, Wr, P1/1814/93
Frances, widow, Durley, Burbage, 1715, W, P11/114
Church als Holiday, Frideswide, widow, Wootton B., 1681-83, AB (2), I, P3/C/433, 468
Gabriel, yeo., Highway, 1645, AB, I, P1/C/205
Gabriel, yeo., Wootton B., 1677, I, W, P3/C/399
Geo., yeo., Beanacre, Melk., 1679, I, W, P2/C/679
Geo., jun., Hungerford, Berks., 1748, AB, P23/606
Geo., yeo., Aldbourne, 1801, W, P1/1801/60, P1/15Reg/276
Hannah, sp., Overton, 1816, W, P3/1816/2
Hy., labourer, Kennet, Overton, 1756, W, P1/C/874, P1/11Reg/199
Isaac, yeo., Beanacre, Melk., 1739, W, P2/C/1188
Isaac, yeo., Braydon Side, Brinkw., 1788, comm, I, W (2 different), P3/C/1101
Jacob, yeo., White Heath, Burton Hill, Malm., 1768, W, P3/C/1003
Jas., Charlton nr Malm., 1672, AB, P3/C/356
Jn., Durley, Burbage, 1606, W (damaged), P1/C/35
Jn., husb., E. Stowell, Wilcot, 1637, AB, I, P3/C/225
Jn., husb., Overton & Oare, 1683, I, W, P3/C/469
Jn., Tockenham Wick, 1690, AB, I, P3/C/543
Jn., yeo., Durley, Burbage, 1715, AB, I (2), T (3 - Jn. C., son of decd, aged 13, elected as his guardian Gabriel Blanchard 3 Dec 1716; Eliz. Long 7 Dec & re-elected her 26 Feb 1717), W, P11/115
Jn., Purton, 1730, AB, P3/C/800
Jn., [shoemaker], Brinkw., 1730, AB, I (2), P3/C/799
Jn., carp., E. Stowell, Wilcot, 1739, W, P3/C/848
Jn., miller, Clatford, Preshute, 1743, W, P1/C/795, P1/9Reg/271B
Jn., sen., butcher, Lea and Cleverton, 1773, W, P1/C/978, P1/13Reg/25

Jn., innholder, Ludg., 1777, W, P2/C/1390
Jn., yeo., Burbage, 1791, W, P11/249
Jn., pig butcher, Malm., 1797, W, P3/C/1132
Jn., labourer, Axford, Rams., 1806, W, P5/1806/9, P5/19Reg/155B
Jn., labourer, S. Burcombe, 1813, W, Wr, P2/1813/41
Jn., smith and farrier, Hungerford, Berks., 1823, W, P23/910
Jn., yeo., Harepath, Burbage, 1834, O, W, Wr, P11/287
Jos., S. Leaze, Wrou., 1729, AB, P3/C/781
Lemuel, miller, Oak Hill, Froxfield, 1709, I, W, P3/C/671
Lucy, widow, Marl. St My., 1686, I, W, P1/C/380
Mgt., widow, Burderop, Chiseldon, 1618, I, W, P3/C/93
My., widow, Broad H., 1694, AB, comm, I, P3/C/571
My., widow, Devizes, 1695, I, W, P1/C/449
My., sp., Sutton C., Berks., 1717, W, P1/C/574, P1/6Reg/133A
My., sp., Malm., 1779, AB, ren, W, P3/C/1061
My., widow, Aldbourne, 1811, AB, Wr, P1/1811/52
My., sp., W. Overton, 1812, W, Wr, P3/1812/12
Nich., yeo., Durley, Burbage, 1634, I, W (GVS), P5/1634/30, P5/12Reg/275
Nich., sen., yeo. *or* gent., Chaddington, Lydiard T., 1694, AB, I, W, P3/C/572-73
Nich., Avington &, Lydiard T., 1742, W, Wr, P3/C/867
Rd., husb., Durley, Burbage, 1570, W, P5/2Reg/65C
Rd., husb., Lydiard M., 1606, I, W (NEP), P3/C/22
Rd., jun., yeo., Tockenham Wick, 1664, I, NW (NEP), P3/C/301
Rd., yeo., Tockenham Wick, 1677, I, W, P3/C/400
Rd., tailor, Seend, Melk., 1693, comm, I, W, P2/C/828
Rd., Fieldings, Westport St My., 1734, AB, P3/C/822
Rd., maltster, Newbury, Berks., 1735, AB, I, P1/C/733
Rd., yeo., Milbourne, Malm., 1764, W, P3/C/977
Rd., yeo., Aldbourne, 1856, aff, O, W, Wr, P3/1856/19
Robt., yeo., Clyffe P., 1618, I, W (NEP), P3/C/94
Chearch, Robt., husb., Hurst, Berks., 1641, W, P5/14Reg/24A
Robt., Wootton B., 1683, AB, I, P3/C/470
Robt., sen., Aldbourne, 1693, I, W (NEP), P3/C/557
Robt., sen., yeo., Lea, L. and Cleverton, 1693, I, W, P3/C/562
Robt., yeo., Overton, 1757, W, P3/C/944
Robt., yeo., Brinkw., 1764, W, P3/C/978
Robt., yeo., Aldbourne, 1774, comm, W, P3/C/1037
Roger, Berwick B., 1706, AB, P26/528
Sarah, widow, Blewbury, Berks., 1801, W, P5/1801/16, P5/18Reg/320B
Thos., carp., Winterbourne, Chieveley, Berks., 1628, I, W, P1/C/130
Chearch, Thos., husb., Hurst, Berks., 1641, I, W, P5/1641/24
Thos., Rowde, 1668, AB, I, P3/C/316
Thos., yeo., Purton, 1669, AB, comm, I, NW, P3/C/327
Thos., Tockenham Wick, 1674, AB, a/c, comm, I, P3/C/371
Thos., yeo., W. Overton, 1696, AB, I, ren, Wr, P3/C/592
Thos., Amesb., 1739, AB, ren, P2/C/1186
Thos., sen., yeo., Duxford, Hinton Waldrist, Berks., 1741, I, W, P1/C/780, P1/9Reg/92
Wm., Lydiard T., 1608, AB, P3/C/31
Wm., no abode stated, [c1613?], I, W (NEP *or* indication of date), P3/C/67
Wm., Hankerton, 1617, I, NW, P3/C/86
Wm., Lydiard M., 1620, I, W, P3/C/108
Wm., yeo., Rodbourne C., 1638, AB, NW, P3/C/229
Wm., yeo., Clyffe P., 1661, comm, W, P3/C/275, P3/3Reg/33
Wm., Compton B., 1686, AB, I, P1/C/1117
Wm., carp., Overton, 1688, AB, I, P3/C/528
Wm., labourer, Stanford in the Vale, Berks., 1726, W, P1/C/646, P1/7Reg/99
Wm., E. Stowell, Wilcot, 1737, AB, comm, P3/C/836
Wm., Sal., 1743, AB, Wr, P4/1743/6
Wm., Cherhill, 1757, AB, P26/952
Churchill, Agnes, widow, Sherb., Dorset, 1799, comm, req, W, copy W, P5/1799/6, P5/18Reg/272B

Ann, widow, Corton, Boyton, 1721, W, P2/C/1041
Chas., gent., Fordington, Dorset, 1723, comm, W, P15/107
Chas., Mere, 1855, AB, aff, comm, Wr, P5/1855/7
Chris., Corton, Boyton, 1733, W, P2/C/1156
Cicely, Stratton, Dorset, 1610, AB, T (unnamed children), P5/1609/12, P5/9Reg/21C
Edwd., yeo., Milton upon Stour, Gillingham, Dorset, 1850, comm, W, Wr, P27/1/763
Jn., sen., yeo., Corton, Boyton, 1689, I, W, P2/C/792
Jn., yeo., Corton, Boyton, 1728, W, P2/C/1092
Jn., yeo., Lt. Coxwell, Gt. Faringdon, Berks., 1746, W, P5/1746/14
Jn., yeo., Corton, Boyton, 1815, W, Wr, P2/1815/74
My., sen., sp., Corton, Boyton, 1663, W, P1/C/258
My., widow, Warm., 1844, AB, comm, Wr, P2/1844/79
Rawlins, tanner, Mere, 1568, W, P5/2Reg/34C
Thos., Mere, 1579, I, W, P5/1579/16, P5/3Reg/136B
Thos., Sal., 1728, AB, P4/1728/8
Wm., Mere, 1724, AB, P5/1724/23
Wm., Fordington, Dorset, 1729, AB, W, P15/111
Wm., yeo. *or* gent., Warm., 1770, W, P1/C/957, P1/12Reg/303
Wm., Corton, Boyton, 1829, AB, comm, P2/1829/26
Wm., gardener, Warm., 1841, W, Wr, P2/1841/39
Wm., Warm., 1844, AB, comm, Wr, P2/1844/56, 78
see also Rawlins als C.
Churchman, Wm., yeo., Hurst, Berks., 1827, W, Wr, P5/1827/8
Churchouse, Joan, widow, Beer Hackett, Dorset, 1617, I, W, P5/1617/11, P5/9Reg/190C
Jn., Beer Hackett, Dorset, 1581, I, W, P5/1580/18, P5/4Reg/15B
Robt., Pierston, Gillingham, Dorset, 1579, W, P27/1Reg/38A
Churchowse, Thos., yeo., Beer Hackett, Dorset, 1611, comm, I, NW, copy NW, P5/1610/11, P5/9Reg/26D
Churly, Alice, widow, Uffc., Devon, 1733, W, P20/1/187
Grace, sp., Uffc., Devon, 1755, W, P5/1755/7
My., widow, Uffc., Devon, 1804, W, P20/1/280
Nich., gent., Uffc., Devon, 1784, W, P20/1/268
Nich., yeo., Uffc., Devon, 1841, O, W, Wr, P20/1/323
Churme, Wm., Westport St My., [1570], W (NEP), P1/1Reg/125A
Chute, Jn., Chards., Devon, 1717, AB, P14/123
Cicell *see* Cecil
Cimmer *see* Kimber
Cissell *see* Cecil
Clace *see* Clase
Clacer, Alice, Highway, 1625, I, W, P1/C/117
Clack, Agnes, widow, Marden, 1563, I, W, P2/C/27, P2/4Reg/111A
Chas., shoemaker, Swindon, 1849, O, W, Wr, P3/1849/7
Eliz., widow, Broughton G., 1812, W, Wr, P2/1812/28
Jas., Marden, 1619, I, W, P1/C/91
Jas., sen., tailor, Devizes St My., 1736, W, P1/C/743, P1/8Reg/156
Jn., yeo., Marden, 1709, I, W, P2/C/955
Jn., marine (d. on HMS *Triton*), Devizes, 1747, AB, P1/C/820
Jn., tailor, New Park St., Devizes St My., 1775, W, P1/C/985, P1/13Reg/65B
Jn., yeo., Wedh., Urchf., 1781, W, P2/C/1417
Jn., Devizes St Jn., 1801, W, P1/1801/3, P1/15Reg/224
Rd., sen., husb., Atworth, Bradford A., 1714, I, W, P1/C/556, P1/5Reg/437
Rd., yeo., Aston U., Blewbury, Berks., 1734, I, W, P5/1734/13
Rd., Atworth, Bradford A., 1781, W, P2/C/1415
Sarah, widow, Broughton G., 1800, W, P2/1800/27
Thos., cordw., Chilton, Berks., 1735, W, P1/C/729, P1/7Reg/651
Thos., farmer, Atworth, Bradford A., 1777, W, P2/C/1391
Wm., yeo., Aston Tirrold, Berks., 1711, AB, I, ren, P1/C/525
Clacy, Clasy, Anth., cordw., Westb., 1702, AB, I, P25/1702/2
Clavy, Hy., husb., Mere, 1588, I, W, P5/1588/8, P5/5Reg/14
My., widow, Chute, 1750, W, P7/145
Robt., labourer, Chute, 1693, I, W, P7/83

Robt., bach., Chute, 1735, AB, P7/129
Simon, labourer, Chute, 1706, W, P7/100
Clafford, Clafford form. Morris, Ann, widow, Chipp., 1709, AB, I (re all 3 people), P3/C/672
Claggett, Jn., writing master, Warm., 1729, W, P2/C/1098
Clandfield, Sarah, Appleton, Berks., 1763, W, P1/C/927, P1/12Reg/133
Clanville, Thos., husb., Eastrop, Highw., 1624, I, W, P10/1624/1
Clapcott, Cath., widow, Sutton Poyntz, Dorset, 1728, I, W, P5/1728/21, P5/16Reg/178B
Joan, widow, Sutton Poyntz, Dorset, 1622, I, W, P5/1622/12, P5/10Reg/131
Jn., Sutton Poyntz, Dorset, 1679, AB, P18/25
Robt., Sutton Poyntz, Dorset, 1684, a/c, P18/26
Clapp, Jn., yeo., Hackpen, Uffc., Devon, 1819, W, Wr, P20/1/88
Clapton, Geo., Bodenham, Nunton and B., 1606, AB, note of AB, P2/C/214
Clare, Alice, Reading, Berks., 1711, note of probate at PCC, P1/5Reg/175A
Ambrose, husb., Beam., Dorset, 1703, AB, I, NW, P17/140
Ann, widow, Warm., 1746, W, P2/C/1236
Ann, widow, Heytes., 1748, AB, Wr, P5/1748/6
Anth., yeo., Knook, 1704, W, P5/1704/13
Chris., shoemaker, Beam., Dorset, 1634, comm, I, NW, P17/21
Chris., yeo., Beam., Dorset, 1694, AB, I, P17/342
Edwd., Warm., 1678-79, AB, a/c, I, P2/C/677
Edwd., yeo., Strode, Netherb., Dorset, 1690, AB, I, P17/316
Eleanor, widow, Sal., 1748, W, P4/1748/2
Jane, widow, Devizes, 1813, W, Wr, P1/1813/2
Joan, widow, Beam., Dorset, 1662, I, W, P5/1662/31
Jn., Netherb., Dorset, 1586, AB, P5/4Reg/130A
Jn., miller, Clennam Mill, Netherb., Dorset, 1589, AB, I, P5/1589/11, P5/5Reg/62A
Jn., husb., S. Bowood, Netherb., Dorset, 1616, I, W, P5/1616/15
Jn., gent., Marl. St Peter and St Paul, 1628, AB, I, L, NW, P1/C/135
Jn., weaver, Chilmark, 1681, AB, I, P2/C/699
Jn., Warm., 1698, AB, I, P2/C/877
Jn., vintner, Warm., 1703, W, P2/C/908
Jn., yeo., Strode, Netherb., Dorset, 1703, I, W, P17/151
Jn., weaver, Chilmark, 1732, W, P2/C/1145
Jn., maltster, Warm., 1755, W, P2/C/1289
Jn., gent., Devizes, 1794, AB, comm, P3/C/1122
Jn., Devizes, 1798, AB, ren, P1/C/1100, P1/15Reg/141A
Jonathan, plumber, Warm., 1701, AB, I, W, P2/C/895
Julian, widow, Chilmark, 1573, W, P2/5Reg/163D
Philip, Fonthill B., 1569, W, P2/5Reg/64
Philip, Ditchampton, Wilton, 1615, AB, a/c, I, P2/C/284, P2/8Reg/279B
Clare als Miller, Rd., Beam., Dorset, 1600, AB, I, P5/1600/13, P5/6Reg/249A
Rd., minister, Shottesbrooke, Berks., 1686, AB, I, P1/C/1116
Sam., mercer, Beam., Dorset, 1718, W, P17/377
Thos., carp., Netherb., Dorset, 1664, I, W (NEP), P30/44
Clare als Dominick, Wm., Chilmark, 1546, AB, P2/2Reg/18C
Wm., tailor, Netherb., Dorset, 1694, I, W, P17/339
Wm., clothier, Beam., Dorset, 1725, W, P5/1725/13, P5/16Reg/114C
Wm., gent., Heytes., 1726, AB, W, P5/1725/19, P5/16Reg/128A
Wm., Warm., 1742, AB, P2/C/1219
Wm., Warm., 1762, AB, P2/C/1312
see also Dominick als C.
Clargo, Ann, widow of shopkeeper, Warm., 1778, W, P2/C/1399
Rd., Chr. M., 1663, AB, comm, I, P1/C/264
Rd., shopkeeper, Warm., 1778, W, P2/C/1395
Clark, Abijah, yeo., Tisb. (form. of Fonthill B.), 1785, W, P2/C/1434
Clarke, Abraham, mariner, Lyme R., Dorset, 1634, comm, I (detailed incl. part shares in ships' cargoes), W (GVS), P5/1634/31, P5/12Reg/296
Clarke, Abraham, Enmore Grn, Motc., Dorset, 1683, I, P19/43
Clarke, Abraham, yeo., Dauntsey, 1741, W, P3/C/862
Abraham, Brinkw., 1764, AB, P3/C/979

Abraham, yeo., Alderton, 1811, W, Wr, P3/1811/28
Abraham, Kington St M., 1816, AB, comm, Wr, P3/1816/47
Abraham, bach., Westport St My., 1850, AB, Wr, P3/1850/40
Clarke, Adam, sen., cordw., Malm., 1702, I, W (NEP), P3/C/638
Clarke, Adam, sen., Malm., 1729, I, W, P1/C/681, P1/7Reg/317A
Aeneas, yeo., Collingbourne K., 1798, note of probate, W, P3/C/1137
Clerke, Agnes, widow, Grimstone, Stratton, Dorset, 1588, W, P5/5Reg/21C
Clerk als Pearce, Agnes, Mkt. L., 1602, AB, I, P2/C/189
Clarke, Agnes, widow, Martin, Hants, 1603, AB, note of AB, P2/C/192
Clarke, Agnes, widow, Wilton, Gt. Bedwyn, 1638, I, W, P5/1638/18, P5/13Reg/91
Clarke, Agnes, widow, Brinkw., 1640, I, W, P3/C/251
Clarke, Alice, widow, Wilton, Gt. Bedwyn, 1581, I, W, P5/1581/3, P5/4Reg/23B
Clarke als Wickwar, Alice, widow, Calne, 1588, AB, I, W, P5/1588/10, P5/5Reg/46B
Clarke, Alice, widow, Brinkw., 1629, AB, I, NW, P3/C/160
Clarke, Alice, sp., Croucheston, Bishopstone S., 1640, AB, P2/C/480
Clarke, Alice, widow, Shitterton, Bere R., Dorset, 1677, I, W, P5/1677/15
Clarke, And., sen., wheeler, Marl., 1663, I, W, P1/C/263
Ann, widow, Purton, 1665, I, W, P3/C/302
Clarke, Ann, widow, Bishopstone N., 1679, I, W, P5/1679/15
Clarke, Ann, sen., widow, Timbrell Lane, Downton, 1704, I, W, P2/C/914
Clarke, Ann, Lyneham, 1747, AB, P1/C/824
Clarke, Ann, widow, Steeple A., 1748, comm, W, P2/C/1251
Ann, widow, Collingbourne K., 1799, W, P3/C/1140
Ann, widow, Heddington, 1841, comm, W, Wr, P3/1841/1
Ann, widow, Greenway, Tockenham, 1848, W, Wr, P1/1848/35
Ann, sp., Corsham, 1852, AB, O, W, P29/3Reg/323, P29/1800-1857/47
Clarke, Anth., Martin, Hants, 1598, AB, P2/C/163
Anth., husb., Clyffe P., 1633, I, P3/C/184
Clarke, Arthur, Swindon, 1683, AB, P1/C/369
Clarke, Azarias, Shitterton, Bere R., Dorset, 1665, I, note, W, P5/1665/19
Benj., yeo., Purton, 1778, W, P3/C/1057
Benj., Bourton, Gillingham, Dorset, 1827, W, Wr, P27/1/678
Clarke, Betty, widow, Chipp., 1755, AB, P3/C/938
Clarke, Betty, sp., Caundle Marsh, Dorset, 1809, W, P5/1809/4
Clarke, Caleb, Lyme R., Dorset, 1821, AB, Wr, P5/1821/36
Cath., Sal., 1646, I, W, P1/C/213
Clarke, Cath., widow, Beam., Dorset, 1720, I, W, P17/385
Cath., wife, Sal., 1730, AB, P4/1729/9
Clarke, Chas., yeo., Hannington, 1694, comm, I, W, P3/C/574
Clarke, Chas., mariner on HMS *Nottingham*, Sal., 1713, AB, P4/1713/1
Chas., yeo., Hannington, 1737, W, P3/C/837
Clerk, Christian, widow, Westwood, 1579, W, P2/5Reg/330A
Clarke, Christian, Wilton, Gt. Bedwyn, 1620, I, W, P5/1620/13, P5/10Reg/2
Clerke, Christian, widow, Milton L., 1714, AB, P3/C/690
Clerke, Chris., Seend, Melk., 1571, W, P1/1Reg/31C
Dan., Wootton B., 1682, I, W, P3/C/450
David, sen., yeo., Studley, Calne, 1836, comm, W, Wr, P26/1425
Clarke, Dorothy, widow, Calne, 1675, W, P26/234
Clarke, Dorothy, Martin, Hants, 1695, AB, P2/C/853
Dorothy, widow, Smithcot, Dauntsey, 1741, W, P3/C/861
Clarke, Edith, widow, Woolley, Bradford A., 1580, W, P2/5Reg/360C
Clarke, Edmd., Charminster, Dorset, 1674, AB, comm, P5/1674/22
Clarke, Edmd., Eisey, 1693, AB, I, Wr, P3/C/563
Clarke, Edmd., jun., bach., Eisey, 1752, AB, P3/C/917
Clarke, Edwd., Idmiston, 1585, I, W, P2/C/65, P2/7Reg/19C
Clarke, Edwd., maltster, Damerham, Hants, 1735, I (detailed), W, P1/C/724, P1/7Reg/622
Clarke, Edwd., gent., Abingdon, Berks., 1773, W, P1/C/968, P1/12Reg/481
Edwd., Bishopstone S., 1795, AB, P1/C/1085, P1/14Reg/620A
Clerke, Eleanor, sp. *or* widow, Haxton, Fittleton, 1689-90, AB, W (2) (described as sp. 1688 & widow 1689), P2/C/794
Clarke, Eleanor, widow, Marl., 1694, I, W, P1/C/432

Clarke, Eliz., widow, Bere R., Dorset, 1617, I, W, P5/1617/7, P5/9Reg/190A
Clarke, Eliz., widow, Pewsey, 1667, I, W, P3/C/311
Clarke, Eliz., widow, Homington, 1708, W, P24/582
Clarke, Eliz., widow, Grittenham, Brinkw., 1715, W, P3/C/696
Eliz., Marl., 1717, AB, P1/C/571
Eliz., widow, Oxbridge, Netherb., Dorset, 1720, I, W, P17/380
Clarke, Eliz., widow, Beam., Dorset, 1722, W, P5/1722/10, P5/16Reg/65B
Clarke, Eliz., widow, Trowb., 1730, W, P1/C/695, P1/7Reg/405
Clarke, Eliz., widow, Lyme R., Dorset, 1737, AB, I, P5/1737/13
Clarke, Eliz., widow, Eisey, 1739, W, P3/C/849
Clarke, Eliz., widow, Winkfield, Berks., 1759, W, P1/C/899, P1/11Reg/382
Clarke, Eliz., widow, Hilp., 1767, AB, P2/C/1339
Eliz., widow, Sal., 1850, W, Wr, P4/1850/16
Clarke, Frances, sp., Clyffe P., 1675, AB, P3/C/376
Frances, widow, Sonning, Berks., 1805, W, P5/19Reg/130
Clarke, Francis, husb., Idmiston, 1625, I, W, P2/C/351
Clarke, Francis, tailor, Brinkw., 1674, AB, comm, I, P3/C/372
Clerke, Francis, Clyffe P., 1682, AB, P3/C/452
Francis, sen., yeo., Brinkw., 1750, W, P1/C/842, P1/10Reg/393
Clarke, Francis, Brinkw., 1756, AB, P1/C/887
Clarke, Francis, yeo., Eye and Dunsden, Sonning, Berks., 1769, W, P5/1769/6
Francis, widow, Sonning, Berks., 1805, W, P5/1805/12
Clarke, Geoff., husb., Brinkw., 1611, I, W (NEP), P3/C/59
Geoff., Brinkw., 1636, I, P3/C/215
Clerke, Geo., Hurst, Berks., 1543, W, P5/20Reg/47B
Clarke, Geo., yeo., Croucheston, Bishopstone S., 1667, comm, I, W, P2/C/569
Clarke, Geo., pinmaker, Marl., 1668, AB, I, P1/C/285
Clarke, Geo., yeo., Martin, Hants, 1682, I, W, P2/C/715
Clarke, Geo., blacksmith, Tockenham Wick, 1684, I, W, P3/C/483
Geo., Corsley, 1724, AB, P2/C/1058
Geo., Binfield, Berks., 1811, W, Wr, P1/1811/73
Geo., weaver, Ditchampton, Wilton, 1847, D, W, Wr, P2/1847/66
Clarke, Giles, husb., Over C., Dorset, 1605, AB, a/c, I, copy I, T, P5/1604/4, P5/8Reg/25A
Clarke, Giles, yeo. *or* tailor, Chelworth, Crudwell, 1682, I, W, P3/C/451
Clarke, Giles, tailor, Chelworth, Crudwell, 1726, W, P3/C/760
Clarke, Giles, carp., Newbury, Berks., 1808, W, Wr, P1/1808/114
Clarke, Hannah, widow, Brinkw., 1838, O, W, Wr, P3/1838/58
Clarke, Harry, Warm., 1590, W, P2/C/1513
Clarke, Hy., Cholderton, 1575, W, P2/5Reg/220D
Clarke, Hy., husb., Over C., Dorset, 1589, I, W, P5/1589/6, P5/5Reg/57C
Clarke, Hy., Warm., 1597, AB, P2/C/142
Clarke, Hy., husb., Sevenhampton, Highw., 1613, NW, P5/1613/12, P5/9Reg/97B
Clerk, Hy., husb., Sevenhampton, Highw., 1614, comm, W, P1/C/65
Clarke, Hy., Trowb., 1625, I, W, P22/1/2
Clarke, Hy., yeo., Brinkw., 1672, I, W, P3/C/357
Clarke, Hy., dyer, Mere, 1675, AB, a/c, I, P5/1675/16, P5/1676/11
Clarke, Hy., sen., dyer, Mere, 1691, AB, I, W, P5/1691/11
Clarke, Hy., sen., carp., Beam., Dorset, 1692, AB, I, P17/334
Clarke, Hy., Hamptworth, Downton, 1714, W, P2/C/989
Clarke, Hy., Chipp., 1720, AB, I, P3/C/732
Hy., sen., husb., The Earldoms, Whitep., 1741, I, W, P1/C/773, P1/9Reg/41
Clarke, Hy., yeo., Whitep., 1766, W, Wr, P2/C/1331
Hy., ironmonger, Hungerford, Berks., 1771, comm, W, P23/736
Hy., blanketmaker, Gastard, Corsham, 1790, W, P3/C/1107
Clarke, Hy., Whitep., 1815, AB (re property in W.; no abode stated), P2/1815/83
Hy., Kington St M., 1834, AB, comm, court proceeding, W, Wr, P3/1834/41
Clarke, Hester, sp., Rodbourne, Malm., 1734, W, P3/C/823
Isaac, Stockley, Calne, 1820, req, W, Wr, P26/1335
Clarke, Isaac, gent., Rowde, 1837, O, W, Wr, P3/1837/74
Isaac, Tockenham Wick, 1847, AB, I, Wr, P3/1847/20

Clarke, Isabel, widow, Keevil, 1577, W, P2/C/45, P2/5Reg/288B
Clarke, Jas., Crudwell, 1629, AB, P3/C/161
Clarke, Jas., yeo., Hannington, 1679, I, P3/C/417
Clarke als Eliott, Jas., mercer, Wrou., 1698, I, W, P3/C/601
Clarke, Jas., Calne, 1720, AB, P26/641
Jas., gent., Devizes, 1758, W, P1/C/892, P1/11Reg/366
Clarke, Jas., yeo., Caundle Marsh, Dorset, 1773, W, P5/1773/13, P5/17Reg/67B
Clarke, Jas., innholder, Theale, Tilehurst, Berks., 1779, W, P1/C/1015, P1/13Reg/275B
Jas., gent., Sherston, 1812, W, Wr, P3/1812/37
Clerk, Jane, Bere R., Dorset, 1611, AB (3), a/c, comm, P5/1610/15, P5/1611/6, P5/9Reg/54A
Clarke als Paties, Jane, widow, Calne, 1634, AB, I(GVS), P5/1634/70
Clarke, Jane, widow, Devizes, 1688, I, W, P1/C/386
Clarke, Jane, Easton, 1711, W, P1/C/515, P1/5Reg/43
Jane, widow, Odstock, 1742, W, P1/C/789, P1/9Reg/220A
Joan, Bere R., Dorset, 1611, AB, P5/9Reg/50C
Joan, Calne, 1636, I, W, P26/59
Clarke als Habberly, Joan, widow, Clyffe P., 1636, AB, I, P3/C/216
Clarke, Joan, widow, Coombe, Donhead St My., 1637, I, W, P2/C/456
Clerke als Betford, Joan, widow, Halstock, Dorset, 1638, AB, comm, P5/1637/6, P5/13Reg/146A
Clarke, Joan, wife, Marl., 1703, AB, comm, P1/C/480
Joan, Hannington Wick, 1723, W, P1/C/614, P1/6Reg/456A
Clarke, Jn., Westwood, 1561, I, W, P2/C/16, P2/4Reg/87C
Jn., Rushall, 1561, I, W, P2/C/14, P2/4Reg/81D
Clerke, Jn., servant to Thos. Sowthe, W. Amesb., 1561, I, P2/C/15
Clarke, Jn., Seend, Melk., 1563, I, W, P2/C/30, P2/4Reg/145A
Clarke, Jn., Gt. Bedwyn, 1572, W, P5/3Reg/4D
Clerk als Pearce, Jn., Mkt. L., 1573, W, P2/5Reg/173B
Clarke als Wickwar, Jn., yeo., Calne, 1583, AB, I, W, P5/1583/10, P5/4Reg/59A
Clarke, Jn., Grimstone, Stratton, Dorset, 1585, W, P5/4Reg/103C
Clarke, Jn., Martin, Hants, 1587, AB, ren, NW, P2/7Reg/70C
Clerk, Jn., carp., Marl., 1593, I (2), P1/C/9
Clarke als Williams, Jn., Upton L., 1597, a/c (very detailed & long), P2/C/141
Clarke, Jn., shoemaker, Marl., 1604, W, P1/C/20
Clerke, Jn., Shalbourne, Berks. *or* Wiltshire, [1609], W. Date of probate not given., P23/1003
Clarke, Jn., husb., Wilton, Gt. Bedwyn, 1610, I, W, P5/1610/14, P5/9Reg/18
Clarke, Jn., Aldbourne, 1624, AB, a/c, I, P3/C/128
Clarke, Jn., yeo., Long Newnton, 1624, I, W, P3/C/129
Clarke, Jn., blacksmith, Highw., 1627, I, P10/1627/1
Clarke, Jn.?, Homington, 1630, AB, P2/C/396
Jn., Martin, Hants, 1631, AB, a/c, I, P2/C/405
Clarke, Jn., clerk and parson, Nether C., Dorset, 1631-33, AB, I, ren, P5/1631/34, P5/1633/12, P5/11Reg/169A
Clarke, Jn., sen., Sandhurst, Berks., 1644, AB, comm, I, P5/1644/9, P5/14Reg/66B
Clarke, Jn., baker, Devizes, 1644, AB, comm, P1/C/202
Jn., Wilton, Gt. Bedwyn, 1648, comm, I, W, P21/1/69
Jn., mason, Pewsey, 1663, comm, I, W, P3/C/291
Jn., gent., Nunton, N. and Bodenham, 1670, W, P2/C/600
Clarke, Jn., yeo., Mkt. L., 1672, AB, I, P2/C/628
Clarke, Jn., jun., Easton, 1673, AB, a/c, I, P3/C/365
Jn., clerk and vicar, Malm., 1676, AB, I, ren, P3/C/387
Clarke, Jn., jun., pinmaker, Marl. St My., 1681, AB, comm, I, ren (2), W, P1/C/353
Clarke, Jn., sen., yeo., Easton, 1681, I, W, P3/C/434
Clarke, Jn., Wilton, 1683, AB, I, P2/C/732
Clerke, Jn., Keevil, 1685, AB, P2/C/759
Clarke, Jn., Homington, 1687, AB, P24/711
Clarke, Jn., husb., Brinkw., 1687, AB, I, ren, P3/C/519
Clarke, Jn., pinmaker, Marl., 1691, W, P1/C/413
Jn., jun., baker, Devizes, 1694, comm, I, W, P1/C/436
Clarke, Jn., yeo., Downton, 1694, I, W, P2/C/844
Clarke, Jn., sen., baker, Devizes St Jn., 1697, I, W, P1/C/452
Clarke, Jn., sen., yeo., Winkfield, Berks., 1701, I (detailed), W, P1/C/473, P1/4Reg/165

Clarke, Jn., tailor, Wootton B., 1702, I, W, P3/C/639
Clarke, Jn., husb., Ogbourne St And., 1705, comm, I, W, P5/1705/15
Clarke, Jn., baker, Lyme R., Dorset, 1709, W, P16/179
Jn., blacksmith, Gillingham, Dorset, 1711, AB, I, P27/1/184
Clarke, Jn., sen., butcher, Wilton, 1711, AB (2), ren, W, P1/C/531, P1/5Reg/240
Clarke, Jn., yeo., Woodminton, Bower C., 1711, W, P1/C/528, P1/5Reg/205
Clarke, Jn., Chitterne St My., 1714, AB, P1/C/541
Clarke, Jn., butcher, Beam., Dorset, 1715, W, P17/242
Clarke, Jn., carp., Beam., Dorset, 1716, W, P17/365
Jn., yeo., Purton Stoke, 1719, I, W, P3/C/720
Clarke, Jn., sen., wheelwright, Marl., 1720, W, P1/C/605, P1/6Reg/354
Clarke als Warren, Jn., Marl. St My., 1721, I, W, P1/C/608, P1/6Reg/376A
Clarke, Jn., butcher, Chieveley, Berks., 1723, AB, ren, P1/C/626
Clarke, Jn., gardener, Reading, Berks., 1723, AB, I, P1/C/623
Jn., yeo., Easton, 1727, comm, W, Wr, P3/C/765
Jn., Downton, 1728, W, P2/C/1093
Clarke, Jn., labourer, Brinkw., 1728, AB, I, P3/C/775
Clarke, Jn., glazier, Steeple A., 1729, AB, I, P1/C/683
Clarke, Jn., yeo., Holt, Bradford A., 1730, comm, W, P2/C/1114
Clarke, Jn., baker, Trowb., 1731, AB, I, P1/C/699
Clarke, Jn., Fovant, 1734, AB, I, P2/C/1162
Jn., Compton, Berks., 1741, W, P1/C/779, P1/9Reg/85
Clarke, Jn., Damerham, Hants, 1745, AB, I, P2/C/1229
Clarke, Jn., yeo., Burbage, 1757, W, P11/210
Clarke, Jn., yeo., Chelworth, Crudwell, 1762, W, P3/C/966
Clarke, Jn., Hilp., 1767, AB, P2/C/1338
Clarke, Jn., Devizes, 1768, AB, P1/C/952
Clarke, Jn., yeo., Lacock & Corsham, [1770], W (property in C.), P29/C/23, P29/2Reg/129
Clarke, Jn., sen., gent., Halstock, Dorset, 1771, comm, W, P16/336
Jn., blacksmith, Gillingham, Dorset, 1772, W, P27/1/478, P27/3Reg/167
Clarke, Jn., rector, Padworth, Berks., 1777, W, P1/C/1001, P1/13Reg/181A
Jn., sen., yeo., Bishopstone S., 1779, W, P1/C/1009, P1/13Reg/224A
Jn., E. Hanney, W. Hanney, Berks., 1792, AB, comm, P1/C/1074, P1/14Reg/461A
Clarke, Jn., gent., Caundle Marsh, Dorset, 1797, W, P5/1797/8, P5/18Reg/247B
Jn., yeo., Grittenham, Brinkw., 1800, W, P3/1800/31
Jn., dancing master, Malm., 1802, req, W, copy W, P3/1802/69
Clarke, Jn., gent., Halstock, Dorset, 1808, AB, comm, W, P16/368
Jn., sen., Draycot C., 1815, W, Wr, P3/1815/40
Jn., Westcourt, Burbage, 1833, AB, O, Wr, P11/286
Clarke, Jn., Silver St., Lyme R., Dorset, 1835, O, W, P16/411
Jn., gent., Sal., 1847, W, Wr, P4/1847/7
Clarke, Jn., yeo., Wick, Preshute, 1850, D, O, W, Wr, P1/1850/7
Jn., yeo., Gt. Somerford (form. of Dauntsey), 1852, O, W, Wr, P3/1852/26
Clarke, Jn. *see also* Jn. Weare
Jn. Imber, carp., Boscombe, 1845, D, note, W, Wr, P2/1845/26
Clarke, Jos., gent., Halstock, Dorset, 1746, I (detailed), W, P5/1746/15
Clarke, Jos., yeo., Purton, 1828, W, Wr, P3/1828/3
Joyce, widow, Easton Grey, 1738, W, P1/C/761, P1/8Reg/333A
Clarke, Judith, minor, Mere, 1691, T, P5/1691/12
Clarke, Laura, widow, Bushton, Clyffe P., 1622, I, W, P3/C/114
Clarke, Lawr., butcher and yeo., Bradfield, Berks., 1720, I, W, P1/C/600, P1/6Reg/310B
Clarke, Levi, Sherston, 1693, AB, P1/C/431
Clarke, Love, widow, Sherb., Dorset, 1774, AB, comm, P5/1774/3
Clarke, Mgt., widow, Gt. Bathampton, Steeple L., 1635, I, W, P2/C/428, P2/9Reg/44A
Clarke, Mgt., widow, Hannington, 1730, W, P3/C/801
Mgt., sp., Hannington, 1773, W, P3/C/1033
Clarke, Margery, widow, W. Yatton, Yatton K., 1667, I, W, P3/C/312
Martha, widow, Trowb., 1714, comm, W, P1/C/201, P1/5Reg/464B
Martha, widow, Castle C., 1719, AB, I, P28/8
Clarke, My., widow, Sal. St Mart., 1611, I, W, P4/1611/10

My., widow, Brinkw., 1641, I, W, P3/C/262
Clarke, My., widow, Devizes, 1646, AB, comm, I, P1/C/217
Clarke als Hughs, My., widow, Codf. St My., 1650, I, W, P1/C/231
Clarke, My., widow, Lyme R., Dorset, 1772, AB, comm, P16/338
My., widow, Sal. (form. of Bedminster, Somerset), 1836, AB, Wr, P4/1836/18
My. Wilkins, widow, Brinkw., 1797, I, W, P3/C/1133
Clarke, Matthew, yeo., Ham, 1639, I, W (damaged), P3/C/241
Clarke, Matthew, yeo., Wilton, Gt. Bedwyn, 1670, I, W, P21/2/12
Clarke, Maud, widow, N. Bradley, 1592, AB, I, P2/C/113
Clarke, Michael, gent., Easton, 1686, comm, ren, W, P3/C/504
Clarke, Michael, sen., livier, Compton, Enford, 1728, I, W, P2/C/1090
Clarke, Nathan, yeo., Brinkw., 1813, W, Wr, P3/1813/29
Clerke, Nich., Westb., 1560, W. No date of probate, P1/2Reg/99C
Clarke als Wickwar, Nich., husb., Calne, 1593, I, T, W, P5/1593/27, P5/6Reg/34C
Clarke, Nich., husb., Grimstone, Stratton, Dorset, 1615, AB, comm, I, T, P5/1615/6, P5/9Reg/166C
Clarke, Nich., husb., Downton, [1676], I, W, P2/C/665
Clarke, Peter, shoemaker, Sal. St Thos., 1636, I, W, P4/1636/5
Clarke, Peter, gardener, Theale, Tilehurst, Berks., 1750, I, W, P1/C/836, P1/10Reg/329
Peter, gent., Devizes, 1752, comm, W, P1/C/847, P1/10Reg/491B
Clarke, Prudence, widow, Hannington, 1733, W, P3/C/814
Clarke, Rd., Amesb., 1558, W, P2/3Reg/84C
Clarke, Rd., husb., Clyffe P., 1592, I, W, P1/C/3
Clarke, Rd., Warm., 1599, I, W, P2/C/172
Clarke, Rd., Broad H., 1604, I, W, P3/C/10
Rd., yeo., Brinkw., 1628, I, W, P1/C/168
Clarke, Rd., tailor, Beam., Dorset, 1638, I, W, P5/1638/19, P5/13Reg/76
Clarke, Rd., sen., yeo., Hannington, 1665, I, ren, W, P3/C/303
Clarke, Rd., miller, Milbourne, Malm., 1676, AB, I, P3/C/388
Clarke, Rd., Hannington, 1688, AB, I, P3/C/529
Clarke, Rd., Maiden B., 1689, AB, I, P2/C/795
Clarke, Rd., pinmaker, Marl. St My., 1697, I, W, P1/C/454
Clarke, Rd., Pewsey, 1700, AB (2), I, P3/C/620
Clarke, Rd., Sonning, Berks., 1710, AB, I, P5/1710/27
Rd., Melk., 1727, AB, P2/C/1083
Clarke, Rd., maltster, Crickl. St My., 1733, W, P3/C/815
Rd., yeo., Charlton nr Malm., 1733, W, P3/C/813
Clarke, Rd., Crickl. St My., 1762, AB, P3/C/967
Rd., twister, Corsley, 1766, W, P2/C/1330
Clarke, Rd., gent., Hannington Wick, 1767, W, P3/C/1000
Rd., Marl., 1808, AB, Wr, P1/1808/2
Clarke, Rd., Boscombe, 1816, AB, D, W, Wr, P2/1816/18
Clarke, Rd., farmer, Bradford A. (form. of Monkton F.), 1852, W, Wr, P2/1852/37
Clerke, Robt., vicar, Charl. nr. P., 1559, W, P2/3Reg/162A
Clerke, Robt., vicar, Chitterne AS, 1567, W, P2/5Reg/5C
Clarke, Robt., no abode stated, brother is of Bremhill, 1600, AB, P2/C/175
Clarke, Robt., yeo., Lydiard M., 1627, AB, a/c, I, W, P3/C/149
Clarke, Robt., husb., Sopworth, 1636, I, W, P3/C/217
Clarke, Robt., gent., Brinkw., 1674, AB, a/c, I, P3/C/373
Clarke, Robt., clerk and rector, Barford St Mart., 1677, AB, I (detailed), ren, P1/C/334
Clarke, Robt., rector, Barford St Mart., 1713, AB, P1/C/538
Robt., barber, Malm., 1772, W, P3/C/1024
Robt., Gillingham, Dorset, 1784, AB, P27/1/518, P27/3Reg/237
Robt., maltster, Sherb., Dorset, 1799, W, Wr, P5/1799/4, P5/18Reg/278B
Clarke, Robt., labourer, Castleton, Dorset, 1814, W, Wr, P5/1814/6
Robt., carp., Malm. Abbey, 1851, O, W, Wr, P3/1851/15
Clarke als Hiller, Roger, Murcott, Crudwell, 1632, AB, a/c, I, P3/C/181
Roger, labourer, Wilsford nr Pewsey, 1745, W, P2/C/1227
Clarke, Sam., shopkeeper, Lyme R., Dorset, 1748-49, AB, election of guardians, ren, T, P5/1749/13, P16/300
Clarke, Sarah, widow, Brinkw., 1669, I, W, P3/C/328
Sarah, widow, Melk., 1745, AB, comm, P2/C/1230

Sarah, Wokefield, Stratfield M., Berks., 1795, comm, W, P1/C/1078, P1/14Reg/613
Clarke, Sibyl, widow, Hill D. & Horningsham, 1728, W (bequest to poor widows of Dissenting Congregation at Ho.), P5/1728/22, P5/16Reg/161C
Clarke, Steph., Netherb., Dorset, 1697, I, W, P17/118
Clarke, Steph., Sal., 1698, AB, P4/1697/3
Steph., blacksmith, Milton upon Stour, Gillingham, Dorset, 1840, W, Wr, P27/1/731
Clarke, Susanna, widow, Stanton St Q., 1684, I, W, P3/C/493
Clarke, Susanna, widow, Ashbury, Berks., 1635, AB, I (detailed), P1/C/157
Clerke, Thos., Keevil, 1567, W, P2/5Reg/20B
Clerke, Thos., Long Burton, Dorset, 1573, AB, P5/3Reg/23D
Clarke, Thos., Keevil, 1585, W, P2/7Reg/5A
Clarke, Thos., Bradford A., 1591, I (detailed), W, P2/C/90
Clarke, Thos., sen., Croucheston, Bishopstone S., 1593, AB, I, P2/C/119
Clerke, Thos., Lydiard T., 1610, AB, P3/C/47
Clerke, Thos., sen., Sherston, 1617, I, W, P3/C/87
Thos., sen., Wilton, Gt. Bedwyn, 1623, AB, I, P5/1622/16, P5/10Reg/156A
Clarke, Thos., yeo., Homington, 1623, I, W, P2/C/332
Clarke, Thos., husb., Westport St My., 1638, I, W, P3/C/230
Thos., Bere R., Dorset, 1639, L, P5/1639/23
Thos., no abode stated (exhibited at Sal.), 1639, I, P5/1639/24
Clarke, Thos., husb., Grimstone, Stratton, Dorset, 1668, I, W, P5/1668/18
Clerke, Thos., Alderbury, 1669, AB, P26/162
Clarke, Thos., yeo., Wilton, Gt. Bedwyn, 1669, AB, I, note, ren, P5/1669/9
Clarke als Hillier, Thos., yeo., Murcott, Crudwell, 1671, I, W, P3/C/348
Clarke, Thos., baker, Westb., 1671-74, AB, a/c (1674), P25/1671/13
Clarke, Thos., yeo., Woodminton, Bower C., 1674, I, W, P2/C/642
Clarke, Thos., bodicemaker, Chipp., 1675, AB, I, P3/C/377
Clerke, Thos., clerk and rector, Manningford A., 1683, comm, I, W, P1/C/360
Clerk, Thos., gent., Haxton, Fittleton, 1685, I, W, P2/C/756
Clarke, Thos., baker, Lyme R., Dorset, 1689, NW, P16/97
Clarke, Thos., yeo., Martin, Hants, 1689-90, AB, a/c, I, ren, P2/C/793
Clarke, Thos., sen., yeo., Odstock, 1693, AB, I, P2/C/836
Clarke, Thos., sen., sergemaker, Devizes, 1702, I, W, P1/C/478, P1/4Reg/215
Clarke, Thos., Marl. St My., 1716, AB, P1/C/562
Clarke, Thos., gent., Wallingford, Berks., 1720, W, P1/C/597, P1/6Reg/297A
Thos., Pensworth, Downton, [1721], W, P2/C/1048
Clarke, Thos., Beam., Dorset, 1734, AB, P5/1734/14
Clarke, Thos., yeo., Odstock, 1734, W, P2/C/1160
Clarke, Thos., Bradford A., 1737, AB, P2/C/1181
Thos., yeo., Bere R., Dorset, 1740, W, Wr, P5/1740/16
Clarke, Thos., Bradfield, Berks., 1756, AB, ren, P1/C/878
Clarke, Thos., butcher, Gillingham, Dorset, 1767, W, P27/1/458, P27/3Reg/143
Clarke, Thos., pattenmaker, Sherb., Dorset, 1774, AB, comm, P5/1774/4
Clarke, Thos., Trowb., 1775, AB (2), P1/C/986
Thos., weaver, Idmiston, 1786, W, P1/C/1045, P1/14Reg/84A
Thos., woolcomber, Charlton nr Malm., 1789, W, P3/C/1103
Thos., sen., husb., Hebden Farm, Luckington, 1809, W, P3/1809/35
Thos., widower, Lyneham, 1813, W, Wr, P3/1813/68
Clerk, Thomasine, widow, Long Burton, Dorset, 1581, I, W, P5/1580/17, P5/4Reg/17A
Clarke, Thomasine, Grimstone, Stratton, Dorset, 1676, AB, I, P5/1676/9
Clarke, Walter, husb., Trowb., 1639, AB, I, W, P22/2/41
Clarke, Walter, baker, Sherston, 1641, AB, I, ren, P1/C/189
Clarke, Walter, clerk and minister, Alvediston, 1648, AB, I (2), P2/C/541
Clarke, Walter, Brinkw., 1689, AB, comm, I, P3/C/536
Clarke, Walter, Sherston, 1693, AB, comm, P1/C/430
Clarke, Walter, carp., Seend, Melk., 1767, W, P2/C/1337
Walter, farmer, Brinkw., 1810, W, Wr, P3/1810/20
Clarke, Walter Long, rector, Whaddon, 1736, AB, P1/C/741
Clerk, Wm., Cholderton, 1526, W, P1/2Reg/93A
Wm., Lyme R., Dorset, 1593, AB, P5/1593/88, P5/6Reg/50C, 128A

Clerk, Wm., sailor, Lyme R., Dorset, 1593, AB, I, W, P5/1593/26, P5/6Reg/49
Clarke, Wm., husb., Shalbourne, 1594, I, W, P5/1594/15, P5/6Reg/73B
Clarke als Patie, Wm., no abode stated, 1632, AB, P3/C/182
Wm., sen., yeo., Brinkw., 1639, I, W, P3/C/242
Clarke, Wm., yeo., W. End, Brinkw., 1661, AB, comm, I, NW, P3/C/276, P3/3Reg/10A
Clarke, Wm., yeo., W. Crudwell, 1683, I, W, P3/C/471
Clarke, Wm., yeo., Sunton, Collingbourne K., 1704, I, W, P3/C/646
Clarke, Wm., Fonthill G., 1705, AB, P2/C/925
Wm., Easton Grey, 1718, W, P3/C/713
Wm., Bere R., Dorset, 1719, AB, P5/1719/14
Clarke, Wm., yeo., Brinkw., 1724, W, P3/C/750
Clarke, Wm., Odstock, 1725, AB, I, P2/C/1071
Wm., Bishopstone S., 1729, AB, P2/C/1109
Clarke, Wm., gent., Halstock, Dorset, 1734, comm, W, P16/274
Clarke, Wm., yeo., Eddington, Hungerford, Berks., 1738, I, W, P23/533
Wm., Easton Grey, 1740, W, P3/C/853
Wm., Ardington, Berks., 1741, W, P1/C/778, P1/9Reg/87
Clarke, Wm., tailor, Westport St My., 1748, W, P3/C/894
Wm., maltster, Bishopstone S. (d. of wounds received at Wilton), 1750, AB, NW, P1/C/837, P1/10Reg/322
Clarke, Wm., cordw., Kintbury, Berks., 1756, W, P1/C/876, P1/11Reg/231
Wm., chapman, Kintbury, Berks., 1759, W, P1/C/903, P1/11Reg/415
Wm., labourer, Winterborne K., Dorset, 1761, W (draft, holograph), W (NEP), P5/1761/5
Clarke, Wm., Hilp., 1767, AB, P2/C/1340
Wm., yeo., Corston, Malm., 1769, W, P3/C/1014
Wm., Broughton G., 1773, W, Wr, P2/C/1364
Wm., weaver, Rowde, 1781, comm, W, P3/C/1071
Wm., tailor, Collingbourne K., 1787, W, P3/C/1093
Wm., yeo., Bishopstone S., 1792, W, P1/C/1066, P1/14Reg/371
Wm., yeo., Stockley, Calne, 1803, W, P5/1803/32, P5/19Reg/60
Wm., yeo., Wantage, Berks., 1822, comm, W, Wr, P23/899
Wm., Collingbourne K. (effects at Devizes), 1841, AB, comm, Wr, P1/1841/10
Zachary, Martin, Hants, 1729, W, P2/C/1103
see also Bayly als C.; Champion als C.; Elliott als C.; Felys als C.; Gilbert als C.; Hiller als C.; Miall/Mihill als C.; Morris als C.; Paty als C.; Robertson als C.; Rogerson als C.; Shakespear als C.; Warren als C.
Clase, Anth., yeo., Knook, 1626, D, I, W, P5/1626/8, P5/11Reg/1B
Clace, Joan, widow, Heytes., 1716, I, W, P5/1716/16, P5/15Reg/334
Jn., sen., husb., Corton, Boyton, 1580, I, W, P2/C/56, P2/6Reg/5B
Clace, Jn., husb., Chitterne AS, 1592, W, P2/C/114
Jn., husb., Knook, 1602-08, AB, I, W, P5/1601/10, P5/7Reg/28D
Clace, Jn., yeo., Longleat (in Longbridge D.), Horningsham, 1667-68, AB, a/c, I, P2/C/574
Jn., day labourer, Trowb., 1729, W, P1/C/691, P1/7Reg/384
Maud, widow, Tytherington, Heytes., 1587, I, W, P5/1587/12, P5/5Reg/11A
Robt., husb., Tytherington, Heytes., 1595, I, T, W, P5/1595/15, P5/6Reg/101A
Walter, Corton, Boyton, 1594, I, W, P2/C/126
Clace, Wm., Corsley, 1730, W, P2/C/1119
Clasy *see* Clacy
Clattrie *see* Tompkins als C.
Claver *see* Cleaver
Clavering, Robt., clerk and rector, Marl. St Peter and St Paul, 1773, W, P1/C/983, P1/13Reg/49B,
Clavy *see* Clacy
Clay, Cley, Jn., Devizes St Jn., 1563, W (lacking part along right side) (NEP), P1/2Reg/158B
Jn., yeo., Easton Grey, 1775, W, P3/C/1043
Claydon, Cleydon, Amy, widow, Broad C., 1579, I (2), W, P2/C/51, P2/5Reg/353E
Jn., husb., Broad C., 1573, W, P2/5Reg/171C
Cleydon, Thos., Farnham, Tollard Royal, Dorset, 1581, W, P2/6Reg/49B
Cleydon, Wm., husb., Stoke F., [1596], I, P2/C/137
see also May nee C.
Clayton, Hannah, Reading, Berks., 1732, W, P1/C/706, P1/7Reg/482A
Sarah, widow, Reading, Berks., 1817, W, Wr, P1/1817/71
Cleal, Jn., carp., Lyme R., Dorset, 1852, comm, W, Wr, P16/449

Cleaveland *see* Cleveland
Cleavely *see* Cleverly
Cleaver, Hy., pawnbroker, Warm., 1836, comm, W, P2/1836/11
Claver, Robt., husb., Clapton, Kintbury, Berks., 1625, I, W, P1/C/113
Cleaver *or* Clever als Lawrence, Thos., sen., yeo., Wawcott, Kintbury, Berks., 1759, AB, W, P1/C/896, P1/11Reg/377B
Cleaverly *see* Cleverly
Clee, Hy., yeo., Heytes., 1742, W, Wr, P5/1742/8
Cleeter, Geo., sen., yeo., Uffcott, Broad H., 1728, W, P3/C/776
Hercules, tailor, Hurst, Berks., 1710, W, P5/1710/29, P5/15Reg/157
Jn., Uffcott, Broad H., 1684, AB, I, W, P3/C/484
Jn., Froxfield, 1686, AB, I, P3/C/505
My., sp., Broad H., 1753, W, P1/C/864, P1/11Reg/115
Robt., Purton, 1639, AB, I, P3/C/243
Clitter, Thos., wheelwright, Froxfield, 1671, I, W, P1/C/311
Wm., husb., Overtown, Wrou., 1804, comm, W, P3/1804/18
Cleeveland *see* Cleveland
Cleft *see* Clift
Clefton *see* Clifton
Clelford, Clilvard, Edith, sp., Maiden B., 1604, AB, P2/C/206
Geo., gardener, W. Lavington, 1731, W, P1/C/697, P1/7Reg/418
Jn., brickmaker, Mkt. L., 1771, W, P2/C/1358
Clellard, Wm., husb., Mere, 1574, W, P5/3Reg/48C
Clements, Clement, Abraham, baker, Bradford A., 1631, I, W, P2/C/402, P2/9Reg/64A
Clement, Alice, widow, Tisb., 1557, W, P2/3Reg/29B
Clement, Alice, widow, Gt. Cheverell, 1558, W, P2/3Reg/92C
Clement, Alice, widow, Stratford Tony, 1600, AB, W, P2/C/178
Clement, Alice, widow, Mere, 1619, I, W, P5/1618/6, P5/9Reg/220B
Clement, Alice, widow, Wantage, Berks., 1738, W, P23/527
Clemence, Alice *see also* Wm. Fry
Clement, Ann, widow, Grove, Wantage, Berks., 1683, I, W, P23/117
Clement, Ann, widow of Robt., chandler, Wantage, Berks., 1706, I, W, P23/282
Clement, Ann, widow, Wantage, Berks., 1724, W, P23/431
Ann, widow, Bishopstone N., 1727, I, W, P6/111
Ann, widow, Newbury, Berks., 1729, W, P1/C/680, P1/7Reg/285A
Clement, Ann, widow, late of Bath but effects at Box, 1792, AB, comm, I, P3/C/1115
Ann Charlotte, sp., Rams., 1856, aff, O, W, Wr, P5/1856/14
Anth., jun., husb., Nursteed, Bps. C., 1683, W, P24/762
Clement, Cath., widow, Donhead St My., 1733, W, P2/C/1150
Clement, Christian, widow, All C., 1681, W, P3/C/435
Clement, Cicely, widow, Gt. Cheverell, 1586, I, T, W, P2/C/69, P2/7Reg/32A
David, widow, Trowb., 1856, AB, aff, O, Wr, P1/1856/19
Clement, Dorothy, widow, Wantage, Berks., 1716, I, W, P5/1716/22, P5/15Reg/351A
Clement als Horsman, Edmd., Hindon, 1613, I, W, P1/C/51
Clement, Edwd., Wingfield, 1622, AB, a/c, comm, I, P1/C/109
Clement, Edwd., maltster, Mere, 1691, AB, I, P5/1691/17
Clement, Edwd., Reading, Berks., 1808, AB, Wr, P1/1808/130
Clement, Eliz., Westwood, 1633, I, W, P2/C/421
Eliz., sp., Lyneham, 1665, comm, I, W, P3/C/304
Clement, Francis, yeo., Holt, Bradford A., [1667], I, W, P2/C/568
Geo., Sal., 1710, AB, P4/1710/6
Clement, Hy., dyer, Stratford Tony, 1625, I, W, P2/C/349
Clement, Hy., Grove, Wantage, Berks., 1662, I, W, P5/1662/29
Clement als Fowler, Hy., sen., husb., Rowde & All C., 1681, AB, I, P3/C/436
Clement, Hy., widower, Eddington, Hungerford, Berks., 1857, AB, aff, D, O, Wr, P5/1857/16
Clement, Jas., Mere, 1815, AB, Wr, P5/1815/17
Clement, Jas., carp., Mere, 1823, I, W, P5/1823/32
Clement, Jeremy, husb., All C., 1631, AB, I, P1/C/140
Clement, Jerome, pointmaker, Ludwell, Donhead St My., [1670], I, W, P2/C/603
Clement, Joan, widow, Hurst, Berks., 1567, W, P5/2Reg/24B
Clement, Joan, Gt. Cheverell, 1622, I, W, P2/C/324

Joan, sp., Corston, Malm., 1714, W, P3/C/689
Clement, Jn., sen., Gt. Cheverell, 1557, W, P2/3Reg/42A
Clement, Jn., Chilmark, 1559, AB, P2/3Reg/170A
Clement, Jn., Downton, 1560, W, P2/4Reg/44D
Clement, Jn., husb., Wallmead, Tisb., 1560, W, P2/4Reg/31B
Clement, Jn., husb., Mere, 1564, W, P5/1Reg/44A
Clement, Jn., Hurst, Berks., 1566, W, P5/1Reg/71A
Clement, Jn., Stratford Tony, 1570, AB, P2/5Reg/104C
Clement, Jn., Sal. St Edmd., 1587, AB, P4/Reg/31B
Clement, Jn., yeo., Farnborough, Berks., 1611, I, W, P1/C/46
Clement, Jn., yeo., Gt. Cheverell, 1631, AB, comm, I, W, P2/C/404
Clement, Jn., Gt. Cheverell, 1639, I, W, P2/C/470
Clement, Jn., husb., Over Zeals, 1647-48, AB, I (2 copies), L, P5/1647/3, P5/14Reg/100A
Clement, Jn., Hindon, 1671, AB, I, P2/C/614
Jn., sen., vict. and blacksmith, Wokm., Berks., 1671, comm, I, W (signature cut away), P5/1671/21
Clement, Jn., husb., Wantage, Berks., 1678, I, W, P23/81
Clements als Brown, Jn., joiner, Heale, Woodford, 1681, W, P13/3/5
Clement, Jn., tanner, Wantage, Berks., [1702], W (fine decorative work on 1st line, green & black ink). No date of probate., P23/246
Clement, Jn., Mere, 1703, AB, I, P5/1703/6
Clement, Jn., yeo., Wantage, Berks., 1712, W, P23/325
Clement, Jn., chandler, Wantage, Berks., 1714, I, W, P23/337
Jn., Wokm., Berks., 1715, AB, comm, P5/1715/14
Clement, Jn., cordw., Wantage, Berks., 1727, W, P23/451
Clement, Jn., glover, Wantage, Berks., 1728, I, W, P5/1728/23, P5/16Reg/196
Jn., gelder, Wokm., Berks., 1735, W, P5/1735/12
Clement, Jn., tailor, Wantage, Berks., 1735, W, P23/506
Clement, Jn., gardener, Wantage, Berks., 1745, W, P23/581
Clement, Jn., yeo., Ditteridge, 1751, AB, ren, P3/C/910
Jn., Wilsford nr Pewsey, 1767, AB, I, P1/C/948
Jn., yeo. *or* land surveyor, Avebury, 1798, note of probate, W, P3/C/1138
Clement, Jn., Newtown, Hungerford, Berks., 1827, AB, comm, Wr, P23/931
Clement, Jn., Eddington, Hungerford, Berks., 1857, AB, aff, O, Wr, P5/1857/14
Jos., gent., Trowb., 1814, comm, W, Wr, P1/1814/60
Judith, wife, Sal., 1738, AB, I, P1/C/753
Mgt., widow, Wokm., Berks., 1725, comm, W, P5/1725/17, P5/16Reg/127B
Clement, Martha, widow, Mere, 1717, W, P5/1717/10, P5/15Reg/399B
Clement, My., widow, Gt. Cheverell, 1640, I, W, P2/C/487
Clement, My., widow, Mere, 1711-12, AB, W, P5/1711/19, P5/15Reg/279
Clement, My., sp., Sal. The Close (form. of Baverstock), 1780, W, P2/C/1408
My., widow, Sal., 1828, W, Wr, P4/1828/2
Clement, Maud, widow, Chards., Devon, 1570, W, P5/2Reg/77B
Clement, Michael, yeo., Coombe Farm, Donhead St My., 1674, comm, I, W, P1/C/316
Clement, Nich., husb., Mere, 1600, AB, T, W, P5/1600/14, P5/6Reg/239, 240A
Clement, Nich., husb. *or* yeo., Grove, Wantage, Berks., 1674, AB, I, P23/48
Clement, Nich., sen., yeo., Grove, Wantage, Berks., 1677, I, W, P23/68
Clement, Nich., butcher, Wantage, Berks., 1689, W, P23/169
Clement, Nich., yeo., Wantage, Berks., 1778, W, P23/766
Patience, widow, Trowb., 1820, comm, req, W, Wr, P1/1820/139
Clement, Paul, clerk and rector, Nether C., Dorset, 1707, AB, comm, I, P5/1707/14
Clement, Pearce, husb., Stratford Tony, 1588, AB, I, T, W, P2/C/76, P2/7Reg/126A
Clements als King, Phoebe, yeo.'s wife, Liddington, 1735, AB, P3/C/826
Clement, Rebecca, widow, Wantage, Berks., 1671, cert, I, W, P23/28
Clement, Rd., yeo., Westwood, 1588, W, P2/7Reg/141B
Clement, Rd., yeo., Westwood, 1594, I, W, P2/C/130
Rd., weaver, Wokm., Berks., 1638, I, W, P5/1638/20, P5/13Reg/126
Clemence, Rd., yeo., Barkham, Berks., 1692, I, W, P1/C/421
Clement, Rd., maltster, Mere, 1711-12, AB, ren, W, P5/1711/20, P5/15Reg/280
Clement, Rd., yeo., Studley, Trowb., 1765, comm, W, P1/C/935, P1/12Reg/161
Clement, Robt., husb., Tisb., 1555, W, P2/1Reg/97B

Clement, Robt., husb., Keevil Wick, 1594, I, W, P2/C/128
Clemond, Robt., tanner, Mere, 1635, AB, a/c, bond to pay debt, deed of gift, I (2), P5/1634/5, P5/12Reg/170B
Clement, Robt., bailiff, Wantage, Berks., 1668, AB, I, P23/1
Clement, Robt., tallow chandler, Wantage, Berks., 1688, I, W, P5/1688/20
Clement, Robt., All C., 1701, AB, comm, I (2), P1/C/471, P3/C/629
Clement, Robt., potter, Wantage, Berks., 1705-08, AB, I, W, P23/276, 292
Robt., clerk, Ogbourne St Geo., 1717, W, P23/359
Clement, Robt., innholder, Wantage, Berks., 1718-24, AB, I, W, P23/368, 419
Robt., yeo., Avebury, 1797, note of probate, W, P3/C/1134
Clement, Robt., butcher, Wantage, Berks., 1801, W, P23/825
Clement, Sarah, widow, Wantage, Berks., 1683, W, P23/122
Steph., E. Kennett, 1841, AB, O, Wr, P3/1841/11
Clement, Susan, sp., Melk., [1640], I, W, P2/C/490
Clement als Tabarar, Thos., Hindon, 1545, W (NEP), P2/1Reg/58B
Thos., Bulford, 1581, AB, P2/6Reg/21A
Clement, Thos., baker, Bradford A., 1636, I, W, P2/C/441
Clement, Thos., yeo., Wantage, Berks., 1678, I, W, P23/82
Thos., Purton, 1684, AB, I, P3/C/485
Thos., jun., Sal., 1695, AB, P4/1695/12
Clement, Thos., sen., cordw., Wantage, Berks., 1695, I, W, P5/1695/19
Thos., cordw., Inkpen, Berks., 1698, I, W, P1/C/464
Thos., yeo., Inkpen, Berks., 1698, W, P1/3Reg/124
Thos., Sal., 1706, I, P4/1706/14
Clemence, Thos., cordw., Bishopstone N., 1710, W (small measuring about 5 by 7 inches), P5/1710/28, P5/15Reg/178
Thos., vicar, Idmiston, 1747, comm, W, P2/C/1243
Thos., carp., Sal., 1822, W, Wr, P4/1822/8
Clement, Tristram, tailor, Childrey, Berks., 1689, I, W, P1/C/397
Clement, Walter, sen., husb., Semley, 1552, I, W, P2/C/8, P2/2Reg/161A
Clement, Wm., Chilmark, 1557, W, P2/3Reg/65
Clemence, Wm., tailor, Highw., 1579, W, P5/1579/19, P5/3Reg/144A
Clement, Wm., tailor, Stratford Tony, 1591, I, W, P2/C/98
Clement, Wm., Keevil Wick, 1640, I, W, P2/C/486
Clement, Wm., sen., yeo., Wantage, Berks., 1669, I, W, P23/4
Clement, Wm., husb., Grove, Wantage, Berks., 1686, AB, I, P23/148
Wm., Sal., 1701, AB, I, P4/1701/6
Wm., hellier, Sal., 1714, W, P4/1714/1
Clement, Wm., weaver, Wantage, Berks., 1722, I, W, P5/1722/11, P5/16Reg/76B
Clement, Wm., bricklayer, Wantage, Berks., 1743, W, Wr, P5/1743/17
Wm., yeo., Ogbourne St And., 1777, W, P23/762
Wm., yeo., Beckhampton, Avebury, 1804, comm, W, P3/1804/16
see also Brown(e) als C.; Tabor als C.
Clemm *see* Steadman als C.
Clempson, Ann, widow, Sal., 1723, AB, P4/1723/4
Clench, Ann, widow, Winterborne M., Winterborne K., Dorset, 1580, AB (in minority of Thos., George, Wm., Phillip, Lucy & Eliz. C.), P5/4Reg/6B
Ann, Winterborne M., Winterborne K., Dorset, 1587, a/c (2), I, T (re Wm., Philip, Eliz. & Lucy C., children of Ann & Wm., decd), P5/1587/45
Ann, Stourpaine, Dorset, 1695, I, W, P24/519
Ann, widow, Winterborne M., Winterborne K., Dorset, 1726, AB, W, P5/1726/14, P5/16Reg/134C
Collette, widow, Southbrook, Bere R., Dorset, 1622, I, W, P5/1622/13, P5/10Reg/137
Edwd., yeo., Winterborne M., Winterborne K., Dorset, 1629, AB, comm, I, T, W, P5/1628/29, P5/11Reg/17C
Geo., Stourpaine, Dorset, 1724, W, P24/871
Joan, widow, Hurst, Berks., 1554, W, P5/20Reg/130A
Jn., Winterborne K., Dorset, 1684, AB, I, P5/1683/17
Jn., clothier, Bere R., Dorset, 1684, AB, I, P5/1684/12
Jn., Stourpaine, Dorset, 1695, AB, P24/518
Clinch, Jn., Long Wittenham, Berks., 1756, AB, P1/C/880
Jn., sen., clothier, Bere R., Dorset, 1777, W, P5/1777/6, P5/17Reg/146
Joshua, sen., yeo., Winterborne M., Winterborne K., Dorset, 1704, I, W, P5/1704/11
Miriam, widow, Stourpaine, Dorset, 1734, W, P24/926

Philippa, widow, Shitterton, Bere R., Dorset, 1698, I, W, P5/1698/20
Reynold, gent., Oborne, Dorset, 1693, AB, comm, W, P5/1693/13
Robt., mercer, Bere R., Dorset, 1612, AB, comm, I (2), P5/1612/14, P5/9Reg/64B
Thos., carp., Stourpaine, Dorset, 1774, W, P24/1140
Timothy, Bere R., Dorset, 1769, AB, comm, P5/1769/7
Wm., Bere R., Dorset, 1577, I, P5/1576/11
Wm., Winterborne M., Winterborne K., Dorset, 1577, AB, P5/3Reg/101A
Wm., Winterborne M., Winterborne K., Dorset, 1580, AB (in minority of Thos., George, Wm., Phillip, Lucy & Eliz. C.), P5/4Reg/6A
Wm., Winterborne M., Winterborne K., Dorset, 1587, AB, P5/4Reg/139B
Clerdew, Alice, widow, Crickl. St S., 1727, W, P3/C/766
Joan, widow, Crickl. St S., 1638, I, W, P3/C/231
Jn., yeo., Crickl. St S., 1604, I, W, P3/C/11
Jn., barber surgeon *or* innholder, Crickl. St S., 1702, I, W, P3/C/640
My., sp., Crickl. St S., 1626, I, W, P3/C/142
Wm., innholder, Crickl. St S., 1696, I, W, P3/C/593
Clere, Rd., priest, Wasing, Berks., 1561, institution to rectory, P1/1Reg/79D
Clerk, Clerke *see* Clark
Cleve, Cleves, Eliz., widow, Mere, 1626-27, I, W, P5/1626/7, P5/11Reg/4
Eliz., widow, Purton, 1689, comm, I, W, P3/C/537
Cleves, Geo., Lyme R., Dorset, 1667, AB, P16/10
Jn., Gillingham, Dorset, 1563, W, P27/1Reg/13C
Jn., mason, Mere, 1618, I, W, P5/1618/8, P5/9Reg/218B
Cleves, Robt., husb., Britford, 1585, I, W, P5/1585/8, P5/4Reg/102A
Robt., fuller, Mere, 1591, AB, I, W, P5/1591/14, P5/5Reg/106C
Cleveland, Cleaveland, Ann, widow, Devizes St Jn., 1781, AB, P1/C/1024
Christian, widow, Ashbury, Berks., 1677, I, W, P1/C/328
Cleaveland, Jane, minor, Devizes St Jn., 1781, app. of guardian, bond to secure goods, P1/C/1025
Cleaveland, Jn., staymaker, Devizes St My., 1747, AB (2), W, P1/C/832, P1/10Reg/198
Cleaveland, Rd., Baynton, Edington, 1784, comm, W, P2/C/1430
Cleaveland, Rd., shopkeeper, Lacock, 1796, W, P3/C/1129
Cleeveland, Sarah, widow, Pott. (effects at Bradford A.), 1780, W, P2/C/1409
Cleaveland, Thos., carp., Bradford A., 1844, O, W, Wr, P2/1844/6
Cleaveland, Wm., sen., gent., Devizes St Jn. (form. of Lacock), 1781, AB, comm, W, P1/C/1023, P1/13Reg/329A
Clevelodd *see* Adlam als Clevelodd
Clever *see* Cleaver
Cleverly, Geo., cordw., Broughton G., 1805, W, P2/1805/1
Cleverley, Jn., Arborfield, Berks., 1601, AB, I, W, P5/1601/13, P5/7Reg/27B
Cleavely, Jn., clerk and rector, Sutton V., 1680, a/c (very detailed), AB, comm, I (very detailed), P1/C/352
Jn., mason, Calne, 1842, AB, comm, ren, W, Wr, P26/1458
Cleaverly, My., sen., widow, Sutton V. & Kingston D., 1687, AB, copy AB, I (2), W, P2/C/775
Thos., husb., Heddington, 1745, AB, I, W, P3/C/884
Thos., Gt. Somerford, 1807, AB, Wr, P3/1807/11
Cleves *see* Cleve
Cley *see* Clay
Cleydon *see* Claydon
Clidesdale als Hidden, Edwd., yeo., W. Shefford, Berks., 1747, W, P1/H/1048, P1/10Reg/124
Jn., Hungerford, Berks., 1685, AB, I, P5/1685/27
see also Hidden als C.
Clifford, Alice, widow, Ashton K., 1603, I, W (NEP), P3/C/7
Ann, widow, Sal., 1777, AB, P4/1777/8
Anth., husb., Sonning, Berks., 1633, AB, comm, I, P5/1632/17, P5/12Reg/159C
Clifford als Bartlemew, Avis, widow, Spirthill, Bremhill, 1611, W (NEP), P3/C/60
Bethia, widow, Wootton B., 1790, comm, W, P3/C/1108
Dorothy, widow, Cleverton, Lea and C., 1765, W, P3/C/987
Esther, widow, Elcombe, Wrou., 1726, W, P3/C/761
Francis, yeo., Ardington, Berks., 1723, AB, I, P1/C/617
Francis, carp., Lockeridge, Overton, 1774, L, W, P3/C/1038
Hy., Leigh, Ashton K., 1633, I, ren, P3/C/185
Hy., yeo., Somerford K., 1779, W, P1/C/1013, P1/13Reg/247

Hy., Ashton K. (late of Somerford K.), 1814, AB, comm, Wr, P3/1814/10
Hester, widow, St. Martins St., Marl. St My., 1774, AB, I, P1/C/984
Jeremiah, Brinkw., 1729, W, P3/C/782
Jeremiah, sen., yeo., Brinkw., 1744, W, P1/C/808, P1/9Reg/393B
Joan, widow, Elcombe, Wrou., 1687, I, W, P3/C/520
Jn., Gt. Wishford, 1615, AB, I, P2/C/280, P2/8Reg/260B
Jn., Dilton M., Westb., 1736, AB, P25/1736/7
Jn., sen., Latton, 1743, AB, P3/C/874
Jn., pipemaker, Oxford St., Marl. St My., 1749, W, P1/C/835, P1/10Reg/252
Jn., yeo., Ashton K., 1751, W, P3/C/911
Jn., collarmaker, *The Three Tuns Inn*, Wootton B., 1777, comm, W, P3/C/1054
Jn., Shaw, Lydiard M., 1788, W, P3/C/1102
Jos., sen., Stockley, Calne, 1810, AB, comm, P26/1278
My., sp., Figh., 1729, W, P26/645
My., Overton, 1766, AB, P3/C/994
My., widow, Ashton K., 1803, W, Wr, P3/1803/15
My., widow, Crickl. St S., 1830, W, Wr, P3/1830/27
Maurice, husb., Elcombe, Wrou., 1630, I, W, P3/C/167
Philip, yeo., Westb. L., 1812, O, W, P25/1813/7
Rd., Ashton K., 1668, I, NW, P3/C/317
Rd., weaver, Gt. Wishford, 1668, AB, I, P2/C/579
Rd., shoemaker, Sal., 1773, W, note (NEP), P4/1773/10
Robt., husb., Elcombe, Wrou., 1630, I, NW, P3/C/168
Robt., yeo., Elcombe, Wrou., 1697, I, W, P3/C/600
Robt., sen., farmer, Upton S., 1803, W, P2/1803/10
Ruth, widow, Winterbourne M., 1739, W, P3/C/850
Sam., cordw., Gt. Bedwyn, 1670, I, W, P21/2/6
Sam., Winterbourne M., 1735, AB, P3/C/827
Sam., shopkeeper, Cholderton, 1841, W, Wr, P2/1841/28
Thos., broad weaver, Chilmark, 1596, AB, I, P2/C/140
Thos., yeo., Lockeridge, Overton, 1731, AB, I, P3/C/791
Thos., Amesb., 1758, AB, P2/C/1299
Wm., yeo., Elcombe, Wrou., 1673, AB, a/c, I, P3/C/366
Wm., cordw., Gt. Bedwyn, 1677, I, W, P21/2/50
Wm., jun., Calne, 1689, AB, comm, I, P26/378
Wm., sen., Lockeridge, Overton, 1701, AB, I, P3/C/630
Wm., shopkeeper, Marl., 1749, AB, I, P1/C/834
Wm., dealer in cards, Ashton K., 1785, W, P3/C/1086
Wm., Lockeridge, Overton, 1822, AB, Wr, P3/1822/33
Wm., yeo., Calne, 1841, W, Wr, P26/1454
Clift, Ann, sp., Sal., 1813, W, Wr, P4/1813/5
Arthur, cordw., Beam., Dorset, 1716, I, W, P17/367
Eliz., widow, Quidh. (effects at Sal.), 1844, AB, Wr, P1/1844/5
Eliz., widow, Trowb., 1856, aff, O, W, Wr, P1/1856/20
Eliz. Talver, sp., Prospect House, Rowde, 1857, AB, aff, comm, Wr, P3/1857/39
Jas., Westb., 1708, AB, P25/1708/11
Jas., butcher, Westb., 1737, W, P25/1737/4
Jas., butcher, Chitterne St My., 1739, AB, I, P2/C/1196
Joan, Coombe, Beam., Dorset, 1686, AB, I, W, P17/91
Jn., handle setter, Westb., 1742, W (sermon to be given in Presbyterian Meeting House), P25/1742/4
Jn., gent., Hilcott, N. Newnton, 1829, W, Wr, P1/1829/55
Jos., Baptist minister, N. Bradley, 1828, comm, W, P2/1828/51
Martha, widow, Sal., 1783, AB, ren, P1/C/1034
My. Ann, sp., Chirton, 1854, AB, aff, O, Wr, P2/1854/73
Nich., sen., yeo., Westb., 1683, W, P25/1683/5
Nich., butcher, Westb., 1691, AB, I, P25/1691/6
Philip, sen., vict., Westb., 1687, I, W, P25/1687/7
Philip, yeo., Deptford, Wylye, 1806, AB, W, P2/1806/56
Robt., husb., Coombe, Beam., Dorset, [1680], W (NEP), P17/289
Sam., butcher and mercer, Westb. L., 1722, AB, I (detailed), P25/1722/6

Sam., Sal., 1766, AB, P4/1766/10
Sarah, Netherb., Dorset, 1702, AB, I, P17/142
Cleft, Thos., carp., Hurst, Berks., 1632, I, W, P5/1632/16, P5/12Reg/101
Cleft, Thos., yeo., Luccombe, Netherb., Dorset, 1696, AB, I, NW, P17/356
Thos., Heytes., 1746, AB, P5/1746/16
Thos., labourer, Norton B., 1845, O, W, Wr, P2/1845/9
Cleft, Thomasine, widow, Netherb., Dorset, 1720, W, P17/384
Wm., sen., joiner, Netherb., Dorset, 1709, AB, I, P17/181
Wm., shoemaker, Beam., Dorset, 1710, AB, I, P5/1710/30
Cleft, Wm., yeo., Netherb., Dorset, 1711, AB, I, P17/206
Wm., minor, Chitterne St My., 1739, T (son of Jas. C. d. 1739?), P2/C/1198
Wm., butcher, Steeple A., 1744, W, P1/C/809, P1/9Reg/420B
Wm., yeo., Yondover, Netherb., Dorset, 1785, W, P5/1785/8, P5/18Reg/33
Wm., gent., Durrington, 1832, O, W, Wr, P1/1832/33
Wm., butcher, Chirton, 1834, comm, W, Wr, P2/1834/22
Clifton, Ann, widow, W. Overton, 1764, W, P3/C/980
Ann, sp., Overton, 1765, AB, comm, P3/C/988
Anth., sen., Lt. Bedwyn, 1635, I, W, P5/1635/22, P5/12Reg/236C
Anth., yeo., Lt. Bedwyn, 1662, AB, comm, I, P5/1662/23
Eliz., widow, Lt. Bedwyn, 1669, I, W, P5/1669/12
Clefton *or* Clifton, Hy., yeo., Burridge Heath, Lt. Bedwyn, 1609, I, W, P5/1609/14, P5/8Reg/154C
Hy., Overton, 1682, comm, W, P3/C/453
Jas., Sal., 1850, AB, Wr, P4/1850/1
Jn., no abode stated, but widow is of Gt. Bedwyn, 1635, AB, I, P21/1/18
Rd., husb., Longcott, Shrivenham, Berks., 1631, I, W, P1/C/141
Solomon, Gt. Bedwyn, 1619, I, W, P5/1619/13, P5/9Reg/228C
Thos., Burridge Heath, Lt. Bedwyn, 1612, cert, I, P3/C/63
Thos., Overton, 1676, AB, a/c, I, P3/C/389
Thos., yeo., Preshute, 1685, I, W, P1/C/373
Thos., Overton, 1736-75, AB (3), comm, P3/C/828
Clilvard *see* Clelford
Clinch *see* Clench
Clinton, Ralph, husb., Stoke F., 1610, I, W, P2/C/244, P2/8Reg/146
Clissold, Dan., Marl., 1833, AB, Wr, P1/1833/6
Clisild, Eliz., sp., Fisherton A., 1761, AB, P2/C/1310
Clisild, Frances, widow, Fisherton A., 1753, W, P1/C/858, P1/11Reg/71
Clisild, Sarah, sp., Fisherton A., 1754, AB, a/c, I, P2/C/1284
Clissell, Thos., rugmaker, Calne, 1726, I, W, P26/708
Clitter *see* Cleeter
Clode, Jn., clerk, Chards., Devon, 1638, I, W, P5/1638/21, P5/13Reg/71B
Walter, husb., Tytherleigh, Chards., Devon, 1626, comm, I, W, P5/1625/17, P5/10Reg/190A
Clore, Jn., sen., yeo., Warm., 1646, W, P2/C/524
My., widow, Netherb., Dorset, [1669], W, P17/87
Clothier, Caleb, yeo., Fordington, Dorset, 1791, W, P5/1791/5, P5/18Reg/169A
Osmund, husb., Sherb., Dorset, 1611, I, P5/1611/7
Clotterbooke *see* Clutterbuck
Clotworthy, Eliz., Caundle Marsh, Dorset, 1767, W, P5/1767/12
Clough, Hy., currier, Sal., 1842, W, Wr, P1/1842/75
My., widow, Froxfield, 1807, req, W, Wr, P3/1807/70
Clove, Alice, widow, Kingston D., 1580, W, P2/5Reg/363C
Cloves, Jas., shepherd, Maiden B., 1601, AB, I, P2/C/183
Mgt., widow, Monkton D., 1621, I, W, P2/C/323
Wm., husb., Kingston D., 1576, I, T, W, P2/C/41, P2/5Reg/270A
Clowde, Clowdes, Gilbt., husb., Hungerford, Berks., 1662, AB, comm, I, L, NW, P5/1662/22
Jn., E. Knoyle, 1558, W, P2/3Reg/92A
Robt., husb., Devizes Grn, Devizes St Jas., Devizes, 1575, I, W, P5/1574/5, P5/3Reg/54B
Clunn, Nich., clerk, Sal. The Close, 1630, I, W, P5/1630/2, P5/11Reg/157
Clutterbuck, Clotterbooke, Eliz., sp., Tollard Royal, 1758, AB, comm, P2/C/1295
Clutton, Sibyl, widow, Bradford A., 1663, AB, comm, I, P1/C/266
Susan, sp., Bradford A., 1707, I, W, P2/C/942

Wm., Bradford A., 1648, AB, I, P2/C/537
Coad, Frances, widow, Lyme R., Dorset, 1701, I, W, P5/1701/14
Frances, sp., Lyme R., Dorset, 1724, W, P16/233
Coates, Chris., husb., Leigh, Ashton K., 1622, AB, I, NW, P3/C/115
Jas., wheelwright, Brokenb., 1846, O, W, Wr, P3/1846/13
Coat, Jn., miller, Fordington, Dorset, 1744, W, P15/135
Jn., yeo., Littleton Drew, 1803, W, Wr, P3/1803/55
Mgt., widow, Reading, Berks., 1717, W, P1/C/578, P1/6Reg/108
Martha, widow, Nettleton, 1837, W, Wr, P3/1837/51
My., sp., Wantage, Berks., 1672, AB, I, P23/29
Coats, Rd., yeo., Nettleton, 1796, W, Wr, P3/C/1130
Rd., innkeeper and vict., *The Pack Horse Inn*, Corsham, 1822, AB, W, Wr, P3/1822/23
Thos., yeo., Nettleton, 1847, O, W, Wr, P3/1847/46
Coats, Wm., labourer, Arborfield, Berks., 1810, comm, W, Wr, P5/1810/4
Wm., yeo., Nettleton, 1824, W, Wr, P3/1824/33
Wm., Wallingford St Leonard, Berks., 1829, AB, Wr, P1/1829/106
Coats, Wm., Corsham, 1846, W, Wr, P3/1846/23
see also Baker als C.
Cobb, Chris., husb., Hurst, Berks., 1604, I, W, P5/1604/6, P5/8Reg/18
Edwd., yeo., E. Coulston, 1692, AB, I, P1/C/417
Joan, widow, Sherb., Dorset, 1595, AB, I, W, P5/1594/21, P5/6Reg/92
Jn., Keevil, 1560, AB, P2/4Reg/35D
Jn. *see also* Jn. Parry
Nich., lockier, Sherb., Dorset, 1582, W, P5/4Reg/40C
Nich., smith, Sherb., Dorset, 1582, I, T, P5/1582/16
Philip, Norton B., 1552, L (about his NW), W, P2/C/7, P2/2Reg/161B
Rd., priest, Aldbourne, 1558, institution to vicarage, P1/1Reg/7E
Rd., Gt. Durnford, 1627-28, I, W, P5/1627/7, P5/11Reg/6A
Sarah, widow, Chitterne St My., 1669, AB, P2/C/588
Thos., husb., Alvediston, 1648, I, W, P2/C/538
Cobb als Iddols, Thos., yeo., Westport St My. (form. of Corston), 1852, W, Wr, P3/1852/31
Una, widow, Sherb., Dorset, 1612, AB, I, W, P5/1612/11, P5/9Reg/58A
Wm., husb., Gt. Durnford, 1619, I, W, P5/1618/9, P5/9Reg/224
Wm., cordw., Sutton C., Berks., 1695, AB, I, ren, P1/C/438
Cobbams *see* Cobham
Cobbock *see* Coppock
Cobden, Jn., fidler[fiddler?], Whitep., 1733, I, W, P2/C/1148
Jn., Whitep., 1832, AB, Wr, P2/1832/30
Cobern *see* Colbourne
Cobery *see* Coborowe
Cobham, Jas., clerk and rector, Patney, 1708, W, P1/C/505
My., Hurst, Berks., 1674, AB, P5/1674/19
Cobbams, Robt., husb., Hurst, Berks., 1665, AB, I, P5/1665/20
Thos., fisherman, Hurst, Berks., 1687, I, W, P5/1689/12
Cobley, Robt., sen., yeo., Witcomb, Hilmarton, 1684, I, W, P3/C/486
Coborne *see* Cobourne
Coborowe, Hy., husb., Ashbury, Berks., 1616, I, W, P1/C/77
Cobery, Jn., yeo., Tockenham, 1685, W, P3/C/496
Cobourne *see* Colbourne
Cobwell, Rd., labourer, Thatcham, Berks., 1635, AB, I, P1/C/170
Cock, Jn., yeo., Halstock, Dorset, 1573, W, P5/3Reg/20E
Mgt., widow, Lacock, 1567, W (NEP), P1/1Reg/41A
Nathaniel, yeo., Easthampstead, Berks., 1738, comm, W, P1/C/748, P1/8Reg/201B
Ralph, Cookham, Berks., 1735, W, P1/C/732, P1/8Reg/16
Rd., W. Dean, 1630, AB, I, P2/C/391
Thos., sen., carp., Winkfield, Berks., 1763, W, P1/C/919, P1/12Reg/69
Wm., Sal., 1618, AB, I, P4/1618/3
see also Atkins als C.
Cockarell *see* Cockerell
Cockell, Anth., yeo., Compton B., 1782, W, P3/C/1077

Cockle, Bridget, widow, Stanton St Q., 1756, W, P1/C/888, P1/11Reg/318
Cockle, Cath., widow, Codf. St P., 1610-13, AB, a/c, court paper, I, T, P2/C/264, P2/8Reg/112B
Cockle, Eliz., widow, Hawkeridge, Westb., 1734, AB, P25/1734/1
Eliz., Chapmanslade, Corsley, 1758, W, P2/C/1297
Cockle, Hy., yeo., Tinh., Edington, 1613, AB, I, P1/C/54
Hy., Westb., 1842, AB, O, Wr, P1/1842/15
Cockle, Jas., vict., Westb., 1737, W, P25/1737/5
Cockle, Jas., Stanton St Q., 1747, AB, P1/C/817
Jane, clothier's wife, Chapmanslade, Corsley, 1764, AB, P2/C/1321
Cockle, Jn., husb., Crockerton, Longbridge D., 1555, W, P2/1Reg/94D
Jn., husb., Codf. St P., 1607, I, W, P2/C/223
Jn., mason, Calne, 1675, AB, I, P26/232
Cockle, Jn., Westb., 1679, AB, comm, P25/1679/2
Cockle, Jn., mason, Kington St M., 1688, I, W, Wr, P3/C/530
Cockle, Jn., husb., Hawkeridge, Westb., 1711, AB, P25/1711/14
Cockle, Jn., clothier, Westb., 1732, W, P25/1732/2
Cockle, Jn., yeo., Stanton St Q., 1749, W, P3/C/902
Jn., Dilton M., Westb., 1832, AB, Wr, P25/1832/1
Cockle, My., widow, Chalford, Westb., 1747, W, P25/1747/2
Cockle, My., widow, Hilmarton, 1816, comm, W, Wr, P3/1816/34
Cockhill, My., widow, Heywood, Westb. (effects at Warm.), 1847, AB, O, W, Wr, P2/1847/4
Nich., broad weaver, Hawkeridge, Westb., 1685, I, W (copy with grant of probate), p25/1685/15
Rd., husb., Edington, 1583, W, P2/6Reg/78B
Cockle, Rd., [clothier], Westb., 1763, a/c (very detailed), AB, I (very detailed - ref. to room over school), P25/1763/8
Cockles, Sarah, widow, Trowb., 1797, W, P1/15Reg/21
Cockell, Sarah, Dilton M., Westb., 1841, W, Wr, P25/1841/5
Cockle, Thos., Codf. St P., 1558, W, P2/3Reg/89D
Thos., husb., Gt. Cheverell, 1567, I, W, P2/C/37, P2/5Reg/23A
Cockle, Thos., Warm., 1607, AB, I, P2/C/227
Cockle, Thos., Imber, 1628, AB, I, P2/C/380
Cockle, Thos., roof mason, Lyneham, 1675, I, NW, P3/C/378
Cockle, Thos., Heywood, Westb., 1699, I, P25/1699/10
Cockle, Thos., yeo., Westb., 1733, W, P25/1733/3
Cockle, Thos., farmer, Leighs Marsh, Dilton, Westb., 1736, AB, W, P25/1736/1
Cockle, Wm., yeo., Hawkeridge, Westb., 1644, AB, I, W, P25/1644/5
Wm., [haberdasher], Westb., 1676, I (detailed), NW, P25/1676/6
Cockle, Wm., Westb., 1722, I, T, P25/1722/5
Cockle, Wm., Littleton P., 1788, AB, P1/C/1053
Cockerell, Agnes, widow, Stockton, 1585-86, I, W, P2/C/68, P2/7Reg/29
Ambrose, Stockton, 1614, a/c, P2/C/278
Cockrell, Ambrose, yeo., Stockton, 1640, I, W, P2/C/488
Cockrill, Ambrose, yeo., Stockton, 1682, AB, I, NW, P2/C/713
Cockrell, Ann, widow, Redlynch, Downton, 1845, aff, D, W, Wr, P2/1845/16
Cockrell, Jacob, vict., Warm. (form. of Rode, Somerset), 1801, W, P1/1801/23, P1/15Reg/245C
Jeremiah, shepherd, Codf. St My., 1684, I, NW, P2/C/734
Cockrell, Jn., husb., Stockton, 1637, I, W, P2/C/451
Cockarell, Jn., Sal., 1694, AB, I, P4/1694/13
Cockrell, Louisa, sp., N. Bradley, 1840, comm, W, Wr, P2/1840/34
Robt., Stockton, 1557, W, P2/3Reg/23B
Cockrell, Steph., builder, Warm., 1850, W, Wr, P2/1850/34
Cockrell, Wm., innholder, *The New Inn*, Warm., 1793, W, P2/C/1470
Cockrell, Wm., Redlynch, Downton, 1826, I, O, W, Wr, P2/1826/22
Cockes *see* Cox
Cockett, Rd., W. Lavington, 1711, AB, I, P1/C/511
Susanna, sp., Edington, 1641, I, W, P2/C/501
Cockey, Ann, brazier's wife, Bradford A., 1753, AB, P2/C/1280
Ann, widow, Thornford, Dorset, 1779, W, P5/1779/2, P5/17Reg/165A
Anth., apothecary, Sal., 1664, I, W, P4/1663/1
Chris., yeo., Warm., 1834, comm, W, Wr, P2/1834/4
Edwd., baker, Sal. St Thos., 1738, I, NW, P4/1637/5

Elias, blacksmith, Sal., 1629, AB, I, P4/1629/8
Lewis, Warm., 1714, AB, P2/C/993
My., widow, Sal., 1721, W, P4/1721/8
My., sp., Sal. The Close, 1747, AB, W, P5/1747/5
Cocky, Thos., tailor, Marl., 1591, I, P1/C/1
Wm., [shoemaker], Sal. St Edmd., 1613, AB, I (damaged), P4/1613/2
Wm., apothecary, Sal., 1705, O, W, P1/C/494
Cockhill *see* Cockell
Cockin, Wm., husb., Eddington, Hungerford, Berks., 1641, I, W, P5/1641/19, P5/14Reg/12
Cockle *see* Cockell
Cockrell, Cockrill *see* Cockerell
Cocks *see* Cox
Cocky *see* Cockey
Codd, Codd als Priest, Geo., Bere R., Dorset, 1590, AB, I, P5/1590/13, P5/5Reg/78C
Jas., priest, Whaddon, 1550, institution to rectory on death of Foxe, P2/2Reg/108C
Jas., priest, Stapleford, 1551, institution to perpetual curacy on resignation of [Wm.] Toppyng, P2/2Reg/138A
Jas., priest, Codf. St My., 1561, institution to rectory, P1/1Reg/75C
Jas. *see also* Jn. Corell, clerk, Whaddon
Codrinton, Jn., gent., Sutton M., 1633-35, AB, I, ren, P2/C/415, 434
Coe, David, furrier, Sal., 1813, W, Wr, P4/1813/12
Jn., yeo., Purton, 1694, AB, comm, I (2 - 1 a copy)., P3/C/576
Coely *see* Calley
Coffin, Darby, tailor, S. Wraxall, 1564, I, W, P2/C/1512, P2/4Reg/174C
Hy., Bere R., Dorset, 1579, I, W, P5/1579/18, P5/3Reg/122B
My., Alvediston, 1632-33, AB, I, P2/C/414, P2/9Reg/37A
My., widow, Stourton, 1728, W, P2/C/1088
Rd., Stourton, 1713, AB, P2/C/986
Thos., Bere R., Dorset, 1597, AB, I, P5/1597/18, P5/6Reg/163B
Coffin als Darby, Thos., weaver, S. Wraxall, 1607, AB, I, W, P2/C/220
Coffen, Walter, husb., Hamptworth, Downton, 1710-29, AB, I, W, P2/C/965, 1112
Cogan, Coggins, Chris., merchant, Lyme R., Dorset, 1634, I, W. Proved at the Metropolitan visitation to Dorchester, P5/1634/32, P5/12Reg/293
Coggins, Eleanor, widow, Lyme R., Dorset, 1628, AB, W, P5/1628/24, P5/11Reg/64C
Jn., tailor, Lyme R., Dorset, 1627, AB, I (2 copies), P5/1627/8, P5/11Reg/7D
My., Chards., Devon, 1675, AB, I, P14/15
My., widow, Coaxden, Chards., Devon, 1721, AB, comm, LA, ren, W, P14/89
Nich., sen., mariner, Lyme R., Dorset, 1635, AB, I, T (re Nich. C., jun.), W, P5/1635/16, P5/12Reg/224B
Nich., mariner, Lyme R., Dorset, 1668, AB, I, ren, P5/1668/15
Patience, widow, Lyme R., Dorset, 1694, I (2 - 1 a copy), W, P16/127
Rd., Chards., Devon, 1708, AB, comm, I, P14/107
Coggins, Simon, Lyme R., Dorset, 1583, AB, P5/1583/7, P5/4Reg/58F
Cogen, Wm., husb., Netherb., Dorset, 1714, I, W, P17/221
Coggeswell *see* Cogswell
Coggins *see* Cogan
Cogswell, Alice, widow, Tytherton L., Chipp., 1618, AB, I, P3/C/95
Ann, widow, Trowb., 1820, W, Wr, P1/1820/123
Ann, widow, Pott., 1837, AB, comm, W, Wr, P1/1837/5
Benj., shopkeeper, Trowb., 1799, comm, W, P1/C/1104, P1/15Reg/182B
Jas., clothw., Westb. L., 1700, AB, I, P25/1700/8
Jas., yeo., Hilp. Marsh, 1712, W, P2/C/979
Jas., chapman, dealer and tailor, Trowb., 1764, AB, ren, P1/C/932
Jas., Trowb., 1821, AB, comm, Wr, P1/1821/6
Jas., weaver, Trowb., 1837, aff, O, W, Wr, P1/1837/25
Jn., Trowb., 1768, AB, P1/C/949
Jn., shoemaker, Melk., 1790, W, P2/C/1458
Mgt., widow, Melk., 1764, AB, W, P2/C/1320
Coggeswell, Margery, widow, Ludbourne, Westb., 1651, AB, I, ren, P1/C/234
Nich., sen., Speen, Berks., 1732, AB, comm, P1/C/714
Philip, sen., linen draper, High St., Chipp., 1649, W, P1/C/226
Sam., Trowb., 1835, aff, comm, W, Wr, P1/1835/3

Steph., [Westb.] (NBI), 1609, I, P30/33
Thos., Tytherton L., Chipp., 1617, AB, I, P3/C/88
Thos., gent., Hilp., 1827, comm, W, Wr, P2/1827/14
Coggeswell, Wm., yeo., Stormore, Dilton, Westb., 1635, I (5 appraisers named with their occupations), W, P25/1635/3
Wm., shopkeeper, Trowb., 1778, W, P1/C/1002, P1/13Reg/188A
Coke, Coke als Richardson, Edith, widow, Purton, 1570, W (NEP), P1/1Reg/57B
Edwd., broad weaver, Melk., 1607, AB, I, note of AB, P2/C/221
Geo., Bere R., Dorset, 1641, AB, I, P5/1641/17, P5/14Reg/26C
Cokes, Joan, widow, Martin, Hants, 1570, W, P2/5Reg/91B
Coke als Chandler, Jn., Quidh., [1559], AB, P2/C/9
Jn., jun., Steeple L., 1605, a/c, P2/C/207
Cokes, Jn., sen., husb., Bere R., Dorset, 1721, W, P5/1721/9, P5/16Reg/59A
Jn., yeo., Gillingham, Dorset, 1763, W, P27/1/438, P27/3Reg/101
Cokes, Matthew, Bere R., Dorset, 1665, AB, I, P5/1665/21
Rd., Milston, [1680], I, P2/C/686
Cokes, Robt., Charlton, Downton, 1537, W (NEP), P2/1Reg/2B
Cokes, Ruth, widow, Bere R., Dorset, 1725, AB, P5/1725/14
Coke als Chandler, Walter, Quidh., 1558, AB, P2/3Reg/129C
Wm., Gillingham, Dorset, 1747, AB, P27/1/391, P27/3Reg/48B
Wm., yeo., Gillingham, Dorset, 1844, O, ren, W, Wr, P27/1/741
see also Cook *or* C.
Cokeman, Edwd., husb., Knook, 1564, W, P5/1Reg/24B
Giles, husb., Knook, 1562, W, P5/1Reg/8B
Coker, Coker als Beach, Agnes, Horningsham, 1605, AB, I (incomplete), P5/1605/12
Ann, gentlewoman, Orcheston St My., 1610, W, P2/C/241
Benj., clerk and rector, Kingston D. (form. of Marston Bigott, Somerset), 1742, AB, W, P1/C/790, P1/9Reg/223B
Edmd. Ludlow, rector, Kingston D., 1711, AB, P1/C/529
Eliz., widow, Seend, Melk., 1642, I, copy I, W, copy W, P2/C/508
Eliz., sp., Longford, Britford, 1737, W, P24/917
Hy., yeo., Ditchampton, Wilton, 1721, W, P2/C/1047
Hy., yeo., Poulshot, 1748, W, P2/C/1248
Jane, widow, Ash, Stourpaine, Dorset, 1633, I, W, P24/241
Jn., sen., gent., Ash, Stourpaine, Dorset, 1612, I (dated 1598), W, P24/122
My., widow, Ditchampton, Wilton, 1730, AB, P2/C/1115
My., widow, Sal. The Close, 1742, W, Wr, P5/1742/10
Coker als Beach, Michael, Horningsham, 1605, AB, P5/8Reg/31B
Nich., sen., yeo., Poulshot, 1733, W, P2/C/1155
Rebecca, widow, Chipp., 1738, W, P3/C/843
Rd., Orcheston St My., 1602, I, W, P2/C/191
Robt., gent., Baverstock, 1612, AB, I, P2/C/269
Robt., sen., Ash, Stourpaine, Dorset, 1630, monition, P24/1428
Wm., gent., Ash, Stourpaine, Dorset, 1670, AB, comm, P24/387
Cokes *see* Coke
Colbeach, Martha, widow, Purton, 1726, W, P1/C/642, P1/7Reg/80
Colbern *see* Colbourne
Colbert, Thos., Lyme R., Dorset, 1674, AB, comm, P5/1674/20
Colbord, Jn., husb., Over C., Dorset, 1610, AB, I (2), W (2), P5/1609/19, P5/9Reg/4D
Colbourne, Agnes, widow, Lacock, 1609, W, P3/C/39
Colebourn, Ann, sp., Mere, 1745-77, AB, ren, W (made 1745) (NEP), but original dated 1777, P5/1777/4, P5/17Reg/137
Colborne, Ann, widow, Chipp., 1843, O, W, Wr, P3/1843/31
Colborne, Benj., Notton, Lacock, 1680, AB, I, P1/C/344
Colborne, Cath., widow, Chipp., 1754, W, P3/C/932
Cobourne, Dorothy, widow, Mere, 1691, AB, I, P5/1690/11
Colbern, Dorothy, widow, Long Burton, Dorset, 1707, I, W, P5/1707/15, P5/15Reg/29
Colborne, Eliz., widow, Over C., Dorset, 1620, I, W, P5/1620/14, P5/10Reg/10
Colborne, Eliz., sp., Long Burton, Dorset, 1697, AB, comm, I, P5/1697/10
Colborne, Eliz., widow, Ogbourne St Geo., 1698, I, W, P5/1698/21
Colborne, Eliz., widow, Lacock, 1740, AB, P3/C/854
Colborne, Eliz., sp., Calne, 1756, AB, W, P26/946
Colborne, Frances, widow, Calne, 1756, AB, P26/947

Colborne, Hy., sen., yeo., Charlton nr Malm., 1641, I, W, P3/C/263
Colborne, Hy., sen., Lacock, 1735, W, P1/C/722, P1/7Reg/606B
Colborne, Isaac, Lacock, 1639, comm, NW, P3/C/236
Jas., Twyford, Hurst, Berks., 1836, AB, O, ren, Wr, P5/1836/35
Colborne, Joan, widow, Lacock, 1682, AB, I, W, P3/C/454
Cobern, Jn., sen., cordw., Whitep., 1819, W, Wr, P2/1819/12
Colborne, Jos., gent., Ogbourne St Geo. & Lacock, 1689, comm, I (2), W, P5/1689/13
Colborne, Jos., tallow chandler, Chipp., 1742, AB, comm, P3/C/865
Colborne, Jos., gent. and bach., Lacock, 1743, AB, P3/C/875
Colborne, Jos., Corsham, 1752, marriage licence, P29/2Reg/64C
Colborne, My., sen., widow, Lacock, 1702, I, W, P3/C/641
Colborne, My., widow, Lacock, 1726, AB, W, P1/C/652, P1/7Reg/119B
Rachel, widow, Bourton, Gillingham, Dorset, 1844, O, W, Wr, P27/1/743
Colborne, Rd., husb., Bradford A., 1552, I, W, P2/C/5, P2/2Reg/158D
Robt., Lacock, 1608, I, W (NEP), P3/C/32
Colborne, Robt., Long Burton, Dorset, 1626, AB, comm, I, P5/1626/10
Colborne, Robt., sen., clothier, Lacock, 1694, comm, I, W, Wr, P3/C/577
Colborne, Robt., apothecary, Chipp., 1776, W, P1/C/992, P1/13Reg/103A
Colborne, Sam., clothier, Lacock, 1721, AB, ren, P3/C/735
Colebourn, Sarah, sp., Mere, 1720, W, P5/1720/13, P5/16Reg/45B
Cobern, Sarah, sp., Wilton, 1851, W, Wr, P1/1851/30
Colborne, Thos., Broughton G., 1563, I, W, P2/C/31, P2/4Reg/150
Colborne, Thos., husb., Croucheston, Bishopstone S., [1675], I, W, P2/C/657
Colborne, Thos., sen., dyer, Gastard, Corsham, 1678, I, W, P3/C/407
Cobourne, Thos., sen., linen weaver, Mere, 1691, W, P5/1691/14
Colborne, Thos., dyer, Lacock, 1699, AB, comm, I, P3/C/608
Colborne, Thos., minor, Calne, 1723, T, P3/C/745
Colbron, Thos., gent., Seend, Melk., 1728, W, P2/C/1096
Colborne, Thos., gent., Gastard, Corsham, 1745, W (2 - 1 a copy), P3/C/885
Cobern, Thos., Damerham, Hants, 1808, W, Wr, P2/1808/4
Thos., labourer, Damerham, Hants, 1857, aff, W, Wr, P2/1857/3
Coborne, Wm., [blacksmith], Hannington, 1678, AB, I, P3/C/406
Colborne, Wm., druggist, Chipp., 1794, comm, W, P3/C/1123
see also Corbin
Colcell *see* Colsell
Colchester als Watts, Wm., broad weaver, Kington L., 1641, AB, I, P3/C/264
Coldery *see* Couldry
Coldwell, My., widow, Sal., 1751, W, P1/C/844, P1/10Reg/450B
Robt., Sal., 1743, AB, Wr, P4/1743/9
Thos., canon resident of Sal. Cathedral and MA, Sal. The Close, 1619, AB, a/c (2), I, ren, P5/1618/5
Cole *see* Coles
Colebourn *see* Colbourne
Coleman, Colman, Ann, widow, Heddington, 1682, AB, I, P3/C/456
Ann, widow, Highw., 1750, W, P10/1750/5
Bridget, widow, Devizes, 1706, AB, nomination, T, P1/C/498
Cath., widow, Berwick B., 1668, AB, I, W, P26/151
Colman, Chris., Ashton K., 1573, W, P1/1Reg/130C
Colman, Dorothy, widow, Mere, 1701, AB, I, P5/1701/10
Edwd., Bremhill, 1700, comm, W, P3/C/621
Colman, Edwd., labourer, Rams., 1709, I, W, P5/1709/8, P5/15Reg/119
Edwd., Pott., 1762, AB, W, P1/C/914, P1/12Reg/26
Edwd., cordw., Swindon, 1776, W, P1/C/995, P1/13Reg/108B
Colman, Eleanor, widow, Wrou., 1615, W, P3/C/78
Colman, Eleanor, widow, Broad Town, Clyffe P., 1681, I, W, P3/C/437
Eleanor, widow, Horningsham, 1706, AB, P5/1706/6
Coleman als Hooper, Eliz., widow, Wedh., Urchf., 1600, AB, I, W, P2/C/179
Coulman, Eliz., widow, Kington L., 1611, W, P3/C/61
Eliz., widow, Hullavington, 1675, AB, I, P3/C/379
Colman, Eliz., widow, Elcombe, Wrou., 1683, AB, comm, I, ren, W, P3/C/472
Colman, Eliz., widow, Mildenhall, 1686, I, W, P1/C/1115

Eliz., widow, Highw., 1715, W (NEP), P10/1715/1
Eliz., widow, Marl., 1760, AB, P1/C/911
Francis, yeo., Maiden B., 1797, W, P2/C/1483
Francis, 19 Friday St., Cheapside, London, 1841, comm, W, Wr, P3/1841/33
Geo., innholder and saddler, Sal., 1645, AB, I (detailed), ren, P1/C/206
Geo., yeo., Elcombe, Wrou., 1681, I, W, P3/C/438
Geo., Elcombe, Wrou., 1779, W, P1/C/1014, P1/13Reg/243
Hy., Devizes, 1645, AB, comm, P1/C/204
Hy., Lockeridge, Overton, 1714, AB, P1/C/557
Hy., mercer, Highw., 1722, W, P5/1722/13, P5/16Reg/72B
Jas., yeo., Lt. Cheverell, 1789, W, P1/C/1059, P1/14Reg/287
Jas., yeo., Horningsham, 1824, W, Wr, P5/1824/36
Colman, Jane, Chr. M., 1618, W, P3/C/97
Joan, widow, Bowditch, Chards., Devon, 1590, I, W, P5/1590/14, P5/5Reg/84E
Joan, widow, Hungerford, Berks., 1598, AB, a/c, P5/1597/22, P5/6Reg/193D
Joan, widow, Marl., 1663, AB, P1/C/259
Colman, Joan, sp., Elcombe, Wrou., 1678, I, W, P3/C/408
Joan, widow, Sal., 1696, W, P4/1696/8
Jn., Dorset, 1583, I, P5/1583/8
Collman, Jn., husb., Bowditch, Chards., Devon, 1583, W, P5/4Reg/67A
Jn., husb., Bowditch, Chards., Devon, 1590, I, W, P5/1589/13, P5/5Reg/65D
Jn., husb., Wedh., Urchf., 1591, I, W, P2/C/91
Colman, Jn., no abode stated, 1606, I, W, P1/C/33
Jn., sen., carp., Worton, Pott., 1662, AB, I, P1/C/243
Jn., carp., Berwick B., 1667, AB, I, P5/1667/18
Jn., Mere, 1683, AB, I, P5/1683/8
Jn., cordw., Pewsey, 1692, I, W (NEP), P3/C/558
Jn., servant in husbandry, Newtown, Durnford, 1705, NW (NEP), P9/32
Jn., carp., Worton, Pott., 1711, AB, I, P1/C/533
Jn., Sal., 1718, AB, P4/1718/14
Jn., sen., Kington St M., 1736, W, P3/C/829
Jn., Worton, Pott., 1736, AB, comm, P1/C/744
Jn., yeo., Kington St M., 1776, comm, W, P3/C/1051
Jn., dairyman, Southbroom, 1820, AB, W, Wr, P24/1283
Jn., sen., yeo., Horningsham, 1825, W, Wr, P5/1825/16
Jn., pawnbroker, Westb., 1855, declaration, O, W, Wr, P25/1855/3
Jos., Sutton B., 1778, AB, P3/C/1058
Colman, Lionel, Broad Town, Clyffe P., 1661, comm, W, P3/C/278, P3/3Reg/21
Collman, Mariam, widow, Aldbourne, 1678, I, W, P3/C/411
Martha, widow, Aldbourne, 1773, W, P1/C/972, P1/12Reg/504
Colman, My., widow, Worton, Pott., 1666, I, W, P1/C/278
My., yeo.'s wife, Kington St M., 1721, AB, P3/C/736
My., sp., Devizes, 1724, W, P1/C/630, P1/7Reg/48
My., sp., Marl., 1755, AB, P1/C/868
My., minor, Chiseldon, 1821, app. of guardian, T, P3/1821/10
Nathaniel, jun., yeo., Sutton B., 1694, AB, comm, I, P3/C/578
Colman, Nathaniel, yeo., Sutton B., 1700, W, P3/C/623
Colman, Nathaniel, yeo., Sutton B., 1753, comm, W, P3/C/926
Collman, Nich., shoemaker, Sal., 1633, I, W, P4/1632/6
Paul, Mkt. L., 1636, I, NW, P2/C/440
Paul, maltster, Mkt. L., 1709, W, P2/C/961
Paul, Pott., 1719, AB, deed of gift, I, ren, P1/C/585
Philip, mercer, Devizes, 1700, AB, comm, I (detailed), P1/C/467
Philip, yeo., Maiden B., 1768, W, P2/C/1344
Colman, Rd., husb., Clyffe P., 1569, W, P1/2Reg/86A
Colman, Rd., husb., Easterton, Mkt. L., 1674, I, W, P2/C/643
Rd., husb., Pott., 1698, W, P1/C/456
Rd., linen draper, Marl., 1713, W, P1/C/536, P1/5Reg/295
Rd., yeo., Broomfield, Yatton K., 1777, comm, W, P1/C/1000, P1/13Reg/170
Robt., Gt. Durnford, 1620, AB, admr's cert, P5/1620/17

Robt., yeo., Kington L., 1627, I, W, P3/C/150
Colman, Robt., Wedh., Urchf., 1647, I, P2/C/535
Robt., maltster, Mkt. L., 1717, I, W, P2/C/1016
Colman, Robt., labourer, Tidcombe and Fosbury, 1771, W, P3/C/1020
Robt., W. Lavington, 1844, AB, O, Wr, P1/1844/30
Robt., yeo., Horningsham, 1849, note, W, Wr, P5/1849/7
Sam., labourer, Pott., 1710, I, W, P1/C/509, P1/5Reg/21B
Cowleman, Sibyl, widow, Broad H. & Clyffe P., 1675, I, W, P3/C/390
Colman, Steph., yeo., Aldbourne, 1727, AB, bargain & sale (making provision for wife & children after his death), P3/C/768
Steph., yeo., Shalbourne, Berks., 1771, W, P23/737
Coleman als Deverell, Susanna, Bradford A., 1715, AB, comm, P2/C/999
Coulman, Thos., yeo., Axford, Rams., 1588, I, W, P5/1588/11, P5/5Reg/32A
Colman, Thos., sen., yeo., Ogbourne St Geo., 1608, W, P5/8Reg/111A
Thos., [carp.], Berwick B., c1612?, W (undated), P3/C/64
Thos., Aldbourne, 1623, AB, a/c, I, P3/C/122
Thos., Chards., Devon, 1635, AB, comm, I, P5/1635/15, P5/12Reg/157C
Colman, Thos., Lyneham, 1666, AB, I, P1/C/280
Colman, Thos., yeo., Hullavington, 1682, comm, W, P3/C/458
Thos., yeo., Elcombe, Wrou., 1682, comm, I, W, P3/C/457
Thos., yeo., Ogbourne St Geo., 1690, I, W, P5/1690/12
Thos., saddler, Sal., 1695, W, P4/1694/7
Thos., gent., Marl. St My., 1741, W, P1/C/786, P1/9Reg/142
Colman, Thos., Sutton B., 1748-53, AB, comm, W, P3/C/895
Thos., sen., yeo., Aldbourne, 1772, W, P3/C/1025
Thos., currier, Marl. (property in Manton, Preshute), 1822, AB, comm, P1/1822/9
Thos., yeo., Aldbourne, 1803, W, Wr, P3/1803/66
Colman, Walter, Bulford, 1553, AB, P2/2Reg/173C
Colman, Walter, sen., gent., Kington L., 1676, AB, ren, I, P3/C/391
Colman, Walter, yeo., Kington L., 1676, AB, a/c, I, P3/C/392
Walter, carp., Pott., 1691, I, W, P1/C/411
Collman, Wm., husb. *or* yeo., Thornhill, Clyffe P., [c1603?], I, W, P3/C/8
Cooleman, Wm., Chiseldon, [c1618?], I, W (undated), P3/C/99
Colman, Wm., yeo., Hullavington, 1633, I, W, P3/C/187
Wm., sen., Marl., 1649, AB, I, P1/C/227
Wm., carp., Berwick B., 1666, I, W, P1/C/281
Wm., yeo., Pewsey, 1689, AB, a/c, I, ren, P3/C/538
Wm., cordw., Bradford A., 1693-94, AB, a/c, comm, I, P2/C/829
Wm., husb., Berwick St Jas., 1697, AB, I, P1/C/451
Wm., Horningsham, 1706, I, W, P5/1706/7
Colman, Wm., yeo., Pott., 1728, W, P1/C/659, P1/7Reg/193
Wm., gent., Cotmarsh, Broad H., 1736, W, P3/C/830
Wm., yeo., Horningsham, 1739, comm, W, Wr, P5/1739/13
Wm., yeo., Lt. Cheverell, 1776, W, P2/C/1387
Wm., yeo., Warm., 1782, W, P1/C/1029, P1/13Reg/362
Zachary, Avell Cross, Hurst, Berks., 1680, I, W, P5/1680/9
see also Lander als C.
Colenut, Robt., Bere R., Dorset, 1597, AB, I, P5/1597/20, P5/6Reg/164A
Coles, Cole, Abel, Lydiard M., 1768, AB, P3/C/1004
Agnes, widow, no abode stated, [1567], I, P2/C/35
Agnes, widow, Chitterne AS, 1597, I, W, P2/C/150
Cole, Alice, widow, Netherb., Dorset, 1677, AB, I, P17/273
Alice, widow, Elston, Orcheston St Geo., 1695, I, W, P2/C/850
Alice, widow, Winterbourne S., 1719, W, P2/C/1025
Cole, Alice, widow, Baulking, Uffington, Berks., 1720, I, W, P1/C/598, P1/6Reg/294
Ann, widow, Lacock, 1679, AB, W, P3/C/418
Cole, Ann, sp., Rodbourne C., 1682, AB, P3/C/455
Ann, widow, Bloxworth, Dorset, 1801, W, P5/1801/20, P5/18Reg/323B
Augustine, Netherb., Dorset, 1684, AB, P17/240
Barnaby, sen., gent., Woodfalls, Downton, 1720, W, P2/C/1032

Benj., baker, Wallingford, Berks., 1680, I, W, P1/C/340
Cole, Betty, widow, Kington L., 1855, aff, O, W, Wr, P3/1855/48
Cole, Castle, innkeeper, *The Blue Lion*, Sal., 1693, AB, I, P4/1692/13
Cole als Carswell, Cath., Uffc., Devon, 1549, W, P20/Reg/40
Cole, Cath., widow, Stanton Fitzwarren, 1635, I, W, P3/C/205
Chas., Middlehill, Box, 1787, AB, comm, P3/C/1094
Cole, Chas., Yatton K., 1853, O, W, Wr, P3/1853/66
Cole, Dan., clothier, Littleton Drew, 1776, W, P1/C/994, P1/13Reg/102
Cole, Dan., publican, Devizes, 1846, O, W, Wr, P1/1846/36
Cole, Dinah, widow, Reading, Berks., 1753, W, P1/C/855, P1/11Reg/38
Cole, Dorcas, widow, Downton, 1675, AB, P1/C/319
Cole, Dorothy, widow, Stanton Fitzwarren, 1639, I, W, P3/C/244
Cole, Edith, widow, Stanton Fitzwarren, 1604, I, W, P3/C/12
Cole, Edith, sp., Britford, 1828, AB, P24/1315
Cole, Edmd., Uffc., Devon, 1629, AB, a/c, comm, I, P5/1628/33, P5/11Reg/20B
Edmd., cardmaker, Trowb., 1678, AB, comm, I, P2/C/675
Edwd., tanner, Trowb., 1712, W, P2/C/978
Cole, Edwd., glover, Reading St My., Berks., 1714, AB, I, P1/C/547
Cole, Edwin, plumber and glazier, Corsham, 1856, aff, W, Wr, P3/1856/38
Eleanor, Fonthill B., 1694, AB, P2/C/847
Cole, Elias, tailor, Beam., Dorset, 1767, W, P5/1767/13
Eliz., W. Harnham, 1615, AB, P5/9Reg/154D
Eliz., widow, Whitep., 1666, I (detailed), W, P1/C/282
Eliz., sp., *The Forrester*, Westb., 1707, W (list of clothes & valuables), P25/1707/1
Cole, Eliz., widow, Bratton, Westb., 1718, I ((2 - 1 itemised), NW, P25/1718/2
Cole, Eliz., widow, Reading, Berks., 1747, AB, comm, P1/C/833
Cole, Eliz., sp., Kington St M., 1757, AB, P3/C/945
Eliz., widow, Maddington, 1780, W, P2/C/1413
Eliz., widow, Crickl. St S., 1806, W, Wr, P3/1806/54
Cole, Eliz., widow, Chipp., 1807, W, Wr, P3/1807/1
Cole, Eliz., bach., Bowden Farm, Lacock, 1844, W, Wr, P3/1844/60
Frances, widow, Reading, Berks., 1723, W, P1/C/622, P1/7Reg/8A
Cole, Francis, Burbage, 1741, W, P11/183
Cole, Francis, labourer, Derry Hill, Pewsham, 1843, D, O, W, Wr, P5/1843/6
Coules, Gabriel, tiler and plasterer, Chipp., 1717, W, P3/C/707
Geo., yeo., Winterbourne S., 1700, I, W, P2/C/889
Geo., yeo., Elston, Orcheston St Geo., 1720, I, W, P2/C/1029
Cole, Geo., yeo., Uffc., Devon, 1756, W, P20/1/231
Cowles, Giles, husb., Tockenham Wick, 1640, AB, I, ren, W, P3/C/254
Giles, yeo., Orcheston St My., [1675], I, copy I, W, P2/C/652
Hy., Sal., 1614, AB, I, P4/1614/6
Hy., husb., Southwick, N. Bradley, 1631, I, copy I, W, copy W, P2/C/403, P2/9Reg/62A
Hy., Brigmerston, Milston, 1680, AB, P2/C/685
Hy., Sal., 1691, AB, I, P4/1691/10
Hy., clothw., Trowb., 1724, W, P1/C/631, P1/7Reg/41A
Cole, Hy., innholder, Rams., 1724, AB, W, P5/1724/19, P5/16Reg/104B
Hy., Trowb., 1746, AB, P1/C/814
Hy., Wootton R., 1759, W, P3/C/950
Cole, Hy., labourer, Derry Hill, Pewsham, 1849, W, Wr, P5/1849/8
Cole, Isaac, surgeon, Marl., 1671, AB, I (detailed), ren, W, P1/C/305
Jas., Downton, 1593, AB, I, P2/C/1518
Cole, Jas., husb., Stanton Fitzwarren, 1622, I, W, P1/C/110
Jas., clothw., Trowb., 1730, W, P1/C/693, P1/7Reg/399
Cole, Jas., waggoner, Cherhill (form. of Chipp.), 1733, I, W, P26/770
Cole, Jasper, Easton Grey, 1726, AB, P3/C/762
Joan, Hurst, Berks., 1609, AB, P5/8Reg/160A
Cowles, Joan, Trowle, Bradford A., 1619, I, W, P1/C/195
Joan, widow, Witherington Farm, Standlynch, Downton, 1631, I, W, P2/C/399
Cole, Joan, widow, Chiseldon, 1641, I, W, P3/C/265
Joan, widow, Kellaways, 1692, I, W, P3/C/556

Jn., baker, Devizes, 1561, W. No date of probate given., P1/2Reg/103 (incomplete: page 104 is missing)
Cole, Jn., Chitterne AS, 1596, AB, I, W, P2/C/139
Cole als Kerswell als Cashere, Jn., Uffc., Devon, 1596, AB, a/c, I, P5/1595/11
Jn., Hurst, Berks., 1609, AB, comm, P5/1609/16
Cole, Jn., tanner, Marl., 1626, I, W, P1/C/164
Cowles, Jn., glover, Gt. Faringdon, Berks., 1628, I, W, P5/1628/18, P5/11Reg/95
Cole, Jn., blacksmith, Tockenham, 1636, I, W, P3/C/218
Cowles, Jn., Brinkw., 1638, I, W, P3/C/232
Jn., yeo., Dinton, 1639, I, W, P2/C/474
Coules, Jn., weaver, Charlton, 1647, I, W, P1/C/220
Cole, Jn., Bratton, Westb., 1671, I, W, P25/1671/3
Jn., yeo., Fonthill B., 1676, I, W, P2/C/661
Jn., tanner, Lacock, 1677, AB, I, P1/C/332
Cole, Jn., yeo., Wantage, Berks., 1684, I, W, P23/131
Cole, Jn., Burbage, 1700, AB, I, P11/85
Cole, Jn., yeo., Devizes, 1726, comm, W, P1/C/636, P1/7Reg/67B
Jn., yeo., Gt. Trowle, Bradford A., 1728, W, P2/C/1094
Jn., E. Harnham, Britford, 1732, AB, P5/1732/9
Jn., yeo., Maddington, 1756, W, P1/C/882, P1/11Reg/268A
Jn., yeo., Gt. Trowle, Bradford A., 1768, W, P2/C/1345
Jn., clothw., Trowb., 1769, AB, P1/C/953
Jn., edge toolmaker, Fisherton A., 1769, W, P2/C/1348
Jn., tanner, Westb., 1769, W, P25/1769/1
Jn., gardener, Bradford A., 1775, W, P2/C/1382
Jn., labourer, Landford, 1792, W, P2/C/1469
Cole, Jn., Bloxworth, Dorset, 1797, AB, P5/1797/6, P5/18Reg/256A
Cole, Jn., yeo., Burbage, 1797, W, P11/229
Cole, Jn., Wylye, 1803, AB, P2/1803/28
Cole, Jn., clerk, Overton, 1810, AB, comm, P3/1810/10
Jn., Amesb., 1814, AB, P1/1814/151
Cole, Jn., Pewsham, 1823, AB, Wr, P5/1823/31
Jn., Breamore, Hants (effects at Fisherton A.), 1823, AB, Wr, P2/1823/16
Cole, Jn., gunsmith, Devizes, 1835, O, W, P1/1835/119
Cole, Jonathan, yeo., Euridge, Colerne, 1762, W, P3/C/968
Cole *or* Cowell, Jos., Lyme R., Dorset, 1733, AB, comm, P16/272
Cole, Lucian, haberdasher, Eastcourt, Crudwell, 1802, W, P3/1802/50
Cole, Luke, yeo., Eastcourt, Crudwell, 1828, L, W, Wr, P3/1828/58
Cole, Mgt., widow, Milston, 1672, I, W, P2/C/627
Mgt., widow, Dinton, 1682, AB, I, P2/C/706
Mgt., widow, Trowb., 1730, W, P1/C/694, P1/7Reg/398B
My., Wedh., Urchf., 1679, AB, P2/C/681
My., widow, Trowb., 1717, comm, W, P2/C/1011
My., widow, Fisherton A., 1773, W, P2/C/1366
My., widow, Downton, 1785-93, AB (2), ren, P2/C/1436
Cole, Matthew, Allington, Chipp., 1719, W, P3/C/721
Matthew, Fonthill G., 1748-49, AB (3 - 1 revoked as dau minor), I, P2/C/1252
Michael, tailor, Marl. St Peter and St Paul, 1612, AB, P1/C/49
Cole, Nathaniel, yeo., Chr. M., 1780, W, P3/C/1064
Peter, tanner, Downton, 1693, W, P2/C/835
Peter, mercer, Downton, 1776, W, P1/C/989, P1/13Reg/86
Ralph, blacksmith, Avell Cross, Hurst, Berks., 1704, I, W, P5/1704/10
Cole, Reynold, husb., Winterborne M., Winterborne K., Dorset, 1610, I, W, P5/1610/13, P5/9Reg/19B
Cole, Rd., Uffc., Devon, 1567, W, P5/2Reg/17B
Cole, Rd., Steeple A., 1571, AB, P2/5Reg/116C
Cole als Barnarde, Rd., husb., Monkton F., 1598, I, W, P2/C/159
Rd., Hamptworth, Downton, 1616, AB, I, P1/C/80
Cole, Rd., sen., husb., Anderson, Dorset, 1671, I, W, P5/1671/17
Cole, Rd., sen., yeo., Uffc., Devon, 1687, AB, comm, NW, P20/1/104
Cole, Rd., husb., Shalbourne (form. of Linkenholt, Hants), 1722, I, W, P5/1722/12, P5/16Reg/71B
Rd., husb., Whitep., 1731, W, P2/C/1127

Cole, Rd., corn dealer, Derry Hill, Pewsham, 1825, comm, W, Wr, P5/1825/29
Robt., Bradford A., 1576, AB, P2/5Reg/261B
Robt., clerk, Dinton, 1583, W, P2/6Reg/90C
Cole, Robt., tanner, Marl. St Peter and St Paul, 1603, AB, I, W, P1/C/18
Robt., Minety, 1608, AB, P3/C/29
Robt., Trowle, Bradford A., 1615, AB, I, P2/C/281, P2/8Reg/262B
Robt., sen., husb., Teffont M., 1631, I, W, P2/C/400
Robt., husb., W. Lavington, 1662, AB, comm, I, P1/C/255
Robt., Maddington, 1670, AB, a/c, I, ren, P2/C/601
Robt., yeo., Elston, Orcheston St Geo., 1690, I, W, P2/C/800
Robt., Maddington, 1725, AB, P2/C/1063
Coules, Robt., sen., tiler, Chipp., 1729-73, AB, I, W (d. 1729, but goods left unadmd until 1773), P3/C/784
Cole, Robt., yeo., Chaddington, Lydiard T., 1785, W, P3/C/1087
Roger, sen., Dinton, 1630, AB, a/c, I, P2/C/392
Roger, yeo., Fonthill B., 1705, AB, I, P2/C/915
Cole, Roger, sen., tailor, Swindon, 1806, W, Wr, P3/1806/26
Cole, Sam., yeo., Uffc., Devon, 1751, W, P20/1/217
Cole, Sarah, sp., Burbage, 1797, W, P5/1797/10, P5/18Reg/233
Couls, Sarah, sp., Bishopstone N., 1799, AB, W, P6/138
Cole, Sarah, widow, Row Moor Farm, Lydiard M., 1853, aff, comm, W, Wr, P3/1853/57
Cole, Simon, Sandy Lane, Calne, 1820, W, Wr, P26/1337
Cole, Steph., yeo., Lydiard M., 1793, W, P3/C/1118
Cole, Susanna, widow, Devizes, 1743, W, P1/C/791, P1/9Reg/239
Thos., husb., Coombe B., 1609, I, copy I, W, P5/1609/17, P5/9Reg/6C
Cole, Thos., Badbury, Chiseldon, 1633, AB, I, P3/C/186
Thos., yeo., N. Bradley, 1635, I, W, P2/C/431, P2/9Reg/90C
Cole als Barnard, Thos., husb., Bratton, Westb., 1643, I, W, P25/1643/2
Thos., yeo., Elston, Orcheston St Geo., 1664, I, ren, W, P2/C/557
Thos., yeo., Dinton, 1667, I, W, P2/C/572
Thos., oatmealmaker, Hurst, Berks., 1683, I, W, P5/1683/14
Cole, Thos., yeo., Bratton, Westb., 1711, AB, I, P25/1711/18
Thos., yeo., Maddington, 1717, W, P2/C/1008
Cole, Thos., yeo., Kington St M. (form. of Chipp.), 1834, comm, W, Wr, P3/1834/10
Cole, Thos., yeo., Plaitford, 1844, AB, Wr, P2/1844/3
Thos., yeo., Axe Farm, Chards., Devon, 1857, AB, aff, Wr, P14/234
Cole, Thos. Paine, yeo., Ogbourne St Geo., 1839, comm, W, Wr, P23/997
Ursula, sp., Upavon, 1801, W, P1/1801/66, P1/15Reg/283
Wm., Dinton, 1607, AB, I, W, P2/C/224
Cole, Wm., husb., Anderson, Dorset, 1614, I, W, P5/1614/16, P5/9Reg/135A
Cole, Wm., Medbourne, Liddington, 1618, AB, I, ren, P3/C/96
Cole, Wm., husb., Orcheston St My., 1636, I, W, P2/C/439
Wm., yeo., Whitep., 1646, AB, I, ren, P2/C/523
Wm., yeo., Hamptworth, Downton, 1676, I, W, P2/C/658
Wm., yeo., Stratton St Mgt., 1680, AB (2), P3/C/428-29
Wm., baker, New Windsor, Berks., 1680, AB, I, P1/C/339
Cole, Wm., innkeeper, Burbage, 1682, W, P11/48
Wm., yeo., Gt. Trowle, Bradford A., 1686, I, W, P2/C/774
Cole, Wm., yeo., Dinton, 1689, AB, I, P1/C/403
Wm., jun., yeo., Dinton, 1693, AB, I, P2/C/826
Wm., sen., carp., Reading, Berks., 1698, I, W, P1/C/459, P1/3Reg/53
Wm., [publican], Westb., 1700, AB, I (detailed), P25/1700/10
Cole, Wm., gent., Sal., 1704, AB, I, ren, P1/C/483, P4/1704/14
Cole, Wm., Wrou., 1718, I, W, P3/C/714
Cole, Wm., grocer, Reading, Berks., 1726, AB, I (detailed), P1/C/644
Wm., saddler, Trowb., 1727, W, P1/C/656, P1/7Reg/165
Cole, Wm., Burbage, 1739, I, W, P11/170
Wm., grocer, Fovant, 1758, W, P2/C/1296
Cole, Wm., yeo., Burbage, 1773, W, Wr, P5/1773/14, P5/17Reg/63B
Wm., Downton, 1798, AB, P2/C/1487
Wm., Bere R., Dorset, 1801, AB, W, P5/1801/24, P5/18Reg/324C

Cole, Wm., Corsham, 1813, AB, comm, Wr, P3/1813/15
Cole, Wm., gent., Sal., 1823, W, Wr, P4/1823/2
Cole, Wm., Milford, Sal. St Mart., 1832, AB, Wr, P4/1832/5
Cole, Wm., painter and glazier, Corsham, 1835, W, P29/1800-1857/28, P29/3Reg/285
Wm., yeo., Seend, Melk., 1847, D, W, Wr, P2/1847/31
Cole, Wm., out of business, Burton, Nettleton, 1854, aff, D, O, W, Wr, P3/1854/5
see also Carswell als C.; Coole; Crooke als C.; Stevens als C.; Wilkins als C.
Colestone *see* Colstone
Coley *see* Calley
Colfox, Hy., yeo., Over C., Dorset, 1716, I, W, P5/1716/18, P5/15Reg/337A
Coulfox, Jn., yeo., Bowood, Netherb., Dorset, 1628, comm, I, W, P5/1628/31, P5/11Reg/15A
Robt., Chards., Devon, 1666, AB, comm, P14/21
Coling *see* Collins
Colivord *see* Culliford
Collant, Eliz., widow, Beam., Dorset, 1675, I, NW, P17/282
Eliz., widow, S. Bowood, Netherb., Dorset, 1702, I, W, P17/146
Hannah, widow, Pavelands, Netherb., Dorset, 1735, AB, I, P17/458
Jn., yeo., Beam., Dorset, 1676, I, NW, P5/1676/15
Matthew, Netherb., Dorset, 1731, AB, P17/448
Thos., sen., yeo., S. Bowood, Netherb., Dorset, 1692, I, W, P17/333
Thos., Netherb., Dorset, 1726, AB, P17/423
Wm., Netherb., Dorset, 1708, I, W, P17/173
Collar *see* Coller
Collens *see* Collins
Coller, Abigail, widow, Bradford A., 1752, AB, I, P2/C/1268
Ann, widow, Atworth, Bradford A. (late of Kington St M.), 1624, I, W, P2/C/339
Collor, Anna, widow, Chr. M., 1744, comm, W, P1/C/799, P1/9Reg/315
Edith, widow, Rodbourne, Malm., 1666, I, W, P3/C/307
Hester, widow, Sherston, 1839, aff, O, W, Wr, P3/1839/26
Jas., gent., Kington St M., 1825, W, Wr, P3/1825/51
Jas., Bremhill, 1845, AB, O, Wr, P3/1845/5
Joan, widow, Hullavington, 1669, AB, P3/C/329
Joan, widow, Ford, N. Wraxall, 1677, I, W, P3/C/401
Job, yeo., Kington L., 1815, W, Wr, P3/1815/75
Collar, Jn., broad weaver, Trowle, Bradford A., 1766, W, P2/C/1333
Collar, Jn., cordw., Bradford A., 1799, AB, comm, ren, P2/C/1497
Jn., gent., Kington St M., 1811, W, Wr, P3/1811/21
Jos., Tytherton L., Chipp., 1852, aff, O, W, Wr, P3/1852/14
Lucy, widow, Langley Burrell, 1699, I, W, P3/C/609
Margery, widow, Kington L., 1633, I, W, P3/C/188
My., wife, Wootton B., 1670, AB, comm, W, P3/C/340
Miriam, widow, Sutton B., 1760, W, P3/C/953
Rd., Kington L., 1605, W, P3/C/19
Rd., Ford, N. Wraxall, 1613, I, W, P3/C/68
Rd., husb., Rodbourne, Malm., 1620, I (damaged & not definitely linked to W), W, P3/C/109
Sam., vict., Chipp., 1821, W, Wr, P3/1821/30
Thos., labourer, Chr. M., 1622, I, W, P3/C/116
Thos., carp., Newtown, Bradford A., 1726, W, P1/C/653, P1/7Reg/146B
Thos., Kington L., 1727, W, P3/C/767
Thos., gent., Kington St M., 1811, W, Wr, P1/1811/93
Collar, Walter, Trowb., 1734, AB, P1/C/720, P1/7Reg/596B
Wm., Chr. M., 1604, I, W, P3/C/13
Wm., Kington L., 1609, W, P3/C/40
Wm., Kington St M., 1613, AB, I (detailed), P1/C/56
Wm., husb., Sutton B., 1614, W, P1/C/72
Wm., yeo., Kington St M., 1620, a/c, comm, W (damaged), P1/C/101
Wm., husb., Sutton B., 1629, I, W, P3/C/162
Wm., husb., N. Wraxall, 1633, AB, I, P3/C/189
Wm., Kington L., 1691, AB, I, P3/C/550
Wm., mercer, Sutton B., 1692, I, W, P1/C/418

Wm., weaver, Sutton B., 1760, AB, W, P3/C/952
Collar, Wm., cordw., Bradford A., 1846, O, W, Wr, P2/1846/16
Collerne *see* Cullerne
Colles *see* Collis
Colleton, Francis *see* Thos. Stafford
Collett, Agnes, widow, Conock, Chirton, 1603, I, W, P2/C/197
Alice, widow, S. Wraxall, 1592, I, W, P2/C/117
Ann, widow, Urchf., 1668, AB, I, P1/C/288
Anth., Gt. Chalfield, 1602, I, P2/C/185
Benj., innholder, Corsham, [1798], W, P29/C/24, P29/2Reg/216
Brian, yeo., Patney, 1669, I, W, P2/C/592
Edmd., yeo., Wedh., Urchf., 1723, comm, I, W, P1/C/618, P1/6Reg/404A
Eliz., widow, S. Wraxall, 1785, W, P2/C/1433
Francis, yeo., Byde Mill, Corsham, 1772, W, P3/C/1026
Francis, yeo., Corsham, 1855, aff, W, Wr, P3/1855/23
Hannah, S. Wraxall, [1680], I, P2/C/687
Hy., yeo., Badbury Wick, Chiseldon, 1662, I, W, P3/C/284
Hy., sen., yeo., Trowb., 1779, comm, W, P1/C/1005, P1/13Reg/214
Hester, widow, Wedh., Urchf., [1682], I, W, P2/C/708
Jas., sen., yeo., Wedh., Urchf., 1646, AB, I, ren, P2/C/530
Jas., yeo., Langley Burrell, 1699, AB, I, P3/C/610
Jane, widow, Badbury Wick, Chiseldon, 1685, W, P3/C/497
Joan, widow, Conock, Chirton, [1636], I, W, P2/C/445
Joan, widow, Sal. St Edmd., 1673, I, W, P4/1672/15
Jn., Wedh., Urchf., 1549, W, P2/2Reg/102A
Jn., husb., S. Wraxall, 1585, W, P2/6Reg/140B
Jn., Conock, Chirton, 1592, I, W, P2/C/116
Jn., husb., S. Wraxall, 1620, I, W, P2/C/318
Jn., clothw., Lt. Trowle, Trowb., 1652, AB, comm, I, P1/C/207
Jn., yeo., Whaddon Pitts, Hilp., 1692, AB, I, P1/C/415
Jn., clothier, Bradford A., [1694], W, P2/C/839
Jn., carp., S. Wraxall, 1698, I, W, P2/C/874
Jn., yeo., Lt. Chalfield, 1698, comm, I, W, P1/C/466, P1/3Reg/203
Jn., wheelwright and carp., S. Wraxall, 1775, W, P2/C/1383
Jn., sen., gent., Hullavington, 1831, W, Wr, P3/1831/30
Jn., farmer, S. Wraxall, 1837, W, Wr, P2/1837/64
Jn., Nettleton, 1842, AB, Wr, P3/1842/21
Jn., baker, Hilp., 1848, O, W, Wr, P2/1848/20
Jonathan, carp., Leigh, Bradford A., 1808, W, Wr, P1/1808/33
Jos., gent., Easton Piercy, Kington St M., 1809, W, Wr, P3/1809/52
My., widow, Wedh., Urchf., 1731, W, P2/C/1128
Matthew, gent. [and silversmith *or* jeweller], Sal., 1668, AB, a/c, I, ren, P4/1667/24
Rebecca, widow, Bromham, 1681, AB, I, P3/C/439
Coolett, Rd., S. Wraxall, 1540, W (NEP), P2/1Reg/28B
Rd., husb., Wedh., Urchf., 1592, I, W, P2/C/101
Rd., husb., Marl. St Peter and St Paul, 1671, I, W, P1/C/302
Robt., All C., [1581], W (NEP), P3/1Reg/16B
Robt., Conock, Chirton, 1587, W, P2/7Reg/81B
Robt., husb., Urchf., 1611, I, NW, P2/C/255
Robt., yeo., Urchf., 1636, I, W, P2/C/448
Robt., blacksmith, Broad H., 1636, AB, I, W, P3/C/219
Robt., yeo., Wedh., Urchf., 1663, AB, I, P2/C/554
Robt., shepherd, Shrewton, 1663, AB, comm, I, P2/C/551
Robt., yeo., Chiseldon, 1672, AB, I, P3/C/358
Robt., yeo., Wedh., Urchf., 1683, AB, I, W, P2/C/733
Sam., gent., Landsend, Langley, Chipp., 1744, W, P1/C/807, P1/9Reg/398
Simon, yeo., Box, 1695, AB, comm, I, P3/C/583
Steph., glover, Highw., 1635, I, W, P5/1635/24, P5/12Reg/176
Steph., yeo., Easton Piercy, Kington St M., 1852, D, O, W, Wr, P3/1852/52
Thos., Wedh., Urchf., 1549, W, P2/2Reg/85A

Thos., S. Wraxall, 1650, AB, P1/C/228
Thos., broad weaver, S. Wraxall, 1671, I, W, P1/C/303
Thos., W. Lavington, 1706, AB, P1/C/496
Thos., carp., S. Wraxall, 1732, W, P1/C/708, P1/7Reg/520B
Thos., perukemaker, Bradford A., 1739, comm, W, P2/C/1197
Thos., Blackmore, Melk., 1785, AB, comm, P2/C/1431
Wm., sen., husb., Wedh., Urchf., 1592, I, W, P2/C/106
Wm., Shrewton, [1612], W, P2/C/266
Wm., husb., Conock, Chirton, 1626, I, W, P2/C/367
Wm., yeo., Badbury Wick, Chiseldon, 1661, AB, comm, I, P3/C/277, P3/3Reg/7B
Wm., Sal., 1667, AB, I, P4/1667/8
Wm., husb., S. Wraxall, 1672, I, P2/C/631
Wm., yeo., Bromham, 1675, I, NW, P3/C/380
Wm., carp., Monkton F., 1693-94, AB, a/c, I, P2/C/838
Wm., yeo., Broughton G., 1725, I, W, P2/C/1065
Wm., Poole Keynes, 1828, O, W, Wr, P3/1828/30
Wm., Oaksey, 1841, AB, comm, Wr, P3/1841/52
Colley *see* Culley
Collier, Agnes, widow, Winterbourne S., 1597, AB, I, W, P2/C/144
Agnes, Chards., Devon, 1689, AB, I, P14/69
Ann, widow, Urchf., [1670], I, W, P2/C/608
Ann, widow, Winterbourne S., 1681, I, W, P1/C/354
Ann, widow, Sal. The Close, 1722, W, P5/1722/14, P5/16Reg/61C
Cath., widow, Sherb., Dorset, 1697, I, W, P5/1697/5
Chas., yeo., Winterbourne S., 1764, W, P2/C/1319
David, blacksmith, Gt. Faringdon, Berks., 1622, I, W, P5/1622/15, P5/10Reg/109
Edith, widow, Urchf., 1714, W, P2/C/991
Edwd., Maddington, 1648, I, W, P2/C/539
Edwd., yeo., Hill D., 1694, I, W, P2/C/849
Edwd., Reading, Berks., 1747, AB, P1/C/821
Edwd., yeo., Sutton V., 1766-68, AB, a/c, app. of guardian, comm, I (very detailed), T, P2/C/1334
Eleanor, sp., Gt. Durnford, 1700, AB, P9/29
Eliz., widow, Hungerford, Berks., 1717, AB, P5/1717/9
Eliz., widow, Twyford, Hurst, Berks., 1760, acceptance of guardianship with app. of proctors, AB, app. of guardian, comm, W, P5/1760/6
Hy., Alton P., Dorset, 1683, AB, I, P5/1683/10
Hy., Shalbourne, 1749, AB, I, P23/613
Jas., innholder, Crickl. St S., 1798, W, P1/C/1093, P1/15Reg/50B
Jas., weaver, Dilton M., Westb., 1823, W, P25/1823/6
Jane, widow, Brigmerston, Milston, 1712, I, W, P2/C/976
Jane, widow, Chards., Devon, 1741, AB, comm, P14/155
Jennifer, widow, Sal. The Close, 1747, W, P5/1747/6
Jn., Durley, Burbage, 1579, AB, I, T, P5/1578/11, P5/3Reg/118B
Jn., yeo. and husb., Maddington, 1643, I, W, P2/C/514
Jn., Lyme R., Dorset, 1678-79, AB, a/c, comm, I, ren, P5/1678/10, P5/1679/12
Jn., yeo., Winterbourne S., [1686], I, W, P2/C/773
Jn., yeo., Sutton V., 1692, AB, W, P1/C/427
Jn., sen., Ford, Laverstock, 1722, AB, I, W (incomplete bond on reverse), P4/1721/11
Jn., yeo., Sutton V., 1832, W, Wr, P2/1832/39
Jos., clerk and parson, Steeple L., 1636, I, W, P1/C/171
Jos., Reading, Berks., 1792, AB, P1/C/1070, P1/14Reg/414A
Letitia, widow, Heytes., 1799, AB, ren, W, P5/1799/7, P5/18Reg/272A
My., widow, Maddington, 1692, I, W, P2/C/824
My., sp., Sal., 1789, W, P1/C/1054, P1/14Reg/213
Nathaniel, husb., Chards., Devon, 1668, I, W, P14/18
Nathaniel, yeo., Chards., Devon, 1685, I, W, P14/56
Nathaniel, carp., Chards., Devon, 1703, AB, I, P14/97
Nathaniel, Chards., Devon, 1734, AB, P5/1734/15
Nich., Winterbourne S., 1614, I, W, P1/C/67
Nich., yeo., Brigmerston, Milston, 1751, W, P2/C/1267

Rd., Trowb., 1663, AB, P1/C/268
Rd., Hungerford, Berks., 1702, AB, ren, P23/247
Rd., dealer and chapman, Bishopstone N., 1728, AB (2), I (his widow & admx, Susanna, d. before AB completed), P6/113
Rd., yeo., Sutton V., 1760, W, P2/C/1306
Rd., yeo., Sutton V., 1818, W, Wr, P2/1818/40
Robt., husb., Winterbourne S., 1583, I, W, P2/C/61, P2/6Reg/102
Robt., husb., Sal., 1677, AB, I, P4/1677/5
Sam., glazier, Warm., 1804, AB, comm, W, P1/1804/35
Sarah, painter's widow, Hungerford, Berks., 1688, AB, I, P5/1688/21
Susan, Winterbourne S., 1721, AB, P2/C/1039
Susanna, widow, Bishopstone N., 1729, AB, P6/118
Thos., sen., husb., Urchf., 1637, I, W, P2/C/455
Thos., clothier, Devizes, 1670, AB, I, P1/C/297
Thos., no abode stated - proved at Crickl., 1679, I, W (2), P3/C/419
Thos., yeo., Ashton K., 1778, W, P3/C/1059
Wm., Winterbourne S., 1693, AB, I, P2/C/837
Wm., yeo., Sal., 1697, W, P4/1697/8
Wm., Trowb., 1755, AB, P1/C/870
Wm., Hurst, Berks., 1757, AB, P5/1757/6
Wm., schoolmaster, Farley, Alderbury, 1769, W, P26/1032
Colliford *see* Culliford
Colling *see* Collins
Collingbourn, Collingbourne, Ann, sp., Lt. Somerford, 1837, O, W, Wr, P3/1837/63
Caleb, Brinkw., 1851, AB, O, Wr, P3/1851/21
Chas., baker, Melk., 1802, comm, W, P2/1802/21
Chas., Melk., 1812, AB, comm, ren, W, Wr, P2/1812/62
Collingborn, Eleanor, wife, Lt. Somerford, 1807, AB, comm, Wr, P1/1807/23
Collingborn, Eliz., widow, Lt. Somerford (form. of Dauntsey), 1776, I, NW (NEP), P30/41
Collingborne, Francis, Lt. Somerford, 1700, I, W, P3/C/624
Collingborne, Francis, Cleverton, Lea and C., 1734, W, P3/C/824
Collingborn, Francis, yeo., Brinkw., 1786, W, P3/C/1091
Collingbourne, Francis, Corston, Malm., 1812, AB, comm, Wr, P3/1812/24
Collingborn, Hy., yeo., Stanton St Q., 1766, W, P3/C/995
Collingborne, Jacob, yeo., Cleverton, Lea and C., 1798, W, P1/C/1099, P1/15Reg/114
Jas. Sartain, minor, Holt, Bradford A., 1800-09, AB, app. of guardian, T (re Jas. Sartain C. ex. of W of his late grandfather, Jas. Sartain), comm, Wr, P2/1800/20, 22, P2/1809/67
Collingborn, Jasper, yeo., Lt. Somerford, 1791, W, P3/C/1112
Collingbourne, Jn., Rodbourne, Malm., 1733, AB, P3/C/816
Collingborn, Jn., yeo., Lt. Somerford, 1775, W, P3/C/1044
Collingborne, Joyce, widow, Lt. Somerford, 1706, I, W, P3/C/658
Collingborne, Priscilla, widow, Garsdon, 1767, W, P3/C/1001
Collingborn, Priscilla, widow, Stanton St Q., 1776, W, P1/C/993, P1/13Reg/104
Collingborne, Thos., yeo., Lea and Cleverton, 1760, W, P3/C/954
Collingborn, Thos., yeo., Dauntsey, 1773, W, P3/C/1034
Thos., baker, Holt, Bradford A., 1798, W, P2/C/1488
Collins, Abraham, husb., Hurst, Berks., 1682, I, P5/1682/22
Agnes, widow, Stanford in the Vale, Berks., 1631, comm, I, W, P1/C/142
Alice, Coombe B., 1573, W, P5/3Reg/24D
Collings, Alice, Netheravon, [1608], I (incomplete - total only), W, P12/15
Alice, widow, E. Grimstead, W. Dean, 1619, I, W, P1/C/88
Allef, innholder, Horningsham, 1853, comm, W, Wr, P5/1853/13
Collens, Ann, widow, Fordington, Dorset, 1677, I, W, P15/25-26
Ann, widow, Netheravon, [1686], AB (gives monarch's name as Chas., in error for Jas.), I, W, P12/124
Collings, Ann, sp., Bradford A., 1797, comm, W, P2/C/1482
Colling, Anth., Gt. Bedwyn, 1715, AB, P21/7/20
Anth., labourer, Broad H., 1719, I, W, P3/C/722
Anth., Clapton, Kintbury, Berks., 1773, comm, W, P1/C/982, P1/13Reg/45B
Collens, Benj., clothw., Fisherton A., 1729, W, P1/C/661, P1/7Reg/210B
Benj., gent., Devizes, 1752, AB, ren, P1/C/849
Chas., Winterslow, 1733, AB, I, P2/C/1159

Chas., labourer, Winterslow, 1779, W, P2/C/1401
Chas., labourer, Winterslow Common, 1799, W, P2/C/1500
Chas., labourer, Boxford, Berks., 1835, O, W, P1/1835/31
Christian, widow, Roke, Bere R., Dorset, 1692, I, W, P5/1692/17
Christian, widow, Reading, Berks., 1738, W, P1/C/755, P1/8Reg/269
Collens, Chris., Chards., Devon, 1615, I, W, P5/1615/5, P5/9Reg/156B
David, widower, Sutton B., 1844, AB, Wr, P3/1844/37
Collens, Denise, widow, Whitep., 1685, AB, I, P2/C/755
Dennis, collarmaker, Barford St Mart., 1588, W, P2/7Reg/119A
Dorothy, widow, Farnham, Tollard Royal, Dorset, 1610, I, W, P2/C/247, P2/8Reg/139B
Edmd., sen., Codf. St P., 1711, I, W, P1/C/532, P1/5Reg/241
Edwd., husb., Idmiston, 1572, W, P2/5Reg/138B
Collens, Edwd., carp., Hurst, Berks., 1682, AB, I, ren, W, P5/1682/24
Edwd., carp., Hurst, Berks., 1718, W, P5/1718/8, P5/15Reg/410B
Edwd., carp., Wokm., Berks., 1746, W, P5/1746/17
Edwd., plumber and glazier, Hungerford, Berks., 1836, O, W, Wr, P5/1836/15
Edwd. Hearn, bach., Easton, 1847, AB, comm, Wr, P3/1847/33
Eleanor, Mkt. L., 1715, AB, I, P2/C/997
Eleanor, widow, Fonthill B., 1799, W, Wr, P2/C/1496
Collens, Eliz., widow, Hurst, Berks., 1572, W, P5/2Reg/114A
Eliz., widow, Stapleford, 1605, AB, a/c, I, note of AB, P2/C/211
Collens, Eliz., widow, Stapleford, 1681, I, W, P2/C/703
Eliz., Enmore Grn, Motc., Dorset, 1684, AB, P19/44
Eliz., Grove, Wantage, Berks., 1727, W, P23/452
Eliz., widow, Gt. Faringdon, Berks., 1728, AB, P5/1728/25, P5/16Reg/213B
Collings, Eliz., widow, Bradford A., 1797, AB, comm, P2/C/1480
Eliz., widow, Bremilham, 1814, W, Wr, P1/1814/122
Eliz., sp., Laverstock, 1817, AB, Wr, P2/1817/4
Frances, widow, Sonning, Berks. (*also* of Hurst), 1685, I, W, P5/1685/20
Francis, Fordington, Dorset, 1692, AB, comm, P15/48
Geoff., Devizes St Jn., 1681, AB, comm, I, P1/C/356
Geo., Stapleford, 1595, AB, I, P2/C/131, P2/7Reg/144B
Geo., clothw., Seend, Melk., [1668], W, P2/C/584
Grace, sp., Reading, Berks., 1759, W, P1/C/898, P1/11Reg/386B
Collins als Dymer, Helen, Burbage, 1569, AB, P5/2Reg/39A
Hy., E. Grimstead, W. Dean, 1580, I, NW, P2/C/59, P2/6Reg/17B
Hy., yeo., W. Ginge, E. Lockinge, Berks., 1628, AB, I, P1/C/129
Collens, Hy., husb., E. Grimstead, W. Dean, 1635, I, W, P2/C/430, P2/9Reg/52B
Hercules, blacksmith, Stanford in the Vale, Berks., 1789, AB, W, P1/C/1058, P1/14Reg/253
Isaac, Brixton D., 1835, O, W, P2/1835/31
Isaac, gardener, Sutton B., 1857, aff, O, W, Wr, P3/1857/4
Jas., Maiden B., 1626, AB, I, P2/C/359
Collens, Jas., Fordington, Dorset, 1681, AB, I, P15/37
Jas., weaver, Mill St., Fordington, Dorset, 1735, I, W (NEP), P5/1735/13
Jas., yeo., Corsley, 1835, W, Wr, P1/1835/72
Collings, Jas., butcher, Devizes, 1837, O, W, Wr, P1/1837/28
Jas., Brixton D., 1848, AB, comm, Wr, P2/1848/4
Jane, widow, Fordington, Dorset, 1717, AB, W, P15/96
Jane, widow, Fisherton A., 1729, AB, P2/C/1110
Joan, widow, Sherrington, 1624, I, W, P2/C/347
Coolins, Jn., Winterbourne S., 1538, W, P2/1Reg/17B
Jn., Fovant, 1558, W, P2/3Reg/89B
Jn., Hungerford, Berks., 1575, I, P5/1575/12
Jn., Coombe B., 1582, I, T, W, P5/1582/14, P5/4Reg/31C
Jn., yeo., Ludg., 1605, I, NW, P2/C/213
Jn., Britford, 1607, AB, P24/9
Jn., N. Wraxall, 1608, NW, P3/C/33
Jn., W. Harnham, 1608, AB, I, W, P5/1608/8, P5/8Reg/129
Jn., weaver, Warm., 1618, I, W, P2/C/305
Collens, Jn., Stratford Tony, 1619, AB, P2/C/311

Jn., yeo., Yondover, Netherb., Dorset, 1622, AB, comm, NW, P5/1622/19
Jn., Stapleford, 1624, AB, I, P2/C/335
Jn., carp., Hurst, Berks., 1636, AB, a/c, I, P5/1636/15, P5/13Reg/2A
Collens, Jn., Chards., Devon, 1637, AB, P14/197
Jn., husb., Stapleford, 1645, I, P2/C/520
Jn., bricklayer, Swallowfield, Shinfield, Berks., 1662, AB, I, P1/C/246
Jn., tailor, Hurst, Berks., 1663, I, W, P5/1663/15
Jn., yeo., Hurst, Berks., 1672, I (detailed), W, P5/1672/6
Jn., yeo., Stapleford, [1674], I, W, P2/C/647
Jn., maltster, Netheravon, 1680, AB, I, P12/112
Jn., yeo. *or* innholder, Sherston, 1685, I, W, P3/C/498
Jn., sen., Chute Forest, Chute, 1689, AB, I, P7/75
Jn., bricklayer, Greenham, Thatcham, Berks., 1695, I, W, P1/C/445
Jn., sen., yeo., Frilford, Marcham, Berks., 1698, I, W, P1/C/463, P1/3Reg/92
Collens, Jn., yeo., Peaks Wood, Aldbourne, 1699, I, W, P3/C/611
Jn., yeo., Sedgehill, 1724, AB, I, ren, P2/C/1059
Jn., cordw., Ruscombe, Berks., 1727, W, P5/1727/7, P5/16Reg/153B
Jn., husb., Kingston Bagpuize, Berks., 1729, AB, I, W, P1/C/670, P1/7Reg/241A
Jn., innkeeper, Knook, 1737, W, Wr, P5/1737/14
Jn., E. Knoyle, 1739, AB, comm, P2/C/1195
Jn., sen., glazier, Devizes, 1739, W, P1/C/770, P1/8Reg/408
Collens, Jn., gardener, Mere, 1742, W, Wr, P5/1742/12
Jn., carp., Hurst, Berks., 1744, W, Wr, P5/1744/11
Jn., yeo., Motc., Dorset, 1774, W, P27/1/488, P27/3Reg/184
Jn., bach., Gt. Cheverell, 1778, AB, P2/C/1396
Jn., servant to Wm. Beckford of Fonthill House, Fonthill G., 1783, comm, W, P1/C/1031, P1/13Reg/413B
Jn., sen., maltster, Abingdon, Berks., 1789, W, P1/C/1057, P1/14Reg/257
Jn., weaver, Sal., 1795, W, P4/1795/6
Jn., vict., Trowb., 1802, AB, comm, ren, W, P1/1802/3, P1/15Reg/362
Jn., gardener, Westb., 1810, W, P25/1810/3
Jn., Abingdon, Berks., 1814, AB, P1/1814/103
Jn., Betterton, E. Lockinge, Berks., 1827, comm, ren, W, Wr, P1/1827/4
Jn., gent., Easton, 1839, O, W, Wr, P3/1839/29
Jn. Edmd.s, gent., Trowb., 1851, W, Wr, P1/1851/50
Jonathan, yeo., Frilford, Marcham, Berks., 1753, W, P1/C/852, P1/11Reg/9
Jos., yeo., Stapleford, 1692, comm, I, W, P2/C/819
Jos., gardener, Wokm., Berks., 1750, W, P5/1750/6
Jos., yeo., Knook, 1779, AB, W, P5/1779/5, P5/17Reg/182C
Jos., yeo., Stoford, S. Newton, 1788, AB (2), app. of guardians, P2/C/1450
Judith, widow, Hungerford, Berks., 1625, AB, a/c, I, order to accountant, P5/1625/15
Mgt., widow, Maiden B., [1633], I, W, P2/C/419
Collens, Margery, widow, Netherb., Dorset, 1672, I, W, P17/129
Margery, Netherb., Dorset, 1685, AB, P5/1685/25
Margery, Steeple L. (late of Elston), 1709, W, P2/C/954
Collens, Mark, wheeler, Aldbourne, 1678, I, W, P3/C/410
Mark, Aldbourne, 1679, AB, I, P3/C/420
Mark, yeo., Aldbourne, 1722, AB, I, P3/C/739
Mark, yeo., Aldbourne, 1783, W, P1/C/1036, P1/13Reg/457
My., widow, Broad H., 1630, I, W, P3/C/169
My., widow, Brinkw., 1682, AB, P3/C/459
My., widow, Sedgehill, 1741, AB, ren, P2/C/1210
My., sp., Sal., 1742, AB, P4/1742/7
My., widow, Upton L., 1765, W, P2/C/1326
My., widow, Stockton, 1842, O, W, Wr, P2/1842/6
[Penelope], widow, Brightwalton, Berks., 1671, I, W (christian name not stated, taken from bishop's transcripts), P1/C/308
Peter, Snailscraft, Netherb., Dorset, 1568, W, P5/2Reg/32A
Petronel, wife of Jn. C. & form. widow of Giles Mills, Netherb., Dorset, 1606, AB, I, P5/1606/12, P5/8Reg/65C
Collens, Philip, husb., Wick, Bps. C., [1621], deed of gift, P24/74
Philip, yeo., Sherston, 1635, I, W, P1/C/155
Rd., W. Dean, 1612, I, T, P2/C/267

Rd., yeo., Speen, Berks., 1680, AB, comm, I, P1/C/350
Collens, Rd., sen., Alderbury, 1685, I, W, P26/329
Rd., yeo., Collingbourne K., 1688, I, W, P1/C/394
Rd., woolcomber, Calne, 1690, AB, I, P26/389
Rd., butcher, Broad St., Reading, Berks., 1717, W, P1/C/577, P1/6Reg/92
Rd., apothecary, Malm., 1718, I, W, P3/C/715
Collings, Rd., maltster, Aughton, Collingbourne K., 1742, I, W, P3/C/869
Rd., yeo., Chute, 1744, W, P7/139
Collings, Rd., innholder and maltster, Collingbourne K., 1760, W, P1/C/909, P1/11Reg/480A
Rd., Marl. St My., 1765, W, P1/C/933, P1/12Reg/154A
Rd., Aldbourne, 1771, AB, P3/C/1018
Rd., sen., yeo., Compton, Berks., 1779, W, P1/C/1008, P1/13Reg/220B
Rd., Downton, 1798, W, P2/C/1491
Rd., yeo., Corsley, 1799, comm, W, P2/C/1498
Rd., Brixton D., 1800, W, P2/1800/19
Robt., husb., N. Wraxall, 1571, W (NEP), P1/1Reg/81B
Robt., husb., Bloxworth, Dorset, 1614-15, I, W, P5/1614/18, P5/9Reg/158B
Robt., Keevil, 1672, AB, comm, P2/C/621
Robt., Fordington, Dorset, 1681, AB, a/c, I, P15/54
Robt., yeo., Sutton C., Berks., 1695, I (detailed), W, P1/C/441
Robt., yeo., Peaks Wood, Aldbourne, 1700, AB, I, P3/C/622
Roger, Downton, 1614, I, W, P1/C/68
Collens, Sam., yeo., Beam., Dorset, 1745, W, P17/498
Sam., Laverstock, 1792, AB, P1/C/1071, P1/14Reg/468B
Sarah, sp., Newbury, Berks., 1720, W, P1/C/602, P1/6Reg/341
Silvester, widow, Sherston, 1718, I, W, P3/C/716
Steph., Sherrington, 1604, AB, I, P2/C/204
Steph., Brixton D., 1669, AB, I, P2/C/593
Steph., Sherrington, 1676, AB, I, ren, P2/C/666
Steph., broad weaver, Longbridge D., 1731, W, P2/C/1129
Thos., husb., Coombe B., 1603, AB, I, W, P5/1603/21, P5/8Reg/2A
Collens, Thos., husb., Broad H., 1610, W, P3/C/48
Collings, Thos., N. Wraxall, 1623, I, NW, P3/C/123
Thos., yeo., Aldbourne, 1629, AB, a/c, I, P3/C/157
Thos., husb., Hurst, Berks., 1641, AB, I, P5/1641/18, P5/14Reg/23B
Thos., sen., Stapleford, 1663, AB, I, P2/C/553
Collens, Thos., Sal., 1685, AB, P4/1685/3
Thos., yeo., Aldbourne, 1698, comm, I, W, P3/C/602
Thos., yeo., Elston, Orcheston St Geo., 1706, I, W, P2/C/929
Thos., jun., husb., Aldbourne, 1709, I, W (NEP), P3/C/673
Thos., Berwick St Jas., 1734, AB, P1/C/721, P1/7Reg/599B
Thos., cooper, Wantage, Berks., 1742, W, P23/564
Thos., Westport St My., 1784, AB, P3/C/1082
Collings, Thos., labourer, Collingbourne K., 1825, W, Wr, P3/1825/48
Thos., vict., Fisherton A. (form. of Southampton St Michael), 1827, W, Wr, P2/1827/54
Collings, Thos., Horningsham, 1835, AB, comm, Wr, P5/1835/27
Thos., shopkeeper and timber dealer, Pitton, Alderbury, 1837, W, Wr, P26/1431
Thos., gent., Gillingham, Dorset, 1840, W, Wr, P27/1/729
Walter, husb., Bloxworth, Dorset, 1617, I, NW, P5/1617/6, P5/9Reg/190B
Walter, yeo., Sedgehill, 1704, I, W, P2/C/913
Wm., Broad C., 1540, I, W (NEP), P30/40
Wm., Idmiston, 1546, AB, P2/2Reg/18B
Wm., Fordington, Dorset, 1588, AB, P5/5Reg/23A
Wm., husb., Bulford, 1611, AB, I, NW, P2/C/254
Wm., yeo., Snailscraft, Netherb., Dorset, 1613, I, W, P5/1613/13, P5/9Reg/94A
Collens, Wm., Wick, Bps. C., 1614, I, P24/96
Wm., husb., Bloxworth, Dorset, 1615, I, W, P5/1615/3, P5/9Reg/157A
Wm., Sal. St Mart., 1624, AB, a/c (2), I, P4/1624/7
Wm., sen., husb., Coombe B., 1631, I, NW, P5/1631/20, P5/11Reg/163A
Wm., husb., Stapleford, 1631, W, P2/C/406, P2/9Reg/72

Wm., yeo., Hurst, Berks., 1635, I, W, P5/1635/25, P5/12Reg/196B
Collens, Wm., Chards., Devon, 1638, AB, I, P14/198
Collens, Wm., Westbrook, Boxford, Berks., 1638, AB, a/c, I, P1/C/178
Wm., yeo., Fordington, Dorset, 1671, I, W, P5/1671/16
Wm., chandler, Chute, 1673, I (detailed), W, P7/44
Wm., carrier, Wick, Bps. C., 1674, I, W, P24/440
Collens, Wm., Hurst, Berks., 1682, AB, P5/1682/23
Wm., Clyffe P., 1687, AB, comm, P3/C/521
Wm., sen., butcher, Devizes St My., 1687, I, W, P1/C/391
Wm., yeo., Stanford in the Vale, Berks., 1689, I, W, P1/C/396
Wm., yeo., Fordington, Dorset, 1690, AB, I, P15/59
Wm., weaver, Sal., 1701, I, W, P1/C/477, P1/4Reg/205
Wm., yeo., Stapleford & Upton L., 1716, AB, I, W, P1/C/565, P1/6Reg/15
Wm., gent., Berwick St Jas., 1720, AB, ren, P1/C/586
Wm., yeo., Grove, Wantage, Berks., 1725, W, P5/1725/11, P5/16Reg/123B
Wm., Sal., 1740, W, P4/1740/11
Wm., yeo., Upton L., 1759, W, P2/C/1303
Wm., Mere, 1763, O, W, P5/1763/3
Wm., supervisor of excise, Warm., 1769, comm, W, P2/C/1350
Wm., W. Hagbourne, Berks., 1770, AB, P1/C/956
Wm., vict., Compton, Berks., 1779, W, P1/C/1007, P1/13Reg/222
Coling, Wm., farmer, Sugworth Farm, Radley, Berks., 1829, W, Wr, P1/1829/107
Wm., yeo., Childrey, Berks., 1835, O, W, Wr, P1/1835/75
Wm., labourer, Littleton P., 1842, O, W, Wr, P1/1842/82
Wm., cordw., Sal., 1850, D, W, Wr, P4/1850/2
Wm., servant, Sal., 1853, aff, W, Wr, P4/1853/14
see also Ward als C.
Collinson, My., widow, Donhead St A. (form. of Heytes.), 1778, W, P2/C/1394
Collis, Hy., sen., yeo., Allweston, Folke, Dorset, 1721, I, W, P5/1721/7, P5/16Reg/58A
Colles, Hy., yeo., Long Burton, Dorset, 1729, W, P5/1729/11, P5/16Reg/238
Hy., blacksmith, Allweston, Folke, Dorset, 1737, I, W, Wr, P5/1737/8
Hy., Cowesfield, Whitep., 1794, W, P2/C/1475
Jas., blacksmith, Allweston, Folke, Dorset, 1684, I, NW, P5/1684/11
Jas., Long Burton, Dorset, 1760, W, P5/1760/7
Jas., yeo., N. Wootton, Dorset, 1845, D, W, Wr, P5/1845/21
Collis als Wilkins, Jn., husb., Bulford, 1552, W, P2/2Reg/151A
Jn., husb., Malm., 1570, W, P1/1Reg/21C, 113B
Jn., husb., Whitep., 1651, AB, I, W, P1/C/232
Jn., farmer, Gillingham, Dorset, 1841, W, Wr, P27/1/734
Rd., sen., parchmentmaker, Sherb., Dorset, 1609, I, W, P5/1608/9, P5/8Reg/142A
Rd., carp., Sal., 1766, W, P4/1766/7
Colles, Thos., husb., Berwick St Leonard, [1562?], I, P2/C/21
Thos., yeo., Butterwick, Folke, Dorset, 1737, W, P5/1737/15
Wm., priest, E. Coulston, 1553, institution to rectory on death of Watson, P2/2Reg/167B
Wm., Berwick St Leonard, 1556, W, P2/1Reg/112B
Wm., Sherb., Dorset, 1711, AB, P5/1711/21
Collman *see* Coleman
Collor *see* Coller
Colls *see* Coles
Collymor *see* Cullimore
Collyprist, Wm., innholder, Warm., 1749, W, P2/C/1254
Colman *see* Coleman
Colmer, Jn., Shatcombe, Netherb., Dorset, 1632, I, W (NEP), P17/17
Jos., Netherb., Dorset, 1638, AB, I, P5/1638/22, P5/13Reg/78A
Robt., husb., Shatcombe, Beam., Dorset, 1588, NW, P5/5Reg/24D
Colsell, Amy, sp., Bodenham, Nunton and B., 1739, W, P2/C/1187
Dennis, gent., Britford & Sal. The Close, 1631, I (detailed), W, P24/260
Colstone, Chris., husb., Upton L., 1675, I, W, P2/C/649
Cowlstone, Edmd., shepherd, Ashton K., 1620, comm, I, W, P3/C/110
Cowlstone, Francis, husb., Ashton K., 1627, I, W, P3/C/151

Coulston, Geo., W. Lavington, 1729, AB, P1/C/690
Hy., husb., Lt. Cheverell, 1625, AB, I, P2/C/354
Jn., yeo., Gt. Cheverell, [1680], I, W, P2/C/689
Colestone, Jn., yeo., Imber, 1683, comm, I, W, P1/C/365
Coulston, Jn., bach., Poulshot, 1808, comm, W, Wr, P2/1808/32
Marian, widow, Lt. Cheverell, [1627], I, W, P2/C/371
My., widow, Poulshot, 1786, W, P1/C/1050, P1/14Reg/136
Philip, shepherd, Swallowcliffe, 1616, AB, I, P5/1616/12, P5/9Reg/173B
Rd., Ashton K., 1640, I, NW, P3/C/252
Thos., smith, Lt. Cheverell, 1575, AB, I, P2/C/38, P2/5Reg/241B
Coulston, Thos., shoemaker, Melk., 1732, W, P2/C/1137
Colestone, Wm., yeo., N. Bradley, 1720, I, W, P1/C/591, P1/6Reg/245B
Colthurst, Chris., Mkt. L., 1625, AB, I, P1/C/161
Edwd., clerk and vicar, Tilsh., 1599, I, W, P2/C/166
Colverhouse *see* Culverhouse
Colvill, Sarah, sp., Melk., 1775, AB, P2/C/1377
Wm., clerk and rector, Corsley, 1764, AB, P1/C/931
Comage, Christian, widow, Fovant, 1706, I, W, P2/C/932
David, clerk, Fovant, 1685, comm, I, W, P2/C/746
Geo., Compton C., 1663, AB, I, P1/C/267
Combes, Combe, Alexander, yeo., Chiseldon, 1661, comm, I, W, P3/C/279
Alexander, yeo., Chiseldon, 1661, W, P3/3Reg/7A
Coombes, [?Alice], Homington, 1611, a/c. Not the same person as P24/94, P24/80
Coombes, Alice, Homington, 1614, AB. Not the same person as P24/80., P24/94
Combe als Hillary, Amy, widow, Netherb., Dorset, 1691, AB, I, P17/330
Combe, Ann, widow, Farnham, Tollard Royal, Dorset, 1625, I, W, P2/C/350
Combe, Anth., clerk and vicar, Tisb., 1645, I, W, P2/C/522
Coombes, Anth., husb., Norton B., 1710, W, P2/C/970
Combe, Audrey, widow of Jn., Mere, 1598, I, T, W, P5/1597/21, P5/6Reg/196
Coombe, Benj., Thornford, Dorset, 1735, AB, P5/1735/14
Coombes, Benj., yeo., Enmore Grn, Motc., Dorset, 1792, W, Wr, P19/192
Combe, Cath., widow, Chiseldon, 1671, I, W, P3/C/349
Coombs, Cath., widow, Alvediston, 1682, I, W, P2/C/697
Combe, Chas., yeo., Sedgehill, 1672, I, W, P2/C/625
Combe, Chas., yeo., Sedgehill, 1680, I, W, P1/C/351
Chas., Sal., 1692, AB, I, P4/1692/5
Edmd., yeo., Pierston Farm, Gillingham, Dorset, 1613, W (NEP), P1/C/50
Comes, Edwd., Chute, 1567, AB, P5/2Reg/7D
Coombes, Edwd., Heytes., [1616], AB not granted, I, P5/1616/16
Coombes, Edwd., sen., Sal., 1699, AB, I, P4/1698/4
Coombs, Edwd., yeo., Kingston D., 1818, W, Wr, P2/1818/3
Coombe, Eliz., widow, Enmore Grn, Motc., Dorset, 1603, I, W, P5/1603/14, P5/7Reg/71A
Combe, Eliz., Stop, Fonthill G., 1685, AB, P2/C/757
Eliz., widow, Sal., 1709, AB, I, P4/1709/6
Eliz., Corsley, 1716, AB, P2/C/1000
Coombes, Eliz., Ryme I., Dorset, 1809, AB, Wr, P5/1809/44
Eliz., sp., Highw., 1820, AB, Wr, P10/1820/4
Coombe, Francis, sailor, Lyme R., Dorset, 1634, I, W, P16/470, P5/12Reg/289B
Combe, Frideswide, widow, Stop, Fonthill G., [1682], W, P2/C/707
Geo., Plaitford, 1606, AB, I, P1/C/30
Coombs, Geo., cordw., Mere, 1792, W, P5/1792/7
Coombs, Harriet, sp., Sal., 1829, AB, D, P4/1829/7
Coombs, Helen, sp., Sal., 1829, AB, D, P4/1829/8
Coombs, Isaac, Corsley, 1827, AB, Wr, P2/1827/29
Coombe, Jas., sen., yeo., Milton, Berks., 1711, I, W, P1/C/522, P1/5Reg/169
Coombe, Jas., yeo., Milton, Berks., 1732, W, P1/C/704, P1/7Reg/452
Coombs, Jas., yeo., S. Newton, 1741, W, P1/C/787, P1/9Reg/193
Coombs, Jas., Westb., 1800, AB, P25/1800/5
Jas., maltster, Tisb., 1832, W, Wr, P2/1832/19
Coombs, Jas., Tisb., 1846, AB, Wr, P2/1846/68

Coombs, Jas., widower, Stratford Tony, 1848, D, W, Wr, P1/1848/61
Coombs, Jas. Morris, bookseller, Chipp., 1820, W, Wr, P1/1820/80
Coombs, Jane, sp., Woolley, Bradford A., 1799, W, P2/C/1493
Comes, Joan, widow, Heytes., 1648, I, W, P5/1648/4, P5/14Reg/106D
Coombe, Joan, Uffc., Devon, 1725, AB, P5/1725/16
Combe, Jn., jun., Bourton, Gillingham, Dorset, 1561, W, P27/1Reg/10A
Combe, Jn., sen., Bourton, Gillingham, Dorset, 1561, W, P27/1Reg/9B
Comes, Jn., sen., Bently Parcill, Burbage, 1597, I, W, P5/1597/17, P5/6Reg/182A
Combe, Jn., yeo., S. Bowood, Netherb., Dorset, 1597, I, P5/1597/25
Combe, Jn., sen., yeo., Tisb., 1600, I (detailed), W, P2/C/180
Combes als Roche, Jn., yeo., Heytes., 1608, W, P5/8Reg/133B
Coombe, Jn., sen., weaver, N. Wootton, Dorset, 1631-32, I, NW, P5/1631/29, P5/12Reg/24
Coombe, Jn., yeo. and broad weaver, Warm., 1643, I, W, P2/C/513
Combe, Jn., yeo., Chicksgrove, Tisb., 1670, AB, I, ren, P2/C/610
Coombe, Jn., yeo., N. Wootton, Dorset, 1679, I, W, P5/1679/18
Coombs, Jn., musician, Sal., 1680, AB, I (detailed description of public house; rooms are named Bear, Lion, Rose, Dolphin, & Hart), P1/C/347
Coombes, Jn., yeo., Corsley, 1682, I, W, P2/C/721
Coombes, Jn., Bere R., Dorset, 1688, AB, I, P5/1688/16
Coombes, Jn., clerk, Ludg., 1691, AB, I, P2/C/807
Combe, Jn., yeo., Wambrook, Somerset, 1700, I, W, P14/91
Combe, Jn., yeo., Wick, Tisb., 1703, W, P2/C/905
Coombe als Davis, Jn., sackclothmaker, Beam., Dorset, 1710, D, NW, O, P5/1710/31, P5/15Reg/203
Coombes, Jn., Bodenham, Nunton and B., 1726, AB, I, P1/C/637
Coombs, Jn., yeo., Studley, Trowb., 1776, comm, W, P1/C/987, P1/13Reg/69A
Coombs, Jn., farmer, Berwick St Jas., 1779, W, P2/C/1404
Jn., sen., tailor, Devizes St My., 1783, comm, W, P1/C/1040, P1/14Reg/44
Coombs, Jn., Ludg., 1788, AB, P2/C/1447
Coombs, Jn., weaver, Bradford A., 1799, W, P2/C/1492
Coombs, Jn., Stapleford, 1801-05, aff (2 re 2 cods), D (several), W, P1/1801/118, P1/15Reg/336B
Coombs, Jn., weaver, N. Bradley, 1824, AB, W, Wr, P2/1824/47
Coombes, Jn. *see also* Thos. Gray
Coombe, Jos., yeo., Enmore Grn, Motc., Dorset, 1732, AB, ren, W, P19/123
Coombs, Jos., Kingston D., 1823, AB, Wr, P1/1823/57
Joyce, mealman, Sal., 1741, W, P1/C/784, P1/9Reg/135
Coombe, Lancelot, yeo., Tisb., 1680, AB, I, P1/C/348
Lawr., Fordington, Dorset, 1662, AB, P5/1662/27
Coombs, Luke, innholder, Wilton, 1727, W, P2/C/1080
Coombs, Luke, bach., Bulbridge, Wilton, 1824, AB, Wr, P2/1824/63
Margery, fuller's wife, S. Newton, 1732, W, P2/C/1143
Coombes, My., Sal. The Close, 1697, AB, P5/1697/7
Coombs, My., sp., Sal., 1721, W, P4/1721/4
Coombes, My., sp., Winterborne K., Dorset, 1789, W, P5/1789/3, P5/18Reg/124
Coombs, My., widow, Heywood Cleaves, Westb., 1813, O, W, Wr, P25/1813/4
Combe, Matthew, yeo., Tisb., 1665, I, W, P2/C/564
Matthew, husb., Stourton, 1672, AB, I, P2/C/630
Matthew, sen., Tisb., 1823, AB, P2/1823/30
Coombe, Moses, Grovely, Barford St Mart. (form. of Shaftesbury, Dorset), 1836, W, P2/1836/66
Comes, Nich., Warm., 1604, I, W, P2/C/205
Combe, Philip, widow, Tisb., 1677, I, W, P1/C/327
Coombs, Philip, sen., baker, Heytes., 1730, W, P5/1730/13
Combe, Philippa, Tisb., 1731, W, P2/C/1133
Coombes, Ralph, Horningsham, 1605, AB, I, W, P5/1605/10, P5/8Reg/29C
Combe, Rebecca, sp., Chilton F., 1740, W, P3/C/855
Rd., Wantage, Berks., 1631, AB, P5/1631/31, P5/12Reg/44A
Rd., sen., Bere R., Dorset, 1639, AB, comm, I, P5/1639/19, P5/13Reg/199D
Rd., husb., Alvediston, 1684, AB, NW, P2/C/745
Rd., Martin, Hants, 1742, I, W, P2/C/1218
Coombs, Rd., yeo., Berwick St Jas., 1799, W, P1/C/1105, P1/15Reg/193
Coombs, Rd., gardener, Sal., 1831, W, Wr, P4/1831/3

Coombes, Robt., Barford St Mart., 1588, AB, P2/C/71, P2/7Reg/114C
Robt., Durley, Burbage, 1598, AB, T (children: Margery, Thomasine & Eliz. C.), P5/1598/53, P5/6Reg/203A
Combe, Robt., yeo., Chiseldon, 1642, I, W (NEP), P3/C/271
Coombs, Robt., yeo., Swindon, 1662, AB, I, W, P1/C/248
Coombes, Roger, sen., yeo., Alvediston, 1670, I, W, P2/C/611
Combe, Sam., Netherb., Dorset, 1684, AB, I, P17/236
Coombe, Sarah, sp., Lyme R., Dorset, [1636], W (NEP), P5/1636/61
Coombs, Sarah, sp., Woolley, Bradford A., 1786, W, P2/C/1439
Coombs, Sarah, wife, Warm., 1824, AB, Wr, P2/1824/69
Coombs, Steph., [farmer], Dunge Farm, Steeple A., 1791-93, AB, a/c, comm (2), L, receipt, witness statement, P2/C/1463
Combe, Susanna, Farnham, Tollard Royal, Dorset, [1629], I, W, P2/C/386
Coombe, Susanna, sen., widow, Warm., [1644], NW, P2/C/517
Combe, Thos., Chiseldon, [1587], W (NEP), P3/1Reg/4
Combe, Thos., yeo., Chicksgrove, Tisb., 1593, I, T, W, P2/C/122
Coombe, Thos., Bridzor, Tisb., 1614-16, AB, a/c, I, P2/C/277, P2/8Reg/238A
Thos., clerk and vicar, Urchf., 1686, AB, I, P1/C/1114
Coombs, Thos., clothw., Westb. L., 1705, W, P25/1705/2
Coombs, Thos., broad weaver, Trowb., 1759, comm, W, P1/C/895, P1/11Reg/373B
Coombs, Thos., labourer, Broad C., 1820, W, Wr, P2/1820/17
Combe, Tristram, Thornford, Dorset, 1636, AB, a/c, I, P5/1636/13, P5/12Reg/255B
Combe, Tristram, mercer, Tisb., 1696, AB, I, P2/C/861
Coombes, Tristram, Beer Hackett, Dorset, 1699, AB, I, P5/1699/9
Walter, Sal. St Thos., 1679, AB, I, P4/1679/4
Walter, Wilton, 1714, AB, P1/C/544
Combe, Wm., Bourton, Gillingham, Dorset, 1561, W, P27/1Reg/9A
Coombe, Wm., sen., Yetm., Dorset, 1593, W, P5/6Reg/18B
Combe, Wm., sen., Enmore Grn, Motc., Dorset, 1593, AB, I, W, P5/1592/18
Combe, Wm., husb., Chards., Devon, 1605, W, P5/1605/16, P5/8Reg/81A
Coombes, Wm., [shoemaker], Southbrook, Bere R., Dorset, 1617, AB (severely damaged), comm, I (severely damaged), P5/1617/10, P5/9Reg/216E
Comes, Wm., husb., Chute, 1619, I, W, P5/1619/89, P5/10Reg/37B
Combe, Wm., yeo., Farnham, Tollard Royal, Dorset, 1620, I, W, P2/C/316
Combe, Wm., gent., Chicksgrove, Tisb., 1660, AB, comm, P1/C/236
Wm., innholder, Sal. St Edmd., 1674, AB, I, P4/1674/3
Coombe, Wm., yeo., Enmore Grn, Motc., Dorset, 1697, AB, I, P19/79
Coombes, Wm., gent., Southbrook, Bere R., Dorset, 1708, I (detailed), W, P5/1708/21, P5/15Reg/81
Coombs, Wm., serge weaver, Warm., 1709, I, W, P2/C/952
Combe, Wm., yeo., Chiseldon, 1714, W, P3/C/691
Coombe, Wm., yeo., Wambrook, Somerset, 1726, W, P14/137
Coombs, Wm., sen., broad weaver, Bradford A., 1776, W, P1/C/991, P1/13Reg/93A
Coombe, Wm., widower, Enmore Grn, Motc., Dorset, 1789, W, P19/187
Coombs, Wm., Sal., 1791, AB, P4/1791/8
Coombs, Wm., yeo., N. Bradley, 1813, AB, comm, W, P2/1813/62
Coombs, Wm., gent., Woolley, Bradford A., 1816, W, Wr, P2/1816/69
Coombs, Wm., Sal., 1819, AB, P4/1819/2
Coombs, Wm., gunmaker, Sal., 1823, W, Wr, P1/1823/19
Coombs, Wm., Martin, Hants, 1845, AB, aff, D, W, Wr, P1/1845/48
see also Hillary als C.; Richards als C.
Comden *see* Camden
Comely *see* Comley
Comer, Comer, Wm., husb., Anderson, Dorset, 1579, AB, P5/1579/13, P5/3Reg/147B
Comes *see* Combes
Comfort, Comfort, Marian, widow, Edington, 1597, I, P2/C/154
Comfort, Wm., husb., Edington, 1581, W, P2/6Reg/27B
Comfrey, Cumfrey, Jas., Sutton Poyntz, Dorset, 1573, AB, P5/3Reg/20C
Comfrey, Thos., Sutton Poyntz, Dorset, 1609, AB, I, T, P5/1609/15, P5/8Reg/164C
Comin, Coming, Comings *see* Cummins
Comley, Comly, Aldhelm, yeo., Gt. Somerford, 1636, I, W, P3/C/220
Aldhelm, yeo., Rodbourne, Malm., 1639, I, W, P3/C/245
Aldhelm, labourer *or* yeo., Gt. Somerford, 1733, I, W, P3/C/817

Comly, Betty, widow, Nettleton, 1802, W, P3/1802/70
Eliz., widow, Corsham, 1687, AB, I, W, P29/C/11, P29/1Reg/238B
Frances, widow, Gt. Somerford, 1684, AB, I, P3/C/495
Comly, Geoff., Gt. Somerford, 1750, AB, P3/C/905
Comly, Jas., gent., W. Kington, 1854, O, W, Wr, P3/1854/43
Comly, Jane, widow, Devizes, 1687, I, W, P1/C/390
Comly, Joan, widow, Chipp., 1630, I, W, P3/C/170
Jn., Gt. Somerford, 1570, W, P1/1Reg/122D
Comly, Jn., Chipp., 1617, I, W, P3/C/89
Jn., sen., yeo., Startley Farm, Gt. Somerford, 1634, I, W, P1/C/148
Jn., mercer, Corsham, 1684, AB, I, W, P29/C/8, P29/1Reg/221B
Jn., Melk., 1698, AB, I, P2/C/876
Rd., yeo., Startley, Gt. Somerford, 1634, I, W, P3/C/202
Comly, Robt., Startley, Gt. Somerford, 1637, AB, a/c, I, P3/C/226
Sabina, widow, late of Fairford but left goods at Castle Eaton, 1751, W, P3/C/912
Comely, Sarah *see* Edith Tawney
Theophilus, yeo., Gt. Somerford, 1763, W, P3/C/973
Cumly, Theophilus, Gt. Somerford, 1782, W, P1/C/1030, P1/13Reg/382
Thos., cordw., Gt. Somerford, 1626, I, W, P3/C/146
Thos., husb., Rodbourne, Malm., 1679, AB, I, P3/C/421
Comly, Thos., woolcomber, Gt. Somerford, 1723, W, P1/C/613, P1/6Reg/454
Comly, Thos., Sopworth, 1816, W, Wr, P3/1816/51
Comly, Wm., yeo., Nettleton, 1800, W, Wr, P3/1800/28
Comly, Wm., yeo., W. Kington, 1854, aff, O, W, Wr, P3/1854/60
Comlin, Cumlyn, Dorothy, widow, Lt. Cheverell, 1635, I, W, P1/C/159
Hugh, W. Lavington, 1625, comm, I, W, P1/C/111
Cumlyn, Hugh, Sal., 1727, AB, P4/1727/7
Joan, widow, Erlestoke, 1628, comm, I, W, P2/C/378
Cumlyn, Judith, Lt. Cheverell, 1625, I, W, P1/C/118
Philip, Lt. Cheverell, 1609, AB, I, T, P2/C/231, P2/8Reg/73B
Comlyn, Sarah, sp., Sal. The Close, 1722, AB, P5/1722/15
Cumlyn, Silas, hatter, Sal., 1717, W, P4/1717/12
Cumlyn, Silas, tailor, Sal., 1784, W, P4/1784/7
Cumlyn, Susanna, sp., Lt. Cheverell, 1720, AB, P2/C/1031
Comlyn, Wm., hatter, Sal., 1732, AB, I, P4/1732/5
Comly *see* Comley
Comlyn *see* Comlin
Commerford, Rd., Devizes, 1688, AB, P1/C/393
Commin *see* Cummins
Compas, Thos., Seend, Melk., 1597, AB, I, P2/C/151
Compton, Adam, Clyffe P., 1740, W, P3/C/856
Alice, widow, Erlestoke, 1705, I, W, P2/C/926
Ann, widow, Shitterton, Bere R., Dorset, 1826, AB, comm, W, Wr, P5/1826/10
Anna, widow, Netheravon, 1819, W, Wr, P12/213
Arthur, Warm., 1739, AB, P2/C/1191
Chris., sen., cordw., Chitterne AS, 1746, W, P2/C/1237
Dan., gent., Urchf., 1781, comm, W, P2/C/1419
David, Bere R., Dorset, 1751, AB, P5/1751/6
David, gardener, Sal., 1807, W, P4/1807/5
David, carp., Bere R., Dorset, 1809, W, Wr, P5/1809/41
Edmd., shepherd, Idmiston, 1561, I, W, P2/C/13, P2/4Reg/63A
Edwd., husb., Chitterne St My., 1581, W, P2/6Reg/31B
Eliz., Chitterne AS, 1663, I, W, P1/C/257
Eliz., widow, Chitterne AS, 1705, I, W, P2/C/928
Eliz., widow, Martin, Hants, 1721, I, W, P2/C/1044
Eliz., widow, Reading, Berks., 1723, W, P1/C/621, P1/7Reg/7
Eliz., sp., Winterborne K., Dorset, 1733, W, P5/1733/18
Eliz., widow, Martin, Hants, 1734, I, W, P2/C/1165
Eliz., sp., Devizes St Jn., 1737, W, P1/C/746, P1/8Reg/194
Eliz., widow, Chitterne AS, 1759, W, P1/C/908, P1/11Reg/476

Eliz., widow, Bere R., Dorset, 1810, AB, W, Wr, P5/1810/22
Eliz., Garsdon, 1824, W, Wr, P3/1824/21
Eliz., sp., Devizes, 1825, W, Wr, P1/1825/12
Eliz., widow, Avon, Stratford sub C., 1850, W, Wr, P4/1850/12
Eliz., sp., Stert, Urchf., 1852, W, Wr, P1/1852/3
Emanuel, husb. and widower, Croucheston, Bishopstone S., 1790, W, P2/C/1460
Geo., husb., Martin, Hants, 1559, W, P2/4Reg/42B
Geo., yeo., Westwood, 1617, I, W, P2/C/299
Geo., gent., Benham Lovell, Speen, 1723, W, P1/C/624, P1/7Reg/18A
Geo., Martin, Hants, 1732, W, P1/C/711, P1/7Reg/544B
Geo., vict., Wantage, Berks., 1814, W, P23/872
Geo., bach., Bodenham, Nunton and B., 1855, AB, aff, Wr, P1/1855/56
Hy., husb., Bulford, 1593, I, T, W, P2/C/120
Hy., bach., Laverstock, 1844, AB, comm, court proceedings (2), Wr, P2/1844/48
Hester, widow and licenced brewer and retailer of beer, Sherston, 1854, aff, L, W, Wr, P3/1854/26
Humphrey, husb., Chitterne AS, 1625, AB, a/c, I, P1/C/112
Isaac, Heytes., 1853, AB, Wr, P5/1853/11
Isabel, Chitterne AS, 1562, AB (in minority of Edith & Eliz. C.), I, W, P2/C/20, P2/4Reg/93C
Isabel, widow, Chitterne St My., 1589, I, W, P2/C/84
Jas., bach., Chisenbury, Enford, 1793, AB, P2/C/1473
Jas., poulterer, Sal., 1810, W, P4/1810/2
Jas., yeo., Fisherton A., 1851, W, Wr, P1/1851/28
Jas., Chitterne St My., 1851, AB, comm, court proceeding, Wr, P2/1851/22, 27
Compton form. Hewitt, Jane, labourer's wife, Bishopstone S., 1753, AB, P2/C/1276
Joan, Orcheston St Geo., 1748, W, P2/C/1250
Jn., Chitterne St My., 1557, W, P2/3Reg/19A
Jn., Chitterne AS, 1559, W, P2/3Reg/184A
Jn., sen., husb., Wick, Bps. C., 1603, req, W, P24/10
Jn., tailor, Tidpit, Martin, Hants, 1614, I, W, P2/C/275, P2/8Reg/234
Jn., husb., Tidpit, W. Martin, Hants, 1615, I, W, P2/C/282, P2/8Reg/264B
Jn., husb., Chitterne AS, [1623], I, W, P2/C/331
Jn., husb., Devizes St Jn., 1629, I, W, P1/C/134
Jn., husb., Martin, Hants, 1632, I, W, P2/C/409
Jn., husb., Fritham, Bramshaw, Hants, 1664, AB, I, P24/321
Jn., yeo., Rushall, 1674, I, W, P2/C/644
Jn., maltster, Rowde, 1675, AB, I, P3/C/381
Jn., weaver, Bere R., Dorset, 1695, AB, I, W, P5/1695/20
Jn., Chitterne AS, 1711, AB, I, P1/C/517
Jn., yeo., Norton B., 1720, W, P2/C/1030
Jn., Martin, Hants, 1727, AB, P2/C/1079
Jn., tailor, Steeple L., 1732, W, P2/C/1139
Jn., Monkton D., 1741, AB, W, P2/C/1214
Jn., wheelwright, Bere R., Dorset, 1773, W, P5/1773/15, P5/17Reg/71
Jn., yeo., Chitterne AS, 1792, W, P1/C/1073, P1/14Reg/444
Jn., woodman to the Earl of Ilchester, Plaitford, 1810, W, Wr, P2/1810/6
Jn., plumber and glazier, Heytes., 1817, comm, W, Wr, P5/1817/9
Jn., yeo., Bishopstrow, 1822, W, Wr, P2/1822/38
Jn., clock and watchmaker, Calne, 1837, comm, ren, W, Wr, P26/1430
Jn., labourer, Bishopstone S., 1839, W, Wr, P2/1839/23
Jn., farmer, Brixton D., 1846, comm, W, Wr, P2/1846/24
Jos., Orcheston St Geo., 1730-32, AB, P2/C/1113, 1140
Jos., minor, Netheravon, 1733, T, P5/1733/17
Jos., minor, Orcheston St Geo., 1734, T (Jos., aged 16, appoints new guardian), P2/C/1169
Jos., yeo., Lacock, 1795, W, P1/C/1081, P1/14Reg/547
Jos., Charlton, Downton (form. of Britford), 1806, W, P2/1806/14
Jos., farmer, Warm., 1857, aff, W, Wr, P2/1857/33
Josias, weaver, E. Harnham, Britford, 1690, I (detailed), W, P24/726
Maria, sp., Sal. (form. of Netherh. & Fisherton A.), 1849, AB, Wr, P4/1849/18
Mark, Chitterne AS, 1732, AB, W, P2/C/1142
My., widow, Martin, Hants, 1624, I, W, P2/C/334

My., widow, Chitterne AS, 1803, W, P2/1803/23
My., Upavon, 1829, AB, Wr, P1/1829/150
Matthew, Wedh., Urchf., 1773, AB, P1/C/966
Maud, widow, Bulford, 1626, I, W, P2/C/361
Nich., Berwick St Jas., 1666, AB, I, P2/C/565
Parnell, widow, Martin, Hants, 1563, I, W, P2/C/28, P2/4Reg/114B
Peter, Imber, 1637, AB, I, P2/C/449
Rd., husb., Martin, Hants, 1570, W, P2/5Reg/108A
Rd., sen., linen weaver, Martin, Hants, 1698, I, W, P2/C/873
Rd., Chitterne, 1705, W, P2/C/923
Rd., yeo., Newnham, Sutton V., 1731, W, P2/C/1130
Rd., gent., Netheravon, 1779, W, P12/196
Robt., yeo., Chitterne AS, 1714, AB, I, P1/C/551
Robt., yeo., Ashton G., Codf. St P., 1771, W, P2/C/1357
Robt., yeo., Codf. St My., 1830, W, Wr, P2/1830/78
Roger, shepherd, Brixton D., 1611, I, W, P2/C/251
Sam., maltster, Erlestoke, 1695, I, W, P2/C/855
Sarah, sp., Littlecote, Rams., 1721, W, P5/1721/5, P5/16Reg/53B
Sarah, wife, Calne, 1837, AB, W, Wr, P26/1436
Sarah, sp., Corsley, 1851, D, W, Wr, P1/1851/43
Sibyl, widow, Brixton D., 1617, I, W, P2/C/297, P2/8Reg/316D
Steph., Steeple L., 1732, AB, P2/C/1141
Thos., yeo., Martin, Hants, 1714, I, W, P1/C/539, P1/5Reg/305
Thos., minor, Orcheston St Geo., 1740, T (no decd named), P2/C/1201
Thos., Chitterne St My., 1785, AB, app. of guardian, T, P1/C/1041
Thos., Chr. M., 1790, AB, P3/C/1109
Thos., Chitterne St My., 1821, AB, Wr, P2/1821/64
Thos., E. Knoyle, 1833, W, Wr, P2/1833/42
Wm., husb., Kingston D., 1583, I, W, P2/C/64, P2/6Reg/109B
Wm., husb., Bulford, 1619, NW, P1/C/98
Wm., Brixton D., 1628, AB, a/c, I, P2/C/382
Wm., yeo., Martin, Hants, 1685, AB, I, P2/C/762
Wm., W. Harnham, 1715, W, P5/1715/15, P5/15Reg/328B
Wm., yeo., Martin, Hants, 1716, I (detailed), W, P1/C/563, P1/6Reg/9B
Wm., husb., Winterborne K., Dorset, 1730, W, P5/1730/10
Wm., minor, Orcheston St Geo., 1734-35, T (2) (Wm. aged 12 in 1734, appoints new guardians; no mention of decd), P2/C/1166
Wm., servant, Sal. St Edmd., 1763, AB, aff, W, P1/C/930, P1/12Reg/142B
Wm., maltster, Chitterne St My., 1771, W, P2/C/1355
Wm., yeo., Shitterton, Bere R., Dorset, 1803, W, P5/1803/52, P5/19Reg/85
Wm., shopkeeper, Chitterne St My., 1848, W, Wr, P1/1848/44
Wm. Burbidge, gent., E. Knoyle, 1845, W, Wr, P2/1845/27

Conant, Alice, sp., Sal. The Close, 1745, W, P5/1745/5
Cunnant, Jn., miller, Uffc., Devon, 1695, I, W, P5/1695/21

Concience, Concience als Read, Jn., innholder, Wick, Bps. C., 1699, AB, I, P24/561
see also Read als C.

Conduit, Cunditt, Agnes, widow, Keevil, 1594, I, W, P2/C/127
Cunditt, Edith, widow, Hinton, Steeple A., 1621, I, NW, P2/C/1507
Edwd., husb., Winterbourne D., 1629, I, W, P7/29
Cunditt, Eliz., sp., Sal., 1792, AB, P1/C/1072, P1/14Reg/470B
Cunditt, Joan, widow, Keevil (ex. lives in Corsham), 1686, I, W, P29/C/10
Condit, Jn., Lyme R., Dorset, 1622, AB, I, P5/1622/18, P5/10Reg/127D
Jn., Gt. Durnford, 1800, AB, P5/1800/9, P5/18Reg/291B
Cunditt, Jn., yeo., Steeple A., 1825, comm, W, Wr, P2/1825/60
Cunditt, Mgt., Gt. Durnford, 1647, I, W, P5/1647/4, P5/14Reg/98
Cunditt, Rd., Imber, late 16th C., W (NEP), P3/1Reg/37B
Cunditt, Rd., yeo., Gt. Durnford, 1645, I, W, P5/1645/6, P5/14Reg/80B
Cunditt, Rd., yeo., Lt. Durnford, 1673, I, W, P5/1673/45
Cunditt, Rd., [husb.?], Gt. Durnford, 1716, I, W (NEP), P9/40
Cunditt, Rd., labourer, Newton T., 1771, W, P2/C/1361

Robt., Chilmark, 1618, AB, P2/C/308
Roger, Semington, Steeple A., 1697, I, W, P2/C/869
Cunditt, Steph., Keevil, 1599, I, W, P2/C/170
Thos., Gt. Durnford, 1608, AB, I, P5/1607/14, P5/8Reg/109A
Thos., cordw., Folly Lane, Melk., 1752, comm, W, P2/C/1272
Cunditt, Walter, Keevil, 1587, W, P2/7Reg/79A
Cunditt, Wm., sen., Durnford, 1739, AB, ren, Wr, P5/1739/14
Wm., yeo., Folly Lane, Melk., 1751, W, P2/C/1263
Cunditt, Wm., Cholderton, 1770, AB, P1/C/958
Wm., blacksmith, Gt. Woodford, 1841, O, W, Wr, P5/1841/5
Coney, Eleanor, widow, Deptford, Wylye, 1684, W, P1/C/366
Konney, Morgan, yeo., Lacock, 1667, AB, comm, I, P3/K/71
Robt., brickmaker, Sal. The Close, 1848, W, Wr, P5/1848/11
Connell, Rd., Brinkw. & Lydiard T., 1700, I, W, P3/C/625
Connop, My., sp., W. Lavington, 1734, AB, P1/C/718
My., widow, W. Lavington, 1734, AB, P1/C/717
Norris, gent., W. Lavington, 1738, AB, ren, P1/C/765
Rd., W. Lavington, 1736, AB, P1/C/742
Conscience *see* Concience
Constable, Alice, widow, Wanb., 1826, AB, Wr, P3/1826/27
Edwd., blacksmith, Sutton C., Berks., 1704, I (detailed), W, P1/C/489
Edwd., yeo., Tockenham, 1728, W, P3/C/777
Eliz., widow, Chaddington, Lydiard T., 1632, I, W, P3/C/183
Eliz., sp., Purton, 1702, W, P3/C/642
Jn., Wrou., 1822, AB, comm, Wr, P3/1822/9
Rd., Radley, Berks., 1759, AB, P1/C/900
Rd., yeo., Wanb., 1823, comm, W, Wr, P3/1823/4
Robt., Ewen, Kemble, 1693, AB, P3/C/564
Wm., Ewen, Kemble, 1614, AB, I, P3/C/72
Conway, Eliz., sp., Hatchlands, Netherb., Dorset, 1803, W (& cod), P5/1803/53, P5/19Reg/87
Eliz., Binghams, Netherb., Dorset, 1813, O, W, P17/600
Geo., clerk and rector, Wilton, 1754, AB (2), ren, W, P1/C/866, P1/11Reg/147
Hannah, widow, Malm., 1711, I, W (NEP), P3/C/679
Joan, wife, Netherb., Dorset, 1764, AB, P17/559
Jn., gent., Beam., Dorset, 1745, W, P17/497
Jos., Beam., Dorset, 1697, AB, I, P17/122
Jos., Beam., Dorset, 1738, AB, P17/469
Jos., Beam., Dorset, 1750, AB, P17/517
Jos., cordw., Enmore Grn, Motc., Dorset, 1751, W, P19/149
My., widow, Beam., Dorset, 1676, I, W, P5/1676/13
Thos., sen., gent., Coombe, Beam., Dorset, 1757, W, P17/534
Wm., innholder, Enmore Grn, Motc., Dorset, 1696, AB, I, P19/71
Cooe, Chas., Sal., 1825, AB, Wr, P4/1825/3
Jn., Britford, 1719, AB, I, P24/632
Jn., Britford, 1779, AB, P24/1121
Sarah, sp., Bodenham, Nunton and B., 1850, AB, D, O, W, Wr, P2/1850/54
Cook, Cooke, Agnes, widow, Rams., 1618, I, W, P5/1618/7, P5/9Reg/219A
Alexander, farmer, Chards., Devon, 1726, W, P14/138
Cook als Somerset, Alice, widow, Clatford, Preshute, 1697, I, W, P1/C/455
Cooke, Ann, widow, Latton, 1640, I, W, P3/C/253
Cooke, Ann, widow, Erlestoke, 1691, I, W, P2/C/816
Ann, widow, Cholsey, Berks., 1729, I, W, P1/C/666, P1/7Reg/254B
Ann, widow, Codf. St My., 1753, AB, P2/C/1273
Ann, sp., Shalbourne, Berks., 1768, AB, ren, P23/722
Cooke, Anth., clothier, Sal., 1677, AB, a/c, I, P4/1677/7
Cooke, Arthur, Bps. C., 1723, I, W, P24/881
Baldwin, tailor, Langley Burrell, 1768, comm, W, P3/C/1005
Betty, sp., Latton, 1811, W, Wr, P3/1811/13
Cooke, Cath., widow, Hurst, Berks., 1677, AB, I, P5/1677/12
Cath., widow, Bps. C., 1701, I, W, P24/552

Charity, sp., Keevil, 1834, W, Wr, P2/1834/30
Cooke, Chas., sen., shepherd, Idmiston, 1694, I, W, P2/C/841
Chas., sen., shepherd, Idmiston, 1731, I, W, P2/C/1132
Chas., farmer, Drynham, N. Bradley, 1816, comm, W, Wr, P2/1816/66
Chas., blacksmith, Chute, 1833, O, W, Wr, P5/1833/13
Chas., Chapmanslade, Corsley, 1845, AB, Wr, P1/1845/81
Cooke, Chris., yeo., Codf. St My., 1689, comm, I, NW, P2/C/791
Chris., clothw., Damerham, Hants, 1714, I, W, P1/C/542, P1/5Reg/333A
Cicely, widow, Chr. M., 1635, I, W, P3/C/206
Dan., Aldbourne, 1809, W, Wr, P3/1809/42
David, sen., whitesmith, Reading, Berks., 1832, W, Wr, P1/1832/111
Cooke, Dorothy, widow, Lyme R., Dorset, 1638, I, W, P5/1638/23, P5/13Reg/101
Ebenezer Hy., attorney's clerk, Devizes, 1841, comm, W, Wr, P1/1841/9
Cooke, Edith, widow, Lacock, 1602, W, P3/1Reg/78
Cooke, Edith, widow, Wantage, Berks., 1638, AB, a/c, I, P5/1638/24, P5/13Reg/140A
Cooke, Edith, widow, Latton, 1752, AB, P3/C/918
Cooke, Edith, sp., Horton, Bps. C., 1778, AB, P24/1127
Cooke, Edmd., shepherd, Hackpen, Chiseldon, 1665, I, W, P3/C/305
Cook als Somerset, Edmd., yeo., Pewsey, [1708], W (NEP), P3/C/668
Edmd., yeo., Chiseldon, 1746, W, P3/C/891
Edmd., baker, Marl., 1781, affs (3), W, P1/C/1027, P1/13Reg/331
Cook als Somerset, Edwd., Wilton, Gt. Bedwyn, 1578, T, W, P5/1578/13, P5/3Reg/103C
Cooke, Edwd., husb., Heytes., 1585, AB, I, T, P5/1584/6, P5/4Reg/101A
Cooke, Edwd., yeo., Foxham, Bremhill, 1636, I, W, P3/C/221
Cooke, Edwd., yeo., Foxham, Bremhill, 1678, AB, a/c, comm, I, P3/C/412
Edwd., mercer, Trowb., 1692, I, W, P1/C/200
Cook als Somerset, Eleanor, widow, Wilton, Gt. Bedwyn, 1670, I, W, P5/1670/52
Cooke, Eliza, minor, Laverstock, 1845, app. of guardian, O, T (Eliza & Wm. C. are grandchildren of Wm. C. decd), P1/1845/65-66
Eliz., widow, Chute, 1706, W, P7/99
Cooke, Eliz., widow, Amesb., 1732, AB, P2/C/1144
Eliz., widow, Beam., Dorset, 1753, W, P17/523
Cooke, Eliz., yeo.'s wife, Sal., 1765, W, P4/1765/3
Cooke, Eliz., Marl., 1786, AB, P1/C/1048
Eliz., widow, Yatton K., 1813, W, Wr, P3/1813/30
Eliz., sp., Latton, 1817, W, Wr, P3/1817/25
Eliz., sp., Latton, 1838, O, W, Wr, P3/1838/21
Cooke, Eliz. Bailey, sp., Collingbourne K., 1829, AB, Wr, P3/1829/6
Cooke, Gabriel, Idmiston, 1697, AB, I, P2/C/864
Cooke, Geo., yeo., Foxham, Bremhill, 1662, I, W, P1/C/252
Cooke, Geo., sen., butcher, Chute, 1705, comm, W, P7/93
Geo., blacksmith, Chute, 1769, W, P7/164
Geo., tailor, Marl., 1825, W, Wr, P1/1825/14
Geo., yeo., Crudwell, 1857, aff, O, W, Wr, P3/1857/32
Cooke, Giles, N. Bradley, 1581, W, P2/6Reg/28A
Giles, Stratfield M., Berks., 1738, AB, P1/C/757
Grace, widow, Codf. St My., 1754, W, P2/C/1283
Cook als Hacker, Gregory, Fisherton A., 1594, AB, I, P2/C/125
Cooke, Hy., Rams., 1599, W, P5/1599/5, P5/6Reg/244A
Cooke, Hy., yeo., Milborne Stileham, Bere R., Dorset, 1631, AB, comm, I, P5/1631/21, P5/11Reg/163B
Hy., spurrier, Sal., 1636, AB, I (detailed), P4/1636/3
Cooke, Hy., Milborne Stileham, Bere R., Dorset, 1639, AB, P5/1639/18, P5/13Reg/165B
Cooke, Hy., yeo., Sutton V., 1641, AB, a/c, I, P2/C/494
Cooke, Hy., butcher, Ludg., 1647, AB, P2/C/531
Cooke, Hy., husb., Erlestoke, 1647, AB, I, ren, P2/C/532
Cooke, Hy., Erlestoke, 1675, AB, I, P2/C/656
Cooke, Hy., bellowsmaker, Sal., 1676, AB, a/c, I (2), P4/1676/12
Hy., pattenmaker, Sal., 1687, AB, I, W, P4/1687/3
Cooke, Hy., yeo., Erlestoke, 1698, W, P2/C/875
Hy., tailor, Uffington, Berks., 1738, W, P1/C/754, P1/8Reg/255

Hy., Sal., 1745, W, P4/1745/10
Hy., gent., Collingbourne D., 1825, W, Wr, P21/12/44
Cooke, Hugh, carp., Devizes St My., 1640, I, W, P1/C/187
Cooke, Humphrey, sen., yeo., Upper Stratton, Stratton St Mgt., 1683, I, W, P1/C/362
Cooke, Jas., innkeeper, Froxfield, 1720, AB, I, P1/C/594
Jas., brazier, Calne, 1736, comm, W, P26/789
Cooke, Jane, widow, Quemerford, Calne, 1662, W, P26/108
Cooke, Jane *see* Joan *or* Jane, 1682
Cooke, Jane, widow, Amesb., 1689, I, W, P2/C/797
Cooke, Jane, widow, Donhead St A., 1690, AB, I, W, P2/C/801
Cooke, Jane, widow, Newbury, Berks., 1723, AB, P1/C/609
Jane, widow, Nursteed, Bps. C., 1773, AB, P24/1143
Jane, widow, Devizes, 1800, W, P1/1800/16, P1/15Reg/218
Jane, widow, Lockeridge, Overton, 1814, AB, comm, P1/1814/46
Cooke, Jane, Marl., 1838, comm, W, Wr, P1/1838/4
Jane, widow, Aldbourne, 1854, aff, L, O, W, Wr, P3/1854/52
Cooke, Jasper, Lacock, 1601, W, P3/1Reg/53C
Cook *or* Coke, Joan, Bere R., Dorset, 1589, AB, I, P5/1589/9
Cooke, Joan, widow, Gt. Cheverell, 1597, I, W, P2/C/147
Cooke, Joan *or* Jane, widow, Chiseldon, 1682, I, W, P3/C/460
Joan, widow, Farley, Alderbury, 1763, W, P26/996
Joanna, sp., Trowb., 1854, aff, O, W, Wr, P1/1854/2
Cooke, Jn., Bere R., Dorset, 1589, AB, P5/5Reg/54A
Cooke, Jn., miller, Steeple L., 1592, I, T, W, P2/C/110
Cooke, Jn., husb., Latton, 1606, W, P1/C/36
Cooke, Jn., sen., Steeple L., 1616, AB, P2/C/291
Cooke, Jn., sen., Erlestoke, 1625, I, W, P2/C/355
Cooke, Jn., Dilton, Westb., 1638, AB, I, P25/1638/8
Cooke, Jn., Rams., 1639, AB, I, P5/1639/22, P5/13Reg/185A
Cooke, Jn., yeo., Wilton, 1643, I, P30/39
Cooke, Jn., gent., Pott., 1669, AB, I, P1/C/296
Cooke, Jn., spurrier, Sal., 1669, AB, a/c, I (detailed), P4/1669/16
Cooke, Jn., yeo., Luckington, 1670, I, W, P3/C/341
Cook als Somerset, Jn., yeo., Urchf., 1677, AB, I, P2/C/669
Cook als Somerset, Jn., Lt. Bedwyn, 1682, AB, P5/1682/25
Jn., husb., Stockton, 1683, NW, P2/C/726
Cooke, Jn., husb., Wilton, Gt. Bedwyn, 1683, I, P5/1682/27
Cooke, Jn., sen., miller, Howe Mill, Rams., 1683, I, W, P5/1683/12
Cook als Garmy, Jn., sen., butcher, Hungerford, Berks., 1684, I, W, P23/130
Cooke, Jn., clothier, Bewley, Lacock, 1690, I, W, P3/C/545
Cooke, Jn., sen., collarmaker, Codf. St My., 1692, I, W, P1/C/428
Cooke, Jn., yeo., Farley, Alderbury, 1693, ren, W, P26/415
Jn., yeo., Bourton, Bps. C., 1701, AB, I, P24/553
Jn., Fisherton A., 1702, W, P2/C/897
Cooke, Jn., sen., Farley, Alderbury, 1703, I, W, P26/497
Cooke, Jn., Chute, 1703, AB, I, P7/90
Jn., jun., butcher, Ludg., 1706, I, W, P2/C/931
Jn., collarmaker, Heytes., 1708, AB, I, P5/1708/20
Cooke, Jn., Ludg., 1709, AB, I, P2/C/958
Jn., jun., Poulshot, 1710, NW, P2/C/969
Jn., vicar, Hullavington, 1710, AB, I, P3/C/678
Cooke, Jn., minor, Farley, Alderbury, 1713, T, P26/578
Cooke, Jn., husb., Baynton, Edington, 1716, AB, L, ren, P2/C/1007
Cooke, Jn., broad weaver, Sutton V., 1717, NW, P2/C/1013
Jn., yeo., Quemerford, Calne, 1720, I (detailed), W, P26/633
Cooke, Jn., yeo., Chilton F., 1720, W, P1/C/588, P1/6Reg/204
Jn., clothw., Bradford A., 1721, W, P2/C/1045
Cooke, Jn., sen., yeo., Latton, 1726, W, P1/C/655, P1/7Reg/155
Jn., tripe seller, Sal., 1729, W, P4/1729/4
Cooke, Jn., sen., fellmonger, Devizes, 1738, W, P1/C/750, P1/8Reg/211

Jn., vict., Hippenscombe, 1738, AB, I (detailed), W, P1/C/747
Jn., yeo., Collingbourne K., 1738, W, P1/8Reg/200
Cooke, Jn., sen., gent., Alderbury, 1741, W, P26/824
Jn., labourer, E. Coulston, 1742, AB, I, P2/C/1225
Jn., collarmaker, Codf. St My., 1751, AB, W, P2/C/1262
Cooke, Jn., Farley, Alderbury, 1755, AB, P26/938
Jn., cooper and innholder, Chute, 1756, W, P7/150
Jn., labourer, Chute, 1756, W, P7/152
Jn., sen., hatmaker, Abingdon, Berks., 1770, W, P1/C/961, P1/12Reg/361A
Jn., yeo., Collingbourne D., 1797, W, P21/11/42
Cooke, Jn., bach., Westb., 1802, AB, P25/1802/6
Jn., cordw., Erlestoke, 1808, W, Wr, P2/1808/10
Jn., Ashton K., 1816, W, Wr, P3/1816/33
Jn., yeo., Swindon, 1816, comm, W, Wr, P3/1816/15
Jn., Ashton K., 1819, W, Wr, P3/1819/52
Cooke, Jn., Overton, 1819, AB, comm, Wr, P3/1819/41
Jn., yeo., Manton, Preshute, 1821, comm, W, Wr, P1/1821/10
Jn., cordw., Chipp., 1829, W, Wr, P1/1829/102
Cooke, Jn., shoemaker, Sal., 1830, AB, W, Wr, P4/1830/8
Cooke, Jos., draper, Wantage, Berks., 1698, AB, I (detailed), P23/229
Cooke, Jos., yeo., Trowb., 1726, W, P1/C/654, P1/7Reg/150
Jos., labourer, Damerham, Hants, 1746, D, I, NW (never saw final W & only made draft by mouth - written up too late for him to sign), P2/C/1235
Jos., Upton S., 1774, AB, P2/C/1369
Cooke, Julian, widow, no abode stated, 1605, I, W, P3/C/20
Cooke, Leonard, Sal. St Thos., 1685, AB, I, ren, P4/1685/7
Levi, yeo., Wanb., 1837, W, Wr, P3/1837/27
Cooke, Mgt., sp., Chr. M., 1635, I, W, P3/C/207
Cooke, Mgt., Wilton, Gt. Bedwyn, 1648, AB, P21/1/72
Cooke, Mgt., widow, Chards., Devon, 1709, W, P14/111
Mgt., widow, Sal., 1732, W, P1/C/712, P1/7Reg/545
Cooke, Margery, widow, Foxham, Bremhill, 1684, I, W, P3/C/487
Mark, husb., Ludg., 1791, W, P2/C/1461
My., widow, Latton, 1741, W, P3/C/863
My., wife, Wootton B., 1744, AB, P1/C/797
My., Chute, 1837, comm, W, Wr, P7/205
My., widow, Devizes, 1839, AB, comm, Wr, P1/1839/4
Cooke, Matthew, gent., Farley, Alderbury, 1690, I, W, P26/377
Maurice, butcher, Wrou., 1793, comm, W, P3/C/1119
Michael, sen., Bps. C., 1719, AB, comm, W, P24/638
Michael, gent., W. Overton, 1722, AB, I, P3/C/740
Cooke, Michael, minor, Overton, 1724, T, P3/C/751
Michael, yeo., Horton, Bps. C., 1744, W, P24/968
Michael, jun., yeo., W. Overton, 1780, W, P3/C/1065
Michael, gent., W. Overton, 1783, W, P1/C/1037, P1/13Reg/498
Miriam, Latton, 1798, W, Wr, P3/C/1139
Cooke, Nathaniel, sailor, Lyme R., Dorset, 1636, AB, a/c, I, P16/471
Cooke, Nathaniel, fuller, Bratton, Westb., 1663, AB, I, P25/1663/8
Cooke, Patience, clothier's wife, Chipp., 1727, AB, P3/C/770
Cooke, Peter, tailor, Damerham, Hants, 1614, I, W, P2/C/276, P2/8Reg/236A
Cooke, Rachel, widow, Poulshot, 1728, W, P2/C/1095
Cooke, Ralph, Sherb., Dorset, 1740, W, Wr, P5/1740/21
Cooke, Ralph, maltster, Collingbourne K., 1771, W, P3/C/1021
Rebecca, yeo.'s widow, Chiseldon, 1764, W, P3/C/981
Rebecca, sp., Ashton K., 1839, O, W, Wr, P3/1839/16
Cooke, Rd., vicar of Charlton, Charl. nr. P., 1592, I, W, P2/C/118
Koock, Rd., weaver, Leighs Marsh, Dilton, Westb., 1636, I, W, P25/1636/7
Cooke, Rd., Wantage, Berks., 1675, AB, I, P23/52
Cooke, Rd., butcher, Chute, 1691, I, W, P7/82
Cooke, Rd., gent., Nether St., Bromham, 1707, AB, I (2 - 1 a copy)., P3/C/663

Rd., sen., butcher, Ludg., 1712, W, P2/C/981
Rd., Langley Burrell, 1718, AB, I, P3/C/717
Cooke, Rd., sen., yeo., Horton, Bps. C., 1739, comm, W, P24/900
Rd., vict., Nursteed, Bps. C., 1762, W, P24/1103
Rd., publican, Twyford, Hurst, Berks., 1765, W, P5/1765/9
Rd., Motc., Dorset, 1802, W, P27/1/575
Rd., dairyman, Poulshot, 1827, O, W, Wr, P2/1827/18
Cooke, Rd., brushmaker, Sal., 1838, W, Wr, P4/1838/7
Rd., Clatford, Preshute, 1853, AB, O, Wr, P1/1853/15
Cooke, Robt., yeo., Werg, Mildenhall, 1618, I, W (both damaged), P3/C/98
Cooke, Robt., Foxham, Bremhill, 1630, I, W, P3/C/171
Cooke, Robt., tailor, Wilton, Gt. Bedwyn, 1641, I, W, P5/1641/25, P5/14Reg/10A
Cooke, Robt., clothier, Melk., 1647, I, W, P2/C/534
Cook als Somerset, Robt., yeo., Wilton, Gt. Bedwyn, 1678, AB, comm, I, W (NEP), P21/2/55
Cooke, Robt., Amesb., 1685, AB, a/c, I, P2/C/749
Robt., Bere R., Dorset, 1689, AB, P5/1689/14
Robt., Bratton, Westb., 1690, AB, I (ref. to millhouse), P25/1690/5
Robt., sen., yeo., Chards., Devon, 1699, AB, I, P14/88
Robt., yeo., Chards., Devon, 1715, I, W, P14/132
Robt., butcher, Chute, 1717, W, P7/112
Robt., innholder, Speenhamland, Berks., 1750, W, P1/C/840, P1/10Reg/368
Robt., yeo., Hullavington, 1814, W, Wr, P1/1814/110
Roger, Foxham, Bremhill, 1610, W, P3/C/49
Cooke, Sam., Newbury, Berks., 1708, AB, P1/C/502
Cooke, Sam., Bewley, Lacock, 1723, AB, comm, P3/C/752
Cooke, Sam., apothecary, Wantage, Berks., 1726, W, P23/438
Cooke, Sam., Trowb., 1734, AB, comm, P1/C/719, P1/7Reg/596A
Sam., brazier, Wootton B., 1740, AB, cit, L, P3/C/857
Sam., yeo., Tytherton L., Chipp., 1785, W, P3/C/1088
Sarah, widow, Chards., Devon, 1716, I, W, P5/1716/21, P5/15Reg/343A
Sarah, Idmiston, 1783, W, P1/C/1033, P1/13Reg/423B
Sarah, widow, Chards., Devon, 1787, W, P14/190
Sarah, sp., W. Grimstead, 1826, W, Wr, P1/1826/40
Simon, Coate, Bps. C., 1794, comm, W, P24/1218
Cooke, Steph., husb., Gt. Cheverell, 1574, W, P2/5Reg/211B
Cooke, Steph., miller, Rams., 1635, I, W, P5/1635/30, P5/12Reg/265
Cooke, Susanna, widow, Erlestoke, 1670, I, W, P2/C/604
Cook als Kingman, Susanna, widow, Gillingham, Dorset, 1689, I, P27/1/112
Susanna, Foxham, Bremhill, 1693, W (NEP), P3/C/565
Susanna, widow, Horton, Bps. C., 1770, AB, P24/1073
Cooke, Susanna, widow, Sal., 1841, AB, Wr, P1/1841/1
Cooke, Thos., husb., S. Wraxall, 1572, W, P2/5Reg/153
Cook *or* Coke, Thos., dyer, Mere, 1578-79, I, T, W, P5/1578/12, P5/3Reg/107A
Cooke, Thos., Donhead St A., 1579, W, P2/5Reg/342A
Cooke, Thos., fuller, Mount Mill, Sutton V., 1610, I, W, P2/C/243, P2/8Reg/140A
Thos., gent., Horton, Bps. C., 1620, deed of gift, D, P24/61
Cooke, Thos., Chards., Devon, 1622, AB, I, NW, P5/1622/14
Cooke, Thos., tailor, Damerham, Hants, 1633, I, W, P2/C/418, P2/9Reg/31B
Cooke, Thos., husb., Steeple L., [1635], I, W, P2/C/433, P2/9Reg/87
Cooke, Thos., dyer, Bere R., Dorset, 1668, I, W, P5/1668/14
Cooke, Thos., Gillingham, Dorset, 1670, AB, P27/1/38
Cooke, Thos., Bps. C., 1674, AB, I, P24/445
Cooke, Thos., Bps. C., 1680, I, W, P24/420
Cooke, Thos., Damerham, Hants, 1682, AB, I, P2/C/716
Cooke, Thos., [shoemaker], Wantage, Berks., 1696, AB, I (incomplete), P5/1696/12
Cooke, Thos., yeo., Chards., Devon, 1701, AB, I, P5/1701/13
Cooke, Thos., yeo., Upper Stratton, Stratton St Mgt., 1715, I, W, P3/C/697
Cooke, Thos., gent., Shaw Dean, Shaw cum Donnington, Berks., 1726, W, P1/C/649, P1/7Reg/108B
Thos., [haberdasher], Highw., 1729, AB, I, P10/1729/1
Thos., yeo., Latton, 1729, W, P3/C/783

Thos., sen., Ludg., 1739, AB, P2/C/1194
Cooke, Thos., Pewsey, 1752, O, W, P3/C/919
Thos., Chute, 1756, AB, P7/151
Thos., yeo., Latton, 1765, W, P3/C/989
Cooke, Thos., Ludg., 1773, AB, P1/C/977
Thos., Figh., 1800, AB, P26/1227
Cooke, Thos., gent., E. Hanney, W. Hanney, Berks., 1801, W, P1/1801/56, P1/15Reg/271
Thos., yeo., Latton, 1802, W, P3/1802/6
Thos., Aldbourne, 1803, AB, P3/1803/20
Thos., widower, Poulton, 1811, AB, Wr, P1/1811/47
Thos., blacksmith, Chute, 1819, O, W, Wr, P7/194
Thos., labourer, Bratton, Westb., 1828, comm, W, Wr, P25/1828/5
Cooke, Tryphena, Collingbourne D., 1821, W, Wr, P21/12/41
Cooke, Wm., Sherb., Dorset, 1587, AB, P5/4Reg/147A
Cooke, Wm., husb., Swallowcliffe, 1597, AB, I, W, P5/1596/19, P5/6Reg/146B
Wm., sen., yeo., Bothampstead, Hampstead N., Berks., 1611, I, W, P1/C/45
Cooke, Wm., collarmaker, Codf. St P., [1626], I, W, P2/C/360
Cooke, Wm., Wilton, Gt. Bedwyn, 1639, I, W, P21/1/43
Cooke, Wm., Chute, 1639, AB, I, P7/21
Cooke, Wm., weaver, Erlestoke, 1664, AB, I, P2/C/556
Cooke, Wm., Rams., 1674, AB, a/c, I, P5/1674/21
Cooke, Wm., fanmaker, Hurst, Berks., 1677, W, P5/1677/10
Cooke, Wm., tailor, Sherb., Dorset, 1684, AB, comm, I, ren, W, P5/1684/21
Cooke, Wm., yeo., Ashton G., Codf. St P., 1705, I, W, P2/C/922
Cooke, Wm., Amesb., 1715, AB, P2/C/998
Wm., Collingbourne D., 1720, W, P21/8/3
Cooke, Wm., Farley, Alderbury, 1728, W, P26/731
Wm., W. Field, Latton, 1729, W, P3/C/785
Wm., sen., yeo., Latton, 1730, W, P3/C/802
Wm., Collingbourne D., 1748, W, P21/10/3
Wm., Sal., 1755, AB, P4/1755/4
Wm., labourer, Collingbourne D., 1773, W, P21/11/4
Cooke, Wm., baker, Devizes, 1787, AB, comm, ren, W, P1/C/1055, P1/14Reg/174A
Wm., cordw., Erlestoke, 1802, W, P2/1802/75
Wm., yeo., Latton, 1802, W, P3/1802/19
Wm., yeo., Yatton K., 1811, W, Wr, P3/1811/23
Wm., Chipp., 1814, AB, P1/1814/112
Wm., Haydon Wick, Rodbourne C., 1825, W, Wr, P3/1825/64
Wm., yeo., Broad C., 1826, W, Wr, P1/1826/26
Cooke, Wm., labourer, Milford & Laverstock, 1845, AB, O, W, Wr, P1/1845/66
Wm., Warm., 1847, AB, comm, Wr, P2/1847/16
Wm., yeo., Westfield Farm, Latton, 1848, O, W, Wr, P3/1848/39
see also Garmy als C.; Hooper als C.; Kingman als C.; Roberts als C.; Somerset als C.
Cookman, Alice, sp., Heytes., 1608, I, draft W, W, P5/1607/15, P5/8Reg/108C
Giles, husb., Ebbesborne Wake, 1717, W, P2/C/1018
Cuckman, Jn., Boyton, 1559, AB, P2/3Reg/170B
Jn., husb., Whitep., 1585, W, P2/6Reg/139C
Jn., Broad C., 1733, AB, P2/C/1157
My., widow, Britford, 1822, W, Wr, P24/1290
Matthew, Bower C., 1728, AB, P2/C/1089
Cookney, Ann, Lyme R., Dorset, 1696, AB, P16/141
Jn., husb., Chards., Devon, 1662, AB, comm, I, L (the author, Rd. Luce, comments on political & church affairs with ref. to both locality & nation), ren, P5/1662/24
Jn., butcher, Lyme R., Dorset, 1811-16, AB, comm (2), W, Wr, P16/376, 383
Nich., butcher, Sal. St Thos., 1633, I, NW, P4/1633/3
Rd., Lyme R., Dorset (d. at sea), 1729, AB, comm, P16/253
Rd., butcher, Lyme R., Dorset, 1810, comm, W, P16/371
Robt., sen., ship's carp., Lyme R., Dorset, 1717, W, P16/206
Roger, Sal., 1664, AB, I, P4/1664/11
Cuckney, Roger, Fisherton A., 1713, AB, P2/C/988

Thos., Chards., Devon, 1690, AB, I, P14/72
Cooksey, Ann, widow, Pott., 1685, I, W, P1/C/371
Cucksey, Arthur, sen., tailor, Scots Lane, Sal., 1695, I, W, P1/C/442
Jane, sp., Cadley Farm, Pott., 1738, W, P1/C/749, P1/8Reg/208
Jn., sen., yeo., Cadley Farm, Pott., 1709, I, W, P1/C/507, P1/5Reg/10
Cuxey, Jn., clothier, Sal., 1716, AB, ren, W, P4/1716/10
Jn., sen., yeo., Cadley Farm, Pott., 1723, I (detailed), W, P1/C/612, P1/6Reg/427
Jn., sen., gent., Cadley Farm, Pott., 1785, comm, W, P1/C/1043, P1/14Reg/62
Jos., Pott., 1785, AB, comm, P1/C/1042
Jos., yeo., Coate, Bps. C., 1837, W, Wr, P24/1354
Cuxey, Sam., clothw., Horningsham (form. of Frome Selwood, Somerset), 1732, W, P5/1732/12
Thos., yeo., Swindon, 1663, I, W, P3/C/292
Thos., yeo., Bromham, 1738, W, P1/C/762, P1/8Reg/330B
Walter, husb., Erlestoke, 1592, I, W, P2/C/115
Wm., no abode stated, 1664, AB, P1/C/269
Wm., Bromham, 1764, AB, P3/C/982
Coole, Alice, widow, Lt. Somerford, 1613, I, W, P3/C/69
Ann, widow, S. Burcombe, 1773, W, P2/C/1365
Edmd., shepherd, Ansty, 1683, AB, I, P2/C/728
Edmd., Linley, Tisb., 1764, W, P2/C/1317
Geo., Devizes, 1803, AB, Wr, P1/1803/8, P1/15Reg/389
Jane, widow, Lt. Somerford, 1665, I, W, P3/C/306
Jane, widow, Devizes, 1805, W, P1/1805/4
Joan, widow, Broad C., 1596, I, W, P2/C/135
Jn., Broad C., 1583, I, T, W, P2/C/62, P2/6Reg/104A
Jn., yeo., Lt. Somerford, 1633, I, W, P3/C/190
Jn., yeo., Lt. Somerford, 1643, AB, L, P1/C/192
Jn., husb., Wrou., 1682, I, W, P3/C/461
Jn., Stratford Tony, 1709, AB, P2/C/950
Jos., sen., clothier and bacon dealer, Devizes, 1796, comm, W, P1/C/1087, P1/15Reg/5
Matthew, miller, S. Burcombe, 1771, W, P2/C/1356
Cool, Nemiah, husb., S. Marston, 1722, W, P5/1722/16, P5/16Reg/73B
Peter, Devizes, 1685, AB, P1/C/370
Peter, brickmaker, Devizes, 1815, O, W, Wr, P1/1815/3
Cools, Rd., Standlynch, Downton, 1680, AB, I, P2/C/690
Robt., sen., yeo., Semley, 1688, I, W, P2/C/783
Cool, Sam., W. Harnham, 1831, AB, P8/84
Steph., husb., Broad C., 1612, I, W, P2/C/265
Susanna, sp., Brinkw., 1676, I, W, P3/C/393
Thos., Maddington, [1562], I, P2/C/22
Thos., Stratton St Mgt., [1584], W (NEP), P3/1Reg/6C
Wm., Hilmarton, 1602, I, W, P1/C/16
Wm., Minety, 1675, AB, I, P3/C/382
see also Coles
Cooleman *see* Coleman
Coolett *see* Collett
Cooley *see* Cully
Coolins *see* Collins
Coolly *see* Cowley and Cully
Cools *see* Coole
Coombe, Coombes, Coombs *see* Combes
Coope, Mgt., widow, Southwick, N. Bradley, 1580, I, W, P2/C/57, P2/6Reg/11C
Wm., Southwick, N. Bradley, 1587, W, P2/7Reg/82A
Wm., husb., Southwick, N. Bradley, 1602, AB, I, W, P2/C/190
Cooper, Abel, sawyer, Sal., 1672, AB, I, P4/1672/3
Cowper, Agnes, widow, Corsley, 1571, W, P2/5Reg/120B
Agnes, widow, Winterslow, 1623, I, W, P2/C/330
Cowper, Alice, widow, Stapleford, 1556, W, P2/3Reg/6A
Ambrose, clothw., Bradford A., 1774, comm, I, W, P2/C/1372
And., blacksmith, Coombe B., 1705, W, P2/C/921

Ann, widow, Gt. Woodford, 1681, I, W, P13/3/4
Ann, widow, W. Lavington, 1681, AB, comm, L, P1/C/355
Ann, Rabson Farm, Winterbourne Bassett, 1694, W, P3/C/579
Ann, widow, N. Tidworth, 1722, W, P2/C/1053
Ann, sp. and [farmer], Brixton D., 1797, W, P2/C/1484
Ann, sp., Aldbourne, 1828, AB, comm, Wr, P3/1828/39
Bridget, sp., Rowde, 1688, AB, comm, I, P3/C/531
Chas., Redlynch, Downton, 1851, AB, Wr, P2/1851/30
Charlotte, widow, Rams., 1837, comm, D, W, Wr, P5/1837/8
Christian, widow, Dinton, 1727, W, P2/C/1081
Edmd., Wokm., Berks., 1583, AB, I, P5/1583/9, P5/4Reg/70A
Edmd., yeo., Pott., 1646, I, W, Wr, P1/C/215
Coper, Edwd., Greenham, Thatcham, Berks., 1616, AB, I, P1/C/79
Edwd., joiner, Sal., 1623, I, NW, P4/1622/5
Edwd., draper, Highw., 1626, I, W, P10/1626/4
Edwd., sen., yeo., Gt. Woodford, 1679, I, W, P5/1679/16
Edwd., Gt. Woodford, 1682, AB, I, P5/1682/21
Edwd., Winterslow, 1733, AB, P2/C/1152
Edwd., sen., yeo., E. Winterslow, 1789, W, Wr, P1/C/1061, P1/14Reg/293
Edwd., Porton, Idmiston, 1790, AB, P2/C/1457
Elias, husb., Pott., 1619, comm, I, W, P1/C/99
Eliz., widow, Upton, Blewbury, Berks., 1603, AB, I, W, P5/1603/16, P5/7Reg/82C
Eliz., widow, Crockerton, Longbridge D., 1639-41, AB, a/c, I, P2/C/472
Eliz., widow, Figh., 1662, AB, I, W, P26/111
Eliz., widow, Yattendon, Berks., 1674, I, W, P1/C/318
Cooper form. Bacon, Eliz., shopkeeper's wife, Wincanton, Somerset but leaving effects at Plaitford, 1755, AB, P2/C/1287
Eliz., widow, W. Grimstead, 1769, W, P2/C/1351
Eliz., sp., Farleigh Wick, Monkton F., 1801, W, Wr, P2/1801/16
Frances, widow, N. Tidworth, 1807, W, P2/1807/32
Francis, yeo., Shalbourne, 1673, I, W (damaged and part lost), P5/1673/10
Francis, bricklayer, Milton L., 1775, comm, W, P3/C/1045
Francis, Ham, 1782, AB, P1/C/1028
Geoff., Boyton, 1674, AB, I, P2/C/638
Geo., husb., Winterbourne M., 1625, AB, a/c (both George C. & Simon Ponting), I, P3/C/137
Geo., yeo., Heddington, 1794, W, P3/C/1124
Geo., draper, Melk., 1841, O, W, Wr, P2/1841/5
Cowper, Gilbt., clerk and vicar, Wanb., 1746, AB, ren, W, P3/C/892
Hy., Netherb., Dorset, 1674, I, P17/270
Hy., sen., Shalbourne, 1720, W, P23/383
Hy., yeo., Whitep., 1783, W, P2/C/1424
Humphrey, yeo., Ham, 1729, I, W, P1/C/1122, P1/7Reg/222B
Humphrey, Ham, 1739, AB, comm, NW, P1/C/768, P1/8Reg/379B
Isaac, surgeon, Collingbourne D., 1810, W, P21/12/25
Jas., Bushton, Clyffe P., 1663, AB, I, P1/C/265
Jas., yeo., Upavon, 1687, AB, I, ren, P1/C/384
Jas., yeo., Tilsh., 1701, W, P2/C/894
Jas., groom to the Earl of Suffolk, Charlton nr Malm., 1775, W, P3/C/1046
Jane, widow, Downton, 1697, W, P2/C/866
Jane, widow, Southcott, Pewsey, 1789, comm, W, P1/C/1062, P1/14Reg/335
Jane, sp. *or* widow, Ham, 1792, W, P3/C/1116
Jasper, husb., W. Lavington, 1667, AB, comm, I, P1/C/283
Joan, Downton, 1617, AB, P2/C/296
Cooper als Kew, Joan, Alton Pr., 1711, AB, P1/C/518
Joan, widow, Milton L., 1758, W, P3/C/949
Joel, yeo., Brixton D., 1780, W, P2/C/1407
Jn., Milston, 1557, AB, W, P2/3Reg/34A, 60C
Jn., sen., Figh., 1562, AB, P5/1Reg/3C
Cowper, Jn., Milston, 1562, AB, P2/4Reg/110B
Cooper als Rogers, Jn., Farley, Alderbury, 1565, AB, P5/1Reg/61A
Jn., Upton, Blewbury, Berks., 1570, W, P5/2Reg/69C

Jn., Milston, 1573, W, P2/5Reg/166A
Jn., Hindon, 1583, W, P2/6Reg/78A
Jn., Figh., [1590], W (NEP), P3/1Reg/32B
Jn., sen., carrier, Corsley, 1601, I, W, P2/C/1505
Jn., Bourton, Bps. C., 1606, a/c, P24/11
Jn., husb., Collingbourne D., 1621, AB, I, P21/1/6
Jn., Malm., 1623, AB, a/c, I, P3/C/124
Jn., husb., Netheravon, 1624, W, P5/1624/7, P5/10Reg/176
Jn., thatcher, Gt. Cheverell, 1625, I, W, P2/C/353
Jn., yeo., Chisenbury, Enford, 1628, I, W, P1/C/133
Cowper, Jn., cook, Maiden B., 1640, I, W, P2/C/491
Jn., sen., Donhead St A., 1644, AB, I (for Jn. & his wife Alice), P2/C/516
Jn., sen., husb., Codf. St My., 1671, AB, I, W (for Jn. & his wife My.), P2/C/618-19
Jn., husb., Longbridge D., 1673, I, NW, P2/C/634
Jn., yeo. and maltster, Downton, [1675], I, W, P2/C/655
Jn., husb., Alton Pr., 1681, AB, I, P3/C/440
Jn., yeo., Charl. nr. P., [1685], I, W, P2/C/760
Jn., sen., market spinner, Urchf., 1695, I, W, P2/C/854
Jn., husb. and yeo., Newton T., 1697, I, W, P2/C/870
Jn., labourer, Wantage, Berks., 1697, I, W, P23/222
Jn., yeo., Shalbourne, 1716, I, W, P5/1716/24, P5/15Reg/356B
Jn., Ebbesborne Wake, 1717, W, P2/C/1017
Jn., Woodford, 1729, I, W, P13/4/23
Jn., bach., Newbury, Berks., 1729, AB, P1/C/676
Jn., sen., yeo., W. Dean, 1731, W, P2/C/1136
Jn., Winterslow, 1733, AB, W, P2/C/1153
Jn., Downton, 1741, AB, P2/C/1211
Jn., Newton T., 1744, AB, P1/C/813
Jn., blacksmith, N. Tidworth, 1749, W, P2/C/1256
Jn., gent., E. Winterslow, 1749, W, P2/C/1255
Jn., sen., husb., Wokm., Berks., 1755, W, P5/1755/9
Jn., E. Grimstead, W. Dean, 1776, W, P2/C/1385
Jn., Whitep., 1787, AB, P2/C/1443
Jn., blacksmith, N. Tidworth, 1791, W, P2/C/1464
Jn., gent., Sal., 1799, receipt, req, W, copy W, P4/1799/11
Jn., yeo., Poulshot, 1799, W, P2/C/1494
Jn., yeo., Hurst, Berks., 1804, W, P5/1804/6, P5/19Reg/99
Jn., yeo., W. Dean, 1812, W, Wr, P2/1812/11
Jn., Poulshot, 1826, AB, P2/1826/20
Jn., yeo., Sindlesham, Hurst, Berks., 1832, AB, aff, O, W, Wr, copy W, P5/1832/17
Jn., Trowb., 1842, AB, aff, comm, Wr, P1/1842/11
Jn., Broxmore, Whitep., 1845, AB, D, W, Wr, P1/1845/77
Jos., broad weaver, Bradford A., 1752, AB, ren, P2/C/1269
Jos., Urchf., 1756-65, AB, W, P1/C/885, P2/C/1325, P1/11Reg/290B
Jos., Downton, 1776, AB, P2/C/1384
Jos., Crookham, Thatcham, Berks., 1779, AB, P1/C/1019
Joyce, widow, Durrington, 1853, AB, D, ren, W, Wr, P2/1853/11
Julian, widow, Gt. Cheverell, 1628, I, T, P1/C/126
Lawr., Wantage, Berks., 1573, W, P5/3Reg/11F
Lawr., yeo., Tilsh., 1705, W, P2/C/920
Leonard, husb., Gt. Wishford, 1682, AB, I, P2/C/711
Magdalen, widow, Collingbourne D., 1625, I, NW, P21/1/11
Mgt., sp., Sal., 1714, W, P4/1714/3
Mgt., widow, Frankleigh, Bradford A., 1758, W, P2/C/1298
Margery, Seend Row, Melk., 1621, I, W, P2/C/322
Margery, Poulshot, 1624, AB, I, P2/C/338
Martha, minor, Sal., 1691, T (no decd named), P4/1691/9
Martha, widow, Odstock, 1805, comm, note, W, P2/1805/16
Mart., husb., Charl. nr. P., 1607-15, AB, a/c, I, P2/C/226
My., widow, Codf. St My., 1671, AB, I, W, P2/C/618-19

My., sp., Sal., 1706, W, P4/1706/3
My., widow, Bradford A., 1718, AB, P2/C/1021
My., sp., All C., 1756, AB, comm, P3/C/943
My., widow, Shalbourne, 1758, W, P5/1758/12
My., sp., Chiseldon, 1780, AB, P3/C/1066
My., widow, Collingbourne D., 1819, W, Wr, P21/12/38
Matthew, Aston Tirrold, Berks., 1759, W, P1/C/901, P1/11Reg/395
Meshach, vict., Bradford A., 1722, I, W, copy W, P2/C/1051
Michael, widow, Salterton, Durnford, 1571, W, P1/1Reg/91
Nathan, vicar, Chirton, 1727, AB, I, P2/C/1078
Nathan, sen., gent., Coate, Bps. C., 1741, AB, W (d. 1732), P24/957
Nathaniel, husb., Compton, Enford, 1681, AB, I, P2/C/695
Nathaniel, spinner, Figh., 1687, AB, I, P26/361
Ralph, labourer, Downton, 1817, W, Wr, P2/1817/11
Coper, Rd., husb., Durrington, 1558, W, P2/3Reg/123B
Rd., husb., Gt. Cheverell, 1569, W, P2/5Reg/76C
Coper, Rd., E. Grimstead, W. Dean, 1589, I, W, P2/C/86
Cooper als Rogers, Rd., [brewer], Sal. St Thos., 1613, AB, a/c, I, P4/1613/9
Rd., W. Grimstead, 1614, AB, P2/C/274
Rd., husb. and yeo., Hurst, Berks., 1632, I, W, copy W, P5/1632/18, P5/12Reg/97
Rd., sen., collarmaker, Urchf., 1664, I, W, P1/C/274
Rd., Finchampstead, Berks., 1708, AB, P1/C/504
Rd., yeo., Gt. Wishford, 1710, I, W, P2/C/964
Rd., clerk and curate, Bishopstone S., 1714, NW, P1/C/545, P1/5Reg/333B
Rd., Shropshire Marsh, Lydiard T., 1731, AB, P3/C/792
Rd., blacksmith, Heytes., 1782, W, P5/1782/7, P5/17Reg/237B
Rd., Winnersh, Hurst, Berks., 1789, W, P5/1789/2, P5/18Reg/131
Cowper, Robt., Brigmerston, Milston, 1551, AB, P2/2Reg/128B
Cowper, Robt., Charl. nr. P., 1564, I, W, P2/C/1511, P2/4Reg/176A
Robt., husb., Winterslow, 1591, I, W, P2/C/100
Robt., Donhead St A., 1600, AB, I, W, P2/C/177
Robt., Salterton, Durnford, 1600, AB, I, W, P5/1599/6, P5/6Reg/237C
Robt., Sonning, Berks., 1639, AB, NW, P5/1639/20, P5/13Reg/212A
Robt., Wootton B., 1669, AB, I, P3/C/330
Robt., yeo., Brixton D., 1690, I, W, P2/C/805
Robt., mercer, Bradford A., 1732, comm, W, P1/C/702, P1/7Reg/444A
Robt., grocer, Sal., 1739, W, Wr, P4/1738/3
Robt., sen., labourer, Downton, 1747, W, P2/C/1241
Robt., yeo., Brixton D., 1747, W, P1/C/826, P1/10Reg/180B
Robt., gent., Rabson, Winterbourne Bassett, 1761, W, P3/C/960
Roger, Collingbourne K., 1649, AB, comm, P1/C/222
Sampson, yeo., Rabson Farm, Winterbourne Bassett, 1688, I, W, Wr, P3/C/532
Sam., gent., Winterbourne Bassett, 1748, W, P3/C/896
Sarah, widow, Crockerton, Longbridge D., 1719, AB, I, ren, P2/C/1026
Solomon, Calne, 1772, AB, P26/1055
Steph., husb., Longbridge D., 1577, AB, I, T, P2/C/46, P2/5Reg/297C
Susanna, sp., Netherb., Dorset, 1672, comm, I, copy W, W, P17/97
Susanna, widow, Gt. Woodford, 1694, AB, I (dated 1682), P13/3/21
Thos., Wokm., Berks., 1544, W, P5/20Reg/55
Thos., Salterton, Durnford, [1571], W, P1/1Reg/130B
Coper, Thos., Figh., 1580, AB, P26/1479, P5/3Reg/151C
Thos., Sunton, Collingbourne K., 1603, I, W, P3/C/9
Thos., Netheravon, 1607, AB, I, P12/13
Thos., Lt. Trowle, Trowb., 1614, I, W, P22/2/15
Thos., husb., Quidh., 1635, I, W, P1/C/158
Thos., husb., Longbridge D., 1637, AB, a/c, I, P2/C/454
Thos., husb., Bradfield, Berks., 1645, AB, comm, I (detailed), NW, P1/C/209
Thos., sen., yeo., Bradford A., 1683, comm, W, P2/C/725
Thos., Porton, Idmiston, 1686, AB, I, P2/C/771
Thos., shoemaker, Sal., 1687, AB, I (detailed), P4/1686/6

Thos., Crockerton, Longbridge D., 1691, AB, P2/C/811
Thos., gent., Milford, Sal. St Mart., 1697, I, W, P4/1696/3
Thos., rope winder *or* cordw., All C., 1704, I, W, P3/C/647
Thos., tailor, Porton, Idmiston, 1709, I, ren, W, P2/C/956
Thos., Brixton D., 1710, AB, I, P2/C/968
Thos., sen., gent., Upper Clatford, Hants (form. of Figh.), 1729, W, P26/739
Thos., sen., Figh., 1754, AB, L, P26/933
Thos., Marl., 1756, AB, comm, P1/C/873
Thos., gent., Ablington, Figh., 1756, W, Wr, P26/939
Thos., husb., Heddington, 1763, comm, W, P3/C/974
Thos., Bradford A., 1775, AB, P2/C/1379
Thos., grocer, Sal., 1806, AB, LA, P4/1806/3
Thos., yeo., Wokm., Berks., 1831, W, Wr, P5/1831/11
Thos., Bramshaw, Hants, 1834, AB, Wr, P24/1338
Thos., innkeeper, Malm., 1850, O, W, Wr, P3/1850/48
Thos., bricklayer, Sal., 1853, W, Wr, P4/1853/9
Walter, Donhead St A., 1617, I, T, P2/C/300
Warborough, widow, Quidh., 1663, AB, I, P1/C/261
Cowper, Wm., Landford, 1545, W (NEP), P2/1Reg/54A
Wm., Durrington, 1562, W (incomplete), P1/2Reg/144B
Wm., sen., shepherd, Burbage, 1595-96, AB, I, P5/1595/12, P5/6Reg/119A
Coppar als Rogers, Wm., E. Grimstead, W. Dean, 1619, I, W, P2/C/312
Wm., husb., Upton, Blewbury, Berks., 1628, AB, I, P5/1628/21, P5/11Reg/83B
Wm., husb. *or* yeo., Netheravon, 1628, I, W, P5/1628/26, P5/11Reg/55
Wm., Netheravon, 1634, AB, app. of guardian, P5/1634/7
Wm., husb., E. Grimstead, W. Dean, 1641, I, W, P2/C/497
Wm., husb., Charl. nr. P., 1643, comm, I, W, P2/C/511
Wm., yeo., Marl., 1646, AB, comm, P1/C/212
Wm., husb., Ham, 1661-62, I, W, P3/C/280, P3/3Reg/13A
Wm., Brixton D., 1672, AB, P2/C/624
Wm., worsted comber, Urchf., 1677, I, W, P1/C/323
Wm., clothw., Newbury, Berks., 1683, I, W, P1/C/361
Wm., Stratton St Mgt., 1684, I, W, P3/C/488
Wm., yeo., Sandhurst, Berks., 1686, I, W, P5/1686/18
Wm., minor, Sal., 1690, T (no decd named), P4/1689/16
Wm., Milton L., 1702, AB, I, P3/C/643
Wm., Charl. nr. P., 1709, AB, P2/C/960
Wm., Winterbourne Bassett, 1717, AB, P3/C/705
Wm., yeo., Lockeridge, Overton, 1718, I, W (2 - 1 a copy), P3/C/718
Wm., yeo., Bishopstone N., 1726, AB, I, W, P6/107
Wm., E. Grimstead, W. Dean, 1732, AB, P1/C/700
Wm., sen., cordw., Manton, Preshute, 1751, AB, W, P1/C/845, P1/10Reg/467
Wm., Figh., 1756, AB, P26/943
Wm., blacksmith, Pott., 1762, W, P1/C/913, P1/12Reg/21A
Wm., bricklayer, Milton L., 1768, W, P3/C/1006
Wm., yeo., Stert, Urchf., 1772, AB, P1/C/965
Wm., yeo., E. Grimstead, W. Dean, 1798, W, P2/C/1490
Wm., gent., Tilsh., 1804, W, Wr, P1/1804/10
Wm., carp., Wokm., Berks., 1833, W, Wr, P5/1833/17
Wm., coal carrier, Warm. Common, 1835, W, P1/1835/73
Wm., yeo., Steeple A., 1847, comm, W, Wr, P2/1847/51
see also Gyne nee C.; Rogers als C.; Woolridge als C.
Coosner *see* Cusner
Cooth, Jonathan, Sherb., Dorset, 1677, AB, comm, P5/1676/14
Josias, gent., Sherb., Dorset, 1672, AB, comm, I, P5/1671/24
Couthe, Rd., husb., Newnham, Sutton V., 1571, W, P1/1Reg/29C
Cope, Edmd., bach., Wrou., 1719, AB, I, P3/C/723
Copes, Edwd., Gt. Bedwyn, 1706, AB, P21/6/36
Jn., N. Bradley, 1559, W, P2/3Reg/161B
Jn., husb., Wrou., 1621, I, NW, P3/C/112

Jn., yeo., Chiseldon, 1681, AB, ren, W, P3/C/441
Jn., sen., wheelwright, Eastrop, Highw., 1693, AB, I, P10/1693/7
Jn., yeo., Hungerford, Berks., 1761, W, P5/1761/6
Jos., Marl. St My., 1810, AB, Wr, P1/1810/4
Letitia *see* Letitia Wilton
Rd., yeo., Wrou., 1713, I, W, P3/C/685
Rd., Gt. Bedwyn, 1717, I, W, P21/7/31
Rd., yeo., Brail Farm, Gt. Bedwyn, 1728, I, W, P21/8/43
Sam., Foxham, Bremhill, 1731, W, P3/C/793
Thos., yeo., Foxham, Bremhill, 1725, AB, I, P3/C/756
Wm., Box, 1625, AB, P3/C/136
Coper *see* Cooper
Copes *see* Cope
Copinger, Jn., Sal., 1614, W, copy W, P4/1613/17
Copland, Aaron, yeo., Wokm., Berks., 1832, comm, W (& cod), Wr, P5/1832/18
Grace, sp., Ewin's Hill, Aldbourne, 1764, W, P3/C/983
Joan, sp., Stratton St Mgt., 1639, AB, a/c, I, P3/C/246
Jn., innholder, Marl., 1711, I, W, P1/C/520, P1/5Reg/149
Robt., yeo., Stratton St Mgt., 1675, I, W, P3/C/383
Steph., blacksmith, Sal., 1712, W, P4/1712/4
Wm., mason, Rams., 1837, W, Wr, P5/1837/17
Coplin, Ephraim, labourer, Aldbourne, 1815, W, Wr, P3/1815/24
Jos., yeo., Aldbourne, 1747, W, P1/C/825, P1/10Reg/131
Copp, Hy., N. Bradley, 1571, W, P2/5Reg/132
Joan, widow, Bradford A., 1646, AB, comm, I, P2/C/525
Robt., yeo., Bradford A., 1634, I, W, P1/C/152
Thos., sen., husb., Bradford A., 1646, comm, I, T, P2/C/528
Coppage, Chas., labourer, Chelworth, Crickl. St S., 1727, W, P3/C/769
Wm., husb., Chelworth, Crickl. St S., 1684, I, W, P3/C/489
Coppar *see* Cooper
Coppock, My., widow, Fordington, Dorset, 1704, AB, I, P15/72
Wm., Fordington, Dorset, 1730, AB, P15/119
Copson, Rd., sen., clerk, Brinkw., 1732, W, P1/C/713, P1/7Reg/547A
Copson, Rd., Malm., 1756, AB, P1/C/886
Coram, Jn., husb., Uffc., Devon, 1631, I, W, P5/1631/27, P5/12Reg/15B
Corban *see* Corbin
Corbar, Jn., Ogbourne St Geo., 1566, W, P5/2Reg/11A
Corbett, Corbett als Davis, Edith, widow, Crockerton, Longbridge D., 1603, I, W, P2/C/196
Corbett als Davis, Jn., Warm., [1692], W, P2/C/817
Rd., weaver, Warm., 1585, W, P2/7Reg/10A
Corbett als Davis, Sarah, widow, Warm., 1726, W, P2/C/1073
Thos., yeo., Crockerton, Longbridge D., [1626], I, W, P2/C/364
Thos., maltster, Sonning, Berks., 1754, W (& cod), P5/1754/4
see also Davis als C.
Corbin, Agnes, widow, Lyme R., Dorset, 1638, comm, I, W, P5/1638/25, P5/13Reg/147
Corban, Jn., Whitep., 1768, W, P2/C/1342
Jn., Sherb., Dorset, 1825, W (& cod), Wr, P5/1825/22
Corban, Rd., Whitep., 1782, W, P2/C/1422
see also Colbourne
Corderoy, Cordery, Ann, sp., Earley, Sonning, Berks., 1700, AB, I, P5/1700/10
Ann, sp., Blewbury, Berks., 1718, W, P5/1718/7, P5/15Reg/409B
Cordery, Ann, widow, Blewbury, Berks., 1735, W, P5/1735/15
Dorothy, widow, Tilehurst, Berks., 1714, I, W, P1/C/549, P1/5Reg/364
Eliz., widow, Compton C., 1636, AB, a/c, I, P2/C/442
Cordery, Frances, widow, Hurst, Berks., 1644, AB, P5/1644/11, P5/14Reg/68A
Francis, gent., Chute, 1716, I, W, P7/107
Hy., miller, Blewbury, Berks., 1706, I, W, P5/1706/8
Jas., sen., gent., Compton C., 1628, I (detailed), W, P1/C/124
Joan, widow, All C., 1686, AB, P3/C/506
Cordery, Jn., yeo., Earley, Sonning, Berks., 1641, I, W, P5/1640/13, P5/13Reg/271C

Jn., gent., Chute, 1669, I, W, P7/39
Jos., farmer, Blewbury, Berks., 1855, aff, O, W, Wr, P5/1855/4
My., widow, Chute, 1689, I, W, P7/71
Cordery, My., innkeeper and widow, Reading St Lawr., Berks., 1798, AB, ren, P1/C/1095, P1/15Reg/62A
Ralph, yeo., Aston U., Blewbury, Berks., 1729, I, W, P5/1729/12, P5/16Reg/233
Rd., husb., Lt. Coxwell, Gt. Faringdon, Berks., 1600, AB, I, P5/1600/17, P5/6Reg/270
Robt., Devizes St Jn., 1627, I, W, P1/C/167
Cordery, Robt., yeo., Hurst, Berks., 1644, AB, I, W, P5/1644/10, P5/14Reg/66C
Cordery, Sam., glazier, Reading, Berks., 1798, W, P1/C/1091, P1/15Reg/35B
Sarah, widow, Blewbury, Berks., 1818, W, Wr, P5/1818/17
Thos., Sulhamstead Bannister, Berks., 1635, AB, a/c, I, proclamation, P1/C/160
Thos., yeo., Aston U., Blewbury, Berks., 1733, AB, I, P5/1733/19
Cordray, Thos. *see also* Wm. Cox
Cordery, Wm., Hurst, Berks., 1543, W, P5/20Reg/47A
Cordery, Wm., All C., 1711, AB, P1/C/530
Corell, Jn., priest, Whaddon, 1551, institution to rectory on resignation of [Jas.] Codde, P2/2Reg/138D
Corendon, Jn., yeo., Rams., 1613, I, NW, P1/C/57
Corfe, Corse, Jn., Sal., 1743, AB, Wr, P4/1743/11
Jn., dancing master, Sal., 1772, AB, W, P4/1772/16
Lucretia, sen., widow, Amesb., 1756, W (very detailed bequests), P2/C/1291
Robt. Cary, Sal., 1824, W, Wr, P4/1824/4
Corfield, Jane, widow, Sal. The Close, 1790, W, P2/C/1456
Wm., Sal. The Close (effects at Wilton), 1787-90, AB (2), P2/C/1444
Corke, Edmd., yeo., Kemble, 1733, AB, NW, P3/C/818
Jane, wife, Uffc., Devon, 1780, AB, court paper, W (Jn. C., husband of decd, agrees to AB being granted to Jn. Dunn, whose late wife, Rebecca, was sole ex. of Jane C.'s W who d. without having executed it)., P20/1/266
Philip, cordw., Uffc., Devon, 1776, W, P5/1776/10, P5/17Reg/127
Corker *see* Simkins als C.
Corless *see* Careles
Corme, Cicely, seamstress, Long Burton, Dorset, 1604, NW, P5/8Reg/6A
Cicely, sp., Holnest, Dorset, 1604, AB, I, NW, P5/1603/23
Robt., potter, Holnest, Dorset, 1580, W, P5/4Reg/2C
Robt., tucker, Stratton, Dorset, 1611, AB, I, W, P5/1610/10, P5/9Reg/49A
Thos., potter, Holnest, Dorset, 1579, I, W, P5/1579/15, P5/3Reg/131B
Thos., Holnest, Dorset, 1593, AB, I, T, W, P5/1593/25, P5/6Reg/43A
Walter, Holnest, Dorset, 1590, I, T, W, P5/1590/15, P5/5Reg/75A
see also Bartlett als C.
Corne, Jn., yeo., W. Ashton, Steeple A., 1691, AB, comm, I, P2/C/808
Miles, shepherd, Berwick St Jas., 1627, I, W, P1/C/166
Rd., shepherd, Stapleford, 1575, W, P2/5Reg/214C
Thos., yeo., Stapleford, 1636, I, W, P2/C/435, P2/9Reg/89D
Wm., S. Newton, 1586, W, P2/7Reg/48C
Cornelius, Bridget, Steeple L., 1588, AB, P2/7Reg/122A
Deborah, sp., Sal., 1784, W, P4/1784/3
Edwd., rector, Wingfield, 1687, AB, P1/C/377
Frances, widow, Sal., 1758, W, P4/1758/7
Hugh, Steeple L., 1571, W, P2/5Reg/114B
Jn., husb., Steeple L., 1580, I (2), T, W, P2/C/54, P2/5Reg/354B
Jn., Coombe B., 1589, AB, I, W, P5/1589/7, P5/5Reg/61A
Jn., gent., Wingfield, 1688, AB, I, P2/C/785
Jn., yeo., Netherb., Dorset, 1700, W, P17/136
Thos., Sal., 1720, AB, P4/1719/16
Wm., Steeple L., 1558, W, P2/3Reg/84B
Corner *see* Carver; Lewis als C.
Cornish, Edwd., yeo., Gillingham, Dorset, 1740, I, W, Wr, P27/1/357, P27/3Reg/8
Flower, shoemaker, Warm., 1640, NW, P2/C/492
Geo., Westb., 1721, AB, P25/1722/1
Hy., Stapleford, 1789, AB, P2/C/1454
Hy., bach., Stapleford, 1840, AB, Wr, P2/1840/55
Jane, Bishopstrow, 1726, W, P2/C/1077

Jn., yeo., Uffc., Devon, 1636, comm, I, W, P5/1636/16, P5/12Reg/252D
Jn., yeo., Gillingham, Dorset, 1735, I, W, Wr, P27/1/337
Martha, widow, Dinton, 1761, AB, P2/C/1309
My., sp., Malm. (form. of Chipp.), 1855, aff, O, W, Wr, P3/1855/6
Nathaniel, yeo., Westb., 1730, AB, ren, P25/1730/2
Wm., currier, Sal., 1584, NW, P4/Reg/26
Cornish als Duff, Wm., tailor, Marl. St My., 1685, I, ren, W, P1/C/372
see also Guddridge als C.; Taylor als C.
Cornock *see* Curnick
Cornwell, Alice, widow, Sal., 1631, AB, I, W, P4/1631/8
Cornelius, gardener, Sal., 1699, I (2), W, P4/1698/1
Eliz., widow, Sal., 1699, W, P4/1699/6
Cornwall, Jn., miller, Sal., 1629, I, W, P4/1629/11
Cornwall, Rd., Marl. St My., 1630, I, W, P1/C/136
Cornwall, Rd., shoemaker, Marl. St My., 1644, AB, comm, I, W, P1/C/197
Thos., Sonning, Berks., 1734, AB, I, P5/1734/16
Thomasine, yeo., Purton, 1682, AB, I, P3/C/462
Cornwall, Wm., minister of the gospel, Avebury, 1847, comm, W, Wr, P3/1847/48
Corp, Ann, Westb. L., 1836, O, W (bequest to minister of W.L. Baptist church), Wr, P25/1836/1
Corpe, Dan., Sherb., Dorset, 1708, W, P5/1708/22, P5/15Reg/79
Corpe, Dorothy, widow, Sherb., Dorset, 1720, W, P5/1720/14, P5/16Reg/48B
Eliz., widow, Longbridge D., 1831, W, Wr, P2/1831/66
Corpe, Jn., sen., [shoemaker], Sherb., Dorset, 1691, AB, I, P5/1691/15
Corpe, Margery, sp., Sherb., Dorset, 1678, AB, comm, I, P5/1678/14
Michael, yeo., Longbridge D., 1828, O, W, Wr, P2/1828/63
Corpe, Rd., cordw., Sherb., Dorset, 1698, comm, I, W, P5/1697/11
Wm., Maiden B., 1761, AB, P2/C/1311
Corr, Alan, Aldbourne, 1686, AB, I, P3/C/507
Alice, Aldbourne, 1713, AB, valuation cert, P3/C/686
Jn., bellfounder, Aldbourne, 1715, I, W, P3/C/699
Robt., Aldbourne, 1725, AB, P3/C/757
Robt., minor, Aldbourne, 1735, comm, T, P1/C/723
Wm., gunsmith, Aldbourne, 1669, comm, I, W, P3/C/331
Wm., bellfounder, Aldbourne, 1719, I, W, P3/C/724
Corry, Jn., Sherb., Dorset, 1799, AB, P5/1799/3, P5/18Reg/280B
Corse *see* Corfe
Corster *see* Coster
Cortas, Corties, Cortis *see* Curtis
Corton, Corton *or* Courtney, Eliz., widow, Uffc., Devon, 1626, I, W, P20/1/7
Thos., sen., Uffc., Devon, 1595, I, W, P5/1594/20, P5/6Reg/91C
Corver *see* Carver
Corviser, Wm., vicar, Rams., 1586, I, W, P5/1586/6, P5/4Reg/131B
Cosen, Cosens *see* Cousins
Cosh, Agnes, widow, Bere R., Dorset, 1693, I, W, P5/1693/14
Jn., carp., Bere R., Dorset, 1687, I, W, P5/1687/11
Cosham, Jos., maltster, Marl., 1724, W, P1/C/634, P1/7Reg/50
Cosier, Hy., [blacksmith], Sal., 1692, AB, I, P4/1691/14
Hy., blacksmith, Sal., 1733, AB, I, ren, P4/1733/14
Cozier, Robt., husb., Whitep., 1674, I, W, P2/C/641
Cosker *see* Coster
Cossam, Jas., husb., Shrewton, 1660, AB, I, note of probate, W, P2/C/543
Costar, Costard *see* Coster
Costen, Geo., glover, Wokm., Berks., 1588, W, P5/1587/10, P5/5Reg/2A
Causten, Jn., Crickl. St S., [1600], W (NEP), P3/1Reg/45C
Custins, Jn., Ditchampton, Wilton, 1668, I, P2/C/582
Castan, Mgt., widow, Crudwell, [1602], W (NEP), P3/1Reg/98B
Caston *or* Custon, Wm., yeo., Hungerford, Berks., 1598, AB, I, W, P5/1598/10, P5/6Reg/199B
see also Costen *or* C.; Fry als C.
Coster, Costard, Agnes, widow, Rushall, 1695, I, W, P2/C/851
Alice, widow, Fittleton, 1735, W, P1/C/738, P1/8Reg/102

Ann, widow, Grittenham, Brinkw., 1832, AB, comm, Wr, P1/1832/15
Costard, Cath., widow, Fisherton A., 1666, I, copy I, W, P2/C/566
Chas., stage coachman, Marl., 1834, AB (2), comm, O, W, Wr, P1/1834/17
Costar, Chris., Fisherton A., 1643, I, W, P1/C/190
Dorothy, widow, Mildenhall, 1672, AB, W, P3/C/359
Dorothy *see also* Jn. Sparrow
Edwd., yeo., Mildenhall, 1682, I, W, P3/C/463
Edwd., Mildenhall, 1705, I, W, P3/C/653
Edwd., husb., Ogbourne St Geo., 1714, W, P23/338
Costerd, Eliz., widow, Buckland, Berks., 1677, I, W, P1/C/325
Eliz., widow, Shrewton, 1738, AB, P2/C/1185
Eliz., widow, Hungerford, Berks., 1745, AB, P23/589
Eliz., widow, Speenhamland, Berks., 1835, AB, comm, Wr, P1/1835/16
Harry, yeo., Upavon, 1840, O, W, Wr, P2/1840/22
Costard, Hy., husb., Charl. nr. P., 1611, I, W, P2/C/253
Costard, Hy., Charl. nr. P., 1686, AB, I, P2/C/767
Hy., cabinetmaker and upholsterer, Sal., 1797, W, P4/1797/11
Jas., sen., Marl., 1715, AB, P1/C/559
Joanna, widow, Sal., 1799, AB, app. of guardian, T, P4/1800/8-9
Costard, Jn., Colthrop, Thatcham, Berks., 1561, W. No date of probate, P1/2Reg/102A
Costerd, Jn., husb., Stratton St Mgt., 1615, I, W, P3/C/79
Costard, Jn., yeo., Conock, Chirton, 1661, comm, I, P2/C/547
Costard, Jn., Charl. nr. P., [1680], I, W, P2/C/693
Costerd, Jn., yeo., Rushall, 1692, AB, I, P2/C/821
Costard, Jn., yeo., Burcombe, 1705, I, W, P2/C/927
Jn., Bower C., 1723, AB, P2/C/1054
Costar, Jn., Stockley, Calne, 1726, AB, I, ren, P26/709
Costard, Jn., yeo., Aston U., Blewbury, Berks., 1740, I, W, Wr, P5/1740/15
Jn., wheelwright, Fittleton, 1754, W, P2/C/1285
Costar, Jn., sen., yeo., Tubney, Berks., 1756, W, P1/C/881, P1/11Reg/247B
Jn., gent., W. Dean, 1800, AB, W, P2/1800/99-100
Jos., joiner, Mildenhall, 1670, AB, I, P3/C/342
Costard *or* Coster, Mgt., widow, Mildenhall, 1671, I, W, P1/C/304
Corster, Margery, widow, Mildenhall, 1690, AB, P3/C/546
My., widow, Mildenhall, 1727, W, P3/C/771
Costard, Melior, widow, N. Burcombe, 1707, AB, W, P2/C/940
Nathaniel, yeo., Shrewton, 1691, I, W, P2/C/814
Nathaniel, innholder, Shrewton, 1733, W, P2/C/1147
Oliver, gent., W. Dean, 1810, W, Wr, P2/1810/52
Robt., watchmaker, Newbury, Berks., 1750, W, P1/C/841, P1/10Reg/367
Robt., labourer, Chute Forest, Chute, 1783, W, P7/176
Robt., labourer, Collingbourne K., 1820, W, Wr, P1/1820/52
Sarah, widow, Sal., 1797, W, P4/1797/16
Costar, Steph., yeo., Stockley, Calne, 1822, W, Wr, P26/1342
Costard, Susanna, Charl. nr. P., [1680], I, NW. Place not given, but *see* P2/C/693, P2/C/694
Thos., Lt. Bedwyn, 1742, AB, P21/9/43
Thos., sen., yeo., Grittenham, Brinkw., 1818, W, Wr, P3/1818/24
Thos., yeo., Grittenham, Brinkw., 1832, comm, W, Wr, P3/1832/10
Costard, Wm., husb., Stratton St Mgt., 1608, I, W (NEP), P3/C/34
Wm., blacksmith, Charnham St., Hungerford, Berks., 1684, AB, comm, I, P5/1684/10
Wm., sen., Rushall (form. of Burcombe), 1711, AB, P1/C/510
Costar, Wm., sen., yeo., Stockley, Calne, 1713, I, W, P5/1713/20, P5/15Reg/363A
Wm., weaver, Marl. (form. of Swindon), 1715, I, W, P1/C/560, P1/5Reg/477
Wm., yeo., Pitton, Alderbury, 1724, I, W, P26/697
Wm., yeo., Conock, Chirton, 1727, I, W, P2/C/1085
Wm., clerk and curate, Fittleton, 1733, I, W, P2/C/1158
Cosker, Wm., maltster, Sal., 1772, AB, W, P4/1772/9
Wm., Fittleton, 1778, AB, P2/C/1398
Wm., wine cooper, Sal., 1788, W, P4/1788/10
Wm., clothier, Sal., 1790, W, P4/1790/13

Wm., farmer and shopkeeper, Upavon, 1803, W, P2/1803/73
Costrell, Chas., yeo., Sonning, Berks., 1633, AB, I, W, P5/1633/11, P5/12Reg/144A
Cotmore *see* Cottmore
Coton *see* Cotton
Cott, Jn., Lacock, 1755, W, P3/C/939
Cottam, Cottam *or* Cottom, Jn., weaver, Sal., 1742, W, P4/1742/12
Cottell *see* Cottle
Cotten *see* Cotton
Cotterell, Abraham, yeo., Waltham St Lawr., Berks., 1795, W, P1/C/1083, P1/14Reg/570
Agnes, widow, Uffc., Devon, 1670, I (date lost through decay), W (made 1655, but endorsed 1670; an Agnes C. was buried U. 3 Jun 1670), P20/1/61
Ambrose, weaver, Uffc., Devon, 1645, I, W, P20/1/40
Ann, widow, Codf. St P., 1781, W, P2/C/1420
Anth., Bulford, 1558, I, W, P2/C/1510, P2/3Reg/96B
Crispin, yeo., Warfield, Berks., 1625, I (detailed), W, P1/C/115
Cotterill, Edwd., Salterton, Durnford, 1629, AB, I, P5/1628/30, P5/11Reg/17B
Cotterill, Eliz., widow, Wokm., Berks., 1706, W, P5/1706/9
Cotterill, Hugh, Easthampstead, Berks., 1692, AB, ren, P1/C/422
Hugh, yeo., Easthampstead, Berks., 1723, I, W, P1/C/620, P1/7Reg/5A
Cotterill, Jane, sp., Blewbury, Berks., 1726, AB, P5/1725/20
Cotterill, Joan, Wokm., Berks., 1543, W, P5/20Reg/42D
Jn., Dinton, 1610, W, P2/8Reg/108
Jn., Teffont M., 1610, I, W, P2/C/238
Jn., Uffc., Devon, 1815, AB, comm, P20/1/301
Jn., yeo., Easthampstead, Berks., 1829, W, Wr, P1/1829/115
Cotterill, My., widow, Blewbury, Berks., 1718, W, P5/1718/6, P5/15Reg/409A
My., widow, Codf. St P., 1797, W, P2/C/1485
Philip, yeo., Teffont M., 1694, I, W, P2/C/845
Cotterill, Philip, yeo., Teffont M., 1714, AB, I, P2/C/996
Rachel, Sal. The Close, 1709-10, W, P5/1709/9, P5/15Reg/141B
Cotterill, Rd., yeo., Easthampstead, Berks., 1714, W, P1/C/550, P1/5Reg/355
Cotterill, Rd., vict., Shrewton, 1756, W, P1/C/879, P1/11Reg/265
Robt., Barford St Mart., 1548, AB, P2/2Reg/58C
Simon, Bulford, 1540, I, W (NEP), P30/38
Simon, husb., Barford St Mart., [1559], I, P2/C/11
Thos., Bulford, 1584, AB, P2/6Reg/127D
Thos., yeo., Uffc., Devon, 1597, AB, I, W, P5/1596/17, P5/6Reg/140C
Thos., shoemaker, Codf. St P., 1780, W, P2/C/1411
Wm., Teffont M., 1550, W, P2/2Reg/109A
Wm., Dinton, 1667, W, P2/C/570
Cotterill, Wm., Boyton, 1682, I, W, P2/C/714
Wm., yeo., Uffc., Devon, 1692, I, W, P5/1692/15
Cottle, Ann, widow, Ashley, Bradford A., 1729, AB, W, P1/C/682, P2/C/1108
Benj., tallow chandler, Bradford A., 1674, comm, I, W, P2/C/639
Edwd., sen., yeo., Box, 1762, W, P3/C/969
Eliz., Seagry, 1668, AB, P1/C/295
Eliz., widow, Bradford A., 1746, AB, P2/C/1233
Eliz., widow, Hilp., 1804, comm, W, P2/1804/25
Frances, sp., Swindon, 1762, AB, P3/C/970
Geo., sen., husb., Westb., 1665, I, W, P25/1665/3
Geo., collier, Westb., 1695, AB, a/c, I, P25/1695/7
Geo., bach., Box, 1785, AB, P3/C/1089
Geo., yeo., Corsham, 1803, I, W, P29/1800-1857/4, P29/3Reg/234
Isaac, Hullavington, 1714, W, P3/C/692
Jas., yeo., Box, 1831, comm, W, P3/1831/2
Jas., minor, Monkton F., 1843, court proceeding, O, T (children of Jeremiah C., decd), P2/1843/6
Jane, widow, Bearfield, Bradford A., 1746, AB, W, P2/C/1232
Jeremiah, yeo., Farleigh Wick, Monkton F., 1791, W, P2/C/1465
Jeremiah, Monkton F., 1843, AB, O, Wr, P2/1843/7
Cottell, Jn., carp., Ditteridge, 1662, comm, I, W, P3/C/285

Jn., Box, 1691, AB, comm, ren, P3/C/559
Jn., sen., Stanton St Q., 1705, AB, I, P3/C/654
Jn., carp., Box, 1715, AB, I, P3/C/698
Cottell, Jn., yeo., Folly Lane, Melk., 1720, I, W, P2/C/1034
Jn., carp., Ashley, Bradford A., 1725, I, W, P2/C/1069
Jn., sen., Ashley, Bradford A., 1753, AB, W, P2/C/1277-78
Jos., sen., tallow chandler, Trowb., 1738, W, P1/C/763, P1/8Reg/340B
Jos., tallow chandler, Hilp., 1774, AB, comm, P2/C/1374
Lawr., Lacock, 1705, AB, P3/C/655
Lawr., carp., Ashley, Box, 1717, W, P3/C/706
My., widow, Monkton F., 1747, W, P2/C/1244
My., widow, Box, 1809, comm, W, Wr, P3/1809/24
Moses, yeo., Winsley, Bradford A., 1740, W, P2/C/1205
Moses, Winsley, Bradford A., 1774, AB, P2/C/1367
Rd., chandler, Bradford A., 1664, AB, comm, I (detailed), NW, P1/C/270
Rd., Bradford A., 1676, AB, comm, P2/C/662
Rd., carp., Ditteridge, 1677, I, NW, P3/C/402
Rd., clothier, Corsham, 1728, marriage licence, P29/2Reg/54C
Rd., sen., *The Red Hat*, Trowb., 1751, W, P1/C/846, P1/10Reg/471A
Rd., Frankleigh, Bradford A., 1751, AB, P2/C/1260
Rd., Box, 1757, AB, P3/C/946
Cottell, Thos., broad weaver, Bradford A., 1742, W, P2/C/1216
Thos., broad weaver, Bradford A., 1746, AB, I, P2/C/1231
Thos., Winsley, Bradford A., 1764, AB, P2/C/1368
Thos., carp., Kingsdown, Box, 1791, W, P3/C/1113
Thos., gent., Monkton F., 1803, W, P2/1803/60
Cuttle, Wm., Blackland, Calne, 1638, AB, a/c, I, P26/76
Cottell, Wm., Box, 1639, I, W, P3/C/248
Cottell, Wm., Monkton F., 1714, AB, P2/C/990
Wm., yeo., Farleigh Wick, Monkton F., 1734, W, P2/C/1164
Wm., yeo., Pewsham Forest, 1750, W, P3/C/906
Wm., innholder, Trowb., 1768, AB, ren, P1/C/950
Wm., coal merchant, Trowb., 1829, W, Wr, P1/1829/3
Wm., Bemerton, Fugg. St Peter, 1852, AB, Wr, P2/1852/27
Cottmore, Ann, Shippon, Abingdon, Berks., 1732, W, P1/C/703, P1/7Reg/458A
Cotmore, Edmd., wheelwright, Ashton K., 1766, W, P3/C/996
Cottmore als Maale, Hugh, day labourer, Ashton K., 1676, comm, I, W, P3/C/394
Cottmore als Maale, Jane, widow, Ashton K., 1676, I, W, P3/C/395
Cottom *see* Cottam *or* C.
Cotton, Cotten, Abraham, sen., yeo., Hurst, Berks., 1731, W, P5/1731/16
Anth., Ashton K., 1609, AB, P3/C/41
Cotten, Dan., yeo. and butcher, Calne, 1728, I, W, P5/1728/24, P5/16Reg/184D
Edwd., Tisb., 1731, AB, P2/C/1122
Hy., chanter of Sal. Cathedral, Sal. The Close, 1626, a/c, I (on reverse a/c of Thos. Randell of Fisherton Anger re free quartering on his own yard & Chantry yard since 1 Aug 1644, & contribution he paid to garrison of Langford until 24 Mar 1645), P5/1626/11
Cotten, Humphrey, Tisb., 1585, I, T, W, P2/C/66, P2/7Reg/22A
Humphrey, yeo., Tisb., 1638, AB, P2/C/457
Cotten, Humphrey, Tisb., [1685], I, W, P2/C/758
Humphrey, grocer, Downton, 1725-26, I, T, W, P2/C/1070
Isaac, sen., vict., Calne, 1748, AB, W, P26/887
Cotten, Jas., butcher, Calne, 1738, W, P26/803
Jane, widow, Reading, Berks., 1713, W, P5/1713/18
Cotten, Jn., tailor, Tisb., 1607, I, W, P2/C/222
Jn., Devizes, 1689, AB, I, P1/C/399
Jn., gent., Manningford Bohun, 1775, comm, W, P3/C/1047
Mgt., widow, Devizes, 1682, W, P1/C/357
My., widow, Manningford Bohun, 1779, W, P1/C/1018, P1/13Reg/292
My., widow, Wilton, 1780, W, P2/C/1406
Coton, Rd., priest, Fonthill G., 1552, institution to rectory on resignation of [Robt.] Teyntour, P2/2Reg/145C

Rowland, doctor of physic, Warm., 1752, W, P2/C/1271
Thos., yeo., Sherb., Dorset, 1613, I, W, P5/1613/16, P5/9Reg/108A
Thos., sen., yeo., Finchampstead, Berks., 1773, W, P1/C/970, P1/12Reg/488B
Walter, Warm., 1580, AB, I, P2/C/55, P2/5Reg/356C
Wm., tanner, Warm., 1627, I, T, W, P2/C/372
Cotten, Wm., Sherston, 1639, AB, I, P3/C/247
Cottsall, Hy., Sonning, Berks., 1636, I, W, P5/1636/14, P5/13Reg/4
Wm., husb., Hurst, Berks., 1640, AB, I, P5/1640/10, P5/13Reg/252A
Couch, Dan., yeo., Leigh, Bradford A. (form. of Chapmanslade), 1789, comm, W, P2/C/1453
Cowch, Edwd., butcher, N. Bradley, 1588, I, T, W, P2/C/77
Edwd., yeo. and husb., Thoulstone, Upton S., 1590, I, W, P2/C/88
Eliz., widow, Chapmanslade, Corsley, 1610, I, NW, P2/C/237, P2/8Reg/105A
Jas., Durrington, 1835, AB, ren, P1/1835/36
Couch als Tucker, Joan, sp., Westb. L., 1681, AB, I, P25/1680/12
Jn., Chapmanslade, Corsley, 1591, I, T, W, P2/C/99
Couch als Tucker, Margery, widow, Westb., 1678, comm, I, W, P25/1678/6
Couch als Tucker, Nich., shepherd, Warm., 1706, I, W, P2/C/934
Nich., copyholder, Figh., 1752, W, P26/909
Cowch, Rd., yeo., N. Bradley, 1611, AB, I (detailed), P2/C/250
Cowch, Rd., Fisherton A., 1626, AB, I, P2/C/358
Couch als Tucker, Robt., gent., Westb. L., 1698, AB, ren, P25/1698/6
Wm., gent., Corston, Malm., 1719, W, P3/C/725
Wm. Tucker, sawyer, Wingfield, 1846, AB, O, ren, W, Wr, P2/1846/59
see also Tucker als C.
Couldry, Jn., sen., yeo., Draycot Moor, Longworth, Berks., 1698, AB, I, copy W, P1/C/462, P1/3Reg/214
Jn., sen., labourer, Marcham, Berks., 1744, I, W, P1/C/805, P1/9Reg/368A
Moses, labourer, Marcham, Berks., 1744, W, P1/C/804, P1/9Reg/368B
Rebecca, Draycot Moor, Longworth, Berks., 1698, AB, T, P1/C/461
Rd., tailor, Fyfield, Berks., 1747, W, P1/C/828, P1/10Reg/91
Coules *see* Coles
Coulman *see* Coleman
Couls *see* Coles
Coulsey, Edith, widow, New Windsor, Berks., 1744, I, W, P1/C/803, P1/9Reg/364B
Coulson, Ann, Melk. (form. of Whaddon), 1849, D, O (2), W, Wr, P2/1849/38
Coulston *see* Colstone
Coultridge, Thos., labourer, Shinfield, Berks., 1805, note, W, P1/1805/2
Courage, Roger, Gillingham, Dorset, 1682, I, P27/1/66
Courtenay *see* Courtney
Courtis *see* Curtis
Courtley, Eliz., widow, Imber, 1664, AB, I, P2/C/559
Courtlow, Courtlow als Stabbin, Ann, widow, Imber, 1638, I, W, P1/C/176
Courtlow als Stabbin, Ann, widow, Imber, 1696, I, W, P2/C/858
Edwd., husb., Chitterne AS, 1602, I, W, P2/C/186
Courtlow als Stabbin, Eliz., Imber, 1703, AB, ren, P2/C/906
Courtlow, Joan, widow, no abode stated, 1596, I, P2/C/1519
Jn., husb., Imber, 1558, W, P2/3Reg/131C
Courtlow als Stabbin, Jn., husb., Chitterne AS, 1612, I, W, P2/C/270
Courtlow als Stabbin, Jn., Imber, 1627, comm, I, W, P2/C/374
Courtlow als Stabbin, Jn., Imber, 1635, comm, I (2), W, P2/C/429
Courtlow als Stabbin, Jn., Imber, 1645, I, W, P2/C/519
Jn., husb., Imber, 1673-74, AB, a/c, I, P2/C/633
Courtlow als Stabbin, Jn., Imber, 1706, AB, comm, P2/C/935
Courtlow, Thos., Chitterne AS, 1559, W, P2/3Reg/182C
Thos., clothier, Sal., 1672, NW (NEP), P4/1672/19
Courtney, Ann, sp., Sal., 1771, W, P4/1771/9
Cass *see* Clace
Chas., Sal., 1701, AB, I, P1/C/476
Chris., Codf. St P., 1586, W, P2/C/70, P2/7Reg/60B
Clace *or* Cass, widow, Sal. The Close, 1708, AB, I, P5/1708/23
Eliz., widow, Sal. St Mart., 1678, I, W, P4/1678/20

Gregory, Edington, 1642, AB, I, NW, P2/C/507
Jn., Gillingham, Dorset, 1602, I, P27/1/4
Jn., sen., stationer, bookbinder and bookseller, Sal., 1683, AB, I, P1/C/363
Jn., Sal., 1712, AB, P4/1712/15
Jn., Sal., 1719, AB, P4/1718/29
Jn., bookseller, Sal., 1722, AB, I, P4/1722/14
Jn., sen., Sal., 1730, AB, P4/1730/13
Jos., Warm., 1801, AB, P2/1801/35
My., sp., Sal., 1718, AB, P4/1718/9
Rebecca, widow, Clarendon Park, 1782, AB, P4/1782/3
Wm., Tollard Royal, [1627], I, P2/C/368
Wm., bookseller, Sal. The Close, 1708, W, P5/1708/24, P5/15Reg/86
Courtenay, Wm., Lyme R., Dorset, 1714, AB, P16/198
Wm., weaver, Sal., 1739, W, Wr, P4/1738/4
see also Corton *or* C.; Miles form. C.
Courtroll, Cartrowll, Thos., Westrop, Highw., 1594, I, W, P5/1594/16, P5/6Reg/83B
Cousins, Couzens, Chas., baker, Berwick B., 1817, W, Wr, P26/1313
Cozens, Chas., tailor, Netheravon, 1834, L, O, copy W, Wr (original removed from Sarum Registry 1844, to be proved PCC), P12/221
Cosens, Christian, widow, Fordington, Dorset, 1619, AB, I, W, P5/1619/46, P5/10Reg/57B
Cosens, Christian, widow, Enmore Grn, Motc., Dorset, 1741, W, P19/131
Cosens, Cicely, widow, Grimstone, Stratton, Dorset, 1620, I, W, P5/1620/12, P5/10Reg/7
Cozens, Dan., baker, All C., 1730, W, P3/C/804
Cosens, Edith, widow, Sal., 1694, I, W, P4/1693/14
Cosens, Edmd., Grimstone, Stratton, Dorset, 1603, I, NW, P5/1603/13, P5/7Reg/65B
Eliz., widow, Abingdon, Berks., 1723, AB, I, P1/C/616
Cozens, Francis, Etchilhampton, 1749, AB, P3/C/903
Cosens, Gervase, weaver, Wilton, 1673, I, NW, P2/C/635
Cozens, Grace, widow, Stratton, Dorset, 1707, W, P5/1707/16, P5/15Reg/45
Cussens, Hy., yeo., Whithay, Netherb., Dorset, 1689, AB, I, W, P17/310
Cozens, Hy., Bps. C., 1742, comm, W, P24/988
Cousens, Jane, tailor's widow, Heytes., 1814, comm, W, Wr, P5/1814/13
Couzens, Jane, Durrington, 1834, cert, O, W, Wr, P2/1834/20
Cosens, Joan, widow, Grimstone, Stratton, Dorset, 1600, I, W, P5/1600/11, P5/6Reg/245A
Cosen, Jn., jun., Fordington, Dorset, 1573, I, W, P30/32, P5/3Reg/18D
Cozens, Jn., Preston, Dorset, 1588, AB, P5/5Reg/23B
Caissons, Jn., husb., Grimstone, Stratton, Dorset, 1611, W, P5/1611/8
Cosens, Jn., sen., no abode stated but includes elm in St Edmd.'s churchyard, Sal., c1635, I, P4/1635/6
Cussins, Jn., yeo., Quidh., 1684, AB, I, P2/C/736
Cussens, Jn., husb., Netherb., Dorset, 1690, AB, I, P17/314
Jn., weaver, Wilton, 1780, W, P2/C/1412
Couzins, Jn., blacksmith, Berwick B., 1833, comm, W, Wr, P26/1407
Cozens, Jos., tailor, Netheravon, 1837, W, Wr, P12/225
Cozens, Judith, widow, All C., 1736, AB, W, P3/C/831
Cosens, Julian, Preston, Dorset, 1583, I, W, P5/1582/15, P5/4Reg/60C
Couzens, Leonard, blacksmith, Easton, 1845, O, W, Wr, P1/1845/9
My., widow, Amesb., 1729, W, P2/C/1100
Cosens, My., sp., Beam., Dorset, 1744, W, P17/494
Cosens, Nich., Fordington, Dorset, 1562, AB, P5/1Reg/4B
Cosen, Philip, husb., Grimstone, Stratton, Dorset, 1611, I, W, P5/1610/12, P5/9Reg/49B
Cosens, Reyner, clerk, Mere, 1834, AB, comm, Wr, P5/1834/5
Cousens, Rd. Young, gent., Heytes., 1846, W (& cod), Wr, P5/1846/7
Cosens, Robt., gent., Lyme R., Dorset, 1735, comm, W, P16/276
Couzens, Robt., timber dealer, Bromham, 1841, W, Wr, P3/1841/24
Cozens, Sarah, Corsham, 1770, AB, P29/2Reg/136
Cousens, Sarah, sp., Longbridge D., 1809, AB, ren, Wr, P2/1809/53
Cosen, Thos., Hamptworth, Downton, 1546, W (NEP), P2/1Reg/63A
Cosen, Thos., Damerham, Hants, 1586, W, P2/7Reg/43A
Cosen, Thos., husb., Hamptworth, Downton, 1629-30, AB, a/c, P2/C/389
Thos., Amesb., 1719, AB, P2/C/1023

Cousens, Thos., Bishopstone S., 1734, W, P2/C/1167
Cousens, Thos., sen., gent., Heytes., 1802, W, P5/1802/14, P5/19Reg/13
Cosen, Wm., husb., Hamptworth, Downton, 1558, W, P2/3Reg/80B
Cosen, Wm., sen., Fordington, Dorset, 1590, AB, a/c, I, W, P5/1589/12, P5/5Reg/68C
Cosens, Wm., Netherb., Dorset, 1625, I, W, P5/1625/16, P5/10Reg/265
Cosens, Wm., miller, Fordington, Dorset, 1681, comm, I, W, P15/55
Wm., Amesb., 1710, AB, P2/C/966
Wm., Amesb., 1719, AB, P2/C/1024
Cozens, Wm., tailor, Netheravon, 1747, W, P12/177
Wm., Southwick, N. Bradley, 1769, AB, I, P2/C/1349
Cozens, Wm., Netherb., Dorset, 1829, AB, comm, P17/608
Cozens, Wm., master of the workhouse, Devizes, 1838, AB, O, W, Wr, P1/1838/13
see also Wheeler als C.
Couslade *see* Cowslade
Cousnell, Cousnell als Cozener, Thos., husb., Bradford A., 1633, AB, a/c, I, P2/C/417
Cousner *see* Cozener
Couthe *see* Coothe
Couzens, Couzins *see* Cousins
Covances, Chris., Fovant, [1620], I, W (buried 1619), P2/C/317
Cove, Alexander, Kingston D., 1546, W, P2/2Reg/7B
Betty, sp., Ashton K., 1739, AB, I, P3/C/851
Cath., widow, Oaksey, 1715, I, W, P3/C/700
Eliz., widow, Wantage, Berks., 1832, W, Wr, P23/964
Ellen, widow, Charlton nr Malm., 1684, I, W, P3/C/490
Harry, Ashton K., 1784, AB, P3/C/1083
Hy., yeo., Ashton K., 1596, W (NEP), P3/C/2
Hy., yeo., Ashton K., 1604, I, W, P3/C/14
Hy., slater, Purton, 1683, I, W, P3/C/473
Hy., tiler, Ashton K., 1737, W, P3/C/838
Hy., Easton Grey, 1748, AB, P3/C/897
Hy., Easton Grey, 1776, AB, P3/C/1052
Hy., Easton Grey, 1796, AB, P3/C/1131
Jas., bach. and husb., Minety, 1694, AB, I, P3/C/575
Jas., sen., pig jobber, Crickl. St S., 1774, W, P3/C/1039
Jn., yeo., Ashton K., 1622, I, W, P3/C/117
Jn., yeo., Lydiard M., 1689, AB, I, P1/C/408
Jn., yeo., Crickl. St S., 1749, AB, W, P3/C/904
Jn., miller, Easton Grey, 1803, W, P3/1803/38
My., widow, Ashton K., 1803, W, P3/1803/14
My., sp., Amesb., 1844, comm, W, Wr, P2/1844/45
Robt., Purton, 1706, I, W, P3/C/659
Thos., Charlton nr Malm., 1668, AB, I, P1/C/294
Thos., yeo., Charlton nr Malm., 1682, I, W, P3/C/464
Thos., tiler, Ashton K., 1794, comm, W, P3/C/1125
Timothy, sen., slater and plasterer, Ashton K., 1802, W, P3/1802/41
Timothy, slater and plasterer, Ashton K., 1856, aff, O, W, Wr, P3/1856/17
Wm., Amesb., 1805, AB, comm, P2/1805/37
Wm., carrier, Amesb., 1813, W, Wr, P2/1813/32
Covell, Alice, widow, Urchf., 1582, AB, NW, P2/6Reg/60B
Jn., Urchf., 1571, W, P2/5Reg/130B
Coventry, Benj., Highw., 1700, AB, P10/1700/1
Eleanor, widow, W. Lavington, 1603, I, W, P1/C/19
Joan, widow, Purton, 1622, I, W, P3/C/118
Jn., yeo., Wanb., 1689, I, W, P3/C/533
Jn., Wanb., 1809, W, Wr, P3/1809/20
Jn. *see also* Robt. Oliver
Jn. Humphris, Latton, 1832, AB, comm, Wr, P1/1832/101
Jos., yeo., Wrou., 1751, W, P3/C/913
Maria, Right Honourable Lady, Cumberwell, Bradford A., 1785, W, P2/C/1432
My., widow, Wanb., 1673, I, W, P3/C/367

Rd., farmer, Lydiard M., 1684, I, W, P3/C/491
Thos., yeo., Rodbourne C., 1678, AB, a/c, I, P3/C/413
see also Smart als C.
Covey, Jas., Newton T., 1570, AB, P2/5Reg/82D
Jn., Brigmerston, Milston, 1547, W, P2/2Reg/36B
Jn., jun., gent., Hungerford, Berks., 1673, AB, I, P5/1673/9
Wm., Deptford, Wylye, 1663, I, W, P2/C/552
Coward, Agnes, sp., Codf. St P., 1627, I, note of deed of gift, W, P2/C/375
Agnes, widow, Mere, 1662, I, W, P5/1662/26
Alice, cardmaker's wife, Westb., 1684, AB, comm (wife & children of Nich. C.), P25/1684/3
Arthur, turner, White Hill, Mere, 1663, I, W, P5/1663/16
Bridget, widow, Westb., 1677, I, W, P25/1677/5
Chris., turner, Woodlands, Mere, 1693, AB, I, P5/1693/12
Edmd., husb., Plaitford, 1725, W, P2/C/1067
Edmd., baker, Amesb., 1751, W, P2/C/1261
Edmd., Amesb., 1778, AB, P2/C/1393
Eliz., Boyton, 1591, I, W, P2/C/94
Eliz., widow, Sherb., Dorset, 1723, I, W, P5/1723/7, P5/16Reg/84A
Eliz., widow, Warm., 1728, AB, I, P2/C/1086
Eliz., widow, Mere, 1761, W, P5/1761/7
Ellen, widow, Sedgehill, 1586, W, P2/7Reg/46A
Hy., husb., Corton, Boyton, 1571, W, P1/1Reg/119A, P2/5Reg/119D
Hy., broad weaver, Devizes, 1643, W, P1/C/194
Hy., labourer, Fifield, 1821, O, W, Wr, P3/1821/5
Jas., tailor, Westb., 1706, W, P25/1706/5
Jas., excise officer, Devizes St Jn., 1731, W, P1/C/698, P1/7Reg/416B
Jane, widow, Chaddenwick, Mere, 1620, I, W, P5/1620/15
Jane, widow, Mere, 1750, AB, P5/1750/8
Jane, widow, Amesb., 1784, W, P2/C/1429
Joan, widow, Mere, 1620, W, P5/10Reg/11D
Joan, widow, Gillingham, Dorset, 1666, AB, W, P27/1/27
Jn., sen., Sedgehill, 1569, W, P2/5Reg/68A
Jn., sen., Sedgehill, 1579, T (children: Mgt., Edith & Walter C.), W, P2/C/49, P2/5Reg/335D
Jn., yeo., Wyke, Gillingham, Dorset, 1582, AB, a/c, I, W, P27/2Reg/8B
Jn., sen., yeo., Sedgehill, 1592, I, T, W, P2/C/102
Jn., husb., Chaddenwick, Mere, 1597, AB, I, W, P5/1597/24, P5/6Reg/178A
Jn., sen., Sedgehill, 1598, AB, I, W, P2/C/164
Jn., husb., Britford, 1606, AB, I, W, P24/12
Jn., Corton, Boyton, 1612, AB, NW, P2/C/268
Jn., yeo., Sedgehill, 1614, NW, P2/8Reg/218D
Jn., tailor, Sherb., Dorset, 1624, I, W, P5/1624/9, P5/10Reg/236C
Jn., linen weaver, Mere, 1641, AB, I, NW, P5/1641/20, P5/14Reg/41B
Jn., sen., cardmaker, Westb., 1669, I, W, P25/1669/2
Jn., hosier, Mere, 1684, AB, I, P5/1683/16
Jn., cardmaker, Westb., 1709, I, W, P25/1709/5
Jn., innholder, Sal., 1720, W, P4/1720/4
Jn., linen weaver, Mere, 1726, W, P5/1726/13, P5/16Reg/131A
Jn., sen., wheelwright, Mere, 1731, W, P5/1731/18
Jn., butcher, Sherb., Dorset, 1736, W, P5/1736/9
Jn., sen., maltster, Longstreet, Enford, 1767, W, P1/C/944, P1/12Reg/229A
Jn., jun., Sherb., Dorset, 1770, W, P5/1770/11, P5/17Reg/16B
Jn., yeo., Martin, Hants, 1778, W, P2/C/1392
Jn., maltster, Enford, 1822, W, Wr, P2/1822/34
Jos., husb., Alton P., Dorset, 1724, comm, W, P5/1724/20, P5/16Reg/92B
Julian, widow, Mere, 1605, AB, I, W, P5/1604/5, P5/8Reg/38B
Martha, sp., Sal., 1661, I, draft NW, P4/1661/12
My., sp., Wilton, 1800, AB, P2/1800/26
My., widow, Burdens Ball, Wilton, 1809, W, Wr, P2/1809/40
Maurice, Wilton & Ugford, 1696, AB, I, P1/C/450
Maurice, Wilton, 1792, AB, P2/C/1468

Melior, widow, Mere, 1695, I, W, P5/1695/13
Nich., sen., Westb., 1681, I, W, P25/1681/7
Randall, White Hill, Mere, 1601, AB, I, W, P5/1601/14, P5/7Reg/12C
Robt., Mere, 1725, W, P5/1725/18
Robt. *see*dsman, Wilton, 1842, W, Wr, P1/1842/30
Simon, Plaitford, 1671, AB, I, P2/C/617
Thos., Chilmark, 1571, W, P2/5Reg/134A
Thos., Mere, 1583, AB, I, P5/1582/17, P5/4Reg/58D
Thos., weaver, Studley, Trowb., 1637, I, W, P22/2/28
Thos., Ugford, S. Newton, 1667-68, AB, a/c, I, P2/C/571
Thos., clerk and vicar, Bucklebury, Berks., 1686, comm, I (detailed), W, P1/C/383
Thos., yeo., Sedgehill, 1707, W, P2/C/938
Thos., yeo., Mere, 1793, W, P5/1793/4, P5/18Reg/190B
Tippinga, widow, Devizes, 1763, W, P1/C/915, P1/12Reg/32
Walter, Sherb., Dorset, 1773, AB, comm, P5/1773/16, P5/17Reg/49C
Wm., Chilmark, 1548, W, P2/2Reg/63A
Wm., Sedgehill, 1596, I, T, P2/C/1520
Wm., husb., Downton, [1669], W, P2/C/595
Wm., W. Knoyle, 1697, AB, I, P2/C/865
Wm., vict., Sherb., Dorset, 1767, W, P5/1767/14
Wm., carp., Mere, 1825, note, W, Wr, P5/1825/3
Cowborough, Cowborough, Alice, widow, Garsdon, 1610, W, P3/C/51
Cowbrick, Cowbrick, Jane, sp., Tubney, Berks., 1753, W, P1/C/853, P1/11Reg/5
Cowch *see* Couch
Cowdall *see* Cadle
Cowdry, Ann, widow, Arborfield, Berks., 1741, AB, Wr, P5/1741/5
Cowdrey, Ann *see also* Jane Cox
Cuthbert, Downton, 1569, W, P2/5Reg/77D
Edwd., yeo., Gt. Wishford, 1787, W, P2/C/1442
Cowdrey, Eliz. *see* Jane Cox
Cowdery, Jas., sen., Amesb., 1745, W, P2/C/1228
Jane, widow, Burghfield, Berks., 1808, W, Wr, P1/1808/103
Jane *see also* Jane Cox
Cowdrey, Joan, widow, Tilehurst, Berks., 1686, AB, I, quitclaim, P1/C/1113
Jn., yeo., Avon, Sopley, Hants (exs from Wishford), [1643], copy W, P2/C/512
Jn., yeo., Barford St Mart., 1682, AB, I, P2/C/723
Jn., innholder, *The Saracen's Head*, Reading, Berks., 1686, comm, NW, P1/C/382
Cowderoy, Jn., salesman, Wokm., Berks., 1749, W, P5/1749/16
Cowdrey, Jn., shoemaker, Wilton, 1778, W, P2/C/1397
My., widow, S. Newton, 1820, W, Wr, P2/1820/26
Cowdrey, My. *see also* Jane Cox
Cowdery, Ralph, Grazeley, Sulhamstead Abbots, Berks., 1662, I, W, P1/C/245
Cowdery, Rd., yeo., Sulhamstead Bannister, Berks., 1779, W, P1/C/1016, P1/13Reg/278
Cowdrey, Robt., husb., Wilton, 1664, AB, I, W, P1/C/275
Cowdrey, Susanna *see* Jane Cox
Cowderey, Thos., Warm., 1740, AB, P2/C/1200
Ursula, Barford St Mart., 1688, AB, I, P2/C/788
Cauderay, Wm., Sal. St Edmd., 1571, W, P1/1Reg/31B
Cowdrey, Wm., jun., Wilton, 1703, W, P2/C/909
Wm., husb., Gt. Wishford, 1707, I, W, P2/C/939
Cowdrey, Wm., sen., Wilton, 1710, W, P2/C/971
Cowdery, Wm., Brimpton, Berks. (form. of St Mart. in the Fields, Middlesex), 1729, W, P1/C/678, P1/7Reg/273A
Wm., yeo., Gt. Wishford, 1751, W, P2/C/1259
Cowderoy, Wm., Woolhampton, Berks., 1759, AB, P1/C/897
Wm., yeo., S. Newton (form. of Wishford), 1800, AB, W, P2/1800/102
Cowell, Jn. Flower, watchmaker, Sal. (form. of St And. Holborn, London), 1755, W, P1/C/871, P1/11Reg/188
see also Cole *or* C.
Cowleman *see* Coleman
Cowles *see* Coles
Cowley, Ann, widow, Purton, 1614, I, W (NEP), P3/C/73

Ann, sp., Pewsey, 1700, W, P3/C/626
Cawlie, Beatrice, widow, Lyme R., Dorset, 1616, I, W, P5/1616/14
Cowley *or* Cowling, Chas., carp., Sevenbridges, Crickl. St S., 1731, AB, I, W, P3/C/794
Eliz., widow, Leigh, Ashton K., 1633, AB, I, P3/C/191
Hugh, yeo., E. Garston, Berks., 1776, W, P1/C/996, P1/13Reg/113
Joan, widow, Mere, 1574, I, W, P5/1574/4, P5/3Reg/35B
Joan, widow, Pewsey, 1639, AB, a/c, I, P3/C/249
Jn., husb., Woodlands, Mere, 1617, I, W, P5/1617/9, P5/9Reg/191B
Jn., yeo., Mere, 1640, I, W, P5/1640/9, P5/13Reg/257
Jn., yeo., Ashton K., 1800, W, P3/1800/22
Jn., widower, Hullavington, 1856, AB, aff, O, Wr, P3/1856/61
Josias, yeo. *or* tailor, Pewsey, 1689, AB, I, ren, P3/C/539
Leonard, yeo., Woodlands, Mere, 1609, AB, I, W, P5/1609/13, P5/8Reg/138B
My., sp., Pewsey, 1640, I, W, P3/C/255
My., widow, Crickl. St S., 1815, ren, W, Wr, copy W, P3/1815/23
Ralph, Wadswick, Box, 1627, AB, a/c, I, P3/C/153
Coolly, Rd., husb., Purton, 1610, W, P3/C/50
Rd., yeo., Leigh, Ashton K., 1793, W, P3/C/1120
Thos., Leigh, Ashton K., 1611, I, W, P1/C/44
Thos., sen., tanner, Mere, 1631, I, W, P5/1631/23, P5/12Reg/29
Thos., husb., Ashton K., 1633, I, W, P3/C/192
Thos., sen., Mere, 1681, AB, I, P5/1681/8
Thos., miller, Howe Mill, Rams., 1827, W (& cod), Wr, P5/1827/20
Wm., husb., Slimbridge, Gloucs, 1599, W (NEP), P3/C/4
Wm., Westrop, Highw., 1605, AB, I, P5/1605/13, P5/8Reg/36A
Wm., baker, Rams., 1818, comm, W, Wr, P5/1818/10
Wm., innkeeper, Winterbourne D., 1855, aff, W, Wr, P7/214
see also Goodcheap als C.
Cowlstone *see* Colstone
Cowly *see* Cowley
Cowper *see* Cooper
Cowrine, Robt., potter, Holnest, Dorset, 1580, I, P5/1580/15
Cowsey *see* Cawsey
Cowslade, Ann, sp., Donnington, Berks., 1814, W, Wr, P1/1814/95
Couslade, Bennet, blacksmith, Sal., 1685, AB, I, P4/1685/2
Chas., Sal., 1749, AB, P4/1749/7
My., tailor's widow, Sal., 1753-54, W, P1/C/850, P1/11Reg/143B
Moses, 1679, I (2 - 1 copy has details of exhibition at Subdean's court), P4/1679/28
Susanna, sp., Sal., 1819, W, Wr, P4/1819/10
see also Batt als C.
Cox, Adam, Chilton, Berks., 1622, AB, a/c, comm, I, P1/C/108
Agnes, widow, Alderton, 1624, I, W, P3/C/130
Agnes, widow, Halstock, Dorset, 1695, I, W, P16/135
Alexander, yeo., Chr. M., 1671, I, W, P3/C/350
Alexander, Chr. M., 1707, AB, I, P3/C/664
Ambrose, yeo., Berwick St Leonard, 1620, comm, I, W, P1/C/106
Ambrose, yeo., Bemerton, Fugg. St Peter, 1682, I, W, P2/C/718
And., labourer, Teffont M., 1724, AB, W, P2/C/1056
Ann, sp., Nash Hill, Lacock, 1662, AB, P3/C/286, P3/3Reg/14A
Ann, widow, Chute, 1664, I, W, P7/35
Ann, Huntingford, Gillingham, Dorset, 1698, W, P27/1/136
Ann, Mere, 1713, AB, P5/1713/23
Barbara, widow, Speenhamland, Berks., 1717, AB, I, ren, W, P1/C/576, P1/6Reg/140B
Cath., widow, Ashton K., 1643, W, P1/C/191
Cath., widow, Chr. M., 1679, I, W, P3/C/422
Cath., widow, Bradford A., 1779, W, P2/C/1402
Christian, widow, Halstock, Dorset, 1638, AB, NW, P5/1638/26, P5/13Reg/73B
Chris., Teffont M., 1724, AB, W, P2/C/1055
Clement, husb., Charlton, Downton, 1610, I, NW, P2/C/240, P2/8Reg/123D
Dan., husb., Marl., 1676, I, W, P1/C/320

David, tallow chandler, Wilton, 1744, W, P1/C/796, P1/9Reg/278
Dorothy, Kingston D., 1636, I, W, P2/C/438, P2/9Reg/94
Dorothy, widow, Tilsh., 1692, I (detailed), W, P1/C/425
Edmd., sexton, W. Mills, Newbury, Berks., 1760-67, W, P1/C/940, P1/12Reg/236
Edwd., husb., Newton, Whitep., 1633, I, W, P2/C/422
Edwd., yeo., Berwick St Leonard, 1661, AB, I, P2/C/544
Edwd., yeo., Whitley, Reading, Berks., 1695, I, W, P1/C/440
Edwd., ironmonger, Sal., 1706, W, P4/1706/1
Edwd., yeo., Compton Beauchamp, Berks., 1723, AB, I, P1/C/615
Edwd., wheelwright, Silver St., Reading St Giles, Berks., 1738, W, P1/C/756, P1/8Reg/281
Edwd., Pott., 1740, AB, P1/C/771
Edwd., yeo., E. Harnham, Britford, 1742, W, P24/987
Edwd., Inkpen, Berks., 1773, W, P1/C/976, P1/13Reg/28
Edwd., Trowb., 1789, AB, P1/C/1060
Edwd., innkeeper, Trowb., 1856, aff, D, O, W, Wr, P1/1856/12
Eleanor, widow, Trowb., 1797, comm, W, P1/C/1089, P1/15Reg/22
Eliz., widow, Easton, Bps. C., 1601, I (dated 1597), P24/13
Eliz., widow, Seend Grn, Melk., 1610, I, W, P2/C/239, P2/8Reg/111A
Eliz., widow, Ogbourne St Geo., 1629, I, W, P5/1629/16, P5/11Reg/23B
Eliz., sp., Chards., Devon, 1640, AB, W, P14/7
Eliz., widow, Lyme R., Dorset, 1691, AB, I, P16/110
Eliz., widow, Sal., 1694, W, P4/1694/14
Eliz., widow, Beam., Dorset, 1703, I, W, P17/154
Eliz., Bps. C., 1708, I, W, P24/574
Eliz., widow, Uffington, Berks., 1711, W, P1/C/523, P1/5Reg/162
Eliz., Bps. C., 1743, W, P24/976
Eliz., Sal., 1757, NW, P4/1757/4
Eliz., widow, Leigh, Yetm., Dorset, 1826, W, P19/234
Frances, widow, Lyme R., Dorset, 1668, I, W, P5/1668/17
Frances, sp., Sonning, Berks., 1671, W, P5/1671/18
Coxe, Frances Ann, sp., Hungerford, Berks., 1824, AB, comm, P23/917
Francis, sen., yeo., Mannington, Lydiard T., 1699, W, P3/C/613
Francis, Badbury, Chiseldon, 1766, W, P3/C/997
Frederick, accountant, Trowb., 1845, D, note, O, W, Wr, P1/1845/21
Frideswide, widow, Lyford, W. Hanney, Berks., 1606, I, W, P1/C/32
Gabriel, vict., Melk., 1687, AB, I, W, P2/C/778
Gabriel, fuller, Bradford A., 1725, I, W, P2/C/1066
Geo., Gillingham, Dorset, 1704, AB, P27/1/155
Geo., stone cutter, Swindon, 1787, W, P3/C/1095
Gertrude, widow, Westertown, N. Wraxall, 1721, I, W, P3/C/737
Grace, widow, Atworth, Bradford A., 1727, AB, P2/C/1084
Grace, sp., Gillingham, Dorset, 1828, comm, W, Wr, P27/1/685
Kockes, Hy., Donhead St My., 1552, W, P2/2Reg/153B
Hy., Ogbourne St Geo., 1629, AB, comm, I, P5/1629/17, P5/11Reg/23A
Hy., yeo., Aston U., Blewbury, Berks., 1667, I, W, P5/1667/14
Hy., clerk, Boscombe, 1679, AB, I, W, P1/C/335
Hy., N. Bradley, 1680, AB, comm, I, P2/C/684
Hy., yeo., Halstock, Dorset, 1690, I, W, P16/102
Hy., butcher, Melk., 1699, AB, I, P2/C/881
Hy., yeo., Cholsey, Berks., 1723, I, W, P1/C/619, P1/7Reg/1B
Hy., tailor, Badbury, Chiseldon, 1737, W, P3/C/839
Hy., serge weaver, Beam., Dorset, 1748, I, W, P17/511
Hy., sen., Amesb., 1798, AB, P1/C/1101, P1/15Reg/141B
Hy., bach., Luckington, 1802, AB, P3/1802/15
Hugh, broad weaver, Melk., 1614, AB, a/c, I, P1/C/70
Hugh, yeo., Tilsh., [1688], I, W, P2/C/782
Hugh, jun., porter, Lyme R., Dorset, 1704, I, W, P16/168
Hugh, yeo., Lyme R., Dorset, 1710, W, P5/1710/32, P5/15Reg/198B
Hugh, tailor, Lyme R., Dorset, 1751, AB, W, P16/308
Isaac, Orange Grove, Devizes, 1844, aff, O, W, Wr, P1/1844/22

Isabel, widow, Allington, 1595, I, W, P2/C/132, P2/7Reg/150B
Jas., Membury, Rams., 1670, AB, comm, I (2 - 1 copy), P5/1669/10
Jas., Chards., Devon, 1675, I, P14/42
Jas., yeo., Stanford in the Vale, Berks., 1677, AB, I, P1/C/330
Jas., yeo., W. Hanney, Berks., 1711, I, W, P1/C/524, P1/5Reg/163A
Jas., W. Hanney, Berks., 1750, AB, P1/C/839
Jas., Milton upon Stour, Gillingham, Dorset, 1792, W, P27/1/546
Jas., gent., Enford, 1800, W, P2/1800/45
Jas., yeo., Maiden B. (late of Brixton D.), 1800, W, P2/1800/66
Jas., vict., Trowb., 1822, W, Wr, P1/1822/12
Jas., yeo., Steeple A., 1853, D, O, W, Wr, P2/1853/17
Jane, widow, Westrop, Highw., 1583-95, AB, I (detailed), P5/1595/13, P10/1593/1
Jane, Bremhill, 1664, AB, P3/C/299
Jane, Lockerley, Mottisfont, Hants, 1711, T (legatees of the decd: Susanna, Jane, Eliz., Ann & My. Cowdrey, minors), P2/C/973
Jane, sp., Rowde (form. of Walcot, Bath, Somerset), 1851, W, Wr, P1/1851/51
Cockes, Joan, widow, Charlton, Downton, 1557, W, P2/3Reg/67A
Joan, widow, Durrington, 1614, AB, a/c, P2/C/273, P2/8Reg/206C
Joan, Westrop, Highw., 1632, I, P10/1632/1
Joan, sp., Bishopstone N., 1663, I, NW, P6/36
Joan, widow, Gillingham, Dorset, 1690, I, P27/1/120
Joan, widow, Wanb., 1695, I, W, Wr, P3/C/584
Joan, sp., Bps. C., 1719, W, P24/635
Cockes, Jn., Poulshot, 1549, W (NEP), P2/2Reg/86A
Jn., Brook, Bramshaw, Hants, 1565, W, P5/1Reg/43A
Cocks, Jn., Bramshaw, Hants, 1570, W, P5/2Reg/62
Jn., Netherb., Dorset, 1572-73, I, W, P5/1572/4, P5/3Reg/23B
Jn., sen., Tilsh., 1592, W, P1/C/7
Jn., yeo., Stratton St Mgt., 1592, I, P1/C/4
Jn., Seend, Melk., 1598, W, P2/C/161
Jn., herdsman, no abode stated, c1600, I, P2/C/1524
Jn., Gt. Faringdon, Berks., 1607, AB, P5/8Reg/103A
Jn., husb., Hurst, Berks., 1610, W, P5/9Reg/29A
Jn., shepherd, Durrington, 1610, AB, I, P2/C/242, P2/8Reg/128C
Cockes, Jn., husb., Codf. St P., 1611, AB, I, P2/C/258
Jn., shepherd, Stanton Fitzwarren, 1612, AB, comm, I, P3/C/65
Jn., sen., weaver, E. Fogham, Box, 1613, I, W (NEP), P3/C/70
Jn., yeo., Sal., 1616, W, P4/1616/2
Jn., sen., Easton, Bps. C., 1620, I, W, P24/60, P5/1629/11
Jn., weaver, Fogham, Box, 1624, AB, I, W, P3/C/131
Jn., N. Wraxall, 1627, I, W, P3/C/152
Jn., husb., Chute, 1631, I, W, P7/30
Jn., sen., husb., Lt. Somerford, 1633, I, W, P3/C/193
Jn., sen., W. Shefford, Berks., 1635, I, W, P1/C/169
Jn., yeo., Corsham, [1635], W, P29/C/4
Jn., yeo., Purton Stoke, 1638, I, W, P3/C/233
Jn., yeo., Wrou., 1643, AB, a/c, I, ren, P1/C/196, P3/C/272
Jn., yeo., Bremhill, 1649, AB, I, P1/C/223
Jn., yeo., W. Shefford, Berks., 1668, I, W, P1/C/292
Jn., fuller, Melk., 1670, I, W, P2/C/606
Jn., miller, Hurst, Berks., 1672, AB, I, P5/1672/5
Jn., vict., Liddington, 1683, I, W, P3/C/474
Jn., sen., Chute, 1690, I, W, P7/76
Jn., Box, 1691, AB, comm, P3/C/551
Jn., Charlton, Downton, 1694, AB, P2/C/840
Jn., tailor, Warm., 1694, comm, I, W, P2/C/843
Jn., goldsmith, Sal. St Thos., 1695, I (detailed), W, P4/1694/1
Jn., maltster, Sutton C., Berks., 1695, AB, I, ren, P1/C/439
Jn., yeo., Halstock Leigh, Dorset, 1700, I, W, P16/159
Jn., labourer, Lt. Hinton, 1701, I, W, P3/C/632

Jn., yeo., Draycot Foliat, 1701, I, W, P3/C/631
Jn., gent., Bourton, Shrivenham, Berks., 1704, AB, I (detailed), ren, P1/C/488
Jn., miller, Dauntsey, 1708, I, W, P3/C/669
Jn., Newbury, Berks., 1720, AB, I, P1/C/601
Jn., Lyme R., Dorset, 1720, AB, P16/215
Jn., labourer, Wanb., 1722, I, W, P3/C/741
Jn., yeo., Beam., Dorset, 1724, W, P17/413
Jn., Kingston Lisle, Sparsholt, Berks., 1726, AB, P1/C/645
Jn., Hurst, Berks., 1727, AB, I, P5/1727/10
Jn., waggoner, Rams., 1729, AB, I, P5/1729/13, P5/16Reg/237A
Jn., yeo., Compton, Berks., 1729, W, P1/C/677, P1/7Reg/273B
Jn., yeo., Lyme R., Dorset, 1738, I, W, Wr, P5/1738/13
Jn., tobacconist, Lyme R., Dorset, 1752, W, P5/1752/7
Jn., clothw., Chipp., 1753, AB, ren, P1/C/860
Jn., gent., Axford Farm, Rams., 1753, W, P5/1753/4
Jn., yeo., Letcombe Regis, Berks., 1763, AB, a/c, I, W, P1/C/929, P1/12Reg/137A
Jn., shopkeeper and miller, Pewsey, 1770, W, Wr, P3/C/1016
Jn., W. Tithing, Lt. Hinton, 1771, AB (2), comm, ren, W (2 - 1 a copy), P3/C/1022
Jn., gardener, Shellingford, Berks., 1773, comm, W, P1/C/979, P1/13Reg/26
Jn., clerk, Sal. The Close, 1779, AB, P5/1779/6, P5/17Reg/181C
Jn., Chr. M., 1797, W, P3/C/1135
Jn., yeo., Thornford, Dorset, 1807, W, Wr, P5/1807/8
Jn. *see also* Wm. Watts
Jos., publican, Melk., 1844, O, W, Wr, P2/1844/70
Judith, husb.'s widow, Wanb., 1666, AB, I, P3/C/308
Judith, widow, Fyfield, Berks., 1767, W, P1/C/947, P1/12Reg/252B
Lawr., sen., yeo., Huntingford, Gillingham, Dorset, 1690, I, W, P27/1/119
Lawr., yeo., Gillingham, Dorset, 1708, I, W, P27/1/173
Lucy, widow, Pewsey, 1765, AB, P3/C/990
Cocks, Mgt., widow, Hurst, Berks., 1628, I, W, P5/1628/22, P5/11Reg/78B
Martha, widow, Beam., Dorset, 1729, W, P17/435
My., widow, Chr. M., 1629, I, W, P3/C/163
My., widow, Easton, Bps. C., 1691, comm, I, W, P24/716
My., widow, Hampstead Marshall, Berks., 1704, I, W, P1/C/491
My., widow, Eaton Hastings, Berks., 1714, W, P1/C/554, P1/5Reg/385B
My., widow, Beam., Dorset, 1748, W, P17/510
My., widow, Badbury, Chiseldon, 1753, W, P3/C/927
My., sp., Beam., Dorset, 1757, W, P17/537
My., widow, Lyme R., Dorset, 1802, comm, W, Wr, P16/360
My., widow, Swindon, 1802, comm, W, P3/1802/74
My., sp., Burbage, 1822, W, Wr, P11/271
My., sp., Keevil, 1836, W, P2/1836/64
My. Ann, sp., Fordington, Dorset, 1855, AB, aff, O, Wr, P15/60
Matthew, Leigh, Yetm., Dorset, 1766, AB, comm, P19/163
Matthew, Leigh, Yetm., Dorset, 1788, AB, P5/1788/6, P5/18Reg/109A
Maud, widow, Codf. St P., 1635, I, W, P1/C/156
Nathaniel, mason, Trowb., 1756, W, P1/C/883, P1/11Reg/303
Nathaniel, W. Leigh, Halstock, Dorset, 1769, comm, W, P16/332
Nich., Norton B., 1556, W, P2/3Reg/4D
Nich., tailor, Box, 1617, AB, I (2 - 1 a copy), P3/C/90
Nich., yeo., Milton upon Stour, Gillingham, Dorset, 1740, AB (in minority of ex.), W, P27/1/354, P27/3Reg/12
Paul, sen., Ufton Nervet, Berks., 1692, AB, comm, I, P1/C/426
Philip, mariner, Lyme R., Dorset, 1744, W, P16/286
Philippa, Bps. C., 1692, AB, I, P24/538
Phoebe, sp., Lt. Hinton, 1787, W, P3/C/1096
Ralph, yeo., Alderton, 1616, W, P1/C/82
Ralph, Beam., Dorset, 1690, I, W, P17/320
Rebecca, sp., Rabson, Winterbourne Bassett, 1765, W, P3/C/991
Rd., tailor, Sherston, [1602], W (NEP), P3/1Reg/97A
Rd., N. Wraxall, 1609, W, P3/C/42

Rd., Charlton, Downton, 1610, AB, P2/C/234
Rd., Sutton M., 1614, AB, P1/C/66
Rd., Charlton, Downton, [1630?], W, P2/C/393
Rd., sen., Sevenhampton, Highw., 1631, I, P10/1631/1
Rd., yeo., Chr. M., 1634, I, W, P3/C/203
Rd., sen., yeo., Chards., Devon, 1635, comm, I, W, P5/1635/29, P5/12Reg/264
Rd., yeo., Chr. M., 1641, I, W, P3/C/266
Rd., yeo., Bps. C., 1735, comm, W, P24/937
Rd., carp., Wantage, Berks., 1764, W, P5/1764/9
Rd., yeo., Keevil, 1790, W, P2/C/1455
Rd., yeo., Mackney, Brightwell, Berks., 1792, W, P1/C/1069, P1/14Reg/410B
Rd., yeo., Heytes., 1843, W, Wr, P5/1843/9
Robt., Westb., 1570, AB, P5/2Reg/84B
Robt., husb., Lyme R., Dorset, 1630, AB, NW, P5/11Reg/128C
Robt., husb., Holt, Kintbury, Berks., 1680, AB, I, P1/C/349
Robt., Lyme R., Dorset, 1691, W, P16/111
Robt., Sal., 1693, AB, a/c, I (detailed), P4/1692/12
Robt., yeo., Heddington, 1693, I, W, P3/C/566
Robt., butcher, Elwell, Netherb., Dorset, 1737, W, P17/535
Roger, Allington, 1587, W, P2/7Reg/86B
Roger, Sal. The Close, 1630, AB, I, P5/1629/12, P5/11Reg/101A
Rowland, tailor, Sherston, 1638, I, W, P3/C/234
Rubeth, sp., Chards., Devon, 1732, AB, comm, P5/1732/10
Ruth, widow, Chr. M. sojourning at Malm., 1633, AB, I, W, P3/C/194
Sarah, widow, Cholsey, Berks., 1729, AB, P1/C/687
Cox form. Denslow, Sarah, Netherb., Dorset, 1765, AB, P17/557
Sarah, widow, Lt. Hinton, 1778, W, P3/C/1060
Cockes, Sarah, widow, Trowb., 1797, comm, W, P1/C/1088
Steph., husb., Allington, 1608, W, P2/8Reg/15
Susanna, widow, Lower Elwell, Netherb., Dorset, 1759, W, P17/538
Cockes, Thos., Seend, Melk., 1559, W, P2/3Reg/173A
Cox als Randoll, Thos., Widhill, Crickl. St S., 1566, court papers, W (NEP), P30/30
Thos., Inmarsh, Seend, Melk., 1589, I (2), NW, P2/C/83
Cox als Somerset, Thos., husb., Thornford, Dorset, 1589, I, W, P5/1589/5, P5/5Reg/61C
Thos., Fisherton A., 1605, AB, P1/C/21
Thos., husb., Purton, 1609, W, P3/C/43
Thos., sen., Chr. M., 1615, AB, I, P3/C/80
Thos., husb., Wrou., 1618, comm, I, W, P3/C/100
Thos., Wanb., 1620, AB, T, P1/C/102
Thos., yeo., Aston U., Blewbury, Berks., 1623, comm, I, W, P5/1622/17, P5/10Reg/159B
Thos., Sevenhampton, Highw., 1624, comm, I, W (badly damaged), P10/1624/5
Thos., husb., Britford, 1635, AB, I, P24/236
Thos., Netherb., Dorset, [1639], W, P17/42
Thos., yeo., Strongyeate, Netherb., Dorset, [1665], W, P17/81
Thos., yeo., Corsham, 1677, I, NW, P29/C/7
Thos., clerk, Winterborne Thompson, Dorset, 1678, comm, I, W, P5/1678/9, 11
Thos., wheelwright, Aston U., Blewbury, Berks., 1684, I, NW, P5/1684/14
Thos., sen., yeo., Ogbourne St Geo., 1685, I, W, P5/1685/22
Thos., yeo., Buckland, Berks., 1686, I, W, P1/C/1112
Thos., shoemaker, Axford, Rams., 1689, AB, I, ren, W, P5/1689/15
Thos., Lockeridge, Overton, 1720, AB, P1/C/593
Thos., higler, Hurst, Berks., 1729, W, P5/1729/14, P5/16Reg/235A
Thos., Ludg., 1730, AB, P2/C/1118
Thos., Biddestone St Nich., 1732, AB, P3/C/810
Thos., Overton, 1836, comm, W, Wr, P3/1836/10
Thomasine, widow, Devizes, 1671, I (detailed), W, P1/C/298
Thomasine, widow, Chilton F., 1685, I, W, P3/C/499
Toby, yeo., Hampton, Highw., 1633, I, W, P10/1633/2
Cox als Somerset, Tristram, Thornford, Dorset, 1601, I, T, W, P5/1600/68
Kockes, Wm., Sutton V., 1550, W, P2/2Reg/92B

Cockes, Wm., Fisherton A., 1558, AB, P2/3Reg/140B
Cockes, Wm., bach., Downton, 1559, W, P2/4Reg/6E
Wm., Heytes., 1560, I, P5/1560/3
Wm., servant to Thos. Cordray, Chute, 1566, W, P5/2Reg/10A
Wm., sen., Ashton K., 1591, I (detailed), P1/C/2
Wm., husb., Portland, Halstock, Dorset, 1594, AB, I, W, copy W, P16/467
Cox als Somerset, Wm., Thornford, Dorset, 1595, AB, I, T, P5/1594/22, P5/6Reg/93A
Wm., Halstock, Dorset, 1600, W, P5/6Reg/251A
Wm., Chr. M., 1606, I, W, P1/C/28
Wm., sen., gent. *or* farmer, Ashton K., 1624, comm, I (detailed), W, P3/C/132
Wm., husb., Britford, 1628, I, W, P24/224
Wm., yeo., Chr. M., 1631-33, AB, a/c, I (2 - 1 a copy), note, quitclaim, W, P3/C/177, 195
Wm., blacksmith, Holnest, Dorset, 1668, AB, I, NW, P5/1668/20
Wm., Tilsh., 1676, AB, I, P2/C/663
Wm., Mere, 1678-79, AB, a/c, I, P5/1678/6, P5/1679/11
Wm., yeo., Ludg., 1683, I, W, P2/C/727
Wm., Hampstead Marshall, Berks., 1686, AB, I, P1/C/1111
Wm., Gillingham, Dorset, 1695, I, P27/1/132
Wm., yeo., Berwick St Jn., 1701, AB, I, ren, P2/C/891
Wm., Halstock, Dorset, 1711, AB, P16/188
Wm., sen., tallow chandler, Gillingham, Dorset, 1726, W, P27/1/282
Wm., Brinkw., 1735, AB, I, P1/C/735
Wm., husb., Lt. Hinton, 1735, AB, ren, W, P1/C/739, P1/8Reg/123
Wm., gent. *or* yeo., Aldbourne, 1737, comm, W, P3/C/840
Wm., seaman, Lyme R., Dorset (d. on HMS *Victory*), 1745, AB, P16/291
Wm., Teffont M., 1748, AB, P2/C/1249
Wm., Sutton Poyntz, Dorset, 1764, AB, P18/6
Wm., yeo., W. Tithing, Lt. Hinton, 1772, AB, req, W, copy W, P3/C/1027
Wm., miller, Newbury, Berks., 1776, W, P1/C/997, P1/13Reg/112B
Wm., Bps. C., 1782, AB, comm, P24/1188
Wm., farmer, Keevil, 1817, W, Wr, P1/1817/84
Wm., blacksmith, Waytown, Netherb., Dorset, 1818, W, Wr, P5/1818/31
Wm., shopkeeper, Marl. St My., 1826, W, Wr, P1/1826/97
Williams, widow, Portland, Halstock, Dorset, 1600, I, W, P5/1600/15
see also Dike (Dyke) als C.; Somerset als C.
Coxesden, Baldwin, Chards., Devon, 1596, AB, P5/1596/18, P5/6Reg/139A
Coxhead, Ann, widow, Newbury, Berks., 1705-08, W, P1/C/492, P1/4Reg/290
Ann, widow, Sal., 1794, W, P4/1794/5
Benj., yeo., Mere Farm, Mildenhall, 1790, W, P3/C/1110
Eliz., widow, Hungerford, Berks., 1685, comm, I, W, P5/1685/26
Eliz., widow, Hungerford, Berks., 1829, AB, comm, P23/951
Jn., weaver, High Close, Hungerford, Berks., 1680, comm, I (detailed), W, copy W, P5/1680/8
Jn., sen., yeo., Shinfield, Berks., 1767, W, P1/C/945, P1/12Reg/245A
Jos., yeo., Charnham St., Hungerford, Berks., 1706, comm, W, P5/1706/10, P5/15Reg/2
Jos., Hungerford, Berks., 1771, AB, P23/738
Jos., Rams., 1823, W, Wr, P5/1823/2
My., widow, Hungerford, Berks., 1805, comm, W, P23/844
Peter, Rowde, 1616, AB, I, P1/C/81
Rd., yeo., Charnham St., Hungerford, Berks., 1701, comm, W, P5/1701/12
Rd., yeo., Hungerford, Berks., 1719, AB, I, P5/1719/17
Robt., sen., yeo., Charnham St., Hungerford, Berks., 1689, I, W, P23/170
Robt., yeo., Sanden Fee, Hungerford, Berks., 1750, W, P23/622
Sarah, widow, Rams., 1829, O, W, Wr, P5/1829/3
Sarah, sp., Hungerford, Berks., 1835, AB, comm, P23/979
Wm., sen., yeo., Charnham St., Hungerford, Berks., 1712, W, P23/326
Wm., mason, Hungerford, Berks., 1726, I, W, P23/439
Wm., innholder, Hungerford, Berks., 1761, W, P23/692
Wm., cabinetmaker, Hungerford, Berks., 1794, comm, W, P23/799
Coxhole, Simon, Haydon, Dorset, 1588, I, T, W, P5/1588/7, P5/5Reg/12A
Coxon, Wm., chapman, Reading, Berks., 1753, W, P1/C/854, P1/11Reg/31

Coy, Jn., gent., Sal., 1775, W, P4/1775/10
Cozener, Cousner *or* Wheeler, Alice, widow, Worton, Pott., 1595, AB, I (detailed), W, P1/C/10
Geo., tailor, Westb. L., 1712, I, W (NEP), P25/1713/5
My., sp., Westwood, [1675], I, NW, P2/C/654
Cusner, My., widow, Westb. L., 1705, I, W, P25/1705/3
Cuzner, Sarah, widow, Sherb., Dorset, 1813, W, Wr, P5/1813/13
Coosnar, Thos., innholder, St Mgt., Preshute, 1563, W (NEP), P1/2Reg/152
Cusner, Thos., Leighs Marsh, Dilton, Westb., 1700, W, P25/1700/6
Cursner, Thos., yeo., Melk., 1730, W, P2/C/1117
Thos., Dilton M., Westb., 1821, O, W, Wr, P25/1821/1
see also Cousnell als C.
Cozens *see* Cousins
Cozier *see* Cosier
Crabb, [...], Sal., 1619, a/c, P4/1619/12
Agnes, widow, Netherb., Dorset, 1679, I, W, P5/1679/13
Crabb als Taylor, Aldhelm, husb. *or* yeo., Charlton nr Malm., 1635, I, W, P3/C/208
Alice, widow, N. Bradley, 1603, I, W, P2/C/195
And., vict., Netherb., Dorset, 1678, AB, I, P17/276
Arthur, yeo., Whitecross, Netherb., Dorset, 1714, AB, W, P17/219
Arthur, linen weaver, Whitecross, Netherb., Dorset, 1723, W, P17/407
Edith, Easton, 1637, AB, a/c, P3/C/227
Edith, widow, Marl. St My., 1686, AB (2), I, ren, W, P1/C/375
Eleanor, widow, Kingsland, Netherb., Dorset, 1609, AB, I, W, P5/1609/18, P5/9Reg/1A
Eliz., sp., Netherb., Dorset, 1666, I, NW (NEP), P30/37
Eliz., widow, Whitecross, Netherb., Dorset, 1725, W, P5/1725/15, P5/16Reg/114A
Eliz., sp., Liverpool, Lancashire (effects at Southwick, N. Bradley), 1853, AB, court proceedings (2), D (2), O, Wr, P2/1853/44
Ezekiel, yeo., Woolcombs, Netherb., Dorset, 1696, comm, W, P5/1696/10
Frances, sp., Whitecross, Netherb., Dorset, 1736, I, W, P17/460
Geo., Mere, 1630, AB, P5/11Reg/132A
Geo., tailor, Fonthill B., 1704, W, P2/C/912
Hannah, sp., S. Bowood, Netherb., Dorset, 1738, I, W, P17/465
Hannah, sp., Whitecross, Netherb., Dorset, 1751, W, P17/518
Hy., clothier, Hilp., 1756, W, P1/C/884, P1/11Reg/302
Hester, widow, Trowb., 1824, W, Wr, P1/1824/13
Hugh, yeo., Beam., Dorset, 1632, AB, a/c, I, P17/8
Hugh, Netherb., Dorset, 1665, I, W, P5/1665/22
Hugh, Furleigh Cross, Netherb., Dorset, 1672, comm, I, W, P17/131
Hugh, Netherb., Dorset, 1684, I, W, P17/232
Isaac, clothier, N. Bradley, 1683-84, AB, a/c, bonds to pay legacies (2), I, P2/C/737
Jas., Marl. St My., 1685, AB, I, P1/C/374
Jane, widow, Southwick, N. Bradley, 1641, AB, I, P2/C/504
Joan, widow, Kershay, Netherb., Dorset, 1573, I, W, P5/1573/7, P5/3Reg/23C
Joan, widow, Chards., Devon, 1746, W, P5/1746/18
Jn., Netherb., Dorset, 1564, W, P5/1Reg/42B
Jn., husb., N. Bradley, 1577, I, T, W (damaged), P2/C/42, P2/5Reg/288A
Jn., Netherb., Dorset, 1597, AB, P5/6Reg/161D
Jn., yeo., Southwick, N. Bradley, 1618, I, T, P2/C/303
Jn., yeo. and tailor, Southwick, N. Bradley, 1668, I, W, P1/C/290
Jn., yeo., Netherb., Dorset, 1671-75, comm, I (1675), W, O (1671), P17/96
Jn., shearman, Beam., Dorset, 1680, I, W, P17/288
Jn., yeo., Atram, Netherb., Dorset, 1689, I (detailed), W, P17/312
Jn., Hungerford, Berks., 1697, AB, comm, I, P5/1697/9
Jn., Netherb., Dorset, 1700, AB, I, P17/134
Jn., vict., Quidh., 1767, W, P2/C/1335
Mgt., widow, Netherb., Dorset, 1609, I, W, P5/1609/20, P5/9Reg/50B
Martha, widow, Studley, Trowb., 1724, AB, ren, W, P1/C/629, P1/7Reg/38B
My., widow, Chards., Devon, 1669, I, NW, P14/27
My., sp., Atram, Netherb., Dorset, 1689, I, W, P17/311
My., widow, Marl., 1693, W, P1/C/429

My., widow, Netherb., Dorset, 1720, W, P17/387
My., sp., Netherb., Dorset, 1727, W, P17/431
Nich., Kingston, Netherb., Dorset, 1595, AB, W, P17/639, P5/6Reg/113
Robt., bach., N. Bradley, 1637, AB, cert, comm, I, P2/C/450
Robt., Netherb., Dorset, 1663, AB (unsigned), P17/19
Roger, yeo., Morgansland, Netherb., Dorset, 1709, comm, I, W, P5/1709/10, P5/15Reg/138B
Roger, Netherb., Dorset, 1710, AB, P17/198
Sarah, Marl., 1736, W, P1/C/745, P1/8Reg/172A
Simon, sen., yeo., N. Bradley, 1717-20, AB, I, W, P1/C/587, P2/C/1014
Simon, tailor, Southwick, N. Bradley, 1749, W, P2/C/1253
Thos., Netherb., Dorset, 1601, AB, I, W, P5/1601/9, P5/7Reg/19
Thos., clothw., Southwick, N. Bradley, 1681, comm, I, W, P2/C/700
Thos., carp., Southwick, N. Bradley, [1685], I, W, P2/C/748
Thos., N. Bradley, 1697-98, AB, comm, P2/C/868, 872
Walter, vict., Netherb., Dorset, 1600, W, P5/1600/10, P5/6Reg/252C
Walter, Easton, 1640, I, W (NEP), P3/C/256
Walter, freemason, Southwick, N. Bradley, 1640-41, a/c, I, W, P2/C/483
Walter, sen., vict., Netherb., Dorset, 1663, I, W (NEP), P30/36
Walter, sen., vict., Netherb., Dorset, 1710, I, W, P17/190
Wm., Southwick, N. Bradley, 1627, I, W, P2/C/376
Wm., Netherb., Dorset, 1712, W, P17/207
Wm., sen., clothw., Trowb., 1717, AB, comm, ren, W, P1/C/581, P1/6Reg/157
Wm., yeo., Easton, 1741, W, P1/C/777, P1/9Reg/68A
Craddock, Credock, Hy., Bourton, Gillingham, Dorset, 1728, AB, I, P27/1/294
Morgan, yeo., Luckington, 1626, I, W, P3/C/144
Rd., yeo., Minety, 1634, I, W, P1/C/147
Steph., gent., Mere, 1639, AB, I, P5/1639/21, P5/13Reg/210C
Craft, Dorothy, widow, Bradford A., 1610, W, P2/C/1506, P2/8Reg/134B
Craft als Simkins, Ellen, widow, Ashton G., Codf. St P., 1638, I, W, P2/C/463
Crafte als Simkins, Philip, yeo., Ashton G., Codf. St P., 1635, I, P30/35
see also Iles als C.
Cragg, Crugge, Jn., Uffc., Devon, 1564, W, P5/1Reg/40B
Jn., rector, N. Tidworth, 1665, AB, comm, I, P1/C/277
Crugge, Rd., Smythnycott, Uffc., Devon, 1553, W, P20/Reg/63
Craker *see* Crocker
Cramborne, Chris., lay vicar of Sal. Cathedral, Sal. The Close, 1587, I, NW, P5/1587/11, P5/4Reg/154A
Cramm, Thos., Damerham, Hants, 1671, W, P2/C/616
Crandole, Jn., husb., Arborfield, Berks., 1580, I, W, P5/1580/14, P5/4Reg/7D
Crandon, Jn., Wambrook, Somerset, 1565, W, P5/1Reg/46A
Jn., Wambrook, Somerset, 1675, I, P14/34
Jn., Wambrook, Somerset, 1775, AB, O, P14/182
Wm., Chards., Devon, 1633, AB, comm, I, P5/1634/6, P5/12Reg/170A
Wm., Chards., Devon, 1709, AB, comm, I, P14/108
Crane, Alice, widow, Sal., 1637, I, W, P4/1637/6
And., parchmentmaker, Sal. St Mart., 1628, I, P4/1627/23
Lucy, sp., Wantage, Berks., 1802, W, P23/830
Martha, sp., Sherb., Dorset, 1763, comm, W, P5/1763/4
Wm., sen., clerk, Britford, 1674, I, W, P24/438
Wm., vict., Wantage, Berks., 1812, W, Wr, P5/1812/9
Cranford, Rd., yeo., Stratfield M., Hants, 1698, W, P1/3Reg/65
Crapon, Crapon als Buy, Arthur, yeo., Pewsey, 1671, AB, I, P3/C/351
Crapen, Frances, Marl. St My., 1703, AB, P1/C/479
Thos., clerk, Stanton St B., 1687, W, P3/C/522
Crasby *see* Crosby
Crase, Crause *see* Cruse
Craven, Benj., weaver, Sal., 1790, W, Wr, P4/1790/11
Wm., grocer, Sal., 1789, W, P4/1789/3
Crawford, Rd., yeo., Stratfield M., Berks., 1698, I, W, P1/C/457
Crawly, Dan., yeo., Mkt. L., 1768, W, P2/C/1343
Hy., husb., Calne, 1611, W, P26/9

Hy., yeo., Mkt. L., [1689], I, W, P2/C/790
Rd., Odstock, 1605, W, P2/C/210
Cray, Alexander, gent., Horningsham, 1697, AB, P5/1697/8
Crey, Eleanor, widow, Trowb., 1719, comm, W, P1/C/583, P1/6Reg/175A
Crey, Jn., tailor, Bradford A., 1705, W, P2/C/917
Crey, Rd., Corsley, 1640, AB, P2/C/485
Rd., blacksmith, Beedon, Berks., 1744, AB, I, P1/C/801
Thos., Bradford A., 1558, AB, P2/3Reg/99B
Thos., sen., blacksmith, Compton, Berks., 1756, W, P1/C/875, P1/11Reg/197
Wm., Horningsham, 1716, comm, W, P5/1716/20, P5/15Reg/347B
Wm., tailor, Bradford A., 1721, W, P2/C/1037
Creaker *see* Crocker
Creature, Jn., Sonning, Berks., 1744, AB, Wr, P5/1744/12
Credock *see* Craddock
Creech, Ann, minor, Ogbourne St Geo., 1701, T, P5/1701/15
Creetch, Wm., husb., Bere R., Dorset, 1614, I, W (original damaged), P5/1613/11, P5/9Reg/127B
Wm., sen., yeo., Ogbourne St Geo., 1735, W, P23/508
Creed, Bennet, Sal., 1680, AB, I, P4/1680/21
Edwd., Barford St Mart., 1575, AB, P2/5Reg/232B
Edwd., Barford St Mart., 1585, AB, P2/6Reg/139A
Eliz., widow, Reading St Lawr., Berks., 1716, W, P1/C/567, P1/6Reg/49
Geo., wheelwright, Amesb., 1775, W, P2/C/1380
Jn., husb., Netherh., 1554, W (NEP), P2/1Reg/100B
Jn., Barford St Mart., 1599, note of AB, P2/C/173
Jn., Barford St Mart., 1615, AB, P2/8Reg/251B
Jn., jun., mariner, Lyme R., Dorset, 1637, AB, I, P16/475
Jn., basketmaker, Sal., 1704, W, P4/1704/3
Jn., E. Lockinge, Berks., 1722, AB, comm, P1/C/607
Jn., bach., Crickl. St S., 1815, AB, Wr, P3/1815/59
My., widow, Barford St Mart., 1594, I (detailed), W, P2/C/123
Robt., Sal., 1584, AB, P4/Reg/22D
Robt., Reading St Lawr., Berks., 1674, AB, I, P1/C/315
Robt., sen., yeo., Charminster, Dorset, 1749, W, P5/1749/15
Thos., carp., Amesb., 1846, AB, Wr, P2/1846/34
Walter, Sal., 1622, AB, P4/1622/8
see also Luffe nee C.
Crees *see* Cruse
Creetch *see* Creech
Cresbin, Chresbin als Snook, Christian, Gillingham, Dorset, 1582, AB, P27/2Reg/8A
Jn., butcher, Gillingham, Dorset, 1577, W, P27/1Reg/33A
Cresby *see* Crosby
Cretall *see* Crutwell
Crew, Ann, Highw., 1669, AB, P10/1669/5
Arthur, sen., gent., Stroud Farm, Lacock, 1678, I, W, P3/C/414
Arthur, broad weaver, Chipp., 1700, I, W, P3/C/627
Arthur, gent., Beanacre, Melk., 1712, I, W, P2/C/980
Bart., yeo., Notton, Lacock, 1679, AB, comm, I, P3/C/423
Bart., Dauntsey, 1730, I, W, P3/C/805
Bridget, widow, Notton, Lacock, 1715, I, W, P3/C/701
Edwd., glover, Lacock, 1640, I, W, P3/C/258
Edwd., butcher, Lacock, 1679, AB, I, P3/C/424
Edwd., Marl. St My., 1688, AB, I, P1/C/392
Edwd., Lacock, 1725, AB, I, P3/C/759
Edwd., Bradford A., 1729, AB, I, P2/C/1104
Edwd., blacksmith, Chr. M., 1783, AB, W, P1/C/1039, P1/14Reg/2
Eliz., widow, Lacock, 1609, W, P3/C/44
Eliz., widow, Lacock, 1640, comm, I, NW, P3/C/257
Eliz., widow, Bradford A., 1827, W, Wr, P2/1827/31
Giles, Brokenb., 1699, AB, comm, P3/C/614
Hy., S. Newton, 1687, AB, a/c, P2/C/776

Jas., Sal. St Edmd., 1701, AB, P1/C/474
Jas., butcher, Lacock, 1724, AB, I, P3/C/753
Jas., sen., blacksmith, Chr. M., 1760-61, AB, W, P3/C/955, 961
Jas., broad weaver, Bearfield, Bradford A., 1803, W, P2/1803/21, P2/1805/50
Jeremiah, burler, Limpley Stoke, Bradford A., 1722, W, P2/C/1052
Joan, widow, Chedglow, Crudwell, 1614, I, W (NEP), P3/C/74
Joan, Bewley, Lacock, 1729, AB, comm, P1/C/684
Joanna, sp., Lacock, 1678, AB, Wr, P3/C/415
Jn., Bourton, Gillingham, Dorset, 1578, W, P27/1Reg/35A
Jn., shoemaker, Lacock, 1613, W, P3/C/71
Jn., yeo. *or* carp., Chedglow, Crudwell, 1633, I, W, P3/C/196
Jn., Beanacre, Melk., 1682, I, W, P2/C/710
Jn., shoemaker, Bradford A., 1711, AB, I, P2/C/975
Jn., yeo., Bromham, 1761, W, P3/C/962
Jn., gent., Devizes, 1809, W, Wr, P1/1809/3
Jn., Devizes, 1839, AB, comm, Wr, P1/1839/60
Jos., Avill's Farm, Corsham, 1723, AB, comm, P3/C/746
Crewes, Leonard, weaver, Castleton, Dorset, 1625, AB, I, L, W, P5/1625/22, P5/10Reg/276A
Mgt., widow, Lacock, 1723, W, P3/C/747
Martha, widow, Wootton B., 1745, W, P3/C/887
My., sen., widow, Lacock, 1688, I, W, Wr, P3/C/534
My., widow, Lacock, 1730, I, W, P3/C/806
My., widow, Chr. M., 1799, AB, P1/C/1103, P1/15Reg/177
Rd., yeo., Lacock, 1604, I, W, P3/C/15
Rd., Lacock, 1690, AB, P3/C/547
Robt., tanner, Chipp., 1669, AB, a/c, comm, I, P3/C/332
Robt., tailor, Lacock, 1684, I, W, P3/C/492
Robt., glover, Lacock, 1738, W, P1/C/767, P1/8Reg/371
Roger, gent., Lacock, 1716, W, P3/C/703
Sam., sen., gent., Bewley, Lacock, 1726, W, P1/C/651, P1/7Reg/122
Sam., blacksmith, Chr. M., 1780, AB, W, P3/C/1067
Thos., yeo., Lacock, 1686, comm, I, W, P3/C/508
Thos., innholder, Wootton B., 1740, comm, W, P3/C/858
Walter, sen., clothw., Limpley Stoke, Bradford A., [1682], W, P2/C/712
Wm., sen., tailor, Lacock, 1664, I, W (NEP), P3/C/300
Wm., yeo., Gt. Somerford, 1787, W, P3/C/1097
see also Bishop als C.
Crey *see* Cray
Cribb, Chris., Thornford, Dorset, 1584, I, W, P5/1583/11, P5/4Reg/78C
Geo., yeo., Southbrook, Bere R., Dorset, 1684, I, W, P5/1684/13
Joan, sen., widow, Thornford, Dorset, 1588, W, P5/5Reg/26B
Thos., labourer, Sherb., Dorset, 1597, AB, I, P5/1597/26, P5/6Reg/154C
Cribson, Augustine, mariner, Lyme R., Dorset, 1701, W (2 - 1 a copy), P16/161
Criche, Rd., Gillingham, Dorset, 1570s?, court proceedings (absolution from excommunication to Rd. C. & Ann Sanger), P27/1Reg/37C
Crichell, Edmd., Leigh, Yetm., Dorset, 1600, I, W, P5/1600/16, P5/6Reg/252B
Chritchell, Jas., yeo., Sherb., Dorset, 1776, W, P5/1776/11, P5/17Reg/124B
Crichett, Jn., wheeler, Mere, 1564, W, P5/1Reg/25A
Crickesby, Nich., millward, Bps. C., 1586, W, P5/4Reg/126A
Nich., miller and servant, Southbroom, 1586, AB, I, P24/1438
Crimell, Wm., sen., Fordington, Dorset, 1595, I, W, P5/1595/14, P5/6Reg/106A
Crine, Cryne, Edmd., husb., Fovant, 1597, AB, W, P2/C/155
Edwd., tallow chandler, Tisb., 1699, AB, I, ren, P2/C/882
Hy., husb., Fovant, 1638, I, W, copy W, P2/C/458
Hy., Fovant Stroud, 1690, AB, P2/C/803
Hy., vict., Fovant, 1746, W, P2/C/1239
Hy., gent., Winterslow, 1808, comm, W, Wr, P2/1808/27
Cryne, Jn., Sutton M., 1559, W, P2/3Reg/153B
Cryne, Jn., husb., Over Zeals, 1618, AB, I, P5/1618/10, P5/10Reg/34B
My., widow, Fovant, 1763, W, P1/C/926, P1/12Reg/131

Cripps, Alice, widow, Berwick B., 1608-09, AB, I, W, P5/1608/40, P5/8Reg/131B
Ambrose, Elston, Orcheston St Geo., 1741, AB, P1/C/775
And., gent., Calne, 1723, W, P26/675
Ann, widow, Marl., 1680, I, W, P1/C/341
Ann, widow, Chiseldon, 1725, AB, P3/C/758
Ann, sp., Brinkw., 1730, AB, W, P3/C/807
Ann, widow, Hurst, Berks., 1673, I, W, P5/1673/8
Avis, yeo.'s wife, Winkfield, Berks., 1770, AB, W, P1/C/964, P1/12Reg/373
Chas., Wootton B., 1755, AB, comm, P3/C/940
Chas., gent., Wootton B., 1840, W, Wr, P3/1840/31
Edwd., mercer, Brinkw., 1720, W, P1/C/592, P1/6Reg/262A
Edwd., yeo., Burghfield, Berks., 1729, AB, ren, P1/C/675
Edwd., tailor, Rodbourne C., 1731, a/c, I, W, P3/C/795
Eliz., sp., Marl., 1720, W, P1/C/595, P1/6Reg/269
Francis, gent., Wootton B., 1676, I, W, P3/C/396
Geo., yeo., Berwick B., 1679, AB, comm, W, P5/1679/19
Hy., brazier, Upavon, 1688, I, copy I, W, P2/C/784
Jane, widow, Conock, Chirton, [1686], I, W, P2/C/766
Joan, widow, Wootton B., 1687, AB, P3/C/523
Jn., Wootton B., 1670, AB, I, P3/C/343
Jn., yeo., Aston U., Blewbury, Berks., 1717, I, W, P5/1717/11, P5/15Reg/396B
Jn., sen., yeo., Chiseldon, 1746, W, P3/C/893
Jn., sen., baker, Brinkw., 1748, W, P3/C/898
Jn., baker, Brinkw., 1768, W, P3/C/1008
Jos., yeo., Berwick B., 1683, W, P26/300
Mgt., widow, Berwick B., 1692, I, W, P5/1692/18
Mgt., sp., Devizes, 1760, W, P1/C/912, P1/11Reg/489B
My., widow, Shrewton, 1826, AB, Wr, P1/1826/131
Matthew, yeo., Sindlesham, Hurst, Berks., 1632, AB, a/c, comm, I, P5/1632/14, P5/12Reg/92A
Matthew, husb., Hurst, Berks., 1667, AB, I, P5/1667/15
Philip, carp., Buckland, Berks., 1726, W, P1/C/647, P1/7Reg/104B
Ralph, yeo., Sindlesham, Hurst, Berks., 1606, I (detailed), W, P1/C/24
Rd., sen., Gt. Faringdon, Berks., 1573, W, P5/3Reg/11A
Rd., blacksmith, W. Kennett, Avebury, 1671, I, W, P3/C/352
Rd., carp., Sindlesham, Hurst, Berks., 1695, AB, I, P5/1695/16
Rd., baker, Wootton B., 1743, W, P3/C/876
Rd., yeo., Brinkw., 1752, W, P3/C/920
Robt., farmer, Stanford Dingley, Berks., 1814, W, Wr, P1/1814/88
Robt. Gouldisborough, gent., Shrewton, 1786, W, P2/C/1438
Thos., yeo., Berwick B., 1579, I, W, P5/1579/21, P5/3Reg/144B
Thos., husb., Poulton, 1630, AB, I, P3/C/172
Thos., yeo., Dauntsey, 1677, AB, I, W, P1/C/333
Thos., sen., yeo., W. Kennett, Avebury & Berwick B., 1679, AB, W, P3/C/425
Thos., gent., Corton, Boyton, [1679], W, P2/C/683
Thos., Chiseldon, 1687, AB, I, P3/C/524
Thos., Marl., 1689, AB, I, P1/C/401
Thos., blacksmith, Milton L., 1753, W, P3/C/928
Thos., maltster, Mildenhall, 1766, W, P1/C/937, P1/12Reg/170
Thos., yeo., Wootton B., 1768, W, P3/C/1009
Thos., Shrewton, 1811, AB, Wr, P1/1811/31
Timothy, sen., gent., Wootton B., 1663, I, W, P3/C/293
Timothy, Wootton B., 1686, AB, ren, P3/C/509
Valentine, husb., Chiseldon, 1705, I, W, P3/C/656
Wm., husb., Berwick B., 1591, AB, I, W, P5/1590/17, P5/5Reg/95A
Wm., jun., Chiseldon, 1633, I, W, P3/C/197
Wm., baker, Wootton B., 1707, I, W, P3/C/665
Wm., Orcheston St Geo., 1737, AB, P2/C/1176
see also Oatridge als C.
Crisp, Jas., sen., vict., Bradford A., 1832, O, W, Wr, P1/1832/42
Jas., vict., Bradford A., 1845, D, W, Wr, P1/1845/27

Thos., yeo., Surrendell Farm, Hullavington, 1792, W, P1/C/1068, P1/14Reg/394
Wm., sen., yeo., Surrendell, Hullavington, 1779, W, P1/C/1012, P1/13Reg/240
Criswick, Jas., Sherb., Dorset, 1852, AB, D, ren, Wr, P5/1852/16
Croad *see* Crode
Crocheat, Thos., carp., Wylye, 1603, I, note of AB, NW, P2/C/201
Crock, Hy., husb., Atworth, Bradford A., 1592, I, W, P1/C/5
My., widow, Ogbourne St Geo., 1693, I, W, P23/185
Crocker, Croker, Eliza Crosbie, sp., Beam., Dorset, 1855, aff, comm, W, Wr, P17/629
Eliz., widow, Upavon, 1705, I, W, P2/C/924
Croker, Eliz., brazier's widow, Sal., 1771, W, P4/1771/6
Craker, Eliz., widow, Sutton C., Berks., 1773, W, P1/C/980, P1/13Reg/33
Francis, yeo., Binfield, Berks., 1835, W, P1/1835/97
Hy., husb., Winterborne K., Dorset, 1730, W, P5/1730/11
Jas., yeo., Butterwick, Folke, Dorset, 1763, I, W, P5/1763/5
Jas., yeo., Holt, Kintbury, Berks., 1826, comm, W, Wr, P1/1826/127
Joan, widow, Bere R., Dorset, 1667, AB, I, P5/1667/13
Jn., tailor, Whitep., 1630-37, I, T, W, P2/C/395, 452, P2/9Reg/118
Jn., Amesb., 1686, AB, P2/C/768
Jn., yeo., Hampstead Marshall, Berks., 1701, AB, I, P1/C/472
Creaker, Jn., Chr. M., 1745, AB, comm, P3/C/888
Jn., plumber and glazier, Amesb., 1777, W, P2/C/1388
Jn., sen., Wormstall Farm, Kintbury, Berks., 1798, AB, P1/C/1097, P1/15Reg/76A
Croker, Jn., yeo., Nash Hill, Lacock, 1799, comm, W, Wr, P3/C/1141
Jn., vict., Sandy Lane, Chipp., 1815, W, Wr, P3/1815/39
Jn., bach., Sherb., Dorset, 1856, AB, aff, comm, Wr, P5/1856/1
Jos., husb., Bere R., Dorset, 1641, I, W, P5/1641/21, P5/14Reg/25B
Jos., sen., tailor, Bere R., Dorset, 1700, I, W, P5/1700/8
Croker, Jos., yeo., Nash Hill, Lacock, 1825, comm, W, Wr, P3/1825/5
My., sp. and chapwoman, Bere R., Dorset, 1708, AB, I, P5/1708/25
Croker, Nich., Nethermore, Chipp., 1822, AB, Wr, P3/1822/26
Robt., Bere R., Dorset, 1641, AB, I, P5/1641/22, P5/14Reg/26A
Croker, Sam., brazier, Sal., 1766, W, P4/1766/11
Thos., yeo., Upavon, [1688], I, W, P2/C/789
Toby, husb., Marl., 1648, I, W, P1/C/218
Crockford, And., yeo., Sonning, Berks., 1641, I, W, P5/1641/23, P5/14Reg/23C
Ann, widow, Twyford, Hurst, Berks., 1665, AB, I, W, P5/1665/23
Eliz., widow, Sonning, Berks., 1583, W, P5/4Reg/72A
Eliz., widow, Hurst, Berks., 1743, AB, Wr, P5/1743/19
Hannah, sp., Hurst, Berks., 1727, W, P5/1727/8, P5/16Reg/154B
Hy., Sonning, Berks., 1594, AB, a/c, I, T, P5/1594/19, P5/6Reg/90A
Hy., collar and harnessmaker, Twyford, Hurst, Berks., 1663, I, W, P5/1663/17
Hy., sen., yeo., Hurst, Berks., 1727, I (detailed), W, P5/1727/9, P5/16Reg/154A
Humphrey, jun., husb., Hungerford, Berks., 1689, AB, I, P23/171
Isabel, widow, Sonning, Berks., 1583, I, P5/1582/12
Joan, widow, Twyford, Hurst, Berks., 1677, I, W, P5/1677/11
Jn., glover, Charnham St., Hungerford, Berks., 1661, comm, I, W, P5/1661/9
Jn., yeo., Hurst, Berks., 1752, W, P5/1752/10
Lucy, yeo.'s wife, Hurst, Berks., 1674, comm, W, P5/1674/23
Ralph, Sonning, Berks., 1545, W, P5/20Reg/63
Ralph, husb., Hinton, Hurst, Berks., 1631, I, W, P5/1631/33, P5/12Reg/62
Rd., husb., Hurst, Berks., 1604-08, I, W, P5/1603/20, P5/8Reg/4A
Thos., Sonning, Berks., 1571, AB, P5/2Reg/116D
Thos., yeo., Hurst, Berks., 1605, W, P5/8Reg/47
Thos., yeo., Hurst, Berks., 1616, AB, I, W, P5/1605/11
Thos., clerk and vicar, Fisherton D., 1634, I (detailed), W, P1/C/153
Thos., yeo., Hurst, Berks., 1675, I, W, P5/1675/13
Wm., Sonning, Berks., 1574, W, P5/3Reg/43B
Wm., ropemaker, Twyford, Hurst, Berks., 1615, W, P5/9Reg/120C
Wm., sen., baker, Waltham St Lawr., Berks., 1795, W, P1/C/1084, P1/14Reg/578
Crode, Croad, Ann, sp., Donhead St A., 1807, AB, comm, W, P2/1807/64

Thos., sen., husb., Currenden, Halstock, Dorset, 1719-21, W, comm, I, copy W (written on reverse of draft licence), P5/1719/15, P16/223
Thos., gent., Mangerton, Netherb., Dorset, 1789, W, P17/579, P5/18Reg/135
Crofts, Thos., weaver, Frys Bottom, Longbridge D., 1837, comm, W, Wr, P2/1837/57
Wm., Longbridge D., 1682, AB, P2/C/717
Croke *see* Crook
Croker *see* Crocker
Cromall *see* Cromwell
Crombe, Crome *see* Croome
Cromewell *see* Cromwell,
Crompe *see* Crump
Cromwell, Agnes, widow, Erlestoke, 1616, I, W, P1/C/85
Ann, widow, Pott., 1719, I, ren, W, P1/C/584, P1/6Reg/186A
Chris., Erlestoke, 1636, I, W, P2/C/436, P2/9Reg/93B
Chris., yeo., Erlestoke, 1732, I, W, P1/C/710, P1/7Reg/530
Edwd., Erlestoke, [1640], I, W, P2/C/479
Edwd., sen., yeo., Erlestoke, [1688], I, W, P2/C/781
Edwd., yeo., Erlestoke, 1721, W, P2/C/1038
Exlie, yeo., Erlestoke, 1715, AB, I, ren, P2/C/1001
Grace, widow, Erlestoke, 1663, AB, P2/C/555
Hy., yeo., Erlestoke, 1649, I, W, P1/C/225
Jas., shopkeeper, Westwood, 1832, O, W, Wr, P1/1832/141
Cromall, Jn., husb., Erlestoke, 1576, W, P2/5Reg/268B
Cromewell, Jn., wheeler, Gt. Somerford, 1606, W (NEP), P3/C/23
Crumwell, Jn., currier, Malm., 1640, I, W, P3/C/259
Jn., Gt. Somerford, 1670, AB, P3/C/344
Crumwell, Jn., Pott., 1713, AB, P1/C/537
Jn., gent., Roundway, Bps. C., 1746, W, P24/1067
Mgt., widow, Pott., 1634, I, W, P1/C/150
My., widow, Westwood, 1833, O, W, Wr, P2/1833/78
Nich., yeo., Pott., 1688, I, W, P1/C/385
Nich., Pott., 1732, AB, P1/C/715
Philip, clothw., Bedborough, Bps. C., 1749, W, P24/1055
Philip, Westwood, 1800, AB, P2/1800/96
Rd., husb., Startley, Gt. Somerford, 1637, I, W, P3/C/228
Rd., husb., Stanton St B., 1692, W, P1/C/419
Rd., Westwood, 1711, AB, I, P1/C/519
Thos., sen., yeo., Roundway, Bps. C., 1712, I, W, P24/692
Wm., clerk and vicar, Stanton St B., 1602, W (NEP), P3/C/5
Crooch *see* Crouch
Crook, Croke, Alice, widow, Urchf., 1548, W, P2/2Reg/65B
Crooke, Alice, widow, Monkton F., 1587, W, P2/7Reg/100A
Crooke, Alice, widow, E. Kennett, 1609, W, P3/C/45
Crooke, Ann, widow, Hodson, Chiseldon, 1612, W (NEP), P3/C/66
Crooke, Ann, widow, Langley Burrell, 1666, AB, I, W, P1/C/279
Crooke, Ann, widow, Swindon, 1676, I, NW, P3/C/397
Ann, widow, Easterton, Mkt. L. (form. of Crookwood Farm, Urchf.), 1770, W, P1/C/959, P1/12Reg/324A
Ann, sp., Rowde, 1785, W, P3/C/1090
Ann, widow, Chipp., 1824, W, Wr, P3/1824/48
Ann, sp., Hinton, Steeple A., 1833, cert, W, Wr, P2/1833/76
Anth., yeo., Tytherton L., Chipp., 1837, comm, W, Wr, P3/1837/60
Benj., Etchilhampton, 1772, W, P3/C/1028
Benj., breechesmaker, Bedborough, Bps. C., 1786, W, P24/1171
Benj., sen., Etchilhampton, 1813, AB, Wr, P3/1813/49
Crooke, Betty, Fisherton A., 1695, AB, P2/C/852
Cath., sp., Tytherton L., Chipp., 1728, comm, W, P3/C/778
Cath., widow, Tytherton L., Chipp., 1809, W, Wr, P3/1809/58
Cath., sp., Tytherton L., Chipp., 1853, O, W, Wr, P3/1853/14
Crooke, Christian, Ham, [1609], W (NEP), P3/C/35
Crooke, Cicely, S. Wraxall, 1617, I, W, P2/C/302

Crooke, David, yeo., S. Wraxall, 1636-41, AB, court paper, I, P2/C/437, 495
Crooke, Edith, widow, Langley Burrell, 1630, W, P3/C/173
Crooke, Edmd. *or* Edwd., weaver, Langley Burrell, 1624, I, W, P3/C/133
Edwd., yeo., Tytherton L., Chipp., 1696, I, W (damaged), P3/C/594
Edwd., gent., Tytherton L., Chipp., 1743, W, P3/C/877
Crooke, Eliz., widow, Urchf., [1684], I, W, P2/C/738
Eliz., widow, Shaw, Melk., 1728, I, W, P2/C/1091
Eliz., widow, Rockley, Ogbourne St And., 1743, AB, I, Wr, P5/1743/18
Eliz., widow, Eastrop, Highw., 1765, W, P10/1765/1
Eliz., widow, Ogbourne St Geo., 1770, W, P5/1770/12, P5/17Reg/4A
Eliz., sp., Bps. C. (effects at Bromham), 1792, AB, comm, P3/C/1117
Eliz., widow, Whitep., 1849, D, W, Wr, P2/1849/14
Croke, Grace, widow, Steeple A., 1677, I, W, P1/C/322
Hannah, sp., Seend, Melk., 1811, comm, W, Wr, P1/1811/124
Hannah, widow, Calne, 1835, comm, W, Wr, P26/1414
Hannah, sp., Boreham, Warm. (form. of Bishopstrow), 1844, O, W, Wr (where erroneously called widow), P2/1844/14
Hy., Broad B., Highw., 1673, AB, a/c, comm, I, P10/1673/1
Hy., yeo., Hinton, Steeple A., 1806, W, P2/1806/45
Jacob, vict., Holt, Bradford A., 1773, AB, comm, ren, P1/C/981
Jacob, yeo., Ludg., 1846, O, W, Wr, P2/1846/29
Crooke, Jas., yeo., Highw., 1675, comm, I, NW, P10/1675/3
Jas., scribbler, Devizes, 1813, AB, O, Wr, P1/1813/1
Crooke, Jane, Langley Burrell, 1619, I, W, P1/C/92
Crooke, Jane, widow, Urchf., [1712], W, P2/C/977
Jane, widow, Poulshot, 1782, W, P2/C/1421
Crooke, Jn., Langley Burrell, 1596, W (NEP), P3/C/1
Crooke, Jn., yeo., Steeple A., 1606, W, P2/C/217
Crooke, Jn., husb., Lt. Hinton, 1638, AB, a/c, I. L, P3/C/235
Crooke als Hood, Jn., husb., Urchf., 1676, comm, I, W, P2/C/659
Crooke, Jn., sen., fellmonger, Urchf., 1684, AB, comm, I (2), W, P2/C/731, 735, 744
Crooke, Jn., yeo., Urchf., 1691, AB, I, P2/C/809
Jn., husb., Wilcot, 1692, AB, comm, I, P1/C/416
Crooke, Jn., yeo., Steeple A., [1694], I, W, P2/C/848
Jn., vict., Keevil, 1742, AB, I, P2/C/1217
Jn., yeo., Ogbourne St Geo., 1742, AB, I, ren, P23/565
Crooke, Jn., tinman, Devizes, 1746, W, P1/C/815, P1/10Reg/34B, 56
Jn., cordw., Bradford A., 1759, W, P1/C/907, P1/11Reg/457B
Jn., Ogbourne St And., 1780, AB, P23/770
Jn., yeo., Bromham (form. of Urchf. where W was made), 1808, W, Wr, P1/1808/47
Jn., Monkton F., 1840, AB, comm, Wr, P2/1840/37
Jn., yeo., Avebury, 1844, note, O, W, Wr, P3/1844/20
Jn. Manning, Swindon (effects at Ogbourne St Geo. ; form. of Maidenhead, Berks.), 1838, aff, W, Wr, P23/995
Jn. Mannings, maltster, Ogbourne St Geo., 1824, AB, W, P23/918
Crooke, Jos., Urchf., 1740, I, W, P2/C/1209
Jos., baker, Avill's Farm, Corsham, 1768, W, P3/C/1010
Jos., Melk., 1819, comm, W, Wr, P2/1819/73
Jos., yeo., Easterton, Mkt. L. (form. of Pott.), 1831, O, W, Wr, P2/1831/26
Ludovic, yeo., Shaw, Melk., 1700, I, W, P2/C/884
Marian, widow, Pott., 1646, I, W, P1/C/214
Martha, sp., Wrou., 1783, AB, W, P1/C/1032, P1/13Reg/419A
Martha, widow, Melk., 1820, AB, comm, Wr, P2/1820/11
My., servant to Jn. Hungerford, Cadenham, Bremhill, 1618, I, W, P3/C/101
Crooke, My., Baldham, Keevil, 1636, I, W, P2/C/443
My., widow, Devizes St Jn., 1755, W, P1/C/872, P1/11Reg/192
My., sp., Chr. M., 1769, W, P3/C/1015
My., widow, Sandy Lane, Calne, 1772, W, P26/1054
My., sp., Bromham, 1823, W, Wr, P1/1823/49
My., widow, Broughton G., 1825, comm, W, Wr, P2/1825/39
My., sp., Thornhill, Clyffe P., 1838, D, O, W, Wr, P3/1838/20
My., sp., Tytherton L., Chipp., 1847, O, W, Wr, P3/1847/44

Crooke, Maud, widow, S. Wraxall, 1591, I, W, P2/C/93
Crooke, Obadiah, cordw., Erlestoke, 1731, W, P2/C/1124
Crooke, Oliver, Hodson, Chiseldon, 1720, AB, comm, P1/C/589
Croke, Peter, S. Wraxall, 1557, W, P2/3Reg/49C
Philip, Sandy Lane, Calne, 1749, AB, Wr, P5/1749/12
Philip, mason, Avebury, 1775, W, P3/C/1048
Rd., husb., Wootton R., 1685, W, P3/C/500
Crooke, Rd., Wootton B., 1687, AB, comm, P3/C/525
Rd., Sandy Lane, Calne, 1796, AB, comm, P26/1203
Rd., gent., Aldbourne, 1805, req, W, P3/1805/14
Croke, Robt., S. Wraxall, 1537, I, W, P30/29
Crooke als Hood, Robt., Urchf., 1670, AB, P2/C/598
Crooke, Robt., maltster, Urchf., 1742, W, P2/C/1220
Robt., tailor, Mildenhall, 1767, W, P1/C/942, P1/12Reg/206
Robt., Rowde, 1801, AB, comm, P3/1801/9
Robt., bricklayer, Marl., 1812, W, Wr, P1/1812/11
Robt., Urchf., 1837, AB, Wr, P2/1837/79
Sarah, widow, Chipp., 1775, comm, W, P3/C/1049
Sarah, widow, Seend, Melk., 1786, W, P1/C/1046, P1/14Reg/94
Simon, gent., Flaxlands, Lydiard T., 1820, W, Wr, P1/1820/118
Crooke, Steph., sen., Steeple A., 1640, I, W, P2/C/493
Steph., carp., Avebury, 1805, W, P3/1805/31
Steph., carp., Avebury, 1833, O, W, Wr, P3/1833/9
Crooke als Colls, Thos., sen., yeo., Ogbourne St Geo., 1562, W, P5/1Reg/15
Crooke, Thos., S. Wraxall, 1594, AB, I, W, P2/C/1515
Crooke, Thos., Ogbourne St And., 1603, I, T, NW, P5/1603/19, P5/7Reg/88B
Crooke, Thos., Hodson, Chiseldon, 1605, W (NEP), P3/C/21
Crooke, Thos., yeo., Steeple A., 1625, I, W, P2/C/352
Crooke, Thos., yeo., Hodson, Chiseldon, 1628, AB, a/c, I, P3/C/158
Thos., shepherd, Burbage, 1634, AB, I (GVS), P5/1634/33
Crooke als Hood, Thos., husb., Seend, Melk., 1665, I, copy I, W, P2/C/562
Crooke, Thos., sen., yeo., Hodson, Chiseldon, 1668, AB, I, W, P3/C/318
Thos., jun., currier, Sal., 1680, AB, I, P1/C/337
Crooke, Thos., baker, Urchf., 1682, AB, I, ren, P2/C/709
Crooke, Thos., husb., Hodson, Chiseldon, 1685, I, W, P3/C/503
Thos., Highw., 1723, AB, P10/1723/4
Thos., Seend, Melk., 1732, AB, P2/C/1138
Thos., yeo., Pewsey, 1744, W, P3/C/881
Thos., jun., miller, Wrou., 1774, comm, req, W, copy W, P3/C/1040
Crooke, Thos., breechesmaker, Urchf., 1790, W, P2/C/1459
Thos., Rowde, 1809, AB, comm, Wr, P3/1809/15
Thos., gent., Chipp., 1824, W, Wr, P3/1824/27
Crooke, Wm., shearman, Marl. St My., 1610, AB (2), comm, P1/C/41
Wm., Brixton D., 1618, I, T, P2/C/306
Crooke, Wm., sen., mason, Ogbourne Maizey, 1678, AB, I, P23/83
Wm., Ogbourne St And., 1692, AB, I, P5/1692/20
Wm., yeo., Beanacre, Melk., [1692], I, W, P2/C/818
Wm., Chiseldon, 1729, AB, I, P3/C/786
Wm., mason, Ogbourne St And., 1730, W, P23/472
Crooke, Wm., yeo., Urchf., 1741, W, P2/C/1212
Wm., Eastrop, Highw., 1750, W, P10/1750/2
Wm., carp., Avebury, 1754, W, P3/C/933
Wm., sen., tailor, Urchf., 1770, comm, W, Wr, P2/C/1354
Wm., clothw., Seend, Melk., 1771, comm, W, P2/C/1359
Wm., gent., Tytherton L., Chipp., 1805, W, Wr, P3/1805/25
Wm., yeo., Ogbourne St Geo., 1812, W (& cod), Wr, P5/1812/2
Wm., yeo., Tytherton L., Chipp., 1816, W, Wr, P3/1816/24
Wm., yeo., Urchf., 1823, W, Wr, P1/1823/52
Wm., grocer, Trowb., 1825, comm, W, Wr, P1/1825/5
Wm., carp., Whitep., 1832, W, Wr, P2/1832/8

Wm., widower, Hinton, Steeple A., 1848, AB, O, Wr, P2/1848/32
see also Hood als C.; Pryer form. C.
Croome, Crome, Agnes, widow, Tilsh., 1555, W, P2/1Reg/82B
Agnes, widow, Gt. Wishford, 1616, I, W, P2/C/290, P2/8Reg/294A
Agnes, widow, Malm., 1631, I, W, P3/C/178
Chas., sen., yeo., Woodb., 1763, W, P1/C/925, P1/12Reg/121B
Chas., yeo., Bps. C., 1769, W, P24/1080
Dorothy, Crockerton, Longbridge D., 1753, AB, P2/C/1279
Edwd., yeo., Crockerton, Longbridge D., 1670-74, AB, a/c, I, P2/C/609, 645
Edwd., cordw., Bratton, Westb., 1678, AB, I, P25/1678/11
Eliz., widow, Brokenb., 1754, W, P3/C/934
Croom, Geo., gardener, Melk., 1814, W, Wr, P1/1814/80
Croom, Geo., vict., Sal., 1855, a/c, aff, D, W (on pre-printed form), Wr, P4/1855/4
Jas., yeo., Malm., 1617, I, W, P3/C/91
Jas., Lea, L. and Cleverton, 1771, W, P3/C/1023
Croom, Jas., innholder, Tisb., 1802, W, P2/1802/72
Joan, widow, Bratton, Westb., 1633, I, W, P25/1633/1
Joan, widow, Tisb., [1677], I, W, P2/C/671
Crombe, Jn., Tilsh., 1552, I, W, P2/C/6, P2/2Reg/159B
Crome, Jn., Tilsh., 1577, I, W, P2/C/44, P2/5Reg/290A
Jn., yeo., Gt. Wishford, 1602, AB, I, W, P2/C/187
Crome, Jn., husb., Stoford, S. Newton, 1697, W, P2/C/871
Jn., Longbridge D., 1703, AB, P2/C/911
Crome, Jn., sen., Bratton, Westb., 1704, I, W, P25/1704/8
Jn., Tisb., 1771, AB, P2/C/1360
Jn., [harnessmaker and slaymaker], Bromham, 1781, W, P3/C/1072
Jn., perukemaker and innholder, Malm., 1825, D, O, W, Wr, P3/1825/39
My., sp., Malm., 1727, AB, comm, P3/C/772
Nathan, Woodb., 1797, AB, comm, P3/C/1136
Rebecca, Malm., 1709, AB, P3/C/674
Robt., Hartham, Corsham, 1663, I, W, P3/C/294
Robt., sen., carp., Woodb., 1696, I, W, P3/C/595
Robt., Woodb., 1700, I, W, P3/C/628
Robt., clothier, W. Harnham, 1714, W, P5/1713/19, P5/15Reg/382
Robt., Brokenb., 1722, I, W, P3/C/742
Croom *or* Crumb, Sarah, widow, Bittlesea Farm, Chr. M., 1745, W, P3/C/889
Sarah, sp., Wilsford with Lake, 1797, W, P13/5/12
Thos., yeo., Sal., 1620, I, W, P4/1620/4
Thos., yeo., Erlestoke, 1666, I, W, P2/C/567
Thos., woolstapler, Crockerton, Longbridge D., 1722, W, P2/C/1050
Thos., Crockerton, Longbridge D., 1755, AB, P2/C/1288
Walter, Sal. St Edmd., 1626, AB, a/c, I (3), P4/1626/7
Crome, Wm., Tisb., 1670, AB, I, NW, P2/C/599
Wm., miller, W. Harnham, 1745, W, P8/101
Crooms, Wm., Amesb., 1783, AB, comm, P2/C/1426
Croppe, Croope, Jn., Wambrook, Somerset, 1613, I, W, P5/1613/14, P5/9Reg/92C
Rd., husb., Bulford, 1587, W, P2/7Reg/77B
Simon, husb., Bulford, 1562, I, W, P2/C/26, P2/4Reg/103C
Wm., husb., Amesb., 1561, AB, I, W, P2/C/18, 1509, P2/4Reg/88A
Crosby, Crasby, Ann, widow, Badbury, Chiseldon, 1667, I, W, P3/C/313
Crasby, Eliz., widow, Axford, Rams., 1696, I, W, P5/1696/9
Eliz., widow, Westb., 1804, O, W, P25/1804/6
Cresby, Jn., husb., Badbury, Chiseldon, 1619, I, W (NEP), P3/C/104
Jn., Chiseldon, 1645, AB, comm, I, P1/C/208
Jn., [weaver], Rams., 1694, AB, I, P5/1694/35
Cresby, Jn., sen., yeo., Badbury, Chiseldon, 1701, I, W, P3/C/633
Cresby, Jn., yeo., Badbury, Chiseldon, 1718, W, P3/C/719
Cresby, Jn., yeo., Badbury, Chiseldon, 1768, AB, ren, W, P3/C/1007
Cresby, Jn., yeo., Badbury, Chiseldon, 1802, comm, note, W, P3/1802/66
Crossby, Margery, widow, Rams., 1715, I, W, P5/1715/16, P5/15Reg/315A

Thos., sen., Axford, Rams., 1677, I, W, P5/1677/13
Thos., yeo., Axford, Rams., 1683, I, W, P5/1683/11
Thos., weaver, Rams., 1732, AB, I, P5/1731/17
Tryphena, sp., Sal., 1751, W, P4/1751/2
Chreasby, Wm., carp., Badbury, Chiseldon, 1611, W (NEP), P3/C/58
Crosdall, Geoff., Pewsey, 1606, AB, P3/C/24
Cross, Crosse, Agnes, widow, Uffc., Devon, 1564, W, P5/1Reg/33A
Alexander, Corsley, 1820, AB, Wr, P2/1820/20
Ann, widow, Coombe B., 1835, AB, P8/88
Ann, widow, Mere, 1852, comm, W, Wr, P5/1852/8
Dan., yeo., Easthampstead, Berks., 1729, W, P1/C/672, P1/7Reg/263
Crosse, Eliz., widow, Uffc., Devon, 1635, AB, I, P5/1635/21, P5/12Reg/217
Eliz., widow, Maiden B., 1743, W, P2/C/1222
Francis, sen., currier, Beam., Dorset, 1688, AB, I, P17/305
Hy., Laverstock, 1824, AB, Wr, P2/1824/52
Humphrey, Uffc., Devon, 1549, W, P20/Reg/41
Humphrey, innholder, Fisherton A., 1810, W, Wr, P2/1810/42
Jas., butterman, Erlestoke, 1737, AB, W, P2/C/1179
Jas., Grittleton, 1839, aff, O, W, Wr, P3/1839/3
Jas., labourer, Ludwell, Donhead St My., 1848, aff, W, Wr, P2/1848/45
Jn., curate, Maddington, 1545, W (NEP), P2/1Reg/56C
Crosse, Jn., Uffc., Devon, 1570, W, P5/2Reg/76A
Jn., tailor, Lyme R., Dorset, 1667, I, W, P16/11
Jn., servant to Mrs Hutin, Warm., 1851, W, Wr, P2/1851/15
Jos., yeo., E. Knoyle, 1765, W, P2/C/1324
Jos., Coombe B., 1835, AB, W, P8/89
Crosse, Mgt., widow, Allweston, Folke, Dorset, 1576, I, W, P5/1576/12, P5/3Reg/78A
Crosse, Michael, yeo. *or* husb., Wadswick, Box, 1668, comm, I, W, P3/C/319
Reuben, labourer, E. Harnham, Britford, 1828, AB, W, P24/1314
Crosse, Robt., weaver, Crickl. St S., 1626, AB, I, P3/C/145
Crosse, Thos., Uffc., Devon, 1628, comm, I, NW, P5/1628/25, P5/11Reg/11D
Thos., tanner, Maiden B., 1733, I, W, P2/C/1151
Thos., Sherb., Dorset, 1795, AB, W, Wr, P5/1795/2, P5/18Reg/215B
Thos., shopkeeper, Luckington, 1804, W, P3/1804/21
Wm., yeo., Enford, 1545, W, P2/1Reg/63B
Crosse, Wm., Keevil, 1568, W, P2/5Reg/36B
Crosse, Wm., clothier, Devizes St Jn., 1605, I, W, P1/C/22
Crosse, Wm., sen., yeo., Uffc., Devon, 1667, I, W, P20/1/55
Crosse, Wm., Uffc., Devon, 1683, AB, I, P20/1/97
Wm., sen., yeo., Sutton M., 1788, W, P2/C/1445
Wm., gent., Turleigh, Winsley, Bradford A., 1793, AB, comm, ren, W, P2/C/1474
Wm., pork butcher and gardener, Chipp., 1814, AB, W, Wr, P3/1814/25
Crossby *see* Crosby
Crosse *see* Cross
Crossley, Ann, jun., sp., Abingdon, Berks., 1773, W, P1/C/967, P1/12Reg/469B
Crosswell, Jn., Wokm., Berks., 1567, W, P5/2Reg/26B
Rd., Newbury, Berks., 1823, AB, comm, Wr, P1/1823/13
Crottall *see* Crutwell
Crouch, And., widow, Bemerton, Fugg. St Peter, 1691, I, NW, P2/C/810
Ann, widow, Collingbourne K., 1772, AB, P3/C/1029
Avis, widow, Mere, 1635, AB, I, ren, W, P5/1635/28, P5/12Reg/263
Cath., widow, Deptford, Wylye, 1582-92, AB, a/c, I, W (3 copies), P2/C/107, P2/6Reg/76A
Chris., sen., yeo., Barford St Mart. (described as of Winterborne St Mart.), 1706, I, W, P2/C/937
Chris., grocer, Fovant Stroud, 1721, W, P2/C/1036
Chris., sen., yeo., Barford St Mart., 1780-92, AB, W, P2/C/1405, 1467
Edmd., husb., Codf. St My., 1591, AB, I, W, P2/C/97
Edmd., Codf. St My., 1624, AB, P2/C/345
Edmd., blacksmith, Codf. St My., 1634, I, W, P2/C/423, P2/9Reg/32
Edmd., yeo., Codf. St P., 1661, comm, I, W, P2/C/545
Edmd., Barford St Mart., 1788, AB, P2/C/1448

Edmd., vict., *The Running Horse*, Sal., 1840, W, Wr, P4/1840/1
Eliz., Deptford, Wylye, 1580, W, P2/6Reg/3B
Eliz., Longbridge D., 1598, I, W, P2/C/158
Eliz., sp., Fonthill B., 1724, AB, P2/C/1057
Hy., Codf. St My. & Sal., 1646, caveat, L (to Mr Hill at S. to find W of Wm. Bithum, written on reverse), P2/C/527
Isaac, sen., Bradford A., 1792, W, P1/C/1067, P1/14Reg/382
Jas., Gillingham, Dorset, 1760, W, P27/1/425, P27/3Reg/84
Crowch, Jn., Upton L., c1538, W (NEP), P2/1Reg/4D
Crowch, Jn., Oxenwood, Shalbourne, 1571, W, P5/2Reg/94C
Jn., Wexcombe, Grafton, 1587, I, T, W, P5/1586/5, P5/4Reg/139D
Jn., carp., Longbridge D., 1599, I, W, P2/C/171
Crowch, Jn., yeo., Knook, 1648, I, W, P5/1648/3, P5/14Reg/103A
Jn., sen., cardmaker, Sal., 1668-69, AB, W, copy W, P4/1668/7, P4/1669/1
Jn., husb., Codf. St P., 1680, I, W, P2/C/692
Jn., yeo., Motc., Dorset, 1680, I, W, P27/1/61
Jn., yeo., Codf. St P., 1687, I, W, P2/C/779
Jn., Motc., Dorset, 1701, AB, P27/1/139
Jn., Codf. St My., 1707-14, AB, P2/C/941, 992
Crowch, Jn., husb., Corsley, 1709, W, P2/C/959
Jn., cooper, Collingbourne K., 1738, W, P1/C/764, P1/8Reg/344
Jn., Barford St Mart., 1758, AB, P2/C/1300
Crowch, Jn., clerk, Upton L., 1769, W, P2/C/1352
Jn., mealman, Lt. Cheverell, 1770, W, P2/C/1353
Jn., yeo., Motc., Dorset, 1799, W, P27/1/564
Jn., yeo., Whitep., 1805, W, P2/1805/52
Jn., bach., Wylye, 1836, AB, P2/1836/50
Jos., gardener, Newcastle town, Tisb., 1823, I, W, Wr, P2/1823/2
Joyce, sp., Ogbourne St Geo., 1757, AB, P23/674
Judith, widow, Stockton, 1669, AB, I (d. 1658), P2/C/589
Crowch, Mgt., widow, Upton L., 1563, I, W, P2/C/29, P2/4Reg/121
Crooch, Mgt., widow, Ludg., 1641, AB, W, P2/C/502-03
Martha, sp., Norton B., 1755, AB, P2/C/1290
My., widow, Barford St Mart., 1793, W, P2/C/1472
Crowch, Nich., yeo., Gt. Bedwyn, 1616, I, W, P5/1616/13, P5/9Reg/177
Nich., yeo., Barford St Mart., 1736, a/c, I, W, P2/C/1172
Nich., yeo., Barford St Mart., 1814, W, Wr, P1/1814/55
Rd., Deptford, Wylye, 1565, W (bequest to roofing nave of chapel at D.), P2/4Reg/215B
Rd., Codf. St P., 1572, W, P2/5Reg/144D
Rd., yeo., Longbridge D., [1627], I, W, P2/C/377
Crowch, Rd., gent., Tytherington, Heytes., 1671, I, W (both damaged), P5/1671/22
Rd., Pewsey, 1729, AB, comm, P3/C/787
Rd., blacksmith, Pewsey, 1738, AB, I, P1/C/760
Rd., husb., Crawlboys, Collingbourne D., 1763, comm, W, P1/C/917, P1/12Reg/54B
Crowch, Robt., husb., Radley, Berks., 1592, I (top part is missing), W, P1/C/6
Sam., Dinton, 1845, AB, Wr, P1/1845/53
Crowch, Steph., gent., Tytherington, Heytes., 1755, W, P5/1755/10
Steph., bach., Sal., 1810, AB, P4/1810/11
Steph., labourer, Motc., Dorset, 1823, W, Wr, P27/1/665
Steph., carp., Barford St Mart., 1830, W, P2/1830/9
Crowch, Thos., Gt. Cheverell, 1559, AB, P2/3Reg/174D
Thos., husb., Codf. St My., 1624-25, AB, a/c, I, P2/C/343
Thos., yeo., Codf. St P., 1665, I, W, P2/C/561
Thos., Ludg., 1685, AB, a/c, I, ren, P2/C/752
Thos., Collingbourne K., 1733, W, P3/C/819
Tristram, yeo., Codf. St P., 1612, I, W, P2/C/259
Tristram, Codf. St P., 1729, W, P1/C/686, P1/7Reg/354
Wm., Codf. St My., 1580, W, P2/6Reg/13B
Crooch, Wm., Crockerton, Longbridge D., [1622], I, W, P2/C/327
Crooch, Wm., shepherd, Ludg., 1641, AB, I (for Wm. & his wife Mgt.), W, P2/C/502-03
Wm., Ashton G., Codf. St P., 1670, I, W (NEP), P1/C/299

Wm., joiner, Sal. St Thos., 1672, AB, I, P4/1671/17
Wm., sen., tailor, Wexcombe, Grafton, 1689, I, W, P21/4/42
Crowch, Wm., clerk, Steeple A., 1707, W, P2/C/943
Wm., sen., yeo., Gillingham, Dorset, [1713], W, P27/1/200
Wm., tailor, Wexcombe, Grafton, 1726, I, W, P21/8/30
Wm., Gillingham, Dorset, 1727, AB, P27/1/283
Wm., shoemaker, Whitep., 1767, AB, P2/C/1336
Wm., mealman and baker, Lt. Cheverell, 1786, W, P2/C/1441
Wm., baker, Rowde, 1790, W, P3/C/1111
Wm., innkeeper, Sal., 1841, W, Wr, P1/1841/27
Wm., labourer, Wylye, 1841, W, Wr, P2/1841/30
Winifred, widow, Codf. St My., 1712, W, P2/C/982
Croucher *see* Crutcher
Crouchfield *see* Crutchfield
Crow, Honour, widow, Lyme R., Dorset, 1685, AB, P16/82
Nathaniel, husb., Kemble, 1752, W, P3/C/921
Thos., yeo., Sherston, [1712], W (NEP), P3/C/682
Crowch *see* Crouch
Crowdy, Geo. Hy., bach., Swindon, 1847, AB, comm, Wr, P3/1847/12
Theodora, sp., Swindon, 1847, AB, comm, Wr, P3/1847/13
Crowter, Edwd., clothw., Trowb., 1741, W, P1/C/788, P1/9Reg/197
Edwd., shopkeeper, Back St., Trowb., 1773, W, P1/C/975, P1/13Reg/16
Jos., sen., Trowb., 1743, W, P1/C/792, P1/9Reg/247A
Croyden, Thos., yeo., Uffc., Devon, 1670, AB, I, ren, P20/1/62
Cru *see* Crew
Crugge *see* Cragg
Crumb, Jn., sen., Wilcot, 1614, I, W, P1/C/74
see also Croom *or* C.
Crumly, Wm., gent., Fisherton A., 1831, W, P2/1831/16
Crump, Ann, Mere, 1695, W, P5/1695/22
Crompe, Giles, vicar, S. Newton, 1733-39, AB (2), comm, W, P2/C/1149
Jas., jun., gent., Charlcote, Bremhill, 1666, AB, I, P3/C/309
Jas., clerk, Calne, 1684, I, W, P26/318
Jeremiah, gent., Calne, 1688, AB, comm, I (very detailed), P26/365
Crompe, Jn., Mere, 1639, AB, comm, P5/1639/25, P5/13Reg/221A
Crompe, My., widow, Stoford, S. Newton, 1740, W, P2/C/1199
Thos., yeo., Calne, 1827, W, Wr, P5/1827/30
Wm., Mere, 1671, AB, I, P5/1671/20
Crumplehore, Crumpler, Edith, Winterborne K., Dorset, 1633, AB, P5/1633/13, P5/12Reg/163A
Crumpler, Jn., sen., yeo., Winterborne K., Dorset, 1752, AB, W, P5/1752/8
My., widow, Winterborne K., Dorset, 1595, AB (in minority of Thos. C.), a/c, W, P5/1595/17, 52, P5/6Reg/111C
Rd., Winterborne K., Dorset, 1595, AB (in minority of Thos. C.), I, W, P5/1595/17-18, P5/6Reg/111B
Thos., Winterborne K., Dorset, 1570, W, P5/2Reg/73C
Wm., sen., yeo., Winterborne K., Dorset, 1614, I, W, P5/1614/17, P5/9Reg/135B
Crumwell *see* Cromwell
Cruse, Edith, widow, Beckhampton, Avebury, 1754, W, P3/C/935
Crusse, Edmd., Urchf., 1646, AB, I, P2/C/526
Edwd., cutler, Sal., 1710, AB, I, NW, P4/1710/2
Crase, Emma, widow, Long Burton, Dorset, 1605, AB, I, W, P5/1605/14, P5/8Reg/37
Crause, Jn., Long Burton, Dorset, 1590, AB, I, W, P5/1590/16, P5/5Reg/79C
Jn., Beckhampton, Avebury, 1752, AB, P3/C/922
Jn., blacksmith, Avebury, 1762, W, P3/C/971
Jn., Hodson, Chiseldon, 1824, AB, comm, Wr, P3/1824/41
Crees, Jn., miller and farmer, Maiden B., 1857, aff, D, W, Wr, P2/1857/34
My., sp., Sal., 1742, AB, P4/1742/15
Robt., brewer, Sal., 1738, W, P1/C/752, P1/8Reg/234
Thos., yeo., Upper Lambourn, Berks., 1823, W, Wr, P1/1823/104
Wm., Lydiard T., 1631, I, NW, P1/C/139
Wm., blacksmith, Aldbourne, 1829, W, Wr, P1/1829/138
Crutcher, Croucher, Jane, widow, Avill's Farm, Corsham, 1791, AB, P3/C/1114

Croucher, Lucy, widow, Hamptworth, Downton, 1716, W, P2/C/1003
Croucher, My., wife, Didmarton, Gloucs (form. of Netheravon & effects there), 1760, AB, comm (form. known as My. Rolfe, widow), P1/C/910
Rd., baker, Wootton B., 1686, I, NW, P3/C/510
Rd., Lydiard T., 1757, AB, comm, P3/C/947
Crutchfield, Thos., Wallingford, Berks., 1747, AB, P1/C/830
Crouchfield, Wm., Blewbury, Berks., 1751, AB, P5/1751/7
Crutchman, Crutchman, Simon, Farley, Alderbury, 1574, AB, P5/3Reg/47B
Crutwell, Clement, sen., butcher, Wokm., Berks., 1757, W, P5/1757/7
Crottall, Jn., Wokm., Berks., 1602, AB, I, P5/1601/15, P5/7Reg/33B
Jn., bach., Wokm., Berks., 1750, AB, P5/1750/7
Cretall, Rd., Wokm., Berks., 1619, AB, I, P5/1619/45, P5/10Reg/42A
Wm., Wokm., Berks., 1697, AB, I, P5/1697/6
Wm., Wokm., Berks., 1751, AB, P5/1751/8
Cryer, Rd., Sherb., Dorset, 1582, AB, T (children: Jn., Wm. & My. C.), P5/1581/4, P5/4Reg/30A
Cryne *see* Crine
Cuckman *see* Cookman
Cuckney *see* Cookney
Cucksey *see* Cooksey
Cuddimore, Abigail, widow, Sal., 1713, W, P4/1713/11
Ann Askue, widow, Wilton, 1667, AB, P2/C/577
Christian, widow, Ditchampton, Wilton, 1639, AB, I, P2/C/471
Jn., butcher, Ditchampton, Wilton, 1706, I, W, P2/C/930
Cue, Benj., yeo., Wrou., 1767, W, P1/C/943, P1/12Reg/202B
Eleanor, widow, Hilmarton, 1673, AB, I, ren, P3/K/85
Eliz., widow, Avebury, 1671, I, W, P3/K/84
Jas., yeo., Wrou., 1682, I, W, P3/C/465
Jas., wheelwright, Compton B., 1691, I, W, P3/C/552
Jas., yeo., Fyfield, Overton, 1743, W, P3/C/878
Jn., sen., husb., E. Kennett, 1604, I, W, P3/C/16
Jn., jun., E. Kennett, 1641, AB, I, P3/C/267
Jn., husb., Yatesbury, 1661, comm, I, W, P3/C/281, P3/3Reg/38B
Jn., yeo., Wrou., 1691, I, W, P3/C/553
Jn., Earley, Sonning, Berks., 1714, AB, P5/1714/7
Jn., yeo., Lockeridge, Overton, 1719, I, W, P3/C/726
Jn., yeo., Wrou., 1751, W, P3/C/914
Jn., sen., Calne, 1799, AB, P26/1225
Jn., wheelwright, Calne, 1836, O, W, Wr, P5/1836/19
Margery, widow, Compton B. (property at Calne), 1740, W, P26/820
Martha, widow, Avebury, 1733, AB, I, P3/C/820
My., widow, Fyfield, Overton, 1744, AB, P1/C/806
Rd., sen., Avebury, 1629, I, NW, P3/K/39
Thos., wheelwright, Compton B., 1717, I, W, P3/C/708
Walter, farmer, Bishopstone N., 1834, AB, W, Wr, P6/156
Wm., sen., Calne, 1793, AB, comm, P26/1193
see also Kew
Cuffe, Adam, Zeals, 1675, AB, a/c, I, P5/1675/12
Ann, widow, Cuff's Corner, Calne, 1680, W, P26/264
Cuff, Ann, widow, E. Knoyle, 1846, D, W, Wr, P2/1846/37
Basil, sp., Stourton, 1725, AB, P2/C/1064
Caleb, Bere R., Dorset, 1721, W, P5/1721/8, P5/16Reg/58B
Christine, widow, Broughton G., 1570, AB, P2/5Reg/89E
Eliz., widow, Box, 1630, I, W, P3/C/174
Eliz., Horningsham, 1691, AB, P5/1691/13
Eliz., Folke, Dorset, 1736, W, P5/1736/10
Francis, Stourton, 1672, AB, a/c, I, P2/C/623
Cuff, Hy., Corsley, 1716, W, P2/C/1002
Cuff, Jas., widower, Corsley, 1848, AB, Wr, P1/1848/46
Jeremiah, maltster, Sherb., Dorset, 1685, W, I, P5/1685/28
Joan, widow, Sherb., Dorset, 1689, comm, I, W, P5/1689/16

Jn., Stourton, 1669, AB, P2/C/587
Cuff, Michael, clothw., N. Bradley, [1689], I, W, P2/C/798
Nathaniel, E. Knoyle, 1846, AB, O, Wr, P2/1846/3
Rd., Broughton G., 1560, T (child: Michael C.), W, P2/C/12, P2/4Reg/59
Rd., yeo., Stourton, 1716, AB, I, P2/C/1004
Robt., yeo., Long Burton, Dorset, 1718, AB, I (detailed), P5/1718/9
Cuff, Thos., gent., Corsley, 1830, W, Wr, P2/1830/33
Cuff, Thos., minor, Corsley, 1848, app. of guardian, court proceeding, O, T (children of Jas. C., decd), P1/1848/45-46
Wm., servant to Sir Giles Pole, Broad H., 1569, W, P1/1Reg/104A, P1/2Reg/96A
Wm., yeo., Stourton, 1726, W, P2/C/1076
Cuffin, Cuffin als Jones, Hy., yeo., Appleton, Berks., 1631, I, W, P1/C/144
Cuffly, Jane, widow, Padworth, Berks., 1717, I, W, P1/C/573, P1/6Reg/97
Cugley, My., widow, Milbourne, Malm., 1695, I, W, Wr, P3/C/585
Rd., husb., Milbourne, Malm., 1684, I, W, P3/C/494
Cuin, Cuin als Besse, Jane, wife, Lyme R., Dorset, 1702, AB, P16/160
Sam., husb., Lyme R., Dorset, 1735, I (detailed), W, P5/1735/16
Cull, Eliz., widow, Corsham, 1629, W, P29/1Reg/120B
Jn., glover, Corsham, 1614, I, P29/C/2
Jn., Corsham, 1653, AB, P29/1Reg/149A
Steph., husb., Broad C., 1551, W, P2/2Reg/120C
Thos., Maddington, 1562, W, P2/4Reg/95C
see also Baker als C.; Gregory als C.
Cullam *see* Cullum
Cullerne, Cullurne, Ann, sp., Melk., 1781, W, P2/C/1414
Cullern, Hy., Chelworth, Crickl. St S., 1772, AB, P3/C/1030
Jas., yeo., Calcutt, Crickl. St S., 1821, AB, comm, Wr, P1/1821/1, P3/1821/3
Cullerne als Haynes, Joan, Marl., 1660, AB, comm, P1/C/239
Collerne, Jn., Ogbourne St And., 1567, AB, P5/2Reg/26F
Jn., Eastrop, Highw., 1594, T, W, P5/1594/17, P5/6Reg/81B
Jn., sen., tanner, Garsdon, 1670, I, W, P3/C/345
Jn., yeo., Broad B., Highw., 1835, W, P10/1835/1
Cullern, Jn., widower, New Swindon, Swindon, 1848, AB, comm, Wr, P3/1848/56
Rachel, widow, Abingdon, Berks., 1766, W, P1/C/938, P1/12Reg/171A
Collerne, Robt., Ogbourne Maizey, 1639, I, W, P5/1639/101
Cullurne, Robt., Malm., 1706, I, W, P3/C/660
Cullurne, Robt., bach., Malm., 1751, AB, P3/C/915
Cullurne, Robt., Malm., 1763, AB, P3/C/975
Thos., draper, Malm., 1695, W, Wr, P3/C/586
Cullurn, Thos., distiller, Malm., 1701, I, W, P3/C/634
Cullern, Wm., husb., Chiseldon, 1669, I, W, P3/C/333
Culley *see* Cully
Culliford, Ann, sp., Uffc., Devon, 1752, AB, ren, P5/1752/9
Edwd., shoemaker, Sal., 1682, I, W, P4/1682/20
Colliford, Jn., husb., Uffc., Devon, 1594, I, W, P5/1594/14, P5/6Reg/65A
Jn., Uffc., Devon, 1626, I, NW, P20/1/9
Jn., innholder, *Rainbow Inn*, Uffc., Devon, 1728, AB, W, P5/1728/26, P5/16Reg/176
Jn., jun., innholder, Uffc., Devon, 1734, W, P5/1734/19
Jn., Uffc., Devon, 1740, W, Wr, P5/1740/20
Colivord, Millicent, Plaitford, 1592, I, P1/C/8
Rd., gent., Stourton, 1689, AB, comm, I, P1/C/409
Culliver, Robt., Plaitford, 1571, AB, P1/1Reg/23F
Colliford, Thos., Calne, 1564, AB, P5/1Reg/54E
Wm., chandler, Warm., 1678, I, W, P2/C/672
Cullimore, Alice, widow, N. Wraxall, 1647, AB, comm, P1/C/219
Dan., gent., Sherston, 1685, W, P3/C/501
Hy., jun., yeo., Slaughterford, 1673, AB, P3/C/368
Martha, sp., W. Yatton, Yatton K., 1787, W, P3/C/1098
My., sp., Corsham, 1628, W, P29/1Reg/115B
Rd., Sherston, 1648, AB, comm, P1/C/221
Rd., Yatton K., 1729, AB, P3/C/788

Callimore, Sarah, widow, Yatton K., 1732, AB, I, P1/C/709
Collymor, Thos., Calne, 1563, AB, P5/1Reg/4C
Thos., Calne, 1607, AB (in minority of Hy. & Robt. C.), I, T, P5/1607/18, P5/8Reg/94A
Thos., Yatton K., 1688, AB, I, Wr, P3/C/535
Thos., maltster, Slaughterford, 1704, AB, I, P3/C/648
Thos., fuller, Slaughterford, 1730, W, P3/C/808
Thos., yeo., Slaughterford, 1731, AB, W, P3/C/796
Thos., yeo., W. Yatton, Yatton K., 1762, W, P3/C/972
Thos., Marl. St Peter and St Paul, 1792, AB, P1/C/1075, P1/14Reg/467A
see also Walker form. C.
Cullis, Jonathan, Corsham, 1714, marriage licence, P29/2Reg/10B
Rd., husb., Stock St., Calne, 1705, W, P26/518
Culliver *see* Culliford
Cullum, Jn., Charlton, Wantage, Berks., 1734, AB, I, P5/1734/17
Cullam, Robt., collarmaker, Kingston Bagpuize, Berks., 1820, AB, W, Wr, P1/1820/90
Thos., yeo., E. Lockinge, Berks., 1735, W, P1/C/730, P1/7Reg/645
Cullurn, Cullurne *see* Cullerne
Cully, And., Collingbourne K., 1614, I, W, P1/C/75
And., yeo., Aughton, Collingbourne K., 1670, I, W, P3/C/346
And., sen., blacksmith, Froxfield, 1694, I, W, P3/C/580
And., blacksmith, Froxfield, 1719, AB, I, P3/C/727
Culley, And., Marl. St My., 1730, AB, P1/C/692
Ann, widow, Sal., 1775, AB, W, P4/1775/17
Christian, widow, Froxfield, 1709, I, W, P3/C/675
Dan., husb., Gt. Amesb., [1675], I, W, P2/C/651
Culley, Edwd., Collingbourne K., 1614, I, W, P1/C/73
Edwd., sen., yeo., Aughton, Collingbourne K., 1678, I, W, P3/C/416
Edwd., husb., Collingbourne K., 1686, AB, I, P1/C/1110
Edwd., Chute, 1706, comm, W, P7/98
Culley, Edwd., Marl. St My., 1715, W, P1/C/561, P1/5Reg/476A
Edwd., bach., Collingbourne K., 1794, AB, P3/C/1126
Culley, Eliz., widow, Chute, 1734, AB, ren, W, P5/1734/18
Francis, tailor, Collingbourne K., 1775, W, P3/C/1050
Cooley, Giles, sen., yeo., Calne, 1668, AB, W, Wr, P5/1668/16
Coolly *or* Cully, Hy., no place visible but I exhibited at Marl., 1691, I, W, P1/C/412
Culley, Jas., gent., Burbage, 1817, comm, ren, W, Wr, P11/267
Culley, Jas., yeo., Lt. Bedwyn, 1853, D, O, W, Wr, P5/1853/4
Colley, Jane, widow, Marl., 1724, AB, I, P1/C/633
Jn., husb., E. Grimstead, W. Dean, 1579, I (2), T, W, P2/C/50, P2/5Reg/339C
Jn., yeo., Sunton, Collingbourne K., 1689, I, W, P3/C/540
Jn., labourer, Ludg., 1713, I, W, P2/C/985
Culley, Jn., yeo., Whitley, Reading, Berks., 1729, W, P1/C/674, P1/7Reg/267B
Jn., marine on Neptune, Sal., 1775, AB, W, P4/1775/18
Culley, Jos., yeo., Purton Stoke, 1854, AB, O, W, Wr, P3/1854/3
Matthew, yeo., Fovant Stroud, 1716, W, P2/C/1006
Culley, Phoebe, widow, Purton, 1853, AB, aff, O, Wr, P3/1853/47
Culley, Rd., Bulford, 1579, W, P2/5Reg/353F
Rd., labourer, W. Grafton, 1705, I, W, P21/6/21
Robt., Sal., 1724, I, P4/1724/26
Culley, Roger, husb., Bulford, 1579, I (detailed), W, P2/C/52
Culley, Sarah, sp., Melk., 1827, AB, comm, Wr, P2/1827/5
Simon, Bramshaw, Hants, 1836, aff, O, W, P24/1345
Culley, Steph., yeo., Easton, 1843, W, Wr, P3/1843/40
Culley, Thos., shepherd, N. Tidworth, 1602, AB, I, NW, P2/C/184
Colley, Thos., sen., vict., Trowb., 1731, a/c, copy AB, D (2), I, W, P1/C/696, P1/7Reg/415
Thos., cordw., Marl. St My., 1758, W, P1/C/893, P1/11Reg/367
Culley, Ursula, Froxfield, 1726, AB, P1/C/650
Wm., W. Dean, 1548, W, P2/2Reg/54A
Wm., farmer, Easton, 1828, W, Wr, P3/1828/37
Culley, Wm., yeo., Easterton, Mkt. L., 1836, O, W, P2/1836/72

Culpeper, Edmd., clerk and vicar, Milton, Berks., 1626, comm, I, W, P1/C/163
Culver, Culver als Culverhouse, Dorothy, widow, Reading, Berks., 1708, W, P1/C/500
Jn., husb. and yeo., Wokm., Berks., 1701, I, W, P5/1701/9
Jn., Chards., Devon, 1767, W, P5/1767/15
Culverhouse, Agnes, Chapmanslade, Dilton, Westb., 1639, I, W, P25/1639/4
Cath., widow, Chapmanslade, Corsley, 1744, W, P1/C/810, P1/9Reg/429A
Edwd., Trowb., 1753, AB, P1/C/863
Jn., blacksmith, Chapmanslade, Dilton, Westb., 1694, I, W, P25/1694/7
Jn., sen., baker, N. Bradley, 1713, W, P2/C/984
My., widow, N. Bradley, 1736, W, P2/C/1173
Rd., sen., blacksmith, Chapmanslade, Dilton, Westb., 1631, I, W, P25/1631/1
Rd., blacksmith, Warm., 1662, AB, I, P2/C/550
Rd., blacksmith, Chapmanslade, Dilton, Westb., 1713, W, P25/1713/11
Thos., Chapmanslade, Dilton, Westb., 1644, AB, I, P25/1644/6
Colverhouse, Wm., blacksmith, Sal., 1617, I, W, P4/1617/9
Wm., baker, Chapmanslade, Corsley, 1711, W, P2/C/974
Wm., gent., Hilp., 1831, W, Wr, P2/1831/11
see also Culver als C.
Culverwell, Jn., yeo., Chards., Devon, 1797, W, P5/1797/7, P5/18Reg/251
Cumber, Jn., carp., Theale, Tilehurst, Berks., 1716, AB, I, P1/C/566
Cumfrey *see* Comfrey
Cumly *see* Comley
Cumlyn *see* Comlin
Cummins, Commin, Agnes, widow, no abode stated, 1619, AB, I, Wr (found together & note on Wr assumes connection), P3/C/105
Charlotte, widow, Hungerford, Berks. (form. of Henley in Buttermere), 1856, AB, aff, comm, D, W, Wr, P5/1856/7
Comin, Dorothy, widow, Blewbury, Berks., 1691, AB, I, P5/1691/16
Cummin, Edwd., Gt. Bedwyn, 1729, AB, P21/8/46
Cumming, Edwd., Gt. Bedwyn, 1754, AB, P21/10/24
Cumming, Eliz., widow, Gt. Bedwyn, 1694, AB, I, W (not signed; preamble in different hand), P21/5/28
Geo., bach., Chitterne St My., 1795, W, P2/C/1477
Comyn, Hy., Crudwell, [1606], W (NEP), P3/2Reg/12B
Coming, Hy., sen., yeo., Crudwell, [1690], W (NEP), P3/C/544
Comyn, Joan, Crudwell, 1625, I, W, P1/C/162
Comyn, Jn., day labourer, Wootton B., 1570, W, P1/1Reg/20D, 115B
Comyn, Jn., yeo., Crudwell, 1638, I, W, P1/C/179
Jn., brickmaker, Gt. Bedwyn, 1671, AB, I, P21/2/24
Cumming, Jn., yeo., Gt. Bedwyn, 1694, O, W, P21/5/21
Cummin, Jn., Gt. Bedwyn, 1754, AB, P21/10/23
Commins, Jn., shepherd, Steeple L., 1806, W, Wr, P2/1806/78
Commings, Jos., yeo., Devizes Grn, Bps. C., 1811, W, P24/1255
Commin, My., Crudwell, 1699, W, P3/C/612
Comings, My., widow, Damerham, Hants, 1713, AB, I, P2/C/987
Commings, My., yeo.'s wife, Devizes Grn, Devizes St Jas., Devizes, 1800, app. of proctor, W, P1/1800/5, P1/15Reg/203
Commin, Rd., yeo., Aston Tirrold, Berks., 1720, AB, I, P1/C/599
Coming, Robt., clerk, Wingfield, 1620, AB, a/c, I, req, P1/C/103
Sarah, widow, Eastcott, Urchf., 1842, O, W, Wr, P2/1842/15
Comin, Wm., Blewbury, Berks., 1677, AB, a/c, I, T (re My. C. & Ann Warner *or* C., minors), P5/1677/9
Cumin, Wm., Blewbury, Berks., 1712, AB, P5/1712/19
see also Warner *or* C.
Cumner, Cath., widow, Rams., 1788, W, P5/1788/8, P5/18Reg/106
Jn., carp., Chiseldon, 1763, W, P1/C/923, P1/12Reg/126A
Jn., Preshute, 1801, AB, Wr, P1/1801/128, P1/15Reg/354A
Jos., innholder, Rams., 1780, W, P5/1780/5, P5/17Reg/197B
Jos., yeo., Rams., 1810, W, Wr, P5/1810/7
Rd., yeo., Sal., 1769, W (only cod survives), P4/1769/16
Wm., weaver, W. St., Aldbourne, 1795, W, P1/C/1082, P1/14Reg/557
Cundick, Jn., Winterbourne E., 1718, AB, P2/C/1022
Cunditt *see* Conduit
Cunnant *see* Conant

Cunnick *see* Curnick
Cunny, Eliz., Warm., 1595-96, AB (2), I, NW, P2/C/134, P2/7Reg/146D
Cur *see* Curr
Curle, Anna Maria, minor, no abode stated, 1695, T, P1/C/437
Jn., gent., Buttermere, 1663, AB, comm, I (detailed), P1/C/262
Kerle, Jn., labourer, Alton B., 1794, W, Wr, P3/K/269
Walter, esquire, Buttermere, 1686, I, W, P1/C/1109
Wm., jun., bach., Compton B., 1844, AB, note, O, Wr, P3/1844/21
Carle *or* Cearle, Wm., yeo., Studley, Trowb., 1855, AB, aff, D (2), O (2), W, Wr, P1/1855/62
Curme *see* Bartlett als Curme; Corme
Curnick, Cunnick, Chas., Reading, Berks., 1708, AB, P1/C/503
Cunnick, Eliz., widow, Reading, Berks., 1714, AB, P1/C/548
Jas., gardener, Seend Row, Melk., 1745, W, P2/C/1226
Jas., yeo., Beanacre, Melk., 1793, W, P2/C/1471
Cornock *or* Curnick, Robt., Limpley Stoke, Bradford A., 1564, AB, I, W, P2/C/32, P2/4Reg/174B
Robt., yeo., Beanacre, Melk., 1811, W, Wr, P1/1811/130
Curr, Agnes, widow, Shalbourne, 1607, I, W, P5/1607/13, P5/8Reg/98
Alice, widow, Shalbourne, Berks., 1607, W, P23/1001
Bart., husb., Shalbourne, 1591, I, W, P5/1591/15, P5/5Reg/112A
Cath., widow, Sanden Fee, Hungerford, Berks., 1661, comm, I, W, P5/1661/10
Dorothy, widow, Holt, Kintbury, Berks., 1687, comm, I, W, P1/C/376
Eliz., widow, Helm House, Helm, Hungerford, Berks., 1586, AB, I, W, P5/1585/17, P5/4Reg/124D
Hy., husb., Horton, Bps. C., 1671, I, W, P24/379
Jn., jun., yeo., Charnham St., Hungerford, Berks., 1601-02, AB, I, W, P5/1601/12, P5/7Reg/10A
Jn., Holt, Kintbury, Berks., 1686, AB, P1/C/381
Jn., Hungerford, Berks., 1706, W, P23/283
Margery, widow, Hungerford, Berks., 1635, AB, I, W, P5/1635/18, P5/12Reg/239B
Margery, widow, Sanden Fee, Hungerford, Berks., 1704, I, W, P5/1704/9
Ralph, Rams., 1565, W, P5/1Reg/61D
Robt., rector, Ham, 1561, W (NEP), P1/2Reg/140B
Thos., sen., husb., Sanden Fee, Hungerford, Berks., 1613, I, NW, P5/1613/15, P5/9Reg/102A
Thos., yeo., Sanden Fee, Hungerford, Berks., 1699, I, W, P23/233
Thos., Hungerford, Berks., 1714, AB, P5/1714/8
Thos., farmer, W. Woodhay, Berks., 1835, W, Wr, P1/1835/104
see also Cary als C.
Currant, Edwd., yeo., Wyats, Bromham, 1838, O, W, Wr, P3/1838/56
Currier, Hy., cooper, Sal., 1681, AB, I, P4/1681/29
Roger, husb., Cloatley, Hankerton, 1618, I, W, P3/C/102
Curry, My., widow, Sherb., Dorset, 1823, AB, Wr, P5/1823/12
Rd., shepherd, Maddington, 1587, I, W, P2/C/72, P2/7Reg/110C
Cursell, Jas., sen., yeo., Aldermaston, Berks., 1692, I, W, P1/C/423
Kersill, Jn., mason, E. Hendred, Berks., 1741, AB, ren, W, P1/K/210, P1/9Reg/18
Rd., Aston U., Blewbury, Berks., 1600, AB, I, P5/1600/18, P5/7Reg/3A
Kersill, Wm., Highw., 1742, W, P10/1742/4
Cursner *see* Cozener
Curtis, Agnes *or* Agatha, widow, Broughton G., 1673, AB, comm, I, P2/C/636
Alexander, tailor, Broad C., 1614, W, P2/8Reg/222A
Alice, widow, Seend, Melk., 1575, W, P2/5Reg/222B
Alice, widow, Sonning, Berks., 1613, I, W, P1/C/62
Alice, sp., Chipp., 1856, AB, aff, O, Wr, P3/1856/14
Ambrose, alehouse keeper, Sal., 1703, AB, I, P4/1702/2
Ann, widow, Chetnole, Yetm., Dorset, 1703, AB, I, P19/88
Ann, Blewbury, Berks., 1730, AB, P5/1730/12
Ann, widow, Milton, Berks., 1744, comm, W, P1/C/812, P1/9Reg/436B
Ann, widow, Mere, 1760, W, P5/1760/8
Courtis, Anth., husb., Box, 1623, I, W, P3/C/125
Cortas, Anth., husb., Pott., 1709, W, P1/C/508, P1/5Reg/1A
Barbara, sp., Malm., 1805, W, P3/1805/39
Bart., labourer, Farnborough, Berks., 1683, AB, I, P1/C/364
Benj., vict., Hullavington, 1845, O, W, Wr, P3/1845/4

Betty, sp., Warm., 1832, comm, W, Wr, P1/1832/12
Bridget, widow, Box, 1630, I, W, P3/C/175
Cath., widow, Lus Hill, Castle Eaton, 1609, W, P3/C/46
Curtoys, Chas., Sal., 1786, AB, P1/C/1052
Christabella, widow, Downton, 1794, W, P2/C/1476
Christian, widow, Bloxworth, Dorset, 1605, AB, comm, I, W, P5/1605/9, P5/8Reg/28A
Chris., Woodlands, Mere, 1686, AB, I, P5/1686/19
Chris., builder, Westb. Town, 1854, declaration, O, W, Wr, P25/1854/3
Clement, tailor, Sonning, Berks., 1612, comm, I, W, P5/1612/13, P5/9Reg/77C
Cuthbert, Woodlands, Mere, 1612, I, W, P5/1612/12, P5/9Reg/73
Dan., blacksmith, Axford, Rams., 1689, AB, I, P5/1689/17
Deborah, widow, Axford, Rams., 1690, I (NEP), P5/1690/13
Edwd., cordw., Westb. L., 1825, O, W, Wr, P25/1825/9
Edwd., plasterer, Warm. Common, 1827, aff, W, Wr, P2/1827/41
Eliz., widow, Hankerton, 1610, W, P3/C/52
Eliz., widow, Fisherton A., 1779-83, AB, W, P2/C/1403
Geo., Britford, 1585, I, W, P24/170, P5/4Reg/99B
Geo., carp., Downton, 1639, AB, a/c, I, P2/C/476
Cortis, Geo., innholder, Barford St Mart., 1725, W, P2/C/1062
Hannah, widow, Tilehurst, Berks., 1708, comm, W, P1/C/506
Helen, widow, Hurst, Berks., 1573, W, P5/3Reg/15B
Hy., tailor, Broad C., 1565, W, P2/4Reg/199A
Hy., Charlton nr Malm., 1692, AB, P3/C/560
Hy., gent., Castle Eaton, 1730, AB, comm, W, P3/C/809
Hy., labourer, Milbourne, Malm., 1743, W, P3/C/879
Hy., Bishopstone N., 1803, AB, comm, P6/143
Hy., cordw., Charlton, Wantage, Berks., 1803, W, Wr, P23/836
Humphrey, yeo., Buck Hill, Calne, 1675, AB, comm, I, P26/231
Jas., innholder, Sherb., Dorset, 1753, W, P5/1753/5
Jas., bacon factor, Devizes, 1810, W, Wr, P1/1810/13
Jas., labourer, Lt. Somerford, 1837, W, Wr, P3/1837/41
Jane, widow, Norton B., 1648, I, W, P2/C/536
Jane, widow, Corsham, 1665-66, I, W, P29/C/6, P29/1Reg/173B
Jane, widow, Downton, 1667, I, W, P2/C/573
Jane, Sutton C., Berks., 1779, W, P1/C/1010, P1/13Reg/229A
Jemima, sp., Chipp., 1856, AB, aff, O, Wr, P3/1856/13
Joan, widow, Seend Row, Melk., 1609, AB, a/c, I, P2/C/232, P2/8Reg/79C
Joan, Over C., Dorset, 1671, I, W, P5/1671/19
Jn., husb., Seend, Melk., 1559, W, P2/3Reg/172A
Jn., Kingston D., 1561, AB, P2/4Reg/73C
Jn., Seend, Melk., 1589, I, P2/C/82
Jn., yeo., Kingston D., 1600, I, W, P2/C/174
Jn., husb., Castle Eaton, 1604, I, W (NEP), P3/C/17
Jn., sen., husb., Hankerton, 1610, W, P3/C/53
Jn., gent., Reading, Berks., 1631, AB, I, P1/C/143
Jn., Keevil, 1632, AB, P2/C/408
Curtis als Horton, Jn., blacksmith, Stratton St Mgt., 1633, I, W, P3/C/198
Jn., servant, Eye and Dunsden, Sonning, Berks., 1663, AB, I, P5/1663/18
Jn., Over C., Dorset, 1670, AB, I, P5/1670/6
Jn., Sherb., Dorset, 1676, AB, P5/1676/12
Jn., carp., Sal., 1679, I, W, P4/1679/2
Jn., Hankerton, 1680, I, W, P1/C/345
Jn., sen., blacksmith, Stratton St Mgt., 1698, I, W, P3/C/603
Jn., sen., husb., Boreham, Warm., 1701, I, W, P2/C/893
Jn., horse driver, Hankerton, 1707, AB, I, P3/C/666
Jn., cooper, Warm., 1717-28, AB, W, P2/C/1012, 1097
Jn., Sutton C., Berks., 1735, AB, comm, P1/C/740
Jn., blacksmith, E. Lockinge, Berks., 1735, W, P1/C/731, P1/7Reg/644
Jn., sen., scribbler, Devizes St Jn., 1768, W, P1/C/951, P1/12Reg/284A
Jn., jun., Sal., 1781, AB, P4/1781/2

Jn., yeo., Britford, 1782, W, P24/1190
Jn., sen., yeo., The Common, Warm., 1786, AB, ren, W, P1/C/1051, P1/14Reg/159
Jn., Devizes, 1801, W, Wr, P1/1801/104, P1/15Reg/321B
Jn., sen., gardener, The Common, Warm., 1817, W, Wr, P2/1817/26
Jn., Sutton V., 1842, AB, comm, Wr, P2/1842/25
Jn., yeo., Hullavington, 1851, D, O, W, Wr, P3/1851/26
Jn., Netherb., Dorset, 1857, AB, aff, comm, Wr, P17/386
Jonathan, yeo., Enmore Grn, Motc., Dorset, 1710, AB, I, P5/1710/33
Jos., gardener, The Common, Warm., 1792, AB, W, P1/C/1064, P1/14Reg/368
Jos., Wargrave, Berks., 1798, AB, P1/C/1096, P1/15Reg/63A
Jos., Warm. Common, 1822, comm, W, Wr, P2/1822/22
Jos., plasterer, Mill Lane, Lyme R., Dorset, 1855, AB, D, W, Wr, P16/461
Mgt., widow, Whitep., 1610, AB, I, P2/C/246, P2/8Reg/145C
Margery, widow, Boreham, Warm., 1708, W, P2/C/948
Martha, sp., Marcham, Berks., 1695, AB, I, P1/C/444
My., widow, The Common, Warm., 1736, AB, P2/C/1174
My., widow, Downton, 1850, W, Wr, P2/1850/21
Matthew, maltster, Wilton, [1667], I, W, P2/C/576
Michael, yeo., Castle Eaton, 1668, AB, I, W, P3/C/320
Michael, Longbridge D., 1699, AB, P2/C/879
Nich., husb., Hurst, Berks., 1603, W, P5/7Reg/77B
Nich., husb., Atworth, Bradford A., 1615, W, P2/8Reg/249
Nich., yeo., Lus Hill, Castle Eaton, 1621, I, W, P3/C/113
Nich., sen., yeo., Hannington, 1699, I, W, P3/C/615
Nich., yeo., Hannington, 1737, W, P3/C/841
Courtis, Nich., yeo., Boreham, Warm., 1763, W, P1/C/924, P1/12Reg/125B
Courtis, Ralph, husb., Bower C., 1624, I, W, P2/C/344
Rebecca, widow, The Common, Warm., 1792, W, P1/C/1065, P1/14Reg/369
Courtis, Rd., husb., Maiden B., 1634, I, W, P2/C/426
Rd., Milton, E. Knoyle, 1640, comm, I, W, P2/C/482
Rd., jun., yeo., Wootton B., 1674, AB, I, P1/C/313
Rd., sen., Easton Grey, 1690, I, W, P3/C/548
Rd., cooper, Downton, 1696, AB, W, P2/C/857
Rd., Easton Grey, 1701, AB, I, P3/C/635
Rd., no abode stated, 1708, W, copy W, P1/C/501
Rd., yeo., Britford, 1740, W, P24/995
Rd., miller, Fordington, Dorset, 1774, W, P15/147
Rd., butcher, Burton Hill, Malm., 1801, W, P1/1801/77, P1/15Reg/294
Rd., yeo., Ashton K., 1804, W, P1/1804/131
Rd., minor, Fisherton A., 1811, app. of guardian, T (son of Jn. C. of, Seend, decd), P2/1811/31
Robt., sen., husb., Upton L., 1599, AB, W, P2/C/168
Corties, Robt., Halstock, Dorset, 1603, AB, I, P5/1603/24, P5/7Reg/70B
Courtis, Robt., broad weaver, Melk., 1613, I, W, P1/C/61
Robt., husb., Kingston D., 1616, AB, I, W, P1/C/84
Robt., Woodlands, Mere, 1633, AB, I, P5/1633/10, P5/12Reg/146C
Robt., husb., Heytes., 1640, I, W, P5/1640/8, P5/13Reg/260B
Robt., yeo., Hungerford, Berks., 1661, comm, I (discoloured & damaged), W, P5/1661/11
Robt., sen., yeo., Kingston D., 1680, I, W, P2/C/688
Robt., Kingston D., 1703-04, AB, a/c, I, P2/C/904
Robt., yeo., Charlton, Wantage, Berks., 1722, I, W, P5/1722/17, P5/16Reg/76C
Robt., blacksmith and husb., Ogbourne St Geo., 1731, I, W (& cod), P5/1731/15
Robt., merchant tailor, Mere, 1732, W, P5/1732/11
Robt., linen weaver, Gillingham, Dorset, 1750, W, P27/1/398, P27/3Reg/58
Robt., Gillingham, Dorset, 1760, AB, P27/1/424, P27/3Reg/87
Roger, husb., Bere R., Dorset, 1626, I, P5/1626/6
Sarah, Hannington, 1766, AB, P3/C/998
Sarah, widow, Fordington, Dorset, 1776, W, P15/151
Sarah, widow, Warm. Common, 1827, AB, W, Wr, P2/1827/38
Sarah, widow, Warm. Common, 1832, W, Wr, P2/1832/7
Thos., Box, 1570, W (NEP), P1/1Reg/118A

Thos., Longbridge D., 1587, AB, P2/7Reg/90C
Thos., husb., Cowesfield, Whitep., 1600, AB, I, W, P2/C/1523
Thos., yeo., Cloatley, Hankerton, 1626, I, W, P3/C/147
Thos., husb., Broughton G., 1672, comm, I, W, P2/C/622
Thos., miller, Sherb., Dorset, 1698, I, W, P5/1698/18
Thos., yeo., Mangerton, Netherb., Dorset, 1709, I, W, P17/186
Courtis, Thos., sen., woollen weaver, Conrish, Mere, 1713, W, P5/1713/24, P5/15Reg/372A
Thos., innholder, Fisherton A., 1724, I, W, P2/C/1060
Thos., tailor, Sal. St Thos., 1740, AB, I, Wr, P4/1740/19
Thos., fellmonger and glover, Newbury, Berks., 1741, W, P1/C/781, P1/9Reg/101
Thos., sen., yeo., Mere, 1742, W, Wr, P5/1742/11
Thos., carp., Netherb., Dorset, 1770, W, P17/561
Thos., yeo., Mere, 1774, W, P5/1774/5, P5/17Reg/78
Thos., miller, Sutton Poyntz, Dorset, 1803, W, P18/18
Thos., Mere, 1808, AB, Wr, P5/1808/4
Thos., shoemaker, Dilton M., Westb. (Providence Chapel, Penknap ; some beneficiaries in Canada), 1851, comm, W (bequest to promote singing in P.C.), Wr, P25/1851/1
Walter, husb., Martin, Hants, 1638, I, NW, P2/C/466
Walter, Fisherton A., 1783, AB, P2/C/1425
Wm., Castleton, Dorset, 1585, AB, P5/4Reg/107A
Wm., Seend Row, Melk., 1597, I, W, P2/C/156
Wm., husb., Ewen, Kemble, 1602, I, W, P1/C/12
Wm., Heytes., 1603, I, W, P5/1603/15, P5/7Reg/75A
Wm., yeo., Wokm., Berks., 1611, AB, I, P5/1611/9
Wm., yeo., Castle Eaton, 1624, I, W, P3/C/134
Wm., Box, 1625, AB, NW, P3/C/138
Wm., yeo., Ashley, Box, 1641, comm, I, NW, P3/C/268
Courtis, Wm., yeo., Kingston D., 1642, I, W, P2/C/506
Wm., Sal., 1664, AB, I, P1/C/271
Wm., gent., Durnford, 1674, AB, I, P9/14
Wm., yeo., Bromham, 1675, W, P3/C/384
Wm., yeo., Sutton Poyntz, Dorset, 1680, I, P30/34
Wm., carp., Rams., 1682, I, W, P5/1682/26
Wm., Lambourn Woodlands, Berks., 1686, I, W, P1/C/1108
Wm., yeo., Maiden B., [1688], I, W, P2/C/780
Courtis, Wm., Crockerton, Longbridge D., 1696, I, W, P2/C/862
Wm., Kingston D., 1699, I, W, P2/C/880
Curtoys, Wm., sen., gent., Blewbury, Berks., 1724, W, P5/1724/21, P5/16Reg/96C
Courtis, Wm., widower, Swindon, 1730, AB, comm, P3/C/803
Wm., Sherb., Dorset, 1749, AB, Wr, P5/1749/18
Wm., millwright, Fisherton A., 1765, W, P2/C/1323
Wm., sen., gardener, Warm., 1777, W, P2/C/1389
Wm., gardener, The Common, Warm., 1804, W, P2/1804/29
Wm., millwright, Fisherton A., 1812, W, Wr, P2/1812/55
Wm., cattle dealer, Downton, 1832, W, Wr, P2/1832/20
Courtis, Wm., tanner, Semington, Steeple A., 1832, comm, W, Wr, P1/1832/9
Curver *see* Carver
Cusler, Rd. *see* Thomas Freeman
Cusner *see* Cozener
Cusse, Aldhelm, yeo., Stanton Fitzwarren, 1604, I, W, P3/C/18
Dorothy, widow, Inglesham, 1686, I, W, P3/C/511
Edmd., husb., S. Marston, 1591, I, W, P5/1591/17, P5/5Reg/120B
Edwd., gent., Winterbourne G., 1838, W, Wr, P2/1838/2
Eliz., widow, S. Marston, 1591, AB, I, W, P5/1591/16, P5/5Reg/120C
Hy., Pewsey, 1668, AB, P3/C/321
Hy., Fyfield, Milton L., 1669, AB, P3/C/334
Jas., bach., Sal. (form. of Milton L.), 1850, AB, Wr, P4/1850/9
Jane, widow, Ford, Winterbourne G., 1740, W, P2/C/1207
Jane, widow, Durnford, 1822, AB, Wr, P9/106
Joan, widow, Purton, 1614, AB, I, W, P3/C/75

Jn., yeo., S. Marston, 1603, AB, I, W, P5/1603/18, P5/7Reg/87
Jn., labourer *or* husb., Stratton St Mgt., 1673, I, W, P3/C/369
Jn., innkeeper, Old Castle House, Stratford sub C., 1844, D, W, Wr, P1/1844/26
Jn., farmer, Idmiston, 1845, W, Wr, P1/1845/62
Cuss, My. Grinfield, wife, Crickl. St My., 1836, O, W, Wr, P3/1836/1
Cuss, Neville, maltster, Crickl. St S., 1835, O, W, P3/1835/6
Peter Courtenay, farmer, Winterbourne G., 1824, W, Wr, P2/1824/58
Rd., Chiseldon, 1661, AB, comm, I, P3/C/282
Sam., gent., Ford, Winterbourne G., 1734-37, AB, ren, P2/C/1168
Sam., minor, Ford, Winterbourne G., 1737-38, AB, ren, T, P2/C/1178
Sarah, widow, Stanton Fitzwarren, 1677, AB, P3/C/403
Thos., husb., Stratton St Mgt., 1625, I, W, P1/C/121
Wm., sen., S. Marston, 1616, W, P5/1616/17
Wm., gent., Woodlands, Mildenhall, 1668, AB, I, P3/C/322
Wm., jun., miller and yeo., Winterbourne G., 1774, W, P2/C/1371
Wm., yeo., Winterbourne E., 1775, W, P2/C/1381
Cuss, Wm., yeo., Crickl. St My., 1837, W, Wr, P3/1837/34
Cuss, Wm., Latton, 1853, AB, aff, comm, D, W, Wr, P3/1853/58
Cussell *see* Cassell
Cussens, Cussins *see* Cousins
Cust, Jos., Fordington, Dorset, 1822, AB, O, Wr, P15/180
Custins, Custon *see* Costen
Cuthbert, Cuttberd, Geo., mercer, Bradford A., 1573, W, P2/5Reg/174D
Geo., yeo., Wanb., 1825, W, Wr, P3/1825/20
Jn., glazier, Lt. Hinton, 1781, W, P3/C/1073
Cuthbertson, Bennet, Sal., 1791, AB, P4/1791/1
Cutler, Abraham, pauper, Burghfield, Berks., 1695, AB, I, P1/C/447
Augustine, maltster, Holyport, Bray, Berks., 1711, I, W, P1/C/527, P1/5Reg/183
Eliz. *or* Eliza, sp., Sal., 1840-55, AB, aff, D, Wr (d. 1840, but AB not applied for, as thought no estate worth admg), P4/1855/6
Ellen, widow, Stourpaine, Dorset, 1612, I, W, P24/117
Jane, widow, Collingbourne D., 1662, AB, comm, I, NW, P1/C/242
Jn., sen., yeo., Figh., 1611, W, P26/10
Jn., labourer, Remenham, Berks., 1613, AB, I, P1/C/64
Jn., husb., Ash, Stourpaine, Dorset, 1670, AB, a/c, comm, I, P24/381
Jn., Hurst, Berks., 1728, AB, P5/1728/27, P5/16Reg/200C
Lewis, bach., Ashton K., 1611, W, P3/C/62
My., widow, Melk., 1783, AB, ren, W, P1/C/1035, P1/13Reg/440
Rd., Maddington, 1559, W, P2/3Reg/146B
Rd., sailor (d. serving in the Royal Navy), Damerham, Hants, 1779, AB, P1/C/1003
Robt., bargeman, Hurley, Berks., 1613, I, W, P1/C/63
Sam., widower, Wilton, 1855, AB, aff, Wr, P1/1855/6
Thos., sen., clothier, Sal., 1685, W, P4/1685/14
Cutler als Smith, Thos., jun., weaver and shopkeeper, Wilton, 1754, a/c, I (2 - very detailed), W, P2/C/1282
Cutler als Smith, Thos., weaver, Wilton, 1775, W, P2/C/1375
Wm., yeo., Cookham, Berks., 1619, I, W, P1/C/96
Wm., Tilehurst, Berks., 1686, AB, I, P1/C/1107
Wm., yeo., Warm., 1836, W, P2/1836/28
see also Smith als C.
Cuttberd *see* Cuthbert
Cutter, Francis, tallow chandler, Edington, 1690-91, AB, I, P2/C/804
Cutteris, Susan, widow, New Windsor, Berks., 1714, I, W, P1/C/552, P1/5Reg/353A
Cutting, Alexander, Devizes, 1668, AB, comm, I, P1/C/287
Dan., gent., Devizes St My., 1717, comm, W, P1/C/580, P1/6Reg/112
Joan, widow, Devizes, 1718, I (detailed), W, P1/C/582, P1/6Reg/159
Nathan, vict., Devizes, 1767, AB, W, P1/C/941, P1/12Reg/189
Sarah, widow, Devizes, 1759, AB, P1/C/894
Cuttle *see* Cottle
Cutts, Edwd., Chiseldon, 1703, I, W, P3/C/645
Rd., sen., yeo., Bytham, Ogbourne St Geo., 1689, AB, I, P23/172

Rd., yeo., Bytham, Ogbourne St Geo., 1691, AB, I, P5/1691/10
Cuxey *see* Cooksey
Cuzner *see* Cozener
Cyford *see* Siffard

D..., Wm., Etchilhampton, 1576, W (NEP), P1/D/1
Dabram, Edmd., mason, Wrou., 1619, comm, I, W, P3/D/37
Thos., Caundle Marsh, Dorset, 1630, AB, NW, P5/11Reg/135A
Dabynott, Dobenett, Joan, widow, Chards., Devon, 1567, W, P5/1Reg/81B
Thos., husb., Crowlway, Chards., Devon, 1585, AB, I, W, P5/1584/7, P5/4Reg/100
Thos., yeo., Chards., Devon, 1637, AB, I, W, P14/199
Daccombe, Hy., Winterborne K., Dorset, 1613, I, W, P5/1613/17, P5/9Reg/132C
Jn., husb., N. Wootton, Dorset, 1640, AB, I, P5/1640/15, P5/13Reg/233B
Thos., Easton Basset, Donhead St A., 1640, I, NW, P2/D/217
Dade, Agnes, Warm., 1598, AB, P1/D/8
Geoffrey, Warm., 1598, I, P2/D/55
Dafter, Ann, widow, Bradford A., 1796, W, P2/D/722
Richd., yeo., Lower Chelworth Grn, Crickl. St S., 1844, comm, W, Wr, P3/1844/49
Daggle, Nich., gent., Enmore Grn, Motc., Dorset, 1729, W, P19/117
Dainton, Chas., N. Bradley, 1787, AB, P2/D/704
Jn., Bradford A., 1704, AB, I, P2/D/438
Jn., broad weaver, Whitehill, Bradford A., 1710, W, P2/D/467
Jos., N. Bradley, 1795, AB, comm, P1/D/440, P1/14Reg/610A
Deynton, Mgt., widow, Purton, 1601, W, P3/1Reg/59
Thos., N. Bradley, 1787, AB, P2/D/705
Thos., weaver, N. Bradley, 1854, aff, O, W, Wr, P2/1854/60
Daintrey *see* Dantry
Dakins *see* Deakins
Dalby, Ann, widow, Corsham, 1632, W, P29/D/7, P29/1Reg/123C
Betty, widow, Sherston, 1778, W, P3/D/429
My., sp., Sal. The Close (form. of Rothwell, Northamptonshire), 1795, W, P5/1795/4, P5/18Reg/208A
see also Forster alias D.
Dale, Edwd., Bramshaw, Hants, 1675, AB, a/c, I, P24/437
Hugh, Chilhampton, S. Newton, 1547, W, P2/2Reg/45A
Humphrey, vicar, Compton C., 1565, AB, P2/4Reg/214B
Jn., Warm., 1583, W, P2/6Reg/110B
Jn., yeo., Marl., 1683, I, W, P1/D/156
Richd., husb., Fisherton A., 1575, I, W, P2/D/11, P2/5Reg/244F
Thos., Whitep., 1559, AB, P2/4Reg/7D
Dalimear *see* Dalmer
Dalimere *see* Dallimore
Dallen, Jn., Slaughterford, [1588], W (NEP), P3/1Reg/38C
Dallyn, Thos., shopkeeper, Westb., 1812, W, P25/1812/6
Daller, Rebecca, Bray, Berks., 1711, AB, P1/D/238
Dalley, Edwd., Bradford A., 1586, I, W, P2/D/27, P2/7Reg/35A
Eliz., widow, Bradford A., 1600, AB, I, W, P2/D/62
Joan, widow, Chards., Devon, 1640, AB, I, P14/9
Jn., Maiden B., 1794, AB, P2/D/718
Richd., Chards., Devon, 1573, W, P5/3Reg/21F
Dulley, Richd., sen., Woodley, W. and Sandford, Berks., 1731, W, P5/1731/22
Roger, Rowde, 1641, AB, ren, P3/D/106
Wm., Bradford A., 1585, W, P2/7Reg/4C
Wm., sen., gent., Ridge, Chilmark, 1809, W, P2/1809/90
Dalliber, Anthony, Sherb., Dorset, 1564, AB, P5/1Reg/54G
Jonathan, yeo., Chards., Devon, 1767, W, P5/1767/16
Dallimore, Humphrey, priest, Water Eaton, Latton, 1557, institution to vicarage, P1/1Reg/4A
Dalimere, Isaac, carp., Avoncliff, Westwood, 1808, W, Wr, P1/1808/32
Richd., sen., hosier, Devizes, 1629, W, P1/D/53
Wm., farmer, Staverton, Trowb., 1849, D, O, W, Wr, P1/1849/15
Dallyn *see* Dallen

Dalman *see* Dalmon
Dalmer, Dammer, Ambrose, sen., yeo., Butterwick, Folke, Dorset, 1728, W, P5/1728/28, P5/16Reg/181A
Edith, widow, Seend, Melk., 1574, W, P2/5Reg/185B
Geo., husb., Keevil, 1643-46, AB, a/c, I, P2/D/231
Jane, baker's widow, Avill's Farm, Corsham, 1787, comm, W, P3/D/449
Joan, widow, Seend, Melk., 1631, I, W, P2/D/163
Damore, Joan, widow, Keevil, 1648, I, W, P2/D/243
Jn., Seend, Melk., 1575, AB, P2/5Reg/228B
Jn., Seend, Melk., 1587, AB, P2/7Reg/79C
Jn., Seend, Melk., 1635, I, W, P1/D/74
Dawmore, Jn., yeo., Chr. M., 1640, I, W, P3/D/105
Jn., yeo., Seend Row, Melk., 1671, comm, I, W, P2/D/281
Jn., Seend, Melk., 1720, AB, comm, P1/D/265
Jn., yeo., Keevil, 1734, comm, W, P2/D/555
Jn., common brewer, Avill's Farm, Corsham, 1787, comm, W, P3/D/450
Jonathan, yeo., Staverton, Trowb., 1751, W, P2/D/615
Mgt., widow, Bromham, 1619, I, W, P3/D/38
Margery, Bulk., Keevil, 1609, AB, W, P2/D/86, P2/8Reg/76
My., widow, Melk., 1756, AB, P1/D/378
Maurice, innholder, Chipp., 1779, W, P3/D/431
Richd., sen., Bulk., Keevil, 1609, AB, I, W, P2/D/85, P2/8Reg/52B
Richd., Keevil, 1641, W, P2/D/219
Dalmer *or* Dawmore, Richd., Marston, Pott., 1646, AB, comm, I, P1/D/88
Richd., sen., yeo. and husb., Keevil, 1669, I, W, P2/D/271
Robt., yeo., Seend Row, Melk., 1671, AB, comm, I, W, P2/D/282
Robt., yeo., Bradford A., 1738, AB, I, P2/D/571
Simon, yeo., Seend, Melk., 1615, I, W, P2/D/108, P2/8Reg/270B
Dalimear, Susanna, widow, Keevil, 1760, comm, I, W, P2/D/631
Thos., yeo., Seend Row, Melk., 1612, I, W, P2/D/102
Walter, yeo., Seend, Melk., 1563, I, W, P2/D/4, P2/4Reg/124
Wm., Seend, Melk., 1566, W, P2/4Reg/230B
Wm., Bulk., Keevil, 1626, I, T, P2/D/149
Wm., barber, Steeple A., 1722, W, P2/D/511
Dalmore, Wm., yeo., Gt. Cheverell, 1724, I, W, P2/D/523
Damer, Wm., clothworker, Lyme R., Dorset, 1731, AB, I, P5/1731/24
Damer, Wm., Monkton F., 1832, AB, Wr, P2/1832/14
Dalman, Dalmon *see* Dolman
Dalmore *see* Dalmer
Dalton, Edwd., husb., Fyfield, Berks., 1808, W, Wr, P1/1808/94
Thos., Wantage, Berks., 1791, AB, P5/1791/6, P5/18Reg/164A
Dolton, Thos., gardener, Speenhamland, Berks., 1801, W, P1/1801/43, P1/15Reg/263
Damenick *see* Dominick
Damer *see* Dalmer
Damett *see* Dammett
Damlick, Betty, widow, Amesb., 1805, W, P2/1805/58
Thos., Durnford & Chilmark, 1795, AB, P2/D/720
Dammer *see* Dalmer
Dammett, Domett, Emanuel, yeo., Chards., Devon, 1710, I, W, P5/1710/34, P5/15Reg/197
Geo., husb., Axnoller, Beam., Dorset, 1610, comm, I, W, P5/1610/16, P5/9Reg/27A
Geo., sen., blacksmith, Beam., Dorset, 1707, I, NW, P5/1707/17, P5/15Reg/39A
Dummott, Jn., Chards., Devon, 1582, AB, I, P5/1582/19, P5/4Reg/38C
Domet, Jn., victualler, Chards., Devon, 1633, comm, I, W, P5/1633/16, P5/12Reg/160
Damett, Marian, widow, Axnoller, Beam., Dorset, 1663, I, W (NEP), P30/51
Damett, My., wife, Beam., Dorset, 1760, AB, P17/546
Dematt alias Stephens, Richd., Beam., Dorset, 1769, AB, P17/560
Dematt, Richd., gent., Beam., Dorset, 1783, W, P17/575
Domett, Sam., yeo., Alton P., Dorset, 1766, W, P5/1766/6
Domet, Sam., yeo., Chards., Devon, 1796, comm, W, P14/193
Dematt, Sarah, widow, Devizes (form. of St Bride's, London), 1772-73, req, copy W, P1/D/412, P1/12Reg/432
Dumett, Sarah, widow, Uffc., Devon, 1773, AB, O, P20/1/258

Damore *see* Dalmer
Dampee, Dampee alias Hayward, Jn., yeo., Lacock, [1709], W (NEP), P3/D/270
Dampier, Joel, yeo., Wambrook, Somerset, 1847, comm, W, Wr, P14/227
Jn., clerk (Revd), Codf. St P., 1839, comm, W, Wr, P1/1839/66
Sam., widower, Sherb., Dorset, 1766, AB, P5/1766/9
Thos., husb., Sherb., Dorset, 1641, I, T (re Ann D., minor), W, P5/1641/27, P5/14Reg/37
Thos., husb., Sherb., Dorset, 1707, I, W, P5/1707/18, P5/15Reg/30
Dampney, Grace, widow, Boys Hill, Holnest, Dorset, 1822, comm, W, Wr, P5/1822/12
Jn., yeo., Boys Hill, Holnest, Dorset, 1822, comm, W, Wr, P5/1822/1
Dampney *or* Darghbeny, Jn., Maiden B., 1747, AB, I, P1/D/357
Damsell, Wm., husb., Westport St My., [1617], I, W (NEP), P3/D/30
Damyon, Jn., Sutton Poyntz, Dorset, 1576, I, W, P5/1576/13, P5/3Reg/81B
Dance, Daunce, Ann, sp., Sal., 1719, W, P4/1719/4
Anthony, husb., Crofton, Gt. Bedwyn, 1634, I, W (GVS), P5/1634/37, P5/12Reg/277
Benj., mariner (of the Lion man of war), Whittonditch, Rams., 1747, W, P5/1747/7
Edwd., Collingbourne D., 1685, I, W, P21/4/16
Geo., innholder, Pewsey, 1767, AB, ren, P3/D/407
Isaac, shopkeeper, Rams., 1807, W, Wr, P5/1807/18
Daunce, Jas., husb., Whitep., 1559, W, P2/4Reg/25B, 27A
Jas., Collingbourne D., 1784, AB, P21/11/26
Jane, widow, Mildenhall, 1793, AB, P3/D/457
Jn., Wilton, Gt. Bedwyn, 1624, I, W, P21/3/7
Jn., labourer, Gt. Bedwyn, 1740, AB, I (2 - 1 a copy), Wr, P5/1740/27
Jn., yeo., Sanham Grn, Hungerford, Berks., 1818, W, Wr, P23/882
Kitty, labourer's wife, Marridge Hill, Rams., 1855, AB, aff, O, Wr, P5/1855/1
Daunce, Margery, Gt. Bedwyn, 1568, AB, P5/2Reg/2B
My., widow, Crofton, Gt. Bedwyn, 1631, AB, I, P21/3/16
My., widow, proved at Gt. Bedwyn, 1639, I, W, P21/1/44
Daunce, Michael, Rams., 1737, AB, P5/1737/16
Deance, Richd., husb., Marl., 1625, I, W, P1/D/44
Daunce, Richd., weaver, Marl. St My., 1635, I, W, P1/D/70
Daunce, Robt., Shalbourne, 1569, W, P5/2Reg/39C
Daunce, Robt., Sal., 1715, W, P4/1715/7
Daunce, Robt., Sal., 1759, W, P1/D/386, P1/11Reg/420B
Robt., miller, Werg Mill, Mildenhall, 1768, W, P3/D/409
Sarah, apothecary's wife, Marl., 1732, AB, P1/D/305
Thos., Collingbourne D., 1635, I, W, P21/1/16
Thos., tiler, Marl., 1701, I, W, P1/D/207, P1/4Reg/92
Thos., Axford, Rams., 1736, AB, P5/1736/11
Thos., Marl., 1743, AB, P1/D/343
Thos., Crowood, Rams., 1831, AB, O, W, Wr, P5/1831/1
Daunce, Wm., Gt. Bedwyn, 1566, W, P5/1Reg/77B
Daunce, Wm., tailor, Marl. St My., 1632, AB, I, P1/D/63
Wm., tiler, Marl., 1751, W, P1/D/374, P1/10Reg/460
Dancey, Dansey, Amos, yeo., Easton Grey, 1769, W, P3/D/413
Dancy, Andrew, farmer, Kellaways, 1828, W, Wr, P3/1828/26
Christian, widow, Atworth, Bradford A., 1811, comm, W, Wr, P2/1811/4
Dancy, Eliz., widow, Bradford A., 1857, aff, W, Wr, P2/1857/13
Dansey, Fanny, sp., Swindon, 1781, W, P3/D/437
Dansey, Geo., lieutenant 66th Regiment of Foot, Swindon, 1765, W, P3/D/399
Jn., bach., Atworth, Bradford A., 1812, AB, comm, Wr, P2/1812/4
Dansey, Lucy, sp., Swindon, 1781, W, P3/D/438
Richd., labourer, Easton Grey, 1787, W, P3/D/451
Dancy, Sam., carp., Pickwick, Corsham, 1750, W, P3/D/375
Dansey, Sarah, sp., Swindon, 1792, W, P3/D/455
Dansey, Thos., gent., Swindon, 1781, comm, W (2 - 1 a copy), P3/D/439
Wm., yeo., Atworth, Bradford A., 1798, comm, W, P1/D/446, P1/15Reg/161
Wm., farmer, Westlands Farm, Melk., 1849, O, W, Wr, P2/1849/17
Dancock, Wm., Sherb., Dorset, 1644, AB, comm, I, P5/1643/2, P5/14Reg/62D
Dancy *see* Dancey

Dandett, Wm. Thos., lay vicar of Salisbury Cathedral, Sal. The Close, 1748, AB, I, W, Wr, P5/1748/7
Dando, Thos., re property at Limpley Stoke & Bradford A., 1823, AB, comm, P2/1823/22
Dandridge, Agnes, widow, Blewbury, Berks., 1638, AB, I, P5/1638/27, P5/13Reg/139B
Edwd., Blewbury, Berks., 1716, AB, P5/1716/25
Francis, husb., Blewbury, Berks., 1631, AB, I, P5/1631/37, P5/12Reg/82A
Jn., yeo., Aston U., Blewbury, Berks., 1602, AB, I, W, P5/1602/12, P5/7Reg/34B
Jn., shoemaker, Blewbury, Berks., 1632, AB, I, P5/1632/19, P5/12Reg/105A
Matthew, yeo., E. Hendred, Berks., 1808, W, Wr, P1/1808/97
Robt., yeo., Blewbury, Berks., 1663, I, W (both damaged), P5/1663/19
Thos., sen., oatmealman and yeo., Blewbury, Berks., 1641, I, W, P5/1641/101, P5/14Reg/5B
Dandy, Eliz., widow, Urchf., 1624, I, W, P2/D/136
Dawndy, Thos., Urchf., 1553, W, P2/2Reg/180B
Thos., jun., husb., Urchf., 1611, I, P2/D/100
Thos., husb., Urchf., 1618, I, W, P2/D/120
Dangerfield, Edwd., sen., baker, Marl., 1709, AB, I, P1/D/232
Edwd., joiner, Marl., 1736-38, W, P1/D/323, P1/8Reg/377
Jn., husb., Whitep. and Lockerley, Hants, 1616, I, W, P2/D/111, P2/8Reg/313A
Jn., yeo., Wootton R., 1763, W, P1/D/394, P1/12Reg/99B
My., widow, Wootton R., 1776, W, P1/D/418, P1/13Reg/135
My., widow, Devizes St My., 1857, aff, O, W, Wr, P1/1857/4
Melior, widow, Sal., 1684, I, NW, P4/1683/6
Richd., Calne, 1597, AB, a/c, T, P5/1597/29, P5/6Reg/161A
Richd., baker, Marl., 1671, I, W, P1/D/128
Richd., sen., baker, Marl., 1750, W, P1/D/367, P1/10Reg/390
Robt., bach., Avebury, 1760, AB, P3/D/390
Thos., gent., Devizes, 1840, comm, W, Wr, P1/1840/23
Wm., Cherhill, 1591, I, W, P5/1591/18, P5/5Reg/125A
Wm., Yatesbury, 1740, AB, P3/D/349
Wm., gent., Bradford A., 1744, comm, W, P2/D/589
Daniel, Daniell, Adam, E. Lockinge, Berks., 1614, AB, a/c, copy of court paper, I, P1/D/24
Alice, Mere, 1595, AB, P5/1595/20, P5/6Reg/98
Daniell, Alice, widow, E. Lockinge, Berks., 1613, I, W, P1/D/23
Daniell, Ann, widow, Corsham, 1614, AB, I, LA, P29/D/4
Daniell, Ann, widow, Notton, Lacock, [1665], I, W (NEP), P3/D/123
Ann, sp., Upton S., [1686], W, P2/D/365
Daniell, Ann, sp., Trowb., 1709, I, W, P2/D/456
Daniell, Avis, widow, Boyton, 1614, I, W, P2/D/105
Daniell, Chris., yeo., Norridge, Upton S., 1636, AB, a/c, I (very detailed), P2/D/193
Daniell, Chris., sen., yeo., Thoulstone, Upton S., 1664, I, W, P2/D/254
Daniell, Chris., husb., Fittleton, 1693, I, W, P2/D/398
Chris., jun., yeo., Thoulstone, Upton S., 1693, AB, I, P2/D/400
Chris., Horningsham, 1775, AB, P5/1775/6, P5/17Reg/84C
Daniell, Cicely, widow, Beanacre, Melk., 1639, comm, I, W, P2/D/210
Daniell, Edith, Maiden B., 1546, W (NEP), P2/1Reg/78A
Daniell, Edwd., yeo., Ludg., 1677, I, W, P2/D/311
Daniell, Eleanor, widow, Norridge, Upton S., 1663, comm, W, P2/D/252
Daniell, Eleanor, sp., Upton S., 1710, W, P2/D/461
Daniell, Eliz., widow, Teffont M., 1601, I, W (NEP), P1/D/9
Eliz., Warm., 1696, AB, P2/D/407
Eliz., Upton S., 1719, AB, P2/D/501
Daniell, Evan, yeo., Ludg., 1732, AB, W, P1/D/306, P1/7Reg/449A
Francis, Drayton, Abingdon, Berks., 1795, AB, P1/D/441, P1/14Reg/562C
Daniels, Francis, Corsley, 1828, AB, W, Wr, P2/1828/10
Gabriel, yeo., Brook, Westb., 1789, W, P25/1789/2
Daniell, Geo., husb., Baycliff, Horningsham, 1581, W, P2/6Reg/30B
Daniell, Geo., husb., Upton S., 1621, comm, I, NW, P2/D/130
Geo., yeo., Rushall, 1795, W, P2/D/721
Daniell, Gregory, fletcher, Sherb., Dorset, 1593, I, W, P5/1593/30, P5/6Reg/38C
Hy., yeo., Beam., Dorset, 1597, AB, I, W, P5/1597/32, P5/6Reg/171A
Daniell, Hy., [yeo.], Dinton, 1626, I, W, P2/D/147

Hy., sen., yeo., Beam., Dorset, 1705, W, P17/160
Hy., Beam., Dorset, 1727, AB, P17/429
Daniell, Hy., yeo., Beam., Dorset, 1745, W, P17/499
Hugh, Sherb., Dorset, 1686, AB, I, P5/1686/21
Isaac, sen., yeo., Beam., Dorset, 1727, NW, P17/430
Jas., Beam., Dorset, 1698, I, W, P17/124
Jas., attorney, Beam., Dorset, 1711, I, W, P17/202
Daniell, Jas., victualler, Beam., Dorset, 1724, W, P17/412
Jas., yeo., Beam., Dorset, 1731, W, P5/1731/25
Daniels, Jas., spinner, Trowb., 1822, W, Wr, P1/1822/3
Daniels, Jane, sp., Littleton Drew, 1854, AB, aff, O, Wr, P3/1854/19
Daniell, Joan, widow, Sherb., Dorset, 1594-95, AB, I, P5/1594/27, P5/6Reg/91A
Daniell, Joan, widow, Burbage, 1597, W, P5/1597/34, P5/6Reg/182B
Daniell, Joan, widow, Beam., Dorset, 1753, W, P17/530
Daniell, Jn., yeo., Upton S., 1570, W, P2/5Reg/94A
Daniell, Jn., Burbage, 1589-96, AB, W, P5/1589/16, P5/5Reg/54C
Daniell, Jn., shepherd, Boyton, 1605, AB, I, P2/D/76
Daniell, Jn., husb., Dinton, 1608, AB, I, W, P2/D/81, P2/8Reg/33B
Daniell, Jn., husb., Berwick St Leonard, 1625, I, W, P1/D/43
Daniell, Jn., husb., Beam., Dorset, 1629, AB, a/c, comm, I, P5/1628/34, P5/11Reg/22A
Daniell, Jn., cook, Barton, Kintbury, Berks. (form. of Newport, Essex), 1638, AB, I, L, P1/D/77
Daniell, Jn., Upton S., [1663], I, P2/D/251
Daniell, Jn., Upton S., 1676, AB, P2/D/298
Daniell, Jn., yeo., Goods, Corsham, 1676, AB, I, ren, P29/D/15, P29/1Reg/206B
Daniell, Jn., sen., yeo., Castle C., 1690, I, W, P3/D/215
Jn., Warm., 1695, AB, comm, ren, P2/D/403
Dannel, Jn., brickmaker, Brokerswood, N. Bradley, 1706, W, P2/D/448
Daniell, Jn., yeo., Lyme R., Dorset (form. of Axminster, Devon), 1706, I, W, P16/169
Daniell, Jn., sen., tailor, Imber, 1707, W, P2/D/450
Jn., sen., yeo., Beam., Dorset, 1721, AB, W, P17/394-95
Daniell, Jn., Imber, 1732, AB, P1/D/304
Jn., Castle C., 1737, AB, P28/16
Jn., shepherd, E. Hanney, W. Hanney, Berks., 1756, W, P1/D/379, P1/11Reg/262
Jn., maltster, Warm., 1774, AB, comm, ren, W, P2/D/666
Jn., Warm., 1797, AB, P2/D/728
Jn., yeo., Drayton, Abingdon, Berks., 1814, W, Wr, P1/1814/105
Jn., Charlton, 1818, AB, Wr, P2/1818/49
Daniels, Jn., Corsley, 1822, AB, Wr, P2/1822/67
Daniell, Jn., Warm., 1824, AB, Wr, P2/1824/26
Daniell, Jn., sen., gent., Westb., 1828, comm, W, Wr, P25/1828/1
Daniels, Jn., gent., Westb., 1856, declaration, W, Wr, P25/1856/2
Daniell, Jos., Imber, 1815, AB, Wr, P2/1815/77
Lucy, widow, Woodford and Sal., 1727, W, P13/4/20
Daniell, Mgt., widow, Sal., 1612, AB, I, P4/1612/7
Daniell, Margery, widow, Upton S., 1676, comm, W, P2/D/296
Daniell, My., widow, S. Newton, 1628, AB, I, W, P2/D/154
Daniell, My., widow, Mere, [1632], I, copy I, W, copy W, P5/1632/20
Daniell, My., sen., widow, Imber, 1713, W, P2/D/481
My., widow, Beam., Dorset, 1733, W, P17/455
My., widow, Brook Common, Dilton, Westb., 1792, AB, O, P25/1792/1
Daniels, My., sp., Pewsey, 1854, AB, aff, L, O, Wr, P3/1854/18
Daniell, Nich., tucker, Sherb., Dorset, 1605, AB, I, T, P5/1605/18, P5/8Reg/26A
Daniell, Nich., gent., Dinton, 1709, comm, W, P2/D/458
Daniell, Nich., gent., Sutton B., 1726, AB, comm, W, P3/D/314
Phyllis, Sherb., Dorset, 1595, AB, P5/1594/26, P5/6Reg/90D
Daniell, Ralph, yeo., Dinton, 1597, I, W, P2/D/52
Daniell, Ralph, yeo., Dinton, 1673, I (very detailed), W, P2/D/289
Daniell, Richd., Maiden B., 1554, W, P2/2Reg/183C
Daniell, Richd., Upton S., 1560, W, P2/4Reg/39F
Daniell, Richd., yeo., S. Newton, 1624, I, W, P2/D/141

Daniell, Richd., Sal. St Edmd., 1634, a/c, I, P1/D/66
Robt., Corsham, 1635, AB, P29/D/8
Robt., Steeple L., 1708, AB, P2/D/454
Daniell, Robt., Castle C., 1720, AB, I, W, P28/11
Dannel, Sarah, widow, Brokerswood, N. Bradley, 1707, W, P2/D/449
Daniell, Sarah, widow, Warm., 1775, W, P2/D/670
Daniell, Sarah, widow, Wantage, Berks., 1831, O, W, Wr, P23/952
Daniell, Simon, Bradford A., 1630, AB, I, P2/D/160
Daniell, Susanna, widow, Warm., 1808, AB, Wr, P1/1808/63
Daniell, Thos., Sal. St Thos., 1587, W, P4/Reg/29E
Daniell, Thos., yeo., Corsham, 1601, W, P29/D/2, P29/1Reg/50A
Daniell, Thos., sen., Collingbourne K., 1630, AB, I, ren, P3/D/77
Daniell, Thos., husb., Sunton, Collingbourne K., 1675, I, W, P3/D/158
Daniels, Thos., Upton S., 1762, AB, P2/D/635
Daniell, Thos., gardener, Warm. Common, 1822, W, Wr, P2/1822/37
Daniell, Thos., plumber and glazier, Westb., 1831, O, W, Wr, P25/1831/4
Daniell, Wm., grocer, Sal. St Martin, 1626, I, NW, P4/1626/21
Daniell, Wm., yeo., Teffont M., 1639, I, W, P2/D/204
Daniell, Wm., yeo. and gent., Dinton, 1715, I, W, P2/D/487
Dannel, Wm., sen., husb., Downton, 1725-26, I, W, P1/D/280, P1/7Reg/75B
Wm., yeo., Rushall, 1830, W, P2/1830/44
see also Gregory alias D.

Dann, Ann, widow, Mildenhall, 1761, W, P3/D/393
Edwd., bach., Heytes., 1834, AB, Wr, P5/1834/3
Daun, My., widow, Heytes., 1744, AB, Wr, P5/1744/13
My., widow, Heytes., 1835, AB, O, Wr, P5/1835/2
Richd. *see also* Edwd. Fricker
Wm., Heytes., 1787, AB, P5/1787/4, P5/18Reg/75

Dannel *see* Daniel

Dansey *see* Dancey

Dantry, Eliz., widow, Lambourn, Berks., 1707-08, W, P1/D/221, P1/4Reg/294
Hy., miller, Leverton, Chilton F., 1641, I, W, P3/D/107
Dauntrey, Jn., Aldbourne, 1569, W (NEP), P1/1Reg/107A
Daintrey, Sibyl, widow, Gt. Faringdon, Berks., 1635, AB, I, NW, P5/1635/34, P5/12Reg/181
Thos., innholder, Marl., 1734, W, P1/D/311, P1/7Reg/599C

Danvers, Edwd., gent., Charlcote, Bremhill, 1694, comm, I, W, P3/D/228
Jas., apothecary, Westb., 1722, W, P25/1722/4

Darby, Bartholemew, Beam., Dorset, 1570, W, P5/2Reg/78B
Derby, Eliz., Gt. Somerford, 1558, W (NEP), P1/1Reg/111C
Derby, Eliz., Gt. Somerford, 1570, W, P1/1Reg/25B
Francis, sen., Sherb., Dorset, 1722, AB, I, P5/1722/18
Derby, Francis, Sherb., Dorset, 1730, AB, P5/1730/16
Jeremiah, clothier, Sherb., Dorset, 1692, I, W, P5/1692/22
Jn., Hurst, Berks., 1541, W, P5/20Reg/24
Jn., carp., Gt. Bedwyn, 1685, I, W, P5/1685/30
Jn., maltster, Highw., 1771, comm, W (member of Friendly Society at H.), P10/1771/5
Jn., excise officer, Lyme R., Dorset, 1813, W, P16/378
Derby, My., widow, Sherb., Dorset, 1719, W, P5/1719/25, P5/16Reg/19A
Derby, Thos., vicar, Damerham, Hants, 1699, AB, comm, I, P2/D/416
Thos., Ruscombe, Berks., 1728, W, P5/1728/29, P5/16Reg/205B
Wm., mercer, Highw., 1748, AB, W, P10/1748/1
Wm., carp., Ashton K., 1762, W, P3/D/394
see also Coffin alias D.

Dare, Frances, widow, Lyme R., Dorset, 1721, W, P16/224
Gertrude, Lyme R. and Uplyme, Dorset, 1690, W, P16/103
Jn., Lyme R., Dorset, 1696, AB, P16/142
My., widow, Lyme R., Dorset, 1687, AB, P16/94
Rachel, widow, Lyme R., Dorset, 1798, AB, comm, W (2), P16/357
Dayer, Robt., Sandhurst, Berks., 1709, W, P5/1709/11, P5/15Reg/121
Wm., sen., mariner, Lyme R., Dorset, 1668, I, W, P5/1668/26

Darely *see* Darley
Darghbeny *see* Dampney *or* D.
Dark, Ann, widow, Devizes, 1771, W, P1/D/410, P1/12Reg/417
Deborah, widow, Chr. M., 1815, AB, comm, Wr, P3/1815/18
Edwd. Jefferys, yeo., Broughton G., 1824, W, Wr, P2/1824/44
Eliz., Wilton, 1618, T (ex. of the decd: Francis Davis, minor), P2/D/118
Isaac, yeo., Broughton G., 1819, AB, comm, ren, W, Wr, P2/1819/6
Jane, sp., Biddestone St Peter, 1619, I, W (NEP), P3/D/39
Joan, widow, Corsham, 1650, AB, I, W, P29/D/10
Jn., mercer, Warm., 1600, AB, I, P2/D/64
Jn., carp., Biddestone St Peter, 1621, I, W, P3/D/45
Jn., Upavon, 1624, AB, I, P2/D/142
Jn., yeo., Biddestone St Peter, 1690, I, W, P3/D/216
Jn., sievemaker, Castle C., 1764, W, P3/D/397
Jn., yeo., Broughton G., 1781, W, P2/D/683
Jn., Chr. M., 1814, AB, comm, P1/1814/72
Jn., tailor, Keevil, 1825, W, Wr, P2/1825/12
My., widow, Mkt. L., 1828, W, Wr, P2/1828/31
Richd., weaver, Corsham, 1643, W, P29/D/9, P29/1Reg/142
Sam., shopkeeper, Devizes, 1770, W, P1/D/403, P1/12Reg/384A
Stephen, gent., Broughton G., 1789, W, P2/D/708
Stephen, Maiden B., 1815, AB, comm, Wr, P2/1815/19
Stephen, gent., Gastard, Corsham, 1837, W, P29/1800-1857/29, P29/3Reg/287
Thos., Corsham, 1608, AB, I, W, P29/D/3, P29/1Reg/63A
Thos., no abode stated, 1674, AB, I, P3/D/155
Thos., carp., Biddestone St Nich., 1720, I, W, P1/D/266
Thos., sen., carp., Biddestone St Nich., 1760, comm, D (several), W, P3/D/391
Wm., husb., Biddestone St Peter, [1641], NW (NEP), P3/D/108
Darknell, Benj., sadler and harnessmaker, Rams., 1845, O, W, Wr, P5/1845/7
Darley, Jas., architect, Hullavington, 1822, W, Wr, P3/1822/22
Darley, Jas. Jos., Hullavington, 1825, AB, P3/1825/55
Richd., wheeler, Netheravon, 1628, I, W, P12/57
Darling, Phoebe, widow, Wantage, Berks., 1699, I, W, P23/234
Richd., sen., victualler, Wantage, Berks., 1694, I, W, P23/207
Durling, Thos., Reading, Berks., 1741, AB, P1/D/341
Wm., Buckland, Berks., 1763, AB, P1/D/395
Darnford *see* Durnford
Dart, Robt., Gt. Bedwyn, 1588, AB, I, W, P5/1588/15, P5/5Reg/31B
Robt., Mkt. L., 1778, AB, P2/D/677
Darter, Asher [male], Ashton K., 1817, AB, O, Wr, P3/1817/24
Thos., yeo., Garsdon, 1687, AB, I, P3/D/202
Darville *see* Dorvill
Dash, Eliz., sp., Calne, 1682, AB, I, W, P5/1682/31
Harriet, wife, Milbourne, Malm., 1816, AB, Wr, P3/1816/10
Jn., yeo., Malm., 1839, O, W, Wr, P3/1839/14
Robt., yeo., Clack, Lyneham, 1854, aff, comm, W, Wr, P3/1854/56
Sam., victualler, Wootton B., 1836, comm, W, Wr, P3/1836/5
Dashwood, Edmd., Sal. St Edmd., 1690, AB, I, P4/1690/15
Eliz., widow, Sal., 1702, AB, I, P4/1702/12
Nathaniel, physician, Gillingham, Dorset, 1667, a/c, P27/1/779
Wm., clerk, Enborne, Berks., 1734, W, P1/D/312, P1/7Reg/596C
Dassell *see* Dossell
Daston *see* Dauston
Daton, Amy, widow, Bps. C., 1733, W, P24/952
Edwd., yeo., St Mgt., Preshute, 1750, W, P1/D/368, P1/10Reg/386
Jn., maltster, Marl., 1741, W, P1/D/333, P1/9Reg/218A
Robt., gardener, Wick, Bps. C., 1730, comm, W, P24/826
see also Dawton
Daughter, My., sp., Crickl. St S., 1803, AB, W, P3/1803/8
Tobias, yeo., Cloatley, Hankerton, 1770, AB, W, P1/D/404, P1/12Reg/325B

Wm., Chelworth, Crickl. St S., 1774, W, P3/D/425
Daunce *see* Dance
Dauntrey *see* Dantry
Dauntsey, Aquila, Corsham, 1718, marriage licence, P29/2Reg/28A
Dauntsey, Avis, widow, N. Bradley, 1559, W, P2/3Reg/165C
Dauntsey, Giles, gent., N. Bradley, 1551, W, P2/2Reg/122C
Dauntsey, Sarah, sp., Corsham, 1835, AB, comm, P3/1835/10
Dauston, Daston, Ann, sp., Hampstead N., Berks., 1811, W, Wr, P1/1811/63
Edwd., Grove, Wantage, Berks., 1686, AB, I, W, P23/149
Dawsten, Richd., sen., yeo., W. Hanney, Berks., 1701, I, W, P1/D/203, P1/4Reg/122
Dawsten, Roger, Gt. Faringdon, Berks., 1573, W, P5/3Reg/11B
see also Pearce alias D.
Dave, Jn., [yeo.], Durrington, 1593, AB, I, W, P2/D/42
Davenant, Cath., sp., Landford, 1694, W, P2/D/402
Jn., minor, Dauntsey, 1675, AB (Philip Butcher, guardian of 4 named minors to admr), P3/B/658
Jn. (bishop of Salisbury) *see* Roger Humfreys
Davenport, Ann, widow, Sal., 1741, AB, ren (2), Wr, P4/1740/2
Hy., vintner, Sal., 1737, W, Wr, P4/1737/20
Davers, Jn., Odstock, 1588, I, W, P2/D/31
Daves *see* Davis
Davey *see* Davy
Davidge, Eliz., wife, Teffont M., 1843, AB, Wr, P2/1843/41
Hy., Quidh., 1703, AB, P2/D/437
Jas., Upavon, 1814, AB, Wr, P2/1814/19
Jn., shoemaker, Allweston, Folke, Dorset, 1692, AB, I, P5/1692/23
Jn., Sal., 1704, AB, P4/1704/5
Jn., cordw., Folke, Dorset, 1761, W, P5/1761/8
Jos., cordw., Allweston, Folke, Dorset, 1742, I, W, Wr, P5/1742/13
Joshua, Madjeston, Gillingham, Dorset, 1734, I, W, P27/1/330, P27/3Reg/2
Richd., husb., Fovant, 1619, I, W, P1/D/36
Thos., sen., Motc., Dorset, 1717, W, P27/1/221
Thos., innholder, Collingbourne D., 1743, W, P21/9/46
Thos., Sherb., Dorset, 1824, AB, Wr, P5/1824/28
Wm., bach., Collingbourne D., 1732, AB, P1/D/310
Davids, Thos., sackcloth weaver, Abingdon, Berks., 1795, W, P1/D/442, P1/14Reg/560
Davis, Alfred, yeo., Bromham, 1831, comm, W, P3/1831/44
Alice, widow, Sal. St Martin, 1595, AB, I, W, P1/D/7
Alice, widow, Sherston, 1621, I, W, P3/D/46
Alice, widow, Steeple L., 1633, NW, P2/D/178
Alice, widow, Nettleton, 1633, I, W, P3/D/85
Alice, widow, Broad C., 1681, AB, I, P2/D/335
Ambrose, W. Grimstead, 1713, AB, P2/D/484
Andrew, scribbler, Westb., 1736, I, W, P25/1736/2
Ann, widow, Westport St My., 1606, W, P3/2Reg/11A
Ann, widow, W. Grafton, 1665, I, W, P5/1665/24
Ann, widow, Durnford, 1682, I, W, Wr, P5/1682/28
Davies, Ann, gentlewoman, Maiden B., 1693, I, W, P2/D/399
Ann, sp., Steeple A., 1714, W, P1/D/252, P1/5Reg/446A
Ann, sp., Long Newnton, 1720, AB, I, P3/D/293
Ann, widow, Chicksgrove, Tisb., 1769, AB, a/c, I (very detailed), P2/D/652
Ann, widow, Calne, 1774, AB, W, P26/1069
Ann, Sonning, Berks., 1801, AB, P5/1801/22, P5/18Reg/324A
Anthony, sen., tailor, Westb., 1688, I, W, P25/1688/4
Avis, widow, Sherrington, 1710, W, P2/D/464
Bartholemew, Bradford A., 1567, AB, P2/5Reg/4B
Bridget, widow, Nettleton, 1639, I, W, P3/D/100
Cath., Chr. M., 1572, W (NEP), P1/1Reg/37B
Cath., widow, Pott., 1851, AB, O, Wr, P1/1851/39
Chas., Stourton, 1698, I, W, P2/D/414
Chas., Crickl. St S., 1765, AB, comm, P3/D/400

Daves, Christian, widow, Netheravon, 1626, I, W, P12/50
Christian, wife, Sal., 1802, AB, P4/1802/8
Chris., cordw., Haydon, Dorset, 1780, W, P5/1780/6, P5/17Reg/199C
Clement, husb., Homanton, Maddington, 1646, W, Wr, P2/D/236
Dan., Charlton nr Malm., 1750, AB, P1/D/369
Dan., stonemason, Colerne, 1816, W, Wr, P3/1816/16
Dan., Hungerford, Berks., 1826, AB, O, P23/924
Dathan, yeo., Nether St., Bromham, 1853, aff, O, W, Wr, P3/1853/59
Davis alias Powell, David, tailor, W. Kington, 1688, comm, I, W, P3/D/205
David, Hilmarton, 1746, AB, P3/D/364
Dorothy, Maiden B., 1609, I, copy I, W, copy W, P2/D/82, P2/8Reg/34A
Dorothy, widow, Sal. The Close, 1693, I (detailed), W, P5/1693/17
Edith, sp., Lt. Woodford, 1661, I, W, P5/1661/12
Edith, widow, E. Stowell, Wilcot, 1704, AB, I, P3/D/258
Davies, Edmd., blacksmith, Corston, Malm., [1637], I, W (NEP), P3/D/93
Davis alias Taylor, Edmd., Brinkw., 1646, AB, I, P1/D/87
Davis alias Simes, Edwd., husb., Maiden B., [1627], I, W, P2/D/152
Edwd., Binfield, Berks., 1631, ren, P1/D/54
Edwd., yeo., Woodley, W. and Sandford, Berks., 1663, I, W (both damaged), P5/1663/20
Davis alias Taylor, Edwd., yeo., Brinkw., 1673, AB, comm, P3/D/149
Edwd., yeo., Teffont E., 1678, I, W, P2/D/315
Davies, Edwd., Stert, Urchf., 1684, AB, P1/D/160
Davies, Edwd., blacksmith, Homington, 1706, W, P24/592
Edwd., Teffont E., 1711, AB, P1/D/239
Edwd., Lydeway, Urchf., 1715, AB, I, P2/D/486
Edwd., sen., Trowb., 1735, AB, P1/D/315
Edwd., maltster, Biddestone St Nich., 1736, comm, W, P3/D/343
Edwd., innholder, Mere, 1765, W, P5/1765/10
Edwd., Wylye, 1784, AB, ren, P2/D/692
Edwd., Bps. C., 1805, AB, P24/1235
Eleanor, widow, Gt. Woodford, 1695, I, W, P5/1695/23
Eliz., widow, Stratford sub C., 1592, W, P1/D/4
Davis alias Powell, Eliz., widow, Alderton, 1627, I, W, P3/D/64
Eliz., widow, Pickwick, Corsham, 1675, I, W, P29/D/14, P29/1Reg/205B
Eliz., mercer's widow, Trowb., 1707, W, P2/D/451
Eliz., sp., Steeple A., 1718, I, W, P2/D/497
Eliz., wife, Calne, 1731, AB (form. Eliz. James), P26/754
Davies, Eliz., widow, Sal., 1750, AB, ren, P4/1750/3
Eliz., Bradford A., 1756, AB, P1/D/380
Eliz., Calne, 1757, AB, P26/958
Ephraim, Atworth, Bradford A., 1710, AB, I, P2/D/466
Ephraim, yeo., Farley, Alderbury, 1773, W, P1/D/414, P1/13Reg/30
Frances, widow, Broad Town, Clyffe P., 1700-02, AB, I, L, P3/D/240, 251
Francis, woollen weaver, Sal. St Martin, 1594, AB, I (2), W, P1/D/5
Francis, widow, Sal., 1679, AB, I, ren, W, P4/1679/7
Francis, Bloxworth, Dorset, 1681, AB, comm, I, W, P5/1681/9
Francis, yeo., Kingswood, Gloucs, 1811, W, Wr, P3/1811/20
Francis *see* Eliz. Dark
Geoffrey, Chilhampton, S. Newton, 1710-11, W, P1/D/234, P1/5Reg/31
Geoffrey, Stert, Urchf., 1760, AB, P1/D/390
Davies, Geo., husb., Broughton G., 1637, AB, I, NW, P2/D/194
Geo., Semington, Steeple A., 1639, a/c (2 - 1 for food & clothing for 3 children in minority), P2/D/209
Geo., Westport St My., 1673, AB, comm, P3/D/150
Geo., gent., Netton, Durnford, 1676, W (NEP), P30/50
Geo., gent., Lt. Woodford, 1727, AB, I, P5/1727/12
Geo., barber, Sal., 1729, W, P1/D/289, P1/7Reg/345B
Geo., cordw., Highw., 1773, W, P10/1773/1
Geo., bach., Warm., 1801, AB, P2/1801/31
Geo., shopkeeper, Urchf., 1839, comm, W, Wr, P2/1839/20
Geo., carp. and joiner, New St., Sal., 1852, W, Wr, P4/1852/10

Davies, German, weaver, Horningsham, 1578, I, W, P5/1578/14, P5/3Reg/106B
Giles, husb., Clapcote, Grittleton, 1649, comm, I, W, P1/D/93
Hannah, gent., Calne, 1801, W, P26/1234
Hannah, sp., Hungerford, Berks., 1829, W, P23/946
Harry, Maiden B., 1596?, I, W, copy W, P2/D/49
Davies, Hy., yeo., Woolley, Bradford A., [1623], I, W, P2/D/132
Hy., Chicksgrove, Tisb., 1631, a/c, P2/D/165
Hy., [yeo.], Chicksgrove, Tisb., 1640, I, W (2), P2/D/214
Hy., yeo. and husb., Buckham Mill, Beam., Dorset, 1669, I, W, P5/1669/15
Hy., Bradford A., 1676, AB, I, P2/D/303
Hy., Teffont E., [1679], NW, P2/D/322
Davis alias Snow, Hy., sen., labourer, Westport St My., 1721, AB, I, ren, P3/D/295
Hy., sen., yeo., Chicksgrove, Tisb., 1734, W, P2/D/553
Davies, Hy., Ansty, 1760, W, P2/D/629
Hester, widow, *The Bear*, Westb., 1836, O, W, Wr, P25/1836/4
Hugh, yeo., Manningford Bruce, 1629, I, W, P3/D/73
Isaac, yeo., Brokenb., 1680, I, W, P3/D/176
Davies, Isabel, widow, Corston, Malm., 1627, I, W, P3/D/65
Jas., Atworth, Bradford A., 1685, AB, I, P2/D/356
Jas., Atworth, Bradford A., 1713, AB, P2/D/479
Jas., Trowle, Bradford A., 1721, I, W, P2/D/508
Jas., Maiden B., 1721, AB, P2/D/733
Jas., W. Ashton, Steeple A., 1725, AB, P2/D/526
Jas., yeo., Chitterne St My., 1740, comm, W, P2/D/578
Jas., Bradford A., 1744, AB, P1/D/344
Jas., mason, Castle C., 1755, W, P3/D/386
Davies, Jas., innholder, Warm., 1803, W, P2/1803/42
Jas., servant, *The Bear Inn*, Devizes, 1810, AB, comm, W, Wr, P1/1810/11
Jas., sen., yeo., Woodley and Sandford, Berks., 1818, W, Wr, P5/1818/20
Jas., sadler, Warm., 1842, W, Wr, P1/1842/47
Davies, Jas., Wylye, 1846, AB, Wr, P2/1846/38
Davies, Jas., Deptford, Wylye, 1855, AB, aff, ren, Wr, P1/1855/46
Jane, widow, Charlton nr Malm., 1616, I, W (both on same sheet), P3/D/29
Jane, widow, Chieveley, Berks., 1616, I, W, P1/D/30
Jane, sp., W. Kington, 1709, I, W, P3/D/269
Jane, Plaitford, 1726, AB, P1/D/283
Jane, Devizes, 1851, AB, comm, Wr, P1/1851/33
Jasper, yeo., Purton, 1706, I, W, P3/D/263
Jennifer, widow, Tisb., 1787, AB, P2/D/703
Joan, widow, Wilton, 1610, AB, I (*also* for Jn. Chatwell of Wilton, 1610. Cath. C. was admr for her husband & for Joan D., her mother in law, W, P2/D/99 (& P2/C/249)
Joan, widow, Stratford sub C., 1631, AB, I, P4/1631/15
Joan, widow, Nettleton, 1631, AB, I, P1/D/55
Joan, widow, Marl., 1671, comm, W, P1/D/129
Joan, Lockeridge, Overton, 1691, AB, I, P3/D/223
Joan, widow, Bapton, Fisherton Delamare, 1692, I, W, P1/D/176
Joan, widow, Westb., 1702, I, W (NEP), P25/1702/5
Joan, widow, Horton, Bps. C., 1714, W, P24/678
Joan *see also* Jn. Chatwell
Jn., husb., Durrington, 1548, W, P2/2Reg/53A
Jn., husb., Tisb., 1550, W, P2/2Reg/117A
Daves, Jn., yeo., Fovant, 1563, I, W, P2/D/5, P2/4Reg/151
Jn., husb., Durrington, 1566, W, P2/5Reg/2D
Jn., Tisb., 1575, AB, P2/5Reg/233C
Jn., carrier, Trowb., 1575, AB, a/c, P22/2/2, P5/3Reg/72A
Jn., Chicksgrove, Tisb., 1580, AB, P2/6Reg/16A
Devys, Jn., Sal. St Thos., 1587, AB, P4/Reg/29D
Jn., weaver, Bradford A., 1590, I, W, P2/D/38
Jn., yeo., Steeple A., 1590, I, W, P2/D/37
Jn., Gt. Bedwyn, 1592, I, W, P5/1592/19, P5/6Reg/2A

Jn., jun., yeo., Stratford sub C., 1594, I, P1/D/6
Jn., Stanton St Q., [1602], W (NEP), P3/1Reg/99B
Davis alias Powell, Jn., husb., Alderton, [1605], W (NEP), P3/D/4
Davies, Jn., Corston, Malm., 1609, AB, W, P3/D/11
Jn., Nettleton, 1623, I, W, P3/D/56
Davies, Jn., husb., Upton S., 1626, I, W, P2/D/145
Jn., yeo., Stratford sub C., 1626, I, W, P4/1626/18
Davis alias Symes, Jn., yeo., Longbridge D., 1626, I, W, P2/D/148
Jn., clothmaker, Woolley, Bradford A., 1627, I, W, P2/D/153
Jn., shepherd, Broad H., 1630, AB, a/c, I, W, P3/D/78
Davies, Jn., yeo., Corston, Malm., 1631, I, W, P3/D/82
Jn., blacksmith, Hullavington, 1636, I, W, P3/D/88
Daves, Jn., Horningsham, 1637, I, P5/1637/8
Jn., baker, Marl., 1661, AB, comm, I, P1/D/99
Jn., tailor, Malm., 1665, comm, I, W, P3/D/124
Jn., husb., Luckington, 1666, AB, I, ren, W, P1/D/115, 130
Jn., Chicksgrove, Tisb., [1666?], AB, I, ren (all fragmentary), P1/D/114
Jn., no abode stated, 1667, record of caveats, P3/D/128
Jn., yeo., Bapton, Fisherton Delamare, 1668, I, W, P2/D/266
Jn., blacksmith, Ogbourne St A., 1677, comm, I, W, P5/1677/16
Jn., Heytes., 1682, AB, P5/1682/37
Jn., Downton, 1686, AB, P1/D/164
Jn., labourer, S. Newton, 1686, AB, I, P2/D/367
Jn., Bapton, Fisherton Delamare, 1692, AB, I, P2/D/391
Jn., Fisherton A., 1695, AB, P2/D/405
Jn., maltster, Marl., 1706, W (NEP), P1/D/219
Jn., distiller, Luckington, [1710], I, W (NEP), P3/D/272
Jn., Wilton, 1713, AB, P2/D/482
Jn., broad weaver, Westb. Town, 1715, AB, I, P25/1715/1
Jn., carp., Nettleton, 1723, I, W, P1/D/272, P1/6Reg/449A
Jn., Corsham, 1726, I, P29/D/19
Jn., Downton, 1728, AB, P1/D/287
Jn., sailor on HMS *Edinburgh*, Plaitford, 1745, AB, P2/D/592
Jn., victualler, *Dolphin Inn*, Devizes, 1760, W, P1/D/391, P1/11Reg/483
Jn., Oxenwood, Shalbourne, 1767, AB, P5/1767/17
Jn., Marl., 1769, AB, P1/D/402
Jn., Pewsey, 1772, AB, P3/D/422
Jn., broad weaver, Beanacre, Melk., 1779, W, P2/D/679
Jn., yeo., Downton, [1781], W, P2/D/684
Jn., sen., yeo., Winterbourne S., 1785, AB, W, P2/D/694
Jn., sen., yeo., Sutton M., [1785], W, P2/D/693
Jn., yeo., Netton, Durnford, 1785, W, P5/1785/10, P5/18Reg/8
Jn., gent., Davis's House alias The Wore, Calne, 1786, W, P26/1151
Jn., butcher, Bradford A., 1788, W, P2/D/706
Jn., shopkeeper, Marden, 1789, W, P1/D/433, P1/14Reg/288
Jn., Reading St Giles, Berks., 1792, AB, P1/D/436, P1/14Reg/443A
Jn., Chirton, 1798, AB, P2/D/730
Jn., clerk, Marl., 1806, W, Wr, P1/1806/15
Jn., bricklayer, Milford, Sal. St Martin, 1821, W, Wr, P4/1821/3
Jn., labourer, Manningford A., 1826, W, Wr, P1/1826/101
Jn., Manningford A., 1840, AB, O, Wr, P1/1840/26
Jn., dairyman, Castleton, Dorset, 1842, comm, W, Wr, P5/1842/35
Jonathan, Bourton, Gillingham, Dorset, 1809, W, P27/1/602
Jos., Bucklebury, Berks., 1726, AB, P1/D/284
Jos., Charlton nr Malm., 1750, AB, P3/D/376
Jos., yeo., Longstreet, Enford, 1812, W, P2/1812/53
Davith, Julian, widow, Broad C., 1559, W, P2/3Reg/169B
Lancelot, clothworker, Sal., 1667, I, W, P4/1667/16
Lawr., husb., Alderton, 1638, I, W, P1/D/78
Lucy, widow, Warm., 1852, W, Wr, P2/1852/78

Mgt., widow, W. Kington, 1729, AB, P3/D/324
Mgt., widow, Heytes., 1852, comm, W, Wr, P5/1852/17
My., Gt. Bedwyn, 1633, I, W, P21/3/22
My., sp., Sherston, 1671, AB, a/c, I, P3/D/141
My., Pott., 1684, AB, I, P1/D/161
My., sp., Sherston, 1695, I, NW, P1/D/182
My., widow, Calne, 1702, I (detailed), W, P26/486
My., sp., Marl., 1708, I, W, P1/D/227
Daves, My., widow, Chilmark, 1723, W, P1/D/271, P1/6Reg/419B
My., widow, Froxfield Almshouse, 1725, AB, I, P3/D/313
My., Homington, 1737, W, P24/927
My., Stockley, Calne, 1750, W, P26/903
My., widow, Hilmarton, 1773, W, P3/D/423
My., Downton, 1782, W, P2/D/687
My., sp., Fisherton A., 1794, AB, D, W, P2/D/719
My., widow, Beanacre, Melk., 1798, W, P1/D/447, P1/15Reg/119
My., sp., Bromham, 1806, AB, Wr, P3/1806/49
My., widow, Shalbourne, 1813, comm, W, P23/864
My., widow, Horningsham, 1814, AB, comm, Wr, P5/1814/12
My., widow, Marl., 1816, W, Wr, P1/1816/9
Davies, My., widow, Froxfield Almshouse, 1842, O, W, Wr, P3/1842/22
My. Ann, widow, Malm., 1848, AB, court proceeding, O, T, Wr, P3/1848/13-14
Matthew, gent., Chicksgrove, Tisb., 1687, AB, I (very detailed listing over 100 book titles), ren, P2/D/370
Matthew, yeo., Stockton, 1693, I, W, P1/D/181
Matthew, grocer, Sal., 1766, W, P4/1766/3
Davies, Matthew, jun., gent., Warm., 1823, ren, W, Wr, P1/1823/56
Molly, clothier's wife, Devizes, 1742, AB, P1/D/342
Davis alias Griffith, Nathaniel, [dyer], Bromham, 1628, AB, I, P3/D/72
Nathaniel, shoemaker, W. Kington, 1688, AB, I, P3/D/206
Nich., husb., Broad C., 1557, W, P2/3Reg/25D
Davis alias Corbett, Nich., Crockerton, Longbridge D., 1594, I, W, P2/D/45
Nich., broad weaver, Sherston, 1673, I, W, P3/D/151
Paul, Marl., 1639, W, P1/D/84
Petronel, widow, Bremhill, 1660, AB, P3/D/113
Philip, Garsdon, 1620, AB, P3/D/44
Philip, yeo., Nettleton, 1675, comm, I, W, P3/D/159
Philip, Chicksgrove, Tisb., 1742, AB, I, P2/D/582
Philip, yeo., Alderbury, 1776, W, P26/1082
Rebecca, widow, Maiden B., 1687, NW, P2/D/374
Davis *or* Davith, Richd., husb., Damerham, Hants, 1566, W, P2/4Reg/220A
Richd., [blacksmith], Maiden B., 1579, W, P2/5Reg/334B
Davies, Richd., Stourpaine, Dorset, 1608, AB, P24/154
Davies, Richd., husb., Nettleton, 1609-10, I, W, P2/D/93, P3/D/12
Richd., Burnford, Bramshaw, Hants, 1620, I, P24/62
Davies, Richd., husb., Corston, Malm., 1623, I, W (2 - not identical), P3/D/57
Richd., husb., Longbridge D., 1640, I, W, P2/D/211
Richd., parchmentmaker, Warm., [1666], W, P2/D/260
Richd., Avebury, 1668, AB, I, P3/D/130
Daves, Richd., blacksmith, Burbage, 1669, I, W, P11/20
Richd., Charl. nr. P., 1695, AB, I, P1/D/183
Richd., Charl. nr. P., 1703, AB, P2/D/436
Richd., Ogbourne St A., 1706, AB, ren, P5/1706/11
Richd., Chitterne AS, 1722, AB, P2/D/515
Richd., tailor, Minety, 1728, comm, W, P1/D/288, P1/7Reg/197
Richd., gardener, Littleton P., 1740-41, I, W, P1/D/329, P1/9Reg/12
Richd., Charl. nr. P., 1763, AB, P1/D/396
Richd., Crickl. St S., 1771, AB, P3/D/417
Richd., shopkeeper, Wilton, 1850, W, Wr, P2/1850/12
Robt., Tisb., 1570, AB, P2/5Reg/100C
Robt., Horningsham, 1610, AB, I, W, P5/1610/17, P5/9Reg/44

Robt., yeo., Charlton nr Malm., 1616, I, W, P1/D/31
Robt., husb., Over Stratton, Stratton St Mgt., 1629, I, W, P3/D/74
Davies, Robt., Marl. St My., 1663, AB, I, P1/D/103
Robt., broad weaver, Bremhill, 1663, I, W, P3/D/116
Robt., Stourton, 1668, I, W, P2/D/265
Robt., Sherston, 1689, AB, I (detailed), ren, P1/D/168
Robt., husb., Yatton K., 1690, I, W, P3/D/217
Robt., blacksmith, Tilsh., 1696, I, W, P2/D/406
Robt., yeo., Steeple A., [1699], I, W, P2/D/415
Robt., Avill's Farm, Corsham, 1735, AB, comm, P3/D/340
Robt., clothworker, Westb., 1736, AB, I, P25/1736/3
Robt., Manton, Preshute, 1760, W, P1/D/392, P1/11Reg/484
Robt., Box, 1765, AB, P3/D/401
Robt., labourer, Broad H., 1816, W, Wr, P3/1816/8
Robt., gent., Trowb., 1823, comm, W, Wr, P1/1823/32
Davis alias Morris, Roger, blacksmith, Marl., 1665, I, W, P1/D/112
Sam., gent., Bradford A., 1820, O, W, Wr, P1/1820/27
Sam., Ansty, 1826, W, Wr, P5/1826/1
Sarah, widow, Minety, 1697, I, W, P3/D/236
Sarah, widow, Devizes, 1704, W, P1/D/210
Sarah, glazier's widow, Trowb., 1720, W, P1/D/268, P1/6Reg/251
Sarah, sp., Brokenb., 1722, AB, I, W, P3/D/299
Sarah, sp., Devizes, 1732, W, P1/D/307, P1/7Reg/516B
Sibyl, widow, Warm., 1688-91, AB, court paper, W, P2/D/376
Susanna, Alvediston, 1703, AB, P2/D/435
Susanna, sp., Devizes, 1749, W, P1/D/365, P1/10Reg/246
Thos., miller, Maiden B., 1576, W, P2/5Reg/276A
Davies, Thos., Durrington, 1589, I, T, P2/D/735
Thos., husb., Netheravon, 1627-30, a/c, bond to pay legacy (1630), I (1627), receipts (2), P12/54
Davis alias Taylor, Thos., Brinkw., 1633, court paper, P3/D/86
Thos., husb., Semington, Steeple A., 1636, comm, I, W, P2/D/186, P2/9Reg/103B
Davis alias Powell, Thos., Kington St M., 1637, AB, I, P3/D/92
Davis alias Taylor, Thos., yeo., Brinkw., 1639, I, W, P3/D/101
Thos., sen., weaver, Littleton P., 1666, I (2 - 1 a copy), W, P1/D/116
Thos., gent., Malm., 1667, I, W, P3/D/129
Davis alias Powell, Thos., Alderton, 1670, AB, P3/D/135
Thos., yeo., Sherston, 1671, comm, I, W, P1/D/131
Thos., miller, Coombe, Enford, 1684, AB, I, P2/D/349
Thos., Calne, 1688, AB, P26/369
Thos., yeo., Fisherton A., 1699, W, P2/D/418
Davies, Thos., sen., yeo., Stanford in the Vale, Berks., 1708, I (2 - 1 a copy), W, P1/D/226
Thos., yeo., Easton Town, Sherston, 1726, W, P3/D/315
Davies, Thos., yeo., Homington, 1728, W, P24/841
Thos., gent., Tytherton L., Chipp., 1765, W, P3/D/403
Thos., mole catcher, Marden, 1768, comm, W, P2/D/649
Thos., plumber and glazier, Calne, 1772, W, P26/1052
Thos., gardener, Enmore Grn, Motc., Dorset, 1810, W, P27/1/603
Thos., gent., Westb., 1821, O, W, Wr, P25/1821/2
Thos., Motc., Dorset, 1830, AB, comm, Wr, P27/1/692
Thos., Sal., 1847, AB, ren, Wr, P4/1847/10
Thos., yeo., Urchf., 1848, note, W, Wr, P2/1848/50
Thos., innkeeper, Easterton, Mkt. L., 1853, D, O, W, Wr, P2/1853/35
Thos., carp., Milford, Sal. St Martin, 1857, aff, W, Wr, P4/1857/6
Thos. Jn., carp. and builder, Sal. St Edmd., 1837, W, Wr, P4/1837/7
Walter, blacksmith, Codf. St P., 1647, I, W, P2/D/240
Walter, edge toolmaker, Sherrington, 1703, I, W, P2/D/433
Davis alias Corbett, Wm., yeo., Longbridge D., 1607, I, W, P2/D/78
Wm., Chieveley, Berks., 1614, NW (NEP), P1/D/25
Wm., husb., Luckington, 1614, I, W, P1/D/26
Davis alias Taylor, Wm., yeo., Brinkw., [1619], I (2), W (NEP), P3/D/40

Wm., clerk and vicar, Marden, [1636], I, W, P2/D/184
Davies, Wm., sen., yeo., Bewley, Lacock, 1638, comm, I, W, P3/D/96
Wm., sen., weaver, Hannington, 1662, comm, I, W, P1/D/100
Wm., parchmentmaker, Warm., 1676, I, NW, P2/D/299
Wm., yeo., Chetnole, Yetm., Dorset, 1677, I, W, P19/37
Wm., sen., tailor, Sutton M., [1677], W, P2/D/312
Wm., husb., Stanton Fitzwarren, 1680, comm, I, W, P3/D/177
Wm., Gt. Bedwyn, 1682, AB, I, P5/1682/35
Wm., husb., Ditchampton, Wilton, 1683, AB, I, P2/D/342
Wm., glazier, Downton, [1684], W, P2/D/352
Wm., yeo., Sutton M., 1686, W, P2/D/364
Wm., husb., Quidh., 1693, I, W, P2/D/393
Wm., yeo., E. Stowell, Wilcot, 1700, I, W, P3/D/241
Wm., jun., yeo., N. Wraxall, 1704, AB, I, T, P1/D/211, P3/D/259
Wm., tailor, Chilmark, 1705, AB, I, P2/D/443
Wm., Ludg., 1706, AB, P2/D/446
Wm., Homington, 1717, AB, I, P24/647
Wm., wheelwright, Winterslow, 1734, I, W, P2/D/554
Davies, Wm., labourer, Manton, Preshute, 1735, W, P1/D/314, P1/8Reg/39
Daves, Wm., sen., blacksmith, Haxton, Fittleton, 1737, I, W, P2/D/569
Wm., gent., Radley, Berks., 1747, W, P1/D/358, P1/10Reg/88
Wm., yeo., Lyneham, 1748, W, P3/D/370
Wm., sen., yeo., Whitley Farm, Calne, 1757, W, P26/954
Wm., Haxton, Fittleton, 1761, AB, P2/D/633
Wm., Whitley Farm, Calne, 1772, AB, P26/1056
Wm., Bradford A., 1772, AB, P2/D/660
Wm., yeo., Bradford A., 1783, comm, W, P1/D/424, P1/14Reg/31
Wm., Downton, 1787, AB, P2/D/700
Wm., Milborne Stileham, Bere R., Dorset, 1790, cert, W, P5/1790/7, P5/18Reg/140
Wm., innkeeper, *The Castle Inn*, Warm., 1797, AB, W, P2/D/727
Wm., jun., Pott., 1801, AB, LA, P1/1801/122
Wm., Warm., 1803, AB, P2/1803/43
Wm., Bromham, 1805, comm, W, P3/1805/6
Davies, Wm., victualler, Wantage, Berks., 1808, W, P23/854
Davies, Wm., blacksmith, Winterbourne G., 1811, AB, W, Wr, P1/1811/129
Wm., esquire, Fisherton D., 1816, comm, W, Wr, P2/1816/51
Wm., yeo., Tilehurst, Berks., 1823, O, W, Wr, P1/1823/90
Wm., woolworker, Poulshot, 1825, comm, W, Wr, P2/1825/6
Wm., timber dealer, Lye Hill, Burbage, 1844, comm, D, W, Wr, P11/297
Wm., bach., E. Town, W. Ashton, Steeple A., 1857, AB, aff, comm, Wr, P2/1857/4
Zachary, yeo., Cloatley, Hankerton, 1692, I, W, P3/D/226
see also Coombe alias D.; Corbett alias D.; Laws alias D.; Lewse alias D.; Powell alias D.; Sergeant alias D.; Silvester alias D.; Smith alias D.; Tayler alias D.
Davisey, Anthony, Wilton, 1773, AB, P2/D/662
Davison, Alexander, Devizes, 1736, AB, I, P1/D/320
Hester, widow, Devizes, 1758, AB, P1/D/385
Joan, widow, N. Bradley, 1666, comm, NW, P1/D/117
Jn., yeo., Ryme I., Dorset, 1741, AB, comm, W, P5/1740/24
Jn., apothecary, Trowb., 1746, W, P1/D/355, P1/10Reg/21A
Jn., Trowb., 1749, AB, P1/D/366
Davith *see* Davis
Davy, Agnes, widow, Stourpaine, Dorset, 1612, I, W, P24/121
Alexander, husb., Stourton, 1561, W, P2/4Reg/70C
Eliz., Lyme R., Dorset, 1611, AB, P5/9Reg/57A
Emma, Barias, Stourton, 1591, I, W, P2/D/41
Giles, maltster and brewer, Lyme R., Dorset, 1817, comm, W, Wr, P16/386
Davey, Isaac, mariner, Lyme R., Dorset, 1709, I, W, P16/180
Jane, Lyme R., Dorset, 1709, AB, P16/181
Jane, widow, Mere, 1818, W, Wr, P5/1818/34
Joan, widow, Monkton D., 1564, I, W, P2/D/7, P2/4Reg/184D

Joan, widow, Lyme R., Dorset, 1592, AB, I, W, P5/1592/21, P5/5Reg/134
Joan, widow, Stourton, 1632, I, W, P2/D/168, P2/9Reg/25A
Jn., husb., Durnford, 1571, W, P1/1Reg/92A
Jn., tucker, Crockerton, Longbridge D., 1577, W, P2/5Reg/292B
Jn., sen., husb., Uffc., Devon, 1600, AB, I, NW, P5/1600/21, P5/6Reg/247C
Jn., gent., Sal. The Close, 1624, AB, I, P5/1624/10
Jn., sen., Lyme R., Dorset, 1639, AB, comm, P5/1639/26, P5/13Reg/204A
Jn., jun., gent., Avill's Farm, Corsham, 1700, AB, comm, note, P3/D/242
Jn., Lyme R., Dorset, 1720, W, P16/216
Davey, Jn., millman [fuller], Lyme R., Dorset, 1841, comm, W, Wr, P16/429
My., widow, Lyme R., Dorset, 1670, AB, P5/1670/7
My., widow, Lyme R., Dorset, 1696, I, W, P16/143
Maud, widow, Tisb., 1570, W, P2/5Reg/92D
Morgan, Sherb., Dorset, 1675, AB, I, P5/1675/18
Philip, husb., Grimstone, Stratton, Dorset, 1637, comm, I, L, W (original sent to PCC), P5/1636/18, P5/12Reg/248C
Richd., esquire, Sal. The Close, 1673, copy W (NEP), P5/1673/46
Richd., Lyme R., Dorset, 1745, AB, comm, P16/287
Richd. Churchill, gent., Lyme R., Dorset, 1824, comm, W, Wr, P5/1824/37
Robt., Stourton, 1623, I, W, P2/D/133
Robt., yeo., Grimstone, Stratton, Dorset, 1662, W, P5/1662/34
Robt., Lyme R., Dorset, 1688, AB, P5/1688/26
Davey, Robt., yeo., Wambrook, Somerset, 1783, W, P5/1783/4, P5/17Reg/255A
Simon, Uffc., Devon, 1648, I, P20/1/41
Davey, Solomon, cooper, Lyme R., Dorset, 1621-22, I (2), W, copy W, P5/1621/8, P5/10Reg/128B
Thos., Uffc., Devon, 1570, W, P5/2Reg/76B
Thos., clerk, Holt, Bradford A., 1618, I, W, P2/D/119
Thomasine, widow, Lyme R., Dorset, 1710, W, P16/182
Wm., E. Kennett, 1608, AB, I, P1/D/19
Davy alias Mathew, Wm., yeo., Church Speen, Speen, Berks., 1620, I (damaged), W, P1/D/37
Wm., Halstock, Dorset, 1622, I, W, P5/1622/22, P5/10Reg/125B
Wm., Grimstone, Stratton, Dorset, 1676, AB, I, W, P5/1676/16
Wm., husb., Uffc., Devon, 1714, I, W, P20/1/148
Daw, Amy, widow, Fordington, Dorset, 1756, W, P15/144
Andrew, husb., Compton, Enford, 1693, I, NW, P2/D/397
Basil, widow, Downton, 1730, AB, P2/D/545
Bridget, widow, Chitterne AS, 1669, I, NW, P2/D/272
Christian, widow, Bere R., Dorset, 1587, AB, I, W, P5/1587/13, P5/4Reg/144B
Edith, widow, Enford, 1599, I, W, P2/D/59
Edwd., Gt. Faringdon, Berks., 1564, AB, P5/1Reg/54C
Dawes, Eliz., sp., Charnham St., Hungerford, Berks., 1719, W, P5/1719/21, P5/16Reg/24A
Dawes, Hy., Sonning, Berks., 1743, AB, comm, W, Wr, P5/1742/14
Hy., Sherston, 1828, W, Wr, P3/1828/59
Jas., yeo., Haydon, Dorset, 1781, AB, comm, W, P5/1781/4, P5/17Reg/205
Jas., thatcher, Longstreet, Enford, 1843, comm, W, Wr, P2/1843/24
Dawys, Joan, former nun in Amesbury Priory, Amesb., 1541, I, W (NEP), P30/47
Joan, Chetnole, Yetm., Dorset, 1567, W, P5/2Reg/19C
Jn., yeo., Turners Puddle, Dorset, 1628, I, W, P5/1628/36, P5/11Reg/72C
Dawes, Jn., gent., Sal., 1664, AB, I, P1/D/106
Dawes, Jn., yeo., Hannington, 1795, AB, W, P3/D/459
Dawes, Jn., tailor, Ashton K., 1808, W, Wr, P1/1808/126
Jn., thatcher, Enford, 1810, AB, W, Wr, P2/1810/71
Jn., Chards., Devon, 1811, AB, comm, P14/205
Dawes, Judith, widow, Sal., 1695, I, W, P4/1694/12
Martha, widow, Haydon, Dorset, 1753, W, P5/1753/7
Michael, cutler, Sherb., Dorset, 1615, I, W, P5/1615/8
Nich., shepherd, Boyton, [1729], W, P2/D/540
Peter, Stockley, Bere R., Dorset, 1595, AB, I, T, P5/1595/23, P5/6Reg/107A
Philip, labourer, E. Knoyle, 1845, O, W, Wr, P1/1845/7
Richd., cordw., Stockton, [1691], I, W, P2/D/383
Dawes, Richd., yeo., Chelworth, Crickl. St S., 1721, W, P3/D/296

Richd., yeo., Fordington, Dorset, 1755, comm, W, P5/1755/13
Dawys, Robt., Maiden B., 1541, I, W, P30/48
Thos., Durrington, 1576, I, W, P2/D/13, P2/5Reg/261A
Dowes, Thos., Fifield, Enford, 1583, I, T, W, P2/D/25, P2/6Reg/96C
Thos., Enford, 1588, W, P2/7Reg/126D
Dawes, Thos., Wokm., Berks., 1619, I, W, P5/1619/18, P5/10Reg/45A
Thos., labourer, Ludg., 1753, W, P1/D/375, P1/11Reg/62
Dawes, Thos., gent., Fisherton A., 1851, W, Wr, P1/1851/10
Thos., sen., thatcher, Longstreet, Enford, 1856, aff, comm, W, Wr, P2/1856/25
Dawes, Walter, yeo., Crickl. St S., 1771, W, P3/D/418
Wm., husb., Stockwood, Dorset, 1609, AB, I, T, P5/1609/24, P5/9Reg/4A
Wm., yeo., Enford, 1662, I, W, P2/D/247
Wm., husb., Earley, Sonning, Berks., 1663, AB, I, P5/1663/21
Wm., yeo., Enford, [1673], I, P2/D/288
Wm., Downton, 1710, AB, I, P1/D/235
Wm., yeo., Stanley, Chipp., 1724, W, P3/D/306
Dawes, Wm., labourer, Hannington, 1727, W, P3/D/317
Wm., yeo., Enmore Grn, Motc., Dorset, 1807, comm, W, P19/213
see also Earls alias D.
Dawers *see* Dowers
Dawes *see* Daw
Dawkins, Anthony, yeo., Britford, 1667, AB, I, W, P24/347
Dan., carp., Barford St M., 1841, W, Wr, P2/1841/11
Geo., gent., N. Burcombe (bequest of hospital of St Jn., Ditchampton), 1563, I, W, P2/D/2, P2/4Reg/111B
Jas., Lyme R., Dorset, 1688, AB, I, P16/96
Jas., smith, Dinton, 1814, W, Wr, P2/1814/26
Jn., Enford, 1734, AB, a/c, I, P2/D/557
Jn., shopkeeper, Wilton, 1745, W, P2/D/596
Jos., Wilton, 1717, AB, I, P2/D/490
Martha, widow, Wilton, 1747, W, P2/D/601
My., Dinton, 1741, W, P2/D/581
My., widow, Wilton, 1746, AB, P2/D/599
Philip, Downton, 1686-87, AB, a/c, I, P2/D/368
Ralph, Sandhurst, Berks., 1682-83, AB, a/c, I, P5/1682/32, P5/1683/18
Richd., carp., Downton, 1741, W, P1/D/332, P1/9Reg/48B
Richd., Sal. The Close, 1825, AB, Wr, P5/1825/2
Robt., Burcombe, 1585, grant of AB as recipient now adult, P2/7Reg/17B
Robt., sen., gent., Burcombe, 1636, AB, P2/D/188
Robt., husb., Teffont M., 1692, I, W, P2/D/388
Robt., Chilmark, 1693, AB, P2/D/394
Robt., yeo., Dinton, 1718, W, P2/D/496
Stephen, Wilton, 1749, AB, P2/D/610
Thos., yeo., Newtown, Durnford, 1681, AB, I, W, P5/1681/11
Thos., sen., yeo., Dinton, 1740-41, W, P1/D/330, P1/9Reg/21
Thos., Chute, 1746, AB, P5/1746/19
Wm., carp., Downton, 1775, AB, P2/D/669
Wm., wheelwright, Dinton, 1825, W, Wr, P2/1825/5
see also Pavy alias D.
Dawks, Dawks alias Limner, Thos., priest and curate, Alvediston, 1571, W, P1/1Reg/92B
Dawley, Dowley, Barbara, widow, Bulford, 1672, NW, P2/D/284
Dawley *or* Dowley, Jn., innholder, Sal. St Edmd., 1614, AB, I (detailed), P4/1614/7
Dowley, Roger, husb., Bulford, 1635, I, P1/D/75
Thos., Chitterne St My., [1633], I, W, P2/D/176
Dawling *see* Dowling
Dawmore *see* Dalmer
Dawndy *see* Dandy
Dawson, Edwd., Wantage, Berks., 1702, I, W, P23/249
Francis, clerk and parson, Binfield, Berks., 1628, W, P1/D/49
Hy., gent., Sal., 1766, W, P4/1766/16
Jos., carp., Appleton, Berks., 1829, W, Wr, P1/1829/105

Joshua, victualler, Wantage, Berks., 1755, W, P5/1755/11
My., widow, Wantage, Berks., 1764, W, P5/1764/10
Oliver, yeo., Grove, Wantage, Berks., 1729, W, P23/462
Richd., yeo., Grove, Wantage, Berks., 1711, I, W, P23/316
Thos., yeo., S. End, Bradfield, Berks., 1701, comm (to Quaker, who made her declaration), I, W, P1/D/202, P1/4Reg/20
Wm., Codf. St P., 1545, W (NEP), P2/1Reg/61B
Dawsten *see* Dauston
Dawton, Edwd., pewterer, Sal. St Thos., 1615, I, W, P4/1615/16
Edwd., sen., Preshute, 1711, AB, P1/D/240
Jn., bellfounder, Sal. St Edmd., 1638, AB, I, P1/D/79
see also Daton
Dawys *see* Daw
Day, Alice, widow, Smithcot, Dauntsey, 1704, AB, comm, I, P3/D/260
Andrew, Fovant, 1693, AB, I, P2/D/395
Ann, sp., Devizes, 1692, AB, P1/D/177
Anthony, Stratton St Mgt., 1801, W, P1/1801/67, P1/15Reg/284
Anthony, yeo., Stratton St Mgt., 1818, W, Wr, P3/1818/17
Barbara, sp., Boscombe, 1636, AB, a/c, I, P2/D/185, P2/9Reg/89C
Chas., carp., Lt. Somerford, 1729, W, P1/D/290, P1/7Reg/359
Chas., collarmaker & sadler, Rams., 1778, W, P5/1778/6, P5/17Reg/153A
Days, Dan., yeo., Swindon, 1783, W, P3/D/443
Edwd., W. Grimstead, 1685, note of AB, P2/D/354
Edwd., yeo., Hook, Lydiard T., 1700, alleg, I, W, P3/D/243
Eleanor, widow, Upton, Blewbury, Berks., 1670, I, W, P5/1670/10
Eliz., Fovant, 1712, AB, P2/D/475
Eliz., widow, Thatcham, Berks., 1795, AB, P1/D/443, P1/14Reg/527B
Eliz., minor, Knook, 1806, app. of guardian, T (niece of My. D.), P5/1806/10, P5/19Reg/156A
Francis, locksmith, Highw., 1699, I, W, P10/1698/2
Francis, Dinton, 1729, AB, P2/D/541
Francis, weaver, Quidh., 1756, court paper, W, P2/D/621
Gamaliel, clerk, Hampstead Marshall, Berks., 1670, AB, comm, P1/D/126
Hannah, sp., Collingbourne D., 1805, W, P21/12/13
Hy., Hurst, Berks., 1704, AB, I, P5/1704/73
Hy., gardener, Bassett Down, Lydiard T., 1719, I, W, P3/D/287
Hy., alehouse keeper, Everleigh, 1781, W, P3/D/440
Jane, widow, Wootton B., 1670, comm, I, W, P3/D/136
Jane, sp., Sal., 1825, AB, comm, Wr, P4/1825/1
Joan, widow, Boscombe, [1632], I, W, P2/D/167
Joan, sp., Sal., 1682, AB (2), I, P4/1681/7
Joan, widow, Wilsford with Lake, 1691, I, W, P13/3/15
Jn., husb., Amesb., 1558, W, P2/3Reg/112A
Jn., husb. & labouring man, Bishopstone N., 1576, I, W, P5/1576/14, P5/3Reg/89F
Jn., yeo., Boscombe, 1646, I, W, P1/D/89
Jn., Eddington, Hungerford, Berks., 1666, AB, comm, P5/1666/12
Jn., clothier, Wilton, 1676, AB, I, P2/D/301
Jn., currier, Devizes St Jn., 1687, AB, W, P1/D/167
Jn., fuller, Crabb Mill, Lea and Cleverton, 1706, AB, I, P3/D/264
Jn., gent., Wilsford with Lake, 1714, W, P13/4/5
Jn., yeo., Eddington, Hungerford, Berks., 1725, I, W, P5/1725/23, P5/16Reg/118C
Jn., schoolmaster, Fovant Stroud, 1743, W, P2/D/587
Jn., gent., Wilsford with Lake, 1753, AB, comm, P13/4/36
Jn., yeo., Steventon, Berks., 1773, W, P1/D/415, P1/12Reg/470
Jn., bricklayer, Woodley, W. and Sandford, Berks., 1776, W, P5/1776/12, P5/17Reg/115
Jn., yeo., Stratton St Mgt., 1809, comm, W, Wr, P3/1809/41
Jn., Wormwood, Box, 1825, AB (2), comm (2), Wr, P3/1825/40
Jn., Hindon, 1849, D, W, Wr, P2/1849/23
Jos., plumber and glazier, Pewsey, 1853, comm, W, Wr, P3/1853/11
Lionel, silk weaver, Abingdon, Berks., 1695, I, W, P1/D/184
Martha, widow, Lt. Somerford, 1811, AB, Wr, P3/1811/18
Martin, husb., Gt. Amesb., 1559, W, P2/3Reg/159A

My., sp., Lt. Somerford, 1728, I, W, P3/D/323
My., widow, Downton, 1775, W, P2/D/673
My., sp., Knook, 1806, AB, P5/1806/11, P5/19Reg/156B
My., sp., Fovant, 1851, aff, D, W, Wr, P1/1851/65
My., widow, Mkt. L., 1856, aff, D, O, W, Wr, P2/1856/35
My. Ann, widow, Wilton, 1852, W, Wr, P2/1852/1
Miles, shoemaker, Marl., 1571, W, P1/1Reg/30A
Nathaniel, husb., Compton C., 1770, W, P1/D/405, P1/12Reg/378B
Nich., yeo., Newton, Whitep., 1641, AB, a/c, I, P2/D/225
Obadiah, jun., carp. and bach., Lt. Somerford, 1708, AB, I, P3/D/266
Obadiah, carp., Lt. Somerford & Burton Hill, 1715, I, W, P3/D/279
Obadiah, Hannington, 1747, AB, I, P3/D/368
Ralph, yeo., Stratton St Mgt., 1843, comm, W, Wr, P3/1843/26
Rebecca, widow, Swindon, 1750, W, P1/D/371, P1/10Reg/309
Richd., baker, Highw., 1689, I, P10/1689/1
Richd., cordw., Fovant Stroud, 1721, AB, comm, ren, P2/D/507
Richd., carp., Chelworth, Crickl. St S., 1727, I (2 - 1 a copy), W, P3/D/318
Richd., fellmonger, Sal., 1765, W, P4/1765/18
Richd., yeo., Buscot, Berks., 1783, W, P1/D/425, P1/13Reg/401
Robt., Landford, 1611, AB, I, P2/D/97, P2/8Reg/160C
Robt., maltster, Amesb., [1690], I, W, P2/D/382
Robt., husb., Downton, 1770, W, P2/D/654
Robt., sen., yeo., Hindon, 1772, W, P2/D/657
Sam., innholder, Swindon, 1694, AB, I, P3/D/229
Sam., yeo., Clarendon Park, 1712, W, P4/1711/7
Sarah, widow, Crabb Mill, Lea and Cleverton, 1720, I, W, P3/D/294
Thos., yeo., Boscombe, 1631, I (very detailed), W, P2/D/166, P2/9Reg/75A
Thos., Smithcot, Dauntsey, 1663, AB, I, P3/D/117
Thos., husb., Soley, Chilton F., 1673, AB, I, P3/D/152
Thos., sen., yeo., Bourton, Shrivenham, Berks., 1677, I, W, P1/D/142
Thos., baker, Highw., 1693, I, W, P10/1692/5
Thos., sen., fellmonger, Sal., 1724, W, P4/1724/20
Thos., surgeon, Malm., 1739, comm, W, P3/D/347
Thos., Stratton St Mgt., 1768, AB, P3/D/410
Thos., Down Ampney, Gloucs & Castle Eaton, 1795, AB, comm, P1/D/444, P1/14Reg/535A
Thos., carrier, Chipp., 1847, AB, O, W, Wr, P3/1847/47
Thos., beer house keeper, Rams., 1854, aff, O, W, Wr, P5/1854/13
Walter, Caundle Marsh, Dorset, 1617, AB, I, P5/1617/13, P5/9Reg/214A
Wm., miller and dyer, Dauntsey, 1670, I (detailed), W, P3/D/137
Wm., yeo., E. Lockinge, Berks., 1735, W, P1/D/316, P1/7Reg/647
Wm., husb., Inglesham, 1739, W, P3/D/348
Wm., millwright, Fovant, 1741, W, P1/D/334, P1/9Reg/202
Wm., Avon Farm, Chipp., 1812, AB, Wr, P3/1812/4
Wm., Gt. Somerford, 1831, W, P3/1831/33
see also Grant alias D.
Dayer *see* Dare
Days *see* Day
Deacon, Abraham, sen., collarmaker, E. Ilsley, Berks., 1786, W, P1/D/432, P1/14Reg/101
Ann, Keevil, 1692, AB, comm, P2/D/389
Ann, innholder's widow, Newbury, Berks., 1770, W, P1/D/406, P1/12Reg/369
Chris., broad weaver, Heywood, Westb., 1641, I, W, P25/1641/4
David, husb., Westbrook, Gt. Faringdon & Shellingford, Berks., 1692, comm, I, W, P1/D/178
Edwd., husb., Westbrook, Gt. Faringdon, Berks., 1601, AB, I, W, P5/1601/16, P5/7Reg/13
Francis, sen., collarmaker, Amesb., 1733, AB (2), I, W, copy W, P2/D/552
Geo., Westb., 1669, AB, P25/1669/3
Geo., broad weaver, Fairwood, Dilton, Westb., 1729, AB, W (NEP), P25/1729/13
Hy., Burbage, 1702, I, W, P11/88
Hy., broad weaver, N. Bradley, 1713, I, W, P2/D/477
Hy., sen., hatter and yeo., Hurst, Berks., 1721, I (2), W, P5/1721/11, P5/16Reg/55B
Hy., hatter, Hurst, Berks., 1723, W, P5/1723/8, P5/16Reg/89A

Hy., husb., Burbage, 1733, AB, court paper (re revocation of probate 1727 in favour of will of 1733), L, note, O, W, copy W, P11/137
Hugh, sen., yeo., Durley, Burbage, 1672, W, P11/67
Hugh, Durley, Burbage, 1711, I, W, P11/103
Jas., widower, Lt. Hinton, 1843, AB, comm, Wr, P3/1843/44
Joan, widow, Heywood, Westb., 1669, W, P25/1669/5
Jn., clerk, Cholderton, 1558, W, P2/3Reg/133C
Jn., tiler, Warm., 1702, I, W, P2/D/428
Jn., clerk and rector, Gt. Chalfield, 1707, AB, P1/D/222
Jn., yeo., Oare, Wilcot, 1712, I, W, P3/D/275
Jn., clothworker, Westb., 1764, W, P25/1764/3
Jn., yeo., Downend, Chieveley, Berks., 1804, W, P1/1804/58
Jn., N. Bradley, 1818, AB, comm, W, Wr, P2/1818/46
Lizzy, widow, Wanb., 1816, W, Wr, P3/1816/20
Margery, widow, Gt. Faringdon, Berks., 1613, W, P5/1613/24, P5/9Reg/114C
Nich., tiler, Westb., 1675, I, W, P25/1675/8
Richd., Westb., 1579, AB, P5/1579/24, P5/3Reg/137C
Richd., Heywood, Westb., 1639, AB, I (very detailed, ref. to millhouse), P25/1639/8
Richd., bach., Heywood, Westb., 1689, AB, I, P25/1689/13
Richd., yeo., Carswell, Buckland, Berks., 1744, W, P1/D/345, P1/9Reg/381C
Richd., Wanb., 1809, AB, Wr, P3/1809/28
Robt., husb., Heywood, Westb., 1614, I, W, P25/1614/3
Robt., Hardenhuish, 1646, AB, comm, I, P1/D/90
Robt., Chiseldon, 1807, AB, comm, Wr, P3/1807/2
Thos., sen., tiler, Warm., 1701, I, W, P2/D/427
Thomasine, widow, Heytes., 1687, I, W, P5/1687/13
Wm., yeo., Heywood, Westb., 1616, I (part missing), W, P25/1616/4
Wm., Heytes., 1674, AB, a/c, I, P5/1674/24
Wm., sen., baker, Seend, Melk., 1701, I, W, P2/D/426
Wm., Seend, Melk., 1711, AB (2), I, P1/D/241
Wm., Dilton, Westb., 1725, AB, P25/1724/14
Deakins, Dakins, Dan., Dinton, 1734, AB, P2/D/558
Richd., barber, Abingdon, Berks., 1686, W, P1/D/450
Dakins, Thos., Newtown, Durnford, 1649, AB, P9/6
Deane, Agnes, widow, Hurst, Berks., 1576, W, P5/3Reg/75B
Agnes, widow, Chirton, 1616, a/c, P2/D/741
Alice, Wokm., Berks., 1543, W, P5/20Reg/33
Alice, Sonning, Berks., 1610, AB, P5/9Reg/37C
Deanes, Alice, Rowde, 1617, I, W, P3/D/31
Ambrose, Monkton D., 1623, AB, I, P2/D/134
Andrew, Broad C., 1681, I, W, P2/D/331
Andrew, Broad C., 1703, AB, I, P2/D/429
Ann, Conock, Chirton, 1613, AB, P2/8Reg/193C
Ann, widow, Heytes., 1762, W, P5/1762/9
Ann, widow, Heytes., 1685, AB, I, ren, W, P5/1685/31
Arthur, Marl., 1617, I, W, P1/D/35
Brian, husb., Chirton, 1578, I, T, W, P2/D/18, P2/5Reg/301A
Cath., Wokm., Berks., 1635, W, P5/1635/36, P5/12Reg/201A
Chris., carp., Wokm., Berks., 1599, I, W, P5/1599/7, P5/6Reg/232
Dan., husb., Broad C., 1641, AB, I, P2/D/226
Dorothy, widow, Notton, Lacock, 1735, W, P3/D/341
Duby, Lacock, 1641, AB, P3/D/109
Deans, Edith, sp., Monkton D., 1640, I, W, P2/D/218
Edwd., cooper, Warm., 1605, I, T, W, P2/D/738
Edwd., barber, Sal., 1686, AB, I, NW, P4/1686/18
Edwd., yeo., Heytes., 1718, I, W, P5/1718/11, P5/15Reg/413
Edwd., innholder, Sal., 1723, W, P4/1722/8
Dean, Edwd., Heytes., 1738, AB, Wr, P5/1738/14
Eleanor, widow, Conock, Chirton, 1590, I, W, P2/D/39
Eliz., widow, Sal., 1613, AB (damaged), P4/1613/18

Eliz., widow, Gt. Bedwyn, 1623, AB, I, P21/3/2
Eliz., widow of Wm., husb., Wokm., Berks., 1707, AB, ren, W, P5/1707/19, P5/15Reg/3
Eliz., widow, Broad C., 1726, AB, I, P2/D/530
Geo., tailor, Wokm., Berks., 1634, comm, I, W, P5/1633/15, P5/12Reg/164A
Geo., Hurst, Berks., 1698, AB, I, P5/1698/23
Dean, Geo., Hilp., 1842, AB, O, Wr, P1/1842/26
Hy., gent., Oxenwood, Shalbourne, 1682, I, W, P5/1682/34
Hy., clerk, Sutton Poyntz, Dorset, 1777, W, P18/14
Isaac, clothier, Wambrook, Somerset (form. of Tatworth, Chard, Somerset), 1833, W, Wr, P14/217
Jas., yeo., Wedh., Urchf., 1669, I, W, P2/D/268
Jas., shoemaker, Wedh., Urchf., 1728, W, P2/D/536
Dean, Jas., Rodbourne, Malm., 1833, AB, Wr, P3/1833/22
Deans, Jane, widow, Warm., 1616, I, P1/D/32
Jane, sp., Wokm., Berks., 1747, AB, P5/1747/8
Joan, sp., Tidcombe and Fosbury, [1623], I, W (NEP), P3/D/59
Joan, Worton, Pott., 1636, AB, I (2), P1/D/76, P2/D/189
Joel, Woodley, W. and Sandford, Berks., 1664, AB, I, P5/1664/8
Jn., yeo., Chirton, 1576, I, W, P2/D/12, P2/5Reg/258C
Jn., Sal. St Thos., 1584, AB, P4/Reg/23B
Jn., Sonning, Berks., 1605, AB, P5/1605/19, P5/8Reg/29B
Dean, Jn., husb., Wedh., Urchf., 1605, AB, I, P1/D/14
Jn., husb., Conock, Chirton, 1610, I, W, P2/D/77, 91, P2/8Reg/118A
Jn., Gt. Bedwyn, 1623, I, W, P21/3/3
Jn., tailor, Broad C., 1638, I, W, P1/D/80
Jn., Pott., 1646, AB, P1/D/91
Jn., Lyneham, 1662, AB, I, P1/D/101
Jn., husb. *or* yeo., Aughton, Collingbourne K., 1666, comm, I, W, P3/D/119
Jn., carp., Lt. Woodford, 1668, W, P13/2/2
Jn., sen., plumber, Lacock, 1677, I, W, P1/D/143
Jn., Hurst, Berks., 1682, AB, I, P5/1682/33
Jn., cooper, Heytes., 1682, I, W, P5/1682/29
Jn., gent., Pewsey, 1716, AB, I, P1/D/258
Deans, Jn., Heytes., 1759, W, P5/1759/6
Jn., victualler, Sonning, Berks., 1780, W, P5/1780/7, P5/17Reg/191
Dean, Jn., yeo., Swindon, 1798, W, P1/D/448, P1/15Reg/96
Jos., broommaker, Wokm., Berks., 1833, W, Wr, P5/1833/18
Kinborough, widow, Warm., 1677, I, W, P2/D/310
Mgt., widow, Broad C., 1684, I, W, P2/D/346
My., widow, Lyme R., Dorset, 1695, I, W, P5/1695/24
Dean, My., widow, Sal., 1738, W, Wr, P4/1738/8
Richd., Wokm., Berks., 1554, W, P5/20Reg/124
Richd., Wokm., Berks., 1579, I, T, W, P5/1579/22, P5/3Reg/141A
Richd., cooper, Sal. St Thos., 1674, AB, I, P4/1673/16
Richd., Uffington, Berks., 1695, AB, I, P1/D/185
Dean, Richd., Sal., 1728, AB, P4/1727/17
Dean, Richd., bach. and cooper, Heytes., 1750, AB, a/c, I, P5/1750/10
Richd., farmer, Chards., Devon, 1835, W, P14/218
Dean, Robt., currier, Chipp., 1690, I, W, P3/D/218
Dean, Robt., gent., Imber, 1826, W, Wr, P1/1826/126
Salathiel, sen., yeo., Aughton, Collingbourne K., 1668, I, W, P1/D/120
Salathiel, Collingbourne K., 1675, AB, P3/D/157
Salathiel, yeo., Sutton M., 1685, AB, I, W, P2/D/359
Dean, Salathiel, sen., yeo., Aughton, Collingbourne K., 1719, I, W, P3/D/288
Dean, Salathiel, yeo., Collingbourne K., 1757, W, P3/D/388
Sam., Sandhurst, Berks., 1671, I, W, P5/1671/25
Sarah, widow, Hurst, Berks., 1711, AB, comm, P5/1711/22
Sarah, servant, Lyme R., Dorset, 1829, O, W, P16/402
Simon, Earley, Sonning, Berks., 1593, I, W, P5/1593/31, P5/6Reg/47B
Dean, Susanna, widow, W. Tockenham, Lyneham, 1680, I, W, P1/D/149
Thos., Broad C., 1604, I, P2/D/73

Thos., sen., yeo., Anfields Cross, Hurst, Berks., 1604, AB, I, W, P5/1604/7, P5/8Reg/15
Thos., Wokm., Berks., 1617, AB, comm, I, P5/1617/12, P5/9Reg/214B
Thos., Wokm., Berks., 1626, I, W, P5/1626/13, P5/10Reg/313
Dean, Thos., husb., Wokm., Berks., 1689, AB, I, P5/1689/18
Deans, Thos., husb., All C., 1697, comm, I, W, P3/D/237
Dean, Thos., yeo., Chandler's Farm, Sulham, Berks., 1814, comm, W, Wr, P1/1814/36
Walter, joiner, Lyme R., Dorset, 1614, AB, I (detailed), W, P5/1614/19, P5/9Reg/137B
Wm., carp., Monkton D., 1593, I, W, P2/D/44
Wm., Castleton, Dorset, 1604, comm, I, W, P5/1604/8, P5/8Reg/20
Wm., Lyme R., Dorset, 1610, I, P5/1610/18
Deans, Wm., Rowde, 1633, I, W, P3/D/87
Wm., carp., Wokm., Berks., 1638, AB, I, W, P5/1638/28, P5/13Reg/128
Wm., Sulhamstead Abbots, Berks., 1664, AB, I (both damaged), P1/D/107
Deans, Wm., sen., cooper, Heytes., 1667, I, W, P5/1666/13
Wm., Chiseldon, 1675, AB, I, P3/D/160
Wm., Notton, Lacock, 1686, AB, I, P3/D/200
Deans, Wm., cooper, Heytes., 1732, I, W, P5/1732/13
Dean, Wm., yeo., Broad C., 1763, W, P2/D/638
Wm., fisherman, Sonning, Berks., 1790, W, P5/1790/6, P5/18Reg/151
Dean, Wm., shopkeeper, Swindon, 1815, W, Wr, P3/1815/26
Dean, Wm., labourer, Warm., 1832, W, Wr, P1/1832/64
Zachary, yeo., Downton, 1588, W, P2/7Reg/123A
Dear, Alice, widow, Damerham, Hants, 1688, I, W, P2/D/378
Ann, widow, Sal. The Close, 1720, W, P5/1720/15, P5/16Reg/41
Ann, widow, Woodford, 1840, W, Wr, P5/1840/7
Charlotte, widow, Netton, Durnford, 1847, W, Wr, P9/120
Edith, widow, Gt. Wishford, 1638, I, W, P2/D/203
Edmd., Wootton R., 1607, W, P3/D/7
Edwd., sen., bricklayer, Pewsey, 1773, W, P1/D/416, P1/12Reg/503B
Eliz., Sal. The Close, 1749, W, Wr, P5/1749/19
Eliz., sp., Winterbourne S., 1844, AB, Wr, P2/1844/77
Hy., husb., Hanging L., 1680, I, W, P2/D/325
Isaac, Woodford, 1725, AB, P5/1725/21
Jas., yeo., Fonthill B., 1678, I, W, P2/D/314
Jas., bach., Sal., 1770, AB, P1/D/407
Jas., Netton, Durnford, 1826, W, Wr, P9/111
Jn., Blackland, Calne, 1569, W, P5/2Reg/55C
Deare, Jn., sen., husb., Gt. Wishford, 1614, W, P2/8Reg/218B
Jn., carp., Gt. Wishford, 1638, comm, I, note of AB, W, P2/D/200
Jn., carp., Woodford, 1668, I, P5/1668/22
Jn., brickmaker, Pewsey, 1752, W, P3/D/383
Jn., yeo., Gt. Durnford, 1797, W, P5/1797/13, P5/18Reg/246
Lucy Ann, wife of Richd., Durnford, 1803, AB, P5/1803/30, P5/19Reg/58B
Deare, Mgt., widow, Dinton, 1670, comm, W, P2/D/276
My., widow, Heale, Woodford, 1741, W, P13/4/31
Richd., jun., carp., Quidh., 1665, I, W, P2/D/257
Richd., carp., Gt. Wishford, 1674, I, W, P2/D/293
Richd., yeo., St Mgt., Preshute, 1748, W, P1/D/364, P1/10Reg/216
Richd., yeo., Idmiston, 1787, W, P2/D/702
Richd., yeo., Gt. Durnford, 1816, W, Wr, P9/104
Robt., carp., Gt. Woodford, 1694, W, P13/3/20
Robt., Woodford, 1727, W, P13/4/21
Robt., shepherd and bach., Sal. (form. of Woodford), 1849, AB, D, Wr, P4/1849/10
Robt. King, Pewsey, 1848, comm, D, W, Wr, P1/1848/36
Roger, Pewsey, 1722, AB, P3/D/300
Sam., day labourer, Bottwellsford, N. Newnton, 1698, W, P1/D/194, P1/3Reg/195
Sam., The Earldoms, Whitep., 1719, W, P2/D/494
Sam., labourer, Redlynch, Downton, 1856, aff, W, Wr, P2/1856/29
Thos., sen., Gt. Wishford, 1647, AB, I, P2/D/239
Thos., sen., yeo., Stratford sub C., 1667, deed of gift, P4/1667/22

Thos., husb. *or* yeo., Collingbourne K., 1680, I, W, P3/D/178
Thos., Gt. Wishford, 1697, AB, P2/D/412
Thos., labourer, Gt. Wishford, 1760, W, P2/D/630
Wm., Stapleford, 1686, AB, I, P2/D/363
Wm., Durrington, 1777, AB, comm, P2/D/676
Dearlove, Thos., sen., yeo., Brightwalton, Berks., 1801, W, Wr, P1/1801/123, P1/15Reg/341
Wm., cordw., Sonning, Berks., 1826, W, Wr (2), P5/1826/11
Wm., yeo., E. Hendred, Berks., 1826, comm, W, Wr, P1/1826/4
Deavin, Chris., yeo., Pewsey, 1784, comm, W, P3/D/444
Jos., innholder, Pewsey, 1798, AB, comm, W, P3/D/462
My., wife, Marl., 1842, AB, O, Wr, P1/1842/13
Sam., Marl., 1761, AB, P1/D/393
Devyn, Wm., Ruscombe, Berks., 1595, I, T, W, P5/1595/22, P5/6Reg/103B
Wm., sen., yeo. and husb., Hurst, Berks., 1685, I, W, P5/1685/29
Debbutt, Thos., Dunsden Grn, Sonning, Berks., 1705, AB, comm, I, P5/1705/16
DeBeare, DeBeare *or* Abeare, Francis, Hare Hatch, Wargrave, Berks., 1677, AB, comm, I, P1/D/144
Debnam, Eleanor, widow, Warm., 1710, W, P2/D/463
Dedman, Ezekiel, Warm., 1672, W (damaged), P2/D/286
Isaac, ironmonger, Warm., 1764, W, P2/D/642
Dednam, Jn., baker, Warm., 1617, I, ren, NW, P2/D/115
Wm., whitesmith, Warm., 1773, AB, ren, P2/D/663
Dee, Ann, Sal., 1769, W, P4/1769/12
David, sawyer, Sal., 1681, AB, I, ren, P4/1680/13
David, [owner of lime kilns], Sal., 1730, AB, I, P4/1730/5
Jn., yeo., Liberty of Newland, Hurst, Berks., 1591, AB, I, W, P5/1591/19, P5/5Reg/117A
Jonas, blacksmith, Ruscombe, Berks., 1716, I, W, P5/1716/26, P5/15Reg/355A
Thos., Hurst, Berks., 1547, W, P5/20Reg/91
Deecker *see* Deeker
Deedman, Jane, sp., W. Dean, 1848, AB, Wr, P1/1848/74
Deeke, Anna, widow, Seend Row, Melk., 1743, copy W, P2/D/586
Bartholomew, Seend, Melk., 1739, W, P2/D/573
Eliz., widow, Kington L., 1702, I, W, P3/D/252
Geoffrey, yeo., Kington L., 1684, I, W, P3/D/192
Deek, Geoffrey, gent., Kington L., 1762, W, P3/D/395
Deek, Geoffrey, maltster and baker, Hullavington, 1780, W, P3/D/433
Jas., Kington St M., 1714, W, P1/D/253, P1/5Reg/424A
Joan, widow, Kington L., 1705, I, W, P3/D/261
Jn., Fifield, Enford, 1611, AB, I, P2/D/95, P2/8Reg/156A
Jn., maltster, Chipp., 1688, I, W, Wr, P3/D/208
Jonathan, sen., clothier, Kington L., 1700, I, W, P3/D/244
Jonathan, gent., Kington L., 1717, I, W, P3/D/285
Jonathan, yeo., Kington L., 1726, I (2 - 1 is just a total), W, P3/D/316
Jos., Kington L., 1677, AB, I, P3/D/165
Margery, Kington L., 1615, I, W, P3/D/25
Sarah, sp., Kington St M., 1725, comm, I, W, P3/D/307
Deeks, Thos., Eastcourt, Crudwell, 1671, AB, I, P3/D/142
Deek, Wm., sen., Kington L., 1694, AB, I, P3/D/230
Wm., yeo., Nettleton, 1719, I, W, P3/D/289
see also Dicke
Deeker, Deecker, Agnes, widow, Alton P., Dorset, 1616, I, W, P5/1616/20
Jn., Alton P., Dorset, 1635, AB, I, P5/1635/31, P5/12Reg/228A
Roger, sen., Alton P., Dorset, 1600, AB, I, P5/1600/19, P5/6Reg/242A
Deeks *see* Deeke
Deem, Thos., sen., cordw., Chards., Devon, 1842, W, Wr, P5/1842/27
Deemer, Deemer alias Pound, Wm., blacksmith, Moredon, Rodbourne C., 1641, I, W, P3/D/110
Deepe, Baptist, E. Winterslow, 1636, AB, P2/D/192
Joan, widow, Whitep., 1638, AB, I, NW, P2/D/198
Rowland, husb., E. Winterslow, 1637, I, W, P2/D/195
Wm., yeo., Winterslow, [1672], I, W, P2/D/287
Deerham *see* Derham

Deering, Deeringe alias Meech, Edwd., Charminster, Dorset, 1606-07, AB, I, W, P5/1606/31, P5/8Reg/59
Ralph, husb., Bere R., Dorset, 1596, AB, I, W, P5/1596/21, P5/6Reg/125C
Defey, Eliz., widow, Fordington, Dorset, 1684, AB, P15/42
Deighton, Chris., Sal. The Close, 1682, NW, P5/1681/12
Dorothy, widow, Leigh, Ashton K., 1680, I, W, P3/D/179
Deighton alias Whiting, Hy., yeo., Leigh, Ashton K., 1625, I, NW, P3/D/66
Jane, widow, Minety, 1678, AB, I, NW, P3/D/168
Deighton alias Whiting, Jn., yeo., Leigh, Ashton K., 1648, I, NW, P1/D/92
Jn., Leigh, Ashton K., 1743, AB, comm, P3/D/361
Jn., yeo., Leigh, Ashton K., 1751, AB, W, P3/D/377
Deighton alias Whiting, Mgt., widow, Leigh, Ashton K., 1628, I, NW, P3/D/71
Richd., Shrewton, 1722, AB, P2/D/514
Wm., yeo. *or* husb., Minety, 1667, I, W, P3/D/127
Wm., sen., yeo., Minety, 1677, AB, a/c, I, P3/D/166
Wm., yeo., Minety, 1681, AB, I, P3/D/183
Delafield, Susanna, yeo.'s wife, N. Newington, Oxfordshire, 1783, W, P2/D/689
Delamere, Alexander, yeo., Seend, Melk., 1794, W, P2/D/717
Delawney, Jacob, dairyman, Swindon, 1847, comm, W, Wr, P3/1847/7
Dell, Amy, Wrou., 1610, W, P3/D/17
Jn., yeo., Broad H., [1642], I, W (NEP), P3/D/111
Deller, Eliz., widow, Bray, Berks., 1664, I, NW, P1/D/108,
Diller, Jn., sen., carrier, Lyme R., Dorset, 1832, O, W, Wr, P16/407
Wm., yeo. and husb., Bray & Clewer, Berks., 1708, I, W, P1/D/228
DeLuce, Geo., Speenhamland, Berks., 1779, W, P1/D/422, P1/13Reg/255
Deluke, Jn., jun., Bramshaw, Hants, 1633, AB, P24/242
Dematt *see* Dammett
Demay, Peter, yeo., Bratton, Westb., 1855, declaration, O, W, Wr, P25/1855/2
Denby, Jn., miller, Wantage, Berks., 1698, I, W, P5/1698/22
Dench, Edwd., husb., Newton T., 1661, I, W, P2/D/246
Edwd., labourer *or* gardener, Idmiston, 1671, I, W, P1/D/132
Edwd., Idmiston, 1724, AB, I, P2/D/734
Hy., husb., Boscombe, 1608, I, W, P1/D/20
Hy., sen., Winterslow, 1670, court papers, NW, P2/D/274
Hy., yeo., E. Grimstead, W. Dean, 1710, I, W, P2/D/465
Jn., tailor, Longstreet, Enford, 1625, I, W, P2/D/143
Thos., Fittleton, 1601, AB, note of AB, P2/D/67
Thos., collarmaker, Woodb., 1685, I, W, P3/D/197
Wm., husb., Fittleton, 1559, W, P2/3Reg/152C
Denchfield, Thos., Sonning, Berks., 1699, AB, I, P5/1699/11
Denham, Agnes, widow, Sherb., Dorset, 1615, AB, I, P5/1615/11, P5/9Reg/160B
Hy., haberdasher, Sal., 1626, AB, I, P4/1626/15
Robt., husb., Sherb., Dorset, 1627, I, W, P5/1627/13, P5/11Reg/40A
Dinham, Sarah, widow, Uffc., Devon, 1797, W, P5/1797/12, P5/18Reg/254A
Thos., buttonmaker, Sherb., Dorset, 1706, AB, comm, I, P5/1706/12
Wm., weaver, Sal., 1615, I, W, P4/1615/4
Denis *see* Dennis
Denison *see* Dennison
Denly, Dan., yeo., Rodbourne, Malm., 1855, aff, D, O, W, Wr, P3/1855/21
Jas., farmer, Castle C., 1849, O, W, Wr, P3/1849/22
Joshua, cordw., Bishopstone N., 1799, W, P6/136
Ruth, wife, Castle C., 1839, comm, W, Wr, P3/1839/36
Denman, Alice, widow, Inglesham, 1639, I, W, P3/D/102
Alice, widow, Westrop, Highw., 1694, AB, I, P10/1694/6
Ambrose, blacksmith, Westrop, Highw., 1626, AB, I, W, P10/1626/2
Geo., tailor, Chards., Devon, 1630, W, P5/11Reg/127A
Jas., wheelwright, Eddington, Hungerford, Berks., 1679, AB, I, P5/1679/26
Joan, widow, Upper Inglesham, 1635, I, W, P1/D/71
Jn., husb., Inglesham, 1610, AB, I, W, P3/D/9, 18
Jn., cordw., Highw., 1705, I, W, P10/1705/3
Richd., yeo., Highw., 1745, AB, P10/1745/6

Sibyl, widow, Chards., Devon, 1605, NW, P5/1605/20, P5/8Reg/79
Wm., husb., Highw., 1588, I, W, P10/1588/2, P5/5Reg/10A
Wm., jun., husb., Chards., Devon, 1643, AB, I, W, P14/13
Wm., cordw., Westrop, Highw., 1683, I, W, P10/1683/2
Denmead, Sarah, shopkeeper, Corsley, 1827, W, Wr, P2/1827/55
Wm., Corsley, 1557, W, P2/3Reg/55A
Wm., shopkeeper, Corsley, 1797, W, P2/D/726
Wm., yeo., Corsley, [1628], I (incomplete), W, P2/D/155
Dennen *see* Denning
Dennes, Denness *see* Dennis
Dennett, Dennis, Martin, Hants, 1849, AB, Wr, P2/1849/47
Jn., Wilton, 1686, AB, P2/D/362
Jn., Winterbourne G., 1723, W, P2/D/519
Jn., gent., Wilton, 1732, W, P2/D/547
Martha, widow, Wilton, 1746, W, P2/D/598
Thos., sen., gent., Sal. The Close, 1693, W, P5/1693/19
Thos., gent., Wilton, 1724, AB, ren, W, P1/D/281, P1/7Reg/40A
Denning, Amy, widow, Chards., Devon, 1806, W, Wr, P5/1806/28
Ann, widow, Sherb., Dorset, 1834, AB, comm, Wr, P5/1834/14
Benj., Chards., Devon, 1842, W, Wr, P5/1842/28
Chas., yeo., Chards., Devon, 1800, W, P5/1800/25, P5/18Reg/298
Dennen, Colin, tailor, Wallingford, Berks., 1689, AB, I, P1/D/169
Edwd., yeo., Chards., Devon, 1661, comm, I, W, P5/1661/13
Eliz., sp., Sherb., Dorset, 1853, AB, comm, Wr, P5/1853/6
Francis, Uffc., Devon, 1807, AB, comm, P20/1/284
Hy., whitesmith, Sherb., Dorset, 1805, W, P5/1805/16, P5/19Reg/138
Jn., sen., husb., Chards., Devon, 1680, I, W, P14/46
Jn., Uffc., Devon, 1795, AB, comm, P20/1/271
Richd., sen., parish clerk, Chards., Devon, 1800, W, P5/1800/26, P5/18Reg/299
Richd., yeo., Chards., Devon, 1828, W, Wr, P14/213
Dinning, Thos., innholder, Sherb., Dorset, 1724, AB, I, P5/1724/25
Wm., yeo. *or* cooper, Malm., 1678, I, W, P3/D/169
Dinning, Wm., innholder, Sherb., Dorset, 1720, AB, I, P5/1719/23
Wm., Lyme R., Dorset, 1735, AB, P5/1735/17
Wm., sen., victualler, Sherb., Dorset, 1772, comm, W, P5/1772/4, P5/17Reg/38
Wm., Lyme R., Dorset, 1782, AB, P5/1782/8, P5/17Reg/239B
Wm., gunsmith, Sherb., Dorset, 1835, W, Wr, P5/1835/16
Dennis, [...], widow, W. Dean, [1677], I (same admrs as Thos. D., P2/D/306), P2/D/307
Ann, Landford, 1698, AB, P1/D/195
Ann, widow, W. Dean, 1718, I, W, P2/D/498
Anna *see* Hannah
Benj., yeo., Hungerford, Berks., 1727, W, P3/D/319
Betty, surgeon's widow, Sal., 1811, W, Wr, P4/1811/3
Dennes, Cicely, Poole Keynes, 1690, I, P3/D/219
Dorothy, widow, Newtown, Hungerford, Berks., 1693, I, W, P23/186
Edmd., maltster, W. Dean, 1699-1709, AB, I, W, P2/D/419, 459
Denis, Eleanor, widow, W. Dean, 1560, W, P2/4Reg/55B
Giles, sen., yeo., Landford, [1666], I, W, P2/D/258
Hannah *or* Anna, widow, Landford, 1697-1701, court papers, W, Wr, P2/D/409
Hy., jun., gent., Crickl. St S., 1742, W, P3/D/355
Hy., sen., Crickl. St S., 1751, AB, P3/D/378
Jas., Hatch, Tisb., 1799, W, P2/D/731
Jane, widow, Trowb., 1783, AB, ren, P1/D/426
Denis, Jn., Hurst, Berks., 1580, I, W, P5/1580/19, P5/4Reg/2A
Jn., tailor, W. Dean, 1630, I, NW, P2/D/161, P2/9Reg/76A
Jn., sen., yeo., E. Grimstead, W. Dean, 1644, I, W, P2/D/233
Jn., blacksmith, Alderbury, 1669, I, W, P26/172
Jn., sen., yeo., Alderbury, 1735, W, P26/788
Jn., blacksmith, Wantage, Berks., 1743, W, Wr, P5/1743/20
Jn., sen., baker and confectioner, Sal., 1824, W, P4/1824/3

Jos., Trowb., 1776, AB, comm, P1/D/419
Denis, Lawr., W. Dean, 1601, I, W, P2/D/68
Martha, widow, W. Grimstead, 1711, AB, I, P2/D/469
Dennes, Martha, widow, Farnham, Tollard Royal, Dorset, 1738, W, P4/1737/21
My., sp., Sal. St Edmd., 1758, W, P4/1758/12
Rebecca, widow, Wantage, Berks., 1746, AB, P5/1746/20
Richd., blacksmith, W. Grimstead, 1705, AB, I, P2/D/442
Richd., Tisb., 1801, W, P2/1801/14
Roger, Aldbourne, 1661, AB, comm, P3/D/114, P3/3Reg/12A
Rowland, clerk, Sal. The Close, 1755-59, AB, P5/1755/14, P5/1759/7
Sibyl, widow, W. Dean, 1617, I, W, P2/D/113, P2/8Reg/324
Denis, Stephen, tailor, W. Grimstead, 1647, I, W, P2/D/238
Stephen, W. Grimstead, 1688, I, W, P2/D/375
Stephen, W. Grimstead, 1699, AB, I, P2/D/420
Stephen, W. Grimstead, 1713, AB, P2/D/480
Thos., yeo., W. Dean, 1601, AB, I, W, P2/D/69
Thos., yeo., Crickl. St S., 1616, comm, O, I, W, P3/D/26
Thos., blacksmith, Gt. Hidden & Newtown, Hungerford, Berks., 1676, I, W, P5/1676/19
Thos., yeo., W. Dean, 1677, I, P2/D/306
Thos., Landford, 1681, AB, I, P2/D/334
Thos., blacksmith, Gt. Hidden, Hungerford, Berks., 1681, I, W, P23/105
Thos., Landford, 1736, AB, P2/D/563
Thos., Wantage, Berks., 1742, AB, L, P23/566
Wm., shepherd, Aldbourne, 1611, AB, P3/D/21
Wm., W. Dean, 1709, AB, P2/D/457
Wm., blacksmith, Uffington, Berks., 1770, W, P1/D/408, P1/12Reg/363
Denness, Wm., yeo., Eastridge, Rams., 1839, W, Wr, P5/1839/21
Dennison, Betty, wife, Beam., Dorset, 1756, AB, comm, P17/533
Denison, Robt., Westb., 1813, AB, comm, P25/1813/5
Denny, Thos., weaver, Crickl. St My., 1688, W, Wr, P3/D/207
Wm., Sal. St Thos., 1697, AB, P4/1697/5
Denslow, Ann, sp., Beam., Dorset, 1729, W, P17/425
Jn., Beam., Dorset, 1625, I, W, P5/1625/26, P5/10Reg/267B
Denslow alias Baily, Jn., Netherb., Dorset, 1751, AB, P17/519
Denslow alias Bayly, Paul, yeo., Fole, Netherb., Dorset, 1690, I, W, P17/317
Richd., innholder, Beam., Dorset, 1708, AB, I, P17/176
Denslow alias Baily, Thos., yeo., Lyme R., Dorset, 1607, AB, comm, I, P5/1607/22, P5/8Reg/87A
see also Bailey alias D.; Cox form. D.
Dent, Jn., Calne, 1718, AB, I, P26/619
My., sp., Newbury, Berks., 1756, W, P1/D/381, P1/11Reg/226
Wm., tailor, Beam., Dorset, 1688, AB, I, P5/1688/23
Denton, Jn., Milton, Berks., 1832, W, Wr, P1/1832/107
Thos., E. Hatch, Tisb., 1720, AB, comm, notification (admr took his O in York Minster), P1/D/269
Deper *see* Diper
Derant *see* Durrant
Derby *see* Darby
Derham, Agnes, widow, Chiseldon, 1627, I, W, P3/D/67
Anthony, husb., Bloxworth, Dorset, 1635, I, W, P5/1635/32, P5/12Reg/227A
Edith, widow, Bloxworth, Dorset, 1636, I, W, P5/1636/19, P5/13Reg/30B
Edwd., victualler, Devizes, 1729, AB, W, P1/D/291, P1/7Reg/333B
Edwd., gardener, Wick, Bps. C., 1780, AB, comm, P24/1119
Jn., yeo., Brinkw., 1671, I, W, P3/D/143
Jn., Devizes, 1832, AB, W, Wr, P1/1832/89
Mgt., sp., Lyneham, 1822, comm, W, Wr, P3/1822/40
Matthew, husb., Bloxworth, Dorset, 1679, AB, I, P5/1679/20
Oliver, Wrou., 1746, AB, P3/D/365
Richd., husb., Brinkw., 1631, I, W, P3/D/83
Richd., Dauntsey, 1665, AB, I, P3/D/125
Stephen, hempdresser, Marl. St My., 1711, I, W, P1/D/242, P1/5Reg/253B
Deerham, Thos., husb., Chiseldon, [1607], W (NEP), P3/D/8

Thos., clerk, Highw., 1702, bond (re withdrawal of W of (made 1702 - date of death not stated), as evidence in court case by Dennis Huntingdon, son in law - bond recites contents), P10/1702/6
Wm., yeo., Snodshill Lane, Chiseldon, 1841, comm, W, Wr, P3/1841/48
Derrenc, Derrent *see* Durrant; *see also* Baylie alias Derrenc
Derrett, Thos., shopkeeper, Bradford A., 1766, W, P2/D/646
Derriman, Jn., Holnest, Dorset, 1746, W, P5/1746/21
Derrington, Jn., Hilp., 1611, I, W, P2/D/96
Jn., Bulk., Keevil, 1639, AB, I, W, P2/D/207
Wm., yeo., Hilp., 1635, I, copy I, W, P2/D/182
Descrambes, Jn., Shellingford, Berks., 1738, AB, I, P1/D/324
Deson, Phyllis, widow, Bradford A., 1842, O, W, Wr, P2/1842/3
Wm., victualler, Bradford A., 1826, W, Wr, P2/1826/9
Devall, Joan, widow, Bere R., Dorset, 1640, AB, I, P5/1640/16, P5/13Reg/227B
Roger, Bere R., Dorset, 1624, I, W, P5/1624/13, P5/10Reg/240B
Devenish, Joan, widow, Charminster, Dorset, 1686, AB, I, P5/1686/20
Peter, smith, Charminster, Dorset, 1592, I, T, W, P5/1592/23, P5/5Reg/133B
Richd., gent., Chetnole, Yetm., Dorset, 1692, AB, comm, I, P19/63
Tristram, Chetnole, Yetm., Dorset, 1669, I, W (badly damaged), P5/1668/23
Wm., Charminster, Dorset, 1569, AB, P5/2Reg/43C
Devenshire, Wm., yeo., Stanford in the Vale, Berks., 1729, W, P1/D/292, P1/7Reg/297
Deverell, Ann, widow, Hilp., 1691, AB, I, P2/D/385
Ann, sp., Haugh, Winsley, Bradford A., 1746, W, P2/D/597
Ann, widow, Pinkney, Sherston, 1801, comm, W, P3/1801/1
Anthony, Cumberwell, Bradford A., 1596, I, W, P2/D/47
Anthony, Saunders, Bradford A., 1662, comm, I, W, P1/D/104
Anthony, broad weaver, Bradford A., [1697], I, W, P2/D/410
Cath., sp., Devizes, 1695, W, P1/D/186
Dan., Langley Burrell, 1684, AB, I, P3/D/193
Dan., broad weaver, Limpley Stoke, Bradford A., 1719, comm, I, W, P2/D/499
Dan., broad weaver, Limpley Stoke, Bradford A., 1785, comm, W, P2/D/696
Edith, widow, Willesley, Sherston, 1703, comm, I, W, P3/D/255
Elias, yeo., Ugford, S. Newton, 1723-39, AB, W, P2/D/518, 572
Eliz., widow, Sherston, 1819, comm, W, Wr, P3/1819/60
Francis, Wilton, 1670, AB, P2/D/277
Geo., clothworker, Hilp., 1729, I, W, P1/D/293, P1/7Reg/320B
Grace, widow, Keevil, 1705, I, W, P1/D/217
Hy., Bradford A., 1560, W, P2/4Reg/30A
Hy., labourer, Melk., 1620, I, W, P2/D/125
Hy., Keevil, 1685, AB, I, P2/D/357
Deverell *or* Deveral, Hester, widow, Sal., 1767, W, P4/1767/1
Hugh, Zeals, 1769, W, P5/1769/8
Jas., Imber, 1605, AB, I, W, P1/D/15
Jeremiah, broad weaver, Bradford A., 1813, W, P2/1813/16
Jn., Bradford A., 1580, I, W, P2/D/21, P2/6Reg/8B
Jn., husb., Keevil, 1676, AB, I, P2/D/300
Jn., Bradford A., 1677, AB, I, P2/D/309
Jn., clothier, Monkton F., 1687, I, W, P2/D/373
Jn., husb., Willesley, Sherston, 1689, comm, I, W, P3/D/214
Jn., broad weaver, Limpley Stoke, Bradford A., [1691], I, W, P2/D/386
Jn., clothier, Winsley, Bradford A., 1703, AB, a/c, I, P2/D/434
Jn., Hilp., 1723, AB, P2/D/517
Jn., yeo., Frankleigh, Bradford A., 1727-36, AB (2), comm, ren, P2/D/533
Jn., broad weaver, Bradford A., 1758, W, P2/D/625
Jn., yeo., S. Wraxall, 1789, AB, app. of guardian, comm, T, P2/D/707
Jn., broad weaver, Winsley, Bradford A., 1790, W, P2/D/711
Jn., builder, Holt, Bradford A., 1849, D, O, W, Wr, P2/1849/30
Mgt., Melk., 1598, AB, I, W, P2/D/57
My., widow, Monkton F., 1728, W, P2/D/538
Matthew, broad weaver, S. Wraxall, 1703, I, W, P2/D/430
Nathaniel, yeo., Sherston, 1681, I, W, P3/D/184

Rebecca, widow, Bradford A., 1721, W, P2/D/505
Richd., Imber, 1576, AB, P2/5Reg/269C
Richd., sen., husb., Limpley Stoke, Bradford A., 1614, I, W, P1/D/27
Richd., yeo., Hilp., 1689, AB, comm, I, P1/D/170
Richd., yeo., Hannington, 1722, AB, P3/D/301
Robt., maltster, Hilp., 1706, I, W, P2/D/445
Robt., yeo., Box, 1783, W, P1/D/427, P1/14Reg/7
Roger, husb., Frankleigh, Bradford A., 1549, W, P2/2Reg/78
Roger, yeo. *or* innholder, Bradford A., 1662, I, W, P1/D/102
Roger, Fisherton A., 1679, AB, I, P2/D/320
Roger, butcher, Bradford A., 1722, AB, I, P2/D/512
Sam., husb., Hannington, 1679, I, W, P3/D/171
Simon, yeo. and cordw., Bradford A., [1679], I, W, P2/D/324
Thos., sen., husb., Nettleton, [1614], I, W, P3/D/24
Thos., yeo., Willesley, Sherston, 1626, I, W, P3/D/63
Thos., Nettleton, 1683, AB, P3/D/190
Thos., Sherston, 1791, W, P3/D/454
Thos. Wm., jun., tailor, Sherston, 1831, comm, W, P3/1831/49
Walter, carp., Horningsham, 1590, I, T, W, P5/1590/18, P5/5Reg/89A
Wm., yeo., S. Wraxall, 1773, W, P2/D/664
Wm., S. Wraxall, 1822, AB, comm, Wr, P2/1822/29
Deverall, Wm., Bromham, 1835, AB, comm, P1/1835/33
see also Coleman alias D.
Devotion *see* Dyer alias Devotion
Devyn *see* Deavin
Devys *see* Davis
Dew, Abraham, broad weaver, Westb., 1822, O, W, Wr, P25/1822/5
Abraham, pork butcher, Marsh, Westb., 1830, O, W, Wr, P25/1830/1
Alexander, yeo. and miller, Gomeldon, Idmiston, 1671, I, W, P2/D/283
Alice, widow, Crockerton, Longbridge D., 1748, W, P2/D/603
Ann, widow, Sparsholt, Berks., 1683, AB, I, P1/D/157
Ann, widow, Sutton V., [1687], W, P2/D/371
Ann, widow, Blackland, Calne, 1842, W, Wr, P5/1842/18
Ann, widow, Hanging L., 1848, AB, Wr, P1/1848/38
Beatrice, widow, Horningsham, 1602, AB, I, W, P5/1602/13, P5/7Reg/41B
Benj., widow, Motc., Dorset, 1766, AB, P27/1/453, P27/3Reg/127A
Bennet, W. Hanney, Berks., 1714, AB, P1/D/254
Bridget, Sal., 1716, AB, P1/D/259
Caroline, cook and sp., Sal. (form. of W. Harnham), 1849, D, W, Wr, P4/1849/13
Chris., sen., miller, Laverstock, 1648, I, W, P2/D/242
Chris., yeo., W. Grimstead, 1686, AB, I, P1/D/165
Edith, widow, E. Knoyle, 1558, W, P2/3Reg/99A
Edwd., Sutton V., 1576, W, P2/5Reg/269D
Edwd., yeo., Aston Tirrold, Berks., 1753, W, P1/D/376, P1/10Reg/518
Francis, sen., husb., Hanging L., [1676], W, P2/D/304
Francis, Steeple L., 1705, AB, ren, P2/D/444
Francis, mason, Hanging L., 1716, I, W, P2/D/488
Geo., yeo., Rowde, 1828, W, Wr, P3/1828/42
Grace, widow, Teffont M., 1778, W, P2/D/678
Hy., plasterer, Warm., 1726, W, P2/D/531
Hy., tiler, Warm., 1799, AB, ren, W, P2/D/732
Hy. *or* Harry, yeo., E. Hendred, Berks., 1616, I, W, P1/D/33
Jane, widow, Sutton V., 1722, W, P2/D/516
Jn., Norton B., 1539, W (NEP), P2/1Reg/1A
Jn., Middleton, Norton B., 1561, W, P2/4Reg/73B
Jn., E. Knoyle, 1571, W, P2/5Reg/125F
Jn., husb., Imber, 1583, I, T, W, P2/D/26, P2/6Reg/105B
Jn., husb., Knighton, Broad C., 1598, I, W, P2/D/56
Jn., Horningsham, 1598, AB, I, W, P5/1598/14, P5/6Reg/212B
Jn., Upton S., 1618, comm, I, W, P2/D/117

Jn., yeo., Crockerton, Longbridge D., [1627], I, W, P2/D/151
Jn., Fovant, [1681], I, P2/D/332
Jn., jun., Sutton V., 1697, AB, P2/D/408
Jn., innholder, Warm., 1724, W, P2/D/524
Jn., tailor, Dinton, 1727, W, P2/D/534
Jn., yeo., S. Moreton, Berks., 1747, W, Wr, P1/D/359, P1/10Reg/87
Jn., yeo., Hanging L., 1796, W, Wr, P2/D/724
Jn., wheelwright, Burdens Ball, S. Newton, 1833, W, Wr, P2/1833/62
Jn., weaver, Stormore, Dilton, Westb., 1841, W, Wr, P25/1841/8
Julian, widow, Norton B., 1563, I, W, P2/D/3, P2/4Reg/119A
My., widow, Crockerton, Longbridge D., 1640, I, W, P2/D/216
My., widow, Swallowcliffe, 1679, AB, I, P5/1679/23
My., broad weaver, Dilton M., Westb., 1819, W, Wr, P25/1819/5
Nich., husb., N. Tidworth, ?1556, W, P2/1Reg/102A
Ralph, husb., Norton B., 1606, I, W, P1/D/17
Richd., Norton B., 1561, W, P2/4Reg/74A
Richd., husb., Middleton, Norton B., 1610, I, W, P2/D/92, P2/8Reg/104
Richd., cordw., E. Knoyle, 1684, I, W, P2/D/348
Richd., tailor, Dinton, 1850, aff, W, Wr, P2/1850/44
Roger, husb., Norton B., 1611, I, W (damaged), P1/D/22
Simon, Norton B., 1569, W, P2/5Reg/62B
Stephen, Newnham, Sutton V., 1622, I, W, P2/D/131
Stephen, Crockerton, Longbridge D., 1708, AB, I, P2/D/452
Thos., Warm., c1540, W, P30/60
Thos., Norton B., 1580, I, W, P2/D/22, P2/6Reg/12B
Thos., husb., Broad C., 1587, W, P2/7Reg/90D
Thos., yeo., Heytes., 1593-94, I, W, P5/1593/32, P5/6Reg/22C
Thos., husb., Broad C., 1629, I, copy I, W, P2/D/157
Thos., Bishopstrow, 1649, L (refers to deed of 1641 & dispute between 2 sons), P2/D/244
Thos., yeo., Broad C., 1667, I, P2/D/263
Thos., wheelwright, Sutton V., 1719, W, P2/D/500
Thos., cordw., Steeple L., 1725, W, P2/D/528
Thos., Wokm., Berks., 1732, AB, P5/1732/53
Thos., tailor, Swallowcliffe, 1756, W, P5/1756/8
Wm., husb., E. Knoyle, 1556, W, P2/1Reg/105A
Wm., Mkt. L., [1562], I, P2/D/6
Wm., husb., Broad C., 1643, AB, a/c, I, P2/D/229
Wm., sen., yeo., Swallowcliffe, 1673-78, AB, I, W, P5/1673/11, P5/1678/12
Wm., Norton B., 1685, AB, I, P2/D/358
Wm., herdsman, Marl., 1696, W, P1/D/191
Wm., Swallowcliffe, 1732, AB, P5/1732/14
Wm., innholder, Teffont M., 1766, AB, P2/D/648
Wm., E. Hanney, W. Hanney, Berks., 1795, W, P1/D/445, P1/14Reg/524B
Wm., yeo., Tinh., Edington, 1822, comm, W, Wr, P2/1822/28
see also Tame/Taine alias D.
Dewcane, Wm., Sal. St Edmd., 1562, W, P1/2Reg/131
Dewcy *see* Ducie
Dewden *see* Dowding
Dewdney *see* Dowdney
Dewell, Francis, innholder, Reading St My., Berks., 1616, AB, I (rooms in inn are named), P1/D/34
Hy., gent., Shaw, Lydiard M., 1731, W, P3/D/331
Duell, Isaac, yeo., Redlynch, Downton, 1851, D, W, Wr, P2/1851/14
Jn., clerk, Lydiard T., 1684, AB, comm, I, P3/D/194
Richd., gent., Binfield, Berks., 1704, I, W, P1/D/212
Duell, Thos., yeo., Fifield, Bray, Berks., 1776, ren, P1/D/421
see also Dowle
Dewey, Andrew, clothworker, Bere R., Dorset, 1688, AB, I, P5/1688/25
Andrew, clothier, Bere R., Dorset, 1743, W, Wr, P5/1743/21
Azariah, labourer, E. Knoyle, 1855, aff, O, W, Wr, P2/1855/13
Dorothy, widow, Chute, 1736, AB, P7/133

Edwd., Donhead St A., 1796, AB, P2/D/723
Eleanor, widow, Donhead St A., 1802, AB, comm, P2/1802/15
Eliz., widow, Warm., 1782, W, P2/D/686
Joan, widow, Bere R., Dorset, 1712, I, W, P5/1712/23, P5/15Reg/301A
Jn., maltster, Sal. The Close, 1670, AB, I, P5/1670/9
Jn., Collingbourne D., 1706, AB, P21/6/33
Jn., yeo., Longbridge D., 1759, W, P1/11Reg/474
Jn., labourer, E. Knoyle, 1838, W, Wr, P2/1838/24
Mgt., Homington, 1574, W, P24/322, P5/3Reg/32C
Thos., miller, Coombe, Enford, 1721, W, P2/D/506
Thos., miller, Coombe, Enford, 1748, W, P2/D/607
Wm., Mkt. L., 1563, W, P2/4Reg/129
Wm., Ludg., 1632, I, W, P2/D/170, P2/9Reg/25C
Wm., yeo., Chute, 1712, W, P7/102
Wm., tailor, Sal., 1721, AB, I, P4/1721/5
Wm., Brixton D., 1742, AB, P2/D/584
Wm., sen., Chute, 1752, W, P5/1752/11
see also Ward form. D.
Dewland *see* Duland
Dewley, Thos., Keevil, 1561, I, W, P2/D/23, P2/4Reg/88D
Dewling *see* Duland
Dewsome, Jn., Chilton F., [1608], W (2 - 1 a copy) (NEP), P3/D/10
Deymond *see* Dymond
Deynton *see* Dainton
Diaper *see* Diper
Dibben, Edwd., hairdresser, Sherb., Dorset, 1833, W, Wr, P5/1833/24
Geo., husb., Tollard Royal, 1618, I, W, P2/D/122
Jn., Winterborne K., Dorset, 1609, I, W, P5/1609/23, P5/8Reg/160B
Dibbens, Nich., blacksmith, Corsley, 1641, I, W, P2/D/224
Richd., yeo., Tollard Royal, [1701], W, P2/D/425
Dibbins, Richd., glazier, Crickl. St My., 1806, W, Wr, P3/1806/12
Thos., husb., Charlton, Donhead St My., 1624, comm, I, W, P2/D/135
Thos., yeo., Tisb., 1806, comm, W, Wr, P2/1806/77
Dibbins, Thos., plumber and glazier, Crickl. St S., 1832, W, Wr, P3/1832/1
Wm., Charlton, Donhead St My., 1609, I, NW, P2/D/87, P2/8Reg/80B
Wm., mercer, Sherb., Dorset, 1772, AB, comm, ren, W, P5/1772/5, P5/17Reg/36A
Dibbes, Wm., Turners Puddle, Dorset, 1572, AB, P5/3Reg/5A
Dibbins *see* Dibben
Dibble, Edwd. *or* Edmond, husb., Bapton, Fisherton Delamare, 1694, AB, I, P2/D/401
Dibden, Cath., widow, Bramshaw, Hants, 1814, W, P24/1269
Jn., sen., Bramshaw, Hants, 1781, AB, W, P24/1116
Moses, sen., labourer, Bramshaw, Hants, 1856, AB, aff, D, W, Wr, P24/1419
Wm., husb., Bramshaw, Hants, 1830, W, P24/1321
Dibley, Ann, sp., Boxford, Berks., 1692, I, W, P1/D/179
Eleanor, widow, Bucklebury & Thatcham, Berks., 1674, I, W, P1/D/137
Eleanor, sp., Landford, 1747, W, P2/D/604
Eliz., gent.'s widow, Newtown, Hungerford, Berks., 1803, W, P5/1803/37, P5/19Reg/68
Jas., butcher, Speenhamland, Berks., 1741, AB, I, P1/D/335
Martha, widow, Blewbury, Berks., 1761, W, P5/1761/9
Thos., Chieveley, Berks., 1744, AB, P1/D/346
Thos., Speenhamland, Berks., 1829, AB, Wr, P1/1829/120
Diccox, Diccocks, Charity, widow, N. Tidworth, 1614, W, P2/8Reg/230A
Geo., glover, Chipp., 1686, AB, comm, I, P3/D/201
Dickok, Thos., yeo., Collingbourne K., 1622, AB, a/c, I, P3/D/51
Dicey, Hy., yeo., Sandhurst, Berks., [1626-30?], W (deed of gift 1626) (NEP), but context suggests 1630, P5/11Reg/145C
Joan, Hurst, Berks., 1690, AB, comm, P5/1690/14
Dicke, Dick, Alice, widow, Eastcourt, Crudwell, 1609, W, P3/D/15
Dick, Ann, widow, Devizes, 1675, AB, I, P1/D/140
Dick, Ann, widow, Hankerton, 1677, AB, comm, I, L, P1/D/146
Dicks, Ann, widow, Warm., 1763, comm, W, P1/D/397, P1/12Reg/55B

Dycke, Nich., husb., Milston, 1559, W, P2/3Reg/160C
Dick, Benj., joiner, Bradford A., 1646, AB, I, P2/D/235
Dick, Benj., gent., Westwood, 1764, comm, W, P2/D/640
Dick, Cath., widow, Allington, All C., 1679, I, W, P3/D/175
Cath., sp., N. Bradley, 1706, I, W, P2/D/447
Dick, Dan., Wrou., 1799, req, W, copy W, P3/D/463
Dick, Edwd., Horton, Bps. C., 1603, AB, I, P24/14
Dick, Edwd., husb., Mere, 1603, I, W, P5/1603/25, P5/7Reg/73B
Dick, Edwd., victualler *or* innholder, Bradford A., 1668, I, W, P1/D/121
Dick, Edwd., yeo., Allington, All C., 1679, AB, comm, I (2 - 1 a copy)., P3/D/172
Dick, Edwd., schoolmaster, Bradford A., 1689, comm, W, P2/D/380
Dick, Eleanor, widow, Limpley Stoke, Bradford A., 1701, I, W, P1/D/204, P1/4Reg/46
Dicks, Eliz., widow, Shalbourne, Berks., 1686, I, W, P23/150
Dick, Geoffrey, Kington L., 1604, I, W, P3/D/3
Dick, Geoffrey, husb., Hankerton, 1624, I, W, P3/D/60
Dickes, Geo., Whaddon, 1668, I, NW, P1/D/122
Dickes, Geo., joiner, Bradford A., 1695, comm, W, P1/D/188
Dick, Gilbert, husb., Newton T., 1575, W, P2/D/9, P2/5Reg/237C
Dick, Giles, jun., labourer, Eastcourt, Crudwell, 1795, AB, comm, P3/D/460
Dycke, Hy., yeo., Sherb., Dorset, 1629, AB, I, P5/1629/13, P5/11Reg/103A
Dick, Jas., N. Bradley, 1605, I, T, P2/D/75
Dicks, Jas., Warm., 1733, AB, NW, P2/D/549
Dicks, Jas., Longbridge D., 1775, app. of guardian, P2/D/672
Dicks, Jas., yeo., Westb., 1826, O, W, Wr, P25/1826/3
Dicks, Jas., yeo., Beanacre, Melk., 1830, AB, W, Wr, P2/1830/74
Dick, Joan, widow, Horton, Bps. C., 1607, comm, I, W, P24/167
Dycke, Jn., Monkton D., 1557, W, P2/3Reg/20C
Dycke, Jn., husb., Horton, Bps. C., 1579, W, P5/3Reg/120B
Jn., husb., Netheravon, 1588, I, W, P12/235, P5/5Reg/4C
Jn., Fifield, Enford, 1600, W, P2/D/61
Dick, Jn., sen., yeo., Hankerton, 1625, I, W, P3/D/62
Jn., shoemaker, Woolley, Bradford A., 1635, comm, I, copy NW (2), P2/D/179
Jn., brewer, Bradford A., 1641, I, W, P2/D/223
Jn., yeo., Fifield, Enford, 1661, I, W, P2/D/245
Dick, Jn., Chisenbury, Enford, 1677, I, P1/D/145
Jn., broad weaver, Coombe Bottom, Bradford A., 1712, AB, comm, I, P2/D/471
Dicks, Jn., gent., N. Bradley, 1822, comm, W, Wr, P2/1822/14
Dicks, Jonathan, gardener, Newton T., 1747, W, P2/D/600
Dicks, Judith, widow, Melk., 1727, W, P2/D/532
Dick, Mgt., sp., Hankerton, 1707, I, W, P3/D/265
Dycke, Margery, widow, Enford, 1589, I, T, W, P2/D/34
Dick, My., widow, Bps. C., 1625, AB, a/c, I, P24/174
Dickes, My., widow, Whaddon, 1671, I, W, P1/D/133
Dicks, My., widow, Bremhill, 1705, AB, I, P3/D/262
Ralph, Fifield, Enford, 1585, W, P2/7Reg/2C
Richd., weaver, Wilton, 1641, AB, I, P2/D/222
Richd., cordw., Longstreet, Enford, 1679, AB, I, P2/D/319
Richd., clothworker, Bradford A., 1682, comm, I, W, P2/D/340
Dicks, Richd., clothworker, Bradford A., 1729, W, P1/D/294, P1/7Reg/330A
Richd., sen., clothier, Limpley Stoke, Bradford A., 1740, W, P2/D/579
Richd., yeo., Hilmarton, 1749, W, P3/D/373
Robt., Horton, Bps. C., 1602, I (detailed), P24/15
Dickes, Robt., broad cloth weaver, Woolley, Bradford A., 1802, W, P2/1802/59
Sibyl, widow, Bradford A., 1701, AB, I, P2/D/424
Susan, widow, Seend, Melk., 1612, I, W, P2/D/103
Thos., husb., Netheravon, 1606, I, W, P12/14
Thos., husb., Fifield, Enford, 1613, W, P2/8Reg/194A
Thos., jun., husb. *or* yeo., Eastcourt, Crudwell, 1621, I, W, P3/D/47
Thos., husb., Netheravon, [1630], I, W, P12/63
Dick, Thos., Chisenbury, Enford, 1639, AB, I, P12/80

Thos., sen., yeo. *or* husb., Netheravon, 1663, I, W, P1/D/105
Dick, Thos., yeo., Eastcourt, Crudwell, 1693, AB, I, P3/D/227
Thos., tailor, Crudwell, 1767, W, P3/D/408
Thos., victualler, Winsley, Bradford A., 1825, comm, W, Wr, P2/1825/2
Wm., Winsley, Bradford A., 1574, W, P2/5Reg/185A, P2/5Reg/206C
Wm., husb., Bedborough, Bps. C., 1610, I, W, P24/141
Wm., husb., Fifield, Enford, 1619-20, a/c, I, T, P2/D/124
Wm., Eastcourt, Crudwell, 1628, AB, a/c, I, ren, P1/D/50
Dickes, Wm., broad weaver, Hinton, Steeple A., 1677, AB, I, P2/D/308
Wm., Fifield, Enford, [1698?], I, P1/D/21
Wm., joiner, Bradford A., 1700, comm, W, P2/D/422
Wm., sen., yeo., Rushall, 1704, W, P2/D/439
Dickes, Wm., maltster, Edington, 1714, W, P2/D/485
Wm., Rushall, 1723, AB, P1/D/273
Dicks, Wm., Bishopstrow, 1836, AB, comm, D, W, P2/1836/15
see also Deeke
Dickens, Edwd., yeo., Britford, 1621, W, P24/63
Hugh, Britford, 1617, I, W, P24/86
Dickenson, Edmd., maltster, Wallingford, Berks., 1695, AB, comm, I, P1/D/187
Geo., wheelwright, Waltham St Lawr., Berks., 1744, W, P1/D/347, P1/9Reg/350B
Robt., yeo., Hook, Lydiard T., 1617, I, W, P3/D/35
Robt., Chirton, 1681, AB, P2/D/330
Walter, clerk, S. Newton, 1681, AB, I, P2/D/329
Dickinson, Wm., gent., Uffc., Devon, 1836, O, W, Wr, P5/1836/9
Dicker, Dyker, Hy., yeo., Chetnole, Yetm., Dorset, 1688, AB, I, P5/1688/24
Diker, Jn., Sutton Poyntz, Dorset, 1594, AB, I, T, P5/1594/24, P5/6Reg/59B
My., Long Burton, Dorset, 1689, AB, comm, I, P5/1689/19
Thos., gent.'s servant and bach., Netherb., Dorset, 1833, comm, W, Wr, P5/1833/34
Dyker, Wm., Erlestoke, 1561, W, P2/4Reg/70B
Dyker, Wm., yeo., Long Burton, Dorset, 1679, AB, comm, I, P5/1679/24
Wm., sen., Long Burton, Dorset, 1705, AB, comm, P5/1705/17
Wm., draper, Woolhampton, Berks., 1804, W, P1/1804/57
Dickes *see* Dicke
Dickinson *see* Dickenson
Dickman, Ann, widow, Fyfield, Overton, 1723, AB, I (applies to both people), P3/D/303
Jn., blacksmith, Redlynch, Downton, 1813, W, Wr, P2/1813/47
Jn. Brewer, Redlynch, Downton, 1766, AB, P2/D/644
Dikeman *or* Dickman, Matthew, yeo., Corsham, 1673, AB, I, P29/D/13, P29/1Reg/200A
Robt., yeo., Rowde, 1779, W, P3/D/432
Thos., sen., weaver, Newtown, Enford, 1703, I, W, P2/D/431
Thos., weaver, Enford, 1739, AB, ren, P2/D/574
Wm., Marl. St My., 1682, AB, comm, P1/D/155
Wm., husb., Shalbourne, 1807, W, Wr, P23/851
Dickok *see* Diccox
Dicks *see* Dick
Dickson *see* Dixon
Didding, Jas., clothier, Castle C., 1838, O, W, Wr, P3/1838/7
Diffield, Jn., husb., Bulk., Keevil, 1574, W, P2/5Reg/189B
Dyffold, Ralph, Mkt. L., 1578?, W, P2/D/19
Thos., Enford, 1570, W, P2/5Reg/90D
Thos., husb., Bulk., Keevil, 1574, W, P2/5Reg/189C
Wm., sen., market spinner, Whitley, Melk., 1713-14, I, W, P1/D/251, P1/5Reg/306
Digby, Wm. (5th Baron) *see* Mgt. Barnard
Digges, Richd., esquire, Purton, 1672, I, W, P3/D/145
Diggrey, Hugh, vintner, Sal., 1667, W, P1/D/119
Dike *see* Dyke
Dikeman *see* Dickman
Diker *see* Dicker
Dilleket, Wm., chandler, Fisherton A., 1785, W, P2/D/695
Dill *see* Oldis alias D.

Diller *see* Deller
Dillinge, Nich., husb., Chards., Devon, 1581, I, W, P5/1581/7, P5/4Reg/24B
Robt., Chards., Devon, 1567, W, P5/2Reg/19A
Wm., husb., Chettishall, Chards., Devon, 1593, I, W, P5/1592/24, P5/6Reg/17A
Dilly, Eliz., widow, Stourpaine, Dorset, 1612, I, W, P24/120
Diment, Diment alias Andrews, Jn., Halstock, Dorset, 1791, AB, comm, P16/351
Dimock, Ann, husb.'s wife, Charlton, Downton, 1749, W, P2/D/611
Martin, Bradford A., 1600, AB, T (W of Martin D. proved 1584), P2/D/66
Richd., Gt. Chalfield, 1611, T (unnamed children), P2/D/98
Dimor *see* Dymer
Dinham *see* Denham
Dinning *see* Denning
Dinsdel, Christian, widow, Sal., 1797, W, P4/1797/20
Diper, Diaper, Alice, widow, Cholderton, 1621, I, W, P2/D/127
Eliz., sp., Marridge Hill, Rams., 1616, I, W, P5/1616/19
Hy., Allington, 1554, W, P2/2Reg/196B
Hugh, Lt. Bedwyn, 1581, AB, P5/1580/20, P5/4Reg/11B
Jn., Sunton, Collingbourne K., [1580], W (NEP), P3/1Reg/41C
Lawr., Collingbourne K., 1560, W. No date of probate, P1/2Reg/108A
Mgt., widow, Laverstock, 1571, W, P2/5Reg/111B
Diaper, Richd., husb., Cholderton, 1635, I, W, P2/D/181
Robt., Aldbourne, 1696, AB, I, P3/D/234
Stephen, Cholderton, 1598, AB, I, W, P2/D/58
Deper, Thos., husb., Laverstock, 1559, W, P2/3Reg/152D
Thos., husb., Fittleton, 1618, I (incomplete), W, P2/D/123
Vincent, husb., Preston, Aldbourne, 1649, I, W, P1/D/94
Wm., yeo., Sunton, Collingbourne K., 1630, I, W, P3/D/79
Dippen, Thos., baker, Marl., 1591, I, W (NEP), P1/D/2
Dirdoe, Dirdoe alias Martin, Cicely, wife *or* widow (unclear which) of Jas. M., Mere, 1596, AB, note, P5/1596/22, P5/6Reg/128B
Eliz., widow, Milton, Gillingham, Dorset, [1702], W, P27/1/143
Frances, sp., Milton, Gillingham, Dorset, 1734, W, P27/1/324
Hy., esquire, Gillingham, Dorset, 1724, AB, P27/1/263
Hy. White, gent., Bourton, Gillingham, Dorset, [1707], W, P27/1/164
Jn., gent., E. Knoyle, 1695, I, W, P2/D/404
Robt., Milton, Gillingham, Dorset, 1582, NW, P27/2Reg/13
Thos., husb., Sal., 1722, I, W, P4/1722/15
Diser, Jn., Sal., 1685, AB, I, P4/1685/9
Dishon *see* Diston
Dismore, Alexander, innholder, Rams., 1731, I (detailed), W, P5/1731/21
Alexander, wheelwright, Hungerford, Berks., 1765, W, P23/707
Ann, widow, Froxfield, 1742, I, W, P3/D/356
Ann, widow, Rams., 1744, AB, Wr, P5/1744/14
Christian, widow, Lockeridge, Overton, 1680, I, W, P1/D/150
Dysmer, Chris., yeo., Fyfield, Overton, 1602, W, P3/1Reg/87A
Dorothy, Marl. St My., 1707, AB, I, P1/D/223
Edwd., yeo., Lambourn, Berks., 1705, comm, W, P1/D/218
Edwd., yeo., Rudge, Froxfield, 1723-24, cert, comm, I, note, W, P1/D/274, P1/7Reg/38A
Edwd., baker, Gt. Bedwyn, 1734, W, P5/1734/20
Eleanor, widow, Crofton, Gt. Bedwyn, 1684, AB, I, P21/4/9
Jane, widow, Overton, 1690, comm, I, NW, P3/D/220
Jn., baker, Gt. Bedwyn, 1694, AB, I, P21/5/30
Jonathan, Hungerford, Berks., 1743, AB, I, Wr, P5/1743/22
Richd., sen., yeo., Rudge, Froxfield, 1638, comm, I, W, P3/D/97
Richd., yeo., Crofton, Gt. Bedwyn, 1665, I, W, P5/1665/25
Richd., Lockeridge, Overton, 1688, comm, I, W, P3/D/209
Richd., gent., Rams., 1732, I, W, P5/1732/15
Richd., gent., Rams., 1742, AB, comm, ren, W, P5/1741/8
Dysmore, Thos., husb., Haxton, Fittleton, 1614, I, W, P1/D/28
Thos., W. Overton, 1683, AB, I, P3/D/191

Thos., weaver, Lockeridge, Fyfield, 1695, AB, I, W, P3/D/232
Wm., parchmentmaker, Marl., 1639, I, W, P1/D/85
see also Dymer; Greenaway alias D.
Disney, Richd., yeo., Durnford, 1692, W, P9/24
Dison *see* Dyson
Diston, Jn., clerk and vicar, Hullavington, 1675, I, NW, P3/D/161
Dishon or D., Wm., wheelwright, Westrop, Highw., 1694, AB, comm, I, P10/1693/8, P10/1694/8
Ditchine, Wm., turner, Stratfield M., Berks., 1635, I, W, P1/D/73
Ditton, Abraham, jun., gent., Wilton, 1668, I, W, P1/D/123, P2/D/264
Eliz., Sal., 1618, AB, I, P4/1618/20
Humphrey, sen., gent., Wilton, 1633, I, W, P2/D/172, P2/9Reg/26, 27
Humphrey, Sal., 1685, AB, P1/D/190
Jn., miller, Wilton, 1639, AB, a/c, I, P2/D/208
Dix, Dan., Leigh Delamere, 1711, I, W, P1/D/243, P1/5Reg/99
Jane, sp., N. Bradley, 1621, I, T, W, P2/D/129
Thos., husb., Wexcombe, Grafton, 1621, I, W, P5/1620/19, P5/10Reg/15A
Wm., husb., Imber, 1683, I, W, P1/D/158
Dixon, Adam, Sal. St Edmd., 1622, AB (2), libel, W, P4/1622/10
Agnes, widow, Sal., 1625, I, W, P1/D/45
Ann, widow, Ogbourne St Geo., 1641, W, P23/1012
Ann, widow, Ogbourne St Geo., 1694, I, W, P5/1694/36
Ann, widow, Rams., 1735, I, W, P5/1735/18
Ann, apothecary's widow, Swindon, 1757, W, P3/D/389
Ann, widow, Britford, 1820, AB, W, Wr, P24/1284
Benj., yeo., Rams., 1787, W, P5/1787/5, P5/18Reg/84
Dickson, Edith, widow, Whitep., 1635, I, W, P1/D/72
Edwin, Sal., 1849, AB, Wr, P4/1849/25
Elias, yeo., Rams., 1730, AB, W, P5/1730/17
Eliz., widow, Brinkw., 1742, W, P3/D/357
Hannah, sp., Rams., 1778, W, P5/1778/5, P5/17Reg/151
Dickson, Hy., Abingdon St Helen, Berks., 1695, AB, P1/D/189
Hy., gardener, Calne, 1747, AB, P26/869
Honour, widow, Studley, Bremhill, 1725, W, P3/D/311
Jn., Collingbourne K., 1622, AB, I, P3/D/52
Jn., sen., yeo., Aldbourne, 1636, I, W, P3/D/89
Jn., sen., fellmonger, Rams., 1708, W, P5/1708/26, P5/15Reg/58
Jn., Rams., 1718, AB, I, P5/1718/10
Jn., Whaddon, 1744, W, P1/D/348, P1/9Reg/417A
Jn., apothecary, Swindon, 1756, W, P1/D/382, P1/11Reg/283B
Jn., late a servingman, but now out of business, Bodenham, Nunton and B., 1848, W, Wr, P1/1848/59
Matthew, tailor, Crudwell, 1823, W, Wr, P1/1823/145
Matthew, tailor, Avebury, 1850, AB, D, O, W, Wr, P3/1850/20
Peter, gardener, Devizes St My., 1689, AB, I, P1/D/171
Richd., yeo., Rams., 1748, W, Wr, P5/1748/8
Robt., Ogbourne St Geo., 1741, AB, P23/553
Robt., Marl., 1794, AB, P1/D/439, P1/14Reg/506A
Robt., Axford, Rams., 1842, AB, O, Wr, P5/1842/30
Robt., wine merchant, Marl., 1853, O, W, Wr, P1/1853/17
Thos., Rams., 1579, I, W, P5/1579/23, P5/3Reg/138A
Thos., Ogbourne St Geo., 1582, AB, I, W, P5/1582/18, P5/4Reg/47
Thos., yeo., Ogbourne St Geo., 1666, AB, I, request for AB, P5/1665/26
Thos., Aldbourne, 1671, AB, I, P1/D/141
Thos., tailor, Rams., 1723, AB, I, P5/1723/9
Thos., innholder, Studley, Bremhill, 1724, W (2 - 1 a copy), P3/D/308
Thos., Aldbourne, 1832, AB, Wr, P1/1832/102
Wm., yeo., Ogbourne St Geo., 1689, AB, comm, I, P5/1689/20
Dobbs, Agnes, widow, Brinkw., 1603, I, W, P3/D/1
Chris., husb., Nursteed, Bps. C., 1575-76, AB, I (2), T, W, copy W, P5/1575/13, P5/3Reg/53D, 54A, 73A
Dan., Ludg., 1818, AB, Wr, P2/1818/69
Dorcas, widow, S. Wraxall, 1725, W, P2/D/527

Hy., yeo., Upton S., 1603, I, W, P2/D/72
Joan, widow, Ludg., 1672, I, W, P2/D/285
Jn., carp., Ludg., 1628, I, W, P2/D/156
Nich., tailor, Malm., 1605, I, W, P3/D/5
Richd., Netheravon, 1634, I, P5/1634/34
Richd., husb., Garsdon, 1637, I, W, P3/D/94
Richd., yeo., Ludg., 1733, W, P1/D/308, P1/7Reg/570
Robt., surgeon, Devizes, 1685, AB, comm, I, ren, P1/D/162
Thos., yeo., Ludg., 1736, W, Wr, P2/D/562
Thos., shopkeeper, Ludg., 1797, W, P2/D/725
Wm., husb., Charlton & Garsdon, 1630, I, W, P3/D/80
Wm., yeo., Ludg., 1737, W, P2/D/567
Wm., Ludg., 1770, W, P2/D/655
Dobby, Margery, sp., Corsham, 1689, AB, I, P29/D/17, P29/1Reg/241C
Dobenett *see* Dabynott
Dober, Arthur, Holnest, Dorset, 1609, I, W, P5/1609/21, P5/8Reg/141F
Christian, sp., Holnest, Dorset, 1681, AB, comm, I, P5/1681/10
Edith, widow, Holnest, Dorset, 1620, AB, I, W, P5/1620/18, P5/10Reg/81
Edwd., husb., Holnest, Dorset, 1675, I, W, P5/1675/17
Jethro, yeo., Hermitage, Dorset, 1680, AB, comm, I, P5/1680/10
Joan, widow, Holnest, Dorset, 1669, AB, comm, I, P5/1669/14
Jn., Chetnole, Yetm., Dorset, 1593, AB, I, W, P5/1592/25, P5/6Reg/16C
Jn., Holnest, Dorset, 1626, AB, a/c, I, P5/1626/12, P5/10Reg/326B
Jn. the middle, potter, Holnest, Dorset, 1668, AB, I (detailed), NW, P5/1668/24
Jn., sen., husb., Holnest, Dorset, 1676, I, NW, P5/1676/17
Jn., husb., Hermitage, Dorset, 1717, W, P5/1717/12, P5/15Reg/407A
Robt., Holnest, Dorset, 1673, AB, comm, I, ren, P5/1673/12
Thos., Holnest, Dorset, 1589, AB, I, P5/1589/15, P5/5Reg/52A
Thos., jun., miller, Sherb., Dorset, 1623, I, W, P5/1623/9, P5/10Reg/217
Thos., miller, Sherb., Dorset, 1638-39, comm, W, P5/1638/29, P5/13Reg/112B
Dobles *see* Lawrence alias D.
Dobson, Eliz., widow, Overton, 1748, AB, I, P3/D/371
Geo., sen., victualler, Newbury St., Preshute, 1689, AB, ren, W, P1/D/172
Geo., jun., chandler, Marl., 1709, I, W, P1/D/233
Dopson, Geo., Worton, Pott., 1746, AB, I, W, P1/D/356, P1/10Reg/19B
Dopson, Hannah, Lockeridge, Overton, 1721, I, W (2 - 1 a copy), P3/D/292
Hy., Barnards St., Sal. St Martin, 1843, D, W, Wr, P1/1843/10
Jn., Lt. Bedwyn, 1571, W, P5/2Reg/106C
Jn., Froxfield, 1819, W, Wr, P3/1819/17
Nich., Fyfield, Overton, 1701, I, W, P1/D/206, P1/4Reg/73
Nich., yeo., Lockeridge, Overton, 1810, comm, W, Wr, P3/1810/40
Richd., Netheravon, 1634, W, P5/1634/35, P5/12Reg/274B
Robt., curate, Horningsham, 1625, I, W, P5/1625/25, P5/10Reg/284
Thos., yeo., Savernake Forest, 1717, AB, I, W, P21/7/28
Wm., sen., yeo., Slade End, Brightwell, Berks., 1625, I, O, W, P1/D/46
Wm., yeo., Slade End, Brightwell, Berks., 1677, AB, L (2), P1/D/147
Dockerell, Richd., yeo., Wootton B., 1716, I, W, P3/D/283
Dockett, Lucy, widow, Preston, Dorset, 1587, I, W, P5/1587/46, P5/4Reg/144A
Dodall, Jn., smith, Longbridge D., 1562, W, P2/5Reg/36C
Dodd, Jn., innholder, Sal., 1742, W, P4/1742/13
Jn., surgeon, Trowb., 1800, AB, comm, ren, P1/1800/15, P1/15Reg/217B
Robt., W. Hanney, Berks., 1559, W. No date of probate given, P1/2Reg/102B
Thos., Woolhampton, Berks., 1753, AB, P1/D/377
Thos., Stratford sub C., 1781, AB, P4/1781/11
Doddrell, Wm., master, Bere R., Dorset, 1613, I, W, P5/1613/20, P5/9Reg/87A
Dodge, Hy., weaver, Uffc., Devon, 1717, comm, W, P20/1/159
Jos., glover, Sherb., Dorset, 1712, W, P5/1712/22, P5/15Reg/293
Dodimead, Hugh, yeo., Hudswell, Corsham, 1689, I, W, P29/D/16, P29/1Reg/246
Jas., shoemaker, Sherb., Dorset, 1735, W, P5/1735/19
Jn., carp., Berwick St Jn., 1769, W, P2/D/650

Jn., cordw., Warm., 1819, AB, comm, W, Wr, P2/1819/7
Moses, broad weaver, Dilton M., Westb., 1773, AB, W, P25/1773/2
Walter, cordw., Warm., 1640, I, W, P2/D/212
Dodington, Chas., mason, Mere, 1837, W, Wr, P5/1837/16
Chris., gent., Burton, Mere, 1688, AB, a/c, I, P5/1687/12
Susanna, Maiden B., 1741, W, P1/D/337, P1/9Reg/46
Wm., gent., Woodlands, Mere, 1578-96, AB (2 - 1 of goods left unadmd by decd's father, Sir Chris. D.), a/c, I, P5/1578/15, P5/1588/13, P5/1596/20, P5/3Reg/108A, P5/5Reg/49C, P5/6Reg/143A
Dodshon, Jn., Marl., 1621, comm, I, W (all documents badly damaged), P1/D/39
Dodwell, Ann, widow, Shottesbrooke, Berks., 1750, W, P1/D/372, P1/10Reg/342
Doe, Alexander, clothier, Wantage, Berks., 1699, I, W, P23/235
Alice, widow, Letcombe Regis, Berks., 1704, W, P1/D/213
Ann, Richmond, Surrey (proved at Wantage), 1751, W, P23/631
David, weaver, Wantage, Berks., 1685, I, W, P23/151
Deborah, widow, Lower Stratton, Stratton St Mgt., 1719, I, W, P3/D/290
Edwd., yeo., Wantage, Berks., 1699, I, W, P23/236
Jas., widower, Donnington, Berks., 1801, W, P1/1801/44, P1/15Reg/264
Jn., E. Lockinge, Berks., 1602, I, W (NEP), P1/D/11
Jn., harnessmaker, Ashampstead, Basildon, Berks., 1717, I, W, P1/D/263, P1/6Reg/131
Mgt., widow, Wantage, Berks., 1616, AB, I, W, P5/1616/18
My., wife, Aston U., Blewbury, Berks., 1823, app. of proctors, W, Wr, P5/1823/20
Philip, yeo., Lt. Coxwell, Gt. Faringdon, Berks., 1663, I, W, P5/1662/33
Doo, Richd., joiner, Wantage, Berks., 1598, I, W, P5/1597/33, P5/6Reg/193E
Richd., husb., Wantage, Berks., 1613, I, W, P5/1613/18, P5/9Reg/104A
Richd., yeo., Wantage, Berks., 1685, I, W, P23/145
Wm., sen., Blewbury, Berks., 1753, AB, I, P5/1752/12
Wm., sen., victualler, Blewbury, Berks., 1784, W, P5/1784/4, P5/17Reg/260
Doggerill *see* Doggrell
Doggett, Chris., Sutton Poyntz, Dorset, 1579, I, T, W, P5/1579/25, P5/3Reg/124D
Cicely, widow, Bradford A., 1624, AB, I, P2/D/137
Edwd., Bradford A., 1597, AB, I, P2/D/50
Jn., broad weaver, Bradford A., 1643, I, W, P2/D/230
Thos., baker, Bradford A., 1564, W, P2/4Reg/176D
Thos., publican, Marl., 1835, O, W, P1/1835/6
Wm., broad weaver, Westwood, 1598, I, W, P2/D/54
Wm., publican, Marl., 1837, W, Wr, P1/1837/18
Doggrell, Christian, sp., Huntingford, Gillingham, Dorset, 1829, comm, W, P27/1/688
Jn., Bedborough, Bps. C., 1671, I, P24/378
Jn., Gillingham, Dorset, 1728, AB, P27/1/293
Jn., yeo., Gillingham, Dorset, 1834, comm, W, Wr, P27/1/702
Robt., Pierston, Gillingham, Dorset, 1576, W, P27/1Reg/31B
Doggerill, Thos., jun., husb., Wolverton, Zeals, 1678, I, W, P5/1678/13
Doggerill, Thos., yeo., Wolverton, Zeals, 1684, AB, I, P5/1684/15
Thos., yeo., Gillingham, Dorset, 1816, W, Wr, P27/1/635
Wm., yeo., Gillingham, Dorset, 1840, W, Wr, P27/1/732,
Dogood *see* Twogood (Toogood) alias D.
Dolbury, Agnes, Yetm., Dorset, 1567, W, P5/2Reg/20A
Dolden, Jn., Chilmark, 1789, AB, W, P2/D/709
Dole, Ann, widow, Warm., 1840, comm, W, Wr, P2/1840/15
Edwd., Worton, Pott., 1710, AB, P1/D/236
Hugh, Hawkeridge, Westb., 1633, I, NW, P25/1633/4
Jas., Warm., 1833, AB, Wr, P2/1833/36
Joan, widow, Lt. Cheverell, 1675, I, W, P2/D/295
Jn., husb., Lt. Cheverell, 1571, W, P1/1Reg/95A
Doole, Jn., Erlestoke, 1633, I, W, P2/D/173
Jn., yeo., N. Bradley, 1800, W, P2/1800/97
Jn., Horningsham, 1814, AB, Wr, P5/1814/23
My., widow, Bradford A., 1816, W, Wr, P2/1816/40
Philip, husb., Lt. Cheverell, 1622, I, W, P1/D/40
Doole, Philip, Hawkeridge, Westb., 1633, I, NW, P25/1633/5

Philip, N. Bradley, 1711, AB, P2/D/468
Sarah, sp., Westb., 1730, AB, comm, P25/1730/6
Wm., husb., Lt. Cheverell, 1591, I, W (NEP), P1/D/3
Wm., Heytes., 1668, AB, P5/1668/27
Dolel, Jacob, pastry cook, Westb., 1812, W, Wr, P25/1812/4
Doleman *see* Dalman
Dolen, Doling *see* Dowling
Dolman, Doleman, Andrew, Netheravon, 1632, I, W, P12/69
Ann, sp., Sal., 1792, AB, P1/D/437, P1/14Reg/470A
Eliz., widow, Netheravon, 1678, I, W, P5/1678/15
Dooleman, Hy., husb., Cleverton, Lea and C., 1617, I, W (2), P3/D/32
Jas., builder, High St., Sal. St Thos., 1856, aff, W, Wr, P4/1856/2
Joan, Lyme R., Dorset, 1637, I, W (NEP), P30/54
Joan, widow, Netheravon, 1638, AB, I, NW, P5/1638/30, P5/13Reg/103C
Jn., sen., husb., Netheravon, 1605, AB, I, P5/1604/9
Jn., husb., Chieveley, Berks., 1668, AB, W, P1/D/125
Jn., sen., butcher, Calne, 1719, I, W, P26/627
Jn., butcher, Calne, 1721, W, P26/655
Dalman, Juliana, widow, Broad H., 1847, AB, O, Wr, P5/1847/3
Margery, widow, Ebbesborne Wake, 1612, AB, P2/D/101
Martin, cooper, Lyme R., Dorset, 1631, AB, I, P5/1631/36, P5/12Reg/9C
Dalmon, My., Fittleton, 1762, AB, P2/D/637
Matthew, tailor, Netheravon, 1709, I, NW, P12/143
Richd., yeo., Malm., 1702, AB, I, P3/D/253
Thos., innholder, Hungerford, Berks., 1570, W, P5/2Reg/63A
Thos., cooper, Lyme R., Dorset, 1677, W, P16/48
Doleman, Thos., bach., Sal., 1785, AB, P4/1785/5
(Sir) Thos. *see also* Wm. Checker
Tristram, innholder, Hungerford, Berks., 1619, AB, I, P5/1619/49, P5/10Reg/37D
Walter, Netheravon, 1617, AB, I, P12/34
Doleman, Walter, wheelwright, Malm., 1618, I, W, P3/D/36
Walter, sen., butcher, Calne, 1709, I, W, P26/553
Wm., Netheravon, 1583, AB, I, P5/1583/12, P5/4Reg/70B
Wm., coal merchant, Rushy Platt, Swindon, 1849, comm, W, Wr, P3/1849/37
Dolton *see* Dalton
Domer *see* Dummer
Domet, Domett *see* Dammett
Domin, Jos., Longbridge D., 1847, W, Wr, P2/1847/12
Dominick, Damenick, Alice, widow, Chilmark, 1541, I, W (NEP), P30/53
Dominy alias Clare, Eleanor, widow, Fisherton A., 1677, AB, I, W, P2/D/305
Dominy, Emma, widow, Stourpaine, Dorset, 1688, comm, I, W, P24/784
Jas., yeo., Milton, E. Knoyle, 1680, I, W, P1/D/151
Jas., gent., Milton, E. Knoyle, 1686, I, W, P1/D/166
Dominick alias Clare, Jn., clerk, Fonthill B., 1620, a/c (2), AB, I (2), P1/D/38
Dominy, Nich., Winterbourne D., 1690, AB, I, P7/74
Dominick alias Clare, Philip, Ridge, Chilmark, 1610, AB, P2/D/90, P2/8Reg/83A
Philip, Chilmark, [1675], I, P2/D/297
Randall, gent., E. Knoyle, 1665, I, W, P2/D/255
Dominy, Sarah, sp., Wrou., 1717, AB, P3/D/284
see also Clare alias D.; Wheeler alias D.
Donaldson, Robt., sen., tea dealer, Wrou., 1825, comm, W, Wr, P3/1825/15
Robt., grocer, Wrou., 1833, comm, W, Wr, P3/1833/35
Donden *see* Dunden
Donnam *see* Dunham
Donne, Abraham, cooper, Enmore Grn, Motc., Dorset, 1845, comm, W, Wr, P19/251
Andrew, scrivener, Sherb., Dorset, 1679, I, W, P5/1679/22
Jn., jun., Uffc., Devon, 1624, I, W, P20/1/4
Jn., husb., Fovant, 1637, AB, I, P2/D/197
Philip, mariner (taken sick at Plymouth), Lyme R., Dorset, 1628, I, W, P5/1628/37, P5/11Reg/65C
Wm., Dinton, 1581, W, P2/6Reg/22B

Wm., sen., yeo., Fovant, [1629], I, P2/D/158
Wm., yeo., Fovant, 1669-79, AB, I, W, P2/D/267, 323
Donning *see* Dunning
Donwyke *see* Dunnick
Doo *see* Doe
Dooche *see* Dutch
Doole *see* Dole
Dooleman *see* Dolman
Doosell, Doosell alias Brewer, Eliz., widow, Chipp., 1612, W, P3/D/22
Dopson *see* Dobson
Dorchester, Ann, widow, Wick Farm, Lacock, 1664, comm, W, P3/D/121
Ann, yeo.'s widow *or* sp., Etchilhampton, 1685, I, W, P3/D/199
Ann, widow, Etchilhampton, 1734, W, P3/D/338
Cath., widow, Devizes, 1704, W, Wr, P1/D/214
Cath., minor, Devizes, 1744, AB, I, P1/D/349
Dan., Wick, Bps. C., 1705, AB, I, P24/598
Edwd., Lyme R., Dorset, 1594, I, W, P5/1594/25, P5/6Reg/67C
Jane, widow, Bourton, Gillingham, Dorset, 1738, AB, W, P27/1/348
Jane, sp., Mkt. L., 1777, W, P2/D/675
Jn., Lyme R., Dorset, 1597, I, W, P5/1597/30, P5/6Reg/158B
Dorsetar, Jn., Wick, Bps. C., 1603, I, P24/16
Jn., yeo., Etchilhampton, 1671, AB, I, P3/D/144
My., widow, Etchilhampton, 1742, AB, P3/D/359
Robt., yeo., Etchilhampton, 1694, I, W, P3/D/231
Robt., Etchilhampton, 1724, I, W, P3/D/309
Robt., leather breechesmaker, Devizes, 1847, O, W, Wr, P1/1847/1
Roger, Etchilhampton, 1700, W, P3/D/245
Roger, jun., Devizes, 1730, AB, P1/D/303
Roger, haberdasher, Etchilhampton (late of Devizes), 1736, W, P3/D/344
Susanna, sp., Devizes, 1739, comm, W, P1/D/328, P1/8Reg/381
Wm., yeo., Etchilhampton, 1672-82, AB, I, W, P3/D/146, 186
Wm., gent., Etchilhampton, 1721, comm, court paper, I, ren, W, P3/D/297
Wm., yeo., Etchilhampton, 1725, AB, I, ren, W, P3/D/312
see also Merewether form. D.
Dore, Ann, widow, Lydiard T., 1741, W, P1/D/336, P1/9Reg/168
Ann, widow, Lydiard T., 1806, W, Wr, P3/1806/28
Cath., widow, Wrou., 1742, W, P3/D/360
Edwd., sen., yeo., Haywood Farm, Chilton F., 1692, I, W, P1/D/180
Eliz., widow, Haywood Farm, Chilton F., 1701, W, P1/D/208, P1/4Reg/107
Hannah, widow, Sal., 1783, W, P1/D/428, P1/14Reg/20
Hy., husb., Wanb., 1680, comm, I, W, P3/D/180
Hy., collarmaker *or* yeo., Liddington, 1703, I, W, P3/D/256
Dore alias Sawyer, Jas., butcher, Minety, 1627, W, P3/D/69
Jane, sp., Lydiard T., 1722, W, P3/D/302
Jane, widow, Furze Hill, Speen, Berks., 1826, W, Wr, P1/1826/86
Jn., husb., E. Garston, Berks., 1628, I, W, P1/D/51
Jn., sen., yeo., Welford, Berks., 1680, I, W, P1/D/152
Jn., Aldbourne, 1696, AB, I, P3/D/235
Jn., yeo., Upper Stratton, Stratton St Mgt., 1715, I, W, P3/D/280
Jn., Lydiard M., 1716, W, P1/D/260, P1/6Reg/63
Jn., yeo., Wrou., 1738, W, P3/D/346
Jn., Swindon, 1768, AB, comm, P3/D/411
Jn., cheese factor, W. Leaze, Wrou., 1785, AB, W, P3/D/446
Jn., yeo., Wanb. & Stratton St Mgt., 1820, AB, comm, Wr, P1/1820/16
Jn., labourer, Broad B., Highw., 1839, W, Wr, P5/1839/18
Lawr., yeo., Purton, 1781, W, P3/D/441
Martha, widow, Wrou., 1766, W, P3/D/402
My., widow, Aldbourne, 1700, I, W, P3/D/246
My., sp., W. Leaze, Wrou., 1810, O, W (& cods), Wr, P3/1810/42
My., widow, Purton, 1812, comm, W, Wr, P3/1812/40

Peter, yeo., Lydiard M., 1740, W, P3/D/350
Peter, Swindon, 1780, AB, P3/D/434
Richd., yeo., Burbage, 1671, I, W, P11/30
Richd., yeo., Lydiard T., 1723-30, AB, W, P3/D/304, 327
Richd., yeo., Mannington, Lydiard T., 1794, ren, W, P3/D/458
Richd., Newbury, Berks., 1826, AB, Wr, P1/1826/89
Robt., baker and maltster, Purton, 1802, W, P3/1802/42
Robt., maltster, Purton, 1818, comm, W, Wr, P3/1818/7
Stephen *see also* Eliz. Bainton
Stephen, sen., yeo., Burbage, 1723, I, W, P11/160
Stephen, gent., Burbage, 1733, AB, I, W, P11/138
Stephen, minor, Burbage, 1761, AB, P11/215-16
Thos., yeo., Longcott, Shrivenham, Berks., 1701-02, W, P1/D/205, P1/4Reg/210
Wm., husb., Hoe Benham, Welford, Berks., 1622, AB, a/c, I, P1/D/41
Wm., Wrou., 1733, W, P3/D/334
Wm., yeo., Lydiard T., 1815, comm, W, Wr, P3/1815/7
Wm., baker, Swindon, 1816, comm, ren, W, Wr, P3/1816/42
Dorell *see* Dorrill
Dorman, Eliz., widow, Malm., 1819, W, Wr, P3/1819/24
My., sp., Hurst, Berks., 1625, I, NW, P5/1625/24, P5/10Reg/249B
Richd., cutter, Malm., 1721, I, W, P3/D/298
Richd., maltster and capital burgess, Malm., 1789, W, P3/D/452
Richd., silversmith, Malm., 1799, W, P3/D/464
Richd., Malm., 1823, AB, comm, Wr, P1/1823/45
Thos., sen., Clack, Lyneham, 1785, AB, P3/D/447
Wm., sen., yeo., E. Hanney, W. Hanney, Berks., 1756, AB, W, P1/D/383, P1/11Reg/263B
Dormer, Jn., gent., Chute, 1620, AB, P7/14
Wm., yeo., E. Hanney, W. Hanney, Berks., 1792, W, P1/D/438, P1/14Reg/435
Dorney, Edwd., feltmaker, Hurst, Berks., 1693, W, P5/1693/18
Dornford *see* Durnford
Dorrill *see* Durrell
Dorrington, Jn., Warm., 1543, ren, W (NEP), P2/1Reg/44A
Jn., gent., Collingbourne K., 1619, comm, I, W, P3/D/41
Wm., Collingbourne K., 1609, W, P3/D/13
Dorset, Jn., innholder, Halstock, Dorset, 1724, comm, I, W, P16/230
Dorsetar *see* Dorchester
Dorvill, Martha, widow, Sal., 1712, AB, P4/1712/18
Darville, Susanna, sp., Sal. St Thos., 1749, W, P4/1749/2
Dory, Geo., shear grinder, Bradford A., 1763, AB, ren, P1/D/398
Jn., common brewer, Bradford A., 1772, W, P2/D/656
Dossell, Jn., innholder and victualler, Milford, Sal. St Martin, 1775, W, P4/1775/16
Doswell, Jn., Warm., 1816, AB, P2/1816/34
Dassell, Thos., merchant, Lyme R., Dorset, 1627, AB, I, P5/1627/12, P5/11Reg/7C
Thos., sen., blacksmith, Winterbourne D., 1688, AB, I, P7/69
Thos., yeo., Winterbourne D., 1721, I, W, P7/116
Dotchin, Richd., woollen draper, Abingdon, Berks., 1668, AB, comm, I, P1/D/124
Dotheridge, Jn., jun., Wokm., Berks., 1668, AB, I, P5/1668/25
Jn., labourer, Wokm., Berks., 1741, AB, comm, ren, Wr, P5/1741/6
Dotrell, Agnes, widow, Bere R., Dorset, 1615, W, P5/1615/10, P5/9Reg/154A
Doublell, Nich., currier, Sal. St Thos., 1614, AB, I, W, P4/1614/1
Douce *see* Dowse
Doughty, Douty, Abednego, weaver, Newbury, Berks., 1747, I, W, P1/D/360, P1/10Reg/119
Alice, widow, Wylye, [1680], I, W, P2/D/326
Eliz., widow, Fisherton D., 1618, I, W, P2/D/116
Eliz., widow, Steeple L., 1853, AB, I, note, Wr, P2/1853/31
Douty, Harriet, widow, Wilton, 1856, AB, aff, D, W, Wr, P2/1856/9
Doufty, Jas., Sal., 1829, AB, Wr, P1/1829/155
Dowty, Jane, S. Newton, 1772, W, P2/D/661
Joel, vicar, Fisherton D., [1613], W (NEP), P2/8Reg/195
Joel, Fisherton D., [1647], I, P2/D/241

Douty, Joel, jun., Dinton, 1828-29, AB, P2/1828/66, P2/1829/10
Jn., Speenhamland, Berks., 1711, AB, comm, I, P1/D/244
Dowty, Jn., sen., labourer, Alderbury, 1835, valuation (2), W, Wr, P26/1415
Jn., Sal., 1840, AB, Wr, P4/1840/6
Peter, weaver, Sal., 1771, AB, W, P4/1771/11
Wm., Fisherton D., 1787, AB, P2/D/701
Dowty, Wm., Woodford, 1810, AB, P13/6/5
Douty, Wm., collar and harnessmaker, Dinton, 1837, W, Wr, P2/1837/54
Douglas, Jas., farrier, Sal., 1830, W, P4/1830/16
Jn., blacksmith, Hurst, Berks., 1731, I, W, P5/1731/23
Wm., Enmore Grn, Motc., Dorset, 1711, AB, ren, P19/95
Wm., wheelwright, Wokm., Berks., 1809, W, Wr, P5/1809/26
Douling *see* Doling
Dounam *see* Dunham
Douphrate, Jonathan, clerk and bach., W. Dean, 1852, AB, Wr, P2/1852/63
Douty *see* Doughty
Dove, Alice, widow, Teffont, 1557, W, P2/3Reg/28B
Alice, widow, Fovant, 1664, I, W, P1/D/109
Ann, widow, Newbury, Berks., 1738, W, P1/D/325, P1/8Reg/292A
Ann, widow, Downton, 1798, W, P1/D/449, P1/15Reg/151
Dan., gent., Hungerford, Berks., 1698, comm, W, P5/1698/24
Dan., Shalbourne, 1729, W, P23/463
Eliz., wife of Morgan, Gillingham, Dorset, 1732, W, P27/1/310
Hannah, widow, Sal. The Close, 1794, W, P5/1794/8, P5/18Reg/207
Hy., Pythouse, Tisb., 1689, AB, comm, P2/D/379
Hy., sen., cordw., Hamptworth, Downton, 1703, I, W, P2/D/432
Humphrey, yeo., Fovant, 1628, I, P2/D/159
Jas., husb., Fovant, 1638, AB, I, P2/D/202
Jn., husb., Fovant, 1570, W, P2/5Reg/82B
Jn., husb., Teffont E., 1576, I, W, P2/D/15, P2/5Reg/265A
Jn., Chr. M., 1633, AB, I, T, P1/D/64
Mgt., widow, Chr. M. & Wrou., 1636, I, W, P3/D/90
My., sp., Sal. The Close, 1789, W, P5/1789/5, P5/18Reg/126
Peter, gent., Pythouse, Tisb. & Milford, 1682, AB, I (very detailed, ref. to brick kiln), P2/D/337
Richd., cordw., Downton, 1724, W, P2/D/520
Thos., Teffont M., 1548, W, P2/2Reg/56B
Wm., Chr. M., 1602, I, W (NEP), P1/D/12
Doverd, Jn., yeo., Yarnfield, Maiden B., Somerset, 1741, W, P2/D/580
Doverdale, Thos., clerk and rector, Castle Eaton, 1696, AB, P1/D/192
Dovey, Dan., Eddington, Hungerford, Berks., 1851, AB, O, Wr, P5/1851/8
Edwd., Salterton, Durnford, 1597, AB, I, W, P5/1597/28, 35, P5/6Reg/162A
Francis, butcher, Kington L., 1708, comm, W, P1/D/229
Jane, widow, Biddestone St Nich., 1756, I, W, P1/D/384, P1/11Reg/316
Jn., yeo., Hartham, Corsham, 1836, W, Wr, P3/1836/40
My., widow, Chr. M., 1677, comm, I, W, P3/D/167
Richd., butcher, Chr. M., 1676, AB, a/c, comm, I, P3/D/163
Richd., Chr. M., 1733, W, P3/D/333
Walter, Gt. Bedwyn, 1563, AB, P5/1Reg/14B
Wm., butcher, Chr. M., 1684, AB, comm, I, P3/D/195
Wm., druggetmaker, Kington L., 1719, I, W, P3/D/291
Dowce *see* Dowse
Dowch *see* Dutch
Dowdall, Alice, widow, Longbridge D., 1631, I, W, P1/D/58
Dowdell, Andrew, yeo., Over C., Dorset, 1679, AB, I, W, P5/1679/21
Dowdell, Andrew, yeo., Over C., Dorset, 1751, W, P5/1751/10
Augustine, tailor, Heytes., 1635, AB, I, NW, P5/1635/35, P5/12Reg/203A
Cath., widow, Heytes., 1640, AB, I, W, P5/1640/14, P5/13Reg/260A
Harry, Mkt. L., 1575, W, P2/D/10, P2/5Reg/241D
Jn., husb., Longbridge D., 1609, I, W, P2/D/80, P2/8Reg/55A
Jn., tailor, Over C., Dorset, 1637, I, W, P5/1637/9, P5/13Reg/46C

Joshua, yeo., Over C., Dorset, 1696, I, W, P5/1696/14
Joshua, Over C., Dorset, 1724, AB, P5/1724/24
Dowdell, Martha, sp., Codf. St P., 1848, W, Wr, P2/1848/41
Matthew, sen., yeo., Over C., Dorset, 1691, I, W, P5/1691/20
Richd., tailor, Stockton, 1633, I, T, W, P2/D/177
Dowden *see* Dowding
Dowdeswell, Thos., yeo., Poulton, 1716, W, P1/D/262, P1/6Reg/66A
Dowding, Agnes, widow, Wedh., Urchf., 1559, W, P2/3Reg/177C
Ann, widow, Bratton, Westb., 1686, I, W, P25/1686/2
Ann, widow, Trowb., 1772, AB, comm, P1/D/413
Dowden, Ann, sp., Roke Farm, Bere R., Dorset, 1847, W, Wr, P5/1847/18
Dowden, Caroline, sp., Roke Farm, Bere R., Dorset, 1847, AB, Wr, P5/1847/21
Chris., husb., Mere, 1630, I, W, P5/1629/14, P5/11Reg/35A
Dowden, Chris., Mere, 1719, AB, P5/1719/24
Dowden, Chris., yeo., Littleton P., 1736-37, W, P1/D/321, P1/8Reg/174
Chris., sen., linen weaver, Mere, 1787, W, P5/1787/6, P5/18Reg/87B
Eliz., widow, Stanton St Q., 1778, W, P3/D/430
Eliz., wife of Wm. (*also* since decd), Gillingham, Dorset, 1790, AB, P27/1/540
Geo., yeo., Bourton, Gillingham, Dorset, 1806, W, P27/1/587
Geo., bach., Maiden B., 1851, AB, O, Wr, P1/1851/11
Hannibal, Mere, 1633, AB, I, P5/1633/14, P5/12Reg/146D
Jas., husb., Urchf., [1633], I, W, P2/D/175
Jas., innholder, Mere, 1840, AB, comm, ren, W, Wr, P5/1840/2
Jn., Wedh., Urchf., [1557], W, P2/3Reg/24A
Jn., husb., Wedh., Urchf., 1588, AB, W, P2/7Reg/128B
Dowden, Jn., Horningsham, 1592, I, W, P5/1592/20, P5/6Reg/3A
Jn., husb., Littleton P., 1601, I, W, P1/D/10
Jn., victualler and grazier, Gillingham, Dorset, 1784, W (decorative pen-work), P27/1/519, P27/3Reg/235
Jn., Mere, 1848, D, O, W, Wr, P5/1848/5
Dowden, My., widow, W. Lavington, 1747, W, P1/D/362, P1/10Reg/192
Maud, Urchf., 1616, a/c, P2/D/739
Richd., mason, Tisb., 1615, I, W, P2/D/106
Dowden, Richd., freemason, Keevil, 1638, I, W, P1/D/81
Robt., W. Knoyle, 1581, T (children: Jn. & Jane D.), W, P2/D/24, P2/6Reg/37B
Sam., clothier, Westb., 1856, declaration, O, W, Wr, P25/1856/1
Dowden, Sarah, widow, Roke Farm, Bere R., Dorset, 1847, note, W (& cod), Wr, P5/1847/19
Dewden, Thos., Bere R., Dorset, 1624, AB, a/c, P5/1624/11
Thos., yeo., Gillingham, Dorset, 1730-32, AB, comm, I, W, P27/1/307, 318
Wm., Tisb., 1616, AB, I, T, P2/D/112, P2/8Reg/315A
Dowden, Wm., sen., yeo., W. Lavington, 1670, comm, W, P1/D/127
Wm., labourer, Gillingham, Dorset, 1790, W, P27/1/539, P27/3Reg/270
Wm., grocer, Sal., 1853, D (2), W, Wr, P4/1853/16
Dowdney, Agnes, sp., Uffc., Devon, 1642-47, I, W (d.1642, proved 1647), P20/1/38
Ann, widow, Uffc., Devon, [1708], W (NEP), P20/1/164
Arthur, sen., tailor, Uffc., Devon, 1688, AB, I, P5/1688/27
Baptist, husb., Uffc., Devon, 1690, I, W, P20/1/119
Bartholemew, Uffc., Devon, 1647, AB, I, P20/1/33
Charity, widow, Uffc., Devon, 1625, AB, P5/1624/12
Denise, widow, Uffc., Devon, 1635, I, W, P5/1635/33, P5/12Reg/215
Eliz., widow, Uffc., Devon, 1551, W, P20/Reg/48
Dewdney, Eliz., widow, Mere, 1840, W, Wr, P5/1840/9
Ellen, widow, Uffc., Devon, 1575-76, I, W, P5/1575/14, P5/3Reg/74A
Francis, yeo., Uffc., Devon, 1673, AB (2), I, ren (2), P20/1/75
Jas., husb., Uffc., Devon, 1713, W, P5/1713/25, P5/15Reg/376B
Jane, widow, Uffc., Devon, 1606, I, W, P5/1606/15, P5/8Reg/65B
Joan, sp., Uffc., Devon, 1678, AB, I, P20/1/89
Joan, sp., Uffc., Devon, 1692, I, W, P5/1692/24
Jn., sen., husb., Foxell, Uffc., Devon, 1545, W, P20/Reg/30-31
Jn., Uffc., Devon, 1573, AB, P5/3Reg/21E
Jn., Southill *or* Sowell, Uffc., Devon, 1593, AB, I, W, P5/1592/22, P5/6Reg/15A

Jn., yeo., Uffc., Devon, 1662, I, NW, P5/1662/36
Jn., Uffc., Devon, 1727, AB, P20/1/183
Jn., husb., Uffc., Devon, 1759, W, P20/1/234
Jn., yeo., Gillingham, Dorset, 1789, W, P27/1/533, P27/3Reg/260
Mgt., widow, Uffc., Devon, 1662, I, W, P5/1662/35
Nich., Southill, Uffc., Devon, 1613, AB, I, P5/1613/21, P5/9Reg/79C
Nich., Foxell, Uffc., Devon, 1647, AB, I, P20/1/35
Robt., sen., Uffc., Devon, 1552, W, P20/Reg/51B
Dowell *see* Dowle
Dowers, Jas., sen., husb., Ashton K., 1727, W, P3/D/320
Jas., clothier's servant/maltster, Sal., 1752, AB, D, NW, P4/1752/9
Dawers *or* Dowers alias Brewer, Richd., husb. *or* yeo., Gomeldon, Idmiston, 1633, I, W (made 1625 proved 1633), P2/D/174, P2/9Reg/2
Ruth, widow, Pewsey, 1839, AB, comm, Wr, P1/1839/13
Wm., labourer, Chirton, 1839, comm, W, Wr, P1/1839/12
see also Brewer alias D.
Dowes *see* Daw
Dowland, Edwd., Gillingham, Dorset, 1669, AB, P27/1/36
Jn., clerk, Chitterne St My., 1735, comm, W, P2/D/560
Jn., yeo., Melk. Forest, 1821, comm, W, Wr, P2/1821/7
Robt., gent., Pott., 1851, O, W, Wr, P1/1851/75
Thos., shopkeeper, Bere R., Dorset, 1826, I, W (NEP), P5/1826/19
Wm., Hamp, Gillingham, Dorset, 1581, W, P27/2Reg/5B
Dowle, Alexander, baker, Hindon, [1664], I, W, P2/D/253
Alexander, Chicklade, 1716, comm, NW, P1/D/261, P1/6Reg/69A
Edith, Hindon, 1588, AB, T, W, P2/D/30, P2/7Reg/123B
Edith, widow, Chicklade, 1717, W, P2/D/493
Edwd., Grimstone, Stratton, Dorset, 1784, AB, P5/1784/3, P5/17Reg/258A
Hy., Chicklade, [1691], I, W, P2/D/387
Hy., Chicklade, 1740, AB, P2/D/577
Dowles, Jas., victualler, Hindon, 1748, W, P2/D/608
My., widow, Wingfield, [1617], I, W, P2/D/114
Richd., Leigh, Yetm., Dorset, 1567, W, P5/2Reg/20B
Robt., husb., Oborne, Dorset, 1588, I, W, P5/1588/14, P5/5Reg/10D
Dowell, Sarah, widow, Southwick, N. Bradley, 1766, W, P2/D/647
Wm., innholder, Sal., 1636, I, W, P4/1636/4
Wm., Binfield, Berks., 1747, W, P1/D/363, P1/10Reg/104
see also Dewell
Dowley *see* Dawley
Dowling, Alice, Ogbourne St A., 1757, AB, P5/1757/8
Ann, widow, Gt. Bedwyn, 1747, W, P21/9/57
Dawling, Chris., tailor, Sal., 1662, AB, P4/1661/17
Doling, Edwd., gent., Stop, Fonthill G., 1671-87, AB, I, W, P2/D/280, 328, 372
Edwd., Axford, Rams., 1694, AB, I, P5/1694/37
Eliz., widow, Sal., 1836, AB, Wr, P4/1836/7
Dawling, Grace, Yarmouth, Isle of Wight (leaving effects at Fittleton), 1845, AB, Wr, P1/1845/47
Hy., Durrington, 1772, AB, P2/D/658
Dowlin, Jn., tailor, Reading, Berks., 1723, W, P1/D/275, P1/7Reg/10A
Dolen, Jn., Gt. Durnford, 1730, W, P9/49
Mgt., widow and innholder, Chipp., 1803, W, P3/1803/67
Martha, widow, Durrington, 1786, W, P2/D/697
Robt., Sherston, 1612, AB, I, W (2 - 1 a copy, attached to the I), P3/D/23
Sam., Chipp., 1802, AB, P3/1802/58
Doling, Thos., Netherb., Dorset, 1608, W, P5/8Reg/134
Dolen, Thos., yeo., Pillempsay, Netherb., Dorset, 1712, I, W, P17/211
Doling, Walter, yeo. and husb., Southwick, N. Bradley, 1662, AB, I, P2/D/249
Doling, Walter, yeo., Pillempsay, Netherb., Dorset, 1680, I, W, P17/287
Wm., husb., Luckington, 1623, I, W, P3/D/58
Dollin, Wm., husb., Binfield, Berks., 1631, I, W, P1/D/57
Douling *or* Dawling, Wm., yeo., Gt. Durnford, 1671-75, AB, I, P9/12, P9/127

Wm., Pillempsay, Netherb., Dorset, 1682, AB, I, P17/249
Dolling, Wm., Motc., Dorset, 1721, AB, P27/1/251
Wm., yeo., Durrington, 1758, W, P2/D/624
Wm., Durrington, 1784, AB, P2/D/691
Wm., farmer, Buckland, Berks., 1826, comm, W, Wr, P1/1826/24
Wm., yeo., Buckland Marsh Farm, Berks., 1830, comm, W, Wr, P1/1830/2
Down, (Colonel) *see* Wm. Bugden
Alice, widow, Burcombe, 1596, AB, I, NW, P2/D/46
Chas., yeo., Trent & Sherb., Dorset, 1798, W, P5/1798/7, P5/18Reg/265A
Eliz., widow, Chisenbury, Enford, 1626, AB, I, P2/D/150
Eliz., widow, Mere, 1750, W, P5/1750/11
Eliz., sp., Devizes, 1767, AB, P1/D/399
Eliz., widow, Devizes, 1775, W, P1/D/417, P1/13Reg/59B
Eliz., widow, Mere, 1824, W, Wr, P5/1824/25
Downes, Giles, yeo., N. Tidworth, 1721, I, W, P2/D/503
Jas., Orcheston, 1547, W, P2/2Reg/26
Downes, Jas., husb., Gt. Amesb., 1686, NW, P2/D/366
Jas., hatter, Warm., 1809, AB, W, Wr, P2/1809/35, 75
Jas., widower, Mere, 1853, AB, aff, O, Wr, P5/1853/21
Downes, Jas. Francis Edwd., Avill's Farm, Corsham, 1744, AB, P1/D/351
Jeremy, husb., S. Burcombe, 1639, AB, comm, I, P2/D/206
Joan, widow, Shrewton, 1548, W, P2/2Reg/53B
Joan, widow, W. Hatch, Tisb., 1667, I, W, P2/D/262
Jn., Orcheston St My., 1559, W, P2/3Reg/155C
Jn., Smallbrook, Warm., 1601, I, W, P30/49
Jn., S. Newton, 1605, AB, I, P2/D/74
Jn., yeo., Hatch, Tisb., 1724?, W, P2/D/521
Downes, Jn., maltster, Speenhamland, Berks., 1725-26, comm, W, P1/D/282, P1/7Reg/73
Downes, Jn., maltster, Sal., 1780, W, P4/1780/6
Jn., Sherb., Dorset, 1801, AB, P5/1801/19, P5/18Reg/323A
Jonas, sen., innkeeper, Sherb., Dorset, 1844, comm, W, Wr, P5/1844/11
Jonathan, Whitep., 1740, AB, P2/D/576
Jos., yeo., Burcombe, 1826, W, Wr, P2/1826/8
Margery, Wilton, 1685, AB, I, P2/D/360
My., widow, Mere, 1743, W, Wr, P5/1743/24
Michael, edge toolmaker, Mere, 1684, I, W, P5/1683/19
Rachel, widow, Gillingham, Dorset, 1775, AB, P27/1/495, P27/3Reg/197A
Richd., priest, Baverstock, 1551, institution to rectory. On death of Onion alias Evan, P2/2Reg/136B
Richd., yeo., Littlecott, Enford, 1693, I, W, P2/D/396
Richd., blacksmith, Newell Hill, Sherb., Dorset, 1856, aff, I, note, W, Wr, P5/1856/8
Robt., N. Tidworth, 1590, I, T, P2/D/736
Robt., white clothier, Sherb., Dorset (late of Milborne Port, Somerset), 1748, W, Wr, P5/1748/9
Sam., Uffc., Devon, 1693, AB, P20/1/123
Sam., gent., Trowb., 1715, AB, I, ren, W, P1/D/257, P1/5Reg/487
Thos., yeo., Sutton V., 1545, W (NEP), P2/1Reg/78B
Thos., husb., Maddington, 1558, W, P2/3Reg/130B
Thos., Fifield, Enford, 1575, W, P2/5Reg/219B
Thos., husb., S. Burcombe, 1593, I, T, W, P2/D/43
Thos., husb., Fifield, Enford, 1626, I, W, P2/D/146
Thos., husb., Netheravon, [1626], I, W, P12/51
Thos., yeo., Gillingham, Dorset, 1775, AB, W, P27/1/496, P27/3Reg/195B
Thos., clothier and woolstapler, Corsley, 1817, W, Wr, P1/1817/43
Wm., husb., Haydon, Dorset, 1670, AB, comm, NW, P5/1670/8
Wm., Corsley, 1721, AB, P2/D/504
Wm., baker, Sherb., Dorset, 1770, comm, W, P5/1770/13, P5/17Reg/5A
Wm., innkeeper, Warm., 1835, comm, W, Wr, P1/1835/68
Wm. Pitman, post horse master, Warm., 1854, aff, ren, W, Wr, P2/1854/34
see also Buckland alias D.; Wilshere alias D.
Downbill, Nich., husb., Crickl. St S., [1619], I, NW (NEP), P3/D/42
Downer, Humphrey, Coombe B., 1663, AB, I, P5/1663/22

Jn., yeo., Rams., 1580, AB, P5/1579/27, P5/3Reg/147E
Mark, Charlton, Downton, 1840, W, Wr, P2/1840/42
Phoebe, Woodgreen, Hants, 1833, AB, Wr, P2/1833/20
Wm., blacksmith, Odstock, 1638, I, W, P2/D/201
see also Carpenter alias D.
Downes *see* Down
Downey, Geo., yeo., Nonsuch Farm, Bromham, 1844, O, W, Wr, P3/1844/52
Downham, Ambrose, husb., E. Stowell, Wilcot, 1685, W, P3/D/198
Eliz., widow, Biddestone St Nich., 1741, comm, W, P3/D/353
Geo., husb., Oare, Wilcot, 1684, I, W, P3/D/196
Jn., tailor, Winterbourne M., 1735, W, P3/D/342
Luke, yeo., Wilcot, 1631, I, NW, P3/D/84
Thos., maltster, Greenham, Thatcham, Berks., 1783, W, P1/D/429, P1/13Reg/475B
Downing, Alice, widow, Whitep., 1669, I, W, P2/D/270
Jn., hair weaver, Hamptworth, Downton, 1646, AB, I, P2/D/237
Wm., sen., yeo., Chipp., 1835, W, P3/1835/35
Downton, Aldhelm, Yatton K., 1617, I, W, P3/D/33
Christian, widow, Winterbourne S., 1645, I, W, P2/D/234
Chris., labourer, Sherston, 1733, W, P3/D/335
Geo., yeo., Winterbourne S., 1609, AB, I, W, P2/D/84, P2/8Reg/45B
Geo., sen., yeo., Winterbourne S., 1676, W, P2/D/302
Geo., labourer, Winterbourne S., 1733, I, W, P2/D/551
Isaac, draper, Wilton, 1856, aff, W, Wr, P2/1856/39
Joan, widow, Winterbourne S., 1589, AB, I, W, P2/D/33
Joan, widow, Enmore Grn, Motc., Dorset, [1703], W, P19/89
Jn., sen., Winterbourne S., 1577, I, W, P2/D/16, P2/5Reg/279B
Jn., Thornford, Dorset, 1590, AB, I, W, P5/1590/19, P5/5Reg/83C
Jn., clerk, Beer Hackett, Dorset, 1626, comm, I, W, P5/1626/14, P5/10Reg/195B
Jn., Thornford, Dorset, 1638, AB (re both Jn. D., & Agnes his wife), comm, L, P5/1638/31, P5/13Reg/103B
Jn., yeo., Winterbourne S., 1684-86, AB, comm, I, W, P2/D/353, 369
Jn., yeo., Leigh, Yetm., Dorset, 1686, AB, ren, P19/52
Jn., husb., Winterbourne S., 1744, W, P2/D/590
Jn., labourer, Winterbourne S., 1772, W, P2/D/659
Richd., yeo., Winterbourne S., 1770, W, P2/D/653
Richd., yeo., Winterbourne S., 1801, W, Wr, P1/1801/134, P1/15Reg/359
Ruth, widow, Winterbourne S., 1713, AB, P2/D/478
Sam., husb., Ford, Laverstock, 1698, W, P2/D/413
Sam., husb., Winterbourne S., 1748, a/c, I, note of debt, receipt, W, P2/D/602
Thos., husb., Thornford, Dorset, 1614, I, W, P5/1614/21, P5/9Reg/115B
Thos., Maddington, 1638, I, W, P2/D/199
Thos., sen., yeo., Chetnole, Yetm., Dorset, 1665, I, W, P5/1665/27
Thos., gent., Chetnole, Yetm., Dorset, 1696, comm, W, P19/73
Thos., sen., Ford, Laverstock, 1735, AB, P1/D/318
Thos., yeo., Leigh, Yetm., Dorset, 1815, W, Wr, P5/1815/7
Wm., sen., husb., Leigh, Yetm., Dorset, 1595, AB, I, W, P5/1595/21, P5/6Reg/104
Wm., Leigh, Yetm., Dorset, 1665, AB, I, P5/1665/28
Dowse, Agnes, widow, Marten, Grafton, 1582-88, I, W, P5/1588/16, P5/4Reg/56A
Alice, Lt. Bedwyn, 1590, AB, I, P5/1590/21, P5/5Reg/93B
Alice, widow, Wingfield, 1620, AB, I, NW, P2/D/126
Alice, widow, Urchf., 1724, I, W, P2/D/522
Ann, Easterton, Mkt. L., 1826, AB, Wr, P1/1826/112
Ann, widow, Easterton, Mkt. L., 1835, O, W, Wr, P1/1835/25
Eliz., E. Grimstead, W. Dean, 1735, AB, P2/D/561
Eliz., widow, Bulk., Keevil, 1787, W, P2/D/699
Geo., mealman, Worton, Pott., 1855, aff, D, O, W, Wr, P1/1855/59
Hy., Devizes, 1708, AB, P1/D/230
Jas., Easterton, Mkt. L., 1831, AB, O, Wr, P2/1831/53
Joan, widow, Easterton, Mkt. L., 1678, I, W, P2/D/316
Jn., yeo., Marten, Grafton, 1575, I, W, P5/1574/6, P5/3Reg/55C
Jn., yeo. and husb., Easterton, Mkt. L., 1662, I, W, P2/D/250

Dowce, Jn., sen., husb. and yeo., N. Heath, Chieveley, Berks., 1674, I, W, P1/D/138
Jn., yeo., Easterton, Mkt. L., 1716, W, P2/D/489
Jn., Marston, Pott., 1768, AB, P1/D/401
Jn., victualler, Hampstead Marshall, Berks., 1779, W, P1/D/423, P1/13Reg/253
Jn., sen., yeo., Easterton, Mkt. L., 1817, W, Wr, P1/1817/11
Jn., victualler, Easterton, Mkt. L., 1826, W, Wr, P2/1826/11
Jn., publican, Lydeway, Urchf., 1856, aff, W, Wr, P2/1856/69
Leonard, Trowb., 1609, AB (in minority of Agnes D.), I (2), T, P2/D/89, P2/8Reg/66A
Lucy, widow, Sal., 1709, AB, P4/1709/20
My., widow, Longstreet, Enford, 1600, I, W, P2/D/63
My., widow, Gt. Cheverell, 1800, W, Wr, P2/1800/94
Merrell, widow, Easterton, Mkt. L., 1824, W, Wr, P2/1824/81
Michael, yeo., E. Grimstead, W. Dean, 1682, I, W, P2/D/341
Nich., Stratford sub C., 1709, AB, P4/1709/17
Rachel, wife, Bps. C., 1730, AB, P24/821
Richd., gent., Highw., 1612, AB, comm, W, P5/1611/10
Richd., Orcheston St My., 1624, I, T, P2/D/138
Richd., sen., yeo., Eastcott, Urchf., 1712, W, P2/D/474
Richd., gent., Fisherton A., 1758, AB, ren, W, P2/D/628
Douce, Robt., husb., Haxton, Fittleton, 1630, comm, W, P2/D/162, P2/9Reg/121
Robt., W. Dean, 1635, AB, a/c - a/c is for Robt. only, admin. for Robt. & Sibyl D., P2/D/180
Robt., sen., E. Grimstead, W. Dean, 1732, W, P1/D/309, P1/7Reg/536A
Robt., sen., yeo., Gt. Cheverell, 1748, I, W, P2/D/606
Robt., E. Grimstead, W. Dean, 1755, AB, P2/D/620
Robt., Gt. Cheverell, 1790, AB, P2/D/710
Robt., carp., Devizes, 1816, W, Wr, P1/1816/18
Robt., gardener, Easterton, Mkt. L., 1835, W, P1/1835/115
Robt., gent., Mkt. L., 1855, aff, O, W, Wr, P2/1855/2
Robt., Enford, 1553-58, AB, W, P2/2Reg/176B, P2/3Reg/132B
Sibyl, W. Dean, 1635, AB, P2/9Reg/105C
Thos., husb., Longstreet, Enford, 1597, AB, I, W, P2/D/53
Thos., jun., husb., Enford, 1600, AB (My. & Thos. D.), I, W, P2/D/65
Thos., husb., Shalbourne, Berks., 1605, I, W (NEP), P30/55
Thos., husb., Wexcombe, Grafton, 1628, I, W, P5/1628/35, P5/11Reg/100C
Thos., yeo., Chilton F., 1670, AB, I, P3/D/138
Thos., victualler, Newbury, Berks., 1747, AB, I, P1/D/361
Thos., yeo., Easterton, Mkt. L., 1815, W, Wr, P2/1815/81
Thos., yeo., Mkt. L., 1837, O, ren, W, Wr, P2/1837/8
Thos., woolcomber, Urchf., 1666-67, AB, comm, I, P2/D/261
Wm., sen., Urchf., 1615, I, W, P2/D/107, P2/8Reg/278B
Wm., Marl. St My., 1631, I (damaged), P1/D/59
Wm., Wick, Bps. C., 1667, AB, comm, I (detailed), P24/355
Douce, Wm., yeo., Braydon Forest, Crickl. St S., 1691, I, NW, P3/D/224
Wm., yeo., Gt. Cheverell, 1806, W, P2/1806/79
Dowsell, Jn. Brain, yeo., Chelworth, Crickl. St S., 1843, comm, W, Wr, P3/1843/41
Dowswell, My., widow, Purton, 1748, AB, W, P3/D/372
Dowty *see* Doughty
Drake, Andrew, joiner, Lyme R., Dorset, 1721, AB, I, P16/225
Dan., weaver, Rowde, 1741, W, P3/D/354
Eliz., widow, Chipp., 1711, W, P1/D/245, P1/5Reg/75
Francis, clerk, Englefield, Berks., 1741-45, AB, comm, W (2 - 1 copy), P1/D/338, P1/9Reg/127, P1/10Reg/4A
Francis, victualler, *The Cross Keys Inn*, Rowde, 1766, W, P3/D/405
Fulk, clerk and parson, Fifield Bavant, 1606, AB, P1/D/18
Jas., broad weaver, Pewsham Forest, 1682, I, W, P3/D/188
Jn., Shrewton, 1559, W, P2/3Reg/162D
Lydia, widow, Rowde, 1740, W, P3/D/351
Nathaniel, sen., tailor, Rowde, 1714, W, P3/D/278
Nathaniel, tailor, Rowde, 1727, W, P3/D/321
Nathaniel, innholder, Rowde, 1773, W, P3/D/424
Richd., yeo., W. Dean, 1792, W, P2/D/714

Simon, husb., Ludg., 1625, I, W, P1/D/47
Thos., minor, Sal., 1695, T. No decd named, P4/1695/10
Wm., shoemaker, Chipp., 1605, I, NW, P3/D/6
Draper, Alice, Broad H., 1629, I, W, P3/D/75
Ambrose, yeo., Mkt. L., 1743-55, AB, W, P2/D/588
Andrew, glover, Melk., 1713, I, W, P2/D/476
Benj., yeo., Tilehurst, Berks., 1832, W, Wr, P1/1832/114
Betty, widow, Marl., 1827, comm, W, Wr, P1/1827/24
Chris., [yeo.], no abode stated, [1642], copy I (very detailed), P2/D/228
Dan., carp., Mkt. L., 1815, W, Wr, P2/1815/40
David, shoemaker, Urchf., 1857, aff, O, W, Wr, P2/1857/51
Edwd., chandler, Maiden B., 1636, comm, I, W, P2/D/191
Edwd., Longbridge D., 1699, AB, P2/D/417
Edwd., Studley, Lydiard T., 1708, AB, I, P1/D/231
Eliz., widow, Netheravon, 1733, AB, I, P5/1733/20
Eliz., widow, Marl., 1845, AB, O, Wr, P1/1845/88
Gabriel, Maiden B., 1699, AB, P2/D/421
Geo., sen., wheelwright, Purley & Pangbourne, Berks., 1664, I, W, P1/D/110
Dreaper, Geo., [servant], Box, 1715, W, P3/D/281
Geo., blacksmith, Buckland, Berks., 1826, W, Wr, P1/1826/75
Gifford, yeo., Netheravon, 1841, W, Wr, P12/228
Hannah, singlewoman, Netheravon, 1778, W, P12/195
Jas., Melk., 1640, I, W, P2/D/213
Jas., sen., broad weaver, Melk., 1673, I, W (damaged), P2/D/291
Jas., plumber, glazier and innholder, Theale, Tilehurst, Berks., 1783, W, P1/D/430, P1/13Reg/463
Jn., husb., Wrou., 1621, I, W, P3/D/48
Jn., yeo., Cotmarsh, Broad H., 1668, I, W, P3/D/131
Jn., sen., glover, Horningsham, 1672, I, W, P5/1672/7-8
Jn., Warm., 1719, AB, P2/D/502
Jn., yeo., Easterton, Mkt. L., 1766, W, P2/D/645
Jn., brickmaker, Urchf., 1774, W, P2/D/667
Jn., W. Lavington, 1810, AB, Wr, P1/1810/15
Jn., yeo., Gore Farm, Mkt. L., 1827, aff, O, W, Wr, P2/1827/58
Jos., keeper of Devizes Bridewell, Devizes, 1817, comm, W, Wr, P1/1817/37
Leonard, yeo., Easterton, Mkt. L., 1806, AB, P2/1806/16
My., sp., Maiden B., 1712, W, P2/D/472
My. Ann, Purton, 1841, AB, O, Wr, P3/1841/32
Miriam, singlewoman, Maiden B., 1749, W, P2/D/609
Philip, wheelwright, Sal., 1792, W, P4/1792/5
Richd., shepherd, The Weir, Broad H., [1619], I, W (on same sheet) (NEP), P3/D/43
Richd., Sal., 1629, I, W, P4/1628/16
Richd., sen., yeo. and husb., Longbridge D., 1670, I, W, P2/D/275
Richd., yeo., Studley, Lydiard T., 1672, AB, I, P3/D/148
Richd., Maiden B., 1679, I, W, P2/D/321
Richd., Fisherton A., 1704, I, W, P1/D/215
Robt., weaver, Melk., 1618, I, T, P2/D/121
Robt., Warm., 1774, AB, comm, P2/D/668
Sam., cardmaker, Warm., 1773, AB, ren, P2/D/665
Stephen, yeo., Easterton, Mkt. L., 1826, W, Wr, P2/1826/33
Stephen, innkeeper, Mkt. L., 1853, AB, O, ren, W, Wr, P2/1853/8
Thos., sen., broad weaver, Easterton, Mkt. L., [1681], I, W, P2/D/327
Thos., sen., cowkeeper, New Windsor, Berks., 1729, AB, W, P1/D/296, P1/7Reg/266
Thos., Easterton, Mkt. L., 1763, AB, P2/D/639
Thos., Lydiard M., 1827, AB (2), LA, Wr, P3/1827/69
Thos., widower, Easterton, Mkt. L., 1857, AB, aff, O, Wr, P2/1857/60
Walter, weaver, Melk., 1616, I, W, P2/D/109, P2/8Reg/328
Wm., sen., broad weaver, Easterton, Mkt. L., [1691], I, W, P2/D/384
Wm., innholder, Warm., 1798, W, P2/D/729
Drayton, Thos., yeo., Chards., Devon, 1815, W, Wr (2), P5/1815/25
Dreaper *see* Draper

Dredge, Betty, sp., Warm., 1821, AB, comm, W, Wr, P2/1821/24
Charlotte, widow, Boreham, Warm., 1856, aff, O, W, Wr, P2/1856/22
Chris., yeo., Corton, Boyton, 1803, W, P2/1803/4
Dan., Warm., 1793, AB, comm, P2/D/715
Edwd., tailor, Monkton D., 1810, W, P2/1810/34
Eliz., widow, S. Newton, 1857, AB, aff, Wr, P2/1857/28
Enos, Gt. Wishford, 1829, AB, Wr, P1/1829/39
Hy., bach., Horningsham, 1852, AB, Wr, P5/1852/15
Jas., Warm., 1735, AB, ren, P2/D/559
Jas., brewer and timber merchant, Horningsham, 1838, comm, W (& cod), Wr, P5/1838/12
Jane, widow, Warm., 1793, AB, comm, ren, W, P2/D/716
Jn., husb., Brixton D., 1564, I, W, P2/D/740, P2/4Reg/177C
Jn., yeo. and husb., Whitbourne, Corsley, [1621], I, W, P2/D/128
Jn., Longbridge D., 1636, I, P2/D/190
Jos., Horningsham, 1782, AB, P5/1782/9, P5/17Reg/237A
My., widow, Monkton D., 1819, AB, comm, Wr, P2/1819/16
Paul, husb., Newnham, Sutton V., 1603, I, P2/D/70
Richd., labourer, Brixton D., 1579, W, P2/5Reg/335A
Robt., yeo., Corsley, 1632, I, W, P2/D/169, P2/9Reg/115
Solomon, bach., Steeple L., 1856, AB, aff, Wr, P2/1856/28, 50
Thos., broad weaver, Sal., 1661, AB, P4/1661/8
Thos., shopkeeper, Gt. Wishford, 1803, W, P2/1803/1
Tristram, husb., Corton, Boyton, 1634, I, W, P1/D/67
Tristram, husb., Norton B., 1709, NW, P2/D/460
Wm., gent., S. Newton, 1823, W, Wr, P1/1823/135
Wm., innkeeper, Boreham, Warm., 1848, I (2), W, Wr, P1/1848/6
Dresser, Richd., carp., Sal., 1785, W, P4/1785/11
Drew, Anthony, Rowde, 1743, W, P3/D/362
Arney, Brinkw., 1790, W, Wr, P3/D/453
Avis, widow, Poulshot, 1697, I, W, P2/D/411
Benj., jun., gent., Baverstock, 1666-70, AB, a/c, comm, I, ren (badly damaged), P1/D/118, P2/D/273
Christian, Ogbourne St A., 1571, W, P5/2Reg/96C
Edwd., Fonthill G., 1737, AB, W, P2/D/570
Eliz., widow, Heddington, 1682, I, W, P3/D/189
Eliz., widow, Devizes St Jn., 1690, I, W, P1/D/173
Geo., gent., Brook, Bramshaw, Hants, 1631, AB, a/c, I, P24/261
Geo., yeo., Chelworth, Crickl. St S., 1825, W, Wr, P3/1825/75
Hy., Corsham, 1617, AB, a/c (mentions charges due for time he could not work), I, copy I, P29/D/5
Hy., gent., Poulshot, 1678, AB, a/c, I, P2/D/313
Hugh, Lyme R., Dorset, 1612, AB, I, P5/1612/17, P5/9Reg/64A
Isaac, sen., labourer, Bourton, Bps. C., 1776, W, P24/1134
Isaac, carp., Bourton, Bps. C., 1802, comm, W, Wr, P24/1229
Jas., tiler and plasterer, Castle C., 1822, W, Wr, P3/1822/28
Joan, husb., W. Dean, 1554, W, P2/2Reg/186B
Joan, Liddington, 1717, I, P30/56
Jn., sen., husb., W. Dean, 1578, AB, I, NW, P2/D/20
Jn., Whitep., 1589, AB, P2/D/32
Jn., Horton, Bps. C., 1683, AB, P24/763
Jn., labourer, Bps. C., 1696, W, P24/506
Jn., yeo., Kintbury, Berks., 1735, alleg, sentence, W, P1/D/319, P1/8Reg/125
Jn., N. Newnton, 1769, AB, P3/D/414
Jn., sen., miller, Horton, Bps. C., 1795, W, P24/1214
My., widow, Bere R., Dorset, 1588, W, P5/5Reg/20C
My., widow, Rowde, [1664], W (NEP), P3/D/122
My., [Devizes] (NBI), 1665, I, P1/D/113
Mildred, widow, Devizes, 1638, I, NW, P1/D/82
Nathaniel, grocer, Devizes, 1685, AB, I, P1/D/163
Nich., Sherston, 1569, W (NEP), P1/1Reg/106A
Nich., Sherston, 1622, AB, a/c, I, P3/D/53
Philip, husb., Idmiston, 1558, AB, W, P2/3Reg/98D

Richd., yeo. and husb., Preston, Dorset, 1597, AB, I, W, P5/1597/31, P5/6Reg/166B
Richd., cutler, Abingdon, Berks., 1744, W, P1/D/352, P1/9Reg/365B
Richd., Cothill, Marcham, Berks., 1817, W, Wr, P1/1817/28
Robt., Devizes St My., 1634, I, NW, P1/D/68
Robt., gent., Devizes, 1671, AB, comm, I, P1/D/134
Robt., woollen draper, Devizes, 1696, AB, I, P1/D/193
Robt., wheelwright, Melk., 1759, W, P1/D/388, P1/11Reg/463
Robt., Winterborne K., Dorset, 1762-63, W (not proved), P5/1762/10
Roger, husb., Sherston, 1622, I, W, P3/D/54
Thos., yeo., Sutton Poyntz, Dorset, 1579, AB, I, W, P5/1579/26, P5/3Reg/127A
Drew alias Hunt, Thos., Marl. St My., 1638, AB, P1/D/83
Thos., sen., shepherd, Horton, Bps. C., 1670, I, W, P24/396
Thos., yeo., Heddington, 1680, comm, W, P3/D/181
Thos., collarmaker, Twyford, Hurst, Berks., 1712, I, W, P5/1712/25, P5/15Reg/304B
Thos., carp., Seend, Melk., 1738, W, P1/D/326, P1/8Reg/360
Thos., Castle C., 1803, AB, P3/1803/57
Wm., [yeo.], Crockerton, Longbridge D., 1586, I, W, P2/D/28, P2/7Reg/38B
Wm., blacksmith, Easton Grey, 1631, I, W, P1/D/60
Wm., esquire, Cripps Farm, Yatesbury, 1708, AB (2), I (2), note, ren, W, P3/D/267
Wm., Long Newnton, 1729, AB, P1/D/297
see also Austin alias D.; Lewes alias D.
Drewett, Agnes, widow, Patney, 1603, I, W, P2/D/71
Ann, widow, Bratton, Westb., 1763, AB, W, P25/1763/2
Anthony, miller, Box, 1751, AB, comm, ren, W, P3/D/379
Anthony, Colerne, 1780, AB, P3/D/435
Anthony, baker and malster, Colerne, 1839, W, Wr, P3/1839/35
Drueatt, Benj., sen., yeo., Marlstone, Bucklebury, Berks., 1783, W, P1/D/431, P1/13Reg/479
Benj., yeo., Soley, Chilton F., 1825, W, Wr, P3/1825/70
Brian, husb., Patney, 1628, I, W, P1/D/52
Dan., Colerne, 1729, AB, P1/D/298
Edwd., Bradford A., 1624, AB, P2/D/140
Edwd., yeo., Patney, 1733, W, P2/D/548
Edwd., gent., Etchilhampton, 1775, W, P3/D/426
Edwd., Trowb., 1790, AB, P1/D/435
Edwd., yeo., Patney, 1790, W, P2/D/712
Eliz., sp., Berwick B., 1692, I, W, P5/1692/21
Eliz., widow, Marston, Pott., 1837, O, W, Wr. form. Eliz. May, sp., P1/1837/27
Geo., gent., Colerne, 1785, comm, W, P3/D/448
Geo., baker and maltster, Colerne, 1852, comm, D, W, Wr, P3/1852/7
Hy., tailor, Westb., 1749, AB, ren, P25/1749/3
Hy., Westb., 1763, AB (W missing), P25/1763/1
Isaac, bach., Box, 1751, AB, comm, P3/D/380
Jas., Edington, 1816, AB, comm, Wr, P2/1816/16
Jas., Tinh., Edington, 1833, AB, O, Wr, P2/1833/11
Jane, widow, Ashton Crofts, W. Ashton, Steeple A., 1779, W, P2/D/680
Jasper, wire drawer, Bradford A., 1681, AB, I, P2/D/336
Jesse, Hilp., 1848, AB, O, Wr, P2/1848/44
Joan, widow, Lt. Coxwell, Gt. Faringdon, Berks., 1588, I, W, P5/1588/12, P5/5Reg/16
Joan, widow, Patney, 1625, I, W, P2/D/144
Joan, widow, Bradford A., 1683, comm, I, NW, P2/D/344
Joan, Westb., 1747, AB, P25/1747/6
Jn., Patney, 1572, W, P2/5Reg/155A
Jn., fellmonger, Westb., 1681, AB, I (detailed), P25/1681/1
Jn., Patney, [1698?], note (dismisses need for probate, as goods worh less than £5), P1/D/196
Jn., cordw., Box, 1702, W, P3/D/254
Jn., shoemaker, Box, 1711, comm, W, P1/D/246, P1/5Reg/266
Jn., sen., fellmonger, Westb., 1721, req, W, I (detailed), P25/1721/9
Jn., sen., gent., Patney, 1765, W, P2/D/643
Jonathan, labourer, Tinh., Edington, 1849, D, W, Wr, P2/1849/1
Lydia, widow, Colerne, 1751, W, P3/D/381

Mgt., widow, Box, 1768, W, P3/D/412
Margery, widow, Patney, 1771, W, P3/D/419
My., Westb., 1738, AB, P25/1738/2
My., sp., Westb., 1802, AB, P25/1802/2
Peter, sen., clothier, Colerne, 1733, W, P3/D/336
Peter, Colerne, 1818, W, Wr, P3/1818/32
Philip, Widbrook, Bradford A., 1577, I, W, P2/D/17, P2/5Reg/291A
Richd., husb., Widbrook, Bradford A., 1587, I, T, W, P2/D/29, P2/7Reg/107B
Richd., labourer, Box, 1690, I, W, P3/D/221
Richd., tailor, Westb., 1731, W, P25/1731/1
Richd., labourer, Tinh., Edington, 1819, AB, W, Wr, P2/1819/71
Stephen, Tinh., Edington, 1600, T (children: My., Agnes, Alice, Eliz. D.), P2/D/60
Thos., Box, 1701, AB, Wr, P3/D/248
Thos., cordw., Crickl. St S., 1730, W, P3/D/328
Thos., cordw. *or* shoemaker, Box, 1734, I, W, P3/D/339
Walter, husb., Edington, 1553, I, W, P2/D/1, P2/2Reg/169B
Wm., yeo., Widbrook, Bradford A., 1625, I, W, P1/D/48
Wm., Tinh., Edington, 1637, AB, P2/D/196
Wm., sen., yeo., Widbrook, Bradford A., 1664, AB, comm, I, P1/D/111
Wm., Wrou., 1668, AB, comm, I, P3/D/132
Wm., yeo., Bratton, Westb., 1707, I, W, P25/1707/3
Wm., Box, 1729, AB, P3/D/325
Wm., joiner, Westb., 1747, AB, P25/1747/7
Wm., labourer, Tinh., Edington, 1800, W, P2/1800/42
Wm., gent., Colerne, 1813, W, Wr, P3/1813/63
Wm., sawyer, Trowb., 1834, AB, aff, O, ren, W, Wr, P1/1834/19
Wm., labourer, Tinh., Edington, 1840, W, Wr, P2/1840/25
Drie *see* Dry
Dring, Rawlins, master of arts, Sherb., Dorset, 1703, W, P5/1703/7
Drinkwater, Ann, widow, Semington, Steeple A., 1632, I, W, P2/D/171, P2/9Reg/111
Cath., Broughton G., 1737, W, P2/D/568
Eliz., widow, Melk., 1734, AB, P2/D/556
Geo., Semington, Steeple A., 1607, AB, I, note of admon, P2/D/79
Geo., maltster, Melk., 1750, AB, W, P2/D/613
Geo., maltster, Melk., 1776, comm, W, P2/D/674
Hy., husb. *or* yeo., Yatton K., 1715, AB, I, ren, P3/D/282
Jn., husb., Wingfield, 1651, AB, I, P1/D/96
Jn., Wingfield, 1686, AB, P2/D/361
Jn., Trowb., 1734, AB, P1/D/313
My., widow, Yatton K., 1756, ren, P30/57
Nich., baker, Chipp., 1711, I, W, P3/D/274
Robt., yeo., Melk., 1723, W, P1/D/276, P1/6Reg/445
Robt., Trowb., 1736, AB, P1/D/322
Robt., apothecary, Trowb., 1767, AB, comm, P1/D/400
Ruth, widow, Melk., 1762, AB, P2/D/636
Sarah, widow, Semington, Steeple A., 1757-62, AB, a/c (3), I (2), P1/D/451, P2/D/622
Sarah, widow, Melk., 1833, W, Wr, P2/1833/75
Timothy Maton, gent., Semington, Steeple A., 1755, W, P2/D/619
Wm., maltster, Yatton K., 1753, comm, W, P3/D/384
Driver, Alice, widow, Chelworth, Crudwell, 1670, I, W, P3/D/139
Eliz., widow, Norton, 1674, W, P3/D/156
Giles, yeo., Ashton K., 1639, I, W, P3/D/103
Jn., Corsham, [1564], W (NEP), P29/1Reg/6B
Jn., sen., yeo., Ashton K., 1669, AB, I, W, P3/D/134
Jn., yeo., Norton, 1672, I, W, P3/D/147
Jn., sen., yeo., Ashton K., 1709, W, P3/D/271
Mgt., widow, Corsham, [1566], W (NEP), P29/1Reg/7
Richd., yeo., Oaksey, 1704, I, W, P1/D/216
Druce, Abel, Bradford A., 1662, AB, comm, P2/D/248
Drew, yeo., Turleigh, Winsley, Bradford A., 1621, I, P30/59

Hy., smith, Winkfield, Berks., 1729, AB, ren, W, P1/D/299, P1/7Reg/370
Druse, Hugh, yeo., N. Bradley, 1624, I, W, P2/D/139
Jn., sen., yeo., Ashley, Bradford A., 1612, W, P2/D/104, P2/8Reg/175
Jn., yeo., Brook, Westb., 1651, AB, I, P1/D/97
Jn., husb., Haugh, Winsley, Bradford A., 1684, comm, I, W, P2/D/350
Mgt., widow, Bradford A., 1631, AB, I, W, copy NW, P2/D/164, P2/9Reg/60C
My., widow, Leigh, Bradford A., 1717, comm, W, P2/D/492
Richd., yeo., Turleigh, Winsley, Bradford A., 1708, I, W, P2/D/453
Wm., Turleigh, Winsley, Bradford A., 1587, W, P2/7Reg/85A
Wm., shoemaker, Bradford A., 1643, AB, I, P2/D/232
Drueatt *see* Drewett
Drury, Drew, Riddlesworth Hall, Norfolk (to be buried at Steeple A.), 1698-99, comm, W, P1/D/197, P1/3Reg/162
Eleanor, yeo.'s *or* maltster's widow, Marl., 1745, I, W, P1/D/354, P1/10Reg/9
Jos., victualler, *The Pelican Inn*, Froxfield, 1764, W, P3/D/398
Nich., Ludg., 1741, AB, comm, P1/D/339
Robt., Froxfield, 1780, AB, P3/D/436
Druse *see* Druce
Dry, Cath., widow, Netherb., Dorset, 1622, AB, I, NW, P5/1622/21, P5/10Reg/119A
Drie, Hy., sen., husb., Elwell, Netherb., Dorset, 1607, AB, a/c, comm, I, P5/1607/21, P5/8Reg/93A
Dryden, Robt., chapman, Hungerford, Berks., 1766, W, P23/714
Thos., shopkeeper, Abingdon, Berks., 1835, AB, P1/1835/91
Dryer, Edith, Sutton Poyntz, Dorset, 1568, W, P5/2Reg/29E
Jn., Sutton Poyntz, Dorset, 1568, W, P5/2Reg/29D
Maud, Sutton Poyntz, Dorset, 1568, W, P5/2Reg/29C
Nich., Preston, Dorset, 1609, I, P5/1609/25
Dubben, Wm., Holnest, Dorset, 1801, AB, comm, P5/1801/3, P5/18Reg/313A
Ducie, Dewcy, Jas., dyer, Sal., 1787, W, P4/1787/2
Jn., N. Bradley, 1609, AB, P2/8Reg/80E
Dewcy, Jn., yeo., Longbridge D., 1759, W, P1/D/387
Thos., N. Bradley, 1609, AB, I, P2/D/88
Ducisme, Jn., Boxford, Berks., 1711, AB, P1/D/247
Duck, Abel, carp., Pickwick, Corsham, 1842, W, P29/1800-1857/36, P29/3Reg/301
Alice, widow, Wrou., 1627, I, W, P3/D/70
Ambrose, fuller, Quemerford, Calne, 1734, I (detailed), W, P26/781
Ann, widow, Stock St., Calne, 1705, I (detailed), W, P26/516
Anthony, weaver, Swindon, 1609, W, P3/D/14
Chris., tinker, Warm., 1572, W, P2/5Reg/140A
Chris., yeo., Wrou., 1616, alleg, I, NW, P3/D/27
Chris., Wrou., 1770, AB, P3/D/416
Edwd., jun., Marl. St Peter and St Paul, 1678, AB, comm, P1/D/148
Edwd., Marl., 1698, I, note (dismisses need for probate, as goods worth under £5), P1/D/198
Edwd., Calne, 1705, W, P26/519
Edwd., timber merchant, Notton, Lacock, 1776, W, P1/D/420, P1/13Reg/99
Eliz., widow, Marl., 1680, I, W, P1/D/153
Emma, widow, Mynte, Corsham, 1667, I, W, P29/D/12, P29/1Reg/181
Emma, sp., Corsham, 1767, W, P29/D/20, P29/2Reg/107
Duck *or* Ducke, Hy., Netherb., Dorset, 1609, AB, a/c, P5/1609/22, P5/8Reg/151A
Jn., Calne, 1567, AB, P5/2Reg/27D
Jn., husb., Wrou., 1610, I, NW, P3/D/20, 28
Jn., yeo., Wrou., 1666, I, W, P3/D/126
Jn., yeo., Wrou., 1679, AB, a/c, I, P3/D/173
Jn., sen., yeo., Wrou., 1719, I, W, P3/D/286
Jn., jun., tucker, Calne, 1727, W, P26/716
Jn., carp., Lacock, 1732, I, W, P3/D/332
Jn., Wrou., 1747, AB, P3/D/369
Jn., Wrou., 1771, W, P3/D/420
Jn., labourer, Chilton F., 1825, comm, W, Wr, P3/1825/1
Jn., yeo., Wrou., 1829, W, Wr, P1/1829/134
Lawr., yeo., Corsham, 1655, AB, I, P29/D/11, P29/1Reg/154A
Lawr., yeo., Mynte, Corsham, 1724, AB, I, W, P29/D/18

Margery, widow, Horton, Bps. C., 1563, W, P5/1Reg/19A
Nich., yeo., Imber, 1728, W, P2/D/537
Robt., Bps. C., 1563, AB, P5/1Reg/20B
Robt., husb., Corsham, 1593, draft W (incomplete), W, P29/D/1, P29/1Reg/37
Susanna, widow, Calne, 1705, I, P26/517
Thos., Wilsford nr Pewsey, 1567, AB, P2/5Reg/9C
Thos., Curzon St., Calne, 1597-98, W, P5/1597/27, P5/6Reg/155D
Thos., blacksmith, Wrou., 1639, AB, a/c, I, P3/D/104
Thos., Lacock, 1754, AB, P3/D/385
Wm., Corsham, 1631, AB, I, P29/D/6
Wm., Ogbourne St Geo. (d. at Slinfold, Sussex), 1641, I, NW, P5/1641/26, P5/14Reg/13
Wm., Lacock, 1750, AB, P1/D/370
Wm., blacksmith and farmer, Heddington, 1831, O, W, P3/1831/7
see also Trent alias D.
Ducker, My., sp., Oaksey, 1723, AB, P3/D/305
Duckett, Alexander, labourer, Highw., 1636, I, NW, P10/1636/2
Martha, widow, Hartham, Corsham, 1695, comm, I (detailed), W, P3/D/233
Ducock, Ann, widow, Highw., 1630, I, W, P10/1630/3
Robt., yeo., Highw., 1619, AB, comm, I, P5/1620/16, P5/10Reg/3A
Dudden, Jacob, sen., common brewer, Warm., 1808, AB, ren, W, Wr, P1/1808/31
Dudds, Wm., tailor, Allington, 1726-27, W, P1/D/285, P1/7Reg/161B
Wm., yeo., Allington, 1818, AB (re property in A.), P2/1818/31
Dudley, Ann, widow, Sherb., Dorset, 1775, W, P5/1775/7, P5/17Reg/96
Chas., attorney at law, Wilton, 1829, W, Wr, P1/1829/63
Chris., sen., Upton L., 1641, AB, P2/D/220
Harriet, widow, Wilton, 1836, W, P2/1836/6
Hy., clerk, Broad H., 1697, I, W, P3/D/238
Dudman, Jn., sen., Chute, 1689, AB, W, P7/72
Dudman, Jonathan, Sal. St Thos., 1784, W, P4/1784/9
Dudman, My., widow, Newbury, Berks., 1770, W, P1/D/409
Dudman, Richd., Marl., 1826, W, Wr, P1/1826/2
Dudmarsh, Edwd., yeo., Enborne, Berks., 1602, I, W, P1/D/13
Dudmarsh, My., widow, Newbury, Berks., 1770, W, P1/12Reg/349A
Duell *see* Dewell
Duelyn *see* Duland
Duff, Joan, widow, Marl. St My., 1690, AB, I (form. Joan Eagleford, widow), P1/D/174
Duff, Jos., maltster, Marl. St My., 1700-01, comm, I, W, P1/D/201, P1/3Reg/270
see also Cornish alias D.
Duffett, Richd., Sherb., Dorset, 1588, AB, P5/5Reg/25B
Thos., Devizes, 1811, AB, comm, ren, Wr, P1/1811/119
Duffing, Eliz., widow, Wokm., Berks., 1569, I, Wr (endorsed in later hand 'Ex court of the Chancellor of the University of Oxford'), P5/1569/1
Rowland, Wokm., Berks., 1569, AB (re both Rowland & Eliz. D.), P5/2Reg/55B
Duffine, Walter, husb., Ditteridge, 1668, I, W, P3/D/133
Dufosee, Anthony, Wilton, 1787, W, P2/D/698
Dugdale, Chris., rector, Codf. St P., 1633, I, W, P1/D/65
Eliz., widow, Codf. St P., 1640, AB, a/c, I, P2/D/215
Thos., yeo., Seend, Melk., 1685, AB, I, P2/D/355
Dugmore, Jn., clerk, Compton C., 1634, I, W, P1/D/69
Dugoe, Jn., husb., Collingbourne K., 1676, AB, a/c, I, P3/D/164
Robt., husb., Durrington, 1611, AB (re Robt. D., jun.), a/c, I, W, P2/D/94, P2/8Reg/155C
Wm., Crickl. St My., 1630, AB, I, P3/D/81
Duke, Andrew, Bulford, 1678-82, AB, a/c, I, P2/D/317, 339
Fanny, widow, Hungerford, Berks., 1826, comm, W, Wr, P23/929
Geo., (Mr), no abode stated but probably Durnford, 1655-59, a/c, P30/61
Geo., Durnford, 1676, AB, P9/82
Geo., esquire, Lake, Wilsford with L., 1693, AB, I, P13/3/17
Jn., yeo., Lake, Wilsford with L., 1574, W, P5/3Reg/35C
Jn., esquire, Sal., 1671, AB, P1/D/135
Judith, Teffont, 1541, W (NEP), P30/46A

My., sp., S. Marston, 1762, AB, comm, W, P10/1762/2
Thos., glover, Reading, Berks., 1631, I, W, P1/D/61
Dukes, Winifred, sp., Avill's Farm, Corsham, 1691, AB, P3/D/225
see also Robins alias D.
Duland, Bridget, widow, Homington, 1681, I, W, P24/415
Dewland, Eliz., widow, Coombe B., 1681, I, W, P2/D/333
Eliz., widow, Leigh, Yetm., Dorset, 1798, comm, W, P19/201
Dewland, Hy., yeo., Charminster, Dorset, 1778, W, P5/1778/4, P5/17Reg/150
Hy., Leigh, Yetm., Dorset, 1794, AB, comm, P19/194
Duelyn, Joan, dau of Eliz. D. alias Truslowe, Coombe B., 1590, AB, I, NW, P5/1590/20, P5/5Reg/73B
Dewling, Jn., Stourpaine, Dorset, 1662, AB, comm, P24/331
Jn., sen., yeo., Homington, 1670, I, NW, P24/385
Jn., yeo., Charminster, Dorset, 1682, I, W, P5/1682/30
Dewland, Jn., husb., Homington, 1687, I, W (2 - 1 is NW), P24/797
Dulin, Jn., fuller, Uffc., Devon, 1690, I, W, P20/1/115
Dewling, Mark, Stourpaine, Dorset, 1638, AB, I, P24/296
Dewland, Mark, yeo., Charminster, Dorset, 1795, W, P5/1795/5, P5/18Reg/218A
Dewling, Richd., Coombe B., 1569, W, P5/2Reg/44A
Thos., farmer, Leigh, Yetm., Dorset, 1792, W, P19/191
Dulley *see* Dalley
Dumett *see* Dammett
Dummer, Ann, Lacock, 1637, AB, P3/D/95
Domer, Anthony, shopkeeper, Lacock, 1742, W, P3/D/358
Edwd., broad weaver, Lacock, 1638, I, NW, P3/D/98
Geo., yeo., Lacock, 1679, I, W, P3/D/174
Domer, Hy., Lacock, 1729, AB, I, P1/D/295
Jn., broad weaver, Lacock, 1617-21, AB, I, NW, P3/D/34, 49
Domer, Jn., labourer, Notton, Lacock, 1750, W, P1/D/373, P1/10Reg/396
Nich., husb., Keevil, 1575, W, P2/5Reg/223C
Nich., Bradford A., 1722, AB, W, P2/D/513
Nich., broad weaver, Paxcroft, Steeple A., 1724, comm, definitive sentence, D, W, P2/D/525
Robt., broad weaver, Bradford A., 1682, I, W, P2/D/338
Wm., weaver, Lacock, 1638, court paper (2), I (damaged & part is lost), W, P3/D/99
Wm., Chipp., 1823, AB, comm, Wr, P1/1823/12
Dummott *see* Dammett
Dunckerton *see* Dunkerton
Duncomb, Jn., clerk and rector, Beer Hackett, Dorset, 1691, AB, comm, P5/1691/19, 21
Sarah, widow, Kington St M., 1771, comm, W (2 - 1 a copy), P3/D/421
Dunden, Robt., husb., Maiden B., 1616, AB, I, P2/D/110
Donden, Thos., Maiden B., 1591, I, W, P2/D/40
Dundsdon *see* Dunsdon
Dunford, Eliz., widow, Gillingham, Dorset, 1679, I, P27/1/60
Jane, sp., Longbridge D., 1764, W, P2/D/641
Jn., cordw., Marl., 1825, W, Wr, P1/1825/11
Thos., farmer, Gt. Cheverell, 1847, comm, W, Wr, P2/1847/68
Dunham, Alice, widow, Sherb., Dorset, 1627, AB, W, P5/1627/11
Francis, husb., Sherb., Dorset, 1638, AB, I, W (NEP), P5/1638/33, P5/13Reg/83
Jas., yeo., Limbry, Netherb., Dorset, 1798, comm, W, P17/585
Donnam, Jn., husb., Sherb., Dorset, 1600, AB, I, P5/1600/22, P5/7Reg/5A
Dounam, Jn., husb., Lillington, Dorset, [1607], I, W, P5/1607/20, P5/8Reg/115B
Jn., husb. and yeo., Sherb., Dorset, 1679, AB, comm, I, W, P5/1679/25
Jn., sen., yeo., Broadenham Farm, Netherb., Dorset, 1776, AB, comm, W, P5/1776/13, P5/17Reg/123B
Jn., Netherb., Dorset, 1812, AB, comm, P17/598
Judith, widow, Lillington, Dorset, 1722, W, P5/1722/19, P5/16Reg/63B
Martha, widow, Netherb., Dorset, 1776, W, P5/1776/14, P5/17Reg/107A
Martin, Sherb., Dorset, 1615, AB, I, P5/1615/12
My., widow, Limbry, Netherb., Dorset, 1847, O, W, Wr, P17/618
Matthew, Sherb., Dorset, 1615, AB, P5/9Reg/161A
Richd., yeo., Lillington, Dorset, 1701, AB, I, P5/1701/19
Wm., Clifton Maybank, Dorset, 1802, AB, comm, P5/1802/11, P5/19Reg/10A

Dunhead, Wm., husb., Sal., 1698, W, P1/D/199, P1/3Reg/25
Dunkerton, Joan, widow, Stratford sub C., 1741, W, P1/D/340, P1/9Reg/75
Robt., Stratford sub C., 1734, AB, P4/1733/19
Dunckerton, Wm., Calne, 1577, AB, P5/1576/15, P5/3Reg/100B
Dunmon, Dan., shepherd, Sutton Poyntz, Dorset, 1769, AB, P18/10
Dunn, Ambrose, gent., Chipp., 1765, W, P3/D/404
Ambrose, joiner, Chipp., 1809, AB, comm, P3/1809/9
Ann, widow, Trowb., 1808-12, req, copy W, Wr, P1/1808/123
Edwd., feltmaker, Crickl. St S., 1769, W, P3/D/415
Eliz., Bishopstone N., 1741, AB, P6/128
Eliz., sp., Uffc., Devon, 1782, comm, W, Wr, P5/1782/10, P5/17Reg/225
Eliz., widow, Gillingham, Dorset, 1847, comm, W, Wr, P27/1/749
Geo., Sutton M., 1670, I, W, P2/D/279
Hy., woolcomber, Uffc., Devon, 1745, W, P20/1/212
Hy., Uffc., Devon, 1774, W, P20/1/261
Hy., gent., Uffc., Devon, 1821, W, Wr, P5/1821/33
Jas., husb., Warm., 1710, W, P2/D/462
Jn., woollen weaver, Gillingham, Dorset, 1666, I, W, P27/1/22
Jn., blacksmith, Uffc., Devon, 1688, I, W, P20/1/108
Jn., Gillingham, Dorset, 1710, AB, P27/1/185
Jn., Halstock, Dorset, 1727, NW, P16/245
Jn., Wanb., 1729, W, P1/D/300, P1/7Reg/286A
Jn., Uffc., Devon, 1743, AB, Wr, P5/1743/25
Jn., innholder, Chipp., 1760, W, P3/D/392
Jn., sen., yeo., Uffc., Devon, 1762, W, P20/1/241
Jn., gent., form.of Halberton, Devon, 1764, W, P5/1764/11
Jn., linen weaver, Pierston, Gillingham, Dorset, 1773, W, P27/1/482, P27/3Reg/178
Jn., yeo., Uffc., Devon, 1817, AB, comm, W, P20/1/306
Jn., yeo., Stratton St Mgt., 1826, W, Wr, P1/1826/99
Jn., yeo., Uffc., Devon, 1842, comm, W, Wr, P20/1/324
Jn. *see also* Jane Corke
Jos., Gillingham, Dorset, 1749, AB, I, P27/1/392, P27/3Reg/57
Justin, widow, Uffc., Devon, 1697, I, W, P20/1/132
My., Uffc., Devon, 1695, AB, P20/1/121
My., widow, Newton T., 1737, W, P2/D/565
My., widow, Gillingham, Dorset, 1769, AB, P27/1/465, P27/3Reg/150A
My., singlewoman, Pierston, Gillingham, Dorset, 1781, AB, P27/1/508, P27/3Reg/219A
Maurice, cordw., Wanb., 1733, W, P3/D/337
Maurice, husb., Wanb., 1745, W, P3/D/363
Rachel, widow, Halstock, Dorset, 1765, AB, W, P16/328
Rebecca, wife, Uffc., Devon, 1780, a/c, P20/1/267
Rebecca *see also* Jane Corke
Richd., Newton T., 1711, AB, P1/D/248
Robt., labourer, Bishopstone N., 1749, W, Wr, P5/1749/20
Thos., Uffc., Devon, 1696, AB, P20/1/131
Wm., [blacksmith], Wanb., 1673, AB, I, P3/D/153
Wm., yeo., Uffc., Devon, 1747, W, P20/1/214
Wm., yeo., Brinsham, Netherb., Dorset, 1827, W, Wr, P5/1827/47
Wm., Gillingham, Dorset, 1841, W, Wr, P27/1/733
Dunnen *see* Dunning
Dunnett, Sarah, widow, Uffc., Devon, 1773, AB, P5/17Reg/48B
Dunnick, Alice, widow, Bradford A., 1742, W, P2/D/583
Dunwick, Chas., Bradford A., 1725, AB, P2/D/529
Jane, widow, Edington, 1680, comm, I, W, P1/D/154
Dunnock, Martin, Trowle, Bradford A., 1585, W, P2/6Reg/139B
Donwyke, Stephen, husb., Tinh., Edington, 1597, I, W, P2/D/51
Dunwick, Thos., husb., Tinh., Edington, 1609-14, AB, a/c, I, T, W, P2/D/83, P2/8Reg/42
Thos., fuller, Edington, [1636], I, W, P2/D/183
Dunning, Chas., Bere R., Dorset, 1732, AB, comm, P5/1732/16
Chris., basketmaker, Chapmanslade, Corsley, 1823, W, Wr, P2/1823/8

Dunnen, Eliz., widow, Ashton G., Codf. St P., 1791, W, P2/D/713
Geo., gent., Beam., Dorset, 1724, W, P17/404
Hy., doctor of physic, Beam., Dorset, 1763, comm, W, P17/553
Hy., Beam., Dorset, 1801, AB, P17/587
Jn., Boyton, 1550, W, P2/2Reg/112B
Dunning *or* Donning, Jn., Hawkeridge, Westb., 1581, I, T, W, P5/1581/6, P5/4Reg/20C
Jn., Horningsham, 1720, AB, P5/1720/16
Jn., yeo., Codf. St P., 1753, W, P2/D/617
Dunning *or* Donning, Nich., Sherrington, 1567, I, W, P2/D/8, P2/5Reg/24A
Nich., yeo., Bere R., Dorset, 1712, I, W, P5/1712/24, P5/15Reg/302A
Dunnen, Richd., husb., Ashton G., Codf. St P., 1780, W, P2/D/681
Robt., N. Bradley, 1641, AB, I, P2/D/221
Robt., fellmonger, Sherb., Dorset (form. of Cerne Abbas, Dorset), 1854, AB, aff, Wr, P5/1854/8
Sarah, widow, Codf. St P., 1754, W, P2/D/618
Sarah, widow, Chapmanslade, Dilton, Westb., 1827, W, Wr, P25/1827/2
Donning, Thos., Westb., 1572, W, P5/3Reg/1B
Thos., cordw., Westb., 1669, AB, ren, P25/1669/16
Thos., sen., yeo., Southwick, N. Bradley, 1721, I, W, P1/D/270, P1/6Reg/373
Wm., N. Bradley, 1642, a/c (2), AB, comm, I, P2/D/227
Wm., husb., Corsley, 1690, I, W, P2/D/381
Wm., broad weaver, Southwick, N. Bradley, 1743, AB, I, P2/D/585
Wm., gent., Beam., Dorset, 1753, W, P17/525
see also Raymond alias D.
Dunnock *see* Dunnick
Dunsdon, Ann, widow, Steeple A., 1801, comm, W, P2/1801/9
Ann, widow, Steeple A., 1846, D, O, W, Wr, P2/1846/32
Ann, widow, Corsham, 1855, AB, aff, comm, Wr, P3/1855/42
Eliz., widow, Steeple A., 1809, W, P2/1809/1
Geo., yeo., Corsham, 1836, O, W, Wr, P3/1836/52
Geo., bach., Corsham, 1853, AB, comm, Wr, P3/1853/2
Harriet, sp., Steeple A., 1810, W, Wr, P2/1810/55
Jas., yeo., Bromham, 1842, W, Wr, P1/1842/54
Jas., yeo., Gastard, Corsham, 1844, W, P29/1800-1857/39, P29/3Reg/308
Jn., yeo., Steeple A., 1722, comm, W, P2/D/509
Jn., Steeple A., 1801, AB, comm, P2/1801/10
Jn., bach. and yeo., Steeple A., 1851, D, O, ren, W, Wr, P1/1851/23
Martha, widow, Corsham, 1854, AB, aff, O, Wr, P3/1854/22
My., widow, Wilton, Gt. Bedwyn, 1743, W, Wr, P5/1743/23
Richd., yeo., Upper Lambourn, Berks., 1714, W, P1/D/255, P1/5Reg/398B
Richd., yeo., Gt. Bedwyn, 1757, AB, W, P21/10/38
Thos., sen., yeo., Standen, Hungerford, Berks., 1725, W, P5/1725/22, P5/16Reg/118A
Thos., Steeple A., 1758, AB, W, P2/D/626
Thos., Gastard Farm, Corsham, 1857, AB, aff, comm, Wr, P3/1857/22
Wm., maltster, Steeple A., 1739, W, P2/D/575
Wm., bach., Steeple A., 1822, AB, Wr, P2/1822/42
Wm., late plumber and glazier, Steeple A., 1834, W, Wr, P2/1834/31
Wm., yeo., Linley's Farm, Corsham, 1848, D, O, W, Wr, P3/1848/42
Dunsford, Stevenson *see* Sarah Calbreath
Dunster, David, sen., builder, Silver St., Lyme R., Dorset, 1843, comm, W, Wr, P16/431
Dunster, David, builder, Sherb. Lane, Lyme R., Dorset, 1844, comm, W, Wr, P16/437
Dunster, Jonathan, labourer, Chards., Devon, 1846, aff, comm, O, W, Wr, P14/226
Dunster, Richd., cooper, Chards., Devon, 1623, I, W, P5/1622/23, P5/10Reg/148A
Dunster, Wm., fuller, Bere R., Dorset, 1721, W, P5/1721/12, P5/16Reg/59C
Dunt, My., widow, Sonning, Berks., 1723, I, W, P5/1723/10, P5/16Reg/87A
Dunt, Thos., husb., Sonning, Berks., 1719, AB, I, P5/1719/22
Duntan, Thomasine, no abode stated, but in peculiar of Sonning, [1539], court proceedings (against Thomasine D. - - on a charge of incontinence with Sir Walter Stoner), P5/20Reg/11B
Dunwick *see* Dunnick
Dupe, Chris., yeo., Sal., 1671, AB, a/c, I, W, P4/1670/27
Du Plessis, Jn. Bernard, Devizes, 1706, AB, I, P1/D/220

Durber, Joan, widow, N. Wraxall, 1631, I, W, P1/D/62
Durck, Agnes & Jn. *see* Jn. & Agnes Peach
Durdaunt, Jn., Donhead St My., 1540, I, W, P30/52A, 58
Durden, Chas., Hermitage, Dorset, 1836, AB, note, req, W, Wr, P5/1836/24
Durham, Jn., labourer, Urchf., 1596, I, copy I, W, copy W, P2/D/48
Durling *see* Darling
Durman, Abraham, husb., Gt. Bedwyn, 1591, W, P5/5Reg/110A
Ellen, widow, Collingbourne K., 1621, I, W, P3/D/50
Wm., Lt. Bedwyn, 1613, AB, comm, I, P5/1613/23, P5/9Reg/151A
Durman *or* Thurman, Wm., husb., Heddington, 1622, AB, I, P3/D/55
Durndell, Thos., chandler, Kemble, 1609, W, P3/D/16
Durnel, Jn., labourer, Kemble, 1801, W, P3/1801/16
Durnford, Alice, widow, Wilcot, 1700, W, P3/D/247
Ann, sp., Burbage, 1710, I, W, P11/99
Ann, widow, Burbage, 1715, W, P11/112
Dan., Swindon, 1824, comm, W, Wr, P3/1824/11
Edwd., Wilcot, 1712, AB, P3/D/276
Dornford, Eliz., Longbridge D., 1713, AB, P2/D/483
Eliz., Coate, Bps. C., 1760, W, P24/1110
Eliz., widow, Southbroom, 1855, aff, O, W, Wr, P24/1412
Francis, husb., W. Stowell, Alton Pr., 1688, I, W, P3/D/211
Francis, yeo., E. Grafton, 1718, W, P21/7/32
Giles, yeo., Burbage, 1722, I, W, P11/126
Giles, yeo., Burbage, 1742, W, P11/189
Darnford, Harry, husb., Coworth, Old Windsor, Berks., 1562, W (NEP), P1/2Reg/139A
Hy., W. Stowell, Alton Pr., 1682, I, W, P3/D/187
Jane, widow, Tisb., 1748, AB, P2/D/605
Dornford, Jn., Wilcot, 1663, AB, I, P3/D/118
Jn., husb., Wilcot, 1688, AB, I, ren, Wr, P3/D/210
Jn., carp., Gillingham, Dorset, 1689, I, W, P27/1/113
Jn., yeo., W. Grafton, 1720, W, P21/8/7
Jn., yeo., All C., 1730, W, P3/D/330
Jn., yeo., All C., 1775, W, P3/D/427
Jn., yeo., Stert, Urchf., 1783, W, P2/D/690
Jn., Sal., 1811, AB, P4/1811/7
Jn., blacksmith, Bedborough, Bps. C., 1831, O, W, Wr, P24/1324
Jn., yeo., Chirton, 1836, W, Wr, P2/1836/39
Jos., yeo., Hindon, 1750, W, P2/D/614
Margery, widow, All C., 1714, W, P1/D/256, P1/5Reg/439B
Martha, sp., Sal., 1737, W, Wr, P4/1737/17
My., widow, Rushall, 1745, AB, I, P2/D/591
My., sen., widow, All C., 1766, AB, W, P3/D/406
My., singlewoman, Collingbourne D., 1819, W, Wr, P21/12/39
Richd., sen., innholder, Sal., 1681, I, W, P4/1680/14
Richd., carp. and wheelwright, Swindon, 1824, comm, W, Wr, P3/1824/12
Robt., schoolmaster, Hindon, 1729, W, P1/D/301, P1/7Reg/378
Solomon, yeo., All C., 1744, W, P1/D/353, P1/9Reg/410B
Thos., yeo., W. Grafton, 1638, I, W, P5/1638/32, P5/13Reg/106E
Thos., husb. *or* yeo., All C., 1687, I, W, P3/D/204
Thos., sen., All C., 1740, AB, I, P3/D/352
Thos., Etchilhampton, 1751, AB, comm, P3/D/382
Thos., yeo., Burbage, 1780, W, P11/241
Dornford, Wm., husb., Bere R., Dorset, 1608, I, W, P5/1607/19, P5/8Reg/127
Dornford *or* Durnford, Wm., sen., labourer, Urchf., 1744, W, P1/D/350, P1/9Reg/421
Wm., Bottlesford, Wilsford nr Pewsey, 1844, comm, L, W (made 1827 but not proved until death of widow), Wr, P3/1844/6
Durnton, Abraham, Gt. Bedwyn, 1591, I, W, P5/1591/20
Durrant, Derrent, Eleanor, widow, Bere R., Dorset, 1626, I, W, P5/1626/15, P5/10Reg/201
Geo., Hermitage, Dorset, 1821, AB, Wr, P5/1821/31
Derrent, Jn., blacksmith, Gt. Somerford, 1627, I, W, P3/D/68

Derrent, Nich., blacksmith, Gt. Somerford, 1631, I, W, P1/D/56
Derant, Richd., husb., Bere R., Dorset, 1590, I, W, P5/1589/17, P5/5Reg/69A
Sarah, widow, Hermitage, Dorset, 1842, W, Wr, P5/1842/22
Durrell, Ann, wife, Gt. Bedwyn, 1757, AB, P21/10/35
Dorrill, Bridget, widow, Gt. Bedwyn, 1726, W, P21/8/26
Dorrill, Edith, widow, Ashton K., 1610, W, P3/D/19
Edwd., yeo., Gt. Bedwyn, 1723, I, W, P21/8/19
Dorell, Eliz., dame, Lt. Hinton, [1581], W (NEP), P3/1Reg/16C
Francis, labourer, Swindon, 1704, AB, I, P3/D/257
Dorrill, Gilbert, husb., Ashton K., [1603], I, W (NEP), P3/D/2
Joan, widow, Bishopstone N., 1726, I (2), W, P6/106
Jos., sen., husb., Gt. Bedwyn, 1760, W, P21/10/56
Dorrill, Sarah, widow, Bishopstone N., 1701, I, W, P5/1701/17
Wm., Upavon, 1636, AB, I, P2/D/187
Wm., yeo., Bishopstone N., 1685, I, W, P6/61
Dorrill, Wm., Bishopstone N., 1708, I, W, P6/102
Wm., Gt. Bedwyn, 1715, AB, comm, I, P21/7/25
Wm., cordw., Gt. Bedwyn, 1726, AB, I, ren, P21/8/27
Wm., sen., cordw., Gt. Bedwyn, 1741, I, W, P21/9/34
Durston, Alexander, Lyme R., Dorset, 1588-89, AB, a/c, P5/1589/14, P5/5Reg/23D
Dutch, Ann, widow, Gt. Cheverell, 1856, AB, aff, comm, ren, W, Wr, P2/1856/64
Benj., ironfounder, Warm., 1833, W, Wr, P2/1833/37
Benj., ironfounder, Warm., 1852, W, Wr, P2/1852/79
Dooche, Christmas, Mythe, Mapperton, Dorset, 1588, AB, P5/5Reg/24C
Dan., Sutton V., 1749, AB, P2/D/612
Edmd., Sutton V., 1789, AB, P1/D/434
Dowch, Isabel, widow, Mythe, Mapperton, Dorset, 1598, AB, I, P5/1598/13, P5/6Reg/213A
Jas., carp., Gt. Cheverell, 1856, aff, comm, W, Wr, P2/1856/49
Jn., broad weaver, Sutton V., 1736, AB, W, P2/D/566
Jonas, Sutton V., 1808, W, Wr, P2/1808/46
Dutton, Anthony, Bemerton, Fugg. St Peter, 1581, AB, W, P2/6Reg/40A
Dyars *see* Dyer
Dycke *see* Dicke
Dyer, Alice, widow, Fifield, Enford, 1586, W, P2/7Reg/33B
Alice, widow, Sal., 1666, AB, P4/1666/15
Alice, widow, Heytes., 1694, AB, I, P5/1694/33
Ann, widow, Sal., 1768, D, W, P4/1768/5
Ann, widow, Sal., 1780, W, P4/1780/9
Ann, widow, Sal., 1796, AB, ren, P4/1796/2
Benj., innholder, Longbridge D., 1729, W, P2/D/539
Bridget, widow, W. Kennett, Avebury, 1629, I, W, P3/D/76
Bridget, widow, Westb., 1719, AB, I, P25/1719/6
Cath., sp., Gt. Wishford, 1730, AB, P2/D/544
Dorothy, widow, Enford, 1652, I, W, P1/D/98
Edith, widow, Heytes., 1675, I, NW, P5/1675/19
Edwd., victualler, Upton S., 1733, W, P2/D/550
Eleanor, widow, Sherb., Dorset, 1730, I, W, P5/1730/15
Geo., gent., Heytes., 1661, AB, I, NW, P5/1661/14
Geo., sen., woolstapler, Corton, Boyton, 1711, I, W, P1/D/249, P1/5Reg/236
Geo., woolstapler, Steeple A., 1712, AB, I, P2/D/473
Geo., Upton L., 1718, AB, I, W, P2/D/495
Geo., sen., yeo., Heytes., 1730, W, P5/1730/14
Geo., farmer, Heytes., 1745, W, P5/1745/6
Geo., woolstapler, Tytherington, Heytes., 1766, W, P5/1766/7
Geo., Sal., 1772, AB, P4/1772/14
Geo., widower, Winterbourne S., 1852, AB, Wr, P2/1852/71
Hannah, sp., Trowb., 1827, AB, Wr, P1/1827/29
Hy., yeo., Stanton St B., 1664, I, W, P3/D/120
Hy., broad weaver, Fovant, 1711, AB, I, P2/D/470
Hy., sen., yeo., Sedgehill, 1751, W, P2/D/616

Hugh, husb., Chicklade, 1639, AB, I, P2/D/205
Jas., N. Bradley, 1561, AB, P2/4Reg/81C
Jas., victualler, Hungerford, Berks., 1682, I, W, P5/1682/36
Jas., gent. and rector, Devizes, 1691, AB, I, P1/D/175
Jas., clothworker, Heytes., 1735, AB, I, W, P5/1735/20
Jas., Hullavington, 1746, AB, P3/D/367
Jas., Kington L., 1797, AB, P3/D/461
Jas., gent., Kingston D., 1804, W, Wr, P1/1804/115
Jas., shopkeeper, Sherb., Dorset, 1851, W, Wr, P5/1851/18
Joan, widow, Halstock, Dorset, 1701, comm, I, W, P5/1701/18
Joan, widow, Wilton, 1710-11, W, P1/D/237, P1/5Reg/32B
Dyars, Jn., [draper], Highw., 1589, I, W, P10/1589/1, P5/5Reg/60B
Jn., Marl., 1625, AB, P1/D/42
Jn., Heytes., 1681, AB, I, P5/1681/13
Jn., yeo., Hinton Waldrist, Berks., 1698, I, W, P1/D/200, P1/3Reg/111
Jn., Halstock, Dorset, 1699, AB, comm, I, P5/1699/10
Jn., gardener, Fovant, 1709, I, NW, P2/D/455
Jn., Corton, Boyton, 1723, NW, P1/D/277, P1/6Reg/421B
Jn., yeo., Heytes., 1737, a/c, I, W, Wr, P5/1737/17
Jn., collarmaker, Shalbourne, 1755, W, P5/1755/12
Jn., jun., shepherd, E. Stowell, Wilcot, 1755, AB, ren, P3/D/387
Jn., yeo., Sal., 1757, W, P4/1757/2
Jn., yeo., Rodmead Farm, Maiden B., 1758, comm, W, P2/D/627
Jn., sen., blacksmith, Tisb., 1775, AB, ren, W, P2/D/671
Jn., carp., Trowb., 1823, AB, comm, ren, W, Wr, P1/1823/2
Jn., blacksmith, Amesb., 1833, W, Wr, P2/1833/47
Jn., labourer, Bourton, Gillingham, Dorset, 1853, W, Wr, P27/1/766
Leonard, mercer and yeo., Wilton, 1665, I, W, P2/D/256
Luke, Tisb., 1671, AB, P1/D/136
Mgt., widow, Long Burton, Dorset, 1614, AB, comm, I, T, W, P5/1614/20, P5/9Reg/149
Mgt., sp., Patney (form. of London), 1726, W, P1/D/286, P1/7Reg/130B
Margery, widow, Chipp., 1737, comm, W, P3/D/345
Martin, yeo., Lacock, 1670, AB, W, P3/D/140
My., widow, Fovant, 1729, I, W, P2/D/542
My., widow, Fovant Stroud, 1745, W, P2/D/595
My., Shalbourne, Berks., 1760, AB, P23/696
My., widow, Kington St M., 1819, W, Wr, P3/1819/27
My., widow, Brixton D., 1840, comm, W, Wr, P2/1840/13
Matthew, oatmealmaker, Southcott, Pewsey, 1644, I, W, P1/D/86
Matthew, woolstapler, Warm., 1728, AB, W, P2/D/535
Maurice, Downton, 1692, AB, I, P2/D/390
Ralph, Fovant Wood, 1684, AB, I, P2/D/351
Ralph, sen., wool tryer, Upton L., 1720, I, W, P1/D/267, P1/6Reg/203
Ralph, clothworker, Upton L., 1724, AB, I, P1/D/278
Ralph, Upton L., 1745, AB, P2/D/593
Ralph, woolstapler, Upton L., 1759, W, P1/D/389, P1/11Reg/381
Richd., W. Kennett, Avebury, 1649, AB, a/c, I (2), L, P1/D/95
Richd., labourer, Pewsey, 1674, comm, I, W, P1/D/139
Richd., sen., yeo., Corton, Boyton, 1684, I, W, P2/D/343, 347
Richd., yeo., Ham, 1688, AB, I, P3/D/212
Richd., Sal. St Edmd., 1693, AB, I, P4/1692/18
Richd., clothworker, Bishopstrow, 1711, AB, I (mentions burling loft), P1/D/250
Richd., sen., labourer, Gt. Wishford, 1738, W, P1/D/327, P1/8Reg/376B
Richd., woolstapler, Corton, Boyton, 1780, W, P2/D/682
Richd., labourer, Gt. Wishford, 1807, W, Wr, P2/1807/60
Richd., gent., Sal., 1855, aff, W, Wr, P1/1855/29
Robt., Hurst, Berks., 1543, W, P5/20Reg/45A, 49
Robt., Fifield, Enford, 1574, AB, P2/5Reg/201A
Robt., Fittleton, 1589, AB, I, P2/D/35
Robt., cooper, Heddington, 1636, AB, I, P3/D/91

Robt., woolstapler, Corton, Boyton, 1705, I, W, P2/D/441
Simon, shepherd, Stanton St B., 1605, I, W, P1/D/16
Simon, linen draper, Calne, 1730, W, P26/755
Simon, sen., cordw., Heytes., 1785, W, P5/1785/9, P5/18Reg/39
Susanna, singlewoman, Enford, 1722, W, P2/D/510
Susanna, widow, Hungerford, Berks., 1840, comm, W, Wr, P23/998
Theophilus, Corton, Boyton, 1666, AB, P2/D/259
Theophilus, Sal., 1724, AB, P4/1724/13
Thos., Arborfield, Berks., 1555, W, P5/20Reg/144A
Thos., Fittleton, 1569, AB, P2/5Reg/69B
Thos., husb., Kingston D., 1573, W, P2/5Reg/176A
Thos., yeo., Enford, [1670], I, W, P2/D/278
Thos., husb. *or* shepherd, Fyfield, Milton L., 1678, I, W, P3/D/170
Thos., yeo., Hinton Waldrist, Berks., 1701, I, W, P1/D/209, P1/4Reg/128
Thos., shepherd, Fyfield, Milton L., 1701, W, copy W, P3/D/249
Thos., Enford, 1704, AB, I, P2/D/440
Thos., labourer, Imber, 1717, NW, P2/D/491
Thos., gent., Purton Stoke, 1749, AB, W, P3/D/374
Walter, Ogbourne St Geo., [1577], W (NEP), P3/1Reg/20C
Walter, sen., cooper, Wilton, 1669, I, W, P2/D/269
Walter, cooper, Wilton, 1674, I, W, P2/D/294
Walter, Wilton, 1683, AB, P2/D/345
Wm., Enford, 1560, AB, P2/4Reg/54B
Wm., Ditchampton, Wilton, 1590, I, W, P2/D/36
Dyer alias Devotion, Wm., yeo., Hazelbury, Box, 1661, comm, I, L, W, P3/D/115, P3/3Reg/17A
Wm., sen., carp., Westb., 1665, comm, NW, P25/1665/4
Wm., weaver, Wilton, 1673, AB, I, P2/D/292
Wm., [shopkeeper], Wilton, 1678, AB, I, P2/D/318
Wm., Dinton, 1730, W, P2/D/546
Wm., Chute, 1731, W, P7/128
Wm., Lyme R., Dorset, 1735, AB, comm, P5/1735/21
Wm., broad weaver, Fovant Stroud, 1745, AB, W, P2/D/594
Wm., draper, Shalbourne, Berks., 1800, W, P23/822
Wm., Heytes., 1803, AB, P5/1803/54, P5/19Reg/90A
Wm., Tisb., 1806, AB, P2/1806/1
Wm., blacksmith, Winterbourne S., 1806, W, Wr, P2/1806/68
Wm., Stockton, 1847, W, Wr, P2/1847/73
see also Hews (Hughes) alias D.; Levier alias D.; Lyther alias D.
Dyett, Ann, widow, Heytes., 1751, W, P5/1751/11
Anthony, Heytes., 1750, W, Wr, P5/1750/9
Barnett, Martin, Hants, 1782, AB, P2/D/688
Edith, Bere R., Dorset, 1622, AB, I, P5/1622/20
Eliz., widow, Bere R., Dorset, 1573, W, P5/3Reg/16B
Geoffrey, Bere R., Dorset, 1573, W, P5/3Reg/16A
Geo., husb. and labourer, Chamberlayne, Bere R., Dorset, 1613, I, W, P5/1613/22, P5/9Reg/83C
Geo., yeo., Bratton, Westb., 1707, W (NEP), P25/1707/6
Hy., Martin, Hants, 1781, AB, P2/D/685
Jas., shoemaker, Sal., 1703, W, P4/1703/1
Joan, Winterborne K., Dorset, 1567, W, P5/2Reg/13C
Jn., husb., Winterborne K., Dorset, 1576, W, P5/3Reg/97C
Jn., yeo., Bere R., Dorset, 1595, AB, a/c, T, W, copy W, P5/1595/19, P5/6Reg/99B
Jn., sen., yeo., Bere R., Dorset, 1616, I, W, P5/1615/9, P5/9Reg/167
Jn., mercer, Bere R., Dorset, 1639, I (detailed), W, P5/1639/28, P5/13Reg/213B
Jn., Bere R., Dorset, 1662, AB, I, P5/1662/32
Luke, blacksmith, Heytes., 1701, AB, I, ren, Wr, P5/1701/16
Luke, Heytes., 1740, W, Wr, P5/1740/25, 28
My., sp., Downton (form. of Sixpenny Handley, Dorset), 1693, I, W, P2/D/392
Maud, widow, Alton P., Dorset, 1613, I, W, P5/1613/19, P5/9Reg/87B
Nich., blacksmith, Norton B., 1701, AB, I, P2/D/423
Nich., blacksmith, Heytes., 1738, W, Wr, P5/1738/15

Wm., husb., Bere R., Dorset, 1600, I, W, P5/1600/20, P5/6Reg/244C
Wm., Bere R., Dorset, 1639, AB, I, P5/1639/27, P5/13Reg/215B
Dyffold *see* Diffield
Dyke, Alice, widow, Bedborough, Bps. C., 1791, W, P24/1154
Dike, Andrew, Knook, 1729, W, P5/1729/15, P5/16Reg/217B
Dike, Ann, sp., Sal., 1671, AB, I, P4/1670/20
Ann, widow, Poulshot, 1817, AB, Wr, P1/1817/88
Dike alias Cox, Anna, Warm., 1688, AB, P2/D/377
Dike, Benj., cordw., Chipp., 1746, W, P3/D/366
Christian, widow, Woodb., 1730, AB, P3/D/329
Dan., gent., Stanton St B., 1729, comm, W, P3/D/326
Dan., jun., gent., Sal., 1742, D, W, P4/1742/19
Eliz., widow, Coate, Bps. C., 1693, I, W, P24/530
Francis, Allington, All C., 1707, AB, ren, P1/D/224
Geoffrey, husb., Allington, All C., 1701, I, W, P3/D/250
Geo., Poulshot, 1815, AB, comm, Wr, P2/1815/9
Hy., Thornford, Dorset, 1741, AB, Wr, P5/1741/7
Jerome, gent., Woodb., 1782, W, P3/D/442
Joan, Ablington, Figh., 1582, AB, P26/1483, P5/4Reg/55B
Jn., husb., Chirton, 1576, I, W, P2/D/14, P2/5Reg/265B
Jn., Westwood, 1593, T (children: Jn., Alice & Edwd. D.), P2/D/737
Jn., sen., yeo., Wick Mill, Bps. C., 1685, I, W, P24/808
Jn., Bps. C., 1715, AB, P24/672
Jn., yeo., Haxton, Fittleton, 1729, I, W, P2/D/543
Dike, Jn., carp., Limpley Stoke, Bradford A., 1761, AB, comm, ren, W, P2/D/634
Jn., Manningford Bruce, 1775, AB, P3/D/428
Jonathan Waterman, Woodb., 1792, AB, P3/D/456
Margery, widow, Stanton St B., 1727, W, P3/D/322
My., widow, Woodb., 1681, AB, comm, NW, P3/D/185
My., widow, Chipp., 1688, comm, I, W, P3/D/213
My., All C., 1708, W, P3/D/268
My., [widow], Netheravon, 1769, AB, W, P12/191
My., widow, Sal., 1770, AB, P4/1770/3
My., sp., Sherb., Dorset, 1846, AB, Wr, P5/1846/11
Dike, Richd., cordw., Chipp., 1784, W, P3/D/445
Robt., Calne, 1812, AB, Wr, P5/1812/6
Robt., gardener, Bedborough, Bps. C., 1831, AB, comm, ren, W, Wr, P24/1323
Sarah, widow, Pewsey, 1690, I, W, P3/D/222
Dike, Simon, yeo., Rowde, 1642, I, W, P3/D/112
Susanna, widow, Nursteed, Bps. C., 1740, AB, W, P24/1003
Susanna, sp., Woodb. (form. of Devizes), 1823, W, Wr, P1/1823/149
Thos., yeo., Woodb., 1673, AB, a/c (lengthy & detailed), comm, I, ren, W, P3/D/154
Thos., blacksmith, Netheravon, 1689, I, W, P12/130
Thos., sen., gent., Woodb., 1717, I, W, P1/D/264, P1/6Reg/150
Thos., gent., Woodb., 1729, W, P1/D/302, P1/7Reg/352
Thos., Upavon, 1736, AB, P2/D/564
Thos., Upavon, 1757, AB, comm, P2/D/623
Dike, Thos., gent., Bradford A., 1769, W, P2/D/651
Dike, Thos., Limpley Stoke, Bradford A., 1826, O, W, Wr, P1/1826/39
Thos., Bloxworth, Dorset, 1841, AB, comm, Wr, P5/1841/2
Thos. Webb, gent., Winterbourne D., 1755, W, P7/149
Wm., husb., Fifield, Enford, 1673, I, W, P2/D/290
Wm., sen., yeo., Bromham, 1681, comm, I, W, P3/D/182
Dike, Wm., carp., Bradford A., 1735, W, P1/D/317, P1/8Reg/134
Wm., Gt. Woodford, 1792, AB, P13/5/9
Wm., Woodb., 1815, AB, comm, D, ren, W, Wr, P3/1815/60
Wm., Sal. St Martin, 1817, AB, Wr, P4/1817/2
Dykes, Wm., Newton T., 1822, AB, Wr, P2/1822/72
see also Bartlett lately called D.
Dyker *see* Dicker

Dykes *see* Dyke
Dymer, Ann, widow, N. Moreton, Berks., 1707, W, P1/D/225
Dymore, Edwd., yeo., Fyfield, Overton, 1725, I, W, P3/D/310
Dymmer, Eleanor, widow, Calne, 1572, W, P5/3Reg/2A
Dymore, Eliz., sp., Fyfield, 1740-41, W, P1/D/331, P1/9Reg/15
Isaac, yeo., Fyfield, Overton, 1698, I, W, P3/D/239
Dymore, Jas., yeo., Fyfield, Overton, 1800, W, P3/1800/52
Dimor, Jn., husb., Fittleton, 1575, W, P2/5Reg/217B
Jn., husb., Fyfield, Overton, 1615, I (damaged), W (NEP), P1/D/29
Jn., Lockeridge, Overton, 1624, AB, a/c, I, P3/D/61
Dymore, Nich., Lockeridge, Overton, 1712, AB, I (2 - 1 a copy), P3/D/277
Nich., E. Overton, W. Overton, 1763, AB, comm, P3/D/396
Robt., husb., Lockeridge, Overton, 1675, I, W (damaged), P3/D/162
Dymore, Thos., yeo., Fyfield, Overton, 1802, req, W, P3/1802/28
see also Collins alias D.; Dismore
Dymond, Deymond, Hannah, sp., Lyme R., Dorset, 1694, W, P16/128
Thos., barber, Sal., 1667, I, W, P4/1667/14
Dymore *see* Dymer
Dymott, Jn., Charlton, Downton, 1761, W, P2/D/632
Jn., baptist minister, Hilp., 1848, O, W, Wr, P2/1848/15
Dyos, Roger, vicar, Lt. Bedwyn, 1582, AB, I, W, P5/1582/20, P5/4Reg/52C
Dysley, Jn., priest, Bishopstone, 1560-61, collation to prebend, P1/1Reg/79A
Dysmer, Dysmore *see* Dismore
Dyson, Jn., Marl., 1724, AB, P1/D/279
Dison, Jn., sen., yeo., Littlecote, Rams., 1740, AB, ren, W, P5/1740/26
Dison, Jn., cordw., Marl., 1771, W, P1/D/411, P1/12Reg/416B
Roger, yeo., Mildenhall, 1710, W, P3/D/273

Eacott, Edwd., sen., husb., Warm., [1701], I, W, P2/E/249
Jas., shearman, Trowb., 1853, D, O, W, Wr, P1/1853/7
Eccott, Jn., sen., labourer, Warm., 1696, AB, I, ren, P2/E/241
Jn., sen., gardener, Warm., 1710, W, P2/E/268
Jn., yeo., Warm., 1775, W, P2/E/387
Jn., yeo., Wootton B., 1792, W, P3/E/307
Eccott, My., widow, Warm., 1748, W, P2/E/339
Eccott, Richd., Warm., 1631, I, copy I, W, copy W, P2/E/109, P2/9Reg/66A
Richd., bodicemaker, Devizes, 1685, I, W, P1/E/119
Ecut, Thos., Westport St My., 1628, I, W, P3/E/47
Thos., plumber and glazier, Chipp., 1778, W, P3/E/289
Ecut, Wm., Westport St My., 1618, I, W, P3/E/29
Ecut, Wm., labourer, Eisey, 1685, I, W, P3/E/130
Wm., Warm., 1720, W, P1/E/178, P1/6Reg/236
Eccott, Wm., gardener, Warm., 1774, AB, P2/E/386
Wm., baptist minister, Southwick, N. Bradley, 1850, D, O, W, Wr, P2/1850/53
Eades, Ann, sp., Devizes, 1794, AB, P1/E/293, P1/14Reg/503A
David, alehouse keeper, Hurst, Berks., 1771, comm, W, P5/1771/6, P5/17Reg/31A
Edde, Eliz., Amesb., 1551, AB, P2/2Reg/122B
Jas., carp., Devizes, 1790, W, P1/E/286, P1/14Reg/349
Jas., hatter, Sal. St Edmd., 1822, W, Wr, P4/1822/6
Edes, Jn., Ditteridge, 1572, W. No date of probate., P1/1Reg/53A
Edes, Jn., Warm., 1616, AB, I, P1/E/20
Edes, Jn., Sal. St Thos., 1678, I, W, P4/1678/12
Jn., jun., carp., Devizes, 1767, W, P1/E/261, P1/12Reg/271
Jn., carp., Devizes, 1776, W, P1/E/273, P1/13Reg/91B
Thos., carp., Devizes, 1790, W, P1/E/287, P1/14Reg/353
Edes, Wm., yeo., Lydiard T., 1626, W, P3/E/41
Edes, Wm., sen., innholder, Devizes, 1738, W, P1/E/219, P1/8Reg/239
Eadleam *see* Adlam
Eadney *see* Edney
Eagleford, Joan *see* Joan Duff

Eagles, Jn., yeo., Sevenhampton, Highw., 1752, I, W, P10/1752/1
Thos., gent., Wilton, 1651, AB, I, P1/E/78
Eagle, Thos., Sal., 1717, AB, P4/1717/14
Eagleton, Eggelton, Chris., yeo., Burbage, 1826, W, P11/281
Jas., yeo., Broad B., Highw., 1828, AB, W, P10/1828/3
Jn., Bishopstone N., 1833, AB, O, W, Wr, P6/155
Ealey *see* Ely
Ealless *see* Ellis
Ealmes *see* Elmes
Ealy *see* Ely
Eames, Eliz., W. Dean, 1695, T (legatee of the decd: My. Hibberd, minor), P2/E/239
Geo., baker, Calne, 1639, I, P5/1639/102
Isaac, Bradford A., 1752, AB, comm, P2/E/348
Eymes alias Yemes, Joan, Chipp., 1613, AB, comm, I, P3/E/13
Jn., Fordington, Dorset, 1662, AB, I, P5/1662/39
Jonathan, Fordington, Dorset, 1702, AB, I, P15/67
Jonathan, Bere R., Dorset, 1720, AB, P5/1720/17
Lucy, widow, Fordington, Dorset, 1665, AB, I, P5/1665/29
My., widow, Bere R., Dorset, 1727, W, P5/1727/13, P5/16Reg/147B
Peter, clothworker, Bradford A., 1769, W, P2/E/380
Eme?, Richd., Gillingham, Dorset, 1664, AB, P27/1/16
Thos., physician, Trowb., 1693, comm, I, W, P2/E/232
Warborough, widow, Bradford A., 1778, W, P2/E/395
Wm., sen., fuller, Lyme R., Dorset, 1625, I, W, P5/1625/28, P5/10Reg/274D
Eamor *see* Amor
Earle, Agnes, widow, Patney, 1629, I, W, P2/E/102
Agnes *see also* Ann
Alice, widow, Corston, Malm., 1616, I, W, P3/E/22
Ann, widow, Corston, Malm., 1631, I, W, P1/E/38
Ann, widow, Hammonds, Chipp., 1674, I, W, P3/E/98
Earl, Ann, widow, Compton, Enford, 1738, AB, I, W, P2/E/322
Ann *or* Agnes, widow, Sunton, Collingbourne K., 1663, I, W, P3/E/74
Ann *see also* Wm. Riley
Anthony, Holt, Bradford A., 1616, AB, I, P2/E/79, P2/8Reg/303A
Benj., yeo., Shaw, Melk., 1730, AB, I, P2/E/307
Brian, no abode stated, [1628], I, P2/E/101
Dan., Collingbourne D., 1682, W, P21/2/79, P21/4/2
Edwd., Collingbourne D., 1690, I, W, P21/5/3
Edwd., mercer, Ludg., 1698, AB, comm, I, P1/E/143
Edwd., yeo., Burton Hill, Malm., 1706, AB, I, P3/E/175
Edwd., yeo., Corston, Malm., 1820, W, Wr, P3/1820/13
Eliz., Cules Parcill, Burbage, 1597-98, AB (crossed out), I, T, W, P5/1597/36, P5/6Reg/182C, 203C
Earls alias Dawes, Eliz., widow, Inkpen, Berks., 1638, I, W, P1/E/55
Eliz., widow, Corston, Malm., 1677, I, W, P3/E/108
Francis, Sunton, Collingbourne K., 1699, AB, I, P3/E/161
Francis, gent., Stanham, Chute, 1718, W, P7/113
Francis, yeo., Collingbourne K., 1740-41, W, P1/E/224, P1/9Reg/14B
Geo., blacksmith, Collingbourne D., 1740-41, I, W, P1/E/225, P1/9Reg/14A
Earl, Geo., labourer, Trowb., 1820, W, Wr, P1/1820/51
Giles, yeo., Eastcourt, Crudwell, [c1614], W (NEP), P3/E/18
Hester, sp., Collingbourne K., 1733, AB, P3/E/211
Earl, Hezekiah, carp. and shopkeeper, Bradford A., 1819, W, Wr, P2/1819/60
Isaac, yeo., Melk., 1811, comm, W, Wr, P2/1811/12
Jas., Collingbourne K., 1616, AB, I, P3/E/23
Jas., schoolmaster and yeo., Whitley, Melk., 1724, I, W, P2/E/295
Jas., tailor, Melk., 1770, W, P2/E/381
Earl, Jas., bach., Seend, Melk., 1826, AB, Wr, P1/1826/110
Jas., baker, Seend, Melk., 1845, O, W, Wr, P1/1845/17
Jane, widow, Corston, Malm., 1749, W, P3/E/240
Joan, widow, Holt, Bradford A., 1679, comm, I, W, P2/E/193

Joan, sp., Corston, Malm., 1691, comm, I, W, P3/E/151
Joan, widow, Shaw, Melk., 1730, AB, W, P2/E/306
Jn., Patney, 1558, W, P2/3Reg/106B
Jn., Collingbourne K., 1570, W (NEP), P1/1Reg/117C
Jn., Patney, 1574, W, P2/5Reg/204A
Jn., yeo., Crudwell, [1613], I, W (NEP), P3/E/15
Jn., yeo., Patney, 1616, I, W, P1/E/19
Jn., yeo., Corston, Malm., 1626, AB, a/c, I, NW, P3/E/40
Jn., Imber, 1631, I, W, P2/E/108, P2/9Reg/62B
Jn., Lyneham, 1644, AB, I (detailed), P1/E/66
Jn., sen., yeo., Holt, Bradford A., 1645, AB, comm, ren, W, P2/E/145
Jn., sen., gent., Holt, Bradford A., 1667, I, W, P2/E/255
Earl, Jn., sen., husb., Manningford A., 1691, I, W, P3/E/150
Jn., baker, Holt, Bradford A., 1735, comm, W, P1/E/207, P1/8Reg/127
Jn., yeo., E. Coulston, 1736, W, P2/E/319
Jn., tailor, Melk., 1763, AB, comm, P2/E/368
Jn., baker, Corsham, 1808, comm, W, Wr, P3/1808/24
Jn., miller, Sonning, Berks., 1821, comm, W, Wr, P5/1821/4
Jn., carp., Seend, Melk., 1825, W, Wr, P2/1825/38
Jn. *see also* Wm. Riley
Jos., Collingbourne D., 1705, AB, I, W, P21/6/27
Earl, Jos., Melk., 1734, AB, P2/E/316
Lawr., Holt, Bradford A., 1714, AB, ren, P2/E/278
Marmaduke, shepherd, Sunton, Collingbourne K., 1635, I, W, P3/E/57
Martha, widow, Collingbourne D., 1680, AB, I, P21/2/71
My., widow, Seend, Melk., 1837, AB, Wr, P2/1837/80
Maud, widow, Patney, 1598, W (value of I given), P1/2Reg/161A
Maurice, baker, Seend Row, Melk., 1793, comm, W, P2/E/418
Maurice, baker, Seend Row, Melk., 1825, W, Wr, P2/1825/47
Mercy, widow, re property in Holt, Bradford A. ; no abode stated, 1814, AB, comm, P2/1814/14
Richd., husb., Corston, Malm., 1609, W, P3/E/7
Richd., Arborfield, Berks., 1616, AB, comm, I, P5/1616/23, P5/9Reg/217B
Richd., yeo., Corston, Malm., 1665, I, W, P3/E/76
Richd., Whitep., 1670s?, I, P2/E/185
Richd., Chute, 1734, AB (2), P5/1734/21
Robt., husb., Brokenb., [1610], W (NEP), P3/E/8
Robt., Whitep., 1638, I, W, P1/E/58
Robt., Chirton, 1703, AB, P2/E/254
Earl, Robt., yeo., Holt, Bradford A., 1808, W, Wr, P1/1808/30
Roger *see* Wm. Riley
Thos., blacksmith, Collingbourne D., 1626, AB, I, W, P21/1/12
Thos., yeo., Collingbourne D., 1671, AB, I, P21/2/20
Thos., yeo., Corston, Malm., 1676, I, W, P3/E/103
Thos., yeo., Upavon, 1716, I, W, P2/E/283
Thos., clerk and vicar, Malm., 1749, W, P3/E/238
Earl, Thos., yeo., Trowb., 1771, W, P1/E/267, P1/12Reg/410
Thos., gent., Sal., 1855, aff, cert, W, Wr, P4/1855/1
Erles, Walter, Sal., 1644, AB, I, P1/E/67
Wm., labourer, Cules Parcill, Burbage, 1597, I, W, P5/1597/37, P5/6Reg/155A
Wm., Patney, 1606, I, W, P1/E/8
Wm., husb., Collingbourne K., 1623, I, W, P3/E/37
Wm., yeo., Eastcourt, Crudwell, 1632, I, W, P3/E/52
Wm., weaver, Holt, Bradford A., 1648, AB, NW, P2/E/151
Wm., sen., yeo., Shaw, Melk., 1672, I, W, P2/E/179
Wm., gent., Holt, Bradford A., [1676], W, P2/E/187
Wm., yeo., Shaw, Melk., [1700], I, W, P2/E/248
Wm., yeo., Stanton St Q., 1714, D, I, W, P1/E/164, P1/5Reg/468B
Wm., tailor, Seend, Melk., 1737, AB, ren, P2/E/321
Wm., Corston, Malm., 1749, W, P3/E/239
Earl, Wm., Malm., 1792, W, P1/E/288, P1/14Reg/387

Earl, Wm., husb., Leigh, Bradford A., 1814, W, Wr, P1/1814/40
Earlesman, Dan., joiner, Sal., 1699, I, W, P4/1699/3
Earls *see* Earle
Early, Agnes, widow, Arborfield, Berks., 1620, I, W, P5/1616/24, P5/10Reg/76A
Anthony, Lt. Bedwyn, 1625, AB, a/c, I, P5/1625/27, P5/10Reg/295A
Anthony, Lt. Bedwyn, 1661, AB, comm, P5/1661/15
Dan., shearman, Hungerford, Berks., 1641, I, W, P5/1641/28, P5/14Reg/10C
Hugh, [carp.], Bedwyn Brail, Gt. Bedwyn, 1592-93, AB, I, P5/1592/27, P5/5Reg/143F
Jane, widow, Standen, Hungerford, Berks., 1680, AB, comm, P5/1680/13
Joan, Gt. Bedwyn, 1676, AB, I, P5/1676/20
Jn., vicar, Maiden B., [1552], I, P2/E/3
Jn., yeo., Gt. Bedwyn, 1670, AB, I, P21/2/10
Jn., yeo., Newtown, Shalbourne, 1744, W, P21/9/50
Nich., Chisbury, Lt. Bedwyn, 1633, I, W, P21/3/24
Richd., sen., gent., Damerham, Hants, 1646, caveat, P2/E/148
Thos., husb., Marten, Grafton, 1585, AB, I, W, P5/1585/6, P5/4Reg/108C
Thos., Sal. St Edmd., 1628-29, AB, I, P4/1628/9, P4/1629/10
Wm., innholder, Sal., 1624, I, W, P4/1624/5
Wm., yeo., Lt. Bedwyn, 1746, W, P5/1746/22
Wm., labourer, Gt. Bedwyn, 1752, AB, ren, P5/1752/15
Earney, Jn., husb., Downton, 1709, W, P2/E/265
Ears, Hy., widower, Bere R., Dorset, 1847, AB, comm, Wr, P5/1847/23
Earth, Wm., [rector], Mildenhall, 1619, W (damaged), P1/E/23
Earwood *see* Erwood
Eason, Thos., innholder, Zeals, 1727, W, P5/1726/15, P5/16Reg/143B
East, Ann, sp., Sandford, Abingdon, Berks., 1811, W, Wr, P1/1811/74
Edwd., yeo., Charlcote, Bremhill, 1720, I, W, P1/E/179, P1/6Reg/260
Jn., wheelwright, Theale, Tilehurst, Berks., 1735, W, P1/E/208, P1/8Reg/11B
Este, Richd., Ditchampton, Wilton, 1597, I, T, W, copy W, P2/E/47
Thomasine, Sonning, Berks., 1679, AB, P5/1679/27
Wm., sen., husb., Sonning, Berks., 1615, W, P5/9Reg/122B
Eastbrooke, Eliz., Uffc., Devon, 1638, I, NW, P5/1638/34, P5/13Reg/70
Easter, My., widow, Stourpaine, Dorset, 1696, AB, W, P24/508
My., Stourpaine, Dorset, 1742, W, P24/984
Eastfield, Thos. Dan., cordw., Hurst, Berks., 1805, W, P5/1805/1
Eastgate, Estgate, Avis, Teffont E., 1608, AB, P2/E/64
Estgate, Jas., Teffont E., 1608, AB, I, P2/E/62
Jas., baker, Warm., 1751, W, P2/E/344
Jn., shopkeeper, Warm., 1733, W, P2/E/315
Estgate, Philip, currier, Newbury, Berks., 1680, AB, I, P1/E/114
Eastman, Eastmond, Ann, widow, N. Hidden, Hungerford, Berks., 1693, I, W, P23/187
Eastmond *or* Esment, Edwd., N. Hidden, Hungerford, Berks., 1685, I, W, P5/1685/33
Eastmond, Edwd., yeo., Hidden, Hungerford, Berks., 1731, I, W, P5/1731/27
Eastmond, Eliz., widow, Hidden, Hungerford, Berks., 1704, I, W, P5/1704/16
Eastmond, Eliz., widow, Newtown, Hungerford, Berks., 1752, W, P5/1752/13
Esther, sp., Downton, 1797, AB, ren, P2/E/424
Eastment, Geo., Judith, Halstock, Dorset, 1764, W, P5/1764/12
Hannah, Milbrook, Hants (leaving effects at, Seend, Melk.), 1805, AB, P2/1805/47
Hester, widow, Downton, 1761, W, P2/E/361
Eastmond, Isaac, yeo., Lt. Hinton, 1728, AB, I, P3/E/207
Estmond, Joan, widow, N. Wootton, Dorset, 1579, I, W, P5/1579/28, P5/3Reg/133A
Jn., sen., husb., Nunton and Bodenham, 1562, I, W, P2/E/8, P2/4Reg/117
Jn., husb., Downton, 1565, W, P2/4Reg/193B
Jn., E. Harnham, Britford, 1588, I, W, P5/1587/15, P5/5Reg/4A
Jn., Nunton, N. and Bodenham, 1633, AB, comm, P2/E/116, P2/9Reg/13C
Jn., fisherman and husb., Downton, 1663, I, W, P2/E/159
Eastman *or* Easton, Jn., shepherd, Corton, Boyton, [1684], I, W, P2/E/209
Jn., shoemaker, Sal., 1686, I (detailed), W, P1/E/122
Estmond, Jn., Chards., Devon, 1687, AB, I, P14/68
Eastmond, Jn., yeo., Hidden, Hungerford, Berks., 1697, AB, comm, I, P5/1697/13

Jn., carp., Downton, 1699, W, P2/E/245
Jn., basketmaker, Downton, 1719, I, W, P2/E/287
Jn., yeo., Bemerton, Fugg. St Peter, 1723, W, P1/E/188, P1/6Reg/405
Jn., weaver, Downton, 1735, I, W, P1/E/209, P1/8Reg/116
Jn., basketmaker, Downton, 1744, W, P1/E/231, P1/9Reg/434A
Jn., Downton, 1763, AB, appt of guardian, P1/E/254
Jn., Downton, 1791, AB, P2/E/415
Eastment, Jn., carp., Maiden B., 1838, W, Wr, P2/1838/25
Jos., Downton, 1778-88, AB (2), P2/E/393, 414
Eastmond, Mgt., widow, Sal. (form. of Downton), 1673, I, W, P4/1673/9
My., sp., Downton, 1636, I, W, P2/E/124
Estmond, My., widow, Chards., Devon, 1691, AB, I, P14/78
My., widow, E. Harnham, Britford, 1693, AB, I, ren, P24/527
My., sp., Bemerton, Fugg. St Peter, 1731-32, W, P1/E/199, P1/7Reg/442
Moses, yeo., Nunton, N. and Bodenham, 1693, I, W, P2/E/231
Nathaniel, bed tickmaker, Downton, 1798, W, P2/E/425
Estmond, Peter, Downton, 1554, W, P2/2Reg/191
Peter, N. Wootton, Dorset, 1603, AB, I, P5/1603/27
Estmond, Richd., Fovant, 1590, AB, P2/E/30
Richd., Downton, 1620, I, T, P2/E/87
Eastmond, Richd., yeo., Hidden, Hungerford, Berks., 1672, AB, I, P23/30
Eastmond, Richd., yeo., Hungerford, Berks., 1744, W, P23/576
Estmond, Robt., scrivener, Wantage, Berks., 1641, AB, I, P5/1641/30, P5/14Reg/2B
Roger, Charlton, Downton, 1547, W (NEP), P2/1Reg/71B
Roger, yeo., Charlton, Downton, 1605, AB, I, W (damaged), P1/E/4
Roger, sen., yeo., Charlton, Downton, 1610, I, W (2), P2/E/68, P2/8Reg/125A
Sarah, widow, Downton, 1780, W, P2/E/398
Susanna, widow, Downton, 1740, I, W, P2/E/324
Estmond, Thos., Wantage, Berks., 1572, W, P5/2Reg/110B
Estmond, Thos., gent., Chards., Devon, 1686, I, W, P14/63
Thos., carp., Downton, 1735, W, P1/8Reg/133
Eastment, Thos., cordw., Mere, 1742, AB, I, ren, W, P5/1741/10
Walter, Nunton, N. and Bodenham, 1575, AB, P2/5Reg/232A
Walter, yeo., Bodenham, Nunton and B., 1608-09, court papers, I, W, P2/E/65, P2/8Reg/39C
Walter, yeo., Bodenham, Nunton and B., 1639-45, AB, I, W, P2/E/137, 144
Eastmond, Wm., Britford, 1671, NW, P24/382
Wm., sen., shoemaker, E. Harnham, Britford, 1688, AB, I, P24/777
Wm., sen., tailor, E. Harnham, Britford, 1706, I, W, P24/593
Wm., sen., bacon and cheese factor; boot and shoe dealer, E. Harnham, Britford, 1745, AB, guardianship bond, I (very detailed), P24/966
Eastmead, Hy., Sonning, Berks., 1686, AB, I, P5/1686/22
Estmead, Jn., surgeon, Urchf., 1619, I, W, P1/E/24
Estmead, Matthew, bach., Calne, 1669, comm, W, P26/170
Thos., sen., mason, Westport St My., 1705, I, W, P3/E/170
Wm., broad weaver, Chipp., 1720, W, P3/E/190
Eastment, Eastmond *see* Eastman
Easton, Alice, widow, Sal., 1707, AB, P4/1706/6
Ann, widow, Corton, Boyton, [1689], I, P2/E/222
Edwd., broad weaver, Semley, 1611, AB, I, NW, P2/E/69
Frances, widow, Mere, 1684, AB, I, P5/1684/17
Eston, Jas., yeo., Crockerton, Longbridge D., 1638, AB, I, P2/E/131
Jas., shoemaker, Sal., 1724, I, ren, W, P4/1724/5
Jas., coal merchant, Sal., 1800, W, P4/1800/1
Jn., weaver, Teffont E., 1572, W, P2/5Reg/148A
Easton alias Mayo, Jn., weaver, Teffont E., 1592, I, W, P2/E/36
Jn., Sal., 1719, AB, P4/1719/8
My., sp., Sal. St Martin, 1760, AB, W, P4/1760/6
Richd., yeo., Sal. St Edmd., 1645, AB, I (includes a shuffle board room), P1/E/69
Thos., rector, Beechingstoke, 1716, I, W, P1/E/169, P1/6Reg/32B
Thos., Teffont E., 1764, AB, P2/E/370

Thos., yeo., Teffont E., 1784, AB, W, P2/E/403
Wm., weaver, Teffont E., 1629, AB, P2/E/104
see also Eastman *or* E.
Eastwood, Thos., yeo. and innholder, Blewbury, Berks., 1696, I, W, P5/1696/15
Eatall *see* Eatwell
Eateman, Chris., Mere, 1638-39, AB, I, P5/1638/35, P5/13Reg/152A
Eaton, Ambrose, Sal., 1667, AB, I, P4/1667/26
Cath., widow and gentlewoman, Wilton, 1662, I, W, P1/E/80
Eton, Geo., scrivener, no abode stated, c1635, I, P30/63
Isaac, haberdasher, Mere, 1614, I, W, P5/1614/22, P5/9Reg/148D
Jeremiah, yeo., Sal. The Close, 1664, I, W, P1/E/87
Jn., husb., Orcheston St My., 1560, I, W, P2/E/6, P2/4Reg/52A
Jn., barber, Marl. St Peter and St Paul, 1629, I (detailed), W, P1/E/37
Jn., yeo., Britford, 1633, I (detailed), W, P24/239
Jn., Britford, 1672, AB, I, P24/468
Jn., yeo., Britford, 1716, I, P24/655
Jn., butcher, Chipp., 1809, W, Wr, P3/1809/62
Richd., Marl. St Peter and St Paul, 1632, W, P1/E/45
Richd., Biddestone St Nich., 1732, AB, I, W, P1/E/200, P1/7Reg/510A
Susanna, widow, Warm., 1810, W, Wr, P2/1810/35
Thos., servingman, Chute, 1611, AB, I, P7/5
Thos., sen., dealer in bacon, Chipp., 1773, comm, W, P3/E/276
Thos., sen., baker and maltster, Chipp., 1775, comm, W, P3/E/280
Walter, vintner, Sal. St Thos., 1641, AB, ren, P4/1640/4
Wm., weaver, Corsham, 1593, draft W, W (on reverse lease of meadow in C., Wm. E. to Thos. E., his son. 1593), P29/E/1, P29/1Reg/36
Eattel *see* Eatwell
Eattes, Thos., Lyme R., Dorset, 1609, AB, P5/8Reg/168C
Eatwell, Etwall, Ann, sp., Bps. C., 1694, I, W, P24/523
Ann, tailor's wife, Marl., 1706, AB, P1/E/153
Ann, sp., Calne, 1766, AB, P26/1016
Ettwall, Bridget, widow, Bourton, Bps. C., 1706, W, P24/591
Bridget, sp., Yatesbury, 1708, comm, W, P1/E/155
Ettwall, Bridget, widow, Horton, Bps. C., 1755, W, P24/1019
Etwell, Cath., Etchilhampton, 1753, W, P1/E/248, P1/11Reg/108B
Dan., labourer, Clyffe P., 1768, W, P3/E/271
Edith, widow, Winterbourne M., 1635, I, W, P1/E/51
Etwall, Edith, widow, Bourton, Bps. C., 1673, I, W, P24/457
Ettwall, Edith, widow, Bourton, Bps. C., 1721, W, P24/897
Eatall, Edwd., husb., Marl., 1672, AB, I, P1/E/103
Edwd., sen., blacksmith, Calne, 1784, W, P26/1142
Eatall, Eliz., widow, Purton, 1728-29, W, P1/E/194, P1/7Reg/208
Eatall, Florence, widow, Castle Eaton, 1635, I, W, P1/E/52
Francis, yeo., Littlecote, Rams., 1720, I, W, P5/1720/18, P5/16Reg/42A
Francis, blacksmith, Calne, 1746, W, P5/1746/23
Francis, Calne, 1758, AB, comm, P5/1758/13
Francis, ironmonger, Calne, 1835, comm, W, Wr, P26/1422
Grace, widow, Chipp., 1706, W, P3/E/176
Jas., farmer, Cherhill, 1849, AB, D, O, W, Wr, P5/1849/2
Ettwall, Jane, widow, Allington, All C., 1685, I, W, P3/E/136
Etwall, Joan, sp., Eastcott, Urchf., 1678, W, P2/E/188
Joan, widow, Winterbourne M., 1684, AB, I, W, P3/E/122-23
Eatall, Jn., yeo., Castle Eaton, 1624, I, W, P3/E/38
Etwall, Jn., sen., yeo., Bourton, Bps. C., 1689, I, W, P24/734
Jn., innholder, Chipp., 1700, comm, W, P3/E/163
Eatall, Jn., Wootton B., 1705, I, P3/E/171
Eatall, Jn., yeo., Purton, 1711, I (2 - 1 a copy), W, P3/E/180
Eatall, Jn., sen., Wootton B., 1720, W, P3/E/191
Jn., yeo., Winterbourne M., 1721, I, W, P3/E/193
Ettwall, Jn., yeo., Horton, Bps. C., 1730, I, W, P24/820

Ettwell, Jn., yeo., Bourton, Bps. C., 1735, W, P24/933
Ettwell, Jn., yeo., Horton, Bps. C., 1743, W, P24/977
Jn., Winterbourne M., 1744, W, P1/E/232, P1/9Reg/286A
Etwall, Jn., doctor, Sal., 1747, req, W, copy W, P4/1747/10
Eatall, Jn., yeo., Stanton Fitzwarren, 1747, W, P3/E/233
Jn., yeo., Castle Eaton, 1752, W, P3/E/249
Jn., cordw., Berwick B., 1764, W, P5/1764/13
Jn., cordw., Berwick B., 1778, W, P26/1094
Eattel, Jn., maltster, Conock, Chirton, 1798, AB, W, P1/E/298, P1/15Reg/38B
Jn., mason, Cherhill, 1851, O, W, Wr, P5/1851/13
Eatwall *or* Etwall, Jos., Berwick B., 1671, AB, comm, I (detailed), P26/184
Etwall, Lucy, widow, Bourton, Bps. C., 1759, comm, W, P24/1113
Ettwall, Margery, Horton, Bps. C., 1713, AB, P24/710
My., sp., Calne, 1830, comm, W (& cod), Wr, P5/1830/10
Eatwall, Ralph, sen., yeo., Bourton, Bps. C., 1661-62, AB, comm (2), I (2), W, P24/332-33
Ettwall, Ralph, yeo., Horton, Bps. C., 1720, I, W, P24/687
Ettwall, Ralph, yeo., Bourton, Bps. C., 1736-38, AB, comm, W, P24/914, 925
Richd., husb., Winterbourne M., 1687, I, W, P3/E/140
Richd., maltster, Ashton K., 1696, a/c, I, W, P3/E/158
Eatwell *or* Etwell, Robt., sen., husb., Horton, Bps. C., 1613, I (detailed), W, P24/103
Robt., Winterbourne M., 1640, AB, a/c, I, P3/E/63
Ettwall, Robt., sen., yeo., Allington, All C., 1683, I, W, P3/E/120
Ettwell, Robt., farmer, Sharcott, Pewsey, 1850, comm, W, Wr, P3/1850/45
Eatwall, Ruth, sp., Coate, Bps. C., 1679, I, W, P24/477
Sarah, widow, Winterbourne M., 1721, I, W, P3/E/194
Susanna, widow, Winterbourne M., 1752, AB, P3/E/251
Eatall, Thos., labourer, Godsell Farm, Bremhill, 1677, I, W (NEP), P1/E/111
Ettwall, Thos., clerk and vicar, Bps. C., 1683, comm, I, W, P24/764
Thos., yeo., Winterbourne M., 1685, AB, I, W, P3/E/129
Eatwall, Thos., sen., Bps. C., 1687, AB, P1/E/125
Thos., clothworker, Melk., 1726, I, W, P2/E/300
Ettwall, Thos., yeo., Horton, Bps. C., 1734, W, P24/946
Etwell, Thos., labourer, Etchilhampton, 1751, W, P3/E/247
Eatwall, Thos., maltster, Marl., 1778, W, P1/E/276, P1/13Reg/190
Ettwell, Thos., sen., yeo., Bourton, Bps. C., 1817, W, Wr, P24/1278
Ettwell, Thos., Mkt. L., 1831, AB, comm, P2/1831/56
Thos., carp., Broad H., 1841, AB, Wr, P3/1841/20
Eatwall *or* Etwall, Wm., yeo., Horton, Bps. C., 1624, I, W, P24/187
Eatwall, Wm., yeo., Coate, Bps. C., 1667, I, ren, W, P24/354
Ettwall, Wm., vicar, Ogbourne St Geo., 1669, I (library valued at £60), W, P23/6
Wm., blacksmith, Berwick B., 1731, AB, ren, P26/752
Wm., yeo., Lyneham, 1779, comm, W, P3/E/291
see also Russ alias E.
Eave *see* Eve
Eavence *see* Evans
Eayears, Eayers *see* Ayers
Eaylford *see* Alford
Eayres *see* Eyre
Ebber *see* Harbin alias E.
Ebdy *see* Abdy
Ebony, My., widow, Sal. St Edmd., 1732, I, W, P1/E/201, P1/7Reg/540A
Ebrall, Chris., tallow chandler, Devizes, 1784, W, P1/E/281, P1/14Reg/55
Ebsworth, Jn., millwright, Crickl. St S., 1614, I, W, P1/E/15
Eburne, Jas., clerk and minister, Bramshaw, Hants, 1675, I, W, P24/439
Eccott *see* Eacott
Ecton, Jn., Ludg., 1580, I, W, P2/E/20, P2/6Reg/8C
Wm., Downton, 1552, W, P2/2Reg/158B
Ecutt *see* Eacott
Edalls *see* Iddolls
Edbrook, Robt., grocer, Warm., 1849, W, Wr, P2/1849/26

Edde *see* Eades
Eddington *see* Edington
Eddolls *see* Iddolls
Eden, Benj., Devizes, 1829, W, Wr, P1/1829/50
Giles, Devizes, 1779, AB, P1/E/277
Jas., sen., coachmaker, Southbroom, 1831, AB, comm, ren, W, P24/1325
Eden alias Hellier, Jn., husb., Devizes St My., 1664, AB, I, W, P1/H/352
Jn., cordw., Devizes, 1852, W, Wr, P1/1852/24
Jn., coach builder, Devizes St My., 1856, aff, O, W, Wr, P1/1856/24
Jos., sen., butcher, Devizes, 1760, AB, W, P1/E/250, P1/11Reg/487A
Jos., Devizes, 1773, AB, comm, P1/E/268
Jos., gent., Poulshot, 1824, comm, D, W, Wr, P2/1824/7
Mgt., widow, Devizes, 1842, AB, O, ren, W, Wr, P1/1842/20
My., widow, Sal., 1847, AB, Wr, P4/1847/2
Richd., hellier, Devizes St My., 1717, W, P1/E/175, P1/6Reg/118
Richd., baker, Sal., 1825, W, Wr, P4/1825/2
Robt., woolcomber, Devizes, 1775, W, P1/E/271, P1/13Reg/68
Sarah, sp., Poulshot, 1825, AB, comm, D, W, Wr, P2/1825/29
Thos., yeo., Wick, Bps. C., 1804, W, P24/1233
Wm., gardener, Devizes, 1696, AB, ren, P1/E/141
Wm., gardener, Nursteed, Bps. C., 1763, comm, W, P24/1098
Wm., dyer, Devizes, 1768, AB, P1/E/263
Wm., yeo., Southbroom, 1836, O, W, P24/1346
Wm., coachmaker, Southbroom, 1838, O, W, Wr, P24/1358
see also Hilliar alias E.
Edes *see* Eades
Edgare, Edgar, Ann *see* Chas. Lee
Isabel, widow, Alderbury, 1572, W, P5/2Reg/115F
Edge, Ann, widow, Devizes, 1716, W, P1/E/170, P1/6Reg/6
Edgecombe, Betty, widow, Chipp., 1817, W, Wr, P1/1817/60
Eliz., sp., Malm., 1828, O, W, Wr, P3/1828/51
Jas., gingerbread baker and bach., Malm., 1748, AB, I, P3/E/235
Jn., labourer, Enborne, Berks., 1808, W, Wr (2), P1/1808/115
Nathaniel, Malm., 1733, AB, I, P3/E/213
Edgell, Jn., butcher, Trowb., 1792, comm, W, Wr, P1/E/289
Wm., gent., Trowb., 1840, O, W, Wr, P1/1840/3
Edginton, Jn., sen., yeo., Harwell, Berks., 1770, W, P1/E/264, P1/12Reg/361B
Edington, Agnes, widow, Idmiston, 1681, AB, I, P2/E/200
Amy, widow, Buttermere, 1631, I, W, P1/E/39
Eddington, Edwd., husb., Ludg., 1603, I, W, P2/E/58
Edwd., husb., Ludg., 1648, I, W, P2/E/152
Jas., Ludg., 1680, AB, comm, I, P2/E/195
Jane, widow, Idmiston, 1710, W, P2/E/269
Jn., yeo., Ludg., 1713, W, P2/E/277
Mgt., widow, Idmiston, 1633, I, W, P2/E/115, P2/9Reg/7
Richd., Collingbourne D., 1634, I, W, P1/E/47
Richd., jun., Ludg., 1667, AB, I, copy I, P2/E/167
Richd., Ludg., 1669, I, W, P2/E/174
Robt., sen., day labourer, Idmiston, 1627, I, W, P2/E/100
Robt., husb., Buttermere, 1629, I, W, P3/E/48
Eddington, Robt., Ludg., 1646, AB, I, ren, P2/E/147, 153
Robt., sen., husb., Idmiston, 1667, I, W, P2/E/165
Robt., Sal., 1681, AB, P4/1681/10
Robt., bach., Collingbourne K., 1695, AB, I, P3/E/155
Eddington *or* Edington, Wm., shepherd, Idmiston, 1632, I, W, P2/E/110, P2/9Reg/25B
Wm., Bourton, Gillingham, Dorset, 1682, I, P27/1/67
Wm., husb., Idmiston, 1707, I, W, P2/E/259
Edlin, Michael, clerk and parson, Ham, 1633, AB, comm, I (all damaged), P1/E/46
Thos., sen., yeo., Aston U., Blewbury, Berks., 1746, W, P5/1746/24
Edmay *see* Edney

Edmonds, Abraham, Fittleton, 1827, AB, Wr, P2/1827/71
Ann, sp., Lyneham, 1803, W, P3/1803/53
Edments alias Partridge, Ann (possibly Amy), widow, Lyme R., Dorset, 1611, W, P5/9Reg/56B
Bartholomew, maltster, Newbury, Berks., 1698, W, P1/E/144, P1/3Reg/133
Cath., sp., Sal. The Close, 1708-09, W, P5/1708/27, P5/15Reg/102B
Edmunds, David, Sherb., Dorset, 1845, AB (2), O (2), Wr, P5/1845/31
Edmonds alias Carter, Edith, widow, Gillingham, Dorset, 1572, W, P27/1Reg/27B
Edmd., Bishopstone N., 1685, NW, P5/1685/32
Eliz., widow, Broughton G., 1614, I, W, P1/E/16
Eliz., widow, Sal., 1739, req, W, P4/1739/1
Giles, Chicklade, 1806, AB, Wr, P2/1806/40
Hannah, sp., Oare, Wilcot, 1823, W, P3/1823/18
Hy., Broughton G., 1626, AB, I, P2/E/98
Hy., vicar, Netherb., Dorset, 1708, I, note, ren, P17/180
Hester, widow, Oare, Wilcot, 1807, W, P1/1807/24
Jacob, Clack, Lyneham, 1747, AB, comm, P3/E/234
Jacob, Chr. M., 1781, AB, P3/E/292
Edmunds, Jas., Chicklade, 1785, AB, P2/E/406
Jane, widow, Bishopstone N., 1735, W, P6/123
Edmunds, Joan, widow, Britford, 1570, W, P5/2Reg/58B
Jn., husb., Stapleford, 1580, I, W, P2/E/19, P2/6Reg/7E
Edmunds, Jn., tailor, Corsham, 1619, I, LA, P29/E/2
Edmunds, Jn., Ludg., 1623, T (unnamed children), P2/E/92
Edmunds alias Sayer *or* Sawyer, Jn., Aughton, Collingbourne K., 1634, AB, a/c, I, NW, P3/E/56
Jn., broad weaver, Steeple A., 1645, AB, I, P2/E/146
Jn., blacksmith, Oare, Wilcot, 1674, AB, I, NW, P1/E/105
Edmunds, Jn., yeo., N. Hinksey, Berks., 1686, I, W, P1/E/304
Jn., Baydon, 1692-93, AB, a/c, I, P5/1692/26, P5/1693/20
Jn., blacksmith, Hurst, Berks., 1702, AB, comm, I, P5/1702/25
Edmonds alias Holloway, Jn., Milston, 1721, AB, P2/E/290
Jn., innholder, Devizes, 1721, W (ill with smallpox), P1/E/185, P1/6Reg/382
Edmunds, Jn., blacksmith, E. Knoyle, 1723, comm, W, P1/E/189, P1/6Reg/411B
Jn., yeo., Hannington Wick, 1723, W, P3/E/197
Jn., Wilcot, 1737, W, P3/E/219
Jn., Oare, Wilcot, 1751, W, P3/E/244
Jn., Porton, Idmiston, 1762, AB, W, P2/E/365
Jn., Highw., 1780, AB, P10/1780/1
Jn., Sandy Lane, Heddington, 1794, W, Wr, P3/E/310
Jn., yeo., Long Burton, Dorset, 1812, W, Wr, P5/1812/22
Jn., yeo., Oare, Wilcot, 1855, aff, comm, W, Wr, P3/1855/3
Jn., widower, Bradford A., 1857, AB, aff, O, Wr, P2/1857/2
Julian, Warm., 1616, AB, P2/E/78
Martha, widow and sp., Ebbesborne Wake, 1707, I, W, P2/E/260
My., widow, Chicklade, 1793, AB, note, P2/E/420
Edmunds, Nich., Downton, 1547, W, P2/2Reg/30
Edmunds, Nich., Broughton G., 1586, I, W, P2/E/24, P2/7Reg/37B
Nich., victualler, Bradford A., 1751, AB, ren, P2/E/346
Edmunds, Oliver, Lyneham, 1613, AB, P1/E/11
Edmunds alias Lawrence, Richd., [yeo.], Oare in Huish, Wilcot, 1634, AB, a/c, I, P1/E/48
Edmunds, Richd., yeo., Stock, Gt. Bedwyn, 1646, W, P21/1/61
Richd., [farmer], Ford, Laverstock, 1684, AB, I, P4/1684/14
Richd., Baydon, 1686, I, NW, P5/1686/23
Richd., sen., yeo., Oare, Wilcot, 1735, W, P1/E/210, P1/8Reg/45
Richd., Oare, Wilcot, 1741, W, P3/E/227
Edmon, Richd., labourer, Hamptworth, Downton, 1791, W, P2/E/416
Richd., maltster, Oare, Wilcot, 1799, comm, W, Wr, P3/E/313
Edmunds, Robt., yeo., Stratford sub C., 1628, I, W, P4/1628/8
Robt., clothworker, Sal., 1672, I, W, P4/1672/13
Robt., Britford, 1680, AB, I (detailed), ren, W, P24/426
Edmunds, Robt., W. Harnham, 1747, W, P8/38

Roger, weaver, Heddington, 1731, I, W, P3/E/210
Edmunds, Ruth, widow, Baydon, 1695, AB, I, P5/1695/25
Edmunds, Stephen, sen., yeo., Baydon, 1695, I, W, P5/1695/26
Stephen, bach., Pewsey, 1831, AB, O, P3/1831/16
Edmunds, Susanna, widow, Milford, Sal. St Martin, 1754, AB, P4/1754/5
Thos., weaver, Broughton G., 1597, I, W, P2/E/48
Edmunds, Thos., husb., Bulk., Keevil, [1617], I, W, P2/E/82
Thos., husb., Ogbourne St A., 1634, AB, I (2) (GVS), P5/1634/36
Thos., Wanb., 1636, AB, I, P3/E/58
Edmunt, Thos., yeo., Netherb., Dorset, 1636, I, W, P17/33
Edmunds alias Sayer *or* Sawyer, Thos., yeo., Aughton, Collingbourne K., 1639, I, W (damaged), P3/E/62
Thos., yeo., Collingbourne K., [c1650], W (NEP), P3/E/70
Thos., husb., Collingbourne K., 1672, AB, I, P3/E/91
Edmunds, Thos., sen., husb., Ogbourne St A., 1677, I, W, P23/69
Thos., gardener, Stratford sub C., 1771, W, P4/1771/1
Valerius, Yatesbury, 1619, AB, P1/E/25
Valerius, Yatesbury, 1627, AB, comm, O, W (damaged), P1/E/34
Edmund alias Carter, Wm., Gillingham, Dorset, 1570, W, P27/1Reg/21D
Wm., clerk, Gt. Amesb., 1624, I, W, P2/E/93
Edmunds alias Lawrence, Wm., sen., husb. and yeo., Wilton, Gt. Bedwyn, 1670, I, W, P21/2/9
Wm., blacksmith, E. Knoyle, 1681, I, W, P2/E/201
Wm., labourer, Whaddon, 1703, I, W, P2/E/251
Edmunce, Wm., labourer, Eastrop, Highw., 1716, W, P5/1716/28, P5/15Reg/350D
Wm., husb., Sal., 1754, W, P4/1754/7
Edmunds, Wm., minors, Sherb., Dorset, 1845, T, P5/1845/30
Edmondson, Ann, widow, Sevenhampton, Highw., 1688, I, W, P5/1688/28
Edmunce, Edmund, Edmunds, Edmunt *see* Edmonds
Edney, Alfred, minor, Whitep., 1843, AB, Wr, P2/1843/38
Alice, widow, Durrington, 1557, W, P2/3Reg/8C
Ann, widow, Devizes, 1639, AB, I, W, P1/E/60
Idny, Chas., yeo., Durrington, 1639, I, W, P2/IJ/112
Cudbury, yeo.'s widow, Steeple L., 1673, I, W, P2/E/182
Edmd., husb., Steeple L., 1623, I, W, P2/E/91
Jas., yeo. *or* innholder, Devizes, 1638, I, W, P1/E/59
Idny, Jn., husb., Durrington, 1590, I, P2/IJ/23
Eadney, Jn., Amesb., 1610, I, W, P2/E/429, P2/8Reg/138A
Edney alias Hooper, Jn., yeo., Luckington, 1664, AB, I, P1/E/88
Jn., blacksmith, Marl. St My., 1762, W, P1/E/252, P1/12Reg/30A
Martha, Collingbourne D., 1727, W, P21/8/33
Maud, widow, Durrington, 1621, I, W, P2/E/88
Nich., husb., Steeple L., 1660, AB, a/c, I, P2/E/156
Idny, Richd., brewer, Sal. St Martin, 1636, AB, I, NW, P4/1636/7
Idny, Richd., [blacksmith], Marl., 1668, AB, comm, I, P1/IJ/88
Richd., gent., Marl., 1714, I, W, P1/E/165, P1/5Reg/417
Edmay alias Hooper, Robt., weaver, Luckington, 1601, W, P3/1Reg/63A
Idny, Robt., husb., Durrington, 1671, I, W, P2/IJ/149
Sarah, widow, Marl., 1718, I, W, P1/E/176, P1/6Reg/162B
Sibyl, widow, Swindon, 1679, I, W, P3/E/110
Edney alias Hooper, Simon, blacksmith, Corsham, 1700, I, P29/E/3
Idny, Thos., yeo., Durrington, 1640, I, W, P2/IJ/117
Idny, Thos., sen., yeo., Durrington, 1662, I, W, P1/IJ/72
Thos., yeo., Swindon, 1674, comm, I, W, P3/E/99
Thos., [blacksmith], Marl., 1692, AB, I, P1/E/127
Thos., sen., blacksmith, Marl., 1708, AB, I, P1/E/156
Thos., yeo., Collingbourne D., 1718, W, P21/7/35
Walter, husb., Stoke F., 1644, I, W, P2/E/142
Eadney, Wm., Durrington, 1582, W, P2/6Reg/65C
Edome, Alexander, Downton, 1715, AB, I, P2/E/282
Edridge, Hy., blacksmith, Stapleford, 1684, AB, I, P2/E/211
Humphrey, Sherrington, 1593, I, W, P2/E/40

Jn., husb., Sherrington, 1610-15, AB, a/c, I, P2/E/67, P2/8Reg/123C
Mgt., widow, Sherrington, 1621, I, W, P2/E/428
Robt., Sherrington, 1593, I, W, P2/E/43
Edridge *or* Etheredge, Thos., Bradford A., 1567, W, P2/5Reg/6A
Edsall, Cicely, Downton, 1678, AB, P2/E/192
Jn., blacksmith, Downton, 1669, I, P2/E/175
Jn., blacksmith, Downton, 1674, AB, I, P1/E/106
Jn., Downton, 1678, AB, P2/E/191
Jn., Downton, 1720, AB, P1/E/180
Simon, blacksmith, Downton, 1727, W, P2/E/301
Valentine, blacksmith, Downton, 1709, W, P2/E/264
Edsons, Peter, Lacock, 1638, I, NW, P1/E/56
Edwards, Abraham, Devizes, 1692, AB, ren, P1/E/128
Edward, Abraham, husb., Chards., Devon, 1703, I, W, P14/98
Agnes, sp., Norton B., 1631, I, W, P1/E/40
Alice, Hannington, 1570, W (NEP), P1/1Reg/57A
Edwards alias Brewer, Alice, widow, Malm., 1668, I, W, P3/E/80
Alice, widow, Eisey, 1679, I, W, P3/E/111
Alice, widow, Bramshaw, Hants, 1679, I (detailed), W, P24/473
Alice, widow, Carters, Colerne, 1692, comm, I, W, P1/E/129
Alice, widow, Wedh., Urchf., 1745, AB, P2/E/335
Amram, maltster, Mkt. L., 1783, W, P1/E/280, P1/13Reg/452
Ann, widow, Wedh., Urchf., 1636, AB, a/c, I copy I, P2/E/121
Ann, widow, Urchf., 1705, alleg, I, W, P2/E/258
Ann, widow, Norton B., 1712, W, P2/E/274
Ann, gent.'s widow, Rams., 1803, W, P5/1803/36, P5/19Reg/64B
Ann, widow, Chipp., 1810, W, Wr, P3/1810/32
Ann, widow, Rams., 1814, W, Wr (2), P5/1814/22
Ann, Trowb., 1823, W, Wr, P1/1823/51
Anthony, husb., Wanb., 1688, I, W, P3/E/144
Anthony, yeo., Brinkw., 1716, AB, I, P3/E/186
Anthony, Wilton, Gt. Bedwyn, 1773, W, P21/11/5
Anthony, Wilton, Gt. Bedwyn, 1822, W, Wr, P5/1822/3
Avis, widow, Wedh., Urchf., 1707, W, P2/E/261
Benj., sen., yeo., Bramshaw, Hants, 1666, I (detailed), W, P24/375
Benj., cardmaker, Chipp., 1756, W, P3/E/255
Brian, Stanton St B., 1619, I, W (on same sheet), P3/E/30
Brian, maltster, Westb., 1759, W, P25/1759/3
Bridget, Burbage, 1736, W, P11/131
Chas., butcher, Wrou., 1680, AB, I, P1/E/113
Chas., mail coachman, Warm., 1839, W, Wr, P1/1839/42
Christian, widow, Bramshaw, Hants, 1718, I (detailed), W, P24/640
Chris., yeo., Bramshaw, Hants, 1612, I, P24/109
Chris., shearman, Bishopstone N., 1629, I, W, P6/9
Edith, widow, Westb., 1618, I, W, P25/1618/4
Edmd., [clothworker], Brook, Westb., 1661, AB, I, P25/1661/2
Edwd., Fonthill B., 1611, a/c (damaged), AB, I, P1/E/9
Edwd., yeo., Brinkw., 1697, I, W, P3/E/159
Edwd., Wilton, Gt. Bedwyn, 1722, AB, I, P5/1722/20
Edwd., Stourton, 1786, AB, appt of guardian, P1/E/282
Edwd., yeo., Wedh., Urchf., 1796, W, P2/E/423
Edwd., innkeeper, Urchf., 1820, comm, W, Wr, P1/1820/144
Edwd.s, widower, Lt. Hinton, 1846, AB, aff, O, Wr, P3/1846/7
Elias, yeo., Liddington, 1676, AB, I, P3/E/104
Eliz., Steeple L., 1547, W, P2/2Reg/47B
Eliz., Wrou., 1619, I, W, P3/E/32
Eliz., widow, Conock, Chirton, 1622, deed of gift, I, P2/E/90
Eliz., widow, Brook, Westb., 1669, AB, I (clothworker's tools), W, P25/1669/9
Edwards alias George, Eliz., yeo. and widow, Lt. Cheverell, 1704, I, W, P2/E/256
Eliz., clothier's widow, Trowb., 1718, W, P2/E/286

Eliz., widow, Sal., 1723, W, P4/1722/9
Eliz., widow, Malm., 1760, W, P3/E/262
Eliz., widow, Wedh., Urchf., 1767, AB, P1/E/256
Eliz., widow, Corsham, 1771, W, P29/E/5, P29/2Reg/146
Eliz., widow, Biddestone St Nich., 1773, AB, P3/E/277
Eliz., wife, Avill's Farm, Corsham, 1783, AB, comm, P3/E/298
Eliz., sp., Purton, 1798, comm, W, P1/E/299, P1/15Reg/54
Eliz., widow, Highw., 1823, W, P10/1823/3
Francis, yeo., Biddestone, 1700, AB, I, P3/E/164
Francis, clothworker, Bradford A., 1745, W, P2/E/336
Francis, gent., Devizes, 1748, W, P1/E/239, P1/10Reg/228
Francis, labourer, N. Tidworth, 1752, W, P2/E/349
Francis, yeo., Milbourne, Corsham, 1794, W, P3/E/311
Geo., husb., Norton B., 1613, I, W, P1/E/12
Geo., Enmore Grn, Motc., Dorset, 1662, I, W, P5/1662/38
Geo., husb., Hamptworth, Downton, 1663, I, W, P2/E/158
Geo., cooper, Wootton B., 1727, W, P3/E/202
Geo., cloth dresser, Bradford A., 1780, comm, O (2), W, P2/E/397
Geo., Winterbourne E., 1806, AB, Wr, P2/1806/54
Geo., shopkeeper, Chipp., 1812, W, Wr, P3/1812/1
Edwards alias Price, Geo., Warm., 1842, W, Wr, P2/1842/12
Grace, widow, Bradford A., 1730, W, P2/E/309
Grace, sen., widow, Manningford Bohun, 1777, W, P3/E/288
Hannah Taylor, excise officer's wife, Allweston, Folke, Dorset, 1826, W (& cod), Wr, P5/1826/8
Hy., husb., Tinh., Edington, 1625, AB, a/c, comm, I, P1/E/30
Hy., yeo., Bramshaw, Hants, 1662, I (2), P24/310
Hy., yeo., S. Newton, 1713, W, P2/E/276
Hy., yeo. *or* tailor, W. Kington, 1720, I, W, P3/E/192
Hy., E. Harnham, Britford, 1738, W, Wr, P5/1738/16
Hy., Swindon, 1751, AB, comm, P3/E/245
Hy., collarmaker, Highw., 1787, AB, note, P10/1787/1
Hy., yeo., N. Leaze, Rodbourne C., 1798, comm, W, P1/E/300, P1/15Reg/55
Hy., bach., Wanb., 1820, AB, comm, Wr, P3/1820/19
Hy., farmer, Upper Stratton, Stratton St Mgt., 1855, aff, comm, W, Wr, P3/1855/18
Hester, Westb., 1756, W, P25/1756/2
Hugh, Fisherton A., 1567, AB, P2/4Reg/239G
Isaac, tobacco pipemaker, Lyme R., Dorset, 1716, W, P5/1716/27, P5/15Reg/342C
Israel, sp., Chr. M., 1706, W, P3/E/177
Jas., yeo., Wedh., Urchf., 1644-47, AB, a/c (2), comm (2), court paper, I (2), ren, P2/E/143, 149
Jas., yeo., Semley, 1687, comm, I, W, P2/E/219
Jas., yeo., Wedh., Urchf., 1690, AB, I, P2/E/225
Jas., Corsham, 1730, marriage licence, P29/2Reg/58B
Edward, Jas., Corsham, 1778, AB, P29/2Reg/162
Jas., Lydiard T., 1828, AB, comm, Wr, P3/1828/7
Jas., yeo., Wilton, Gt. Bedwyn, 1841, comm, W, Wr, P5/1841/19
Jane, widow, Reybridge, Lacock, 1685, AB, I, L, P3/E/131
Jane, sp., Box, 1722, W, P3/E/196
Jean, sen., Wanb., 1684, W, P3/E/124
Jeremiah, Horningsham, 1728, AB, I, P5/1728/30, P5/16Reg/165A
Joan, widow, Fonthill B., 1634, W, P2/E/117
Joan, widow, Tinh., Edington, 1642, I, W, P2/E/140
Joan, widow, Wedh., Urchf., 1664, I, W, P2/E/161
Joan, widow, Colerne, 1683, comm, I, W, P3/E/117
Joan, widow, Corsley, 1723, AB, P2/E/292
Joan, widow, Crickl. St S., 1748, I, P3/E/236
Jn., Edington, c1538, W (NEP), P2/1Reg/2C
Jn., Norton B., 1558, W, P2/3Reg/119B
Jn., clerk, Gt. Horningsham, 1575, I, W, P5/1575/15, P5/3Reg/70A
Jn., husb., Barford St M., 1588, I, W, P2/E/26, P2/7Reg/120B
Jn., carp., Chirton, 1599, I, W, P2/E/55

Jn., sen., Norton B., 1605, AB, comm, I, O, P1/E/5
Jn., weaver, Chards., Devon, 1608, W, P5/8Reg/117B
Jn., husb., Wedh., Urchf., 1610, W, P2/8Reg/132C
Jn., tailor, Hannington, [c1617], I, NW (NEP), P3/E/25
Jn., miller, Stanton Fitzwarren, 1637, AB, a/c, I, P3/E/61
Jn., weaver, Norton B., 1643, AB, I, P1/E/62
Jn., sen., yeo., Eisey, 1662, I, W, P1/E/82
Jn., Wanb., 1672, I, W, P3/E/92
Jn., cordw., Lacock, 1673, I, W, P3/E/96
Jn., Eisey, 1676, I, P3/E/105
Jn., Stapleford, 1684, AB, P2/E/210
Jn., N. Tidworth, 1686, AB, I, P2/E/216
Jn., yeo., Wanb., 1686, W, P1/E/303
Jn., yeo., Norton B., [1689], I, W, P2/E/223
Jn., clothworker, Westb., 1696, AB, I, P25/1696/8
Jn., Broughton G., 1697, I, W, P2/E/243
Jn., yeo., Westb., 1702, AB, I (ref. to looms in millhouse), P25/1702/6
Jn., Bramshaw, Hants, 1708, AB, I, P24/578
Jn., yeo., Bishopstrow, 1711, W, P2/E/271
Jn., yeo., Norton B., 1711, W, P1/E/160, P1/5Reg/62
Jn., grocer, Sal., 1712, AB, P4/1712/16
Jn., wheelwright, Wilcot, 1715, AB, I, P3/E/184
Jn., linen draper, Chipp., 1716, I, W, P3/E/187
Jn., Sal. The Close, 1723, AB, P5/1723/11
Jn., yeo., Giddeahall, Yatton K., 1725, I, W, P3/E/200
Jn., Westb., 1727, AB, P25/1727/3
Jn., Maiden B., 1731, W, Wr, P2/E/310
Jn., carp. and widower, N. Tidworth, 1732, AB, I, P1/E/202
Jn., scribler, Trowb., 1738, comm, W, P1/E/220, P1/8Reg/240B
Jn., Sevenhampton, Highw., 1741, W, P10/1741/1
Jn., Gillingham, Dorset, 1743, AB, P27/1/370, P27/3Reg/30A
Jn., husb., Rodbourne C., 1751, W, P3/E/246
Jn., yeo., Thickwood, Colerne, 1754, W, P3/E/253
Jn., yeo., Liddington, 1758, W, P3/E/257
Jn., clerk, Wilton, 1759, W, P2/E/358
Jn., carp., Gillingham, Dorset, 1763, W, P27/1/436, P27/3Reg/99
Jn., gent., Slaughterford, 1767, W, P1/E/257, P1/12Reg/223
Jn., Stourton, 1769, W, P2/E/378
Jn., plumber and glazier, Corsham, [1771-1830], req (by bishop of Salisbury of W of Jn. E., wrongfully proved by Peculiar Court of Corsham in 1771), W, P29/E/8, P29/2Reg/144, P29/1800-1857/24
Jn., gent., Thickwood, Colerne, 1775, W, P3/E/282
Jn., yeo., Barnhill, Clyffe P., 1776, comm, W, P3/E/285
Jn., gent., Seend, Melk., 1777, W, P2/E/388
Jn., gent., Warm., 1777, W, P2/E/390
Jn., plumber and glazier, Hindon, 1778, W, P2/E/394
Jn., gent., Moor, Corsham, 1788, W, P3/E/302
Jn., Lt. Hinton, 1792, AB, P1/E/290, P1/14Reg/396
Jn., bach., Westb., 1793, AB, P25/1793/3
Jn., gent., Biddestone, 1798, W, P1/E/301, P1/15Reg/106C
Jn., yeo., Wilton, Gt. Bedwyn, 1798, W, P21/11/45
Jn., Eastcott, Urchf., 1813, W, Wr, P2/1813/21
Jn., yeo., Wedh., Urchf., 1817, W, Wr, P1/1817/114
Jn., fellmonger, Ashton K., 1825, O, W, Wr, P3/1825/47
Jn., yeo., Wilton, Gt. Bedwyn, 1827, O, W, Wr, P5/1827/7
Jn., shopkeeper, Chalford, Westb., 1828, W, Wr, P25/1828/4
Jn., yeo., Highw., 1830, note, O, W, P5/1830/12
Jn., tailor, Sal., 1837, W, Wr, P4/1837/1
Jn., Bratton, Westb., 1841, AB, Wr, P25/1841/9
Jn. Hitchman, yeo., Cherhill (form. of Broad B.), 1844, O, W, Wr, P5/1844/16
Jos., Bramshaw, Hants, 1716, AB, P24/656

Jos., Notton, Lacock, 1738, W, P3/E/222
Jos., labourer, W. Harnham, 1834, W, P8/86
Judith, widow, Enmore Grn, Motc., Dorset, 1818, comm, W, Wr, P5/1818/22
Lawr., yeo., Biddestone, 1812, comm, W, Wr, P3/1812/21
Lizzy, widow, Hannington Wick, 1809, comm, W, Wr, P3/1809/71
Marianne, widow, Baynton, Edington, 1553, I, W, P2/E/4, P2/2Reg/168C
Mark, aleman, Bromham, 1752, W, P3/E/248
Martha, Corsham, 1782, AB (re Martha & Jane E.), P29/2Reg/166B
Martha Ann My., widow, Corsham, 1785, W, P29/E/7, P29/2Reg/185
My., virgin, Sindlesham, Hurst, Berks., 1670, I, W, P5/1670/12
My., widow, Chards., Devon, 1705, AB, I, P14/102
My., widow, Notton, Lacock, 1734, I, W, P3/E/216
My., widow, Slaughterford, 1744, W, P1/E/233, P1/9Reg/414
My., widow, Gillingham, Dorset, 1785, W, P27/1/523, P27/3Reg/243
My., widow, Urchf., 1814, W, Wr, P2/1814/16
My., shopkeeper's wife, Chalford, Westb., 1823, AB, Wr, P25/1823/1
My., widow, Devizes Grn, Bps. C., 1835, W, P24/1344
My., widow, Calne, 1837, comm, W, Wr, P26/1439
My., widow, S. Marston, 1841, comm, W, Wr, P10/1841/1
My., sp., Highw., 1789, AB, P10/1789/2
Nathaniel, woolbroker, Trowb., 1826, AB, comm, W, Wr, P1/1826/144
Nathaniel, yeo., Charlton, 1826, W, Wr, P2/1826/2
Nich., husb., Over Stratton, Stratton St Mgt., 1624, I, W, P3/E/39
Nich., Maddington, 1638, I, W, P2/E/133
Nich., Brook, Westb., 1646, AB, I, P25/1646/1
Nich., Hurst, Berks., 1662, AB, comm, P5/1662/37
Nich., Westb., 1743, W, P25/1743/11
Oliver, Devizes, 1701, AB, P1/E/147
Oliver, Melk., 1795, AB, comm, P2/E/422
Peter, carp., N. Tidworth, 1738, W, P2/E/323
Philip, cardmaker, Chipp., 1775, W, P3/E/283
Phyllis, widow, Highw., 1758, AB, P10/1758/1
Prudence, widow, Norton B., 1684, W, P2/E/208
Richd., Ham, 1663, AB, comm, P3/E/75
Richd., carp., Collingbourne D., 1672, AB, I, P21/2/30
Richd., blacksmith, Sindlesham, Hurst, Berks., 1723, I, W, P5/1723/12, P5/16Reg/88C
Richd., sen., Wokm., Berks., 1752, AB, P5/1752/14
Richd., Lyme R., Dorset, 1753, AB, W, P16/312
Richd., yeo., Queen Laines Farm, Highw., 1795, ren, P10/1795/1
Robt., sen., yeo., Wedh., Urchf., 1633, I, W, P2/E/111
Robt., jun., Wedh., Urchf., 1665, AB, I, P2/E/163
Robt., jun., grocer, Wedh., Urchf., [1686], I, W, P2/E/215
Robt., husb., Stockton, 1690, comm, I, W, P2/E/224
Robt., yeo., Wichehazel, Urchf., 1694, I, W, P2/E/234
Robt., yeo., Wedh., Urchf., 1703?, W, P2/E/252
Robt., Landford, 1709, W, P2/E/263
Robt., Pewsey, 1714, AB, P3/E/182
Robt., yeo., Notton, Lacock, 1739, AB, W, P3/E/223
Robt., carp., N. Tidworth, 1744, W, P2/E/333
Robt., Wedh., Urchf., 1745, AB, P2/E/334
Robt., glazier, Hindon, 1752, AB, deed of gift, P2/E/347
Robt., Lacock, 1753, W, P1/E/243, P1/11Reg/127
Robt., yeo., Biddestone St Nich., 1756, W, P3/E/256
Robt., Bradford A., 1758, AB, P2/E/356
Robt., bach., Tilsh., 1813, AB, comm, Wr, P2/1813/31
Sam., yeo., Thickwood, Colerne, 1709, I, W, P3/E/178
Sam., cordw., Lyme R., Dorset, 1759, W, P16/322
Sam., gent., Avill's Farm, Corsham, 1759-86, AB (3), comm, ren, P3/E/261
Sarah, widow, Eastcott, Urchf., 1827, W, Wr, P2/1827/45
Sarah, widow, Highw., 1832, W, Wr, P10/1832/1

Stephen, Lyme R., Dorset, 1829, O, W, Wr, P16/401
Susanna, widow, Codf. St P., 1715, W, P2/E/281
Thos., Edington, 1560, W, P2/4Reg/61B
Edwards alias G..., Thos., Westb., 1560, W. No date of probate, P1/2Reg/98B
Thos., husb., Norton B., 1597, AB, I, W, P2/E/49
Thos., sen., weaver, Highw., 1630, I, W, P10/1630/5
Thos., sen., Wanb., 1668, I, W, P1/E/96
Thos., husb., Manningford A., 1672, I, W, P3/E/93
Thos., clerk and vicar, W. Lavington, 1673, comm, I, W, P1/E/104
Thos., yeo., Wanb., 1675, comm, I, W, P3/E/100
Thos., tailor, Crickl. St S., 1681, AB, I, W, P3/E/115
Thos., yeo., Wedh., Urchf., [1686], I, W, P2/E/213
Thos., sen., yeo., Westb., 1700, I, W, P25/1700/3
Thos., maltster, Devizes, 1702-03, I, W, P1/E/150, P1/4Reg/254
Thos., Mkt. L., 1705, AB, I, P2/E/257
Thos., Norton B., 1709, AB, P2/E/266
Thos., sen., cordw., Castle Lane, Rams., 1713, I, W, P5/1713/27, P5/15Reg/365C
Thos., carp., Sonning, Berks., 1718, W, P5/1718/12, P5/15Reg/411
Thos., clothier, Trowb., 1718, W, P2/E/285
Thos., Malm., 1727, AB, P3/E/203
Thos., Wrou., 1727, W, P3/E/204
Thos., sen., gent., Wanb., 1728, comm, W, P3/E/206
Thos., Wedh., Urchf., 1729, AB, I, P1/E/195
Edwards alias George, Thos., gent., Pott., 1735, W, P1/E/211, P1/8Reg/137
Thos., Wanb., 1739, AB, P3/E/224
Thos., sen., husb., Pewsey, 1740, AB, W, P3/E/225
Thos., yeo., Slaughterford, 1740, W, P3/E/226
Thos., carp., N. Tidworth, 1741, W, P2/E/328
Thos., sen., yeo., Lt. Hinton, 1744, W (NEP), P30/62
Thos., Collingbourne K., 1754, AB, P3/E/254
Thos., labourer, Gt. Bedwyn, 1758, W, P5/1758/14
Thos., clerk and bach., Sal. The Close, 1759, AB, ren, P5/1759/8
Thos., Crookwood in Pott., Urchf., 1760, AB, comm, P1/E/251
Thos., yeo., Sharcott, Pewsey, 1772, W, P3/E/275
Thos., carp., Gillingham, Dorset, 1774, W, P27/1/489, P27/3Reg/188
Thos., bach., Hampton, Highw., 1778, AB, comm, ren, P10/1778/2
Thos., yeo., Colerne, 1782, W, P3/E/297
Thos., yeo., Lt. Hinton, [1790-1829], AB, comm, court proceedings (3 as estate unadm., 1829), req, W, copy W, Wr, P3/E/305, P3/1829/9
Thos., Badbury, Chiseldon, 1792, W (NEP), P1/E/291, P1/14Reg/399
Thos., yeo., Lt. Hinton, 1794, W, P3/E/312
Thos., husb., Clarendon Park, 1799, W, P4/1799/19
Thos., Hindon, 1803, AB, P2/1803/83
Thos., maltster, Avebury, 1806, W, Wr, P3/1806/65
Thos., yeo., Lt. Hinton, 1814, comm, W, Wr, P1/1814/67
Thos., blacksmith, Urchf., 1827, AB, W, Wr, P2/1827/48
Thos., cooper, Gillingham, Dorset, 1848, comm, W, Wr, P27/1/756
Thomasine, widow, Bramshaw, Hants, 1663, I (4), T, NW, P24/309
Timothy, Sal. St Thos., 1711, W, P1/E/161, P1/5Reg/51
Uriel, cordw., Trowb., 1816, comm, W, Wr, P1/1816/4
Walter, yeo., Chelworth, Crickl. St S., 1670, AB, I, P3/E/85
Walter, maltster *or* yeo., Biddestone St Nich., 1695, comm, I, W, Wr (damaged), P3/E/156
Walter, yeo., Notton, Lacock, 1753, W, P3/E/252
Walter, yeo., S. Marston, 1800, W, P10/1800/1
Wm., Highw., 1564, W, P5/1Reg/51C
Wm., husb., Chards., Devon, 1591, I, W, P5/1591/22, P5/5Reg/102C
Wm., sen., Rams., 1599, AB, I, P5/1598/15, P5/6Reg/221B
Wm., Fonthill G., 1625, AB, I, P2/E/95
Wm., clerk and rector, Stanton Fitzwarren, 1625, I, W, P1/E/31
Wm., tailor, Bishopstrow, 1637, I, W, P2/E/126

Wm., Norton B., 1639, a/c, P2/E/136
Wm., sen., shoemaker, Devizes, 1643, comm, I, W, P1/E/63
Wm., husb., Urchf., 1662, AB, comm, I, P1/E/81
Wm., jun., Wanb., 1668, I, P1/E/305
Wm., clerk, Latton, 1671, I, W, P3/E/90
Wm., husb., Collingbourne K., 1672, AB, I, L, ren, P3/E/94
Wm., Castleton, Dorset, 1681, I, W, P5/1681/14
Edwards alias Browne, Wm., no abode stated, 1683, AB, P3/E/118
Wm., husb., Fovant, 1683, AB, I, P2/E/203
Wm., husb., Bishopstrow, 1694, I, W, P2/E/237
Wm., scrivener, Crickl. St S., 1694, I, W, P3/E/153
Wm., labourer, Burbage, 1697-99, AB, I, W, P11/81, 84
Wm., jun., N. Tidworth, 1707, AB, P2/E/262
Wm., sen., wheelwright, Gillingham, Dorset, 1707, AB, I, W, P27/1/166
Wm., Shaw, Lydiard M., 1724, AB, I, P3/E/199
Wm., carp., N. Tidworth, 1724, I, W, P2/E/296
Wm., mariner and shipwright, Lyme R., Dorset, 1727, I, W, P16/246
Wm., glover, Speenhamland, Berks., 1732, W, P1/E/203, P1/7Reg/486B
Wm., yeo., Even Swindon, 1746, W, P3/E/232
Wm., tailor, Crickl. St S., 1748, AB, W, P3/E/237
Wm., yeo., Colerne, 1749, W, P3/E/241
Wm., Fovant, 1750, AB, P2/E/342
Wm., yeo. and bach., Liddington, 1760, AB, ren, P3/E/263
Wm., carp., Gillingham, Dorset, 1763, AB, W, P27/1/437, P27/3Reg/97
Wm., yeo., Manningford Bohun, 1764, W, P2/E/369
Wm., collarmaker, Wilton, Gt. Bedwyn, 1765, W, P21/10/64
Wm., Burbage, 1767, AB, comm, W, P5/1767/18
Wm., cardmaker, Chipp., 1778, W, P3/E/290
Wm., cordw., Colerne, 1782, W, P1/E/279, P1/13Reg/392
Wm., yeo., Burbage, 1798, W, Wr, P11/230
Wm., Ford, N. Wraxall, 1801, AB, comm, P2/1801/24
Wm., Ludg., 1817, AB, Wr, P2/1817/14
Wm., innholder, Enmore Grn, Motc., Dorset, 1818, W, Wr, P19/223
Wm., yeo., Manningford Bohun, 1842, comm, W, Wr, P2/1842/2
Wm. Howitt, medical practitioner and doctor in medicine, Fovant, 1843, AB, court proceedings (2), D, ren, W, Wr, P2/1843/54
Wolstan, druggetmaker, Devizes, 1719, AB, comm, ren, W, P1/E/177, P1/6Reg/187A
see also George alias E.
Eeles *see* Eyles
Egerton, Wm., joiner, Arborfield, Berks., 1662, I, W, P5/1662/40,
Eggar, My., widow, Trowb., 1854, aff, O, W, Wr, P1/1854/5
Eggelton *see* Eagleton
Eggerdon, Francis, Netherb., Dorset, 1685, AB, I, P17/231
Hugh, Netherb., Dorset, 1640, AB, a/c, I, P17/54
Eggon, My., widow, Netherb., Dorset, 1749, AB, P5/1749/21
Eglen, Eglen alias Boucher, Jane, sp., Sal. (form. of Yeovil, Somerset), 1802, AB, comm (form. Jane Jackson), P4/1802/11
Egrige, Wm., Gt. Faringdon, Berks., 1576-77, AB, T (child: Richd. E.), P5/1576/16, P5/3Reg/89C
Egton, Wm., Downton, [1552?], I, P2/E/2
Eilot *see* Elliott
Ekins, My., widow, Bere R., Dorset, 1775, W, P5/1775/8, P5/17Reg/98B
Elborough, Agnes, widow, Purton, [1613], I, W (NEP), P3/E/12
Ann, widow, Purton, 1617, AB, a/c, I, P3/E/26
Ann, Purton, 1683, AB, P1/E/115
Arthur, yeo., Purton, 1643, comm, I, W, P1/E/64
Edith, widow, Purton, 1570, W, P1/1Reg/22B
Harriet, sp., Speen, Berks., 1820, W, Wr, P1/1820/111
Jn., mason, Swindon, 1783, W, P3/E/299
Jn., yeo., Purton, 1806, comm, W, Wr, P3/1806/9
Eldbrough, Richd., bach., Purton, 1767, AB, P3/E/270
Sarah, widow, Stratton St Mgt., 1813, AB, comm, Wr, P3/1813/46

Thos., husb., Lydiard T., [1583], W (NEP), P3/1Reg/6B
Thos., butcher, Purton, [1605], W (NEP), P3/E/2
Thos., yeo., Purton, 1662, comm, I, W, P3/E/73
Wm., yeo., Purton, 1682, I, W, P3/E/116
Elby, Robt., Netherb., Dorset, 1690, AB, I, P17/313
Elcock, Ellcock, Ann, widow, Alderbury, 1667, AB, I, P26/137
Hy., yeo., Sal. The Close, 1704, W, P5/1704/18
Jas., yeo., E. Harnham, Britford, 1798, W, P24/1201
Jn., yeo., Whaddon, Alderbury, 1758, W, P26/961
Moses, yeo., Whaddon, Alderbury, 1775, AB, P26/1080
Thos., sen., yeo., Whaddon, Alderbury, 1691, I, W, P26/398
Thos., Whaddon, Alderbury, 1736, AB, P26/790
Thos., bach., Coombe B. (form. of Whaddon, Alderbury), 1758, AB, P5/1758/15
see also Alcock
Elcombe, Jn., yeo., W. Hagbourne, Berks., 1753, W, P1/11Reg/11
Elcott, Thos., Wylye, 1559, AB, P2/3Reg/163D
Eldbrough *see* Elborough
Elderfield, Francis, sen., yeo., Harwell, Berks., 1711, I, W, P1/E/162, P1/5Reg/167
Richd., yeo., Harwell, Berks., 1695, I, W (NEP), P1/E/136
Elderton, Edwd., maltster, Figh., 1716, I (detailed), W, P26/602
Eliz., sp., S. Newton, 1699, I, W, P2/E/244
Eliz., widow, Sal., 1722, AB, P4/1722/21
Frances Henrietta, Warm., 1829, W, P4/1829/5
Jas., clothworker, Sal., 1667, I, NW, P4/1667/20
Jas., S. Newton, 1691, AB, P2/E/229
Jas., yeo., S. Newton, 1710, W, P2/E/270
Jas., yeo., Hawkeridge, Westb., 1730, W, P25/1729/11
Jn., sen., gent., Sutton V., 1667, AB, comm, I, W, P2/E/171
Jn., gent., Bewden, Orcheston St Geo., 1695, I (damaged), W, P1/E/137
Jn., gent., Orcheston St My., 1727, W, P2/E/302
Jn., auctioneer, Sal., 1825, req, W, copy W, Wr, P4/1825/4
Jos., Sal., 1832, AB (re property in High St., S.), O, P1/1832/22
Jos., baker, Sal., 1845, AB, ren, W, Wr, P1/1845/76
Eldridge, Edwd., yeo., Sevenhampton, Highw., 1768, W, P10/1768/3
Eliz., widow, Abingdon, Berks., 1795, W, P1/E/294, P1/14Reg/563
Francis, Chapelrow, Bucklebury, Berks., 1735, W, P1/E/212, P1/8Reg/30
Geo., yeo., *The Franchise*, Downton, 1850, D, W, Wr, P2/1850/11
Henrietta, widow, Wantage, Berks., 1806, comm, W, Wr, P5/1806/20
Jas., sen., yeo., Hamptworth, Downton, 1827, W, Wr, P2/1827/15
Jas., pig butcher, Southbroom, 1838, O, W, Wr, P24/1356
Jn., Wokm., Berks., 1583, I, W, P5/1583/13, P5/4Reg/62B
Jn., yeo., Cholsey, Berks., 1738, W, P1/E/221, P1/8Reg/250
Jonathan, maltster, Abingdon, Berks., 1732, W, P1/E/204, P1/7Reg/459
My., Sal., 1768, W, P4/1768/7
Richd., yeo., Cholsey, Berks., 1674, I, W, P1/E/107
Richd., tailor, Wokm., Berks., 1704, W, P5/1704/15
Thos., bellfounder, Wokm., Berks., 1593, AB, a/c, I, P5/1593/33, P5/6Reg/37B
Thos., Steventon, Berks., 1628, AB, a/c, I, P1/E/35
Thos., Ufton Nervet, Berks., 1662, AB, I, P1/E/83
Thos., Cholsey, Berks., 1683, AB, I, P1/E/116
Thos., Poulton, 1758, AB, P3/E/258
Thos., pork butcher, Devizes, 1840, O, W, Wr, P1/1840/12
Thos., yeo., Whitehorn Hill, Whitep., 1851, D, W, Wr, P2/1851/8
Thos., pork butcher, Devizes St My., 1854, AB, aff, O, W, Wr, P1/1855/2
Wm., sen., joiner, Wokm., Berks., 1609, AB, I, W, P5/1608/11, P5/1609/29, P5/8Reg/151D
Wm., husb., Poulton, 1670, I, NW, P3/E/88
Wm., Henwick Farm, Thatcham, Berks., 1763, W, P1/E/258, P1/12Reg/90B
Elem *see* Elmes
Elery *see* Ellery
Elford, Ann, widow of Sam., innholder, White Hart Inn, Sherb., Dorset, 1818, W, Wr, P5/1818/24

Hannah, sp., Chetnole, Yetm., Dorset, 1745, AB, I, P19/141
Hannah, sp., Chetnole, Yetm., Dorset, 1758, AB, P5/1758/16
Jane, sp., Fordington, Dorset, 1824, W, Wr, P5/1824/38
Jn., sen., yeo., Chetnole, Yetm., Dorset, 1638, I, W, P5/1638/36, P5/13Reg/79
Jn., clerk, Ryme I., Dorset, 1664, AB, comm, I, ren, P5/1664/9
Jn., Chetnole, Yetm., Dorset, 1731, I, W, P5/1731/28
Jonathan, Chetnole, Yetm., Dorset, 1722, AB, P5/1722/21
Jos., labourer, Chetnole, Yetm., Dorset, 1727, AB, ren, P19/114
Leah, widow, Chetnole, Yetm., Dorset, 1774, AB, P19/175
Matthew, Chetnole, Yetm., Dorset, 1765, AB, P19/160
Matthew, Chetnole, Yetm., Dorset, 1807, AB, P19/210
Maud, widow, Seend, Melk., 1613, AB, I, P1/E/13
Philip, Chetnole, Yetm., Dorset, 1689, comm, T, P19/55
Sam., innholder, *The White Hart Inn*, Sherb., Dorset, 1814, W, Wr, P5/1814/5
Simon, Burbage, 1741, AB, P11/181
Wm., gent., Chetnole, Yetm., Dorset, 1768, W, P19/165
Wm., gent., Chetnole, Yetm., Dorset, 1813, comm, W, P19/220
Wm., gent., Chetnole, Yetm., Dorset, 1827, comm, W, Wr, P19/237
see also Alford
Elisander, Elixander *see* Alexander
Elkins, […], widow, no abode stated, 1681, a/c, P2/E/197
Edwd., blacksmith, E. Grafton, 1743, W, Wr, P5/1743/26
Hy., dairyman, Newton Farm, Whitep., 1844, cert, W, Wr, P2/1844/67
Jas., clothworker, Westb., 1738, W, P25/1738/1
Jas., servant, Compton B., 1835, comm, W, P3/1835/17
Jane, widow, Wokm., Berks., 1773, W, P5/1773/17, P5/17Reg/58A
Jn., husb., E. Grafton, 1637, I, NW, P21/1/32
Jn., miller, Compton C., 1648, I, W, P2/E/150
Jn., sen., yeo., Compton C., 1773, W, P1/E/269, P1/12Reg/463A
Jn., schoolmaster, Reading, Berks., 1814, comm, W, Wr, P1/1814/35
Matthew, Hamptworth, Downton, 1678, AB, I, P2/E/190
Robt., yeo., Compton C., 1674, I, W, P2/E/184
Robt., Gt. Bedwyn, 1760, W, P21/10/53
Roger, innholder, Whitep., 1668, AB, I, W, P1/E/97
Thos., yeo., Compton C., 1715-19, AB, I, ren, P2/E/280, 289
Thos., Compton C., 1800, AB, P2/1800/58
Wm., yeo., Barkham, Berks., 1735, W, P1/E/213, P1/8Reg/17
Wm., clothworker, Penleigh Marsh, Dilton, Westb., 1736, AB, ren, Wr, P25/1736/5
Wm., yeo., Compton C., 1760, W, P2/E/359
Wm., gamekeeper, Clarendon Park, 1835, W, Wr, P5/1835/3
Ellaway *see* Elloway
Ellcock *see* Elcock
Ellen, Eliz., widow, Devizes, 1795, AB, P1/E/295, P1/14Reg/595A
Eliz., widow, Calne, 1840, AB, comm, Wr, P26/1445
Elling, Geo., gent., Sutton V., 1843, D, ren, W, Wr, P2/1843/12
Illen, Hugh, Mere, 1598, AB, a/c, P5/1597/62, P5/6Reg/197B
Elling, Hugh, Mere, 1680, I, W, P5/1680/12
Jas., victualler, Devizes, 1823, W, Wr, P1/1823/151
Jas., Devizes, 1835, AB, comm, P1/1835/117
Elling, Jane, widow, Sutton V., 1787, W, P2/E/410
Illing, Jn., sen., cordw., Mere, 1703, I, W, P5/1703/20
Elling, Jn., sen., maltster, Mere, 1730, comm, W, P5/1730/18
Jn., bach., Devizes, 1814, AB, P1/1814/139
Elling, Jn. Snelgrove, Sutton V., 1842, AB, Wr, P2/1842/5
Elling, Jos., butcher, Sal., 1788, W, P4/1788/6
Illing, Mgt., widow, Over Zeals, 1662, I, W, P5/1662/68
Elling, My., widow, Mere, 1724, AB, I, P5/1724/26
Elling, Robt., Mere, 1722, AB, P5/1722/22
Elling, Robt., woolstapler, Sutton V., 1842, W, Wr, P1/1842/76
Sarah, widow, Devizes, 1842, O, W, Wr, P1/1842/83

Thos., brickmaker and limeburner, Devizes Grn, Devizes St Jas., Devizes, 1791, W, P3/E/306
Wm., limeburner, Devizes Grn, Bps. C., 1845, aff, W, Wr, P24/1375
see also Allen
Ellery, Hugh, currier, Amesb., 1736, AB, I, P2/E/317
Isaac, pig killer, Sutton B., 1853, O, W, Wr, P3/1853/22
My., widow, Over C., Dorset, 1618, AB, I, T, W, P5/1618/12, P5/10Reg/31B
Elery, My., widow, Leigh, Yetm., Dorset, 1770, W, P5/1770/14, P5/17Reg/16A
Illery, Wm., husb., Charminster, Dorset, 1613, comm, I, W, P5/1612/25, P5/9Reg/89B
see also Jennings alias Hillary *or* E.
Elles *see* Ellis
Ellesdon *see* Elstone
Elleson *see* Ellison
Ellet, Ellett *see* Elliott
Elling *see* Ellen
Ellington, Christian, widow, Poulshot, 1628, I, W, P1/E/36
Clement, widow, Bulk., Keevil, 1585, AB, I, P2/E/22, P2/7Reg/20C
Eliz., sp., Poulshot, 1663, AB, I, P2/E/160
Hy., husb., Keevil, 1558, W, P2/3Reg/95C
Joan, widow, Seend, Melk., 1660, comm, I, W, P2/E/154
Jn., Poulshot, 1564, I, W, P2/E/11, P2/4Reg/168B
Jn., husb., Chitterne AS, 1596, AB, I, W, P2/E/46
Jn., husb., Poulshot, 1613, I, W, P2/E/73, P2/8Reg/191A
Jn., no abode stated, but vicar of Chitterne St Mary witness & bequests to both C. churches., 1616, W, P1/E/21
Jn., yeo., Poulshot, 1660, comm, I, W, P2/E/155
Mgt., husb.'s widow, Chitterne AS, 1619, I, W, P2/E/84
Thos., Bulk., Keevil, 1570, W, P2/5Reg/88A
Thos., husb., Poulshot, 1631, I, W, P2/E/107, P2/9Reg/65A
Thos., yeo., Poulshot, 1692, AB, I, W, P2/E/230
Wm., Bulk., Keevil, 1583, I, W, P2/E/21, P2/6Reg/106A
Wm., sen., husb., Poulshot, 1589, I (2), W, P2/E/28
Elliott, Agnes, widow, Edington, 1572, W, P2/5Reg/144C
Elliot, Agnes, widow, Ditchampton, Wilton, 1584, W, P2/6Reg/117A
Elliott alias Clarke, Alice, widow, Aldbourne, 1631, I, W, P1/E/41
Alice, woolstapler's wife, Devizes, 1696, W, P1/E/142
Alice, widow, Chipp., 1710-11, I, W, P1/E/158, P1/5Reg/37
Ann, widow, Wokm., Berks., 1637, I (christian name not given), W, P5/1637/10, P5/13Reg/36
Ann, sp., Lacock, 1685, comm, I, W, P3/E/132
Elliot, Ann, widow, Ansty, Horningsham, 1687, I, W, P5/1687/14
Ann, Quemerford, Calne, 1726, AB, P5/1725/24
Ann, widow, Fisherton A., 1779, W, P1/E/278, P1/13Reg/215B
Elliott alias Hill, Benj., yeo., Lacock, 1680, NW, P3/E/112
Cath., widow, Burcombe, 1590, I, W, P2/E/31
Elliot, Cath., widow, Martin, Hants, 1591, I, W, P2/E/32
Chas., cabinetmaker, Sal., 1747, W, P1/E/238, P1/10Reg/41A, 64B
Christian, Stourton, 1836, AB, comm, P2/1836/37
Chris., Compton C., 1570, T (children: Jn., Joan & Mgt. E.), W, P2/E/14, P2/5Reg/96A
Edith, Odstock, 1597, I, W, P2/E/50
Edmd., shoemaker and innholder, Sal., 1680, I (detailed), W, P4/1679/20
Edwd., Barford St M., 1555, W, P2/1Reg/96B
Edwd., Barford St M., c1590, a/c, P30/66
Elliot, Edwd., Upton L., 1777, AB, P2/E/391
Elliot, Eleanor, widow, Steeple A. & Poulshot, 1615, I, W, P2/E/74, P2/8Reg/260D
Eliz., sp., Sal. St Thos., 1612, I, P4/1612/22
Elliot, Eliz., widow, Broad C., 1668, I, W, P1/E/98
Elliot, Eliz., broad weaver's widow, Trowb., 1757, W, P1/E/249, P1/11Reg/341
Eliz., widow, Chipp., 1807, AB, Wr, P3/1807/33
Ellen, widow, Compton C., 1635, I, W, P1/E/53
Frances, widow, S. Burcombe, 1682, AB, I, copy I, P2/E/202
Francis, husb., Compton C., 1638, I, W, P2/E/132
Francis, yeo. and husb., Boreham, Warm., 1687, AB, I, W, P2/E/218

Francis, [pattenmaker], Devizes, 1692, AB, comm, I, P1/E/130
Francis, maltster, Rowde, 1730, W, P3/E/208
Geo., broad weaver, Keevil, 1620, I, W, P2/E/85
Geo., blacksmith, Lacock, 1646, AB, comm, I, P1/E/72
Goddard, grocer, Sal., 1671, AB, P4/1671/7
Hy., chandler *or* soap boiler, Bradford A., 1679, AB, comm, I, P2/E/194
Eilot *or* Ellott, Hy., gunsmith, Calne, 1683, I (detailed), W, P26/301
Hy., yeo., E. Knoyle, 1789, AB, W, P1/E/284, P1/14Reg/198
Isabella, widow, Winterbourne G., 1753, W, P2/E/352
Elliot, Jabez, broad weaver, Trowb., 1763, W, P1/E/253, P1/12Reg/136
Jas., Compton C., 1550, W, P2/2Reg/107A
Jas., Compton C., 1579, W, P2/5Reg/352
Jas., labourer, Heytes., 1587, I, T, W, P5/1587/47, P5/4Reg/141A
Jas., sen., husb., Compton C., 1626, I, W, P2/E/97
Elliott alias Furkes, Jas., Oborne, Dorset, 1648, I, W, P5/1647/5, P5/14Reg/100B
Jas., Compton C., 1668, I, W, P2/E/172
Jas., serge weaver, Keevil, 1716, W, P1/E/171, P1/6Reg/13
Jas., shopkeeper, Warm., 1729, AB, ren, P1/E/196
Jas., baker, Biddestone St Nich., 1850, O, W, Wr, P3/1850/43
Jane, widow, Ratfyn, Amesb., 1580, W, P2/E/18, P2/5Reg/367A
Joan, Ratfyn, Amesb., 1558, AB, W, P2/E/5, P2/3Reg/109, P2/4Reg/28C
Jn., Ratfyn, Amesb., 1558, W, P2/3Reg/107B
Jn., [clothworker], Wilton, 1558, W, P2/3Reg/98A
Jn., Ditchampton, Wilton, 1559, AB, W, P2/4Reg/10C
Jn., husb., Tilsh., 1559, W, P2/4Reg/6B
Jn., Martin, Hants, 1563, W, P2/4Reg/122A
Elliot, Jn., husb., Compton C., 1563, I, W, P2/E/9, P2/4Reg/116B
Jn., Tilsh., 1564-69, AB, T (2, children: Jn. & Robt. sons of Jn. E. of Tilshead, & *also* heirs of Jn. & Joan E. of Amesbury, decd. Both documents struck through), P2/4Reg/184A, P2/5Reg/56A
Jn., farmer [of the rectory], Steeple L., 1568, W (bequests of tithes; to be buried in chancel), P2/5Reg/47
Jn., Donhead St My., 1582, W, P2/6Reg/74A
Elliot, Jn., husb., Odstock, 1592, I, W, P2/E/35
Jn., Boreham, Warm., 1593, I, W, P2/E/41
Elliott alias Hill, Jn., Tilsh., 1595, AB, I, W, P2/E/44, P2/7Reg/143B
Jn., yeo., Compton C., 1629, I, W, P2/E/103
Jn., tailor, Homington, 1637, I, W, P24/285
Elliot, Jn., baker, Marl., 1664, I, W, P1/E/89
Elliott alias Clarke, Jn., Bishopstone N., 1670, comm, I, P6/32
Elliot, Jn., husb., Beam., Dorset, 1671, W, P5/1671/26
Jn., gent., Wanb., 1679, AB, comm, P3/E/109
Jn., Boreham, Warm., 1684, AB, I, P2/E/207
Elliot, Jn., innholder, Sal., 1689, I (detailed), W, P4/1689/5
Jn., yeo., Sutton V., 1689, AB, I, ren, P1/E/126
Jn., Quidh., 1715, AB, I, P2/E/279
Jn., bricklayer, Fisherton A., 1769, AB, cert, W, P2/E/377
Jn., labourer, E. Knoyle, 1845, cert, note, W, Wr, P2/1845/7
Julius, yeo., Marston, Pott., 1677, AB, I, P1/E/109
Mgt., widow, Donhead St My., 1588, W, P2/7Reg/118C
Mgt., widow, Compton C., 1618, I, W, P2/E/83
Ellet, Mgt., widow, S. Burcombe, [1636], I, P2/E/122
Mgt., widow, Longbridge D., 1669, AB, P2/E/173
Elliott nee Haggard, Martha, gent.'s wife, Wanb., 1715, AB, I, P3/E/185
Elliot, Martha, widow, Chipp., 1760, AB, W, P3/E/264
My., Sal., 1731, W, P4/1730/22
My., widow, Milborne Stileham, Bere R., Dorset, 1785, W, P5/1785/11, P5/18Reg/43
Richd., Barford St M., 1541, I, W, P30/65
Richd., weaver, Steeple A., 1584, W, P2/6Reg/130A
Elliott alias Clarke, Richd., husb., Baydon, 1603, AB, W, P5/1603/26, P5/7Reg/61
Elliot, Richd., Sal. St Thos., 1626, AB, P4/1626/20
Elliot, Richd., blacksmith, Lake, Wilsford with L., 1638, comm, I, NW, P5/1638/39, P5/13Reg/112A

Richd., sen., clothworker, Lt. Horningsham, 1691, I, W, P5/1690/15
Richd., sen., yeo., Keevil, 1712, W, P2/E/275
Richd., Horningsham, 1730, AB, P5/1730/19
Richd., yeo., Whitep., 1748, W, P2/E/337
Elliott alias Clarke, Robt., Rams., 1564, W, P5/1Reg/51B
Robt., Tilsh., 1569, AB, P2/5Reg/56B
Robt., husb., Burcombe, 1575, I, W, P2/E/16, P2/5Reg/245A
Robt., smith, Amesb., 1581, W, P2/6Reg/54A
Robt., Gt. Wishford, 1596, I, W, P2/E/45
Robt., broad weaver, Keevil, 1633, I, NW, P2/E/112
Robt., husb., Burcombe, 1663, I, W, P1/E/86
Robt., husb., Beam., Dorset, 1676, I, W, P5/1676/21
Robt., cutler, Chipp., 1713, W, P3/E/181
Robt., Sal., 1716, AB, I, P1/E/172
Elliot, Robt., innholder, Hungerford, Berks., 1726, W, P23/440
Robt., whitesmith, Chipp., 1776, W, Wr, P3/E/286
Robt., Sparsholt, Berks., 1808, AB, Wr, P1/1808/91
Sam., cutler, Chipp., 1697, W, P3/E/160
Sam., Malm., 1734, AB, I (2 - 1 a copy), P3/E/217
Sam., whitesmith, Chipp., 1758, W, P3/E/259
Ellett, Stephen, no abode stated; proved at Chipp., 1614, I, W, P1/E/17
Elyet, Thos., clerk and parson, Lillington, Dorset, 1572-73, I, W, P5/1572/1, P5/3Reg/28B
Elliot, Thos., husb., Tinh., Edington, 1616, I, W, P2/E/80
Elliot, Thos., husb., Crudwell, 1631, AB, I, W, P1/E/42
Elliot, Thos., husb., Chilton F., 1634, I, W, P1/E/50
Thos., Stoford, S. Newton, [1636], I, W, P2/E/120
Elliot *or* Ellet, Thos., sen., Wanb., 1684, I, W, P3/E/125
Elliott alias Hill, Thos., yeo., Rowde, 1695, I, W, P1/E/139, P1/6Reg/216
Thos., sen., yeo., Studley, Trowb., 1720, W, P1/E/181
Thos., gent., Rowde, 1730, W, P3/E/209
Elliot, Thos., Corsley, 1742, AB, P2/E/331
Thos., clothworker, Bradford A., 1751, W, P2/E/345
Thos., Chipp., 1753, AB, P1/E/244
Thos., yeo., Sal., 1836, W, Wr, P4/1836/14
Walter, Compton C., 1559, W, P2/3Reg/174E
Wm., Wokm., Berks., 1573, W, P5/3Reg/13C
Wm., sen., Hurdcott, Barford St M., 1574, AB, P2/5Reg/179C
Wm., husb., Britford, 1580, I, W, P5/1580/21, P5/4Reg/7B
Wm., Donhead St My., 1611, NW, P2/E/70
Wm., Compton C., 1631, AB, I, P1/E/43
Elliot, Wm., Sal. The Close, 1639, AB, I, P5/1638/37, P5/13Reg/158
Wm., yeo., Southwick, N. Bradley, 1665, AB, I, P2/E/164
Wm., yeo., Wanb., 1685, I, W, P3/E/133
Wm., Boreham, Warm., 1693, AB, P2/E/233
Wm., sen., yeo., Corsley, 1752, W, P2/E/350
Elliot, Wm., innkeeper, Bridzor, Tisb., 1800, comm, W, Wr, P2/1800/81
Wm., yeo., Earley, Sonning, Berks., 1807, W, Wr, P5/1807/4
see also Clarke alias E.; Furkes/Furks alias E.
Ellis, Agnes, widow, Bourton, Gillingham, Dorset, 1690, I, W, P27/1/121
Ann, sp., Bulk., Keevil, 1842, W, Wr, P1/1842/56
Anthony, clerk and vicar, Rodbourne C., 1626, AB, court papers, O, P1/E/33, P3/E/42
Anthony, glover, Marston Meysey & Crickl., 1705, AB, P3/E/172
Ellis alias Mere, Barbara, gent.'s wife, Swallowfield, Shinfield, Berks., 1710, AB, P1/E/159
Betty, widow, Keevil Wick, 1816, W, Wr, P2/1816/25
Christian, widow, Thornford, Dorset, 1605-06, I, W, P5/1604/10, P5/8Reg/74B
Chris., glazier, Marl., 1683, AB, comm, I, P1/E/117
Chris., yeo., Marston, Pott., 1685, I, W, P1/E/120
Chris., Marl., 1695, T (child: Chris. E., jun.), P1/E/138
Edith, widow, Quidh., Wrou., 1604, I, P3/E/1
Edith, yeo.'s wife, Stert, Urchf., 1721, W, P1/E/186, P1/6Reg/379A

Edwd., gent., Gt. Amesb., 1685, AB, I, P2/E/212
Edwd., husb., Quidh., 1686, AB (2), I, W, P1/E/123
Edwd., yeo., Winlaim, Pierston, Gillingham, Dorset, 1720, I, W, P27/1/230
Eleanor, widow, Steeple A., 1769, W, P2/E/379
Ealless, Eliz., widow, Bemerton, Fugg. St Peter, 1690, AB, I, P2/E/226
Eliz., widow, Castleton, Dorset, 1799, AB, P5/1799/8, P5/18Reg/278A
Emma, widow, Gillingham, Dorset, 1728, W, P27/1/291
Francis, Whaddon, Alderbury, 1672, I, W, P26/198
Francis, tailor, Marston, Pott., 1721, I, W, P1/E/187, P1/6Reg/376B
Giles, yeo., Bourton, Gillingham, Dorset, 1664, W, P27/1/17
Hy., Faulston, Bishopstone S., 1630, I, W, P2/E/105
Isaac, yeo., Marston, Pott., 1776, W, P1/E/274, P1/13Reg/136
Jacob, labourer, Pott., 1847, D, note, O, W, Wr, P1/1847/6
Jas., clothworker, Southwick, N. Bradley, 1664, AB, I, ren, P2/E/162
Jas., Steeple A., 1755, AB, P2/E/354
Jas., yeo., Whaddon, 1803, W, P2/1803/50
Joan, widow, N. Wootton, Dorset, 1611, I, copy I, W, P5/1610/19, P5/9Reg/48B
Jn., Quidh., 1542, W (NEP), P2/1Reg/32A
Jn., Pott. Wick, 1607, AB, I, W, P1/E/7
Jn., Thornford, Dorset, 1618, AB, I, T, W, P5/1618/11, P5/10Reg/30B
Jn., yeo., Stourton, 1620, I, W, P1/E/29
Elles, Jn., jun., Marston, Pott., 1634, I, W, P1/E/49
Jn., Marston, Pott., 1649, AB, comm, I, P1/E/76
Jn., yeo., Gillingham, Dorset, 1667, I, P27/1/28
Jn., husb., Sal., 1677, AB, I, P4/1677/11
Jn., yeo., Marston, Pott., 1720, W, P1/E/182, P1/6Reg/361
Jn., Corsham, 1740, AB, L, W, copy W, P29/E/4
Jn., barber, Avill's Farm, Corsham, 1741, W, P1/E/226, P1/9Reg/163
Jn., Bourton, Gillingham, Dorset, 1748, AB, P27/1/395, P27/3Reg/52
Jn., Keevil, 1751, AB, comm, P2/E/343
Jn., Hungerford, Berks., 1825-27, AB (2), comm, P23/921
Jn., bach., Keevil, 1833, AB, comm, Wr, P2/1833/10
Ells, Jos., cordw., Kintbury, Berks., 1770, W, P1/E/265, P1/12Reg/344
Jos., yeo., Whitep. (form. of Donhead St My.), 1847, I, W, Wr, P2/1847/72
My., widow, Uffc., Devon, 1677, court paper, NW, P20/1/83
My., widow, Stert, Urchf., 1686, I, W, P1/E/306
Philip, miller *or* yeo., Stert, Urchf., 1670, I, W, P1/E/101
Philip, Stert, Urchf., 1713, AB, P1/E/163
Richd., Quidh., 1592, I, T, W, P2/E/38
Richd., sadler, Sal., 1626, AB, I, P4/1626/12
Ellis alias Baker, Richd., Wootton R., 1701, AB, a/c, I (2 - 1 a copy), P3/E/168
Richd., yeo., Hurst, Edington, 1703, I, W, P2/E/253
Richd., grazier, Edington, 1781, comm, W, P2/E/399
Elles, Robt., husb., Bemerton, Fugg. St Peter, 1688, W, P2/E/221
Sam., Bulk., Keevil, 1808, AB, Wr, P2/1808/47
Sarah, widow, Stert, Urchf., 1726, W, P1/E/192, P1/7Reg/141
Elles, Susanna, widow and sadler, Sal., 1641, I, W, P4/1640/3
Thos., Sonning, Berks., 1569, W, P5/2Reg/54B
Thos., Broughton G., 1586, I, W, P2/E/23, P2/7Reg/37A
Thos., sen., N. Wootton, Dorset, 1639, AB, I, P5/1639/29, P5/13Reg/176D
Thos., Bourton, Gillingham, Dorset, [1714], W, P27/1/202
Thos., gent., Stert, Urchf., 1723, W, P1/E/190, P1/7Reg/33B
Thos., yeo., Hurst, Edington, 1753, W, P1/E/245, P1/11Reg/128
Thos., Keevil, 1793, AB, P2/E/421
Thos., innholder, Castleton, Dorset, 1795, W, P5/1795/6, P5/18Reg/214B
Thos., carp., Sherb., Dorset, 1831, W, Wr, P5/1831/14
Thos., yeo., Hurst Farm, Keevil, 1844, W, Wr, P2/1844/85
Wm., Bourton, Gillingham, Dorset, 1572, W, P27/1Reg/28A
Wm., [narrow weaver], Bratton, Westb., 1665, AB, I, P25/1665/5
Elles, Wm., husb., Beam., Dorset, 1674, I, P17/269

Wm., sen., Alderbury, 1677, I, W, P26/249
Wm., Donhead St My., 1710, AB, P2/E/267
Wm., bach., Alderton, 1750, AB, P3/E/243
Wm., yeo., Bulk., Keevil, 1829, W, P2/1829/27
Wm., dairyman, Keevil, 1842, O, W, Wr, P1/1842/102
Ellisander *see* Alexander
Ellison, Edmd., Minety, 1795, W, P1/E/296, P1/14Reg/548B
Elleson, Edmd., yeo., Minety, 1831, W, Wr, P3/1831/65
Eleanor, Erlestoke, 1694, AB, P2/E/236
Eliz., widow, Purton, 1781, W, P3/E/293
Hy., Swindon, 1793, AB, comm, P3/E/309
Honour, widow, Fordington, Dorset, 1846, AB, comm, O, W, Wr, P15/186
Elleson, Jn., Lydiard T., 1714, comm, I, W, P3/E/183
Jn., yeo., Grittenham, Brinkw., 1749, W, P3/E/242
Jn., yeo., Dauntsey, 1847, O, W, Wr, P3/1847/30
My., widow, Swindon, 1813, W, Wr, P3/1813/23
My., widow, Ashton K., 1857, AB, aff, O, Wr, P3/1857/35
Sam., Ashton K., 1857, AB, aff, O, Wr, P3/1857/13
Thos., Eastcott, Swindon, 1815, AB, comm, Wr, P3/1815/15
Wm., yeo., Chaddington, Lydiard T., 1836, W, Wr, P3/1836/57
Ellott *see* Elliott
Elloway, Adam, mason, Warm., 1800, comm, W, Wr, P2/1800/70
Amy, widow, Rams., 1825, AB, W, Wr, P5/1825/15
Eylwaye, Edwd., Bishopstrow, 1593, AB, I, W, P2/E/42
Eliz., Warm., 1771, AB, a/c (2), I, P2/E/384
Elloaway, Eliz., widow, Sutton V., 1818, W, Wr, P2/1818/70
Fanny, widow, Warm., 1821, W, Wr, P2/1821/28
Jas., mason, Warm., 1761, W, P2/E/362
Ellaway, Jane, widow, Rams., 1673, AB, I, W, P5/1673/13
Ellaway, Jn., sen., yeo., E. Hendred, Berks., 1811, comm, W, Wr, P1/1811/136
Ellaway, Jn., E. Hendred, Berks., 1826-28, AB (2), comm (2), court proceeding, Wr, P1/1826/31
Ellaway, Richd., husb., Marridge Hill, Rams., 1672, I, W, P5/1672/10
Elloway *or* Allaway, Richd., husb., Lt. Somerford, 1752, comm, W, P3/E/250
Thos., innholder, Warm., 1764, W, P2/E/371
Ellaway, Thos., E. Hendred, Berks., 1773, W, P1/E/270, P1/12Reg/475A
Wm., mason, Warm., 1795, comm, W, P1/E/297, P1/14Reg/607
see also Alloway; Tanton alias E.
Elloy *see* Alley
Ells *see* Ellis
Elly *see* Alley
Elmes, Arthur, wheelwright, Teffont M., 1665, AB, I, P1/E/90
Elms, Betty, widow, Seend, Melk., 1762, AB, comm, P2/E/366
Eliz., widow, Nash Hill, Lacock, 1727, I, W, P3/E/205
Elms, Geo., widower, Bremhill, 1847, AB, comm, Wr, P3/1847/16
Ealmes [Ellmes], Grace, widow, Steeple A., 1687, a/c, copy AB, a/c, I, P2/E/217
Jas., Seend, Melk., 1761, AB, comm, P2/E/364
Jn., yeo., Stourpaine, Dorset, 1582, AB, I, W, P24/1441, P5/4Reg/32A
Elem *or* Ealmes, Jn., carp., Baydon, 1665, I, W, P5/1665/30
Elms, Jn., drover, Gillingham, Dorset, 1715, AB, I, P27/1/206
Martha, widow, Aldworth, Berks., 1716, I, W, P1/E/173, P1/6Reg/55A
Elms, My., widow, Gillingham, Dorset, 1738, AB, Wr, P27/1/349
Ralph, carp., Teffont M., 1639, AB, I, P2/E/135
Robt., husb., Tollard Royal, 1561-63, AB, I, W, P2/E/10, P2/4Reg/87D, 153B
Elms, Robt., drover, Gillingham, Dorset, 1723, W, P27/1/260
Robt., Melk., 1771, AB, comm, P2/E/383
Elms, Sam., jun., husb., Bradfield, Berks., 1744, W, P1/E/234, P1/9Reg/356A
Elms, Sam., yeo., Bradfield, Berks., 1753, W, P1/E/246, P1/11Reg/37A
Thos., Broad C., 1586, W, P2/7Reg/43B
Elme, Thos., Semley, 1600, AB, I, P2/E/56
Elme alias Helmes, Thos., gent., Maiden B., 1639, AB, I, P2/E/138

Elms, Thos., sen., carp., Charlcote, Bremhill, 1680, I, W, P3/E/113
Elms, Thos., private marine of the 82nd co. Portsmouth Division, Corsham, 1783, W, P29/E/6, 9, P29/2Reg/180
Elms, Wm., Dinton, 1575, W, P2/5Reg/217C
Wm., husb., Bradfield, Berks., 1707, I, W (NEP), P1/E/154
Wm., tinker *or* metalman, Reybridge, Lacock, 1716, I, W, P3/E/188
Elms, Wm., yeo., Lower Hyde, Bere R., Dorset, 1728, W, P5/1728/31, P5/16Reg/181B
see also Gingell form. E.
Elock, Richd., husb., Whaddon, Alderbury, 1702, I, W, P26/485
Elphy, Jn., grocer, Seagry, 1686, AB, ren, P1/E/307
Elsbury *see* Aylesbury
Elstone, Francis, gent., Hungerford, Berks., 1571, W, P5/2Reg/98A
Elsdon, Joan, widow, Lyme R., Dorset, 1581, W, P5/4Reg/11C
Ellesdon, Jn., gent., Lyme R., Dorset, 1668, AB, comm, ren, P5/1668/28
Allston, My., sp., Reading, Berks., 1714, D (draft), L (4 - dispute over court fees), note of cost of probate, copy W, P1/A/225, P1/5Reg/372
Ellesdon, Nich., [fuller], Lyme R., Dorset, 1592-93, AB (widow, Olive E.), I, P5/1592/26, 29, P5/6Reg/6B
Robt., Odstock, 1667, AB, I, O, P2/E/168
Roger, [sadler], Marl., 1593, AB, I, P1/E/1
Ellesdon, Sarah, widow, Lyme R., Dorset, 1677, W, P16/49
Elswood, Clement, husb., Fordington, Dorset, 1714, I, W, P15/71
Wm., Fordington, Dorset, 1705, AB, I, P15/73
Eltenton, Hannah, widow, Chilton F., 1831, comm, W, Wr, P3/1831/11
Jn., Chilton F., 1803, AB, P3/1803/21
Elton, Edwd., Collingbourne D., 1728, AB, notification, T (My. E., widow), P21/8/40
Edwd., grocer, Rams., 1739, W, P5/1739/15
Eliz., widow, Henley, Buttermere, 1631, I, W, P1/E/44
Eliz., widow, Swindon, 1726, W, P1/E/193, P1/7Reg/117A
Jacob, Blewbury, Berks., 1669, AB, cert, I, P5/1669/17
Joan, sp., Chute, 1741, W, P7/135
Jn., Gt. Bedwyn, 1696, AB, I, P21/5/35
Jn., Winterbourne E., 1736, AB, P2/E/318
Eltorne, Jn., yeo., W. Hagbourne, Berks., 1753, W, P1/E/247
Martha, widow, Wanb., 1709, I, W, P3/E/179
Richd., Tidcombe and Fosbury, 1684, AB, comm, I, P3/E/126
Robt., yeo., Soley, Chilton F., 1669, comm, I, W, P3/E/83
Thos., husb., Soley, Chilton F., 1619, I, NW, P1/E/26
Elton alias Martin, Thos., sen., husb., Henley, Buttermere, 1630, I, W, P3/E/50
Thos., carp., Wanb., 1692, AB, I, P1/E/131
Thos., Crofton, Gt. Bedwyn, 1713, AB, I, P5/1713/26
Elton alias Martin, Thos., yeo., Buttermere, 1717, I, W, P3/E/189
Thos., yeo., Porton, Idmiston, 1765, AB, P2/E/373
Thos., Ham, 1807, AB, Wr, P3/1807/55
Walter, brewer, Draycot C., [1619], I, W (NEP), P3/E/33
Wm., yeo., Ham, 1662, AB, I, P1/E/84
Wm., carp., Marl., 1666, AB, I (both damaged), P1/E/91
Wm., Ham, 1758, W, P3/E/260
see also Martin alias E.
Elver, Nich., innkeeper, Castle C., 1678, I, P28/3
Elwes, Jn., knight, N. Standen, Hungerford, Berks., 1680, AB (2), I (effects at other Berkshire locations *also* listed), P5/1680/11
Ely, Ann, widow, Slaughterford, 1820, AB, comm, Wr, P1/1820/48
Cornelius, labourer, Enford, 1741, copy AB, a/c (2), I, copy I (2), P2/E/327
Ealy, Eliz., widow, Compton B., 1823, W, Wr, P3/1823/11
Eliz. Caroline Gale, sp., Calne, 1832, AB, comm, ren, Wr, P26/1401
Hy., woollen draper, Chipp., 1641, I, W, P3/E/65
Jas., brewer, Sal., 1690, W, copy W, P4/1690/5
Jas., labourer, Westrop, Highw., 1853, D (2), O, W, Wr, P10/1853/1
Joan, widow, Foxham, Bremhill, 1615, AB, a/c, I, P3/E/20
Joan, widow, Langley Burrell, 1673, comm, I, W, P3/E/97
Jn., sen., husb., Cherhill, 1593, I, W, P5/1592/28, P5/6Reg/19B

Jn., yeo., Grittleton, 1648, I, W, P1/E/75
Jn., yeo., Malm., 1688, I, W, P3/E/145
Ealy, Jn., barber, Wantage, Berks., 1703, AB, P23/259
Jn., Winterslow, 1724, AB, P2/E/293
Jn., yeo., Warm., 1761, W, P2/E/363
Jn., Berwick St Jas., 1775, AB, comm, ren, P1/E/272
Margery, widow, 1602, W, P3/1Reg/52
My., gent.'s widow, Chipp., 1672, AB, a/c, I, P3/E/95
Nich., clerk and parson, Winterslow, 1635, D, I (detailed), W, P1/E/54
Rachel, widow, Langley Burrell, 1705, I, W, P3/E/173
Richd., gent., Chipp., 1676, I, probated copy of W, P3/E/106
Ealey, Richd., yeo., Netton, Durnford, 1822, O, W, Wr, P9/105, 873/266
Richd., yeo., Hannington Wick, 1835, W, P1/1835/89
Robt., Chipp., 1620, AB, I, P3/E/34
Robt., Langley Burrell, 1738, AB, P1/E/222
Robt., yeo., Slaughterford, 1760, W, P3/E/265
Robt., sen., yeo., Studley, Calne, 1825, W, Wr, P26/1357
Thos., Foxham, Chr. M., 1618, I, W, P3/E/31
Thos., labourer, Winterslow, 1731, AB, I, ren, P2/E/312
Wm., sen., woollen draper, Chipp., 1633, AB, a/c, I (detailed), P3/E/54
Wm., yeo., Hardenhuish, 1792, W, P3/E/308
Emans *see* Yeomans *or* E.
Ember *see* Imber
Emberle, Emberlin *see* Emblen
Emberry *see* Embury
Emblen, Cath., widow, Westb., 1769, AB, P25/1769/8
Jane, widow, Bramshaw, Hants, 1688, I, W, P24/778
Emlyng *or* Emlin, Jn., Westb., 1575, I, W, P25/1575/3, P5/3Reg/65B
Jn., yeo., Fritham, Bramshaw, Hants, 1686, I, W, P24/803
Jos., Bramshaw, Hants, 1711, AB, P24/703
Emberlin, My. Ann, widow, Marl., 1848, W, Wr, P1/1848/57
Embling, Richd., miller, Friars Mill, Shrivenham, Berks., 1817, W, Wr, P1/1817/61
Emberle, Robt., Bramshaw, Hants, 1679, AB, I, P24/474
Sarah, sp., Sal., 1753, AB, W (detailed description of clothing), P4/1753/5
Emlyn, Stephen, yeo., Fritham, Bramshaw, Hants, 1630, AB, surety bond, I, P24/207
Stephen, maltster, Bramshaw, Hants, 1686, AB, I, W, P24/802
Wm., Westb., 1768-72, AB, P25/1768/4, P25/1772/3
Emberlin, Wm., chemist, Marl., 1856, aff, W, Wr, P1/1856/15
Embury, Emberry, Ann, Devizes St My., 1699, I, W, P1/E/146, P1/3Reg/239
Chas., Purton, 1833, AB, Wr, P3/1833/42
Embris, Hy., clerk and rector, Thornford, Dorset, 1743, comm, W, Wr, P5/1743/27
Jn., sen., brickmaker, Purton, 1807, W, Wr, P3/1807/21
Richd., Devizes, 1685, comm (Edwd. E.), I, W, P1/E/121
Embry, Thos., yeo., Ashton K., 1725, AB, a/c, I, legal opinion, P3/E/201
Eme *see* Eames
Emerly, Jn., Bramshaw, Hants, 1665, I, W, P24/346
Emerson, Eleanor, widow, Lacock, 1810, AB, O, W, Wr, P3/1810/29
Emery, Emery alias Sturney, Agnes, widow, Semley, 1570, W, P2/5Reg/81B
Ann, widow, Landford, 1760, W, Wr, P2/E/360
Isaac, bach., Bradford A., 1786, AB, comm, P2/E/407
Jn., Burdsall, Tisb., 1591, I, P2/E/33
Jn., yeo., Landford, 1671, I, W, P1/E/102
Jn., yeo., Landford, 1753, W, P2/E/351
Jn., joiner, Landford, 1786, AB, W, P2/E/409
Margery, widow, Landford, 1598, I, W, P2/E/52
Richd., Underdown, Bremhill, 1627, AB, I, P3/E/46
Richd., Semley, 1567, W, P2/5Reg/30E
Robt., yeo., Landford, 1626, I, W, P2/E/99
Wm., husb., Plaitford, 1551, I, W, P2/E/1, P2/2Reg/138B
Wm., husb., Siderow, Bremhill, [1606], I, W (NEP), P3/E/3

Wm., Brook, Bramshaw, Hants, 1607, AB, P24/168
Emett *see* Emmett
Emlin *see* Emblen
Emly, Chas., yeo., Alderton, 1700, I, W, P3/E/165
Edith, widow, Sal., 1787, W, P4/1787/5
Eleanor, widow, Alderton, 1613, a/c (2), AB, I (2), ren, P3/E/16
Giles, yeo., Crudwell, 1750, W, P1/E/240, P1/10Reg/405
Joan, widow, Alderton, 1616, AB, I, P1/E/22
Lydia, widow, Crudwell, 1769, W, P3/E/272
Roger, yeo., Brokenb., 1737, AB, I, P3/E/220
Wm., yeo., Brokenb., 1733, W, P3/E/214
Emlyn, Emlyng *see* Emblen
Emm, Agnes, widow, Sutton V., 1589, I, W, P2/E/29
Agnes, widow, Sutton V., 1616, I, W, P2/E/81, P2/8Reg/315B
Benj., yeo., Bratton, Westb., 1803, W, Wr, P25/1803/1
Jas., Edington, 1811, AB, Wr, P1/1811/50
Jas., yeo., Bratton, Westb., 1833-46, AB, O (2), W (2), Wr (2), P25/1833/8, P25/1846/5
Jn., husb., Sutton V., 1581, W, P2/6Reg/31A
Jn., yeo., Keevil, 1702, I, W, P2/E/250
Jn., Warm., 1768, AB, P2/E/375
Jos., yeo., Bratton, Westb., 1845, O, W, Wr, P25/1845/2
My., widow, Bratton, Westb., 1846, AB, O, Wr, P25/1846/4
Stephen, Ebbesborne Wake, 1788, AB, ren, NW, P2/E/413
Thos., yeo., Ashton G., Codf. St P., 1730, AB, I, ren, P2/E/308
Wm., blacksmith, Bratton, Westb., 1725, W, P25/1725/6
Emmett, Ann, widow, Melk., [1718], W, P2/E/284
Ann, sp., Trowb., 1742, W, P1/E/229, P1/9Reg/234
Chris., Trowb., 1735, AB, P1/E/214
Amyatt, Dan., weaver, Kington L., 1707, W, P1/A/202
Dan., yeo., Bremhill, 1781, W, P3/E/294
Emmetts alias Taylor, Eleanor, Sal., c1670, W (NEP), P4/1670/28
Amiat, Francis, brickmaker, Westb., 1705, AB, I, P25/1705/10
Geo., Sonning, Berks., 1735, AB, P5/1735/22
Amyatt, Jas., weaver, Kington L., 1721, W, P3/A/291
Emmetts alias Taylor, Joan, widow, Malm., 1614, I, W, P3/E/19
Emett, Joan, widow, Rams., 1625, I, W, P5/1624/14, P5/10Reg/182A
Jn., Rams., 1613, I, NW, P5/1613/25, P5/9Reg/142A
Amiat, Jn., gent., Westb., 1674, I, W, P25/1674/5
Jn., jun., Calne, 1684, AB, P26/319
Emett, Jn., mason, Blackland, Calne, 1695, AB, I, W, P5/1695/33
Amiat, Jn., yeo., Westb., 1704, W, P25/1704/7
Jn., Trowb., 1742, AB, P1/E/230
Jn., broad weaver, Trowb., 1746, W, P1/E/237, P1/10Reg/24, 42B
Jn., innholder, *The New Bear*, Chipp., 1750, AB, W, P1/E/241, P1/10Reg/326
Jn., Melk., 1826, AB, comm, Wr, P2/1826/3
Jos., victualler, Clack, Lyneham, 1825, W, Wr, P3/1825/74
Emmetts, Margery, widow, Crickl. St S., 1605, I, W, P1/E/6
Nathaniel, Westb., 1747, AB, P25/1747/5
Nich., baker, Melk., [1612], I, W, P2/E/71
Nich., Pewsham Forest, 1710, AB, P5/1710/35
Nich., Chipp., 1737, AB, comm, P3/E/218
Peter, yeo., Studley, Calne, 1696, W, P26/437
Emmott, Philip, W. Dean, 1786, AB, comm, P2/E/408
Ralph, cordw., Trowb., 1730, AB, W, P1/E/197, P1/7Reg/407
Emmott, Ruth, sp., Binfield Heath, Sonning, Berks., 1734, W, P5/1734/22
Susanna, widow, Studley, Calne, 1700, I, W, P26/472
Thos., broad weaver, Melk., 1639, AB, I, P2/E/134
Thos., yeo., Melk., [1691], I, W, P2/E/228
Amiat, Wm., Westb., 1693, a/c, P25/1693/11
see also Taylor alias E.

Empson, Wm., gent., Gt. Wishford, 1742, W, P2/E/330
Emsbury *see* Amesbury
Emysdall, Jn., priest, Ashley, 1561, institution to rectory, P1/1Reg/75B
End *see* Ind
Endall, Nich., smith, Wantage, Berks., 1571, W, P5/2Reg/99A
Enfield, Wm., esquire, Whitley Farm, Calne, 1731, I, W, P5/1731/26
England, Jn., clerk, Sherb., Dorset, 1724, W, P5/1724/27, P5/16Reg/101C
My., widow, Wilton (form. of Lyme R.), 1846, W, Wr, P2/1846/23
England alias Whinyard, Robt., yeo., Henley, Box, 1626, I, W, P3/E/43
Sarah, widow, Sal., 1823, W, P4/1823/1
Thos., Chipp., 1640, AB, P3/E/64
Thos., W. Harnham, 1709, AB, I, P8/16
Thos., schoolmaster, Wilton (form. of Lyme R.), 1846, W, Wr, P2/1846/21
Wm., innholder, Calne, 1719, comm, W, P5/1719/29, P5/16Reg/11B
Wm., yeo., Alderbury, 1809, W, P26/1275
see also Whunyard alias E.
Englebert, Ann, widow, Sherb., Dorset, 1590, AB, P5/1590/22, P5/5Reg/70B
Englefield *see* Inglefield
English, Geo., yeo., Mildenhall, 1689, AB, comm, P3/E/148
My., widow, Boys Hill, Holnest, Dorset, 1801, comm, W, P5/1801/6, P5/18Reg/315A
Thos., labourer, Marl., 1702, I, W, P1/E/149, P1/4Reg/212
Wm., tailor, Wokm., Berks., 1723, W, P5/1723/13, P5/16Reg/88B
Ennis, Inness, Bartholomew, sen., wheelwright, Cumnor, Berks., 1801, W, P1/1801/33, P1/15Reg/254B
Christian, widow, Sal., 1744, AB, Wr, P4/1743/2
Enock, Enock, Jos., Crickl. St My., 1781, W, P3/E/295
Enos, Barbara, widow, Lacock, 1684, I, W, P3/E/127
Ensor, Jn., yeo., Sherb., Dorset, 1806, W, Wr, P5/1806/24
My., yeo.'s widow, Sherb., Dorset, 1813, O, W, Wr, P5/1813/18
Enstance, Edwd., Grittleton, 1667, I, W, P3/E/78
Jn., yeo., Grittleton, 1675, I, W, P3/E/101
Jn., Bencroft Farm, Bremhill, 1677, AB, a/c, comm, I, ren, P1/E/110
My., widow, Grittleton, 1700, I, W, P3/E/166
Enton *see* Hinton
Erbery, Eliz., Whaddon, 1683, W, P2/E/205
Erbery alias Hind, Hy., Haydon, Dorset, 1587, I, W, P5/1587/48, P5/4Reg/143B
Jn., jun., Warm., 1582, AB, P2/E/427
Erbery alias Hine, Jn., Haydon, Dorset, 1616, I, W, P5/1616/22
Mgt., Bradford A., 1610, T (unnamed children), P2/Y/15
Thos., Sherb., Dorset, 1627-28, I, W, P5/1628/38, P5/11Reg/61
Erles *see* Earle
Ernle, Ernley, […] *see* Wm. Chasy, clerk
Edwd., gent., Whetham, Calne, 1670, comm, W, P26/177
Ernly, Eliz., widow, Dilton M., Westb., 1742, W, P25/1742/9
Ernly, Joan, widow, Dilton M., Westb., 1695, I, W, P25/1695/3
Ernly, Jn., vicar, N. Bradley, 1552, AB, P2/2Reg/166E
Jn., esquire, Brimslade Farm, Savernake, 1738, AB, W, P1/E/223, P1/8Reg/220
Mgt., widow of baronet, Conock, Chirton, 1736, AB, W, P1/E/217, P1/8Reg/165
Ernly, Richd., yeo., Dilton M., Westb., 1682, AB, I, ren, P25/1682/4
Ernly, Richd., Dilton M., Westb., 1737, W, P25/1737/1-2
Ernly, Thos., gent., Leighs Marsh, Dilton, Westb., 1675, AB, I, P25/1675/7
Thos., gent., Eastcourt, Crudwell, 1694, AB, I, P3/E/154
Thos., gent., Purton, 1695, I, W, P3/E/157
Ernly, Thos., collier, Leighs Marsh, Dilton, Westb., 1701, D, I, sentence, W, P25/1701/9
Thos., gent., Wedh., Urchf., 1740, AB, comm, note, W, P2/E/325
Walter, Maddington, 1692, AB, comm, P1/E/132
Walter, baronet, Conock, Chirton, 1732, AB, comm, W, copy W, P1/E/205, P1/7Reg/550
Ernly, Wm., yeo., Dilton, Westb., 1704, W, P25/1704/3
Wm. *see also* Eliz. Puttoll
Errington, Gerard, gent. [and haberdasher], Sal., 1677, a/c, I (detailed), W, P4/1677/19
Nich., gent., Salterton, Durnford, 1605, I, W, P5/1605/22, P5/8Reg/33D

Richd., husb., Idmiston, 1729-31, AB (3), ren, W, P2/E/305, 311
Erwin, David, Uffc., Devon, 1743, AB, Wr, P5/1743/28
Erwood, Annabel, widow, Devizes, 1730-31, W, P1/E/198, P1/7Reg/413B
Erwood *or* Earwood, Edwd., clothier, Devizes, 1714, I, W, P1/E/166, P1/5Reg/446B
Edwd., gardener, Devizes, 1812, W, Wr, P1/1812/4
Jas., gardener, Devizes, 1735, AB, alleg, inty, W, P1/E/215, P1/8Reg/136
Jn., yeo., Orcheston St Geo., 1712, W, P2/E/273
Jn., yeo., Nunton, N. and Bodenham, 1771, W, P2/E/382
Jn., Bps. C. (form. of Devizes), 1833, AB, comm, Wr, P24/1331
My., widow, Devizes, 1735, W, Wr, P1/E/216, P1/8Reg/135
Richd., Mkt. L., 1612, I, W, P2/E/72, P2/8Reg/173A
Richd., husb., W. Grimstead, 1662, AB, I, P1/E/79
Richd., Alderbury, 1663, I, W, P26/115
Richd., shepherd, Orcheston St Geo., 1681, I, W, P2/E/196
Earwood, Richd., husb., W. Grimstead, 1683, AB, I, P2/E/204
Earwood, Richd., yeo., W. Grimstead, 1731, W, P2/E/314
Wm., maltster, Devizes, 1666, I, W, P1/E/92
Wm., Devizes, 1832, AB, comm, W, Wr, P1/1832/130
Escott, Chris., husb., Upton S., 1637, AB, I, NW, P2/E/127
Estcourt, Eliz., widow, Swinley Farm, Kington St M., 1686, AB, I, P3/E/138
Hy., Melk., 1683, AB, I, P2/E/206
Iskett, Hy., Brook, Westb., 1738, AB, P25/1738/4
Escott alias Heward, Joan, widow, Upton S., 1577-78, W, P2/E/431, P2/5Reg/303A
Estcourt, Richd., gent., Lt. Somerford, 1641, comm, I, W (damaged items), P3/E/66
Hescot, Richd., Elston, Orcheston St Geo., 1676, AB, P2/H/740
Estcourt, Richd., gent., Swinley Farm, Kington St M., 1687, AB, comm, I (very detailed), P3/E/139
Escourt, Richd., Ladydown Farm, Bradford A., 1704, W, P1/E/151
Arscott *or* Escot, Wm., tailor, Uffc., Devon, 1700, I, W, P20/1/138
Wm., surgeon, Pott., 1724, W, P1/E/191, P1/7Reg/44A
Esdall, Wm., shearman, Swallowfield, Shinfield, Berks., 1625, I, W, P1/E/32
Esington *see* Essington
Esment *see* Eastman *or* E.
Essex, Goodman, sen., Newbury, Berks., 1714, AB, P1/E/167
Margery, widow, Bulford, 1575, W, P2/5Reg/234A
Robt., Bulford, 1562, AB, I, P2/E/7, P2/4Reg/94C
Thos., gent., Thatcham, Berks., 1638, I, W, P1/E/57
Essgar, Wm., yeo., Pewsham Forest, 1685, I, W, P3/E/134
Essington, Alice, widow, Goatacre, Hilmarton, 1692, I, W, P1/E/133
Chas., gent., Kington St M., 1676, AB, a/c, I, P3/E/107
Edith, widow, Goatacre, Hilmarton, 1670, I, W, P3/E/86
Eliz., widow, Calne, 1760, W, P26/974
Frances, widow, Stanley Abbey, Bremhill, 1745, W, P3/E/230
Henrietta, sp., Worton, Pott., 1827, AB, comm, Wr, P1/1827/10
Hy., Goatacre, Hilmarton, 1614, AB, I, P3/E/17
Lucy, widow, Peckingell, Langley Burrell & Kington St M., 1683, I, W, P3/E/119
Esington, Stephen, stone mason, Malm., 1841, W, Wr, P3/1841/43
Walter, butcher, Oaksey, 1641, AB, I, ren, P1/E/61
Walter, clothier, Goatacre, Hilmarton, 1763, W, P1/E/259, P1/12Reg/33
Wm., Goatacre, Hilmarton, 1626, I (detailed), W, P3/E/44
Wm., yeo., Goatacre, Hilmarton, 1670, I, W, P3/E/87
Wm., Peckingell, Langley Burrell & Kington St M., 1685, AB (2), comm, I, P3/E/135
Wm., bach., Malm., 1825, AB, Wr, P3/1825/59
Estcourt *see* Escott
Este *see* East
Estgate *see* Eastgate
Estmead *see* Eastmead
Estment, Estmond *see* Eastman
Eston *see* Easton
Etheredge, Thos., soldier in 77th Regt of Foot, Sal., 1794, AB, O, P4/1794/6
see also Edridge *or* E.

Eton *see* Eaton
Ettry, Hartry, Dorothy, sp., Sal., 1722, W, P4/1722/18
Hannah, widow, Horton, Bps. C., 1788, W, P24/1165
Hierom, carp., Bps. C., 1797, W, P24/1208
Joel, Horton, Bps. C., 1786, W, P24/1169
Hattrie, Jn., E. Harnham, Britford, 1588, AB, I, P24/1432, P5/5Reg/4B
Attry, Thos., yeo., Warfield, Berks., 1729, W, P1/A/283, P1/7Reg/269B
Ettwall, Ettwell, Etwall, Etwell *see* Eatwell
Eustice, Eustis *see* Hustis
Evans, Alice, widow, Wilton, 1621, W, P2/E/89
Andrew, Bromham, 1602, W, P3/1Reg/51B
Ann, sp., Malm., 1721, W, P3/E/195
Arthur, gent., Wantage, Berks., 1692, W, P23/181
Evance, Bridget, widow, Burbage, 1735, AB, I, P5/1735/23
Charlotte Ann, widow, Lyme R., Dorset, 1806, comm, W, P16/366
Edmd., Dunsden, Sonning, Berks., 1630, I, P5/1630/3
Ivans *or* Evans, Edwd., Keevil, 1578, I, W, P2/IJ/11, P2/5Reg/305C
Edwd., wheelwright, Wokm., Berks., 1746, W, P5/1746/25
Evance, Eliz., widow, Erlestoke, [1615], W, P2/E/75
Eliz., yeo.'s widow, Wrou., 1801, W, Wr, P3/1801/14
Eliz., sp., Wrou., 1811, AB, comm, Wr, P1/1811/117
Eliz., widow, Sal., 1856, D, W, Wr, P4/1856/3
Ellen, Bromham, 1642, AB, P3/E/67
Francis, Burbage, 1718, AB, I, P11/119
Francis, wheelwright, Ashton K., 1743, W, P3/E/229
Geo., yeo. and victualler, Sherb., Dorset, 1605-09, AB, I, T (child of decd: Geo. E., jun.), W, P5/1605/55, P5/1609/27, P5/8Reg/141E
Eveness *or* Eavines, Geo., yeo., Milford, Sal. St Martin, 1678, AB, a/c, I, ren, P4/1677/20
Evance, Hy., blacksmith, Erlestoke, 1599, W, P2/E/53
Evens, Hy., yeo., Kemble, 1680, AB, I, P3/E/114
Hy., husb., Kemble, 1693, AB, I, P3/E/152
Hy., yeo., Moredon, Rodbourne C., 1773, W, P3/E/278
Hy., yeo., Paven Hill, Purton, 1832, comm, W, Wr, P1/1832/45
Jas., Lyme R., Dorset, 1680, AB, P16/58
Jane, sp., Wrou., 1811, AB, comm, Wr, P1/1811/103
Eavence, Jean, widow, Westb., 1726, W, P25/1725/3
Jenkin, husb., W. Lavington, 1645, AB, I, W, P1/E/70
Joan, widow, Sherb., Dorset, 1609, AB, I, T, P5/1609/26, P5/8Reg/141C
Joan, widow, Keevil, 1624, I, W, P2/E/94
Jn., Keevil, 1569, AB, P2/5Reg/50D
Jn., Pott., 1571, W, P1/1Reg/92C
Jn., husb., Calne, 1573, I, W, P5/1573/8, P5/3Reg/25A
Evinges, Jn., Boreham, Warm., 1598, I, W, P2/E/51
Jn., Wilton, 1602, AB, I, W, P2/E/57
Jn., husb., Keevil, 1619, I, W, P1/E/27
Evance, Jn., husb., Steeple A., 1620, I, W, P2/E/86
Jn., weaver, Bromham, 1632, I, W, P3/E/53
Jn., Bromham, 1668, AB, I, P3/E/81
Jn., sen., clothworker, Reading, Berks., 1701, AB, I, P1/E/148
Jn., gent., Wantage, Berks., 1704, W, P5/1704/14
Jn., butcher, Rams., 1714, AB, I, ren, P5/1714/9
Evenes, Jn., Barkham, Berks., 1714, W, P1/E/168, P1/5Reg/359A
Jn., Mere, 1775, W, P5/1775/9
Jn., Zeals, 1775, W, P5/17Reg/94A
Jn., Donhead St My., 1782, W, Wr, P2/E/401
Jn., miller, Latton, 1789, W, P3/E/303
Jn., Sal. St Thos., 1806, AB, W, P4/1806/7
Jn., tobacconist, Holborn, London (& Haydon, Rodbourne C.), 1821, AB (re property in R.C.), comm, P3/1821/8
Jn., labourer, Wokm., Berks., 1834, comm, W, Wr, P5/1834/2
Jn., baker and grocer, Sherston, 1851, D, O, W, Wr, P3/1851/54

Evans alias Powell, Mgt., widow, Westb., 1677, AB, I, P25/1677/1
Mgt., widow, Marl. St Peter and St Paul, 1679, I, W (NEP), P1/E/112
Evens, My., widow, Downton, 1686, AB, P2/E/214
Owen, chapman, Devizes, 1674, I, W, P1/E/108
Richd., glover, Malm., 1668, I, W, P3/E/82
Richd., yeo., Winterbourne S., 1766, W, P2/E/374
Robt., Westb., 1618, AB, I, P25/1618/2
Robt., clerk and rector, Ludg., 1619, W (NEP), P1/E/28
Robt., mason, E. Harnham, Britford, 1625, AB, a/c, I (2 - 1 a copy), P24/173
Robt., Bps. C., 1629, AB, comm, I, P24/212
Robt., wheelwright, Ashton K., 1773, AB, ren, P3/E/279
Roger, Melk., 1636, comm, I, W, P2/E/118, P2/9Reg/103A
Sam., yeo., Milford, Sal. St Martin, 1728, W, P4/1728/10
Susanna, widow, Town, Malm., 1840, O, W, Wr, P3/1840/49
Thos., baker, Malm., 1630, I, W, P3/E/51
Evens, Thos., Marl., 1667, comm, W, P1/E/95
Thos., innkeeper, Sal., 1668, AB, I (detailed), P4/1667/29
Evance, Thos., blacksmith, Erlestoke, 1673, AB, I, P2/E/181
Evans alias Powell, Thos., sen., weaver, Westb., 1685, AB, I, W, P25/1685/6
Thos., sen., mercer, Malm., 1688, I, W, P3/E/146
Thos., victualler, Wantage, Berks., 1691, AB, I, P5/1691/23
Thos., Wilton, 1695, AB, ren, P1/E/140
Thos., Malm., 1700, AB, P3/E/167
Thos., Burbage, 1705, AB, I, P11/95
Thos., Rodbourne C., 1733, AB, P3/E/215
Evens, Thos., Chards., Devon, 1739, W, P14/154
Thos., gent., Elcombe, Wrou., 1832, comm, W, Wr, P3/1832/11
Wm., priest, Latton, 1560, institution to vicarage, P1/1Reg/81A
Wm., Devizes, 1613, AB, P1/E/14
Wm., W. Lavington, 1630, W, copy W, P2/E/106
Wm., tailor, Westb., 1708, AB, I, P25/1708/6
Wm., Faulston, Bishopstone S., 1793, AB, P2/E/419
Wm., clerk, Lyme R., Dorset, 1804, comm, W, P16/364
see also Onion alias E.; Ovens
Eve, Eves, Agnes, widow, Mkt. L., 1615, deed of gift, W, P2/E/77, P2/8Reg/288B
Alice, widow, Gt. Wishford, 1596, I, W, P2/E/426
Alice, widow, Gt. Wishford, 1643, I, W, P1/E/65
Edmd., husb., Gt. Wishford, 1608, AB, I, W, P2/E/63
Hy., Heytes., 1585, AB, I, W, P5/1585/21, P5/4Reg/127A
Eave, Hy., tailor, Heytes., 1683, AB, I, P5/1682/38
Eves, Jas., Mkt. L., 1633, I, W, P2/E/113
Jn., Gt. Wishford, 1586, I, copy I, W, P2/E/25, P2/7Reg/41C
Eves, Jn., Berwick St Jas., 1593, I, W, P2/E/39
Jn., yeo., Gt. Wishford, 1716, AB, I, P1/E/174
Jn., gent., Sal., 1792, W, P1/E/292, P1/14Reg/448
Eves, Matthew, shepherd, Orcheston St Geo., 1676, AB, I, P2/E/186
Ralph, Tytherington, Heytes., 1576-77, AB, P5/1576/17, P5/3Reg/91A
Thos., curate, Dinton, 1556, W, P2/1Reg/110A
Thos., Heytes., 1562, W, P5/1Reg/4D
Eves, Thos., smith, Wokm., Berks., 1566, W, P5/1Reg/72A
Eves, Thos., Mkt. L., 1611, W, P1/E/10
Eves, Wm., Urchf., 1565, W, P2/4Reg/213A
Wm., yeo., Gt. Wishford, 1726, W, P2/E/299
Wm., gent., Gt. Wishford, 1741, W, P1/E/227, P1/9Reg/44
Ives, Wm., yeo., Woodley, W. and Sandford, Berks., 1761, W, P5/1761/25
Wm., yeo., Donhead St A., 1782, W, Wr, P2/E/402
Eveleigh *see* Everley
Evelle, Chas., Stourton, 1750, AB, W, P2/E/341
My., widow, Stourton, 1670, AB, P2/E/177
Wm., Stourton, 1749, AB, W, P2/E/340

Evemay, Ithimay, Alice, widow, Rudge, Froxfield, 1628, I, W, P1/IJ/40
Evymay, Roger, yeo., Rudge, Froxfield, 1626, I, W, P3/E/45
Sam., wheelwright, Bramshaw, Hants, 1710, AB, I, P24/706
Evendon, Hy., tailor, Sonning, Berks., 1637, I, W, P5/1637/11, P5/13Reg/45
Jn., tailor, Sonning, Berks., 1608, W, P5/1608/10, P5/8Reg/115C
see also Juden alias E.
Evenes, Eveness, Evens *see* Evans
Evenson, Obadiah, innholder, *The Bell Inn*, Chipp., 1738, W, P3/E/221
Everall, Edith, widow, Chilhampton, S. Newton, 1640, I, NW, P2/E/139
Jn., Chilhampton, S. Newton, 1636, I, NW, P2/E/123
Everett, Everit, Aaron, tailor, Martin, Hants, 1637, D, inty, I, sentence, W, P2/E/129
Abraham, yeo., Mapperton, Dorset, 1734, W, P5/1734/23
Alice, widow, Hazeldon, Tisb., 1817, comm, W, Wr, P2/1817/19
Ann, widow, Heytes., 1739, W, Wr, P5/1739/16
Everatt, Bartholomew, glover, Draycot C., 1629, I, NW, P3/E/49
Everard, Brian, yeo., Kington St M., 1688, comm, I, W, P3/E/147
Everard, Cath., widow, Corsley, 1781, W, P2/E/400
Charlotte, Salterton, Durnford, 1857, AB, O, Wr, P9/125
Edith, Upton L., 1599, AB, I, W, P2/E/54
Everet, Edith, widow, Sal. St Martin, 1665, AB, I, W, P4/1664/1
Edwd., yeo., Gillingham, Dorset, 1707, AB, I, P27/1/165
Everard alias Webb, Eliz., widow, Durley, Burbage, 1747, AB, I, P11/198
Francis, yeo., Tytherington, Heytes., 1756, comm, I, W, P5/1756/33
Geoffrey, spurrier, Sal., 1720, W, P1/E/183, P1/6Reg/228
Geo., All C., [1607], W (NEP), P3/E/4
Hy., labourer, Durnford, 1856, O, W, Wr, P9/124
Everatt alias Webb, Jas., Durley, Burbage, 1764, W, P5/1764/14
Everett alias Randall, Joan, widow, Tidcombe and Fosbury, 1670, I, W, P3/E/89
Everatt, Jn., Thatcham, Berks., 1561, W. No date of probate given, P1/2Reg/105B
Evered, Jn., [smith], Enmore Grn, Motc., Dorset, 1593, AB, I, T, P5/1592/30, P5/6Reg/19A
Everit, Jn., Charlton, Downton, 1610, AB, P2/E/66, P2/8Reg/90A
Evered, Jn., shepherd, Sal., 1612, I, P4/1612/23
Everett alias Randall, Jn., Tidcombe and Fosbury, 1614-15, AB, a/c, I, W (a/c & W on one sheet), P1/E/18, P3/E/21
Everard, Jn., tailor, Heytes., 1639, AB, I, P5/1639/30, P5/13Reg/215A
Evered, Jn., pinmaker, Sal., 1647, W (damaged), P1/E/74
Evered, Jn., yeo., Enmore Grn, Motc., Dorset, 1680, comm, W, P19/39
Evered, Jn., Laverstock, 1695, AB, P2/E/238
Everard alias Webb, Jn., yeo., Durley, Burbage, 1703, I, W, P11/90
Jn., yeo., Damerham, Hants, 1712, I, W, P2/E/272
Everitt, Jn., Tytherington, Heytes., 1730, W, P5/1730/20
Jn., labourer, Overton, 1810, W, Wr, P3/1810/12
Everet, Jos., Laverstock, 1724, W, P2/E/294
Evered, My., widow, Martin, Hants, 1670, NW, P2/E/178
Evered, My., widow, Laverstock, 1754, W, P4/1754/1
My., widow, Bradford A., 1838, AB, comm, Wr, P2/1838/35
Nathaniel, gent., Crockerton, Longbridge D., 1823-33, AB, W, Wr (2), P1/1823/48, P2/1833/66
Evered alias Webb, Noah, Draycot, Chiseldon, 1642, I, W, P3/E/69
Rees, yeo., Hazeldon, Tisb., 1801, W, Wr, P1/1801/110, P1/15Reg/329
Rees, yeo., Wardour, Tisb., 1838, W, Wr, P2/1838/1
Richd., grocer, Devizes, 1777, W, P1/E/275, P1/13Reg/172
Everatt, Robt., yeo., Kington L., [1642], I, W (NEP), P3/E/68
Everatt, Robt., husb., Kington L., 1665, I, NW, P3/E/77
Everard, Robt., jun., sheer grinder, Whitbourne, Corsley, 1778, W, P2/E/396
Evered alias Webb, Stephen, yeo., Rams., 1623, I, W, P5/1622/29, P5/10Reg/148B
Evered alias Webb, Stephen, Draycot, Chiseldon, 1667, W, P3/E/79
Everett alias Webb, Stephen, yeo., Rams., 1670, I, W, P5/1669/16
Everight, Thos., miller, Tilehurst, Berks., 1698, comm, I, W, P1/E/145, P1/3Reg/31
Thos., yeo., Wargrave, Berks., 1763, W, P1/E/260, P1/12Reg/67B
Thos., yeo., Tisb., 1829, W, Wr, P2/1829/21
Wm., husb., Kington L., 1675, comm, D, I, W, P3/E/102

Averad alias Webb, Wm., yeo., Wootton R., 1698, I, W, P3/A/239
Wm., Fisherton A., 1787, AB, P2/E/411
Wm., bach., Fovant, 1855, AB, aff, Wr, P2/1855/14
see also Newman alias E.; Webb alias E.
Everidge, Jn., yeo., Chisenbury, Enford, 1681, I, W, P12/114
Robt., husb., Durrington, 1725, AB, W, P2/E/297-98
Everight, Everit, Everitt *see* Everett
Everley, Christian, widow, Fisherton D., 1574, W, P2/5Reg/212B
Everly, David, Hill D., 1767, AB, P5/1767/19
Eveleigh, Eliz., sp., The Palace, The Close, Sal., 1683, W, P1/E/118
Eveleigh, Francis, gent., Uffc., Devon, 1754, W, P20/1/224
Jane, Wylye, 1728, W, P2/E/303
Jane, sp. and baker, Wylye, 1742, AB, I, W, P2/E/332
Everly, Joan, widow, Sal., 1668, AB, P4/1667/32
Everly, Jn., innholder, Sherb., Dorset, 1740, W, Wr, P5/1740/29
Eveleigh, Jn., mercer, Lyme R., Dorset, 1804, comm, W, P16/363
Jn., sen., baker, Ashton G., Codf. St P., 1819, W, Wr, P2/1819/2
Richd., yeo., Wilton, 1644, I, W, P2/E/141
Walter, Fisherton D., 1567, AB, P2/5Reg/10B
Wm., yeo., Wylye, 1670, AB, I, P2/E/176
Everly, Wm., Tytherington, Heytes., 1719, AB, P5/1719/27
Everton, David, clothier, Sal., 1670, I, W, P4/1670/17
Jas., victualler, Melplash, Netherb., Dorset, 1640, I, NW, P17/52
Jas., yeo., Sherb., Dorset, 1714, W, P5/1714/10, P5/15Reg/389B
Thomasine, widow, Sherb., Dorset, 1729, AB, W, P5/1729/16, P5/16Reg/245C
Every *see* Avery
Eves *see* Eve
Evinges *see* Evans
Evymay *see* Evemay
Ewen, Ann, sp., Stratton & Swindon, 1683, I, W, P3/E/121
Ewens, Ann, widow, Ruscombe, Berks., 1683, AB, P5/1683/20
Ewence, Edwd., blacksmith, Compton C., 1802, W, P2/1802/54
Yowing, Hy., husb., Charlton nr Malm., [1611], I, W (NEP), P3/Y/7
Ewens, Humphrey, husb., Waltham St Lawr., Berks., 1692, AB, I, P1/E/134
Yewen, Jas., Haydon Wick, Rodbourne C., [1609], W (NEP), P3/Y/5
Ewens, Jane, Ruscombe, Berks., 1683, AB, comm, P5/1682/39
Yeowens, Jn., husb., Eye and Dunsden, Sonning, Berks., 1609, I, W, P5/1609/93, P5/8Reg/157
Ewens, Jn., Hurst, Berks., 1617, AB, I, P5/1617/14, P5/9Reg/216B
Jn., Liddington, 1662, AB, I, P1/E/85
Jn., yeo., Draycot Foliat, 1705, I, W, P3/E/174
Ewens, Jn., yeo., Axnoller, Beam., Dorset, 1719, W, P5/1719/28, P5/16Reg/18B
Youen, Jn., sen., maltster, Aston U., Blewbury, Berks., 1755, W, P5/1755/61
Youen, Jn., Aston U., Blewbury, Berks., 1779, AB, P5/1779/28, P5/17Reg/181B
Yewin, Jn. *see also* Joan Kitchen
Ewens, Margery, widow, Axnoller, Beam., Dorset, 1724, W, P17/414
Michael, yeo., Wantage, Berks., 1675, I, W, P23/53
Ewens, Oliver, Ruscombe, Berks., 1750, AB, P5/1750/12
Ewens, Richd., Enford, 1812, AB, Wr, P2/1812/22
Ewence, Robt., Gt. Wishford, 1839, W, Wr, P2/1839/33
Roger, husb., Eastcott, Swindon, 1620, I, W (damaged), P3/E/35
Roger, gent., Draycot Foliat, 1723, W, P3/E/198
Ewens, Thos., sen., Sindlesham, Hurst, Berks., 1622, I, W, P5/1622/24, P5/10Reg/108
Thos., Fawley, Berks., 1666, AB, I (both damaged), P1/E/93
Thos., yeo., Winterbourne M., 1704, AB, I, release, W, P1/E/152, P3/E/169
Thos., Chr. M., 1771, AB, P3/E/273
Yewen, Wm., carp., Calcutt, Chilton F., 1630, I, W, P3/Y/16
Ewin, Wm., yeo., Axford, Rams., 1670, I, W, P5/1670/11
Wm., labourer, Swindon, 1687, I, W, P3/E/142
Youen, Wm., Aston U., Blewbury, Berks., 1720, AB, I, P5/1720/62
Wm., stone cutter, Swindon, 1763, W, P3/E/267

Ewens, Wm., blacksmith, Marden, 1770, W, P1/E/266, P1/12Reg/324B
Ewens, Wm., Everleigh, 1785, AB, P3/E/300
Ewence, Wm., blacksmith, Teffont M., 1849, W, Wr, P2/1849/10
Ewer, Chris., gent., Clarendon Park, 1680, a/c, I (detailed), W, P4/1680/4
Hy., Highw., 1762, AB, comm, P10/1762/3
Philemon, Sal., 1848, AB, Wr, P1/1848/37
Richd., gent., Highw., 1678, AB, I, P10/1678/2
Thos., sen., yeo., Highw., 1714, W (NEP), P10/1714/1
Ewin *see* Ewen
Exall, Alexander, innholder, Sherb., Dorset, 1604, AB, I, P5/1604/11, P5/8Reg/11B
Hugh, yeo., Pinford, Castleton, Dorset, 1602, I, W, P5/1601/17, P5/7Reg/32A
Stephen, Sherb., Dorset, 1605, AB, P5/1605/21, P5/8Reg/30A
Exell, Thos., miller, Over C., Dorset, 1712, W, P5/1712/26, P5/15Reg/292
Exden *see* Exten
Exell *see* Exall
Exham, Robt., Chipp., 1613, AB, I, P3/E/14
Thos., glover, Chipp., 1569, W, P1/2Reg/86B
Wm., Chipp., 1618, AB, I, P3/E/28
Exton, Exden, Agnes, widow, Sutton V., 1638, AB, I, P2/E/130
Extin, Alice, widow, Gillingham, Dorset, 1691, I (on dorse is record of proceedings in manorial court of Gillingham, re writ of right of dower, Frances Hurman vs Wm. Bowles & others, 1694), P27/1/126
Exten, Alice, widow, Warm., 1692, AB, comm, I, W, P1/E/135
Ann, brewer's widow, Tytherington, Heytes., 1704, I (2 - detailed 2nd I relates to Robt. E.), W, P5/1704/19
Chas., cordw., Westport St My., 1689, AB, I, P3/E/149
Chas., gent., Malm., 1787, W, P3/E/301
Exden, Edwd., husb., Gt. Horningsham, 1580, I, W, P5/1580/22, P5/4Reg/6C
Exden, Eliz., widow, Codf. St P., 1559-60, AB, W, P2/4Reg/8C, 51B
Exten, Francis, tailor, Tisb., 1615, AB, a/c, I, P2/E/76, P2/8Reg/274A
Exten, Geoffrey, yeo., Tytherington, Heytes., 1706, AB, I, P5/1706/13
Exten, Geoffrey, innholder, Warm., 1720, W, P1/E/184, P1/6Reg/234
Geoffrey, butcher, Warm., 1758, W, P2/E/355
Hannah, widow, Westport St My., 1750, W, P1/E/242, P1/10Reg/401C
Hy., Horningsham, 1691, W, P5/1691/22
Isaac, maltster, Westport St My., 1745, W, P3/E/231
Exten, Jane, gent.'s wife, Bishopstrow, 1785, W, P2/E/404
Exden, Joan, widow, Horningsham, 1602, AB (2), I, W, P5/1602/14, P5/7Reg/36D
Exden, Jn., husb., Longbridge D., 1564, AB, P2/E/13, P2/4Reg/192C
Exten, Jos., yeo., Tytherington, Heytes., 1767, W, P5/1767/20
Jos., Warm., 1827, W, Wr, P2/1827/70
Libbeus, Warm., 1686, AB, I, P1/E/124
Margery, widow, Warm., 1741, W, P1/E/228, P1/9Reg/136
Exten, My., Sutton V., 1672, AB, P2/E/180
Exten, My., widow, Erlestoke, 1740, W, P2/E/326
Exten, My., widow, Heytes., 1756, W, P5/1756/9
My., wife, Warm., 1816, W, P2/1816/33
My., sp., Lyme R., Dorset, 1844, comm, W, Wr, P16/436
Exten, Nich., Horningsham, 1634, I, W, P5/1634/8, P5/12Reg/166B
Extin, Peter, Gillingham, Dorset, 1670, AB, P27/1/39
Richd., Tytherington, Heytes., 1672, AB, P5/1672/9
Exten, Richd., yeo., Heytes., 1719, W, P5/1719/26, P5/16Reg/33B
Exten, Richd., Heytes., 1721, AB, P5/1721/13
Exten, Richd., Bishopstrow, 1821, AB, W, Wr, P2/1821/31
Exden, Robt., Leighs Marsh, Dilton, Westb., 1665, AB, P25/1665/6
Robt., yeo., Tytherington, Heytes., 1692, W, P5/1692/25
Robt., sen., yeo., Tytherington, Heytes., 1712, AB, I, P5/1712/27
Roger, weaver, Horningsham, 1638, I, W, P5/1638/40, P5/13Reg/109
Exten, Susanna, widow, Leighs Marsh, Dilton, Westb., 1683, AB, I, P25/1683/3
Exden, Thos., broad weaver, Leighs Marsh, Dilton, Westb., 1675, AB, I, NW, P25/1675/5
Exten, Thos., sen., gent., Warm., 1785, W, P2/E/405
Thos., yeo., Knook, 1792, W, P5/1792/8, P5/18Reg/185

Thos., yeo., Boreham, Warm., 1823, comm, W, Wr, P1/1823/10
Eyers *see* Ayers
Eyles, Oyles, Alice, widow, Deptford, Wylye, 1576, W, P2/5Reg/246B
Amelia, widow, Collingbourne K., 1781, AB, P3/E/296
Anthony, carp., Oare, Wilcot, 1762, W, P3/E/266
Edith, widow, Wanb., 1818, L, W, Wr, P3/1818/11
Eyles alias Hicks, Edwd., husb., Wylye, 1564, I, W, P2/E/12, P2/4Reg/161A
Eeles, Edwd., yeo., Ditchampton, Wilton, 1681, I, W, P2/E/199
Oyles, Frideswide, Bapton, Fisherton Delamare, 1581, W, P2/6Reg/20A
Geo., husb., Lydiard M., 1611, W, P3/E/11
Geo., yeo., Holt, Bradford A., 1777, AB, P2/E/392
Eyles nee Jeffery, Hannah, sp., Sherb., Dorset, 1807, W, Wr, P5/1807/9
Hannah, sp., Rams., 1830, O, W, Wr, P5/1830/6
Eyles alias Hicks, Hy., yeo., Bapton, Fisherton Delamare, 1605, AB, I, W, P2/E/61
Hy., husb., Burghfield, Berks., 1666, comm, I, W (damaged), P1/E/94
Eyles alias Hicks, Hy., yeo., Stockton, 1722, I, W, P2/E/291
Oyles, Jas., Bapton, Fisherton Delamare, 1582, W, P2/6Reg/77A
Eyles alias Hicks, Jas., yeo., Stockton, 1667, a/c, I, W, P2/E/169
Jas., yeo., Bapton, Fisherton Delamare, 1668, AB, I, P1/E/99
Jas., Bapton, Fisherton Delamare, 1700, AB, I, P2/E/246
Jas., Chisbury, Lt. Bedwyn, 1758, AB, P5/1758/17
Jane, widow, Melk., 1777, AB, P2/E/389
Oyles alias Hicks, Jn., Bapton, Fisherton Delamare, 1572, W, P2/5Reg/142B
Ayles alias Hicks, Jn., Wylye, 1613, AB, a/c, P2/A/98, P2/8Reg/189A
Ailes, Jn., Berwick St Jn., 1801, req, copy W, Wr, P1/1801/100, P1/15Reg/318
Jn., Oare, Wilcot, 1824, W, Wr, P3/1824/42
Jos., wheelwright, Marl. St Peter and St Paul, 1767, W, P1/E/262, P1/12Reg/268B
Jos., coal dealer, Stratton St Mgt., 1841, comm, W, Wr, P3/1841/25
Ayles, My., widow, Ditchampton, Wilton, 1628, AB, P2/A/145
My., widow, Wanb., 1733, AB, I, P3/E/212
My., widow, Bradford A., 1741, W, P2/E/329
My., widow, Atworth, Bradford A., 1768, W, P2/E/376
My., widow, Holt, Bradford A., 1798, W, P1/E/302, P1/15Reg/42
Robt., Haydon Wick, Rodbourne C., 1825, I, O, W, Wr, P3/1825/66
Robt., gardener, Rode, N. Bradley, 1841, comm, W, Wr, P2/1841/8
Ayles, Thos., Stockton, 1628, I, W, P2/A/144
Eeles, Thos., husb., Waltham St Lawr., Berks., 1702, W, P5/1702/16
Thos., Corsham, 1715, marriage licence, P29/2Reg/19B
Thos., Atworth, Bradford A., 1731, AB, comm, P2/E/313
Thos., yeo., Beanacre, Melk., 1765, W, P2/E/372
Thos., Collingbourne K. (with land & goods in Collingbourne D.), 1774, W, P21/11/7
Thos., yeo., Shurnhold, Melk., 1791, comm, W, P2/E/417
Thos., Winsley, Bradford A., 1800, AB, comm, P2/1800/72
Ayles, Thos., yeo., Motc., Dorset, 1812, comm, W, P27/1/616
Thos., carp., Collingbourne K., 1844, AB, O, Wr, P3/1844/43
Wm., sen., yeo., Fisherton D., 1694, I, W, P2/E/235
Wm., Coate, Liddington, 1708, AB, I, P1/E/157
Wm., Collingbourne K., 1732, AB, P1/E/206
Wm., Crudwell, 1744, AB, P1/E/235
Wm., Wick Farm, Lacock, 1765, W, P3/E/268
Wm., Crudwell, 1771, AB, P3/E/274
Wm., staymaker, Lambourn, Berks., 1786, W, P1/E/283, P1/14Reg/89
Wm., Hinton Charterhouse, Somerset (leaving effects at Melk.), 1843, W, Wr, P2/1843/48
see also Hicks alias E.
Eylowe *see* Alow
Eylward *see* Aylward
Eylwaye *see* Elloway
Eymes *see* Eames
Eymons, Wm., husb., Eastcourt, Shalbourne, 1565, W, P5/1Reg/59A
Eynells *see* Aynoll

Eynes *see* Haynes
Eyng, Jn., sen., tailor, Heytes., 1582, I, P5/1582/21
Eyre, Eyres *see* Ayers

Fabian, Agnes, widow, Froxfield, 1634, I, W, P1/F/78
Jn., sadler, Chipp., 1631, I, W, P1/F/66
Jn., yeo., Froxfield, 1640, AB, I, P3/F/88
Jn., yeo. *or* husb., Froxfield, 1663, comm, I, note, W, P3/F/102
Jn., yeo., Nettleton, 1738, comm, W, P3/F/354
Wm., wine cooper, Nettleton, 1695, AB, I, P3/F/226
Facy, Wm., Uffc., Devon, 1673, D, I, W, P20/1/74
see also Vaisey
Faggott, Frances, tailor, Burbage, 1588, AB, I, NW, W (2 - 1 crossed out & annotated void), P5/1588/18, P5/5Reg/11C
Fairbeard, Ann, widow, Long Wittenham, Berks., 1747, AB, I, W, P1/F/387, P1/10Reg/95
Fairclough, Sarah, widow, Frome Selwood, Somerset, 1729?, W, P2/F/469
Fairechild, Ann, widow, Eastbury, Lambourn, Berks., 1714, W, P1/F/252, P1/5Reg/399
Jn., Aldbourne, 1649, I, W, P1/F/110
Vairchild, Jn., husb., Aldbourne, 1669, I, W, P3/UV/25
Fair *see* Fayre
Fairthorne, Amy, widow, Soley, Chilton F., 1645, ren (Wm. Hamlin renounces admon), P1/F/100
Cath., sp., Watchfield, Shrivenham, Berks., 1735, AB, ren, P1/F/335
Faythorne *or* Fethorne, Edwd., Clyffe P., 1669, AB, I, P3/F/122
Fairthorne *or* Fetterne alias Smith, Eliz., mantuamaker, Wanb., 1752, W, P3/F/382
Faythorne, Hy., yeo., Soley, Chilton F., 1645, AB, NW, P1/F/99
Fethorne alias Haywood, Jn., blacksmith, Rams., 1594, AB, I, W, P5/1594/28, P5/6Reg/74A
Fethorne alias Heyward, Roger, blacksmith, Rams., 1619, AB, I, T, P5/1619/53, P5/10Reg/37A
Fethorne alias Haywood, Thos., jun., Chilton F., [1606], I, W, P1/F/15
Faythorne, Thos., Chilton F., [1608], W, Wr (NEP), P3/F/7
Thos., gent. *or* yeo., Eastcott, Swindon, 1730, I, W, P3/F/323
Wm., apothecary, Wootton B., 1774, W, P3/F/417
Faithfull, Dan., brickmaker, Kintbury, Berks., 1814, W, Wr, P1/1814/94
Jane, Ham, 1614, I, W, P3/F/24
Richd., Hannington, 1734, W, P3/F/341
Faldo, Edmd., innholder, Froxfield, 1808, W, Wr, P1/1808/85
Falkner *see* Fawconer
Falside, Jas., Heytes., 1744, AB, Wr, P5/1744/18
Fancy, Chris., Turners Puddle, Dorset, 1682, I, NW, P5/1682/41
Fanner, Jn., husb., Charlton, Donhead St My., 1616, AB, I, P1/F/44
Wm., husb., Donhead St My., 1626, W, P2/F/130
Wm., carpet drawer, Wilton, 1773, W, P1/F/463, P1/12Reg/451
Fanning, Oliver, Trinity Hospital, Sal., 1626, I, W, P4/1626/22
Fanstone, Audrcy, widow, Downton, 1629, I, P2/F/141
Edmd., gent., Downton, 1633, AB, I, ren, P1/F/74
Edmd., gent., Downton, 1648, I, W, P2/F/217
Jn., gent., Downton, 1640, AB, a/c, I, P2/F/192
Jn., sen., yeo., Wick, Downton, 1788, W, P2/F/642
Jn., maltster, Downton, 1803, W, P2/1803/79
Ralph, yeo., Wick, Downton, 1797, W, P2/F/664
Richd., yeo., Martin, Hants, 1795, AB, ren, P2/F/653
Farely *see* Farley
Fares *see* Ferris
Farewell *see* Farwell
Faris *see* Ferris
Farley, Alexander, Codf. St My., 1603, AB, I, W, P2/F/65
Anthony, husb., Codf. St My., 1615, I, W, P2/F/98
Anthony, Codf. St My., [1682], I, P2/F/301
Cath., widow, Stockton, [1725], W, P2/F/456
Chris., Heytes., 1597, AB, P5/1597/42, P5/6Reg/159A
Edwd., yeo., Boyton, 1689, AB, I, P2/F/342
Eleanor, widow, Fovant Stroud, 1685, I, W, P2/F/319

Joan, widow, Codf. St My., 1638, I, W, P2/F/176
Jn., Codf. St My., 1597, I, W, P2/F/43
Jn., Codf. St My., 1608, T (children: Alexander, Eliz. & Edith F.), P2/F/76
Jn., cordw., Stockton, 1711, I, W, P1/F/249, P1/5Reg/263
Jn., cordw., Stockton, 1795, W, Wr, P2/F/655
Jn., Sherrington, 1683?, I, P2/F/303
Nathaniel, labourer, Heytes., 1741, AB, ren, W, P5/1741/19
Thos., Stockton, 1562, W, P2/4Reg/107A
Thos., sen., collarmaker, Fovant Stroud, 1685, comm, I, W, P2/F/321
Thos., tailor, Boyton, 1690-91, comm, I, NW, P2/F/346
Timothy, husb., Upton L., 1639, I, W, P2/F/191
Farely, Timothy, sen., yeo., Upton L., 1697, I, W, P2/F/377
Farely, Wm., Enford, 1569, AB, P2/5Reg/68B
Wm., yeo., Heytes., 1691, I, W, P5/1691/25
Farlow, Jn., jun., innholder, Froxfield, 1711, I, W, P3/F/272
Farmer, Alexander, yeo., Stanford in the Vale, Berks., 1683, I, W, P1/F/164
Anna Maria, widow, Hurst, Berks., 1803, W, P5/1803/22, P5/19Reg/51
Anthony, husb., Swindon, 1569, W, P1/1Reg/105B, P1/2Reg/89
Anthony, husb., Eastcott, Swindon, 1614, I, W, P1/F/39
Anthony, Huish, 1634, I, W, P1/F/73
Anthony, Even Swindon, 1734, AB, P3/F/342
Benj., butcher, Twyford, Hurst, Berks., 1809, W, Wr, P5/1809/24
Cath., sp., Lockeridge, Overton, 1667, AB, P3/F/112
Christian, widow, Manningford A., 1640, I, W, P3/F/89
Edwd., tailor, Swindon, 1695, I, P3/F/227
Edwd., yeo., Westlecott, Swindon, 1718, W, P3/F/286
Edwd., ale draper and labourer, Hungerford, Berks., 1759, W, P23/683
Eleanor, widow, Marl., [1677], I, W, P1/F/150
Eliz., baker's wife, Swindon, 1720, AB, P3/F/295
Francis, stone cutter, Swindon, 1733, W, P3/F/337
Farmer alias Hayward, Geo., tailor, Clyffe P., [1607], W (NEP), P3/F/4
Giles, yeo., Calne, 1662, I, W, P26/107
Harriet, sp., Hole Farm, Lyme R., Dorset, 1840, comm, W, Wr, P16/427
Hy., yeo., High Swindon, 1614, I, W, P1/F/38
Hy., yeo., Swindon, 1636, AB, a/c, I, P3/F/74
Hy., yeo., Stanton St B., 1705, comm, I, W, P3/F/246
Jas., Marten, Grafton, 1812, AB, comm, Wr, P5/1812/34
Farmer alias Hazel, Joan, widow, Bagnor, Speen, Berks., 1714, I, W, P1/F/255, P1/5Reg/392
Jn., husb., Ropewind, Shalbourne, 1597, AB, I, W, P5/1597/38, P5/6Reg/183
Jn., husb., Swindon, 1604, I, W, P1/F/9
Jn., yeo., Stanton St B., 1605, AB, P1/F/12
Jn., husb., Ridge, Chilmark, 1616, I, W, P1/F/42
Farmer alias Holloway, Jn., yeo., Swindon, 1661, comm, I, W, P3/F/101, P3/3Reg/15B
Jn., yeo., Langley Burrell, 1663, AB, I, P3/F/103
Jn., Horsehall Hill, Lt. Bedwyn, 1689, I, W, P21/4/35
Jn., Shalbourne, Berks., 1714, AB, I, P23/339
Jn., butcher, Milton L., 1722, AB, ren, W, P3/F/298
Jn., Gt. Bedwyn, 1728, AB, P5/1728/32, P5/16Reg/211D
Jn., victualler, Avebury, 1817, W, Wr, P1/1817/81
Jn., yeo., Shalbourne, 1674, I, W, P5/1674/25
Lucy, widow, Wokm., Berks., 1817, W (& cod), Wr, P5/1817/8
Margery, widow, Woodb., 1692, AB, I, P3/F/213
Martha, widow, Eaton Hastings, Berks., 1738, AB, I, P1/F/346
Farmer alias Hazel, My., Enborne, Berks., 1668, I, W, P1/F/136
My., widow, Horsehall Hill, Lt. Bedwyn, 1733, W, P5/1733/21
Nathaniel, Marl., 1673, AB, I, P1/F/143
Praxy, widow, Stanton St B., 1706, W, P3/F/250
Rebecca, widow, Langley Burrell, 1735, W, P1/F/333, P1/8Reg/82
Richd., husb., Swindon, 1615, I, W, P3/F/29
Richd., Gt. Faringdon, Berks., 1639, AB, I, P5/1639/34

Richd., Gt. Somerford, 1672, AB, P3/F/138
Richd., stone cutter, Swindon, 1686, AB, I, P1/F/521
Richd., clothier, Devizes, 1692, I, W, P1/F/197
Farmer alias Holloway, Richd., yeo., Swindon, 1692, AB, comm, I, ren, P3/H/714
Richd., blacksmith, Wantage, Berks., 1697, AB, I (2), ren, W, P23/223
Farmer alias Hazel, Richd., servant in husbandry, Kintbury, Berks., 1729, W, P1/F/308, P1/7Reg/278
Richd., blacksmith, Wantage, Berks., 1754, W, P23/650
Richd., stone cutter, Swindon, 1763, AB, W, P3/F/400
Richd., Swindon, 1773, AB, comm, P1/F/464
Richd., Shalbourne, Berks., 1776, AB, comm, P5/1776/15, P5/17Reg/131D
Richd., yeo., Hurst, Berks., 1801-02, W, P5/1802/1, P5/18Reg/326B
Robt., husb., Shalbourne, 1582, I, W, P5/1582/23, P5/4Reg/45D
Robt., carp., Stratton St Mgt., 1604, AB, I, LA, NW, P29/F/2
Robt., tailor, Lambourn, Berks., 1628, I, W, P1/F/57
Ruth, widow, Devizes, 1742, W, P1/F/364, P1/9Reg/218B
Farmer alias Hazel, Thos., husb., Church Speen, Speen, Berks., 1611, I, W, P1/F/28
Thos., Westbrook, Gt. Faringdon, Berks., 1638, I, W, P5/1638/41, P5/13Reg/138
Farmer alias Hayward, Thos., yeo., Wood St., Clyffe P., 1643, comm, I, W, P1/F/95
Farmer alias Holloway, Thos., yeo., Swindon, 1667, W, P3/F/113
Thos., sen., innholder (Hart Inn), Wantage, Berks., 1672, AB, I (mentions shop, 34 pairs of shoes, leather & lasts), P23/31
Thos., husb., Collingbourne K., 1681, I, W, P3/F/167
Thos., innholder, Wantage, Berks., 1687, AB, a/c, I, P23/158
Thos., Devizes, 1695, AB, I, P1/F/204
Thos., Windsor, Berks., 1720, AB, P1/F/276
Thos., yeo., Crickl. St S., 1728, W, P3/F/314
Thos., butcher, Woodb., 1730, W, P3/F/324
Farmer-Smith, Thos., sadler, Wootton B., 1811, comm, W, P1/1811/125
Wm., husb., W. Ashton, Steeple A., 1559, W, P2/3Reg/179C
Wm., labourer, Stanton St B., [1584], W (NEP), P3/1Reg/5C
Farmer alias Hayward, Wm., Hilmarton, 1601, W, P3/1Reg/66B
Wm., husb., Swindon, 1609, W, P3/F/11
Wm., husb., Collingbourne K., 1620, I, W, P1/F/50
Wm., husb., Collingbourne D., 1629, I, W (refs. to fittings in house & equipment in farm buildings), P21/3/13
Wm., husb., Stanton St B., 1630, I, W, P3/F/60
Wm., Stanton St B., 1668, AB, I, ren, P3/F/118
Wm., yeo., Bagden, Savernake, 1670, comm, I, W, P21/2/17
Wm., jun., Woodb., 1691, AB, I, P3/F/209
Wm., husb., Compton B., 1694, AB, comm, I, P3/F/221
Wm., yeo., Stanton St B., [1707], W, P1/F/235
Wm., Lt. Bedwyn, 1727, AB, P21/8/32
Wm., innholder, Sal., 1727, W, P4/1726/12
Wm., yeo., Eastcott, Swindon, 1764, W, P3/F/401
Wm., yeo., Shalbourne, Berks., 1772, comm, W, P23/747
Wm., miller, Littleton P., 1799, W, Wr, P1/F/520, P1/15Reg/189
Wm., Littleton Mill, W. Lavington, 1830, O, W, Wr, P1/1830/20
Fermor, Wm., yeo., Clack, Lyneham, 1852, D, O, W, Wr, P3/1852/33
see also Hayward alias F.; Holloway alias F.
Farnell, Edwd., gent., Fonthill G., 1733, W, P2/F/492
Jn., husb., Tisb., 1545, W (NEP), P2/1Reg/67B
Jn., husb., Tisb., 1620, AB, I, W, P2/F/111
Jn., husb., Sedgehill, 1641, AB, I, NW, P1/F/94
Leonard, yeo., Tisb., 1629, AB, I, W, P2/F/143
Margery, widow, Tisb., 1570, AB, P2/5Reg/94E
Marian, widow, Tisb., 1623-26, AB, a/c, W, P2/F/121, 135
Melior, sp., Milton, E. Knoyle, 1629, I, note of probate W, P2/F/142
Robt., husb., E. Knoyle, 1580, W, P2/6Reg/16C
Robt., jun., husb., E. Knoyle, 1603, I, NW, P2/F/63
Robt., E. Knoyle, 1629, AB, a/c, P2/F/138
Robt., yeo., Milton, E. Knoyle, 1677, AB, I, P2/F/281
Wm., Tisb., 1607, AB, I, P2/F/72

Farnham, Thos., blacksmith, Wambrook, Somerset, 1636, I, W (NEP), P30/67
Farnwell, Fernewell alias Goldneye, Adam, yeo., Chipp., 1571, W, P1/1Reg/35B
Farnwell alias Gouldney, Hy., yeo., Chipp., 1641, I, W, P3/F/95
Farr, Agnes, widow, Chirton, 1618, AB, I, P2/F/100
Ann, widow, Sal., 1820, W, Wr, P1/1820/132
Ann, widow and housekeeper to Revd Gorges Pauline Lowther of Longford, Derbyshire, Orcheston St Geo., 1836, W, Wr, P2/1836/29
Chas., Sal., 1808, AB, Wr, P4/1808/4
Dan., Nettleton, 1817, AB, Wr, P1/1817/59
Dorothy, widow, Horningsham, 1641, I, W (& cod), P5/1641/31, P5/14Reg/42B
Edmd., coachmaker, Sal. & S. Newton, 1845, AB, court proceeding, O, P2/1845/23
Edwd., husb., Grittleton, 1616, I, W, P3/F/31
Edwd., Horningsham, 1639, I, W, P5/1639/31, P5/13Reg/174
Eliz., sp., Urchf., 1648, AB, allegs, I, NW, P2/F/212
Eliz., sp., Beam., Dorset, 1732, W, P5/1731/31
Eliz., widow, Sal., 1776, W, P1/F/471, P1/13Reg/87A
Francis, yeo., Surrendell, Hullavington, 1687, I, W, P3/F/190
Jas., yeo., Brokerswood, N. Bradley, 1818, W, Wr, P2/1818/45
Jas., cooper, Beam., Dorset, 1821, AB, comm, W, Wr, P5/1821/11
Jane, widow, Chipp., 1714, I, W, P1/F/256, P1/5Reg/470
Joan, widow, Urchf., 1600, AB, I, NW, P2/F/56
Joan, sp., Sal. St Thos., 1614-18, AB, NW, P4/1614/5, P4/1618/14
Jn., Chirton, 1564, I, W, P2/F/676, P2/4Reg/168A
Jn., sen., weaver, Horningsham, 1634, AB, IGVS, P5/1634/38
Jn., schoolmaster, Sal., 1760, W, P4/1760/8
Jn., yeo., E. Tithing, Lt. Hinton, 1762, W, P3/F/396
Jn., yeo., Chirton, 1764, W, P2/F/569
Jn., Sal., 1798, W, Wr, P1/F/519, P1/15Reg/172
Jos., Westb., 1771, W, P25/1771/3
Lawr., yeo., Lt. Hinton, 1762, AB, W, P3/F/397
Mgt., widow, Chirton, 1666, AB, P2/F/233
My., widow, Grove, Wantage, Berks., 1671, I, W, P5/1671/28
Nathaniel, Horningsham, 1733, AB, P5/1733/22
Nathaniel, Horningsham, 1785, AB, P5/1785/12, P5/18Reg/11A
Nich., husb., Cutteridge, N. Bradley, 1689, I, NW, P2/F/341
Nich., glover, Sal., 1707, W, P2/F/402
Nich., haberdasher, Uffc., Devon, 1782, W, P5/1782/11, P5/17Reg/240
Prudence, widow, Uffc., Devon, 1798, comm, W, P20/1/272
Richd., tailor, Ashbury, Berks., 1743, W, P1/F/367, P1/9Reg/243
Farr alias Lincy, Robt., Chipp., 1618, I, W, P3/F/34
Robt., Beam., Dorset, 1700, AB, P17/132
Thos., yeo. *or* husb., Tulwick, Grove, Wantage, Berks., 1669, I, W, P23/7
Thos., Chipp., 1711, AB, I, P3/F/269
Wm., gent., Lyme R., Dorset, 1677, W, P16/50
Wm., Horningsham, 1680, I, NW, P5/1680/14
Wm., innholder, Chipp., 1710, AB, I, ren, P3/F/267
Wm., clothier, Chipp., 1743, L, req, W, copy W, P3/F/366
Farrant, Farrant, Dan., Sal., 1742, W, P4/1742/8
Farrant, Hy., plasterer, Lyme R., Dorset, 1840, comm, W, Wr, P16/425
Farrat, Jas., thatcher, Sedgehill, 1795, W, P2/F/652
Farrent, Jn., labourer, Broad C., 1699, I, W, P2/F/383
Farrent, Robt., yeo., Chards., Devon, 1797, W, P5/1797/14, P5/18Reg/252
Farrenden *see* Farrington
Farrent *see* Farrant
Farrer, Agnes, widow, Hurst, Berks., 1628, I, W, P5/1628/39, P5/11Reg/78A
Farrer, Richd., yeo., Hurst, Berks., 1671, I, W, P5/1671/30
Farrer, Richd., Twyford, Hurst, Berks., 1681, AB, I, P5/1681/16
Farrer, Robt., yeo., Twyford, Hurst, Berks., 1624, AB, I, P5/1624/17, P5/10Reg/227A
Farrer *or* Furrer, Thos., carp., Hurst, Berks., 1624, I, W, P5/1624/16, P5/10Reg/223
Farrington, Farrenden, Alice, widow, Harding Farm, Gt. Bedwyn, 1694, I, W (to be buried in linen), P21/5/25

Farrington, Chas., yeo., Ashton K., 1746, a/c, I, W, P3/F/370
Farrington, Chas., yeo., Ashton K., 1777, W, P3/F/420
Farrenden, Dan., victualler, Hungerford, Berks., 1746, W, P5/1746/26
Farrington, Eliz., sp., Ashton K., 1781, W, P3/F/428
Farrenden, Jn., yeo., Shalbourne, Berks., 1726, W, P23/441
Farrenden, Richd., yeo., Harding Farm, Gt. Bedwyn, 1673, I, W, P21/2/34
Farrow, Forrow, Hy., brickmaker, Fisherton A., 1728, W, P2/F/466
Farrow, Jos., butcher, Newbury, Berks., 1726, comm, W, P1/F/291, P1/7Reg/69B
Farrow, Lawrence, butcher, Thatcham, Berks., 1695, AB, I, ren, P1/F/208
Forrow, My., widow, Fisherton A., 1748-52, AB (2), W, P2/F/530, 541
Farthing, Avis, widow of Jn., Gillingham, Dorset, 1562, W, P27/1Reg/12A
Edith, widow, Zeals, 1723, W, P5/1723/14, P5/16Reg/85B
Eli, tinman, Bourton, Gillingham, Dorset, 1811, W, P27/1/613
Geo., Gillingham, Dorset, 1728, AB, LA, P27/1/240
Jn., Gillingham, Dorset, 1560, W, P27/1Reg/7C
Jn., Porridge Hill, Gillingham, Dorset, 1580, W, P27/2Reg/5A
Nich., tailor, Bourton, Gillingham, Dorset, 1683, I, P27/1/74
Renatus, Hindon, 1761, AB, P2/F/559
Farwell, Andrew, husb., Alton P., Dorset, 1606, I, draft W, formal W, P5/1606/17, P5/8Reg/58B
Farewell, My., widow, Southwick, N. Bradley, 1724, W, P2/F/449
Fast, Cath., sp., Lacock, 1819, W, Wr, P3/1819/28
Jn., ironmonger, Lacock, 1782, W, P1/F/488, P1/13Reg/386
Fathers, Jn., sen., Nether C., Dorset, 1582, I, W, P5/1582/22, P5/4Reg/39C
Thos., cooper, Sherb., Dorset, 1625, I, NW, P5/1625/34, P5/10Reg/277A
Wm., Hill D., 1698, AB, comm, P5/1698/27
Fatt, Geo., blacksmith, Edington, 1732, W, P1/F/320, P1/7Reg/520A
Hannah, widow, Westb., 1813, AB, P25/1813/1
Jas., yeo., Westb., 1830, AB, comm, ren, W, Wr, P25/1830/8
Jn., sen., blacksmith, Edington, 1723, ren, W, P1/F/285, P1/6Reg/444B
Jos., blacksmith, Edington, 1831, W, Wr, P2/1831/32
Faulkner *see* Fawconer
Faulls *see* Fowle
Fauntleroy, Edwd., Bere R., Dorset, 1578-79, AB, I, P5/1578/16, P5/1579/31, P5/3Reg/113B
Eleanor, sp., Font le Roi, Folke, Dorset, 1695, comm, W, P5/1695/36
Jn., esquire, Font le Roi, Folke, Dorset, 1699, bond to deliver W, W, copy W, P5/1698/26
Susanna, widow, Font le Roi, Folke, Dorset, 1699, comm, W, P5/1699/12
Faux, Ann, widow, Ashton K., 1672, I, W, P3/F/139
Eliz., widow, Westport St My., 1744, I, W, P1/F/375, P1/9Reg/399B
Hy., Malm., 1764, W, P3/F/402
Thos., husb., Ashton K., 1670, AB, I, P3/F/128
Wm., carp. *or* sawyer, Ashton K., 1684, I, W, P3/F/180
Fawcett, Jn., Sal., 1680, AB, P1/F/157
Fawconer, Ann, widow, Sal., 1677, I (2), W, P4/1677/14
Ann, widow, Sal., 1737, AB, P4/1737/2
Edwd., clerk, Sal., 1669, AB, I, P4/1669/14
Frances, sp., Sal., 1777, W, Wr, P4/1777/6
Frances, widow, Sal., 1778, W, P4/1778/8
Faulkner, Geo., grocer, Padworth, Berks., 1835, AB, W, P1/1835/100
Jn., Sal. St Thos., 1619, AB, I, P4/1618/7
Falkner, Jn., husb., Gt. Trowle, Bradford A., 1677, I, W, P1/F/151
Falkner, Jn., tailor, Corsham, 1698-99, AB, I, P29/F/8, P29/1Reg/270A
Faulkner, Jn., farmer, Monkton F., 1776, W, P2/F/602
Faulkner, Jos., auctioneer, Charnham St., Hungerford, Berks., 1831, comm, W, Wr, P23/956
My., wife, Sal., 1668, W, P4/1668/1
Paul Sindry, hosier, Sal., 1774, W, P4/1774/1
Sam., hosier, Sal., 1767, W, P4/1767/7
Sam., shoemaker, Sal., 1818, AB (limited), P4/1818/10
Sarah, widow, Sal., 1724, W, P2/F/454
Wm., rector, Stratford Tony, 1719, AB, I, P1/F/268
Fawkes, Jas., plumber and glazier, Highw., 1837, O, W, Wr, P10/1837/3

Jn. Packer, Crickl. St S., 1854, AB, aff, O, ren, W, Wr, P3/1854/8
Sarah, widow, Crickl. St My., 1852, O (2 - 1 affirmation by Quaker), W, Wr, P3/1852/20
Thos., sen., blacksmith, Ashton K., 1641, I, W, P3/F/94
Thos., yeo., Ashton K., 1719, I, W, P3/F/290
Thos., Crickl. St S., 1804, W, P3/1804/5
Fawler *see* Fowler
Fawn, My., singlewoman, Berwick St Jn., 1838, W, Wr, P2/1838/41
Thos., schoolmaster, Wilton, 1716, I, W, P2/F/421
Wm., clerk and minister, Biddestone St Peter, 1621, I (detailed), W, P3/F/38
Fay, Geo., sen., wheelwright, Collingbourne K., 1735, W, P3/F/347
Jeremy, Collingbourne D., 1624-29, I, note of admon, P21/1/10
My., widow, Collingbourne K., 1805, AB, comm, P3/1805/30
Richd., Collingbourne D., 1679, I, W, P21/2/59
Robt., weaver, Collingbourne D., 1623, I, W, P21/1/9
Timothy, maltster, Collingbourne D., 1691, I, W, P21/5/7
Timothy, maltster, Collingbourne D., 1754, AB, W, P21/10/19, 27
Timothy, Devizes, 1842, AB, comm, W, Wr, P1/1842/1
Walter, Collingbourne D., 1690, AB, I, P21/5/6
Fayre, Jn., Wokm., Berks., 1581, AB, P5/1581/8, P5/4Reg/24D
Faythorne *see* Faithorne
Feake, Eliz., apothecary's wife, Sal., 1737, W, Wr, P4/1736/16
Jn., Sal., 1700, W, P4/1700/8
Fear, Jn., gent., Tisb., 1729, W, P1/F/315, P1/7Reg/346B
Philip, husb., Fordington, Dorset, 1634, I, W, P5/1634/9, P5/12Reg/290B
Richd., husb., Linley, Tisb., 1612-16, AB, a/c, I, P2/F/92, P2/8Reg/185B
Stephen, Fordington, Dorset, 1720, AB, P15/102
Wm., Fordington, Dorset, 1693, AB, I, P15/62
Feats, Feats alias Hughes, Amy, widow, Calstone W., 1692, comm, I, W (scribe is rector of C.), P5/1691/26
Feats alias Hughes, Geo., Calne, 1580, AB, I, P5/1579/29, P5/3Reg/148A
Feats alias Hughes, Jn., sen., Calstone W., 1681, I, W, P26/276
Feats alias Hughes, Michael, fuller, Bremhill, 1679, I, W, P3/F/161
Feats alias Hughes, Pauncefoot, yeo., Calne, 1688, I, W, P5/1688/29
Feats alias Pargis, Robt., Warm., 1612?, NW, P2/F/90
Pheates alias Hewes, Thos., husb., Calstone W., 1588, AB, I, W, P5/1588/50, P5/5Reg/43A
see also Hughes/Hewes alias F.; Pargis alias F.
Feazard *see* Fezard
Febburd, Edwd., Sal., 1761, AB, P4/1761/11
Jn., surgeon, Sal., 1743, W, P4/1743/4
Febin, Emma, sp., Sal., 1678, I, NW, P4/1678/8
Feeldoun *see* Fielding
Fegg *see* Figg
Felder *see* Fielder
Felepes *see* Phelps
Fell, Isaac, labourer, Heddington, 1806, W, Wr, P3/1806/51
Susanna, widow, Steventon, Berks., 1750, W, P1/F/402, P1/10Reg/350B
Fellepes *see* Phelps
Fellowes, Chas., Sal., 1828, AB, P4/1828/4
Clarissa, wife, Sal., 1836, AB, Wr, P4/1836/10
Fellows, Hannah, widow, Sherb., Dorset, 1813, W, Wr, P5/1813/10
Feltham, Agnes, widow, Fovant Stroud, 1683, I, W, P2/F/304
Veltham, Cicely, 1594, I (badly damaged), P30/218
David, yeo., Fovant, 1626, I, W, P2/F/132
David, gent., Sutton M., 1682, I, W, P2/F/300
David, yeo., Fovant, 1709, W, P2/F/405
David, woolstapler, Donhead St My., 1722, W, P2/F/441
David, Coombe B., 1794, AB, P8/67
Edwd., husb., Fonthill B., 1620, I, W, P1/F/49
Edwd., yeo., Quidh., 1665, I, W, P2/F/231
Edwd., painter, Sal., 1806, req, W, copy W, P4/1806/1
Eleanor, widow, Teffont E., 1691, AB, P2/F/350

Eliz., sp., Atworth, Bradford A., 1611, I, W, P1/F/26
Eliz., widow, Chitterne AS, 1846, D, W, Wr, P2/1846/55
Francis, Hilp., 1571, AB, P2/5Reg/126B
Geo., Quidh., 1684-91, AB, I, W, P2/F/307, 351
Geo., yeo., Hilp., 1844, O, W, Wr, P2/1844/15
Humphrey, husb., Holt, Bradford A., 1557, W, P2/3Reg/68E
Jas., sen., Fonthill B., 1645, T (child: Jas. F., jun.), P2/F/207
Jas., sen., yeo., Winterslow, 1666, I, W, P2/F/235
Jas., yeo., E. Winterslow, 1670, AB, I, P2/F/252
Jas., Stourpaine, Dorset, 1724, AB, I, P24/870
Jas., yeo., Winterslow, 1740, W, P2/F/509
Jas., Plaitford (form. of Winterslow), 1805, AB, P2/1805/32
Jas., innholder, Downton, 1813, W, Wr, P2/1813/40
Jas., butcher, Chitterne AS, 1848, D (2), W, Wr, P2/1848/42
Joan, widow, Fonthill B., 1638, I, W, P2/F/177
Joan, Fonthill B., 1647, W, P2/F/215
Joan, widow, Quidh., 1663, I, W, P2/F/229
Joan, widow, Fovant Stroud & Sutton M., 1712, I, W, P2/F/413
Jn., Fonthill B., 1551, W, P2/2Reg/119A
Jn., Quidh., 1622, AB, I, P2/F/117
Jn., yeo., Fovant, 1632, AB, a/c, I, P2/F/153
Jn., innholder, Sal., 1785, W, P4/1785/13
Jos., sen., carp., Wokm., Berks., 1776, W, P5/1776/16, P5/17Reg/114
Lawr., singleman, Fovant, 1705, AB, I, P2/F/397
Feltham alias Beaver, My., Wokm., Berks., 1731, a/c, P5/1730/24
Matthew, Fisherton A., 1811, AB, Wr, P1/1811/111
Robt., Fovant, 1553, W, P2/2Reg/181B
Robt., Fonthill B., 1554, W, P2/2Reg/188A
Robt., husb., Berwick St Leonard, 1638, AB, I, P2/F/183
Robt., yeo. and husb., Fonthill B., 1645, I, W, P2/F/208
Robt., sen., yeo., Fovant, 1646, AB, a/c, I, P2/F/209
Robt., sen., weaver, Fovant, 1679, comm, W, P2/F/290
Robt., Wokm., Berks., 1725, W, P5/1725/26, P5/16Reg/124A
Sam., joiner, Fisherton A., 1770, AB, ren, W, P1/F/456, P1/12Reg/312A
Sarah, Fisherton A., 1765, AB, P2/F/575
Sarah, widow, Plaitford, 1786, W, P1/F/499, P1/14Reg/84B
Thos., husb., S. Wraxall, 1570, W, P2/5Reg/89A
Thos., sen., Atworth, Bradford A., 1590, I, note of admon, T, I (very detailed), P2/F/25
Thos., Fonthill B., 1630, I (2), P2/F/147
Thos., sen., yeo., Fonthill B., 1667, AB, I, W, P2/F/239
Thos., yeo., Sutton M., 1669, W, P2/F/246
Thos., Fisherton D., 1686, AB, P2/F/326
Thos., Fovant, 1692, W, P1/F/194
Thos., clothworker, Fugg. St Peter, 1694, AB, I, P2/F/357
Thos., yeo., Fovant, 1697, AB, W, P2/F/374
Thos., yeo., Sutton M., 1733, W, P2/F/489
Thos., baker, Sal., 1750, W, P4/1750/8
Thos., yeo., Coombe B., 1761-62, W, P5/1761/10, P8/51
Thos., innholder, Donhead St A., 1820, comm, W, Wr, P1/1820/131
Thos., Codf. St P., 1855, AB, aff, Wr, P2/1855/28
Walter, yeo., Fonthill B., 1583, I, W, P2/F/21, P2/6Reg/104B
Wm., butcher, Trowb., 1631, I, W, P1/F/65
Wm., Fovant, 1633, AB, a/c, I, receipt, W, P2/F/155, P2/9Reg/22A
Wm., husb., Fonthill B., 1639, I, NW, P2/F/186
Wm., broadweaver, Gastard, Corsham, 1675, AB, I, P29/F/6, P29/1Reg/205A
Wm., yeo., Fovant Stroud, 1696, W, P2/F/371
Feltoe, Ann, sp., Bradford A., 1785, W, P2/F/635
Walter, slaymaker, Bradford A., 1761, W, P2/F/562
Felton, My., sp., Malm. (form. of Shortwood), 1815, W, Wr, P3/1815/35
My., widow, Thatcham, Berks., 1823, W, Wr, P1/1823/100

Thos., yeo., Leigh, Ashton K., 1727, W, P3/F/313
Felys *see* Fillis
Fending, Jn., New Windsor, Berks., 1729, AB, I, P1/F/304
Fennell, Venell, Agnes, widow, Hilp., 1559, AB, P2/3Reg/161D
Agnes, widow, Steeple A., 1589, I, W, P2/F/22
Andrew, husb., Steeple A., 1621, W, P2/F/671
Ann, widow of Jas., Brook, Westb., 1683, I, W, P25/1683/7
Edith, widow, Brook, Westb., 1637, I, W, P25/1637/5
Eliz., jun., Hilp., 1616, I, NW, P2/F/99
Eliz., widow, Hilp., 1638, I, W, P2/F/181
Vennell, Geo., Chipp., 1855, aff, O, W, Wr, P3/1855/19
Fennell *or* Vennell, Hy., broad weaver, Brook, Westb., 1631, I, W, P25/1631/5
Hy., Sal., 1669, AB, I, P4/1669/17
Jas., weaver, Brook, Westb., 1683, I, W, P25/1683/6
Vennell, Jas., broad weaver, Winsley, Bradford A., 1722, I, W, copy W, P2/UV/93
Jn., husb., Hilp., 1574, W, P2/5Reg/205C
Venell, Jn., husb., Steeple A., 1576, I, W, P2/UV/3, P2/5Reg/258A
Jn., Hilp., 1613, I, W, P2/F/93, P2/8Reg/189F
Vennell, Jn., Leighs Marsh, Dilton, Westb., 1632, I (loom), NW, P25/1632/6
Jn., Brook, Westb., 1681, AB, I, P25/1680/3
Jn., Turleigh, Winsley, Bradford A., 1708, AB, P1/F/237
Jn., Bradford A., 1718, AB, I, P2/F/425
Jn., Winsley, Bradford A., 1747, W, P1/F/392, P1/10Reg/169
Jn., Westbrook, Bromham, 1752, AB, P3/F/383
Vennell, Jn., broad weaver, Leigh, Bradford A., 1784, W, P2/UV/119
Vennell, Jn., broad weaver, Winsley, Bradford A., 1792, W, P2/UV/121
Vennell, Jn., yeo., Bradford A., 1851, O, W, Wr, P1/1851/21
Richd., broad weaver, Bratton, Westb., 1637, I, W, P25/1637/1
Thos., shepherd, W. Dean, [1599], I, NW, P2/F/54
Vennell, Thos., cordwainer, Westb., 1665, AB, P25/1665/7
Vennell, Thos., sen., labourer, Sanden Fee, Hungerford, Berks., 1726, W, P23/446
Thos., yeo., Hilp., 1732, I, W, P1/F/321, P1/7Reg/529
Venell, Thos., yeo., Inglesham, Berks., 1741, W, P1/UV/68, P1/9Reg/148B
Venell, Walter, husb., Hilp., 1558, W, P2/3Reg/115A
Veinell, Wm., carp., Winsley, Bradford A., 1617, I, W, P2/UV/26
Vennell, Wm., yeo., Seend, Melk., 1713, W, P2/UV/87
Wm., Bromham, 1778, comm, W, P3/F/423
Wm., victualler and cordw., Devizes, 1782, W, P1/F/484, P1/13Reg/337
Fenner *see* Venner
Feppen, Jn., Chards., Devon, 1585, W, P5/4Reg/105B
Ferebee, Agnes, widow, Poulton, 1619, I, W, P1/F/48
Alice, widow, Poulton, 1672, AB, I, W, P3/F/140
Ann, widow, Chipp., 1671, AB, comm, I, W, P3/F/133
Bridget, widow, Seend, Melk., 1633, I, W, P2/F/158
Chas., yeo., Oaksey, 1767, W, P1/F/452, P1/12Reg/263B
Edmd., husb., Poulton, 1609, W, P3/F/12
Edmd., husb., Poulton, 1681, AB, a/c, I, P3/F/168
Geo., clerk and vicar, Bps. C., 1624, AB, a/c, comm, I, ren, P24/175
Hy., husb., Poulton, 1635, I, W, P3/F/72
Richd., yeo., Crudwell, 1702, I, W, P3/F/241
Richd., blacksmith and bach., Latton, 1709, AB, I, P3/F/262
Richd., farmer, Kemble, 1828, O, W, Wr, P3/1828/50
Ferfield, Alice, widow, All C., 1564, W. No date of probate, P1/2Reg/145A
Jn., All C., [1570], W (NEP), P1/1Reg/124A
Fergison, Ann, widow, Bishopstone N., 1723, I (2), W, P6/104
Feriman *see* Ferryman
Fermor *see* Farmer
Fernewell *see* Farnwell
Fernley, Simon, Bradford A., 1563, W, P2/4Reg/173A
Ferrers *see* Ferris

Ferrett, Grace, Bradford A., 1743, W, P2/F/517
Ferret, Jane, widow, Fonthill B., 1822, W, Wr, P2/1822/35
Thos., Calne, 1597, T, W, P5/1597/120, P5/6Reg/190C
Thos., mercer, Bradford A., 1729, W, P1/F/313, P1/7Reg/332A
Ferris, Abel, yeo., Worton, Pott., 1735, I, W, P1/F/327, P1/7Reg/603B
Abel, Bremhill, 1792, AB, P1/F/510, P1/14Reg/470C
Agnes, widow, Sutton B., 1621, I, W, P3/F/41
Alice, widow, Bulk., Keevil, 1697, AB, comm, I, W, P2/F/375
Anthony, gent., Ashton K., 1634, AB (2), award, court paper, I, P1/F/80
Anthony, Ashton K., 1734, AB, P3/F/343
Betty, widow, Bremhill, 1808, W, Wr, P3/1808/14
Chas., [mercer, grocer and apothecary], Crickl. St S., 1685, AB, I, P3/F/183
Chris., plumber, Bradford A., 1731, W, P2/F/485
Cornelius, W. Tockenham, Lyneham, 1737, AB, comm, P3/F/351
Edith, widow, Chr. M., [1612], I, W (2) (NEP), P3/F/20
Edmd., husb., Bulk., Keevil, [1687], I, W, P2/F/335
Edwd., gent., Ashton K., 1623, AB, a/c, I, P3/F/44
Edwd., Wrou., 1640, I, W, P3/F/90
Elias, sen., apothecary, Malm., 1701, AB, I, ren, W, P3/F/238-39
Elias, Sutton B., 1705, AB, comm, I, P1/F/229
Eliz., widow, Rodbourne, Malm., 1718, W, P3/F/287
Eliz., widow, Bulk., Keevil, 1728, W, P2/F/464
Eliz., widow, Sutton B., 1740-52, AB, W, P3/F/358
Eliz., widow, Devizes, 1760, AB, P1/F/433
Eliz., widow, Reading, Berks., 1770, W, P1/F/460, P1/12Reg/374A
Eliz., widow, Seend, Melk., 1805, AB, W, P2/1805/56
Ellen, Sutton B., 1621, I, W, P3/F/42
Frances, widow, Sutton B., 1681, comm, I, W, P3/F/166
Francis, yeo., Sutton B., 1769, W, P3/F/412
Francis, shopkeeper, Kington St M., 1840, W, Wr, P3/1840/37
Faris, Francis, blacksmith, Tollard Royal, 1842, W, Wr, P1/1842/72
Geo., sen., baker, Ashton K., 1694, W, P3/F/222
Hannah, widow, Devizes, 1829, AB, comm, Wr, P1/1829/28
Harry, yeo., Foxham, Bremhill, 1800, W, P3/1800/8
Hy., Sutton B., 1617, I, W, P3/F/32
Hy., Sutton B., 1635, I, W, P1/F/82
Hy., Sutton B., 1693, AB, I, P3/F/217
Hy., millwright and blacksmith, Giddeahall, Yatton K., 1806, W, P3/1806/60
Isaac, yeo., Sutton B., 1677, I, NW, P3/F/157
Isaac, Sutton B., 1688, I, W, P3/F/199
Isaac, dairyman, Rowde, 1840, comm, W, Wr, P3/1840/22
Isaac, dairyman, Easton Piercy, Kington St M., 1856, AB, aff, O, W, Wr, P3/1856/47
Jas., Dauntsey, 1836, AB, Wr, P3/1836/28
Jane, widow, Dauntsey, 1732, W, P3/F/335
Joan, widow, Malm., 1701, W, P1/F/220, P1/4Reg/202
Jn., sen., carp., Horton, Bps. C., 1670, I, W, P24/395
Jn., Chr. M., 1685, AB, I, W (damaged), P3/F/184
Jn., clerk, Sutton B., 1689, I, W, P1/F/179
Jn., Ashton K., 1693, I, W, Wr, P3/F/218
Jn., plumber, Chipp., 1711, I, W, P3/F/270
Jn., Wootton B., 1713, AB, comm, P3/F/274
Jn., yeo., Mannings Hill, Calne, 1722, W, P26/668
Jn., Seend, Melk., 1730, AB, P2/F/475
Jn., Chr. M., 1733, AB, P3/F/338
Jn., Worton, Pott., 1758, AB, P1/F/426
Jn., gent., Warm., 1797, W, P2/F/665
Jn., broad weaver, Dilton M., Westb., 1799, W, P25/1799/3
Jn., miller, Chalford, Westb., 1802, O, W, P25/1802/9
Jn., Warm., 1811, AB, Wr, P1/1811/108
Jos., victualler, maltster, grocer & baker, Wootton B., 1833, comm, W, Wr, P3/1833/4

Mgt., widow, Horton, Bps. C., 1679, I, W, P24/476
Martha, widow, Warm., 1800, AB, comm, D, W, P2/1800/89
My., widow, Ashton K., 1713, I, W, P3/F/275
My., yeo.'s widow, Lyneham, 1730, W, P3/F/325
Michael, yeo., Lyneham, 1730, W, P3/F/326
Philip, Chapmanslade, Dilton, Westb., 1733, AB, P25/1733/6
Fares, Richd., Maiden B., 1597, I, W, P2/F/48
Richd., carp., Horton, Bps. C., 1708, AB, I, P24/575
Richd., yeo., Lyneham, 1720, I (2 - 1 a copy), W, P3/F/296
Richd., jun., yeo., Ashton K., 1729, AB, comm, ren, W, P3/F/319
Richd., sen., yeo., Ashton K., 1729, AB, comm, W, P3/F/318
Robt., sen., yeo., Whitlands, Dauntsey, 1702, I, W, P3/F/242
Robt., yeo., Tockenham Court Farm, Lyneham, 1725, W, P3/F/305
Robt., yeo., Lyneham, 1730, W, P3/F/327
Robt., yeo., Sutton B., 1754, AB, a/c, I, ren, P3/F/386
Robt., Chr. M., 1810, AB, Wr, P3/1810/47
Sam., sen., yeo., Keevil, 1743, W, P2/F/519
Sam., yeo., Bulk., Keevil, 1788, W, P2/F/641
Sam., gent., Bulk., Keevil, 1830, W, P2/1830/38
Sarah, widow, Whaddon, 1805, W, P2/1805/45
Sarah, widow, Tollard Royal, 1857, aff, O, W, Wr, P2/1857/27
Simon, yeo., Chr. M., 1824, W, Wr, P3/1824/53
Susanna, sp., Chipp., 1737, W, P3/F/350
Ferrers, Thos., Sal. St Martin, 1613, bond to secure goods, P4/1613/6
Thos., carp., Allington, All C., 1728, W, P3/F/315
Thos., carp., Allington, All C., 1730, W, P3/F/328
Thos., Ashton K., 1738, AB, P1/F/350
Thos., Winterbourne Bassett, 1745, AB, comm, P3/F/367
Thos., husb., Dauntsey, 1767, W, P1/F/450, P1/12Reg/220B
Thos., yeo., Bradford A., 1770, comm, W, P2/F/587
Thos., yeo., Keevil Wick, 1775, W, P2/F/599
Thos., yeo., Oldfield, Buscot, Berks., 1776, W, P1/F/475, P1/13Reg/128
Thos., yeo., Rowde, 1782, W, P1/F/487, P1/13Reg/374
Thos., yeo., Holt, Bradford A., 1807, W, Wr, P2/1807/25
Thos., labourer, Dauntsey, 1814, W, Wr, P1/1814/127
Thos., yeo., Sutton B., 1817, W, Wr, P1/1817/52
Thos., Sutton B., 1832, AB, comm (2), O, T, Wr, P3/1832/6-7
Thos., Dauntsey, 1850, AB, O, Wr, P3/1850/49
Uriah, yeo., S. Wraxall, 1856, aff, O, W, Wr, P2/1856/36
see also Oram alias F.
Ferry, Ferry, Thos., jun., hellier, Lyme R., Dorset, 1669, AB, I, P16/18
Ferryman, Virriman, Bridget, widow, Coleshill, Berks., 1613, I, W, P1/UV/7
Ferryman, Geo., [shoemaker], Sonning, Berks., 1729, AB, I, P5/1729/17, P5/16Reg/236A
Ferryman, Hugh, gent., Sonning, Berks., 1693, AB, ren, P5/1693/24
Feriman, Wm., Longcott, Shrivenham, Berks., 1763, W, P1/F/443, P1/12Reg/67A
Ferthing *see* Farthing
Fethorne *see* Faithorne
Fettiplace, Petyplace *or* Phettiplace, Agnes, widow, Fisherton A., 1559, AB, P2/3Reg/158D
Alexander, sen., gent., Letcombe Regis, Berks., 1680, I, W, P1/F/155
Edwd., gent., Crickl. St S., 1729, AB, P3/F/320
Grace, widow, Homington, 1739, W, P24/910
J[...] (male), Fisherton A., 1594, I, W, P2/F/670
My., widow, Buckland, Berks., 1686, I, W, P1/F/522
Pelipace, Thos., Fisherton A., 1555, W, P2/1Reg/97A
Thos., yeo., Homington, 1672, I, W, P24/460
Phettiplace, Wm., glazier, Sal., 1649, W, P1/P/196
Fever, Betty, widow, Stratton, Dorset, 1781, AB, P5/1781/5, P5/17Reg/203B
Edwd., Beam., Dorset, 1622, AB, P5/1622/28, P5/10Reg/27C
Hy., Stratton, Dorset, 1768, AB, comm, I, P5/1768/6
Few, Alexander, husb., Coate, Bps. C., 1686, I, W, P24/805

Eliz., widow, W. Lavington, 1847, I, W, Wr, P1/1847/11
Geoffrey, tanner, Maiden B., 1665, AB, I, W, P1/F/130
Jas., Pott., 1828, AB, comm, Wr, P1/1828/12
Jas., Worton, Pott., 1857, aff, D, O, W, Wr, P1/1857/11
Richd., blacksmith, Urchf., 1633, I, W, P2/F/156
Susanna, Devizes, 1685, AB, comm, W, P1/F/171
Thos., husb., Coate, Bps. C., 1606, W, P1/F/20
Thos., Littleton P., 1837, O, W, Wr, P1/1837/9
Wm., yeo., Bromham, 1796, W, P3/F/445
Fewell, Thos., Chards., Devon, 1587, AB, I, P5/1587/50, P5/4Reg/142C
Fewkes *see* Foulkes
Fewster, My., yeo.'s wife, Ewen, Kemble, 1685, AB, I, P3/F/185
Fuester, Richd., labourer, Moredon, Rodbourne C., 1729, AB, I, P3/F/322
Fuester, Richd., Moredon, Rodbourne C., 1751, AB, P3/F/381
Fezard, Eliz., widow woman, Tisb., 1613, W, P2/8Reg/204A
Hy., yeo., Tisb., 1673, I, W, P2/F/267
Feazard, Jn., yeo., Tisb., [1687], I, W, P2/F/333
Jn., jun., Tisb., 1722, AB, P2/F/672
Jn., sen., Tisb., 1722, AB, P2/F/443
Lawr., Tisb., [1609], court paper, inty, I, copy I, W, P2/F/79
Lawr., Tisb., 1697, W, P2/F/373
Lucretia, Tisb., 1703, AB, P2/F/392
Richd., yeo., Tisb., 1639, I, W, P2/F/187
Richd., gent., Donhead St A., 1714, W, P1/F/253, P1/5Reg/308
Fiander, Jas., Shrewton, 1780, AB, P2/F/620
My., widow, Idmiston, 1742, AB, P2/F/514
see also Butt nee F.; Fye alias F.
Fibb *see* Fripp alias Fibb
Fickotts *see* Fitchett
Fidkin, Ann, widow, Warm., 1783, W, P1/F/491, P1/13Reg/423A
Richd., Martin, Hants, 1747, AB, W, P2/F/528
Robt., innholder, Warm., 1758, W, P2/F/553
Fidler, Chas., Newbury, Berks., 1827, AB, comm, ren, Wr, P1/1827/3
Edwd., sen., brickmaker, Newbury, Berks., 1763, comm, W, P1/F/441, P1/12Reg/47
Eliz., widow *or* wife, Collingbourne K., 1627, I, W, P3/F/55
Eliz., widow, Collingbourne D., 1731, W, P21/8/63
Eliz., widow and sp., Tidcombe, T. and Fosbury, 1810, W, Wr, P3/1810/8
Geo., Shaw cum Donnington, Berks., 1832, AB, Wr, P1/1832/120
Jn., Marten, Grafton, 1665, comm, I, surrender of caveat, NW, P5/1665/31
Jn., Netheravon, 1742, AB, P12/174
Jn., labourer, Collingbourne K., 1800, W, P3/1800/3
Jn., Alton Pr., 1836, AB, aff, O, Wr, P3/1836/19
Matthew Rivers, grocer, Codf. St My., 1857, aff, W, Wr, P2/1857/35
Reynold, husb., Gt. Bedwyn, 1621, I, W, P5/1621/9, P5/10Reg/22
Robt., husb., Collingbourne D., 1611, AB, W, P1/F/29
Robt., yeo., Rowde, 1838, W, Wr, P3/1838/71
Stephen, yeo., Fifield, Enford, 1729, I, W, P1/F/301, P1/7Reg/222A
Stephen, shopkeeper, Alton Pr., 1841, comm, W, Wr, P3/1841/12
Thos., Tidcombe, T. and Fosbury, 1667, I, W, P3/F/114
Thos., parish clerk, Collingbourne K., 1689, I, W, P3/F/200
Thos., yeo., Tidcombe, T. and Fosbury, 1694, I, W, P3/F/223
Thos., sen., brickmaker, Pewsey, 1736, AB, ren, W, P3/F/349
Thos., Hippenscombe, 1756-59, AB, W, P1/F/416, 431, P1/11Reg/196
Thos., brick burner, Clay Hill, Thatcham, Berks., 1798, W, P1/F/517, P1/15Reg/71
Thos., Alton Pr., 1829, AB, comm, Wr, P3/1829/5
Thos., Codf. St My., 1845, AB, ren, Wr, P1/1845/59
Wm., yeo., Collingbourne D., 1711, I, W, P1/F/243, P1/5Reg/54
Wm., E. Grimstead, W. Dean, 1735, AB, P2/F/496
Wm., sen., yeo., Etchilhampton, 1799, W, P3/F/450
Wm., Wylye, 1823, W, Wr, P1/1823/11

Wm., Woodb., 1857, AB, aff, O, Wr, P3/1857/44
see also Moxham alias F.
Fido, Jn., clerk, Hilp., 1723, W, P1/F/283, P1/6Reg/429
My., sp., Biddestone St Peter, 1828, W, Wr, P3/1828/23
Fidsall, Jas., glover, Mkt. L., 1620, AB, I, P2/F/112
My., Devizes, 1697, AB, P1/F/210
Fitzall, Richd., woolcomber, Devizes, 1692, AB, I, ren, P1/F/189
Field, Field alias Jude, Aldery (male), N. Wootton, Dorset, 1671, comm, I, NW, P5/1671/32
Ann, widow, Wokm., Berks., 1704, I, W, P5/1704/20
Ann, widow, Sherb., Dorset, 1738, W, Wr, P5/1738/17
Ann, widow, Chicklade, 1791, W, P2/F/648
Anthony, Eddington, Hungerford, Berks., 1667, AB, P5/1666/14
Anthony, sen., yeo., Eddington, Hungerford, Berks., 1718, I, W, P23/369
Anthony, yeo., Hungerford, Berks., 1732, AB, I, P23/481
Bartholomew, Kintbury, Berks., 1608, I, W, P1/F/22
Chas., Trowb., 1772-82, W, P1/F/489, P1/13Reg/404B
Chris., husb., Hoe Benham, Welford, Berks., 1680, I, W, P1/F/154
Edith, widow, Easton, Corsham, 1606, AB, I, W, P29/F/3, P29/1Reg/57
Fields, Eliz., widow, W. Hanney, Berks., 1602, I, W, P1/F/7
Eliz., widow, Newbury, Berks., 1780-86, W, P1/F/500, P1/14Reg/118
Francis, maltster, N. Moreton, Berks., 1763, W, P1/F/444, P1/12Reg/77
Geo., yeo., Hampstead & Kintbury, Berks., 1726, I, summary I, W, P1/F/290, P1/7Reg/68B
Gideon, N. Wootton, Dorset, 1625, AB, a/c, comm, I, P5/1625/32, P5/10Reg/288A
Jacob, Thatcham, Berks., 1729, AB, I, P1/F/305
Jas., sen., collarmaker, Hindon, 1697, AB, I, W, P2/F/379
Jas., jun., Hindon, 1747, AB, W, P1/F/384, P2/F529, P1/10Reg/69A
Jas., Gt. Bedwyn, 1770, AB, P5/17Reg/4D
Jas., victualler, Rams., 1770, AB, comm, ren, P5/1770/15
Jas., Hanging L., 1831, AB, comm, Wr, P2/1831/57
Joan, widow, N. Wootton, Dorset, 1682, I, W, P5/1682/40
Jn., sen., Kingston D., 1541, I, W (NEP), P30/71
Jn., collarmaker, Devizes St Jn., 1683, AB, I, P1/F/165
Jn., Wokm., Berks., 1710, AB, I, P5/1710/36
Jn., Brightwell, Berks., 1726, AB, P1/F/294
Jn., shopkeeper, Clewer, New Windsor, Berks., 1726, W, P1/F/295, P1/7Reg/97
Jn., cordw., Wokm., Berks., 1727, AB, W, P5/1727/15, P5/16Reg/156B
Jn., Sherb., Dorset, 1756, AB, P5/1756/10
Jn. *see also* Jane Lamborn
Martha, yeo.'s wife, Chilton F., 1800, AB, W, P3/1800/1
My., widow, Wantage, Berks., 1772, W, P23/746
My., victualler, Newbury, Berks., 1798, W, P1/F/516, P1/15Reg/78
My., sp., Trowb., 1803, AB, Wr, P1/1803/12, P1/15Reg/392C
My., lady, re property in Whitep., 1816, AB (d. wife of Sir Chas. F.), LA, Wr, P2/1816/71
Maud, widow, Corsham, 1654, AB, I, W, P29/F/5, P29/1Reg/153
Nathaniel, clerk, Stourton, 1668, I, W, P1/F/134
Nich., tailor, Wokm., Berks., 1694, AB, I, ren, P5/1694/1
Richd., sen., yeo., N. Moreton, Berks., 1698, I, W, P1/F/213, P1/3Reg/103
Richd., collarmaker, Warm., 1700, AB, I, ren, P2/F/387
Richd., carp., Aston U., Blewbury, Berks., 1717, I, W, P5/1717/13, P5/15Reg/396C
Sam., yeo., Aston U., Blewbury, Berks., 1731, AB, I, P5/1731/29
Sam., yeo., Long Wittenham, Berks., 1763, W, P1/F/438, P1/12Reg/36A
Sam., yeo., Aston U., Blewbury, Berks., 1766, W, P5/1766/10
Sam., glazier, Wantage, Berks., 1766, W, P23/715
Sarah, widow, Wokm., Berks., 1695, W, P5/1695/28
Thos., Wokm., Berks., 1689, AB, P5/1689/21
Thos., yeo., Eddington, Hungerford, Berks., 1733, AB, I, P23/496
Thos., blacksmith, Sherb., Dorset, 1734, AB, I, P5/1734/24
Thos., yeo., Whistley, Hurst, Berks., 1738, I, W, Wr, P5/1738/18
Thos., sen., victualler, Newbury, Berks., 1747, W, P1/F/390, P1/10Reg/118
Thos., yeo., Broughton G., 1756, AB, ren, P1/F/422

Thos., sen., Newbury, Berks., 1776, AB, ren, P1/F/473
Timothy, Broughton G., 1744, AB, P1/F/376
Wm., Kingston D., 1610, AB, I, P2/F/82, P2/8Reg/107A
Wm., wheelwright, Hungerford, Berks., 1693, I, W, P23/188
Wm., sen., blacksmith, Newbury, Berks., 1698, W, P1/F/214, P1/3Reg/137
Wm., Chute, 1745, AB, P7/143
Wm., yeo., Eddington, Hungerford, Berks., 1745, W, P23/590
Wm., tailor, Hoe Benham, Welford, Berks., 1750, W, P1/F/397, P1/10Reg/299
Wm., Langley Burrell, 1852, comm, D, W, Wr, P3/1852/25
see also Gellyjohn *or* Jellijohn alias F.
Fielden *see* Fielding
Fielder, Filder, Amy, Sonning Eye, Berks., 1571, AB, P5/2Reg/102C
Jas., Kingswood, Gloucs, 1812, AB, Wr, P3/1812/9
Jn., Sandhurst, Berks., 1618, I, W, P5/1618/13, P5/9Reg/200
Jn., E. Grimstead, W. Dean, 1738, W, P2/F/505
Jn., yeo., Plaitford, 1819, W, Wr, P2/1819/66
Jos., Bramshaw, Hants, 1784, AB, P24/1181
Jos., Bramshaw, Hants, 1827, AB, Wr, P24/1308
My., sp., Sal., 1720, AB, P1/F/270
Felder, Robt., husb., Sonning, Berks., 1572, W, P5/2Reg/113B
Robt., yeo., Ufton Nervet, Berks., 1662, AB, I, NW, P1/F/116
Sarah, widow, Gt. Bedwyn, 1767, W, P5/1767/21
Thos., rector, Luckington, 1564, W (made temp. Edwd. VI), P1/2Reg/128B
Thos., Sherston, 1626, AB, I, P3/F/51
Tobias, [yeo.], Rushall, 1609, AB, comm, I, L, P2/F/80, P2/8Reg/62D
Wm., Sandhurst, Berks., 1754, AB, P5/1754/6
Fieldew, Cath., Beam., Dorset, 1709, AB, P17/193
Eliz., widow, Beam., Dorset, 1728, AB, P5/1728/33, P5/16Reg/160B
Peter, sadler, Beam., Dorset, 1705, AB, I, P17/161, 196
Velldew, Wm., miller, Chards., Devon, 1683, I, W, P14/51
Fielding, Feeldoun, Israel, baker, Pott., 1716, I, W, P1/F/263, P1/6Reg/45A
Israel, Pott., 1764, AB, P1/F/447
Fielden, Robt., baker, Pott., 1668, AB, I, P1/F/137
Fields *see* Field
Fifield, Benj., Broad C., 1781, W, P2/F/624
Eliz., widow, Broad C., 1778, AB, P2/F/612
Jn., Broad C., 1778, AB, W, P2/F/613
Roger, Motc., Dorset, 1571, W, P27/1Reg/26C
Thos., husb., Gastard, Corsham, 1637, W, P29/F/4, P29/1Reg/134B
Wm., clerk; reverend, Minety, 1747, W, P1/F/383, P1/10Reg/66
Wm., clerk, Sherston, 1769, AB, P3/F/413
Fifoot *see* Pippatt
Fiford, Wm., carp., Sal., 1826, W, Wr, P1/1826/48
Figeon, Cath., widow, Bourton, Winterbourne S., 1583, W, P2/6Reg/95
Robt., vicar, Winterbourne S., 1580-83, T (children: My. & Margery F.), W, P2/F/19, P2/6Reg/9B
Figge, Ambrose, sen., gent., Nunton, N. and Bodenham, 1638, AB, I, P2/F/185
Figge alias Payne, Eliz., Nunton, N. and Bodenham, 1603, AB, comm, P2/F/61
Matthew, Nunton, N. and Bodenham, 1575, W, P2/5Reg/236A
Figes, Richd., ironmonger, Sal., 1830, W, Wr, P4/1830/6
Robt., soldier form. shoemaker, Sal., 1644, AB, NW, P1/F/97
Fegg, Wm., baker, Kington St M., 1679, AB, comm, I, P3/F/162
Figgins, Benj., cordw., Reading, Berks., 1720, W, P1/F/277, P1/6Reg/312
Edmd., gardener, Westb., 1679, AB, comm, I, P25/1679/3
Eliz., widow, Broughton G., 1751, AB, P2/F/536
Hy., gardener, Wick, Bps. C., 1729, W, P24/828
Hy., gardener, Wick, Bps. C., 1786, W, P24/1172
Joan, widow, Bishopstrow, 1721, W, P2/F/437
Jn., gardener, Devizes, 1715, W, P1/F/259, P1/5Reg/491
Mgt., widow, Devizes, 1709, AB, P1/F/240
My., widow, Devizes, 1752, comm, W, P1/F/408, P1/10Reg/481

Figgens, Matthew, gent., Devizes, 1708, comm, I, W, P1/F/238
Matthew, gardener, Devizes, 1743, AB, ren, W, P1/F/369, P1/9Reg/265B
Robt., gardener, Warm., [1680], a/c, NW, P2/F/292
Thos., Devizes, 1721, AB, I, P1/F/282
Thos., innholder, Devizes, 1739, comm, W, P1/F/352, P1/8Reg/393
Thos., gent., Chipp., 1809, AB, comm, P3/1809/8
Vincent, woolstapler and maltster, Devizes, 1755, W, P1/F/415, P1/11Reg/189B
Wm., gardener, Warm., 1719, AB, I, W, P2/F/432
Wm., gardener, Devizes, 1732, I, W, P1/F/322, P1/7Reg/531A
Filder *see* Fielder
Fildown, Hy., sen., yeo., Quemerford, Calne, 1690, I, W, P26/394
Richd., Quemerford, Calne, 1727, W, P26/715
Filer, Fyler, Jn., rector, Stockton, 1730, AB, I (detailed catalogue of books), W, P1/F/317, P1/7Reg/390
Sam., Stockton, 1704, AB, P2/F/394
Filkes, Ann, widow, Rowde, 1629, I, W, P3/F/59
Ann, widow, Rowde, 1682, AB, P3/F/172
Philkes, Edmd., Mkt. L., 1569, W, P2/5Reg/80C
Edwd., Mkt. L., 1710, W, P2/F/410
Eliz., widow, All C., 1668, comm, W, P3/F/120
Eliz., Mkt. L., 1697, AB, P2/F/380
Hannah, widow, Mkt. L., 1722, W, P2/F/440
Hannah, widow, Devizes, 1735, AB, P1/F/337
Jacob, clerk and vicar, Box, 1694-95, AB, comm, I, ren, W, P3/F/224, 228
Jas., gent., Devizes, 1742, W, P1/F/365, P1/9Reg/223D
Jane, clerk's widow, Box, 1701, W, P1/F/219, P1/4Reg/43
Joan, widow, Rowde, 1669, AB, P3/F/124
Jn., husb., All C., 1626, I, W, P3/F/52
Jn., yeo., Rowde, 1630, I, W, P3/F/61
Jn., sen., husb., Mkt. L., 1645, I, W, copy W, Wr, P2/F/206
Jn., Devizes, 1689, AB, I, P1/F/185
Jn., sen., yeo., Mkt. L., 1695, I, W, P2/F/363
Jn., gent., Devizes, 1760, AB, P1/F/434
Jn., gent., Devizes, 1782, AB, comm, P1/F/490
Jos., woolstapler, Devizes, 1750, AB, W, P1/F/396
Joshua, mercer, Devizes, 1682, I, P1/F/158
Mgt., widow, All C., 1629, I, W, P3/F/58
My., widow, Nursteed, Bps. C., 1636, I, W, P24/52
My., widow, Devizes, 1698, W, P1/F/211
My., sp., Devizes, 1759, req, copy W, P1/F/432, P1/11Reg/473
Richd., yeo., Rowde, 1669, I, W, P3/F/125
Richd., yeo., Mkt. L., 1678, I, W, P2/F/285
Robt., Rowde, 1646, AB, comm, P1/F/102
Susanna, widow, Devizes, 1662, I, W, P1/F/119
Thos., apothecary and gent., Devizes, 1675, AB, comm, I, P1/F/147
Wm., gent., Mkt. L., 1741, copy W, W, P1/F/355, P1/9Reg/187
Fillis, Jn., Warm., 1596, AB, P2/F/673
Jn., Melk., 1781, AB, comm, P2/F/623
Felys, Thos., Bishopstrow, 1548, W, P2/2Reg/55B
Felys alias Clarke, Thos., N. Bradley, 1550, W, P2/2Reg/98B
Fylis, Thos., Draycot C., 1570, W (lengthy preamble), P1/1Reg/109A
Fillis alias Miller, Thos., yeo., Cotmarsh & Ham, Broad Town, 1634, I, W, P3/F/69
Phillis alias Miller, Wm., yeo., Cotmarsh, Broad H., 1646, a/c, AB, comm, I, P1/P/175
Wm., Seend, Melk., 1798, AB, P2/F/667
Fillkins, Richd., tailor, Upton, Blewbury & Kingston Bagpuize, Berks., 1735, I, W, P1/F/332, P1/8Reg/5
Fillol, Eleanor, Abingdon, Berks., 1628, AB, comm, P1/F/59
Filmore, Philmore, Mgt., widow, Lydiard T., 1670, I, W, P3/P/322
Peter, yeo., Lydiard T., 1662, AB, I, P1/F/117
Philmore, Peter, Lydiard T., 1702, I, W, P3/P/569
Wm., husb., Ashton K., 1571, W (NEP), P1/1Reg/48
Filpes *see* Phelps

Finch, [male], son of Jn., no abode stated, [1602], NW (NEP) No christian name given (decd's father & son both called Jn.), P3/1Reg/109B
Ann, widow, Bishopstone N., 1679, AB, deed of gift, P5/1679/31
Caroline, widow, Laverstock, 1838, W, Wr, P2/1838/19
Finch alias Sidy, Chas., cordw., Milford, Sal. St Martin, 1772, W, P4/1772/3
Chris., carp., New Bracknell, Warfield, Berks., 1711, W, P1/F/248, P1/5Reg/175B
Eliz., widow, Wingfield, 1701, W, P1/F/221, P1/4Reg/162
Gray, clothier, Newbury, Berks., 1773, W, P1/F/468, P1/12Reg/493B
Jas., yeo., Marridge Hill, Rams., 1665, I, W, Wr, P5/1665/32
Jas., labourer, Devizes, 1763, W, P1/F/442, P1/12Reg/52B
Jane, widow, Aldbourne, 1707, I, W, P3/F/256
Jn., sen., carp., Warfield, Berks., 1662, I, W, P1/F/124
Jn., husb., Bishopstone N., 1671, AB, I, P5/1671/29
Jn., yeo., Waltham St Lawr., Berks., 1747, W, P1/F/389, P1/10Reg/99
Jn., innholder, Sal., 1788, W, P4/1788/2
Jn., sen., yeo., Baydon, 1811, ren, W, P5/1811/22
Jn., Baydon, 1829, AB, aff, comm, P5/1829/4
Jn., Baydon, 1834, AB, aff, O, Wr, P5/1834/4
Jn., yeo., Baydon, 1695, I, W, P5/1695/35
Finch alias Aldridge, Martha, widow, Sotwell, Wallingford St Leonard, Berks., 1695, I, W, P1/F/203
My., widow, Marridge Hill, Rams., 1674, comm, I (detailed), W, P5/1674/27
My., widow, Baydon, 1832, AB, comm, Wr, P5/1832/2
Ralph, yeo., Marridge Hill, Rams., [1626], W, P5/1626/17
Robt., Marridge Hill, Rams., 1661, AB, I, P5/1661/16
Finch alias Sidy, Sarah, widow, Milford, Sal. St Martin, 1777, W, P4/1777/1
Simon, mealman, Reading, Berks., 1735, W, P1/F/334, P1/8Reg/25
Stephen, sen., yeo., Baydon, 1750, W, P5/1750/14
Stephen, yeo., Baydon, 1768, W, P5/1768/7
Stephen, yeo., Baydon, 1856, aff, O, W (& cod), Wr, P5/1856/6
Susan, Rams., 1677, comm, I, NW, P5/1677/17
Wm., carp., Hurst, Berks., 1588, I, W, P5/1588/17, P5/5Reg/38B
Wm., Liberty of Newland, Hurst, Berks., 1635, AB, I, P5/1635/40, P5/12Reg/196A
Wm., Wokm., Berks., 1693, AB, I, P5/1693/25
Wm., Binfield, Berks., 1756, AB, P1/F/420
Wm., yeo., Baydon, 1771, W, P5/1771/7, P5/17Reg/24B
Finchthwaite, Cath., widow, Marl., 1676, W, P1/F/148
Finmore, Margery, widow, Childrey, Berks., 1689, I, W, P1/F/181
Finnamory *see* Fynamorry
Fipoot *see* Pippatt
Firebeard, My., Short St., Dilton, Westb., 1741, comm, I (valuation only), W (NEP), P25/1741/2
Firkes *see* Furks
Fish, Ann, widow, Devizes, 1815, O, W, Wr, P1/1815/2
Jn., Fisherton D., 1574, W, P2/5Reg/209A
Jonas, Devizes, 1800, AB, P1/1800/20, P1/15Reg/222A
Jonas, shopkeeper, Devizes, 1815, AB, O, W, P1/1815/5
Simon, tailor, Sal., 1632, I, P4/1632/17
Thos., Broad C., 1579, AB, I, P2/F/15, P2/5Reg/353A
Fisher, Adam, tailor, Sal., 1639, AB, a/c (returned from misc. W series), I, P4/1639/13
Ann, sp., Liddington, 1685, AB, comm, P3/F/186
Ann, widow, Rams., 1727, AB, I, W, P5/1727/16, P5/16Reg/157A
Cath., widow, Westrop, Highw., 1738, I, W, P10/1738/2
Chas., clerk, Lyme R., Dorset, 1853, aff, comm, W, Wr, P16/453
Edwd., linen weaver, Mere, 1646, AB, I, P5/1645/7, P5/14Reg/86B
Eleanor, widow, Aston U., Blewbury, Berks., 1684, I, W, P5/1684/20
Eliz., sp., Sal., 1671, I, NW, P1/F/141
Eliz., widow, Avebury, 1672, I, W, P3/F/141
Eliz., sp., Marl. St My., 1720, W, P1/F/272, P1/6Reg/202
Gabriel, Fordington, Dorset, 1592-97, AB, a/c, P5/1592/33, P5/5Reg/137B
Geo., yeo., Poole Keynes, 1756, W, P1/F/423, P1/11Reg/305
Geo., Lacock, 1758, AB, P3/F/391

Geo., weaver, Bearfield, Bradford A., 1841, O, W, Wr, P2/1841/46
Geo., blacksmith, S. Marston, 1848, D, O, W, Wr, P10/1848/1
Hy., Newbury, Berks., 1729, AB, P1/F/306
Jas., Wantage, Berks., 1665, AB, P5/1665/33
Jas., gent., Enmore Grn, Motc., Dorset, 1666, comm, W, P19/7
Jas., yeo., Semley, 1671, I, NW, P2/F/258
Jas., jun., maltster, Shellingford, Berks., 1720, W, P1/F/275, P1/6Reg/291A
Jas., labourer, Gt. Bedwyn, 1762, W, P21/10/58
Jas., Bearfield, Bradford A., 1796, AB, comm, P2/F/657
Jas., carp., Pott., 1828, W, Wr, P1/1828/18
Jane, widow, Liddington, 1679, comm, I, W, P3/F/163
Joan, Wokm., Berks., 1543, cit (to exhibit W, & accept *or* renounce probate), P5/20Reg/42A
Joan, widow, Sherb., Dorset, 1689, AB, comm, W (2 - 1 copy), P5/1689/22
Jn., husb., Blewbury, Berks., 1597, a/c, W, P5/1597/119, P5/6Reg/188B
Jn., gent., Fernham, Shrivenham, Berks., 1631, AB, comm, I, P1/F/64
Jn., gent., West Hall, Stratton, Dorset, 1681, I, W, P5/1681/15
Jn., gent., Sherb., Dorset, 1689, AB, comm, I, ren, P5/1689/23
Jn., grocer, Mere, 1690, AB, I, ren, Wr, P5/1690/19
Jn., sen., cooper, Highw., 1697, I, note, W, P10/1697/1
Jn., sen., Highw., 1700, AB, I, P10/1700/3
Jn., gent., Chute, 1706, W, P7/96
Jn., minister, Westport St My., 1713, I, W, P3/F/276
Jn., Poole Keynes, 1722, AB, I, P3/F/299
Jn., labourer, Winterslow, 1726, AB, I, P1/F/292
Jn., Welford, Berks., 1735, AB, P1/F/339
Jn., labourer, Chilton F., 1739, AB, I (2 - 1 a copy), P3/F/355
Jn., Pott., 1743, W, P1/F/368, P1/9Reg/254
Jn., broad weaver, Cockstile, Bradford A., 1765, W, P2/F/574
Jn., Thatcham, Berks., 1776, W, P1/F/474, P1/13Reg/116
Jn., surgeon of the Royal Navy, Sherb., Dorset, 1803, comm, note, copy W, P5/1803/16, P5/19Reg/45
Jn., millman, Bradford A., 1814, W, Wr, P1/1814/137
Fisher alias Wason, Jn., gent., Bradford A., 1832, O, W, Wr, P1/1832/21
Jn., miller, Poole Keynes, 1848, comm, W, Wr, P3/1848/20
Jn. *see also* Rabidge Winchell & Sibyl Tanner
Jos., miller, Hungerford, Berks., 1741, I, W, Wr, P5/1741/14
Jos., blacksmith, Stratton St Mgt., 1850, O, W, Wr, P3/1850/22
My., widow, Bradford A., 1811, W, Wr, P2/1811/13
Money, builder, Sal., 1839, W, Wr, P1/1839/10
Philip, Trowb., 1819, AB, comm, Wr, P1/1819/4
Richd., labourer, E. Grafton, 1721, I, W, P21/8/11
Richd., linen weaver, Mere, 1685, AB, I, P5/1685/34
Robt., cooper, Highw., 1597, AB, I, P5/1597/43, P5/6Reg/155C
Robt., tailor, St Nich.'s Hospital, The Close, Sal., 1601, I, W, P5/1601/18, P5/7Reg/22A
Robt., yeo., Fawley, Berks., 1628, I, W, P1/F/56
Robt., yeo., Semley, [1692], I, W, P2/F/354
Robt., Hamptworth, Downton, 1749, AB, P2/F/532
Robt., labourer, Stourpaine, Dorset, 1837, aff, W, Wr, P24/1351
Roger, Tidpit, Martin, Hants, 1675, AB, P2/F/276
Roger, Pott., 1760, AB, P1/F/435
Sam., gent., Grimstone, Stratton, Dorset, 1687, AB, I, P5/1687/15
Sarah, widow, Poole Keynes, 1763, AB, W, P1/F/446, P1/12Reg/141
Sarah, widow, Pott., 1843, AB, O, Wr, P1/1843/8
Thos., Bray, Berks., 1613, I, W, P1/F/37
Thos., sen., husb., Pott. Wick, 1631, I, W, P1/F/71
Thos., yeo., E. Kennett, 1668, I, W, P1/F/133
Thos., labourer, Rams., 1708, W, P5/1708/28, P5/15Reg/55
Thos., Sherb., Dorset, 1743, AB, comm, Wr, P5/1743/29
Thos., Pott., 1745, W, P1/F/380, P1/10Reg/10
Wm., Stratford Tony, 1559, W, P2/3Reg/158C
Wm., weaver, Bradford A., 1604, I, W, P2/F/66

Wm., yeo., Sherb., Dorset, 1629, I, W, P5/1629/20, P5/11Reg/110B
Wm., yeo., Hamptworth, Downton, 1720, W, P1/F/271, P1/6Reg/200A
Wm., gent., Ashley, Bradford A., 1796, W, P2/F/658
Wm., broad weaver, Bradford A., 1796, W, P2/F/659
Fishlake, Agnes, widow, Eastcott, Urchf., 1571, W, P2/5Reg/122C
Eliz., widow, Fisherton A., 1774, W, P2/F/594
Fanny, sp., Sal., 1806, W, P4/1806/6
Jn., sen., maltster, Durnford, 1688, I, W, P5/1688/31
Fishlock, Jn., husb., W. Grafton, 1736, I, W, P21/9/15
Fishlock, Jn., husb., W. Grafton, 1799, W, notes, P21/11/48
Richd., Horton, Bps. C., 1565, W, P5/1Reg/65C
Richd., husb., Eastcott, Urchf., 1592, I, W, P2/F/29
Fishlock, Richd., husb., Shrewton, 1633, I, W, P2/F/161, P2/9Reg/29B
Richd., clerk, Lymington, Hants (holds parsonage of Fisherton), 1754, W, P1/F/413, P1/11Reg/148
Fishlock, Richd., yeo., Rowde Hill, 1760, W, P3/F/394
Fishlock, Robt., Savernake Park, 1670, AB, a/c, comm, court paper, I, P1/F/139
Fishlock, Robt., Marl., 1695, AB, I, P1/F/198
Fishlock, Robt., labourer, Etchilhampton, 1821, W, Wr, P3/1821/15
Robt., Quidh., 1848, W, Wr, P2/1848/5
Thos., sen., husb., Coate, Bps. C., 1687, I, W, P24/788
Fishlock, Thos., husb., Coate, Bps. C., 1703, I, W, P24/609
Wm., Eastcott, Urchf., 1559, W, P2/4Reg/5A
Fishlock, Wm., Erlestoke, 1664, AB, I, P2/F/230
Fishlock, Wm., labourer, Winterbourne Bassett, 1830, O, W, Wr, P3/1830/21
Fitch, Robt., gent., Leigh, Ashton K., 1632, AB, a/c, I, P3/F/67
Fitchett, Geo., Barford St M., 1593, I, W, P2/F/36
Fickotts, Jn., Rams., 1667, AB, comm, P5/1667/19
Fitchew, Geo., yeo., Chelworth, Crickl. St S., 1766, W, P3/F/407
Geo., carp. and builder, Crickl. St S., 1836, W, Wr, P3/1836/55
Jn., feltmaker, Crickl. St My., 1684, I, W, P3/F/181
Thos., feltmaker, Purton Stoke, 1731, W, P3/F/332
Thos., Crickl. St S., 1735, AB, P1/F/340
Thos., yeo., Latton, 1735, W, P3/F/348
Wm., hatmaker, Crickl. St My., 1729, W, P1/F/309, P1/7Reg/292
Fitz, Edwd., maltster, Teffont M., 1776, W, P1/F/476, P1/13Reg/138B
Jn., sen., gent., Chilmark, 1782, W, P2/F/625
Mgt., widow, Warm., 1829, W, Wr, P1/1829/16
Richd., gent., Chilmark, 1696, W, P2/F/369
Richd., grocer, Sal., 1820, W, Wr, P1/1820/134
Robt., Teffont M., 1730, AB, P2/F/474
Thos., Dinton, 1772, AB, W, P2/F/591
Walter, gent., Teffont M., [1680], W, P2/F/291
Walter, gent., Teffont M., 1778, W, Wr, P2/F/608
Fitzall *see* Fidsall
Fitzhugh, Robt., gent., Corsley, 1622, AB, comm, I, P2/F/119
Fitzjames, Francis, gent., Long Burton, Dorset, 1737, W, Wr, P5/1737/19
Jn., gent., Long Burton, Dorset, 1688, AB, I, P5/1688/30
Sarah, widow, Long Burton, Dorset, 1741, W, P5/1741/12
Flacher *see* Fletcher
Flagge, Robt., husb., Caundle Marsh, Dorset, 1608-09, I, W, P5/1608/12, P5/8Reg/140
Flaggett, Wm., Newbury, Berks., 1756, AB, P1/F/421
Flanner, Thos., Warfield, Berks., 1792, W, P1/F/508, P1/14Reg/413
Flannigan, Ann, cook, Trowb., 1854, aff, comm, W, Wr, P1/1855/3
Flatcher *see* Fletcher
Flay, Geo., Calne, 1812, AB, comm, P26/1286
Geo., baker, Calne, 1855, comm, O, W, Wr, P26/1466
Walter, victualler, Calne, 1843, O, W, Wr, P5/1843/28
Feacher *see* Fletcher
Fleet, Dan., husb., Mere, 1639, I, NW, P5/1639/33, P5/13Reg/211B
Edwd., linen weaver, Mere, 1739, W, Wr, P5/1739/18

Joan, widow, Gillingham, Dorset, 1745, W, P27/1/379, P27/3Reg/40
Jn., [weaver], Mere, 1702, AB, I, P5/1702/17
My., widow, Alderbury, 1737, AB, P26/797
Nich., linen weaver, Woodlands, Mere, 1701, I, W, P5/1701/20
Thos., shepherd, Longbridge D., 1598, AB, I, W, P2/F/51
Wm., yeo., Clarendon Park, 1648, I, W, P1/F/107
Wm., Alderbury, 1671, AB, P26/196
Fleetwood, Cath., sp., Alderbury, 1756-58, AB, W, P26/951, 965
Chris., Stapleford, 1706, W, P2/F/400
Chris., Stapleford, 1764, AB, P2/F/570
Chris., yeo., Charlton, Downton, 1778, W, P2/F/606
Eliz., widow, Coombe B., 1814, W, P8/76
Joan, sp., Chipp., 1675, a/c, comm, W, P3/F/149, 152
Jn., Chipp., 1666-74, AB (2 - 1 goods unadmd & for daus Joan & Mgt.), a/c, comm, I (2), P3/F/110, 149
Mgt., Chipp., 1674, a/c, P3/F/149
Tristram, pavior, Chipp., 1618, I, W, P3/F/35
Wm., Chipp., 1766, AB, comm, P3/F/408
see also Bungey nee F.
Fleming, Fleman, Alice, Upton L., 1716, AB, I, P2/F/422
Harry, blademaker, Sal., 1784, W, P4/1784/4
Fleman, Hy., sen., carp., Stockton, [1687], I, ren, P2/F/331
Fleman, Hy., carp., Stockton, 1726, W, P2/F/459
Isaac, carp., Deptford, Wylye, 1819, W, Wr, P2/1819/1
Jas., wheelwright, Heytes., 1820, comm, W, Wr, P5/1820/7
Jas., carp., Stockton, 1850, AB, draft D, D, I, W, Wr, P2/1850/59
Jn., glover, Sal. (form. of Marl.), 1612-13, AB (damaged), I, P1/F/30, P4/1613/19
Jn., carp. and wheelwright, Stockton, 1810, W, Wr, P2/1810/2
Jn. Reece, bach., Devizes, 1857, AB, aff, Wr, P1/1857/16
Jonas, Upton L., 1778, AB, P2/F/607
Martin, carp., Stockton, 1758, W, P2/F/552
My., widow, Stockton, 1769, W, P2/F/584
My., widow, Wilton, 1784, W, P2/F/633
Fleman, Nich., sen., carp., Stockton, 1724, W, P2/F/447
Nich., Stockton, 1788, W, P2/F/640
Thos., husb., Snodshill, Chiseldon, 1673, AB, I, NW, P3/F/145
Fleman, Thos., wheeler, Upton L., 1697, AB, I, P2/F/378
Thos., victualler, Quidh., 1780, W, P2/F/619
Wm., jun., Garsdon, [1614], I, W (NEP), P3/F/25
Wm., wheeler, Stockton, 1803, W, P2/1803/33
Fletcher, Flatcher, Ann, widow, Swindon, 1691, AB, I, P3/F/210
Ann, widow, W. Kington, 1728, AB, I, P3/F/316
Ann, widow, Sal., 1778, AB, P4/1778/6
Anthony, Corston, Malm., 1636, AB, I, P3/F/75
Arthur, parson, Pertwood, 1631, I, T, W, P1/F/63
Dan., yeo. and gent., Crickl. St S., 1756, W, P1/F/424, P1/11Reg/326
Edmd., yeo., Calcutt, Crickl. St S., 1826, O, W, Wr, P3/1826/15
Isaac, dairyman, Tisb., 1799, AB, ren, W, P2/F/668
Jas., blacksmith, Sonning, Berks., 1710, W, P5/1710/37, P5/15Reg/154B
Jn., sen., yeo., Swindon, 1673, comm, W, P3/F/146
Fleacher [Flatcher], Jn., sen., Upton L., 1685, I, W, P2/F/317
Jn., Hullavington, 1716, I, W, P1/F/262, P1/6Reg/32A
Jn., tucker, Sal., 1733, AB, I, P1/F/325
Jn., clothworker, Sal., 1752, W, P4/1752/3
Jn., innholder, Devizes, 1782, W, P1/F/485, P1/13Reg/339A
Jn., Sal., 1792, AB, P4/1792/8
Leonard, gent., Sal., 1767, AB, ren, W, P4/1767/2
Mgt., sp., Calcutt, Crickl. St S., 1833, W, Wr, P3/1833/43
Marian, widow, Tinh., Edington, 1635, AB, I, P2/F/167, P2/9Reg/51C
Peter, husb., Broad C., 1602, I, W, P2/F/58
Philip, Binfield, Berks., 1750, AB, P1/F/401

Rebecca, widow, Abingdon, Berks., 1801, W, P1/1801/50, P1/15Reg/268A
Richd., husb., Tinh., Edington, [1619], I, W, P2/F/108
Richd., Sal., 1710, W, P4/1710/4
Flatcher, Robt., Monkton D., [1557], W (title & part of 1st line only), P2/3Reg/10B
Robt., barber, Reading, Berks., 1756, W, P1/F/417, P1/11Reg/216
Thos., Reading, Berks., 1744, AB, P1/F/373
Flacher, Wm., Monkton D., 1556, W, P2/1Reg/105B
Wm., sen., cordw., Abingdon, Berks., 1662, AB, I, W, P1/F/115
Wm., Kemble, 1670, AB, I, P3/F/129
Wm., sen., cloth weaver, Swindon, 1673, AB, I, W, P3/F/150
Flatcher, Wm., yeo., Swindon, 1687, I, W, P3/F/191
Flacher, Wm., yeo., W. Kington, 1725, I, W, P3/F/306
Flatcher, Wm., grocer, Swindon, 1726, W, P3/F/310
Wm., bach. and clerk, Donhead St A., 1809, AB, Wr, P1/1809/8
Flewell, Ann, Liddington, 1687, W, P3/F/192
Ann, surgeon's widow, Devizes, 1744, comm, W, P1/F/370, P1/9Reg/280
Christian, widow, Farnham, Tollard Royal, Dorset, 1618, I, W, P2/F/101
Christian, widow, Farnham, Tollard Royal, Dorset, 1743, W, P2/F/518
Eliz., sp., Devizes, 1739, W, P1/F/351, P1/8Reg/387
Eliz., sp., Wolverton, Hants (leaving effects at Marl.), 1854, AB, aff, comm, Wr, P1/1854/11
Flowell, Hy., Liddington, 1689, AB, I, P1/F/183
Jane, widow, Badbury, Chiseldon, 1681, AB, I, P3/F/170
Jn., miller, Wrou., 1697, I, W, P3/F/232
Jn., surgeon and bonesetter, Liddington, 1728, W, P3/F/317
Jn., surgeon, Shalbourne, Berks., 1732, W, P23/482
Jn., surgeon, Tilsh., 1763, AB, P1/F/439
Margery, widow, Elcombe, Wrou., 1725, AB, P3/F/307
Stephen, Farnham, Tollard Royal, Dorset, 1731, AB, I, ren, P2/F/484
Thos., yeo., Wrou., 1610, W, P3/F/16
Wm., Elcombe, Wrou., 1718, I, W, P3/F/288
Wm., surgeon, Shalbourne, 1733, W, P5/1733/23
Wm., surgeon, Devizes, 1742, comm, W, P1/F/366, P1/9Reg/233
Flewellen, Dorothy, widow, Slaughterford, 1724, AB, I, P3/F/302
Joan, widow, Devizes & Rowde, 1636, AB, I, P1/F/87
Llewellyn, Jn., Edington, [1540], W, P2/L/1
Jn., Slaughterford, 1724, AB, P3/F/303
Jn., narrow weaver, Slaughterford, 1733, I, W, P3/F/339
Flexall, Flexall alias Watson, Thos., blacksmith, Abingdon, Berks., 1635, I, W, P1/F/86
Flexon, Jn., yeo., Wytham, Berks., 1707, I, W, P1/F/233
Sarah, widow, Sutton C., Berks., 1695, AB, I, P1/F/205
Flinger, Nich., yeo., Milton, Gillingham, Dorset, 1683, I, P27/1/81
Flint, Gregory, Fisherton A., 1619, AB, I, P2/F/104
Flippen, Andrew, yeo., W. Amesb., [1687], I, W, P2/F/330
Joan, widow, W. Amesb., [1688], I, W, P2/F/339
Wm., Semley, 1743, AB, I, P2/F/522
Flood, Edmd., Lyme R., Dorset, 1681, I, P16/67
Jn., mason, Lyme R., Dorset, 1686, I, W, P16/83
Jn., clerk and minister, Crickl. St S., 1704, I, W, P3/F/245
My., widow, Sal., 1676, W, P4/1676/2
My., widow, Crickl. St S., 1720, W, P3/F/297
Nich., husb. and labourer, Whitep., 1639, I, W, P2/F/189
Fludd, Jn., tailor, Erlestoke (pressed to serve the Queen at Newhaven Le Havre, France), 1563, I, W, P2/F/228, P2/4Reg/172C
Fludd, Richd., tanner, Sal. St Edmd., 1622, AB, I (2), W (2), P4/1622/9
Sarah, widow, Lyme R., Dorset, 1691, I, W, P16/112
Simon, sen., mason, Lyme R., Dorset, 1683, I, W, P16/68
Fludd, Thos., Erlestoke, 1543, W (NEP), P2/1Reg/41A
Flooks, Fluke, Chas., loom carp., Trowb., 1839, comm, W, Wr, P1/1839/5
Jn. Cue, baker, Tinh., Edington, 1821, W, Wr, P2/1821/35
Jos., Tinh., Edington, 1739, AB, P2/F/507

Jos., baker, Tinh., Edington, 1783, comm, W, P1/F/492, P1/13Reg/439B
Jos., miller and baker, Tinh., Edington, 1856, aff, D, O, W, Wr, P2/1856/10
Lydia Gaisford, sp., Tinh., Edington, 1856, AB, aff, O, Wr, P2/1856/65
Martha, sp., Tinh., Edington, 1828, comm, W, Wr, P2/1828/55
My., sp., Berwick St Jn., 1735-37, AB, a/c, I, P2/F/497
Florence, Jn., sen., broad weaver, Bradford A., [1619], I, W, P2/F/105
Florence alias Toller, Matthew, husb., Winterborne K., Dorset, 1581, I, T, W, P5/1581/9, P5/4Reg/20A
Flory, Edwd., yeo., Wexcombe, Grafton, 1625, I, W, P5/1625/29, P5/10Reg/296
Eliz., widow, Oxenwood, Shalbourne, 1681, AB, I, P23/106
Eliz., widow, Wexcombe, Grafton, 1715, I, W, P21/7/23
Jane, widow, Collingbourne D. (form. of Wexcombe, Grafton), 1721, W, P21/8/12
Joan, widow, Ludg., 1715, W, P2/F/416
Jn., husb., Wexcombe, Grafton, 1610, I, W, P5/1609/31, P5/9Reg/20A
Jn., Wexcombe, Grafton, 1636, AB, I, P21/1/27
Jn., yeo., Wootton R., 1689, AB, I, P1/F/182
Jn., yeo., Wootton R., 1726, W, P1/F/296, P1/7Reg/115
Jn., Wootton R., 1747, AB, P3/F/371
Flurry *or* Flory, My., Froxfield, 1634, AB, I, P1/F/76, P3/F/70
Richd., husb., Wexcombe, Grafton, 1679, I, W, P21/2/60
Richd., Wexcombe, Grafton, 1698, comm, I, W, P21/5/41
Thos., Wexcombe, Grafton, 1624, AB, I, P5/1623/10, P5/10Reg/167B
Thos., yeo., Wootton R., 1706, I, W, P3/F/251
Wm., husb., Wexcombe, Grafton, 1636, AB, a/c, I, P21/1/29
Wm., Wexcombe, Grafton, 1702, I, W, P21/6/8
Flowell *see* Flewell
Flower, Alice, widow, Melk., 1596, AB, L, P2/F/40
Alice, widow, Easterton, Mkt. L., 1666, I, W, P2/F/236
Alice, widow, Melk., 1669, I, W, P2/F/243
Alice, minister's widow, W. Knoyle, [1685], I, W, P2/F/324
Alice, widow, Ashton G., Codf. St P., [1695], I, W, P2/F/362
Ann, widow, W. Ashton, Steeple A., 1636, I, W, P2/F/171
Ann, widow, Beanacre, Melk., 1671, I, W, P2/F/257
Ann, Upton L., 1729, W, P1/F/316, P1/7Reg/380A
Ann, widow, Norton B., 1836, comm, W, P2/1836/58
Anthony, yeo., Bps. C., 1689, AB, I (detailed), ren, W, P24/727
Bartholomew, Urchf., 1611, AB, P2/F/674, P2/8Reg/159C
Benj., clerk, Chipp., 1709, W, P3/F/263
Christine, widow, Melk., 1560, W, P2/4Reg/33C
Clare, farmer, Compton B., 1831, comm, W, Wr, P3/1831/59
Cornelius, scribler, Devizes, 1783, W, P1/F/495, P1/14Reg/12
Dorothy, widow, W. Lavington, 1591, I, W, P1/F/2
Edith, widow, Littleton, Steeple A., 1641, I, W, P2/F/201
Edmd., husb., Conkwell, Winsley, Bradford A., 1680, I, W, P2/F/293
Edmd., yeo., Cherhill, 1769, W, P26/1033
Edmd., Lockeridge, Overton, 1818, AB, comm, Wr, P3/1818/6
Edmd., farmer, Cherhill, 1831, W, P26/1391
Edwd., Worton, Pott., 1622, I, W, P1/F/52
Edwd., husb., Hurst, Berks., 1635, I, W, P5/1635/39, P5/12Reg/201B
Edwd., yeo., Beanacre, Melk., 1662, comm, I, copy W, P1/F/114
Edwd., sen., clothier, Beanacre, Melk., 1663, I, W, P2/F/225
Edwd., Easterton, Mkt. L., 1670-72, AB, a/c, comm, I, P2/F/263
Edwd., mason, Devizes, 1758, W, P1/F/427, P1/11Reg/364B
Edwin, bach., Netton, Durnford (leaving effects at Sal.), 1846, AB, Wr, P1/1846/14
Eliz., Melk., 1557, W, P2/3Reg/61A
Eliz., sp., Pott., 1686, AB, P1/F/175
Eliz., widow, Mere, 1698, I, W, P5/1698/25
Eliz., widow, Heytes., 1761, W, P5/1761/11
Eliz., sp., Sal., 1773, W, P1/F/466, P1/12Reg/462
Eliz., yeo.'s wife, Nunton, N. and Bodenham, 1778, W, P2/F/609
Enoch, yeo., Corsham, 1711, I, W, P29/F/9

Enoch, carp., Atworth, Bradford A., 1801, W, P1/1801/14, P1/15Reg/236
Frances, widow, Rushall, 1732, AB, W, P1/F/323, P1/7Reg/553A
Frances, sp., Imber, 1800, D, W, P2/1800/40
Francis, Purley, Berks., 1741, AB, P1/F/361
Geo., esquire, Worton, Pott., 1746, W, P1/10Reg/29
Geo., gent., Worton, Pott., 1746, AB, ren, W, P1/F/382, P1/10Reg/48
Geo., yeo., Netton, Durnford, 1824, W, Wr, P5/1824/6
Goyne, yeo., Imber, [1686], I, W, P2/F/328
Hy., W. Lavington, 1591, I, W (fragment), P1/F/1
Hy., sen., yeo., W. Ashton, Steeple A., 1705, I, W, P1/F/226
Hy., yeo., Codf. St P. & Netheravon, 1723, I, summary I, W, P1/F/287, P1/7Reg/30A
Hy., tailor, Durnford, 1733, W, P5/1733/24
Hy., yeo., W. Ashton, Steeple A., 1735, W, P1/F/338, P1/8Reg/90
Hy., victualler, Maiden B., 1737, AB, ren, P2/F/503
Hy., Southbroom, 1750, AB, P24/1049
Hy., yeo., Coombe B., 1776, W, P8/56
Hy., labourer, Maiden B., 1816, W, Wr, P2/1816/23
Hy., yeo., Melk. Park Farm, 1842, comm, W, Wr, P2/1842/9
Flower form. Smith, Hester, wife, Calne, 1771, AB, P26/1039
Isaac, yeo., Heytes., 1746, AB, ren, P5/1746/27
Isaac, yeo., Heytes., 1782, W, P5/1782/12, P5/17Reg/215B
Isaac, gent., Norton B., 1836, comm, W, P2/1836/43
Jas., Poulshot, 1670, AB, I, P2/F/254
Jas., Poulshot, 1690, AB, comm, P2/F/344
Jas., yeo., Neston, Corsham, 1768, W, P29/2Reg/119
Jas., yeo., Ridge, Chilmark, 1813, D, W, Wr, P2/1813/35
Jane, widow, Marl., 1753, W, P1/F/411, P1/11Reg/131
Jane, widow, Devizes, 1760, W, P1/F/436, P1/11Reg/490
Joan, Littleton, Steeple A., 1604, AB, P2/F/67
Joan, widow, Holt, Bradford A., [1630], I, W, P2/F/151
Jn., Worton, Pott., 1571, W (NEP), P1/1Reg/88C, 112
Jn., husb., Littleton, Steeple A., 1603, I, W, P2/F/62
Jn., weaver, Bulk., Keevil, 1609-14, AB, a/c, I, T, P2/F/78, 97, P2/8Reg/52C
Jn., Bulk., Keevil, 1625, D, W, P2/F/128
Jn., sen., Bulk., Keevil, 1630-31, AB, a/c, I, W, P2/F/146, P2/9Reg/76B
Jn., yeo., Melk., 1637, I, W, P2/F/173
Jn., gent. *or* yeo., Pott., 1671, AB, comm, I, NW, P1/F/142
Jn., vicar, W. Knoyle, 1684, AB, comm, I, P2/F/312
Jn., gent., W. Lavington, 1689, I, W, P1/F/184
Jn., husb., Rockley, Ogbourne St A., 1691, I (dated 1684), W, P5/1691/28
Jn., tailor, Sal., 1695-98, AB, W, P1/F/202, 212, P1/3Reg/12
Jn., gent., Worton, Pott., 1700, W, P1/F/218, P1/3Reg/265
Jn., Steeple A., 1701, AB, P2/F/390
Jn., sen., labourer, Devizes, 1703-05, AB, I, P1/F/224, 230
Jn., yeo., Corsham, 1714, I, W, P29/F/10
Jn., Sal., 1716, AB, P4/1716/14
Jn., yeo., Corsham, 1716, W, P29/2Reg/17
Jn., esquire, W. Grimstead, 1750, AB, W, P1/F/395, P1/10Reg/272
Jn., gent., Beanacre, Melk., 1753, W, P1/F/409, P1/11Reg/49
Jn., yeo., Seend, Melk., 1765, W, P2/F/577
Jn., schoolmaster, Calne, 1805, W, Wr, P26/1252
Jn., blacksmith, Earley, Sonning, Berks., 1815, W, Wr, P5/1815/15
Jn., yeo., Coombe B., 1833, W, Wr, P5/1833/30
Jonathan, gent., Chitterne St My., 1744, W, P1/F/371, P1/9Reg/287
Jonathan, Heytes., 1768, AB, P5/1768/8
Jonathan, farmer, Maddington, 1820, W, Wr, P2/1820/31
Jos., gent., W. Ashton, Steeple A., 1730, W, P2/F/476
Jos., gent., Bratton, Westb., 1850, comm, W, Wr, P25/1850/2
Lawr., original index gives abode as ? Norton B., 1597, I, P2/F/44
Lawr., husb. and yeo., Sulham, Berks., 1664, I, W, P1/F/127

Lucy, widow of clerk, Chipp., 1712, I (mentions school), W, P3/F/273
Mgt., widow, W. Lavington, 1631, I, W, P1/F/60
Mgt., widow, Chipp., 1671, comm, I, W, P3/F/134
Mgt., sp., Devizes, 1682, AB, comm, I, P1/F/159
Mgt., widow, Bradford A., 1705, comm, W, P2/F/401
Mgt., widow, Devizes St Jn., 1705, W, P1/F/231
Marian, widow, Rowde, [1608], W (NEP), P3/F/8
My., widow, Melk., [1667], I, W, P2/F/238
My., widow, Steeple A., 1724, W, P2/F/453
My., widow, Bratton, Westb., 1802, O, W, P25/1802/4
Nich., broad weaver, Woodrow, Melk., 1625, I, W, P1/F/55
Nich., Littleton, Steeple A., 1633, W, P2/F/163
Nich., gent., Sal., 1634, I, NW, P1/F/77
Obadiah, yeo., Littleton P., 1702, I, W, P1/F/222, P1/4Reg/213
Obadiah, grocer, Chitterne AS, 1726, W, P1/F/297, P1/7Reg/153A
Obadiah, Heytes., 1756, AB, P5/1756/11
Obadiah, Heytes., 1764, AB, P5/1764/15
Obadiah, victualler, Heytes., 1809, W, Wr, P5/1809/5
Obadiah, widower, Warm., 1851, AB, comm, Wr, P1/1851/16
Peter, victualler, Cherhill, 1783, W, P26/1126
Philip, Imber, 1771, AB, P2/F/589
Richd., husb., Steeple A., 1559, W, P2/3Reg/150A
Richd., Keevil, 1611-14, AB, a/c, NW, P2/F/96, P2/8Reg/156C
Richd., husb., Norton B., 1640, I, W, P2/F/195
Richd., innholder, Pickwick, Corsham, 1689, I, W, P29/F/7, P29/1Reg/245
Richd., victualler, Milborne Stileham, Bere R., Dorset, 1690, AB, I, P5/1690/18
Richd., cordw., Upton L., 1708, I, W, P2/F/404
Richd., Pickwick, Corsham, 1714, marriage licence, P29/2Reg/4A
Richd., yeo., Corsham, 1742, W, P29/F/12
Robt.?, victualler, Melk., 1602, I, P2/F/59
Robt., yeo., W. Lavington, 1611, I, W, P1/F/25
Robt., Rowde, 1631, I, W, P1/F/68
Robt., sen., broad weaver, Melk., 1643, AB, comm, I (2), P2/F/204
Robt., Newtown, Melk., 1647, AB, P2/F/214
Robt., yeo., Bulk., Keevil, [1700], I, W, P2/F/385
Roger, Sal., 1683, AB, P4/1683/3
Ruth, Imber, 1705, AB, P2/F/398
Ruth, widow, Whaddon, 1800, W, P2/1800/80
Sampson, physician, Alderton, 1691, AB, I, P3/F/208
Sam., yeo., Corsham, 1750, W, P29/F/13, P29/2Reg/60
Sam., yeo., Chipp., 1795, AB, W, P3/F/444
Sam., carp., Atworth, Bradford A., 1828, W, Wr, P2/1828/33
Sarah, widow, Lockeridge, Overton, 1827, W, Wr, P3/1827/26
Flowers, Sarah, widow, Sonning, Berks., 1843, W, Wr, P5/1843/20
Stephen, yeo., W. Lavington, 1662, I, W, P1/F/113
Stephen, yeo., Lt. Cheverell, 1676, I, W, P2/F/278
Stephen, yeo., Bulk., Keevil, 1732, W, P1/F/319, P1/7Reg/516A
Stephen, Newtown, Melk., 1765, AB, P2/F/576
Stephen, yeo., Whaddon, 1774, W, P2/F/597
Susan, Chittoe, Bps. C., 1606, W, P1/F/19
Susan, sp., Melk., 1619, I, W, P2/F/110
Susanna, widow, Poulshot, 1678, AB, comm, I, P2/F/283
Susanna, widow, Calne, 1812, W, Wr, P26/1284
Susanna, widow, Calne, 1828, AB, comm, O, ren, Wr, P26/1366
Thos., husb., Melk., 1557, W, P2/3Reg/21B
Thos., husb., Bulk., Keevil, 1572, W, P2/5Reg/152B
Thos., Chitterne AS, 1611, AB, P2/F/86, P2/8Reg/155A
Thos., yeo., Melk., 1618, I (very detailed), P2/F/102
Thos., Imber, 1625-26, AB, a/c, I, P2/F/126
Thos., fuller, Quidh., 1647, T (children: Thos. & Alice F.), P2/F/213

Thos., gent., Melk., 1647, I, W, P2/F/210
Thos., sen., gent., Beanacre, Melk., 1677, I, W, P2/F/280
Thos., yeo., Bulk., Keevil, 1694, I, W, P2/F/358
Thos., sen., gent., Beanacre, Melk., 1741, W, P1/F/362, P1/9Reg/177
Thos., writing master, Westb. L., 1741, AB, W, P25/1741/7
Thos., Beanacre, Melk., 1752, AB, comm, P2/F/540
Thos., Whaddon, 1757, AB, comm, P2/F/550
Thos., yeo., Inmarsh, Seend, Melk., 1764, comm, W, P2/F/572
Thos., sen., yeo., Nunton, N. and Bodenham (form. of Titchfield, Hants), 1807, AB, W, P2/1807/62
Thomasine, widow, Melk., 1593, I (2), W, copy W, P2/F/32
Tristram, gent., W. Ashton, Steeple A., 1605, I, W, P1/F/11
Tristram, [clothier], Maiden B., 1715, AB, I (very detailed), P2/F/417
Wm., weaver, Melk., 1579, W, P2/5Reg/330C
Wm., yeo., W. Lavington, 1607, W, P1/F/21
Wm., sen., broad weaver, Semington, Steeple A., 1608, AB, I, W, P2/F/77, P2/8Reg/31B
Wm., yeo., Bulk., Keevil, 1626, I, NW, P2/F/137
Wm., yeo., Box, 1668, I, W, P3/F/121
Wm., sen., barber surgeon, Melk., 1669, AB, I, P2/F/248
Wm., jun., surgeon, Melk., 1669, I, P2/F/247
Wm., husb., Compton, Enford, 1684, AB, I, P2/F/313
Wm., yeo., Littleton P. & Orcheston St My., W. Lavington, [1687], I, W, P2/F/334
Wm., Melk., 1688, AB, I, P2/F/338
Wm., Imber, 1705, AB, P2/F/399
Wm., baker, Marl. St My., 1740, I, W, P1/F/353, P1/8Reg/420
Wm., yeo., Gt. Durnford, 1781, W, P9/84
Wm., collarmaker, Lockeridge, Overton, 1800, W, P3/1800/39
Wm., gent., Bulk., Keevil, 1824, comm, W, Wr, P2/1824/36
Wm., yeo., Cherhill, 1824, W, Wr, P5/1824/9
Wm., weaver, Seend, Melk., 1828, W, Wr, P2/1828/59
Wm., gent., Newtown, Melk., 1845, W, Wr, P1/1845/38
Wm., farmer, Cherhill, 1855, O, W, Wr, P26/1468
see also Shergold alias F.
Floyd, Cath., widow, Wootton B., 1696, AB, I, W, P3/F/229
Eliz., gardener's widow, Reading, Berks., 1759, W, P1/F/429, P1/11Reg/383
Evans, Brightwell, Berks., 1638, AB, I, P1/F/89
Jn., clothier, Steeple A., 1566, W, P2/4Reg/233A
Jn., weaver, Sal. St Thos., 1633, AB, a/c, I, P4/1632/16
Sarah, widow, Whittonditch, Rams., 1823, AB, Wr, P5/1823/24
Thos., clerk and vicar, Wootton B., 1670, I, W, P3/F/130
Wm., Bradford A., 1806, AB, comm, P2/1806/33
Fluce, Ann, widow, Crickl. St S., 1748, I, W, P3/F/373
Flues, Anthony, carp., Purton, 1690, AB, I, P3/F/203
Jn., carp., Crickl. St S., 1719, W, P3/F/291
Jn., bach., Swindon, 1749, AB, P3/F/375
My., widow, Crickl. St S., 1746, W, P3/F/372
Fludd *see* Flood
Fluddier, Jn., husb., Upton, Blewbury, Berks., 1637, I, W, P5/1637/12, P5/13Reg/68
Flues *see* Fluce
Fluke *see* Flooks
Flurry *see* Flory
Foach, Edwd., cordw. *or* shoemaker, Easton, 1687, I, W, P3/F/193
Edwd., sen., Easton, 1726, W, P3/F/311
Edwd., yeo., Savernake Park, 1774, W, note (explaining delay in spending probate), P21/11/8
Foche, Emma, Mkt. L., 1566, AB, P2/4Reg/239F
Foche, Jn., Ludg., 1577, I, T, W, P2/F/10, P2/5Reg/295A
Foche, Jn., husb., Pewsey, 1602, W, P3/1Reg/104
Foche, Jn., Preshute, 1632, I, NW, P1/F/72
Richd., husb., Sharcott, Pewsey, 1616, I, W, P1/F/43
Foche, Richd., Easton, 1666, AB, I, P3/F/111
Stephen, maltster, Marl., 1762, W, P1/F/437, P1/12Reg/16B

Foakes *see* Foulkes
Foard *see* Ford
Foche *see* Foach
Foley, Francis, farmer, Ashton G., Codf. St P., 1797, W, P2/F/661
Folliott, Follett, Alexander, husb., Downton, 1746, W, P2/F/525
Follett, Alice, widow, Lyme R., Dorset, 1606, comm, I, W, copy W, P5/1606/16, P5/8Reg/83A
Folliot, Avis, sp., Broad C., 1643, AB, I, P2/F/205
Follett, Chas., yeo., Chards., Devon, 1740, W, Wr, P5/1740/32
Edwd., blacksmith, Mkt. L., 1764, W, P2/F/571
Gilbert, Chitterne St My., 1807, AB, Wr, P2/1807/46
Folliatt alias Taylor, Hy., Stratford Tony, 1557, W, P2/3Reg/50C
Folliot, Hy., yeo., Hare Warren, Wilton, 1664, AB, I, W, P1/F/129
Hy., farmer, Monkton D., 1795, W, P2/F/656
Hy., gent., Hill D., 1809, AB, W, P5/1809/6
Jas., E. Knoyle, 1845, D, O, W, Wr, P2/1845/13
Follett, Jane, Stratford Tony, 1560, W, P2/4Reg/49A
Jane, widow, Maiden B., 1780, W, P2/F/615
Folliatt, Jn., yeo., Stratford Tony, 1636, I, W, P2/F/170
Folliatt, Jn., yeo., Broad C., 1638, I, NW, P2/F/179
Folliatt, Jn., Broad C., 1701, AB, I, ren, P2/F/389
Folliot, Jn., sen., yeo., Pertwood, 1749, W, P2/F/533
Keturah, widow, E. Knoyle, 1830, AB, comm, P2/1830/46
My., widow, Monkton D., 1803, W, P2/1803/45
Follitt, Richd., yeo., Broad C., 1785, W, P2/F/637
Follett, Robt., Lower Wambrook, Somerset, 1783, W, P14/188
Follett, Sam., gent., Lyme R., Dorset, 1825, AB, comm, P16/393
Folliatt, Walter, yeo., Broad C., 1594, I, T, W, P2/F/37
Walter, Maiden B., 1780, AB, P2/F/616
Folliatt, Wm., Stratford Tony, 1572, AB, P2/5Reg/159E
Wm. Hy., minor, Hill D., 1809, T, P5/1809/7
Fook, Fooke, Fooks *see* Foulkes
Foord *see* Ford
Foot, Ann, widow, Berwick St Jn., 1802, W, P2/1802/17
Ann, widow, Charlton, Donhead St My., 1846, comm, W, Wr, P2/1846/26
Asher [male], Donhead St My., 1824-33, AB (2), comm (2), O, Wr, P2/1824/50, P2/1833/15
Betty, widow, Fovant, 1814, W, Wr, P1/1814/28
Eliz., widow, Devizes, 1687, AB, P1/F/176
Eliz., widow, Tisb., 1740, W, P2/F/513
Eliz., widow, Charlton, Donhead St My., 1781, W, P2/F/622
Emma, sp., Oborne, Dorset (form. of Odstock), 1842, W, Wr, P1/1842/80
Fortune, widow, Donhead St My. (form. of Gussage St Michael, Dorset), 1803, W, P2/1803/59
Hy., Fovant, 1760, AB, P2/F/557
Hy. Mitchell, surgeon and apothecary, Fovant, 1803, AB, ren, W, P2/1803/55
Hester, widow, Berwick St Jn., 1791, W, P2/F/645
Jas., Bridgwater but leaving effects at Berwick St Jn., 1779, AB, P1/F/478
Jas., gent., Sal. The Close, 1829, W, Wr, P5/1829/9
Jn., miller, Bishopstone S., 1584, W, P2/6Reg/132B
Jn., [blacksmith], Ludwell, Donhead St My., 1610, I, W, P2/F/81, P2/8Reg/86B
Jn., blacksmith, Elston, Orcheston St Geo., 1661, AB, I, P2/F/220
Jn., sen., gent., Charlton, Donhead St My., 1751, W, P2/F/535
Jos., glover, Donhead St My., 1767, I, W, P2/F/583
Jos., sen., Berwick St Jn., 1792, AB, P2/F/649
Jos., yeo., Charlton, Donhead St My., 1810, W, Wr, P2/1810/17
Joshua, Berwick St Jn., 1775, AB, P2/F/598
Joshua, Berwick St Jn., 1824, AB, comm, LA, O, Wr, P2/1824/49
Joshua, Berwick St Jn., 1833, AB, O, W, P2/1833/14
Margery, widow, Keevil, 1634, I, W, P2/F/165
My., widow, Donhead St My., 1743, AB, W, P2/F/521
My., gentlewoman and widow, Berwick St Jn., 1816, W, Wr, P2/1816/27
My., widow, Bradford A., 1843, O, W, Wr, P2/1843/3

My., labourer's wife, Sherb., Dorset (form. of Poyntington, Dorset), 1849, AB, comm, D, W, Wr, P5/1849/12
Robt., yeo., Cumberwell, Bradford A., 1671, comm, W, P2/F/259
Robt., Sherb., Dorset, 1683, AB, comm, P5/1683/21
Robt., gent., Devizes, 1687, AB, P1/F/177
Robt., maltster, Bradford A., 1715, AB, I, ren, P2/F/418
Robt., yeo., Bourton, Gillingham, Dorset, 1755, W, P27/1/411, P27/3Reg/72
Robt., Berwick St Jn., 1762, AB, P2/F/563
Robt., Donhead St My., 1837, AB, O, Wr, P2/1837/65
Sarah, Bradford A., 1718, AB, comm, P2/F/426
Sarah, widow, Lower Bridmore, Berwick St Jn., 1796, AB, W, P2/F/660
Sarah, widow, Charlton, Donhead St My., 1818, comm, W, Wr, P2/1818/68
Thos., husb., Sherb., Dorset, 1592, AB, I, P5/1592/31, P5/5Reg/143C
Thos., tanner, Mere, 1703, AB, I, P5/1703/12
Thos., Charlton, Donhead St My., 1774, AB, ren, P2/F/596
Thos., Charlton, Donhead St My., 1783, AB, P2/F/632
Thos., yeo., Charlton, Donhead St My., 1788, definitive sentence, W, P1/F/503, P1/14Reg/346
Thos., woolstapler, Quidh., 1793, W, P2/F/650
Thos., yeo., Charlton, Donhead St My., 1816, W, Wr, P2/1816/49
Thos., woolstapler, Quidh., 1817, W, Wr, P1/1817/20
Wm., weaver, Keevil (d. at Lent Assizes in Sal.), 1623, I, NW, P2/F/120
Wm., blacksmith, Ludwell, Donhead St My., [1674], I, P2/F/271
Wm., sen., maltster, Sherb., Dorset, 1742, W, P5/1741/11
Wm., Donhead St My., 1823, AB, comm, Wr, P2/1823/15
Wm., woolstapler, Quidh., 1823, AB, W, Wr, P2/1823/9
Footner, Jn., innkeeper, Sal., 1798, W, P1/F/515, P1/15Reg/139
Ford, Abraham, yeo., Ditteridge, 1843, comm, W, Wr, P3/1843/33
Agnes, Tinh., Edington, 1608, AB, I, T, P2/F/75, P2/8Reg/30A
Agnes, Crickl. St S., 1612, AB, I, P3/F/21
Alice, widow, Tinh., Edington, 1574, W, P2/5Reg/196B
Alice, widow, Urchf., 1574, W, P2/5Reg/182A
Alice, widow, Tinh., Edington, 1619, I, W, P2/F/109
Alice, widow, Seend, Melk., 1631, I, W, P1/F/70
Alice, Mere, 1641, AB, P5/13Reg/282C
Alice, widow, Over Zeals, 1641, AB, I, P5/1641/32
Alice, widow, Fordington, Dorset, 1681, I, W, P15/56
Ann, Sal., 1714, AB, P4/1714/4
Ann, widow, Monkton D., 1803, W, P2/1803/41
Ann, widow, Overton, 1850, O, W, Wr, P3/1850/54
Foord, Anthony, Ashley, Box, 1607, AB, P3/F/5
Anthony, yeo., Lt. Cheverell, 1661, comm, I, W, P2/F/221
Betty, widow of licensed victualler, *The White Hart Inn*, Colerne, 1844, comm, W, Wr, P3/1844/65
Cath., widow, Winterborne K., Dorset, 1746, W (NEP), P5/1746/28
Chas. Thos., Bemerton, Fugg. St Peter, 1838, AB, Wr, P2/1838/43
Christian, widow, Woodlands, Mere, 1627, I, W, P5/1627/14, P5/11Reg/8A
Christian, widow, Sal. St Thos., 1685, AB, I, P4/1685/13
Foord, Christian, widow, Sal., 1716, W, P4/1716/12
Chris., sen., yeo., Compton C., 1682-92, I (2), W (2), P2/F/299, 355
Chris., woolcomber, Eastcott, Urchf., 1703, I, W, P2/F/391
Dorcas, yeo.'s wife, Box, 1684, AB, P3/F/182
Foord, Dorothy, Damerham, Hants, [1594], I, W, P2/F/34-35
Dorothy, widow, Downton, 1683, I, W, P2/F/305
Edith, widow, Pott., 1754, W, P1/11Reg/153
Foord, Edwd., jun., yeo., Damerham, Hants, 1667, AB, I, W, P2/F/240
Edwd., blacksmith, Gt. Woodford, 1688, AB, I, P13/3/12
Foord, Edwd., Mere, 1707, AB, I, P5/1707/20
Foard, Edwd., yeo., Mere, 1728, W, P5/1728/34
Foord, Edwd., yeo., Mere, 1772, W, P5/1772/6, P5/17Reg/46C
Edwd., soldier, Longbridge D., 1780, W, P2/F/617, P5/16Reg/168B
Edwd., Devizes, 1841, AB, comm, Wr, P3/1841/3
Eleanor, widow, Durrington, [1675], I, W, P2/F/277

Eliz., widow, Damerham, Hants, 1562, I, W, P2/F/3, P2/4Reg/99A
Eliz., widow, Stourpaine, Dorset, 1731, I, W, P24/816
Eliz., widow, Kingsdown, Box, 1731-52, AB (2), P3/F/333
Eliz., widow, Beam., Dorset, 1744, W, P17/496
Eliz., widow, Bucklebury, Berks., 1795, W, P1/F/512, P1/14Reg/581
Eliz., widow, W. Kington, 1797, W, Wr, P3/F/447
Eliz., widow, Devizes, 1832, W, Wr, P1/1832/11
Ellen, Rushall, 1730?, W, P2/F/472
Frances, widow, Damerham, Hants, 1629, AB, I, T, P2/F/139
Frances, sp., Milton upon Stour, Gillingham, Dorset, 1704, W, P27/1/581
Frances, widow, Amesb., 1722, W, P2/F/444
Francis, husb., Compton C., 1670, AB, I, NW, P2/F/253
Geo., yeo., Willesley, Sherston, 1687, AB, comm, I, P3/F/194
Geo., butcher, Seend, Melk., 1832, W, Wr, P2/1832/34
Geo., E. Knoyle, 1851, AB, O, Wr, P2/1851/6
Giles, Luckington, 1646, comm, I, W, P1/F/103
Hy., husb., Chipp., [1571], W (NEP), P1/1Reg/133B
Foord, Hy., Damerham, Hants, 1593, AB, I (joint with Dorothy F.), W, P2/F/34-35
Hy., yeo. and carp., Old Bracknell, Easthampstead, Berks., 1638, I, W, P1/F/92
Hy., carp. and builder, Teffont M., 1852, D, W, Wr, P2/1852/9
Foard, Humphrey, sen., victualler, Chipp., 1681, I, W, P3/F/169
Jas., Stourpaine, Dorset, 1711, AB, P24/697
Jas., belonging to HMS *Sunderland*, Trowb., 1746, comm, W (written in holograph at sea), P1/F/381, P1/10Reg/26B, 45A
Foord, Jas., cooper, Lyme R., Dorset, 1751, AB, O, P16/309
Foord, Jas., yeo., Brunton, Collingbourne K., 1765, W, P3/F/405
Jas., Overton, 1850, AB, O, Wr, P3/1850/55
Jas., shopkeeper, Hanging L., 1853, I (detailed), W, Wr, P2/1853/43
Jane, Urchf., 1703, AB, P2/F/393
Jane, sp., Corsham, 1718, I, W, P29/F/11, P29/2Reg/27B
Jane, widow, Pott., 1786, W, P1/F/498, P1/14Reg/81
Joan, widow, Urchf., 1570, W, P2/5Reg/90C
Joan, widow, Beam., Dorset, 1622, AB, I, W, P5/1622/26, P5/10Reg/119B
Joan, widow, Lt. Cheverell, [1622], I, NW, P2/F/118
Joan, widow, Urchf., [1634], I, W, P2/F/164
Joan, widow, Woodlands, Mere, 1703, I, W, P5/1703/11
Fords, Joan, widow, Somerford K., 1717, I, W, P3/F/282
Joanna, widow, Lyme R., Dorset, 1772, AB, comm, P16/339
Jn., Heywood, Westb., 1565, W, P5/1Reg/45A
Jn., sen., husb., Woodlands, Mere, 1570, W, P5/2Reg/60B
Jn., Durrington, 1580, W, P2/F/18, P2/6Reg/8D
Foord, Jn., blacksmith, Durrington, 1604, AB, I, W, P2/F/64
Jn., yeo., proved at Reading, Berks., 1613, I, W (damaged), P1/F/36
Jn., yeo., Tinh., Edington, 1621, I, P2/F/115
Ford alias Smith, Jn., Damerham, Hants, 1622, I, W, P2/F/116
Foord, Jn., yeo., Chicklade, [1623], deed of gift, P2/F/123
Jn., husb., Urchf., 1633, I, W, P2/F/157
Jn., shoemaker, Beam., Dorset, 1635, AB, comm, I, P5/1634/10, P5/12Reg/170C
Jn., husb., Gurston, Broad C., 1638, AB, a/c, I, P2/F/184
Foord, Jn., sen., husb., Damerham, Hants, 1670, I, W, P2/F/251
Jn., Amesb., 1692, AB, I, P2/F/353
Jn., husb., Compton C., 1692, I, W, P2/F/356
Jn., yeo., Box, 1696, I, W, P3/F/230
Jn., Mere, 1714, W, P5/1714/12, P5/15Reg/388C
Jn., yeo., Turners Puddle, Dorset, 1719, AB, W, P5/1719/30, P5/16Reg/12B
Foord, Jn., yeo., Durrington, 1722, W, P2/F/445
Jn., yeo., E. Winterslow, 1729, AB, W, P2/F/467
Foord, Jn., Edington, 1731, W, P2/F/479
Jn., yeo., Muston Farm, Winterborne K., Dorset, 1731, W, P5/1731/32
Jn., Durrington, 1734, AB, P1/F/326
Foord, Jn., yeo., Fonthill B., 1736-38, a/c (2), AB, I, W, P2/F/504

Jn., Rushall, 1738, AB, P1/F/344
Jn., brickmaker, Pott., 1741, W, P1/F/356, P1/9Reg/24
Jn., sen., yeo., Box, 1748, W, P3/F/374
Fords, Jn., Bridge, Colerne, 1757, W, P3/F/388
Jn., gent., Box, 1775, W, P3/F/418
Jn., yeo., Shaw Farm, Melk., 1787, W, P2/F/638
Jn., yeo., Pott., 1789, comm, W, P1/F/505, P1/14Reg/333
Jn., yeo., Wincanton, Somerset (effects at Milton, Gillingham, Dorset), 1799, W, P27/1/565
Jn., farmer, Pott., 1841, AB, Wr, P1/1841/19
Jn., blacksmith and farrier, Maiden B., 1843, comm, W, Wr, P2/1843/34
Jn. *see also* Sarah Tudgy
Jos., Heywood, Westb., 1698, AB, I, P25/1698/8
Jos., yeo., Westb., 1734, W, P25/1734/6
Joy, widow, Marston, Pott., 1754, W, P1/F/414
Luke, wheeler, Monkton D., 1793, W, Wr, P2/F/651
Ford alias Smith, Mgt., Damerham, Hants, 1562-63, AB, I, P2/F/6
Mgt., widow, Keevil, 1566, W, P2/4Reg/225B, P5/3Reg/148D
Mgt., widow, Lt. Cheverell, 1663, I, W, P2/F/226
Ford alias Smith, Margery, widow, E. Harnham, Britford, 1580, I, W, P5/1580/23, P2/4Reg/119D
Margery, widow, Beam., Dorset, 1756, AB, ren, P17/532
Maria, sp., Fugg. St Peter, 1845, AB, Wr, P1/1845/78
Martha, Coulston, Edington, 1619, AB, P1/F/47
Martha, widow, Alvediston, 1821, AB, Wr, P2/1821/12
My., widow, Gt. Woodford, 1689, I, W, P13/3/13
Foord, My., widow, Durrington, 1724, W, P2/F/452
My., widow, Penleigh Mill, Dilton, Westb., 1781, W, P25/1781/3
My., widow, Wardour, Tisb., 1846, W, Wr, P2/1846/18
Michael, yeo., Chicklade, 1673, AB, I, P2/F/266
Michael, Fonthill B., 1735-38, AB, W, P2/F/498
Michael, yeo., Colerne, 1743, comm, W, P3/F/363
Michael, baker, Pickwick, Corsham, 1798, W, P3/F/449
Foord, Michael, sen., farmer and maltster, Collingbourne K., 1826, W, Wr, P1/1826/34
Nathaniel, hatmaker, Amesb., 1714, I, W, P2/F/414
Nich., Westb., 1560, W. No date of probate given, P1/2Reg/100B
Nich., sen., yeo., Damerham, Hants, 1679, comm, I, NW, P2/F/287
Nich., yeo., Damerham, Hants, 1684, AB, a/c, I, P1/F/166
Oswald, husb., Tinh., Edington, 1612, AB, I, W, P2/F/87
Peter, Rushall, 1743, AB, P2/F/520
Philip, bach., Urchf., 1640, W, P2/F/194
Foard, Philip, yeo., Biddestone St Peter, 1750, W, P3/F/378
Reuben, yeo., Berwick St Leonard, 1684, I, W, P2/F/308
Foord, Reuben, Hindon, 1719, W, P2/F/431
Richd., sen., husb., Compton C., 1682, I, W, P2/F/302
Richd., clerk, Odstock (d. in town gaol), 1683, AB, I (includes detailed list of books), P1/F/167
Richd., sen., husb. and musician, Westrop, Highw., 1694, AB, I, P10/1694/3
Richd., innholder, Highw., 1744, W, P10/1744/1
Richd., sen., linen weaver, Wolverton, Zeals, 1752, W, P5/1752/19
Richd., labourer, Holyport, Bray, Berks., 1767, W, P1/F/451, P1/12Reg/246
Richd., linen weaver, Wolverton, Zeals, 1772, W, P5/1772/7, P5/17Reg/39B
Robt., husb., Keevil, 1574, W, P2/5Reg/210B
Robt., husb., Aston U., Blewbury, Berks., 1600, I, W, P5/1600/23, P5/7Reg/2A
Robt., shoemaker, Mere, 1636, AB, I, P5/1636/21, P5/13Reg/15A
Foord, Robt., sen., husb., Downton, 1676, comm, I, W, P2/F/279
Robt., yeo., Beam., Dorset, 1688, W, P5/1688/32
Robt., tallow chandler, Sal., 1703, AB, I (detailed), P4/1702/4
Robt., husb., Downton, 1710, AB, I, W, P2/F/409
Robt., yeo., Collingbourne K., 1717, I, W, P3/F/283
Robt., yeo., Compton C., 1717, I, W, P2/F/423
Robt., cooper, Worton, Pott., 1720, I, summary I, W, P1/F/274, P1/6Reg/241
Foord, Robt., yeo., Tinh., Edington, 1731, deed of gift, I, P2/F/482

Foord, Robt., d. on HMS *Ipswich*, man of war at Gibraltar, E. Knoyle, 1740, AB, ren, P2/F/511
Robt., hog butcher and baker, Pott., 1783, W, P1/F/493, P1/14Reg/14
Robt., bacon factor, Devizes, 1832, W, Wr, P1/1832/10
Robt., Highw., 1839, AB, O, ren, Wr, P5/1839/7
Robt., weaver, Broughton G., 1839, W, Wr, P1/1839/51
Sam., sen., blacksmith, Colerne, 1729, I, W, P1/F/312
Foord, Sarah, widow, Woodlands, Mere, 1723, W, P5/1723/15, P1/7Reg/317B, P5/16Reg/82A
Sarah, widow, Gillingham, Dorset, 1774, AB, P27/1/490, P27/3Reg/195A
Sarah, widow, Chipp., 1847, W, Wr, P3/1847/23
Stephen, yeo., N. Wraxall, 1804, W, Wr, P1/1804/90
Susan, widow, Sal. The Close, 1768, W, P5/1768/9
Susanna, widow, Sal. (form. of Burdens Ball, Wilton), 1832, W, Wr, P1/1832/132
Susanna, widow, Colerne, 1838, W, Wr, P3/1838/51
Forde alias Tyler, Thos., Tinh., Edington, 1559, I, W, P2/F/2, P2/3Reg/149B
Thos., Compton C., 1578, W, P2/5Reg/314C
Thos., yeo., Haydon, Dorset, 1635, AB, I, P5/1635/38, P5/12Reg/208A
Thos., Codf. St My., 1647, I, W, copy W, P2/F/211
Foord, Thos., linen weaver, Mere, 1661, I, NW, P5/1661/17
Thos., Fordington, Dorset, 1662, AB, I, P5/1662/46
Thos., Fordington, Dorset, 1668, AB, I, P15/12
Foord, Thos., yeo., White Waltham, Berks., 1695, I, W, P1/F/206
Fords, Thos., yeo., Somerford K., 1709, I, W, P3/F/264
Thos., yeo., Stourpaine, Dorset, 1713, W, P24/682
Thos., husb., Biddestone St Peter, 1753, W, P1/F/410, P1/11Reg/89
Thos., yeo., Milton upon Stour, Gillingham, Dorset, 1806, W, P27/1/585
Thos., Calne, 1828, comm, W, P26/1371
Thomasine, widow, Tinh., Edington, 1624, W, P2/F/125
Walter, Seend, Melk., 1594, I, W, P2/F/38
Wm., husb., Urchf., 1574, W, P2/5Reg/211A
Foord, Wm., husb., Edington, 1583, W, P2/6Reg/78C
Foord, Wm., husb., Upavon, 1605, AB, I, W, I (very detailed), P2/F/69
Wm., Damerham, Hants, 1612, AB, I, P2/F/89
Wm., sen., husb., Woodlands, Mere, 1613, AB, I, P1/F/32
Foord, Wm., shoemaker, Hindon, 1626, I, W, P2/F/133
Wm., mariner *or* sailor, Lyme R., Dorset, 1634, AB, comm, I, T (re Jn. F.), W, P16/477, P5/12Reg/297B
Wm., husb., Compton C., 1636, I, W, P2/F/169, P2/9Reg/98D
Wm., tanner, Westb., 1636, I, W, P25/1636/3
Foard, Wm., broad weaver, Seend Row, Melk., 1637, I, W, P2/F/175
Wm., cordw., Hindon, 1666, AB, I, P2/F/234
Foord, Wm., yeo., W. Kington, 1683, I, W, P3/F/176
Wm., yeo., Tinh., Edington, [1685], I, W, P2/F/320
Wm., Maiden B., [1690], W, P2/F/343
Wm., Maiden B., 1695, W, P2/F/366
Wm., sen., carp., Binfield Heath, Sonning, Berks., 1703, AB, I, P5/1703/9
Wm., Mere, 1705, AB, I, P5/1705/18
Wm., yeo., Colerne, 1709, AB, I, ren, P3/F/265
Wm., tailor, Tisb., 1710, W, P2/F/408
Wm., yeo., Englefield, Berks., 1711, W, P1/F/246, P1/5Reg/189
Wm., baker, Trowb., 1741, AB, W, P1/F/359, P1/9Reg/66
Foord, Wm., yeo., Mere, 1741, AB, I, Wr, P5/1741/13
Wm., tailor, Stapleford, 1752, W, P2/F/539
Wm., tailor, Stapleford, 1766, a/c, copy a/c, I, copy I, W, P2/F/578
Wm., yeo., Mere, 1772, W, P5/1772/8, P5/17Reg/46A
Foord, Wm., cooper, Tinh., Edington, 1777, W, P2/F/605
Wm., Bucklebury, Berks., 1779, AB, W, P1/F/480, P1/13Reg/267
Wm., yeo., Gt. Wishford, 1785, W, P2/F/636
Wm., yeo., Burton, Mere, 1807, W, Wr, P5/1807/2
Wm., W. Knoyle, 1811, AB, W, P1/1811/123
Wm., *The White Hart Inn*, Colerne, 1831, comm, W, Wr, P3/1831/8
Wm., butcher, Seend, Melk., 1839, D, O, W, Wr, P2/1839/6

see also Hutchens alias F.; Symes alias F.; Tudgy alias F.; Webb form. F.
Forder, Anthony, Sal. St Edmd., 1644, AB, P4/1644/1
Bartholomew, Long Burton, Dorset, 1665, AB, comm, P5/1665/34
Edmd., mercer, Highw., 1692, cit, W, P10/1692/3
Jn., yeo., Winterslow, 1779, AB, P2/F/614
Jn., blacksmith, Hurdcott, Winterbourne E., 1791, AB, ren, P2/F/646
My., widow, W. Dean, 1742, W, P2/F/515
Phyllis, widow, Stratford sub C. (form. of W. Dean), 1829, W, Wr, P4/1829/2
Sarah, widow, Endless St., Sal., 1845, W, Wr, P1/1845/1
Thos., shoemaker, W. Dean, 1778, AB, W, P2/F/610
Thos., Newton T., 1786, AB, grant of admon, P1/F/502
Wm., blacksmith, Winterslow, 1769, W, P2/F/585
Wm., W. Dean, 1808, W, Wr, P1/1808/8
Fordom, Robt., Amesb., 1565, W, P2/4Reg/190B
Fords *see* Ford
Forehead, Forhead, Ann, widow, Ley St., Mere, 1693, I, W, P5/1693/21
Jn., Milford, Sal. St Martin, 1791, AB, P4/1791/9
Foreman *see* Forman
Forevil, Jas., labourer, Bere R., Dorset, 1804, W, P5/1804/15
Foreward *see* Forward
Forget, Jane, sometime nun of Wilton Abbey, Mere, 1588, I, W, P5/1588/19, P5/5Reg/28A
Forhead *see* Forehead
Forlick, Jn., husb., Chilmark, 1686, NW, P2/F/325
Formage *see* Furmidge
Forman, Ann, sp., Calne, 1744, AB, comm, P26/857
Arthur, chandler, Calne, 1673, AB, a/c, comm, I, ren, P26/210
Foreman, Cicely, widow, Calne, 1687, AB, I, P26/357
Edwd., Warm., 1753, AB, P2/F/544
Foreman, Eliz., Twerton, Somerset (leaving effects at Warm.), 1841, AB, O, Wr, P2/1841/62
Geo., gent., Calne, 1755, W, P5/1755/15
Foreman, Geo., gent., Calne, 1809, W, P5/1809/19
Grace, widow, Calne, 1666, I (detailed), NW, P26/132
Foreman, Grace, widow, Warm., 1810, W, Wr, P2/1810/47
Foreman, Hester, widow, Warm. Common, 1819, comm, W, Wr, P2/1819/67
Foreman, Joan, Calne, 1692, AB, P5/1691/27
Foreman, Jn., husb., Quidh., 1601, I, W, P2/F/57
Jn., yeo., Calne, 1631, I, NW, P26/41
Jn., linen draper, Calne, 1669, I, W, P26/160
Jn., sen., grocer and victualler, Calne, 1732, comm, W, P26/771
Jn., innholder, Devizes (late of Poulshot), 1750, AB, W, P2/F/534
Foreman, My., widow, Quidh., 1605, AB, I, W, I (very detailed), P2/F/68
Foreman, Rachel, sp., Studley, Bremhill, 1809, AB, Wr, P3/1809/40
Richd., Fugg. St Peter, 1558, W, P2/3Reg/75A
Foreman, Richd., yeo., The Common, Warm., 1801, W, P2/1801/38
Roger, Hill D., 1588, AB, P5/5Reg/30D
Thos., gent., Rodbourne, Malm., 1678, AB, a/c, I, P3/F/158
Foreman, Walter, sen., Calne, 1685, AB, comm, I (detailed), P26/334
Walter, mercer, Calne, 1724, W, P26/694
Walter, Calne, 1746, AB, P5/1746/30
Wm., husb., Quidh., 1566, W, P2/4Reg/236C
Wm., jun., butcher, Calne, 1597, AB, a/c, W, P5/1596/23, P5/6Reg/150B
Wm., sen., yeo., Calne, 1599, AB, I, W, P5/1598/16, P5/6Reg/215A
Wm., jun., Calne, 1605, AB, P5/1605/23, P5/8Reg/31A
Wm., yeo., Calne, 1666, I, W, P26/133
Forrest, Anthony, Horningsham, 1625, AB, a/c, I, P5/1625/31
Eliz., widow, Sherb., Dorset, 1672, I, NW, P5/1672/12
Jas., baker and grocer, Trowb., 1856, aff, O, W, Wr, P1/1856/3
Jn., sen., Horningsham, 1671, AB, P5/1671/31
Jos., yeo., Sherb., Dorset, 1626-30, AB, a/c, court paper, D, I, ren, NW, sentence, P5/1626/16, P5/1629/18, P5/1630/4, P5/10Reg/327B, P5/11Reg/103B

Thos., Trowb., 1636, AB, I, P1/F/88
Wm., gardener, Warm., 1710, W, P2/F/406
Forrester, Abraham, gent., Sherb., Dorset, 1663, AB, comm, I (2 - 1 is damaged, in 2 pieces), P5/1663/23
Abraham, physician, Sherb., Dorset, 1746, W, P5/1746/29
Isaac, apothecary, Sherb., Dorset, 1634, AB, I(GVD), P5/1634/39
Martha, Cowesfield, Whitep., 1685, AB, P2/F/322
Robt., gent., Sherb., Dorset, 1695, AB, comm, I, ren, P5/1695/27, 58
Forrow *see* Farrow
Forsbury, Lionel, Rams., 1587, AB, T (children: Jn., Jas. & Agnes F.), P5/1587/49, P5/4Reg/142D
Forschew, Richd., yeo., Loscombe, Netherb., Dorset, 1681, I, P17/257
Forse, Jn., husb., Uffc., Devon, 1662, W (NEP), P20/1/44
Forsey, Christian, widow, Netherb., Dorset, 1662, I, W, P5/1662/45
Jn., butcher, Chards., Devon, 1845, D, W, Wr, P5/1845/18
Richd., yeo., Luccombe, Netherb., Dorset, 1742, W, P17/481
Robt., yeo., Netherb., Dorset, 1632, W, P17/14
Forsith, Cath., Devizes St Jn., 1712, AB, I, P1/F/250
Nich., Devizes, 1698, AB, I, P1/F/217
Nich., gent., Devizes, 1766, W, P1/F/449, P1/12Reg/185
Fort, [...], place lost, but is Sal., 1614, W (half-missing), P4/1614/3
Ann, widow, Mere, 1753, W, P5/1753/8
Benj., Wilton, 1718, AB, P2/F/429
Eliz., widow, W. Dean, 1736, AB, P2/F/499
Hugh, Wilton, 1623, AB, I, NW, P2/F/122
Jas., sen., feltmaker, Sal., 1681-1727, I, W, P4/1681/8, P4/1727/6
Jn., woollen weaver, Sherb., Dorset, 1610, AB, I, P5/1610/20, P5/9Reg/41C
Osmund, parchmentmaker and widower, Sherb., Dorset, 1611, I, NW, P5/1611/11, P5/9Reg/55A
Philip, bach., Coombe B., 1800, AB, P5/1800/36, P5/18Reg/308A
Richd., Sal. The Close, 1724, W, P5/1724/28, P5/16Reg/102A
Robt., Wilton, 1718, AB, W, P2/F/428
Stephen, Wilton, 1721, AB, I, P2/F/435
Wm., Semington, Steeple A., 1630, AB, P2/F/148
Fortescue, Fortiscue, Francis, sen., yeo., Baulking, Uffington, Berks., 1779, W, P1/F/482, P1/13Reg/295
Jn., Dry Sandford, Abingdon, Berks., 1801, AB, P1/1801/46, P1/15Reg/265B
Fortiscue, Wm., sen., yeo., Buckland, Berks., 1763, W, P1/F/440, P1/12Reg/45B
Forth, Edwd., cordw., Mkt. L., 1718, AB, I, P2/F/427
Grace, widow, Devizes, 1788, W, P1/F/501, P1/14Reg/183
Nathaniel, Durnford, 1695, AB, I, P9/30
Thos., provision merchant, Bradford A., 1852, O, W, Wr, P2/1852/5
Forth alias Taylor, Wm., yeo., Winterbourne G., 1686, I, W, P2/F/329
Fortiscue *see* Fortescue
Fortune, Dan., labourer, Chipp., 1768, W, P3/F/410
Giles, Crofton, Gt. Bedwyn, 1701, AB, P21/6/3
Jn., shepherd, S. Newton, 1590, I, W, P2/F/24
Jn., Amesb., 1637, AB, P2/F/174
Jn., labourer, Donhead St A., 1836, W, P2/1836/4
Richd., Seend, Melk., 1575, W, P2/5Reg/222C
Forty, Ann, widow, Fisherton A., 1849, D, W, Wr, P2/1849/32
Eliz., widow, Hungerford, Berks., 1641, I, W, P23/1013
Jas., husb., S. Marston, 1721, W, P10/1721/7
Thos., coachmaker, Marl., 1836, W, P1/1836/13
Forward, Agnes, widow, Woodlands, Mere, 1606, AB, I, W, P1/F/17
Forwarde, Alice, servant to her aunt Avis F., Mere, 1571, W, P5/2Reg/91B
Avis, widow, Ley St., Mere, 1588, AB, I, W, P5/1587/16, P5/4Reg/155B
Cath., sp., Draycot Fitzpaine, Wilcot, 1671, I, W, P1/F/140
Christian, Woodlands, Mere, 1614, I, W, P5/1613/28, P5/9Reg/126
Chris., sen., yeo., Mere, 1640, AB, a/c, I, P5/1640/17, P5/13Reg/261A
Dorothy, widow, Woodlands, Mere, 1638, I, W, P5/1638/42, P5/13Reg/115B
Dorothy, widow, Lyemarsh and Woodlands, Mere, 1679, I, W, P5/1679/29
Edwd., Woodlands, Mere, 1618, W, P5/10Reg/33
Edwd., sen., husb., Woodlands, Mere, 1618, I, W, P5/1618/14

Edwd., woollen draper, Woodlands, Mere, 1618, AB, I, W, P5/1618/15, P5/9Reg/211A
Eliz., widow, Mere, 1710, W, P5/1710/38
Eliz., widow, Wolverton, Zeals, 1711, W, P5/15Reg/220
Geo., shopkeeper, Mere, 1812, W, Wr, P5/1812/14
Giles, gent., Zeals, 1757, W, P5/1757/9
Giles, linen weaver, Wolverton, Zeals, 1792, W, P5/1792/9, P5/18Reg/176
Hannah, widow, Wolverton, Zeals, 1768, W, P5/1768/10
Hy., husb., Mere, 1662, AB, I, P5/1662/42
Hy., Hindon, 1725, AB, P2/F/457
Foreward, Joan, widow, Mere, 1567, W, P5/1Reg/83B
Jn., sen., Woodlands, Mere, 1596, AB, I, W, P5/1596/24, P5/6Reg/138B
Jn., Woodlands, Mere, 1614, AB, I, P5/1614/23, P5/9Reg/148C
Jn., White Marsh, Mere, 1614, AB, I, T, P5/1614/24, P5/9Reg/132B
Jn., husb., Mere, 1616, I, W, P5/1616/26
Jn., yeo., Woodlands, Mere, 1619, I, W, P5/1619/21, P5/10Reg/60C
Jn., Mere, 1718, AB, P5/1718/13
Jn., sen., linen weaver, Mere, 1727, W, P5/1727/14, P5/16Reg/146A
Jn., linen weaver, Mere, 1729, I, W, P5/1729/18, P5/16Reg/221D
Judith, sp., Mere, 1737, AB, P5/1737/18
Magdalen *see* Maud
My., widow, Bourton, Gillingham, Dorset, 1829, comm, W, P27/1/689
Maud *or* Magdalen, servant, Mere, 1607, AB, W, P5/1607/24, P5/8Reg/88B
Michael, linen weaver, Mere, 1728, W, P5/1728/35, P5/16Reg/168C
Rachel, widow, Abingdon, Berks., 1741, W, P1/F/360, P1/9Reg/80
Richd., Mere, 1570, AB, P5/2Reg/59B
Robt., husb., Mere, 1574, W, P5/3Reg/47D
Robt., sen., thatcher, Lyemarsh, Mere, 1686, I, W, P5/1686/24
Robt., thatcher, Mere, 1723, W, P5/1723/16, P5/16Reg/82B
Roger, thatcher, Mere, 1693, AB, I, P5/1693/23
Sarah, widow, Sal. St Edmd., 1661, I, W, P4/1661/3
Sarah, minors, no abode stated, 1670, T, P5/1669/18
Susanna, Mere, 1692, I, W, P5/1692/28
Thos., husb., Ley St., Mere, 1564, W, P5/1Reg/43B
Thos., husb., Mere, 1571, W, P5/2Reg/91A
Thos., sen., husb., Mere, 1629, I, W, P5/1629/21, P5/11Reg/29
Thos., yeo., White Marsh, Mere, 1664, AB, I, P5/1664/10
Thos., Abingdon, Berks., 1747, AB, P1/F/388
Walter, linen weaver, Wolverton, Zeals, 1705, I, ren, W, P5/1705/19
Wm., Mere, 1576, I, T, W, P5/1576/18, P5/3Reg/76D
Wm., Barrow St., Mere, 1590, I, T, W, P5/1590/23, P5/5Reg/80D
Wm., yeo., Ley St., Mere, 1596, I, W, P5/1596/25, P5/6Reg/126D
Wm., Uffc., Devon, 1692, AB, P5/1692/29
Wm., linen weaver, Mere, 1811, AB, W, Wr, P5/1811/23
Foskett, Alice, widow, Charlton nr Malm., 1598, W (value of I given), P1/2Reg/162A
Alice, widow, Milbourne, Malm., 1638, I, W, P3/F/82
Ann, widow, Charlton nr Malm., 1614, I, W, P1/F/40
Eliz., Brinkw., [1584], W, P3/1Reg/2
Eliz., widow, Brinkw., 1615, I, W, P3/F/30
Eliz., widow, Charlton nr Malm., 1672, I, W, P3/F/142
Jn., Milbourne, Malm., 1637, I, W, P3/F/79
Walter, Brinkw., 1618, AB, a/c, I, P3/F/36
Walter, schoolmaster, Brinkw., 1719, W, P1/F/269, P1/6Reg/190
Vosket, Wm., Foxham, Bremhill, [1590], W (NEP), P3/1Reg/40B
Fossett, Ann, widow, Sal., 1686, AB, P4/1685/33
Thos., yeo., Sonning, Berks., 1763, W, P5/1763/6
Foster, Aaron, yeo., Sal., 1775, W, P4/1775/4
Aaron, gent., Farley, Alderbury, 1836, W, Wr, P26/1426
Forster, Alice, widow, Wootton B., 1734, comm, W, P3/F/344
Forster alias Dalby, Ann, Avill's Farm, Corsham, 1632, AB, NW, P3/F/65
Ann, widow, Bapton, Fisherton Delamare, 1691, I, W, P2/F/347

Benj., Newbury, Berks., 1689, AB, comm, I, P1/F/180
Benj., yeo., Horningsham, 1802, AB, W, P5/1802/10, P5/19Reg/9
Cath., widow, Bapton, Fisherton Delamare, 1707, I, W, P2/F/403
Chas. Sellwood, Castle St., Sal., 1847, I, W, Wr, P4/1847/9
Eleanor, widow, Stapleford, 1596, W, P2/F/41
Eliz., widow, Horningsham, 1725, W, P5/1725/25, P5/16Reg/109C
Eliz., sp., Wootton B., 1735, W, P1/F/336, P1/8Reg/44
Foster *or* Forster, Eliz., Hurst, Berks., 1755, W, P5/1755/21
Eliz., widow, Trowb., 1818, comm, W, Wr, P1/1818/7
Emblin, widow, Newbury, Berks., 1744, W, P1/F/372, P1/9Reg/329
Forster, Geo., Trowb., 1790, AB, comm, P1/F/507
Hy., Westb., 1694, I, W, P25/1694/9
Hy., Mere, 1697, AB, I, P5/1697/14
Forster, Honour, sp., Wootton B., 1739, comm, W, P3/F/356
Isabel, widow, Stapleford, 1544, W (NEP), P2/1Reg/51B
Forster, Isabella, widow, Wootton B., 1759, W, P1/F/428, P1/11Reg/378
Jas., Gt. Faringdon, Berks., 1603, I (2 - 1 damaged), receipt, P5/1602/15, 18
Jas., Sherb., Dorset, 1674, AB, P5/1674/26
Forster, Jas., innholder, Wootton B., 1732, comm, W, copy W, P1/F/324, P1/7Reg/565B
Jas., clerk and vicar, Britford, 1787, W, P24/1168
Jas., Sal., 1789, AB, L, W, P4/1789/7
Forster, Jas., glover, Speenhamland, Berks., 1789, W, P1/F/504, P1/14Reg/237
Forster, Jas., clothier, Warm., 1800, W, P2/1800/68
Jn., Bapton, Fisherton Delamare, 1579, I, W, P2/F/16, P2/5Reg/348B
Jn., Stanley, Chipp., 1706, AB, I, P3/F/252
Jn., weaver, Sal., 1713, AB, P4/1713/2
Forster, Jn., Sherb., Dorset, 1721, AB, P5/1721/14
Jn., Sherb., Dorset, 1766, AB, comm, P5/1766/11
Forster, Jn., Warm., 1800, AB, P2/1800/64
Jn., yeo., Horningsham, 1828, note, W, Wr, P5/1828/24
Mgt., sp., Westb., 1638, I, W, P25/1638/1
Mgt., sp., Ruscombe, Berks., 1639, AB, I, P5/1639/32, P5/13Reg/193B
Mgt., widow, Westb., 1672, AB, I, P25/1672/3
Margery, widow, Sherb., Dorset, 1672, I, W, P5/1672/11
Forster, My., widow, Malm., 1732, AB, P3/F/336
My., weaver's widow, Sal., 1801, W, P1/1801/12, P1/15Reg/235A
My., widow, Sal., 1809, AB, W, P4/1809/3
Forster, Nich., weaver, Westbrook, Gt. Faringdon, Berks., 1607, I, W, P5/1607/23, P5/8Reg/103C
Peter, husb., Gt. Horningsham, 1562, W, P5/1Reg/16
Philip, Bapton, Fisherton Delamare, [1640], I, W, P2/F/197
Philip, yeo., Edington, 1720, I, draft I, W, P1/F/273, P1/6Reg/245A
Rebecca, Mere, 1693, AB, P5/1693/26
Richd., Wilton, 1612, AB, I, P2/F/88
Richd., sen., husb., Trowb., 1645, I, W, P1/F/101
Richd., yeo., Eye and Dunsden, Sonning, Berks., 1676, I, W, P5/1676/22
Richd., yeo., Bapton, Fisherton Delamare, [1697], I, W, P2/F/376
Robt., mercer, Mere, 1593, AB, I, P5/1593/34, P5/6Reg/34E
Robt., yeo., Sherb., Dorset, 1616, I, W, P5/1616/27
Robt., Horningsham, 1636, AB, P5/1636/20, P5/13Reg/15C
Robt., yeo., Sherb., Dorset, 1645, AB, I, ren, W, P5/1644/12
Robt., innholder, Westb., 1661, comm, I, W (part missing), P25/1661/4
Robt., [innkeeper], *The Bear*, Westb., 1680, AB, comm, I, W, P25/1680/13
Robt., Westb., 1693, AB, P25/1693/8
Forster, Robt., Horningsham, 1750, AB, comm, P5/1750/13
Sarah, Mere, 1693, AB, P5/1693/22
Silvester, husb., Sherb., Dorset, 1584, I, T, W, P5/1583/14, P5/4Reg/73C
Silvester, parchmentmaker, Sherb., Dorset, 1602, I, W, P5/1602/17, P5/7Reg/41A
Thos., husb., Bapton, Fisherton Delamare, 1608, W, P2/8Reg/12B
Thos., Sherb., Dorset, 1620, AB, P5/1620/20, P5/10Reg/11A
Thos., Horningsham, 1629, I, W, P5/1629/19, P5/11Reg/101B

Thos., sen., Westb., 1646, AB, I, P25/1646/2
Thos., yeo., Bapton, Fisherton Delamare, 1678, I, W, P2/F/284
Thos., carp., New Windsor, Berks., 1689, AB, comm, I, P1/F/187
Thos., clerk, Clyffe P., 1719, I, W, P3/F/292
Forster, Thos., bach., Wootton B., 1757, AB, P3/F/389
Thos., Horningsham, 1827, AB, O, W, Wr, P5/1827/57
Thos., former butler but now living independently, Ansty (form. of Compton C.), 1854, aff, W, Wr, P5/1854/5
Thos., sen., Mere, 1645-46, AB, P5/1645/8, P5/14Reg/86C
Thomasine, widow, Sherb., Dorset, 1678, comm, I, W, P5/1678/16
Wm., weaver, Sherb., Dorset, 1573, W, P5/3Reg/28C
Wm., Sherb., Dorset, 1597, AB, I, P5/1597/45, P5/6Reg/161C
Wm., Brixton D., 1619, AB, I, P2/F/106
Forster, Wm., gent., Avill's Farm, Corsham, 1673, W, P3/F/147
Forster, Wm., husb., Dinton, 1743, AB, a/c, I, P2/F/516
Forster, Wm., gent., Easthampstead, Berks., 1756, W, P1/F/419, P1/11Reg/210
Wm., yeo., Eye and Dunsden, Sonning, Berks., 1806, W, P5/1806/2, P5/19Reg/148
Forster, Wm., Woodley, W. and Sandford, Berks., 1814, AB, Wr, P5/1814/4
Forster, Wm., Limpley Stoke, Bradford A., 1818, AB, comm, Wr, P2/1818/13
Wm., carrier and shopkeeper, Compton C., 1827, W, Wr, P2/1827/72
Wolstan, Mere, 1638, AB, P5/1638/43, P5/13Reg/118A
see also Bannister alias F.; Knight alias F.; Smith alias F.; Wild alias F.
Foulkes, Fooks, Cath., widow, Netherb., Dorset, 1694, I, W, P17/331
Fook, Eliz., widow, Beam., Dorset, 1731, W, P5/1730/25
Fooks, Eliz., widow, Sutton Poyntz, Dorset, 1791, W, P5/1791/7, P5/18Reg/169C
Fook, Hugh, tailor, Beam., Dorset, 1729, W, P17/440
Foulks, Jane, wife, Sal., 1727, W, P4/1727/10
Fook, Jn., sen., butcher, Sherb., Dorset, 1619, AB, I, P5/1619/52, P5/10Reg/54C
Fook, Jn., victualler, Sherb., Dorset, 1625, AB, I, P5/1625/33, P5/10Reg/278A
Foakes, Jn., gent., Fonthill B., 1824, W, Wr, P2/1824/55
Mark, Horningsham, 1811, W, Wr, P5/1811/9
Fewkes, My., widow, Berhills Farm, Studley, Calne, 1739, W, P26/813
Fewkes, Matthew, minor, Studley, Calne, 1675, appt of guardian, P3/F/153
Foulks, Richd., gent., Sal., 1727, W, P4/1727/8
Fewkes, Richd., yeo., Berhills Farm, Studley, Calne, 1738, W, P26/805
Fooks, Robt., no abode stated, [1669], I, P2/F/245
Fook, Sibyl, widow, Sherb., Dorset, 1604, AB, I, W, P5/1604/13, P5/8Reg/19C
Foulke, Thos., yeo., Calne, 1620, I, W, P5/1619/20, P5/9Reg/231
Fooks, Thos., blacksmith, Sutton Poyntz, Dorset, 1819, W, Wr, P18/20
Fooks, Thos., Preston, Dorset, 1701, W, P5/1701/21
Fooks, Thomasine, sp., Sutton Poyntz, Dorset, 1804, W, P18/19
Fook, Walter, husb., Sherb., Dorset, 1604, I, W, P5/1604/12, P5/8Reg/9A
Fooks, Walter, jun., gent., Beam., Dorset, 1671, I (damaged), W, P5/1671/27
Fooks, Walter, innholder, Beam., Dorset, 1679, W, P5/1679/28
Fook, Wm., sen., yeo., Chetnole, Yetm., Dorset, 1594, AB, I, W, P5/1594/29, P5/6Reg/58A
Fook, Wm., sen., yeo., Sherb., Dorset, 1597, AB (2), I, NW, P5/1597/39, 41, P5/6Reg/176C, 193B
Foakes, Wm., yeo., Fonthill B., 1807, W, P1/1807/17
Found, Jn., labourer, Mildenhall, 1764, W, P3/F/403
Fouracres, Julian, husb.'s wife, Sherb., Dorset, 1760, AB, P5/1760/9
Fouthrop, Jonathan, Stoford, S. Newton, 1787, D, W, P2/F/639
Fowcher, Parnell, widow, W. Dean, 1590, I, W, P2/F/23
Walter, E. Grimstead, W. Dean, 1558, W, P2/3Reg/135A
Fowle, Alice, widow, All C., 1716, I (2 - 1 a copy), W, P3/F/281
Fowell, Ann, widow, Avill's Farm, Corsham, 1768, comm, W, P3/F/411
Vowles, Bartholomew, Ebbesborne Wake, 1617, I, T, P2/UV/25
Benj., Allington, All C., 1777, AB, P3/F/421
Cath., sp., Stanton St B., 1707, AB, comm, I, P3/F/257
Fowles, Cath., widow, Sal., 1733, AB, W, P4/1733/1
Cath., widow, Wick, Bps. C., 1814, AB, P24/1267
Dan., yeo., Stanton St B., 1837, O, W, Wr, P3/1837/15
Fowles, Edmd., weaver and size boiler, Sal. St Edmd., 1790, W, P4/1790/20

Edwd., Stanton St B., 1628, I, NW, P3/F/56
Fowles, Edwd., husb., Stockton, 1678, I, W, P2/F/282
Edwd., Stanton St B., 1679, AB, I, P3/F/164
Edwd., yeo., Manningford A., 1717, AB, W, P1/F/265, P1/6Reg/110
Edwd., gent., Manningford A., 1784-87, comm, W, P3/F/430, 437
Fowles, Frances, tailor, Sal., 1730, AB, I, W, P4/1730/17
Frances, widow, Wick, Bps. C., 1810, O, W, P24/1252
Fowles, Geoffrey, sen., yeo., Allington, All C., 1752, W, P3/F/385
Fowles, Geo., gent., Sal. The Close, 1728, AB, ren, W, P5/1728/36, P5/16Reg/210D
Fowles, Geo., sen., merchant tailor, Sal., 1732, W, P4/1732/1
Fowles, Geo., gent., Sal. The Close, 1744, req, W, copy W, Wr, P5/1744/15
Grace, widow, Stanton St B., 1602, W, P3/1Reg/91
Fowles, Hy., Whitep., 1638, I, NW, P2/F/182
Hy., Stanton St B., 1710, W, P1/F/241, P1/5Reg/243
Fowles, Hy., cordw., Short St., Dilton, Westb., 1851, comm, W, Wr, P25/1851/2
Jane, widow, Durrington, 1750, AB, comm, P1/F/400
Jane, sp., Easterton, Mkt. L., 1783, AB, W, P2/F/630
Joan, Sonning, Berks., [1542], W (NEP), P5/20Reg/38B
Faulls, Joan, widow, Winterborne K., Dorset, 1569, W, P5/2Reg/56B
Joan, widow, Allington, All C., 1698, I, W, P3/F/234
Jn., husb., Stanton St B., 1613, I, W, P1/F/31
Voule, Jn., Bramshaw, Hants, 1631, I, W, P24/269
Jn., sen., yeo., All C., 1706, I (2 - 1 a copy), W, P3/F/253
Jn., gent., Easterton, Mkt. L., 1783, AB, W, P2/F/631
Jn., gardener, Wick, Bps. C., 1836, W, P24/1347
Fowles, Jos., gent., Rams., 1731, W, P5/1731/30
Jos., Wick, Bps. C., 1814, AB, P24/1268
My., widow, Allington, All C., 1773, W, P3/F/416
Michael, Lacock, 1789, AB, comm, P3/F/443
Rebecca, widow, Manningford A., 1787, W, P3/F/438
Richd., labourer, Newtown, Shalbourne, 1576, NW, P5/3Reg/86C
Richd., Gt. Bedwyn, 1625, I, W, P5/1625/30, P5/10Reg/295B
Fowell, Richd., clerk and vicar, Avill's Farm, Corsham, 1750, comm, W, P1/F/405, P1/10Reg/438B
Fowles, Robt., yeo., Chapmanslade, Dilton, Westb., 1745, W, P25/1745/7
Fowles, Robt., yeo., Fisherton D., 1785, W, P2/F/654
Sarah, widow, Stanton St B., 1698, W, P1/F/215, P1/3Reg/174
Vowle, Thos., W. Dean, 1597, AB, I, W, P2/UV/13
Thos., yeo. *or* husb., Allington, All C., 1682, I, W, P3/F/174
Thos., yeo., Allington, All C., 1752, AB, P3/F/384
Thos., Allington, All C., 1760, AB, W, P3/F/395
Thos., victualler and gardener, Wick, Bps. C., 1780, comm, W, P24/1118
Thos., gent., Durrington, 1783, W, P2/F/629
Wm., husb., Stanton St B., [1584], W (NEP), P3/1Reg/5B
Wm., sen., gent. *or* yeo., Nether St., Bromham, 1687, I, W, P3/F/195
Wm., sen., yeo., All C., 1705, I, W, P3/F/247
Wm., Haxton, Fittleton, 1731, AB, P2/F/480
Wm., Devizes St Jn., 1769, AB, I, P1/F/454
Wm., clerk and rector, All C., 1770, comm, W, P1/F/462, P1/12Reg/386B
see also Bolsom alias V.; Pargis alias F.
Fowler, Anthony, Aldbourne, 1771, AB, ren, P3/F/414
Benj., Stanford in the Vale, Berks., 1801, AB, P1/1801/54, P1/15Reg/270A
Dan., Beam., Dorset, 1736, AB, P17/463
Edwd., Broad B., Highw., 1736, AB, I, P10/1736/2
Eliz., sp., Westb., 1704, I, W, P25/1704/9
Fawler, Geoffrey, butcher, Hungerford, Berks., 1569, W, P5/2Reg/46A
Geo., carp. and wheelwright, E. Overton, W. Overton, 1855, aff, W, Wr, P3/1855/52
Giles, yeo., Garford, Marcham, Berks., 1698, comm, I, W, P1/F/190, P1/3Reg/4
Hannah, widow, Marl., 1740, W, P1/F/354, P1/9Reg/6
Hester, linen draper, Marl., 1751, W, P1/F/407, P1/10Reg/466
Isaac Jn., auctioneer and inn keeper, Lyme R., Dorset, 1847, D, O, W, Wr, P16/445

Israel, widow, Marl. St My., 1685, W, P1/F/172
Jas., carp., Overton, 1826, W, Wr, P3/1826/29
Jane, widow, Devizes, 1688, I, W, P1/F/523
Jeremy, Poulton, 1683, comm, I, W, P3/F/177
Joan, widow, Aldbourne, 1667, comm, I, W, P3/F/115
Jn., priest, Chute & Chisenbury, 1558, collation to prebend, P1/1Reg/7D
Fawler *or* Fowler, Jn., woollen draper, Hungerford, Berks., 1607, AB, W, P5/1607/61, P5/8Reg/97B
Fawler, Jn., husb., Chilton F., 1618, I, W, P1/F/45
Fawler, Jn., Chilton F., 1635, AB, a/c, I, P3/F/73
Jn., innkeeper, Sherb., Dorset, 1638, AB, I, P5/1638/44, P5/13Reg/82B
Fawler, Jn., maltster, Hungerford, Berks., 1662, AB, comm, I, P5/1662/43
Jn., jun., linen draper, Marl. St Peter and St Paul, 1723-29, AB, comm, I (detailed), W, P1/F/288, 300, P1/7Reg/206B
Jn., innholder, Beckhampton, Avebury, 1745, I, W, P3/F/368
Jn., Stratton St Mgt., 1786, AB, P3/F/434
Jn., surgeon and apothecary, Devizes, 1840, comm, W, Wr, P1/1840/7
Lemuel, clerk, Stratton St Mgt., 1634, I, W, P3/F/71
Lemuel, innholder *or* yeo., W. Kennett, Avebury, 1671, AB, I, ren, P3/F/135
Lemuel, Devizes, 1685, AB, comm, I, P1/F/174
My., widow, Calne, 1635, I, W, P26/50
Matthias, Marl. St Peter and St Paul, 1696, AB, P1/F/209
Michael, sen., yeo., Sonning, Berks., 1716, L, W (now sojourner at dau, Mercy Lovegrove), P5/1716/29, P5/15Reg/355C
Philip, weaver, Calne, 1607, AB, I, P5/1607/25, P5/8Reg/89B
Richd., clerk, Calne, 1632, I, P30/68
Richd., husb., Chr. M., 1639, I, NW, P3/F/84
Richd., Aldbourne, 1663, AB, comm, I, P3/F/104
Fawler, Robt., tanner, Chilton F., 1683, AB, I, ren, P3/F/178
Robt., Groundwell, Blunsdon St Andrew, 1692, AB, I, P3/F/214, P10/1692/1
Fawler, Robt., sen., Chilton F., 1715, I, P3/F/280
Robt., chandler, Wantage, Berks., 1720, I (detailed), W, P23/384
Fawler, Robt., yeo., Chilton F., 1760, W, P3/F/393
Robt., yeo., Oare, Wilcot, 1835, W, P1/1835/109
Sam., carp., Avebury, 1740, W, P3/F/359
Susanna, widow, Broad B., Highw., 1802, AB, comm, P10/1802/1
Susanna, sp., Collingbourne K., 1805, AB, P3/1805/35
Thos., yeo., Aldbourne, 1621, W, P3/F/39
Thos., linen draper, Marl. St My., 1702, AB, comm, I, P1/F/223
Thos., innholder, Calne, 1735, W, P26/783
Thos., yeo., Broad B., Highw., 1775, W, P10/1775/1
Thos., yeo., Broad B., Highw., 1792, AB, comm, P10/1792/1
Wm., Lowden, Chipp., 1609, W, P3/F/13
Wm., clerk, Berwick B., 1631, AB, I, P5/1631/38, P5/12Reg/39B
Wm., shearman, Marl., [1668], W, P1/F/135
Wm., Hawkeridge, Westb., 1693, AB, I, P25/1693/9
Wm., alehouse keeper, Avebury, 1765, W, P3/F/406
see also Clement alias F.
Fowles *see* Fowle
Fownes, Meliora, widow, Netherh., 1778-79, comm, req, copy W, P2/F/611
Thos., gent., Marl., 1662, I, W, P1/F/112
Fox, [...] *see* James Codd, clerk, Whaddon
Adam, farmer, Thornford, Dorset, 1850, case (includes copy W & copy deed of gift), deed of gift, D, form of O, O, ren (2), W, Wr, P5/1850/6
Ann, sp., Sherb., Dorset, 1730, W, P5/1730/22
Anthony, Trowle, Bradford A., [1624], I, W, P2/F/124
Baruch, apothecary, Sherb., Dorset, 1720, W, P5/1720/20, P5/16Reg/46B
Brian, Winterbourne G., 1612, AB, I, P2/F/91
Edmd., yeo., Cowesfield, Whitep., [1665-73], I, W, P2/F/232, 269
Edwd., W. Dean, 1642, I, P2/F/202
Eliz., widow, Warm., 1744, AB, P1/F/377
Eliz., widow, Hungerford, Berks., 1801, comm, W, P23/824
Geo., sen., yeo., Trowle, Bradford A., [1668], I, P2/F/241

Geo., innkeeper, Sal., 1768, W, P4/1768/10
Hy., gent., Sal., 1663, AB, I, P1/F/122
Hy., shepherd, Flamston, Bishopstone S., 1663, AB, I, P2/F/227
Hy., Westport St My., 1730, W. Not proved., P3/F/329
Jas., Whitep., 1773, AB, P1/F/465
Jas., carp., Hungerford, Berks., 1828, W, P23/937
Jane, widow, New Windsor, Berks., 1729, comm, W, P1/F/303, P1/7Reg/228B
Joan, Trowle, Bradford A., 1594, I, W, P2/F/39
Jn., Bradford A., 1558, W, P2/3Reg/87B
Jn., Trowle, Bradford A., 1590, I, copy I (2), W, P2/F/26
Jn., Wanb., 1740, AB, P3/F/360
Jn., tailor, Tilehurst, Berks., 1756, W, P1/F/418, P1/11Reg/203
Jn., victualler, Melk., 1791, W, P2/F/647
Jn., grocer, Melk., 1818, W, Wr, P2/1818/42
Voxe, My., widow, Bradford A., 1621, I, P2/UV/29
Nathaniel, tobacconist, Sherb., Dorset, 1720, W, P5/1720/19, P5/16Reg/48A
Philip, husb., Mere, 1589, I, W, P5/1589/18, P5/5Reg/51A
Richd., parson, Whaddon, 1549, W, P2/2Reg/83A
Stephen, yeo., Sal. The Close, 1683, I, W, P1/F/169
Stephen, innholder, Warm., 1737, W, P2/F/501
Stephen, yeo., Whitep., 1837, W, Wr, P2/1837/30
Stephen, Cowesfield, Whitep., 1856, aff, W, Wr, P2/1856/23
Thos., labourer, Twyford, Hurst, Berks., 1635, I, W, P5/1635/37, P5/12Reg/197
Thos., yeo., Cowesfield, Whitep., 1639, I, W, P2/F/188
Thos., blacksmith, Ebbesborne Wake, 1752, W, P2/F/538
Thos., cordw., Rams., 1847, D (2), O (2), W (& cod), Wr, P5/1847/24
Wm., Chute, 1628, I, W, P5/1628/42, P5/11Reg/10
Wm., parish clerk, Sal., 1677, W, P4/1677/18
Wm., labourer, Donnington, Berks., 1823, W, Wr, P1/1823/101
Wm., cordw., Rams., 1835, comm, W, Wr, P5/1835/25
Foxanger, Jas., Britford, 1692, AB, I, P24/537
Foxly, Emma, widow, Ashton K., 1634, I, W, P1/F/75
Jas., husb., Ashton K., 1622, I, W, P3/F/43
Foye, Jas., priest, Upavon, 1557, institution to vicarage, P1/1Reg/6C
Jn., Chetnole, Yetm., Dorset, 1585, W, P5/4Reg/106B
Foyle, Hy., Swallowcliffe, 1753, AB, P5/1752/18
Jas., Tisb., 1844, AB, Wr, P2/1844/65
Jn., sen., husb., Dinton, 1752, W, P2/F/542
Foyell, Jn., Shrewton, 1789, AB, ren, P2/F/643
Wm., Ebbesborne Wake, 1669, AB, P2/F/250
Wm., sen., yeo., Bower C., 1724, W, P2/F/451
Wm., yeo., Bower C., 1734, W, P2/F/495
Frame, Abigail, Broomfield, Yatton K., 1705, I, W, P3/F/248
Freem, Hy., yeo., Broomfield, Yatton K., 1742, W, P3/F/364
Freem, Hy., innholder, Yatton K., 1744-86, AB, comm, W, P3/F/436
Jas., yeo., Trowb., 1797, comm, W, P1/F/514, P1/15Reg/10
Jn., husb., Charlton nr Malm., 1609, I, W (both on same sheet), P3/F/14
Freame, Jn., Broomfield, Yatton K., 1692, AB, I, P3/F/215
Freem, Jn., yeo., Easton Piercy, Kington St M., 1717, W, P3/F/284
Freame, Jn., sen., yeo., Cromhall, Kington St M., 1729, W, P1/F/311, P1/7Reg/312
Jn., tailor, Seagry, 1830, O, W, Wr, P3/1830/37
Freeme, Jonathan, woolstapler, Devizes, 1718, AB, W, P1/F/267, P1/6Reg/168
Freem, My., widow, Kington St M., 1731, W, P3/F/334
Freeme, Phyllis, widow, Devizes, 1705, W, P1/F/227
Freeme, Rebecca, sp., Devizes, 1705, W, P1/F/228
Robt., yeo., Dauntsey, 1663, I, W, P3/F/105
Freame, Ruth, widow, Avill's Farm, Corsham, 1786, AB, P3/F/435
Freame, Sam., staymaker, Corsham, 1786, W, P29/F/15, P29/2Reg/188
Thos., Dauntsey, 1665, AB, I, P3/F/109
Wm., husb., Garsdon, 1652, AB, comm, I, P1/F/111

Frampton, Alice, sp., Hermitage, Dorset, 1833, AB, comm, W, Wr, P5/1833/11
Helena, widow, W. Harnham, 1819, W, Wr, P8/79
Jas., carp. and builder, Swindon, 1848, comm, W, Wr, P3/1848/1
Jn., shepherd, Warm., 1619, I, W, P2/F/107
Jn., husb., Tidpit, Martin, Hants, 1699, I, W, P2/F/382
Jn., wheelwright, Anderson, Dorset, 1703, AB, ren, W, P5/1703/10, P5/1704/22
Jn., Bloxworth, Dorset, 1704, AB, I, P5/1704/21
Jn., Stratford sub C. (*also* of Plympton, Devon), 1765, AB, P4/1765/13
Jn., Anderson, Dorset, 1767, W, P5/1767/22
Lucy, sp., Fisherton A., 1821, W, Wr, P2/1821/9
Mgt., Bloxworth, Dorset, 1722, AB, P5/1722/23
My., widow, Anderson, Dorset, 1777, W, P5/1777/7, P5/17Reg/134B
Richd., yeo., Stratford Tony, 1808, req, W, Wr, P2/1808/25
Robt., yeo., Bere R., Dorset, 1729, W, P5/1729/19, P5/16Reg/225B
Thos., yeo., Sal., 1664, I, W, P1/F/125
Thos., vicar, Broad H., 1753, W, P1/F/412, P1/11Reg/143A
Thos., Longbridge D., 1768, AB, P2/F/582
Walter, Martin, Hants, 1719, AB, P2/F/430
Wm., yeo., Milford, Sal. St Martin, 1708, AB, I, P1/F/234
Wm., Bloxworth, Dorset, 1730, AB, P5/1730/23
Wm., yeo., Fordington, Dorset, 1778, W, P15/156
Frances *see* Francis
Franch *see* French
Francis, Alexander, Bradford A., 1686, AB, I, P2/F/327
Ann, widow, Stapleford, 1699, AB, I, NW, P2/F/384
Ann, widow, E. Ilsley, Berks., 1779, W, P1/F/479, P1/13Reg/257B
Ann, widow, N. Bradley, 1822, comm, W, Wr, P2/1822/26
Ann, sp., Sal. (form. of Maddington), 1849, W, Wr, P4/1849/3
Cath., widow, W. Stowell, Alton Pr., 1751, AB, W, P3/F/380
Dan., N. Bradley, 1818, AB, comm, Wr, P2/1818/1
David, Easterton, Mkt. L., 1733, AB, W, P2/F/488
David, carp., Easterton, Mkt. L., 1756, LA, W, P2/F/549
Edwd., yeo., Aldbourne, 1726, W, P3/F/312
Edwd., victualler, Westb. L., 1727, W, P25/1727/2
Frances, Edwd., Rams., 1753, W, P5/1753/9
Edwd., yeo., N. Bradley, 1782, W, P2/F/626
Edwd., Norris Hill Farm, N. Bradley, 1854, aff, O, W, Wr, P2/1854/44
Elias, gent., Berwick St Jas., 1682, W, P1/F/160
Eliz., widow, Bodenham, Nunton and B., 1672, AB, W, P2/F/260
Eliz., widow, Westb. L. (to be buried in the Upper Meeting house), 1831, O, W, Wr, P25/1833/4
Eliz., widow, Southwick, N. Bradley, 1855, aff, W, Wr, P1/1855/52
Eliz., servant to Hy. Chever, W. Lavington, c1570, W (NEP); undated, P1/1Reg/43A
Emma, Stapleford, 1687, AB, P2/F/336
Geo., Asserton, Berwick St Jas., 1666, I, W, P1/F/132
Hy., Sal. St Thos., 1621, AB, I, P4/1621/9
Jacob, gent., Westb. L., 1814, O, W, Wr, P25/1814/5
Jas., yeo., N. Bradley, 1810, AB, W, Wr, P2/1810/54
Jas., N. Bradley, 1820, AB, comm, Wr, P1/1820/55
Jas., labourer, Southwick, N. Bradley, 1857, aff, O, W, Wr, P2/1857/16
Jane, widow, Abingdon, Berks., 1747, AB, I, P1/F/386
Jeremiah, yeo., N. Bradley, 1773, W, P2/F/592
Jeremiah, yeo., N. Bradley, 1819, W, Wr, P2/1819/51
Frances, Joan, widow, Hanging L., 1592, AB, I, P2/F/28
Job, yeo., N. Bradley, 1779, W, P1/F/483, P1/13Reg/302
Job, innkeeper and farmer, Westb. L., 1849, AB, comm, ren, W, Wr, P25/1849/1
Frances, Jn., servant in husbandry, Smallbrook, Warm., 1573, W, P2/5Reg/167A
Jn., Upton, Blewbury, Berks., 1579, I, T, W, P5/1579/32, P5/3Reg/141C
Frances, Jn., Allington, 1604, I, W, P3/F/1
Jn., husb., Bodenham, Nunton and B., 1671, I, W, P2/F/256
Jn., sen., husb., Gt. Wishford, 1681, I, W, P2/F/296

Jn., carp., Brook, Westb., 1684, AB, I, P25/1684/8
Jn., Manton, Preshute, 1692, AB, comm, P1/F/191
Jn., Broad C., 1696-1700, AB, P2/F/368, 386
Jn., blacksmith, Sal., 1702, AB, I, P4/1702/7
Jn., Penleigh, Dilton, Westb., 1711, AB, I, P25/1711/13
Jn., millwright, Westb. L., 1714, I, W, P25/1714/11
Frances, Jn., shopkeeper, Ebbesborne Wake, 1735, W, P1/F/329, P1/7Reg/627B
Jn., Homington, 1737, AB, P24/920
Jn., victualler, Horningsham, 1763, W, P5/1763/7
Jn., Hanging L., 1767, W (NEP), P30/69
Jn., Eye and Dunsden, Sonning, Berks., 1823, AB, Wr, P5/1823/14
Jn., N. Bradley, 1839, O, W, Wr, P2/1839/30
Jn., Devizes, 1846, AB, O, Wr, P1/1846/33
Jos., yeo., N. Bradley, 1805, W, P2/1805/39
Josiah, bach., Barford St M., 1855, AB, aff, Wr, P2/1855/21
Frances, Mgt., widow, Marl. & Manton, Preshute, 1693, AB, I, P1/F/200
My., widow, W. Harnham, 1755, AB, I, P8/42
My., widow, Codf. St P., 1832, AB, Wr, P2/1832/10
Melchisadech, clerk, Lt. Hinton, 1635, I, W, P1/F/85
Richd., sen., yeo., Rams., 1755, W, P5/1755/16
Richd., labourer, N. Bradley, 1775, W, P2/F/600
Richd., draper, Marl., 1790, W, P1/F/506, P1/14Reg/342
Francies, Richd., yeo., Codf. St P., 1822, W, Wr, P2/1822/55
Sarah, widow, Southwick, N. Bradley, 1846, comm, W, Wr, P2/1846/4
Stephen, husb., Hanging L., 1607-08, a/c, I, T, P2/F/73
Frances, Stephen, yeo., Hanging L., 1733, I, W, P2/F/487
Frances, Thos., Hanging L., 1576, W, P2/5Reg/250A
Frances, Thos., [weaver], Dilton, Westb., 1630, AB, I, P25/1630/1
Thos., Hanging L., 1663, AB, I, P1/F/123
Thos., sen., burler, Westb. L., 1691, I, NW, P25/1691/4
Frances, Thos., Benham Valence, Speen, Berks., 1692, I, W, P1/F/195
Thos., W. Stowell, Alton Pr., 1734, W, P3/F/345
Thos., [hatter], Abingdon, Berks., 1735, AB, I, P1/F/330
Thos., Appleford, Sutton C., Berks., 1763, AB, P1/F/445
Thos., Sonning Common, Berks., 1835, W, Wr, P5/1835/22
Frances, Wm., Yatesbury, 1594, I, W, P5/1594/30, P5/6Reg/87B
Wm., Marl., 1785, AB, P1/F/496
Wm., innkeeper, Devizes, 1824, W, Wr, P1/1824/10
see also Matthews alias F.
Francome *see* Frankham
Frank, Amos, yeo., Uffc., Devon, 1664, I, W, P20/1/48
Amos, Uffc., Devon, 1681, AB, P20/1/95
Jn., curate, Idmiston, 1564, AB, I, P2/F/675, P2/4Reg/171C
Jos., Uffc., Devon, 1715, AB, P20/1/154
Susanna, Uffc., Devon, 1697, AB, P20/1/133
Frank alias Mason, Susanna, sp., Overton, 1617, I, W, P3/F/33
see also Mason alias F.
Frankham, Cath., widow, Allington, Chipp., 1624, I, W, P3/F/48
Hy., husb., Allington, Chipp., 1623, I, W, P3/F/45
Joan, widow, Allington, Chipp., 1632, I, W, P3/F/66
Jn., yeo., Charlton nr Malm., 1671, I, W, P3/F/136
Frankam, Jn., yeo., Charlton nr Malm., 1687, I, W, P3/F/196
Francome, Jn., widower, Minety, 1705, AB (2), P3/F/249
Francome, Jn., yeo., Purton, 1815, W, Wr, P3/1815/32
Francome, Jos., yeo., Minety, 1855, aff, comm, W, Wr, P3/1855/40
Francome, Richd., gent., Purton, 1797, W, Wr, P3/F/448
Robt., tailor, Chittoe, Bps. C., 1638, I, W, P24/302
Sam., Corsham, 1714, marriage licence, P29/2Reg/10A
Thos., yeo., Charlton nr Malm., 1669, AB, comm, I, P3/F/126
Francome, Thos., yeo., Braydon (form. of Minety), 1718, I, W, P3/F/293

Francome, Wm., yeo., Chittoe, Bps. C., 1795, comm, W, P24/1215
Frankland, Jn., cloth dresser, Sal., 1844, D, W, Wr, P1/1844/6
Franklin, Alexander, yeo., Downton, 1545, W (NEP), P2/1Reg/53
Alice, widow, Newbury, Berks., 1664, AB, I, W, P1/F/126
Alice, widow, Sherston, 1708, I, W, P3/F/260
Ann, widow, Downton, 1554, W, P2/2Reg/190C
Ann, widow, Broad H., [1604], I, W (NEP), P3/F/2
Ann, widow, Broad H., 1626, I, W, P3/F/53
Ann, widow, Overton, 1671, I, W, P3/F/137
Anthony, husb., Milton L., 1602, W, P3/1Reg/68A
Franlyn, Anthony, proved at Newbury, Berks., 1686, I, W, P1/F/524
Benj., husb., Broad B., Highw., 1681, comm, I, W, P10/1681/3
Benj., sen., tailor, Wootton B., 1780, W, P3/F/426
Benj., tailor, Wootton B., 1838, comm, W, Wr, P3/1838/52
Christian, widow, Marl. St My., 1604, W, P1/F/8
Chris., maltster, Purton, 1707, I, W, P3/F/258
Cicely, widow, Wokm., Berks., 1609, AB, I, W, P5/1609/30, P5/8Reg/146A
Dan., gent., Sutton V., 1629-32, I, W, P2/F/144, 154
Dorothy, widow, Wrou., [1612], W (NEP), P3/F/22
Dorothy, widow, Broad H., 1679, AB, P3/F/165
Edith, schoolmaster's widow, Bromham, [1642], I, W (NEP), P3/F/98
Edwd., jun., broad weaver, Melk., 1633, I, NW, P2/F/162
Edwd., yeo., Overton, 1663, AB, comm, I, P3/F/106
Edwd., gent., Grove Farm, Mildenhall, 1674, AB, I, P3/F/151
Edwd., mason, Pott., 1690, AB, I, P1/F/188
Edwd., Overton, 1698, I, W, P3/F/235
Edwd., Overton, 1704, AB, I, P1/F/225
Edwd., sergemaker, Melk., 1704, AB, I, ren, P2/F/395
Edwd., fuller, Lady Down Mill, Trowb., 1817, comm, W, Wr, P1/1817/102
Eleanor, Broad H., [1590], W (NEP), P3/1Reg/36B
Eliz., widow, Sal., 1761, W, P4/1761/13
Eliz., widow, Cholswell, Abingdon, Berks., 1770, W, P1/F/457, P1/12Reg/354A
Eliz., widow, Calne, 1772, comm, W, P26/1060
Eliz., sp., Crickl. St S., 1787, W, Wr, P3/F/439
Francis, yeo., E. Everleigh, Everleigh, 1745, W, P3/F/369
Francis, bach., Everleigh, 1759, AB, comm, P3/F/392
Francis, yeo., Lacock, 1806, W, Wr, P3/1806/62
Geo., Devizes St Jn., 1635, I, W, P1/F/83
Geo., Broad H., 1682, AB, comm, I, P3/F/175
Geo., sen., Everleigh, 1701, I, W, P3/F/240
Geo., tailor, Steeple A., 1729, W, P2/F/470
Geo., yeo., Everleigh, 1747, W, P1/F/391, P1/10Reg/135
Gilbert, yeo., Purton, 1639, I, W, P3/F/85
Giles, gent., Wrou., 1639, comm, I, W, P3/F/86
Grace, Allington, Chipp., undated, late 16th C., W (NEP), P3/1Reg/34A
Henrietta Maud, widow, Abingdon, Berks., 1826, W, Wr, P1/1826/76
Hy., Fisherton A., 1567, AB, P2/5Reg/4D
Hy., Milton L., 1614, I, P3/F/27
Hy., gent., Sherston, 1686, I (detailed), ren, W, P3/F/188
Jas., miller, E. Kennett, 1623, I, W, P3/F/46
Jas., Gt. Bedwyn, 1698-99, AB (2 - 2nd in 1699 as widow d. before admg), I, P21/5/40
Jas., Everleigh, 1735, AB, P1/F/328
Frauncklen, Joan, Gt. Bedwyn, 1613, AB, P5/1613/27, P5/9Reg/97A
Joan, widow, Sherston, 1614, I, W, P3/F/26
Frankling, Joel, yeo., Reading, Berks., 1817, W, Wr, P1/1817/66
Jn., Chaddington, Lydiard T., 1563, W, P1/2Reg/124A
Jn., Castleton, Dorset, 1574, AB, P5/3Reg/32A
Jn., Sherb., Dorset, 1574, AB, P5/3Reg/46D
Jn., Sonning, Berks., 1591, AB, P5/5Reg/118
Jn., Sonning, Berks., 1591, AB, I, P5/1591/24

Jn., husb., Coulston, Edington, 1597, I, W, P2/F/47
Jn., clothier, Calne, 1630, I, W, P26/39
Jn., no abode stated, 1635, I, W, P2/F/168, P2/9Reg/84D
Frankling, Jn., Sherston & Crickl. St S., 1638-41, AB, I, P1/F/90, P3/F/96
Jn., Sherston, 1646, AB, court paper, P3/F/100
Jn., tailor, Wootton B., 1648, AB, I, NW (d. of plague), P1/F/108
Jn., Seend, Melk., 1669, AB, P2/F/249
Jn., yeo., Sutton V., [1675], I, W, P2/F/275
Jn., freemason, Box, 1693, I, W, P3/F/219
Jn., sen., mason, Melk., 1697, AB, I, P2/F/381
Jn., gent., Woodb., 1710, AB, P3/F/268
Jn., yeo., Purton, 1723, AB, I, P3/F/301
Jn., gent., Woodb., 1725, W, P3/F/308
Jn., rough mason, Seend, Melk., 1726, W, P2/F/458
Jn., yeo., Lydiard M., 1852, O, W, Wr, P3/1852/47
Jonathan, blanketmaker and innholder, Avill's Farm, Corsham, 1749, AB, I, ren, P3/F/376
Judith, widow, Devizes St My., 1748, AB, ren, W, P1/F/394, P1/10Reg/217
Lucy Ann, widow, Ham, 1842, AB, comm, Wr, P3/1842/16
Margery, widow, Grove & Wantage, Berks. form.of Uffington, Berks., 1716, I, W, P5/1716/30, P5/15Reg/353A
My., widow, Longcott, Shrivenham, Berks., 1711, I, W, P1/F/245, P1/5Reg/133A
My., widow, Sal., 1721, I, W, P4/1721/17
My., widow, Compton, Enford, 1734, W, P2/F/494
My., sp., Melk., 1745, AB, comm, I, P2/F/524
Micah, sen., husb., Compton, Enford, 1772, W, P2/F/442
Nich., Thornhill, Clyffe P., 1686, AB, I, P3/F/189
Peregrine, yeo., Bromham, 1670, comm, I, W, P3/F/131
Philip, gent., Marl., 1683, AB, I, ren, W, P1/F/161
Philip, Sherston, 1706, AB, P3/F/254
Frankling, Priscilla, singlewoman, Melk., 1757, comm, W, P2/F/551
Rebecca, widow, Overton, 1706-15, AB (2), I, W, P3/F/255
Richd., Seend Marsh, Melk., 1571, W, P2/5Reg/117C
Richd., sawyer, Marl. St My., 1598, grant of admon, I, P1/F/6
Richd., yeo., Sherston, 1608, I, W, P3/F/9
Richd., schoolmaster, Bromham, [1642], I, W (NEP), P3/F/99
Richd., yeo., Broad H., 1647, AB, comm, I, P1/F/105
Richd., gent., Wrou., 1673, AB, comm, I, P3/F/148
Richd., Overton, 1713, W, P3/F/277
Richd., gent., Wrou., 1744, comm, W, P1/F/374, P1/9Reg/382B
Richd., victualler, Poulshot, 1752, W, P2/F/543
Robt., yeo., Melk., 1670, AB, ren, P2/F/255
Robt., fuller, Devizes, 1741, W, P1/F/363, P1/9Reg/213
Robt., carp., Steeple A., 1744, W, P1/F/379, P1/9Reg/410A
Robt., Lydiard M., 1809, AB, Wr, P3/1809/67
Robt., Devizes, 1817, AB, Wr, P1/1817/87
Sam., mason, Seend Row, Melk., 1716, AB, I, ren, P1/F/264
Frankling, Sam., yeo., Melk. Common, 1798, comm, W, P2/F/666
Sarah, widow, Woodb., 1676, AB, I, P3/F/155
Sarah, sp., Marl., 1796, W, P1/F/513, P1/15Reg/1
Thos., yeo., Sutton V., 1586, W, P2/7Reg/54B
Thos., yeo., Chaddington, Lydiard T., 1605, I, W, P1/F/14
Thos., fuller, Bromham, 1630, I, NW, P3/F/62
Thos., Pott., 1680, I, W, P1/F/156
Thos., Stratford sub C., 1688, AB, P4/1688/14
Thos., Bishopstone N., 1703, I, W, P6/89
Thos., yeo., Fawley, Berks., 1720, I, W, P1/F/279, 284, P1/6Reg/322B
Thos., Sal. The Close, 1754, AB, P5/1754/5
Frankling, Thos., yeo., Marcham, Berks., 1770, W, P1/F/459, P1/12Reg/366
Walter, Wokm., Berks., 1591-92, AB, I, W, P5/1591/25, P5/1592/32, P5/5Reg/132
Wm., husb., Eddington, Hungerford, Berks., 1585, I, W, P5/1585/3, P5/4Reg/111
Wm., innholder, Castleton, Dorset, 1609, AB, I, P5/1609/32, P5/9Reg/7A

Frankling, Wm., tanner, Dilton, Westb., 1615, a/c, I, P25/1615/3
Wm., yeo. *or* husb., Hook, Lydiard T., 1621, I, W, P3/F/40
Wm., husb., Warm., 1633, I, W, P2/F/160
Wm., yeo., Sutton V., 1695, comm, I, W, P1/F/207
Wm., Broad H., 1699, AB, P3/F/236
Wm., New Windsor, Berks., 1723, AB, P1/F/286
Wm., Hook, Lydiard T., 1729, W, P1/F/310, P1/7Reg/282B
Wm., yeo., Melk., 1732, W, P2/F/486
Wm., yeo., Sutton V., 1736-86, note of admon, W, P2/F/500
Wm., Gt. Bedwyn, 1782, AB, P21/11/23
Wm., carp., Lydiard M., 1798, W, P1/F/518, P1/15Reg/95
Wm., maltster, Stanford in the Vale, Berks., 1820, W, Wr, P1/1820/11
Frapell, Gowen, sen., husb., Berwick St Jas., 1685, I, W, P1/F/173
Frapwell, Gowen, Berwick St Jas., 1716, AB, P1/F/260
My., wife, Berwick St Jas., 1708, AB, P1/F/239
Frasier, Eliz., widow, Sherb., Dorset, 1808, W, Wr, P5/1808/10
Frauncklen *see* Franklin
Frawley, Robt., bookkeeper, Trowb., 1836, comm, W, Wr, P1/1836/6
Fray, Ann, sp., Milford, Sal. St Martin, 1815, W, P4/1815/6
Frey, Anthony, tanner, Blewbury, Berks., 1691, AB, I, ren, W, P5/1691/24
Edwd., mason, Tisb., 1784, W, P2/F/634
Jas., plasterer, Tisb., 1799, W, P2/F/669
Jn., Burghfield, Berks., 1638, AB, I, P1/F/91
Frey, Mgt., widow, W. Kennett, Avebury, 1692, I, W, P3/F/216
see also Fry
Frayling, Ann, widow, Heddington Wick, 1697, W, P3/F/233
Cath., widow, Chipp. (form. of Calne), 1738, AB, comm, W, P1/F/349, P1/8Reg/350
Chas., Odell, Bedfordshire (leaving effects at Calne), 1841, AB, comm, Wr, P26/1453
Geo., victualler, Bremhill, 1838, comm, W, Wr, P3/1838/14
Geo., butcher, Calne, 1848, O, W, Wr, P5/1848/18
Hannah, widow, Calne, 1846, comm, W, Wr, P5/1846/2
Hannah, sp., Calne, 1849-50, AB (2), O (2), Wr, P5/1849/11, P5/1850/14
Hy., innholder, *The Black Boy*, Calne, 1726, W, P26/711
Jn., sen., husb., Heddington, 1631, I, W, P1/F/67
Jn., sen., butcher, Calne, 1687, I, W, P26/363
Jn., gent., Heddington Wick, 1689, comm, I, W, P3/F/201
My., widow, Heddington, 1737, W, P3/F/352
Rachel, widow, Calne, 1663, AB, I, NW, P5/1663/24
Robt., Heddington, 1737, AB, comm, P3/F/353
see also Stevens alias F.
Freame *see* Frame
Frebbins, Frebence *see* Fribbins
Frecke *see* Freke
Freegard, Chas., yeo., Melk., 1809, W, Wr, P2/1809/20
Geo., yeo., Dauntsey, 1840, W, Wr, P3/1840/40
Hy., Charlton nr Malm., 1844, AB, O, Wr, P3/1844/3
Jas., Naish House, Bremhill, 1806, comm, W, P3/1806/42
Jas., farmer, Whitley, Melk., 1856, aff, comm, W, P2/1856/42
Job, retired boot and shoemaker, Calne, 1851, comm, W, Wr, P5/1851/4
Jn., Charlcote, Bremhill, 1837, comm, W, Wr, P3/1837/17
Jn., Lacock, 1838, AB, O, ren, Wr, P3/1838/54
Freem *see* Frame
Freeman, Ann, widow *or* wife, Wrou., 1687, I, W, P3/F/197
Benj., Wrou., 1724, AB, P3/F/304
Cath., widow, Castle Eaton, 1685, I, W, P3/F/187
Charity, Marl., 1684, AB, I, P1/F/170
Chris., maltster, Marl., 1712, AB, I, P1/F/254
Dan., Rams., 1616, AB, I, P5/1616/25, P5/9Reg/173A
Eleanor, widow, Chilton, Berks., 1611, AB, I, P1/F/27
Eleanor, Crudwell, [1611], W (NEP), P3/F/19

Eliz., widow, Rams., 1640, I, W, P5/1640/19, P5/13Reg/255
Eliz., widow, Sal., 1776, W, P4/1776/6
Eliz., widow, Walcot, Swindon, 1825, comm, W, Wr, P3/1825/6
Geo., clothier, Bradford A., 1776, W, P2/F/603
Giles, sen., skinner, Sal. St Thos., 1669, I, W, P4/1668/2
Giles, Sal., 1694, AB, P4/1693/12
Hy., Steeple L., 1571, W (ref. to wintering of sheep), P1/1Reg/31A
Hy., proved at Reading, Berks., 1625, I, W, P1/F/54
Jas., broad weaver, Westwood, 1827, W, Wr, P2/1827/1
Jn., Twyford, Hurst, Berks., 1543, W, P5/20Reg/46C
Jn., husb., Upton, Blewbury, Berks., 1612-13, I, W, P5/1612/18, P5/9Reg/105A
Jn., Wrou., 1640, I, W, P3/F/92
Jn., Sal. The Close, 1673, AB, I, P5/1673/15
Jn., sen., weaver, Wrou., 1681, I, W, P3/F/171
Jn., Wrou., 1687, AB, I, ren, W, P3/F/198
Jn., gent., Highw., 1714, W, P10/1714/3
Jn., yeo., Coate, Liddington, 1788, W, P3/F/441
Jn., yeo., Walcot, Swindon, 1823, comm, W, Wr, P1/1823/141
Martha, innholder, Lyme R., Dorset, 1807, comm, W, P16/367
Ralph, innholder, Lyme R., Dorset, 1794, W, P5/1794/9, P5/18Reg/204B
Robt., husb., Wokm., Berks., 1709, W, P5/1709/12, P5/15Reg/132
Robt., maltster, Marl., 1736, W, P1/F/341, P1/8Reg/161B
Rowland, yeo., Ewen, Kemble, 1667, comm, I, W, P3/F/116
Sam., Sal., 1770, AB, P1/F/455
Thos., sen., Rams., 1628, AB, a/c, I, P5/1627/16, P5/11Reg/43F
Thos., victualler, Sal., 1758, W, P4/1758/8
Thos., tinplate worker, Sal., 1764, W, P4/1764/2
Thos., Waltham St Lawr., Berks., 1804, W (living at house of Richd. Cusler), P1/1804/49
Thomasine, widow, Sal., 1706, W, P1/F/232
Wm., yeo., Charlton, Donhead St My., 1662, I, W, P1/F/121
Freemantle, Alice, widow, Winterbourne E., 1696, AB, I, P2/F/372
Ann, widow, Fisherton A., 1759, W, P2/F/554
Benj., yeo., Fisherton A., 1738, W, P1/F/345, P1/8Reg/227
Jn., sen., Heytes., 1730, W, P5/1730/21
Richd., yeo., Laverstock, [1695], I, W, P2/F/367
Robt., yeo., Boscombe, 1721, W, P2/F/438
Robt., gent., Idmiston (late of Boscombe), 1783, W, P2/F/628
Wm., yeo., Winterbourne E., [1694], I, W, P2/F/361
Wm., yeo., Hurdcott, Winterbourne E., 1715, W, P2/F/419
Wm., tucker, Sal., 1742, W, P4/1742/18
Wm., tucker, Sal., 1745, W, P4/1745/12
Freeme *see* Frame
Freepens *see* Fribbins
Freestone, Hy., Hindon, 1620, AB, I, P1/F/51
Jonathan, day labourer, Wilton, 1689, I, W, P2/F/340
Robt., husb. [and fellmonger], Westb. L., 1615, AB, I, P25/1615/1
Roger, Westb., 1570, W, P5/2Reg/83A
Thos., Sal., 1612, AB, P4/1611/6
Wm., Hindon, 1684, AB, I, P2/F/309
Freke, Dorothy, Fordington, Dorset, 1670, I, W, P15/15
Geo., gent., Gillingham, Dorset, 1686, I, P27/1/90
Jane, Gillingham, Dorset, 1783, W, P27/1/513, P27/3Reg/230
Jn., gent., Gillingham, Dorset, 1711, I, W, P27/1/186
My., widow, Fordington, Dorset, 1720, I, copy I, P15/77
Ralph, esquire, Hannington, 1762, AB, comm, ren, P3/F/398
Robt., Fordington, Dorset, 1641, AB, I, P5/1641/34, P5/14Reg/29A
Frick, Thos., yeo., Sedgehill, [1683], I, P2/F/306
Thos., yeo., Whitchurch, Malm., 1833, W, Wr, P3/1833/45
Frick *or* Frecke, Wm., yeo., Warm., 1563, I, W, P2/F/7, P2/4Reg/123B
Wm., weaver, Fordington, Dorset, 1704, AB, I, P15/69

French, Alice, widow, Kingston D., 1586, W, P2/7Reg/60A
Edith, Halstock, Dorset, 1597, AB, P5/1597/44, P5/6Reg/161B
Frances, husb. (Hy.)'s daughter, Sherb., Dorset, 1610, AB, I, W, P5/1610/21
Francis, druggist, Abingdon, Berks., 1773, W, P1/F/469, P1/12Reg/459B
Francis, husb., Shalbourne, 1785, comm, W, P23/781
Grace, widow, Chards., Devon, 1734, W, P5/1734/25
Hy., Sherb., Dorset, 1610, AB, P5/9Reg/43A
Hy., husb., Warm., 1633, I, P2/F/159
Hy., Halstock, Dorset, 1669, AB, P16/19
Jas., husb. *or* yeo., Long Wittenham, Berks., 1683, I, W, P1/F/162
Joan, Sherb., Dorset, 1612, AB, P5/1611/13, P5/9Reg/61C
Jn., Kingston D., 1542, W (NEP), P2/1Reg/39D
Jn., Hill D., 1555, W, P2/1Reg/97C
Jn., husb., Halstock, Dorset, 1591, I, W, P5/1591/26, P5/5Reg/102A
Jn., husb., Kingston D., 1596, I, W, P2/F/42
Jn., Warm., 1760, AB, comm, P2/F/558
Jn., victualler, Blue Boar Inn, Wantage, Berks., 1776, W, P5/1776/17, P5/17Reg/112B
Jn., publican, Stanford Dingley, Berks., 1804, W, P1/1804/52
Jn., yeo., Upton S., 1807, W, Wr, P2/1807/11
Jos., labourer, Streatley, Berks., 1759, W, P1/F/430, P1/11Reg/399A
Julian, widow, Halstock, Dorset, 1628, I, P5/1628/41
My., widow, Horningsham, 1740, AB, Wr, P5/1740/30
Otho, labourer, Sherb., Dorset, 1700, I, W, P5/1700/11
Robt., husb., Kingston D., 1571, W, P2/5Reg/133B
Robt., Bere R., Dorset, 1619, AB, I, T, P5/1619/51, P5/10Reg/56B
Robt., Alton P., Dorset, 1640, AB, P5/1640/18, P5/13Reg/256B
Robt., clerk, S. Newton, 1681, AB, I, P2/F/298
Robt., husb., Chards., Devon, 1704, AB, comm, I, P14/100
Thos., clerk, Haydon, Dorset, 1635, I, W, P5/1635/41, P5/12Reg/204B
Thos., gent., Haydon, Dorset, 1662, AB, I, W (undated; not witnessed *or* signed), P5/1662/51
Wm., sen., butcher, Halstock, Dorset, 1619, I, W, P5/1619/50, P5/10Reg/52
Wm., sen., Halstock, Dorset, 1661, I, W, P5/1661/18
Wm., Haydon, Dorset, 1685, AB, P5/1685/35
Wm., husb., Long Wittenham, Berks., 1732, AB, I, P1/F/318
Freshwater, Robt., plumber and glazier, Calne, 1793, comm, W, P26/1188
Frewin, Christian, widow, Eye and Dunsden, Sonning, Berks., 1677, I, W, P5/1677/18
Edwd., pewterer, Reading, Berks., 1711, W, P1/F/247, P1/5Reg/178
Francis, yeo., Bishopsland, Sonning, Berks., 1689, I, W, P5/1689/24
Geo., Sonning, Berks., 1697, AB, P5/1697/15
Jn., yeo., Westridge, Streatley, Berks., 1631, bond to pay legacy, I, NW, P1/F/69
Jn., yeo., Eye and Dunsden, Sonning, Berks., 1690, I, W, P5/1690/16
Mgt., widow, Eye and Dunsden, Sonning, Berks., 1690, AB, comm, I, P5/1690/17
My., sp., Blewbury, Berks., 1632, AB, I, P5/1632/21, P5/12Reg/105B
Thos., sen., carp., Blewbury, Berks., 1644, I (2) (NEP), P5/1644/30
see also Quoke alias F.
Frey *see* Fray
Fribbins, Dorothy, widow, Manton, Preshute, 1693, AB, I, P1/F/199
Freepens, Eleanor, sp., Pewsey, 1838, AB, O, Wr, P3/1838/61
Jn., blacksmith, Manton, Preshute, 1683, AB, I, P1/F/168
Jn., blacksmith, Wantage, Berks., 1704, AB, I, P23/270
Fribbence, Maria, sp., Pewsey, 1839, AB, comm, Wr, P1/1839/20
Frebence, Richd., tailor, E. Stowell, Wilcot, 1640, I, W, P3/F/91
Frebence, Robt., E. Kennett, 1633, I, W, P3/F/68
Frebbins, Robt., tailor, E. Kennett, 1672, AB, a/c, I, P3/F/143
Robt., St Mgt., Preshute, 1692, AB, I, P1/F/193
Wm., Marl., 1591, I, P1/F/3
Frippens, Wm., yeo., Westcourt, Burbage, 1720, I, W, P11/303
Frick *see* Freke
Fricker, Aldred, husb., Sutton V., 1563, AB, I, copy I (2), P2/F/5, P2/4Reg/122B
Alice, widow, Westb., 1725, W, P25/1725/2

Ambrose, Ridge, Chilmark, 1610, AB, I, P2/F/84, P2/8Reg/119B
Ambrose, husb., Ridge, Chilmark, 1631, I, W, P1/F/61
Ambrose, Lt. Bathampton, Steeple L., [1684], I, W, P2/F/311
Ambrose, jun., tailor, Orcheston St My., 1738-40, AB, W, P1/F/343, P2/F/512, P1/8Reg/203
Ann, widow, Tisb., 1751, W, P2/F/537
Arthur, yeo., Baverstock, 1637, AB, I, P2/F/172
Cath., widow, Westb., 1700, I, W, P25/1700/4
Cath., widow, Atworth, Bradford A., 1753, AB, comm, ren, W, P2/F/545
Chris., yeo., W. Knoyle, 1727, AB, W, P1/F/298, P1/7Reg/173
Chris., yeo., Chitterne AS, 1822, comm, W, Wr, P2/1822/6
Edith, Chilmark, 1569, AB, P2/5Reg/50C
Edwd., yeo., E. Hatch, Tisb., 1649, I (very detailed), W, P2/F/218
Edwd., yeo., Tisb. (bastardy bond for Hester Abbott of Heytes. vs Richd. Dann, 1727, on reverse of ren), 1731, AB, ren, P2/F/477
Edwd., yeo., Norrington, Alvediston, 1738, W, P1/F/347, P1/8Reg/343
Edwd., yeo., Ridge, Chilmark, 1740, AB, W, P2/F/508
Edwd., gent., Imber, 1814, comm, W, Wr, P2/1814/35
Eliz., widow, Ridge, Chilmark, 1610, I, W, P2/F/83, P2/8Reg/109A
Eliz., widow, Westb., 1731, W, P25/1730/8
Eliz., widow, Sal., 1747, AB, I, P1/F/385
Eliz., widow, Donhead St My., 1769, W, P2/F/586
Ellen, widow, E. Hatch, Tisb., 1608, W, P2/8Reg/12A
Francis, shoemaker, Castle C., 1817, W, Wr, P3/1817/16
Geo., yeo., Alton Pr., 1648, AB, I, P1/F/109
Geo., Southcott, Pewsey, 1681, AB, comm, I, P3/F/173
Geo., Winterbourne S., 1681, AB, I, P2/F/295
Geo., Donhead St A., 1815, W, Wr, P2/1815/14
Gideon, baker, Rode, N. Bradley, 1780, W, P2/F/618
Gideon, millwright, Bradford A., 1842, comm, W, Wr, P1/1842/39
Harriet, singlewoman, Sutton M., 1852, D, W, Wr, P2/1852/4
Hy., Baverstock, 1587, W, P2/7Reg/89C
Hy., Nippred, Tisb., 1638, AB, a/c, P2/F/178
Hy., yeo., Sal., 1668, AB, I, P4/1667/31
Hy., yeo., W. Knoyle, 1704, I, W, P2/F/396
Hy., husb., W. Stour, Dorset, 1710, W, P2/F/407
Hy., labourer, Steeple L., 1739, W, P2/F/506
Hy., bach., Mere, 1768, AB, P5/1768/11
Hy., clerk, Sutton M., 1793, W, P1/F/511, P1/14Reg/475
Hy., Melk., 1804, AB, P1/1804/13
Isaac, serge weaver, Biddestone St Nich., 1739, I, W, P3/F/357
Jas., barber, Biddestone St Nich., 1762, W, P3/F/399
Jas., broad weaver, Dilton M., Westb., 1787, W, P25/1787/2
Jane, widow, Baverstock, 1634, I, W, P1/F/81
Jane, singlewoman, Baverstock, 1700, W, P2/F/388
Jane, widow, Milton, Gillingham, Dorset, 1733, AB, W, P27/1/325
Jn., [yeo.], Fovant, 1563, I, W, P2/F/4, P2/4Reg/115C
Jn., husb., E. Hatch, Tisb., 1578, I, T, W, P2/F/14, P2/5Reg/320
Jn., husb., Fovant, 1581, W, P2/6Reg/21C
Jn., yeo., Alton Pr., 1610, W, P3/F/17
Jn., husb., Sedgehill, 1641, comm, I, W, P2/F/200
Jn., Donhead St My., 1684, AB, I, P2/F/314
Jn., Tisb., 1695, AB, I, P1/F/201
Jn., Hindon, 1721, AB, P2/F/436
Jn., collarmaker, Wylye, 1731, W, P2/F/483
Jn., sen., broad weaver, Biddestone, 1734, W, P3/F/346
Jn., shopkeeper, Whitep., 1761, AB, P2/F/560
Jn., broad weaver, Biddestone St Nich., 1772, W, P3/F/415
Jn., Gillingham, Dorset, 1783, AB, P27/1/514, P27/3Reg/228B
Jn., Tisb. (form. of Stour Provost, Dorset), 1819, W, Wr, P2/1819/28
Julian, Tisb., 1587, W, P2/7Reg/94A

Julian, sp., Fovant, 1744, W, P2/F/523
Martha, N. Bradley, 1781, W, P2/F/621
Martha, widow, Sutton M., 1847, W, Wr, P2/1847/48
My., widow, Baverstock, 1593, I, W, P2/F/31
My., schoolmistress, Whitep., 1797, W, Wr, P2/F/663
Matthew, tailor, Maiden B., [1684], I, W, P2/F/316
Nich., tailor, Maiden B., 1631, I, P2/F/150
Philip, Sedgehill, 1672, AB, ren, P2/F/262
Philip, jun., maltster, Donhead St My., 1763, W, P2/F/567
Philip, yeo., Donhead St My., 1768, W, P2/F/581
Richd., husb., Maddington, 1557, W, P2/3Reg/29C
Richd., Ridge, Chilmark, 1581, W, P2/6Reg/44B
Richd., yeo., Ridge, Chilmark, 1662, AB, I, P2/F/222
Richd., yeo., Donhead St My., 1662, comm, I, W, P2/F/224
Richd., sen., yeo., Donhead St My., 1719, I, W, copy W with probate, P2/F/439
Richd., Sal., 1731, AB, I, P4/1731/17
Richd., innholder, Hindon, 1759, W, P2/F/555
Roger, cordw., Westb., 1713, W, P25/1713/9
Roger, innholder, Westb., 1724, W, P25/1724/7
Sam., yeo., Midway, Wingfield, 1773, W, P2/F/593
Sam., handlestockmaker, Rode, N. Bradley, 1839, AB, O, W, Wr, P2/1839/39
Sarah, sp., Southcott, Pewsey, 1703, I, W, P3/F/243
Sarah, widow, Biddestone St Peter, 1742, W, P3/F/365
Sarah, widow, Imber, 1814, AB, comm, W, Wr, P2/1814/36
Sarah, widow, Sal. (form. of Downton), 1847, cert, W, Wr, P4/1847/15
Thos., Tisb., 1569, W, P2/5Reg/52A
Thos., yeo., Heytes., [1675], W, P2/F/272
Thos., Sedgehill, 1684, AB, P2/F/315
Thos., cordw., Westb., 1698, I, W, P25/1698/13
Thos., maltster, Greenhills, Westb., 1708, W, P25/1708/14
Thos., Wylye, 1738, comm, W, P1/F/342, P1/8Reg/204
Thos., yeo., Sedgehill, 1754, W, P2/F/546
Thos., broad weaver, Dilton M., Westb., 1760, W, P25/1760/9
Thos., barber and innholder, Whitep., 1765, AB, I, P2/F/573
Thos., Ridge, Chilmark, 1772, W, P2/F/590
Thos., Warm., 1777, AB, P2/F/604
Thos., baker, Knook, 1818, W, Wr, P5/1818/5
Thos., sen., yeo., Ridge, Chilmark, 1833, W, Wr, P2/1833/30
Thos., yeo., Sutton M., 1854, aff, D, W, Wr, P2/1854/26
Thos., gent., Chilmark, 1857, AB, aff, D, O, Wr, P2/1857/12
Thos. *see also* My. Holloway
Walter, Tisb., 1557, W, P2/3Reg/70A
Walter, yeo., Baverstock, 1626, AB, a/c, comm, I, P2/F/129
Wm., yeo., E. Hatch, Tisb., 1661, I, W, P2/F/219
Wm., husb., E. Knoyle, 1692, I, W, P2/F/352
Wm., yeo., Ridge, Chilmark, 1711, W, P2/F/411
Wm., yeo., Biddestone St Nich., 1757, W, P3/F/390
Wm., gent., Sal., 1794, req, W, copy W, P4/1794/8
Wm., Knook, 1811, AB, Wr, P5/1811/8
Wm., sen., yeo., Donhead St My., 1816, W, Wr, P2/1816/61
see also Lanfear form. F.
Frickerjukes, Richd., mariner on HMS *Sunderland*, E. Knoyle, 1749, W, P2/F/531
Friend, Dorothy, sp., Sal. The Close, 1706, NW, P5/1706/14
Dorothy, widow, Sal., [1706], W, P4/1706/10
Eliz., Sal., 1674, AB, P1/F/144
Geo., innholder, Wilton, 1672, AB, I, copy I, P2/F/261
Hy., servant to Wm. Petty-Fitzmaurice, 1st Marquess of Landsdowne and 2nd Earl of Shelburne (d.1805), Bowood, 1810, AB, W, Wr, P5/1810/1
Hy., bach., Plaitford, 1821, AB, Wr, P2/1821/10
Joan, widow, W. Lavington, 1669, AB, I, NW, P1/F/138

My., widow, Wilton, 1672-75, AB, a/c (2), W, P2/F/265
My., widow, Wilton, 1728, W, P2/F/462
My., sp., Wilton, 1814, W, P2/1814/10
Robt., chandler, Sal., 1670, AB, I, P4/1670/10
Robt., sen., soap boiler, Sal., 1671, a/c, I, W (not proved), P4/1671/21
Robt., broad weaver, Bradford A., 1720, comm, W, P1/F/281, P1/6Reg/350A
Sarah, widow, Plaitford, 1804, W, P1/1804/138
Friend alias Hayward, Thos., N. Bradley, 1571, W, P2/5Reg/131B
Wm., Old Windsor, Berks., 1628, I, W, P1/F/58
Wm., Bramshaw, Hants (form. of Winkton, Christchurch, Hants), 1679, I, W, P24/478
see also Hayward alias F.
Fripp, Hy., husb., Woodlands, Mere, 1709, W, P5/1709/13, P5/15Reg/114
Frippe, Jerome, husb., Gillingham, Dorset, 1567, W, P27/1Reg/19A
Frippe, Jn., Gillingham, Dorset, 1560, W, P27/1Reg/7B
Jn., Tollard Royal, 1580, AB, I, T, W, P2/F/17, P2/5Reg/358B
Jn., Westb., 1757, AB, P25/1757/1
Jn., maltster, Westb., 1763, W, P25/1763/6
Margery, widow, Westb., 1763, W, P25/1763/7
My., Westb., 1813, O, W, P25/1813/6
Oliver, Wylye, 1695, AB, P2/F/364
Phripp, Rachel, Gillingham, Dorset, 1848, AB, comm, Wr, P27/1/755
Frippe, Robt., Gillingham, Dorset, 1562, W, P27/1Reg/14A
Phripp, Robt., yeo., Bugley, Gillingham, Dorset, 1679, I, P27/1/55
Phripp, Robt., Gillingham, Dorset, 1791, AB, P27/1/544
Phripp, Robt., gent., Gillingham, Dorset, 1804, W, P27/1/580
Phripp, Robt., Gillingham, Dorset, 1820, W, Wr, P27/1/651
Sarah, Milton L., 1690, AB, I, P3/F/204
Phripp, Sarah, widow, Bugley, Gillingham, Dorset, 1707, AB, I, P27/1/169
Fripp alias Fibb, Wm., Milton L., 1690, AB, comm, I, P3/F/205-06
Wm., yeo., Bugley, Gillingham, Dorset, 1729, AB, I, P27/1/298
Phripp, Wm., chairmaker, Gillingham, Dorset, 1767, W, P27/1/462, P27/3Reg/139
Phripp, Wm., yeo., Bugley, Gillingham, Dorset, 1767, W, P27/1/463, P27/3Reg/135
Phripp, Wm., baker, Gillingham, Dorset, 1788, W, P27/1/535, P27/3Reg/255
Wm., Westb., 1807, AB, P25/1807/1
Phripp, Wm., Gillingham, Dorset, 1819, comm, W, Wr, P27/1/647
Frippens *see* Fribbins
Frith, Agnes, widow, Hindon, 1638, I, W, P2/F/180
Alice, Hindon, 1548, W (NEP), P2/2Reg/40A
Frith alias Bracher, Ann, Wilsford nr Pewsey, 1740, AB, P2/F/510
Ann, widow, Wootton B., 1778, AB, W, P3/F/424
Ann, minors, Whitep., 1806, comm, T (children of Wm. F.), P2/1806/18-19
Freeth, Chas., yeo., Garsdon, 1708, I, W, P3/F/261
Freeth, Chas., yeo., Gt. Somerford, 1821, W, Wr, P3/1821/24
Edwd., carp., Hindon, 1625, AB, I, P2/F/127
Edwd., husb., Hindon, 1631, I, W, P1/F/62
Frances, widow, Mere, 1727, AB, ren, W, P5/1727/17, P5/16Reg/157C
Harry *or* Hy., butcher, Mere, 1770, W, P5/1770/16, P5/17Reg/15A
Hugh, yeo., Winterbourne E., 1630, I, W, P2/F/149
Jas., Mere, 1689, AB, I, P5/1689/25
Freeth, Jane, Sonning, Berks., 1546, W, P5/20Reg/76A
Freeth, Joan, widow, Mere, 1695, I, W, P5/1695/34
Jn., husb., Mere, 1602, I, W, P5/1602/16, P5/7Reg/38A
Jn., yeo., Warm., 1685, AB, I, P2/F/318
Freeth, Jn., Bremhill, 1787, AB, P3/F/440
Freeth, Jn., Patterdown, Corsham, 1833, W, Wr, P3/1833/30
Martha, widow, Mere, 1776, AB, paper, P5/1776/18, P5/17Reg/131E
My., widow, Hindon, 1724, AB, P2/F/448
My., widow, Hindon, 1755, AB, P2/F/547
Maud, widow, Hindon, 1578, I, W, P2/F/11, P2/5Reg/302A
Philip, maltster, Mere, 1708, AB, I, P5/1708/29

Robt., sen., yeo., Wilsford nr Pewsey, 1635, I, W, P1/F/84
Robt., sen., yeo., Wilsford nr Pewsey, [1684], I, W, P2/F/310
Robt., labourer, Old Court, Wootton B., 1691, AB, I, P3/F/212
Robt., yeo., Wootton B., 1778, AB, W, P3/F/425
Roger, Wootton B., 1718, AB, P3/F/289
Freeth, Roger, Wootton B., 1730, W, P3/F/330
Freeth, Sarah, widow, Crudwell, 1842, AB, Wr, P3/1842/14
Freeth, Susanna, wife, Chipp. (form. of Wootton B.), 1850, W, Wr, P3/1850/33
Thos., Hindon, 1539, W (NEP), P2/1Reg/40A
Thos., yeo., Wilsford nr Pewsey, 1774, AB, comm, P2/F/595
Wm., Hindon, 1542, W (NEP), P2/1Reg/44B
Wm., Hindon, 1574, W, P2/5Reg/178A
Wm., Hindon, 1618, AB, I, P2/F/103
Wm., baker, Hindon, 1642, AB, I, P2/F/203
Freeth, Wm., yeo., Patterdown, Corsham, 1781, W, P3/F/429
Freeth, Wm., yeo., Garsdon, 1784, W, P3/F/431
Freeth, Wm., yeo., Corsham, 1806, comm, W, Wr, P3/1806/47
Wm., yeo., Whitep., 1806, W, P2/1806/18
Freeth, Wm., Westb., 1814, AB, P25/1814/4
Fritwell, Judith, Ardington Wick, Berks., 1613, I, W, P1/F/33
Robt., yeo., Ardington, Berks., 1615, I, W, P1/F/34
Frizell, My., Alderbury, 1838, W, Wr, P26/1440
Frizer, Thos., yeo., Eye and Dunsden, Sonning, Berks., 1830, W, Wr, P5/1830/22
Frogley, Alexander, tobacconist, Wantage, Berks., 1702, I, W, P23/250
Jn., clothworker, Wantage, Berks., 1691, AB, I, P23/178
Jn., sen., clothier, Wantage, Berks., 1735, W, P23/509
Martha, sp., Wantage, Berks., 1680, I, W, P23/84
My., maltster's wife, Long Wittenham, Berks., 1770, W, P1/F/458, P1/12Reg/357B
Froome, Frome, Dorothy, sp., Sal. The Close, 1822, AB, D, W (& cod), Wr, P5/1822/18
Edwd., yeo., Woolhampton, Berks., 1770, W, P1/F/461, P1/12Reg/372B
Froom, Eliz., widow, Woolhampton, Berks., 1726, W, P1/F/293, P1/7Reg/96B
Jane, widow, Sal. The Close, 1696, W, P5/1696/16
Jn., exhibited at Reading, Berks., 1592, I, P1/F/4
Jn., gent., Dodding, Bere R., Dorset, 1642, AB, ren, P5/1642/9, P5/14Reg/45B
Jn., gent., Bere R., Dorset, 1663, definitive sentence, inty, I, W, P5/1662/44
Jn., carp., Baydon, 1710, I, W, P5/1710/39, P5/15Reg/181
Froom, Jn., Winterbourne, Berks., 1750, AB, P1/F/399
Frome, My., sp., Sal., 1691, NW, P4/1691/11
Frome, My., sp., Sal., 1707, AB, ren, P4/1707/9
Frome, Thos., gent., Sal., 1734, W, P4/1733/17
Thos., shoemaker, Marl., 1852, AB, Wr, P1/1852/9
Frost, Hy., Stratfield M., Berks., 1779, AB, P1/F/481
Jn., yeo., Draycot C., 1783, W, P1/F/494, P1/13Reg/497
My. Ann, sp., Shripple, Idmiston, 1855, AB, aff, Wr, P1/1855/57
Robt., rector, Pewsey, 1724, AB, P1/F/289
Thos., joiner, Wilton, 1762, AB, ren, P2/F/566
Froud, Abraham, mercer, Sal., 1751, W, P4/1750/11
Frowde, Agnes, widow, West Hall, Stratton, Dorset, 1589, I, W, P5/1589/20, P5/5Reg/55B
Alice, widow, Wilton, 1719, ren, W, P4/1719/1
Ann, widow, Sal., 1735, a/c, W, P1/F/331, P1/7Reg/634
Frowde, Anthony, yeo., Rollestone, 1662, I, T, W, P2/F/223
Dorothy, widow, Alderbury, 1694, I, W, P26/425
Frowde, Edith, widow, Sal., 1723, I, W, P4/1722/2
Edwd., sen., gent., Tinh., Edington, 1715, W, P2/F/415
Frowd, Edwd., gent., Sedgehill, 1744, W, P1/F/378, P1/9Reg/439B
Edwd., maltster, Tinh., Edington, 1756, AB, W, P2/F/548
Frowd, Edwd., gent., Brixton D., 1776, comm, W, P1/F/477, P1/13Reg/157
Frowd, Eleanor, sp., Bratton, Westb., 1776, comm, W, P25/1776/2
Eliz., widow, Edington, 1750, AB, P1/F/404
Eliz., widow, Sal., 1773, W, P4/1773/5

Frowde, Ellen, widow, Sedgehill, 1586, W, P2/7Reg/43C
Frowde, Jas., yeo., Netton, Durnford, 1718, AB, P9/41
Jas., yeo., Tinh., Edington, 1750, comm, W, P1/F/398, P1/10Reg/320
Jn., yeo., Sedgehill, 1675, I, NW, P1/F/146
Jn., sen., Alderbury, 1681, I, W, P26/285
Frowd, Jn., yeo., Foxham, Bremhill, 1693, AB, I, W, P3/F/220
Jn., gent., Rollestone, 1719, AB, ren, Wr, P2/F/434
Frowd, Jn., cutler, Sal., 1735, I, W, Wr, P4/1735/9
Frowd, Jn., maltster, Tinh., Edington, 1782-84, comm, D (several), draft W (shorthand), W (3), P1/F/497, P1/14Reg/46
Frowd, Jn., yeo., N. Bradley, 1819, W, Wr, P2/1819/40
Frowde, Lawr., yeo., Swallowcliffe, 1728, W, P5/1728/37, P5/16Reg/161B
Mgt., widow, Sal., 1778, W, P4/1778/14
My., widow, Sal., 1828, W, Wr, P4/1828/1
Frowde, Nich., yeo., Sal., 1703, W, P4/1703/7
Frowde, Nich., shopkeeper, E. Knoyle, 1714-15, comm, I, W, P1/F/258, P1/5Reg/489A
Nich., yeo., Alderbury, 1724, W, P26/701
Nich., yeo., Quidh., 1731, W, P2/F/478
Richd., grocer, Sal., 1774, W, P4/1774/8
Robt., weaver, Sal., 1713, I, W, P4/1713/9
Robt., shopkeeper, Winchester St., Sal. St Edmd., 1760, W, P4/1760/4
Frowd, Sarah, wife, Sal., 1726, AB, W, P4/1725/16
Stephen, Damerham, Hants, 1730, W, P2/F/473
Thos., Sedgehill, 1681, AB, a/c, I, P2/F/297
Thos., Edington, 1733, AB, P2/F/491
Frowde, Wm., clothworker *or* clothier, Sal., 1682, AB, a/c, I, P4/1682/22
Wm., Damerham, Hants, 1731, W, P2/F/481
Wm., clothier, Sal., 1731, W, P4/1730/28
see also Parsons alias F.
Fry, Abraham, Alderbury, 1820, AB, Wr, P26/1333
Alexander, yeo., Corston, Malm., 1638, I, W, P3/F/83
Alice, widow, Brinkw., 1670, I, W, P3/F/132
Andrew, cordw., Downton, 1723, W, P2/F/446
Ann, Lyme R., Dorset, 1672, I, W, P16/33
Ann, sp., Sal. St Martin, 1692, AB, I, W, P1/F/192
Ann, widow, Heytes., [1724], deed of gift (NEP), P5/1723/45
Ann, sp., Ashton K. (form. of Marylebone), 1848, D, O, W, Wr, P3/1848/45
Anthony, mercer, Brinkw., 1636, I, W, P3/F/76
Anthony, sen., mason, Lt. Somerford, 1678, I, W, P3/F/159
Anthony, yeo., Quemerford, Calne, 1699, I, W, P26/462
Arabella, Downton, 1728, AB, P2/F/463
Benj., Sal., 1751, W, P4/1751/18
Betty, widow, Ashton K., 1843, I, O, W, Wr, P3/1843/13
Chas., gardener, Hurst, Berks., 1724, W, P5/1724/29, P5/16Reg/104A
Chas., innkeeper, Corston, Malm., 1831, W, Wr, P3/1831/64
Dan., in Royal Navy on the Romney, Netherb., Dorset, 1707, AB, P5/1707/21
David, labourer, Nettleton, 1785, W, P3/F/433
Edmd., baker, Malm., [1613], I, W (NEP), P3/F/23
Edmd., fellmonger, Malm., 1719, W, P3/F/294
Edmd., mason, Malm., 1749, W, P3/F/377
Edwd., Sal. St Edmd., 1689, AB, P1/F/178
Edwd., *The Almshouse*, Longbridge D., 1797, W, P2/F/662
Edwd., Eastcourt, Crudwell, 1830, AB, O, Wr, P3/1830/18
Edwd., sen., Chiverliers Farm, Chipp., 1851, comm, W, Wr, P3/1851/43
Eliz., sp., Ryme I., Dorset, 1596, AB, I, P5/1596/26, P5/6Reg/126B
Eliz., Sutton V., ?1666, AB, W (fragmentary), P1/F/131
Eliz., widow, Foxham, Bremhill, 1740, W, P3/F/361
Eliz., sp., Brinkw., 1741, comm, W, P1/F/358, P1/9Reg/63
Eliz., widow, Sal., 1795, W, P4/1795/7
Fry alias Bloxham, Eliz., widow, Malm., 1810, comm, W, Wr, P3/1810/39
Ellen, widow, Blewbury, Berks., 1570, W, P5/2Reg/70A

Francis, yeo., Bramshaw, Hants, 1847, aff, W, Wr, P24/1387
Geo., Alton Pr., 1619, AB, I, P1/F/46
Geo., Compton C., 1629, AB, I, P2/F/140
Geo., yeo., Lacock, 1703, I, W, P3/F/244
Hy., husb., Maddington, 1591, I, W, P2/F/27
Hy., Redlynch, Downton, 1626, AB, I, P2/F/131
Hy., labourer, Crudwell, 1637, I, NW, P3/F/80
Hy., Brinkw., 1750, AB, P3/F/379
Hy., woolstapler, Quemerford, Calne, 1781, W, P26/1115
Hugh, yeo., Midgham, Thatcham, Berks., 1720, I, W, P1/F/280, P1/6Reg/330A
Jas., tailor, Shinfield, Berks., 1664, AB, comm, I, P1/F/128
Jas., bricklayer, Sal. St Edmd., 1768, W, P4/1768/8
Jas., gent., Mere, 1806, comm, W, P5/1806/33
Jas., Pitton, Alderbury, 1832, AB, Wr, P26/1400
Jane, widow, Bere R., Dorset, 1734, AB, I, W (2), P5/1734/26
Jane, widow, Ashgrove, Donhead St My., 1746, AB, comm, ren, W, P2/F/527
Joan, widow, W. Grimstead, 1555, W, P2/1Reg/19
Joan, widow, Sal., 1700, AB, I, P4/1699/1
Joanna, sp., Calstone W., 1752, comm, W, P5/1752/17
Jn., Hamptworth, Downton, 1550, W, P2/2Reg/105C
Jn., Everleigh, 1605, AB, I, P1/F/10
Jn., husb., Westport St My., [1607], I, W (NEP), P3/F/6
Jn., yeo., Winterbourne Bassett, 1626, I, W, P3/F/54
Jn., sen., husb., Brinkw., 1630, I, W, P3/F/63
Jn., sen., Kington St M., 1639, I, W, P3/F/87
Jn., yeo., Brinkw., 1664, I, W, P3/F/108
Jn., yeo., Stert, Urchf., 1678, AB, I, P1/F/152
Jn., fuller, Blackland, Calne, 1685, I (detailed), W, P26/330
Jn., Netherb., Dorset, 1696, AB, I, P17/355
Jn., parchmentmaker, Sal., 1700, W, P4/1700/11
Jn., ropemaker, Shitterton, Bere R., Dorset, 1708, AB, I (detailed), P5/1708/30
Jn., mason, Lt. Somerford, 1708, I (2), W, P1/F/236, P1/4Reg/282
Jn., Wilton, 1711, AB, P1/F/242
Jn., sen., grocer, Devizes, 1711, W, P1/F/244, P1/5Reg/120A
Jn., yeo., Foxham, Bremhill, 1713, AB, I, P3/F/278
Jn., yeo., Brinkw., 1740, W, P3/F/362
Jn., Sal., 1750, AB, P4/1750/4
Jn., Wick, Lacock, 1750, W, P1/F/403, P1/10Reg/408
Jn., sen., Calstone W., 1760, AB, W, P26/980
Jn., Pitton, Alderbury, 1761, AB, I, P26/981
Jn., victualler, Sal., 1767, W, P4/1767/11
Jn., shopkeeper, Sutton B., 1776, AB, W, P3/F/419
Jn., Sutton B. (property in Chipp.), 1828, AB, O, P3/1828/71
Jn., yeo., Cadenham, Bremhill, 1830, comm, W, Wr, P3/1830/1
Jn., sen., yeo., Cowage, Calne, 1834, comm, ren, W, Wr, P26/1411
Jn., widower, Pitton, 1843, AB, Wr, P1/1843/31
Jn., sen., farmer, Fritham, Bramshaw, Hants, 1843, I, W, Wr, P24/1370
Jn., yeo., Lacock, 1847, W, Wr, P3/1847/26
Jos., Foxley, 1725, NW, P3/F/309
Jos., minor, Foxley, 1733, T, P3/F/340
Jos., tailor, Blewbury, Berks., 1757, comm, W, P5/1757/10
Jos., clerk, Upavon, 1759, AB, ren, P2/F/556
Jos., labourer, Bradford A. (form. of Broughton G.), 1809, W, Wr, P2/1809/68
Jos., basketmaker, Sal., 1824, W, Wr, P4/1824/9
Jos., sen., yeo., Alderbury, 1824, W, Wr, P26/1349
Jos., yeo., Grittenham, Brinkw., 1831, comm, W, P3/1831/53
Julian, widow, Westport St My., 1636, I, W, P3/F/77
Lydia, widow (occupation -sp.), Mere, 1715, W, P5/1715/17, P5/15Reg/322B
Mgt., widow, Mere, 1724-25, I, W, P5/1724/30, P5/16Reg/106A
Mgt., Draycot C., 1755, W, P3/F/387

Mgt., widow, Ashton K., 1784, W, P3/F/432
Margery, sp., Earley, Sonning, Berks., 1631-32, AB, P5/1631/39, P5/12Reg/66A
My., widow, Slaughterford, 1696, AB, I, W, P3/F/231
My., Calne, 1699, AB, I, P26/465
My., sp., Crickl. St S., 1729, I, W, P3/F/321
My., sp., Sutton B., 1764, W, P3/F/404
My., widow, Lacock, 1788, W, P3/F/442
My., sp., Sal., 1826, W, Wr, P4/1826/2
My. Pullen, sp., Bremhill, 1856, aff, O, W, Wr, P3/1856/25
Michael, Brinkw., 1628, AB, a/c, I, P3/F/57
Michael, yeo., Brinkw., 1678, AB, I, P3/F/160
Michael, Lt. Somerford, 1730, AB, I, P3/F/331
Peter, Biddestone St Peter, 1850, O, W, Wr, P3/1850/24
Ralph, Damerham, Hants, 1559, W (incomplete) (NEP), P2/4Reg/10B
Rebecca, sp., Scots Lane, Sal., 1816, D, W, Wr, P4/1816/4
Richd., Downton, 1598, AB, P2/F/49
Richd., innholder, Codf. St P., 1605, I, W, P2/F/71
Fry alias Caston, Richd., husb., Crudwell, 1608, I, W, P3/F/10
Richd., shoemaker, Bere R., Dorset, 1617, I, W, P5/1617/17, P5/9Reg/192
Richd., Cleverton, Lea and C., 1636, AB, a/c, I, P3/F/78
Richd., Wootton B., 1637, AB, I, P3/F/81
Richd., shepherd, Urchf., 1638, AB, I, P1/F/93
Richd., baker, Sal., 1707, I, W, P4/1707/6
Richd., sen., yeo., Ashton K., 1767, W, P1/F/453, P1/12Reg/270A
Richd., sen., mercer, Calne, 1772, comm, W, P26/1059
Richd., Bere R., Dorset, 1781, AB, P5/1781/6, P5/17Reg/213B
Richd., yeo., Ashton K., 1796, W, P3/F/446
Richd., yeo., Ashton K., 1820, W, Wr, P1/1820/33
Richd. *see also* Wm. Trickey
Robt., Broad H., 1609, W, P3/F/15
Robt., yeo., Corston, Malm., [1619], I, W (NEP), P3/F/37
Robt., Inglesham, 1623, court paper, P3/F/47
Robt., Sutton V., 1648, alleg, court papers, cit (3), I (2), W, P2/F/216
Robt., cordw., Westport St My., 1669, I, W, P3/F/127
Robt., cordw., Lt. Somerford, 1672, AB, I, P3/F/144
Robt., shepherd, Sutton V., 1711, W, P2/F/412
Robt., innholder, Lacock, 1729, W, P1/F/302, P1/7Reg/228A
Robt., Sal., 1746, AB, P4/1746/1
Robt., Stratton St Mgt., 1767, AB, P3/F/409
Robt., innholder, Lacock, 1777, W, P3/F/422
Ruth, widow, Chr. M., 1844, O, W, Wr, P3/1844/42
Sam., innholder, Warm., 1664, W (NEP), P30/70
Sam., yeo., Brinkw., 1722, AB, I, P3/F/300
Sam., tailor, Mere, 1724, AB, W, P5/1724/31, P5/16Reg/100C
Sam., tailor, Mere, 1770, W, P5/1770/17, P5/17Reg/1B
Sam., Stanton St Q., 1826, W, Wr, P1/1826/68
Sarah, widow, Sal., 1677, I, W, P1/F/149
Sarah, minor, Sal., 1764, T (no decd named), P4/1764/4
Sarah, widow, Winchester St Maurice, Hants, 1790, receipt, W, copy W, P4/1790/15
Stephen, Ashgrove, Donhead St My., 1738, AB, comm, P1/F/348
Susanna, widow, Netherb., Dorset, 1716, I, NW, P5/1716/31, P5/15Reg/340A
Thos., Brokenb., [1581], W (NEP), P3/1Reg/17B
Thos., Enford, 1593, AB, I, NW, P2/F/33
Thos., husb., Enford, 1597, W, P2/F/46
Thos., husb., Earley, Sonning, Berks., [1625], I, L, ren, W, P5/1625/35, P5/10Reg/243
Thos., carp., Westport St My., 1630, I, W, P3/F/64
Thos., sen., W. Kennett, Avebury, 1667, AB, P3/F/117
Thos., shepherd, Sutton V., 1675, comm, I, W, P2/F/273
Thos., rough mason, Brook, Westb., 1677, I, W, P25/1677/2
Thos., husb., Charlton nr Malm., 1690, AB, I, P3/F/207

Thos., innholder, W. Kennett, Avebury, 1691, comm, I, W, P3/F/211
Thos., sen., baker, Mere, 1692, AB, I, P5/1692/27
Thos., Charlton nr Malm., 1694, AB, ren, P3/F/225
Thos., mason, Lt. Somerford, 1707, I, W, P3/F/259
Thos., innholder, W. Kennett, Avebury, 1709, AB, I, P3/F/266
Thos., widower, Lydiard M., 1711, W, P3/F/271
Thos., minor, Bere R., Dorset, 1723, AB, P5/1723/17
Thos., bricklayer, Pitton, Alderbury, 1723, I, W, P26/670
Thos., sen., cork cutter, Shitterton, Bere R., Dorset, 1752, W, P5/1752/16
Thos., Enford, 1761, AB, P2/F/561
Thos., Uffc., Devon, 1769, AB, P20/1/251
Thos., sen., bricklayer, Wilton, 1771, W, P2/F/588
Thos., gent., Sal., 1802, W, P4/1802/14
Thos., bricklayer, Wilton, 1805, W, P2/1805/3
Thos., labourer, Mere, 1807, W, Wr, P5/1807/5
Thos., yeo., Cadenham, Bremhill, 1831-32, AB (2), comm (2), ren, W, Wr, P3/1831/61
Thos., gardener, Broughton G., 1837, W, Wr, P2/1837/50
Timothy, mason, Brinkw., 1683, AB, I, W, P3/F/179
Walter, Halstock, Dorset, 1627, I, ren, P5/1627/15
Wm., husb., Calstone W., 1589, I, T, W, P5/1589/19, P5/5Reg/51C
Wm., Calne, 1613, I, W, P5/1613/26, P5/9Reg/130A
Wm., [blacksmith], Brinkw., 1625, I, P3/F/49
Wm., sen., yeo., Crickl. St S., 1625, I, W, P3/F/50
Wm., baker, Sal. St Martin, 1626, I, NW, P4/1626/10
[Fry], Wm., yeo., Marl. St My. & M. St Peter & St Paul, 1633, I, W (surname missing; probably Wm. F. who married Alice Clemence in 1613, had six children alive in 1632 when he d.), P1/F/526
Wm., Lt. Somerford, 1641, I, W, P3/F/97
Wm., parchmentmaker, Sal., 1644, AB, I, P1/F/98
Wm., husb., Gt. Somerford, 1663, AB, I, P3/F/107
Wm., husb., Axford, Rams., 1663, I, W (damaged), P5/1663/25
Wm., yeo., Brinkw., 1675, I, W, P3/F/154
Wm., yeo., Bewley, Lacock, 1686, I, W, P1/F/525
Wm., [blacksmith], Brinkw., 1689, AB, I, P3/F/202
Wm., sen., clothworker, Sutton B., 1698, I, W, P1/F/216, P1/3Reg/172
Wm., maltster, Westport St My., 1699, W, P3/F/237
Wm., pipemaker, Marl., 1712, I, W, P1/F/251, P1/5Reg/277B
Wm., yeo., Stratford sub C., 1734, W, P4/1734/1
Wm., yeo., Brinkw., 1741, AB, comm, W, P1/F/357, P1/9Reg/62
Wm., sen., maltster, Pitton, Alderbury, 1745, W, P26/863
Wm., yeo., Highw., 1747, AB, P10/1747/2
Wm., cork cutter, Bere R., Dorset, 1787, W, P5/1787/7, P5/18Reg/82
Wm., bricklayer, Sal., 1796, W, P4/1796/7
Wm., glover, Crickl. St S., 1803, req, W, P3/1803/9
Wm., Crickl. St S., 1812, AB, P3/1812/22
Wm., yeo., Stanton St Q., 1827, AB, ren, Wr, P3/1827/43
Wm., yeo., Chr. M., 1836, W, Wr, P3/1836/36
Zephaniah, jun., clothier, Chipp., 1717, AB, I, P3/F/285
see also Fray; Urche alias F.

Fryer, Fryar, […] *see* Wm. Augustine
Aaron, Downton, 1782, AB, P1/F/486
Bennet, miller, Uffc., Devon, 1581, AB, I, P5/1581/10, P5/4Reg/23C
Cicely, widow, Whaddon, 1577, W, P2/5Reg/289B
Edith, widow, Keevil, 1694, AB, I, P2/F/360
Edwd., sen., yeo., Steeple A., 1688, I, W, P2/F/337
Eliz., widow, Steeple A., 1691, I, W, P2/F/349
Eliz., widow, Sal., 1705, W, P4/1705/3
Eliz., widow, Hilp., 1734, comm, I, W, P2/F/493
Francis, husb., Uffc., Devon, 1664, I, NW, P20/1/49
Grace, widow, Hilp., 1613, comm, I, copy I, W, copy W, P2/F/95, P2/8Reg/192A
Hy., husb., Pascroft, Whaddon, [1631], I, W, P2/F/152

Hy., Bemerton, Fugg. St Peter, 1679, AB, I, P2/F/289
Isaac, sen., baker, Sal., 1690, AB, W, P4/1689/15
Jane, widow, Wingfield, 1762, comm, W, P2/F/565
Joan, widow, Sutton V., 1563, W, P2/4Reg/131C
Jn., sen., Hilp., [1613], I, W, P2/F/94, P2/8Reg/190
Jn., Maiden B., 1669, AB, P2/F/244
Jn., sen., yeo., W. Ashton, Steeple A., 1672, I, W, P2/F/264
Jn., yeo., Seend, Melk., [1679], I, W, P2/F/288
Jn., husb., Compton C., 1690, I, W, P2/F/345
Fryers, Jn., gardener and yeo., Westrop, Highw., 1692, I, W, P5/1692/30
Jn., blacksmith, Bemerton, Fugg. St Peter, 1716-19, AB (2), I (2), P1/F/261, P2/F/433
Jn., sen., carp., W. Ashton, Steeple A., 1727, W, P2/F/460
Jn., yeo., W. Ashton, Steeple A., 1766, W, P2/F/579
Fryers, Jn., Highw., 1794, AB, comm, P5/1794/10, P5/18Reg/201A
Jn., bach., Downton, 1855, AB, aff, Wr, P1/1855/32
My., widow, Trowb., 1694, AB, P2/F/359
My., widow, Fritham, Bramshaw, Hants, 1723, W, P24/876
Nich., husb., Seend, Melk., 1627, I, W, P2/F/136
Richd., Sherston, [1614], I, W (NEP), P3/F/28
Richd., innholder, Sal., 1653, I, P4/1653/1
Richd., yeo., Studley, Trowb., 1776, comm, W, P1/F/470, P1/13Reg/76B
Robt., sen., yeo., Steeple A., 1691, I, W, P2/F/348
Robt., tallow chandler, Hilp., 1746, W, P2/F/526
Fryer alias Barnard, Roger, carp., Hilp., 1674, AB, comm, I, NW, P2/F/268
Stephen, Mere, 1739, AB, Wr, P5/1739/17
Thos., Chilmark, 1555, W, P2/1Reg/25A
Walter, E. Knoyle, 1598, AB, I, P2/F/52
Wm., Whaddon, 1559, W, P2/3Reg/175B
Wm., Hilp., 1599, I, W, P2/F/53
Wm., sen., carp., Hilp., 1674, I, W, P2/F/270
Wm., Hilp., 1685, AB, I, P2/F/323
Wm., tallow chandler, Hilp., 1727, W, P2/F/461
Wm., Steeple A., 1762, W, P2/F/564
Fuce, Geo., blacksmith, Moulsford, Cholsey, Berks., 1776, W, P1/F/472, P1/13Reg/120
Fues, Jn., Fullaway, All C., 1608, AB, I, P1/F/23
Jn., husb., Swindon, 1647, comm, W, P1/F/106
Jn., blacksmith, Blewbury, Berks., 1742, W (NEP), P5/1741/15
Wm., husb., Swindon, 1640, I, W, P3/F/93
Wm., blacksmith, Blewbury, Berks., 1724, AB, P5/1724/32
Wm., Wantage, Berks., 1755, AB, P23/662
Wm., victualler, Wantage, Berks., 1791, W, P5/1791/8, P5/18Reg/163
Fudge, Ann, widow, Chetnole, Yetm., Dorset, 1816, AB, comm, Wr, P19/222
Jacob, Lyme R., Dorset (form. of Bridport), 1836, AB, P16/415
Jane, widow, Melk., 1801, comm, W, P2/1801/27
Fydge, Jn., Idmiston, 1551, W, P2/2Reg/126C
Jn. Cookney, butcher, Lyme R., Dorset, 1836, O, W, Wr, P5/1836/33
Fuidge, My., sp., Semington, Steeple A., 1764, AB, P2/F/568
Silvester, butcher, Shitterton, Bere R., Dorset, 1839, W, Wr, P5/1839/12
Thos., clerk, Melk., 1782, AB, comm, P2/F/627
Thos., Chetnole, Yetm., Dorset, 1800, AB, P19/202
Fuidge, Wm., Westb. L., 1740, AB, P25/1740/5
Fues *see* Fuce
Fuester *see* Fewster
Fugger, Thos., tiler, Kington St M., 1713, I, W, P3/F/279
Fuidge *see* Fudge
Fulbrook, Ann, widow, Brightwalton, Berks., 1692, I, W, P1/F/196
Benj., yeo., Newtown, Hungerford, Berks., 1823, comm, W, P23/914
Francis, yeo., Burghfield, Berks., 1720, W, P1/F/278, P1/6Reg/313
Francis, Shinfield, Berks., 1747, AB, comm, P1/F/393
Gabriel, victualler, Welford, Berks., 1792, W, P1/F/509, P1/14Reg/421

Jn., bach. and yeo., Trindledown, W. Shefford, Berks., 1729, I, W, P1/F/307, P1/7Reg/274
Jn., Ogbourne St A., 1766, AB, comm, ren, P23/716
Richd., sen., yeo., Newtown, Hungerford, Berks., 1748, W, P23/607
Richd., labourer, Newtown, Hungerford, Berks., 1813, comm, W, P23/868
Thos., farmer, Newtown, Hungerford, Berks., 1804, W, P23/840
Wm., Brightwalton, Berks., 1674, AB, I, P1/F/145
Fulford, Edwd., [blacksmith], Damerham, Hants, 1557, W, P2/3Reg/20A
Geo., innholder, Sal., 1683, AB, I, P4/1683/4
Geo., maltster, Downton, 1729, W, P1/F/299, P1/7Reg/205
Geo., Barford St M., 1737, AB, I, P2/F/502
Geo., Whitep., 1851, AB, D, W, Wr, P1/1851/6
Joan, widow, Stenhall, Uffc., Devon, 1731, W, P5/1731/33
Jos., labourer, Downton, 1854, aff, W, Wr, P2/1854/9
My., widow, Idmiston, 1730, AB, P2/F/471
Robt., shoemaker, Whitep., 1847, W, Wr, P2/1847/24
Stephen, shoemaker, Sal., 1836, cert, W, Wr, P4/1836/2
Wm., Downton, 1718, AB, P2/F/424
Fulker, Joan, widow, proved at Newbury, Berks., 1606, W, P1/F/18
Fullaway, Ann, widow, Edington, 1687, AB, I, P2/F/332
Jn., labourer, Crickl. St S., 1780, W, P3/F/427
Richd., Malm. (form. of Wootton B.), 1842, AB, O, Wr, P1/1842/98
Thos., blacksmith, Malm., 1662, AB, I, W, P1/F/118
Fuller, Alice, Sonning, Berks., 1617, AB, P5/1617/16, P5/9Reg/215A
Benj., Milton, Berks., 1773, W, P1/F/467, P1/12Reg/474A
Jas., gent., Arborfield, Berks., 1850, O, W, Wr, P5/1850/4
Jn., Devizes St My., 1593, I, W, P1/F/5
Jn., Sherb., Dorset, 1598, I (2), NW, P5/1598/17, P5/6Reg/202B
Jn., husb., Sonning, Berks., 1603, W, P5/1603/29, P5/7Reg/75B
Jn., husb., Calcot, Tilehurst, Berks., 1613, I, NW, P1/F/35
Jn., linen draper's son, Devizes, 1615, W, P1/F/41
Jn., labourer, Westridge, Streatley, Berks., 1625, I, W, P1/F/53
Jos., yeo., Standen, Hungerford, Berks., 1698, AB, I, P5/1697/16
My., widow, Marston, Pott., 1683, AB, I, P1/F/163
My., Devizes, 1757, AB, P1/F/425
Peter, yeo., Tilehurst, Berks., 1643, AB, comm, I, P1/F/96
Robt., butcher, Bradford A., 1600, AB, I, P2/F/55
Simon, Twyford, Hurst, Berks., 1638, AB, I, P5/1638/46, P5/13Reg/124B
Wm., worsted comber, Marston, Pott., 1662, AB, I, P1/F/120
Fulmoore, Edith, widow, Eastrop, Highw., 1588, I, W, P10/1588/3, P5/5Reg/9B
Fulway, Jn., husb., Urchf., 1558, AB, T (child: Gracian F.), P2/F/1, P2/3Reg/136B
Jn., E. Kennett, 1610, W, P3/F/18
Philip, Urchf., 1556, W, P2/3Reg/1C
Roger, husb., Chirton, 1578, I, T, P2/F/13
Fulwood, Jn., Gt. Faringdon, Berks., 1567, AB, P5/2Reg/26E
Furbar, Francis, Charminster, Dorset, 1740, AB, comm, Wr, P5/1740/31
Francis, Charminster, Dorset, 1782, AB, P5/1782/13, P5/17Reg/218A
Furby, Thos., Plaitford, 1733, AB, P2/F/490
Furks, Christian, widow, Oborne, Dorset, 1622, I, W, P5/1622/25, P5/10Reg/171B
Furks alias Eliot, Hy., Oborne, Dorset, 1661, comm, I, W, P5/1661/19
Firkes, Jas., husb., Oborne, Dorset, 1630, W, P5/11Reg/136
Richd., yeo., Oborne, Dorset, 1611-12, I, W, P5/1611/12, P5/9Reg/59B
see also Elliott alias F.
Furmidge, Hy., yeo., Winterborne K., Dorset, 1736, W, P5/1736/12
Formage, Thos., husb., Winterborne K., Dorset, 1603, AB, I, W, P5/1603/28, P5/7Reg/63A
Furnell, Agnes, widow, Chilmark, 1610, I, W, P2/F/85, P2/8Reg/123B
Alice, widow, Ridge, Chilmark, 1605, AB, I, W, P2/F/70
Furnell alias Rogers, Alice, widow, Chilmark, 1640, I, W, P2/F/199
Ann, Chilmark, 1583, W, P2/F/20, P2/6Reg/100A
Furnall, Brian, bach., Trowb., 1844, AB, comm, Wr, P1/1844/2
Cath., widow, Marl., 1750, AB, P1/F/406

Furnell alias Rogers, Cicely, widow, Sedgehill, 1679, I, W, P2/F/286
Edith, Chitterne AS, 1574, W, P2/5Reg/196A
Edwd., husb., Chitterne AS, 1602, I, W, P2/F/60
Elias, labourer, Chicksgrove, Tisb., 1845, O, W, Wr, P2/1845/22
Gregory, husb., Chitterne AS, 1597, AB, I, W, P2/F/45
Jas., Stratford sub C., 1828, AB, P4/1828/5
Joan, Chitterne AS, 1606?, caveat, P1/F/16
Joan, widow, Marl. St Peter and St Paul, 1634, AB, I, P1/F/79
Jn., Chilmark, 1578, I, W, P2/F/12, P2/5Reg/313A
Furnell alias Rogers, Jn., Hindon, 1587, AB, P2/7Reg/76A
Jn., husb., Heytes., 1597, AB, I, W, P5/1597/40, P5/6Reg/179C
Furnell alias Rogers, Jn., yeo., Chilmark, 1639, I, W, P2/F/190
Jn., husb. and labourer, Sherrington, [1640], I, W, P2/F/198
Jn., sen., cheese factor, Marl., 1718, AB, I, W, P1/F/266, P1/6Reg/166
Jn., Wylye, 1724, AB, I, P2/F/450
Furnall, Jn., Ansty (late of Chilmark), 1725, W, P2/F/455
Jn., Steeple L., 1729, AB, I, ren, P1/F/314
Jn., tailor, Chilmark, 1809, W, Wr, P2/1809/55
Jos., cheese factor, Marl., 1810, W, Wr, P1/1810/2
Lucy, widow, Upton L., 1696, AB, I, W, P2/F/370
Furnell alias Rogers, My., sp., Chilmark, 1626, AB, I, W (2), NW, P2/F/134
My., Marl., 1715, AB, P1/F/257
Furnall, Nich., husb., Ditchampton, Wilton, 1767, AB, W, P2/F/580
Richd., Chilmark, 1592, I, W, P2/F/30
Robt., labourer, Chicksgrove, Tisb., 1845, O, W, Wr, P2/1845/21
Stephen, yeo., Sherrington, 1667, I, W, P2/F/237
Susanna, wife, Chitterne AS, 1830, AB, P2/1830/10
Thos., Wylye, 1564, I, W, P2/F/8, P2/4Reg/161B
Thos., husb., Chilmark, 1565, W, P2/4Reg/191B
Thos., Chilmark, 1598, AB, I, W, P2/F/50
Furnell alias Rogers, Walter, Swallowcliffe, 1638, AB, I, P5/1638/47, P5/13Reg/106C
Furnell alias Rogers, Walter, Swallowcliffe, 1661, AB, P5/1661/20
Walter, Chilmark, 1675, AB, P2/F/274
Furnell alias Rogers, Walter, Chilmark, 1695, I, W, P2/F/365
Furnell alias Rogers, Walter, yeo., Teffont M., 1728, W, P2/F/465
see also Rogers alias F.
Furnes, Eliz., widow, Lyme R., Dorset, 1628, AB, P5/1628/40, P5/11Reg/65A
Furnival, Jn., Wantage, Berks., 1706, AB, I, ren, P23/284
Richd., yeo., Charlton, Wantage, Berks., 1672, I, W, P23/32
Richd., jun., Charlton, Wantage, Berks., 1707, AB, I, P5/1707/22
Richd., yeo., Charlton, Wantage, Berks., 1710, I, W, P5/1710/40, P5/15Reg/164
Furrer *see* Farrer
Furs *see* Furze
Fursby, Constance, Britford, 1638, I (detailed), W, P24/307
Joan, Wick, Downton, 1608, I, W, P1/F/24
Joan, widow, Downton, 1635, AB, a/c, alleg, court paper, I, P2/F/166, P2/9Reg/98B
Jn., husb., Homington, 1608, I, W, P2/F/74
Peter, Britford, 1630, I (detailed) (buried at B. 30 Sep 1630), P24/267
Wm., husb., Downton, 1554, W, P2/2Reg/190B
Wm., Downton, 1577, W, P2/F/9, P2/5Reg/280D
Wm., yeo., Broad H., 1676, AB, ren, P3/F/156
Fursden, Eliz., widow, Uffc., Devon, 1670, AB, I, P20/1/59
Geo., yeo., Uffc., Devon, 1664, I, W, P20/1/50
Furze, Furs, Eliz., sp., Wilton, 1766, W, P1/F/448, P1/12Reg/166B
Peter, husb., Wilcot, [1591], W (NEP), P3/1Reg/34B
Fussell, Hy., no abode stated, 1620, I, P2/F/114
Hy. Down, gent. and clerk, Glastonbury, Somerset (effects at Corsley), 1843, O, W, Wr, P2/1843/59
Jn., gent., Grovely Lodge, Barford St M., 1668, AB, I, P2/F/242
Wm., gent., Clarendon Park, 1678-81, I, T (child: Eliz. F. - not decd's dau), W, P4/1678/9, P4/1681/19
Futcher, Edwd., sen., Fisherton A., 1680-81, I, W, P1/F/153, P2/F/294

Isaac, E. Grimstead, W. Dean, 1841, AB, Wr, P2/1841/42
Vocher, Jn., E. Grimstead, W. Dean, 1592, I, T, W, P2/UV/11
Jn., no abode stated, 1630, I, P2/F/145
Kingston, sen., wheelwright, Fisherton A., 1716, W, P2/F/420
My., widow, Fisherton A., 1729, AB, P2/F/468
Robt., Bodenham, Nunton and B., 1790, AB, P2/F/644
Robt., sen., yeo., E. Grimstead, W. Dean, 1849, W, Wr, P2/1849/56
Thos., widower, E. Grimstead, W. Dean, 1775, W, P2/F/601
Thos., gent., Sal., 1817, W, Wr, P1/1817/10
Fydge *see* Fudge
Fye, Fye alias Fiander, Eliz., widow, Maddington, 1814, AB, W, Wr, P2/1814/1
Fyler *see* Filer
Fylis *see* Fillis
Fylppe *see* Phelps
Fynamorry, Roger *see* Wm. Berryman
Fynge, Nich., Corsham, 1589, W, P29/F/1

G… *see* Edwards alias G…
Gabbett, Gabbett alias Benjamin, Chris., Highw., 1637, AB, I (illegible), Wr, P10/1637/6
Giles, yeo., Broad B., Highw., 1608-09, AB, I, W, P5/1608/14, P5/8Reg/132D
Gabbett alias Benjamin, Robt., yeo., Broad B., Highw., 1735, W, P10/1735/2
Gabbett alias Benjamin, Wm., yeo., Broad B., Highw., 1664, comm, I, W, P5/1664/11
see also Benjamin alias G.
Gabell, Mgt., wife, Abingdon, Berks., 1729, AB, I, W, P1/G/455, P1/7Reg/255
Gaby, Chas., bach., Bromham, 1779, AB, P1/G/707
Hy. Headly, Calne, 1834, AB (2), comm, ren, Wr, P26/1410
Jacob, sen., yeo., Bencroft Hill Farm, Bremhill, 1795, AB, cert, draft cert, W, P1/G/754, P1/14Reg/595B
Jas., yeo., Chittoe, Bps. C., 1832, W, Wr, P24/1327
Gawby, Jn., husb., Bromham, 1628, AB, a/c, I, P3/G/101
Gabye, Jn., broad weaver, Broughton G., [1686], I, P2/G/500
Jn., sen., serge weaver, Bromham, 1720, I, W, P3/G/467
Jn., Bromham, 1724, I, W, P3/G/486
Robt., yeo., Bromham, 1671, AB, comm, I, P1/G/222
Robt., Bromham, 1721, I, W, P3/G/468
Robt., Calne, 1786, AB, P26/1150
Sarah, sp., St Edith's Marsh, Bromham, 1840, W, Wr, P3/1840/19
Sarah, widow, Devizes, 1843, O, W, Wr, P1/1843/24
Susanna, widow, Bromham, 1815, AB, Wr, P3/1815/13
Walter, gent., Nether St., Bromham, 1784, W, P3/G/733
Wm., sen., husb., Bromham, 1703, W, P3/G/415
Wm., sen., yeo., Roundway, Bps. C., 1739, W, P24/908
Wm., yeo., Bromham, 1760, W, P3/G/664
Wm., Devizes St Jn., 1831, W, Wr, P1/1831/5
Gadfield *see* Gatfield
Gaffray *see* Jeffreys
Gage, Ann, wife, Sal., 1710, AB, P4/1710/11
Geo., yeo., Sal., 1710, W, P4/1708/11
Jn., sen., gardener, Lyme R., Dorset, 1829, aff, O, W, P16/403
Margery, widow, Netheravon, 1639, AB, a/c, I, L, P12/78
Sam., chandler, Chipp., 1672, AB, I, W, P3/G/222
Gagg, Alice, widow, Hankerton, 1631, I, W, P1/G/108
Edwd., husb., Sherston, 1625, AB, list of debts, NW, P3/G/88
Jn., sen., yeo., Hankerton, 1603, I, W, P3/G/1
Jos., Hankerton, 1756, AB, comm, P3/G/656
My., widow, Hankerton, 1771, W, P3/G/696
Richd., husb., Hankerton, 1613, I, W (NEP), P3/G/28
Robt., sen., yeo., Froxfield, 1698, I, W, P1/G/309, P1/3Reg/157
Susanna, widow, Hankerton, 1631, I, W, P1/G/110
Thos., husb., Hankerton, 1563, W, P1/2Reg/121D
Thos., husb., Hankerton, 1623, I, W, P3/G/76

Wm., Hankerton, 1670, AB, I, P3/G/207
Wm. Pearce, Colerne, 1836, AB, comm, Wr, P3/1836/9
Wm. Pearce, Colerne, 1852, AB, comm, Wr, P3/1852/55
Gaich *see* Gutch
Gailer, Gailor *see* Gaylard
Gaisford, Ann, sp., Melk., 1731, AB, comm, P2/G/764
Ann, widow, Bulk., Keevil, 1820, O, W, Wr, P1/1820/20
Edmd., Keevil, 1559, W, P2/3Reg/170D
Edmd., Gt. Cheverell, 1730, I, W, P2/G/758
Eliz., Keevil, 1758, W, P2/G/910
Geo., Bulk., Keevil, [1641], I (2), W, P2/G/290
Jas., yeo., Keevil, 1725, W, P2/G/735
Jas., spinner, Trowb., 1837, D, O, W, Wr, P1/1837/26
Jeremiah, yeo., Poulshot, 1731, W, P2/G/768
Jn., yeo., Bulk., Keevil, 1642, AB, I, W, P2/G/295
Jn., Bulk., Keevil, 1700, AB, ren, P2/G/584
Jn., gent., Bulk., Keevil, 1720-22, AB, I, P1/G/404, P2/G/711
Jn., widower, Worton, Pott., 1724, AB, I, draft I, P1/G/435
Jn., cordw., Bulk., Keevil, 1734, W, P2/G/788
Jn., maltster, Bulk., Keevil, 1745-65, AB, W, P2/G/849
Jn., Trowb., 1753, AB, ren, P1/G/604
Jn., Poulshot, 1757, W, P2/G/904
Jn., yeo., Warm., 1790, W, P2/G/1051
Jn., sen., gent., Wick, Bps. C., 1805, comm, W, P24/1240
Jn., yeo., Southwick, N. Bradley, 1820, W, Wr, P1/1820/128
Jn., Bulk., Keevil, 1823, W, P2/1823/26
Jn., postmaster, Trowb., 1845, O, W, Wr, P1/1845/32
Jn. Collier, sen., carp. and wheelwright, Warm., 1836, W, Wr, P2/1836/30
Jonathan, yeo., Melk., 1677, I, W, P2/G/409
My. Ann, wife, Warm. (form. of Weston, nr Bath, Somerset), 1844, aff, O, req, W, Wr, P2/1844/54
Rebecca, sp., Holt, Bradford A., 1833, AB, O, Wr, P2/1833/26
Richd., Marston, Pott., 1722, AB, comm, I, P1/G/414
Robt., Bulk., Keevil, 1747, AB, comm, P1/G/575
Roger, gent., Bulk., Keevil, 1758-62, AB, comm, P2/G/908, 929
Sam., Bulk., Keevil, 1690, AB, I, P2/G/526
Sam., Keevil, 1714, AB, P2/G/667
Sarah, widow, Marston, Pott., 1731, AB, comm, P1/G/477
Stephen, gent., Marston, Pott., 1689, I, W, copy W, P1/G/269
Stephen, gent., Bulk., Keevil, 1710-33, comm, W, P2/G/787
Stephen, Bratton, Westb., 1753, AB, P25/1753/2
Stephen, gent., Bulk., Keevil, 1763-81, AB, W, P2/G/934
Stephen, labourer, Bulk., Keevil, 1766, W, P2/G/952
Thos., husb., Bulk., Keevil, 1608, I, W, P2/G/129, P2/8Reg/35B
Tuck, yeo., Bulk., Keevil, 1790, W, P2/G/1052
Tuck, farmer, Bulk., Keevil, 1844, D, W, Wr, P2/1844/43
Wm., sen., yeo., Bulk., Keevil, 1598, W (NEP), P30/72
Wm., yeo., Bulk., Keevil, 1637, I, W, P2/G/266
Wm., husb., Pickwick, Corsham, 1654, AB, I, P29/G/13, P29/1Reg/149C
Wm., broad weaver, Bulk., Keevil, 1668-74, I (2), W (2), P2/G/352, 382
Wm., yeo., Bulk., Keevil, 1669, I, W, P2/G/356
Wm., Bulk., Keevil, 1685, AB, I, P2/G/488
Wm., yeo., Poulshot, 1729, W, P1/G/463, P1/7Reg/319
Wm., gent., Bulk., Keevil, 1755, W, P2/G/894
Wm., gardener, Whitehill, Bradford A., 1774, W, P2/G/980
Gaispur *see* Gesper
Gaitch *see* Gutch
Gaite *see* Gates
Galby, Wm., weaver, Calne, 1566, W, P5/2Reg/9C
Gale, Agnes, singlewoman, Devizes, 1602, I, W, P1/G/6
Alice, widow, Kington L., 1688-89, AB, comm, P3/G/322, 334

Andrew, bricklayer, Sunton, Collingbourne K., 1703, AB, I, P3/G/414
Ann, widow, Foghamshire, Chipp., 1602, W, P3/1Reg/69B
Ann, widow, Oare, Wilcot, 1631, I, W, P1/G/113
Ann, widow, Chipp., 1670, AB, I, P3/G/208
Ann, widow, Chipp., 1674, AB, P3/G/230
Ann, widow, Kington St M., 1736, AB, ren, W, P3/G/564
Ann, widow, N. Wraxall, 1744, W, P1/G/561, P1/9Reg/438C
Ann, widow, Melk., 1757, AB, comm, P2/G/902
Ann, widow, Malm., 1769, AB, comm, P3/G/692
Ann, wife, Beam., Dorset, 1813, AB, comm, P17/599
Ann, sp., Cold Harbour, Hinton, Steeple A., 1846, comm, W, Wr, P2/1846/13
Anthony, clothworker, Bradford A., 1795, W, P1/G/757, P1/14Reg/633
Avis, widow, Elcombe, Wrou., 1681, I, W, P3/G/275
Betty *or* Eliz., Lockeridge, Overton, 1835, O, W, Wr, P3/1835/5
Cath., sp., Sutton B., 1674, I, W, P3/G/231
Chas., yeo., Sutton B., 1667, AB, comm, I, W, P3/G/190
Chas., yeo., Alderton, 1703, I, W, P3/G/416
Chas., sen., yeo., Corston, Malm., 1730, W, P3/G/524
Chas., Bremhill, 1778, AB, P3/G/714
Chas., carp. and wheelwright, Biddestone St Nich., 1826, W, Wr, P1/1826/55
Chris., yeo., Allington, 1699, I, W, P1/G/314, P1/3Reg/221
Dan., Rebel, Clyffe P., 1671, I, W, P3/G/219
Gale alias Arden, Dan., Clyffe P., 1722, I, W, P3/G/472
Dan., yeo., Sutton B., 1772, W, P3/G/699
Dorcas, widow, Chipp., 1766, W, P3/G/680
Dorothy, wife of grocer, Gt. Bedwyn, 1805, W, P21/12/12
Edith, widow, Notton, Lacock, 1614, I (very detailed), P3/G/34
Edmd., surgeon, Chipp., 1618, I, W, P3/G/54
Edmd. Estcourt, clerk and rector, Long Newnton, 1770, comm, W, P1/G/679, P1/12Reg/380
Edwd., yeo., Foghamshire, Chipp., 1612, W (2), P3/G/22
Edwd., husb., Foxham, Bremhill, 1633, I, W, P3/G/129
Edwd., feltmaker, Chipp., 1666, AB, I, P1/G/202
Edwd., yeo., Charlton nr Malm., 1672, I, W, P3/G/223
Edwd., broad weaver, Chipp., 1689, AB, comm, I, P1/G/274, P3/G/335
Edwd., yeo., Sunton, Collingbourne K., 1696, I, W, P3/G/377
Edwd., jun., yeo., Chr. M., 1706-07, W (2), P3/G/421, 426
Edwd., yeo., Charlton nr Malm., 1743, W, P3/G/600
Edwd., gent., Studley, Bremhill, 1744, comm, W, P1/G/560, P1/9Reg/429B
Edwd., Cleverton, Lea and C., 1747, I, W, P3/G/620
Edwd., Bratton, Westb., 1750, AB, P25/1750/4
Edwd., sen., yeo., Stanley Abbey, Bremhill, 1779, AB, W, P1/G/708, P1/13Reg/209A
Edwd., Chr. M., 1784, AB, P3/G/734
Eleanor, widow, Bulidge, Kington St M., [1613], I, W (NEP), P3/G/29
Eliz., widow, Reybridge, Lacock, [1619], I, W (NEP), P3/G/58
Eliz., Sutton B., 1678, AB, P3/G/254
Eliz., widow, Everleigh, 1773, W, P1/G/689, P1/12Reg/508
Eliz., widow, Bremhill (form. of Calne), 1802, W, P3/1802/56
Eliz., widow, Corsham, 1845, ren, W, P29/3Reg/316, P29/1800-1857/41
Eliz. *see also* Betty
Francis, yeo., Allington, 1661, a/c, W, P2/G/327
Gale alias Palmer, Francis, yeo., Sutton B., 1678, I, NW, P3/G/255
Geo., minors, Littlecott, Hilmarton, 1851, comm, court paper, D, note, T, P5/1851/1
Grace, widow, Corston, Malm., 1734, W, P3/G/557
Grace, sp., Hinton, Steeple A., 1744, AB, I, P1/G/559
Grace, widow, Clyffe P., 1826, W, Wr, P3/1826/13
Hy., cordw., Chipp., 1701, W, P3/G/401
Hy., labourer, Hinton, Steeple A., 1749, W, P2/G/873
Isaac, yeo., Foxham, Bremhill, 1721, AB, I (2 - 1 a copy), P3/G/469
Isaac, sen., gent., Corston, Malm., 1727, W, P3/G/502
Isaac, Kington St M., 1732, W, P1/G/483, P1/7Reg/506B

Isaac, gent., Allington, Chipp., 1778, W, P3/G/715
Isaac, Kington St M., 1801, AB, P1/1801/81, P1/15Reg/303A
Isaac, Thornhill, Clyffe P., 1810, W, Wr, P3/1810/52
Isaac, Calne (form. of Littlecott, Hilmarton), 1851, AB, note, O, Wr, P5/1851/2
Isaac, Pott., 1857, aff, O, W, Wr, P1/1857/15
Jacob, sen., yeo., Corston, Malm., 1723, W, P3/G/483
Jacob, gent., Corston, Malm., 1772, W, P3/G/700
Jas., Netherb., Dorset, 1778, AB, P17/571
Jas., clothdresser, Bradford A., 1806, W, P2/1806/7
Jane, widow, Melk., 1762, AB, P2/G/926
Jasper, Sutton B., 1665, comm, I, W (badly damaged), P1/G/197
Jasper, sen., yeo., Sutton B., 1685, W, P3/G/299
Joan, widow, Studley, Calne, 1688, I, W, P5/1688/35
Joan, widow, Chipp., 1724, AB, I (2 - 1 a copy), P3/G/487
Jn., Oare, Wilcot, 1604, I, W, P3/G/3
Jn., husb., Rebel, Clyffe P., 1612, I, P3/G/26
Jn., husb., Studley, Calne, 1612, I, W, P26/23
Jn., husb., Ashton K., 1621, AB, a/c, I, P3/G/67
Jn., tailor, Hilmarton, 1627, AB, I, P3/G/100
Jn., sen., yeo., Chipp., 1630, I, W, P3/G/111
Jn., yeo. and husb., N. Tidworth, 1631, I, W, P2/G/235
Jn., yeo., Sutton B., 1631, I, NW, P3/G/116
Jn., husb., Charlton nr Malm., 1637, I, W, P3/G/147
Jn., Sal., 1645, AB, P1/G/152
Jn., sen., husb., Sutton B., 1648, AB, I, W, P1/G/161
Jn., gent., Chipp., 1669, AB, P3/G/198
Jn., yeo., Sutton B., 1676, AB, comm, I, P3/G/240
Jn., carp., Chr. M., 1681, AB, I, P3/G/276
Gale *or* Geale, Jn., Charlton nr Malm., 1685, AB, comm, I (comm & I on same sheet), P3/G/302
Jn., sen., yeo., Burbage, 1694, AB, I, P11/77
Jn., Loscombe, Netherb., Dorset, 1696, AB, I, P17/353
Jn., labourer, Wokm., Berks., 1731, W, P5/1731/34
Jn., yeo., Elcombe, Wrou., 1733, W, P3/G/547
Jn., yeo., Hinton, Steeple A., 1734, W, P2/G/791
Jn., Wootton R., 1736, AB, ren, P3/G/565
Jn., Wokm., Berks., 1737, AB, P5/1737/22
Jn., Collingbourne D., 1743, AB, P21/9/44
Jn., yeo., Everleigh, 1743, comm, W, P3/G/601
Jn., merchant tailor, Bushton, Clyffe P., 1744, W, P1/G/558, P1/9Reg/379B
Jn., yeo., Alderton, 1758, W, P3/G/660
Jn., clothworker, Chipp., 1766, W, P3/G/681
Jn., Bushton, Clyffe P., 1767, AB, P3/G/685
Jn., yeo., Cocklebury, Langley Burrell, 1767, req, copy W, W, P1/G/659, P1/12Reg/222A
Jn., yeo., Beanacre, Melk., 1771, AB, comm, ren, W, P2/G/967
Jn., wheelwright, Grittleton, 1781, W, P3/G/726
Jn., cloth dresser, Melk., 1797, I, W, P2/G/1072
Jn., bach., Corston, Malm., 1812, AB, comm, Wr, P3/1812/23
Jn., bricklayer, Lockeridge, Overton, 1813, W, Wr, P3/1813/11
Jn., *The Seven Stars*, Bottlesford, Wilsford nr Pewsey, 1831, AB, comm, W, copy W (seems made because of poor legibility of original), P2/1831/40
Jn., sen., carp., Lacock, 1842, comm, W, Wr, P3/1842/18
Jos., beer brewer, Sal. St Martin, 1623, W, P4/1623/4
Jos., yeo., Dauntsey, 1689, comm, I, W, P3/G/336
Jos., bach., Studley, Calne, 1817, AB, Wr, P26/1317
Jos., brasier and widower, Chipp., 1843, AB, Wr, P3/1843/46
Judith, widow, Foxham, Bremhill, 1716, I, W, P3/G/452
Martha, sp., Chipp., 1688, AB, W, Wr, P3/G/323
Martha, barber surgeon's wife, Marl., 1698, W, P1/G/304
Martha, sp., Devizes, 1833, O, W, Wr, P1/1833/3
Gale *or* Geale, My., widow, Hilmarton, 1641, AB, I, W, P3/G/165

My., widow, Calne, 1663, AB, comm, P26/114
My., widow, Sutton B., 1668, AB, comm, I, NW, P1/G/209
My., widow, Charlton nr Malm., 1692, AB, I, W, P3/G/355
My., Foxham, Bremhill, 1696, I, W, P3/G/378
My., widow, Ogbourne St Geo., 1708, AB, I, P23/293
My., widow, Jays, Chipp., 1715, W, P3/G/446
My., widow, Wootton R., 1760, W, P3/G/665
My., widow, Chr. M., 1764, W, P3/G/674
My., widow, Froxfield later Burbage, 1768, AB, ren, W, P11/227
My., widow, Trowb., 1785, comm, W, P1/G/728, P1/14Reg/73
My., sp., Rowde, 1811, comm, O, W, Wr, P3/1811/1
My., victualler, Clyffe P., 1835, comm, W, P1/1835/116
Michael, tailor, Alton Pr., 1790, AB, comm, W, P3/G/750
Nich., husb., Langley Burrell, 1617, AB, a/c, I, P3/G/44
Nich., Pewsham Forest, 1719, AB, P3/G/463
Nich., blacksmith, Chipp., 1743, ren, W, P3/G/602
Nich., Winterborne K., Dorset, 1790, W, P5/1790/8, P5/18Reg/158A
Peter, Corston, Malm., 1711, I (2 - 1 a copy), W, P3/G/436
Peter, yeo., Corston, Malm., 1800, W, P3/1800/32
Rachel, sp., Cold Harbour, Hinton, Steeple A., 1851, O, W, Wr, P1/1851/3
Ralph, husb., Sutton B., 1620, AB, a/c, I, P3/G/60
Ralph, cordw., Chipp., 1685, I, W, P3/G/300
Ralph, yeo., Chr. M., 1726, AB, I, P1/G/448
Ralph, yeo., Chr. M., 1775, W, P3/G/704
Ralph, yeo., Chr. M., 1823, W, Wr, P1/1823/131
Richd., yeo., Reybridge, Lacock, 1620-21, AB (2), comm, I, W, P3/G/61, 68
Richd., husb., Monkton F., 1635, I, W, P1/G/127
Richd., Clyffe P., 1645, W, P1/G/151
Richd., yeo., Chipp., 1670, AB, comm, I, P3/G/209
Richd., Sandhurst, Berks., 1679, AB, I, P5/1679/37
Richd., yeo., Rebel, Clyffe P., 1697, AB, I, P3/G/384
Richd., yeo., Jays, Chipp., 1701, I, NW, P3/G/402
Gale *or* Gearle, Richd., husb. and yeo., Wokm., Berks., 1721, I, W, P5/1721/15
Richd., yeo., Everleigh, 1726, W, P3/G/499
Richd., Clyffe P., 1730, AB, P3/G/525
Richd., Forest Gate, Chipp., 1747, comm, W, P1/G/577, P1/10Reg/193
Richd., Chittoe, Bps. C., 1752, AB, P24/1029
Richd., shopkeeper, Alton Pr., 1785, W, P3/G/737
Richd., Stanley, Chipp., 1802, W, P3/1802/53
Richd., sadler, Corsham, [1804], W, P29/1800-1857/8, P29/3Reg/241
Richd., yeo., Stanley Abbey, Bremhill, 1807, AB, ren, P3/1807/67
Richd., Alton Pr., 1834, aff, W, Wr, P3/1834/14
Robt., yeo., Reybridge, Lacock, 1617, I, W, P3/G/45
Robt., yeo., Chipp., 1675, AB, a/c, I, P3/G/233
Robt., husb., Wokm., Berks., 1694, I, W, P5/1694/2
Robt., narrow weaver, Chr. M., 1726, AB, I, NW, P1/G/450, P1/7Reg/146A
Robt., Corston, Malm., 1804, AB, P1/1804/100
Robt., Chipp., 1715, AB, P3/G/447
Gale *or* Geal, Roger, yeo. *or* husb., Oare, Wilcot, 1700, I, W, P3/G/398
Ruth, widow, Chipp., 1811, W, Wr, P1/1811/91
Sadler, gent., Allington, All C., 1772, W, P3/G/701
Sarah, widow, Chipp., 1703, comm, I, W, P3/G/417
Sarah, widow, Milbourne, Malm., 1810, W, Wr, P3/1810/45
Sarah, sp., Corston, Malm., 1815, W, Wr, P3/1815/37
Sarah, widow, Standen, Chute, 1834, W, Wr, P7/203
Stephen, builder, Burbage, 1824, W, P11/276
Susanna, widow, Elcombe, Wrou., 1736, W, P3/G/566
Susanna, widow, Lyneham, 1748, AB, W, P3/G/623
Susanna, gardener's wife, Chipp., 1808, W, Wr, P1/1808/80
Thos., Melk., 1603, I, W, P2/G/113

Thos., sen., yeo., Notton, Lacock, 1612, AB, comm, I, W, P3/G/23-24
Gale alias Savage, Thos., Westb. L., 1667, NW, P25/1667/3
Thos., Elcombe, Wrou., 1677, AB, a/c, comm, I, P3/G/249
Thos., clothworker, Melk., 1735, comm, W, P1/G/510, P1/8Reg/141B
Thos., yeo., Stanley Abbey, Bremhill, 1741, comm, W, P3/G/590
Thos., gent., Beanacre, Melk., 1741, W, P1/G/542, P1/9Reg/167
Thos., Alderton, 1767, W, P1/G/660, P1/12Reg/221A
Thos., gent., Melk., 1792, comm, W, P2/G/1058
Thos., gent., Crofton, Gt. Bedwyn, 1840, note, O, W, Wr, P5/1840/5
Thos., farmer, Broad Town, Clyffe P., 1857, aff, comm, W, Wr, P3/1857/5
Wm., sen., yeo., Chipp., 1592, I, W, P1/G/2
Wm., *The George*, Calne, 1595-1604, I, definitive sentence, P5/1604/14
Wm., husb., Avon, Chr. M., 1616, I, W, P1/G/59
Wm., yeo., Chipp., 1630, I, W, P3/G/112
Wm., yeo., Bulidge, Kington St M., 1632, I, W, P3/G/123
Wm., Pewsey, 1637, AB, a/c, I, P3/G/148
Wm., cordw., Lacock, 1644, court paper, I, ren, P1/G/153
Wm., Langley Burrell, 1668, comm, I, P3/G/195
Wm., Chr. M., 1670, AB, comm, I, ren, P3/G/210
Wm., Oare, Wilcot, 1675, AB, I, P3/G/234
Wm., maltster, Chipp., 1680, I, W, P1/G/240
Wm., yeo., Chute, 1700, I, W, P7/52
Wm., grocer, Chipp., 1708, AB, comm, ren (2), P3/G/429
Wm., Chipp., 1714, AB, comm, P1/G/380
Wm., Wokm., Berks., 1737, AB, P5/1737/23
Wm., Wexcombe, Grafton, 1744, AB, P21/9/48
Wm., clerk and vicar, Clyffe P., 1745, AB, comm, ren, P3/G/608
Wm., Wokm., Berks., 1748, W, Wr, P5/1748/10
Wm., Corston, Malm., 1751, AB, I, P3/G/637
Wm., labourer, Alton Pr., 1753, W, P1/G/606, P1/11Reg/109
Wm., yeo., Cocklebury, Langley Burrell, 1770, req, W, copy W, P3/G/694
Wm., yeo., Westrop, Highw., 1781, W, P10/1781/1
Wm., yeo., Crofton, Gt. Bedwyn, 1784, W, P21/11/24
Wm., widower, Hullavington, 1811, AB, Wr, P1/1811/88
Wm., gent., Corston, Malm., 1813, W, Wr, P3/1813/59
Wm., labourer, Clyffe P., 1818, W, Wr, P3/1818/30
Wm., workhouse governor, Netherb., Dorset, 1827, W, Wr, P5/1827/44
Wm., W. Kington, 1834, W, Wr, P3/1834/21
Wm., yeo., Durley, Burbage, 1838, W, Wr, P11/295
see also Geale; Godwin alias G.
Galer *see* Gaylard
Gallaway, Eliz., widow, Devizes, 1709, AB, P1/G/352
Hy., serge clothier, Devizes, 1704, AB, I, P1/G/325
My., widow, Froxfield, 1735, AB, P1/G/496
Gilloway, Wm., Tilsh., 1597, AB, NW, P2/G/83
Galle, Chris., Wilcot, 1620, I (2 - 1 a copy), P3/G/62
Edmd., Stanton St Q., 1602, W, P3/1Reg/94
Mgt., widow, Ashton K., 1636, I, W, P3/G/140
Galler *see* Gaylard
Galley, Jas., Sal. St Thos., 1613, AB, P4/1613/13
Gally, Jas., Sherb., Dorset, 1764, W, P5/1764/16
Galli, Octavio Lawr., painter, Rams., 1723, I, W, P5/1723/18, P5/16Reg/85D
Galli, Sarah, widow, Rams., 1744, W, Wr, P5/1744/16
Gallimore, Humphrey, butcher, Wootton B., 1681, I, W, P3/G/277
Jn., vicar, Chiseldon, 1617, AB, I (2 - 1 a copy), P3/G/46
Jn., clerk and vicar, Chiseldon, 1642, AB, I, P3/G/167
Jn., gent., Wootton B., 1733, W, P3/G/548
Jn., gent., Wootton B., 1830, AB, comm, D, Wr, P3/1830/10
Timothy, Wootton B., 1687, AB, I, P3/G/313
Wm., clerk, Swindon, 1662, AB, comm, I, P3/G/175

Gallington, Ann, widow, Devizes, 1746, W, P1/G/562, P1/10Reg/20
Eliz., sp., Devizes, 1782, W, P1/G/719, P1/13Reg/368
Jos., Devizes, 1724, AB, P1/G/436
Jos., blacksmith, Bedborough, Bps. C., 1762, W, P24/1104
Gallop *see* Gollop
Gally *see* Galley
Galpin, Jos., rector, Caundle Marsh, Dorset, 1760, AB, P5/1760/10
Nich., yeo., Enmore Grn, Motc., Dorset, 1821, comm, W, Wr, P19/227
Sam., sen., yeo., Beam., Dorset, 1828, comm, W, P17/606
Wm., Sal., 1666, AB, P4/1665/1
Galton, Alice, widow, Bere R., Dorset, 1593, I, T, W, P5/1593/35, P5/6Reg/46A
Edmd., husb., Bloxworth, Dorset, 1665, AB, I, NW, P5/1665/35
Goulton, Eliza Oliver, dressmaker and sp., Lyme R., Dorset, 1855, aff, comm, D, W, Wr, P16/457
Eliz., widow, Bere R., Dorset, 1631, I, W, copy W, P5/1631/44, P5/12Reg/1
Eliz., Winterborne K., Dorset, 1680, AB, I, P5/1680/16
Eliz., sp., Wilton, 1854, AB, aff, D, W, Wr, P2/1854/15
Galtons, Emma, widow, Bere R., Dorset, 1622, I, W, P5/1622/32, P5/10Reg/138
Hubert, husb. *or* yeo., Winterborne K., Dorset, 1620, AB, I, T, W, P5/1620/25, P5/10Reg/5
Hubert, sen., Winterborne K., Dorset, 1674, AB, I, ren, P5/1674/29
Hubert, yeo., Kingston, Dorset (form. of Hinton St Geo., Somerset), 1677, I, W, P5/1677/22
Joan, widow, Bere R., Dorset, 1593, I, W, P5/1592/34, P5/6Reg/21B
Jn., Bere R., Dorset, 1569, W, P5/2Reg/34D
Jn., Winterborne K., Dorset, 1571, W, P5/2Reg/94B
Jn., husb., Bere R., Dorset, 1616, AB, comm, I, P5/1616/31, P5/9Reg/179B
Ralph, husb., Bere R., Dorset, 1628, I, W, P5/1628/49, P5/11Reg/73
Richd., sen., yeo., Burcombe, 1769, W, P2/G/959
Robt., Bere R., Dorset, 1579, I, W, P5/1579/30, P5/3Reg/122C
Robt., Bere R., Dorset, 1619, AB, comm, I, P5/1618/16, P5/9Reg/229C
Gaulton, Thos., husb., Bere R., Dorset, 1613, I, W, P5/1613/29, P5/9Reg/84
Gaulton, Thos., Hilp., 1727, AB, P2/G/741
Thos., widow, Fovant, 1816, W, P2/1816/45
Gamble, Gamboll, David, blacksmith, Malm., 1635, AB, a/c, I, P3/G/135
Jas., clothworker, Bradford A., 1770, W, P1/G/668, P1/12Reg/314A
Jn., stone mason, Nursteed, Bps. C., 1798, comm, W, P24/1202
Michael, clothworker, Seend Cleeve, Melk., 1819, comm, W, Wr, P2/1819/19
Sarah, widow, Nursteed, Bps. C., 1807, W, P24/1246
Gamboll, Thos., broad weaver, Malm., 1615, I, W, P3/G/39
Gamblin, Chas., yeo., Corton, Boyton, 1799, W, P2/G/1079
Gambling, Robt., innkeeper, Whitep., 1835, W, P1/1835/52
Gamboll *see* Gamble
Game, Ann, widow, S. Bowood, Netherb., Dorset, 1738, AB, P17/466
Francis, sen., yeo., S. Bowood, Netherb., Dorset, 1755, W, P5/1755/17
Hy., yeo., S. Bowood, Netherb., Dorset, 1711, AB, I, P17/203
Games, My., sp., Bowden, Lacock, 1707, AB, comm, ren, P1/G/341
Peter, Allweston, Folke, Dorset, 1705, W, P5/1705/20
Susanna, widow, Haydon, Dorset, 1699, AB, I, NW, P5/1699/14
Thos., yeo., Haydon, Dorset, 1719, I, W, P5/1719/36, P5/16Reg/20A
Thos., yeo., Sherb., Dorset, 1820, comm, W, Wr, P5/1820/2
Wm., sen., Haydon, Dorset, 1683-85, AB (2), comm, I (2), W, P5/1683/22, P5/1685/40
Wm., yeo., S. Bowood, Netherb., Dorset, 1744, AB, I, P17/491
Gamedge, Richd., husb., Chards., Devon, 1682-84, I, W (NEP), P30/73
Thos., mariner, Lyme R., Dorset, 1622, AB, I, P5/1622/34, P5/10Reg/127B
Games *see* Game
Gamlin, Gamlyn, Jas., linen weaver and yeo., Wolverton, Zeals, 1667, I (detailed), W, P5/1667/20
Gamlyn, Sam., innholder, Fisherton A., 1748, W, P2/G/862
Wm., Mere, 1624, AB, P5/1624/19, P5/10Reg/168A
Gammon, Alice, widow, Wantage, Berks., 1711, W, P23/317
Alice, Oare, Wilcot, 1725, W, P3/G/491
Anthony, yeo., St Mgt., Preshute, 1720, I, W, P1/G/406, P1/6Reg/350B
Gamman, Eliz., widow, Eastcourt, Burbage, 1748, W, P11/204

Gammons, Jn., Overton, 1728, AB, P3/G/509
Jn., gardener, Burbage, 1738, I, W, P11/163
Gamman, My., Grafton, 1765, W, P21/10/67
Richd., glazier, Thatcham, Berks., 1704, I, W, P1/G/331
Gamon, Robt., E. Kennett, 1691, AB, I, Wr (badly damaged), P3/G/349
Sarah, sp., Thatcham, Berks., 1759, AB, P1/G/624
Thos., yeo., E. Hagbourne, Berks., 1735, W, P1/G/501, P1/7Reg/662B
Wm., weaver, Blewbury, Berks., 1591, AB, I, W, P5/1591/27, P5/5Reg/119A
Wm., plumber, Wantage, Berks., 1695, I, W, P23/218
Ganaway, Chris., jun., yeo., Damerham, Hants, 1716, W, P2/G/674
Chris., yeo., Damerham, Hants, 1723, W, P1/G/431, P1/7Reg/27C
Jn., sen., labourer, Damerham, Hants, 1766, W, P2/G/953
Thos., sen., yeo., Damerham, Hants, 1725, W, P2/G/729
Gander, Jn., tailor, Sherb., Dorset, 1722, AB, I, P5/1722/24
Penelope, widow, Sherb., Dorset, 1797, AB, comm, P5/1797/15, P5/18Reg/257A
Gandy, Alice, widow, Farley, Alderbury, 1780, AB, ren, W, P26/1104
Edwd., yeo., Sal. St Martin, 1664, I, W, P4/1664/12
Jas., husb., Loosehanger, Downton, 1699, I, W, P2/G/571
Gandy *or* Candy, Jn., Westb., 1637, AB, I, P25/1637/4
Robt., Downton, 1695, AB, I, P2/G/551
Simon, Quidh., 1606, I, W, P1/G/18
Susan, widow, Quidh., 1615, I, W, copy W, P2/G/171, P2/8Reg/292B
Wm., Reading St My., Berks., 1704, AB, P1/G/330
Gane, Anna Maria, sp., Melk., 1837, AB, ren, Wr, P2/1837/48
Geyne, Avis, widow, Bere R., Dorset, 1615, AB, I, NW, P5/1615/13, P5/9Reg/156A
Eliza, sp., Amesb., 1849, AB, D, Wr, P2/1849/53
Eliz., widow, Corsley, 1810, AB, Wr, P2/1810/19
Geyne, Gilbert, Newton T., 1613, W, P2/G/159
Hy., Chicklade, 1593, note of admon, P2/G/65
Jas., grocer, Melk., 1838, AB, Wr, P2/1838/23
Joan, widow, Corsham, 1812, comm, W, Wr, P3/1812/20
Job, builder, Trowb., 1817, W, Wr, P1/1817/83
Jn., clerk and rector, Berwick St Jn., 1747, W, P1/G/576, P1/10Reg/184
Jn., Gillingham, Dorset, 1826, W, Wr, P27/1/675
Jos., yeo., Heytes., 1742, W, Wr, P5/1742/17
My., Berwick St Leonard, 1625, AB, I, P1/G/94
Richd., Imber, 1635, AB, I, P2/G/255, P2/9Reg/51B
Geyne, Thos., husb., Bere R., Dorset, 1610, W, P5/9Reg/46
Wm., yeo., Hungerford, Berks., 1678, I, W, P23/85
Wm., tailor, Hullavington, 1825, W, Wr, P3/1825/28
see also Gawen
Gange, Jos., Halstock, Dorset, 1836, comm, W, P16/412
My., widow, Uffc., Devon, 1732, I, W, P20/1/186
Ganger *see* Genger
Gannet, Edwd., bricklayer, Sal., 1698, W, P4/1697/4
Richd., vicar choral and clerk, Sal. The Close, 1623, AB, I, P5/1622/30, P5/10Reg/143A
Gantlett *see* Gauntlett
Ganway, My., widow, Beam., Dorset, 1710, I, NW, P17/191
Gapper, Frances, sp., Sal., 1791, W, P4/1791/6
Jane Burton, widow, Sherb., Dorset, 1816, W, Wr, P5/1816/8
My., sp., Stapleton, Somerset (effects at Fittleton), 1786, AB, P2/G/1034
Gapping, Ann, Ryme I., Dorset, 1710, W, P5/1710/48, P5/15Reg/195A
Gardner, Agnes, widow, Stockton, 1638, I, W, P2/G/271
Alice, widow, S. Hinksey, Cumnor, Berks., 1692, W, P1/G/281
Gardener, Andrew, Charlcote, Bremhill, 1729, W, P3/G/519
Gardener, Ann, widow, Whitep., 1802, AB, P2/1802/13
Arnold, baker, Sal., 1665, W, P4/1665/8
Gardiner, Chas., yeo., Nunton, N. and Bodenham, 1764, W, P2/G/941
Chas., yeo., Pitton, Alderbury, 1794, note (rough valuation), W, P26/1198
Chas., Slaughterford, 1817, W, Wr, P1/1817/50

Gardiner, Chris., gent., Tinh., Edington, [1642], I, W, P2/G/302
Gardiner, Chris., gent., Tinh., Edington, [1667], I, P2/G/348
Gardiner, Chris., baker, Sal., 1688, AB, NW, P4/1688/16
Chris., barber, Sherb., Dorset, 1693, W, P5/1693/27
Chris., yeo., Pascroft, Whaddon, 1714, I, W, P2/G/669
Gardiner, Dan., husb., Whaddon, Alderbury, 1665, I, W, P26/127
Gardiner, Dan., yeo., W. Grimstead, 1681, a/c, I, W, P2/G/435
Dan., Laverstock, 1701, ren, W, P2/G/590
Gardiner, Dorothy, sp., Sal. The Close, 1679, AB, I, P5/1679/36
Edith, widow, Bere R., Dorset, 1559-61, AB, W, P1/2Reg/109C-D
Edwd., maltster, Warm., 1783, W, P2/G/1020
Gardiner, Eliz., Upham, Aldbourne, 1563, W, P1/2Reg/126A
Eliz., sp., Warm., 1679, I, W, P2/G/419
Gardiner, Eliz., wife, Alderbury, 1730, W, P26/747
Gardiner, Eliz., widow, Bradfield, Berks., 1747, AB, P1/G/571
Gardiner, Eliz., sp., Wilton, 1798, AB, P1/G/761, P1/15Reg/38A
Gardner alias Gardiner, Eliz., widow, Whitep., 1853, W, Wr, P2/1853/40
Fanny, widow, Whitep., 1855, AB, aff, Wr, P1/1855/28
Gardiner, Frances, sp., Sal. The Close, 1681, W, P5/1681/18
Gardener, Geo., Warm., 1752, AB, ren, P2/G/885
Gardiner, Geo., carp., Bodenham, Nunton and B., 1804, W, P1/1804/40
Gardiner, Geo., shopkeeper, Whitep., 1828, W, Wr, P2/1828/7
Geo., Whitep., 1831, AB, Wr, P2/1831/38
Hy., Upham, Aldbourne, 1669, AB, comm, I, P3/G/199
Jas., N. Bradley, 1705, AB, P2/G/612
Jas., widower, Stratford Tony, 1799, W, P2/G/1080
Gardnar, Jas., yeo., Manningford Bruce, 1853, comm, W, Wr, P3/1853/5
Jane, gent.'s wife, Warm., 1779, W, P1/G/709, P1/13Reg/212
Gardener, Jenny, widow, Whitep., 1758, AB, P2/G/913
Jn., husb., Wedh., Urchf., 1571-75, AB, W, P1/1Reg/128A, P2/5Reg/231C
Gardener, Jn., Liddington, 1602, I, W, P1/G/7
Gardiner, Jn., yeo., Upham, Aldbourne, 1604, I, W, P3/G/4
Gardiner, Jn., Liddington, 1614, I, P1/G/51
Jn., tailor, Stockton, 1617, AB, I, P2/G/175, P2/8Reg/320B
Gardener, Jn., baker, Sal., 1626, AB, I, W, P4/1626/9
Jn., glover, Wootton B., 1669, I, W, P3/G/200
Gardiner, Jn., yeo., Dartfords Wood, Norton B., 1672, I, W, P2/G/368
Gardiner, Jn., yeo., Liddington, 1674-78, AB, comm, I, P3/G/232, 256
Jn., yeo., Inglesham, Berks., 1679, comm, I, W, P3/G/263
Jn., gent., Tinh., Edington, 1720, W, P2/G/702
Jn., yeo., Tytherton L., Chipp., 1728, I, W, P3/G/510
Jn., clothworker, Westb. L., 1731, AB, I, P25/1731/4
Jn., Bradford A., 1766, AB, P2/G/951
Gardener, Jn., Burghfield, Berks., 1770, AB, P1/G/675
Gardiner, Jn., yeo., Tytherton L., Chipp., 1772, W, P3/G/702
Gardener, Jn., Bodenham, Nunton and B., 1777, W, P2/G/993
Gardener, Jn., labourer, Minety, 1837, aff, O, W, Wr, P3/1837/64
Jn., coal merchant, Wootton B., 1852, O, W, Wr, P3/1852/24
Jos., carp., Crickl. St S., 1838, comm, W, Wr, P3/1838/59
Lucy, widow, Leigh, Bradford A., 1750, AB, P1/G/583
Mgt., widow, Upton L., 1562, I, W, P2/G/10
Gardiner, Mgt., sp., Ashton K. & Purton, 1622, AB, I, P3/G/71
Mgt., sp., Liddington, 1742, W, P3/G/594
Gardiner, Margery, widow, Bratton, Westb., 1640, I (ref. to cost of burial), P25/1640/9
Gardiner, Margery, widow, Liddington, 1689, W, P3/G/324
Gardiner, My., widow, Chipp., 1693, I, W, P3/G/360
Gardiner, My., Bulk., Keevil, 1764, AB, P2/G/936
My., widow, Gt. Wishford, 1810, W, P2/1810/8
Gardener, My., sp., Slaughterford, 1823, W, Wr, P1/1823/60
Gardiner, My., sp., Whitep., 1853, D, W, Wr, P2/1853/39

Gardener alias Lame, Matthew, wheelwright, Warm., 1747, W, P2/G/860
Moses, labourer, Poulshot, 1773, AB, W, P2/G/977
Oswald, W. Grimstead, 1690, AB, P2/G/525
Richd., sen., Britford, 1573, W, P5/3Reg/16C
Richd., baker, Warm., [1614], I, W, P2/G/163
Gardener, Richd., husb., Aldbourne, 1628, AB, comm, I, P1/G/104
Richd., Compton C., 1646, AB, P2/G/310
Gardiner, Richd., gent., Broughton G., 1676, I, W, P2/G/397
Gardiner, Richd., linen draper, Sal., 1681, AB, P4/1680/16
Gardiner, Richd., sen., Bradford A., 1722, AB, P2/G/714
Gardener, Richd., sen., tailor, Bradfield, Berks., 1741, W, P1/G/539, P1/9Reg/120
Gardener *or* Gardner, Ruth, widow, Wilton, 1803, AB, P2/1803/65
Gardiner, Stephen, Aldbourne, 1683, AB, I, P3/G/285
Stephen, yeo., Lyneham, 1734, W, P3/G/558
Gardener, Stephen, Netherton, Fyfield, Berks., 1763, W, P1/G/635, P1/12Reg/45A
Gardener, Thos., Upton L., 1552, I, W, P2/G/2, P2/2Reg/159A
Gardiner, Thos., Cherhill, 1631, I, W (no religious preamble), P5/1631/43, P5/12Reg/40A
Thos., miller, Chr. M. & Cadenham, 1662, comm, I, W, P3/G/176
Thos., glover, Tytherton L., Chipp., 1663, I, W, P3/G/177
Thos., sen., tailor, Warm., 1676, I, W, P2/G/400
Gardiner, Thos., husb., Baydon, 1693, AB, I, NW, P5/1692/34
Gardiner, Thos., bach., Liddington, 1695, AB, I, Wr, P3/G/373
Gardiner, Thos., yeo., Tytherton L., Chipp., 1702, I, W, P3/G/406
Gardiner, Thos., yeo., Foxham, Bremhill, 1728, I, W, P3/G/511
Gardiner, Thos., yeo., Whitep., 1753, I, W, P2/G/891
Thos., Warm., 1780, AB, P2/G/1005
Thos., shopkeeper, Whitep., 1835, W, P2/1835/16
Wm., baker, Warm., 1567, I, W, P2/G/21, P2/5Reg/24B
Gardiner, Wm., yeo., Liddington, 1622, I, W, P3/G/72
Gardiner, Wm., husb., Liddington, 1630, I, W, P3/G/113
Wm., sen., yeo., Ogbourne St Geo., 1662, comm, W, P5/1662/47
Gardiner, Wm., baker, Wilton, 1669, AB, I, P2/G/354
Gardiner, Wm., baker, Sal., 1672, AB, a/c, I, P4/1672/5
Wm., baker, Sal., 1710, W, P4/1710/8
Gardener, Wm., sadler, Warm., 1752, comm, W, P2/G/888
Wm., Wilton, 1785, W, P2/G/1031
Wm., Bradford A., 1793, AB, comm, P2/G/1062
Wm., tailor, Sherb., Dorset, 1804, D, W, P5/1804/14, P5/19Reg/112
Gardiner, Wm., labourer, Bodenham, Nunton and B., 1806, W, P2/1806/17
see also Garner *or* G.; Lamb alias G.; Wall alias G.
Gare, Robt., priest, Upton L., 1550, W (to rectory), P2/2Reg/111B
Garland, Anthony, tucker, Westb., 1575, AB, I, P25/1575/2, P5/3Reg/57B
Hy., yeo., Yondover, Netherb., Dorset, 1744, W, P17/488
Richd., Fordington, Dorset, 1573, W, P5/3Reg/18C
Robt., weaver, Brook, Westb., 1679, AB, I, P25/1679/9
Tobias, clothworker, Westwood, 1720, I (books listed), W, P1/G/399, P1/6Reg/210
Wm., clothworker, Sherb., Dorset, 1684, I, W, P5/1684/22
Garlick, Ann, widow, Broad Town, Clyffe P., 1700, AB, I, P3/G/397
Beata, widow, Hyam Farm, Westport St My., 1746, W, P3/G/615
Benj., watchmaker, Malm., 1833, AB (re property in M.), comm, P3/1833/13
Dan., sen., Kintbury, Berks., 1795, W, P1/G/755, P1/14Reg/583C
Dan., Brokenb., 1837, AB, O, Wr, P3/1837/14
Dan. Jn. Bennet, Westport St My., 1817, AB, comm, Wr, P1/1817/2
Edwd., yeo. *or* farmer, Westport St My., 1712, I, W, P3/G/437
Edwd., tanner, Sal., 1797, AB, W, P4/1797/9
Eliz., widow, Broad Town, Clyffe P., 1620, I, W, P3/G/59
Eliz., widow, Marl., 1698, I, W, P1/G/313, P1/3Reg/150
Eliz., widow, Westport St My., 1798, AB, T (children: Geo. & Eliz. G.), W, P3/G/770
Geo., Marl. St My., 1644, AB, NW, P1/G/147
Giles, farmer and tanner, Gilboa Farm, Brokenb., 1814, W, P1/1814/131

Harry, yeo., Thornhill, Westport St My., 1825, comm, W, Wr, P3/1825/12
Jas., butcher, Malm., 1821, W, Wr, P3/1821/23
Jn., carp., Broad Town, Clyffe P., 1631, I, list of debts, W, P3/G/117
Jn., yeo., Cherhill, 1708, AB, I, ren, P26/545
Jn., Broad B., Highw., 1723, W, P10/1723/8
Jn., maltster, Westport St My., 1802, W, P3/1802/47
Jn., yeo., Leigh, Ashton K. (form. of Brokenb.), 1849, D, O, W, Wr, P3/1849/36
Lucy, sp., Milbourne, Malm., 1776, W, P3/G/705
My., widow, Ashton K., 1739, W, P3/G/579
My., widow, Backbridge, Westport St My., 1757, W, P3/G/658
My., widow, Pott., 1827, W, Wr, P1/1827/11
Nathaniel, gent., Westport St My., 1737, AB, comm, P3/G/567
Rachel, sp., Malm., 1836, AB, Wr, P3/1836/62
Richd., Broad Town, Clyffe P., 1610, W, P3/G/16
Richd., gent., Cotmarsh, Clyffe P., 1688, I, W, P3/G/325
Richd., sen., yeo., Broad Town, Clyffe P., 1717, AB, I, ren, P3/G/457
Richd., yeo., Hyam Farm, Westport St My., 1742, W, P3/G/595
Richd., gent., Clyffe P., 1779, W, P3/G/718
Richd., tanner, Westport St My., 1789, AB, ren, W, P3/G/747
Robt., yeo., Ludg., 1587, W, P2/7Reg/74A
Robt., Broad Town, Clyffe P., 1644-45, AB, comm, I (damaged), P1/G/154, P3/G/170
Robt., butcher, Oak Well, Poole Keynes, 1741, W, Wr, P1/G/541, P1/9Reg/170A
Robt., shopkeeper, Avebury, 1819, W, Wr, P3/1819/11
Roger, Broad Town, Clyffe P., [1688], I, W, P1/G/268
Thos., victualler, Marl., 1686, I, W, P1/G/261
Thos., Clyffe P., 1717, AB, P3/G/458
Thos., Charlton nr Malm., 1724, AB, P3/G/488
Thos., Brokenb., 1737, AB, P3/G/569
Thos., cordw., Malm., 1737, W, P3/G/568
Thos., tanner, Westport St My., 1770, W, P1/G/670, P1/12Reg/331
Thos., butcher, Malm., 1799, W, Wr, P3/G/772
Wm., yeo., Broad Town, Clyffe P., 1688, AB, comm, I, P3/G/326
Wm., innholder, Lambourn, Berks., 1733-34, W, P1/G/492, P1/7Reg/588
Wm., farmer, Broad Town, Clyffe P., 1768, W, P3/G/688
Wm., shoemaker, Wood Street Lane, Wootton B., 1836, W, Wr, P3/1836/29
Garmy, Garmy, Jn., Hungerford, Berks., 1606, I, NW, P1/G/17
Germy *or* Garmy alias Cook, Thos., sen., Hungerford, Berks., 1661, AB, comm, NW (very fragile), P5/1661/21
Garmy alias Cook, Thos., butcher, Hungerford, Berks., 1694, AB, I, P23/208
see also Cook alias G.
Garn *see* Gurn
Garner, Garner *or* Gardiner, Hy., baker, Castle C., 1669-70, AB, I, W, P28/1
Jn., yeo., Purton, 1691, comm, I, W, P3/G/350
Jn., yeo., Newton, Whitep., [1711], I, W, P2/G/643
Robt., S. Marston, 1664, AB, I, P5/1664/12
Thos., Leigh, Bradford A., 1786, W, P2/G/1035
Wm., Bradford A., 1791, AB, comm, P2/G/1054
Garnett, Thos., Enford, 1553, W, P2/2Reg/171A
Wm., priest, Fisherton D., 1557, institution to vicarage, P1/1Reg/4B
Wm., vicar, Fisherton D., 1564, AB, I, P2/G/17, P2/4Reg/182B
Garnsey, Sarah, sen., widow, Uffc., Devon, 1746, W, P5/1746/31
Thos., gent., Bodmiscombe, Uffc., Devon, 1821, AB, appt of proctors, comm, W, Wr, P5/1821/45
Garoway *see* Garraway
Garrard *see* Gerrard
Garrat, Garratt *see* Garrett
Garraway, Garoway, Ralph, Hurst, Berks., 1647, AB, P5/14Reg/92C
Richd., yeo., Avebury, 1688, I, W, Wr, P3/G/327
Garrett, Ambrose, Maddington, 1806, AB, Wr, P2/1806/66
Ann, widow, Cottles, Atworth, Bradford A., 1705, comm, W, P2/G/618
Ann, Martin, Hants, 1725, AB, P2/G/734
Chas., Dilton M., Westb., 1854, declarations, O, W, Wr, P25/1854/5

Jarrett, Christian, widow, Warm., 1609, AB, I, W, P2/IJ/48, P2/8Reg/38
Jarrett, Edith, widow, Yatesbury, 1585, I, W, P3/IJ/1, P5/4Reg/119C
Garret, Edmd., Martin, Hants, 1593, I, T, P2/G/69
Garret, Edmd., yeo., Martin, Hants, 1683, I, W, P2/G/465
Garrat, Eliz., widow, Martin, Hants, 1559, W, P2/4Reg/10D
Eliz., widow, Kingston Lisle, Sparsholt, Berks., 1616, AB, I, P1/G/58
Eliz., sp., Gt. Faringdon, Berks., 1633-34, comm, I (2), W (2), NW, P5/1633/20, P5/12Reg/319
Garret, Eliz., widow, Tytherington, Heytes., 1759, AB, P5/1759/9
Francis, Maddington, 1815, AB, P2/1815/24
Hy., blacksmith, Kingston D., 1724, W, P2/G/726
Hy., blacksmith, Sutton V., 1740, W, P2/G/822
Hy., Horningsham, 1774, AB, comm, P5/1774/6, P5/17Reg/84B
Jarred, Jane, widow, Devizes, 1830, AB, Wr, P1/1830/10
Garret, Joan, widow, Downton, 1613, I, W, P1/G/38
Joel, yeo., Hill D., 1823, W, Wr, P5/1823/30
Jn., Damerham, Hants, 1558, W, P2/3Reg/83D
Jn., husb., Martin, Hants, 1558, W, P2/3Reg/111A
Jn., yeo., Compton C., 1613-15, AB, I, req, W, P2/G/160, P2/8Reg/196B
Jn., shoemaker, Sal., 1683, AB, I, ren, P1/G/252
Jn., yeo., Martin, Hants, 1695, I, W, P1/G/300
Jn., blacksmith, Seend Row, Melk., 1762, AB, ren, P2/G/928
Jn., Mkt. L., 1764, AB, P2/G/935
Jn., innholder, Sal., 1810, W, P4/1810/9
Jn., blacksmith, Corton, Boyton, 1817, W, Wr, P2/1817/24
Garritt, Jonathan, fuller, Westb., 1754, AB, ren, P25/1754/7
Garritt, Jos., fuller, Westb., 1746, W, P25/1746/1
Jarrett, Mgt., widow, Malm., 1665, I, W, P3/IJ/88
Garratt, My., widow, Warm., 1702, AB, I, P2/G/592
Nich., Damerham, Hants, 1557, W, P2/3Reg/10C
Garret alias Carret, Richd., Wick, Bps. C., 1668, AB, comm, I, P24/374
Garret, Richd., blacksmith, Wilton, 1746, W, Wr, P2/G/853
Richd., Corton, Boyton, 1781, AB, P2/G/1011
Richd., yeo., Dilton M., Westb., 1855, aff, O, W, Wr, P25/1855/1
Jarrett, Roger, Yatesbury, 1594, I, W, P5/1594/44, P5/6Reg/87A
Thos., Damerham, Hants, 1558, W, P2/3Reg/138A
Jarrett, Thos., cordw., Manton & Marl. St My., 1705, I, W, P1/IJ/139
Garrott, Thos., sen., yeo., Bockhampton, Lambourn, Berks., 1723, W, P1/G/425, P1/6Reg/464
Garrett alias Johnson, Thos., Motc., Dorset, 1728, AB, P27/1/292
Thos., blacksmith, Monkton D., 1847, W, Wr, P2/1847/44
Walter, Martin, Hants, 1639, AB, I, P2/G/284
Walter, rector, Everleigh, 1716, AB, comm, P1/G/389
Wm., Martin, Hants, 1648, AB, P2/G/317
Wm., sen., plumber, Warm., 1672, I (very detailed), W, P2/G/369
Garratt, Wm., sen., plumber, Warm., 1681, W, P2/G/445
Garret, Wm., blacksmith, Sutton V., 1693, I, W, P2/G/540
Garratt, Wm., Rams., 1702, AB, P5/1702/19
Garratt, Wm., yeo., Woodley, W. and Sandford, Berks., 1704, comm, I, W, P5/1703/13
Garrish, Wm., Hilp., 1716, AB, P2/G/680
Wm., blacksmith, Keevil, 1719, AB, ren, P2/G/696
Wm., Sutton V., 1733, AB, P2/G/781
Garrat, Wm., sen., innkeeper, Tilsh., 1766, W, P1/G/654, P1/12Reg/169B
Wm., Corton, Boyton, 1768, AB, P2/G/956
see also Gerrard
Gartherell, Gartrell *see* Gatrell
Gasard, Chas., gent., Alderton, 1734, W, P3/G/559
Gaskins, Hy., New Windsor, Berks., 1708, AB, I, P1/G/346
Gasney *see* Gosney
Gasper *see* Gesper
Gasse *see* Gast
Gassett *see* Jessett

Gast, Jane, sp., Lt. Burton, Long Burton, Dorset, 1692, AB, I (2), P5/1692/31
Jn., gent., Leigh, Yetm., Dorset, 1677, I, P19/35
Jn., sen., yeo., Lt. Burton, Long Burton, Dorset, 1677, comm, I, W, P5/1677/19
Jn., yeo., Leigh, Yetm., Dorset, 1698, W, P19/81
Gasse, Jn., yeo., Lt. Burton, Long Burton, Dorset, 1701, I, W, P5/1701/22
Jn., gent., Leigh, Yetm., Dorset, 1717, W, P19/102
Jn., wine merchant, Sal., 1791, W (detailed), P4/1791/4
Sarah, widow, Long Burton, Dorset, 1717, I, W, P5/1717/16, P5/15Reg/402
Thos., victualler, Leigh, Yetm., Dorset, 1566, W, P5/1Reg/69C
Thos., Leigh, Yetm., Dorset, 1635, AB, I, P5/1635/45, P5/12Reg/208B
Gaston, Robt., Bray, Berks., 1662, I, W, P1/G/177
Gastrell, Alice, widow, Monkton F., 1639, I, NW, P2/G/280
Edmd., gent., Monkton F., 1626, AB, comm, I (very detailed), P2/G/212
Jas., gent., Kington St M., 1679, AB, I, W, P3/G/264
Jas., yeo., Swinley Farm, Kington St M., 1725, comm, W, P3/G/492
Jn., [Luckington] (NBI), 1635, I, P3/G/136
Jn., gent., Charlton nr Malm., 1694, AB, I, P3/G/366
Mgt., widow, Langley Burrell, 1638, I, T, W, P1/G/138
My., widow, Allington, Chipp., 1735, W, P3/G/562
Thos. Stevens, gunsmith, Malm., 1794, aff, comm, W, P3/G/761
Walter, gent., Sherston, 1627, comm, I, W, P3/G/97
Gatch *see* Gaich
Gatehouse, Chas., Steeple L., 1758, AB, P2/G/906
Chas., cheese factor and shopkeeper, Sal., 1814, W, Wr, P1/1814/45
Eliz., minors, Sal., 1800, appt of guardian, P4/1800/12
Geo., gardener, Motc., Dorset, 1764, W, P27/1/443, P27/3Reg/117
Hy., Hanging L., 1856, AB, aff, O, Wr, P2/1856/51
Jane, widow, Mere, 1796, W, P5/1796/4, P5/18Reg/224A
Jeremiah, sen., linen weaver, Motc., Dorset, 1684, I, P27/1/82
Jeremiah, sen., Motc., Dorset, 1710, AB, P27/1/187
Jn., yeo., Mere, 1785, W, P5/1785/13, P5/18Reg/29
Jn., innholder, *The Plume of Feathers*, Sal., 1800, D, NW, P4/1800/13
Roger, Motc., Dorset, 1574, W, P27/1Reg/29A
Gethowse, Wm., Motc., Dorset, 1562, W, P27/1Reg/12C
Wm., Motc., Dorset, 1727, AB, P27/1/284
Gately, Geatly, Ann, widow, Stratford sub C., 1734, AB, Wr, P4/1734/8
Gethly, Chris., Penleigh, Dilton, Westb., 1698, AB, ren, P25/1698/3
Getly, Hy., blacksmith, E. Knoyle, 1703, W, P2/G/598
Getly, Hy., yeo., Milton, E. Knoyle, 1769, W, P2/G/962
Gatley, Jn., husb., Hawkeridge, Westb., 1627, I, W, P25/1626/5
Geatly, Jn., yeo., Bradford A., 1697, AB, comm, I, P2/G/566
Getly, Jn., farrier, Warm., 1722, W, P2/G/716
Gateley *or* Geatly, Jn., yeo., Stratford sub C., 1737, I, W, Wr, P4/1737/19
Gatley, My., Chicklade, 1705, AB, P2/G/619
Getly, Robt., husb., Upton, E. Knoyle, 1682, I, W, P2/G/455
Gattley, Roger, Gt. Bedwyn, 1582, AB, I, T, P5/1582/25, P5/4Reg/45C
Gatley, Thos., E. Knoyle, 1607, I, W, copy I, note about NW, P2/G/125
Gatley, Thos., Hungerford, Berks., 1710, AB, comm, P5/1710/41
Geatly, Thos., yeo., Stratford sub C., 1730, W, P4/1729/12
Getly, Thos., sen., bricklayer, Marl., 1750, W, P1/G/593, P1/10Reg/447
Getly, Thos., yeo., E. Knoyle, 1763, W, P1/G/636, P1/12Reg/42B
Getley, Wm., blacksmith, Milton, E. Knoyle, 1664, W, P1/G/188
Wm., maltster, Mkt. L., 1714, W, P2/G/668
Gater, Eliz., widow, Milbourne, Malm., 1676, I, W, P3/G/241
Jn., Milbourne, Malm., 1730, AB, P3/G/526
Geater, Martha, widow, Froxfield, 1780, AB, P3/G/722
Gator, Richd., husb., Milbourne, Malm., 1638, I, W, P3/G/153
Geater, Roger, gent., Ludg., 1785, W, P2/G/1024
Gates, Chris., miller, Wokm., Berks., 1724, W, P5/1724/33, P5/16Reg/95A
Edmd., husb., Hurst, Berks., 1604, NW, P5/1604/15, P5/8Reg/19B

Gatte, Elias, husb. and shepherd, Bower C., 1625, I, W, P1/G/92
Eliz., widow, Arborfield, Berks., 1690, W, P5/1690/68
Isabel, widow, Dunsden, Sonning, Berks., 1574, W, P5/3Reg/42B
Jane, widow, Liberty of Newland, Hurst, Berks., 1689, AB, I, P5/1689/26
Robt., yeo., Wokm., Berks., 1631, comm, I, NW, P5/1631/125
Robt., yeo., Wokm., Berks., 1743, W, Wr, P5/1743/30
Thos., yeo., Arborfield, Berks., 1682, AB, I, T (re Thos. G.), W, P5/1682/44
Thos., husb., Wokm., Berks., 1760, W, P5/1760/11
Ursula, Hurst, Berks., 1705, AB, P5/1705/21
see also Griffen alias G.
Gatfield, Gatfield *or* Gadfield, Jas., schoolmaster, Hurst, Berks., 1727, W, P5/1727/20, P5/16Reg/156A
Jn., Devizes St Jn., 1623, AB, I, P1/G/80
Gadfield, Thos. Dan., cordw., Hurst, Berks., 1805, W, P5/19Reg/117B
Gatherell *see* Gatrell
Gatley *see* Gately
Gator *see* Gater
Gatrell, Gartrell, Christian, widow, Hindon, 1722, W, P2/G/715
Gartrell, David, servant to Jas. Wise, Chitterne, 1716, NW, P2/G/679
David, sen., carp., Chilmark, 1792, W, P2/G/1056
Gartherell, Dorothy, Fonthill G., 1692, AB, P2/G/537
Gatterell, Eliz., Fonthill B., 1783, AB, P2/G/1018
Gatherell, My., widow, Gasper, Stourton, [1687], W, P2/G/505
Richd., yeo., Fonthill G., 1708, W, P1/G/345, P1/4Reg/284
Richd., Fonthill G., 1728, W, P2/G/746
Gartrell, Sam., sen., Fonthill B., 1750, W, P2/G/879
Gattrell, Sam., yeo., Fonthill B., 1808, W, Wr, P2/1808/39
Gatherell, Thos., carp., Stourton, [1683], I, W, P2/G/471
Wm., Fonthill G., 1736, AB, ren, P2/G/804
Gatte *see* Gates
Gatten *see* Gayton
Gatterell *see* Gatrell
Gattley *see* Gatley
Gattrell *see* Gatrell
Gaulton *see* Galton
Gaunt, Hugh, husb., Chirton, 1579, I, W, P2/G/33, P2/5Reg/343D
Gauntlett, Ann, sp., Sal., 1679, AB, I, P4/1679/5
Gauntlet, Denise, widow of Jn., jun., Pensworth, Downton, 1561, W, P2/4Reg/61C
Geo., Mkt. L., 1844, AB, O, Wr, P2/1844/8
Geo., widower, Redlynch, Downton, 1850, AB, Wr, P2/1850/1
Giles, bach., Plaitford, 1747, AB, P2/G/861
Gauntlet, Hy., yeo., Wick, Downton, 1614, W, P2/8Reg/207
Hy., Sal., 1676, AB, I, P4/1676/5
Hy., baker, Sal., 1695, W, P4/1695/13
Gantlett, Hy., yeo., Plaitford, 1705, AB, W, P1/G/334
Hy., yeo., Downton, 1729, W, P2/G/753
Hy., innholder, Devizes, 1776, AB, ren, P1/G/701
Jane, widow, Plaitford, 1711, AB, I, P1/G/368
Gauntlet, Jn., sen., husb., Pensworth, Downton, 1558-59, I (very detailed), W, P2/G/6, P2/3Reg/139C, P2/4Reg/19C
Gauntlet, Jn., jun., no abode stated, 1562, AB (re Thos. son of Jn. & his widow Denise G.), T, P2/4Reg/104A
Jn., Amesb., 1631, AB, a/c, I, P2/G/236
Gauntlet, Jn., yeo., Pensworth, Downton, 1631, I, W, P1/G/106
Jn., innholder, Downton, 1633, I, W, P2/G/251, P2/9Reg/8
Jn., gent., Sal., 1677, AB, I, P1/G/233
Jn., yeo., Downton, [1679], I, W, P2/G/421
Gantlett, Jn., shoemaker, Pensworth, Downton, 1702, AB, I, ren, P2/G/579, 591
Gantlett, Jn., Downton, 1713, AB, P2/G/662
Jn., baker, Wilton, 1716, ren, W, P2/G/683
Jn., minor, Downton, 1722, T, P2/G/718
Jn., gent., Brinkw., 1743, comm, W, P3/G/603
Gantlett, Jn., baker, Wilton, 1752, W, P2/G/886

Jn., Downton, 1799, AB, P2/G/1078
Gauntlet, Jn., baker, Mkt. L., 1802, W, P2/1802/31
Jn., baker, Mkt. L., 1838, O, W, Wr, P2/1838/57
Jos., maltster, Downton, 1756, W, P2/G/896
Jos., yeo., Ardington Wick, Berks., 1811, comm, W, Wr, P1/1811/23
Gauntlet, Mgt., widow, Downton, 1619, I, NW, P2/G/187
Mgt., Sal., 1631, I, W, P4/1631/2
Gantlett alias Gauntlett, Martha, sp., Lea, L. and Cleverton, 1843-49, AB, O, Wr, P3/1843/1, P3/1849/32
My., widow, Wick, Downton, 1705, I, W, P2/G/614
Gantlett, My., Coombe B., 1720, I, W, P8/18
My., widow, Downton, 1760, AB, ren, W, P2/G/918
Gauntlet form. Barton, My., Sedgehill, 1772, AB, P2/G/975
Maurice, yeo., Wick, Downton, 1632, I, W, P2/G/239
Maurice, baker, Wilton, 1753, W, P2/G/889
Gauntlet, Richd., yeo., Pensworth, Downton, 1573, W, P2/5Reg/175A
Gantlett, Richd., Plaitford, 1720, AB, P2/G/701
Roger, gent., Garsdon, 1681-1718, AB, I, W, P3/G/278
Gauntlett *or* Gantlet, Roger, Pensworth, Downton, 1682, I, W, P2/G/452
Gantlett, Roger, Cleverton, Lea and C., 1732, AB, P1/G/479
Roger, sen., gent., Lt. Somerford, 1766, W, P3/G/682
Roger, yeo., Lea and Cleverton, 1798, W, P1/G/766, P1/15Reg/109
Gauntlet, Thos., Downton, 1606, AB, I, ren, P2/G/121
Thos., sen., maltster, Downton, 1721, I, W, P2/G/707
Gawby *see* Gaby
Gawen, Abel, clothier, Tinh., Edington, [1641], W, P2/G/291
Agnes, Tinh., Edington, 1558, W, P2/3Reg/81B
Ann *or* Agnes, widow, Tinh., Edington, 1647, caveat, note of probate, P2/G/314
Gowen, Ann, widow, Grittleton, 1788, W, P3/G/746
Cath., widow, Norrington, Alvediston, 1628, W, P2/G/222
Cath., widow, Wilton, 1730, AB, P2/G/760
Gawen *or* Gane, Edmd., gent., Berwick St Jn., 1564, I, W, P2/G/20, P2/4Reg/186B
Eliz., Poulshot, 1683, AB, I, P2/G/463
Gowen, Eliz., sp., Westport St My., 1745, I, W, P3/G/612
Geoffrey, gent., Westb., 1803, O, W, Wr, P25/1803/3
Hy., gent., W. Grimstead, 1574, W, P2/5Reg/197B
Hy., sen., yeo., Ebbesborne Wake, 1685, I, W, P2/G/485
Hy., Poulshot, 1689, AB, comm, P2/G/524
Hy., jun., Tollard Royal, 1705, AB, I, P2/G/610
Gowen, Hy., sergemaker, Broughton G., 1712, AB, I, W, P2/G/653
Hy., yeo., Ebbesborne Wake, 1742, W, P2/G/828
Hy., Ebbesborne Wake, 1771, AB, P2/G/970
Gawen *or* Gayne, Jane, widow, Calne, 1632, W, P26/42
Jn., yeo., Edington, 1549, W, P2/2Reg/91C
Jn., gent., Bodenham, Nunton and B., 1585, W, P2/7Reg/1D
Jn., Edington, 1594, AB, I, note of admon, P2/G/71
Jn., Crickl. St S., 1614, AB, court paper, P3/G/35
Jn., Hawkeridge, Westb., 1711, I, W (endorsed 'a Quaker protested') (NEP), P25/1711/11
Gowen, Jn., Broughton G., 1728, AB, I, P2/G/748
Jn., tanner, Westb., 1754, W, P25/1754/5
Mgt., widow, Heywood, Westb., 1669, I, W, P25/1669/18
Gowen *or* Gawen, Mgt., widow, Hawkeridge, Westb., 1714, I, W, P25/1714/12
My., sp., Hullavington, 1708, I, W, P3/G/430
Maud, widow, Edington, 1559, AB, W, P2/3Reg/154C, 155A
Gowen, Nathaniel, broad weaver, Westb., 1733, W, P25/1733/5
Nich., gent., Warm., 1631, AB, I, P1/G/114
Rachel, widow, Westb., 1728, W, P25/1728/3
Goen, Richd., Foxham, Bremhill, 1670, AB, I, P3/G/213
Gowen *or* Goeing, Robt., barber, Wilton, 1666, W, P2/G/344
Roger, husb., Alderton, [1605], W (NEP), P3/G/5
Sarah, widow, Westb., 1764, W, P25/1764/1

Thos., sen., yeo., Woodlands, Calne, 1591, W, P5/5Reg/97C
Thos., Etchilhampton, 1616, I, W, P3/G/41
Gouinge *or* Gouene, Thos., husb., Steeple A., 1645, I, W, P2/G/309
Thos., Steeple A., 1648, AB, NW, P2/G/316
Thos., gent., Heywood, Westb., 1668, comm, I, W, P25/1668/8
Gowen, Thos., yeo., Foscote, Grittleton, 1737, I, W, P3/G/573
Wm., blacksmith, Wilton, 1570, AB, W, P2/5Reg/101D, 104A
Wm., gent., Hurdcott, Barford St M., 1682, AB (2), P2/G/458
Wm., Westb., 1685, AB, I, P25/1685/4
Wm., Sal., 1709, AB, P4/1709/18
see also Bevan form. G.; Gane
Gawler *see* Gaylard
Gay, Agnes, widow, Heddington, 1572, W (NEP), P1/1Reg/56C
Francis, N. Bradley, 1683, I, W, P2/G/468
Geo., Corsham, 1833, AB, Wr, P3/1833/51
Hy., clothier, Uffc., Devon, 1686, I, W, P20/1/107
Gey, Hugh, yeo., Tilsh., 1664, I, W, P2/G/331
Jn., sen., husb., Hankerton, 1571, W, P1/1Reg/87B
Geye, Jn., husb., Winterborne K., Dorset, 1588, W, P5/5Reg/20A
Gayes, Jn., Halstock, Dorset, 1596-97, AB, I, P5/1596/30, P5/6Reg/151A
Gey *or* Gye, Jn., sen., wheeler, Calne, 1608, AB, I, P5/1608/13
Jn., weaver, Broughton G., [1627], I, NW, P2/G/217
Gey, Jn., yeo., Tilsh., 1671, a/c, I, W, P1/G/221
Jn., jun., clothier, Uffc., Devon, 1685, AB, comm, I, P20/1/102
Jn., broad weaver, Westwood, 1711, AB, ren, W, P1/G/357, P1/5Reg/113
Jn., Steeple A., 1782, AB, P2/G/1012
Ghey, Jn., butcher, Silver St., Trowb., 1792, comm, W, P1/G/744, P1/14Reg/433B
Jn., Easton Grey, 1827, AB (2), Wr, P3/1827/31
Jn., mason, Corsham, 1834-41, W, P29/1800-1857/26, P29/3Reg/294
Ghey, Jos., farmer, Littleton, Semington & Steeple A., 1848, D, O, W, Wr, P1/1848/70
Mgt., widow, Uffc., Devon, 1701, I, W, P5/1701/24
Ghey, Martha, widow, Trowb., 1801, W, P1/1801/7, P1/15Reg/228
My., widow, Bere R., Dorset, 1812, AB, comm, Wr, P5/1812/36
Matthew, clerk, Lyme R., Dorset, 1734, W, P5/1734/27
Nathaniel, yeo., Cocklebury, Langley Burrell, 1738, W, P1/G/525, P1/8Reg/319
Nich., Broughton G., 1570, W, P2/5Reg/111A
Nich., Pott., 1608, I, W, P1/G/27
Nich., weaver, Broughton G., 1676, comm, W, P2/G/399
Gey, Philip, Tilsh., 1679, AB, P2/G/429
Richd., labourer, Kington St M., 1752, W, P3/G/640
Robt., Lyme R., Dorset, 1710, AB, P16/183
Ghey, Sam., yeo., Rooks Nest Farm, Pewsham, 1850, W (& cod), Wr, P5/1850/7
Gey, Stephen, gent., Tilsh., [1681], I, W, P2/G/436
Gey, Thos., sen., no abode stated, 1530, W (NEP), P30/79
Thos., yeo., Broughton G., [1623], W, P2/G/202
Thos., yeo., Broughton G., 1714, W, P1/G/381, P1/5Reg/439A
Thos., stone mason, Corsham, 1800, W, P3/1800/18
Thos., mason, Corsham, 1853, O, W, Wr, P3/1853/13
Gey, Wm., Broad C., 1544, W (NEP), P2/1Reg/50B
Gey, Wm., [carp.], Rowde, 1623, I, W, P3/G/77
Wm., Swindon, 1818, AB, Wr, P3/1818/48
see also Guy
Gaylard, Gawler, Cecily, widow, Winterborne K., Dorset, 1705, AB, I, P5/1704/30
Gailor, Christian, jun., sp., Sherb., Dorset, 1698, comm, NW, P5/1697/17
Christian, widow, Sherb., Dorset, 1700, I, W, P5/1700/12
Geo., Sherb., Dorset, 1684, AB, I, P5/1684/18
Gailer, Hy., Sutton B., 1762, AB, P3/G/670
Jas., brazier, Sherb., Dorset, 1761, W, P5/1761/12
Gaylard *or* Galer, Jn., blacksmith, Chards., Devon, 1627, AB, I, P5/1627/17, P5/11Reg/7A
Galler *or* Gawler, Jn., tailor, Winterborne K., Dorset, 1728, W, P5/1728/38, P5/16Reg/211E

Gawler, My., widow, Winterborne K., Dorset, 1742, W, Wr, P5/1742/15
Galler, Richd., husb., Bere R., Dorset, 1583, I, W, P5/1582/29, P5/4Reg/58C
Sam., Sherb., Dorset, 1741, AB, Wr, P5/1741/17
Gayne *see* Gawen *or* G.
Gayton, Chas., widower, Trowb., 1857, AB, aff, O, ren, Wr, P1/1857/8
Chris., weaver, Hilp., 1671, W, P2/G/366
Gatten, Chris., Hilp., 1687, AB, comm, P2/G/502
Jacob, weaver, Trowb., 1799, W, P1/G/772, P1/15Reg/174
Wm., labourer, E. Town, W. Ashton, Steeple A., 1729, I, W, P2/G/754
Gaze, My., sp., Sherston, 1852, O, W, Wr, P3/1852/49
Sarah, widow, Sherston, 1855, aff, O, W, Wr, P3/1855/27
Gealard *see* Gillard
Geale, Agnes, widow, Chr. M., 1611, I, W, P1/G/34
Alice, widow, Bremhill, 1609, W, P3/G/13
Alice, Alton Pr., 1618, I, W, P3/G/55
Arthur, Yatton K., 1690, AB, I, P3/G/343
Edmd., Preston, Dorset, 1597-98, AB, copy I, I, T, W, P5/1597/51, P5/6Reg/191D, 203B
Edwd., Underdown, Bremhill, [1607], I, W (on same sheet) (NEP), P3/G/6
Edwd., yeo., Foxham, Bremhill, 1617, I, W, P3/G/47
Hy., husb., Loscombe, Netherb., Dorset, 1663, I, W, P17/640
Joan, widow, Sutton B., 1612, I, W, P3/G/25
Joan, sp., Chr. M., 1634, I, W, P1/G/120
Jn., Sutton B., 1614, AB, comm, I, P3/G/36
Jn., husb., Alton Pr., 1616, comm (2), I, W, P3/G/42
Jn., yeo., Avon, Chr. M., 1635, I, W, P3/G/137
Jn., sen., yeo., Loscombe, Netherb., Dorset, 1662, I, W, P5/1662/49
Josiah, weaver, N. Wraxall, 1741, W, P1/G/543, P1/9Reg/162
Julian, widow, Sutton B., 1618, I, W, P3/G/56
Leonard, Sutton, 1617, I, W, P3/G/48
Gell, Mgt., Bremhill, 1571, W (NEP), P1/1Reg/84C
Geall, Martha, Beam., Dorset, 1715, W, P17/363
Ralph, husb., Sutton B., [1613], I, W (NEP), P3/G/30
Ralph, yeo., Sutton B., 1647, I, W, P1/G/156
Richd., yeo., Sandhurst, Berks., 1607, AB, I, P5/1607/28, P5/8Reg/101B
Richd., yeo., Sandhurst, Berks., 1696, W, P5/1696/17
Thos., husb., Chr. M., 1628, I, W, P3/G/102
Thos., yeo., Chr. M., 1669, I, W, P3/G/201
Gele, Thos., innkeeper, Chipp., 1733, comm, W, P3/G/549
Gele, Wm., Brinkw., 1563, W, P1/2Reg/126B
Wm., yeo., Dean Farm, Oaksey, 1798, W, Wr, P3/G/771
see also Gale
Geane, Stephen, yeo., Whately, Beam., Dorset, 1715, W, P17/285
Geare, Edmd., yeo., Clifton Maybank, Dorset, 1713, AB, I, P5/1713/30
Geere, Richd., yeo., Halstock, Dorset, 1676, AB, comm, I, P5/1676/23
Geere, Thos., butcher, Damerham, Hants, 1681, AB, I, W, P1/G/244
Thos., sackclothmaker, Perhay, Netherb., Dorset, 1725, W, P5/1725/28, P5/16Reg/113A
Gearell, Jn., Netheravon, 1588, I, W, P5/1588/23, P5/5Reg/18C
Gearing, Emmot, widow, Pinkney, Sherston, 1678, I, W, P3/G/257
Jane, widow, Hannington, 1764, W, P3/G/675
Joan, Pinkney, Sherston, 1624, W, P3/G/84
Jn., gent., Pinkney, Sherston, 1677, comm, I, W, P3/G/250
Gerring, Jos., yeo., Hannington, 1717, W, P3/G/459
Richd., gent., Fittleton, 1645, AB, I, P2/G/308
Thos., gent., Pinkney, Sherston, 1622, comm, I (very detailed), W, P3/G/73
Thos., Pinkney, Sherston, 1643, AB (2), note, P3/G/168
Gerring, Thos., Letcombe Regis, Berks., 1832, AB, Wr, P1/1832/108
Wm., Watchfield, Shrivenham, Berks., 1726, AB, P1/G/445
Gearle *see* Girle
Geary, Geerie, Hugh, maltster, Cookham, Berks., 1625, I, W, P1/G/86
Robt., edge toolmaker, Milford, Sal. St Martin, 1783, W, P4/1783/5

Gerey, Thos., Wantage, Berks., 1713, AB, P5/1713/31
Geater *see* Gater
Geatly *see* Gately
Geboll *see* Jeboult
Geddes, (Dr) *see* Philip Wayte
Gee, Abel, yeo., Pewsham Forest, 1756, AB, W, P1/G/619, P1/11Reg/311
Abraham, Lt. Hinton, 1852, D, O, W, Wr, P3/1852/50
Eliz., minors, Bromham, 1830, comm, court proceeding, T, P3/1830/44
Geo., Bromham, 1830, AB, comm, Wr, P3/1830/43
Geo., shopkeeper, Bromham, 1856, AB, aff, O, Wr, P3/1856/42
Jas., Bromham, 1852, AB, O, Wr, P3/1852/37
Jn., coachmaker, Marl., 1794, W, P1/G/747, P1/14Reg/506B
My., widow, Pewsham Forest, 1776, W, P5/1776/19, P5/17Reg/121
My., widow, Marl., 1800, W, P1/1800/4, P1/15Reg/202
Jee, Stephen, blacksmith, Everleigh, 1795, AB, W, P3/IJ/314
Jee, Wm., jobber, Ludg., 1819, W, Wr, P2/1819/42
see also Jay
Geere *see* Geare
Geerie *see* Geary
Gefford *see* Gifford
Geffres, Geffreys *see* Jefferies
Geffreyson, Wm., Yatesbury, 1561, W, P5/1Reg/9B
Gegg *see* Gigg
Gele, Gell *see* Geale
Gellett *see* Gillett
Gelley, Gelly *see* Jelly
Gellicos *see* Jellicots
Gellyjohn *see* Jellijohn
Genens *see* Jennings
Gengell *see* Gingell
Genger, Jn., labourer, Winterbourne S., 1736, comm, I, W, P2/G/803
Ganger, Philip, husb., Winterbourne S., 1720, AB, I, P1/G/403
Genis, Wm., carp., Woodrow, Melk., 1570, W, P2/5Reg/86B
Genkins *see* Jenkins
Gennance, Gennings *see* Jennings
Gent, Edith, sp., Langley Burrell, 1664, I, W, P3/G/180
Eliz., sp., Devizes, 1754, W, P1/G/607, P1/11Reg/146
Hy., innholder, Calne, 1696, AB, I (detailed), ren, P26/442
Jane, sp., Devizes, 1827, AB, Wr, P1/1827/22
Jn., clothier, Devizes, 1774, W, P1/G/695, P1/13Reg/57
Mgt., widow, Calne, 1667, I, W, P26/130
My., sp., Devizes, 1762, W, P1/G/639, P1/12Reg/28
My., widow, Sherb., Dorset, 1829, W, Wr, P5/1829/14
Sam., Sherb., Dorset, 1799, req, W, P5/1799/10, P5/18Reg/279B
Gentle, Wm., yeo., Leverton, Chilton F., 1701, I, W, P1/G/318, P1/4Reg/79
George, Agnes, widow, Imber, 1552, W, P2/2Reg/148B
Agnes, widow, Steeple A., 1567, W, P2/5Reg/19A
Alexander, maltster, E. Knoyle, 1743, AB, ren, P2/G/840
Alice, widow, Lt. Bedwyn, [c1616], valuation, P1/G/56
Ann Maria, sp., Wanb., 1856, aff, D, W, Wr, P3/1856/1
Benet, widow, Ashton K., 1610, W, P3/G/18
Cath., Westb., 1565, W, P5/1Reg/60B
Chris., yeo., Erlestoke, 1683, AB, I, ren, P2/G/464
Cicely, widow, no abode stated, 1596, I, P2/G/74
David, yeo., Axford, Rams., 1842, O, W, Wr, P5/1842/9
Edmd., Highw., 1675, comm, W, P10/1675/1
Edwd., yeo., W. Woodhay, Berks., 1625, I, W, P1/G/85
Edwd., Highw., 1676, I, P10/1676/1
Edwd., yeo., Eastcott, Urchf., 1822, W, Wr, P2/1822/27
George alias Knight, Eliz., Gillingham, Dorset, 1562, LA, P27/1Reg/12B

Eliz., sp., Westb., 1678, AB, comm, I, P25/1678/7
Eliz., widow, Whittonditch, Rams., 1689, I, W, P5/1689/27
Eliz., widow, Steeple A., 1735, W, P1/G/504, P1/8Reg/78B
George alias Edwards, Eliz., widow, Westb., 1777, W, P25/1777/4
Geo., Longbridge D., 1558, W, P2/3Reg/119A
Hy., blacksmith, Devizes, 1673, NW, P1/G/225
Hy., sen., E. Knoyle, 1682, I, W, P2/G/457
Hugh, Brixton D., 1735, AB, P2/G/797
Humphrey, weaver, Seend, Melk., 1590, I, W, P2/G/51
George alias Edwards, Humphrey, yeo., Tilsh., 1700, I, W, P2/G/581
George alias Edwards, Humphrey, Corton, Boyton, 1713, AB, P2/G/656
Jacob, Preshute, 1833, AB, Wr, P1/1833/16
Jas., yeo., W. Lockinge, Wantage, Berks., 1681, AB, I, P23/107
Jas., Boreham, Warm., 1704, AB, P2/G/607
Jas., broad weaver, N. Bradley, 1788, W, P2/G/1039
Jas., turner, Gillingham, Dorset, 1832, W, Wr, P27/1/699
George alias Edwards, Jane, widow, W. Lavington, 1671, I, W, P1/G/213
Jane, widow, Minety, 1728, W, P3/G/512
George alias Edwards, Jean, gentlewoman, Worton, Pott., 1686, W, P1/G/264
Joan, widow, Bere R., Dorset, 1576, I, P5/1576/19, P5/3Reg/83C
Joan, widow, Bere R., Dorset, 1587, comm, I, draft I, W, P5/1587/19, P5/4Reg/152A
Joan, widow, Steeple A., 1698, W, P2/G/567
George alias Edwards, Joan, widow, Easterton, Mkt. L., 1699, AB, I, P2/G/574
Jn., Tilsh., 1542-43, W (NEP), P2/1Reg/30B
Jn., sen., miller, Longbridge D. (form. of Bishopstrow), 1569, I, W, P2/G/22, P2/5Reg/61B
Jn., Erlestoke, 1588, AB, P2/7Reg/133C
Jn., clerk, Berwick St Jas., 1598, I, W, P2/G/94
Jn., day labourer, Trowb., 1611, I, W, P1/G/36
George alias Edwards, Jn., yeo., Orcheston St My., 1665, I, W, P2/G/337
Jn., yeo., Gt. Bedwyn, 1704, I, W, P5/1704/26
Jn., grocer, Erlestoke, 1719, W, P2/G/697
Jn., yeo., Chedglow, Crudwell, 1722, I, W, P3/G/475
Jn., Horningsham, 1727, AB, P5/1727/19
George alias Edwards, Jn., yeo., Tilsh., 1737, note, W (2 different), P3/G/570
George alias Edwards, Jn., gent., Tilsh., 1777, W, P2/G/996
George alias Edwards, Jn., clerk, Tilsh., 1782, W, P1/G/718, P1/13Reg/360
Jos., sen., cordw., Horningsham, 1739, W, Wr, P5/1739/19
Jos., yeo., Elmdown, Rams., 1761, W, P5/1761/13
Lydia, sp., Sal., 1826, AB, W, Wr, P1/1826/27
Mgt., widow, Rams., 1769, W, P5/1769/9
My., widow, Maddington, 1601, AB, I, W, P2/G/105
My., Crockerton, Longbridge D., 1607, I, W, P2/G/124
My., widow, Erlestoke, 1737, W, P2/G/807
My., widow, Maddington, 1741, AB, P1/G/531
My., widow, Erlestoke, 1746, W, P2/G/851
Nich., sen., yeo., Whittonditch, Rams., 1675, I, W, P5/1675/20
Philip, Pott., 1676, AB, P1/G/230
George alias Edwards, Philip, yeo., Bradford A., 1718, W, P2/G/691
George alias Edwards, Rebecca, sp., Lt. Cheverell, 1707, I, W, P2/G/626
Richd., N. Bradley, 1625, AB, I, P2/G/208
Richd., labourer, Everleigh, 1781, W, P3/G/727
Robt., husb., Maddington, 1588, I, W, P2/G/41
Robt., W. Lavington, 1649, AB, I, P1/G/166
George alias Edwards, Robt., yeo., Lt. Cheverell, [1688], I, W, P2/G/520
Robt., Gillingham, Dorset, 1724, AB, P27/1/262
Robt., husb., Horningsham, 1725, W, P5/1725/27, P5/16Reg/109B
George alias Edwards, Robt., victualler, Bratton, Westb., 1769, W, P25/1769/4
Robt. Willshire, yeo., Sutton Poyntz, Dorset, 1824, O, W, P18/22
George alias Edwardes, Thos., husb., Tilsh., 1574, W, P2/5Reg/200B
Thos., husb., Wrou., 1681, AB, I, P3/G/279

Thos., weaver, Wilton, 1733, W, P2/G/784
Thos., miller, E. Coulston, 1754, AB, comm, P2/G/892
Thos., ironmonger, Wantage, Berks., 1771, D, W, P23/739
Thos. Whitlock, gent., Brixton D., 1745, W, P2/G/848
Wm., Bulk., Keevil, 1621, I, W, P2/G/199
Wm., yeo., Maddington, [1632], I, W, P2/G/244
Wm., Maddington, 1641, AB, I, P2/G/292
George alias Edwards, Wm., yeo., Marston, Pott., 1713-16, AB, I, LA, P1/G/371, 388
Wm., butcher, Farnham, Tollard Royal, Dorset, 1742, AB, P2/G/831
Wm., yeo., Maddington, 1769, W (damaged), P2/G/960
Wm., corn chandler, Reading, Berks., 1801, W, P1/1801/37, P1/15Reg/257
Wm., yeo., Gillingham, Dorset, 1809, W, P27/1/601
Wm., Collingbourne K., 1820, AB, Wr, P3/1820/8
Wm., Maddington, 1824, AB, Wr, P2/1824/6
Wm., Netton, Durnford, 1836, AB, ren, Wr, P9/116
Wm., farmer, Upper Stratton, Stratton St Mgt., 1837, W, Wr, P3/1837/35
Wm., weaver, Dilton M., Westb., 1840, declaration, O, W, Wr, P25/1840/1
see also Edwards alias G.; Thomas alias G.
Gerard *see* Gerrard
Gerey *see* Geary
Gerish *see* Gerrish
Gerle *see* Gearle
German, Thos., miller, Landford, 1802, W, P2/1802/24
Germy *see* Garmy
Gerner *see* Garner
Gerrard, Gerrett, Agnes, widow, Bere R., Dorset, 1585, W, P5/4Reg/103A
Gerrett *or* Garrett, Agnes, widow, Damerham, Hants, 1610, AB, I, P2/G/143, P2/8Reg/130A
Gerratt, Alexander, brewer, Warm., 1829, W, Wr, P2/1829/29
Garrard, Ann, widow, Thornhill, Clyffe P., 1636, AB, a/c, I, P3/G/141
Gerard, Ann, widow, Sutton Poyntz, Dorset, 1641, AB, I, P5/1640/22, P5/13Reg/270A
Ann, widow, Fonthill G., 1801, AB, P2/1801/15
Jerrett, Anthony, Homington, 1729, AB, I, P24/829
Garrard, Cath., widow, Inkpen, Berks., 1664, I, W, P1/G/192
Garrard, Cath., gent.'s widow, Thornhill, Clyffe P., 1729, W, P3/G/520
Gerrett, Chas., maltster, Warm., 1773, W, P1/G/685, P1/12Reg/455A
Gerrett, Chas., Charlock Hill Farm, Hill D., 1847, AB, Wr, P5/1847/22
Garrard, Dan., gent., Burghfield, Berks., 1714, AB, W, P1/G/373, P1/5Reg/358
Gerritt, Dan., weaver, Horningsham, 1818, AB, W, Wr, P5/1818/36
David, Stop, Fonthill G., 1615, NW, P2/8Reg/246B
Jerrard, David, husb., Hanging L., 1711, W, P2/IJ/230
Gerritt, Edmd., shearman, Warm., 1797, W, P2/G/1071
Garrard, Edwd., vicar, Mere, 1695, AB, I, P5/1695/38
Edwd., husb., N. Wootton, Dorset, 1695, NW, P5/1695/30
Edwd., joiner, Fonthill G., 1711, W, P1/G/366, P1/5Reg/222
Edwd., maltster, Ansty, 1724, W, P2/G/727
Edwd., plumber and glazier, Wilton, 1807, W, Wr, P2/1807/37
Eliz. Flower Carter, widow, Fisherton A., 1846, W, Wr, P2/1846/36
Girrit, Geo., sen., yeo., Horningsham, 1743, W, Wr, P5/1743/32
Gerard, Gregory, Tisb., c1540, I, P30/80
Gerritt, Hannah, sp., Warm., 1835, W, P2/1835/12
Jerrard, Hy., Tisb., 1559, AB, W, P2/4Reg/28E
Jerrard, Hy., Tisb., 1574, W, P2/5Reg/194E
Hy., husb., Bere R., Dorset, 1599, AB, I, W, P5/1598/18, P5/6Reg/216A
Jerratt, Hy., sen., yeo., Warm., 1600, AB, I, W, P2/G/101, P2/IJ/34
Jerrard, Hy., sen., yeo., W. Hatch, Tisb., 1639, I, W, P2/IJ/108
Jarard, Hy., sen., yeo., Warm., 1639, AB, I, P2/IJ/110
Jarard, Hy., Lyndhurst, Hants, [1644], I (2), P2/IJ/132
Jerrard, Hy., Fonthill G., 1646, T, NW, P2/IJ/128
Jerratt, Hy., husb., Fovant Stroud, 1718, AB, I, P2/IJ/248
Jerrard, Hy., yeo., Tisb., 1726, W, P2/IJ/265

Gerratt, Hy., yeo., Sutton V., 1732, W, P2/G/776
Gerrat, Hy., labourer, Barford St M., 1757, I, W, P2/G/899
Jerrard, Hy., carp., Swallowcliffe, 1763, W, P5/1763/13
Hilary, husb., Halstock, Dorset, 1756, W, P16/315
Gerard, Humphrey, Bulford, [1687], I, W, P2/G/509, P2/IJ/194
Isaac, butcher, Beam., Dorset, 1710, I, W, P5/1710/42, P5/15Reg/208
Jas., architect, Ansty, 1737, W, P1/G/516, P1/8Reg/183A
Jerrard, Jas., Ansty, 1805, AB, P5/1805/4
Jerrard, Jas., Bramshaw, Hants, 1806, AB, P5/19Reg/119B
Garrard, Jane, widow, Thornhill, Clyffe P., 1685, I, W, P3/G/301
Jerrard, Jane, widow, Cholderton, 1779, W, P2/IJ/350
Jerrard, Joan, Bere R., Dorset, 1630, AB, P5/11Reg/137A
Joan, widow, Collingbourne K., 1665, I, W, P3/G/182
Garrard, Joanna, widow, Rams., 1687, I, W, P5/1687/17
Jerrard, Jn., Tisb., 1576, AB, I, W, P2/IJ/9, P2/5Reg/262
Gerrett, Jn., Bower C., 1593, I, W, P2/G/66
Jerrard *or* Jerrod, Jn., surgeon, Bere R., Dorset, 1619, I, W, P5/1619/62, P5/10Reg/56C
Jerrard, Jn., carp., W. Knoyle, 1619, AB, I, W, P2/G/185, P5/1618/19
Jerratt, Jn., Stop, Fonthill G., 1622, AB, I, P1/IJ/34
Jerratt, Jn., carp., W. Knoyle, 1636, AB, I, P2/IJ/104
Gerrard *or* Jerret, Jn., sen., Bere R., Dorset, 1666, AB, I, ren, P5/1665/36
Jerrard, Jn., yeo., Fonthill G., 1703, I, W, P2/IJ/333
Garrard, Jn., brazier, Wantage, Berks., 1717-32, AB (2), I (his widow, My., d.1732 without having admd all goods), P23/360, 483
Jn., Ansty, 1722, AB, I, P2/G/719
Gerratt, Jn., Upton L., 1738, AB, P1/G/514
Jerrard, Jn., Fonthill G., 1752, AB, P2/IJ/309
Jerrard, Jn., yeo., Fonthill G., 1764, W, P2/IJ/329
Jn., miller, Sutton M., 1783, W, P2/G/1015
Garrard, Jn., Chilmark, 1785, AB, P2/G/1027
Jerrard, Jn., yeo., Fonthill G., 1789, aff, D, W, P1/IJ/289, P1/14Reg/308
Jn., stone mason, Sherb., Dorset, 1793, W, P5/1793/6, P5/18Reg/191B
Jerrard, Jn., Ansty, 1804, AB, P5/1804/16, P5/19Reg/114A
Jerard, Jn., gent., Fisherton A., 1812, W, Wr, P2/1812/61
Jerrard, Jn., Fovant, 1826, AB, Wr, P2/1826/6
Jn., yeo., Beam., Dorset, 1836, O, W, Wr, P5/1836/30
Garrard, Lucy, sp., Mannington, Lydiard T., 1689, AB, I, P3/G/337
Gerard, Mgt., widow, Sutton Poyntz, Dorset, 1570, W, P5/2Reg/74D
Jorots *or* Jerratt, Margery, Preston, Dorset, 1582, AB, I, W, P5/1582/34, P5/4Reg/36A
Jerrard, Martha, widow, Fonthill G., 1733, AB, I, P2/IJ/275
Martha, widow, Swallowcliffe, 1810, AB, Wr, P5/1810/23
Jerrard, My., milliner, Coombe B. (form. of Sal.), [1783], W (NEP), P5/1783/8
Jerard, My., widow, Fisherton A., 1813, W, Wr, P2/1813/3
Matthew, Tisb., 1747, AB, P1/G/567
Gerritt, Moses, gardener, Warm. Common, 1821, W, Wr, P2/1821/61
Nich., husb., Preston, Dorset, 1589, AB, I, W, P5/1589/24, P5/5Reg/64D
Jerratt, Nich., Collingbourne K., 1757, AB, P3/IJ/271
Gerard, Richd., Preston, Dorset, 1591, AB, I, W, P5/1591/21, P5/5Reg/101B, P5/6Reg/23A
Gerrett, Richd., Longbridge D., 1829, AB, Wr, P1/1829/80
Jerrard, Richd., weaver, Fonthill G., 1731-34, AB (2), I (2), P2/IJ/273, 279
Gerard alias Hiscock, Robt., Fonthill G., 1547, W, P2/2Reg/41C
Robt., yeo., Netherb., Dorset, 1721, I, W, P17/402
Robt. Edwd., E. Harnham, Britford, 1855, AB, aff, Wr, P24/1415
Garrard, Roger, gent., Thornhill, Clyffe P., 1610, AB, court paper, P3/G/17
Jerrard, Sam., labourer, Fonthill G., 1779, W, P1/IJ/276, P1/13Reg/210
Jerrett, Sarah, widow, Ansty, 1793, W, P5/1793/8, P5/18Reg/190A
Silas, yeo., Semley, 1753, W, P1/G/601, P1/11Reg/63
Gerrett, Stephen, Downton, 1611, AB, a/c, P2/G/148
Garrard, Thos., gent., Thornhill, Clyffe P., 1666, AB, I, ren, W, P3/G/185
Gerard, Thos., Burghfield, Berks., 1714, W, P1/G/374, P1/5Reg/357

Garrard, Thos., gent., Thornhill, Clyffe P., 1729, W, P1/G/461, P1/7Reg/291
Gorrard, Thos., yeo., Thatcham, Berks., 1735, W, P1/G/508, P1/8Reg/131
Thos., blacksmith, Ansty, 1767, AB, ren, P2/G/954
Garrard, Thos., brazier, Wantage, Berks., 1767, W, P23/767
Jerrard, Thos., Fovant, 1805, W, P2/1805/19
Jerrard, Walter, husb., Billhay, Tisb., 1586, W, P2/7Reg/49B
Garrard, Wm., Clyffe P., 1561, AB, P1/2Reg/112B
Gerratt, Wm., butcher, Downton, 1667, AB, I, P2/G/349
Wm., butcher, Beam., Dorset, 1695, AB, I, P5/1695/39
Gerrett, Wm., Horningsham, 1769, AB, P5/1769/10
Gerrett, Wm., blacksmith, Sutton V., 1779, W, P1/G/705, P1/13Reg/201
see also Arnold alias G.; Garrett
Gerring *see* Gearing
Gerrish, Gyrishe, Agnes, widow, Melk., 1560, W, P2/4Reg/54A
Alice, Broughton G., 1596, AB, P2/G/100
Ann, widow, Broughton G., 1694, AB, I, P2/G/546
Gerish, Anthony, gent., Broughton G., [1663], W, P2/G/329
Bridget, widow, Hilp., 1715, AB, P2/G/671
Chas., Bradford A., 1702, AB, cert, P1/G/322
Edwd., yeo., Gt. Chalfield, 1677, AB, I, P2/G/406
Edwd., yeo., Broughton G., 1831, W, Wr, P2/1831/63
Girishe, Eliz., widow, Broughton G., 1578, I, W, P2/G/28
Eliz., widow, Dilton, Westb., 1745, W, P25/1745/8
Geo., Westwood, 1640, I, W, P2/G/289
Geo., yeo., Marston, Pott., 1729, I, W, P1/G/472, P1/7Reg/383B
Gifford, Hilp., 1691, AB, I, P2/G/530
Grace, sp., Hawkeridge, Westb., 1843, O, W, Wr, P25/1843/1
Hannah, widow, Westb., 1830, O, W, Wr, P25/1830/2
Gireshe, Hy., no abode stated, 1602?, I, P2/G/109
Gerish, Hy., Bromham, 1733, I, P30/76
Jas., victualler, Bradford A., 1834, O, W, Wr, P2/1834/8
Gyrishe, Jerome, clothier, Broughton G., 1579, AB, I, W, P2/G/31, P2/5Reg/340A
Joan, Broughton G., 1670, AB, comm, P2/G/358
Gyrishe, Jn., Melk., 1560, W, P2/4Reg/48A
Gerish, Jn., yeo., Melk., 1618, AB, comm, I, W, P2/G/183
Jn., jun., gent., Melk., 1626, AB, I, P2/G/211
Jn., sen., gent., Broughton G., 1635, AB, comm, P2/G/258, P2/9Reg/105A
Jn., yeo., Shaw, Melk., 1687, I, W, P2/G/511
Jn., yeo., Broughton G., 1725, AB, P2/G/730
Jn., Broughton G., 1732, AB, L, ren, P1/G/485
Jn., sen., victualler, Melk., 1793, W, P2/G/1063
Jn., victualler, Melk., 1804, W, P1/1804/105
Jn., licensed victualler, *The New Inn*, Seend, 1838, comm, W, Wr, P2/1838/59
Jn., Lacock, 1849, AB, O, Wr, P3/1849/3
Jn., carp., Broughton G., 1849, W, Wr, P2/1849/21
My., widow, Bromham, 1809, W, P3/1809/2
Richd., weaver, Shaw, Melk., 1615-17, AB, a/c, alleg, comm, court papers, inty, NW, P2/G/177
Richd., clothworker, Melk., 1728, AB, I, P2/G/745
Gerish, Robt., Seend, Melk., 1634, AB, a/c (2), I, P1/G/123
Roger, butcher, Atworth, Bradford A., 1763, AB, ren, W, P1/G/647, P1/12Reg/114A
Gerish, Thos., sen., yeo., Broughton G., 1619, I, W, P1/G/67
Thos., yeo., Semington, Steeple A., 1740, W, P2/G/821
Gerish, Thos., Bromham, 1790, comm, W, P3/G/751
Thos., Ashley, Bradford A., 1801, comm, W, P1/1801/29, P1/15Reg/252
Ursula, widow, Melk., 1632, I, W, P2/G/243, P2/9Reg/113
Gerish, Wm., jun., weaver, Shaw, Melk., 1602, AB (2), I (2), I (very detailed), P2/G/111
Gyrishe, Wm., yeo., Shaw, Melk., 1604, I (very detailed), W, P2/G/116
Gerish, Wm., husb., Broughton G., 1611, I, W, P1/G/32
Gerish, Wm., yeo., Seend, Melk., 1632, AB, a/c, I, ren, P2/G/245
Wm., yeo., Hilp., 1715, AB, comm, I, P2/G/670

Wm., Westb., 1737, AB, P25/1737/6
Wm., yeo., Bradford A., 1781, W, P2/G/1007
Gerritt *see* Gerrard
Gervase, Gervis *see* Jervis
Gesper, Alice, widow, Fovant, 1580, AB, W, P2/5Reg/364B
Gaispur, Edwd., Fovant, 1732, AB, P2/G/774
Eliz., sp., Quidh., 1750, W, P1/G/591, P1/10Reg/433
Gasper, Giles, husb., Fovant, 1588-91, AB, a/c, NW, T (children: Edwd. & Joan G.), P2/G/40, 54, P2/7Reg/125B
Gasper, Giles, yeo., Fovant, [1677], I, W, P2/G/405
Gasper, Hy., Fovant, 1620, AB, I, P2/G/197
Hy., yeo., Fovant, 1622, AB, I, W, P1/G/79
Hy., Fovant Stroud, [1679], I, W, P2/G/425
Gasper, Joan, widow, Fovant, 1589, I, W, P2/G/42
Gespar, Jn., husb., Fovant, 1576, W, P2/5Reg/257C
Jn., yeo., Fovant, 1665, I, W, P2/G/341
Gasper, My., Fovant (d. in London), 1682, AB, I, P2/G/453
Gesper alias Matt, My., Quidh., 1748, AB, P2/G/863
Gasper, Sarah, sp., St Giles, Aldgate, London (exs of Broad C. & Fovant), 1683, I, W, P2/G/466
Sarah, widow, Hindon, 1742, W, P2/G/835
Thos., Hindon, 1720, W, P2/G/703
Gesse *see* Jesse
Geste *see* Guest,
Gethly *see* Gately
Gethowse *see* Gatehouse
Gethurst, Augustine, joiner, Fonthill G., 1676, I, W, P2/G/392
Getley, Getly *see* Gately
Gettene *see* Jeton
Getter, Jos., Gt. Somerford, 1767, W, P1/G/661, P1/12Reg/222B
Gewly, Sarah, widow, Winterbourne Bassett, 1732, W, P3/G/542
Gey, Geye *see* Gay
Geyne *see* Gane
Ghey *see* Gay
Ghost, Barnaby, blacksmith, Sal., 1660, AB, I, P4/1660/1
Gost, Thos., yeo., Bramshaw, Hants, 1681, I, W, P24/411
Giare, Jonathan, clerk and vicar, Chipp., 1681, comm, I, W, P3/G/280
Gibb *see* Gibbs
Gibberd, My., wife of Timothy, Wantage, Berks., 1747, AB, P23/598
Gibbard, Richd., Southmoor, Longworth, Berks., 1832, AB, W, Wr, P1/1832/110
Gibbard, Robt., Pott., 1633, I, W, P1/G/117
Walter, Durrington, 1664, AB, I, P1/G/191
Gibben, Gibbens *see* Gibbons
Gibberd *see* Gibbard
Gibbons, [female], Corsham, 1685, caveat (Jas. ?Peirce of C. against W of sister, whose 1st name not given), P29/1Reg/229A
Gibbens, Alice, widow, S. Wraxall, 1631, I, NW, P1/G/116
Gibbins, Alice, widow, Baydon, 1678, W, P5/1678/18
Ann, widow, Aldbourne, 1689, AB, I, P3/G/338
Gibbins, Anthony, innholder, Wadswick, Box, 1689, I, W, P3/G/339
Anthony, innholder, Box, 1767, W, P1/G/662, P1/12Reg/213B
Gibbins, Audrey, widow, Witcomb, Hilmarton, 1631, I, W, P1/G/109
Christian, widow, Mere, 1565, W, P5/1Reg/55B
Dan., Marl., 1754, AB, P1/G/608
Gibbins, Dan., blacksmith, Overton, 1841, O, W, Wr, P3/1841/4
Gibben, Edwd., Fittleton, 1668, I, W, P1/G/207
Gibbins, Edwd., S. Wraxall, 1674, I, W, copy NW, P2/G/384
Gibbins, Eliz., widow, Whitley, Melk., [1684], I, W, P2/G/476
Frances, widow, Bradford A., 1697, comm, W, P2/G/562
Frances, widow, Sherb., Dorset, 1699, AB, comm, ren, W, P5/1699/13
Gibbens, Geo., Idmiston, 1615, I, W, P2/G/167, P2/8Reg/268
Jane, wife, S. Wraxall, 1732, AB, I, P1/G/484

Gibbins, Joan, widow, S. Wraxall, 1681, I, W, P2/G/443
Joan, widow, Bowden Hill, Lacock, 1816, comm, W, Wr, P3/1816/32
Jn., Corsham, 1563, W, P29/1Reg/13
Gibbins, Jn., husb., Baydon, 1580, I, T, W, P5/4Reg/3A, P5/1580/25
Gibbins, Jn., Bishopstone N., 1597, AB, I, W, P5/1597/122, P5/6Reg/188D
Gibbins, Jn., husb., Hilmarton, 1609, W, P3/G/14
Gibbens, Jn., sen., Corsham, 1626, AB, I, W, P29/G/9, P29/1Reg/105B
Jn., sen., yeo., Ridge, Corsham, 1656, AB, I, draft I (incomplete), W, P29/G/14, P29/1Reg/159A
Jn., sen., yeo., Pond Close, Corsham, 1677, comm, I, W, P1/G/232
Gibbins, Jn., yeo., Aldbourne, 1687, I, W, P3/G/314
Jn., yeo., Ridge, Corsham, 1691, AB, I, copy I, ren, W, P29/G/20, P29/1Reg/250
Jn., sen., clothier, Corsham, 1700, AB, I, ren, P29/G/21, P29/1Reg/274A
Jn., innholder *or* yeo., Box, 1715, I, W, P3/G/448
Jn., Wootton R., 1724, AB, P3/G/489
Jn., sen., yeo., Sherston & Gt. Somerford, 1733, AB, ren, P3/G/550
Jn., sen., husb., Bray, Berks., 1741, W, P1/G/538, P1/9Reg/122
Jn., Melk., 1758, AB, comm, P2/G/911
Gibbens, Jn., Winterbourne D., 1796, AB, P7/181
Jn., labourer, Whaddon, 1823, W, Wr, P1/1823/119
Gibbens, Jos., yeo., Maiden B., 1685, AB, I, W, P2/G/487
Jos., clothier, Lippiatts, Corsham, [1687], W, P29/1Reg/237
Gibbins, Leonard, husb., S. Wraxall, 1587, AB, I, P2/G/38, P2/7Reg/110D
Gibbens, Leonard, clerk, Seend, Melk., [1612], I, P2/G/153
Mgt., widow, Bishopstone N., 1614, I, W, P5/1613/32, P5/9Reg/131E
Gibbins, Mgt., widow, Upavon, 1660, I, W, P2/G/322
Mgt., sp., Corsham, 1703, I, W, P29/G/23
Gibbins, My., S. Wraxall, [1680], I, P2/G/433
My., widow, Box, 1739, W, P3/G/580
Priscilla, Stratford upon Avon, Warwickshire (leaving effects at Melk.), 1839, AB, comm, Wr, P1/1839/16
Gibbins, Richd., Baydon, 1594, AB, I, W, P5/1594/31, P5/6Reg/75A
Gibbens, Richd., husb., Idmiston, 1638, I, W, P2/G/272
Richd., innholder, Sal., 1775, W, P4/1775/11
Gibbins, Robt., Gt. Cheverell, 1559, W, P2/4Reg/3B
Gibbens, Robt., yeo., Kingston D., 1629, I, T, W, P2/G/228
Gibbon, Robt., gent., Sherb., Dorset, 1730, W, P5/1730/29
Sarah, widow, Chapel Plaster, Box, 1712, AB, I, W (living in former chapel), P3/G/438
Stephen, Wilsford with Lake, 1616, I, W, P5/1616/28
Gibbens, Stephen, yeo., Baydon, 1673, comm, I, W, P5/1672/16
Gibbens, Swithin, yeo., Overton (form. of Marl.), 1782, W, P1/G/720, P1/13Reg/438
Thos., yeo., W. Knoyle, [1719], W, P2/G/695
Thos., Oxford carrier, Porton, Idmiston, 1790, W, P2/G/1050
Thos., carrier, Sal., 1797, W, P4/1797/1
Wm., Corsham, 1687, AB, P29/G/19
Gibbens, Wm., yeo., Marl., 1741, W, P1/G/544, P1/9Reg/206
Wm., innholder, Bradford A., 1800, W, P2/1800/7
Wm., Holt, Bradford A., 1801, W, P1/1801/91, P1/15Reg/309A
Wm., innholder, Bradford A., 1806, W, Wr, P2/1806/71
Wm., Box, 1815, AB, W, Wr, P3/1815/45
Gibbole *see* Jeboult
Gibbs, Abel, yeo., N. Bradley, 1808, W, Wr, P1/1808/23
Agatha, widow, Corsham, 1632, I, W, copy W, P29/G/12, P29/1Reg/123B
Ann, widow, Bishopstone N., 1685, I, W, P5/1685/36
Ann, sp., Westb., 1808, O, W, P25/1808/3
Ann, widow, Hungerford, Berks., 1808, comm, W, P23/856
Anthony, gent., Warm., 1668, AB, I, ren, P2/G/355
Benj., millwright, Downton, 1730, I, W, P2/G/756
Chas., carp. and victualler, Quemerford, Calne, 1819, W, Wr, P26/1323
Chas., Lt. Hinton, 1831, AB, comm, Wr, P3/1831/74
Dulcimer, Sal., 1727, W, P4/1727/5
Edith, widow, Westb., 1730, W, P25/1730/1

Edmd., no abode stated, [1685], I, P2/G/489
Edmd., Fugg. St Peter, 1687-89, AB, a/c, I, P2/G/513
Edwd., husb., Mere, 1623, I, W, P5/1623/11, P5/10Reg/211
Edwd., Charlton, Wantage, Berks., 1746, W, P5/1746/32
Edwd., yeo., Dilton M., Westb., 1832, declaration, O, W, Wr, P25/1832/6
Gibes, Eliz., widow, Bere R., Dorset, 1678, I, NW, P5/1678/17
Eliz., widow, Grove, Wantage, Berks., 1704, AB, I, P5/1704/27
Eliz., widow, Hullavington, 1804, AB, P1/1804/103
Emma, sp., Corsham, 1686, AB, I, W, P29/G/18, P29/1Reg/229D
Everist, widow, Melk., 1765, affirmation, comm, W (Quaker), P2/G/942
Francis, cooper, Sal., 1634, I, W, P1/G/121
Francis, husb., Wantage, Berks., 1758, AB, W (decd's exx, Edith Skinner, d. before admg estate), P23/677
Francis, baker and maltster, Ashton K., 1762, W, P3/G/671
Francis, yeo., Orcheston St My., 1769, W, P2/G/961
Francis, coachman, Buck Hill, Calne, 1771, AB, W, P26/1043
Francis, gent., Orcheston St My., 1813-20, AB, comm, ren, W, Wr, P2/1813/36, P2/1820/41
Francis, Quemerford, Calne, 1822-28, AB (3), aff, comm, O, Wr, P26/1339, 1372
Gabriel, Sal., 1616, T (child: Alice G.), P4/1616/1
Gabriel, mason, Yatton K., 1671, I, W, P1/G/216
Geo., apothecary, Westb., 1691, AB, I (total value of goods only), ren, P25/1691/1
Geo., Pott., 1762, AB, comm, P1/G/640
Grace, jun., sp., Charminster, Dorset, 1673, AB, comm, NW, P5/1673/16
Grace, widow, Charminster, Dorset, 1676, I, W, P5/1676/24
Hy., husb., Ogbourne Maizey, 1672, comm, I, NW, P5/1672/13
Hy., Woodley, W. and Sandford, Berks., 1677, bond to return W, I, W (damaged), copy W, P5/1677/25
Gibbs alias Sheppard, Hy., yeo., Bulk., Keevil, 1721, I, W, P2/G/710
Hy., yeo., Bulk., Keevil, 1741, W, P2/G/824
Isaac, Melk., 1802, AB, comm, P2/1802/42
Jas., tucker, Marl. St My., 1639, AB, a/c, comm, I, P1/G/139
Jas., cordw., Trowb., 1774, W, P1/G/694, P1/13Reg/51
Jas., gent., Sharcott, Pewsey, 1827, W, Wr, P3/1827/68
Jane, sp., Westb., 1808, O, W, P25/1808/2
Joan, widow, Clack, Lyneham, 1676, I, W, P3/G/242
Joan, widow, Sonning, Berks., 1683, I, W, P5/1683/25
Jn., Boyton, 1568, W, P2/5Reg/46A
Gibb, Jn., Corsham, [1576], W (NEP), P29/G/1
Jn., Swallowcliffe, 1580, I, W, P5/1579/35, P5/3Reg/147H
Jn., yeo., Moor, Corsham, 1592, AB, W, P29/G/2-3, P29/1Reg/, 2931
Jn., sen., yeo., Moor, Corsham, 1626, AB, I, W, P29/G/8, P29/1Reg/106
Jn., husb., Corsham, 1628, W, P29/1Reg/117B
Gibes, Jn., fuller, Bremhill, 1639, AB, I, W, P3/G/156
Jn., yeo., Sonning, Berks., 1645, comm, I, W, P5/1644/13, P5/14Reg/77A
Jn., Ditchampton, Wilton, 1665, AB, P2/G/335
Jn., Gillingham, Dorset, 1668, AB, a/c, P27/1/32
Jn., Bishopstone N., 1669, I, W, P6/29
Jn., maltster *or* yeo., Lacock, 1669, I, W, P3/G/202
Jn., Ridge, Corsham, 1670, AB, I, P29/G/17, P29/1Reg/193B
Jn., Bishopstrow, 1684, AB, P2/G/477
Jn., sen., gent., Gillingham, Dorset, 1684, I, P27/1/83
Gibbs alias Sheppard, Jn., yeo., Bulk., Keevil, [1688], I, W, P2/G/523
Jn., yeo., Yatton K., 1703, W, P3/G/418
Jn., husb., Wantage, Berks., 1710, W, P5/1710/43, P5/15Reg/168
Jn., sen., yeo., Imber, 1724, W, P2/G/725
Jn., Broad C., 1762, AB, I, P2/G/927
Jn., Reading, Berks., 1767, AB, P1/G/663
Jn., Imber, 1797, AB, P2/G/1073
Jn., Bradford A., 1809, AB, comm, Wr, P2/1809/51
Jn., grocer, Westb., 1816, W, Wr, P25/1816/6
Jn., Purton, 1851, AB, O, Wr, P3/1851/37
Jonathan, N. Bradley, 1756, AB, P1/G/617

Gibb, Jonathan, dealer in horses, Corsham, 1768, AB, P29/2Reg/110
Jos., gent., Quidh., 1816, W, Wr, P2/1816/12
Jos., yeo., Stowford, Wingfield, 1852, I, W, Wr, P2/1852/22
Lionel, jun., shoemaker, Limpley Stoke, Bradford A., 1706, AB, I, P2/G/621
Lucy, widow, Corsham, 1595, W, P29/1Reg/40B
Mgt., widow, Fugg. St Peter, 1665, I, W, P2/G/340
My., widow, Gt. Cheverell, 1698, I, W, P1/G/306, P1/3Reg/223
My., Mkt. L., 1717, AB, P2/G/688
My., widow, N. Bradley, 1808, AB, comm, Wr, P2/1808/2
My., wife, Sal., 1811, AB, Wr, P1/1811/37
My., Lea, L. and Cleverton, 1823, W, Wr, P1/1823/140
Matthew, sen., Fugg. St Peter, 1635, I, W, P1/G/125
Osmund, yeo., Westwood, 1665, AB, I, NW, P2/G/336
Gibbs alias Sheppard, Philip, yeo., Trowb., 1635, I, W, P22/1/31
Ralph, Bishopstone N., 1628, I, W, P5/1628/43, P5/11Reg/96A
Richd., husb., Boyton, 1608, I, W, P1/G/28
Richd., wheeler, Wantage, Berks., 1628, I, W, P5/1628/44, P5/11Reg/88B
Richd., baker, Sal., 1638, AB, I, P4/1638/5
Richd., yeo., Wantage, Berks., 1677, AB, I, P23/70
Richd., yeo., Wantage, Berks., 1711, AB, I, P23/319
Richd., yeo., Ogbourne St A., 1723, W, P5/1723/19, P5/16Reg/85C
Richd., mason, Malm., 1727, AB, comm, I, P3/G/503
Richd., tallow chandler, Wantage, Berks., 1738, W, P23/534
Richd., yeo., Wantage, Berks., 1768, W, P23/723
Richd., Bishopstrow, 1793, AB, comm, P2/G/1060
Robt., husb., Badbury, Chiseldon, 1602, I, W, P1/G/9
Robt., sen., Bere R., Dorset, 1664, I (2), W, P5/1664/13
Robt., [Mere] (NBI), [1669], I, P5/1669/19
Robt., yeo., Bowden Farm, Burbage, 1685, I, W, P5/1685/38
Robt., barber, Wantage, Berks., 1742, W, P23/567
Roger, Marl., 1636, I, W, P1/G/133
Sam., yeo., Hawkeridge, Westb., 1639, I (detailed), W, P25/1639/15
Stephen, sword cutler, Sal., 1690, I, W, P4/1690/14
Thos., Boyton, 1622, I, W, P1/G/77
Thos., sen., yeo., Fugg. St Peter, [1676], I, W, P2/G/391
Thos., husb., Sonning, Berks., 1688, AB, I, P5/1688/33
Thos., yeo., Fugg. St Peter, 1695, I, W, P1/G/297
Thos., Newtown, Burghclere, Hants, 1716, AB, P1/G/393
Thos., yeo., Melk., 1718, W, P2/G/692
Thos., marine in Hon Brig.Powlett's Regt. and on Pembroke, Sal., 1747, W, P4/1746/9
Thos., yeo., Imber, 1748, I, W, P2/G/865
Thos., Bradford A., 1752, AB, I, P2/G/884
Thos., Reading, Berks., 1767, AB, P1/G/664
Thos., Sal., 1769, AB, P4/1769/11
Thos., woolstapler, Devizes, 1777, W, P1/G/703, P1/13Reg/175
Thos., Devizes, 1791, AB, P1/G/742, P1/14Reg/360A
Thos., yeo., Imber, 1791, W, P2/G/1053
Thos., yeo., Cutteridge, N. Bradley, 1806, W, P2/1806/28
Ursula, widow, Fugg. St Peter, 1682, I, W, P2/G/456
Valentine, painter, Devizes, 1730, W, P1/G/473, P1/7Reg/404
Wm., labourer, Urchf., 1594, I, W, P2/G/70
Wm., husb., Ogbourne St A., 1606, I, W, P1/G/21
Gibes, Wm., yeo., Lydiard T., 1664, I, W, P1/G/193
Wm., yeo., Rudside, Corsham, 1669-70, AB, I, P29/G/16, P29/1Reg/191B
Wm., yeo., Gt. Cheverell, 1679, I, W, P2/G/426
Wm., Badbury, Chiseldon, 1683, AB, I, P3/G/286
Wm., Wootton B., 1691, AB, P3/G/354
Wm., tailor, Mkt. L., 1704, W, P2/G/608
Wm., Highw., 1762, W, P10/1762/1
Wm., yeo., Bulk., Keevil, 1767, W, P2/G/955

Wm., farmer, Orcheston St Geo., 1776, W, P2/G/985
Wm., miller, Rams., 1805, W, P5/1805/9, P5/19Reg/125
Wm., shopkeeper, Chipp., 1820, W, Wr, P1/1820/75
Wm., widower, Lyme R., Dorset, 1854, AB, aff, O, Wr, P16/456
see also Shepeard alias G.; Shotough alias G.
Gibson, Ann, no abode stated, [1618], I, P2/G/181
Bennet, [broad weaver], Wingfield, 1635, I, W, P1/G/128
Edwd., clothworker, Trowb., 1725-26, I, W, P1/G/438, P1/7Reg/59B
Gibson alias May, Hy., blacksmith, Seend, Melk., 1607, I, W, P2/G/122
Hester, widow, Wingfield, 1729, W, P1/G/467, P1/7Reg/318
Isaac, widower, Seend, Melk., 1789, W, P1/G/740, P1/14Reg/281
Jn., Berwick St Jas., 1751, AB, P1/G/596
Rachel, widow, Seend, Melk., 1809, W, Wr, P2/1809/49
Sam., labourer, Melk., 1821, W, Wr, P2/1821/42
Thos., Sal. St Thos., 1611, AB, P4/1611/12
Thos., Ufton Nervet, Berks., 1698, note of value of goods, P1/G/311
Timothy, Sal., 1803, AB, P4/1803/5
Wm., Netherh., 1610, AB, I, T, P2/G/145, P2/8Reg/144A
Wm., yeo., Wingfield, 1788, W, P2/G/1040
see also Maye alias G.
Gid, Leonard, Fyfield, Milton L., 1609, I, P3/G/12
Giddings, Gidden, Abraham, Warm., 1705, AB, ren, P2/G/615
Alexander, Urchf., 1761, AB, comm, P2/G/921
Ann, widow, Urchf., 1750, W, P2/G/878
Ann, widow, Devizes, 1829, AB, O, Wr, P1/1829/9
Benj., New Park Cottage, Southbroom, 1829, aff, O, W, P24/1316
Cary, sen., yeo., Urchf., 1695, I, W, P2/G/552
Cary, Urchf., 1747, W, P1/G/574, P1/10Reg/183
Chas., yeo., Sherrington, 1707, W, P2/G/623
Chas., sen., yeo., Stert, Urchf., 1723, I, W, P1/G/415, P1/6Reg/397
Chas., breechesmaker, Urchf., 1826, W, Wr, P2/1826/34
Chas., gent., Netheravon (form. of Urchf.), 1833, W, Wr, P5/1833/8
Gidding, Edwd., Urchf., 1598, I, note of admon, T, P2/G/95
Edwd., sen., yeo. and miller, Chirton, 1686, I, W, P2/G/495
Edwd., Mkt. L., 1702, AB, I, P2/G/594
Edwd., Urchf., 1776, AB, P2/G/988
Edwd., Draycot C., 1836, AB, Wr, P3/1836/71
Giddens, Eleanor, widow, Marston, Pott., 1710, I, W, P1/G/354, P1/5Reg/18
Gidding, Eliz., widow, Pott., 1597, AB, P1/G/5
Eliz., sp., Southbroom, 1790, W, P24/1156
Eliz., sp., Stert, Urchf., 1840, O, W, Wr, P1/1840/4
Eliz., sp., Badminton, Gloucs (leaving effects at Chipp.), 1852, aff, O, W, Wr, P3/1852/46
Eunice, widow, Urchf., 1822, AB, Wr, P2/1822/21
Geo., Urchf., 1681, AB, P2/G/446
Geo., yeo., Urchf., 1812, W, P2/1812/66
Geo., labourer, Urchf. Bottom, 1855, aff, D, W, Wr, P2/1855/38
Gracian, widow, Urchf., 1672, I, W, P2/G/372
Henrietta Caroline, sp., Stert, Urchf., 1840, O, W, Wr, P1/1840/5
Humphrey, sen., yeo., Urchf., 1735, W, P1/G/507, P1/8Reg/103
Jas., Wedh., Urchf., 1730, AB, W, P2/G/757
Jas., yeo., Urchf., 1785, W, P2/G/1028
Jas., yeo., Urchf., 1833, W, Wr, P2/1833/29
Jas., Stert, Urchf., 1841, AB, comm, Wr, P1/1841/24
Jas., gent., Nursteed, Bps. C., 1844, O, W, Wr, P24/1373
Jas., yeo., Bratton, Westb., 1849, comm, declaration, W, Wr, P25/1849/5
Jane, widow, Urchf., 1803, AB, comm, P2/1803/88
Joan, widow, Urchf., 1666, I, W, P1/G/203
Joan, Urchf., 1687, AB, P2/G/515
Joan, Mkt. L., 1716, AB, P2/G/682
Jn., yeo., Urchf., 1681, I, W, P2/G/440

Jn., sen., yeo., Wedh., Urchf., 1683, I, W, P2/G/462
Jn., woolcomber, Urchf., 1693, comm, I, W, P2/G/541
Jn., clerk and vicar, Charl. nr. P., 1702, I, W, P2/G/596
Jn., yeo., Wedh., Urchf., 1703, I, W, P2/G/600
Jn., tailor, Chirton, 1708, AB, I, copy I, P1/G/344
Jn., Urchf., 1716, AB, P2/G/678
Jn., Urchf., 1721, AB, P2/G/709
Jn., Urchf., 1744, AB, P1/G/549
Jn., Rowde, 1758, AB, P3/G/661
Jn., yeo., Urchf., 1763-71, comm, L, W, P1/G/645, P1/12Reg/118A
Jn., sen., gent., Stert, Urchf., 1781, W, P1/G/716, P1/13Reg/322
Giddance, Jn., gardener, Warm., 1785, W, P2/G/1026
Jn., carp., Urchf., 1801, W, P1/1801/94, P1/15Reg/311
Giddings alias Barton, Jn., Easterton, Mkt. L., 1807, W, P1/1807/9
Jn., Urchf., 1817, AB, P1/1817/90
Jn., yeo., Larborough Farm, Pott., 1831, O, W, Wr, P1/1831/8
Jn., gent., Devizes, 1835, W, Wr, P1/1835/122
Jn., gent., Stert, Urchf., 1841, AB, ren, W, Wr, P1/1841/18
Josiah, Urchf., 1813, W, Wr, P2/1813/48
Mgt., widow, Urchf., 1636, I, W, P2/G/260
My., widow, Urchf., 1695, comm, W, P1/G/293
My., widow, Stert, Urchf., 1725, W, P1/G/439, P1/7Reg/66
My., widow, Urchf., 1739, AB, I, P2/G/814
My., widow, Urchf., 1850, AB, aff, O, Wr, P2/1850/55
Moses, cheese dealer, Chisenbury, Enford, 1818, W, Wr, P2/1818/57
Guiding, Robt., broad weaver, Winsley, Bradford A., 1713, W, P2/G/663
Robt., Urchf., 1751, W, P2/G/883
Robt., yeo., Nursteed, Bps. C., 1769, W, P24/1081
Robt., yeo., Urchf., 1802, W, P2/1802/49
Robt., thatcher, Urchf., 1850, AB (2), aff, D (2), O (2), W, Wr (2), P2/1850/6, 58
Sarah, Urchf., 1758, W, P2/G/909
Sarah, breechesmaker's wife, Urchf., 1789, W, P1/G/739, P2/G/1042, P1/14Reg/282
Sarah, widow, Urchf., 1798, W, P1/G/767, P1/15Reg/126
Sarah, widow, Urchf., 1849, O, W, Wr, P2/1849/8
Thos., yeo., Urchf., 1811, W, Wr, P1/1811/18
Gidding, Wm., weaver, Winsley, Bradford A., 1590, I, W, P2/G/49
Gidding, Wm., weaver, Bradford A., 1593, I, W, P2/G/67
Wm., soapmaker, Urchf., 1682, AB, I, W, P2/G/450
Wm., Conock, Chirton, 1682-83, AB, a/c, I, P2/G/449
Giddens, Wm., yeo., Netheravon, 1722, W, P5/1721/17, P5/16Reg/61A
Wm., husb., Patney, 1749, comm, W, P2/G/869
Wm., sen., labourer, Southbroom, 1790, W, P24/1157
Wm., collarmaker, Heytes., 1799, W, P5/1799/9, P5/18Reg/283B
Wm., Bps. C., 1823, AB, Wr, P24/1296
Wm., sen., Calne, 1847, W, Wr, P5/1847/13
see also Stevens nee G.
Gilbert *see* Gybburd *or* G.
Giessen, Robt., cordw., Sal., 1829, req, W, copy W, Wr, P4/1829/6
Gifford, Bartholemew, yeo., Shrewton, [1680], I, W, P2/G/432
Chas. Francis, rector, Rushall, 1708, AB, ren, P1/G/348
Eleanor, widow, Grimstone, Stratton, Dorset, 1603, AB, I, W, P5/1603/30, P5/7Reg/65A
Giffard, Eliz., widow, Devizes, 1793, W, P1/G/745, P1/14Reg/485C
Geo., vicar, Downton, 1721, AB, P2/G/706
Jefferd, Hy., sen., builder and house carp., Lyme R., Dorset, 1830, W, Wr, P5/1830/36
Jefferd, Hy. Parkin, Lyme R., Dorset, 1839, AB, aff, O, Wr, P16/423
Humphrey, innholder, Swan Inn, Cheap St., Sherb., Dorset, 1834, W, Wr, P5/1834/9
Joan, carp.'s widow, Laverstock, 1563, AB, P2/4Reg/155B, 159A
Gefford, Joan, widow, Keevil, [1618], I, P2/G/182
Jn., husb., Laverstock, 1563, I, W, P2/G/11, P2/4Reg/118
Jn., husb., Baydon, 1610, W, P5/9Reg/27C

Jn., yeo., Baydon, 1627, I, W, P5/1627/18, P5/11Reg/44A
Gifford alias Jeffery, Jn., brewer, Sal., 1639, I, W, P4/1638/12
Jn., gent., Warm., [1712], I, W, P2/G/648
Jos., gent., Sal., 1729, W, P1/G/468, P1/7Reg/362
Mgt., widow, Monkton D., 1618, I, W, P2/G/179
Philip, gardener, Corsham, 1732, W, P29/G/22
Thos., husb., Stratton, Dorset, 1566, W, P5/1Reg/68B
Thos., gent., Boreham, Warm., 1575, W, P2/5Reg/235B
Thos., husb., Grimstone, Stratton, Dorset, 1588, W, P5/5Reg/21B
Thos., Baydon, 1695, I, W, P5/1695/31
Giffard, Thos., ironmonger, Devizes, 1740, comm, W, P1/G/530, P1/9Reg/5
Giffard, Thos., rector, Rushall, 1747, W, P1/G/566, P1/10Reg/35, 57
Wm., Plaitford, 1582, W, P2/6Reg/57B
Wm., tailor, Bodenham, Nunton and B., 1628, I, W, copy I, copy W, P2/G/220, P2/9Reg/59A
Wm., yeo., Baydon, 1628, I, W, P5/1628/45, P5/11Reg/98
Wm., husb., Bodenham, Nunton and B., 1662, AB, I, NW, P1/G/180
Wm., Fordington, Dorset, 1752, AB, P5/1752/20
Giffard, Wm., gent., Charl. nr. P. (d. at Badminton, Gloucs), 1783, AB, ren, P2/G/1016
Giffard, Yate, apothecary, Devizes, 1782, comm, W, P1/G/722, P1/13Reg/404A
Gigg, Edwd., husb., Gt. Bedwyn, 1692, AB, I, P5/1692/37
Edwd., tiler, Colerne, 1838, W, Wr, P3/1838/50
Giggs, Frideswide, widow, Gt. Bedwyn, 1727, AB, I, P21/8/38
Geo., Gt. Bedwyn, 1704, AB, I, P21/6/18
Giggs, Joan, widow, Lt. Bedwyn (abode at Froxfield Almshouse struck out), 1715, AB, I (2 - 1 with several sums owed decd), P21/7/22
Jos., miller, Gt. Bedwyn, 1706, I, W, P21/6/28
Giggs, Thos., husb., Rushall, 1574, W, P2/5Reg/192B
Gegg, Thos., husb., Gt. Bedwyn, 1695, AB, I, P21/5/32
Wm., Wilton, Gt. Bedwyn, 1741, W, P21/9/33
Gilbert, Adrian, esquire, Wilton, 1628, AB, a/c, I (?step-brother of Sir Walter Ralegh), P1/G/102
Agnes, widow, Patney, 1597, I, W, P2/G/82
Agnes, Rowde, 1626, I, W, P3/G/91
Gilbard, Alice, widow, Sutton V., 1558, AB, I, P2/G/3, P2/3Reg/77B
Alice, widow, Rollestone, 1569, W, P2/5Reg/52C
Angel, yeo., Chaddington, Lydiard T., 1733, W, P3/G/551
Gilbert alias Clarke, Ann, Lacock & Chipp., 1623, AB, a/c, I, P3/G/78
Ann, widow, Urchf., 1694, I, W, P2/G/547
Gilberd, Ann, Kingston D., 1723, W, P1/G/421, P1/6Reg/421C
Gilbard, Ann, widow, Gt. Bedwyn, 1737, W, P21/9/19
Ann, widow, Tilsh., 1832, W, P2/1832/6
Anthony, husb., Durrington, 1590, I, W, P2/G/50
Bartholomew, Tollard Royal, 1714, AB, I, P1/G/382
Brian, Shrewton, 1627-28, AB, a/c, I (2), W, P2/G/215
Cath., widow, Steeple A., 1763, AB, comm, P2/G/930
Gilberd, Chas., husb., Rollestone, 1610, I, copy I, W, P2/G/144, P2/8Reg/141
Chas., husb., Aldbourne, 1679, I, W, P3/G/265
Chas., gent., Shrewton, 1728, W, P2/G/749
Chas., yeo., Gt. Durnford, 1765, W, P9/78
Chas., yeo., Durrington, 1773, W, P1/G/686, P1/12Reg/461B
Edwd., Ebbesborne Wake, 1579, W, P2/5Reg/338D
Gilbart, Edwd., Stert, Urchf., 1597, I, P2/G/84
Edwd., beer drawer, Gt. Faringdon, Berks., 1679, I (includes two gross of tobacco pipes), W, P5/1679/38
Edwd., blacksmith, Fittleton, 1720, W, P1/G/402, P1/6Reg/212
Edwd., farmer, Poulshot, 1838, comm, W, Wr, P2/1838/58
Eliz., widow, Rowde, 1629, I, W, P3/G/105
Eliz., sp., W. Camel, d. at Caundle Marsh, Dorset, 1633, I, W (2), P5/1633/22, P5/12Reg/155C
Eliz., widow, Winterbourne S., 1664, I, W, P2/G/334
Eliz., widow, Shrewton, 1683, I, W, P2/G/472
Eliz., widow, Knook, 1729, AB, P5/1729/20, P5/16Reg/221A
Eliz., Maiden B., 1731, AB, P2/G/769

Eliz., widow, Purton, 1748, W, P3/G/624
Eliz., widow, Sutton V., 1785, comm, W, P2/G/1029
Gabriel, tailor, Longbridge D., 1749, I, W, P2/G/870
Geo., Aldbourne, 1636, AB, I, P3/G/142
Geo., Knook, 1687, AB, I, P5/1687/18
Geo., gent., Keevil, 1695, AB, I, W, P2/G/554
Geo., Edington, 1711, AB, comm, P1/G/355
Geo., gent., Keevil, 1790-91, AB, W, P2/G/1049, 1059
Geo., yeo., Keevil, 1829, O, W, Wr, P1/1829/17
Giles, yeo., Bratton, Westb., 1635, I, W, P25/1634/2
Giles, yeo., Bratton, Westb., 1643, I, W, P25/1643/3
Helena, widow, Laverstock, 1691, AB, P2/G/534
Hy., husb., Benham, Speen, Berks., 1721, W, P1/G/412, P1/6Reg/374
Gilbert alias Netten, Hester, widow, Berwick St Jas., 1735, W, P1/G/499, P1/7Reg/637B
Gybburd *or* Giddurd, Humphrey, Rowde, 1619, I, W, P1/G/69
Jane, widow, Keevil, 1794, W, P2/G/1065
Joan, widow, Sutton V., 1586, W, P2/7Reg/53B
Joan, widow, Sonning, Berks., 1633, I, W, copy W, P5/1633/21, P5/12Reg/144B
Joanna, sp., Britford (form. of Kimpton, Hants), 1813, W, Wr, P2/1813/24
Jn., Sutton V., 1557, W, P2/3Reg/46A
Jn., Maddington, 1558, W, P2/3Reg/139A
Jn., Sutton V., 1569, W, P2/5Reg/62A
Jn., husb., Porton, Idmiston, 1586, W, P2/7Reg/65B
Jn., Kingston D., 1597, I, NW, P2/G/86
Gilberd, Jn., sen., husb., Rollestone, 1609, I, W, P2/G/131, P2/8Reg/75
Jn., husb., Conock, Chirton, 1619, I, W, P1/G/68
Jn., Rowde, [1619], W, P1/G/66
Jn., victualler, Sonning, Berks., 1628, AB, a/c, I, P5/1628/47, P5/11Reg/76
Jn., Porton, Idmiston, 1631, AB (re bequest of Wm. G. to brother Jn.), release (2), P2/G/224, 238
Jn., yeo., Sutton V., 1637, I, W, copy I, copy W, P2/G/269
Jn., husb., Winterbourne S., 1642, I, W, P2/G/301
Jn., yeo., Shrewton, 1679, I, W, P2/G/428
Jn., gent., Sal., 1680, AB, I, ren, P4/1680/9
Jn., scrivener, Sal., 1680, AB, I (detailed), ren, P4/1679/21
Jn., Upton L., [1681], I, P2/G/437
Jn., cordw., Stert, Urchf., 1685, AB, comm, I, P1/G/257
Jn., husb., Aldbourne, 1692, comm, I, W, P1/G/278
Jn., sen., gent., Addeston, Maddington, 1693, I, W, P1/G/277
Jn., [huntsman *or* warrener], Aldbourne, 1694, AB, I, P3/G/367
Jn., tailor, Longbridge D., 1700, W, P2/G/583
Jn., yeo., Shrewton, 1705, I, W, P2/G/611
Jn., carp., Chirton, 1714, I, W, P1/G/372, P1/5Reg/336
Jn., jun., Winterbourne S., 1721, W, P1/G/413, P1/6Reg/380
Gilbard, Jn., innholder, Maddington, 1722, W, P2/G/717
Jn., cooper, Devizes St My., 1723, AB, I, P1/G/432
Jn., yeo., Conock, Chirton, 1723, AB, I, P1/G/423
Jn., maltster, Knook, 1729-30, AB, I, W, P5/1729/21, P5/1730/26, P5/16Reg/221B
Jn., cordw., Longbridge D., 1746, AB, W, P2/G/858
Jn., yeo., Fisherton D., 1748, W, P2/G/867
Jn., sen., yeo., Fisherton D., 1789, W, P1/G/734, P1/14Reg/206
Jn., baker, Rams., 1792, W, P5/1792/10, P5/18Reg/178B
Jn., yeo., Newtown, Durnford, 1796, W, P9/93
Jn., yeo., Crudwell, 1804, comm, W, Wr, P1/1804/6, P1/15Reg/399
Jn., Berwick St Jas., 1807, W, Wr, P1/1807/28
Jn., dairyman, Poulshot, 1807, W, P2/1807/18
Jn., gent., Swindon, 1814, AB, comm, P1/1814/153
Jn., yeo., Fisherton D., 1833, W, Wr, P2/1833/74
Jn., Rushall, 1838, O, W, Wr, P2/1838/34
Jos., tailor, Longbridge D., 1719, I, W, P2/G/694
Jos., sawyer, Gt. Bedwyn, 1737, W, P21/9/18

Jos., Warm., 1805, AB, P2/1805/20
Margery, Elcombe, Wrou., 1726, AB, P1/G/447
Martha, widow, Urchf., 1819, AB, comm, Wr, P2/1819/3
My., widow, Conock, Chirton, 1631-33, I, W, P2/G/237, 249
My., widow, Childrey, Berks., 1714, I, W, P1/G/376, P1/5Reg/379
My., widow, Devizes, 1734, W, P1/G/493, P1/7Reg/595
My., widow, Marden, 1738, AB, P1/G/519
My., Marden, 1757, AB, P2/G/898
My., Wantage, Berks., 1757, W, P23/675
My., widow, Corsham, 1772, W, P29/G/24, P29/2Reg/152
My., widow, Durrington, 1789, W, P2/G/1043
My., sp., Horton, Bps. C., 1826, AB, O, P24/1306
My., sp., Chirton, 1827, O, W, Wr, P2/1827/19
Maurice, husb., Longbridge D., [1640], I, W, P2/G/286
Gilbard, Nich., Urchf., 1547, W, P2/2Reg/74A
Nich., husb., Stert, Urchf., 1571, W, P2/5Reg/115C
Nich., Elcombe, Wrou., 1721, AB, I (2 - 1 a copy), P3/G/470
Nich., Hindon, 1741, AB, P2/G/825
Paul, maltster, Urchf., 1701, I, W, P2/G/586
Ralph, husb., Chirton, 1583, W, P2/6Reg/107A
Gilberd, Richd., Shrewton, 1600, AB, I, P2/G/103
Richd., husb., Urchf., 1614, W, P2/8Reg/225B
Richd., yeo., Longbridge D., 1615, AB, I, W, P2/G/169
Richd., yeo., Patney, 1642-48, AB, a/c, comm, I, P2/G/297, 315
Richd., Aldbourne, 1667, AB, comm, I, P3/G/188
Gilberd, Richd., yeo., Benham, Speen, Berks., 1674, AB, I, W, P1/G/227
Richd., husb., Upton L., 1675, I, P2/G/387
Richd., Aldbourne, 1702, AB, I, P3/G/407
Gilbart, Richd., weaver, Wantage, Berks., 1741, W, P23/554
Robt., coalburner, Downton, 1610, I, copy I, T, P2/G/136
Robt., Edington, 1639, AB, I, P2/G/279
Gilbert alias Netten, Robt., tailor, Shrewton, 1653, I, W, P1/G/173
Gilbert alias Netten, Robt., yeo., Shrewton, 1668, AB, I, P2/G/353
Robt., labourer, Benham Valence & Marsh Benham, Speen, Berks., 1692, I, W, P1/G/280
Robt., Codf. St My., 1744, AB, P2/G/845
Robt., Urchf., 1793, AB, P2/G/1061
Sam., Shrewton, 1777, AB, P2/G/994
Sam., labourer, Fonthill G., 1808, W, Wr, P1/1808/54
Sarah, widow, Warm., 1781, W, P2/G/1010
Sarah, widow, Marl., 1782, W, P1/G/721, P1/13Reg/437
Sarah, widow, Warm., 1808, AB, Wr, P1/1808/60
Susanna, Aldbourne, 1697, AB, I, P3/G/385
Gilberd, Thos., Rollestone, 1549, W, P2/2Reg/88B
Thos., Longbridge D., 1561, W, P2/4Reg/71A
Thos., shepherd, Fifield Bavant, 1580, I, W, P2/G/35, P2/5Reg/368B
Thos., husb., Longbridge D., 1599, I, W, P2/G/99
Thos., husb., Chirton, 1605, W, P2/G/115
Thos., day labourer, Bemerton, Fugg. St Peter, 1606, I, W, P2/G/118
Thos., sen., husb., Rollestone, 1639, I, W, P2/G/275
Thos., thatcher, Kingston D., 1639, deed of gift, I, NW, P2/G/278
Thos., sen., husb., Chirton, 1660, comm, I, W, P2/G/320
Thos., yeo., Maddington, 1661, I, W, P2/G/326
Gilbart alias Netton, Thos., yeo., Rollestone, 1666, AB, I, P2/G/342
Gilbert alias Netten, Thos., sen., yeo., Berwick St Jas., 1689, AB, I, W, P1/G/271
Thos., yeo., Durrington, [1694], W, P2/G/545
Thos., Berwick St Jas., 1703, AB, P1/G/323
Thos., carp., Rodbourne C., 1711, I, W, P1/G/358, P1/5Reg/141
Thos., Wilton, 1712, AB, P2/G/650
Thos., yeo., Monkton D., 1723, W, P1/G/420, P1/6Reg/422
Thos., Longbridge D., 1727, AB, P2/G/742

Thos., carp. and victualler, Devizes, 1736, W, P1/G/513, P1/8Reg/170
Thos., yeo., Durrington, 1748, W, P2/G/868
Thos., gent., Aughton, Collingbourne K., 1771, W, P3/G/697
Thos., yeo., Winterbourne S., 1776, W, P1/G/698, P1/13Reg/147
Thos., yeo., Durrington, 1781, W, P2/G/1009
Thos., Idmiston, 1783, AB, P2/G/1017
Thos., gent., Collingbourne K., 1807, W, Wr, P3/1807/50
Thos., gent., Longbridge D., 1808, W, Wr, P2/1808/19
Thos., labourer, Berwick St Jas., 1810, D, W, Wr, P1/1810/7
Gilbard, Wm., husb., Maddington, 1548, W, P2/2Reg/59A
Wm., Durrington, 1571, W, P2/5Reg/130A
Wm., husb., Patney, 1579, W, P2/5Reg/331A
Wm., yeo., Chirton, 1610, I, W, P2/G/137, P2/8Reg/116A
Wm., Upton L., 1621, I, T, W, P2/G/196
Wm., Fisherton A., 1628, AB, I, P2/G/224
Wm., yeo., Porton, Idmiston, 1631, D, I, W, P1/G/115
Wm., Patney, 1636, AB, a/c, I, P2/G/261
Wm., apothecary, Sal., 1637, AB, I (detailed), P4/1637/11
Wm., Chirton, 1660, AB, comm, I, P2/G/321
Wm., butcher, Sal., 1664, W, P1/G/189
Wm., Devizes, 1665, AB, P1/G/198
Wm., husb., Urchf., 1677, AB, I, W, P2/G/407
Wm., sen., gent., Maddington, 1704, W, P2/G/605
Wm., Conock, Chirton, 1740, W, P2/G/817
Wm., gent., Maddington, 1744, W, P1/G/551, P1/9Reg/285
Gilbart, Wm., sen., yeo., Aldbourne, 1747, W, P1/G/573, P1/10Reg/139
Wm., Fonthill G., 1757, AB, P2/G/903
Wm., Hindon, 1758, AB, P2/G/915
Gilbord, Wm., Marl., 1776, AB, P1/G/702
Wm., shopkeeper, Urchf., 1815, W, P2/1815/12
Gilbart, Winifred, widow, Durrington, 1594, I, W, P2/G/55
see also Gybburd *or* G.; Lybbin alias G.; Netton alias G.; Webb alias G.
Gildon, Christian, widow, Mere, 1583, I, W, P5/1583/15, P5/4Reg/62A
Edith, Mere, 1601, AB, I, P5/1601/20
Edwd., Woodlands, Mere, 1598, AB, a/c, I, P5/1598/23
Gyldon, Hugh, Mere, 1582, AB, I, T, P5/1582/28, P5/4Reg/42B
Jn., Mere, 1579, I, W, P5/1579/20, P5/3Reg/135B
Gyldon, Peter, Mere, 1569, W, P5/2Reg/43D
Richd., yeo., Mere, 1616, W, P5/1616/30
Richd., Gillingham, Dorset, [1679], W, P27/1/52
Gyldon, Roger, husb., Zeals, 1571, W, P5/2Reg/108C
Thos., Mere, 1598-1601, AB (2 - 1 re Thos. G. & Edith his wife), P5/6Reg/215B, P5/7Reg/17A
Gyldon, Thos., Over Zeals, 1599, AB, I, P5/1598/20
Gyldon, Wm., Calne, 1569, AB, P5/2Reg/43E
Gyldon, Wm., husb., Mere, 1609, AB, I, T, P5/1609/35, P5/9Reg/6A
Giles, Gilles, Agnes, Eisey, 1648, AB, P1/G/162
Ann, widow, Heytes., 1811, W, Wr, P5/1811/1
Ann, sp., Sutton V., 1826, AB, Wr, P2/1826/10
Gyles, Anthony, labourer, Buckland, Berks., 1741, AB, I, P1/G/536
Gyles, Avis, widow, Maddington, 1608, AB, I, P2/G/127
Gyles, Blanch, widow, Over C., Dorset (*also* of Longburton), 1624, AB, I, P5/1624/18, P5/10Reg/232
Chas., widower, Stockton, 1857, AB, aff, O, Wr, P2/1857/47
Chris., Corston, Malm., 1727, W, P3/G/504
Cornelius, innkeeper, Wylye, 1850, W, Wr, P2/1850/48
Dan., gardener, Warm. Common, 1831, O, W, P2/1831/24
Edmd., joiner, Ashton K., 1619, I, W, P1/G/70
Gyles, Edwd., wheelwright, Ashton K., 1679, I, NW (both on same document), P3/G/272
Edwd., yeo., Garsdon, 1692, I, W, P3/G/356
Edwd., sen., yeo., Stanford in the Vale, Berks., 1729, AB, I, P1/G/454
Edwd., victualler, Brinkw., 1770, W, P3/G/695

Edwd., yeo., Purton, 1786, comm, W, P1/G/732, P1/14Reg/174B
Edwd., bach., Purton, 1814, AB, comm, P1/1814/76
Eliz., widow, Woolstone, Uffington, Berks., 1723, AB, I, P1/G/426
Francis, shopkeeper, Sutton C., Berks., 1786, W, P1/G/730, P1/14Reg/125B
Giles, butcher, Grove, Wantage, Berks., 1837, O, W, Wr, P23/992
Gyles, Gillett, husb., Over C., Dorset, 1601, AB, I, W, P5/1601/22
Gyles alias Soper, Gillian, widow, Hinton, Hurst, Berks., 1596, I, NW, P5/1596/29, P5/6Reg/132A
Gyles, Hy., yeo., Wokm., Berks., 1640, I, W, P5/1640/21, P5/13Reg/245
Gyles, Hy., [tanner], Maddington, 1732, AB, I, P2/G/777
Hy., carp., Bishopstrow, 1817, W, Wr, P1/1817/44
Humphrey, collarmaker, Maddington, 1693, AB, I, W, P2/G/539
Humphrey, Maddington, 1743, W, P2/G/839
Humphrey, jun., Steeple L., 1812, AB, Wr, P2/1812/5
Humphrey, Steeple L., 1829, AB, P2/1829/33
Isaac, yeo., Thornhill Farm, Westport St My., 1787, attestation, W, P3/G/743
Jas., yeo., Chilton F., 1774, W, P3/G/703
Jas., collar and harnessmaker, Littleton P., 1836, W, Wr, P1/1836/21
Gyles, Joan, widow, Ashton K., 1640, I, W, P3/G/164
Gyell, Jn., singleman, Damerham, Hants, 1571, W, P2/5Reg/128B
Jn., joiner, Corsham, 1627, AB, W, P29/G/11, P29/1Reg/108
Jn., husb., Ashton K., 1630, AB, a/c, I, P3/G/114
Jn., yeo., Ashton K., 1676, I, W, P3/G/248
Gyles, Jn., sen., Warm., 1680, AB, comm, I, P1/G/241
Jn., yeo., Farnborough, Berks., 1692, I, ren, W, P1/G/284
Jn., shearman, Warm., [1694], I, NW, P2/G/544
Gyles, Jn., S. Moreton, Berks., 1708, ren, P1/G/347
Gyles, Jn., jun., butcher, Wantage, Berks., 1730, W, P23/473
Jn., tallow chandler, Ashton K., 1739, I, W, P3/G/581
Jn., yeo., Wantage, Berks., 1770, W, P5/1770/18, P5/17Reg/7
Jn., harnessmaker, Littleton P., 1838, O, W, Wr, P1/1838/19
My., widow, Hanging L., 1683-84, a/c (2), AB, I, P2/G/467
My., widow, Ashton K., 1733, AB, P3/G/552
My., Thornhill Farm, Westport St My., 1787, W, P3/G/744
My. Ann, sp., Grove, Wantage, Berks., 1835, AB, comm, P23/980
Matthew, smith, Hannington, 1634, I, W, P3/G/132
Matthew, yeo., Marridge Hill, Rams., 1723, NW, P5/1723/20, P5/16Reg/86A
Matthew, farmer, Ewin's Hill, Aldbourne, 1826, AB, O, W, Wr, P1/1826/139
Merrick, yeo., Downton, 1662, I, W, P1/G/182
Giles alias Soper, Oliver, Ruscombe, Berks., 1642, AB, P5/14Reg/48B
Gyles, Richd., clerk and parson, Stockwood, Dorset, 1632, AB, a/c, I, NW, P5/1632/23, P5/12Reg/111C
Richd., widow, Marl., 1696, AB (re Ann), I (re Ann & Richd.), P1/G/301
Richd., butcher, Purton, 1715-22, AB, ren, W, P3/G/449, 476
Richd., Whitep., 1826, AB, Wr, P1/1826/12
Richd., gent., Chitterne St My. (form. of Shercott, Pewsey), 1850, comm, W, Wr, P2/1850/64
Gyles, Robt., Hurst, Berks., 1614, AB, I, P5/1614/25, P5/9Reg/117D
Robt., Milborne Stileham, Bere R., Dorset, 1633, I (NEP), P5/1633/64
Robt., staymaker, Bradford A., 1753, W, P1/G/603, P1/11Reg/69B
Robt., Gt. Cheverell, 1766, AB, P2/G/948
Robt., collarmaker, Steeple L., 1834, W, Wr, P2/1834/21
Sarah, wife of Jn., yeo., Wantage, Berks., 1754, AB, P23/651
Stephen, S. Newton, 1731, AB, P2/G/767
Gyles, Thos., yeo., Calne, 1572, W, P5/3Reg/2B
Gyles, Thos., Bulford, 1701, AB, I, P2/G/588
Thos., butcher, Wantage, Berks., 1711, AB, I, P23/318
Thos., yeo., Gt. Coxwell, Berks., 1723, I, O, W, P1/G/430, P1/7Reg/27B
Wm., labourer, Maddington, 1573, W, P2/5Reg/164B
Gilles, Wm., Eisey, [1607], W (NEP), P3/G/7
Wm., yeo., Hinton, Hurst, Berks., 1613, I, W, P5/1613/35, P5/9Reg/80
Wm., collarmaker, Maddington, 1661, I, W, P2/G/323
Wm., husb., Hanging L., 1681, I, W, P2/G/439

Wm., mason, Hanging L., 1771, AB, W, P2/G/968
Wm., yeo., Crickl. St S., 1780, W, P3/G/723
Wm., labourer, Shaw, Lydiard M., 1791, W, P3/G/754
Wm., butcher, Purton, 1796, W, P3/G/762
Wm., collarmaker, Littleton P., 1816, W, Wr, P1/1816/19
Wm., sen., yeo., Littleton P., 1817, W, Wr, P1/1817/4
Wm., yeo., Hanging L., 1820, W, Wr, P1/1820/22
Wm., tallow chandler, Ashton K., 1823, comm, W, Wr, P3/1823/16
Wm., collarmaker, Heytes., 1831, W, Wr, P5/1831/18
Zachary, day labourer, Crickl. St S., 1712, I, P3/G/439
see also Soper alias G.; Taylor alias G.
Gilgrass, Gilgrace, Eliz., widow, Basildon, Berks., 1680, AB, I, P1/G/237
Jn., Stanford in the Vale, Berks., 1726, AB, P1/G/446
Gilham *see* Gillam
Gill, Agnes, widow, Tinh., Edington, [1629], W, P2/G/227
Ann, Wokm., Berks., 1662, AB, I, P5/1662/54
Gills, Anthony, blacksmith, Inglesham, 1621, I, W, P3/G/69
Cath., widow, Gt. Cheverell, [1688], W, P2/G/517
Chas., Chetnole, Yetm., Dorset, 1805, AB, P5/1805/19, P5/19Reg/143
Chris., Gt. Cheverell, 1566, W, P2/4Reg/234A
Chris., husb., Gt. Cheverell, 1601, I, W, P2/G/104
Chris., yeo., Gt. Cheverell, [1627], I, NW, P2/G/213
Chris., sen., Gt. Cheverell, 1647, AB, I, P2/G/312
Gille, Edwd., W. Lavington, 1746, AB, P1/G/565
Eliz., widow, Gt. Cheverell, 1634, I, W, P2/G/252
Geo., yeo., Shatcombe, Beam., Dorset, 1732, W, P17/453
Giles, mercer, Reading, Berks., 1726, W, P1/G/444, P1/7Reg/98A
Hy., yeo., Uffc., Devon, 1663, AB, I, P20/1/47
Hy., Sutton Poyntz, Dorset, 1774-78, AB, copy W (original sent to Dean of Sarum's Registrar, Mr Powell, on 4 Sep 1774), W (proved there), P5/1777/25, P18/11, 13
Jn., W. Ashton, Steeple A., 1566, W, P2/4Reg/223A
Gills, Jn., shepherd, Ashton K., 1615, AB, I, P3/G/40
Jn., husb., Tinh., Edington, 1628, comm, I, W, P1/G/97
Jn., yeo., Uffc., Devon, 1691, AB, I, P20/1/118
Gills, Mark, Sal., 1807, AB, Wr, P1/1807/12
My., widow, Uffc., Devon, [1607], I, W, P20/1/43
My., widow, Gt. Cheverell, 1635, I, W, P2/G/257, P2/9Reg/85A
Richd., Uffc., Devon, 1713, AB, I (detailed), P5/1713/34
Richd., sergemaker, Craddock, Uffc., Devon, 1744, W, P20/1/205
Robt., sen., yeo., Uffc., Devon, 1676, I, W, P5/1676/25
Robt., yeo., Holcombe Rogus & Uffc., Devon, 1707, comm, W, P5/1707/23, P5/15Reg/48
Robt., miller, Sutton Poyntz, Dorset, 1765, AB, P18/7
Stephen, husb., Gt. Cheverell, 1614, I, W, P1/G/43
Stephen, weaver, Wilsford nr Pewsey, [1622], I, W, P2/G/201
Thos., Sherb., Dorset, 1626, AB, I, P5/1625/38
Thos., glover, Lt. Titchborne, Whitep., 1678, AB, I, P2/G/417
Thos., yeo., Ryme I., Dorset, 1809, W, Wr, P5/1809/1
Gills, Tilly, widow, Upper Inglesham, 1623, I, W, P3/G/79
Walter, Chards., Devon, 1573, W, P5/3Reg/22A
Wm., clerk and parson, Finchampstead, Berks., 1593, I, W, P1/G/4
see also Gillett; Sutton alias G.
Gillam, Edmd., yeo., Purton, 1645, comm, I, W, P1/G/149
Jn., Ashton K., 1666, AB, I, P3/G/186
Jn., carp., Wantage, Berks., 1681, AB, I, W (ex. dau My. Wheler), P23/108
Jn., yeo., Purton & Lydiard M., 1684, I, W, P3/G/288
Gillham, Jn., Hindon, 1741, AB, P2/G/823
Gillham, Richd., butcher, Hurst, Berks., 1628, AB, I, P5/1628/46, P5/11Reg/82B
Gilham, Richd., Hindon, 1712, AB, P2/G/647
Wm., Pott., 1669, AB, comm, P1/G/211
Gillard, Jas., Uffc., Devon, 1819, W, Wr, P20/1/308

Jn., Nether C., Dorset, 1764, AB, P5/1764/17
Owen, yeo., Brook Ways Gate, Westb., 1703, W (NEP), P25/1703/4
Gealard, Thos., husb., Uffc., Devon, 1677, NW, P20/1/79
Gille *see* Gill
Gilles *see* Giles
Gillett, Edith, widow, Boscombe, 1607, I, W, P2/G/123
Eliz., widow, Avoncliff, Westwood, 1737, W, P2/G/808
Geo., victualler, Trowb., 1797, W, P1/G/760, P1/15Reg/26
Geo., carp. and joiner, Trowb., 1846, W, Wr, P1/1846/18
Giles, husb., Over C., Dorset, [1601], W (date of probate not given), P5/7Reg/25B
Gillett *or* Jollate, Jas., Mere, 1670, AB, I, P5/1670/13
Jellett, Jas., Bloxworth, Dorset, 1807, AB, Wr, P5/1807/16
Gillet, Jane, widow, W. Lavington, 1751, AB, T, P1/G/595
Joan, widow, Over C., Dorset, 1605, AB, I, W, P5/1604/16, P5/8Reg/24C
Jn., husb., Horton, Bps. C., 1770, W, P24/1071
Gillott, Mgt., wife, Coombe, Donhead St My., 1542, W (NEP), P2/1Reg/55
Gillet, My., widow, Wambrook, Somerset, 1743, W, Wr, P5/1743/31
My., widow, Trowb., 1837, O, W, Wr, P1/1837/1
Gillet, Matthew, Wambrook, Somerset, 1746, AB, NW, P5/1746/49
Philip, gent., Trowb., 1842, comm, W, Wr, P1/1842/10
Gillet, Richd., yeo., Chards., Devon, 1742, AB, I, P14/178
Gillet, Robt., glover, Westbrook, Gt. Faringdon, Berks., 1635, I, W, P5/1635/43, P5/12Reg/187
Gylett alias Smith, Stephen, Warm., 1588, AB, P2/7Reg/124A
Stephen, butcher, Chards., Devon, 1742, comm, W, P14/157
Thos., Devizes, 1671, AB, P1/G/212
Gillet, Thos., clothworker, Trowb., 1750-54, AB, W, P1/G/610, P1/11Reg/162
Gellett, Wm., Boscombe, 1564, AB, P2/4Reg/182C
Gillet, Wm., Gillingham, Dorset, 1571, W, P27/1Reg/26A
Wm., yeo., Wambrook, Somerset, 1741, AB, I (1740, is of goods of widow G. lately decd), ren, P14/158
see also Carter alias G. alias Smith; Gill
Gillham *see* Gillam
Gillingham, Geo., blacksmith, Allweston, Folke, Dorset, 1784, W, P5/1784/5, P5/17Reg/261
Joan, widow, Long Burton, Dorset, 1672, comm, I, W, P5/1671/33
Jn., yeo., Long Burton, Dorset, 1704, I, W, P5/1704/29
Jn., yeo., Bere R., Dorset, 1777, AB, P5/1777/9, P5/17Reg/133B
Jn., Bere R., Dorset, 1685, AB, I, P5/1685/39
Magdalen, minor, Bere R., Dorset, 1707, T, P5/1707/24
My., sp., Teffont E., 1625, I, W, P1/G/82
My., widow, Sal., 1806, AB, D, NW, P4/1806/12
Richd., no abode stated, [1611?], W, P2/G/149
Thos., Tisb., 1684, AB, P2/G/483
Thos., cordw., Bere R., Dorset, 1704, AB, W, P5/1704/25
Thos., jun., cordw., Bere R., Dorset, 1705, AB, comm, W, P5/1705/41
Thos., labourer, Winterborne K., Dorset, 1777, W, P5/1777/8, P5/17Reg/145
Wm., blacksmith, Allweston, Folke, Dorset, 1780, comm, W, P5/1780/8
Wm., blacksmith, Folke, Dorset, 1790, W, P5/17Reg/187C
Gillman, Ann, widow, Holt, Bradford A., 1832, AB, W, Wr, P2/1832/33
Gilman, Anthony, sen., carp., Isbery, Lambourn, Berks., 1701, I, W, P1/G/316, P1/4Reg/26
Jn., clothworker, Wantage, Berks., 1671, AB, comm, I, P5/1671/39
Gilman, Jn., sen., yeo., Lambourn, Berks., 1711, I, W, P1/G/364, P1/5Reg/200
Jn., Highw., 1746, AB, P5/1746/33
Jn., Stratton St Mgt., 1779, AB, P3/G/719
Gilman, Jn., farmer, Lambourn, Berks., 1823, W, Wr, P1/1823/148
Gilman, Martin, bach., Ashton K., 1629, I, W, P3/G/106
Gilman, Richd., yeo., Stratton St Mgt., 1714, I, W, P1/G/379, P1/5Reg/405A
Robt., husb., Stratton St Mgt., 1730, W, P3/G/527
Sam., Trowb., 1818, comm, W, Wr, P1/1818/9
Wm., yeo., Stratton St Mgt., 1730, W, P3/G/528
Wm., joiner, Highw., 1754, W, P3/G/648
Gillmore, Agnes, sen., widow, Rams., 1626, I, W, P5/1626/18

Gilmore, Andrew, bookbinder, Sal., 1810, W, P4/1810/12
Gilmore, Dorothy, widow, Aldbourne, 1606, I, W, P1/G/24
Gilmore, Eliz., Wick Farm, Wootton R., 1688, I, W, Wr, P3/G/328
Gilmore, Eliz., widow, Rams., 1717, AB, I, P5/1717/17
Frances, sp., Marl., 1777, AB, P1/G/704
Francis, yeo. and gent., Elmdown Farm, Rams., 1691, comm, I (detailed), W, P5/1691/29
Gilmore, Hannah, sp., Gt. Somerford, 1839, AB, Wr, P3/1839/20
Jane, widow, Stock, Gt. Bedwyn, 1705, W, P21/6/25
Joan, Marl., 1697, AB, I, P1/G/302
Gilmore, Jn., Rams., 1631, AB, P5/1631/46, P5/11Reg/169B
Gilmore, Jn., Rams., 1641, AB, P5/1641/33, P5/13Reg/282B
Jn., gent., Elmdown Farm, Rams., 1673, AB, I, W, P5/1673/20
Jn., sen., gent., Marl., 1742, W, P1/9Reg/232
Jn., sen., gent., Marl., 1750, AB, W, P1/G/548
Gilmore, Jos., Marl., 1728, AB, P1/G/453
My., widow, Sal., 1741, I, W, P1/G/535, P1/9Reg/68B
My., widow, Marl., 1751, a/c, comm, I, W, P1/G/594, P1/10Reg/449
Gilmore, Sarah Jane, sp., S. Marston, 1856, AB, aff, comm, Wr, P10/1856/2
Gilmore, Stephen, tanner and gent., Marl., 1681, I, W, P1/G/247
Susanna, Marl. (but d.at Chute Forest), 1788, AB, P1/G/733
Gilmore, Thos., sen., tailor, Wrou., 1673, I, W, P3/G/227
Gilmore, Thos., jun., tailor, Wrou., 1694, comm, I, W, P3/G/368
Gilmore, Thos., Marl., 1728, AB, I, P1/G/452
Gilmore, Thos., butcher, Gt. Somerford, 1838, AB, ren, Wr, P3/1838/49
see also Woolley alias G.
Gillott *see* Gillett
Gillow, Joan, widow, E. Harnham, Britford, 1615, I, W, P24/92
Jn., Sal., 1714, AB, P4/1714/8
Margery, Britford, 1611, I, W, P24/132
Mark, collar and harnessmaker, Sal., 1804, W, P4/1804/5
My., widow, E. Harnham, Britford, 1674, I, W, P24/442
Richd., E. Harnham, Britford, 1606, I, W, P24/17
Richd., Britford, 1637, I, P2/G/268
Susanna, widow, Sal., 1734, W, P4/1733/18
Thos., Sal. The Close, 1681, AB, I, P5/1681/17
Wenslay, jun., Sal., 1725, AB, I (detailed), P4/1725/1
Wm., sen., husb., E. Harnham, Britford, 1617, I, W, P24/81
Wm., Britford, 1664, AB, I, P24/340
Wm., Sal., 1682, ren, P4/1682/23
Gilloway *see* Gallaway
Gills *see* Gill
Gilman *see* Gillman
Gilmar, Gilmore *see* Gillmore
Gilpin, Eliz., widow, Kington St M., 1755, AB, comm, P3/G/651
Gine, Gyne, Agnes, widow, Allington, 1612, I, W, P2/G/156
Gyne nee Cooper, Cath., wife, Sal. St Edmd., 1693, AB, I, P4/1693/3
Gyne, Edwd., Newton T., 1561, W, P2/4Reg/66C
Gyne, Geo., yeo., S. Newton, [1684], I, NW, P2/G/480
Gyne, Hy., husb., Bulford, 1545, W (NEP), P2/1Reg/67A
Joan, widow, Compton, Enford, 1633, AB, a/c, I (joint probate, Robt.'s W unadmd by his widow), P2/G/250
Gyne, Jn., Newton T., 1602, AB, I, W, P2/G/108
Gynes, Jn., clerk, Easton Grey, 1616, I, W, P1/G/54
Gyne, Jn., yeo., Newton T., [1687], I, W, P2/G/514
Gynes, Peter, S. Newton, 1712, AB, P2/G/651
Gyne, Richd., Bulford, c1542, W (NEP), P2/1Reg/42B
Gyne, Richd., yeo., Compton, Enford, 1630, I, W, P2/G/233
Gines *or* Guines, Richd., sen., yeo., Compton, Enford, 1682, I, W, P2/G/447
Gyne, Robt., husb., Durrington, 1610, I, W, P2/G/142, P2/8Reg/128D
Gyne, Thos., Alton, Figh., 1558, W, P2/3Reg/129D
Gyne, Thos., Bulford, 1564, AB, P2/4Reg/173D

Guynes, Thos., Compton, Enford, 1597, I, NW, P2/G/87
Gingell, Adam, Cocklebury, Langley Burrell, 1640, I, W, P3/G/162
Agnes, widow, Chipp., 1632, I, W, P3/G/124
Agnes, widow, Luckington, 1671, AB, comm, I, P3/G/220
Amy, widow, Corsham, 1619, AB, I, W, P29/G/6, P29/1Reg/85B
Gingel, Ann, widow, Garsdon, 1648, I, W, P1/G/163
Gingel, Ann, widow, Chr. M., 1732, W, P1/G/489, P1/7Reg/558
Anthony, Langley Burrell, 1634, I, P3/G/133
Dan., yeo., Hartham, Corsham, 1697, comm, I, W, P3/G/386
Dan., Atworth, Bradford A., 1824, AB, Wr, P2/1824/72
Edwd., maltster, Clack, Lyneham, 1676, I, W, P3/G/243
Edwd., sadler, Chipp., 1687, AB, I, P3/G/315
Eleanor, widow, Chr. M., 1661, comm, I, W, P3/G/171, P3/3Reg/18B
Eleanor, widow, Brinkw., 1672-75, AB, a/c, I, P3/G/224
Eliz., widow, Kington St M., 1728, W, P3/G/513
Eliz., widow, Chr. M., 1740, W, P3/G/585
Gingel, Geo., Clack, Lyneham, 1797, AB, P3/G/766
Grace, sp., Chipp., 1752, W, P3/G/641
Hy., yeo., Chr. M., 1703, I, W, P3/G/419
Hy., labourer *or* yeo., Westport St My., 1722, I, W, P3/G/477
Isaac, blacksmith, Chipp., 1680, AB, I, P3/G/273
Jacob, yeo., Chr. M., 1812, W, Wr, P3/1812/3
Jas., yeo., Marl., 1801, W, P1/1801/61, P1/15Reg/278
Jas., yeo., Melk., 1805, comm, W, P2/1805/13
Jane, widow, Alderton, 1690, I, W, P3/G/344
Jn., husb., Chr. M., 1625, AB, I, W, P1/G/93
Jn., yeo., Kington L., 1633, I, W, P3/G/130
Jn., Chr. M., 1639, a/c, P3/G/155
Jn., Chr. M., 1677, I, W, P3/G/251
Jn., Hullavington, 1692, AB, P3/G/357
Jn., broad weaver, Kington L., 1694, I, W, P3/G/369
Jn., labourer, Hullavington, 1697, AB, I, P3/G/387
Jn., husb., Langley Burrell, 1712, I, W, P3/G/440
Gingel, Jn., Malm., 1752, AB, P3/G/642
Jn., gent., Latton, 1767, W, P1/G/658, P1/12Reg/203
Jn., Box, 1782, AB, P1/G/717
Jn., Latton, 1801, AB, D, W, Wr, P1/1801/133, P1/15Reg/358
Jn., mealman, E. Tytherton, Bremhill, 1855, aff, D, O, W, Wr, P1/1855/21
Jonathan, Corston, Malm., 1754, AB, P3/G/649
Jos., Malm., 1782, AB, P3/G/731
Martha, widow, Clack, Lyneham, 1785, req, W, copy W, P3/G/738
My., widow, Chr. M., 1684, AB, I, W, P3/G/289
Nich., yeo., Kington L., 1647, comm, I, W, P1/G/155
Ralph, sen., Chr. M., 1628, AB, I, P3/G/103
Ralph, sen., yeo., Chr. M., 1666, comm, I, W, P1/G/200
Ralph, sen., yeo., Chr. M., 1685, I, W, P3/G/304
Ralph, Chr. M., 1730, AB, P3/G/529
Richd., yeo., Kington L., 1623, AB, I, W, P3/G/80
Richd., yeo. *or* husb., Alderton, 1663, I, W, P3/G/178
Robt., broad weaver, Kington L., 1677, AB, I, P3/G/252
Robt., yeo., Chr. M., 1837, W, Wr, P3/1837/49
Gingell form. Elmes, Sarah, yeo.'s wife, Melk. (form. of Lacock), 1794, W, P2/G/1066
Gingel, Sarah, widow, Lacock, 1830, W, Wr, P3/1830/59
Thos., Chr. M., 1620, I, W, P3/G/63
Thos., yeo., Sheldon, Chipp., 1679, comm, I, W, P3/G/266
Thos., sen., serge weaver *or* sergemaker, Malm., 1702, I, W, P3/G/408
Gengell, Thos., serge weaver, Malm., 1722, W, P3/G/474
Thos., scribler, Devizes, 1740, W, P1/G/529, P1/8Reg/429
Walter, husb., Kington L., 1638, I, W, P3/G/154
Walter, yeo., Malm., 1661, comm, I, W, P3/G/174, P3/3Reg/10B

Walter, tailor *or* yeo., Brinkw., 1672, AB, a/c, I, P3/G/225
Wm., yeo., Eastcourt, Crudwell, 1625, I, W, P3/G/89
Wm., labourer *or* husb., Bromham, 1695, I, W, P1/G/299
Wm., sen., weaver, Stanley, Bremhill (Standly in Chipp.), 1729, AB, I, P1/G/462
Wm., yeo., Clack, Lyneham, 1779, comm, W, P3/G/720
Wm., yeo., Nash House Farm, Bremhill, 1828, W, Wr, P3/1828/64
Wm., labourer, Bowerhill, Melk., 1842, AB, Wr, P1/1842/55
Wolfram, Hullavington, 1628, AB, a/c, court paper, I, P3/G/104
Wolfram, tailor, Hullavington, 1692, I, W, P3/G/358
Ginn, Jn., coach man, Shipton, Oxfordshire, but d. at Kington St M., 1773, W, P1/G/691, P1/13Reg/7A
Gipson, Walter, Wingfield, 1759, W, P2/G/916
Girdler, Eliz., Sal., 1605, AB, I, P1/G/13
Hy., Calne, 1666, AB, P26/125
Joan, Sal., 1605, AB, I, P1/G/12
Jn., Sal., 1587, W, P4/Reg/30
Jn., carp., Hurst, Berks., 1726, I, W, P5/1726/16, P5/16Reg/139A
Nich., innkeeper, Calne, 1622, AB, I (detailed), P5/1622/31, P5/10Reg/136B
Phyllis, widow, Scots Lane, Sal., 1632, AB, a/c, I, P4/1631/13
Gridler *or* Greller, Sarah, Sal., 1662, I, W, P4/1661/16
Thos., carp., Hurst, Berks., 1711, I, W, P5/1711/23, P5/15Reg/259
Wm., husb., Wokm., Berks., 1755, W, P5/1755/18
Gireshe, Girishe *see* Gerrish
Girle, Benj., bricklayer, Newton T., 1779, W, P1/G/706, P1/13Reg/202
Edwd., Newton T., 1674, I, W, P2/G/380
Jane, Corsham, 1669-70, AB, I, P29/G/15, P29/1Reg/190
Gearle, Jn., wheeler, Ludg., 1663, I, W, P2/G/328
Jn., sen., shoemaker, Milton L., 1744, W, P1/G/557, P1/9Reg/383
Jos., Newton T., 1738, W, P2/G/809
Jos., Newton T., 1776, W, P2/G/986
Jos., bricklayer, Newton T., 1779, W, P2/G/1001
Gerle, Marmaduke, husb., Fifield, Enford, 1615, AB, comm, I, W, P2/G/170, P2/8Reg/282B
Nich., mason, Newton T., 1635, I, NW, P2/G/254
Richd., Enford, 1627, AB, P2/G/219
Gearle, Richd., Sal., 1686, I, W, P4/1685/27
Richd., sen., wheelwright, Upavon, 1713, W, P2/G/659
Gearle, Richd., husb., Wokm., Berks., 1721, W, P5/16Reg/54B
Thos., Sal. St Thos., 1691, AB, P4/1691/5
Thos., innholder, Sherb., Dorset, 1719, AB, I, P5/1719/31
Wm., Marl., 1717, AB, P1/G/395
Wm., maltster, Newton T., 1781, W, P2/G/1008
see also Gale *or* G.
Girritt *see* Gerrard
Giver *see* Gover
Glade, Geo., yeo., Chitterne AS, 1571, W, P1/1Reg/94B
Jn., Wambrook, Somerset, 1590, AB, I, W, P5/1590/24, P5/5Reg/85B
Jn., Wambrook, Somerset, 1627, AB, P5/11Reg/2B
Jn., Wambrook, Somerset, 1718, W, P14/129
Roger, yeo., Wambrook, Somerset, 1568, W, P5/2Reg/33A
Glanville, Glanfield, Joan, widow, Charminster, Dorset, 1617, AB, I, T, W, P5/1617/18, P5/9Reg/186
My., widow, Abingdon, Berks., 1835, O, W, P1/1835/35
Winifred, widow, Broad H., 1676, W, P3/G/244
Glasby, Emma, Bere R., Dorset, 1671, AB, I, P5/1671/34
Wm., husb., Hyde, Bere R., Dorset, 1666, AB, I, P5/1666/16
Wm., Hyde, Bere R., Dorset, 1714, AB, P5/1714/11
Glaskadine, Jn., tailor, Lea, L. and Cleverton, 1647, comm, I, W, P1/G/158
Robt., labourer, Seagry, 1737, comm, W, P3/G/571
Glasgooden, Thos., Lea, L. and Cleverton, 1622, I, W, P3/G/74
Glass, Glasse, Agnes, widow, Sharcott, Pewsey, 1626, I, W, P3/G/94
Ann, sp., N. Newnton, 1744, AB, P1/G/553
Ann, widow, Sandy Lane, Calne, 1747, W, P3/G/621

Ann, sp., Trowb., 1831, AB, comm, ren, W, Wr, P1/1831/10
Benj., Worton, Pott., 1836, AB, comm, P1/1836/17
Edmd., Tidcombe and Fosbury, 1651, I, W, P1/G/170
Glasse, Edwd., Chipp., 1742, AB, comm, P3/G/596
Glasse, Eliz., widow, Sharcott, Pewsey, 1665, W, P3/G/183
Eliz., widow, Tidcombe and Fosbury, 1751, W, P3/G/638
Eliz., widow, Pewsey, 1778, W, P3/G/716
Glasse, Geoffrey, carp., Durrington, 1678, AB, I, P2/G/415
Glasse, Hannah, Poulshot, 1710, W, P2/G/641
Glasse, Hy., Upavon, 1648, AB, P1/G/164
Hy., Purton, 1803, AB, P3/1803/3
Jas., yeo., Worton, Pott., 1785, W, P1/G/727, P1/14Reg/60B
Jane, sp., Five Lanes, Pott., 1850, O, W, Wr, P1/1850/9
Glasse, Jn., yeo., Sharcott, Pewsey, 1685, AB, a/c, I, ren, P3/G/305
Jn., Pott., 1705, AB, P1/G/336
Jn., Erlestoke, 1713, AB, I, P2/G/664
Glasse, Jn., gent., Sharcott, Pewsey, 1726, W, P3/G/500
Jn., maltster, Melk., 1734-35, AB, ren, T (child: Barbara G.), P1/G/495, P2/G/789
Jn., yeo., Five Lanes, Pott., 1818, W, Wr, P1/1818/8
Jn., Pott., 1822, AB, comm, Wr, P1/1822/1
Jos., Pott., 1829, AB, comm, Wr, P1/1829/15
Jos., Devizes, 1855, aff, O, W, Wr, P1/1855/30
Mariam, widow, Melk., 1817, AB, W, P2/1817/23
My., miller's widow, Latton, 1802, W, P3/1802/30
My., wife, Pott., 1850, O, W, Wr, P1/1850/10
Moses, gent., Devizes (form. of Pott.), 1850, O, W, Wr, P1/1850/2
Glasse, Peter, husb., Sutton M., 1611, AB, I, NW, P2/G/150
Philip, glover, Devizes, 1715, AB, I, P1/G/385
Glasse, Richd., Sal., 1705, W, P4/1705/2
Richd., Pott., 1730, AB, I, summary I, P1/G/475
Richd., clerk and vicar, Purton, 1748, comm, W, P3/G/625
Glasse, Robt., husb., Urchf., 1558, W, P2/3Reg/108A
Robt., innholder, Sandy Lane, Calne, 1741, comm, W, P3/G/591
Robt., yeo., Pott., 1809, W, Wr, P1/1809/1
Robt., gent., Five Lanes, Pott., 1845, O, W, Wr, P1/1845/3
Susanna, widow, Pott., 1827, O, W, Wr, P1/1827/1
Thos., cordw., Upavon, 1680, I, W, P1/G/242
Thos., sen., yeo., Tidcombe, T. and Fosbury, 1740, I (2 - 1 a copy), W, P3/G/586
Thos., Tidcombe, T. and Fosbury, 1759, AB, P1/G/629
Thos., yeo., Tidcombe, T. and Fosbury, 1770, W, P1/G/678, P1/12Reg/379A
Thos., miller, Latton, 1784, W, P3/G/735
Uriah, Poulshot, 1750, AB, deed of gift, P2/G/880
Uriah, yeo., Bowerhill, Melk., 1807, comm, W, P2/1807/72
Glasse, Wm., sen., miller, W. Lavington, 1685, I, W, P1/G/258
Wm., sen., Pott., 1729, I, W, P1/G/464, P1/7Reg/342A
Wm., Pott., 1738, AB, I, W, P1/G/526, P1/8Reg/328A
Glasspoole, Wm., clerk, Sherb., Dorset, 1799, comm, W, P5/1799/11, P5/18Reg/273B
Glaven, Cath., W. Grimstead, 1557, W, P2/3Reg/34C
Gleed, [...], no abode stated, 1571, W (NEP), P1/1Reg/88B
Agnes, widow, Purton, [1614], I, W (NEP), P3/G/37
Ambrose, Lydiard T., 1765, AB, comm, P3/G/679
Glyde, Ann, widow, Marl., 1695, I, W, P1/G/294
Ann, widow, Purton, 1713, AB, I, P3/G/442
Anthony, husb., Purton, [1589], W (NEP), P3/1Reg/30
Bennet, husb., Paven Hill, Purton, 1624, AB, I, P3/G/85
Bennet, husb., Lydiard M., 1667, AB, I, W, P1/G/217
Cath., widow, S. Marston, 1718, W, P10/1718/2
Chris., husb., Purton, [1607], W (NEP), P3/G/8
Glide, Elias, Wilton, 1703, AB, I, P2/G/599
Glide, Elias, clothier, Bulbridge, Wilton, 1714, W, P1/G/384, P1/5Reg/453

Eliz., widow, Charlton nr Malm., 1632, I, W (both on same sheet), P3/G/125
Frances, sp., Purton, 1729, I, W, P3/G/521
Francis, Littleton Drew, 1685, AB, I, P3/G/306
Glide, Geo., yeo., Broad B., Highw., 1730, W, P10/1730/6
Glyde, Gilbert, Long Burton, Dorset, 1617, AB, I, P5/1617/19, P5/9Reg/215B
Isaac, tallow chandler, Ashton K., 1784, W, P3/G/736
Glide, Jas., Barford St M., 1591, I, P2/G/57
Glide, Jane, widow, Burbage, 1703, I, W, P11/92
Joan, sp., Crudwell, 1625, I, W, P1/G/90
Jn., Charlton nr Malm., 1570, W (NEP), P1/1Reg/41C
Glyde, Jn., Sherb., Dorset, 1612, AB, I, ren, P5/1611/15, P5/9Reg/60B
Glyde, Jn., yeo., Barford St M., 1613, alleg, deed of gift, P2/G/157
Jn., sen., yeo., Paven Hill, Purton, 1621, I, W, P3/G/70
Glyde, Jn., husb., Marl., 1628, AB, I, L, P1/G/103
Jn., yeo., Paven Hill, Purton, 1631, I, W, P3/G/119
Jn., Purton, 1636, AB, a/c, I, P3/G/143
Jn., sen., yeo., S. Marston, 1665, I, W, P5/1665/37
Glyde, Jn., blacksmith, Sherb., Dorset, 1683, I, W, P5/1683/23
Jn., yeo., Webb's Wood, Lydiard T., 1685, I, W, P3/G/307
Glide, Jn., sen., grocer, Burbage, 1689, I, W, P11/71
Jn., yeo., S. Marston, 1712, W, P10/1712/3
Glyde, Jn., sen., shopkeeper, Burbage, 1720, I, W, P11/121
Jn., Littleton Drew, 1748, W, P3/G/626
Jn., bach., Latton, 1799, AB, O, P3/G/773
Glyde, Jn., labourer, Sherb., Dorset, 1852, W, Wr, P5/1852/25
Maurice, yeo., Latton, 1797, W, P3/G/767
Maurice, Latton, 1815, AB, Wr, P3/1815/6
Nich., Purton, 1786, comm, W, P3/G/740
Richd., yeo., Purton, 1667, I, W, P3/G/191
Robt., husb., Charlton, 1625, I, W, P1/G/91
Susanna, Groundwell, Blunsdon St Andrew, 1702, W, P3/G/409
Glyde, Thos., yeo., Ryme I., Dorset, 1698, AB, comm, I, P5/1698/28
Glyde, Thos., sen., chandler, Marl., 1708, comm, W, P1/G/342, P1/4Reg/272
Thos., thatcher, Lydiard T., 1800, W, P3/1800/23
Thos., farmer, Charlton nr Malm., 1852, O, W, Wr, P3/1852/57
Wm., glover, Purton, 1661, AB, I, W, P3/G/172, P3/3Reg/29
Wm., Purton, 1680, AB, P3/G/274
Wm., jun., Purton Stoke, 1741, AB, P3/G/592
Glyde, Wm., shopkeeper, Marl., 1762, W, P1/G/637, P1/12Reg/30B
Glendining, Sarah, widow, Sal., 1846, comm, W, Wr, P1/1846/4
Glenn, Robt., Warm., 1761, AB, comm, P2/G/920
Glew, Wm., wheeler, Chipp., 1689, I, W, P3/G/329
Glide *see* Gleed
Glinsford, Alice, Melk., 1565, W, P2/4Reg/197B
Glisson, Eliz., Tisb., 1725, W, P2/G/736
Gliston, Jos., clerk, Caundle Bishop, Dorset, 1753, W, P5/1753/10
Glover, Chas., woollen draper, Chipp., 1684, AB, I, P3/G/290
Christine, Damerham, Hants, 1560, AB, P2/4Reg/31C-D
Edwd., Damerham, Hants, 1559, W, P2/4Reg/7B
Eliz., widow, Chipp., 1713, W, P3/G/443
Eliz., widow, Sherb., Dorset, 1736, W, P5/1736/13
Geo., no abode stated, 1685, I, W, P2/G/492
Hy., sen., Mere, 1753, I, W, P5/1753/11
Hester, sp., Mere, 1802, W, P5/1802/15, P5/19Reg/14
Jas., gent., Dunheads Lodge, Motc., Dorset, 1729, AB, ren, P27/1/300
Jas., yeo., Westb., 1850, AB, aff, comm, declaration, W, Wr (d.1833), P25/1850/6
Jn., draper, Reading, Berks., 1744, W, P1/G/555, P1/9Reg/348
Jn., gent., Sherb., Dorset, 1780, W, P5/1780/9, P5/17Reg/196B
Nich., yeo., Kington St M., 1684, comm, I, W, P3/G/291
Robt., glover, Marl., 1663, comm, I, W, P1/G/185

Sam., Burton Hill, Malm., 1663, I, W, P3/G/179
Semei, collar and harnessmaker, Mere, 1813, W (& cod), Wr, P5/1813/9
Valentine, Sherb., Dorset, 1705, comm, copy of monition, receipt, P5/1705/23
Wm., Martin, Hants, 1663, I, W, P1/G/183
Wm., Marl., 1669, AB, P1/G/210
see also Wright alias G.
Gloyne, Jas., carrier, Sherb., Dorset, 1814, W, Wr, P5/1814/7
Glyde *see* Gleed
Goad, Jos., grocer, Reading, Berks., 1704, AB, I, P1/G/329
Goard, Goord, Alice, widow, Semley, [1621], I, P2/G/195
Gourde, Jn., yeo., Coombe, Donhead St My., 1630, I, W, P2/G/231
Jn., yeo., Uffc., Devon, 1707, W, P5/1707/25, P5/15Reg/39B
Gurd, Jn., pointmaker, Donhead St My., 1716, W, P2/G/676
Gurd, Jn., Donhead St My., 1752, AB, P2/G/887
Gurd, Jn., Charlton, Downton, 1813, AB, comm, Wr, P2/1813/61
Guard, Jn., Overton (leaving effects at Devizes), 1830, AB, Wr, P1/1830/16
Martha, widow, Uffc., Devon, 1744, W, P20/1/208
Gurd, Martha, widow, Donhead St My., 1750, AB, P2/G/877
Gurd, Martha, sp., Bristol, Gloucs (effects at Donhead St My.), 1761, W, P2/G/922
Gurd, My., widow, Donhead St My., 1740, W, P2/G/819
Goord, Thos., Semley, 1563, I, W, P2/G/15, P2/4Reg/173C
Gurd, Thos., blacksmith, Donhead St My., 1720, NW, P2/G/700
Gurd, Thos., Sixpenny Handley, Dorset (but late of Donhead St My.), 1729, I, W, P1/G/465, P1/7Reg/351B
Gurd, Thos., Donhead St My., 1856, AB, aff, D, O, Wr, P2/1856/66
Gourde, Warner, fuller, Donhead St My., [1611], W, P2/G/147
Gurd, Wm., cordw., Donhead St A., 1826, W, Wr, P1/1826/14
Goatley, Gotley, Ann, widow, Avon, Chr. M., 1764, W, P3/G/677
Goatley (nee Dear), Ann, yeo.'s wife, St Mgt., Preshute, 1771, W, P1/G/682
Gotley, Ann, sp., Avon, Chr. M., 1794, comm, I, W, P3/G/760
Geo., yeo., St Mgt., Preshute, 1771, W, P1/G/681, P1/12Reg/394, 396
Jn., innholder, Rams., 1663, AB, I, P5/1663/26
Jn., Chilton F., 1756, AB, P1/G/616
Jn., yeo., Letcombe Bassett, Berks., 1766, AB, comm, P1/G/655
Goatly, Jn., farmer, Sanham Grn, Hungerford, Berks., 1805, comm, W, P23/850
Jn., tailor, Speenhamland, Berks., 1820, W, Wr, P1/1820/112
Gotley, Jos., Foxham & Avon, Chr. M., 1797, I, W, P3/G/769
Goatly, My., widow, Mildenhall, 1745, W, P3/G/609
Richd., yeo., Letcombe Regis, Berks., 1763, W, P1/G/643, P1/12Reg/76
Thos., yeo., St. Martins St., Marl. St My., 1762, AB, a/c, I, P1/G/634
Thos., carp., Marl., 1804, W, P1/1804/86
Wm., labourer, Eddington, Hungerford, Berks., 1751, I, W, P23/632
Goblett, Jn., day labourer, Laverstock, 1598, AB, I, NW, P2/G/92
Godby *see* Goodbee
Goddard, Abigail, widow, Castle Eaton, 1734, W, P3/G/560
Amy, widow, Blewbury, Berks., 1664, I, W, P5/1664/14
Andrew, Bemerton, Fugg. St Peter, 1697, AB, I, P2/G/561
Ann, Bishopstone N., 1675, W, P6/43
Anthony, gent., Clyffe P., 1606, W, P3/2Reg/3
Anthony, gent., Clyffe P., 1643-47, AB, a/c, I, P1/G/143, 157
Cath., widow, Sal. St Edmd., 1698, AB, P1/G/305
Christian, sp., Sal., 1800, W, P4/1800/3
Cicely, widow, Blewbury, Berks., 1633, I, NW, P5/1633/17, P5/12Reg/130B
Dan., Bramshaw, Hants, 1743, AB, P24/978
David, Donhead St My., 1742, AB, P2/G/834
David, Donhead St My., 1823, AB, comm, Wr, P1/1823/129
David, Warm., 1831, AB, comm, Wr, P2/1831/9
Edith, Welford, Berks., 1606, I, W, P1/G/22
Edith, widow, Enford, 1690, AB, I, P2/G/527
Edmd., gent., Sal. The Close, 1617, W, P5/1616/29
Edmd., Hartham, Corsham, 1633, comm, I, W, P3/G/131

Edwd., gent., Berwick B., 1626, comm, I, W, P5/1626/20, P5/10Reg/199
Edwd., sen., gent., Hartham, Corsham, 1643, I, W, P1/G/145
Edwd., gent., Mere, 1666, AB, I, P5/1666/15
Edwd., gent., Aldbourne, 1667, comm, W, P3/G/192
Edwd., yeo., Alton P., Dorset, 1668, I, W, P5/1668/30
Edwd., clerk, Clyffe P., 1811, AB, comm, Wr, P3/1811/29
Godderd, Eliz., widow, Sedgehill, 1564, I, W, P2/G/16, P2/4Reg/187B
Eliz., widow, Mere, 1668, I, W, P5/1668/32
Eliz., widow, Westb., 1721, AB, P25/1721/5
Eliz., widow of Jn., Ogbourne St Geo., 1732, AB, NW, P23/485
Eliz., sp., Swindon, 1760, AB, P3/G/666
Eliz., widow, Earley, Sonning, Berks., 1790, AB, cert, comm, ren, W, Wr, P5/1790/9, P5/18Reg/157B
Eliz., widow, Grove, Wantage, Berks., 1831, AB, comm, Wr, P23/955
Goddard alias Hurst, Frances, wife, Marl., 1665, AB, P1/H/342
Frances, sp., Mere, 1679, I, W, P5/1679/39
Godderd, Frances, widow, Blewbury, Berks., 1679, AB, I, P5/1679/34
Gabriel, fuller, Mount Mill, Sutton V., [1614], I, W, P2/G/164
Geo., yeo., Crookham, Thatcham, Berks., 1750, W, P1/G/587, P1/10Reg/370
Geo., brewer, Donhead St My., 1847, W, Wr, P2/1847/2
Hannah, widow, Charlton nr Malm., 1722, W, P3/G/478
Howell, yeo., Oaksey, 1725, W, P3/G/493
Howell, Crudwell, 1764, AB, P3/G/676
Isaac, maltster, Donhead St My., 1798, comm, W, P1/G/771, P1/15Reg/168B
Jas., yeo., Stourpaine, Dorset, 1777, AB, P24/1129
Jas., Sal., 1781, note, W, P4/1781/1
Jas., yeo., Semley, 1856, aff, comm, W, Wr, P2/1856/37
Jane, Tisb., 1694, AB, I, P2/G/542
Jane, widow, Blewbury, Berks., 1716, W, P5/1716/33, P5/15Reg/353B
Joan, Sedgehill, 1605, AB, I, P2/G/119
Godderd, Joan, Marl., 1618, AB, I, P1/G/65
Jn., Sedgehill, 1558, W, P2/3Reg/112C
Jn., Urchf., 1559, W, P2/3Reg/183F
Jn., Thatcham, Berks., 1611, AB, I, P1/G/35
Jn., Welford, Berks., 1614, I, W, P1/G/47
Jn., husb., Donhead St My., 1633, AB, I, P2/G/248
Jn., gent., N. Hidden, Hungerford, Berks., 1672, AB, P23/33
Jn., E. Knoyle, 1673, I, P2/G/378
Jn., Upton L., 1673, I, NW, P2/G/375
Jn., gent., Swindon, 1678, I, W, Wr, P3/G/258
Jn., husb., Ogbourne St Geo., 1680, I, W, P23/99
Jn., Manton, Preshute, 1685, AB, comm, I, P1/G/256
Jn., yeo., Charlton nr Malm., 1697, W, P3/G/388
Jn., sen., shepherd and yeo., Blewbury, Berks., 1704, I, W, P5/1704/24
Jn., barber, Sal., 1709, W, P4/1708/3
Jn., tailor, Sandhurst, Berks., 1714, W, P5/1714/13, P5/15Reg/385A
Jn., Donhead St My., 1721, AB, P2/G/704
Jn., yeo., Gillingham, Dorset, 1725, W, P27/1/271
Jn., yeo., Ogbourne St Geo., 1732, W, P23/484
Jn., Blewbury, Berks., 1739, W, Wr, P5/1739/20
Jn., yeo., Wokefield, Stratfield M., Berks., 1789, W, P1/G/736, P1/14Reg/226
Jn., sen., yeo., Semley, 1819, W, Wr, P2/1819/23
Jn., bach., Winterbourne Bassett (leaving effects at Marl.), 1851, AB, comm, Wr, P1/1851/76
Jos., tailor and shopkeeper, Yattendon, Berks., 1773, W, P1/G/688, P1/12Reg/493A
Mgt., widow, Bishopstone N., 1635, I, W, P5/1635/42, P5/12Reg/173A
Mgt., widow, Stockley, Calne, 1748, W, P26/890
Martha, Donhead St My., 1714, AB, P1/G/383
My., widow, Netherh., 1683, I, W, P2/G/459
My., Berwick B., 1692, AB, comm, P5/1691/30
My., widow, Swindon, 1789, comm, W, P3/G/748
My., widow, Sal., 1796, W, P4/1796/1

Nathan, sen., yeo., Earley, Sonning, Berks., 1778, W, P5/1778/7, P5/17Reg/154
Nich., gent., Mere, 1669, AB, comm, NW, P5/1669/20
Penelope, sp., Tollard Royal, 1639, W, P2/G/274
Peter, Farnham, Tollard Royal, Dorset, 1587, W, P2/7Reg/86A
Philip, vicar, Beenham Valence, Berks., 1686, I, W, P1/G/260
Richd., rector, Castle Eaton, 1683, AB, P1/G/251
Richd., esquire, Clatford, Preshute, 1685, bond to deliver up W, comm, L, W, P1/G/259
Richd., yeo., Marlstone, Bucklebury, Berks., 1723, I, W, P1/G/427, P1/7Reg/2A
Richd., orangeman, Marl., 1750, W, P1/G/592, P1/10Reg/437
Sarah, sp., Marl., 1714, W, P1/G/378, P1/5Reg/406A
Sarah, widow, Sal., 1724, W, P4/1723/1
Sarah, sp., Sal., 1745, W, P4/1745/9
Thos., Donhead St A., 1578, AB, I, W, P2/G/30, P2/5Reg/319C
Thos., shepherd, Upton L., 1612, a/c, I, T, P2/G/155
Thos., Bishopstone S., 1664, AB, I, L, P1/G/190
Thos., gent., Hidden, Hungerford, Berks., 1672, I, W (AB, 1686 exx. d. without fully admg goods), P23/34, 152
Thos., butcher, Bishopstone N., 1675, AB, P6/42
Thos., gent., Beckhampton, Avebury, 1687, W (NEP), P3/G/316
Thos., yeo., Oaksey, 1728, W, P3/G/514
Thos., cooper, Oaksey, 1732, W, P3/G/543
Thos., husb., Bishopstone N., 1744, I, P6/132
Thos., Chieveley, Berks., 1750, AB, P1/G/588
Thos., Aldbourne, 1779, AB, P1/G/713
Thos., yeo., Swallowfield, Shinfield, Berks., 1835, W, P1/1835/95
Thos., tanner, Rams., 1852, D, O, W, Wr, P5/1852/24
Thos. Ryall, farmer, Heywood, Westb., 1857, declarations, O, W, Wr, P25/1857/5
Vincent, yeo., Crookham, Thatcham, Berks., 1662, I, W, P1/G/178
Walter, yeo., Charlton, Donhead St My., 1670, I, W, P2/G/360
Wm., yeo., Sedgehill, 1586, W (grant of probate incomplete), P2/7Reg/44
Wm., Sherb., Dorset, 1589, AB, I, P5/1589/21, P5/5Reg/59A
Wm., husb., Flamston, Bishopstone S., 1605, I, W, P2/G/117
Wm., Westrop, Highw., 1607, AB, I, P5/1607/26, P5/8Reg/105A
Wm., gent., Clyffe P., 1627, AB, P3/G/99
Wm., no abode stated, [1678?], I, P2/G/412
Wm., Marl. St Peter and St Paul, 1679, AB, a/c, comm, I, P1/G/235
Wm., yeo., Ogbourne St Geo., 1682, comm, I, W, P5/1682/45
Wm., clerk, N. Wraxall, 1712, W, P1/G/369, P1/5Reg/268
Wm., yeo., Flamston, Bishopstone S., 1713, AB, I, P2/G/655
Wm., farrier, Sherb., Dorset, 1720, I, W, P5/1720/22
Wm., gent., Castle Eaton, 1756, W, P1/G/621, P1/11Reg/328
Wm., yeo., Preshute, 1797, W, P1/G/759, P1/15Reg/17
Godden, [male], Homanton, Maddington, 1614, a/c, P2/G/162
Gooding, Agnes, Wokm., Berks., 1543-44, court proceedings (re alleg of fornication between Agnes G. & Jn. (Richd. erased) Abbott, P5/20Reg/43B, 45B, 51A, 53
Alexander, husb., Winterbourne G., 1692, I, W, P2/G/536
Alexander, Winterbourne E., 1701, AB, P2/G/587
Gooden, Ann, widow, Oborne, Dorset, 1846, AB, Wr, P5/1846/15
Benj., glover, Sal., 1729, W, P4/1729/1
Godding, Betty, widow, Chiseldon, 1823, AB, comm, W, Wr, P3/1823/3
Godding, Cath., widow, Haydon Wick, Rodbourne C., 1700, I, NW, P3/G/399
Dennis, Easterton, Mkt. L., 1838, O, W, Wr, P2/1838/4
Gooden, Eleanor, widow, Sherb., Dorset, 1588, I, W, P5/1587/22, P5/5Reg/2B
Ellen, widow, Langley Burrell, 1572, W (NEP), P1/1Reg/40A
Godding, Grace, widow, Ashton K., 1733, W, P3/G/553
Grecian, widow, Stert, Urchf., 1812, O, W, Wr, P1/1812/18
Hy., husb., Langley Burrell, 1606, I, W, P1/G/25
Hy., Langley Burrell, 1620, AB, a/c, I, P3/G/64
Godding, Hy., baker, Ashton K., 1728, I, W, P3/G/515
Hugh, currier, Lyme R., Dorset, 1635, AB, I, P5/1635/44, P5/12Reg/224A
Gooding, Humphrey, clerk and parson, Easthampstead, Berks., 1622, AB, a/c, I, W, P1/G/78

Gooding, Isabel, widow, Wokm., Berks., 1540-43, W (dispute over alleged omission of certain bequest), P5/20Reg/15A, 35B
Jas., miller, Stert, Urchf., 1791, comm, W, P2/G/1055
Jas., widower, Stert, Urchf., 1806, AB, Wr, P1/1806/12
Jas., Five Lanes Mill, Pott., 1838, AB, comm, Wr, P1/1838/5
Godding, January, Chelworth, Crickl. St S., 1681, I, W, P3/G/281
Jenny, Stert, Urchf., 1806, AB, Wr, P1/1806/13
Joanna, sp., Pewsey, 1843, W, Wr, P3/1843/45
Gooden, Jn., sen., Sherb., Dorset, 1587, AB, I, T, P5/1587/21, P5/4Reg/153B
Gooding, Jn., Wokm., Berks., 1601, AB, I, P5/1601/19, P5/7Reg/12B
Jn., no abode stated, 1616, I, P1/G/61
Jn., weaver, Sal. St Edmd., 1620, AB, I, W, P4/1620/9
Gooden, Jn., husb., Sherb., Dorset, 1662, I (2), W (including fragment of copy I), P5/1662/48
Gooding, Jn., gent., Wokm., Berks., 1668, I, W, P5/1668/31
Jn., Hilp. Marsh, 1727, W, P2/G/743
Godding alias Batt, Jn., Easterton, Mkt. L. (late of Guy's Hospital, London), 1814, AB, comm, P1/1814/53
Godding, Jn., labourer, Ashton K., 1842, O, W, Wr, P3/1842/31
Mgt., Sal., 1612, I, W, P4/1612/20
Gooding, Nathaniel, labourer, E. Stowell, Wilcot, 1801, W, P3/1801/7
Gooding, Richd., Wokm., Berks., 1543, W, P5/20Reg/43A
Richd., Langley Burrell, 1630, I, W, P3/G/115
Richd., Lt. Cheverell, 1746, AB, P2/G/857
Godden alias Godwyn, Robt., husb., Haydon Wick, Rodbourne C., 1620, I, W, P1/G/74
Robt., husb., Purton, 1629, AB, I, W, P3/G/107
Stephen, shopkeeper, Pewsey, 1839, comm, W, Wr, P1/1839/27
Gooding, Thos., husb., Wokm., Berks., 1540, W, P5/20Reg/32
Gooding, Thos., Wokm., Berks., 1621, AB, I, P5/1621/11, P5/10Reg/100A
Goden, Thos., yeo., Calstone W., 1632, AB, I, W, P26/44
Goding, Thos., W. Grimstead, [1678], I, P2/G/418
Gooding, Thos., ironmonger, Wokm., Berks., 1690, W, P5/1690/20
Thos., hatter, Devizes, 1801, comm, W, Wr, P1/1801/131, P1/15Reg/355B
Thos., Devizes, 1812, AB, comm, Wr, P1/1811/2
Wm., Keevil, 1695, AB, comm, I, P1/G/290
Godding, Wm., sen., baker, Ashton K., 1701, I, W, P1/G/317, P1/4Reg/84
see also Godwin *or* G.
Godderd *see* Goddard
Godding, Goden *see* Godden
Godfrey, Abraham, gardener, Whitep., 1697, I, W, P2/G/560
Alice, widow, Sal., 1639, W, P4/1638/8
Godfry, Ann, widow, Steeple L., 1623, AB, P2/G/203
Ann, widow, Sal., 1755, W, P4/1755/1
Bartholomew, yeo., Kintbury, Berks., 1635, I, W, P1/G/129
Cath., widow, Grove, Wantage, Berks., 1755, I, W, P23/663
Godfry, Edwd., yeo., Salterton, Durnford, 1636, I, W, P5/1636/22, P5/12Reg/254B
Edwd., Fritham, Bramshaw, Hants, 1638, comm, I, W (W & I dated 1634), P24/282
Edwd., sen., Coombe B., 1729, AB, I, P8/29
Eliz., widow, Sal., 1687, I, W, P4/1685/30, P4/1687/14
Frances, widow, E. Hanney, W. Hanney, Berks., 1714, I, W, P1/G/375, P1/5Reg/386
Geo., pinmaker, Sal. St Martin, 1638, AB, I, P4/1638/7
Geo., milliner, Sal., 1706, I (very detailed), P4/1706/13
Godfry, Hy., Uffc., Devon, 1593, AB, I, T, P5/1593/36, P5/6Reg/34D
Jas., gardener, Streatley, Berks., 1792, W, P1/G/743, P1/14Reg/436
Jereyal, carp., E. Hanney, W. Hanney, Berks., 1767, AB, I, P1/G/665
Jereyal, carp. and joiner, W. Hanney, Berks., 1773, W, P1/G/687, P1/12Reg/476
Joan, wife, Lyme R., Dorset, 1672, AB, comm, P16/29
Godfer, Joan, jun., Marl. St Peter and St Paul, 1687, AB, I, P1/G/266
Godfer, Joan, [Marl. St Peter and St Paul] (NBI) (but son is of Huish), 1689, AB, P1/G/272
Jn., weaver, Sal., 1746, W, P4/1746/8
Jn., yeo., E. Hanney, W. Hanney, Berks., 1756, W, P1/G/614, P1/11Reg/260
Jn., Sal., 1762, W, P4/1762/7

Jn., yeo., Uffc., Devon, 1846, comm, D, W, Wr, P20/1/328
Godfry, Joshua, stone cutter, Sherb., Dorset, 1664, I, W, P5/1664/15
Martha, widow, Grove, Wantage, Berks., 1800, comm, W, P5/1800/3, P5/18Reg/287
Godfry, Martin, husb., Childrey, Berks., 1605, I, W, P1/G/14
Godfry, My., widow, Netheravon, 1785, W, P5/1785/14, P5/18Reg/6
Philip, glover, Devizes, 1637, I, W, P1/G/134
Philip, Devizes, 1662, AB, P1/G/176
Richd., gent., Sal., 1631, I, W, P1/G/107
Godfry, Richd., husb., Easthampstead, Berks., 1738, W, P1/G/517, P1/8Reg/277
Roger, cook, Sal., 1677, a/c (2), AB, I, P4/1676/16
Sam., sen., yeo., Netheravon, 1731, W, P12/159
Thos., Bradford A., 1556, W, P2/3Reg/2B
Godfry, Thos., weaver, Hilp., 1570, W, P2/5Reg/99B
Godfry, Thos., Salterton, Durnford, 1607, I, W, P5/1606/19, P5/8Reg/82B
Thos., yeo., Trowle, Bradford A., 1608, I, W, P2/G/128, P2/8Reg/22A
Thos., husb., Gt. Coxwell, Berks., 1625, I, W, P1/G/83
Thos., yeo., Hungerford, Berks., 1673, AB, comm, I, P5/1673/17
Wm., yeo., N. Tidworth, 1628, I, W, copy W, P2/G/225
Wm., cook, Sal., 1710, W, P4/1710/9
Godfry, Wm., labourer, Botley Pound, Cumnor, Berks., 1717, I, W, P1/G/396, P1/6Reg/130
Godfry, Wm., minor, Netheravon, 1738, T, P12/167
Wm., sen., carp., W. Hanney, Berks., 1763, W, P1/G/642, P1/12Reg/73
Godfry, Wm., Warm., 1813, AB, Wr, P2/1813/17
see also Pine nee G.
Goding *see* Godden
Godly, Jn., yeo., Staverton, Trowb., 1639, I, W, P1/G/141
Godman *see* Goodman
Godpath, Hy., tailor, Melbourne, Bratton, Westb., 1614, W (buried 12 May 1613), P25/1614/7
Godsell, Anthony, blacksmith, Bradford A., 1708, W, P2/G/628
Jane, widow, Bradford A., [1636], I, W, P2/G/262
Godshill, Jn., smith, Bradford A., 1598, AB, I, P2/G/96
Richd., no abode stated, c1640, I, P30/74
Ruth, widow, Corsley, 1663, I, W, P2/G/330
Godshill, Wm., blacksmith, Bradford A., 1597, I, W, P2/G/80
Godward, Edwd., fuller, Westb., 1636, I, W, P25/1636/8
Eliz., widow, Chilton F., 1686, AB, I, P1/G/265
Israel, yeo., Chipp., 1702, W, P3/G/411
Jn., weaver, Sal. St Edmd., 1634, I, W, P1/G/119
Jn., Brimpton, Berks., 1671, court paper, P1/G/219
Godwin, Abigail, widow, Malm., 1762, AB, P3/G/672
Alexander, yeo., Hurdcott, Winterbourne E., 1673, AB, I, P2/G/379
Alexander, Sal., 1739, AB, Wr, P4/1739/11
Alice, widow, Gillingham, Dorset, 1785, W, P27/1/524, P27/3Reg/239
Andrew, tailor, Rowde, 1719, W, P3/G/464
Ann (*or* Nancy), widow, Gillingham, Dorset, 1820, comm, W, Wr, P27/1/648
Ann, widow, Melk., 1841, AB, Wr, P2/1841/55
Ann, sp., Quobwell, Malm. St Paul, 1846, AB, O, Wr, P3/1846/20
Anthony, Westb., 1765, AB, P25/1765/4
Cath., widow, Lambourn, Berks., 1829, W, Wr, P1/1829/12
Chas., yeo., St Mgt., Preshute, 1662, AB, I, P1/G/175
Chas., cordw., Purton, 1782, W, P3/G/732
Chas., farmer, Easton Grey, 1852, O, W, Wr, P3/1852/27
Chris., yeo., Homanton, Maddington, 1765, W, P2/G/943
David, yeo., Poole Keynes, 1813, W, Wr, P3/1813/61
David, gent., Malm., 1814, W, Wr, P1/1814/123
Edmd., yeo., Maddington, 1701, W, P2/G/585
Goodwin, Edwd., yeo., Poulshot, 1713, I, W, P2/G/654
Edwd., yeo., Wanb., 1771, AB, W, P3/G/698
Edwd., Gillingham, Dorset, 1813, AB, P27/1/617
Eleanor, sp., Westwood, 1702, AB, W, P2/G/593

Eleanor, widow, Stanton St B., 1723, W, P1/G/418, P1/6Reg/413
Eliz., widow, Homanton, Maddington, 1667, AB, I, W, P2/G/347
Eliz., widow, Chipp., 1687, AB, P3/G/317
Eliz., Stanley, Chipp., 1697, W, P3/G/389
Eliz., widow, Sal. The Close (form. of Weeke, Hants), 1740, W, Wr, P5/1740/35
Eliz., widow, Stanley, Chipp., 1759, W, P1/G/630, P1/11Reg/445A
Eliz., widow, Poulshot, 1804, AB, ren, W, P1/1804/130
Eliz., sp., Sal., 1820, W, P1/1820/61
Eliz., sp., Coulston, Edington, 1833, AB, O, Wr, P2/1833/45
Francis, Draycot C., 1641, AB, I, P3/G/166
Francis, rough mason, Westwood, 1675, I, W, P2/G/385
Geo., Bemerton, Fugg. St Peter, 1648, I, W, P2/G/318
Geo., yeo., Gillingham, Dorset, 1771, W, P27/1/475, P27/3Reg/157B
Geo., Homington, 1809, AB, P24/1251
Geo., gardener, Westport St My., 1846, O, W, Wr, P3/1846/42
Giles, gent., Durnsford, Mildenhall, 1689, AB, I, W, P3/G/340
Godden, yeo., Ford, Laverstock, 1710, W, P2/G/642
Hy., Stanley, Chipp., 1696, AB, I, P3/G/379
Goodwin, Hy., wheelwright, Drayton, Abingdon, Berks., 1704, comm, W, P1/G/324
Hy., vicar, Stratton St Mgt., 1742, W, P3/G/597
Hy., innkeeper, Lyneham, 1848, comm, W, Wr, P3/1848/57
Howell, yeo., Cloatley, Hankerton, 1840, O, W, Wr, P3/1840/15
Hugh, yeo., Draycot C., 1679, AB, I, P3/G/267
Jas., butcher, Gillingham, Dorset, 1836, W, P27/1/711
Jas., yeo., Holt, Bradford A., 1841, comm, W, Wr, P2/1841/32
Jane, widow, Overton, [1602], W (NEP), P3/1Reg/82
Jane, widow, Keevil Wick, 1695, I, W, P1/G/296
Jeremiah, yeo., Rodbourne, Malm., 1706, AB, I, ren, P3/G/422
Jeremiah, yeo., Blackacre Farm, Holt, Bradford A., 1778, W, P2/G/997
Jeremy, sen., yeo., Rodbourne, Malm., 1695, I, W, P3/G/374
Joan, widow, Wanb., 1730, AB, P3/G/531
Joan, widow, Staverton, Trowb., 1766, W, P1/G/656, P1/12Reg/179A
Goodwin, Jn., Sandhurst, Berks., 1562, W, P5/1Reg/7C
Jn., Whitep., 1572, W, P2/5Reg/150D
Jn., sen., yeo., Grove Farm, Mildenhall, 1601, W, P3/1Reg/65
Jn., Malm., 1616, AB, P1/G/62
Goodwin, Jn., carrier, Beam., Dorset, 1633, AB, I, P5/1633/18, P5/12Reg/159B
Goodwin *or* Godwin, Jn., Lyme R., Dorset, 1663, AB, comm, P5/1663/27
Jn., Upper Westwood, [1670-76], I, W, P2/G/362, 404
Goodwin, Jn., innholder, Remenham, Berks., 1686, I, W, P1/G/774
Jn., husb., Motc., Dorset, 1712, AB, I, P27/1/197
Jn., Lyme R., Dorset, 1724, AB, comm, P16/231
Jn., Hilp., 1730, AB, I, P2/G/759
Goodwin, Jn., painter stainer, Wokm., Berks., 1732, W, P5/1732/17
Jn., Crickl. St My., 1741, W, P3/G/593
Jn., yeo., Stock St., Calne, 1743, W, Wr, P5/1743/33
Jn., sen., yeo., Rodbourne, Malm., 1752, W, P3/G/643
Jn., gent., Bremilham, 1761, W, P3/G/669
Jn., innholder, Holt, Bradford A., 1776, AB, comm, P2/G/987
Jn., victualler, Holt, Bradford A., 1785, W, P2/G/1025
Jn., butcher, Blewbury, Berks., 1795, W, P5/1795/7, P5/18Reg/211
Jn., yeo., Milbourne, Malm., 1798, W, P1/G/770, P1/15Reg/135
Jn., Crickl. St S., 1813, AB, Wr, P3/1813/55
Jn., farmer, Berwick St Jas., 1817, O, W, Wr, P1/1817/1
Jn., Allington, All C., 1822, AB, Wr, P3/1822/16
Jn., Cloatley, Hankerton, 1837, AB, O, Wr, P3/1837/75
Jn., widower, Crickl. St S., 1856, AB, aff, comm, Wr, P3/1856/23
Jn. Hunt, yeo., Holt, Bradford A., 1833, O, W, Wr, P2/1833/6
Jonathan, yeo., Holt, Bradford A., 1713, W, P2/G/658
Jonathan, Stanley, Chipp., 1749, W, P3/G/634

Jonathan, Bradford A., 1757, AB, P2/G/901
Jos., yeo., Crudwell, 1730, AB, comm, P3/G/532
Jos., broad weaver, Whitehill, Bradford A., 1730, W, P2/G/762
Jos., S. Wraxall, 1733, AB, I, P2/G/780
Jos., cooper, Malm., 1829, W, Wr, P3/1829/32
Kezia, sp., Heytes., 1836, W (& cods), Wr, P5/1836/6
Godwin alias Gale, Mgt., yeo.'s wife, Rodbourne, Malm., 1691, AB, P3/G/351
Mgt., widow, Holt, Bradford A., 1725, W, P2/G/732
Margery, widow, Rodbourne, Malm., 1669, I, W, P3/G/203
Mark, Fisherton A., 1770, AB, P2/G/964
My., widow, Sandy Lane, Calne, 1695, I, NW, P5/1695/37
My., widow, Lt. Somerford, 1743, W, P3/G/604
My., widow, Maddington, 1756, W, P2/G/895
My., Devizes, 1763, AB, P1/G/646
Goodwin, My., widow, Bracknell, Warfield, Berks., 1770, W, P1/12Reg/370B
Michael, husb., Westwood, 1637, I, NW, P2/G/264
Nathaniel, Chipp., 1670, AB, I, ren, P3/G/212
Nathaniel, clerk, Bps. C., 1704, AB, comm, P24/602
Nathaniel, jun., linen draper, Malm., 1745, W, P3/G/610
Nich., carp., Hardenhuish, 1678, AB, I, P3/G/260
Philip, Lacock, 1684, AB, comm, P3/G/292
Philip, shoemaker, Foghamshire, Chipp., 1735, W, P1/G/506, P1/8Reg/75A
Philip, glazier, Lambourn, Berks., 1808, W, P1/1808/42
Philip, Purton, 1829, W, Wr, P1/1829/68
Phyllis, widow, Bishoper Farm, Hankerton, 1833, W, Wr, P3/1833/27
Godwin *or* Godding, Richd., yeo., Easton Piercy, Kington St M., 1634, AB, a/c, I, P3/G/134
Richd., yeo., Homanton, Maddington, 1723, I, W, P1/G/417, P1/6Reg/404B
Richd., cordw., Chipp., 1729, I, W, P3/G/522
Richd., yeo., Homington, 1741, ren, W, P1/G/534, P1/9Reg/43
Robt., Homanton, Maddington, 1628, I, W, P2/G/221
Robt., Winterbourne S., 1687, AB, I, P2/G/504
Robt., Oaksey, 1710, AB, P3/G/434
Sarah, sp., Downton, 1852, aff, W, Wr, P2/1852/54
Susanna, widow, Stanton St B., 1698, I, W, P3/G/391
Susanna, widow, Stratton St Mgt., 1731, AB, P3/G/538
Susanna, sp., Wanb., 1746, AB, P3/G/616
Thos., bishop of Bath and Wells, d.at Wokm., Berks., 1591, AB (2 - limited & to secure goods), a/c, bond to collect goods, I, P5/1590/26, P5/5Reg/94B-95C
Goodwin, Thos., Hilmarton, 1667, I, NW, P3/G/193
Thos., Stanton St B., 1673, AB, a/c, comm, I, P3/G/228
Thos., wheeler, Chipp., 1680, AB, I, P1/G/239
Thos., sen., blacksmith, Harwell, Berks., 1692, I, W, P1/G/282
Thos., Sandy Lane, Calne, 1694, AB, comm, P26/422
Thos., yeo., Stanton St B., [1707], W, P1/G/340
Thos., gent., Ford Farm, Bradford A., 1714, W, P2/G/665
Thos., hair weaver, Marl., 1715, W, P1/G/386, P1/5Reg/489B
Thos., serge weaver, Kington L., 1735, W, P1/G/498, P1/7Reg/637A
Thos., Kington L., 1748, AB, comm, P3/G/627
Thos., collarmaker, Calne, 1754, W, P26/928
Thos., cordw., Ogbourne St A., 1776, W, P5/1776/20, P5/17Reg/122B
Thos., yeo., Gillingham, Dorset, 1814, AB, ren, W, P27/1/628
Thos., bach., Crickl. St S., 1819, AB, Wr, P3/1819/51
Thos., victualler, Burton Hill, Malm., 1838, O, W, Wr, P3/1838/69
Thos. Miles, minor, Berwick St Jas., 1812, T, P1/1812/16
Unity, widow, Holt, Bradford A., 1789, AB, P2/G/1044
Walter, Kington L., 1725, W, P3/G/494
Wm., husb. *or* yeo., Haydon Wick, Rodbourne C., 1685, I, W, P3/G/309
Wm., Hardenhuish, 1689, AB, I, P3/G/341
Goodwin, Wm., yeo., Stratfield M., Berks., 1704, I, W, P1/G/328
Wm., Bradford A., 1714, AB, P2/G/666

Wm., Stratton St Mgt., 1723, AB, P3/G/484
Goodwin, Wm., labourer, Wokm., Berks., 1724, W, P5/1724/34, P5/16Reg/93A
Wm., yeo., Motc., Dorset, 1732, I, W, P27/1/319
Wm., Lt. Somerford, 1743, W, P3/G/605
Wm., Axford, Rams., 1748, AB, Wr, P5/1748/11
Wm., Chipp., 1755, AB, comm, P3/G/652
Wm., Staverton, Trowb., 1794, comm, W, P1/G/746, P1/14Reg/501B
Wm., Fonthill B., 1806, AB, Wr, P2/1806/70
Wm., gent., Gillingham, Dorset, 1807, W, P27/1/593
Wm., yeo., Bishoper Farm, Hankerton, 1817, W, Wr, P3/1817/18
Wm., Charlton nr Malm., 1824, W, Wr, P3/1824/52
see also Godden alias G.; Goodwin *or* G.
Goen *see* Gawen
Goff, Goffe *see* Gough
Golborn, Wm., chemist and druggist, Sal., 1836, W, Wr, P4/1836/1
Gold *see* Gould
Golden *see* Golding
Goldenham, Jn., Wick, Southbroom, 1707, AB, I, P24/588
Goldesbrough *see* Goldisborough
Goldesney *see* Golsney
Goldhawke, Wm., sen., New Windsor, Berks., 1704, AB, comm, I, L, P1/G/337
Goldiker, Eliz., Cholderton, 1593, AB, I, W, P2/G/68
Golding, Agnes, widow, Netheravon, 1588, AB, I, W, P12/236, P5/5Reg/1A
Agnes *see also* Ann
Goulding, Ann, widow, Downton, 1855, AB, aff, Wr, P2/1855/15
Golden, Ann *or* Agnes, widow, Sutton V., 1676, I, W, P2/G/398
Guilden, Edwd., Mere, 1598, AB, P5/6Reg/200C
Goulding, Edwd., barber, Gt. Faringdon, Berks., 1674-76, AB, a/c, I (detailed), P5/1674/28, P5/1676/26
Goulden, Eliz., widow, Donhead St A., 1820, AB, Wr, P2/1820/29-30
Geo., serge weaver, Warm., 1673, I, W, P2/G/377
Goulding, Geo., yeo., Downton, 1772, W, P2/G/976
Goulden, Geo., Fisherton A., 1796, AB, comm, ren, P2/G/1069
Goulding, Geo., Downton, 1799, AB, P2/G/1077
Goulding, Geo., glover, Downton, 1847, O, W, Wr, P2/1847/6
Goulding, Hannah, widow, Broom, Swindon, 1766, W, P3/G/683
Jas., weaver, Sal., 1738, W, P4/1738/16
Jn., Axford, Rams., 1563, W, P5/1Reg/22B
Jn., weaver, Wokm., Berks., 1594, AB, I, W, P5/1594/32, P5/6Reg/57
Goulden, Jn., husb., Wootton R., 1681, I, W, P3/G/282
Goulding, Jn., Broom Farm, Swindon, 1729, AB, P3/G/523
Goulding, Jn., gent., Broughton G., 1732, W, P1/G/488, P1/7Reg/547B
Jn., sen., gent., Netherb., Dorset, 1742, W, P17/483
Goulding, Jn., gent., Broughton G., 1756, W, P1/G/618, P1/11Reg/298
Jn., Stanford in the Vale, Berks., 1798, AB, ren, P1/G/762, P1/15Reg/39A
Golden, Jn., Donhead St A., 1812, AB, Wr, P2/1812/33
Jn., butcher, Haydon, Dorset, 1828, O, W, Wr, P5/1828/22
Goulding, Jn., innkeeper, Downton, 1843, W, Wr, P2/1843/44
Jn. Reynolds, yeo., Letcombe Regis, Berks., 1798, W, P1/G/764, P1/15Reg/92
Goulden, Mgt., widow, Warm., 1696, I, W, P2/G/558
Margery, widow, Axford, Rams., 1586, AB, I, P5/1586/7, P5/4Reg/136B
Martha, yeo.'s wife, Letcombe Regis, Berks., 1738, W, P1/G/520, P1/8Reg/262
Goulding, My., widow, Devizes, [1688], W, P1/G/267
Golden, My., Sherb., Dorset, 1696, AB, comm, P5/1696/18
My., widow, Wokm., Berks., 1754, W, P5/1754/9
My., sp., Beam., Dorset, 1764, W, P17/555
Golden, Nich., currier, Sherb., Dorset, 1771, W, P5/1771/8, P5/17Reg/32A
Golding *or* Golden, Peter, sen., maltster, Sherb., Dorset, 1706, I, W, P5/1706/15
Golden, Peter, sen., maltster, Sherb., Dorset, 1740, W, Wr, P5/1740/36
Peter, maltster, Sherb., Dorset, 1751, W, P5/1751/12
Richd., sen., weaver, Stockton, 1637, I, W, P2/G/267

Golden, Richd., shoemaker, Devizes, 1644, AB, comm, P1/G/148
Golding *or* Golden, Richd., husb., Stockton, [1679], I, W, P2/G/422
Richd., maltster, Bromham, 1690, I, W, P3/G/345
Richd., barber, Highw., 1726, W, P10/1726/3
Goulding *or* Golden, Richd., sen., wheeler, Wilcot, 1748, W, P1/G/581, P1/10Reg/225A
Robt., Axford, Rams., 1584, AB, I, P5/1584/8, P5/4Reg/92A
Golden, Robt., Foxham, Bremhill, 1745, AB, P3/G/611
Sarah, widow, Wokm., Berks., 1809, W, Wr, P5/1809/25
Goulden, Sarah, minors, Donhead St My., 1820, T (grandchildren of Eliz. G.), P2/1820/29-30
Thos., son of rector, N. Tidworth, 1560, AB, P2/4Reg/48C
Thos., Allington (Idmiston crossed out), 1571, AB, P2/G/23, P2/5Reg/128A
Goulding, Thos., gent., Seend Park, Melk., 1664, I, W, P2/G/333
Thos., Downton, 1727, AB, P2/G/744
Valentine, miller, Devizes St Jn., 1614, I, NW, P1/G/53
Goulding, Walter, sen., husb., Devizes, 1683, AB, comm, I, P1/G/248
Walter, chairmaker, Sal., 1764, W, P4/1764/3
Wm., Upton L., 1635, I, W, P2/G/256, P2/9Reg/51D
Wm., maltster, Wantage, Berks., 1765, comm, W, P23/708
Goldisborough, Gouldisborough, Alice, widow, Slade Farm, Bradford A., 1710, W, P2/G/633
Augustus, gent., Shrewton, 1608, W, P1/G/29
Gouldisborough, Bridget, widow, Shrewton, 1726, W, P2/G/738
Goldsbury alias Turvile, Eliz., E. Knoyle, 1678, AB, P2/G/414
Eliz., widow, Shrewton, 1766, W, P2/G/949
Jn., gent., Milton, E. Knoyle, 1664, AB, comm, I, P2/G/332
Goldisbrough, Jn., gent., Mere, 1728, AB, ren, P5/1728/40, P5/16Reg/210B
Jn., clerk rector, Berwick St Jas., 1731, AB, P1/G/476
Goldsborough, My., widow, Upton, E. Knoyle, 1674, I, W, P2/G/381
Gouldisborough, Robt., gent., Shrewton, 1633, I, W, P2/G/246, P2/9Reg/23C
Goldisbrough, Robt., Mere, 1713, AB, P5/1713/33
Gouldisborough, Robt., gent., Shrewton, 1739, W, P2/G/813
Goldsbrough, Robt., Bourton, Gillingham, Dorset, 1831, AB, comm, P27/1/695
Wm., Wedh., Urchf., 1685, AB, I, W, P2/G/493
Goldsbrough, Wm., gent., Mere, 1721, W, P5/1721/16, P5/16Reg/56C
Goldney, Gouldney, Adam, clothier, Chipp., 1684, comm, I, W, P3/G/293
Anna, widow, Chipp., 1720, comm, W, P1/G/400, P1/6Reg/207
Chas., victualler, Chipp., 1828, W, Wr, P3/1828/24
Gouldney, Gabriel, sen., clothier, Chipp., 1670, I, W, P3/G/216
Gouldney, Gabriel, clothier, Chipp., 1684, I, W, P3/G/294
Gouldney, Hy., yeo., Chipp., 1625, W, P3/G/90
Gouldney, Hy., clothier, Chipp., 1696, comm, I, ren, W, Wr, P3/G/381
Gouldney, Jn., Devizes, 1676, AB, P1/G/231
Gouldney, Jn., sen., clothier, Chipp., 1724, W, copy W, P3/G/490
My., sp., Chipp., 1737, AB, ren, P3/G/572
My., milliner, Bath (all goods at Chipp.), 1753, I (detailed), W, P3/G/647
Sarah, widow, Chipp., 1814, W, Wr, P1/1814/111
see also Farnwell alias G.
Goldring, Hester, widow, Warm., 1852, AB, cert, comm, Wr, P2/1852/2
Jn., Wilton, 1586, AB, P2/7Reg/31A
Gouldring, Jn., Holnest, Dorset, 1671, AB, comm, I, P5/1671/38
Thos., sailor form. serving on man of war Stratford, Enmore Grn, Motc., Dorset, 1741, AB, Wr, P5/1740/33
Wm., Holnest, Dorset, 1620, AB, I, P5/1620/23, P5/10Reg/77B
Goldsborough *see* Goldisborough
Goldsmith, Dorothy, sp., Marl., 1743, AB, copy req, copy W, P1/G/546, P1/9Reg/250B
Jn., gent., Avebury, 1641, AB, ren, W, P1/G/142
Marmaduke, shoemaker, Earley, Sonning, Berks., 1585, I, T, W, P5/1585/24, P5/4Reg/114A
Thos., Sonning, Berks., 1546, W, P5/20Reg/71B
Goldstone, Goldstone *or* Goulstone, Edmd., Swallowcliffe, 1692, AB, I, P5/1692/32
Golstone, Philip, husb., Swallowcliffe, 1619, I, W, P5/1619/24, P5/9Reg/226B
Golstone, Wm., Corsley, 1557, W, P2/3Reg/55B
Goldwin, Jn., organist, Windsor Castle, Berks., 1720, W, P1/G/405, P1/6Reg/305B

Goldwyer, Eliz., widow, Sal., 1798, W, P1/G/768, P1/15Reg/141C
Thos., Edington, 1563, I, W, P2/G/19, P2/4Reg/156A
Golle, Mgt., widow, Bower C., 1596, I, W, P2/G/76
Golledge, Cath., widow, Trowb., 1639, I, W, P1/G/140
Gulledge, Edwd., Nether C., Dorset, 1840, AB, comm, Wr, P5/1840/6
Gabriel, tiler, Lacock, 1755, W, P3/G/653
Jn., weaver, Trowb., 1632, I, W. No date of probate, P22/1/26
Roger, victualler, Chapmanslade, Corsley, 1751, W, P2/G/882
Wm., Amesb., 1573, W, P2/5Reg/174C
Wm., sen., tiler and plasterer, Lacock, 1732, I, W, P3/G/544
Gollesney *see* Golsney
Gollop, Cath., sp., Beam., Dorset, 1734, AB, P5/1734/28
Gallop, Hy., gent., Lyme R., Dorset, 1634, AB, comm, I, P5/1634/40
Gallop, Jn., gent., Netherb., Dorset, 1682, AB, P17/251
Gallop, Jos., Anderson, Dorset, 1827, W (endorsed: 'not to be proved'), Wr, P5/1827/64
Joshua, yeo., Bere R., Dorset, 1737, AB, W, P5/1737/21
Joshua, Bloxworth, Dorset, 1807, AB, Wr, P5/1807/14
Gallop, Richd., butcher and husb., Bere R., Dorset, 1730, W, P5/1730/27
Richd., bach., Beam., Dorset, 1734, AB, P5/1734/29
Roger, merchant, Netherb., Dorset, 1712, I (detailed), W, P17/208
Sarah, widow, Strode, Netherb., Dorset, 1705, W (NEP), P17/642
Gallop, Simon, innholder, Ford, N. Wraxall, 1722, AB, I, P3/G/473
Susanna, wife, Lillington, Dorset, 1750, AB, comm, P5/1750/15
Gallop, Theobald, sp., Seagry, 1631, I, W, P3/G/118
Thos., gent., Strode, Netherb., Dorset, 1727, court paper, W, P17/427
Thos., gent., Lillington, Dorset, 1749, AB, comm, ren, Wr, P5/1749/24
Thos., gent., Caundle Marsh, Dorset, 1758, req, W, copy W, P5/1758/18
Thos., gent., Caundle Marsh, Dorset, 1789, W, P5/1789/6, P5/18Reg/128
Gallop, Thos., butcher, Bloxworth, Dorset, 1791, AB, comm, W, P5/1791/9, P5/18Reg/171
Wm., sen., esquire, Caundle Marsh, Dorset, 1775, W, P5/1775/10, P5/17Reg/89
Golsney, Alice, Folke, Dorset, 1627, AB, P5/1627/20, P5/11Reg/43A
Ann, widow, Haydon, Dorset, 1632, AB, I, P5/1632/25, P5/12Reg/110B
Ann, widow, Haydon, Dorset, 1640, AB, P5/1640/20, P5/13Reg/270B
Edith, widow, Holnest, Dorset, 1660, I, NW, P5/1660/1
Hy., yeo., Folke, Dorset, 1632, W, P5/12Reg/118
Goldesney, Jn., Gillingham, Dorset, 1562, W, P27/1Reg/11C
Gollesney, Jn., husb., Haydon, Dorset, 1581, I, W, P5/1580/27, P5/4Reg/15C
Jn., yeo., Folke, Dorset, 1633, I, W, P5/1632/22
Jn., gent., Holnest, Dorset, 1679-80, AB, a/c, I, ren, P5/1679/32, P5/1680/15
Sam., gardener, Haydon, Dorset, 1813, W, Wr, P5/1813/6
Thos., weaver, N. Wootton, Dorset, 1603, AB, I, W, P5/1603/31, P5/7Reg/60C
Thos., labourer, Haydon, Dorset, 1735, I, W, P5/1735/25
Wm., jun., Holnest, Dorset, 1640, AB, P5/13Reg/225A
Wm., sen., Holnest, Dorset, 1640, AB, I, P5/1640/24
Wm., maltster, Sal., 1653, I, W, P1/G/172
Wm., yeo., Holnest, Dorset, 1660, AB, W, P5/1660/3
Wm., jun., labourer, Haydon, Dorset, 1730, I, W, P5/1730/30
Golstone *see* Goldstone
Gomeldon, Gomelton *see* Gumbleton
Gonne, Sam., gent., Pewsey, 1670, AB, I, ren, P3/G/214
Wm., clerk, Marden, 1685, I, W, P2/G/486
Gonstone *see* Gunstone
Good, Alexander, Broad C., 1558, W, P2/3Reg/101A
Alice, sp., Bower C., 1736, W, P2/G/801
Goode, Andrew, bricklayer, Hurst, Berks., 1689, I, W, P5/1689/29
Goode, Andrew, bricklayer, Hurst, Berks., 1722, AB, I, W, P5/1722/25, P5/16Reg/80A
Bartholemew, husb., Broad C., 1608, W, P2/8Reg/16A
Chas., gent., Broad C., 1813, W, Wr, P2/1813/12
Dorothy, minor, Broad C., 1705, T, P2/G/613
Eliz., sp., Devizes, 1742, comm, W, P1/G/547, P1/9Reg/230

Eliz., sp., Broad C., 1803, W, P2/1803/76
Frances, widow, Ufton Nervet, Berks., 1671, AB, I, P1/G/215
Harry, gent., Broad C. Farm, 1776, W, P1/G/697, P1/13Reg/89
Hy., yeo., Broad C., [1671], I, W, P2/G/367
Hy., Broad C., 1702, AB, I, P2/G/602
Hy., gent., E. Hatch, Tisb., 1746, AB, I, ren, P2/G/852
Isaac, Gt. Woodford, 1681, AB, a/c, I, P13/3/3
Jas., yeo., Yatesbury, 1694, AB, I, P3/G/371
Jane, sp., Yatesbury, 1664, AB, a/c, I, P1/G/195
Jane, widow, Sal., 1688, I, NW, P4/1688/11
Jane, widow, Stoke F., 1706, W, P2/G/620
Joan, widow, Mount Sorrell, Broad C., 1630, W, P2/G/234
Jn., husb., Broad C., 1597, AB, I, W, P2/G/79
Jn., Broad C., 1609, I, W, P2/G/132, P2/8Reg/78C
Jn., yeo., Yatesbury, 1683, I, W, P3/G/287
Jn., gent., Broad C., 1795, W, P2/G/1067
Lucretia, Broad C., 1709, W, P2/G/630
Mgt., sp., Sal. The Close, 1688, W, P5/1687/16
My., minor, Broad C., 1723, T (bond for My. dau of Ralph & My. - mother d. 1709), P2/G/1083
Ralph, gent., Broad C., 1699, I, W, P2/G/572
Ralph, gent., Devizes, 1761, W, P1/G/633, P1/12Reg/11
Goode, Robt., tailor, Bere R., Dorset, 1592, AB, I, W, P5/1592/38
Roger, gent., Bower C., 1757, W, P2/G/900
Goode, Sam., Sulhamstead, Berks., 1695, comm, W, P1/G/291
Susanna, widow, Broad C., 1703, I, W, P2/G/603
Thos., Sal. St Martin, 1633, AB, P4/1633/16
Thos., husb., Barford St M., 1667, I, W, P2/G/345
Thos., yeo., Yatesbury, 1675, AB, I, P3/G/235
Thos., yeo., Yatesbury, 1711, W, P1/G/365, P1/5Reg/264
Thos., Hurst, Berks., 1750, AB, P5/1750/16
Thos., labourer, Netherh., 1845, W, Wr, P1/1845/22
Wm., broad weaver, Wilton, 1606, D, W, P1/G/26
Wm., sen., yeo., Yatesbury, 1614, I, W, P5/1613/36, P5/9Reg/128B
Wm., sen., Barford St M., 1681, I, W, P2/G/438
Wm., sen., yeo., Wanb., 1709, W, P3/G/432
see also Hellier alias G.
Goodall, Ananias, Froxfield, 1785, W, P3/G/739
Ann, dairy woman, Worton, Pott., 1831, W, Wr, P1/1831/7
Anthony, Farnborough, Berks., 1686, AB, I, P1/G/773
Edwd., Ludg., 1598, I, W, P2/G/91
Eliz., widow, Oak Hill, Froxfield, 1790, comm, W, P3/G/752
Geo., bach. of divinity and rector, Padworth, Berks., 1704, W (contains catalogue of books to form library for use of rectors of P.), P1/G/332
Geo., Easton, 1714, AB, P3/G/445
Jn., Chisenbury, Enford, 1542, W (NEP), P2/1Reg/35
Goodale, Jn., husb., Enford, 1560, AB, W (probate crossed out & annotated void), P2/1Reg/110B
Jn., Ludg., 1587-88, I, W, P2/G/39, P2/7Reg/117C
Goodale, Jn., Allington, 1621, AB, a/c, P2/G/198
Goodale, Jn., husb., Allington, 1639, I, W, P2/G/277
Jn., yeo., Easton, [1675], W, P1/G/229
Goodale, Richd., Ludg., 1564, I, W, P2/G/1084, P2/4Reg/174A
Richd., yeo., Urchf., 1681, I, W, P2/G/442
Goodale, Simon, yeo., Pott., 1712, AB, ren, P1/G/370
Goodale, Stephen, bach., Idmiston, 1679, I, W, P2/G/420
Goodale, Thos., Coombe, Fittleton, 1557, W, P2/3Reg/17C
Thos., gent., Sal., 1823, O, W, Wr, P1/1823/136
Goodale, Wm., husb., Longstreet, Enford, 1596, AB, I, P2/G/77
Goodale, Wm., husb., Easton, 1622, AB, I, P3/G/75
Wm., yeo., Easton, 1702, I, W, P3/G/410
Goodanter, Christian, widow, Hurst, Berks., 1625, I, W, P5/1625/40, P5/10Reg/247B

Ralph, Hurst, Berks., 1567, W, P5/2Reg/25D
Goodbee, Godby, Abraham, innholder, Trowb., 1720, W, P1/G/407, P1/6Reg/363
Ann, Hurdcott, Winterbourne E., 1732, W, P2/G/773
Godby, Ann, sp., Crickl. St S., 1834, W, Wr, P3/1834/8
Benj., yeo., Hurdcott, Winterbourne E., 1730, W, P2/G/755
Godby, Edwd., baker, Chipp., 1636, I, W, P3/G/144
Godby, Edwd., maltster, Chipp., 1685, comm, I, W, P3/G/308
Hy., yeo., Bishopsdown Farm, Laverstock, 1712, W, P4/1711/1
Hy., gent., Sal., 1725, W, P4/1725/3
Godby, Hy., farmer, Broad Town, Clyffe P., 1799, note of probate, W, P3/G/774
Godby, Joan, sp., Chipp., 1716, I, W, P3/G/453
Goodboy, Jn., husb., Sulham, Berks., 1692, AB, I, P1/G/283
Goodby, Jos., yeo., Netton, Durnford, 1730, AB, ren, NW, P9/47
Godby, My., sp., Chipp., 1694, AB, I, ren, P3/G/370
Godby, Richd., jun., common carrier, Trowb., 1818, comm, W, Wr, P1/1818/3
Godby, Robt., farmer, Trowb., 1771, AB, W, P1/G/683, P1/12Reg/402
Thos., Milford, Sal. St Martin, 1753, AB, P4/1753/7
Wm., gent., Stratford sub C., 1733, W, P4/1733/3
Goodcheap, Eliz., widow, Chipp., 1747, W, P3/G/622
Hugh, mason, Chipp., 1690, AB, I, P3/G/346
Hugh, mason, Chipp., 1756, W, P3/G/657
Jn., Easton Grey, [1579], W (NEP), P3/1Reg/41B
Wm., rough mason, Chipp., 1699, I, W, Wr, P3/G/393
Goodcheap alias Cowly, Winifred, widow, Easton Grey, 1669, I, W, P3/G/205
Goodchild, Hy., yeo., Liberty of Newland, Hurst, Berks., 1601, AB, I, W, P5/1601/21, P5/7Reg/17C
Jas., Hurst, Berks., 1813, AB, Wr, P5/1813/3
Jn., bricklayer, Ruscombe, Berks., 1819, W, Wr, P5/1819/13
Jos., blacksmith, Swallowfield, Shinfield, Berks., 1835, W, Wr, P1/1835/99
Susanna, widow, Finchampstead, Berks., 1680, AB, I, P1/G/238
Thos., yeo., Hurst, Berks., 1761, W, P5/1761/14
Thos., Marl. St My., 1828, AB, comm, Wr, P1/1828/2
Goode *see* Good
Goodeares *see* Goodyear
Gooden *see* Godden
Goodenough, Ambrose, husb., Coleshill, Berks., 1614, comm, I, W, P1/G/49
Ann, sp., Sherston, 1693, W, P3/G/361
Anthony, harnessmaker, Damerham, Hants, 1731, W, P2/G/766
Cicely, widow, Malm., 1672, AB, comm, I, ren, P3/G/226
Edith, widow, Sherston, 1678, I, W, P3/G/261
Eliz., sen., widow, Pott., 1572, AB, W, P1/1Reg/55A
Eliz., widow, Winterbourne S., 1777, AB, W, P2/G/995
Jn., husb., Ebbesborne Wake, 1574, W, P2/5Reg/177B
Jn., Marston, Pott., 1631, I, W, P1/G/111
Jn., tallow chandler, Warm., 1743, W, P2/G/842
My., widow, Warm., 1773, W, P2/G/978
Richd., husb., Foxley, 1636, I, NW, P3/G/145
Robt., yeo., Pott. Wick, 1636, I, W, P1/G/132
Robt., carp., Foxley, 1676, I, NW, P3/G/245
Stephen, sen., yeo., Winterbourne S., 1746, W, P1/G/563, P1/10Reg/25, 43
Stephen, gent., Winterbourne S. (late of Lacock), 1761, AB, P2/G/923
Thos., Donhead St A., 1618, I, W, copy NW, P2/G/178
Ursula, jun., widow, Donhead St A., 1634, I, W, P1/G/122
Goodfellow, Alexander, yeo., Britford, 1717, W, P24/646
Eliz., widow, Laverstock, 1739, AB, P2/G/812
Eliz., widow, Coombe B., 1819, W, Wr, P8/80
Francis, fisherman, Britford, 1615, I, W, P24/93
Francis, Britford, 1679, AB, I, P24/472
Francis, Sal. The Close, 1784, W, P5/1784/7, P5/17Reg/256C
Geo., yeo., Chilmark, 1682, I, W, P2/G/448
Geo., Teffont E., 1713, AB, P2/G/661

Geo., Fovant, 1723, AB, I, P1/G/416
Geo., Fonthill B., 1763, AB, P2/G/933
Hannah, widow, Codf. St P., 1780, W, P2/G/1003
Harry, husb., Ebbesborne Wake, 1566, W, P2/4Reg/236A
Hy., yeo., Compton C., 1673-76, AB, a/c, I, P2/G/374, 403
Hy., miller, Teffont E., 1719, I, W, P2/G/698
Hy., miller, Teffont E., 1789, W, P2/G/1046
Hy., sawyer, Fovant, 1850, W, Wr, P2/1850/60
Isaac, Britford, 1684, AB, I, P24/739
Jas., maltster, Downton, 1744, W, P2/G/844
Jn., Britford, 1601, I, P24/18
Jn., Ebbesborne Wake, 1609, comm, I, T, P2/G/130
Jn., Bishopstone S., 1609, AB, P2/8Reg/62B
Jn., Sal. The Close, 1638, AB, I, P5/1637/14, P5/13Reg/66A
Jn., freemason, E. Harnham, Britford, 1704, I, W, P5/1704/28
Jn., Homington, 1734, AB, W, P24/940
Jn., gent., Teffont E., 1809, req, W, Wr, P2/1809/44
Jn., yeo., Fovant, 1848, W, Wr, P1/1848/68
Jos., Laverstock, 1738, AB, P2/G/810
Jos., mariner on *The Captain*, ship of war, Sal., 1761, AB, P4/1761/5
Lucy, widow, E. Harnham, Britford, 1717, W, P5/1717/14, P5/15Reg/405C
Mgt., widow, Britford, 1609, I, W, P24/150
Martha, widow, Amesb., 1800, W, Wr, P2/1800/85
My., widow, Fovant Stroud, 1778, W, P2/G/1000
Matthew, gent., Sal., 1776, W, P4/1776/1
Richd., Bemerton, Fugg. St Peter, 1685, AB, P2/G/491
Richd., tailor, Fovant, 1723, AB, I, P2/G/723
Robt., Bemerton, Fugg. St Peter, 1701, AB, P1/G/321
Sam., Sal., 1723-28, I, W, P4/1723/5, P4/1728/4
Sarah, widow, Sal., 1779, W, P1/G/712, P1/13Reg/288A
Susanna, widow, Compton C., 1670, AB, I, W, P2/G/361
Thos., shoemaker, Sal., 1686, AB, I, ren, P4/1685/29
Thos., bricklayer, E. Harnham, Britford, 1715, W, P5/1715/18, P5/15Reg/328A
Thos., weaver, Wilton, 1733, W, P2/G/786
Thos., glazier, Sal., 1754, W, P4/1754/2
Thos., yeo., Milford, Sal. St Martin, 1780, W, P4/1780/16
Thos., stationer, bookbinder and bookseller, Sal. St Thos., 1790, W (2), P4/1790/10
Wm., Britford, 1628, I, W, P24/223
Wm., Fovant, 1742, AB, P2/G/836
Wm., carp., Fovant, 1773, W (note that lodged in Archd Sarum), P1/12Reg/447
Wm., yeo., Fovant, 1773-92, AB, W, P2/G/979
Wm., yeo., Pitton, Alderbury, 1775, AB, W, P26/1072
Wm., Fovant, 1789, AB, P1/G/741
Wm., yeo., Fovant, 1835, W, Wr, P1/1835/40
Wm., miller, Boreham, Warm., 1837, comm, W, Wr, P2/1837/20
Goodhalt *see* Wastfield alias G.
Goodhind, My., widow, Bemerton, Fugg. St Peter, 1716, I, W, P2/G/681
Wm., yeo., Bemerton, Fugg. St Peter, [1691], I, W, P2/G/531
Gooding *see* Godden
Goodman, Agnes, widow, Langley Burrell, 1617, I, W, P3/G/50
Ann, sp., Pewsey, 1722, W, P3/G/479
Ann, sp., Westrop, Highw., 1799-1805, AB, W, P10/1799/2, P10/1805/1
Anthony, Sharcott, Pewsey, 1733, AB, I, P3/G/554
Bernard, farrier, Uffington, Berks., 1830, comm, W, Wr, P1/1830/3
David, yeo., Lyneham, 1732, comm, W, P1/G/478, P1/7Reg/438
Dorothy, sp., Sharcott, Pewsey, 1708, W, P3/G/431
Godman, Geoffrey, Allington, All C., 1606, I, W, P1/G/19
Godman, Geoffrey, Manningford A., 1635, AB, I, P3/G/138
Geoffrey, sen., Allington, All C., 1693, AB, I, P3/G/362
Geoffrey, yeo., Lacock (form. of Allington All C.), 1713, comm, I, W, P3/G/441

Geoffrey, yeo., Sharcott, Pewsey, 1730, W, P3/G/533
Geo., husb., Chiseldon, 1755, W, P3/G/654
Godman, Hy., sen., yeo., Sharcott, Pewsey, 1689, I, W, P1/G/273
Hy., yeo., W. Sharcott, Pewsey, 1721, W, P3/G/471
Godman, Honour, sp., All C., 1670, AB, I, P3/G/211
Humphrey, Goatacre, Hilmarton, 1637, I, W, P3/G/149
Humphrey, broad weaver, W. Tockenham, Lyneham, 1682, AB, comm, I, P3/G/283
Humphrey, Lyneham, 1738, AB, P3/G/576
Godman, Jane, widow, All C., 1667, AB, comm, I, W, P3/G/189
Jane, widow, Easton, 1800, AB, P3/1800/14
Joan, widow, Goatacre, Hilmarton, 1632, W (2), P3/G/126
Joan, widow, Wantage, Berks., 1676, AB, I, P23/60
Godman, Jn., sen., Allington, All C., 1629, I, W, P3/G/108
Godman, Jn., yeo. *or* miller, Sharcott, Pewsey, 1666, I, W, P3/G/187
Godman alias Goodman, Jn., sen., yeo., Allington, All C., 1671, AB, I, P3/G/221
Godman, Jn., sen., yeo., Sharcott, Pewsey, 1678, AB, I, W, Wr, P3/G/259
Jn., sen., yeo., Allington, All C., 1693, I, W, P3/G/363
Jn., Lyme R., Dorset, 1697, AB, P16/147
Jn., victualler, Fordington, Dorset, 1733, W, P15/122
Godman, Jn., Sharcott, Pewsey, 1751, W, P3/G/639
Jn., sen., chairmaker, Bewley Common, Lacock, 1777, W, P3/G/707-08
Jn., yeo., Easton, 1797, W, P3/G/768
Jn., gent., Fyfield, Overton, 1853, O, W, Wr, P3/1853/69
Jonathan, yeo., Farnborough, Berks., 1773, W, P1/G/692, P1/13Reg/22
Godman, Jos., butcher, Wanb., 1730, W, P3/G/530
Martha, widow, Clack, Lyneham, 1675, I, W, P3/G/236
My., widow, Goatacre, Hilmarton, 1693, I, W, P3/G/364
My., widow, Allington, All C., 1699-1746, AB (2), I, W, P3/G/394
My., widow, Bracknell, Warfield, Berks., 1770, AB, ren, W, P1/G/676
Maurice, farmer, Greenham, Thatcham, Berks., 1821, AB, O, ren, Wr, P1/1821/17
Robt., husb., Bouden, Bromham, 1611, I, W, P1/G/33
Robt., mercer, Clack, Lyneham, 1670, I, W, P3/G/215
Sarah, widow, Trowb., 1786, comm, W, P1/G/729, P1/14Reg/104
Stephen, Devizes Grn, Bps. C., 1781, AB, comm, P24/1114
Thos., yeo., Witcomb, Hilmarton, 1686-87, comm, I, W, Wr, P1/G/262, P3/G/318
Thos., yeo., Spillman's Farm, Hilmarton, 1697, I, W, P3/G/390
Thos., miller, Crofton, Gt. Bedwyn, 1797, W (& cod), P5/1797/19, P5/18Reg/231
Wm., yeo., Allington, All C., 1668, I, W, P3/G/196
Wm., shoemaker, Trowb., 1779, W, P1/G/715, P1/13Reg/301A
Wm., jun., labourer, Basildon, Berks., 1808, W, Wr, P1/1808/101
see also Godman alias G.
Goodridge, Alexander, yeo., Uffc., Devon, 1610, I, W, P5/1610/23, P5/9Reg/22A
Alice, widow, Uffc., Devon, 1567, W, P5/2Reg/27E
Anthony Gregory, architect and surveyor, Sherb., Dorset, 1854, aff, W, Wr, P5/1854/14
Arthur, Corsham, 1587, W, P29/1Reg/25A
Cuthbert, Sal., 1618, AB, I (? incomplete), P4/1618/2
Jn., Northcott, Uffc., Devon, 1553, W, P20/Reg/59
Jn., Ruscombe, Berks., 1582, AB, I, P5/1582/26, P5/4Reg/49B
Jn., Ruscombe, Berks., 1585, I, W, P5/1585/2, P5/4Reg/115A
Jn., carp., Mkt. L., 1626, I, W, P2/G/209
Nich., Ruscombe, Berks., 1544, W, P5/20Reg/60
Nich., Uffc., Devon, 1567, W, P5/2Reg/18B
Richd., yeo., Uffc., Devon, 1663, I, W (2 - 1 more detailed than the other), P20/1/45
Richd., gent., Allweston, Folke, Dorset, 1693, W, P5/1693/28
Thos., basketmaker, Ruscombe, Berks., 1628, I, W, P5/1628/48, P5/11Reg/77
Wm., Horningsham, 1592, AB, I, W, P5/1592/36, P5/6Reg/2C
Wm., husb., Uffc., Devon, 1669, AB, I, P20/1/56
Wm., Sal., 1773, AB, P1/G/693
see also Gutteridge
Goodrose, Goodrous, Francis, Boreham, Warm., 1634, comm, I, W, P2/G/253

Francis, sen., Boreham, Warm., 1670, AB, comm, P2/G/363
Wm., gent., Boreham, Warm., [1674], I, W, P2/G/383
Goodson, Geo., husb., Coleshill, Berks., [1612], W, P1/G/37
Goodwin *see* Godwin
Goodyear, Hy., clerk and curate, Bulford, 1610, AB, I, T, NW, P2/G/138, P2/8Reg/113A
Hy., blacksmith, Marston, Pott., 1684, AB, I, P1/G/255
Jn., shoemaker, Poulshot, 1630, I, W, P2/G/230, P2/9Reg/81A
My., widow, Poulshot, 1619, I, W, P2/G/186
Goodeares, Sam., Poulshot, 1702, AB, I, P2/G/595
Sam., yeo., Marston, Pott., 1705, I, W, P1/G/335
Wm., curate, Poulshot, 1613, I, P1/G/42
Gooes *see* Goss
Goord *see* Goard
Gootheridge *see* Gutteridge
Gordon, Jn., rector, Lt. Cheverell, 1735, AB, P1/G/509
Mgt., widow, Froxfield Almshouse, 1746, I, W, P3/G/617
My., widow, Wingfield, 1815, AB, comm, Wr (form. My. Mullings, widow), P2/1815/7
Thos., Wingfield, 1804, AB, comm, P1/1804/42
Gore, Alice, Broughton G., 1570, W, P2/5Reg/95D
Cecily, widow, Trowb., 1627, I, W, P22/1/10
Edith, widow, Broughton G., 1559, W, P2/3Reg/154A
Eliz., widow, Chipp., 1752, comm, W, P3/G/644
Jas., preacher of the gospel, Bradford A., 1798, W, P1/G/769, P1/15Reg/150B
Jas., tea dealer, Endless St., Sal., 1854, aff, W, Wr, P4/1854/6
Joan, Broughton G., 1705, AB, I, ren, P2/G/617
Jn., husb., Steeple A., 1568, W, P2/5Reg/36A
Jn., husb., Keevil, 1598, I, W, P2/G/98
Jn., weaver, Broughton G., 1785, AB, ren, P2/G/1032
Nich., yeo., Broughton G., 1610, AB, comm, I, W, P2/G/140, P2/8Reg/117
Nich., sen., fuller, Broughton G., [1670], W, P2/G/359
Nich., yeo., Broughton G., 1675, comm, I, W, P2/G/386
Nich., clothier, Broughton G., 1697, I, W, P2/G/563
Richd., blacksmith, Fonthill G., 1782, W, P2/G/1014
Robt., Lt. Somerford, 1635, I, W, P3/G/139
Thos., Broughton G., 1550, W, P2/2Reg/104B
Thos., gent., Sherston, 1603, I, W, P3/G/2
Thos., yeo., Broughton G., 1640, I, W, P2/G/288
Thos., yeo., Broughton G., 1683, AB, comm, I, P2/G/460
Thos., Uffc., Devon, 1798, AB, comm, ren, P20/1/274
Thos., Uffc., Devon, 1830, limited admon, O, Wr, P5/1830/17
Thos., yeo., Broughton G., 1854, aff, O, W, Wr, P2/1854/23
Wm., Franklyn, Broughton G., 1542, W (NEP), P2/1Reg/45B
Wm., yeo., Broughton G., 1584, W, P2/6Reg/113F
Wm., husb., Trowle, Bradford A., 1598, W, P2/G/89
Wm., yeo., Broughton G., 1616, I, W, P1/G/60
Wm., sen., husb., Paxcroft, Steeple A., [1619], I, W, P2/G/188
Wm., husb., Hudswell, Corsham, 1621-22, AB, W, P29/G/7, P29/1Reg/99
Wm., yeo., Broughton G., 1671, AB, comm, NW, P2/G/365
Goring, Jos., dairyman, Enmore Grn, Motc., Dorset, 1830, W, Wr, P5/1830/26
Gorman, Agnes, widow, Longbridge D., 1620, I, T, P2/G/190
Edwd., husb., Warm., 1647, I, T, NW, P2/G/313
Jn., husb. and shepherd, Maiden B., 1589, I, W, P2/G/43
Goroway *see* Gorway
Gorrard *see* Gerrard
Gorton, Edmd., jun., Highw., 1683, W, P10/1683/4
Jane, widow, Highw., 1675, AB, comm, P10/1675/6
Jn., baker, Highw., 1746, AB, I, ren, P5/1746/34
My., widow, Highw., 1675, I, W, P10/1675/4
Richd., innholder, Highw., 1675, AB, I (named rooms in inn), P10/1675/5
Richd., blacksmith, Eastrop, Highw., 1727, AB, W, P10/1727/1, 4

Thos., blacksmith, Highw., 1593, AB, I, W, P5/1593/37, P5/6Reg/35B
Thos., sen., victualler, Highw., 1662, I, W, P5/1662/53
Gorway, Agnes, widow, Hurst, Berks., 1632, AB, a/c, I, P5/1631/40, P5/11Reg/175A
Andrew, Hurst, Berks., 1585, I, W, P5/1584/9, P5/4Reg/98B
Chris., Hurst, Berks., 1564, W, P5/1Reg/75D
Goroway, Chris., husb., Twyford, Hurst, Berks., 1627, I, W, P5/1627/21, P5/11Reg/49A
Eliz., widow, Hurst, Berks., 1566, W, P5/1Reg/72C
Eliz., widow, Hinton, Hurst, Berks., 1573, W, P5/3Reg/5D
Faith, widow, Wootton B., 1619, I, W, P1/G/71
Joan, Hurst, Berks., 1548, W, P5/20Reg/97B
Jn., Hurst, Berks., 1539, W, P5/20Reg/4
Ralph, Twyford, Hurst, Berks., 1588, I, W, P5/1588/24, P5/5Reg/36
Goroway, Ralph, shoemaker, Twyford, Hurst, Berks., 1647, AB, comm, I, P5/1647/6
Richd., Hurst, Berks., 1554, W, P5/20Reg/127
Richd., yeo., Hurst, Berks., 1615, W, P5/9Reg/121
Richd., Hurst, Berks., 1545-48, W, P5/20Reg/71A, 96
Thos., Hurst, Berks., 1546, W, P5/20Reg/72B
Thos., yeo., Hurst, Berks., 1598, AB, I, W, P5/1598/19, P5/6Reg/205
Wm., yeo., Wootton B., 1607, I, W, P3/G/9, P3/2Reg/17B
Gosemore *see* Gosmore
Goslett, Ann, widow, Sherston, 1728, W, P3/G/516
Arthur, yeo., Sherston, 1701, W, Wr, P3/G/403
Chas., yeo., Foxham, Bremhill, 1702, I, W, P3/G/405
Dorothy, widow, Sherston, 1693, I, W, P3/G/365
Hester, sp., Sherston, 1690, AB, P3/G/348
Jas., Devizes, 1604, T (children: Jn. & Jas. G.), P1/G/11
Jn., yeo., Sherston, 1701, I, W, P3/G/404
Philip, Sherston, 1786, W, P3/G/741
Wm., yeo., Sherston, 1682, W, P3/G/284
Wm., sen., servant, Littlecote, Rams., 1730, AB, I, ren, P5/1730/28
Gosling, Andrew, curate, Stert, Urchf., 1547, W, P2/2Reg/74B
Eliz., widow, Swindon, 1824, W, Wr, P3/1824/17
Francis, Chute, 1627, AB, P7/13
Francis, widower, Chute, 1723, AB, I, P7/118
Jn., Bloxworth, Dorset, 1625, I (2), P5/1625/37
Jn., Collingbourne K., 1643, AB, a/c, I, P3/G/169
Jn., yeo., Lt. Bedwyn, 1667, I, W, P5/1667/23
Jn., sen., yeo., Shrivenham, Berks., 1674, comm, I, W, P1/G/228
Jn., shopkeeper, Swindon, 1796, comm, W, P3/G/763
Jn., cordw., Tidcombe, T. and Fosbury, 1796, W, P3/G/764
Jn., gent., Swindon, 1831, comm, W, Wr, P3/1831/62
Robt., rugweaver, Reading, Berks., 1723, W, P1/G/428, P1/7Reg/8B
Rowland, Gillingham, Dorset, 1580, LA, P27/2Reg/1B
Thos., cordw., Chute, 1693, AB, I, P7/59
Thos., Hankerton, 1837, AB, Wr, P3/1837/83
Wm., Bloxworth, Dorset, 1575, AB, P5/3Reg/52C
Wm., husb., Ogbourne St A., 1575, W, P5/3Reg/51A
Wm., Ham, 1602, W, P3/1Reg/93B
Wm., sen., husb., Ham, 1623, I, W, P3/G/81
Gosmore, Edith, sp., Chr. M., 1699, comm, I, W, P3/G/395
Gosemore, Nich., husb., Sherston, 1614, I, W, P1/G/44
Richd., Milbourne, Malm., 1647, I, W, P1/G/159
Wm., Sherston, 1679, AB, P3/G/268
Gosney, Betty, sp., Sherb., Dorset, 1811, comm, W, Wr, P5/1811/21
Jn., husb., Barford St M., 1665, AB, I, P2/G/339
Michael, husb., Haydon, Dorset, 1629, I, W, P5/1629/23, P5/11Reg/106A
Richd., Barford St M., 1628, a/c (2), AB, comm, I, proclamation, P1/G/99
Gasney, Wm., Sal., 1853, AB, Wr, P4/1853/11
Gossney, Wm. Geo., schoolmaster, Bedwin St., Sal., 1848, appt of proctor, D, ren, W, Wr, P4/1848/4
Goss, Ann, widow, Pott., 1825, AB, Wr, P1/1825/8

Jn., sen., Lyme R., Dorset, 1589, I, T, W, P5/1589/23, P5/5Reg/55D
Jn., sen., yeo., Bramshaw, Hants, 1638, I, W, P24/292
Jos., clerk and apparitor, Pott., 1819, W, Wr, P1/1819/13
Richd., husb., Plaitford, 1559, W, P2/4Reg/14C
Thos., husb., Bramshaw, Hants, 1560, W, P2/4Reg/50A
Gooes, Wm., Burnford, Bramshaw, Hants, 1577, I, W, P5/1576/22, P5/3Reg/101D
Wm., sen., husb., Over C., Dorset, 1597, I, W, P5/1597/49, P5/6Reg/174C
Gossney *see* Gosney
Gost *see* Ghost
Goswell, Edmd., Hurst, Berks., 1569, W, P5/2Reg/52C
Jn., Hurst, Berks., 1547, W, P5/20Reg/87
Mgt., widow, Hurst, Berks., 1545, W, P5/20Reg/66B
My., sp., Sindlesham, Hurst, Berks., 1829, AB, O, Wr, P5/1829/11
Ralph, yeo., Hurst, Berks., 1573, W, P5/3Reg/15C
Ralph, Hurst, Berks., 1630-31, AB, a/c, P5/1631/126, P5/11Reg/148
Robt., Swallowfield, Shinfield, Berks., 1776, AB, P1/G/699
Thos., Hurst, Berks., [1550], W (NEP), P5/20Reg/114B
Wm., Hurst, Berks., 1556, W, P5/20Reg/149A
Gotfer, Gotfer alias Pearce, Robt., husb., Benham, Speen, Berks., 1619, I, W, P1/G/73
Gothard, Wm., labourer, Langham, Gillingham, Dorset, 1783, W, P27/1/515, P27/3Reg/229
Gothridge *see* Gutteridge
Gotley *see* Goatley
Gouene *see* Gawen
Gough, Cath., widow, Sal., 1719, W, P4/1718/24
Goff, Chas., Tidpit, Martin, Hants, 1625-27, AB, a/c, I, P2/G/207
Goffe, Chris., glover, Gillingham, Dorset, 1683, I, P27/1/76
Eleanor, widow, Mere, 1677, I, NW, P5/1677/24
Eliz., widow, Sal., 1692, I, W, P4/1692/7
Eliz., Devizes, 1766, W, P1/G/657, P1/12Reg/180A
Goffe, German, Halstock, Dorset, 1629, AB, a/c, I, P5/1629/22, P5/11Reg/20C
Goffe, German, Halstock, Dorset, 1735, AB, P5/1735/24
Hugh, woollen draper, Devizes, 1754, W, P1/G/609, P1/11Reg/154
Jacob, labourer, Catcomb, Hilmarton, 1791, W, P3/G/756
Jane, widow, Gt. Cheverell, 1630, W, P2/G/229, P2/9Reg/78
Jane, widow, *The Crown Inn*, Red Hill, Calne, 1781, W, P26/1116
Jane, Pewsham Forest, 1788, AB, P5/1788/10, P5/18Reg/96A
Goffe, Jerome, yeo., Stockton, 1675, I, W, P2/G/388
Goffe, Joan, widow, Fonthill G., 1543, W (NEP), P2/1Reg/40B
Joan, clerk's wife, Erlestoke, 1709, W, P1/G/351, P1/5Reg/9
Goffe, Joan, widow, Stockton, 1721, W, P2/G/705
Goffe, Joan, sp., Halstock, Dorset, 1738, AB, I, paper (2), W, Wr (2), P5/1738/19
Joan, widow, W. Lavington, 1741, W, P1/G/532, P1/9Reg/20
Jn., innholder, Sal. St Edmd., 1561-62, W, P1/2Reg/128C, 130
Goffe alias Thomas, Jn., Damerham, Hants, 1590, I, W, P2/G/52
Jn., Sal., 1696, AB, ren, P4/1695/4
Jn., Trowle, Bradford A., 1722, AB, P2/G/712
Jn., yeo., Compton B., 1727, I, W, P3/G/505
Goffe, Jn., Halstock, Dorset, 1728, AB, P5/1728/39, P5/16Reg/170A
Goff, Jn., victualler, Reading, Berks., 1741, W, P1/G/540, P1/9Reg/110
Jn., W. Lavington, 1746, AB, P1/G/564
Goff, Jn., Bourton, Gillingham, Dorset, 1781, AB, P27/1/509, P27/3Reg/219B
Jn., yeo., Chipp., 1854, AB, D, O, Wr, P3/1854/14
Jos., yeo., Upton S., 1783, W, P2/G/1019
Judith, widow, Mildenhall, 1725, W, P3/G/495
Mgt., widow, Whitbourne, Corsley, 1586, W, P2/7Reg/55A
Goffe, Martha, widow, Halstock, Dorset, 1740, W, Wr, P5/1740/34
Martha, widow, Sandy Lane, Calne, 1791, W, P3/G/757
My., widow, E. Tytherton, Bremhill, 1669, I, W, P3/G/204
My., Chr. M., 1690, AB, comm, I, P3/G/347
My., widow, Derry House, Pewsham, 1713, AB, I, P5/1713/29

My., widow, Bourton, Gillingham, Dorset, 1839, W, Wr, P27/1/722
Matthew, victualler, Redhill, Pewsham, 1758, W, P3/G/662
Nathaniel, currier, Devizes, 1769, W, P1/G/667, P1/12Reg/284B
Nathaniel, innkeeper, Warm., 1786, W, P1/G/731, P1/14Reg/152
Peter, Halstock, Dorset, 1597, AB, I, P5/1597/48, P5/6Reg/176A
Goffe alias Thomas, Peter, yeo., Damerham, Hants, 1707, AB, W, P2/G/627
Richd., Burton Hill, Malm., 1739, W, P1/G/528, P1/8Reg/390B
Richd., Catcomb, Hilmarton, 1829, AB, comm, Wr, P3/1829/8
Goffe, Robt., yeo., Catcomb, Hilmarton, 1696, I, W, P3/G/380
Robt., goldsmith, Marl., 1706, W, P1/G/338
Robt., Compton B., 1718, AB, P3/G/460
Robt., husb., W. Lavington, 1732, W, P1/G/487, P1/7Reg/525A
Goffe, Robt., Goatacre, Hilmarton, 1742, W, P3/G/598
Roger, cordw., Shaftesbury, Dorset (effects at Damerham), 1785, W, P2/G/1030
Sarah, wife, Plaitford, 1815, AB, P2/1815/43
Sarah, widow, Grittenham, Brinkw., 1854, AB, aff, D, O, ren, Wr, P3/1854/16
Silas, carp., Warm., 1830, W, P2/1830/34
Susanna, widow, All C., 1665, comm, I, W, P3/G/184
Thos., Corsley, 1580, W, P2/5Reg/361B
Thos., labourer, Wantage, Berks., 1687, AB, I, P23/159
Goffe, Thos., yeo., Stockton, [1690], I, P2/G/528
Thos., Chr. M., 1692, AB, P3/G/359
Goffe, Thos., victualler, Mere, 1698, AB, comm, I, P5/1697/18
Goffe, Thos., Wylye, 1719, AB, P2/G/699
Thos., sen., yeo., Catcomb Farm, Hilmarton, 1815, comm, W, Wr, P3/1815/80
Thos., Grittenham, Brinkw., 1837, AB, comm, Wr, P3/1837/16
Goffe, Wm., Bremhill Grove, Bremhill, 1663, comm, I, W, P1/G/186
Goffe, Wm., yeo., Mere, 1672, I, W, P5/1672/14
Wm., goldsmith, Marl., 1695, W, P1/G/287
Wm., weaver, Compton B., 1698, I, W, P3/G/392
Wm., yeo., Milbourne, Malm., 1702, AB, ren, P3/G/412
Goffe, Wm., Gillingham, Dorset, 1737, AB, Wr, P27/1/353
Gough alias Thomas, Wm., sen., cordw., Damerham, Hants, 1747, W, P2/G/859
Wm., sen., Marl., [1794], AB, P1/14Reg/501A
Wm., goldsmith, Marl., 1759, AB, limited AB, comm, P1/G/625
Wm., Stockley, Calne, 1779, AB, P5/1779/7, P5/17Reg/168A
Wm., Calne, 1801, AB, P26/1232
Wm., Bourton, Gillingham, Dorset, 1815, AB, P27/1/631
Wm., broker, Bradford A., 1837, AB, O, ren, W, Wr, P2/1837/88
Wm., carp. and joiner, Calne, 1849, comm, W, Wr, P5/1849/17
see also Thomas alias G.
Gouinge *see* Gawen
Gould, Golde, Alice, widow, Bere R., Dorset, 1589, AB, I, W, P5/1588/26, P5/5Reg/47B
Ann Rhodes, Sal., 1844, AB, Wr, P1/1844/9
Gold, Chas., husb., Aldbourne, 1750, W, P1/G/589, P1/10Reg/385
Chas., yeo., Beer Hackett, Dorset, 1797, W, P5/1797/17
Gold, Constance, Edith & Edmd. *see* Jn. Reeves
Gold, Edwd., Devizes, 1605, AB, I, P1/G/16
Gould *or* Gold, Edwd., yeo., Donhead St My., 1662, AB, I, P1/G/181
Eliz., widow, Donhead St My., 1718, W, P2/G/690
Gold, Eliz., singlewoman, Broad C., 1756, W, P1/G/612, P1/11Reg/201A
Eliz., widow, Bower C., 1825, AB, Wr, P2/1825/31
Flora, sp., Durnford, 1845, D, note, W, Wr, P5/1845/11
Geo., victualler, Bere R., Dorset, 1621, comm, I, W, P5/1621/10, P5/10Reg/21
Geo., grocer, Chipp., 1748, W, P3/G/628
Geo., yeo., Chipp., 1802, W, P3/1802/54
Hy., husb., Bere R., Dorset, 1634, AB, I(GVD), P5/1634/41
Hy., Downton, [1679], I, W, P2/G/423
Jas., Donhead St My., 1786, AB, P2/G/1033
Jas., yeo., Beer Hackett, Dorset, 1797, W, P5/18Reg/249

Jane, widow, Donhead St A., [1676], I, W, P2/G/390
Jane, widow, E. Stowell, Wilcot, 1706, AB, I, P3/G/423
Jane, widow, Bower C., 1737, W, P2/G/806
Jane, widow, Fisherton A., 1766, W, P2/G/950
Jane, Woolbridge, Dorset (effects at Longbridge D.), 1832, AB, Wr, P1/1832/139
Joel, rodman, Aldermaston, Berks., 1832, comm, W, Wr, P1/1832/138
Jn., husb., Holnest, Dorset, 1607, AB, a/c, comm, I, P5/1606/18, P5/8Reg/86B, 93E
Jn., carp., Bere R., Dorset, 1627, AB, I, T, W, P5/1627/22, P5/11Reg/36B
Gold, Jn., sen., husb., Bere R., Dorset, 1638, AB, I, W, P5/1638/49, P5/13Reg/88C
Jn., husb., Bere R., Dorset, 1640, I, W, P5/1640/25, P5/13Reg/268B
Jn., husb., Overton, 1661, I, W, P3/G/173, P3/3Reg/22B
Gold, Jn., yeo., Kingston Bagpuize, Berks., 1671, I, W, P1/G/218
Gold *or* Gould, Jn., yeo., Bower C., 1683, AB, I, W, P2/G/461
Jn., sen., Shitterton, Bere R., Dorset, 1685, AB, I, ren, P5/1685/37
Gold, Jn., Sonning, Berks., 1738, AB, Wr, P5/1738/20
Jn., yeo., Warm., 1743, W, P2/G/843
Jn., sen., Bere R., Dorset, 1754, W, P5/1754/10
Jn., glover, Mere, 1755, AB, ren, P5/1755/19
Jn., sen., Bere R., Dorset, 1761, W, P5/1761/15
Jn., yeo., Bower C., 1769, W, P2/G/958
Jn., sen., Nether C., Dorset, 1804, W, P5/19Reg/101
Jn., jun., Nether C., Dorset, 1804, W, P5/1804/8
Jn., innholder, Chipp., 1811, W, Wr, P1/1811/97
Jn., Bere R., Dorset, 1825, W, Wr, P5/1825/24
Jn., Bere R., Dorset, 1830, O, W, Wr, P5/1830/2
Jn., blacksmith, Bower C., 1839, W, Wr, P2/1839/21
Gold, Jos., yeo., Damerham, Hants, 1717, W, P2/G/684
Jos., Damerham, Hants, 1731, AB, I, P2/G/770
Jos., Cholsey, Berks., 1732, AB, P1/G/480
Jos., Broad C., 1750, W, P2/G/876
Joshua, yeo., Middleton, Norton B., 1734, W, P2/G/790
Josiah, yeo., Broad C., 1804, W, P2/1804/17
Josiah, mason, Ebbesborne Wake, 1839, W, Wr, P2/1839/4
Lawr., fishmonger, Sal., 1614, I, W (damaged), P4/1614/4
Gold, Magdalen, widow, Sal., 1692, I, NW, P1/G/276
Martha, widow, Chipp., 1803, AB, P3/1803/56
My., widow, Bere R., Dorset, 1640, I, W, P5/1640/23, P5/13Reg/227C
My., widow, Langdon, Beam., Dorset, 1756, W, P17/520
My., widow, Mere, 1774, W, P5/1774/7, P5/17Reg/79A
My., sp., Sal. The Close, 1798, W, P5/1798/8, P5/18Reg/270A
My., widow, Thornford, Dorset, 1843, comm, D, W, Wr, P5/1843/27
Nich., yeo., Bower C., 1736, W, P2/G/799
Nich., yeo., Bower C., 1772, W, P2/G/973
Rebecca, widow, Broad C., 1762, W, P2/G/925
Gold *or* Gould, Richd., husb., Ogbourne St A., 1677, I, W, P5/1677/21
Richd., Stourpaine, Dorset, 1741, AB, I, W, P24/993
Richd., yeo., Bower C., 1822, W, Wr, P2/1822/1
Robt., husb., Bloxworth, Dorset, 1588, I, W, P5/1588/20, P5/5Reg/15B
Robt., tailor, Bere R., Dorset, 1592-93, AB, W, P5/6Reg/10A, 11B
Robt., Dauntsey, 1705, AB, I, P3/G/420
Gold, Robt., sen., yeo., Wokefield, Stratfield M., Berks., 1726, I, W, P1/G/442, P1/7Reg/90A
Robt., yeo., Broad C., 1737-52, req., copy W, P2/G/802
Roger, Bere R., Dorset, 1613, I, W, P5/1613/31, P5/9Reg/86
Sampson, yeo., Bere R., Dorset, 1805, W, P5/1805/17, P5/19Reg/139
Sarah, dame and widow, Sal., 1733, AB, ren (2), P1/G/491
Thos., husb., Bere R., Dorset, 1609-10, I, W, P5/1610/25, P5/8Reg/161B
Thos., yeo., Berwick St Jn., 1639, I, W, P2/G/283
Gold, Thos., yeo., Donhead St A., 1646, AB, I, P2/G/311
Thos., yeo., Donhead St A., 1664, AB, I, P1/G/194
Gold, Thos., Bodenham, Nunton and B., 1682, AB, I, P2/G/451

Thos., yeo., Donhead St A., 1749, W, P2/G/875
Thos., wheelwright, Chipp., 1752, W, P3/G/645
Thos., Sutton M., 1754, W, P2/G/893
Thos., clothworker, Chipp., 1759, W, P3/G/663
Thos., baker, Bere R., Dorset, 1784, W, P5/1784/6, P5/17Reg/258C
Thos., yeo., Donhead St A., 1827, I, W, Wr, P2/1827/65
Thos., yeo., Aldbourne, 1836, comm, W, Wr, P3/1836/73
Wm., tailor, Mere, 1620-21, I, W, P5/1620/26, P5/10Reg/96
Wm., Stratton, Dorset, 1663, AB, comm, I, P5/1663/28
Wm., Barford St M., 1730, AB, P2/G/761
Wm., yeo., Stallen, Nether C., Dorset, 1763, W, P5/1763/8
Wm., yeo., Nether C., Dorset, 1769, W, P5/1769/11
Wm., maltster and baker, Chipp., 1786, W, P3/G/742
Wm., tanner, Pound Hill, Corsham, 1824, W, Wr, P3/1824/47
Wm., Thornford, Dorset, 1831, AB, comm, Wr, P5/1831/3
Wm., woollen draper, Sal., 1848, note, W, Wr, P4/1848/5
Wm., sen., bach., Aldbourne, 1849, AB, comm, Wr, P3/1849/24
see also Hawkins alias G.; Lockyer alias G.
Goulden *see* Golding
Goulder, Thos., yeo., Reading St My., Berks., 1711, W, P1/G/361, P1/5Reg/174
Goulding *see* Golding
Gouldisborough *see* Goldisborough
Gouldney *see* Goldney
Gouldring *see* Goldring
Goulstone *see* Goldstone
Goulton *see* Galton
Gourde *see* Goard
Goustone *see* Gunstone
Gover, Avis, widow, Nether C., Dorset, 1632, AB, P5/1632/24, P5/12Reg/111B
Giver, Hy., husb., Beer Hackett, Dorset, 1620, I, W, P5/1620/24, P5/10Reg/8
Joan, widow, Sherb., Dorset, 1584, I, P5/1584/10, P5/4Reg/92B
Jn., carp., Stratton, Dorset, 1585, NW, P5/4Reg/104B
Mgt., widow, Eastrop, Highw., 1603, note, W, draft NW, P5/1603/32, P5/7Reg/86A
Richd., carrier, Beam., Dorset, 1696, I, W, P17/357
Simon, Eastrop, Highw., 1588, I, W, P5/1588/22 (noticed missing, 27.8.2004), P10/1588/4, P5/5Reg/8D
Walter, sen., parchmentmaker, Sherb., Dorset, 1612, I, W, P5/1611/17, P5/9Reg/57C
Wm., Nether C., Dorset, 1618, AB, I, P5/1618/17
Govis *see* Jervis
Gowden, Joel, yeo., Compton C., 1807, W, Wr, P2/1807/9
Gowen *see* Gawen
Gower, Sarah, sp., Mere, 1741, W, Wr, P5/1741/16
Gowre, Wm., Corsham, 1622, note of probate, P29/1Reg/92B
Gowge *see* Gudge
Gowle, Wm., husb., Stratton, Dorset, 1592-97, AB, a/c, I, T, P5/1592/37, P5/1597/46, P5/6Reg/6A
Gowre *see* Gower
Grace, Agnes, widow, Newton T., 1586, I, W, P2/G/37, P2/7Reg/30B
Edwd., sen., miller, Fordington, Dorset, 1713, AB, ren, W, P5/1713/35, P5/15Reg/378B
Eliz., widow, Sal., 1755, AB, W, P4/1755/8
Eliz., sp., Manningford Bruce, 1756, W, P1/G/615, P1/11Reg/267
Eliz., sp., Collingbourne D., 1824, W, Wr, P21/12/42
Hy., carp., Sal., 1744, W, P4/1743/12
Jn., Amesb., 1606, I, W, P1/G/20
Jn., Newton T., 1614, I, W, P1/G/40
Jn., carp., Compton C., 1796, AB, W, P2/G/1068
Jn., yeo., Winterslow, 1824, W, P2/1824/86
Jos., tailor, Pidgeons House, Blewbury, Berks., 1848, D, O, W, Wr, P5/1848/17
Malachi, Blewbury, Berks., 1852, O, W, Wr, P5/1852/5
Margery, widow and shopkeeper, Manningford Bruce, 1767, AB, W (ren on back), P3/G/686
Maurice, carp., Sal., 1732, AB, I, ren, P4/1732/7
Richd., Urchf., 1550, W, P2/2Reg/104A

Richd., innholder, Amesb., 1592, a/c, I, T, P2/G/64
Robt., yeo., Collingbourne D., 1843, W, Wr, P1/1843/27
Sam., gent., Manningford Bruce, 1735, W, P3/G/563
Thos., husb., Newton T., 1579, W, P2/5Reg/328A
Thos., sen., Netheravon, 1821, W, Wr, P5/1821/26
Timothy, labourer, Gt. Amesb., 1640, I, W, P2/G/287
Wm., E. Harnham, Britford, 1682, AB, I, P24/408
Wm., yeo., Compton C., 1744, W, P1/G/552, P1/9Reg/295
Wm., sen., yeo., Manningford Bruce, 1748, W, P3/G/629
Grafton, Hy., sexton, Sal. St Edmd., 1621, I, W, P4/1621/13
Jn., Horton, Bps. C., 1625, AB, I (2), NW, P24/178
Mgt., Sonning, Berks., 1554, court proceedings (penance imposed on Mgt. G. for fornication), P5/20Reg/117A
Mgt., sp., Devizes, 1668, I, W, P1/G/206
My., Sal., 1676, AB, a/c, I, P4/1676/11
Richd., Marl., 1626, AB, W, P1/G/96
Richd., Bourton, Bps. C., 1632, AB, a/c (2), guardianship bond (2), I, P24/250
Richd., maltster, Sal., 1674, AB, a/c, I, P4/1674/11
Graham, My., widow, Trowb., 1836, AB, comm, P1/1836/19
Robt., apothecary, Sal., 1740, W, P4/1740/3
Robt., grocer, Wantage, Berks., 1800, comm, W, P23/821
Robt., victualler, Trowb., 1816, W, Wr, P1/1816/14
Rose, widow, Calne, 1753, W, P26/914
Wm., cheesemonger, Reading, Berks., 1738, W, P1/G/522, P1/8Reg/278
Wm., maltster, Patford St., Calne, 1749, W, P5/1749/23
Graile, David, yeo., Garsdon, 1640, I, W, P3/G/163
Grayle, Hy., tucker, Malm., 1620, I, W (2 - 1 a copy), P3/G/65
Grayle, Hy., tucker *or* fuller, Westport St My., 1637, I, W, P3/G/150
Richd., shoemaker, Castleton, Dorset, 1583, I, W, P5/1583/17, P5/4Reg/65
Grayle, Thos., sen., Sherb., Dorset, 1613, AB, P5/1613/37, P5/9Reg/110D
Graily, Grayley, Jn., Durrington, 1572, W, P2/5Reg/151B
Grayley, Robt., yeo., Tinh., Edington, 1676, AB, I, P2/G/393
Grayley, Robt., yeo., Netherh., 1723, AB, ren, P1/G/419
Robt., maltster, Netherh., 1739, W, P2/G/811
Robt., yeo., Netherh., 1776, W, P2/G/989
Robt., maltster and farmer, Netherh., 1812, W, Wr, P2/1812/30
Robt., yeo., Alton Pr., 1827, W, Wr, P3/1827/4
Grainge *see* Grange
Grainger *see* Granger
Grammet, Grammet als Akerman, Alice, yeo.'s wife, Milton L., 1687, AB, P3/G/319
Ann, Marl. St My., 1688, I, NW, P1/G/775
Jn., labourer, Milton L., 1684, I, W, P3/G/295
Grannett, Thos., Enborne, Berks., 1723, AB, W, P1/G/429, P1/7Reg/27A
Thos., Boxford, Berks., 1770, AB, P1/G/674
Wm., Wootton R., 1592, AB, I, W, P1/G/3
Wm., millwright, Gt. Bedwyn, 1675, I, W, P21/2/44
Grandier, Mgt., widow, Sal., 1695, AB, I, P1/G/286
Grange, Grainge, Michael, stone mason, Malm., 1830, W, Wr, P3/1830/54
Richd., Sherb., Dorset, 1768, AB, comm, W, P5/1768/12-13
Robt., Chards., Devon, 1606, I, NW, P5/1606/20, P5/8Reg/69B
Susanna, innholder's widow, Sherb., Dorset, 1787, W, P5/1787/8, P5/18Reg/79
Thos., husb., Long Burton, Dorset, 1600, AB, I, P5/1600/24, P5/6Reg/254C
Granger, Andrew, labourer, Purton, 1852, comm, W, P3/1852/28
Ann, widow, Holnest, Dorset, 1682, comm, I, W, P5/1681/19
Benj., thatcher, Long Burton, Dorset, 1832, W, Wr, P5/1832/6
Grainger, Chas., yeo., Minety, 1829, W, Wr, P3/1829/29
Chris., yeo., Holnest, Dorset, 1664, I, W, P5/1664/16
Chris., Stourpaine, Dorset, 1694, AB, comm, P24/521
Chris., yeo., Haydon, Dorset, 1698, I, W, P5/1698/31
Chris., Stourpaine, Dorset, 1721, AB, comm, P24/892
Grainger, Edith, widow, Thornhill, Clyffe P., 1601, W, P3/1Reg/54B

Eliz., widow, Bushton, Clyffe P., 1632, I, W, P3/G/127
Eliz., widow, Haydon, Dorset, 1696, comm, I, W, P5/1696/19
Eliz., accountant's wife, Uffc., Devon (form. of Milverton, Somerset), 1836, AB, O, Wr, P5/1836/8
Hy., yeo., Haydon, Dorset, 1673, comm, I, W, P5/1672/15
Hy., yeo., Holnest, Dorset, 1705, I, W, P5/1705/22
Hy., sen., Holnest, Dorset, 1714, AB, I, P5/1714/14
Hugh, yeo., Holnest, Dorset, 1667, I, W, P5/1667/22
Hugh, yeo., Court House Farm, Thornford, Dorset, 1781, comm, W, P5/1781/7, P5/17Reg/214C
Joan, Haydon, Dorset, 1682, AB, comm, P5/1682/46
Jn., ex. of Calne, 1597, W, P5/1597/47
Jn., husb., Over C., Dorset, 1611, I, W, P5/1612/19, P5/9Reg/47
Jn., yeo., Over C., Dorset, 1677, I, W, P5/1677/23
Jn., sen., Holnest, Dorset, 1683, AB, comm, I, P5/1683/26
Jn., Billings Lane, Holnest, Dorset, 1709, W, P5/1709/14, P5/15Reg/107
Lucy, widow, Cuff's Corner, Calne, 1783, W, P26/1137
Moses, sen., yeo., Calne, 1766, W, P26/1017
Moses, yeo., Melk., 1784, W, P2/G/1022
Moses, yeo., Melk., 1801, comm, W, P2/1801/19
Noah, husb., Holnest, Dorset, 1679, W, P5/1679/30
Robt., Enmore Grn, Motc., Dorset, 1827, W, Wr, P5/1827/41
Robt., sen., yeo., Cuff's Corner, Calne, 1830, AB, ren, W, Wr, P26/1379
Robt., weaver, Poulshot, [1687], I, W, P2/G/506
Sam., cooper, Enmore Grn, Motc., Dorset, 1849, AB, comm, Wr, P19/256
Simon, Thornford, Dorset, 1841, AB, Wr, P5/1841/14
Granger alias Stevens, Thos., yeo., Dauntsey Park, 1643, I, W, P1/G/146
Thos., sen., Haydon, Dorset, 1719, I, W, P5/1719/37, P5/16Reg/19C
Thos., yeo., Haydon, Dorset, 1757, W, P5/1757/11
Thos., yeo., Haydon, Dorset, 1773, AB, comm, W, P5/1773/18, P5/17Reg/49D
Thos., Cuff's Corner, Calne, 1783, AB, W, P26/1136
Thos., yeo., Melk. Forest, 1805, comm, W, P2/1805/5
Wm., chandler, Calne, 1597, AB, I, P5/1597/54, P5/6Reg/159C
Wm., yeo., Ham, Broad Town, 1618, I, W, P3/G/57
Wm., husb., Long Burton, Dorset, 1620, I, W, P5/1620/22, P5/10Reg/76B
Wm., husb., Bagshot, Shalbourne (*also* of Hungerford, Berks.), 1720, I (2), W, P5/1720/21, P5/16Reg/43A
Wm., yeo., Cuff's Corner, Calne, 1762, W, P26/990
Wm., yeo., Sherb., Dorset, 1776, W, P5/1776/21, P5/17Reg/124A
Wm., yeo., Rodwell Farm, Hilmarton, 1795, W, P1/G/750, P1/14Reg/538
Wm., sen., farmer, Garsdon, 1828, W, Wr, P3/1828/63
Grannett *see* Gramett
Grant, Grant alias Day, Alice, Devizes, 1698, AB, P1/G/303
Alice, widow, Chitterne AS, 1773, W, P1/G/690, P1/12Reg/466A
Amy, Farleigh Wick, Monkton F., 1610, alleg, copy NW, P2/G/135
Ann, widow, Easterton, Mkt. L., 1808, W, Wr, P1/1808/48
Ann, sp., Winterbourne S., 1854, aff, W, Wr, P2/1854/75
Anna, widow, Mkt. L., 1837, O, W, Wr, P2/1837/60
Betty *see* Eliz.
Christian, widow, Sherb., Dorset, 1625, I, W, P5/1625/39, P5/10Reg/278B
Chris., weaver, Holt, Bradford A., 1626-27, a/c, I, copy I, T, NW, P2/G/210
Edith, Holt, Bradford A., 1602, I, P2/G/110
Edith, widow, Bishopstrow, 1733, AB, P2/G/785
Graunt, Edmd., Melk., 1610, T (unnamed children), P2/G/146
Edmd., clothworker, Leigh, Bradford A., 1704, I, W, P2/G/609
Edmd., gent., S. Wraxall, 1771, comm, W, P2/G/971
Graunt, Edwd., Whitley, Melk., 1610, AB, P2/8Reg/144B
Graunt, Edwd., yeo., Rodbourne, Malm., 1685, AB, I, P3/G/310
Eleazar, innkeeper, Rowde, 1762, W, P3/G/673
Eliz., widow, Bishopstrow, 1636, I, T, W, P2/G/259
Eliz., Avill's Farm, Corsham, 1647, W, P1/G/160
Eliz., widow, Rowde, 1780, W, P3/G/724
Eliz. *or* Betty, widow, Corsley, 1833, W, Wr, P2/1833/38

Geo., sen., yeo., Monkton F., 1642, AB, I, P2/G/296
Geo., yeo., Farleigh Wick, Monkton F., [1683], I, W, P2/G/473
Geo., clothier, Newtown, Bradford A., 1743, W, P2/G/837
Geo., sen., yeo., Westb., 1767, W, P25/1767/5
Geo., staymaker, Calne, 1771, W, P26/1042
Geo., yeo., Worton, Pott., 1829, O, W, Wr, P1/1829/10
Geo., wheelwright, Chapmanslade, Dilton, Westb., 1839, comm, W, Wr, P25/1839/1
Geo., farmer, Winterbourne S., 1840, W, Wr, P2/1840/4
Hy., Hawkeridge, Westb., 1644, comm, I, W, P25/1644/2
Hy., sen., yeo., Westb. L., 1732, W, P25/1732/1
Jacob, yeo., Winterbourne S., 1853, W, Wr, P2/1853/38
Jas., ropemaker, Malm., 1857, aff, O, W, Wr, P3/1857/21
Jane, Chitterne AS, 1818, AB, P2/1818/12
Jane, Chitterne AS, 1828, AB, P2/1828/21
Joan, widow, Holt, Bradford A., 1590, W, P2/G/48
Joan, widow, Stockton, [1687], a/c, W, P2/G/501
Joan, widow, Chipp., 1695, AB, I, P3/G/375
Graunt, Jn., husb., Erlestoke, 1606, I, W, P2/G/120
Jn., Holt, Bradford A., 1607, I, P2/G/126
Jn., Holt, Bradford A., 1627, AB, I, P2/G/214
Jn., shepherd, Lockeridge, Overton, 1627, I, W, P3/G/98
Graunt, Jn., husb., Erlestoke, 1642, I, W, P2/G/298
Jn., Hindon, 1682, AB, P2/G/454
Jn., Westwood, 1686, AB, P2/G/496
Graunt, Jn., weaver, Leighs Marsh, Dilton, Westb., 1690, I, W, P25/1690/6
Jn., feltmaker, Chipp., 1691, AB, ren, P3/G/352
Jn., Monkton F., 1709, AB, P2/G/629
Jn., weaver, Bradford A., 1710, W, P2/G/632
Jn., surgeon, Devizes, 1715, AB, I, P1/G/387
Jn., yeo., Staverton Wick, Trowb., 1717, I, NW, P2/G/686
Jn., Monkton F., 1724, AB, P1/G/434
Grant alias Bedford, Jn., broad weaver, Warm., 1728, W, P2/G/752
Jn., scribbler, Trowb., 1773, W, P1/G/780
Jn., labourer, Westb., 1778, W, P25/1778/4
Jn., carp., Mkt. L., 1824, W, Wr, P2/1824/79
Jn., sen., clerk, Chitterne AS, 1828, W, Wr, P2/1828/22
Jn., yeo., Shrewton, 1849, W, Wr, P2/1849/36
Jos., Longbridge D., 1743, AB, P2/G/838
Jos., plasterer, Warm., 1829, W, Wr, P2/1829/28
Leonard Bishop, gent., Easterton, Mkt. L., 1833, O, W, Wr, P2/1833/19
Mgt., widow, S. Wraxall, 1716, W, P2/G/677
Mark, Holt, Bradford A., 1575, W, P2/5Reg/218C
Mark, husb., Holt, Bradford A., 1598, I, W, P2/G/90
Mark, weaver, Studley, Trowb., 1628, I, W, P1/G/100
My., sp., Leigh, Bradford A., 1680, I, W, P1/G/243
My., widow, Tilsh., 1852, O, W, Wr, P2/1852/59
Nathaniel, slaymaker, Bradford A., 1766, AB (2), comm, P2/G/945
Richd., Holt, Bradford A., 1598, AB, I, P2/G/93
Richd., gent., Leigh, Bradford A., 1763, W, P1/G/644, P1/12Reg/120
Robt., yeo., Bradford A., 1689, I, W, P2/G/522
Robt., woolstapler, Bishopstrow, 1720, AB, I, ren, P1/G/401
Robt., scribler, Bradford A., 1766, AB, note, W, P2/G/946
Robt., bach., Lyneham, 1814, note, W, Wr, P3/1814/26
Roger, ropemaker, Westport St My., 1832, W, Wr, P1/1832/77
Sarah, sp., Bradford A., 1742, comm, W, P2/G/833
Grant alias Gunhill, Sarah, sp., Bratton, Westb., 1839, O, W, Wr, P25/1839/2
Sarah, widow, Hurst, Berks., 1840, W, Wr, P5/1840/19
Susanna, widow, Trowb., 1730, AB, P1/G/474
Graunt, Thos., Maddington, 1578, I, W, P2/G/27
Thos., Bradford A., 1578, AB (void, as decd had goods in several dioceses), P2/5Reg/319A

Graunt, Thos., husb., Erlestoke, 1591, I, W, P2/G/60
Thos., innholder, Sherb., Dorset, 1623, I, NW, P5/1623/12, P5/10Reg/212B
Graunt, Thos., Edington, 1639, a/c, P2/G/281
Thos., Hindon, 1680, AB, P2/G/431
Thos., blacksmith, Collingbourne K., 1711, AB, I, ren, P1/G/356
Thos., *The Grove*, Westb., 1845, comm, declaration, W, Wr, P25/1845/1
Thos., labourer, Snap, Aldbourne, 1846, aff, death cert., O, W, Wr, P3/1846/1
Walter, yeo., Monkton F., 1685, AB, a/c, I (2), P2/G/503
Walter, Bradford A., 1725, AB, P2/G/733
Walter, yeo., Staverton, Trowb., 1753, W, P1/G/599, P1/10Reg/508A
Wm., Bradford A., 1553, AB, P2/2Reg/172B
Wm., Tidpit, Martin, Hants, 1628, I, W, P2/G/226
Wm., Staverton, Trowb., 1678, AB, comm, P2/G/413
Wm., Bishopstrow, 1684, AB, I, P2/G/478
Wm., rough mason, Bradford A., 1718, W, P2/G/689
Wm., Widbrook, Bradford A., 1724, AB, W, P2/G/724
Wm., Mkt. L., 1761, AB, P2/G/919
Wm., yeo., Bratton, Westb., 1763, W, P25/1763/3
Wm., scribler, Trowb., 1765, W, P1/G/651, P1/12Reg/158
Wm., victualler, Westb., 1770, W, P25/1770/4
Wm., victualler, Warm., 1772, W, P2/G/974
Wm., butcher, Bratton, Westb., 1782, W, P25/1782/3
Wm., Dilton, Westb., 1785, AB, P25/1785/4
Wm., gent., Bourton Farm, Maddington, 1821, W, Wr, P2/1821/55
Wm., sen., Chapmanslade, Dilton, Westb., 1852, declaration, O, W, Wr, P25/1852/1
see also Applegate *or* Appledore alias G.
Grantham, Frances, widow, Seend, Melk., 1704, W, P1/G/327
Joan, widow, Seend, Melk., 1716, W, P1/G/392, P1/6Reg/39B
Jn., yeo., W. Dean, 1703, I, W, P2/G/597
My., Whitep., 1711, AB, P2/G/644
My., sp., Devizes, 1852, AB, O, ren, Wr, P1/1852/11
Peter, yeo., Seend, Melk., 1704, comm, I, W, P2/G/604
Peter, yeo., Seend, Melk., 1713, W, P2/G/660
Richd., sen., wheelwright, Woodspeen, Speen, Berks., 1692, I, W, P1/G/279
Grantland, Dorothy, wife, Uffc., Devon, 1752, W (form. widow of Chris. Knowlman *or* Knowman of Culmstock, Devon, sergemaker), P5/1752/23
Hugh, Uffc., Devon, 1574, W, P5/3Reg/30C
Jn., sen., yeo., Uffc., Devon, 1670, I, W, P20/1/60
Jn., sen., yeo., Uffc., Devon, 1725, W (& cod), P5/1725/29, P5/16Reg/115C
Jn., yeo., Uffc., Devon, 1752, W, P5/1752/22
Jn., Uffc., Devon, 1764, AB, P20/1/243
Wm., sen., yeo., Uffc., Devon, 1800, W, P5/1800/31, P5/18Reg/302B
Grape, Robt., jerseyman, Wokm., Berks., 1597, I, W, P5/1597/121, P5/6Reg/186C
Grately *see* Jarvis alias G.
Graunt *see* Grant
Grave, Cath., widow, Warfield, Berks., 1729, AB, I, P1/G/459
Dan., yeo., Warfield, Berks., 1711, W, P1/G/359, P1/5Reg/185B
Jn., yeo., Warfield, Berks., 1729, I, W, P1/G/457, P1/7Reg/269A
Rebecca, jun., widow, Warfield, Berks., 1729, AB, I, P1/G/460
Wm., yeo., Warfield, Berks., 1698, AB, I, P1/G/307
see also Hook alias G.
Gravell, Grevill, Eleanor, widow, Sherb., Dorset, 1615, I, W, P5/1615/14, P5/9Reg/165A
Francis, cordw., Coombe B., 1793, W, P8/68
Jane, widow, Burcombe, 1686, AB, P2/G/497
Jn., Barford St M., 1732, W, P1/G/490, P1/7Reg/565A
Jn., Coombe B., 1737, AB, P5/1737/24
Jn., Barford St M., 1749, AB, P2/G/871
Grivel, Jn., labourer, Crudwell, 1823, W, Wr, P1/1823/78
Richd., Rollestone, 1597, AB, I, P2/G/78
Gravell alias Burton, Robt., husb., Stoford, S. Newton, 1602, AB, I, W, P2/G/107

Thos., labourer, Coombe B., 1843, D, W, Wr, P8/92
Walter, yeo., S. Burcombe, [1687], I, W, P2/G/510
Wm., yeo., S. Burcombe, 1684, I, W, P2/G/482
Wm., sen., yeo., Barford St M., 1710, I, W, P2/G/640
Gravenar, Geo., Hilp., 1597, I, W, P2/G/81
Graves *see* Grave
Gray, Abigail, widow, Alderbury, 1704, AB, I, ren, W, P26/504
Agnes, widow, Semley, 1671, I, W, P2/G/364
Alexander, sen., labourer, Swindon, 1707, I, W, P3/G/427
Alexander, Swindon, 1752, AB, P3/G/646
Alexander, yeo., Netherh., 1775-90, AB, W, P2/G/981
Grey, Alice, widow, Baverstock, 1597, AB, I, W, P2/G/88
Grey, Alice, widow, Wilton, 1613, I (very detailed), W, P2/G/158
Arthur, yeo., Coombe B., 1734, AB, ren, P5/1734/30
Arthur, blacksmith, Melk., 1771-75, AB, comm, W, P2/G/972, 983
Betty, sp., Mere, 1810, W, Wr (2), P5/1810/13
Cath., Tisb., 1672, AB, P2/G/370
Cath., widow of chandler, Tisb., 1731, W, P2/G/765
Chas., petty chapman, Swindon, 1706, AB, I, P3/G/424
Chas., Sal., 1802, AB, P4/1802/12
Chas., miller, Urchf., 1817, comm, W, Wr, P1/1817/111
Chris., gent., Wilton, 1661, I, W (fragment), P2/G/324
Dan., yeo., Ford, Laverstock, 1734, W, P2/G/795
Dan., Ford, Laverstock, 1742, W, P2/G/826
Dan., rakemaker, Semley, 1764, W, P2/G/938
Dan., Semley, 1809, AB, Wr, P2/1809/69
David, yeo., Semley, 1787, W, P2/G/1038
Dorothy, widow, Wilton, 1645, AB, I, W, P2/G/305
Grey, Edith, widow, Semley, 1579, W, P2/5Reg/336A
Edith, widow, Teffont M., 1592, I, W, P2/G/63
Edith, widow, Foxley, 1679, I, W, P3/G/269
Grey, Edmd., husb., E. Hatch, Tisb., 1558, W, P2/3Reg/127B
Edmd., Martin, Hants, 1712, AB, W, P2/G/645
Edmd., Toyd Farm, Martin, Hants, 1742, AB, P2/G/832
Grey, Edwd., linen weaver, Semley, 1643, AB, I, ren, P2/G/303
Eliz., widow, Semley, 1614, AB, I, P2/G/165, P2/8Reg/246C
Eliz., widow, Coate, Liddington, 1706, AB, I, P3/G/425
Grey, Eliz., widow, E. Hatch, Tisb., 1721, W, P2/G/708
Eliz., widow, W. Harnham, 1739, W, P8/35
Eliz., widow, Maddington, 1776, W, P2/G/984
Eliz., sp., Downton, 1784, AB, P2/G/1023
Eliz., widow, Sal., 1850, AB, Wr, P2/1850/62
Frances, shepherd and husb., Ford, Laverstock, 1695, I, W, P1/G/289
Geo., yeo., Calstone W., 1614, I, W, P5/1614/26, P5/9Reg/133A
Grey, Geo., yeo., Semley, 1677-79, AB, alleg, I, W, P2/G/408, 430
Geo., jun., Calstone W., 1719, AB, I, W, P5/1719/32, P5/16Reg/21C
Grey, Geo., farmer, Alderbury, 1765, W, P26/1010
Geo., yeo., Bourton, Gillingham, Dorset, 1813, W, P27/1/620
Geo., yeo., Britford, 1828, W, Wr, P24/1310
Grey, Geo., tailor and salesman, Trowb., 1831, W, Wr, P1/1831/13
Gray alias Tomkins, Hannah, sadler's wife, Marl., 1710, AB, P1/G/353
Hy., Wilton, 1628, AB, I, P2/G/223
Hy., husb., Coate, Liddington, 1639, I, W, P3/G/157
Hy., [stone mason], Badbury Wick, Chiseldon, 1676, AB, a/c, I, P3/G/246
Hy., yeo., N. Burcombe, 1681, AB, a/c, I, P2/G/441
Grey, Hy., S. Burcombe, 1687, AB, P2/G/507
Hy., stone cutter, Badbury, Chiseldon, 1696, AB, I, P3/G/382
Hy., yeo., Chicksgrove, Tisb., 1798, W, P2/G/1074
Jas., Downton, 1704, AB, P2/G/606
Jas., Chicksgrove, Tisb., 1748, W, P2/G/866

Jas., yeo., E. Knoyle, 1784, W, P2/G/1021
Jas., Tisb. & Semley, 1806, AB, comm, P2/1806/34
Jas., weaver, Devizes, 1810, comm, W, Wr, P1/1810/3
Jas., smith, Fisherton A., 1812, W, Wr, P2/1812/46
Jas., gent., Netherh., 1820, W, Wr, P1/1820/30
Jas., Britford, 1826-37, AB (2), T, Wr (2), P24/1304
Jas., yeo., Tisb., 1830, W, Wr, P2/1830/56
Jas., gent., Devizes, 1831, O, W, Wr, P1/1831/15
Jas., smith, Fisherton A., 1848, AB, D, W, Wr (d. 1812), P2/1848/28
Jas., sen., yeo., E. Knoyle, 1848, comm, W, Wr, P2/1848/23
Jane, widow, Damerham, Hants, 1620, I, W, P2/G/189
Jane, sp., Sal., 1665, I, W, P4/1665/7
Jane, widow, Badbury Wick, Chiseldon, 1684, I, W, P3/G/296
Jane, widow, Amesb., 1710, W, P2/G/634
Jane, widow, Sal., 1767, AB, P4/1767/10
Jasper, Homington, 1676, AB, I, P24/492
Jasper, jun., tailor, Coombe B., 1713, W, P5/1713/28, P5/15Reg/361B
Joan, widow, Wilton, 1537, W (NEP), P2/1Reg/2A
Joan, widow, Sutton Poyntz, Dorset, 1593, W, P5/1592/39, P5/6Reg/20B
Joan, widow, Semley, 1597, AB, I, W, P2/G/85
Joan, Semley, 1668, I, W, P2/G/350
Joan, widow, Wilton, 1676-82, AB, a/c, P2/G/402
Joel, millwright, Fisherton A., 1849, W, Wr, P2/1849/42
Jn., Semley, 1562-63, I, W, P2/G/18, P2/4Reg/95B
Jn., husb., Teffont M., 1589, I, W, P2/G/45
Jn., Preston, Dorset, 1591, I, W, P5/1591/28, P5/5Reg/100C
Jn., sen., yeo., Semley, 1602, AB, I (2), W, P2/G/112
Grey, Jn., Coate, Liddington, 1608, I, W, P1/G/30
Jn., E. Ilsley, Berks., 1619, I, W, P1/G/72
Jn., husb., Tilsh., 1666, AB, I, P2/G/343
Jn., tailor, Homington, 1674, I, NW, P24/449
Jn., gunsmith, Wilton, 1683, I, W, P2/G/470
Jn., sen., tanner, Shaw, S. cum Donnington, Berks., 1683, I, W, P1/G/249
Jn., blacksmith, Swindon, 1688, AB, I, P3/G/331
Jn., yeo. *or* husb., Coate, Liddington, 1688, I, W (2 - 1 a copy), P3/G/330
Jn., yeo., Upper Stratton, Stratton St Mgt., 1716, AB, I, ren, W, P1/G/390, P1/6Reg/65
Jn., chandler, Tisb., 1723, I, W, P2/G/722
Grey, Jn., gent., Edington, 1723, W, P1/G/422, P1/6Reg/437
Jn., yeo., Over Stratton, Stratton St Mgt., 1730, W, P3/G/534
Jn., sen., Brightwalton, Berks., 1738, AB, P1/G/523
Jn., cordw., Baverstock, 1740, W, P2/G/818
Jn., apothecary, Crickl. St S., 1745, W, P3/G/613
Jn., yeo., Fifield, Bray, Berks., 1753, W, P1/G/602, P1/11Reg/69A
Jn., wheelwright, Fisherton A., 1758, a/c, I, W, P2/G/914
Jn., victualler, Bromham, 1776, W, P3/G/706
Jn., blacksmith, Melk., 1794, comm, W, P2/G/1064
Jn., yeo., Winkfield, Berks., 1795, W, P1/G/753, P1/14Reg/573B
Jn., yeo., Chicksgrove, Tisb., 1820, D (2), W, Wr, P1/1820/120
Jn., hardware man, Sal. St Thos., 1831, W, Wr, P4/1831/5
Jos., yeo., Bishopstone N., 1801, O, W, Wr, P6/141
Grey, Lawr., tailor, Melplash, Netherb., Dorset, 1684, AB, I, P17/234
Lawr., Donhead St A., 1717, AB, I, P2/G/685
Magdalen, widow, Homington, 1677, a/c, appt of guardian, I, T, W, P24/486
Mgt., widow, Over Stratton, Stratton St Mgt., 1740, W, P3/G/588
Grey, Martha, widow, Bps. C., 1750, req, W, P24/1051
Martha, sp., Sal., 1759, AB, P4/1759/7
My., widow, Semley, 1694, AB, I, W, P2/G/549
Grey, My., widow, Edington, 1710, I, W, P2/G/635
My., sp., Coombe B., 1713, I, W, P5/1713/36, P5/15Reg/380B
Grey, My., widow, Chiseldon, 1713, I (2 - 1 a copy), W, P3/G/444

My., widow, Ford, Laverstock, 1744, W, P2/G/846
My., widow, Semley, 1780, W, P2/G/1004
My., widow, E. Knoyle, 1799, AB, P2/G/1075
My., widow, Semley, 1811, W, Wr, P2/1811/26
My. Ann, sp., Britford, 1855, aff, W, Wr, P24/1416
Matthew, Swindon, 1694, AB, comm, P3/G/372
Matthew, Earley, Sonning, Berks., 1718, AB, I, P5/1718/14
Matthew, yeo., Tisb., 1776, W, P1/G/696, P1/13Reg/75
Grey, Maurice, weaver, Westb., 1615, AB (not completed), I, P25/1615/9
Nich., yeo., Horningsham, 1590, AB, I, W, P5/1590/25, P5/5Reg/81B, 84B
Philip, Longbridge D., 1728, AB, P2/G/747
Richd., weaver, N. Bradley, 1616, AB, I, P1/G/63
Richd., labourer, E. Ilsley, Berks., 1714, AB, I, P1/G/377
Grey, Richd., Westport St My., 1820, AB, Wr, P1/1820/137
Grey, Robt., vicar, E. Hagbourne, Berks., 1686, I, W, P1/G/778
Robt., yeo., Coate, Liddington, 1699, AB, I, P3/G/396
Robt., sadler, Swindon, 1779, W, P3/G/721
Roger, labourer, Barrow St., Mere, 1810, W, P5/1810/12
Sam., tailor, Highw., 1688, AB, I (detailed), P5/1688/34
Sam., Over Stratton, Stratton St Mgt., 1737, AB, W, P3/G/574
Sam., gent., Upper Stratton, Stratton St Mgt., 1781, W, P3/G/728
Sam., yeo., Purton, 1781, W, P3/G/729
Sander, husb., Netherh., 1807, W, Wr, P2/1807/53
Sarah, sp., Newbury, Berks., 1704, AB, P1/G/326
Sarah, widow, Sutton M. (form. of Chicksgrove), 1810, W, Wr, P2/1810/63
Sarah, widow, Fisherton A., 1848, AB, D, Wr, P2/1848/29
Simon, yeo., Semley, 1634, I, NW, P1/G/124
Grey, Stephen, Semley, 1567, W, P2/5Reg/9A
Susanna, widow, Netherh., 1789, W, P2/G/1045
Thos., husb., Semley, 1554, W, P2/2Reg/192B
Thos., E. Hatch, Tisb., 1610, AB, I, T, P2/G/141, P2/8Reg/121A
Thos., clothier, Westb. L., 1617, I, W, P25/1617/7
Thos., servant to Jn. Coombes, Codf. St My., 1632, AB, I, NW, P2/G/241, P2/9Reg/37C
Thos., Tisb., 1642, I, copy I, P2/G/294
Thos., gent. and clothier, Wilton, 1642, I, NW, P2/G/299
Thos., jun., Tisb., 1644, AB, I, P2/G/304
Thos., Sal., 1671, AB, P4/1670/24
Thos., sen., sadler, Newbury, Berks., 1671, I, W, P1/G/220
Thos., yeo., Semley, 1677, I (2), W, P2/G/410, 577
Thos., innholder, Gt. Amesb., 1679-80, AB, a/c, I, P2/G/427
Thos., S. Wraxall, 1681, AB (2), P2/G/444
Grey, Thos., gent., Edington, 1707, I, W, P2/G/624
Thos., yeo., Berwick St Jn., 1710, W, P2/G/638
Thos., sen., clerk, Wanb., 1725, W, P3/G/496
Thos., yeo., Over Stratton, Stratton St Mgt., 1730, W, P3/G/535
Thos., Coombe B., 1732, AB, P5/1732/18
Grey, Thos., yeo., Winkfield, Berks., 1738-50, AB, W, P1/G/521, 585, P1/8Reg/286
Thos., husb., Winterbourne E., 1751, W, P2/G/881
Thos., Netherh., 1790, AB, P2/G/1048
Thos., yeo., Foxleigh Grn, Bray, Berks., 1795, W, P1/G/752, P1/14Reg/569
Thos., thatcher, Heddington, 1802, comm, W, Wr, P3/1802/2
Grey, Walter, Semley, [1546], W, P2/2Reg/24B
Walter, clothier, Wilton, 1557, W, P2/3Reg/38C
Grey, Walter, E. Hatch, Tisb., 1558, W, P2/3Reg/127C
Walter, Semley, 1574, W, P2/5Reg/179A
Grey, Walter, husb., Baverstock, 1592, AB, I, W, P2/G/61
Walter, Town, Wilton, 1611-16, AB (2), I (2), W, P2/G/172, P2/8Reg/154B, 312B
Walter, no abode stated, [1672], I, P2/G/371
Grey, Walter, Whitley, Melk., 1686, AB, I, W, P2/G/498
Walter, yeo., Semley, 1694, I, W, P2/G/548

Walter, yeo., Sal. The Close, 1704, I, W, P5/1703/14
Grey, Wm., Semley, 1558, W, P2/3Reg/90B
Grey, Wm., clothier, Wilton, [1600], W, P2/G/1082, P2/8Reg/114C
Wm., husb., Homington, 1612, I, W, P24/111
Wm., sen., wheeler, Wilton, 1648, I, W, P2/G/319
Wm., innholder, Wilton, 1675, I, W, P2/G/389
Wm., sen., blacksmith, Swindon, 1677, I, W, P3/G/253
Wm., innholder, Gt. Amesb., 1680, AB, I, P2/G/434
Grey, Wm., yeo., Bridzor, Tisb., [1685], I, W, P2/G/490
Grey, Wm., E. Hatch, Tisb., 1699, AB, P2/G/570
Wm., Semley, 1708, AB, I, copy I, P1/G/343
Wm., sen., E. Ilsley, Berks., 1711, AB, I, P1/G/363
Wm., husb., Bishopstone N., 1720, I, P6/83
Wm., yeo., Homington, 1724, W, P24/867
Wm., Martin, Hants, 1728, AB, P2/G/751
Wm., Whitep., 1732, AB, P2/G/772
Wm., innholder, Swindon, 1746, W, P3/G/618
Grey, Wm., yarnmaker, Urchf., 1761, W, P2/G/924
Wm., yeo., Elston, Orcheston St Geo., 1764, W, P2/G/937
Wm., yeo., Barrow St., Mere, 1788, W, P5/1788/9, P5/18Reg/108
Wm., landlord, Bromham, 1806, AB, ren, W, Wr, P3/1806/43
Wm., yeo., Stert, Urchf., 1831, W, Wr, P1/1831/2
Wm., publican, Stratford sub C., 1857, aff, D, W, Wr, P4/1857/5
Wolstan, sen., Mere, 1636, AB, I, P5/1636/23, P5/13Reg/14A
see also Simpsion alias G.
Grayer, Ann, sp., Sal. (form. of S. Newton & Whitep.), 1851, AB, cert, D, W, Wr, P4/1851/5
Mgt., widow, Whitep. (form. of Landford), 1853, AB, aff, cert, Wr, P2/1853/72
Grayle *see* Graile
Grayley *see* Grailey
Greast *see* Grist
Greate, Greete, Hy., husb., Winterslow, 1610, AB, I, W, P2/G/133, P2/8Reg/83D
Margery, widow, Winterslow, 1623, AB, P2/G/204
Greatrex, Francis, vicar, Keevil, 1618, I, W, P2/G/184
Thos., yeo., Keevil, 1678, AB, I, ren, P2/G/416
Greatwood, Francis, Corsley, 1788, note of admon, P2/G/1041
Geoffrey, broad weaver, Edington, [1692], I, W, P2/G/538
Geo., Corsley, 1741, AB, P2/G/827
Jas., yeo., Corsley, 1805, W, P2/1805/33
Jn., tailor, Corsley, 1694, I, W, P2/G/550
Mgt., widow, Edington, 1710, W, P2/G/639
Greaves, Andrew, vicar, Westb., 1640, AB, comm, I (detailed; ref. to library of books), P25/1640/1
Green, Adam, sen., yeo., Leigh, Ashton K., 1715, I, W, P3/G/450
Adam, cordw., Wantage, Berks., 1800, W, P5/1800/12, P5/18Reg/292C
Greene, Agnes, widow, Stratton, Dorset, 1582, I, W, P5/1582/27, P5/4Reg/35A
Greene, Agnes, widow, Downton, 1615, W, P2/8Reg/247A
Greene, Alice, Norton B., 1591, I, W. Identified from note, P2/G/58
Greene, Alice, widow, Upton S., [1620], I, W, P2/G/191
Alice, sp., Froxfield, 1626, I, W, P3/G/95
Greene, Alice, widow, Bulford, [1678], copy I, P2/G/411
Greene, Ambrose, husb., Coleshill, Berks., 1614, W, P1/G/48
Greene, Ambrose, sen., maltster, Westrop, Highw., 1677, W, P10/1677/2
Green alias Alexander, Amy, N. Newnton, 1732, AB, P3/G/545
Ann, widow, Fosbury, Tidcombe and F., 1687, AB, I, W, P3/G/320
Greene, Ann, widow, Sal., 1688, AB, I, P4/1687/13
Ann, sp., Wootton B., 1695, I, W, P3/G/376
Greene, Arthur, Wootton B., 1636, AB, I, P3/G/146
Greene, Avis, Corsley, 1592, I, P2/G/62
Avis, sp., Southbroom, 1639, I, NW, P24/288
Bathsheba, sp., Charminster, Dorset, 1802, W, P5/1802/12, P5/19Reg/10A
Benj., sen., yeo., Charminster, Dorset, 1742, W, Wr, P5/1742/16

Betty, widow, Tisb., 1807, W, Wr, P2/1807/1
Greene, Cath., widow, Axford, Rams., 1689, I, W, P5/1689/28
Cath., widow, Tollard Royal, 1821, W, Wr, P2/1821/13
Chas., organ builder, Sal., 1779, W (co-habiting with Ann Holliday), P4/1779/3
Greene, Christian, widow, Bulford, 1632, I, W, P2/G/240
Greene, Chris., Upton S., 1611, T (child: Agnes G.), P2/G/151
Chris., yeo., Upton S., 1690, W, P2/G/529
Chris., gent., Gillingham, Dorset, 1722, AB, I, P27/1/253
Chris., Gillingham, Dorset, 1751, AB, P27/1/401, P27/3Reg/63B
Cicely, widow, Berwick St Leonard, 1699, W, P2/G/575
Greene, Denise, widow, Wick, Downton, 1562, I, W, P2/G/9, P2/4Reg/99C
Dionisia, sp., Chicksgrove, Tisb., 1778, W, P2/G/999
Greene, Edith, widow, W. Knoyle, 1587, AB, W, P2/7Reg/76B
Edmd., Hilmarton, 1750, W, P1/G/590, P1/10Reg/422
Edmd., sen., yeo., Compton B., 1777, W, P3/G/709
Greene, Edwd., [grocer], Sal. St Thos., 1613, AB, I, P4/1613/3
Greene, Edwd., E. Knoyle, 1616-19, AB, a/c, I, P2/G/173, P2/8Reg/314
Greene, Edwd., clerk rector, E. Lockinge, Berks., 1673, AB, comm, P1/G/223
Greene, Edwd., sen., yeo., Bapton, Fisherton Delamare, 1706, W, P2/G/622
Edwd., Tisb., 1742, AB, P2/G/829
Edwd., gent., Tisb., 1770, W, P2/G/963
Edwd., widower, Fovant, 1819, W, Wr, P2/1819/22
Edwd., husb., Highw., 1820, W, Wr, P10/1820/2
Eleanor, widow, Mkt. L., 1845, D, note, O, W, Wr, P1/1845/71
Greene, Eliz., widow, Sal., 1677, AB, P4/1677/12
Greene, Eliz., widow, Westrop, Highw., 1679, I, W, P10/1679/1
Eliz., Nether C., Dorset, 1698, W, P5/1698/30
Greene, Eliz., widow, Charminster, Dorset, 1703, I, W, P5/1703/16
Eliz., widow, Manningford, 1739, W, P3/G/582
Eliz., widow, Blewbury, Berks., 1743, comm, W (& cod), Wr, P5/1743/34
Eliz., widow, Sal., 1744, AB, W, P1/G/550, P1/9Reg/284B
Eliz., widow, Leigh, Ashton K., 1748, comm, W, P3/G/630
Eliz., sp., Tisb., 1778, AB, P2/G/998
Eliz., wife, Fonthill B., 1843, AB, Wr, P2/1843/40
Greene, Ellen, Amesb., 1560, AB, P2/4Reg/54E
Ellen Eliz., sp., Gillingham, Dorset, 1854, aff, comm, W, Wr, P27/1/774
Frances, widow, Bishopstone N., 1708, I, W, P6/101
Greene, Francis, clerk and rector, E. Coulston, 1738, AB, comm, P1/G/527
Greene, Gabriel, Westb., 1575, AB, I, P25/1575/5, P5/3Reg/65A
Greene, Geoffrey, Brunton, Collingbourne K., 1614, I, W, P1/G/52
Greene, Geo., sen., blacksmith, Over Zeals, 1622, I, NW, P5/1622/33
Greene, Geo., jun., blacksmith, Over Zeals, 1622, NW, P5/10Reg/114A
Greene, Geo., Barford St M., 1705, AB, P2/G/616
Geo., Colerne, 1726, AB, P3/G/501
Geo., Tollard Royal, 1786, D, W, P2/G/1036
Geo., Tollard Royal, 1823, AB, Wr, P1/1823/132
Greene, Giles, Wokm., Berks., 1613, AB, I, T, P5/1613/30, P5/9Reg/101B
Greene, Giles, yeo., Baverstock, 1615, I (very detailed), W, P2/G/166, P2/8Reg/275
Greene, Giles, clothworker, Warm., 1676, AB, I, P2/G/396
Giles, husb., Barford St M., 1723, I, W, P2/G/720
Giles, widower, Upton S., 1734, AB, P2/G/792
Greene, Gregory, husb., Bulford, 1574, W, P2/5Reg/177D
Hatton, glover, Westbrook, Gt. Faringdon, Berks., 1725, W, P5/1725/30, P5/16Reg/122A
Greene, Hy., Sal., 1618, AB, I, P4/1618/9
Greene, Hy., yeo., Charminster, Dorset, 1662, AB, I, P5/1662/50
Hy., sen., yeo., Bishopstone N., 1669, comm, I, W, P6/31
Greene, Hy., clerk rector, Blunsdon St Andrew, 1677, comm, I, W, P1/G/234
Greene, Hy., yeo., Charminster, Dorset, 1684, I, W, P5/1684/23
Hy., butcher and shopkeeper, Bishopstone N., 1778, W, P5/1778/9, P5/17Reg/161
Hy., Uffc., Devon, 1797, W, P5/1797/16, P5/18Reg/255

Hy., Mkt. L., 1828, AB, W, Wr, P2/1828/52
Hy., innkeeper, Milford, Sal. St Martin, 1838, W, Wr, P4/1838/13
Hy., grocer, Highw., 1843, comm, W, Wr, P10/1843/1
Hugh, labourer, Chaddleworth, Berks., 1620, I, W, P1/G/76
Greene, Jas., yeo., Barford St M., [1687], I, W, P2/G/516
Greene, Jas., Sal., 1700, AB, a/c, I (2), P4/1700/5
Jas., distiller, Sal., 1729, AB, I, P4/1729/5
Jas., Reading, Berks., 1779, AB, P1/G/711
Jas., beadle, Sal., 1793, W, P4/1793/3
Jas. Goddard, shoemaker, Donhead St My., 1848, comm, D, W, Wr, P2/1848/13
Greene, Jane, widow, Upton S., [1627], I, P2/G/218
Jane, widow, Eastrop, Highw., 1686, AB, comm, I, P10/1686/8
Jane, widow, Cholswell, Abingdon, Berks., 1779, W, P1/G/714, P1/13Reg/296
Greene, Jean, sp., W. Kennett, Avebury, 1722, W, P3/G/480
Greene, Joan, Corsley, 1569, W, P2/5Reg/71B
Greene, Joan, widow, Blewbury, Berks., 1614, I, W, P5/1613/33, P5/9Reg/128A
Greene, Joan, sp., Nether C., Dorset, 1698, I, W, P5/1698/29
Greene, Jn., Corsley, 1558, W, P2/3Reg/95A
Greene, Jn., Stourton, 1565, AB, P2/4Reg/209B, 213C
Greene, Jn., husb., Bulford, 1576, W, P2/5Reg/250B
Greene, Jn., Nether C., Dorset, 1582, AB, P5/4Reg/32B
Greene, Jn., broad weaver, Heddington, 1614, AB, I, P3/G/38
Greene, Jn., sen., Heytes., 1619, I, W, P5/1619/25, P5/10Reg/63B
Greene, Jn., Collingbourne K., 1626, I, W, P3/G/96
Jn., husb., Froxfield, 1626, I, W, P3/G/92
Greene, Jn., husb., Corsley, [1627], I, W, P2/G/216
Grine, Jn., Mkt. L., 1637, AB, I, P2/G/270
Greene, Jn., Marston, Pott., 1639, I (2), W, P2/G/282
Greene, Jn., sen., husb., Blewbury, Berks., 1639, I, W, P5/1639/36, P5/13Reg/186C
Greene, Jn., yeo., Minety, 1639, AB, a/c, I, P3/G/158-59
Greene, Jn., jun., yeo., Nether C., Dorset, 1641, I, W, P5/1641/35, P5/14Reg/38
Jn., husb., Bedborough, Bps. C., 1665, AB, I, P24/364
Greene, Jn., yeo., Nether C., Dorset, 1670, AB, I, T (re Jn. & Hugh G.), W (& cod), P5/1670/14
Greene, Jn., Horningsham, 1672, AB, I, P5/1672/17
Greene, Jn., husb., Barford St M., 1683, AB, I, P2/G/469
Greene, Jn., Stourton, 1684, AB, P2/G/481
Greene, Jn., joiner, Sal., 1703, W, P4/1703/6
Jn., sen., linen weaver, Gillingham, Dorset, 1707, I, W, P27/1/167
Greene, Jn., Blewbury, Berks., 1710, W, P5/1710/44, P5/15Reg/161
Jn., yeo., Bps. C., 1713, I (2 - 1 a copy), W, P24/685
Jn., baker, Gt. Faringdon, Berks., 1719, W, P5/1719/33, P5/16Reg/25D
Jn., Sutton B., 1720, AB, I, P1/G/408
Jn., N. Newnton, 1723, W, P1/G/424, P1/6Reg/430A
Jn., sen., joiner, Mkt. L., 1726, AB, I, ren, P1/G/440
Greene, Jn., baker, Crickl. St S., 1738, W, P3/G/577
Jn., yeo., Fisherton D., 1740, comm, W, P2/G/816
Jn., Mkt. L., 1745, AB, P2/G/847
Jn., yeo., Cumnor, Berks., 1747, AB, P1/G/568
Jn., yeo., Bishopstone N., 1753, comm, W, P5/1752/24
Jn., labourer, Wantage, Berks., 1756, W, P23/666
Jn., Sal., 1764, AB, P4/1764/6
Jn., Tisb., 1766, W, P2/G/947
Jn., yeo., Abingdon, Berks., 1766, W, P1/G/653, P1/12Reg/162
Jn., Mkt. L., 1770, AB, P2/G/965
Jn., carp., Sal., 1773, W, P4/1773/8
Jn., Mkt. L., 1779, AB, P2/G/1002
Jn., yeo., Gillingham, Dorset, 1808, W, P27/1/596
Jn., Donhead St My., 1813, W, Wr, P2/1813/64
Jn., yeo., Hilmarton, 1833, comm, W, Wr, P3/1833/41
Jn., blacksmith, Gillingham, Dorset, 1834, O, W, Wr, P27/1/703

Jn., yeo., Castleton, Dorset, 1846, W, Wr, P5/1846/12
Jn., Charminster, Dorset, 1853, AB, aff, comm, Wr, P5/1853/25
Jn., widower, Stourton, 1854, AB, aff, Wr, P2/1854/3
Jos., Charminster, Dorset, 1703, comm, W, P5/1703/15
Jos., miller, Charminster, Dorset, 1809, W, Wr, P5/1809/31
Jos., baker, Wrou., 1849, comm, W, Wr, P3/1849/30
Jos., miller, Charminster, Dorset, 1853, AB, comm, D, W, Wr, P5/1853/1
Lawrence, W. Woodhay, Berks., 1729, AB, comm, I, W, P1/G/469, P1/7Reg/367A
Mgt., widow, Barford St M., [1684], I, W, P2/G/479
Greene, Margery, widow, Woodspeen, Speen, Berks., 1606, I, W, P1/G/23
Margery, widow, Bratton, Westb., 1635, AB, P25/1635/2
Martha, sen., widow, Corsham, 1838, W, Wr, P3/1838/47
My., widow, Leigh, Ashton K., 1718, W, P3/G/461
My., widow, Wokm., Berks., 1723, I, W, P5/1723/21, P5/16Reg/88A
My., widow, Kingstone Winslow, Ashbury, Berks., 1729, W, P1/G/456, P1/7Reg/251A
My., widow, Ansty, 1733, AB, P2/G/779
My., widow, Thatcham, Berks., 1735, W, P1/G/502, P1/8Reg/35B
My., widow, Sutton B., 1742, AB, comm, P3/G/599
My., widow, Marnhull, Dorset (leaving effects at Gillingham, form. of Madson, Dorset), 1742, AB, ren (2), W, P27/1/366, P27/3Reg/19
My., singlewoman, Melk., 1782, AB, ren, W, P2/G/1013
My., widow, Sal., 1799, W, P4/1799/12
My., sp., Ansty, 1826, W, Wr, P5/1826/15
Greene, Meriam, widow, Coleshill, Berks., 1695, I, W, P1/G/292
Greene, Morgan, Lyme R., Dorset, 1636, AB, a/c, P16/472
Greene, Nathaniel, yeo., Barford St M., 1696, I, W, P2/G/557
Greene, Nich., husb., Mkt. L., 1667, I, W, P2/G/346
Peter, yeo., Ansty Farm, 1814, W (& cod), P5/1814/15
Greene, Philip, husb., Eastcourt, Crudwell, 1628, comm, I, W, P1/G/101
Philip, cabinetmaker, Devizes, 1812, W, Wr, P1/1812/14
Rebecca, widow, Wokm., Berks., 1832, W, Wr, P5/1832/16
Greene, Richd., Downton, [1592], W, P1/G/1
Greene, Richd., Aldbourne, 1625, AB, I, P1/G/87, 89
Greene, Richd., yeo., Rivar, Shalbourne, 1662, AB, I, P5/1662/52
Greene, Richd., shepherd, Widhill, Crickl. St S., 1668, NW, P1/G/208
Richd., husb., Minety, 1675, I, W, P3/G/237
Richd., yeo., Motc., Dorset, 1687, I, W, P27/1/102
Greene, Richd., Manningford Bohun, [1687], I, W, P2/G/508
Greene, Richd., linen weaver, Gillingham, Dorset, 1690, I, P27/1/123
Richd., sen., yeo., Bedborough, Bps. C., 1692, I, W, P24/536
Richd., linen weaver, Gasper, Stourton, 1704, comm, D, I, W, P1/G/333
Richd., sen., gent. *or* yeo., Hilcott, N. Newnton, 1715, I, W, P3/G/451
Richd., gent., Hilcott, N. Newnton, 1722, comm, W, P3/G/481
Richd., yeo., Minety, 1732, AB, I, P3/G/546
Greene, Richd., Leigh Delamere, 1741, AB, P1/G/533
Greene, Richd., cooper, Sal., 1741, W, P4/1740/1
Richd., Warm., 1746, AB, P2/G/850, 854
Richd., gent., Sal., 1752, AB, P4/1752/6
Richd., sen., yeo., Barford St M., 1771, W, Wr, P2/G/969
Richd., Reading, Berks., 1776, W, P1/G/700, P1/13Reg/131B
Richd., yeo., Barford St M., 1800, AB, note, ren, W, P2/1800/29
Gryne, Robt., Baverstock, 1550, AB, P2/2Reg/118B
Robt., Wedh., Urchf., 1581, NW, P2/6Reg/26B
Greene, Robt., sen., yeo., Blewbury, Berks., 1605, AB, I, W, P5/1605/27, P5/8Reg/39B
Greene, Robt., husb., Upton S., 1614, W, P2/8Reg/210B
Greene, Robt., Bratton, Westb., 1617, I, W. No note of probate, P25/1617/6
Greene, Robt., sen., yeo., Blewbury, Berks., 1636, I, W, P5/1636/24, P5/13Reg/7B
Greene, Robt., joiner, Sal., 1682, AB, I, P4/1682/19
Robt., sen., blacksmith, Stourton, [1688], I, W, P2/G/518
Robt., cordw., Ashampstead, Basildon, Berks., 1747, W, P1/G/569, P1/10Reg/82

Robt., Chiseldon, 1756, AB, P1/G/620
Roger, husb., Horningsham, 1682, W, P5/1682/43
Sam., cooper, Sal., 1724, AB, I, P4/1724/2
Sam., Horningsham, 1736, W, P5/1736/14
Sam., basketmaker, Sal., 1737, W, Wr, P4/1737/9
Sarah, widow, Barford St M., 1712, W, P2/G/646
Sarah, widow, Abingdon, Berks., 1735, W, P1/G/500, P1/7Reg/649
Simon, weaver, Heddington, 1612, W, P3/G/27
Simon, Ditchampton, Wilton, 1742, W, P2/G/830
Greene, Stephen, Sal. St Edmd., 1613, AB, P4/1613/1
Greene, Stephen, yeo., Abingdon, Berks., 1625, I, W, P1/G/84
Susan, widow, Bedborough, Bps. C., 1667, comm, I, W, P24/350
Susan, sp., Salt Lane, Sal. St Edmd., 1835, W, Wr, P4/1835/1
Greene, Susanna, sp., Sal., 1684, AB, I, P4/1683/11
Susanna, Sal., 1726, W, P4/1725/13
Greene, Thos., Gillingham, Dorset, 1560s-70s, court proceedings (matrimonial case), P27/1Reg/1
Greene, Thos., Ogbourne Maizey, 1591, AB, a/c, I, P5/1591/30, P5/5Reg/111B
Greene, Thos., Heytes., 1591, I, T, W, P5/1591/29, P5/5Reg/108A
Greene, Thos., Wokm., Berks., 1596, AB, I, P5/1596/28, P5/6Reg/135B
Thos., blacksmith, Bedborough, Bps. C., 1616, I, W, P24/88
Greene, Thos., husb., Lydiard M., 1617, I, W, P3/G/52
Greene, Thos., W. Knoyle, 1621, a/c, I, P2/G/193
Greene, Thos., Sal., 1625, AB, I, P4/1625/5
Greene, Thos., mercer, Gt. Bedwyn, 1634, AB, I (2)(GVS), P5/1634/42
Greene, Thos., yeo., Langham, Gillingham, Dorset, 1665, AB, T (re Chris. G., minor), W, P27/1/23
Greene, Thos., husb., Fosbury, Tidcombe and F., 1667, I, W, P3/G/194
Thos., Imber, 1670-72, AB, a/c, comm, I, copy I, P2/G/373
Greene, Thos., Gillingham, Dorset, 1673, AB, P27/1/45
Greene, Thos., grocer, Gt. Bedwyn, 1682, I, W, P21/4/3
Greene, Thos., sen., yeo., Blewbury, Berks., 1686, I, W (book titles given in W), P5/1686/25
Thos., Gt. Coxwell, Berks., 1701, AB, cert, I, P1/G/319
Greene, Thos., goldsmith, Sal., 1715, W, P4/1715/4
Thos., yeo., Blewbury, Berks., 1727, W, P5/1727/18, P5/16Reg/149B
Thos., carp., Leigh, Ashton K., 1750, AB, ren, P1/G/584
Thos., Sal., 1752, AB, W, P4/1752/2
Thos., innholder, Charminster, Dorset, 1756, comm, W, P5/1756/13
Thos., yeo., Water Eaton, Latton, 1757, W, P3/G/659
Thos., Gt. Faringdon, Berks., 1761, AB, P5/1761/16
Thos., yeo., Goatacre, Hilmarton, 1764, W, P3/G/678
Greene, Thos., chandler and soapboiler, Westb. L., 1782, W, P25/1782/2
Thos., plumber and glazier, Newbury, Berks., 1783, W, P1/G/725, P1/13Reg/469B
Thos., Collingbourne K., 1787, AB, P3/G/745
Thos., victualler, Corsham, 1807, W, P29/1800-1857/12, P29/3Reg/249
Thos., Corsham, 1823, AB, P29/3Reg/266, P29/1800-1857/20
Thos., gent., Newbury, Berks., 1823, comm, W, Wr, P1/1823/20
Thos., gardener, Abingdon, Berks., 1829, W, Wr, P1/1829/109
Thos., Tollard Royal, 1830, AB, W, P2/1830/4
Thos. Skeates, bach., Sal., 1818, AB, Wr, P4/1818/6
Greene, Timothy, Lt. Hinton, 1678, I, Wr, P3/G/262
Greene, Walter, Quidh., 1590, AB, P2/G/46
Greene, Walter, Coombe B., 1611, AB, P5/1611/14
Walter, N. Bradley, 1763-64, AB (2), P2/G/932
Wellman, fishmonger, Gt. Faringdon, Berks. (form. of St Giles, Holborn, Middlesex), 1734, W, P5/1734/31
Greene, Wm., husb., Wick, Downton, 1557, W, P2/3Reg/11A
Greene, Wm., butcher, W. Knoyle, 1560-63, I, W (NEP), P2/G/12, P2/4Reg/136A
Greyne, Wm., Semley, 1561, AB, I, copy I, note of admon, P2/G/8, P2/4Reg/82E
Greene, Wm., yeo., Teffont M., 1580, I, W, P2/G/34, P2/5Reg/366
Greene, Wm., innholder, Gt. Faringdon, Berks., 1588, I, T, W, P5/1588/21, P5/5Reg/39B
Greene, Wm., sen., husb., Froxfield, [1610], W (NEP), P3/G/19
Greene, Wm., husb., Bulford, 1628, I, W, P1/G/98

Wm., farrier, Bps. C., 1636, I, W, P24/287
Greene, Wm., yeo., Minety, 1664, I, NW, P3/G/181
Greene, Wm., husb., Charminster, Dorset, [1665], W (NEP), P5/1665/38
Greene, Wm., yeo., Baverstock, [1679], I, W, P2/G/424
Greene, Wm., Ham, 1684, cert, P1/G/254
Greene, Wm., sen., yeo. and blacksmith, Stourton, [1691], I, W, P2/G/535
Greene, Wm., joiner, Wokm., Berks., 1698, W, P5/1698/32
Wm., Wokm., Berks., 1713, AB, comm, P5/1713/37
Wm., yeo., Bishopstone N., 1716, W, P6/75
Greene, Wm., glover, Gt. Faringdon, Berks., 1719, AB, I, P5/1719/34
Wm., Southbroom, 1724, AB, I, P24/866
Wm., Sal., 1726, AB, P4/1726/3
Wm., yeo., Tisb., 1726, W, P2/G/739
Wm., Dinton, 1727, AB, P2/G/740
Wm., Trowb., 1742, AB, P1/G/545
Wm., victualler, Amesb., 1777, W, P2/G/991
Wm., Barford St M., 1795, AB, P1/G/756, P1/14Reg/620B
Wm., gent., Sal., 1812, AB (limited), P4/1812/9
Wm., farmer, Gillingham, Dorset, 1829, W, P27/1/687
Wm., carp., Sal., 1836, W, Wr, P4/1836/3
Wm., sen., Hindon, 1838, AB, T (his children), Wr, P2/1838/47-48
see also Bailey *or* G.; Greenway alias G.; Guy alias G.
Greenall *see* Greenhill
Greenaugh, Edmd., yeo., Purton, 1629, I, W, P3/G/109
Joyce, widow, Purton, 1638, I, W, P1/G/135
Greenoff, Richd., Coscote, E. Hagbourne, Berks., 1783, W, P1/G/724, P1/13Reg/486
Greenaway, Ann, sp., Uffcott, Broad H., 1691, AB, I, P3/G/353
Greenaway alias Dismore, Ann, Rams., 1741, AB, Wr, P5/1740/23
Ann, widow, Radley, Berks., 1789, W, P1/G/737, P1/14Reg/252
Crispin, victualler, Broad H., 1750, W, P3/G/636
Grinaway, Dan., maltster, Colerne, 1746, W, P3/G/619
Greenway, David, mason, Colerne, 1725, I, W, P3/G/497
Greenway, David, yeo., Colerne, 1836, W, Wr, P3/1836/37
Greenway, Edwd., Broad H., 1631, AB, I, P3/G/120
Edwd., Preshute, 1683, I, W, P1/G/253
Edwd., labourer, Stanford Dingley, Berks., 1735, AB, I, P1/G/503
Eliz., widow, Sal., 1725, W, P4/1724/21
Greenway, Eliz., sp., Colerne, 1727, W, P3/G/506
Eliz., widow, Clyffe P., 1731, W, P3/G/539
Greenaway alias Ponting, Frances, victualler, Marl., 1757, AB, ren, P1/G/622
Grinway, Francis, mason, Ford, N. Wraxall, 1698, I, W, P1/G/310, P1/3Reg/170
Francis, sen., cordw., Bushton, Clyffe P., 1739, comm, W, P3/G/583
Francis, innholder, Marl., 1752, AB, ren, W, P1/G/597, P1/10Reg/480
Grinaway, Francis, mason, Colerne, 1759, W, P1/G/632, P1/11Reg/446
Francis, Hullavington, 1781, AB, P3/G/730
Greenway, Geo., Ogbourne St Geo., 1611, I, W (NEP), P30/77
Geo., yeo., Broad H., [1617], I, W, P3/G/51
Greenway, Geo., victualler, Calne, 1754, W, P26/932
Geo., Calne, 1809, AB, comm, Wr, P5/1809/42
Joan, Ogbourne St Geo., 1720, AB, comm, P23/385
Joan, widow, Preshute, 1721, AB, comm, P1/G/411
Greenway, Jn., patron, Froxfield, 1561, institution to vicarage, P1/1Reg/78A
Greenway, Jn., vicar, Netheravon, 1587, W, P5/4Reg/150A
Greneway, Jn., clerk and vicar, Netheravon, 1587, AB, I, W, P5/1587/18, queried
Jn., husb., Charlton nr Malm., 1639, I, W, P3/G/160
Jn., yeo., Broad B., Highw., 1670, comm, W, P10/1670/2
Jn., yeo., Bremhill, 1689, comm, W, P3/G/332
Jn., chapman, Sal., 1690, I, W, P4/1690/8
Greenway, Jn., yeo., Uffcott, Broad H., 1695, I, W, P1/G/298
Greenway, Jn., glover, Marl., 1709, I, W, P1/G/350, P1/5Reg/6B

Jn., joiner, Sal., 1733, W, P4/1733/15
Jn., innholder, Broad H., 1735, W, P1/G/505, P1/8Reg/54
Jn., maltster, Hungerford, Berks., 1762-73, AB (widow Eliz. d. without admg), ren, W, P23/697, 754
Jn., mason, Colerne, 1790, AB, comm, ren, P3/G/753
Jn., dealer, Clyffe P., 1812, W, Wr, P3/1812/18
Greenway, Jn., yeo., Colerne, 1833, W, Wr, P3/1833/53
Jn., shopkeeper, Haydon Wick, Rodbourne C., 1845, O, W, Wr, P3/1845/36
Greenway alias Green, Jn., Chipp., 1850, D (draft), W (NEP), P3/1850/61
Jn., Stratton St Mgt., 1856, aff, comm, W, Wr, P3/1856/24
Jos., glover, Marl., 1762, W, P1/G/638, P1/12Reg/29
Greenway, My., clerk's wife, Sal. The Close (form. of Kimpton, Hants), 1739, W, Wr, P5/1739/21
My., Wrou., 1747, AB, P1/G/572
Nich., Preshute, 1686, AB, I, P1/G/263
Nich., glover, Marl., 1694, I, W, P1/G/776
Greenway, Nich., yeo., Clyffe P., 1709, AB, I, P3/G/433
Priscilla, Marl., 1758, W, P1/G/623, P1/11Reg/357
Richd., Sal., 1687, AB, I, P4/1687/7
Greenway, Robt., yeo., E. Ginge, W. Hendred, Berks., 1605, AB, I, W, P1/G/15
Greenway, Robt., gent., Swindon, 1740, AB, P3/G/587
Grinaway, Sam., Colerne, 1689, AB, I, P3/G/342
Sam., Bradford A., 1730, AB, P2/G/763
Sarah, widow, Sal., 1735, W, Wr, P4/1734/14
Sarah, Sal. St Thos., 1737, W, Wr, P4/1736/13
Sarah, sp., Sal., 1745, AB, P4/1745/5
Greenway, Sarah, widow, Hullavington, 1789, W, P1/G/738, P1/14Reg/276A
Susanna, widow, Yatesbury, 1814, W, Wr, P1/1814/119
Thos., parchmentmaker, Charlton nr Malm., 1662, I, W, P1/G/179
Thos., Marl., 1663, I, W, P1/G/187
Greenway, Thos., Clevancy, Hilmarton (buried at Mayglass, Wexford, Ireland), 1673, AB, burial cert., ren, P3/G/229
Thos., yeo., Thornhill, Clyffe P., 1685, comm, I, W, P3/G/311
Thos., glover, Marl. St Peter and St Paul, [1707], I, W, P1/G/339
Thos., yeo., Steventon, Berks., 1741, W, P1/G/537, P1/9Reg/89
Greenway, Thos., clerk, Uffc., Devon, 1746, AB, P5/1746/35
Greenway, Thos., Colerne, 1804, AB, comm, P3/1804/26
Thos., Grove, Wantage, Berks., 1830, AB, comm, Wr, P5/1830/7
Wm., miller, Tidpit, Martin, Hants, 1666, AB, I, P1/G/199
Greenway, Wm., sen., husb., Marl., 1667, AB, NW, P1/G/205
Wm., sen., Calne, 1690, I, W, P26/388
Wm., butcher, Wanb., 1718, I, W, P3/G/462
Wm., husb., Eastrop, Highw., 1734, W, P5/1734/32
Wm., husb. and labourer, Sandy Lane, Calne, 1741, I, W, P26/825
Wm., sen., yeo., Even Swindon, 1840, comm, W, Wr, P3/1840/25
Greene *see* Green
Greenfield, Agnes, widow, Enmore Grn, Motc., Dorset, 1641, AB, I, P5/1641/36, P5/14Reg/35A
Grinfield, Ann, sp., Crickl. St S., 1748, W, P3/G/633
Grinfield, Ann, Marl. St My., 1747-48, comm, D, W, P1/G/578, P1/10Reg/205
Grinfield, Edwd., esquire, Ogbourne St Geo., 1759, W, P5/1759/10
Edwd., apothecary, Marl., 1763, comm, W, P1/G/649, P1/12Reg/31
Edwd., apothecary, Marl., 1825, AB (re property in M.), comm, P1/1825/4
Jn., gent., Beam., Dorset, 1716, AB, I, W, P5/1716/32, P5/15Reg/340B
Nathaniel, clerk, Maiden B., 1617, AB, I, P2/G/176
Phillipine, widow, Marl. St My., 1682, I, W, P1/G/246
Richd., woollen draper, Marl., 1662, AB, comm, I, P1/G/174
Grinfield, Richd., gent., Manningford Bohun, 1743, AB, comm, ren, W, P2/G/841
Grinfield alias Thomas, Robt., Marl. St Peter and St Paul, 1614, W, P1/G/46
Grinsfield, Thos., Tinh., Edington, 1574, W, P2/5Reg/199B
Thos., yeo., Edington, 1581, AB, P2/G/36, P2/6Reg/36A
Grinfield, Thos., Marl. St Peter and St Paul, 1650, AB, I, P1/G/167
Grinfield, Thos., innholder, Marl. (form. of Preshute), 1674, I, W, P1/G/226
Thos., apothecary, Warm., 1700, AB, W, P2/G/580

Grinfield, Wm., clerk, Burbage (vicar of Buckland, Berks., 1771), 1783, comm, W, P11/244
Wm., farmer, Motc., Dorset, 1821, W, Wr, P27/1/656
Greenham, Jane, widow, Leigh, Yetm., Dorset (form. of W. Chelbury, Dorset), 1790, W, Wr, P19/190
Greenhill, Anthony, fuller, N. Bradley, 1652, I, W, P1/G/171
Benj., farmer, Whitaker's Farm, Southwick, N. Bradley, 1855, AB, aff, O, ren, W, Wr, P1/1855/63
Edwd., butcher, Edington, 1586, W, P2/7Reg/38A
Grenhill, Edwd. *see* Wm. Pitman
Eliz., widow, Southwick, N. Bradley, 1734, AB, ren, W, P2/G/794
Frances, Westb. L., 1690, AB, comm, I, P25/1690/7
Hy., yeo., Hawkeridge, Westb., 1693, I, W, P25/1693/1
Jas., Westrop, Highw., 1766, AB, P10/1766/2
Jn., victualler and butcher, Westb., 1667, I (detailed), W, P25/1667/2
Jn., Bromham, 1695, AB, comm, P1/G/288
Jn., Westb. L., 1741, AB, a/c, I, note, P25/1741/10
Jn., gent., Southwick, N. Bradley, 1812, W, P2/1812/42
My., widow, N. Bradley, 1668, AB, comm, I, W, P2/G/351
Nich., Westb., 1565, W, P5/1Reg/60A
Richd., yeo., Southwick, N. Bradley, [1691], I, W, P2/G/532
Richd., gent., Southwick, N. Bradley, 1771, W, P2/G/966
Ruth, sp., Corsley, 1763, W, P1/G/648, P1/12Reg/128
Sam., yeo., Penleigh, Dilton, Westb., 1778, W, P25/1778/3
Greenhill *or* Greenall, Thos., Steeple A., 1613-14, AB, a/c, P2/G/161, P2/8Reg/193A
Thos., sen., farmer, E. Town, W. Ashton, Steeple A., 1830, comm, W, Wr, P2/1830/77
Greening, Ann *or* Agnes, sp., Buckland, Berks., 1686, I, W, P1/G/777
Hy., yeo., Fordington, Dorset, 1683, I, W, P15/39
Jas., yeo., Aston U., Blewbury, Berks., 1769, W, P5/1769/12
Jn., husb., N. Wootton, Dorset, 1610, AB, a/c, I, P5/1610/22, P5/9Reg/41A
Jn., Fordington, Dorset, 1731, AB, P5/1731/35
Richd., bodicemaker, Gt. Faringdon, Berks., 1692, I, W, P5/1692/36
Walter, husb., N. Wootton, Dorset, 1612, I, W, P5/1611/16, P5/9Reg/57D
Wm., Sherb., Dorset, 1582, I, W, P5/1582/24, P5/4Reg/41A
Wm., Netherb., Dorset, 1684, AB, comm, I, P17/239
Greenland, Edwd., brickmaker, Westb., 1797, W (provision for blind son), P25/1797/6
Edwin, gent., Westb., 1854, declaration, O, W, Wr, P25/1854/2
Geo., brickmaker, Westb., 1841, W, Wr, P25/1841/3
Hy., brick and tilemaker, Westb., 1804, W, P25/1804/4
Jesse, brick and tilemaker, Westb., 1853, comm, W, Wr, P25/1853/4
Jn., Edington, 1559, W, P2/3Reg/149A
Jn., sen., pipemaker, Marl., 1737, W, P1/G/515, P1/8Reg/177B
Jn., Marl., 1765, AB, P1/G/650
Jn., gardener, Westb., 1829, O, W, P25/1829/3
My., widow, Westb., 1827, AB, comm, Wr, P25/1827/2
Richd., pipemaker, Devizes St My., 1736, I, W, P1/G/511, P1/8Reg/160
Richd., clothworker, Bradford A., 1749, AB, ren, P2/G/872
Richd., Westb., 1778, W, P25/1778/2
Richd., brickmaker, Westb., 1816, W, P25/1816/5
Robt., bricklayer, Bridewell St., Devizes St Jn., 1855, aff, D, O, W, Wr, P1/1855/22
Sam., yeo., Westb., 1826, O, W, Wr, P25/1826/6
Sarah, sp., Chapmanslade, Dilton, Westb., 1841, AB, comm, Wr, P25/1841/4
Wm., husb., Wingfield, 1560, W, P2/4Reg/43B
Wm., sen., Wingfield, 1563, AB, P2/4Reg/138A
Greenleaf, Jn., Bere R., Dorset, 1661, AB, P5/1661/22
Greenman, Alice, sp., Lyneham, 1730, W, P1/G/471, P1/7Reg/402
Dan., mason, Castle C., 1793, ren, W, P3/G/759
David, dairyman, Dauntsey, 1854, aff, O, W, Wr, P3/1854/32
Gabriel, Hullavington, 1777, W, P3/G/710
Jn., yeo., Melk., 1661, I, W, P2/G/325
Jos., yeo., Lt. Somerford, 1832, aff, W, Wr, P3/1832/3
Robt., Langley Fitzurse, Kington St M., 1836, W, Wr, P3/1836/61
Thos., farmer, Hullavington, 1823, W, P3/1823/21

Greenoff *see* Greenaugh
Greenway *see* Greenaway
Greenwood, Chas., farmer and victualler, Crickl. St S., 1848, comm, W, Wr, P3/1848/52
Dorothy, widow, Newbury, Berks., 1690, I, W, P1/G/270
Eliz., sp., Sal., 1758, AB, P4/1758/5
Hannah, widow, Sal., 1680, AB, I, P4/1679/16
Hy., yeo., E. Winterslow, 1694, I, W, P2/G/553
Joan, widow, E. Winterslow, 1635, I, W, P1/G/130
Jn., tanner, Chipp., 1727, comm, W, P3/G/507
Richd., husb., E. Winterslow, 1591, AB, I, P2/G/59
Thos., husb., Winterslow, 1578, I, P2/G/29
Thos., Blewbury, Berks., 1585, AB, P5/1585/23, P5/4Reg/118A
Thos., Winterslow, 1697, AB, I, ren, P2/G/565
Greete *see* Greate
Greetham, Hy., clerk rector, Enborne, Berks., 1674, D, I, L, W, P1/G/224
Greethurst, Robt., yeo., Winkfield, Berks., 1770, W, P1/G/677, P1/12Reg/375
Grefen *see* Griffin
Gregory, Agnes, widow, Bishopstone N., 1573, W, P5/3Reg/10B
Agnes, husb., Hurst, Berks., 1599, AB (2), I, P5/1598/22
Agnes, widow, Castle Eaton, 1629, I, W, P3/G/110
Alice, widow, Gt. Bedwyn, 1585, AB, P5/1585/22, P5/4Reg/122C
Alice, widow, Box, 1610, AB, P3/G/20
Alice, widow, Pickwick, Corsham, 1627, AB, I, W, P29/G/10, P29/1Reg/109
Andrew, cordw., N. Moreton, Berks., 1750, I, W, P1/G/586, P1/10Reg/356
Ann, widow, Hungerford, Berks., 1631, discharge of ex., P5/1631/47
Ann, sp., Twyford, Hurst, Berks., 1827, AB, Wr, P5/1827/18
Benj., Wantage, Berks., 1710, I, W, P23/311
Betty, sp., Calne, 1848, aff, W, Wr, P5/1848/9
Brian, Melk., 1780, AB, P2/G/1006
Cath., widow, Studley, Trowb., 1631, I, W, P1/G/112
Chas., Bromham, 1851, AB, comm, D, W, Wr, P1/1851/73
Denise, widow, Winkfield, Berks., 1638, AB, I, P1/G/137
Edmd., no abode stated, 1670, W (NEP), P3/G/217
Edmd., yeo., Savernake Park, 1681, AB, a/c, comm, court paper, I, P1/G/245, P11/24
Edmd., Stitchcombe, Mildenhall, 1754, AB, comm, P3/G/650
Edwd., Lyme R., Dorset, 1681, W, P16/63
Eliz., sp., Sherb., Dorset, 1782, W, P5/1782/14, P5/17Reg/227
Francis, sen., yeo., Grove, Wantage, Berks., 1674, AB, I, W, P23/49-50
Francis, cutler, Marl., 1748, I (detailed incl.shop goods), W, P1/G/580, P1/10Reg/214
Geo., Devizes St Jn., 1603, AB, P1/G/10
Geo., haberdasher, Marl., 1817, req, W, Wr, P1/1817/80
Hy., clerk and parson, Sherrington, 1634, I, W, P1/G/118
Hy., Twyford, Hurst, Berks., 1829, AB, O, Wr, P5/1829/22
Grigory alias Leach, Isaac, yeo., Rudge, Froxfield, 1780, W, P3/G/725
Jas., tailor, Chiseldon, 1829, W, Wr, P1/1829/133
Jas., gent., Corsham, 1843, aff, W, Wr, P3/1843/25
Jas., Calne, 1853, AB, O, Wr, P5/1853/8
Jas., innkeeper, *The George Inn*, Sandy Lane, Chipp., 1856, aff, W, Wr, P3/1856/34
Joan, widow, Sonning, Berks., 1583, W, P5/4Reg/72B
Gregory alias Daniel, Joan, widow, Sherb., Dorset, 1594, AB (2 - in 1 name later altered to Phyllis dau of Gregory D. in error, caused by confusion with P5/6Reg/90D), P5/1594/33, P5/6Reg/90B
Joan, Burbage, 1644, W, P11/15
Jn., yeo., Wokm., Berks., 1564, W, P5/1Reg/49A
Jn., Laverstock, 1565, AB, P2/4Reg/194A
Jn., Sonning, Berks., 1574, W, P5/3Reg/43C
Jn., Burbage, 1579, I, NW, P5/1579/34, P5/3Reg/138C
Jn., husb., Bulmershe, Sonning, Berks., 1591, I, W, P5/1591/32, P5/5Reg/116B
Jn., husb., Hurst, Berks., 1599-1600, AB (re Jn. & Agnes G.), W, P5/6Reg/219, 241B
Grigory, Jn., husb., Studley, Trowb., 1610, I, W, P1/G/31
Jn., Corsham, 1616, I, P29/G/5

Gregory alias Cull, Jn., bricklayer, Chilton F., 1725, W, P3/G/498
Jn., Lt. Bedwyn, 1744, W, P21/9/47
Jn., Reading, Berks., 1747, AB, P1/G/570
Jn., bricklayer, Chilton F., 1755, W, P3/G/655
Jn., bach., Melk., 1818, AB, P2/1818/4
Grigory, Jn., miller, Westbrook Mill, Bromham, 1826, W, Wr, P1/1826/114
Jos., scribler, Melk., 1795, W, Wr, P1/G/751, P1/14Reg/548A
Jos., Marl. (with goods in Wilcot), 1844, AB, alleg, comm, O, Wr, P3/1844/19, 29
Grigory, Mgt., widow, Burbage, 1597, AB, I, W, P5/1597/53, P5/6Reg/152F
Grigory, Martin, Castle Eaton, 1620, I, W, P1/G/75
My., widow, Hungerford, Berks., 1625, I, W, P5/1625/36, P5/10Reg/297B
My., New St., Sal., 1669, I, W, P4/1669/11
Michael, husb., Chards., Devon, 1668, I, W, P5/1668/29
Nich., Chipp., 1722, I (2), W, P3/G/482
Richd., sen., yeo., Wantage, Berks., 1671, I, W, P5/1671/36
Richd., yeo., Wantage, Berks., 1709, I, W, P23/294
Richd., Whitep., 1847, AB, ren, Wr, P2/1847/19
Robt., Sutton Poyntz, Dorset, 1593, AB, I, P5/1592/35
Robt., husb., Bere R., Dorset, 1599-1605, I, T (child: Thos. G.), W, P5/1599/8, P5/1605/26, P5/6Reg/223
Robt., husb., Hurley, Berks., 1616, AB, I, P1/G/57, 64
Robt., Ash, Stourpaine, Dorset, 1636, AB, comm, I, P24/53
Robt., Bray, Berks., 1729, AB, P1/G/458
Robt., gent., Devizes, 1841, O, W, Wr, P1/1841/2
Stephen, innholder, Sal., 1748, AB, W, P4/1748/4
Susanna, widow, Burbage, 1704, W, P5/1704/23
Thos., Netheravon, 1589, AB, I, P12/240, P5/5Reg/50C
Grigory, Thos., Haydon Wick, Rodbourne C., 1675, I, W, P3/G/238
Grigory, Thos., Lt. Bedwyn, 1708, AB, I, P21/6/45
Thos., Oak Hill, Froxfield, 1745, AB, P3/G/614
Thos., labourer, Hungerford, Berks., 1749, AB, ren, P23/614
Thos., labourer, Reading, Berks., 1759, W, P1/G/627, P1/11Reg/388A
Wm., sen., Holnest, Dorset, 1580, I, W, P5/1580/26, P5/3Reg/149A
Wm., Borough, Sonning, Berks., 1591, AB, I, W, P5/1591/31, P5/5Reg/112B
Wm., gardener, Newbury, Berks., 1717, W, P1/G/397, P1/6Reg/142
Wm., bricklayer, Chilton F., 1734, AB, I, P3/G/561
Wm., Chr. M., 1748, W, P3/G/631
Wm., gent., Hannington, 1778, W, P3/G/717
Wm., yeo., Studley, Calne, 1800, note of admon, W, P5/1800/34, P5/18Reg/306B
Wm., yeo., Sands Farm, Calne, 1846, note, W, Wr, P5/1846/21
Wm., sen., Sandridge Hill, Melk., 1852, AB, D, O, Wr, P2/1852/17
see also Leach alias G.; Persons alias G.
Greinshere, Thos., Gt. Amesb., 1688, AB, I, P2/G/519
Greller *see* Girdler
Greneway *see* Greenway
Grenhill *see* Greenhill
Grevill *see* Gravell
Grey *see* Gray
Greyne *see* Green
Gridler *see* Girdler
Grier, Alexander, yeo. and husb., Hamptworth, Downton, 1732, I, W, P2/G/778
Griffen *see* Griffin
Griffeth *see* Griffith
Griffin, Abraham, clerk, Garsdon, 1689, AB, P1/G/275
Agnes, widow, Steeple A., 1615, I, W, P2/G/168
Griffen, Ann, widow, Enford, 1732, I, W, P1/G/486, P1/7Reg/531B
Griffen, Ann, sp., Heath Hill, Steeple A., 1737, W, P2/G/805
Ann, sp., Avebury, 1739, AB, comm, I, P3/G/584
Ann, Latton, 1749, W, P3/G/635
Anthony, weaver, Steeple A., 1602, I, W, P1/G/8
Cath., widow, Sherb., Dorset, 1591, AB, P5/5Reg/96A

Griffen, Chas., Trowb., 1829, W, Wr, P1/1829/145
David, tucker, Warm., [1621], I, NW, P2/G/194
David, cooper, Malm., 1731, W, P3/G/540
Denise, widow, Warm., 1710, W, P2/G/637
Griffen alias Gaite, Edith, widow, Westb., 1687, AB, I, P25/1687/3
Edwd., Porton, Idmiston, 1612, T (unnamed children), P2/G/152
Edwd., cordw., Enford, 1719, I, W, P2/G/693
Edwd., yeo., Latton, 1770, W, P1/G/671, P1/12Reg/336A
Eliz., widow, Fisherton A., 1783, W, P1/G/726, P1/14Reg/29
Elnard *or* Ellen, E. Kennett, 1609, W, P3/G/15
Griffen, Frances, sp., Croucheston, Bishopstone S., 1736, W, P1/G/512, P1/8Reg/150
Francis, maltster, Steeple A., 1823, W, Wr, P1/1823/79
Griffen, Geo., yeo., All C., 1676, I, W, P3/G/247
Griffen, Geo., Netheravon, 1748, AB, P12/178
Hannah, widow, Beckhampton, Avebury, 1777, W, P3/G/711
Hy., yeo., N. Tidworth (of T. but goods left there & Newton T.), 1614, I, W, P1/G/50
Hy., husb., Tilsh., 1638, AB, I, W, P2/G/273
Jas., shopkeeper, Kington St M., 1834, W, Wr, P3/1834/32
Jane, widow, Kellaways, 1684, I, W, P3/G/297
Jane, sp., Warm., 1726, AB, P2/G/737
Jane, widow, Avebury, 1728, I, W, P3/G/517
Jane, widow, Malm., 1808, W, P1/1808/82
Joan, widow, Sherb., Dorset, 1591, AB, P5/1591/33
Jn., Teffont E., 1638, AB, I, P1/G/136
Jn., yeo., Garsdon, 1651, I, W, P1/G/169
Grefen, Jn., husb., Bloxworth, Dorset, 1664, I, W, P5/1664/17
Jn., sen., Tytherton L., Chipp., 1668, AB, a/c, comm, court paper, I, receipt (2), P3/G/197
Griffen, Jn., yeo., Steeple A., 1676, I, W, P2/G/394
Jn., Allington, 1685, AB, P3/G/312
Jn., innholder, Avebury, 1716, I, W, Wr, P3/G/454
Jn., yeo., Avebury, 1723, I, W, P3/G/485
Jn., clothier, Trowb., 1724, AB, W, P1/G/433, P1/7Reg/36A
Jn., gent., Avebury, 1734, AB, W, P3/G/555
Jn., Kington St M., 1768, AB, P3/G/689
Griffen, Jn., Trowb., 1770, AB, I, P1/G/680
Jn., innholder, Wilton, 1775, W, P2/G/982
Jn., Kington St M., 1791, AB, P3/G/755
Jn., Clarendon Park, 1837, AB, Wr, P5/1837/3
Jonathan, cooper, Avill's Farm, Corsham, 1760, W, P3/G/667
Jonathan, shopkeeper, Malm., 1798, W, P1/G/765, P1/15Reg/116B
Jos., yeo., Avebury, 1719-33, AB (2), comm, I, W, P3/G/465, 518, 556
Jos., husb., Beckhampton, Avebury, 1748, W, P3/G/632
Lucy, widow, Nether C., Dorset, 1855, aff, O, W, Wr, P5/1855/15
Lydia, wife, Ogbourne St Geo., 1749, AB, Wr, P5/1749/22
Mgt., widow, Malm., 1711, W, P1/G/367, P1/5Reg/226
My., widow, Wantage, Berks., 1754, W, P23/652
Griffen, My., widow, Netheravon, 1757, AB, P12/182
Peter, yeo., Avebury, 1702, I, W, P3/G/413
Richd., yeo., Faulston, Bishopstone S., 1716, I, W, P2/G/675
Richd., yeo., Faulston, Bishopstone S., 1733, I, W, P2/G/783
Griffen, Robt., shepherd, Patney, 1628, I, W, P1/G/105
Sibyl, widow, Gt. Faringdon, Berks., 1639, I, W (damaged), P5/1639/35
Griffen, Silas, parish clerk, Steeple A., 1833, W, Wr, P2/1833/35
Simon, Alvediston, 1640, AB, NW, P2/G/285
Griffen, Stephen, currier, Warm., 1696, comm, I, W, P2/G/555
Thos., Clyffe P., 1613, AB, P1/G/39
Griffen, Thos., Netheravon, 1702, I, W, P12/139
Thos., yeo., Avebury, 1716, I, W, P1/G/391, P1/6Reg/46
Thos., barber, Mkt. L., 1717, W, P2/G/687
Thos., gent., Ogbourne St Geo., 1763, W, P23/702

Thos., gent., Avebury, 1814, W, Wr, P3/1814/16
Timothy, Avebury, 1710, I, W, P3/G/435
Walter, sen., yeo., Clewer, New Windsor, Berks., 1717, W, P1/G/398, P1/6Reg/93
Wm., Enford, 1558, W, P2/3Reg/78B
Wm., sen., Steeple A., 1563-64, I, W, P2/G/14, P2/4Reg/131B
Wm., weaver, Steeple A., 1596, I, W, P2/G/75
Wm., Teffont M., 1642, AB, I, P2/G/300
Wm., Malm., 1684, AB, I, P3/G/298
Wm., cooper, Malm., 1779, W, P1/G/710, P1/13Reg/241
Wm., Malm., 1789, AB, P3/G/749
Griffen, Wm., labourer, Steeple A., 1830, AB, O, W, Wr, P2/1830/61
Wm., widower, Sal., 1856, AB, aff, Wr, P4/1856/5
see also Suter alias G.
Griffith, Ann, widow, Trowb., 1727, W, P1/G/451, P1/7Reg/180
Jn., Beam., Dorset, 1593, I, T, W, P5/1593/38, P5/6Reg/44A
Gruffith, Jn., cardmaker, Reading, Berks., 1695-1714, AB, comm (2), I, W, P1/G/295
Griffiths, Jn., hoopmaker, Warm., 1820, W, Wr, P1/1820/68
Richd., MA and vicar, Idmiston, 1617, I, W, P2/G/174, P2/8Reg/318
Robt., Steeple A., 1589, I, W, P2/G/44
Robt., Trowb., 1721, AB, note, P1/G/410
Griffiths, Robt., gent., Marl. & Wootton B., 1841, AB, comm, P3/1841/51
Thos., sen., yeo., Blewbury, Berks., 1620, I, W, P5/1620/21, P5/10Reg/3B
see also Davis alias G.
Grigg, Geo., Warm., 1585, AB, P2/6Reg/141A
Sam., sen., gent., Newbury, Berks., 1823, W, Wr, P1/1823/110
Stephen, sen., Newbury, Berks., 1770, W, P1/G/672, P1/12Reg/349B
Griggs, Thos., husb., Chetnole, Yetm., Dorset, 1679, I, W, P5/1679/33
Grigory *see* Gregory
Grimer, Ann, widow, Wootton B., 1675, I, W, P3/G/239
Geoffrey, Clyffe P., 1679, AB, P3/G/270
Grymer, Jas., vicar, Chitterne St My., 1567, ren, W, P2/5Reg/28A
Grymer, Jn., Chitterne AS, 1596, AB, P2/G/73
Richd., yeo., Wootton B., 1670, comm, I, L, NW, P3/G/218
Grimes, Ann, sp., Keevil, 1748, W, P2/G/864
Grymes, Jas., Purton, 1796, AB, P3/G/765
Grimess, Joan, widow, Purton, 1744, AB, P3/G/607
Grymes, Jn., yeo., Purton, 1825, comm, W, Wr, P3/1825/38
Martha, sp., Woodb., 1836, AB, O, Wr, P3/1836/16
Nehemiah, Woodb., 1844, req, copy W, Wr, P3/1844/64
Richd., yeo., Allweston, Folke, Dorset, 1692, AB, comm, I, P5/1692/33
Grymes, Richd., yeo., Ashcombe Farm, Caundle Marsh, Dorset, 1763, W, P5/1763/9
Thos., Woodb., 1852, W, Wr, P3/1852/13
Grinaway *see* Greenaway
Grindy *see* Grundy
Grine *see* Green
Grinfield *see* Greenfield
Grinnell, Jn., yeo., Friars Farm, Shrivenham, Berks., 1789, W, P1/G/735, P1/14Reg/209B
Grinsfield *see* Greenfield
Grinter, Grinter *or* Grinster, Jn., Beam., Dorset, 1679, AB, I, ren, P5/1679/35
Grinway *see* Greenaway
Grissell, Thos., yeo., Sal., 1625, I, ren, P4/1624/16
Grist, Ann, Bradford A., 1735, AB, P2/G/796
Ann, sp., Bishopstone N., 1842, W, Wr, P5/1842/17
Edith, widow, Bulford, 1699, I, W, P2/G/573
Edwd., broad weaver, Lacock, 1635, I, W, P1/G/126
Edwd., Lacock, 1730, W, P3/G/536
Edwd., broad weaver, Westb., 1823, W, Wr, P25/1823/4
Esther, wife, Bradford A., 1844, O, W, Wr, P2/1844/31
Frances, widow, Reybridge, Lacock, 1730, W, P3/G/537
Geo., carp., Bradford A., 1820, O, W, Wr, P2/1820/23

Grace, baker's widow, Lacock, 1720-21, W, P1/G/409, P1/6Reg/370
Hy., sen., husb. and labourer, Warm., 1691, I, W, P2/G/533
Hy., sen., Bulford, 1698, W, P2/G/569
Jas., husb., Bulford, 1665, I, W, P2/G/338
Jas., yeo., Bulford, 1748, W, P1/G/579, P1/10Reg/206
Jas., servant to Wm. Batt, esquire, Coombe B. (master of Nunton, Bodenham), 1754, W, P5/1754/7
Jas., carp., Melk., 1796, AB, comm, W, P2/G/1070
Jas., Bishopstone N., 1823, AB, Wr, P6/151
Jas., carp., Melk., 1850, AB, O, W, Wr, P2/1850/23
Joan, widow, Lacock, 1639, I, W, P3/G/161
Jn., Lacock, 1688, AB, I, Wr, P3/G/333
Jn., baker, Lacock, 1716, AB, comm, court paper, I, ren (2), W, P3/G/455
Jn., joiner, Laverstock, 1756, W, P2/G/897
Greast, Jn., mariner on Intrepid, (Captain) Jn. Hale, Sal., 1764, probate copy of W, P4/1764/8
Jn., yeo., Bulford, 1799, W, P2/G/1076
Jos., Wylye, 1700, AB, P2/G/582
Jos., baker, Heytes., 1798, W, P5/1798/10, P5/18Reg/259
Judith, widow, Bradford A., 1789, W, P2/G/1047
Grysse, Mgt., Melk., 1574, W, P2/5Reg/187A
Gryst, My., widow, Wylye, 1701, NW, P2/G/589
My., widow, Sal., 1757, AB, P4/1757/12
Reuben, Langham Farm, N. Bradley, 1848, AB, Wr, P1/1848/48
Richd., baker and clerk, Lacock, 1731, I, W, P3/G/541
Richd., pastry cook, Bradford A., 1819, W, Wr, P2/1819/37
Robt., Westb. L., 1825, AB, O, W, Wr, P25/1825/14
Sarah, widow, Horningsham, 1820, AB, comm, Wr, P5/1820/16
Thos. Duffett, carp., Westb. L., 1848, W, Wr, P25/1848/3
Walter, husb., Newton T., 1670, NW, P2/G/357
Wm., sen., baker, Leigh, Bradford A., 1733, W, P2/G/782
Grivel *see* Gravell
Grome, Agnes, widow, S. Wraxall, 1583, W, P2/6Reg/84A
Thos., husb., S. Wraxall, 1565, W, P2/4Reg/206A
Wm. *see* Ellis Lanham
Grose, Elias, schoolmaster, Marl., 1810, W, Wr, P1/1810/8
Eliz., sp., Sal., 1817, W, Wr, P4/1817/5
Mgt., sp., Marl., 1795, AB, W, P1/G/758, P1/14Reg/634A
Grove, Ann, yeo.'s widow, Burghfield, Berks., 1744, W, P1/G/556, P1/9Reg/346
Groves, Benj., Halstock, Dorset, 1765, AB, P16/329
Eliz., Wantage, Berks., 1692, AB, P5/1692/35
Groves, Helen, widow, Grove, Wantage, Berks., 1594, I, W, P5/1594/34, P5/6Reg/80
Jas., Reading, Berks., 1798, AB, P1/G/763, P1/15Reg/58B
Groves, Jas., thatcher, Beam., Dorset, 1853, comm, W, Wr, P17/624
Jane, widow, Waltham St Lawr., Berks., 1726, W, P1/G/443, P1/7Reg/95B
Joan, widow, Hungerford, Berks., 1605, I, W, P5/1605/24, P5/8Reg/26B
Jn., jun., gardener, Sal., 1663, I, W, P4/1663/12
Jn., servant to Doctor Blagrove, Longworth, Berks., 1698, AB, I, P1/G/308
Jn., gent., Martin, Hants, 1723, W, P2/G/721
Groves, Lucy, wife, Swindon, 1855, AB, aff, O, Wr, P3/1855/11
My., widow, Sal., 1666, NW, P4/1666/13
My., widow, Wantage, Berks., 1697, I, W, P23/219
My., widow, Ruscombe, Berks., 1707, W, P5/1707/26, P5/15Reg/5
Richd., yeo., White Waltham, Berks., 1711, AB, I, P1/G/362
Richd., yeo., Ruscombe, Berks., 1713, W, P5/1713/32, P5/15Reg/370A
Richd., jun., yeo., Stonewall, White Waltham, Berks., 1732, W, P1/G/481, P1/7Reg/479A
Groves, Richd., thatcher, Beam., Dorset, 1838, comm, W, Wr, P17/611
Robt., Ludg., 1583, W, P2/6Reg/105A
Robt., esquire, Donhead St A., 1664, comm, I, W, P1/G/196
Robt., gent., Baulking, Uffington, Berks., 1698-99, comm, I, W, P1/G/312, P1/3Reg/206
Robt., carp., Fernham, Longcott, Shrivenham, Berks., 1808, W, Wr, P1/1808/93
Simon, Hurley, Berks., 1744, I, W, P1/G/554, P1/9Reg/363A

Thos., Ruscombe, Berks., 1609, AB, P5/1609/33, P5/8Reg/151B
Thos., husb., Martin, Hants, 1612, AB, I, W, P2/G/154
Thos., Waltham St Lawr., Berks., 1645, comm, I, P1/G/150
Thos., gent., Martin, Hants, 1645, I, P2/G/307
Thos., Sal., 1667, W, P4/1666/19
Thos., innholder, Wantage, Berks., 1685, I, W, P23/146
Thos., Ruscombe, Berks., 1686, AB, I, P5/1686/26
Thos., yeo., Swallowfield, Shinfield, Berks., 1711, AB, I, P1/G/360
Thos., Martin, Hants, 1713, AB, I, P2/G/657
Thos., yeo., Ruscombe, Berks., 1733, AB, comm, W, P5/1733/25
Thos., jun., yeo., Stonewall Farm, White Waltham, Berks., 1738, W, P1/8Reg/272
Thos., sen., yeo., Stonewall Farm, White Waltham, Berks., 1738, W, P1/G/518
Thos., victualler, Pewsey, 1773, W, P1/G/684, P1/12Reg/452
Groves, Wm., glover, Hungerford, Berks., 1588, AB, I, P5/1588/25, P5/5Reg/33A
Wm., Arborfield, Berks., 1596, AB, a/c, I, P5/1596/31, P5/6Reg/138F
Wm., yeo., Minety, 1614, I, W, P1/G/45
Wm., gent., Bower C., 1632-36, AB, a/c, W, copy W, P2/G/242, 263, P2/9Reg/106B
Wm., clerk, Poulshot, 1666, AB, comm, I, P1/G/201
Wm., sen., Waltham St Lawr., Berks., 1686, AB, I, P1/G/779
see also Arnold alias G.
Grover, Ann, sp., Calne, 1851, O, W, Wr, P5/1851/5
Edwd., husb., Hurst, Berks., 1677, AB, I, P5/1677/20
Humphrey, Downton, 1857, aff, D, W, Wr, P2/1857/40
Jn., Highw., 1720, AB, P10/1720/2
Groves *see* Grove
Growte, Nich., Bere R., Dorset, 1570, AB, P5/2Reg/73D
Grubb, Jane, widow, Pott., 1708, comm, I, W, P1/G/349
Grubbe, Mgt., sp., Pott., 1750, comm, req, copy W, W, P1/G/582, P1/10Reg/266
Stephen, bach., Calne, 1852, AB, O, Wr, P5/1852/21
Grubbe, Thos., baker and maltster, Chipp., 1768, W, P3/G/690
Grubham, Geo., yeo., Chards., Devon, 1763, W, P14/162
Geo., sen., Chards., Devon, 1838, AB, comm, Wr, P14/222
Jn., husb., Pound St., Lyme R., Dorset, 1697, I, W, P16/148
Gruffith *see* Griffith
Grundy, Grindy, Cath., widow, Chedglow, Crudwell, 1623, I, W, P3/G/82
Eliz., widow, Stanton Fitzwarren, [1601], W (NEP), P3/1Reg/90B
Grindy, Giles, yeo., Charlton nr Malm., 1707, ren, P3/G/428
Jn., E. Stowell, Wilcot, 1571, W, P1/1Reg/128B
Grindy, Jn., husb., Bishopstone N., 1599, I, W, P5/1598/21, P5/6Reg/214C
Jn., husb., Stratton St Mgt., 1616, I, W, P3/G/43
Jn., tailor, Stratton St Mgt., 1617, I, W, P3/G/53
Jn., tanner, Marl., 1624, I, W, P1/G/81
Grindy, Jn., tanner, Marl. St My., 1625, AB, W, P1/G/95
Jn., yeo., Stratton St Mgt., 1679, W, P3/G/271
Mgt., widow, Stratton St Mgt., 1631, I, W, P3/G/121
Margery, widow, Liddington, 1623, I, W, P3/G/83
Nich., Norton, 1613, AB, W, P3/G/32
Grindy, Robt., husb., Chedglow, Crudwell, [1613], I, W (NEP), P3/G/31
Wm., sen., husb., Ninnocks, Rams., 1607, I, W, P5/1607/27, P5/8Reg/132B
Wm., husb., Liddington, 1613, W, P3/G/33
Grunsell, Thos., Plaitford, 1614, AB, I, P1/G/41
Grymer *see* Grimer
Grymes *see* Grimes
Gryne *see* Green
Grysse, Gryst *see* Grist
Guard *see* Goard
Gudderidge, Guddridge *see* Gutteridge
Gudge, Gowge, Jn., sen., husb., Beam., Dorset, 1611, I, W, P5/1610/24, P5/9Reg/50A
Jn., husb., Beam., Dorset, 1632, AB, I, P17/9
Jn., yeo., Shatcombe, Beam., Dorset, 1678, AB, I, P17/272

My., widow, Netherb., Dorset, 1723, W, P17/409
Richd., coachman, Sal., 1735, W, P1/G/497, P1/7Reg/626
Guest, Eliz., widow, Ashton K., 1795, comm, W, P1/G/749, P1/14Reg/551
Hy., Leigh, Ashton K., 1767, AB, comm, P3/G/687
My., widow, Norton, 1769, W, P3/G/693
Robt., Kemble, 1696, AB, I, P3/G/383
Guess, Robt., husb., Earley, Sonning, Berks., 1747, W, P5/1747/9
Geste, Thos., cutler, Sherb., Dorset, 1699, W, P5/1699/15
Thos. Robt., artist, Sal., 1819, W, P4/1819/6
Wm., Norton, 1760, W, P3/G/668
Gugo, Robt., Durrington, 1566, AB (of a minor's estate), P2/4Reg/220C
Guiding *see* Giddings
Guilden *see* Golding
Guilford, Thos., husb., Ashton K., 1607, I, W, P3/G/10
Guill *see* Gill
Guilliams, Jn., clerk and vicar, S. Burcombe, 1601, AB, I, W, P2/G/106
Guines *see* Gine
Guire *see* Gwyer
Guley, Agnes, widow, Yarnbrook, N. Bradley, 1581, W, P2/6Reg/29B
Amy, widow, Sharcott, Pewsey, 1844, O, W, Wr, P3/1844/53
Anthony, serge weaver, Snarlton, Steeple A., 1722, W, P2/G/713
Anthony, Trowb., 1753, AB, comm, P1/G/598
Cath., sp., N. Bradley, 1604, AB, I, P2/G/114
Edwd., broad weaver, Yarnbrook, N. Bradley, 1663, comm, NW, P1/G/184
Edwd., Broad Town, Broad H., 1700, AB, I, P3/G/400
Eliz., Trowb., 1755, AB, ren, P1/G/611
Francis, serge weaver, Paxcroft, Steeple A., 1676, AB, I, P2/G/395
Gifford, victualler, Yarnbrook, N. Bradley, 1768, AB, ren, W, P2/G/957
Jas., Yarnbrook, N. Bradley, 1590, I, W, P2/G/47
Jas., Trowle, Bradford A., 1810, AB, comm, Wr, P2/1810/64
Jn., tailor, Warm., 1600, I, W, P2/G/102
Jn., weaver, Yarnbrook, N. Bradley, 1630, AB, I, copy I, P2/G/232
Richd., W. Ashton, Steeple A., 1697, AB, I, P2/G/559
Walter, draper, Warm., 1554, W, P2/2Reg/192A
Wm., sen., Sharcott, Pewsey, 1835, comm, W, P1/1835/118
Gull, Robt., yeo., Speen, Berks., 1738, W, P1/G/524, P1/8Reg/297
Gulledge *see* Golledge
Gulliford, Joan, widow, Mere, 1739, AB, Wr, P5/1739/22
Joan, widow, Hilp., 1759, W, P2/G/917
Jn., Hilp., 1749, AB, comm, P2/G/874
Walter, Maiden B., 1725, W, P2/G/728
Gulliver, Chas., yeo., Crockerton, Longbridge D., 1767, W, P1/G/666, P1/12Reg/259B
David, labourer, Cherhill, 1704, I, W, P26/507
Harry, Mere, 1778, AB, P5/1778/8, P5/17Reg/156C
Isaac, yeo., Semington, Steeple A., 1765, W, P2/G/944
Jacob, Semington, Steeple A., 1792, AB, comm, P2/G/1057
Jean, widow, Hinton, Steeple A., 1712, I, W, P2/G/649
Jn., blacksmith, Deptford, Wylye, 1610, I, NW, P2/G/139, P2/8Reg/119A
Jn., carp., Deptford, Wylye, [1686], I, ren, W, P2/G/494
Jn., yeo., Hinton, Steeple A., 1712, I, W, P2/G/652
Jn., Steeple A., 1776, AB, P2/G/990
Jos., wheelwright, Mere (form. of St Marylebone, Middlesex), 1719, W, P5/1719/35, P5/16Reg/32C
Margery, Deptford, Wylye, 1618, I, NW, P2/G/180
My., widow, Mere, 1710, AB, P5/1710/45
Richd., yeo., Mere, 1707, W, P5/1707/27, P5/15Reg/26
Thos., Wylye, 1584, AB, P2/6Reg/138A
Thos., yeo., Semington, Steeple A., 1696, I, W, P2/G/556
Walter, yeo., Longbridge D., 1684, I, W, P2/G/484
[illegible], Mere, 1710, AB, P5/1710/46
[illegible] Semington, Steeple A., 1842, AB, comm, Wr, P2/1842/8

Gulwell, Francis, Luckington, 1570, W (NEP), P1/1Reg/118B
Jn., yeo., Alderton, 1687, I, W, P3/G/321
Gum, Rebecca, widow, Seend, Melk., 1840, W, Wr, P2/1840/49
Roger, yeo., Seend, Melk., 1703, AB, I, P2/G/601
Gumbleton, Ann, sp., Britford, 1742, W, P24/986
Edwd., labourer, Sal., 1620, AB, I, P4/1720/5
Hy., blacksmith, Long Burton, Dorset, 1665, AB, I, P5/1665/39
Hy., yeo., Stourpaine, Dorset, 1720, W, P24/628
Gomeldon, Joan, Britford, 1587, I, W, P5/1587/20, P5/4Reg/142E
Jn., innholder, Sal., 1671, I (detailed), W, P4/1670/21
Jn., blacksmith, Britford, 1705, AB, I (2 - 1 records working materials & tools), P24/594
Jonathan, innkeeper, Sal., 1702, W, P4/1702/8
Gumbelton, Jonathan, blacksmith, Britford, 1747, W, P24/1061
Gomelton, Robt., Britford, 1579, I (part missing), W, P5/1578/17, P5/3Reg/105B
Gomelton, Robt., Britford, 1581, AB, P5/1580/24, P5/4Reg/1D
Robt., blacksmith, W. Grimstead, 1764, W, P2/G/939
Gomeldon, Roger, sen., yeo., Porton, Idmiston, [1546-47], I, W, P2/G/1, P2/2Reg/33
Gomelton, Roger, yeo., Idmiston, 1560, W, P2/4Reg/42A
Sarah, sp., Charlton, Donhead St My., 1834, W, Wr, P2/1834/38
Susan, widow, Sal., 1727, W, P4/1726/11
Susanna, Sal., 1683, AB, P1/G/250
Susanna, sp., Sal., 1729, W, P1/G/466, P1/7Reg/357B
Thos., husb., Britford, 1638, I, W, P24/432
Gummer, Ann, N. Wootton, Dorset, 1759, AB, P5/1759/11
Gundry, Cath., widow, Calne, 1804, AB, P26/1247
Edmd., Beam., Dorset, 1708, AB, P17/171
Fanny, wife, Sherb., Dorset, 1754, AB, P5/1754/8
Francis, bach., Sherb., Dorset, 1798, AB, comm, ren, P5/1798/9, P5/18Reg/261A
Jn., woolstapler, Calstone W., 1761, AB, ren, W, P5/1761/18
Jn., gent., Quemerford, Calne, 1816, W, Wr, P26/1307
Maria, sp., Calne, 1846, AB, comm, Wr, P5/1846/6
Martha, sp., Calne, 1846, note, O, W, Wr, P5/1846/8
Peter, bach., Calne, 1803, AB, P26/1241
Peter, yeo., Stock St., Calne, 1808, note, W, P26/1270
Peter, gent., Southbroom, 1845, O, W, Wr, P24/1376
Gundrey, Ralph, Hindon, 1572, W, P2/5Reg/146A
Robt., husb., Netherb., Dorset, 1688, I, W, P17/307
Robt., yeo., Waytown, Netherb., Dorset, 1726, W, P17/424
Robt., Sherb., Dorset, 1816, AB, comm, O, P5/1816/13
Sam., grocer, Lyme R., Dorset, 1759, W, P16/323
Wm., sen., clothier, Bere R., Dorset, 1735, AB, I, NW, P5/1735/26
Gunhill *see* Gunnell
Gunn, Jn., Warm., 1687, AB, I, P2/G/512
Thos., cooper, Sal., 1620, AB, I, P4/1620/11
Wm., Sal. St Thos., 1616, AB, I, P4/1615/9
Gunnell, Ann, widow, Borough, Sonning, Berks., 1744, comm, W, Wr, P5/1744/17
Eliz., widow, Sonning, Berks., 1797, W, P5/1797/18, P5/18Reg/240
Jn., yeo., Aldworth, Berks., 1716, I, W, P1/G/394, P1/6Reg/73
Jn., yeo., E. Hagbourne, Berks., 1753, I, W, P1/G/600, P1/10Reg/520
Richd., husb., Borough, Sonning, Berks., 1737, W, Wr, P5/1737/20
Richd., Sonning, Berks., 1761, AB, P5/1761/17
see also Grant alias G.
Gunning, Jn., Westb., 1565, W, P5/1Reg/58A
Jn., Warm., 1710, W, P2/G/636
Lettice, widow, Westb., 1576, AB, I, W, P5/1576/20, P5/3Reg/91D
Thos., sen., baptist minister, Downton, 1843, AB, W, Wr, P2/1843/31
Gunstone, Agnes, widow, Westb., 1575, I, W, P25/1575/1, P5/3Reg/56C
Gonstone *or* Goustone, Agnes, Westb., 1580, AB, NW, P5/1580/28, P5/3Reg/150
Ann, widow, E. Tisb., 1855, aff, W, Wr, P1/1855/31
Anthony, Dilton, Westb., 1730, AB, P25/1730/13

Edwd., plumber and glazier, Tisb., 1804, W, P1/1804/126
Geo., innholder, Hindon, 1735-40, AB, W, P1/G/494, P2/G/820, P1/7Reg/611
Gunston, Geo., Westb., 1828, AB, O, P25/1828/2
Grecian, widow, Beanacre, Melk., 1736, W, P2/G/800
Gunston, Hannah, widow, Hindon, 1753, W, P2/G/890
Jas., Melk., 1849, D, W, Wr, P2/1849/27
Jn., mason, Whitley, Melk., 1842, W, Wr, P1/1842/29
My., widow, Dilton M., Westb., 1729, AB, P25/1729/9
Gunston, My., widow, Edington, 1764, comm, W, P2/G/940
Matthias, husb., Heywood, Westb., 1708, I, W, P25/1708/13
Ruth, widow, Tisb., 1795, AB, appt of guardian, T, W, P1/G/748, P1/14Reg/593
Gunston, Solomon, yeo., Edington, 1753, W, P1/G/605, P1/11Reg/123
Gunston, Solomon, victualler, Speenhamland, Berks., 1770, W, P1/G/673, P1/12Reg/347A
Wm., sen., yeo., Edington, 1641, I, W, P2/G/293
Wm., E. Coulston, Edington, 1670-73, AB, comm, I, ren, P2/G/376, 576
Wm., Heywood, Westb., 1671, I, W, P25/1671/12
Wm., yeo., Heywood, Westb., 1676, AB, I, P25/1676/8
Wm., yeo., Edington, 1686, AB, I, P2/G/499
Wm., yeo., Beanacre, Melk., 1729, AB, I, P1/G/470
Gunston, Wm., Melk., 1734, AB, P2/G/793
Gunte, Jn., Sal. St Martin, 1562, W (NEP), P1/2Reg/133B
Richd., husb., Mere, 1565, W, P5/1Reg/54H
Gunter, Anthony, glover, Marl., 1625, I, W, P1/G/88
Wm., Marl. St My., 1636, AB, a/c, I, proclamation, P1/G/131
Wm., gent., Milton L., 1637, AB, P3/G/151
Guppy, Ann, widow, Sal., 1844, AB, Wr, P1/1844/11
Ann, sp., Sherb., Dorset (form. of Alnwick), 1856, AB, aff, O, Wr, P5/1856/13
Chas., Chetnole, Yetm., Dorset, 1798, W, P19/200
Chris., Halstock, Dorset, 1761, AB, P5/1761/19
Eliz., widow, Melplash, Netherb., Dorset, 1730, W, P17/442
Eliz., Wilton, 1756, AB, P1/G/613
Eliz., widow, Halstock, Dorset, 1810, comm, W, P16/372
Hy., yeo., Portland, Halstock, Dorset, 1627, AB, I, P5/1627/19, P5/11Reg/44B
Jn., gent., Seend, Melk., 1676, I, W, P2/G/401
Jn., Chards., Devon, 1691, AB, a/c, P14/74
Jn., yeo., Melplash, Netherb., Dorset, 1701, AB, I, P5/1701/23
Jn., gent., Canonhold, Melk., 1725, W, P2/G/731
Jn., husb., Halstock, Dorset, 1754, AB, I, P16/313
Margery, widow, Lyme R., Dorset, 1628, AB, I, P5/1628/50, P5/11Reg/70C
My., widow, Halstock, Dorset, 1770, AB, P5/17Reg/4C
My., widow, Chards., Devon, 1770, AB, comm, P5/1770/19
Rebecca, sp., Melk., 1735, AB, comm, W, P2/G/798
Richd., Halstock, Dorset, 1630-31, comm, I, W, P5/1631/42, P5/11Reg/180B
Richd., gent., Sandridge Hill, Melk., 1697, W, P2/G/564
Robt., Chards., Devon, 1730, I, W, P14/145
Robt., butcher, Halstock, Dorset, 1781, W, P16/346
Robt., yeo., Leigh, Yetm., Dorset, 1826, W, Wr, P19/236
Sam., sen., yeo., Halstock, Dorset, 1768, W, P16/331
Simon, innholder, Castleton, Dorset, 1729, AB, I, P5/1729/22, P5/16Reg/243A
Thos., jun., Chards., Devon, 1636, a/c, NW (NEP), P30/78
Thos., yeo., Chards., Devon, 1644, AB, alleg, comm, inty, I, process, definitive sentence, W (disputed), P5/1644/14, P5/14Reg/70
Thos., sen., yeo., Chards., Devon, 1711, I, W, P14/114
Thos., sen., schoolmaster, Chards., Devon, 1713, AB, I, W, P5/1713/38, P5/15Reg/378A
Thos., Chards., Devon, 1740, AB, I (detailed), Wr, P5/1740/37
Thos., Chards., Devon, 1751, AB, P14/167
Thos., yeo., Currenden, Halstock, Dorset, 1781, W, P16/347
Wm., husb., Alston, Chards., Devon, 1577, I, W, P5/1576/21, P5/3Reg/100D
Wm., chandler, Halstock, Dorset, 1600, I, W, P5/1600/26, P5/6Reg/252A
Gurd *see* Goard

Gurn, Garn, Thos., wheelwright, Sevenhampton, Highw., 1854, aff, O, W, Wr, P10/1854/1
Wm., yeo., Seend, Melk., 1827, O, W, Wr, P2/1827/56
Gurnard, Agnes *see* Alexander Shifford, P2/8Reg/87A
Gutch, Gatch, Andrew, yeo., Winterborne K., Dorset, 1717, I (2 - 1 a copy), L, W, P5/1717/15, P5/15Reg/403A
Christian, widow, Donhead St My., 1610, AB, I, P2/G/134
Clement, Tisb., 1563, I, W, P2/G/13, P2/4Reg/126A
David, tailor, Tisb., 1623, I, T, W, P2/G/205, 578
Edith, widow, Bemerton, Fugg. St Peter, 1583, W, P2/6Reg/111
Eliz., Tisb., 1581, W, P2/6Reg/23
Geo., Bemerton, Fugg. St Peter, 1568, AB, P2/5Reg/43B
Gaitch, Jas., mariner (on board *The George*, ship hired by the Royal Navy), Lyme R., Dorset, 1691, I, W, P16/117
Gaitch, Jane, sp., Lyme R., Dorset (form. of Uplyme, Devon), 1842, AB, O, Wr, P5/1842/20
Jn., Tisb., 1572, AB, P2/5Reg/159F
Lawr., fuller, Ludwell, Donhead St My., 1591, I (very detailed), W, P2/G/56
Melior, wife, Corsley, 1842, AB, O, Wr (form. Melior Moore, spinster), P1/1842/78
Nich., day labourer, Tisb., [1622], NW, P2/G/200
Gaich, Richd., tailor, Lyme R., Dorset, 1684, I, W, P16/79
Gaich, Wm., carp. (form. shipwright aboard HMS *Constant Warwick*), Lyme R., Dorset, 1690, I, W, P16/104
Gutteridge, Gothridge, Agnes, widow, Ruscombe, Berks., 1633-37, AB, I, W, P5/1633/19, P5/1637/13, P5/12Reg/135
Gothridge, Agnes *see also* Thos. Maynard
Jane, Mkt. L., 1746, AB, I, P2/G/855
Guddridge alias Cornish, Joan, widow, Trowb., 1567, W, P5/1Reg/85B
Gothridge, Jn., yeo., Ruscombe, Berks., 1671-74, AB, a/c, I (2), W, P5/1671/37, P5/1674/30
Guttridge, Jn., husb., Purley, Berks., 1701, I, W, P1/G/320, P1/4Reg/163
Gudderidge, Jn., Purton, 1727, AB, P3/G/508
Jn., Mkt. L., 1812, AB, Wr, P2/1812/35
Guttridge, My., widow, Abingdon, Berks., 1759, W, P1/G/628, P1/11Reg/393A
Gudderidge, Reynold, baker, Sonning, Berks., 1609, I, W, P5/1608/15, P5/8Reg/144C
Gothridge, Thos., sen., Ruscombe, Berks., 1674, AB, I, P5/1674/31
Guttridge, Wm., Purley, Berks., 1759, AB, W, P1/G/626, P1/11Reg/389
see also Goodridge
Guy, Gye, [...], bailiff, Malm., 1571, W (NEP), P1/1Reg/87D
Gyes, Agnes, widow, Longbridge D., 1558, W, P2/3Reg/75D
Gye, Agnes, widow, Tilsh., 1595, AB, I, W, P2/G/72, P2/7Reg/140B
Gye, Agnes, widow, Mkt. L., [1715], W, P2/G/673
Gye, Ann, Rowde, 1624, I, W, P3/G/87
Ann, widow, Avill's Farm, Corsham, 1770, W, P1/G/669, P1/12Reg/328
Anthony, sen., maltster, Chipp., 1716, W, P3/G/456
Anthony, bach., Corsham, 1722, marriage licence, P29/2Reg/43E
Anthony, butcher, Avill's Farm, Corsham, 1777, W, P3/G/712
Barnaby, husb., Allington, Chipp., 1651, comm, I, NW, P1/G/168
Benj., brazier, Sal., 1706, W, P4/1706/5
Bennet, husb., Bere R., Dorset, 1711, comm, W, P5/1711/24, P5/15Reg/271
Gye, Brian, sen., Bps. C., 1736, W, P24/929
David, husb., Longbridge D., 1623, I, W, P2/G/206
David, Bere R., Dorsct, 1671, AB, I, P5/1671/35
David, mason, Bere R., Dorset, 1695, AB, I, W, P5/1695/40
Gye, Edith, Bere R., Dorset, 1589, I, W, P5/1589/22, P5/5Reg/65B
Gye, Edwd., husb., Chitterne AS, 1645, AB, I, P2/G/306
Gye, Edwd., Chitterne AS, 1694, I, W, P2/G/543
Gye, Edwd., sen., Mkt. L., 1715, comm, W, P2/G/672
Gye, Edwd., yeo., Chitterne AS, 1731, W, P2/G/771
Gye, Edwd., Mkt. L., 1732, AB, P2/G/775
Gye, Edwd., Mkt. L., 1783, AB, P1/G/723
Eliz., widow, Collingbourne K., 1626, I, W, P3/G/93
Esther, widow, Gt. Bedwyn, 1732, I, memo, W, P21/8/69
Geo., Horningsham, 1838, W, Wr, P5/1838/1
Gye, Grace, widow, Chitterne AS, 1728, W, P2/G/750
Hannah, widow, Chipp., 1817, comm, W, Wr, P1/1817/107
Hy., baker, Kington St M., 1759, W, P1/G/631, P1/11Reg/447

Isaac, Westb., 1631, AB, I, P25/1631/3
Gye alias Greene, Jas., Collingbourne K., 1570, W, P1/1Reg/20A, 96B
Gye, Jas., farmer and shopkeeper, Heddington, 1843, comm, O, W, Wr, P3/1843/29
Jane, sp., Avill's Farm, Corsham, 1768, W, P3/G/691
Jasper, Bere R., Dorset, 1670, I, W, P5/1670/15
Jeremiah, Horningsham, 1786, AB, comm, P5/1786/4, P5/18Reg/58A
Gye, Jeremiah, Fiddington, W. Lavington, 1837, W, Wr, P1/1837/22
Gye, Jerome, Woodwate, Steeple A., 1688, AB, I, P2/G/521
Gye, Jn., Chirton, 1554, W, P2/2Reg/187C
Gye, Jn., sen., Tilsh., 1574, W, P2/5Reg/213B
Guy alias Greene, Jn., husb., Collingbourne K., 1620, AB, a/c (2), I, ren, P3/G/66
Jn., Bromham, 1624, I, W, P3/G/86
Jn., Bere R., Dorset, 1682, AB, I, P5/1682/42
Gye, Jn., yeo., Chitterne St My., 1698, I, W, P2/G/568
Jn., yeo., Pott., 1699, AB, I, W, P1/G/315, P1/3Reg/261
Gye, Jn., sen., maltster, Mkt. L., 1746, W, P2/G/856
Gye, Jn., Mkt. L., 1758, AB, P2/G/912
Jn., Corsham, 1768, AB, P29/2Reg/114
Gye, Leonard, Shitterton, Bere R., Dorset, 1584, I, W, P5/1583/16, P5/4Reg/78A
Leonard, Foulcombe, Bere R., Dorset, 1598, AB, I, W, P5/1597/52, P5/6Reg/198A
Gye, My., widow, Winterborne K., Dorset, 1596, AB, I, W, P5/1596/27, P5/6Reg/122C
My., widow, Bere R., Dorset, 1683, AB, I, P5/1683/24
My., widow woman, Bradford A., 1799, W, P2/G/1081
Meliora Olivia, widow, Calne, 1819, AB, comm, ren, W, Wr, P26/1321
Richd., vicar, Collingbourne K., 1611, AB, P3/G/21
Richd., Westb., 1754, AB, P25/1754/4
Robt., Bere R., Dorset, 1831, AB, O, W, Wr, P5/1831/2
Sam., Horningsham, 1752, AB, P5/1752/21
Sam., butcher, Avill's Farm, Corsham, 1777, W, P3/G/713
Stephen, carrier, N. Bradley, 1683, AB, I, P2/G/474
Susan, Marl., 1667, AB, I, W, P1/G/204
Gyes, Thos., yeo., Longbridge D., 1557, W, P2/3Reg/8B
Thos., yeo., Burton Hill, Malm., 1608, W, P3/G/11
Gye, Thos., yeo., White Lovington, Bere R., Dorset, [1613], W, P5/1613/34
Thos., yeo., Brunton, Collingbourne K., 1637, I, W, P3/G/152
Thos., widower, Beam., Dorset, 1857, AB, aff, comm, Wr, P17/630
Gye, Wm., vicar, Bower C., Broad C. and Alveston, 1575, W, P2/5Reg/232E, 237B
Wm., sen., Marl., 1616, AB, a/c, P1/G/55
Wm., husb., Sutton B., 1631, W, P3/G/122
Wm., Bradford A., 1726, AB, P1/G/449
Wm., sen., butcher, Avill's Farm, Corsham, 1743, comm, W, P3/G/606
Wm., butcher, Avill's Farm, Corsham, 1766, W, P3/G/684
Wm., Bere R., Dorset, 1788, AB, P5/1788/11, P5/18Reg/91A
Wm., Devizes, 1823, AB, Wr, P1/1823/14
Wm., Corsham, 1831, AB, comm, P3/1831/1
see also Gay
Guyatt *see* Gyatt,
Gwyer, Andrew, maltster, Sal., 1712, W, P4/1712/8
Ann, widow, Gillingham, Dorset, 1690, W, [illegible]
Chris., husb., E. Knoyle, 1707, W, P2/G/625
Eliz., widow, Sal., 1719, W, P4/1719/13
Geo., tailor, Nether Zeals, 1609, AB, I, T, W, P5/1609/34, [illegible]
Gwyer, Jacob, Lower Lodge Farm, Downton, 1758, W, P2/G/907
Gwyer, Jacob, yeo., Lodge Farm, Downton, 1803, AB, W, P2/1803/2
Gwyer, Jacob, yeo., Woodfalls, Downton, 1851, W, Wr, P1/1851/38
Jerman, Beer Hackett, Dorset, 1675, AB, a/c, I, P5/1675/21
Guire, Joan, widow, Over Zeals, 1579, I, W, P5/1579/33, P5/3Reg/136A
Gwyer, Jn., tailor, Mere, 1575, AB, I, P5/1575/16, P5/3Reg/56A
Gwyer, Jn., yeo., Over Zeals, 1612, I, W, P5/1612/20, P5/9Reg/75B
Gwyer, Jn., sen., husb., Over Zeals, 1631, I, W, P5/1631/45, P5/12Reg/31

Gwyer, Jn., husb., Stoke F., 1692, I, W, P1/G/285
Gwyer, Jn., yeo., Lodge Farm, Downton, 1787, W, P2/G/1037
Guyear, My., widow, Marl. (form. of Overton), 1765, W, P1/G/652, P1/12Reg/150B
Gwyer, My., widow, *The Drove*, Downton, 1777, W, P2/G/992
Richd., Sherb., Dorset, 1781, AB, P5/1781/8, P5/17Reg/213A
Robt., Sal., 1633, AB, I, P4/1633/19
Robt., mason, Zeals, 1667, AB, I, P5/1667/21
Thomasine, widow, Zeals, 1634, AB, I(GVS), P5/1634/43
Wm., Gillingham, Dorset, 1684, I, P27/1/75
Wm., Overton, 1738, AB, P3/G/578
Wm., yeo., Newtown, Hungerford, Berks., 1802, W, P23/831
Guyne *see* Gwynn
Guynes *see* Gine
Guyther, Wm., Sal., 1710, AB, P4/1709/19
Gwariar, Peter, rector, Pertwood (to be buried in chancel before picture of St Peter; refers to month's mind), 1557, W, P1/1Reg/15
Gwinnett, Ann, widow, Ashton K., 1726, W, P1/G/441, P1/7Reg/103A
Isaac, clerk and vicar, Ashton K., 1719, comm, I, W, P3/G/466
Jn., clerk, rector and widower, Ashley, 1724, AB, comm, ren (2), P1/G/437
Gwyer *see* Guyer
Gwynn, Guyne, Edith, widow, Netheravon, 1593, I, W, P12/241, P5/6Reg/13B
Geo., fustianmaker, Aldbourne, 1791, W, P3/G/758
Geo., watchmaker, Rams., 1823, W, Wr, P5/1823/17
Gwyn, Hugh, vicar, Shrewton, 1553, AB, P2/2Reg/179C
Joan, widow, Durrington, 1633, I, W, P2/G/247
Jn., Newton T., 1528, W (incomplete copy) (NEP), P2/1Reg/15A
Guyne, Jn., shepherd, Netheravon, 1591, AB, I, W, P5/1591/34, P5/5Reg/108D
Jn., Netheravon, 1631, W, P12/66
Jn., Aldbourne, 1740, W, P3/G/589
Jn., gardener, Aston Tirrold, Berks., 1763, W, P1/G/641, P1/12Reg/78A
Jonathan, gardener, Earley, Sonning, Berks., 1742, W, Wr, P5/1742/18
My., widow, Wilton, 1684, I, W, P2/G/475
Philip, clerk, Wilton, 1678, comm, W, P1/G/236
Wm., husb., Netheravon, [1678], court paper, I, T, W (date of probate missing, damaged), P12/111
Wm., sen., mason, Aldbourne, 1732, W, P1/G/482, P1/7Reg/497A
Wm., sen., Aldbourne, 1737, AB, P3/G/575
Wm., fustian manufacturer, Aldbourne, 1806, W, Wr, P3/1806/37
Gyatt, Guyatt, Sarah, widow, Sal. St Edmd., 1825, W, Wr, P4/1825/13
Thos., Bishopstone S., 1576, AB, I, W, P2/G/24
Thos., Bishopstone S., 1576, W, P2/5Reg/275A
Walter, Broad C., 1561, I, W, P2/G/7, P2/4Reg/81A
Gybburd *see* Gilbert
Gye *see* Guy
Gyell *see* Giles
Gyes *see* Guy
Gyett *see* Gyatt
Gyldon *see* Gildon
Gyles *see* Giles
Gyllett *see* Gillett
Gyne, Gynes *see* Gine
Gynner *see* Jenner
Gyrishe *see* Gerrish

H..., Jn., husb., Speen, Berks., 1664, NW, P1/H/348
Habberly, Haboly alias Clarke, Cath., widow, Clyffe P., 1610, W, P3/H/54
see also Clarke alias H.
Habbott *see* Abbott
Habgood *see* Hopgood
Haboly *see* Habberley
Haccombe *see* Hackham

Hachmane *see* Hatchman
Hackens *see* Hawkins
Hacker, Edwd., Abingdon, Berks., 1747, AB, P1/H/1034
Eliz., sp., Fonthill G., 1766, W, P2/H/1485
Hocker, Eliz., widow, Uffc., Devon, 1779, W, P20/1/263
Hucker, Geo., Bloxworth, Dorset, 1747, AB, P5/1747/12
Geo., shoemaker, Sal., 1813, W, P4/1813/13
Isaac, baker and carrier, Broad H., 1851, D (2), O, W, Wr, P1/1851/69
Jas., Avill's Farm, Corsham, 1814, AB, comm, W, Wr, P1/1814/143
Hucker, Jn., Lyme R., Dorset, 1567, AB, P5/1Reg/86C, P5/2Reg/25C
Haker, Jn., Warm., 1628, I, NW, P2/H/405
Hucker, Jn., carp., Bloxworth, Dorset, 1726, I, W, P5/1726/19, P5/16Reg/134B
Jn., yeo., Tisb., 1776, W, P1/H/1237, P1/13Reg/88B
Jn., tailor, Broad H., 1842, comm, W, Wr, P3/1842/12
Hocker, Jos., Reading, Berks., 1744, W, P1/H/1015, P1/9Reg/344
Jos., carp., Hindon, 1844, W, Wr, P2/1844/20
Martha, Fonthill G., 1836, AB, comm, P2/1836/69
Hocker, My., widow, Reading, Berks., 1750, W, P1/H/1068, P1/10Reg/331
Hacker alias King, Richd., Reading, Berks., 1698, AB, P1/H/600
Robt., shopkeeper, Lea, L. and Cleverton (abode Lea, Garsdon), 1830, O, W, Wr, P3/1830/12
Hacker alias King, Thos., sen., yeo., Reading, Berks., 1680, I, W, P1/H/449
Hocker, Wm., white bread baker, Uffc., Devon, 1779, AB, W, P20/1/264
see also Cook alias H.
Hackett, Hockett, Jn., sen., Derry Hill, Bowood, 1820, W, Wr, P26/1329
My., sp., Charminster, Dorset, 1764, AB, comm, W, P5/1764/18
Hockett, Nich., husb., Reading, Berks., 1662, I, W, P1/H/319
Hockett (*or* Hoggett), Wm., glover, Lyme R., Dorset, 1629-34, comm, I (2), copy W, NWGVS, P5/1631/50
Hackham, Arthur, yeo. *or* husb., Fordington, Dorset, 1679, I, W, P15/27, P5/12Reg/9A, 297A
Arthur, Fordington, Dorset, 1742, AB, P15/132
Eleanor, widow, Fordington, Dorset, 1664, I, W, P15/10
Haccombe, Geo., Chards., Devon, 1628, AB, I, P5/1628/56, P5/11Reg/70B
Jas., yeo., Fordington, Dorset, 1720, W, P15/103
Jas., yeo., Fordington, Dorset, 1729, W, P15/115
Joan, widow, Chards., Devon, 1638, I, NW, P14/6
Jn., yeo., Bere R., Dorset, 1714, W, P5/1714/15, P5/15Reg/386A
Nathaniel, yeo., Fordington, Dorset, 1721, AB, ren, W, P15/104
Nathaniel, bach., Fordington, Dorset, 1730, AB, P15/120
Richd., yeo., Fordington, Dorset, 1710-11, quitclaim, W, P5/1710/47, P15/88
Wm., yeo., Fordington, Dorset, 1746, W, P5/1746/36
Hackman, Leonard, no abode stated, 1684, AB, I, P2/H/838
Hackwell, Jas., shoemaker, Lyme R., Dorset, 1635, I, W, P5/1635/48, P5/12Reg/225
Thos., mariner, Lyme R., Dorset, 1597, AB, I, P5/1597/57, P5/6Reg/168C
Huckwell, Thos., clothier, Wantage, Berks., 1797, AB, W, P5/1797/21, P5/18Reg/237B
Hackwood, Eliz., widow, Sherb., Dorset, 1636, I, W, P5/1636/25, P5/13Reg/27
Jn., Lyme R., Dorset, 1667, AB, P16/12
Susanna, widow, Lyme R., Dorset, 1684, I, NW, P16/80
Haddon *see* [illegible]
Haddrell, Benj., yeo., [illegible]pton B., 1813, W, Wr, P3/1813/36
Haddrill, Geoffrey, Mkt. L., [illegible], AB, I, W, P2/H/195
Geo., yeo., Pewsham, 1707, I (2), W, P3/H/874
Haddrill, Jas., sen., Kington L., 1805, [illegible] P3/1805/24
Haddrill, Jas., yeo., Kington L., 1856, aff, O, W, Wr, P3/1856/45
Joyce, widow, Nocketts Hill, Pewsham, 1710, I, W, P3/H/903
Mark, yeo., Pewsham, 1676, I, W, P3/H/516
Hadnam, Chas., sen., Kington St M., 1721, AB, P3/H/976
Marian, Hullavington, 1620, a/c (2), AB, I, P3/H/146
Wm., husb., Kington St M., 1619, I, W, P1/H/128
Hagemann, Chas. (*or* Lawr., servant, Chirton (native of Hanover), 1835, W, P2/18[illegible]
Haggard, Edwd., gent., Bourton, Shrivenham, Berks., 1720, W, P1/H/760, P1/6Reg/340B
Geo., innholder, Swindon, 1666, AB, comm, I, P3/H/396

Geo., innholder, Swindon, 1729, W, P3/H/1053
Hy., yeo., Wanb., 1675-84, comm, I, W, P3/H/489, 588
Hy., Marl., 1760, AB, P1/H/1156
Hester, sp., Swindon, 1763, W, P3/H/1344
Jas., mason, Elcombe, Wrou., 1835, W, P3/1835/25
Jn., Uffington, Berks., 1695, AB, I, P1/H/578
Hagger, Jn., innholder, Sal., 1728, W (NEP), P4/1728/33
Jn., yeo., Swanhill, Wanb., 1730, W, P3/H/1067
Jn., Highw., 1755, AB, I, P10/1755/1
My., sp., Swindon, 1744, W, P3/H/1201
My., sp., Highw., 1758, AB, P10/1758/2
My., sp., Swindon, 1759, AB, P1/H/1140
Richd., yeo., Coate, Liddington, 1669, AB, comm, I, P3/H/405
Robt., innholder *or* innkeeper, Swindon, 1691, I, W, P3/H/685
Simon, yeo., Purton, 1667, AB, I, P3/H/383
Simon, grocer *or* mercer, Wanb., 1683, AB, comm, I, ren, P3/H/579
Simon, mercer, Wanb., 1695, AB, ren, P3/H/750
Simon, collarmaker, Tinh., Edington, 1803, W, P2/1803/68
Thos., fuller, Turners Puddle, Dorset, 1637, AB, comm, NW, P5/1637/18, P5/13Reg/49B
Thomasine, widow, Swindon, 1725, W, P3/H/1012
see also Elliott nee H.
Haggett, Eliz., Hardington, Somerset (effects at Wilton), 1786, AB, P2/H/1624
Hailstone, Halston, Cath., widow, Idstone, Ashbury, Berks., 1614, comm, I, W, P1/H/95
Jn., farmer, Pewsey, 1811, W, P3/1811/6
Jn., sen., yeo., Pewsey, 1814, comm, W, Wr, P3/1814/11
Robt., labourer, Manningford A., 1743, W, P3/H/1200
Thos., husb., Wokm., Berks., 1682, I, W, P5/1682/52
Halston, Wm., Westrop, Highw., 1671, I, NW, P5/1671/43
Haimes, Haine, Haines, Hains *see* Haynes
Hake, Wm., Chards., Devon, 1688, AB, I, P5/1688/39
Hakens *see* Hawkins
Haker *see* Hacker
Hakings, Hakins *see* Hawkins
Halcomb, Hulcomb, Edwd., Charminster, Dorset, 1726, AB, P5/1726/21
Jn., sen., yeo., Rowde, 1709, I, W, P3/H/886
Jn., Rowde, 1720, AB, I, P1/H/761
Jn., yeo., Rowde, 1740, W, P3/H/1165
Richd., sen., yeo., Chirton, 1710, I, W, P2/H/1083
Susanna, banker's wife, Marl., 1813, AB (with O), D, W, Wr, P1/1813/12
Wm., butcher, Chirton, 1709, I, W, P2/H/1072
Wm., gent., Devizes, 1802, W, P3/1802/10
Hale, Alexander, sen., yeo., Stanford in the Vale, Berks., 1738, AB, I, P1/H/964
Alice, widow, Highw., 1579, I, W, P5/1579/40, P5/3Reg/120A
Hales, Alice, widow, Westb., 1639, a/c, I, P25/1639/12
Ambrose, yeo., Kingston D., 1718, W, P2/H/1151
Hales, Ann, sp., Winterborne K., Dorset, 1743, W, Wr, P5/1743/36
Ann, widow, *The Black Dog Inn*, W. Lavington, 1828, O, req, W, Wr, P1/1828/17
Hales, Anthony, husb., Blackland, Calne, 1582, AB, I, W, P5/1582/30, P5/4Reg/52A
Hale alias Carpenter, Anthony, husb., Haydon Wick, Rodbourne C., 1631, I, W, P1/H/190
Anthony, fuller, Stock St., Calne, 1664, AB, comm, P26/119
Anthony, Calne, 1757, AB, P26/959
Anthony, butcher, Calne, 1780, W, P26/1111
Arnold, husb., Wick, Bps. C., 1694, AB, I, ren, P24/525
Hales, Banister, husb., Westb., 1666, AB, I, P25/1666/3
Benj., broad weaver, Melk., 1733, W, P2/H/1267
Benj., yeo., Wood St., Calne, 1790, W, P26/1167
Benj., sen., cheese factor, Calne, 1807, comm, W, P26/1263
Betty, widow, Melk., 1741, AB, P1/H/994
Charlotte, singlewoman, Cholderton, 1837, W, Wr, P2/1837/22
Hayles, Chris., [Hannington] (NBI), 1677, I, W, P3/H/518

Hales, Dan., jun., gent., Sal. St Martin, 1647, AB, P1/H/289
Hales, Dan., yeo., Brook, Westb., 1668, AB, comm, I, P25/1668/1
David, yeo., Charlcote, Bremhill, 1665, AB, comm, I, P3/H/366
Hales, Edith, widow, Westb., 1616, AB (2), I, P25/1616/2
Edith, sp., Sherston, 1705, I, W, P3/H/852
Hayle, Edmd., Hullavington, 1634, I, W, P3/H/279
Hales, Edwd., fuller, Dilton, Westb., 1627, AB, a/c, I, P25/1626/6
Edwd., farrier, Devizes St Jn., 1731, I, W, P1/H/884, P1/7Reg/420A
Edwd., tanner, Malm., 1751, req, W, copy W, P3/H/1260
Eleanor, widow, Ogbourne St A., 1765, W, P23/709
Hales, Eliz., widow, Highw., 1685, comm, I, W, P10/1685/5
Eliz., sp., Sherston, 1731, AB, P3/H/1083
Hales, Eliz., widow, Bradford A., 1768, W, P2/H/1507
Eliz., widow, Winkfield, Berks., 1792, W, P1/H/1326, P1/14Reg/415
Francis, baker, Westb. L., 1685, W, P25/1685/11
Hales, Francis, Corsham, 1730, marriage licence, P29/2Reg/58A
Geo., jun., bach., Tinh., Edington, 1852-55, AB, aff, D, O (3), W, Wr (2), P2/1852/6, P2/1855/8
Hy., Cholderton, 1837, AB, Wr, P2/1837/24
Jas., Haydon Wick, Rodbourne C., [1605], W (NEP), P3/H/9
Jas., yeo., Kennington, Sunningwell, Berks., 1811, W, Wr, P1/1811/75
Jas., widower, Southbroom, 1852, AB, appt of guardian, O, T, Wr, P24/1405
Hales, Joan, widow, Westb., 1645, AB, I, P25/1645/1
Jn., husb., Devizes, 1593, I, W, P1/H/13
Jn., gent., Sal., 1626, W, P4/1626/5
Jn., Blackland, Calne, 1632, I, P26/45
Hales, Jn., weaver, Westb., 1670, NW, P25/1670/1
Jn., husb., Whetham, Calne, 1673, I, NW, P26/214
Hales, Jn., collier, Brook, Westb., 1686, I, W, p25/1686/1
Hales, Jn., yeo., Gastard, Corsham, 1687, AB, I, W, P29/H/60, P29/1Reg/236
Hales, Jn., gent., Castle Eaton, 1689, AB, I, P1/H/522
Hales, Jn., jun., [wheelwright], Westb., 1693, AB, I (detailed), P25/1693/5
Hales, Jn., shearman, Boreham, Warm., 1712, W, P2/H/1098
Jn., silk throwster, Charlcote, Bremhill, 1743, W, P3/H/1189
Jn., yeo., Longcott, Shrivenham, Berks., 1750, AB, I, P1/H/1066
Hales, Jn., Westb., 1774, AB, P25/1774/2
Jn., W. Lavington, 1776, W, P1/H/1236, P1/13Reg/88A
Jn., Brinkw., 1786, AB, P3/H/1469
Jn., W. Lavington, 1800, AB, P1/1800/2, P1/15Reg/200
Jn. *see also* Jn. Greast
Jos., yeo., Shaw, Melk., 1848, comm, W, Wr, P1/1848/26
Hales, Margery, widow, Westb., 1689, I, W, P25/1689/8
Marian, sp., Devizes, 1692, I, W, P1/H/547
Hales, Martin, weaver, Chards., Devon, 1630, AB, comm, T (damaged - re Eliz. H.), NW, P5/1630/6, P5/11Reg/130D, 155A
My., widow, Melk., 1741, AB, comm, I, P2/H/1331
Hales, My., widow, Westb., 1795, AB, P25/1795/1
Matthew, mercer, Sherston, 1696, W, P3/H/756
Moses, chapman, Devizes, 1765, W, P1/H/1179, P1/12Reg/159A
Hales, Nich., broad weaver, Westb., 1636, I, W, P25/1636/4
Hales, Nich., bach., Corsham, 1722, marriage licence, P29/2Reg/43C
Hayles, Richd., Bratton, Westb., 1568, W, P5/2Reg/34B
Hayles, Richd., carp., N. Bradley, 1590, I, W, P2/H/106
Hales, Robt., chapman, Fisherton A., 1638, I, W, P2/H/508
Robt., sen., husb., Blackland, Calne, 1673, AB, comm, I, P26/201
Robt., sen., blacksmith, Calne, 1724, AB, W, P26/704
Robt., blacksmith, Calne, 1743, AB, P26/841
Robt., W. Lavington, 1829, AB, O, Wr, P1/1829/164
Roger, sen., miller, Cherhill, 1697, I, W, P26/445
Roger, yeo., Cherhill, 1748, AB, I, L, note (on torn out page from Moore's Almanack records date of birth of Roger H., 1740 & date & time of birth of Roger H., 1765), ren, W, I (detailed), P26/881

Hayles alias Skipper, Thos., tailor, Marl., 1647, W, P1/H/288
Thos., broad weaver, Whitley, Melk., 1648, I, W, P2/H/598
Hales, Thos., [shoemaker], Westb., 1672, AB, I, P25/1672/13
Hales, Thos., Highw., 1700, AB, P10/1700/2
Hales, Thos., Amesb., 1731, W, P2/H/1254
Thos., Ogbourne St A., 1743, AB, Wr, P5/1743/35
Thos. Phillips, Devizes Grn, Bps. C., 1781, AB, comm, P24/1117
Hales, Wm., husb., Bratton, Westb., 1572, W, P5/3Reg/1D
Hale alias Carpenter, Wm., husb., Eastcott, Swindon, 1619, I, W, P1/H/132
Hales, Wm., Corsham, 1640, W, P29/1Reg/137
Wm., blacksmith, Calne, 1641, I, W, P5/1641/37, P5/14Reg/6B
Wm., Cotmarsh, Broad H., 1666, AB, I, P3/H/375
Hales, Wm., fuller, Westb., 1669, I, NW, P25/1669/6
Hales, Wm., Tinh., Edington, 1677, AB, P1/H/438
Wm., sen., broad weaver, Shaw Hill, Melk., [1684], I, W, P2/H/834
Wm., bach. and gent.'s servant, Chipp., 1690, AB, P3/H/670
Wm., Melk., 1696, AB, I, P2/H/960
Hales, Wm., sen., millwright, Brook, Westb., 1719, I, W, P25/1719/10
Hales, Wm., bach., Dilton, Westb., 1772, AB, P25/1772/5
Wm., victualler, *The Royal Oak*, Wick, Bps. C., 1775, W, P24/1137
Hales, Wm., yeo., Westb., 1802, O, W, P25/1802/5
Hales, Wm., widower, Urchf., 1816, AB, P2/1816/3
Wm., widower, Bradford A., 1852, AB, O, Wr, P2/1852/13
Wm., grocer, Trowb., 1854, aff, O, W, Wr, P1/1854/14
see also Hall *or* H.; Heale
Haley, Hy., curate, Swallowcliffe, 1562, AB, P5/1Reg/7E
Halfacre, Francis, yeo., Wokm., Berks., 1702, I, W, P5/1702/24
Francis, yeo., Wokm., Berks., 1712, W, P5/1712/31, P5/15Reg/302C
My., widow, Wokm., Berks., 1708, W, P5/1708/31, P5/15Reg/66
Susanna, widow, Wokm., Berks., 1713, W, P5/1713/42, P5/15Reg/369B
Halfe, Jn., Uffc., Devon, 1570, W, P5/2Reg/75D
Halfpenny, Wm., tailor, Mkt. L., 1847, O, W, Wr, P2/1847/62
Haling, Geo., sen., yeo., Luckington, 1634, I, W, P3/H/277
Hallings, Jn., husb., Luckington, 1621, I, W, P3/H/155
Hall, Agnes, widow, Marridge Hill, Rams., 1588, I, W, P5/1588/31, P5/5Reg/32C
Agnes, widow, Mildenhall, 1628, I, W, P1/H/171
Alexander, gent., Eelemore Hall, Durham (having property in diocese of Sal.), 1646, comm, L, note, ren, P1/H/275
Alice, widow, Ashton K., 1630, I, W, P3/H/235
Alice, widow, Melk., 1637, I, W, P2/H/486
Alice, widow, Chr. M., 1757, AB, W, P3/H/1300
Andrew, labourer, Fordington, Dorset, 1774, AB, W, Wr, P15/148
Barbara, widow, High St., Sal. St Thos., [1635], acquittance, I (NEP), P1/H/1367
Cath., widow, Canonhold, Melk., 1635, I, W, P1/H/219
Chas., Castle C., 1680, AB, P3/H/540
Chas., innholder, Fisherton A., 1692, W, P2/H/928
Chas., gardener, Savernake Park (form. of Oare, Wilcot), 1845, O, W, Wr, P5/1845/2
Chris., Earley, Sonning, Berks., 1674, I, W, P5/1674/34
Chris., yeo., Earley, Sonning, Berks., 1731, W, P5/1731/39
Dan., husb., Longcott, Shrivenham, Berks., 1729, W, P3/H/1054
Drew, husb., Inglesham, Berks., 1629, I, W, P3/H/221
Edith, Sherb., Dorset, 1666, I, W, P5/1665/40
Edmd., sen., baker, Ashton K., [1612], I, W (NEP), P3/H/75
Edmd., Gammons Corner, Chute, 1709, AB, I, P7/101
Edwd., yeo., Hurst, Berks., 1591, AB, I, W, P5/1591/35, P5/5Reg/117B
Edwd., E. Harnham, Britford, 1604, I, P24/55
Edwd., sen., E. Harnham, Britford, 1614, I (incorrectly dated), W (buried 28 May 1614), P24/101
Edwd., wheeler, Westb. L., 1703, I, W (NEP), P25/1703/6
Edwd., parchmentmaker, Sal., 1721, W, P4/1720/15
Edwd., yeo., Wilton, Gt. Bedwyn, 1760, W, P21/10/55
Eliz., widow, Tidcombe, T. and Fosbury, 1701, AB, I, W, P3/H/803

Eliz., Wokm., Berks., 1712, AB, P5/1712/30
Eliz., Bramshaw, Hants, 1760, AB, P24/1111
Eliz., minors, Sonning, Berks., 1808, T, P5/1808/8
Felix, broad weaver, Dilton M., Westb., 1819, W, Wr, P25/1819/4
Fortune, widow, Fisherton A., 1683, AB, P2/H/825
Frances, no abode stated, [c1616], I, W, P1/H/102
Francis, sen., weaver, Sal. St Martin, 1733, W, P4/1733/16
Francis, plumber, Mkt. L., 1768, W, P2/H/1506
Francis, cordw., Sal., 1813, W, Wr, P4/1813/10
Geo., tailor, Sal. St Thos., 1670, I, W, P4/1670/11
Geo., brick and tilemaker, Studley Grn, Trowb., 1839, O, req, W, Wr, P1/1839/3
Hy., Sonning, Berks., 1619-20, AB, I, P5/1619/57, P5/10Reg/9A, 47A
Hy., Chilton F., [c1620], a/c, P3/H/147
Hy., Gt. Bedwyn, 1731, AB, I, P21/8/66
Hy., bach., Gillingham, Dorset, 1838, AB, Wr, P27/1/718
Honour, sp., Hankerton, 1831, AB, comm, P3/1831/48
Humphrey, victualler, Froxfield, 1680, AB, comm, I, P3/H/541
Isaac, Nettleton, 1814, AB, P1/1814/114
Jas., priest, Stanton Fitzwarren, 1558, institution to rectory, P1/1Reg/6I
Jas., gent., Chipp., 1751, W, P3/H/1261
Jas., fuller, Ludbourne Mill, Westb., 1786, comm, W, P25/1786/1
Jas., tiler and plasterer, Westb. L., 1799, W, note (requests return of this W & that of Thos. Austin), P25/1799/4
Jas., widower, Sal., 1811, AB, Wr, P1/1811/116
Jane, widow, Studley, Calne, 1635, I, W, P26/49
Joan, widow, Baydon, 1603, I, W, P5/1603/38, P5/7Reg/88A
Joan, Limpley Stoke, Bradford A., 1619, AB, I, P2/H/334
Joan, widow, Calne, 1674, I, W, P26/220, P2/H/717
Hall *or* Hale, Joan, widow, Charlcote, Bremhill, 1697, AB, comm, I, ren, P3/H/765
Joan, widow, Overton, 1703, I, W, P3/H/836
Jn., husb., Limpley Stoke, Bradford A., 1556, W, P2/3Reg/4C
Jn., servant to Jn. Boland, Sutton V., 1569, W, P2/5Reg/77A
Jn., husb., Shalbourne, 1575, W, P5/3Reg/52B
Jn., husb., Gt. Cheverell, 1583, I, W, P2/H/67, P2/6Reg/86B
Jn., freemason, Marridge Hill, Rams., 1586, AB, I, W, P5/1586/9, P5/4Reg/132A
Jn., Bradford A., [1597], I, P2/H/160
Jn., Purton, 1606, AB, court paper, I, P1/H/36
Jn., Beanacre, Melk., 1609, I, W, P2/H/255, P2/8Reg/73C
Jn., Purton, 1611, NW, P3/H/65
Jn., Wootton B., 1627, AB, P3/H/209
Jn., basketmaker, Ward's Cross, Hurst, Berks., 1634, AB, I, NW. Proved at the Metropolitan Visitation to Reading, P5/1634/44, P5/12Reg/318
Jn., grocer, Melk., 1636, I, W, P2/H/475
Jn., Westcott, Swindon, 1639, AB, I, P3/H/311
Jn., husb., Whitecroft, Dilton, Westb., 1639, I (includes burial cost), W, P25/1639/5
Jn., Minety, 1675, I, W, P3/H/490
Jn., yeo., Laverstock, [1679], W, P2/H/764
Jn., sen., broad weaver, Limpley Stoke, Bradford A., 1715, W, P2/H/1127
Jn., husb., Chute, 1716, I, W, P5/1716/34, P5/15Reg/333A
Jn., Kemble, 1734, AB, P3/H/1120
Jn., Chr. M., 1735, W, P1/H/934, P1/8Reg/60
Jn., tailor, Laverstock, 1736, W, P2/H/1291
Jn., parchmentmaker, Sal., 1744, W, P1/H/1002, P1/9Reg/296
Jn., yeo., Gidley Farm, Peasemore, Berks., 1753, W, P1/H/1091
Jn., Gt. Bedwyn, 1759-63, AB (2), P21/10/41, 60
Jn., millwright, Westb. L., 1794, comm, W, P25/1794/2
Jn., gardener, Westb. L., 1797, W, P25/1797/3
Jn., schoolmaster, Tilehurst, Berks., 1798, W, P1/H/1351, P1/15Reg/64B
Jn., farmer, Eye and Dunsden, Sonning, Berks., 1820, W, Wr, P5/1820/15
Jn., victualler, Marl., 1823, W, Wr, P1/1823/112
Jos., Ashton K., 1625, AB, I, P3/H/193

Jos., yeo., Nettleton, 1744, W, P1/H/1019, P1/9Reg/396B
Jos., yeo., Sal., 1771, W, P4/1771/7
Jos., yeo., Nettleton, 1799, comm, W, P3/H/1534
Jos., Shrivenham, Berks. & Swindon, 1817, AB, comm, P3/1817/6
Manuel, wheelwright, Westb. L., 1756, W, P25/1756/4
Mgt., widow, Sal., 1741, W, P4/1741/12
Mgt., widow, Buckland, Berks., 1789, AB, P1/H/1319
Martha, sp., Trowb., 1827, W, Wr, P1/1827/27
My., Earley, Sonning, Berks., 1620, I, P5/1619/58
My., widow, Tidcombe, T. and Fosbury, 1642, AB, P3/H/336
My., widow, Newbury, Berks., 1698, comm, I, W, P1/H/593, P1/3Reg/17
My., Gt. Bedwyn, 1748, AB, P21/10/7
My., widow, Sonning, Berks., 1764, AB, P5/1764/19
Nich., Stoke & Melk., 1558, W, P2/3Reg/81E
Osmund, Boyton, 1537, W (NEP), P2/1Reg/6B
Rebecca, sp., Sherston, 1756, AB, W, P3/H/1296
Richd., husb. *or* yeo., Winterslow, 1563, I, copy I, W, P2/H/26, P2/4Reg/147B
Hall alias Baker, Richd., Gt. Faringdon, Berks., 1570, W, P5/2Reg/71D
Richd., yeo., Alton B., 1619, AB, I, P3/H/138
Richd., yeo., Yatesbury, 1731, AB, ren, P3/H/1084
Richd., Bucklebury, Berks., 1732, AB, P1/H/899
Richd., Sonning, Berks., 1808, AB, Wr, P5/1808/7
Richd., wheelwright, Wokm., Berks., 1828, W, Wr, P5/1828/14
Robt., husb., Sonning, Berks., 1607, AB, I, W, P5/1607/29, P5/8Reg/99B
Robt., husb., Minety, 1633, I, W, P3/H/271
Robt., Calne, 1640, W, P5/1640/79
Robt., tailor, Lacock, 1704, I, W, P1/H/631
Robt., yeo., Chelworth, Crickl. St S., 1719, I, W, P3/H/965
Robt., [tanner], Gt. Bedwyn, 1760, AB, I, P21/10/50
Roger, husb., Dilton, Westb., 1672, AB, I, NW, P25/1672/1
Roger, gent., Sudden Park, Gt. Bedwyn, 1736, W, P21/9/11
Roger, husb., Bucklebury, Berks., 1738, W, P1/H/961, P1/8Reg/293
Sam., yeo., Gillingham, Dorset, 1785, W, P27/1/525, P27/3Reg/241
Sarah, widow, Watchfield, Shrivenham, Berks., 1732, W, P1/H/889, P1/7Reg/457
Sarah, widow, Hankerton, 1809, AB, Wr, P3/1809/34
Sarah, widow, Westb. L., 1819, AB, comm, W, Wr, P25/1819/1
Scory, wheelwright, Overton, 1724, W, P3/H/1005
Sibyl, widow, Westb. L., 1724, W, P25/1724/9
Stephen, sen., husb., Marridge Hill, Rams., 1628, AB, I, P5/1628/52, P5/11Reg/99A
Susan, widow, Corsham, 1699, AB, I, P29/H/72, P29/1Reg/272A
Susanna, widow, Wilton, Gt. Bedwyn, 1735, AB, I, P21/9/10
Susanna, sp., Sonning, Berks., 1806, W (& cod), Wr (2), P5/1806/31
Susanna, widow, Westb., 1835, W, Wr, P25/1835/5
Thos., husb., Baydon, 1578, I, W, P5/1578/18, P5/3Reg/109B
Thos., loader, Easton Grey, 1609, AB, W, P3/H/45
Thos., gent., Sherb., Dorset, 1616, I, W, P5/1616/35
Thos., Sherb., Dorset, 1661, AB, comm, P5/1661/23
Thos., Sherb., Dorset, 1667, AB, P5/1667/24
Thos., husb., Wokm., Berks., 1669, W, P5/1669/24
Thos., Sonning, Berks., 1677, AB, comm, I, W (damaged), P5/1677/26
Thos., Kemble, 1682, AB, I, ren (I & ren on same sheet), P3/H/562
Thos., yeo., Gammons Corner, Chute, 1684, I, W, P7/63
Thos., yeo., Overton, 1687, comm, I, W, P3/H/629
Thos., Tidcombe, T. and Fosbury, 1691, AB, I, ren, P3/H/686
Thos., yeo., Shalbourne, 1703, I, W, P23/260
Thos., sen., Inglesham, 1720, AB, I, P3/H/973
Thos., Sal., 1728, AB, P4/1728/7
Thos., sen., husb. *or* yeo., Wilton, Gt. Bedwyn, 1734, I, W, P5/1734/33
Thos., yeo., Littlecote, Rams., 1738, W, P5/1738/21
Thos., Westb. L., 1774, AB, P25/1774/3

Thos., innholder, Downton, 1775, AB, P2/H/1548
Thos., yeo., Hurst, Berks., 1794, W, P5/1794/12, P5/18Reg/200A
Thos., farmer, Arborfield, Berks., 1803, W, P5/1803/56, P5/19Reg/91
Thos., Hurst, Berks., 1823, AB, Wr, P5/1823/27
Thos., Arborfield, Berks., 1824, AB, Wr, P5/1824/15
Thos., yeo., Broad B., Highw., 1839, comm, W, Wr, P10/1839/1
Wm., Melk., 1581, AB, P2/H/66
Wm., husb., Winnersh, Hurst, Berks., 1604, I, W, P5/1604/17, P5/8Reg/7A
Wm., joiner, Wokm., Berks., 1627, I, W, P5/1627/25, P5/11Reg/48
Wm., fuller, Bradford A., 1631, W, P2/H/425
Wm., sen., Melk., 1634, I, W, P2/H/462
Wm., husb., Greenham, Thatcham, Berks., 1662, AB, I, P1/H/326
Wm., yeo., Melk., 1664, a/c, comm, W, P2/H/625
Wm., Wexcombe, Grafton, 1677, AB, I, P21/2/51
Wm., gent., Avill's Farm, Corsham, 1682, AB, I (detailed), P3/H/563
Wm., E. Harnham, Britford, 1682-90, AB, a/c, I, P5/1681/26, P5/1690/22
Wm., husb., Swallowfield, Shinfield, Berks., 1714, I, W, P1/H/698, P1/5Reg/359B
Hall alias Blisset, Wm., Wilton, 1728, AB, ren, P2/H/1232
Wm., cordw., Chipp., 1748, W, P3/H/1231
Wm., clothier and druggetmaker, Calne, 1755, W, P5/1755/24
Wm., maltster, Alderton, 1759, AB, ren, W, P1/H/1146, P1/11Reg/443
Wm., gent., Crickl. St S., 1780, W, P3/H/1433
Wm., yeo., Sonning, Berks., 1783, W, Wr, P5/1783/5, P5/17Reg/245A
Wm., miller, Dun Mill, Hungerford, Berks., 1786, W, P23/783
Wm., yeo., Cloatley, Hankerton, 1793, W, P3/H/1504
Wm., sen., gent., Steeple A., 1806, W, Wr, P2/1806/61
Wm., Blunsdon St Andrew, 1812, W, Wr, P3/1812/27
Wm., blacksmith, Westb. L., 1836, O, W, Wr, P25/1836/3
Wm., Cloatley, Hankerton, 1838, O, W, Wr, P3/1838/5
Wm., victualler, Chipp., 1853, W, Wr, P3/1853/33
Wm., yeo., Brinkw., 1857, aff, court proceeding, D, W, Wr, P3/1857/53
see also Phelps alias H.
Halladay *see* Holliday
Hallam, Hallom, Ann, widow, Snelling Farm, Turners Puddle, Dorset, 1701, AB, I, P5/1701/32
Jn., Snelling Farm, Turners Puddle, Dorset, 1694, AB, I, P5/1694/3
Hallen, Thos., Chipp., 1684, AB, I, P3/H/589
Hallett, Charlotte, dressmaker and sp., Sal., 1848, AB, ren, W, Wr, P4/1848/3
Dan., Netherb., Dorset, 1691, AB, a/c, I, P17/327
Dan., yeo., Netherb., Dorset, 1698, I, W, P5/1698/34
Denise, widow, Netherb., Dorset, 1564, W, P5/1Reg/42A
Edwd., Beam., Dorset, 1632, AB, comm, I, P5/1632/29, P5/12Reg/84C
Erasmus, Netherb., Dorset, 1640, I, W, P17/55
Fanny, sp., Beam., Dorset, 1852, comm, W, Wr, P17/622
Geo., yeo., Melplash, Netherb., Dorset, 1721, W, P17/393
Grace, widow, Halstock, Dorset, 1669, AB, I, P16/20
Hannibal, husb., Haydon, Dorset, 1730, AB, I, P5/1730/37
Hy., Wooth, Netherb., Dorset, 1707, comm, W, P5/1707/28, P5/15Reg/23
Jas., Halstock, Dorset, 1682, AB, I, P5/1682/48
Jas., innholder, Kingsland, Netherb., Dorset, 1702, I, W, P17/145
Jas., mariner late of the Eltham man of war, Beam., Dorset, 1748, AB, Wr, P5/1748/12
Jane, widow, Fovant, 1777, W, P2/H/1563
Joan, widow, Beam., Dorset, 1573, I, W, P30/90, P5/3Reg/23A
Joan, widow, Pineapple, Netherb., Dorset, 1724, I, W, P17/419
Joan, widow, Netherb., Dorset, 1727, AB, W, P17/426
Jn., husb., Netherb., Dorset, 1599, AB, I, P5/1599/10, P5/6Reg/235B
Jn., gent., Netherb., Dorset, 1698, AB, I, P5/1698/35
Jn., yeo., Coombe, Beam., Dorset, 1723, W, P17/405
Jn., Beam., Dorset, 1747, AB, P17/503
Jn., gent., Perhay, Netherb., Dorset, 1788, W (& cod), P5/1788/12, P5/18Reg/114
Joshua, yeo., Winterborne M., Winterborne K., Dorset, 1670, I, W, P5/1670/24

Mgt., widow, Melplash, Netherb., Dorset, 1681, I, W, P17/263
Martha, Beam., Dorset, 1758, AB, comm, P5/1758/19
Hollett, Nich., Barford St M., 1714, AB, P2/H/1120
Robt., Netherb., Dorset, 1568, W, P5/1Reg/86B
Robt., Netherb., Dorset, 1575-76, I, T, W, P5/1576/23, P5/3Reg/62B
Robt., Shitterton, Bere R., Dorset, 1588, I, W, P5/1587/23, P5/5Reg/5B
Robt., yeo., Melplash, Netherb., Dorset, 1664, AB, I, P17/79
Robt., yeo., Pineapple, Netherb., Dorset, 1725, W, P17/421
Sarah, Netherb., Dorset, 1710, AB, P17/195
Sarah, sp., Sal., 1841, AB, Wr, P1/1841/3
Stephen, sen., yeo., Melplash, Netherb., Dorset, 1679-80, AB (2), I, W, P5/1679/41, P17/290
Stephen, Bidlake, Netherb., Dorset, 1684, I, W, P17/237
Stephen, yeo., Melplash, Netherb., Dorset, 1716, W, P5/1716/38, P5/15Reg/339B
Thos., Mangerton, Netherb., Dorset, 1600, AB, I, P5/1600/34, P5/6Reg/250B
Thos., Ford, Netherb., Dorset, 1695, AB, I, P17/349
Thos., widow, Beam., Dorset, 1702, AB, P17/148
Thos., butcher, Beam., Dorset, 1725, AB, P5/1725/35
Thos., Fovant, 1776, AB, P2/H/1556
Thos., Fovant, 1780, W, P2/H/1583
Hollett, Wm., Burcombe, 1628-29, AB, a/c, I, P2/H/404
Wm., weaver, Beam., Dorset, 1637, AB, comm, I, P17/34
Wm., joiner, Netherb., Dorset, 1774, comm, W, P17/565
Halleway *see* Holloway
Halley *see* Holly
Hallick *see* Haylock
Halliday *see* Holliday
Hallings *see* Haling
Hallis *see* Hollis
Hallock *see* Haylock
Hallom *see* Hallam
Halock *see* Haylock
Halse, Halse *or* Halsey, Hy., Lyme R., Dorset, 1732, W, P16/269
Halston *see* Hailstone
Halys *see* Hollis
Ham, Geo., Ufton Nervet, Berks., 1729, AB, I, P1/H/857
Hy., yeo., Over C., Dorset, 1690, AB, I, P5/1690/23
Jas., hatter, Sal., 1738, W, Wr, P4/1738/6
Joan, widow, Stratfield M., Berks., 1704, I, W, P1/H/634
Jn., clothworker, Lyme R., Dorset, 1712, W, P16/194
My., widow, Sal., 1754, W, P4/1754/10
Nanny, Beenham Valence, Berks., 1835, AB, comm, ren, P1/1835/42
Richd., sen., labourer, Whitep., 1699, AB, ren, P1/H/606
Thos., Chetnole, Yetm., Dorset, 1709, AB, NW, P19/93
Wm., sen., Whitep., 1638, I, W, P2/H/500
Wm., shoemaker, Sal., 1781, W, P4/1781/5
Wm., shoemaker, Sal., 1786, W, P4/1786/2
Wm., Whitep., 1569, W, P2/5Reg/54
Haman, Hamance, Hamand, Hamant *see* Hammond
Hamar, Hy., yeo., Sonning, Berks., 1645, comm, I, W, P5/1644/15, P5/14Reg/76A
Hambidge, Eliz., sp., Sherston, 1805, W, P3/1805/22
Geo., Buscot, Berks., 1756, AB, P1/H/1115
Martha, widow, Buscot Wick, Buscot, Berks., 1817, comm, W, Wr, P1/1817/32
Hanbridge, Robt., no abode stated, 1603, I, W, P3/H/2
Hambridge, Robt., yeo., Sherston & Wortley, Gloucs, 1788, W, Wr, P3/H/1477
Sarah, sp., Eaton Hastings, Berks., 1798, W, P1/H/1355, P1/15Reg/85
Hambridge, Wm., yeo., Buscot Wick, Buscot, Berks., 1804, comm, W, P1/1804/135
Hambleden, Jn., clothworker, Wokm., Berks., 1669, I, P5/1669/23
Jn., sen., blacksmith, Wokm., Berks., 1727, W, P5/1727/22, P5/16Reg/155A
Jn., husb., Wokm., Berks., 1758, W, P5/1758/20
Hamblen *see* Hamlen

Hamblett *see* Hamlet
Hamblin *see* Hamlen
Hambridge *see* Hambidge
Hamden, Jas., yeo., Stratfield M., Berks., 1720, I, W, P1/H/773, P1/6Reg/304A
Hames, Alice, widow, Monkton F., [1689], I, W, P2/H/902
Eliz., widow, Stourpaine, Dorset, 1785, AB, P24/1178
Jn., Mkt. L., 1612-13, AB, I, W, P2/H/293, P2/8Reg/170A
Haume, Nich., Eastcott, Urchf., 1547, W, P2/2Reg/19
Hame, Richd., Eastcott, Urchf., 1559, W, P2/4Reg/4B
Hame, Wm., Eastcott, Urchf., 1571, NW, P2/5Reg/131A
Hamilton, (Captain) *see* Ambrose Osmistone
Jn., parchmentmaker, Sal., 1795, W, P4/1795/5
My., sp., Abingdon, Berks., 1776, AB, P1/H/1245
Sarah, Warm., 1738, AB, comm, P1/H/955,
Hamlen, Hamlin, Ann, widow, Melk., 1773, W, P1/H/1228, P1/13Reg/21
Hamblen, Chas., Eddington, Hungerford, Berks., 1753, AB, P23/640
Dan., yeo., Stanton St B., 1725, I, W, P3/H/1013
Hamling, Edwd., Chards., Devon, 1669, I, W (NEP), P5/1669/30
Hamlin, Eliz., widow, Burghfield, Berks., 1668, I, W, P1/H/387
Hamblen, Geo., servant to Revd Massey, vicar of Warm., Warm., 1799, AB, ren, P2/H/1691
Isaac, yeo., Pewsey (form. of Marden), 1813, comm, W, Wr, P3/1813/67
Hamlin, Jas., yeo., Sherb., Dorset, 1759, W, P5/1759/12
Hamlin, Jane, widow, Marridge Hill, Rams., 1595, AB, I, W, P5/1595/26, P5/6Reg/100
Jane, sp., Devizes Grn, Bps. C., 1851, O, W, Wr, P24/1404
Hamlin, Jn., sen., Rams., 1563, W, P5/1Reg/23A
Hamlin, Jn., yeo., Rams., 1591, AB, I, P5/1590/27, P5/5Reg/96F
Hamlin, Jn., Stanton St B., 1694, AB, I, P3/H/738
Jn., Nether St., Bromham, 1857, aff, D, O, W, Wr, P3/1857/10
Hamblin, Mgt., Sherb., Dorset, 1683, AB, comm, P5/1682/49
Martha, widow, Stanton St B., 1822, W, Wr, P3/1822/42
Hamlin, My., widow, Stanton St B., 1709, I, W, P3/H/887
Hamblin, My., sp., Newbury, Berks., 1798, W, P1/H/1353, P1/15Reg/73B
Hamlin, Richd., husb., Stanton St B., 1621, I, W, P3/H/156
Richd., Melk., 1775, AB, P2/H/1546
Hamlin, Robt., husb., Marridge Hill, Rams., 1600, AB, I, W, P5/1600/27, P5/6Reg/262
Sam., sen., Stanton St B., 1684, I, NW, P3/H/591
Sarah, widow, Sal., 1782, AB, comm, ren, W, P4/1782/6
Hamblin, Sarah, widow, Chilton F., 1855, AB, aff, O, Wr, P1/1855/17
Hamblin, Simon, Marl. St Peter and St Paul, 1717, AB, I, P1/H/737
Hamlin, Simon, sadler, Marl., 1756, AB (2), ren, P1/H/1127
Hamlin, Stephen, Sal. (form. of Whitsbury, Wiltshire, now Hants), 1811, AB, P4/1811/4
Hamblin, Thos., carp., Chards., Devon, 1634, AB, I(GVD), P5/1634/45
Wm., miller, Coombe, Enford, 1686, I, W, P1/H/498
Wm., yeo., Stanton St B., 1720, W, P1/H/763, P1/6Reg/268
Hamblin, Wm., innholder, Marl., 1748, W, P1/H/1056, P1/10Reg/238
Wm., Melk., 1763, AB, P1/H/1173
Hamlin, Wm. *see also* Amy Fairthorne
Hamlet, Eliz., widow, Milbourne, Malm., 1766, W, P3/H/1356
Hamblett, Joan, widow, Minety, 1809, W, Wr, P3/1809/63
Jn., Milbourne, Malm., 1752, AB, P3/H/1268
Hamblett, Sarah, sp., Minety, 1833, AB, O, Wr, P3/1833/1
Hamlin, Hamling *see* Hamlen
Hammaton, Wm., yeo., Mount Scipett Farm, Bray, Berks., 1798, W, P1/H/1347, P1/15Reg/36
Hammond, Hammon, Ann, widow, Lydiard M., 1614, I, W, P3/H/98
Ann, widow, Marl., 1789, W, P1/H/1320, P1/14Reg/320
Ann, leather parer's wife, Sherb., Dorset (form. of Yeovil, Somerset), 1847, AB, comm, Wr, P5/1847/6
Betty, Sal. The Close, 1770, AB, P5/17Reg/4B
Betty, sp., E. Harnham, Britford, 1770, AB, P5/1770/20
Hammon, Cath., widow, Marl., 1683, AB, I, P1/H/468
Chas., yeo., Sanham Grn, Hungerford, Berks., 1764, W, P5/1764/20

Hamon, Edwd., ropemaker, Highw., 1607, AB, I, P1/H/49
Hammons *or* Hamand, Eliz., widow, Kellaways, 1669, comm, I, W, P3/H/406
Hammel, Eliz., widow, Motc., Dorset, 1737, W, Wr, P27/1/346
Heyman, Francis, Uffc., Devon, 1638, I, P5/1637/16
Geo., Easton, 1745, W, P3/H/1214
Hy., stationer, Sal., 1670, W, P4/1669/3
Hammand, Hy., worsted comber, Brinkw., 1691, AB, I, P3/H/687
Hammonds, Isaac, farmer, Underdown, Bremhill, 1838, W, Wr, P3/1838/42
Hammonds, Jacob, dairyman, Hanger, Bremhill, 1849, AB, comm, W, Wr, P3/1849/10
Hamyn, Jas., paymaster of late 1st garrison battalion, Holt, Bradford A., 1832, O, W, Wr, P2/1832/1
Hamon, Jn., husb., Lambourn Woodlands, Berks., 1606, I, W, P1/H/45
Hamon, Jn., husb., Lydiard M., 1611, I, W, P1/H/65
Jn., yeo., Foxham, Bremhill, 1632, I, W, P3/H/252
Hamon, Jn., Warfield, Berks., 1683, AB, I, P1/H/480
Hammon, Jn., Devizes, 1697, AB, P1/H/591
Hamont *or* Hamond, Jn., broad weaver, Gt. Faringdon, Berks., 1698, I, W, P5/1698/36
Hammans, Jn., Forest Gate, Melk., 1733, I, W, P2/H/1268
Jn., yeo., Allweston, Folke, Dorset, 1733, W, P5/1733/26
Jn., Aldbourne, 1768, AB, P3/H/1370
Hammans, Jn., yeo., Lyford, W. Hanney, Berks., 1792, req, copy W, W, P1/H/1327, P1/14Reg/458
Jn., yeo., Bushton, Clyffe P., 1839, W, Wr, P1/1839/52
Margery, widow, Grittenham, Brinkw., 1711, W, P3/H/913
Hammon, Martin, Sal. (form. of the University of Oxford), 1624, I, W, P4/1624/12
Hammonds, My., widow, Westport St My., 1730, W, P3/H/1078
My., Marl., 1749, AB, P1/H/1057
Haman, Mordecai, parish clerk, Shaw, S. cum Donnington, Berks., 1773, W, P1/H/1222, P1/12Reg/490A
Hamond, Richd., Wokm., Berks., 1541, W, P5/20Reg/22
Haymond, Richd., husb., Lambourn Woodlands, Berks., 1613, I, W, P1/H/79
Richd., sen., Foxham, Bremhill (& Gotshill), 1617, I, W, P3/H/118
Hammons, Richd., Foxham, Bremhill (& Cadenham), 1624, I, W, P3/H/184
Richd., yeo., Grittenham, Brinkw., 1674, AB, comm, I, P1/H/421
Hammans, Robt., husb., Foxham, Bremhill, 1629, I, W, P3/H/220
Hammons *or* Hamant, Robt., yeo., Gotshill, Bremhill, 1641, I (2), W, P3/H/327
Robt., sen., Winterbourne M., 1742, W, P3/H/1179
Hammons, Robt., Lyford, W. Hanney, Berks., 1798, AB, P1/H/1356, P1/15Reg/82C
Thos., yeo., Sherb., Dorset, 1812, W, Wr, P5/1812/19
Hamman, Wm., sen., husb. *or* yeo., Hodson, Chiseldon, 1640, I, W, P3/H/318
Hammon, Wm., Sherb., Dorset, 1661, comm, I, NW, P5/1661/24
Hamance, Wm., yeo., Gotshill, Bremhill, 1684, I, W, P3/H/590
Wm., Mildenhall, 1731, I, W, P3/H/1085
Hampshire, Edmd., Marden, 1717, AB, P2/H/1146
Jn., husb., Marden, 1558, W, P2/3Reg/123A
Richd., yeo., Foxham, Bremhill, 1744, W, P3/H/1202
Hampton, Abel, yeo., Gt. Cheverell, 1822, AB, W, Wr, P2/1822/17
Assincrete, gent., Shalbourne, Berks., 1623, I, W (NEP), P30/91
Cath., sp., Gt. Wishford, 1631, I, W, P2/H/428
Denise, widow, Marston, Pott. (form. of W. Lavington), 1825, comm, W, Wr, P1/1825/1
Edwd., Worton, Pott., 1704, AB, I, P1/H/627
Edwd., feltmaker and hatter, Mkt. L., 1706, I, W, P2/H/1044
Eleanor, sp., Southbroom, 1837, comm, W, Wr, P24/1353
Eliz., widow, Brigmerston, Milston, 1786, W, P1/H/1298, P1/14Reg/83
Grace, widow, Lt. Cheverell, 1757, W, P2/H/1427
Jas. Neate, bach., Plymouth, N. America (leaving effects at Devizes, Pott. & W. Lavington), 1838, AB, comm, Wr, P1/1838/6
Jn., jun., husb., Gt. Wishford, 1614-15, I, W, P2/H/303, P2/8Reg/260C
Jn., husb., Gt. Wishford, 1631-32, AB, I, NW, P2/H/429, 439
Jn., Gt. Cheverell, 1704, W, P2/H/1032
Jn., husb., Gt. Cheverell, 1708, I, W, P2/H/1061
Jn., gent., Lt. Cheverell, 1758, W, P2/H/1437
My., widow, Mkt. L., 1748, AB, L, ren, W, P1/H/1053, P1/10Reg/207

My., widow, Devizes, 1849, AB, D, O, W, Wr, P1/1849/18
Paul, labourer, Gt. Cheverell, 1706, AB, I, P2/H/1046
Richd., cordw., Newbury, Berks., 1683, AB, I, P1/H/473
Robt., tailor, Sal., 1625, I, NW, P1/H/162
Robt., sen., yeo., Worton, Pott., 1733, AB, ren, W, P1/H/918, P1/7Reg/571A
Robt., sen., yeo., Pott., 1756, W, P1/H/1119, P1/11Reg/279B
Robt., sen., Pott., 1798, comm, W, P1/H/1359, P1/15Reg/171
Sarah, widow, Worton, Pott., 1710, AB, ren, W, P1/H/662, P1/5Reg/16
Thos., Gt. Wishford, 1557, W, P2/3Reg/38A
Wm., W. Lavington, 1792, AB, P1/H/1322, P1/14Reg/364
Wm., sen., carp., Pott. Wick, 1849, D, O, W, Wr, P1/1849/16
Hamyn *see* Hammond
Han *see* Hann
Hanbridge *see* Hambidge
Hanbury *see* Henbury
Hanby, Hy., Corsham, [1577], W (NEP), P29/1Reg/17A
Thos., Sal. St Martin, 1583, AB, P4/Reg/22B
Hancock, Abigail, Westb., 1688, W, P25/1688/7
Handcock, Agnes, widow, Steeple A., 1693, I, W, P2/H/939
Alice, widow, Bromham, 1619, W, copy W, P4/1619/4
Alice, widow, Steeple L., 1646, AB, I, P2/H/580
Ambrose, Elcombe, Wrou., 1629, AB, a/c, I, P3/H/222
Amery, blacksmith, Tinh., Edington, [1617], I, W, P2/H/319
Andrew, [veyner *or* vener], Melk., 1559, W, P2/3Reg/176D, 184B
Ann, sp., Chittoe, Bps. C., 1684, I, W, P24/746
Ann, widow, Marl., 1685, I, W, P1/H/489
Ann, widow, Malm., 1748, comm, W, P3/H/1232
Ann, sp., Keevil, 1845, O, W, Wr, P2/1845/6
Benedict, yeo., Quemerford, Calne, 1668, I, W, P5/1667/30, P26/140
Betty, sp., Malm., 1729, AB, P3/H/1055
Cecilia, widow, Lippiatts, Corsham, 1755, AB, P29/2Reg/80B
Handcock, Christian, sp., Westwells, Corsham, 1685, AB, I, W, P29/H/57, P29/1Reg/227
Handcock, Christian, widow, Westwells, Corsham, 1686, AB (2 - 2nd bond not executed), I, W, P29/H/59, P29/1Reg/234
Chris., victualler, Speenhamland, Berks., 1763, W, P1/H/1161, P1/12Reg/39B
Cornelius, yeo., Woodhill Park, Clyffe P., 1697, I, W, P3/H/766
Edwd., weaver, Hinton, Steeple A., 1591, I, W, P1/H/2
Edwd., Woodrow, Melk., 1611, AB, P2/H/275, P2/8Reg/152B
Edwd., broad weaver, Hinton, Steeple A., 1625, I, W, P1/H/169
Edwd., shoemaker, Corsham, 1663-64, AB, I, P29/H/42, P29/1Reg/169A
Handcock, Edwd., Corsham, 1739, W, P29/H/113
Edwd., yeo., Pewsham, 1802, W, P5/1802/13, P5/19Reg/12
Eliz., widow, Quemerford, Calne, 1668, I, W, P5/1668/36
Eliz., widow, Chipp., 1841, AB, O, Wr, P3/1841/46
Ellis, husb., Steeple A., 1598, I, T, NW, P2/H/179
Handcock, Francis, sen., limeburner, Marl., 1712, I, W, P1/H/686, P1/5Reg/278
Frederick, bach., Malm., 1851, AB, Wr, P3/1851/50
Frideswide, widow, Hinton, Steeple A., 1714, I, ren, W, P2/H/1118
Geo., sen., yeo., Hinton, Steeple A., 1681, I, W, P2/H/798
Geo., sen., tailor, Hinton, Steeple A., 1695, I, W, P1/H/575
Geo., Steeple A., 1722, AB, P2/H/1190
Geo., yeo., Hinton, Steeple A., 1734, a/c, copy a/c, I, copy I, W, P2/H/1277
Geo., Hindon, 1762, W, P2/H/1453
Harry, tucker, Broughton G., 1579, W, P2/5Reg/331C
Hester, widow, Warm., 1700, AB, P2/H/995
Hugh, yeo., Malm., 1741, W, P3/H/1171
Handcock, Isaac, Ashton K., 1815, W, P3/1815/22
Jas., weaver, Hinton, Steeple A., 1598, AB, I, W, P2/H/172
Jas., sen., yeo., Bromham, 1630, I, W, P3/H/236
Jas., sen., yeo., Keevil, 1676, I, W, P2/H/737
Jas., yeo., Keevil, 1682, I, NW, P2/H/809

Jas., Westb., 1704, AB, P25/1704/4
Jas., baker, Chalford, Westb., 1708, I, W, P25/1708/1
Handcock, Jas., gent., Lippiatts, Corsham, 1715, I, W, P29/H/92, P29/2Reg/18B
Jas., yeo., Westbrook, Bromham, 1722, I, W, P3/H/984
Jas., yeo., Sutton B., 1797, W, P3/H/1521
Jas., cordw., Chipp., 1807, comm, W, Wr, P3/1807/38
Jane, widow, Chalford, Westb., 1708, I, W, P25/1708/5
Jane, widow, Pewsham Forest, 1816, W, Wr, P3/1816/13
Jane, widow, Pewsham, 1850, AB, comm, court proceeding, W, P3/1850/57
Jeremiah, yeo., Chittoe, Bps. C., 1677, I, W, P24/487
Joan, widow, Corsham, 1547, W, P29/1Reg/3A
Joan, widow, Bromham, 1619, W, P1/H/119
Joan, widow, Foxham, Bremhill, 1671, comm, I, W, P3/H/447
Joan, widow, Warm., 1707, AB, W, P2/H/1057
Joan, widow, Steeple A., 1714, AB, P1/H/708
Jn., Corsham, [1479], W (Latin - 17th century transcript). Date of probate not given, P29/1Reg/1B
Jn., Steeple A., 1557-59, AB, W, P2/3Reg/68C, P2/4Reg/19A
Jn., tailor, Melk., 1558, W, P2/3Reg/110A
Jn., Pickwick, Corsham, 1580, W, P29/1Reg/18B
Jn., Broughton G., 1587, NW, P2/7Reg/81A
Jn., W. Ashton, Steeple A., 1588, W, P2/7Reg/129B
Jn., weaver, Hinton, Steeple A., 1600, I, W, P2/H/190
Jn., husb., W. Ashton, Steeple A., [1612], I, W, P2/H/287
Jn., sen., husb., Hinton, Steeple A., 1636, deed of gift, I, P2/H/473
Jn., Staverton, Trowb., 1637, AB, I, W, P22/2/33
Jn., broad weaver, Hinton, Steeple A., 1664, I, NW, P1/H/356
Jn., mercer, Westb., 1664, AB, comm, I, P25/1664/6
Jn., sen., yeo., Lippiatts, Corsham, 1667, AB, I, W, P29/H/43
Jn., husb., Wanb., 1670, comm, I, W, P3/H/426
Jn., apothecary and doctor, Sal., 1682, I, W, P4/1682/5
Jn., yeo., Craysmarsh, Melk., [1685], I, W, P2/H/861
Handcock, Jn., yeo., Lippiatts, Corsham, 1692-93, caveat, I, W, P29/H/67, P29/1Reg/258B, 259
Jn., cordw., Melk., 1696, AB, D, I, W, P2/H/966
Jn., sen., yeo., Warm., 1705, comm, W, P2/H/1040
Jn., shoemaker, Marl., 1715, W, P1/H/718, P1/5Reg/476B
Jn., yeo., Pewsham, 1722, I, W, P3/H/985
Jn., yeo., Woodley, W. and Sandford, Berks., 1726, AB, W, P5/1726/17, P5/16Reg/140A
Jn., Speenhamland, Berks., 1729, W, P1/H/859, P1/7Reg/279A
Handcock, Jn., gent., Westwells, Corsham, 1733, W, P29/H/109
Jn., yeo., Pewsham Forest, 1733, W, P3/H/1105
Jn., Pewsham Forest, 1783, AB, P5/17Reg/243B
Handcock, Jn., Langley Burrell, 1789, W, P1/H/1312, P1/14Reg/277
Jn., gent., Westwells, Corsham, 1791, comm, W, P3/H/1497
Jn., Bremhill, 1807, AB, Wr, P1/1807/8
Jn., Lt. Hinton, 1838, comm, W, Wr, P3/1838/28
Jn., yeo., Chipp., 1838, comm, W, Wr, P3/1838/10
Jonathan, broad weaver, Leighs Marsh, Dilton, Westb., 1711, I, W (NEP), P25/1711/6
Jonathan, brazier, Marl., 1765, W, P1/H/1180, P1/12Reg/160A
Jos., jun., mason, Malm., 1722, W, P3/H/986
Jos., sen., mason, Malm., 1723, W, P3/H/1000
Jos., glazier, Malm., 1749, W, P3/H/1243
Mgt., widow, Steeple A., 1557, W, P2/3Reg/41C
Mgt., sp., Bromham & Devizes, 1619, I, W, P1/H/137
Mgt., Martin, Hants, 1677, AB, I, P2/H/747
Martha, widow, Sal., 1709, W, P4/1709/14
Martha, widow, Bremhill & Corsham, 1739, AB, I, P3/H/1157
Martha, widow, Trowb., 1745, AB, comm, P1/H/1028
My., widow, Steeple A., 1620, I, W, P1/H/140
My., widow, Gastard, Corsham, 1684, AB, I, W, P29/H/56, P29/1Reg/222B
My., sp., Pewsham Forest, 1816, W, P3/1816/14

Matthew, yeo., Keevil, 1717, AB, I, ren, P2/H/1140
Maud, widow, Woodrow, Melk., 1568, W, P2/5Reg/40A
Millicent, widow, West Field, Corsham, 1782, W, P1/H/1279, P1/13Reg/390
Millicent, Corsham, 1806-07, I, W, P29/1800-1857/11, P29/3Reg/253
Nathaniel, Corsham, 1694, note, P29/1Reg/263A
Nathaniel, clerk, Compton C., 1717, W, P2/H/1144
Nich., Hinton, Steeple A., 1585, W, P2/7Reg/3B
Richd., Wrou., 1571, W, P1/1Reg/129C
Richd., Warm., 1579, W, P2/5Reg/349
Richd., Hinton, Steeple A., 1598, AB, I, W, P2/H/171
Richd., husb., Monkton D., 1609, I, NW, P2/H/252, P2/8Reg/55B
Richd., yeo., Corsley, 1676, I, W, P2/H/732
Richd., Corsham, 1715, marriage licence, P29/2Reg/10F
Richd., Avill's Farm, Corsham, 1794, AB, comm, P3/H/1509
Robt., husb., Steeple A., 1567, W, P2/5Reg/14B
Robt., husb., Codf., 1606, AB, I, note of admon, P2/H/230
Robt., broad weaver, Quemerford, Calne, 1612, AB, a/c, I, W, P26/20
Robt., yeo., Steeple A., 1619, I, W, P1/H/126
Robt., weaver, Steeple A., 1623, I, W, P2/H/367
Robt., Ashton K., 1625, AB, P3/H/194
Robt., Wootton B., 1685, AB, I, P3/H/604
Handcock, Robt., broad weaver, Steeple A., 1711, W, P1/H/671, P1/5Reg/104
Robt., maltster, Devizes, 1728, comm, W, P1/H/840, P1/7Reg/194B
Robt., stone mason, Box, 1824, W, Wr, P3/1824/35
Sarah, widow, Netherh., 1663, AB, P1/H/337
Sarah, widow, Devizes, 1741, AB, comm, copy W, P1/H/996, P1/9Reg/203
Sarah, widow, Marl., 1774, AB, comm, P1/H/1232
Sarah, widow, Chipp., 1784, W, P3/H/1451
Stephen, Warm., 1579, I, P2/H/56
Thos., husb., Elcombe, Wrou., [1581], W (NEP), P3/1Reg/7B
Thos., jun., husb., Hinton, Steeple A., [1611], I, W, P2/H/284
Thos., husb., Steeple A., 1619, I, W, P2/H/341
Thos., E. Harnham, Britford, 1640, I (NEP), P5/1640/78
Thos., Marl., 1684, AB, I, P1/H/487
Handcock, Thos., clerk and rector, Chilmark, 1684, I, W, P1/H/478
Thos., mercer, Westb., 1684, I, W, P25/1684/7
Handcock, Thos., sen., yeo., Westwells, Corsham, 1684, I, W, P3/H/592
Thos., wool worker, Chalford, Westb., 1702, W, P25/1703/1
Thos., gent., Westwells, Corsham, 1728, W, P3/H/1044
Thos., Westport St My., 1752, AB, P3/H/1269
Thos., coach master, Marl., 1783, W, P1/H/1282, P1/13Reg/394
Walter, husb., Steeple A., 1584, W, P2/6Reg/131
Wm., weaver, Bromham, 1604, NW, P3/1Reg/53B
Wm., yeo., Steeple A., 1614, W, P2/8Reg/221B
Wm., yeo., Tinh. Mill (described as in Steeple A.), Edington, [1628], I, P2/H/397
Wm., Wanb., 1677, AB, comm, I, P3/H/517
Wm., Steeple A., 1679, AB, P2/H/765
Wm., Steeple A., 1705, AB, P2/H/1037
Handcock, Wm., sen., Kington L., 1720, W, P1/H/765, P1/6Reg/264B
Wm., Avill's Farm, Corsham, 1731, AB, comm, P3/H/1086
Wm., mason, Malm., 1733, W, P3/H/1106
Wm., yeo., Chittoe, Bps. C., 1733, W, P24/928
Wm., yeo., Corsham, 1768, W, P29/H/117, P29/2Reg/116
Wm., Seagry, 1772, W, P3/H/1393
Wm., Pewsham Forest, 1783, AB, ren, P5/1783/6
Wm., innholder, Warm., 1830, W, P2/1830/6
see also Bartlett alias H.; Ritchwell alias H.; Weekes alias H.
Hancorne, Ann, widow, Corsham, 1690, I, W, P29/H/63, P29/1Reg/248
Thos., son of Thos., gent., Corsham, 1662, AB, P29/1Reg/165
Thos., gent., Corsham, 1689, AB, I, W, P29/H/62, P29/1Reg/243A

Hand, Agnes, widow, Leigh Delamere, [1603], W (incomplete) (NEP), P3/1Reg/114
Ann, widow, Shaw, Melk., 1687, comm, I, W, P2/H/883
Hands, Benj., innholder, Baydon, 1715, I, W, P5/1715/19, P5/15Reg/329
Cornelius, Castle C., 1697, AB, comm, P3/H/767
Cornelius, Castle C., 1722, AB, P3/H/987
Edith, sp., Kellaways, 1633, I, W (although described as sp., W mentions 8 children), P3/H/266
Jn., bach., Lyneham, 1711, AB, I, P3/H/914
Jn., yeo., Pickwick, Corsham, 1722-24, AB, I, W, P29/H/103, P29/2Reg/44
Mgt., widow, Slaughterford, 1669, comm, I, W, P3/H/407
Martha, widow, E. Tytherton, Bremhill, 1709, I, W, P3/H/888
Rebecca, sp., Clack, Lyneham, 1832, W, P1/1832/82
Thos., Sevington, Leigh Delamere, [1582], W (NEP), P3/1Reg/15B
Thos., Charlcote, Bremhill, 1604, I, P3/H/7
Wm., yeo., Kellaways, 1669, comm, I, W, P3/H/408
Wm., yeo., Tytherton L., Chipp., 1670, AB, comm, I, P3/H/427
Handcock *see* Hancock
Hands *see* Hand
Handy, Ann, widow, Malm., 1690, I, W, P3/H/671
Edwd., Malm., 1669, AB, I, P3/H/409
Hundy, Felix, [shopkeeper], Liddington, 1641, AB, I, P3/H/335
Jane, Rodbourne, Malm., 1669, I, W, P3/H/410
Hundy, Joan, Liddington, 1638, AB, I, P1/H/235
Hundy, Jn., husb., Urchf., 1574, W, P2/5Reg/210A
Jn., gent., Rodbourne, Malm., 1788, W, P3/H/1478
Jn., Malm., 1810, AB, P3/1810/21
Jn. Weeks, yeo., Rodbourne, Malm., 1857, aff, O, W, Wr, P3/1857/7
Paul, yeo., Cleverton, Lea and C., 1842, O, W, Wr, P3/1842/15
Hundy, Richd., Rushall, 1557, AB, P2/3Reg/33B
Richd., gent., Gt. Somerford, 1844, O, W, Wr, P3/1844/56
Thos., baker, Malm., 1747, W, P1/H/1040, P1/10Reg/148
Thos., sen., gent., Rodbourne, Malm., 1826, W, Wr, P1/1826/65
Thos., sen., gent., Rodbourne, Malm., 1838, O, W, Wr, P3/1838/74
Hundy, Wm., husb., Liddington, 1629, I, W, P3/H/233
Hanham, Hannum, Betty, widow, Calne, 1804, AB, P26/1249
Betty, widow, Oborne, Dorset, 1827, comm, W, Wr, P5/1827/12
Chas., weaver, Ditchampton, Wilton, 1737, W, P2/H/1296
Hannum, Edwd., Calne, 1705, AB, P26/521
Hannam, Eliz., widow, Wilton, 1746, W, P2/H/1360
Hannam, Eliz., sp., Gillingham, Dorset (of Shaftesbury, Dorset in 1807), 1808, W, P27/1/598
Hannam, Francis, yeo., Gillingham, Dorset, 1720, I, W, P27/1/244
Hannam, Joan, widow, Gillingham, Dorset, 1731, I, W, P27/1/311
Hannam, Joan, widow, Pierston, Gillingham, Dorset, 1764, W, P27/1/444, P27/3Reg/119
Jn., victualler, Sherb., Dorset, 1747, W, P5/1747/10
Jn., weaver, Ditchampton, Wilton, 1773, W, P2/H/1536
Jn., yeo., Sherb., Dorset, 1782, W, P5/1782/15, P5/17Reg/228
Hannam, Jn., blacksmith, Easton, 1807, comm, W, Wr, P3/1807/69
Jn. *see also* Sarah Tudgy
Hannam, Josiah, mealman, Gillingham, Dorset, 1828, W, P27/1/681
Hannam, Love, Gillingham, Dorset, 1820, comm, W, Wr, P27/1/650
Hannam, Mgt., Sal., 1612, AB, I, P4/1612/11
Hannam, Martha, sp., Wilton, 1773, W, P2/H/1537
Hannam, Martin *see* Roger Martin
Morgan, Gillingham, Dorset, 1689, I, P27/1/114
Hannam, Philip, innholder, E. Knoyle, 1802, W, P2/1802/27
Hannum, Rachel, widow, Chr. M., 1724, AB, I, P3/H/1006
Hannam, Robt., joiner, Calne, 1691, AB, I, P26/399
Hannum, Robt., carp., Bremhill (form. of Tytherton Kellaways), 1824, comm, W, Wr, P3/1824/37
Hannam, Roger, Warm., 1561, W, P2/4Reg/73A
Hannam, Stephen, miller, Gillingham, Dorset, 1780, W, P27/1/507, P27/3Reg/216
Hannum, Susan, publican and widow, Calne, 1705, I (detailed), P26/523

Thos., victualler, Mere, 1748, AB, ren, Wr, P5/1748/13
Hannam, Thos., draper, Marl. (form. of Winchcomb, Gloucs), 1848, O, W, Wr, P1/1848/4
Wm., Sherb., Dorset, 1811, AB, Wr, P5/1811/14
Hankins, Hankin, Abigail, sp. and grocer, Thatcham, Berks., 1744, W, P1/H/1013, P1/9Reg/333
Frances, Lillington, Dorset, 1697, I, NW, P5/1697/19
Jn., gent., Thornford, Dorset, 1725, comm, W, P5/1725/31, P5/16Reg/107A
Jn., sen., Lillington, Dorset, 1727, W, P5/1727/21, P5/16Reg/145A
My., widow, Lillington, Dorset, 1736, W, P5/1736/15
Hankinson, Hugh, Marl., 1717, W, P1/H/747, P1/6Reg/152B
Hanks, Dyer, tailor, Malm., 1765, W, P3/H/1353
Edith, sp., Westport St My., 1693, AB, P3/H/719
Edwd., Abingdon, Berks., 1735, AB, P1/H/928
Eleanor, widow, Westport St My., 1628, I, W, P3/H/217
Eleanor, sp., Malm., 1834, AB, Wr, P3/1834/40
Eliz., wife, Malm., 1819, AB, comm, Wr, P3/1819/4
Francis, yeo., Garsdon, 1729, AB, I, P3/H/1057
Francis, Westport St My., 1785, W, P3/H/1460
Geo., sadler, Malm., 1850, O, W, Wr, P3/1850/6
Hy., currier, Westport St My., 1753, W, P1/H/1100, P1/11Reg/136
Hy., Marshfield (but having effects at Malm.), 1772, AB (2), P3/H/1394
Jas., Malm., 1741, AB, P3/H/1172
Jn., tailor, Malm., 1732, W, P1/7Reg/501B
Jn., Malm., 1801, AB, comm, P1/1801/30, P1/15Reg/253A
My., widow, Malm., 1811, W, Wr, P3/1811/16
Michael, Wanb., 1719, W, P3/H/966
Nich., husb., Westport St My., 1603, I, W, P3/H/3
Nich., butcher, Westport St My., 1733, W, P3/H/1107
Nich., boot and shoemaker, Malm., 1832, W, Wr, P1/1832/73
Rachel, widow, Westport St My., 1756, W, P1/H/1120, P1/11Reg/315
Sarah, widow, Westport St My., 1849, AB, comm, court proceeding, D, Wr, P3/1849/33
Susanna, sp., Malm., 1834, AB, W, Wr, P3/1834/39
Thos., Westport St My., 1739, AB, P3/H/1159
Thos., tailor, Malm. Abbey, 1771, AB, W, P3/H/1389
Thos., capital burgess, Westport St My., 1807, W, Wr, P3/1807/25
Wm., butcher, Westport St My., 1749, W, P3/H/1244
Wm., sen., labourer, Hartley, Winsley, Bradford A., 1808, W, Wr, P2/1808/14
Hanley, Hanly, Dorcas, Froxfield, 1761, W, P3/H/1323
Sam., gent., Lower Studley, Trowb., 1831, W, Wr, P1/1831/12
Hann, Benson, Holnest, Dorset, 1766, AB, I, P5/1766/12
Geoffrey, husb., Over C., Dorset, 1636, I, W, P5/1636/31, P5/13Reg/22
Isaac, yeo., Holnest, Dorset, 1857, aff, comm, D, W, Wr, P5/1857/6
Jas., yeo., Over C., Dorset, 1702, I, W, P5/1702/22
Han, Jane, widow, Holnest, Dorset, 1683, AB, comm, I, P5/1683/28
Jane, widow, Amesb., 1838, W, Wr, P2/1838/55
Joyce *see* Joyce Tomes
Mgt., widow, Hayway, Over C., Dorset, 1696, AB, I, W, P5/1696/20
My., widow, Castleton, Dorset, 1719, W, P5/1719/38, P5/16Reg/10A
My., Thornford, Dorset, 1742, AB, Wr (form. My. Ring, widow), P5/1742/21
Han, Thos., sen., husb., Holnest, Dorset, 1666, AB, I, P5/1666/18
Wm., Holnest, Dorset, 1811, AB, Wr, P5/1811/16
Wm., gent., Langham, Gillingham, Dorset, 1819, comm, W, Wr, P27/1/642
see also Haynes
Hannaford, Wm., bach., Gillingham, Dorset, 1794, AB, comm, ren, P27/1/553
Hannah, Jn., labourer, Gt. Amesb., 1706, I, W, P2/H/1051
Hannam *see* Hanham
Hanney, Hanny, Edwd., tiler, Leigh, Bradford A., 1712, comm, W, P2/H/1096
Jane, widow, Trowb., 1749, W, P1/H/1059, P1/10Reg/255
Jn., [tucker], Bradford A., 1581, W, P2/6Reg/41B
My., widow, Limpley Stoke, Bradford A., 1836, O, W, P2/1836/51
Hanny, Robt., Bradford A., 1758, AB, P2/H/1436

Hanny, Wm., weaver, Trowle, Bradford A., 1780, AB, P2/H/1585
Hannington, Ann, widow, Warm., 1707, W, P2/H/1060
Cath., widow, Burghfield, Berks., 1795, AB, P1/H/1341, P1/14Reg/575B
Edwd., basketmaker, Warm., 1707, AB, ren, W, P2/H/1058
Edwd., victualler, Reading, Berks., 1798, W, P1/H/1349, P1/15Reg/68
Francis, Wokm., Berks., 1669, AB, I, NW, P5/1669/25
Geo., shopkeeper, Burghfield, Berks., 1779, W, P1/H/1265, P1/13Reg/279
Wm., joiner, Peach St., Wokm., Berks., 1731, W, P5/1731/48
Wm., chairmaker, Warm., 1734, W, P2/H/1274
Hannold, Hannold alias Hannon, Richd., baker, Calne, 1608, I, P5/1608/16
Hannum *see* Hanham
Hanny *see* Hanney
Hansford, Johanna, widow, Gillingham, Dorset, 1756, W, P27/1/414, P27/3Reg/75
Jn., Hamp, Gillingham, Dorset, 1683-86, I (probate 1686), P27/1/77
Jn., Gillingham, Dorset, 1730, AB, I, P27/1/303
Sarah, sp., Gillingham, Dorset, 1775, W, P27/1/497, P27/3Reg/197B
Wm., Gillingham, Dorset, 1744, AB, I, P27/1/377, P27/3Reg/35A
Hansley, Abraham, Marl. St My., 1709, W, P1/H/658, P1/5Reg/8A
Hanson, Jn., gent., Bradfield, Berks., 1738, W, P1/H/960, P1/8Reg/270A
Lewis, mercer, Blewbury, Berks., 1603, I, NW, P5/1602/19, P5/7Reg/55B
Thos., Newtown, Shalbourne, 1753, AB, P23/641
Thos., stone mason, Speenhamland, Berks., 1817, W, Wr, P1/1817/76
Hapgood *see* Hopgood
Harbard, Harbart *see* Herbert
Harben *see* Harbin
Harber, Thos., bricklayer, Bray, Berks., 1677, AB, I, P1/H/440
Wm., Sevenhampton, Highw., 1713, AB, P10/1712/4
Harbert *see* Herbert
Harbin, Joan, widow, Charminster, Dorset, 1628, I, W, P5/1628/60, P5/11Reg/60B
Jn., Charminster, Dorset, 1667, AB, comm, W, P5/1667/27
Jn., jun., Charminster, Dorset, 1667, AB, I, NW, P5/1667/28
Jn., gent. & schoolmaster, Dorchester & Beam., Dorset, 1712, I, W, P17/205
Jn., Bloxworth, Dorset, 1726, AB, P5/1726/35
Jn., yeo., Charminster, Dorset, 1730, I, note, P5/1729/71
Harbin alias Ebber, Mgt., widow, Charminster, Dorset, 1669, AB, comm, I, P5/1669/22
Morgan, husb., Charminster, Dorset, 1594, I, W, P5/1594/36, P5/6Reg/60B
Sam., buttonmaker, Sherb., Dorset, 1695, AB, I, P5/1695/44
Harben, Thos., innholder, Sherb., Dorset, 1789, AB, comm, ren, P5/1789/7, P5/18Reg/138
Wm., Burton, Charminster, Dorset, 1694, comm, W, P5/1694/4
Wm., Charminster, Dorset, 1713, AB, P5/1713/47
Harburd, Harbutt *see* Herbert
Harcourt, My., widow, Fisherton A., 1795, W, P1/H/1337, P1/14Reg/594
Thos., linen weaver, Wolverton, Zeals, 1677, I, NW, P5/1677/30
Valentine, linen weaver, Wolverton, Zeals, 1701, I, W, P5/1701/25
Wm., gardener, Fisherton A., 1789, W, P1/H/1311, P1/14Reg/212
Hardcastle, Dorothy, Mere, 1728, AB, P5/1728/41, P5/16Reg/211B
Jn., gent., Ewen, Kemble, 1662, AB, comm, I, P3/H/345
Jn., yeo., Kemble, 1663, I, W, P3/H/352
Hardekin *see* Hardikin
Hardeman *see* Hardiman
Harden *see* Harding
Hardikin, Hardekin, Anthony, Seend, Melk., 1628, AB, I, P2/H/398
Hardikin alias Atkins, Jn., gent., Seend, Melk., 1612-16, a/c, comm, I, T, P2/H/290
Hardkins, My., widow, Baldham, Keevil, 1624, I, W, P2/H/373
Simon, yeo., Seend, Melk., 1665, AB, comm, I, P2/H/632
Hardiman, Edwd., Bower C., 1620, AB, a/c, I, P1/H/138
Edwd., sen., husb., Bower C., [1697], W, P2/H/970
Edwd., yeo., Bower C., 1718, W, P2/H/1154
Edwd., Bower C., 1742, AB, P2/H/1333
Edwd., blacksmith, Bower C., 1841, W, Wr, P2/1841/2

Jas., Tisb., 1766, AB, I, P2/H/1487
Hardyman, Jane, sp., Devizes, 1802, comm, W, P1/1802/15, P1/15Reg/372
Hardyman, Jane, wife, Swindon, 1804, AB, comm, P1/1804/121
Hardmon, Jn., Bower C., 1546, W, P2/2Reg/17
Hardeman, Jn., Tisb., 1614-16, AB, a/c, W, P2/H/1699
Hardeman, Jn., Coombe B., 1715, AB, I, P5/1715/20
Hardeman, Jn., yeo., Damerham, Hants, 1816, W, Wr, P2/1816/20
My., Bower C., 1732, AB, I, P1/H/887, P2/8Reg/224
Hardeman, Peter, Bower C., 1586, W, P2/7Reg/47B
Hardyman, Thos., esquire, Lydiard T., 1733, W, P3/H/1108
Hardyman, Walter, esquire, Swindon, 1774, W, P3/H/1405
Harding, Abraham, yeo., Manningford Bruce, 1671, comm, I, W, P3/H/448
Abraham, yeo., Etchilhampton, 1708, AB, I, P1/H/656
Abraham, Patney, 1736, AB, P2/H/1286
Abraham, yeo., Stanley, Chipp., 1802, AB, W, P3/1802/71
Hardinge, Agnes, widow, Sunton, Collingbourne K., 1563, W, P1/2Reg/124B
Hardinge, Agnes, widow, Durrington, 1581, W, P2/6Reg/24B
Agnes, widow, Lt. Hinton, [1609], W (NEP), P3/H/41
Hardinge, Agnes, widow, Orcheston St My., 1611, W, P2/H/281, P2/8Reg/161B
Hardinge, Agnes, widow, Over Stratton, Stratton St Mgt., 1613, W, P29/1Reg/59B
Harden, Alexander, labourer, Boscombe, 1781, W, P2/H/1592
Alice, widow, Durrington, 1559, W, P2/3Reg/158B
Alice, widow, Sutton M., 1627, I, W, P2/H/386
Harden, Alice, widow, Chitterne St My., 1645, I, W, P2/H/576
Harden *or* Harding, Alice, widow, Gillingham, Dorset, 1671, AB, P27/1/42
Alice, widow, Eastcourt, Crudwell, 1672, I, W, P3/H/462
Alice, wife [of Robt.], Gillingham, Dorset, 1718, AB, P27/1/223
Ann, daughter of Willliam, Durrington, 1559, W, P2/3Reg/163C
Hardinge, Ann, widow, Over Stratton, Stratton St Mgt., 1613, AB, I, P29/H/17
Hardinge, Ann, widow, Sal., 1630, I, W, P4/1629/15
Ann, Broughton G., [1678], I, W, P2/H/762
Ann, sen., widow, Inglesham, 1702, W, P3/H/814
Ann, sp., Crudwell, 1704, W, P3/H/844
Ann, widow, Westport St My., 1725, AB, comm, W, P3/H/1014
Ann, widow, Collingbourne K., 1725, W, P3/H/1015
Ann, widow, Mere, 1749, W, Wr, P5/1749/25
Ann, sp., Broughton G., 1781, W, P2/H/1595
Ann, widow, Bradford A., 1822, W, Wr, P2/1822/44
Hardinge, Anthony, Pewsey, 1605, W, P3/H/10
Anthony, Swindon, 1709, AB, I, P3/H/889
Arthur, Chirton, 1723, AB, P2/H/1198
Benj., W. Lavington, 1745, AB, I, P1/H/1029
Benj., labourer, Tytherington, Heytes., 1801, W (& cod), P5/1801/9, P5/18Reg/316B
Harden, Cath., widow, Enford, 1639, I, W, P2/H/519
Chas., brickmaker, Clarendon Park, 1770, W, P5/1770/21, P5/17Reg/1C
Dan., innholder, Bradford A., 1751, W, P2/H/1402
Dan., Chitterne AS, 1811, AB, Wr, P2/1811/5
Dan., Sal., 1818, AB, Wr, P4/1818/13
David, gent., Dunkirk, Rowde, 1856, aff, O, W, Wr, P3/1856/29
Deborah, sp., Limpley Stoke, Bradford A., 1830, W, Wr, P2/1830/79
Edmd., husb., Fittleton, 1671, I, T, W, P1/H/413
Edwd., Wantage, Berks., 1723, AB, P23/420
Harden, Edwd., sen., yeo., Amesb., 1732, W, P1/7Reg/536B
Edwd., jun., Amesb., 1776, AB, P2/H/1557
Edwd., sen., Amesb., 1776, AB, P2/H/1559
Edwd., carp., Ham, 1780, aff (2), comm, D, W, P3/H/1434
Edwd., Trowb., 1826, AB, comm, Wr, P1/1826/17
Eliz., widow, Broad C., 1559, W, P2/3Reg/146C
Hardin, Eliz., sp., Burbage, 1664, W, P5/1664/18
Harding alias North, Eliz., widow, Bishopstone N., 1687, AB, I, P6/66

Eliz., widow, Bradford A., 1805, W, P2/1805/73
Eliz., Hindon, 1824, W, Wr, P2/1824/85
Ellis, husb., Chitterne AS, 1641, I, W, P2/H/551
Ellis, Waltham St Lawr., Berks., 1680, AB, I, P1/H/451
Frances, Anderson, Dorset, 1708, AB, P5/1708/32
Francis, Orcheston St My., 1708, AB, I, P1/H/657
Francis, Bishopstone S., 1763, AB, P2/H/1461
Gabriel, Orcheston St My., 1639, I, W, copy W, P2/H/525
Geo., clothier, Broughton G., 1666, AB, ren, P1/H/373
Geo., Orcheston St My., 1728, AB, P2/H/1221
Geo., tallow chandler, Bere R., Dorset, 1757, W, P5/1757/12
Grace, widow, Holt, Bradford A., 1745, comm, W, P2/H/1354
Hannah, widow, Westwood, 1729, W, P2/H/1235
Hannah *see also* Hannah Morgan
Hy., sen., clothier, Broughton G., 1666, I, W, P1/H/370
Hy., innholder, Abingdon, Berks., 1683, I, NW, P1/H/482
Hy., gent., Broughton G., 1751, W, P2/H/1396
Hy., gent., Broughton G., 1774, W, P2/H/1541
Hy., victualler, Bradford A., 1800, W, P2/1800/74
Hy., widower, Fonthill G., 1815, AB, Wr, P2/1815/1
Hardinge, Jas., husb. *or* shepherd, Mere, 1631, comm, I, W, P5/1631/41, 52, P5/11Reg/170
Hardinge, Jas., husb., Charnham St., Hungerford, Berks., 1670-77, AB (his widow d. without admg), I, W, P23/8, 71
Jas., blacksmith, Westport St My., 1722-24, comm, I, W, P3/H/988, 1007
Jas., Mere, 1802, AB, P5/1802/16, P5/19Reg/15
Jas., staymaker, Bradford A., 1809-12, AB, comm, Wr, P2/1809/50, P2/1812/57
Jas., yeo., Melk. Forest, 1831, AB, D, O, W, Wr, P2/1831/20
Jas., grocer, Trowb., 1841, O, W, Wr, P1/1841/5
Jas., Chipp., 1848, AB, O, Wr, P3/1848/47
Jane, widow, Collingbourne K., 1689, AB, P3/H/659
Jane, widow, Calne, 1709, W, P26/562
Jane, widow, Mere, 1710, W, P5/1710/49, P5/15Reg/214
Jane, sp., Holt, Bradford A., 1745, AB, comm, W, P2/H/1352
Hardinge, Jane, widow, Bradford A., 1821, W, Wr, P2/1821/46
Jeremiah, innholder, Melk., 1780, comm, W, P2/H/1586
Harden, Jerome, husb., Chitterne St My., 1644, I, W, P2/H/568
Hardinge, Joan, widow, Enford, 1566, W (NEP), P1/1Reg/32C, 93C
Joan, Collingbourne K., 1613, W, P1/H/77
Jn., Broughton G., 1551, W, P2/2Reg/129B
Hardinge, Jn., Durrington, 1570, AB, P2/5Reg/94G
Hardinge, Jn., Easton Grey, [1570], W (NEP), P1/1Reg/121C
Hardinge, Jn., husb., Wantage, Berks., 1574, W, P5/3Reg/40B
Jn., husb., Wantage, Berks., 1603, AB, I, P5/1603/36
Hardinge, Jn., innkeeper, Steeple A., 1603, I, W, P2/H/212
Jn., sen., Orcheston St My., 1610, I, W, P2/H/260, P2/8Reg/83C
Hardinge, Jn., Donnington, Berks., 1613, I, W, P1/H/78
Jn., husb., Hinton, Steeple A., 1614, W, P2/8Reg/221A
Jn., yeo., Badbury, Chiseldon, 1616, I, W, P1/H/112
Hardinge, Jn., Gomeldon, Idmiston, 1617, AB, I, P2/H/321
Jn., sen., yeo. *or* husb., Winterbourne M., 1618, comm, I, W, P3/H/129
Jn., yeo., Longcott, Shrivenham, Berks., 1619, I, W, P1/H/134
Jn., sen., Sunton, Collingbourne K., 1623, I, W, P3/H/174
Hardinge, Jn., clothier, Broughton G., 1624, comm, I, W, P2/H/375
Hardinge, Jn., yeo., Southwick, N. Bradley, 1631, I, W, P1/H/188
Jn., day labourer, Wexcombe, Grafton, 1636, I, NW, P21/1/30
Jn., husb., Aughton, Collingbourne K., 1636, I, W, P3/H/282
Jn., yeo., Winterbourne Bassett & Monkton, 1637, AB, a/c, I, P3/H/293
Jn., Enford, 1638, I, W, P2/H/499
Jn., yeo., Shalbourne, 1670, I, W, copy W, P5/1670/25
Jn., Chiseldon, 1674, AB, I, P3/H/483
Hardinge, Jn., Longcott, Shrivenham, Berks., 1680, AB, I, P1/H/453

Jn., butcher, Wantage, Berks., 1680, AB, a/c, I, P23/100
Jn., yeo., Orcheston St Geo., 1682, AB, P2/H/806
Hardinge, Jn., sen., cooper, Hindon, [1689], I, W, P2/H/900
Jn., yeo., Cole Park, Malm., 1691, I, W, P3/H/689
Jn., gent., Charlton, Wantage, Berks., 1693, I, W, P23/189
Jn., husb., Enford, 1693, I, W, P2/H/937
Jn., husb. and innkeeper, Baydon, 1695, I, W, P5/1695/48
Jn., yeo., Wick, Bps. C., 1695, AB, I, P24/511
Jn., sen., broad weaver, Holt, Bradford A., 1697, I, W, P2/H/981
Jn., gent., Ashley, Box, 1700, I, W, P3/H/792
Jn., yeo., Collingbourne K., 1708, I, W, P3/H/879
Harden, Jn., Southbroom, 1718, AB, P24/642
Hardin, Jn., maltster, Devizes, 1720, W, P1/H/778, P1/6Reg/362B
Jn., yeo., Lt. Hinton, 1722, W, P3/H/989
Jn., Milton, Gillingham, Dorset, 1742, I, P27/1/365
Jn., husb., Milton, Gillingham, Dorset, 1744, W, P27/1/378, P27/3Reg/32
Jn., yeo., Bloxworth, Dorset, 1746, AB, W, P5/1746/38
Jn., [carp.], Wilton, Gt. Bedwyn, 1747, AB, I, P21/9/61
Jn., gunsmith, Abingdon, Berks., 1750, W, P1/H/1071, P1/10Reg/363
Harden, Jn., mariner, Lyme R., Dorset, 1782, AB, O, P5/1782/16, P5/17Reg/239C
Jn., yeo., Wilton, Gt. Bedwyn, 1786, W, P21/11/29
Jn., shopkeeper, Hindon, 1789, W, P2/H/1640
Jn., Chicklade, 1806, AB, ren, P2/1806/11
Jn., Rodbourne C., 1830, AB, comm, Wr, P3/1830/17
Jn., labourer, Stanley, Langley Burrell, 1835, O, W, P1/1835/32
Jn., yeo., Wanb., 1837, W, Wr, P3/1837/37
Jn., quartermaster in 3rd Regiment of Foot, Trowb., 1839, aff, O, W, Wr, P1/1839/68
Jn., bach., Bishopstone S., 1848, AB, Wr, P1/1848/20
Hardin, Jonathan, sen., Penton Mewsey, Hants (effects at Bulford), 1780, W, P2/H/1589
Jos., Malm., 1673, I, W, P3/H/472
Jos., rope, twine and sacking manufacturer, Fisherton A., 1855, aff, W, Wr, P2/1855/25
Julian, sp., Sherb., Dorset, 1630, AB, P5/1629/24, P5/11Reg/34C
Lucy, sp., Inglesham, 1702, W, P3/H/815
Harden, Luke, cooper, Hindon, 1770, W, P2/H/1525
Mgt., widow, Mere, 1638, I, W, P5/1638/57, P5/13Reg/117
Harden, Mgt., Hill D., 1669, I, P5/1669/21
Mgt., widow, Amesb., 1735, W, P2/H/1281
Mgt., widow, Maddington, 1781, W, P2/H/1596
Margery, widow, Wootton B., 1705, AB, comm, P3/H/853
Marian, widow, Steeple A., 1606, AB, I, W, P1/H/40
Harden, Marmaduke, W. Lavington, 1729, AB, I, P1/H/879
My., widow, Winterbourne M., 1672, I, W, P3/H/463
My., widow, Sal., 1721, AB, I (detailed), ren, W, P4/1721/12
My., widow, Bishopstone N., 1731, AB, I, W, P5/1731/36
Harden, My., widow, Bloxworth, Dorset, 1746, W, P5/1746/37
My., widow, Bradford A., 1773, W, P1/H/1230, P1/13Reg/34A
My., wife, Wootton B., 1818, AB, W, Wr, P3/1818/47
My., Bishopstone S., 1836, AB, P2/1836/10
My. *see also* Jn. Sparrow
My. Ann, widow, Hilmarton, 1853, AB, aff, O, Wr, P3/1853/62
Michael, labourer, Gillingham, Dorset, 1791, comm, W, P27/1/542
Hardinge, Nich., Durrington, 1578, I, W, P2/H/52, P2/5Reg/316B
Hardin, Nich., gardener, Sal., 1613, I, W, P4/1613/7
Nich., yeo., Badbury, Chiseldon, 1636, I, W, P3/H/283
Paul, yeo., Bradford A., 1789, comm, W, P2/H/1646
Philip, gent., Eastcourt, Crudwell, 1673, I, W, P3/H/473
Rebecca, widow, Trowb., 1802, AB, W, Wr, P1/1802/6, P1/15Reg/364
Hardinge, Richd., Farley, Alderbury, 1569, AB, P5/2Reg/45A
Hardinge, Richd., yeo., Bushton, Clyffe P., 1613, I, W, P1/H/80
Richd., W. Kennett, Avebury, 1627, AB, a/c, I, P3/H/210

Richd., yeo., Pewsey, 1678, AB, I, P3/H/524
Richd., yeo., Wantage, Berks., 1694, I, W, P23/209
Richd., haywarden, Pewsey, 1709, AB, I, P3/H/890
Richd., Wilton, Gt. Bedwyn, 1732, AB, P21/8/71
Richd., Charlcote, Bremhill, 1772, W, P3/H/1395
Robt., husb., Maddington, 1558, W, P2/3Reg/144A
Harden, Robt., Sutton M., 1561, I, W, P2/H/12, P2/4Reg/86A
Harden, Robt., Collingbourne K., 1611, W, P3/H/66
Robt., Bishopstone N., 1630, I, W, P6/15
Harding alias North, Robt., yeo., Badbury, Chiseldon, 1630, a/c, I, W, P3/H/237
Robt., sen., husb., Sutton V., [1638], I, W, P2/H/502
Harden *or* Harding, Robt., Sutton M. & Chicksgrove, Tisb., 1651, I, W, P1/H/301
Robt., Chelworth, Crudwell, 1675, AB, a/c, I, P3/H/491
Harding alias North, Robt., Bishopstone N., 1681, I, W, P6/55
Robt., Chiseldon, 1687, AB, I, ren, P3/H/630
Harden, Robt., Orcheston St My., 1690, AB, P2/H/911
Robt., sen., Gillingham, Dorset, 1703, AB, P27/1/148
Robt., linen weaver, Pierston, Gillingham, Dorset, 1733, AB, W, P27/1/326
Robt., Berwick St Jas., 1740, AB, T, P1/H/973
Robt., innholder, Melk., 1761, W, P2/H/1449
Robt., Chr. M., 1813, AB, comm, Wr, P3/1813/13
Robt., yeo., Chilton F., 1841, AB, comm, ren, W, Wr, P3/1841/34
Roger, Sal. St Martin, 1621, AB, I, P4/1620/5
Harding alias North, Roger, yeo., Wootton B., 1636, I, W, P3/H/284
Sam., carp., Trowb., 1850, W, Wr, P1/1850/16
Sam., coal agent, Chipp. (form. of Henry St., Bristol ; agent for Wethered, Cossham & Bendall coal proprietors of Shortwood & Pucklechurch Collieries nr Bristol), 1857, aff, D, O, W, Wr, P3/1857/31
Harden, Sarah, widow, Southbroom, 1722, AB, P24/887
Sarah, wife, Box, 1741, AB, I, P1/H/987
Sarah, widow, Hilmarton, 1749, AB, P3/H/1245
Sarah, widow, Corsham, 1839, W, Wr, P3/1839/17
Sarah, sp., Gt. Trowle, Bradford A., 1844, AB, O, Wr, P1/1844/13
Thos., husb., Enford, 1563, I, W, P2/H/21, P2/4Reg/114C
Hardinge, Thos., Broughton G., 1566, W, P2/4Reg/224A
Hardinge, Thos., Orcheston St My., 1598, I, W, P2/H/178
Thos., husb., Enford, 1602, I, W, P2/H/208
Thos., yeo., Compton, Enford, 1645, I, NW, P2/H/574
Thos., Pewsey, 1699, AB, I, P3/H/778
Harden, Thos., yeo., Chitterne St My., 1701, W, P2/H/1005
Thos., yeo., Pierston, Gillingham, Dorset, [1706], W, P27/1/161
Thos., Wootton B., 1709, AB, I, P3/H/891
Thos., Trowb., 1712, AB, P2/H/1104
Thos., yeo., Holt, Bradford A., 1712, AB, comm, I, P2/H/1102
Thos., husb., Ogbourne St Geo., 1714, W, P23/340
Thos., yeo., Badbury Wick, Chiseldon, 1718, W, P3/H/954
Thos., cordw., Bishopstone S., 1723, AB, P1/H/790
Thos., yeo., Pierston, Gillingham, Dorset, 1727, W, P27/1/285
Thos., Westwood, 1729, AB, P1/H/876
Thos., Holt, Bradford A., 1734, AB, P2/H/1275
Thos., Hindon, 1737, AB, P2/H/1301
Harden, Thos., mason, Sutton M., 1741, W, P2/H/1330
Thos., yeo., E. Challow, Letcombe Regis, Berks., 1776, note, W, P1/H/1242, P1/13Reg/129B
Thos., Orcheston St Geo., 1781, AB, P2/H/1590
Thos., yeo., Croucheston, Bishopstone S., 1781, W, P2/H/1593
Thos., Bishopstone S., 1788, AB, P2/H/1636
Thos., Aldbourne, 1804, AB, P1/1804/87
Thos., Trowb., 1807, AB, comm, Wr, P1/1807/29
Thos., Bishopstone S., 1820, AB, Wr, P1/1820/63
Thos., Wilton, Gt. Bedwyn, 1823, bond to secure goods, P5/1823/29
Thos., Church St., Mere, 1828, O, W, Wr, P5/1828/3

Hardinge, Walter, Enford, 1615, AB, I, T, P2/H/309, P2/8Reg/279A
Wm., husb., Durrington, 1557, W, P2/3Reg/72A
Wm., Hinton, Steeple A., 1578, I, P2/H/50
Hardinge, Wm., husb., Durrington, 1578, W, P2/5Reg/316A
Hardinge, Wm., sen., Holt, Bradford A., 1593, I, W, P2/H/129
Hardinge, Wm., yeo., Holt, Bradford A., [1612], I, W, P2/H/286
Wm., yeo., Winkfield, Berks., 1614, I, W, P1/H/84
Hardinge, Wm., [Preshute] (NBI) (but all debts owing in Marl.), [c1616], I, P1/H/101
Wm., labourer, Wedh., Urchf., 1631, I, W, P2/H/431
Wm., Badbury, Chiseldon, 1632, AB, a/c, I, P3/H/253
Harden, Wm., husb., Enford, 1638, I, W, P1/H/229
Wm., Stourton, 1665, AB, comm, P2/H/634
Wm., Wootton B., 1665, I, W, P3/H/368
Harden, Wm., husb., Lt. Hinton, 1672, I, W, P3/H/461
Hardinge, Wm., yeo., Fonthill B., 1672, a/c, I, W, P2/H/695
Wm., yeo., Ashley, Box, 1675, I, W, P3/H/492
Wm., sen., clothier, Broughton G., 1678, comm, W, P2/H/754
Wm., yeo., Mere, 1684-85, AB, a/c, I, P5/1684/33, P5/1685/48
Wm., schoolmaster, Tisb., 1703, W, P2/H/1016
Harden, Wm., Holt, Bradford A., 1710, W, P2/H/1077
Wm., gent., Tisb., 1711, I, P2/H/1093
Wm., clothworker, Trowb., 1717, W, P1/H/736, P1/6Reg/124
Wm., Holt, Bradford A., 1720, AB, P2/H/1171
Wm., yeo., Broughton G., 1722, I, W, P2/H/1187
Wm., yeo. and bach., Wantage, Berks., 1722, AB, I, P5/1722/26
Wm., yeo., Box, 1732, W, P3/H/1099
Wm., yeo., Mere, 1738, W, Wr, P5/1738/22
Wm., maltster, Ewen, Kemble, 1749, W, P3/H/1246
Wm., sen., butcher, Box, 1768, W, P3/H/1371
Wm., Bradford A., 1778, AB, comm, P2/H/1576
Wm., tailor, Sutton M., 1781, W, P2/H/1600
Wm., Newbury, Berks., 1798, AB, P1/H/1352, P1/15Reg/72A
Wm., shoemaker, Trowb., 1813, W, Wr, P1/1813/3
Wm., sen., yeo., Mere, 1836, W, Wr, P5/1836/27
Wm., yeo., Wanb., 1846, comm, W, Wr, P3/1846/21
see also Lilly form. H.; North alias H.
Hardkins *see* Hardikin
Hardwick, Thos., Sal. The Close, 1681, AB, P5/1680/21
Hardy, Christmas, yeo., Grimstone, Stratton, Dorset, 1697, AB, I, P5/1697/20
Giles, Sutton Poyntz, Dorset, 1581, I, T (children: Jn., Wm., Christian, Avice & David H.), W, P5/1580/29, P5/1581/13, P5/4Reg/21A
Hugh, yeo., Thornford, Dorset, 1681, I, W, P5/1681/29
Hugh, gent., Long Burton, Dorset, 1729, W, P5/1729/23, P5/16Reg/236D
Jn., Sutton Poyntz, Dorset, 1581, I, W, P5/1581/11, P5/4Reg/21B
Jn., shepherd, Alton P., Dorset, 1594, I, T, W, P5/1594/35, P5/6Reg/59C
Jn., Charminster, Dorset, 1691, I, W, P5/1691/35
Jn., labourer, Preston, Dorset, 1731, W, P5/1731/42
Jn., no abode stated, 1746, I (joint I of goods of both persons), P30/89
Jn., Charminster, Dorset, 1769, AB, P5/1769/13
Jn., widower, Lyme R., Dorset, 1771, AB, ren, P16/337
Lancelot, Beam., Dorset, 1682, AB, I, P5/1682/50
Mgt., Bere R., Dorset, 1759, W, P5/1759/13
Nich., yeo., Grimstone, Stratton, Dorset, 1677, I, W, Wr, P5/1677/27
Richd., Beam., Dorset, 1721, AB, P17/401
Robt., Bere R., Dorset, 1723, AB, I, P5/1723/22
Thos., Shitterton, Bere R., Dorset, 1615, I, W, P5/1614/27, P5/9Reg/152A
Thos., sen., yeo., N. Mapperton, Dorset, 1632, I, W, P17/5
Wm., apothecary, Lyme R., Dorset, 1692, AB, I, P5/1692/39
Wm., yeo., Grimstone, Stratton, Dorset, 1732, comm, W, P5/1732/20
Hardyman *see* Hardiman

Hare, Jas., butcher, Chapmanslade, Dilton, Westb., 1749, W, P25/1749/4
Jn., gent., Collingbourne K., 1725, W, P21/8/24
Jn., Short St., Dilton, Westb., 1743, AB, P25/1743/9
Heyre, Richd., husb., Sonning, Berks., 1591, I, W, P5/1591/39, P5/5Reg/115A
Richd., yeo., Leigh, Yetm., Dorset, 1826, comm, W, Wr, P19/232
Hares, Robt., yeo., Bulk., Keevil, 1667, I, W, P1/H/376
Robt., yeo., Enmore Grn, Motc., Dorset, 1826, W, P19/235
Wm., Lyme R., Dorset, 1743, W, Wr, P5/1742/22
Harewell, Harwell, Edwd., sen., yeo., Hankerton, 1671, comm, I, W, P3/H/450
Eliz., widow, Crudwell, 1744, W, P3/H/1203
Geo., gent., Crudwell, 1727, W, P3/H/1031
Geo., Crudwell, 1769, AB, P3/H/1382
Harewell alias Trinder, My., baker's wife, Leigh, Ashton K., 1729, AB, P3/H/1056
Harwell, My., widow, Gillingham, Dorset, [1770], W, P27/1/471
Rebecca, gent.'s wife, Crudwell, 1700, AB, P3/H/793
Harford, Abimelech, sen., Draycot C., 1696, AB, I, W, P3/H/757
Agnes, Bishopstone S., 1570, W, P2/5Reg/101C
Harvard, Alice, widow, Ludg., 1605, AB, I, note of admon, P2/H/228
Edith, Steeple L., [1611], I, P2/H/276
Eleanor, widow, Heale, Woodford, 1597, AB, I, W, P13/1/4, P5/6Reg/160A
Eliz., widow, Netton, Bishopstone S., 1641, I, W, P2/H/550
Harvard, Geo., carrier, Foghamshire, Chipp., 1623, AB, I, P3/H/175
Giles, Netton, Bishopstone S., 1640, AB, a/c, I, P2/H/544
Hy., husb., Chute, 1686, I, W, P7/66
Jn., sen., Bishopstone S., 1559, W, P2/4Reg/11A
Jn., husb., Bishopstone S., 1568, W, P2/5Reg/41A
Jn., Stratford Tony, 1584, W, P2/6Reg/120B
Jn., Edington, 1591, I, W, P2/H/112
Jn., husb., Lt. Wittenham, Berks., 1622, I, W, P1/H/156
Harvard, Jn., broad weaver, Chipp., 1664, comm, I, W, P1/H/353
Harfett, Jn., Quidh., 1683, AB, P2/H/827
Jn., [clothworker], Castle C., 1690, AB, I, P3/H/672
Jn., narrow weaver, Broughton G., 1739, I, W, P2/H/1311
Jn., carp. and shopkeeper, Dauntsey, 1748, AB, a/c, comm, I, W, P3/H/1235
Jos., N. Bradley, 1790, AB, comm, P2/H/1651
Lucy, Sherb., Dorset, 1756, W, P5/1756/14
My., widow, Bishopstone S., 1664, I, W, P1/H/355
Harvard, My., widow, Chipp., 1686, AB, comm, I, P3/H/622
My., widow, N. Bradley, 1791, W, P2/H/1656
Matthew, husb., Ford, Laverstock, 1701, W, P2/H/1002
Richd., Bradford A., 1587, I (only note of probate & total), W, P2/H/80, P2/7Reg/83B
Richd., tailor, Ludg., 1601, AB, I, W, P2/H/193
Harfutt, Richd., husb., Purton, [1608], W (NEP), P3/H/31
Richd., Dauntsey, 1689, AB, I, P3/H/660
Robt., innholder, Sal., 1663, I, W, P4/1662/4
Robt., weaver, Chipp., 1693, AB, I, ren, P3/H/717
Robt., Castle C., 1745, AB, P3/H/1215
Sarah, widow, Holt, Bradford A., 1752, W, P2/H/1403
Susan, widow, Dauntsey, 1704, I, W, P3/H/845
Thos., Netton, Bishopstone S., 1594, I, T, NW, P2/H/136
Thos., sen., husb., Chute, 1605, I, W, P5/1605/31, P5/8Reg/44
Harverd, Thos., husb., Steeple A., 1620, I, W, P1/H/141
Thos., Quidh., 1743, AB, P2/H/1344
Thos., gent., Broad C., 1851, W, Wr, P2/1851/3
Wm., Ditchampton, Wilton, 1548, W, P2/2Reg/63B
Wm., tiler, Foghamshire, Chipp., 1624, I, W, P3/H/185
Harvard, Wm., husb., Lt. Wittenham, Berks., 1631, I, W, P1/H/192
Wm., sen., broad weaver, Corsley, 1670, AB, I, NW, P2/H/676
Wm., sen., yeo., Netton, Bishopstone S., 1681, comm, I, W, P2/H/790
Wm., husb., Netton, Bishopstone S., [1697], I, W, P2/H/973

Wm., carp., Holt, Bradford A., 1747, W, P2/H/1367
Wm., broad weaver, Studley, Trowb., 1760, W, P1/H/1155, P1/11Reg/489A
see also Ley alias H.
Hargett, Edmd., yeo., Hullavington, 1636, I, NW, P3/H/286
Hy., yeo., Gt. Somerford, 1676, I, W, P3/H/500
Hargoll, Geo., Fisherton A., 1624, AB, a/c, I, P2/H/376
Hargraves, Jn., victualler, Avoncliff, Westwood, 1807, W, Wr, P2/1807/7
Haring *see* Herring
Harland, Wm., wheelwright, Marden, 1739, W, P1/H/952
Harle, Jn., sen., labourer, Lt. Coxwell, Gt. Faringdon, Berks., 1707, I, W, P5/1707/29
Wm., Melk., 1581, AB, P2/6Reg/53A
Harman, Arman, Ann, widow (*or* sp.), Wootton B., 1674, AB, I, ren, W, P1/A/136
Ann, widow, Mkt. L., 1764, W, P2/H/1474
Hearman, Benj., E. Hanney, W. Hanney, Berks., 1826, W, Wr, P1/1826/30
Edwd., Calne, 1737, AB, I, P26/799
Arman, Edwd., farmer, Chiseldon, 1804, W, P1/1804/117
Arman, Eliz., widow, Wootton B., 1678, I, W, P3/A/158
Hurman, Frances *see* Alice Extin
Arman, Gabriel, [draper], Wootton B., 1670, comm, I, W, P3/A/130
Arman, Jane, widow, Wootton B., 1780, W, P3/A/461
Jn., Enford, 1587, W, P2/7Reg/87B
Jn., broad weaver, Warm., 1643, I, W, P2/H/563
Jn., sen., yeo., Stock St., Calne, 1682, comm, I (detailed), W, P26/296
Jn., Calne, 1706, AB, P26/531
Jn., sen., victualler, Studley, Calne, 1724, W, P26/687
Hearman, Jn., sen., yeo., E. Hanney, W. Hanney, Berks., 1753, W, P1/H/1094, P1/11Reg/57
Jn., Crockerton, Longbridge D., 1756, W, P2/H/1420
Jn., maltster, Mkt. L., 1759, comm, W, P1/H/1145, P1/11Reg/421A
Jn., yeo., Keevil, 1796, W, Wr, P2/H/1681
Jn., Ditchampton (described as in Burcombe), Wilton, 1797, AB, P2/H/1685
Jn., victualler, Ditchampton, Wilton, 1831, W, Wr, P2/1831/27
Arman, Jn., Chiseldon, 1854-55, AB, aff, comm, court proceeding, P3/1854/67, P3/1855/53
Harmon, Jos., yeo., Purton, 1692, AB, I, P3/H/706
Leah, widow, Crickl. St S., 1844, comm, W, Wr, P3/1844/8
Herman, My., widow, Cholsey, Berks., 1741, AB, I, draft I, P1/H/980
My., widow, Ditchampton, Wilton, 1803, W, P2/1803/20
Maurice, husb., Bishopstrow, 1637, AB, I, P2/H/494
Oliver, maltster, Witcomb, Hilmarton, 1702, comm, I, ren, W, P3/H/817
Phoebe, widow, Ditchampton, Wilton, 1857, aff, W, Wr, P2/1857/61
Arman, Richd., blacksmith, Wootton B., 1688, AB, I, W, Wr, P3/A/203
Richd., chandler, Devizes, 1693, AB, comm, I, ren, I (detailed), P1/H/558
Richd., maltster, Sonning, Berks., 1812, req, W, copy W, Wr, P5/1812/1
Arman, Richd., labourer, Chiseldon, 1834, W, Wr, P3/1834/53
Arman, Robt., flaxdresser, Wootton B., 1668, AB, I, NW, P3/A/118
Arman, Robt., sailor, Wootton B., 1758, AB, P3/A/410
Arman, Sarah, widow, Hodson, Chiseldon, 1838, W, Wr, P3/1838/34
Sarah, sp., Berwick St Jn., 1843, AB, D, W, Wr, P2/1843/22
Sarah, widow, Ditchampton, Wilton, 1848, W, Wr, P1/1848/67
Thos., Stourpaine, Dorset, 1608, I, W, P24/158
Arman, Thos., mercer, Wootton B., 1697, I, W, P3/A/233
Arman, Thos., joiner, Marl., 1736, AB, I, ren, P1/A/316
Arman, Thos., sen., blacksmith, Wootton B., 1776, comm, W, P3/A/452
Thos., yeo., Crickl. St S., 1799, AB, W, P3/H/1535
Thos., labourer, Crickl. St S., 1844, aff, comm, W, Wr, P3/1844/15
Hurman, Wm., gent., Motc., Dorset, 1690, I, W, P27/1/124
Arman, Wm., blacksmith, Chiseldon, 1749, W, P3/A/389
Wm., bach. & seaman on HMS *Sappho*, Marl., 1820, AB, Wr, P1/1820/113
Harmer, Geo., sen., tailor, Moredon, Rodbourne C., 1702, I, W, P3/H/816
Richd., Chipp., 1636, I, ren, P3/H/285
Wm., Chipp., 1625, AB, a/c, I, P3/H/195

Harmon *see* Harman
Harmswood, Ralph, sen., [Ufton Nervet, Berks.]; admrs from Ufton & Sulhampstead, Berks., 1668, AB, P1/H/389
Harner *see* Horner
Harnest, Grace, sp., Keevil, [1683], I, W, P2/H/824
Harnett *see* Hornett
Harny, Edwd., ostler, Lyme R., Dorset, 1716, W, P5/1716/42, P5/15Reg/344A
Harold *see* Harrold
Harper, Andrew, blacksmith, Westport St My., 1638, I, P1/H/233
Ann, Sal., 1727, AB, P4/1727/3
Barbara, widow, Crickl. St S., 1717, W, P3/H/948
Dominic, Rowde, 1615, I, W, P3/H/104
Eliz., widow, Colerne, 1729, I, W, P3/H/1060
Harper alias Willis, Geo., joiner, Chipp., 1678, I, NW, P3/H/525
Hy., yeo., Letcombe Regis, Berks., 1741, I, W, P1/H/981, P1/9Reg/88
Hy., gardener, Corsham, 1800-03, I, W, P29/1800-1857/5, P29/3Reg/230
Jas., sen., yeo., Rowde, 1717, I, W, P3/H/949
Jas., cooper, Marl., 1799, W, P1/H/1361, P1/15Reg/192
Jane, widow, Crickl. St My., 1702, AB, comm, I, P3/H/818
Joan, widow, Rowde, 1615, I, W, P3/H/105
Joan, widow, Rowde, 1621, I, W, P3/H/157
Joan, widow, Kington St M., 1625, I, W, P3/H/196
Jn., Urchf., 1557, AB, P2/3Reg/27C
Jn., tailor, Hilmarton, 1661, I, W, P3/H/338, P3/3Reg/23B
Jn., jun., Chilton F., 1684, AB, I, P3/H/593
Jn., sen., carp., Chilton F., 1685, I, W, P3/H/606
Jn., Avebury, 1706, I, W, P3/H/860
Jn., freemason, Colerne, 1718, I, W, P3/H/955
Jn., tailor, Chilton F., 1749, AB, ren, W, P3/H/1247
Jn., cordw., Crickl. St S., 1763, W, P1/H/1169, P1/12Reg/98B
Jn., carp., Monkton F., 1799, W, P2/H/1690
Jonathan, yeo., Lyneham, 1748, W, P3/H/1233
Mgt., widow, N. Bradley, 1696, NW, P2/H/962
Margery, widow, Hannington Wick, 1619, I, W, P1/H/121
Harper alias Hicks, My., wife, Pott., 1639, AB, I, P1/H/244
Harpur, My., sp., Devizes, 1798, AB, comm, P1/H/1346, P1/15Reg/30A
My., widow, Wallingford St Peter, Berks., 1795, W, P1/H/1332, P1/14Reg/523A
My., sp., Trowb., 1835, comm, W, P1/1835/136
Matthew, shoemaker, Sal., 1687, W, P4/1687/6
Richd., Netheravon, 1579, I, W, P5/1579/36, P5/3Reg/146A
Richd., sen., Netheravon, 1633, I, W, P12/72
Richd., N. Bradley, 1691, comm, I, W, P2/H/919
Richd., Westb., 1725, AB, P25/1725/1
Richd., yeo., Rowde, 1826, AB, Wr, P1/1826/107
Robt., joiner, Gt. Faringdon, Berks., 1662, AB, I, P5/1662/56
Robt., Broad B., Highw., 1685, AB, P5/1685/41
Robt., joiner, Crickl. St S., 1689, I, W, P3/H/661
Robt., Crickl. St S., 1729, W, P1/H/845, P1/7Reg/227
Robt., Avill's Farm, Corsham, 1732, W, P1/H/905, P1/7Reg/510B
Robt., yeo., Rowde, 1735, W, P1/H/935, P1/8Reg/106
Robt., salesman, Devizes, 1816, W, Wr, P1/1816/6
Susanna, widow, W. Tockenham, Lyneham, 1759, AB, ren, W, P1/H/1147, P1/11Reg/451
Thos., blacksmith, Kington St M., [1619], I, W (NEP), P3/H/139
Thos., day labourer, Clevancy, Hilmarton, 1626, I, NW (on same document), P3/H/201
Thos., Milbourne, Malm., 1670, AB, court paper, I, P3/H/429
Thos., Fiddington, W. Lavington, 1670, AB, I, P1/H/398
Thos., shopkeeper, Inkpen, Berks., 1756, W, P1/H/1109, P1/11Reg/245
Wm., Rowde, 1606, W, P3/2Reg/13B
Wm., sen., yeo., Hannington Wick, 1616, I, W, P3/H/116
Wm., husb., Hannington, 1636, I, W, P3/H/287
Wm., [carp.], Hannington, 1676, I, W, P3/H/501

Wm., sen., yeo., Rowde, 1701, I, W, Wr, P3/H/804
Harpur, Wm., Rowde, 1745, W, P3/H/1216
Harpoole, Chris., clerk, Bishopstone N., 1603-04, I, W, P5/1603/39, P5/8Reg/3B
Harpur *see* Harper
Harraway, Alice, widow, E. Grimstead, W. Dean, 1709, W, P2/H/1069
Harroway, Eliz., widow, E. Grimstead, W. Dean, [1689], I, W, P2/H/904
Harraway alias Berkshire, Jn., W. Dean, 1552, W, P2/2Reg/157C
Harroway, Jn., husb., E. Grimstead, W. Dean, 1623, AB, I, W (2), NW, P2/H/366
Jn., yeo., E. Grimstead, W. Dean, 1672, I, W, P2/H/692
Harroway, Jn., Pitton and Farley, 1680, NW (NEP), P30/81
Harroway, Jn., husb., Farley, Alderbury, 1680, I, W, P26/273
Jn., Melchet Park, 1687, AB, I, P5/1686/31
Jn., butcher, Devizes, 1771, W, P1/H/1214, P1/12Reg/411
My., widow, Urchf., 1845, O, W, Wr, P1/1845/15
Harway alias Berkshire, Richd., E. Grimstead, W. Dean, 1573, W, P2/5Reg/165B
Harway alias Berkshire, Thos., E. Grimstead, W. Dean, 1558, W, P2/3Reg/133A
Thos., E. Grimstead, W. Dean, 1585, AB, I, W, P2/H/72, P2/7Reg/20B
Thos., Easton, Bps. C., 1850, AB, O, Wr, P24/1399
Wm., E. Grimstead, W. Dean, 1620-21, AB, I (2), W (2), P2/H/344, 349
Wm., husb., Whitep., 1639, I, NW, P2/H/509
Wm., sen., E. Grimstead, W. Dean, 1641, I, W, P1/H/250
Harway, Wm., Whitep., 1669, AB, P2/H/657
Harroway, Wm., sen., husb., Farley, Alderbury, 1671, W, P26/193
Harroway, Wm., no abode stated; possibly Farley, Alderbury, [1677], I, P2/H/745
Harroway, Wm., yeo., Farley, Alderbury, 1681, I, W, P26/283
Wm., blacksmith, Britford, 1682, AB, I, W, P24/405
Wm., sen., victualler, Lydeway, Urchf., 1767, W, P2/H/1492
Wm., victualler and maltster, Urchf., 1781, W, P2/H/1599
Harrell, Harrill, Edwd., Hankerton, 1681, AB, comm, I (with typed transcripts of documents), P3/H/551
Horrill, Francis, labourer, Purton, 1724, W, P3/H/1011
Harrell, Wm., baker, Steeple A., 1757, AB, comm, ren, P2/H/1428
see also Burbidge alias H.
Harres *see* Harris
Harrett, My., minors, Baydon, 1714, T, P5/1713/48
Harrey *see* Harry
Harries *see* Harris
Harrill *see* Harrell
Harring *see* Herring
Harrington, Herrington, Agnes, widow, Wantage, Berks., 1569, AB, P5/2Reg/48F
Benj., schoolmaster, Longbridge D., 1812, req, W, Wr, P2/1812/39
Edwd., Warm., 1750, AB, P1/H/1063
Herrington, Geo., farmer, Bower C., 1844, W, Wr, P2/1844/50
Herrington, Hy., Bower C., 1748, W, P2/H/1371
Herrington, Hy., yeo., Bower C., 1803, W, P2/1803/37
Herrington, Hy., Whitep., 1852, D, W, Wr, P2/1852/75
Jane, sp., Mudeford, Hants (effects at Sal.), 1855, AB, aff, Wr, P1/1855/61
Jn., innholder, Maidenhead, Berks., 1625, I, W, P1/H/221
Sarah, sp., Bower C., 1825, AB, note, Wr, P2/1825/49
Thos., chairmaker, W. St., Wilton, 1830, AB, P2/1830/68
Wm., Bower C., 1728, W, P2/H/1225
Harris, Abraham, Sal., 1705, AB, I, P1/H/638
Abraham, miller, Wrou., 1808, AB, W, Wr, P3/1808/21
Agnes, widow, Stapleford, 1575, W, P2/5Reg/246A
Agnes, sp., Hankerton, 1616, I, W, P1/H/109
Agnes, widow, Westb., 1631, AB, I, P25/1631/4
Harrish, Agnes, widow, Eastcott, Swindon, 1639, I, W, P3/H/312
Agnes, widow, Charlton, 1646, AB, I, ren, W, P1/H/269
Aldhelm, mason, Westb. L., 1682, I (2), W, P25/1682/15
Aldhelm, mason, Penleigh Marsh, Dilton, Westb., 1685, I, W, P25/1685/3
Aldhelm, yeo., Westb., 1742, W, P25/1742/1

Alfred, minor, Avebury (form. of Milton L.), 1857, appt of guardian, court proceeding, O, T, P3/1857/62
Alice, Keevil, 1548, AB, P2/2Reg/54B
Alice, widow, Imber, 1559, W, P2/3Reg/163B
Alice, widow, N. Bradley, 1566, W, P2/4Reg/227C
Alice, widow, Dinton, 1608, AB, I, W, P2/H/240
Alice, widow, Keevil, 1610, I, W, P2/H/263, P2/8Reg/97B
Alice, widow, W. Ashton, Steeple A., 1641, I, W, P2/H/549
Andrew, chandler, Lacock, 1637, I, W, P3/H/294
Andrew, husb., Bower C., 1682, comm, I, W, P2/H/807
Harrish, Ann, sp., Eastcott, Swindon, 1640, I, W, P3/H/319
Ann, sp., Chards., Devon, 1666, AB, P14/16
Ann, widow, Chards., Devon, 1674, I, W, P14/39
Ann, widow, Tilsh., [1676], I, W, P2/H/730
Ann, widow, Devizes, 1690, I, W, P1/H/531
Ann, widow, Beechingstoke, 1710, comm, I, W, P3/H/904
Ann, Warm., 1727, AB, P2/H/1216
Ann, widow, S. Wraxall, 1728, AB, ren, W, P2/H/1228
Ann, sp., Corsham, 1733, W (made 1724; 1733 at foot - not specifically stated that this refers to probate), P29/H/104
Ann, widow, Compton C., 1779, W, P1/H/1269, P1/13Reg/297
Ann, widow, Martin, Hants, 1785, W, P2/H/1616
Ann, widow, Sal., 1785, W, P4/1785/16
Ann, Berwick St Jn., 1786, W, P2/H/1623
Ann, widow, Calne, 1809, comm, W, Wr, P5/1809/10
Ann, widow, Lyme R., Dorset, 1834, AB, aff, O, W, Wr, P16/409
Ann, widow, Woodford, 1835, AB, Wr, P13/6/13
Ann, widow, Sal. St Edmd., 1835, W, Wr, P1/1835/9
Anthony, labourer, Littlecote, Rams., 1720, W, P5/1720/24, P5/16Reg/38
Augustine, yeo., Stapleford, 1572-74, W, P2/5Reg/158A, 177C
Augustine, yeo., Stapleford, 1579, AB, I, W, P2/H/55, P2/5Reg/338B
Augustine, husb., Uppington, Stapleford, 1639, AB, I, P2/H/518
Benj., yeo., Ardington, Berks., 1738, W, P1/H/956, P1/8Reg/254
Benj., tiler, Trowb., 1759, comm, W, P1/H/1135, P1/11Reg/369A
Benj., carp., Enmore Grn, Motc., Dorset, 1808, W, P19/214
Benj., gent., Trowb., 1835, comm, req, W, Wr, P1/1835/49
Betty *or* Eliz., singlewoman, Bradford A., 1789, W, P1/14Reg/298
Betty, widow, Sal., 1809, W, P4/1809/5
Betty, widow, Bowerhill, Melk., 1844, W, Wr, P2/1844/41
Cath., widow, Sherb., Dorset, 1611, AB, comm, I, P5/1611/23, P5/9Reg/96A
Cath., widow, Malm. Abbey, 1694, W, P3/H/739
Cath., widow, All C., 1707, I, W, P3/H/875
Charity, widow, Bugley, Warm., 1672, W, P2/H/701
Chas., baker, Sal., 1778, W, P4/1778/12
Chas., gent., Chipp., 1807, W, P3/1807/37
Chas., Haxton, Fittleton, 1809, AB, W, Wr, P2/1809/58
Chas., yeo., Haxton, Fittleton, 1833, W, Wr, P2/1833/32
Christian *see* Christian Stillman
Chris., yeo., Melk., 1790, W, P2/H/1649
Chris., yeo., Seend Row, Melk., 1816, comm, W, Wr, P2/1816/15
Cicely, widow, Bulk., Keevil, 1637, I, W, P2/H/495
Cicely, widow, Brinkw., 1691, I, W, P3/H/690
Cressida, widow, Beanacre, Melk., [1693], I, W, P2/H/930
Damason (?Thomasine), widow, Gt. Cheverell, 1614, I, W, P1/H/89
Dan., Keevil, 1641, AB, I, P2/H/548
Dan., Goatacre, Hilmarton, 1714, AB, I, P1/H/693
Deborah, sp., Netheravon, 1841, AB, Wr, P12/226
Edith, widow, Mere, 1629, AB, I, P5/1629/25, P5/11Reg/21A
Harris alias Cabbell, Edith, Rode, N. Bradley, 1744, AB, P2/H/1347
Edmd., Tilsh., 1645, comm, W, P2/H/571
Edwd., tailor, Bulk., Keevil, 1693, I, W, P2/H/936
Edwd., sen., yeo., Stockley, Calne, 1717, I, W, P26/609

Edwd., Sherston, 1721, W, P3/H/977
Edwd., Enmore Grn, Motc., Dorset, 1726, AB, P19/112
Edwd., Bulk., Keevil, 1754, AB, P2/H/1408
Edwd., sen., yeo., Knighton, Beer Hackett, Dorset, 1755, W, P5/1755/31
Edwd., Patney, 1765, AB, P2/H/1481
Eleanor, widow, Keevil, 1633-34, I, W, P2/H/455, P2/9Reg/5A
Eleanor, sp., Charlton nr Malm., 1669, AB, I, W, P3/H/411
Elias, Stapleford, [1675], I, P2/H/728
Elisha, widow, Longworth, Berks., 1783, AB, P1/H/1284
Eliz., All C., [1604], power of attorney, P2/H/222
Eliz., widow, Swindon, [1611], I, W (NEP), P3/H/67
Eliz., widow, Inmarsh, Seend, Melk., 1613, I, P1/H/81
Eliz., Chamberlayne, Bere R., Dorset, 1671, AB, I, P5/1671/40
Eliz., sp., Gt. Cheverell, 1671, W, P2/H/687
Eliz., widow, Gt. Bedwyn, 1693, I, W, P21/5/17
Eliz., widow, Winterbourne G., 1702, I, W, P2/H/1008
Eliz., Bulk., Keevil, 1762, AB, P2/H/1460
Eliz., singlewoman, Bradford A., 1789, W, P1/H/1315
Eliz., Charlton, Donhead St My. (form. of Semley), 1810, W, Wr, P2/1810/68
Eliz., widow, Dilton M., Westb., 1814, W, P25/1814/1
Eliz., widow, Swindon, 1814, W, Wr, P1/1814/140
Eliz., sp., Milbourne, Malm., 1853, D, O, W, Wr, P3/1853/36
Eliz. *see also* Betty
Ellen, Bower C., 1685, AB, P2/H/847
Emma, Bishopstone N., 1694, W, P6/84
Florence, widow, Uffington, Berks., 1692, I, W, P5/1692/43
Frances, yeo.'s wife, Chisbury, Lt. Bedwyn, 1806, W, P5/1806/34
Francis, Bulk., Keevil, 1644-45, AB, I, ren, P2/H/570
Francis, yeo., Stratfield M., Berks., 1732, W, P1/H/892, P1/7Reg/469
Geo., husb., Winterborne K., Dorset, 1606, AB, W, P5/1606/24, P5/8Reg/57B
Geo., Orcheston St Geo., 1624, AB, I, P2/H/377
Geo., blacksmith, Westover, Beer Hackett, Dorset, 1632, I, W, P5/1632/28, P5/12Reg/112B
Geo., yeo., Orcheston St Geo., 1667, I, W, P2/H/647
Geo., Damerham, Hants, 1669-70, AB, a/c, P2/H/665
Geo., yeo., Ryme I., Dorset, 1693, I, W, P5/1693/31
Geo., yeo., Gillingham, Dorset, 1694, W, P27/1/131
Geo., yeo., Martin, Hants, 1695, AB, I, P1/H/571
Geo., yeo., Winterborne K., Dorset, 1716, W, P5/1716/43, P5/15Reg/344C
Geo., yeo., Yatton K., 1727, I, W (2 - 1 a copy), P3/H/1032
Geo., Sal. St Edmd., 1728, AB, I, P4/1728/16
Geo., Martin, Hants, 1744, AB, P1/H/1005
Geo., yeo., Holnest, Dorset, 1748, W, Wr, P5/1748/14
Geo., Knighton, Figh., 1760, AB, P26/972
Geo., yeo., Holnest, Dorset, 1796, W, P5/1796/6, P5/18Reg/222A
Geo., Burton Hill, Malm., 1806, W, Wr, P3/1806/11
Geo., widower, Coombe B., 1846, AB, note, O, T (re decd's children: Emma, Eliz., Edwin, Geo. & Giles H.), Wr, P8/94
Geo., blacksmith, Woodford, 1848, W, Wr, P13/6/18
Gideon, Chards., Devon, 1667, I, P14/24
Gilbert, Baydon, 1571, AB, P5/2Reg/92D
Gilbert, parchmentmaker, Sal. St Edmd., 1628, AB, I, P4/1627/1
Giles, Maddington, 1740, W, P2/H/1322
Hannah, victualler's wife, Westb. L., 1837, AB, O, Wr, P25/1837/3
Hy., jun., Yatton K., 1620, AB, I, P3/H/148
Hy., yeo., Martin, Hants, 1648, I, W, P2/H/596
Hy., sadler, Calne, 1676, AB, comm, I (detailed), P26/241
Hy., sen., yeo., Shrewton, 1704, W, P2/H/1024
Hy., yeo., Shrewton, 1726, W, P1/H/831, P1/7Reg/154B
Hy., Netheravon, 1787, AB, P12/199
Hy., yeo., Boreham, Warm., 1793, comm, W, P2/H/1666
Hester, widow, Avebury (form. of Milton L.), 1857, AB, aff, Wr, P3/1857/63

Higgins, rector, Woodb., 1753, AB, ren, comm, P1/H/1095
Huddie, Corsham, 1642, AB, P29/H/35
Humphrey, W. Grimstead, 1557, W, P2/3Reg/63A
Isaac, yeo., Malm., 1751, AB, W, P3/H/1262
Isabel, widow, Lt. Hinton, 1710, I (2 - 1 a copy), W, P3/H/905
Jacob, linen draper, Sal., 1709, AB, P4/1709/10
Jas., Kingsdown, Box, [1638], I, W (NEP), P3/H/303
Jas., tailor, Box, 1675, alleg, I, W (2 - not identical), NW, P3/H/493
Jas., yeo., Bradford A., 1718, comm, W, P2/H/1147
Jas., sen., bellman *or* beadman, Chipp., 1733, AB, I, W, P3/H/1109
Jas., labourer, Gastard, Corsham, 1781, W, P29/H/121, P29/2Reg/164
Jas., yeo., Fordington, Dorset, 1788, W, P15/167
Jas., shepherd, Lt. Woodford, 1805, W, P13/6/4
Jas., yeo., Dilton M., Westb., 1809, W, Wr, P25/1809/1
Jas., cordw., Sal., 1817, W, Wr, P4/1817/4
Jas., yeo., Bowerhill, Melk., 1818, W, Wr, P2/1818/41
Jas., innkeeper and grazier, Westb. L., 1837, O, W, Wr, P25/1837/4
Jas., Salterton, Durnford, 1839, AB, Wr, P9/117
Jas., jun., Fordington, Dorset, 1840, AB, O, Wr, P15/184
Jas., yeo., Fordington, Dorset, 1841, AB, comm, copy W, Wr, P15/185
Jas., Woodford, 1854, AB, aff, Wr, P13/6/22
Jas., bach., Seend, Melk., 1854, AB, aff, O, Wr, P2/1854/5
Jane, Lacock, 1664, AB, I, W, P3/H/358
Jane, widow, Gt. Cheverell, 1691, comm, ren, W, P1/H/536
Jane, widow, Foxham, Bremhill, 1730, I, W, P3/H/1068
Jane, widow, Hankerton, 1741, I, W, P3/H/1173
Jane, Bradford A., 1814, AB, comm, Wr, P2/1814/27
Jane, widow, Britford, 1834, W, Wr, P24/1339
Jeremiah, Gt. Bedwyn, 1674, AB, I, P5/1674/35
Jeremiah, Marl., 1771, AB, P1/H/1215
Jeremiah, yeo., Snarlton Farm, Melk., 1849, comm, W, Wr, P2/1849/9
Joan, widow, Damerham, Hants, 1559, W, P2/3Reg/171E
Joan, widow, Allweston, Folke, Dorset, 1596, W, P5/1596/34, P5/6Reg/123B
Joan, widow, Rodbourne, Malm., 1615, I, W, P3/H/106
Joan, Rodbourne C., 1629, AB, I, P3/H/224
Joan, widow, Damerham, Hants, 1642, AB, P2/H/555
Joan, widow, Martin, Hants, 1646, AB, I, W, P2/H/584
Joan, widow, Minety, 1646, I, W, P1/H/280
Joan, widow, Bishopstone N. & Lt. Hinton, 1691, I, W, P3/H/688
Joan, sp., Clyffe P., 1698, I, W, P1/H/604, P1/3Reg/185
Joan, widow, Martin, Hants, 1698, AB, I, P1/H/605
Harris alias Hoskins, Joan, widow, Squirrels Down, Netherb., Dorset, 1730, W, P17/445
Harries, Jn., Bishopstone S., 1549, W, P2/2Reg/81A
Jn., Martin, Hants, 1549, W, P2/2Reg/87A
Jn., Bower C., 1558, W, P2/3Reg/126A
Jn., priest, Stapleford, 1561, institution to vicarage, P1/1Reg/76C
Jn., Sherrington, 1567, W, P2/5Reg/29A
Jn., vicar, Stapleford, 1571, T (children: Jn., Thos., Geo., Nich. & Chris. H.), W, P2/H/37, P2/5Reg/125C
Jn., Westwood, 1574, AB, P2/5Reg/189D
Jn., Amesb., 1578, I, W, P2/H/53, P2/5Reg/315B
Jn., Keevil, 1581, W, P2/6Reg/46
Jn., husb., Winterborne M., Winterborne K., Dorset, 1591, I, W, P5/1590/28, P5/5Reg/93C
Jn., sen., husb., Dinton, 1593, I, T, W, P2/H/127
Jn., yeo., Chisbury, Lt. Bedwyn, 1593, I, T, NW, P5/1592/44, P5/6Reg/15B
Jn., sen., yeo., Gt. Cheverell, 1604, AB, W, P2/H/216
Harris alias Hoskins, Jn., Beam., Dorset, 1606, W, P5/8Reg/69A
Jn., Martin, Hants, 1607, AB, I, W. Proved at manorial court of Damerham & Martin, then exhibited at the Archdeaconry court, P2/H/247
Jn., labourer, Hannington, 1608, W, P3/H/33
Jn., husb., Martin, Hants, 1609, AB, W, P2/8Reg/43C

Jn., cutler, Chipp., 1612, W, P3/H/78
Jn., husb., Martin, Hants, 1619, I, W, P2/H/343
Jn., All C., 1620, I, W, P3/H/149
Jn., clerk and curate, Hilcott, N. Newnton, 1621, I, W, P3/H/158
Jn., yeo., Bulk., Keevil, 1621, I, W, P2/H/350
Jn., Lt. Bedwyn, 1628, I, W (NEP), P30/93
Jn., husb., Berwick B., 1631, W (not strictly W, more assignment), P30/94
Jn., sen., yeo., E. Tytherton, Bremhill, 1631, I, W, P1/H/189
Jn., Martin, Hants, 1632, AB, a/c, I, W, copy NW, P2/H/435, 443
Jn., Brokenb., 1632, I, W, P3/H/254
Jn., sen., yeo., Kellaways, 1634, AB, I, W, P3/H/278
Jn., jun., yeo., W. Ashton, Steeple A., 1637, AB, a/c, I, L, W, P2/H/485
Jn., yeo., Plaitford, 1638, I, W, P2/H/507
Jn., Baydon, 1640, I, W, P5/1640/28, P5/13Reg/254C
Jn., yeo., Bulk., Keevil, 1640, I, W, P2/H/541
Jn., gent., Lacock, 1662, AB, I, ren, W, P3/H/346
Jn., mercer, Devizes, 1664, I, W, P1/H/344
Jn., husb., Keevil, 1667, AB, P1/H/375
Jn., husb., Winterborne M., Winterborne K., Dorset, 1669, AB, comm, I, ren, P5/1669/28
Jn., yeo., Kellaways, 1669, AB, comm, I, P3/H/412
Jn., weaver, Grove, Wantage, Berks., 1672, AB, I, P23/35
Jn., yeo., Martin, Hants, 1672, I, W, P2/H/693
Jn., husb., Horningsham, 1678, I, W, P5/1678/24
Harris *or* Herres, Jn., yeo., Chards., Devon, 1678-79, AB, D (booklet), I, W (2), P14/37, 40, P5/1678/25, P5/1679/44
Jn., [Horningsham] (NBI), [1678], I, P2/H/752
Jn., Rams., 1681, AB, I, P5/1681/31
Jn., carp., Heytes., 1681, I, W, P5/1681/23
Jn., yeo., All C., 1681, I, W, P3/H/553
Jn., sen., yeo., Yatton K., 1681-83, AB, comm, I, W, P3/H/552, 580
Jn., Bower C., 1684, AB, P2/H/845
Jn., tailor, Edington, 1686, I, W, P1/H/1366
Jn., gent., Devizes, 1693, comm, ren, W, P1/H/560
Jn., blacksmith, Alderbury, 1696, AB, I, P26/438
Jn., sen., yeo., Bremhill Wick, 1696, W, P3/H/758
Jn., yeo., Wyfield, Boxford, Berks., 1701, I, W, P1/H/614, P1/4Reg/101
Jn., Chamberlayne's Farm, Bere R., Dorset, 1702, AB, I, P5/1702/18
Jn., Steeple A., 1705, AB, P2/H/1031
Jn., sen., Homington, 1705, AB, I, P24/601
Jn., Grove, Wantage, Berks., 1707, I, W, P5/1707/31, P5/15Reg/9
Harris alias Turner, Jn., Wilton, 1711, AB, P1/H/663
Jn., Mildenhall, 1712, AB, I, P3/H/917
Jn., Boxford, Berks., 1723, AB, I, P1/H/801
Jn., yeo., Boreham, Warm., 1724, W, P2/H/1204
Jn., Marl. St My., 1726, AB, W, P1/H/821, P1/7Reg/118A
Jn., W. Harnham, 1727, W, P8/25
Jn., sen., glazier, Heytes., 1731, I, W, P5/1731/45
Jn., sen., yeo., Purton, 1732, W, P3/H/1100
Jn., yeo., Rams., 1733, W, P5/1733/27
Jn., sen., yeo., Winterborne K., Dorset, 1741, W, P5/1741/23
Jn., woolstapler, Haxton, Fittleton, 1744, W, P2/H/1348
Jn., gent., E. Garston Woodlands, Berks., 1756, AB, comm, ren, W, P1/H/1118, P1/11Reg/273
Jn., labourer, Elmdown Farm, Rams., 1757, W, P5/1757/13
Jn., Westb. L., 1760, W, P25/1760/6
Jn., yeo., Peasemarsh, Gillingham, Dorset, 1762, W, P27/1/432, P27/3Reg/95B
Jn., yeo., Yatton K., 1768, W, P3/H/1372
Jn., yeo., Middleton Farm, Norton B., 1777, W, P2/H/1565
Jn., sawyer, Whitep., 1779, W, P2/H/1578
Jn., sen., yeo., Winterborne K., Dorset, 1780, cert, W, P5/1780/10, P5/17Reg/203A
Jn., yeo., Milton upon Stour, Gillingham, Dorset, 1792, W, P27/1/547
Jn., yeo., Rams., 1795, W, copy W, P5/1795/8, P5/18Reg/219B

Jn., maltster, Sopworth, 1804, comm, W, P3/1804/4
Jn., butcher, Dilton M., Westb., 1814, W, P25/1814/2
Jn., miller, Wrou., 1815, W, P3/1815/19
Jn., soldier, Westb., 1818, AB, P25/1818/2
Jn., Haxton, Fittleton, 1826, AB, Wr, P1/1826/6
Jn., yeo., Turleigh, Winsley, Bradford A., 1829, AB, comm, W, Wr, P1/1829/54
Jn., farmer, Alton, Figh., 1833, AB, Wr, P26/1405
Jn., Haxton, Fittleton, 1840, AB, Wr, P2/1840/20
Jn., capital burgess, Malm., 1852, D, O, W, Wr, P3/1852/2
Jos., Rams., 1673, AB, P5/1673/22
Jos., Rams., 1687, AB, P5/1686/30
Jos., tailor, Leigh, Yetm., Dorset, 1766, W, P19/162
Jos., carp., Leigh, Yetm., Dorset, 1808, W, P19/217
Jos., dairyman, Hannington Wick, 1852, comm, ren, W, Wr, P3/1852/12
Lawr., yeo., Winterborne K., Dorset, 1764, W, P5/1764/21
Leonard, husb., Mere, 1570, W, P5/2Reg/88C
Lewis, Winterbourne E., 1596, T (child: Ann H.), P2/H/154
Lydia, widow, Fonthill G., 1820, W, Wr, P2/1820/32
Mgt., widow, Sal., 1698, W, P1/H/594, P1/3Reg/34
Mgt., widow, Tytherton Kellaways, Bremhill, 1714, I, W, P3/H/935
Martha, sp., Eastcott, Swindon, 1687, AB (2), comm, P3/H/631
My., widow, Damerham, Hants, 1621, I, W, P2/H/355
My., widow, All C., 1638, I, W, P3/H/304
My., widow, Stapleford, 1663, AB, P2/H/623
My., widow, Bulk., Keevil, 1685, I, W, P2/H/858
My., widow, All C., 1691, I, W, P3/H/691
My., widow, Preshute, 1692, AB, I, P1/H/546
My., widow, Alderbury, 1699, I, W, P26/461
My., widow, Atworth, Bradford A., 1707, comm, W, P2/H/1054
My., widow, Beam., Dorset, 1708, W, P17/177
My., widow, Beam., Dorset, 1724, I, W, P17/411
My., singlewoman, Gillingham, Dorset, [1745], W, P27/1/380
My., sp., Devizes, 1756, W, P1/H/1123, P1/11Reg/294
My., sp., Rams., 1758, AB, W, P5/1758/21
My., widow, Rams., 1767, W, P5/1767/24
My., widow, Reading, Berks., 1820, req, W, Wr, P1/1820/6
My., widow, Warm., 1843, comm, W, Wr, P2/1843/49
My., victualler's wife, Westb., 1844, O, W, Wr, P25/1844/3
My. Ann, Sal., 1846, AB, Wr, P1/1846/23
Maud, widow, Stapleford, 1569, W (mother of vicar of S.), P2/5Reg/67B
Melior, sp., Imber, 1690, AB, P2/H/914
Melior, sp., Devizes, 1748, W, P1/H/1055, P1/10Reg/221
Moses, shopkeeper, Downton, 1803, W, Wr, P2/1803/31
Nathaniel, druggetmaker, N. Bradley, 1739, W, P2/H/1310
Harres, Nich., husb., Tilsh., 1557, W, P2/3Reg/26D
Owen, husb., Netton, Bishopstone S., 1588, I, NW, P2/H/82, P2/7Reg/118B
Paul, Limpley Stoke, Bradford A., 1819, AB, comm, Wr, P2/1819/21
Peter, Warm., 1637, I, W, P2/H/492
Peter, maltster, Warm., 1722, W, P2/H/1194
Peter, wheelwright, Kingston Bagpuize & Draycot Moor, Longworth, Berks., 1741, I, W, P1/H/982, P1/9Reg/84
Philip, Westwood, 1571, AB, P2/5Reg/131C
Philip, widow, Eastcott, Swindon, [1605], W (NEP), P3/2Reg/6A
Praxed, widow, Orcheston St Geo., 1633, W, P2/H/449, P2/9Reg/28
Praxy, sp., Westb., 1730, W, P25/1730/3
Ralph, sen., maltster, Beam., Dorset, 1740, W, Wr, P5/1740/41
Rebecca, sp., Edington, 1827, AB, comm, Wr, P2/1827/32
Reynold *or* Reginald, Chamberlayne's Farm, Bere R., Dorset (*also* of Winterborne K., Dorset), 1667, AB, comm, I, P5/1668/33
Richd., Martin, Hants, 1557, W, P2/3Reg/35B
Richd., carp., Hawkeridge, Westb., 1572, W, P5/3Reg/1C

Harres, Richd., [weaver], Warm., 1576, W, P2/5Reg/256B
Richd., husb., Hawkeridge, Westb., 1579, I, W, P5/1579/42, P5/3Reg/118D
Richd., Martin, Hants, 1587, AB, P2/7Reg/84C
Richd., husb., Eastcott, Swindon, 1601, W, P3/1Reg/57B
Richd., husb., Bishopstone S., 1602, AB, I, W, P2/H/204
Richd., shepherd, Deptford, Wylye, 1602, AB, I, W, P2/H/207
Richd., husb., Winterborne M., Winterborne K., Dorset, 1603, AB, I, P5/1603/34, P5/7Reg/63B
Richd., Keevil, 1622, AB, I, P2/H/357
Richd., gent., Damerham, Hants, 1639-40, AB, a/c, I, P2/H/523
Richd., yeo., Conock, Chirton, 1678, I, W, P2/H/758
Richd., yeo., Sutton M., 1720, W, P1/H/758, P1/6Reg/213
Richd., yeo., Hankerton, 1729, W, P1/H/867, P1/7Reg/302
Richd., victualler, Downton, 1744, W, P1/H/1006, P1/9Reg/307
Richd., yeo., Hamptworth, Downton, 1810, W, Wr, P2/1810/5
Richd., Westport St My., 1812, W, Wr, P3/1812/7
Robt., yeo., Stratton, Dorset, 1567, W, P5/2Reg/15A
Robt., yeo., Seend, Melk., 1581, W, P2/6Reg/28B
Robt., Lt. Bedwyn, 1589, AB, P5/1589/26, P5/5Reg/50D
Robt., Foxham, Bremhill, 1636, AB, a/c, I (last 2 on same sheet), P3/H/288
Robt., yeo., Martin, Hants, 1640, I, W, P2/H/535
Robt., sen., rector and clerk, Milston, 1663, I, W, P1/H/313
Robt., sen., yeo., Lt. Hinton, 1666, comm, I, W, P3/H/376
Robt., yeo., Beanacre, Melk., 1674, I, W, P2/H/698, 721
Robt., Broughton G., 1676, AB, ren, P2/H/739
Robt., sen., husb., Lt. Hinton, [1677], I, W, P1/H/439
Robt., husb., Stitchcombe, Mildenhall, 1680, I, W, P1/H/454
Robt., Martin, Hants, 1681, AB, I, P2/H/794
Robt., jun., E. Tytherton, Bremhill, 1691, AB, I, P3/H/692
Robt., Bradford A., 1693, AB, comm, P2/H/931
Robt., yeo., Alderton, 1694, I, W, P3/H/740
Robt., maltster, Beam., Dorset, 1695, AB, I, P17/344
Robt., gent., Tytherton Kellaways, Bremhill, 1713, I, W, P3/H/925
Robt., yeo., Aldermaston, Berks., 1717, W, P1/H/745, P1/6Reg/100
Robt., yeo., Bishopstone N., 1728, I, W, P5/1728/42, P5/16Reg/191B
Robt., Westb. L., 1742, AB, P25/1742/10
Robt., sen., butcher, Beam., Dorset, 1745-46, AB, comm, W, P5/1746/39, P17/500
Robt., woodman, E. Grimstead, W. Dean, 1757, W, P2/H/1421
Robt., Westb., 1771, AB, O, P25/1771/5
Roger, husb., Eastcott, Swindon, 1638, comm, I, W, P3/H/305
Ruth, widow, Figh., 1787, AB, P26/1152
Sam., husb., Lt. Hinton, 1701, I, W, P1/H/611, P1/4Reg/76
Sam., Sherb. & Pimperton, Dorset, [1707], I (consists largely of unpaid legacy from uncle, Jn. Byrt of P.), P5/1707/30
Sam., Sherb., Dorset, 1710, AB, P5/1710/50
Sam., tailor, Marl., 1746, W, P1/H/1033, P1/10Reg/21B
Sam., baker, Westb., 1773, AB, I (detailed), P25/1773/4
Sam., widower, Gillingham, Dorset, 1844, AB, O, ren, Wr, P27/1/742
Sarah, widow, Yatton K., 1691, I, W, P3/H/693
Sarah, widow, Shefford Woodlands, W. Shefford, Berks., 1756, W, P1/H/1110, P1/11Reg/243B
Sarah, widow, Calne, 1802, W, P26/1238
Sarah, widow, Figh., 1807, W, P26/1264
Sarah, widow, Rams., 1827, AB, aff, O, Wr, P5/1827/2
Silas, heelcutter, Donhead St My., 1810, comm, W, Wr, P2/1810/73
Simon, yeo., Amesb., 1736, W, P2/H/1288
Stephen, Westb., 1614, I, W, P25/1614/2
Stephen, sen., mason, Coldharbour, Dilton ?, Westb., 1684, I, W, P25/1684/4
Stephen, fuller, Westb. L., 1690, I, W, P25/1690/4
Stephen, labourer, Widhill, Crickl. St S., 1702, AB, I, P3/H/819
Stephen, Westb., 1770, AB, P25/1770/1
Stephen, blacksmith, Farley, Alderbury, 1773, AB, P26/1064
Stephen, Dilton, Westb., 1781, AB, P25/1781/2

Stephen, Westb., 1805, O, W, P25/1805/2
Susanna, widow, Westb. L., 1771, AB, P25/1771/2
Harries, Susanna, widow, Blewbury, Berks., 1785, W, P5/1785/16, P5/18Reg/19
Thos., servant to (Mr) Wrestley of Britford, Britford, 1576, W, P24/1435, P5/3Reg/96A
Thos., weaver, Sutton V., 1580, I, W, P2/H/64, P2/6Reg/13A
Thos., husb., Lt. Cheverell, 1603, AB, I, W, P2/H/210
Thos., E. Tytherton, Bremhill, 1608, I, W, P3/H/32
Thos., Charlton nr Malm., 1612, AB, I, P3/H/77
Thos., husb., Martin, Hants, 1623-26, AB, I, W, P2/H/361, 382
Thos., Swallowcliffe, 1638, AB, I, P5/1638/51, P5/13Reg/106B
Thos., Aldbourne Chase, 1646, I, NW, P1/H/276
Thos., gent., Orcheston St Geo., 1661-63, AB, a/c, I (detailed), P2/H/607
Thos., gent., Gt. Cheverell, 1665, comm, W, P2/H/631
Thos., yeo., Orcheston St Geo., [1668], I, W, P1/H/392
Thos., yeo., Stock and Ford, Gt. Bedwyn, 1671, AB, ren, P21/2/27
Thos., Crofton, Gt. Bedwyn, 1673, AB, consent (Jeremiah H., uncle), I, P21/2/35
Thos., gent., Imber, 1673, comm, I, W, P1/H/420
Thos., innholder, Sal., 1676, AB, P4/1676/1
Thos., Holt, Bradford A., 1681, AB, comm, P2/H/787
Thos., husb., Crofton, Gt. Bedwyn, 1685, I, W, P21/4/12
Thos., N. Bradley, 1686, AB, I, P2/H/870
Thos., Imber, 1690, AB, P2/H/913
Thos., Sutton V., 1690, AB, P2/H/912
Thos., yeo., Enmore Grn, Motc., Dorset, 1696, I, W, P19/72
Thos., husb., Chards., Devon, 1718, AB, I, P14/128
Thos., alehouse keeper, Easton Grey, 1731, W, P3/H/1087
Thos., sen., combmaker, Sal., 1739, W, P4/1739/7
Thos., Bradford A., 1742, AB, caveat, P2/H/1337
Thos., sen., scribler, Devizes, 1757, W, P1/H/1130, P1/11Reg/349A
Thos., innholder, Chipp., 1762-75, AB (2), W, P3/H/1335
Thos., yeo., Compton C., 1778, W, P2/H/1573
Thos., labourer, E. Grimstead, W. Dean, 1782, W, P1/H/1272, P1/13Reg/340
Thos., innholder, E. Harnham, Britford, 1783, W, P24/1184
Thos., yeo., Rams., 1783, W, P5/1783/7, P5/17Reg/246
Thos., Warm., 1785, AB, P2/H/1618
Thos., Bradford A., 1792, AB, comm, P2/H/1662
Thos., yeo., Haxton, Fittleton, 1802, W, P2/1802/67
Thos., glazier, Warm., 1816, W, Wr, P2/1816/72
Thos., jun., hairdresser, Devizes, 1821, W, Wr, P1/1821/7
Thos., Devizes, 1828, AB, Wr, P1/1828/6
Thos., yeo., Netheravon, 1829, W, Wr, P12/219
Thos., labourer, Luckington, 1833, W, Wr, P3/1833/25
Thos., farmer, Lt. Woodford, 1834, W, Wr, P13/6/12
Thos., labourer, Gastard, Corsham, 1856-57, W, P29/1800-1857/50, P29/3Reg/327
Thos. Pollern, yeo., Figh., 1802, W, P26/1236
Timothy, cordw., Winterbourne E., 1691, AB, I, P2/H/922
Timothy, wheelwright, Martin, Hants, 1810, W, Wr, P2/1810/1
Townsend, Tytherton Kellaways, Bremhill, 1703, I, W, P3/H/837
Ursula, Devizes, 1747, AB, P1/H/1042
Vincent, Hatts Farm, Semley, 1806, I (photocopy - original in private custody), W, P2/1806/38
Walter, husb., Imber, 1550, W, P2/2Reg/102B
Walter, weaver, Marl., 1593, I (part missing), W, P1/H/10
Walter, husb., S. Wraxall, 1677, comm, I, L, copy W, NW, P1/H/441
Wm., Keevil, 1546, W (NEP), P2/1Reg/70A
Wm., Imber, 1564, W, P2/4Reg/188A
Wm., yeo., Orcheston St Geo., 1570, T (children: Thos., Wm., My., Agnes & Maud H.), W, P2/H/31, P2/5Reg/104D
Wm., Stapleford, 1573, AB, P2/5Reg/176D
Wm., Westb., 1579, I, W, P5/1579/43, P5/3Reg/137A
Wm., Orcheston St Geo., 1584, AB, P2/6Reg/125A
Wm., jun., husb., Stapleford, 1586-88, T (children: Joan, Mgt. & Ann H.), W, P2/H/86, P2/7Reg/32B

Wm., Eastcott, Swindon, [1607], W (NEP), P3/H/28
Wm., sen., yeo., Bulk., Keevil, [1610], W, P2/H/268
Wm., butcher, Sherb., Dorset, 1610, AB, comm, I, T, P5/1610/30, P5/9Reg/43B
Wm., tailor, Damerham, Hants, 1616, AB, comm, I, W, P2/H/313, P2/8Reg/311
Wm., Allweston, Folke, Dorset, 1617, AB, comm, I, T, P5/1616/34, P5/9Reg/213C
Wm., Rodbourne, Malm., 1622, I, W, P3/H/167
Wm., yeo., Keevil, 1629, I, W, P2/H/411
Wm., Bremhill Wick, 1633, I, W, P3/H/267
Wm., Marden, 1636, AB, I, P2/H/477
Wm., husb., Wexcombe, Grafton, 1636, AB, a/c, I, P21/1/28
Harris alias Plot, Wm., Woodb., 1641, AB, I, P3/H/329
Wm., Chards., Devon, 1661, AB, P5/1661/25
Wm., yeo., Bremhill Wick, 1671, AB, I, ren, P3/H/449
Wm., yeo., Blewbury, Berks., 1673, AB, I, P5/1673/21
Wm., yeo., Stapleford, 1674, I, W, P2/H/719
Wm., Imber, 1684, AB, P2/H/831
Wm., Bower C., 1684, AB, I, ren, P2/H/844
Wm., gent., Leigh, Yetm., Dorset, 1684, I, W, P5/1684/24
Wm., miller, Werg, Mildenhall, 1687, I, W, P3/H/633
Wm., sen., sawyer, Malm., 1687, I, W, P3/H/632
Wm., Stapleford, 1689, AB, a/c, P2/H/905
Wm., Keevil, 1694, AB, I, P2/H/944, 954
Wm., yeo., Beechingstoke, 1699, I, W, P3/H/779
Wm., carp., Netherb., Dorset, 1701, AB, I, P17/141
Wm., gent., Malm. Abbey, 1702, I, W, P3/H/821
Wm., yeo., Lt. Hinton, 1702, AB, I, P3/H/820
Wm., Marston, Pott., 1709, W, P2/H/1074
Wm., yeo., Yatton K., 1737, W, P3/H/1135
Wm., Fisherton A., 1738, a/c, I, W, P1/H/969, P1/8Reg/358A
Wm., yeo., N. Tidworth, 1750, W, P1/H/1064, P1/10Reg/324
Wm., Haxton, Fittleton, 1760, AB, P2/H/1446
Wm., Westport St My., 1763, AB, P3/H/1345
Wm., maltster, Whitbourne, Corsley, 1773, W, P2/H/1534
Wm., weaver, Donnington, Berks., 1783, AB, W, P1/H/1289, P1/13Reg/473
Wm., limeburner, Sherb., Dorset, 1825, W (& cod), Wr, P5/1825/23
Wm., Hindon, 1827, AB, Wr, P2/1827/9
Wm., W. Hanney, Berks., 1832, AB, comm, Wr, P1/1832/131
Wm., yeo., Westrop, Corsham, 1833, comm, W, Wr, P3/1833/37
Wm., sen., Britford, 1844, AB, Wr, P24/1371
Wm., yeo., Haxton, Fittleton, 1853, AB, W, Wr, P2/1853/2
see also Bew alias H.; Harrison *or* H.; Hoskins alias H.; Palmer alias H.; Tucker alias H.; Vyall (Viles) alias H.
Harrison, Aaron, yeo., Sedgehill, 1820, W, Wr, P1/1820/54
Alice, widow, Gt. Amesb., 1629, I (very detailed), W, P2/H/406
Ann, ironmonger's widow, Sal., 1700, W, P4/1700/12
Arthur, yeo. and gent., Devizes St Jn., 1640, I, W, P1/H/245
Brightweed, [female], Sal. St Edmd., 1595, AB, I (documents relate to both Brightweed & Jn. H.), P1/H/17
Cath., Amesb., 1715, AB, P2/H/1125
Chris., tailor, Maddington, 1587, I, T, W, P2/H/78, P2/7Reg/109B
Edwd., Charlton nr Malm., 1763, AB, P1/H/1171
Gilbert *see* Alice Lackington
Harry, miller, Crickl. St S., 1748, W, P3/H/1234
Harry, Latton, 1777, AB, comm, P3/H/1419
Hy., vicar, Maddington, 1570, W, P2/5Reg/92B
Harrison alias Bowdiche, Honour, wife of Lionel, Chards., Devon, 1580, AB, P5/1580/30, P5/3Reg/155A
Hugh, tailor, E. Harnham, Britford, 1621, I, W, P24/64
Hugh, Devizes St My., 1638, AB, I, P1/H/239
Jas., Reading St Lawr., Berks., 1708, AB, I, P1/H/651
Jas., Cowesfield, Whitep., 1816, AB, Wr, P2/1816/64
Jane, widow, Amesb., 1705, W, P2/H/1035
Jn., canon residentiary, Sal. The Close, 1605, W, P24/19

Jn., Waltham St Lawr., Berks., 1674, AB, P1/H/427
Jn., woollen draper, Reading, Berks., 1683, comm, W, P1/H/472
Jn., Stratfield M., Berks., 1798, W, P1/H/1350, P1/15Reg/66
Jn., jun., tinplate worker, Reading, Berks., 1801, AB (limited), P1/1801/120
Margery, widow, Aldbourne, 1667, AB, I, NW, P3/H/384
My., widow, Downton, 1716, I, W, P2/H/1129
Nich., sen., cordw., Gt. Amesb., 1660, I, W, P2/H/604
Harrison *or* Harris, Richd., Brokenb., 1606, I, W, P3/H/16, P3/2Reg/10B
Richd., sen., no abode stated, 1608, I, W, P1/H/57
Richd., weaver, Downton, 1714, I, W, P2/H/1119
Richd., Sal., 1746, W, P4/1746/5
Richd., Reading, Berks., 1747, AB, P1/H/1038
Richd., mariner serving on HMS *Chester*, Sal., 1750, req, W, copy W, P4/1750/6
Richd., gardener, Dinton, 1799, W, P2/H/1687
Robt., sen., Gt. Amesb., 1688-94, AB (2), I, W, P2/H/893, 953
Thos., Sal., 1595, bond to deliver legacy, P1/H/16
Wm., tailor, Amesb., 1541, W (NEP), P30/87
Wm., Gt. Amesb., 1577, W, P2/H/46, P2/5Reg/287B
Harrison alias Wasdile, Wm., husb., Hamptworth, Downton, 1640, I, W, P2/H/536
Wm., Devizes, 1681, AB, comm, I, P1/H/465
Wm., Tilehurst, Berks., 1698, AB, comm, P1/H/595
Wm., grocer, Newbury, Berks., 1723, W, P1/H/803, P1/7Reg/13B
Wm., shopkeeper, Amesb., 1749, AB, P2/H/1385
Wm., labourer, Fovant Stroud, 1781, W, P2/H/1591
Wm., yeo., Beam., Dorset, 1815, W, Wr, P5/1815/23
Wm., Gillingham, Dorset, 1821, AB, Wr, P27/1/653
Harrod, Mgt., Devizes St My., 1564, W, P1/2Reg/153A
Harrold, Bridget, widow, Ham, 1634, I, W, P1/H/195
Harold, Edwd., printer and druggist, Marl., 1824, W, Wr, P1/1824/3
Harold, Geo., Corsham, 1592-93, W, P29/H/6, P29/1Reg/27
Geo., mercer, Crickl. St S., 1727, AB, I, W, P3/H/1033
Harold, Jas., Wilton, 1563, AB, I, P2/H/27, P2/4Reg/159B
Jn., Corsham, 1581, W, P29/1Reg/23A
Jn., Bishopstone S., 1590, I, T, W, P2/H/104
Harold, Jn., husb., Ham, 1628, I, W, P1/H/177
Jn., Westwood, 1769, AB, comm, P2/H/1510-11
Mgt., widow, Purton, 1627, AB, I, W, P3/H/211
Ralph, butcher, Marl. St My., 1629, AB, a/c, I, ren, P1/H/180
Harold, Robt., yeo., Ham, 1693, AB, I, P3/H/718
Wm., husb., Compton B., [1567], W (NEP), P3/1Reg/31
Thos., Marten, Grafton, 1597, AB, a/c, I, P5/1596/39
Thos., Gt. Bedwyn, 1597, AB, P5/6Reg/142C
Harrole, Thos., Purton Stoke, 1616-21, AB, a/c, comm, I, copy I, P1/H/116, 148
Harold, Thos., weaver, Corsham, 1621, I, P29/H/25
Wm., clerk, Compton B., 1636, I, W, P3/H/289
Wm., yeo., Biddestone, 1682, AB, I, P3/H/564
Wm., woolcomber, Brinkw., 1722, W, P3/H/990
Harroway *see* Harraway
Harry, Eliz., sp., Tinh., Edington, 1854, aff, W, Wr, P2/1854/35
Geo., Chapmanslade, Dilton, Westb., 1824, AB (2), O, P25/1824/3
Jn., Sherston, 1800, AB, P3/1800/60
Robt., rector, Manningford Bruce, 1570, AB, P1/1Reg/23E
Thos., innholder, Sal., 1662, AB, I, P4/1661/15
Harrey, Wm., jun., husb., Stapleford, 1585, W, P2/H/75
Wm., sen., farmer, Luckington, 1769, W, P3/H/1383
Wm., labourer, Limehouse but left effects at Sutton B., 1807, req, W, Wr, P3/1807/45
Hart, Alice, widow, Bere R., Dorset, 1612, AB, I, W, P5/1612/22, P5/9Reg/62B
Alice, widow, Fittleton, 1685, AB, I, P2/H/850
Ann, minors, Marl., 1684, T, P1/H/488
Benj., broad weaver, Frankleigh, Bradford A., 1848, O, W, Wr, P2/1848/34

Chris., husb., Inglesham, 1641, I, W, P3/H/330
Dan., Sandridge Hill, Melk., 1745, AB, I, P2/H/1355
Dan., Woolmore, Melk., 1788, AB, comm, W, P2/H/1631
Edwd., yeo., Durweston & Stourpaine, Dorset, 1785, W (bequest to married dau Eliz. Bower of S.), P24/1175
Eliz., widow, Tinh., Edington, 1639, AB, I, NW, P2/H/513
Hart alias Hort, Eliz., widow, Norton, 1668, I, W, P3/H/397
Eliz., widow, Beam., Dorset, 1719, W, P5/1719/43, P5/16Reg/18A
Eliz., widow, Clevancy, Hilmarton, 1784, W, P3/H/1452
Francis, Foxley, 1690, AB, P3/H/673
Francis, yeo., Dauntsey, 1808, W, Wr, P1/1808/69
Geo., yeo., Brinkw., 1796, W, P3/H/1514
Gowen, wine cooper, Malm., 1723, W, P3/H/1001
Hannah, widow, Brinkw., 1802, comm, W, P3/1802/35
Hannah, wife, Bradford A., 1836, AB, P2/1836/35
Harry, brazier, Malm., 1779, W, P3/H/1430
Jas., clothier, Lyme R., Dorset, 1747, AB, P16/294
Jas., Nether C., Dorset, 1769, AB, comm, P5/1769/14
Jas., weaver, Bearfield, Bradford A., 1843, O, W, Wr, P2/1843/1
Jeremiah, Seend, Melk., 1703, AB, ren, P2/H/1017
Joan, widow, Tinh., Edington, 1610, I, W, P2/H/274, P2/8Reg/133
Joan, widow, Fittleton, 1615, I, W, P2/H/306, P2/8Reg/263
Joan, widow, Highw., 1623, I, W, P10/1623/2
Joan, yeo., Beam., Dorset, 1723, W, P17/408
Jn., Seend, Melk., 1559, W, P2/3Reg/167A
Jn., no place, but contains ref. to animal in Poulshot Marsh, 1599, I, W, P2/H/1700
Jn., sen., husb., Nether C., Dorset, 1635, I, W, P5/1635/83, P5/12Reg/205
Jn., sen., yeo., Stallen, Nether C., Dorset, 1682, W, P5/1682/47
Jn., maltster, Figh., 1684, AB, I, P26/324
Jn., Beam., Dorset, 1706, AB, P17/167
Jn., sen., yeo., Stallen, Nether C., Dorset, 1714, I, W, P5/1714/16, P5/15Reg/390A
Jn., Nether C., Dorset, 1726, AB, P5/1726/22
Jn., sen., joiner, Lyme R., Dorset, 1752, W, P5/1752/25
Jn., Clevancy, Hilmarton, 1782-84, AB (2), P1/H/1280
Jn., linenmaker, Nether C., Dorset, 1786, comm, W, P5/1786/5, P5/18Reg/66
Jn., Westb. L., 1816, AB, P25/1816/1
Jn., Hungerford, Berks., 1817, AB, Wr, P23/880
Jn., labourer, Nether C., Dorset, 1824, O, W, Wr, P5/1824/41
Jos., mariner (late of HMS *Torbay*), Lyme R., Dorset, 1743, W, Wr, P5/1743/37
Jos., gent., Sherb., Dorset, 1769, W, P5/1769/15
Lucy, labourer's wife, Long Burton, Dorset, 1812, AB, Wr, P5/1812/38
My., widow, Haxton, Fittleton, 1669, I, W, P2/H/656
My., widow, E. Stowell, Wilcot, 1708, I, W, P3/H/880
My., widow, Bazills, Melk., 1769-70, draft AB, a/c (2), I, P2/H/1522
Morgan, Sherb., Dorset, 1741, W, Wr, P5/1741/22
Nich., Corsham, 1592, AB, P29/H/4, P29/1Reg/26B
Nich., husb., Nether C., Dorset, [1602], deed of gift, P5/1601/24
Paul, clothier, Limpley Stoke, Bradford A., 1723, I, summary I, W, P1/H/787, P1/6Reg/402
Philip, husb., Sutton V., 1559, W, P2/3Reg/165A
Priscilla, widow, Lyme R., Dorset, 1669, W, P16/21
Reynold, innkeeper and yeo., Bere R., Dorset, 1608, I, W, P5/1608/17, P5/8Reg/126
Richd., Edington, 1589, I, W, P2/H/88
Richd., clothier, Beam., Dorset, 1708, W, P17/174
Richd., Beam., Dorset, 1724, AB, P17/417
Richd., yeo., Lea, L. and Cleverton, 1853, AB, O, ren, W, Wr, P3/1853/17
Richd., Newent, Gloucs, 1857, AB, aff, note, O, Wr, P3/1857/33
Robt., husb., Castleton, Dorset, 1615, I, W, P5/1614/30, P5/9Reg/150A
Robt., yeo., Foxley, [1615], I, W (NEP), P3/H/107
Robt., Nether C., Dorset, 1645, AB, comm, I, P5/1644/16, P5/14Reg/82B
Robt., innholder, Castleton, Dorset, 1676, I, W, P5/1676/30
Robt., Witcomb, Hilmarton, 1785, AB, P3/H/1461

Sam., jun., miller, Sherb., Dorset, 1730, W, P5/1730/35
Sam., maltster, Sherb., Dorset, 1743, W, Wr, P5/1743/40
Sarah, widow, Castleton, Dorset, 1778, W, P5/1778/10, P5/17Reg/157
Sarah, widow, Gt. Somerford, 1820, W, Wr, P1/1820/81
Sarah, Grittenham, Brinkw., 1854, AB, aff, O, Wr, P3/1854/7
Simon, yeo., Highw., 1609, comm, I, W, P5/1609/37, P5/8Reg/158
Stephen, yeo., Seend, Melk., 1848, comm, W, Wr, P1/1848/31
Thos., husb., Sherston, 1606, W (2 - 1 a copy), P3/H/17
Thos., yeo., Fittleton, 1662, I, W, P2/H/614
Thos., sen., yeo., Lyme R., Dorset, 1672, comm, W, P16/34
Thos., fuller, Calstone W., 1681, AB, comm, I, P3/H/554
Thos., yeo., Stallen, Nether C., Dorset, 1690, AB, I, P5/1690/21
Thos., sen., yeo., Figh., 1747, W, P26/871
Thos., yeo., Goatacre, Hilmarton, 1784, W, P3/H/1453
Thos., labourer, Pott., 1819, W, P1/1819/15
Thos., labourer, Hilmarton, 1824, W, Wr, P3/1824/23
Thos., Westport St My., 1847, AB, O, Wr, P3/1847/37
Thos. Geoffrey, yeo., Sherb., Dorset, 1795, W, P5/1795/9, P5/18Reg/212B
Walter, Edington, 1587, W, P2/7Reg/98A
Walter, yeo., Bowerhill, Melk., 1760, W, P2/H/1448
Wm., yeo., Cook St., Chipp., 1562, W (NEP), P1/2Reg/135A
Wm., Bps. C., 1568, AB, P5/2Reg/29F
Wm., yeo., Seend, Melk., 1638, AB, a/c, I, P1/H/232
Wm., Seend, Melk., 1671, AB, I, P1/H/405
Wm., Beam., Dorset, 1706, AB, P17/164
Wm., Old Windsor, Berks., 1723, AB, P1/H/798
Wm., cordw., Chipp., 1723, AB, I, W, P1/H/795, P1/6Reg/455
Wm., yeo., Castleton, Dorset, 1764, W, P5/1764/22
Wm., Melk., 1769, AB, P2/H/1521
Wm., gent., Sherb., Dorset, 1792, comm, W, P5/1792/11, P5/18Reg/174A
Wm., clothier, Bradford A., 1807, W, Wr, P2/1807/19
see also Woodman form. H.
Harten, Roger, mole catcher, Whitep., 1732, I, W, P2/H/1264
Hartfield, Andrew, sen., Bagshot, Shalbourne, 1675-81, AB, a/c, I, P5/1675/25, P5/1679/47, P5/1680/23, P5/1681/21
Andrew, miller, Pewsey, 1711, W, P3/H/915
Roger, millward, Mildenhall, 1703, W, P3/H/838
Hartford, Harthforth, Edmd., S. Newton, 1540, I, W (NEP), P30/92
Hartford alias Samuel, Hy., tailor, Westb., 1644, AB, I, P25/1644/8
Hartforth, Jn., sen., Bishopstone S., [1559?], I, P2/H/7
Jn., Ebbesborne Wake, 1583, AB, P2/6Reg/113B
Jn., yeo., Heale, Woodford, 1634, I, W. Proved at Metropolitan Visitation to Salisbury, P5/1634/46, P5/12Reg/285B
Richd., Castle C., [1583], W (NEP), P3/1Reg/3A
Richd., carp., Fonthill B., 1607, AB, comm, I, note of admon, W, P2/H/235
Thos., husb., Cleverton, Lea and C., 1621, I, W, P3/H/159
Hartgill, Arthur, gent., W. Knoyle, 1639, AB, comm, P2/H/521
Dorothy, Maiden B., 1609, AB, I, P2/H/248, P2/8Reg/46C
Eliz., minors, Zeals, 1821, T, Wr, P5/1821/44
Jn., yeo., Stourton, 1819, W, Wr, P2/1819/18
Jn., Zeals, 1821, AB (2), Wr, P5/1821/43
My., sp., Mere, 1742, AB, I, Wr, P5/1741/20
Hartington *see* Hortington
Hartland, My., widow, Chipp., 1753, AB, ren, W, P1/H/1098, P1/11Reg/104A
Hartry *see* Ettry
Hartwell, Hannah, widow, Sonning, Berks., 1709, W, P5/1709/15, P5/15Reg/123A
Jn., Maidenhead, Berks., 1628, I, W, P1/H/178
Richd., clerk, Blewbury, Berks., 1677, I, W, P5/1677/29
Richd., Sonning, Berks., 1744, AB, Wr, P5/1744/19
Harvard *see* Harford
Harvest, Eliz., widow, Rowde, 1671, I, W, P1/H/404
Eliz. *see also* Sarah

Eliz., widow, Devizes, 1693, comm, I, W, P1/H/561
Joan, widow, Urchf., [1622], I, W, P2/H/359
Jn., gent., Pott., [1671], copy W, P1/H/416
Jn., gent., Keevil, [1692], I, ren, W, P2/H/924
Jn., yeo., Urchf., 1730, W, P2/H/1249
Jn., yeo., Urchf., 1753, W, P1/H/1099, P1/11Reg/108A
Mgt., widow, Coombe B., 1634, AB, I(GVS), P5/1634/47
Philip, gent., Devizes St Jn., 1690, comm, I, W, P1/H/528, 535
Rebecca, widow, Pott., 1663, I, NW, P1/H/339
Richd., Urchf., 1551, W, P2/2Reg/123B
Richd., Coombe B., 1628, AB, I, P5/1628/59, P5/11Reg/57A
Roger, husb., Urchf., 1621, I, W, P2/H/351
Sarah (*or* Eliz. in AB), sp., W. Lavington, 1673, AB, comm, I, NW, P1/H/419
Sarah, widow, Keevil, 1716, W, P2/H/1136
Susan, sp., Pott., 1662, AB, comm, P1/H/318
see also Smith alias H.
Harvet, Sarah, sp., Marston, Pott., 1814, W, Wr, P1/1814/4
Harvey, Harvy, Agnes, E. Knoyle, 1546, AB, P2/H/1
Alice, widow, Bower C., 1590, I, W, P2/H/111
Betty, widow, Malm., 1834, AB, comm, Wr, P3/1834/51
Cath., widow, Sal. The Close, 1675, W, P5/1675/28
Dorothy, widow, Stourpaine, Dorset, 1732, W, P24/962
Harvy, Edmd., Broad C., 1727, AB, P2/H/1219
Edwd., Sal. The Close, 1674, AB, P5/1674/36
Edwd., Sal. The Close, 1690, AB, P5/1689/30
Frances, Farnham, Tollard Royal, Dorset, 1744, W, P1/H/1008, P1/9Reg/308
Geo., Charlton nr Malm., 1699, AB, I, ren, P3/H/780
Harvy, Geo., sen., woollen weaver, Chards., Devon, 1701, I, W, P14/93
Geo., Water Eaton, Latton, 1772, AB, P3/H/1396
Geo., innkeeper, Coombe St., Lyme R., Dorset, 1843, comm, W, Wr, P16/433
Grace, Calne, 1745, AB, P26/860
Hy., yeo., Farnham, Tollard Royal, Dorset, [1689], I, W, P2/H/901
Harvy, Hugh, Broad C., 1584, W, P2/6Reg/134B
Jas., Westb., 1782, AB, appt of proctor, P25/1782/1
Joanna, Bradford A., 1766, AB, comm, P2/H/1483
Jn., Marl. St Peter and St Paul, 1564, W (value of I given), P1/2Reg/147A
Jn., sadler, Sherb., Dorset, 1593, AB, I, P5/1593/40, P5/6Reg/40D
Jn., yeo., Imber, 1701, AB, I, ren, W, P1/H/619, P1/4Reg/189
Jn., Chards., Devon, 1704, AB, I, P5/1704/34
Jn., yeo., S. Marston, 1730, W, P10/1730/2
Jn., Holnest, Dorset, 1744, AB, Wr, P5/1744/20
Jn. Edwd., minor, Malm., 1834, appt of guardian, comm, T, P3/1834/50
Jos., Crickl. St S., 1815, AB, Wr, P3/1815/82
Lawr., labourer, Bemerton, Fugg. St Peter, 1740, W, P2/H/1320
Mgt., widow, Zeals (form. of St Jas. Bristol), 1601, AB, I, W, P5/1600/29, P5/7Reg/6
Harvy, Margery, Sutton M., 1580, AB, P2/H/60, P2/5Reg/369B
My., sp., Sal., 1744, W, P4/1744/1
Hervey, My., widow, S. Marston, 1795, AB, comm, P10/1795/2
Paul, Marl., 1820, AB, Wr, P1/1820/115
Harvy, Phillippa, Chards., Devon, 1728, W, P5/1728/44, P5/16Reg/173A
Reginald, sawyer, Horningsham, 1569, W, P5/2Reg/37B, 56D
Richd., broad weaver, Bradford A., 1716, AB, I, P2/H/1132
Richd., Tollard Royal, 1727, AB, P2/H/1218
Richd., gent., Bradford A., 1852, D, O, W, Wr, P2/1852/49
Richd., yeo., S. Marston, 1758, W, P5/1758/22
Harvy, Robt., husb., Over Zeals, 1587, I, T, W, P5/1586/8, P5/4Reg/138C
Robt., broad weaver, Heywood, Westb., 1643, I, W, P25/1643/4
Robt., sen., yeo., Bradford A., [1688], I, W, P2/H/898
Robt., yeo., Bradfield, Berks., 1732, comm, I, W, P1/H/916
Robt., yeo., Bradford A., 1733, W, P1/7Reg/567

Harvy, Roger, sen., Stourpaine, Dorset, 1680, I, W, P24/418
Sam., weaver, Alston, Chards., Devon, 1728, W, P5/1728/43, P5/16Reg/174A
Sarah, Bradford A., 1733, W (NEP), P30/95
Stephen, Farnham, Tollard Royal, Dorset, 1589, I, T, W, P2/H/92
Harvy, Thos., Codf. St P., 1564, W, P2/4Reg/185E
Harvy, Thos., Sherrington, 1584, W, P2/6Reg/133A
Thos., wool breaker, Erlestoke, 1684, AB, I, P2/H/839
Hervey, Thos., yeo., Sherrington, 1699, I, W, P2/H/963, 986
Thos., broad weaver, Bradford A., 1739, AB, ren, P2/H/1315
Uriah, mariner, Church St., Lyme R., Dorset, 1811, comm, W, P16/374
Wm., broad weaver, Bearfield, Bradford A., 1745, W, P2/H/1351
Wm., minister of the Gospel, Bearfield, Bradford A., 1804, W, P2/1804/13
Wm., innkeeper, Warm., 1837, W, Wr, P2/1837/85
Harvill, Denis, Sutton Poyntz, Dorset, 1579, AB, I, NW, P5/1578/26, P5/3Reg/115C
Harvy *see* Harvey
Harward *see* Harwood
Harway *see* Harraway
Harwell *see* Harewell
Harwin, Jn., sen., yeo. and shoemaker, Lacock, 1641, comm, I, W, P1/H/249
Harwood, Alice, widow, Throope, Bishopstone S., 1686, I, W, P2/H/866
Ambrose, sen., yeo., Swallowcliffe, 1718, W, P5/1718/17, P5/16Reg/7B
Ambrose, Linley, Tisb., 1749, W, P2/H/1382
Ambrose, gent., Homington, 1822, W, Wr, P24/1287
Ann, widow, Swallowcliffe, 1674, I, W, P5/1674/37
Ann, widow, Quidh., 1797, AB, P2/H/1682
Chas., Mr, Sal., 1747, AB, I, P4/1746/11
Chas., maltster and innkeeper, Coombe B., 1855, AB, aff, ren, W, Wr, P8/99
Chris., yeo., Faulston, Bishopstone S., 1698, I, W, P2/H/985
Chris., hatter, Sal., 1769, W, P4/1769/17
Eliz., widow, Tisb., 1763, W, P1/H/1162, P1/12Reg/40B
Eliz., widow, Coombe B., 1831, W, P8/85
Hy., hatter, Sal., 1765, W, P4/1765/16
Jas., yeo., Beenham Valence, Berks., 1698, W, P1/H/598, P1/3Reg/45
Jas., N. Tidworth, 1788, AB, P2/H/1635
Jn., yeo., Throope, Bishopstone S., 1691, AB, I, P2/H/916
Jn., carp., Homington, 1713, AB, I, P24/683
Jn., jun., Coombe B., 1716, AB (2), I, W, P5/1716/41, P5/15Reg/346C
Jn., yeo., Coombe B., 1722, W, P5/1722/27, P5/16Reg/81A
Jn., yeo., Tisb., 1767, W, P2/H/1501
Jn., yeo., Coombe B., 1768, W, P8/50
Jn., yeo., Stratford Tony, 1784, W, P2/H/1609
Jn., yeo., Coombe B., 1819, W, Wr, P8/81
Jn., bach., Coombe B., 1835, AB, P8/87
Harward, Joshua, clerk, Shrewton, 1757, receipt, req, copy W, W, P1/H/1132, P1/11Reg/340B
My., widow, Throope, Bishopstone S., 1701, I, W, P2/H/1003
My., widow, Swallowcliffe, 1720, AB, P5/1720/28
Harward, My., widow, Wanb., 1728, AB, I, P3/H/1046
My., widow, Stratford Tony, 1785, W, P2/H/1613
My., widow, Chilmark, 1841, AB, Wr, P2/1841/25
Matthew, Anderson, Dorset, 1798, AB, P5/1798/11, P5/18Reg/267A
Peter, bach., Bishopstone N., 1690, AB, P6/91
Rachel, Homington, 1735, I, W, P24/936
Richd., Sal., 1680, AB, I, P4/1680/19
Harward, Robt., Wanb., 1686, AB, I, P3/H/623
Sarah, widow, Homington, 1805, W, P24/1241
Thos., husb., Amesb., 1671, AB, I, P1/H/411
Thos., yeo., Imber, 1702, W, P2/H/1012
Thos., yeo., E. Knoyle, 1766, W, P2/H/1486
Thos., yeo., Coombe B., 1771, W, P8/53
Wm., husb., Flamston, Bishopstone S., 1635, AB (to pay legacy), I, W, P1/H/224

Wm., yeo., Throope, Bishopstone S., 1683, I, W, P2/H/826
Wm., yeo., Imber, 1685, I, W, P2/H/855
Wm., tailor, Stockton, 1744, AB, I, P1/H/1003
Wm., farmer, Swallowcliffe, 1757, W, P5/1757/14
Wm., yeo., Stratford Tony, 1767, W, P2/H/1497
Wm., sen., yeo., Homington, 1770, AB, W, P24/1072
Wm., Heytes., 1803, W, P5/1803/14, P5/19Reg/41
Wm., farmer, Homington, 1829, W, Wr, P24/1317
Wm., gent., Chilmark, 1837, W, Wr, P2/1837/81
Hascer *see* Hasker
Hascoll *see* Haskell
Hascott *see* Haskett
Hasel *see* Hasell
Haseland, Hazeland, Edwd., sen., miller, Woodb., 1688, I, W, P3/H/652
Edwd., millward, Woodb., 1709, W, P3/H/892
Hazeland, Edwd., yeo., Whitley, Melk., 1796, comm, W, P2/H/1680
Hazeland, Eliz., Marden, 1750, AB, P1/H/1065
Hazeland, Eliz., widow, Devizes, 1836, O, W, P1/1835/2
Hazeland, Jn., sen., carp. and wheelwright, Wilcot, 1803, O, W, P3/1803/6
Hazeland, Jn., Devizes, 1816, AB, Wr, P1/1816/12
Matthew, Hilmarton, 1643, AB, comm, P1/H/258
Hazeland, Thos., baker, Woodb., 1786, W, P3/H/1470
Hazeland, Thos., wheelwright, Marden, 1808, comm, W, Wr, P2/1808/34
Hasland, Wm., Bps. C., 1626, I, W (buried at Bishops Cannings 24 Mar 1626), P24/228
Hasland, Wm., Woodb., 1631, I, W, P1/H/193
Hazeland, Wm., wheelwright, Marden, 1739, W, P1/8Reg/379A
Hazeland, Wm., gent., Woodb., 1786, W (& cods), P3/H/1471
Hazeland, Wm., Melk., 1836, AB, comm, P1/1836/1
Haseldon, Jn., no abode stated, context suggests Uffc., Devon, 1570, W, P5/2Reg/76D
Hasell, Hazel, Bartholomew, sen., yeo., Charney Bassett, Longworth, Berks., 1738, W, P1/H/957, P1/8Reg/251
Hazell, Benj., yeo., Etchilhampton, 1706, I, W, P3/H/872
Hazell, Benj., Urchf., 1787, W, P2/H/1626
Hazell, Benj., yeo., Urchf., 1808, W, Wr, P2/1808/36
Heasell, Edwd., yeo., Bower C., 1827, W, Wr, P2/1827/12
Heasell, Edwd., Gravesend, Kent (leaving effects at Bower Chalk), 1843, AB, Wr, P2/1843/52
Hazell, Eliz., widow, Bucklebury, Berks., 1767, W, P1/H/1192, P1/12Reg/238
Hazle, Jn., sen., labourer, Lt. Coxwell, Gt. Faringdon, Berks., 1707, W, P5/15Reg/11
Hasel, Jn., yeo., Hoe Benham, Welford, Berks., 1720, W, P1/H/775, P1/6Reg/332
Hazell, Jn., wheelwright, Etchilhampton, 1725, comm, W, P3/H/1017
Jn., Burbage, 1742, AB, I, P11/188
Hazell, Jn., millwright, Etchilhampton, 1743, AB, I, ren, P3/H/1190
Hasel, Jn., sen., Broad C. (late of Fyfield), 1769, AB, W, P2/H/1518
Hazell, Jn., yeo., Greenham, Thatcham, Berks., 1770, W, P1/H/1208, P1/12Reg/338
Heasel, Jn., Bower C., 1774, W, P2/H/1542
Hazell, Jn., Urchf., 1799, W, P2/H/1693
Hazell, Jn., farmer, Whittonditch, Rams., 1827, W, Wr, P5/1827/21
Jos., victualler, Thatcham, Berks., 1770, AB, W, P1/H/1207, P1/12Reg/337B
Heasell, Jos., coach carver, Sal., 1799, W, P4/1799/9
Hazle, Leonard, yeo., Grove, Wantage, Berks., 1762, W, P23/698
Hazell, My., Upavon, 1761, AB, P2/H/1452
Richd., husb., Bremhill, 1670, I, W, P3/H/430
Hazill, Richd., vicar, Compton, Berks., 1683, AB, comm, I, P1/H/486
Hazell, Richd., Charney Bassett, Longworth, Berks., 1729, AB, P1/H/848
Hazell, Richd., yeo., Rams., 1854, aff, O, W, Wr, P5/1854/12
Robt., miller, Newbury, Berks., 1683, I, W, P1/H/474
Hazel, Sarah, widow, Easton, Welford, Berks., 1801, W, P1/1801/42, P1/15Reg/262B
Hazell, Stephen, yeo., Upavon, 1740-61, AB, W, P2/H/1325
Hazell, Thos., sen., yeo., Lt. Coxwell, Gt. Faringdon, Berks., 1743, W, Wr, P5/1743/38
Hazell, Thos., All C., 1791, AB, P3/H/1498
Thos., sen., yeo., Benham, Speen, Berks., 1795, W, P1/H/1342, P1/14Reg/585

Wm., sen., yeo., Childrey, Berks., 1614, I, W, P1/H/93
Hazell, Wm., yeo., Wantage, Berks., 1717, I, W, P23/361
Hazel, Wm., Easton, 1747, AB, LA (LA cancelled), P1/H/1043
Hazell, Wm., Easton, 1752, AB, W, P1/H/1084, P1/10Reg/485B
Hazel, Wm., yeo., Lt. Coxwell, Gt. Faringdon, Berks., 1752, AB, W, P5/1752/30
Hazell, Wm., sen., yeo., Whittonditch, Rams., 1778, W, P5/1778/11, P5/17Reg/160C
Hazell, Wm., labourer, Langley Burrell, 1817, W, Wr, P3/1817/21
see also Farmer alias H.
Haskell, Ann, sp., E. Knoyle, 1854, D (2), O, W, Wr, P2/1854/21
Edith, sp., Donhead St My., [1688], I, W, P2/H/890
Edwd., Sal., 1767, AB, P1/H/1183
Haskall, Francis, Abbot's Court, Winterborne K., Dorset, 1705, comm, I, W, P5/1704/37
Geo., Sal., 1830, W, Wr, P4/1830/1
Jas., Donhead St A., 1807, AB, comm, Wr, P2/1807/3
Jas., blacksmith, Donhead St A., 1821, W, Wr, P2/1821/27
Jn., yeo., Charlton, Donhead St My., 1637, I (very detailed), W, P2/H/481
Jn., gent., Donhead St My., 1731, W, P2/H/1259
Jn., blacksmith, Horningsham, 1846, D, W, Wr, P5/1846/18
Morgan, yeo., W. Hatch, Tisb., 1668, I, NW, P2/H/654
Richd., husb., Quidh., 1747, AB, W, P2/H/1369
Robt., Alvediston, 1717, AB, P2/H/1142
Sarah, sp., Donhead St A., 1818, W, Wr, P2/1818/2
Haskoll, Sebastian, Donhead St My., 1830, AB, comm, Wr, P2/1830/28
Hascoll, Wm., husb., Semley, 1568, W, P2/5Reg/31C
Hasker, Bernard, yeo., Pen Close, Chieveley, Berks., 1662, I, W, P1/H/323
Hascer, Thos., Lt. Cheverell, 1595, AB, P2/7Reg/144A
Haskett, Hascott, Hugh, Winterbourne D., 1591, I, W, P2/H/113
Jn., gent., Alton P., Dorset, 1730, W, P5/1730/38
Hascott, Richd., husb., Gt. Amesb., 1630, I, copy I, W, copy W, P2/H/424, P2/9Reg/122B
Sarah, widow, Gt. Amesb., 1687, AB, I, P2/H/877
Stephen, merchant, Sal., 1695, W, P1/H/579
Haskins *see* Hoskins
Haskoll *see* Haskell
Haslam, Jane, widow, Hindon, 1840, AB, Wr, P2/1840/10
Hasland *see* Haseland
Haslett, Jn., mole catcher, Whitep., 1748, AB, I, P2/H/1375
Hasley, Jn., Hurst, Berks., 1567, W, P5/2Reg/24A
Hasling, Susanna, widow, E. Kennett, 1668, AB, I, W, P3/H/398
Hassard *see* Hazard
Hasten, Judith, widow, Whitep., 1760, W, P2/H/1447
Haster, Susanna, widow, Lt. Cheverell, 1598, I, W, P2/H/180
Thos., Lt. Cheverell, 1595, AB, P2/H/141
Hastny, Edwd., Corsham, 1587, W, P29/1Reg/25B
Hatch, Abner, labourer, Bramshaw, Hants, 1855, aff, W, Wr, P24/1418
Cornelius, blacksmith, Ruscombe, Berks., 1728, W, P5/1728/46, P5/16Reg/207A
Edwd., Wargrave, Berks., 1770, AB, P1/H/1211
Jn., yeo., Gillingham, Dorset, 1783, W, P27/1/516, P27/3Reg/231
Margery, widow, Hurst, Berks., 1619, AB, I, P5/1619/56, P5/10Reg/46A
Nich., sen., yeo., Bramshaw, Hants, 1701, I, W, P24/550
Robt., Burbage, 1579, W, P5/3Reg/139A
Sarah, widow, Bramshaw, Hants, 1760, court paper, W, P24/1108
Simon, sen., farmer, Bray Wick, Berks., 1698, I, W, P1/H/601, P1/3Reg/70
Thos., White Waltham, Berks., 1611, AB, P1/H/67
Thos., husb., White Waltham, Berks., 1708, AB, I, P1/H/650
Wm., Hungerford, Berks., 1666, AB, P5/1665/41
Wm., blacksmith, Ruscombe, Berks., 1698, W, P5/1698/37
Wm., Bray, Berks., 1729, AB, P1/H/855
Wm., Cookham, Berks., 1753, W, P1/H/1093, P1/11Reg/39
Wm., sen., yeo., Bramshaw, Hants, 1754, W, P24/1022
Wm., sen., Bramshaw, Hants, 1778, W, P24/1123

Hatcher, Hy., woodman, Farley, Alderbury, 1840, W, Wr, P26/1446
Robt., yeo., Broad B., Highw., 1803, W, P5/1803/27, P5/19Reg/55
Thos., carp., Downton, [1699], W, P2/H/988
Thos., Water Eaton (Eisey), Latton, 1727, AB, P3/H/1034
Wm., E. Knoyle, 1857, aff, D, O, W, Wr, P2/1857/46
Hatchett, Ann, widow, Sal. St Thos., 1765, W, P4/1765/7
Jn., Gillingham, Dorset, 1573, court proceedings (adultery case), P27/1Reg/2
Robt., husb., Froxfield, 1683, I, W, P3/H/581
Thos., sen., yeo., Brinkw., 1671, I, W, P3/H/452
Thos., tailor, Brinkw., 1673, AB, a/c, I, P3/H/474
Hatchman, Agnes, widow, Netheravon, 1640, AB, I, P12/82
Benj., glover, Netheravon, 1647, I, NW, P12/87
Benj., Netheravon, 1709, AB, I, P5/1709/16
Benj., yeo., Netheravon, 1749, W, P5/1749/28
Benj., yeo., Netheravon, 1766, W, P12/188
Jn., Netheravon, 1620, I, P12/41
Jn., blacksmith, Netheravon, 1674-76, AB, a/c, I, P5/1674/32, P5/1676/28
My., widow, Netheravon, 1639, I, W, P12/81
Nathaniel, innholder, Netheravon, 1648, AB, I, P12/88
Nathaniel, Durrington, 1718, AB, P2/H/1156
Phineas, Netheravon, 1728, AB (unsigned), P12/155
Robt., sen., yeo., Netheravon, 1682, I, W, P12/116
Robt., bach., Netheravon, 1687, AB, I, W, P5/1687/19
Simon, blacksmith, Netheravon, 1625, I, W, P5/1625/41, P5/10Reg/186B
Simon, baker, Pott., 1664, AB, I, P1/H/354
Hachmane, Thos., husb., Netheravon, 1594, AB, I, W, P5/1593/39, P5/6Reg/54A
Hate, Thos., Quidh., [1550?], I, P2/H/3
Hater *see* Hatter
Hatfield *see* Hutfield
Hathaway, Alice, widow, Hullavington, 1606, I, W (NEP), P3/H/18
Hathway, Eleanor, widow, Tockenham Wick, 1837, comm, W, Wr, P3/1837/20
Hathway, Eliz., widow, Grittleton, 1694, I, W, P3/H/742
Hathway, Francis, clerk and rector, Hatford, Berks., 1671, comm, I, W, P1/H/417
Hathway, Harry, Tockenham Wick, 1825, AB, Wr, P3/1825/31
Hathway, Richd., yeo., Grittenham, Brinkw., 1857, aff, O, W, Wr, P3/1857/17
Robt., Hullavington, [1602], W (NEP), P3/1Reg/97B
Hathway, Robt., husb., Foxham, Bremhill, 1640, I, W, P3/H/320
Hathway, Thos., Tockenham Wick, 1833, AB, comm, Wr, P3/1833/56
Hathaway *or* Hathway, Wm., husb., Stanton St Q., 1671, I, W, P3/H/451
Wm., Stanton St Q., 1691, I, W, P3/H/694
Hatherell, Avis, widow, Gt. Somerford, 1641, AB, I, P3/H/331
Hathrill, Edmd., labourer, Calne, 1638, I, W, P26/65
Edmd., husb., Gt. Somerford, 1639, I, W, P3/H/313
Edwd., yeo., Marten, Grafton, 1721, W, P21/8/10
Eliz., widow, Langley Burrell, 1618, AB, a/c, I, P3/H/130
Jas., innholder, Sutton B., 1729-36, a/c, I, W, P1/H/841, P1/7Reg/210A
Hawtrell, Jn., wheelwright, Wokm., Berks., 1573, W, P5/3Reg/16D
Jn., Langley Burrell, [1617], I, W (NEP), P3/H/119
Jn., innholder, Chr. M., 1666, I, W, P1/H/371
Jn., weaver, Chipp., 1797, W, P3/H/1522
Hathrill, Jn., Nables Farm, Draycot C., 1839, comm, W, Wr, P3/1839/11
Hathrill, Jn., Aldbourne, 1857, AB, aff, O, Wr, P3/1857/6
Marian, widow, Chr. M., [1618], I, W (NEP), P3/H/131
Michael, Chr. M., 1620, AB, I, P3/H/150
Robt., Sutton B., 1801, W, P1/1801/72, P1/15Reg/287B
Thos., husb., Bps. C., 1608, I, W, P24/152
Thos., yeo., Lower Seagry, 1633, comm, I, W, P3/H/268
Wm., yeo., Bremhill, 1738, W, P3/H/1154
Hatherley, Simon, Bloxworth, Dorset, 1718, AB, P5/1718/18
Hathorne, Ann, sp., Wokm., Berks., 1669, I, P5/1669/26

Haythorne, Eliz., widow, Fordington, Dorset, 1696, I, W, P15/49
Haythorne, Randall, Fordington, Dorset, 1693, W, P15/45
Hathrill *see* Hatherell
Hathway *see* Hathaway
Hatkins *see* Atkins
Hatt, Ann, Chilton F., 1606, AB, I, P1/H/43
Ann, widow, Ogbourne St Geo., 1698, I, W, P5/1698/33
Ann, widow, Brightwalton, Berks., 1704, AB, W, P1/H/629
Anthony, barber, Marl., 1638, I, W, P1/H/242
Anthony, yeo., Wanb., 1771, W, P3/H/1390
Anthony, Wanb., 1807, AB, Wr, P3/1807/49
Cath., sp., Badbury, Chiseldon, 1841, AB, O, Wr, P3/1841/50
Chris., husb., Stratton St Mgt., 1630, AB, W, P29/H/28, P29/1Reg/121A
Edwd., Liddington, 1782, AB, P3/H/1443
Eliz., widow, Swindon, 1822, comm, W, Wr, P3/1822/11
Giles, sen., yeo., Broad B., Highw., 1713, I, ren, W, P3/H/926
Jane, Hullavington, 1782, AB, P1/H/1273
Joel, gent., Reading, Berks., 1817, W, Wr, P1/1817/69
Jn., Chiseldon, [1570], W, P1/1Reg/124C
Jn., Wilton, Gt. Bedwyn, 1629, I, W, P5/1628/51, P5/11Reg/17A
Jn., husb., Aldbourne, 1631, I, W, P3/H/246
Jn., yeo. and bach., Snodshill, Chiseldon, 1695, AB, appt of admr, I, P1/H/568
Jn., yeo., Liddington, 1729, W, P1/H/860, P1/7Reg/289B
Jn., yeo., Gidley Farm, Peasemore, Berks., 1753, W, P1/11Reg/19
Jn., sen., Aldbourne, 1809, AB, Wr, P3/1809/46
Jn., yeo., Westlecott, Wrou., 1829, comm, W, Wr, P1/1829/77
Jn., Badbury, Chiseldon, 1856, AB, aff, comm, Wr, P3/1856/56
Mgt., widow, Broad B., Highw., 1694, AB, comm, P10/1694/1
Mgt., widow, Devizes, 1717, W, P1/H/746, P1/6Reg/115
Martha, wife, North St., Westminster St Jn., London (leaving effects at Overton), 1851, AB, comm, W, Wr, P1/1851/74
Richd., Shalbourne, 1567-70, AB, W, P5/2Reg/64B, 90B
Richd., yeo., Snap, Aldbourne, [1606], W (NEP), P3/H/19
Robt., yeo., Snodshill, Chiseldon, 1700, I, W, P3/H/794
Stephen, tailor, Gt. Bedwyn, 1602, I, W, P5/1602/20, P5/7Reg/43A
Stephen, husb., Wilton, Gt. Bedwyn, 1615, I, W, P5/1614/28, P5/9Reg/151B
Thos., yeo., Snap, Aldbourne, 1633, I, W, P3/H/269
Thos., husb., Thrupp, Gt. Faringdon, Berks., 1638, I, W, P5/1638/58, P5/13Reg/139A
Thos., sen., yeo., Snap, Aldbourne, 1684, I, W, P3/H/594
Thos., Rowde, 1688, AB, I, P3/H/651
Thos., yeo., Eastcott, Swindon, 1780, W, P3/H/1435
Thos., yeo., Liddington, 1781, W, P3/H/1438
Thos., maltster, Swindon, 1806, comm, W, P3/1806/13
Wm., husb., Ham, 1646, I, W, P1/H/278
Wm., sen., butcher, Speenhamland, Berks., 1720, AB, I, ren, W, P1/H/776, P1/6Reg/340A
Wm., Swindon, 1822, AB, comm, Wr, P3/1822/41
Wm., yeo., Medbourne, Liddington, 1854, aff, comm, W, Wr, P3/1854/37
Hatter, Alice, widow, Poulshot, 1628, W, P1/H/175
Christian, widow, Poulshot, 1589, I, W, P2/H/97
Geo., husb. and yeo., Chirton, [1680], I, W, P2/H/780
Hy., husb., Poulshot, 1620, I, W, P1/H/142
Joan, widow, Chirton, 1610, I, W, P2/H/264, P2/8Reg/96B
Jn., sen., husb., Chirton, 1592, I, W, P2/H/119
Jn., labourer, Stonen Bridge, Wilcot, 1804, W, P3/1804/27
Jn., yeo., Lt. Cheverell, 1823, W, Wr, P2/1823/21
Jos., yeo., Lyneham, 1801, W, P1/1801/68, P1/15Reg/285
Jos., Burbage, 1834, AB, comm, P11/289
Mgt., widow, Poulshot, 1606, W, P1/H/50
Roger, sen., labourer, Chirton, 1716, W, P1/H/727, P1/6Reg/33
Sarah *see* Sarah Yates
Susan, Poulshot, 1639, I, W, P2/H/528

Hater, Wm., husb., Poulshot, 1623, I, W, P2/H/364
Hatton, Eliz., widow, Crickl. St My., 1624, a/c, I (both on same sheet), P3/H/186
Jane, Leigh, Ashton K., 1668, AB, comm, P3/H/399
Jn., Gt. Bedwyn, 1850, AB, O, Wr, P5/1850/9
Luke, gent., Charlton nr Malm., 1633, AB, I, P3/H/270
My., widow, Binfield, Berks., 1750, W, P1/H/1067, P1/10Reg/338
My., wharfinger and coal merchant's widow, Gt. Bedwyn, 1849, note, O, W, Wr, P5/1849/18
Richd., Pewsey, 1632, AB, I, P3/H/256
Sarah, widow, Childrey, Berks., 1729, AB, I, summary I, W, P1/H/851, P1/7Reg/245
Thos., wharfinger and coal merchant, Gt. Bedwyn, 1847, note, O, W, Wr, P5/1847/1
Hattrie *see* Ettry
Haume *see* Hames
Havell, Eliz., widow, Reading, Berks., 1829, W, Wr, P1/1829/116
Philip, Uffc., Devon, 1594, I, W, P5/1594/37, P5/6Reg/63B
Havenoe, Wm., no abode stated, [1630], I, P2/H/420
Haviland, Jn., weaver, Sal., 1660, AB, I, P4/1660/5
My., widow, Broad B., Highw., 1816, W, Wr, P10/1816/2
Havis *see* Avis
Haw *see* Hawes
Haward *see* Hayward
Hawarden *see* Haywarden
Haway *see* Hayward
Hawcer *see* Hawker
Hawes, Clarges, Rams. and ship Devonshire, 1707, AB, comm, P5/1707/32
Eliz., sp., Wokm., Berks., 1755, W, P5/1755/26
Geo., Charlton nr Malm., 1851, AB, O, Wr, P3/1851/1
Hy., rector and clerk, Wilton, 1759, AB, W, P1/H/1138, P1/11Reg/377A
Hy., clerk, Box (form. of Bitton, Gloucs), 1798, W, P3/H/1530
Jn., sen., husb., Rams., 1643, AB, comm, I, P5/1643/3, P5/14Reg/58B
Mgt., Wokm., Berks., 1691, AB, P5/1691/31
My., widow, Wokm., Berks., 1724, W, P5/1724/35, P5/16Reg/94C
Rachel Frances, sp., Sal., 1830, AB, Wr, P4/1830/3
Hawe, Thos., gent., Wokm., Berks., 1706, W, P5/1706/16
Thos., clerk, Rams., 1718, AB, P5/1718/16
Haw, Wm., innholder, Wokm., Berks., 1663, AB, I (damaged), P5/1663/30
Hawes *or* Hawe, Wm., maltster, Wokm., Berks., 1675, AB, a/c, I, P5/1675/30
Hawkens *see* Hawkins
Hawker, Jas. Hunt, Bere R., Dorset, 1846, AB, comm, D, W, Wr, P5/1846/3
Jn., Kershay, Netherb., Dorset, 1664, AB, I, P17/76
Margery, clothworker's wife, Sal., 1700, W, P4/1700/13
Richd., Lyme R., Dorset, 1600, AB, I, P5/1600/32, P5/6Reg/247A
Hawcer, Robt., clothworker, Sal., 1621, I, W, P4/1621/7
Thos., woollen weaver, Woodlands, Mere, 1619, I, W, P5/1619/30, P5/10Reg/60A
Wm., tanner, Kershay, Netherb., Dorset, [1690], I, W (NEP), P17/324
Hawkes, Alice, widow, Purton, 1667, comm, D, I, W, P3/H/385
Ann, widow, Ashton K., 1725, I, W, P3/H/1016
Ann, widow, Shorncote, 1779, comm, W, P1/H/1264, P1/13Reg/290
Hawkes alias Stephens, Anthony, sen., yeo., Marl., 1607, I, W, P1/H/54
Benj., shopkeeper, Sal., 1787, W, P4/1787/8
Christian, widow, Bere R., Dorset, 1667, comm, I, W, P5/1667/29
Deborah, sp., Garsdon, 1647, I, T, NW, P1/H/285
Eliz., widow, Somerford K., 1738, AB, W, P1/H/962, P1/8Reg/312B
Hester, Ogbourne St A., 1691, AB, P5/1691/38
Hawkes alias Stephens alias Martyn, Joan, widow, Ogbourne St A., 1636, AB, P5/1636/34, P5/13Reg/15B
Jn., yeo., Ogbourne St A., 1691, I, W, P5/1691/39
Hawks, Jn., Shorncote, 1693, AB, I, Wr, P3/H/720
Jn., Ogbourne St A., 1701, AB, P5/1701/30
Jn., yeo., Medbourne, Liddington, 1701, AB, I, P3/H/805
Hawks, Jn., yeo., Ashton K., 1712, I, W, P3/H/918
Jn., Wokm., Berks., 1725, AB, I (no valuation given), P5/1725/39

Hawks, Jn., tailor, Malm., 1732, I, W, P1/H/904
Hawks, Richd., Wantage, Berks., 1573, AB, P5/3Reg/11E
Richd., clerk, Wanb., 1682, I, W, P3/H/566
Richd., yeo., Somerford K., 1814, W, Wr, P1/1814/68
Robt., yeo., Shorncote, 1702, AB, I, P3/H/822
Robt., yeo., Ashton K., 1717, I, W, P3/H/950
Sam., gent., Marl., 1725, W, P1/H/814, P1/7Reg/63B
Hawks, Thos., Kington L., 1598, W (value of I given), P1/2Reg/162B
Thos., no abode stated, [1646], I, W, P1/H/283
Thos., Marl., 1689, AB, comm, P1/H/527
Wm., yeo., Ogbourne St A., 1694, AB, a/c, I, P23/210
Wm., yeo., Shorncote, 1700, I, W, P3/H/795
Wm., Shorncote, 1768, W, P3/H/1373
see also Pearce alias H.
Hawkesbury, Wm., miller, Bere R., Dorset, 1640, AB, I, P5/1640/27, P5/13Reg/256A
Hawkeswell, Eulalia *see* Esther Howell
Lamont, clerk, Longbridge D., 1760, W, P2/H/1444
Hawkesworth, Ann, widow, Beanacre, Melk., 1733, W, P2/H/1266
Chas. Thos., grocer, Hungerford, Berks., 1814, comm, W, P23/873
Peter, yeo., Beanacre, Melk., 1723, I, W, P2/H/1200
see also Butler alias H.
Hawkins, Adam, yeo., Brinkw., [1664], I, W (NEP), P3/H/359
Adam, Chipp., 1666, AB, I, P3/H/377
Hawkings, Agnes, Chr. M., 1571, W, P1/1Reg/36A
Alice, widow, Minety, 1669, AB, P3/H/413
Ann, widow, no abode stated, 1709, I, P30/88
Ann, wife, Warm., 1805, AB, P2/1805/43
Ann, sp., Collingbourne K., 1837, AB, O, Wr, P3/1837/59
Benj., farmer, Wokm., Berks., 1755, W, P5/1755/27
Chas., Hardenhuish, 1674, AB, P1/H/433
Dan., yeo., Kington L., 1701, I, W, Wr, P3/H/806
Edith, widow, Kington L., 1605, I, W, P1/H/27
Edith, widow, Kington L., 1616, I, W, P1/H/110
Edwd., gent., Chipp., 1689, AB, P3/H/662
Edwd., Melk., 1748, comm, W, P2/H/1381
Eleanor, widow, Chipp., 1700, W, P3/H/796
Eleanor, sp., Wilton, Gt. Bedwyn, 1705, W, P21/6/29
Hawkens, Eliz., widow, Tilehurst, Berks., 1611, I, W, P1/H/66
Eliz., widow, Purton, 1620, I, W, P3/H/151
Eliz., singlewoman, Kemble, 1625, I, W, P1/H/166
Eliz., widow, Savernake Forest, 1676, AB, I, P3/H/502
Eliz., sp., Wilcot, 1834, AB, O, Wr, P3/1834/48
Francis, yeo., Hinton, Steeple A., [1675], I, W, P2/H/723
Hakens, Francis, Hazeldon, Tisb., 1763, W, P2/H/1465
Francis, Charlton, Donhead St My., 1781, AB, P2/H/1598
Geoffrey, broad weaver, Corsley, 1704, AB, P2/H/1028
Geo., yeo., Chr. M., 1667, comm, I, W, P3/H/386
Geo., Seagry, 1676, AB, ren, W, Wr, P3/H/503
Harry, clothier, Chipp., 1692, AB, I, P3/H/707
Harry, clothier, Chipp., 1714, W, P1/H/706, P1/5Reg/429
Hawkins alias Gold, Hugh, Bathampton, Steeple L., 1662, AB, P2/H/619
Isaac, yeo., W. Yatton, Yatton K., 1732, I, W, P1/H/903, P1/7Reg/502
Jas., broad weaver, Corsham, 1700, AB, I, P29/H/74, P29/1Reg/274B
Jas., sen., butcher, Abingdon, Berks., 1735, W, P1/H/927, P1/7Reg/648
Jas., shepherd, Bowood, 1818, W, Wr, P5/1818/15
Jas., butcher, Keevil, 1828, comm, W, Wr, P2/1828/58
Hawkins alias Lightfoot, Jane, widow, Gt. Bedwyn, 1671, I, W, P21/2/23
Jane, widow, Manningford A., 1723, W, P3/H/1002
Hawkings, Joan, sp., Bushton, Clyffe P., 1609, NW, P3/H/42
Jn., Wilsford nr Pewsey, 1587, I, W, P2/H/79, P2/7Reg/99A

Jn., Wilsford nr Pewsey, 1598?, W, P2/H/169
Jn., Calstone W., 1612, I, W, P26/18
Jn., pewterer, Sal., 1612, AB, I, W, P4/1611/4
Hakings, Jn., husb., Corston, Malm., 1616, I, W, P3/H/115
Jn., clerk and vicar, Kemble, 1621, I, W, P3/H/161
Jn., husb., Wilton, Gt. Bedwyn, 1646, AB, I, W, P21/1/64
Jn., sen., Warm., 1650, AB, comm, I, P1/H/299
Jn., pewterer, Sal., 1667, I, W, P4/1666/5
Jn., yeo., Rowde, 1671, AB, comm, I, W, P3/H/453
Jn., yeo., Wexcombe, Grafton, 1673, AB, I, ren, P21/2/37
Jn., maltster *or* gent., Chipp., 1683, AB, comm, I, P3/H/582
Jn., innholder, Warm., 1701, T (child: Chris. H.), W, P1/H/610, P2/H/1001
Jn., Shippon, Abingdon, Berks., 1708, AB, I, P1/H/652
Jn., Chards., Devon, 1725, AB, I, P5/1725/36
Jn., ironmonger, Abingdon, Berks., 1729, W, P1/H/852, P1/7Reg/236
Jn., jun., yeo., Marcham, Berks., 1729, W, P1/H/875, P1/7Reg/360B
Jn., sen., yeo., Minety, 1729, W, P1/H/866, P1/7Reg/299B
Jn., sen., Tidcombe, T. and Fosbury, 1734, W, P3/H/1122
Jn., Wilton, Gt. Bedwyn, 1738, AB, P21/9/20
Jn., yeo., Wexcombe, Grafton, 1745, W, P5/1745/7
Jn., linen weaver, Warm., 1754, W, P2/H/1405
Jn., Melk., 1756, AB, P2/H/1419
Jn., innholder, Warm., 1761, W, P2/H/1450
Jn., yeo., Inkpen, Berks., 1805, W, Wr, P1/1805/12
Jn., mason, Warm., 1813, W, Wr, P2/1813/37
Jn., innkeeper, Wootton B., 1820, comm, W, Wr, P3/1820/9
Jn., Pickwick, Corsham, 1826, AB, comm, Wr, P3/1826/3
Jn., publican, Marl., 1828, W, Wr, P1/1828/9
Jn., labourer, Manton, Preshute, 1834, W, Wr, P1/1834/24
Jn., hairdresser, Wilton, 1835, W, P2/1835/30
Jn., Stockcloses, Aldbourne, 1839, AB, comm, Wr, P3/1839/2
Jn., yeo., Wootton B., 1854, aff, comm, W, Wr, P3/1854/55
Jos., broad weaver, W. Yatton, Yatton K., 1687, AB, I, ren, P3/H/634
Hackens, Jos., husb., Hinton, Steeple A., 1689, I, W, P1/H/515
Jos., cordw., Steeple A., 1734, W, P2/H/1276
Jos., Preshute, 1751, AB, P1/H/1083
Lawr., Luckington, 1648, AB, a/c, I, P1/H/291
Leonard, yeo., Minety, 1638, I, W, P3/H/306
Leonard, jun., Minety, 1702, AB, comm, I, Wr, P3/H/823
Leonard, yeo., Minety, 1706, I, W, P3/H/861
Leonard, gent., Oaksey, 1820, comm, W, Wr, P3/1820/1
Mgt., widow, Oaksey, 1744, W, P1/H/1027, P1/9Reg/438B
Martha, wife of Edwd., Gillingham, Dorset, 1818, W, Wr, P27/1/640
My., widow, Ham, 1667, AB, I, P3/H/387
Hawkins alias Ruddle, My., sp., Horton, Bps. C., 1682, I, W, P24/407
My., widow, Kington St M., 1690, AB, comm, I, P3/H/674
Hawkens, My., Marl., 1703, AB, P1/H/624
Hawkens, My., widow, Ram Alley, Burbage, 1734, W, P3/H/1123
My., wife, Calne, 1790, AB, P26/1172
Michael, yeo., Brinkw., 1668, I, W, P3/H/400
Nich., Wilton, Gt. Bedwyn, 1722, AB, cert, I, P5/1722/28
Nich., Tisb., 1762, AB, P2/H/1455
Hawkins alias Gold, Osmund, Wilsford nr Pewsey, 1637, AB, a/c, I, P2/H/483
Ralph, Sutton M., 1646, AB, P2/H/582
Rebecca, widow, W. Grimstead, 1742, AB, W, P2/H/1338
Richd., weaver, Norton B., 1594, I, W, P2/H/138
Richd., Kington L., [1609], W (NEP), P3/H/44
Richd., Kington L., 1669, comm, I, W, P3/H/414
Richd., sen., innholder, Warm., 1672, I (detailed), W, P2/H/691
Richd., husb. and yeo., Barford St M., 1685, I, W, P2/H/848

Richd., yeo., Marl., 1706, I, W, P1/H/640
Richd., Warm., 1722, AB, P2/H/1192
Richd., Midgham, Thatcham, Berks., 1726, W, P1/H/820, P1/7Reg/106B
Richd., Gt. Bedwyn, 1733, AB, P21/9/4
Richd., tailor, Trowb., 1741, W, P1/H/992, P1/9Reg/172B
Hawkens, Richd., Donhead St My., 1815, AB, comm, Wr, P2/1815/54
Robt., yeo., Chipp., 1611, W, P3/H/68
Robt., yeo., Purton, 1615, I, W, P3/H/108
Robt., sen., Wilton, Gt. Bedwyn, 1633, I, P21/1/14
Robt., shoemaker, Marl. St My., 1635, comm, I, W, P1/H/209
Hawkins alias Lightfoot, Robt., yeo., Wilton, Gt. Bedwyn, 1644, I, W, P21/1/56
Robt., Bremhill, 1665, AB, P1/H/365
Robt., sen., yeo., Wilton, Gt. Bedwyn, 1703, I, W, P21/6/15
Robt., yeo., Grittenham, Brinkw., 1706, I, W, P3/H/862
Robt., esquire and bach., Hardenhuish, 1709, AB, I (detailed), ren, P3/H/893
Robt., Tidcombe, T. and Fosbury, 1739, AB, P3/H/1158
Robt., yeo., Martin, Hants, 1741, AB, I, P1/H/977
Robt., Steeple A., 1762, AB, P2/H/1454
Robt., brickmaker, Bedwyn Brail, Gt. Bedwyn, 1766, W, P21/10/68
Robt., grocer, Sal., 1768, W, P4/1768/6
Robt., yeo., Gt. Bedwyn, 1779, W, P5/1779/8, P5/17Reg/173
Robt., yeo., Gt. Bedwyn, 1802, W, P21/12/3
Robt., Uffc., Devon, 1833, AB, Wr, P5/1833/22
Roger, Enmore Grn, Motc., Dorset, 1669, I, P19/16
Hakins alias Gold, Roger, Wilsford nr Pewsey, 1702, AB, I, P2/H/1010
Sam., carp., Westrop, Corsham, 1837, W, Wr, P3/1837/78
Sarah, widow, Stockcloses, Aldbourne, 1837, comm, W, Wr, P3/1837/72
Sarah, sp., Sal. The Close, 1842, AB, Wr, P5/1842/1
Thos., Kington St M., 1609, AB, P3/H/43
Thos., Chr. M., 1614, AB, I, proclamation, P1/H/96
Hawkens, Thos., sen., ploughwright, Gastard, Corsham, 1618, AB, I, W, P29/H/21, P29/1Reg/81B
Thos., weaver, Bishopstrow, 1619, I, T, P2/H/337
Thos., husb. and yeo., Cleverton, Lea and C., 1625, I, W, P1/H/220
Thos., vintner, Sal., 1636, AB, a/c, I (2), I (detailed), P4/1636/12
Thos., carrier, N. Bradley, 1638, AB, I, P2/H/506
Thos., Langley Burrell, 1646, AB, P1/H/271
Hawkins alias Tinker, Thos., victualler, Devizes, 1646, AB, comm, I, P1/H/272
Thos., yeo., Wilton, Gt. Bedwyn, 1694, W, P21/5/23
Thos., yeo. *or* husb., Kington L., 1694, I, W, P3/H/743
Thos., gent., Hardenhuish, 1697, I, W, P3/H/768
Thos., Poulshot, 1705, AB, P2/H/1034
Thos., Wexcombe, Grafton, 1715, W, P21/7/24
Thos., yeo., Urchf., 1716, W, P2/H/1134
Thos., yeo., Wexcombe, Grafton, 1724, W, P21/8/23
Thos., yeo., Collingbourne D., 1789, comm, W, P21/11/31
Walter, carp., Poulshot, 1572, W (working tools listed), P2/5Reg/143A
Hawkins alias Gold, Wm., Wilsford nr Pewsey, 1566, W, P2/4Reg/224B
Wm., jun., silk weaver, Sherb., Dorset, 1667, I, P5/1667/31
Wm., shoemaker, Minety, 1672, AB, I, P3/H/464
Wm., husb., Purton, 1677, I, NW, P3/H/526
Wm., butcher and victualler, Devizes, 1698, I, W, P1/H/592
Wm., Southwick, N. Bradley, 1703, I, W, P2/H/1018
Wm., husb., Brimpton, Berks., 1714, AB, I, P1/H/701
Wm., yeo., Frilford, Marcham, Berks., 1756, AB, ren, W, P1/H/1116, P1/11Reg/263A
Wm., Pott., 1764-67, AB (2), P1/H/1177
Wm., Tidcombe, T. and Fosbury, 1767, AB, P1/H/1188
Wm., Gt. Bedwyn, 1773, W, P5/1773/19, P5/17Reg/62
Wm., innholder, Wootton B., 1797, I, W, P3/H/1523
Wm., Urchf., 1801, AB, P2/1801/7
Hawkens, Wm., farmer, Sutton M., 1820, W, Wr, P2/1820/38

Wm., Calne, 1826, AB, Wr, P26/1360
Wm., maltster, Angel Inn, High St., Wootton B., 1836, comm, W, Wr, P3/1836/46
Hawkins alias Shipton, Wm., wheelwright, Gt. Somerford, 1849, O, W, Wr, P3/1849/15
Zachariah, weaver, Wilton, 1848, W, Wr, P1/1848/43
see also Lightfoot alias H.; Tinker alias H.
Hawks *see* Hawkes
Hawksworth *see* Hawkesworth
Hawkyer, Wm., Uffc., Devon, 1706, W, P20/1/144
Hawly, Wm., gardener, Melk., 1722, I, W, copy W, P2/H/1191
Hawson *see* Howson
Hawthorne, Hawten, Geo., Rodbourne, Malm., 1621, AB, a/c, I (2), P3/H/160
Hawtine, Geo., yeo., Startley, Gt. Somerford, 1668, comm, I, W, P1/H/388
Hawtaine, Hy., [clothier], Devizes St Jn., 1685, AB, I, P1/H/493
Jn., gent., Hawthorn, Warfield & Hurst, Berks., 1645, comm, I, W, P1/H/263
Hawthyn, Margery, widow, Rodbourne, Malm., 1625, I, W, P3/H/197
Stephen, Wokm., Berks., 1614, AB, comm, I, P5/1614/29, P5/9Reg/143A
Hawtrell *see* Hatherell
Hay *see* Hayes
Hayard *see* Hayward
Haycock, Jos., Chipp., 1775, AB, comm, P3/H/1409
Haycraft, Dionysius, yeo., Fyfield, Berks., 1747, W, P1/H/1035, P1/10Reg/92A
Haycroft, Thos., brick burner, Welford, Berks., 1750, W, P1/H/1072, P1/10Reg/369B
Hayden, Ann, widow, Idmiston, 1593, I, W, P2/H/126
Benj., yeo., S. Newton, 1728, I, W, P2/H/1223
Benj., merchant, Netherh., 1756, W, P2/H/1417
Benj., yeo., Durrington, 1804, W, P2/1804/8
Heydon, Bernard, husb., Wambrook, Somerset, 1631, I, W, P5/1631/51, P5/12Reg/5B
Cuthbert, husb., Gt. Amesb., 1643, AB, I, P2/H/567
Geo., sen., broad weaver, Netherh., 1695-96, I, T (child: Rebecca H.), W, P2/H/957, 968
Haydon, Geo., Netherh., 1731, AB, a/c, P2/H/1253
Haydon, Hy., Idmiston, 1558, AB, P2/3Reg/129B
Heydon, Jas., yeo., Littleworth, Gt. Faringdon, Berks., 1671, I, W, P5/1671/44
Haydon, Jas., perfumer, Sal., 1818, W, Wr, P4/1818/14
Jas., N. Bradley, 1837, AB, O, ren, Wr, P2/1837/3
Jennifer, widow, Maddington, 1832, W, Wr, P1/1832/129
Jn., yeo., Amesb., 1704, I, W, P2/H/1025
Jn., victualler, Tilsh., 1766, AB, I, P2/H/1488
Jn., Netherh., 1769, AB, P2/H/1512
Haydon, Leonard, yeo., Wambrook, Somerset, 1622, I, W, P5/1622/36, P5/10Reg/124
Haydon, Nich., Bathampton, Steeple L., 1661, AB, I, W, P2/H/608
Nich., Gt. Bathampton, Steeple L., 1666, AB, P2/H/636
Heydon, Petronel, widow, Wambrook, Somerset, 1638, AB, I, T (re Bernard, Mgt. & Thomasine H.), P5/1638/54, P5/13Reg/73A
Robt., Martin, Hants, 1588, AB, I, W, P2/H/85, P2/7Reg/137A
Robt., broad weaver, Wilton, 1665, AB, P2/H/628
Robt., miller, Lt. Woodford, 1846, W, Wr, P13/6/15
Haydon, Sarah, sp., Lyme R., Dorset, 1837, AB, O, Wr, P16/416
Haydon, Simon, husb., Wambrook, Somerset, 1622, comm, I, W, P5/1622/35, P5/10Reg/129
Heyden, Thos., yeo., Lake, Wilsford with L., 1623-24, I, W, P5/1623/15, P5/10Reg/166A
Haydon, Thos., Milston, 1682, I, P2/H/803
Thos., Brigmerston, Milston, 1757, W, P2/H/1424
Thos., minors, Netherh., 1827, T, P2/1827/74
Wm., Britford, 1605, AB, W, P24/20
Haydon, Wm., bach., Wanb., 1736, AB, I, P3/H/1130
Wm., gent., Milston, 1811, W, Wr, P1/1811/126
Wm., Netherh., 1827, AB, W, Wr, P2/1827/73
Wm., Durrington, 1847, D, W, Wr, P2/1847/42
Haydes, Eliz., Fordington, Dorset, 1573, AB, P5/3Reg/19D
Haydock, Thos., esquire, Bury Blunsdon, Highw., 1612, I, P5/1612/21
Haydon *see* Hayden

Hayes, ?, husb., Winterslow, [1607], W, P2/H/241
Abraham, Ashton G., Codf. St P., [1684], I, P2/H/829
Abraham, yeo., Ditchampton, Wilton, 1686, AB, I, W, P1/H/496
Abraham, weaver, Wilton, 1743, I, W, P2/H/1342
Alexander, Winterslow, 1551, AB, P2/2Reg/121B
Hays, Alexander, Sherston, 1638, I, W, P1/H/237
Alexander, tailor, Sherston, 1703, I (informative re tailoring), W, P3/H/839
Alice, widow, Kingston D., 1673, I, W, P2/H/715
Hayse, Ann, widow, Tytherington, Heytes., 1684, I, W, P5/1684/30
Anstis, Inkpen, Berks., 1622, AB, I, P1/H/155
Christian, widow, Sherston, 1671, I, W, P3/H/454
Hay, Christian, widow, Shalbourne, 1710, I, W, P5/1710/51, P5/15Reg/189
Chris., yeo., Wilton, 1679, I, W, P2/H/772
Edith, widow, Quidh., 1666, I, W, P2/H/637
Hay alias Archard, Edith, widow, Hankerton, 1729, AB, ren, W, P1/H/846, P1/7Reg/305
Hays, Edwd., yeo., Enmore Grn, Motc., Dorset, 1742, AB, P19/133
Edwd., sen., cooper, Chetnole, Yetm., Dorset, 1804, comm, W, P19/206
Haye, Eliz., Pewsey, 1563?, W (undated, but context suggests 1563), P1/2Reg/121C
Eliz., widow, Odstock, [1685], W, P2/H/863
Eliz., widow, Enmore Grn, Motc., Dorset, 1771, W, P19/169
Geo., Wilton, 1852, AB, Wr, P2/1852/32
Gilbert, Chute Forest, Chute, 1822, AB, Wr, P7/197
Hayes alias Archard, Giles, yeo., Hankerton, 1718, I, W, P3/H/956
Hy., clerk and vicar, Sherston, 1678, AB, a/c, I (last 2 on same sheet), P3/H/527
Hy., rector, Castle C., 1715, AB, P1/H/715
Hy., gent., Devizes, 1733, appt of proctor, comm, ren, P1/H/917
Hy., gent., Devizes, 1765, W, P1/H/1178, P1/12Reg/151B
Hy., labourer, Westport St My., 1848, D, W, Wr, P3/1848/35
Isaac, chapman, Aldbourne, 1614, AB, I, NW, P3/H/99
Isaac, Littleton Drew, 1717, AB, I, P3/H/951
Jas., maltster, Warm., 1739, W, P2/H/1314
Jas., gent., Fisherton A., 1851, D, W, Wr, P1/1851/8
Joan, widow, Laverstock, 1632, I, W, P2/H/444, P2/9Reg/47
Joan, tailor's widow, Sherston, 1704, I, W, P3/H/846
Joanna, widow, Marl., 1685, W, P1/H/494
Joel, butcher, Chards., Devon, 1803, W, P5/1803/50, P5/19Reg/83
Jn., brewer, Wilton, 1558, I, W, P2/H/6, P2/3Reg/122C
Jn., clerk and parson, Lydiard M., 1571, W, P1/1Reg/29A
Jn., Hungerford, Berks., 1582, AB, I, T, P5/1582/32, P5/4Reg/49A
Jn., husb., Brinkw., [1607], W (NEP), P3/H/26
Jn., broad weaver, Trowb., 1611, I, W, P1/H/61
Jn., sen., Wilton, 1627, AB, I, P2/H/392
Hay, Jn., tailor, Corsham, 1632, I, P29/H/31
Jn., sen., White Hill, Mere, 1635, AB, a/c, I, P5/1635/46, P5/12Reg/172A
Jn., clerk, Overton, 1635, AB, I, P1/H/213
Jn., yeo., Durley, Burbage, 1640, I, W, P11/12
Jn., Sal. St Martin, 1667, ren, P4/1667/33
Hayes alias Archard, Jn., sen., yeo., Crudwell, 1672, AB, I, P3/H/465
Jn., Kingston D., 1676, AB, I, P2/H/735
Jn., yeo., Chisbury, Lt. Bedwyn, 1679, comm, I, W, P21/2/64
Jn., butcher, Sherston, 1686, a/c (2), AB, comm, I, P3/H/625
Jn., yeo. *or* husb., Nettleton, 1686, I, W, P3/H/624
Hay, Jn., sen., yeo., Shalbourne, 1702, I, W, P23/251
Hay, Jn., yeo., Shalbourne, 1719, W, P5/1719/41, P5/16Reg/24B
Hays alias Archard, Jn., yeo., Crudwell, 1732, W, P3/H/1101
Jos., jun., labourer, Chute, 1702-06, AB, I, W, P7/88, 95
Hay alias Archard, Joyce, widow, Crudwell, 1634, AB, I, P1/H/199
Mgt., widow, Durley, Burbage, 1661, AB, I, P5/1661/26
Margery, widow, Chisbury, Lt. Bedwyn, 1639, I, W, P21/1/53
My., sp., Sonning, Berks., 1681, comm, W, P5/1680/22

My., widow, Devizes, 1760, AB, P1/H/1154
Matthew, woolstapler, Knook (form. of Corton, Boyton), 1701, I, W, P5/1701/31
Haye, Peter, currier, Sal., 1736, W, Wr, P4/1736/9
Philip, miller, Sherston, 1729, W, P3/H/1058
Richd., yeo., Wilton, 1672, court papers, I, W, P2/H/703
Richd., husb. and yeo., Baverstock, [1675], I, W, P2/H/724
Richd., yeo., Inkpen, Berks., 1741, W, P1/H/984, P1/9Reg/109
Richd., yeo., Longbridge D., 1777, W, P2/H/1571
Haye, Robt., innholder, Sherston, 1607, W, P3/2Reg/15A
Robt., Kingston D., 1721, AB, P2/H/1185
Robt., Sherston, 1811, W, Wr, P1/1811/84
Hayse, Roger, Tytherington, Heytes., 1663, AB, I, P5/1662/63
Hay, Sam., the Honourable, Cliffe Hall, Mkt. L., 1847, AB, O, Wr, P2/1847/70
Hay alias Archard, Sarah, yeo.'s wife, Eastcourt, Crudwell, 1692, W, P3/H/708
Stephen, husb., Quidh., 1635, I, W, P2/H/469
Thos., yeo., Savernake Forest, Burbage, 1576, W, P5/3Reg/97A
Hey, Thos., yeo., Lt. Bedwyn, 1587, I, W, P5/1587/51, P5/4Reg/145B
Thos., Wilton, 1613, AB, a/c, I, P1/H/69
Thos., sen., mercer *or* chapman, Aldbourne, 1614, I, W, P3/H/100
Thos., mercer, Aldbourne, 1688, I, W, P3/H/650
Hay, Thos., tailor, Marl., 1689, I, W, P1/H/519
Thos., curate, Alton B., 1698, AB, I, P3/H/774
Thos., yeo., Winterbrook, Cholsey, Berks., 1750, W, P1/H/1070, P1/10Reg/352
Thos., Winterbourne G., 1777, AB, P2/H/1570
Thos., yeo., Durley, Burbage, 1695, I, W, P5/1695/49
Wm., Winterslow, 1576, W, P2/5Reg/272A
Wm., no abode stated, 1596, note of admon, P2/H/155
Hayse, Wm., husb., Tytherington, Heytes., 1603, AB, I, W, P5/1603/35, P5/7Reg/74A
Wm., Broad C., 1630, AB, a/c, P2/H/423
Wm., husb., Laverstock, 1632, I, W, P2/H/440, P2/9Reg/60B
Hayse, Wm., husb., Knook, 1636, I, W, P5/1636/28, P5/12Reg/255D
Wm., baker, Marl., 1641, I, W, P1/H/254
Wm., husb., Ditchampton, Wilton, 1645, I, T, W, P2/H/577
Wm., sen., gent., Devizes St My., 1684, I, W, P1/H/490
Wm., Devizes, 1700, AB, P1/H/607
Wm., Hampstead Marshall, Berks., 1708, AB, I, P1/H/648
Wm., gent., Devizes, 1714-15, W, P1/H/713, P1/5Reg/472
Wm., weaver, Wilton, 1777, W, P2/H/1567
Wm., woolcomber, Tetbury, Gloucs & Crudwell, 1789, AB, comm, ren, P3/H/1487
Wm., labourer, Sherston, 1812, note, W, Wr, P3/1812/47
see also Archard alias H.; Nicholls alias H.
Hayle, Hayles *see* Hale
Haylock, Alice, Motc., Dorset, 1709, AB, P27/1/179
Bartholomew, Sal. St Edmd., 1663, I, W, P4/1663/8
Dorothy, widow, Motc., Dorset, 1676, AB, NW, P27/1/49
Hy., yeo., Ebbesborne Wake, 1631, I, W, P2/H/434, P2/9Reg/117B
Jas., clothworker, Sal. St Thos., 1638, AB, I, P4/1638/17
Joan, widow, Ebbesborne Wake, 1604, AB, I, P2/H/218
Haylock *or* Halock, Jn., Donhead St My., 1552, I, W, P2/H/5, P2/2Reg/162C
Jn., Tisb., 1589, I (very detailed), T, W, P2/H/93
Jn., labourer, Broad C., 1707, AB, I, P2/H/1056
Jn., yeo., Ansty, 1716, W, P1/H/724, P1/6Reg/21
Hallick, Jn., Tisb., 1716, AB, P2/H/1130
Jn., Tisb., 1718, AB, P2/H/1148
Richd., Tisb., 1670, AB, a/c, P2/H/670
Richd., Tisb., 1730, W, P2/H/1246
Susan, widow, Sal., 1674, AB, I, W, P4/1673/12
Hallock, Thos., Hindon, 1686, AB, I, P2/H/868
Thos., Semley, 1726, NW, P2/H/1213
Wm., husb., Ebbesborne Wake, 1604, AB, I, W, P2/H/219

Wm., innholder, Sal., 1675, AB, a/c, I, ren, P4/1675/12
Wm., no abode stated, [1675], I, P2/H/729
Hayme, Alice, widow, Semley, 1624, I, W, P2/H/371
Dorothy, widow, Groves Place, Donhead St My., [1674], I, W, P2/H/720
Eliz., widow, Motc., Dorset, 1738, AB, I, Wr, P27/1/350
Jn., Wolverton, Zeals, 1585, AB, P5/4Reg/107D
Jn., Kingston D., 1675, AB, I (2), W, P2/H/727
Phineas, grocer, Donhead St My., 1660, AB, I, ren, P2/H/605
Robt., tailor, Groves Place, Donhead St My., 1671, comm, I, W, P2/H/680
Haymond *see* Hammond
Haynes, Agnes, widow, Crickl. St My., [1607], W (NEP), P3/H/27
Alexander, milliner, Fisherton A., 1632, AB, NW, P2/H/438
Alexander, bellfounder, Sal., 1637, I, W, P4/1637/8
Hayne, Alice, widow, Donhead St A., 1562, W, P2/4Reg/107C
Haine, Alice, widow, Sherb., Dorset, 1676, AB, I, P5/1675/23
Haines, Alice, sp., Latton (form. of Cirencester, Gloucs), 1817, comm, W, Wr, P1/1817/110
Hains, Ann, Buscot, Berks., 1692, W, P1/H/552
Ann, widow, Netheravon, 1735, AB, P12/162
Ann, widow, Ashton K., 1735, I, W, P3/H/1126
Arthur, collarmaker, Sal., 1661, AB, I, P4/1661/6
Hayne, Benj., Sherb., Dorset, 1638, AB, I, P5/1638/52, P5/13Reg/84A
Haines, Bridget, widow, Alderton, 1632, I, W, P3/H/261
Edith, widow, Gt. Somerford, 1626, I, W, P3/H/202
Hayns, Edwd., sen., husb., Figh., 1671, I, W, P26/183
Haines, Edwd., gardener, Warm., 1701, I, W, P2/H/1006
Haines, Edwd., victualler, Warm., 1777, W, P2/H/1566
Haines, Edwd., Warm., 1789, AB, P2/H/1641
Hains, Edwd., Warm., 1824, AB, Wr, P2/1824/4
Eleanor, widow, Crickl. St S., 1608, I, P1/H/56
Eynes, Eliz., widow, Biddestone St Nich., [1601], W, P3/1Reg/84
Haines, Eliz., widow, Steeple L., 1638, I, NW, P2/H/504
Hayne, Eliz., Holnest, Dorset, 1679, AB, I, P5/1679/45
Eliz., widow, Bugley, Warm., 1713, I, W, P2/H/1110
Haines, Eliz., widow, Hannington, 1764, W, P3/H/1350
Haines, Francis, carp., New Windsor, Berks., 1714, I, draft I, W, P1/H/697, P1/5Reg/353B
Haines, Frederick, silversmith, Sherb., Dorset, 1856, aff, W, Wr, P5/1856/10
Garrett, yeo., Ford, Laverstock, 1663, AB, I, P1/H/336
Geoffrey, miller, Friars Mill, Shrivenham, Berks., 1662, I, W, P1/H/322
Geo., weaver, Alderton, [1610], W (NEP), P3/H/55
Hy., husb., Corsley, 1684, AB, comm, I, NW, P2/H/837
Haines, Hy., Warm., 1804, AB, P2/1804/22
Hains, Jas., yeo., Hannington, 1713, W, P3/H/924
Haines, Jas., Trowb., 1734, AB (2), P1/H/923, P1/7Reg/597B
Haines, Jas., Warm., 1789, AB, P2/H/1643
Haines, Jas., baker and farmer, Erlestoke, 1823, W, Wr, P2/1823/7
Haimes, Jas., Gillingham, Dorset, 1828, W, P27/1/683
Hains, Jemima, widow, Warm., 1805, AB, P2/1805/42
Haines, Joan, widow, Abingdon, Berks., 1605, I, W, P1/H/31
Joan, widow, Bemerton, Fugg. St Peter, 1680, AB, I, P2/H/781
Haines, Jn., yeo., Reading, Berks., 1620, I, W, P1/H/145
Jn., Sal., 1628, AB, I, P4/1628/10
Haines *or* Hayme, Jn., husb., Steeple L., 1635, I, W, P2/H/467, P2/9Reg/52A
Jn., no abode stated, 1666, I, P30/86
Haines, Jn., yeo., Hannington, 1681, I, W, P3/H/550
Haines, Jn., [brewer], Blewbury, Berks., 1731, AB, I, P5/1731/40, P5/1732/54
Haines, Jn., E. Harnham, Britford, 1732, AB, P5/1732/19
Hayne, Jn., Stratton, Dorset, 1736, AB, comm, P5/1736/16
Haines, Jn., yeo., Winterbourne G., 1750, W, P1/H/1062, P1/10Reg/304
Haines, Jn., Crickl. St S., 1814, AB, comm, P1/1814/38
Hains, Jn., gent., Crickl. St S., 1823, W, Wr, P1/1823/115

Haines, Jn., yeo., Aldbourne, 1830, O, W, Wr, P3/1830/63
Jos., collarmaker, St Nich.'s Hospital, The Close, Sal., 1658, I, P4/1658/1
Jos., shoemaker, Netheravon, 1746, W, P5/1746/40
Lewis, yeo., Netheravon, 1737, W, P12/164
Haines, Martha, widow, Wantage, Berks., 1787, comm, W, P23/784
Heynes, My., widow, Figh., 1681, I, W, P26/279
Hains, Melior, widow, Longbridge D., 1721, W, P1/H/780, P1/6Reg/372A
Michael, gardener, Baverstock, 1694, I, W, P2/H/941
Haines, Michael, yeo., Maggot Mill Farm, Highw., 1771, comm, W, P10/1771/1
Haine, Nich., Bere R., Dorset, 1581, I, W, P5/1581/12, P5/4Reg/32D
Olive, widow, Ashton K., 1739, AB, P3/H/1161
Oliver, blacksmith, Ashton K., 1727, W, P3/H/1035
Phineas, bach., Sal., 1683, AB, I, P1/H/471
Richd., blacksmith, Ashton K., 1689, I, W, P3/H/663
Haines, Richd., yeo., Hannington Wick, 1712, W, P3/H/916
Richd., collarmaker, Crickl. St S., 1727, AB, I, W, P3/H/1036
Richd., Wanb., 1738, AB, P3/H/1155
Haines, Richd., Netheravon, 1805, W, P12/207
Hayns, Richd., Westb., 1811, AB, P25/1811/1
Haines, Richd., shoemaker and shopkeeper, Burcombe, 1849, W, Wr, P2/1849/16
Hayne, Robt., sen., Donhead St A., 1546, W (incomplete) (NEP), P2/2Reg/41B
Robt., Hungerford, Berks., 1637, W (abode missing but Robt. H., aged over 100, buried in H. 1637), P30/84
Robt., yeo., Corsley, 1688, I, W, P2/H/897
Haines, Robt., husb., Pott., 1701, I, W, P1/H/612
Haines, Robt., sen., farmer, Chisenbury, Enford (described as being of Chisenbury, Netheravon), 1711, I, W., P5/1711/25, P5/15Reg/241B
Haines, Robt., sen., blacksmith, Ashton K., 1737, W, P3/H/1134
Robt., Figh., 1742, AB, I, P26/837
Hayns, Robt., maltster, Ashton K., 1770, W, P1/H/1205, P1/12Reg/335
Robt., Corsley, 1821, W, Wr, P2/1821/48
Sam., dyer, Bulk., Keevil, 1681, AB, I, P2/H/789
Haines, Sarah, sp., Figh. (form. of Sal.), 1815, AB, P26/1300
Hayne, Thos., Hurst, Berks., 1540, W, P5/20Reg/19A
Hayne, Thos., Enmore Grn, Motc., Dorset, 1604, AB, I, W, P5/1604/18, P5/8Reg/10A
Thos., husb., Gt. Somerford, [1611], I, W (NEP), P3/H/69
Thos., yeo., Netheravon, 1726, AB, I, P12/153
Haines, Thos., innholder, Wantage, Berks., 1762, comm, W, P23/703
Thos., sen., gent., Netherton, Fyfield, Berks., 1767, W, P1/H/1194, P1/12Reg/254A
Haines, Thos., labourer, Aldbourne, 1803, W, P3/1803/23
Heyne, Walter, Semley, 1571, W, P1/1Reg/27A
Hayne, Wm., Donhead St A., 1574, W, P2/5Reg/203B
Hayne, Wm., yeo., Donhead St My., 1602, I, W (2), NW, P2/H/203
Hayne, Wm., yeo., Holnest, Dorset, 1616, comm, I, W, P5/1616/33, P5/9Reg/179A
Haines, Wm., Netheravon, 1665, AB, I, P12/93
Wm., yeo., Sal., 1678, AB, W, P4/1678/7
Wm., sergemaker, Melk., 1685, AB, I, P2/H/852
Wm., fuller and dyer, Keevil, 1701, W, P2/H/1004
Haines, Wm., dyer, Bulk., Keevil, 1704, I, W, P1/H/628
Wm., Netheravon, 1732, AB, P5/1732/21
Hains, Wm., labourer, Crickl. St S., 1769, AB, W, P3/H/1381
Haines, Wm., baker, Lacock, 1816, W, Wr, P3/1816/29
Haines, Wm., Somerford K., 1853, AB, O, Wr, P3/1853/43
see also Cullerne alias H.; Hann; Lennard alias H.
Hayord *see* Hayward
Hays, Hayse *see* Hayes
Haysome, Avis, widow, Bere R., Dorset, 1670, AB, comm, I, P5/1670/18
Dorcas, widow, Anderson, Dorset, 1697, I, W, P5/1696/22
Eliz., widow, Rams., 1752, W, P5/1752/27
Jn., widow, Martin, Hants, 1662, AB, a/c, I, P2/H/616
Jn., husb., Kingston D., 1669, AB, I, P2/H/666

Robt., clerk and rector, Lt. Langford, 1694, AB, I, P1/H/564
Thos., Shitterton, Bere R., Dorset, 1662, AB, I, P5/1662/66
Hayter, Heyter, [male], Chitterne St My., 1616, a/c, P2/H/1698
Abigail, widow, Teffont E., 1676, I, W, P2/H/731
Alice, widow, Downton, 1737, AB, P2/H/1304
Ambrose, Hurdcott, Winterbourne E., 1765, AB, I, P2/H/1478
Andrew, Wilton, 1726, AB, I, P1/H/829
Ann, widow, Wylye, 1765, W, P2/H/1480
Ann, esquire's widow, Sal. The Close (leaving goods at Lea), 1812, AB, Wr, P3/1812/15
Anthony, yeo., Barford St M., 1645, AB, I, P2/H/575
Anthony, tailor, Heytes., 1685, I, W, P5/1685/52
Anthony, yeo., Chitterne AS, 1758, W, P2/H/1430
Augustine, clerk and rector, Sutton M., 1709-10, AB (2), I (2), P1/H/660
Augustine, yeo., Salterton, Durnford, 1724, W, P9/42
Augustine, Landford, 1833, AB, W, Wr, P2/1833/79
Betty, widow, Dinton, 1791, AB, P2/H/1654
Cath. *see also* Eliz.
Chas., Witherington Farm, Standlynch, Downton, 1748, AB, P2/H/1378
Edwd., husb., Ugford, S. Newton, 1631, AB, I, petition, P1/H/186
Edwd., blacksmith, W. Grimstead, [1677], I, P2/H/744
Edwd., bach., Dinton, 1823, W, Wr, P2/1823/25
Eliz., Teffont E., 1637, I, NW, P2/H/482
Eliz., widow, Chitterne St My., 1643, I, W, P2/H/565
Eliz., widow, Chitterne St My., 1667, I, W, P2/H/645
Eliz. *or* Cath., widow, Gt. Wishford, [1681], I, W, P2/H/792
Eliz., widow, Tytherington, Heytes., 1716, W, P5/1716/35, P5/15Reg/335A
Eliz., widow, Witherington Farm, Standlynch, Downton, 1729, AB, P1/H/874
Eliz., widow, Newton T., 1810, AB, Wr, P2/1810/29
Emma, widow, Winterbourne G., 1828, W, Wr, P2/1828/56
Fortune, widow, Wylye, 1695, I, W, P2/H/958
Heyter, Geo., yeo., Tisb., 1593?, W, P2/H/133
Haytor, Geo., yeo., Ugford, S. Newton, 1732, W, P2/H/1263
Geo., cooper, Gillingham, Dorset, 1782, W, P27/1/510, P27/3Reg/225
Geo. Holmes, Tisb., 1819, AB, Wr, P2/1819/46
Hannah, widow, Salterton, Durnford, 1739, W, Wr, P9/54
Hannah, widow, Brown St., Sal., 1855, aff, W, Wr, P4/1855/8
Harry, Dinton, 1811, AB, Wr, P2/1811/15
Hy., Clarendon Park, 1667, a/c (2), AB, I, P4/1666/1
Hy., sen., yeo., Witherington Farm, Standlynch, Downton, 1719, I, W, P2/H/1170
Jas., cordw., Wilton, 1722, I, W, P2/H/1196
Jas., gent., Sal., 1748, AB, P4/1748/14
Jas., Sal. (leaving effects at Hazelbury, Box), 1790, AB, P3/H/1492
Jane, Wilton, 1647, I, W, P2/H/585
Jane, sp., Dinton, 1647, AB, I, NW, P2/H/592
Joan, widow, Barford St M., 1622, W, copy W, P2/H/360
Joan, widow, Monkton D., 1640, AB, I, P2/H/537
Heyter, Jn., Teffont E., 1558, W, P2/3Reg/111C
Jn., Hindon, 1558, AB, P2/3Reg/101F
Jn., Longbridge D., 1559, W, P2/3Reg/179B
Heytor, Jn., husb., Chitterne St My., 1567, W, P2/5Reg/24C
Jn., Odstock, 1569, AB, P2/5Reg/69A
Jn., S. Newton, 1569, AB, P2/5Reg/80B
Jn., husb., Dinton, 1609, AB, I, W, P2/H/254, P2/8Reg/70B
Jn., Ugford, S. Newton, 1613, W, P1/H/70
Jn., sen., yeo., Britford, 1632, AB, I (detailed), W, P24/258
Jn., husb., Wick, Downton, 1637, AB, a/c, I, P2/H/488
Jn., sen., Chitterne St My., 1642, AB, I, P2/H/560
Jn., yeo., Dinton, 1670, I, W, P2/H/669
Jn., Barford St M., 1670-71, AB, a/c, P2/H/675
Jn., Baverstock, 1692, AB, I, P2/H/927

Jn., yeo., Gt. Wishford, 1695, I, W, P2/H/955
Jn., Wilton, 1703, AB, P2/H/1021
Jn., Whitep., 1711, AB, P1/H/681
Jn., Horningsham, 1727, AB, I, P5/1727/24
Jn., tailor, Zeals, 1728, AB, consent, I, W, P5/1728/47, P5/16Reg/209B
Jn., Amesb., 1739, AB, I, P2/H/1312
Jn., Dilton M., Westb., 1739, W, P25/1739/1
Jn., clothworker, Bradford A., 1751, W, P2/H/1399
Jn., yeo., Witherington Farm, Standlynch, Downton, 1755, W, P2/H/1411
Jn., Downton, 1758, AB, P2/H/1434
Jn., Gt. Durnford, 1758, W, P5/1758/23
Jn., yeo., Barford St M., 1760, W, P2/H/1445
Jn., yeo., Dinton, 1767, AB, P2/H/1498
Jn., sen., haycutter, Warm., 1802, W (father of Jn. H., P2/1802/78), P2/1802/77
Jn., sen., haycutter, The Common, Warm., 1802, W, Wr (son of Jn. H. P2/1802/77), P2/1802/78
Jn., Salterton, Durnford, 1804, W, P9/99
Jn., maltster, Teffont M., 1815, W, Wr, P2/1815/47
Jn., Gillingham, Dorset, 1826, comm, W, Wr, P27/1/670
Jn., gent., Scots Lane, Sal., 1842, aff, W, Wr, P1/1842/16
Jos., Sal., 1777, AB, P1/H/1251
Leonard, Gt. Wishford, 1612-16, AB, a/c, I, T, P2/H/296, P2/8Reg/186A
Heyter, Lucy, widow, E. Knoyle, 1552, I, W, P2/H/4, P2/2Reg/163A
Lucy alias Rebecca, sp., Sal., 1847, D, W, Wr, P4/1847/13
Mgt., widow, Winterbourne E., 1584, W, P2/6Reg/136B
Mgt., widow, Sal., 1661, I, W, P4/1661/13
My., widow, Chute, 1671, I, W, P5/1671/42
My., sp., Teffont E., [1687], I, W, P2/H/884
My., widow, Pitton, Alderbury, 1737, W, P26/798
My., widow, Downton, 1758, W, P2/H/1432
My., Durnford, 1760, W, P9/73
My., sp., W. Harnham, 1790, W, P4/1790/6
My., widow, Downton, 1832, AB, Wr, P2/1832/38
My., wife, Sal., 1840, W, Wr, P1/1840/22
Moses, Clarendon Park, 1799, AB, P4/1799/5
Nich., Winterbourne E., 1619, AB, P2/H/332
Heyter, Nich., yeo., Barford St M., [1679], I, W, P2/H/771
Nich., Sal., 1693, AB, P4/1692/16
Nich., sen., Barford St M., 1712, W, P2/H/1095
Nich., Barford St M., 1738, AB, I, P1/H/954
Richd., Ditchampton, Wilton, 1621, W, P2/H/354
Richd., yeo., Britford, 1626, AB, a/c, I, P24/172
Richd., husb., Barford St M., 1628, comm, I, copy I, T, W, copy W, P2/H/403
Richd., yeo., W. Grimstead, 1684, AB, I, W, P2/H/835
Richd., yeo., Motc., Dorset, 1698-1700, a/c, appt of guardian, court paper, I, note, T (dispute between brothers, guardians of his children, & his widow, remarried to Robt. Lilly, re admon of estate), P27/1/140
Richd., Winterbourne E., 1737, AB, P2/H/1295
Robt., yeo., Fugg. St Peter, 1629, I, W, P2/H/407
Robt., sen., husb., Dinton, 1638, I, W, P1/H/230
Robt., Wylye, 1678, I, W, P2/H/761
Robt., yeo., Wylye, 1718, I, W, P2/H/1155
Robt., sen., cordw., Dinton, 1751, W, P2/H/1400
Robt., shoemaker, Dinton, 1766, W, P2/H/1484
Saul, Codf. St P., 1696, AB, I, P2/H/965
Sibyl, Britford, 1611, I, W, P24/138
Stephen, Barford St M., 1760, AB, P2/H/1443
Stephen, Stratford sub C., 1782, W, P4/1782/11
Susanna, Stratford sub C., 1782, W, P4/1782/10
Susanna, widow, Salterton, Durnford, 1784, W, P9/88
Susanna, widow, Sal., 1835, W, P1/1835/46
Thos., Odstock, 1558, W, P2/3Reg/74A

Heyter, Thos., husb., Gt. Horningsham, 1563, W, P5/1Reg/23C
Heyter, Thos., potter, Studley, Calne, 1570, W, P5/2Reg/84C
Heiter *or* Heyter, Thos., Monkton D., 1616, W, P1/H/108
Thos., yeo., Ugford, S. Newton, 1623, I, W, P2/H/365
Thos., yeo., Winterbourne E., 1639, I, W, P2/H/511
Thos., gent., Chute, 1664, I, NW, P7/34
Thos., yeo., Gt. Wishford, 1681, AB, a/c, I, ren, P2/H/799
Thos., husb., Bapton, Fisherton Delamare, 1714, W, P1/H/710, P1/5Reg/452A
Thos., carp., W. Lavington, 1736, W, P1/H/945, P1/8Reg/168
Thos., gent., Dilton M., Westb., 1739, W, P25/1739/10
Thos., yeo., Wylye, 1753, W, P1/H/1086, P1/10Reg/511
Thos., gent., Wylye, 1795, W, P2/H/1676
Thos., Ashcombe, Berwick St Jn., 1804, AB, P1/1804/15
Thos., carp., Salterton, Durnford, 1836, D, O, W, Wr, P9/115
Haytor, Walter, tailor, Huntingford, Gillingham, Dorset, [1713], W, P27/1/199
Wm., Tisb., 1542, W (NEP), P30/96
Wm., Winterbourne E., 1583, W, P2/6Reg/97A
Wm., yeo., Lt. Langford, 1585, T (children: Thos., Eliz., Thomasine & My. H.), W, P2/H/69, P2/7Reg/14
Wm., Downton, 1698, AB, P1/H/597
Wm., Britford, 1710, AB, ren, W, P24/707
Wm., yeo., Clarendon Park, 1716, W, P5/1716/47, P5/15Reg/357B
Wm., Sal., 1719, AB, P4/1718/31
Wm., Downton, 1729, AB, I, P2/H/1236
Wm., bach., Durnford, 1784, AB, P9/87
Wm., innholder, Imber, 1792, W, P1/H/1325, P1/14Reg/412
Wm., esquire, Newton T., 1805, W, P2/1805/61
Wm., sen., haycutter, The Common, Warm., 1819, W, Wr, P2/1819/34
Wm., Kington L., 1827, AB, Wr, P3/1827/61
Haytery, Haytery, Francis, Sal., 1685, AB, I, P4/1685/16
Haythorne *see* Hathorne
Haytor *see* Hayter
Hayward, Haward, (Mr) *see* Geo. Symons
Abraham, labourer, Gt. Bedwyn, 1731, I, W, P21/8/67
Heywood, Agnes, widow, Wokm., Berks., 1567, W, P5/2Reg/25E
Agnes, Patney, 1576, I, W, P2/H/42, P2/5Reg/268A
Heyward, Agnes, widow, Calne, 1577, I, W, P5/1576/24, P5/3Reg/100C
Haward, Agnes, Hinton, Steeple A., 1605, I, W, P1/H/34
Heyward, Agnes, widow, Charlton nr Malm., 1610, W, P3/H/58
Heyward, Alice, widow, Sonning, Berks., 1591, I, W, P5/1591/40, P5/5Reg/113B
Heyward, Alice, Corsham, 1603, W, P29/1Reg/51
Alice, widow, Swallowcliffe, 1611, AB, a/c, comm, T, W, copy W, P5/1611/18, P5/9Reg/54C
Alice, Easterton, Mkt. L., 1663, AB, P2/H/621
Alice, sp., Calne, 1763, W, P26/999
Ambrose, maltster, Lacock, 1776, W, P1/H/1248, P1/13Reg/145
Andrew, Corsham, [1584], W, draft W, P29/H/1
Ann, widow, Calne, 1665, AB, comm, I, W, P5/1665/42, P26/117
Ann, sp., Calne, 1719, comm, W, P26/628
Ann, sp. and gentlewoman, Chirton, 1757, comm, W, P2/H/1423
Ann, widow, Broughton G., 1775, AB, P2/H/1551
Ann, widow, Wilsford nr Pewsey, 1830, O, W, Wr, P2/1830/23
Ann, widow, Chipp., 1847, W, Wr, P3/1847/21
Ann, widow, Westport St My., 1848, court proceeding, D, O, W, Wr, P3/1848/54
Ann, widow, Sutton B., 1849, W, Wr, P3/1849/21
Anthony, yeo., Seend, Melk., 1789-96, receipt, W, P1/H/1317, P1/14Reg/303
Heyward, Avis, widow, Thornhill, Clyffe P., 1612, W, P3/H/84
Hayward alias Simms, Avis, widow, Beechingstoke, 1630, AB, a/c, I, P3/H/238
Basil, widow, Ryme I., Dorset, 1700, I, W, P5/1700/13
Benj., Beechingstoke, 1731, AB (2), comm, P3/H/1088
Benj., Hankerton, 1763, AB, P3/H/1346
Benj., weaver, Yarnbrook, N. Bradley, 1824, W, Wr, P2/1824/48

Betty *see* Betty Wood
Brian, sen., Pewsey, 1673, I, NW, P3/H/475
Brian, yeo., Whitehorn Hill, Whitep., [1686], I, W, P2/H/873
Brian, yeo., Lt. Cheverell, 1713, W, P2/H/1109
Brian, bach., Corsham, 1722, marriage licence, P29/2Reg/43F
Brian, yeo., Hilcott, N. Newnton, 1729, AB, I, W, P1/H/871, P1/7Reg/336
Brian, yeo., Wilsford nr Pewsey, 1775, ren, W, P2/H/1552
Heyward, Cath., widow, Bushton, Clyffe P., 1592, I, NW, P1/H/6
Cath., Bishopstone N., 1622, AB, I, P5/1622/37, P5/10Reg/110A
Chas., yeo., Chipp., 1839, W, Wr, P3/1839/18
Christian, Brinkw., 1627, AB, P3/H/212
Heyward, Chris., Goods, Corsham, 1595, W, P29/1Reg/42A
Chris., Sedgehill, 1627, AB, I, P2/H/391
Chris., Purton, 1670, AB, I, P3/H/432
Cicely, widow, Croucheston, Bishopstone S., 1585, I, W, P2/H/70
Edith, Whitley, Melk., 1611, AB, I, P2/H/279
Edmd., Patney, 1574, W, P2/5Reg/194A
Edmd., miller, Corsham, [1638], W, P29/H/34
Edmd., husb., Milbourne, Malm., 1649, I, W, P1/H/295
Edwd., yeo., Bishopstone S., 1581, W, P2/6Reg/45C
Heyward, Edwd., Bps. C., 1588, I, W, P5/1587/26, P5/5Reg/7B
Edwd., gent., Croucheston, Bishopstone S., 1636, I, W, P2/H/476
Edwd., gent., Croucheston, Bishopstone S., 1664, AB, I, P1/H/347
Edwd., yeo., Tilsh., [1697], I, W, P2/H/972
Edwd., yeo., Tilsh., 1707, W, P2/H/1052
Edwd., sen., yeo., Nethermore (in Chipp.), Pewsham, 1714, W, P1/H/707, P1/5Reg/428A
Heyward, Edwd., broad weaver, Pickwick, Corsham, 1728, I, P29/H/106
Edwd., Petersfinger, Corsham, 1740, AB, W, P3/H/1166
Edwd., sen., yeo., Corsham, 1749, W, P29/H/116
Edwd., blacksmith, Hankerton, 1778, W, P3/H/1423
Edwd., gent., Corsham, 1802, I, P29/1800-1857/2
Edwd., labourer, Rudloe, Box, 1810, W, Wr, P3/1810/31
Edwd., yeo., Corsham, 1815, W, P29/1800-1857/16, P29/3Reg/256
Edwd., farmer, Broad B., Highw., 1844, O, W, Wr, P3/1844/41
Heyward, Edwd. *see also* Jn. Purnell
Eleanor, widow, Milbourne, Malm., 1667, I, W, P3/H/388
Elias, woolstapler, Upton L., 1721, I, W, P2/H/1181
Elisha, Melk., 1848, AB, comm, Wr, P1/1848/10
Eliz., widow, Idmiston, 1617, I, W, P2/H/318, P2/8Reg/321
Hayward alias Burrough, Eliz., widow, Gt. Woodford, 1639, I, W, P13/1/19
Eliz., [Gt. Somerford] (NBI), [1671], I, P2/H/689
Eliz., widow, Nether St., Bromham, 1673, I, W, P3/H/476
Eliz., widow, Mannings Hill, Calne, 1715, I, W, P26/591
Eliz., widow, City, Melk., 1716, W, P2/H/1135
Eliz., widow, Manningford A., 1730, W, P3/H/1069
Eliz., Boscombe, 1741, W, P1/H/975, P1/9Reg/17
Eliz., widow, Calne, 1744, AB, comm, Wr, P5/1744/21
Eliz., Roundway, Bps. C., 1753, W, P24/1028
Eliz., sp., Devizes, 1795, AB, P1/H/1336, P1/14Reg/532A
Eliz., sp., Beechingstoke, 1823, comm, W, Wr, P1/1823/126
Eliz., sp., Seend, Melk., 1826, AB, comm, Wr, P1/1826/44
Eliz., widow, Ryme I., Dorset, 1830, W, Wr, P5/1830/30
Eliz. *see also* Eliz. Wood
Ellen, widow, Broughton G., 1562, I, W, P2/H/15, P2/4Reg/96D
Francis, yeo., Beechingstoke, 1728, AB, W, P3/H/1047
Gabriel, broad weaver, Melk., 1663, AB, comm, I, NW, P2/H/622
Geo., yeo., Corsham, 1635, I (2 - not quite identical), W, P29/H/32, P29/1Reg/131
Geo., yeo. *or* broad weaver, Charlton nr Malm., 1694, I, W, P3/H/744
Hayward *or* Hayord, Geo., yeo., Charlton nr Malm., 1698, AB, I, P3/H/775
Geo., sen., broad weaver, Lacock, 1711, I, W, P1/H/683, P1/5Reg/255

Geo., husb., Chaddington, Lydiard T., 1772, W, P3/H/1398
Geo., cardmaker, Calne, 1801, note, W, P26/1233
Heywood, Geo., Devizes, 1819, AB, Wr, P1/1819/7
Geo., yeo., Seend, Melk., 1824, W, Wr, P2/1824/82
Geo., Sherb., Dorset, 1826, AB, O, Wr, P5/1826/13
Giles, gent., Ryme I., Dorset, 1810, comm, W, Wr, P5/1810/25
Harris, yeo., Corsham, 1804, W, P3/1804/22
Harry, Wilsford nr Pewsey, 1856, AB, aff, O, Wr, P2/1856/4
Hy., Fovant, 1546, W (NEP), P2/1Reg/71A
Hy., husb., Lt. Cheverell, 1569, W, P2/5Reg/76A
Heyward, Hy., Sonning, Berks., 1574, W, P5/3Reg/41B
Hy., mason, Milbourne, Malm., 1618, I, W, P3/H/132
Hy., Whitchurch Canonicorum, Dorset, [1635], I, W, P2/H/468
Hy., husb., Mkt. L., 1662, I, W, P2/H/617
Hy., sen., yeo., Corsham, [1692], W, P29/1Reg/266
Hy., yeo., Manningford A., 1695, I, W, P1/H/577
Heyward, Hy., sen., yeo., Corsham, 1696, I, W, P29/H/69
Hy., tailor, Stockham Marsh, Bremhill, 1714, I, ren, W, P3/H/936
Hy., Hankerton, 1717, AB, P3/H/952
Hy., Lt. Cheverell, 1717, AB, P2/H/1145
Hy., maltster, Manningford A., 1719, I, W, P3/H/967
Heyward, Hy., jun., baker, Corsham, 1727, I, W, P29/H/105, P29/2Reg/52A
Hy., sen., yeo., Gastard, Corsham, 1737, W, P29/H/107
Hy., gent., Warm., 1855, aff, W, Wr, P1/1855/35
Hezekiah, bach., Melk., 1844, AB, comm, Wr, P2/1844/19
Hugh, husb., Durnford, 1617, I, W, P5/1617/21, P5/10Reg/163B
Humphrey, servant to Thos. Ashlocke, Heytes., 1572, W, P5/3Reg/2C
Humphrey, parish clerk, Brinkw., 1821, AB, comm, W, Wr, P3/1821/12
Isaac, Reybridge, Lacock, 1778, W, P3/H/1424
Heyward, Isabel, Steeple A., 1545, W (NEP), P2/1Reg/74B
Isabella, Sutton B., 1708, AB, I, P1/H/645
Jacob, cordw., Melk., 1718, AB, I, P2/H/1159
Jacob, husb., Bassett Down, Lydiard T., 1801, W, Wr, P3/1801/20
Jas., husb., Patney, 1543, W, P2/1Reg/28A
Jas., husb., Bower C., 1595, I (2), W, P2/H/145, P2/7Reg/146E
Jas., Heytes. (d. at Upton L.), 1666, W, P2/H/640
Jas., Anderson, Dorset, 1714, AB, P5/1714/17
Heyward, Jas., sen., yeo., Corsham, 1722, AB, I, copy I, W, P29/H/101, P29/2Reg/39
Jas., victualler and baker, Enmore Grn, Motc., Dorset, 1785, W, P19/185
Jas., yeo., Dilton M., Westb., 1808, O, W, P25/1808/7
Jas., mason, Sherb., Dorset, 1845-47, AB, W, Wr, P5/1845/20, P5/1847/16
Jas., Silver St., Trowb., 1850, D, O, W, Wr, P1/1850/8
Jane, widow, Heddington, 1690, I, W, P3/H/675
Jane, widow, Reybridge, Lacock, 1720, W, P1/H/767, P1/6Reg/258
Jane, sp., Chelworth, Crickl. St S., 1730, W, P3/H/1070
Jane, singlewoman, Corsham, 1816, AB, P29/1800-1857/19, P29/3Reg/264
Jane, widow, Sandfurlong, Broad H., 1830, comm, W, Wr, P3/1830/2
Jane, widow, Mkt. L., 1845, aff, W, Wr, P1/1845/19
Hayward form. James, Joan, widow, Melk., 1757, AB, P2/H/1426
Jn., sen., husb., Odstock, 1557, W, P2/3Reg/9B
Jn., sen., Melk., 1558, W, P2/3Reg/81D
Heyward, Jn., husb., Beanacre, Melk., 1570, W, P2/5Reg/98A
Jn., smith, Downton, 1573, W, P2/5Reg/167C
Jn., Odstock, 1575, W, P2/5Reg/215B
Jn., Thingley, Corsham, 1580, W, P29/1Reg/18A
Jn., Enmore Grn, Motc., Dorset, 1595, I, W, P5/1595/27, P5/6Reg/105A
Jn., husb., Odstock, 1596, W, P2/H/151
Jn., husb., Hinton, Steeple A., 1602, I, W, P1/H/23
Hayward alias Friend, Jn., weaver and husb., Westwood, 1603, a/c, I, W, P2/H/214, 317
Jn., Purton, 1622, I, P3/H/168

Hayward alias Farmer, Jn., yeo., Wood St., Clyffe P., 1622, I, W, P1/H/152
Jn., weaver, Westrop, Corsham, 1631, NW, P29/H/30, P29/1Reg/122B
Jn., tailor, Corsham, 1633, NW, P29/1Reg/125
Jn., husb., Orcheston St Geo., 1634, AB, caveat, I, P2/H/461
Jn., husb., Bloxworth, Dorset, 1636, AB, court paper, P5/1636/26, P5/13Reg/30A
Haward, Jn., sen., yeo., Hurst, Berks., 1637, W, P5/1637/22, P5/13Reg/40
Jn., Upton L., 1642, I, W, P2/H/553
Jn., sen., broad weaver, Melk., 1652, I, W, P1/H/305
Jn., Avebury, 1661-70, AB, comm, I, NW, P3/H/339, 433, P3/3Reg/28B
Hayward alias Farmer, Jn., yeo., Heddington Wick, 1669, I, W, P3/H/415
Jn., yeo., Heddington Wick, 1671, AB, I, P1/H/406
Jn., Urchf., 1693, AB, I, P2/H/935
Heyward, Jn., jun., broad weaver, Gastard, Corsham, 1693, AB, I, P29/H/66, P29/1Reg/258C
Jn., yeo., Winterbourne E., 1697, I, W, P2/H/980
Heyward alias Roberts, Jn., cordw., Crickl. St My., 1702, I, W, P3/H/824
Jn., sen., yeo., Chirton, 1703, I, W, P2/H/1019
Jn., yeo., Whitley, Melk., 1712, I, W, P2/H/1099
Jn., yeo., Semley, 1712, W, P2/H/1097
Jn., gent., Chirton, 1718, W, P2/H/1158
Haywood, Jn., Westb., 1727, AB, P25/1727/1
Jn., Newton T., 1730, AB, P2/H/1250
Jn., gent., Littlecott, Enford, 1751, W, P2/H/1395
Jn., labourer, Eastcourt, Crudwell, 1778, W, P3/H/1425
Jn., Orcheston St My., 1779, AB, P2/H/1579
Jn., Marden, 1800, AB, P2/1800/54
Jn., Monk's Farm, Corsham, 1804, AB, P1/1804/99
Jn., clothier, Trowb., 1808, W, Wr, P1/1808/88
Jn., innholder, Chipp., 1825, comm, W, Wr, P3/1825/42
Jn., All C., 1831, AB, comm, P3/1831/17
Jn., Ridge Side, Corsham, 1844, AB, aff, comm, W, Wr, P3/1844/28
Jonas, Corsham, 1818, W, Wr, P3/1818/40
Jos., Beechingstoke, 1711, AB, P1/H/667
Jos., Beechingstoke, 1750, AB, P3/H/1257
Jos., Melk., 1757, AB, P2/H/1425
Jos., gent., Beechingstoke, 1767, comm, W, P1/H/1199, P1/12Reg/260
Jos., yeo., Chitterne AS, 1767, W, P2/H/1495
Jos., gent., Hilcott, N. Newnton, 1793, AB, W, Wr, P3/H/1505
Lawr., yeo., Corsham, 1667, I, W, P29/H/44
Lawr., yeo., Tilsh., 1737, W, P2/H/1305
Lawr., yeo., Westb., 1780, W, P25/1780/3
Lawr., Westb., 1792, AB (W missing), P25/1792/3
Hayard, Lettice, widow, Stourpaine, Dorset, 1614, I, W, P24/100
Lot, Stanton St Q., 1836, AB, aff, W, Wr (with list of household goods), P3/1836/33
Lucy, widow, Rowde, 1707, I, W, P3/H/876
Lydia, widow, Chr. M., 1797, W, P3/H/1524
Mgt., widow, Avebury, 1665, I, W, P3/H/369
Mgt., widow, Purton Stoke, 1723, AB, I, W, P3/H/1003
Mgt., widow, Calne, 1734, W, P5/1734/34
Margaretta, widow, Orcheston St My., 1777, W, P2/H/1572
Heyward *or* Hayard, Margery, widow, Charlton nr Malm., 1638, I, W, P3/H/308
Margery, widow, Poulshot, 1721, W, P2/H/1177
Martha, Nettleton, 1765, O, W, P3/H/1354
Haway, My., Chalford, Westb., 1617, AB, P25/1617/8
My., widow, Mkt. L., [1680], I, W, P2/H/777
My., widow, Monkton F. (form. of Chirton), 1718, comm, W, P2/H/1153
My., widow, Hilcott, N. Newnton, 1729, AB, I, P1/H/870
My., widow, Marden, 1735, AB, P1/H/938
My., widow, Bere R., Dorset, 1742, W, Wr, P5/1742/19
My., cardmaker, Calne, 1783, W, P26/1130
My., Brinkw., 1840, O, W, Wr, P3/1840/11

My., wife, Melk., 1854, AB, aff, L, O, Wr, P2/1854/14
Nich., Atworth, Bradford A., 1568, W, P2/5Reg/39A
Haywood, Nich., chapman, N. Heath, Chieveley, Berks., 1776, W, P1/H/1240, P1/13Reg/119
Noah, bach., Corsham, 1810, AB, Wr, P3/1810/51
Haywood, Philip, innholder and yeo., Lyme R., Dorset, 1606, AB, I, W, P5/1606/22, P5/8Reg/64A
Heyward, Philip, Chirton, 1618, AB, comm, I, P2/H/331
Philip, [farmer], Gt. Durnford, 1711, AB, I, P5/1711/26
Philip, sen., cordw., City, Melk., 1711, comm, I, W, P2/H/1087
Philip, Upavon, 1715, AB, P2/H/1121
Philip, Mkt. L., 1729, AB, comm, P1/H/847
Philip, yeo., Bradford A., 1760, W, P1/H/1151, P1/11Reg/481A
Philip, Orcheston St My., 1763, comm, W, P2/H/1468
Philip, yeo., Chirton, 1790, W, P2/H/1648
Richd., Upton S., 1559, W, P2/3Reg/168B
Richd., yeo., Croucheston, Bishopstone S., 1605, AB, I, W, P2/H/229
Richd., yeo., no abode stated, c1614, W, P1/H/82
Richd., husb., Latton, 1628, I, W, P3/H/218
Hayward alias Simms, Richd., Beechingstoke, 1629, I, W, P3/H/225
Richd., yeo., Beanacre, Melk., 1629, comm, I, W, P2/H/410
Richd., yeo., Patney, 1676, I, W, P2/H/736
Richd., baker, Latton, 1679, comm, I, W, P3/H/536
Richd., gent., Roundway, Bps. C., 1702, W, P24/611
Richd., yeo., Urchf., 1725, W, P2/H/1208
Richd., tailor, Latton, 1753, W, P3/H/1271
Richd., farmer, Wilsford nr Pewsey, 1787, AB, W, P2/H/1627
Richd., Bradford A., 1815, AB, comm, Wr, P2/1815/58
Richd., gent., Marden, 1824, comm, W, Wr, P2/1824/53
Richd., yeo., Chirton, 1844, W, Wr, P2/1844/42
Richd., confectioner, Marl., 1856, aff, O, W, Wr, P1/1856/4
Robt., Upton L., 1559, W, P2/4Reg/18A
Robt., husb., Atworth, Bradford A., 1570, W, P2/5Reg/101A
Haywood, Robt., Bower C., 1570, W, P2/5Reg/83A
Robt., Swallowcliffe, 1611, AB, W, P5/1611/19, P5/9Reg/54B
Robt., yeo., Tinh., Edington, 1616, I, W, P1/H/107
Robt., yeo., Upton L., [1666], I, W, P2/H/638
Robt., Garsdon, 1668, I, W, P3/H/401
Robt., Urchf., [1677], I, W, P2/H/746
Robt., yeo., Chirton, [1680], I, W, P2/H/779
Robt., yeo., Mkt. L., 1692, AB, I, ren, P2/H/925
Robt., Melk., 1694, AB, I, P2/H/951
Robt., Remenham, Berks., 1695, AB, P1/H/580
Robt., maltster, Mkt. L., 1727, W, P2/H/1217
Robt., sen., gent., Roundway, Bps. C., 1736, W, P24/924
Robt., yeo., Chirton, 1782, W, P1/H/1277, P1/13Reg/367
Robt., sen., yeo., Roundway, Bps. C., 1815, W, Wr, P24/1271
Robt., yeo., Chirton, 1824, W, Wr, P2/1824/80
Robt., yeo., Hilp., 1835, comm, W, Wr, P1/1835/50
Robt., labourer, Hannington, 1848, O, W, Wr, P3/1848/50
Roger, husb., Holt, Bradford A., 1570, W, P2/5Reg/83C
Roger, miller, Stockwood, Dorset, 1595, I, W, P5/1595/30, P5/6Reg/109A
Roger, husb., Rams., 1702, I, W, P5/1702/23
Roger, yeo., Cherhill, 1706, W, P26/535
Haward, Rowland, clerk, parson and gent., Arborfield, Berks., 1609, AB, comm, I, T, P5/1609/43, P5/9Reg/15B
Haywood, Sarah, widow, Westb., 1784, W, P25/1784/2
Sarah, widow, Wilsford nr Pewsey, 1799, W, P2/H/1692
Sibyl, widow, Croucheston, Bishopstone S., 1585, W, P2/7Reg/18
Stephen, labourer, Purton, 1815, W, Wr, P3/1815/2
Thos., Semley, 1569, W, P2/5Reg/63E
Thos., husb., Ditchampton, Wilton, 1579, AB, I, T, P2/H/57, P2/5Reg/353D
Thos., Ditchampton, Wilton, 1590, notes of AB (2), a/c, P2/H/108

Thos., day labourer, Bemerton, Fugg. St Peter, [1605], W, P2/H/224
Thos., tailor, Corsham, 1622, W, P29/1Reg/92C, 100A
Heyward, Thos., husb., Charlton nr Malm., 1623, I, W (on same sheet), P3/H/177-78
Hayward alias Simms, Thos., Etchilhampton, 1632, I, W, P3/H/257
Heyward, Thos., mason, Garsdon, 1634, I, W, P1/H/198
Thos., timberman, Melk., 1634, I, W, P1/H/202
Thos., yeo., Charlton nr Malm., 1640, I, W, P1/H/294
Thos., Lt. Cheverell, 1648, AB, comm, I, P2/H/594
Thos., yeo., Ryme I., Dorset, 1676, comm, I, NW, P5/1676/27
Thos., husb., Beechingstoke, 1677, I, W, P3/H/519
Thos., goldsmith, Sal., 1678, W, P4/1677/1
Thos., Enmore Grn, Motc., Dorset, 1680, AB, comm, I, P5/1680/27
Thos., Westwood, 1683, I, P2/H/821
Thos., jun., Lt. Cheverell, 1683, I, W, P2/H/822
Thos., sen., gent., West Amesb., 1689, W, P1/H/526
Thos., Chr. M., 1695, AB, I, Wr, P3/H/751
Thos., sen., yeo., Lt. Cheverell, [1700], I, W, P2/H/996
Thos., yeo., Beechingstoke, 1701, I, W, P3/H/807
Haierd, Thos., Urchf., 1713, W, P2/H/1111
Thos., innholder, Melk., 1740, AB, comm, ren, P2/H/1321
Haywood, Thos., Westb., 1742, W, P25/1742/5
Thos., shoemaker, Lt. Cheverell, 1751, W, P2/H/1394
Thos., mason, Nettleton, 1757, W, P3/H/1301
Thos., clothworker, Trowb., 1790, W, P1/H/1321, P1/14Reg/348
Thos., Portsmouth, Hants (effects at Longbridge D.), 1792, AB, P2/H/1663
Thos., yeo., Corsham Side, Corsham, 1806, W, P29/1800-1857/10, P29/3Reg/248
Haywood, Thos., innholder, Sal., 1821, W, Wr, P4/1821/2
Thos., gent., Hungerford, Berks., 1823, AB (re residue of term of 500 years in property in H.), comm, P23/905
Thos., Horton, Bps. C., 1828, AB, O, W, P24/1312
Thos., bach., Brinkw., 1834, AB, O, Wr, P3/1834/47
Walter, yeo., Fonthill G., 1726, W, P1/H/828, P1/7Reg/147B
Wm., Lt. Cheverell, 1553, W, P2/2Reg/181A
Wm., husb., Broughton G., 1558, W, P2/3Reg/114D
Wm., Calne, 1568, AB, P5/2Reg/28A
Wm., Warm., 1571, W, P2/5Reg/120A
Wm., Lt. Cheverell, 1572, W, P2/5Reg/142C
Wm., shepherd, Avebury, 1610, comm, I, W, P3/H/56
Wm., tailor, Corsham, 1612, I, NW, P29/H/16, P29/1Reg/70A
Hayward alias Barnaby, Wm., tailor, Warm., 1613, I, NW, P1/H/73
Heyward, Wm., mason, Garsdon, [1613], I, W, P3/H/93
Hayward alias Farmer, Wm., yeo., Bushton, Clyffe P., 1620, AB, a/c, I, P3/H/152
Wm., yeo., Melk., 1628, I, W, P2/H/401
Wm., yeo., Westwood, 1633, I, W, P2/H/453
Heyward, Wm., mason, Brinkw., 1639, I, W, P3/H/315
Wm., yeo., Upton L., 1640, W, P2/H/533
Wm., Melk., 1648, I, W, P2/H/597
Wm., yeo., Swindon & Cotmarsh, 1664, AB, I, P1/H/351
Wm., sen., gent., Heale, Woodford, 1672, AB, ren, W (2 - 1 a copy), P13/2/1
Wm., jun., Hilcott, N. Newnton, 1676, AB, a/c, I, P3/H/504
Wm., Upper Westwood, 1679, I, W, P2/H/774
Wm., yeo., Hilcott, N. Newnton, 1681, I, W, P3/H/557
Wm., Somerford K., 1686, AB, I, P1/H/1362
Wm., gent., Stourpaine, Dorset, 1687, AB, I, P24/785
Wm., yeo., Purton Stoke, 1690, AB, comm, I, P3/H/676
Wm., baker, Sutton B., 1693, W (2 - 1 a copy), P3/H/721
Wm., yeo., Rowde, 1694, I, W, P3/H/745
Wm., husb., Gt. Bedwyn, 1704, AB, W, P21/6/19
Wm., yeo., Gt. Bedwyn, 1704, AB, I, P5/1704/31
Heyward, Wm., shopkeeper, Corsham, 1715, I, W, P29/H/94, P29/2Reg/15B
Wm., gent., Marden, 1729, W, P1/H/869, P1/7Reg/324

Wm., Earlscourt, Wanb., 1737, AB, P3/H/1136
Wm., yeo., Clarendon Park, 1763, W, P4/1763/3
Wm., yeo., Broughton G., 1776, AB, P2/H/1554
Wm., sen., yeo., Bradford A., 1783, W, P1/H/1285, P1/13Reg/399
Wm., gent., Marden, 1807, W, Wr, P1/1807/21
Wm., yeo., Kemble, 1813, W, Wr, P3/1813/56
Wm., yeo., Gt. Cheverell, 1835, O, W, P1/1835/14
Wm., Trowb., 1836, comm, W, Wr, P1/1836/2
see also Barnard alias H.; Dampee alias H.; Faithorne/Fethorne alias H.; Farmer alias H.; Friend alias H.; Roberts alias H.; Symmes alias H.; Westrop alias H.; Wood (Woods) form. H.
Haywarden, Heywarden, Hy., [blacksmith], Chr. M., 1625, AB, I, P3/H/198
Joan, widow, Chr. M., 1680, I, W, P3/H/542
Hawarden, Jn., Devizes Grn, Bps. C., 1607, I, NW, P24/164
Jn., Chr. M., 1640, AB, I, P3/H/321
Jn., yeo., Sutton B., 1685-1703, AB, bond to pay legacy, I, W, P1/H/507, P3/H/607, 840
Walter, blacksmith, Chr. M., 1669, I, W, P3/H/416
Haywood *see* Hayward
Hazard, Hazard alias Bledwin, Edwd., husb., Stourpaine, Dorset, 1576, I, W, P24/1434, P5/3Reg/80B
Jn., Shitterton, Bere R., Dorset, 1688, AB, I, P5/1688/41
Jn., tailor, Drove Hill, Donhead St My., [1688], I, W, P2/H/894
Hassard, Jn., Bere R., Dorset, 1720, I, W, P5/1720/27, P5/16Reg/49D
Jn., Barford St M., 1728, W, P2/H/1224
Jn., tailor, Barford St M., 1736, W, P2/H/1293
My., widow, Shitterton, Bere R., Dorset, 1718, comm, W, P5/1718/15, P5/15Reg/408A
Richd., Milborne Stileham, Bere R., Dorset, 1663, AB, comm, I, P5/1663/29
Hazard alias Bluding, Robt., yeo., Milborne Stileham, Bere R., Dorset, 1688, AB, I, P5/1688/40
Thos., yeo., W. Knoyle, 1729, I, W, P2/H/1238
Thos., Bemerton, Fugg. St Peter, 1825, AB, Wr, P2/1825/11
Hazzard, Wm., carp., S. Burcombe, 1827, W, Wr, P2/1827/21
Hazel *see* Hasell
Hazeland *see* Haseland
Hazell, Hazle *see* Hasell
Hazzard *see* Hazard
Head, Adam, gent., Chilton, Berks., 1729, W, P1/H/853, P1/7Reg/233
Hedd, Agnes, Alton Pr., 1571, W, P1/1Reg/33C
Alexander, Pitton, Alderbury, 1688, AB, I, W, P26/366
Alexander, innholder, Sal., 1741, W, P4/1741/6
Alice, widow, W. Stowell, Alton Pr., 1631, AB, NW, P1/H/185
Alice, widow, Wilsford with Lake, 1647, AB, I, W, P5/1647/8, P5/14Reg/93B
Hedd, Amy, widow, Gt. Woodford, 1633, I, W, P13/1/14
Ann, widow, Box, 1662, AB, I, W, P1/H/332
Anthony, Durley, Burbage, 1639, I, NW, P11/9
Anthony, yeo., Wootton R., 1692, I, W, P3/H/709
Anthony, Collingbourne K., 1754, AB, P3/H/1277
Augustine, husb., Easton, 1702, AB, I, P3/H/825
Cath., sp., Amesb., 1700, NW, P2/H/998
Cath., widow, Marl., 1842, W, Wr, P1/1842/62
Chas., yeo., Alton B., 1685, comm, I, NW, P3/H/608
Chas., husb., W. Stowell, Alton Pr., 1740, W, P3/H/1167
Chas., baker, Marl., 1773, W, P1/H/1220, P1/12Reg/460
Chas., carp., Westrop, Highw., 1831, W, P10/1831/1
Clement, Easton, 1615, AB, I, W, P3/H/109
Dorothy, widow, Wilcot, 1742, W, P3/H/1180
Ebenezer, clothier, Leigh and Woolley, Bradford A., 1781, W, P2/H/1597
Edith, widow, Cloatley, Hankerton, 1608, W, P3/H/34
Heade, Edith, widow, W. Stowell, Alton Pr., 1671, comm, I, W, P3/H/455
Edwd., yeo., Easton, 1688, I, Wr, P3/H/653
Edwd., clerk, Latton, 1725, W, P3/H/1018
Edwd., Newbury, Berks., 1744, AB, P1/H/1011
Edwd., S. Marston, 1764, AB, Wr, P5/1764/23

Edwd., clerk, Wanb., 1803, AB, Wr, P3/1803/1
Eliz., widow, Boscombe, 1600, AB, I, W, P2/H/191
Eliz., widow, Huish, 1690, W, P3/H/677
Eliz., widow, W. Stowell, Alton Pr., 1756, W, P1/H/1122, P1/11Reg/295
Francis, gent., Chipp., 1796, W, P3/H/1515
Francis, upholsterer and auctioneer, Chipp., 1827, W, Wr, P3/1827/39
Heade, Geoffrey, W. Stowell, Alton Pr., 1632, AB, I, P3/H/258
Geoffrey, Box, 1766, AB, P3/H/1357
Geo., yeo., Gt. Woodford, 1636, I, W, P13/1/17
Geo., Ludg., 1639, AB, P2/H/526
Giles, yeo., Stanton Fitzwarren, 1713, W, P3/H/927
Hannah, widow, Ogbourne St Geo. (of Marl., 1804), 1810, comm, W, P23/860
Hy., clerk, Amesb., 1748, AB, P2/H/1377
Hugh, yeo., Lt. Woodford, 1621-22, I, W, P5/1621/12, P5/10Reg/25C
Isabel, W. Stowell, Alton Pr., 1622, AB, I, P3/H/169
Jas., yeo., Winterbourne, Chieveley, Berks., 1674, I, W, P1/H/426
Jas., Woodford, 1680, AB, P13/2/6
Jas., yeo., Winterbourne, Chieveley, Berks., 1759, W, P1/H/1143, P1/11Reg/414A
Jane, sp., Sal. (form. of Ibsley, Fordingbridge, Hants), 1848, AB, D, W, Wr, P4/1848/2
Heade, Jerome, husb., Wilsford with Lake, 1574, I, W, P5/1574/8, P5/3Reg/34C
Jiffard, Box, 1847, AB, comm, Wr, P3/1847/38
Hedd, Jn., husb., Coombe B., 1564, W, P5/1Reg/35B
Hedd, Jn., husb., Stapleford, 1564, I, W, P2/H/28, P2/4Reg/179A
Hedd, Jn., Boscombe, 1570, AB, P2/5Reg/107D
Hedd, Jn., husb., W. Stowell, Alton Pr., 1592, W, P1/H/7
Hedd, Jn., husb., Lake, Wilsford with L., 1593, I, W, P5/6Reg/48, P13/1/3
Jn., Wootton R., 1622, I, NW, P3/H/170
Jn., husb., W. Stowell, Alton Pr., 1627, I, W, P3/H/213
Jn., Wilsford with Lake, 1630, I, W, P13/1/12
Hedd, Jn., yeo., Huish, 1635, AB, court paper, D, I, W, P1/H/208
Jn., freemason, Middlehill, Box, 1637, I, W, P3/H/295
Jn., W. Stowell, Alton Pr., 1638, I, W, P1/H/236
Jn., freemason, Box, 1640, I, W, P3/H/322
Jn., hatter, Easton, 1685, I, P3/H/609
Jn., yeo., W. Overton, 1687, I, W, P3/H/635
Jn., yeo., Leckhampstead, Chieveley, Berks., 1695, I, W, P1/H/576
Jn., E. Ilsley, Berks., 1701, note of probate, P1/H/616
Jn., Pitton, c1708, W (buried 1708 - parish register) (NEP), P30/85
Jonathan, sen., Chipp., 1737, W, P3/H/1137
Jonathan, mason, Chipp., 1754, W, P3/H/1278
Jos., Box Quarries, 1852, D, O, W, Wr, P3/1852/40
Lawr., Newbury, Berks., 1756, W, Wr, P1/H/1111, P1/11Reg/225
Hedd, Lucy, widow, Wilsford with Lake, 1634, I, WGVS, P5/1634/48, P5/12Reg/270B
Mgt., Stert, Urchf., 1663, AB, I, P1/H/340
Mgt., widow, Badbury, Chiseldon, 1665, I, W, P3/H/370
Margery, Brigmerston, Milston, 1629, I, W, P2/H/412
Martha, wife, Reading St Giles, Berks., 1741, W, P1/H/999, P1/9Reg/45
My., sp., Charlton nr Malm., 1630, I, W (both on same sheet), P3/H/239
My., widow, W. Stowell, Alton Pr., 1707, I, W, P1/H/642
My., midwife, Haxton, Fittleton, 1750, W, P2/H/1389
Heade, Matthew, yeo., W. Stowell, Alton Pr., 1622, I, W, P3/H/171
Matthew, Winterbourne Bassett, 1646, AB, comm, P1/H/273
Matthew, Wilcot, 1647, AB, I, P1/H/282
Matthew, Wilcot, 1732, W, P1/H/900, P1/7Reg/495B
Philip, yeo., Enborne, Berks., 1662, AB, I, P1/H/325
Richd., sen., Whaddon, Alderbury, 1716, W, P26/600
Richd., husb., Easton, 1720, I, W, P3/H/974
Richd., carp., Crookham, Thatcham, Berks., 1750, AB, W, P1/H/1073, P1/10Reg/379
Richd., yeo., Leckhampstead, Chieveley, Berks., 1756, W, P1/H/1112, P1/11Reg/227
Richd., Gt. Wishford, 1780, AB, P2/H/1584

Richd., Pewsey, 1796, AB, P3/H/1516
Robt., yeo., Woodford, 1628, W, P13/1/7
Robt., yeo., Gt. Amesb., 1632, I, P2/H/441
Robt., sen., yeo., Whaddon, Alderbury, 1822, W, Wr, P26/1340
Hedd, Stephen, Stapleford, 1550, W, P2/2Reg/116A
Susan, widow, Oare, Wilcot, 1720, W, P1/H/768, P1/6Reg/283B
Hedd, Thos., Coombe B., 1581, AB, P5/1580/31, P5/4Reg/12A
Thos., Collingbourne K., 1702, a/c, I, W, P3/H/826
Thos., baker, Chipp., 1731, W, P3/H/1089
Thos., victualler, Chipp., 1798, W, P3/H/1531
Thos., baker, Marl., 1840, W, Wr, P1/1840/9
Vincent, Wilcot, 1664, AB, I, P3/H/360
Vincent, husb., W. Stowell, Alton Pr., 1695, I, W, P1/H/567
Vincent, yeo., Manningford A., 1742, comm, W, P3/H/1181
Vincent, yeo., Marl., 1783, W, P1/H/1290, P1/13Reg/488
Hedd, Wm., jun., Gt. Woodford, 1588, AB, I, W, P13/1/1, P5/5Reg/13A
Heade, Wm., Lake, Wilsford with L., 1592-93, AB, I, P5/1592/46, P5/6Reg/7A
Hedd, Wm., [Huish] (NBI), 1608, I, W, P3/H/37
Hedd, Wm., Brigmerston, Milston, 1612, I, W, P2/H/294, P2/8Reg/184A
Wm., sen., yeo., Gt. Woodford, 1617, I, W, P5/1617/20, P5/9Reg/188A
Wm., yeo., Charlton nr Malm., 1618, I, W (both on same sheet), P3/H/133
Heade, Wm., yeo., Wilcot, [1619], I, W (NEP), P3/H/140
Heade, Wm., husb., Netheravon, [1640], I, W (NEP), P12/79
Wm., husb., Wootton R., 1661, AB, comm, I, P3/H/340
Heade, Wm., husb. *or* yeo., W. Stowell, Alton Pr., 1672, I, W, P3/H/466
Wm., husb., Pitton, Alderbury, 1675, I, W, P26/223
Wm., yeo., Easton, 1680, W, I (NEP), P3/H/1542
Wm., husb., Wilcot, 1702, AB, I (2 - 1 a copy), NW, P3/H/827
Wm., freemason, Chipp., 1705, I, W, P3/H/855
Wm., minor, Alderbury, 1708, T, P26/538
Wm., W. Stowell, Alton Pr., 1732, W, P3/H/1102
Wm., gent., Whaddon, Alderbury, 1743, W, P26/842
Wm., yeo., Pitton, Alderbury, 1748, W, P26/888
Wm., Chipp., 1755, W, P3/H/1287
Wm., yeo., Horningsham, 1774, W, P5/1774/8, P5/17Reg/75A
Wm., Marl. St My., 1834, W, Wr, P1/1834/22
Wm., innkeeper, Charlton, 1846, O, W, Wr, P2/1846/30
see also Reeves alias H.
Headach, Joan, [1539], court proceedings, P5/20Reg/11A
Jn., Frilsham, Berks., 1732, AB, P1/H/897
Lucy, widow, Bradfield, Berks., 1680, AB, I, P1/H/448
Thos., Hurst, Berks., 1539, W, P5/20Reg/2A
Thos., Hawkridge, Bucklebury, Berks., 1729, AB, W, P1/H/858, P1/7Reg/270B
Heade *see* Head
Headidge, Hedditch, Hy., Gillingham, Dorset, 1684, I, P27/1/84
Hedditch, Jn., sen., Ham Common, Gillingham, Dorset, 1804, W, P27/1/579
Thos., yeo., Wokm., Berks., 1711, W, P5/1711/27, P5/15Reg/267
Hedeage *or* Hedah, Vincent, Sulham, Berks., 1686, I, W, P1/H/1364
Hedditch, Wm., Bourton, Gillingham, Dorset, 1773, AB, P27/1/483, P27/3Reg/170
Hedditch, Wm., yeo., Gillingham, Dorset, 1839, W, Wr, P27/1/723
Heading, Amelia, widow, Hill Farm, Chawley, Cumnor, Berks., 1808, W, Wr, P1/1808/99
Jn., sen., yeo., Grove, Wantage, Berks., 1712, W, P23/327
Jn., yeo., Grove, Wantage, Berks., 1732, W, P23/486
Thos., yeo., Grove, Wantage, Berks., 1758, W, P23/678
Heady *see* Verdue alias H.
Heale, Alexander, Stanford, Berks., 1763, AB, P1/H/1164
Ambrose, Maiden B., 1697, AB, I, P2/H/969
Heal, Ambrose, sen., Milton upon Stour, Gillingham, Dorset, 1812, W, P27/1/615
Heal, Edmd., clothworker, Bradford A., 1736, W, P2/H/1290
Eliz., widow, Sandy Lane, Calne, 1766, AB, P26/1015

Herne, Hester, widow, Netheravon, 1696, I, W, P12/135
Hester, Netherb., Dorset, 1726, AB, P17/422
Isaac, tallow chandler, Netherb., Dorset, 1741, W, P17/477
Hearne, Jas., Crofton, Gt. Bedwyn, 1591, I, T, W, P5/1591/37, P5/5Reg/110C
Hearne, Jas., husb., Marten, Grafton, 1672, W (NEP), P21/4/1
Hearne, Joan, widow, Netherb., Dorset, 1592, AB, I, P5/1592/42, P5/5Reg/140A
Hearne, Joan, sp., Netherb., Dorset, 1608, I, W, P5/1608/19, P17/1, P5/8Reg/117A
Herne, Jn., husb., Netherb., Dorset, 1592-93, AB, I, T, P5/1592/47, P5/6Reg/5A
Hearne, Jn., Allington, 1611, comm, I, W, P1/H/62
Herne, Jn., sen., yeo., Netheravon, 1621, I, L, W, P12/43
Herne, Jn., tailor, Netheravon, 1626, I, W, P12/52
Herne, Jn., sen., yeo., Choulston, Figh., 1667, I, W, P26/134
Hearne, Jn., baker, Netheravon, 1675, I, NW, P12/109
Herne, Jn., yeo., Netheravon, 1678, I, W, P12/110
Hearne, Jn., sen., potter, Beam., Dorset, 1695, AB, W, P17/346
Herne, Jn., sergemaker, Beam., Dorset, 1695, I, W, P5/1695/32
Herne, Jn., tailor, Ablington, Figh., 1700, I, W, P26/469
Herne, Jn., yeo., Bulford, 1710, I, W, P2/H/1079
Hern, Jn., yeo., Netheravon, 1712, I, W, P12/146
Hearne, Jn., sergemaker, Beam., Dorset, 1716, AB, I (detailed & clearly written), P5/1716/39
Hearne, Jn., yeo., Ash, Netherb., Dorset, 1721, AB, I, P17/397
Hearne, Jn., gent., Mangerton, Netherb., Dorset, 1729, W, P17/428
Herne, Jn., gent., Devizes, 1770, W, P1/H/1212, P1/12Reg/382B
Herne, Jn., Fittleton, 1774, AB, ren, P2/H/1540
Hearne, Jos., yeo., Netherb., Dorset, 1678, AB, I, P17/277
Mgt., widow, Rodbourne, Malm., 1693, AB, I, P3/H/722
Herne, My., sp., Norton, 1678, W, P3/H/530
Herne, My., widow, Netheravon, 1709, I, W, copy W, P12/144
Hearne, My., widow, Beam., Dorset, 1719, I, W, P5/1719/44, P5/16Reg/17B
My., widow, Kershay, Netherb., Dorset, 1736, W, P17/461
My., widow, Netherb., Dorset, 1762, I (detailed), W, P17/548
Herne, Nathaniel, sen., yeo., Choulston, Figh., 1694, W, P26/420
Hearnes, Richd., Wantage, Berks., 1569, AB, P5/2Reg/48D
Richd., husb., Netheravon, 1663, I, W, P12/91
Herne, Richd., yeo., Lake, Wilsford with L., 1679, I, W, P13/1/26, P13/2/5
Herne, Richd., Netherb., Dorset, 1725, AB, P5/1725/34
Herne, Richd., yeo., Netheravon, 1725, W, P5/1725/37, P5/16Reg/116B
Hearne, Robt., tailor, Sherb., Dorset, 1672, AB, I, P5/1672/23
Herne, Sam., clerk, Corsham, 1716, AB, P29/H/97, P29/2Reg/18A
Sam., tailor, Netherb., Dorset, 1743, W, Wr, P5/1743/39
Sam., carp., Beam., Dorset, 1845, comm, W, Wr, P17/616
Hern, Sarah, yeo.'s wife, Chilton F., 1777, AB, P3/H/1422
Herne, Sarah, widow, Trowb., 1820, comm, W, Wr, P1/1820/150
Herne, Simon, yeo., Netheravon, 1628, I, W, P12/56
Hearne, Thos., Camesworth, Netherb., Dorset, 1597, AB, I, NW, P5/1597/58, P5/6Reg/170B
Hearne, Thos., sen., yeo., Netheravon, 1598, AB, I, W, P12/3
Hearne, Thos., Netheravon, 1610, AB, a/c, I, P12/19
Hearne, Thos., Collingbourne D., 1612, I, W, P1/H/68
Hearne, [Thos.], husb., Netherb., Dorset, 1635, I [christian name from burial register], P17/29
Thos., Netherb., Dorset, 1640, AB, P17/48
Thos., yeo., Netheravon, 1690, I, W, P12/133
Thos., Lt. Somerford, 1741, AB, P3/H/1176
Hearne alias Starr, Walter, Allington, Chipp., 1632, I, W, P3/H/260
Herne, Wm., Netherb., Dorset, 1591, AB, I, W, P5/1591/38, P5/5Reg/102D
Hearne, Wm., Corsley, 1626, AB, I, P2/H/383
see also Starr alias H.
Hearth, Abraham, tailor, Everleigh, 1753, W, P3/H/1272
Ann, widow, Steeple A., 1685, I, W, P2/H/860
Hearth *or* Heath, Frances, minor, Baydon, 1681, T, P5/1681/27
Jacob, Lyneham, 1696, AB, I (applies to both people), P3/H/760

Robt., Lt. Hinton, 1662, I, W, P1/H/328
Heasel, Heasell *see* Hasell
Heath, Agnes, widow of Humphrey, baker, Wokm., Berks., 1619, I, W, P5/1619/55, P5/10Reg/42E
Alice, widow, Ashton G., Codf. St P., 1602, I, W, P2/H/200
Alice, wife, Seagry, 1827, AB, Wr, P3/1827/14
Alice *see also* Alice Iles, P1/6Reg/364B
Andrew, sen., yeo., Clack, Lyneham, 1720, W, P1/H/779
Andrew, yeo., Clack, Lyneham, 1725, I, W, P3/H/1019
Andrew, Lt. Somerford, 1735, AB, P1/H/932
Andrew, tailor, Clack, Lyneham, 1797, W, P3/H/1525
Andrew, tailor, Devizes, 1812, W, Wr, P1/1812/9
Andrew, mealman, Quemerford, Calne, 1819, W, Wr, P26/1322
Ann, widow, Clack, Lyneham, 1723, comm, W, P3/H/1004
Ann, Clack, Lyneham, 1726, W, P1/H/822, P1/7Reg/120
Ann, sp., Sal., 1751, W, P4/1751/5
Ann, sp., Lt. Hinton, 1786, W, P3/H/1472
Ann, widow, Dauntsey, 1851, AB, O, Wr, P3/1851/2
Benj., husb., Gt. Ham, Lt. Hinton, 1758, W, P3/H/1309
Benj., Marl., 1820, AB, comm, Wr, P1/1820/114
Betty, widow, Kington L., 1768, comm, W, P3/H/1374
Cath., widow, Sevenhampton, Highw., 1625, AB (in minority of ex.), a/c, comm, I, W, P5/1625/46, P5/1628/53, P5/10Reg/204, P5/11Reg/82C
Cath., Stratton St Mgt., 1641, AB, P1/H/252
Cath., widow, Swindon, 1670, I, W, P3/H/434
Dan., sen., Lt. Hinton, 1666, comm, I, W, P3/H/378
Dan., yeo., Lt. Hinton, 1706, I (2 - 1 a copy), W, P3/H/863
Edmd., yeo., Whaddon, Alderbury, 1681, AB, I, P26/291
Edmd., tallow chandler, Sal., 1744, W, P1/H/1009, P1/9Reg/317
Hethe, Eliz., widow, Chitterne St My., 1559, W, P2/3Reg/169C
Heath alias Bayly, Eliz., yeo.'s wife, Swindon, 1674, AB, comm, I, P3/H/484
Eliz., sp., Lt. Hinton, 1775, W, P3/H/1410
Frances, sp., Gt. Somerford, 1836, AB, O, Wr, P3/1836/12
Francis, Marl. St My., 1695, AB, P1/H/583
Geo., Wick, Bps. C., 1834, AB, comm, Wr, P24/1337
Grace, sp., Lt. Hinton, 1784, comm, W, P3/H/1454
Harry, Gt. Somerford, 1837, W, Wr, P3/1837/44
Hy., woollen draper, Swindon, 1730, W, P3/H/1072
Heithe, Humphrey, yeo., Chitterne St My., 1558, W, P2/3Reg/137B
Humphrey, Wokm., Berks., 1592, AB, I (2), P5/1592/43
Jas., yeo., Amesb., 1660, AB, comm, I, P1/H/308
Jas., yeo., Whaddon, 1745, W, P4/1745/3
Jas., cabinetmaker, Sutton B., 1854, aff, O, W, Wr, P3/1854/36
Jane, widow, Swindon, 1726, comm, W, P1/H/816, P1/7Reg/82A
Joan, widow, Lt. Hinton, 1669, I, W, P3/H/417
Jn., Milston, 1567, AB, P2/5Reg/28B
Jn., Wokm., Berks., 1600, AB, I, P5/1600/35, P5/7Reg/5B
Jn., Amesb., 1627, court paper, I, NW, P2/H/395
Jn., sen., weaver, Gt. Cheverell, 1628, I, W, P1/H/176
Jn., innholder, Marl., 1637, AB, a/c, court paper, I, proclamation, P1/H/227
Jn., husb., Stanton Fitzwarren, 1639, I, W, P3/H/314
Jn., clothworker, Wokm., Berks., 1640, I, W, P5/1640/30, P5/13Reg/244
Jn., no abode stated, 1647, I, W, P1/H/286
Jn., yeo., Bremhill Wick, 1666, I, W, P1/H/369
Jn., yeo., Clack, Lyneham, 1702, I, W, P3/H/828
Jn., collarmaker, Westbrook, Boxford, Berks., 1770, AB (2), comm, P1/H/1206
Jn., staymaker, Gt. Somerford, 1777, W, P3/H/1420
Jn., Westbrook, Boxford, Berks., [1792], AB (undated), P1/14Reg/433A
Jn., tallow chandler and grocer, Corsham, 1846, comm, W, Wr, P3/1846/15
Jos., surgeon, Swindon, 1711, AB, I, ren, P1/H/664
Jos., tailor, Welford, Berks., 1711, W, P1/H/680, P1/5Reg/199

Jos., servant man, Marl., 1843, comm, D, ren, W, Wr, P1/1843/33
Joyce, widow, Wick, Southbroom, 1692, AB, I, P1/H/550
Julian, widow, Burbage, 1591, I, W, P5/1591/36, P5/5Reg/109
Mgt., widow, Lt. Hinton, 1610, W, P3/H/57
Mgt., widow, Lt. Hinton, 1623, I, W, P3/H/176
Martha, widow, Swindon, 1753, AB, P1/H/1102
My., widow, Bremhill Wick, 1688, I, W, P3/H/654
My., Lt. Hinton, 1775, W, P3/H/1411
Matthew, tailor, Sutton B., 1845, W, Wr, P3/1845/26
Maurice, Milston, 1599, I, W, P2/H/182
Philip, Lt. Bedwyn, 1622, AB, I, P5/1622/38, P5/10Reg/133A
Ralph, Hampstead Marshall, Berks., 1801, AB, O, P1/1801/21, P1/15Reg/245A
Ralph, Calne, 1811, AB, P26/1282
Richd., shepherd, Horton, Bps. C., 1672, I, W, P24/465
Richd., shepherd, Horton, Bps. C., 1680, AB, I, P24/424
Richd., jun., Wick, Southbroom, 1691, AB, comm, I, P24/715
Richd., silk weaver, Swindon, 1710, I, W, P3/H/906
Heyzth, Robt., husb., Milston, 1558, W, P2/3Reg/104C
Robt., Burbage, 1579, I, W, P5/1579/38
Robt., husb., Blackland, Calne, 1588, I, W, P5/1588/27, P5/5Reg/45A
Robt., sen., husb., Lt. Hinton, 1608-09, W, P3/H/35, 46
Robt., husb., Lt. Hinton, 1634, I, W, P1/H/196
Robt., sen., yeo., Upper Stratton, Stratton St Mgt., 1667, I, W, P3/H/389
Robt., Stratton St Mgt., 1678, AB, a/c, P3/H/528
Robt., yeo., Lt. Hinton, 1684-89, I, W, P3/H/596, 664
Robt., yeo., Stratton St Mgt., 1725, W, P3/H/1020
Robt., apothecary, Swindon, 1730, W, P3/H/1073
Susanna, Corsham, 1823, W, Wr, P1/1823/65
Thos., husb., Swindon, 1606, W, P3/2Reg/8B
Thos., Lt. Hinton, 1614, I, P3/H/101
Thos., husb., Over Stratton, Stratton St Mgt., 1621, I, W, P3/H/162
Thos., sen., blacksmith, Wokm., Berks., 1671, I (detailed), W, P5/1671/45
Thos., sen., yeo., Swindon, 1676, AB, a/c, I, P3/H/506
Thos., Urchf., 1685, AB, I, P2/H/851
Thos., yeo., Even Swindon, 1695, I, W, P3/H/752
Thos., labourer, Horton, Bps. C., 1704, I, W, P24/612
Thos., sen., Swindon, 1729-33, AB (2), P3/H/1061, 1110
Thos., sen., grocer, Calne, 1732, W, P26/766
Thos., grocer, tallow chandler and soap-boiler, Corsham, 1813, W, Wr, P3/1813/37
Thos., Gt. Somerford, 1833, comm, D, W, Wr, P3/1833/36
Wm., husb., Ashton G., Codf. St P., 1601, I, W, P2/H/196
Wm., Gt. Cheverell, 1601, I, W, P2/H/197
Wm., fletcher, Sal., 1616, AB, I, P4/1615/7
Wm., rector, Landford, 1624, I, P1/H/160
Wm., yeo., Bremhill Wick, 1627, I, W, P3/H/214
Wm., sen., yeo., Lt. Hinton, 1661, comm, I, W, P3/H/341, P3/3Reg/20
Wm., sen., Swindon, 1662, AB, I, P1/H/329
Wm., Wokm., Berks., 1663, comm, W, P5/1662/62
Wm., Gt. Cheverell, 1672, AB, I, P2/H/702
Wm., sen., clothworker, Swindon, 1687, I, W, P3/H/636
Wm., Charlton nr Malm., 1701, AB, I, P3/H/808
Wm., sen., woollen draper, Swindon, 1708, I, W, P3/H/881
Wm., sen., bellowsmaker, Crookwood, Urchf., 1716, I, W, P1/H/726, P1/6Reg/24B
Wm., Swindon, 1734, AB, P3/H/1124
Wm., Milton, Berks., 1798, W, P1/H/1354, P1/15Reg/84
Wm., linen draper, Swindon, 1800, W, P3/1800/56
Wm., labourer, Swindon, 1832, W, Wr, P3/1832/17
see also Hearth *or* H.
Heather, Dan., brickmaker, Corsley, 1684, AB, I, W, P2/H/828
Henrietta, sp., Sherston, 1761, AB, P3/H/1324

Hether, Joan, widow, Hurst, Berks., 1541-43, cit (Oliver Boswell to accept *or* renounce admon), W, P5/20Reg/20C, 39B
Hyther, Mgt., Sonning, Berks., 1554, court proceedings (penance imposed on her for fornication), P5/20Reg/118A
Hether, Thos., Monkton D., 1546, W, P2/2Reg/5
Heathfield, Lucy, widow, Uffc., Devon, 1639-40, I, NW, P20/1/28
Heaven, Wm., Chipp., 1800, AB, P3/1800/65
Heavill *see* Hevill
Hebberd *see* Hibbard
Hebbes *see* Hobbs
Hebbet *see* Hibbard
Hebblewhite, Eliz., schoolmistress, Wantage, Berks., 1826, W, Wr, P23/930
Hebborne, Heborn, Susanna, widow, Frilford, Marcham, Berks., 1767, W, P1/H/1198, P1/12Reg/251A
Thos., Sherston, 1570, W, P1/1Reg/39A
Hebditch, Hidditch, Dorothy, widow, Pierston, Gillingham, Dorset, 1706, W, P27/1/158
Florence, widow, Zeals, 1684, W, P5/1684/31
Francis, shoemaker, Sherb., Dorset, 1612, I, NW, P5/1611/21, P5/9Reg/60A
Hibditch, Jas., sen., yeo., Sherb., Dorset, 1709, W, P5/1709/17, P5/15Reg/108
Hibditch, Jas., sen., yeo., Sherb., Dorset, 1720, AB, I, P5/1720/26
Hibditch, Jeremiah, yeo., Sherb., Dorset, 1757, W, P5/1757/15
Hibditch, Joan, widow, Zeals, 1750, W, P5/1749/27
Hebdich, Jn., yeo., Zeals, 1685, I, W, P5/1685/53
Jn. *see* Agnes Mogge, P5/10Reg/216B
Richd., yeo., Folke, Dorset, 1623, AB, I, P5/1623/16
Richd., Nether Zeals, 1681, AB, a/c, I (2), P5/1680/20
Hipdich, Sam., seaman of the Lightning Bomb vessel, Sherb., Dorset, 1746, AB, P5/1746/43
Thos., Sherb., Dorset, 1638, AB, a/c, comm, P5/1637/15, P5/13Reg/104B
Thos., yeo., Over Zeals, 1725, W, P5/1725/33, P5/16Reg/111B
Thos., weaver, Sherb., Dorset, 1793, W, P5/1793/7, P5/18Reg/191A
Thos., labourer, Castleton, Dorset, 1798, W, P5/1798/13, P5/18Reg/262A
Heborn *see* Hebborne
Hechekocke *see* Hitchcock
Hedah *see* Headidge
Hedd *see* Head
Hedditch, Hedeage *see* Headidge
Hedges, Agnes, widow, Wrou., [1606], W, P3/2Reg/5
Ann, Broad H., 1614, AB, P1/H/83
Edwd., sen., yeo., Charnham St., Hungerford, Berks., 1704, I, W, P5/1704/32
Eliz., widow, Avill's Farm, Corsham, 1777, W, P3/H/1421
Francis, turner, Reading, Berks., [1707], W, P1/H/643
Gabriel, blacksmith, Welford, Berks., 1645, AB (relates to both G. & his wife My.), I, P1/H/267
Geo., yeo., Wootton B., 1690, AB, comm, ren, P3/H/678
Geo., labourer, Blagrove, Wrou., 1827, W, Wr, P3/1827/58
Harry, labourer, Brinkw., 1772, W, P3/H/1397
Hy., Estcourt, Lt. Hinton, 1674, AB, comm, I, P3/H/485
Hedgis, Hy., husb., Bishopstone N., 1681, I, P6/57
Hy., labourer, Shrivenham, Berks., 1747, I, W, P1/H/1049, P1/10Reg/129A
Hy., yeo., Lydiard Marsh, Lydiard T., 1758, W, P3/H/1310
Hedges alias Parsons, Jane, widow, Eisey, 1629, I, W, P3/H/226
Jane, Henley, Buttermere, 1737, W, P3/H/1138
Joan, widow, Steeple A., 1574, W, P2/5Reg/188B
Hedgus, Joan, widow, Aldbourne, 1677, I, W, P3/H/520
Hedgis, Joan, widow, Bishopstone N., 1684, a/c (2), court paper, I, P6/65
Jn., Steeple A., 1572, W, P2/5Reg/144B
Jn., Semington, Steeple A., 1595, AB, P2/H/147, P2/7Reg/153B
Jn., sen., husb., Buttermere, 1612, AB, a/c, I, P3/H/80
Jn., husb., Wrou., 1625, I, W, P3/H/199
Jn., yeo., Henley, Buttermere, 1648, I, W, P1/H/293
Jn., yeo., Henley, Buttermere, 1678, comm, W, P3/H/529
Hedges *or* Hodges, Jn., sen., blacksmith, Bucklebury, Berks., 1683, comm, I, W, P1/H/475
Jn., blacksmith, Newbury, Berks., 1689, AB, I, P1/H/518
Jn., blacksmith, Devizes, 1689, AB, W, P1/H/529

Jn., carp., Clatford Park, Preshute, 1696, comm, I, W, P5/1696/21
Jn., yeo., Chiseldon, 1706-07, I, W, P3/H/877, P30/100
Jn., tanner, Charnham St., Hungerford, Berks., 1719, AB, ren, P5/1719/47
Jn., miller, Werg, Mildenhall, 1737, W, P3/H/1139
Jn., Letcombe, Berks., 1753, W, P1/H/1087, P1/10Reg/512A
Jn., sen., Highw., 1806, W, P10/1806/1
Hedges *or* Hodges, Jos., Bearfield, Bradford A., 1805, AB, P1/1805/13
Mgt., widow, Westb. L., 1607, I, W (NEP), P25/1607/2
Margery, widow, Estcourt, Lt. Hinton, 1699, I, W, Wr, P3/H/781
My., Wanb., 1746, AB, P3/H/1222
Hedges alias Whitaker, My., widow, Trowb., 1765, AB, ren, I, P1/H/1181
My., sp., Marl., 1844, W, Wr, P1/1844/37
Michael, husb., Ham, 1630, I, NW, P3/H/240
Nich., Hannington, 1618, I, W, P3/H/134
Richd., yeo., Charlton nr Malm., 1626, I, W, P3/H/203
Richd., Box, 1636, I, W, P3/H/290
Richd., yeo., Calcutt, Crickl. St S., 1670, comm, I, W, P3/H/435
Richd., yeo., Worton, Pott., 1691, AB, I, P1/H/534
Richd., yeo., Henley, Buttermere, 1719, I, W, P3/H/968
Hedges alias Leacy, Robt., yeo., Lt. Hinton, 1617, I, W, P3/H/120
Robt., Aldbourne, [1665], W (NEP), P3/H/371
Sarah, sp., Kemble, 1748, AB, P3/H/1236
Stephen, Mildenhall, 1800, AB, P3/1800/68
Susanna, Purton, 1744, W, P3/H/1204
Thos., millwright, Westb. L., 1578-79, I, T, W, P5/1578/19, P5/3Reg/116
Thos., Wrou., 1616, I, W, P1/H/113
Thos., shepherd, Liddington, 1626, I, NW, P3/H/204
Thos., bach., Clatford, Preshute, 1661, AB, I, P1/H/310
Thos., yeo., Penny Quicks, Charnham St., Hungerford, Berks., 1706, AB, I, P23/285
Thos., yeo., Lydiard T., 1761, W, P3/H/1325
Thos., Bowden Hill, Lacock, 1768, AB, P3/H/1375
Thos., esquire, Alderton, 1783, W, P1/H/1291, P1/14Reg/3
Walter, Wingfield, 1630-32, comm, I, W, copy W, P2/H/602
Wm., husb., Ogbourne St Geo., 1684, I, W, P23/132
Wm., cordw., Avill's Farm, Corsham, 1740, W, P3/H/1168
Wm., yeo., Lydiard T., 1773, comm, W, P3/H/1403
Wm., yeo., Mannington, Lydiard T., 1814, W, Wr, P3/1814/24
Wm., yeo., Melk., 1830, W, Wr, P2/1830/76
see also Adee alias H.; Parsons alias H.
Hegish *see* Parsons alias Hegish
Hegnell *see* Hignell
Hehuslman *see* Hillman
Heighington, Jn., gent., Winterbourne S., [1694], I, P2/H/942
Jn., yeo., Winterbourne S., 1720, AB, W, P2/H/1174
Heighmore *see* Highmore
Heighmore *see* Highmore
Heiter *see* Hayter
Heithe *see* Heath
Hele *see* Heale
Helier, Helierd *see* Hillier
Hell *see* Heale
Hellaker *see* Hilliker
Hellary *see* Hillary
Hellear *see* Hillier
Heller *see* Hiller
Hellery *see* Hillary
Hellier *see* Hillier
Hellings, Robt., Uffc., Devon, 1704, AB, I, P5/1704/33
Hellman *see* Hillman
Hellyar, Hellyer *see* Hillier

Helm *see* Helme
Helman *see* Hillman
Helme, Ann, Gillingham, Dorset, 1729, AB, P27/1/297
Chris., yeo., Teffont E., 1628, I, W, P2/H/400
Eleanor, widow, Ridge, Chilmark, 1732, W, P1/7Reg/449B
Jane, widow, Idmiston, 1735-49, AB (2), P2/H/1283
Joan, widow, Chilmark, 1590, I, P2/H/102
Jn., yeo., Stockton, 1673, AB, I, P2/H/711
Helms, Jn., Ridge, Chilmark, 1786, AB, P2/H/1625
Helms, Jos., shopkeeper, Stockton, 1694, AB, I, P2/H/945
Mgt., widow, Chilmark, 1634, AB, I, W, P2/H/457, P2/9Reg/14B
Mgt., sp., Sal., 1672, NW, P4/1672/6
My., sp., Gillingham, Dorset, 1730, AB, req, W, P27/1/290, 301
Helm, My., widow, Chilmark, 1845, I, W, Wr, P1/1845/57
Ralph, Stapleford, 1593, I, W, P2/H/128
Richd., Ridge, Chilmark, 1610, AB, I, P2/H/261, P2/8Reg/84A
Richd., sen., yeo., Stockton, 1705, I, W, P2/H/1030
Richd., Stockton, 1712, AB, I, ren, P2/H/1103
Helmes, Robt., butcher, Gillingham, Dorset, 1721, AB, I, P27/1/247
Ursula, widow, Coombe B., 1720, W, P8/20
Wm., gent., Ridge, Chilmark, 1711, I, W, P2/H/1088
Wm., gent., Chilmark, 1724, AB, P2/H/1206
Wm., sen., yeo., Ridge, Chilmark, 1734, W, P2/H/1272
Wm., yeo., Ridge, Chilmark, 1739, W, P2/H/1313
Helm, Wm., yeo., Ridge, Chilmark, 1801, W, P1/1801/8, P1/15Reg/229
see also Elme alias H.
Helps, Christian, widow, Hilp., 1564, I, W, P2/H/1697, P2/4Reg/175A
Christian, widow, Wilsford nr Pewsey, 1751, AB, comm, P2/H/1397
David, [weaver], Rowde Hill, 1761, I, W, P3/H/1326
David, S. Wraxall, 1845, AB, Wr, P1/1845/45
Eliz., widow, Wootton B., 1769, comm, W, P3/H/1384
Eliz., wife, Bath, Somerset, 1819, W, Wr, P1/1819/6
Hilpes, Ellen, widow, Holt, Bradford A., 1573, W, P2/5Reg/161C
Geo., husb., Rowde, 1682, AB, ren, P3/H/567
Hy., Wilsford nr Pewsey, 1713, AB, I, P3/H/928
Jas., yeo., Corsham, 1827-28, comm (2), D (4), O, W, Wr (probate complicated by additions & deletions made to W), P3/1828/10, P29/1800-1857/22
Hilpes, Jn., sen., broad weaver, Holt, Bradford A., 1610, AB, a/c, court paper, I (2), P2/H/267, P2/8Reg/123A
Hilpes, Jn., weaver, Holt, Bradford A., 1619, I, W, P2/H/336
Jn., Holt, Bradford A., 1694, AB, I, P2/H/950
Jn., weaver, Wilsford nr Pewsey, 1744, W, P1/H/1021, P1/9Reg/409A
Jn., sen., yeo., Melk., 1745, W, P2/H/1356
Jn., Bradford A., 1763, AB, I, P2/H/1462
Jn., grocer, Trowb., 1836, O, W, P1/1836/4
My., widow, Wilsford nr Pewsey, 1750, W, P1/H/1078, P1/10Reg/420B
My., widow, Trowb., 1836, O, W, P1/1836/18
Hilpes, Richd., broad weaver, Bradford A., 1635, I, W, P1/H/211
Richd., sen., miller, Rangebourne Mill, Pott., 1734-35, W, P24/930, 945
Robt., husb., Shalbourne, Berks. & Wiltshire, 1677, AB, I, P23/72
Sam., yeo., Chapel Knapp, Corsham, 1855, aff, O, W, Wr, P3/1855/8
Thos., Heywood, Westb., 1711, AB, I, P25/1711/9
Thos., Collingbourne D., 1733, W, P1/H/919, P1/7Reg/571B
Thos., Trowb., 1767, AB, P1/H/1191
Hilpes, Walter, Holt, Bradford A., 1559, W, P2/4Reg/27C
Hilpes, Walter, weaver, Gastard, Corsham, 1663, AB, I, P29/H/41, P29/1Reg/166
Hilpes, Wm., weaver, Holt, Bradford A., 1649, comm, I, W, P2/H/600
Wm., husb., Rowde, 1676, I, W, P3/H/507
Wm., Rowde, 1681, AB, a/c, I, P3/H/555
Helsam, Sam., yeo., Colerne, 1714, comm, I, W, P1/H/696, P1/5Reg/350
Helsen, Hilsen, Ann, Quidh., 1715, I, W, P2/H/1123

Helsen [Hilson], Hy., Quidh., 1708, I, W, P2/H/1063
Hely *see* Healy
Hembury, Himbury, Matthew, Trill, Clifton Maybank, Dorset, 1818, AB, comm, Wr, P5/1818/35
Hembry, Nich., Stratford Tony, 1667, AB, I, P1/H/378
Thos., carrier, Bourton, Gillingham, Dorset, 1826, W, Wr, P27/1/673
Hemerford, Jas., clerk and vicar, Purton, 1630, I, W, P3/H/241
Hemery, Joan, widow, Holnest, Dorset, 1628, AB, I (2), W, copy W, P5/1628/58, P5/11Reg/59
Hymory, Roger, husb., Holnest, Dorset, 1624, I, W, P5/1624/22, P5/10Reg/233B
Susanna, widow, Calne, 1834, comm, W, Wr, P26/1413
Hemming, Heming, Edwd., esquire, collector of the excise, Marl. (form.of Gloucester), 1737, req, copy W, W, P1/H/946, P1/8Reg/178
Jn., husb., Beanacre, Melk., 1573, W, P2/5Reg/162D
Jn., Broughton G., 1589, I, W, P2/H/95
Heming, Jn., husb., Lacock, 1619, I, NW, P1/H/127
Jn., yeo., Beanacre, Melk., 1732, I, W, P1/H/908, P1/7Reg/527A
Nich., Melk., 1583, W, P2/6Reg/83B
Hemmin, Richd., sacking manufacturer, Abingdon, Berks., 1801, W, P1/1801/51, P1/15Reg/268B
Robt., husb., Littleton, Steeple A., 1559, W, P2/3Reg/181A
Heming, Thos., Ebbesborne Wake, 1635, I, W, P2/H/466, P2/9Reg/51A
Wm., Beanacre, Melk., 1608, AB, P2/8Reg/9A
Henbery *see* Henbury
Henbest, Eliz., widow, Bramshaw, Hants, 1845, aff, W, Wr, P24/1378
Jn., jun., Bramshaw, Hants, 1635, AB, a/c, P24/235
Jn., sen., yeo., Fritham, Bramshaw, Hants, 1836, W, P24/1348
Osmund, yeo., Bramshaw, Hants, 1739, W, P24/903
Richd., sen., Bramshaw, Hants, 1682, I, W, P24/773
Robt., sen., Bramshaw, Hants, 1717, I, W, P24/649
Robt., Bramshaw, Hants, 1745, AB, P24/967
Robt., sen., yeo., Bramshaw, Hants, 1812, W, P24/1257
Robt., cordw., Bramshaw, Hants, 1832, O, I, W, Wr, P24/1328
Thos., Trowb., 1756, AB, P1/H/1124
Ursula, widow, Bramshaw, Hants, 1812, W, P24/1259
Wm., yeo., Bramshaw, Hants, 1686, AB, I, P24/794
Wm., Bramshaw, Hants, 1832, AB, Wr, P24/1330
Henbury, Ann, widow, Gillingham, Dorset, 1761, W, P27/1/429, P27/3Reg/93
Edwd., sen., Lotborne, Gillingham, Dorset, 1697, AB, court paper, ren, P27/1/133
Edwd., Gillingham, Dorset, 1735, AB, Wr, P27/1/338
Edwd., bach., Gillingham, Dorset, 1765, AB, P27/1/449, P27/3Reg/126B
Henbery, Eliz., widow, Gillingham, Dorset, 1721, W, P27/1/245
Jn., Gillingham, Dorset, 1720, AB, P27/1/238
Hanbury, Nich., gent., Sandhurst, Berks., 1673, AB, I (detailed, damaged), P5/1673/18
Walter, yeo., Hamp, Gillingham, Dorset, 1580-81, W, P27/2Reg/3A, 6B
Henchman, Jn., clerk, Sherb., Dorset, 1699, W, P5/1699/16
Hendan *see* Hendon
Hende *see* Hendy
Henden *see* Hendon
Henderson, Wm., baker and shopkeeper, Haxton, Fittleton, 1818, W, Wr, P2/1818/55
Hendley, Hendly *see* Henley
Hendon, Hinden, Abigail, Lyneham, 1769, AB, P3/H/1385
Henden, Ann, widow, Bradford A., 1825, AB, O, Wr, P2/1825/53
Henden, Jas., butcher, Rowde, 1703, AB, I, ren, P3/H/841
Jn., bach., Lyneham, 1785, AB, P3/H/1464
Hendan, Wm., butcher, Clack, Lyneham, 1747, W, P1/H/1045
Wm., butcher, Clack, Lyneham, 1747, W, P1/10Reg/137
Wm., sen., maltster, Clack, Lyneham, 1789, W, P1/H/1314, P1/14Reg/275
Hendy, Abraham, butcher, Box, 1614, I, W, P1/H/90
Hende, Angel, sp., Over Zeals, 1681, AB, I, W, P5/1680/28
Ann, widow, Worton, Pott., 1670, I, W, P2/H/672
Ann, sp., Chute Forest, Chute, 1758, AB, P5/1758/24
Hindy, Chas., tailor, Rushall, 1723, W, P1/H/792

Edith, widow, Zeals, 1570, W, P5/2Reg/81A
Edwd., husb., Over Zeals, 1626, a/c, I, W, P5/1626/23
Edwd., husb., Mere, 1626, W, P5/10Reg/328
Jas., Trowb., 1834, AB, O, Wr, P1/1834/5
Jn., sen., husb., Trowle, Bradford A., 1618, I, W, P2/H/325
Jn., husb., Winsley, Bradford A., 1620, I, W, P1/H/139
My., sp., Zeals, 1662, I, W, P5/1662/61
Philip, yeo. and husb., Zeals, 1604-05, I, W, P5/1604/22, P5/8Reg/24A
Robt., carp., Chute Forest, Chute, 1777, W, P7/171
Sibyl, widow, Mere, 1610, I, NW, P5/1610/32
Thos., sen., carp., Chute, 1731, W, P5/1731/43
Wm., husb., Mere, 1568, W, P5/2Reg/34A
Wm., husb., Winsley, Bradford A., 1581, W, P2/6Reg/25B
Hindy, Wm., carp., Collingbourne K., 1724, W, P3/H/1009
Hening *see* Henning
Henley, Henly, Adam, Grittenham, Brinkw., 1780, req, W, Wr, P3/H/1436
Henly, Alexander, yeo., Brinkw., 1676, AB, a/c, I, P3/H/508
Henly, Chris., weaver, Wootton B., 1633, I, W, P3/H/272
Henly, Eleanor, sp., Sonning, Berks., 1744, W, Wr, P5/1744/22
Henly, Francis, gent., Hullavington, 1786, W, P3/H/1473
Henly, Geoffrey, yeo., Brinkw., 1638, AB, a/c, I, P3/H/307
Hy., esquire, Colway, Lyme R., Dorset, 1684, AB, comm, ren, P16/81
Henly, Hy., upholsterer, Malm., 1722, I, W, P3/H/991
Hy., weaver, Crickl. St S., 1726, W, P3/H/1027
Henly, Jacob, yeo., Langley Burrell, 1822, W, Wr, P3/1822/24
Jas., Marl. & Vernham, Andover, Hants, 1825, O, W (in form of L to Robt. Alexander of V.), Wr, P1/1825/15
Joan?, Alderton, 1621, a/c (person & place taken from previous endorsement), P1/H/147
Henly, Jn., blacksmith, Tidcombe, T. and Fosbury, 1626, I, W, P3/H/205
Jn., Sal., 1774, AB, P4/1774/3
Henly, Jn., yeo., Brinkw., 1775, W, P3/H/1412
Henly, Jn., Goatacre, Hilmarton, 1824, AB, Wr, P3/1824/50
Henly, Mgt., sp., Grittenham, Brinkw., 1786, W, P1/H/1308, P1/14Reg/143B
My., widow, Colway, Lyme R., Dorset, 1710, I (very detailed), W, P16/184
Hendley, My., school mistress, Lacock, 1760, W, P3/H/1318
Henly, Maurice, shoemaker, Wootton B., [1605], W (NEP), P3/H/12, P1/7Reg/524A
Hendly, Robt., butcher, Wootton B., 1732, W, P1/H/906
Robt., Wootton B., 1751, AB, P3/H/1264
Hensley, Sarah, widow, Fyfield Wick, Berks., 1782, W, P1/H/1274
Henly, Sarah, sp., Wootton B., 1805, W, P3/1805/28
Hendly, Stephen, mariner, Lyme R., Dorset, 1686, W, P16/88
Thos., doctor of physic, Lyme R., Dorset, 1740, AB, comm, ren, Wr, P5/1740/39
Henly, Thos., sen., yeo., Tockenham Wick, 1772, W, P3/H/1399
Henly, Thos., yeo., Preston, Lyneham, 1793, W, P3/H/1506
Henly, Thos., gent., Lyneham, 1849, O, W, Wr, P3/1849/8
Henly, Thos. Peter, Heywood Farm, Kington St M., 1856, AB, aff, Wr, P3/1856/35
Wm., weaver, Wootton B., 1605, W, P3/H/11
Hendly, Wm., yeo., Brinkw., 1618, I, W, P3/H/135, P1/7Reg/471
Hendly, Wm., yeo., Wootton B., 1708, I (2 - 1 a copy), W, P3/H/882
Henly, Wm., husb. and bach., Winkfield, Berks. (form. of Windlesham, Surrey), 1732, W, P1/H/893
Henly, Wm., butcher, Wootton B., 1770, W, P1/H/1213, P1/12Reg/385
Henly, Wm., sen., Studley, Calne, 1827, comm, W, Wr, P26/1365
Henly, Wm., yeo., Pond Close Farm, Corsham, 1856, aff, W, Wr, P3/1856/37
Henlow, Geo., gent., Calne, 1678, I (detailed), W, P26/253
Henly *see* Henley
Henman, Wm., clerk and vicar, Netherb., Dorset, 1608, AB, I, W, P5/1608/18, P5/8Reg/118
Hennesey, Dan., Amesb., 1703, AB, P2/H/1023
Henning, Hinning, Ann, widow, Ebbesborne Wake, 1639, I, W, P1/H/243
Edmd., gent., Mere, 1739, comm, W, Wr, P5/1739/23
Hening, Eliz., sp., Wick, Lacock, 1606, I, W, P1/H/41
Jn., yeo., Bramshaw, Hants, 1811, W, P24/1254

Robt., Steeple L., 1590, I, T, W, P2/H/110
Hennor, Ann, sp., Easton Grey, 1729, W, P3/H/1059
Hinner, Jn., yeo., N. Wraxall, 1634, I, W, P1/H/201, P1/13Reg/359
Hensley *see* Henley
Henson, Humphrey, bach. [and weaver], Uffc., Devon, 1662, I, W, P5/1662/65
Henson, Sam. *see* Wm. Trickey
Henstridge, Jn., mason, Donhead St A., 1856, aff, D, W, Wr, P2/1856/45
Henstridge, Wm., Hindon, 1588, I, T, W, P2/H/83, P2/7Reg/121
Hentage, Robt., Trowb., 1816, AB, comm, Wr, P1/1816/16
Henton *see* Hinton
Henvill, Agnes, widow, Fordington, Dorset, 1603, AB, I, W, P5/1603/33
Henvill, Jn., bach., Netherb., Dorset, 1807, AB, comm, P17/594
Henvill, Philip, clerk, Damerham, Hants, 1805, AB, comm, ren, P2/1805/70
Henville, Sampson, carp., Anderson, Dorset, 1825, W (NEP), P5/1825/30
Henvill, Susanna, Netherb., Dorset, 1720, AB, P17/389
Henwood *see* Hinwood
Henyll, Wm., Fisherton D., 1590, I, W, P2/H/107
Herbert, Harbert, Cath., widow, Crickl. St S., 1685, AB, I, W, P3/H/605
Harbert, Edwd., yeo., Longworth, Berks., 1701, AB, I, P1/H/620
Harbard, Hy., Woolhampton, Berks., 1614, I, W, P1/H/85
Harbert, Hy., blacksmith, Sevenhampton, Highw., 1685, AB, I, P10/1685/1
Hy., Kingston Bagpuize, Berks., 1756, W, P1/H/1113, P1/11Reg/253B
Hy., sen., yeo., Hannington Bridge, 1826, W, Wr, P1/1826/69
Harbart, Jane, widow, Kemble, 1614, I, P1/H/86
Jane, widow, Southmoor, Longworth, Berks., 1804, W, P1/1804/75
Jn., silk weaver, late of Whitechapel, now of Bristol (d. at Marl.), 1725, W, P1/H/812, P1/7Reg/61
Jn., Swindon, 1730, AB, P3/H/1074
Harbert, Jn., baker, Ashton K., 1734, W, P3/H/1121
Jn., yeo. and cordw., Kingston Bagpuize, Berks., 1750, AB, agreement, W, P1/H/1069, P1/10Reg/365
Jn., yeo., Eastcourt, Crudwell, 1759, W, P3/H/1314
Jn., gardener, Wantage, Berks., 1769, W, P23/748
Jn., gardener, Wantage, Berks., 1814, W, P23/871
Harbutt, Mgt., widow, Wantage, Berks., 1685, I, W, P5/1685/42
Harbert, Robt., tailor, Wootton B., [1611], I, W (NEP), P3/H/76
Harbert, Robt., Crickl. St S., 1665, AB, I, P3/H/367
Harbard *or* Herberd, Thos., Wokm., Berks., 1543, W, P5/20Reg/35C
Harburd, Thos., husb., Sulham, Berks., 1638, I, W, P1/H/231
Herbert *or* Harbut, Thos., tiler, Purton, 1699, I, W, P3/H/782
Harbart, Thos., harnessmaker, E. Challow, Letcombe Regis, Berks., 1763, W, P1/H/1160, P1/12Reg/34
Thos., Pott., 1846, AB, O, Wr, P1/1846/22
Harbutt, Wm., yeo., Crickl. St My., 1754-73, AB, comm, W, P3/H/1276
Wm., Wallingford, Berks., 1763, AB, P1/H/1163
Wm., sen., shepherd, Aston U., Blewbury, Berks., 1767, W, P5/1767/23
Herbeart, Wm., yeo., Avebury, 1779, W, P3/H/1431
Wm., Chieveley, Berks., 1823, AB, Wr, P1/1823/107
Hercomb, Chas., bach., Shalbourne, 1829, AB, comm, P23/945
Hercombe, Hy., Gt. Bedwyn, 1687, AB, I, P21/4/28
Hercombe, Jn., sen., yeo., Borough, Gt. Bedwyn, 1763, W, P21/10/62
Jn., sen., yeo., Gt. Bedwyn, 1797, W, P5/1797/22, P5/18Reg/234A
My., widow, Collingbourne K., 1856, AB, aff, comm, D, W, Wr, P3/1856/66
Hurcombe, Sam., Brokenb., 1737, AB, P3/H/1153
Hurcombe, Thos., yeo., Charlton nr Malm., 1636, AB, I, P3/H/281
Hurcombe, Thos., blacksmith, Gt. Bedwyn, 1706, W, P21/6/32
Hercombe, Thos., labourer, Gt. Bedwyn, 1775, W, P21/11/9
Wm., jun., yeo., Collingbourne K., 1835, AB, comm, W, Wr, P1/1835/19-20
Wm., Chisbury, Lt. Bedwyn, 1838, AB, O, ren, Wr, P5/1838/14
Heriat *see* Herriet
Herin *see* Herring
Heritage, Jn., yeo., Seend, Melk., 1791, W, P2/H/1657
Jonathan, blacksmith, Keevil, 1722, W, P2/H/1189

My., clothier's wife, Trowb., 1792-94, comm, W, P1/H/1329, P1/14Reg/507B
Rachel, sp., Trowb., 1822, comm, W, Wr, P1/1822/19
Robt., carp., Trowb., 1846, O, W, Wr, P1/1846/1
Herman *see* Harman
Hern, Herne *see* Hearne
Heron, Edith, Charl. nr. P., 1557, W, P2/3Reg/43C
Jn., gent., Wantage, Berks., 1676, I, W (refers to books of physic, especially one written by testator), P23/62
Richd., tailor, Wantage, Berks., 1694, I, W, P23/211
Herrage *see* Herridge
Herres *see* Harris
Herridge, Jas., roper, Gillingham, Dorset, 1837, W, Wr, P27/1/714
Herrage, Jane, widow, Hurst, Berks., 1810, W, Wr, P5/1810/11
Thos., Gillingham, Dorset, 1776, AB, P27/1/500, P27/3Reg/201B
Herriet, Herriot, Jas., bach., Mkt. L., 1854, AB, aff, O, Wr, P2/1854/53
Jn., weaver, N. Bradley, 1549, W, P2/2Reg/79B
Herriot, Jn., weaver, N. Bradley, 1606, AB, I, P1/H/37
Herriot, Jn., jun., Devizes St My., 1637, I, W, P1/H/226
Heriat, Jn., yeo., Buttermere (of Vernham's Dean, Hants, at time of making W), 1735, W, P3/H/1127
Herriot, Wm., sen., broad weaver, Devizes, 1643-46, AB, W, P1/H/256, 281
Herring, Ann, sp., Swindon, 1774, W, P3/H/1406
Ann, widow, Aldbourne, 1846, aff, O, W, Wr, P3/1846/40
Cath., widow, Coleshill, Berks., 1723, W, P1/H/796, P1/6Reg/466
Chas., Elcombe, Wrou., 1744, W, P3/H/1206
Chris., maltster, Swindon, 1716, I, W, P1/H/725, P1/6Reg/41
Edwd., yeo., Crickl. St S., 1748, W, P3/H/1237
Eliz., widow, Wanb., 1680, I, W, P3/H/543
Francis, feltmaker, Marl., 1662, comm, I, NW, P1/H/311
Francis, feltmaker, Marl., 1681, comm, I, W, P1/H/459
Francis, wheelwright, Wanb., 1806, W, Wr, P3/1806/25
Hannah, widow, Swindon, 1814, AB, P1/1814/83
Hy., sen., labourer, Chittoe, Bps. C., 1799, W, P24/1195
Jane, widow, Wrou., 1838, W, Wr, P3/1838/36
Joan, widow, Marl., 1672, I, W, P1/H/418
Jn., yeo., Wanb., 1662, comm, I, W, P3/H/348
Jn., yeo., Elcombe, Wrou., 1664, AB, I, P3/H/361
Jn., sen., Stratton St Mgt., 1668, AB, I, P1/H/390
Jn., sen., yeo., Stratton St Mgt., 1670, I, W, P3/H/436
Jn., yeo., Wanb., 1682, I, W, P3/H/568
Haring, Jn., sen., Chittoe, Bps. C., 1693, AB, I, W, P24/534
Jn., Stratton St Mgt., 1714-15, AB, I, P29/H/93, P29/2Reg/15A
Harring, Jn., Chittoe, Bps. C., 1717, AB, I, W, P24/652
Hearing, Jn., Elcombe, Wrou., 1727, W, P3/H/1037
Jn., gent., Swindon, 1744, W, P3/H/1207
Jn., maltster, Swindon, 1745, comm, W, P3/H/1217
Jn., yeo., Swindon, 1797, W, P3/H/1526
Jn., carp., Crickl. St S., 1808, W, P1/1808/50
Jn., property in Wanb. ; no abode stated, 1817, AB, comm, P3/1817/4
Jn., farmer, Wokm., Berks., 1821, comm, W, Wr, P5/1821/47
Jn., gent., Swindon, 1830, O, W, Wr, P3/1830/35
Jn., labourer, Wanb., 1844, comm, W, Wr, P3/1844/10
Lawr., yeo., Stratton St Mgt., 1674, I, W, P3/H/486
Mgt., widow, Wanb., 1698, W, P3/H/776
Margery, widow, Elcombe, Wrou., 1693, I, W, Wr, P3/H/724
Martha, widow, Liddington, 1685, W, P3/H/610
Martha, widow, Wanb., 1724, W, P3/H/1008
Martha, sp., Devizes, 1796, AB, P1/H/1345, P1/15Reg/4A
My., Chiseldon, 1781, W, P3/H/1440
My., widow, Shaw, Lydiard M., 1788, W, P3/H/1479
Miles, barber, Swindon, 1685, I, W, P3/H/611
Reynold, yeo., Stratton St Mgt., 1637, AB, a/c, I, P3/H/296

Richd., The Marsh, Swindon, 1675, AB, I, W, P3/H/494
Richd., upholder *or* upholsterer, Liddington, 1687, AB, I, ren, P3/H/637
Richd., chandler *or* mercer, Swindon, 1710, I, W, P3/H/907
Richd., husb., Wanb., 1733, W, P3/H/1111
Richd., Lydiard M., 1760, AB, P3/H/1319
Richd., yeo., Studley, Lydiard T., 1798, W, P1/H/1357, P1/15Reg/104
Harring, Robt., Lacock, 1728, AB, P3/H/1045
Harring, Robt., Bromham, 1760, AB, W, P3/H/1317
Sarah, widow, Bagshot, Shalbourne, 1812, W, Wr, P5/1812/11
Susanna, widow, Stratton St Mgt., 1676, I, W, P3/H/509
Thos., yeo., Wanb., 1680, I, W, P3/H/544
Thos., sen., Wanb., 1686, AB, I, P3/H/626
Thos., yeo., Wanb., 1699, W, P3/H/783
Thos., yeo., Liddington, 1763, W, P3/H/1347
Thos., yeo., Chaddington, Lydiard T., 1769, W, P3/H/1386
Thos., yeo., Chiseldon, 1791, req, W, copy W, P3/H/1499
Wm., Wanb., 1704, AB, I, P3/H/847
Wm., blacksmith, Stratton St Mgt., 1719, W, P3/H/969
Harring, Wm., Chittoe, Bps. C., 1740, AB, comm, P24/901
Herin, Wm., day labourer, Rodbourne, Malm., 1744, AB, W, P3/H/1205
Wm., yeo., Crickl. St S., 1764, W, P3/H/1351
Herrington *see* Harrington
Herriot *see* Herriet
Hersent, Peter, rector, Barford St M., 1758, W, P1/11Reg/352
Peter, clerk, Sal., 1758, W, P1/H/1133
Hersie, Christian, widow, Malm., 1668, I, W, P3/H/402
Hervey *see* Harvey
Hescot *see* Escott
Heskin, Heskins *see* Hoskins
Hester, Martha, widow, Dean Court, Cumnor, Berks., 1767, I, W, P1/H/1195, P1/12Reg/252A
Robt., bach., Westb., 1710, AB, I (ref. to sign & signpost), P25/1710/4
Hetch *see* Hatch
Hethe *see* Heath
Hether *see* Heather
Hetherthorne, Alexander, S. Newton, 1559, W, P2/3Reg/171A, P2/4Reg/2A
Hetheron, Alexander, Gt. Wishford, 1576, AB, P2/H/40
Alexander, Chilhampton, S. Newton, 1576, AB, P2/5Reg/249B
Christian, Ditchampton, Wilton, 1602, AB, I, note of admon, P2/H/205
Hetherthorne *or* Hetheron, Edmd., yeo., S. Newton, 1558-63, T (child: Agnes H., dau), W, P2/3Reg/131A, P2/4Reg/139C
Hetheron, Eliz., Chilhampton, S. Newton, 1563, W, P2/4Reg/140
Wm., yeo., Gt. Wishford, 1596, AB, I, W, P2/H/153
Hevill, Denise, widow, Gt. Bathampton, Steeple L., 1626-27, a/c, I, T, P2/H/385
Eliz., widow, Edington, 1686-87, AB, a/c, I, P2/H/869
Francis, yeo., Knook, 1691, I, W, P5/1691/34
Hy., yeo., Bratton, Westb., 1641, I, W (NEP), P25/1641/10
Jn., Edington, 1567, I, W, P2/H/30, P2/5Reg/7B
Jn., husb., Edington, 1605-11, AB, a/c, I, P2/H/227
Jn., husb., Gt. Bathampton, Steeple L., 1626, AB, I, P2/H/381
Oswald, Edington, 1584, W, P2/6Reg/129B
Heavill, Oswald, yeo., Edington, 1668, I, W, P2/H/651
Stephen, Bratton, Westb., 1689, AB, I, P25/1689/15
Wm., sen., gent., Bratton, Westb., 1642, AB, a/c, I, note (agreement appointing admr), P25/1642/1
Wm., Westb., 1739, W, P25/1739/6
Heward, Jn., Whitley, Melk., 1589, I, W, P2/H/96
Richd., Swallowfield, Shinfield, Berks., 1717, W, P1/H/743, P1/6Reg/99A
see also Escott alias H.
Hewchin *see* Hutchins
Hewer, Francis, yeo., Wanb., 1789, W, P3/H/1488
Francis, yeo., Wanb., 1830, W, Wr, P3/1830/25
Geo., Westport St My., 1831, AB, P3/1831/34

Jn., yeo., Wanb., 1842, comm, W, Wr, P3/1842/13
Thos., Grittleton, 1812, AB, Wr, P3/1812/2
see also Rodbourn alias H.
Hewes *see* Hughes
Hewett, Abraham, yeo., Kington L., 1698, W, P3/H/777
Alice, widow, Sherston, 1614, I, W, P1/H/88
Alice, widow, Horningsham, 1685, AB, I, P5/1685/44
Anchoret, Sal., 1682, AB, P4/1682/3
Ann, Sutton B., 1713, AB, P3/H/929
Edith, widow, Erlestoke, 1597, I, W, P2/H/162
Edith, widow, Mere, 1620, I, W, P5/1620/28, P5/10Reg/12B
Edwd., husb. and yeo., Croucheston, Bishopstone S., 1606, I, W, P2/H/231
Edwd., yeo., Croucheston, Bishopstone S., 1662, I, W, P1/H/316
Edwd., Wilton, 1766, W, P2/H/1491
Edwd., butcher, Swallowfield, Shinfield, Berks., 1817, W, Wr, P1/1817/68
Eliz., widow, Codf. St My., 1622, I, W, P2/H/356
Hewitt, Francis, Theale, Tilehurst, Berks., 1786, AB, P1/H/1305
Hewitt, Geo., watchmaker, Marl., 1807, W, Wr, P1/1807/25
Gilbert, clerk, Codf. St My., 1613, I, W, P1/H/72
Hy., yeo., Uffc., Devon, 1824, W, Wr, P5/1824/31
Jas., Grittleton, 1818, AB, comm, Wr, P3/1818/5
Jeremiah, Grittleton, 1746, AB, P3/H/1223
Jeremy, husb., Malm., 1680, AB, I, P3/H/549
Joan, widow, Faulston, Bishopstone S., 1713, I, W, P2/H/1115
Jn., yeo. and innholder, Sal. St Martin, 1594, AB, I, copy I, NW, P1/H/12
Jn., mason, Sherston, [1596], W (NEP), P3/H/1
Jn., Devizes St Jn., 1597, AB, I, P1/H/20
Jn., husb., Orcheston St My., 1604, AB, I, W, P2/H/220
Huatt, Jn., tailor, Fyfield, Overton, 1606, W, P1/H/48
Hwet, Jn., Rowde, 1612, W, P3/H/83
Jn., husb., Burton, Mere, 1612, W, P5/9Reg/74
Jn., yeo., Burton, Mere, 1612, comm, I, W, P5/1611/22
Hewitt, Jn., yeo., Burton, Mere (*also* of Woodlands, Mere), 1639, I, NW, P5/1639/38, P5/13Reg/210A
Hewitt, Jn., yeo., Mere, 1680, comm, I, W, P5/1680/26
Jn., yeo., Bishopstone S., 1701, W, P2/H/1007
Jn., woolcomber *or* worstedcomber, Malm., 1705, I, W, P3/H/856
Hewitt, Jn., Mere, 1711, AB, P5/1711/28
Hewett *or* Hewlett, Jn., Gillingham, Dorset, 1718, AB, P27/1/228
Hewitt, Jn., yeo., Bere R., Dorset, 1732, W, P5/1732/22
Jn., Faulston, Bishopstone S., 1736, AB, P2/H/1285
Jn., Grittleton, 1779, AB, P1/H/1261
Jn., baker, Uffc., Devon, 1815, W, Wr, P20/1/302
Jn., Old Windsor, Berks., 1829, AB, O, Wr, P1/1829/66
Jn., gent., Martin, Hants, 1841, W, Wr, P2/1841/17
Huatt, Mgt., widow, Mere, 1686, I, W, P5/1686/28
Martha, sp., Westb., 1789, W, P25/1789/1
My., carp.'s widow, Stanford in the Vale, Berks., 1756, W, P1/11Reg/256
My., widow, Stanford in the Vale, Berks., 1756, W, P1/H/1114
My., sp., Wokm., Berks., 1823, AB, Wr, P5/1823/15
Rendall, Bishopstone S., 1754, AB, P2/H/1404
Richd., labourer, Bishopstone S., 1822, W, Wr, P2/1822/58
Robt., Wet Lane, Mere, 1602, I, W, P5/1602/22, P5/7Reg/48
Robt., broad weaver, Kington L., 1628, I, NW, P3/H/219
Robt., Kington L., 1681, I, W, P3/H/556
Hewitt, Robt., Bourton, Gillingham, Dorset, 1756, W, P27/1/416, P27/3Reg/74
Sarah, widow, Kington L., 1743, W, P3/H/1191
Sarah, widow, Bishopstone S., 1829, AB, Wr, P1/1829/64
Thos., husb., Erlestoke, 1573, W, P2/5Reg/162C
Hewitt, Thos., Mere, 1590, I, T, W, P5/1589/28, P5/5Reg/65E
Hewitt, Thos., Zeals, 1662, AB, I, memo, P5/1662/60

Thos., Zeals, 1691, AB, I, P5/1690/24
Thos., Bishopstone S., 1714, AB, ren, P2/H/1116
Thos., Bishopstone S., 1740, AB, P2/H/1323
Thos., yeo., Bishopstone S., 1765, W, P2/H/1479
Hewitt, Wm., cordw., Mere, 1748, W, Wr, P5/1748/16
Wm., woollen draper, Devizes, 1761, comm, W, P1/H/1157, P1/12Reg/7A
Wm., bach., Uffc., Devon, 1827, AB, comm, P20/1/315
see also Compton form. H.
Hewish *see* Huish
Hewitt *see* Hewett
Hewlett, Hewlett alias Wheeler, Alice, widow, Crickl. St S., 1687, I, W, P3/H/645
Betty, widow, Sherb., Dorset, 1812, comm, W, Wr, P5/1812/35
Cath., widow, Sal., 1737, W, P4/1736/17
Hulett, Christian, widow, Winterborne K., Dorset, 1639, I, W, P5/1638/53, P5/13Reg/152C
Dan., gent., Berwick St Jas., [1671-81], AB, W, P1/H/414, P1/H/460
Drew, husb., Corton, Boyton, 1595, AB, I, W, P2/H/142, P2/7Reg/145B
Drew, yeo., Heytes., 1643, comm, I, W, P5/1643/8, P5/14Reg/60F
Drew, sen., husb., Knook, 1670-72, I (2), W (2), P5/1670/16, P5/1671/47
Drew, Bishopstrow, 1712, AB, comm, P1/H/685
Edwd., gent., Chetnole, Yetm., Dorset, 1728, W, P5/1728/50, P5/16Reg/160C
Edwd., Boyton, 1744, AB, P1/H/1007
Eliz., sp., Sal., 1730, AB, P4/1730/9
Frances, widow, Knook, 1735, AB, P5/1735/27
Frances, widow, Heytes., 1738, W, Wr, P5/1738/24
Hugh, sen., yeo., Heytes., 1675-78, I (2), W (2), P5/1675/24, P5/1678/26
Hulett, Jas., wheeler, Crickl. St S., 1624, I, W, P3/H/192
Hulett, Jn., Winterbourne S., 1568, W, P2/5Reg/38B
Jn., Winterborne K., Dorset, 1571, W, P5/2Reg/93C
Jn., labourer, Corton, Boyton, 1595, I, W, P2/H/143, P2/7Reg/146A
Jn., Sal. St Thos., 1618, I (returned from misc W series), P4/1618/21
Jn., clerk, Bulbridge, Wilton, 1660, I, W, P2/H/603
Jn., sen., yeo., Leigh, Yetm., Dorset, 1685, I, W, P19/46
Hulett, Jn., Earley, Sonning, Berks., 1725, AB, P5/1725/38
Jn., gent., Chetnole, Yetm., Dorset, 1778, W, P19/178
Joyce, cordw., Sal., 1687, W, P4/1687/4
Joyce, glazier, Sal., 1731, W, P4/1731/12
Lewis, yeo., Knook, 1680, I, W, P5/1680/25
Hulett, Mgt., widow, Sherb., Dorset, 1626, AB, a/c, I, P5/1626/22, P5/10Reg/322A
Hulett, Mgt., widow, Fisherton D., 1648, AB, court paper, I, W, P2/H/595
My., widow, Boyton, 1610, AB, T (unnamed children), P2/H/269, P2/8Reg/143A
My., widow, Knook, 1680, I, W, P2/H/782
My., widow, Chetnole, Yetm., Dorset, 1745, W, P19/142
Nich., Sal., 1664, AB, P4/1663/2
Hulett, Philip, husb., Britford, 1680, I, W, P24/431
Rachel, sp., Warm. & Shaftesbury, Dorset, 1694, I, W, P1/H/565
Hulett, Richd., husb., Heytes., 1599, AB, a/c, I, T, P5/1599/9, P5/6Reg/233B
Robt., husb., New Court, Downton, 1668, I, W, P2/H/653
Roger, sen., clerk, Homington, 1666, I, W, P24/363
Hulett, Stephen, husb., Knook, 1591, I, W, P5/1591/44, P5/5Reg/96E
Stephen, yeo., Heytes., 1646, AB, P5/1646/2, P5/14Reg/91B
Hulett, Stephen, Winterborne K., Dorset, 1678, AB, I, P5/1678/23
Thos., yeo., Sherb., Dorset, 1608, AB, I, W, P5/1608/20, P5/8Reg/122B
Thos., Bere R., Dorset, c1550-1620, W, copy W (damaged), P5/1585/43
Hulett, Thos., yeo., Bere R., Dorset, 1613, AB, ren, P5/1613/43, P5/9Reg/79E
Thos., cordw., Enmore Grn, Motc., Dorset, 1747, W, P19/145
Timothy, yeo., Enmore Grn, Motc., Dorset, 1716, W, P5/1716/37, P5/15Reg/337B
Hulett, Wm., Asserton, Berwick St Jas., 1538, W (NEP), P2/1Reg/4A
Hulett, Wm., husb., Corton, Boyton, 1558, W, P2/3Reg/117A
Hulett, Wm., sen., husb., Asserton, Berwick St Jas., 1559, W, P2/3Reg/145A
Wm., Asserton, Berwick St Jas., 1574, W, P2/5Reg/180A

Howlet, Wm., Bloxworth, Dorset, 1632, I, NW, P5/1632/27, P5/12Reg/122B
Wm., yeo., Knook, 1639, I, W, P5/1639/39, P5/13Reg/204B
Wm., Winterborne K., Dorset, 1672, AB, I, P5/1672/20
Hulett, Wm., tailor, Sal., 1674, I, NW, P4/1674/4
Hulett, Wm., husb., Heytes., 1677, I, W, P5/1677/31
Wm., yeo., Chetnole, Yetm., Dorset, 1706, I, W, P19/90
see also Hewett *or* H.
Hews, Hewse *see* Hughes
Hewson *see* May alias H.
Hewster, Wm., jun., Stapleford, 1591, AB, W, P2/H/116
Wm., clerk, Sal. St Martin, 1632, AB, NW, P4/1632/12
Hewstes, Hewstice, Hewstone *see* Hustis
Hex, Sam., seaman (d. serving in Royal Navy), Lyme R., Dorset, 1741, AB, P16/278
Hey *see* Hay
Heychins *see* Hutchins
Heyden, Heydon *see* Hayden
Heyford, Arthur, jun., bach., Wokm., Berks., 1755, AB, P5/1755/28
Joan, widow, Barkham, Berks., 1695, comm, I, W, Wr, P5/1695/45
Heyle *see* Heale
Heyman *see* Hammond
Heymore, Rose, widow, Hungerford, Berks., 1669, AB, comm, I, P5/1669/27
Heyne, Heynes *see* Haynes
Heyre *see* Hare
Heyter, Heytor *see* Hayter
Heyward *see* Hayward
Heywarden *see* Haywarden
Heywood *see* Hayward
Hiam, Hyem, Jn., yeo., Brimpton, Berks., 1631, I, NW, P1/H/191
Wm., innholder, Trowb., 1778, AB, W, P1/H/1253, P1/13Reg/191A
Hiatt *see* Hyatt
Hibbard, Hibbert, Alexander, S. Burcombe, 1634, AB, I, P2/H/460, P2/9Reg/43B
Hibberd, Alice, widow, Foghamshire, Chipp., 1639, I, W, P3/H/316
Hibbert, Ambrose, husb., Corsham, 1623, AB, W, P29/H/26, P29/1Reg/94C, 102
Hibberd, Amy, Baverstock, 1713, AB, P2/H/1112
Hibberd, Ann, widow, Ugford, S. Newton, 1615, I, W, P2/H/311, P2/8Reg/262C
Hibbert, Ann, Chicklade, 1725, AB, P2/H/1212
Hibberd, Ann, widow, Barford St M., 1759, AB, W, P2/H/1441
Hibberd, Ann, widow, Sal., 1799, W, P4/1799/8
Hibberd, Ann, widow, Sal., 1835, AB, Wr, P4/1835/2
Hibbert, Augustine, farmer, Steeple L., 1681, I, W, P2/H/793
Hibberd, Chas., innholder, Stapleford, 1744, W, P2/H/1349
Hibbert, Chas., farmer, Winterbourne S., 1818, W, Wr, P2/1818/15
Hibberd, Chas., bach., Sal., 1849, AB, Wr, P4/1849/23
Hibberd, Chris., Barford St M., 1619, a/c, I, T, P2/H/338
Hibberd, Chris., yeo., Barford St M., 1713, I, W, P2/H/1114
Hibberd, Dan., Woodb., 1726, AB, P3/H/1028
Hibberd, Dan., Barford St M., 1729, AB, P2/H/1239
Hibberd, Dorothy, widow, All C., 1766, W, P3/H/1359
Hibberd, Edith, widow, Netherh., 1558, W, P2/3Reg/128C
Hibbert, Edith, widow, All C., 1693, AB, I, P3/H/725
Hibberd, Edmd., Netherh., 1628, AB, comm, I, P2/H/399
Edwd., Ashley, 1601, W, P3/1Reg/62A
Hibberd, Edwd., Tisb., 1840, AB, Wr, P2/1840/12
Hibberd, Elias *or* Ellis, husb., S. Burcombe, 1601-09, AB, I (2), W, P2/H/199, 250, P2/8Reg/50A
Elias *or* Ellis, Wilton, 1670-78, AB, a/c, I, P2/H/679, 755
Eliz., widow, Seagry, 1569, W, P1/1Reg/96B, P1/2Reg/90B
Hibberd, Eliz., widow, Netherh., 1635, I, W, P1/H/210
Hibberd, Eliz., Steeple A., 1685, AB, P2/H/862
Hibberd, Eliz., widow, Chipp., 1689, I, W, P1/H/523
Hibberd, Francis, shepherd, Milton, Berks., 1634, I, T, W, P1/H/200

Hibberd, Francis, W. Grafton, 1673, AB, I, P21/2/41
Geoffrey, blacksmith, All C., 1722, AB, I, P3/H/992
Hibbert, Geo., husb., Winterbourne S., 1735, I, W, P1/H/941, P1/8Reg/118A
Hibberd, Geo., yeo., Winterbourne S., 1764, W, P2/H/1472
Hibberd, Geo., Bishopstone S., 1771, AB, P2/H/1530
Hibbert, Geo., yeo., Winterbourne S., 1801, W, P2/1801/39
Hibberd, Hy., husb., Fisherton A., 1623, W, P2/H/369
Hibbert, Hy., sen., Wokm., Berks., 1730, W, P5/1730/31
Hy., Lt. Somerford, 1738, AB, comm, P3/H/1156
Hy., linen weaver, Woodlands, Mere, 1701, I, W, P5/1701/28
Jas., Wilton, 1681, AB, a/c, I, P2/H/801
Hibberd, Jas., Barford St M., 1730, W, P2/H/1248
Hibberd, Jas., weaver, Barford St M., 1737, AB, I, W, P2/H/1302
Hibbert, Jas., copyholder, Waltham St Lawr., Berks., 1753, W, Wr, P1/H/1092, P1/11Reg/40
Hibberd, Jas., yeo., Coombe B., 1783, W, P8/61
Hibberd, Jas., dairyman, Netherh., 1845, W, Wr, P2/1845/3
Hibberd, Jane, sp., Tisb., 1857, AB, aff, O, Wr, P2/1857/26
Joan, widow, Wilton, 1593, AB, I, P2/H/131
Hibberd, Joan, widow, Ashley, [1607], W (NEP), P3/H/29
Hibberd, Joan, widow, Bapton, Fisherton Delamare, 1613, AB, NW, P2/H/298, P2/8Reg/188B
Hibberd, Joan, widow, Winterbourne S., 1683, I, W, P2/H/819
Hibbert, Joan, widow, Compton C., 1715, I, W, P2/H/1124
Hibberd, Joan, widow, Burcombe, 1729, W, P2/H/1234
Hibberd, Jn., sen., Netherh., 1550, W, P2/2Reg/94B
Hibbert, Jn., Codf. St P., 1550, W (NEP), P2/2Reg/130A
Hibberd, Jn., yeo., Compton, Enford, 1601, AB, I, W, P2/H/198
Hibbert, Jn., Poulshot, 1605, I, W, P2/H/225
Hibberd, Jn., yeo., Hankerton, [1605], W (NEP), P3/H/13
Hibberd, Jn., sen., husb., S. Burcombe, 1607, I, W, P2/H/239
Jn., All C., 1609, AB, P3/H/50
Hebberd, Jn., blacksmith, Fisherton A., 1613, I, W, P1/H/71
Hibberd, Jn., husb., Crickl. St S., 1622, I, W, P1/H/151
Hibberd, Jn., sen., yeo., Seagry, 1662, comm, I, W, P1/H/330
Hibberd, Jn., husb., Fonthill B., 1669, AB, I, P2/H/663
Hibbert, Jn., carp., Winterbourne S., 1681, I, W, P2/H/786
Hibberd, Jn., Codf. St P., 1687, AB, I, P2/H/885
Hibberd, Jn., yeo., Netherh., 1699, AB, I, P2/H/991
Hibberd, Jn., Sal., 1715, AB, P4/1715/15
Jn., yeo., Coombe B., 1717, I (detailed), W, P5/1717/20, P5/15Reg/395A
Jn., yeo., Coombe B., 1721, W, P8/19
Jn., sen., yeo., Seagry, 1722, I, W, P3/H/993
Hibberd, Jn., blacksmith, All C., 1727, W, P3/H/1038
Hibbert, Jn., sen., yeo., Chicklade, 1733, W, P2/H/1269
Hibberd, Jn., Compton C., 1735, AB, I, P1/H/940
Jn., yeo., Lydiard T., 1736, W, P3/H/1132
Hibberd, Jn., tailor, Hindon, 1739, AB, I, P2/H/1316
Hibberd, Jn., All C., 1744, AB, P3/H/1208
Hibberd, Jn., sen., baker and maltster, Kington St M., 1745, AB (2), comm, ren, P3/H/1218
Hibberd, Jn., Woodb., 1751, AB, P3/H/1259
Hebberd, Jn., W. Harnham, 1752, W, P5/1752/29
Jn., gent., Erlestoke, 1757, comm, W, P2/H/1422
Hibberd, Jn., weaver, Burcombe, 1763, W, P2/H/1464
Hibberd, Jn., yeo., Cumberwell, Bradford A., 1764, comm, W, P2/H/1469
Hibberd, Jn., Netherh., 1767, AB, P2/H/1500
Hibberd, Jn., shoemaker, Sutton M., 1767, AB, I, P2/H/1496
Jn., yeo., Chipp., 1778, W, P3/H/1426
Hibberd, Jn., Kington L., 1786, AB, P1/H/1301
Hibberd, Jn., yeo., Amesb., 1788, W, P2/H/1637
Hibberd, Jn., Sal. St Martin, 1789, W, P1/H/1318, P1/14Reg/311
Hibberd, Jn., gent., Laverstock, 1795, W, P2/H/1674

Hibbert, Jn., cordw., Woodb., 1796, W, P3/H/1517
Hibberd, Jn., labourer, Porton, Idmiston, 1811, AB, W, Wr, P1/1811/121
Hibberd, Jn., yeo., Bishopstone S., 1814, W, Wr, P2/1814/17
Hibberd, Jn., Corsley, 1830, AB, O, P2/1830/52
Hibberd, Jn., chimney sweep, Sal., 1833, W, Wr, P4/1833/2
Hibberd, Jn., innkeeper, Pott., 1855, aff, O, W, Wr, P1/1855/64
Hibberd, Jn., Woodb., 1856, AB, aff, O, Wr, P3/1856/10
Jos., Urchf., 1793, AB, P2/H/1670
Jos., carp., Corsham, 1856, W, P29/1800-1857/49, P29/3Reg/324B
Hibberd, Laurana, widow, W. Harnham, 1729, AB, P8/31
Hibberd, Lewis, bach., Sal., 1849, AB, Wr, P4/1849/22
Hebberd, Mgt., widow, W. Harnham, 1760, W, P8/46
Hibberd, Margery, widow, All C., 1624, I, W, P3/H/187
Hibberd, Maria, sp., Sutton M., 1842, W, Wr, P1/1842/79
Hibbert, Martha, gent.'s widow, Sutton C., Berks., 1711, W, P1/H/676, P1/5Reg/172
Hibberd, My., widow, Seagry, 1665, comm, I, W, P3/H/372
My., wife of Jas., Corsham, [1742], W, P29/H/114
Hibberd, My., widow, Hamptworth, Downton, 1776, W, P2/H/1560
Hibberd, My., widow, Winterbourne E., 1808, AB, Wr, P2/1808/33
Hibberd, My. *see also* Eliz. Eames, P2/8Reg/137C
Hibberd, Michael, S. Burcombe, 1610, AB, I, W, P2/H/270
Hibberd, Moses, thatcher, S. Burcombe, 1833, W, Wr, P2/1833/58
Hibberd, Nich., Sutton M., 1827, AB, Wr, P2/1827/67
Noah, victualler, Marl., 1853, O, W, Wr, P1/1853/3
Hibberd, Rebecca, sp., Chipp., 1696, W, P3/H/761
Hibberd, Richd., Burcombe, 1577, AB, I, P2/H/45
Hibbert, Richd., Burcombe, 1577, AB, P2/5Reg/285B
Richd., Burcombe, 1580, AB, T (children: Jn., Thos., Alice, Joan & Florence H.), P2/H/63, P2/6Reg/7D
Richd., husb., Netherh., 1598, I, W, P2/H/168
Hibberd, Richd., Ugford, S. Newton, 1620, I, T, P2/H/347
Hibberd, Richd., glover, Foghamshire, Chipp., 1633, I, W, P3/H/276
Hibberd, Richd., Netherh., 1638, I, NW, P2/H/505
Hibbert, Richd., S. Marston, 1646, AB, comm, I, P10/1646/1
Hibberd, Richd., tailor, Sal., 1653, I, P4/1653/2
Hibberd, Richd., Teffont M., 1666, AB, P2/H/639
Hibberd, Richd., yeo., S. Burcombe, [1678], I, W, P2/H/756
Hibberd, Richd., yeo., Seagry, 1686, comm, I, W, P3/H/627
Hibberd, Richd., yeo., Compton C., 1692, I, W, P2/H/926
Hibbert, Richd., sen., broad weaver, S. Burcombe, 1705, I, W, P2/H/1036
Hibberd, Richd., Barford St M., 1711, I, W, P2/H/1089
Richd., All C., 1726, AB, I, P1/H/824
Hibbert, Richd., butcher, Wokm., Berks., 1727, I, W, P5/1727/23, P5/16Reg/155B
Hibberd, Richd., yeo., All C., 1750, I, W, P1/H/1080, P1/10Reg/423
Hebberd, Richd., Downton, 1759, AB, W, P2/H/1438
Hibbert, Richd., sen., butcher, Wokm., Berks., 1772, AB, W, P5/1772/10
Hibberd, Richd., millwright, Compton C., 1777, W, P2/H/1569
Hibberd, Richd., Sutton B., 1811, AB, Wr, P3/1811/22
Robt., Winterbourne S., 1680, AB, I, P1/H/446
Hebberd, Robt., fishmonger, Pott., 1715, I, W, P1/H/716, P1/5Reg/479B
Hebberd, Robt., labourer, Downton, 1741, W, P1/H/978, P1/9Reg/50
Hebberd, Robt., Downton, 1764, note of admon, W, P2/H/1473
Hibberd, Robt., Sal., 1803, AB (to brothers, widow being mentally ill), cert, P4/1803/8
Hibberd, Robt., carp., Urchf., 1815, W, P2/1815/21
Hibberd, Roger, yeo., Netherh., 1734, W, P2/H/1280
Hebberd, Ruth, widow, Wilton, 1683, I, W, P2/H/817
Hibberd, Sam., shoemaker, Overton, 1742, W, P3/H/1183
Hebberd, Sam., Langley Wood, 1760, AB, P1/H/1152
Hibberd, Sam., Tisb., 1834, AB, Wr, P2/1834/1
Hebberd, Sarah, widow, Wilton (form. of Barford St M.), 1729, W, P2/H/1240
Hibberd, Sarah, widow, Bishopstone S., 1773, W, P2/H/1535

Sarah, widow, Overton, 1781, W, P3/H/1327
Hibberd, Sibyl, sp., Malm., 1785, AB, P3/H/1462
Hibberd, Simon, Ugford, S. Newton, 1612, I, P2/H/291
Hibberd, Stephen, husb., Netherh., 1553, W, P2/2Reg/178B
Stephen, Barford St M., 1608, AB, P2/8Reg/22B
Hibberd, Stephen, yeo., Fonthill B., 1671, I, W, P2/H/685
Hibberd, Stephen, yeo., Barford St M., 1679, I, W, P2/H/775
Hibbert, Stephen, Barford St M., 1718, W, P2/H/1149
Hibberd, Stephen, bach., Tisb., 1833, AB, Wr, P2/1833/52
Hibberd, Thos., Sutton V., 1563, AB, P2/4Reg/133B
Hibberd, Thos., yeo., Wilton, 1606, I, W, P1/H/51
Hibbert, Thos., yeo., Wilcot, 1613, W, P3/H/94
Thos., husb., Chelworth, Crickl. St S., 1626, I, P3/H/206
Hibberd, Thos., shoemaker, Wilton, 1637, I, W, P2/H/491
Hibberd, Thos., husb., S. Burcombe, 1640, I, W, P2/H/539
Hibbert, Thos., yeo., Ugford, S. Newton, 1642, AB, I, copy I, P2/H/558
Hibberd, Thos., Codf. St P., 1664, AB, ren, P2/H/626
Hibbert, Thos., Marl., 1666, AB, comm, I, P1/H/374
Hibbert, Thos., Newton T., 1673, AB, I, P2/H/704
Thos., hellier, Sal. St Martin, 1681, I, W, P4/1681/26
Hibberd, Thos., labourer, Winterbourne S., 1712, AB, I, P2/H/1100
Hibberd, Thos., sen., innholder, Stapleford, 1728, W, P2/H/1229
Hibberd, Thos., mason, Pott., 1736, W, P1/H/944, P1/8Reg/161A
Hibberd, Thos., victualler, Chipp., 1753, W, P1/H/1097, P1/11Reg/99
Hebbet, Thos., butcher, Wokm., Berks., 1759, W, P5/1759/14
Thos., butcher, Kington L., 1778, W, P3/H/1427
Hibberd, Thos., All C., 1803, AB, W, P3/1803/5
Hibbert, Thos., labourer, Wokm., Berks. (form. of Wisley, Surrey), 1834, aff, note, O, W, Wr, P5/1834/17
Thos., West Field, Corsham, 1855, aff, D, W, Wr, P3/1855/25
Wilks, yeo., Fonthill B., 1718, W, P2/H/1152
Hibberd, Wm., husb., S. Newton, 1580, I, W, P2/H/61, P2/6Reg/2A
Hibberd, Wm., jun., husb., All C., 1685, AB, comm, I, P3/H/613
Hibberd, Wm., Sutton C., Berks., 1695, note of probate, P1/H/582
Hibberd, Wm., broad weaver, S. Burcombe, 1697, I, W, P2/H/974
Hibberd, Wm., weaver, S. Burcombe, 1714, AB, I, P1/H/695
Hibberd, Wm., yeo., W. Harnham, 1725, W, P5/1725/32, P5/16Reg/107C
Hibberd, Wm., clothworker, Westwood, 1737, I, W, P2/H/1306
Hibberd, Wm., labourer, Winterbourne S., 1764, W, P2/H/1471
Hibberd, Wm., shepherd, Winterbourne S., 1764, W, P2/H/1470
Hibberd, Wm., innholder, Sal., 1766, W, P4/1766/12
Wm., All C., 1775-81, AB (2), W, P3/H/1413
Hibberd, Wm., Tisb., 1785, AB, P2/H/1620
Hibberd, Wm., yeo., W. Grimstead, 1792, W, P2/H/1659
Hibberd, Wm., gent., W. Harnham, 1796, W, P8/70
Wm., barber, Melk., 1799, W, P2/H/1695
Wm., cordw., Corsham, [1803], I, W (NEP), P29/1800-1857/3, P29/3Reg/236
Hibberd, Wm., yeo., Pott. Wick, 1829, W, Wr, P1/1829/147
Hibberd, Wm., Tisb., 1851, AB, Wr, P1/1851/19
see also Jeffery alias H.
Hibditch *see* Hebditch
Hickes *see* Hicks
Hickets, Hickett *or* Higgett, Edwd., Erlestoke, 1580, AB, I, P2/H/58, P2/5Reg/359A
Jn., sen., husb., Starrs Bridge, Westb., 1694, I (detailed), W, P25/1694/10
Martha, widow, Westb., 1716, I, W, P25/1716/3
Stephen, labourer, Littleton P., 1759, W, P1/H/1149, P1/11Reg/459A
Hickman, Ann, widow, Bulford, 1725, W, P2/H/1207
Ann, widow, Kington St M., 1769, W, P3/H/1387
Dan., E. Kennett, 1720, AB, P1/H/769
Dan., carp., Norton B., 1793, comm, W, P2/H/1667
Dan., yeo., Warm., 1840, AB, comm, W, Wr, P2/1840/45

Dorothy, widow, Bromham, 1693, AB, I, ren, W, P3/H/726
Edmd., clerk, Sal. The Close, 1728, W, P4/1728/14
Eliz., widow, Haxton, Fittleton, 1647, I, W, P2/H/587
Eliz., widow, W. Knoyle, 1682, I, W, P2/H/812
Eliz., widow, Warm., 1841, comm, W, Wr, P2/1841/54
Emma, Homington, 1607, AB, P24/165
Jas., Warm., 1838, AB, comm, Wr, P2/1838/10
Jn., husb., Haxton, Fittleton, 1609, I, W, P2/H/253, P2/8Reg/62C
Jn., Corsham, 1688, AB, I, copy I, P29/H/61, P29/1Reg/241D
Jn., [miller], Bromham, 1691, AB, comm, I, P3/H/695
Jn., miller, Bulford, 1696, I, W, P2/H/964
Jn., Kington St M., 1731, AB, P3/H/1090
Jn., farrier, Chute, 1744, AB, W, P7/140
Jn., husb., Hilp., 1746, W, P2/H/1362
Luke, Longstreet, Enford, 1636, I, NW, P2/H/471, P2/9Reg/98C
My., widow, Longstreet, Enford, 1702, W, P2/H/1013
My., sp., Bulford, 1720, W, P2/H/1173
Nich., yeo., Stapleford, 1729, I, W, P2/H/1233
Richd., husb., Fittleton, 1599, AB, I, W, P2/H/187
Richd., husb., Haxton, Fittleton, 1661, I, NW, P2/H/610
Robt., Fittleton, 1559, W, P2/3Reg/157E
Sam., Warm., 1754, AB, P2/H/1407
Sarah, widow, E. Kennett, 1752, W, P3/H/1270
Simon, Haxton, Fittleton, 1598, W, P2/H/175
Susanna, widow, Collingbourne K., 1744, AB, W, P3/H/1209
Thos., rector, Upton L., 1666, AB, comm, P1/H/366
Thos., sen., yeo., Sunton, Collingbourne K., 1706, W, P3/H/864
Thos., Fovant, 1779, W, P2/H/1577
Thos., yeo., Collingbourne K., 1741-42, AB, W, P3/H/1177, 1184
Wm., sen., husb., Haxton, Fittleton, 1619, I, W, P2/H/340
Wm., Bulford, 1736, AB, a/c, I, P2/H/1287
Wm., husb. *or* yeo., Collingbourne K., 1737, I, W, P3/H/1140
Wm., yeo., Chapmanslade, Dilton, Westb., 1793, comm, W, P25/1793/1
Hickocks, Wm., husb., Rams., 1638, I, W, P5/1638/55, P5/13Reg/99
Hicks, Ann, widow, Bishopstone N., 1633, W, P6/17
Ann, widow, Gomeldon, Idmiston, 1733, W, P2/H/1270
Dan., sen., yeo., Bromham, 1681, comm, I, W, P3/H/558
Dan., innholder, Bradford A., 1721, W, P2/H/1178
Dorothy, widow, S. Wraxall, 1718, W, P2/H/1160
Hix, Edmd., husb., Clevancy, Hilmarton, 1610, AB, NW, P3/H/60
Hix, Edwd., baker, E. Knoyle, [1684], I, W, P2/H/843
Hickes, Eleanor, widow, Paxcroft, Steeple A., [1675], I, W, P2/H/722
Eleanor, widow, Hindon, 1735, AB, ren, W, P1/H/942, P1/8Reg/141A
Hickes, Geoffrey, yeo., Semington, Steeple A., 1646, AB, a/c, I, P2/H/581
Hickes, Geoffrey, Steeple A., 1673, I, W, P2/H/707
Geoffrey, jun., baker and maltster, Seend, Melk., 1751, comm, W, P2/H/1391
Geoffrey, baker, Seend, Melk., 1753, AB, ren, W, P1/H/1101, P1/11Reg/102
Geo., Westwood, 1763, AB, P2/H/1466
Hy., joiner, Sal., 1695, W, P1/H/581
Hy., yeo., Bromham, 1754, W, P3/H/1279
Hy., butcher and victualler, Amesb., 1767, W, P2/H/1493
Humphrey, Calne, 1714, AB, I, P26/584
Hickes, Jacob, broad weaver, Frankleigh, Bradford A., 1706, W, P2/H/1050
Hickes, Jas., yeo., Lydiard M., 1693, W, P3/H/727
Jane, widow, Calstone W., 1698, I, W, P26/457
Jasper, husb., Gillingham, Dorset, 1720, ren, W, P27/1/243
Joan, widow, Ashton K., 1630, AB, I, W, P3/H/242
Hickes, Joan, sp., Crickl. St My., 1665, I, W, P3/H/373
Jn., Preston, Dorset, 1594, AB, I, W, P5/1594/38, P5/6Reg/62A
Jn., Bishopstone N., 1625, I, P6/1

Hicks alias Eyles, Jn., Steeple L., 1640, AB, I, P2/H/543
Jn., [turner], Sal. St Thos., 1670, AB, I, P4/1670/7
Jn., tailor, Steeple A., 1678, I, W, P2/H/760
Jn., fellmonger, Blewbury, Berks., 1688, AB, comm, I, ren, P5/1688/43
Jn., fuller, Calstone W., 1697, I, W, P26/444
Jn., Reading, Berks., 1698, AB, comm, P1/H/596
Jn., sen., yeo., Calne, 1715, I, W, P26/592
Jn., E. Knoyle, 1719, AB, I, P2/H/1167
Jn., sen., fuller, Calstone W., 1720, AB, I, P26/636
Hicks alias Eyles, Jn., Fisherton D., 1726, AB, P2/H/1214
Jn., yeo., Longcott, Shrivenham, Berks., 1729, W, P1/H/862, P1/7Reg/296
Jn., yeo., Atworth, Bradford A., 1730, AB, I, P2/H/1241
Hix, Jn., Bromham, 1733, AB, I, P3/H/1113
Jn., Studley, Calne, 1733, AB, P26/775
Jn., yeo., Tytherton L., Chipp., 1735, W, P1/H/926, P1/7Reg/635B
Jn., Urchf., 1737, AB, P2/H/1294
Jn., surgeon and apothecary, Melk., 1775, AB, a/c, I, W, P2/H/1553
Jn., yeo., Bromham, 1781, W, P3/H/1441
Jn., farmer, Upavon, 1843, W, Wr, P2/1843/29
Jos., Bromham, 1760, W, P3/H/1320
Mgt., Amesb., 1741, AB, P2/H/1332
Martin, bach., Bishopstone N., 1706, AB, I, P6/94
Hix alias Eyles, My., widow, Stockton, 1729, I, summary I, W, P1/H/878, P1/7Reg/377B
My., widow, Landford, 1799, W, P2/H/1688
Hix, Matthew, Hanging L., 1802, AB, P2/1802/63
Hix, Nich., wheelwright, Urchf., 1684, AB, I, W, P2/H/832
Hix, Nich., Urchf., 1698, AB (2), comm, P2/H/982
Oliver, yeo., Bishopstone N., 1686, I, W, P6/64
Hickes, Richd., [tucker], Chr. M., [c1619], I, W (NEP), P3/H/141
Hickes, Richd., Chr. M., 1646, AB, comm, I, P1/H/270
Hicks alias Eyles, Richd., yeo., Hanging L., 1662, W, P2/H/613
Richd., yeo., Lt. Coxwell, Gt. Faringdon, Berks., 1663, AB, I, P5/1662/57
Richd., fuller, Lacock, 1690, I, W, P3/H/681
Richd., fuller, Calstone W., 1708, I (detailed), W, P26/547
Hicks alias Eyles, Richd., yeo., Steeple L., 1712, I, W, P2/H/1101
Hickes, Richd., yeo., Whitley, Melk., 1737, ren, W, P2/H/1298
Richd., Hanging L., 1766, W, P2/H/1490
Hix alias Eyles, Robt., husb. and yeo., Fisherton D., 1638, I, NW, P1/H/240
Hickes alias Eyles, Robt., Deptford, Wylye, 1667, I, W, P2/H/648
Robt., yeo., W. Lavington, 1716, I, W, P1/H/721, P1/6Reg/3
Sam., Bromham, 1670, I, W, P3/H/437
Sam., baker, Bromham, 1716, AB, W, P1/H/732, P1/6Reg/71A
Sam., Keevil, 1790, AB, comm, P2/H/1647
Hickes, Stephen, clothier, Lacock, 1646, W, P1/H/268
Hickes, Thos., yeo., Alton Pr., 1680, I, NW, P3/H/545
Hix, Thos., yeo., Paxcroft, Steeple A., [1687], W, P2/H/879
Thos., yeo., Stanley, Chipp., 1692, AB, I, ren, W, P3/H/710
Thos., sen., fuller, W. Lavington, 1694-96, AB, I, W, P1/H/563, 585
Thos., Calstone W., 1721, AB, P26/651
Thos., Seend, Melk., 1789, AB, comm, P2/H/1644
Thos., yeo., Landford, 1797, W, P2/H/1684
Tobias, Blewbury, Berks., 1674, W, P5/1674/38
Hickes, Walter, yeo., Chelworth, Crickl. St S., 1622, I, W, P3/H/172
Walter, Hindon, 1719, W, P2/H/1162
Hickes, Wm., Quidh., 1545, W (NEP), P2/1Reg/59C
Hix, Wm., Bishopstone N., 1593, I, W, P5/1593/42, P5/6Reg/38A
Hix, Wm., husb., Ashton K., [1610], I, W (NEP), P3/H/61
Wm., glover, Blewbury, Berks., 1629, I, W, P5/1629/26, P5/11Reg/115B
Hickes, Wm., Chiseldon, 1629, AB, I, P3/H/228
Hickes, Wm., husb., Bere R., Dorset, 1633, I, NW, P5/1633/23, P5/12Reg/154

Wm., Calstone W., 1716, W, P26/605
Hicks alias Eyles, Wm., yeo., Gomeldon, Idmiston, 1719, I, W, P2/H/1163
Wm., butcher, Amesb., 1734, W, P2/H/1273
see also Androws alias H.; Eyles alias H.; Harper alias H.
Hickson, Eliz., innkeeper, Amesb., 1785, W, P2/H/1614
Joan, widow, Britford, 1665, NW, P24/317
Jn., innholder, E. Harnham, Britford, 1683, AB, a/c, I (detailed), ren, P24/753
Jn., cooper, Amesb., 1796, W, P2/H/1679
Hixon, My., sp., Gillingham, Dorset, 1773, W, P27/1/484, P27/3Reg/172
Hixon, My., widow, Sedgehill, 1811, comm, W, Wr, P1/1811/133
Matthew, husb., Britford, 1663, I, W, P1/H/338
Robt., cooper, Amesb., 1763, W, P1/H/1175, P1/12Reg/134
Hixon, Robt., yeo., Gillingham, Dorset, 1767, W, P27/1/460, P27/3Reg/134
Hixon, Sarah, sp., Gillingham, Dorset, 1787, W, P27/1/530, P27/3Reg/253
Thos., husb., Britford, 1661, AB, I (2), P24/280
Thos., sen., cordw., E. Harnham, Britford, 1683, I, W, P24/755
Thos., barber, Amesb., 1720, I, W, P1/H/777, P1/6Reg/353
Thos., brandy merchant, Amesb., 1796, W, P2/H/1678
Wm., cutler, Amesb., 1580, W, P2/H/1588
Wm., gent., Amesb., 1837, comm, W, Wr, P2/1837/28
Hidden, Hidden alias Clidesdale, Edwd., Eddington, Hungerford, Berks., 1602, AB, I, P5/1602/21, P5/7Reg/44A
Hiding, Edwd., Baydon, 1699, I, W, P5/1699/18
Hidden alias Clidesdale, Jn., Chilton F., 1623, I, W, P3/H/179
Jn., Hungerford, Berks., 1710, AB, P5/1710/52
Hidden alias Chidsden, Thos., yeo., Baydon, 1720, W, P5/1720/25, P5/16Reg/39A
see also Clidesdale alias H.
Hidditch *see* Hebditch
Hide *see* Hyde
Hiding *see* Hidden
Hieron, Hierne, Bartholomew, gent., Whitchurch, Malm., 1703, W, P3/H/842
Hiron, Jn., yeo., Idmiston, 1733, AB, I, P1/H/920
Hiron, Jn., Idmiston, 1768, AB, P2/H/1502
Wm., yeo., Rodbourne, Malm., 1676, AB, a/c, I, P3/H/510
Hiett *see* Hyatt
Higdon, Jn., Wokm., Berks., 1545, W, P5/20Reg/68A
Jn., yeo., Semley, 1548, W, P2/2Reg/38B
Higg *see* Higgs
Higgence, Higgens *see* Higgins
Higges *see* Higgs
Higgett *see* Hickett
Higgins, Higgens, Andrew, Collingbourne D., 1684, AB, P21/4/10
Ann, widow, Stratford sub C., 1762, W, P4/1762/16
Higgons, Ann, widow, Shellingford, Berks., 1776, W, P1/H/1243, P1/13Reg/125
Avis, Donhead St My., 1557, W, P2/3Reg/33C
Chas., carp., Marcham, Berks., 1732, W, P1/H/891, P1/7Reg/465B
David, weaver, Chipp., 1623, I, W, P3/H/180
Edwd., weaver, Chipp., 1638, I, W, P3/H/309
Eliz., widow, Rode Hill, Somerset, 1825, W, Wr, P2/1825/61
Francis, yeo. *or* husb., Buckland, Berks., 1747-51, AB, comm, W, P1/H/1036, P1/10Reg/90
Geo., Chipp., 1610, W, P3/H/59
Higgence, Hy., broad weaver, Chipp., 1678, I, W, P3/H/531
Hy., yeo., Chards., Devon, 1809, req, W, copy W, Wr, P5/1809/39
Higgin, Jn., sen., Donhead St My., 1543, W (NEP), P2/1Reg/44C
Higgens, Jn., Corsley, 1578, I, copy I, W, P2/H/49, P2/5Reg/306C
Jn., Chr. M., 1606, I, W (2), P3/H/20
Jn., carp., Marcham, Berks., 1698, I, W, P1/H/602, P1/3Reg/100
Jn., [nurseryman *or* gardener], Sal. St Edmd., 1736, AB, a/c, I, Wr, P4/1736/4
Jn., carp., Marcham, Berks., 1763, W, P1/H/1166, P1/12Reg/83
Jn., blacksmith, Blewbury, Berks., 1802, W, P5/19Reg/6
Martha, widow, Rushall, 1704, AB, I, P2/H/1026

Richd., Wantage, Berks., 1576, I, W, P5/1576/26, P5/3Reg/89A
Higgens, Richd., N. Newnton, 1748, AB, P3/H/1238
Richd., Everleigh, 1795, AB, P1/H/1343, P1/14Reg/617A
Richd., yeo., Wootton R., 1795, W, P1/H/1340, P1/14Reg/552
Higgens, Thos., Chr. M., 1613, AB, P3/H/95
Higgons, Thos., husb., N. Newnton, 1633, I, W, P3/H/273
Thos., weaver, Chipp., 1640, I, W, P3/H/323
Thos., shepherd, Drayton, Abingdon, Berks., 1668, comm, I, W, P1/H/393
Higgens, Thos., yeo., Hilcott, N. Newnton, 1687, AB, comm, I, P3/H/638
Thos., carp., Stratford sub C., 1777, W, P4/1777/3
Thos., grocer, maltster and brewer, Sal. St Martin, 1836, W, Wr, P4/1836/16
Thos., yeo., Clench, Milton L., 1854, AB, aff, D (2), ren, W, Wr, P3/1854/68
Ursula, widow, Chipp., 1709, I, W, P3/H/894
Wm., sen., thatcher, Chipp., 1682, I, W, P3/H/569
Wm., yeo., Chipp., 1687, AB, I, P3/H/639
Higgons, Wm., surgeon and physician, Rushall, 1697, I, W, P2/H/976
Higgens, Wm., bach., Hannington, 1766, AB, P3/H/1358
Wm., farmer, Kingston D., 1856, aff, W, Wr, P2/1856/32
see also Newport alias H.
Higgs, Higges, Eliz., Earley, Sonning, Berks., 1605, AB, I, W, P5/1605/30, P5/8Reg/49
Hy., husb., Basildon, Berks., 1606, I, W, P1/H/38
Jas., bucketmaker, Cold Ash, Thatcham, Berks., 1763, W, P1/H/1168, P1/12Reg/92
Jn., Hurst, Berks., 1569, W, P5/2Reg/53A
Higges, Jn., husb., Sonning, Berks., 1570, W, P5/2Reg/68C
Jn., husb., Ward's Cross, Hurst, Berks., 1598, AB, I, P5/1598/25, P5/6Reg/206B
Jn., yeo., Hurst, Berks., 1730, W, P5/1730/32
Jn., Redlynch, Downton, 1795, AB, P2/H/1677
Julian, widow, Swallowfield, Shinfield, Berks., 1625, I, W, P1/H/164
Lettice, Bisham, Berks., 1692, AB, comm, I, P1/H/551
Moses, yeo., Wokm., Berks., 1724, AB, W, P5/1724/37, P5/16Reg/92C
Moses, Sherston, 1838, AB, O, Wr, P3/1838/3
Moses, butcher, Sherston, 1857, aff, D, O, W, Wr, P3/1857/23
Higges, Nich., Hurst, Berks., 1540, W, P5/20Reg/19B
Higges, Ralph, Ruscombe, Berks., 1573, W, P5/3Reg/15A
Higges, [Richd.], Hurst, Berks., 1605, I (damaged - evidence that it belongs with W is circumstantial), W [chr.name from burial register], P5/1605/29
Richd., sen., basketmaker, Hurst, Berks., 1716, W, P5/1716/45, P5/15Reg/354C
Richd., sen., basketmaker, Hurst, Berks., 1728, W, P5/1728/51, P5/16Reg/202B
Richd., W. Hanney, Berks., 1753, I, W, P1/H/1088, P1/10Reg/517
Higges, Stephen, husb., Tilehurst, Berks., 1602, I, W, P1/H/24
Thos., Earley, Sonning, Berks., 1607, AB, I, W, P5/1607/31, P5/8Reg/102A
Thos., sen., yeo., Upton, Blewbury, Berks., 1670, comm, I, W, P5/1670/22
Thos., labourer, Paccombe, Downton, 1828, W, Wr, P2/1828/11
Wm., cooper, Basildon, Berks., 1717, AB, I, W, P1/H/744, P1/6Reg/107
Higg, Wm., labourer, Whistley, Hurst, Berks., 1827, W, Wr, P5/1827/19
Wm., cordw., Broad B., Highw., 1852, aff, O, W, Wr, P10/1852/1
Higham, Jas., postmaster, Marl., 1804-05, cert, comm, W, copy W, P1/1804/150
Jn., salesman, Marl., 1725, W, P1/H/811, P1/7Reg/60
Jn., Marl., 1756, AB, P1/H/1129
My., salesman's widow, Marl., 1746, W, P1/H/1030, P1/10Reg/15B
My., sp., Marl., 1763, W, P1/H/1170, P1/12Reg/111B
Richd., victualler, Marl., 1746, W, P1/H/1032, P1/10Reg/23A
Thos., salesman, Marl., 1729, W, P1/H/861, P1/7Reg/289A
Thos., salesman, Marl., 1737, W, P1/H/949, P1/8Reg/195
Highett *see* Hyatt
Highman, Wm., shopkeeper, Sal., 1793, W, P4/1793/7
Highmore, Heighmore, Eliz., Bishopstone S., 1719, W, P2/H/1168
Francis, Bishopstone S., 1711, AB, P2/H/1091
Jn., Thornford, Dorset, 1791, AB, P5/1791/10, P5/18Reg/172A
Nathaniel, gent., Thornford, Dorset, 1769, W, P5/1769/17

Susanna, sp., Donhead St My., 1820, AB, comm, Wr, P1/1820/57
Highwood, Richd., tailor, Sal. St Thos., 1633, I, W, P4/1633/5
Hignell, Jn., Crickl. St S., 1626, AB, P3/H/207
Hegnell, Robt., yeo., Crickl. St S., 1755, W, P3/H/1288
Ursula, farmer's wife, Crickl. St S., 1675, AB, P3/H/496
Wm., maltster, Crookham, Thatcham, Berks., 1763, W, P1/H/1167, P1/12Reg/85
Higton, Mgt., widow, Trowb., 1817, AB, Wr, P1/1817/85
Hilary *see* Hillary
Hilbert, Richd., sen., butcher, Wokm., Berks., 1772, W, P5/17Reg/42
Hilberd, Thos., sen., Netherh., 1544, W (NEP), P2/1Reg/51A
Hilcock, Giles, Sal., 1766, W, P4/1766/5
Hildesley, Chris., Woolhampton, Berks., 1614, AB, I, P1/H/92
Eliz., widow, Beenham Valence, Berks., 1605, I, W, P1/H/30
Eliz., widow, Sonning, Berks., 1681, I, W, P5/1681/30
Richd., Sonning, Berks., 1680, AB, I, P5/1680/17
Robt., Wokefield, Stratfield M., Berks., 1625, I, W, P1/H/163
Hill, (Mr) *see* Hy. Crouch, P1/7Reg/543
Adam, Ansty, 1732, AB, W, P1/H/912
Alice, Corsley, 1567, W, P2/5Reg/8B
Alice, widow, Mere, 1572, W, P5/3Reg/3C
Hill alias Tucker, Alice, widow, Sal., 1595, AB, P1/H/14
Alice, Berwick St Leonard, [1677], I, P2/H/748
Amy, widow, Winterborne K., Dorset, 1683, AB, I, W, P5/1683/27
Amy, widow, Welford, Berks., 1711, AB, I, P1/H/682
Andrew, yeo., Dilton, Westb., 1648, AB, I, P25/1648/1
Andrew, tailor, Netherb., Dorset, 1701, AB, I, P5/1701/29
Andrew, clothworker, Marsh, Westb., 1725, W, P25/1725/5
Ann, widow, Compton B. (leaving effects at Calne), 1755, AB, ren, W, P26/937
Ann, widow, Latton, 1809, AB, Wr, P3/1809/16
Ann, widow, Damerham, Hants, 1822, W, Wr, P2/1822/33
Ann, widow, Easton Town, Sherston, 1837, W, Wr, P3/1837/84
Ann, widow, Kemble, 1664, I, W, P3/H/362
Anthony, carp., Pott., 1643, I, W, P1/H/259
Anthony, jun., yeo., Dilton, Westb., 1663-64, comm, I (detailed), W, P25/1663/6, P25/1664/2
Anthony, dyer, Westb. L., 1699, I, W, P25/1699/4
Bartholomew, tanner, Westport St My., 1699, comm, I, W, P3/H/785
Benj., Lyme R., Dorset, 1687, AB, P16/95
Benj., yeo., Dilton M., Westb., 1832, AB, O, ren, summons (to produce W at assizes 1867), W, Wr, P25/1832/4
Betty, widow, Wrou., 1790, W, P3/H/1493
Bridget, widow, Littleton P., 1748, AB, P1/H/1054
Cath., widow, Marl. St My., 1720, AB, I, P1/H/752
Chas. Brown, gent., Lt. Somerford, 1851, O, ren, W, Wr, P3/1851/27
Chris., Gt. Cheverell, 1606, AB, P2/H/236
Chris., weaver, Heytes., 1606, AB, I, NW, P1/H/39
Chris., yeo., Upton S., 1638, I, W, P2/H/498
Chris., husb., Winterborne K., Dorset, 1682-84, AB, comm, I, T, P5/1682/57, P5/1684/32
Chris., clothworker, Melk., 1770, W, P1/H/1203, P1/12Reg/315
Dan., labourer, Fyfield, Milton L., 1715, I, W, P3/H/940
Dan., Fordington, Dorset, 1754, W, P15/140
Dan., cordw., Trowb., 1795, W, P1/H/1330, P1/14Reg/514
Dan., servant to Thos. Winkworth of Hidden Farm, Hungerford, Hungerford, Berks., 1809, W, Wr, P5/1809/28
Edwd., no abode stated, 1597, W, P1/H/19
Edwd., yeo., Netherh., 1641, AB, P1/H/253
Edwd., Stratford Tony, 1681, I, W, P2/H/784
Edwd., gent., Rodbourne C., 1730, W, P3/H/1075
Eleanor, widow, Twyford, Hurst, Berks., 1627, I, W, P5/1627/24, P5/11Reg/46B
Eliz., Mkt. L., 1597, I, W, P2/H/163
Eliz., widow, Horningsham, 1616, I, W, P5/1616/36
Eliz., widow, Ham, 1623, I, W, P3/H/181
Eliz., Stratfield M., Berks., 1625, I, W, P1/H/165

Eliz., widow, Dilton, Westb., 1665, comm, W (a/c of debts due on back), P25/1665/8
Eliz., singlewoman, Short St., Dilton, Westb., 1713, AB, P25/1713/2
Eliz., widow, Sal., 1720, copy W, W, P1/H/756, P1/6Reg/195
Eliz., widow, Malm., 1730, AB, P3/H/1076
Eliz., widow, Westb. L., 1779, AB, P25/1779/3
Eliz., yeo.'s wife, Allington, All C., 1798, AB, P3/H/1532
Eliz., widow, Devizes St Jn., 1810, W, Wr, P1/1810/5
Ephraim, Biddesden, Ludg., 1671, AB, I, P1/H/403
Francis, yeo., Woodhouse Farm, Horningsham, 1856, aff, W, Wr, P5/1856/16
Geo., yeo., Uffc., Devon, 1712, W, P20/1/146
Geo., Berwick St Jn., 1812, AB, W, Wr, P2/1812/63
Giles, Shalbourne, Berks., 1708, I, W, P23/295
Harriet, sp., Quidh. (form. of Swallowcliffe), 1797, W, P2/H/1686
Hy., Mkt. L., 1582, W, P2/6Reg/71B
Hy., Preston, Dorset, 1609, AB, I, T, P5/1609/39, P5/8Reg/165B
Hy., Minety, 1613, I, W, P1/H/76
Hy., Bere R., Dorset, 1667, AB, I, P5/1667/25
Hy., tucker, Minety, 1667, AB, I, P3/H/390
Hy., yeo., Wylye, 1704, inty, I, sentence, W, P2/H/1029
Hy., Mere, 1737, AB, NW, P5/1737/27
Hy., yeo., Stratford Tony, 1740, W, P2/H/1326
Hy., yeo., Hankerton, 1744, W, P1/H/1017, P1/9Reg/390B
Hester, widow, Keevil, 1725, I, W, P2/H/1209
Hugh, husb., Heytes., 1699, I, W, P5/1699/19
Hill alias Phelps, Jas., Netherb., Dorset, 1632, I, P17/13
Jas., Berwick St Jas., 1710, AB, P1/H/659
Jas., Devizes, 1757, AB, P1/H/1131
Jane, widow, E. Town, W. Ashton, Steeple A., [1687], W, P2/H/881
Jane, widow, Lyme R., Dorset, 1719, W, copy W, P5/1719/45, P5/16Reg/14C
Jane, widow, Gillingham, Dorset, 1723, W, P27/1/258
Joan, widow, Bruton, Somerset, 1632, I, L, receipt, P2/H/446
Jn., Poulshot, 1559, AB, P2/3Reg/183C
Jn., tailor, Westb. L., 1576, I, W, P5/1576/27, P5/3Reg/91B
Jn., blacksmith, Gillingham, Dorset, 1596, I, P27/1/1
Jn., Downton, 1598, AB, I, P2/H/177
Jn., fletcher, Chipp., 1606, I, W, P3/H/21
Jn., sen., yeo., Rod St., Corsley, 1608, W, P2/8Reg/5B
Jn., W. Harnham, 1613, comm, W, P5/1613/39, P5/9Reg/83B
Jn., Bathampton, Steeple L., 1616-17, AB, a/c (2), I, P2/H/314, P2/8Reg/306C
Jn., W. Harnham, 1617, W, copy W, P4/1617/8
Jn., weaver, Ham, [1619], I, W (NEP), P3/H/142
Jn., shepherd, Britford, 1624, AB, I, P24/184
Jn., tanner, Sherb., Dorset, 1624, AB, I, P5/1624/21, P5/10Reg/233A
Jn., yeo., Corsley, 1631, I, W, P2/H/430, P2/9Reg/69
Jn., Donhead St My., 1636, AB, comm, I, P2/H/474
Jn., yeo., Whitep., 1643, AB, I, P2/H/566
Jn., Collingbourne K., 1668, AB, I, W, P1/H/391
Jn., yeo., Ryme I., Dorset (*also* of Dorchester Prison), 1668, I, W, P5/1668/34
Jn., Poulshot, 1672, I, W, P2/H/697
Jn., yeo., Heytes., 1684, AB, I, P5/1684/29
Jn., Rams., 1686, I, NW, P5/1686/75
Jn., Malm., 1690, AB, I, P3/H/682
Jn., sen., gardener, Devizes St My., 1702, W, P1/H/621, P1/4Reg/217
Jn., sen., Westb. L., 1709, AB, I, P25/1709/6
Jn., yeo., Gasper, Stourton, 1711, I, W, P2/H/1092
Jn., gardener, Devizes, 1719, I, copy I, W, P1/H/754, P1/6Reg/188
Jn., yeo., Compton B., 1722, I, W, P3/H/994
Jn., Hindon, 1728, AB, P2/H/1231
Jn., sen., victualler, Devizes, 1729, I, W, P1/H/873, P1/7Reg/342B
Jn., Stratford Tony, 1729-35, AB, W, P1/H/842, P2/H/1282

Jn., Hindon, 1740, AB, I, L, P2/H/1329
Jn., innholder, Sal., 1740, AB, I (detailed), Wr, P4/1740/20
Jn., wheelwright, Mildenhall, 1744, AB, P3/H/1210
Jn., victualler, Devizes, 1750, W, P1/H/1081, P1/10Reg/444B
Jn., yeo., Uffc., Devon, 1756, W, P20/1/230
Jn., Charlton, Downton, 1758, AB, ren, P2/H/1429
Jn., mariner on the Tilbury man of war, Sal., 1759, AB, W, P1/H/1144, P1/11Reg/420A
Jn., yeo., Westb., 1764, W, P25/1764/2
Jn., sadler, Uffc., Devon, 1765, W, P20/1/245
Jn., broad weaver, Wags Mill, Westb., 1772, W, P25/1772/4
Jn., labourer, Pott., 1775, W, copy W (& note of cost), P1/H/1234, P1/13Reg/60B
Jn., sen., yeo., Keevil, 1776, W, P2/H/1561
Jn., cordw., Damerham, Hants, 1820, W, Wr, P1/1820/14
Jn., yeo., Poulton, 1825, W, Wr, P3/1825/63
Jn., Bushton, Clyffe P., 1833, AB, O, Wr, P3/1833/14
Jn., gent., Calne, 1842, comm, W, Wr, P26/1461
Jn., tallow chandler, Malm., 1848, O, W, Wr, P3/1848/5
Jn., Thickthorn Farm, Lyneham, 1856, AB, aff, comm, Wr, P3/1856/20
Jn. Coventry, yeo., Wrou., 1758, AB, P3/H/1311
Jolliffe, Downton, 1747, AB, P2/H/1368
Jonas, barber surgeon, Devizes St My., 1631, I, W, P1/H/184
Jonas, gardener, Devizes, 1701, AB, I, L, P1/H/609
Jonas, gardener, Devizes, 1744, W, P1/H/1024, P1/9Reg/407B
Jonathan, Cholderton, 1672, W, P2/H/694
Jonathan, [Sal. Cathedral] (NBI), 1714, AB, P1/H/711
Jonathan, Sal., 1715, AB, P4/1715/13
Jonathan, bach., Stock St., Calne, 1761, AB, comm, P5/1761/20
Jos., Lacock, 1732, I, W, P1/H/901, P1/7Reg/503A
Jos., scribler, Trowb., 1743, AB, W, P1/H/1001, P1/9Reg/271A
Jos., yeo., Wrou., 1790, AB, W, P3/H/1494
Jos., Bps. C., 1823, AB, Wr, P24/1295
Jos., Uffc., Devon, 1830, W, Wr, P5/1830/37
Jos. *see also* Isaac Veals
Julian, widow, Chipp., 1606, I, W, P3/H/22
Margery, widow, Warm., 1567, W, P2/5Reg/13D
Margery, widow, Chipp., 1611, AB, P3/H/71
Martha, widow, Upton S., 1665, I, W, P2/H/629
Martha, widow, Bratton, Westb., 1740, W, P25/1740/1
My., widow, Compton B., 1663, I, W, P1/H/334
My., widow, Gillingham, Dorset, 1682, I, P27/1/68
My., widow, Sal. St Martin, 1692, I, W, P4/1692/3
My., widow [*or* tanner], Westport & Marl., 1699, I (lists tanning goods), W, P3/H/786
My., Keevil, 1719, AB, I, P2/H/1164
My., widow, Wantage, Berks., 1723, AB, P23/421
My., widow, Hurst, Berks., 1733, W, P5/1733/28
My., widow, Horningsham, 1771, W, P5/1771/9, P5/17Reg/31B
My., widow, Froxfield Almshouse, 1818, W, Wr, P3/1818/50
My. Ann, sp., Easton Town, Sherston, 1845, W, Wr, P3/1845/28
Matthew, apothecary, Sal., 1667, I, P4/1667/34
Matthew, woolcomber, Uffc., Devon, 1756, W, P20/1/233
Maud, widow, Rod St., Corsley, 1616, I, W, P1/H/115
Maud, widow, Longbridge D., 1625, I, T, W, P2/H/379
Michael, Upton S., 1567, W, P2/5Reg/13C
Nich., yeo., Corsham, 1623, AB, W, P29/H/27, P29/1Reg/100B
Nich., weaver, Corsham, 1623, note of probate, P29/1Reg/93B
Nich., Upton S., 1697, AB, I, P2/H/977
Osmund, Upton L., 1557, AB, P2/3Reg/23C
Osmund, sen., barber, Mere, 1673, comm, I, NW (damaged), P5/1673/19
Paul, plumber, Wokm., Berks., 1815, comm, grant of probate, W, P5/1815/1
Philip, fellmonger, Hurst, Berks., 1682-83, AB, a/c, I, P5/1682/54, P5/1683/29

Philip, innholder, *The Dragon*, Rams., 1686, I (detailed), W, P5/1686/29
Priscilla, widow, Wrou., 1841, AB, O, Wr, P3/1841/27
Prudence, widow, Devizes, 1719, comm, W, P1/H/749, P1/6Reg/172
Rachel, widow, N. Heath, Chieveley, Berks., 1808, W, Wr, P1/1808/113
Randall, yeo., Quidh., 1751, W, P2/H/1392
Rebecca, widow, Ryme I., Dorset, 1682, AB, comm, P5/1682/58
Richd., Warm., 1559, W, P2/3Reg/163A
Richd., Westb., 1559, W. No date of probate given, P1/2Reg/101A
Richd., Hurst, Berks., 1615, AB, P5/9Reg/124A
Richd., tanner, Sal. St Martin, 1628, AB, I, W, P4/1627/15
Richd., Sal., 1630, AB, P4/1630/10
Richd., yeo., Swindon, 1630, I, W (part missing), P3/H/243
Richd., yeo., Bruton, Somerset, [1632], deed of gift, req, P2/H/448
Richd., Heytes., 1643, comm, I, W, P5/1643/7, P5/14Reg/60E
Richd., parchmentmaker, Sal. St Martin, 1681, I, P4/1681/31
Richd., sen., tanner, Sal., 1689-90, AB, I, W, P4/1689/7, P4/1690/13
Richd., gent., Baverstock, 1690, I, W, P2/H/909
Richd., clerk and canon, Sal. The Close, 1695, W, P5/1695/42
Richd., husb., Compton B., 1710, I, W, P3/H/908
Richd., yeo., Stratford Tony, 1711, W, P1/H/666, P1/5Reg/46
Richd., Quidh., 1713, AB, P2/H/1113
Richd., Sal., 1724, AB, P4/1723/11
Richd., Alderbury, 1728, AB, P26/729
Richd., jun., wheelwright, Cholsey, Berks., 1738, W, P1/H/958, P1/8Reg/245
Richd., sen., husb., Cholsey, Berks., 1738, W, P1/H/959, P1/8Reg/246A
Richd., yeo., Wyke Farm, Sherb., Dorset, 1769, W, P5/1769/18
Richd., clothdresser, Melk., 1779, W, P2/H/1581
Richd., Widdenham Farm, Colerne, 1806, AB, comm, Wr, P3/1806/14
Robt., Corsley, 1564, I, W, P2/H/1696, P2/4Reg/188B
Robt., husb., Horningsham, 1626, I, W, P5/1625/45, P5/10Reg/190B
Robt., shepherd, Britford, 1665, I, NW, P24/365
Robt., Corsley, 1671, AB, I, P1/H/412
Hills, Robt., gent., Wootton B., 1673, AB, I, ren, W, P3/H/477
Robt., husb., Horningsham, 1679, I, W, P5/1679/40
Robt., sen., yeo., Goatacre, Hilmarton, 1697, I, W, P3/H/769
Robt., innholder, Marl., 1703, comm, W, P1/H/625, P1/4Reg/244
Robt., yeo., Goodleigh, Uffc., Devon, 1711, comm, W, P20/1/145
Robt., yeo., Leverton, Chilton F., 1738, AB, I, ren, P1/H/951
Robt., yeo., Catcomb, Hilmarton, 1785, W, P3/H/1463
Roger, yeo., Charlton, Wantage, Berks., 1679, I, note (re safekeeping of AB), P23/95
Ruth, widow, Preston, Rams., 1708, W, P5/1708/33, P5/15Reg/56
Sam., sen., husb., Chilton F., 1662, I, W, P1/H/327
Sarah, Leigh, Ashton K., 1674, AB, I, P1/H/429
Sarah, widow, Maiden B., 1678, I, W, P2/H/750
Sarah, widow, Dilton, Westb., 1719-22, AB (on death of ex.), I, W, P25/1718/4, P25/1722/3
Sarah, sp., W. Harnham, 1730, W, P8/32
Sarah, widow, Lacock, 1747, AB, ren, W, P3/H/1227
Sarah, widow, Wrou., 1810, AB, P3/1810/17
Sarah, sp., Malm., 1811, W, Wr, P1/1811/100
Sarah, widow, Rowde, 1838, comm, W, Wr, P3/1838/23
Stephen, yeo., Upton S., 1642, comm, I, W, P2/H/561
Stephen, yeo., Brook, Westb., 1704, W, P25/1704/11
Stephen, Brook, Westb., 1730, AB, P25/1730/14
Susanna, widow, Leighs Marsh, Dilton, Westb., 1679, I, W, P25/1679/8
Susanna, Marl. St My., 1691, AB, I, P1/H/541
Susanna, widow, N. Bradley, 1755, AB, ren, P2/H/1414
Thos., Hungerford, Berks., 1575, I, NW, P5/1575/17, P5/3Reg/59B
Thos., Crockerton, Longbridge D., 1599, I, W, P2/H/185
Thos., day labourer, Hungerford, Berks., 1604, I, P5/1603/42
Thos., Leighs Marsh, Dilton, Westb., 1616, I, W, P25/1616/3

Thos., sen., yeo., Upton S., 1634, comm, I, W, P1/H/194
Thos., sen., Bruton, Somerset, 1634, T (children: Thos. & Jas. H.), P2/H/458
Thos., sen., [saddle and harnessmaker], Gt. Faringdon, Berks., 1664, I (detailed), W, P5/1664/21
Thos., tailor, Compton Comberwell, Compton B., 1669, I, W, P3/H/419
Thos., Gillingham, Dorset, 1676, AB, P27/1/50
Thos., no abode stated, 1677, I, P2/H/742
Thos., yeo., Gillingham, Dorset, 1687, I, W, P27/1/103
Thos., tobacco pipemaker, Fisherton A., 1710, W, P2/H/1081
Thos., Horningsham, 1713, AB, P5/1713/43
Thos., Fordington, Dorset, 1713, I, P5/1713/46
Thos., Gillingham, Dorset, 1715, AB, P27/1/207
Thos., Preston, Rams., 1715, AB, P5/1715/21
Thos., clothworker, Leighs Marsh, Dilton, Westb., 1717-19, AB, I (£1,251), W, P25/1717/5, P25/1719/8
Thos., tallow chandler, Lambourn, Berks., 1747, W, P1/H/1050, P1/10Reg/125
Thos., innholder and maltster, Gt. Bedwyn, 1766, W, P21/10/70
Thos., Devizes, 1783, AB, P1/H/1293
Thos., yeo., Calne, 1784, comm, W, P26/1141
Thos., Southbroom, 1797, AB, W, P24/1210
Thos., Pott., 1803, AB (2), comm, Wr, P1/1803/1, P1/15Reg/379A
Thos., Devizes, 1828, AB, comm, Wr, P1/1828/4
Thos., yeo., Aldbourne, 1835, comm, W, Wr, P3/1835/3
Walter, husb., Stourton, 1635, a/c, I, W (all on one page), P1/H/214
Wm., husb., Ebbesborne Wake, 1557, W, P2/3Reg/37A
Wm., N. Bradley, 1570, W, P2/5Reg/100A
Wm., Tinh., Edington, 1572, W, P2/5Reg/154D
Wm., husb., Norridge, Warm., 1574, W, P2/5Reg/189E
Wm., sen., tailor, Poulshot, 1597, I, W, P2/H/166
Wm., husb., Longbridge D., 1606, I, W, P2/H/233
Wm., tailor, Corsley, [1626], I, W, P2/H/387
Wm., tailor, Winterbourne D., 1638, I, W, P7/23
Wm., tailor, Poulshot, [1639], I, W, P2/H/529
Hill alias Millard, Wm., shoemaker, Chipp., 1641, AB, I, P3/H/332
Wm., tailor, Wylye, 1646, AB, I, W, P2/H/583
Wm., carp., Pott., 1653-54, W (NEP), P1/H/306
Wm., clothworker, W. Harnham, 1663, AB, I, NW, P5/1663/32
Wm., Collingbourne K., 1680, AB, I, P3/H/546
Wm., fellmonger, Malm., 1699, I, W, Wr, P3/H/787
Wm., Hodson, Chiseldon, 1709, AB, I, ren (written on reverse of I), P3/H/895
Wm., yeo., Keevil, 1711, I, W, P2/H/1086
Wm., yeo., Gillingham, Dorset, 1712, W, P27/1/189
Wm., Laverstock, 1713, AB, P2/H/1107
Wm., glazier, Lyme R., Dorset, 1715, W, P16/203
Wm., butcher, Marl. St Peter and St Paul, 1719, AB, I, P1/H/753
Wm., yeo., Latton, 1754, AB, P3/H/1280
Wm., turnpikekeeper, Keevil, 1766, comm, W, P2/H/1489
Wm., scribler, Trowb., 1775, W, P1/H/1235, P1/13Reg/64B
Wm., labourer, Pott., 1780, W, P1/H/1271, P1/13Reg/315
Wm., sen., yeo., Crickl. St My., 1784, comm, W, P3/H/1455
Wm., yeo., Seend, Melk., 1786, W, P1/H/1306, P1/14Reg/133A
Wm., Latton, 1799, AB, O, P3/H/1537
Wm., bach., Malm., 1807, AB, Wr, P3/1807/63
Wm., bach., Highw., 1820, AB, comm, note, Wr, P10/1820/3
Wm., Derry Hill, Pewsham, 1825, AB, comm, ren, Wr, P5/1825/6
Wm., whipmaker, Sal., 1851, W, Wr, P4/1851/2
Wm., plumber, glazier and painter, Devizes St My., 1851, O, W, Wr, P1/1851/42
see also Elliott alias H.
Hillar *see* Hiller
Hillard, Adam, mercer, Bradford A., 1631, comm, I, W, P1/H/183
Walter, husb., Charminster, Dorset, 1582, AB, I, W, P5/1582/31, P5/4Reg/34C
Heillard *or* Heillyer, Wm., Oare, Wilcot, 1608, I, NW (both on same document), P3/H/36

Hillary, Ann, widow, Nether C., Dorset, 1754, AB, P5/1754/11
Dan., Sherb., Dorset, 1737, AB, P5/1737/28
Eliz., widow, Over C., Dorset, 1751, W, P5/1750/17
Ephraim, yeo., Nether C., Dorset, 1770, W, P5/1770/22, P5/17Reg/2A
Jas., sen., yeo., Stallen, Nether C., Dorset, 1712, I, W, P5/1712/29, P5/15Reg/296
Jas., Leigh, Yetm., Dorset, 1733, AB, P19/124
Hilary, Jas., Enmore Grn, Motc., Dorset, 1757, AB, I, P19/152
Jn., Nether C., Dorset, 1579, I, W, P5/1579/37, P5/3Reg/131A
Jn., yeo., Meerhay, Beam., Dorset, 1595-96, AB, I, W, P5/1595/28, P5/1596/33, P5/6Reg/102
Jn., husb., Nether C., Dorset, 1634, AB, I, W. Proved at the Metropolitan Visitation to Dorchester, P5/1634/49, P5/12Reg/295A
Jn., sen., maltster, Nether C., Dorset, 1715, I, W, P5/1715/22, P5/15Reg/323, P30/99
Jn., yeo., Nether C., Dorset, 1715-16, I (2), W, P5/1716/36, P5/15Reg/336B
Jn., linen weaver, Over C., Dorset, 1746, W, P5/1746/42
Jos., bookbinder and stationer, Sal., 1775, W, P4/1775/3
Joshua, labourer, Nether C., Dorset, 1763, W, P5/1763/10
Hellary, Maurice, yeo., Nether C., Dorset, 1707, comm, I, W, P5/1707/33, P5/15Reg/22
Hilary, Nich., yeo., Nether C., Dorset, 1661, AB, appt of guardians, comm, I, W, P5/1661/31
Richd., shoemaker, Sal., 1672, AB, a/c, I, P4/1671/19
Robt., yeo., Nether C., Dorset, 1762, W, P5/1762/12
Hellary, Sarah, widow, Bishopstone N., 1711, I, W, P6/97
Susanna, widow, Nether C., Dorset, 1812, W, Wr, P5/1812/24
Hilary, Thos., husb., Nether C., Dorset, 1639, AB, I, T (re Ann Hatkins, minor), W, P5/1639/40, P5/13Reg/179
Hilary, Thos., yeo., Nether C., Dorset, 1667, I, W, P5/1667/33
Hillery, Thos., Nether C., Dorset, 1686, AB, comm, P5/1686/34
Thos., Over C., Dorset, 1747, AB, P5/1747/11
Wm., blacksmith, Sherb., Dorset, 1638, AB, L, ren, P5/1637/19, P5/13Reg/65C
Wm., husb., Sherb., Dorset, 1681, AB, comm, I, ren, W, P5/1681/25
Hillary alias Coombe, Wm., Netherb., Dorset, 1685, AB, I, P17/309
Wm., sen., yeo., Nether C., Dorset, 1714, AB, I, W, P5/1714/18, P5/15Reg/391A
Hellary, Wm., tailor, Nether C., Dorset, 1738, W, P5/1738/23
Hellery, Wm., Nether C., Dorset, 1748, AB, Wr, P5/1748/15
see also Combe alias H.; Jennings alias H. *or* Ellery
Hiller, Ann, sp., Manningford Bruce, 1662, AB, I, P3/H/349
Ann, widow, Bottle, Beechingstoke, 1731, W, P3/H/1091
Edith, Lt. Cheverell, 1572, AB, P2/5Reg/159G
Healer alias Grant, Edwd., husb., W. Tockenham, Lyneham, 1711, I, W, P1/H/670, P1/5Reg/90
Hillar, Eliz., widow, Manningford A., 1750, W, P1/H/1074, P1/10Reg/387
Eliz., wife, Trowb., 1772, AB, comm, P1/H/1217
Francis, yeo., Bottle, Beechingstoke, 1678, AB, a/c, I, ren, Wr, P3/H/532
Heller, Giles, [Netherbury, Dorset] (NBI), 1679, I, P30/82
Hiller alias Clarke, Jn., W. Crudwell, 1605, I, W, P1/H/29
Jn., yeo., Murcott, Crudwell, 1713, I, W, P3/H/930
Jn., Manningford A., 1746, W, P3/H/1224
Jn., gent., Allington, All C., 1776, comm, W, P3/H/1416
Jn., maltster, shearman and baker, Trowb., 1800, AB, comm, W, P1/1800/11, P1/15Reg/215
Mgt., Manningford A., 1629, W, P3/H/229
Maurice, yeo., E. Kennett, 1691, I, W (2), P3/H/696
Rebecca, widow, Bottle, Beechingstoke, 1681, AB, I, P3/H/559
Rebecca, sp., Bottle, Beechingstoke, 1762, AB, W, P3/H/1336
Richd., Manningford A., 1617, I, W, P3/H/123
Richd., Devizes, 1701, AB, P1/H/608
Richd., gent., Devizes, 1708, AB, W, P1/H/655
Robt., shepherd, Kingston D., 1586, W, P2/7Reg/63B
Healer alias Grant, Robt., Sopworth, [1611], W (NEP), P3/H/70
Ruth, Marl. St My., 1711, AB, P1/H/674
Sam., Murcott, Crudwell, 1743, W, P3/H/1192
Sarah, sp., Trowb., 1815, comm, W, P1/1815/4
Thos., Hurst, Berks., 1569, AB, P5/2Reg/51B
Thos., yeo., Devizes, 1623, comm, I, W, P1/H/157

Hillar, Thos., husb., Alcombe, Box, 1634, I, W, P1/H/197
Hiller *or* Hillier, Thos., Calne, 1721, AB, I, P26/652
Timothy, gent., Manningford A., 1741, W, P1/H/989, P1/9Reg/192B
Hillar, Wm., Boyton, 1548, W, P2/2Reg/69B
Wm., [gunsmith and swordmaker], Marl., 1616, I, W, P1/H/114
Wm., yeo., Sherston, 1729, W, P1/H/868, P1/7Reg/313A
Wm., parchmentmaker, Malm., 1754, W, P3/H/1281
see also Clarke alias H.; Hillier
Hillery *see* Hillary
Hillgrove, Alice, widow, Sedgehill, 1574, W, P2/5Reg/208B
Dorothy, widow, Sedgehill, 1615, I, W, P2/H/307, P2/8Reg/266B
Isaac, Sedgehill, 1724, W, P2/H/1205
Jane, widow, W. Knoyle, 1669, AB, I, P2/H/658
Jn., yeo., Lawn, Gillingham, Dorset, 1740, W, Wr, P27/1/358, P27/3Reg/10
Jn., yeo., Sedgehill, [1669-79?], AB, I, P2/H/660, 769
Wm., husb., Sedgehill, 1571, W, P2/5Reg/118C
Wm., husb., Sedgehill, 1650, I, W, P1/H/300
Hillier, Hilliar, Abraham, yeo., W. Knoyle, 1825, W, Wr, P2/1825/62
Hellier, Agnes, widow, Chipp., 1612, NW (2 - both on same sheet), P3/H/81
Hellier, Alan, grocer, Newbury, Berks., 1735, I, W, P1/H/939, P1/8Reg/115
Alexander, gardener, Gloucester, Gloucs (but belonging to Society of Gentlemen, Tradesmen &c, Marl. & leaving goods there & at Winterbourne Bassett), 1772, comm, W, copy W, P1/H/1218, P1/12Reg/431
Helliard, Ambrose, yeo., Gt. Cheverell, 1622, I, W, P1/H/153
Helliar, Andrew, maltster, Sal., 1684, I, W, P4/1683/1
Hellier, Ann, Manningford A., 1609, AB, P3/H/47
Hellier, Ann, Britford, 1674, I, NW, P24/447
Ann, widow, Bottle, Beechingstoke, 1705, I, W, P3/H/857
Hilliar, Ann, widow, Warm., 1743, W, P2/H/1340
Ann, widow, Devizes, 1771, W, P1/H/1216, P1/12Reg/414
Ann, sp., Warm., 1831, W, P2/1831/49
Helliar, Anthony, Escott, Chute, 1636, AB, I, L (undated, re failure of admrs to meet, & pay relevant fees (he d. 1633, but they did not sign bond until 1636), W, P7/32
Hellyar, Anthony, no abode stated, but admr of Enborne, Berks., 1641, T (re Hy. H., son of decd.), P1/H/255
Helliar, Anthony, bricklayer, Wootton R., 1676, AB, a/c, I, P3/H/511
Hilliard, Anthony, sen., yeo., Fosbury, Tidcombe and F., 1709, AB, I, P3/H/897
Hellier, Anthony, Milford, Sal. St Martin, 1738, AB, Wr, P4/1738/17
Helliar form. Kittle, Betty, widow, Sherb., Dorset, 1823, comm, W (& cods), Wr, P5/1823/5
Cath., wife, Seend, Melk., 1855, AB, aff, court proceeding, O, Wr, P2/1855/19, 34
Chas., bricklayer, Devizes, 1827, W, Wr, P1/1827/21
Chas., carp., Seend, Melk., 1851, comm, W, Wr, P2/1851/2
Hellier, Edmd., husb., Oare, Wilcot, [1609], W (NEP), P3/H/48
Helliard, Edwd., husb., Witcomb, Hilmarton, 1621, I, W, P3/H/163
Hilliar, Edwd., yeo., Goatacre, Hilmarton, 1710, AB, I, ren, W, P3/H/896
Edwd., W. Knoyle, 1739, W, P2/H/1309
Edwd., Tockenham Wick, 1831, AB, comm, Wr, P3/1831/3
Edwd., Marl. St My., 1837, AB, Wr, P1/1837/16
Hellier, Eliz., widow, Leckhampstead, Chieveley, Berks., 1608, I, W, P1/H/55
Helliar, Eliz., Wilton, 1710, AB, P2/H/1080
Hellyar, Eliz., sp., Bere R., Dorset, 1728, W (very small), P5/1728/48, P5/16Reg/182A
Hellier, Eliz., widow, Highw., 1736, AB, P10/1736/5
Eliz., yeo.'s wife, Atworth, Bradford A., 1804, appt of proctor, W, P1/1804/31
Helliar, Eliz., widow, Chards., Devon, 1813, comm, W, P14/207
Hellier, Eliz., widow, Uffc., Devon, 1828, O, W, P20/1/316
Frances, widow, Hilmarton, 1853, AB, O, Wr, P3/1853/8
Hellier, Francis, husb., Marcham, Berks., 1763, AB, W, P1/H/1165, P1/12Reg/75A
Helliar, Geo., mason, Wootton R., 1689, I, W, P3/H/665
Geo., labourer, W. Kennett, Avebury, 1706, I, W, P3/H/865
Hilliar, Geo., bricklayer, E. Stowell, Wilcot, 1728, W, P3/H/1048
Geo., maltster, Avon, Chr. M., 1739, comm, W, P3/H/1160
Hannah, widow, Tockenham Wick, 1832, AB, comm, Wr, P3/1832/24

Hellier, Hy., Westb., 1607, AB, P25/1607/1
Hellyer, Hy., yeo., Wokm., Berks., 1630, I, W (damaged), P5/1630/7, P5/11Reg/138
Hellyer, Hy., husb. and yeo., Devizes, 1635, I, W, P1/H/217
Hy., yeo., Brickworth, Whitep., 1718, W, P2/H/1150
Hy., carp. and joiner, Rowde, 1845, W, Wr, P1/1845/42
Isaac, Devizes, 1801, AB, comm, P1/1801/16, P1/15Reg/241A
Helliar, Jas., husb., Wootton R., 1693-1711, AB (2), P3/H/723
Hilliard, Jas., Purton, 1731, AB, cit, I, P3/H/1092
Hilliard, Jas., surgeon, Burbage, 1743, AB (to creditors re My., Sarah, Hannah, Rachel & Eliz. H., daus), W (endorsed with ren of trustees), P11/190
Jas., Bowden Hill, Lacock, 1826, AB, Wr, P1/1826/130
Hilliar, Jas., Rams., 1841, AB, comm, Wr, P5/1841/1
Jas., bach., St Pancras, London (eaving effects at, Seend, Melk.), 1844, AB, comm, Wr, P2/1844/22
Jane, widow, Manningford A., 1757, AB, comm, P3/H/1303
Hellier, Joan, widow, Corton, Boyton, 1579, W, P2/5Reg/334A
Hellier alias Good, Joan, yeo.'s wife, Bremhill, 1663, AB, comm, P3/H/351
Joan, sp., Hilp., 1668, AB, P1/H/382
Hellier alias Champlate, Joan, widow, Sal., 1711, AB, P4/1711/9
Helliar, Jn., husb., Wokm., Berks., 1547, W, P5/20Reg/100A
Hellier, Jn., butcher, Eastrop, Highw., 1597, AB, I, P5/1597/123, P5/6Reg/189B
Hellicot, Jn., Lyme R., Dorset, 1609, I, T, P5/1609/41
Hellier, Jn., yeo., Purcum, Wokm., Berks., 1609-11, AB, a/c, agreement, comm, I, T, W, P5/1610/26, P5/9Reg/21A
Helliar, Jn., Purcum, Wokm., Berks., 1613, W (dated 1617, in error), P5/9Reg/113
Helliar, Jn., Minety, 1620, AB, a/c, I, P3/H/164
Hellier, Jn., Sal., 1626, AB, a/c, P4/1626/13
Helliar, Jn., weaver, Calne, 1634, I, W, P26/48
Hellyar, Jn., husb., Heytes., 1638, AB, I, P5/1638/59, P5/13Reg/114B
Hellyar, Jn., yeo., Milton, E. Knoyle, 1640, I, W, P2/H/532
Hellyar, Jn., jun., no abode stated but admrs both of Marl., 1641, AB, I, P1/H/251
Hellyer, Jn., Burbage, 1663, I, P5/1663/31
Hellier, Jn., carp., Sherb., Dorset, 1664, W (NEP), P5/1664/20
Helliar, Jn., Burbage, 1668, I, P5/1668/37
Hellier, Jn., Hilp., 1670, AB, P2/H/674
Helierd *or* Helier, Jn., Sal., 1673, AB, I, P4/1673/2
Hellier, Jn., feltmaker, Lyme R., Dorset, 1692, W, P5/1692/40
Hilliar alias Eden, Jn., Devizes, 1696, AB, P1/H/588
Hilliar, Jn., miller, Wilton, 1697, I, W, P2/H/978
Hellyer, Jn., sergemaker, Lyme R., Dorset, 1704, AB, comm, I, ren, P5/1704/35
Jn., Beechingstoke, 1706, AB, I, P3/H/866
Jn., Netherb., Dorset, 1721, AB, P17/399
Hilliar, Jn., W. Knoyle, 1729, AB, P2/H/1237
Hilliar, Jn., labourer, Laverstock, 1749, W, P2/H/1387
Hellier, Jn., Sutton C., Berks., 1770, AB, P1/H/1209
Jn., Lt. Hinton, 1779, AB, P1/H/1262
Jn., cordw., Netheravon, 1805, W, P12/206
Jn., yeo., W. Knoyle, 1809, W, Wr, P2/1809/74
Jn., collarmaker, Upavon, 1827, W, Wr, P2/1827/57
Hellyer, Jos., sen., Lyme R., Dorset, 1686, W, P16/89
Hellyer, Jos., bellman, Lyme R., Dorset, 1749, AB, ren, P16/306
Helliar, Lawr., Sherb., Dorset, 1670, AB, comm, P5/1670/19
Hellier, Lettice, widow, Avon, Chr. M., 1677, comm, I, W, P3/H/521
Hellier, Lucy, widow, Avon, Chr. M., [1612], I, W (NEP), P3/H/82
Hellier, Mgt., widow, Penn, Hilmarton, 1613, W (2), P3/H/92
Helliard, Mgt., widow, Sal., 1683, I, W, P4/1683/15
Helliar, Margery, widow, Collingbourne D., 1690, I, W, P21/5/4
Helliard, My., Burbage, mid to late 17th C., W. No date *or* evidence of probate, P11/31
Hillyar, My., widow, White Waltham, Berks., 1689, I, W, P1/H/517
Helliar, My., widow, Sharcott, Pewsey, 1700, I, W, P3/H/797
Hellyar, My., widow, Halstock, Dorset, 1736, I, W, P5/1736/17
Hilliard, My., widow, Chieveley, Berks., 1759, W, P1/H/1137, P1/11Reg/376

My., sp., Sherston, 1767, W, P3/H/1366
My., widow, Netheravon, 1814, W (NEP), P12/212
Nich., glover *or* labourer, Blewbury, Berks., 1629, AB, I, P5/1629/27, P5/11Reg/115A
Helliar, Nich., hatter, Lyme R., Dorset, 1682, AB, I, P16/59
Hityard, Paul, baker, Sherb., Dorset, 1574, I, T, W, P5/1573/2, P5/3Reg/31E
Hellier, Priscilla, sp., Sal., 1711, I, W, P4/1711/11
Hillyer, Richd., Fyfield, Overton, [1611], NW (NEP), P3/H/72
Helliar, Richd., husb., Malm., 1615, I, W, P3/H/110
Hellier, Richd., Hungerford, Berks., 1640, AB, I, P23/1018
Hellyar, Richd., yeo., Stop, Fonthill G., 1641, AB, I, P1/H/248
Richd., husb., Hilmarton, 1668, AB, I, P3/H/403
Helliard, Richd., yeo., Alderbury, 1694, AB, I, W, P26/424
Richd., sen., gent., Devizes, 1696, I, W, P1/H/587
Hilliar, Richd., yeo., Clevancy, Hilmarton, 1712, I, W, P3/H/920
Hilliar, Richd., Hilmarton, 1775, AB, P3/H/1414
Helliar, Robt., Ford, Laverstock, 1598, AB, I, P2/H/174
Hilliar, Robt., Hullavington, 1603, I, NW, P3/H/5
Robt., yeo., Bremhill, 1677, AB, I, W, P3/H/522
Hellier, Robt., Gt. Cheverell, 1678, I, W, P2/H/751
Hellier, Robt., clothworker, Southwick, N. Bradley, [1688], I, W, P2/H/888
Helliard, Robt., yeo., Alderbury, 1692, comm, I, W, P26/404
Hellier alias Chiseldean, Roger, sen., day labourer, Heddington, 1721, I, W, P3/H/978
Roger, carp., Seend, Melk., 1811, W, Wr, P2/1811/17
Roger, carp., Seend, Melk., 1841, O, W, Wr, P2/1841/9
Roger, yeo., Seend, Melk., 1852, O, W, Wr, P2/1852/65
Hilliar, Sam., Sherston, 1729, AB, I, P3/H/1062
Sam., Nether C., Dorset, 1796, AB, P5/1796/5, P5/18Reg/226B
Sarah, widow, Willesley, Sherston (late of Wallsworth), 1705, I, W, P3/H/858
Hilliar, Sarah, widow, Burbage, 1706, I, W, P11/96
Hilliar, Sarah, widow, Fittleton, 1795, W, Wr, P1/H/1333, P1/14Reg/521
Helliar, Stephen, shoemaker, Hungerford, Berks., 1669, AB, comm, I, P5/1669/29
Helliar, Susanna, widow, Sherb., Dorset, 1802, comm, W, P5/1802/3, P5/19Reg/2
Helliar, Temperance, widow, Furleigh Cross, Netherb., Dorset, 1641, AB, I, P5/1641/38, P5/14Reg/33G
Hellyer, Thos., shepherd, Idmiston, 1633, I, W, P2/H/454, P2/9Reg/6
Helliar, Thos., Calne, 1638, a/c, I (NEP), P5/1638/128
Hellier, Thos., Netherb., Dorset, 1640, W, P17/60
Hellier, Thos., haberdasher, Sal., 1668, AB, I, NW, P4/1668/14
Hellier, Thos., jun., yeo., Bremhill, 1669, I, W, P3/H/418
Hellyer, Thos., husb., Hungerford, Berks., 1682, AB, comm, I, P5/1682/59
Helliard *or* Hilliard, Thos., sen., yeo., Collingbourne D., 1682, I, W, P21/2/81
Hellyar, Thos., sen., blacksmith, Alton P., Dorset, 1685, I, W, P5/1685/43
Hillyard, Thos., clothworker, Newbury, Berks., 1686, AB, comm, I, P1/H/500
Hilliar, Thos., yeo., Compton B., 1722, I, W, P3/H/995
Hilliard, Thos., yeo., Burbage, 1727, W, P11/171
Thos., yeo., Murcott, Crudwell, 1729, W, P3/H/1063
Hilliar, Thos., yeo., Bottle, Beechingstoke, 1735, W, P1/H/937, P1/8Reg/99
Hellier, Thos., marine in Hon.Sir Andrew Agnew's Regt. on board the Tilbury, Devizes, 1749, W, Wr, P1/H/1058, P1/10Reg/244
Hilliar, Thos., yeo., Badbury, Chiseldon, 1804, W, P1/1804/82
Hellier, Thos., yeo., Uffc., Devon, 1818, W, Wr, P5/1818/25
Hillyard, Thos., carp., Sutton C., Berks., 1826, W, Wr, P1/1826/77
Hilliar, Thos., W. Knoyle, 1832, AB, Wr, P1/1832/56
Hilliar, Thos., Netheravon, 1842, AB, O, W, Wr, P12/229
Thos., yeo., Chr. M., 1845, O, W, Wr, P3/1845/31
Thos., gent., Savernake Park, 1849, W, Wr, P5/1849/6
Hellier, Thomasine, widow, Manningford A., 1664, I, W, P1/H/343
Helliard, Walter, yeo., E. Grimstead, W. Dean, 1628, I, W, P2/H/402
Hellier, Wm., Downton, 1590, T (children: Roger & Hugh H.), P2/H/109
Helliar, Wm., no abode stated but admr is of Gt. Bedwyn, 1592, AB., P1/H/8
Hellier, Wm., Manningford A., 1604, I, W, P3/H/8

Hellier, Wm., yeo., Charlton nr Malm., [1609], I, W (both on same sheet) (NEP), P3/H/49
Hellyer, Wm., Hilp., 1625, I, W, P1/H/168
Hellier, Wm., hivemaker, Stockley, Calne, 1636, AB, I, P26/57
Helliar, Wm., yeo., Kingston D., 1674, I, W, P1/H/423
Hellear, Wm., gent., Wootton R., 1714-15, comm, W, P1/H/691, P1/5Reg/309
Helliard, Wm., mason, Wootton R., 1715, I, NW, P3/H/939
Wm., sen., yeo., Seend Park, Melk., 1716, W, P2/H/1131
Hilliard, Wm., Burbage, 1760, W, P11/214
Wm., yeo., Avebury, 1774, W (NEP), P3/H/1407
Hellyar, Wm., gent., Sherb., Dorset, 1794, W, P5/1794/11, P5/18Reg/201D
Hellyar, Wm., carp., Sherb., Dorset, 1821, AB, W, Wr, P5/1821/28
Wm., Fosbury, Tidcombe and F., 1846, AB, comm, Wr, P3/1846/2
Wm., labourer, Avebury, 1851, O, W, Wr, P1/1851/35
see also Champ alias H.; Chisleton alias H.; Eden alias H.; Hiller
Hilliker, Jas., yeo., Upton L., 1769, W, P2/H/1523
Hellaker, Jn., Lyme R., Dorset, 1609, AB, P5/8Reg/169A
Sam., Marl., 1785, W, P1/H/1296, P1/14Reg/69
Hillis, Jn., Whitep., 1634, AB, I, P1/H/203
Hillman, Alexander, yeo., Ford, N. Wraxall, 1722, AB, I, P3/H/996
Ann, widow, Devizes, 1692, W, P1/H/544
Ann, sp., Trowb., 1813, W, Wr, P1/1813/8
Chas., Trowb., 1820, AB, W, Wr, P1/1820/47
Denise, widow, Durnford, 1648, I, NW, P5/1648/5, P5/14Reg/105D
Eliz., sp., Devizes, 1740, W, P1/H/974, P1/9Reg/2
Geo., sen., carp., Wingfield, 1826, W, Wr, P2/1826/26
Gervase, Quidh., 1674, AB, I, P1/H/422
Hugh, Devizes, 1667, AB, comm, P1/H/381
Hugh, innholder, Devizes, 1681, I, W, P1/H/464
Isaac, Dilton M., Westb., 1829, O, W, Wr, P25/1829/4
Jas., innholder, Devizes, 1716, W, P1/H/728, P1/6Reg/43B
Jas., leather seller, Trowb., 1743, comm, W, P1/H/998, P1/9Reg/241
Jas., grocer, Trowb., 1834, W, Wr, P1/1834/15
Jane, widow, Lower Marsh, Westb., 1693, AB, I (detailed), P25/1693/10
Jane, Brook, Westb., 1739, W, P25/1739/7
Helman, Jn., Uffc., Devon, 1551, W, P20/Reg/47A
Hehuslman *or* Hellman, Jn., husb., Gt. Wishford, 1576, W, P2/H/41, P2/5Reg/260C
Hellman, Jn., tucker, Trowle, Bradford A., 1603, I, W, P2/H/213
Jn., tailor, Wylye, 1640, AB, I, P2/H/545
Helman, Jn., innholder, Warm., 1646, I, W, P2/H/579
Jn., broad weaver, Dilton, Westb., 1672, I, W, P25/1672/9
Jn., yeo., Brook, Westb., 1708, I, W, P25/1708/10
Jn., Wylye, 1735, W, P2/H/1284
Lucy, sp., Devizes, 1739, comm, W, P1/H/972, P1/8Reg/406
Hillman nee Reason, Mgt., Trowb., 1785, AB, P1/H/1297
My., widow, Wingfield, 1845, AB, Wr, P1/1845/39
Priscilla, widow, Trowb., 1793, W, P1/H/1328, P1/14Reg/493
Rawlins, Gt. Amesb., 1673, I, W, P2/H/708
Robt., yeo., Gt. Wishford, 1639, I, W, P2/H/522
Robt., Upton L., 1675, AB, P2/H/725
Robt., yeo., Trowle, Bradford A., 1779, W, P1/H/1260, P1/13Reg/238
Roger, innholder, Wylye, 1751, W, P2/H/1390
Ruth, sp., Warm., 1671, I, W, P2/H/686
Sarah, sp., Limpley Stoke, Bradford A., 1827, AB, O, Wr, P2/1827/2
Thos., Wylye, 1580, W, P2/5Reg/365B
Thos., Warm., 1638, I, W, P2/H/497
Wm., Westb., 1730, AB, I, P25/1730/5
Wm., Winterbourne G., 1814, AB, comm, P1/1814/50
Wingfield, Sal. St Thos., 1822, AB, Wr, P4/1822/5
Hills *see* Hill
Hillyar, Hillyard, Hillyer *see* Hillier

Hilpes *see* Helps
Hilsdon, Hilsden alias Burdge, Jn., butcher, Warm., 1632-37, AB, a/c, I, W, P2/H/437, 480
Nich., labourer, Buckland, Berks., 1729, I, W, P1/H/849, P1/7Reg/254A
Hilsen *see* Helsen
Hilton, Ann, sp., Hurst, Berks., 1693, W, P5/1693/29
Edwd., fellmonger, Wokm., Berks., 1741, W, Wr, P5/1741/21
Eliz., Wokm., Berks., 1742, W, Wr, P5/1742/20
Jn., sen., Ludg., 1631-33, AB, a/c, I, P2/H/426, 464
Hilwood, Wm., Downton, 1783, W, P1/H/1287, P1/13Reg/456
Himbury *see* Hembury
Himman, Sam., bodicemaker, Westb., 1724, W, P25/1724/1
Hinchliffe, Wm., victualler, Hurst, Berks., 1807, comm, W, Wr, P5/1807/3
Hinckley, Hester, widow [and innholder], Sal. St Edmd., 1667, AB, a/c, I, P4/1667/1
Hinde, Alice, wife, Blewbury, Berks., 1705, W, P5/1705/24
Ann, widow, Rams., 1709, I, W, P5/1709/18, P5/15Reg/120
Edwd., husb., Rams., 1675, AB, I, P5/1675/29
Hugh, clerk and vicar, Chitterne AS, 1643, I, W, P2/H/564
Jn., husb., Warm., 1592, I, W, P2/H/124
Jn., clerk and vicar, Rowde, 1689, comm, I, W, P3/H/667
Hind, Jn., sen., High St., Rams., 1713, W, P5/1713/41, P5/15Reg/365A
Richd., glover, Rams., 1599, AB (not completed), W, P5/1598/24, P5/6Reg/224B
Thos., husb., Rams., 1711, I, W, P5/1711/30, P5/15Reg/249
Hind, Thos., Fisherton A., 1731, AB, ren, P2/H/1255
Hind, Thos., yeo., Rams., 1766, W, P5/1766/13
see also Erbery alias H.
Hinden *see* Hendon
Hinder, Ann, widow, Latton, 1687, I, W, P3/H/640
Ann, widow, Purton, 1836, comm, W, Wr, P3/1836/51
Christian, widow, Swindon, 1842, O, W, Wr, P3/1842/30
Edwd., jun., mason, Latton, 1682, I, W, P3/H/570
Edwd., sen., tailor, Latton, 1684, I, W, P3/H/598
Edwd., Latton, 1702, AB, I, P3/H/829
Francis, husb., Crickl. St S., 1701, AB, I, P3/H/809
Hy., Purton, 1807, W, P3/1807/23
Joanna, sp., Lydiard M., 1799, AB, comm, P3/H/1538
Jn., jun., carp., Latton, [1619], I, W (NEP), P3/H/143
Jn., carp., Latton, [1641], I, W (NEP), P3/H/333
Jn., sen., tailor, Crickl. St My., 1720, I, W, P3/H/975
Jn., mason, Latton, 1721, I, W, P3/H/979
Jn., mason, Latton, 1749, W, P3/H/1250
Martha, widow, Latton, 1685, AB, I, P3/H/614
Thos., blacksmith, Purton, 1846, comm, W, Wr, P3/1846/16
Thos. Elbrough, Purton, 1812, W, Wr, P3/1812/34
Walter, sen., mason, Latton, 1747, W, P3/H/1228
Wm., yeo., Purton Stoke, 1825, W, Wr, P3/1825/61
Wm., Lydiard M., 1833, AB, Wr, P3/1833/18
Hindley, Chris., clerk, Manningford Bruce, 1679, AB, I, P1/H/445
Rose Amzer, widow, Mere, 1816, W, Wr, P5/1816/3
Sarah, sp., Manningford Bruce, 1702, W, P3/H/830
Hindy *see* Hendy, P1/6Reg/424B
Hine, Ann, widow, Kington L., 1667, comm, W, P3/H/391
Benj., jun., Avill's Farm, Corsham (of Easton Piercy, Corsham), 1676, AB, P3/H/512
Benj., Kington St M., 1689, AB, P1/H/512
Jonathan, Wantage, Berks., 1754, AB, P23/653
Jos., innholder, Kington St M., 1673, I, W, P3/H/478
My., widow, E. Lockinge, Berks., 1776, W, P1/H/1239, P1/13Reg/111
Richd., clerk and vicar, Kington St M., 1663, I, W, P3/H/353
Richd., Kington St M., 1689, AB, comm, P1/H/511
Robt., yeo., Caundle Bishop, Dorset, 1822, W, Wr, P5/1822/19
Thos., yeo., Bourton, Gillingham, Dorset, 1848, D, O, W, Wr, P27/1/759

Wm., Bugley, Warm., 1583, W, P2/6Reg/108C
Hinksman *see* Hinxman
Hinner *see* Hennor
Hinning *see* Henning
Hinton, Henton, Agnes, Corton, Boyton, 1591, AB, I, W, P2/H/118
Alice, widow, Broad B., Highw., 1669, I, W, P10/1669/3
Ann, widow, Werfield, Warm., 1682, AB, I, P2/H/813
Ann, widow, Warm., 1771, W, P2/H/1531
Cath., widow, Sherrington, 1642, comm, I, W, P2/H/554
Chas., victualler, Bradford A., 1739, W, P2/H/1318
Chris., Corton, Boyton, 1589, I, W, P2/H/91
Chris., husb., Keevil Wick, 1597, I, W, P2/H/161
Chris., Corton, Boyton, 1631, I, W, P2/H/432, P2/9Reg/71B
Henton, Chris., no abode stated, [1681], I, P2/H/788
Chris., sen., yeo., Corton, Boyton, 1770, AB, W, P2/H/1526
Chris., yeo., Corton, Boyton, 1799, AB, W, Wr, P2/H/1694
Chris., Ewen, Kemble, 1807, W, Wr, P1/1807/19
Dan., Sutton V., 1684, AB, P2/H/840
Dan., Bayclift Farm, Hill D., 1748, W, Wr, P5/1748/17
Dan., clothier, Bradford A., 1814, W, Wr, P1/1814/61
Henton, Edith, maid, Corton, Boyton, 1592, I, W, P2/H/120
Henton, Edith, widow, Sutton V., 1683, I, W, P1/H/484
Edwd., Sutton V., 1836, AB, comm, ren, P2/1836/60
Eleanor, widow, Codf. St P., 1689, I, W, P1/H/516
Henton, Eliz., Keevil Wick, 1601, I, notes of admon, T, P2/H/161, 194
Eliz., gent., Aldbourne, 1646, I, W, P1/H/277
Giles [female], widow, Aldbourne, 1624, AB, I, NW, P3/H/188
Henton, Jane, widow, Studley, Calne, 1569, AB, P5/2Reg/60C, P5/11Reg/103C
Henton, Joan, widow, Chirton, 1589, W, P2/H/100
Henton, Joan, widow, Sutton V., 1592, I, W, P2/H/121
Henton, Joan, widow, Sutton V., 1607, I, W, P2/H/238
Joan, widow, Sherb., Dorset, 1629, I, W, P5/1629/28
Henton, Jn., Whitep., 1549, W, P2/2Reg/73B, P5/3Reg/143A
Henton, Jn., Sutton V., 1556, W, P2/1Reg/107B
Henton, Jn., husb., Sutton V., 1559, AB, W, P2/4Reg/9A
Henton, Jn., Corton, Boyton, 1571, AB, W, P2/H/34, P2/5Reg/120C
Henton, Jn., Tytherington, Heytes., 1579, AB, P5/1578/20, P5/3Reg/115D
Jn., Gt. Faringdon, Berks., 1579, AB, I, W, P5/1579/44
Jn., sen., gent., Sutton V., 1597, AB, I, W, P2/H/158
Henton, Jn., husb., Sutton V., 1603, W, P2/H/215, P2/8Reg/138B, 252C
Henton, Jn., Sutton V., 1606, I, W, P2/H/234
Jn., shepherd, Chisenbury, Enford, 1610-15, AB (in minority of Jn. H., jun.), T (child: Jn. H., jun.), W, P2/H/272
Jn., husb., Chirton, 1619, I, W, P2/H/342
Henton, Jn., Westwood, 1629, AB, P2/H/413
Jn., husb., Sutton V., 1635, I, W, P2/H/465
Henton, Jn., yeo., Corton, Boyton, 1645, I, W, P2/H/572, P2/9Reg/48B
Jn., sen., gent., Sutton V., 1651, I, W, P1/H/302
Jn., yeo., Ashton G., Codf. St P., 1669, AB, I, P2/H/661
Jn., yeo., Minety, 1682, I, W, P3/H/571
Jn., gent., Sutton V., 1686, AB, I, P2/H/867
Henton, Jn., yeo., Hamptworth, Downton, 1694, I, W, P2/H/949
Jn., clothier, Bishopstrow, 1699, I, W, P2/H/993
Jn., sen., yeo., Sutton V., 1702, I, W, P2/H/1014
Jn., yeo., Corton, Boyton, 1721, W, P2/H/1183
Jn., jun., Ashton G., Codf. St P., 1732, W, P1/H/914, P1/7Reg/552A
Jn., sen., schoolmaster, Ashton G., Codf. St P., 1732, AB, W, P2/H/1262
Jn., woolcomber, Sutton V., 1768, W, P2/H/1503
Jn., shopkeeper, Bishopstrow, 1775, W, P2/H/1547
Jn., Sutton V., 1792, aff, W, P2/H/1664
Jn., yeo., Crickl. St My., 1792, W, P3/H/1503

Jn., weaver, Ditchampton, Wilton, 1811, W, Wr, P1/1811/26
Jn., yeo., Sutton V., 1812, W, Wr, P2/1812/37
Jn., tailor, Chitterne, 1851, W, Wr, P1/1851/26
Josias, gent., Sutton V., 1775, W, P2/H/1550
Leonard, innholder, Barford St M., 1839, W, Wr, P2/1839/8
Mgt., sp., Devizes, 1715, I, W, P1/H/719, P1/5Reg/490
Martha, widow *or* gentlewoman, Earlscourt, Wanb., 1637, I, W, P3/H/299
Martha, widow, Broad B., Highw., 1694, AB, I, P10/1694/4
My., Chirton, 1629, AB, P2/H/414
My., widow, Ashton G., Codf. St P., [1687], I, W, P2/H/875
My., widow, Minety, 1730, W, P3/H/1077
My., sp., Warm., 1771, AB, P2/H/1527
Henton, Philip, husb., Sutton V., [1620], I, W, P2/H/345
Henton, Richd., Tilsh., 1558, AB, P2/3Reg/140A
Henton, Richd., jun., Marden, 1578-81, I, W, P2/H/51
Richd., husb., Poulshot, 1597, I, W, P2/H/157, P2/5Reg/245C, P2/6Reg/43A
Richd., husb., Sutton V., 1599, AB, I, W, P2/H/183
Richd., yeo., Corton, Boyton, 1683, I, W, P2/H/816
Richd., farmer, Rye Hill Farm, Hill D., 1798, W, P5/1798/12, P5/18Reg/270B
Robt., yeo., Sutton V., 1662, I, W, P2/H/615
Robt., widow, Idmiston, 1820, AB, P1/1820/66
Henton, Roger, Chirton, 1575, I, W, P2/H/39, P1/10Reg/406
Henton, Roger, husb., Warm., 1588, AB, I, P2/H/84, P2/7Reg/124B
Somerset, yeo., Ashton K., 1750, W, P1/H/1076
Stephen, no abode stated, 1589, I, P2/H/98
Stephen, Sutton V., 1627, AB, a/c, I, P2/H/388
Stephen, Heytes., 1728, AB, I, P5/1727/26
Susanna, widow, Codf. St My., [1691], I, NW, P2/H/915
Enton, Thos., husb., Sutton V., 1546, W, P2/2Reg/9B
Henton, Thos., husb., Corton, Boyton, 1571, T (children: Wm., Maud, Avis & Agnes H.), W, P2/H/35, P2/5Reg/121A
Henton, Thos., yeo., Sutton V., 1602, AB, I, P2/H/206
Henton, Thos., labourer *or* husb., Devizes, 1621, I, W, P1/H/149
Thos., yeo., Latton, 1666, AB, I, W, P3/H/379
Thos., Latton, 1725, AB, P3/H/1021
Thos., Minety, 1740, AB (2), comm, I, L, T, P3/H/1169
Thos., glazier, Crickl. St S., 1814, W, P1/1814/52
Henton, Walter, husb., Tytherington, Heytes., 1561, T (children: Alice, Walter, Chris. & Cicely H.), P5/1561/2
Henton, Walter, husb., Tytherington, Heytes., 1581, I, W, P5/1581/14, P5/4Reg/22B
Hinton *or* Henton, Walter, Sutton V. & Warm., 1619, AB, comm, I, W, P1/H/122
Warborough, Boyton, 1604, AB, note of admon, P2/H/221
Henton, Wm., Corton, Boyton, 1548, W, P2/2Reg/69C
Henton, Wm., Sutton V., 1555, W, P2/1Reg/92C
Henton, Wm., husb., Corton, Boyton, 1581-89, AB (2), acquittance, I (2), W, P2/H/87, 99, P2/7Reg/112B
Wm., gent., Earlscourt, Wanb., 1592, W, P1/H/9, P5/7Reg/62B
Wm., Minety, 1687, I, W, P3/H/641
Wm., baker, N. Bradley, 1697, comm, W, P2/H/979
Wm., weaver, Gt. Wishford, 1731, I, W, P2/H/1256
Wm., yeo., Eisey, 1788, note, W, Wr, P3/H/1480
Wm., sen., weaver, Ditchampton, Wilton, 1793, W, P2/H/1665
Wm., sen., weaver, Ditchampton, Wilton, 1821, W, Wr, P2/1821/23
Wm., Lyneham, 1828, AB, comm, Wr, P1/1828/20
Wm., weaver, Ditchampton, Wilton, 1836, W, P2/1836/38
Wm., tallow chandler, Crickl. St S., 1838, O, W, Wr, P3/1838/25
Wm., schoolmaster, Lyneham, 1844, comm, W, Wr, P3/1844/4
see also Oborne alias H.

Hinwood, Alice, widow, Monkton D., 1821, W, Wr, P2/1821/49
Henwood, Ann, widow, Collingbourne D., 1687, I, W, P21/4/24
Ann, sp., Deptford, Wylye, 1810, AB, Wr, P2/1810/51
Chas., butcher, Lt. Somerford, 1716, AB, comm, I, P3/H/945
Henwood, Chas., Compton B., 1757, AB, P3/H/1302

Henwood, Christian, widow, Pitton, Alderbury, 1698, AB, P26/454
Chris., blacksmith, Codf. St My., 1824, W, Wr, P2/1824/34
Eliz., widow, Deptford, Wylye, 1756, W, P2/H/1415
Henwood, Hugh, cordw., Fisherton D., 1674, AB, I, ren, P1/H/431
Henwood, Hugh, Bapton, Fisherton Delamare, 1680, AB, W, P2/H/776
Jas., Wylye, 1809, AB, Wr, P2/1809/21
Jas., Deptford, Wylye, 1837, AB, Wr, P2/1837/23
Henwood, Jn., yeo., Charney Bassett, Longworth, Berks., 1680, I, W, P1/H/452
Henwood, Jn., Pitton, Alderbury, 1709, AB, P26/558
Jn., blacksmith, Steeple L., 1750, AB, I, W, P2/H/1388, P5/16Reg/208A
Jn., gent., Gt. Wishford, 1755, W, P2/H/1413
Jn., yeo., Gt. Wishford, 1785, W, P2/H/1621
Jn., yeo., Gt. Wishford, 1803, W, P2/1803/75
Henwood, Patience, widow, Hurst, Berks., 1728, W, P5/1728/49
Henwood, Robt., warrener, Hurst, Berks., 1753, W, P5/1753/13
Henwood, Robt., yeo., Hurst, Berks., 1772, W, P5/1772/9, P5/17Reg/41
Sam., Wylye, 1825, AB, Wr, P2/1825/40
Henwood, Thos., Porton, Idmiston, 1618, I, W, P2/H/322
Thos., Deptford, Wylye, 1765, AB, P2/H/1476
Thos., maltster, Gt. Wishford, 1809, W, Wr, P2/1809/30
Thos., Stratford sub C., 1810, AB, P4/1810/3
Wm., clerk, Hungerford, Berks., 1670, AB, comm, I, P23/17
Henwood, Wm., Pitton, Alderbury, 1677, AB, P26/247
Wm., yeo., Gt. Wishford, 1724, W, P2/H/1202
Wm., Monkton D., 1820, W, Wr, P2/1820/27
Wm., blacksmith, Whitep., 1826, W, Wr, P2/1826/28
Wm., W. Dean, 1849, D, W, Wr, P2/1849/35
Hinxman, Edwd., W. Dean, 1785, W, P2/H/1617
Eliz., widow, W. Dean, 1790, W, Wr, P2/H/1650
Hy., Winterslow, 1784, AB, D, W, P1/H/1295, P1/14Reg/58
Hinksman, Thos., W. Dean, 1744, W, P1/H/1004
Thos., mercer, Sal., 1803, W, P4/1803/1, P1/9Reg/304
Wm., Sal., 1777, AB, ren, P4/1777/5
Wm., mercer and haberdasher, Sal., 1806, W, P4/1806/5
Hipdich *see* Hebditch
Hippersley *see* Hippisley
Hippes, Edith, widow, Coombe B., 1624, W, P5/10Reg/171A
Hippisley, Jn., gent., Stanton Fitzwarren, 1691, comm, I, W, P3/H/697
My., Lambourn, Berks., 1720, AB (2), P1/H/694
Richd., gent., Lambourn, Berks., 1666, AB, comm, P1/H/372
Hippersley, Robt., gent., Old Park, Devizes St Jn., 1616, T (children: Dorothy, My. & Robt. H.), P1/H/118
Thos., gent., Hampton, Highw., 1706, W, P10/1706/2
Thos., West Tithing, Lt. Hinton, 1771, req, W, copy W, P3/H/1391
Thos. Somner, gent., Purton, 1733, W, P3/H/1112
Hipstone, Hipstone alias Mayes, Jn., Westb., 1721, AB, P25/1721/7
Hiron *see* Hieron
Hiscock, Abel, yeo., Stert, Urchf. (form. of Coate), 1856, aff, O, W, Wr, P1/1856/11
Agnes, widow, Wick, Mkt. L., 1585, W, P2/7Reg/6B
Hiscox, Agnes, widow, Allington, All C., 1624, I, W, P3/H/189
Hiscox, Agnes, widow, Gt. Cheverell, 1647, I, W, P2/H/588
Alice, widow, Hilp., 1632, AB, I, P2/H/442
Ambrose, W. Harnham, 1695, AB, I, P8/5
Hiscocks, Andrew, husb., Whitep., 1745, W, P2/H/1353
Ann, widow, Melk., 1811, AB, comm, Wr, P2/1811/11
Anthony, Bps. C., 1708, AB, P24/580
Cath., sp., Allington, All C., 1709, I, W, P3/H/898
Chris., yeo., Mkt. L., [1699], W, P2/H/987
Chris., husb., Tisb., 1702, AB, I, P2/H/1011
Dan., yeo., Allington, All C., 1749, AB, ren, P3/H/1251
Dorothy, widow, Minety, 1716, I, W, P3/H/946

Edith, widow, Hilp., 1568, W, P2/5Reg/35A
Edwd., smith, Barford St M., 1599, I, W, P2/H/184
Edwd., Keevil, 1625, I, W, P1/H/167
Edwd., maltster, Limpley Stoke, Bradford A., 1708, I, W, P2/H/1064
Edwd., yeo., Rowde, 1833, W, Wr, P3/1833/49
Eliz., widow, Tisb., 1705, W, P2/H/1039
Eliz., Gillingham, Dorset, 1711, AB, P27/1/190
Eliz., Minety, 1731, W, P3/H/1093
Eliz., yeo.'s wife, Manningford A., 1766, AB, P3/H/1360
Eliz., widow, Rowde, 1807, W, Wr, P1/1807/15
Francis, yeo., Hilp., 1705, I, W, P2/H/1038
Geoffrey, jun., husb., Allington, All C., 1693, AB, I, P3/H/729
Hiscock *or* Hitchcock, Geoffrey, sen., husb., Allington, All C., 1693, AB, comm, I, W, P3/H/728
Geo., husb., Haygrove, Warm., 1676, a/c, I, P2/H/741
Geo., yeo., Minety, 1697, I, W, P3/H/770
Hy., All C., 1569, W, P1/1Reg/105A, P1/2Reg/93B
Hy., sen., yeo., Allington, All C., 1663, comm, I, W, P3/H/354
Hy., Allington, All C., 1687, AB, I, P3/H/642
Hy., yeo., All C., 1691, I, W, P3/H/698
Hy., yeo., Bedborough, Bps. C., 1714, W, P24/679
Hy., Devizes, 1741, AB, P1/H/976
Hy., yeo., Chipp., 1815, note, W, Wr, P3/1815/3
Hiscocks, Hugh, maltster, Gt. Amesb., [1685], I, W, P2/H/859
Jane, widow, Maddington, 1694, AB, I, W, P2/H/943
Jane, widow, Hilp., 1717, I, W, P2/H/1138
Jane, widow, Urchf., 1759, comm, W, P1/H/1139, P1/11Reg/379
Jeremiah, yeo., Calstone W., 1747, W, P26/868
Joan, widow, Donhead St My., 1572, W, P2/5Reg/155D
Hiscocks, Joan, sp., All C., 1637, I, NW, P3/H/300
Joan, widow, Allington, 1692, AB, comm, I, P3/H/711
Jn., Donhead St My., 1558, W, P2/3Reg/105B
Jn., tucker, Keevil, 1608, W, P2/H/242, P2/8Reg/21C
Hiscocks, Jn., Hilp., 1611, I, W, P1/H/63
Jn., yeo., Wilcot, 1612, a/c, court paper, I, W, P3/H/85
Hiscox, Jn., Seend, Melk., 1614, T (unnamed children), P2/H/299
Jn., Mere, 1615, AB, comm, I, P5/1614/31, P5/9Reg/166A
Hitchcock *or* Hiscock, Jn., Marl., 1630, AB, I, P1/H/181
Hiscox, Jn., Lt. Somerford, 1631, AB, a/c, I, P3/H/248
Jn., Allington, All C., 1634, I, W, P1/H/206
Hiscocks, Jn., baker, Goatacre, Hilmarton, 1674, AB, a/c, I, P3/H/487
Jn., husb., Over Zeals, 1681, comm, I, W, P5/1681/22
Jn., yeo., Pewsham Forest, 1682, AB, I, P3/H/572
Hiscocks, Jn., maltster, Sal. St Edmd., 1683, AB, I, ren, P1/H/470
Jn., mercer, Pewsey, 1685, AB, a/c, I, P3/H/615
Jn., Southbroom, 1693, AB, comm, I, P24/533
Jn., yeo., Rowde, 1702, AB, I, ren, P3/H/831
Jn., yeo., Sutton V., 1713, W (NEP), P30/97
Jn., Allington, All C., 1735, W, P1/H/936, P1/8Reg/107
Jn., yeo., Rowde, 1737, W, P3/H/1141
Jn., Wilton, 1738, AB, P2/H/1308
Hiscocks alias Hitchcock, Jn., Netheravon, 1753, AB, P5/1753/12
Jn., Lacock, 1768, AB, P3/H/1376
Jn., yeo., Minety, 1773, W, P1/H/1226, P1/13Reg/8
Jn., gent., W. Stowell, Alton Pr., 1783, comm, W, P3/H/1447
Jn., gent., Aldbourne, 1797, AB, ren, W, P3/H/1527
Jn., yeo., Rowde, 1854, aff, O, W, Wr, P3/1854/34
Jn., gent., All C., 1856, aff, O, W, Wr, P3/1856/32
Jonathan, husb., Lt. Cheverell, 1705, I, W, P2/H/1041
Jos., sen., husb., Stockley, Calne, 1736, W, P26/795
Hissocks, Jos., Stratford sub C., 1738, AB, Wr, P4/1738/11

Jos., yeo., Stockley, Calne, 1748, AB, ren, P26/877
Jos., innholder, Malm., 1768, AB, W, P3/H/1377
Jos., sen., yeo., Minety, 1776, W, P3/H/1417
Jos., yeo., Minety, 1799, W, P3/H/1539
Hiscocks, Jos., sen., weaver, Melk., 1808, comm, W, Wr, P1/1808/40
Jos., Melk., 1829, AB, comm, Wr, P1/1829/30
Hiscocks alas Chapman, Joyce, sp., Grittenham, Brinkw., 1671, AB, comm, I, P3/H/456
Joyce, widow, Devizes Grn, Bps. C., 1679, comm, I, W, P24/471
Hiscocks, Martha, widow, Broad C., 1847, W, Wr, P2/1847/63
Hiscock *or* Hiscox, My., widow, Chaddenwick, Mere, 1688, I, W, P5/1688/42
My., widow, Limpley Stoke, Bradford A., 1717, W, P2/H/1141
My., widow, Holt, Bradford A., 1719, W, P2/H/1169
Hiscox, My., widow, Bradford A., 1736, W, P2/H/1289
Hiscocks, My., widow, Westb. L., 1762, W, P25/1762/1
My., sp., Lackham, Lacock, 1767, W, P3/H/1367
My., sp., Devizes, 1831, aff, comm, W, Wr, P1/1831/9
Hiscox, Maurice, shepherd, All C., 1623, I, W, P3/H/182
Michael, sen., wheelwright, Hilp., 1814, W, Wr, P1/1814/69
Nathaniel, clothworker, Melk., 1772, AB, W, P2/H/1533
Hiscox, Nich., Pott., 1605, I, P1/H/33
Philadelphia, sp., Devizes, 1741-42, W, P1/H/997, P1/9Reg/216
Philip, husb., Lt. Trowle, Trowb., 1559, W, P2/4Reg/3D
Phyllis, widow, Bedborough, Bps. C., 1758, W, P24/1010
Richd., Bradford A., 1591, I, copy I, P2/H/114
Hiscocks, Richd., Allington, All C., [1611], W (NEP), P3/H/73
Richd., dyer, Atworth, Bradford A., 1634, I, W, P2/H/463
Richd., Barford St M., 1641, a/c, P2/H/547
Richd., yeo., Bromham, 1718, I, W, P3/H/957
Richd., sen., yeo., Coate, Bps. C., 1792, W, P24/1221
Robt., Devizes St Jn., 1628, NW, P1/H/179
Robt., Horton, Bps. C., 1632, AB, I, P24/252
Robt., labourer, Seend, Melk., 1633, I, W, P2/H/450
Robt., sen., husb., Stockley, Calne, 1670, W, P26/178
Robt., smith, E. Harnham, Britford, 1683, I, W, P5/1682/61
Robt., yeo., Mere, 1712, W, P5/1712/28, P5/15Reg/288
Robt., sen., gardener, Bedborough, Bps. C., 1718, I, W, P24/643
Robt., grazier, Devizes, 1746, comm, W, P1/H/1031, P1/10Reg/27, 45B
Hiscox, Robt., Melk., 1799, AB, P2/H/1689
Roger, yeo., W. Stowell, Alton Pr., 1664, I, W, P3/H/363
Ruth, All C., 1835, W, P3/1835/13
Sam., Calstone W., 1725, AB, comm, P26/703
Hiscocks, Sam., maltster, Turleigh, Winsley, Bradford A., 1739, W, P2/H/1317
Sarah Axford, Cherhill, 1837, AB, Wr, P26/1434
Hiscocks, Simon, farmer, Heywood Farm, Westb., 1828, W, Wr, P25/1828/3
Hiscocks, Simon, miller, Norleaze, Westb. (form. of Congresbury, Somerset), 1846, AB, O, ren, W, Wr, P25/1846/3
Stephen, sen., yeo., Calstone W., 1663, comm, I, W, P5/1662/59
Stephen, yeo., Fowlswick Farm, Chipp., 1718, I, W, P3/H/958
Hiscock *or* Hiscox, Stephen, Calne, 1733, I, W, P26/773
Hiscox, Susanna, sp., Grittenham, Brinkw., 1664, I, W, P3/H/364
Susanna, widow, Bedborough, Bps. C., 1711, I, W, P24/700
Hiscocks, Susanna, Rodbourne C., 1832, AB, W, Wr, P3/1832/18
Thos., tucker, Erlestoke, 1608, W, P2/H/244, P2/8Reg/17
Thos., Rowde, 1629, I, W, P3/H/230
Thos., broad weaver, Langley Burrell, 1688, AB, I, P3/H/655
Thos., Melk., 1693, AB, I, P2/H/934
Thos., yeo., All C., 1741, W, P1/H/993, P1/9Reg/170B
Hiscocks, Thos., Trowb., 1832, AB, Wr, P1/1832/63
Wm., Mkt. L., 1589, I, W, P2/H/90
Hiscox, Wm., yeo., Allington, All C., 1623, I, W, P3/H/183
Hiscocks *or* Hitchcock, Wm., husb., W. Stowell, Alton Pr., 1637, I, W, P3/H/298

Wm., yeo., Chaddenwick, Mere, 1678, I, W, P5/1678/19
Wm., yeo., Stapleford, 1688, AB, I, W, P2/H/887
Wm., servant to Jas. Chubbe, Odstock, 1693, AB, I, P2/H/933
Wm., sen., yeo., Bedborough, Bps. C., 1702, I, W, P24/547
Hiscox, Wm., yeo., Bedborough, Bps. C., 1735, W, P24/932
Hiscocks, Wm., yeo., Manningford Bohun, 1756, W, P1/H/1121, P1/11Reg/299
Wm., sen., victualler, Whitep., 1761, W, P2/H/1451
Wm., yeo., Motc., Dorset, 1765, W, P27/1/450, P27/3Reg/122
Wm., miller, Moredon, Rodbourne C., 1850, O, W, Wr, P3/1850/1
see also Gerard alias H.; Stafford alias H.
Hiscutt, Joel, Longbridge D., 1793, AB, P2/H/1668
Jn., yeo., Crockerton, Longbridge D., 1823, W, P2/1823/28
Richd., sen., broad weaver, Crockerton, Longbridge D., 1716, W, P1/H/733, P1/6Reg/76
Hisey *see* Hissey
Hiskens, Hiskens *see* Hoskins
Hislop, Francis, linen draper, Bradford A., 1770, comm, W, P2/H/1524
Hissey, Hisey, Jn., Gt. Faringdon, Berks., 1641, I, W, P5/1641/39, P5/14Reg/3A
Jn., yeo., Longworth, Berks., 1795, W, P1/H/1338, P1/14Reg/602
Maurice, yeo., Buttermere, 1848, comm, W, Wr, P3/1848/4
Robt., E. Hagbourne, Berks., 1717, AB, P1/H/739
Hissocks *see* Hiscock
Hitchcock, Agnes, widow, Mkt. L., 1618, AB, I, W, P2/H/326
Agnes, Erlestoke, 1630, I, W, P2/H/421
Agnes, widow, Manton, Preshute, 1634, AB, I, P1/H/207
Betty, widow, Swindon, 1811, W, Wr (2), P1/1811/54
Edmd., gent., Manningford Bohun, 1802, W, P2/1802/55
Edwd., baker, Marl., 1725, W, P1/H/813, P1/7Reg/65A
Edwd., Manton, Preshute, 1735, W, P1/H/931, P1/8Reg/52
Edwd., yeo., Uffc., Devon, 1759, AB, P20/1/237
Edwd., sen., baker, Marl., 1774, W, P1/H/1233, P1/13Reg/53
Eliz., sp., W. Stowell, Alton Pr., 1786, W, P3/H/1474
Harry, sen., gent., Mkt. L., 1830, W, P3/1830/3
Harry, yeo., Chitterne AS, 1852, O, W, Wr, P2/1852/26
Jas., fuller, Lyme R., Dorset, 1711, I (detailed), W, P16/189
Jas., maltster, Avebury, 1803, AB, W, Wr, P3/1803/7
Jas., yeo., Calne, 1808, W, Wr, P26/1272
Jas., yeo., Dauntsey, 1848, D, O, W, Wr, P3/1848/36
Joan, widow, Sherb., Dorset, 1626, I, W, P5/1626/21, P5/10Reg/324
Joan, widow, Goatacre, Hilmarton, 1680, AB, I, P3/H/547
Joan, mistress, Marl., 1692, AB, comm, P1/H/557
Hysshecokes, Jn., Mkt. L., 1557, W, P2/3Reg/49B
Jn., All C., 1619, I, W (on same sheet), P3/H/144
Jn., tailor, Manton, Preshute (form. of Marl.), 1686, W, P1/H/1365
Jn., Marl. St Peter and St Paul, 1708, I, W, P1/H/646
Jn., yeo., Goatacre, Hilmarton, 1767, W, P1/H/1190, P1/12Reg/221C
Jn., yeo., Fittleton Farm, 1815, W, Wr, P2/1815/49
Jn., Kington St M., 1820, W, Wr, P1/1820/83
Jn., gent., Avebury, 1828, O, W, Wr, P3/1828/43
Maria, sp., Calne, 1824, W, Wr, P5/1824/3
Marian, widow, Manton, Preshute, 1645, comm, I, W, P1/H/266
My., widow, Woodb., 1697, W, P3/H/771
My., widow, Goatacre, Hilmarton, 1781, W, P3/H/1442
My., sp., Avebury, 1829, W, Wr, P1/1829/11
Michael Pontin, gent., Avebury, 1838, O, W, Wr, P3/1838/64
Ralph, thatcher, Goatacre, Hilmarton, 1823, comm, W, Wr, P3/1823/5
Robt., yeo., Manton, Preshute, 1616, I, W, P1/H/111
Robt., Wootton R., 1691, AB, I, P3/H/699
Robt., Woodb., 1704, AB, P1/H/635
Roger, yeo., Huish, 1683, AB, I, P3/H/583
Roger, E. Stowell, Wilcot, 1728, AB, P3/H/1049

Roger, Winterbourne M., 1801, AB, comm, P3/1801/4
Hitchcock *or* Hiscock, Rosamond, widow, Redhill, Pewsham, 1687, AB, I, W, P3/H/643
Rose, yeo.s wife, Manningford A., 1743, W, P3/H/1193
Simon Pile, gent., All C., 1850, court proceeding, req, W, Wr, P3/1850/58
Hechekocke, Thos., no abode stated, 1559, I, P2/H/16
Thos., husb., Seend, Melk., 1562, W, P2/4Reg/96C
Thos., fletcher, Sherb., Dorset, 1603, I, T, NW, P5/1603/40, P5/7Reg/89F
Thos., yeo., Basildon, Berks., 1664, AB, I, ren, P1/H/350
Wm., sen., Allington, All C., 1619, I, W, P3/H/145
Wm., sen., husb., Manton, Preshute, 1663, I, W, P1/H/341
Wm., fuller, Uffc., Devon, 1665, I, P5/1665/43
Wm., gent., Preshute, 1670, AB, comm, I, P1/H/399
Wm., yeo., W. Stowell, Alton Pr., 1704, I, W, P3/H/848
Wm., yeo., W. Stowell, Alton Pr., 1730, W, P3/H/1079
Wm., Marl., 1784, AB, P1/H/1294
Wm., gent., W. Stowell, Alton Pr., 1812, AB, W, Wr, P3/1812/10
Wm., gent., W. Stowell, Alton Pr., 1820, W, Wr, P1/1820/76
Wm., yeo., Winterbourne M., 1786, W, P3/H/1475
Zenobia, widow, Preshute, 1670, AB, a/c, comm, I, P1/H/400
see also Chapman alias H.; Hiscocks alias/*or* H.
Hitchens, Agnes, widow, Luckington, 1664, comm, I, NW, P1/H/358
Hitchings, Chas. Trimnell, bach., Sherston, 1817, W, Wr, P3/1817/20
Jane, yeo.'s wife, Rowde, 1779, AB, ren, W, P1/H/1257
Hitchins, Joan, Corsham, 1670, AB, I, P29/H/46, P29/1Reg/193A
Hitchens *or* Hutchins, Jn., miller, Limpley Stoke, Bradford A., 1614, I, W, P2/H/301
Jn., yeo., Rowde, 1782, W, P3/H/1444
Hitchins, Stephen, yeo., Manningford A., 1842, comm, W, Wr, P3/1842/20
Wm., no abode stated, 1631, I, P2/H/427
Hitchins, Wm., victualler, Devizes, 1836, O, W, P1/1836/16
Hitchman, Jn., Rowde, 1615, I, P3/H/111
Thos., yeo., Broad B., Highw., 1761, W, P10/1761/1
Hitt, Andrew, butcher, Beam., Dorset, 1594, AB, I, P5/1594/40
Giles, gent., Beam., Dorset, 1761, comm, W, P5/1761/21
Humphrey, Beam., Dorset, 1776, AB, comm, P5/1776/23, P5/17Reg/131C
Sam., yeo., Beam., Dorset, 1731, AB, ren, P5/1731/37
Thos., Beam., Dorset, 1758, note, W, P17/536
Hityard *see* Hilliard
Hix *see* Hicks
Hixon *see* Hickson
Hoane *see* Hone
Hoare, Hoor, Ann, Lyme R., Dorset, 1669, NW., P16/22
Hore, Ann, sp., Sal., 1742, AB, P4/1742/9
Hoare alias Bowyer, Audrey, sp., Chr. M., 1625, AB, a/c, I, NW, P3/H/200
Hore, Benj., husb., Laverstock, 1758, W, Wr, P2/H/1433
Hore, Cath., widow, Yondover, Netherb., Dorset, 1716, I, W, P17/366
Hoar, Chas., Hankerton, 1809, AB, comm, Wr, P3/1809/44
Constantine, yeo., Meerhay, Beam., Dorset, 1723, AB, I, P17/406
Dan., yeo., E. Knoyle, 1785, W, P2/H/1615
Hore, Eliz., widow, Oborne, Dorset, 1640, I, W, P5/1640/31, P5/13Reg/232A
Eliz., widow, White Waltham, Berks., 1732, W, P1/7Reg/473B
Hore, Eliz., widow, Sal., 1747, W, P4/1747/2
Hoar, Eliz., sp., Lyme R., Dorset, 1748, AB, P16/301
Eliz., sp., Sunninghill, Berks., 1783, W, P1/H/1288, P1/13Reg/469A
Eliz., widow, Sutton C., Berks., 1820, W, Wr, P1/1820/91
Hoar, Francis, yeo., Meerhay, Beam., Dorset, 1721, W, P17/392
Geo., Devizes, 1845, AB, O, Wr, P1/1845/2
Hy. *see* Thos. Burree
Hoar, Jas., yeo., Chards., Devon, 1804, comm, W (made 1754), P14/201
Hore/Whore alias Bowyer, Jn., Mere, 1616, AB, I, P5/1616/32, P5/9Reg/178B
Hore, Jn., esquire, Netherb., Dorset, 1687, I, W (NEP), P2/H/880, P17/301

Hoar, Jn., Chards., Devon, 1704, AB, I, P5/1704/36
Hoor, Jn., Lyme R., Dorset, 1747, AB, P16/296
Hoar, Jn., labourer, Bourton, Shrivenham, Berks., 1747, W, P1/H/1046, P1/10Reg/129B
Hoar, Jn., wheelwright, Beam., Dorset, 1802, comm, W, P17/588
Jn., tailor, Broad St., Lyme R., Dorset, 1843, comm, W, Wr, P16/434
Hoar, Jonathan, bargemaster, Wallingford, Berks., 1786, W, P1/H/1299, P1/14Reg/123
Whore, Leonard, mason, Bere R., Dorset, 1602, AB, W, P5/1602/42, P5/7Reg/51C
Mgt., Sal. St Thos., 1633, AB, I, P4/1633/18
Hoar, My., wife, Chards., Devon, 1742, W, P14/179
Maud, widow, Lt. Coxwell, Gt. Faringdon, Berks., 1635, I, W, P5/1635/47, P5/12Reg/186
Obadiah, Marcham, Berks., 1729, AB, P1/H/850
Whore, Ralph, Stratton, Dorset, 1599, a/c, AB, I, P5/1599/36, P5/6Reg/234B
Hore, Richd., Clack, Lyneham, 1601, W, P3/1Reg/76A
Hore, Richd., Oborne, Dorset, c1608?, W (undated) (NEP), P5/8Reg/115A
Richd., innholder, Marl., 1729, W, P1/H/880, P1/7Reg/386B
Whore, Roger, Shitterton, Bere R., Dorset, 1602, AB, I, P5/1602/43, P5/7Reg/36B
Whore, Thos., Shitterton, Bere R., Dorset, 1616, I, W, P5/1615/38, P5/9Reg/171A
Thos., grocer, Melk., 1820, comm, W, Wr, P1/1820/146
Hoar, Thomasine, widow, Chards., Devon, 1731, AB, P5/1731/46
Timothy, yeo., Chards., Devon, 1803, W, P5/1803/49, P5/19Reg/82
Hore, Wm., sen., yeo., Corsley, 1545, W (NEP), P2/1Reg/51C
Hore, Wm., husb., Fernham, Shrivenham, Berks., 1619, I, W, P1/H/133
Hore, Wm., husb., Oborne, Dorset, 1636, I, W, P5/1636/30, P5/13Reg/24A
Hore, Wm., gent., Ham, 1683, I, W, P1/H/483
Hore, Wm., blacksmith, Blewbury, Berks., 1711, AB, comm, ren, P5/1711/31
Wm., Lt. Coxwell, Gt. Faringdon, Berks., 1722, I, W, P5/1722/29, P5/16Reg/75B
Hoar, Wm., Oxenwood, Shalbourne, 1743, AB, Wr, P5/1743/41
Wm., Beam., Dorset, 1811, AB, note, P17/597
see also Barber alias H.
Hobbs, Hobbes, Agnes, widow, Chittoe, Bps. C., 1611-15, AB, a/c, W, P24/134-35
Hobbes, Agnes, widow, Drayton, Abingdon, Berks., 1614, I, W, P1/H/97
Alexander, Chilton F., 1721, W (NEP), P3/H/980
Alice, widow, Sherston, 1685, comm, W, P3/H/616
Hobbes, Ann, widow, Coombe, Enford, 1639, I, W, P2/H/527
Ann, widow, Devizes, 1782, W, P1/H/1276, P1/13Reg/366
Avery, carp., Sutton C., Berks., 1711, I, W, P1/H/678, P1/5Reg/158A
Hobbes, Cath., tailor's wife, Sal., 1626, I, W, P4/1626/11
Cath., widow, Devizes St My., 1680, I, W, P1/H/456
Chas., carp., Abingdon, Berks., 1776, AB, ren, W, P1/H/1244, P1/13Reg/129A
Chas., grocer, Abingdon, Berks., 1795, W, P1/H/1331, P1/14Reg/515
Edith, widow, Westport St My., 1710, I, W, P3/H/909
Edwd., tailor, Gt. Cheverell, 1621, I, W, P2/H/352
Edwd., almsman form. victualler, Lyme R., Dorset, 1633, AB (re Edwd. & Joan H.), L, P5/1632/26, P5/12Reg/84A
Edwd., serge weaver, Malm., 1689, I, W, P3/H/668
Edwd., All C., 1693, AB, P3/H/730
Edwd., cordw., Calne, 1752, W, P26/913
Hobbes, Eleanor, widow, Westport St My., 1683, I (2), W (1 I relates to Wm. & other & W to Eleanor), P1/H/476
Eleanor, widow, Barkham, Berks., 1808, W, Wr, P1/1808/108
Eliz., gent.'s wife, no abode stated but husband is of Tetbury, Gloucs, 1675, AB, P1/H/435
Eliz., widow, Amesb., 1692, AB, I, P1/H/548
Eliz., widow, Westport St My., 1761, W, P3/H/1328
Eliz., widow, Coombe B., 1790, AB, P8/65
Ellen, Landford, [1598?], I, P2/H/173
Ellen, widow, Landford, [1612], W, P2/H/288
Francis, gent., Westport St My., 1638, I, P1/H/228
Hobbes, Francis, yeo., Westport St My., 1668, I, W, P3/H/404
Hobbes, Francis, yeo., Sherston, 1670, I, W, P3/H/438
Giles, collier, Landford, 1711, I, W, P1/H/665, P1/5Reg/40
Giles, yeo., Whitep., 1744, W, Wr, P1/H/1026, P1/9Reg/436A
Giles, sen., collier, Landford, [1681], I, W, P2/H/791

Hy., Westport St My., 1669, AB, comm, I, P3/H/420
Hobbes, Hugh, Charl. nr. P., 1610, I, W, P2/H/262, P2/8Reg/84B
Israel, maltster, New Windsor, Berks., 1726, W, P1/H/817, P1/7Reg/91B
Israel, maltster, New Windsor, Berks., 1732, AB, comm, W, P1/H/911, P1/7Reg/537
Jas., thatcher, Lacock, 1737, comm, W, P3/H/1142
Jas., Lt. Hinton, 1796, W, P3/H/1518
Jane, Wylye, 1674, a/c, P2/H/718
Jane, sp., Shrewton, 1789, AB, ren, P1/H/1310
Joan, widow, Fritham, Bramshaw, Hants, 1566, W, P5/1Reg/66D
Hobbes, Joan, widow, Longbridge D., 1598, I, W, P2/H/170
Hobbes, Joan, widow, Sutton V., 1603, I (very detailed), W, P2/H/211
Hobbes, Joan, widow, Chittoe, Bps. C., 1617, AB, P24/79
Joan, widow, Sherston, 1715, I, W, P3/H/941
Hobbes, Jn., Sutton V., 1557, W, P2/3Reg/41A
Hobbes, Jn., Bramshaw, Hants, 1562, W, P5/1Reg/10A
Hobbes, Jn., husb., Sutton V., 1573, W, P2/5Reg/163B
Hobbes, Jn., weaver, Longbridge D., 1589, I, T, W, P2/H/101
Hobbes, Jn., weaver, Longbridge D., 1608, I, W, P2/H/245, P2/8Reg/29A
Hobbs alias Absolon, Jn., husb., Gt. Durnford, 1613, I, W, copy W, P5/1613/42, P5/9Reg/96B, 127A
Hobbes, Jn., Fritham, Bramshaw, Hants, 1622, AB, a/c, I, P24/194
Hebbes, Jn., husb., Oborne, Dorset, 1634, I, W. Proved at the Metropolitan visitation at Dorchester, P5/1634/11, P5/12Reg/290A
Hobbes, Jn., barber, Sherb., Dorset, 1636, I, W, P5/1636/27, P5/13Reg/26C
Jn., collier, Plaitford, 1638, I, NW, P1/H/238
Jn., miller, Coombe, Enford, [1645], I, W, P2/H/573
Jn., Brook, Bramshaw, Hants, 1646, I, W, P24/277
Hobbes, Jn., yeo., Stert, Urchf., 1662, comm, I, W, P1/H/315
Jn., sen., butcher, Coate, Bps. C., 1668, surety bond, I, W, P24/372
Hobbes, Jn., husb., Urchf., 1668, I, T, W, P2/H/655
Jn., yeo., Gt. Cheverell, 1669, I, W, P2/H/664
Hobbes, Jn., Amesb., 1671, I, NW, P2/H/681
Jn., yeo., Newtown, Hungerford, Berks., 1676, AB, I, NW, P5/1675/22, P5/1676/31
Hobbs alias Absolon, Jn., Gt. Durnford, 1677, AB, I, P9/17
Jn., Easterton, Mkt. L., 1683, AB, P2/H/820
Jn., Easterton, Mkt. L., 1696, AB, I, P2/H/961
Jn., Ardington, Berks., 1711, AB, I, P1/H/675
Jn., Bramshaw, Hants, 1717, AB, P24/654
Jn., yeo., Hidden, Hungerford, Berks., 1736, W, P23/522
Jn., sen., yeo., Easterton, Mkt. L., 1746, W, P2/H/1363
Jn., jun., labourer, Drayton, Abingdon, Berks., 1759, W, P1/H/1141, P1/11Reg/405A
Jn., yeo., Sutton C., Berks., 1767, W, P1/H/1197, P1/12Reg/251B
Jn., victualler, *The Royal Oak*, Swindon, 1772, W, P3/H/1400
Jn., yeo., Mkt. L., 1779, W, P2/H/1580
Hobbes, Jn., yeo., Bray, Berks., 1826, W, Wr, P1/1826/81
Hobbis, Jn., Grove, Wantage, Berks., 1831, AB, comm, Wr, P23/954
Jos., Newtown, Hungerford, Berks., 1764, draft W, W, P5/1764/24
Hobbes, Mgt., widow, Charl. nr. P., 1605, AB, I, P2/H/226
Mgt., widow, Marl. St Peter and St Paul, 1690, W, P1/H/532
Mgt., shopkeeper, Garford, Marcham, Berks., 1835, O, W, P1/1835/7
Hobbes, Margery, widow, Bugley, Warm., 1623, I, W, P2/H/363
Margery, widow, Coate, Bps. C., 1670, AB, process, W, P24/393
Margery, widow, Lyme R., Dorset, 1690, AB, I, W, P16/98
Margery, widow, Chittoe, Bps. C., 1703, I, W, P24/541
Mark, miller, Coombe, Enford, 1623, I, W, P2/H/362
Mark, sen., yeo., Winterbourne D., 1671, I, W, P7/42
My., Erlestoke, 1681, AB, comm, P1/H/462
Nich., Lyme R., Dorset, 1606, AB, I, P5/1606/21, P5/8Reg/65A
Nich., yeo., Sherston, 1663, AB, I, P3/H/355
Nich., labourer, Wingfield, 1837, AB, aff, O, W, Wr, P2/1837/19
Peter, W. *or* Mkt. L., 1738, W, P1/H/967, P1/8Reg/332

Hobbys, Philip, yeo., Teffont E., 1542, W, P2/H/2, P2/1Reg/36
Phillippa, widow, Sherb., Dorset, 1648, AB, I (includes Spanish money with pieces of broken silver), P5/1648/6, P5/14Reg/106A
Hobbes, Richd., husb., Urchf., 1581, T (children: Richd., Alice & Eliz. H.), W, P2/H/65, P2/6Reg/36C
Richd., Bramshaw, Hants (but no parish of abode recorded), 1635, W, P24/234
Richd., husb., Urchf., 1637, I, W, P2/H/496
Hobbes, Richd., husb., Idmiston, 1673, I, W, P2/H/714
Richd., yeo., Newton T., 1709, I, W, P2/H/1068
Richd., yeo., Marl., 1714, W, P1/H/705, P1/5Reg/416
Richd., yeo., Aldbourne, 1721, W, P3/H/981
Hobbes, Robt., Urchf., 1572, W, P2/5Reg/148E
Robt., collier, Landford, 1591, I, T, P2/H/115
Robt., Fullaway, All C., 1614, I, P1/H/91
Robt., cordw., Westport St My., 1706, I (2 - 1 a copy), W, P3/H/867
Robt. Nash, Stert, Urchf., 1827, AB, comm, Wr, P1/1827/25
Roger, Bramshaw, Hants, 1562, W, P5/1Reg/12B
Hobbes, Roger, Mkt. L., 1573, W, P2/5Reg/163A
Hobbes, Roger, yeo., Fritham, Bramshaw, Hants, 1608, I, W, P24/159
Sarah, widow, Hidden, Hungerford, Berks., 1716, AB, W, P5/1716/44
Simon, Bere R., Dorset, 1672, comm, I, W, P5/1672/19
Stephen, Warm., 1616, AB, a/c, I, P1/H/103
Stephen, Devizes, 1675, AB, I, P1/H/436
Hobbes, Thos., Gt. Bedwyn, 1557, W, P1/1Reg/13
Hobbes, Thos., Longbridge D., 1594, AB, I, W, P2/H/139
Thos., shepherd, Aldbourne, 1603, I, W, P3/H/6
Hobbes, Thos., sen., Chittoe, Bps. C., 1611-15, AB, a/c, I, T, W, P24/135
Thos., Plaitford, 1618, AB, I, P2/H/324
Thos., yeo., Foxley, 1637, I, W, P3/H/301
Thos., jun., Chittoe, Bps. C., 1668, AB, comm, P24/368
Thos., gent. *or* yeo., Fisherton D., 1668, AB, comm, P1/H/385
Hobbes, Thos., mason, Westport St My., 1670, I, W, P3/H/439
Thos., limeburner, Fisherton A., 1679, AB, I, W, P2/H/773
Thos., servant to (Hon) Madam Thynne, Broughton G., 1685, I, W, P2/H/846
Thos., miller, Baldham, Keevil, 1692, AB, cert, I, P1/H/555
Thos., jun., yeo., Hidden, Hungerford, Berks., 1695, AB, I, P5/1695/47
Thos., sen., yeo., N. Hidden, Hungerford, Berks., 1695, AB, I, W, P5/1695/43
Thos., Sherston, 1701, I, W, P3/H/810
Thos., sen., yeo., Hidden, Hungerford, Berks., 1714, W, P23/341
Thos., jun., Hidden, Hungerford, Berks., 1716, AB, comm, P5/1716/46
Thos., Chute, 1730, AB, P7/126
Thos., sen., yeo., Westport St My., 1730, W, Wr, P3/H/1080
Hobbes, Thos., currier, Westport St My., 1747, W, P3/H/1229
Thos., sen., yeo., N. Hidden, Hungerford, Berks., 1747, W, P23/599
Thos., publican, Whitep. (form. of Sal.), 1848, W, Wr, P2/1848/40
Walter, Longbridge D., 1619, I, T, P2/H/333
Hobbes, Wm., jun., Wilsford nr Pewsey, 1574, W, P2/5Reg/179D
Hobbes, Wm., Charl. nr. P., 1594, I, W, P2/H/135
Hobbes, Wm., weaver, Bromham, [1605], W (NEP), P3/H/14
Wm., Malm., 1608, AB, P3/H/38
Hobbes, Wm., husb., Highw., 1610, I, W, P5/1609/42, P5/9Reg/129A
Wm., weaver, Bromham, 1624, I, W, P3/H/190
Hobbes, Wm., clothier, Malm., 1632, I, W, P3/H/262
Wm., husb., Shute, Longbridge D., 1666, AB, I, P1/H/367
Hobbes, Wm., gardener, Devizes, 1667, I, W, P1/H/377
Wm., husb., Marl. St Peter and St Paul, 1667, AB, I, P1/H/380
Wm., butcher, Coate, Bps. C., 1670, AB, I, W, P24/398
Wm., rector, Sherrington, 1670, I, W, P1/H/397
Wm., N. Hidden, Hungerford, Berks., 1693, AB, comm, P5/1692/41
Wm., mason, Westport St My., 1694, W, P3/H/746
Wm., sen., gardener, Sanden Fee, Hungerford, Berks., 1701, W, P5/1701/26

Wm., sen., collier, Bramshaw, Hants, 1706, I, W, P24/590
Wm., butcher, Bps. C., 1752, AB, I, P24/1040
Wm., yeo., Baydon, 1779, W, Wr, P5/1779/9, P5/17Reg/163
Hobbis, Wm., Grove, Wantage, Berks., 1802, AB, P23/829
Wm., gardener, Easterton, Mkt. L., 1811, W, Wr (2), P1/1811/44
see also Absolon alias H.
Hobby, Jane, widow, Wylye, 1669, AB, P2/H/668
Hobdey, Richd., Gt. Faringdon, Berks., 1710, AB, I, P5/1710/55
Hobgood *see* Habgood
Hocker *see* Hacker
Hockett *see* Hackett
Hockley, Humphrey, Bishopstone N., 1694, AB, I, P6/88
Jas. Hy., Worton, Pott., 1839, AB, O, Wr, P1/1839/11
Jn., yeo., Fyfield, Milton L., [1606], W (NEP), P3/H/23
Jos., wheelwright, Marl., 1691, AB, I, P1/H/537
Hodde, Christian, widow, Wokm., Berks., 1567, W, P5/2Reg/26A
Hodder, Agnes, widow, Bapton, Fisherton Delamare, 1618, I, W, P2/H/327
Ann, widow of yeo., Aldbourne, 1846, O, W, Wr, P3/1846/39
Chas., Sherb., Dorset, 1803, AB, P5/1803/2, P5/19Reg/24B
Geo., Winterbourne S., 1706, AB, P2/H/1043
Jane, widow, Axford, Rams., 1705, I, W, P5/1705/25
Hodder alias Sidway, Jn., Netherb., Dorset, 1576, AB, P5/1576/28, P5/3Reg/84C
Jn., gent., Farley, Netherb., Dorset, 1774, comm, W, P17/566
My., singlewoman, Aldbourne, 1837, comm, W, Wr, P3/1837/7
Maud, widow, Gt. Cheverell, 1599, AB, I, W, P2/H/188
Ralph, sen., husb., Teffont M., 1639, I, W, P2/H/530
Robt. Lewis, husb., Holnest, Dorset, 1811, W, Wr, P5/1811/17
Roger, Teffont, 1541, I, W (NEP), P30/83
Thos., Gt. Cheverell, 1597, W, P2/H/164
Thos., Sherb., Dorset, 1612, AB, I, NW, P5/1611/20, P5/9Reg/59A
Thos., Sherb., Dorset, 1830, AB, O, Wr, P5/1830/13
Thos., Aldbourne, 1841, AB, comm, Wr, P3/1841/29
Wm., husb., Teffont M., [1615], I, P2/H/308
Wm., Leigh, Yetm., Dorset, 1671, AB, I, W, P5/1671/41
Hodding, Edwd. Davis, yeo., Odstock, 1849, W, Wr, P2/1849/19
Jn., gent., Sal., 1824, W, Wr, P4/1824/6
My., widow, Sal., 1737, W, P4/1737/13
Richd., husb., Speen, Berks., 1683, AB, I, P1/H/477
Thos., Sal., 1724, AB, P4/1724/6
Thos., Sal., 1755, AB, P4/1755/9
Thos., tucker, Sal., 1796, W, P4/1796/6
Hoddinott, Christian, widow, Sherb., Dorset, 1573, W, P5/3Reg/23E
Eliz., sp., Sherb., Dorset, 1782, comm, D, W, P5/1782/17, P5/17Reg/238B
Gustavus, buttonmaker, Sherb., Dorset, 1787, comm, W, P5/1787/9, P5/18Reg/73
Hy., Sherb., Dorset, 1637, AB, P5/1637/20, P5/13Reg/65A
Jas., yeo., Sherb., Dorset, 1803, W, P5/1803/45, P5/19Reg/77B
Jas., gent., Sherb., Dorset, 1807, W, Wr, P5/1807/6
Jas., Sherb., Dorset, 1829, AB, comm, Wr, P5/1829/15
Jn., Sherb., Dorset, 1613, AB, I, P5/1613/41, P5/9Reg/110A
Jn., jun., upholsterer, Sherb., Dorset, 1768, ren, P5/1768/14
Jn., Sherb., Dorset, 1770, AB, P5/1770/23, P5/17Reg/15B
Jn., hosier, Sherb., Dorset, 1781, W, P5/1781/10, P5/17Reg/211
Jn., carp., Sherb., Dorset, 1852, comm, W, Wr, P5/1852/1
Julian, widow, Sherb., Dorset, 1637, AB, P5/1637/17, P5/13Reg/51A
My., widow, Sherb., Dorset, 1780, AB, comm, P5/1780/11, P5/17Reg/199B
Robt., yeo., Sherb., Dorset, 1629, AB, a/c, comm, I, P5/1629/29, P5/11Reg/20D
Thos., gent. [and innholder], Sherb., Dorset, 1681, AB, I, W, P5/1681/28
Thos., scrivener, Sherb., Dorset, 1725, AB, P5/1725/40
Thos., sen., yeo., Sherb., Dorset, 1828, W, Wr, P5/1828/8
see also King nee H.

Hodges, Ann, sp., Wilcot, 1681, AB, I, NW, P3/H/560
Chas., shoemaker, Sal., 1723, AB, I, P1/H/804
Edith, widow, Stallen, Nether C., Dorset, 1688, I, W, P5/1688/38
Francis, labourer, Kingsdown, Box, 1804, W, P1/1804/93
Giles, shoemaker, E. Tytherton, Bremhill, 1856, aff, O, W, Wr, P3/1856/53
Hy., blacksmith, Stanford Dingley, Berks., 1606, I, W, P1/H/47
Hy., sen., yeo., Latton, 1709, I, W, P3/H/899
Hy., Speenhamland, Berks., 1756, AB, comm, P1/H/1105
Hugh, esquire, Sherb., Dorset, 1712, W, P5/1712/32, P5/15Reg/310B
Jas., maltster, Warm., 1724, W, P2/H/1201
Jas., Sal., 1770, AB, NW, P4/1770/1
Jane, sp., Milton L., 1848, W, Wr, P1/1848/55
Hogges, Jn., Preston, Dorset, 1561, W, P5/1Reg/3A
Hodge, Jn., Uffc., Devon, 1589, I, W, P5/1589/27, P5/5Reg/50B
Jn., [clothworker], Leighs Marsh, Dilton, Westb., 1669, AB, I (detailed), P25/1669/10
Jn., sergemaker, Ashley, Bradford A., 1716, W, P2/H/1133
Jn., Enmore Grn, Motc., Dorset, 1728, AB, P5/1728/52, P5/16Reg/184C
Jn., yeo., Nether C., Dorset, 1758, W, P5/1758/25
Jn., Sal., 1776, AB, P4/1776/3
Jn., farmer, Bremhill Wick, 1820, W, Wr, P1/1820/71
Jos., sen., yeo., Enmore Grn, Motc., Dorset, 1716, W, P5/1716/40, P5/15Reg/345C
Jos., Bearfield, Bradford A., 1801, AB, comm, P1/1801/25, P1/15Reg/247A
Margery, widow, Westb. L., 1632, I, W, P25/1632/3
Margery, widow, Leigh, Yetm., Dorset, 1731, W, P5/1731/44
My., widow, Enmore Grn, Motc., Dorset, 1724, AB, I, P19/110
My., widow, Latton, 1732, I, W, P3/H/1103
My., widow, Wootton R., 1737, AB, comm, ren, W, P3/H/1143
My., Over C., Dorset, 1756, AB, P5/1756/15
Philadelphia, Leighs Marsh, Dilton, Westb., 1683, comm, I, W, P25/1683/1
Rebecca, widow, Sherb., Dorset, 1808, W, Wr, P5/1808/11
Sarah, Wilcot, 1710, AB, I, P3/H/910
Thos., bricklayer, Arborfield, Berks., 1572, W, P5/2Reg/115C
Thos., Nether C., Dorset, 1673, AB, a/c, comm, I, P5/1673/23
Thos., Nether C., Dorset, 1714, AB, I, P5/1714/19
Thos., yeo., Nether C., Dorset, 1748, W, Wr, P5/1748/18
Thos., Latton, 1756, AB, P3/H/1297
Thos., yeo., Latton, 1761, W, P3/H/1329
Thos., maltster, Mkt. L., 1762, a/c, I, W, P2/H/1457
Hodge, Thos., maltster, Marl., 1780, W, P1/H/1270, P1/13Reg/304B
Thos., Nether C., Dorset, 1806, AB, comm, P5/1806/8, P5/19Reg/155A
Wm., clerk & vicar, Ogbourne St A., 1574, W, P5/3Reg/47C
Hodge, Wm., tailor, Uffc., Devon, 1669, AB, I, P20/1/57
Wm., esquire, late of Sherston (now of Wellington, Herefordshire), 1685, W, P3/H/617
Hogges, Wm., yeo., Rushall, 1691, I, W, P2/H/917
Wm., yeo., Over C., Dorset, 1705, cert, comm, W, P5/1704/38
Wm., gent., Sopworth, 1729, comm, W, P1/H/877, P1/7Reg/377A
Wm., yeo., Leigh, Yetm., Dorset, 1730, comm, W, P19/121
Wm., cordw., Kellaways, 1831, W, P3/1831/35
see also Hedges *or* H.; Lacy alias H.
Hodgetts, Diana, wife, Woodb., 1825, AB, Wr, P3/1825/45
Hodging *see* Hodding
Hodgkin, Ann, sp., Kington St M., 1742, W, P3/H/1185
Frances, Alderbury, 1668, AB, I, P26/144
Hodkins, Joan, widow, Corsley, 1673, I, W, P2/H/705
Hodgson, Wm., minor, Downton, 1809, appt of guardian, court proceeding, T (son of Jn. & Sarah H., decd; *also* nephew of Wm. Mowland of Downton), P2/1809/26
Hodkins *see* Hodgkin
Hodman, Edmd., husb., Arborfield, Berks., 1591, I, W, P5/1591/41, P5/5Reg/115B
Thos., Arborfield, Berks., 1566, W, P5/1Reg/70B
Hodson, Ann, Devizes, 1748, AB, P1/H/1052

Elias, Chards., Devon, 1684, AB, I, P14/57
Geo., proved at Calne, 1638, I, P5/1637/54
Jas., cooper, Chipp., 1772, W, P3/H/1401
Jos., carp., Chipp., 1738, comm, W, P1/H/950, P1/8Reg/209
Richd., weaver, Kington L., 1626, AB, I, P3/H/208
Robt., weaver *or* yeo., Langley Burrell, 1678, I, W, P3/H/533
Sarah, carp.'s wife, Chipp., 1741, AB, P3/H/1178
Stephen, Dauntsey, 1719, I, W, P3/H/970
Stephen, carp., Chipp., 1747, W, P1/H/1039, P1/10Reg/149A
Susanna, widow, Chipp., 1762, W, P3/H/1337
Wm., schoolmaster, Dauntsey, 1751, W, P3/H/1265
Hody, Ann, sp., Sal. The Close, 1744, W, Wr, P5/1744/23
Hoff *see* Huff
Hoford *see* Holford
Hogarth, Robt., brazier, Wantage, Berks., 1823, comm, W, Wr, P23/908
Hoggard *see* Vivian alias H.
Hoggers, Hoggers alias King, Thos., Worton, Pott., 1722, AB, P1/H/782
Hogges *see* Hodges
Hoggett *see* Hockett
Holborne *see* Oborne
Holborow, Agnes, no abode stated, but possibly Chipp. area, 1617, NW, P3/H/124, P5/12Reg/9A, 297A
Alexander, yeo., Sherston, 1732, W, P3/H/1104
Alexander, clerk, Sherston, 1743, comm, W, P3/H/1194
Ann, widow, Sherston, 1692, I, W, P3/H/712
Ann, sp., Biddestone St Peter & St Andrew, 1816, AB, Wr, P3/1816/46
Dan., mason, Luckington, 1700, I, NW, P3/H/798
Dan., yeo., Alderton, 1720, W, P1/H/762, P1/6Reg/259B
Dan., Luckington, Sherston, 1744, W, P3/H/1212
Dan., mason, Luckington, 1754, W, P3/H/1282
Holbrough, Edwd., dyer and victualler, Chipp., 1720, W, P1/H/766, P1/6Reg/259A
Eliz., widow, Sherston, 1743, comm, W, P3/H/1195
Geo., labourer and bach., Derry Hill, Pewsham (leaving effects at Chipp.), 1854, AB, aff, Wr, P3/1854/29
Hannah, sp., Biddestone St Nich., 1814, W, Wr, P1/1814/118
Hy., yeo., Wick, Sherston, 1755, W, P3/H/1289
Jn., Luckington, 1631, AB, I, P3/H/249
Holbrow, Jn., yeo., Sherston, 1634, I, NW, P1/H/205
Holbrough, Jn., dyer, Chipp., 1685, W, P3/H/618
Jn., mason, Luckington, 1725, comm, I, W, P3/H/1022
Jos., yeo., Sherston, 1733, W, P3/H/1114
Jos., freemason, Luckington, 1742, W, P3/H/1186
Jos., yeo., W. Yatton, Yatton K., 1799, W, P3/H/1540
Martha, widow, Luckington, 1747, W, P1/H/1047, P1/10Reg/152
My., widow, Alderton, 1565, W, P1/1Reg/47B
Rees, yeo., Luckington, 1688, I, W, P3/H/656
Holbrow, Richd., yeo., Foscote, Grittleton, 1663, I, W, P3/H/356
Holbrow, Richd., yeo., Turleigh, Winsley, Bradford A., 1800, W, P2/1800/3
Thos., mason, Luckington, 1670, I, NW, P3/H/440
Holbrow, Thos., sen., yeo., Nethermore, Pewsham, 1773, W, P3/H/1404
Holbrow, Thos., Lacock, 1822, AB, O, W, Wr, P3/1822/36
Holbrow, Thos., victualler, Chipp., 1829, AB, W, Wr, P1/1829/97
Wm., husb., Sherston, [1607], W (NEP), P3/H/30
Hulbrough, Wm., Upavon, 1661, AB, I, P2/H/606
Wm., farmer, W. Kington, 1805, W, Wr, P3/1805/29
Holbrook, Edwd., tailor, Foxham, Bremhill (form. of Wade St., Gloucester), 1724, I, W, P3/H/1010
Jn., Fisherton D., 1559, W, P2/3Reg/170E
Jn., Corsham, [1567], W (NEP), P29/1Reg/8
Jn., Longbridge D., 1580, AB, NW, P2/5Reg/364A
Jn., stay and corset manufacturer, Sal., 1851, W, Wr, P1/1851/40
Mgt., widow, Martin, Hants, 1571, W, P2/5Reg/128C
My., widow, Foxham, Bremhill, 1676, AB, I, P3/H/513

Robt., husb., Damerham, Hants, 1551, W, P2/2Reg/120A
Thos., husb., Mere, 1568, W, P5/2Reg/5B
Thos., Warm., 1592, I, P2/H/123
Thos., quarrier, Corsham, [1607], W, P29/H/13
Thos., yeo., Foxham, Bremhill, 1689, I, NW, P1/H/525
Holbrough, Holbrow *see* Holborow
Holcott, Wm., Wilton, 1593, AB, I, P2/H/130
Holdaway *see* Holway
Holden, Holding, My., widow, Rowde, 1664, AB, a/c, comm, I, P1/H/360
Robt., merchant, Lyme R., Dorset, 1685, I, W, P5/1685/50
Thos., husb., Ham, 1622, I, W, P1/H/154
Holder, Jane, sp., Devizes, 1779, AB, P1/H/1267-68
Jn., millman, Colerne, 1809, W, Wr, P3/1809/38
My., innholder, N. Wraxall, 1737, W, P3/H/1144
Sarah, Wadswick, Box, 1842-65, O, W, writ (for W to be produced at Wilts Assizes, Jun 1865), Wr, P3/1842/26
Thos., husb., N. Wraxall, 1712, I, W, P3/H/921
Holdest, Ann, widow, N. Bradley, 1776, AB, P2/H/1562
Holdeway *see* Holway
Holding *see* Holden
Hole, Benj., yeo., Nettleton, 1702, AB, I, P3/H/832
Benj., serge weaver, Littleton Drew, 1754, W, P3/H/1283
Eliz., widow, Nettleton, 1719, I, W, P3/H/971
Jn., husb., Alderton, 1696, AB, I, P3/H/763
Jn., yeo., Nettleton, 1706, AB, I, P3/H/868
Holegge *see* Hollidge
Holes *see* Hollis
Holford, Ann, sp., Melk., 1801, AB, comm, ren, P1/1801/18, P1/15Reg/242A
Edmd., curate, Tidcombe, T. and Fosbury, 1589, I, W, P1/H/514
Edmd., gent., Tidcombe, T. and Fosbury, 1691, AB, I, P3/H/700
Hoford alias Holford, Wm., miller, Sherston, 1622, I, NW, P1/H/150
Holiday, Holladay *see* Holliday
Holland, Alice, widow, Winterborne K., Dorset, 1634, I, W. Proved at the Metropolitan Visitation to Dorchester, P5/1634/50, P5/12Reg/295B
Brian, clerk, Heytes., 1730, AB, I, P5/1730/36
Dan., yeo., Long Burton, Dorset, 1729, W, P5/1729/24, P5/16Reg/217D
Dorothy, widow, Chipp., 1726, comm, W, P1/H/823, P1/7Reg/125A
Hollands, Eliz., widow, Stratfield M., Berks., 1717, AB, I, P1/H/741
Jn., clothier, Beckington, Somerset, 1618, I, W, P2/H/328
Jn., clothworker, Fordington, Dorset, 1681, AB, I, P15/38
Jn., esquire, Chipp., 1723, AB, P1/H/794
Jn., Sherb., Dorset, 1827, AB, comm, Wr, P5/1827/62
Jn., Uffc., Devon, 1797-1800, W, P5/1797/20, P5/1800/4, P5/18Reg/254B, 289A
My., sp., Enborne, Berks., 1811, W, Wr, P1/1811/36
Nathaniel, bach. (d. at sea), Lyme R., Dorset, 1748, AB, O, P16/295
Sam., miller, Bere R., Dorset, 1816, comm, W, Wr, P5/1816/16
Thos., husb., Winterborne K., Dorset, 1630, NW, P5/11Reg/137B
Thos., sen., minister, Amesb., 1680, I, W, P1/H/458
Hollard, Jn., Netherb., Dorset, 1695, AB, P17/343
My., widow, Hingsdon, Netherb., Dorset, 1694, I, W, P17/110
Hollard alias Silk, My., widow, Hingsdon, Netherb., Dorset, 1753, W, P17/524
Hollard alias Silk, Thos., tailor, Waytown, Netherb., Dorset, 1606, I, W, P5/1606/26
Thos., Lyme R., Dorset, 1778, W, P16/344
see also Silk alias H.
Hollaway *see* Holloway
Hollegge *see* Hollidge
Hollery, Holree, Ann, Manton, Preshute, 1691, I, W, P1/H/542
Hollerre, Jn., Ogbourne St A., 1719, I, W, P5/1719/40, P5/16Reg/23B
Richd., husb., Manton, Preshute, 1698, AB, I, P1/H/590
Wm., husb., Beckhampton, Avebury, 1727, W, P3/H/1039
Holles *see* Hollis

Hollett *see* Hallett
Holley *see* Holly
Holliar *see* Hollyer
Hollick, Betty, widow, Shrivenham, Berks., 1817, W, Wr, P1/1817/23
Holliday, Halladay, Ann, widow, Eastcott, Urchf., 1700, I, W, P2/H/994
Halliday, Ann, widow, Bradford A., 1708, W, P2/H/1062
Ann *see also* Chas. Green, P1/4Reg/141
Halladay, Anselm, Figh. (form. of Newbury, Berks.), 1712, AB, P26/572
Halliday, Charlotte, sp., Sutton V., 1831, AB, comm, P2/1831/47
Halliday, Edwd., gent., Sutton V., 1758, W, P2/H/1431
Eliz., widow, Fernham, Shrivenham, Berks., 1701, W, P1/H/617
Holiday, Eliz., widow, W. Challow, Letcombe Regis, Berks., 1756, AB, comm, P1/H/1107
Holiday, Francis, Steeple A., 1559, AB, P2/3Reg/180C
Francis, labourer, Milton L., 1670, AB, I, P3/H/441
Holiday, Geoffrey, Milton L., 1713, I, W, P3/H/931
Geoffrey, Shropshire Marsh, Lydiard T., 1715, AB, I, O, P3/H/942
Holiday, Geoffrey, Corsham, 1716, marriage licence, P29/2Reg/19D
Geoffrey, Chisbury, Lt. Bedwyn, 1739, AB, P21/9/28
Geoffrey, maltster, Corsham, [1797], W, P29/H/123, P29/2Reg/220
Giles, sen., yeo., Wedh., Urchf., 1703, I, W, P2/H/1020
Halliday, Giles, gent., Wedh., Urchf., 1731, AB, W, P2/H/1258
Halliday, Giles, Sutton V., 1828, AB, comm, P2/1828/9
Halliday, Jane, widow, Sutton V. (leaving effects at Knook), 1781, W, P5/1781/9, P5/17Reg/203C
Jn., Wrou., 1609, AB, P3/H/51
Jn., carp., Milton L., 1646, I, W, P1/H/279
Jn., yeo. *or* carp., Milton L., 1679, I, W, P3/H/537
Jn., yeo. *or* husb., Purton Stoke, 1701, I, W, P3/H/811
Jn., Sherston, 1729, AB, P1/H/865
Holladay, Jn., yeo., Hazel Hill, Lydiard T., 1730, W, P3/H/1081
Jn., yeo., Bushton, Clyffe P., 1771, W (2 - 1 a copy), Wr, P3/H/1392
My., widow, Hook, Lydiard T., 1661, comm, I, W, P3/H/342, P3/3Reg/16
Halliday, My., widow, Wedh., Urchf., 1717, W, P2/H/1139
Halliday, My., widow, Warm., 1724, W, P2/H/1203
Michael, sen., yeo., Lt. Coxwell, Gt. Faringdon, Berks., 1710, W, P5/1710/56, P5/15Reg/171
Halladay, Paul, Figh., 1731, AB, I, P26/762
Halliday, Rebecca, sp., Sutton V., 1830, AB, comm, P2/1830/1
Halliday, Rebecca Ann, widow, Sutton V., 1841, comm, W, Wr, P2/1841/1
Richd., Brixton D., 1720, AB, I, P2/H/1175
Richd., Purton, 1727, AB, comm, W, P3/H/1040
Halliday, Richd., Tinh., Edington, 1766, AB, P2/H/1482
Robt., S. Marston, 1721, AB, P10/1721/5
Robt., Purton, 1758, AB, P3/H/1312
Holiday, Thos., carp., Hook, Lydiard T., 1661, I, W, P3/H/343, P3/3Reg/25B
Holiday, Thos., Allington, Chipp., 1748, W, P3/H/1239
Thos., sen., baker, Purton, 1767, comm, W, P3/H/1368
Thos., Purton, 1802, W, Wr, P3/1802/67
Wm., yeo., Purton, 1714, AB, W, P3/H/937
Halliday, Wm., clothier, Bradford A., 1755, comm, W, P2/H/1410
see also Church alias H.; Wilkins form. H.
Hollidge, Grace, widow, All C., 1784, W, P3/H/1457
Hollegge, Jn., cordw., Swindon, 1699, AB, I, P3/H/788
Jn., Marl., 1855, AB, aff, Wr, P1/1855/38
Hollidge, Jn. Bewley, tailor, Wedh., Urchf. (late of Trowb.), 1788, W, P2/H/1634
Hollegge, Nich., shoemaker, Swindon, 1684, AB, I, P3/H/599
Holegge, Wm., cordw., Swindon, 1694, I, W, P3/H/747
Hollier *see* Hollyer
Hollis, Honour, sp., Sal., 1677, I, W, P4/1677/13
Jas., husb., Calne, 1689, AB, I, P26/382
Halys, Jn., carp., Norton B., 1550, W, P2/2Reg/105A
Hollyse, Jn., bailiff, Bradford A., 1588, W, P2/7Reg/131B

Jn., gent., Devizes, 1683, AB, I, P1/H/469
Jn., Devizes, 1706, AB, P1/H/637
Jn., gent., Devizes, 1732, W, P1/H/909, P1/7Reg/532
Jn., gent., Seagry, 1742, W (2 - 1 is copy), P3/H/1187
Martha, widow, Hurst, Berks., 1682, W, P5/1682/53
My., widow, Devizes, 1705, W, P1/H/639
Hallis, Nathan, cook, Mere, 1643, I, W, P5/1643/5, P5/14Reg/58A
Peter, Wilton, 1706, W, P2/H/1049
Robt., Seagry, 1729, AB, comm, W, P3/H/1064
Robt., yeo., Seagry, 1810, W, Wr, P3/1810/19
Holes *or* Hollyes, Simon, husb., Teffont M., 1586, I, W, P2/H/76, P2/7Reg/41A
Susanna, sp., Seagry, 1753, AB, comm, P3/H/1273
Thos., husb., Wokm., Berks., 1634, I, W. Proved at the Metropolitan Visitation to Reading, P5/1634/51, P5/12Reg/313
Thos., tanner, Emmbrook, Wokm., Berks., 1643, AB, comm, I, P5/1643/6, P5/14Reg/60B
Holles, Ultra, widow, Seagry, 1728, AB, P3/H/1050
Hollister, Ann, widow, Wootton B., 1692, I, W, P1/H/556
Eliz., sp., *The Limekiln*, Wootton B., 1744, W, P1/H/1020, P1/9Reg/404
Gabriel, grazier, Wootton B., 1715, I, W, P3/H/943
Hester, widow, Wootton B., 1735, AB, comm, P3/H/1128
Jn., gent., Wootton B., 1705, W, P3/H/859
Timothy, tallow chandler, Lacock, 1678, AB, a/c, I, P3/H/534
Wm., gent., Wootton B., 1726, AB, I, W, P1/H/832, P1/7Reg/156
Wm., gent., Wootton B., 1800, W, P3/1800/24
Holloway, Adam, broad weaver, Stanmead & Stockham Marsh, Bremhill, 1671, comm, I, ren, NW, P3/H/457
Alice, widow, Corsley, 1644, AB (2), comm, I, P2/H/569
Alice, widow, Mkt. L., [1688], I, W, P2/H/891
Amelia, sp., Horton, Bps. C., 1851, O, W, Wr, P24/1403
Ann, Wokm., Berks., 1638, W, P5/13Reg/129B
Ann, widow, Sonning, Berks., 1638, I, W, P5/1638/62
Ann, widow, Wilsford nr Pewsey, 1673, I, W, P2/H/710
Ann, Swindon, 1699, I, W, P3/H/789
Ann, widow, Leverton, Chilton F., 1725, W, P3/H/1023
Ann, widow, Mkt. L., 1744, W, P1/H/1025, P1/9Reg/433B
Ann, widow, St Edith's Marsh, Bromham, 1794, W, P3/H/1510
Holloway *or* Holdway, Arthur, Damerham, Hants, 1563, I, W, P2/H/22, P2/4Reg/123C
Bernard, yeo., Martin, Hants, 1662, AB, P2/H/612
Bernard, yeo., Burbage, 1738, AB, P11/164
Cath., sp., Bucklebury, Berks., 1635, AB, I, P1/H/223
Cath., widow, Calne, 1708, AB, I, P26/544
Cath., widow, Tisb., 1734, AB, P2/H/1278
Dan., tailor, Bedborough, Bps. C., 1751, W, P24/1044
Dan., wheelwright, Stratfield M., Berks., 1820, W, Wr, P1/1820/102
Edith, widow, Preston, Lyneham, 1609, W, P3/H/52
Edith, Wilsford nr Pewsey, 1679, AB, I, P2/H/767
Edwd., husb., Bremhill, 1662, AB, I, NW, P1/H/333
Edwd., sen., yeo., Purton, 1671, I, W, P3/H/458
Edwd., Purton, 1674, AB, I, P1/H/428
Edwd., Marston, Pott., 1703, AB, I, P1/H/626
Edwd., yeo., Etchilhampton, 1716, AB, I, P3/H/947
Edwd., Calne, 1754, AB, P26/931
Eleanor, Britford, 1604, I, W, P24/21
Eliz., widow, Mkt. L., 1682, I, W, P2/H/808
Eliz., widow, Westb., 1720, I, W, P25/1720/3
Eliz., wife, Rams., 1760, W, P5/1760/12
Florence, widow, Britford, 1613, I, W, P24/102
Francis, linen weaver, Martin, Hants, 1674, I, W, P2/H/716
Francis, yeo., Burbage, 1728, AB, I, P11/150
Gabriel, husb., Mkt. L., [1640], I, W, P2/H/534
Gabriel, yeo., Mkt. L., 1737, W, P2/H/1307
Geo., Hurst, Berks., 1569, AB, P5/2Reg/51C

Geo., yeo., Chilton F., 1755, W, P3/H/1290
Grace, widow, Manningford Bohun, 1749, W, P2/H/1384
Gracian, sp., Wilsford nr Pewsey, 1664, I, W, P2/H/624
Hy., husb., Cotmarsh, Clyffe P., 1619, I, W, P1/H/130
Hester, widow, Newton T., 1822, AB (2), Wr, P2/1822/18
Hugh, Wilsford nr Pewsey, 1560, W, P2/4Reg/32D
Hugh, carp., Corsley, 1637-46, cit, I, W, P2/H/493
Hugh, husb., Winterslow, 1664, I, W, P1/H/346
Hugh, yeo., Mkt. L., 1670, I, W, P2/H/677
Humphrey, cordw., Mkt. L., [1642], I, W, P2/H/556
Hollway, Jas., jun., yeo., Lawmore, Uffc., Devon, 1760, W, P20/1/239
Jas., yeo., Tisb., 1792, W, P2/H/1661
Jas., weaver, Westb., 1818, O, W, Wr, P25/1818/3
Jas., yeo., Yatton K., 1835, AB, O, ren, W, P3/1835/15
Joan, Edington, 1565, W, P2/4Reg/191D
Joan, widow, Gt. Woodford, 1595, AB, I, W, P5/1595/29, P5/6Reg/108B
Joan, Compton C., 1609, AB, P2/H/256, P2/8Reg/79B
Joan, widow, All C., 1612, W, P3/H/86
Job, schoolmaster, Trowb., 1799-1800, W, P1/H/1360, P1/15Reg/173B
Jn., Ludg., 1572, W, P2/5Reg/137C
Jn., Damerham, Hants, 1611, W, P2/H/277, P2/8Reg/158B
Jn., sen., yeo., Corsley, 1614, I, W, P1/H/94
Jn., husb., Purton, 1617, AB, W, P3/H/125
Jn., husb., Fovant, 1619, I, W, P2/H/335
Jn., Purton, 1621, a/c, P3/H/166
Jn., Britford, 1626, AB, a/c, surety bond, I, proclamation, ren, P24/227
Jn., husb., Mkt. L., [1640], I, W, P2/H/524
Jn., All C., 1651, I, NW, P1/H/303
Jn., bricklayer, Sal. St Thos., 1665, I, W, P4/1665/4
Hollaway alias Farmer, Jn., yeo., Swindon, 1675, I, W, P3/H/497
Holloway alias Farmer, Jn., Swindon, 1692, AB, P3/H/713
Jn., Mkt. L., 1709, AB, P2/H/1070
Jn., Idmiston, 1720, AB, P2/H/1172
Jn., yeo., Binfield, Berks., 1723, I, W, P1/H/799, P1/7Reg/10B
Jn., yeo., Soley, Chilton F., 1731, W, P3/H/1094
Jn., yeo., Wilton, 1746, W, P2/H/1364
Jn., Pott., 1747, AB, P1/H/1044
Hollwey, Jn., yeo., Upton S., 1748, W, P2/H/1373
Jn., Chapmanslade, Corsley, 1759, AB, comm, P2/H/1440
Jn., dairyman, Littlecott, Hilmarton, 1762, W, Wr, P3/H/1338
Jn., Devizes, 1763, AB, P1/H/1172
Jn., yeo., St Edith's Marsh, Bromham, 1775, AB, W, P3/H/1415
Jn., carp., Sal., 1788, W, P4/1788/8
Jn., yeo., Bulford, 1789, W, P1/H/1316, P1/14Reg/205
Jn., Idmiston, 1790, AB, P2/H/1652
Jn., sen., innholder, Whitep., 1794, W, P2/H/1673
Jn., yeo., Alderston Farm, Whitep., 1804, W, Wr, P2/1804/21
Jn., minor, Newton T., 1822, T (son of Hester H.), P2/1822/18-19
Jn., gent., Devizes, 1843, O, W, Wr, P1/1843/22
Jos., Trowb., 1749, W, P1/10Reg/259
Julian, widow, Mkt. L., 1640, I, W, P2/H/540
Mgt., widow, Gt. Amesb., 1665, I (very detailed), W, P2/H/633
Mgt., Marden, 1670, AB, P2/H/671
Marian, Fovant, 1626, I, W, P2/H/380
My., Mere, 1663, AB, P5/1662/58
My., sp., Mkt. L., 1665, I, NW, P2/H/630
My., widow, Restrop, Purton, 1691-93, AB (2), court paper, W, P3/H/701, 731
My., widow, Mkt. L., 1715, AB, P2/H/1126
My., widow, Trowb., 1730, W, P1/H/881, P1/7Reg/397
My., widow, All C., 1733, W, P3/H/1115

My., widow, Thornford, Dorset, 1832, AB, comm, Wr, P5/1832/3
My., widow, Rushall, 1833, AB, comm, Wr, P2/1833/24
My. Anna Fricker, minor, Chilmark, 1857, appt of guardian, court proceeding, O, T (My. H. is residuary legatee of Thos. Fricker), P2/1857/11
Holloway alias Farmer, Miles, yeo., Swindon, 1663, I, W, P3/H/357
Hollwey, Nich., yeo., Dilton, Westb., 1703, I, W, P25/1703/5
Oliver, Swindon, 1735, AB, I, P1/H/924
Peter, Damerham, Hants, 1571, W, P2/5Reg/135F
Hollway, Peter, strawjoiner, Uffc., Devon, 1718, W, P20/1/160
Ralph, yeo., Highway, 1615, I, W, P3/H/112
Ralph, husb., Barrow St., Mere, 1629, AB, I, NW, P5/1629/30, P5/11Reg/113A
Richd., jun., husb., Damerham, Hants, 1562, I, W, P2/H/14, P2/4Reg/93A
Richd., Damerham, Hants, 1570, AB, P2/5Reg/89D
Richd., All C., 1622, I, W (on same sheet), P3/H/173
Richd., Mkt. L., 1645, AB, comm, I, P2/H/578
Richd., yeo., Purton, 1693, comm, I, W, P3/H/732
Richd., Mkt. L., 1694, AB, P2/H/946
Richd., labourer, Tilehurst, Berks., 1714, AB, I, P1/H/699
Richd., yeo., Marden, 1740, W, P2/H/1324
Richd., Chilton F., 1743, AB, P3/H/1196
Richd., sen., gent., Marden, 1775, W, P2/H/1549
Richd., gent., Eddington, Hungerford, Berks., 1810, comm, W, P23/859
Richd., Newton T., 1819, AB, Wr, P2/1819/10
Robt., husb., Purton Stoke, 1620, I, W, P3/H/153
Robt., husb., Blackland, Calne, 1625, I, W, P5/1625/42, P5/10Reg/304C
Robt., Chilton F., 1632, AB, P3/H/263
Robt., sen., husb., Notton, Lacock, 1633, I, W, P3/H/274
Robt., husb., Gt. Bedwyn, 1666, AB, I, ren, P5/1665/44
Robt., Moorshall Farm, Kington St M., 1680, AB, a/c, I, P3/H/548
Robt., yeo., Leverton, Chilton F., 1691, I, W, P3/H/702
Robt., Binfield, Berks., 1695, AB, comm, P1/H/572
Hollaway, Robt., Moorshall Farm, Kington St M., 1696, AB, I, P3/H/762
Robt., tailor, Dilton M., Westb., 1705, I, NW, P25/1705/13
Robt., Haywood Farm, Chilton F., 1789, W, P3/H/1489
Sam., cordw., Thornford, Dorset, 1836, W, Wr, P5/1836/21
Sarah, widow, Devizes, 1779, W, P1/H/1258, P1/13Reg/234
Sarah, sp., Westb., 1811, W, P25/1811/3
Sarah, widow, Westb., 1825, O, W, Wr, P25/1825/12
Stephen, sen., yeo., Sheldon, Chipp., 1689, comm, I, W, P3/H/669
Stephen, yeo., Middlehill Farm, Chipp., 1706, AB, W, P3/H/869
Stephen, clothworker, Brokers Gate, Westb., 1743, W, P25/1743/5
Stephen, carp., Rushall, 1829, W, Wr, P2/1829/15
Stephen, Woodb., 1830, AB, comm, Wr, P3/1830/42
Susanna, widow, Tisb., 1824, AB, P2/1824/87
Thos., Britford, 1611, I, W, P24/131
Thos., [weaver], Sal., 1633, AB, I, P4/1633/22
Thos., husb., Bradfield, Berks., 1635, AB, a/c, I, P1/H/222
Thos., sen., yeo., Leverton, Chilton F., 1662, AB, comm, I, P3/H/350
Thos., husb., Blake's Farm, Rams., 1663, AB, I, P5/1663/33
Thos., clerk, Kemble, 1706, I, W, P3/H/870
Thos., Burbage, 1740, W, P11/176
Thos., sen., gent., Bedborough, Bps. C., 1750, W, P24/1052
Thos., wheelwright, Devizes, 1779, AB, W, P1/H/1259, P1/13Reg/235
Thos., Westb. L., 1797, AB, comm, P25/1797/1
Thos., labourer, Seend Cleeve, Melk., 1808, W, Wr, P2/1808/1
Thos., Manningford A., 1836, AB, O, Wr, P3/1836/72
Holloway *or* Allaway, Unity, widow, Wokm., Berks., 1703, AB, comm, I, P5/1703/18
Walter, All C., 1695, I, W, P3/H/753
Halleway, Wm., Wilsford nr Pewsey, 1583, I (2), T, W, P2/H/68, P2/6Reg/85
Wm., husb., Gt. Woodford, 1589, AB, W, P5/1589/25, P5/5Reg/63C

Wm., tailor, Netheravon, 1604, I, release, P12/8
Wm., Chapmanslade, Corsley, 1610, AB, a/c, I, P2/H/259, P2/8Reg/83B
Wm., Clyffe P., 1610, AB, P3/H/62
Wm., Clack, Lyneham, [c1612], W (NEP), P3/H/87
Wm., Catcomb, Hilmarton, 1637, AB, a/c, I, P3/H/302
Wm., Chapmanslade, Corsley, 1668, AB, comm, I, P2/H/649
Wm., husb., Mkt. L., 1679, I, W, P2/H/766
Wm., All C., 1693, AB, I, P3/H/733
Wm., yeo., Marden, 1703, I, W, P2/H/1022
Wm., sen., yeo., Manningford Bohun, 1725, W, P2/H/1210
Wm., tailor, Devizes, 1728, W, P1/H/839, P1/7Reg/189
Wm., tailor, Bedborough, Bps. C., 1741, W, P24/990
Wm., W. Hatch, Tisb., 1743, AB, P2/H/1339
Wm., yeo., W. Overton, 1744, W, P1/H/1016, P1/9Reg/382A
Wm., yeo., All C., 1745, W, P3/H/1219
Wm., Uffc., Devon, 1755, I, P30/101
Wm., gent., Manningford Bohun, 1762, comm, W, P2/H/1459
Wm., yeo., Littlecott, Hilmarton, 1762, AB, ren, P3/H/1339
Wm., Idmiston, 1771, AB, I, P2/H/1529
Wm., Chipp., 1783, AB, comm, P3/H/1448
Wm., yeo., Thornford, Dorset, 1821, W, Wr, P5/1821/3
see also Edmonds alias H.; Farmer alias H.; Holway; New form. H.
Holly, Holly alias Pope, Ann, labourer's wife, Lyneham, 1731, AB, P3/H/1095
Ann, Calne, 1828, W, P26/1370
Elijah, shopkeeper, Netherh., 1850, W, Wr, P2/1850/37
Eliz., wife, Calne, 1753, AB, P26/917
Geo., Beanacre, Melk., 1818, W, Wr, P2/1818/26
Jas., shoemaker, Quidh., 1824, W, Wr, P2/1824/71
Jn., sen., sawyer, Calne, 1696, comm, I, W, P26/435
Jn., sen., yeo., Studley, Calne, 1710, I, W, P26/566
Holley, Jn., yeo., Court Farm, Damerham, Hants, 1778, W, P2/H/1574
Jn., yeo., Ashton K., 1827, O, W, Wr, P3/1827/22
Halley, Lydia, widow, Warm., 1820, comm, W, Wr, P1/1820/148
Holley, My., wife, Wilton, 1729-30, AB, P1/H/843, 882
Robt., weaver, Wilton, 1767, AB, W, P2/H/1499
Thos., barber, Chipp., 1697, I, W, P3/H/772
Thos., minor, Coombe B., 1727, T, P8/26
Thos., Studley, Calne, 1801, AB, P26/1230
Hollyer, Holliar, Chas., Sal., 1705, AB, P4/1704/4
Hollier, Chas., Wilton, 1713, AB, P2/H/1108
Hollier, Jn., blacksmith, Sonning, Berks., 1667, AB, I, P5/1667/26
Holliar, Jn., turner, Shinfield, Berks., 1683, AB, I, P1/H/481
Jn., Shinfield, Berks., 1698, I, W, P1/H/543, 599, P1/3Reg/72
Hollier, Robt., Sonning, Berks., 1674, AB, P5/1674/33
Hollyes *see* Hollis
Hollyman, Lionel, Boyton, 1609, I, P1/H/60
Hollyse *see* Hollis
Holman, Edith, widow, Sherb., Dorset, 1596-97, W, P5/1596/37, P5/6Reg/145B
Howman, Hy., sen., yeo., Fordington, Dorset, 1641, I, W (damaged), P5/1641/41, P5/14Reg/27B
Hy., yeo., Fordington, Dorset, 1679, I, W, P15/28
Hy., husb., Berwick B., 1600-01, AB, I, W, P5/1600/28, P5/6Reg/240B
Thos., Fordington, Dorset, 1685, AB, P15/44
Holme *see* Holmes
Holmed, Richd., Sal. St Thos., undated but c1560, W (NEP), P1/2Reg/108C
Holmer *see* Homer
Holmes, Alice, Sal. St Thos., 1561, W (NEP), P1/2Reg/132B
Ann, widow, Ablington, Figh., 1716, I (detailed), W, P26/598
Cath., widow, Sal., 1623, W, P4/1623/1
Homes, Chris., clothier, Broughton G., 1602, I, W, P2/H/201
Homes, Dulcibella, widow, Sal. The Close, 1638, I, W, P5/1638/61, P5/13Reg/145

Homes, Edwd., maltster, Wootton B., 1819, W, Wr, P3/1819/21
Holme, Eleanor, widow, Ridge, Chilmark, 1732, comm, W, P1/H/888
Francis, E. Garston, Berks., 1692, AB, P1/H/554
Homes alias Poytheras, Francis, Manton, Preshute, 1720, W, P1/H/770, P1/6Reg/284B
Francis, Durrington, 1737, AB, P2/H/1297
Holmes alias Pidris, Francis, barber, Marl., 1743, AB, comm, P1/H/1000
Geo., yeo., Bagshot, Shalbourne, 1638, I, W, P5/1638/60, P5/13Reg/140B
Geo., wheelwright, Ablington, Figh., 1668, I, W, P26/143
Geo., labourer, Ablington, Figh., 1748, D, W, P26/882
Geo., yeo., Elmdown, Rams., 1785, W, P5/1785/15, P5/18Reg/27
Hy., husb., Brigmerston, Milston, 1652, W, P1/H/304
Jas., carp., Figh., 1681, AB, I, W, P26/280
Jas., Figh., 1728, AB, P26/725
Jas., W. Lavington, 1731, AB, P1/H/883
Jas., shopkeeper, Littleton P., 1789, W, P1/H/1309, P1/14Reg/185
Jane, widow, Bagshot, Shalbourne, 1686, AB, comm, I, P5/1686/32
Joan, widow, Figh., 1647, I, W. Not the same testatrix as P26/97, P26/99
Joan, widow, Figh., 1647, W. Not the same testatrix as P26/99, P26/97
Joan, widow, Figh., 1676-78, AB, I, P26/244, 255
Jn., yeo., Broad C., 1574, W, P2/5Reg/181D
Jn., husb., Martin, Hants, 1619, I, W, P1/H/124
Jn., husb., Blewbury, Berks., 1625, AB, I, P5/1625/43, P5/10Reg/304A
Jn., Bower C., 1627, AB, I, P2/H/393
Jn., gent. & cathedral organist., Sal. The Close, 1629, I (musical instruments), W, P5/1628/54, P5/11Reg/16
Jn., sen., yeo., Bagshot, Shalbourne, 1666, comm, W, P5/1666/17
Jn., sen., yeo., Figh., 1674, I, W, P26/222
Jn., yeo., Bagshot, Shalbourne, 1681, AB, a/c, comm, I, P5/1680/19
Jn., Ablington, Figh., 1709, AB, P26/554
Jn., yeo., Bere R., Dorset, 1734, W, P5/1734/35
Jn., gent., Fisherton A., 1824, W, Wr, P2/1824/64
Jn., grocer, Littleton P., 1836, AB, P1/1836/22
Jn., yeo., Ogbourne St Geo., 1843, O, W, Wr, P5/1843/3
Jn., yeo., Littleton P., 1851, L, O, W, Wr, P1/1851/37
Homes, Martha, widow, Froxfield, 1827, comm, W, Wr, P3/1827/3
My., widow, Wootton B., 1825, W, Wr, P3/1825/65
My., widow, Ogbourne St Geo., 1855, O, W, Wr, P5/1855/17
Nich., carp., Figh., 1724, W, P26/684
Phyllis, sp., Longford, Britford, 1739, AB, NW, P24/906
Richd., yeo., Compton, Berks., 1662, I, W, P1/H/324
Richd., husb., Figh., 1687, AB, I, P26/359
Richd., sen., maltster, Durrington, 1732, I, W, P1/H/885, P1/7Reg/433A
Homes, Richd., narrow weaver, Dilton M., Westb., 1741, W, P25/1741/6
Richd., shopkeeper, Littleton P., 1811, W, Wr, P1/1811/118
Sarah, widow, W. Lavington, 1759, W, P1/H/1150, P1/11Reg/479
Sarah, widow, Littleton P., 1815, W, Wr, P1/1815/1
Stephen, W. Harnham, 1805, AB, P8/74
Susanna, sp., Figh., 1681, I, W, P26/275
Home, Susanna, Corsham, 1774, AB, P29/2Reg/131
Thos., sen., Sal. St Edmd., 1619, I, W, P4/1619/3
Thos., maltster, Sal., 1715, AB, I (detailed), P4/1715/8
Thos., yeo., Sal., 1731, W, P4/1730/23
Thos., cordw., Burbage, 1751, W, P11/206
Homes, Thos., gent., Chipp., 1788, W, P3/H/1481
Homes, Thos., Box, 1791, W, P3/H/1500
Thos., cordw., Burbage, 1791, W, P11/248
Thos., widower, Wootton R., 1854, AB, aff, court proceeding, D, O, W, Wr, P3/1854/38
Vincent, labourer, Reading St Lawr., Berks., 1711, AB, I, P1/H/679
Wm., Southwick, N. Bradley, 1671, AB, comm, P1/H/410
Wm., sen., husb., Figh., 1671, W, P26/195
Homes, Wm., husb., Westb. L., 1687, AB, I, P25/1687/6

Wm., husb., Figh., 1716, I, W, P26/603
Wm., labourer *or* yeo., Hurley, Berks., 1720, I, W, P1/H/774, P1/6Reg/306
Wm., excise officer, Milbourne, Malm. (form. of Minety), 1833, W, Wr, P3/1833/21
Holree *see* Hollery
Holt, Collibery, widow, Hurst, Berks., 1633, I, W, P5/1633/24, P5/12Reg/136B
Dan., basketmaker, Twyford, Hurst, Berks., 1814, AB, W, Wr (2), P5/1814/14
Hugh, Sonning, Berks., 1634-35, AB, a/c, I. Exhibited at the Metropolitan Visitation to Reading, P5/1634/55, P5/1635/52, P5/12Reg/316B
Jn., husb., Hurst, Berks., 1627, I, W, P5/1627/23, P5/11Reg/49B
Jn., Uffc., Devon, 1700, AB, P20/1/161
My., widow, Sal., 1672, I, W, P4/1671/12
Michael, carp., Hurst, Berks., 1709, W, P5/1709/19, P5/15Reg/126
Stephen, Colemans More, Earley, Sonning, Berks., 1592, I, W, P5/1592/45, P5/6Reg/1A
Thos., sen., Reading St My., Berks., 1717, AB, I, P1/H/742
Thos., Bishopsdown, Milford, Sal., 1810, AB, P4/1810/8
Holton, (Captain) *see* Jn. Oram
Edwd., sen., butcher, Warm., [1688], W, P2/H/899
Edwd., gardener, Warm., 1822, O, W, Wr, P2/1822/40
Francis, flaxdresser, Wokm., Berks., 1709, W, P5/1709/20, P5/15Reg/133
Houlton, Jas., Wokm., Berks., 1814, AB, Wr, P5/1814/1
Jane, widow, Warm., 1650, AB, I, W, P1/H/296
Houlton, Jn., flaxdresser, Wokm., Berks., 1677, AB, comm, I, P5/1677/28
Houlton, Jn., tailor, Wokm., Berks., 1731, W, P5/1731/38
Houlton, Jn., vicar, Chitterne AS, 1743, AB, comm, ren, P2/H/1343
Houlton, My., widow, Seend, Melk., 1730, comm, W, P2/H/1247
Houlton, Nathaniel, esquire, Seagry, 1754, comm, W, P3/H/1284
Houlton, Nich., yeo., Longbridge D., 1721, W, P2/H/1176
Richd., Sonning, Berks., 1567, AB, P5/2Reg/25B
Houlton, Richd., sen., cordw., *The Cock and Bowl*, Market Place, Wokm., Berks., 1751, W, P5/1751/13
Richd., victualler, The Common, Warm., 1792, W, P2/H/1658
Thos., clothworker, Sonning, Berks., 1619, I, W, P5/1619/27, P5/10Reg/45B
Thos., Sal., 1640, I, P4/1639/16
Wm., Warm., 1831, comm, W, P2/1831/23
Holway, Avis, widow, Maiden B., 1552, W, P2/2Reg/149B
Beaton, sp., Uffc., Devon, 1768, AB, O, P20/1/250
Holwey, Denise, widow, Westb., 1708, I, W, P25/1708/8
Holdway, Edwd., husb., Stoford, S. Newton, 1667, I, W, P2/H/643
Holdway, Grace, sp., Westb., 1723, AB, P25/1723/4
Holdaway, Jas., S. Newton, 1730, AB, P2/H/1243
Holdeway, Jas., blacksmith, Boscombe, 1840, W, Wr, P2/1840/8
Holdoway, Jeremiah, gardener, Westb., 1827, W, Wr, P25/1827/6
Holwey, Joan, sp., Westb., 1676, I, W, P25/1676/3
Jn., Damerham, Hants, 1558, W, P2/3Reg/141A
Holdway, Jn., shepherd, Tilsh., 1604, AB, I, P2/H/217
Holdway, Jn., husb., Westb., 1629, I, P25/1629/5
Holwey, Jn., gent., Norton B., 1648, AB, I, P2/H/599
Holdaway, Jn., Trowb., 1803, AB, comm, Wr, P1/1803/6, P1/15Reg/388B
Nich., W. Dean, 1563, AB, I, W, P2/H/20, P2/4Reg/112A
Peter, yeo., Uffc., Devon, 1728, W, P5/1728/53, P5/16Reg/174D
Peter, Uffc., Devon, 1799, AB, comm, P20/1/273
Holwey, Richd., Whitbourne, Corsley, 1621, W, P2/H/353
Holdaway, Richd., pensioner, Chalford, Westb., 1843, O, W, Wr, P25/1843/3
Holdway, Robt., Wilton, Gt. Bedwyn, [1569], W (year of probate omitted), P5/2Reg/67A
Holdway, Susanna, wife, Westcott Farm, Swindon, 1855, AB, aff, comm, Wr, P3/1855/14
Holdway, Thos., husb., Chitterne AS, 1608, W, P2/8Reg/3C
Holdway, Thos., weaver, S. Newton, 1669, AB, I, P2/H/659
Holdway, Thos., husb., Tilsh., [1694], I, W, P2/H/948
Holdoway, Thos., yeo., Bemerton, Fugg. St Peter, 1698, I, W, P2/H/975
Holdway, Thos., sen., scribler, Westb., 1702, I, W, P25/1702/3
Wm., mason, Uffc., Devon, 1734, I, W, P5/1734/36

Wm., Uffc., Devon, 1755, AB, P5/1755/23
Holdway, Wm., Ham, 1807, AB, comm, T (children: Jn. & Henrietta H.), Wr, P3/1807/13
Wm., Uffc., Devon, 1821, W, Wr, P5/1821/6
see also Holloway
Holwell, Holwill, Florence, widow, Uffc., Devon, 1624, I, W, P20/1/6
Holwill, Humphrey, Uffc., Devon, 1613, I, W, P5/1613/38, P5/9Reg/92A
Jn., weaver, Whiterow, Trowb., 1808, W, Wr, P1/1808/122
Jn., jun., Stowford, Wingfield, 1820, AB, comm, Wr, P2/1820/25
Maria, sp., Studley, Trowb., 1837, O, W, Wr, P1/1837/15
Thos., weaver, N. Bradley, 1800, W, P2/1800/32
Holwey *see* Holway
Holwill *see* Holwell
Holyoak, Jn., innholder and cordw., Highw., 1749, W, Wr, P5/1749/26
Hombie *see* Humby
Home *see* Holmes
Homer, Howmar, Agnes, widow, Bere R., Dorset, 1572, W, P5/2Reg/116B
Bartholomew, sen., Bere R., Dorset, 1663, I (2), P5/1663/34
Edith, widow, Bere R., Dorset, 1687, I, W, P5/1687/20
Giles, Bere R., Dorset, 1830, notes, O, W, Wr, P5/1830/15
Jas., Downton, 1702, AB, P2/H/1009
Jn., yeo., Bere R., Dorset, 1682, I, W, P5/1682/51
Jn., tailor, Bere R., Dorset, 1685, W, P5/1685/45
Holmer, Robt., husb., Bere R., Dorset, 1628, AB, a/c, I, P5/1628/55, P5/11Reg/71C
Robt., yeo., Downton, 1680, I, W, P1/H/457
Holmer, Thos., sen., husb., Bere R., Dorset, 1609, W, P5/1609/38, P5/8Reg/162
Wm., sen., yeo., Bere R., Dorset, 1732, W, P5/1732/23
Homes *see* Holmes
Hondy, Edwd., Urchf., 1557, W, P2/3Reg/42C
Hone, Hoane, Eliz., widow, White Waltham, Berks., 1732, I, W, P1/H/896
Nathaniel, shoemaker, Marl. St My., 1665, I, W, P1/H/363
Nathaniel, Marl. St My., 1696, I, W, P1/H/586
Hoane, Wm., yeo., Hurst, Berks., 1817, W, Wr, P5/1817/6
Honeman, Wm., husb., Maiden B., 1575, I, W, P2/H/43, P2/5Reg/242C
Honey, Geo., Shitterton, Bere R., Dorset, 1591, I, W, P5/1591/42, P5/5Reg/99B
Hunny, Hy., Charlton, Donhead St My., 1585, I, T, W, P2/H/74, P2/7Reg/24B
Hy., Donhead St My., 1686, AB, I, ren, P1/H/502
Hony, Hy., jun., Donhead St My., 1753, W, P1/H/1096, P1/11Reg/75
Hony, Jos., Donhead St My., 1768, W, P2/H/1508
Robt., husb., Charlton, Donhead St My., 1563, I, W, P2/H/24, P2/4Reg/145B
Hunny, Thos., Shitterton, Bere R., Dorset, 1614, comm, I, W, P5/1613/40, P5/9Reg/134
Honeyborne, Honeybone, Ann, widow, Wanb., 1807, comm, W, Wr, P1/1807/16
Honybunn alias Honybone, Cath., Netherb., Dorset, 1712, W, P17/212
Hy., yeo., Winterborne K., Dorset, 1717, AB, I, P5/1717/19
Honeybone, Jane, widow, Medbourne, Liddington, 1670, comm, W, P3/H/442
Honeybone, Jn., miller, Wanb., 1733, AB, I, P3/H/1116
Nich., yeo., Winterborne K., Dorset, 1714, I, W, P5/1714/20, P5/15Reg/392A
Richd., yeo., Winterborne K., Dorset, 1713, AB, W, P5/1713/45, P5/15Reg/379C
Robt., Anderson, Dorset, 1740, AB, Wr, P5/1740/40
Honeybone, Thos., Corston, Malm., 1751, AB, P3/H/1266
Honeybone, Thos., clockmaker, Wanb., 1807, AB, W, Wr, P3/1807/16
Thomasine, widow, Bere R., Dorset, 1561, AB, P5/1Reg/2B
Wm., Winterborne K., Dorset, 1561, W, P5/1Reg/2A
Honibone, Wm., innholder, Reading, Berks., 1732, W, P1/H/894, P1/7Reg/480A
Honeybone, Wm., watchmaker, Wanb., 1807, W, Wr, P3/1807/15
Honeybone, Wm. Couch, miller, Corston, Malm., 1753, W, P3/H/1274
Honeyfield, Wm., Gillingham, Dorset, 1793, AB, P27/1/551
Honeywell, Eliz., widow, Downton, 1824, AB, Wr, P2/1824/25
Hy., Downton, 1824, AB, Wr, P2/1824/30
Honywill, Jn., draper and grocer, Trowb., 1817, ren, W, Wr, P1/1817/97
Honywill, My., minors, Devizes, 1846, appt of guardian, court proceeding, O, T (children of Sarah H.), P1/1846/19

Richd., Downton, 1821, AB, Wr, P2/1821/1
Honywill, Sarah, widow, Devizes, 1846, AB, Wr, P1/1846/20
Wm., chairmaker, Downton, 1810-24, AB, W, P2/1810/3, P2/1824/24
Honywill, Wm., Devizes, 1844, AB, O, Wr, P1/1844/27
Honeywood, My., widow, E. Harnham, Britford, 1817, AB, W, P24/1277
Honibone *see* Honeyborne
Honnycot, Wm., Woodlands, Mere, 1611, I, W, P5/1610/27, P5/9Reg/48C
Honycot, Wm., Sherb., Dorset, 1761, AB, P5/1761/22
Honour, Gabriel, yeo., Bulmershe, Sonning, Berks., 1684-85, AB, a/c, I, P5/1684/34, P5/1685/49
Honte *see* Hunt
Hony *see* Honey
Honybone, Honybunn *see* Honeyborne
Honycot *see* Honnycot
Honywill *see* Honeywell
Hood, Hood alias Crooke, Alice, widow, Urchf., 1669, I, W, P2/H/667
Ambrose, Coate, Bps. C., 1754, AB, P24/1024
Ambrose Jn., gent., Bedborough, Bps. C., 1832, W, Wr, P24/1329
Ann, widow, Chipp., 1786, W, P1/H/1307, P1/14Reg/143A
Arthur, yeo., Heddington, 1683, AB, I, P3/H/584
Arthur, gent., Poulton, 1735, W, P3/H/1129
Arthur, upholsterer, Beam., Dorset, 1739, W, P17/471
Edith, widow, Sherb., Dorset, 1619, AB, P5/1619/54
Hood alias Crooke, Edith, widow, Urchf., 1619, I, W, P1/W/77
Hood alias Crooke, Edwd., husb., Wedh., Urchf., 1622, W, P2/W/278
Eliz., widow, N. Wootton, Dorset, 1610, W, P5/9Reg/40B
Francis, victualler, Westb., 1785, W, P25/1785/2
Hy., jun., Plaitford, 1682, AB, appt of guardian, I, P2/H/805
Hy., yeo., Plaitford, 1788, W, P2/H/1633
Isabel, widow, N. Wootton, Dorset, [1610], I, W, P5/1610/31
Jas., Lacock, 1768, AB, P3/H/1378
Jas., yeo., Heddington, 1831, W, P3/1831/54
Jane, widow, Stert, Urchf., 1689, W, P1/H/509
Jane, widow, Poulton, 1739, AB, comm, W, P3/H/1162
Jn., husb., N. Wootton, Dorset, 1592, I, T, W, P5/1592/40, P5/5Reg/137C
Hood alias Crooke, Jn., sen., Urchf., 1606, AB, I, W, P2/W/181, P2/H/232
Hood alias Crooke, Jn., sen., husb., Urchf., 1637, I, T, W, P2/W/385
Jn., yeo., Calstone W., 1669, comm, W, P26/110
Jn., Heddington, 1737, AB, note, P3/H/1145
Jn., yeo., Studley House, Studley, Calne, 1792, comm, W, P26/1182
Margery, widow, Coate, Bps. C., 1720, AB, P24/624
Martha, widow, Plaitford, 1849, W, Wr, P2/1849/34
My., Westb., 1758, AB, P25/1758/1
Maud, Mkt. L., [1611?], I, W, P2/H/278
Michael, yeo., Calstone W., 1694, AB, comm, I, W (2), P5/1694/40
Nich., Keevil, 1576, W, P2/5Reg/269A
Nich., yeo., Wedh., Urchf., 1596, I, W, P2/H/148
Philip, sen., widow, Calstone W., 1683, I, W, P26/310
Richd., yeo., Hullavington, 1704, I, W, P1/H/630
Richd., mason, Studley, Bremhill, 1713, AB, comm, I, W, P3/H/932
Robt., Bulford, 1557, W, P2/3Reg/60B
Hood alias Crooke, Robt., sen., husb., Urchf., 1619, I, W, P2/W/259
Robt., sen., yeo., Stert, Urchf., 1689, comm, I, W, P1/H/508
Robt., yeo., Chirton, 1700, I, W, P2/H/997
Robt., yeo., Coate, Bps. C., 1722, I, W, P24/886
Sam., yeo., Netherb., Dorset, 1805, comm, W, P17/592
Stephen, labourer, Chirton, 1702, AB, I, W, P2/H/1015
Thos., Charl. nr. P., 1569, W, P2/5Reg/75C
Hood alias Crooke, Thos., wheeler, Wingfield & Monkton F., 1615, D, I, W, P2/W/238, P2/8Reg/287B
Hood alias Crooke, Thos., sen., Urchf., 1626, I, W, P2/W/297
Thos., Stockley, Calne, 1686, W, P26/340

Thos., sen., yeo., Coate, Bps. C., 1714, AB, I, P24/677
Thos., yeo., Chirton, 1731, W, P2/H/1257
Thos., yeo., Bps. C., 1735, W, P24/935
Thos., yeo., Loxwell, Chipp., 1794, W, P3/H/1511
Hood alias Crooke, Wm., husb., Urchf., 1615, I, W, P2/W/237, P2/8Reg/267
Wm., tailor, Trowb., 1615, I, NW, P1/H/99
Wm., Lacock, 1640, AB, P3/H/324
Hood alias Crooke, Wm., yeo., Urchf., 1668, comm, W, P1/H/394
Wm., Bremhill, 1702, AB, P3/H/833
Wm., Chipp., 1785, AB, P3/H/1465
Wm., labourer, Chipp., 1789, W, P3/H/1490
Wm., yeo., Loxwell, Chipp., 1815, W, Wr, P3/1815/77
Wm., wheelwright, Plaitford, 1849, W, Wr, P2/1849/33
see also Crooke alias H.; Monkton alias H.
Hooke, Hook, Ann, miller's wife, Malm., 1766, AB, P3/H/1361
Hooks, Chas., Thornford, Dorset, 1813, AB, Wr, P5/1813/2
Edith, widow, Sal. The Close, 1643, I, W, P5/1643/9, P5/14Reg/69B
Edwd., Grittenham, Brinkw., 1700, AB, comm, ren, P3/H/799
Hook nee Spencer, Eliz., pastry cook's wife, Devizes, 1809, AB, comm, Wr, P1/1809/11
Hooks, Eliz., sp., Thornford, Dorset, 1857, AB, aff, comm, Wr, P5/1857/12
Eustace, gent., Shinfield, Berks., 1664, comm, W, P1/H/362
Giles, yeo., Purton, 1666, AB, I, P3/H/380
Hook, Israel May, minor, Malm., 1766, appt of guardian, P3/H/1362
Hook alias Graves, Jas., carp., Uffc., Devon, 1846, AB, comm, W, Wr, P20/1/327
Hook, Jn., apparitor, Malm., 1822, W, Wr, P3/1822/20
Leonard, gent., Sonning, Berks., 1625, AB, a/c, I, P5/1625/47, P5/10Reg/247A
Wm., Lyme R., Dorset, 1824, AB, comm, Wr, P16/391
Hooker, Agnes, Netheravon, 1621, I, L, W, P12/45
Dorothy, widow, Downton, 1755, W, P2/H/1409
Jn., Mere, 1567, W, P5/2Reg/11C
Jn., sen., Downton, 1638, AB, I, P2/H/503
Jn., Downton, 1763, AB, P2/H/1463
Jn., Winterslow, 1773, AB, P1/H/1219
Wm., yeo., Downton, 1776, W, P1/H/1249, P1/13Reg/152A
Hooks *see* Hooke
Hookway, Walter, blacksmith, Uffc., Devon, 1822, W, Wr, P20/1/310
Wm., husb., Uffc., Devon, 1745, W, P20/1/213
Hoole, Jn., Nettleton, [1612], NW (NEP), P3/H/88
Hoole *or* Howell, Jordan, husb., Eastmanstreet, Calne, 1604, AB, I, W, P5/1604/19, P5/8Reg/8
Hoope, Joan, widow, Bere R., Dorset, [1643-44], a/c, P5/1643/20
Hooper, Agnes, Wokm., Berks., 1589, I, W, P5/1589/30, P5/5Reg/52B
Alice, widow, Chards., Devon, 1614-34, I, W. Proved at the Metropolitan Visitation to Dorchester, P5/1634/52, P5/12Reg/291
Alice, widow, Mere, 1701, AB, I, P5/1701/27
Ann, widow, Stoford, S. Newton, 1630, W, P2/H/416
Hooper alias Axbridge, Ann, Corsham, 1649, AB, I (2), W (2), P29/H/122, P29/1Reg/144B
Ann, Edington, 1736, W, P2/H/1292
Ann, widow, Boreham, Warm., 1789, AB, P2/H/1645
Ann, widow, St Ann's St., Sal. St Martin, 1854, cert, D, O, W, Wr, P4/1854/2
Arthur, Monkton D., 1593, I, copy I, P2/H/132
Arthur, yeo., Sherb., Dorset, 1763, W, P5/1763/12
Bridget, Melk., 1769, AB, P2/H/1517
Chas., E. Knoyle, 1814, AB, Wr, P2/1814/31
Christian, widow, Stockton, 1602, AB, I, W, P1/H/25
Edith, widow, Chapmanslade, Dilton, Westb., 1637, AB, I, W, P25/1637/6
Edmd., yeo., Dilton, Westb., 1827, O, W, Wr, P25/1827/7
Eliz., widow, Sal. The Close, 1572, AB, P5/3Reg/5C
Eliz., widow, Stockton, 1611-14, AB, a/c, P2/H/280, P2/8Reg/161A
Eliz., widow, Pewsey, 1749, W, P3/H/1252
Eliz., widow, Bratton, Westb., 1777, W, P25/1777/7

Eliz., widow, Chute (leaving effects at Newbury), 1804, D, W, P1/1804/22
Geo., husb., Ebbesborne Wake, 1706, AB, I, P2/H/1048
Geo., yeo., Dilton, Westb., 1833, AB, O, ren, W, Wr, P25/1833/7
Geo., yeo., Beam., Dorset, 1845, comm, W, Wr, P17/615
Hannah, widow, Warm., 1740, W, P2/H/1328
Hannah, sp., Westb., 1815, W, P25/1815/1
Harry, farmer, W. Lavington, 1848, O, W, Wr, P1/1848/58
Hy., gent., Sal. The Close, 1606, W, P24/22
Hy., clothier, Sherb., Dorset, 1641, AB, comm, I, P5/1640/26, P5/13Reg/275A
Hy., maltster, Sherb., Dorset, 1694, comm, I, W, P5/1693/30
Hy., yeo., Westwells, Corsham, 1803, AB, I, W, P3/1803/12
Hy., Bishopstrow, 1824, AB, Wr, P2/1824/38
Herbert, Sal., 1811, bond to collect goods, P4/1811/2
Humphrey, Wokm., Berks., 1588, AB, I, W, P5/1588/29, P5/5Reg/37B
Jas., wool breaker, Lyme R., Dorset, 1754, W, P16/314
Jas., Tilsh., 1848, AB, O, Wr, P2/1848/12
Jane, sp., Sal., 1683-86, I, W, P5/1682/60, P5/1684/25, P5/1686/35
Jane, widow, Bishopstone S., 1813, W, Wr, P2/1813/56
Joan, widow, Winterbourne S., 1637, I, W, P2/H/490
Jn., Stockton, 1609, AB, I, W, P2/H/258, P2/8Reg/49B
Jn., husb., Corsley, 1640, I, W, P2/H/531
Jn., Mere, 1675, AB, I, P5/1675/26
Jn., Bonnishe, Sonning, Berks., 1675-76, AB, a/c, comm, I, P5/1675/27, P5/1676/29
Jn., sen., yeo., Edington, 1679, comm, I, W, P2/H/763
Jn., yeo., Mere, 1683, I, NW, P5/1683/31
Jn., Brigmerston, Milston, 1688, I, W, P2/H/896
Jn., yeo., Chapmanslade, Corsley, 1744, W, P2/H/1346
Jn., yeo., Edington, 1748, comm, W, P2/H/1376
Jn., labourer, Zeals, 1766-73, D, O (incorporates witness's memory of W contents, made about 19 years before), W, P5/1766/14, P5/1773/20, P5/17Reg/72A
Jn., yeo., Whitley, Melk., 1784, W, P2/H/1607
Jn., linen draper, Mere, 1801, W, P5/1801/21, P5/18Reg/323C
Jn., sen., victualler, Devizes Grn, Bps. C., 1807, W, P24/1245
Jn., gent., Bugley, Gillingham, Dorset, 1814, W, P27/1/626
Jn., Marl. St Peter and St Paul, 1830, AB, Wr, P1/1830/11
Jn., gent., Pewsey, 1836, comm, W, Wr, P3/1836/15
Jn., Downton, 1839, AB, Wr, P1/1839/30
Mgt., Mkt. L., 1582, W, P2/6Reg/71A
Mgt., widow, Milston, 1616, NW, P1/H/106
Mgt., sp., Corsley, 1813, W, Wr, P2/1813/19
Margery, widow, Wedh., Urchf., 1641, I, W, P2/H/552
My., Hanging L., 1729, AB, P1/H/844
Hopper, Maud, widow, Bratton, Westb., 1616, I, W. No note of probate, P25/1616/6
Nich., Wokm., Berks., 1620, comm, I, W, P5/1619/26, P5/10Reg/1A
Hooper alias Cooke, Nich., yeo., Uffc., Devon, 1809, W, Wr, P5/1809/38
Ralph, yeo., Edington, 1721, W, P2/H/1179
Ralph, Dilton M., Westb., 1744, AB, P25/1744/2
Richd., yeo., Pewsey, 1766, W, P3/H/1363
Richd., Corsley, 1789, AB, comm, P2/H/1642
Richd., farmer, Bishopstrow, 1791, W, P2/H/1653
Richd., gent., Pewsey, 1799, aff, W, P3/H/1541
Robt., husb., Chitterne St My., 1614, W, P2/H/302, P2/8Reg/247B
Howper, Robt., husb., Wedh., Urchf., 1627, I, W, P2/H/390
Robt., Ditchampton, Wilton, 1640, AB, I, P2/H/542
Robt., husb., Wedh., Urchf., 1647, W, P2/H/591
Robt., husb., Bratton, Westb., 1692, I, W, P25/1692/5
Hopper *or* Hooper, Robt., Salterton, Durnford, 1705, I, W, P9/33
Robt., yeo., Salterton, Durnford, 1726, AB, I, ren, P9/45
Robt., yeo., Pewsey, 1737, W, P3/H/1146
Robt., yeo., Pewsey, 1782, comm, W, P3/H/1445

Robt., Westb. L., 1787, AB, P25/1787/1
Robt., yeo., W. Lavington, 1811, W, Wr, P1/1811/120
Robt., farmer, Imber, 1826, O, W, Wr, P1/1826/42
Hooper *or* Hopper, Roger, tailor, Britford, 1630, I, W, P24/206
Sarah, sp., Westwells, Corsham, 1803, I, W, P3/1803/11
Susanna, sp., Warm., 1808, W, Wr, P1/1808/62
Susanna, sp., Corsley, 1815, W, Wr, P2/1815/2
Thos., husb., Chards., Devon, 1588, W, P5/5Reg/24B
Thos., sen., Brigmerston, Milston, 1600, I, W, P2/H/192
Thos., innholder, Trowb., 1732, I, W, P1/H/907, P1/7Reg/528
Thos., farmer, Semington, Steeple A., 1845, D, O, W, Wr, P1/1845/68
Hoper, Walter, Longbridge D., 1546, W, P2/2Reg/6A
Wm., gent., Corsley, 1609, AB, I, P2/H/257, P2/8Reg/79A
Hooper *or* Hopper, Wm., blacksmith, Wick, Bps. C., 1633, I, W, P24/244
Wm., yeo., Winterbourne D., 1662, I, W, P7/33
Wm., sen., Easton, 1664, I, W, P3/H/365
Wm., potter, Hurst, Berks., 1664, I, W, P5/1664/22
Wm., Corsley, 1671, AB, P2/H/683
Wm., yeo., Smithcot, Dauntsey, 1675, I, W, P3/H/498
Wm., sen., yeo., Whitbourne, Corsley, 1682, AB, a/c, I, W, P2/H/804
Wm., potter, Hurst, Berks., 1694, I, W, P5/1694/5
Wm., linen weaver, Woodlands, Mere, 1695, AB, I, P5/1695/46
Wm., yeo., Bishopstrow, 1742, W, P2/H/1335
Wm., yeo., Rollestone, 1782, W, P2/H/1603
Wm., yeo., Boreham, Warm., 1785, W, P2/H/1622
Wm., miller, Upton S., 1787, W, P2/H/1628
Wm., yeo., Pewsey Farm, 1791, W, P3/H/1501
Wm., gent., Westb., 1802, D, O, W, P25/1802/8
Wm., Semley, 1803, AB, P2/1803/27
Wm., blacksmith, Dilton M., Westb., 1807, W, P25/1807/3
Wm., millman, Westb., 1812, W, P25/1812/3
Wm., shear grinder, Trowb., 1820, comm, W, Wr, P1/1820/2
Wm., property in Pewsey ; no abode stated, 1830, AB, O, Wr, P3/1830/66
Wm., farmer, Warminster Bottom Farm, W. Lavington, 1834, W, Wr, P1/1834/8
Wm., farmer, Shrewton, 1841, W, Wr, P2/1841/24
Wm. Wilkins, Redlands Farm, Westb., 1825-27, AB (2), comm, O, Wr, P25/1825/15
see also Burgh alias H.; Coleman alias H.; Edney alias H.; Rosier alias H.
Hoor *see* Hoare
Hoord, Hored, Jas., Sal., 1770, AB, W, P4/1770/6
Thos., Fritham, Bramshaw, Hants, 1608, AB, P24/160
Hope, Amos, clothier, Rowde, 1673, I, W, P3/H/479
Chris., [shoemaker], Westb., 1634, AB, I, P25/1634/1
Eliz., Pott., 1728, AB, P1/H/838
Eliz., sp., Marl., 1754, AB, comm, P1/H/1103
Eliz., sp., Devizes, 1755, AB, comm, P1/H/1104
Francis, clothier, Rowde, 1663, AB, P1/H/335
Francis, woolcomber, Rowde, 1669, AB, I, P3/H/421
Hannah, sp., Uffc., Devon, 1811, W, P20/1/297
Jn., victualler, Blewbury, Berks., 1661, AB, comm, I, P5/1661/28
Moses, yeo., Rowde, 1683, comm, I, W, P3/H/585
Robt., cordw., Devizes St My., 1619, I, W, P1/H/129
Sarah, widow, Cholsey, Berks., 1766, AB, P1/H/1182
Susanna, widow, Rowde, 1684, I, W, P3/H/600
Thos., worsted comber, Rowde, 1718, W, P3/H/959
Thos., Bromham, 1763, W, P3/H/1348
Wm., alehouse keeper, Cholsey, Berks., 1759, W, P1/H/1142, P1/11Reg/405B
Hoper *see* Hooper
Hopgood, Ann, widow, Sal., 1830, W, Wr, P4/1830/15
Habgood, Betty, widow, Crickl. St S., 1805, AB, P3/1805/32
Habgood, Edith, widow, Sal., 1632, I, W, P4/1632/10

Hapgood, Edwd., sen., Chute, 1682, I, W, P5/1682/56
Edwd., yeo., Chute, 1722, W, P5/1721/21, P5/16Reg/60D
Habgood, Edwd., yeo., Latton, 1727, W, P3/H/1030
Habgood, Edwd., Collingbourne K., 1777, AB, comm, P3/H/1418
Habgood, Edwd., Chelworth, Crickl. St S., 1794, W, P3/H/1508
Hapgood, Eliz., widow, Chute, 1640, I, NW, P7/20
Eliz., widow, Donnington, Berks., 1753, AB, comm, P1/H/1085
Geo., Sal., 1830, AB, Wr, P4/1830/10
Habgood, Isaac, yeo., Bower C., 1825, W, Wr, P2/1825/8
Habgood, Isaac, Bower C., 1847, AB, Wr, P2/1847/61
Jas., cordw., Wilton, 1714, I, W, P1/H/692, P1/5Reg/319A
Jas., Wilton, 1741, AB, P2/H/1334
Habgood, Jas., yeo., Latton, 1790, W, P3/H/1491
Joan, widow, Chute, 1736, W, P7/131
Habgood, Jn., husb., Chute, [1559], W (NEP), P5/1Reg/3B
Habgood, Jn., Chute, 1564, W, P5/1Reg/34B
Jn., N. Tidworth, 1633-34, comm, I, NW, P2/H/456, P2/9Reg/36A
Hapgood, Jn., sen., yeo., Aughton, Collingbourne K., 1670, I, W, P3/H/428
Hapgood, Jn., yeo., Chute, 1692, I, W, P5/1692/44
Jn., yeo., Chute, 1726, W, P7/121
Jn., weaver, Wilton, 1765, AB, W, P2/H/1477
Jn., innholder, Milford, Sal. St Martin, 1770, W, P4/1770/2
Jn., Chute, 1831, AB, O, P7/200
Habgood, My., widow, Latton, 1702, W, P3/H/813
Habgood, My., widow, Bower C., 1857, aff, W, Wr, P2/1857/50
Hapgood, Nich., husb., Chute, 1609, AB, I, W, P7/2
Habgood, Philip, yeo., Chelworth, Crickl. St S., 1804, W, P1/1804/33
Habgood, Philip, Braydon, Purton, 1811, AB, Wr, P3/1811/11
Hapgood, Richd., sen., husb., Chute, 1636, I, W, P7/25
Hapgood, Richd., yeo., Shaw, Chute, 1677, I, W, P7/46
Hapgood *or* Hobgood, Robt., yeo., Collingbourne K., 1629, I, W, P3/H/223
Habgood, Sarah, widow, Bower C. (form. of Ebbesborne Wake), 1810, W, Wr, P2/1810/72
Sidney, Downton, 1856, aff, W, Wr, P2/1856/17
Thos., husb., Winterbourne E., 1568, W, P2/5Reg/46B
Hapgood, Thos., husb. *or* yeo., Chute, 1596-7, I, W, P7/217, P5/6Reg/152A
Thos., feltmaker, Sal., 1645, I, P4/1645/1
Hobgood, Thos., Shaw, Chute, 1661, comm, I (damaged & fragile), W, P5/1661/27
Thos., sen., labourer, Chute, 1717, I, W, P7/111
Thos., yeo., Wexcombe, Grafton, 1726, I, W, P21/8/28
Thos., Burbage, 1745, AB, P11/195
Habgood, Thos., tailor, Crickl. St S., 1762, W, P3/H/1334
Thos., miller, Overton, 1783, W, P1/H/1283, P1/13Reg/395A
Thos., Chute, 1831, AB, aff, O, P7/202
Thos., carp., Standen, Chute, 1849, comm, W, Wr, P7/210
Wm., husb., Winterbourne E., 1574, W, P2/5Reg/196C
Hapgood, Wm., sen., yeo., Brunton, Collingbourne K., 1641, I, W, P3/H/328
Hapgood, Wm., Collingbourne K., 1674, AB, I, P3/H/482
Wm., yeo. *or* labourer, Speen, Berks., 1701, I, W, P1/H/615, P1/4Reg/98
Wm., Stapleford, 1718, AB, I, P2/H/1161
Hobgood, Wm., Brunton, Collingbourne K., 1744, W, P3/H/1211
Wm., Wilton, 1749, AB, P2/H/1380
Habgood, Wm., sen., tailor, Collingbourne K., 1758, W, P3/H/1308
Hopkins, Alice, widow, Corsley, 1695, W, P1/H/574
Ann, widow, Clyffe P., 1682, I, W, P3/H/573
Ann, widow, Highway, 1709, I, W, P3/H/900
Ann, widow, Melk., 1709, W, P2/H/1071
Ann, sp., Lyneham, 1832, AB, comm, Wr, P3/1832/8
Anthony, broad weaver, Corsley, 1677, I, W, P2/H/743
Anthony, weaver, Ditchampton, Wilton, 1822, I, W, Wr, P2/1822/10
Benj., yeo., Gt. Somerford, 1807, W, P3/1807/26

Chris., Mere, 1579-80, AB, I, P5/1579/41, P5/3Reg/147C
Edwd., husb., Mere, 1572, W, P5/3Reg/3B
Edwd., yeo., Broad H., 1699, AB, I, P3/H/790
Edwd., yeo., Wootton B., 1701, comm, W (2 - 1 is copy), P3/H/812
Edwd., Gt. Bedwyn, 1728, AB, P5/1727/25
Edwd., Broad Town, Clyffe P., 1748, AB, I, W, P3/H/1240
Edwd., watchmaker, Bradford A., 1803, comm, W, P2/1803/57
Eliz., widow, Elston, Orcheston St Geo., 1715, W, P2/H/1128
Eliz., Lockeridge, Overton, 1735, W, P1/H/930, P1/8Reg/41
Eliz., widow, Sal., 1743, W, P4/1742/2
Eliz., widow, Bushton, Clyffe P., 1749, W, P3/H/1253
Eliz., widow, Hungerford, Berks., 1783, W, P23/774
Hopkins *or* Hotkins, Ellis, husb., Stockton, 1633, I, W, P2/H/451, P2/9Reg/30B
Frances, sp., Clyffe P., 1699, AB, I, W, P3/H/791
Francis, yeo., Clevancy, Hilmarton, 1666-68, court papers, W, P1/H/384, P3/H/381
Francis, yeo., Steventon, Berks., 1759, W, P1/H/1136, P1/11Reg/374
Francis, gent., E. Ginge, W. Hendred, Berks., 1773, W, P1/H/1221, P1/12Reg/467
Francis, sen., yeo., Wootton B., 1778, W, P3/H/1428
Gilbert, yeo., Elston, Orcheston St Geo., 1718, inty, I, W, P2/H/1157
Hopkins alias Legg, Grace, Milston, 1717, W, P2/H/1137
Guy, sen., Swindon, 1672, I, W, P3/H/467
Guy, stone cutter, Swindon, 1687, I, W, P3/H/644
Guy, stone cutter, Swindon, 1782, W, P3/H/1446
Hy., Mere, 1587, AB, I, P5/1587/52, P5/4Reg/144D
Hy., husb., Steventon, Berks., 1720, I, W, P1/H/771, P1/6Reg/289A
Hy., hosier, Alton P., Dorset, 1809, AB, comm, W, Wr, P5/1809/17
Jas., blacksmith, Wilton, 1764, W, P2/H/1475
Hopkens, Jas., labourer, Baverstock, 1783, AB, W, P1/H/1286, P1/13Reg/413A
Jas., Swallowfield, Shinfield, Berks., 1823, AB, Wr, P1/1823/91
Jas., [broad weaver], Marsh, Westb., 1825, comm, W, Wr, P25/1825/7
Jas., farmer, Grittleton, 1830, AB, W, P3/1830/57
Jas., plumber and glazier, Crickl. St S., 1844, O, W, Wr, P3/1844/18
Jeremiah, Mkt. L., 1742, AB, P2/H/1336
Jerome, yeo., Elston, Orcheston St Geo., 1695, I, W, P2/H/956
Joan, widow, Corsley, 1685, AB, I, P2/H/853
Jn., Donhead St A., 1571, W, P2/5Reg/122B
Jn., Corsley, 1585, I (2), NW, P2/H/73, P2/7Reg/20A
Jn., Nether Zeals, 1588, I, T, NW, P5/1587/24, P5/5Reg/27F
Jn., tanner, Wokm., Berks., 1596, AB, I, W, P5/1596/32, P5/6Reg/130
Jn., Stanford in the Vale, Berks., 1620, I, W, P1/H/143
Jn., yeo., Steventon, Berks., 1662, W, P1/H/321
Jn., sen., yeo., Whitbourne, Corsley, 1662, I, W, P2/H/618
Hopkins [Hodkins], Jn., jun., clothworker, Bradford A., 1681, AB, I, P2/H/795
Jn., yeo., Clevancy, Hilmarton, 1683, I, W, P3/H/586
Hopkins [Hotkins], Jn., yeo., Chapmanslade, Corsley, 1691, I (2), W, P2/H/918
Jn., yeo., Dauntsey, 1694, I, W, P3/H/748
Jn., Thornford, Dorset, 1700, AB, I, P5/1700/14
Jn., Nether C., Dorset, 1703, AB, P5/1703/17
Jn., yeo., Duxford, Hinton Waldrist, Berks., 1717, I, W, P1/H/740, P1/6Reg/128
Jn., Clyffe P., 1723-24, comm, W, P1/H/793, P1/6Reg/447
Jn., singleman, Thornford, Dorset, 1728-29, AB, comm, I (2 - 1 a copy), P5/1728/54, P5/1729/25, P5/16Reg/217C, 218A
Jn., sen., yeo., Clevancy, Hilmarton, 1737, W, P3/H/1147
Jn., clothworker, Corsley, 1756, AB, W, P1/H/1117, P1/11Reg/272A
Jn., yeo., Thornhill, Clyffe P., 1762, W, P3/H/1340
Jn., Kington St M., 1763, AB, a/c, I, P3/H/1349
Jn., gent., Bremhill, 1767, W, P1/H/1189, P1/12Reg/219
Jn., Devizes, 1769, AB, P1/H/1201
Jn., tailor, Chr. M., 1772, W, P3/H/1402
Jn., Rams., 1781, AB, P5/1781/11, P5/17Reg/206A
Jn., maltster, Sutton B., 1794, req, W, copy W, P3/H/1512

Jn., yeo., Brigmerston, Milston, 1809, W, Wr, P2/1809/15
Jn., Clyffe P. & Chiseldon, 1822, AB, comm, Wr, P3/1822/34
Jn., yeo., Chr. M., 1825, AB, W, Wr, P3/1825/54
Jn., wheelwright, Chapmanslade, Corsley, 1844, comm, W, Wr, P2/1844/52
Jn., gent., Westport St My., 1854, aff, O, W, Wr, P3/1854/17
Jonathan, stone cutter, Swindon, 1815, W, Wr, P3/1815/25
Jos., clothworker, Corsley, 1739, W, P2/H/1319
Jos., yeo., Lockeridge, Overton, 1760, W, P3/H/1321
Jos., Goatacre, Hilmarton, 1764, AB, P3/H/1352
Jos., blacksmith, Abingdon, Berks., 1767, W, P1/H/1186, P1/12Reg/250B
Jos., clothworker, Corsley, 1769, W, P2/H/1509
Jos., yeo., Clack, Lyneham, 1796, W, P3/H/1519
Jos., yeo., Chr. M., 1805, W, P3/1805/23
Jos., blacksmith, E. Garston, Berks., 1817, W, Wr, P1/1817/78
Jos., yeo., Chr. M., 1825, W, Wr, P3/1825/49
Jos., farmer, Soley, Chilton F., 1835, O, W, P1/1835/57
Lucy, widow, Thornford, Dorset, 1729, AB, I (2 - 1 a copy), P5/1729/26, P5/16Reg/245B
Mgt., widow, Durley, Burbage, 1597, comm (cancelled), W, P5/1597/56
Margery, widow, Elston, Orcheston St Geo., 1667, I, W, P2/H/641
Martha, widow, Duxford, Hinton Waldrist, Berks., [1690], W, P1/H/533
My., sp., Stock St., Calne, 1670, I, W, P26/181
My., widow, Lockeridge, Overton, 1692, AB, I, W, P3/H/715
My., widow, Duxford, Hinton Waldrist, Berks., 1692, I, W, P1/H/553
My., widow, Dauntsey, 1731, court paper (3), W, P3/H/1096
My., widow, Worton, Pott., 1733, W, P1/H/921, P1/7Reg/574A
My., widow, Wilton, 1767, W, P1/H/1185, P1/12Reg/200A
My., widow, Devizes, 1768, AB, P1/H/1200
Matthew, yeo., Highway, 1671, AB, comm, I, P3/H/459
Matthew, yeo., Dodford Farm, Chr. M., 1722, I, W, P3/H/997
Matthew, yeo., Chr. M., 1766, W, P3/H/1364
Matthew, dairyman, Bishop Fowley, Wootton B., 1807, W, Wr, P3/1807/22
Matthew, Chr. M., 1808, AB, Wr, P1/1808/6
Matthew, Bushey Vowley Farm, Wootton B., 1844, O, W, Wr, P3/1844/11
Nich., clothworker, Corsley, [1685], I, W, P2/H/854
Nich., slaymaker, Marsh, Westb., 1754, W, P25/1754/2
Olive, widow, Bradford A., 1834, O, W, Wr, P2/1834/40
Philip, husb., Mere, 1636, AB, L, P5/1636/29, P5/12Reg/253B
Richd., tailor, Mere, 1578, I, W, P5/1578/21, P5/3Reg/107B
Richd., jun., stone cutter, Swindon, 1703, AB, I, P3/H/843
Richd., feltmaker, Sherb., Dorset, 1729, W, P5/1729/27, P5/16Reg/240B
Richd., bach., Overton, 1747, AB, P3/H/1230
Richd., Mkt. L., 1826, W, Wr, P1/1826/115
Robt., yeo., Dauntsey, 1675, I (2), W, P3/H/499
Robt., clothworker, Chapmanslade, Dilton, Westb., 1708, I, W, P25/1708/3
Robt., sen., stone cutter, Swindon, 1708, W, P3/H/883
Robt., stone cutter, Swindon, 1815, W, Wr, P3/1815/27
Robt., baker in the courts, Trowb., 1845, O, W, Wr, P1/1845/74
Sarah, singlewoman, Westb., 1700, AB, L, P25/1700/9
Sarah, widow, Devizes, 1783, AB, P1/H/1292
Sarah, yeo.'s wife, Lambourn, Berks., 1801, AB, W, P1/1801/40, P1/15Reg/261
Stephen, tallow chandler, Luckington, 1719, AB, I, P3/H/972
Susan, Sal., 1703, AB, P4/1703/10
Hopkins *or* Hotkins, Susanna, widow, Chapmanslade, Dilton, Westb., 1681, AB, I, P25/1680/6
Susanna, Corsley, 1776, W, P2/H/1558
Thos., husb., Wolverton, Zeals, 1565, W, P5/1Reg/56A
Thos., Durley, Burbage, 1597, AB, I, P5/1597/59, P5/6Reg/156B
Thos., Seend, Melk., 1599, AB, P2/H/186
Thos., rough mason, Lockeridge, Overton, 1685-92, AB, I, P3/H/619, 716
Thos., barber and wigmaker, Sal., 1714, W, P1/H/690, P1/5Reg/313
Thos., currier, Lambourn, Berks., 1716, AB, I, P1/H/723

Thos., yeo., Clack, Lyneham, 1807, W, P3/1807/40
Thos., cooper, Leigh, Yetm., Dorset, 1831, W, P19/241
Thos., yeo., Bishop Fowley, Wootton B., 1853, AB, aff, court proceeding, D, O, W, Wr, P3/1853/64-65
Walter, yeo., Sherb., Dorset, 1629, comm, I, W, P5/1628/62, P5/11Reg/20A
Wm., Shrewton, 1548, W, P2/2Reg/57B
Wm., Stockton, 1588, AB, I, T, W, P2/H/81, P2/7Reg/115C
Wm., Durley, Burbage, 1589, AB, I, W, P5/1589/29, P5/5Reg/62B
Wm., husb., Lambourn, Berks., 1606, I, W, P1/H/46
Hopkins alias Reade, Wm., sen., husb., Halstock, Dorset, 1636, I, W, P5/1636/32, P5/13Reg/17
Wm., yeo., Stapleford, 1682-83, a/c, I, W, P2/H/815
Wm., sen., hatter, Sherb., Dorset, 1713, AB, I, ren, P5/1713/39
Wm., yeo., Hilmarton, 1741, W, P1/H/995, P1/9Reg/192A
Wm., barber, Lambourn, Berks., 1744, W, P1/H/1012, P1/9Reg/336
Wm., Corsley, 1748, AB, W, P2/H/1374
Wm., gardener, Mkt. L., 1769, W, P2/H/1516
Wm., Corsley, 1811, AB, comm, Wr, P2/1811/27
Wm., Dilton M., Westb., 1828, O, W, P25/1828/8
Wm., draper, Hungerford, Berks., 1830, O, W, Wr, P5/1830/18
see also Read alias H.
Hopper *see* Hooper
Horden, Edwd., sen., yeo., Amesb., 1732, W, P1/H/910
Horder, Eliz., sp., Donhead St My., 1734, AB, P2/H/1279
Jn., Donhead St My., 1814, AB, comm, P2/1814/2
My., wife, Mkt. L., 1726, AB, P1/H/827
Robt., yeo., Charlton, Donhead St My., 1709, comm, W, P2/H/1067
Robt., sen., yeo., Ludwell, Donhead St My., 1709, AB, comm, W, P2/H/1066
Thos., sen., yeo., Bugley, Gillingham, Dorset, 1664, AB, I, W, P27/1/18
Thos., yeo., Gillingham, Dorset, 1686, I, P27/1/93
Thos., Gillingham, Dorset, 1772, AB, P27/1/479, P27/3Reg/162
Wm., sen., gent., Donhead St My., 1819, W, Wr, P2/1819/45
see also Read form. H.
Hore *see* Hoare
Hored *see* Hoord
Horlock, Anthony, husb., Studley, Trowb., 1637, AB, a/c, I, P22/2/32
Chris., Trowb., 1627, I, NW, P22/1/9
Chris., staymaker, Sal., 1751, W, P4/1750/10
Edith, Warm., 1558-62, AB (in minority of Nich. H.), W, P2/3Reg/74C, P2/4Reg/93E
Edith, widow, Trowb., 1641, I, W, P22/2/44
Jn., weaver, Studley, Trowb., 1574-75, I, W, P22/2/1, P5/3Reg/65D
Jn., Studley, Trowb., 1630, comm, I, W, P22/1/12
Jn., Studley, Trowb., 1637, AB, I, P22/2/29
Luke, weaver, N. Bradley, 1602, AB, I, W, P2/H/209
Margery, widow, N. Bradley, [1617], I, W, P2/H/320
Martha, wife, Sal., 1790, AB, P4/1790/8
Richd., husb., Studley, Trowb., 1622, comm, I, W, Wr, P22/2/25
Robt., Studley, Trowb., 1635, AB, P1/H/215
Thos., Warm., 1557, AB, P2/3Reg/67C
Thos., clothworker, Trowb., 1630, comm, I, W, P22/1/13
Thos., sen., yeo. and weaver, Studley, Trowb., 1639, I, W, P22/2/39
Horlick, Thos., Frowd's Almshouses, Bedwin St., Sal., 1853, O, W, Wr, P4/1853/18
Wm., broad weaver, Hilp., 1741, W, P1/H/991, P1/9Reg/178
Horlor, Geo., apothecary, Wilton, 1775, AB, P2/H/1545
Hormibie *see* Humby
Horn *see* Horne
Hornblow, Robt., Hurst, Berks., 1570, W, P5/2Reg/68A
Roger, Thatcham, Berks., 1671, AB, I, W, P1/H/409
Sam., blacksmith, Broad B., Highw., 1771, AB, W, P10/1771/4
Thos., clothier, Newbury, Berks., 1789, W, P1/H/1313, P1/14Reg/247
Wm., yeo., Charnham St., Hungerford, Berks., 1724, AB, I, P5/1724/38
Horne, Agnes, Marston, Pott., 1607, I, W, P1/H/53

Ann, widow, Lyneham, 1695, W, Wr, P3/H/754
Ann, widow, Swindon, 1805, W, P3/1805/37
Chas., blacksmith, Swindon, 1803, W, P3/1803/64
Horn, Deborah, widow, Rams., 1720, AB, P5/1720/23
Edith, Marston, Pott., 1607, I, W, P1/H/52
Horn, Edith, widow, Marston, Pott., 1635, I, W, P1/H/218
Hurne, Edith, clothier's wife, Trowb. (late of N. Bradley), 1744, W, P1/H/1022, P1/9Reg/411
Edwd., husb. and labourer, Rams., 1699, I, W, P5/1699/17
Edwd., excise officer, Sal., 1770, W, P1/H/1202, P1/12Reg/298B
Eliz., widow, Rams., 1703, comm, W, P5/1703/19
Hy., farmer, Corsham, 1834, W, Wr, P3/1834/58
Jn., husb., Heytes., 1587, I, T, W, P5/1586/13, P5/4Reg/139A
Jn., tilemaker, Wokm., Berks., 1605, I, W, P5/1605/28, P5/8Reg/46C
Jn., Uffc., Devon, 1613, I, W, P5/1612/24, P5/9Reg/92B
Jn., N. Tidworth, 1624, a/c, I, P1/H/159
Jn., yeo., Hurst, Berks., 1634-35, AB, a/c, I. Granted at the Metropolitan Visitation to Reading, P5/1634/53, P5/1635/50
Jn., husb., Gt. Bedwyn, 1646, I, NW, P21/1/66
Jn., jun., apothecary, Sherb., Dorset, 1684, AB, comm, I, P5/1683/30
Jn., sen., cordw., Rams., 1684, I, W, P5/1684/35
Jn., Sherb., Dorset, 1691, AB, comm, P5/1691/33
Jn., yeo., Earley, Sonning, Berks., 1700, I, W, P5/1700/15
Jn., Marston, Pott., 1707, AB, I, P1/H/644
Jn., yeo., Marston, Pott., 1717, AB, I, T, W, P1/H/735, P1/6Reg/125
Jn., farrier, Upavon, 1723, AB, I, ren, P2/H/1199
Horn, Jn., Marston, Pott., 1737, AB, appt of proxy, P1/H/948
Hurne, Jn., Melk., 1802, comm, W, P2/1802/76
Horn, Jn., Worton, Pott., 1829, AB, O, Wr, P1/1829/7
Jos., Wokm., Berks., 1721, AB, I, P5/1721/18
Lawr., gent., Durrington, 1637, I, W, P2/H/489
Lydia, widow, Corsham, 1834, AB, W, Wr, P3/1834/59
Mgt., widow, Rams., 1700, I, W, P5/1700/17
My., widow, Sal., 1781, W, P4/1781/7
My., widow, Swindon, 1804, W, P1/1804/136
My., Martin, Hants, 1833, aff, cert, W, Wr, P2/1833/43
Horne alias Johnson, Michael, widow, Sal. (form. of Andover, Hants), 1675, AB, I, W, P4/1674/18
Peter, Sherb., Dorset, 1615, AB, comm, I, T, P5/1615/15, P5/9Reg/166B
Peter, Sherb., Dorset, 1647, AB, I, P5/1647/7, P5/14Reg/93A
Richd., Marston, Pott., 1597, I, W, P1/H/22
Horn, Richd., labourer, Stoford, S. Newton, 1751, I, W, P2/H/1393
Robt., victualler, Reading St My., Berks., 1689, AB, I, P1/H/520
Horn, Robt., sen., blacksmith, Stoford, S. Newton, 1710, I, W, P2/H/1085
Horn, Robt., yeo., Stoford, S. Newton, 1769, W, P2/H/1519
Robt., Winterslow, 1811, W, Wr, P2/1811/6
Horn, Ruth, widow, Stoford, S. Newton, 1780, W, P2/H/1582
Thos., husb., Gt. Bedwyn, 1591, I, T, W, P5/1591/43, P5/5Reg/111A
Thos., Sherb., Dorset, 1603, AB, I, P5/1603/37, P5/7Reg/89E
Thos., Marston, Pott., 1611, I, W, P1/H/64
Thos., yeo., Pickwick, Corsham, 1611, I, copy I, P29/H/14
Thos., Marston, Pott., 1669, AB, P1/H/395
Thos., sen., yeo., Corsham, 1678, AB, I, P29/H/51, P29/1Reg/209A
Thos., clothworker, Bradford A., 1682, AB, comm, I, P2/H/811
Thos., yeo., Rams., 1684, I, W, P5/1684/26
Thos., shearman, Marl., 1686, AB, I, P1/H/495
Horn, Thos., Corsham, 1705, I, P29/H/79
Thos., Corsham, 1731, I, P29/H/108
Horne alias Buckland, Thos., Ogbourne St A., 1731, AB, P5/1731/41
Horn, Thos., collarmaker, Sanden Fee, Hungerford, Berks., 1741, W, P23/555
Horn, Thos., farmer, Brightwalton, Berks., 1820, W, Wr, P1/1820/110
Thos., yeo., Tilehurst, Berks., 1823, W, Wr, P1/1823/28
Thos., yeo., Westrop, Corsham, 1830, W, P3/1830/58

Tobias, Liberty of Newland, Hurst, Berks., 1726, AB, W, P5/1726/20, P5/16Reg/138A
Hurne, Valentine, shepherd, Netheravon, 1664, I, W, P12/92
Wm., husb., Stratton St Mgt., [1611], W (2 - 1 a copy) (NEP), P3/H/74
Wm., yeo., Melk., 1670, AB, comm, I, P2/H/678
Wm., Bradford A., 1693, AB, P1/H/559
Wm., chandler, Corsham, 1711, I, W, P29/H/86
Horn, Wm., Limmerhill, Wokm., Berks., 1767, AB, P5/1767/25
Horn, Wm., farmer, Marston, Pott., 1802, W, P1/1802/17, P1/15Reg/375
see also Amesbury/Emsbury alias Horn/Hurne; Buckland alias H.
Horner, Alice, widow, W. Lavington, 1613, AB, I, W, P1/H/74
Cath., widow, Marl., 1662, comm, I, W, P1/H/312
Joan, Amesb. (to be buried in chancel of Downton church), 1550, W, P2/2Reg/97C
Harner, Jn., smith, W. Lavington, 1605, I, W, P1/H/35
Jn., jun., Marl., 1704, AB, P1/H/633
Jn., sen., gent., Marl., 1714, AB, W, P1/H/703, P1/5Reg/420
Harner alias Turner, Jn., husb., Chards., Devon, 1776, AB, W, P5/1776/22, P5/17Reg/129B
Richd., pewterer, Sal., 1595, AB, I, W, P1/H/15
Hornett, David, labourer, Fisherton A., 1843, AB, W, Wr, P2/1843/4
Harnett, Jn., Earldoms Farm, Whitep., 1853, D (2), W, Wr, P2/1853/67
Harnett, Wm., yeo., Whitep., 1838, W, Wr, P2/1838/15
Horrill *see* Harrell
Horsall *see* Horsell
Horse, Ann, widow, Wootton B., 1826, comm, W, Wr, P3/1826/5
Jn., Bucklebury, Berks., 1592, I, P1/H/4
Horseley, Frideswide, widow, Wantage, Berks., 1573, AB, P5/3Reg/12C
Horsell, Abraham, Brinkw., 1829, AB, Wr, P1/1829/85
Bartholomew, sen., cordw. *or* shoemaker, Wootton B., 1702, I, W, P3/H/834
Bartholomew, cordw., Wootton B., 1783, W, P3/H/1449
Bartholomew, sen., yeo., Nore Marsh, Wootton B., 1812, W, Wr, P3/1812/45
Eliz., widow, Brinkw., 1842, O, W, Wr, P3/1842/8
Horsewell, Gabriel, yeo. and bach., Poulton, 1715, comm, I, W, P1/H/714, P1/5Reg/473B
Giles, yeo., Poulton, 1693, I, W, Wr, P3/H/734
Hy., sen., cordw., Wootton B., 1762, W, P3/H/1342
Horsill, Jn., Shalbourne, 1575, W, P5/3Reg/59A
Jn., shoemaker, Avebury, 1769, W, P3/H/1388
Horswell, Mgt., widow, Poulton, 1718, W, P3/H/960
My., Wootton B., 1706, I, P3/H/871
Horsall alias Phillipps, Matthew, labourer, Ham, Broad Town, [1606], I, W (NEP), P3/H/24
Reuben, bach., Chiseldon, 1854, AB, aff, comm, W, Wr, P3/1854/65
Horsall, Richd., husb., Poulton, [1613], I, W (NEP), P3/H/96
Wm., yeo., Wootton B., 1824, W, Wr, P3/1824/16
Horseman *see* Horsman
Horsenail *see* Horsnell
Horsewell *see* Horsell
Horsey, David, Martin, Hants, 1763, W, P1/H/1176, P1/12Reg/129
Dorothy, widow of Wm., esq., Upton, Berwick St Jn. (her husband of Martin, Hants), 1576-77, W, P2/H/44
Eliz., Martin, Hants, 1774, AB, P2/H/1544, P2/5Reg/281
Oliver, gent., Damerham, Hants, 1608-09, I, W. Proved at manorial court of D. & Martin, then exhibited at Archdeaconry court, P2/H/243, P2/8Reg/50B
Oliver, jun., Martin, Hants, 1673, AB, I, P2/H/712, ??
Oliver, sen., gent., Tidpit, Martin, Hants, 1673, I (extract from PCC), P2/H/713
Peter, priest, Winterbourne Bassett, 1560, institution to rectory, P1/1Reg/80B
Peter, Martin, Hants, 1584, W, P2/6Reg/137B
Robt., gent., Tidpit, Martin, Hants, 1627, AB, I, P2/H/396
Solomon, Martin, Hants, 1767, W, P1/H/1184, P1/12Reg/201
Thos., gent., Damerham, Hants, 1560, W, P2/4Reg/35B
Thos., yeo., Winnersh, Hurst, Berks., 1597, AB, I, W, P5/1596/36, P5/6Reg/143B
Wm., esquire, Martin, Hants, 1570, AB, note of seq of goods, P1/1Reg/23B, P2/5Reg/107A
Wm., weaver, Hurst, Berks., 1619, I, W, P5/1619/47, P5/10Reg/41
Horsford, Ann, widow, Drayton, Abingdon, Berks., 1698, I, W, P1/H/603, P1/3Reg/82

Hugh, schoolmaster, Slape, Netherb., Dorset, 1631, I, W, copy W, P5/1631/48, P5/12Reg/21
Hosford, Hugh, Slape Hill, Netherb., Dorset, 1681, I, W, P17/253
Hugh, yeo., Slape, Netherb., Dorset, 1737, I, W, Wr, P5/1737/26
Jn., Netherb., Dorset, 1575, AB (2), T (re Hugh & Jn. H., children), W, P17/633, P5/3Reg/61B
Jn., carp., Netherb., Dorset, 1738, AB, I, P17/468
My., widow, Netherb., Dorset, 1787, W, Wr, P17/577
Sam., yeo., Slape Mill, Netherb., Dorset, 1742, AB, I, P17/482
Wm., sergemaker, Beam., Dorset, 1694, AB, I, P17/112
Wm., yeo., Pipsford, Corscombe, Dorset, 1702, I, W, P17/149
Horsill *see* Horsell
Horsington, Barnabas, Calne, 1703-09, AB (2), I (detailed), P26/499, 559
Eliz., Calne, 1741, W, P26/829
Horsonton, Wm., Westb., 1639, I, P25/1639/11
Horsman, Job, retired yeo., Pond Close, Corsham, 1810, comm, W, Wr, P3/1810/7
Horsman alias Shere, My., widow, Beam., Dorset, 1593, AB, P5/1593/41, P5/6Reg/43B
Horsman alias Smith, Wm., clothworker, Steeple A., [1703], W, P1/H/623
see also Clement alias H.; Reade alias H.
Horsnell, Chris., White Waltham, Berks., 1767, W, P1/H/1193, P1/12Reg/247A
Horsenail, Hy., tailor, Warfield, Berks., 1619, I, W, P1/H/123
Horsnail, Stephen, Warfield, Berks., 1683, I, W, P1/H/479
Horsenail, Stephen, victualler, New Windsor, Berks., 1729, W, P1/H/854, P1/7Reg/268
Horsnail, Wm., shearman, Warfield, Berks., 1664, I, W, P1/H/349
Wm., yeo., Warfield, Berks., 1744, I, W, P1/H/1014, P1/9Reg/363B
Horsnail, Wm., Warfield, Berks., 1773, W, P1/H/1224, P1/12Reg/486A
Horsonton *see* Horsington
Horswell *see* Horsewell
Hort, Horte, Alice, widow, Penn, Hilmarton, 1571, W, P1/1Reg/33B
Alice, widow, Devizes, 1674, I, NW, P1/H/432
Horte, Benj., widower, Martin, Hants, 1723, AB, I, P1/H/788
Chris., Devizes, 1682, AB, I, P1/H/466
Dan., rough mason, Corsham, 1713, I, W, P29/H/89
Dan., yeo., Langley Burrell, 1741, W, P1/H/986, P1/9Reg/160
Edmd., husb., Westport St My., 1670, I, W, P3/H/443
Edmd., yeo., Sherston, 1693, I, W, P3/H/735
Edmd., sen., maltster, Sherston, 1736, W, P3/H/1133
Edwd., clerk, Lt. Cheverell, 1667, AB, I, P1/H/379
Horte, Eliz., widow, Sutton V., 1565, W, P2/4Reg/195B
Horte, Eliz., Seend, Melk., 1575, W, P2/5Reg/222A
Eliz., widow, Whaddon, 1695, AB, comm, I, NW, P2/H/959
Isaac, yeo., Stanton St Q., 1715, W, P3/H/944
Jas., yeo., Westport St My., 1677, I, W, P1/H/444
Horte, Jn., Sutton V., 1565, AB, P2/4Reg/198C
Horte, Jn., yeo., Hanging L., 1612, I, W, P2/H/292
Horte, Jn., husb., Coulston, Edington, 1616, I, W, P1/H/100
Jn., sen., Biddestone St Nich., 1682, I, W, P3/H/574
Jn., husb., Elston, Orcheston St Geo., 1683, AB, I, P2/H/823
Jn., Amesb., 1687, AB, P2/H/882
Jn., mason, Malm., 1700, I, W, P3/H/800
Jn., Calne, 1719, AB, P5/1719/39
Jn., gent., Biddestone St Nich., 1733, comm, W, P3/H/1117
Horte, Jn. *or* Richd., Biddestone, 1614, AB, I, P3/H/102
Horte, Mgt., widow, Hanging L., 1602, AB, I, W, P2/H/202
Mgt., widow, Halcombe, Westport St My., 1688, AB, comm, I, W, P1/H/506
Mgt., widow, Sherston, 1711, AB, I, W, P1/H/669, P1/5Reg/100
My., Teffont E., 1608, AB, I, P2/H/246, P2/8Reg/33A
My., singlewoman, Marl., 1724, W, P1/H/805, P1/7Reg/41B
Horte, Maud, widow, Penn, Hilmarton, [1606], W (NEP), P3/2Reg/13A
Nathaniel, tailor, Sherston, 1708, AB, I, P3/H/884
Richd., yeo., Sherston, 1704, I, W, P3/H/849
Richd. *see also* Jn.

Horte, Robt., Sherston, 1615, AB, P3/H/113
Robt., N. Wraxall, 1617, AB, a/c, I, P3/H/126
Robt., blacksmith, Pewsham Forest, 1667, I, W, P3/H/392
Horte, Robt., blacksmith, Redhill, Pewsham, 1717, AB, L, W, P3/H/953
Robt., yeo., Broad C., 1749, W, P2/H/1386
Horte, Simon, yeo., Charlton nr Malm., [1606], I, W (both on same sheet) (NEP), P3/H/25
Stephen, Broad C., 1733, AB, P2/H/1271
Stephen, yeo., Heytes., 1779, AB, a/c, comm, I, P5/1779/10, P5/17Reg/182B
Horte, Thos., Compton C., 1596, I, NW, P2/H/150
Thos., sen., Draycot C., 1669, I, W, P3/H/422
Thos., victualler, Pewsham, 1738, W, P1/H/965, P1/8Reg/325
Thos., yeo., Wanb., 1803, W, P3/1803/27
Horte *or* Horton, Wm., no abode stated, 1581-82?, W (incomplete) (NEP), P3/1Reg/19A
Horte, Wm., mason, Pinkney, Sherston, 1619, I, W, P1/H/125
Wm., fuller, Stanley, Bremhill, 1672, comm, I, W, P3/H/468
Wm., labourer, Chipp., 1761, W, P3/H/1330
Wm., Melk., 1830, AB, comm, P2/1830/69
see also Hart alias H.
Horter, Jos., Sal., 1735, AB, P1/H/925
Hortington, Hartington, Alice, widow, Uppington, Stapleford, 1639, I, W, P2/H/512
Jn., husb., Stapleford, 1565, AB, W, P2/4Reg/200B
Jn., husb., Stapleford, 1587, W, P2/7Reg/93B
Hartington, Jn., brewer, Wilton, 1606, AB, I, W, P1/H/44
Simon, Stockton, 1574, W, P2/5Reg/206D
Thos., husb., S. Newton, 1635, AB, I, P1/H/212
Horton, Alexander, plumber, E. Harnham, Britford, 1734, W, P5/1734/37
Chas., jun., plumber [and glazier], E. Harnham, Britford, 1686, I, NW, P5/1686/33
Chas., yeo., Badbury, Chiseldon, 1722, AB, I, P3/H/998
Chas., yeo., Badbury, Chiseldon, 1788, W, P3/H/1482
Chas., yeo., Badbury, Chiseldon, 1804, W, P1/1804/83
Edwd., gent., Pott., 1616-20, AB, I, W, P1/H/105, 146
Grace, widow, Devizes, 1719, AB, ren, W, P1/H/751, P1/6Reg/187B
Hannah, widow, S. Marston, 1811, comm, W, P10/1811/2
Hy., miller, Grove, Wantage, Berks., 1746, W, P23/594
Jas., shepherd, Bishopstone N., 1839, W, Wr, P5/1839/17
Joan, Gomeldon, Idmiston, 1585, W, P1/H/1
Jn., gent., Calne, 1604, AB, a/c, I, P5/1603/43, P5/1604/21
Jn., husb., Bishopstone N., 1604, W, P5/1604/20
Jn., day labourer, Bishopstone N., 1629, I, W, P6/8
Jn., labourer, Tilsh., 1701, AB, P2/H/1000
Jn., plumber, E. Harnham, Britford, 1723, W, P5/1723/23, P5/16Reg/91A
Jn., weaver, Berwick St Jas., 1732, I, W, P1/H/913, P1/7Reg/549
Jn., yeo., S. Marston, 1777, W, P10/1777/2
Jn., Dauntsey, 1790, AB, P3/H/1495
My., widow, Newbury, Berks., 1619, I, W, P1/H/135
Robt., yeo., Calne, 1798, comm, W, P26/1214
Sarah, wife, Stratton St Mgt., 1811, W, Wr (2), P1/1811/80
Thos., jun., Bishopstone N., 1594, AB, I, T, W, P5/1594/43, P5/6Reg/81A
Thos., Mere, 1600, I, W, P5/1600/31, P5/6Reg/256C
Thos., Calne, 1610, AB, comm, T, P5/1610/33, P5/9Reg/45A
Thos., sen., husb., Bishopstone N., 1610, I, W, P5/1610/28, P5/9Reg/17
Thos., blacksmith, Purton, [1613], I, W (NEP), P3/H/97
Thos., gent., Broughton G., 1745, AB, comm, P2/H/1357
Thos., shoemaker, Calne, 1766, AB, P26/1014
Thos., cordw., Blackland, Calne, 1788, W, P5/1788/13, P5/18Reg/98
Wm., esquire, Corsham, 1706, I, ren (by son Jn. H.), W (jewels include 24 diamonds & 23 pearls, both set in gold), P29/H/81, P29/1Reg/287
Wm., glazier, E. Harnham, Britford, 1711, AB, I, W, P5/1711/32, P5/15Reg/269
Wm., yeo., N. Bradley, 1809, W, Wr, P2/1809/6
see also Curtis alias H.; Hort *or* H.

Horwell, Jas., husb., Sherb., Dorset, 1644, comm, I, W, P5/1644/17, P5/14Reg/62E
Horwood, Joan, widow, Chute, 1609, I, W, P7/3
Hosea, Jos., weaver, Bearfield, Bradford A., 1812, AB, D, ren, W, Wr, P2/1812/15
Hosey, Elias, sen., clerk, Chipp., 1680, AB, I, P1/H/455
Jn., Gt. Bedwyn, 1581-83, AB, I, W, P5/1581/15, 33, P5/1582/33, P5/4Reg/1C, 57C
Hosford *see* Horsford
Hosier, Jn., yeo., Seagry, 1730, I, W, P3/H/1082
Thos., maltster, Newbury, Berks., 1680, AB, I, ren, P1/H/447
Thos., Hidden, Hungerford, Berks., 1691, AB, I, P5/1691/32
Hoskins, Heskin, Alice, Corsley, 1565, W, P2/4Reg/203B
Haskins, Alice, Crickl. St S., 1694, AB, I, P3/H/741
Andrew, yeo., Gillingham, Dorset, 1731, W, P27/1/312
Heskins, Ann, widow, W. Lavington, 1684, AB, I, W, P1/H/461
Haskins, Bernard, N. Wraxall, 1809, W, Wr, P3/1809/39
Chas., sen., butcher, Beam., Dorset, 1743, I, W, Wr, P5/1743/42
Haskins, Christian, widow, Hilp., 1581, W, P2/6Reg/22A
Dan., Gillingham, Dorset, 1730, AB, P27/1/305
Haskins, Diana, widow, Leigh, Ashton K., 1682, I, W, P3/H/565
Haskins, Edith, Warm., 1594, AB, P2/H/140
Edith, widow, Beam., Dorset, 1596, I, W, P5/1596/38, P5/6Reg/121B
Haskins, Edith, widow, Eastrop, Highw., 1623, W, P5/1623/14
Heskins, Edwd., yeo., Bapton, Fisherton Delamare, 1597, I, T, P2/H/156
Edwd., yeo., Wilton, 1649, I, W, P2/H/601
Edwd., Bapton, Fisherton Delamare, 1706, AB, P2/H/1042
Heskins, Eliz., Gt. Somerford, 1570, W (NEP), P1/1Reg/117B
Heskins, Eliz., sp., Baynton, Edington, 1619, AB, I, NW, P2/H/339
Eliz., widow, Beam., Dorset, 1695, AB, I, P17/347
Heskins, Geo., yeo., Purton, 1675, AB, I, P3/H/495
Hiskens, Geo., Semley, 1791, AB, P2/H/1655
Hy., yeo., Beam., Dorset, 1634, comm, I, NWGVS, P5/1634/54, P5/12Reg/282
Hy., gent., Beam., Dorset, [1666], W, P17/82
Hy., innholder, Beam., Dorset, 1680, AB, I, P17/259
Hy., sackclothmaker, Beam., Dorset, 1700, W, P17/135
Jas., gent., Beam., Dorset, 1677, I, P17/241
Jas., grocer, Gillingham, Dorset, 1819, W, Wr, P27/1/644
Heskins, Jane, widow, Littleton P., 1725, AB, P1/H/810
Joan, Netherb., Dorset, 1640, W, P17/61
Heskins, Joan, widow, Easterton, Mkt. L., 1672, AB, I, W, P2/H/700
Jn., husb., Hilp., 1557, W, P2/3Reg/17A
Heskins, Jn., Byght, Westb., 1570, W, P5/2Reg/83B
Heskins, Jn., Wick, Mkt. L., 1591, I (2), W (2), P2/H/117
Hoskins alias Harris, Jn., gent., Langdon, Beam., Dorset, 1606, AB, I, W, P5/1606/25, P5/9Reg/93A
Heskins, Jn., Warm., 1606, AB, I, P1/H/42
Jn., gent., Langdon, Beam., Dorset, 1613, I, W, P5/1612/23
Heskins, Jn., Devizes St Jn., 1616, AB, I, ren, P1/H/117
Jn., vintner, Beam., Dorset, 1635, AB, a/c, I, P17/24
Jn., mason, Netherb., Dorset, 1635, W, P17/26
Heskins, Jn., yeo., Gt. Somerford, 1637, AB, I, P3/H/297
Heskins, Jn., Devizes St Jn., 1648, AB, P1/H/290
Haskins, Jn., Nursteed, Bps. C., 1672, AB, comm, I, P24/376
Jn., *The White Hart*, Beam., Dorset, 1680, I, P17/255
Heskins, Jn., sen., yeo., W. Lavington, 1681, I, W, P1/H/463
Haskins, Jn., Wantage, Berks., 1682, I, W (legacies include £5 to be divided between 5 named ousted ministers), P23/118
Haskins, Jn., mercer, Keevil, 1689, comm, I, W, P2/H/903
Heskins, Jn., yeo., W. Lavington, 1691, comm, W, P1/H/539
Haskins, Jn., Upton L., 1712, AB, P1/H/684
Hoskins alias Harris, Jn., jun., carp., Ash, Netherb., Dorset, 1717, AB, I, P17/371
Hoskins alias Harris, Jn., sen., carp., Ash, Netherb., Dorset, 1718, comm, W, P17/378
Haskins, Jn., innholder, Calne, 1728, W, P5/1728/45, P5/16Reg/185
Jn., Beam., Dorset, 1732, AB, P17/452

Jn., Beam., Dorset, 1742, AB, comm, Wr, P5/1741/18
Haskins, Jn., yeo., Purton, 1814, W, P3/1814/7
Jos., cordw., Beam., Dorset, 1733, I, W, P17/454
Jos., Beam., Dorset, 1761, AB, P5/1761/23
Haskins, Magdalen, widow, Calne, 1664, W (NEP), P5/1664/19
Haskins *or* Heskins, Mgt., widow, Devizes, 1647, AB, NW, P1/H/287
Margery, sp., Beam., Dorset, 1597, AB, I, NW, P5/1596/35, P5/6Reg/144A
Martha, widow, Gillingham, Dorset, 1834, W, Wr, P27/1/705
My., widow, Beam., Dorset, 1677, I, W, P17/261, 291
My., sp., Lyme R., Dorset, 1695, AB, comm, I, P16/136
Oliver, sergemaker, Beam., Dorset, 1698, W, P17/115
Peter, esquire, Beam., Dorset, 1641, AB, comm, P5/1641/40, P5/13Reg/282D
Priscilla, Beam., Dorset, 1695, AB, I, P17/350
Haskins, Rebecca, gent.'s widow, Keevil, [1690], I, W, P2/H/908
Reynold *or* Reginald, yeo., W. Kington, 1642, AB, I, P3/H/337
Richd., Easterton, Mkt. L., 1580, a/c, W, P2/H/62, P2/6Reg/3A
Heskins, Richd., Mkt. L., 1582, W, P2/6Reg/70C
Heskins, Richd., husb., Purton, 1603, I, W, P3/H/4
Haskings, Richd., Bedborough, Bps. C., 1626, AB, I, P24/229
Richd., Beam., Dorset, 1631, AB, I, NW, P5/1630/5, P5/11Reg/160C
Hiskins, Richd., yeo. and blacksmith, S. Burcombe, 1685, I, W, P2/H/864
Richd., Burcombe, 1721, W, P2/H/1180
Richd., sen., sergemaker, Beam., Dorset, 1739, W, P17/472
Richd., butcher, Beam., Dorset, 1744, W, P17/490
Haskins, Robt., Purton, 1592, I, P1/H/5
Robt., tanner, Beam., Dorset, 1616, I, W, P5/1616/37
Haskins *or* Heskins, Robt., sen., weaver, Calne (& Cherhill & Berwick), 1671, I, notes (info on churchwardens of C., C. & B.), NW, P5/1671/46
Sam., clerk, Cholderton, 1710, W, P1/H/661, P1/5Reg/13
Heskins, Stephen, yeo., Melk., [1687], I, W, P2/H/878
Heskins, Stephen, gardener, Littleton P., 1717-18, I, draft I, W, P1/H/748, P1/6Reg/167B
Heskins, Thos., yeo., Charlton nr Malm., [1596], W (NEP), P3/1Reg/113A
Heskins, Thos., yeo., Devizes, 1619, AB, I, W, P1/H/136
Haskins, Thos., husb., Latton, 1632, I, W, P3/H/255
Hoskins alias Harris, Thos., yeo., Squirrels Down, Netherb., Dorset, 1717, AB, I, P17/370
Haskins, Thos., yeo., Purton, 1828, W, Wr, P3/1828/44
Hoskins alias Harris, Tobias, Netherb., Dorset, 1710, AB, P17/194
Heskin, Wm., yeo., Urchf., 1561, W, P2/4Reg/65A
Wm., Beam., Dorset, 1574-75, AB, I, P5/1574/7, P5/3Reg/49B
Haskins, Wm., sen., [shoemaker], Calne, 1588, I, W, P5/1588/30, P5/5Reg/13B
Haskins, Wm., yeo., Chapmanslade, Corsley, [1611], NW, P2/H/283
Haskins, Wm., Marl. St Peter and St Paul, 1622, I, W, P1/H/158
Heskins, Wm., sen., husb., Purton, 1627, I, W, P3/H/215
Haskins, Wm., husb. *or* yeo., Leigh, Ashton K., 1670, I, W, P3/H/431
Wm., tailor, Bapton, Fisherton Delamare, 1671, AB, I, ren, P1/H/402
Haskins, Wm., sen., cordw., Calne, 1672, I, W, P26/207
Wm., husb., Easterton, Mkt. L., 1672, AB, I, P2/H/690
Haskins, Wm., yeo., Melk., 1680, AB, a/c, I, P2/H/778
Haskins, Wm., Calne, 1683, I (detailed), W, P26/308
Haskins *or* Hoskins, Wm., Lockeridge, Overton, 1741, AB, a/c, I, P3/H/1174
Haskins, Wm., yeo., Upton L., 1769, AB, W, P2/H/1515
see also Harris alias H.
Hostler *see* Ostler
Hother, Eliz., sp., Poole St Jas., Dorset, 1746, W, P5/1746/44
Hotherne, Hy., husb., Wokm., Berks., 1700, AB, I, P5/1700/16
Hotkins *see* Hopkins
Houghton, Jn., clerk, Colerne, 1712, ren, P30/98
Houliston, David, bailiff, Dinton, 1848, W, Wr, P1/1848/19
Houlton *see* Holton
Hounsell, Matthew, yeo., Netherb., Dorset, 1676, I, W, P17/294

Wm., mariner, Lyme R., Dorset, 1634, AB, comm, I(GVS), P5/1634/56
Hount *see* Hunt
House, Howse, Agnes, widow, Hurst, Berks., 1640, I, W, P5/1640/29, P5/13Reg/250B
Howse, Alice, widow, Westb. L., 1615, I, W, P25/1615/7
Ann, widow, Westport St My., 1813, W, Wr, P3/1813/58
Bridget, widow, Sal., 1724, W, P4/1724/7
Chester, weaver, Hurst, Berks., 1681, AB, comm, I, P5/1681/24
Christian, sp., Tinh., Edington, 1855, AB, aff, D, O, W, Wr, P2/1855/11
Cottle, widow, Westb., 1817, W, Wr, P25/1817/3
Edith, widow, Rockbourne, Hants, 1710, W, P2/H/1084
Howse, Eliz., widow, Langley Burrell, 1741, W, P1/H/979, P1/9Reg/95
Eliz., widow, Basildon, Berks., 1779, W, P1/H/1255, P1/13Reg/211
Francis, innholder, Gillingham, Dorset, 1823, comm, W, Wr, P27/1/661
Geo., husb., Thatcham, Berks., 1674, I, W, P1/H/434
Geo., yeo. and widower, Brook, Westb., 1697, I, W, P25/1697/3
Geo., yeo., Caundle Marsh, Dorset, 1854, AB, aff, Wr, P5/1854/9
Hannah, sp., Streatley, Berks., 1741, W, P1/H/983, P1/9Reg/91B
Hy., Westb. L., 1635, AB, I, P25/1635/5
Howse, Isaac, excise officer, Westport St My., 1798, W, P3/H/1533
Howse, Jas., yeo., Somerford K., 1762, W, P3/H/1343
Jas., husb., Sutton V., 1782, W, P1/H/1275, P1/13Reg/363
Jas., labourer, Codf. St My., 1808, W, Wr, P1/1808/20
Jas., innkeeper, W. Lavington, 1842, O, W, Wr, P1/1842/28
Howse, Joan, widow, Poulton, 1695, I, W, Wr, P3/H/755
Howse, Jn., husb., Bishopstone S., 1571, AB, P2/H/36, P2/5Reg/125A
Howse, Jn., Warm., 1590, W, P2/H/103
Howse, Jn., sen., Sal. St Thos., 1645, AB, I, P1/H/265
Jn., [blacksmith], Sal., 1693, AB, I, W, P4/1692/11
Jn., yeo., S. Moreton, Berks., 1747, AB, I, P1/H/1037
Jn., gent., Moulsford, Cholsey, Berks., 1753, W, P1/H/1090, P1/10Reg/521
Jn., labourer, Sutton V., 1763, W, P1/H/1174, P1/12Reg/127
Jonathan, Beckhampton, Avebury, 1755, W, P3/H/1291
Mgt., widow, Sal., 1664, I, W, P1/H/345
Martha, Gillingham, Dorset, 1837, comm, W, Wr, P27/1/717
Howse, My., widow, Sevenhampton, Highw., 1642, I, W, P5/1642/12, P5/14Reg/52C
House *or* Huse, Nich., cooper, Arborfield, Berks., 1626, W, P5/1626/49, P5/10Reg/308
Reynold, Warm., 1630, I, W, P2/H/415
Howse, Richd., yeo., Arborfield, Berks., 1618, comm, I, W, Wr, P5/1618/18, P5/9Reg/221
Howse, Richd., husb. *or* yeo., Sevenhampton, Highw., 1634, I, W, P10/1634/1
Richd., broad weaver, Heywood, Westb., 1641, I, W, P25/1641/3
Howse, Richd., Heywood, Westb., 1671, I, W, P25/1671/10
Richd., sadler, Dilton M., Westb., 1704, W, P25/1704/5
Richd., Sherrington, 1721, AB, I, P2/H/1182
Robt., Wokm., Berks., 1555, marriage licence, bride's name given once as Eliz., once as Agnes, P5/20Reg/133B
Robt., Edington, 1821, AB, W, Wr, P2/1821/11
Howse, Sam., Mkt. L., 1756, AB, P2/H/1416
Sam., bach., Sutton V., 1795, W, P2/H/1675
Sam., sen., carrier, Westb., 1803, O, W, P25/1803/4
Sarah, widow, Beam., Dorset, 1853, comm, W, Wr, P17/632
Howse, Thos., carp., Arborfield, Berks., 1598, AB, I, T, P5/1598/26, P5/6Reg/211A
Howse, Thos., Sherb., Dorset, 1614, AB, P5/1614/3
Howse, Thos., husb., Berwick St Jn., 1637, AB, comm, I, P2/H/484
Thos., Poulton, 1670, AB, I, P3/H/444
Howse, Thos., gent., Corsham, 1735, AB, I, P29/H/110
Thos., yeo., Beam., Dorset, 1853, comm, W, Wr, P17/626
Wm., Westb., 1560, W. No date of probate given, P1/2Reg/107A
Wm., clerk and rector, Brightwalton, Berks., 1722, AB, I, ren, P1/H/784
Wm., yeo., Britford, 1724, W, P24/874
Wm., yeo., Poulton, 1731, AB, W, P3/H/1097
Howse, Wm., victualler, Wantage, Berks., 1825, W, P23/920

How *see* Howe
Howard, Howard, Dorothy, widow, Gt. Amesb., [1691], NW, P2/H/921
Howard, Geo., sen., labourer, Sutton C., Berks., 1770, W, P1/H/1210, P1/12Reg/360
Howard, Hy., clerk [vicar of Burbage], Burbage, 1766, W, P11/222
Howard, Jn., bricklayer, Binfield, Berks., [1707], W, P1/H/641
Howard, Martha, widow, Durrington, 1800, W, P2/1800/98
Howard, Richd., grocer, Reading, Berks., 1756, W, P1/H/1108, P1/11Reg/217A
Howard, Robt., millwright, Amesb., 1686, I, W, P1/H/499
Howard, Wm., cordw., Durrington, 1784, W, P2/H/1612
Howard, Wm., clothworker, Bradford A., 1802, comm, W, P2/1802/66
Howe, How, Anna, widow, Fordington, Dorset, 1742, W, P15/130
How, Jas., carp., Uffc., Devon, 1805, W, P20/1/282
Joan, widow, Uffc., Devon, 1564, W, P5/1Reg/40C
Jn., Uffc., Devon, 1552, W, P20/Reg/53
Jn., Uffc., Devon, 1594, I, W, P5/1594/41, P5/6Reg/64B
Jos., Uffc., Devon, 1743, AB, Wr, P5/1743/43
How alias Tanner, My., widow, Uffc., Devon, 1684, AB, I, P20/1/100
How, My., widow, Downton, 1833, W, Wr, P2/1833/82
How, Richd., clockmaker, Fordington & Dorchester, Dorset, 1715, W (Quaker), P15/92
How, Sarah, sergemaker, Uffc., Devon, 1771, W, P20/1/254
Wm., Colerne, 1809, AB (2), appt of guardian, comm, Wr, P3/1809/21
How, Wm., Marl., 1824, AB, Wr, P1/1824/8
see also Tanner alias H.
Howell, Agnes, widow, Gt. Chalfield, 1547, W (NEP), P2/2Reg/42A
Alice, widow, Holt, Bradford A., 1575, W, P2/5Reg/223A
Alice, widow, Sal. St Martin, 1648, I, W, P1/H/292
Ann, widow, Odstock, 1624, I, W, P2/H/370
Ann, sp., Semington, Steeple A., 1837, comm, W, Wr, P2/1837/17
Chris., Bradford A., 1559, W, P2/3Reg/174A
Chris., husb., Bradford A., 1616-19, AB, a/c, I, T, P2/H/316, P2/8Reg/310B
Chris., fuller, Bradford A., 1676, I, W, P2/H/738
Eliz., widow, Bradford A., 1613, I, W, P1/H/75
Eliz., widow, Sherston, 1690, I, W, P3/H/683
Eliz., Semington, Steeple A., 1722, W, P2/H/1188
Eliz., widow, Dauntsey, 1748, W, P3/H/1241
Esther, servant to Eulalia Hawkeswell, Longbridge D., 1769, W, P2/H/1514
Ethelbert, yeo., Sherston, 1673, comm, I, W, P3/H/480
Ethelbert, yeo., Sherston, 1784, W, P3/H/1458
Ethelbert, sen., yeo., Sherston, 1818, W, Wr, P3/1818/44
Ethelbert, yeo., Sherston, 1848, D, O, W, Wr, P3/1848/53
Francis, Sutton B., 1734, AB, W, P3/H/1125
Geo. Berry, yeo., Kington L., 1851, W, Wr, P3/1851/52
Hy., yeo., Bradford A., 1615, W, P2/8Reg/251A
Hy., carp., Bradford A., 1678, AB, I, P2/H/759
Hy., butcher, Sherston, 1694, I, W, P3/H/749
Hy., husb., Hilp., 1698, comm, W (Quaker), P2/H/984
Hy., Sal., 1707, AB, I, P4/1707/7
Hugh, husb., Corsham, 1617, I, P29/H/20
Jas., yeo., Highway, 1738, W, P1/H/963, P1/8Reg/309B
Jas., yeo., Wanb., 1767, W, P3/H/1369
Jas., yeo., Erlestoke, 1816, comm, W, Wr, P2/1816/57
Jas., Rowde, 1847, AB, aff, Wr, P3/1847/19
Joanna, sp., Seend, Melk., 1788-96, AB, comm (2), W (unadmd in 1788), P2/H/1638
Job, spinner, Paxcroft, Steeple A., 1847, I (summary only), W, Wr, P2/1847/35
Jn., Sherston, 1608, W, P3/H/39
Jn., Wingfield, 1610, AB, I, P2/H/265, P2/8Reg/101A
Jn., Wingfield, 1624, I, NW, P2/H/372
Jn., butcher, Winkfield, Berks., 1720, AB, I, P1/H/772
Jn., butcher, Winkfield, Berks., 1741, W, P1/H/985, P1/9Reg/139
Jn., Sutton V., 1746, AB, I, P2/H/1361

Jn., Sutton B., 1748, AB, P3/H/1242
Jn., jun., baker, Wantage, Berks., 1772, comm, W, P23/749
Jn., Monkton D., 1794, AB, P2/H/1671
Jn., yeo., Compton B., 1809, W, Wr, P3/1809/36
Jn., Hindon, 1827, W, Wr, P2/1827/6
Jn., Fisherton A., 1849, AB, Wr, P2/1849/31
Jos., yeo., Monkton D., 1730-33, a/c, P2/H/1251
Lawr., yeo., Steeple A., 1741, W, P1/H/990, P1/9Reg/182
Lawr., labourer, Steeple A., 1833, W, Wr, P2/1833/31
Lot, Tisb., 1831, AB, P2/1831/46
Mgt., widow, Edington, 1626, I, W, P2/H/384
Margery, widow, Monkton D., 1639, I, W, P2/H/520
My., widow, Sherston, 1729, I, NW, P1/H/864, P1/7Reg/314A
My., singlewoman, Steeple A., 1781, AB, P2/H/1594
Richd., pipemaker, Mere, 1726, W, P5/1726/18, P5/16Reg/132A
Richd., Bradford A., 1806, AB, comm, P2/1806/32
Robt., Sal., 1715, AB, P4/1715/1
Robt., Brixton D., 1722, AB, P2/H/1195
Robt., yeo., Steeple A., 1768, comm, W, P2/H/1504
Robt., Chr. M., 1850, AB, Wr, P3/1850/32
Roger, yeo., Odstock, 1605, AB, I, W, P2/H/223
Thos., Bratton, Westb., 1664, AB, P25/1664/5
Thos., sen., Mere, 1718, AB, P5/1717/18
Thos., yeo., Sherston, 1757, W, P3/H/1304
Wm., Holt, Bradford A., 1570, W, P2/5Reg/83D
Wm., Bradford A., 1605, AB, I, P1/H/32
Wm., carp., Monkton D., 1633, AB, a/c, I, P2/H/452
Wm., yeo., S. Wraxall, 1637, AB, a/c, I, P2/H/487
Wm., Euridge Farm, Colerne, 1819, AB, Wr, P3/1819/57
Wm., Highway, 1836, AB, comm, Wr, P3/1836/74
Wm., yeo., Pewsham, 1840, AB, comm, P26/1449
Wm., Corsham, 1847, O, W, Wr, P3/1847/49
see also Hoole *or* H.
Howes, Martha, widow, Greenham, Thatcham, Berks., 1726, comm, W, P1/H/815, P1/7Reg/71
Thos., weaver, Crickl. St S., 1614, I, W, P3/H/103
Howithropp, Jas., glover, Chipp., 1612, W, P3/H/89
Howlet *see* Hewlett
Howman *see* Holman
Howmar *see* Holmer
Howorth, Jn., Reading, Berks., 1723, AB, P1/H/800
Howper *see* Hooper
Howse *see* House
Housell *see* Howsell
Howsell, Jn., woolstapler, Seend, Melk., 1748, W, P2/H/1379
Howson, Eliz., widow, Buckland, Berks., 1786, AB, P1/H/1304
Hy., gent., Avebury, 1785, W, P3/H/1466
Hawson, My., widow, Buckland, Berks., 1767, AB, P1/H/1196
Robt., sen., Buckland, Berks., 1786, AB, W, P1/H/1303, P1/14Reg/105
Sarah Dyke, gent.'s widow, Avebury, 1787, W, P3/H/1476
Hoyle, Ann, sp., Marl. (form. of Overton), 1850, O, W, Wr, P1/1850/20
Chas., MA and vicar, Overton, 1849, O, W, Wr, P1/1849/2
Hoyte, Hoyte, Ann, widow, Lyme R., Dorset, 1694, AB, NW, P5/1694/6
Huatt *see* Hewett
Huband, Dan., marine store dealer and shopkeeper, Marl., 1853, D (2), W, Wr, P1/1853/25
Jn., marine store and general dealer, Devizes, 1846, O, W, Wr, P1/1846/31
Jn., Calstone W., 1853, W, Wr, P3/1853/30
Hubbard, Hubberd, Jn., Fittleton, 1688, AB, I, ren, P2/H/892
Jn., labourer, Winterbourne S., 1690, I, W, P2/H/910
Hubbert, Jn., Ogbourne St Geo., 1736, W, P23/523
Roger, tailor, Wilton, 1681, I, W, P2/H/800

Hubbert, Wm., Sonning, Berks., 1586, AB, I, P5/1586/12, P5/4Reg/133A
Huby, Eliz., widow, Hurst, Berks., 1625, AB (re both Eliz. & Wm. H. her husband), I, NW, P5/1625/48, P5/10Reg/242B
Huce *see* Hughes
Hucker *see* Hacker
Huckesley, Wm., Wokm., Berks., 1571, AB, P5/2Reg/107B
Huckings, Abraham, woollen draper, Malm., 1708-35, AB, I, W, P3/H/885
Benj., Devizes, 1704, AB, P1/H/632
Eliz., widow, Devizes, 1722, W, P1/H/783, P1/6Reg/385A
Jean, sp., Malm., 1670, I, W, P3/H/445
My., sp., Devizes, 1726, W, P1/H/826, P1/7Reg/126
Robt., cordw., Malm., 1669, I, W, P3/H/423
Robt., woollen draper, Malm., 1718, W, P3/H/961
Huckwell *see* Hackwell
Hudd, Alexander, innholder, Sal. St Edmd., 1643, AB, I, P1/H/260
Ezekiel, yeo., Quemerford, Calne, 1825, W, Wr, P26/1353
Ezekiel, yeo., Quemerford, Calne, 1838, AB, comm, W, Wr, P26/1442
Joan, Bere R., Dorset, 1670, comm, I, NW, P5/1670/17
Joan, widow, Limpley Stoke, Bradford A., 1704, W, P2/H/1027
Hudde, Jn., Studley, Trowb., 1615, I, NW, P1/H/98
Jn., W. Ashton, Steeple A., 1715, AB, P2/H/1122
Jn., sen., blanketmaker, Avill's Farm, Corsham, 1784, W, P3/H/1459
My. Ann, wife, Corsham, 1834, AB, comm, Wr, P3/1834/7
Thos., husb., W. Ashton, Steeple A., 1673, I, W, P2/H/709
Thos., broad weaver, Westwood, [1686], W, P2/H/871
Thos., yeo., Nash Hill, Lacock, 1756, W, P1/H/1126, P1/11Reg/319
Thos., labourer, Nash Hill, Lacock, 1818, W, Wr, P3/1818/42
Wm., sen., baker, Tinh., Edington, 1684, AB, I, W, P2/H/836
Wm., scribler, Limpley Stoke, Bradford A., 1719, W, P2/H/1165
Wm., burler, Limpley Stoke, Bradford A., 1728, AB, W, P2/H/1226
Wm., yeo., Edington, 1729, W, P1/H/872, P1/7Reg/341
Wm., gardener, Hilp. Marsh, 1838, O, W, Wr, P1/1838/16
Hudden, Cath., widow, Worton, Pott., 1671, AB, I, P1/H/401, P2/H/684
Haddon, Eliz., Gt. Faringdon, Berks., 1635, AB, I, T (re Joan Worthen), W, P5/1635/53, P5/12Reg/188
Hugh, broad weaver, Gt. Cheverell, 1638, I, W, P1/H/234
Joan, Gt. Cheverell, 1699, AB, P2/H/989
Hudding, Jn., Gt. Cheverell, 1614, AB, I, P2/H/300
Jn., sen., Worton, Pott., 1646, I, W, P1/H/284
Jn., yeo., Worton, Pott., 1662, AB, comm, I, P1/H/314
Jn., yeo., Worton, Pott., 1687, I, W, P1/H/505
Jn., Pott., 1720, AB, P1/H/755
Jn., mercer, Hungerford, Berks., 1720, W, P23/386
Jn., victualler, Hindon, 1728, W, P2/H/1227
Lawr., Devizes, 1641, I, W, P1/H/247
My., Worton, Pott., 1671, AB, comm, P1/H/415
Michael, Urchf., 1677, AB, I, P1/H/442
Patient, grocer, Pott., 1723, W, P1/H/786, P1/6Reg/396
Robt., mason, Gt. Cheverell, [1688], I, W, P2/H/895
Ruth, widow, Pott., 1719, W, P1/H/750, P1/6Reg/175B
Wm., chapman, Devizes St My., 1675, comm, I, W, P1/H/437
Wm., grocer, Pott., 1685, I, W, P1/H/492
Wm., yeo., Worton, Pott., 1720, AB, I, ren, P1/H/757
see also Somner alias H.
Huddey, Jas., husb., Ebbesborne Wake, 1681, AB (2), I (2), P2/H/797
Hudding *see* Hudden
Hudnall, Martin, carp., Hurst, Berks., 1747, W, P5/1747/13
Hudson, Alice, widow, Sonning form.of Reading, Berks., 1755, W, P5/1755/29
Eliz., widow, Twyford, Hurst, Berks., 1689, I, W, P5/1689/31
Hudson alias Bayly, Geo., [butcher], Twyford, Hurst, Berks., 1684-85, AB, a/c, I, P5/1684/3, P5/1685/47
Jn., butcher, Wokm., Berks., 1662, I, W, P5/1662/67
Jn., baker, Westport St My., 1728, W, P3/H/1051

Jn., yeo., Westport St My., 1855, aff, O, W, Wr, P3/1855/10
My., widow, Malm., 1761, AB, W, P3/H/1331
Nathaniel, servant to Earl of Pembroke, Wilton, 1770, W, P1/H/1204, P1/12Reg/308
Richd., gent., Malm., 1754, AB, W, P3/H/1285
Sam., cordw., Malm., 1733, W, P3/H/1118
Sarah, widow, Rodbourne C., 1830, AB, Wr, P3/1830/48
Thos., butcher, Wokm., Berks., 1709, W, P5/1709/21, P5/15Reg/130
Wm., butcher, Hurst, Berks., 1696, comm, NW, P5/1696/23
Wm., butcher, Hurst, Berks., 1730, W, P5/1730/33
Wm., gent. and capital burgess, Malm., 1761, W, P3/H/1332
Huff, Eliz., widow, Wilton, 1785, AB, W, P2/H/1619
Hoff, Jn., whitesmith, Sherb., Dorset, 1811, AB, W, P5/1811/12
Hoff, Jos., reverend, Martin, Hants, 1740, AB, P2/H/1327
Hoff, Jos., Sherb., Dorset, 1763, AB, P5/1763/11
Thos., Tisb., 1629, AB, I, P2/H/408
Huggill, Francis, butcher, Blewbury, Berks., 1672, AB, I, P5/1672/21
Francis, cordw., Blewbury, Berks., 1735, W, P5/1735/29
Jn., husb. *or* labourer, Blewbury, Berks., 1672, I, W, P5/1672/22
Wm., shopkeeper, Upton, Blewbury, Berks., 1824, W, Wr, P5/1824/11
Huggins, Abraham, cordw., Grittleton, 1712, I, W, P3/H/922
Abraham, maltster, Nettleton, 1746, W, P3/H/1225
Ann, widow, Horningsham, 1756, W, P5/1756/16
Isaac, Grittleton, 1788, AB, comm, P3/H/1483
Jn., blacksmith, Blewbury, Berks., 1802, W, P5/1802/7
My., widow, Nettleton, 1754, W, P3/H/1286
Robt., blacksmith, Grittleton, 1797, W, P3/H/1528
Zachariah, yeo., Hankerton, 1832, W, Wr, P3/1832/19
Hughes, Agnes, widow, Aldermaston, Berks., 1620, I, W, P1/H/144
Hewes, Ambrose, innholder, Sal., 1650, I, W, P1/H/298
Ann, widow, Elcombe, Wrou., 1727, AB, comm, P3/H/1041
Ann, widow, Bremhill Wick, 1814, W, Wr, P1/1814/116
Ann, sp., Corsham, 1826, AB, Wr, P1/1826/54
Hewes, Anthony, yeo., Gillingham, Dorset, 1735, comm, I, W, P27/1/331
Chas., gent., Swindon, 1713, W, P3/H/933
Chas., labourer, Heddington, 1827, W, Wr, P3/1827/17
Hewes, Collissa, widow, Wilton, 1618, I, W, P2/H/329
Dan., yeo., Bremhill Wick, 1829, W, Wr, P1/1829/82
David, roper, Warm., 1754, W, P2/H/1406
Hewse, Denise, widow, Lt. Coxwell, Gt. Faringdon, Berks., 1668, AB, W, P5/1668/35
Hewse, Dorothy, widow, Lt. Coxwell, Gt. Faringdon, Berks., 1682, I, W, P5/1682/55
Hewes, Edwd., gent., Sutton V., 1730, AB, W, P2/H/1244
Huse, Eleanor, widow, Wilton, 1689, D, I, W, P2/H/907
Eliz., widow, Bremhill, 1699, AB, I, P3/H/784
Hewes, Eliz., Calstone W., 1707, AB, I, ren, P26/540
Eliz., widow, Broad H., 1839, W, Wr, P1/1839/54
Emma, servant maid, Charlton nr Malm., 1705, I, W, P3/H/854
Hewes, Frances, mistress, Stratford Tony, 1668, I, P2/H/652
Huse, Geo., Brinkw., 1617, AB, a/c, I, list of debts, P3/H/121, 128
Huce alias Checete, Geo., Charlton nr Malm., 1682, I, P3/H/578
Hewes, Geo., Imber, 1731, AB, P2/H/1252
Geo., yeo., Charlton nr Malm., 1751, AB, comm, ren, P3/H/1267
Geo., Cherhill (form. of Anchor & Hope Inn, Winchester St., Sal.), 1850, W, Wr, P5/1850/16
Huse, Hy., brickmaker, Motc., Dorset, 1739, W, P27/1/351
Hewes, Hy., labourer, Downton, 1746, W, P2/H/1359
Huse, Hy., gardener, Motc., Dorset, 1771, AB, W, P27/1/476, P27/3Reg/161
Hewes, Hester, widow, Malm., 1690, AB, P3/H/679
Isard, Hodson, Chiseldon, 1605, NW, P3/H/15
Jas., scribler, Calne, 1787, W, P26/1153
Jas., S. Marston, 1830, O, W, Wr, P10/1830/1
Huse, Jane, widow, Wrou., 1667, AB, I, W (2 - 1 a copy), P3/H/395

Jane, widow, Wootton B., 1815, comm, W, Wr, P3/1815/64
Jane, widow, S. Marston, 1834, O, W, Wr, P10/1834/1
Hughes alias Feates, Joan, widow, Calstone W., 1597, AB, I, W, P5/1597/55, P5/6Reg/153B
Huse, Joan, widow, Wrou., 1669, AB, I, W, P3/H/425
Joan, widow, E. Town, W. Ashton, Steeple A., 1707, AB, comm, I, P2/H/1053
Jn., clerk, S. Newton, 1597?, lease of vicarage & tithes, P1/2Reg/160
Huise, Jn., Chitterne St My., 1614, AB (re Jordan H.), W, P2/8Reg/242A
Hughes alias Williams, Jn., clerk, Easton, 1631, AB, a/c, I, P3/H/251
Hewes, Jn., mariner, Lyme R., Dorset, 1642, AB (re estate of Jn. H. left unadmd by widow, now *also* decd), comm, I, P5/1642/11, P5/14Reg/45A
Hewes, Jn., yeo., Hodson, Chiseldon, 1684, AB, I, W, P3/H/597
Hews alias Dyer, Jn., jun., husb. and bach., Stapleford, 1684, AB, I, P1/D/159
Hewes, Jn., yeo., Hodson, Chiseldon, 1689, I, W, P1/H/510
Jn., yeo., Walcot, Swindon, 1695, comm, I, W, copy W, P1/H/573
Jn., sadler, Devizes, 1696, W, P1/H/584
Jn., E. Town, W. Ashton, Steeple A., 1706, comm, W, P2/H/1047
Huse, Jn., yeo., Bremhill, 1709, I, W, P3/H/901
Hews, Jn., sievemaker, Calstone W., 1724, I, W, P26/689
Huse, Jn., Ashton K., 1728, AB, I, P3/H/1052
Jn., sen., yeo., Calstone W., 1731, I, W, P5/1731/47
Hews, Jn., yeo., Milton upon Stour, Gillingham, Dorset, 1745, W, P27/1/381, P27/3Reg/36
Hewes, Jn., dairyman, Bowden Hill, Lacock, 1750, I, W, P1/H/1077, P1/10Reg/395
Jn., Castle Eaton, 1766, W, P3/H/1365
Jn., labourer, Broad H., 1815, W, Wr, P3/1815/28
Jn., gent., manor of Westb. Arundell, Warm., 1841, AB, comm, P25/1841/6
Jonathan, butcher, Crickl. St S., 1837, W, Wr, P3/1837/32
Jos., sen., yeo., Alderton, 1753, W, P3/H/1275
Hewes, Margery, widow, Sal., 1663, I, W, P4/1662/3
Hews, My., Sal. St Thos., 1640, AB, P4/1640/5
My., widow, Westport St My., 1732, AB, P1/H/902
Peter, yeo., Winterbourne Bassett, 1779, W, P1/H/1263, P1/13Reg/244
Hews, Randall, Hindon, 1710, AB, P2/H/1078
Hewse, Richd., yeo., Milton, E. Knoyle, 1589, I, W, P2/H/94
Huse, Richd., Sal., 1608, AB, P1/H/58
Huise, Richd., husb., Chitterne St My., 1610, I, W, P2/H/266, P2/8Reg/103
Hewes, Richd., gunsmith, Wootton B., 1677, AB, I, P1/H/443
Hewes, Richd., gunsmith, Malm., 1685-90, AB, I, P3/H/612, 680
Richd., Charlton nr Malm., 1695, AB, comm, I, P1/H/569
Richd., Newbury, Berks., 1708, AB, I, P1/H/649
Huse, Robt., husb., Bemerton, Fugg. St Peter, 1780, W, P2/H/1587
Huse, Sam., yeo., Charlton nr Malm., 1733, AB, I, P3/H/1119
Sarah, Scott's Mill, Bremhill, 1739, W, P3/H/1163
Huse, Hughes *or* Hewes, Sarah, sp., Malm., 1791, W, P3/H/1502
Sarah, sp., Fifield, 1837, W, Wr, P3/1837/31
Sarah, sp., Warm., 1844, AB, Wr, P2/1844/80
Hewse, Thos., Wrou., 1628, I, W, P1/H/172
Hewes, Thos., Lt. Coxwell, Gt. Faringdon, Berks., 1635, I, W, P5/1635/49, P5/12Reg/182A
Hewes alias Feats, Thos., Quemerford, Calne, 1705, AB, I, P26/515
Thos., yeo., Tytherton L., Chipp., 1731, W, P3/H/1098
Huse, Thos., yeo., Wootton B., 1828, O, W, Wr, P3/1828/52
Thos., yeo., E. Tytherton, Bremhill, 1848, W, Wr, P3/1848/30
Hewes, Walter, Hodson, Chiseldon, 1621, I (2), W (2), P3/H/165
Hewes, Wm., husb., E. Knoyle, 1563, W, P2/4Reg/139B
Hewes, Wm., gent., Wilton, 1615, I, W, P2/H/305, P2/8Reg/258
Hewes, Wm., fuller, Bremhill, 1711, I, W, P1/H/672, P1/5Reg/80
Wm., Heddington, 1763, AB, ren, P2/H/1467
Wm., yeo., Cloatley, Hankerton, 1850, O, W, Wr, P3/1850/2
see also Acceley (Ackley) form. H.; Clarke alias H.; Feats alias H.

Huish, Hushe, Thos., husb., Charlton nr Malm., 1640, I, W (both on same sheet), P3/H/326
Thos., mercer, Sal. St Martin, 1645, AB, P1/H/264

Hewish, Wm., E. Knoyle, [1563], I, P2/H/23
Hewish, Wm., bach., Bradford A., 1812, AB, comm, Wr, P2/1812/14
Hulbert, Agnes, widow, Thingley, Corsham, 1604, W, P29/H/12, P29/1Reg/55A
Alice, sp., Corsham, 1638, W, P29/H/33
Alice, widow, Velly Quarr, Corsham, 1690-91, AB, I, copy I, W, P29/H/64, P29/1Reg/253
Amy, Bradford A., 1738, AB, P1/H/953
Ann, widow, Upton S., 1636, AB, I, NW, P2/H/478
Ann, widow, Wootton B., 1710, I (2 - 1 a copy), W, P3/H/911
Ann, sp., Corsham, 1716, I, W, P29/H/98, P29/2Reg/20
Hulbard, Ann, Chelworth, Crudwell, 1744, W, P1/H/1018, P1/9Reg/387B
Anthony, weaver, Wootton B., 1682, I, W, P3/H/575
Cath., widow, Avill's Farm, Corsham, 1761, W, P3/H/1333
Chapman, bach., Ford, N. Wraxall, 1857, AB, aff, O, ren, Wr, P3/1857/14
Chris., husb., Poulshot, 1595, AB, I (2), P2/H/144
Edwd., Easton, Corsham, [1564], W (NEP), P29/1Reg/5
Edwd., husb., Fittleton, 1614, I, W, P1/H/87
Edwd., brazier, Devizes, 1795, AB, comm, W, P1/H/1335, P1/14Reg/533B
Elias, whitesmith, late of Temple & Biddestone, 1768, AB, comm, P3/H/1379
Hulberd, Eliz., Broughton G., 1594, AB, I, W, P2/H/137
Eliz., widow, W. Kington, 1685, I, W, P3/H/620
Eliz., widow, Langley Burrell, 1718, W, P3/H/962
Eliz., milliner, Corsham, 1777, W, P29/H/120, P29/2Reg/161
Eliz., widow, Littleton Drew, 1853, AB, O, Wr, P3/1853/38
Francis, Chr. M., 1726, AB, comm, I, P1/H/830
Francis, Wilton, Gt. Bedwyn, 1729, AB, I, memo, NW, P21/8/47
Hulbatt, Francis, sen., carp., The Grn, Marl. St My., 1734, W, P1/7Reg/583
Geo., Poulshot, 1596-1609, court paper, W, P2/H/167
Geo., tailor and shopkeeper, Biddestone St Nich., 1721, I, W, P3/H/982
Geo., carp., Colerne, 1725, AB, I, P3/H/1024
Geo., gent., Thingley, Corsham, 1759, W, P3/H/1315
Geo., sen., Ford, N. Wraxall, 1847, D, W, Wr, P3/1847/24
Geo., labourer, Biddestone St Nich., 1850, O, W, Wr, P3/1850/44
Gifford, clothier, Corsham, 1697, AB, I, P29/H/70, P29/1Reg/267B
Gifford, yeo., Easton, Corsham, 1710, I, W, P29/H/83
Hulbert alias Pinnell, Grace, wife, Chipp., 1738, AB, P1/H/966
Hannah, sp., Chipping Sodbury, Gloucs (leaving property at Cherhill), 1762, W, P26/991
Hulberd, Hy., Poulshot, 1559, W, P2/3Reg/172C
Hy., [husb. *or* yeo.], Corsham, 1573, W, P29/1Reg/16
Hulberd, Hy., sen., yeo., Sheldon, Chipp., 1612, W, P3/H/90
Hy., carp., Chipp., 1617, I, W, P3/H/127
Hy., yeo., Seend, Melk., 1623, AB, I, W, P2/H/368
Hy., yeo., Easton, Corsham, 1631, AB, I, W, P29/H/29, P29/1Reg/122A
Hy., Swallowcliffe (form. of Helberton), 1661, I, P5/1661/29
Isaac, sen., carp., Pickwick, Corsham, 1676, I, W, P29/H/50, P29/1Reg/206A
Isaac, Pickwick, Corsham, 1711, I, P29/H/85
Isaac, Corsham, 1715, marriage licence, P29/2Reg/10E
Isaac, carp., Pickwick, Corsham, 1716, I, W, P29/H/95, P29/2Reg/24B
Jacob, sen., yeo., Figh., 1740, W, P26/817
Jacob, Lyneham, 1762, AB, P3/H/1341
Jas., cordw., Corsham, 1715-16, AB, I, P29/H/91, P29/2Reg/16B
Jas., wheeler, Hilp., 1727, AB, I, P2/H/1220
Jas., gent., Slade Farm, Bradford A., 1731, W, P2/H/1260
Jas., widower, Avill's Farm, Corsham, 1746, AB, comm, W, P3/H/1226
Jas., tailor, Chipp., 1776, AB, W, P1/H/1238, P1/13Reg/101
Jas., yeo., Folly Lane, Melk., 1810, W, Wr, P2/1810/40
Jane, widow, Westrop, Corsham, 1650, AB, W, P29/H/37, P29/1Reg/145
Jane, widow, Easton, Corsham, 1682, AB, I, P29/H/54, P29/1Reg/214B
Jane, widow, Marl. St My., 1792, W, P1/H/1324, P1/14Reg/373
Joan, widow, Easton, Corsham, 1654, W, P29/1Reg/150
Joan, sp., Hilp., 1697, AB, I, W, P2/H/971

Jn., Poulshot, 1570, AB, P2/5Reg/89F
Jn., Goods, Corsham, 1595, W, P29/H/5, P29/1Reg/42B
Jn., sen., Thingley, Corsham, [1596], W, P29/H/7
Jn., husb., Poulshot, 1597, AB, I, P2/H/159
Jn., Corsham, 1614, AB, P29/H/18
Jn., yeo., Gastard, Corsham, 1639, W, P29/1Reg/135
Jn., Corsham, 1645, LA, P29/1Reg/143B
Jn., sen., yeo., Thingley, Corsham, 1663-64, I, W, P29/H/40, P29/1Reg/171
Jn., sen., Velly, Corsham, 1670-71, AB, I, W, P29/H/45, P29/1Reg/192, 195A
Jn., butcher, Chr. M., 1688, AB, I, P3/H/657
Jn., carp., Marl. St My., [1689], NW, P1/H/521
Jn., yeo., Velly Quarr, Corsham, 1701, W, P29/H/75
Jn., yeo., Thingley, Corsham, 1705, I, W, P29/H/78
Hulbard, Jn., butcher, Seagry, 1711, I, W, P1/H/668, P1/5Reg/94
Jn., yeo., Chipp., 1714, I, W, P3/H/938
Jn., widower, Corsham, 1720, marriage licence, P29/2Reg/31E
Jn., carp., Castle C., 1722, I, ren, P28/12
Jn., maltster, Corsham, 1724, I, W, P29/H/102
Jn., gent., Thingley, Corsham, 1738, W, P29/H/112
Jn., sen., blacksmith, Avill's Farm, Corsham, 1743, W, P3/H/1197
Jn., yeo., Chr. M., 1763, W, P1/H/1159, P1/12Reg/110B
Jn., Avill's Farm, Corsham, 1773, AB, P1/H/1227
Jn., Wick, Bps. C., 1775, AB, P24/1138
Jn., Chipp., 1781, AB, P3/H/1439
Jn., Devizes, 1795, AB, comm, P1/H/1334, P1/14Reg/533A
Jn., yeo., W. Kington, 1811, comm, W, Wr, P3/1811/7
Jn., farmer, W. Lavington, 1853, aff, D, O, W, Wr, P1/1853/19
Jn. Gallimore, Corsham, 1821, AB, ren, Wr, P3/1821/1
Lawr., yeo., Poulshot, 1639, I, W, P2/H/510
Mgt., widow, Corsham, [1598], W (NEP), P29/H/8
Margery, widow, Poulshot, 1667, I, W, P2/H/642
Mark, tailor, Gastard, Corsham, 1620, AB, I, W, P29/H/23, P29/1Reg/86
Martha, widow, Byde Mill, Corsham, 1717, I, copy I, W, P29/H/99, P29/2Reg/26
Hulberd, My., widow, Lacock, 1615, I, W, P3/H/114
My. Ann, sp., Wingfield, 1817, W, Wr, P1/1817/99
Matthew, woollen draper, Corsham (believed d.in Ireland), 1681, AB, note in Latin, I, P29/H/52, P29/1Reg/211C
Matthew, Corsham, 1699, I, W, P29/H/73, P29/1Reg/273
Hulberd, Nich., Gastard, Corsham, 1568, W, P29/H/2, P29/1Reg/9B
Hulbart, Nich., Box, 1569, W (NEP), P1/1Reg/25C
Nich., Box, 1570, W, P1/1Reg/111B
Nich., weaver, Hinton, Steeple A., 1594, I, W, P2/H/134
Nich., yeo., Poulshot, 1596, I (2), W, copy W, P2/H/152
Nich., Marl., 1683, AB, comm, P1/H/467
Oliver, W. Kington, 1785, AB, P3/H/1467
Peter, Sheldon, Chipp., 1650, W, P1/H/297
Richd., weaver, Easton Grey, 1624, I, NW, P3/H/191
Richd., gent., Imber, 1635, I, W, P1/H/225
Richd., sen., husb., Rowde, 1679, I, NW, P3/H/538
Richd., labourer, Biddestone St Nich., 1832, W, Wr, P3/1832/23
Hulberd, Robt., husb., Corsham, 1590, W, draft W, P29/H/3, P29/1Reg/28
Robt., husb., Whitley, Melk., 1668, AB, comm, I, ren, P2/H/650
Robt., husb., Gt. Amesb., 1676, AB, I, P2/H/734
Robt., broad weaver, Corsham, 1683, AB, I, P29/H/55, P29/1Reg/217A
Robt., gent., Ridge, Corsham, 1713, W, P3/H/934
Sarah, widow, Chipp., 1776, AB, P1/H/1250
Sarah, sp., Lippiatts, Corsham, 1818, comm, W, Wr, P3/1818/9
Hulberd, Thos., Poulshot, [1561], I, P2/H/13
Hulberd, Thos., yeo., Russells, Erlestoke, 1561, W (bequest of money to build house on R., E.), P2/4Reg/88E
Thos., Westwells, Corsham, 1603, I, P29/H/11
Hulberd, Thos., yeo., Lacock, 1610, W, P3/H/63

Thos., yeo., Easton, Corsham, 1620, AB, I, W, P29/H/24, P29/1Reg/87
Hulberd, Thos., no abode stated; proved at Sal., 1630, I, P5/1630/8
Thos., husb., Thingley Bridge, Corsham, 1644-45, I, W, P29/H/36, P29/1Reg/143A
Thos., broad weaver, Gastard, Corsham, 1655, AB, I, W, P29/H/38, P29/1Reg/156
Thos., Velly Quarr, Corsham, 1656, AB, I, P29/H/39, P29/1Reg/158A
Thos., husb., Chipp., 1667, AB, comm, I, P3/H/393
Thos., Rowde, 1672, AB, I, P3/H/469
Thos., jun., gent., Easton, Corsham, 1675, AB, I, P29/H/49, P29/1Reg/202A
Thos., sen., gent., Easton, Corsham, 1675, I, W, P29/H/48, P29/1Reg/202B
Thos., yeo., Westrop, Corsham, 1692, AB, W, P29/H/65, P29/1Reg/254
Thos., yeo., Ridge, Corsham, 1697, I, W, P29/H/71, P29/1Reg/267C
Thos., gent., Easton, Corsham, [1704], W, P29/H/77
Thos., market spinner, Pickwick, Corsham, 1708, I, W, P29/H/82
Thos., grocer, Corsham, 1715, I (detailed), W, P29/H/96
Thos., shopkeeper, Corsham, 1716, W, P29/2Reg/16A
Thos., Lippiatts, Corsham, 1718, AB, P29/2Reg/28E
Thos., Brinkw., 1720, AB, P1/H/764
Thos., narrow weaver, Catcomb, Hilmarton, 1721, AB, I, P3/H/983
Thos., Hilmarton, 1729, AB, P1/H/863
Thos., yeo., Pickwick, Corsham, 1771, W, P29/H/118, P29/2Reg/141
Thos., carp., Pickwick, Corsham, 1790, W, P3/H/1496
Thos., innholder, Sutton B., 1823, W, Wr, P1/1823/61
Thos., yeo., Atworth, Bradford A., 1825, W, Wr, P2/1825/35
Thos., Nettleton, 1831, W, P3/1831/38
Thos. Hy., Corsham, 1827, comm, W, Wr, P3/1827/49
Hulberd, Wm., Poulshot, 1543, W (NEP), P2/1Reg/7
Hulberd, Wm., gent., Poulshot, 1559, W, P2/3Reg/180D
Wm., Westrop, Corsham, [1597], W, P29/H/9
Wm., yeo., Rowden, Chipp., late 16th C., W (NEP), P3/1Reg/29
Wm., fuller, Thingley, Corsham, 1616, I, P29/H/19
Wm., yeo., Byde Mill, Corsham, 1681-82, AB, I, P29/H/53, P29/1Reg/212A
Wm., yeo., Easton, Corsham, 1706, I (detailed), W, P29/H/80
Wm., carp., Colerne, 1707, AB, comm, I, P3/H/878
Wm., yeo., Corsham, 1710, AB, I, P29/H/84, P29/1Reg/284B
Wm., yeo., Langley Burrell, 1712, comm, W, P3/H/923
Wm., yeo., Byde Mill, Corsham, 1712, I, W, P29/H/87
Wm., yeo., Westrop, Corsham, 1713, AB, ren, P29/H/88, P29/1Reg/303
Wm., yeo., Rudside, Corsham, 1713-14, I, W, P29/H/90, P29/2Reg/4C
Wm., baker, Corsham, 1728, marriage licence, P29/2Reg/54A
Hulbart, Wm., Brinkw., 1741, AB, P1/H/988
Wm., Chelworth, Crudwell, 1743, AB, comm, P3/H/1198
Wm., gent., Westrop, Corsham, 1772, W, P29/H/119, P29/2Reg/153
Wm., gent., Lippiatts, Corsham, [1787], W, P29/H/124, P29/2Reg/194
Wm., gent., Melk., 1829, W, Wr, P1/1829/98
see also Hurlbatt *or* H.; Pinnell alias H.
Hulbrough *see* Holborow
Hulcomb *see* Halcomb
Hulcup, Amy, widow, Fyfield Wick, Berks., 1723, I, W, P1/H/802, P1/6Reg/463B
Benj., grocer, Wantage, Berks., 1812, W, Wr, P5/1812/10
Jn., yeo., Fyfield, Bray, Berks., 1773, W, P1/H/1223, P1/12Reg/475B
Jos., tallow chandler, Wantage, Berks., 1796, comm, W, P23/804
Richd., yeo., Charney Bassett, Longworth, Berks., 1714, W, P1/H/700, P1/5Reg/388
Thos., Fyfield, Berks., 1726, AB, I, P1/H/818
Hulett *see* Hewlett
Hull, Ann, widow, Gillingham, Dorset, 1730, W, P27/1/304
Ann, wife of Jn., Oborne, Dorset, 1781, AB, P5/1781/12, P5/17Reg/206B
Edith, Butterwick aka Boyes Hill, Haydon *or* Holnest, Dorset, 1640, I, W, P5/1640/32, P5/13Reg/230
Edwd., tailor, Sherb., Dorset, 1625, AB, a/c, I, P5/1625/44, P5/10Reg/288B
Edwd., yeo., Maiden B., [1681], I, W, P2/H/785
Eleanor, Sherb., Dorset, 1582, W, P5/4Reg/42A

Francis, sen., butcher, Chr. M., 1683, AB, I, P3/H/587
Francis, butcher, Kington L., 1688, I, W, P3/H/658
Geo., Mere, 1636, AB, a/c, I, P5/1636/33, P5/12Reg/253C
Geo., [weaver], Mere, 1679-80, AB, a/c, I, P5/1679/43, P5/1680/18
Geo., linen weaver, Mere, 1695, I, NW, P5/1695/41
Geo., thatcher, Oborne, Dorset, 1775, comm, W, P5/1775/11, P5/17Reg/85A
Geo., yeo., Donhead St My., 1851, aff, O, W, Wr, P1/1851/24
Hannah, widow, Chetnole, Yetm., Dorset, 1774, W, P19/173
Hy., yeo., N. Wootton, Dorset, 1638-39, comm, I, NW, P5/1638/56, P5/13Reg/155A
Hy., Chitterne, 1841, AB, Wr, P2/1841/38
Hy. Sampson, Oborne, Dorset, 1772, AB, comm, P5/1772/11, P5/17Reg/47B
Jas., yeo., N. Wootton, Dorset, 1591, I, W, P5/1591/45, P5/5Reg/105
Jas., Semley, 1853, aff, W, Wr, P2/1853/51
Jas., gent., Rowde, 1856, aff, O, W, Wr, P3/1856/30
Jane, sp., Gillingham, Dorset, 1830, W, Wr, P27/1/691
Jasper, Mkt. L., 1669, AB, comm, P2/H/662
Joan, widow, Broughton G., 1560, W. No date of probate given, P1/2Reg/99B
Jn., Hill D., 1592-93, AB, I, T, W, P5/1592/48, P5/6Reg/10B
Jn., husb., Allweston, Folke, Dorset, 1597, I, W, P5/1597/61, P5/6Reg/156D
Jn., Beam., Dorset, 1600, I, T, W, P5/1600/33, P5/6Reg/250C
Jn., husb., Thornford, Dorset, 1604, AB, I, W, P5/1604/23, P5/8Reg/11E
Jn., Boys Hill, Holnest, Dorset, 1619, AB, appt of proctor, I, P5/1619/29, P5/9Reg/229D
Jn., yeo., Bishopstone N., 1678, I, W, P6/45
Jn., jun., Allweston, Folke, Dorset, 1692, I, NW, P5/1692/38
Jn., yeo., Boys Hill, Holnest, Dorset, 1749, W, Wr, P5/1749/30
Jn., yeo., Sherb., Dorset, 1794, W, P5/1794/13, P5/18Reg/201C
Jos., clothier, Frankleigh, Bradford A., 1745, L, W, copy W, P2/H/1358
Jos., sen., butcher, Chr. M., 1783, W, P3/H/1450
Jos., sen., yeo., Chr. M., 1823, W, Wr, P1/1823/64
Jos., widower, Chr. M., 1847, AB, Wr, P3/1847/22
Mgt., widow, Chipp., 1850, O, W, Wr, P3/1850/17
Margery, sp., Gillingham, Dorset, 1610, AB, I, P5/1610/34, P5/9Reg/24B
My., sp., Warm., 1672, AB, NW, P2/H/696
My., Hill D., 1673, AB, P5/1672/18
My., widow, Sherb., Dorset, 1823, W, Wr, P5/1823/7
Matthew, gent., Bere R., Dorset, 1638, I (2 - 1 a draft), ren, P5/1638/50
Matthew, gent., Bere R., Dorset, 1640, AB, I, P5/1640/33, P5/13Reg/226A
Richd., sen., Chr. M., 1620, AB, a/c, I, P3/H/154
Richd., Hill D., 1671, a/c, D, I, P5/1670/73
Richd., Brixton D., 1708, AB, P1/H/654
Richd., butcher, Chr. M., 1720, I, summary I, W, P1/H/781, P1/6Reg/265A
Richd., yeo., Gillingham, Dorset, 1756, W, P27/1/415, P27/3Reg/76
Robt., yeo., Chr. M., 1811, AB, W, Wr, P1/1811/98
Sam., Sherb., Dorset, 1819, AB, Wr, P5/1819/7
Sam., Clack, Lyneham, Chr. M. & Chipp., 1844, AB, comm (re land in C., L., title given from 1732; of C.M. in 1810 & buried there 1843; then living in Ch.), P3/1844/50
Susanna, widow, Worton, Pott., 1714, W, P1/H/709, P1/5Reg/445
Thos., clerk, Caundle Marsh, Dorset, 1586, I, W, P5/1585/26, P5/4Reg/126B
Thos., yeo., Caundle Marsh, Dorset, 1601, AB, I, P5/1601/23, P5/7Reg/22C
Thos., sen., yeo., Caundle Marsh, Dorset, 1635, I, W, P5/1635/51, P5/12Reg/208C
Thos., Bishopstone N., 1672, I, W, P6/164
Thos., Boys Hill, Holnest, Dorset, 1684, AB, comm, I, P5/1684/27
Thos., yeo., Boys Hill, Holnest, Dorset, 1713, I, W, P5/1713/44, P5/15Reg/373A
Hulls, Thos., draper, Westrop, Highw., 1714, W, P10/1714/4
Thos., Brixton D., 1792, AB, P1/H/1323, P1/14Reg/365A
Thos., yeo., Gillingham, Dorset, 1832, comm, W, Wr, P27/1/700
Thos., wheelwright, Sal., 1834, W, Wr, P4/1834/6
Thos., Chr. M., 1842, AB, O, Wr, P3/1842/37
Wm., sen., yeo., Bishopstone N., 1662, comm, I, W, P5/1662/55
Wm., yeo., Worton, Pott., 1685, I, W, P1/H/491

Wm., yeo., Bishopstone N., 1741, AB, W, P6/129
Wm., maltster, Sherb., Dorset, 1750, W, P5/1750/19
Wm., yeo., Chr. M., 1788, AB, W, P3/H/1484
Wm., Sal., 1797, AB, Wr, P4/1797/8
Wm., wheelwright, Nether C., Dorset, 1821, W, Wr, P5/1821/32
see also Wickham alias H.
Humber, Ann, widow, Leigh, Yetm., Dorset, 1771, W, P19/168
Anthony, Brinkw., 1641, AB, I, P3/H/334
Eleanor, widow, Broad H., 1687, I, W, P3/H/646
Eliz., widow, Bodenham, Nunton and B., 1685, I (2), W, P2/H/849
Joan, Britford, 1565, W, P5/1Reg/39A
Jn., husb., Plaitford, 1559, I, W, P2/H/9, P2/4Reg/16B
Jn., blacksmith, Leigh, Yetm., Dorset, 1758, comm, W, P5/1758/26
Mark, Wootton B., 1629, AB, a/c, I, P3/H/231
Philip, sen., yeo., Sutton M., 1609, I, W, P2/H/249, P2/8Reg/48D
Philip, Swallowcliffe, 1666, AB, P5/1665/45
Richd., Broad H., 1638, AB, I, P3/H/310
Richd., Broad H., 1686, comm, W, P1/H/501
Richd., labourer, N. Tidworth, 1784, W, P2/H/1610
Thos., Sutton M., 1550, W, P2/2Reg/110C
Walter, Hindon, 1694, I, W, P2/H/952
Humbleton, Jn. Jas., Malm., 1662, AB, I, P1/H/331
Humby, [...], husb., Pensworth, Downton, 1599, NW, P2/H/181
Ambrose, sen., Downton, 1691, AB, I, P2/H/920
Barnabas, cooper, Downton, 1727, W, P1/H/835, P1/7Reg/168A
Deborah, widow, Downton, 1721, W, P2/H/1186
Elisha, carp., Wilton, 1822, W, Wr, P2/1822/52
Eliz., Pensworth, Downton, 1572, W, P2/5Reg/157A
Eliz., widow, Pensworth, Downton, 1665, cit, P2/H/635
Hy., Downton, 1598, AB, I, W, P2/H/176
Hy., husb., Redlynch, Downton, 1647, AB, I, P2/H/586
Hy., sen., yeo., Pensworth, Downton, 1712, W, P2/H/1105
Hy., farmer, Pensworth, Downton, 1733, W, P2/H/1265
Hy., Pensworth, Downton, 1759, AB, P2/H/1439
Hy., Downton, 1854, AB, aff, O, Wr, P2/1854/45
Jane, widow, Downton, 1773, W, P1/H/1229, P1/13Reg/32
Joan, Britford, 1611, I, W, P24/137
Jn., husb., Britford, 1605, I, W, P24/23
Hombie, Jn., yeo., Pensworth, Downton, 1624, I, W, P2/H/374
Jn., yeo., Redlynch, Downton, 1678, I, W, P2/H/749
Jn., yeo., Pensworth, Downton, [1683], I, W, P2/H/818
Jn., Downton, 1786, AB, P1/H/1300
Jn., blacksmith, Charlton, Downton, 1804, W, P1/1804/5, P1/15Reg/398
Jn., blacksmith, Charlton, Downton, 1824, W, Wr, P2/1824/19
Jn., blacksmith, Downton, 1853, W, Wr, P2/1853/33
Jos., yeo., Downton, 1727, I, W, P2/H/1215
Jos., bach., Longford, Britford, 1729, AB, I, P24/827
Mgt., widow, Charlton, Downton, 1850, AB, Wr, P2/1850/42
My., widow, Downton, 1744-45, AB (2), grant of probate, P2/H/1350
My., sp., Burcombe, 1809, AB, Wr, P2/1809/8
My., widow, Fisherton A., 1829, W, Wr, P1/1829/65
Moses, Downton, 1732, AB, P2/H/1261
Nich., yeo., Pensworth, Downton, 1738, W, P1/H/970, P1/8Reg/358B
Rawbenat, widow, Downton, 1730, W, P2/H/1242
Hormibie, Richd., Redlynch, Downton, 1611, I, W, P2/H/282
Richd., Downton, 1755, AB, P2/H/1412
Robt., Redlynch, Downton, 1633, AB, a/c, I, P2/H/447, P2/9Reg/23B
Robt., Redlynch, Downton, 1647, AB, P2/H/590
Robt., yeo., Downton, 1747, W, P2/H/1366
Sam., blacksmith, Downton, 1737, W, P2/H/1303

Thos., yeo., Downton, 1737, AB, W, P2/H/1299
Thos., sen., Bower C., 1841, W, Wr, P2/1841/41
Wm., husb., Redlynch, Downton, 1566, W, P2/4Reg/238A
Wm., Redlynch, Downton, 1671, AB, I, P2/H/688
Wm., yeo., Black Lane, Downton, 1723, AB, I, ren (2), P1/H/789
Wm., W. Harnham, 1841, AB, Wr, P8/91
Humfrey, Humfry *see* Humphries
Hummes, Lawr., tailor, Clench, Milton L., 1630, I, W, P3/H/244
Humphries, Humphry, Abraham, tiler, Pickwick, Corsham, 1674, I, W, P29/H/47, P29/1Reg/200C
Humphrys, Abraham, tiler and plasterer, Pickwick, Corsham, 1768, AB, ren, W, P3/H/1380
Abraham, widower, Bromham, 1856, AB, aff, O, Wr, P3/1856/27
Humfry, Alice, widow, Swindon, 1629, I, W, P3/H/232
Humphrys, Ambrose, gent., Westrop, Highw., 1772, AB, comm, W, P10/1772/3
Humphreys, Ann, widow, Pickwick, Corsham, 1687, W, P29/1Reg/265B
Humphreys, Ann, widow, Pickwick, Corsham, 1696, I, W, P29/H/68
Humphrey, Ann, widow, Sal., 1728, AB, P4/1728/5
Humphrys, Ann, widow, Melk., 1801, W, P1/1801/90, P1/15Reg/308
Humphris, Ann, sp., Latton, 1812, W, Wr, P3/1812/44
Humphrey, Brian, Patney, 1647, AB, I, P2/H/593
Humphreys, Bridget, widow, Downton, 1699, AB, P2/H/990
Chas., rector, Fonthill B., 1776, W, P1/H/1247, P1/13Reg/141A
Humphry, Chris., Sal., 1639, I, W, P4/1639/7
Humfry, Cicely, widow, Donhead St A., 1630, I, NW, P2/H/418, P2/9Reg/84B
Humphrys, Dan., victualler, Kington St M., 1756, AB, comm, ren, P3/H/1298
Humphreys, David, curate, Homington, 1731, W, P24/815
Humphreys, Edith, sp., Alderton, 1678, AB, I, P3/H/535
Edwd., baker, Sal., 1673, AB, I, NW, P4/1672/17
Humphry, Edwd., yeo., Stockton, 1680, I, W, P2/H/783
Edwd., Edington, 1802, AB, P2/1802/41
Umfries, Eleanor, Gt. Somerford, 1608, AB, P3/UV/3
Humfry, Eleanor, widow, E. Hagbourne, Berks., 1732, W, P1/H/890, P1/7Reg/462
Humphrys, Eleanor, widow, Easton, Corsham, 1737, AB, I, W, P3/H/1149, P29/H/111
Humfry, Eleanor, widow, Blewbury, Berks., 1738, W, Wr, P5/1738/25
Humphry, Eliz., widow, Maddington, 1627, AB, I, P2/H/389
Umfries, Eliz., husb., Purton Stoke, 1633, I, W, P3/UV/20
Humphreys, Eliz., widow, Westb., 1724, W, P25/1724/3
Humphry, Eliz., sp., Kingston D., 1779, ren, W, P1/H/1256, P1/13Reg/283
Humphris, Eliz., wife, N. Bradley, 1804, AB, comm, P2/1804/12
Umphrey, Ellen, widow, W. Kington, 1606, I, W, P1/UV/4
Umphrey, Frances, Amesb., 1620, I, copy W, W, P2/UV/28
Humfry, Frances, blacksmith's widow, Corsley, 1716, W, P1/H/731, P1/6Reg/68
Umphrey, Geo., Edington, 1582, W, P2/6Reg/69A
Humphry, Geo., Donhead St A., [1615], I, P2/H/304
Humphrys, Geo., Latton, 1750, AB, P3/H/1258
Geo., tailor, Bradford A., 1851, O, W, Wr, P1/1851/20
Umphrey, Gilbert, Nettleton, 1641, I, NW, P3/UV/21
Humphry, Gilbert, carp., Mere, 1688, AB, I, P5/1688/37
Humfry, Giles, sen., woollen draper, Chipp., 1639, I, W, P3/H/317
Humphrys, Grace, widow, Westrop, Highw., 1742, W, P10/1742/1
Humphrys, Hy., yeo., Eastrop, Highw., 1688, I (over £650), W, P5/1688/36
Humphry, Hy., sen., rough mason, Upper Stratton, Stratton St Mgt., 1691, comm, I, W, P3/H/703
Humphris, Hy., gent., Eastrop, Highw., 1772, W, P10/1772/4
Hy., labourer, Baulking, Uffington, Berks., 1826, comm, W, Wr, P1/1826/132
Hester, widower, Corsley, 1851, W, Wr, P1/1851/44
Humphrys, Honour, sp., Highw., 1789, note, W, P10/1789/1
Humfrey, Ilbury, yeo., Blewbury, Berks., 1755, I, W, P5/1755/25
Humphrys, Isaac, baker, Chipp., 1756, W, P3/H/1299
Humphrys, Isaac, sen., gent., Chipp., 1765, W, P3/H/1355
Humphreys, Isaac, victualler, Shepton Mallet, Somerset (leaving effects at Stockton), 1833, W, Wr, P2/1833/71
Humphreys, Jas., gent., Westb., 1713, AB, ren, P25/1713/7

Humphrys, Jas., clothier, Easton, Corsham, 1722, AB, ren, P3/H/999
Humphris, Jas., sen., broad weaver, Bowden Hill, Lacock, 1744, W, P1/H/1023, P1/9Reg/407A
Humphrys, Jas., Lacock, 1760, AB, P3/H/1322
Humphrys, Jas., gent., Melk., 1823, comm, W, Wr, P2/1823/13
Jas., grocer, Corsley, 1845, W, Wr, P1/1845/37
Humphris, Jane, widow, Westrop, Highw., 1685, W (NEP), P10/1685/6
Humphrys, Jane, widow, Latton, 1749, AB, I, W, P3/H/1255
Jane, sp., N. Bradley (form. of Beckington, Somerset), 1777, AB, W, P2/H/1568
Humphrys, Job, blacksmith, Corsley, 1769, W, P2/H/1520
Job Cooper, bach., Upper Canada, Canada (effects at Warm.), 1832, AB, O, Wr, P1/1832/142
Humfrey, Jn., Donhead St A., 1559, W, P2/4Reg/17B
Humphrey, Jn., carp., Tinh., Edington, 1562, I, W, P2/H/17, P2/4Reg/96B
Humphry, Jn., husb., W. Kington, 1570, W (NEP), P1/1Reg/54B
Humphry, Jn., Brixton D., 1597, I, W, P2/H/165
Umphrey, Jn., widow, Patney, [1627], I, W (NEP), P2/UV/40
Humphry, Jn., Horningsham, 1641, I, W, P5/1641/42, P5/14Reg/42A
Humphry, Jn., Corsham, 1649, LA, P29/1Reg/144A
Humfry, Jn., Stourton, 1673, AB, a/c, I, P2/H/706
Humfrey *or* Humphreys, Jn., sen., Westb., 1681, I, W, P25/1680/5
Humphreys, Jn., yeo., Bushton, Clyffe P., 1686, AB, I, P3/H/628
Humphreys, Jn., Bps. C., 1689, AB, alleg, comm, I, P24/732
Humphry, Jn., Pewsey, 1689, AB, P1/H/513
Humphrey, Jn., carp., Stourton, 1695, AB, I, P1/H/570
Humphreys, Jn., weaver, Corsham, 1704, AB, P29/H/76, P29/1Reg/283B
Humfry, Jn., carp., Maiden B., 1709, W, P2/H/1065
Humphris, Jn., gent., Broad B., Highw., 1712, W, P10/1712/5
Humfrey, Jn., yeo., Blewbury, Berks., 1736, W, P5/1736/18
Humphris, Jn., sen., mason, Latton, 1743, a/c, aff, cit, I (2), W, P3/H/1199
Humphrys, Jn., Horningsham, 1744, AB, Wr, P5/1744/24
Humphrys, Jn., Brixton D., 1748, W, P2/H/1370
Humphrys, Jn., Latton, 1755, AB, P3/H/1292
Humphrys, Jn., wheelwright, Latton (now resident in city of London), 1758, W, P3/H/1313
Humphris, Jn., husb., Uffcott, Broad H., 1779, W, P3/H/1432
Humphrys, Jn., carp., Malm., 1836, W, Wr, P3/1836/31
Humphris, Jonathan, Tinh., Edington, 1800, W, P2/1800/71
Humfry, Leonard, husb., Maiden B., 1639, AB, I, note, P2/H/515
Humphrys, Leonard, blacksmith, Whitbourne, Corsley, 1748, W, P2/H/1372
Humphrys, Mgt., widow, Eastrop, Highw., 1631, AB, deed of gift (2), W, P5/1631/49, P5/12Reg/73C
Humphris, Mgt., widow, Somerford K., 1729, W, P3/H/1065
My., widow, Broad Town, Clyffe P., 1676, AB, a/c, I, P3/H/514
Humphry, My., W. Yatton, Yatton K., 1685, I, W, P3/H/621
Humphrys, My., widow, Highw., 1759, W, P10/1759/2
My., widow, S. Wraxall, 1848, D, O, W, Wr, P2/1848/36
Humfrey, Michael, husb., Whitbourne, Corsley, 1635, I, copy I, W, P2/H/470
Humfry, Michael, husb., Woodlands, Mere, 1640, AB, a/c, I, P5/1639/37, P5/13Reg/222A
Humphry, Michael, Kingston D., 1716, W, P1/H/729, P1/6Reg/35B
Humphrys, Michael, yeo., Kingston D., 1829, W, Wr, P2/1829/13
Humfry, Nich., Homanton, Maddington, 1593, AB, I, P2/H/125
Umphrey, Nich., widow, Homanton, Maddington, 1626, a/c, P2/UV/41
Humphreys, Nich., Westb., 1739-48, AB (2), P25/1739/4, P25/1748/1
Humfrey, Peter, Sal. St Martin, 1620, I, W, P4/1620/8
Humphrys, Rebecca, widow, Leigh, Ashton K., 1749, W, P3/H/1254
Humphrys, Rebecca, widow, Malm., 1849, D, O, W, Wr, P3/1849/28
Umphrey, Richd., widow, Swindon, 1604, I, W, P3/UV/1
Humphrey, Richd., yeo., Brixton D., 1667, comm, I, NW, P2/H/644
Humfry, Richd., mason, Yatton K., 1677, AB, a/c, I, P3/H/523
Humphrey, Richd., Maiden B., 1686, AB, I, P2/H/865
Humphrey, Richd., Devizes, 1690, AB, comm, P1/H/530
Humphrys, Richd., rector, Draycot C., 1712, AB, P1/H/687
Humphreys, Richd., gardener, Sal., 1719, I, W, P4/1719/6

Humphrys, Richd., yeo., Motc., Dorset, 1729, AB, W, P27/1/287
Humphris, Richd., mason, Westrop, Highw., 1733, W, P10/1733/6
Humphrys, Richd., innholder, Highw., 1745, W, P10/1745/8
Humphreys, Richd., yeo., Uffcott, Broad H., 1757, W, P3/H/1305
Humphrys, Richd., Fonthill G., 1771, AB, W, P2/H/1528
Humphrys, Richd., hairdresser, Highw., 1805, W, P10/1805/2
Humfrey, Robt., Wokm., Berks., 1545, W, P5/20Reg/65B
Humfrey, Robt., Brixton D., 1547, W, P2/2Reg/34
Humfrey, Robt., innholder, Sal., 1595, AB, I, W, P1/H/18
Humfrey, Robt., Shrewton, 1629, I, W, P2/H/409
Robt., yeo., Broad Town, Clyffe P., 1674, I, W, P3/H/488
Humphrys, Robt., innholder, Wantage, Berks., 1722, W, P23/413
Humphrys, Robt., sen., barber, Highw., 1742, W, P10/1742/3
Robt., Highw., 1761, AB, P5/1761/24
Humfreys, Roger, servant to Jn. [Davenant], bishop of Salisbury, Sal. The Close, 1641, W, P5/1641/43
Humphrys, Sarah, scribler's wife, Chipp., 1755, AB, P3/H/1293
Humphrys, Sarah, widow, Chipp., 1774, W, P3/H/1408
Humfry, Stephen, jun., yeo., Fields Court, Corsley, 1710, W, P2/H/1082
Humfry, Stephen, sen., blacksmith, Corsley, 1716, AB, W, P1/H/730, P1/6Reg/67
Humfrey, Theodore, gent., Damerham, Hants, 1630, I, W, P2/H/422
Humfreys, Thos., weaver, Keevil, 1587, I, W, P2/H/77, P2/7Reg/84B
Humfrey, Thos., Patney, 1600, AB, I, W, P2/H/189
Humfrey, Thos., husb., Stratton St Mgt., 1609, W, P3/H/53
Humphrey, Thos., husb., Donhead St My., 1612, AB, I, P2/H/285
Humphry, Thos., yeo., Patney, 1663-64, AB, I, W, P1/H/357, P2/H/620
Humphrey, Thos., husb. and yeo., Kingston D., 1671, I, W, P2/H/682
Humphry, Thos., Nettleton, 1684, AB, I, P3/H/601
Humphreys, Thos., yeo., Allington, Chipp., 1689, I, NW, P1/H/524
Humphrey, Thos., Kingston D., 1691, AB, P2/H/923
Humphrey, Thos., no abode stated, [1693], I, P2/H/940
Humphris, Thos., sen., Broad Town, Clyffe P., 1709, I, W, P3/H/902
Humphris, Thos., glazier, Swindon, 1711, I, W, P1/H/673, P1/5Reg/147
Humphreys, Thos., Corsley, 1714, AB, P2/H/1117
Humphrys, Thos., Stockton, 1719, AB, P2/H/1166
Humphris, Thos., blacksmith, Somerford K., 1725, W, P3/H/1025
Humphrys, Thos., Broad Town, Clyffe P., 1726, AB, P1/H/825
Humfrey, Thos., maltster, Blewbury, Berks., 1733, W, P5/1733/29
Humphrys, Thos., Westb., 1760, AB, P25/1760/5
Humphreys, Thos., clerk and curate, Plaitford, 1762, W, P2/H/1458
Humphrys, Thos., shopkeeper, Stockton, 1784, W, P2/H/1611
Humphris, Thos., Pewsey, 1795, AB, P1/H/1344, P1/14Reg/622A
Humphrys, Thos., shopkeeper, Stockton, 1802, W, P2/1802/51
Humphris, Thorold, yeo., Winterbourne M., 1773, AB, ren, W, P1/H/1225, P1/12Reg/502
Humphry, Timothy, Amesb., 1672, AB, I, P2/H/699
Umphrey, Wm., husb., Orcheston St My., [1550?], I, note of bequests, P2/UV/1
Umphrey, Wm., husb., Patney, 1559, W, P2/4Reg/24A
Humfrey, Wm., sen., Corsham, 1600, AB, NW, P29/H/10
Humfry, Wm., yeo., Pickwick, Corsham, 1618, I, W, P29/H/22, P29/1Reg/82
Humfreys, Wm., sen., yeo., Westb., 1666, AB, comm, I, P25/1666/2
Humphrey, Wm., husb., Heywood, Westb., 1674, AB, a/c, I, P25/1674/3
Humphry, Wm., Collwood, Corsham, 1685, I (dorse shows scribbled names, parts of formularies, Greek & Latin phrases, sketches of decorative letters, a face etc.), NW, P29/H/58
Humfrey, Wm., yeo., Pickwick, Corsham, 1691, I, W, P3/H/704
Humphreys, Wm., Lacock, 1700, AB, I, P3/H/801
Humphry, Wm., yeo., Westwells, Corsham, 1721, AB, I, W, P29/H/100, P29/2Reg/35
Humphris, Wm., quarrier, Swindon, 1737, W, P3/H/1148
Humphrys, Wm., yeo., Westb., 1745, AB, ren, W, P25/1745/10
Humphris, Wm., Rockley, Ogbourne St A., 1752, W, P5/1752/28
Humphrys, Wm., Hindon, 1759, AB, P2/H/1442
Humphrys, Wm., Edington, 1767, AB, P2/H/1494

Humphris, Wm., grocer, Swindon, 1767, AB, ren, W, P1/H/1187, P1/12Reg/205
Humphris, Wm., stone cutter, Swindon, 1778, W, P3/H/1429
Humphreys, Wm., innholder, Kington St M., 1788, W, P3/H/1485
Wm., shopkeeper, Pewsey, 1794, W, P3/H/1513
Humphreys, Wm., carp., Sal., 1808, W, Wr, P1/1808/53
Wm., victualler, Wantage, Berks., 1836, O, W, P23/985
Wm., yeo., Keevil, 1841, W, Wr, P2/1841/36
Wm., gent., Corsley, 1843, comm, W, Wr, P2/1843/5
see also Browne alias H.
Hundy *see* Handy
Hungerford, Anthony, gent., Leigh, Ashton K., 1618, I, W, P3/H/136
Geo., gent., Leigh, Ashton K., 1631, AB, a/c, comm, I, P3/H/250
Jas., Fovant, 1628, AB, I, P1/H/173
Jane, widow, Leigh, Ashton K., 1608, I, W, P3/H/40
Jn., Burton Hill, Malm., 1612, AB, P3/H/91
Jn. *see also* My. Crook
Susanna, dame and widow, Calne, 1693, AB, P26/418
Thos., gent., Kington St M., 1665, I, P3/H/374
Hunkeles *see* Uncles
Hunny *see* Honey
Hunsdon, Alexander, gent., Sal., [1593], W, copy W, P1/H/11
Jn., sen., chandler, Wantage, Berks., 1676, AB, I (detailed), ren, P23/63
Hunt, (widow), Compton, Enford, [1620], I, P2/H/348
Ambrose, Fordington, Dorset, 1588, W, P5/5Reg/22B
Ambrose, sen., Fordington, Dorset, 1662, I, W, P5/1662/64
Ambrose, yeo., Pott., 1668, I, W, P1/H/383
Ambrose, Fordington, Dorset, 1681, AB, a/c, I, P15/36
Ambrose, yeo., Melk., 1738, I, W, P1/H/971, P1/8Reg/367
Andrew, Damerham, Hants, 1634, AB, I, P2/H/459, P2/9Reg/39C
Ann, widow, Figh., 1675, I, W, P26/230
Ann, widow, Studley, Calne, 1677, I, W, P26/246
Ann, Fordington, Dorset, 1686, AB, I, P15/58
Ann, widow, Newbury, Berks., 1726, W, P1/H/819, P1/7Reg/110A
Ann, widow, Marston, Pott., 1737, I, W, P1/H/947, P1/8Reg/189
Ann, minor, Barford St M., 1738, T, P1/H/968
Ann, widow, Broughton G., 1749, W, P2/H/1383
Ann, widow, Marden, 1784, W, P2/H/1608
Ann, widow, Chipp., 1845, O, W, Wr, P3/1845/20
Anthony, husb., Pewsey, 1673, AB, I, P3/H/481
Barnaby, husb., Longbridge D., 1639, I, W, P2/H/514
Bernard, husb., Damerham, Hants, 1563, I, W, P2/H/25, P2/4Reg/147A
Betty, sp., Beam., Dorset, 1855, aff, comm, W, Wr, P17/628
Caleb, yeo., Warm., 1707, I, W, P2/H/1055
Chas., collarmaker, Wanb., 1737, AB, I, P3/H/1150
Christian, Fordington, Dorset, 1600, AB, P5/1600/30, P5/6Reg/246
Chris., tailor, Mere, 1684, I, W, P5/1684/28
Dan., Poulshot, 1743, AB, comm, P2/H/1345
Dan., Bromham, 1783, AB, comm, P1/H/1281
Denise, widow, Pitton, Alderbury, 1679, I, W, P26/267
Dorothy (?), widow, Hodson, Chiseldon, 1629, I, W, P3/H/234
Durant, vicar choral, Sal. The Close, [1671], W (NEP), P4/1671/22
Edith *or* Edna, widow, Marston, Pott., 1630, I, W, P1/H/182
Edith, widow, Sal. The Close, 1681, AB, a/c, I, P5/1681/20
Hunt alias Wilsdon, Edwd., Holnest, Dorset, 1609, AB, P5/9Reg/2
Edwd., Hodson, Chiseldon, 1676, AB, a/c, I, P3/H/515
Edwd., yeo., Beam., Dorset, 1701, W, P17/138
Edwd., husb. and yeo., Baydon, 1710, I, W, P5/1710/57, P5/15Reg/219
Edwd., sen., innkeeper, *The Black Horse*, Cherhill, 1784, W, P26/1139
Edwd., yeo., Ham, 1802, AB, comm, W, P3/1802/77
Edwd., Ham, 1813, AB, comm, P3/1813/52

Edwd., Wrou., 1827, AB, comm, Wr, P3/1827/51
Edwd., farmer, Cherhill, 1836, comm, W, Wr, P26/1424
Eleanor, sp., Wilton, Gt. Bedwyn, 1673, I, NW, P21/2/38
Honte, Eleanor, Beam., Dorset, 1694, W, P17/111
Eleanor, widow, Fordington, Dorset, 1706, W, P15/85
Eliz., widow, Compton Breamore, Compton, Enford, 1590, I (2), W, P2/H/105
Eliz., widow, Fordington, Dorset, 1594, I, W, P5/1594/39, P5/6Reg/62B
Eliz., Cadley, Pott., 1619, AB, a/c, I, W, P1/H/131
Eliz., widow, Winterbourne E., 1630, I, W, P2/H/419
Eliz., widow, Damerham, Hants, [1686], I, W, P2/H/872
Eliz., sp., Marl., 1724, AB, W, P1/H/806, P1/7Reg/51A
Eliz., widow, Bulk., Keevil, 1747, W, P1/10Reg/172, P1/H/1041
Eliz., widow, Newtown, Durnford, 1787, W, P2/H/1629
Eliz., widow, Sal., 1854, aff, W, Wr, P4/1854/8
Geoffrey, husb., Lacock, 1679, I, P3/H/539
Gregory, gent., Stock, Gt. Bedwyn, 1714, I, W, P21/7/17
Hy., yeo., Lt. Hinton, 1687, I, W, P3/H/647
Hy., labourer, Ham, 1737, W, P3/H/1151
Hy., Wootton R., 1756, AB, P1/H/1125
Hy., Enford, 1773, D (2), note, NW, P1/H/1231, P1/13Reg/36
Hy., gent., Littlecott, Enford, 1776, W, P1/H/1246, P1/13Reg/137
Hester, widow, Hilmarton, 1826, comm, W, Wr, P1/1826/133
Hunt alias Robinson, Hugh, wooldriver, Chilton F., 1634, I, NW, P3/H/280
Isaac, sen., weaver, Chittoe, Bps. C., 1742, AB, I, W, P24/979
Isaac, yeo., Beversbrook, Hilmarton, 1780, W, P3/H/1437
Isaac, yeo., Brinkw., 1829, W, Wr, P1/1829/83
Jas., husb., Pitton, Alderbury, 1670, I, W, P26/163
Jas., cooper, Westb., 1752, W, P25/1752/4
Jas., W. Harnham, 1787, AB, P8/63
Jas., carp., Hilmarton, 1823, AB (part crossed out), W, P3/1823/24
Jas., carp., Ludg., 1833, W, Wr, P2/1833/73
Jas., miller, Ludg., 1849, D, W, Wr, P2/1849/51
Jane, widow, Warm., 1815, W, Wr, P2/1815/33
Jane, widow, Brinkw., 1825, W, Wr, P3/1825/35
Jennifer, sp., Pott., 1724, W, P1/H/807, P1/7Reg/51B
Joan, widow, Fordington, Dorset, 1609, AB, I, W, P5/1609/40, P5/8Reg/165C
Joan, Marl. St My., 1691, AB, I, copy I, P1/H/538
Joan, widow, Fordington, Dorset, 1700, I, W, P15/65
Joan, Pott., 1736, W, P1/H/943, P1/8Reg/149B
Job, collarmaker, Broad H., 1808, AB, W, Wr, P1/1808/38
Jn., Court St., Tisb., 1564-65, I, W, P2/H/29, P2/4Reg/166A
Jn., yeo., Woodshaw, Wootton B., 1591, I, W, P1/H/3
Jn., husb., Marston, Pott., 1597, I, W, P1/H/21
Jn., Pott., 1608, I, W, P1/H/59
Jn., yeo., Longbridge D., 1612, I, W, P2/H/295, P2/8Reg/179
Jn., miller, Winterbourne E., 1615, I, W, P2/H/310, P2/8Reg/285
Jn., Cadley, Pott., 1618, AB, a/c, I, P1/H/120
Jn., sen., yeo., Damerham, Hants, 1661, I (detailed), W, P2/H/611
Jn., husb., Figh., 1662, I, NW, P26/109
Hunt alias Taylor, Jn., yeo., Hodson, Chiseldon, 1672, AB, a/c (2), I, P3/H/471
Jn., yeo., Westlecott, Wrou., 1691, AB, I, P3/H/705
Jn., gent., S. Marston, 1695, AB, I, ren, P5/1695/50
Jn., sen., yeo., Marston, Pott., 1701, AB, I, ren, P1/H/613
Jn., yeo., Lopshill, Damerham, Hants, 1708, I, W, P1/H/647, P1/4Reg/288A
Jn., Figh., 1709, I, W, P26/555
Jn., yeo., Lyneham, 1710, I, W, P3/H/912
Jn., sen., yeo., Pott., 1715, I, copy I, W, P1/H/717, P1/5Reg/483B
Jn., gent., Ham, 1720, comm, W, P1/H/759, P1/6Reg/222
Jn., cordw., Marston, Pott., 1724, I, W, P1/H/808, P1/7Reg/52B
Jn., yeo., Damerham, Hants, 1725, W, P2/H/1211

Jn., baker, Pott., 1732, W, P1/H/915, P1/7Reg/560A
Jn., sen., Wanb., 1744, AB, P3/H/1213
Jn., yeo., Ham, 1750, W, P1/H/1075, P1/10Reg/383
Jn., Wanb., 1755, AB, P3/H/1294
Jn., yeo., Broad B., Highw., 1765, W, P10/1765/2
Jn., Bishopstone S., 1782, W, P2/H/1601
Jn., baker, Holt, Bradford A., 1783, W, P2/H/1605
Jn., husb., Brinkw., 1802, W, P3/1802/68
Jn., sen., butcher, Wootton B., 1805, W, P3/1805/19
Jn., yeo., *The Black Horse*, Cherhill, 1807, W, P26/1262
Jn., widower, Amesb., 1814, W, Wr, P1/1814/49
Jn., bach., Gillingham, Dorset, 1821, AB, comm, Wr, P27/1/654
Jn., labourer, Broad H., 1823, W, Wr, P1/1823/116
Jn., gent., Holt, Bradford A., 1825, W, Wr, P2/1825/19
Jn., Melk., 1840, AB, comm, Wr, P2/1840/56
Jn., labourer, Ludwell, Donhead St My., 1844, note, W, Wr, P2/1844/1
Jonas, victualler, Hilmarton, 1850, W, Wr, P3/1850/31
Jos., surgeon, Lambourn, Berks., 1750, AB, ren, W, P1/H/1060, P1/10Reg/293
Jos., tailor, Hilmarton, 1759, comm, W, P3/H/1316
Jos., carp., Hilmarton, 1813, W, Wr, P3/1813/65
Jos., carp. and joiner, Hilmarton (form. of Poole, Dorset), 1836, W, Wr, P3/1836/38
Jos., Marl., 1853, AB, aff, Wr, P1/1853/23
Lawr., sen., yeo., Ham, 1666, AB, comm, I, W, P3/H/382
Leonard, husb., Steeple L., 1558-59, I, W, P2/H/8, P2/3Reg/74B
Hunt alias Robinson, Mgt., widow, Hungerford, Berks., 1634, W, P5/12Reg/301
Martha, sp., Enford, 1713, AB, I, P2/H/1106
Martha, widow, Poulshot, 1751, comm, W, P2/H/1401
My., widow, Malm. Abbey, 1681, I, W, P3/H/561
My., Pott., 1713, AB, P1/H/688
My., widow, Ham, 1729, W, P3/H/1066
My., Ryme I., Dorset, 1734, AB, P5/1734/39
My., widow, Wanb., 1740, AB, comm, I, ren, I (detailed), P3/H/1170
My., widow, Enmore Grn, Motc., Dorset, 1749, W, P5/1749/29
My., widow, Warm., 1779, W, P1/H/1266, P1/13Reg/289
My., widow, Cholsey, Berks., 1784-86, W, P1/H/1302, P1/14Reg/125A
My., sp., Rodbourne C., 1802, W, P3/1802/40
My., widow, Leigh, Yetm., Dorset, 1816, W, P19/221
Matthew, sen., yeo., Ham, 1714, W, P1/H/704, P1/5Reg/418
Matthew, Sheerstocks, Gillingham, Dorset, 1724, NW, P27/1/269
Matthew, labourer, Enmore Grn, Motc., Dorset, 1743, W, Wr, P5/1743/44
Michael, fuller, Bulk., Keevil, 1743, W, P2/H/1341
Nich., yeo., Stock and Ford, Gt. Bedwyn, 1670, I, W, P21/2/19
Philip, maltster, Rowde, 1718, I, W, P3/H/963
Prudence, widow, Wantage, Berks., 1703, W, P23/261
Rachel, sp., Sherb., Dorset, 1755-57, W, copy W (NEP), P5/1755/20, P5/1757/16
Richd., yeo., Compton Breamore, Compton, Enford, 1579, I, T, W, P2/H/54, P2/5Reg/337C
Richd., weaver, Lyme R., Dorset, 1590, I, W, P5/1589/31, P5/5Reg/69C
Hount, Richd., no abode stated, [1676?], I, P2/H/733
Richd., gent., Warm., [1693], I, W, P2/H/929
Richd., sen., gent., Bradfield, Berks., 1729, W, P1/H/856, P1/7Reg/265A
Richd., edge toolmaker, Mere, 1734, W, P5/1734/40
Richd., yeo., Gt. Faringdon, Berks., 1734, I, W, P5/1734/41
Richd., sen., maltster, Everington, Yattendon, Berks., 1744, W, P1/H/1010, P1/9Reg/335
Richd. Matthews, Bps. C., 1817, AB, Wr, P24/1279
Robt., Damerham, Hants, 1560, AB (in minority of Mgt. & Beatrice H.), W, P2/4Reg/44B
Robt., Damerham, Hants, 1570, W, P2/5Reg/82C
Robt., Martin, Hants, 1572, AB, P2/5Reg/156D
Robt., apothecary, Sal., 1678, W, P4/1678/23
Robt., Whitep., 1694, AB, ren, P2/H/947
Robt., blacksmith, W. Common, Horningsham, 1730, W, Wr, P5/1730/34

Robt., Malm., 1737, AB, comm, P3/H/1152
Robt., Broad B., Highw., 1808, W, P10/1808/2
Sam., Dilton M., Westb., 1746, AB, P25/1746/2
Sarah, widow, Mildenhall, 1756, W, P1/H/1128, P1/11Reg/331B
Sarah, widow, Ham, 1802, W, P3/1802/59
Sibyl, widow, Amesb., 1610, NW, P2/H/273, P2/8Reg/139A
Stephen, clothworker, Frankleigh, Bradford A., 1730, W, P2/H/1245
Stephen, sen., innholder, Warm., 1774, W, P2/H/1539
Stephen, gent., Warm., 1854, aff, comm, W, Wr, P2/1854/50
Thos., Wokm., Berks., 1579-80, AB, a/c, I, T, P5/1579/39, P5/3Reg/139C
Thos., Durrington, 1596-1600, AB, I, P2/H/149
Thos., husb., Lyme R., Dorset, 1606, I, W, P5/1606/23, P5/8Reg/61
Thos., mason, Bradford A., 1613, AB, I, P2/H/297, P2/8Reg/185A
Thos., Compton, Enford, 1618, I, W, P2/H/330
Thos., gent., Longstreet, Enford, 1619, I, NW, P2/H/346
Thos., husb., S. Marston, 1627, NW, P10/1627/2
Thos., weaver, Sal., 1628, I, W, P4/1627/16
Thos., husb., Damerham, Hants, 1664-68, AB, a/c, I, W, P2/H/627
Thos., Fordington, Dorset, 1670, AB, comm, I, P5/1670/20
Thos., sen., gent., Marl., 1674, I, W, P1/H/424
Thos., surgeon, Sal. The Close, 1676, AB, copy W, P5/1676/32
Thos., bookseller, Marl., 1692, W, P1/H/545
Thos., gent., Littlecott, Enford, 1695, AB, I, P1/H/566
Thos., Enford, 1711, AB, comm, P2/H/1090
Thos., Donhead St A., 1716, AB, P1/H/722
Thos., sen., weaver, Barford St M., 1717, I, W, P2/H/1143
Thos., yeo., Heytes., 1719-20, W, P5/1719/42, P5/16Reg/34B
Thos., gent., W. Lavington, 1726, W, P1/H/833, P1/7Reg/158
Thos., husb., Damerham, Hants, 1727, W, P1/H/837, P1/7Reg/171A
Thos., yeo., Sherb., Dorset, 1729, W, P5/1729/28, P5/16Reg/246A
Thos., narrow weaver, Barford St M., 1737, W, P2/H/1300
Thos., sen., yeo., Gt. Chalfield, 1746, W, P2/H/1365
Thos., gent., Marl., 1758, AB, P1/H/1134
Thos., Wootton R., 1759, AB, P1/H/1148
Thos., yeo., Enmore Grn, Motc., Dorset, 1769, I, W, P19/164
Thos., Cherhill, 1799, AB, P26/1221
Thos., yeo., Leigh, Yetm., Dorset, 1801, W, Wr, P19/204
Thos., Sal., 1822, AB, Wr, P4/1822/9
Thos., farmer, Wantage, Berks., 1840, O, W, Wr, P5/1840/17
Thos., yeo., Leigh, Yetm., Dorset, 1840, O, W, Wr, P5/1840/3
Wm., Damerham, Hants, 1557, W, P2/3Reg/44B
Wm., tinker, Wokm., Berks., 1588, I, W, P5/1588/28, P5/5Reg/34B
Hunt alias Nicklis, Wm., butcher, Corsley, 1616, AB, I, P2/H/312, P2/8Reg/306B
Wm., Marston, Pott., 1627, I, W, P1/H/174
Wm., Crockerton, Longbridge D., [1639], a/c, P2/H/516
Wm., husb., Marl., 1665, comm, I, W, P1/H/364
Wm., carp., Marston, Pott., 1666, I, W, P1/H/368
Wm., cordw., Malm., 1682, I, W, P3/H/576
Wm., Fordington, Dorset, 1684, AB, I, P15/57
Wm., broad weaver, Westb., 1701, AB, I, P25/1701/6
Wm., Hamptworth, Downton, 1710, AB, P2/H/1076
Wm., Ryme I., Dorset, 1734, I, W, P5/1734/42
Wm., sen., labourer, Wootton B., 1739, comm, W, P3/H/1164
Wm., yeo., Ryme I., Dorset (d. in debtor`s prison in London), 1740, AB, I, ren, Wr, P5/1740/38
Wm., Turners Puddle, Dorset, 1750, AB, P5/1750/18
Wm., Calne, 1753, AB, P26/923
Wm., maltster, Malm., 1757, W, P3/H/1306
Wm., Sal., 1816, AB, P4/1816/1
Wm., Fisherton A., 1819, AB, Wr, P2/1819/15
Wm., yeo., Motc., Dorset, 1822, W, Wr, P27/1/657

Wm., labourer, Broad B., Highw., 1829, W, P10/1829/1
Wm., minor, Wantage, Berks., 1833, AB, O, Wr, P23/967
Wm., victualler, Bradford A., 1833, O, W, Wr, P2/1833/23
Wm., Chapmanslade, Corsley, 1851, D, W, Wr, P1/1851/67
Wm., farmer, Thornford, Dorset, 1854, aff, D, W, Wr, P5/1854/7
Wm. Henly, yeo., Brinkw., 1845, O, W, Wr, P3/1845/12
see also Drew alias H.; Marshall form. H.; Nicholas alias H.; Robinson alias H.; Thompson alias H.; Wilson alias H.
Hunter, Ann, widow, Melk., 1794, W, P2/H/1672
Ann, sp., Melk., 1820, AB, comm, Wr, P1/1820/135
Betty, sp., Melk., 1797, comm, W, P2/H/1683
Edwd., Uffcott, Broad H., 1826, AB, Wr, P3/1826/4
Eleanor, widow, Lyneham, 1726, W, P3/H/1029
Eleanor, sp., Melk., 1806, W, Wr, P2/1806/49
Eliz., sp., Melk., 1820, AB, comm, Wr, P1/1820/136
Frances, widow, Gt. Bedwyn, 1708, W, P5/1708/34, P5/15Reg/73A
Hester, widow, Trowb., 1821, W, Wr, P1/1821/13
Jn., Stanford in the Vale, Berks., 1753, AB, P1/H/1089
Jn., plumber and glazier, Melk., 1762, W, P2/H/1456
Jn., Studley, Lydiard T., 1785, W, P3/H/1468
Jn., Melk., 1803, AB, comm, P2/1803/74
Jn., blacksmith, Trowb., 1836, O, W, Wr, P1/1836/8
Lydia, widow, Trowb., 1839, comm, W, Wr, P1/1839/7
Mgt., Melk., 1834, W, Wr, P2/1834/29
Richd., blacksmith, Swindon, 1693, AB, I, P3/H/737
Robt., cooper, Melk., 1818, comm, W, Wr, P2/1818/48
Sam., soldier, Bradford A., 1818, AB, comm, Wr, P1/1818/1
Thos., yeo., Thornhill, Clyffe P., 1664, I, W, P1/H/361
Thos., tailor, Lyneham, 1702, AB, I, P3/H/835
Thos., plumber and glazier, Avebury, 1749, I, W, P3/H/1256
Thos., sen., yeo., Stanford in the Vale, Berks., 1804, W, P1/1804/73
Thos., blacksmith, Trowb., 1820, comm, W, Wr, P1/1820/4
Thos., blacksmith, Trowb., 1833, W, Wr, P1/1833/8
Wm., mason, Broad H., 1831, W, P3/1831/21
Huntingdon, Huntingdon, Dennis *see* Thomas Derham
Huntingford, Huntingford, Jn., cutler, Devizes, 1778, AB, withdrawal of caveat, P1/H/1252
Huntingford, Thos., clerk, Warm., 1788, AB, comm, P2/H/1632
Huntley, Huntly, Ann, widow, Manningford Bruce, 1837, W, Wr, P3/1837/28
Huntly, Benj., carp., Lyneham, 1700, AB, I, P3/H/802
Huntly, Chas., weaver, Leigh, Bradford A., 1806, W, Wr, P2/1806/24
Geo., yeo., Westb. L., 1784, W, P25/1784/1
Geo., slaymaker, Trowb., 1830, O, W, Wr, P1/1830/17
Joan, widow, Lyneham, 1616, I, W, P3/H/117
Huntly, Jn., blacksmith, Chitterne AS, 1670, W, P2/H/673
Huntly, Jn., sen., husb., Easton, 1687, I, W, P3/H/648
Jn., husb., Winsley, Bradford A., 1706, I, W, P2/H/1045
Jn., yeo., Chitterne St My., 1779, AB, a/c, comm, I, P2/H/1575
Jn., gent., Westb., 1789, W, P25/1789/3
Jn., innholder, Beam., Dorset, 1799, W, P17/584
Huntly, Jn., yeo., Westb., 1802, note, W, P25/1802/7
Jn., yeo., Hilcott, N. Newnton, 1836, comm, W, Wr, P3/1836/43
Jos., dairyman, Littleton P., 1842, AB, Wr, P1/1842/57
Josiah, Chirton, 1855, aff, D, O, W, Wr, P2/1855/30
Huntly, Mark, yeo., Horningsham, 1843, AB, W, Wr, P5/1843/10
Huntly, My., widow, Lyneham, 1671, AB, I, NW, P3/H/460
Peter, shoemaker, Hankerton, 1627, I, NW, P3/H/216
Richd., Bradford A., 1557, AB, P2/3Reg/31B
Huntly, Richd., husb., Winsley, Bradford A., 1614, W, P2/8Reg/220
Richd., sen., broad weaver, Lyneham, 1632, I, W, P3/H/264
Huntly, Richd., jun., joiner, Lyneham, 1632, AB, I (applies to both people), P3/H/265
Huntly, Richd., Lyneham, 1636, AB, a/c, P3/H/292

Huntly, Richd., sen., no abode stated, 1646, comm, I, W, P1/H/274
Huntly, Richd., husb., All C., 1668, comm, W, P1/H/386
Richd., sen., husb., Winsley, Bradford A., 1675, AB, I, P2/H/726
Huntly, Richd., sen., yeo., Lyneham, 1687, AB, comm, I, P3/H/649
Huntly, Richd., sen., weaver, All C., 1718, I, ren, W, P3/H/964
Huntly, Richd., serge weaver, Urchf., 1723, AB, I, W, P1/H/791, P1/6Reg/435B
Richd., yeo., Lyneham, 1742, W, P3/H/1188
Huntly, Richd., blacksmith, Manningford Bruce, 1843, O, W, Wr, P3/1843/5
Robt., husb., Winsley, Bradford A., 1625-26, AB, a/c, I, P2/H/378
Robt., weaver, Melk., 1846, AB, comm, W, Wr, P2/1846/57
Thos., jun., weaver, Preston, Lyneham, 1640, I, W, P3/H/325
Thos., Clack, Lyneham, 1669, AB, I, P3/H/424
Huntly, Thos., Lyneham, 1682, AB, P3/H/577
Thos., husb., Winsley, Bradford A., 1682, comm, I, W, P2/H/810
Thos., Clack, Lyneham, 1690, AB, comm, P3/H/684
Huntly, Thos., plumber and glazier, Clack, Lyneham, 1725, W, P3/H/1026
Thos., Westb., 1768, AB, P25/1768/3
Huntly, Wm., husb., Lyneham, 1684, AB, I, P3/H/602
Wm., baker, Bratton, Westb., 1763, W, P25/1763/9
Wm., gent., Chitterne St My., 1802, W, P2/1802/60
see also Raynor form. H.
Huntmill, David, Blewbury, Berks., 1764, AB, P5/1764/25
Hunton, Richd., esquire, Bushton, Clyffe P., 1625, AB, P1/H/161
Thos., gent., E. Knoyle, [1631], copy I (2), copy W, W, P2/H/433
Virtue, widow, Dorchester, Dorset, 1640, I, W, P2/H/546
Hurcombe *see* Hercomb
Hurd, Bartholomew, Bere R., Dorset, 1744, W, Wr, P5/1744/25
Chas., surgeon, Sal., 1840, W, Wr, P4/1840/5
Jn., Bere R., Dorset, 1733, W, P5/1733/30
Reynold, husb., Bere R., Dorset, 1627, AB, I, P5/1627/26, P5/11Reg/38A
Sam., sen., grocer, Trowb., 1852, O, W, Wr, P1/1852/4
Wm., priest, Gt. Wishford, 1550, institution to rectory on resignation of Portman, P2/2Reg/108B
see also Pearce alias H.
Hurdle, Hurdel, Hy., yeo., Stockton, 1751, W, P2/H/1398
Thos., Bourton, Gillingham, Dorset, 1751, AB, P27/1/402, P27/3Reg/61A
Hurford, Eliz., sp., Uffc., Devon, 1752, W, P5/1752/26
Geo., husb., Uffc., Devon, 1855, aff, comm, W, Wr, P20/1/335
Sarah, sp., Sherb., Dorset, 1734, AB, P5/1734/38
Thos., buttonmaker, Sherb., Dorset, 1685, AB, I, P5/1685/46
Hurket, Dan., Chisenbury, Enford, 1822, W, Wr, P2/1822/45
Hurlbatt, Agnes, Wilton, Gt. Bedwyn, 1622, I, W, P5/1622/39, P5/10Reg/140A
Dorothy, widow, Ogbourne St Geo., 1686, I, W, P5/1686/27
Hurlbatt *or* Hulbard, Edwd., tailor, Swindon, 1674, I, W, P1/H/430
Eliz., widow, Brinkw., 1684, I, W, P3/H/603
Francis, Marl., 1713, AB, I, P1/H/689
Francis, sen., carp., The Grn, Marl. St My., 1734, I, W, P1/H/922
Joan, sp., Brinkw., 1696, I, W, P3/H/764
Jn., Wilton, Gt. Bedwyn, 1619, I, W, P5/1619/28, P5/9Reg/226A
Jn., sen., Ogbourne St A., 1634, I, W. Proved at the Metropolitan Visitation to Devizes, P5/1634/57, P5/12Reg/279
Jn., Wilton, Gt. Bedwyn, 1661, AB, comm, I, P5/1661/30
Jn., husb., Crofton, Gt. Bedwyn, 1684, W (NEP), P21/4/11
Jn., Savernake Park, 1725, AB, P1/H/809
Nich., yeo., Ogbourne St A., 1608, AB, I, W, P5/1607/30, P5/8Reg/109D
Susanna, widow, Marl., 1715, W, P1/H/720, P1/5Reg/493B
Susanna, widow, Marl., 1750, W, P1/H/1082, P1/10Reg/459
Thos., yeo., Ogbourne Maizey, 1616, I, NW, P5/1616/38
Thos., Sandhurst, Berks., 1630, AB, P5/11Reg/126A
Thos., husb., Ogbourne Maizey, 1691, I, W, P5/1691/37
Thos., Marl., 1701, AB, P1/H/618
Thos., Marl., 1760, AB, ren, comm, P1/H/1153

Wm., glover, Brinkw., 1667, I, W, P3/H/394
Wm., Brinkw., 1693, AB, I, P3/H/736
Wm., cordw., Marl., 1804, W, P1/1804/149
Hurle, Ann, widow, Monkton D., 1817, AB, Wr, P2/1817/7
Chas., yeo., Kingston D., [1687], I, W, P2/H/876
Cuthbert, husb., Kingston D., 1583, W, P2/6Reg/87B
Edith, widow, Kingston D., 1634, I, W, P1/H/204
Edwd., weaver, Calne, 1638, AB, I, P26/73
Eleanor, widow, Kingston D., [1688], I, W, P2/H/889
Eliz., widow, Kingston D., 1605, AB, I, W, P1/H/28
Geo., Mkt. L., 1640, I, copy I, P2/H/538
Geo., barber, Melk., 1705, I, W, P1/H/636
Geo., Edington, 1788, AB (2), appt of guardian, comm, P2/H/1639
Geo., butcher, Chipp., 1796, W, P3/H/1520
Grecian, Urchf., 1689, AB, I, P2/H/906
Hester, Maiden B., 1712, AB, P2/H/1094
Joan, widow, Kingston D., 1578, W, P2/5Reg/301C
Joan, widow, Mkt. L., 1616, I, W, P2/H/315
Joan, widow, Kingston D., 1632, AB, I, P2/H/436
Jn., Kingston D., 1578, I, P2/H/48
Jn., husb., Kingston D., 1616, I, W, P1/H/104
Jn., yeo. *or* husb., Kingston D., 1686, a/c (2), draft AB, I, ren, withdrawal of caveat, P1/H/503
Jn., Kingston D., 1827, AB, Wr, P2/1827/82
My., widow, Marl., 1683, appt of ex., I, W, P1/H/485
Peter, sen., yeo. and husb., Kingston D., 1662, I, W, P1/H/317
Peter, yeo., Kingston D., 1699, AB, I, P2/H/992
Peter, yeo., Kingston D., 1721, W, P2/H/1184
Richd., Sutton V., 1837, AB, Wr, P2/1837/58
Robt., husb., Rushall, 1557, W, P2/3Reg/26C
Robt., sen., yeo., Kingston D., 1693, I, W, P2/H/938
Robt., Kingston D., 1696, AB, I (detailed), P2/H/967
Robt., Kingston D., 1709, AB, I, P2/H/1073
Robt., butcher, Chipp., 1807, comm, W, Wr, P3/1807/39
Roger, Kingston D., 1580, I, T, W, P2/H/59, P2/5Reg/367B
Roger, husb., W. Knoyle, 1612, AB, a/c, I, P2/H/289
Roger, yeo., Kingston D., 1636, AB, a/c, I, P2/H/479
Sarah, sp., Marl., 1702, I, W, P1/H/622, P1/4Reg/225
Simon, glover, Marl., 1661, AB, I, P1/H/309
Simon, Marl., 1671, AB, P1/H/407
Simon, Marl. St My., 1687, AB, comm, P1/H/504
Sophia, sp., Trowb., 1835, O, W, P1/1835/135
Thos., husb. *or* yeo., Rushall, 1560, I, W, P2/H/11, P2/4Reg/49C
Thos., yeo., Rushall, 1667, I, W, P2/H/646
Thos., Kingston D., 1682, I, W, P2/H/814
Thos., yeo., Monkton D., 1723, W, P2/H/1197
Thos., yeo., Monkton D., 1756, W, P2/H/1418
Thos., yeo., Stourton, 1774, W, P2/H/1538
Thos., yeo., Monkton D., 1793, W, P2/H/1669
Walter, yeo., Mkt. L., 1678, I, W, P2/H/757
Wm., husb., Kingston D., 1557, W, P2/3Reg/20B
Wm., yeo., Kingston D., 1638, I, W, P2/H/501
Wm., yeo., Kingston D., 1700, AB, I, W, P2/H/999
Wm., yeo., Pott., 1716, I, W, P1/H/734, P1/6Reg/84A
Hurley, Alice, widow, Uffc., Devon, 1628, I, W, P5/1628/61, P5/11Reg/14C
Joan, widow, Uffc., Devon, 1806, W, Wr, P5/1806/27
Jn., yeo., Uffc., Devon, 1744, AB, ren, P20/1/206
Jn., yeo., Uffc., Devon, 1757, W, P20/1/235
Thos., sen., Uffc., Devon, 1626-27, AB, a/c, comm, I, P20/1/13
Thos., fuller, Uffc., Devon, 1628, AB, a/c, I, P5/1628/57, P5/11Reg/64B
Wm., groom, Uffc., Devon, 1619, AB, I, P5/1619/59, P5/10Reg/50B

Wm., gent., Uffc., Devon, 1808, W, P20/1/292
Hurman *see* Harman
Hurne *see* Horne
Hurst, Alexander, yeo., Collingbourne K., 1661, AB, L, P3/H/344
Hust, Alexander, Newton T., 1714, I, W, P1/H/712, P1/5Reg/460A
Anthony, yeo., Chr. M., 1692, I, W, P1/H/549
Dan., Easton Grey, 1735, W, P1/H/933, P1/8Reg/61B
Edwd., Whitep., 1603, I, P1/H/26
Eliz., widow, Whitep., 1558, AB, W, P2/3Reg/86A, 86C, 97A
Eliz., widow, Whitep., 1823, W, Wr, P1/1823/30
Frances, apothecary's wife, Marl., 1668, AB, comm, I, P1/H/396
Isaac, blacksmith, Whitep., 1823, AB, W, Wr, P1/1823/31
Isabel, widow, Whitep., 1560, AB (in minority of Richd. H.), I, P2/H/10, P2/4Reg/26E
Jn., husb., Whitep., 1553, W, P2/2Reg/178C
Jn., Durrington, 1572, W, P2/5Reg/150A
Jn., sen., yeo., Whitep., 1585, I (very detailed), W, P2/H/71, P2/7Reg/27
Jn., Whitep., 1772, AB, P2/H/1532
Jn., brick burner, Whitep., 1822, W, Wr, P2/1822/31
My., widow, Whitep., 1834, O, W, Wr, P2/1834/26
Rebecca, widow, Chr. M., 1704, I, W, P3/H/850
Reuben, gent., Westport St My., 1633, AB, I, P3/H/275
Richd., Whitep., 1558-63, AB, W, P2/3Reg/143, P2/4Reg/123A, 146B
Richd., innholder, Hannington Bridge, 1755, AB, W, P3/H/1295
Richd., Sal., 1777, AB, P4/1777/12
Richd., Speen, Berks., 1826, AB, Wr, P1/1826/88
Robt., blacksmith, Whitep., 1647, W, P2/H/589
Wm., Whitep., 1547, W, P2/2Reg/38A
Wm., sen., husb., Idmiston, [1632], I, W, P2/H/445, P2/9Reg/58
Wm., Cowesfield, Whitep., 1841, AB, Wr, P2/1841/27
see also Goddard alias H.
Husdy, Alice, widow, Grittleton, 1670, AB, P3/H/446
Jn., Langley Burrell, 1704, AB, comm, I, P3/H/851
Husday, Nich., husb., Ryme I., Dorset, 1680, comm, I, W, P5/1680/24
Huse *see* Hughes
Hushe *see* Huish
Husk, Ruth, widow, Fonthill G., 1769, W, P2/H/1513
Husse, Wm., husb., Berwick St Leonard, 1571, AB, T (children: Robt., Cath. & Wm. H.), P2/H/38, P2/5Reg/134B
Hussey, Ambrose, Whitep., 1643, I, W, P2/H/562
Ann, housekeeper to Miss Bayly, Bishopstrow, 1843, comm, W, Wr, P2/1843/32
Betty, widow, Tilsh., 1806, AB, P2/1806/15
Hy., yeo., Landford, 1592, I, T, P2/H/122
Hy., Netherb., Dorset, 1679, AB, I, P5/1679/42
Jas., W. Harnham, 1710, AB, P5/1710/58
Jas., yeo., Uffc., Devon (form. of Nicholashayne Pond, Culmstock), 1836, O, W, Wr, P5/1836/32
Jas. Francis, maltster, Sal. (form. of Netheravon), 1854, AB, aff, Wr, P4/1854/14
Joan, Netherb., Dorset, 1597, AB, P5/1597/60, P5/6Reg/156A
Joan, sp., Wambrook, Somerset, 1694, I, W, P14/83
Jn., Landford, 1550, W, P2/2Reg/106A
Jn., Melplash, Netherb., Dorset, 1585-86, AB, I, P5/1586/10, P5/4Reg/132C
Jn., jun., yeo., Whitep., 1595, AB, I, W, P2/H/146, P2/7Reg/151A
Jn., husb., Landford, 1636, AB, a/c, I, P2/H/472, P2/9Reg/105B
Jn., sen., yeo., Boscombe, 1661, I, W, P2/H/609
Jn., Enmore Grn, Motc., Dorset, 1670, AB, P19/24
Hussey alias Baily, Jn., Chetnole, Yetm., Dorset, 1670, AB, comm, I, P5/1670/21
Husy, Jn., Boscombe, 1685-86, AB, I, P2/H/856, 874
Jn., yeo., Chetnole, Yetm., Dorset, 1693-94, AB, a/c, I (2), P19/64, 69
Jn., labourer, Berwick St Jas., 1722, NW, P1/H/785, P1/6Reg/387A
Jn., farmer, Tilsh., 1842, comm, W, Wr, P2/1842/13
Margery, widow, Downton, 1578, I, W, P2/H/47, P2/5Reg/297D
Margery, widow, Sal., 1754, AB, P4/1754/6

Richd., yeo., Winterborne K., Dorset, 1814, W, Wr, P5/1814/2
Robt., bach., Landford, 1562, I, W, P2/H/18, P2/4Reg/105B
Robt., yeo., Keevil, 1630, I, W, P2/H/417
Robt., husb., Witcha Farm, Rams., 1730, I (detailed), W (NEP), P5/1730/39
Robt., yeo., N. Bradley, 1826, W, Wr, P1/1826/109
Roger, yeo., Wilton, 1607, AB, I, W, P2/H/237
Sarah, widow, Tilsh., 1842, comm, W, Wr, P1/1842/66
Thos., husb., Landford, 1571, AB, W, P2/H/33, P2/5Reg/112B
Wm., bach., Landford, 1562, I, W, P2/H/19, P2/4Reg/109A
Wm., feltmaker, Melplash, Netherb., Dorset, 1638, I, W, P5/1638/63, P5/13Reg/77
Wm., broad weaver, N. Bradley, 1774, W, P2/H/1543
Wm., Tilsh., 1842, AB, Wr, P1/1842/25
Wm. *see also* Jn. Bartlett
see also Bayly alias H.
Hust *see* Hurst
Hustis, Jn., husb., Upton S., 1609, I, W, P2/H/251, P2/8Reg/61A
Hewstis alias Lambart, Jn., Tisb., 1679, AB, I, P2/H/768
Yewstice, Jn., maltster, Calne, 1712, I (detailed), W, P26/571
Hewstice, Lambert, Longbridge D., 1610, AB, I, P2/H/271, P2/8Reg/145B
Mgt., widow, Upton S., 1613, W, P2/8Reg/198
Hustes alias Lambert, Ralph, carp., Longbridge D., 1627, I, W, P2/H/394
Hewstes, Robt., Corsley, 1547, W, P2/2Reg/35C
Yewstice, Thos., Corsley, 1603, AB, I, P2/Y/13
Eustice alias Turner, Wm., Corsley, 1543, W (NEP), P2/1Reg/30A
Eustis, Hewstone *or* Hustus, Wm., sen., Bowood (buried Calne), 1689, AB, I, P26/375
Husy *see* Hussey
Hutchins, Hewchin, Agnes, widow, Sonning, Berks., 1556, W, P5/20Reg/145
Hutchens, Agnes, widow, Stanton St B., 1570, W (NEP), P1/1Reg/126B
Agnes, wife, Ford, Laverstock, 1639, AB, P4/1639/15
Ann, widow, E. Hanney, W. Hanney, Berks., 1711, W, P1/H/677, P1/5Reg/153
Ann, widow, W. Ilsley, Berks., 1732, comm, W, P1/H/886, P1/7Reg/436
Ann, yeo.'s wife, Bucklebury, Berks., 1798, AB, W, P1/H/1358, P1/15Reg/154
Ann, sp., Pickwick, Corsham, 1804, AB, P3/1804/6
Hutchings, Betty, singlewoman, Leigh, Yetm., Dorset, 1796, W, P19/199
Christian, singlewoman, Downend, Chieveley, Berks., 1674, I, W, P1/H/425
Chris., Chards., Devon, 1714, AB, P14/120
David, Southwick, N. Bradley, 1622, AB, I, P2/H/358
Edith, wife, Urchf., 1809, AB, comm, Wr (form. Edith Spencer, sp.), P2/1809/81
Hutchens, Edwd., brickmaker, Marl. St My., 1820, W, Wr, P1/1820/116
Hutchence, Frances, widow, Urchf., 1784, AB, P2/H/1606
Hutchens, Geo., husb., Elcombe, Wrou., 1606, W, P3/2Reg/6B
Hutchans, Geo., sen., farmer, Melchet Park, 1768, W, P2/H/1505
Hutchans, Geo., sen., husb., Plaitford, 1803, W, P2/1803/64
Hutchens, Geo., Plaitford, 1820, AB, Wr, P1/1820/41
Hutchings, Geo., woodman, Castleton, Dorset, 1848, comm, W, Wr, P5/1848/8
Hutchings, Geo., haulier, Marl., 1852, W, Wr, P1/1852/8
Giles, gent., Crane St., Sal., 1667, AB, I, W, P4/1666/6, 25
Hutchens, Hy., husb., Bere R., Dorset, 1586, I, W, P5/1586/11, P5/4Reg/131A
Hutchens, Hugh, husb., Marl., 1692, I, W, P1/H/540
Jas., pewterer, Collingbourne D., 1766, W, P21/10/71
Jas., Ludg., 1831, AB, comm, W, P2/1831/21
Jane, widow, Coate, Bps. C., 1766, AB, P24/1087
Hutchence, Jane, widow, Fyfield, Overton, 1797, W, Wr, P3/H/1529
Hutchens, Joan, widow, Burbage, 1585, I, W, P5/1585/25, P5/4Reg/121D
Hutchin, Jn., Sonning, Berks., 1546, W, P5/20Reg/76B
Hutchens, Jn., carp., Calstone W., 1565, W, P5/1Reg/63C
Hutchens, Jn., Burbage, 1568, W, P5/2Reg/29A
Heychins, Jn., Calstone W., 1568, W, P5/2Reg/60D
Hutchens, Jn., Shaw cum Donnington, Berks., 1571, W (NEP), P1/1Reg/85D
Hutchin, Jn., husb., Thornford, Dorset, 1588, I, W, P5/1587/25, P5/5Reg/3B

Jn., Sonning, Berks., 1610, AB, P5/9Reg/32B
Jn., Beer Hackett, Dorset, 1637, AB, NW, P5/1637/21, P5/12Reg/248A
Jn., Asserton, Berwick St Jas., 1639, AB, I, P1/H/241
Hutchens, Jn., yeo., Chards., Devon, 1668, W, P14/25
Hutchens, Jn., Sal., 1701, I, W, P4/1701/5
Hutchens, Jn., Ludg., 1707, AB, P2/H/1059
Jn., yeo., Chards., Devon, 1719, I, W, P5/1719/46, P5/16Reg/14B
Hutchence, Jn., husb., Henwick, Thatcham, Berks., 1732, W, P1/7Reg/483B
Hutchence, Jn., sen., husb., Yattendon & Henwick, Berks., 1732, I, W, P1/H/898
Jn., sen., yeo., Horton, Bps. C., 1733, AB, ren, P24/949
Hutchings, Jn., serge weaver, Uffc., Devon, 1755, W, P5/1755/22
Hutchings, Jn., yeo., Holnest, Dorset, 1766, W, P5/1766/15
Hutchence, Jn., butcher, Ludg., 1777, W, P2/H/1564
Hutchence, Jn., bricklayer, Urchf., 1782, W, P1/H/1278, P1/13Reg/371
Jn., Fyfield, Overton, 1793, AB, P3/H/1507
Hutchings, Jn., carp., Sal., 1795, W, P1/H/1339, P1/14Reg/605
Jn., yeo., Collingbourne D., 1801, W, P21/12/2
Jn., Ludg., 1826, AB, Wr, P2/1826/13
Jn., brewer, Devizes, 1829, O, W, Wr, P1/1829/2
Jn., miller, Urchf., 1834, W, Wr, P2/1834/13
Jn., stone dresser, Marden, 1839, comm, D, W, Wr, P2/1839/9
Hutchence, Jn., broker, Sal., 1850, W, Wr, P4/1850/6
Jonas Johnson, farmer and brickmaker, Marl., 1852, W, Wr, P1/1852/7
Jos., yeo., Folly Farm, Mildenhall, 1804, W, Wr, P1/1804/94
Jos., innkeeper, painter, glazier and yeo., *The Queen's Head Inn*, Ludg., 1845, D, W, Wr, P1/1845/52
Leonard, Sal., 1661, AB, P4/1661/9
Hutchings, Martha, widow, N. Heath, Chieveley, Berks., 1735, W, P1/H/929, P1/8Reg/36
My., widow, Bere R., Dorset, 1736, AB, I, ren, P5/1736/19
Hutchens, Michael, widow, Marl., 1696, AB, I, W, P1/H/589
Millicent, wife, Devizes, 1827, W, Wr, P1/1827/5
Nathan, butcher, Hurst, Berks., 1709, W, P5/1709/22, P5/15Reg/124
Hutchens, Nich., yeo., Bere R., Dorset, 1733, W, P5/1733/31
Hutchens, Peter, Rushall, 1708, AB, P1/H/653
Rachel, widow, Enmore Grn, Motc., Dorset, 1689, AB, P19/56
Richd., husb., Sonning, Berks., 1567, W, P5/2Reg/25A
Richd., husb., Calstone W., 1609, AB, I, W, P5/1609/36, P5/8Reg/159B
Hutchens, Richd., husb., Draycot C., 1660, I, W, P1/H/307
Richd., Draycot C., 1686, AB, I, P1/H/497
Hutchens, Richd., sen., yeo., E. Hendred, Berks., 1717, I, W, P1/H/738, P1/6Reg/126
Hutchens, Richd., shoemaker, Sal., 1817, W, Wr, P1/1817/22
Hutchence, Robt., clothier, Sal., 1797, W, P4/1797/19
Hutchings, Robt., cordw., Bradford A., 1827, aff, comm, W, Wr, P2/1827/3
Hutchings, Robt., yeo., Over C., Dorset, 1841, W (& cod), Wr, P5/1841/11
Hutchens, Roger, husb., Sonning, Berks., 1603, W, P5/7Reg/55A
Hutchence, Roger, victualler, Ludg., 1679, AB, I, P2/H/770
Hutchens, Sarah, widow, Ludg., 1727, AB, P1/H/836
Hutchings, Sarah, widow, Lyme R., Dorset, 1778, W, P16/345
Stephen, innholder, Sal., 1644, I, W, P1/H/261
Stephen, yeo., Stratford sub C., 1799, W, P4/1799/20
Hutchens, Stephen, Stratford sub C., 1821, AB, Wr, P4/1821/1
Hutchens, Susan, widow, Sonning Eye, Berks., 1634, I, W. Proved at the Metropolitan Visitation to Reading, P5/1634/58, P5/12Reg/316C
Thos., gent., Brinkw., 1630, AB, a/c, I, P3/H/245
Thos., wheelwright, Shalbourne, 1691, AB, I, P5/1691/36
Thos., labourer, Hungerford, Berks., 1694, AB, I, P23/212
Hutchence, Thos., butcher, Ludg., 1705, I, W, P2/H/1033
Thos., Bourton, Gillingham, Dorset, 1787, W, P27/1/531, P27/3Reg/252
Thos., shopkeeper, Devizes, 1837, W, Wr, P1/1837/23
Hutchens, Thos., yeo., Devizes, 1850, note, O, W, Wr, P1/1850/21
Hutchens, Wm., Broad C., 1571-72, AB, W, P2/5Reg/135B, 148D

Wm., husb., Quidh., 1642, NW, P2/H/557
Hutchens alias Ford, Wm., yeo., Rushall, [1684], I, W, P2/H/830
Hutchens, Wm., Enmore Grn, Motc., Dorset, 1722, AB, comm, P5/1722/30
Hutchence, Wm., butcher, Chute, 1769, W, P7/163
Wm., sen., Yattendon, Berks., 1776, AB, ren, P1/H/1241
Hutchens, Wm., butcher, Ludg., 1792, W, P2/H/1660
Hutchens, Wm., labourer, Rowde, 1814, W, Wr, P1/1814/79
Wm. Edgar, bach., Devizes Grn, Bps. C., 1844, AB, O, Wr, P24/1372
see also Allen alias H.; Hitchens *or* H.
Hutfield, Hatfield, Eustace, tailor, Sonning, Berks., 1570, W, P5/2Reg/69B
Frances, wife, Marl., 1762, AB, P1/H/1158
Gabriel, yeo., Winterbourne D., 1719, W, P7/114
Gabriel, yeo., Winterbourne D. (form. of Sal.), 1767, W, P7/162
Huttfield, Geo., yeo., Ogbourne St A., 1737, W, Wr, P5/1737/25
Geo., jun., wigmaker, Sal., 1777, W, P4/1777/13
Geo., barber and wigmaker, Sal., 1779, W, P1/H/1254, P1/13Reg/200
Hester, widow, Ogbourne St A., 1755, W, P5/1755/30
Jn., yeo., Winterbourne G., 1682, I, W, P2/H/802
Hatfield, My., sp., Farley, Alderbury, 1751, W, P26/904
My., widow, Sal., 1802, W, P4/1802/13
Wm., yeo., Winterbourne D., 1750, W, P7/144
Hutin, (Mrs) *see* Jn. Cross
Hutson, Sam., baker, Malm., 1757, W, P3/H/1307
Wm., Malm., 1745, AB, P3/H/1220
Hutt, Jn., Cumnor, Berks., 1723, AB, I, P1/H/797
Jn., basketmaker, Abingdon, Berks., 1756, I, W, P1/H/1106, P1/11Reg/258A
Huttfield *see* Hutfield
Huttoft, Ann, widow, Sal., 1809, AB, P4/1809/6
Wm., Sal., 1748, AB, P4/1748/5
Hutton, Edmd., brazier and tinman, Melk., 1835, comm, W, P2/1835/5
Eliz., widow, Melk., 1684, AB, P2/H/842
Jas., yeo., Melk., 1803, comm, W, P2/1803/26
Joan, widow, Melk., 1681, I, W, P2/H/796
Jn., Pott., 1625, I, P1/H/170
Jn., Melk., 1687, AB, I, W, P2/H/886
Jn., Melk., 1826, AB, D, Wr, P1/1826/8
Jn., Warm., 1827, AB, Wr, P2/1827/42
Jos., sen., yeo., Melk., 1678, I, W, P2/H/753
Jos., yeo., Melk., 1722, W, copy W, P2/H/1193
My., widow, Melk., 1829, AB, comm, P2/1829/22
Robt., parchmentmaker, Sherb., Dorset, 1610, I, W, P5/1610/29, P5/9Reg/20B
Stephen, Melk., 1823, AB, comm, Wr, P1/1823/50
Thos., husb. & widower of Matilda, Edington, 1570, AB, P2/H/32, P2/5Reg/106B
Thos., yeo., Melk., 1782, AB, comm, P2/H/1602
Thos., Melk., 1826, AB, Wr, P1/1826/111
Wm., yeo., Melk., 1684, AB, comm, I, P2/H/841
Huxford, Jn., Bere R., Dorset, 1768, AB, P5/1768/15
Hwet *see* Hewett
Hyatt, Highett, Edwd., labourer, Burbage, 1792, W, P11/250
Eliz., widow, Sherb., Dorset, 1819, W, Wr, P5/1819/6
Highett, Eliz., widow, Burbage, 1835, AB, O, P11/291
Highett, Hannah, sp., Southgrove Farm, Burbage, 1845, O, W, Wr, P11/298
Harry, carp., Chipp., 1784, W, P3/H/1456
Highett, Jas., yeo., Rodmead, Maiden B., 1798, W, P1/H/1348, P1/15Reg/48
Hiett, Jn., Corsley, 1821, AB, Wr, P2/1821/32
Michael, carp., Chipp., 1853, AB, D, L, O, Wr, P3/1853/39
Hyett, Philip, baker, Chute, 1757, W, P7/155
Highett, Philip, husb., Stratton St Mgt. (but late of Sheepstead Farm, Marcham), 1799, W, P3/H/1536
Highett, Philip, bach., Burbage, 1818, W, Wr, P11/268
Richd., Aldbourne, 1631, I, W, P3/H/247

Hyett, Robt., yeo., Marden, 1698, I, W, P2/H/983
Highett, Robt., yeo., Westcourt, Burbage, 1828, AB (re lease of field in B.), O, P11/285
Robt., brazier and innholder, Sherb., Dorset, 1833, W, Wr, P5/1833/28
Highett, Sarah Artiax, sp., Southgrove Farm, Burbage, 1835, W, P11/292
Silas, farmer, Whaddon, 1728, W, P2/H/1230
Hyett, Stephen, yeo., Keevil, 1750, W, P1/H/1079, P1/10Reg/415
Susan, widow, Aldbourne, 1636, W, P3/H/291
Hiatt, Thos., yeo., Sonning, Berks., 1724-25, comm, W, P5/1724/36, P5/16Reg/105B
Hyatt *or* Iatt, Wm., carp., Rams., 1666, a/c, I, W, P5/1665/47
Hyde, Alice, widow, Sal., 1623, W, P4/1623/2
Andrew, Hurst, Berks., 1554, W, P5/20Reg/123A
Hide, Ann, widow, Newbury St., Preshute, 1681, appt of ex., I, W, P1/H/450
Ann, widow, Stitchcombe, Mildenhall, 1706, I, W, P3/H/873
Hide, Ann, Blewbury, Berks., 1710, W, P5/1710/53, P5/15Reg/163
Ann, widow, Stitchcombe, Mildenhall, 1727, AB, W, P3/H/1042
Anna, widow, Hurst, Berks., 1663, W (badly damaged), P5/1663/35
Cath., widow, Wantage, Berks., 1692, W, P5/1692/42
Hide, Cath., widow, Highw., 1702, W, P10/1702/1
Chris., labourer, Hurst, Berks., 1592, I, W, P5/1592/41, P5/5Reg/140B
Edmd., innholder, Highw., 1696, AB, I, P10/1696/2
Edwd., clerk, Sal., 1664, W, P1/H/359
Eliz., widow, Sherb., Dorset, 1772, W, P5/1772/12, P5/17Reg/40B
Eliz., sp., Drayton, Abingdon, Berks., 1814, W, Wr, P1/1814/99
Hide, Gabriel, [baker], Westbrook, Gt. Faringdon, Berks., 1710, AB, I, P5/1710/54
Gabriel, sen., wheelwright, Stratton St Mgt., 1712, I, W, P3/H/919
Gabriel, wheelwright, Stratton St Mgt., 1745, W, P3/H/1221
Geo. Davis, Lyme R., Dorset, 1827, AB, O, Wr, P16/397
Hide, Gillian, widow, Westport St My., 1617, I, W, P3/H/122
Hide, Humphrey, labourer, Wantage, Berks., 1736, W, P23/521
Jane, sp., New St., Sal., 1692, I, W, P4/1691/12
Joanna, sp., Stitchcombe, Mildenhall, 1727, W, P1/H/834, P1/7Reg/166A
Jn., Sherb., Dorset, 1576, AB, P5/1576/25, P5/3Reg/92E
Hide, Jn., wheelwright, Wantage, Berks., 1707, W, P23/296
Hide, Jn., cordw., Hurst, Berks., 1711, W, P5/1711/29
Hide, Jn., esquire, Hyde End, Brimpton, Berks., 1714, W, P1/H/702, P1/5Reg/393B
Jn., marine of the Prince Edward man of war, Sherb., Dorset, 1746, AB, P5/1746/41
Jn., Wantage, Berks., 1748, AB, P23/600
Joshua, yeo., Upper Stratton, Stratton St Mgt., 1803, W, P3/1803/31
Joshua, wheelwright, Stratton St Mgt., 1828, comm, W, Wr, P3/1828/12
Hide, Mandefield *or* Manifield, gent., Sherb., Dorset, 1685, I, W, P5/1685/51
Mgt., sp., Stitchcombe, Mildenhall, 1727, W, P3/H/1043
Nich., Hurst, Berks., 1539, W, P5/20Reg/3
Nich., Waltham St Lawr., Berks., 1662, AB, I, NW, P1/H/320
Hide, Pearce, Chiseldon, 1735, W, P21/9/8
Peter, baker, Sherb., Dorset, 1624, AB, a/c, I, P5/1624/20, P5/10Reg/237
Peter, Sherb., Dorset, 1643, AB, comm, I, P5/1643/4, P5/14Reg/60C
Hide, Ralph, yeo., Hurst, Berks., 1604, AB, W, P5/1603/41, P5/8Reg/4B
Hide, Robt., shoemaker, Sherb., Dorset, 1620, I, W, P5/1620/27, P5/10Reg/79B
Robt., W. Hatch, Tisb., 1642, W, P2/H/559
Robt., wheelwright, Stratton St Mgt., 1788, W, P3/H/1486
Roger, shoemaker, Sherb., Dorset, 1690, AB, comm, I, P5/1689/32
Roger, Sherb., Dorset, 1738, AB, Wr, P5/1738/26
Roger, joiner, Sherb., Dorset, 1751, W, P5/1750/20
Sarah, widow, Stratton St Mgt., 1747, W, P1/H/1051, P1/10Reg/203
Hide, Simon, innholder, Sherb., Dorset, 1735, W, P5/1735/28
Hide, Stephen, St Mgt., Preshute, 1671, AB, I, P1/H/408
Stephen, yeo. *or* gent., Stitchcombe, Mildenhall, 1672, AB, comm (2), I, W, P3/H/470
Stephen, gent., Stitchcombe, Mildenhall, 1697, W, P3/H/773
Thos., Aldbourne, 1618, AB, I, P3/H/137
Hide, Thos., thatcher, Newbury St., Preshute, 1693, W, P1/H/562

Hide, Thos., tanner, Blewbury, Berks., 1721, W, P5/1721/19, P5/16Reg/55C
Hide, Thos., brewer, Reading, Berks., 1732, W, P1/H/895, P1/7Reg/482B
Thos., yeo., Drayton, Abingdon, Berks., 1808, W, Wr, P1/1808/98
Walter, husb., Westport St My., [1610], W (NEP), P3/H/64
Wm., yeo., Hurst, Berks., 1591, I, W, P5/1591/46, P5/5Reg/114B
Hide, Wm., husb., Pewsey, 1689, I, W, P3/H/666
Hide, Wm., S. Newton, 1783, AB, P2/H/1604
Hide, Wm., papermaker and beer seller, Arborfield, Berks., 1848, comm, D, W, Wr, P5/1848/4
Hyem *see* Hiam
Hyett *see* Hyatt
Hymory *see* Hemery
Hysshecokes *see* Hiscock
Hyther *see* Heather

I'Ans, Peter, haberdasher of earthenware, Devizes, 1743, AB, comm, ren, P1/IJ/204
Iatt *see* Hyatt *or* I.; Jatt
Iddols, Alice, Sopworth, [1612], I, W, P3/IJ/21
Chris., yeo., Sherston, 1710, I, W, P3/IJ/190
Eddolls, Edwd., carp., Langley Burrell, 1687, AB, I, W, P3/E/141
Eddolls, Edwd., gent., Chipp., 1743, W, P3/E/228
Eddolls, Eliz., widow, Langley Burrell, 1775, W, P3/E/281
Eddolls, Eliz., widow, Tytherton L., Chipp., 1834, comm, W, Wr, P3/1834/9
Jas., yeo., Hill House Farm, Box, 1835, W, Wr, P1/1835/87
Eddolls, Jn., yeo., Langley Burrell, 1822, W, Wr, P3/1822/49
Jn., yeo., Hill House, Box, 1845, aff, O, W, Wr, P3/1845/2
Eddolls, Magdalen, widow, Kington St M., 1647, comm, NW, P1/E/73
Edalls, Nich., yeo., Wilcot, 1662, I, W, P3/E/72
Philip, husb., Luckington, 1622, I, W, P3/IJ/42
Eddolls, Thos., Milbourne, Malm., 1777, W, P3/E/287
Thos., yeo., Corston, Malm., 1813, W, Wr, P3/1813/25
Wm., sen., rough mason, Sopworth, 1768, W, P3/IJ/284
Wm., innholder, Sherston, 1808, W, Wr, P3/1808/19
see also Cobb alias I.
Idens, Wm., Hindon, 1573, AB, P2/5Reg/167B
Idny *see* Edney
Ilbury, Nich., Blewbury, Berks., 1613, comm, O, W (all documents badly damaged), P1/IJ/15
Nich., yeo., Blewbury, Berks., 1719, W, P5/1719/48, P5/16Reg/26B
Thos., yeo., Blewbury, Berks., 1681, AB, comm, I (over £600), P5/1680/29
Iles, Alice, cordw.'s wife, Wanb., 1689, AB, comm, I (form. Alice Heath), P1/IJ/114, P3/IJ/144
Ann, sp., Lyneham, 1800, W, P3/1800/55
Anthony, S. Wraxall, 1600, I, W, P2/IJ/36
Anthony, sen., carp., Oare, Wilcot, 1682, AB, I, W, P3/IJ/128
Isles, Anthony, tailor, Milton L., 1738, AB, ren, P3/IJ/241
Cath., widow, W. Leaze Farm, Wrou., 1798, comm, W, P1/IJ/299, P1/15Reg/137
Chas., yeo., Atworth, Bradford A., [1691], I, W, P2/IJ/201
Isles, Chas., victualler, Trowb., 1754, W, P1/IJ/226, P1/11Reg/145
Edmd., Cotmarsh, Broad H., 1665, I, W, P3/IJ/87
Eliz., Wanb., 1663, AB, I, P3/IJ/83
Eliz., widow, Hilmarton, 1750, W, P3/IJ/260
Hy., carp., Wanb., 1746, W, P3/IJ/253
Isles, Jas., Trowb., 1755, I, W, P1/IJ/232, P1/11Reg/184A
Jeremiah, innkeeper, Westb. L., 1711, I, W (NEP), P25/1711/1
Joan, widow, Seend, Melk., 1603, AB, I, P2/IJ/40
Jn., Castle Eaton, 1614, I, W, P1/IJ/21
Jn., yeo., Uffington, Berks., 1770, W, P1/IJ/251, P1/12Reg/339B
Jn., slaymaker, Newtown, Bradford A., 1782, W, P2/IJ/360
Jn., farmer, Stratton St Mgt., 1803, W, P3/1803/28
Jn., gent., Studley Grange, Lydiard T., 1821, comm, W, Wr, P3/1821/42
Mgt., widow, Devizes St My., 1631, I, W, P1/IJ/45
My., sp., Wrou., 1770, W, P1/IJ/252, P1/12Reg/332B

Philip, rough mason, Bradford A., 1747, W, P1/IJ/215, P1/10Reg/170
Richd., victualler, Marl. St My., 1757, NW, P1/IJ/233, P1/11Reg/340A
Ilse alias Craft, Robt., husb., Holcombe, Calne, 1574-75, I, W, P26/1484, P5/3Reg/51B
Robt., Downton, 1715, AB, P2/IJ/242
Robt., Marl., 1736, AB, P1/IJ/193
Robt., Goatacre, Hilmarton, 1757, AB, I, P3/IJ/269
Robt., yeo., Walcot, Swindon, 1773, W, P3/IJ/293
Robt., timber dealer, Purton, 1832, W, Wr, P1/1832/100
Roger, husb. *or* yeo., Oare, Wilcot, 1713, I, W, P3/IJ/193
Thos., Seend, Melk., 1559, AB, P2/3Reg/186C
Ilis, Thos., Chitterne AS, 1570, W, P2/5Reg/97B
Thos., S. Wraxall, 1597-1608, AB, I, W, P2/IJ/30
Thos., Westport St My., [1611], W (NEP), P3/IJ/17
Thos., slater, Ashton K., 1636, I, W, P3/IJ/62
Thos., Stratton St Mgt., 1684, AB, I, P3/IJ/133
Thos., sen., Atworth, Bradford A., 1685, AB, I, P2/IJ/187
Thos., Wootton R., 1728, AB, I, P3/IJ/223
Wm., Purton, 1569, W, P1/2Reg/85C
Wm., Malm., 1608, W, P3/IJ/9
Wm., yeo., Forest Gate, Melk., 1635, I, NW, P1/IJ/52
Isles, Wm., Westb., 1701, AB, P25/1701/3
Wm., sen., carp., Oare, Wilcot, 1715, AB, I, P3/IJ/199
Wm., yeo., Rudloe, Box, 1724, comm, W (2 - 1 is copy), P3/IJ/215
Wm., haulier, Crickl. St S., 1857, aff, O, W, Wr, P3/1857/8
Illen *see* Ellen
Illery *see* Ellery
Illing *see* Ellen
Ilse *see* Iles
Ilsley, Bartholemew, Steeple L., 1567, AB, P2/5Reg/11C
Geo., Tilehurst, Berks., 1798, AB, P1/IJ/300, P1/15Reg/62C
Jn., Newbury, Berks., 1714, AB, I, P1/IJ/150
Thos., carp., Tilehurst, Berks., 1829, W, Wr, P1/1829/151
Wm., Theale, Tilehurst, Berks., 1804, AB, P1/1804/50
Ilton, Aaron, yeo., Sonning, Berks., 1722, W, P5/1722/31, P5/16Reg/79A
Ann, widow, Woodley, W. and Sandford, Berks., 1801, AB, P5/1801/13, P5/18Reg/319B
David, Sonning, Berks., 1748, AB, Wr, P5/1748/19
Moses, Sonning, Berks., 1765, AB, P5/1765/11
Imans *see* Yeomans
Imber, Ember, [...], husb., Chitterne AS, 1591, W, P2/E/34
Ember, Alice, widow, Chitterne AS, 1592, I, W, P2/E/37
Edmd., yeo., Upton L., 1664, AB, I, P2/IJ/139
Edmd., Upton L., 1733, AB, P2/IJ/274
Edmd., yeo., Upton L., 1758, W, P2/IJ/320
Edmd., yeo., Sherrington, 1775, W, P2/IJ/341
Edmd., miller, Upton L., 1776, AB, T, W, P1/IJ/270, P1/13Reg/77
Edwd., husb., Tilsh., 1559, AB, W, P2/4Reg/2C
Edwd., husb., Deptford, Wylye, 1610-11, AB, a/c, alleg, I, P2/IJ/56, P2/8Reg/82B
Edwd., Tisb., 1778, AB, P2/IJ/347
Edwd., sen., baker, Sutton V., 1778, W, P2/IJ/348
Edwd., yeo., Sutton V., 1801, W, P1/1801/13, P1/15Reg/235B
Geo., yeo., Sherrington, 1615, I (detailed), W, P2/IJ/62
Geo., yeo., Chitterne AS, 1684, AB, I, W, P2/IJ/183
Geo., yeo., Sherrington, 1738, W, P2/IJ/282
Geo., yeo., Sherrington, 1780, W, P2/IJ/355
Isabel, widow, Chitterne St My., 1558, W, P2/3Reg/80A
Joan, widow, Corton, Boyton, 1628, I, W, P1/IJ/39
Jn., Chitterne St My., 1557, W, P2/3Reg/23A
Jn., jun., Chitterne AS, 1560, W, P2/4Reg/38B
Jn., jun., yeo., Chitterne AS, 1638, comm, I, W, P2/IJ/105
Jn., yeo., Chitterne AS, 1639, I, W, P2/IJ/111

Jn., Heytes., 1682, AB, I, P5/1682/62
Ember, Jn., yeo., Upton L., 1700, AB, I, P2/E/247
Jn., yeo., Sherrington, 1776, W, P2/IJ/345
My., widow, Upton L., 1729, W, P1/IJ/179, P1/7Reg/346A
My., widow, Upton L., 1752, W, P2/IJ/308
Thos., gardener, Sutton V., 1829, AB, O, ren, W, Wr, P2/1829/17
Wm., Chitterne AS, 1581, W, P2/6Reg/44A
Ember, Wm., maltster, Warm., 1755, W, P2/E/353
Wm., husb., Sherrington, 1799, W, Wr, P2/IJ/385
Wm., yeo., Sherrington, 1825, AB, W, Wr, P2/1825/33
Wm., carp., Sutton V., 1832, W, Wr, P2/1832/13
Imray, Jn., Everleigh, 1815, AB, W, Wr, P3/1815/83
Ind, Jonathan, yeo., Callow Hill, Wootton B., 1836, comm, W, Wr, P3/1836/75
Richd., yeo., Whitehill Farm, Wootton B., 1826, W, Wr, P1/1826/102
End, Robt., innholder, Chr. M., 1775, W, P3/E/284
Ind, Robt., Kington St M., 1838, AB, comm, Wr, P3/1838/9
Ind, Wm., yeo., Whitehill Farm, Wootton B., 1813, W, Wr, P3/1813/14
Ind, Wm., bach., Newent, Gloucs, 1854, AB, aff, L, O, Wr, P3/1854/47
Indoe, Wm., butcher, Sal., [1684], I, W, P4/1685/8
Ingerom *see* Ingran
Ingleby, Jane, wife of Stephen, Corsham, 1833, AB, P29/3Reg/283A
Stephen, yeo., Pickwick, Corsham, 1833, AB, O, P29/1800-1857/25
Inglefield, Edwd., yeo., Stanford in the Vale, Berks., 1689, AB, I, P1/IJ/115
Geo., labourer, Sonning, Berks. (late of Binfield, Berks.), 1744, AB, I, Wr, P5/1744/26
Englefield, Jane, widow of baronet, Kington L. (form. of Vasterne, Wootton B.), 1650, I, W, P1/E/77
Inglis, Richd., weaver, Devizes St My., [1572], W (NEP), P1/1Reg/131A
Ingram, Agnes, widow, Codf. St My., 1585, W, P2/7Reg/1B
Agnes, widow, Bapton, Fisherton Delamare, 1597, I, W, P2/IJ/33
Alexander, husb., Winterslow, 1608, W, P2/8Reg/24
Alexander, yeo., Winterslow, 1713, I, W, P2/IJ/236
Amy, widow, Bapton, Fisherton Delamare, 1627, I, W, P2/IJ/83
Ann, widow, Tytherington, Heytes., 1826, W, Wr, P5/1826/3
Ann *or* Nancy, sp., Sherrington, 1836, D, O, W, P2/1836/16
Chris., yeo., Bapton, Fisherton Delamare, 1712, I, W, P2/IJ/234
Dan., tailor, Bapton, Fisherton Delamare, 1719, AB, ren, P2/IJ/253
Deborah, widow, Codf. St My., 1777, AB, ren, W, P2/IJ/346
Edmd., husb., Bapton, Fisherton Delamare, 1569, W, P2/5Reg/63A
Edmd., husb., Bapton, Fisherton Delamare, 1694, I, W, P2/IJ/204
Edmd., Wylye, 1708, AB, P2/IJ/224
Edwd., shepherd, Fonthill B., 1677, I, W, P2/IJ/168
Edwd., bricklayer, Whitep., 1796, W, P2/IJ/382
Eleanor, widow, Gt. Durnford, 1591, I, W, P5/1591/47, P5/5Reg/97A
Elias, yeo., Stoke F., 1730, W, P2/IJ/270
Elias, Broad C., 1805, AB, P2/1805/59
Elias, shopkeeper, Broad C., 1854, aff, W, Wr, P2/1854/20
Eliz., Fisherton D., 1614, W, P2/8Reg/218A
Eliz., widow, Ebbesborne Wake, 1626, AB, I, P2/IJ/80
Eliz., widow, Ebbesborne Wake, 1632, AB, P2/IJ/93, P2/9Reg/37E
Eliz., widow, Codf. St P., 1752, I, W, P2/IJ/307
Eliz., Bapton, Fisherton Delamare, 1774, W, P2/IJ/338
Eliz., widow, Codf. St My., 1815, comm, W, Wr, P2/1815/11
Eliz., sp., Durrington, 1854, D (2), W, Wr, P2/1854/22
Francis, Amesb., 1664, AB, I, P1/IJ/78
Giles, sen., Winterslow, 1624, I, W, P2/IJ/78
Giles, yeo., Codf. St My., 1711, I, W, P2/IJ/231
Hy., Bapton, Fisherton Delamare, 1633, I, copy I, W, P2/IJ/96, P2/9Reg/35B
Hy., yeo., Bapton, Fisherton Delamare, [1684], I, W, P2/IJ/182
Hy., carp., Corton, Boyton, 1738, NW, P1/IJ/194, P1/8Reg/221B
Hy., yeo., Codf. St P., 1762, AB, ren, P2/IJ/324
Hester Turnor, Longbridge D., 1829, W, Wr, P1/1829/42

Jane, sp., Sal., 1851, W, Wr, P4/1851/12
Joan, widow, Bapton, Fisherton Delamare, [1626], I, W, P2/IJ/82
Joan, widow, Codf. St P., 1685, I, W, P2/IJ/186
Jn., Ogbourne St Geo., 1564, W, P5/1Reg/46C
Jn., Winterslow, 1565, AB, P2/4Reg/202A
Jn., Bower C., 1567, W, P2/5Reg/15B
Jn., husb., Woodminton, Bower C., 1592, I, T, W, P2/IJ/25
Jn., Fordington, Dorset, 1603, AB, I, W, P5/1603/44, P5/7Reg/65C
Jn., carp., Sal., 1614, I, P4/1614/9
Jn., yeo., Bapton, Fisherton Delamare, 1646, AB, I, P2/IJ/130
Jn., yeo., Bapton, Fisherton Delamare, 1706, W, P2/IJ/216
Jn., gent., Codf. St My., 1708, AB, I, P2/IJ/225
Jn., Fordington, Dorset, 1724, AB, I, P15/108
Jn., yeo., Bapton, Fisherton Delamare, 1740, W, P2/IJ/286
Jn., widower, Codf. St P., 1740, W, P2/IJ/287
Jn., yeo. *or* gent., Codf. St P., 1741, a/c, I, W, P1/IJ/199, P1/9Reg/209B
Jn., yeo., E. Knoyle, 1760, W, P2/IJ/321
Jn., Codf. St My., 1785, AB, P2/IJ/367
Jn., yeo., Purton, 1789, W, P1/IJ/288, P1/14Reg/224
Jn., Fonthill B., 1824, W, Wr, P2/1824/77
Jos., jun., Fordington, Dorset, 1676, I, P15/22
Mgt., Hindon, 1538, W (NEP), P2/1Reg/4E
Margery, widow, Codf. St P., 1681, I, W, P2/IJ/179
My., sp., Codf. St My., [1639], W, P2/IJ/114
My., sp., Codf. St My., 1642, I, copy I, W, P2/IJ/123
Nancy *see* Ann
Peter, husb., Bower C., 1610, I, W, P2/IJ/53, P2/8Reg/88
Philip, yeo., Codf. St My., 1630, I, P2/IJ/90
Philip, sen., yeo., Codf. St P., 1664, comm, I, W, P1/IJ/79
Philip, Codf. St P., 1681-82, AB, a/c, I, P2/IJ/175
Philip, Codf. St P., 1695, AB, P2/IJ/205
Philip, W. Lavington, 1696, AB, P1/IJ/123
Philip, yeo., Fisherton D., 1720, W, P1/IJ/161, P1/6Reg/221A
Philip, yeo., E. Knoyle, 1727, W, P2/IJ/266
Philip, labourer, Sal., 1836, W, Wr, P4/1836/4
Ingerom, Philippa, sp. and servant, Marl. St My., 1622, I, NW, P1/IJ/33
Phyllis, widow, Bapton, Fisherton Delamare, 1756, AB, P2/IJ/315
Richd., jun., husb., Broad C., 1581, W, P2/6Reg/47C
Richd., Bapton, Fisherton Delamare, 1593, I, W, P2/IJ/28
Richd., husb., Ashton G., Codf. St P., [1633], I, W, P2/IJ/95
Richd., Fordington, Dorset, 1662, AB, I (with a/c), P5/1662/69
Richd., Codf. St My., 1718, AB, P2/IJ/249
Robt., Broad C., 1564, W, P2/4Reg/162B
Robt., Bower C., [1564], I, P2/IJ/5
Robt., husb., Fordington, Dorset, 1672, I, W, P15/18
Robt., yeo., Fordington, Dorset, 1680, I, W, P15/32
Sam., mason, Whitep., 1718, W, P2/IJ/247
Sam., victualler, Westb., 1800, O, W, P25/1800/4
Sarah, widow, Fordington, Dorset, 1679, I, ren, P5/1679/48
Sarah Ann, sp., Sal., 1840, W, Wr, P4/1840/7
Thos., Ebbesborne Wake, 1631, I, W, P2/IJ/91
Thos., victualler, Calne, 1721, AB, I (detailed), P26/653
Thos., yeo., Wylye, 1775, AB, W, P2/IJ/342
Wm., husb., Winterslow, 1565, W, P2/4Reg/201C
Wm., Thornford, Dorset, 1663, comm, I, W, P5/1663/36
Wm., husb., Winterslow, 1682, I, W, P2/IJ/180
Wm., blacksmith, Kingston Bagpuize, Berks., 1716, W, P1/IJ/155, P1/6Reg/62A
Wm., Fisherton D., 1732, AB, P1/IJ/183
Wm., Dinton, 1755, W, P2/IJ/313
Wm., Bapton, Fisherton Delamare, 1756, AB, P2/IJ/314

Wm., widower, Sal., 1762, W, P4/1762/9
Wm., clerk, Fisherton D., 1772, W, P2/IJ/336
Wm., yeo., Fisherton D., 1780, comm, W, P2/IJ/354
Wm., Poulshot, 1845, comm, D, W, Wr, P1/1845/84
Ings, Ann, sp., Sal., 1844, AB, aff, Wr (crossed out & annotated PCC), P1/1844/7
Ann, sp., Sal. St Martin, 1847, D, W (pre-printed W paper), Wr, P4/1847/4
Eliz., widow, Dinton, 1607, AB, I, W, P2/IJ/45
Jn., Dinton, 1558, W, P2/3Reg/83A
Jn., sen., tailor, Heytes., 1582, W, P5/4Reg/45A
Jn., tailor, Heytes., 1588, W, P5/5Reg/29D
Jn., Downton, 1831, W, P2/1831/54
Robt. Hy., bach., Sal., 1855, AB, aff, Wr, P1/1855/26
Silas, sen., glazier, Fovant Stroud, 1722, I, W, P2/IJ/258
Susanna, widow, Everleigh, 1852, AB, O, Wr, P3/1852/42
Thos., Dinton, 1584, AB, P2/6Reg/127C
Walter, husb., Dinton, 1610, AB, I, P2/IJ/54, P2/8Reg/110A
Wm., no abode stated, 1638, I, W, P2/IJ/106
Wm., yeo., Linley Farm, Tisb., 1671, I, W, P1/IJ/100
Wm., husb., Motc., Dorset, 1720, I, W, P27/1/242
Wm., Gt. Wishford, 1787, AB, P2/IJ/371
Wm., tiler and glazier, Gillingham, Dorset, 1791, comm, W, P27/1/543
Wm., glazier, Gillingham, Dorset, 1826, AB, O, ren, W, Wr, P27/1/676
Inness *see* Ennis
Innot, Innot alias Bradbury, Ellen *or* Eleanor, widow, Lyneham, 1663, I, W, P3/IJ/84
Innot alias Bradbury, Francis, Lyneham, 1624, AB, a/c, I, P3/IJ/44
Insell, Jn., yeo., Chelworth, Crickl. St S., 1746, AB, I, P3/IJ/254
Inslate, Inslate *or* Juslate, Nich., sadler, Wokm., Berks., 1572, W, P5/2Reg/111A
Insley, Hannah, Chute, 1789, AB, P7/179
Inwood, Lionel, Lt. Bedwyn, 1681, AB, P21/2/80
Thos., yeo., Sandhurst, Berks., 1685, I, W, P5/1685/54
Ireland, Chas., collier, Bramshaw, Hants, 1685, AB, I, P24/713
Dorothy, widow, Thornford, Dorset, 1679, AB, I, P5/1679/49
Edwd., Farley, Alderbury, 1664, AB, I, P26/121
Eliz., Hurst, Berks., 1693, W, P5/1693/32
Hy., Whitep., 1559, W, P2/3Reg/167B
Hy., Hurst, Berks., 1574, W, P5/3Reg/45B
Jn., husb., Axnoller, Beam., Dorset, [1685], I, W, P17/295
Jn., clothier, Hurst, Berks., 1690, AB, I, P5/1690/25
Jn., Sal., 1704, W, P1/IJ/136
Jn., sen., weaver, Hurst, Berks., 1722, W, P5/1722/32, P5/16Reg/78B
Jn., yeo., Hurst, Berks., 1733, W, P5/1733/32
Jn., yeo., Melbury Horsey aka Melcombe Bingham, Dorset, 1758, W, P5/1758/27
Mgt., widow, Hurst, Berks., 1687, I, W, P5/1687/21
Robt., Plaitford, 1580, W, P2/IJ/13, P2/6Reg/7C
Robt., husb., Farley, Alderbury, 1684, I, W, P26/312
Roger, weaver, Sindlesham, Hurst, Berks., 1671, I, W, P5/1671/48
Roger, Thornford, Dorset, 1685, AB, I, P5/1685/55
Thos., Blunsdon St Andrew, 1614, a/c (3), comm, court paper, I, P3/IJ/25
Thos., costume weaver, Winnersh, Hurst, Berks., 1745, I, W, P5/1745/8
Wm., tailor, Sal. St Martin, 1584, I, W, P4/1584/1, P4/Reg/25B
Wm., cordw., E. Grimstead, W. Dean, 1782, W, P2/IJ/359
Iremonger, Ann, widow, Keevil, 1687, I, W, P2/IJ/195
Ann, sp., Sal., 1707, W, P2/IJ/222
Ann, widow, Bucklebury, Berks., 1711, AB, I, P1/IJ/143
Francis, husb., Wyld Farm, Hampstead N., Berks., 1614, I, W, P1/IJ/20
Jn., rugmaker, Reading, Berks., 1747, AB, W, P1/IJ/216, P1/10Reg/111
Mgt., Grove, Wantage, Berks., 1597, AB, T (children: Joan & Alice I.), P5/1597/125, P5/6Reg/188C
My., widow, Britford, 1681, W, P24/414
My., widow, Reading St Lawr., Berks., 1714, W, P1/IJ/151, P1/5Reg/370
Wm., glover, Newbury, Berks., 1701, I, W, P1/IJ/129, P1/4Reg/5

Ireson, Giles, Curridge, Chieveley, Berks., 1744, AB, I, P1/IJ/206
Jn., Curridge, Chieveley, Berks., 1701, I, W, P1/IJ/130, P1/4Reg/95
Irish, Ann, widow, Sal., 1743, AB, I, P1/IJ/205
Jn., Whitep., 1707, AB, I, P2/IJ/218
Jn., labourer, Whitep., 1763, W, P1/IJ/239, P1/12Reg/57B
Richd., husb., Chards., Devon, 1638, AB, I, P5/1638/45, P5/13Reg/74A
Robt., husb. and labourer, Whitep., 1729, I, W, P2/IJ/268
Wm., Sindlesham, Hurst, Berks., 1597, AB, I, W, P5/1597/63, P5/6Reg/154B
Iron, Jn., Idmiston, 1724, AB, P2/IJ/261
Ironside *see* Bowring nee I., My., 1843
Irving, Urvin, Anstis, widow, Holnest, Dorset, 1640, W, P5/1640/71, P5/13Reg/235B
Jas., Sal., 1729, req, W, copy W, P4/1729/15
Urvin, Jn., husb., Holnest, Dorset, 1640, AB, I, NW, P5/1640/70, P5/13Reg/236A
Isaac, Ann, Lyme R., Dorset, 1755, W, P5/1755/32
Clement, Chitterne, 1616, AB, I, T, P2/IJ/67, P2/8Reg/302C
Hy., Ebbesborne Wake, 1711, AB, P1/IJ/144
Jacob, stone tile quarrier, Kington St M., 1814, W, Wr, P1/1814/126
Jeremiah, yeo., Atworth, Bradford A., 1782, comm, W, P2/IJ/361
Jeremiah, yeo., Broughton G., 1832, O, W, Wr, P1/1832/40
Jn., labourer, Biddestone St Nich., 1830, W, Wr, P3/1830/62
My., widow, Stourpaine, Dorset, 1733, W, P24/951
My., widow, Melk., 1800, AB, comm, P2/1800/1
Maurice, husb., Bishopstrow, 1607, AB, I, P2/IJ/43
Robt., Stourpaine, Dorset, 1720, I, W, P24/620
Wm., sen., Giddeahall, Yatton K., 1753, W, P1/IJ/225, P1/11Reg/88
Wm., yeo., Biddestone St Nich., 1851, W, Wr, P3/1851/48
Isard *see* Izzard
Isgar, Eleanor, sp., Sherston, 1634, I, W, P1/IJ/50
Joan, widow, Sherston, 1640, I, W, P3/IJ/73
Jn., yeo., Sherston, 1646, AB, Wr, P1/IJ/66
Richd., Sherston, 1620, I, W, P3/IJ/38
Thos., yeo., Sherston, 1698, I, W, P3/IJ/163
Wm., no abode stated, late 16th C., W (incomplete & undated) (NEP), P3/1Reg/1
Isgell, Ann, sp., Pewsham Forest, 1709, I, W, P3/IJ/189
Isher, My., Heddington, 1828, AB, comm, Wr, P3/1828/47
Nathaniel, shepherd, Overton, 1706, I, schedule, NW, P3/IJ/185
Wm., labourer, Lydiard T., 1827, comm, W, Wr, P1/1827/26
Iskett *see* Escott
Isles *see* Iles
Isley, Jas., widower, Trowb., 1854, AB, aff, O, Wr, P1/1854/13
Islington, Edwd., Mkt. L., 1758, AB, P2/IJ/318
Itchener, Wm., clerk, Chr. M., 1804, AB, P3/1804/2
Ithimay *see* Evemay
Ivans *see* Evans
Ives *see* Eve
Ivy, Cath., widow, Bucklebury, Berks., 1741, AB, I, P1/IJ/200
Deborah, sp., Sal., 1788, W, P4/1788/13
Eleanor, widow, Sal., 1683, AB, W, P4/1683/8
Eliz., Gt. Bedwyn, 1588, I, P5/1588/33
Eliz., widow, Haxton, Fittleton, [1674], W, P2/IJ/162
Eliz., Wilton, Gt. Bedwyn, 1705, I, P21/6/26
Geo., esquire, Hullavington, 1676, AB, I, P3/IJ/115
Geo., Sal., 1684, AB, ren, P4/1684/8
Jane, Gt. Bedwyn, 1583-88, AB (in minority of Geoffrey Pike), a/c, I, P5/1583/18, P5/1588/32, P5/4Reg/60D
Jane, widow, Fittleton, 1754, W, P2/IJ/311
Jn., yeo., Manningford Bohun, 1661, I, W, P3/IJ/82, P3/3Reg/23A
Jn., gent., Devizes, 1686, W, P1/IJ/112
Jn., mercer, Gt. Bedwyn, 1689, AB, comm, I, ren, P21/4/37
Jn., yeo., Fittleton, 1734, W, P2/IJ/276
Lydia, sp., Hullavington, 1674, comm, NW, P3/IJ/113

Naomi, singlewoman, Fittleton, 1784, AB, P2/IJ/364
Nich., husb., Gt. Bedwyn, 1581-88, AB (in minority of Jane I., for whom T *also* issued), I, T, W, P5/1580/32, P5/4Reg/13B, P5/5Reg/47A
Nich., husb., Gt. Bedwyn, 1646, I, NW, P21/1/65
Richd., priest, Mkt. L., 1553, institution to vicarage on death of Catcote., P2/2Reg/177C
Richd., yeo., Haxton, Fittleton, 1661, I, W, P2/IJ/135
Richd., husb., Chute, 1684, I, W, P7/64
Richd., yeo., Wilton, Gt. Bedwyn, 1699, I, W, P21/5/47
Richd., baker, Reading, Berks., 1744, W, P1/IJ/207, P1/9Reg/345A
Robt., labourer, Wantage, Berks., 1728, W, P5/1728/55, P5/16Reg/194A
Stephen, husb., Seend, Melk., 1645, I, W, P2/IJ/127
Thos., Netheravon, 1567?, W (date incomplete), P5/2Reg/13A
Thos., labourer, Wantage, Berks., 1725, W, P5/1725/42, P5/16Reg/123A
Wm., Gt. Bedwyn, 1748, W, P21/10/4
Ivyleaf, Jn., fuller, Bradford A., [1628], I, W, P2/IJ/85
Ivymay, Wm., husb., Codf. St P., 1609, I, W, P2/IJ/49, P2/8Reg/54
Izzard, Agnes, widow, Lambourn Woodlands, Berks., 1613, I, W, P1/IJ/16
Alice, Rams., 1741, AB, Wr, P5/1740/42
Cath., tanner's widow, Rams., 1772, AB, comm, W, P5/1772/13, P5/17Reg/37
Isard, Jn., Baydon, 1628, a/c, P5/1627/57
Jn., sen., tailor, Rams., 1725, W, P5/1725/41, P5/16Reg/119
Jn., tanner, Rams., 1772, W, P5/1772/14, P5/17Reg/36B
Stephen, mercer, Rams., 1761, W, P5/1761/26
Wm., husb., Chisbury, Lt. Bedwyn, 1599, AB, I, W, P5/1599/11, P5/6Reg/226
Isard, Wm., Wilcot, 1640, I, W, P3/IJ/72
Wm., tailor, Rams., 1691, AB, I, W, P5/1691/40

Jackes *see* Jaques
Jackling, Ann, widow, Devizes, 1690, W (2 - 1 unsigned), P1/IJ/118
Jacklin, Anthony, shopkeeper, Devizes St Jn., [1621], AB, I, W, P1/IJ/29
Wm., woolcomber *or* worsted comber, Devizes, 1690, AB, ren (2), W, P1/IJ/119
Jackman, Cath., widow, Winterslow, 1715, W, P2/IJ/240
Geo., yeo., Grafton, 1749, AB, I, Wr, P5/1749/31
Jn., Knook, 1661, I, P5/1661/32
Jn., E. Grafton, 1820, O, W, Wr, P21/12/40
Rachel, E. Grafton, 1755, AB, P21/10/29
Richd., husb., Whitep., 1603, AB, I, W, P2/IJ/39
Richd., husb. and yeo., Heytes., 1685, I, W (2 - 1 a fair copy), P5/1685/61
Wm., husb., Hamptworth, Downton, 1590, AB, I, W, P2/IJ/24
Wm., sen., yeo., Hamptworth, Downton, 1636, I, W, P2/IJ/100, P2/9Reg/92C
Jackson, Alice, sp., Stanton Fitzwarren, 1604, I, W (NEP), P3/IJ/2
Ambrose, tailor, Nettleton, 1571, W (NEP), P1/1Reg/85C
Ambrose, N. Wraxall, 1638, I, W (2 - 1 a fair copy), P1/IJ/57
Beata, widow, Mkt. L., 1749, W, P2/IJ/300
Cath., widow, Stanton Fitzwarren, 1639, I, W, P3/IJ/69
Cath., widow, Crickl. St My., 1833, W, Wr, P3/1833/39
Chas., yeo., Hawkeridge, Westb., 1824, O, W, P25/1824/1
Jacksons, Christian, widow, Stratton St Mgt., 1629, I, W, P3/IJ/51
Edith, widow, Ashton K., [1611], I, W (NEP), P3/IJ/18
Edwd., dealer in earthen ware, Trowb., 1834, comm, W, Wr, P1/1834/11
Eliz., widow, Wantage, Berks., 1575, I, W, P23/1014, P5/3Reg/66B
Frances, widow, Shalbourne, 1688, comm, I, W, P5/1687/22
Jackson form. Bell, Frances, brewer and sailclothmaker's wife, Marl., 1751, ren, W, P1/IJ/223, P1/10Reg/452
Jacksons, Francis, yeo., Stratton St Mgt., 1699, I, W, P3/IJ/166
Geo., innholder, Fisherton A., 1712, I, W, P2/IJ/232
Gilbert, yeo., Sal., 1615, AB, a/c, P4/1615/1
Hy., sen., husb. and yeo., Shalbourne, 1692, comm, I, W, P5/1692/46
Hy., sen., pedlar *or* chapman, Hungerford, Berks., 1745, AB, I (detailed), ren, W (bequest to wife conditional on her not living with 'her former husband Jn. Beech'), P23/591
Hy., maltster, Mkt. L., 1748, AB, comm, W, P2/IJ/296

Hy., Hilp., Whaddon, Lt. (West) Chalfield & Atworth, Mkt. L., 1828, AB, O, P2/1828/67
Jane *see* Jane Eglen alias Boucher
Joan, Stanton Fitzwarren, 1592, I, P1/IJ/1
Jn., husb., Ashton K., [1604], I, W (NEP), P1/IJ/7
Jn., tailor, Stanton Fitzwarren, 1693, AB, I, P3/IJ/152
Mgt., widow, Watchfield, Shrivenham, Berks., 1602, I, W, P1/IJ/5
Mgt., widow *or* sp., Stratton St Mgt., 1680, AB, ren, W, P3/IJ/121
Mgt., widow, Sal., 1723, AB, I, P4/1722/7
Martha, Abingdon, Berks., 1767, W, Wr, P1/IJ/244, P1/12Reg/249B
My., widow, Stanton Fitzwarren, 1686, I, W, P3/IJ/140
My., widow, Highw., 1714, AB, P10/1714/7
My., sp., Lyme R., Dorset, 1774, W, P16/340
Matthew, Gt. Faringdon, Berks., 1569, W, P5/2Reg/47A
Nich., Stanton Fitzwarren, 1630, AB, I, P3/IJ/55
Jacksons, Nich., sen., Upper Stratton, Stratton St Mgt., 1716, I, W, P29/J/4, P29/2Reg/23
Richd., Calne, 1597, AB, P5/1597/66, P5/6Reg/193C
Richd., Stanton Fitzwarren, 1636, AB, I, P3/IJ/63
Richd., Stanton Fitzwarren, 1673, I, W, P3/IJ/110
Richd., yeo., Hampton, Highw., 1685, I, W, P5/1685/57
Jacksons, Sibyl, widow, Crickl. St S., 1779, W, P3/IJ/300
Thos., miller, Shalbourne, Berks., 1678, AB, I, P23/86
Thos., sen., yeo., Stratton St Mgt., 1680, I, W (2), P3/IJ/122-23
Thos., jun., yeo., Lt. Hidden, Hungerford, Berks., 1753, W, P23/642
Wm., husb., Watchfield, Shrivenham, Berks., 1592, W, P1/IJ/2
Wm., Sonning, Berks., 1604, W, P5/1604/24, P5/8Reg/19A
Wm., Stanton Fitzwarren, 1683, AB, P3/IJ/130
Wm., labourer, Binfield Heath, Sonning, Berks., 1712, I, W, P5/1712/33, P5/15Reg/304A
Wm., clerk and vicar, Aldbourne, 1723, comm, W, P3/IJ/214
Jacob, (Dr) *see* Wm. Mitton
[...], Chitterne AS, 1644, NW, P2/IJ/126
Abigail, widow, Sal., 1690, AB, I, P4/1690/10
Alice, widow, Braydon Forest, Crickl. St S., 1766, comm, W, P3/IJ/282
Andrew, Wootton B., 1620, AB, I, P1/IJ/28
Ann, widow, Wootton B., 1663, AB, comm, I, P3/IJ/85
Ann, widow, Burton Hill, Malm., 1732, W, P3/IJ/232
Ann *see also* Ann Rawlings
Benj., Inglesham, 1683, AB, comm, P3/IJ/131
Benj., gent., Braydon Forest, Crickl. St S., 1732, comm, W, P3/IJ/233
Jacobs, Benj., yeo., Bishopstone N., 1830, comm, W, Wr, P5/1830/25
Bridget, Braydon Forest, Crickl. St S., 1698, AB, P3/IJ/164
Christian, widow, Enmore Grn, Motc., Dorset, 1714, AB, W, P5/1714/21, P5/15Reg/390B
Chris., merchant, Sal., 1631, AB, I, W, P4/1630/12
Edwd., husb., Downton, 1725, W, P2/IJ/262
Edwd., upholsterer, Reading, Berks., 1773, W, P1/12Reg/487A
Eliz., sp., Fordington, Dorset, 1720, AB, comm, P15/100
Eliz., singlewoman, Quidh., 1771, W, P2/IJ/334
Eliz., Crickl. St S., 1803, W, P3/1803/10
Emanuel, yeo., Dauntsey, 1679, comm, I, W, P3/IJ/117
Geo., Landford, 1763, AB, P1/IJ/240
Jas., gent. form. sewingman, Sal. The Close, 1826, a/c, appt of proctor, D (9), I, W, Wr (2), P4/1826/3
Jn., Amesb., 1554, W, P2/2Reg/188B
Jn., Inglesham, 1613, AB, I, P3/IJ/24
Jn., shepherd, Grimstone, Stratton, Dorset, 1629, I, NW, P5/1628/63, P5/11Reg/18C
Jn., weaver, Tockenham, 1641, I, W, P3/IJ/75
Jn., sen., yeo., Swindon, 1669, comm, I, W, P3/IJ/97
Jn., yeo., Avebury, 1670, I, W, P3/IJ/101
Jn., Smithcot, Dauntsey, 1680, AB, a/c, comm, I, P3/IJ/124
Jn., yeo., Westrop, Highw., 1699, AB, I, P10/1699/1
Jn., Mere, 1707, AB, P5/1707/37
Jn., Enmore Grn, Motc., Dorset, 1711, AB, P19/96

Jn., gent., Braydon Forest, Crickl. St S., 1728, AB, comm, Wr, P3/IJ/224
Jn., yeo., Sherb., Dorset, 1737, W, Wr, P5/1737/29
Jn., butcher and cutter, Wrou., 1738, W, P3/IJ/242
Jn., shopkeeper, Lyneham, 1837, W, Wr, P3/1837/79
Jacob alias Annatt, Judith, Sal., 1728, AB, P4/1727/15
Lawr., butcher, Swindon, 1668, AB, comm, I, W, P1/IJ/89
Mgt., widow, Devizes, 1703, W, P1/IJ/135, P1/4Reg/248
My., widow, Clack, Lyneham, 1706, AB, P3/IJ/186
Nathaniel, husb., Mere, 1732, W, P5/1732/24
Oliver, gent., Mere form. of Sal., 1676, AB, I, ren, P5/1676/36
Rachel, Braydon Forest, Crickl. St S., 1696, AB, P3/IJ/161
Rachel, widow, Sal., 1792, W, P4/1792/7
Ralph, Swindon, 1668, AB, comm, I, P1/IJ/90
Reginald, Redford's Bridge, Bremhill, 1669, AB, comm, I, P3/IJ/98
Richd., Netherb., Dorset, 1625, I, W, P5/1625/49, P5/10Reg/268B
Richd., jun., yeo., Clack & Greenhill Farm, Wootton B., 1668, I, W, P1/IJ/91
Richd., yeo., Shropshire Marsh, Lydiard T., 1671, AB, a/c, I, P3/IJ/104
Richd., Clack, Lyneham, 1672, AB, comm, P3/IJ/107
Robt., Eastrop, Highw., 1696, W, P10/1696/3
Robt., yeo., Burton Hill, The Grange, Malm., 1719, comm, I, W, P3/IJ/209
Jacobs, Solomon, [tanner], Sal., 1624, I, W, P4/1624/8
Stephen, yeo., Rams., 1741, W, Wr, P5/1740/45
Thos., husb., Lt. Hinton, 1570, W, P1/1Reg/119B
Thos., husb., Bishopstone S., 1583-84, AB, P2/IJ/15, P2/6Reg/90A, 134A
Thos., yeo., Okus, Swindon, 1666, AB, I, NW, P3/IJ/91
Thos., yeo., Even Swindon, 1668, I, W, P1/IJ/92
Thos., Braydon Forest, Crickl. St S., 1696, AB, P3/IJ/162
Thos., yeo., Blagrove, Wrou., 1699, AB, I, Wr, P3/IJ/167
Jacobs, Thos., husb., Inglesham, Berks., 1713, I, W, P3/IJ/194
Jacobs, Thos., schoolmaster, Wrou., 1818, W, Wr, P3/1818/49
Jacobs alias Kite, Thos., yeo., Haydon Wick, Rodbourne C., 1830, AB, O, ren, W, P3/1830/65
Jacobs, Thos., yeo., Poulton, 1835, D, O, W, P3/1835/8
Jacobs, Thos., gent., Calcutt, Crickl. St S., 1836, W, Wr, P3/1836/20
Wm., Manton, Preshute, 1616, AB, comm, I (badly damaged), P1/IJ/24
Wm., Marridge Hill, Rams., 1688, AB, I, P5/1688/44
Wm., Coombe B., 1725, W, P5/1725/43, P5/16Reg/107B
Jacobs, Wm., Purton, 1804, W, P1/1804/78
Wm., Crickl. St S., 1806, AB, Wr, P3/1806/16
Wm., sen. & jun., husb., Tockenham Wick, 1644-45, AB, I (for both men), W, P1/IJ/62-63
see also Butler form. J.
Jacobson, Philip, Braydon Forest, Crickl. St S., 1692, AB, P3/IJ/149
Jacques *see* Jaques
Jafferis, Jaffery *see* Jeffreys
Jaggerd, Thos., Highw., 1607, AB, P5/8Reg/105B
Jakes *see* Jaques
Jambryn, My., servant to Geo. Pope, clerk and rector, Donhead St My., 1612, AB, I, W, P2/IJ/59
James, Agnes, widow, Bps. C., 1570, W, P5/2Reg/88A
Alice, Purton, 1610, AB, W, P3/IJ/15
Ann, widow, Lyme R., Dorset, 1679, I, W, P16/55
Anthony, Laverstock, 1593, I, T, P2/IJ/27
Benj., sen., Lyme R., Dorset, 1674, I (detailed; fixtures & furniture of market house, bought from corporation of L.R.), W, P5/1674/42
Benj., Beckhampton, Avebury, 1738, W, P1/IJ/195, P1/8Reg/310
Bridget, widow, Mkt. L., 1707, W, P2/IJ/221
Chas., labourer, Melk., 1831, W, P2/1831/30
David, bricklayer, Theale, Tilehurst, Berks., 1832, W, Wr, P1/1832/113
Edmd., gent., Bradfield, Hullavington, 1623, AB, alleg, P3/IJ/43
Edwd., yeo., Sal. (late of Marston Biggott, Somerset), 1792, W, P4/1792/1
Eliz., widow, Calne, 1563, W, P5/1Reg/30A
Eliz., widow, Ogbourne St A., 1672, AB, I, P5/1672/24

Eliz., sp., Wokm., Berks., 1776, W, P5/1776/24, P5/17Reg/104
Eliz., widow, Erlestoke, 1815, W, Wr, P2/1815/82
Eliz. *see also* Eliz. Davis, P5/17Reg/105A
Faith, sp., Wokm., Berks., 1776, W, P5/1776/25
Francis, husb., Hanging L., 1636, I, W, P2/IJ/101
Francis, Reading, Berks., 1683, AB, P1/IJ/110
Francis, Warm., 1788, AB, P2/IJ/372
Geo., baker, Calne, 1639, a/c, W, P26/87
Hy., cordw., Calne, 1723, AB, I (detailed), P26/673
Hy., bricklayer, Aldbourne, 1793, W, P3/IJ/312
Hy., sen., yeo., Fritham, Bramshaw, Hants, 1848, W, Wr, P24/1389
Jas., carp., Reading, Berks., 1753, W, P1/IJ/227, P1/11Reg/32
Jane, widow, Devizes, 1741, comm, NW, P1/IJ/201, P1/9Reg/70A
Jn., priest, W. Dean, 1557, institution to rectory, P1/1Reg/5B
Jn., husb., Mere, 1580-81, I, W, P5/1580/33, P5/4Reg/18A
Jn., sen., baker, Calne, 1594, AB, a/c, I, W, P5/1594/45, P5/6Reg/88E
Jn., jun., husb., Bere R., Dorset, 1597, AB, W, P5/1597/68, P5/6Reg/163A
Jn., husb., Bere R., Dorset, 1606, AB, I, T, W, P5/1605/32, P5/8Reg/51
Jn., husb., Purton, [1606], W (NEP), P3/IJ/7
Jn., husb., Hanging L., 1606, I, W, P2/IJ/42
Jn., N. Tidworth, 1613, T (unnamed children), P2/IJ/60
Jn., husb., Bere R., Dorset, 1615, AB, W, P5/1614/32, P5/9Reg/150B
Jn., sen., plumber, Mkt. L., 1640, I, W, P2/IJ/118
Jn., Lyme R., Dorset, 1641, AB, I, P5/1641/45, P5/14Reg/33D
Jn., Hullavington, 1646, AB, P1/IJ/64
Jn., Berwick St Jn., 1666, AB, P2/IJ/142
Jn., plumber, Mkt. L., 1668, I, W, P2/IJ/146
Jn., sen., linen weaver, Woodlands, Mere, 1674, I, W, P5/1674/43
Jn., W. Lavington, 1687, AB, comm, I, P1/IJ/113
Jn., Stockley, Calne, 1693, AB, I, P26/412
Jn., husb., Ogbourne St A., 1693, I, W, P23/190
Jn., clothier, Sal., 1707, W, P4/1707/1
Jn., Bloxworth, Dorset, 1718, AB, P5/1718/20
Jn., woolstapler, Devizes, 1728, W, P1/IJ/178, P1/7Reg/187B
Jn., W. Lavington, 1729, AB, comm, P1/IJ/180
Jn., Donhead St A., 1752, AB, P2/IJ/310
Jn., Calne, 1763, AB, P26/1001
Jn., Devizes, 1768, AB, P1/IJ/248
Jn., Berwick St Jn., 1783, AB, P2/IJ/363
Jn., baker, Calne, 1790, W, P26/1169
Jn., yeo., Craddock, Uffc., Devon, 1844, comm, W, Wr, P20/1/326
Jos., sen., Lyme R., Dorset, 1670, AB, I, NW, P16/27
Jos., woolstapler, Brinkw., 1770, AB, W, P5/1770/24, P5/17Reg/8B
Jos., carp., Erlestoke, 1837, O, W, Wr, P2/1837/67
Judith, widow, Calne, 1718, AB, I, P26/621
Lawr., yeo., Berwick St Jn., 1594, I, W, P2/IJ/29
Lucy, Lyme R., Dorset, 1695, AB, P16/137
Mgt., widow, Westport St My., 1629, AB, a/c, I, P1/IJ/44, P3/IJ/50
My., widow, Sal., 1715, W, P4/1715/2
My., sp., Sal., 1748, AB, ren, W, P4/1747/6
My., widow, Crickl. St My., 1767, W, P1/IJ/245, P1/12Reg/258A
My. Ann, wife, Berwick St Jn., 1854, AB, aff, O, Wr, P2/1854/42
Melior, Broad C., 1800, D, W, P2/1800/9
Nich., cordw., Stoke tithing, Calne & Calstone W., 1674, I, W, P5/1674/41
Oliver, husb., Sonning, Berks., 1727, W, P5/1727/28, P5/16Reg/152
Richd., yeo., Sulhamstead Bannister, Berks., 1662, AB, I, P1/IJ/73
Richd., yeo., Coate, Bps. C., 1673, AB, I, P24/458
Richd., merchant tailor, N. Bradley, 1690, AB, comm, I (detailed), P2/IJ/200
Richd., sen., cooper, Beam., Dorset, 1715-17, I (2), note of probate, W, P17/222, 293
Richd., yeo., Crickl. St S., 1751, W, P3/IJ/261

Richman, abode lost, 1646, AB, comm (fragments only), P1/IJ/65
James *or* Jeanes, Robt., Lillington, Dorset, 1623, AB, I, record of admon, P5/1622/41, P5/10Reg/143B
Robt., sen., clothier, Reading, Berks., 1662, AB, comm, W, P1/IJ/74
Robt., clothier, Reading, Berks., 1680, comm, W, P1/IJ/105
Robt., yeo., Malm., 1692, AB, I, P3/IJ/150
Robt., silk weaver, Malm., 1729, W, P3/IJ/227
Ruth, widow, Uffc., Devon, 1818, W, Wr, P5/1818/26
James alias Slade, Sam., Uffc., Devon, 1638-40, AB, a/c, I, P20/1/23
Sam., curate, Easton, 1662, I, W, P1/IJ/75
Sam., Uffc., Devon, 1682, AB, I (detailed), ren, P5/1682/63
Sam., yeo., Bloxworth, Dorset, 1764, W, P5/1764/26
Sam., shepherd, Berwick St Jn., 1787, W, P2/IJ/370
Sam., widower, Berwick St Jn., 1856, AB, aff, O, Wr, P2/1856/47
Sarah, widow, Uffc., Devon, 1698, I, W, P5/1698/38
Sibyl, widow, Bradford A., 1779, W, P2/IJ/351
Silas, carp., Bradford A., 1794, W, P2/IJ/380
Stephen, Aldbourne, 1836, AB, comm, ren, Wr, P3/1836/48
Susanna, widow, Froxfield, 1800, AB (2), appt of guardian, P3/1800/10
Thos., weaver, Steeple A., 1559, W, P2/4Reg/23C
James alias Carpenter, Thos., husb., Coombe, Enford, 1595, I, W (NEP), P30/102
Thos., husb., E. Garston, Berks., 1613, I, W, P1/IJ/17
Thos., husb., Milton L., 1672, AB, I, P3/IJ/108
Thos., sen., cordw., Calne, 1717, I, W, P26/610
Thos., husb., Sonning, Berks., 1724-25, L (2), W, P5/1725/44, P5/16Reg/124B
Thos., husb., Stockley, Calne, 1733, W, P26/772
Thos., Bulk., Keevil, 1783, AB, comm, P1/IJ/277
Thos., sailor, Chipp., 1854, aff, D, O, W, Wr, P3/1854/15
Walter, husb., Over C., Dorset, 1589, I, W, P5/1589/32, P5/5Reg/54D
Wm., fuller, Calne, 1638, AB, I, P26/74
Wm., husb., Woodlands, Mere, 1641, I, W, P5/1641/44, P5/14Reg/41A
Wm., Crickl. St My., 1695, AB, I (applies to 2 people), Wr, P3/IJ/160
Wm., Gt. Faringdon, Berks., 1707, AB, P5/1707/34
Wm., Calne, 1717, AB, P26/611
Wm., Bradford A., 1758, AB, P2/IJ/319
Wm., carp., Bradford A., 1776, W, P2/IJ/343
Wm., W. Kington, 1783, AB, P3/IJ/305
Wm., auctioneer, Bradford A., 1785, AB, comm, ren, W, P2/IJ/368
Wm., yeo., Semley, 1786, AB, W, P2/IJ/369
Wm., Donhead St A., 1796, AB, P2/IJ/381
Wm., Winterborne Thompson, Dorset, 1798, AB, P5/1798/14, P5/18Reg/267B
Wm., yeo., Uffc., Devon, 1808, W, Wr, P20/1/291
Wm., carp., Mkt. L., 1830, O, W, Wr, P2/1830/70
Wm., yeo., Melk., 1831, AB, comm, W, P2/1831/50
see also Carpenter alias J.; Hayward form. J.
Janaway *see* Jennaway
Jandell, Jandell *or* Yandall, Jn., Ditchampton, Wilton, 1546, W, P2/2Reg/2A
Janes *see* Jeans
Jankens *see* Jenkins
Janyons, Thos., Maiden B., 1537, W (NEP), P2/1Reg/5A
Jaques, Alice, clerk's wife, Devizes, 1765, AB, P1/IJ/242
Jacques, Anna Maria, widow, Chr. M., 1808, W, Wr, P1/1808/75
Benj., tailor, Sutton B., 1767, W, P1/IJ/246, P1/12Reg/221B
Chas., Warm., 1800, AB, comm, P2/1800/34
Dan., yeo., Luckington, 1851, O, W, Wr, P3/1851/6
Edmd., Grittleton, 1664, AB, I, W, P1/IJ/80
Edmd., Easton Grey, 1728, W, P3/IJ/225
Edwd., yeo., Sevington, Leigh Delamere, 1774, comm, W, P3/IJ/294
Jackes, Eliz., widow, Gt. Amesb., 1610, I, W, P2/IJ/51, P2/8Reg/86A
Eliz., widow, Leigh Delamere, 1635, W, P1/IJ/53
Geo., gent., Chr. M., 1703, I, W, P3/IJ/178

Jacques, Geo., Chr. M., 1804, AB, comm, P1/1804/120
Geo., bach. and gardener, Lacock, 1853, AB, O, ren, Wr, P3/1853/40
Jakes, Jn., Amesb., 1582, W, P2/6Reg/65D
Jakes, Jn., blacksmith, Whitep., 1839, W, Wr, P2/1839/14
Geo., yeo., Cleverton, Lea and C., [1591], W (NEP), P3/1Reg/33B
Hy., Hullavington, [1601], W (NEP), P3/1Reg/98A
Joan, Highw., 1609, T (grandchildren: Thos., Agnes & Joan J.), P5/1609/91
Joan, widow, Milbourne, Malm., 1647, I, W, P1/IJ/68
Joan, widow, Rodbourne, Malm., 1668, comm, I (detailed), W (damaged & part lost), P1/IJ/93
Joan *see also* Thomas Yates
Jn., Grittleton, 1608, AB, P3/IJ/10
Jn., yeo., Milbourne, Malm., [1618], I, W (NEP), P3/IJ/32
Jn., day labourer, Alderton, 1671, I, W, P1/IJ/101
Jn., yeo., Grittleton, 1699, I, W, P3/IJ/168
Jn., butcher, Littleton Drew, 1715-35, AB, I, W, P3/IJ/200
Jacques, Jn., baker and widower, Chipp., 1731, AB, comm, I, P3/IJ/230
Jn., tailor, Sutton B., 1748, W, P3/IJ/256
Jos., yeo., Grittleton, 1681, I, W, P3/IJ/125
Jos., yeo., Alderton, 1742, W, P3/IJ/249
Joyce, widow, Grittleton, 1700, I, W, P3/IJ/173
Kingsman, gent., Langley Burrell, 1765, W, P3/IJ/277
Kingsman, yeo., Yatton Grove, Yatton K., 1804, W, P3/1804/25
Mgt., widow, Littleton Drew & Grittleton, 1704, I, W, P3/IJ/180
Margery, widow, Garsdon, [1605], I, NW, P1/IJ/8
Peter, husb., Corston, Malm., 1617, I, W, P3/IJ/31
Peter, husb., Sherston, 1684, AB, I, P3/IJ/134
Philip, jun., weaver, Garsdon, 1629, I, W, P3/IJ/52
Rebecca, widow, Grittleton, 1733, I, W, P3/IJ/235
Richd., husb. *or* yeo., Garsdon, 1615, I, W, P3/IJ/27
Richd., Grittleton, 1703, AB, I, P3/IJ/179
Robt., Hullavington, 1635, I, W, P1/IJ/54
Jacques, Robt., linen weaver, Gasper, Stourton, 1687, AB, I, P2/IJ/196
Roger, Kington St M., 1683, AB, I, P3/IJ/132
Sam., tailor, Leigh Delamere, [1611], I, W (NEP), P3/IJ/19
Susanna, widow, Alderton, 1744, W, P1/IJ/208, P1/9Reg/396A
Thos., Melk., 1808, AB, comm, Wr, P2/1808/15
Wm., yeo., Sevington, Leigh Delamere, 1704, I, W, P3/IJ/181
see also Blake alias J.
Jarard *see* Gerrard
Jarman, Eliz., widow, Uffc., Devon, 1751, W, P20/1/216
Eliz., sp., Warm., 1800, W, P2/1800/52
Francis, miller, Uffc., Devon, 1751, W, P20/1/219
Hy., haberdasher of hats, Devizes, 1729, W, P1/IJ/181, P1/7Reg/381
Richd., haberdasher of hats, Devizes, 1732, W, P1/IJ/184, P1/7Reg/560B
Richd., victualler, Chipp., 1810, W, Wr, P3/1810/55
Thos., victualler, Chipp., 1765, W, P3/IJ/278
Jarrett *see* Garrett
Jarvill, Richd., yeo., Oakley Grn, Bray, Berks., [1708], I, W (NEP), P1/IJ/140
Jarvis, Jarvis alias Grately, Alice, widow, Tidcombe, T. and Fosbury, 1624, I, W, P3/IJ/45
Eliz., widow, Upavon, 1602, I, W, P2/IJ/38
Eliz., Upavon, 1715, AB, P2/IJ/241
Eliz., widow, Wilsford with Lake, 1718, AB, I (2 - 1 a draft), P13/4/13
Frances, widow, Chards., Devon, 1686, AB, I, P14/67
Grace, sp., Rowde, 1840, AB, Wr, P3/1840/21
Jas., Fovant, 1709, AB, P2/IJ/227
Jas., sen., thatcher, Fovant, 1748, AB, W, P2/IJ/297
Jane, sp., Semington, Steeple A., 1824, comm, W, Wr, P2/1824/65
Joan, widow, Upavon, 1664, I, W, P1/IJ/81
Joan, widow, Donhead St A., 1711, W, P1/5Reg/38
Jn., Chilmark, 1555, W, P2/1Reg/24B

Jn., sen., blacksmith, Fovant, [1635], I, W, P2/IJ/99, P2/9Reg/91
Jn., husb., Fovant, 1639, I, W, P2/IJ/115
Jn., N. Bradley, 1687, AB, I, ren, W, P2/IJ/193
Jn., blacksmith, Fovant, 1823, AB, W, P1/1823/150
Jn., woolstapler, Whistley House, Longbridge D., 1824, comm, W, Wr, P2/1824/29
Jos., clothier, Trowb., 1828, W, Wr, P1/1828/10
Jarvis alias Reeves, Mgt., widow, Wilsford with Lake, 1634, I, WGVS, P5/1634/59, P5/12Reg/270A
Martha, yeo.'s widow, Upavon, 1780, W, P2/IJ/353
Martha, widow, Longbridge D., 1824-25, AB (2), ren, Wr, P2/1824/57
My., widow, Wilsford nr Pewsey, 1820, W, Wr, P1/1820/46
My., widow, Trowb., 1829, AB, O, Wr, P1/1829/49
Maurice, Upavon, 1686, I, W, P2/IJ/190
Jarvis alias Mariner, Richd., bricklayer, Wokm., Berks., 1597, AB, deed of gift, D (3), I (2), sentence, P5/1597/86, P5/6Reg/151C
Richd., miller, Sonning, Berks., 1714-19, AB, I, NW, P5/1714/22, P5/1719/49, P5/15Reg/384D
Robt. Frith, gent., Calne, 1844, comm, W, Wr, P1/1844/24
Simon, Charl. nr. P., 1679, AB, a/c, I, P2/IJ/172
Simon, yeo., Upavon, 1717, W, P2/IJ/246
Simon, yeo., Semington, Steeple A., 1718, AB, I, W, P2/IJ/251
Simon, Wilsford nr Pewsey, 1746, W, P2/IJ/295
Simon, woolstapler, Upavon, 1796, W, Wr, P2/IJ/383
Sophia, sp., Upavon, 1810, W, Wr, P2/1810/18
Susanna, surgeon's widow, Calne, 1843, W, Wr, P5/1843/21
Thos., sen., yeo., Upavon, 1641, a/c (2), AB, I, P2/IJ/121
Thos., yeo., Chisenbury, Enford, 1644, I, W, P2/IJ/125
Thos., Fovant, 1664, I, W, P1/IJ/82
Thos., yeo., Upavon, 1672, I, W, P2/IJ/153
Thos., yeo., Upavon, 1756, W, P2/IJ/316
Jarvis alias Grately, Tobias, yeo., Tidcombe, T. and Fosbury, 1639, I, W, P3/IJ/70
Wm., yeo., Littleton P., 1666, AB, I, ren, W, P1/IJ/86
Wm., Fovant, 1710, AB, P2/IJ/228
Wm., clothier, Avill's Farm, Corsham, 1723, AB, I, P1/IJ/171
Wm., Chr. M., 1743, AB (4), appts of guardian (2), comm, T (child: Eleanor J.), P3/IJ/251
Wm., innholder, Pewsey, 1804, W, P1/1804/85
Wm., Warm., 1811, AB, Wr, P1/1811/106
Wm., Wilsford nr Pewsey, 1833, W, Wr, P2/1833/60
Wm., innkeeper, Pewsey, 1847, comm, W, Wr, P3/1847/11
see also Reeve alias J.
Jason *see* West alias Sason *or* J.
Jatt, Ann, widow, Rams., 1770, W, P5/1770/25, P5/17Reg/21
Jett, Jn., yeo., Wilton, 1558, W, P2/3Reg/97B
Jn., husb., Aldbourne, [1619], I, W (on same sheet) (NEP), P3/IJ/34
Jn., carp., Rams., 1708, W, P5/1708/35, P5/15Reg/61
Jett, Nathan, Gt. Faringdon, Berks., 1704, AB, I, P5/1704/39
Iatt, Sarah, widow, Sal., 1718, W, P4/1718/20
Iatt, Thos., wheelwright, Sal., 1709, I, W, P4/1709/21
see also Jordan alias J.
Jay, Alice, widow, Tisb., 1564-65, I, W, P2/IJ/6, P2/4Reg/166B
Jey, Alice, widow, Tisb., 1587, I, W, P2/IJ/17, P2/7Reg/108A
Anthony, yeo., Sal., 1689, W, P4/1689/2
Jey, Christian, widow, Sal., 1664, I, W, P1/IJ/84
Joyes, Chris., yeo., Woolhampton, Berks., 1680, AB, I, ren, P1/IJ/108
Eliz., sp., Sal., 1747, W, P4/1747/1
Jey, Geoffrey, husb., Bere R., Dorset, 1628, AB, I, P5/1628/64, P5/11Reg/72B
Hy., yeo., Lt. Coxwell, Gt. Faringdon, Berks., 1600, I, W, P5/1600/36, P5/6Reg/269
Hy., shoemaker, Ebbesborne Wake, 1706, W, P2/IJ/217
Jey, Jas., tailor, Lyneham, 1725, W, P3/IJ/219
Jas., Fovant, 1814, AB, P1/1814/29
Jey, Jn., mariner, Lyme R., Dorset, 1669, AB, I, P16/23
Jn., stone mason, Fovant, 1812, W, Wr, P2/1812/45

My., widow, E. Harnham, Britford, 1752, W, P4/1752/10
My., sp., E. Harnham, Britford, 1781, W, P5/1781/13, P5/17Reg/204
Richd., Gt. Faringdon, Berks., 1740, AB, Wr, P5/1740/44
Stephen, yeo., Fovant Stroud, 1763, W, P2/IJ/327
Stephen, shopkeeper and dealer, Everleigh, 1809, W, Wr, P3/1809/50
Thos., Mere, 1565, AB, P5/1Reg/63A
Thos., Fovant, 1823, AB, P1/1823/16
Wm., sen., yeo., Compton C., [1619], W, P2/IJ/72
Jayes, Wm., innholder, Woolhampton, Berks., 1628, I, W, P1/IJ/41
Wm., Compton C., 1667, AB, I, P2/IJ/145
Wm., yeo., Ebbesborne Wake, 1672, AB, I, W, P2/IJ/154
Wm., Compton C., 1673, AB, P2/IJ/155
Wm., Ebbesborne Wake, 1697, AB, P2/IJ/206
Wm., threadman, E. Harnham, Britford, 1736, W, P5/1736/20
Wm., gent., Milton L., 1793, W, P3/IJ/313
Wm., grocer and linen draper, Fovant, 1855, aff, comm, W, Wr, P1/1855/19
see also Jee; Joy
Jeans, Janes, Bernard, sen., yeo., Oborne, Dorset, 1730, W (NEP), P5/1730/42
Bernard, yeo., Chetnole, Yetm., Dorset, 1810, W, Wr, P5/1810/15
Jeanes, Chris., Bower C., 1672, I, W, P2/IJ/151
David, bach., E. Harnham, Britford, 1816, AB, Wr, P24/1275
Jas., Oborne, Dorset, 1811, AB, Wr, P5/1811/15
Jn., butcher, Shitterton, Bere R., Dorset, 1777, AB, ren, P5/1777/10, P5/17Reg/132A
Jos., yeo., Lillington, Dorset, 1835, note, W, Wr, P5/1835/11
Jeanes, Leah, widow, Sherb., Dorset (form. of Minterne Magna, Dorset), 1823, AB, W, Wr, P5/1823/6
Jeanes, Mgt., widow, Lyme R., Dorset, 1679, I, W, P5/1679/50
Mark, Wilton, 1834, AB, Wr, P2/1834/16
Jeynes, Martin, Chards., Devon, 1566, AB, P5/1Reg/69B
Jeanes, My., Donhead St My., 1702, AB, comm, P2/IJ/209
Jeanes, My., wife of Thos., sievemaker, Chetnole, Yetm., Dorset, 1823, W, P19/229
My., wife, Sal., 1849, AB, Wr, P4/1849/19
Jeanes, Richd., husb., Donhead St My., 1702-03, a/c, I, W, P2/IJ/210
Jeanes, Robt., Lillington, Dorset, 1623, AB, I, record of admon, P5/1622/41
Jeanes, Robt., clerk, Bradford A., 1725, AB, I, P2/IJ/263
Jeanes, Sam., cordw., Chetnole, Yetm., Dorset, 1832, W, Wr, P19/244
Jeanes, Thos., Oborne, Dorset, 1732, AB, P5/1732/25
Thos., sen., gent., Bourton, Gillingham, Dorset, 1827, W, Wr, P27/1/677
Jeanes, Thos., yeo., Chetnole, Yetm., Dorset, 1828, comm, W, Wr, P19/247
Jeanes, Walter, barber, Warm., 1705, I, W, P2/IJ/215
Jeanes, Wm., jun., butcher, Sherb., Dorset, 1636, AB, comm, I, P5/1635/55, P5/12Reg/260A
Jeanes, Wm., cordw., Chetnole, Yetm., Dorset, 1826, AB, W, P19/233
see also James *or* J.
Jeblett, Jn., husb., Sandhurst, Berks., 1641, AB, I, W, P5/1641/46, P5/14Reg/22
Jeboult, Hugh, sen., pattenmaker, Sal., 1768, W (NEP), P4/1768/11
Jas., sawyer, Sal., 1771, W, P4/1771/3
Maria, sp., Sal., 1814, AB, P1/1814/71
Geboll *or* Gibbole, Wm., tanner, E. Harnham, Britford, 1639, I, W, P5/1638/48, P5/13Reg/155B
Wm., shoemaker, Sal., 1729, W, P4/1728/32
Jecock, Sam., clerk, Coombe B., 1705, W, P5/1705/26
Jee *see* Gee
Jeeves, Jeeves alias Ricketts, Wm., yeo., Stratton St Mgt., 1834, W, Wr, P3/1834/54
Jeffard *see* Gifford
Jefferies, Jeffrey, (Colonel) *see* Wm. Bugden
Jeffrey, Agnes, widow, Chirton, 1600, AB, P2/IJ/35
Jeffery, Agnes, widow, Sherb., Dorset, 1622, I, W, P5/1622/40, P5/10Reg/115B
Jeffery alias Heskins, Alice, widow, Calne, 1563, W, P5/1Reg/29C
Jeffery, Alice, widow, Hungerford, Berks., 1676, I, W, P5/1676/37
Geffrey, Anastasia, widow, Ebbesborne Wake, 1549, W, P2/2Reg/88A
Jeffery, Ann, widow, Calne, 1677, AB, a/c, comm, I, P26/251
Jeffries, Ann, widow, Ashton K., 1686, AB, I, P3/IJ/141

Jefferys, Ann, widow, Calne, 1715, I, W, P26/594
Ann, clothier's widow, Calne, 1716, comm, W, P5/1716/48, P5/15Reg/358B
Ann, Bremhill, 1726, AB, P1/IJ/177
Jefferys, Ann, sp., Donhead St My., 1781, W, P2/IJ/357
Jeffery, Ann, Beam., Dorset, 1783, AB, P17/573
Jefferis, Ann, mercer's wife, Malm., 1787, W, P3/IJ/308
Jefferis, Ann, widow, Keevil, 1793, W, P2/IJ/378
Jeffery, Anthony, Thornford, Dorset, 1815, AB, Wr, P5/1815/22
Bradford, sen., yeo., Somerford K., 1757, W, P3/IJ/270
Cath., servant, Sal., 1732, NW, P4/1731/21
Chas., maltster, Ashton K., 1720, W, P1/IJ/162, P1/6Reg/359A
Jeffrey, Christian, widow, W. Harnham, 1595, I, NW, P5/1595/32, P5/6Reg/110
Jeffery, Christian, widow, Sal. The Close, 1709-10, I (detailed), W, P5/1709/23, P5/15Reg/142
Gaffray, Chris., husb., Bulk., Keevil, 1621, I, W, P2/G/192
Dan., Eaton Hastings, Berks., 1679, AB, P3/IJ/118
Jeffery, David, Siderow, Bremhill, 1604, I, W (2 - 1 a copy), P3/IJ/3
Jefferys, David, gent., Calne, 1724, AB, I (detailed), P26/690
Jefferys, David, Calne, 1732, AB, comm, P5/1732/26
David, druggetmaker, Whitley, Melk., 1739, W, P2/IJ/283
Jeffries, Dorothy, widow, Chaddington, Lydiard T., 1633, I, W, P3/IJ/61
Jefferys, Edith, widow, Hazeland, Bremhill, 1629, I, W, P3/IJ/53
Jeffery, Edith, widow, Calne, 1676, I, W, P5/1676/34
Jefferis, Edwd., husb., Ashton K., 1682, AB, I, P3/IJ/129
Jefferis, Edwd., Siderow, Bremhill, 1686, I, W, P3/IJ/142
Jefferys, Edwd., Bremhill, 1725, AB, P3/IJ/218
Jefferys, Edwd., sen., yeo., Naish House, Bremhill, 1772, I, W, P3/IJ/291
Edwd., Somerford K., 1824, W, Wr, P3/1824/55
Jefferys, Edwd., bach., Melk., 1844, AB, comm, court proceeding, Wr, P2/1844/12, 64
Eleanor, widow, Purton, [1619], I, W (NEP), P3/IJ/35
Eleanor, widow, Bourton, Gillingham, Dorset, 1725, W, P27/1/274
Jeffrey, Eliza, sp., Sal., 1820, W, Wr, P4/1820/1
Eliz., widow, Ashton K., 1648, AB, P1/IJ/70
Jeffery, Eliz., widow, Sal. St Thos., 1703, AB, I, NW, P4/1703/4
Jeffries, Eliz., gent.'s wife, Somerford K., 1707, AB, I, P3/IJ/187
Jeffery, Eliz., widow, Thornford, Dorset, 1750, W, P5/1750/21
Jeffries, Eliz., widow, Alderbury, 1795, W, P26/1199
Eliz., Dauntsey, 1845, AB, O, Wr, P3/1845/15
Fanny, [sp.], Swindon, 1835, AB, P3/1835/26
Jeffries, Francis, higler, Marl., 1774, W, P1/IJ/268, P1/13Reg/58
Geo., sen., yeo., Minety, 1701, AB, I, P3/IJ/175
Giles, yeo., Purton, 1694, I, W, P3/IJ/157
Jefferys, Grace, widow, Sal. The Close, 1722, AB, I, P5/1722/33
Jeffery, Grace, widow, Haydon, Dorset, 1767, AB, I, W, P5/1767/26
Geffrey, Hy., Ebbesborne Wake, 1557, AB, P2/3Reg/26E
Jeffrey, Hy., husb., Ebbesborne Wake, 1572, W, P2/5Reg/157D
Jeffery, Hy., husb., Baverstock (late of Barford), 1629, I, W, P2/IJ/88
Jeffery, Hy., E. Tytherton, Bremhill, 1633, AB, a/c, comm, I, P3/IJ/60
Hy., yeo., Ebbesborne Wake, 1640, I, W, P2/IJ/120
Jeffery, Hy., yeo., Sal. The Close, 1684, I, W, P5/1683/32
Jeffery, Hy., yeo., Barford St M., 1711, AB, W, P2/IJ/229
Jeffries, Hy., yeo., Easton Grey, 1713, I, W, P3/IJ/195
Jeffery, Hy., Bugley, Warm., 1751, AB, P2/IJ/303
Jeffrey, Hy., Sal., 1819, AB, Wr, P4/1819/1
Jeffery, Hester, sp., Stourton, 1816, AB, P2/1816/30
Jeffrey, Isaac, yeo., Draycot C., 1694, I, W, P3/IJ/158
Jeffery, Jas., Wokm., Berks., 1599, I, P5/1599/13
Jas., husb., Wilton, 1668, AB, P1/IJ/94
Jeffries, Jas., yeo. and bach., Bloxworth, Dorset, 1730, AB, NW, P5/1730/41
Jas. Luckett, bach., Swindon, 1850, AB, O, Wr, P3/1850/3
Jane, yeo.'s widow, Marl. St My., 1747, I, W, P1/IJ/217, P1/10Reg/41B, 65A

Jefferys, Jane, widow, Whitley, Melk., 1751, W, P2/IJ/305
Jeffrey, Joan, Gt. Bedwyn, 1566, W, P5/1Reg/78C
Jeffrey, Joan, widow, Clevancy, Hilmarton, 1606, I, W, P1/IJ/10
Joan, widow, Milford, Sal. St Martin, 1620, I, P4/1620/15
Joan, widow, Highw., 1629, I, W, P10/1629/4
Jeffery, Joan, widow, Dunsden, Sonning, Berks., 1639, I, W, P5/1639/42, P5/13Reg/194
Geffrey, Jn., Ebbesborne Wake, 1541, W, P30/75
Jeffery, Jn., husb., Quidh., 1571, W, P2/5Reg/134C
Jeffrey, Jn., Winterslow, 1578, AB, I, P2/IJ/10, P2/5Reg/298B
Jeffery, Jn., W. Harnham, 1586, AB, I, T, P5/1586/15, P5/4Reg/135A
Jeffery, Jn., Sal. St Martin, 1587, AB, P4/Reg/29A
Jeffery, Jn., sen., husb., W. Harnham, 1595, I, W, P5/1595/31, P5/6Reg/103D
Geffrey, Jn., Lillington, Dorset, 1597, AB, W, P5/1597/50, 65, P5/6Reg/176B
Jn., husb., Purton, [1608], I, W (NEP), P3/IJ/11
Jeffrey, Jn., sen., W. Harnham, 1616, I, W, P5/1616/40, P5/9Reg/174A
Jeffery, Jn., Lillington, Dorset, 1619, I, W, P5/1619/63, P5/10Reg/53B
Jeffreys, Jn., Seagry, [1620], I, W (NEP), P3/IJ/37
Jeffreys, Jn., Hanger, Bremhill, 1627, I, W, P3/IJ/49
Jeffery, Jn., Dunsden, Sonning, Berks., 1629, AB, I, W, P5/1629/31, P5/11Reg/117B
Jeffery, Jn., W. Harnham, 1634, I, WGVS, P5/1634/60, P5/12Reg/284
Jeffery, Jn., husb., Sherb., Dorset, 1645, W, P5/14Reg/85C
Jeffery, Jn., shearman and clothworker, Sherb., Dorset, 1645, comm, I, W, P5/1645/9
Jn., no abode stated, 1649, court paper, P2/IJ/131
Jeffery, Jn., innholder and cordw., Sherb., Dorset, 1665, I, W, P5/1665/48
Jn., husb., Purton, 1666, I, W, P3/IJ/92
Jeffery, Jn., chandler, Calne, 1671, I (detailed), W, P26/189
Jeffries, Jn., sen., yeo., Upper Lillington, Dorset, 1674, I, W, P5/1674/39
Jeffries, Jn., E. Coulston, 1684, AB, I, P2/IJ/184
Jefferys, Jn., yeo., Tytherton Kellaways, Bremhill, 1690, I, W, P3/IJ/146
Jeffery, Jn., clothier, Calne, 1694, AB, comm, I, P26/423
Jeffereys, Jn., coachmaker, Sal., 1700, AB, ren, P4/1700/6
Jefferys, Jn., Sherb., Dorset, 1716, AB, P5/1716/50
Jeffery, Jn., sen., husb., Sherb., Dorset, 1717, AB, a/c, I (2), P5/1717/21
Jn., sergemaker, Avon, Chr. M., 1741, AB, W, P3/IJ/248
Jefferis, Jn., yeo., Poulshot, 1742, W, P2/IJ/291
Jeffery, Jn., husb., Sherb., Dorset, 1743, W, Wr, P5/1743/45
Jefferis, Jn., maltster, Malm., 1748, W, P3/IJ/257
Jeffries, Jn., Charlton nr Malm., 1755, AB, W, P3/IJ/268
Jn., butcher, W. Lavington, 1759, AB, P1/IJ/235
Jefferys, Jn., yeo., Wadswick, Box, 1762, W, P3/IJ/272
Jn., Fisherton A., 1770, AB, P1/IJ/254
Jn., yeo., Draycot Foliat, 1770, comm, W, P1/IJ/253
Jn., victualler, Poulshot, 1776, W, P2/IJ/344
Jn., Burdens Ball, Wilton, 1798, AB, P1/IJ/301, P1/15Reg/39B
Jn., Devizes, 1808, AB, comm, Wr, P1/1808/125
Jeffery, Jn., dyer, Wilton, 1808, W, Wr, P2/1808/7
Jn., farmer, W. Ashton, Steeple A., 1831, comm, W, P2/1831/28
Jefferys, Jn. Gurney, gent., Melk., 1851, W, Wr, P1/1851/70
Jeffery, Jonas, yeo., Bremhill, 1668, AB, I, W, P1/IJ/95
Jonas, Bulk., Keevil, 1794, AB, P2/IJ/379
Jos., yeo., Bloxworth, Dorset, 1728-29, W, P5/1728/56, P5/16Reg/216
Jafferis, Jos., shoemaker, Lydiard M., 1740, W, P3/IJ/246
Jefferis, Jos., Damerham, Hants, 1810, AB, Wr, P2/1810/30
Jos., Wootton B., 1825, AB, comm, Wr, P3/1825/41
Judith, widow, Stockley, Calne, 1698, I, W, P5/1698/39
Jeffery, Leonard, husb., Dunsden, Sonning, Berks., 1596, AB, I, W, P5/1596/40, P5/6Reg/131
Jeffery, Luke, Sal. The Close, 1727, AB, I, P5/1727/27
Jeffrey, Manasses, yeo., Ansty, 1704, W, P1/IJ/137
Mgt., widow, Foxham, Bremhill, 1677, comm, I, NW, P1/IJ/104
Jeffrey, Mgt., widow, Ebbesborne Wake, 1686, I, W, P2/IJ/189

Mgt., widow, Siderow, Bremhill, 1702, W, P3/IJ/177
Geffrey, Margery, widow, Winterslow, 1578, I, W, P2/G/26, P2/5Reg/311C
Martha, widow, Malm., 1815, W, Wr, P3/1815/73
Jeffrey, My., widow, Tytherton Kellaways, Bremhill, 1675, comm, I, W, P3/IJ/114
Jeffries, My., sp., Devizes, 1715, W, P1/IJ/153, P1/5Reg/480
My., widow, Malm., 1768, W, P3/IJ/285
Jeffrey, My., widow, Sal. The Close, 1771, W, P4/1771/12
My., wife, Semington, Steeple A., 1819, AB, Wr, P2/1819/53
My., sp., Devizes, 1836, AB, P1/1836/14
My., widow, My.port St., Devizes, 1852, W, Wr, P1/1852/23
Jeffery, My. *see* My. Moxham, P5/6Reg/9
Jeffery, Nich., W. Harnham, 1592, I, T, W, P5/1592/49
Jeffries, Nich., clerk and parson, Beer Hackett, Dorset, 1636, AB, a/c, comm, I, P5/1636/35, P5/13Reg/12A
Jeffery, Peter, Ebbesborne Wake, 1615-16, AB, a/c, I, T, P2/IJ/65, 69, P2/8Reg/288A
Jeffery, Peter, husb., Swallowcliffe, 1667, I, W, P5/1667/32
Prudence, sp., Draycot Foliat, 1818, comm, W, Wr, P3/1818/10
Jeffries, Ralph, Pangbourne, Berks., 1689, AB, P1/IJ/116
Jefferys, Rebecca, Melk., 1775, AB, comm (Quaker), P2/IJ/340
Jeffery alias Hibberd, Richd., W. Harnham, 1596, AB, a/c, I, P5/1596/41, P5/6Reg/138D
Richd., Netheravon, 1598, AB, I, P12/4
Jeffrey, Richd., tucker, Sherb., Dorset, 1601, AB, I, P5/1601/27, P5/7Reg/18A
Jeffrey, Richd., W. Harnham, 1602, I, W, P5/1601/25, P5/7Reg/30B
Geffrey, Richd., husb., Wyke, Halstock, Dorset, 1606, comm, I, W, P5/1605/25, P5/8Reg/52C
Jeffery, Richd., tanner, Wokm., Berks., 1611, I, P5/1611/24
Jefferis, Richd., yeo., Chaddington, Lydiard T., 1628, I (2), W, P1/IJ/42
Jeffreys, Richd., Bremhill, 1632, AB, I, P3/IJ/59
Jefferis, Richd., yeo., Bremhill, 1673, I, W, P3/IJ/111
Jeffries, Richd., Devizes, 1697, AB, P1/IJ/125
Jeffery, Richd., weaver, Reading, Berks., 1716, W, P1/IJ/154, P1/6Reg/50A
Jefferis, Richd., Siderow, Bremhill, 1730, W, P3/IJ/228
Richd., yeo., Draycot Foliat, 1811, comm, W, Wr, P1/1811/132
Richd., baker, Swindon, 1825, W, Wr, P3/1825/24
Jeffrey, Robt., Sedgehill, 1560, W, P2/4Reg/48D
Jeffery, Robt., husb., Purton, [1610], W (NEP), P3/IJ/16
Robt., Marl., 1632, AB, I (badly damaged), P1/IJ/48
Robt., yeo., Beards, Bremhill, 1636, I, W, P3/IJ/64
Jeffery, Robt., yeo., Eye and Dunsden, Sonning, Berks., 1668, I, W, P5/1668/39
Jeffrey, Robt., yeo., Bencroft, Bremhill, 1670, comm, I, W, P3/IJ/102
Robt., yeo., Bulk., Keevil, 1671, I, W, P2/IJ/150
Robt., yeo., Stockley, Calne, 1686, comm, I (detailed), W, P26/344
Robt., E. Coulston, 1693, AB, I, P2/IJ/202
Jefferys, Robt., yeo. *or* husb., Dauntsey, 1694, I, W, P3/IJ/159
Jeffery *or* Jeffries, Robt., shopkeeper and soapboiler, Calne, 1699, AB, I (detailed), P26/463
Robt., yeo., Bulk., Keevil, 1712, AB, I, P2/IJ/233
Robt., innholder, Rowde, 1735, W, P1/IJ/188, P1/8Reg/98
Jeffreys, Robt., chapman, Marl., 1747, W, P1/IJ/218, P1/10Reg/59B
Robt., yeo., Oxen Leaze Farm, Keevil, 1763, W, P1/IJ/241
Robt., yeo., Bulk., Keevil, 1769, W, P2/IJ/332
Robt., yeo., Poulshot, 1778, W, P2/IJ/349
Robt., yeo., Seend, Melk., [1789], W, P2/IJ/375
Jefferys, Robt., late mealman, Melk., 1805, W, Wr, P2/1805/4
Robt., farmer, Bulk., Keevil, 1831, comm, W, Wr, P2/1831/67
Jeffries, Robt., yeo., Dauntsey, 1840, W, Wr, P3/1840/41
Jeffreys, Roger, chapman, Marl., 1747, W, P1/10Reg/37
Roger, bach., Sal. The Close, 1751, AB, I, P5/1751/14
Jaffery, Rose, widow, Siderow, Bremhill, 1743, W, P3/IJ/250
Jefferys, Sam., yeo., Greenaway Lane, Langley Burrell, 1762, W, P3/IJ/273
Jeffery, Sam. Hart, bach., Sherb., Dorset, 1813, AB, Wr, P5/1813/11
Sarah, Trowb., 1768, AB, P1/IJ/249
Sarah, widow, Trowb., 1773, AB, P1/IJ/260

Sarah, sp., Lydiard T., 1783, W, P3/IJ/306
Jefferis, Sarah, widow, Ashton K., 1809, W, Wr, P3/1809/65
Sarah, widow, Seend, Melk., 1819, W, Wr, P2/1819/72
Sarah, widow, Draycot Foliat, 1837, comm, W, Wr, P3/1837/12
Jefferys, Stephen, Hilmarton, 1835, AB, P1/1835/85
Jefferys, Susanna, sp., Calne, 1668, I, W, P5/1668/40
Jeffrey, Sythe, widow, W. Harnham, 1597-99, I, W, P5/1597/64, P5/6Reg/203D
Jeffrey, Thos., sen., husb., Bulk., Keevil, 1597, AB, I, P2/IJ/32
Jeffery, Thos., tanner, Swallowcliffe, 1608, AB, I, P5/1608/21, P5/8Reg/130A
Jeffery, Thos., husb., Keevil, 1612, W, P2/8Reg/169B
Jefford, Thos., sen., yeo., Chards., Devon, 1671, I, W, P14/33
Jeffery, Thos., yeo., Langley Burrell, 1685, I, W, P3/IJ/136
Jefferys, Thos., maltster, Kington L., 1725, W, P3/IJ/217
Jeffery, Thos., yeo., Ryme I., Dorset, 1739, W, Wr, P5/1739/24
Thos., Biddestone St Nich., 1740, AB, P3/IJ/247
Jeffery, Thos., maltster, Castleton, Dorset, 1760, W, P5/1760/13
Jeffries, Thos., yeo., Oxen Leaze Farm, Keevil, 1763, W, P1/12Reg/124
Jefferys, Thos., yeo., Wadswick, Box, 1770, W, P1/IJ/255, P1/12Reg/388
Thos., yeo., Draycot Foliat, 1773, W, P1/IJ/261, P1/12Reg/507
Jefferys, Thos., baker, Melk., 1776, W, P1/IJ/271, P1/13Reg/71
Jefferys, Thos., Fisherton A., 1791, AB, W, P2/IJ/376
Thos., yeo., Oxen Leaze Farm, Keevil, 1800, W, P2/1800/53
Thos., yeo., Draycot Foliat, 1803, W, Wr, P3/1803/26
Thos., yeo., Draycot Foliat, 1814, comm, W, Wr, P1/1814/155
Thos., cloth dresser, Dilton, Westb., 1825, O, W, Wr, P25/1825/11
Thos., labourer, Wootton B., 1834, aff, O, W, Wr, P3/1834/43
Thos., sadler and harnessmaker, Marl., 1836, O, W, P1/1836/10
Jeffery, Timothy, Sal. St Thos., 1667, AB, a/c, I, P4/1667/13
Walter, sen., baker, Marl., 1641, I, W, P3/IJ/78
Geffrey, Wm., priest, Pewsey, 1558, institution to rectory, P1/1Reg/6J
Geffrey, Wm., Bourton, Gillingham, Dorset, 1563, W, P27/1Reg/16A
Jeffries, Wm., Chaddington, Lydiard T., [1584], W (NEP), P3/1Reg/43B
Jeffrey, Wm., husb., Stratford, 1594, I, W, P1/IJ/3
Jefferson, Wm., Yatesbury, 1599, I, W, P5/1599/12, P5/6Reg/224A
Jeffery, Wm., Ogbourne St A., 1606, AB, (2 - 1 with note of 1612 re widow's situation on reverse), P1/IJ/9, P5/1606/54
Jeffery, Wm., yeo., Hazeland, Bremhill, 1620, I, W, P3/IJ/36
Jeffery alias Hibberd, Wm., W. Harnham, 1623, AB, I, P5/1623/17, P5/10Reg/164B
Jeffries, Wm., shepherd, Gt. Amesb., 1629, I, W, P2/IJ/86
Jeffrey, Wm., sen., Wadswick, Box, 1641, AB, I, P3/IJ/76
Jeffery, Wm., sen., yeo., Siderow, Bremhill, [1642], I, W (NEP), P3/IJ/77
Jeffery, Wm., jun., Bourton, Gillingham, Dorset, 1668, AB, P27/1/33
Jeffery, Wm., carp., Sal., 1670, AB, I, P4/1669/9
Jefferys, Wm., jun., chandler, Calne, 1671, W (damaged), P5/1671/50
Jeffery, Wm., Amesb., 1672, AB, P2/IJ/152
Jeffery, Wm., sen., chandler, Calne, 1672, comm, I, W, P26/199
Wm., sen., chandler, Calne, 1678, I, W, P26/258
Geffres, Wm., Minety, 1685, I, W, P3/G/303
Wm., Chamberlayne's Farm, Bere R., Dorset, 1685, AB, I, W, P5/1685/58
Wm., husb., Barford St M., [1686], I, W, P2/IJ/192
Jeffries, Wm., yeo., Bere R., Dorset, 1687, AB, I, P5/1687/23
Jeffery, Wm., Ogbourne St A., 1697, AB, I (detailed), P5/1697/21
Wm., maltster, Kington L., 1699, comm, W, P3/IJ/169
Jeffery, Wm., yeo., Wadswick, Box, 1718, I, W, P3/IJ/205
Jeffries, Wm., tailor, Devizes, 1722, W, P1/IJ/169, P1/6Reg/383
Jefferys, Wm., Bere R., Dorset, 1723, AB, P5/1723/24
Jafferis, Wm., Avill's Farm, Corsham, 1727, comm, W, P3/IJ/221
Jafferis, Wm., Hackpen Farm, Wrou., 1729, W, P1/IJ/182, P1/7Reg/298
Jeffery, Wm., yeo., Wadswick, Box, 1738, W, P3/IJ/243
Wm., butcher, Poulshot, 1740, W, P2/IJ/288
Wm., Boyton, 1746, AB, comm, I, P2/IJ/294

Jeffery, Wm., gent., Ashley, Box, 1751, a/c, I, W, P3/IJ/263
Jefferys, Wm., sen., yeo., Greenaway Lane, Hardenhuish, 1773, W, P1/IJ/262, P1/13Reg/11A
Wm., Speen, Berks., 1776, AB, P1/IJ/272
Jefferys, Wm., Beckhampton, Avebury, 1776, AB, P1/IJ/273
Jefferys, Wm., Melk. Forest, 1842, O, W, Wr, P2/1842/16
Jeffries, Winifred, widow, Calne, 1701, AB, comm, ren, W, P26/607
Jeffries, Winifred, widow, Calne, 1717, AB, P26/606
Jeffery, Zachariah, yeo., Box, 1717, NW, P3/IJ/204
see also Bayliffe alias J.; Biffin alias J.; Eyles nee J.; Gifford alias J.; Leversuch alias J.
Jeleborn, Jn., Fisherton A., 1713, AB, ren, P2/IJ/238
Jelf, Giles, Kemble, 1738, AB, P3/IJ/244
Jelicot *see* Jellicots
Jelled, Wm., Bloxworth, Dorset, 1731, AB, P5/1731/49
Jellett *see* Gillett
Jellicoe, Joyce, wife, Purton, 1722, I, W, P3/IJ/213
Jellicots, Gellicos, Adam, weaver, Westb., 1649, W, P25/1649/2
Edith, widow, Westb., 1668, I, W, P25/1668/3
Jelicot, Jacob, clothworker, Westb., 1711, AB, I, P25/1711/12
Jellife *see* Jolliffe
Jellijohn, Gellyjohn *or* Jellijohn alias Field, Jn., husb., Littleworth, Gt. Faringdon, Berks., 1638, I, W, P5/1638/64, P5/13Reg/136B
Jelly, Gelly, Alice, widow, Lt. Cheverell, 1590, I, W, P2/G/53
Gelley, Jn., blacksmith, Bourton, Gillingham, Dorset, 1722, W, P27/1/255
Gelly, Jn., edge toolmaker, Bourton, Gillingham, Dorset, 1747, D (2 - 1 used as Wr), W, P27/1/393, P27/3Reg/50
Lawrence, Lt. Cheverell, 1584, AB, P2/6Reg/137A
Jelly *or* Jollyoff, Richd., Sal. St Edmd., 1629, AB, a/c, I, P4/1629/1
Jellyman, Charlotte, papermaker's wife, Downton, 1792, AB, P1/IJ/293, P1/14Reg/467C
My., widow, Downton, 1835, AB, ren, P1/1835/47
Jelphs, Dan., Gt. Somerford, 1751, W, P3/IJ/262
Jeneway *see* Jennaway
Jenkins, Agnes, widow, Devizes, 1603, I, W, P1/IJ/6
Ann, widow, Landford, 1663, AB, I, NW, P2/IJ/137
Ann, widow, Motc., Dorset, 1734, W, P27/1/332
Jenkins alias Morgan, Anthony, yeo., Purton, [1666], I, W (NEP), P3/IJ/93
Jankens, Benj., coach harnessmaker, Sal., 1766, req, W, copy W, P4/1766/8
Cath., Sherston, 1780, aff, W, P3/IJ/301
Chas., petty chapman, Lacock, 1693, ren, P3/IJ/153
Dan., yeo., Stanton St B., 1724, AB, W, P3/IJ/216
David, husb., Oare, Wilcot, 1844, O, W, Wr, P3/1844/5
David, cloth dealer, Trowb., 1853, O, W, Wr, P1/1853/18
Eliz., widow, Ashton K., 1759, W, P1/IJ/236, P1/11Reg/448
Eliz., widow, Ebbesborne Wake, 1849, W, Wr, P2/1849/12
Francis, tailor, Sal. The Close, 1640, AB, a/c, I, P5/1640/35, P5/13Reg/225C
Francis, victualler, Bradford A., 1850, O, W, Wr, P2/1850/45
Hy., carp., Ebbesborne Wake, 1815, W, Wr, P2/1815/59
Jane, Gt. Wishford, 1744, AB, P1/IJ/209
Jeremiah, innholder, Castle C., 1749, W, P3/IJ/258
Joan, sen., widow, Bremhill, 1693, comm, I, W, P3/IJ/154
Jn., labourer, Landford, 1568, W, P2/5Reg/40D
Jn., tailor, Warm., 1580, AB, I, T, P2/IJ/12, P2/5Reg/357A
Jn., husb., Hankerton, 1612, AB, comm, I, W, P3/IJ/22
Jenkins alias Butcher, Jn., husb., Hannington Wick, 1618, I, W, P3/IJ/33
Jn., tailor, Malm., 1704, W, P1/IJ/138
Jn., yeo., Fordington, Dorset, 1755, W, P15/142
Jos., glazier, Hungerford, Berks., 1695, I, W, P5/1695/51
Jos., yeo., Motc., Dorset, 1725, W, P27/1/272
Mgt., widow, Hungerford, Berks., 1708, W, P23/297
My., widow, Castle C., 1773, W, P1/IJ/263, P1/13Reg/4
Robt., Rushall, 1546, W, P2/2Reg/4A
Robt., sen., gent., Bremhill, 1672, I, W, P3/IJ/109

Robt., tailor, Ashton K., 1737, W, P3/IJ/240
Robt., sawyer, Corsham, 1854, aff, O, W, Wr, P3/1854/49
Silvester, widow, Nettleton, 1667, AB, I, W, P3/IJ/94
Stephen, labourer, Oare, Wilcot, 1852, O, W, Wr, P3/1852/39
Thos., Studley, Calne, 1598, AB, I, NW, P5/1597/71, P5/6Reg/194C
Thos., innholder, Malm. Abbey, 1665, comm, I, NW, P3/IJ/89
Genkins, Wm., Hullavington, 1617, I, W, P3/G/49
Wm., yeo., Hullavington, 1676, I, W, P3/IJ/116
Jenkins alias Thomas, Wm., cordw., Chiseldon, 1698, AB, I, P3/IJ/165
Wm., miller, Seend Head, Melk., 1723, W, P1/IJ/172, P1/6Reg/431B
Wm., carp., Ebbesborne Wake, 1801, W, Wr, P1/1801/114, P1/15Reg/333
Wm., carrier, Ebbesborne Wake, 1835, W, P2/1835/8
Wm., yeo., Whaddon, 1838, O, W, Wr, P2/1838/21
Wm., carp., Ebbesborne Wake, 1855, AB, aff, D, W, Wr, P1/1855/16
see also Sutton alias J.
Jenkinson, Godfrey, clerk, Minety, 1705, I, W, P3/IJ/182
Jenkinson, Thos., land surveyor, Letcombe Regis, Berks., 1832, comm, W, P1/1832/127
Jennance *see* Jennings
Jennaway, Jeneway, Arthur, parchmentmaker, Sal., 1706, I, W, P4/1706/2
Francis, husb., Gt. Bedwyn, 1690, I, W, P21/5/5
Janaway, Hy., Eastcourt, Shalbourne, 1567, W, P5/2Reg/23C
Jeneway, Hy., sen., yeo., Shalbourne, 1689, AB, I, ren, P5/1689/33
Jeneway, Jn., Shalbourne, 1680, I, P5/1680/30
Jeneway, Jn., Hungerford, Berks., 1696, W, P5/1696/24
Jennoway, Jn., yeo., Chilton F., 1699, AB, I, P3/IJ/171
Jn., yeo., Normanton (in Gt. Durnford), Wilsford with Lake, 1731, W, P5/1731/50
Jeneway, Jn., Sal., 1795, AB, P4/1795/3
Jeneway, Jn., sen., yeo., Sal., 1820, W, Wr, P1/1820/13
Jennoway, Mgt., widow, Sal., 1707, W, P4/1707/5
Jennoway, Wm., parchmentmaker, Sal., 1678, I, W, P4/1678/18
Jennens *see* Jennings
Jenner, Cath., widow, Lus Hill, Castle Eaton, 1767, W, P3/IJ/283
Edwd., Shrivenham, Berks., 1686, AB, P1/IJ/305
Eleanor, widow, Watchfield, Shrivenham, Berks., 1686, I, W, P1/IJ/306
Eliz., sp., Blunsdon St Andrew (form. of Marston Meysey), 1781, W, P3/IJ/302
Eliz. Lambert, wife, Whetham, Calne, 1830, AB, P26/1385
Hy., clerk, Burbage, 1798, W, P11/256
Gynner, Mgt., widow, Crudwell, 1669, W, P3/G/206
My., sp., Crickl. St S., 1768, AB, comm, P3/IJ/286
Robt., gent. and bach., Lydiard M., 1713-21, AB (2), comm, P3/IJ/196
Robt., Highw., 1809, AB, comm, Wr, P5/1809/14
Sarah, sp., New Windsor, Berks., 1798, O, req, W, copy W, P1/IJ/302, P1/15Reg/58A
Gynner, Thos., yeo., Milbourne, Malm., 1632, I, W, P3/G/128
Thos., yeo., Lt. Hinton, 1731, AB, I, P3/IJ/231
Thos., gent., Chelworth, Crickl. St S., 1809, W, Wr, P3/1809/26
Jennett, Thos., Newbury, Berks., 1622, AB, a/c, I, P1/IJ/35
Jennings, Jennance, Alice, Wokm., Berks., 1615, AB, I, P5/1615/40, P5/9Reg/123A
Alice, widow, Chittoe, Bps. C., 1696, I, W, P24/505
Andrew, sen., blacksmith, Chittoe, Bps. C., 1680, comm, I, W, P24/417
Andrew, blacksmith, Rowde, 1716, W, P1/IJ/156, P1/6Reg/48
Gennings, Ann, widow, Bridzor, Tisb., 1639, I, W, P2/G/276
Ann, widow, Sherston, 1665, AB, I, W, P3/IJ/90
Ann, widow, Rams., 1681, AB, deed of grant, I, P5/1681/33
Ann, widow, Ogbourne St A., 1834, AB, Wr, P23/975
Benj., Sherston, 1829, AB, Wr, P1/1829/87
Cath., widow, Horningsham, 1719, comm, I, W, P5/1719/50, P5/16Reg/31A
Chas., Trowb., 1833, O, W, Wr, P1/1833/4
Charlotte, widow, Ogbourne St A., 1821, W, Wr, P23/892
Jennings alias Hillary *or* Ellery, Clement, clothworker, Amesb., 1671, I, W, P1/G/214
Eliz., widow, Sherston, 1701, I, W, P3/IJ/176

Eliz., widow, Shalbourne, 1750, comm, W, P23/623
Geo., Rams., 1687, AB, I, P5/1686/36
Geo., Easton, 1826, AB, Wr, P1/1826/98
Gillian *or* Julian, widow, Westport St My., 1614, AB, I, P1/IJ/22
Hy., yeo., Easton, 1770, W, P3/IJ/289
Hy., Avill's Farm, Corsham, 1774, AB, P3/IJ/295
Hy., yeo., Eye and Dunsden, Sonning, Berks., 1822, W, Wr, P5/1822/5
Jennens, Jas., Froxfield, 1628, AB, I, ren, P1/IJ/43
Jas., yeo., Collingbourne K., 1685, AB, I, P3/IJ/137
Jas., Compton B., 1736, AB, I, W, P3/IJ/238
Jennens, Jas., Collingbourne K., 1746, AB, comm, P3/IJ/255
Jas., Sal., 1817, AB, Wr, P4/1817/3
Jas., linen draper, Market Place, Trowb., 1824, W, Wr, P1/1824/21
Jas., Sal., 1831-33, AB, Wr, P4/1831/8, P4/1833/4
Jennens, Joan, widow, Bromham, 1606, I, W, P3/IJ/8
Joan, widow, Shinfield, Berks., 1720, W, P1/IJ/163, P1/6Reg/314
Jn., husb., Shrewton, 1567-71, AB, W, P2/IJ/7, P2/5Reg/13A, 29B, 129A
Genens, Jn., husb., Stourton, 1579, I, W, P2/G/32, P2/5Reg/342B
Jn., Shrewton, 1593, I, W, P2/IJ/26
Jn., yeo., Shrewton, 1661, AB, I, P2/IJ/133
Jn., gent., Charlton, Wantage, Berks., 1681, AB, I, P23/109
Jn., tanner, Rams., 1694, W, P5/1693/33
Jn., Sutton B., 1701, AB, P1/IJ/131
Jn., blacksmith, Devizes, 1710, W, P1/IJ/141, P1/5Reg/17B
Jn., Devizes, 1734, AB, P1/IJ/186
Jn., Melk., 1738, AB, P1/IJ/197
Gennings, Jn., gent., Shrewton, 1763, W, P2/G/931
Jn., yeo., Easton, 1765, W, P3/IJ/279
Jn., Manningford Bruce, 1769, AB, P3/IJ/288
Jn., yeo., Wokm., Berks., 1782-83, W, P5/1782/18, P5/17Reg/242
Jn., Chirton, 1809, AB, Wr, P2/1809/77
Jonathan, blacksmith, Chittoe, Bps. C., 1734, W, P24/942
Jos., tanner, Rams., 1711, W, P5/1711/33, P5/15Reg/248
Jos., sen., yeo., Axford Farm, Rams., 1731, W, P5/1731/51
Jos., sen., tanner, Rams., 1743, req, W, copy W (& cod), Wr, P5/1743/46
Jos., Bodenham, Nunton and B., 1781, W, P2/IJ/358
Jos., yeo., Lockeridge, Overton, 1788, AB, W, P3/IJ/310
Joyce, widow, Calne, 1636, I, W, P26/53
Julian *see* Gillian
Martha, widow, Rams., 1749, AB, P5/1749/32
My., widow, Wootton B., 1716, W, P3/IJ/203
My., sp., Easthampstead, Berks., 1753, W, P1/IJ/228, P1/11Reg/33
Gennings, My., widow, Shrewton, 1757, W, P2/G/905
My., widow, Wootton R., 1798, W, P1/IJ/303, P1/15Reg/97
My., widow, Sal., 1833, W, Wr, P4/1833/6
Maud, Shrewton, 1615, I, W, P2/IJ/66, P2/8Reg/293
Moore, yeo., Steeple A., 1664, AB, I, P2/IJ/140
Philip, vicar, Winterbourne M., [1604], I, W (NEP), P3/IJ/4
Gennings, Richd., mason, Shrewton, 1598, W, P2/G/97
Richd., clerk and rector, Calstone W., 1669, comm, W, P1/IJ/98
Robt., sen., wheelwright, Melk., 1639, AB, I, P2/IJ/107
Robt., carp., Sandhurst, Berks., 1676, comm, I, NW, P5/1676/33
Gennings, Robt., sen., innkeeper, *The Bear*, Shrewton, 1710, W, P2/G/631
Jennens, Robt., gent., Collingbourne K., 1738, AB, comm, ren, W, P1/IJ/196, P1/8Reg/356B
Robt., yeo., Savernake Park, 1739, W, Wr, P5/1739/25
Gennings, Robt., Shrewton, 1740, W, P2/G/815
Robt., Shrewton, 1762, AB, P2/IJ/325
Gennings, Robt., farmer, Shrewton, 1829, W, Wr, P2/1829/20
Sibyl, widow, Calstone W., 1669, AB, comm, I, P3/IJ/99
Silas, sen., Shinfield, Berks., 1698, AB, I, P1/IJ/127

Augustus Philmer, gent., Ridge, Chilmark, 1809, W, Wr, P2/1809/63
Betty, widow, Dinton, 1843, W, Wr, P2/1843/13
David, yeo., Chilmark, 1770, W, P1/IJ/256, P1/12Reg/310A
Jes alias Carpenter, Eliz., W. Harnham, 1632, AB, I, P5/1632/31, P5/12Reg/89B
Gesse, Harry, Wilton, 1577, AB, I, W, P2/G/25, P2/5Reg/295B
Jn., gent., Chilmark, [1703], I, W, P2/IJ/211
Jn., gent., Chilmark, 1754, W, P2/IJ/312
Julian, widow, Sutton M., 1588, AB, W, P2/IJ/19, P2/7Reg/135B
Leonard, yeo., Dinton, 1617, I, W, P2/IJ/70
Leonard, gent., Dinton, 1772-80, AB, W, P2/IJ/337
Leonard, Dinton, 1837, AB, comm, ren, Wr, P2/1837/6
Moses, Sal., 1832, AB, Wr, P1/1832/104
Sam., yeo., Dinton, 1831, W, P2/1831/19
Thos., tailor, Cookham, Berks., 1720, I, W, P1/IJ/165, P1/6Reg/316A
Wm., Dinton, 1590, AB, I, W, P2/IJ/22
Wm., sen., Dinton, 1780, W, P2/IJ/356
Wm., gent., Ridge, Chilmark, 1809, W, Wr, P2/1809/41
Wm., farmer, N. Newnton, 1844, comm, W, Wr, P3/1844/48
Jessett, Benj., shopkeeper, Edington, 1815, O, W, Wr, P5/1815/12
Gassett, Hy., Whitep., 1558, I, W, P2/G/4, P2/3Reg/86B
Jonathan, Eddington, Hungerford, Berks., 1835, W, P23/981
Peter, yeo., Kintbury, Berks., 1635, I, W, P1/IJ/55
Richd., sen., yeo., Holt, Kintbury, Berks., 1671, I, W, P1/IJ/102
Thos., labourer, Eddington, Hungerford, Berks., 1759-92, W (made 1759; endorsed 1759 & 1792, but no evidence of probate), P23/790
Walter, yeo., Kintbury, Berks., 1620, I, W, P1/IJ/30
Jessop, Alexander, Beam., Dorset, 1625, AB, I, P5/1625/50, P5/10Reg/267A
Eliz., widow, Beam., Dorset, [1706], W (NEP), P17/170
Jn., husb., Rodbourne, Malm., 1605, I, W, P3/IJ/5
Jn., sen., weaver, Beam., Dorset, 1690, I, W, P17/323
Jos., Beam., Dorset, 1616, I, T, P5/1616/39
Richd., Malm., 1690, AB, P3/IJ/147
Richd., cordw., Chipp., 1762, W, P3/IJ/274
Robt., sen., weaver, Southwick, N. Bradley, 1664, AB, W, P1/IJ/83
Robt., linen weaver, Beam., Dorset, 1707, I, W, P5/1707/36, P5/15Reg/38
Thos., tucker, Westport St My., 1625, I, W, P3/IJ/46
Jester, Jn., innholder *or* gent., Malm., 1705, I, W, P3/IJ/184
Jestigan, Jn., Pensworth, Downton, 1581, AB, P2/IJ/14, P2/6Reg/35A
Jestis *see* Justice
Jesty, Eliz., Enmore Grn, Motc., Dorset, 1778, comm, W, P19/180
Jesty, Robt., yeo., Frankham, Ryme I., Dorset, 1778, W, P5/1778/12, P5/17Reg/158
Jesty, Wm., yeo., N. Wootton, Dorset, 1825, W, Wr, P5/1825/21
Jeton, Jane, widow, Whistley, Hurst, Berks., 1810, W, Wr, P5/1810/10
Gettene, My., widow, Bere R., Dorset, 1619, I, W, P5/1619/22, P5/9Reg/227B
Jett *see* Jatt
Jewell, Jewell alias Stantor, Joan, Landford, 1555, AB, P2/1Reg/94C
Jn., gent., Purton, 1753, comm, W, P3/IJ/266
My., gent.'s wife, Purton, 1747, AB, comm, P1/IJ/219
Wm., sen., cork cutter, Fisherton A., 1835, AB, W, P1/1835/15
see also Neeves alias J.
Jewett, Ann, widow, Marl. St Peter and St Paul, 1692, W, P1/IJ/122
Benj., clerk and rector, Mildenhall (form. of Syon House, Isleworth), 1691, AB, comm, I (2), W, P1/IJ/120
Jey *see* Jay
Jeynes *see* Jeans
Joachim, Cath., sp., Poole Keynes, 1805, W, P3/1805/10
Jocheam, Richd., yeo., Poole Keynes, 1753, W, P1/IJ/229, P1/11Reg/79A
Wm., baker *or* yeo., Brinkw., 1670, AB, comm, I, W, P3/IJ/103
Wm., Minety, 1735, W, P1/IJ/189, P1/8Reg/73
Job, Nich., Uffc., Devon, 1727, W, P20/1/180
Wm., gardener, Uffc., Devon, 1764, W, P5/1764/27

Jobbins, Agnes, widow, Westport St My., 1616, I, W, P3/IJ/30
Edwd., yeo., Sherston, 1850, W, Wr, P3/1850/36
Geo., Westport St My., 1612, W, P3/IJ/23
Jobson, Ann, sp., Reading, Berks., 1744, AB, P1/IJ/210
Jas., brazier, Hindon, 1712, I, W, P2/IJ/235
Jocheam *see* Joachim
Joel *see* Jole
Johnings *see* Thatcher alias J.
Johns, Johans *or* Jones, Agnes, Wedh., Urchf., 1580, W, P2/5Reg/365C
Benj., yeo., Rodbourne C., 1667, I, W, P3/IJ/95
John, Godwin, plumber and glazier, Sal., 1779, W, P4/1779/1
Hy., clerk, Bramshaw, Hants, 1625, I, W, P24/179
Roger, day labourer, Devizes St Jn., 1619, I, W, P1/IJ/27
Johnslin, Eliz., widow, Uffc., Devon, 1765, AB, O, P20/1/244
Robt., Uffc., Devon, 1691, AB, P20/1/120
Johnson, Agnes, widow, Manningford Bruce, 1638, I, W, P3/IJ/67
Alexander, husb. and form. servant, Soley, Chilton F., 1718, I, W, P3/IJ/207
Ann, widow, Sal., 1672, W, P4/1672/1
Ann, widow, Devizes, 1697, comm, W, P1/IJ/126
Ann, vicar's wife, Wanb., 1715, AB, P3/IJ/201
Ann, sp., Beam., Dorset, 1809, AB, comm, Wr, P5/1809/37
Anthony, husb., Manningford Bruce, 1679, I, W, P3/IJ/119
Anthony, Sal., 1735, AB, Wr, P4/1735/6
Bartholomew, no abode stated, [1605], W (NEP), P3/IJ/6
Chas., postmaster, Bradford A., 1853, O, W, Wr, P2/1853/32
Edwd., carp., N. Newnton, 1630, I, W, P3/IJ/56
Johnsons, Edwd., husb., Shaw, Melk., 1666, AB, I, P1/IJ/87
Edwd., sen., yeo., Stapleford, 1703, I, ren, W, P2/IJ/212
Edwd., Rodbourne C., 1721, AB, P3/IJ/212
Edwd., Marl., 1741, W, P1/IJ/202, P1/9Reg/67
Edwd., Burbage, 1791, AB, P5/1791/11, P5/18Reg/162A
Edwd., yeo., Lt. Hinton, 1808, W, P1/1808/87
Eleanor, widow, Hurst, Berks., 1634, AB, appt of guardian (Francis J.), I, WGVS, P5/1634/12, P5/12Reg/321
Eliz., widow, Calne, 1718, comm, W, P5/1718/19, P5/16Reg/1B
Eliz., sp., Hannington Wick, 1771, comm, W, P3/IJ/290
Frances, widow, Avill's Farm, Corsham, 1804, AB, comm, P1/1804/37
Francis, grocer, Sal. St Martin, 1763, W, P4/1763/2
Francis, Sal., 1795, AB, P4/1795/4
Gabriel, keeper of bishop's gaol, Sal., 1625, court proceeding, ren, P4/1625/6
Geo., cook, Sal. St Thos., 1696, AB, I, P4/1695/3
Geo., Sal., 1719, AB, P4/1718/27
Hy., Hurst, Berks., 1630-31, AB, a/c, P5/1631/127, P5/11Reg/130C
Hy., clerk, Devizes, 1681, AB, I, P1/IJ/109
Hester, widow, Malm., 1765, AB, comm, P3/IJ/280
Johnson alias Bockelman, Hugh, glazier, Malm., 1681, I, W, P3/IJ/126
Isaac, yeo., Burbage, 1845, D, O, W, Wr, P5/1845/17
Jacob, yeo., Broad B., Highw., 1768, W, P10/1768/1
Jas., bach., Devizes, 1809, AB, comm, Wr, P1/1809/9
Jane, sp., Stoke F., 1741-42, release by ex., W, P2/IJ/290
Jane, sp., Upton S., 1749, comm, W, P2/IJ/299
Joan, widow, Latton, 1571, W (NEP), P1/1Reg/86A
Jn., glover, Fisherton A., 1561, W, P2/4Reg/88B
Jn., Latton, 1570, W, P1/1Reg/86B
Jn., Winterbourne G., 1573, W, P2/5Reg/169B, P1/14Reg/109B
Jn., Chipp., 1611, W (NEP), P3/IJ/20
Jn., Wilton, Gt. Bedwyn, 1634, AB, I(GVS), P5/1634/61
Jn., tailor, Manningford Bruce, 1636, I, W, P3/IJ/65
Jn., parchmentmaker, Sal., 1646, I, W, P1/IJ/67
Jn., vicar, Overton, 1668, AB, P1/IJ/96
Jn., husb., Melk., 1670, AB, NW, P2/IJ/148

Jn., husb., Wilton, Gt. Bedwyn, 1703, W, P21/6/12
Jn., sen., yeo., Oaksey, 1732, W, P3/IJ/234
Johnson alias Bartholme, Jn., Westport St My., 1736, AB, W, P3/IJ/239
Jn., husb., Shrivenham, Berks., 1770, AB, W, P1/IJ/257, P1/12Reg/353
Jn., butcher, Reading St My., Berks., 1792, W, P1/IJ/294, P1/14Reg/414B
Jn., bach., Pangbourne, Berks., 1798, AB, comm, P1/IJ/304, P1/15Reg/52A
Jn., gent., Bishopstone S., 1799-1807, AB, W, P1/1804/24, P2/1807/79, P2/IJ/384
Jn., captain & adjutant in the Royal Wiltshire Yeomanry Cavalry, Collingbourne K., 1853, O, W, Wr, P3/1853/70
Jonathan, yeo., Wrou., 1778, W, P3/IJ/298
Lewis, Alderbury, 1673, AB, I, NW, P26/212
Lucretia, widow, Sal., 1719, I, W, P4/1718/25
Mgt., widow, Winterbourne G., 1560, I, W, P2/IJ/1, P2/4Reg/50C
Mgt., dau of Jn. J. of Southampton, no abode stated, evidence of I suggests Sal. St Thos., 1583, I, W, P4/Reg/21D
Martha, widow, Sonning, Berks., 1670, I, W, P5/1670/26
My., widow, Fisherton A., [1704], W, P2/IJ/214
Johnsons, My., widow, Crickl. St S., 1777, W, P3/IJ/297
My., widow, Oaksey, 1781, AB, P3/IJ/303
Melior *see* Thos., 1664, P5/10Reg/47C
Nich., Grove, Wantage, Berks., 1619, comm, I, W, P5/1619/61
Peter, shoemaker, Downton, 1566, W, P2/4Reg/236D
Peter, tailor, Sal. St Thos., 1632, I, W, P4/1632/7
Ralph, shoemaker, Binfield Heath, Sonning, Berks., 1600-01, I, W, P5/1601/26, P5/7Reg/11A
Rebecca, widow, Crickl. St S., 1733, W, P3/IJ/236
Rebecca, widow, N. Newnton, 1758, W, P3/IJ/275
Reynold, Hurst, Berks., [1613], I, W (NEP), P1/IJ/19
Richd., basketmaker, Hurst, Berks., 1631, I, W, P5/1631/53, P5/12Reg/67
Richd., Folke, Dorset, 1639, AB, comm, P5/1639/41, P5/13Reg/211A
Richd., Reading St Lawr., Berks., 1713, AB, comm, P1/IJ/149
Robt., Fisherton A., 1559, AB, P2/3Reg/157C
Robt., husb., Upper Inglesham, 1606, I, NW, P1/IJ/11
Robt., leatherdresser, Marl., 1608, court paper, I, sentence, W, P1/IJ/12
Robt., gent., Bowden Park, Lacock, 1669, AB, comm, I, P3/IJ/100
Robt., maltster, Eye and Dunsden, Sonning, Berks., 1673, AB, a/c, I, P5/1673/24
Robt., seaman on the Ipswich man of war, Barford St M., 1744, AB, P2/IJ/292
Robt., barber and wigmaker, Wokm., Berks., 1773, W, P5/1773/21, P5/17Reg/58C
Robt., barber, Wokm., Berks., 1837, comm, W, Wr, P5/1837/11
Sarah, widow, Woodspeen, Speen, Berks., 1804, W, P1/1804/51
Theophilus, yeo., Uffington, Berks., 1701, AB, I, P1/IJ/132
Theophilus, Uffington, Berks., 1720, AB, P1/IJ/159
Thos., sen., yeo., Hurst, Berks., 1590, I, W, P5/1590/29, P5/5Reg/86B
Thos., Sal. The Close, 1602, AB, I, P5/1601/28, P5/7Reg/29A
Thos., Wilton, 1633-34, AB, I, P2/IJ/98, P2/9Reg/5B
Thos., Wokm., Berks., 1641, I, W, P5/1641/47, P5/14Reg/14B
Thos., sen., tailor, Shaw, Melk., 1664, AB, I (relates *also* to his widow, Melior, who d. next day), P1/IJ/85
Thos., sen., Shaw, Melk., 1678, I, W, P2/IJ/169
Thos., clerk and rector, Parsonage House, Yatesbury, 1680, AB, comm, I, P1/IJ/106
Thos., rector, Yatesbury, 1718, AB, P1/IJ/158
Thos., carp., Beanacre, Melk., 1724, W, P2/IJ/260
Thos., Malm. (form. of Tirley, Gloucs), 1727, W, P3/IJ/222
Thos., Barford St M., 1780, W, P2/IJ/352
Thos., pig killer, Crickl. St S., 1784, W, P3/IJ/307
Johnson alias White, Wm., cardmaker, Devizes, 1571, W, P1/1Reg/35A
Wm., Wilton, Gt. Bedwyn, 1646, AB, I, P21/1/63
Johnsons, Wm., yeo., N. Newnton, 1684, I, W, P3/IJ/135
Wm., gent. and bach., Calne, 1722, AB, I, ren, P5/1722/34
Johnsons, Wm., yeo., N. Newnton, 1725, W, P3/IJ/220
Wm., yeo., Westrop, Highw., 1738, W, P10/1738/1
Wm., yeo., W. Harnham, 1751, AB, ren, P8/40
Wm., sen., Oaksey, 1762, W, P3/IJ/276
Wm., yeo., Breach Farm, Easton, 1831, O, W, P3/1831/58

Wm., Lt. Hinton, 1843, comm, seq. bond, Wr, P3/1843/43
see also Barkelman *or* Bartholomew alias J.; Garrett alias J.; Horne alias J.
Jole, Jouls, Joan, widow, Figh., 1687, AB, P26/360
Robt., sen., yeo., Figh., 1686, I, W, P26/339
Robt., sen., Figh., 1719, AB, P26/648
Jouls, Robt., yeo., Figh., 1763, W, P26/997
Joel *or* Jole, Thos., sen., Figh. & Heytes., 1582, I, W, P5/1582/35, P5/4Reg/31B
Wm., Sal. St Edmd., 1633, AB, I, P4/1633/14
Jollate *see* Gillett *or* J.
Jolliffe, Ann, widow, Lt. London, Fifield Bavant, 1745, AB, P2/IJ/293
Geo., innholder, Downton, 1684, AB, W, P2/IJ/171
My., widow, Sal., 1808, W, Wr, P1/1808/49
Joliffe, Richd., husb., Bere R., Dorset, 1591, I, W, P5/1591/48, P5/5Reg/99A
Richd., yeo., Downton, 1630, I, W, P2/IJ/89
Jellife alias Jollife, Thos., Fifield Bavant, 1727, AB, P2/IJ/267
Jolly, Jn., butcher, Newbury, Berks., 1801, W, P1/1801/41, P1/15Reg/262A
Jollycombe, Jollycombe *or* Jollyman, Geo., Sherb., Dorset, 1635, AB, I, P5/1635/54, P5/12Reg/211A
Jollyoff *see* Jelly *or* J.
Jonas, My., widow, Sal., 1707, AB, P4/1707/4
Wm., esquire, Sal. The Close, 1687, AB, cert of admon, P5/1686/37
Wm., Sal. The Close, 1728, AB, P5/1727/29
Jones, Agnes, widow, Lt. Somerford, 1626, I, W, P3/IJ/48
Agnes, widow, Luckington, 1639, I, W, P3/IJ/71
Alice, widow, Axford, Rams., 1668, I, W, P5/1668/38
Amos, yeo., Westrop, Corsham, 1721, AB, I, W, P29/J/5, P29/2Reg/34
Ann, Steeple A., 1609, I, NW, P2/IJ/50, P2/8Reg/73A
Ann, widow, Bradford A., 1723, W, P1/IJ/173, P1/6Reg/424A
Ann, widow, Corsham, 1821, W, Wr, P3/1821/41
Chas., Chipp., 1711, AB, I, P1/IJ/147
Chas., Bps. C., 1719, AB, P24/633
Chas., yeo., Littleton, Steeple A., 1784, AB, comm, W, P2/IJ/365
Chas., yeo., Box, 1829, comm, W, Wr, P3/1829/18
Christian, widow, Corsham, 1633, W, P29/1Reg/124
Cicely, widow, Westb., 1688, I, W, P25/1688/1
Dan., sen., yeo., Britford, 1780, W, P24/1120
Dan., farmer, Colerne, 1808, W, Wr, P3/1808/16
Dan., yeo., Rowde, 1848, comm, D, W, Wr, P3/1848/46
David, yeo., Bisham, Berks., 1613, I, W, P1/IJ/18
Dixon, minor, Calne, 1726, T, P26/647
Dorothy, widow, Bremilham, 1730, AB, I, P3/IJ/229
Edith, widow, Sal., 1648, I, W, P1/IJ/71
Edith, widow, Aldbourne, 1719, W, P5/1719/51, P5/16Reg/32A
Edmd., Lydiard M., 1685, AB, P3/IJ/138
Edwd., sen., freemason, N. Bradley, 1646, I, W, P2/IJ/129
Edwd., mercer and bach., Devizes, 1663, AB, I, P1/IJ/77
Edwd., yeo., N. Bradley, 1673, I, W, P2/IJ/157
Edwd., yeo., N. Bradley, 1685, I, W, P2/IJ/185
Edwd., innholder, Froxfield, 1735, W, P1/IJ/190, P1/8Reg/49
Edwd., sen., labourer, Marl., 1754, W, P1/IJ/231, P1/11Reg/166
Eliz., Netton, Durnford, 1613, AB, I, P5/1613/44, P5/9Reg/131A
Jones alias Adams, Eliz., widow, Littleworth, Gt. Faringdon, Berks., 1634, I, W. Proved at the Metropolitan visitation at Newbury, P5/1634/13, P5/12Reg/300
Eliz., widow, Keevil, 1638, I, W, P1/IJ/59
Eliz., widow, Graunts, Corsham, 1668, W, P29/1Reg/188B
Eliz., widow, S. Wraxall, 1681, AB, comm, P2/IJ/177
Eliz., widow, Wootton B., 1685, AB, ren, P3/IJ/139
Eliz., widow, Clench, Milton L., [1688], W, P3/IJ/143
Eliz., widow, Frankleigh, Bradford A., 1761, comm, W, P2/IJ/322
Eliz., widow, Westb., 1835, AB, comm, P25/1835/4
Francis, victualler, Milford, Sal. St Martin, 1793, W, P4/1793/1

Geo., Easton, 1681, AB, I, P3/IJ/127
Geo., yeo., Colerne, 1714-18, I, W (2 - 1 a copy), P3/IJ/197, 208
Geo., gardener, Reading, Berks., 1801, W, P1/1801/6, P1/15Reg/227B
Geo., Bere R., Dorset, 1831, AB, O, ren, W, Wr, P5/1831/17
Geo., Colerne, 1836, AB, comm, Wr, P3/1836/76
Griffin, husb., Winterborne K., Dorset, 1592, W, P5/1592/50, P5/6Reg/11C
Harriet, wife, Romsey, Hants (leaving effects at Downton), 1835, AB, P1/1835/17
Hy., Allington, 1583, W, P2/6Reg/80A
Hy., Langley Burrell, 1609, W, P3/IJ/12
Hy., sen., Wilton, 1707, W, P2/IJ/223
Hy., grocer, Highw., 1718, W, P10/1718/5
Hy., weaver, Boscombe, 1735-36, W, P1/IJ/191, P1/8Reg/146B
Hugh, Amesb., 1548, W, P2/2Reg/67A
Hugh, Beam., Dorset, 1663, I, W (NEP), P30/103
Humphrey, yeo., Grittenham, Brinkw., 1630, I, W, P3/IJ/58
Humphrey, Castle C., 1664, AB, ren, P3/IJ/86
Jas., weaver, Tucker's Grn, Bromham, 1816, W, Wr, P3/1816/48
Jas., weaver, N. Bradley, 1821, W, Wr, P2/1821/47
Jas., shopkeeper, Nether St., Bromham, 1828, comm, W, Wr, P3/1828/13
Jas., Wantage, Berks., 1835, AB, comm, P23/977
Jane, widow, Hurst, Berks., 1733, AB, P5/1733/33
Jane, Colerne, 1738, comm, W, P1/IJ/198
Jane, widow, Abingdon, Berks., 1811, W, Wr, P1/1811/76
Jane, widow of butcher, Corston, Malm., 1841, W, Wr, P3/1841/39
Jasper, broad weaver, Bradford A., 1768, W, P2/IJ/331
Jean, sp., Colerne, 1738, W, P1/8Reg/334
Jeremiah, Bradford A., 1839, AB, O, Wr, P2/1839/28
Joan, widow, Rushall, 1559, W, P2/3Reg/176F
Joan, widow, Chisenbury, Enford, 1615, AB, I, NW, P2/IJ/64, P2/8Reg/283
Jonesse, Joan, widow, Nettleton, 1616, I, W, P1/IJ/25
Joan, widow, Castle C., 1634, I, W, P1/IJ/51
Joan, widow, Marl., 1641, I, W, P3/IJ/79
Jn., yeo., Goswell, Keevil, 1563, AB, I, P2/IJ/4, P2/4Reg/128A
Jn., Wilton, 1574, W, P2/5Reg/193A
Jn., clerk, S. Wraxall, 1582, W, P2/6Reg/72B
Jn., jun., weaver, N. Bradley, 1584, AB, W, P2/6Reg/120A
Jn., Burbage, 1597, W, P5/1597/67, P5/6Reg/181
Jn., Wedh., Urchf., 1610, AB, I, P2/IJ/55, P2/8Reg/128B
Jn., sen., husb., Nettleton, 1616, AB, I, W, P1/IJ/26
Jn., yeo., Luckington, 1620, AB, I, NW, P3/IJ/39
Jn., Langley Burrell, 1621, I, W, P3/IJ/41
Jn., yeo., Lt. Somerford, 1625, I, W, P3/IJ/47
Jn., yeo., Foscote, Grittleton, 1641, I, W, P3/IJ/80
Jn., broad weaver, Wilton, 1662, I, W, P2/IJ/136
Jn., yeo., Corsham, 1666, AB, I, P29/1Reg/174
Jn., broad weaver, Littleton, Steeple A., 1678, AB, I, P2/IJ/174
Jn., Clarendon Park, 1685, AB, I, P4/1685/4
Jn., Snap, Aldbourne, 1693, AB, comm, P3/IJ/155
Jn., mason, Marl., 1696, I, P1/IJ/124
Jn., husb. and yeo., S. Wraxall, 1697, AB, comm, I, ren, P2/IJ/207
Jn., cordw., Bradford A., 1701, W, P1/IJ/133, P1/4Reg/18
Jn., shepherd, Urchf., [1709], W, P2/IJ/226
Jn., brazier, Chipp., 1711, I, W, P3/IJ/191
Jn., weaver, Derry Hill, Pewsham, 1711, I, W, P3/IJ/192
Jn., tailor, Marl., 1714, I, W, P1/IJ/152, P1/5Reg/466A
Jn., Amesb., 1717, AB, P2/IJ/244
Jn., shepherd, Urchf., 1721, I, W, P2/IJ/255
Jn., widower, Sopworth, 1725, AB, P1/IJ/176
Jn., yeo., Pitton, Alderbury, 1731, W, P26/761
Jn., Sherb., Dorset, 1736, AB, P5/1736/21

Jn., Seend, Melk., 1740, AB, W, P2/IJ/285
Jn., jun., wheelwright, Theale, Tilehurst, Berks., 1744, W, P1/IJ/211, P1/9Reg/355A
Jn., broad weaver, Lacock, 1753, W, P1/IJ/230, P1/11Reg/97
Jn., Whaddon, 1767, AB, W, P1/IJ/247, P1/12Reg/231B
Jn., mercer, Frog & Crow, Highw., 1771, W, P10/1771/2
Jn., Colerne, 1776, AB, P1/IJ/274
Jn., Chilton F., 1782, comm, req, W, P3/IJ/304
Jn., market spinner, Urchf., 1786, W, P1/IJ/282, P1/14Reg/99
Jn., yeo., Southbrook Farm, Rodbourne C., 1788, W, P3/IJ/311
Jn., Bradford A., 1814, AB, comm, Wr, P2/1814/15
Jn., yeo., Stratton St Mgt., 1825, W, Wr, P3/1825/19
Jn., Lt. Hinton, 1828, AB, Wr, P3/1828/33
Jn., dissenting minister, Plymouth Dock, Devon (effects at Birdbush, Donhead St My.), 1830, W, Wr, P2/1830/72
Jn., yeo., Hebden Farm, Luckington, 1831, W, Wr, P3/1831/26
Jn., yeo., Stratton St Mgt., 1835, AB, aff, comm, ren, Wr, P3/1835/16
Jonas, broad weaver, Bearfield, Bradford A., 1792, AB, W, P2/IJ/377
Jos., brazier, Chipp., 1715, W, P3/IJ/202
Jos., butcher, Castle C., 1795, W, P3/IJ/315
Jos., clothworker, Woolley, Bradford A., 1846, O, W, Wr, P2/1846/69
Josias, victualler and butcher, Beam., Dorset, 1692, I, W, P5/1692/45
Judith, Chipp., 1699, AB, P3/IJ/172
Lancelot, yeo., Sutton M., 1740, W, P2/IJ/284
Lewis, Ebbesborne Wake, 1588, AB, I, P2/IJ/21
Lewis, yeo., Pewsey, 1691, I, W, P3/IJ/148
Luke, husb., Hilp., 1575, W, P2/5Reg/223B
Mgt., widow, Hindon, 1717, W, P2/IJ/245
Martha, widow, Woodlands, Mildenhall, 1629, I, W, P3/IJ/54
Martha, sp., Charlton nr Malm., 1765, AB, P3/IJ/281
Martha, widow, Urchf., 1825, W, Wr, P2/1825/36
My., widow, N. Bradley, 1626, AB, a/c, I, W, P2/IJ/81
My., widow, Wilton, 1670, I, W, P2/IJ/147
My., Netherb., Dorset, [1676], W, P17/223
My., widow, Bradford A., 1707, W, P2/IJ/219
My., widow, Wilton, 1795, AB, P1/IJ/298, P1/14Reg/630A
My., widow, Highw., 1798, comm, W, P10/1798/2
My., widow, Fittleton, 1801, W, Wr, P1/1801/105, P1/15Reg/322
My., wife, Luckington, 1823, ren, W, P3/1823/22
My., widow, Alderbury, 1826, AB, Wr, P26/1362
Matthias, Marl., 1785, AB, P1/IJ/281
Maud, widow, Netheravon, 1597, AB, I, W, P12/2
Maurice, tapster, Marl., 1621, AB, NW, P1/IJ/32
Morgan, clerk, Whitep., 1688, I, W, P2/IJ/198
Moses, weaver, Keevil, [1611], I, W, P2/IJ/58
Jones alias Aprice, Nich., Sherb., Dorset, 1592, AB, I, P5/1592/51, P5/5Reg/139A
Nich., Langley Burrell, 1609, AB, P3/IJ/13
Nich., cook, Hindon, 1681, AB, I, P2/IJ/176
Nich., barber, Hindon, 1711, NW, P1/IJ/145, P1/5Reg/225B
Nich., sen., yeo., Stanford in the Vale, Berks., 1732, I, W, P1/IJ/185, P1/7Reg/454B
Nich., Uffc., Devon, 1742, W (NEP), P5/1742/23
Peter, Box, 1668, AB, comm, P3/IJ/96
Rachel, widow, Corsley, 1818, AB, Wr, P2/1818/44
Raymond, Urchf., 1721, AB, I, P2/IJ/256
Raymond, market spinner, Urchf., 1783, W, P1/IJ/278, P1/13Reg/409
Raymond, Southampton, Hants (leaving effects at Mkt. L.), 1817, comm, W, Wr, P2/1817/18
Rees, clerk, Luckington, 1622, I (damaged), W, P1/IJ/36
Rees, yeo., Luckington, 1660, comm, I, W, P3/IJ/81
Richd., clerk, Broughton G., 1572, W, P2/5Reg/152A
Richd., husb., Sutton M., 1572, W, P2/5Reg/140B
Richd., Littleworth, Gt. Faringdon, Berks., 1579, I, W, P5/1579/45, P5/3Reg/142A
Richd., clerk and parson, Stanton St Q., [1585], W (NEP), P3/1Reg/44

Richd., husb., Chisenbury, Enford, 1607, I, W, P2/IJ/44
Richd., yeo. *or* husb., Grittleton, 1620, I, W, P3/IJ/40
Richd., clothier, Reading, Berks., 1631, I, W, P1/IJ/46
Richd., [blacksmith], Devizes St My., 1632, I, W, P1/IJ/49
Richd., husb., Damerham, Hants, 1640, I, W, P2/IJ/116
Richd., innkeeper, Sherb., Dorset, 1640, AB, I, NW, P5/1640/34, P5/13Reg/233C
Richd., N. Bradley, 1643, comm, W, copy W, P2/IJ/124
Richd., feltmaker, Westb., 1662, AB, I, P25/1662/2
Richd., Poulton, 1749, W, P3/IJ/259
Robt., Gt. Faringdon, Berks., 1570, W, P5/2Reg/71C
Robt., innholder, Fisherton A., [1588], W, P2/IJ/20
Robt., Fisherton A., 1612, I (includes the dragon chamber), W, P1/IJ/13
Robt., husb., Sutton M., 1629, I, W, P1/IJ/307
Robt., Draycot C., 1638, AB, I, P3/IJ/68
Robt., yeo., Rodbourne C., 1692, W, P3/IJ/151
Robt., gardener, Westport St My., 1708, AB, I, W, P3/IJ/188
Robt., sen., broad weaver, Southwick, N. Bradley, 1718, I, W, P2/IJ/250
Robt., cook, Hurst, Berks., 1730, W, P5/1730/40
Robt., yeo., Bisham, Berks., 1770, AB, P1/IJ/258
Robt., jun., yeo., Whaddon, 1771, AB, comm, ren, P2/IJ/335
Robt., yeo., Whaddon, 1776, W, P1/IJ/275, P1/13Reg/91A
Robt., miner, Holywell, Flintshire, Wales (residing at Pickwick), 1838, W, Wr, P3/1838/43
Robt., yeo., Stanton St Q., 1846, W, Wr, P3/1846/28
Roger, labourer, Sherston, 1636, I, W, P3/IJ/66
Roger, tallow chandler, Amesb., 1751, AB, I, P2/IJ/306
Sam., tiler, Gt. Somerford, 1770, W, P1/IJ/259, P1/12Reg/325A
Sam., tailor, Corsham, 1820, W, Wr, P1/1820/74
Sarah, sp., Marl., 1699, I, W, P1/IJ/128, P1/3Reg/245
Sarah, widow, Wantage, Berks., 1741, W, Wr, P5/1741/24
Sarah, sp., Wantage, Berks., 1743, AB, W, P5/1742/25
Sarah, E. Hendred, Berks., 1773, AB, P1/IJ/264
Shipway, tanner, Luckington, 1752, AB, W, P3/IJ/264
Stephen, broad weaver, Southwick, N. Bradley, 1723, I, W, P1/IJ/174, P1/6Reg/433A
Stephen, bach., Devizes, 1794, AB, P1/IJ/297, P1/14Reg/503B
Susanna, sp., Sutton B., 1670, AB, comm, I, P3/IJ/105-06
Tacy, mistress, Sal., 1653, NW (2), P4/1653/3
Jonys, Thos., Rushall, 1557, W (2), P2/3Reg/59C, 60A
Thos., husb., Gt. Faringdon, Berks., 1588, I, W, P5/1588/34, P5/5Reg/42B
Thos., Minety, 1606, W, P3/2Reg/14
Thos., husb., Eye and Dunsden, Sonning, Berks., 1610, I, W, P5/1610/35, P5/9Reg/16
Thos., yeo., Littleton Drew, 1615, I, W, P3/IJ/28
Thos., picture drawer, Sal., 1628, I, W, P4/1628/7
Thos., yeo., Hurley, Berks., 1638, I, W, P1/IJ/58
Thos., yeo., Clyffe P., 1640, AB, comm, I, P3/IJ/74
Thos., yeo., Sal., 1661, I, P4/1661/18
Thos., sen., yeo., Keevil, 1668, I, W, P1/IJ/97
Thos., glover, Mere, 1669, comm, I, W, P5/1669/31
Thos., Sutton B., 1670, AB, comm, I, P3/IJ/106
Thos., Littleton, Steeple A., 1678, I, W, P2/IJ/170
Thos., carp., Seend, Melk., 1686, AB, comm, I, P2/IJ/191
Thos., Gillingham, Dorset, 1709, I, W, P27/1/180
Thos., yeo., Colerne, 1719, I, W, P3/IJ/210
Thos., labourer, Fordington, Dorset, 1739, W, P15/125
Thos., clothworker, Melk., 1764, comm, W, P2/IJ/328
Thos., Fittleton, 1773, W, P1/IJ/265, P1/12Reg/465B
Thos., Colerne, 1786, W, P1/IJ/283, P1/14Reg/145A
Thos., labourer, Box, 1816, W, Wr, P3/1816/26
Thos., yeo., Swindon, 1822, W, Wr, P3/1822/18
Thos., butcher, Castle C., 1827, W, Wr, P3/1827/62
Thos., butcher, Corston, Malm., 1840, comm, W, Wr, P3/1840/8

Thos., stone mason, Minety, 1847, O, W, Wr, P3/1847/31
Walter, Jaggards, Corsham, 1582-83, W, P29/J/1, P29/1Reg/22A
Walter, husb., Westwells, Corsham, 1614, AB, I, P29/J/3
Walter, glover, Marl., 1636, I, W, P1/IJ/56
Walter, husb., Melk., 1671, AB, I, P1/IJ/103
Walter, yeo. and surgeon, Melk., 1722, I, W, P2/IJ/257
Jonys, Wm., Winsley, Bradford A., 1562, I, W, P2/IJ/3
Wm., husb., Wedh., Urchf., 1575, W, P2/5Reg/231D
Wm., sen., yeo., Keevil, 1588, W, P2/7Reg/127
Wm., E. Harnham, Britford, 1588-89, AB, P5/1588/36, P5/5Reg/96D
Wm., yeo., Corsham, 1612, AB, W, P29/J/2, P29/1Reg/68
Wm., weaver, Kington L., [1614], I, W (NEP), P3/IJ/26
Wm., husb., Westwood, 1624, AB, I, P2/IJ/77
Wm., sen., Woodlands, Mildenhall, 1630, AB, a/c, I, P3/IJ/57
Wm., husb., Allington, 1633, I, W, P2/IJ/94, P2/9Reg/19A
Wm., fuller, Littleton, Steeple A., 1636, AB, I, P2/IJ/102
Wm., sen., yeo., Pitton, Alderbury, 1676, W, P26/245
Wm., sen., cardmaker, Chipp., 1689, comm, W, P3/IJ/145
Wm., Marl. St My., 1691, W, P1/IJ/121
Wm., Wantage, Berks., 1708, AB, P23/298
Wm., Sal., 1710, I, W, P4/1710/3
Wm., Marl., 1720, AB, P1/IJ/166
Wm., Sal., 1720, bond to pay legacy, P1/IJ/160
Wm., sen., Pitton, Alderbury, 1721, AB, I, P26/656
Wm., yeo., Studley, Bremhill, 1723, AB, I, W, P1/IJ/175, P1/6Reg/453A
Wm., S. Wraxall, 1734, AB, I, P2/IJ/277
Wm., Upton L., 1737, I, W, P2/IJ/280
Wm., tailor, Gillingham, Dorset, 1739, W, Wr, P27/1/355
Wm., yeo., Pountney's House, Bromham, 1739, W, P3/IJ/245
Wm., Wantage, Berks., 1743, AB, Wr, P5/1742/24
Wm., weaver, Foghamshire, Chipp., 1745, W, P3/IJ/252
Wm., maltster, Amesb., 1748, AB, comm, P2/IJ/298
Wm., maltster, Stratton St Mgt., 1752, W, P3/IJ/265
Wm., yeo., Pitton, Alderbury, 1764, W, P26/1006
Wm., mason, E. Hendred, Berks., 1773, AB, W, P1/IJ/266, P1/12Reg/474B
Wm., Melk., 1789, AB, comm, P2/IJ/373
Wm., farmer, Bailey Hill, Baydon, 1791, W, P5/1791/12, P5/18Reg/162B
Wm., innholder, Mere, 1791, W, P5/1791/13, P5/18Reg/165B
Wm., weaver, Southwick, N. Bradley, 1818, W, Wr, P2/1818/9
Wm., yeo., Marl., 1849, O, W, Wr, P1/1849/13
Wm. Blackwell, law stationer, Devizes, 1857, aff, O, W, Wr, P1/1857/14
see also Cuffin alias J.; Johans *or* J.
Joplen, Ann, widow, Aldermaston, Berks., 1786, W, P1/IJ/284
Jopson, Sam., sen., blacksmith, Ebbesborne Wake, 1735, W, P1/IJ/192, P1/7Reg/636
Jordan, Abigail, sp., Trowb., 1751, AB, ren, P1/IJ/224
Alexander, baker, N. Bradley, 1757, W, P2/IJ/317
Jorden, Ambrose, yeo., Keevil Wick, 1631, I, W, P2/IJ/92
Jorden, Ann, widow, Uffc., Devon, 1682, I, W, P20/1/96
Jorden, Ann, sp., Littleton, Steeple A., 1703, I, W, P2/IJ/213
Ann, Devizes, 1788, comm, W, P1/IJ/287, P1/14Reg/187A
Jordan alias Jatt, Bristow, Devizes, 1722, AB, P1/IJ/170
Chris., broad weaver, Malm., 1647, AB, I, P1/IJ/69
Chris., tailor, Erlestoke, 1685, AB, I, W, P2/IJ/188
Jordon, Edwd., Compton B., 1754, comm, W, P3/IJ/267
Edwd., labourer, Seend, Melk., 1773, W, P1/IJ/267, P1/13Reg/14A
Eliz., Allington, 1638, AB, I, P1/IJ/60
Frances, widow, Westb., 1678, I, W, P25/1678/8
Hannah, sp., Chieveley, Berks., 1832, AB, O, Wr, P1/1832/39
Jas., Pott., 1748, AB, P1/IJ/221
Jas., victualler, Highw., 1803, W, P5/1803/35, P5/19Reg/64A

Jane, widow, Latton, 1679, I, W, P3/IJ/120
Jane, widow, Devizes, 1757, W, P1/IJ/234, P1/11Reg/345B
Jane, victualler's wife, Devizes & Bromham, 1772, W, Wr, P3/IJ/292
Jatt, apothecary, Westb., 1767, W, P25/1767/4
Jn., Sal., 1584, AB, P4/Reg/23D
Jn., freemason, High Swindon, 1609, AB, P3/IJ/14
Jn., sen., weaver, Keevil, [1614], W (NEP), P2/8Reg/254
Jorden, Jn., Uffc., Devon, 1670, AB, I, P20/1/63
Jn., fuller, Devizes, 1685, comm, I (detailed), W, P1/IJ/111
Jn., yeo., Luckington, 1693, comm, W, P3/IJ/156
Jn., fuller, Devizes, 1734, AB, I, W, P1/IJ/187, P1/7Reg/593A
Jn., blacksmith, Atworth, Bradford A., 1740-42, AB (2), W, P2/IJ/289
Jn., tailor, Stratton St Mgt., 1747, W, P1/IJ/220, P1/10Reg/201
Jn., Devizes, 1766, AB, P1/IJ/243
Jn., cloth dyer, Hurd Mill, Pott., 1769, AB, ren, W, P1/IJ/250, P1/12Reg/292A
Jn., yeo., Stratton St Mgt., 1796, W, P3/IJ/316
Jn., victualler, Hartmoor, Pott., 1823, AB, comm, ren, W, Wr, P1/1823/54
Jn., blacksmith, Melk., 1837, W, Wr, P2/1837/35
Jorden, Jn. Jatt, dyer, Pott., 1744, W, P1/IJ/212, P1/9Reg/309
Jorden, Jos., yeo., Keevil, 1694, AB, I, P2/IJ/203
Jorden, My., widow, Wingfield, 1719, W, P2/IJ/252
My., widow, E. Kennett, 1733, W (2 - 1 a copy) (NEP), P3/IJ/237
My., sp., Wantage, Berks., 1737, W, P23/528
My., widow, N. Bradley, 1759, W, P1/IJ/237, P1/11Reg/475
Jorden, Matthew, baker, Keevil, 1714, AB, ren, P2/IJ/239
Nich., Keevil, 1551, W, P2/2Reg/133A
Jorden, Nich., yeo., Semington, Steeple A., 1690, I, W, P2/IJ/199
Nich., Keevil, 1723, AB, P2/IJ/259
Jorden, Oliver, Purley, Berks., 1680, AB, P1/IJ/107
Richd., Hindon, 1607, I (very detailed), P2/IJ/46
Richd., cordw., Stratton St Mgt., 1783, W (£1 a year to trustees of Meeting House in Stratton for repairing it & mounds round yard), P1/IJ/279, P1/13Reg/491
Richd., Stratton St Mgt., 1797, AB, P3/IJ/317
Jorden, Robt., yeo., Keevil, 1622, I, W, P1/IJ/37
Robt., Hilp., 1673-74, AB, alleg, I, W, P2/IJ/158
Jorden, Robt., husb., Semington, Steeple A., 1716, W, P1/IJ/157, P1/6Reg/34A
Roger, sen., fuller, Devizes, 1746, W, P1/IJ/214, P1/10Reg/19A
Sam., Broughton G., 1761, W, P2/IJ/323
Sam., Melk., 1804, W, P2/1804/7
Sarah, widow, Pott., 1762, W, P1/IJ/238, P1/12Reg/19A
Jorden, Stephen, yeo., Semington, Steeple A., 1677, AB, I, W, P2/IJ/167
Susanna, sp., Keevil, 1720, W, P2/IJ/254
Jorden, Thos., Whitep., 1561, AB, P2/4Reg/63B
Jorden, Thos., Sal. St Edmd., 1581, AB, P4/Reg/1B
Jorden, Thos., Swindon, 1614, I, W, P1/IJ/23
Thos., butcher, Sal., 1633, AB, I, P4/1633/21
Jorden, Thos., butcher, Stapleford, [1663], I, W, P2/IJ/138
Thos., blacksmith, E. Kennett, 1673, I, W, P3/IJ/112
Jorden, Thos., sen., yeo., Stratton St Mgt., 1714-19, AB, I, W, P3/IJ/198, 211
Thos., Avebury, 1720, AB, I, P1/IJ/167
Thos., yeo., Stratton St Mgt., 1768, W, P3/IJ/287
Thos., victualler, Devizes, 1775, W, P1/IJ/269, P1/13Reg/64A
Walter, Devizes St My., 1594, I, NW, P1/IJ/4
Jorden, Walter, Hilmarton, 1662, AB, P1/IJ/76
Wm., yeo., Sal., 1566, W, P5/1Reg/67A
Jorden, Wm., husb., Keevil, 1569, W, P2/5Reg/71A
Jorden, Wm., yeo., Keevil Wick, 1626, I, note of probate W, P2/IJ/79
Jorden, Wm., husb., Keevil, [1627], I, W, P2/IJ/84
Jorden, Wm., Keevil Wick, 1640, I, W, P2/IJ/119
Jorden, Wm., Keevil Wick, 1677, AB, I, ren, P2/IJ/166

Wm., [shoemaker], Sal. St Thos., 1684, AB, I, P4/1684/10
Wm., roper, Trowb., [1700], W, P2/IJ/208
Wm., tailor, Allington, All C., 1705, I, W, P3/IJ/183
Wm., husb., Wingfield, 1707, ren, W, P2/IJ/220
Wm., Devizes, 1824, AB, Wr, P1/1824/22
Wm., cordw., Erlestoke, 1829, O, W, Wr, P2/1829/23
see also Pearce alias J.; Tanner late J.
Jorots *see* Jerratt
Jose, Ann, widow, Short St., Dilton, Westb., 1639, I, W, P25/1639/6
Joseph, Wm., yeo., Bradford A., 1618, I, W, P2/IJ/71
Jotham, Dan., clothworker, Bradford A., 1751, comm, W, P2/IJ/304
Jn., clothworker, Bradford A., 1827, O, W, P1/1827/7
Thos., clothier, Bradford A., 1806, W, Wr, P2/1806/63
Jouls *see* Jole
Joy, Joye, Ann, widow, Sal., 1797, W, P4/1797/12
Edwd., Lyme R., Dorset, 1698, AB, P16/154
Emma, widow, Fovant, [1673], I, W, P2/IJ/159
Francis, yeo., Fovant, 1666, I, W, P2/IJ/144
Francis, Sal., 1773, AB, ren, P4/1773/4
Harry, Upton S., 1851, AB, comm, Wr, P1/1851/17
Jn., tallow chandler, Gt. Faringdon, Berks., 1685, I, W, P5/1685/56
Jn., Stratton St Mgt., 1728, W, P3/IJ/226
My., widow, Compton C., 1631, I, W, P1/IJ/47
My., widow, Chilton F., 1792, W, P1/IJ/295, P1/14Reg/400
Richd., Tisb., 1557, W, P2/3Reg/70B
Richd., Halstock, Dorset, 1626, I, W, P5/1626/24, P5/10Reg/203
Robt., Bere R., Dorset, 1667, AB, comm, P5/1667/34
Wm., jun., husb., Halstock, Dorset, 1597, AB, I, W, P5/1597/69, P5/6Reg/172B
Wm., sen., husb., Halstock, Dorset, 1597, I, W, P5/1597/70, P5/6Reg/173A
Wm., husb., Halstock Leigh, Dorset, 1632, comm, I, NW, P5/1632/30, P5/12Reg/90B
see also Jay
Joyce, Arnold, yeo., W. Ashton, Steeple A., 1821, comm, W, Wr, P2/1821/19
Barachiah, blacksmith, Marl., 1784, W, P1/IJ/280, P1/14Reg/54
Geo., yeo., Winterborne M., Winterborne K., Dorset, 1711, I, W, P5/1711/34, P5/15Reg/236
Harry, Tisb., 1615, NW, P2/IJ/63
Hy., yeo., Lacock, 1778, W, P3/IJ/299
Hy., yeo., Lacock, 1787, W, P3/IJ/309
Jas., Ash, Stourpaine, Dorset, 1777, AB, P24/1128
Joyes, Jn., yeo., Henwick Farm, Thatcham, Berks., 1711, I, W, P1/IJ/148, P1/5Reg/191
Joys, Jn., blacksmith, Baydon, 1776, W, P5/1776/26, P5/17Reg/103
Jn., sen., gent., Trowb., 1855, aff, D, W, Wr, P1/1855/41
Mgt., widow, Sal., 1671, AB, I, P4/1671/5
Millicent, sp., Corsley, 1641, AB, I, NW, P2/IJ/122
Nimrod, husb., Dilton, Westb., 1665, I, NW, P25/1665/2
Nimrod, Westb., 1766, AB, P25/1766/1
Richd., tailor, Mere, 1609, AB, I, W, P5/1609/44, P5/9Reg/5A
Richd., yeo., Lacock, 1829, W, Wr, P1/1829/99
Thos., Westwood, 1563, W, P2/4Reg/127A
Thos., tailor, Tisb., 1604, AB, I, P2/IJ/41
Thos., Marl., 1832, AB, comm, ren, Wr, P1/1832/2
Wm., gent., Semley, 1678, AB, ren, P2/IJ/173
Wm., yeo., W. Ashton, Steeple A., 1848, comm, W, Wr, P1/1848/27
Wm., innkeeper and brewer, Melk., 1854, aff, O, W, Wr, P2/1854/57
Joye *see* Joy
Joyes *see* Jay
Joyner, Ann, widow, Trowb., 1790, W, P1/IJ/292, P1/14Reg/340
Jn., Downton, 1624, AB, I, ren, P2/IJ/76
Maud, widow, Bere R., Dorset, 1674, AB, I, P5/1674/40
Richd., earthenware seller, Devizes, 1830, W, Wr, P1/1830/8
Ruth, clothworker's wife, Devizes, 1787, AB, P1/IJ/286

Wm., Hilp., 1775, W, P2/IJ/339
see also Booth alias J.; Thomas alias J.
Joys *see* Joyce
Jubbens, Richd., Maiden B., 1731, W, P2/IJ/272
Jubber, Robt., Charminster, Dorset, 1699, AB, P5/1699/22
Wm., innholder, Sal., 1709, AB, I, P4/1708/9
Judd, Judde, Edmd., Shalbourne, 1566, W, P5/1Reg/78A
Edwd., yeo., Lt. Somerford & Rams., 1700, comm, I, W, P3/IJ/174
Edwd., yeo., Burbage, 1734, W, P5/1734/43
Eliz., Winterslow, 1641, I, W, P1/IJ/61
Giles, Winterbourne G., 1623, AB, P2/IJ/75
Jn., Newton T., 1559, W, P2/3Reg/185A
Jude, Jn., sen., husb., Durrington, 1610, AB, comm, I, W, P2/IJ/52, P2/8Reg/92
Jn., clerk, Rams., 1647, comm, I, W, P5/1647/9, P5/14Reg/99C
Jn., sen., blacksmith, Newton T., 1717, W, P2/IJ/243
Jn., Allington, 1730, W, P2/IJ/269
Jn., S. Newton, 1734, AB, comm, P2/IJ/278
Jn., shopkeeper, Winterslow, 1751, W, P2/IJ/301
Jn., yeo., Middle Winterslow, 1782, W, P2/IJ/362
Jn., yeo., Whaddon, Alderbury, 1786, AB, L (2), W, P26/1144
Martha, widow, Sal., 1815, AB, D, note, NW, P4/1815/9
My., Winterbourne D., 1691, AB, P7/79
Maud, widow, Winterbourne G., 1629, NW, P2/IJ/87
Judde *or* Judge, Michael, Newton T., 1576, I, W, P2/IJ/8, P2/5Reg/254B
Nich., Winterbourne D., 1617, I, W, P7/18
Nich., sen., Winterbourne D., 1668, AB, I, P7/38
Nich., [jun.], Winterbourne D., 1691, AB, P7/78
Nich., sen., yeo., Winterbourne D., 1691, AB, W, P7/77
Judde, Peter, yeo., Newton T., 1639, I, W, P2/IJ/113
Richd., husb., Cholderton, 1633, I, W, P2/IJ/97, P2/9Reg/14A
Richd., Shrewton & Tytherley, Hants, 1809, AB, P2/1809/87
Thos., Winterbourne G., 1554, W, P2/2Reg/190A
Jude, Thos., Sal. St Edmd., 1629, I, W, P4/1629/12
Thos., husb., Winterbourne D., 1730, AB, I, P7/125
Thos., common carrier, Petersfinger, Clarendon (described as in Laverstock), 1784, W, P2/IJ/366
Thos., Winterslow, 1837, AB, Wr, P2/1837/51
Thos., widower, E. Grimstead, W. Dean, 1847, AB, Wr, P2/1847/38
Wm., Winterbourne D., 1588, I, W, P5/1587/27, P5/5Reg/1B
Judd alias May, Wm., husb., Hinton, Hurst, Berks., 1600, AB, I, W, P5/1600/37, P5/6Reg/241A
Wm., Winterbourne G., 1619, I, W, P2/IJ/73
Wm., tailor, Winterslow, 1636, I, W, P2/IJ/103
Wm., no abode stated, 1661, I, W, P2/IJ/134
Wm., Idmiston, 1673, AB, I, P2/IJ/156
Wm., Winterbourne G., 1676, AB, I, P2/IJ/165
Wm., Winterslow, 1720, AB, P1/IJ/168
Wm., E. Winterslow, 1725, W, P2/IJ/264
Wm., Whaddon, Alderbury, 1762, AB, P26/992
Wm., Whaddon, Alderbury, 1780, W, P26/1107
Wm., butcher, Sal., 1849, W, Wr, P4/1849/8
see also Field alias J.
Juden, Juden alias Evenden, Jn., tailor, Sonning, Berks., 1625, I, W, P5/1625/51, P5/10Reg/254
Judge, Wm., carp., Welford, Berks., 1744, W, P1/IJ/213, P1/9Reg/321
Wm., Halfway House, Welford, Berks., 1786, W, P1/IJ/285, P1/14Reg/119A
see also Judd *or* J.
Judging, Jn., tailor, Downton, 1557, W, P2/3Reg/47D
Juffs, Wm., Cumnor, Berks., 1789, W, P1/IJ/290, P1/14Reg/313
Jukes, Ann, widow, Gillingham, Dorset, 1810, W, P27/1/606
Chas., farmer, Milton, E. Knoyle, 1854, D, W, Wr, P2/1854/59
Christian, sp., Madjeston, Gillingham, Dorset, 1816-36, W (made 1816, registered 1836), P27/1/709
Eliz., widow, Chicksgrove, Tisb., 1800, W, P2/1800/30

Geo., tallow chandler, E. Knoyle, 1674, AB, I, P2/IJ/161
Geo., shoemaker, Gillingham, Dorset, 1726, NW, P27/1/279
Geo., husb., E. Knoyle, 1730, W, P2/IJ/271
Geo., Zeals, 1731, AB, P5/1731/52
Geo., sen., blacksmith, Landford, 1837, W, Wr, P2/1837/27
Hy., sen., Gillingham, Dorset, 1729, AB, I, P27/1/299
Hy., yeo., Gillingham, Dorset, 1743, W, P27/1/371, P27/3Reg/23B
Hy., yeo., E. Knoyle, 1819, W, Wr, P2/1819/33
Jas., bach., Shalbourne, 1838, AB, Wr, P23/996
Jn., Huntingford, Gillingham, Dorset, 1684, I, P27/1/85
Jn., Zeals, 1699, AB, I, P5/1699/20
Jn., Mere, 1804, AB, P5/1804/20
Jn., gent., Madjeston, Gillingham, Dorset, 1806, comm, W, Wr, P27/1/589
Maria Arundel, sp., Madjeston, Gillingham, Dorset, 1836, W, P27/1/710
Martha, E. Knoyle, 1688, AB, I, P2/IJ/197
My., sp., Wilton, 1848, W, Wr, P2/1848/9
Ralph, Pierston, Gillingham, Dorset, 1684, I, P27/1/88
Ralph, sen., yeo., Madjeston, Gillingham, Dorset, 1730, W, P27/1/306
Ralph, gent., Madjeston, Gillingham, Dorset, 1769, W, P27/1/466, P27/3Reg/151
Sarah, widow, Madjeston, Gillingham, Dorset, 1806-36, W (made 1806, registered 1836), P27/1/708
Thos., yeo., Chicksgrove, Tisb., [1789], W, Wr, P2/IJ/374
Thos., Sal., 1795, AB, comm, W, P4/1795/2
Wm., Dinton, 1836, W, Wr, P2/1836/54
Juler, Wm., Damerham, Hants, 1558, W, P2/3Reg/83C
Jumper, Jumper alias Baldchild, Cornelius, Laverstock, 1558, W, P2/3Reg/102B
Joan, widow, Downton, 1566-69, AB, W, P2/4Reg/237A, P2/5Reg/73A
Wm., yeo., New Court, Downton, 1569, W (to be buried in church by his seat), P2/5Reg/55B
Jupe, Betty, widow, Gillingham, Dorset, 1806, AB, P27/1/590
Edwd., gent., Bourton, Gillingham, Dorset, 1776-78, W, Wr, P27/1/501, 503, P27/3Reg/202, 208
Eliz., widow, Stourton, 1617, I, W, P2/IJ/68
Francis, yeo., Stourton, 1666, AB, I, P2/IJ/143
Francis, Bourton, Gillingham, Dorset, 1733, AB, P27/1/327
Francis, sen., yeo., Stourton, 1766, AB, I, W, P2/IJ/330
Giles, yeo., Bourton, Gillingham, Dorset, [1710], W, P27/1/181
Giles, linen weaver, Bourton, Gillingham, Dorset, 1772, W, P27/1/480, P27/3Reg/169
Giles, yeo., Mere, 1775, W, P5/1775/12, P5/17Reg/101B
Grace, widow, Bourton, Gillingham, Dorset, 1717, W, P27/1/218
Hy., yeo., Burton, Mere, 1732, W, P5/1732/27
Hy., yeo., Burton, Mere, 1811, W, Wr, P5/1811/7
Hy., Burton, Mere, 1836, W, Wr, P5/1836/1
Joan, widow, Coombe B., 1784, AB, P8/62
Jn., yeo. and innholder, Sal., 1615, I, W, P4/1615/3
Jn., Stourton, 1713, AB, P2/IJ/237
Jn., linen weaver, Bourton, Gillingham, Dorset, 1778, W, P27/1/504, P27/3Reg/205
My., [1680], W, P2/IJ/386
My., widow, Whitecliff, Brixton D., 1751, comm, W, P2/IJ/302
My., sp., Mere, 1851, comm, W, Wr, P5/1851/12
Jupp, Reynold, Stourton, 1601, I, W, P2/IJ/37
Robt., Stourton, 1676, I, P2/IJ/164
Robt., Gillingham, Dorset, 1834, W, Wr, P27/1/704
Thos., yeo., Motc., Dorset, 1743, cit, W (exs cited to exhibit W, & accept *or* decline ex'ship), P27/1/372, P27/3Reg/28
Wm., Stourton, 1683, AB, I, P2/IJ/181
Jupp, Wm., yeo., Bourton, Gillingham, Dorset, 1687, I, W, P27/1/104
Wm., yeo., Zeals, 1748, W, Wr, P5/1748/20
Wm., yeo., Gillingham, Dorset, 1842, W, Wr, P27/1/740
Juslate *see* Inslate
Justice, Francis, Sutton C., Berks., 1750, AB, P1/IJ/222
Isaac, gent., Hampstead N., Berks., 1808, W, Wr, P1/1808/112
Jn., mason, Hampstead N., Berks., [1612], W (NEP), P1/IJ/14
Jn., Woodley, W. and Sandford, Berks., 1616, I, T, P5/1616/41

Jn., Northcot, Tilehurst, Berks., 1789, W, P1/IJ/291, P1/14Reg/217
Marline, widow, Sonning, Berks., 1699, I, W, P5/1699/21
Jestis, My., widow, Woodley, W. and Sandford, Berks., 1648, comm, I, W, P5/1648/7, P5/14Reg/103B
Matthew, Tilehurst, Berks., 1741, AB, P1/IJ/203
Matthew, farmer, Sandhurst, Berks., 1776, W, P5/1776/27, P5/17Reg/116B
Matthew, Northcot, Tilehurst, Berks., 1792, W, P1/IJ/296, P1/14Reg/418
Nich., Sonning, Berks., 1588, I, T, W, P5/1588/35
Nich., Twyford, Hurst, Berks., 1588, W, P5/5Reg/37A
Nich., husb. *or* yeo., Purley, Berks., 1620, I, W, P1/IJ/31
Richd., maltster, Brightwell, Berks., 1689, comm, I, W, P1/IJ/117
Justikin, Joan, widow, Alderbury (form. of Langley Wood, Redlynch), 1708, I, W, P26/546
Jos., husb. *or* yeo., Langley Wood, 1703, I, W, P1/IJ/134, P1/4Reg/229
Justins, Edwd., Sherb., Dorset, 1775, AB, P5/1775/13, P5/17Reg/87A
Eliz., widow, Sherb., Dorset, 1757, W, P5/1757/18
Jane, sp., Sherb., Dorset, 1800, W, P5/1800/19, P5/18Reg/295B
Jn., Sherb., Dorset, 1791, AB, P5/1791/14, P5/18Reg/172C
Justin, Robt., butcher, Sherb., Dorset, 1677, AB, I, P5/1677/32
Justy, Jn., woolcomber, Leigh, Yetm., Dorset, 1700, AB, I, NW, P19/85

Kakett, Thos., Wokm., Berks., 1569, AB, P5/2Reg/51A
Kames *see* Keynes
Kate, Kates *see* Keate
Kaynes *see* Keynes
Kays, Thos., brazier, Malm., 1847, W, Wr, P3/1847/55
Keady *see* Caddy
Keale *see* Keele
Keame, Ann, sp., Brightwell, Berks., 1708, AB, I, P1/K/131
Geo., yeo., Brightwell, Berks., 1720, AB, I, P1/K/166
Zachary, yeo., Brightwell, Berks., 1695, AB, I (detailed), ren, P1/K/112
Kearsey, Richd., yeo., Ashley, 1807, W, Wr, P3/1807/24
Keasy, Susanna, farmer's wife, Ashton K., 1715, AB, P3/K/152
Keate, Keats, Ann, widow, N. Bradley, 1807, W, Wr, P2/1807/2
Benj., E. Hagbourne, Berks., 1680, AB, I, P1/K/83
Keat, Cath., widow, Upton, Blewbury, Berks., 1685, I, W, P5/1685/59
Kates, David, Fordington, Dorset, 1746, AB, P15/137
Keat, Dorothy, widow, Fovant Stroud, 1719, W, P2/K/316
Edwd., esquire, Westlecott, Wrou., 1677, AB, I, P3/K/89
Eliz., widow, Rams., 1780, W, P5/1780/12, P5/17Reg/183
Eliz., widow, Hermitage, Dorset, 1808, AB, comm, Wr, P5/1808/5
Kates, Eve, widow, Bere R., Dorset, 1719, I, W, P5/1719/54, P5/16Reg/13A
Francis, Blewbury, Berks., 1699, I, P5/1699/24
Geo., innholder, Devizes, 1714, W, P1/K/151, P1/5Reg/460B
Hy., husb., Stockley, Bere R., Dorset, 1635, AB, I, W, P5/1634/14, P5/12Reg/169B
Hy., husb., Stockley, Bere R., Dorset, 1636, AB, I, LA, W, P5/1635/57, P5/12Reg/260B
Keat, Hugh, gent., Hodcott, W. Ilsley, Berks., 1616, I (detailed), W, P1/K/15
Hugh, yeo., Lillington, Dorset, 1706, I, NW, P5/1706/21
Hugh, yeo., Hermitage, Dorset, 1813, comm, W, P5/1813/8
Jas., yeo., Amesb., 1603, AB, P2/K/73
Jas., vicar, Chards., Devon, 1705, AB, comm, I, ren, W, P14/101
Jas., sen., Chards., Devon, 1722, W, P5/1722/35, P5/16Reg/66C
Keats, Jas., yeo., Harwell, Berks., 1835, O, W, P1/1835/28
Keates, Jas., yeo., Southwick, N. Bradley, 1837, W, Wr, P2/1837/43
Jane, Lillington, Dorset, 1725, AB, P5/1725/46
Jane, wife, Abingdon, Berks., 1750, AB, P1/K/230
Keates, Jane, widow, Wantage, Berks., 1829, aff, O, W, P23/942
Joan, widow, Chards., Devon, 1705, I, W, P14/105
Joan, widow, Blewbury, Berks., 1714, W, P5/1714/23, P5/15Reg/384C
Jn., husb., Rams., 1648, AB, comm, I, P5/1648/14, P5/14Reg/105C
Jn., Upton, Blewbury, Berks., 1670, AB, I, P5/1670/30
Jn., yeo., Fovant, 1689-90, AB, a/c, I, P2/K/254